CPT·PLUS!

A Comprehensive Guide
To Current Procedural
Terminology

Color Coded
2018

ISBN 978-1-943009-89-3 (Coder's Choice®, soft cover)
ISBN 978-1-943009-90-9 (Spiral)
ISBN 978-1-943009-91-6 (e-book)

Practice Management Information Corporation
4727 Wilshire Boulevard
Los Angeles, California 90010
1-800-MED-SHOP
http://pmiconline.com/

Printed in China

INTRODUCTION

CPT® PLUS! 2018 is an enhanced CPT® coding resource which includes all official CPT 2018 codes and complete descriptions plus comprehensive CPT coding instructions, full-color anatomical illustrations, a unique color-coding system to help identify CPT codes subject to special coding rules, and a new and improved alphabetic index.

The CPT coding system includes over 9,000 codes and descriptions for reporting medical services, procedures, supplies and materials. Accurate CPT coding provides an efficient method of communicating medical services and procedures among health care providers, health care facilities, and third party payers and enhances the health care provider's control of the reimbursement process.

The CPT coding system is revised annually by the American Medical Association (AMA). Each year hundreds of additions, changes and deletions are made the CPT coding system. These changes become effective on January 1st. CPT is required by federal law for all health insurance claim forms filed with Medicare, Medicaid, CHAMPUS and Federal Employee Health Plans and is accepted or required by all other third party payers.

CPT® PLUS! 2018 provides valuable instructions, coding tips, and other information to help providers maximize reimbursement while minimizing audit liability. Our objective is to make CPT coding faster, easier and more accurate for medical office, healthcare facility and third party payer coding and billing staff, while setting a new standard for CPT coding references.

James B. Davis, Publisher

DISCLAIMER

This publication is designed to offer basic information regarding coding and reporting of medical services, supplies and procedures using the CPT coding system. The information presented is based on a thorough analysis of the CPT coding system and the experience and interpretations of the editors. Though all of the information has been carefully researched and checked for accuracy and completeness, neither the editors nor the publisher accept any responsibility or liability with regard to errors, omissions, misuse or misinterpretation.

CONTENTS

This page intentionally left blank.

CPT CODING FUNDAMENTALS

CPT® is an acronym for Current Procedural Terminology. Physicians' Current Procedural Terminology, Fourth Edition, known as CPT-4 or more commonly CPT, is a systematic listing of codes and descriptions which classify medical services and procedures. CPT codes are used by physicians, hospitals, and other health care professionals, to report specific medical, surgical and diagnostic services and procedures for statistical and third party payment purposes.

The CPT coding system is maintained by the American Medical Association (AMA) and a revised edition of the CPT book is published each fall. The new CPT codes become effective on January 1st of the following year. The revisions in each new edition are prepared by the CPT Editorial Panel with the assistance of physicians representing all specialties of medicine.

A thorough understanding of the CPT coding system is essential in order to provide accurate reporting of medical services and procedures, maximize payments from third parties, minimize denials, rejections and reductions from third parties, and to protect the medical practice from audit liability.

KEY POINTS REGARDING THE CPT CODING SYSTEM

- *CPT codes describe medical procedures, services and supplies.*

- *All CPT codes are five digit codes.*

- *CPT codes are mandated by federal law for Medicare, Medicaid, CHAMPUS and Federal Employee Health Plan (FEHP) reporting and are accepted or required by all other third party payers.*

- *CPT codes are self-definitive, eg. with the exception of CPT codes for unlisted procedures and/or the few CPT codes which include the term specify in the description, each CPT code number represents the universal definition of the service or procedure.*

- *CPT codes are revised and updated annually by the AMA and the revisions become effective each January 1st. Hundreds of CPT codes are added, changed or deleted each year. All health care professionals, third party payers, and health care facilities must maintain copies of the current code books.*

- *Accurate CPT coding provides an efficient method of communicating medical, surgical and diagnostic services and procedures among health care professionals, health care facilities, and third party payers.*

- *Accurate CPT coding enhances the health care provider's control of the reimbursement process.*

STRUCTURE OF THE CPT CODING SYSTEM

The CPT coding system includes over 7,900 codes and definitions for medical services, procedures and diagnostic tests. Each procedure or service is identified by a five digit code, followed by the definition.

The CPT coding system is divided into eight SECTIONS. The eight sections of are:

Evaluation and Management	99201-99499
Anesthesiology	00100-01999, 99100-99140
Surgery	10021-69990
Radiology (Including Nuclear Med & Dx U/S)	70010-79999
Pathology and Laboratory	80047-89398, 0001U-0017U
Medicine (except Anesthesiology)	90281-99199, 99500-99607
Category II Performance Measurement	0001F-9007F
Category III Emerging Technology	0042T-0504T

Each section of the CPT book includes subsections with anatomic, procedural, condition, or descriptor subheadings. The Evaluation and Management (E/M) section is presented first because 1) these codes are used by virtually all health care providers and 2) are the most frequently used CPT codes.

HOW TO USE THE CPT CODING SYSTEM

A provider or coder using the CPT coding system first chooses the name and associated code of the procedure or service which most accurately identifies and describes the service(s) performed. The provider or coder then chooses names and codes for additional services or procedures. If necessary, modifiers are chosen and added to the selected service and procedure codes. All services or procedures coded must also be documented in the patient's medical record.

According to CPT, "The listing of a service or procedure and its code number in a specific section of the CPT book does not restrict its use to a specific specialty group. Any procedure or service in any section of the CPT coding system may be used to designate the services rendered by any qualified physician or other qualified health care professional."

The codes and descriptions listed in the CPT coding system are those that are generally consistent with contemporary medical practice and being performed by health care professionals in clinical practice. Inclusion in the CPT coding system does not represent endorsement by the American Medical Association of any particular diagnostic or therapeutic procedure. In addition, inclusion or exclusion of a procedure does not imply any health insurance coverage or reimbursement policy.

CPT FORMAT AND CONVENTIONS

DESCRIPTIONS

The descriptions associated with CPT codes have been developed by the AMA to provide complete descriptions of medical services and procedures.

Many CPT descriptions include the definition of basic procedures followed by supplemental descriptions for variations or modifications of the basic procedure. In the CPT coding book, the basic procedure description ends with a semicolon (;), followed by the additional description.

If a CPT description includes the same basic procedure as the preceding listing, the basic procedure is not listed. Only the supplemental description is listed, preceded by an indentation. For example:

25100	Arthrotomy, wrist joint; with biopsy
25105	with synovectomy

SYMBOLS

● *A filled BLACK CIRCLE preceding a CPT code indicates that the code is new to this revision of the CPT coding system. A symbol key appears on all left-hand pages.*

▲ *A filled BLACK TRIANGLE preceding a CPT code indicates that there is a revision to the description. Wherever possible, the revised text is identified with underlining.*

( ) *CPT codes enclosed within parenthesis have been deleted from the CPT coding system and should no longer be used.*

+ *A bold plus sign preceding a CPT code indicates that the code is an "add-on" code and must be listed in addition to the main CPT code.*

⊘ *This symbol preceding a CPT code indicates that the code is exempt from the use of modifier -51.*

Note that a CPT code may be preceded by the add-on, star symbol or modifier-51 exempt symbol, in addition to new or changed code symbols.

COLOR CODING

 Separate procedure. A procedure or service that is normally performed as an integral component of a total service or procedure. CPT codes identified as separate procedure codes should not be coded in addition to the basic procedure code of which it is considered an integral component.

However, if the procedure or service that is usually designated as a separate procedure is performed independently or is considered to be unrelated or distinct from other procedures or services provided at that time, the separate procedure may be coded by itself. The modifier -59 should be added to the separate procedure code to indicate that the procedure is not considered to be a component of another procedure, but is a distinct, independent procedure.

 Unlisted code. Descriptions include the term "unlisted." Use only when a CPT code which specifically describes the service or procedure is unavailable. A report is usually required by third party payers.

 Nonspecific code. Descriptions include the term "specify" instructing the coder to include additional information such as the quadrant, the nerve, the muscle, the level of spine, the number of joints, the type of study, the method of dosimetry, the hormone, the receptor, the assay method, the type of kit, the material injected, the type of tests, the number of tests, the doses provided.

 CCI comprehensive code. Indicates codes identified as comprehensive codes in the Comprehensive Coding Initiative, revised annually. Per CMS rules, all identifiable component procedures are included in the comprehensive code and should not be billed separately to Medicare.

ITALICIZED AND NON-ITALICIZED TEXT

Italicized text is used throughout this publication to distinguish information authored, contributed or otherwise provided by PMIC.

Non-italicized text *is used to distinguish information reproduced verbatim from CPT 2018, published by the American Medical Association.*

SECTION OVERVIEWS

Specific guidelines are presented at the beginning of each of the six sections of the CPT coding system. The guidelines define items that are necessary to interpret and report the procedures and services contained in that section. CPT guidelines also provide explanations regarding terms that apply only to a particular section.

REQUESTS TO UPDATE THE CPT CODING SYSTEM

The American Medical Association (AMA) maintains a CPT Editorial Panel that reviews and approves requests for changes to the CPT coding system. Requests to add, delete or revise specific CPT codes should be addressed to:

CPT Editorial Research & Development
American Medical Association
515 North State Street
Chicago, Illinois 60610

CPT 2018 AVAILABLE IN ELECTRONIC FORMAT

CPT 2018 codes and descriptions with relative value information are available on CD-ROM or as a download. The data files are available in standard ASCII format and may be imported into your billing and health insurance claims software. CPT Plus! 2018 is also available as a PC resident e-book in PDF format. For more information call (800) 633-7467 or visit http://pmiconline.com.

This page intentionally left blank.

CODING & BILLING ISSUES

Most billing, coding and reporting issues involving the CPT® coding system apply generally to all medical specialties and professions. However, there are some specialty specific issues defined in each section of the CPT coding system that apply only to the specific medical specialty represented.

SUPPORTING DOCUMENTATION

Documentation in the patient's medical report must clearly support the procedures, services and supplies coded on the health insurance claim form. Most medical chart reviewers take the position that if something is not documented in the medical record, then the service or procedure was not performed and therefore is not subject to reimbursement.

If a medical practice is selected for an audit by Medicare or other third party payer, the accuracy and completeness of the documentation of the medical records, or lack thereof, will have a significant impact on the outcome of the audit. The current emphasis on "fraud" and "abuse" by Medicare, Medicaid and private third party payer necessitates a review of documentation by all health care professionals.

SPECIAL MEDICARE CONSIDERATIONS

To satisfy Medicare requirements, there must be sufficient documentation in the medical record to verify the services coded and the level of care required. Section 1833(e) of Title XVIII, Social Security Act requires "available information that documents a claim." If there is no documentation to justify the services or level of care, the claim cannot be considered for Medicare benefits.

If there is insufficient documentation to support claims that have already been paid by Medicare, the reimbursement will be considered an overpayment and a refund will be requested by Medicare. Medicare has the authority to review any information, including medical records, when such information pertains to a Medicare claim.

UNLISTED PROCEDURES OR SERVICES

There are services or procedures performed by health care professionals that are not found in the CPT coding system. These services or procedures may be either new procedures which have not yet been assigned a CPT code or simply a variation of a procedure which precludes using the existing CPT code. Each section of the CPT coding system includes codes for reporting these unlisted procedures.

Unlisted procedure codes should not be coded unless the coder has reviewed the CPT coding system carefully to ensure that a more specific code is not available. If a specific CPT code is not located, check for HCPCS codes that may be reportable.

As a rule, a report needs to be enclosed with the health insurance claim form when reporting unlisted procedure codes. Because unlisted procedure codes are subject to manual medical review, payment is usually slower than for normal processing time.

CPT ADDITIONS, CHANGES, AND DELETIONS

Each year hundreds of codes are added, changed or deleted from the CPT coding system. A summary of these changes is found in Appendix B of the CPT code book, which provides a quick reference for coding review. In addition to the summary, these modifications are identified throughout the CPT code book.

ADDITIONS TO THE CPT CODING SYSTEM

New codes are added to the CPT coding system each year. New CPT codes are identified with a small black circle placed to the left of the code number. Examples of new codes found in CPT 2018 include:

- ● **00813** Anesthesia for combined upper and lower gastrointestinal endoscopic procedures, endoscope introduced both prosimal to and distal to duodenum

- ● **74018** Radiologic examination, abdomen; 1 view

CHANGES TO CPT CODE DEFINITIONS

Each year the definitions of many CPT codes are revised. CPT codes with changed definitions are identified with a small black triangle placed to the left of the code number. Examples of CPT codes with changed definitions in CPT 2018 include:

▲ **36140**   Introduction of needle or intracatheter, upper or lower extremity artery

▲ **64550**   Application of surface (transcutaneous) neurostimulator (eg, TENS unit)

The only way to determine exactly what part of the definition has been changed is to compare the current changed definition with the definition from the previous edition of the CPT code book.

DELETIONS FROM THE CPT CODING SYSTEM

Each year some CPT codes are deleted. Deleted CPT codes, and references to replacement codes, if there are any, are enclosed within parentheses. Examples of CPT codes deleted from CPT 2018 include:

(**15732**   **deleted 2017 [2018 edition]. To report myocutaneous or fasciocutaneous flap, use 15733)**

(**71010**   **deleted 2017 [2018 edition]. To report, use 71045)**

NEW SECTIONS AND SUBSECTIONS

New sections and subsections are frequently added to the CPT coding system to reflect changes in technology or medical practice and to provide additional code sequences for special purposes.

Cognitive Assessment and Care Plan Services	99483
Psychiatric Collaborative Care Management Services	99492-99494
General Behavioral Health Integration Care Management	99484
Endovascular Repair of Abdominal Aorta and/or Iliac Arteries	34701-34834
Proprietary Laboratory Analyses	0001U-0017U
Home and Outpatient INR Monitoring Services	93792-93793
Orthotic Management and Training and Prosthetic Training	97760-97763

CATEGORY II PERFORMANCE MEASUREMENT CODES

Category II, Performance Measurement CPT codes, are designed to facilitate outcomes research. This new section was introduced in the 2005 CPT updates. Category II codes include the letter "F" as the fifth digit of the five digit CPT code. These codes are optional, and are not a substitute for Category I codes.

CATEGORY III EMERGING TECHNOLOGY CODES

Temporary codes for emerging technology, services and procedures designed to permit data collection and assessment of new technologies. All Category III codes include the letter "T" as the fifth digit of the five digit CPT code. The inclusion of a specific service or procedure in this section does not imply or endorse clinical efficacy, safety, or applicability to clinical practice.

STARRED PROCEDURES

The star symbol ★ is used to identify codes that may be used to report synchronous (real-time) telemedicine services when appended by modifier 59. Procedures on this list involve electronic communication using interactive telecommunications equipment that includes, at a minimum, audio and video.

90791	90838	90954	92228	93298	96153	98962	99213	99242	99254	99355	0188T
90792	90845	90955	93228	93299	96154	99201	99214	99243	99255	99406	0189T
90832	90846	90957	93229	96040	97802	99202	99215	99244	99307	99407	
90833	90847	90958	93268	96116	97803	99203	99231	99245	99308	99408	
90834	90863	90960	93270	96150	97804	99204	99232	99251	99309	99409	
90836	90951	90961	93271	96151	98960	99205	99233	99252	99310	99495	
90837	90952	92227	93272	96152	98961	99212	99241	99253	99354	99496	

INSTRUCTIONAL NOTES

Notes found in the CPT coding system give instructions for using codes. When selecting a code, look for instructions in the section guidelines for any additional information necessary to code accurately. Also, instructional notes take the form of parenthetical statements and paragraphs, which may appear at the beginning of subsections, headings and subheadings, or above and below the code itself.

DEFINITION OF NEW AND ESTABLISHED PATIENT

Solely to distinguish between new and established patients, professional services are those face-to-face services rendered by physicians and other qualified health care professionals and coded by a specific CPT code(s). A new patient is one who has not received any professional services from the physician/qualified health care professional or another physician/qualified health care professional of the same specialty who belongs to the same group practice, within the past three years. An established patient is one who has received professional services from the physician/qualified health care professional or another physician/qualified health care professional of the same specialty who belongs to the same group practice, within the past three years.

In the instance where a physician/qualified health care professional is on call for or covering for another physician/qualified health care professional, the patient's encounter will be classified as it would have been by the physician/qualified health care professional who is not available.

No distinction is made between new and established patients in the emergency department. Evaluation and Management services in the emergency department category may be coded for any new or established patient who presents for treatment in the emergency department.

PLACE (LOCATION) OF SERVICE

CPT makes specific distinctions for place (location) of service for evaluation and management codes. Place of service may have considerable impact on reimbursement. This list gives CPT code ranges for some specific places of service:

Office or Other Outpatient Services	99201-99215
Hospital Observation Services	99217-99226
Hospital Inpatient Services	99221-99239
Emergency Department	99281-99288
Nursing Facility Services	99304-99318
Domiciliary, Rest Home, or Custodial Care Services	99324-99337
Domiciliary, Rest Home, or Home Care Plan Oversight Services	99339-99340
Home Services	99341-99350
Inpatient Neonatal and Pediatric Critical Care	99466-99480

PLACE OF SERVICE CODES FOR PROFESSIONAL CLAIMS

Listed below are place of service codes and descriptions. These codes should be used on professional claims to specify the entity where service(s) were rendered. Check with individual payers (e.g., Medicare, Medicaid, other private insurance) for reimbursement policies regarding these codes.

Code	*Place Name*	*Place Description*
01	*Pharmacy*	*A facility or location where drugs and other medically related items and services are sold, dispensed, or otherwise provided directly to patients. (Effective 10/1/03)*
02	*Telehealth*	*The location where health services and health related services are provided or received, through a telecommunicatins system. (Effective 1/1/17)*
03	*School*	*A facility whose primary purpose is education.*
04	*Homeless Shelter*	*A facility or location whose primary purpose is to provide temporary housing to homeless individuals (e.g., emergency shelters, individual or family shelters).*

Code	Place Name	Place Description
05	Indian Health Service Free-standing Facility	A facility or location, owned and operated by the Indian Health Service, which provides diagnostic, therapeutic (surgical and non-surgical), and rehabilitation services to American Indians and Alaska Natives who do not require hospitalization.
06	Indian Health Service Provider-based Facility	A facility or location, owned and operated by the Indian Health Service, which provides diagnostic, therapeutic (surgical and non-surgical), and rehabilitation services rendered by, or under the supervision of, physicians to American Indians and Alaska Natives admitted as inpatients or outpatients.
07	Tribal 638 Free-Standing Facility	A facility or location owned and operated by a federally recognized American Indian or Alaska Native tribe or tribal organization under a 638 agreement, which provides diagnostic, therapeutic (surgical and non-surgical), and rehabilitation services to tribal members who do not require hospitalization.
08	Tribal 638 Provider-based Facility	A facility or location owned and operated by a federally recognized American Indian or Alaska Native tribe or tribal organization under a 638 agreement, which provides diagnostic, therapeutic (surgical and non-surgical), and rehabilitation services to tribal members admitted as inpatients or outpatients
09	Prison-Correctional Facility	A prison, jail, reformatory, work farm, detention center, or any other similar facility maintained by either Federal, State or local authorities for the purpose of confinement or rehabilitation of adult or juvenile criminal offenders. (Effective 7/1/06)
10	Unassigned	N/A
11	Office	Location, other than a hospital, skilled nursing facility (SNF), military treatment facility, community health center, State or local public health clinic, or intermediate care facility (ICF), where the health professional routinely provides health examinations, diagnosis, and treatment of illness or injury on an ambulatory basis.
12	Home	Location, other than a hospital or other facility, where the patient receives care in a private residence.
13	Assisted Living Facility	Congregate residential facility with self-contained living units providing assessment of each resident's needs and on-site support 24 hours a day, 7 days a week, with the capacity to deliver or arrange for services including some health care and other services. (Effective 10/1/03)
14	Group Home*	A residence, with shared living areas, where clients receive supervision and other services such as social and/or behavioral services, custodial service, and minimal services (e.g., medication administration). (Effective 10/1/03)
15	Mobile Unit	A facility/unit that moves from place-to-place equipped to provide preventive, screening, diagnostic, and/or treatment services.
16	Temporary lodging	A short-term accomodation such as a hotel, campground, hostel, cruise ship, or resort where the patient receives care, and which is not identified by any other POS code. (Effective 1/1/08)
17	Walk-in retail health clinic	A walk-in retail health clinic, other than an office, urgent care facility, pharmacy, or independent clinic, which is not described by any other POS code, that is located within a retail operation and provides on an ambulatory basis, preventive and primary care services. (Effective 5/1/10)
18	Place of Employment-Worksite	A location, not described by any other POS code, owned or operated by a public or private entity where the patient is employed, and where a health professional provides on-going or episodic occupational medical, therapeutic or rehabilitative services to the individual. (This code is available for use effective January 1, 2013, but not later than May 1, 2013)
19	Off Campus Outpatient Hospital	A portion of an off-campus hospital provider based department which provides diagnostic, therapeutic (both surgical and nonsurgical), and rehabilitation services to sick or injured persons who do not require hospitalization or institutionalization. (Effective 1/1/2016)

Code	Place Name	Place Description
20	Urgent Care Facility	Location, distinct from a hospital emergency room, an office, or a clinic, whose purpose is to diagnose and treat illness or injury for unscheduled, ambulatory patients seeking immediate medical attention. (Effective 1/1/03)
21	Inpatient Hospital	A facility, other than psychiatric, which primarily provides diagnostic, therapeutic (both surgical and non-surgical), and rehabilitation services by, or under, the supervision of physicians to patients admitted for a variety of medical conditions.
22	On Campus— Outpatient Hospital	A portion of a hospital's main campus which provides diagnostic, therapeutic (both surgical and non-surgical), and rehabilitation services to sick or injured persons who do not require hospitalization or institutionalization. (Description change effective 1/1/16)
23	Emergency Room – Hospital	A portion of a hospital where emergency diagnosis and treatment of illness or injury is provided.
24	Ambulatory Surgical Center	A freestanding facility, other than a physician's office, where surgical and diagnostic services are provided on an ambulatory basis.
25	Birthing Center	A facility, other than a hospital's maternity facilities or a physician's office, which provides a setting for labor, delivery, and immediate post-partum care as well as immediate care of new born infants.
26	Military Treatment Facility	A medical facility operated by one or more of the Uniformed Services. Military Treatment Facility (MTF) also refers to certain former U.S. Public Health Service (USPHS) facilities now designated as Uniformed Service Treatment Facilities (USTF).
27-30	Unassigned	N/A
31	Skilled Nursing Facility	A facility which primarily provides inpatient skilled nursing care and related services to patients who require medical, nursing, or rehabilitative services but does not provide the level of care or treatment available in a hospital.
32	Nursing Facility	A facility which primarily provides to residents skilled nursing care and related services for the rehabilitation of injured, disabled, or sick persons, or, on a regular basis, health-related care services above the level of custodial care to other than mentally retarded individuals.
33	Custodial Care Facility	A facility which provides room, board and other personal assistance services, generally on a long-term basis, and which does not include a medical component.
34	Hospice	A facility, other than a patient's home, in which palliative and supportive care for terminally ill patients and their families are provided.
35-40	Unassigned	N/A
41	Ambulance - Land	A land vehicle specifically designed, equipped and staffed for lifesaving and transporting the sick or injured.
42	Ambulance – Air or Water	An air or water vehicle specifically designed, equipped and staffed for lifesaving and transporting the sick or injured.
43-48	Unassigned	N/A
49	Independent Clinic	A location, not part of a hospital and not described by any other Place of Service code, that is organized and operated to provide preventive, diagnostic, therapeutic, rehabilitative, or palliative services to outpatients only. (effective 10/1/03)
50	Federally Qualified Health Center	A facility located in a medically underserved area that provides Medicare beneficiaries preventive primary medical care under the general direction of a physician.
51	Inpatient Psychiatric Facility	A facility that provides inpatient psychiatric services for the diagnosis and treatment of mental illness on a 24-hour basis, by or under the supervision of a physician.

Code	*Place Name*	*Place Description*
52	Psychiatric Facility-Partial Hospitalization	A facility for the diagnosis and treatment of mental illness that provides a planned therapeutic program for patients who do not require full time hospitalization, but who need broader programs than are possible from outpatient visits to a hospital-based or hospital-affiliated facility.
53	Community Mental Health Center	A facility that provides the following services: outpatient services, including specialized outpatient services for children, the elderly, individuals who are chronically ill, and residents of the CMHC's community mental health area who have been discharged from inpatient treatment at a mental health facility; 24-hour a day emergency care services; day treatment, other partial hospitalization services, or psychosocial rehabilitation services; screening for patients being considered for admission to State mental health facilities to determine the appropriateness of such admission; and consultation and education services.
54	Intermediate Care Facility/Mentally Retarded	A facility which primarily provides health-related care and services above the level of custodial care to mentally retarded individuals but does not provide the level of care or treatment available in a hospital or SNF.
55	Residential Substance Abuse Treatment Facility	A facility which provides treatment for substance (alcohol and drug) abuse to live-in residents who do not require acute medical care. Services include individual and group therapy and counseling, family counseling, laboratory tests, drugs and supplies, psychological testing, and room and board.
56	Psychiatric Resident Treatment Center	A facility or distinct part of a facility for psychiatric care which provides a total 24-hour therapeutically planned and professionally staffed group living and learning environment.
57	Non-residential Substance Abuse Treatment Facility	A location which provides treatment for substance (alcohol and drug) abuse on an ambulatory basis. Services include individual and group therapy and counseling, family counseling, laboratory tests, drugs and supplies, and psychological testing.
58-59	Unassigned	N/A
60	Mass Immunization Center	A location where providers administer pneumococcal pneumonia and influenza virus vaccinations and submit these services as electronic media claims, paper claims, or using the roster billing method. This generally takes place in a mass immunization setting, such as, a public health center, pharmacy, or mall but may include a physician office setting.
61	Comprehensive Inpatient Rehabilitation Facility	A facility that provides comprehensive rehabilitation services under the supervision of a physician to inpatients with physical disabilities. Services include physical therapy, occupational therapy, speech pathology, social or psychological services, and orthotics and prosthetics services.
62	Comprehensive Outpatient Rehabilitation Facility	A facility that provides comprehensive rehabilitation services under the supervision of a physician to outpatients with physical disabilities. Services include physical therapy, occupational therapy, and speech pathology services.
63-64	Unassigned	N/A
65	ESRD Treatment Facility	A facility other than a hospital, which provides dialysis treatment, maintenance, and/or training to patients or caregivers on an ambulatory or home-care basis.
66-70	Unassigned	N/A
71	Public Health Clinic	A facility maintained by either State or local health departments that provide ambulatory primary medical care under the general direction of a physician. (effective 10/1/03)
72	Rural Health Clinic	A certified facility which is located in a rural medically underserved area that provides ambulatory primary medical care under the general direction of a physician.

Code	Place Name	Place Description
73-80	Unassigned	N/A
81	Independent Laboratory	A laboratory certified to perform diagnostic and/or clinical tests independent of an institution or a physician's office.
82-98	Unassigned	N/A
99	Other Place/Service	Other place of service not identified above.

HOSPITAL CARE

Hospital services frequently cause reimbursement problems for health care professionals. The three most common coding errors are:

- *More than one physician submits an initial hospital care code for the same patient.*
- *Follow-up hospital visits are coded incorrectly.*
- *Concurrent care visits by multiple specialists are coded improperly.*

If more than one physician is involved in the process of hospitalizing a patient, for example, surgeon and internist, the physicians must decide which is going to actually admit the patient and report the admission services on the health insurance claim form. If both do, the first health insurance claim form to arrive will be processed and paid, and the second will be rejected.

There are valid reasons for visiting a patient more than once daily while hospitalized, however, many physicians and even some insurance billers do not know that subsequent hospital visit codes are for "daily" services. When a physician visits the patient twice in one day, providing a brief level of service each time, the physician or insurance biller may incorrectly report two hospital visit services for the same day, instead of a higher level code incorporating both visits.

Reporting multiple hospital visits provided on the same day separately on the health insurance claim form usually results in either the entire claim being returned for clarification, or the second visit being denied as an apparent duplication. Unfortunately, insurance billers who are unclear on the proper coding of same day hospital visits may simply accept the rejection without question and write-off the unpaid visit as uncollectible.

The CPT coding system clearly defines subsequent hospital care as "per day", meaning daily services. If the physician visits the patient twice in one day, providing the equivalent of "brief" services each time, report the service using the appropriate evaluation and management code that defines the cumulative level of service provided.

HOSPITAL DISCHARGE

The CPT codes for hospital discharge services are evaluation and management code 99238 and 99239, defined as Hospital Discharge Day Management. Hospital discharge services include final examination of the patient, discussion of the hospital stay, instructions for continuing care, and preparation of discharge records. Many health insurance companies do not recognize and/or do not reimburse this CPT code.

Options for the use of these codes include the use of one of the other hospital daily services codes from the evaluation and management series 99231-99233 and perhaps using a code that has a higher value than the routine hospital visit.

REFERRAL

A referral is the transfer of the total care or specific portion of care of a patient from one physician to another. A referral is not a request for consultation. If a patient is referred to the physician for total care or a portion of their care, use evaluation and management visit codes, and other CPT codes if appropriate, to report the services provided. If a patient is sent to the physician for a consultation, use evaluation and management consultation codes to report the services provided.

SEPARATE OR MULTIPLE PROCEDURES

It is appropriate to designate multiple procedures that are rendered on the same date by separate entries. For example: if a proctosigmoidoscopy was performed in addition to a hospital visit, the proctosigmoidoscopy would be considered a SEPARATE procedure and listed in addition to the hospital visit on the health insurance claim form. Another example would be individual medical psychotherapy rendered in addition to a brief subsequent hospital service. In this instance, both services would be coded.

SUPPLIES AND MATERIALS SUPPLIED BY THE PHYSICIAN

The CPT coding system includes specific codes for identifying certain supplies and materials provided by the physician. These supply codes are used to report supplies and materials that are not included in the definition of the basic service.

CPT CODES FOR SUPPLIES AND MATERIALS

92310-92371   Supply of spectacles, contact lenses, low vision aids and ocular prosthesis.

95144-95170   Provision of antigens for allergen immunotherapy.

99070   Supplies and materials (except spectacles) provided by the physician.

99071   Educational supplies, such as books, tapes, and pamphlets, provided by the physician for the patient's education at cost to physician.

PURCHASED DIAGNOSTIC SERVICES

It is common for physicians to bill patients and health insurance companies for diagnostic services that were procured or ordered on behalf of the patient but not actually provided by the ordering physician. It is also common for the ordering physician to "mark-up" the fee for the purchased service prior to billing. This is referred to as <u>global billing</u>.

Medical equipment companies, particularly those offering electrocardiography, pulmonary diagnostic equipment, and other diagnostic equipment, have used this global billing concept in the past as a method of selling physicians a new "profit center" for their practice. Some even provided technicians, who were not employees of the practice, to perform the diagnostic tests in the physicians office. OBRA 1987 placed severe restrictions on global billing of certain diagnostic tests as of March 1, 1988.

The Medicare regulations apply to diagnostic tests other than clinical laboratory tests including, but not limited to: EKGs, EEGs, cardiac monitoring, X-rays and ultrasound. Global billing is allowed only when the billing physician personally performs or supervises the diagnostic procedure. To qualify under the supervision definition, the person performing the test must be an employee or the physician or group. Ownership interest in an outside supplier does not meet the supervision requirement.

Billing for purchased services under the new requirement is complicated. The provider must provide the supplier's name, address, provider number and net charge on the health insurance claim form. In addition, a HCPCS Level III modifier must be coded to indicate that the service was purchased. Billing for global services usually will also require a HCPCS Level III modifier to indicate that the service was not purchased. This requirement does not apply to the professional component of these services if provided separately.

Providers should discontinue billing for the technical component of diagnostic services that were not provided or supervised by the provider as defined in this regulation for the following reasons:

1.   *The provider is no longer making any profit on these procedures;*

2.   *Operating costs are higher due to the increased reporting requirements; and*

3.   *Risk of audit liability is increased if these services are not coded properly.*

UNBUNDLING

Unbundling is defined as reporting multiple CPT codes when one CPT code is sufficient. For example, it is considered unbundling if incidental surgical procedures are coded separately, or office visits for uncomplicated follow-up care are separately coded. This practice often happens unintentionally. However, most third-party payers currently have software in place to catch unbundling when it occurs. When physicians continually break out or itemize services in this manner, they often find themselves under close scrutiny and even the focus of an audit by the insurance company. It is most important to know the guidelines to prevent unbundling when coding and billing for services and/or procedures.

MODERATE (CONSCIOUS) SEDATION

Moderate (also known as conscious) sedation is a drug-induced depression of consciousness during which patients respond purposefully to verbal commands, either alone or with light tactile stimulation. No interventions are required to maintain cardiovascular function or a patent airway, and spontaneous ventilation is adequate. For purposes of reporting, intraservice time of moderate sedation is used to select the appropriate moderate sedation codes 99151, 99152, 99153, 99155, 99156, and/or 99157. Moderate sedation is administered in hospitals, outpatient facilities, for example ambulatory surgery centers, and doctors offices to facilitate procedures such as the following:

- *Breast biopsy*

- *Vasectomy*

- *Minor foot surgery*

- *Minor bone fracture repair*

- *Plastic/reconstructive surgery*

- *Dental prosthetic/reconstructive surgery*

- *Endoscopy*

Procedures That Include Moderate (Conscious) Sedation

The summary of CPT codes that include moderate (conscious) sedation has been removed from CPT. The codes that were previously included here have been revised with the removal of the moderate (conscious) sedation symbol. For information/guidance on reporting moderate (conscious) sedation services with codes formerly listed here, please refer to the guidelines for codes 99151, 99152, 99153, 99155, 99156, 99157.

This page intentionally left blank

2018 ADDITIONS, DELETIONS & REVISIONS

Following is a complete list of all additions, deletions and revisions to the CPT coding system. Indicators to the left of each code define the status of the CPT code as follows:

● Indicates CPT codes that are new to CPT 2018.

▲ Indicates CPT codes that have been revised in CPT 2018.

( ) Indicates CPT codes that have been deleted from CPT 2018.

Evaluation and Management

▲ 99420   Observation care discharge day management (This code is to be utilized to report all services provided to a patient on discharge from outpatient hospital "observation status" if the discharge is on other than the initial date of "observation status." To report services to a patient designated as "observation status" or "inpatient status" and discharged on the same date, use the codes for Observation or Inpatient Care Services [including Admission and Discharge Services, 99234-99236 as appropriate.])

▲ 99218   Initial observation care, per day, for the evaluation and management of a patient which requires 3 key components:

    ● A detailed or comprehensive history;
    ● A detailed or comprehensive examination; and
    ● Medical decision making that is straightforward or of low complexity.

Counseling and/or coordination of care with other physicians, other qualified health care professionals, or agencies are provided consistent with the nature of the problem(s) and the patient's and/or family's needs.

Usually the problem(s) requiring admission to outpatient hospital "observation status" are of low severity. Typically, 30 minutes are spent at the bedside and on the patient's hospital floor or unit.

▲ 99219   Initial observation care, per day, for the evaluation and management of a patient, which requires these 3 key components:

    ● A comprehensive history;
    ● A comprehensive examination; and
    ● Medical decision making of moderate complexity.

Counseling and/or coordination of care with other physicians, other qualified health care professionals, or agencies are provided consistent with the nature of the problem(s) and the patient's and/or family's needs.

Usually the problem(s) requiring admission to outpatient hospital "observation status" are of moderate severity. Typically, 50 minutes are spent at the bedside and on the patient's hospital floor or unit.

▲ 99220   Initial observation care, per day, for the evaluation and management of a patient, which requires these 3 key components:

    ● A comprehensive history;
    ● A comprehensive examination; and
    ● Medical decision making of high complexity.

Counseling and/or coordination of care with other physicians, other qualified health care professionals, or agencies are provided consistent with the nature of the problem(s) and the patient's and/or family's needs.

Usually the problem(s) requiring admission to outpatient hospital "observation status" are of high severity. Typically, 70 minutes are spent at the bedside and on the patient's hospital floor or unit.

(99363   Deleted 2017 [2018 edition]. To report, see 93792, 93793..

(99364   Deleted 2017 [2018 edition]. To report, see 93792, 93793.)

● 99483   Assessment of and care planning for a patient with cognitive impairment, requiring an independent historian, in the office or other outpatient, home or domiciliary or rest home, with all of the following required elements:
    ● Cognition-focused evaluation including a pertinent history and examination;
    ● Medical decision making of moderate or high complexity
    ● Functional assessment (eg, basic and instrumental activities of daily living), including decision-making capacity;
    ● Use of standardized instruments for staging of dementia (eg, functional assessment staging test [FAST], clinical dementia rating [CDR]);
    ● Medication reconciliation and review for high-risk medications;
    ● Evaluation for neuropsychiatric and behavioral symptoms, including depression, including use of standardized screening instrument(s);
    ● Evaluation of safety (eg, home), including motor vehicle operation;
    ● Identification of caregiver(s), caregiver knowledge, caregiver needs, social supports, and the willingness of caregiver to take

on caregiving tasks;
- Development, updating or revision, or review of an Advance Care Plan;
- Creation of a written care plan, including initial plans to address any neuropsychiatric symptoms, neurocognitive symptoms, functional limitations, and referral to community resources as needed (eg, rehabilitation services, adult day programs, support groups) shared with the patient and/or caregiver with initial education and support.

Typically, 50 minutes are spent face-to-face with the patient and/or family or caregiver..

- 99492   Initial psychiatric collaborative care management, first 70 minutes in the first calendar month of behavioral health care manager activities, in consultation with a psychiatric consultant, and directed by the treating physician or other qualified health care professional, with the following required elements:
  - outreach to and engagement in treatment of a patient directed by the treating physician or other qualified health care professional;
  - initial assessment of the patient, including administration of validated rating scales, with the development of an individualized treatment plan;
  - review by the psychiatric consultant with modifications of the plan if recommended;
  - entering patient in a registry and tracking patient follow-up and progress using the registry, with appropriate documentation, and participation in weekly caseload consultation with the psychiatric consultant; and
  - provision of brief interventions using evidence-based techniques such as behavioral activation, motivational interviewing, and other focused treatment strategies

- 99493   Subsequent psychiatric collaborative care management, first 60 minutes in a subsequent month of behavioral health care manager activities, in consultation with a psychiatric consultant, and directed by the treating physician or other qualified health care professional, with the following required elements:
  - tracking patient follow-up and progress using the registry, with appropriate documentation;
  - participation in weekly caseload consultation with the psychiatric consultant;
  - ongoing collaboration with and coordination of the patient's mental health care with the treating physician or other qualified health care professional and any other treating mental health providers;
  - additional review of progress and recommendations for changes in treatment, as indicated, including medications, based on recommendations provided by the psychiatric consultant;
  - provision of brief interventions using evidence-based techniques such as behavioral activation, motivational interviewing, and other focused treatment strategies;
  - monitoring of patient outcomes using validated rating scales; and
  - relapse prevention planning with patients as they achieve remission of symptoms and/or other treatment goals and are prepared for discharge from active treatment.

- 99494   Initial or subsequent psychiatric collaborative care management, each additional 30 minutes in a calendar month of behavioral health care manager activities, in consultation with a psychiatric consultant, and directed by the treating physician or other qualified health care professional (List separately in addition to code for primary procedure)

- 99484   Care management services for behavioral health conditions, at least 20 minutes of clinical staff time, directed by a physician or other qualified health care professional, per calendar month, with the following required elements:
  - initial assessment or follow-up monitoring, including the use of applicable validated rating scales
  - behavioral health care planning in relation to behavioral/psychiatric health problems, including revision for patients who are not progressing or whose status changes;
  - facilitating and coordinating treatment such as psychotherapy, pharmacotherapy, counseling and/or psychiatric consultation; and
  - continuity of care with a designated member of the care team.

Anesthesia

- 00731   Anesthesia for upper gastrointestinal endoscopic procedures, endoscope introduced proximal to duodenum; not otherwise specified

- 00732   Anesthesia for upper gastrointestinal endoscopic procedures, endoscope introduced proximal to duodenum; endoscopic retrograde cholangiopancreatography (ERCP)

  (00740   Deleted 2017 [2018 edition]. To report, see 00731, 00732.)

  (00810   Deleted 2017 [2018 edition]. To report, see 00811, 00812, 00813.)

- 00811   Anesthesia for lower intestinal endoscopic procedures, endoscope introduced distal to duodenum; not otherwise specified

- 00812   screening colonoscopy

- 00813   Anesthesia for combined upper and lower gastrointestinal endoscopic procedures, endoscope introduced both proximal to and distal to the duodenum

  (01180   Deleted 2017 [2018 edition])

  (01190   Deleted 2017 [2018 edition])

  (01682   Deleted 2017 [2018 edition])

Surgery

- 15730   Midface flap (ie, zygomaticofacial flap) with preservation of vascular pedicle(s).

  (15732   Deleted 2017 [2018 edition]. To report myocutaneous or fasciocutaneous flap, use 15733)

● 15733   Muscle, myocutaneous, or fasciocutaneous flap; head and neck with named vascular pedicle (ie, buccinators, genioglossus, temporalis, masseter, sternocleidomastoid, levator scapulae).

▲ 17250   Chemical cauterization of granulation tissue (ie, proud flesh)

● 19294   Preparation of tumor cavity, with placement of a radiation therapy applicator for intraoperative radiation therapy (IORT) concurrent with partial mastectomy (List separately in addition to code for primary procedure).

● 20939   Bone marrow aspiration for bone grafting, spine surgery only, through separate skin or fascial incision (List separately in addition to code for primary procedure).

(29582   Deleted 2017 [2018 edition])

(29583   Deleted 2017 [2018 edition])

● 31241   with ligation of sphenopalatine artery.

▲ 31254   Nasal/sinus endoscopy, surgical with ethmoidectomy; partial (anterior)

▲ 31255   Nasal/sinus endoscopy, surgical with ethmoidectomy; total (anterior and posterior

● 31253   total (anterior and posterior), including frontal sinus exploration, with removal of tissue from frontal sinus, when performed

● 31257   total (anterior and posterior), including sphenoidotomy.

● 31259   total (anterior and posterior), including sphenoidotomy, with removal of tissue from the sphenoid sinus.

▲ 31276   Nasal/sinus endoscopy, surgical, with frontal sinus exploration, including removal of tissue from frontal sinus, when performed

● 31298   with dilation of frontal and sphenoid sinus ostia (eg, balloon dilation).

(31320   Deleted 2017 [2018 edition])

▲ 31645   with therapeutic aspiration of tracheobronchial tree, initial

▲ 31646   with therapeutic aspiration of tracheobronchial tree, subsequent, same hospital stay

▲ 32998   Ablation therapy for reduction or eradication of 1 or more pulmonary tumor(s) including pleura or chest wall when involved by tumor extension, percutaneous, including imaging guidance when performed, unilateral; radiofrequency

● 32994   Cryoablation

● 33927   Implantation of a total replacement heart system (artificial heart) with recipient cardiectomy.

● 33928   Removal and replacement of total replacement heart system (artificial heart).

● 33929   Removal of a total replacement heart system (artificial heart) for heart transplantation (List separately in addition to code for primary procedure).

● 34701   Endovascular repair of infrarenal aorta by deployment of an aorto-aortic tube endograft including pre-procedure sizing and device selection, all nonselective catheterization(s), all associated radiological supervision and interpretation, all endograft extension(s) placed in the aorta from the level of the renal arteries to the aortic bifurcation, and all angioplasty/stenting performed from the level of the renal arteries to the aortic bifurcation; for other than rupture (eg, for aneurysm, pseudoaneurysm, dissection, penetrating ulcer).

● 34702   for rupture including temporary aortic and/or iliac balloon occlusion, when performed (eg, for aneurysm, pseudoaneurysm, dissection, penetrating ulcer, traumatic disruption)

● 34703   Endovascular repair of infrarenal aorta and/or iliac artery(ies) by deployment of an aorto-uni-iliac endograft including pre-procedure sizing and device selection, all nonselective catheterization(s), all associated radiological supervision and interpretation, all endograft extension(s) placed in the aorta from the level of the renal arteries to the iliac bifurcation, and all angioplasty/stenting performed from the level of the renal arteries to the iliac bifurcation; for other than rupture (eg, for aneurysm, pseudoaneurysm, dissection, penetrating ulcer).

● 34704   for rupture including temporary aortic and/or iliac balloon occlusion, when performed (eg, for aneurysm, pseudoaneurysm, dissection, penetrating ulcer, traumatic disruption)

● 34705   Endovascular repair of infrarenal aorta and/or iliac artery(ies) by deployment of an aorto-bi-iliac endograft including pre-procedure sizing and device selection, all nonselective catheterization(s), all associated radiological supervision and interpretation, all endograft extension(s) placed in the aorta from the level of the renal arteries to the iliac bifurcation, and all angioplasty/stenting performed from the level of the renal arteries to the iliac bifurcation; for other than rupture (eg, for aneurysm, pseudoaneurysm, dissection, penetrating ulcer)

● 34706   for rupture including temporary aortic and/or iliac balloon occlusion, when performed (eg, for aneurysm, pseudoaneurysm dissection, penetrating ulcer, traumatic disruption)

● 34707   Endovascular repair of iliac artery by deployment of an ilio-iliac tube endograft including pre-procedure sizing and device selection, all nonselective catheterization(s), all associated radiological supervision and interpretation, and all endograft extension(s) proximally to the aortic bifurcation and distally to the iliac bifurcation, and treatment zone angioplasty/stenting, when performed, unilateral; for other than rupture (eg, for aneurysm, pseudoaneurysm, dissection, arteriovenous malformation)

● 34708   for rupture including temporary aortic and/or iliac balloon occlusion, when performed (eg, for aneurysm, pseudoaneurysm, dissection, arteriovenous malformation, traumatic disruption)

● 34709   Placement of extension prosthesis(es) distal to the common iliac artery(ies) or proximal to the renal artery(ies) for endovascular repair of infrarenal abdominal aortic or iliac aneurysm, false aneurysm, dissection, penetrating ulcer, including pre-procedure sizing and device selection, all nonselective catheterization(s), all associated radiological supervision and interpretation, and treatment zone angioplasty/stenting, when performed, per vessel treated (List separately in addition to code for primary procedure)

● 34710   Delayed placement of distal or proximal extension prosthesis for endovascular repair of infrarenal abdominal aortic or iliac aneurysm, false aneurysm, dissection, endoleak, or endograft migration, including pre-procedure sizing and device selection, all nonselective catheterization(s), all associated radiological supervision and interpretation, and treatment zone angioplasty/stenting, when performed; initial vessel treated

● 34711   each additional vessel treated (List separately in addition to code for primary procedure)

● 34712   Transcatheter delivery of enhanced fixation device(s) to the endograft (eg, anchor, screw, tack) and all associated radiological supervision and interpretation

● 34713   Percutaneous access and closure of femoral artery for delivery of endograft through a large sheath (12 French or larger), including ultrasound guidance, when performed, unilateral (List separately in addition to code for primary procedure)

▲ 34812   Open femoral artery exposure for delivery of endovascular prosthesis, by groin incision, unilateral (List separately in addition to code for primary procedure)

● 34714   Open femoral artery exposure with creation of conduit for delivery of endovascular prosthesis or for establishment of cardiopulmonary bypass, by groin incision, unilateral (List separately in addition to code for primary procedure)

▲ 34820   Open iliac artery exposure for delivery of endovascular prosthesis or iliac occlusion during endovascular therapy, by abdominal or retroperitoneal incision, unilateral (List separately in addition to code for primary procedure)

▲ 34833   Open iliac artery exposure with creation of conduit for delivery of endovascular prosthesis or for establishment of cardiopulmonary bypass, by abdominal or retroperitoneal incision, unilateral (List separately in addition to code for primary procedure)

▲ 34834   Open brachial artery exposure for delivery of endovascular prosthesis, unilateral (List separately in addition to code for primary procedure)

● 34715   Open axillary/subclavian artery exposure for delivery of endovascular prosthesis by infraclavicular or supraclavicular incision, unilateral (List separately in addition to code for primary procedure)

● 34716   Open axillary/subclavian artery exposure with creation of conduit for delivery of endovascular prosthesis or for establishment of cardiopulmonary bypass, by infraclavicular or supraclavicular incision, unilateral (List separately in addition to code for primary procedure)

(34800   Deleted 2017 [2018 edition] To report, see 34701, 34702, 34703, 34704, 34705, 34706, 34707, 34708)

(34802   Deleted 2017 [2018 edition] To report, see 34701, 34702, 34703, 34704, 34705, 34706, 34707, 34708)

(34803   Deleted 2017 [2018 edition] To report, see 34701, 34702, 34703, 34704, 34705, 34706, 34707, 34708)

(34804   Deleted 2017 [2018 edition] To report, see 34701, 34702, 34703, 34704, 34705, 34706, 34707, 34708)

(34805   Deleted 2017 [2018 edition] To report, see 34701, 34702, 34703, 34704, 34705, 34706, 34707, 34708)

(34806   Deleted 2017 [2018 edition] To report, see 34701, 34702, 34703, 34704, 34705, 34706, 34707, 34708)

(34825   Deleted 2017 [2018 edition] To report, see 34709, 34710, 34711)

(34826   Deleted 2017 [2018 edition] To report, see 34709, 34710, 34711)

(34900   Deleted 2017 [2018 edition] To report, see 34707, 34708)

(36120   Deleted 2017 [2018 edition])

▲ 36140   Introduction of needle or intracatheter, upper or lower extremity artery

▲ 36468   Injection(s) of sclerosant for spider veins (telangiectasia), limb or trunk

▲ 36470   Injection of sclerosant; single incompetent vein (other than telangiectasia)

▲ 36471   multiple incompetent veins (other than telangiectasia), same leg

● 36465   Injection of non-compounded foam sclerosant with ultrasound compression maneuvers to guide dispersion of the injectate, inclusive of all imaging guidance and monitoring; single incompetent extremity truncal vein (eg, great saphenous vein, accessory saphenous vein)

● 36466   multiple incompetent truncal veins (eg, great saphenous vein, accessory saphenous vein), same leg

● 36482   Endovenous ablation therapy of incompetent vein, extremity, by transcatheter delivery of a chemical adhesive (eg, cyanoacrylate) remote from the access site, inclusive of all imaging guidance and monitoring, percutaneous; first vein treated

● 36483   subsequent vein(s) treated in a single extremity, each through separate access sites (List separately in addition to code for primary procedure)

(36515   Deleted 2017 [2018 edition]. For therapeutic aphaeresis with extracorporeal immunoadsorption and plasma rein fusion, use 36516)

▲ 36516   with extracorporeal immunoadsorption, selective adsorption or selective filtration and plasma reinfusion

▲ 36908   Transcatheter placement of intravascular stent(s), central dialysis segment, performed through dialysis circuit, including all imaging and radiological supervision and interpretation required to perform the stenting, and all angioplasty in the central dialysis segment (List separately in addition to code for primary procedure)

▲ 38220   Diagnostic bone marrow; aspiration

▲ 38221   biopsy(ies)

● 38222   biopsy(ies) and aspiration(s)

● 38573   with bilateral total pelvic lymphadenectomy and periaortic lymph node sampling, peritoneal washings, peritoneal biopsy(ies), omentectomy, and diaphragmatic washings, including diaphragmatic and other serosal biopsy(ies), when performed

▲ 43112   Total or near total esophagectomy, with thoracotomy; with pharyngogastrostomy or cervical esophagogastrostomy, with or without pyloroplasty (ie, McKeown esophagectomy or tri-incisional esophagectomy)

● 43286   Esophagectomy, total or near total, with laparoscopic mobilization of the abdominal and mediastinal esophagus and proximal gastrectomy, with laparoscopic pyloric drainage procedure if performed, with open cervical pharyngogastrostomy or esophagogastrostomy (ie, laparoscopic transhiatal esophagectomy)

● 43287   Esophagectomy, distal two-thirds, with laparoscopic mobilization of the abdominal and lower mediastinal esophagus and proximal gastrectomy, with laparoscopic pyloric drainage procedure if performed, with separate thoracoscopic mobilization of the middle and upper mediastinal esophagus and thoracic esophagogastrostomy (ie, laparoscopic thoracoscopic esophagectomy, Ivor Lewis esophagectomy)

● 43288   Esophagectomy, total or near total, with thoracoscopic mobilization of the upper, middle, and lower mediastinal esophagus, with separate laparoscopic proximal gastrectomy, with laparoscopic pyloric drainage procedure if performed, with open cervical pharyngogastrostomy or esophagogastrostomy (ie, thoracoscopic, laparoscopic and cervical incision esophagectomy, McKeown esophagectomy, tri-incisional esophagectomy)

(55450   Deleted 2017 [2018 edition] To report, use 55250)

● 55874   Transperineal placement of biodegradable material, periprostatic, single or multiple injection(s), including image guidance, when performed

▲ 57240   Anterior colporrhaphy, repair of cystocele with or without repair of urethrocele, including cystourethroscopy, when performed

▲ 57260   Combined anteroposterior colporrhaphy, including cystourethroscopy, when performed

▲ 57265   with enterocele repair

● 58575   Laparoscopy, surgical, total hysterectomy for resection of malignancy (tumor debulking), with omentectomy including salpingo-oophorectomy, unilateral or bilateral, when performed

▲ 64550   Application of surface (transcutaneous) neurostimulator (eg, TENS unit)

(64565   Deleted 2017 [2018 edition])

● 64912   with nerve allograft, each nerve, first strand (cable).

● 64913   with nerve allograft, each additional strand (List separately in addition to code for primary procedure)

(69820   Deleted 2017 [2018 edition])

(69840   Deleted 2017 [2018 edition])

Radiology

(71010   Deleted 2017 [2018 edition] To report, use 71045)

(71015   Deleted 2017 [2018 edition] To report, use 71045)

(71020   Deleted 2017 [2018 edition] To report, use 71046)

(71021   Deleted 2017 [2018 edition] To report, use 71047)

(71022   Deleted 2017 [2018 edition] To report, see 71047, 71048)

(71023   Deleted 2017 [2018 edition] To report, see 71046, 76000, 76001)

(71030   Deleted 2017 [2018 edition] To report, use 71048)

(71034   Deleted 2017 [2018 edition] To report, see 71048, 76000, 76001)

(71035   Deleted 2017 [2018 edition] To report, see 71046, 71047, 71048)

● 71045   Radiologic examination, chest; single view

● 71046   2 views.

● 71047   3 views

● 71048   4 or more views

(74000   Deleted 2017 [2018 edition]. To report, use 74018)

(74010   Deleted 2017 [2018 edition] To report, see 74019, 74021)

(74020   Deleted 2017 [2018 edition] To report, see 74019, 74021)

● 74018   Radiologic examination, abdomen; 1 view

● 74019   2 views

● 74021   3 or more views

(75658   Deleted 2017 [2018 edition] To report, use 75710)

(75952   Deleted 2017 [2018 edition] To report, see 34701-34711, 0254T)

(75953   Deleted 2017 [2018 edition] To report, see 34701-34711, 0254T)

(75954   Deleted 2017 [2018 edition] To report, see 34701-34711, 0254T)

▲ 76000   Fluoroscopy (separate procedure), up to 1 hour physician or other qualified health care professional time

▲ 76881   Ultrasound, complete joint (ie, joint space and peri-articular soft tissue structures) real-time with image documentation

▲ 76882   Ultrasound, limited, joint or other nonvascular extremity structure(s) (eg, joint space, peri-articular tendon[s], muscle[s], nerve[s], other soft tissue structure[s], or soft tissue mass[es], real-time with image documentation

(77422   Deleted 2017 [2018 edition])

(78190   Deleted 2017 [2018 edition])

Pathology and Laboratory

▲ 80305   Drug test(s), presumptive, any number of drug classes, any number of devices or procedures; capable of being read by direct optical observation only (eg, utilizing immunoassay [eg, dipsticks, cups, cards or cartridges]), includes sample validation when performed, per date of service

▲ 80306   read by instrument assisted direct optical observation (eg, utilizing immunoassay [eg, dipsticks, cups, cards, or cartridges]), includes sample validation when performed, per date of service

▲ 80307   by instrument chemistry analyzers (eg, utilizing immunoassay [eg, EIA, ELISA, EMIT, FPIA, IA, KIMS, RIA]), chromatography (eg, GC, HPLC), and mass spectrometry either with or without chromatography (eg, DART, DESI, GC-MS, GC-MS/MS, LC-MS, LC-MS/MS, LDTD, MALDI, TOF) includes sample validation when performed, per date of service

● 81175   *ASXL1 (additional sex combs like 1, transcriptional regulator)* (eg, myelodysplastic syndrome, myeloproliferative neoplasms, chronic myelomonocytic leukemia), gene analysis; full gene sequence

● 81176   targeted sequence analysis (eg, exon 12)

● 81230   *CYP3A4 (cytochrome P450 family 3 subfamily A member 4)* (eg, drug metabolism), gene analysis, common variant(s) (eg, *2, *22)

● 81231   *CYP3A5 (cytochrome P450 family 3 subfamily A member 5)* (eg, drug metabolism), gene analysis, common variants (eg, *2, *3, *4, *5, *6, *7).

● 81232   *DPYD (dihydropyrimidine dehydrogenase)* (eg, 5-fluorouracil/5-FU and capecitabine drug metabolism), gene analysis, common variant(s) (eg, *2A, *4, *5, *6)

● 81238   *F9 (coagulation factor IX)* (eg, hemophilia B), full gene sequence.

● 81247   *G6PD (glucose-6-phosphate dehydrogenase)* (eg, hemolytic anemia, jaundice), gene analysis; common variant(s) (eg, A, A-).

● 81248   known familial variant(s).

● 81249   full gene sequence.

▲ 81257   *HBA1/HBA2 (alpha globin 1 and alpha globin 2)* (eg, alpha thalassemia, Hb Bart hydrops fetalis syndrome, HbH disease), gene anlysis; common deletions or variant (eg, Southeast Asian, Thai, Filipino, Mediterranean, alpha3.7, alpha4.2, alpha20.5, Constant Spring)

● 81258   known familial variant.

● 81259   full gene sequence

● 81269   duplication/deletion variants.

● 81105   *Human Platelet Antigen 1 genotyping (HPA-1), ITGB3(integrin, beta 3 [platelet glycoprotein IIIa], antigen CD61 [GPIIIa])* (eg, neonatal alloimmune thrombocytopenia [NAIT], post-transfusion purpura), gene analysis, common variant, HPA-1a/b (L33P).

● 81106   *Human Platelet Antigen 2 genotyping (HPA-2), GP1BA (glycoprotein Ib [platelet], alpha polypeptide [GPIba])* (eg, neonatal alloimmune thrombocytopenia [NAIT], posttransfusion purpura), gene analysis, common variant, HPA-2a/b (T145M)

● 81107   *Human Platelet Antigen 3 genotyping (HPA-3), ITGA2B (integrin, alpha 2b [platelet glycoprotein IIb of IIb/IIIa complex], antigen CD41 [GPIIb])* (eg, neonatal alloimmune thrombocytopenia [NAIT], post-transfusion purpura), gene analysis, common variant, HPA-3a/b (I843S)

● 81108   *Human Platelet Antigen 4 genotyping (HPA-4), ITGB3 (integrin, beta 3 [platelet glycoprotein IIIa], antigen CD61 [GPIIIa])* (eg, neonatal alloimmune thrombocytopenia [NAIT], post-transfusion purpura), gene analysis, common variant, HPA-4a/b (R143Q).

● 81109   *Human Platelet Antigen 5 genotyping (HPA-5), ITGA2 (integrin, alpha 2 [CD49B, alpha 2 subunit of VLA-2 receptor] [GPIa])* (eg, neonatal alloimmune thrombocytopenia [NAIT], post-transfusion purpura), gene analysis, common variant (eg, HPA-5a/b (K505E))

● 81110   *Human Platelet Antigen 6 genotyping (HPA-6w), ITGB3 (integrin, beta 3 [platelet glycoprotein IIIa, antigen CD61] [GPIIIa])* (eg, neonatal alloimmune thrombocytopenia [NAIT], post-transfusion purpura), gene analysis, common variant, HPA-6a/b (R489Q)

● 81111   *Human Platelet Antigen 9 genotyping (HPA-9w), ITGA2B (integrin, alpha 2b [platelet glycoprotein IIb of IIb/IIIa complex, antigen CD41] [GPIIb])* (eg, neonatal alloimmune thrombocytopenia [NAIT], post-transfusion purpura), gene analysis, common variant, HPA-9a/b (V837M)

● 81112   *Human Platelet Antigen 15 genotyping (HPA-15), CD109 (CD109 molecule)* (eg, neonatal alloimmune thrombocytopenia [NAIT], post-transfusion purpura), gene analysis, common variant, HPA-15a/b (S682Y).

● 81120   *IDH1 (isocitrate dehydrogenase 1 [NADP+], soluble)* (eg, glioma), common variants (eg, R132H, R132C)

● 81121   *IDH2 (isocitrate dehydrogenase 2 [NADP+], mitochondrial)* (eg, glioma), common variants (eg, R140W, R172M).

● 81283   *IFNL3 (interferon, lambda 3)* (eg, drug response), gene analysis, rs12979860 variant.

● 81334   *RUNX1 (runt related transcription factor 1)* (eg, acute myeloid leukemia, familial platelet disorder with associated myeloid malignancy), gene analysis, targeted sequence analysis (eg, exons 3-8).

● 81328   *SLCO1B1 (solute carrier organic anion transporter family, member 1B1)* (eg, adverse drug reaction), gene analysis, common variant(s) (eg, *5)

● 81335   *TPMT (thiopurine S-methyltransferase)* (eg, drug metabolism), gene analysis, common variants (eg, *2, *3)81346

● 81346   *TYMS (thymidylate synthetase)* (eg, 5-fluorouracil/5-FU drug metabolism), gene analysis, common variant(s) (eg, tandem repeat variant)

● 81361   *HBB (hemoglobin, subunit beta)* (eg, sickle cell anemia, beta thalassemia, hemoglobinopathy); common variant(s) (eg, HbS, HbC, HbE).

● 81362   known familial variant(s)

● 81363   duplication/deletion variant(s)

● 81364   full gene sequence

▲ 81400   Molecular pathology procedure, Level 1 (eg, identification of single germline variant [eg, SNP] by techniques such as restriction enzyme digestion or melt curve analysis)

▲ 81401   Molecular pathology procedure, Level 2 (eg, 2-10 SNPs, 1 methylated variant, or 1 somatic variant [typically using nonsequencing target variant analysis], or detection of a dynamic mutation disorder/triplet repeat

▲ 81403   Molecular pathology procedure, Level 4 (eg, analysis of single exon by DNA sequence analysis, analysis of >10 amplicons using multiplex PCR in 2 or more independent reactions, mutation scanning or duplication/deletion variants of 2-5 exons)

▲ 81404   Molecular pathology procedure, Level 5 (eg, analysis of 2-5 exons by DNA sequence analysis, mutation scanning or duplication/deletion variants of 6-10 exons, or characterization of a dynamic mutation disorder/triplet repeat by Southern blot analysis)

▲ 81405   Molecular pathology procedure, Level 6 (eg, analysis of 6-10 exons by DNA sequence analysis, mutation scanning or duplication/deletion variants of 11-25 exons, regionally targeted cytogenomic array analysis)

▲ 81406   Molecular pathology procedure, Level 7 (eg, analysis of 11-25 exons by DNA sequence analysis, mutation scanning or duplication/deletion variants of 26-50 exons, cytogenic array analysis for neoplasia)

▲ 81432   Hereditary breast cancer-related disorders (eg, hereditary breast cancer, hereditary ovarian cancer, hereditary endometrial cancer); genomic sequence analysis panel, must include sequencing of at least 10 genes, always including BRCA1, BRCA2, CDH1, MLH1, MSH2, MSH6, PALB2, PTEN, STK11, and TP53

● 81448   Hereditary peripheral neuropathies (eg, Charcot-Marie- Tooth, spastic paraplegia), genomic sequence analysis panel, must include sequencing of at least 5 peripheral neuropathy-related genes (eg, BSCL2, GJB1, MFN2, MPZ, REEP1, SPAST, SPG11, SPTLC1).

▲ 81439   Hereditary cardiomyopathy (eg, hypertrophic cardiomyopathy, dilated cardiomyopathy, arrhythmogenic right ventricular cardiomyopathy), genomic sequence analysis panel, must include sequencing of at least 5 cardiomyopathy-related genes (eg, DSG2, MYBPC3, MYH7, PKP2, TTN)

● 81520   Oncology (breast), mRNA gene expression profiling by hybrid capture of 58 genes (50 content and 8 housekeeping), utilizing formalin-fixed paraffinembedded tissue, algorithm reported as a recurrence risk score.

● 81521   Oncology (breast), mRNA, microarray gene expression profiling of 70 content genes and 465 housekeeping genes, utilizing fresh frozen or formalin-fixed paraffinembedded tissue, algorithm reported as index related to risk of distant metastasis.

● 81541   Oncology (prostate), mRNA gene expression profiling by real-time RT-PCR of 46 genes (31 content and 15 housekeeping), utilizing formalin-fixed paraffinembedded tissue, algorithm reported as a diseasespecific mortality risk score

● 81551   Oncology (prostate), promoter methylation profiling by real-time PCR of 3 genes (GSTP1, APC, RASSF1), utilizing formalin-fixed paraffin-embedded tissue, algorithm reported as a likelihood of prostate cancer detection on repeat biopsy.

▲ 82043   urine (eg, microalbumin), quantitative

▲ 82044   urine (eg, microalbumin), semiquantitative (eg, reagent strip assay)

▲ 82042   other source, quantitative, each specimen

(83499   Deleted 2017 [2018 edition])

(84061   Deleted 2017 [2018 edition])

▲ 86003   Allergen specific IgE; quantitative or semiquantitative, crude allergen extract, each

▲ 86005   qualitative, multiallergen screen (sponge card)

● 86008   quantitative or semiquantitative, recombinant or purified component, each.

(86185   Deleted 2017 [2018 edition])

(86243   Deleted 2017 [2018 edition])

(86378   Deleted 2017 [2018 edition])

(86729   Deleted 2017 [2018 edition])

● 86794   Zika virus, IgM

(86822   Deleted 2017 [2018 edition])

(87277   Deleted 2017 [2018 edition])

(87470   Deleted 2017 [2018 edition])

(87477   Deleted 2017 [2018 edition])

(87515   Deleted 2017 [2018 edition])

● 87634   respiratory syncytial virus, amplified probe technique

● 87662   Zika virus, amplified probe technique

(88154   Deleted 2017 [2018 edition])

● 0001U   Red blood cell antigen typing, DNA, human erythrocyte antigen gene analysis of 35 antigens from 11 blood groups, utilizing whole blood, common RBC alleles reported

● 0002U   Oncology (colorectal), quantitative assessment of three urine metabolites (ascorbic acid, succinic acid and carnitine) by liquid chromatography with tandem mass spectrometry (LC-MS/MS) using multiple reaction monitoring acquisition, algorithm reported as likelihood of adenomatous polyps

● 0003U   Oncology (ovarian) biochemical assays of five proteins (apolipoprotein A-1, CA 125 II, follicle stimulating hormone, human epididymis protein 4, transferrin), utilizing serum, algorithm reported as a likelihood score

● 0004U   Infectious disease (bacterial), DNA, 27 resistance genes, PCR amplification and probe hybridization in microarray format (molecular detection and identification of AmpC, carbapenemase and ESBL coding genes), bacterial culture colonies, report of genes detected or not detected, per isolate

● 0005U   Oncology (prostate) gene expression profile by real-time RT-PCR of 3 genes (ERG, PCA3, and SPDEF), urine, algorithm reported as risk score

● 0006U   Prescription drug monitoring, 120 or more drugs and substances, definitive tandem mass spectrometry with chromatography, urine, qualitative report of presence (including quantitative levels, when detected) or absence of each drug or substance with description and severity of potential interactions, with identified substances, per date of service

● 0007U   Drug test(s), presumptive, with definitive confirmation of positive results, any number of drug classes, urine, includes specimen verification including DNA authentication in comparison to buccal DNA, per date of service

● 0008U   Helicobacter pylori detection and antibiotic resistance, DNA, 16S and 23S rRNA, gyrA, pbp1, rdxA and rpoB, next generation sequencing, formalin-fixed paraffin-embedded or fresh tissue, predictive, reported as positive or negative for resistance to clarithromycin, fluoroquinolones, metronidazole, amoxicillin, tetracycline and rifabutin

● 0009U   Oncology (breast cancer), ERBB2 (HER2) copy number by FISH, tumor cells from formalin-fixed paraffin-embedded tissue isolated using image-based dielectrophoresis (DEP) sorting, reported as ERBB2 gene amplified or nonamplified

● 0010U   Infectious disease (bacterial), strain typing by whole genome sequencing, phylogenetic-based report of strain relatedness, per submitted isolate

● 0011U   Prescription drug monitoring, evaluation of drugs present by LC-MS/MS, using oral fluid, reported as a comparison to an estimated steady-state range, per date of service including all drug compounds and metabolites

● 0012U   Germline disorders, gene rearrangement detection by whole genome next-generation sequencing, DNA, whole blood, report of specific gene rearrangement(s)

● 0013U   Oncology (solid organ neoplasia), gene rearrangement detection by whole genome next-generation sequencing, DNA, fresh or frozen tissue or cells, report of specific gene rearrangement(s).

● 0014U   Hematology (hematolymphoid neoplasia), gene rearrangement detection by whole genome nextgeneration sequencing, DNA, whole blood or bone marrow, report of specific gene rearrangement(s)

● 0015U   Drug metabolism (adverse drug reactions), DNA, 22 drug metabolism and transporter genes, real-time PCR, blood or buccal swab, genotype and metabolizer status for therapeutic decision support.

- 0016U   Oncology (hematolymphoid neoplasia), RNA, BCR/ABL1 major and minor breakpoint fusion transcripts, quantitative PCR amplification, blood or bone marrow, report of fusion not detected or detected with quantitation

- 0017U   Oncology (hematolymphoid neoplasia), JAK2 mutation, DNA, PCR amplification of exons 12-14 and sequence analysis, blood or bone marrow, report of JAK2 mutation not detected or detected

Medicine

- 90587   Dengue vaccine, quadrivalent, live, 3 dose schedule, for subcutaneous use

▲ 90651   Human papillomavirus vaccine types 6, 11, 16, 18, 31, 33, 45, 52, 58, nonvalent (9vHPV), 2 or 3 dose schedule, for intramuscular use

- 90756   Influenza virus vaccine, quadrivalent (ccIIV4), derived from cell cultures, subunit, antibiotic free, 0.5 mL dosage, for intramuscular use

- 90682   Influenza virus vaccine, quadrivalent (RIV4), derived from recombinant DNA, hemagglutinin (HA) protein only, preservative and antibiotic free, for intramuscular use

▲ 90620   Meningococcal recombinant protein and outer membrane vesicle vaccine, serogroup B (MenB-4C), 2 dose schedule, for intramuscular use

▲ 90621   Meningococcal recombinant lipoprotein vaccine, serogroup B (MedB-FHbp), 2 or 3 dose schedule, for intramuscular use

- 90750   Zoster (shingles) vaccine (HZV), recombinant, subunit, adjuvanted, for intramuscular use

- 93792   Patient/caregiver training for initiation of home international normalized ratio (INR) monitoring under the direction of a physician or other qualified health care professional, face-to-face, including use and care of the INR monitor, obtaining blood sample, instructions for reporting home INR test results, and documentation of patient's/caregiver's ability to perform testing and report results

- 93793   Anticoagulant management for a patient taking warfarin, must include review and interpretation of a new home, office, or lab international normalized ratio (INR) test result, patient instructions, dosage adjustment (as needed), and scheduling of additional test(s), when performed.

(93982   Deleted 2017 [2018 edition])

- 94617   Exercise test for bronchospasm, including pre- and postspirometry, electrocardiographic recording(s), and pulse oximetry

- 94618   Pulmonary stress testing (eg, 6-minute walk test), including measurement of heart rate, oximetry, and oxygen titration, when performed

(94620   Deleted 2017 [2018 edition]. To report pulmonary stress testing, use 94618)

▲ 94621   Cardiopulmonary exercise testing, including measurements of minute ventilation, CO2 production, O2 uptake and electrocardiographic recordings

▲ 95250   Ambulatory continuous glucose monitoring of interstitial tissue fluid via a subcutaneous sensor for a minimum of 72 hours; physician or other qualified health care professional (office) provided equipment, sensor placement, hook-up, calibration of monitor, patient training, removal of sensor, and printout of recording

- 95249   patient-provided equipment, sensor placement, hookup, calibration of monitor, patient training, and printout of recording

▲ 95251   analysis, interpretation and report

▲ 95930   Visual evoked potentil (VEP) checkerboard or flash testing, central nervous system except glaucoma, with interpretation and report

▲ 96567   Photodynamic therapy by external application of light to destroy premalignant lesions of the skin and adjacent mucosa with application and illumination/activation of photosensitive drug(s), per day

- 96573   Photodynamic therapy by external application of light to destroy premalignant lesions of the skin and adjacent mucosa with application and illumination/activation of photosensitizing drug(s) provided by a physician or other qualified health care professional, per day

- 96574   Debridement of premalignant hyperkeratotic lesion(s) (ie, targeted curettage, abrasion) followed with photodynamic therapy by external application of light to destroy premalignant lesions of the skin and adjacent mucosa with application and illumination/activation of photosensitizing drug(s) provided by a physician or other qualified health care professional, per day

- 97127   Therapeutic interventions that focus on cognitive function (eg, attention, memory, reasoning, executive function, problem solving, and/or pragmatic functioning) and compensatory strategies to manage the performance of an activity (eg, managing time or schedules, initiating, organizing and sequencing tasks), direct (one-on-one) patient contact

(97532   Deleted 2017 [2018 edition]. To report, use 97127)

▲ 97760   Orthotic(s) management and training (including assessment and fitting when not otherwise reported), upper extremity(ies), lower extremity(ies) and/or trunk, initial orthotic(s) encounter, each 15 minutes

▲ 97761   Prosthetic(s) training, upper and/or lower extremity(ies), initial prosthetic(s) encounter, each 15 minutes

(97762   Deleted 2017 [2018 edition]. To report, use 97763)

- 97763   Orthotic(s)/prosthetic(s) management and/or training, upper extremity(ies), lower extremity(ies), and/or trunk, subsequent orthotic(s)/prosthetic(s) encounter, each 15 minutes

Category III Codes

(0051T   Deleted 2017 [2018 edition]. To report, see 33927, 33928, 33929)

(0052T   Deleted 2017 [2018 edition]. To report, see 33927, 33928, 33929)

(0053T   Deleted 2017 [2018 edition]. To report, see 33927, 33928, 33929)

(0178T   Deleted 2017 [2018 edition])

(0179T   Deleted 2017 [2018 edition])

(0180T   Deleted 2017 [2018 edition])

▲ 0254T   Endovascular repair of iliac artery bifurcation (eg, aneurysm, pseudoaneurysm, arteriovenous malformation, trauma, dissection) using bifurcated endograft from the common iliac artery into both the external adn internal iliac artery, including all selective and/or nonselective catheterization(s) required for device placement and all associated radiological supervision and interpretation, unilateral

(0255T   Deleted 2017 [2018 edition]. To report, use 0254T)

(0293T   Deleted 2017 [2018 edition])

(0294T   Deleted 2017 [2018 edition])

(0299T   Deleted 2017 [2018 edition])

(0300T   Deleted 2017 [2018 edition])

(0301T   Deleted 2017 [2018 edition])

(0302T   Deleted 2017 [2018 edition])

(0303T   Deleted 2017 [2018 edition])

(0304T   Deleted 2017 [2018 edition])

(0305T   Deleted 2017 [2018 edition])

(0306T   Deleted 2017 [2018 edition])

(0307T   Deleted 2017 [2018 edition])

(0309T   Deleted 2017 [2018 edition])

(0310T   Deleted 2017 [2018 edition])

▲ 0333T   Visual evoked potential, screening of visual acuity, automated, with report

● 0464T   Visual evoked potential, testing for glaucoma, with interpretation and report

(0340T   Deleted 2017 [2018 edition]. To report, use 32994)

● 0488T   Preventive behavior change, online/electronic structured intensive program for prevention of diabetes using a standardized diabetes prevention program curriculum, provided to an individual, per 30 days

(0438T   Deleted 2017 [2018 edition]. To report, use 55874)

● 0465T   Suprachoroidal injection of a pharmacologic agent (does not include supply of medication)

● 0466T   Insertion of chest wall respiratory sensor electrode or electrode array, including connection to pulse generator (List separately in addition to code for primary procedure)

● 0467T   Revision or replacement of chest wall respiratory sensor electrode or electrode array, including connection to existing pulse generator

● 0468T   Removal of chest wall respiratory sensor electrode or electrode array

● 0469T   Retinal polarization scan, ocular screening with on-site automated results, bilateral

● 0470T   Optical coherence tomography (OCT) for microstructural and morphological imaging of skin, image acquisition, interpretation, and report; first lesion

● 0471T   each additional lesion (List separately in addition to code for primary procedure)

● 0472T   Device evaluation, interrogation, and initial programming of intraocular retinal electrode array (eg, retinal prosthesis), in person, with iterative adjustment of the implantable device to test functionality, select optimal permanent programmed values with analysis, including visual training, with review and report by a qualified health care professional

● 0473T   Device evaluation and interrogation of intraocular retinal electrode array (eg, retinal prosthesis), in person, including reprogramming and visual training, when performed, with review and report by a qualified health care professional

● 0474T   Insertion of anterior segment aqueous drainage device, with creation of intraocular reservoir, internal approach, into the supraciliary space

● 0475T   Recording of fetal magnetic cardiac signal using at least 3 channels; patient recording and storage, data scanning with signal extraction, technical analysis and result, as well as supervision, review, and interpretation of report by a physician or other qualified health care professional

● 0476T   patient recording, data scanning, with raw electronic signal transfer of data and storage

● 0477T   signal extraction, technical analysis, and result

● 0478T   review, interpretation, report by physician or other qualified health care professional

● 0479T   Fractional ablative laser fenestration of burn and traumatic scars for functional improvement; first 100 cm2 or part thereof, or 1% of body surface area of infants and children

● 0480T   each additional 100 cm2, or each additional 1% of body surface area of infants and children, or part thereof (List separately in addition to code for primary procedure)

● 0481T   Injection(s), autologous white blood cell concentrate (autologous protein solution), any site, including image guidance, harvesting and preparation when performed

● 0482T   Absolute quantitation of myocardial blood flow, positron emission tomography (PET), rest and stress (List separately in addition to code for primary procedure)

● 0483T   Transcatheter mitral valve implantation/replacement (TMVI) with prosthetic valve; percutaneous approach, including transseptal puncture, when performed

● 0484T   transthoracic exposure (eg, thoracotomy, transapical)

● 0485T   Optical coherence tomography (OCT) of middle ear, with interpretation and report; unilateral

● 0486T   bilateral

● 0487T   Biomechanical mapping, transvaginal, with report

● 0489T   Autologous adipose-derived regenerative cell therapy for scleroderma in the hands; adipose tissue harvesting, isolation and preparation of harvested cells including incubation with cell dissociation enzymes, removal of non-viable cells and debris, determination of concentration and dilution of regenerative cells

● 0490T   multiple injections in one or both hands

● 0491T   Ablative laser treatment, non-contact, full field and fractional ablation, open wound, per day, total treatment surface area; first 20 sq cm or less

● 0492T   each additional 20 sq cm, or part thereof (List separately in addition to code for primary procedure)

● 0493T   Near-infrared spectroscopy studies of lower extremity wounds (eg, for oxyhemoglobin measurement)

● 0494T   Surgical preparation and cannulation of marginal (extended) cadaver donor lung(s) to ex vivo organ perfusion system, including decannulation, separation from the perfusion system, and cold preservation of the allograft prior to implantation, when performed.

● 0495T   Initiation and monitoring marginal (extended) cadaver donor lung(s) organ perfusion system by physician or qualified health care professional, including physiological and laboratory assessment (eg, pulmonary artery flow, pulmonary artery pressure, left atrial pressure, pulmonary vascular resistance, mean/peak and plateau airway pressure, dynamic compliance and perfusate gas analysis), including bronchoscopy and X ray when performed; first two hours in sterile field

● 0496T   each additional hour (List separately in addition to code for primary procedure)

● 0497T   External patient-activated, physician- or other qualified health care professional-prescribed, electrocardiographic rhythm derived event recorder without 24 hour attended monitoring; in-office connection

● 0498T   review and interpretation by a physician or other qualified health care professional per 30 days with at least one patient-generated triggered event

● 0499T   Cystourethroscopy, with mechanical dilation and urethral therapeutic drug delivery for urethral stricture or stenosis, including fluoroscopy, when performed

● 0500T   Infectious agent detection by nucleic acid (DNA or RNA), human papillomavirus (HPV) for five or more separately reported high-risk HPV types (eg, 16, 18, 31, 33, 35, 39, 45, 51, 52, 56, 58, 59, 68) (ie, genotyping)

● 0501T   Noninvasive estimated coronary fractional flow reserve (FFR) derived from coronary computed tomography angiography data using computation fluid dynamics physiologic simulation software analysis of functional data to assess the severity of coronary artery disease; data preparation and transmission, analysis of fluid dynamics and simulated maximal coronary hyperemia, generation of estimated FFR model, with anatomical data review in comparison with estimated FFR model to reconcile discordant data, interpretation and report

● 0502T   data preparation and transmission

● 0503T   analysis of fluid dynamics and simulated maximal coronary hyperemia, and generation of estimated FFR model

● 0504T   anatomical data review in comparison with estimated FFR model to reconcile discordant data, interpretation and report

This page intentionally left blank

CPT MODIFIERS

The CPT® coding system includes two-digit modifier codes which are used to report that a service or procedure has been "altered or modified by some specific circumstance" without altering or modifying the basic definition or CPT code.

The proper use of CPT modifiers can speed up claim processing and increase reimbursement, while the improper use of CPT modifiers may result in claim delays or claim denials. In addition, using certain CPT modifiers, for example -22, too frequently may trigger a claims audit.

CPT MODIFIERS

-22 Increased procedural services

When the work required to provide a service is substantially greater than typically required, it may be identified by adding modifier -22 to the usual procedure code. Documentation must support the substantial additional work and the reason for the additional work (ie, increased intensity, time, technical difficulty of procedure, severity of patient's condition, physical and mental effort required). **Note**: This modifier should not be appended to an E/M service.

-23 Unusual anesthesia

Occasionally, a procedure, which usually requires either no anesthesia or local anesthesia, because of unusual circumstances must be done under general anesthesia. This circumstance may be reported by adding the modifier -23 to the procedure code of the basic service.

-24 Unrelated evaluation and management service by the same physician or other qualified health care professional during a postoperative period

The physician or other qualified health care professional may need to indicate that an evaluation and management service was performed during a postoperative period for a reason(s) unrelated to the original procedure. This circumstance may be reported by adding the modifier -24 to the appropriate level of E/M service.

-25 Significant, separately identifiable evaluation and management service by the same physician or other qualified health care professional on the same day of the procedure or other service

It may be necessary to indicate that on the day a procedure or service identified by a CPT code was performed, the patient's condition required a significant, separately identified E/M service above and beyond the other service provided or beyond the usual preoperative and postoperative care associated with the procedure that was performed. A significant, separately identifiable E/M service is defined or substantiated by documentation that satisfies the relevant criteria for the respective E/M service to be reported (see Evaluation and Management Services Guidelines for instructions on determining level of E/M service). The E/M service may be prompted by the symptom or condition for which the procedure and/or service was provided. As such, different diagnoses are not required for reporting of the E/M service on the same date. This circumstance may be reported by adding modifier -25 to the approprite level of E/M service. **Note**: This modifier is not used to report an E/M service that resulted in a decision to perform surgery. See modifier -57. For significant, separately identifiable non-E/M services, see modifier -59.

-26 Professional component

Certain procedures are a combination of a physician or other qualified health care professional component and a technical component. When the physician or other qualified health care professional component is reported separately, the service may be identified by adding the modifier -26 to the usual procedure number.

-27 Multiple outpatient hospital evaluation and management encounters on the same date

For hospital outpatient reporting purposes, utilization of hospital resources related to separate and distinct E/M encounters performed in multiple outpatient hospital settings on the same date may be reported by adding modifier -27 to each appropriate level outpatient and/or emergency department E/M code(s). This modifier provides a means of reporting circumstances involving evaluation and management services provided by physician(s) in more than one (multiple) outpatient hospital setting(s) (eg, hospital emergency department, clinic). **Note**: This modifier is not to be used for physician reporting of multiple E/M services performed by the same physician on the same date. For physician reporting of all outpatient evaluation and management services provided by the same physician on the same date and performed in multiple outpatient setting(s) (eg, hospital emergency department, clinic), see Evaluation and Management, Emergency Department, or Preventive Medicine Services codes.

-32   Mandated services

Services related to *mandated* consultation and/or related services (eg, third party payer, governmental, legislative or regulatory requirement) may be identified by adding the modifier -32 to the basic procedure.

-33   Preventive service

When the primary purpose of the service is the delivery of an evidence based service in accordance with a US Preventive Services Task Force A or B rating in effect and other preventive services identified in preventive services mandates (legislative or regulatory), the service may be identified by adding -33 to the procedure. For separately reported services specifically identified as preventive, the modifier should not be used.

-47   Anesthesia by surgeon

Regional or general anesthesia provided by the surgeon may be reported by adding the modifier -47 to the basic service. (This does not include local anesthesia.) **Note**: Modifier -47 would not be used as a modifier for the Anesthesia procedures.

-50   Bilateral procedure

Unless otherwise identified in the listings, bilateral procedures that are performed at the same session, should be identified by adding modifier -50 to the appropriate 5 digit code.

This modifier is reported when bilateral procedures requiring a separate incision are performed during the SAME operative session. Proper reporting of this modifier on the CMS1500 health insurance claim form requires the CPT procedure code to be listed two times: first with no modifier, and the second time with modifier -50.

This modifier may not be used if the definition of the basic procedure code includes the term "bilateral."

-51   Multiple procedures

When multiple procedures, other than E/M services, Physical Medicine and Rehabilitation services, or provision of supplies (eg, vaccines), are performed at the same session by the same individual, the primary procedure or service may be reported as listed. The additional procedure(s) or service(s) may be identified by appending modifier -51 to the additional procedure or service code(s). **Note**: This modifier should not be appended to designated "add-on" codes.

-52   Reduced services

Under certain circumstances a service or procedure is partially reduced or eliminated at the discretion of the physician or other qualified health care professional. Under these circumstances the service provided can be identified by its usual procedure number and the addition of the modifier -52, signifying that the service is reduced. This provides a means of reporting reduced services without disturbing the identification of the basic service. **Note**: For hospital outpatient reporting of a previously scheduled procedure/service that is partially reduced or cancelled as a result of extenuating circumstances or those that threaten the well-being of the patient prior to or after administration of anesthesia, see modifiers -73 and -74 (see modifiers approved for ASC hospital outpatient use).

The intended use of this modifier is to report the reduction of a service without affecting provider profiles maintained by health insurance companies.

Modifier -52 is another frequently misused modifier. Some medical practices mistakenly use modifier -52 to mean "reduced fee" and use it as a discounting method. Not only is this incorrect, the provider may seriously damage their provider profile with health insurance companies. The proper use for modifier -52 is to report that a service was not completed, or some part of a multiple-part service was not performed. A fee reduction may be in order as well; however that is not the primary purpose of the modifier.

-53   Discontinued procedure

Under certain circumstances, the physician or other qualified health care professional may elect to terminate a surgical or diagnostic procedure. Due to extenuating circumstances or those that threaten the well-being of the patient, it may be necessary to indicate that a surgical or diagnostic procedure was started but discontinued. This circumstance may be reported by adding modifier -53 to the code reported by the individual for the discontinued procedure. **Note**: This modifier is not used to report the elective cancellation of a procedure prior to the patient's anesthesia induction and/or surgical preparation in the operating suite. For outpatient hospital/ambulatory surgery center (ASC) reporting of a previously scheduled procedure/service that is partially reduced or cancelled as a result of extenuating circumstances or those that threaten the well-being of the patient prior to or after administration of anesthesia, see modifiers -73 and -74 (see modifiers approved for ASC hospital outpatient use).

-54 Surgical care only

When 1 physician or other qualified health care professional performs a surgical procedure and another provides preoperative and/or postoperative management, surgical services may be identified by adding modifier -54 to the usual procedure number.

-55 Postoperative management only

When 1 physician or other qualified health care professional performed the postoperative management and another performed the surgical procedure, the postoperative component may be identified by adding modifier -55 to the usual procedure number.

-56 Preoperative management only

When 1 physician or other qualified health care professional performed the preoperative care and evaluation and another performed the surgical procedure, the preoperative component may be identified by adding modifier -56 to the usual procedure number.

-57 Decision for surgery

An evaluation and management service that resulted in the initial decision to perform the surgery may be identified by adding the modifier -57 to the appropriate level of E/M service.

-58 Staged or related procedure or service by the same physician or other qualified health care professional during the postoperative period

It may be necessary to indicate that the performance of a procedure or service during the postoperative period was: (a) planned or anticipated (staged); (b) more extensive than the original procedure; or (c) for therapy following a surgical procedure. This circumstance may be reported by adding modifier -58 to the staged or related procedure. **Note**: For treatment of a problem that requires a return to the operating/procedure room (eg, unanticipated clinical condition), see modifier -78.

-59 Distinct Procedural Service

Under certain circumstances, it may be necessary to indicate that a procedure or service was distinct or independent from other non-E/M services performed on the same day. Modifier -59 is used to identify procedures/services, other than E/M services, that are not normally reported together, but are appropriate under the circumstances. Documentation must support a different session, different procedure or surgery, different site or organ system, separate incision/excision, separate lesion, or separate injury (or area of injury in extensive injuries) not ordinarily encountered or performed on the same day by the same individual. However, when another already established modifier is appropriate it should be used rather than modifier -59. Only if no more descriptive modifier is available, and the use of modifier -59 best explains the circumstances, should modifier -59 be used. **Note**: Modifier -59 should not be appended to an E/M service. To report a separate and distinct E/M service with a non-E/M service performed on the same date, see modifier -25.

-62 Two surgeons

When 2 surgeons work together as primary surgeons performing distinct part(s) of a procedure, each surgeon should report his/her distinct operative work by adding modifier -62 to the procedure code and any associated add-on code(s) for that procedure as long as both surgeons continue to work together as primary surgeons. Each surgeon should report the co-surgery once using the same procedure code. If additional procedure(s) (including add-on procedure(s) are performed during the same surgical session, separate code(s) may also be reported with modifier -62 added. **Note**: If a co-surgeon acts as an assistant in the performance of additional procedure(s), other than those reported with the modifier -62, during the same surgical session, those services may be reported using separate procedure code(s) with modifier -80 or modifier -82 added, as appropriate.

-63 **Procedure performed on infants less than 4 kg**

Procedures performed on neonates and infants up to a present body weight of 4 kg may involve significantly increased complexity and physician or other qualified health care professional work commonly associated with these patients. This circumstance may be reported by adding modifier -63 to the procedure number. **Note**: Unless otherwise designated, this modifier may only be appended to procedures/services listed in the 20005-69990 code series. Modifier -63 should not be appended to any CPT codes listed in the Evaluation and Management Services, Anesthesia, Radiology, Pathology/Laboratory, or Medicine sections.

-66 **Surgical team**

Under some circumstances, highly complex procedures (requiring the concomitant services of several physicians or other qualified health care professionals, often of different specialties, plus other highly skilled specially trained personnel, various types of complex equipment) are carried out under the "surgical team" concept. Such circumstances may be identified by each participating individual with the addition of modifier -66 to the basic procedure number used for reporting services.

-73 **Discontinued out-patient procedure prior to anesthesia administration**

Due to extenuating circumstances or those that threaten the well being of the patient, the physician may cancel a surgical or diagnostic procedure subsequent to the patient's surgical preparation (including sedation when provided, and being taken to the room where the procedure is to be performed), but prior to the administration of anesthesia (local, regional block(s) or general). Under these circumstances, the intended service that is prepared for but cancelled can be reported by its usual procedure number and the addition of the modifier -73.

Note: The elective cancellation of a service prior to the administration of anesthesia and/or surgical preparation of the patient should not be reported. For physician reporting of a discontinued procedure, see modifier -53.

-74 **Discontinued out-patient procedure after anesthesia administration**

Due to extenuating circumstances or those that threaten the well being of the patient, the physician may terminate a surgical or diagnostic procedure after the administration of anesthesia (local, regional block(s), general) or after the procedure was started (incision made, intubation started, scope inserted, etc.). Under these circumstances, the procedure started but terminated can be reported by its usual procedure number and the addition of the modifier -74. **Note**: The elective cancellation of a service prior to the administration of anesthesia and/or surgical preparation of the patient should not be reported. For physician reporting of a discontinued procedure, see modifier -53.

-76 **Repeat procedure or service by same physician or other qualified health care professional**

It may be necessary to indicate that a procedure or service was repeated by the same physician or other qualified health care professional subsequent to the original procedure or service. This circumstance may be reported by adding modifier -76 to the repeated procedure or service. **Note**: This modifier should not be appended to an E/M service.

-77 **Repeat procedure by another physician or other qualified health care professional**

It may be necessary to indicate that a basic procedure or service was repeated by another physician or other qualified health care professional subsequent to the original procedure or service. This circumstance may be reported by adding modifier -77 to the repeated procedure or service. **Note**: This modifier should not be appended to an E/M service.

-78 **Unplanned return to the operating/procedure room by the same physician or other qualified health care professional following initial procedure for a related procedure during the postoperative period**

It may be necessary to indicate that another procedure was performed during the postoperative period of the initial procedure (unplanned procedure following initial procedure). When this procedure is related to the first and requires the use of an operating/procedure room, it may be reported by adding modifier -78 to the related procedure. (For repeat procedures, see modifier -76.)

-79 Unrelated procedure or service by the same physician or other qualified health care professional during the postoperative period

The individual may need to indicate that the performance of a procedure or service during the postoperative period was unrelated to the original procedure. This circumstance may be reported by using modifier -79. (For repeat procedures on the same day, see '-76.')

-80 Assistant surgeon

Surgical assistant services may be identified by adding the modifier -80 to the usual procedure number(s).

-81 Minimum assistant surgeon

Minimum surgical assistant services are identified by adding the modifier -81 to the usual procedure number.

-82 Assistant surgeon (when qualified resident surgeon not available)

The unavailability of a qualified resident surgeon is a prerequisite for use of modifier -82 appended to the usual procedure code number(s).

-90 Reference (outside) laboratory

When laboratory procedures are performed by a party other than the treating or reporting physician or other qualified health care professional, the procedure may be identified by adding modifier -90 to the usual procedure number.

-91 Repeat clinical diagnostic laboratory test

In the course of treatment of the patient, it may be necessary to repeat the same laboratory test on the same day to obtain subsequent (multiple) test results. Under these circumstances, the laboratory test performed can be identified by its usual procedure number and the addition of modifier -91. **Note**: This modifier may not be used when tests are rerun to confirm initial results; due to testing problems with specimens or equipment; or for any other reason when a normal, one-time, reportable result is all that is required. This modifier may not be used when other code(s) describe a series of tests results (eg, glucose tolerance tests, evocative/suppression testing). This modifier may only be used for laboratory test(s) performed more than once on the same day on the same patient.

-92 Alternative Laboratory Platform Testing

When laboratory testing is being performed using a kit or transportable instrument that wholly or in part consists of a single use, disposable analytical chamber, the service may be identified by adding modifier 92 to the usual laboratory procedure code (HIV testing 86701-86703, and 87389). The test does not require permanent dedicated space, hence by its design may be hand carried or transported to the vicinity of the patient for immediate testing at that site, although location of the testing is not in itself determinative of the use of this modifier.

-95 Synchronous Telemedicine Service Rendered Via a Real-Time Interactive Audio and Video Telecommunications System

Synchronous telemedicine service is defined as a real-time interaction between a physician or other qualified health care professional and a patient who is located at a distant site from the physician or other qualified health care professional. The totality of the communication of information exchanged between the physician or other qualified health care professional and the patient during the course of the synchronous telemedicine service must be of an amount and nature that would be sufficient to meet the key components and/or requirements of the same service when rendered via a face-to-face interaction. Modifier 95 may only be appended to the services listed in Appendix P of CPT. Appendix P is the list of CPT codes for services that are typically performed face-to-face but may be rendered via a real-time (synchronous) interactive audio and video telecommunications system.

▲ -96 Habilitative services

Habilitative Services: When a service or procedure that may be either habilitative or rehabilitative in nature is provided for habilitative purposes, the physician or other qualified health care professional may add modifier 96 to the service or procedure code to indicate that the service or procedure provided was a habilitative service. Habilitative services help an individual learn skills and functioning for daily living that the individual has not yet developed, and then keep and/or improve those learned skills. Habilitative services also help an individual keep, learn, or improve skills and functioning for daily living.

▲ **-97**   **Rehabilitative services**

Rehabilitative Services: When a service or procedure that may be either habilitative or rehabilitative in nature is provided for rehabilitative purposes, the physician or other qualified health care professional may add modifier 97 to the service or procedure code to indicate that the service or procedure provided was a rehabilitative service. Rehabilitative services help an individual keep, get back, or improve skills and functioning for daily living that have been lost or impaired because the individual was sick, hurt, or disabled.

-99   **Multiple modifiers**

Under certain circumstances two or more modifiers may be necessary to completely delineate a service. In such situations modifier -99 should be added to the basic procedure, and other applicable modifiers may be listed as part of the description of the service.

ANESTHESIA PHYSICAL STATUS MODIFIERS

The Physical Status modifiers are consistent with the American Society of Anesthesiologists ranking of patient physical status, and distinguishing various levels of complexity of the anesthesia provided. All anesthesia services are reported by use of the anesthesia five-digit procedure code (00100-01999) with the appropriate physical status modifier appended. For example, 00100-P1

Under certain circumstances, when another established modifier(s) is appropriate, it should be used in addition to the physical status modifier. i.e., 00100-P4-53

P1   A normal healthy patient

P2   A patient with mild systemic disease

P3   A patient with severe systemic disease

P4   A patient with severe systemic disaease that is a constant threat to life

P5   A moribund patient who is not expected to survive without the operation

P6   A declared brain-dead patient whose organs are being removed for donor purposes

CATEGORY II MODIFIERS

The following performance measurement modifiers may be used with Category II codes to indicate that a service specified in the associated measure(s) was considered byt, due to either medical, patient, or system circumstance(s) documented in the medical record, the service was not provided. These modifiers serve as denominator exclusions from the performance measure. The user should note that not all listed measures provide for exclusions.

Category II modifiers should only be reported with Category II codes—they should not be reported with Category I or Category III codes. In addition, the modifiers in the Category II section should only be used where specified in the guidelines, reporting instructions, parenthetic notes, or code descriptor language listed in the Category II section (code listing and the Alphabetical Clinical Topics Listing).

1P   Performance Measure Exclusion Modifier due to Medical Reasons

Reasons include:
- Not indicated (absence of organ/limb, already received/performed, other)
- Contraindicated (patient allergic history, potential adverse drug interaction, other)
- Other medical reasons

2P   Performance Measure Exclusion Modifier due to Patient Reasons

Reasons include:
- Patient declinde
- Economic, social, or religious reasons

- Other patient reasons

3P Performance Measure Exclusion Modifier due to System Reasons

Reasons include:

- Resources to perform the services not available
- Insurance coverage/payor-related limitations
- Other reason attributable to health care delivery system

Modifier 8P is intended to be used as a reporting modifier to allow the reporting of circumstances when an action described in a measure's numerator is not performed and the reason is not otherwise specified

8P Performance measure reporting modifier—action not performed, reason not otherwise specified

LEVEL II (HCPCS/NATIONAL) MODIFIERS

HCPCS modifiers, defined and managed by The Centers for Medicare and Medicaid Services (CMS), are two digit modifier codes which may be either alpha (all letters) or alphanumeric (letters plus numbers). Some HCPCS modifiers may be used with CPT codes to modify procedures and services on health insurance claim forms filed for Medicare patients. See the most current edition of HCPCS for a complete list.

GENETIC TESTING CODE MODIFIERS

The genetic testing code modifiers have been removed from the CPT code set.

This page intentionally left blank

ANATOMICAL ILLUSTRATIONS

A fundamental knowledge and understanding of basic human anatomy and physiology is a prerequisite for accurate CPT© procedure coding. While a comprehensive treatment of anatomy and physiology is beyond the scope of this text, the large scale, full color anatomical illustrations on the following pages are designed to facilitate the procedure coding process for both beginning and experienced coders.

The illustrations provide an anatomical perspective of procedure coding by providing a side-by-side view of the major systems of the human body and a corresponding list of the most common CPT procedural categories used to report medical, surgical and diagnostic services performed on the illustrated system.

The CPT procedural categories listed on the left facing page of each anatomical illustration are code ranges only and should not be used for coding. These categories are provided as "pointers" to the appropriate section of CPT, where the definitive code may be found.

PLATE 1. SKIN AND SUBCUTANEOUS TISSUE - MALE

Skin, Subcutaneous and Accessory Structures

Incision and Drainage	10040-10180
Debridement	11000-11047
Paring or Cutting	11055-11057
Biopsy	11100-11101
Removal of Skin Tags	11200-11201
Shaving of Lesions	11300-11313
Excision-Benign Lesions	11400-11471
Excision-Malignant Lesions	11600-11646

Nails
	11719-11765

Pilondial Cyst
	11770-11772

Repair (Closure)

Repair-Simple	12001-12021
Repair-Intermediate	12031-12057
Repair-Complex	13100-13160
Adjacent Tissue Transfer	14000-14350
Skin Replacement Surgery	15002-15278
Flaps (Skin and/or Deep Tissues)	15570-15777
Pressure Ulcers	15920-15999
Burns, Local Treatment	16000-16036

Destruction

Destruction, Benign or Premalignant Lesions	17000-17250
Destruction, Malignant Lesions	17260-17286
Mohs' Micrographic Surgery	17311-17315
Other Destruction Procedures	17340-17999

Laboratory Services

Skin Tests, Immunology	86485-86580
Skin Tests, Allergy	95004-95199

Visit and Medicine Services

E/M Services	99201-99499
Special Dermatological Procedures	96900-96999

Male Figure
(Anterior View)

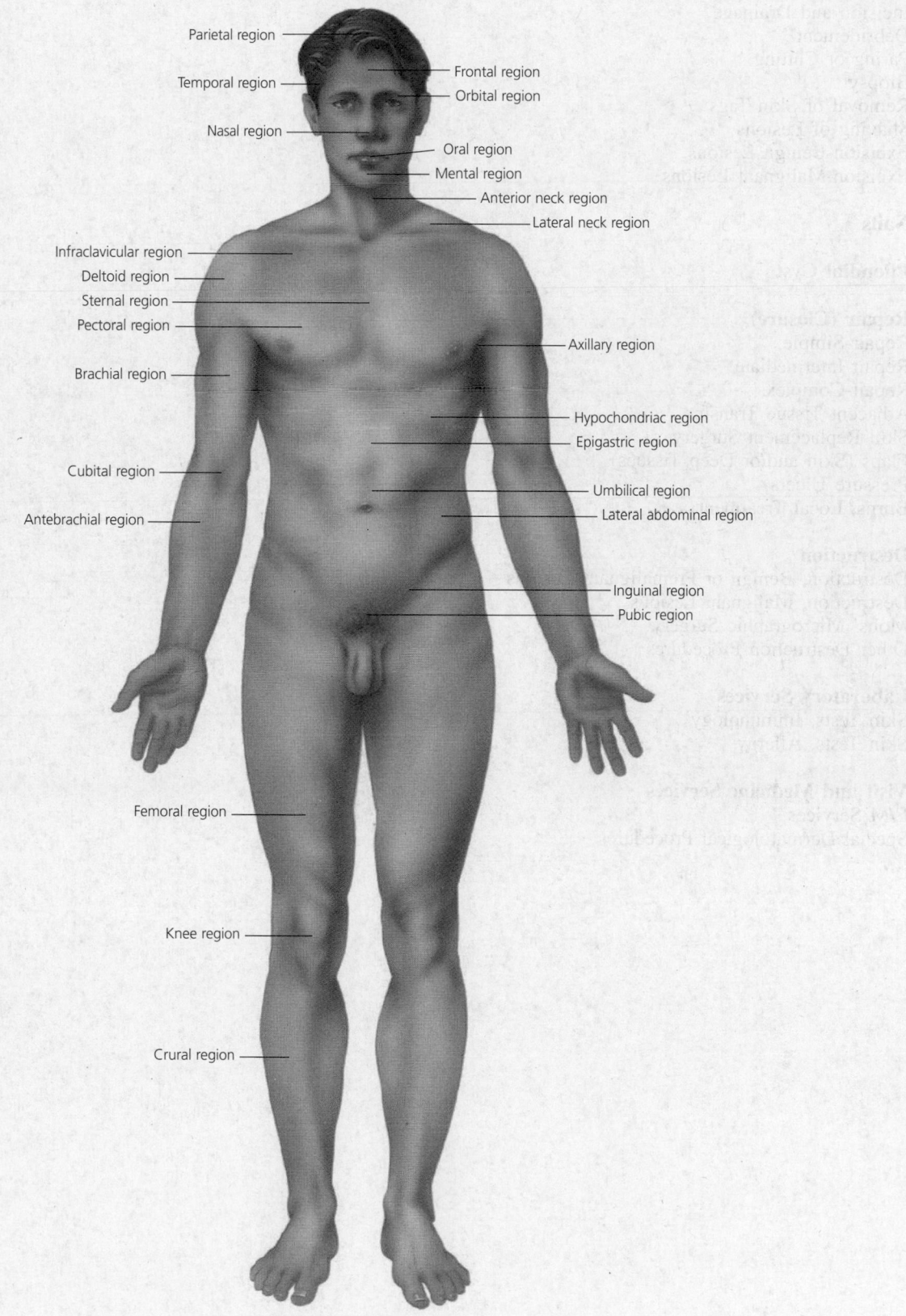

Parietal region

Frontal region

Temporal region

Orbital region

Nasal region

Oral region

Mental region

Anterior neck region

Lateral neck region

Infraclavicular region

Deltoid region

Sternal region

Pectoral region

Axillary region

Brachial region

Hypochondriac region

Epigastric region

Cubital region

Umbilical region

Antebrachial region

Lateral abdominal region

Inguinal region

Pubic region

Femoral region

Knee region

Crural region

PLATE 2. SKIN AND SUBCUTANEOUS TISSUE - FEMALE

Skin, Subcutaneous and Accessory Structures

Incision and Drainage	10040-10180
Debridement	11000-11047
Paring or Cutting	11055-11057
Biopsy	11100-11101
Removal of Skin Tags	11200-11201
Shaving of Lesions	11300-11313
Excision-Benign Lesions	11400-11471
Excision-Malignant Lesions	11600-11646

Nails	11719-11765

Pilondial Cyst	11770-11772

Repair (Closure)

Repair-Simple	12001-12021
Repair-Intermediate	12031-12057
Repair-Complex	13100-13160
Adjacent Tissue Transfer	14000-14350
Skin Replacement Surgery	15002-15278
Flaps (Skin and/or Deep Tissues)	15570-15777
Pressure Ulcers	15920-15999
Burns, Local Treatment	16000-16036

Destruction

Destruction, Benign or Premalignant Lesions	17000-17250
Destruction, Malignant Lesions	17260-17286
Mohs' Micrographic Surgery	17311-17315
Other Destruction Procedures	17340-17999

Laboratory Services

Skin Tests, Immunology	86485-86580
Skin Tests, Allergy	95004-95199

Visit and Medicine Services

E/M Services	99201-99499
Special Dermatological Procedures	96900-96999

Female Figure
(Anterior View)

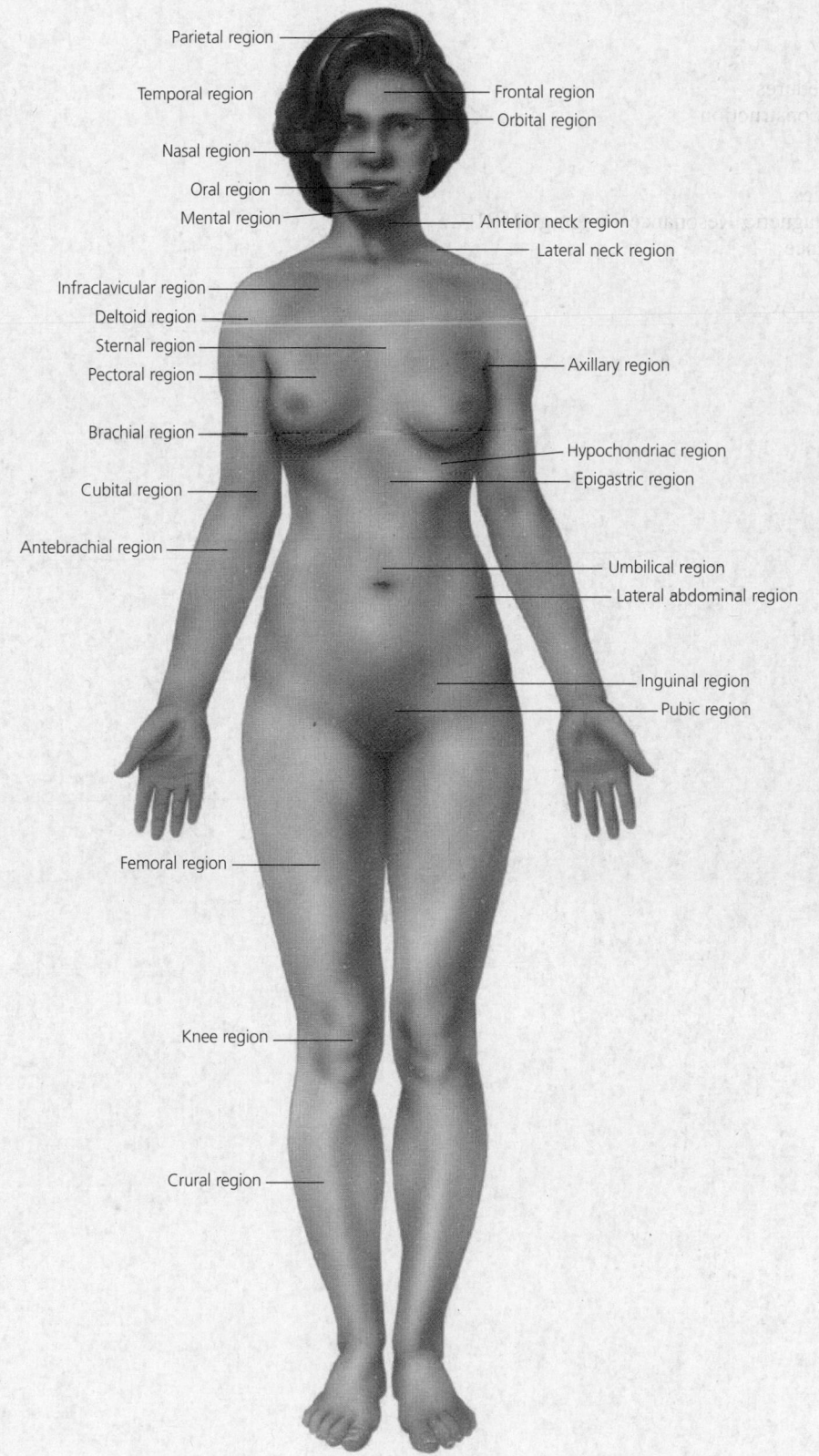

Parietal region

Temporal region

Frontal region

Orbital region

Nasal region

Oral region

Mental region

Anterior neck region

Lateral neck region

Infraclavicular region

Deltoid region

Sternal region

Pectoral region

Axillary region

Brachial region

Hypochondriac region

Cubital region

Epigastric region

Antebrachial region

Umbilical region

Lateral abdominal region

Inguinal region

Pubic region

Femoral region

Knee region

Crural region

PLATE 3. FEMALE BREAST

Breast

Incision	19000-19030
Excision	19081-19272
Introduction	19281-19298
Mastectomy Procedures	19300-19307
Repair and/or Reconstruction	19316-19396
Other Procedures	19499

Radiology Services

Mammography/Magnetic Resonance Imaging (MRI)	77051-77059
Radiologic Guidance	77031-77032
Ultrasound	76645

E/M Services   99201-99499

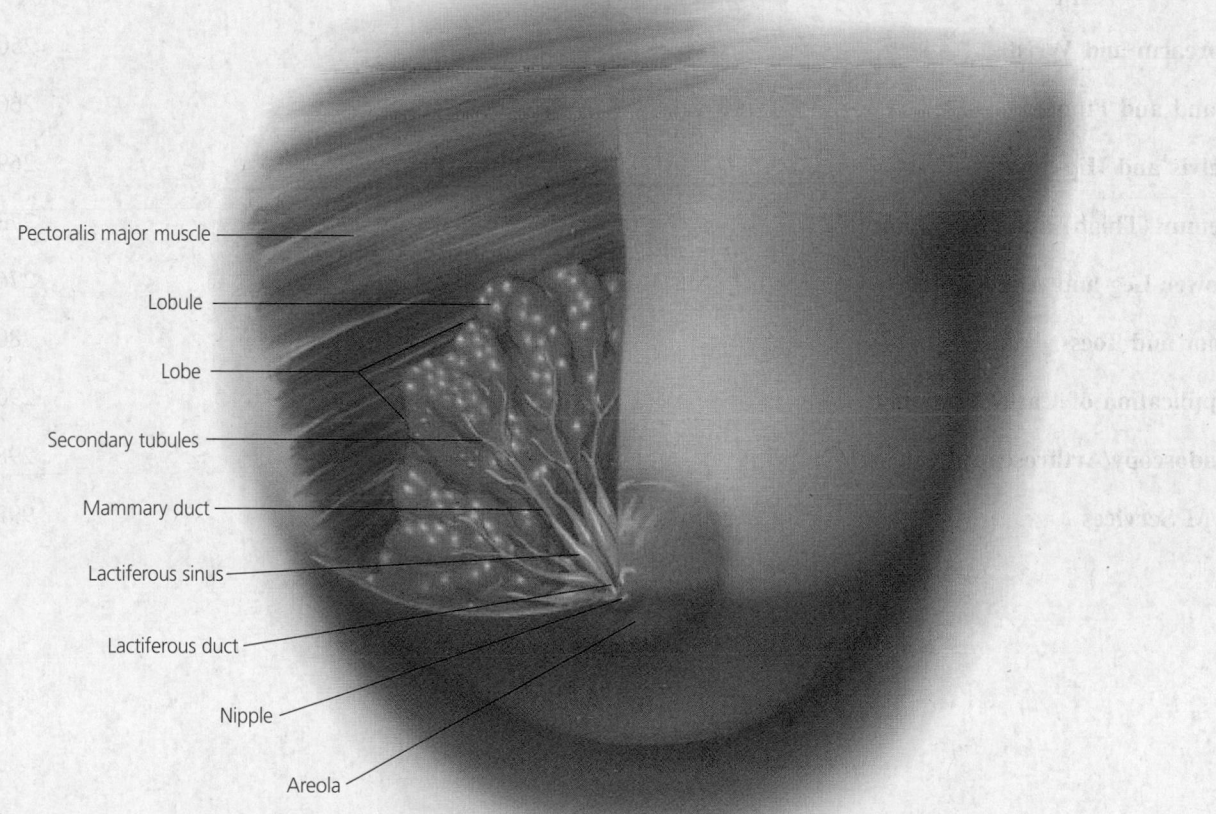

Pectoralis major muscle

Lobule

Lobe

Secondary tubules

Mammary duct

Lactiferous sinus

Lactiferous duct

Nipple

Areola

PLATE 4. MUSCULAR SYSTEM AND CONNECTIVE TISSUE - ANTERIOR VIEW

General	20005-20999
Head	21010-21499
Neck (Soft Tissues) and Thorax	21501-21899
Back and Flank	21920-21936
Spine (Vertebral Column)	22010-22899
Abdomen	22900-22999
Shoulder	23000-23929
Humerous (Upper Arm) and Elbow	23930-24999
Forearm and Wrist	25000-25999
Hand and Fingers	26010-26989
Pelvis and Hip Joint	26990-27299
Femur (Thigh) and Knee Joint	27301-27599
Lower Leg and Ankle Joint	27600-27899
Foot and Toes	28001-28899
Application of Casts/Strapping	29000-29799
Endoscopy/Arthroscopy	29800-29999
E/M Services	99201-99499

Muscular System
(Anterior View)

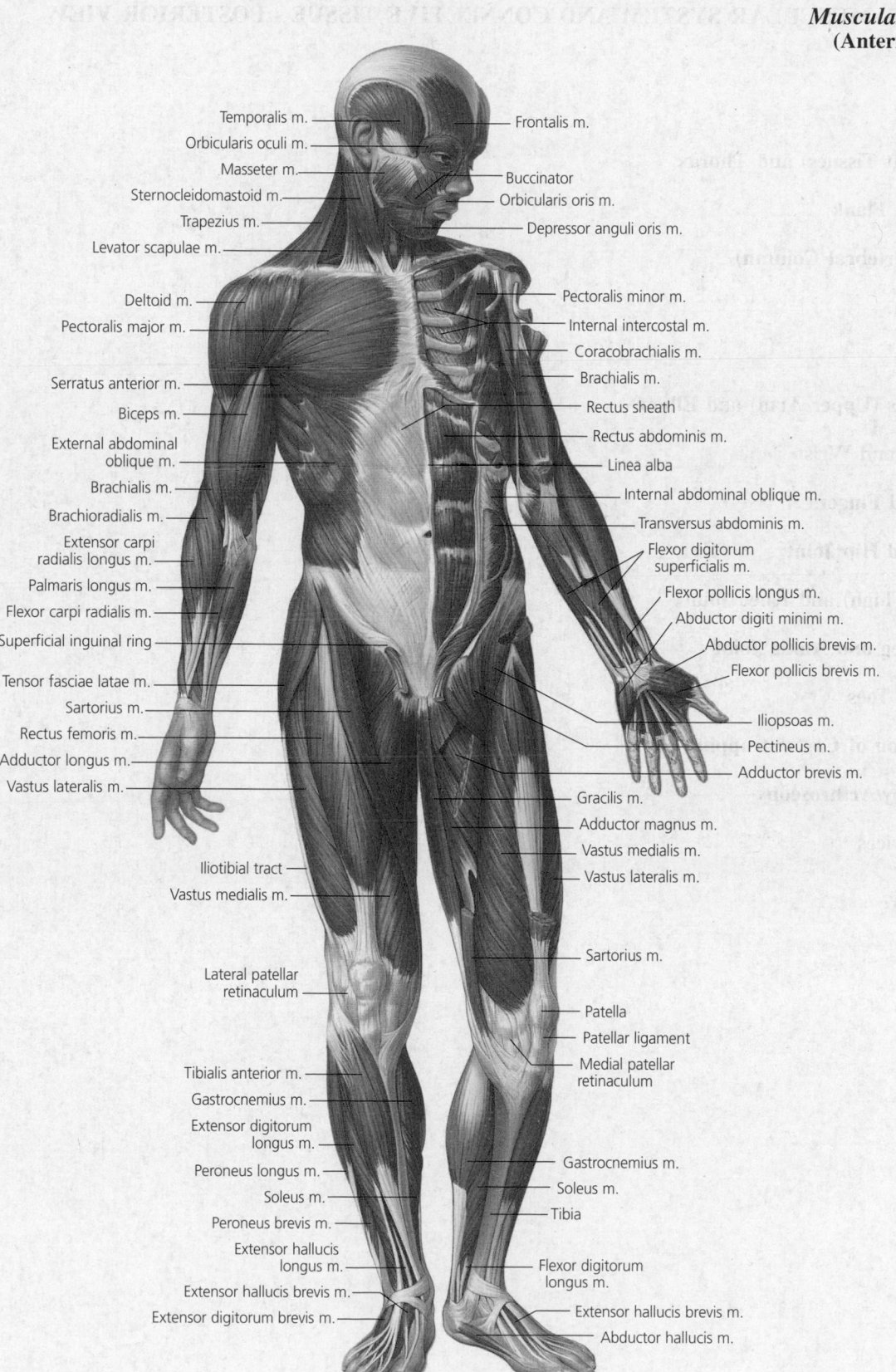

Temporalis m.

Orbicularis oculi m.

Masseter m.

Sternocleidomastoid m.

Trapezius m.

Levator scapulae m.

Deltoid m.

Pectoralis major m.

Serratus anterior m.

Biceps m.

External abdominal oblique m.

Brachialis m.

Brachioradialis m.

Extensor carpi radialis longus m.

Palmaris longus m.

Flexor carpi radialis m.

Superficial inguinal ring

Tensor fasciae latae m.

Sartorius m.

Rectus femoris m.

Adductor longus m.

Vastus lateralis m.

Iliotibial tract

Vastus medialis m.

Lateral patellar retinaculum

Tibialis anterior m.

Gastrocnemius m.

Extensor digitorum longus m.

Peroneus longus m.

Soleus m.

Peroneus brevis m.

Extensor hallucis longus m.

Extensor hallucis brevis m.

Extensor digitorum brevis m.

Frontalis m.

Buccinator

Orbicularis oris m.

Depressor anguli oris m.

Pectoralis minor m.

Internal intercostal m.

Coracobrachialis m.

Brachialis m.

Rectus sheath

Rectus abdominis m.

Linea alba

Internal abdominal oblique m.

Transversus abdominis m.

Flexor digitorum superficialis m.

Flexor pollicis longus m.

Abductor digiti minimi m.

Abductor pollicis brevis m.

Flexor pollicis brevis m.

Iliopsoas m.

Pectineus m.

Adductor brevis m.

Gracilis m.

Adductor magnus m.

Vastus medialis m.

Vastus lateralis m.

Sartorius m.

Patella

Patellar ligament

Medial patellar retinaculum

Gastrocnemius m.

Soleus m.

Tibia

Flexor digitorum longus m.

Extensor hallucis brevis m.

Abductor hallucis m.

PLATE 5. MUSCULAR SYSTEM AND CONNECTIVE TISSUE - POSTERIOR VIEW

General	20005-20999
Head	21010-21499
Neck (Soft Tissues) and Thorax	21501-21899
Back and Flank	21920-21936
Spine (Vertebral Column)	22010-22899
Abdomen	22900-22999
Shoulder	23000-23929
Humerous (Upper Arm) and Elbow	23930-24999
Forearm and Wrist	25000-25999
Hand and Fingers	26010-26989
Pelvis and Hip Joint	26990-27299
Femur (Thigh) and Knee Joint	27301-27599
Lower Leg and Ankle Joint	27600-27899
Foot and Toes	28001-28899
Application of Casts/Strapping	29000-29799
Endoscopy/Arthroscopy	29800-29999
E/M Services	99201-99499

Muscular System
(Posterior View)

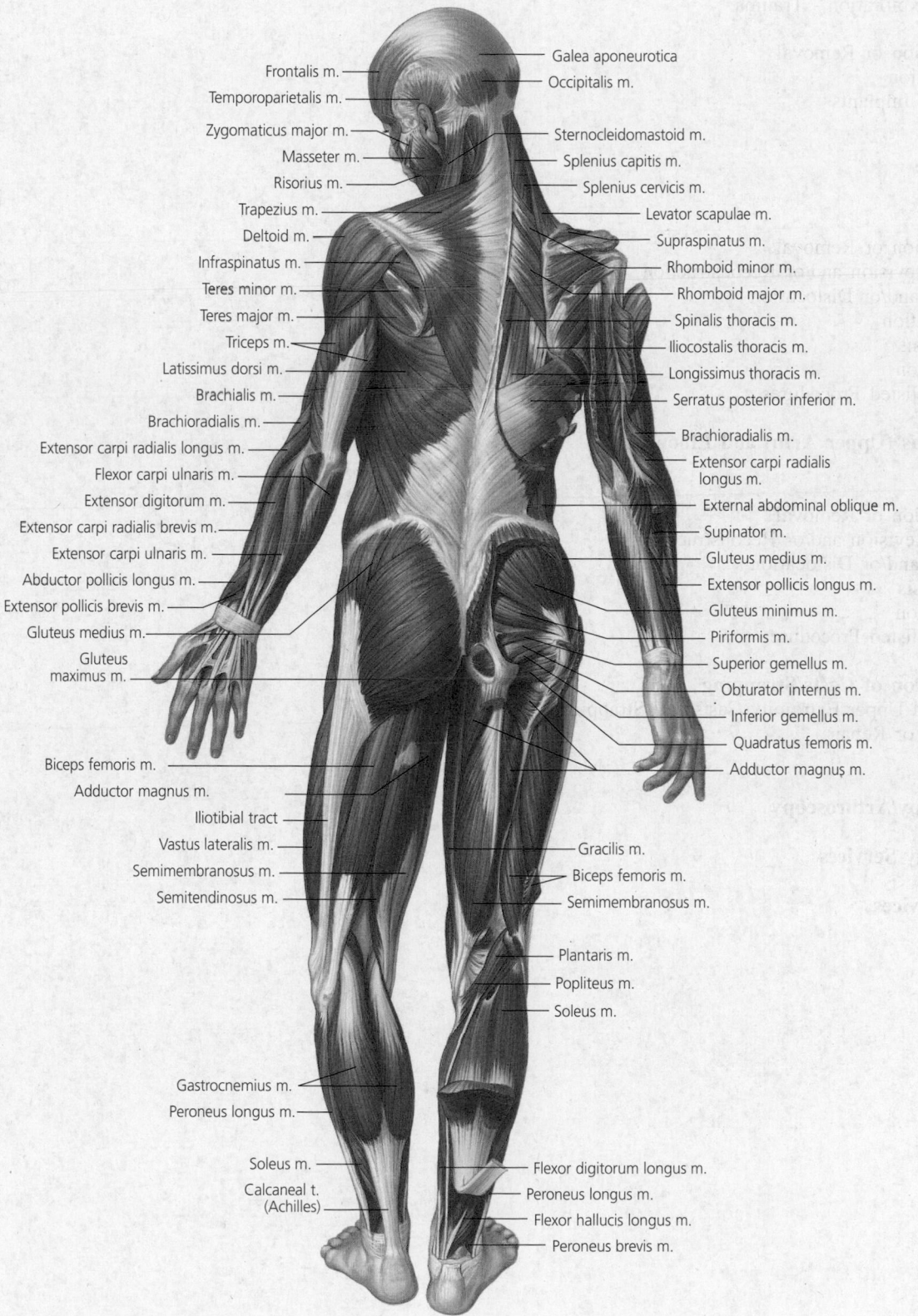

Frontalis m.
Temporoparietalis m.
Zygomaticus major m.
Masseter m.
Risorius m.
Trapezius m.
Deltoid m.
Infraspinatus m.
Teres minor m.
Teres major m.
Triceps m.
Latissimus dorsi m.
Brachialis m.
Brachioradialis m.
Extensor carpi radialis longus m.
Flexor carpi ulnaris m.
Extensor digitorum m.
Extensor carpi radialis brevis m.
Extensor carpi ulnaris m.
Abductor pollicis longus m.
Extensor pollicis brevis m.
Gluteus medius m.
Gluteus maximus m.

Galea aponeurotica
Occipitalis m.
Sternocleidomastoid m.
Splenius capitis m.
Splenius cervicis m.
Levator scapulae m.
Supraspinatus m.
Rhomboid minor m.
Rhomboid major m.
Spinalis thoracis m.
Iliocostalis thoracis m.
Longissimus thoracis m.
Serratus posterior inferior m.
Brachioradialis m.
Extensor carpi radialis longus m.
External abdominal oblique m.
Supinator m.
Gluteus medius m.
Extensor pollicis longus m.
Gluteus minimus m.
Piriformis m.
Superior gemellus m.
Obturator internus m.
Inferior gemellus m.
Quadratus femoris m.
Adductor magnus m.

Biceps femoris m.
Adductor magnus m.
Iliotibial tract
Vastus lateralis m.
Semimembranosus m.
Semitendinosus m.

Gracilis m.
Biceps femoris m.
Semimembranosus m.

Plantaris m.
Popliteus m.
Soleus m.

Gastrocnemius m.
Peroneus longus m.

Soleus m.
Calcaneal t. (Achilles)

Flexor digitorum longus m.
Peroneus longus m.
Flexor hallucis longus m.
Peroneus brevis m.

PLATE 6. MUSCULAR SYSTEM - SHOULDER AND ELBOW

General
Wound exploration - Trauma	20100-20103
Excision	20150-20251
Introduction or Removal	20500-20697
Replantation	20802-20838
Grafts of Implants	20900-20938
Other	20950-20999

Shoulder
Incision	23000-23044
Excision	23065-23220
Introduction or Removal	23330-23350
Repair, Revision and/or Reconstruction	23395-23491
Fracture and/or Dislocation	23500-23680
Manipulation	23700
Arthrodesis	23800-23802
Amputation	23900-23921
Other/Unlisted Procedures	23929

Humerous (Upper Arm) and Elbow
Incision	23930-24006
Excision	24065-24155
Introduction or Removal	24160-24220
Repair, Revision and/or Reconstruction	24300-24498
Fracture and/or Dislocation	24500-24685
Arthrodesis	24800-24802
Amputation	24900-24940
Other/Unlisted Procedure	24999

Application of Casts/Strapping
Body and Upper Extremity Casts and Strapping	29000-29280
Removal or Repair	29700-29750
Other	29799

Endoscopy/Arthroscopy
29805-29838

Radiology Services
73000-73225

E/M Services
99201-99499

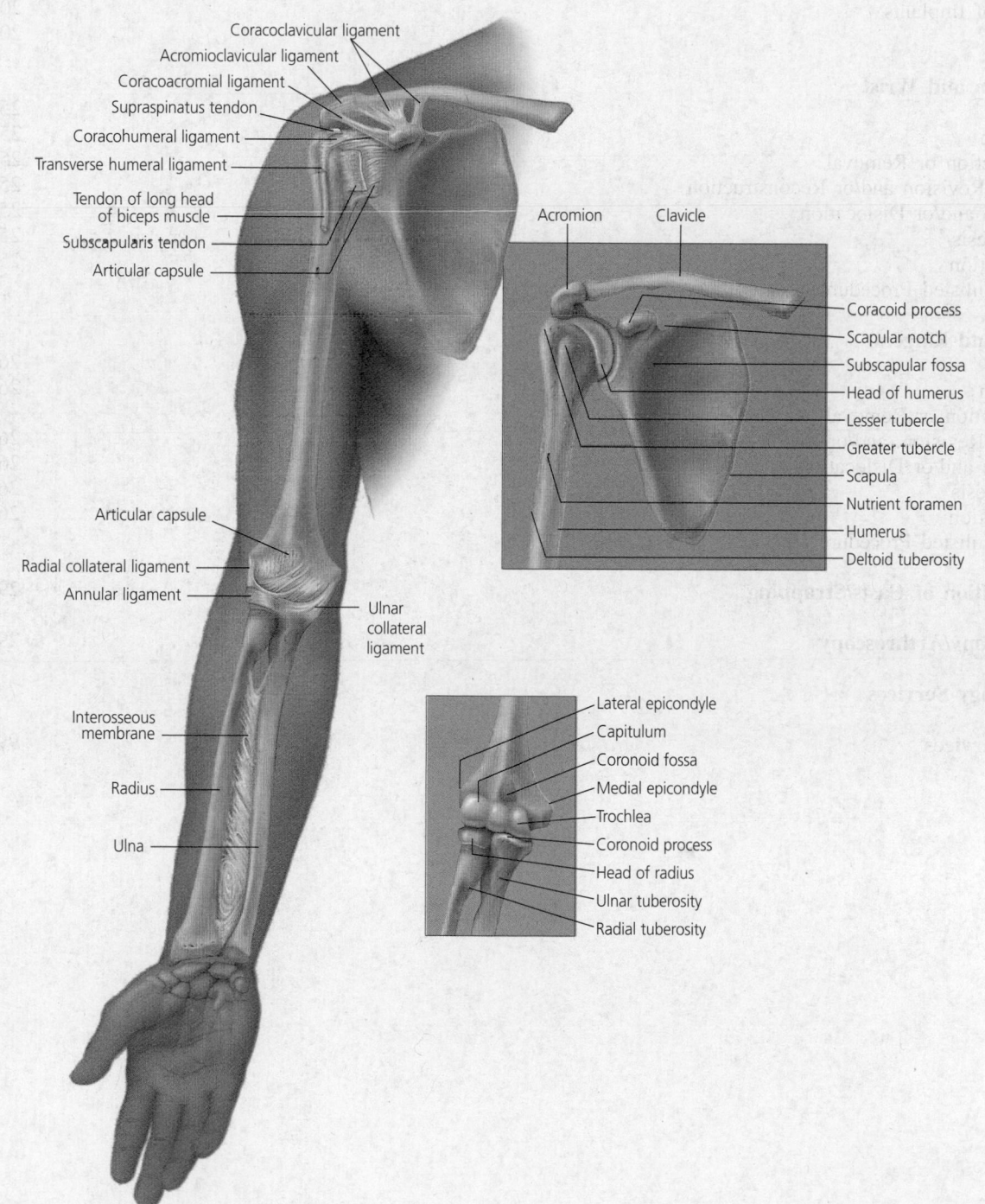

Coracoclavicular ligament
Acromioclavicular ligament
Coracoacromial ligament
Supraspinatus tendon
Coracohumeral ligament
Transverse humeral ligament
Tendon of long head of biceps muscle
Subscapularis tendon
Articular capsule

Acromion
Clavicle

Coracoid process
Scapular notch
Subscapular fossa
Head of humerus
Lesser tubercle
Greater tubercle
Scapula
Nutrient foramen
Humerus
Deltoid tuberosity

Articular capsule
Radial collateral ligament
Annular ligament
Ulnar collateral ligament

Interosseous membrane
Radius
Ulna

Lateral epicondyle
Capitulum
Coronoid fossa
Medial epicondyle
Trochlea
Coronoid process
Head of radius
Ulnar tuberosity
Radial tuberosity

PLATE 7. MUSCULAR SYSTEM - HAND AND WRIST

General
Wound exploration - Trauma	20100-20103
Excision	20150-20251
Introduction or Removal	20500-20697
Replantation	20802-20838
Grafts of Implants	20900-20938
Other	20950-20999

Forearm and Wrist
Incision	25000-25040
Excision	25065-25240
Introduction or Removal	25246-25259
Repair, Revision and/or Reconstruction	25260-25492
Fracture and/or Dislocation	25500-25695
Arthrodesis	25800-25830
Amputation	25900-25931
Other/Unlisted Procedure	25999

Hand and Fingers
Incision	26010-26080
Excision	26100-26262
Introduction or Removal	26320
Repair, Revision, and/or Reconstruction	26340-26596
Fracture and/or Dislocation	26600-26785
Arthrodesis	26820-26863
Amputation	26910-26952
Other/Unlisted Procedure	26989

Application of Casts/Strapping
29000-29280

Endoscopy/Arthroscopy
29840-29848

Radiology Services
73000-73225

E/M Services
99201-99499

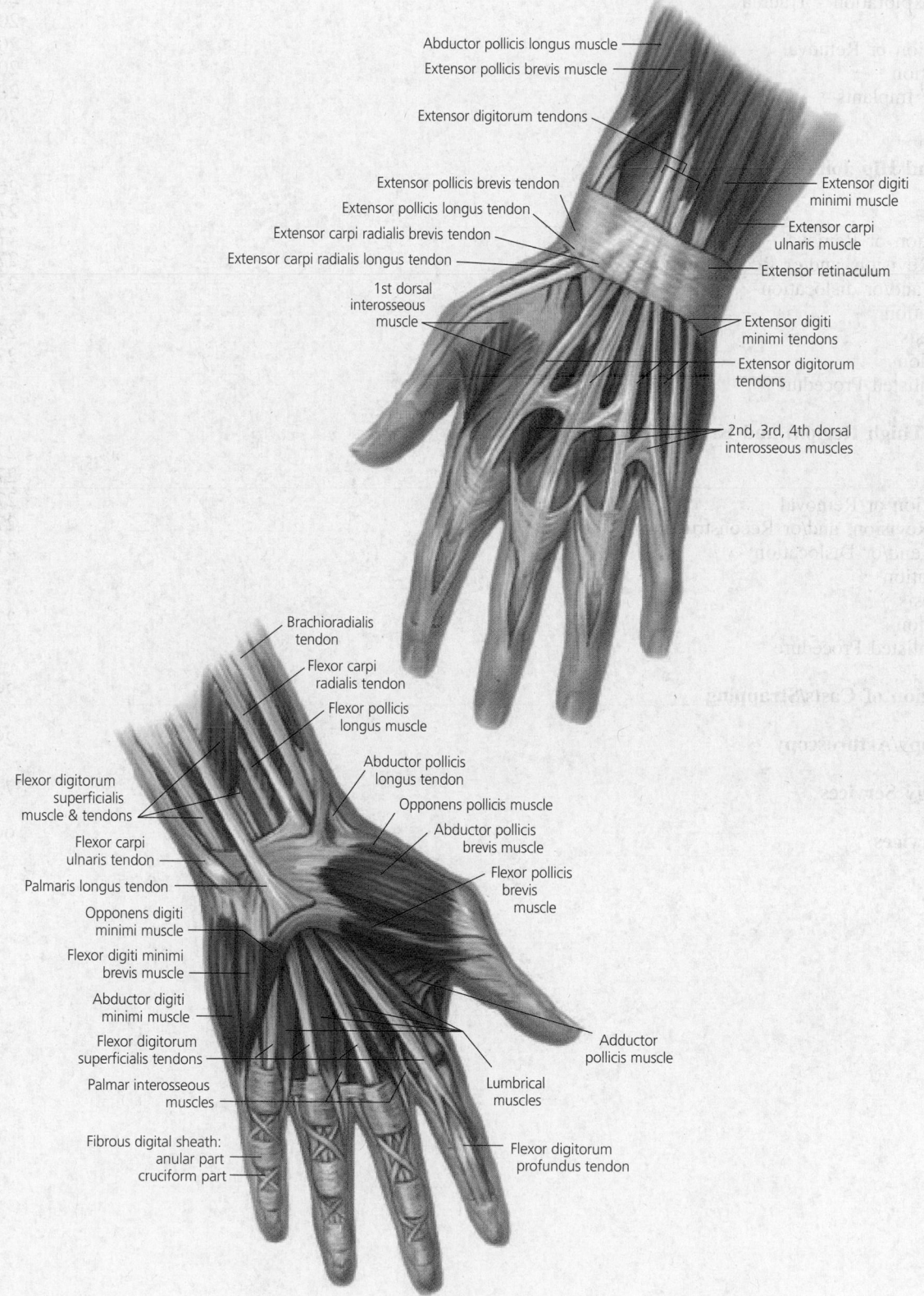

Abductor pollicis longus muscle

Extensor pollicis brevis muscle

Extensor digitorum tendons

Extensor pollicis brevis tendon

Extensor pollicis longus tendon

Extensor carpi radialis brevis tendon

Extensor carpi radialis longus tendon

1st dorsal interosseous muscle

Extensor digiti minimi muscle

Extensor carpi ulnaris muscle

Extensor retinaculum

Extensor digiti minimi tendons

Extensor digitorum tendons

2nd, 3rd, 4th dorsal interosseous muscles

Brachioradialis tendon

Flexor carpi radialis tendon

Flexor pollicis longus muscle

Abductor pollicis longus tendon

Opponens pollicis muscle

Abductor pollicis brevis muscle

Flexor pollicis brevis muscle

Flexor digitorum superficialis muscle & tendons

Flexor carpi ulnaris tendon

Palmaris longus tendon

Opponens digiti minimi muscle

Flexor digiti minimi brevis muscle

Abductor digiti minimi muscle

Flexor digitorum superficialis tendons

Palmar interosseous muscles

Adductor pollicis muscle

Lumbrical muscles

Fibrous digital sheath: anular part cruciform part

Flexor digitorum profundus tendon

PLATE 8. MUSCULOSKELETAL SYSTEM - HIP AND KNEE

General

Wound exploration - Trauma	20100-20103
Excision	20150-20251
Introduction or Removal	20500-20697
Replantation	20802-20838
Grafts of Implants	20900-20938
Other	20950-20999

Pelvis and Hip Joint

Incision	26990-27036
Excision	27040-27080
Introduction or Removal	27086-27096
Repair, Revision, and/or Reconstruction	27097-27187
Fracture and/or dislocation	27193-27269
Manipulation	27275
Arthrodesis	27280-27286
Amputation	27290-27295
Other/Unlisted Procedure	27299

Femur (Thigh Region) and Knee Joint

Incision	27301-27310
Excision	27323-27365
Introduction or Removal	27370-37372
Repair, Revision, and/or Reconstruction	27380-27499
Fracture and/or Dislocation	27500-27566
Manipulation	27570
Arthrodesis	27580
Amputation	27590-27598
Other/Unlisted Procedure	27599

Application of Casts/Strapping
29305-29584

Endoscopy/Arthroscopy
29850-29889

Radiology Services
73500-73725

E/M Services
99201-99499

Hip and Knee
(Anterior View)

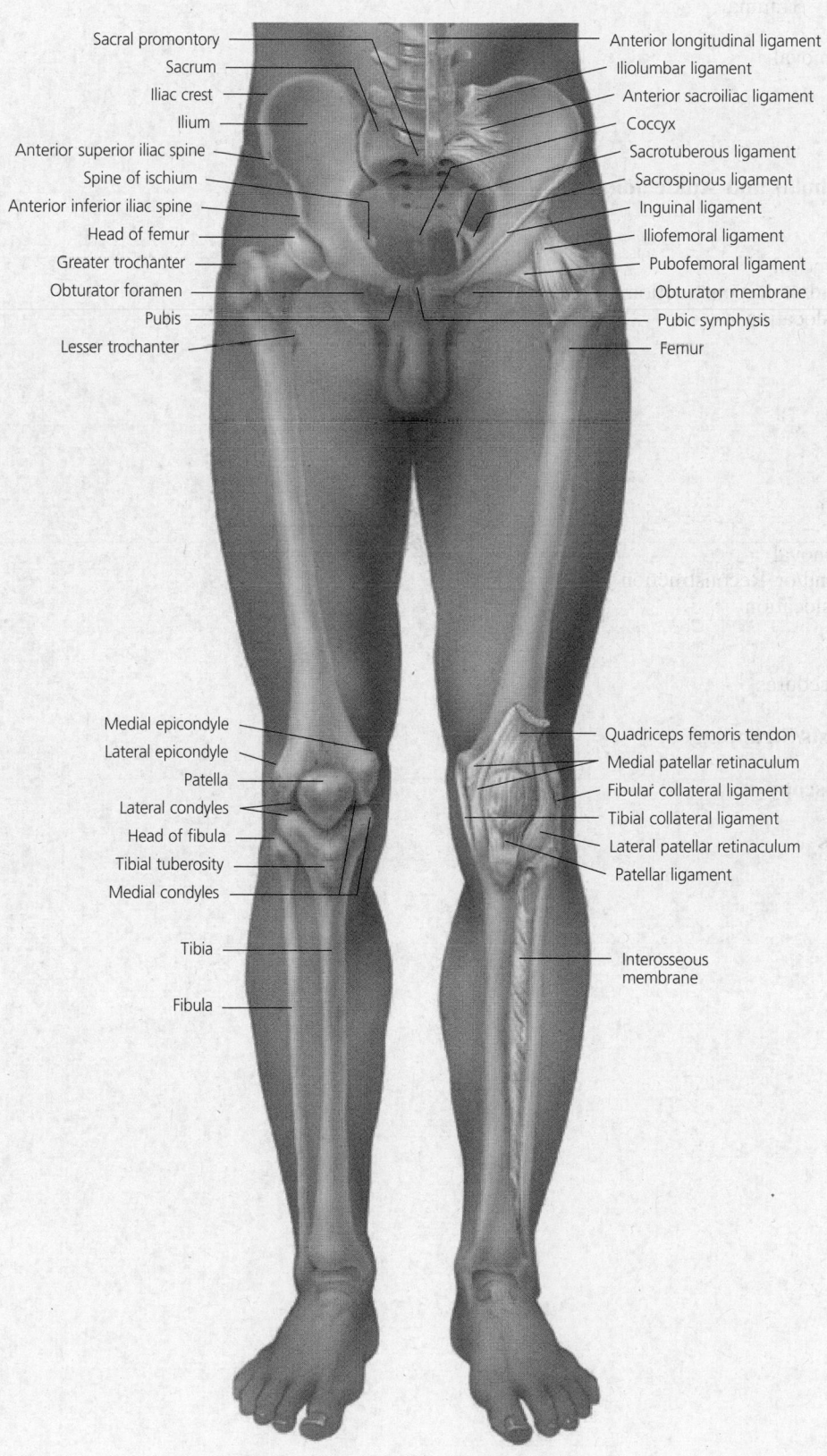

Sacral promontory
Sacrum
Iliac crest
Ilium
Anterior superior iliac spine
Spine of ischium
Anterior inferior iliac spine
Head of femur
Greater trochanter
Obturator foramen
Pubis
Lesser trochanter

Anterior longitudinal ligament
Iliolumbar ligament
Anterior sacroiliac ligament
Coccyx
Sacrotuberous ligament
Sacrospinous ligament
Inguinal ligament
Iliofemoral ligament
Pubofemoral ligament
Obturator membrane
Pubic symphysis
Femur

Medial epicondyle
Lateral epicondyle
Patella
Lateral condyles
Head of fibula
Tibial tuberosity
Medial condyles
Tibia
Fibula

Quadriceps femoris tendon
Medial patellar retinaculum
Fibular collateral ligament
Tibial collateral ligament
Lateral patellar retinaculum
Patellar ligament
Interosseous membrane

PLATE 9. MUSCULOSKELETAL SYSTEM - FOOT AND ANKLE

General
Wound exploration - Trauma	20100-20103
Excision	20150-20251
Introduction or Removal	20500-20697
Replantation	20802-20838
Grafts of Implants	20900-20938
Other	20950-20999

Leg (Tibia and Fibula) and Ankle Joint
Incision	27600-27612
Excision	27613-27647
Introduction or Removal	27648
Repair, Revision and/or Reconstruction	27650-27745
Fracture and/or Dislocation	27750-27848
Manipulation	27860
Arthrodesis	27870-27871
Amputation	27880-27889
Other Procedures	27892-27899

Foot and Toes
Incision	28001-28035
Excision	28043-28175
Introduction or Removal	28190-28193
Repair, Revision, and/or Reconstruction	28200-28360
Fracture and/or Dislocation	28400-28675
Arthrodesis	28705-28760
Amputation	28800-28825
Other/Unlisted Procedures	28890-28899

Application of Casts/Strapping	29305-29584
Endoscopy/Arthroscopy	29891-29999
Radiology Services	73500-73725
E/M Services	99201-99499

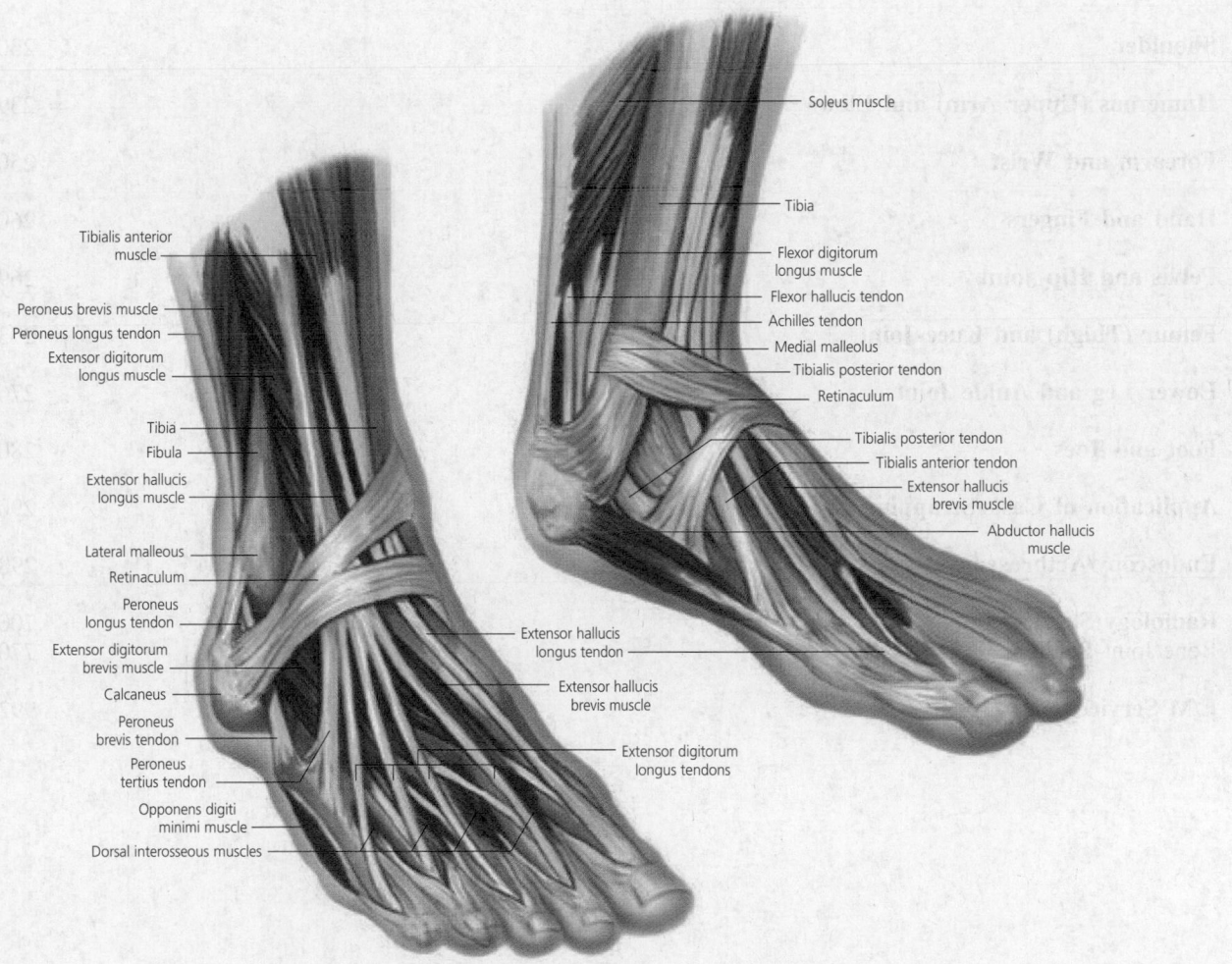

Tibialis anterior muscle

Peroneus brevis muscle

Peroneus longus tendon

Extensor digitorum longus muscle

Tibia

Fibula

Extensor hallucis longus muscle

Lateral malleous

Retinaculum

Peroneus longus tendon

Extensor digitorum brevis muscle

Calcaneus

Peroneus brevis tendon

Peroneus tertius tendon

Opponens digiti minimi muscle

Dorsal interosseous muscles

Extensor hallucis longus tendon

Extensor hallucis brevis muscle

Extensor digitorum longus tendons

Soleus muscle

Tibia

Flexor digitorum longus muscle

Flexor hallucis tendon

Achilles tendon

Medial malleolus

Tibialis posterior tendon

Retinaculum

Tibialis posterior tendon

Tibialis anterior tendon

Extensor hallucis brevis muscle

Abductor hallucis muscle

PLATE 10. SKELETAL SYSTEM - ANTERIOR VIEW

General	20005-20999
Head	21010-21499
Neck (Soft Tissues) and Thorax	21501-21899
Back and Flank	21920-21936
Spine (Vertebral Column)	22010-22899
Abdomen	22900-22999
Shoulder	23000-23929
Humerous (Upper Arm) and Elbow	23930-24999
Forearm and Wrist	25000-25999
Hand and Fingers	26010-26989
Pelvis and Hip Joint	26990-27299
Femur (Thigh) and Knee Joint	27301-27599
Lower Leg and Ankle Joint	27600-27899
Foot and Toes	28001-28899
Application of Casts/Strapping	29000-29799
Endoscopy/Arthroscopy	29800-29999
Radiology Services Bone/Joint Studies	70010-73725 77071-77084
E/M Services	99201-99499

Skeletal System
(Anterior View)

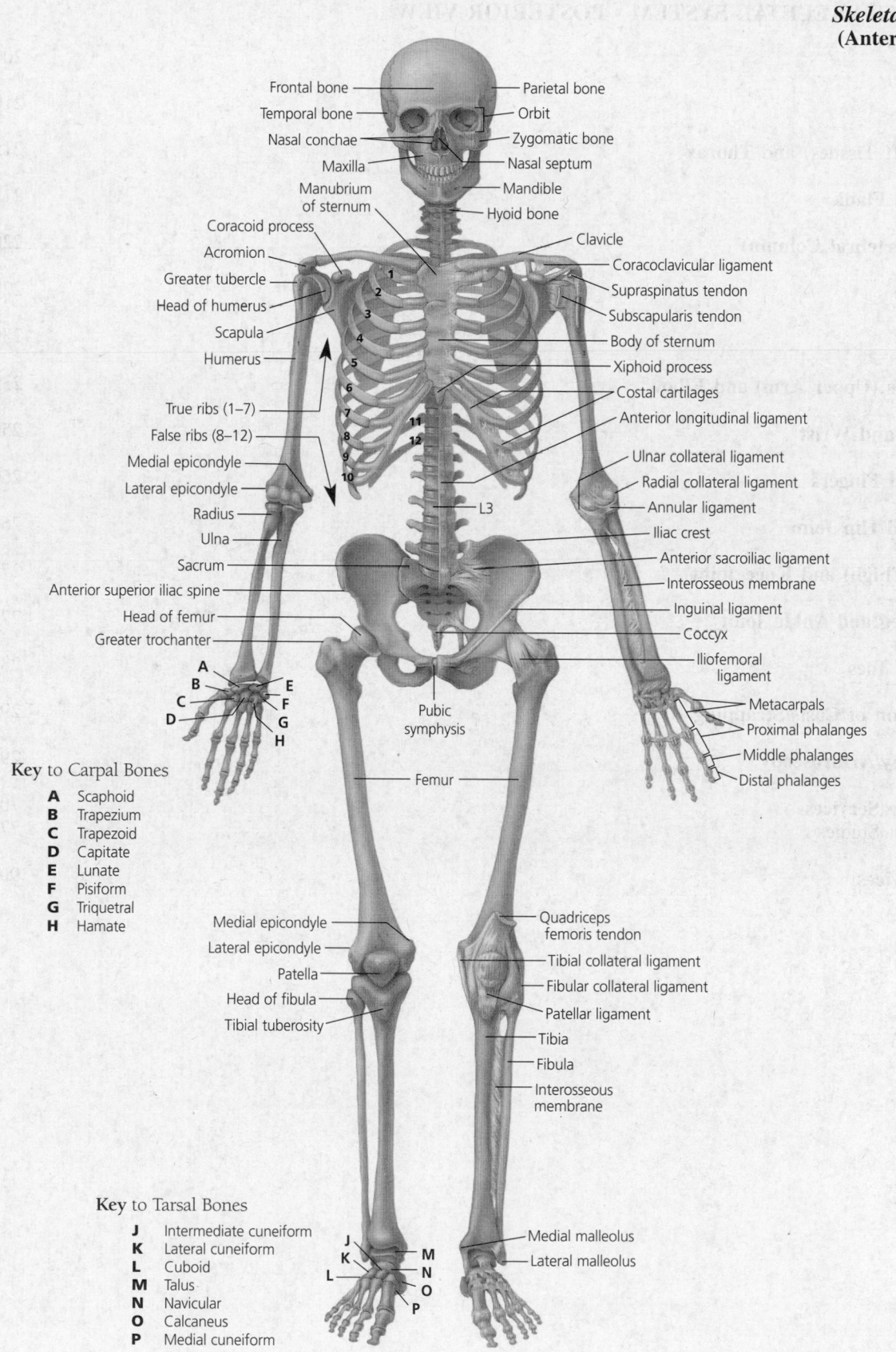

Frontal bone
Temporal bone
Nasal conchae
Maxilla
Manubrium of sternum
Coracoid process
Acromion
Greater tubercle
Head of humerus
Scapula
Humerus
True ribs (1–7)
False ribs (8–12)
Medial epicondyle
Lateral epicondyle
Radius
Ulna
Sacrum
Anterior superior iliac spine
Head of femur
Greater trochanter

Parietal bone
Orbit
Zygomatic bone
Nasal septum
Mandible
Hyoid bone
Clavicle
Coracoclavicular ligament
Supraspinatus tendon
Subscapularis tendon
Body of sternum
Xiphoid process
Costal cartilages
Anterior longitudinal ligament
Ulnar collateral ligament
Radial collateral ligament
Annular ligament
Iliac crest
Anterior sacroiliac ligament
Interosseous membrane
Inguinal ligament
Coccyx
Iliofemoral ligament
Metacarpals
Proximal phalanges
Middle phalanges
Distal phalanges

L3

Pubic symphysis
Femur

Key to Carpal Bones

A Scaphoid
B Trapezium
C Trapezoid
D Capitate
E Lunate
F Pisiform
G Triquetral
H Hamate

Medial epicondyle
Lateral epicondyle
Patella
Head of fibula
Tibial tuberosity

Quadriceps femoris tendon
Tibial collateral ligament
Fibular collateral ligament
Patellar ligament
Tibia
Fibula
Interosseous membrane

Key to Tarsal Bones

J Intermediate cuneiform
K Lateral cuneiform
L Cuboid
M Talus
N Navicular
O Calcaneus
P Medial cuneiform

Medial malleolus
Lateral malleolus

PLATE 11. SKELETAL SYSTEM - POSTERIOR VIEW

General	20005-20999
Head	21010-21499
Neck (Soft Tissues) and Thorax	21501-21899
Back and Flank	21920-21936
Spine (Vertebral Column)	22010-22899
Abdomen	22900-22999
Shoulder	23000-23929
Humerous (Upper Arm) and Elbow	23930-24999
Forearm and Wrist	25000-25999
Hand and Fingers	26010-26989
Pelvis and Hip Joint	26990-27299
Femur (Thigh) and Knee Joint	27301-27599
Lower Leg and Ankle Joint	27600-27899
Foot and Toes	28001-28899
Application of Casts/Strapping	29000-29799
Endoscopy/Arthroscopy	29800-29999
Radiology Services Bone/Joint Studies	70010-73725 77071-77084
E/M Services	99201-99499

Skeletal System
(Posterior View)

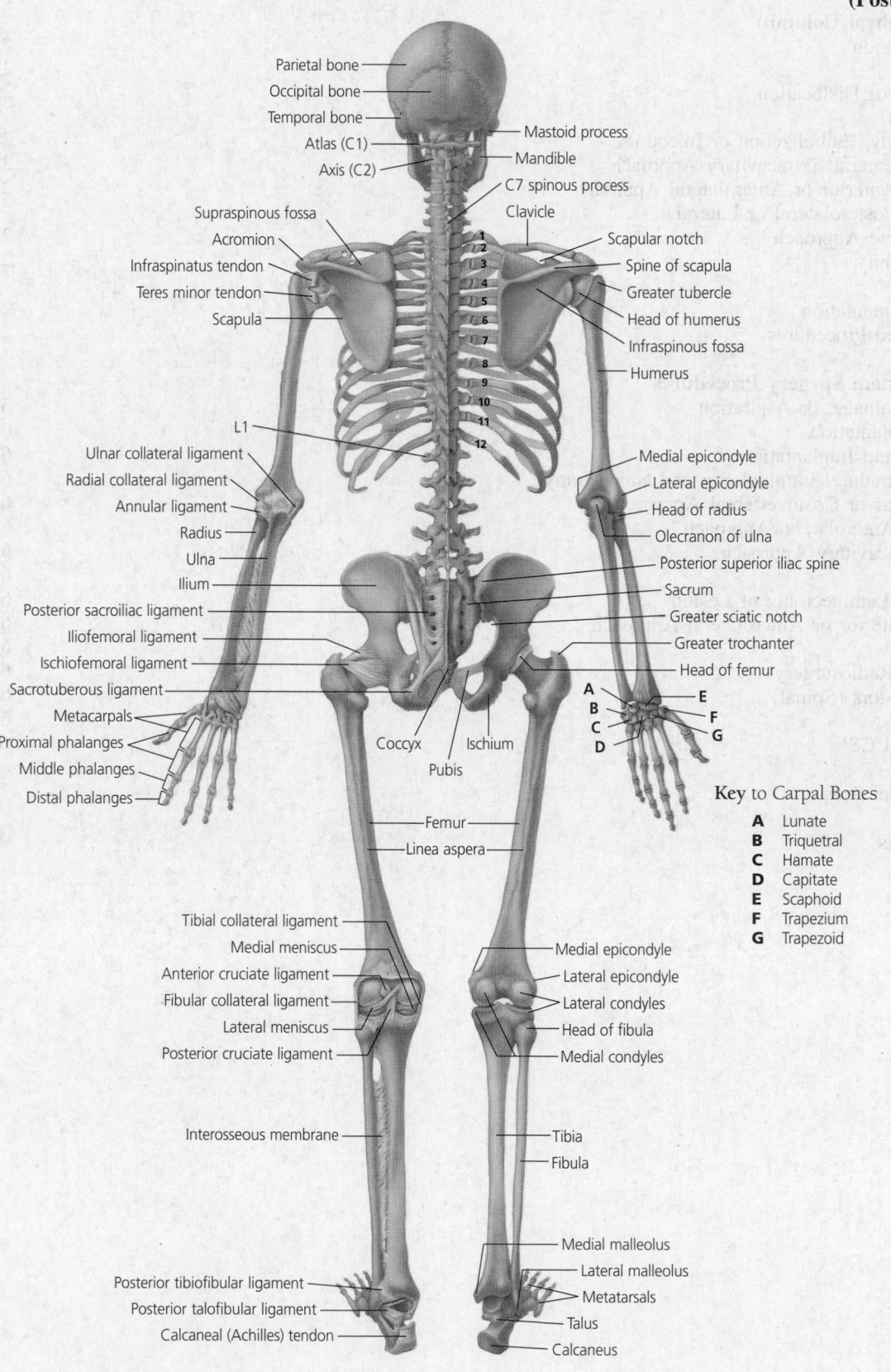

Parietal bone
Occipital bone
Temporal bone
Atlas (C1)
Axis (C2)
Supraspinous fossa
Acromion
Infraspinatus tendon
Teres minor tendon
Scapula
L1
Ulnar collateral ligament
Radial collateral ligament
Annular ligament
Radius
Ulna
Ilium
Posterior sacroiliac ligament
Iliofemoral ligament
Ischiofemoral ligament
Sacrotuberous ligament
Metacarpals
Proximal phalanges
Middle phalanges
Distal phalanges

Mastoid process
Mandible
C7 spinous process
Clavicle
Scapular notch
Spine of scapula
Greater tubercle
Head of humerus
Infraspinous fossa
Humerus
Medial epicondyle
Lateral epicondyle
Head of radius
Olecranon of ulna
Posterior superior iliac spine
Sacrum
Greater sciatic notch
Greater trochanter
Head of femur

Coccyx
Ischium
Pubis

A
B
C
D

E
F
G

Femur
Linea aspera

Tibial collateral ligament
Medial meniscus
Anterior cruciate ligament
Fibular collateral ligament
Lateral meniscus
Posterior cruciate ligament

Medial epicondyle
Lateral epicondyle
Lateral condyles
Head of fibula
Medial condyles

Interosseous membrane

Tibia
Fibula

Posterior tibiofibular ligament
Posterior talofibular ligament
Calcaneal (Achilles) tendon

Medial malleolus
Lateral malleolus
Metatarsals
Talus
Calcaneus

Key to Carpal Bones

A Lunate
B Triquetral
C Hamate
D Capitate
E Scaphoid
F Trapezium
G Trapezoid

57

PLATE 12. SKELETAL SYSTEM - VERTEBRAL COLUMN

Spine (Vertebral Column)

Incision/Excision	22010-22116
Osteotomy	22206-22226
Fracture and/or Dislocation	22305-22328
Manipulation	22505
Vertebral Body, Embolization or Injection	22520-22527
Arthrodesis-Lateral Extracavitary Approach	22532-22534
Arthrodesis-Anterior or Anterolateral Approach	22548-22585
Arthrodesis-Posterolateral or Lateral Transverse Approach	22590-22634
Spine Deformity	22800-22819
Exploration	22830
Spinal Instrumentation	22840-22865
Other/Unlisted Procedures	22899

Nervous System Surgery Procedures

Injection, Drainage, or Aspiration	62263-62319
Catheter Implantation	62350-62355
Reservoir/Pump Implantation	62360-62370
Posterior Extradural Laminotomy or Laminectomy	63001-63051
Transpedicular or Costovertebral Approach	63055-63066
Anterior or Anterolateral Approach	63075-63091
Lateral Extracavitary Approach	63101-63103
Incision	63170-63200
Excision by Laminectomy of Lesion	63250-63295
Excision, Anterior or Anterolateral Approach	63300-63308
Stereotaxis	63600-63615
Stereotactic Radiosurgery	63620-63621
Neurostimulators (Spinal)	63650-63688
Repair	63700-63710
Shunt, Spinal CSF	63740-63746

Radiology Services   72010-72295

E/M Services   99201-99499

Vertebral Column
(Lateral View)

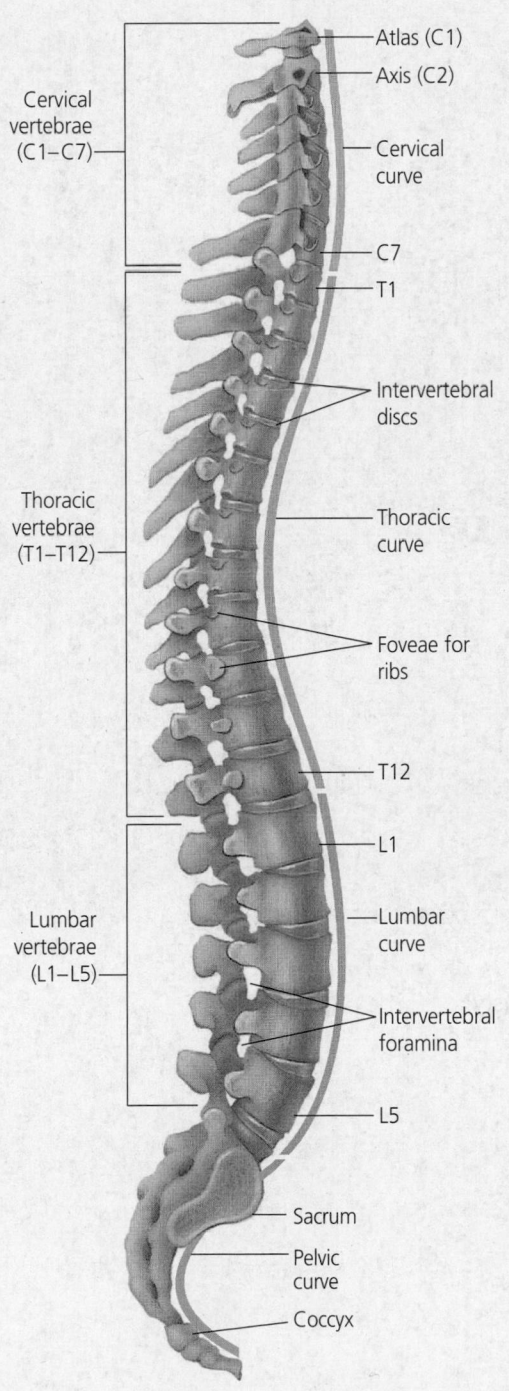

Atlas (C1)

Axis (C2)

Cervical
vertebrae
(C1–C7)

Cervical
curve

C7

T1

Intervertebral
discs

Thoracic
vertebrae
(T1–T12)

Thoracic
curve

Foveae for
ribs

T12

L1

Lumbar
curve

Lumbar
vertebrae
(L1–L5)

Intervertebral
foramina

L5

Sacrum

Pelvic
curve

Coccyx

PLATE 13. RESPIRATORY SYSTEM

Nose

Incision	30000-30020
Excision	30100-30160
Introduction	30200-30220
Removal of Foreign Body	30300-30320
Repair	30400-30630
Destruction	30801-30802
Other	30901-30999

Accessory Sinuses

Incision	31000-31090
Excision	31200-31230
Endoscopy	31231-31297
Other	31299

Larynx

Excision	31300-31420
Introduction	31500-31502
Endoscopy	31505-31579
Repair	31580-31590
Destruction	31595
Other	31599

Trachea and Bronchi

Incision	31600-31614
Endoscopy	31615-31656
Introduction	31715-31730
Excision, Repair	31750-31830
Other	31899

Lungs and Pleura

Incision	32035-32225
Excision/Resection and Removal	32310-32540
Introduction and Removal	32550-32553
Destruction	32560-32562
Thoracoscopy	32601-32674
Repair	32800-32820
Lung Transplantation	32850-32856
Surgical Collapse Therapy; Thoracoplasty	32900-32960
Other	32997-32999

Radiology Services/Chest	71010-71555

E/M Services	99201-99499

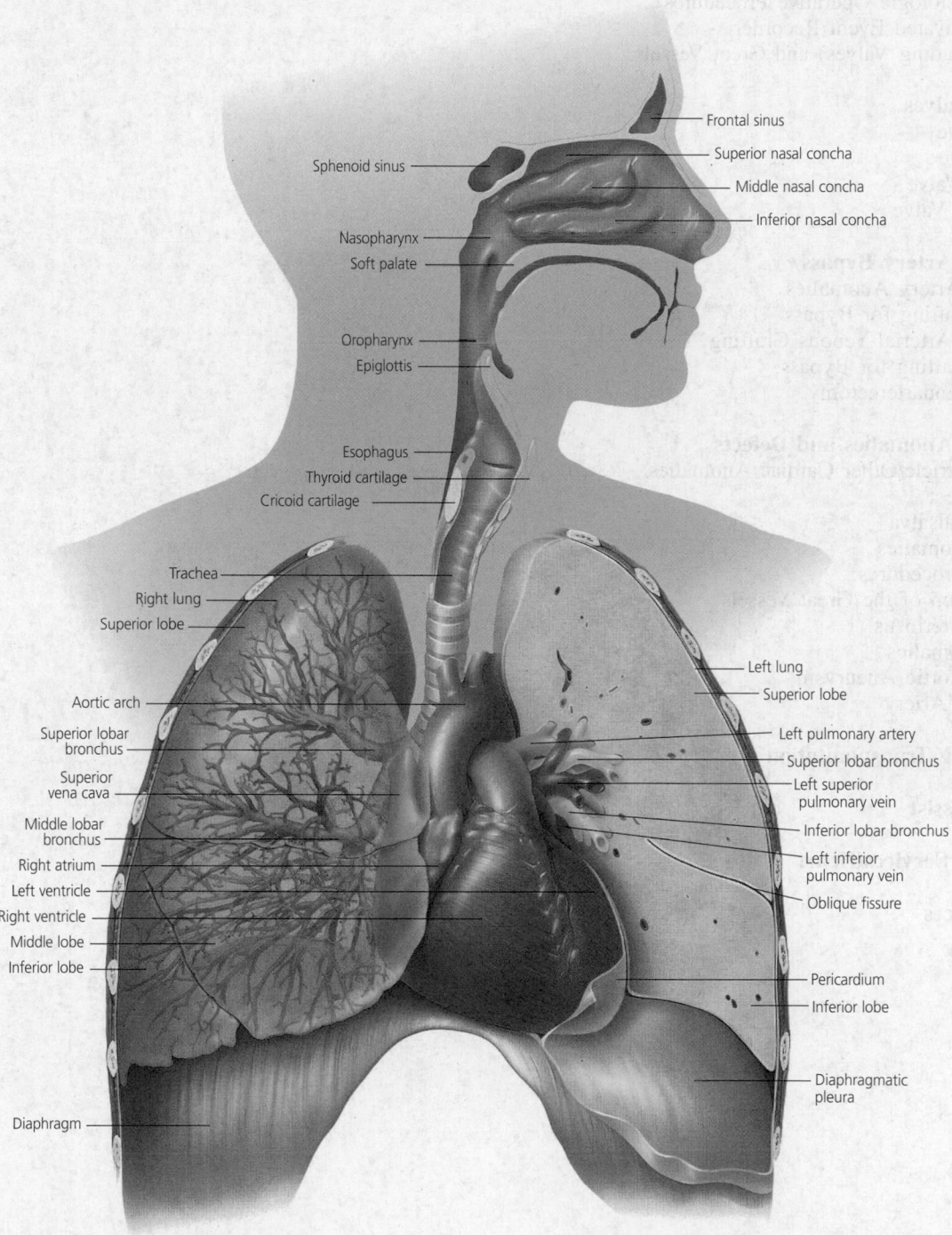

Frontal sinus

Sphenoid sinus

Superior nasal concha

Middle nasal concha

Inferior nasal concha

Nasopharynx

Soft palate

Oropharynx

Epiglottis

Esophagus

Thyroid cartilage

Cricoid cartilage

Trachea

Right lung

Superior lobe

Left lung

Superior lobe

Aortic arch

Left pulmonary artery

Superior lobar bronchus

Superior lobar bronchus

Superior vena cava

Left superior pulmonary vein

Middle lobar bronchus

Inferior lobar bronchus

Right atrium

Left inferior pulmonary vein

Left ventricle

Right ventricle

Oblique fissure

Middle lobe

Inferior lobe

Pericardium

Inferior lobe

Diaphragmatic pleura

Diaphragm

PLATE 14. HEART AND PERICARDIUM

General

Pericardium	33010-33050
Cardiac Tumor	33120-33130
Pacemaker or Defibrillator	33202-33249
Electrophysiologic Operative Procedures	33250-33266
Patient Activated Event Recorder	33282-33284
Heart (Including Valves) and Great Vessels	33300-33335

Cardiac Valves

Aortic Valve	33361-33417
Mitral Valve	33420-33430
Tricuspid Valve	33460-33468
Pulmonary Valve	33470-33478

Coronary Artery Bypass

Coronary Artery Anomalies	33500-33507
Venous Grafting for Bypass	33510-33516
Combined Arterial-Venous Grafting	33517-33530
Arterial Grafting for Bypass	33533-33548
Coronary Endarterectomy	33572

Repair of Anomalies and Defects

Single Ventricle/Other Cardiac Anomalies	33600-33622
Septal Defect	33641-33697
Sinus of Valsalva	33702-33722
Venous Anomalies	33724-33732
Shunting Procedures	33735-33768
Transposition of the Great Vessels	33770-33783
Truncus Arteriosus	33786-33788
Aortic Anomalies	33800-33853
Thoracic Aortic Aneurysm	33860-33877
Pulmonary Artery	33910-33926

Heart/Lung Transplantation	33930-33945
Cardiac Assist	33960-33993
Radiology Services/Heart	75557-75574
E/M Services	99201-99499

Heart
(External View)

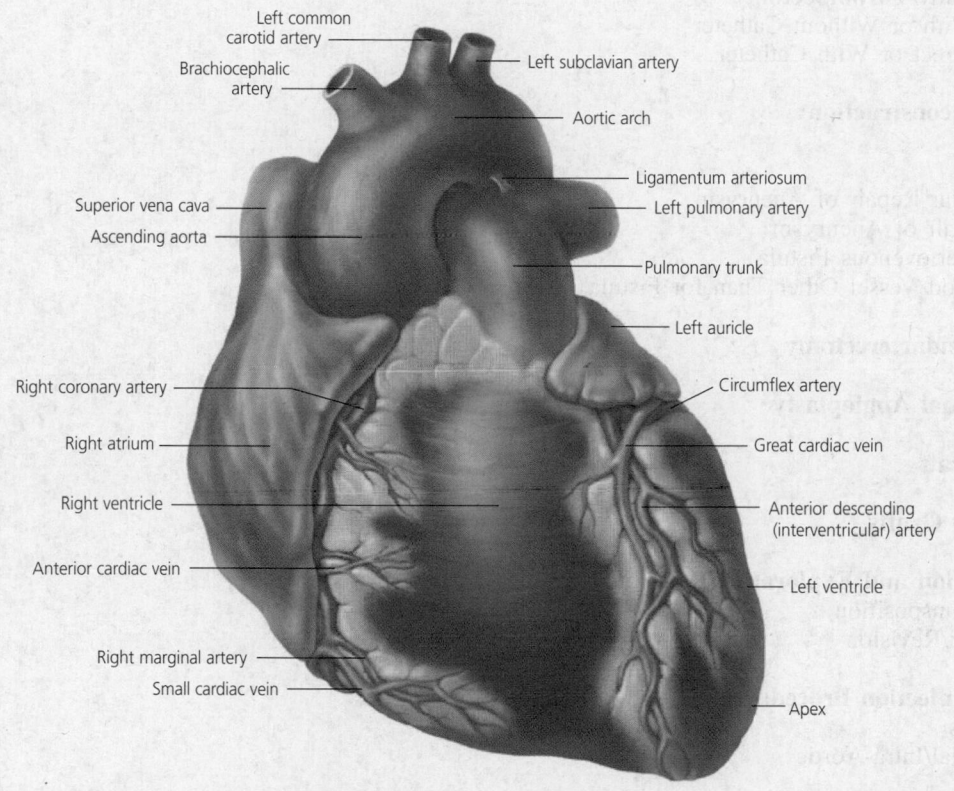

Left common carotid artery

Brachiocephalic artery

Superior vena cava

Ascending aorta

Right coronary artery

Right atrium

Right ventricle

Anterior cardiac vein

Right marginal artery

Small cardiac vein

Left subclavian artery

Aortic arch

Ligamentum arteriosum

Left pulmonary artery

Pulmonary trunk

Left auricle

Circumflex artery

Great cardiac vein

Anterior descending (interventricular) artery

Left ventricle

Apex

Heart
(Internal View)

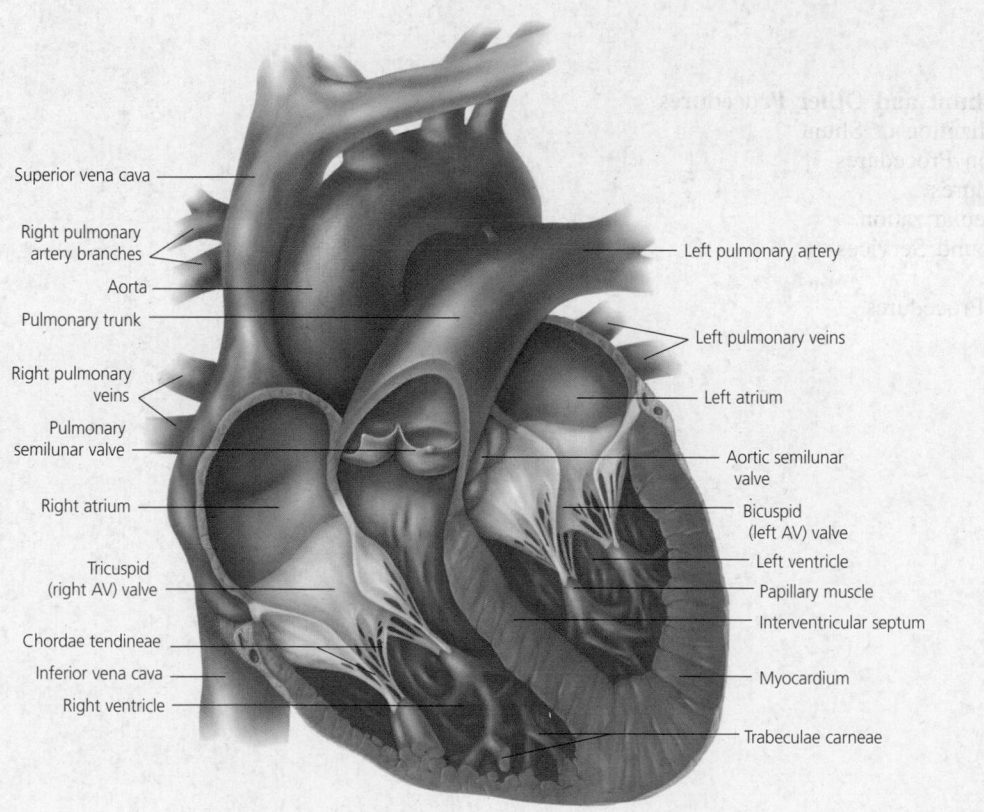

Superior vena cava

Right pulmonary artery branches

Aorta

Pulmonary trunk

Right pulmonary veins

Pulmonary semilunar valve

Right atrium

Tricuspid (right AV) valve

Chordae tendineae

Inferior vena cava

Right ventricle

Left pulmonary artery

Left pulmonary veins

Left atrium

Aortic semilunar valve

Bicuspid (left AV) valve

Left ventricle

Papillary muscle

Interventricular septum

Myocardium

Trabeculae carneae

PLATE 15. CIRCULATORY SYSTEM

Embolectomy/Thrombectomy
Arterial, With or Without Catheter — 34001-34203
Venous, Direct or With Catheter — 34401-34490

Venous Reconstruction — 34501-34530

Repair
Endovascular Repair of Aneurysm — 34800-34900
Direct Repair of Aneurysm — 35001-35152
Repair Arteriovenous Fistula — 35180-35190
Repair Blood Vessel Other Than for Fistula — 35201-35286

Thromboendarterectomy — 35301-35390

Transluminal Angioplasty — 35450-35476

Bypass Graft — 35500-35671

Composite Grafts — 35681-35683

Transposition and Exploration/Revision
Arterial Transposition — 35691-35697
Exploration/Revision — 35700-35907

Vascular Injection Procedures
Intravenous — 36000-36015
Intra-Arterial/Intra-Aortic — 36100-36299
Venous — 36400-36522
Central Venous Access — 36555-36598
Arterial — 36600-36660
Intraosseous — 36680

Cannulization or Shunt and Other Procedures
Intervascular Cannulization or Shunt — 36800-36870
Portal Decompression Procedures — 37140-37183
Transcatheter Procedures — 37184-37216
Endovascular Revascularization — 37220-37235
Intravascular Ultrasound Services — 37250-37251
Endoscopy — 37500-37501
Ligation and Other Procedures — 37565-37799

Radiology Services — 75600-75989

E/M Services — 99201-99499

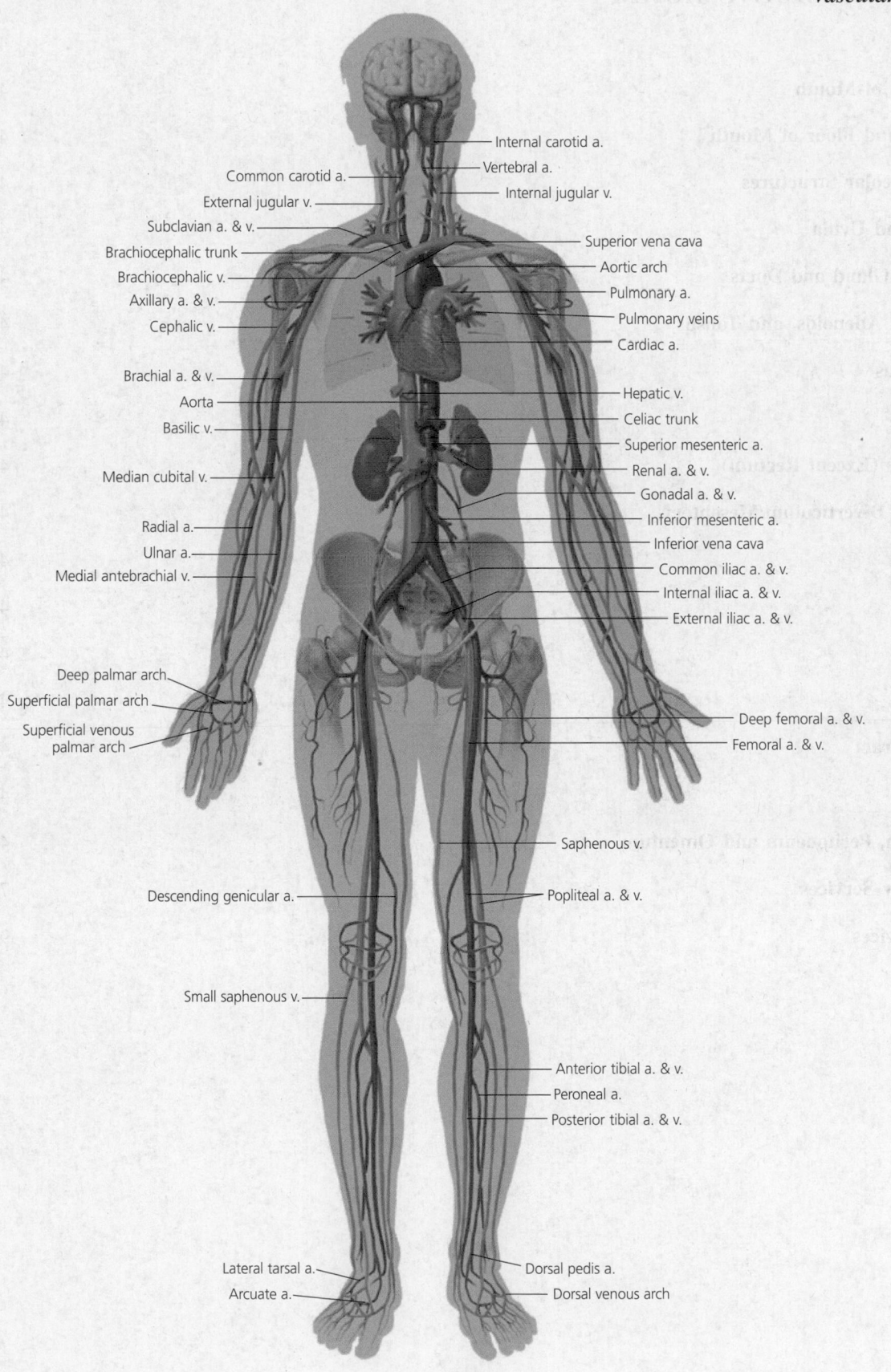

Internal carotid a.
Vertebral a.
Common carotid a.
Internal jugular v.
External jugular v.
Subclavian a. & v.
Superior vena cava
Brachiocephalic trunk
Aortic arch
Brachiocephalic v.
Pulmonary a.
Axillary a. & v.
Pulmonary veins
Cephalic v.
Cardiac a.
Brachial a. & v.
Hepatic v.
Aorta
Celiac trunk
Basilic v.
Superior mesenteric a.
Median cubital v.
Renal a. & v.
Gonadal a. & v.
Radial a.
Inferior mesenteric a.
Ulnar a.
Inferior vena cava
Medial antebrachial v.
Common iliac a. & v.
Internal iliac a. & v.
External iliac a. & v.
Deep palmar arch
Superficial palmar arch
Superficial venous palmar arch
Deep femoral a. & v.
Femoral a. & v.
Saphenous v.
Descending genicular a.
Popliteal a. & v.
Small saphenous v.
Anterior tibial a. & v.
Peroneal a.
Posterior tibial a. & v.
Lateral tarsal a.
Dorsal pedis a.
Arcuate a.
Dorsal venous arch

PLATE 16. DIGESTIVE SYSTEM

Lips	40490-40799
Vestibule of Mouth	40800-40899
Tongue and Floor of Mouth	41000-41599
Dentoalveolar Structures	41800-41899
Palate and Uvula	42000-42299
Salivary Gland and Ducts	42300-42699
Pharynx, Adenoids, and Tonsils	42700-42999
Esophagus	43020-43499
Stomach	43500-43999
Intestines (Except Rectum)	44005-44799
Meckel's Diverticulum/Mesentery	44800-44899
Appendix	44900-44979
Rectum	45000-45999
Anus	46020-46999
Liver	47000-47399
Biliary Tract	47400-47999
Pancreas	48000-48999
Abdomen, Peritoneum and Omentum	49000-49999
Radiology Services	74000-74363
E/M Services	99201-99499

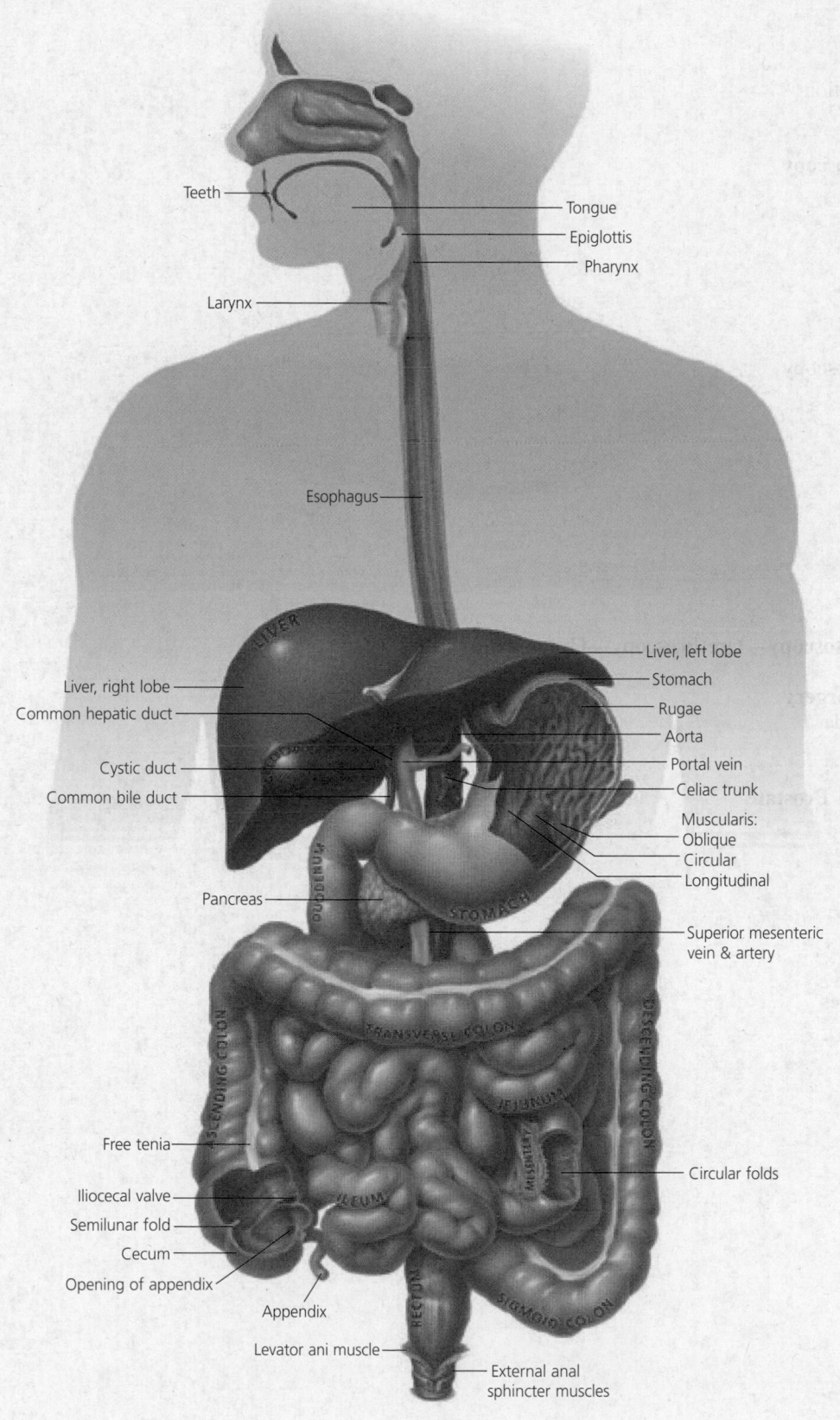

Teeth

Tongue

Epiglottis

Pharynx

Larynx

Esophagus

Liver, left lobe

Liver, right lobe

Stomach

Common hepatic duct

Rugae

Aorta

Cystic duct

Portal vein

Common bile duct

Celiac trunk

Muscularis:

Oblique

Circular

Longitudinal

Pancreas

Superior mesenteric vein & artery

Free tenia

Circular folds

Iliocecal valve

Semilunar fold

Cecum

Opening of appendix

Appendix

Levator ani muscle

External anal sphincter muscles

PLATE 17. GENITOURINARY SYSTEM

Kidney

Incision	50010-50135
Excision	50200-50290
Renal Transplantation	50300-50380
Introduction	50382-50398
Repair	50400-50540
Laparoscopy/Endoscopy	50541-50580
Other	50590-50593

Ureter

Incision	50600-50630
Excision	50650-50660
Introduction	50684-50690
Repair	50700-50940
Laparoscopy/Endoscopy	50945-50980

Bladder

Incision	51020-51080
Removal	51100-51102
Excision	51500-51597
Introduction	51600-51720
Urodynamics	51725-51798
Repair	51800-51980
Laparoscopy	51990-51999

Endoscopy—Cystoscopy—Urethroscopy—Cystourethroscopy

	52000-52010

Transurethral Surgery

Urethra and Bladder	52204-52318
Ureter and Pelvis	52320-52355

Vesical Neck and Prostate

	52400-52700

Urethra

Incision	53000-53085
Excision	53200-53275
Repair	53400-53520
Manipulation	53600-53665

Radiology Services

	74400-74485

E/M Services

	99201-99499

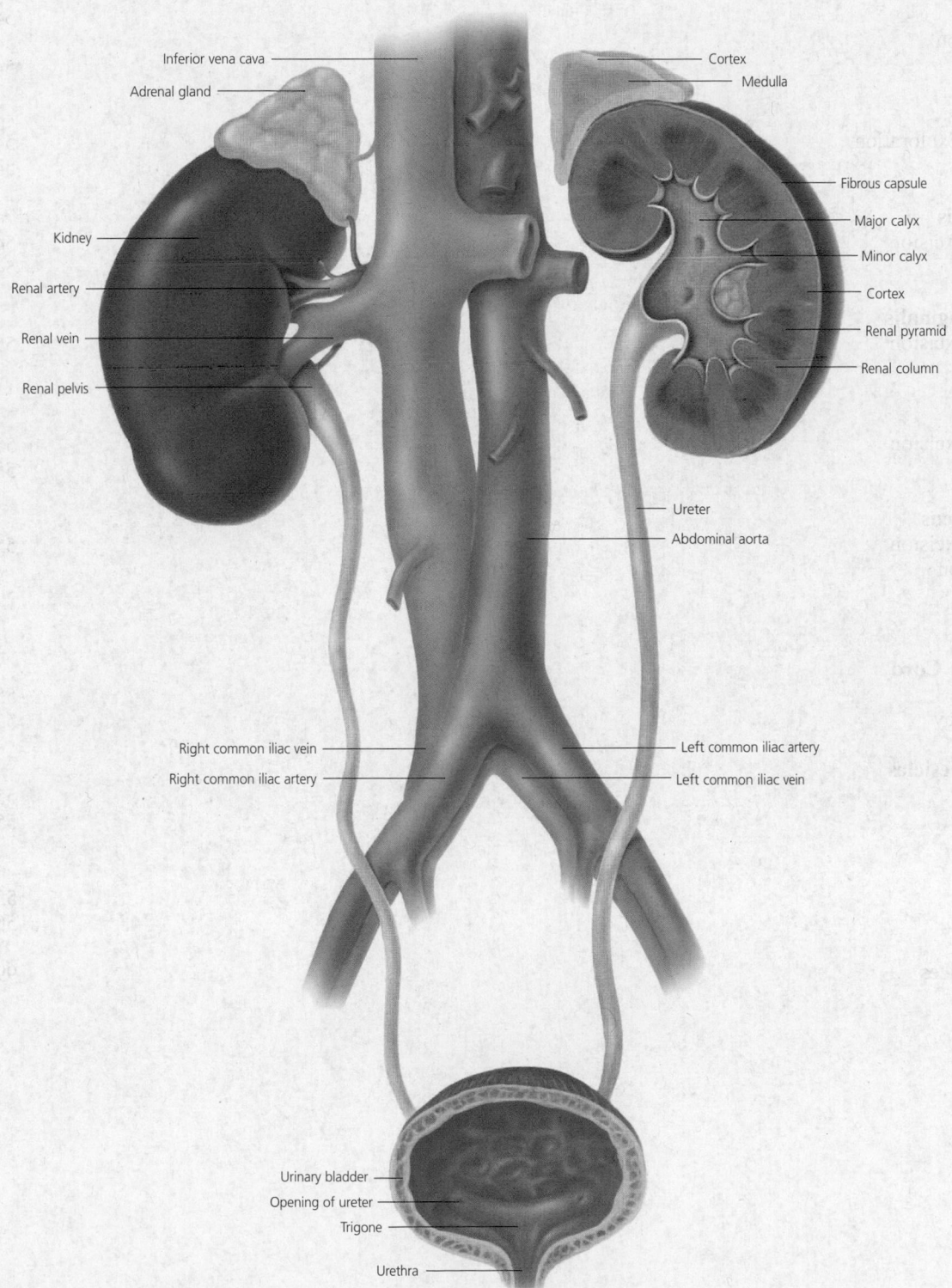

Inferior vena cava

Adrenal gland

Cortex

Medulla

Kidney

Fibrous capsule

Renal artery

Major calyx

Renal vein

Minor calyx

Renal pelvis

Cortex

Renal pyramid

Renal column

Ureter

Abdominal aorta

Right common iliac vein

Left common iliac artery

Right common iliac artery

Left common iliac vein

Urinary bladder

Opening of ureter

Trigone

Urethra

PLATE 18. MALE REPRODUCTIVE SYSTEM

Penis
Incision	54000-54015
Destruction	54050-54065
Excision	54100-54164
Introduction	54200-54250
Repair	54300-54440

Testis
Excision/Exploration	54500-54560
Repair	54600-54680

Epididymis
Incision/Excision	54700-54861
Repair	54900-54901

Tunica Vaginalis
Incision/Excision	55000-55041
Repair	55060

Scrotum
Incision/Excision	55100-55150
Repair	55175-55180

Vas Deferens
Incision/Excision	55200-55250
Introduction	55300
Repair	55400
Suture	55450

Spermatic Cord
Excision	55500-55540
Laparoscopy	55550-55559

Seminal Vesicles
Incision	55600-55605
Excision	55650-55680

Prostate
Incision	55700-55725
Excision	55801-55865

E/M Services
	99201-99499

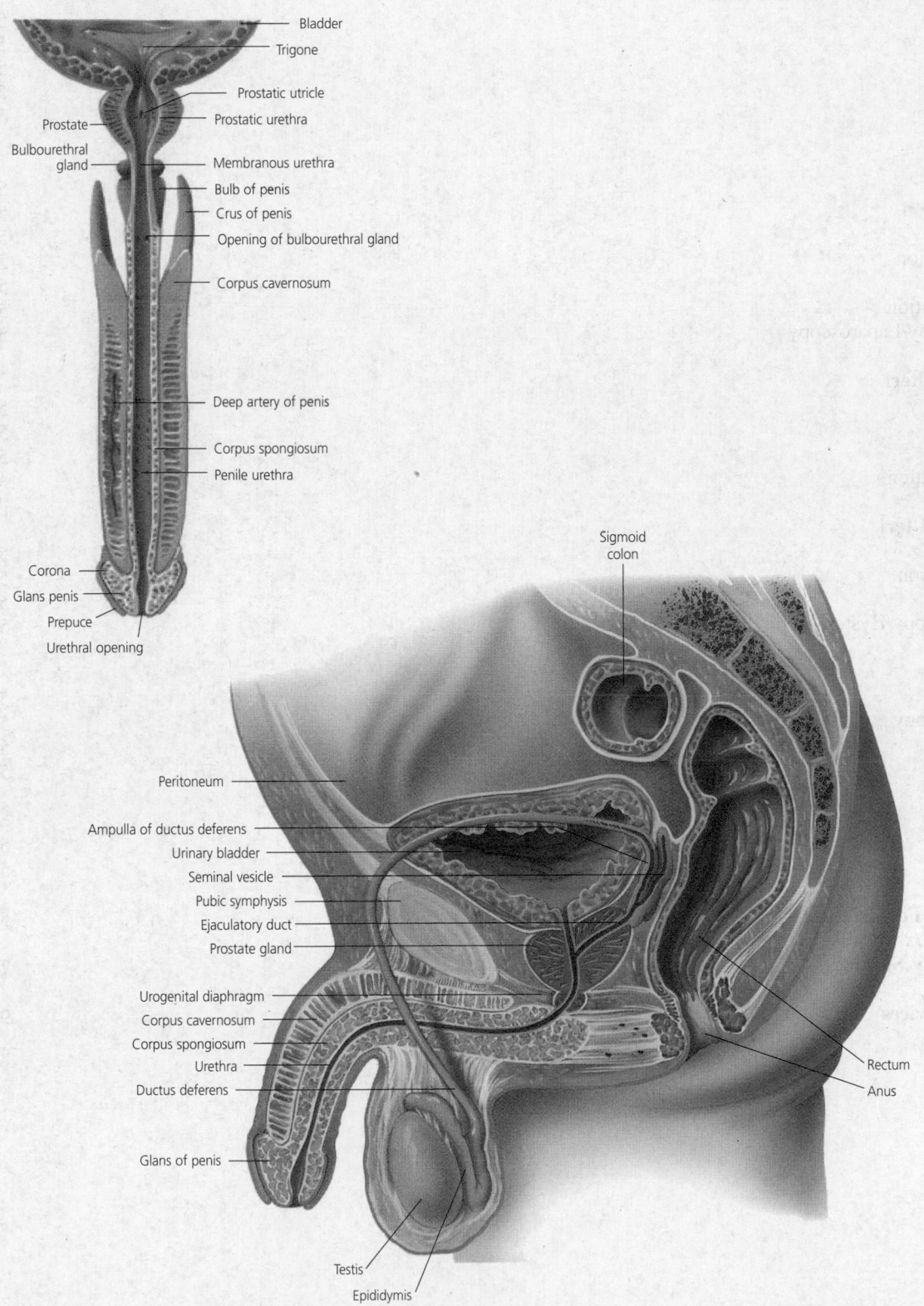

Bladder

Trigone

Prostatic utricle

Prostatic urethra

Prostate

Bulbourethral gland

Membranous urethra

Bulb of penis

Crus of penis

Opening of bulbourethral gland

Corpus cavernosum

Deep artery of penis

Corpus spongiosum

Penile urethra

Corona

Glans penis

Prepuce

Urethral opening

Sigmoid colon

Peritoneum

Ampulla of ductus deferens

Urinary bladder

Seminal vesicle

Pubic symphysis

Ejaculatory duct

Prostate gland

Urogenital diaphragm

Corpus cavernosum

Corpus spongiosum

Urethra

Ductus deferens

Glans of penis

Testis

Epididymis

Rectum

Anus

71

PLATE 19. FEMALE REPRODUCTIVE SYSTEM

Vulva, Perineum and Introitus

Incision	56405-56442
Destruction	56501-56515
Excision	56605-56740
Repair	56800-56810
Endoscopy	56820-56821

Vagina

Incision	57000-57023
Destruction	57061-57065
Excision	57100-57135
Introduction	57150-57180
Repair	57200-57335
Manipulation	57400-57415
Endoscopy/Laparoscopy	57420-57426

Cervix Uteri

Endoscopy	57452-57461
Excision	57500-57558
Repair	57700-57720
Manipulation	57800

Corpus Uteri

Excision	58100-58294
Introduction	58300-58356
Repair	58400-58540
Laparoscopy/Hysteroscopy	58541-58579

Oviduct

Incision	58600-58615
Laparoscopy	58660-58679
Excision	58700-58720
Repair	58740-58770

Ovary

Incision	58800-58825
Excision	58900-58960

In Vitro Fertilization   58970-58999

Radiology Services   74710-74775

E/M Services   99201-99499

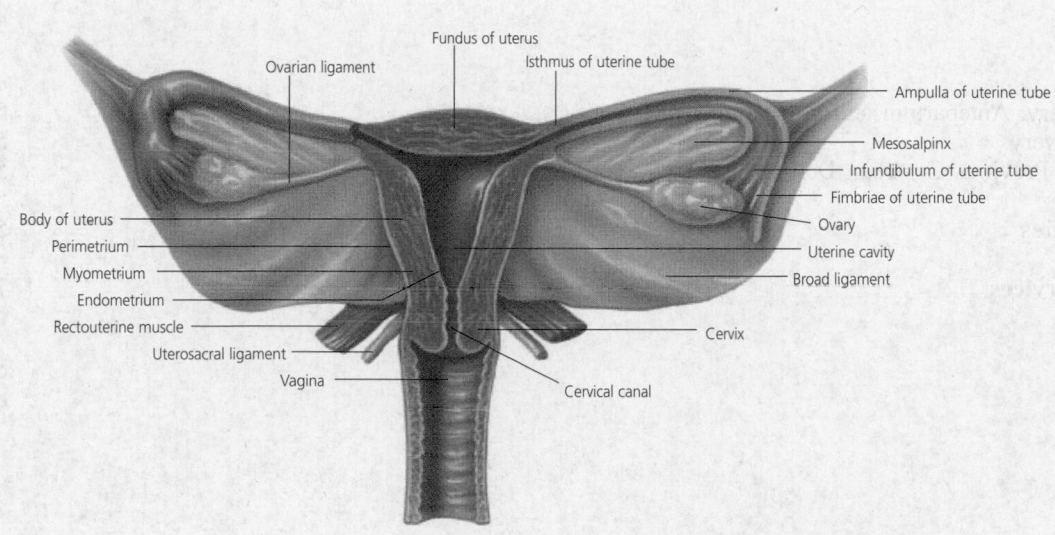

Ovarian ligament
Fundus of uterus
Isthmus of uterine tube
Ampulla of uterine tube
Mesosalpinx
Infundibulum of uterine tube
Fimbriae of uterine tube
Ovary
Body of uterus
Perimetrium
Myometrium
Endometrium
Rectouterine muscle
Uterosacral ligament
Vagina
Uterine cavity
Broad ligament
Cervix
Cervical canal

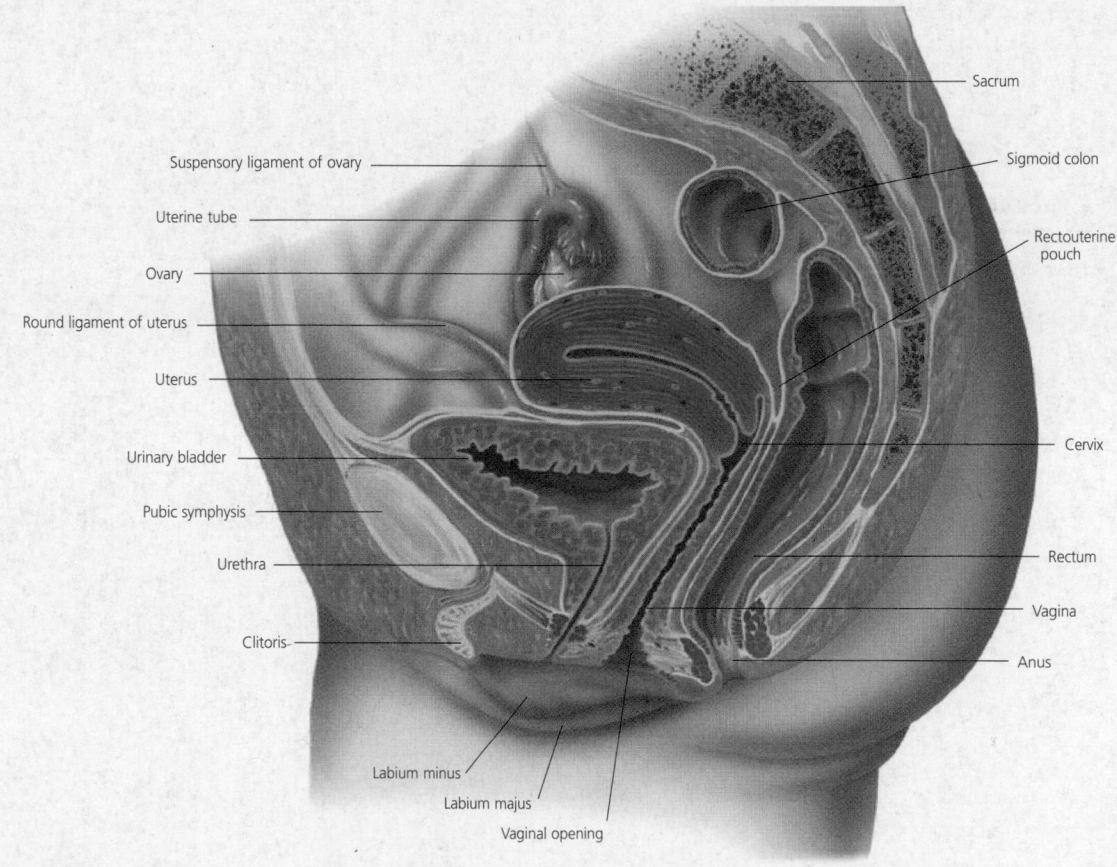

Sacrum
Sigmoid colon
Suspensory ligament of ovary
Uterine tube
Ovary
Round ligament of uterus
Rectouterine pouch
Uterus
Urinary bladder
Pubic symphysis
Urethra
Clitoris
Cervix
Rectum
Vagina
Anus
Labium minus
Labium majus
Vaginal opening

PLATE 20. PREGNANCY, CHILDBIRTH AND THE PUERPERIUM

Antepartum Services

Antepartum Services	59000-59076
Excision	59100-59160
Introduction	59200
Repair	59300-59350

Delivery

Vaginal Delivery, Antepartum and Postpartum Care	59400-59430
Cesarean Delivery	59510-59525
Delivery after Previous Cesarean Delivery	59610-59622
Abortion	59812-59857
Other Procedures	59866-59899

Radiology Services 74710-74775

E/M Services

E/M Services	99201-99499
Newborn Care	99460-99465

Female Reproductive System: Pregnancy
(Lateral View)

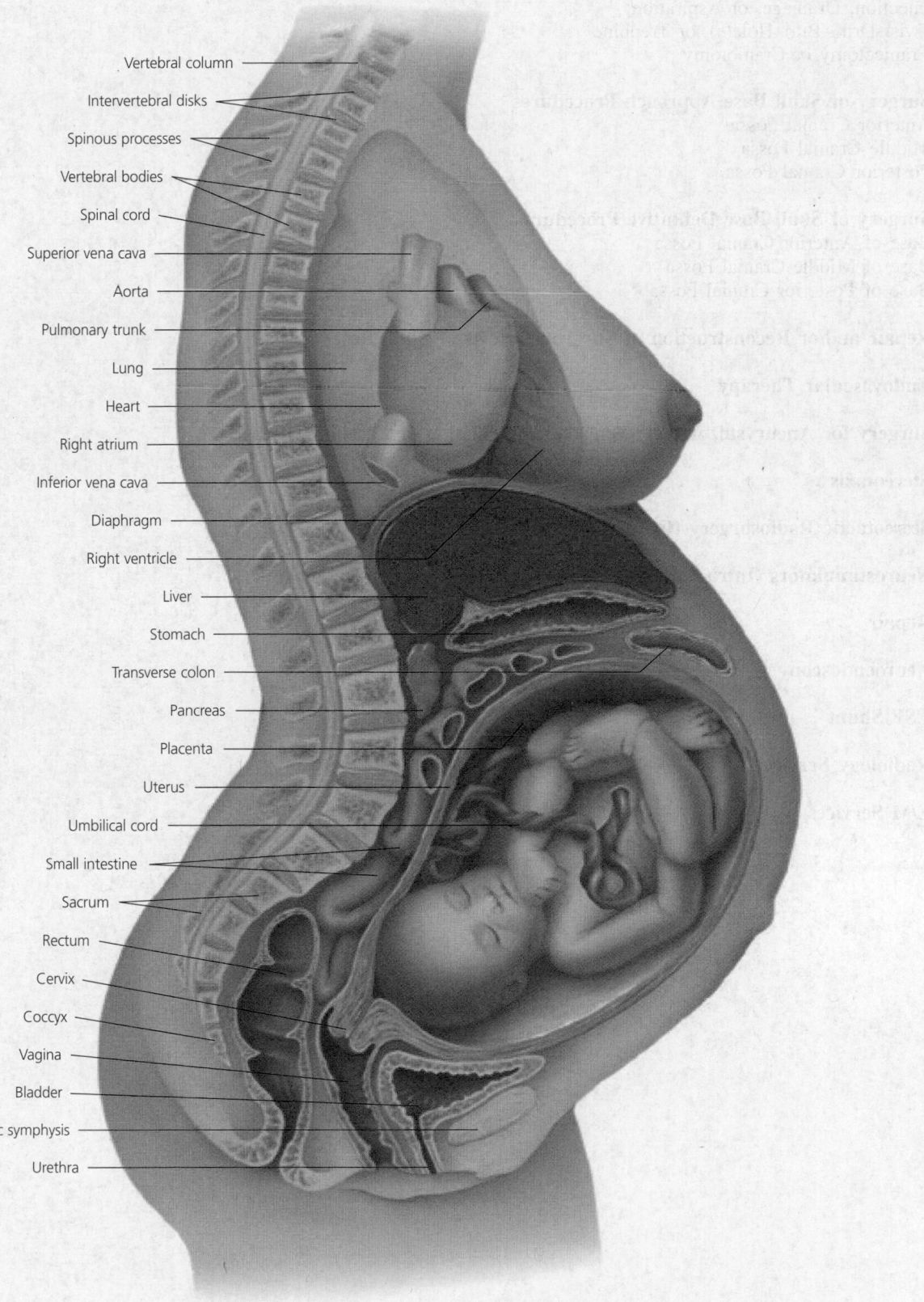

Vertebral column
Intervertebral disks
Spinous processes
Vertebral bodies
Spinal cord
Superior vena cava
Aorta
Pulmonary trunk
Lung
Heart
Right atrium
Inferior vena cava
Diaphragm
Right ventricle
Liver
Stomach
Transverse colon
Pancreas
Placenta
Uterus
Umbilical cord
Small intestine
Sacrum
Rectum
Cervix
Coccyx
Vagina
Bladder
Pubic symphysis
Urethra

PLATE 21. NERVOUS SYSTEM - BRAIN

Skull, Meninges, and Brain
Injection, Drainage, or Aspiration   61000-61070
Twist Drill, Burr Hole(s), or Trephine   61105-61253
Craniectomy or Craniotomy   61304-61576

Surgery of Skull Base Approach Procedures
Anterior Cranial Fossa   61580-61586
Middle Cranial Fossa   61590-61592
Posterior Cranial Fossa   61595-61598

Surgery of Skull Base Definitive Procedures
Base of Anterior Cranial Fossa   61600-61601
Base of Middle Cranial Fossa   61605-61613
Base of Posterior Cranial Fossa   61615-61616

Repair and/or Reconstruction of Surgical Defects of Skull Base   61618-61619

Endovascular Therapy   61623-61642

Surgery for Aneurysm, Arterio-Venous Malformation or Vascular Disease   61680-61711

Stereotaxis   61720-61791

Stereotactic Radiosurgery (Cranial)   61796-61800

Neurostimulators (Intra-Cranial)   61850-61888

Repair   62000-62148

Neuroendoscopy   62160-62165

CSF Shunt   62180-62258

Radiology Services   70010-70559

E/M Services   99201-99499

Brain
(Base View)

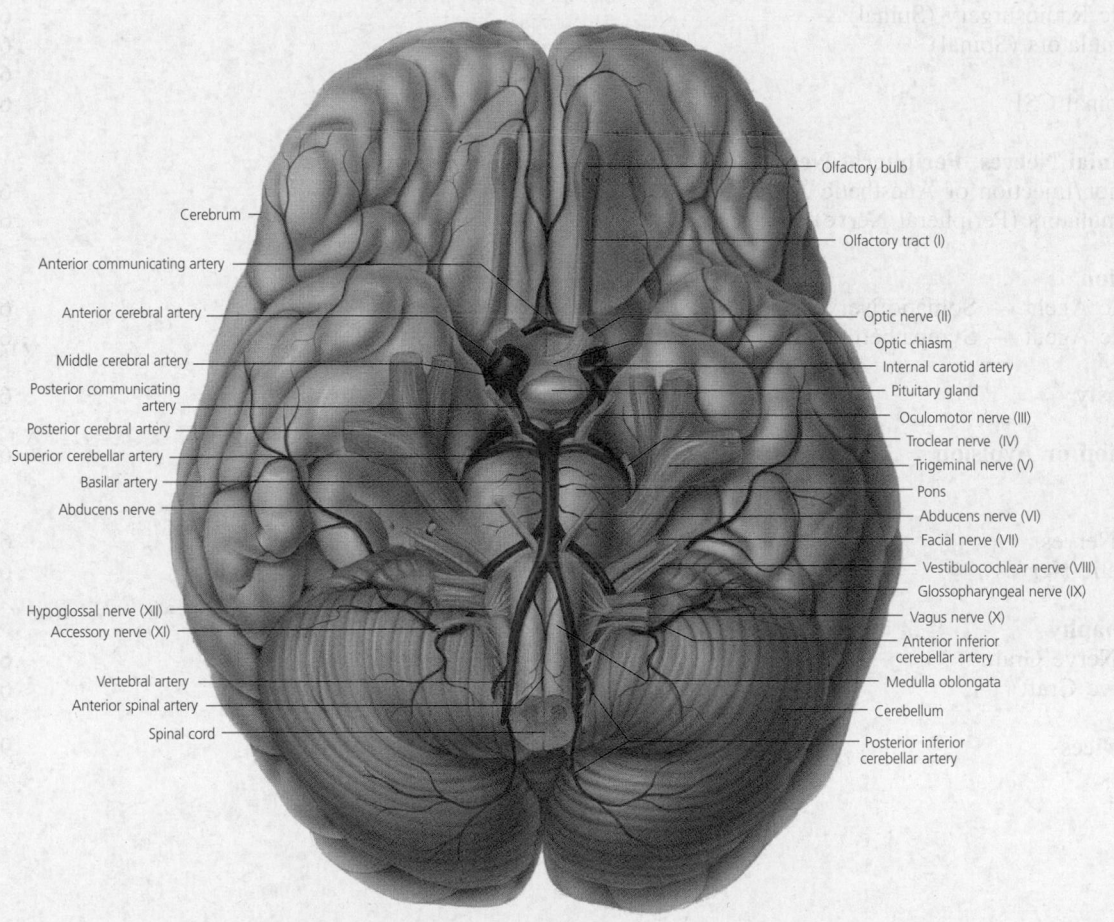

Cerebrum

Anterior communicating artery

Anterior cerebral artery

Middle cerebral artery

Posterior communicating artery

Posterior cerebral artery

Superior cerebellar artery

Basilar artery

Abducens nerve

Hypoglossal nerve (XII)

Accessory nerve (XI)

Vertebral artery

Anterior spinal artery

Spinal cord

Olfactory bulb

Olfactory tract (I)

Optic nerve (II)

Optic chiasm

Internal carotid artery

Pituitary gland

Oculomotor nerve (III)

Troclear nerve (IV)

Trigeminal nerve (V)

Pons

Abducens nerve (VI)

Facial nerve (VII)

Vestibulocochlear nerve (VIII)

Glossopharyngeal nerve (IX)

Vagus nerve (X)

Anterior inferior cerebellar artery

Medulla oblongata

Cerebellum

Posterior inferior cerebellar artery

PLATE 22. NERVOUS SYSTEM

Spine and Spinal Cord

Injection, Drainage or Aspiration	62263-62319
Catheter, Reservoir, Pump Implantation	62350-62370
Posterior Extradural Laminotomy or Laminectomy	63001-63051
Transpedicular or Costovertebral Approach	63055-63066
Anterior or Anterolateral Approach	63075-63091
Lateral Extracavitary Approach	63101-63103
Incision	63170-63200
Excision by Laminectomy of Lesion	63250-63295
Excision, Anterior or Anterolateral Approach Intraspinal Lesion	63300-63308
Stereotaxis	63600-63615
Sterotactic Radiosurgery (Spinal)	63620-63621
Neurostimulators (Spinal)	63650-63688
Repair	63700-63710
Shunt, Spinal CSF	63740-63746

Extracranial Nerves, Peripheral Nerves and Autonomic Nervous System

Introduction/Injection of Anesthetic Agent	64400-64530
Neurostimulators (Peripheral Nerve)	64550-64595

Destruction

Neurolytic Agent — Somatic Nerves	64600-64640
Neurolytic Agent — Sympathetic Nerves	64650-64681

Neuroplasty

	64702-64727

Transection or Avulsion

	64732-64772

Excision

Somatic Nerves	64774-64795
Sympathetic Nerves	64802-64823

Neurorrhaphy

Without Nerve Graft	64831-64876
With Nerve Graft	64885-64911

E/M Services

	99201-99499

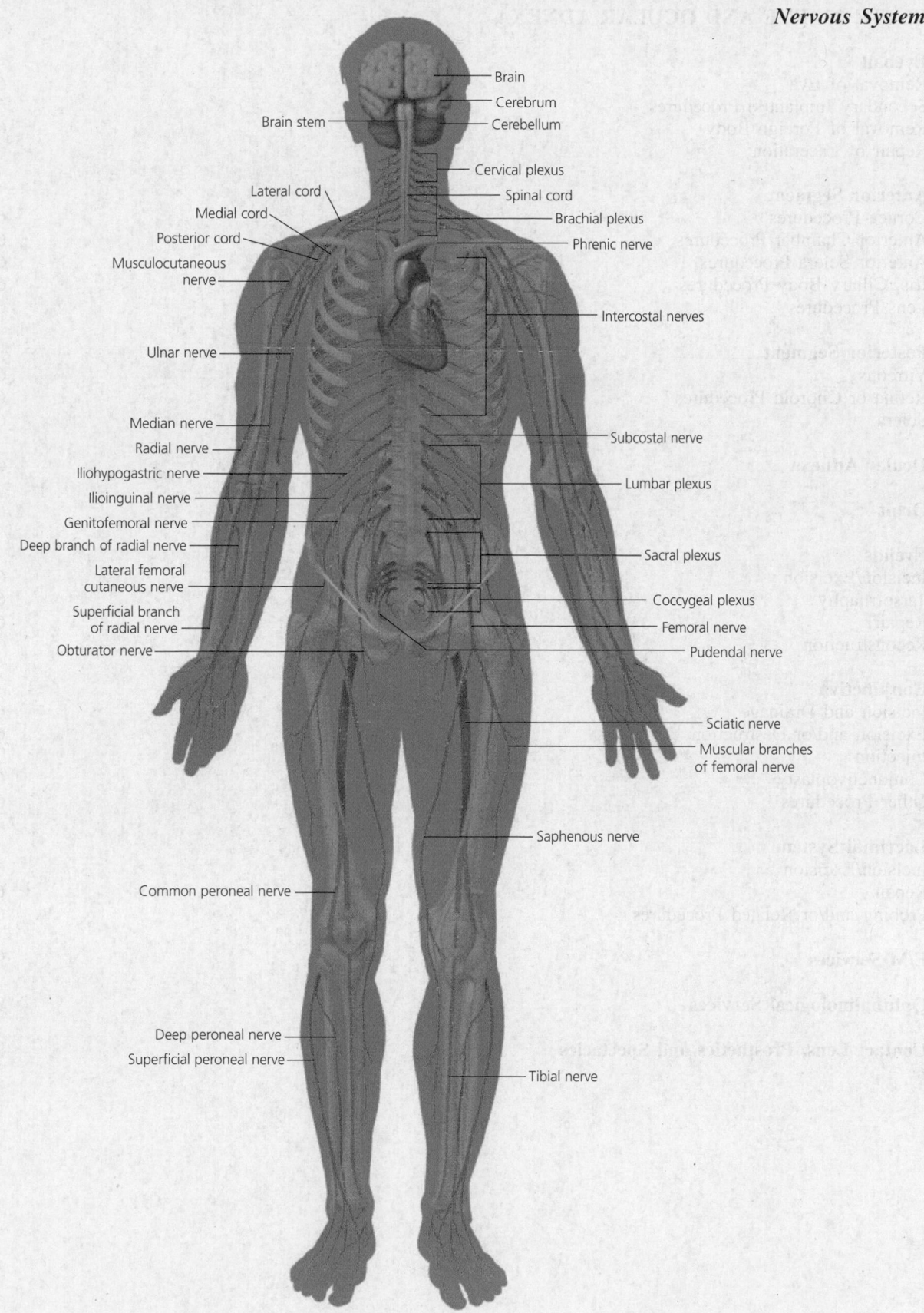

PLATE 23. EYE AND OCULAR ADNEXA

Eyeball
Removal of Eye   65091-65114
Secondary Implant(s) Procedures   65125-65175
Removal of Foreign Body   65205-65265
Repair of Laceration   65270-65290

Anterior Segment
Cornea Procedures   65400-65782
Anterior Chamber Procedures   65800-66030
Anterior Sclera Procedures   66130-66250
Iris, Ciliary Body Procedures   66500-66770
Lens Procedures   66820-66986

Posterior Segment
Vitreous   67005-67043
Retina or Choroid Procedures   67101-67229
Sclera   67250-67255

Ocular Adnexa   67311-67399

Orbit   67400-67599

Eyelids
Incision/Excision   67700-67850
Tarsorrhaphy   67875-67882
Repair   67900-67924
Reconstruction   67930-67975

Conjunctiva
Incision and Drainage   68020-68040
Excision and/or Destruction   68100-68135
Injection   68200
Conjunctivoplasty   68320-68340
Other Procedures   68360-68399

Lacrimal System
Incision/Excision   68400-68550
Repair   68700-68770
Probing and/or Related Procedures   68801-68850

E/M Services   99201-99499

Ophthalmological Services   92002-92287

Contact Lens, Prosthetics and Spectacles   92310-92499

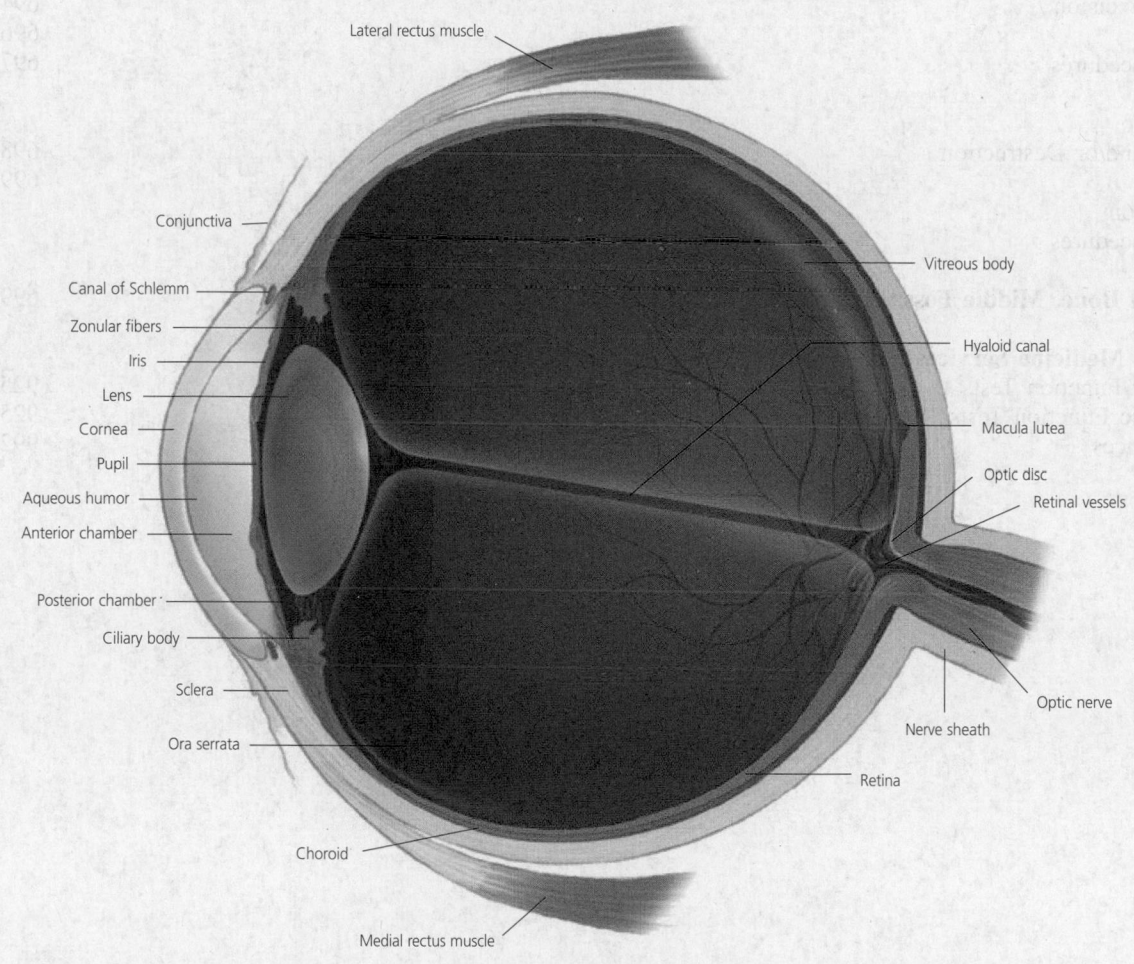

Lateral rectus muscle

Conjunctiva

Canal of Schlemm

Zonular fibers

Iris

Lens

Cornea

Pupil

Aqueous humor

Anterior chamber

Posterior chamber

Ciliary body

Sclera

Ora serrata

Choroid

Medial rectus muscle

Vitreous body

Hyaloid canal

Macula lutea

Optic disc

Retinal vessels

Optic nerve

Nerve sheath

Retina

PLATE 24. AUDITORY SYSTEM

External Ear

Incision	69000-69090
Excision	69100-69155
Removal of Foreign Body	69200-69222
Repair	69300-69320
Other Procedures	69399

Middle Ear

Introduction	69400-69405
Incision/Excision	69420-69554
Repair	69601-69676
Other Procedures	69700-69799

Inner Ear

Incision and/or Destruction	69801-69840
Excision	69905-69915
Introduction	69930
Other Procedures	69949

Temporal Bone, Middle Fossa Approach   69950-69979

Visit and Medicine Services

Vestibular Function Tests	92531-92548
Audiologic Function Tests	92550-92597
E/M Services	99201-99499

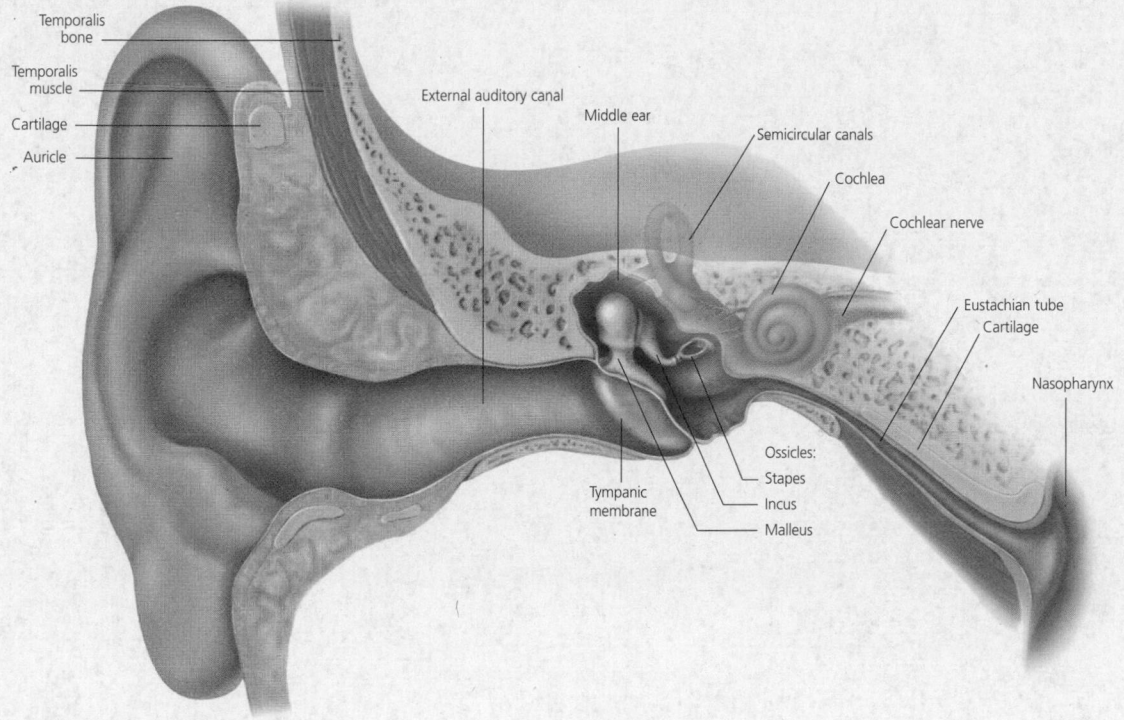

This page intentionally left blank.

EVALUATION & MANAGEMENT GUIDELINES

EVALUATION AND MANAGEMENT (E/M) SERVICES OVERVIEW

The first section of the CPT coding system is the evaluation and management (E/M) section, which includes procedure codes for visits and special care services. Within each subsection, the CPT codes are arranged first by patient category, then by the level of service.

The evaluation and management section of the CPT coding system includes codes for reporting visits, consultations, prolonged service, case management services, preventive medicine services, newborn care, and special services. The section is divided into categories such as office visits, hospital visits and consultations. Most of the categories are further divided into two or more subcategories.

The subcategories for evaluation and management services are further classified into levels of service that are identified by specific codes. The level of service classification is important because the physician work required to provide the service varies by the type of service, the place of service, and the patient's clinical status.

The basic format of the evaluation and management service codes and definitions is the same for most categories.

- *A unique five-digit CPT code number is listed*
- *The place and/or type of service is specified, for example "office consultation"*
- *The content of the service is defined, eg. "comprehensive history and comprehensive examination"*
- *The nature of the presenting problem(s) usually associated with a given level is described.*
- *The time typically required to provide the service is specified.*

EVALUATION AND MANAGEMENT SERVICES SUBSECTIONS

The Evaluation and Management section of the CPT book is divided into the following subsections:

Office or Other Outpatient Services	
New Patient	99201-99205
Established Patient	99211-99215
Hospital Observation Services	
Observation Care Discharge Services	99217
Initial Observation Care	99218-99220
Susbequent Observation Care	99224-99226
Hospital Inpatient Services	
Initial Hospital Care	99221-99223
Subsequent Hospital Care	99231-99233
Observation or Inpatient Care (including	
admission and discharge) Services	99234-99236
Hospital Discharge Services	99238-99239
Consultations	
Office or Other Outpatient Consultations	99241-99245
Inpatient Consultation	99251-99255
Emergency Department Services	99281-99288
Critical Care Services, Adult	99291-99292
Nursing Facility Services	
Initial Nursing Facility Care	99304-99306
Subsequent Nursing Facility Care	99307-99310
Nursing Facility Discharge Services	99315-99316
Other Nursing Facility Services	99318
Domiciliary, Rest Home, or Custodial Care Services	
New Patient	99324-99328
Established Patient	99334-99337

Domiciliary, Rest Home, or Home Care Plan Oversight	99339-99340
Home Services	
New Patient	99341-99345
Established Patient	99347-99350
Prolonged Services	
With Direct Patient Contact	99354-99357
Without Direct Patient Contact	99358-99359
With Physician Supervision	99415-99416
Standby Services	99360
Case Management Services	
Anticoagulent Management	
Medical Team Conferences	99366-99368
Care Plan Oversight Services	99374-99380
Preventive Medicine Services	
New Patient	99381-99387
Established Patient	99391-99397
Counseling Risk Factor Reduction	99401-99429
Non Face-to-Face Physician Services	
Telephone Services	99441-99443
On-line Medical Evaluation	99444
Interprofessional telephone/Internet Consultation	99446-99449
Special Evaluation and Management Services	99450-99456
Newborn Care	99460-99463
Delivery/Birthing Room Attendance and Resuscitation	99464-99465
Inpatient Neonatal Intensive Care Services and Pediatric	
and Neonatal Critical Care Services	99466-99486
Cognitive Assessment and Care Plan SErvices	99483
Care Management Services	
Chronic Care Management	99490
Complex Chronic Care Management	99487, 99489
Psychiatric Collaborative Care Management Services	99492-99494
Transitional Care Management Services	99495-99496
Advance Care Planning	99497-99498
General Behavioral Health Integration Care Management	99484
Other Evaluation and Management Services	99499

All of these subsections have extensive notes that should be reviewed carefully prior to selecting codes for services located within the section.

CLASSIFICATION OF EVALUATION AND MANAGEMENT SERVICES

The E/M section is divided into broad categories such as office visits, hospital visits, and consultations. Most of the categories are further divided into two or more subcategories of E/M services. For example, there are two subcategories of office visits (new patient and established patient) and there are two subcategories of hospital visits (initial and subsequent). The subcategories of E/M services are further classified into levels of E/M services that are identified by specific codes. This classification is important because the nature of work varies by type of service, place of service, and the patient's status.

The basic format of the levels of evaluation and management services is the same for most categories. First, a unique code number is listed. Second, the place and/or type of service is specified, eg, office consultation. Third, the content of the service is defined, eg, comprehensive history and comprehensive examination. Fourth, the nature of the presenting problem(s) usually associated with a given level is described. Fifth, the time typically required to provide the service is specified.

DEFINITIONS OF COMMONLY USED TERMS

Certain key words and phrases are used throughout the Evaluation and Management section. The following definitions are intended to reduce the potential for differing interpretations and to increase the consistency of reporting by physicians in differing specialties. E/M services may also be reported by other qualified health care professionals who are authorized to perform such services within the scope of their practice.

Decision Tree for New vs Established Patients

Received any professional service from the physician or another physician in group of same specialty within the last three years?

- Yes
- No → New patient

Exact same specialty?

- Yes
- No → New patient

Exact same subspecialty?

- Yes
- No → New patient

- Yes → Established
- No → New patient

NEW AND ESTABLISHED PATIENTS

Solely for the purposes of distinguishing between new and established patients, professional services are those face-to-face services rendered by physicians and other qualified health care professionals who may report evaluation and management services reported by a specific CPT code(s). A new patient is one who has not received any professional services from the

physician/qualified health care professional or another physician/qualified health care professional of the exact same specialty and subspecialty who belongs to the same group practice, within the past three years.

An established patient is one who has received professional services from the physician/qualified health care professional or another physician/qualified health care professional of the exact same specialty and subspecialty who belongs to the same group practice, within the past three years. See Decision Tree.

In the instance where a physician/qualified health care professional is on call for or covering for another physician/qualified health care professional, the patient's encounter will be classified as it would have been by the physician/qualified health care professional who is not available. When advanced practice nurses and physician assistants are working with physicians, they are considered as working in the exact same specialty and exact same subspecialties as the physician

No distinction is made between new and established patients in the emergency department. Evaluation and Management services in the emergency department category may be coded for any new or established patient who presents for treatment in the emergency department.

The decision tree on the next page is provided to aid in determining whether to report the E/M service provided as a new or as an established patient encounter.

CHIEF COMPLAINT

A chief complaint is a concise statement describing the symptom, problem, condition, diagnosis or other factor that is the reason for the encounter, usually stated in the patient's words.

CONCURRENT CARE AND TRANSFER OF CARE

Concurrent care is the provision of similar services (eg, hospital visits) to the same patient by more than one physician or other qualified health care professional on the same day. When concurrent care is provided, no special reporting is required. Transfer of care is the process whereby a physician or other qualified health care professional who is providing management for some or all of a patient's problems relinquishes this responsibility to another physician or other qualified health care professional who explicitly agrees to accept this responsibility and who, from the initial encounter, is not providing consultative services. The physician or other qualified health care professional transferring care is then no longer providing care for these problems though he or she may continue providing care for other conditions when appropriate. Consultation codes should not be reported by the physician or other qualified health care professional who has agreed to accept transfer of care before an initial evaluation but are appropriate to report if the decision to accept transfer of care cannot be made until after the initial consultation evaluation, regardless of site of service.

COUNSELING

Counseling is a discussion with a patient and/or family concerning one or more of the following areas:

- Diagnostic results, impressions, and/or recommended diagnostic studies;
- Prognosis;
- Risks and benefits of management (treatment) options;
- Instructions for management (treatment) and/or follow-up;
- Importance of compliance with chosen management (treatment) options;
- Risk factor reduction; and
- Patient and family education. (Psychotherapy, see 90832-90834,90836-90840)

FAMILY HISTORY

A review of medical events in the patient's family that includes significant information about:

- The health status or cause of death of parents, siblings, and children;
- Specific diseases related to problems identified in the Chief Complaint or History of the Present Illness, and/or System Review;
- Diseases of family members which may be hereditary or place the patient at risk.

HISTORY OF PRESENT ILLNESS

A chronological description of the development of the patient's present illness from the first sign and/or symptom to the present. This includes a description of location, quality, severity, timing, context, modifying factors and associated signs and symptoms significantly related to the presenting problem(s).

LEVELS OF EVALUATION AND MANAGEMENT SERVICES

Within each category or subcategory of evaluation and management service, there are three to five levels of evaluation and management services available for reporting purposes. Levels of evaluation and management services are **not** interchangeable among the different categories or subcategories of service. For example, the first level of evaluation and management services in the subcategory of office visit, new patient, does not have the same definition as the first level of evaluation and management services in the subcategory of office visit, established patient.

The levels of E/M services encompass the wide variations in skill, effort, time, responsibility, and medical knowledge required for the prevention or diagnosis and treatment of illness or injury and the promotion of optimal health. Each level of E/M services may be used by all physicians or other qualified health care professionals.

The descriptors for the levels of evaluation and management services recognize seven components, six of which are used in defining the levels of evaluation and management services. These components are:

- History;
- Examination;
- Medical decision making;
- Counseling;
- Coordination of care;
- Nature of presenting problem; and
- Ttime.

The first three of these components (history, examination, and medical decision making) are considered the **key** components in selecting a level of evaluation and management services. (See "Determine the Extent of History Obtained")

The next three components (counseling, coordination of care, and the nature of the presenting problem) are considered **contributory** factors in the majority of encounters. Although the first two of these contributory factors are important evaluation and management services, it is not required that these services be provided at every patient encounter.

Coordination of care with other physicians, other health care professionals, or agencies without a patient encounter on that day is coded using the case management codes.

The final component, time, is discussed in detail later in the chapter.

Any specifically identifiable procedure (ie, identified with a specific cpt code) performed on or subsequent to the date of initial or subsequent evaluation and management services should be reported separately.

The actual performance and/or interpretation of diagnostic tests/studies ordered during a patient encounter are not included in the levels of evaluation and management services. Physician performance of diagnostic tests/studies for which specific CPT codes are available may be reported separately, in addition to the appropriate evaluation and management code. The physician's interpretation of the results of diagnostic tests/studies (ie, professional component) with preparation of a separate distinctly identifiable signed written report may also be reported separately, using the appropriate CPT code with the modifier 26 appended.

The physician or other qualified health care professional may need to indicate that on the day a procedure or service identified by a CPT code was performed, the patient's condition required a significant separately identifiable E/M service above and beyond other services provided or beyond the usual preservice and postservice care associated with the procedure that was performed. The E/M service may be caused or prompted by the symptoms or condition for which the procedure and/or service was provided. This circumstance may be reported by adding modifier 25 to the appropriate level of E/M service. As such, different diagnoses are not required for reporting of the procedure and the E/M services on the same date.

NATURE OF PRESENTING PROBLEM

A presenting problem is a disease, condition, illness, injury, symptom, sign, finding, complaint, or other reason for encounter, with or without a diagnosis being established at the time of the encounter. The evaluation and management codes recognize five types of presenting problems that are defined as follows:

Minimal: a problem that may not require the presence of the physician or other qualified health care professional, but service is provided under the physician's or other qualified health care professional's supervision.

Self-limited or minor: a problem that runs a definite and prescribed course, is transient in nature, and is not likely to permanently alter health status OR has a good prognosis with management/compliance.

Low severity: a problem where the risk of morbidity without treatment is low; there is little to no risk of mortality without treatment; full recovery without functional impairment is expected.

Moderate severity: a problem where the risk of morbidity without treatment is moderate; there is moderate risk of mortality without treatment; uncertain prognosis OR increased probability of prolonged functional impairment.

High severity: a problem where the risk of morbidity without treatment is high to extreme; there is a moderate to high risk of mortality without treatment OR high probability of severe, prolonged functional impairment.

PAST HISTORY

A review of the patient's past experiences with illnesses, injuries, and treatments that includes significant information about:

- prior major illnesses and injuries;
- prior operations;
- prior hospitalizations;
- current medications;
- allergies (eg, drug, food);
- age appropriate immunization status;
- age appropriate feeding/dietary status.

SOCIAL HISTORY

An age appropriate review of past and current activities that includes significant information about:

- marital status and/or living arrangements;
- current employment;
- occupational history;
- military history;
- use of drugs, alcohol, and tobacco;
- level of education;
- sexual history;
- other relevant social factors

SYSTEM REVIEW (REVIEW OF SYSTEMS)

An inventory of body systems obtained through a series of questions seeking to identify signs and/or symptoms that the patient may be experiencing or has experienced. For the purposes of the CPT codebook, the following elements of a system review have been identified:

- Constitutional symptoms (fever, weight loss, etc.)
- Eyes
- Ears, nose, mouth, throat
- Cardiovascular
- Respiratory
- Gastrointestinal
- Genitourinary
- Musculoskeletal
- Integumentary (skin and/or breast)
- Neurological
- Psychiatric
- Endocrine
- Hematologic/lymphatic
- Allergic/immunologic

The review of systems helps define the problem, clarify the differential diagnosis, identify needed testing, or serves as baseline data on other systems that might be affected by any possible management options.

TIME

The inclusion of time in the definitions of levels of E/M services has been implicit in prior editions of the CPT codebook. The inclusion of time as an explicit factor beginning in CPT 1992 is done to assist in selecting the most appropriate level of E/M services. It should be recognized that the specific times expressed in the visit ode descriptors are averages and, therefore, represent a range of times that may be higher or lower depending on actual clinical circumstances.

Time is **not** a descriptive component for the emergency department levels of E/M services because emergency department services are typically provided on a variable intensity basis, often involving multiple encounters with several patients over an extended period of time.Therefore, it is often difficult to provide accurate estimates of the time spent face-to-face with the patient.

Studies to establish levels of E/M services employed surveys of practicing physicians to obtain data on the amount of time and work associated with typical E/M services. Since "work" is not easily quantifiable, the codes must rely on other objective, verifiable measures that correlate with physicians' estimates of their "work." It has been demonstrated that estimations of **intraservice** time (as explained on the next page), both within and across specialties, is a variable that is predictive of the "work" of E/M services. This same research has shown there is a strong relationship between intraservice time and total time for E/M services. Intraservice time, rather than total time, was chosen for inclusion with the codes because of its relative ease of measurement and because of its direct correlation with measurements of the total amount of time and work associated with typical E/M services.

Intraservice times are defined as **face-to-face** time for office and other outpatient visits and as **unit/floor** time for hospital and other inpatient visits. This distinction is necessary because most of the work of typical office visits takes place during the face-to-face time with the patient, while most of the work of typical hospital visits takes place during the time spent on the patient's floor or unit. When prolonged time occurs in either the office or the inpatient areas, the appropriate add-on code should be reported.

Face-to-face time (office and other outpatient visits and office consultations): for coding purposes, face-to-face time for these services is defined as only that time spent face-to-face with the patient and/or family. This includes the time performing such tasks as obtaining a history, performing an examination, and counseling the patient.

Time is also spent doing work before or after the face-to-face time with the patient, performing such tasks as reviewing records and tests, arranging for further services, and communicating further with other professionals and the patient through written reports and telephone contact.

This **non-face-to-face** time for office services—also called pre- and post-encounter time—is not included in the time component described in the evaluation and management codes. However, the pre- and post-non-face-to-face work associated with an encounter was included in calculating the total work of typical services in physician surveys. Thus, the face-to-face time associated with the services described by any evaluation and management code is a valid proxy for the total work done before, during, and after the visit.

Unit/floor time (hospital observation services, inpatient hospital care, initial inpatient hospital consultations, nursing facility): for reporting purposes, intraservice time for these services is defined as unit/floor time, which includes the time present on the patient's hospital unit and at the bedside rendering services for that patient. This includes the time to establish and/or review the patient's chart, examine the patient, write notes, and communicate with other professionals and the patient's family.

In the hospital, pre- and post-time includes time spent off the patient's floor performing such tasks as reviewing pathology and radiology findings in another part of the hospital.

This pre- and post-visit time is not included in the time component described in these codes. However, the pre- and post-work performed during the time spent off the floor or unit was included in calculating the total work of typical services in physician surveys. Thus, the unit/floor time associated with the services described by any code is a valid proxy for the total work done before, during, and after the visit.

UNLISTED SERVICE

An evaluation and management service may be provided that is not listed in this section of CPT. When reporting such a service, the appropriate "Unlisted" code may be used to indicate the service, identifying it by "Special Report" (see section below). The "Unlisted Services" and accompanying codes for the evaluation and management section are as follows:

99429   Unlisted preventive medicine service
99499   Unlisted evaluation and management service

SPECIAL REPORT

An unlisted service or one that is unusual, variable, or new may require a special report demonstrating the medical appropriateness of the service. Pertinent information should include an adequate definition or description of the nature, extent, and need for the procedure; and the time, effort, and equipment necessary to provide the service. Additional items which may be included are complexity of symptoms, final diagnosis, pertinent physical findings, diagnostic and therapeutic procedures, concurrent problems, and follow-up care.

CLINICAL EXAMPLES

Clinical examples of the E/M service codes are provided to assist in understanding the meaning of the descriptors and selecting the correct code. These are listed in Appendix C of the AMA's book. Each example was developed by the specialties shown. The same problem, when seen by different specialties, may involve different amounts of work. Therefore, the appropriate level of encounter should be reported using the descriptors rather than the examples.

HOW TO SELECT A LEVEL OF E/M SERVICE

IDENTIFY THE CATEGORY AND SUBCATEGORY OF SERVICE

The categories and subcategories of codes available for reporting E/M services are shown in Table 1 below.

Table 1: Categories and subcategories of service

Category/subcategory	Code Numbers
Office or other outpatient services	
New patient	99201-99205
Established patient	99211-99215
Hospital observation services	
Observation care discharge services	99217
Initial observation care services	99218-99220
Subsequent observation care	99224-99226
Hospital inpatient services	
Initial hospital care	99221-99223
Subsequent hospital care	99231-99233
Observation or inpatient care (including admission and discharge)	99234-99236
Hospital discharge services	99238-99239
Consultations	
Office or other outpatient consultations	99241-99245
Inpatient consultations	99251-99255
Emergency department services	99281-99288
Critical care services	99291-99292
Nursing facility services	
Initial nursing facility care	99304-99306
Subsequent nursing facility care	99307-99310
Nursing facility discharge services	99315-99316
Other nursing facility services	99318
Domiciliary, rest home or custodial care services	
New patient	99324-99328
Established patient	99334-99337
Domiciliary, rest home or home care plan oversight services	99339-99340
Home services	99341-99350
Prolonged services	
With direct patient contact	99354-99357
Without direct patient contact	99358-99359
With physician or other qualified health care professional supervision	99415-99416
Standby services	99360
Case management services	99366-99368
Care plan oversight services	99374-99380
Preventive medicine services	
New patient	99381-99387
Established patient	99391-99397
Counseling risk factor reduction & behavior change intervention	99401-99429
Non-face-to-face physician services	
Telephone services	99441-99443
Online medical evaluation	99444
Interprofessional telephone/internet consultation	99446-99449
Special E/M services	99450-99456
Newborn care services	99460-99463
Delivery/birthing room attendance and resuscitation	99464-99465

Inpatient neonatal intensive care and pediatric and neonatal critical care services	99466-99486
Cognitive assessment and care plan services	99483
Care management services	99487, 99489, 99490
Psychiatric collaborative care management services	99492-99494
Transitional care management services	99495-99496
Advance care planning	99497-99498
General behavioral health integration care management	99484
Other E/M services	99499

REVIEW THE REPORTING INSTRUCTIONS FOR THE SELECTED CATEGORY OR SUBCATEGORY

Most of the categories and many of the subcategories of service have special guidelines or instructions unique to that category or subcategory. Where these are indicated, eg, "Inpatient Hospital Care," special instructions will be presented preceding the levels of evaluation and management services.

REVIEW THE LEVEL OF E/M SERVICE DESCRIPTORS AND EXAMPLES IN THE SELECTED CATEGORY OR SUBCATEGORY

The descriptors for the levels of evaluation and management services recognize seven components, six of which are used in defining the levels of evaluation and management services. These components are:

- history;
- examination;
- medical decision making;
- counseling;
- coordination of care;
- nature of presenting problem; and
- time.

The first three of these components (ie, history, examination, and medical decision making) should be considered the **key** components in selecting the level of evaluation and management services. An exception to this rule is in the case of visits which consist predominantly of counseling or coordination of care.

The nature of the presenting problem and time are provided in some levels to assist the physician in determining the appropriate level of E/M service.

DETERMINE THE EXTENT OF HISTORY OBTAINED

The extent of the history is dependent upon clinical judgment and on the nature of presenting problems(s). The levels of evaluation and management services recognize four types of history that are defined as follows:

Problem focused: chief complaint; brief history of present illness or problem.

Expanded problem focused: chief complaint; brief history of present illness; problem pertinent system review.

Detailed: chief complaint; extended history of present illness; problem pertinent system review extended to include a review of a limited number of additional systems; **pertinent** past, family, and/or social history **directly related to the patient's problems**.

Comprehensive: chief complaint; extended history of present illness; review of systems which is directly related to the problem(s) identified in the history of the present illness plus a review of all additional body systems; **complete** past, family, and social history.

The comprehensive history obtained as part of the preventive medicine evaluation and management service is not problem-oriented and does not involve a chief complaint or present illness. It does, however, include a comprehensive system review and comprehensive or interval past, family, and social history as well as a comprehensive assessment/history of pertinent risk factors.

DETERMINE THE EXTENT OF EXAMINATION PERFORMED

The extent of the examination performed is dependent on clinical judgment and on the nature of the presenting problem(s). The levels of evaluation and management services recognize four types of examination that are defined as follows:

Problem focused: a limited examination of the affected body area or organ system.

Expanded problem focused: a limited examination of the affected body area or organ system and other symptomatic or related organ system(s).

Detailed: an extended examination of the affected body area(s) and other symptomatic or related organ system(s).

Comprehensive: a general multi-system examination or a complete examination of a single organ system. **Note:** the comprehensive examination performed as part of the preventive medicine evaluation and management service is multisystem, but its extent is based on age and risk factors identified.

For the purposes of these CPT definitions, the following body areas are recognized:

- Head, including the face
- Neck
- Chest, including breasts and axilla
- Abdomen
- Genitalia, groin, buttocks
- Back
- Each extremity

For the purposes of these CPT definitions, the following organ systems are recognized:

- Eyes
- Ears, nose, mouth, and throat
- Cardiovascular
- Respiratory
- Gastrointestinal
- Genitourinary
- Musculoskeletal
- Skin
- Neurologic
- Psychiatric
- Hematologic/lymphatic/immunologic

DETERMINE COMPLEXITY OF MEDICAL DECISION MAKING

Medical decision making refers to the complexity of establishing a diagnosis and/or selecting a management option as measured by:

- the number of possible diagnoses and/or the number of management options that must be considered;
- the amount and/or complexity of medical records, diagnostic tests, and/or other information that must be obtained, reviewed, and analyzed; and
- the risk of significant complications, morbidity, and/or mortality, as well as comorbidities, associated with the patient's presenting problems(s), the diagnostic procedure(s) and/or the possible management options.

Four types of medical decision making are recognized: straightforward; low complexity; moderate complexity; and high complexity. To qualify for a given type of decision making, two of the three elements in Table 2 below must be met or exceeded.

Comorbidities/underlying diseases, in and of themselves, are not considered in selecting a level of evaluation and management services unless their presence significantly increases the complexity of the medical decision making.

Table 2: Complexity of Medical Decision Making

Number of diagnoses or management options	Amount and/or complexity of data to be reviewed	Risk of complications and/or morbidity or mortality	Type of decision making
Minimal	Minimal or none	Minimal	**Straightforward**
Limited	Limited	Low	**Low complexity**
Multiple	Moderate	Moderate	**Moderate complexity**
Extensive	Extensive	High	**High complexity**

SELECT THE APPROPRIATE LEVEL OF EVALUATION AND MANAGEMENT SERVICES BASED ON THE FOLLOWING

1. For the following categories/subcategories, **all of the key components**, (ie, history, examination, and medical decision making), must meet or exceed the stated requirements to qualify for a particular level of evaluation and management service: office, new patient; hospital observation services; initial hospital care; office consultations; initial inpatient consultations; emergency department services; initial nursing facility care; domiciliary care, new patient; and home, new patient.

2. For the following categories/subcategories, **two of the three key components** (ie, history, examination, and medical decision making) must meet or exceed the stated requirements to qualify for a particular level of evaluation and management services: office, established patient; subsequent hospital care; subsequent nursing facility care; domiciliary care, established patient; and home, established patient.

3. When counseling and/or coordination of care dominates (more than 50%) the encounter with the patient and/or family (face-to-face time in the office or other outpatient setting or floor/unit time in the hospital or nursing facility), then **time** shall be considered the key or controlling factor to qualify for a particular level of E/M services. This includes time spent with parties who have assumed responsibility for the care of the patient or decision making whether or not they are family members (eg, foster parents, person acting in locum parentis, legal guardian). The extent of counseling and/or coordination of care must be documented in the medical record.

OTHER DEFINITIONS OF NATURE OF THE PRESENTING PROBLEM

In addition to the above five specific definitions found in the CPT coding system, there are other definitions found in the E.M Service codes used to report Subsequent Hospital Care and Follow-Up Inpatient Consultations. See Table 3 for these additional definitions.

Table 3: Other Definitions of Nature of Presenting Problems

Evaluation and Management Codes	Nature of Presenting Problem(s) Defined	Equivalent To
99231	Stable, recovering or improving	Self-limited or minor
99232	Inadequate response or minor complication	Low to moderate severity
00233	Significant complication or new problem	Moderate to high severity

DIAGNOSTIC TESTS OR STUDIES

The performance of diagnostic tests or studies for which specific CPT codes are available is not included in the levels of evaluation and management services. Any diagnostic tests or studies performed by the physician for which specific CPT codes are available should be coded separately, in addition to the appropriate evaluation and management service code.

EVALUATION AND MANAGEMENT SERVICES MODIFIERS

Evaluation and management services may be modified under certain circumstances. When applicable, the modifying circumstance should be identified by reporting the appropriate modifier code in addition to the basic service. Modifiers which may be used with evaluation and management service codes are:

-24   Unrelated evaluation and management service by the same physician during a postoperative period

-25   Significant, separately identifiable evaluation and management service by the same physician on the same day of the procedure or other service

-32   Mandated services

-52   Reduced services

-57   Decision for surgery

HOW TO CHOOSE EVALUATION AND MANAGEMENT CODE(S)

Choosing the correct evaluation and management service code to report is a nine step process. The most important steps, in terms of both reimbursement and audit liability, are verifying compliance and documentation.

1.   Identify the Category of Service

Where was the patient seen and what category of services were provided?

☐   *Office or Other Outpatient Services*
☐   *Hospital Observation Services*
☐   *Hospital Inpatient Services*
☐   *Consultations*
☐   *Emergency Department Services*
☐   *Pediatric Patient Transport*
☐   *Critical Care Services*
☐   *Neonatal Intensive Care*
☐   *Nursing Facility Services*
☐   *Domiciliary, Rest Home or Custodial Care Services*
☐   *Home Services*
☐   *Prolonged Services*
☐   *Standby Services*
☐   *Case Management Services*
☐   *Care Plan Oversight Services*
☐   *Preventive Medicine Services*
☐   *Special or Other E/M Services*

2.   Identify the Subcategory of Service

Is the patient a new patient or established patient?
Is the service initial care, subsequent care or follow-up?

☐   *New Patient*
☐   *Established Patient*
☐   *Initial Care*
☐   *Subsequent Care*
☐   *Follow-up*

3.   Determine the Extent of History Obtained

What level of history was taken on this patient?

☐   *Problem Focused*
☐   *Expanded Problem Focused*
☐   *Detailed*
☐   *Comprehensive*

4.   Determine the Extent of Examination Performed

What level of physician examination was performed?

☐   Problem Focused
☐   Expanded Problem Focused
☐   Detailed
☐   Comprehensive

5.   Determine the Complexity of Medical Decision Making

What level of medical decision making was required?
☐   Straightforward
☐   Low Complexity
☐   Moderate Complexity
☐   High Complexity

6.   Record the Approximate Amount of Time

How much time was spent either face-to-face with the patient for office visits and consults, or unit or floor time for hospital care, hospital consults, and nursing facilities?

If counseling and/or coordination of care exceeds 50 percent of the total face-to-face physician/patient encounter, then TIME is considered to be the key or controlling factor which qualifies the choice of a particular level of evaluation and management service. The extent of counseling and/or coordination of care must be documented in the medical record.

7.   Verify Compliance with Reporting Requirements

<u>All Three Key Components Required</u>

To report services for new patients, initial care, office or confirmatory consultations, emergency department services, and comprehensive nursing facility assessments, all three key components must meet or exceed the stated requirements.

☐   History component met or exceeded
☐   Examination component met or exceeded
☐   Medical decision making component met or exceeded

<u>Two of Three Key Components Required</u>

To report services to established patients, subsequent or follow-up care, two of the three key components must meet or exceed the stated requirements.

☐   History component met or exceeded; and/or
☐   Examination component met or exceeded; and/or
☐   Medical decision making component met or exceeded

8.   Verify Documentation

Make sure that the medical record includes proper documentation of the history, examination, medical decision making, the nature of the problem(s), the approximate amount of time, and when appropriate, the extent of counseling and/or coordination of care.

9.   Assign the Code

The following is an example of the code selection process.

Table 4: Example of the Code Selection Process

1. Category of Service	*Office*
2. Subcategory	*New patient*
3. History	*Problem focused*
4. Examination	*Problem focused*
5. Medical Decision Making	*Straightforward*
6. Intra-service Time	*10 minutes*
7. Key Components	*Met or exceeded*
8. Documentation	*Met or exceeded*
9. Assign the Code	**99201**

EVALUATION AND MANAGEMENT SERVICES DOCUMENTATION GUIDELINES

Documentation in the medical record of all services provided is critical for reimbursement and audit liability. If the provider reported a service or procedure on the health insurance claim form but did not document it, or document it completely, in the patient's medical records, from the point of view of Medicare or private health insurance company auditors, the service was not performed, can't be reported, and therefore will not be paid for.

Millions of dollars are reclaimed from physicians and other medical professionals annually by Medicare and other third party payers because the medical record documentation does not support the services and procedures reported. Providers can protect their medical practices from audit liability by following the most current documentation guidelines published by CMS.

The following documentation guidelines for evaluation and management services were developed jointly by the American Medical Association (AMA) and CMS. The stated goal of CMS in publishing these guidelines is to provide physicians and health insurance claims reviewers with advice about preparing or reviewing documentation for evaluation and management services.

In developing and testing the validity of these guidelines, special emphasis was placed on assuring that they:

- *are consistent with the clinical descriptors and definitions contained in CPT,*

- *would be widely accepted by clinicians and minimize any changes in record-keeping practices; and*

- *would be interpreted and applied uniformly by users across the country.*

WHAT IS DOCUMENTATION AND WHY IS IT IMPORTANT?

Medical record documentation is required to record pertinent facts, findings, and observations about an individual's health history including past and present illnesses, examinations, tests, treatments, and outcomes. The medical record chronologically documents the care of the patient and is an important element contributing to high quality care. The medical record facilitates:

- *the ability of the physician and other medical professionals to evaluate and plan the patient's immediate treatment, and to monitor his/her health care over time;*

- *communication and continuity of care among physicians and other medical professionals involved in the patient's care;*

- *accurate and timely claims review and payment;*

- *appropriate utilization review and quality of care evaluations; and*

- *collection of data that may be useful for research and education.*

An appropriately documented medical record can reduce many of the hassles associated with claims processing and may serve as a legal document to verify the care provided, if necessary.

WHAT DO THIRD PARTY PAYERS WANT AND WHY?

Because payers have a contractual obligation to enrollees, they may require reasonable documentation that services are consistent with the insurance coverage provided. They may request information to validate:

- *the site of service;*
- *the medical necessity and appropriateness of the diagnostic and/or therapeutic services provided; and/or*
- *that services provided have been accurately reported.*

GENERAL PRINCIPLES OF MEDICAL RECORD DOCUMENTATION

The principles of documentation listed below are applicable to all types of medical and surgical services in all settings. For evaluation and management (E/M) services, the nature and amount of physician work and documentation varies by type of service, place of service and the patient's status. The general principles listed below may be modified to account for these variable circumstances in providing evaluation and management services.

1. *The medical record should be complete and legible.*

2. *The documentation of each patient encounter should include:*
   - *the reason for the encounter as well as relevant history, physical examination findings and prior diagnostic test results;*
   - *an assessment, clinical impression or diagnosis;*
   - *a plan for care; and*
   - *the date and legible identity of the observer.*

3. *If not documented, the rationale for ordering diagnostic and other ancillary services should be easily inferred.*

4. *Past and present diagnoses should be accessible to the treating and/or consulting physician.*

5. *Appropriate health risk factors should be identified.*

6. *The patient's progress, response to and changes in treatment, and revision of diagnosis should be documented.*

7. *CPT and ICD-9-CM codes reported on the health insurance claim form or patient billing statement should be supported by the documentation in the medical record.*

DOCUMENTATION OF EVALUATION AND MANAGEMENT SERVICES

This section provides definitions and documentation guidelines for the three key components of evaluation and management services and for visits which consist predominately of counseling or coordination of care. The three key components—history, examination, and medical decision making—appear in the descriptors for office and other outpatient services, hospital observation services, hospital inpatient services, consultations, emergency department services, nursing facility services, domiciliary care services, and home services. Note that Documentation Guidelines are identified by the symbol •DG.

The E/M descriptors recognize seven components which are used in defining the levels of service. These components are:

- *History*
- *Examination*
- *Medical decision making*
- *Counseling*
- *Coordination of care*
- *Nature of presenting problem*
- *Time*

The first three (i.e., history, examination and medical decision making) are the key components in selecting the level of evaluation and management services. However, with visits that consist predominantly of counseling or coordination of care, time is the key or controlling factor to qualify for a particular level of evaluation and management service.

Because the level of evaluation and management service is dependent on two or three key components, performance and documentation of one component (e.g., examination) at the highest level does not necessarily mean that the encounter in its entirety qualifies for the highest level of evaluation and management service.

These documentation guidelines for evaluation and management services reflect the needs of the typical adult population. For certain groups of patients, the recorded information may vary slightly from that described here.

Specifically, the medical records of infants, children, adolescents and pregnant women may have additional or modified information recorded in each history and examination area.

As an example, newborn records may include under history of the present illness, the details of the mother's pregnancy and the infant's status at birth; social history focused on family structure; family history focused on congenital anomalies and hereditary disorders in the family. In addition, the content of a pediatric examination will vary with the age and development of the child. Although not specifically defined in these documentation guidelines, these patient group variations on history and examination are appropriate.

DOCUMENTATION OF HISTORY

The levels of evaluation and management services are based on four types of history (Problem Focused, Expanded Problem Focused, Detailed, and Comprehensive). Each type of history includes some or all of the following elements:

- *Chief complaint*
- *History of present illness*
- *Review of systems*
- *Past, family and/or social history*

The extent of history of present illness, review of systems and past, family and/or social history that is obtained and documented is dependent upon clinical judgement and the nature of the presenting problem(s).

Present History	Review of Systems	Past, Family or Social History	Type of History
Brief	N/A	N/A	*Problem Focused*
Brief	Problem Pertinent	N/A	*Expanded Problem Focused*
Extended	Extended	Pertinent	*Detailed*
Extended	Complete	Complete	*Comprehensive*

The above chart shows the progression of the elements required for each type of history. To qualify for a given type of history all three elements in the table must be met. (A chief complaint is indicated at all levels.)

●*DG:* *The chief complaint, review of systems and past, family and/or social history may be listed as separate elements of history, or they may be included in the description of the history of the present illness.*

●*DG:* *A review of systems and/or a past, family and/or social history obtained during an earlier encounter does not need to be re-recorded if there is evidence that the physician reviewed and updated the previous information. This may occur when a physician updates his or her own record or in an institutional setting or group practice where many physicians use a common record. The review and update may be documented by:*

- *describing any new review of systems and/or past, family and/or social history information or noting there has been no change in the information; and*

- *noting the date and location of the earlier review of systems and/or past, family and/or social history.*

●*DG:* *The review of systems and/or past, family and/or social history may be recorded by ancillary staff or on a form completed by the patient. To document that the physician reviewed the information, there must be a notation supplementing or confirming the information recorded by others.*

●*DG:* *If the physician is unable to obtain a history from the patient or other source, the record should describe the patient's condition or other circumstance which precludes obtaining a history.*

Definitions and specific documentation guidelines for each of the elements of history are listed below.

CHIEF COMPLAINT

The chief complaint is "a concise statement describing the symptom, problem, condition, diagnosis, or other factor that is the reason for the encounter, usually stated in the patient's words."

●**DG:**   The medical record should clearly reflect the chief complaint.

HISTORY OF PRESENT ILLNESS

The history of present illness is "a chronological description of the development of the patient's present illness from the first sign and/or symptom to the present." It includes the following elements:

- Location
- Quality
- Severity
- Duration
- Timing
- Context
- Modifying factors
- Associated signs and symptoms

Brief and **extended** history of present illnesses are distinguished by the amount of detail needed to accurately characterize the clinical problem(s). A **brief** history of present illness consists of one to three elements of the history of present illness.

●**DG:**   The medical record should describe at least one to three elements of the present illness (history of present illness).

An **extended** history of present illness consists of at least four elements of the history of present illness or the status of at least three chronic or inactive conditions.

●**DG:**   Medical record should describe at least four elements of the present illness (history of present illness), or the status of at least three chronic or inactive conditions.

REVIEW OF SYSTEMS

A review of systems is "an inventory of body systems obtained through a series of questions seeking to identify signs and/or symptoms which the patient may be experiencing or has experienced." For purposes of review of systems, the following systems are recognized:

- Constitutional symptoms (e.g., fever, weight loss)
- Eyes
- Ears, Nose, Mouth, Throat
- Neck
- Cardiovascular
- Respiratory
- Gastrointestinal
- Genitourinary
- Musculoskeletal
- Integumentary (skin and/or breast)
- Neurological
- Psychiatric
- Endocrine
- Hematologic/Lymphatic
- Allergic/Immunologic

101

A **problem pertinent** review of systems inquires about the system directly related to the problem(s) identified in the history of present illness.

●**DG:**   The patient's positive responses and pertinent negatives for the system related to the problem should be documented.

An **extended** review of systems inquires about the system directly related to the problem(s) identified in the history of present illness and a limited number of additional systems.

●**DG:**   The patient's positive responses and pertinent negatives for two to nine systems should be documented.

A **complete** review of systems inquires about the system(s) directly related to the problem(s) identified in the history of present illness plus all additional body systems.

●**DG:**   At least ten organ systems must be reviewed. Those systems with positive or pertinent negative responses must be individually documented. For the remaining systems, a notation indicating all other systems are negative is permissible. In the absence of such a notation, at least ten systems must be individually documented.

PAST, FAMILY AND/OR SOCIAL HISTORY

The past, family and/or social history consists of a review of the following areas:

- Past history: the patient's past experiences with illnesses, operations, injuries and treatments.
- Family history: a review of medical events in the patient's family, including diseases which may be hereditary or place the patient at risk.
- Social history: an age appropriate review of past and current activities.

For certain categories of evaluation and management services that include only an interval history, it is not necessary to record information about the past, family and/or social history. Those categories are subsequent hospital care, follow-up inpatient consultations and subsequent nursing facility care.

A **pertinent** past, family and/or social history is a review of the history area(s) directly related to the problem(s) identified in the history of present illness.

●**DG:**   At least one specific item from any of the three history areas must be documented for a pertinent past, family and/or social history

A **complete** past, family and/or social history is of a review of two or all three of the past, family and/or social history areas, depending on the category of the evaluation and management service. A review of all three history areas is required for services that by their nature include a comprehensive assessment or reassessment of the patient. A review of two of the three history areas is sufficient for other services.

●**DG:**   At least one specific item from two of the three history areas must be documented for a complete past, family and/or social history for the following categories of evaluation and management services: office or other outpatient services, established patient; emergency department; domiciliary care, established patient; and home care, established patient.

●**DG:**   At least one specific item from each of the three history areas must be documented for a complete past, family and/or social history for the following categories of evaluation and management services: office or other outpatient services, new patient; hospital observation services; hospital inpatient services, initial care; consultations; comprehensive nursing facility assessments; domiciliary care, new patient; and home care, new patient.

DOCUMENTATION OF EXAMINATION

The levels of E/M services are based on four types of examination:

- Problem Focused — "a limited examination of the affected body area or organ system."
- Expanded Problem Focused — "a limited examination of the affected body area or organ system and any other symptomatic or related body organ system(s)."
- Detailed — "an extended examination of the affected body area(s) and other symptomatic or related organ system(s)."
- Comprehensive — "a general multi-system examination, or complete examination of a single organ system."

These types of examinations have been defined for general multi-system and the following single organ systems:

- *Cardiovascular*
- *Ears, Nose, Mouth and Throat*
- *Eyes*
- *Genitourinary (Female)*
- *Genitourinary (Male)*
- *Hematologic/Lymphatic/Immunologic*
- *Musculoskeletal*
- *Neurological*
- *Psychiatric*
- *Respiratory*
- *Skin*

A general multi-system examination or a single organ system examination may be performed by any physician regardless of specialty. The type (general multi-system or single organ system) and content of examination are selected by the examining physician and are based upon clinical judgement, the patient's history, and the nature of the presenting problem(s).

The content and documentation requirements for each type and level of examination are summarized below and described in detail in tables beginning on page 116. In the tables, organ systems and body areas recognized by CPT for purposes of describing examinations are shown in the left column. The content, or individual elements, of the examination pertaining to that body area or organ system are identified by bullets (●) in the right column.

Parenthetical examples, (e.g., ...), have been used for clarification and to provide guidance regarding documentation. Documentation for each element must satisfy any numeric requirements (such as "Measurement of any three of the following seven...") included in the description of the element. Elements with multiple components but with no specific numeric requirement (such as "Examination of liver and spleen") require documentation of at least one component. It is possible for a given examination to be expanded beyond what is defined here. When that occurs, findings related to the additional systems and/or areas should be documented.

●DG: *Specific abnormal and relevant negative findings of the examination of the affected or symptomatic body area(s) or organ system(s) should be documented. A notation of "abnormal" without elaboration is insufficient.*

●DG: *Abnormal or unexpected findings of the examination of any asymptomatic body area(s) or organ system(s) should be described.*

●DG: *A brief statement or notation indicating "negative" or "normal" is sufficient to document normal findings related to unaffected area(s) or asymptomatic organ system(s).*

GENERAL MULTI-SYSTEM EXAMINATIONS

To qualify for a given level of multi-system examination, the following content and documentation requirements should be met:

- *Problem Focused Examination — should include performance and documentation of one to five elements identified by a bullet (●) in one or more organ system(s) or body area(s).*
- *Expanded Problem Focused Examination — should include performance and documentation of at least six elements identified by a bullet (●) in one or more organ system(s) or body area(s).*
- *Detailed Examination — should include at least six organ systems or body areas. For each system/area selected, performance and documentation of at least two elements identified by a bullet (●) is expected. Alternatively, a detailed examination may include performance and documentation of at least twelve elements identified by a bullet (●) in two or more organ systems or body areas.*
- *Comprehensive Examination — should include at least nine organ systems or body areas. For each system/area selected, all elements of the examination identified by a bullet (●) should be performed, unless specific directions limit the content of the examination. For each area/system, documentation of at least two elements identified by a bullet is expected.*

SINGLE ORGAN SYSTEM EXAMINATIONS

Variations among single organ system examinations in the organ systems and body areas identified in the left columns and in the elements of the examinations described in the right columns reflect differing emphases among specialties. To qualify for a given level of single organ system examination, the following content and documentation requirements should be met:

- *Problem Focused Examination — should include performance and documentation of one to five elements identified by a bullet (●), whether in a box with a shaded or unshaded border.*

- *Expanded Problem Focused Examination — should include performance and documentation of at least six elements identified by a bullet (●), whether in a box with a shaded or unshaded border.*

- *Detailed Examination — examinations other than the eye and psychiatric examinations should include performance and documentation of at least twelve elements identified by a bullet (●), whether in box with a shaded or unshaded border.*

  Eye and psychiatric examinations should include the performance and documentation of at least nine elements identified by a bullet (●), whether in a box with a shaded or unshaded border.

- *Comprehensive Examination — should include performance of all elements identified by a bullet (●), whether in a shaded or unshaded box. Documentation of every element in each box with a shaded border and at least one element in each box with an unshaded border is expected.*

Documentation of every element in each box with a shaded border and at least one element in each box with an unshaded border is expected.

GENERAL MULTI-SYSTEM EXAMINATION

SYSTEM/BODY AREA	ELEMENTS OF EXAMINATION
Constitutional	• Measurement of any three of the following seven vital signs: 1) sitting or standing blood pressure, 2) supine blood pressure, 3) pulse rate and regularity, 4) respiration, 5) temperature, 6) height, 7) weight (May be measured and recorded by ancillary staff)
	• General appearance of patient (e.g., development, nutrition, body habitus, deformities, attention to grooming)
Eyes	• Inspection of conjunctivae and lids
	• Examination of pupils and irises (e.g., reaction to light and accommodation, size and symmetry)
	• Ophthalmoscopic examination of optic discs (e.g., size, C/D ratio, appearance) and posterior segments (e.g., vessel changes, exudates, hemorrhages)
Ears, Nose, Mouth, Throat	• External inspection of ears and nose (e.g., overall and appearance, scars, lesions, masses)
	• Otoscopic examination of external auditory canals and tympanic membranes
	• Assessment of hearing (e.g., whispered voice, finger rub, tuning fork)
	• Inspection of nasal mucosa, septum and turbinates
	• Inspection of lips, teeth and gums
	• Examination of oropharynx: oral mucosa, salivary glands, hard and soft palates, tongue, tonsils and posterior pharynx
Neck	• Examination of neck (e.g., masses, overall appearance, symmetry, tracheal position, crepitus)
	• Examination of thyroid (e.g., enlargement, tenderness, mass)
Respiratory	• Assessment of respiratory effort (e.g., intercostal retractions, use of accessory muscles, diaphragmatic movement)
	• Percussion of chest (e.g., dullness, flatness, hyperresonance)
	• Palpation of chest (e.g., tactile fremitus)
	• Auscultation of lungs (e.g., breath sounds, adventitious sounds, rubs)
Cardiovascular	• Palpation of heart (e.g., location, size, thrills)
	• Auscultation of heart with notation of abnormal sounds and murmurs
	Examination of:
	• Carotid arteries (e.g., pulse amplitude, bruits)
	• Abdominal aorta (e.g., size, dbruits)
	• Femoral arteries (e.g., pulse amplitude, bruits)
	• Pedal pulses (e.g., pulse amplitude)
	• Extremities for edema and/or varicosities
Chest (Breasts)	• Inspection of breasts (e.g., symmetry, nipple discharge)
	• Palpation of breasts and axillae (e.g., masses or lumps, tenderness)
Gastrointestinal (Abdomen)	• Examination of abdomen with notation of presence of masses or tenderness
	• Examination of liver and spleen

- *Examination for presence or absence of hernia*
- *Examination (when indicated) of anus, perineum and rectum, including sphincter tone, presence of hemorrhoids, rectal masses*
- *Obtain stool sample for occult blood test when indicated*

Genitourinary Male

- *Examination of the scrotal contents (e.g., hydrocele, spermatocele, tenderness of cord, testicular mass)*   *continued*
- *Examination of the penis*
- *Digital rectal examination of prostate gland (e.g., size, symmetry, nodularity, tenderness)*

Genitourinary Female

- *Pelvic examination (with or without specimen collection for smears and cultures), including:*
- *Examination of external genitalia (e.g., general appearance, hair distribution, lesions) and vagina (e.g., general appearance, estrogen effect, discharge, lesions, pelvic support, cystocele, rectocele)*
- *Examination of urethra (e.g., masses, tenderness, scarring)*
- *Examination of bladder (e.g., fullness, masses, tenderness)*
- *Cervix (e.g., general appearance, lesions, discharge)*
- *Uterus (e.g., size, contour, position, mobility, tenderness, consistency, descent or support)*
- *Adnexa/parametria (e.g., masses, tenderness, organomegaly, nodularity)*

Lymphatic

Palpation of lymph nodes in two or more areas:

- *Neck*
- *Axillae*
- *Groin*
- *Other*

Musculoskeletal

- *Examination of gait and station*
- *Inspection and/or palpation of digits and nails (eg clubbing, cyanosis, inflammatory conditions, petechiae, ischemia, infections, nodes)*
- *Examination of joints, bones and muscles of one or more of the following six areas: 1) head and neck; 2) spine, ribs and pelvis; 3) right upper extremity; 4) left upper extremity; 5) right lower extremity; and 6) left lower extremity. The examination of a given area includes:*
- *Inspection and/or palpation with notation of presence of any misalignment, asymmetry, crepitation, defects, tenderness, masses, effusions*
- *Assessment of range of motion with notation of any pain, crepitation or contracture*
- *Assessment of stability with notation of any dislocation (luxation), subluxation or laxity*
- *Assessment of muscle strength and tone (e.g., flaccid, cog wheel, spastic) with notation of any atrophy or abnormal movements*

Skin

- *Inspection of skin and subcutaneous tissue (e.g., rashes, lesions, ulcers)*
- *Palpation of skin and subcutaneous tissue (e.g., induration, subcutaneous nodules, tightening)*

Neurologic

- *Test cranial nerves with notation of any deficits*
- *Examination of deep tendon reflexes with notation of pathological reflexes (e.g., Babinski)*
- *Examination of sensation (e.g., by touch, pin, vibration, proprioception)*

Psychiatric

- *Description of patient's judgment and insight*

Brief assessment of mental status including:

- Orientation to time, place and person
- Recent and remote memory
- Mood and affect (e.g., depression, anxiety, agitation)

CONTENT AND DOCUMENTATION REQUIREMENTS

Level of Exam	Perform and Document:
Problem Focused	One to five elements identified by a bullet.
Expanded Problem Focused	At least six elements identified by a bullet.
Detailed	At least two elements identified by a bullet from each of six areas/systems OR at least twelve elements identified by a bullet in two or more areas/systems.
Comprehensive	Perform all elements identified by a bullet in at least nine organ systems or body areas and document at least two elements identified by a bullet from each of nine areas/systems.

CARDIOVASCULAR EXAMINATION

SYSTEM/BODY AREA	ELEMENTS OF EXAMINATION
Constitutional	• Measurement of any three of the following seven vital signs: 1) sitting or standing blood pressure, 2) supine blood pressure, 3) pulse rate and regularity, 4) respiration, 5) temperature, 6) height, 7) weight (May be measured and recorded by ancillary staff)
	• General appearance of patient (e.g., development, nutrition, body habitus, deformities, attention to grooming)
Head and Face	
Eyes	• Inspection of conjunctivae and lids (e.g., xanthelasma)
Ears, Nose, Mouth and Throat	• Inspection of teeth, gums and palate
	• Inspection of oral mucosa with notation of presence of pallor or cyanosis
Neck	• Examination of jugular veins (e.g., distension; a, v or cannon a waves)
	• Examination of thyroid (e.g., enlargement, tenderness, mass)
Respiratory	• Assessment of respiratory effort (e.g., intercostal retractions, use of accessory muscles, diaphragmatic movement)
	• Auscultation of lungs (e.g., breath sounds, adventitious sounds, rubs)
Cardiovascular	• Palpation of heart (e.g., location, size and forcefulness of the point of maximal impact; thrills; lifts; palpable S3 or S4)
	• Auscultation of heart including sounds, abnormal sounds and murmurs
	• Measurement of blood pressure in two or more extremities when indicated (e.g., aortic dissection, coarctation)
	Examination of:
	• Carotid arteries (e.g., waveform, pulse amplitude, bruits, apical-carotid delay)
	• Abdominal aorta (e.g., size, bruits)
	• Femoral arteries (e.g., pulse amplitude, bruits)
	• Pedal pulses (e.g., pulse amplitude)
	• Extremities for peripheral edema and/or varicosities
Chest (Breasts)	
Gastrointestinal (Abdomen)	• Examination of abdomen with notation of presence (Abdomen) of masses or tenderness
	• Examination of liver and spleen
	• Obtain stool sample for occult blood from patients who are being considered for thrombolytic or anticoagulant therapy
Genitourinary	
Lymphatic	
Musculoskeletal	• Examination of the back with notation of kyphosis or scoliosis
	• Examination of gait with notation of ability to undergo exercise testing and/or participation in exercise programs

	• *Assessment of muscle strength and tone (e.g., flaccid, cog wheel, spastic) with notation of any atrophy and abnormal movements*
Extremities	• *Inspection and palpation of digits and nails (e.g., clubbing, cyanosis, inflammation, petechiae, ischemia, infections, Osler's nodes)*
Skin	• *Inspection and/or palpation of skin and subcutaneous tissue (e.g., stasis dermatitis, ulcers, scars, xanthomas)*
Neurological/Psychiatric	*Brief assessment of mental status including:* • *Orientation to time, place and person* • *Mood and affect (e.g., depression, anxiety, agitation)*

CONTENT AND DOCUMENTATION REQUIREMENTS

Level of Exam	Perform and Document:
Problem Focused	One to five elements identified by a bullet.
Expanded Problem Focused	At least six elements identified by a bullet.
Detailed	At least twelve elements identified by a bullet.
Comprehensive	Perform all elements identified by a bullet; document every element in each box with a shaded border and at least one element in each box with an unshaded border.

EAR, NOSE AND THROAT EXAMINATION

SYSTEM/BODY AREA	ELEMENTS OF EXAMINATION
Constitutional	• Measurement of any three of the following seven vital signs: 1) sitting or standing blood pressure, 2) supine blood pressure, 3) pulse rate and regularity, 4) respiration, 5) temperature, 6) height, 7) weight (May be measured and recorded by ancillary staff) • General appearance of patient (e.g., development, nutrition, body habitus, deformities, attention to grooming) • Assessment of ability to communicate (e.g., use of sign language or other communication aids) and quality of voice
Head and Face	• Inspection of head and face (e.g., overall appearance, scars, lesions and masses) • Palpation and/or percussion of face with notation of presence or absence of sinus tenderness • Examination of salivary glands • Assessment of facial strength
Eyes	• Test ocular motility including primary gaze alignment
Ears, Nose, Mouth and Throat	• Otoscopic examination of external auditory canals and tympanic membranes including pneumo-otoscopy with notation of mobility of membranes • Assessment of hearing with tuning forks and clinical speech reception thresholds (e.g., whispered voice, finger rub) • External inspection of ears and nose (e.g., overall appearance, scars, lesions and masses) • Inspection of nasal mucosa, septum and turbinates • Inspection of lips, teeth and gums • Examination of oropharynx: oral mucosa, hard and soft palates, tongue, tonsils and posterior pharynx (e.g., asymmetry, lesions, hydration of mucosal surfaces) • Inspection of pharyngeal walls and pyriform sinuses (e.g., pooling of saliva, asymmetry, lesions) • Examination by mirror of larynx including the condition of the epiglottis, false vocal cords, true vocal cords and mobility of larynx (Use of mirror not required in children) • Examination by mirror of nasopharynx including appearance of the mucosa, adenoids, posterior choanae and eustachian tubes (Use of mirror not required in children)
Neck	• Examination of neck (e.g., masses, overall appearance, symmetry, tracheal position, crepitus) • Examination of thyroid (e.g., enlargement, tenderness, mass)
Respiratory	• Inspection of chest including symmetry, expansion and/or assessment of respiratory effort (e.g., intercostal retractions, use of accessory muscles, diaphragmatic movement) • Auscultation of lungs (e.g., breath sounds, adventitious sounds, rubs)
Cardiovascular	• Auscultation of heart with notation of abnormal sounds and murmurs • Examination of peripheral vascular system by observation (e.g., swelling, varicosities) and palpation (e.g., pulses, temperature, edema, tenderness)
Chest (Breasts)	
Gastrointestinal (Abdomen)	
Genitourinary	

Lymphatic	● *Palpation of lymph nodes in neck, axillae, groin and/or other location*
Musculoskeletal	
Extremities	
Skin	
Neurological/Psychiatric	● *Test cranial nerves with notation of any deficits*
	Brief assessment of mental status including:
	● *Orientation to time, place and person*
	● *Mood and affect (e.g., depression, anxiety, agitation)*

CONTENT AND DOCUMENTATION REQUIREMENTS

Level of Exam	Perform and Document:
Problem Focused	One to five elements identified by a bullet.
Expanded Problem Focused	At least six elements identified by a bullet.
Detailed	At least twelve elements identified by a bullet.
Comprehensive	Perform all elements identified by a bullet; document every element in each box with a shaded border and at least one element in each box with an unshaded border.

EYE EXAMINATION

SYSTEM/BODY AREA	ELEMENTS OF EXAMINATION

Constitutional

Head and Face

Eyes

- Test visual acuity (Does not include determination of refractive error)
- Gross visual field testing by confrontation
- Test ocular motility including primary gaze alignment
- Inspection of bulbar and palpebral conjunctivae
- Examination of ocular adnexae including lids (e.g., ptosis or lagophthalmos), lacrimal glands, lacrimal drainage, orbits and preauricular lymph nodes
- Examination of pupils and irises including shape, direct and consensual reaction (afferent pupil), size (e.g., anisocoria) and morphology
- Slit lamp examination of the corneas including epithelium, stroma, endothelium, and tear film
- Slit lamp examination of the anterior chambers including depth, cells, and flare
- Slit lamp examination of the lenses including clarity, anterior and posterior capsule, cortex, and nucleus
- Measurement of intraocular pressures (except in children and patients with trauma or infectious disease)
- Ophthalmoscopic examination through dilated pupils (unless contraindicated) of
- Optic discs including size, C/D ratio, appearance (e.g., atrophy, cupping, tumor elevation) and nerve fiber layer
- Posterior segments including retina and vessels (e.g., exudates and hemorrhages)

Ears, Nose, Mouth and Throat

Neck

Respiratory

Cardiovascular

Chest (Breasts)

Gastrointestinal (Abdomen)

Genitourinary

Lymphatic

Musculoskeletal

Extremities

Skin

Neurological/Psychiatric

Brief assessment of mental status including:
- Orientation to time, place and person

• *Mood and affect (e.g., depression, anxiety, agitation)*

CONTENT AND DOCUMENTATION REQUIREMENTS

Level of Exam	*Perform and Document:*
Problem Focused	*One to five elements identified by a bullet.*
Expanded Problem Focused	*At least six elements identified by a bullet.*
Detailed	*At least nine elements identified by a bullet.*
Comprehensive	*Perform all elements identified by a bullet; document every element in each box with a shaded border and at least one element in each box with an unshaded border.*

GENITOURINARY EXAMINATION

SYSTEM/BODY AREA	ELEMENTS OF EXAMINATION
Constitutional	• Measurement of any three of the following seven vital signs: 1) sitting or standing blood pressure, 2) supine blood pressure, 3) pulse rate and regularity, 4) respiration, 5) temperature, 6) height, 7) weight (May be measured and recorded by ancillary staff) • General appearance of patient (e.g., development, nutrition, body habitus, deformities, attention to grooming)
Head and Face	
Eyes	
Ears, Nose, Mouth and Throat	
Neck	• Examination of neck (e.g., masses, overall appearance, symmetry, tracheal position, crepitus) • Examination of thyroid (e.g., enlargement, tenderness, mass)
Respiratory	• Assessment of respiratory effort (e.g., intercostal retractions, use of accessory muscles, diaphragmatic movement) • Auscultation of lungs (e.g., breath sounds, adventitious sounds, rubs)
Cardiovascular	• Auscultation of heart with notation of abnormal sounds and murmurs • Examination of peripheral vascular system by observation (e.g., swelling, varicosities) and palpation (e.g., pulses, temperature, edema, tenderness)
Chest (Breasts)	[See genitourinary (female)]
Gastrointestinal (Abdomen)	• Examination of abdomen with notation of presence of masses or tenderness • Examination for presence or absence of hernia • Examination of liver and spleen • Obtain stool sample for occult blood test when indicated
Genitourinary (male)	• Inspection of anus and perineum Examination (with or without specimen collection for smears and cultures) of genitalia including: • Scrotum (e.g., lesions, cysts, rashes) • Epididymides (e.g., size, symmetry, masses) • Testes (e.g., size, symmetry, masses) • Urethral meatus (e.g., size, location, lesions, discharge) • Penis (e.g., lesions, presence or absence of foreskin, foreskin retractability, plaque, masses, scarring, deformities) Digital rectal examination including: • Prostate gland (e.g., size, symmetry, nodularity, tenderness) • Seminal vesicles (e.g., symmetry, tenderness, masses, enlargement) • Sphincter tone, presence of hemorrhoids, rectal masses
Genitourinary (female)	Includes at least seven of the following eleven elements identified by bullets:

- *Inspection and palpation of breasts (e.g., masses or lumps, tenderness, symmetry, nipple discharge)*
- *Digital rectal examination including sphincter tone, presence of hemorrhoids, rectal masses*

Pelvic examination (with or without specimen collection for smears and cultures) including:

- *External genitalia (e.g., general appearance, hair distribution, lesions)*
- *Urethral meatus (e.g., size, location, lesions, prolapse)*
- *Urethra (e.g., masses, tenderness, scarring)*
- *Bladder (e.g., fullness, masses, tenderness)*
- *Vagina (e.g., general appearance, estrogen effect, discharge, lesions, pelvic support, cystocele, rectocele)*
- *Cervix (e.g., general appearance, lesions, discharge)*
- *Uterus (e.g., size, contour, position, mobility, tenderness, consistency, descent or support)*
- *Adnexa/parametria (e.g., masses, tenderness, organomegaly, nodularity)*
- *Anus and perineum*

Lymphatic	- *Palpation of lymph nodes in neck, axillae, groin and/or other location*
Musculoskeletal	
Extremities	
Skin	- *Inspection and/or palpation of skin and subcutaneous tissue (e.g., rashes, lesions, ulcers)*
Neurological/Psychiatric	*Brief assessment of mental status including:* - *Orientation (e.g., time, place and person) and* - *Mood and affect (e.g., depression, anxiety, agitation)*

CONTENT AND DOCUMENTATION REQUIREMENTS

<u>Level of Exam</u>	<u>Perform and Document:</u>
Problem Focused	*One to five elements identified by a bullet.*
Expanded Problem Focused	*At least six elements identified by a bullet.*
Detailed	*At least twelve elements identified by a bullet.*
Comprehensive	*Perform all elements identified by a bullet; document every element in each box with a shaded border and at least one element in each box with an unshaded border.*

HEMATOLOGIC, LYMPHATIC, AND/OR IMMUNOLOGIC EXAMINATION

SYSTEM/BODY AREA	ELEMENTS OF EXAMINATION
Constitutional	• Measurement of any three of the following seven vital signs: 1) sitting or standing blood pressure, 2) supine blood pressure, 3) pulse rate and regularity, 4) respiration, 5) temperature, 6) height, 7) weight (May be measured and recorded by ancillary staff) • General appearance of patient (e.g., development, nutrition, body habitus, deformities, attention to grooming)
Head and Face	• Palpation and/or percussion of face with notation of presence or absence of sinus tenderness
Eyes	• Inspection of conjunctivae and lids
Ears, Nose, Mouth and Throat	• Otoscopic examination of external auditory canals and tympanic membranes • Inspection of nasal mucosa, septum and turbinates • Inspection of teeth and gums • Examination of oropharynx (e.g., oral mucosa, hard and soft palates, tongue, tonsils, posterior pharynx)
Neck	• Examination of neck (e.g., masses, overall appearance, symmetry, tracheal position, crepitus) • Examination of thyroid (e.g., enlargement, tenderness, mass)
Respiratory	• Assessment of respiratory effort (e.g., intercostal retractions, use of accessory muscles, diaphragmatic movement) • Auscultation of lungs (e.g., breath sounds, adventitious sounds, rubs)
Cardiovascular	• Auscultation of heart with notation of abnormal sounds and murmurs • Examination of peripheral vascular system by observation (e.g., swelling, varicosities) and palpation (e.g., pulses, temperature, edema, tenderness)
Chest (Breasts)	
Gastrointestinal (Abdomen)	• Examination of abdomen with notation of presence of masses or tenderness • Examination of liver and spleen
Genitourinary	
Lymphatic	• Palpation of lymph nodes in neck, axillae, groin, and/or other location
Musculoskeletal	
Extremities	• Inspection and palpation of digits and nails (e.g., clubbing, cyanosis, inflammation, petechiae, ischemia, infections, nodes)
Skin	• Inspection and/or palpation of skin and subcutaneous tissue (e.g., rashes, lesions, ulcers, ecchymoses, bruises)
Neurological/Psychiatric	Brief assessment of mental status including: • Orientation to time, place and person

● *Mood and affect (e.g., depression, anxiety, agitation)*

CONTENT AND DOCUMENTATION REQUIREMENTS

Level of Exam	Perform and Document:
Problem Focused	One to five elements identified by a bullet.
Expanded Problem Focused	At least six elements identified by a bullet.
Detailed	At least twelve elements identified by a bullet.
Comprehensive	Perform all elements identified by a bullet; document every element in each box with a shaded border and at least one element in each box with an unshaded border.

MUSCULOSKELETAL EXAMINATION

SYSTEM/BODY AREA	ELEMENTS OF EXAMINATION
Constitutional	• Measurement of any three of the following seven vital signs: 1) sitting or standing blood pressure, 2) supine blood pressure, 3) pulse rate and regularity, 4) respiration, 5) temperature, 6) height, 7) weight (May be measured and recorded by ancillary staff)
	• General appearance of patient (e.g., development, nutrition, body habitus, deformities, attention to grooming)
Head and Face	
Eyes	
Ears, Nose, Mouth and Throat	
Neck	
Respiratory	
Cardiovascular	• Examination of peripheral vascular system by observation (e.g., swelling, varicosities) and palpation (e.g., pulses, temperature, edema, tenderness)
Chest (Breasts)	
Gastrointestinal (Abdomen)	
Genitourinary	
Lymphatic	• Palpation of lymph nodes in neck, axillae, groin and/or other location
Musculoskeletal	• Examination of gait and station
	• Examination of joint(s), bone(s) and muscle(s)/ tendon(s) of four of the following six areas: 1) head and neck; 2) spine, ribs and pelvis; 3) right upper extremity; 4) left upper extremity; 5) right lower extremity; and 6) left lower extremity. The examination of a given area includes:
	• Inspection, percussion and/or palpation with notation of any misalignment, asymmetry, crepitation, defects, tenderness, masses or effusions
	• Assessment of range of motion with notation of any pain (e.g., straight leg raising), crepitation or contracture
	• Assessment of stability with notation of any dislocation (luxation), subluxation or laxity
	• Assessment of muscle strength and tone (e.g., flaccid, cog wheel, spastic) with notation of any atrophy or abnormal movements
	NOTE: For the comprehensive level of examination, all four of the elements identified by a bullet must be performed and documented for each of four anatomic areas. For the three lower levels of examination, each element is counted separately for each body area. For example, assessing range of motion in two extremities constitutes two elements.
Extremities	[See musculoskeletal and skin]
Skin	• Inspection and/or palpation of skin and subcutaneous tissue (e.g., scars, rashes, lesions, cafe-au-lait spots, ulcers) in four of the following six areas: 1) head and neck; 2) trunk; 3) right upper extremity; 4) left upper extremity; 5) right lower extremity; and 6) left lower extremity.

> *NOTE: For the comprehensive level, all four areas must be examined and documented. For the three lower levels, each body area is counted separately. For example, inspection and/or palpation of the skin and subcutaneous tissue of two extremities constitutes two elements.*

Neurological/Psychiatric	• *Test coordination (e.g., finger/nose, heel/knee/shin, rapid alternating movements in the upper and lower extremities, evaluation of fine motor coordination in young children)*
	• *Examination of deep tendon reflexes and/or nerve stretch test with notation of pathological reflexes (e.g., Babinski)*
	• *Examination of sensation (e.g., by touch, pin, vibration, proprioception)*
	Brief assessment of mental status including
	• *Orientation to time, place and person*
	• *Mood and affect (e.g., depression, anxiety, agitation)*

CONTENT AND DOCUMENTATION REQUIREMENTS

Level of Exam	*Perform and Document:*
Problem Focused	*One to five elements identified by a bullet.*
Expanded Problem Focused	*At least six elements identified by a bullet.*
Detailed	*At least twelve elements identified by a bullet.*
Comprehensive	*Perform all elements identified by a bullet; document every element in each box with a shaded border and at least one element in each box with an unshaded border.*

NEUROLOGICAL EXAMINATION

SYSTEM/BODY AREA	ELEMENTS OF EXAMINATION
Constitutional	• *Measurement of any three of the following seven vital signs: 1) sitting or standing blood pressure, 2) supine blood pressure, 3) pulse rate and regularity, 4) respiration, 5) temperature, 6) height, 7) weight (May be measured and recorded by ancillary staff)* • *General appearance of patient (e.g., development, nutrition, body habitus, deformities, attention to grooming)*
Head and Face	
Eyes	• *Ophthalmoscopic examination of optic discs (e.g., size, C/D ratio, appearance) and posterior segments (e.g., vessel changes, exudates, hemorrhages)*
Ears, Nose, Mouth and Throat	
Neck	
Respiratory	
Cardiovascular	• *Examination of carotid arteries (e.g., pulse amplitude, bruits)* • *Auscultation of heart with notation of abnormal sounds and murmurs* • *Examination of peripheral vascular system by observation (e.g., swelling, varicosities) and palpation (e.g., pulses, temperature, edema, tenderness)*
Chest (Breasts)	
Gastrointestinal (Abdomen)	
Genitourinary	
Lymphatic	
Musculoskeletal	• *Examination of gait and station* *Assessment of motor function including:* • *Muscle strength in upper and lower extremities* • *Muscle tone in upper and lower extremities (e.g., flaccid, cog wheel, spastic) with notation of any atrophy or abnormal movements (e.g., fasciculation, tardive dyskinesia)*
Extremities	*[See musculoskeletal]*
Skin	
Neurological/Psychiatric	*Evaluation of higher integrative functions including:* • *Orientation to time, place and person* • *Recent and remote memory* • *Attention span and concentration* • *Language (e.g., naming objects, repeating phrases, spontaneous speech)* • *Fund of knowledge (e.g., awareness of current events, past history, vocabulary)* *Test the following cranial nerves:*

- *2nd cranial nerve (e.g., visual acuity, visual fields, fundi)*
- *3rd, 4th and 6th cranial nerves (e.g., pupils, eye movements)*
- *5th cranial nerve (e.g., facial sensation, corneal reflexes)*
- *7th cranial nerve (e.g., facial symmetry, strength)*
- *8th cranial nerve (e.g., hearing with tuning fork, whispered voice and/or finger rub)*
- *9th cranial nerve (e.g., spontaneous or reflex palate movement)*
- *11th cranial nerve (e.g., shoulder shrug strength)*
- *12th cranial nerve (e.g., tongue protrusion)*
- *Examination of sensation (e.g., by touch, pin, vibration, proprioception)*
- *Examination of deep tendon reflexes in upper and lower extremities with notation of pathological reflexes (e.g., Babinski)*
- *Test coordination (e.g., finger/nose, heel/knee/shin, rapid alternating movements in the upper and lower extremities, evaluation of fine motor coordination in young children)*

CONTENT AND DOCUMENTATION REQUIREMENTS

Level of Exam	*Perform and Document:*
Problem Focused	One to five elements identified by a bullet.
Expanded Problem Focused	At least six elements identified by a bullet.
Detailed	At least twelve elements identified by a bullet.
Comprehensive	Perform all elements identified by a bullet; document every element in each box with a shaded border and at least one element in each box with an unshaded border.

PSYCHIATRIC EXAMINATION

SYSTEM/BODY AREA	ELEMENTS OF EXAMINATION
Constitutional	• Measurement of any three of the following seven vital signs: 1) sitting or standing blood pressure, 2) supine blood pressure, 3) pulse rate and regularity, 4) respiration, 5) temperature, 6) height, 7) weight (May be measured and recorded by ancillary staff)
	• General appearance of patient (e.g., development, nutrition, body habitus, deformities, attention to grooming)
Head and Face	
Eyes	
Ears, Nose, Mouth and Throat	
Neck	
Respiratory	
Cardiovascular	
Chest (Breasts)	
Gastrointestinal (Abdomen)	
Genitourinary	
Lymphatic	
Musculoskeletal	• Assessment of muscle strength and tone (e.g., flaccid, cog wheel, spastic) with notation of any atrophy and abnormal movements
	• Examination of gait and station
Extremities	
Skin	
Neurological	
Psychiatric	• Description of speech including: rate; volume; articulation; coherence; and spontaneity with notation of abnormalities (e.g., perseveration, paucity of language)
	• Description of thought processes including: rate of thoughts; content of thoughts (e.g., logical vs. illogical, tangential); abstract reasoning; and computation
	• Description of associations (e.g., loose, tangential, circumstantial, intact)
	• Description of abnormal or psychotic thoughts including: hallucinations; delusions; preoccupation with violence; homicidal or suicidal ideation; and obsessions
	• Description of the patient's judgment (e.g., concerning everyday activities and social situations) and insight (e.g., concerning psychiatric condition)
	Complete mental status examination including:
	• Orientation to time, place and person
	• Recent and remote memory
	• Attention span and concentration

- *Language (e.g., naming objects, repeating phrases)*
- *Fund of knowledge (e.g., awareness of current events, past history, vocabulary)*
- *Mood and affect (e.g., depression, anxiety, agitation, hypomania, lability)*

CONTENT AND DOCUMENTATION REQUIREMENTS

Level of Exam	*Perform and Document:*
Problem Focused	*One to five elements identified by a bullet.*
Expanded Problem Focused	*At least six elements identified by a bullet.*
Detailed	*At least nine elements identified by a bullet.*
Comprehensive	*Perform all elements identified by a bullet; document every element in each box with a shaded border and at least one element in each box with an unshaded border.*

RESPIRATORY EXAMINATION

SYSTEM/BODY AREA	ELEMENTS OF EXAMINATION
Constitutional	• Measurement of any three of the following seven vital signs: 1) sitting or standing blood pressure, 2) supine blood pressure, 3) pulse rate and regularity, 4) respiration, 5) temperature, 6) height, 7) weight (May be measured and recorded by ancillary staff)
	• General appearance of patient (e.g., development, nutrition, body habitus, deformities, attention to grooming)
Head and Face	
Eyes	
Ears, Nose, Mouth and Throat	• Inspection of nasal mucosa, septum and turbinates
	• Inspection of teeth and gums
	• Examination of oropharynx (e.g., oral mucosa, hard and soft palates, tongue, tonsils and posterior pharynx)
Neck	• Examination of neck (e.g., masses, overall appearance, symmetry, tracheal position, crepitus)
	• Examination of thyroid (e.g., enlargement, tenderness, mass)
	• Examination of jugular veins (e.g., distension; a, v or cannon a waves)
Respiratory	• Inspection of chest with notation of symmetry and expansion
	• Assessment of respiratory effort (e.g., intercostal retractions, use of accessory muscles, diaphragmatic movement)
	• Percussion of chest (e.g., dullness, flatness, hyperresonance)
	• Palpation of chest (e.g., tactile fremitus)
	• Auscultation of lungs (e.g., breath sounds, adventitious sounds, rubs)
Cardiovascular	• Auscultation of heart including sounds, abnormal sounds and murmurs
	• Examination of peripheral vascular system by observation (e.g., swelling, varicosities) and palpation (e.g., pulses, temperature, edema, tenderness)
Chest (Breasts)	
Gastrointestinal (Abdomen)	• Examination of abdomen with notation of presence of masses or tenderness
	• Examination of liver and spleen
Genitourinary	
Lymphatic	• Palpation of lymph nodes in neck, axillae, groin and/or other location
Musculoskeletal	• Assessment of muscle strength and tone (e.g., flaccid, cog wheel, spastic) with notation of any atrophy and abnormal movements
	• Examination of gait and station
Extremities	• Inspection and palpation of digits and nails (e.g., clubbing, cyanosis, inflammation, petechiae, ischemia, infections, nodes)

Skin	• Inspection and/or palpation of skin and subcutaneous tissue (e.g., rashes, lesions, ulcers)
Neurological/Psychiatric	Brief assessment of mental status including:
	• Orientation to time, place and person
	• Mood and affect (e.g., depression, anxiety, agitation)

CONTENT AND DOCUMENTATION REQUIREMENTS

Level of Exam	Perform and Document:
Problem Focused	One to five elements identified by a bullet.
Expanded Problem Focused	At least six elements identified by a bullet.
Detailed	At least twelve elements identified by a bullet.
Comprehensive	Perform all elements identified by a bullet; document every element in each box with a shaded border and at least one element in each box with an unshaded border.

SKIN EXAMINATION

SYSTEM/BODY AREA	ELEMENTS OF EXAMINATION
Constitutional	• Measurement of any three of the following seven vital signs: 1) sitting or standing blood pressure, 2) supine blood pressure, 3) pulse rate and regularity, 4) respiration, 5) temperature, 6) height, 7) weight (May be measured and recorded by ancillary staff) • General appearance of patient (e.g., development, nutrition, body habitus, deformities, attention to grooming)
Head and Face	
Eyes	• Inspection of conjunctivae and lids
Ears, Nose, Mouth and Throat	• Inspection of lips, teeth and gums • Examination of oropharynx (e.g., oral mucosa, hard and soft palates, tongue, tonsils, posterior pharynx)
Neck	• Examination of thyroid (e.g., enlargement, tenderness, mass)
Respiratory	
Cardiovascular	• Examination of peripheral vascular system by observation (e.g., swelling, varicosities) and palpation (e.g., pulses, temperature, edema, tenderness)
Chest (Breasts)	
Gastrointestinal (Abdomen)	• Examination of liver and spleen • Examination of anus for condyloma and other lesions
Genitourinary	
Lymphatic	• Palpation of lymph nodes in neck, axillae, groin and/or other location
Musculoskeletal	
Extremities	• Inspection and palpation of digits and nails (e.g., clubbing, cyanosis, inflammation, petechiae, ischemia, infections, nodes)
Skin	• Palpation of scalp and inspection of hair of scalp, eyebrows, face, chest, pubic area (when indicated) and extremities Inspection and/or palpation of skin and subcutaneous tissue (e.g., rashes, lesions, ulcers, susceptibility to and presence of photo damage) in eight of the following ten areas: • Head, including the face and • Neck • Chest, including breasts and axillae • Abdomen • Genitalia, groin, buttocks • Back • Right upper extremity

- Left upper extremity
- Right lower extremity
- Left lower extremity

NOTE: For the comprehensive level, the examination of at least eight anatomic areas must be performed and documented. For the three lower levels of examination, each body area is counted separately. For example, inspection and/or palpation of the skin and subcutaneous tissue of the right upper extremity and the left upper extremity constitutes two elements.

- Inspection of eccrine and apocrine glands of skin and subcutaneous tissue with identification and location of any hyperhidrosis, chromhidroses or bromhidrosis

Neurological/Psychiatric   Brief assessment of mental status including:

- Orientation to time, place and person
- Mood and affect (e.g., depression, anxiety, agitation)

CONTENT AND DOCUMENTATION REQUIREMENTS

Level of Exam	Perform and Document:
Problem Focused	One to five elements identified by a bullet.
Expanded Problem Focused	At least six elements identified by a bullet.
Detailed	At least twelve elements identified by a bullet.
Comprehensive	Perform all elements identified by a bullet; document every element in each box with a shaded border and at least one element in each box with an unshaded border.

DOCUMENTATION OF THE COMPLEXITY OF MEDICAL DECISION MAKING

The levels of evaluation and management services recognize four types of medical decision making (straight-forward, low complexity, moderate complexity and high complexity). Medical decision making refers to the complexity of establishing a diagnosis and/or selecting a management option as measured by:

- the number of possible diagnoses and/or the number of management options that must be considered;

- the amount and/or complexity of medical records, diagnostic tests, and/or other information that must be obtained, reviewed and analyzed; and

- the risk of significant complications, morbidity and/or mortality, as well as comorbidities, associated with the patient's presenting problem(s), the diagnostic procedure(s) and/or the possible management options.

The following chart illustrates the progression of the elements required for each level of medical decision making. To qualify for a given type of decision making, two of the three elements in the table must be either met or exceeded.

NUMBER OF DIAGNOSES OR MANAGEMENT OPTIONS

The number of possible diagnoses and/or the number of management options that must be considered is based on the number and types of problems addressed during the encounter, the complexity of establishing a diagnosis and the management decisions that are made by the physician.

Generally, decision making with respect to a diagnosed problem is easier than that for an identified but undiagnosed problem. The number and type of diagnostic tests employed may be an indicator of the number of possible diagnoses. Problems which are improving or resolving are less complex than those which are worsening or failing to change as expected. The need to seek advice from others is another indicator of complexity of diagnostic or management problems.

- **●DG:** *For each encounter, an assessment, clinical impression, or diagnosis should be documented. It may be explicitly stated or implied in documented decisions regarding management plans and/or further evaluation.*

  - *For a presenting problem with an established diagnosis, the record should reflect whether the problem is: a) improved, well controlled, resolving or resolved; or, b) inadequately controlled, worsening, or failing to change as expected.*

  - *For a presenting problem without an established diagnosis, the assessment or clinical impression may be stated in the form of differential diagnoses or as a "possible", "probable", or "rule out" (R/O) diagnosis.*

Number of Diagnoses	Amount of Data to Review	Risk of Complication	Type of Decision Making
Minimal	Minimal or none	Minimal	Straightforward
Limited	Limited	Low	Low Complexity
Multiple	Moderate	Moderate	Moderate Complexity
Extensive	Extensive	High	High Complexity
Each of the elements of medical decision making is described in the text below			

- **●DG:** *The initiation of, or changes in, treatment should be documented. Treatment includes a wide range of management options including patient instructions, nursing instructions, therapies, and medications.*

- **●DG:** *If referrals are made, consultations requested or advice sought, the record should indicate to whom or where the referral or consultation is made or from whom the advice is requested.*

AMOUNT AND/OR COMPLEXITY OF DATA TO BE REVIEWED

The amount and complexity of data to be reviewed is based on the types of diagnostic testing ordered or reviewed. A decision to obtain and review old medical records and/or obtain history from sources other than the patient increases the amount and complexity of data to be reviewed.

Discussion of contradictory or unexpected test results with the physician who performed or interpreted the test is an indication of the complexity of data being reviewed. On occasion the physician who ordered a test may personally review the image, tracing or specimen to supplement information from the physician who prepared the test report or interpretation; this is another indication of the complexity of data being reviewed.

●**DG:** If a diagnostic service (test or procedure) is ordered, planned, scheduled, or performed at the time of the evaluation and management encounter, the type of service, e.g., lab or x-ray, should be documented.

●**DG:** The review of lab, radiology and/or other diagnostic tests should be documented. A simple notation such as "WBC elevated" or "chest x-ray unremarkable" is acceptable. Alternatively, the review may be documented by initialing and dating the report containing the test results.

●**DG:** A decision to obtain old records or decision to obtain additional history from the family, caretaker or other source to supplement that obtained from the patient should be documented.

●**DG:** Relevant findings from the review of old records, and/or the receipt of additional history from the family, caretaker or other source to supplement that obtained from the patient should be documented. If there is no relevant information beyond that already obtained, that fact should be documented. A notation of "Old records reviewed" or "additional history obtained from family" without elaboration is insufficient.

●**DG:** The results of discussion of laboratory, radiology or other diagnostic tests with the physician who performed or interpreted the study should be documented.

●**DG:** The direct visualization and independent interpretation of an image, tracing or specimen previously or subsequently interpreted by another physician should be documented.

RISK OF SIGNIFICANT COMPLICATIONS, MORBIDITY AND/OR MORTALITY

The risk of significant complications, morbidity, and/or mortality is based on the risks associated with the presenting problem(s), the diagnostic procedure(s), and the possible management options.

●**DG:** Comorbidities/underlying diseases or other factors that increase the complexity of medical decision making by increasing the risk of complications, morbidity, and/or mortality should be documented.

●**DG:** If a surgical or invasive diagnostic procedure is ordered, planned or scheduled at the time of the evaluation and management encounter, the type of procedure, e.g., laparoscopy, should be documented.

●**DG:** If a surgical or invasive diagnostic procedure is performed at the time of the evaluation and management encounter, the specific procedure should be documented.

●**DG:** The referral for or decision to perform a surgical or invasive diagnostic procedure on an urgent basis should be documented or implied.

The Table of Risk on the following page may be used to help determine whether the risk of significant complications, morbidity, and/or mortality is minimal, low, moderate, or high. Because the determination of risk is complex and not readily quantifiable, the table includes common clinical examples rather than absolute measures of risk. The assessment of risk of the presenting problem(s) is based on the risk related to the disease process anticipated between the present encounter and the next one. The assessment of risk of selecting diagnostic procedures and management options is based on the risk during and immediately following any procedures or treatment. The highest level of risk in any one category (presenting problem(s), diagnostic procedure(s), or management options) determines the overall risk.

DOCUMENTATION OF AN ENCOUNTER DOMINATED BY COUNSELING OR COORDINATION OF CARE

In the case where counseling and/or coordination of care dominates (more than 50%) of the physician/patient and/or family encounter (face-to-face time in the office or other or outpatient setting, floor/unit time in the hospital or nursing facility), time is considered the key or controlling factor to qualify for a particular level of evaluation and management services.

●**DG:** If the physician elects to report the level of service based on counseling and/or coordination of care, the total length of time of the encounter (face-to-face or floor time, as appropriate) should be documented and the record should describe the counseling and/or activities to coordinate care.

TABLE OF RISK

LEVEL OF RISK	PRESENTING PROBLEM(S)	DIAGNOSTIC PROCEDURES	MANAGEMENT OPTIONS
Minimal	• One self-limited or minor problem, (eg, cold, insect bite, tinea corporis)	• Laboratory tests requiring venipuncture • Chest x-rays • EKG/EEG • Urinalysis • Ultrasound, (eg, echocardiography) • KOH prep	• Rest • Gargles • Elastic bandages • Superficial dressings
Low	• Two or more self-limited or minor problems • One stable chronic illness, (eg, well controlled hypertension, non-insulin dependent diabetes, cataract, BPH) • Acute uncomplicated illness or injury, (eg, cystitis, allergic rhinitis, simple sprain)	• Physiologic tests not under stress, (eg, pulmonary function tests) • Non-cardiovascular imaging studies with contrast,(eg, barium enema) • Superficial needle biopsies • Clinical laboratory tests requiring arterial puncture • Skin biopsies	• Over-the-counter drugs • Minor surgery with no identified risk factors • Physical therapy • Occupational therapy • IV fluids without additives
Moderate	• One or more chronic illnesses with mild exacerbation, progression, or side effects of treatment • Two or more stable chronic illnesses • Undiagnosed new problem with uncertain prognosis, (eg, lump in breast) • Acute illness with systemic symptoms, (eg, pyelonephritis, pneumonitis, colitis) • Acute complicated injury, (eg, head injury with brief loss of consciousness)	• Physiologic tests under stress, (eg, cardiac stress test, fetal contraction stress test) • Diagnostic endoscopies with no identified risk factors • Deep needle or incisional biopsy • Cardiovascular imaging studies with contrast and no identified risk factors, (eg, arteriogram, cardiac catheterization) • Obtain fluid from body cavity, (eg, lumbar puncture, thoracentesis, culdocentesis)	• Minor surgery with identified risk factors • Elective major surgery (open, percutaneous or endoscopic) with no identified risk factors • Prescription drug management • Therapeutic nuclear medicine • IV fluids with additives • Closed treatment of fracture or dislocation without manipulation
High	• One or more chronic illnesses with severe exacerbation, progression, or side effects of treatment • Acute or chronic illnesses or injuries that pose a threat to life or bodily function, (eg, multiple trauma, acute MI, pulmonary embolus, severe respiratory distress, progressive severe rheumatoid arthritis, psychiatric illness with potential threat to self or others, peritonitis, acute renal failure) • An abrupt change in neurologic status, (eg, seizure, TIA, weakness, sensory loss)	• Cardiovascular imaging studies with contrast with identified risk factors • Cardiac electrophysiological tests • Diagnostic endoscopies with identified risk factors • Discography	• percutaneous or endoscopic) with identified risk factors • Emergency major surgery (open, percutaneous or endoscopic) • Parenteral controlled substances • Drug therapy requiring intensive monitoring for toxicity • Decision not to resuscitate or to de-escalate care because of poor prognosis

EVALUATION AND MANAGEMENT CODING VISUAL MATRIX

Many people are visually oriented, which means they perceive and learn better when presented with pictures, graphics, shapes and colors. The following Evaluation and Management Coding Visual Matrix is designed to assist visually oriented readers to quickly grasp the sections and choices available.

The Evaluation and Management Coding Visual Matrix reinforces that each Evaluation and Management code is selected from a choice of 1) history, 2) medical decision making and 3) presenting problem components. Some Evaluation and Management codes include a time unit; measured as either face-to-face time or bedside/floor or unit time.

Color Key   **Significance**

Color	Significance
▉	Components required
▨	History & exam choices
▨	Medical decision making choices
▨	Presenting problem (severity) choices

Office/Other Outpatient Services (New Patients)

Components required: 3 of 3	99201	99202	99203	99204	99205
History & Exam					
Problem focused	●				
Expanded problem focused		●			
Detailed			●		
Comprehensive				●	●
Medical Decision Making					
Straightforward	●	●			
Low			●		
Moderate				●	
High					●
Presenting Problem (Severity)					
Self-limited or minor	●				
Low to moderate		●			
Moderate			●		
Moderate to high				●	●
Typical Time: Face-to-Face	10	20	30	45	60

Office/Other Outpatient Services (Established Patients)

Components required: 2 of 3	99211	99212	99213	99214	99215
History & Exam					
Problem focused		●			
Expanded problem focused			●		
Detailed				●	
Comprehensive					●
Medical Decision Making					
Straightforward		●			
Low			●		
Moderate				●	
High					●
Presenting Problem (Severity)					
Self-limited or minor	●				
Low to moderate		●			
Moderate			●		
Moderate to high				●	●
Typical Time: Face-to-Face	5	10	15	25	40

Initial Observation Care (New/Established Patients)

Components required: 3 of 3	99218	99219	99220
History & Exam			
Detailed or comprehensive	●		
Comprehensive		●	●
Straightforward or low	●		
Moderate		●	
High			●
Presenting Problem (Severity)			
Low	●		
Moderate		●	
High			●
Typical Time: Bedside/Floor/Unit	30	50	70

Subsequent Observation Care (New/Established Patients)

Components required: 2 of 3	99224	99225	99226
History & Exam			
Problem focused	●		
Expanded problem focused		●	
Detailed			●
Medical Decision Making			
Straightforward or low	●		
Moderate		●	
High			●
Presenting Problem (Severity)			
Stable/recovering/improving	●		
Responding inadequately/minor complication		●	
Unstable/significant complication/new problem			●
Typical Time: Bedside/Floor/Unit	15	25	35

Initial Hospital Care (New/Established Patients)

Components required: 3 of 3	99221	99222	99223
History & Exam			
Detailed or comprehensive	●		
Comprehensive		●	●
Straightforward or low	●		
Moderate		●	
High			●
Presenting Problem (Severity)			
Low	●		
Moderate		●	
High			●
Typical Time: Bedside/Floor/Unit	30	50	70

Subsequent Hospital Care (New/Established Patients)

Components required: 2 of 3	99231	99232	99233
History & Exam			
Problem focused	●		
Expanded problem focused		●	
Detailed			●
Medical Decision Making			
Straightforward or low	●		
Moderate		●	
High			●
Presenting Problem (Severity)			
Stable/recovering/improving	●		
Responding inadequately/minor complication		●	
Unstable/significant complication/new problem			●
Typical Time: Bedside/Floor/Unit	15	25	35

Observation/Inpatient Care Services (New/Established Patients)
(Including Admission And Discharge Services)

Components required: 3 of 3	99234	99235	99236
History & Exam			
Detailed or comprehensive	●		
Comprehensive		●	●
Straightforward or low	●		
Moderate		●	
High			●
Presenting Problem (Severity)			
Low	●		
Moderate		●	
High			●
Typical Time:	40	50	55

Office/Other Outpatient Consultations (New/Established Patients)

Components required: 3 of 3	99241	99242	99243	99244	99245
History & Exam					
Problem focused	●				
Expanded problem focused		●			
Detailed			●		
Comprehensive				●	●
Medical Decision Making					
Straightforward	●	●			
Low			●		
Moderate				●	
High					●
Presenting Problem (Severity)					
Self-limited or minor	●				
Low		●			
Moderate			●		
Moderate to high				●	●
Typical Time: Face-to-Face	15	30	40	60	80

Inpatient Consultations (New/Established Patients)

Components required: 3 of 3	99251	99252	99253	99254	99255
History & Exam					
Problem focused	●				
Expanded problem focused		●			
Detailed			●		
Comprehensive				●	●
Medical Decision Making					
Straightforward	●	●			
Low			●		
Moderate				●	
High					●
Presenting Problem (Severity)					
Self-limited or minor	●				
Low		●			
Moderate			●		
Moderate to high				●	●
Typical Time: Bedside/Floor/Unit	20	40	55	80	110

Emergency Department Services (New/Established Patients)

Components required: 3 of 3	99281	99282	99283	99284	99285
History & Exam					
Problem focused	●				
Expanded problem focused		●	●		
Detailed				●	
Comprehensive					●
Medical Decision Making					
Straightforward	●				
Low		●			
Moderate			●	●	
High					●
Presenting Problem (Severity)					
Self-limited or minor	●				
Low to moderate		●			
Moderate			●		
High				●	
High severity/immediate significant threat to life or physiological function					●
Typical Time:	--	--	--	--	--

Initial Nursing Facility Care (New/Established Patients)

Components required: 3 of 3	99304	99305	99306
History & Exam			
Detailed or comprehensive	●		
Comprehensive		●	●
Medical Decision Making			
Straightforward or low	●		
Moderate		●	
High			●
Presenting Problem (Severity)			
Low	●		
Moderate		●	
High			●
Typical Time: Bedside/Floor/Unit	25	35	45

Subsequent Nursing Facility Services

Components required: 2 of 3	99307	99308	99309	99310
History & Exam				
Problem focused	●			
Expanded problem focused		●		
Detailed			●	
Comprehensive				●
Medical Decision Making				
Straightforward	●			
Low		●		
Moderate			●	
High				●
Presenting Problem (Severity)				
Stable/recovering/improving	●			
Responding inadequately to therapy/minor complication		●		
Significant complication/significant new problem			●	
Unstable/significant new problem requiring immediate physician attention				●
Typical Time: Bedside/Floor/Unit	10	15	25	35

Domiciliary, Rest Home, Or Custodial Care Services (New Patient)

Components required: 3 of 3	99324	99325	99326	99327	99328
History & Exam					
Problem focused	●				
Expanded problem focused		●			
Detailed			●		
Comprehensive				●	●
Medical Decision Making					
Straightforward	●				
Low		●			
Moderate			●	●	
High					●
Presenting Problem (Severity)					
Low	●				
Moderate		●			
Moderate to high			●		
High				●	
Unstable/significant new problem requiring immediate attention					●
Typical Time: Face-to-Face	20	30	45	60	75

Domiciliary, Rest Home, or Custodial Care Services (Established Patient)

Components required: 2 of 3	99334	99335	99336	99337
History & Exam				
Problem focused	●			
Expanded problem focused		●		
Detailed			●	
Comprehensive				●
Medical Decision Making				
Straightforward	●			
Low		●		
Moderate			●	
Moderate to high				●
Presenting Problem (Severity)				
Self-limited or minor	●			
Low to moderate		●		
Moderate to high			●	
Moderate to high/unstable/significant new problem				●
Typical Time: Face-to-Face	15	25	40	60

Home Services (New Patients)

Components required: 3 of 3	99341	99342	99343	99344	99345
History & Exam					
Problem focused	●				
Expanded problem focused		●			
Detailed			●		
Comprehensive				●	●
Medical Decision Making					
Straightforward	●				
Low		●			
Moderate			●	●	
High					●
Presenting Problem (Severity)					
Low	●				
Moderate		●			
Moderate to high			●		
High				●	
Unstable/significant new problem					●
Typical Time: Face-to-Face	20	30	45	60	75

Home Services (Established Patient)

Components required: 2 of 3	99347	99348	99349	99350
History & Exam				
Problem focused	●			
Expanded problem focused		●		
Detailed			●	
Comprehensive				●
Medical Decision Making				
Straightforward	●			
Low		●		
Moderate			●	
Moderate to high				●
Presenting Problem (Severity)				
Self-limited or minor	●			
Low to moderate		●		
Moderate to high			●	
Moderate to high/unstable/significant new problem				●
Typical Time: Face-to-Face	15	25	40	60

OFFICE OR OTHER OUTPATIENT SERVICES

The key coding issues are the extent of history obtained, the extent of examination performed, and the complexity of medical decision making. Additional reporting issues include counseling and/or coordination of care, the nature of presenting problem(s), and the duration of face-to-face time spent with the patient and/or family.

CODING RULES

1. *A patient is considered an outpatient until admitted as an inpatient to a health care facility.*

2. *If outpatient evaluation and management services are provided in conjunction with, or result in, an inpatient admission, the service is reported using CPT codes for initial hospital care.*

3. *CPT codes in this section may also be used to report the services provided by a physician to a patient in an observation area of a hospital.*

4. *Laboratory tests, radiology services, and diagnostic or therapeutic procedures performed in conjunction with evaluation and management services are reported in addition to the basic evaluation and management service.*

5. *Supplies and materials provided by the physician over and above those usually included with the evaluation and management or other services rendered may be listed separately. List all drugs, trays, supplies and materials provided.*

The following codes are used to report evaluation and management services provided in the office or in an outpatient or other ambulatory facility. A patient is considered an outpatient until inpatient admission to a health care facility occurs.

To report services provided to a patient who is admitted to a hospital or nursing facility in the course of an encounter in the office or other ambulatory facility, see the notes for initial hospital inpatient care, or initial nursing facility care.

For services provided in the emergency department, see 99281-99285.

For observation care, see 99217-99226.

For observation or inpatient care services (including admission and discharge services), see 99234-99236.

NEW PATIENT

★ **99201** Office or other outpatient visit for the evaluation and management of a new patient, which requires these three key components:

  ● a problem focused history;

  ● a problem focused examination;

  ● straightforward medical decision making.

Counseling and/or coordination of care with other physicians, other qualified health care professionals, or agencies are provided consistent with the nature of the problem(s) and the patient's and/or family's needs.

Usually, the presenting problems are self limited or minor. Typically 10 minutes are spent face-to-face with the patient and/or family.

★ **99202** Office or other outpatient visit for the evaluation and management of a new patient, which requires these three key components:

  ● an expanded problem focused history;

  ● an expanded problem focused examination;

  ● straightforward medical decision making.

Counseling and/or coordination of care with other physicians, other qualified health care professionals, or agencies are provided consistent with the nature of the problem(s) and the patient's and/or family's needs.

Separate Procedure   Unlisted Procedure   CCI Comp. Code   Non-specific Procedure   **137**

Usually, the presenting problem(s) are of low to moderate severity. Typically 20 minutes are spent face-to-face with the patient and/or family.

★ 99203 Office or other outpatient visit for the evaluation and management of a new patient, which requires these three key components:

- a detailed history;

- a detailed examination; and

- medical decision making of low complexity.

Counseling and/or coordination of care with other physicians, other qualified health care professionals, or agencies are provided consistent with the nature of the problem(s) and the patient's and/or family's needs.

Usually, the presenting problem(s) are of moderate severity. Typically 30 minutes are spent face-to-face with the patient and/or family.

★ 99204 Office or other outpatient visit for the evaluation and management of a new patient, which requires these three key components:

- a comprehensive history;

- a comprehensive examination; and

- medical decision making of moderate complexity.

Counseling and/or coordination of care with other physicians, other qualified health care professionals, or agencies are provided consistent with the nature of the problem(s) and the patient's and/or family's needs.

Usually, the presenting problem(s) are of moderate to high severity. Typically 45 minutes are spent face-to-face with the patient and/or family.

★ 99205 Office or other outpatient visit for the evaluation and management of a new patient, which requires these three key components:

- a comprehensive history;

- a comprehensive examination; and

- medical decision making of high complexity.

Counseling and/or coordination of care with other physicians, other qualified health care professionals, or agencies are provided consistent with the nature of the problem(s) and the patient's and/or family's needs.

Usually, the presenting problem(s) are of moderate to high severity. Typically 60 minutes are spent face-to-face with the patient and/or family.

ESTABLISHED PATIENT

99211 Office or other outpatient visit for the evaluation and management of an established patient, that may not require the presence of a physician or other qualified health care professional. Usually, the presenting problem(s) are minimal. Typically, 5 minutes are spent performing or supervising these services.

★ 99212 Office or other outpatient visit for the evaluation and management of an established patient, which requires at least two of these three key components:

- a problem focused history;

- a problem focused examination;

- straightforward medical decision making.

Counseling and/or coordination of care with other physicians, other qualified health care professionals, or agencies are provided consistent with the nature of the problem(s) and the patient's and/or family's needs.

Usually, the presenting problem(s) are self limited or minor. Typically 10 minutes are spent face-to-face with the patient and/or family.

★ 99213 Office or other outpatient visit for the evaluation and management of an established patient, which requires at least two of these three key components:

- an expanded problem focused history;

● New Code ▲ Revised Code + Add-On Code ⊘ Modifier -51 Exempt ★ Telemedicine

- an expanded problem focused examination;
- medical decision making of low complexity.

Counseling and coordination of care with other physicians, other qualified health care professionals, or agencies are provided consistent with the nature of the problem(s) and the patient's and/or family's needs.

Usually, the presenting problem(s) are of low to moderate severity. Typically 15 minutes are spent face-to-face with the patient and/or family.

★ **99214** Office or other outpatient visit for the evaluation and management of an established patient, which requires at least two of these three key components:
- a detailed history;
- a detailed examination;
- medical decision making of moderate complexity.

Counseling and/or coordination of care with other physicians, other qualified health care professionals, or agencies are provided consistent with the nature of the problem(s) and the patient's and/or family's needs.

Usually, the presenting problem(s) are of moderate to high severity. Typically 25 minutes are spent face-to-face with the patient and/or family.

★ **99215** Office or other outpatient visit for the evaluation and management of an established patient, which requires at least two of these three key components:
- a comprehensive history;
- a comprehensive examination;
- medical decision making of high complexity.

Counseling and/or coordination of care with other physicians, other qualified health care professionals, or agencies are provided consistent with the nature of the problem(s) and the patient's and/or family's needs.

Usually, the presenting problem(s) are of moderate to high severity. Typically 40 minutes are spent face-to-face with the patient and/or family.

HOSPITAL OBSERVATION SERVICES

Occasionally a physician will watch or "observe" a patient in an area of an inpatient hospital designated as an "observation" area. This area is frequently located in or near the emergency room, and the observation typically after any acute care is rendered.

The purpose of the observation is to determine if the patient's condition requires inpatient hospitalization. Patients considered under observation status may be discharged from the observation area or admitted to the hospital as an inpatient.

All observation care services are "per day" and should be coded only once per date of service. CPT code 99217 is used to report all services provided on discharge from "observation status" if the discharge is on other than the initial date of "observation status."

The following codes are used to report evaluation and management services provided to patients designated/admitted as "observation status" in a hospital. It is not necessary that the patient be located in an observation area designated by the hospital.

If such an area does exist in a hospital (as a separate unit in the hospital, in the emergency department, etc.), these codes are to be utilized if the patient is placed in such an area.

For definitions of key components and commonly used terms, please see Evaluation and Management Services Guidelines.

OBSERVATION CARE DISCHARGE SERVICES

Observation care discharge of a patient from "observation status" includes final examination of the patient, discussion of the hospital stay, instructions for continuing care, and preparation of dishcarge records. For observation or inpatient hospital care including the admission and discharge of the patient on the same date, see codes 99234-99236 as appropriate.

| | Separate Procedure | | Unlisted Procedure | | CCI Comp. Code | | Non-specific Procedure | **139** |

 **99217** Observation care discharge day management (This code is to be utilized to report all services provided to a patient on discharge from outpatient hospital "observation status" if the discharge is on other than the initial date of "observation status." To report services to a patient designated as "observation status" or "inpatient status" and discharged on the same date, use codes for Observation or Inpatient Care Services [including Admission and Discharge Services, 99234-99236 as appropriate]).

INITIAL OBSERVATION CARE

NEW OR ESTABLISHED PATIENT

The following codes are used to report the encounter(s) by the supervising physician or other qualified health care professional with the patient when designated as outpatient hospital "observation status." This refers to the initiation of observation status, supervision of the care plan for observation, and performance of periodic reassessments. For observation encounters by other physicians, see office or other outpatient consultation codes (99241-99245) or subsequent observation care codes (99224-99226) as appropriate.

To report services provided to a patient who is admitted to the hospital after receiving hospital observation care services on the same date, see the notes for initial hospital inpatient care (later in this section). For observation care services on other than the initial or discharge date, see subsequent observation services codes (99224-99226). For a patient admitted to the hospital on a date subsequent to the date of observation status, the hospital admission would be reported with the appropriate initial hospital care code (99221-99223). For a patient admitted and discharged from observation or inpatient status on the same date, the services should be reported with codes 99234-99236 as appropriate. Do not report observation discharge (99217) in conjunction with a hospital admission (99221-99223).

When "observation status" is initiated in the course of an encounter in another site of service (eg, hospital emergency department, office, nursing facility) all evaluation and management services provided by the supervising physician or other qualified health care professional in conjunction with initiating "observation status" are considered part of the initial observation care when performed on the same date. The observation care level of service reported by the supervising physician or other qualified health care professional should include the services related to initiating "observation status" provided in the other sites of service as well as in the observation setting.

Evaluation and management services including new or established patient office or other outpatient services (99201-99215), emergency department services (99281-99285), nursing facility services (99304-99318), domiciliary, rest home or custodial care services (99324-99337), home services (99341-99350), and preventive medicine services (99381-99429) on the same date related to the admission to "observation status" should **not** be reported separately.

These codes may not be utilized for post-operative recovery if the procedure is considered part of the surgical "package." These codes apply to all evaluation and management services that are provided on the same date of initiating "observation status."

 **99218** Initial observation care, per day, for the evaluation and management of a patient which requires these 3 key components:

- A detailed or comprehensive history;
- A detailed or comprehensive examination; and
- Medical decision making that is straightforward or of low complexity.

Counseling and/or coordination of care with other physicians, other qualified health care professionals, or agencies are provided consistent with the nature of the problem(s) and the patient's and/or family's needs.

Usually, the problem(s) requiring admission to outpatient hospital "observation status" are of low severity. Typically 30 minutes are spent at the bedside and on the patient's hospital floor or unit.

 **99219** Initial observation care, per day, for the evaluation and management of a patient, which requires these 3 key components:

- A comprehensive history;
- A comprehensive examination; and
- Medical decision making of moderate complexity.

Counseling and/or coordination of care with other physicians, other qualified health care professionals, or agencies are provided consistent with the nature of the problem(s) and the patient's and/or family's needs.

Usually, the problem(s) requiring admission to outpatient hospital "observation status" are of moderate severity. Typically 50 minutes are spent at the bedside and on the patient's hospital floor or unit.

 **99220** Initial observation care, per day, for the evaluation and management of a patient, which requires these 3 key components:

- A comprehensive history;
- A comprehensive examination; and
- Medical decision making of high complexity.

Counseling and/or coordination of care with other physicians, other qualified health care professionals, or agencies are provided consistent with the nature of the problem(s) and the patient's and/or family's needs.

Usually, the problem(s) requiring admission to outpatient hospital "observation status" are of high severity. Typically 70 minutes are spent at the bedside and on the patient's hospital floor or unit.

SUBSEQUENT OBSERVATION CARE

All levels of subsequent observation care include reviewing the medical record and reviewing the results of diagnostic studies and changes in the patient's status (ie., changes in history, physical condition, and response to management) since the last assessment.

 99224 Subsequent observation care, per day, for the evaluation and management of a patient, which requires at least 2 of these 3 key components:

- problem focused interval history;
- problem focused examination;
- medical decision making that is straightforward or of low complexity.

Counseling and/or coordination of care with other physicians, other qualified health care professionals, or agencies are provided consistent with the nature of the problem(s) and the patient's and/or family's needs.

Usually, the patient is stable, recovering, or improving. Typically 15 minutes are spent at the bedside and on the patient's hospital floor or unit.

 99225 Subsequent observation care, per day, for the evaluation and management of a patient, which requires at least 2 of these 3 key components:

- an expanded problem focused interval history;
- an expanded problem focused examination;
- medical decision making of moderate complexity

Counseling and/or coordination of care with other physicians, other qualified health care professionals, or agencies are provided consistent with the nature of the problem(s) and the patient's and/or family's needs.

Usually, the patient is responding inadequately to therapy or has developed a minor complication. Typically 25 are spent minutes at the bedside and on the patient's hospital floor or unit.

 99226 Subsequent observation care, per day, for the evaluation and management of a patient, which requires at least 2 of these 3 key components:

- a detailed interval history;·
- a detailed examination
- medical decision making of high complexity.

Counseling and/or coordination of care with other physicians, other qualified health care professionals, or agencies are provided consistent with the nature of the problem(s) and the patient's and/or family's needs.

Usually, the patient is unstable or has developed a significant complication or a significant new problem. Typically 35 minutes are spent at the bedside and on the patient's hospital floor or unit.

HOSPITAL INPATIENT SERVICES

Hospital inpatient services refer to hospital visits during the course of an inpatient hospital stay. The services may be provided by the patient's primary physician and/or other physicians in the event of multiple illnesses or injuries. Evaluation and management codes 99221-99239 are used to report services provided in the hospital. The key coding issues are the extent of history obtained, the extent of examination performed, and the complexity of medical decision making. Additional reporting issues include counseling and/or coordination of care, the nature of presenting problem(s), and the time spent at the bedside and on the patient's facility floor or unit.

CODING RULES

1. *CPT codes defined as Initial Hospital Care are used to report the first hospital inpatient encounter with the patient by the admitting physician.*

2. *The admitting physician should report all service related to the admission provided in all other locations.*

3. *For observation care or inpatient hospital care services provided to patients who are admitted and discharged on the same date, report with CPT codes 99234-99236 from the Observation or Inpatient Care services subsections.*

The following codes are used to report evaluation and management services provided to hospital inpatients. Hospital inpatient services include those services provided to patients in a "partial hospital" setting. These codes are to be used to report these partial hospitalization services. See also psychiatry notes in the full text of the CPT code set.

For definitions of key components and commonly used terms, please see Evaluation and Management Services Guidelines. For Hospital Observation Services, see 99218-99220, 99224-99226. For a patient admitted and discharged from observation or inpatient status on the same date, the services should be reported with codes 99234-99236 as appropriate.

INITIAL HOSPITAL CARE

NEW OR ESTABLISHED PATIENT

The following codes are used to report the first hospital inpatient encounter with the patient by the admitting physician.

For initial inpatient encounters by physicians other than the admitting physician, see initial inpatient consultation codes (99251-99255) or subsequent hospital care codes (99231-99233) as .appropriate.

For admission services for the neonate (28 days of age or younger) requiring intensive observation, frequent interventions, and other intensive care services, see 99477.

When the patient is admitted to the hospital as an inpatient in the course of an encounter in another site of service (eg, hospital emergency department, observation status in a hospital, office, nursing facility), all evaluation and mangement services provided by that physician in conjunction with that admission are considered part of the initial hospital care when performed on the same date as the admission. The inpatient care level of service reported by the admitting physician should include the services related to the admission he/she provided in the other sites of service as well as in the inpatient setting.

Evaluation and management services including new or established patient office or other outpatient services (99201-99215), emergency department services (99281-99285), nursing facility services (99304-99318), domiciliary, rest home, or custodial care services (99324-99337), home services (99341-99350), and preventive medicine services (99381-99397) on the same date related to the admission to "observation status" should **not** be reported separately. For a patient admitted and discharged from observation or inpatient status on the same date, the services should be reported with codes 99234-99236 as appropriate.

 Initial hospital care, per day, for the evaluation and management of a patient which requires these three key components:
- a detailed or comprehensive history;
- a detailed or comprehensive examination; and
- medical decision making that is straightforward or of low complexity.

Counseling and/or coordination of care with other physicians, other qualified health care professionals, or agencies are provided consistent with the nature of the problem(s) and the patient's and/or family's needs.

Usually, the problem(s) requiring admission are of low severity. Typically 30 minutes are spent at the bedside and on the patient's hospital floor or unit.

● New Code   ▲ Revised Code   ✚ Add-On Code   ⊘ Modifier -51 Exempt   ★ Telemedicine

99222 Initial hospital care, per day, for the evaluation and management of a patient, which requires these three key components:

- a comprehensive history;
- a comprehensive examination; and
- medical decision making of moderate complexity.

Counseling and/or coordination of care with other physicians, other qualified health care professionals, or agencies are provided consistent with the nature of the problem(s) and the patient's and/or family's needs.

Usually, the problem(s) requiring admission are of moderate severity. Typically 50 minutes are spent at the bedside and on the patient's hospital floor or unit.

99223 Initial hospital care, per day, for the evaluation and management of a patient, which requires these three key components:

- a comprehensive history;
- a comprehensive examination; and
- medical decision making of high complexity.

Counseling and/or coordination of care with other physicians, other qualified health care professionals, or agencies are provided consistent with the nature of the problem(s) and the patient's and/or family's needs.

Usually, the problem(s) requiring admission are of high severity. Typically 70 minutes are spent at the bedside and on the patient's hospital floor or unit.

99224 This code is out of order. See page 141.

99225 This code is out of order. See page 141.

99226 This code is out of order. See page 141.

SUBSEQUENT HOSPITAL CARE

All levels of subsequent hospital care include reviewing the medical record and reviewing the results of diagnostic studies and changes in the patient's status (i.e., changes in history, physical condition and response to management) since the last assessment.

★ **99231** Subsequent hospital care, per day, for the evaluation and management of a patient, which requires at least two of these three key components:

- a problem focused interval history;
- a problem focused examination;
- medical decision making that is straightforward or of low complexity.

Counseling and/or coordination of care with other physicians, other qualified health care professionals, or agencies are provided consistent with the nature of the problem(s) and the patient's and/or family's needs.

Usually, the patient is stable, recovering or improving. Typically 15 minutes are spent at the bedside and on the patient's hospital floor or unit.

★ **99232** Subsequent hospital care, per day, for the evaluation and management of a patient, which requires at least two of these three key components:

- an expanded problem focused interval history;
- an expanded problem focused examination;
- medical decision making of moderate complexity.

Counseling and/or coordination of care with other physicians, other qualified health care professionals, or agencies are provided consistent with the nature of the problem(s) and the patient's and/or family's needs.

Usually, the patient is responding inadequately to therapy or has developed a minor complication. Typically 25 minutes are spent at the bedside and on the patient's hospital floor or unit.

★  Subsequent hospital care, per day, for the evaluation and management of a patient, which requires at least two of these three key components:

- a detailed interval history;

- a detailed examination;

- medical decision making of high complexity.

Counseling and/or coordination of care with other physicians, other qualified health care professionals, or agencies are provided consistent with the nature of the problem(s) and the patient's and/or family's needs.

Usually, the patient is unstable or has developed a significant complication or a significant new problem. Typically 35 minutes are spent at the bedside and on the patient's hospital floor or unit.

OBSERVATION OR INPATIENT CARE SERVICES (INCLUDING ADMISSION AND DISCHARGE SERVICES)

The following codes are used to report observation or inpatient hospital care services provided to patients admitted and discharged on the same date of sevice. When a patient is admitted to the hospital from observation status on the same date, only the initial hospital care code should be reported. The initial hospital care code reported by the admitting physician or other qualified health care professional should include the services related to the observation status services he/she provided on the same date of inpatient admission.

When "observation status" is initiated in the course of an encounter in another site of service (eg, hospital emergency department, office, nursing facility), all evaluation and management services provided by the supervising physician or other qualified health care professional in conjunction with initiating "observation status" are considered part of the initial observation care when performed on the same date. The observation care level of service should include the services related to initiating "observation status" provided in the other sites of services as well as in the observation setting when provided by the same individual.

For patients admitted to observation or inpatient care and discharged on a different date, see codes 99218-99220, 99224-99226, 99217, or 99221-99223, 99238, and 99239.

 Observation or inpatient hospital care, for the evaluation and management of a patient including admission and discharge on the same date which requires these three key components:

- a detailed or comprehensive history;

- a detailed or comprehensive examination; and

- medical decision making that is straightforward or of low complexity.

Counseling and/or coordination of care with other physicians, other qualified health care professionals, or agencies are provided consistent with the nature of the problem(s) and the patient's and/or family's needs.

Usually the presenting problem(s) requiring admission are of low severity. Typically 40 minutes are spent at the bedside and on the patient's hospital floor or unit.

99235 Observation or inpatient hospital care, for the evaluation and management of a patient including admission and discharge on the same date which requires these three key components:

- a comprehensive history;

- a comprehensive examination; and

- medical decision making of moderate complexity.

Counseling and/or coordination of care with other physicians, other qualified health care professionals, or agencies are provided consistent with the nature of the problem(s) and the patient's and/or family's needs.

Usually the presenting problem(s) requiring admission are of moderate severity. Typically, 50 minutes are spent at the bedside and on the patient's hospital floor or unit.

 Observation or inpatient hospital care, for the evaluation and management of a patient including admission and discharge on the same date which requires these three key components:

- a comprehensive history;

- a comprehensive examination; and

- medical decision making of high complexity.

Counseling and/or coordination of care with other physicians, other qualified health care professionals, or agencies are provided consistent with the nature of the problem(s) and the patient's and/or family's needs.

Usually the presenting problem(s) requiring admission are of high severity. Typically, 55 minutes are spent at the bedside and on the patient's floor or unit.

HOSPITAL DISCHARGE SERVICES

The hospital discharge day management codes are to be used to report the total duration of time spent by a physician for final hospital discharge of a patient. The codes include, as appropriate, final examination of the patient, discussion of the hospital stay, even if the time spent by the physician on that date is not continuous, instructions for continuing care to all relevant caregivers, and preparation of discharge records, prescriptions and referral forms. For a patient admitted and discharged from observation or inpatient status on the same date, the services should be reported with codes 99234-99236 as appropriate.

99238 Hospital discharge day management; 30 minutes or less

99239   more than 30 minutes

(These codes are to be utilized to report all services provided to a patient on the date of discharge, if other than the initial date of inpatient status. To report services to a patient who is admitted as an inpatient and discharged on the same date, see codes 99234-99236 for observation or inpatient hospital care including the admission and discharge of the patient on the same date. To report concurrent care services provided by a individual other than the physician or qualified health care professional performing the discharge day management service, use subsequent hospital care codes [99231-99233] on the day of discharge.)

(For Observation Care Discharge, use 99217)

(For observation or inpatient hospital care including the admission and discharge of the patient on the same date, see 99234-99236)

(For Nursing Facility Care Discharge, 99315, 99316)

(For discharge services provided to newborns admitted and discharged on the same date, use 99463)

CONSULTATIONS

A consultation is a type of evaluation and management service provided at the request of another physician or appropriate source to either recommend care for a specific condition or problem or to determine whether to accept responsibility for ongoing management of the patient's entire care or for the care of a specific condition or problem.

A physician consultant may initiate diagnostic and/or therapeutic services at the same or subsequent visit.

A "consultation" initiated by a patient and/or family, and not requested by a physician or other appropriate source (eg, physician assistant, nurse practitioner, doctor of chiropractic, physical therapist, occupational therapist, speech-language pathologist, psychologist, social worker, lawyer, or insurance company) is not reported using the consultation codes, but may be reported using the office visit, home service, or domiciliary/rest home care codes as appropriate.

The written or verbal request for consult may be made by a physician or other appropriate source and documented in the patient's medical record by either the consulting or requesting physician or appropriate source. The consultant's opinion and any services that were ordered or performed must also be documented in the patient's medical record and sommunicated by written report to the requesting physician or other appropriate source.

If a consultation is mandated (eg, by a third-party payer) modifier 32 should also be reported.

Any specifically identifiable procedure (ie, identified with a specific CPT code) performed on or subsequent to the date of the initial consultation should be reported separately.

If subsequent to the completion of a consultation the consultant assumes responsibility for management of a portion or all of the patient's condition(s), the appropriate Evaluation and Management services code for the site of service should be reported. In the hospital or nursing facility setting, the consulting consultant should use the appropriate inpatient consultation code for the initial encounter and then subsequent hospital or nursing facility care codes. In the office setting, the consultant should use the appropriate office or other outpatient consultation codes and then the established patient office or other outpatient services codes.

To report services provided to a patient who is admitted to a hospital or nursing facility in the course of an encounter in the office or other ambulatory facility, see the notes for Initial Hospital Inpatient Care or Initial Nursing Facility Care. For definitions of key components and commonly used terms, please see Evaluation and Management Services Guidelines.

CODING GUIDELINES

A consultation is the process of taking a history, performing a physical examination, and ordering and interpreting appropriate diagnostic tests for the purpose of rendering an expert opinion about a patient's illness and/or injury. E/M service codes 99241-99275 are used to report office, inpatient, and confirmatory consultation services provided to new or established patients. The key coding issues are the location of the service, the extent of history obtained, the extent of examination performed, and the complexity of medical decision making. Additional reporting issues include counseling and/or coordination of care, the nature of presenting problem(s), and the time, depending on location, spent either face to face with the patient and/or family or at the bedside and on the patient's facility floor or unit.

Coding Rules

1. *The request for a consultation from the attending physician or other appropriate source and the need for a consultation must be documented in the patient's medical record.*

2. *The consultant's opinion and any services that were ordered or performed must be documented in the patient's medical record and communicated to the requesting physician or source.*

3. *Consultations that are initiated by request from the patient and/or family may be reported using codes for confirmatory consultations or office services as appropriate.*

4. *If a confirmatory consultation is required by a third party, such as a Peer Review Organization (PRO), modifier -32 should be added to the basic service.*

5. *Any specifically identifiable procedure performed on or subsequent to the date of the initial consultation is reported separately.*

6. *If the consultant subsequently assumes responsibility for management of all or a portion of the patient's condition(s), then either hospital services or office services are used as appropriate.*

Consultation service codes may not be billed to Medicare for services rendered on or after January 1, 2010. Physicians must use visit/outpatient or inpatient hospital evaluation and management codes to bill Medicare for consultation services. Telehealth consultation may be reported using the appropriate HCPCS G-codes.

Medicare Cross-Walk from Consultation Codes to Outpatient/Hospital Codes

CMS published a cross-walk from consultation codes to outpatient/hospital codes for the purpose of establishing budget neutrality. According to CMS the cross-walks are not billing guidance and physicians should bill the E/M code appropriate for the service provided. For office based consultations, the selection of E/M visit codes is based on whether the patient is a new or established patient. For hospital consultations, the selection of appropriate E/M codes is based on the location of the consultation in either an acute care hospital or nursing home and the level of history, exam, and medical decision making.

Office Consultation Codes			Inpatient Consultation Codes		
Source	Destination	Mapping*	Source	Destination	Mapping*
99241	99201	50%	99251	99221	70%
	99211	50%		99304	30%
99242	99202	50%	99252	99221	35%
	99212	50%		99222	35%
99243	99203	50%		99304	15%
	99213	50%		99305	15%
99244	99204	50%	99253	99222	70%
	99214	50%		99305	30%
99245	99205	50%	99254	99222	35%
	99215	50%		99223	35%
				99305	15%
				99306	15%
			99255	99223	70%
				99306	30%

  ● New Code   ▲ Revised Code   + Add-On Code   ⊘ Modifier -51 Exempt   ★ Telemedicine

Refers to the CMS estimated frequency of conversion from the consultation code to the visit code.

OFFICE OR OTHER OUTPATIENT CONSULTATIONS

NEW OR ESTABLISHED PATIENT

The following codes are used to report consultations provided in the office or in an outpatient or other ambulatory facility, including hospital observation services, home services, domiciliary, rest home or emergency department (see the preceding consultation definition above). Follow-up visits in the consultant's office or other outpatient facility that are initiated by the consultant or patient are reported using the appropriate codes for established patients, office visits (99211-99215), domiciliary, rest home (99334-99337), or home (99347-99350). If an additional request for an opinion or advice regarding the same or a new problem is received from another physician or other appropriate source and documented in the medical record, the office consultation codes may be used again. Services that constitute transfer of care (ie, are provided for the managment of the patient's entire care or for the care of a specific condition or problem) are reported with the appropriate new or established patient codes for office or other outpatient visits, domiciliary, rest home services, or home services.

★ **99241**   Office consultation for a new or established patient, which requires these three key components:

- a problem focused history;
- a problem focused examination; and
- straightforward medical decision making.

Counseling and/or coordination of care with other physicians, other qualified health care professionals, or agencies are provided consistent with the nature of the problem(s) and the patient's and/or family's needs.

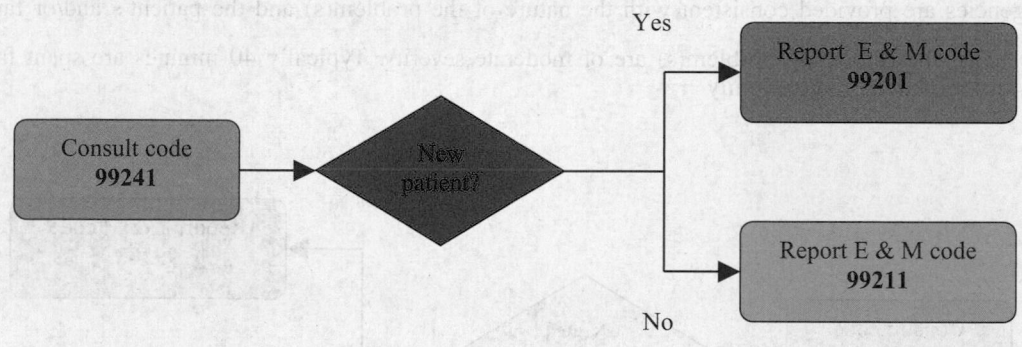

Usually, the presenting problem(s) are self limited or minor. Typically 15 minutes are spent face-to-face with the patient and/or family.

Medicare Cross-Walk:

Report 99201 instead of 99241 for new patients.
Report 99211 instead of 99241 for established patients.

★ **99242**   Office consultation for a new or established patient, which requires these three key components:

- an expanded problem focused history;
- an expanded problem focused examination; and
- straightforward medical decision making.

Counseling and/or coordination of care with other physicians, other qualified health care professionals, or agencies are provided consistent with the nature of the problem(s) and the patient's and/or family's needs.

Usually, the presenting problem(s) are of low severity. Typically 30 minutes are spent face-to-face with the patient and/or family.

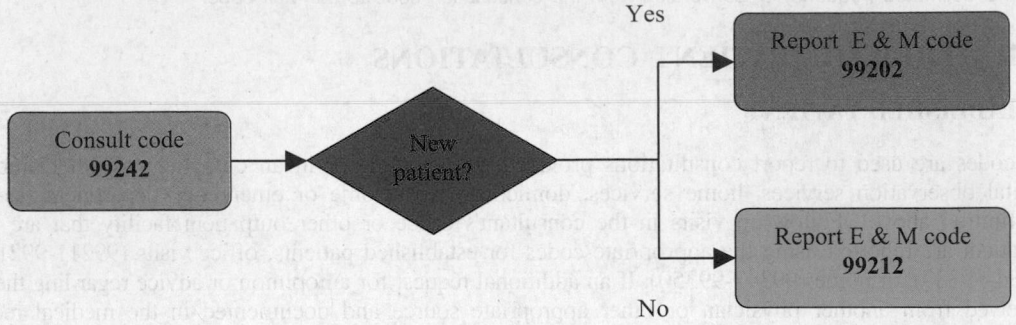

Yes

Consult code
99242

New
patient?

Report E & M code
99202

Report E & M code
99212

No

Medicare Cross-Walk:

Report 99202 instead of 99242 for new patients.
Report 99212 instead of 99242 for established patients.

★ **99243**   Office consultation for a new or established patient, which requires these three key components:

- a detailed history;
- a detailed examination; and
- medical decision making of low complexity.

Counseling and/or coordination of care with other physicians, other qualified health care professionals, or agencies are provided consistent with the nature of the problem(s) and the patient's and/or family's needs.

Usually, the presenting problem(s) are of moderate severity. Typically 40 minutes are spent face-to-face with the patient and/or family.

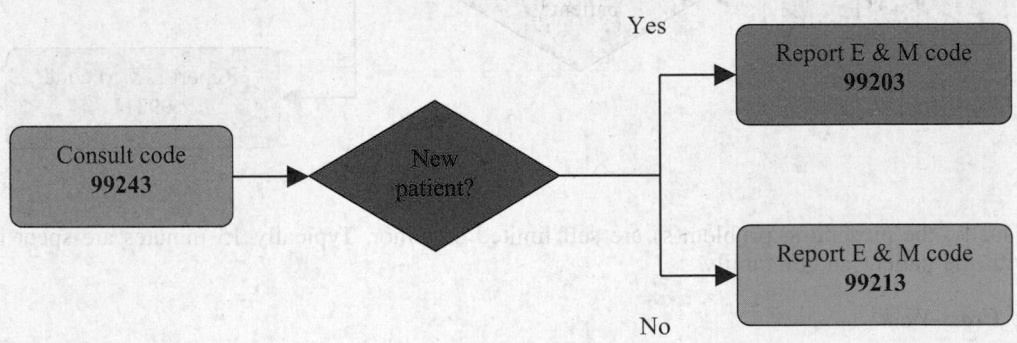

Yes

Consult code
99243

New
patient?

Report E & M code
99203

Report E & M code
99213

No

Medicare Cross-Walk:

Report 99203 instead of 99243 for new patients.
Report 99213 instead of 99243 for established patients

★ **99244**   Office consultation for a new or established patient, which requires these three key components:

- a comprehensive history;
- a comprehensive examination; and
- medical decision making of moderate complexity.

Counseling and/or coordination of care with other physicians, other qualified health care professionals, or agencies are provided consistent with the nature of the problem(s) and the patient's and/or family's needs.

Usually, the presenting problem(s) are of moderate to high severity. Typically 60 minutes are spent face-to-face with the patient and/or family.

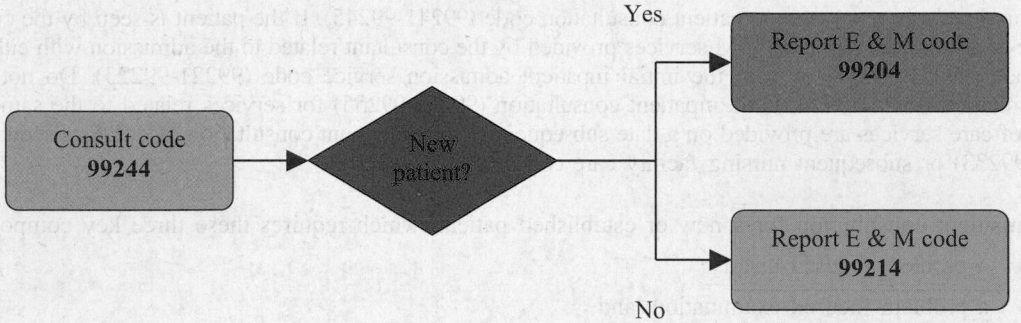

Medicare Cross-Walk:

Report 99204 instead of 99244 for new patients.
Report 99214 instead of 99244 for established patients.

★ **99245**   Office consultation for a new or established patient, which requires these three key components:

- a comprehensive history;
- a comprehensive examination; and
- medical decision making of high complexity.

Counseling and/or coordination of care with other physicians, other qualified health care professionals, or agencies are provided consistent with the nature of the problem(s) and the patient's and/or family's needs.

Usually, the presenting problem(s) are of moderate to high severity. Typically 80 minutes are spent face-to-face with the patient and/or family.

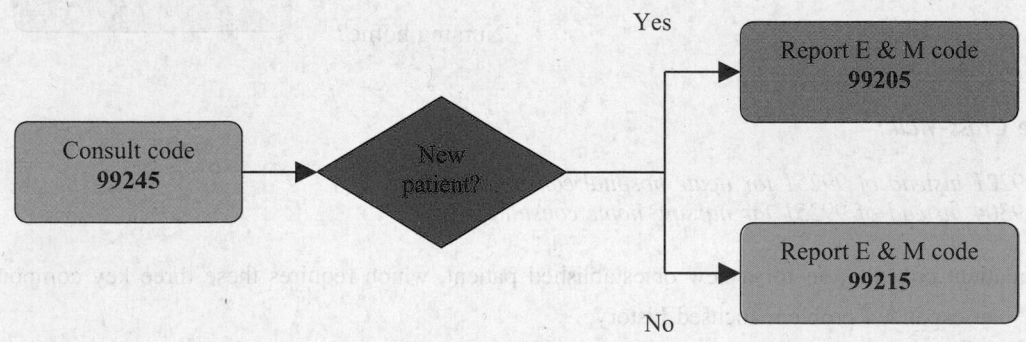

Medicare Cross-Walk:

Report 99205 instead of 99245 for new patients.
Report 99215 instead of 99245 for established patients.

INPATIENT CONSULTATIONS

NEW OR ESTABLISHED PATIENT

The following codes are used to report physician or other qualified health care professional consultations provided to hospital inpatients, residents of nursing facilities, or patients in a partial hospital setting. Only one consultation should be reported by a consultant per admission. Subsequent services during the same admission are reported using Subsequent Hospital Care codes (99231-99233) or Subsequent Nursing Facility Care codes (99307-99310), including services to complete the initial consultation, monitor progress, revise recommendations, or address a new problem. Use subsequent hospital care codes (99231-99233) or subsequent nursing facility care codes (99307-99310) to report transfer of care services.

When an inpatient consultation is performed on a date that a patient is admitted to a hospital or nursing facility, all E/M services provided by the consultant related to the admission are reported with the inpatient consultation service code (99251-99255). If a patient is admitted after an oupatient consultation (office, emergency department, etc.), and the patient is not seen on the unit on the date of admission, only report the outpatient consultation code (99241-99245). If the patient is seen by the consultant on the unit on the date of admission, report all E/M services provided by the consultant related to the admission with either the inpatient consultation code (99251-99255) or with the initial inpatient admission service code (99221-99223). Do not report both an outpatient consultation (99241-99245) and inpatient consultation (99251-99255) for services related to the same inpatient stay. When transfer of care services are provided on a date subsequent to the outpatient consultation, use the subsequent hospital care codes (99231-99233) or subsequent nursing facility care codes (99307-99310).

★ **99251**   Inpatient consultation for a new or established patient, which requires these three key components:

- a problem focused history;
- a problem focused examination; and
- straightforward medical decision making.

Counseling and/or coordination of care with other physicians, other qualified health care professionals, or agencies are provided consistent with the nature of the problem(s) and the patient's and/or family's needs.

Usually, the presenting problem(s) are self limited or minor. Typically 20 minutes are spent at the bedside and on the patient's hospital floor or unit.

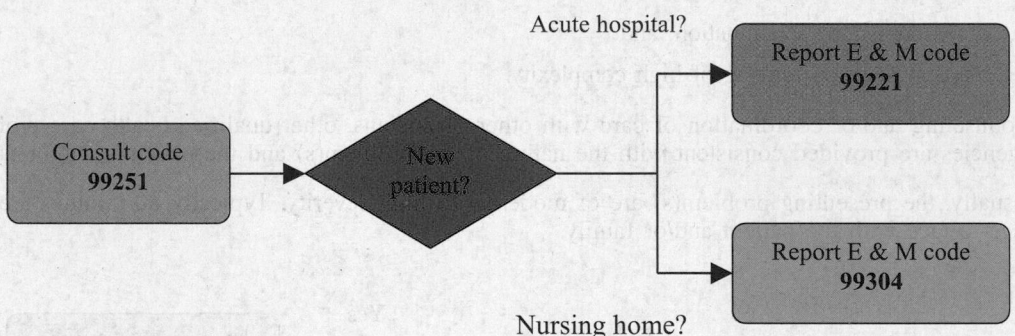

Medicare Cross-Walk:

Report 99221 instead of 99251 for acute hospital consultations.
Report 99304 instead of 99251 for nursing home consultations.

★ **99252**   Inpatient consultation for a new or established patient, which requires these three key components:

- an expanded problem focused history;
- an expanded problem focused examination; and
- straightforward medical decision making.

Counseling and/or coordination of care with other physicians, other qualified health care professionals, or agencies are provided consistent with the nature of the problem(s) and the patient's and/or family's needs.

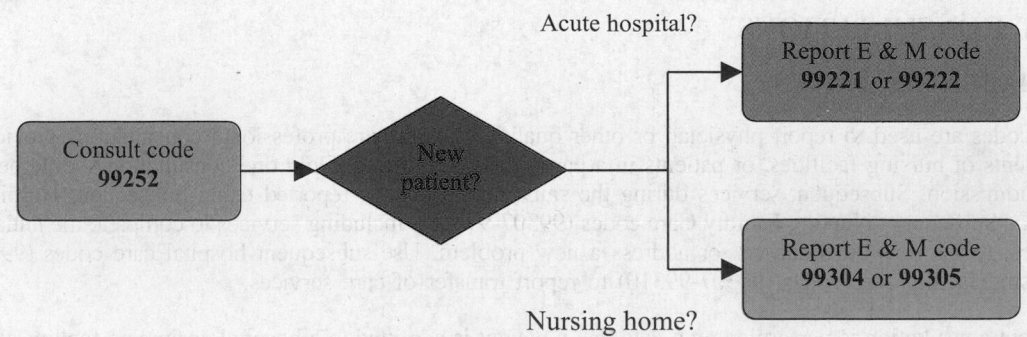

● New Code   ▲ Revised Code   + Add-On Code   ⊘ Modifier -51 Exempt   ★ Telemedicine

Usually, the presenting problem(s) are of low severity. Typically 40 minutes are spent at the bedside and on the patient's hospital floor or unit.

Medicare Cross-Walk:

Report 99221 or 99222 instead of 99252 for acute hospital consultations.
Report 99304 or 99305 instead of 99252 for nursing home consultations.

★ **99253** Inpatient consultation for a new or established patient, which requires these three key components:

- a detailed history;

- a detailed examination; and

- medical decision making of low complexity.

Counseling and/or coordination of care with other physicians, other qualified health care professionals, or agencies are provided consistent with the nature of the problem(s) and the patient's and/or family's needs.

Usually, the presenting problem(s) are of moderate severity. Typically 55 minutes are spent at the bedside and on the patient's hospital floor or unit.

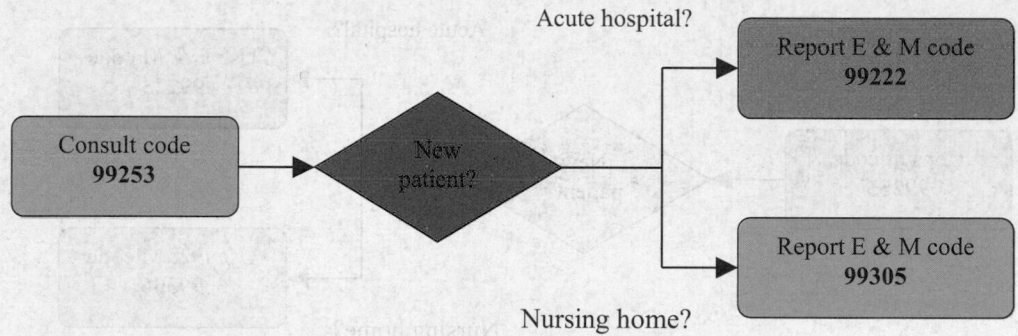

Medicare Cross-Walk:

Report 99222 instead of 99253 for acute hospital consultations.
Report 99305 instead of 99253 for nursing home consultations

★ **99254** Inpatient consultation for a new or established patient, which requires three key components:

- a comprehensive history;

- a comprehensive examination; and

- medical decision making of moderate complexity.

Counseling and/or coordination of care with other physicians, other qualified health care professionals, or agencies are provided consistent with the nature of the problem(s) and the patient's and/or family's needs.

Usually, the presenting problem(s) are of moderate to high severity. Typically 80 minutes are spent at the bedside and on the patient's hospital floor or unit.

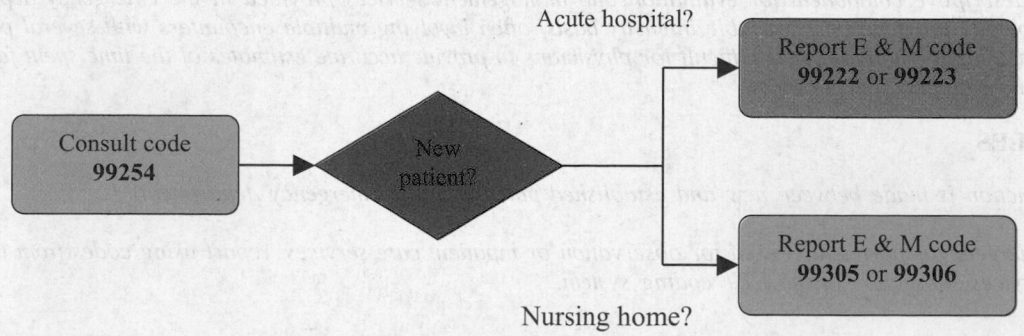

| ■ Separate Procedure | ■ Unlisted Procedure | ■ CCI Comp. Code | ■ Non-specific Procedure | **151** |

★ **99255**   Inpatient consultation for a new or established patient, which requires these three key components:

- a comprehensive history;

- a comprehensive examination; and

- medical decision making of high complexity.

Counseling and/or coordination of care with other physicians, other qualified health care professionals, or agencies are provided consistent with the nature of the problem(s) and the patient's and/or family's needs.

Usually, the presenting problem(s) are of moderate to high severity. Typically 110 minutes are spent at the bedside and on the patient's hospital floor or unit.

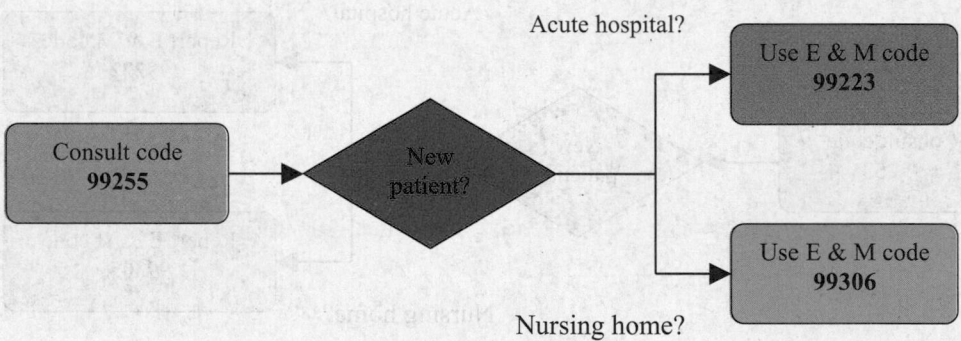

EMERGENCY DEPARTMENT SERVICES

Evaluation and management codes 99281-99288 are used to report services provided to new or established patients in the emergency department. The emergency department is defined as a facility for the treatment of patients with emergent conditions. The emergency department must be attached to a hospital and operate on a 24/7 basis.

The key coding issues for evaluation and management emergency services are the extent of history obtained, the extent of examination performed, and the complexity of medical decision making. Additional reporting issues include counseling and/or coordination of care, and the nature of presenting problem(s).

Time is not a descriptive component for evaluation and management services provided in the emergency department. These services are typically provided on a variable intensity basis, often involving multiple encounters with several patients over an extended period of time. Therefore, it is difficult for physicians to provide accurate estimates of the time spent face-to-face with the patient in the emergency department.

CODING RULES

1.   *No distinction is made between new and established patients in the emergency department.*

2.   *If the emergency department is used for observation or inpatient care services, report using codes from the Observation Care services subsection of the CPT coding system.*

3. *For critical care services provided in the emergency department, use the appropriate codes from the Critical Care subsection of the CPT coding system.*

EMERGENCY DEPARTMENT SERVICES

NEW OR ESTABLISHED PATIENT

The following codes are used to report evaluation and management services provided in the emergency department. No distinction is made between new and established patients in the emergency department.

An emergency department is defined as an organized hospital-based facility for the provision of unscheduled episodic services to patients who present for immediate medical attention. The facility must be available 24 hours a day.

For critical care services provided in the emergency department, see Critical Care notes and 99291, 99292.

For E/M services provided to a patient in an observation area of a hospital, see 99217-99220.

For observation or inpatient care services (including admission and discharge services), see 99234-99236.

99281 Emergency department visit for the evaluation and management of a patient, which requires these three key components:

- a problem focused history;
- a problem focused examination; and
- straightforward medical decision making.

Counseling and/or coordination of care with other physicians, other qualified health care professionals, or agencies are provided consistent with the nature of the problem(s) and the patient's and/or family's needs.

Usually, the presenting problem(s) are self limited or minor.

99282 Emergency department visit for the evaluation and management of a patient, which requires these three key components:

- an expanded problem focused history;
- an expanded problem focused examination; and
- medical decision making of low complexity.

Counseling and/or coordination of care with other physicians, other qualified health care professionals, or agencies are provided consistent with the nature of the problem(s) and the patient's and/or family's needs.

Usually, the presenting problem(s) are of low to moderate severity.

99283 Emergency department visit for the evaluation and management of a patient, which requires these three key components:

- an expanded problem focused history;
- an expanded problem focused examination; and
- medical decision making of moderate complexity.

Counseling and/or coordination of care with other physicians, other qualified health care professionals, or agencies are provided consistent with the nature of the problem(s) and the patient's and/or family's needs.

Usually, the presenting problem(s) are of moderate severity.

99284 Emergency department visit for the evaluation and management of a patient, which requires these three key components:

- a detailed history;
- a detailed examination; and
- medical decision making of moderate complexity.

Counseling and/or coordination of care with other physicians, other qualified health care professionals, or agencies are provided consistent with the nature of the problem(s) and the patient's and/or family's needs.

| | Separate Procedure | | Unlisted Procedure | | CCI Comp. Code | | Non-specific Procedure | **153** |

Usually, the presenting problem(s) are of high severity, and require urgent evaluation by the physician or other qualified health care professional but do not pose an immediate significant threat to life or physiologic function.

 99285 Emergency department visit for the evaluation and management of a patient, which requires these three key components within the constraints imposed by the urgency of the patient's clinical condition and/or mental status:

- a comprehensive history;

- a comprehensive examination; and

- medical decision making of high complexity.

Counseling and/or coordination of care with other physicians, other qualified health care professionals, or agencies are provided consistent with the nature of the problem(s) and the patient's and/or family's needs.

Usually, the presenting problem(s) are of high severity and pose an immediate significant threat to life or physiologic function.

OTHER EMERGENCY SERVICES

In directed emergency care, advanced life support, the physician or other qualified health care professional is located in a hospital emergency or critical care department, and is in two-way voice communication with ambulance or rescue personnel outside the hospital. Direction of the performance of necessary medical procedures includes but is not limited to: telemetry of cardiac rhythm; cardiac and/or pulmonary resuscitation; endotracheal or esophageal obturator airway intubation; administration of intravenous fluids and/or administration of intramuscular, intratracheal or subcutaneous drugs; and/or electrical conversion of arrhythmia.

99288 Physician or other qualified health care professional direction of emergency medical systems (EMS) emergency care, advanced life support

CRITICAL CARE SERVICES

Critical care is the direct delivery by a physician(s) or other qualified health care professional of medical care for a critically ill or critically injured patient. A critical illness or injury acutely impairs one or more vital organ systems such that there is a high probability of imminent or life threatening deterioration in the patient's condition. Critical care involves high complexity decision making to assess, manipulate, and support vital system function(s) to treat single or multiple vital organ system failure and/or to prevent further life threatening deterioration of the patient's condition. Examples of vital organ system failure include, but are not limited to: central nervous system failure, circulatory failure, shock, renal, hepatic, metabolic, and/or respiratory failure. Although critical care typically requires interpretation of multiple physiologic parameters and/or application of advanced technology(s), critical care may be provided in life threatening situations when these elements are not present. Critical care may be provided on multiple days, even if no changes are made in the treatment rendered to the patient, provided that the patient's condition continues to require the level of attention described above.

Providing medical care to a critically ill, injured, or post-operative patient qualifies as a critical care service only if both the illness or injury and the treatment being provided meet the above requirements. Critical care is usually, but not always, given in a critical care area, such as the coronary care unit, intensive care unit, pediatric intensive care unit, respiratory care unit, or the emergency care facility.

Inpatient critical care services provided to infants 29 days through 71 months of age are reported with pediatric critical care codes 99471-99476. The pediatric critical care codes are reported as long as the infant/young child qualifies for critical care services during the hospital stay through 71 months of age. Inpatient critical care services provided to neonates (28 days of age or younger) are reported with the neonatal critical care codes 99468 and 99469. The neonatal critical care codes are reported as long as the neonate qualifies for critical care services during the hospital stay through the 28th postnatal day. The reporting of the pediatric and neonatal critical care services is not based on time or the type of unit (eg, pediatric or neonatal critical care unit) and it is not dependent upon the type of physician or other qualified health care professional delivering the care. To report critical care services provided in the outpatient setting (eg, emergency department or office), for neonates and pediatric patients up through 71 months of age, see the critical care codes 99291, 99292. If the same individual provides critical care services for a neonatal or pediatric patient in both the outpatient and inpatient settings on the same day, report only the appropriate neonatal or pediatric critical care code 99468-99472 for all critical care services provided on that day. Also report 99291-99292 for neonatal or pediatric critical care services provided by the individual providing critical care at one facility but transferring the patient to another facility. Critical care services provided by a second individual of a different specialty not reporting a per day neonatal or pediatric critical care code can be reported with codes 99291-99292. For additional instructions reporting these services, see the Neonatal and Pediatric Critical Care section and codes 99468-99476.

Services for a patient who is not critically ill but happens to be in a critical care unit are reported using other appropriate E/M codes. Critical care and other E/M services may be provided to the same patient on the same date by the same physician.

Critical care and other E/M services may be provided to the same patient on the same date by the same individual.

For reporting by professionals, the following services are included in critical care when performed during the critical period by the physician(s) providing critical care: the interpretation of cardiac output measurements (93561, 93562), chest X-rays (71045, 71046), pulse oximetry (94760, 94761, 94762), blood gases, and information data stored in computers (eg., ECGs, blood pressures, hematologic data [99090]); gastric intubation (43752, 43753); temporary transcutaneous pacing (92953); ventilatory management (94002-94004, 94660, 94662); and vascular access procedures (36000, 36410, 36415, 36591, 36600). Any services performed that are not included in this listing should be reported separately. Facilities may report the above services separately.

Codes 99291, 99292 should be reported for the attendance during the transport of critically ill or critically injured patients older than 24 months of age to or from a facility or hospital. For transport services of critically ill or critically injured pediatric patients 24 months of age or younger, see 99466, 99467.

Codes 99291, 99292 are used to report the total duration of time spent in provision of critical care services to a critically ill or critically injured patient, even if the time spent providing care on that date is not continuous. For any given period of time spent providing critical care services, the individual must devote his or her full attention to the patient and, therefore, cannot provide services to any other patient during the same period of time.

Time spent with the individual patient should be recorded in the patient's record. The time that can be reported as critical care is the time spent engaged in work directly related to the individual patient's care whether that time was spent at the immediate bedside or elsewhere on the floor or unit. For example, time spent on the unit or at the nursing station on the floor reviewing test results or imaging studies, discussing the critically ill patient's care with other medical staff or documenting critical care services in the medical record would be reported as critical care, even though it does not occur at the bedside. Also, when the patient is unable to lacks capacity to participate in discussions, time spent on the floor or unit with family members or surrogate decision makers obtaining a medical history, reviewing the patient's condition or prognosis, or discussing treatment or limitation(s) of treatment may be reported as critical care, provided that the conversation bears directly on the management of the patient.

Time spent in activities that occur outside of the unit or off the floor (eg, telephone calls whether taken at home, in the office or elsewhere in the hospital) may not be reported as critical care since the individual is not immediately available to the patient. Time spent in activities that do not directly contribute to the treatment of the patient may not be reported as critical care, even if they are performed in the critical care unit (eg, participation in administration meetings or telephone calls to discuss other patients). Time spent performing separately reportable procedures or services should not be included in the time reported as critical care time. No individual may report remote real-time interactive video-conferenced critical care services (0188T, 0189T) for the period in which any other physician or qualified health care professional reports codes 99291, 99292.

Code 99291 is used to report the first 30-74 minutes of critical care on a given date. It should be used only once per date even if the time spent by the individual is not continuous on that date. Critical care of less than 30 minutes total duration on a given date should be reported with the appropriate E/M code.

Code 99292 is used to report additional block(s) of time, of up to 30 minutes each beyond the first 74 minutes. (See table)

CORRECT CODING CHART FOR CRITICAL CARE SERVICES

DURATION OF CRITICAL CARE	CODE(S) TO REPORT
less than 30 minutes	appropriate E/M codes
30-74 minutes	99291 once
75-104 minutes	99291 once and 99292 once
105-134 minutes	99291 once and 99292 twice
135-164 minutes	99291 once and 99292 three times
165-194 minutes	99291 once and 99292 four times
195 minutes or longer	99291 and 99292 as appropriate (*see example above*)

CODING RULES

1. *The critical care CPT codes are used to report the total duration of time spent by a physician providing constant attention to a critically ill patient.*

2. *Critical care code 99291 is used to report the first 30-74 minutes of critical care on a given day. It should be reported only once per day even if the time spent is not continuous on that day.*

3. *Critical care 99292 is used to report each additional 30 minutes beyond the first 74 minutes.*

4. *Other procedures which are not considered included in the critical care services, for example, suturing of lacerations, setting of fractures, reduction of joint dislocations, lumbar puncture, peritoneal lavage and bladder tap, are reported separately.*

CRITICAL CARE SERVICES

99291   Critical care, evaluation and management of the critically ill or critically injured patient; first 30-74 minutes

+ **99292**   each additional 30 minutes (List separately in addition to code for primary service)

   (Use 99292 in conjunction with 99291)

NURSING FACILITY SERVICES

The following codes are used to report evaluation and management services to patients in nursing facilities (formerly called skilled nursing facilities [SNFs], intermediate care facilities [ICFs], or long-term care facilities [LTCFs]).

These codes should also be used to report evaluation and management services provided to a patient in a psychiatric residential treatment center (a facility or a distinct part of a facility for psychiatric care, which provides a 24-hour therapeutically planned and professionally staffed group living and learning environment). If procedures such as medical psychotherapy are provided in addition to evaluation and management services, these should be reported in addition to the E/M services provided.

Nursing facilities that provide convalescent, rehabilitative, or long-term care are required to conduct comprehensive accurate, standardized, and reproducible assessments of each resident's functional capacity using a Resident Assessment Instrument (RAI). All RAIs include the Minimum Data Set (MDS), Resident Assessment Protocols (RAPs), and utilization guidelines. The MDS is the primary screening and assessment tool; the RAPs trigger the identification of potential problems and provide guidelines for follow-up assessments.

Physicians have a central role in assuring that all residents receive thorough assessments and that medical plans of care are instituted or revised to enhance or maintain the resident's physical and psychosocial functioning. This role includes providing input in the development of the MDS and a multi-disciplinary plan of care, as required by regulations pertaining to the care of nursing facility residents.

Two major subcategories of nursing facility services are recognized: Initial Nursing Facility Care, and Subsequent Nursing Facility Care. Both subcategories apply to new or established patients.

For definitions of key components and commonly used terms, please see Evaluation and Management Services Guidelines.

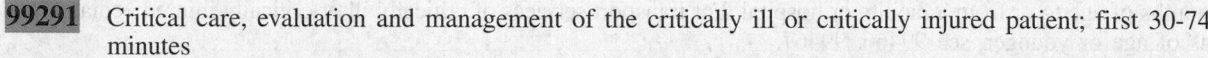

   (For care plan oversight services provided to nursing facility residents, see 99379-99380)

CODING RULES

1. *If a patient is admitted to the nursing facility after receiving services in the physician's office or hospital emergency department, all evaluation and management services are considered inclusive in the initial nursing facility care.*

2. *With the exception of hospital discharge services, evaluation and management service on the same date provided in locations other than the nursing facility that are related to the admission should not be coded separately.*

3. *When reporting these CPT codes to Medicare include the HCPCS Level II modifier -SP or -MP, or HCPCS Level III modifier if specified by the local Medicare carrier.*

INITIAL NURSING FACILITY CARE

NEW OR ESTABLISHED PATIENT

When the patient is admitted to the nursing facility in the course of an encounter in another site of service (eg, hospital emergency department, office), all evaluation and management services provided by that physician in conjunction with that admission are considered part of the initial nursing facility care when performed on the same date as the admission or readmission. The nursing facility care level of service reported by the admitting physician should include the services related to the admission he/she provided in the other sites of service as well as in the nursing facility setting.

Hospital discharge or observation discharge services performed on the same date of nursing facility admission or readmission may be reported separately. For a patient discharged from inpatient status on the same date of nursing facility admission or readmission, the hospital discharge services should be reported with codes 99238, 99239 as appropriate. For a patient discharged from observation status on the same date of nursing facility admission or readmission, the observation care discharge services should be reported with code 99217. For a patient admitted and discharged from observation or inpatient status on the same date, see codes 99234-99236.

(For nursing facility care discharge, see 99315, 99316)

99304 Initial nursing facility care, per day, for the evaluation and management of a patient which requires these three key components:

- a detailed or comprehensive history;
- a detailed or comprehensive examination;
- and medical decision making that is straightforward or of low complexity.

Counseling and/or coordination of care with other physicians, other qualified health care professionals, or agencies are provided consistent with the nature of the problem(s) and the patient's and/or family's needs.

Usually, the problem(s) requiring admission are of low severity. Typically 25 minutes are spent at the bedside and on the patient's facility floor or unit.

99305 Initial nursing facility care, per day, for the evaluation and management of a patient which requires these three key components:

- a comprehensive history;
- a comprehensive examination;
- and medical decision making of moderate complexity.

Counseling and/or coordination of care with other physicians, other qualified health care professionals, or agencies are provided consistent with the nature of the problem(s) and the patient's and/or family's needs.

Usually, the problem(s) requiring admission are of moderate severity. Typically 35 minutes are spent at the bedside and on the patient's facility floor or unit.

99306 Initial nursing facility care, per day, for the evaluation and management of a patient, which requires these three key components:

- a comprehensive history;
- a comprehensive examination;
- and medical decision making of high complexity.

Counseling and/or coordination of care with other physicians, other qualified health care professionals, or agencies are provided consistent with the nature of the problem(s) and the patient's and/or family's needs.

Usually, the problem(s) requiring admission are of high severity. Typically 45 minutes are spent at the bedside and on the patient's facility floor or unit.

SUBSEQUENT NURSING FACILITY CARE

All levels of subsequent nursing facility care include reviewing the medical record and reviewing the results of diagnostic studies and changes in the patient's status (ie, changes in history, physical condition, and response to management) since the last assessment by the physician or other qualified health care professional.

| ■ Separate Procedure | ■ Unlisted Procedure | ■ CCI Comp. Code | ■ Non-specific Procedure | **157** |

★ 99307   Subsequent nursing facility care, per day, for the evaluation and management of a patient, which requires at least two of these three key components:

- a problem focused interval history;
- a problem focused examination;
- straightforward medical decision making.

Counseling and/or coordination of care with other physicians, other qualified health care professionals, or agencies are provided consistent with the nature of the problem(s) and the patient's and/or family's needs.

Usually, the patient is stable, recovering, or improving. Typically 10 minutes are spent at the bedside and on the patient's facility floor or unit.

★ 99308   Subsequent nursing facility care, per day, for the evaluation and management of a patient, which requires at least two of these three key components:

- an expanded problem focused interval history;
- an expanded problem focused examination;
- medical decision making of low complexity.

Counseling and/or coordination of care with other physicians, other qualified health care professionals, or agencies are provided consistent with the nature of the problem(s) and the patient's and/or family's needs.

Usually, the patient is responding inadequately to therapy or has developed a minor complication. Typically 15 minutes are spent at the bedside and on the patient's facility floor or unit.

★ 99309   Subsequent nursing facility care, per day, for the evaluation and management of a patient, which requires at least two of these three key components:

- a detailed interval history;
- a detailed examination;
- medical decision making of moderate complexity.

Counseling and/or coordination of care with other physicians, other qualified health care professionals, or agencies are provided consistent with the nature of the problem(s) and the patient's and/or family's needs.

Usually, the patient has developed a significant complication or a significant new problem. Typically 25 minutes are spent at the bedside and on the patient's facility floor or unit.

★ 99310   Subsequent nursing facility care, per day, for the evaluation and management of a patient, which requires at least two of these three key components:

- a comprehensive interval history;
- a comprehensive examination;
- medical decision making of high complexity.

Counseling and/or coordination of care with other physicians, other qualified health care professionals, or agencies are provided consistent with the nature of the problem(s) and the patient's and/or family's needs.

The patient may be unstable or may have developed a significant new problem requiring immediate physician attention. Typically 35 minutes are spent at the bedside and on the patient's facility floor or unit.

NURSING FACILITY DISCHARGE SERVICES

The nursing facility discharge day management codes are to be used to report the total duration of time spent by a physician or other qualified health care professional for the final nursing facility discharge of a patient. The codes include, as appropriate, final examination of the patient, discussion of the nursing facility stay, even if the time spent on that date is not continuous. Instructions are given for continuing care to all relevant caregivers, and preparation of discharge records, prescriptions and referral forms.

99315   Nursing facility discharge day management; 30 minutes or less

99316   more than 30 minutes

OTHER NURSING FACILITY SERVICES

 99318 Evaluation and management of a patient involving an annual nursing facility assessment, which requires these three key components:

- a detailed interval history;
- a comprehensive examination;
- and medical decision making that is of low to moderate complexity.

Counseling and/or coordination of care with other physicians, other qualified health care professionals, or agencies are provided consistent with the nature of the problem(s) and the patient's and/or family's needs.

Usually, the patient is stable, recovering, or improving. Typically 30 minutes are spent at the bedside and on the patient's facility floor or unitr.

(Do not report 99318 on the same date of service as nursing facility services codes 99304-99316)

DOMICILIARY, REST HOME (eg, BOARDING HOME), OR CUSTODIAL CARE SERVICES

E/M service codes 99324-99340 are used to report services provided to a new or established patient in domiciliary, rest home or custodial care facility. The key coding issues are the extent of history obtained, the extent of examination performed, and the complexity of medical decision making. Additional reporting issues include counseling and/or coordination of care, and the nature of presenting problems.

When reporting these CPT codes to Medicare include HCPCS modifier -SP or -MP to indicate single or multiple patients seen during the visit. Consult the local Medicare intermediary before using these modifiers.

The following codes are used to report evaluation and management services in a facility which provides room, board and other personal assistance services, generally on a long-term basis. These codes include evaluation and management services provided in an assisted living facility, group home, custodial care, and intermediate care facilities.

The facility's services do not include a medical component.

For definitions of key components and commonly used terms, please see Evaluation and Management Services Guidelines.

(For care plan oversight services provided to a patient in a domiciliary facility under the care of a home health agency, see 99374, 99375, and for hospice agency, see 99377, 99378. For care plan oversight provided to a patient under hospice or home health agency care, see 99339, 99340)

NEW PATIENT

 99324 Domiciliary or rest home visit for the evaluation and management of a new patient, which requires these three key components:

- a problem focused history;
- a problem focused examination; and
- straightforward medical decision making.

Counseling and/or coordination of care with other physicians, other qualified health care professionals, or agencies are provided consistent with the nature of the problem(s) and the patient's and/or family's needs.

Usually, the presenting problem(s) are of low severity. Typically 20 minutes are spent with the patient and/or family or caregiver.

99325 Domiciliary or rest home visit for the evaluation and management of a new patient, which requires these three key components:

- an expanded problem focused history;
- an expanded problem focused examination; and
- medical decision making of low complexity.

▮ Separate Procedure	▮ Unlisted Procedure	▮ CCI Comp. Code	▮ Non-specific Procedure	**159**

Counseling and/or coordination of care with other physicians, other qualified health care professionals, or agencies are provided consistent with the nature of the problem(s) and the patient's and/or family's needs.

Usually, the presenting problem(s) are of moderate severity. Typically 30 minutes are spent with the patient and/or family or caregiver.

99326 Domiciliary or rest home visit for the evaluation and management of a new patient, which requires these three key components:

- a detailed history;
- a detailed examination; and
- medical decision making of moderate complexity.

Counseling and/or coordination of care with other physicians, other qualified health care professionals, or agencies are provided consistent with the nature of the problem(s) and the patient's and/or family's needs.

Usually, the presenting problem(s) are of moderate to high severity. Typically 45 minutes are spent with the patient and/or family or caregiver.

99327 Domiciliary or rest home visit for the evaluation and management of a new patient, which requires these three key components:

- a comprehensive history;
- a comprehensive examination; and
- medical decision making of moderate complexity.

Counseling and/or coordination of care with other physicians, other qualified health care professionals, or agencies are provided consistent with the nature of the problem(s) and the patient's and/or family's needs.

Usually, the presenting problem(s) are of high severity. Typically 60 minutes are spent with the patient and/or family or caregiver.

99328 Domiciliary or rest home visit for the evaluation and management of a new patient, which requires these three key components:

- a comprehensive history;
- a comprehensive examination; and
- medical decision making of high complexity.

Counseling and/or coordination of care with other physicians, other qualified health care professionals, or agencies are provided consistent with the nature of the problem(s) and the patient's and/or family's needs.

Usually, the patient is unstable or has developed a significant new problem requiring immediate physician attention. Typically 75 minutes are spent with the patient and/or family or caregiver.

ESTABLISHED PATIENT

99334 Domiciliary or rest home visit for the evaluation and management of an established patient, which requires at least two of these three key components:

- a problem focused interval history;
- a problem focused examination;
- straightforward medical decision making.

Counseling and/or coordination of care with other physicians, other qualified health care professionals, or agencies are provided consistent with the nature of the problem(s) and the patient's and/or family's needs.

Usually, the presenting problem(s) are self-limited or minor. Typically 15 minutes are spent with the patient and/or family or caregiver.

99335 Domiciliary or rest home visit for the evaluation and management of an established patient, which requires at least two of these three key components:

- an expanded problem focused interval history;

- an expanded problem focused examination;
- medical decision making of low complexity.

Counseling and/or coordination of care with other physicians, other qualified health care professionals, or agencies are provided consistent with the nature of the problem(s) and the patient's and/or family's needs.

Usually, the presenting problem(s) are of low to moderate severity. Typically 25 minutes are spent with the patient and/or family or caregiver.

99336 Domiciliary or rest home visit for the evaluation and management of an established patient, which requires at least two of these three key components:

- a detailed interval history;
- a detailed examination;
- medical decision making of moderate complexity.

Counseling and/or coordination of care with other physicians, other qualified health care professionals, or agencies are provided consistent with the nature of the problem(s) and the patient's and/or family's needs.

Usually, the presenting problem(s) are of moderate to high severity. Typically 40 minutes are spent with the patient and/or family or caregiver.

99337 Domiciliary or rest home visit for the evaluation and management of an established patient, which requires at least two of these three key components:

- a comprehensive interval history;
- a comprehensive examination;
- and medical decision making of moderate to high complexity.

Counseling and/or coordination of care with other physicians, other qualified health care professionals, or agencies are provided consistent with the nature of the problem(s) and the patient's and/or family's needs.

Usually, the presenting problem(s) are of moderate to high severity. The patient may be unstable or may have developed a significant new problem requiring immediate physician attention. Typically 60 minutes are spent with the patient and/or family or caregiver.

DOMICILIARY, REST HOME (eg, ASSISTED LIVING FACILITY), OR HOME CARE PLAN OVERSIGHT SERVICES

(For instructions on the use of 99339, 99340, see introductory notes for 99374-99380)

(For care plan oversight services for patients under the care of a home health agency, hospice, or nursing facility, see 99374-99380)

(Do not report 99339, 99340 for time reported with 98966-98969, 99441-99444)

99339 Individual physician supervision of a patient (patient not present) in home, domiciliary or rest home (eg, assisted living facility) requiring complex and multidisciplinary care modalities involving regular physician development and/or revision of care plans, review of subsequent reports of patient status, review of related laboratory and other studies, communication (including telephone calls) for purposes of assessment or care decisions with health care professional(s), family member(s), surrogate decision maker(s) (eg, legal guardian) and/or key caregiver(s) involved in patient's care, integration of new information into the medical treatment plan and/or adjustment of medical therapy, within a calendar month; 15-29 minutes

99340 30 minutes or more

(Do not report 99339, 99340 for patients under the care of a home health agency, enrolled in a hospice program, or for nursing facility residents)

(Do not report 99339, 99340 during the same month with 99487-99489)

(Do not report 99339, 99340 when performed during the service time of codes 99495 or 99496)

HOME SERVICES

The following codes are used to report evaluation and management services provided in a private residence.

For definitions of key components and commonly used terms, please see Evaluation and Management Services Guidelines.

(For care plan oversight services provided to a patient in the home under the care of a home health agency, see 99374-99375, and for hospice agency, see 99377, 99378. For care plan oversight provided to a patient under hospice or home health agency care, see 99339, 99340))

NEW PATIENT

99341 Home visit for the evaluation and management of a new patient, which requires these three key components:

- a problem focused history;
- a problem focused examination; and
- straightforward medical decision making.

Counseling and/or coordination of care with other physicians, other qualified health care professionals, or agencies are provided consistent with the nature of the problem(s) and the patient's and/or family's needs.

Usually, the presenting problem(s) are of low severity. Typically 20 minutes are spent face-to-face with the patient and/or family.

99342 Home visit for the evaluation and management of a new patient, which requires these three key components:

- an expanded problem focused history;
- an expanded problem focused examination; and
- medical decision making of low complexity.

Counseling and/or coordination of care with other physicians, other qualified health care professionals, or agencies are provided consistent with the nature of the problem(s) and the patient's and/or family's needs.

Usually, the presenting problem(s) are of moderate severity. Typically 30 minutes are spent face-to-face with the patient and/or family.

99343 Home visit for the evaluation and management of a new patient, which requires these three key components:

- a detailed history;
- a detailed examination; and
- medical decision making of moderate complexity.

Counseling and/or coordination of care with other physicians, other qualified health care professionals, or agencies are provided consistent with the nature of the problem(s) and the patient's and/or family's needs.

Usually, the presenting problem(s) are of moderate to high severity. Typically 45 minutes ar spent face-to-face with the patient and/or family.

99344 Home visit for the evaluation and management of a new patient, which requires these three components:

- a comprehensive history;
- a comprehensive examination; and
- medical decision making of moderate complexity.

Counseling and/or coordination of care with other physicians, other qualified health care professionals, or agencies are provided consistent with the nature of the problem(s) and the patient's and/or family's needs.

Usually, the presenting problem(s) are of high severity. Typically 60 minutes are spent face-to-face with the patient and/or family.

● New Code ▲ Revised Code + Add-On Code ⊘ Modifier -51 Exempt ★ Telemedicine

99345 Home visit for the evaluation and management of a new patient, which requires these three key components:

- a comprehensive history;

- a comprehensive examination; and

- medical decision making of high complexity.

Counseling and/or coordination of care with other physicians, other qualified health care professionals, or agencies are provided consistent with the nature of the problem(s) and the patient's and/or family's needs.

Usually, the patient is unstable or has developed a significant new problem requiring immediate physician attention. Typically 75 minutes are spent face-to-face with the patient and/or family.

ESTABLISHED PATIENT

 99347 Home visit for the evaluation and management of an established patient, which requires at least two of these three key components:

- a problem focused interval history;

- a problem focused examination;

- straightforward medical decision making.

Counseling and/or coordination of care with other physicians, other qualified health care professionals, or agencies are provided consistent with the nature of the problem(s) and the patient's and/or family's needs.

Usually, the presenting problem(s) are self-limited or minor. Typically 15 minutes are spent face-to-face with the patient and/or family.

99348 Home visit for the evaluation and management of an established patient, which requires at least two of these three key components:

- an expanded problem focused interval history;

- an expanded problem focused examination;

- medical decision making of low complexity.

Counseling and/or coordination of care with other physicians, other qualified health care professionals, or agencies are provided consistent with the nature of the problem(s) and the patient's and/or family's needs.

Usually, the presenting problem(s) are of low to moderate severity. Typically 25 minutes are spent face-to-face with the patient and/or family.

99349 Home visit for the evaluation and management of an established patient, which requires at least two of these three key components:

- a detailed interval history;

- a detailed examination;

- medical decision making of moderate complexity.

Counseling and/or coordination of care with other physicians, other qualified health care professionals, or agencies are provided consistent with the nature of the problem(s) and the patient's and/or family's needs.

Usually, the presenting problem(s) are moderate to high severity. Typically 40 minutes are spent face-to-face with the patient and/or family.

99350 Home visit for the evaluation and management of an established patient, which requires at least two of these three key components:

- a comprehensive interval history;

- a comprehensive examination;

- medical decision making of moderate to high complexity.

Counseling and/or coordination of care with other physicians, other qualified health care professionals, or agencies are provided consistent with the nature of the problem(s) and the patient's and/or family's needs.

Separate Procedure   Unlisted Procedure   CCI Comp. Code   Non-specific Procedure   **163**

Usually, the presenting problem(s) are of moderate to high severity. The patient may be unstable or may have developed a significant new problem requiring immediate physician attention. Typically 60 minutes are spent face-to-face with the patient and/or family.

PROLONGED SERVICES

PROLONGED SERVICE WITH DIRECT PATIENT CONTACT

Codes 99354-99357 are used when a physician or other qualified health care professional provides prolonged service(s) involving direct patient contact that is provided beyond the usual service in either the inpatient or outpatient setting. Direct patient contact is face-to-face and includes additional non-face-to-face services on the patient's floor or unit in the hospital or nursing facility during the same session. This service is reported in addition to the primary procedure (ie, the designated evaluation and management services at any level, code 90837, *Psychotherapy, 60 minutes with patient*, 90847, *Family psychotherapy [conjoint psychotherapy] [with patient present], 50 minutes*) and any other services provided at the same session. Appropriate codes should be selected for supplies provided or other procedures performed in the care of the patient during this period.

Codes 99354-99355 are used to report the total duration of face-to-face time spent by a physician or other qualified health care professional on a given date providing prolonged service in the office or other outpatient setting, even if the time spent by the physician or other qualified health care professional on that date is not continuous. Codes 99356-99357 are used to report the total duration of time spent by a physician or other qualified health care professional at the bedside and on the patient's floor or unit, in the hospital or nursing facility on a given date providing prolonged service to a patient, even if the time spent by the physician or other qualified health care professional on that date is not continuous.

Time spent performing separately reported services other than the E/M or psychotherapy service is not counted toward the prolonged services time.

Code 99354 or 99356 is used to report the first hour of prolonged service on a given date, depending on the place of service.

Either code should be used only once per date, even if the time spent by the physician or other qualified health care professional is not continuous on that date. Prolonged service of less than 30 minutes total duration on a given date is not separately reported because the work involved is included in the total work of the evaluation and management or psychotherapy codes.

Code 99355 or 99357 is used to report each additional 30 minutes beyond the first hour, depending on the place of service. Either code may also be used to report the final 15-30 minutes of prolonged service on a given date. Prolonged service of less than 15 minutes beyond the first hour or less than 15 minutes beyond the final 30 minutes is not reported separately.

The use of the time based add-on codes requires that the primary evaluation and management service have a typical or specified time published in the CPT codebook.

For E/M services that require prolonged clinical staff time and may include face-to-face services by the physician or other qualified health care professional, use 99415, 99416. Do not report 99354 or 99355 with 99415 or 99416.

The following table illustrates the correct reporting of prolonged physician or other qualified health care professional service with direct patient contact in the office setting beyond the usual service time.

TOTAL DURATION OF PROLONGED SERVICES	CODE(S)
less than 30 minutes	Not reported separately
30-74 minutes	99354 once
75-104 minutes	99354 once and 99355 once
105 minutes or more	99354 once and 99355 twice or more for each additional 30 mins.

★+ Prolonged evaluation and management or psychotherapy service(s) (beyond the typical service time of the primary procedure) in the office or other outpatient setting requiring direct patient contact beyond the usual service; first hour (List separately in addition to code for office or other outpatient Evaluation and Management or psychotherapy service)

(Use 99354 in conjunction with 90837, 90847, 99201-99215, 99241-99245, 99324-99337, 99341-99350, 99483)

(Do not report 99354 in conjunction with 99415, 99416)

★+99355   each additional 30 minutes (List separately in addition to code for prolonged physician service)

(Use 99355 in conjunction with 99354)

(Do not report 99355 in conjunction with 99415, 99416)

+ 99356   Prolonged service in the inpatient or observation setting, requiring unit/floor time beyond the usual service; first hour (List separately in addition to code for inpatient Evaluation and Management service)

(Use 99356 in conjunction with codes 99218-99220, 99221-99223, 99224-99226, 99231-99233, 99234-99236, 99251-99255, 99304-99310)

+ 99357   each additional 30 minutes (List separately in addition to code for prolonged physician service)

(Use 99357 in conjunction with 99356)

PROLONGED SERVICE WITHOUT DIRECT PATIENT CONTACT

Codes 99358 and 99359 are used when a prolonged service is provided that is neither face-to-face time in the office or outpatient setting, nor additional unit/floor time in the hospital or nursing facility setting during the same session of an evaluation and management service and is beyond the usual physician or other qualified health care professional service time.

This service is to be reported in relation to other physician or other qualified health care professional services, including evaluation and management services at any level. This prolonged service may be reported on a different date than the primary service to which it is related. For example, extensive record review may relate to a previous evaluation and management service performed earlier and commences upon receipt of past records. However, it must relate to a service or patient where (face-to-face) patient care has occurred or will occur and relate to ongoing patient management. A typical time for the primary service need not be established within CPT code set.

Codes 99358 and 99359 are used to report the total duration of non-face-to-face time spent by a physician or other qualified health care professional on a given date providing prolonged service, even if the time spent by the physician or other qualified health care professional on that date is not continuous. Code 99358 is used to report the first hour of prolonged service on a given date regardless of the place of service. It should be used only once per date.

Prolonged service of less than 30 minutes total duration on a given date is not separately reported.

Code 99359 is used to report each additional 30 minutes beyond the first hour regardless of the place of service. It may also be used to report the final 15 to 30 minutes of prolonged service on a given date.

Prolonged service of less than 15 minutes beyond the first hour or less than 15 minutes beyond the final 30 minutes is not reported separately.

Do not report 99358-99359 for time spent in care plan oversight services (99339, 99340, 99374-99380), home and outpatient INR monitoring (93792, 92793), medical team conferences (99366-99368), on-line medical evaluatinos (99444), or other non face-to-face services that have more specific codes and no upper time limit in the CPT code set. Codes 99358, 99359 may be reported when related to other non face-to-face service codes that have a published maximum time (eg, telephone services).

99358   Prolonged evaluation and management service before and/or after direct patient care; first hour

+ 99359   each additional 30 minutes (List separately in addition to code for prolonged physician service)

(Use 99359 in conjunction with 99358)

(Do not report 99358, 99359 during the same month with 99487-99489)

(Do note report 99358, 99359 when performed during the service time of codes 99495 or 99496)

PROLONGED CLINICAL STAFF SERVICES WITH PHYSICIAN OR OTHER QUALIFIED HEALTH CARE PROFESSIONAL SUPERVISION

Codes 99415, 99416 are used when a prolonged evaluation and management (E/M) service is provided in the office or outpatient setting that involves prolonged clinical staff face-to-face time beyond the typical face-to-face time of the E/M service, as stated in the code description. The physician or qualified health care professional is present to provide direct supervision of the clinical staff. This service is reported in addition to the designated E/M services and any other services provided at the same session as E/M services.

Codes 99415, 99416 are used to report the total duration of face-to-face time spent by clinical staff on a given date providing prolonged service in the office or other outpatient setting, even if the time spent by the clinical staff on that date is not continuous. Time spent performing separately reported services other than the E/M service is not counted toward the prolonged services time.

Code 99415 is used to report the first hour of prolonged clinical staff service on a given date. Code 99415 should be used only once per date, even if the time spent by the clinical staff is not continuous on that date. Prolonged service of less than 45 minutes total duration on a given date is not separately reported because the clinical staff time involved is included in the E/M codes. The typical face-to-face time of the primary service is used in defining when prolonged service time begins. For example, prolonged clinical staff services for 99214 begin after 25 minutes, and 99415 is not reported until at least 70 minutes total face-to-face clinical staff time has been performed. When face-to-face time is noncontiguous, use only the face-to-face time provided to the patient by the clinical staff.

Code 99416 is used to report each additional 30 minutes of prolonged clinical staff service beyond the first hour. Code 99416 may also be used to report the final 15-30 minutes of prolonged service on that date. Prolonged service of less than 15 minutes beyond the first hour or less than 15 minutes beyond the final 30 minutes is not reported separately.

Codes 99415, 99416 may be reported for no more than two simultaneous patients. The use of the time-based add-on codes requires that the primary E/M service has a typical or specified time published in the CPT code set.

For prolonged services by the physician or qualified health care professional, use 99354, 99355. Do not report 99415 or 99416 with 99354 or 99355.

Facilities may not report 99415, 99416.

+  Prolonged clinical staff service (the service beyond the typical service time) during an evaluation and management service in the office or outpatient setting, direct patient contact with physician supervision; first hour (List separately in addition to code for outpatient Evaluation and Management service)

(Use 99415 in conjunction with 99201, 99202, 99203, 99204, 99205, 99211, 99212, 99213, 99214, 99215)

(Do not report 99415 in conjunction with 99354, 99355)

+ **99416**   each additional 30 minutes (List separately in addition to code for prolonged service)

(Use 99416 in conjunction with 99415)

(Do not report 99416 in conjunction with 99354, 99355)

The Total Duration of Prolonged Services Table illustrates the correct reporting of prolonged services provided by clinical staff with physician supervision in the office setting beyond the initial 45 minutes of clinical staff time.

TOTAL DURATION OF PROLONGED SERVICES	CODE(s)
less than 45 minutes	Not reported separately
45-74 minutes	99415 once
75-104 minutes	99415 once and 99416 once
105 minutes or more	99415 once and 99416 twice or more for each additional 30 mins

STANDBY SERVICES

Code 99360 is used to report physician or other qualified health care professional standby services that are requested by another individual and that involve prolonged attendance without direct (face-to-face) patient contact. Care or services may not be provided to other patients during this period. This code is not used to report time spent proctoring another individual. It is also not used if the period of standby ends with the performance of a procedure subject to a surgical package by the individual who was on standby.

Code 99360 is used to report the total duration of time spent on a given date on standby. Standby service of less than 30 minutes total duration on a given date is not reported separately.

Second and subsequent periods of standby beyond the first 30 minutes may be reported only if a full 30 minutes of standby was provided for each unit of service reported.

 99360 Standby service, requiring prolonged attendance, each 30 minutes (eg, operative standby, standby for frozen section, for cesarean/high risk delivery, for monitoring EEG)

(For hospital mandated on call services, see 99026, 99027)

(99360 may be reported in addition to 99460, 99465 as appropriate)

(Do not report 99360 in conjunction with 99464)

CASE MANAGEMENT SERVICES

Case management is a process in which a physician or another qualified health care professional is responsible for direct care of a patient and, additionally, for coordinating, managing access to, initiating, and/or supervising other health care services needed by the patient. .

ANTICOAGULANT MANAGEMENT

(**99363** deleted 2017 [2018 edition]. To report, see 93792, 93793.)

(**99364** deleted 2017 [2018 edition]. To report, see 93792, 93793.)

MEDICAL TEAM CONFERENCES

Medical team conferences include face-to-face participation by a minimum of three qualified health care professionals from different specialties or disciplines (each of whom provide direct care to the patient), with or without the presence of the patient, family member(s), community agencies, surrogate decision maker(s) (eg., legal guardian), and/or caregiver(s). The participants are actively involved in the development, revision, coordination, and implementation of health care services needed by the patient. Reporting participants shall have performed face-to-face evaluations or treatments of the patient, independent of any team conference, within the previous 60 days.

Physicians or other qualified health care professionals who may report evaluation and management services should report their time spent in a team conference with the patient and/or family present using evaluation and management (E/M) codes (and time as the key controlling factor for code selection when counseling and/or coordination of care dominates the service). These introductory guidelines do not apply to services reported using E/M codes (see E/M services guidelines). However, the individual must be directly involved with the patient, providing face-to-face services outside of the conference visit with other physicians, other qualified health care professionals, or agencies.

Reporting participants shall document their participation in the team conference as well as their contributed information and subsequent treatment recommendations.

No more than one individual from the same specialty may report 99366-99368 at the same encounter.

Individuals should not report 99366-99368 when their participation in the medical team conference is part of a facility or organizational service contractually provided by the organizational or facility.

The team conference starts at the beginning of the review of an individual patient and ends at the conclusion of the review. Time related to record keeping and report generation is not reported. The reporting participant shall be present for all time reported. The time reported is not limited to the time that the participant is communicating to the other team members or patient and/or family. Time reported for medical team conferences may not be used in the determination of time for other services such as care plan oversight (99374-99380), home, domiciliary, or rest home care plan oversight (99339-99340), prolonged services (99354-99359), psychotherapy, or any E/M service. For team conferences where the patient is present for any part of the duration of the conference, nonphysician qualified health care professionals (eg, speech-language pathologists, physical therapists, occupational therapist, social workers, dieticians) report the team conference face-to-face code 99366.

MEDICAL TEAM CONFERENCE, DIRECT (FACE-TO-FACE) CONTACT WITH PATIENT AND/OR FAMILY

99366   Medical team conference with interdisciplinary team of health care professionals, face-to-face with patient and/or family, 30 minutes or more, participation by nonphysician qualified health care professional

(Team conference services of less than 30 minutes duration are not reported separately)

(For team conference services by a physician with patient and/or family present, see Evaluation and Management services)

(Do not report 99366 during the same month with 99487-99489)

(Do not report 99366 when performed during the service time of codes 99495 or 99496)

MEDICAL TEAM CONFERENCE, WITHOUT DIRECT (FACE-TO-FACE) CONTACT WITH PATIENT AND/OR FAMILY

99367   Medical team conference with interdisciplinary team of health care professionals, patient and/or family not present, 30 minutes or more; participation by physician

99368   participation by nonphysician qualified health care professional

(Team conference services of less than 30 minutes duration are not reported separately)

(Do not report 99367, 99368 during the same month with 99487-99489)

(Do not report 99367, 99368 when performed during the service time of codes 99495 or 99496)

CARE PLAN OVERSIGHT SERVICES

Care plan oversight services are reported separately from codes for office/ outpatient, hospital, home, nursing facility or domiciliary or non face-to-face services. The complexity and approximate time of the care plan oversight services provided within a 30-day period determine code selection. Only one individual may report services for a given period of time, to reflect the sole or predominant supervisory role with a particular patient. These codes should not be reported for supervision of patients in nursing facilities or under the care of home health agencies unless they require recurrent supervision of therapy.

The work involved in providing very low intensity or infrequent supervision services is included in the pre- and post-encounter work for home, office/outpatient and nursing facility or domiciliary visit codes.

CODING RULES

1.   *Evaluation and management services are not inclusive of care plan oversight services. Care plan oversight is coded separately.*

2.   *Care plan oversight services may be coded only by a single physician for each patient during a specific period of time.*

(For care plan oversight services of patients in the home, domiciliary, or rest home [eg, assisted living facility] see 99339, 99340, and for hospice agency, see 99377, 99378))

(Do not report 99374-99380 for time reported with 98966-98969, 99441-99444)

(Do not report 99374-99378 during the same month with 99487-99489)

(Do not report 99374-99380 when performed during the service time of codes 99495 or 99496)

99374   Supervision of a patient under care of home health agency (patient not present) in home, domiciliary or equivalent environment (eg, Alzheimer's facility) requiring complex and multidisciplinary care modalities involving regular development and/or revision of care plans by that individual, review of subsequent reports of patient status, review of related laboratory and other studies, communication (including telephone calls) for purposes of assessment or care decisions with health care professional(s), family member(s), surrogate decision maker(s) (eg., legal guardian) and/or key caregiver(s) involved in patient's

● New Code   ▲ Revised Code   + Add-On Code   ⊘ Modifier -51 Exempt   ★ Telemedicine

care, integration of new information into the medical treatment plan and/or adjustment of medical therapy, within a calendar month; 15-29 minutes

99375   30 minutes or more

99377   Supervision of a hospice patient (patient not present) requiring complex and multidisciplinary care modalities involving regular development and/or revision of care plans by that individual, review of subsequent reports of patient status, review of related laboratory and other studies, communication (including telephone calls) for purposes of assessment or care decisions with health care professional(s), family member(s), surrogate decision maker(s) (eg, legal guardian) and/or key caregiver(s) involved in patient's care, integration of new information into the medical treatment plan and/or adjustment of medical therapy, within a calendar month; 15-29 minutes

99378   30 minutes or more

99379   Supervision of a nursing facility patient (patient not present) requiring complex and multidisciplinary care modalities involving regular development and/or revision of care plans by that individual, review of subsequent reports of patient status, review of related laboratory and other studies, communication (including telephone calls) for purposes of assessment or care decisions with health care professional(s), family member(s), surrogate decision maker(s) (eg, legal guardian) and/or key caregiver(s) involved in patient's care, integration of new information into the medical treatment plan and/or adjustment of medical therapy, within a calendar month; 15-29 minutes

99380   30 minutes or more

PREVENTIVE MEDICINE SERVICES

The following codes are used to report the preventive medicine evaluation and management of infants, children, adolescents, and adults.

The extent and focus of the services will largely depend on the age of the patient.

If an abnormality is encountered or a pre-existing problem is addressed in the process of performing this preventive medicine evaluation and management service, and if the problem or abnormality is significant enough to require additional work to perform the key components of a problem-oriented E/M service, then the appropriate Office/Outpatient code 99201-99215 should also be reported. Modifier 25 should be added to the Office/Outpatient code to indicate that a significant, separately identifiable evaluation and management service was provided on the same day as the preventive medicine service. The appropriate preventive medicine service is additionally reported.

An insignificant or trivial problem/abnormality that is encountered in the process of performing the preventive medicine evaluation and management service and which does not require additional work and the performance of the key components of a problem-oriented E/M service should not be reported.

The "comprehensive" nature of the Preventive Medicine Services codes 99381-99397 reflects an age and gender appropriate history/exam and is NOT synonymous with the "comprehensive" examination required in Evaluation and Management codes 99201-99350.

Codes 99381-99397 include counseling/anticipatory guidance/risk factor reduction interventions which are provided at the time of the initial or periodic comprehensive preventive medicine examination. (Refer to codes 99401, 99402, 99403, 99404, 99411, and 99412 for reporting those counseling/anticipatory guidance/risk factor reduction internventions that are provided at an encounter separate from the preventive medicine examination.)

(For behavior change intervention, see 99406, 99407, 99408, 99409)

Vaccine/toxoid products, immunization administrations, ancillary studies involving laboratory, radiology, other procedures, or screening tests (eg, vision, hearing, developmental) identified with a specific CPT code are reported separately. For immunization administration and vaccine risk/benefit counseling, see 90460, 90461, 90470-90474. For vaccine/toxoid products, see 90476-90749.

CODING RULES

1.   *The selection of Preventive Medicine codes is mostly dependent upon the age of the patient.*

| Separate Procedure | Unlisted Procedure | CCI Comp. Code | Non-specific Procedure | **169** |

2. *Preventive medicine codes are coded only in the absence of illness. If illness, injury is discovered during provision of a preventive medicine service, office/outpatient evaluation and management codes are coded.*

3. *Immunizations and diagnostic studies involving laboratory or radiology, or other procedures are not included in the preventive medicine service and should be coded separately.*

NEW PATIENT

99381 Initial comprehensive preventive medicine evaluation and management of an individual including an age and gender appropriate history, examination, counseling/anticipatory guidance/risk factor reduction interventions, and the ordering of laboratory/diagnostic procedures, new patient; infant (age under 1 year)

99382 early childhood (age 1 through 4 years)

99383 late childhood (age 5 through 11 years)

99384 adolescent (age 12 through 17 years)

99385 18-39 years

99386 40-64 years

99387 65 years and over

ESTABLISHED PATIENT

99391 Periodic comprehensive preventive medicine reevaluation and management of an individual including an age and gender appropriate history, examination, counseling/anticipatory guidance/risk factor reduction interventions, and the ordering of laboratory/diagnostic procedures, established patient; infant (age under 1 year)

99392 early childhood (age 1 through 4 years)

99393 late childhood (age 5 through 11 years)

99394 adolescent (age 12 through 17 years)

99395 18-39 years

99396 40-64 years

99397 65 years and over

COUNSELING RISK FACTOR REDUCTION AND BEHAVIOR CHANGE INTERVENTION

NEW OR ESTABLISHED PATIENT

These codes are used to report services provided face-to-face by a physician or other qualified health care professional for the purpose of promoting health and preventing illness or injury. They are distinct from evaluation and management (E/M) services that may be reported separately with modifier 25 when performed. Risk factor reduction services are used for persons without a specific illness for which the counseling might otherwise be used as part of treatment.

Preventive medicine counseling and risk factor reduction interventions will vary with age and should address such issues as family problems, diet and exercise, substance use, sexual practices, injury prevention, dental health, and diagnostic and laboratory test results available at the time of the encounter.

Behavior change interventions are for persons who have a behavior that is often considered an illness itself, such as tobacco use and addiction, substance abuse/misuse, or obesity. Behavior change services may be reported when performed as part of the treatment of condition(s) related to or potentially exacerbated by the behavior or when performed to change the harmful behavior that has not yet resulted in illness. Any E/M services reported on the same day must be distinct and reported with modifier 25, and time spent providing these services may not be used as a basis for the E/M code selection. Behavior change services involve

● New Code   ▲ Revised Code   ✚ Add-On Code   ⊘ Modifier -51 Exempt   ★ Telemedicine

specific validated interventions of assessing readiness for change and barriers to change, advising a change in behavior, assisting by providing specific suggested actions and motivational counseling, and arranging for services and follow-up.

For counseling groups of patients with symptoms or established illness, use 99078.

Health and Behavior Assessment/Intervention services (96150-96155) should not be reported on the same day as codes 99401-99412).

Preventive Medicine, Individual Counseling

99401 Preventive medicine counseling and/or risk factor reduction intervention(s) provided to an individual (separate procedure); approximately 15 minutes

99402 approximately 30 minutes

99403 approximately 45 minutes

99404 approximately 60 minutes

Behavior Change Interventions, Individual

★ **99406** Smoking and tobacco use cessation counseling visit; intermediate, greater than 3 minutes up to 10 minutes

★ **99407** intensive, greater than 10 minutes

(Do not report 99407 in conjunction with 99406)

★ **99408** Alcohol and/or substance (other than tobacco) abuse structured screening (eg, AUDIT, DAST), and brief intervention (SBI) services; 15 to 30 minutes

(Do not report services of less than 15 minutes with 99408)

★ **99409** greater than 30 minutes

(Do not report 99409 in conjunction with 99408)

(Do not report 99408, 99409 in conjunction with 96160, 96161)

(Use 99408, 99409 only for initial screening and brief intervention)

Preventive Medicine, Group Counseling

99411 Preventive medicine counseling and/or risk factor reduction intervention(s) provided to individuals in a group setting (separate procedure); approximately 30 minutes

99412 approximately 60 minutes

99415 Code out of order. See page 166.

99416 Code out of order. See page 166.

OTHER PREVENTIVE MEDICINE SERVICES

(**99420** deleted 2016 [2107 edition]. See 96160, 96161)

99429 Unlisted preventive medicine service

NON-FACE-TO-FACE PHYSICIAN SERVICES

TELEPHONE SERVICES

Telephone services are non-face-to-face evaluation and management (E/M) services provided to a patient using the telephone by a physician or other qualified health care professiona, who may report E/M sevices. These codes are used to report episodes of patient care initiated by an established patient or guardian of an established patient. If the telephone service ends with a decision to see the patient within 24 hours or next available urgent visit appointment, the code is not reported; rather the encounter is considered part of the preservice work of the subsequent E/M service, procedure and visit. Likewise, if the telephone call refers to an E/M service performed and reported by that individual within the previous seven days (either requested or unsolicited patient follow-up) or within the postoperative period of the previously completed procedure, then the service(s) are considered part of that previous E/M service or procedure. (Do not report 99441-99443 if reporting 99441-99444 performed in the previous seven days.)

> (For telephone services provided by a qualified nonphysician health care professional who may not report evaluation and management services [eg, speech-language pathologists, physical therapists, occupational therapists, social workers, dieticians], see 98966-98968)

99441 Telephone evaluation and management service by a physician or other qualified health care professional who may report evaluation and management services provided to an established patient, parent, or guardian not originating from a related E/M service provided within the previous 7 days nor leading to an E/M service or procedure within the next 24 hours or soonest available appointment; 5-10 minutes of medical discussion

99442 11-20 minutes of medical discussion

99443 21-30 minutes of medical discussion

> (Do not report 99441-99443 when using 99339-99340, 99374-99380 for the same call[s])

> (Do not report 99441-99443 for home and outpatient INR monitoring when reporting 93792, 93793)

> (Do not report 99441-99443 during the same month with 99487-99489)

> (Do not report 99441-99443 when performed during the service time of codes 99495 or 99496)

ON-LINE MEDICAL EVALUATION

An on-line electronic medical evaluation is a non-face-to-face evaluation and management (E/M) service by a physician to a patient using Internet resources in response to a patient's on-line inquiry. Reportable services involve the physician's personal timely response to the patient's inquiry and must involve permanent storage (electronic or hard coy) of the encounter. This service is reported only once for the same episode of care during a seven-day period, although multiple physicians could report their exchange with the same patient. If the on-line medical evaluation refers to an E/M service previously performed and reported by the physician within the previous seven days (either physician requested or un solicited patient follow-up) or within the postoperative period of the previously completed procedure, then the service(s) are considered covered by the previous E/M service or procedure. A reportable service encompasses the sum of communication (eg, related telephone calls, prescription provision, laboratory orders) pertaining to the on-line patient encounter.

> (For an on-line medical evaluation provided by a qualified nonphysician health care professional, use 98969)

99444 Online evaluation and management service provided by a physician or other qualified health care professional who may report evaluation and management services provided to an established patient or guardian, not originating from a related E/M service provided within the previous 7 days, using the Internet or similar electronic communications network

> (Do not report 99444 when using 99339-99340, 99374-99380 for the same communication[s])

> (Do not report 99444 for home and outpatient INR monitoring when reporting 93792, 93793)

> (Do not report 99444 during the same month with 99487-99489)

> (Do not report 99444 when performed during the service time of codes 99495 or 99496)

INTERPROFESSIONAL TELEPHONE/INTERNET CONSULTATIONS

The consultant should use the following codes to report interprofessional telephone/Internet consultations. An interprofessional telephone/Internet consultation is an assessment and management service in which a patient's treating (eg, attending or primary) physician or other qualified health care professional requests the opinion and/or treatment of a physician with specific specialty expertise (the consultant) to assist the treating physician or other qualified health care professional in the diagnosis and/or management of the patient's problem without the need for the patient's face-to-face contact with the consultant.

● New Code   ▲ Revised Code   + Add-On Code   ⊘ Modifier -51 Exempt   ★ Telemedicine

These services are typically provided in complex and/or urgent situations where a timely face-to-face service with the consultant may not be feasible (eg, geographic distance). These codes should not be reported by a consultant who has agreed to accept transfer of care before the telephone/Internet assessment, but are appropriate to report if the decision to accept transfer of care cannot be made until after the initial interprofessional telephone/Internet consultation.

The patient for whom the interprofessional telephone/Internet consultation is requested may be either a new patient to the consultant or an established patient with a new problem or an exacerbation of an existing problem. However, the consultant should not have seen the patient in a face-to-face encounter within the last 14 days. When the telephone/Internet consultation leads to an immediate transfer of care or other face-to-face service (eg, a surgery, a hospital visit, or a scheduled office evaluation of the patient) within the next 14 days or next available appointment date of the consultant, these codes are not reported.

Review of pertinent medical records, laboratory studies, imaging studies, medication profile, pathology specimens, etc may be required and transmitted electronically by fax or by mail immediately before the telephone/Internet consultation or following the consultation.

The review of this data is included in the telephone/Internet consultation service and should not be reported separately. The majority of the service time reported (greater than 50%) must be devoted to the medical consultative verbal/Internet discussion. This service should not be reported more than once within a 7-day interval.

If more than one telephone/Internet contact(s) is required to complete the consultation request (eg, discussion of test results), the entirety of the service and the cumulative discussion and information review time should be reported with a single code.

The written or verbal request for telephone/Internet advice by the treating/requesting physician or other qualified health care professional should be documented in the patient's medical record, including the reason for the request, and concludes with a verbal opinion report and written report from the consultant to the treating/requesting physician or other qualified health care professional.

Telephone/Internet consultations of less than five minutes should not be reported. Consultant communications with the patient and/or family may be reported using 99441, 99442, 99443, 99444, 98966, 98967, 98968, 98969 and the time related to these services is not used in reporting 99446, 99447, 99448, 99449.

When the sole purpose of the telephone/Internet communication is to arrange a transfer of care or other face-to-face service, these codes are not reported.

The treating/requesting physician or other qualified health care professional may report the prolonged service codes 99354, 99355, 99356, 99357 for the time spent on the interprofessional telephone/Internet discussion with the consultant (eg, specialist) if the time **exceeds 30 minutes** beyond the typical time of the appropriate E/M service performed and the patient is present (on-site) and accessible to the treating/requesting physician or other qualified health care professional. If the interprofessional telephone/Internet assessment and management service occurs when the patient is not present or on-site, and the discussion time **exceeds 30 minutes** beyond the typical time of the appropriate E/M service performed, then the non-face-to-face prolonged service codes 99358, 99359 may be reported by the treating/requesting physician or other qualified health care professional.

(For telephone services provided by a physician to a patient, see 99441, 99442, 99443)

(For telephone services provided by a qualified health care professional to a patient, see 98966, 98967, 98968)

(For an on-line medical evaluation provided by a physician to a patient, use 99444)

(For an on-line assessment and management service provided by a qualified health care professional to a patient, use 98969)

99446 Interprofessional telephone/Internet assessment and management service provided by a consultative physician including a verbal and written report to the patient's treating/requesting physician or other qualified health care professional; 5-10 minutes of medical consultative discussion and review

99447 11-20 minutes of medical consultative discussion and review

99448 21-30 minutes of medical consultative discussion and review

99449 31 minutes or more of medical consultative discussion and review

---

SPECIAL EVALUATION AND MANAGEMENT SERVICES

The following codes are used to report evaluations performed to establish baseline information prior to life or disability insurance certificates being issued. This service is performed in the office or other setting, and applies to both new and established patients When using these codes, no active management of the problem(s) is undertaken during the encounter..

If other evaluation and management services and/or procedures are performed on the same date, the appropriate E/M or procedure code(s) should be reported in addition to these codes.

BASIC LIFE AND/OR DISABILITY EVALUATION SERVICES

99450   Basic life and/or disability examination that includes:

- measurement of height, weight and blood pressure;
- completion of a medical history following a life insurance pro forma;
- collection of blood sample and/or urinalysis complying with "chain of custody" protocols; and
- completion of necessary documentation/certificates.

WORK RELATED OR MEDICAL DISABILITY EVALUATION SERVICES

99455   Work related or medical disability examination by the treating physician that includes:

- completion of a medical history commensurate with the patient's condition;
- performance of an examination commensurate with the patient's condition;
- formulation of a diagnosis, assessment of capabilities and stability, and calculation of impairment;
- development of future medical treatment plan; and
- completion of necessary documentation/certificates and report.

99456   Work related or medical disability examination by other than the treating physician that includes:

- completion of a medical history commensurate with the patient's condition;
- performance of an examination commensurate with the patient's condition;
- formulation of a diagnosis, assessment of capabilities and stability, and calculation of impairment;
- development of future medical treatment plan; and
- completion of necessary documentation/certificates and report.

(Do not report 99455, 99456 in conjunction with 99080 for the completion of Workman's Compensation forms)

NEWBORN CARE SERVICES

The following codes are used to report the services provided to newborns (birth through the first 28 days) in several different settings. Use of the normal newborn codes is limited to the initial care of the newborn in the first days after birth prior to home discharge.

Evaluation and Management (E/M) services for the newborn include maternal and/or fetal and newborn history, newborn physical examination(s), ordering of diagnostic tests and treatments, meetings with the family, and documentation in the medical record.

When delivery room attendance services (99464) or delivery room resuscitation services (99465) are required, report these in addition to normal newborn services E/M codes.

For E/M services provided to newborns who are other than normal, see codes for hospital inpatient services (99221-99233) and neonatal intensive and critical care services (99466-99469, 99477-99480). When normal newborn services are provided by the same individual on the same date that the newborn later becomes ill and receives additional intensive or critical care services, report the appropriate E/M code with modifier 25 for these services in addition to the normal newborn code..

Procedures (eg, 54150, newborn circumcision) are not included with the normal newborn codes, and when performed, should be reported in addition to the newborn services.

When newborns are seen in follow-up after the date of discharge in the office or outpatient setting, see 99201-99215, 99381, 99391 as appropriate.

99460 Initial hospital or birthing center care, per day, for evaluation and management of normal newborn infant

99461 Initial care, per day, for evaluation and management of normal newborn infant seen in other than hospital or birthing center

99462 Subsequent hospital care, per day, for evaluation and management of normal newborn

99463 Initial hospital or birthing center care, per day, for evaluation and management of normal newborn infant admitted and discharged on the same date

(For newborn Hospital discharge services provided on a date subsequent to the admission date, see 99238, 99239)

DELIVERY/BIRTHING ROOM ATTENDANCE AND RESUSCITATION SERVICES

99464 Attendance at delivery (when requested by the delivering physician or other qualified health care professional) and initial stabilization of newborn

(99464 may be reported in conjunction with 99460, 99468, 99477)

(Do not report 99464 in conjunction with 99465)

99465 Delivery/birthing room resuscitation, provision of positive pressure ventilation and/or chest compressions in the presence of acute inadequate ventilation and/or cardiac output

(99465 may be reported in conjunction with 99460, 99468, 99477)

(Do not report 99465 in conjunction with 99464)

(Procedures that are performed as a necessary part of the resuscitation [eg, intubation, vascular lines] are reported separately in addition to 99465. In order to report these procedures, they must be performed as a necessary component of the resuscitation and not as a convenience before admission to the neonatal intensive care unit)

INPATIENT NEONATAL INTENSIVE CARE SERVICES AND PEDIATRIC AND NEONATAL CRITICAL CARE SERVICES

PEDIATRIC CRITICAL CARE PATIENT TRANSPORT

Codes 99466, 99467 are used to report the physical attendance and direct face-to-face care by a physician during the interfacility transport of a critically ill or critically injured pediatric patient 24 months of age or younger. Codes 99485, 99486 are used to report the control physician's non-face-to-face supervision of interfacility transport of a critically ill or critically injured pediatric patient 24 months of age or younger. These codes are not reported together for the same patient by the same physician. For the purpose of reporting 99466 and 99467, face-to-face care begins when the physician assumes primary responsibility of the pediatric patient at the referring facility, and ends when the receiving facility accepts responsibility for the pediatric patient's care. Only the time the physician spends in direct face-to-face contact with the patient during the transport should be reported. Pediatric patient transport services involving less than 30 minutes of face-to-face physician care should not be reported using 99466, 99467. Procedure(s) or services(s) performed by other members of the transporting team may not be reported by the supervising physician.

Codes 99485, 99486 may be used to report control physician's non-face-to-face supervision of interfacility pediatric critical care transport, which includes all twoway communication between the control physician and the specialized transport team prior to transport, at the referring facility and during transport of the patient back to the receiving facility. The "control" physician is the physician directing transport services. These codes do not include pretransport communication between the control physician and the referring facility before or following patient transport. These codes may only be reported for patients 24 months of age or younger who are critically ill or critically injured. The control physician provides treatment advice to a specialized transport team who are present and delivering the hands-on patient care. The control physician does not report any services provided by the specialized transport team. The control physician's non-face-to-face time begins with the first contact by the control physician with the specialized transport team and ends when the patient's care is handed over to the receiving facility team. Refer to 99466 and 99467 for face-to-face transport care of the critically ill/injured patient. Time spent with the individual patient's transport team and reviewing data submissions should be recorded. Code 99485 is used to report the first 16-45 minutes of direction on a given date and should only be used once even if time spent by the physician is discontinuous. Do not report services of 15 minutes or less or any time when another physician is reporting 99466, 99467. Do not report 99485 or 99486 in conjunction with 99466, 99467 when performed by the same physician.

For the definition of the critically injured pediatric patient, see the Neonatal and Pediatric Critical Care Services section.

The non-face-to-face direction of emergency care to a patient's transporting staff by a physician located in a hospital or other facility by two-way communication is not considered direct face-to-face care and should not be reported with 99466, 99467. Physician-directed non-face-to-face emergency care through outside voice communication to transporting staff personnel is reported with 99288 or 99485, 99486 based upon the age and clinical condition of the patient.

Emergency department services (99281-99285), initial hospital care (99221-99223), critical care (99291, 99292), initial date neonatal intensive (99477) or critical care (99468) may only be reported after the patient has been admitted to the emergency department, the inpatient floor, or the critical care unit of the receiving facility. If inpatient critical care services are reported in the referring facility prior to transfer to the receiving hospital, use the critical care codes (99291, 99292)

The following services are included when performed during the pediatric patient transport by the physician providing critical care and may not be reported separately: routine monitoring evaluations (eg, heart rate, respiratory rate, blood pressure, and pulse oximetry), the interpretation of cardiac output measurements (93562), chest X-rays (71045, 71046), pulse oximetry (94760, 94761, 94762), blood gases and information data stored in computers (eg, ECGs, blood pressures, hematologic data) (99090), gastric intubation (43752, 43753), temporary transcutaneous pacing (92953), ventilatory management (94002, 94003, 94660, 94662), and vascular access procedures (36000, 36400, 36405, 36406, 36415, 36591, 36600). Any services performed which are not listed above should be reported separately.

Services provided by the specialized transport team during non-face-to-face transport supervision are not reported by the control physician.

Code 99466 is used to report the first 30 to 74 minutes of direct face-to-face time with the transport pediatric patient and should be reported only once on a given date. Code 99467 is used to report each additional 30 minutes provided on a given date. Face-to-face services of less than 30 minutes should not be reported with these codes.

Code 99485 is used to report the first 30 minutes of non-face-to-face supervision of an interfacility transport of a critically ill or critically injured pediatric patient and should be reported only once per date of service. sOnly the communication time spent by the supervising physician with the specialty transport team members during an interfacility transport should be reported. Code 99486 is used to report each additional 30 minutes beyond the initial 30 minutes. Non-face-to-face interfacility transport of 15 minutes or less is not reported.

(For total body and selective head cooling of neonates, use 99184)

99466 Critical care face-to-face services, during an interfacility transport of critically ill or critically injured pediatric patient, 24 months of age or less; first 30-74 minutes of hands-on care during transport

+ **99467** each additional 30 minutes (list separately in addition to code for primary service)

(Use 99467 in conjunction with 99466)

(Critical care of less than 30 minutes total duration should be reported with the appropriate E/M code)

99485 Supervision by a control physician of interfacility transport care of the critically ill or critically injured pediatric patient, 24 month of age or younger, includes two-way communication with transport team before transport, at the referring facility and during the transport, including data interpretation and report, first 30 minutes.

+ **99486** each additional 30 minutes (List separately in addition to code for primary procedure)

(Use 99486 in conjunction with 99485)

(For physician direction of emergency medical systems supervision for a pediatric patient older than 24 months of age, or at any age if not critically ill or injured, use 99288)

(Do not report 99485, 99486 with any other services reported by the control physician for the same period)

(Do not report 99485, 99486 in conjunction with 99466, 99467 when performed by the same physician)

INPATIENT NEONATAL AND PEDIATRIC CRITICAL CARE

The same definitions for critical care services apply to the adult, child and neonate.

Codes 99468, 99469 may be used to report the services of directing the inpatient care of a critically ill neonate or infant 28 days of age or younger. They represent care starting with the date of admission (99468) for critical care services and all subsequent day(s) (99469) that the neonate remains in critical care. These codes may be reported only by a single individual and only once per calendar day, per patient. Initial inpatient neonatal critical care (99468) may only be reported once per hospital admission. If readmitted for neonatal critical care services during the same hospital stay, then report the subsequent inpatient neonatal critical care code (99469) for the first day of readmission to critical care, and 99469 for each day of critical care following readmission.

The initial inpatient neonatal critical care code (99468) can be used in addition to 99464 or 99465 as appropriate, when the physician or other qualified health care professional is present for the delivery (99464) or resuscitation (99465) is required. Other procedures performed as a necessary part of the resuscitation (eg, endotracheal intubation [31500]) may also be reported separately, when performed as part of the pre-admission delivery room care. In order to report these procedures separately, they must be performed as a necessary component of the resuscitation and not simply as a convenience before admission to the neonatal intensive care unit.

Codes 99471-99476 may be used to report the services of directing the inpatient care of a critically ill infant or young child from 29 days of postnatal age through 5 years of age. They represent care starting with the date of admission (99471, 99475) for pediatric critical care services and all subsequent day(s) (99472, 99476) that the infant or child remains in critical condition. These codes may only be reported by a single individual and only once per calendar day, per patient. Services for the critically ill or critically injured child 6 years of age or older would be reported with the time-based critical care codes (99291, 99292). Initial inpatient critical care (99471, 99475) may only be reported once per hospital admission. If readmitted to the pediatric critical care unit during the same hospital stay, then report the subsequent inpatient pediatric critical care code 99472 or 99476 for the first day of readmission to critical care and 99472 or 99476 for each day of critical care following readmission.

The pediatric and neonatal critical care codes include those procedures listed for the critical care codes (99291, 99292). In addition, the following procedures are also included (and are not separately reported by professionals, but may be reported by facilities) in the pediatric and neonatal critical care service codes (99468-99472, 99475, 99476), and the intensive care services codes (99477- 99480):

Any services performed that are not included in these listings may be reported separately. For initiation of selective head or total body hypothermia in the critically ill neonate, report 99184. Facilities may report the included services separately.

Invasive or non-invasive electronic monitoring of vital signs

Vascular access procedures

> Peripheral vessel catheterization (36000)
> Other arterial catheters (36140, 36620)
> Umbilical venous catheters (36510)
> Central vessel catheterization (36555)
> Vascular access procedures (36400, 36405, 36406)
> Vascular punctures (36420, 36600)
> Umbilical arterial catheters (36660)

Airway and ventilation management

> Endotracheal intubation (31500)
> Ventilatory management (94002-94004)
> Bedside pulmonary function testing (94375)
> Surfactant administration (94610)
> Continuous positive airway pressure (CPAP) (94660)

Monitoring or interpretation of blood gases or oxygen saturation (94760-94762)

Car Seat Evaluation (94780-94781)

■ Separate Procedure ■ Unlisted Procedure ■ CCI Comp. Code ■ Non-specific Procedure **177**

Transfusion of blood components (36430, 36440)

Oral or nasogastric tube placement (43752)

Suprapubic bladder aspiration (51100)

Bladder catheterization (51701, 51702)

Lumbar puncture (62270)

Any services performed which are not listed above may be reported separately.

When a neonate or infant is not critically ill but requires intensive observation, frequent interventions, and other intensive care services, the Continuing Intensive Care Services codes (99477-99480) should be used to report these services.

To report critical care services provided in the outpatient setting (eg., emergency department or office) for neonates and pediatric patients of any age, see the Critical Care codes 99291, 99292. If the same individual provides critical care services for a neonatal or pediatric patient less than 6 years of age in both the outpatient and inpatient settings on the same day, report only the appropriate Neonatal or Pediatric Critical Care codes 99468-99476 for all critical care services provided on that day. Critical care services provided by a second individual of a different specialty not reporting a per-day neonatal or pediatric critical care code can be reported with 99291, 99292.

When critical care services are provided to neonates or pediatric patients less than 6 years of age at two separate institutions by an individual from a different group on the same date of service, the individual from the referring institution should report their critical care services with the critical care codes (99291, 99292) and the receiving institution should report the appropriate initial day of care code 99468, 99471, 99475 for the same date of service.

Critical care services to a pediatric patient six years of age or older are reported with the critical care codes 99291, 99292.

When the critically ill neonate or pediatric patient improves and is transferred to a lower level of care to another individual in another group within the same facility, the transferring individual does not report a per day critical care service. subsequent hospital care (99231-99233) or time-based critical care services (99291-99292) is reported, as appropriate based upon the condition of the neonate or child. The receiving individual reports subsequent intensive care (99478- 99480) or subsequent hospital care (99231-99233) services, as appropriate based upon the condition of the neonate or child.

When the neonate or infant becomes critically ill on a day when initial or subsequent intensive care services (99477-99480), hospital services (99221-99233), or normal newborn services (99460, 99461, 99462) have been performed by one individual and is transferred to a critical care level of care provided by a different individual in a different group, the transferring individual reports either the time-based critical care services performed (99291, 99292) for the time spent providing critical care to the patient, the intensive care service (99477-99480), hospital care services (99221-99233), or normal newborn service ((99460, 99461, 99462) performed, but only one service. The receiving individual reports initial or subsequent inpatient neonatal or pediatric critical care (99468-99476), as appropriate based upon the patient's age and whether this is the first or subsequent admission to the critical care unit for the hospital stay.

When a newborn becomes critically ill on the same day they have already received normal newborn care (99460, 99461, 99462), and the same individual or group assumes critical care, report initial critical care service (99468) with modifier 25 in addition to the normal newborn code.

When a neonate, infant, or child requires initial critical care services on the same day the patient already has received hospital care or intensive care services by the same individual or group, only the initial critical care service code (99468, 99471, 99475) is reported.

Time-based critical care services (99291, 99292) are not reportable by the same individual or different individual of the same specialty and same group, when neonatal or pediatric critical care services (9468-99476) may be reported for the same patient on the same day. Tim-based critical care services (99291, 99292) may be reported by an individual of a different specialty from either the same or different group on the same day that neonatal or pediatric critical care services are reported. Critical care interfacility transport face-to-face (99466, 99467) or supervisory (99485, 99486) services may be reported by the same or different individual of the same specialty and same group, when neonatal or pediatric critical care services (99468-99476) are reported for the same patient on the same day.

No individual may report remote real-time videoconferenced critical care (0188T, 0189T) when neonatal or pediatric intensive or critical care services (99468-99476) are reported.

● New Code   ▲ Revised Code   + Add-On Code   ⊘ Modifier -51 Exempt   ★ Telemedicine

99468 Initial inpatient neonatal critical care, per day, for the evaluation and management of a critically ill neonate, 28 days of age or younger

99469 Subsequent inpatient neonatal critical care, per day, for the evaluation and management of a critically ill neonate, 28 days of age or younger

99471 Initial inpatient pediatric critical care, per day, for the evaluation and management of a critically ill infant or young child, 29 days through 24 months of age

99472 Subsequent inpatient pediatric critical care, per day, for the evaluation and management of a critically ill infant or young child, 29 days through 24 months of age

99475 Initial inpatient pediatric critical care, per day, for the evaluation and management of a critically ill infant or young child, 2 through 5 years of age

99476 Subsequent inpatient pediatric critical care, per day, for the evaluation and management of a critically ill infant or young child, 2 through 5 years of age

INITIAL AND CONTINUING INTENSIVE CARE SERVICES

Code 99477 represents the initial day of inpatient care for the child who is not critically ill but requires intensive observation, frequent interventions, and other intensive care services. Codes 99478-99480 are used to report the subsequent day services of directing the continuing intensive care of the low birth weight (LBW 1500-2500 grams) present body weight infant, very low birth weight (VLBW less than 1500 grams) present body weight infant, or normal (2501-5000 grams) present body weight newborn who does not meet the definition of critically ill but continues to require intensive observation, frequent interventions, and other intensive care services. These services are for infants and neonates who are not critically ill but continue to require intensive cardiac and respiratory monitoring, continuous and/or frequent vital sign monitoring, heat maintenance, enteral and/or parenteral nutritional adjustments, laboratory and oxygen monitoring, and constant observation by the health care team under direct supervision of the physician or other qualified health care professional. Codes 99477-99480 may be reported by a single individual and only once per day, per patient in a given facility. If readmitted to the intensive care unit during the same hospital stay, report 99478-99480 for the first day of intensive care and for each successive day that the child requires intensive care services.

These codes include the same procedures that are outlined in the Neonatal and Pediatric Critical Care Services section and these services should not be separately reported.

The initial day neonatal intensive care code (99477) can be used in addition to 99464 or 99465 as appropriate, when the physician or other qualified health care professional is present for the delivery (99464) or resuscitation (99465) is required. In this situation, report 99477 with modifier 25. Other procedures performed as a necessary part of the resuscitation (eg, endotracheal intubation [31500]) are also reported separately when performed as part of the pre-admission delivery room care. In order to report these procedures separately, they must be performed asa necessary component of the resuscitation and not simply as a convenience before admission to the neonatal intensive care unit.

The same procedures are included as bundled services with the neonatal intensive care codes as those listed for the neonatal (99468, 99469) and pediatric (99471-99476) critical care codes.

When the neonate or infant improves after the initial day and no longer requires intensive care services and is transferred to a lower level of care, the transferring individual does not report a per day intensive care service. Subsequent hospital care (99231-99233) or subsequent normal newborn care (99460, 99462) is reported as appropriate based upon the condition of the neonate or infant. If the transfer to a lower level of care occurs on the same day as initial intensive care services were provided by the transferring individual, 99477 may be reported.

When the neonate or infant is transferred after the initial day within the same facility to the care of another individual in a different group, both individuals report subsequent hospital care (99231-99233) services. The receiving individual reports subsequent hospital care (99231-99233) or subsequent normal newborn care (99462).

When the neonate or infant becomes critically ill on a day when initial or subsequent intensive care services (99477-99480) have been reported by one individual and is transferred to a critical care level of care provided by a different individual from a different group, the transferring individual reports either the time-based critical care services performed (99291-99292) for the time spent providing critical care to the patient, or the initial or subsequent intensive care (99477-99480) services, but not both. The receiving individual reports initial or subsequent inpatient neonatal or pediatric critical care (99468-99476) based upon the patient's age and whether this is the first or subsequent admission to critical care for the same hospital stay.

When the neonate or infant becomes critically ill on a day when initial or subsequent intensive care services (99477-99480) have been performed by the same individual or group, report only initial or subsequent inpatient neonatal or pediatric critical care (99468-99476) based upon the patient's age and whether this is the first or subsequent admission to critical care for the same hospital stay.

For the subsequent care of the sick neonate younger than 28 days of age, but more than 5000 grams who does not require intensive or critical care services, use 99231-99233.

99477 Initial hospital care, per day, for the evaluation and management of the neonate, 28 days of age or less, who requires intensive observation, frequent interventions, and other intensive care services

(For the initiation of inpatient care of the normal newborn, report 99460)

(For the initiation of care of the critically ill neonate, use 99468)

(For initiation of inpatient hospital care of the ill neonate not requiring intensive observation, frequent interventions, and other intensive care services, see 99221-99223)

99478 Subsequent intensive care, per day, for the evaluation and management of the recovering very low birth weight infant (present body weight less than 1500 grams)

99479 Subsequent intensive care, per day, for the evaluation and management of the recovering low birth weight infant (present body weight of 1500-2500 grams)

99480 Subsequent intensive care, per day, for the evaluation and management of the recovering infant (present body weight of 2501-5000 grams)

99485 This code is out of order. See page 176.

99486 This code is out of order. See page 176.

COGNITIVE ASSESSMENT AND CARE PLAN SERVICES

Cognitive assessment and care plan services are provided when a comprehensive evaluation of a new or existing patient, who exhibits signs and/or symptoms of cognitive impairment, is required to establish or confirm a diagnosis, etiology and severity for the condition. This service includes a thorough evaluation of medical and psychosocial factors, potentially contributing to increased morbidity. Do not report cognitive assessment and care plan services if any of the required elements are not performed or are deemed unnecessary for the patient's condition. For these services, see the appropriate evaluation and management code. A single physician or other qualified health care professional should not report 99483 more than once every 180 days.

Services for cognitive assessment and care plan include a cognition-relevant history, as well as an assessment of factors that could be contributing to cognitive impairment, including, but not limited to, psychoactive medication, chronic pain syndromes, infection, depression and other brain disease (eg, tumor, stroke, normal pressure hydrocephalus). Medical decision making includes current and likely progression of the disease, assessing the need for referral for rehabilitative, social, legal, financial, or community-based services, meal, transportation, and other personal assistance services.

● **99483** Assessment of and care planning for a patient with cognitive impairment, requiring an independent historian, in the office or other outpatient, home or domiciliary or rest home, with all of the following required elements:

  ● Cognition-focused evaluation including a pertinent history and examination;

  ● Medical decision making of moderate or high complexity;

  ● Functional assessment (eg, basic and instrumental activities of daily living), including decision-making capacity;

  ● Use of standardized instruments for staging of dementia (eg, functional assessment staging test [FAST], clinical dementia rating [CDR]);

  ● Medication reconciliation and review for high-risk medications;

  ● Evaluation for neuropsychiatric and behavioral symptoms, including depression, including use of standardized screening instrument(s);

  ● Evaluation of safety (eg, home), including motor vehicle operation;

● New Code   ▲ Revised Code   ✛ Add-On Code   ⊘ Modifier -51 Exempt   ★ Telemedicine

- Identification of caregiver(s), caregiver knowledge, caregiver needs, social supports, and the willingness of caregiver to take on caregiving tasks;

- Development, updating or revision, or review of an Advance Care Plan;

- Creation of a written care plan, including initial plans to address any neuropsychiatric symptoms, neurocognitive symptoms, functional limitations, and referral to community resources as needed (eg, rehabilitation services, adult day programs, support groups) shared with the patient and/or caregiver with initial education and support.

Typically, 50 minutes are spent face-to-face with the patient and/or family or caregiver.

(Do not report 99483 in conjunction with E/M services [99201, 99202, 99203, 99204, 99205, 99211, 99212, 99213, 99214, 99215, 99241, 99242, 99243, 99244, 99245, 99324, 99325, 99326, 99327, 99328, 99334, 99335, 99336, 99337, 99341, 99342, 99343, 99344, 99345, 99347, 99348, 99349, 99350, 99366, 99367, 99368, 99487, 99489, 99490, 99495, 99496, 99497, 99498]; psychiatric diagnostic procedures [90785, 90791, 90792]; psychological testing [96103]; neuropsychological testing [96120]; brief emotional/behavioral assessment [96127]; medication therapy management services [99605, 99606, 99607])

99484 This code is out of order. See page 188.

CARE MANAGEMENT SERVICES

Care management services are management and support services provided by clinical staff, under the direction of a physician or other qualified health care professional, to a patient residing at home or in a domiciliary, rest home, or assisted living facility. Services may include establishing, implementing, revising, or monitoring the care plan, coordinating the care of other professionals and agencies, and educating the patient or caregiver about the patient's condition, care plan, and prognosis. The physician or other qualified health care professional provides or oversees the management and/or coordination of services, as needed, for all medical conditions, psychosocial needs, and activities of daily living.

A plan of care must be documented and shared with the patient and/or caregiver. A care plan is based on a physical, mental, cognitive, social, functional, and environmental assessment. It is a comprehensive plan of care for all health problems. It typically includes, but is not limited to, the following elements: problem list, expected outcome and prognosis, measurable treatment goals, symptom management, planned interventions, medication management, community/social services ordered, how the services of agencies and specialists unconnected to the practice will be directed/coordinated, identification of the individuals responsible for each intervention, requirement for periodic review, and when applicable, revision of the care plan.

Codes 99487, 99489, 99490 are reported only **once** per calendar month and may only be reported by the single physician or other qualified health care professional who assumes the care management role with a particular patient for the calendar month.

The face-to-face and non-face-to-face time spent by the clinical staff in communicating with the patient and/or family, caregivers, other professionals, and agencies; revising, documenting, and implementing the care plan; or teaching self-management is used in determining the care management clinical staff time for the month. Only the time of the clinical staff of the reporting professional is counted. Only count the time of one clinical staff member when two or more clinical staff members are meeting about the patient. **Note**: do not count any clinical staff time on a day when the physician or qualified health care professional reports an E/M service (office or other outpatient services 99201, 99202, 99203, 99204, 99205, 99211, 99212, 99213, 99214, 99215, domiciliary, rest home services 99324, 99325, 99326, 99327, 99328, 99334, 99335, 99336, 99337, home services 99341, 99342, 99343, 99344, 99345, 99347, 99348, 99349, 99350).

Care management activities performed by clinical staff typically include:

- communication and engagement with patient, family members, guardian or caretaker, surrogate decision makers, and/or other professionals regarding aspects of care;

- communication with home health agencies and other community services utilized by the patient;

- collection of health outcomes data and registry documentation;

- patient and/or family/caregiver education to support self management, independent living, and activities of daily living;

- assessment and support for treatment regimen adherence and medication management;

- identification of available community and health resources;

- facilitating access to care and services needed by the patient and/or family;

- management of care transitions not reported as part of transitional care management (99495, 99496);

- ongoing review of patient's status, including review of laboratory and other studies not reported as part of an E/M service, noted above;

- development, communication, and maintenance of a comprehensive care plan.

The care management office/practice must have the following capabilities:

- provide 24/7 access to physicians or other qualified health care professionals or clinical staff including providing patients/caregivers with a means to make contact with health care professionals in the practice to address urgent needs regardless of the time of day or day of week;

- provide continuity of care with a designated member of the care team with whom the patient is able to schedule successive routine appointments;

- provide timely access and management for follow-up after and emergency department visit or facility discharge;

- utilize an electronic health record system so that care providers have timely access to clinical information;

- use a standardized methodology to identify patients who require care management services;

- have an internal care management process/function whereby a patient identified as meeting the requirements for these services starts receiving them in a timely manner;

- use a form and format in the medical record that is standardized with in the practice;

- be able to engage and educate patients and caregivers as well as coordinate care among all service professionals, as appropriate for each patient.

E/M services may be reported separately by the same position or other qualified health care professional during the same calendar month. Care management services include care plan oversight services (99339, 99340, 99374–99380), prolonged services without direct patient contact (99358, 99359), home and outpatient INR monitoring (93792, 93793), medical team conferences (99366, 99367, 99368), education and training (98960, 98961, 98962, 99071, 99078), telephone services (99366, 99367, 99368, 99441, 99442, 99443), on-line medical evaluation (98969, 99444), preparation of special reports (99080), analysis of data (99090, 99091), transitional care management services (99495, 99496), medication therapy management services (99605, 99606, 99607) and, if performed, these services may not be reported separately during the month for which 99487, 99489, 99490 are reported. All other services may be reported. Do not report 99487, 99489, 99490 if reporting ESRD services (90951-90970) during the same month. If the care management services are performed within the postoperative period of a reported surgery, the same individual may not report 99487, 99489, 99490.

Care management may be reported in any calendar month during which the clinical staff time requirements are met. If care management resumes after discharge during a new month, start a new period or report transitional care management services (99495, 99496) as appropriate. If discharge occurs in the same month, continue the reporting period or report transitional care management services. Do not report 99487, 99489, 99490 for any post-discharge care management services for any days within 30 days of discharge, if reporting 99495, 99496.

For psychiatric collaborative care management services, see 99492, 99493, 99494.

CHRONIC CARE MANAGEMENT SERVICES

Chronic care management services are provided when medical and/or psychosocial needs of the patient require establishing, implementing, revising, or monitoring the care plan. Patients who receive chronic care management services have two or more chronic continuous or episodic health conditions that are expected to last at least 12 months, or until the death of the patient, and that place the patient at significant risk of death, acute exacerbation/decompensation, or functional decline. Code 99490 is reported when, during the calendar month, at least 20 minutes of clinical staff time is spent in care management activities.

99490   Chronic care management services, at least 20 minutes of clinical staff time directed by a physician or other qualified health care professional, per calendar month, with the following required elements:

- multiple (two or more) chronic conditions expected to last at least 12 months, or until the death of the patient;

- chronic conditions place the patient at significant risk of death, acute exacerbation/decompensation, or functional decline;

- comprehensive care plan established, implemented, revised, or monitored.

(Chronic care management services of less than 20 minutes duration, in a calendar month, or not reported separately)

COMPLEX CHRONIC CARE MANAGEMENT SERVICES

Complex chronic care management services are provided during a calendar month that includes criteria for chronic care management services as well as establishment or substantial revision of a comprehensive care plan; medical, functional, and/or psychosocial problems requiring medical decision making of moderate or high complexity; and clinical staff care management services for at least 60 minutes, under the direction of a physician or other qualified health care professional. Physicians or other qualified health care professionals may not report complex chronic care management services if the care plan is unchanged or requires minimal change (eg., only a medication is changed or an adjustment in a treatment modality is ordered). Medical decision making as defined in the evaluation and management (E/M) guidelines is determined by the problems addressed by the reporting individual during the month.

Patients who require complex chronic care management services may be identified by practice-specific or other published algorithms that recognize multiple illnesses, multiple medication use, inability to perform activities of daily living, requirement for caregiver, and/or repeat admissions or emergency department visits. Typical adult patients who receive complex chronic care management services are treaeted with three or more prescription medications and may be receiving other types of therapeutic interventions (eg., physical therapy, occupational therapy). Typical pediatric patients receive three or more therapeutic interventions (eg., medications, nutritional support, respiratory therapy). All patients have two or more chronic continuous or episodic health conditions that are expected to last at least 12 months, or until the death of the patient, and that place the patient at significant risk of death, acute exaggeration/decompensation, or functional decline. Typical patients have complex diseases and morbidities and, as a result, demonstrate one or more of the following:

- need for the coordination of a number of specialties and services;

- inability to perform activities of daily living and/or cognitive impairment resulting in poor adherence to the treatment plan without substantial assistance from caregiver;

- psychiatric and other medical comorbidities (eg., dementia and chronic obstructive pulmonary disease or substance abuse and diabetes) that complicate their care; and/or

- social support requirements or difficulty with access to care.

Total Duration of Staff Care Management Services	Complex Chronic Care Management
Less than 60minutes	Not reported separately
60 to 89 minutes (1 hr. - 1 hr. 29 min.)	99487
90 to 119 minutes (1 hr. 30 min. - 1 hr. 59 min.)	99487 AND 99489 x 1
120 minutes or more (2 hours or more)	99487 AND 99489 x 2 AND 99489 for each additional 30 minutes

99487 Complex chronic care management services, with the following required elements:

- multiple (two or more) chronic conditions expected to last at least 12 months, or until the death of the patient,

- chronic conditions place the patient at significant risk of death, acute exacerbation/decompensation, or functional decline,

- establishment or substantial revision of a comprehensive care plan,

- moderate or high complexity medical decision-making;

- 60 minutes of clinical staff time directed by a physician or other qualified health care professional, per calendar month.

(Complex chronic care management services of less than 60 minutes duration, in a calendar month, are not reported separately)

(**99488** deleted 2014 [2015 edition]. To report one or more face-to-face visits by the physician or other qualified health care professional that are performed in the same month as 99487, use the appropriate E/M code[s])

+ **99489** each additional 30 minutes of clinical staff time directed by a physician or other qualified health care professional, per calendar month (List separately in addition to code for primary procedure)

(Report 99489 in conjunction with 99487)

(Do not report 99489 for care management services of less than 30 minutes additional to the first 60 minutes of complex chronic care management services during a calendar month)

(Do not report 99487, 99489, 99490 during the same month with 90951-90970, 93792, 93793, 98960–98962, 98966–98969, 99071, 99078, 99080, 99090, 99091, 99339, 99340, 99358, 99359, 99366–99368, 99374–99380, 99441–99444, 99495, 99496, 99605–99607)

99490   This code is out of order. See page 182.

PSYCHIATRIC COLLABORATIVE CARE MANAGEMENT SERVICES

Psychiatric collaborative care services are provided under the direction of a treating physician or other qualified health care professional (see definitions below) during a calendar month. These services are provided when a patient has a diagnosed psychiatric disorder that requires a behavioral health care assessment; establishing, implementing, revising, or monitoring a care plan; and provision of brief interventions. These services are reported by the treating physician or other qualified health care professional and include the services of the treating physician or other qualified health care professional, the behavioral health care manager (see definition below), and the psychiatric consultant (see definition below), who has contracted directly with the treating physician or other qualified health care professional, to provide consultation.

Patients directed to the behavioral health care manager typically have newly diagnosed conditions, may need help in engaging in treatment, have not responded to standard care delivered in a nonpsychiatric setting, or require further assessment and engagement, prior to consideration of referral to a psychiatric care setting. The following definitions apply to this section:

Definitions

Episode of care patients are treated for an episode of care, which is defined as beginning when the patient is directed by the treating physician or other qualified health care professional to the behavioral health care manager and ending with:

- the attainment of targeted treatment goals, which typically results in the discontinuation of care management services and continuation of usual followup with the treating physician or other qualified healthcare professional; or

- failure to attain targeted treatment goals culminating in referral to a psychiatric care provider for ongoing treatment; or

- lack of continued engagement with no psychiatric collaborative care management services provided over a consecutive six month calendar period (break in episode)

A new episode of care starts after a break in episode of six calendar months or more.

Health care professionals refers to the treating physician or other qualified health care professional who directs the behavioral health care manager and continues to oversee the patient's care, including prescribing medications, providing treatments for medical conditions, and making referrals to specialty care when needed. Evaluation and management (E/M) and other services may be reported separately by the same physician or other qualified health care professional during the same calendar month.

Behavioral health care manager refers to clinical staff with a masters-/doctoral-level education or specialized training in behavioral health who provides care management services as well as an assessment of needs, including the administration of validated rating scales, the development of a care plan, provision of brief interventions, ongoing collaboration with the treating physician or other qualified health care professional, maintenance of a registry, all in consultation with a psychiatric consultant. Services are provided both face-toface and non-face-to-face and psychiatric consultation is provided minimally on a weekly basis, typically non-face-to-face.

The behavioral health care manager providing other services in the same calendar month, such as psychiatric evaluation (90791, 90792), psychotherapy (90832, 90833, 90834, 90836, 90837, 90838), psychotherapy for crisis (90839, 90840), family psychotherapy (90846, 90847), multiple family group psychotherapy (90849), group psychotherapy (90853), smoking and tobacco use cessation counseling (99406, 99407), and alcohol and/or substance abuse structured screening and brief intervention services (99408, 99409), may report these services separately. Activities for services reported separately are not included in the time applied to 99492, 99493, 99494.

Psychiatric consultant refers to a medical professional, who is trained in psychiatry or behavioral health, and qualified to prescribe the full range of medications. The psychiatric consultant advises and makes recommendations, as needed, for psychiatric and other medical care, including psychiatric and other medical differential diagnosis, treatment strategies regarding appropriate therapies, medication management, medical management of complications associated with treatment of psychiatric disorders, and referral for specialty services, which are typically communicated to the treating physician or other qualified health care professional through the behavioral health care manager.

The psychiatric consultant typically does not see the patient or prescribe medications, except in rare circumstances. The psychiatric consultant may provide services in the calendar month described by other codes, such as evaluation and management

---

(E/M) services and psychiatric evaluation (90791, 90792). These services may be reported separately by the psychiatric consultant. Activities for services reported separately are not included in the services reported using 99492, 99493, 99494. Do not report 99492 and 99493 in the same calendar month.

Type of Service	Total Duration of Collaborative Care Management Over Calendar Month	Code(s)
Initial - 70 minutes	Less than 36 minutes	Not reported separately
	36-85 minutes (36 minutes - 1 hr. 25 minutes)	99492
Initial plus each additional increment up to 30 minutes	86-116 minutes (1 hr. 26 minutes - 1 hr. 56 minutes)	99492 once AND 99494 once
Subsequent - 60 minutes	Less than 31 minutes	Not reported separately
	31-75 minutes (31 minutes - 1 hr. 15 minustes)	99493
Subsequent plus each additional increment up to 30 minutes	76-105 minutes (1 hr. 16 minutes - 1 hr. 45 minutes)	99493 once AND 99494 once

● **99492** Initial psychiatric collaborative care management, first 70 minutes in the first calendar month of behavioral health care manager activities, in consultation with a psychiatric consultant, and directed by the treating physician or other qualified health care professional, with the following required elements:

- outreach to and engagement in treatment of a patient directed by the treating physician or other qualified health care professional;

- initial assessment of the patient, including administration of validated rating scales, with the development of an individualized treatment plan;

- review by the psychiatric consultant with modifications of the plan if recommended;

- entering patient in a registry and tracking patient follow-up and progress using the registry, with appropriate documentation, and participation in weekly caseload consultation with the psychiatric consultant; and

- provision of brief interventions using evidence-based techniques such as behavioral activation, motivational interviewing, and other focused treatment strategies.

● **99493** Subsequent psychiatric collaborative care management, first 60 minutes in a subsequent month of behavioral health care manager activities, in consultation with a psychiatric consultant, and directed by the treating physician or other qualified health care professional, with the following required elements:

- tracking patient follow-up and progress using the registry, with appropriate documentation;

- participation in weekly caseload consultation with the psychiatric consultant;

- ongoing collaboration with and coordination of the patient's mental health care with the treating physician or other qualified health care professional and any other treating mental health providers;

- additional review of progress and recommendations for changes in treatment, as indicated, including medications, based on recommendations provided by the psychiatric consultant;

- provision of brief interventions using evidence-based techniques such as behavioral activation, motivational interviewing, and other focused treatment strategies;

- monitoring of patient outcomes using validated rating scales; and

- relapse prevention planning with patients as they achieve remission of symptoms and/or other treatment goals and are prepared for discharge from active treatment.

●+**99494** Initial or subsequent psychiatric collaborative care management, each additional 30 minutes in a calendar month of behavioral health care manager activities, in consultation with a psychiatric consultant, and directed by the treating physician or other qualified health care professional (List separately in addition to code for primary procedure)

(Use 99494 in conjunction with 99492, 99493)

TRANSITIONAL CARE MANAGEMENT SERVICES

Codes 99495 and 99496 are used to report transitional care management services (TCM). These services are for a new or established patient whose medical and/or physchosocial problems require moderate or high complexity medical decision making during transitions in care from an inpatient hospital setting (including acute hospital, rehabilitation hospital, long-tem acute care hospital), partial hospital, observation status in a hospital, or skilled nursing facility/nursing facility, to the patient's community setting (home, domiciliary, rest home or assisted living). TCM commences upon the date of discharge and continues for the next 29 days.

TCM is comprised of one face-to-face visit within the specified time frames, in combination with non-face-to-face services that may be performed by the physician or other qualified health care professional and/or licensed clinical staff under his/her direction.

Non-face-to-face services provided by clinical staff, under the direction of the physician or other qualified health care professional, may include:

- communication (with patient, family members, guardian or caretaker, surrogate decision makers, and/or other professionals) regarding aspects of care;

- communication with home health agencies and other community services utilized by the patient;

- patient and/or family/caretaker education to support self-management, independent living, and activities of daily living;

- assessment and support for treatment regimen adherence and medication management;

- identification of available community and health resources;

- facilitating access to care and services needed by the patient and/or family.

Non-face-to-face services provided by the physician or other qualified health care professional may include:

- obtaining and reviewing the discharge information (eg, discharge summary, as available, or continuity of care documents);

- reviewing need for or follow-up on pending diagnostic tests and treatments;

- interaction with other qualified health care professionals who will assume or reassume care of the patient's system-specific problems;

- education of patient, family, guardian, and/or caregiver;

- establishment or reestablishment of referrals and arranging for needed community resources;

- assistance in scheduling any required follow-up with community providers and services.

TCM requires a face-to-face visit, initial patient contact, and medication reconciliation within specified time frames. The first face-to-face visit is part of the TCM service and not reported separately. Additional E/M services provided on subsequent dates after the first face-to-face visit may be reported separately. TCM requires an interactive contact with the patient or caregiver, as appropriate, within two business days of discharge. The contact may be direct (face-to-face), by telephone, or by electronic means. Medication reconciliation and management must occur no later than the date of the face-to-face visit.

These services address any needed coordination of care performed by multiple disciplines and community service agencies. The reporting individual provides or oversees the management and/or coordination of services, as needed, for all medical conditions, psychosocial needs, and activities of daily living support by providing first contact and continuous access.

Medical decision making and the date of the first face-to-face visit are used to select and report the appropriate TCM code. For 99496, the face-to-face visit must occur within 7 calendar days of the date of discharge, and medical decision making must be of high complexity. For 99495, the face-to-face visit must occur within 14 calendar days of the date of discharge, and medical decision making must be of at least moderate complexity.

Type of Medical Decision Making	Face-to-face visit within 7 days	Face-to-face visit within 8 to 14 days
Moderate complexity	99495	99495
High complexity	99496	99495

Medical decision making is defined by the E/M Services Guidelines. The medical decision making over the service period reported is used to define the medical decision making of TCM. Documentation includes the timing of the initial post-discharge communication with the patient or caregivers, date of the face-to-face visit, and the complexity of the medical decision making.

Only one individual may report these services and only once per patient within 30 days of discharge. Another TCM may not be reported by the same individual or group for any subsequent discharge(s) within the 30 days. The same individual may report hospital or observation discharge services and TCM. However, the discharge service may not constitute the required face-to-face visit. The same individual should not report TCM services provided in the postoperative period of a service that the individual reported..

A physician or other qualified health care professional who reports codes 99495, 99496 may not report care plan oversight services (99339, 99340, 99374-99380), prolonged services without direct patient contact (99358, 99359), home and outpatient INR monitoring (93792, 93793), medical team conferences (99366-99368), education and training (98960-98962, 99071, 99078), telephone services (98966-98968, 99441-99443), end stage renal disease services (90951-90970), online medical evaluation services 98969, 99444), preparation of special reports (99080), analysis of data (99090, 99091), complex chronic care coordination services (99487-99489), or medication therapy management services (99605-99607) during the time period covered by the transitional care management services codes.

★ **99495** Transitional care management services with the following required elements:

- Communication (direct contact, telephone, electronic) with the patient and/or caregiver within 2 business days of discharge
- Medical decision making of at least moderate complexity during the service period
- Face-to-face visit withing 14 calendar days of discharge

★ **99496** Transitional care management services with the following required elements:

- Communication (direct contact, telephone, electronic) with the patient and/or caregiver within 2 business days of discharge
- Medical decision making of high complexity during the service period
- Face-to-face visit within 7 calendar days of discharge

(Do not report 99495, 99496 in conjunction with 93792, 93793)

(Do note report 90951-90970, 98960-98962, 98966-98969, 99071, 99078, 99080, 99090, 99091, 99339, 99340, 99358, 99359, 99366-99368, 99374-99380, 99441-99444, 99487-99489, 99605-99607 when performed during the service time of codes 99495 or 99496)

ADVANCE CARE PLANNING

Codes 99497, 99498 are used to report the face-to-face service between a physician or other qualified health care professional and a patient, family member, or surrogate in counseling and discussing advance directives, with or without completing relevant legal forms. An advance directive is a document appointing an agent and/or recording the wishes of a patient pertaining to his/her medical treatment at a future time should he/she lack decisional capacity at that time. Examples of written advanced directives include, but are not limited to, Health Care Proxy, Durable Power of Attorney for Health Care, Living Will, and Medical Orders for Life Sustaining Treatment (MOLST).

When using codes 99497, 99498, no active management of the problems is undertaken during the time period reported.

Codes 99497, 99498 maybe reported separately if the services are performed on the same day as another evaluation and management service (99201–99215, 99217, 99218, 99219, 99220, 99221, 99222, 99223, 99224, 99225, 99226, 99231, 99232, 99233, 99234, 99235, 99236, 99238, 99239, 99241, 99242, 99243, 99244, 99245, 99251, 99252, 99253, 99254, 99255, 99281, 99282, 99283, 99284, 99285, 99304, 99305, 99306, 99307, 99308, 99309, 99310, 99315, 99316, 99318, 99324, 99325, 99326, 99327, 99328, 99334, 99335, 99336, 99337, 99341, 99342, 99343, 99344, 99345, 99347, 99348, 99349, 99350, 99381–99397, 99495, 99496).

99497 Advance care planning including the explanation and discussion of advance directives such a standard forms (with completion of such forms, when performed), by the physician or other qualified health care professional; first 30 minutes, face-to-face with the patient, family members, and/or surrogate.

+ 99498 each additional 30 minutes (List separately in addition to code for primary procedure)

(Use 99498 in conjunction with 99497)

(Do not report 99497 and 99498 on the same date of service as 99291, 99292, 99468, 99469, 99471, 99472, 99475, 99476, 99477, 99478, 99479, 99480, 99483.)

| ▮ Separate Procedure | ▮ Unlisted Procedure | ▮ CCI Comp. Code | ▮ Non-specific Procedure | **187** |

GENERAL BEHAVIORAL HEALTH INTEGRATION CARE MANAGEMENT

General behavioral health integration care management services (99484) are reported by the supervising physician or other qualified health care professional. The services are performed by clinical staff for a patient with a behavioral health (including substance use) condition that requires care management services (face-to-face or non-face-to-face) of 20 or more minutes in a calendar month. A treatment plan as well as the specified elements of the service description is required. The assessment and treatment plan is not required to be comprehensive and the office/practice is not required to have all the functions of chronic care management (99487, 99489, 99490). Code 99484 may be used in any outpatient setting, as long as the reporting professional has an ongoing relationship with the patient and clinical staff and as long as the clinical staff is available for face-to-face services with the patient.

The reporting professional must be able to perform the evaluation and management (E/M) services of an initiating visit. General behavioral integration care management (99484) and chronic care management services may be reported by the same professional in the same month, as long as distinct care management services are performed. Behavioral health integration care management (99484) and psychiatric collaborative care management (99492, 99493, 99494) may not be reported by the same professional in the same month. Behavioral health care integration clinical staff are not required to have qualifications that would permit them to separately report services (eg, psychotherapy), but, if qualified and they perform such services, they may report such services separately, as long as the time of the service is not used in reporting 99484.

- **99484** Care management services for behavioral health conditions, at least 20 minutes of clinical staff time, directed by a physician or other qualified health care professional, per calendar month, with the following required elements:

    - initial assessment or follow-up monitoring, including the use of applicable validated rating scales;

    - behavioral health care planning in relation to behavioral/psychiatric health problems, including revision for patients who are not progressing or whose status changes;

    - facilitating and coordinating treatment such as psychotherapy, pharmacotherapy, counseling and/or psychiatric consultation; and

    - continuity of care with a designated member of the care team.

    (Do not report 99484 in conjunction with 99492, 99493, 99494 in the same calendar month)

    (E/M services, including care management services [99487, 99489, 99490, 99495, 99496], and psychiatric services [90785-90899] may be reported separately by the same physician or other qualified health care professional on the same day or during the same calendar month, but activities used to meet criteria for another reported service do not count toward meeting criteria for 99484)

OTHER EVALUATION AND MANAGEMENT SERVICES

 Unlisted evaluation and management service

● New Code ▲ Revised Code ✚ Add-On Code ⊘ Modifier -51 Exempt ★ Telemedicine

ANESTHESIA OVERVIEW

The second section of the CPT coding system is the anesthesia section, which includes service codes for the delivery of anesthesia. Within each subsection, the CPT codes are arranged by anatomical site.

The Anesthesiologist provides pain relief and maintenance, or restoration, of a stable condition during and immediately following an operation, an obstetric or diagnostic procedure. The Anesthesiologist assesses the risk of the patient undergoing surgery and optimizes the patient's condition prior to, during, and after surgery.

Reporting of anesthesia services is dependent on the third party payer involved. Anesthesia services covered by Medicare are coded using codes from the ANESTHESIA section of the CPT coding system. For most other third party payers, anesthesia services are coded using codes from the SURGERY section of the CPT coding system to describe the major surgical procedure.

Anesthesia services may be coded by anesthesiologists or anesthetists working under the supervision of the anesthesiologist. Anesthesia services include pre- and post-op visits, anesthesia delivery, giving fluids and/or blood needed during a procedure, and monitoring. Anesthesia delivery includes general, regional, supplementing local anesthesia, and other supportive services.

To report moderate (conscious) sedation provided by a physician also performing the service for which conscious sedation is being provided, see codes 99151, 99152, 99153.

When a second physician other than the health care professional performing the diagnostic or therapeutic services provides moderate (conscious) sedation in the facility setting (eg, hospital, outpatient hospital/ ambulatory surgery center, skilled nursing facility), the second physician reports the associated moderate sedation procedure/service 99155, 99156, 99157; when these services are performed by the second physician in the nonfacility setting (eg, physician office, freestanding imaging center), codes 99155, 99156, 99157 would not be reported. Moderate sedation does not include minimal sedation (anxiolysis), deep sedation, or monitored anesthesia care (00100-01999).

KEY POINTS ABOUT ANESTHESIA CODING

1. Time recording for anesthesia services starts with patient preparation for anesthesia induction and ends when the anesthesiologist or anesthetist has completed his/her services and transfers responsibility for postoperative supervision.

2. Consultations and/or other evaluation and management services which are not included in the administration or supervising the administration of anesthesia, regardless of location provided, are reporting using CPT codes from the evaluation and management section of the CPT book.

3. Any supplies and/or materials provided by the anesthesiologist or anesthetist which are not considered to be included in the standard service may be coded separately.

4. Multiple procedures provided on the same date of service should be coded separately.

5. Any service which may be considered rare, unusual, variable or not defined should be supported with a special report which clearly defines the need for the unusual service. These services are generally coded with an unlisted CPT code or by adding modifier -22 to the CPT code which defines the procedure.

ANESTHESIA SERVICE MODIFIERS

A physical status modifier must be added to all CPT codes when reporting anesthesia services. The physical status modifier defines the physical condition of the patient and ranges from a normal health patient to a declared brain-dead patient whose organs are being harvested for a transplant.

PHYSICAL STATUS MODIFIERS

-P1   A normal healthy patient.

-P2   A patient with a mild systemic disease.

-P3   A patient with severe systemic disease.

-P4   A patient with severe systemic disease that is a constant threat to life.

-P5   A moribund patient who is not expected to survive without the operation.

-P6   A declared brain-dead patient whose organs are being removed for donor purposes.

OTHER ANESTHESIA SERVICE MODIFIERS

Under certain circumstances, medical services and procedures may need to be further modified. Other CPT coding system modifiers commonly used with ANESTHESIA services include:

-22   Unusual services

-23   Anesthesia

-32   Mandated services

-51   Multiple procedures

QUALIFYING CIRCUMSTANCES FOR ANESTHESIA

In the case of difficult and/or extraordinary circumstances such as extreme youth or age, extraordinary condition of the patient, and/or unusual risk factors it may be appropriate to report one or more of the following qualifying circumstances in addition to the anesthesia services.

+ 99100   Anesthesia for patient of extreme age, younger than one year and older 70 (List separately in addition to code for primary anesthesia procedure)

            (For procedure performed on infants younger than 1 year of age at time of surgery, see 00326, 00561, 00834, 00836)

+ 99116   Anesthesia complicated by utilization of total body hypothermia (List separately in addition to code for primary anesthesia procedure)

+ 99135   Anesthesia complicated by utilization of controlled hypotension (List separately in addition to code for primary anesthesia procedure)

+ 99140   Anesthesia complicated by emergency conditions (specify) (List separately in addition to code for primary anesthesia procedure)

            (An emergency is defined as existing when delay in treatment of the patient would lead to a significant increase in the threat to life or body part.)

ANESTHESIA CODES

HEAD

00100	Anesthesia for procedures on salivary glands, including biopsy
00102	Anesthesia for procedures on plastic repair of cleft lip
00103	Anesthesia for reconstructive procedures of eyelid (eg, blepharoplasty, ptosis surgery)
00104	Anesthesia for electroconvulsive therapy
00120	Anesthesia for procedures on external, middle, and inner ear including biopsy; not otherwise specified
00124	otoscopy
00126	tympanotomy
00140	Anesthesia for procedures on eye; not otherwise specified
00142	lens surgery
00144	corneal transplant
00145	vitreoretinal surgery
00147	iridectomy
00148	ophthalmoscopy
00160	Anesthesia for procedures on nose and accessory sinuses; not otherwise specified
00162	radical surgery
00164	biopsy, soft tissue
00170	Anesthesia for intraoral procedures, including biopsy; not otherwise specified
00172	repair of cleft palate
00174	excision of retropharyngeal tumor
00176	radical surgery
00190	Anesthesia for procedures on facial bones or skull; not otherwise specified
00192	radical surgery (including prognathism)
00210	Anesthesia for intracranial procedures; not otherwise specified
00211	craniotomy or craniectomy for evacuation of hematoma
00212	subdural taps
00214	burr holes, including ventriculography
00215	cranioplasty or elevation of depressed skull fracture, extradural (simple or compound)

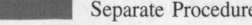

Separate Procedure	Unlisted Procedure	CCI Comp. Code	Non-specific Procedure

00216   vascular procedures

00218   procedures in sitting position

00220   cerebrospinal fluid shunting procedures

00222   electrocoagulation of intracranial nerve

NECK

00300   Anesthesia for all procedures on the integumentary system, muscles and nerves of head, neck, and posterior trunk, not otherwise specified

00320   Anesthesia for all procedures on esophagus, thyroid, larynx, trachea and lymphatic system of neck; not otherwise specified, age 1 year or older

00322   needle biopsy of thyroid

(For procedures on cervical spine and cord, see 00600, 00604, 00670)

00326   Anesthesia for all procedures on the larynx and trachea in children less than 1 year of age

(Do not report 00326 in conjunction with code 99100)

00350   Anesthesia for procedures on major vessels of neck; not otherwise specified

00352   simple ligation

(For arteriography, use 01916)

THORAX (CHEST WALL AND SHOULDER GIRDLE)

00400   Anesthesia for procedures on the integumentary system on the extremities, anterior trunk and perineum; not otherwise specified

00402   reconstructive procedures on breast (eg, reduction or augmentation mammoplasty, muscle flaps)

00404   radical or modified radical procedures on breast

00406   radical or modified radical procedures on breast with internal mammary node dissection

00410   electrical conversion of arrhythmias

00450   Anesthesia for procedures on clavicle and scapula; not otherwise specified

(00452   deleted 2014 [2015 edition])

00454   biopsy of clavicle

00470   Anesthesia for partial rib resection; not otherwise specified

00472   thoracoplasty (any type)

00474   radical procedures (eg, pectus excavatum)

INTRATHORACIC

00500   Anesthesia for all procedures on esophagus

  ● New Code   ▲ Revised Code   + Add-On Code   ⊘ Modifier -51 Exempt   ★ Telemedicine

00520   Anesthesia for closed chest procedures; (including bronchoscopy) not otherwise specified

00522   needle biopsy of pleura

00524   pneumocentesis

00528   mediastinoscopy and diagnostic thoracoscopy not utilizing 1 lung ventilation

(For tracheobronchial reconstruction, use 00539)

00529   mediastinoscopy and diagnostic thoracoscopy utilizing 1 lung ventilation

00530   Anesthesia for permanent transvenous pacemaker insertion

00532   Anesthesia for access to central venous circulation

00534   Anesthesia for transvenous insertion or replacement of pacing cardioverter/defibrillator

(For transthoracic approach, use 00560)

00537   Anesthesia for cardiac electrophysiologic procedures including radiofrequency ablation

00539   Anesthesia for tracheobronchial reconstruction

00540   Anesthesia for thoracotomy procedures involving lungs, pleura, diaphragm, and mediastinum (including surgical thoracoscopy); not otherwise specified

00541   utilizing 1 lung ventilation

(For thoracic spine and cord anesthesia procedures via an anterior transthoracic approach, see 00625-00626)

00542   decortication

00546   pulmonary resection with thoracoplasty

00548   intrathoracic procedures on the trachea and bronchi

00550   Anesthesia for sternal debridement

00560   Anesthesia for procedures on heart, pericardial sac, and great vessels of chest; without pump oxygenator

00561   with pump oxygenator, younger than one year of age

(Do not report 00561 in conjunction with 99100, 99116, and 99135)

00562   with pump oxygenator, age 1 year or older, for all non-coronary bypass procedures (eg. valve procedures) or for re-operation for coronary bypass more than 1 month after original operation)

00563   with pump oxygenator with hypothermic circulatory arrest

00566   Anesthesia for direct coronary artery bypass grafting; without pump oxygenator

00567   with pump oxygenator

00580   Anesthesia for heart transplant or heart/lung transplant

SPINE AND SPINAL CORD

00600   Anesthesia for procedures on cervical spine and cord; not otherwise specified

---

(For percutaneous image-guided spine and spinal cord anesthesia procedures, see 01935, 01936)

00604   procedures with patient in the sitting position

00620   Anesthesia for procedures on thoracic spine and cord; not otherwise specified

(**00622**   deleted 2014 [2015 edition])

00625   Anesthesia for procedures on the thoracic spine and cord, via an anterior transthoracic approach; not utilizing 1 lung ventilation

00626   utilizing 1 lung ventilation

(For anesthesia for thoractomy procedures other than spinal, see 00540-00541)

00630   Anesthesia for procedures in lumbar region; not otherwise specified

00632   lumbar sympathectomy

(**00634**   deleted 2014 [2015 edition])

00635   diagnostic or therapeutic lumbar puncture

00640   Anesthesia for manipulation of the spine or for closed procedures on the cervical, thoracic or lumbar spine

00670   Anesthesia for extensive spine and spinal cord procedures (eg, spinal instrumentation or vascular procedures)

UPPER ABDOMEN

00700   Anesthesia for procedures on upper anterior abdominal wall; not otherwise specified

00702   percutaneous liver biopsy

00730   Anesthesia for procedures on upper posterior abdominal wall

● **00731**   Anesthesia for upper gastrointestinal endoscopic procedures, endoscope introduced proximal to duodenum; not otherwise specified

● **00732**   endoscopic retrograde cholangiopancreatography (ERCP)

(For combined upper and lower gastrointestinal endoscopic procedures, use 00813)

(**00740**   deleted 2017 [2018 edition]. To report, see 00731, 00732.)

00750   Anesthesia for hernia repairs in upper abdomen; not otherwise specified

00752   lumbar and ventral (incisional) hernias and/or wound dehiscence

00754   omphalocele

00756   transabdominal repair of diaphragmatic hernia

00770   Anesthesia for all procedures on major abdominal blood vessels

00790   Anesthesia for intraperitoneal procedures in upper abdomen including laparoscopy; not otherwise specified

00792   partial hepatectomy or management of liver hemorrhage (excluding liver biopsy)

00794   pancreatectomy, partial or total (eg, Whipple procedure)

● New Code   ▲ Revised Code   + Add-On Code   ⊘ Modifier -51 Exempt   ★ Telemedicine

00796   liver transplant (recipient)

(For harvesting of liver, use 01990)

00797   gastric restrictive procedure for morbid obesity

LOWER ABDOMEN

00800   Anesthesia for procedures on lower anterior abdominal wall; not otherwise specified

00802   panniculectomy

(**00810**   deleted 2017 [2018 edition]. To report, see 00811, 00812, 00813.)

● **00811**   Anesthesia for lower intestinal endoscopic procedures, endoscope introduced distal to duodenum; not otherwise specified

● **00812**   screening colonoscopy

(Report 00812 to describe anesthesia for any screening colonoscopy regardless of ultimate findings)

● **00813**   Anesthesia for combined upper and lower gastrointestinal endoscopic procedures, endoscope introduced both proximal to and distal to the duodenum

00820   Anesthesia for procedures on lower posterior abdominal wall

00830   Anesthesia for hernia repairs in lower abdomen; not otherwise specified

00832   ventral and incisional hernias

(For hernia repairs in the infant 1 year of age or younger, see 00834, 00836)

00834   Anesthesia for hernia repairs in the lower abdomen not otherwise specified, under 1 year of age

(Do not report 00834 in conjunction with code 99100)

00836   Anesthesia for hernia repairs in the lower abdomen not otherwise specified, infants less than 37 weeks gestational age at birth and less than 50 weeks gestational age at time of surgery

(Do not report 00836 in conjunction with code 99100)

00840   Anesthesia for intraperitoneal procedures in lower abdomen including laparoscopy; not otherwise specified

00842   amniocentesis

00844   abdominoperineal resection

00846   radical hysterectomy

00848   pelvic exenteration

00851   tubal ligation/transection

00860   Anesthesia for extraperitoneal procedures in lower abdomen, including urinary tract; not otherwise specified

00862   renal procedures, including upper 1/3 of ureter, or donor nephrectomy

00864   total cystectomy

00865   radical prostatectomy (suprapubic, retropubic)

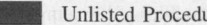

■ Separate Procedure   ■ Unlisted Procedure   ■ CCI Comp. Code   ■ Non-specific Procedure   **195**

| 00866 | adrenalectomy |

| 00868 | renal transplant (recipient) |

(For donor nephrectomy, use 00862)

(For harvesting kidney from brain-dead patient, use 01990)

| 00870 | cystolithotomy |

| 00872 | Anesthesia for lithotripsy, extracorporeal shock wave; with water bath |

| 00873 | without water bath |

| 00880 | Anesthesia for procedures on major lower abdominal vessels; not otherwise specified |

| 00882 | inferior vena cava ligation |

PERINEUM

(For perineal procedures on the integumentary system, muscles and nerves, see 00300, 00400)

| 00902 | Anesthesia for; anorectal procedure |

| 00904 | radical perineal procedure |

| 00906 | vulvectomy |

| 00908 | perineal prostatectomy |

| 00910 | Anesthesia for transurethral procedures (including urethrocystoscopy); not otherwise specified |

| 00912 | transurethral resection of bladder tumor(s) |

| 00914 | transurethral resection of prostate |

| 00916 | post-transurethral resection bleeding |

| 00918 | with fragmentation, manipulation and/or removal of ureteral calculus |

| 00920 | Anesthesia for procedures on male genitalia (including open urethral procedures); not otherwise specified |

| 00921 | vasectomy, unilateral or bilateral |

| 00922 | seminal vesicles |

| 00924 | undescended testis, unilateral or bilateral |

| 00926 | radical orchiectomy, inguinal |

| 00928 | radical orchiectomy, abdominal |

| 00930 | orchiopexy, unilateral or bilateral |

| 00932 | complete amputation of penis |

| 00934 | radical amputation of penis with bilateral inguinal lymphadenectomy |

| 00936 | radical amputation of penis with bilateral inguinal and iliac lymphadenectomy |

● New Code   ▲ Revised Code   ✛ Add-On Code   ⊘ Modifier -51 Exempt   ★ Telemedicine

00938	insertion of penile prosthesis (perineal approach)
00940	Anesthesia for vaginal procedures (including biopsy of labia, vagina, cervix or endometrium); not otherwise specified
00942	colpotomy, vaginectomy, colporrhaphy and open urethral procedures
00944	vaginal hysterectomy
00948	cervical cerclage
00950	culdoscopy
00952	hysteroscopy and/or hysterosalpingography

PELVIS (EXCEPT HIP)

01112	Anesthesia for bone marrow aspiration and/or biopsy, anterior or posterior iliac crest
01120	Anesthesia for procedures on bony pelvis
01130	Anesthesia for body cast application or revision
01140	Anesthesia for interpelviabdominal (hindquarter) amputation
01150	Anesthesia for radical procedures for tumor of pelvis, except hindquarter amputation
01160	Anesthesia for closed procedures involving symphysis pubis or sacroiliac joint
01170	Anesthesia for open procedures involving symphysis pubis or sacroiliac joint
01173	Anesthesia for open repair of fracture disruption of pelvis or column fracture involving acetabulum
(01180	deleted 2017 [2018 edition])
(01190	deleted 2017 [2018 edition])

UPPER LEG (EXCEPT KNEE)

01200	Anesthesia for all closed procedures involving hip joint
01202	Anesthesia for arthroscopic procedures of hip joint
01210	Anesthesia for open procedures involving hip joint; not otherwise specified
01212	hip disarticulation
01214	total hip arthroplasty
01215	revision of total hip arthroplasty
01220	Anesthesia for all closed procedures involving upper 2/3 of femur
01230	Anesthesia for open procedures involving upper 2/3 of femur; not otherwise specified
01232	amputation
01234	radical resection

| Separate Procedure | Unlisted Procedure | CCI Comp. Code | Non-specific Procedure | 197 |

01250	Anesthesia for all procedures on nerves, muscles, tendons, fascia, and bursae of upper leg
01260	Anesthesia for all procedures involving veins of upper leg, including exploration
01270	Anesthesia for procedures involving arteries of upper leg, including bypass graft; not otherwise specified
01272	femoral artery ligation
01274	femoral artery embolectomy

KNEE AND POPLITEAL AREA

01320	Anesthesia for all procedures on nerves, muscles, tendons, fascia, and bursae of knee and/or popliteal area
01340	Anesthesia for all closed procedures on lower 1/3 of femur
01360	Anesthesia for all open procedures on lower 1/3 of femur
01380	Anesthesia for all closed procedures on knee joint
01382	Anesthesia for diagnostic arthroscopic procedures of knee joint
01390	Anesthesia for all closed procedures on upper ends of tibia, fibula, and/or patella
01392	Anesthesia for all open procedures on upper ends of tibia, fibula, and/or patella
01400	Anesthesia for open or surgical arthroscopic procedures on knee joint; not otherwise specified
01402	total knee arthroplasty
01404	disarticulation at knee
01420	Anesthesia for all cast applications, removal, or repair involving knee joint
01430	Anesthesia for procedures on veins of knee and popliteal area; not otherwise specified
01432	arteriovenous fistula
01440	Anesthesia for procedures on arteries of knee and popliteal area; not otherwise specified
01442	popliteal thromboendarterectomy, with or without patch graft
01444	popliteal excision and graft or repair for occlusion or aneurysm

LOWER LEG (BELOW KNEE, INCLUDES ANKLE AND FOOT)

01462	Anesthesia for all closed procedures on lower leg, ankle, and foot
01464	Anesthesia for arthroscopic procedures of ankle and/or foot
01470	Anesthesia for procedures on nerves, muscles, tendons, and fascia of lower leg, ankle, and foot; not otherwise specified
01472	repair of ruptured Achilles tendon, with or without graft
01474	gastrocnemius recession (eg, Strayer procedure)
01480	Anesthesia for open procedures on bones of lower leg, ankle, and foot; not otherwise specified

---

198   ● New Code   ▲ Revised Code   + Add-On Code   ⊘ Modifier -51 Exempt   ★ Telemedicine

01482   radical resection (including below knee amputation)

01484   osteotomy or osteoplasty of tibia and/or fibula

01486   total ankle replacement

01490   Anesthesia for lower leg cast application, removal, or repair

01500   Anesthesia for procedures on arteries of lower leg, including bypass graft; not otherwise specified

01502   embolectomy, direct or with catheter

01520   Anesthesia for procedures on veins of lower leg; not otherwise specified

01522   venous thrombectomy, direct or with catheter

SHOULDER AND AXILLA

Includes humeral head and neck, sternoclavicular joint, acromioclavicular joint, and shoulder joint

01610   Anesthesia for all procedures on nerves, muscles, tendons, fascia, and bursae of shoulder and axilla

01620   Anesthesia for all closed procedures on humeral head and neck, sternoclavicular joint, acromioclavicular joint, and shoulder joint

01622   Anesthesia for diagnostic arthroscopic procedures of shoulder joint

01630   Anesthesia for open or surgical arthroscopic procedures on humeral head and neck, sternoclavicular joint, acromioclavicular joint, and shoulder joint; not otherwise specified

01634   shoulder disarticulation

01636   interthoracoscapular (forequarter) amputation

01638   total shoulder replacement

01650   Anesthesia for procedures on arteries of shoulder and axilla; not otherwise specified

01652   axillary-brachial aneurysm

01654   bypass graft

01656   axillary-femoral bypass graft

01670   Anesthesia for all procedures on veins of shoulder and axilla

01680   Anesthesia for shoulder cast application, removal or repair; not otherwise specified

(01682   deleted 2017 [2018 edition])

UPPER ARM AND ELBOW

01710   Anesthesia for procedures on nerves, muscles, tendons, fascia, and bursae of upper arm and elbow; not otherwise specified

01712   tenotomy, elbow to shoulder, open

01714   tenoplasty, elbow to shoulder

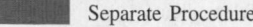 Separate Procedure   Unlisted Procedure   CCI Comp. Code   Non-specific Procedure   **199**

01716	tenodesis, rupture of long tendon of biceps
01730	Anesthesia for all closed procedures on humerus and elbow
01732	Anesthesia for diagnostic arthroscopic procedures of elbow joint
01740	Anesthesia for open or surgical arthroscopic procedures of the elbow; not otherwise specified
01742	osteotomy of humerus
01744	repair of nonunion or malunion of humerus
01756	radical procedures
01758	excision of cyst or tumor of humerus
01760	total elbow replacement
01770	Anesthesia for procedures on arteries of upper arm and elbow; not otherwise specified
01772	embolectomy
01780	Anesthesia for procedures on veins of upper arm and elbow; not otherwise specified
01782	phleborrhaphy

FOREARM, WRIST, AND HAND

01810	Anesthesia for all procedures on nerves, muscles, tendons, fascia, and bursae of forearm, wrist, and hand
01820	Anesthesia for all closed procedures on radius, ulna, wrist, or hand bones
01829	Anesthesia for diagnostic arthroscopic procedures on the wrist
01830	Anesthesia for open or surgical arthroscopic/endoscopic procedures on distal radius, distal ulna, wrist, or hand joints; not otherwise specified
01832	total wrist replacement
01840	Anesthesia for procedures on arteries of forearm, wrist, and hand; not otherwise specified
01842	embolectomy
01844	Anesthesia for vascular shunt, or shunt revision, any type (eg, dialysis)
01850	Anesthesia for procedures on veins of forearm, wrist, and hand; not otherwise specified
01852	phleborrhaphy
01860	Anesthesia for forearm, wrist, or hand cast application, removal, or repair

RADIOLOGICAL PROCEDURES

01916	Anesthesia for diagnostic arteriography/venography

(Do not report 01916 in conjunction with therapeutic codes 01924-01926, 01930-01933)

● New Code   ▲ Revised Code   + Add-On Code   ⊘ Modifier -51 Exempt   ★ Telemedicine

01920 Anesthesia for cardiac catheterization including coronary angiography and ventriculography (not to include Swan-Ganz catheter)

01922 Anesthesia for non-invasive imaging or radiation therapy

01924 Anesthesia for therapeutic interventional radiologic procedures involving the arterial system; not otherwise specified

01925 carotid or coronary

01926 intracranial, intracardiac, or aortic

01930 Anesthesia for therapeutic interventional radiologic procedures involving the venous/lymphatic system (not to include access to the central circulation); not otherwise specified

01931 intrahepatic or portal circulation (eg, transvenous intrahepatic portosystemic shunt(s) (TIPS))

01932 intrathoracic or jugular

01933 intracranial

01935 Anesthesia for percutaneous image guided procedures on the spine and spinal cord; diagnostic

01936 therapeutic

BURN EXCISIONS OR DEBRIDEMENT

01951 Anesthesia for second and third degree burn excision or debridement with or without skin grafting, any site, for total body surface area (TBSA) treated during anesthesia and surgery; less than four percent total body surface area

01952 between four and nine percent of total body surface area

+ **01953** each additional nine percent total body surface area or part thereof (List separately in addition to code for primary procedure)

(Use 01953 in conjunction with code 01952)

OBSTETRIC

01958 Anesthesia for external cephalic version procedure

01960 Anesthesia for vaginal delivery only

01961 Anesthesia for cesarean delivery only

01962 Anesthesia for urgent hysterectomy following delivery

01963 Anesthesia for cesarean hysterectomy without any labor analgesia/anesthesia care

01965 Anesthesia for incomplete or missed abortion procedures

01966 Anesthesia for induced abortion procedures

01967 Neuraxial labor analgesia/anesthesia for planned vaginal delivery (this includes any repeat subarachnoid needle placement and drug injection and/or any necessary replacement of an epidural catheter during labor)

+ **01968** Anesthesia for cesarean delivery following neuraxial labor analgesia/anesthesia (List separately in addition to code for primary procedure performed)

| ▮ Separate Procedure | ▮ Unlisted Procedure | ▮ CCI Comp. Code | ▮ Non-specific Procedure | **201** |

(Use 01968 in conjunction with code 01967)

+ 01969 Anesthesia for cesarean hysterectomy following neuraxial labor analgesia/anesthesia (List separately in addition to code for primary procedure performed)

(Use 01969 in conjunction with code 01967)

OTHER PROCEDURES

01990 Physiological support for harvesting of organ(s) from brain-dead patient

01991 Anesthesia for diagnostic or therapeutic nerve blocks and injections (when block or injection is performed by a different physician or other qualified health care professional); other than the prone position

01992 prone position

(Do not report code 01991 or 01992 in conjunction with 99151, 99152, 99153, 99155, 99156, 99157)

(When regional intravenous administration of local anesthetic agent or other medication in the upper or lower extremity is used as the anesthetic for a surgical procedure, report the appropriate anesthesia code. To report a Bier block for pain management, use 64999.)

(For intra-arterial or intravenous therapy for pain management, see 96373, 96374.)

01996 Daily hospital management of epidural or subarachnoid continuous drug administration

(Report code 01996 for daily hospital management of continuous epidural or subarachnoid drug administration performed after insertion of an epidural or subarachnoid catheter placed primarily for anesthesia administration during an operative session, but retained for post-operative pain management)

01999 Unlisted anesthesia procedure(s)

● New Code ▲ Revised Code + Add-On Code ⊘ Modifier -51 Exempt ★ Telemedicine

SURGERY SECTION OVERVIEW

The third section of the CPT coding system is the surgery section, and it includes surgical procedure codes for all body areas. Within each subsection, the CPT codes are arranged by anatomical site.

It is essential to understand the organization of the CPT surgery section in order to locate the correct procedure code. Understanding other or alternative terms which may apply to a procedure, injury, illness or condition may also make the location of the appropriate procedure easier and faster.

All procedures listed in the surgery section of the CPT book include local, metacarpal/digital block or topical anesthesia if used, the surgical procedure, and normal uncomplicated follow-up care. For diagnostic surgical procedures, follow-up care includes only the care related to recovery from the diagnostic procedure. For therapeutic surgical procedures, follow-up care includes only the care which would usually be included in the surgical service. Any complications resulting in additional services are not considered to be included and should be coded separately.

KEY POINTS ABOUT SURGERY SERVICES

- *Evaluation and management services provided by surgeons in the office, home or hospital, plus consultations and other medical services are coded using evaluation and management service codes.*

- *Any supplies and/or materials provided by the surgeon which are not considered to be included in the standard service may be coded separately.*

GLOBAL SURGICAL PACKAGE

Third-party payers differ in their definition of a surgical or global surgical package concept. Medicare defines the global surgical package as follows:

- *The surgeon's initial evaluation or consultation will be paid separately.*

- *There is a one day preoperative period covered under the global surgical package.*

- *Included in the package are all intraoperative services that are considered to be usual and necessary. Separate billing of these services would be considered unbundling.*

- *Any treatment of complications by the surgeon not requiring a return to the operating room is included in the package.*

- *The surgical package contains a standard 90-day postoperative period which includes all visits to the physician during that time unless the visit is for a totally different reason than that for the surgery.*

- *In cases of organ transplant, immunosuppressive therapy is not included in the global package.*

- *Minor surgical procedures are those with a 0 or 10-day postoperative period, and are excluded from the surgical package definition.*

SPECIAL REPORT

Surgical procedures which are rarely provided, unusual or vary significantly from the standard definition may require a special report. When preparing reports to accompany health insurance claim forms the provider should include a description of the nature, extent, and need for the procedure, and the time, effort, and equipment necessary to provides the service. Try to keep these reports as brief and simple as possible. Additional items which may be needed are:

- *complexity of symptoms*
- *final diagnosis*
- *pertinent physical findings*
- *diagnostic and therapeutic procedures*
- *concurrent problems*
- *follow-up care*

| | Separate Procedure | | Unlisted Procedure | | CCI Comp. Code | | Non-specific Procedure | **203** |

MULTIPLE SURGICAL PROCEDURES

It is common for several surgical procedures to be performed at the same operative session. When multiple procedures are performed on the same day or at the same session, the "major" procedure or service is listed first followed by secondary, additional, or "lessor" procedures or services. CPT modifier -51 is added to all procedures following the first one.

Reporting multiple procedures incorrectly may have a serious impact on reimbursement from health insurance payers. An inexperienced health insurance biller may simply list the procedures on the health insurance claim form in the order dictated or described in the operative report.

There are two critical decisions related to reporting multiple surgical procedures correctly; namely: 1) The order in which the procedures are listed on the health insurance claim form, and 2) whether or not to list the additional procedures with full or reduced fees.

ORDER OF LISTING MULTIPLE PROCEDURES

The first procedure to be listed when reporting services under the multiple procedure rule is the procedure with the highest fee. Additional procedures should be listed in descending order by fee. Modifier -51 should be added to each additional procedure.

All third party payers will reduce the allowance for the additional procedures, typically by 50 percent for the second procedure, and 50 to 75 percent for the third and subsequent procedures. Listing the procedures in descending order by fee minimizes the possibility of an incorrect reduction.

BILLING FULL VERSUS REDUCED FEES

The full fee should be listed for each procedure coded on the health insurance claim form as part of multiple surgical procedures. Third party payers will automatically reduce the allowances for the additional procedures by a specific formula. Listing all multiple procedures with full fees in descending fee order (the procedure with the highest fee first, the procedure with the next highest fee second, et cetera) will result in the maximum total allowable reimbursement for the provider or the insured.

After the maximum benefit has been paid by the health insurance company, the balance remaining, less any patient co-insurance or deductible requirements, should be written off. Note that billing practices vary in different areas of the country. Providers should continue to use the method that is customary or required by third party payers in the provider's practice location.

SEPARATE PROCEDURE

Some surgical procedures are considered to be an integral part of a more extensive surgical procedure. In this circumstance, the integral procedure is not coded. When the integral procedure is performed independently and is unrelated to other services, it should be listed as a "separate procedure."

SURGERY SUBSECTIONS

The SURGERY section of the CPT coding system is divided into 19 subsections:

General	10021-10022
Integumentary System	10030-19499
Musculoskeletal System	20005-29999
Respiratory System	30000-32999
Cardiovascular System	33010-37799
Hemic and Lymphatic Systems	38100-38999
Mediastinum and Diaphragm	39000-39599
Digestive System	40490-49999
Urinary System	50010-53899
Male Genital System	54000-55899
Reproductive System Procedures	55920
Intersex Surgery	55970-55980
Female Genital System	56405-58999
Maternity Care and Delivery	59000-59899
Endocrine System	60000-60699
Nervous System	61000-64999
Eye and Ocular Adnexa	65091-68899
Auditory System	69000-69979
Operating Microscope	69990

● New Code   ▲ Revised Code   + Add-On Code   ⊘ Modifier -51 Exempt   ★ Telemedicine

Each sub-section of the SURGERY section of the CPT coding system is divided into organs then into procedures involving anatomic sites. Each anatomic site is further separated into surgical processes such as incision, excision, repair, removal, amputation, etc.

IMAGING GUIDANCE

When imaging guidance or imaging supervision and interpretation is included in a surgical procedure, guidelines for image documentation and report, included in the guidelines for Radiology (including Nuclear Medicine and Diagnostic Ultrasound) will apply.

SURGERY SECTION MODIFIERS

Due to various circumstances, surgical procedures may be considered to be modified in comparison to the full or complete procedure. Modified procedures are identified by reporting a two-digit modifier to the CPT procedure code(s). The following CPT modifiers may be coded with surgical procedures:

-22   Unusual Procedural Services

-26   Professional Component

-32   Mandated Services

-47   Anesthesia by Surgeon

-50   Bilateral Procedure

-51   Multiple Procedures

-52   Reduced Services

-54   Surgical Care Only

-55   Postoperative Management Only

-56   Preoperative Management Only

-57   Decision for Surgery

-58   Staged or Related Procedure or Service by the Same Physician During the Postoperative Period

-62   Two Surgeons

-66   Surgical Team

-76   Repeat Procedure by Same Physician

-77   Repeat Procedure by Another Physician

-78   Return to the Operating Room for a Related Procedure During the Postoperative Period

-79   Unrelated Procedure or Service by the Same Physician During the Postoperative Period

-80   Assistant Surgeon

-81   Minimum Assistant Surgeon

-82   Assistant Surgeon (when qualified resident surgeon not available)

-90   Reference (Outside) Laboratory

-99   Multiple modifiers

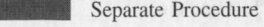 Separate Procedure   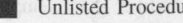 Unlisted Procedure   CCI Comp. Code   Non-specific Procedure   **205**

ADD-ON CODES

Many surgical procedures are performed secondary to primary surgical procedures. These procedures are classified as "additional" or "supplemental" procedures and are designated as "add-on" codes in the CPT coding system. "Add-on" CPT codes are identified in the CPT code book by a black plus sign "+" placed to the left of the code number.

Many of the CPT "Add-on" codes are further identified by phrases included within the descriptions of the definition of the CPT code or include the phrase "(List separately in addition to primary procedure)" following the definition. Examples of CPT codes identified as "add-on" codes include:

+ **11008** Removal of prosthetic material or mesh, abdominal wall for infection (eg, for chronic or recurrent mesh infection or necrotizing soft tissue infection) (list separately in addition to code for primary procedure)

+ **19295** Image guided placement, metallic localization clip, percutaneous, during breast biopsy/aspiration (List separately in addition to code for primary procedure)

MEDICAL AND SURGICAL SUPPLIES

HCPCS Level II codes for medical and surgical supplies, A4000-A4999, may be used to report supplies and materials provided to Medicare patients if the supplies and materials are not considered to be included with or part of the basic service(s) or procedure(s).

SURGERY CODES

GENERAL

(For percutaneous image-guided fluid collection drainage by catheter of soft tissue [eg, extremity, abdominal wall, neck], use 10030)

10021 Fine needle aspiration; without imaging guidance

10022   with imaging guidance

(For placement of percutaneous localization devices [eg, clip, metallic pellet, during breast biopsy], see 19081-19086)

(For radiological supervision and interpretation, see 76942, 77002, 77012, 77021)

(For percutaneous needle biopsy other than fine needle aspiration, see 19081-19086 for breast, 20206 for muscle, 32400 for pleura, 32405 for lung or mediastinum, 42400 for salivary gland, 47000 for liver, 48102 for pancreas, 49180 for abdominal or retroperitoneal mass, 50200 for kidney, 54500 for testis, 54800 for epididymis, 60100 for thyroid, 62267 for nucleus pulposus, intervertebral disc, or paravertebral tissue, 62269 for spinal cord)

(For evaluation of fine needle aspirate, see 88172, 88173)

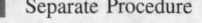 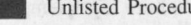

This page intentionally left blank.

● New Code ▲ Revised Code + Add-On Code ⊘ Modifier -51 Exempt ★ Telemedicine

INTEGUMENTARY SYSTEM

SKIN, SUBCUTANEOUS AND ACCESSORY STRUCTURES

INTRODUCTION AND REMOVAL

10030 Image-guided fluid collection drainage by catheter (eg, abscess, hematoma, seroma, lymphocele, cyst), soft tissue (eg, extremity, abdominal wall, neck), percutaneous

(Report 10030 for each individual collection drained with a separate catheter)

(Do not report 10030 in conjunction with 75989, 76942, 77002, 77003, 77012, 77021)

(For image-guided fluid collection drainage, percutaneous or transvaginal/transrectal of visceral, peritoneal, or retroperitoneal collections, see 49405-49407)

Soft tissue marker placement with imaging guidance is reported with 10035 and 10036. If a more specific site descriptor than soft tissue is applicable (eg, breast), use the site-specific codes for marker placement at that site. Report 10035 and 10036 only once per target, regardless of how many markers (eg, clips, wires, pellets, radioactive seeds) are used to mark that target.

10035 Placement of soft tissue localization device(s) (eg, clip, metallic pellet, wire/needle, radioactive seeds), percutaneous, including imaging guidance; first lesion.

+ 10036 each additional lesion (List separately in addition to code for primary procedure)

(Use 10036 in conjunction with 10035)

(Do not report 10035, 10036 in conjunction with 76942, 77002, 77012, 77021)

(To report a second procedure on the same side or contralateral side, use 10036)

INCISION AND DRAINAGE

(For excision, see 11400, et seq)

10040 Acne surgery (eg, marsupialization, opening or removal of multiple milia, comedones, cysts, pustules)

10060 Incision and drainage of abscess (eg, carbuncle, suppurative hidradenitis, cutaneous or subcutaneous abscess, cyst, furuncle, or paronychia); simple or single

10061 complicated or multiple

10080 Incision and drainage of pilonidal cyst; simple

10081 complicated

(For excision of pilonidal cyst, see 11770-11772)

10120 Incision and removal of foreign body, subcutaneous tissues; simple

10121 complicated

(To report wound exploration due to penetrating trauma without laparotomy or thoracotomy, see 20100-20103, as appropriate)

(To report debridement associated with open fracture(s) and/or dislocation(s), use 11010-11012, as appropriate)

10140 Incision and drainage of hematoma, seroma or fluid collection

(If imaging guidance is performed, see 76942, 77012, 77021)

10160 Puncture aspiration of abscess, hematoma, bulla, or cyst

---

Separate Procedure   Unlisted Procedure   CCI Comp. Code   Non-specific Procedure   **209**

(If imaging guidance is performed, see 76942, 77002, 77012, 77021)

10180   Incision and drainage, complex, postoperative wound infection

(For secondary closure of surgical wound, see 12020, 12021, 13160)

DEBRIDEMENT

Wound debridements (11042-11047) are reported by depth of tissue that is removed and by surface area of the wound. These services may be reported for injuries, infections, wounds and chronic ulcers. When performing debridement of a single wound, report depth using the deepest level of tissue removed. In multiple wounds, sum the surface area of those wounds that are at the same depth, but do not combine sums from different depths. For example: When bone is debrided from a 4 sq cm heel ulcer and from a 10 sq cm ischial ulcer, report the work with a single code, 11044. When subcutaneous tissue is debrided from a 16 sq cm dehisced abdominal wound and a 10 sq cm thigh wound, report the work with 11042 for the first 20 sq cm and 11045 for the second 6 sq cm. If all four wounds were debrided on the same day, use modifier 59 with 11042 or 11044 as appropriate.

(For dermabrasions, see 15780-15783)

(For nail debridement, see 11720-11721)

(For burn(s), see 16000-16035)

(For pressure ulcers, see 15920-15999)

11000   Debridement of extensive eczematous or infected skin; up to 10% of body surface

(For abdominal wall or genitalia debridement for necrotizing soft tissue infection, see 11004-11006)

+ 11001   each additional 10% of the body surface, or part thereof (List separately in addition to code for primary procedure)

(Use 11001 in conjunction with code 11000)

11004   Debridement of skin, subcutaneous tissue, muscle and fascia for necrotizing soft tissue infection; external genitalia and perineum

11005   abdominal wall, with or without fascial closure

11006   external genitalia, perineum and abdominal wall, with or without fascial closure

(If orchiectomy is performed, use 54520)

(If testicular transplantation is performed, use 54680)

+ 11008   Removal of prosthetic material or mesh, abdominal wall for infection (eg, for chronic or recurrent mesh infection or necrotizing soft tissue infection) (list separately in addition to code for primary procedure)

(Use 11008 in conjunction with 10180, 11004-11006)

(Do not report 11008 in conjunction with 11000-11001, 11010-11044)

(Report skin grafts or flaps separately when performed for closure at the same session as 11004-11008)

(When insertion of mesh is used for closure, use 49568)

11010   Debridement including removal of foreign material at the site of an open fracture and/or an open dislocation (eg, excisional debridement); skin and subcutaneous tissues

11011   skin, subcutaneous tissue, muscle fascia, and muscle

11012   skin, subcutaneous tissue, muscle fascia, muscle, and bone

(For debridement of skin, ie, epidermis and/or dermis only, see 97597, 97598)

(For active wound care management, see 97597, 97598)

(For debridement of burn wounds, see 16020-16030)

11042 Debridement, subcutaneous tissue (includes epidermis and dermis, if performed); first 20 sq cm or less

(For debridement of skin [ie., epidermis and/or dermis only], see 97597, 97598)

+ 11045 each additional 20 sq cm or part thereof (list separately in addition to code for primary procedure)

(Use 11045 in conjunction with 11042)

11043 Debridement, muscle and/or fascia (includes epidermis, dermis, and subcutaneous tissue, if performed); first 20 sq cm or less

+ 11046 each additional 20 sq cm, or part thereof (list separately in addition to code for primary procedure)

(Use 11046 in conjunction with 11043)

11044 Debridement, bone (includes epidermis, dermis, subcutaneous tissue, muscle and/or fascia, if performed); first 20 sq cm or less

11045 This code is out of order. See page 211.

11046 This code is out of order. See page 211.

+ 11047 each additional 20 sq cm, or part thereof (list separately in addition to code for primray procedure

(Do not report 11042-11047 in conjunction with 97597-97602 for the same wound)

(Use 11047 in conjunction with 11044)

PARING OR CUTTING

(To report destruction, see 17000-17004)

11055 Paring or cutting of benign hyperkeratotic lesion (eg, corn or callus); single lesion

11056 two to four lesions

11057 more than four lesions

BIOPSY

During certain surgical procedures in the integumentary system, such as excision, destruction, or shave removals, the removed tissue is often submitted for pathologic examination. The obtaining of tissue for pathology during the course of these procedures is a routine component of such procedures. This obtaining of tissue is not considered a separate biopsy procedure and is not separately reported. The use of a biopsy procedure code (eg., 11100, 11101) indicates that the procedure to obtain tissue for pathologic examination was performed independently, or was unrelated or distinct from other procedures/services provided at that time. Such biopsies are not considered components of other procedures when performed on different lesions or different sites on the same date, and are to be reported separately.

(For biopsy of conjunctiva, use 68100; eyelid, use 67810)

11100 Biopsy of skin, subcutaneous tissue and/or mucous membrane (including simple closure), unless otherwise listed; single lesion

+ 11101 each separate/additional lesion (List separately in addition to code for primary procedure)

(Use 11101 in conjunction with code 11100)

REMOVAL OF SKIN TAGS

Removal by scissoring or any sharp method, ligature strangulation, electrosurgical destruction or combination of treatment modalities, including chemical destruction or electrocauterization of wound, with or without local anesthesia.

Separate Procedure	Unlisted Procedure	CCI Comp. Code	Non-specific Procedure	**211**

11200 Removal of skin tags, multiple fibrocutaneous tags, any area; up to and including 15 lesions

+ 11201 each additional 10 lesions, or part thereof (List separately in addition to code for primary procedure)

(Use 11201 in conjunction with code 11200)

SHAVING OF EPIDERMAL OR DERMAL LESIONS

Many of the procedure codes listed in the integumentary system subsection of the CPT manual are designated in centimeters or square centimeters. Many physicians document sizes using inches or millimeters. Make sure to verify, and convert if necessary, measurements before assigning a code.

To be able to code lesion removal appropriately, the site, size in centimeters, method of removal and morphology must be documented in the medical record. Always code morphology from the pathology report.

Excision of lesion codes are determined by the diameter of the actual lesion, not the specimen sent to pathology. However, the size of the specimen can be used when the size of the lesion cannot be located in the operative report or elsewhere in the medical record.

When more than one dimension of a lesion is provided in the documentation, select the code based on the largest size. For example, if the dimensions indicated are 3 cm x 2 cm x 1.5 cm, the lesion should be coded as 3 cm. Excision of benign and malignant lesions includes anesthesia and simple repair of the defect site.

Shaving is the sharp removal by transverse incision or horizontal slicing to remove epidermal and dermal lesions without a full-thickness dermal excision. This includes local anesthesia, chemical or electrcauterization ofthe wound. The wound does not require suture closure.

11300 Shaving of epidermal or dermal lesion, single lesion, trunk, arms or legs; lesion diameter 0.5 cm or less

11301 lesion diameter 0.6 to 1.0 cm

11302 lesion diameter 1.1 to 2.0 cm

11303 lesion diameter over 2.0 cm

11305 Shaving of epidermal or dermal lesion, single lesion, scalp, neck, hands, feet, genitalia; lesion diameter 0.5 cm or less

11306 lesion diameter 0.6 to 1.0 cm

11307 lesion diameter 1.1 to 2.0 cm

11308 lesion diameter over 2.0 cm

11310 Shaving of epidermal or dermal lesion, single lesion, face, ears, eyelids, nose, lips, mucous membrane; lesion diameter 0.5 cm or less

11311 lesion diameter 0.6 to 1.0 cm

11312 lesion diameter 1.1 to 2.0 cm

11313 lesion diameter over 2.0 cm

EXCISION OF BENIGN LESIONS

Excision (including simple closure) of benign lesions of skin (eg., neoplasm, cicatricial, fibrous, inflammatory, congenital, cystic lesions) includes local anesthesia. See appropriate size and area below. For shave removal, see 11300 et seq., and for electrosurgical and other methods, see 17000 et seq..

Excision is defined as full-thickness (through the dermis) removal of a lesion, inlcuding margins, and includes simple (non-layered) closure when performed. Report separately each benign lesion excised. Code selection is determined by measuring the greatest clinical diameter of the apparent lesion plus that margin required for complete excision (lesion diameter plus the most

● New Code   ▲ Revised Code   + Add-On Code   ⊘ Modifier -51 Exempt   ★ Telemedicine

narrow margins required equals the excised diameter). The margins refer to the most narrow margin required to adequately excise the lesion, based on the individual judgment. The measurement of lesion plus margin is made prior to excision. The excised diameter is the same whether the surgical defect is repaired in a linear fashion, or reconstructed (eg, with a skin graft).

The closure of defects created by incision, excision, or trauma may require intermediate or complex closure. Repair by intermediate or complex closure should be reported separately. For excision of benign lesions requiring more than simple closure, i.e., requiring intermediate or complex closure, report 11400-11446 in addition to appropriate intermediate (12031-12057) or complex closure (13100-13153) codes. For reconstructive closure, see 15002-15261, 15570-15770. For excision performed in conjunction with adjacent tissue transfer, report only the adjacent tissue transfer code (14000-14302). Excision of lesion (11400-11446) is not separately reportable with adjacent tissue transfer.

> (For destruction [eg, laser surgery, electrosurgery, cryosurgery, chemosurgery, surgical curette] of benign lesions other than skin tags or cutaneous vascular proliferative lesions, see 17110, 17111; premalignant lesions, see 17000, 17003, 17004; cutaneous vascular proliferative lesions, see 17106, 17107, 17108; malignant lesions, see 17260-17286)

> (For excision of cicatricial lesion[s] [eg, full thickness excision, through the dermis], see 11400-11446)

> (For incisional removal of burn scar, see 16035, 16036)

> (For fractional ablative laser fenestration for functional improvement of traumatic or burn scars, see 0479T, 0480T)

11400   Excision, benign lesion including margins, except skin tag (unless listed elsewhere), trunk, arms or legs; excised diameter 0.5 cm or less

11401   excised diameter 0.6 to 1.0 cm

11402   excised diameter 1.1 to 2.0 cm

11403   excised diameter 2.1 to 3.0 cm

11404   excised diameter 3.1 to 4.0 cm

11406   excised diameter over 4.0 cm

> (For unusual or complicated excision, add modifier -22)

11420   Excision, benign lesion including margins, except skin tag (unless listed elsewhere), scalp, neck, hands, feet, genitalia; excised diameter 0.5 cm or less

11421   excised diameter 0.6 to 1.0 cm

11422   excised diameter 1.1 to 2.0 cm

11423   excised diameter 2.1 to 3.0 cm

11424   excised diameter 3.1 to 4.0 cm

11426   excised diameter over 4.0 cm

> (For unusual or complicated excision, add modifier -22)

11440   Excision, other benign lesion including margins (unless listed elsewhere), face, ears, eyelids, nose, lips, mucous membrane; excised diameter 0.5 cm or less

11441   excised diameter 0.6 to 1.0 cm

11442   excised diameter 1.1 to 2.0 cm

11443   excised diameter 2.1 to 3.0 cm

11444	excised diameter 3.1 to 4.0 cm
11446	excised diameter over 4.0 cm

(For unusual or complicated excision, add modifier -22)

(For eyelids involving more than skin, see also 67800 et seq.)

11450	Excision of skin and subcutaneous tissue for hidradenitis, axillary; with simple or intermediate repair
11451	with complex repair
11462	Excision of skin and subcutaneous tissue for hidradenitis, inguinal; with simple or intermediate repair
11463	with complex repair
11470	Excision of skin and subcutaneous tissue for hidradenitis, perianal, perineal, or umbilical; with simple or intermediate repair
11471	with complex repair

(When skin graft or flap is used for closure, use appropriate procedure code in addition)

(For bilateral procedure, add modifier -50)

EXCISION OF MALIGNANT LESIONS

Excision (including simple closure) of malignant lesions of skin (eg., basal cell carcinoma, squamous cell carcinoma, melanoma) includes local anesthesia. (See appropriate size and body area below.) For destruction of malignant lesions of skin, see destruction codes 17260-17286.

The closure of defects created by incision, excision, or trauma may require intermediate or complex closure. Repair by intermediate or complex closure should be reported separately. For excision of malignant lesions requiring more than simple closure, i.e., requiring intermediate or complex closure, report 11600-11646 in addition to appropriate intermediate (12031-12057) or complex closure (13100-13153) codes. For reconstructive closure, see 15002-15261, 15570-15770. For excision performed in conjunction with adjacent tissue transfer, report only the adjacent tissue transfer code (14000-14302). Excision of lesion (11600-11646) is not separately reportable with adjacent tissue transfer.

When frozen section pathology shows the margins of excision were not adequate, an additional excision may be necessary for complete tumor removal. Use only one code to report the additional excision and re-excision(s) based on the final widest excised diameter required for complete tumor removal at the same operative session. To report a re-excised procedure performed to widen margins at a subsequent operative session, see codes 11600-11646, as appropriate. Append modifier 58 if the re-excision procedure is performed during the postoperative period of the primary excision procedure.

11600	Excision, malignant lesion including margins, trunk, arms, or legs; excised diameter 0.5 cm or less
11601	excised diameter 0.6 to 1.0 cm
11602	excised diameter 1.1 to 2.0 cm
11603	excised diameter 2.1 to 3.0 cm
11604	excised diameter 3.1 to 4.0 cm
11606	excised diameter over 4.0 cm
11620	Excision, malignant lesion including margins, scalp, neck, hands, feet, genitalia; excised diameter 0.5 cm or less
11621	excised diameter 0.6 to 1.0 cm
11622	excised diameter 1.1 to 2.0 cm

● New Code ▲ Revised Code + Add-On Code ⊘ Modifier -51 Exempt ★ Telemedicine

11623	excised diameter 2.1 to 3.0 cm
11624	excised diameter 3.1 to 4.0 cm
11626	excised diameter over 4.0 cm
11640	Excision, malignant lesion including margins, face, ears, eyelids, nose, lips; excised diameter 0.5 cm or less
11641	excised diameter 0.6 to 1.0 cm
11642	excised diameter 1.1 to 2.0 cm
11643	excised diameter 2.1 to 3.0 cm
11644	excised diameter 3.1 to 4.0 cm
11646	excised diameter over 4.0 cm

(For eyelids involving more than skin, see also 67800 et seq)

NAILS

(For drainage of paronychia or onychia, see 10060, 10061)

11719	Trimming of nondystrophic nails, any number
11720	Debridement of nail(s) by any method(s); 1 to 5
11721	6 or more
11730	Avulsion of nail plate, partial or complete, simple; single
+ 11732	each additional nail plate (List separately in addition to code for primary procedure)

(Use 11732 in conjunction with code 11730)

11740	Evacuation of subungual hematoma
11750	Excision of nail and nail matrix, partial or complete, (eg, ingrown or deformed nail) for permanent removal;
(11752	deleted 2016 [2017 edition]. See 26236, 28124, 28160)

(For pinch graft, use 15050)

11755	Biopsy of nail unit (eg, plate, bed, matrix, hyponychium, proximal and lateral nail folds) (separate procedure)
11760	Repair of nail bed
11762	Reconstruction of nail bed with graft
11765	Wedge excision of skin of nail fold (eg, for ingrown toenail)

PILONIDAL CYST

| 11770 | Excision of pilonidal cyst or sinus; simple |
| 11771 | extensive |

11772   complicated

(For incision of pilonidal cyst, see 10080, 10081)

INTRODUCTION

11900   Injection, intralesional; up to and including seven lesions

11901   more than seven lesions

(11900, 11901 are not to be used for preoperative local anesthetic injection)

(For veins, see 36470, 36471)

(For intralesional chemotherapy administration, see 96405, 96406)

11920   Tattooing, intradermal introduction of insoluble opaque pigments to correct color defects of skin, including micropigmentation; 6.0 sq cm or less

11921   6.1 to 20.0 sq cm

+ **11922**   each additional 20.0 sq cm or part thereof (List separately in addition to code for primary procedure)

(Use 11922 in conjunction with code 11921)

11950   Subcutaneous injection of filling material (eg, collagen); 1 cc or less

11951   1.1 to 5.0 cc

11952   5.1 to 10.0 cc

11954   over 10.0 cc

11960   Insertion of tissue expander(s) for other than breast, including subsequent expansion

(For breast reconstruction with tissue expander(s), use 19357)

11970   Replacement of tissue expander with permanent prosthesis

11971   Removal of tissue expander(s) without insertion of prosthesis

11976   Removal, implantable contraceptive capsules

11980   Subcutaneous hormone pellet implantation (implantation of estradiol and/or testosterone pellets beneath the skin)

11981   Insertion, non-biodegradable drug delivery implant

11982   Removal, non-biodegradable drug delivery implant

11983   Removal with reinsertion, non-biodegradable drug delivery implant

REPAIR (CLOSURE)

To be able to code wound repair appropriately, the site, length of wound in centimeters and type of repair must be documented in the medical record. Review the definitions of simple, intermediate and complex repair in the current CPT coding system.

Use the codes in this section to designate wound closure utilizing sutures, staples, or tissue adhesives (eg., 2-cyanoacrylate), either singly or in combination with each other, or in combination with adhesive strips. Wound closure utilizing adhesive strips as the sole repair material should be coded using the appropriate E/M code.

● New Code   ▲ Revised Code   + Add-On Code   ⊘ Modifier -51 Exempt   ★ Telemedicine

Definitions

Simple repair is used when the wound is superficial, eg., involving primarily epidermis or dermis, or subcutaneous tissues without significant involvement of deeper structures, and requires simple one layer closure. This includes local anesthesia and chemical or electrocauterization of wounds not closed.

Intermediate repair includes the repair of wounds that, in addition to the above, require layered closure of one or more of the deeper layers of subcutaneous tissue and superficial (non-muscle) fascia, in addition to the skin (epidermal and dermal) closure. Single-layer closure of heavily contaminated wounds that have required extensive cleaning or removal of particulate matter also constitutes intermediate repair.

Complex repair includes the repair of wounds requiring more than layered closure, viz., scar revision, debridement (eg., traumatic lacerations or avulsions), extensive undermining, stents or retention sutures. Necessary preparation includes creation of a limited defect for repairs or the debridement of complicated lacerations or avulsions. Complex repair does not include excision of benign (11400-11446) or malignant (11600-11646) lesions, excisional preparation of a wound bed (15002-15005) or debridement of an open fracture or open dislocation.

Instuctions for listing services at time of wound repair:

1. The repaired wound(s) should be measured and recorded in centimeters, whether curved, angular or stellate.

2. When multiple wounds are repaired, add together the lengths of those in the same classification (see above) and from all anatomic sites that are grouped together into the same code descriptor. For example, add together the lengths of intermediate repairs to the trunk and extremities Do not add lengths of repairs from different groupings of anatomic sites (eg, face and extremities). Also, do not add together lengths of different classifications (eg, intermediate and complex repairs).

When more than one classification of wounds is repaired, list the more complicated as the primary procedure and the less complicated as the secondary procedure, using modifier 59.

3. Decontamination and/or debridement: Debridement is considered a separate procedure only when gross contamination requires prolonged cleansing, when appreciable amounts of devitalized or contaminated tissue are removed, or when debridement is carried out separately without immediate primary closure.

> (For extensive debridement of soft tissue and/or bone, not associated with open fracture(s) and/or dislocation(s) resulting from penetrating and/or blunt trauma, see 11042-11047.)

> (For extensive debridement of subcutaneous tissue, muscle fascia, muscle, and/or bone associated with open fracture(s) and/or dislocation(s), see 11010-11012.)

4. Involvement of nerves, blood vessels and tendons: Report under appropriate system (Nervous, Cardiovascular, Musculoskeletal) for repair of these structures. The repair of these associated wounds is included in the primary procedure unless it qualifies as a complex repair, in which case modifier 59 applies.

Simple ligation of vessels in an open wound is considered as part of any wound closure.

Simple "exploration" of nerves, blood vessels, or tendons exposed in an open wound is also considered part of the essential treatment of the wound and is not a separate procedure unless appreciable dissection is required. If the wound requires enlargement, extension of dissection (to determine penetration), debridement, removal of foreign body(s), ligation or coagulation of minor subcutaneous and/or muscular blood vessel(s) of the subcutaneous tissue, muscle fascia, and/or muscle, not requiring thoracotomy or laparotomy, use codes 20100-20103, as appropriate.

REPAIR — SIMPLE

Sum of lengths of repairs for each group of anatomic sites.

12001 Simple repair of superficial wounds of scalp, neck, axillae, external genitalia, trunk and/or extremities (including hands and feet); 2.5 cm or less

12002 2.6 cm to 7.5 cm

12004 7.6 cm to 12.5 cm

12005 12.6 cm to 20.0 cm

12006	20.1 cm to 30.0 cm
12007	over 30.0 cm
12011	Simple repair of superficial wounds of face, ears, eyelids, nose, lips and/or mucous membranes; 2.5 cm or less
12013	2.6 cm to 5.0 cm
12014	5.1 cm to 7.5 cm
12015	7.6 cm to 12.5 cm
12016	12.6 cm to 20.0 cm
12017	20.1 cm to 30.0 cm
12018	over 30.0 cm
12020	Treatment of superficial wound dehiscence; simple closure
12021	with packing

(For extensive or complicated secondary wound closure, use 13160)

REPAIR — INTERMEDIATE

Sum of lengths of repairs for each group of anatomic sites.

12031	Repair, intermediate of wounds of scalp, axillae, trunk and/or extremities (excluding hands and feet); 2.5 cm or less
12032	2.6 cm to 7.5 cm
12034	7.6 cm to 12.5 cm
12035	12.6 cm to 20.0 cm
12036	20.1 cm to 30.0 cm
12037	over 30.0 cm
12041	Repair, intermediate wounds of neck, hands, feet and/or external genitalia; 2.5 cm or less
12042	2.6 cm to 7.5 cm
12044	7.6 cm to 12.5 cm
12045	12.6 cm to 20.0 cm
12046	20.1 cm to 30.0 cm
12047	over 30.0 cm
12051	Repair, intermediate wounds of face, ears, eyelids, nose, lips and/or mucous membranes; 2.5 cm or less
12052	2.6 cm to 5.0 cm
12053	5.1 cm to 7.5 cm

● New Code   ▲ Revised Code   + Add-On Code   ⊘ Modifier -51 Exempt   ★ Telemedicine

12054	7.6 cm to 12.5 cm
12055	12.6 cm to 20.0 cm
12056	20.1 cm to 30.0 cm
12057	over 30.0 cm

REPAIR — COMPLEX

Reconstructive procedures, complicated wound closure. Sum of lengths of repairs for each group of anatomic sites.

(For full thickness repair of lip or eyelid, see respective anatomical subsections)

13100	Repair, complex, trunk; 1.1 cm to 2.5 cm
	(For 1.0 cm or less, see simple or intermediate repairs)
13101	2.6 cm to 7.5 cm
+ 13102	each additional 5 cm or less (List separately in addition to code for primary procedure)
	(Use 13102 in conjunction with code 13101)
13120	Repair, complex, scalp, arms, and/or legs; 1.1 cm to 2.5 cm
	(For 1.0 cm or less, see simple or intermediate repairs)
13121	2.6 cm to 7.5 cm
+ 13122	each additional 5 cm or less (List separately in addition to code for primary procedure)
	(Use 13122 in conjunction with 13121)
13131	Repair, complex, forehead, cheeks, chin, mouth, neck, axillae, genitalia, hands and/or feet; 1.1 cm to 2.5 cm
	(For 1.0 cm or less, see simple or intermediate repairs)
13132	2.6 cm to 7.5 cm
+ 13133	each additional 5 cm or less (List separately in addition to code for primary procedure)
	(Use 13133 in conjunction with 13132)
(13150	deleted 2013 [2014 edition])
	(For 1.0 cm or less, see simple or intermediate repairs)
13151	Repair, complex, eyelids, nose, ears and/or lips; 1.1 cm to 2.5 cm
13152	2.6 cm to 7.5 cm
+ 13153	each additional 5 cm or less (List separately in addition to code for primary procedure)
	(Use 13153 in conjunction with 13152)
13160	Secondary closure of surgical wound or dehiscence, extensive or complicated
	(For packing or simple secondary wound closure, see 12020, 12021)

Separate Procedure   Unlisted Procedure   CCI Comp. Code   Non-specific Procedure   **219**

ADJACENT TISSUE TRANSFER OR REARRANGEMENT

For full-thickness repair of lip or eyelid, see respective anatomical subsections.

Codes 14000-14302 are used for excision (including lesion) and/or repair by adjacent tissue transfer or rearrangement (eg., Z-plasty, W-plasty, V-Y plasty, rotation flap, random island flap, advancement flap). When applied in repairing lacerations, the procedures listed must be performed by the surgeon to accomplish the repair. They do not apply to direct closure or rearrangement of traumatic wounds incidentally resulting in these configurations. Undermining alone of adjacent tissues to achieve closure, without additional incisions, does not constitute adjacent tissue transfer. See complex repair codes 13100-13160. The excision of a benign lesion (11400-11446) or a malignant lesion (11600-11646) is not separately reportable with codes 14000-14302.

Skin graft necessary to close secondary defect is considered an additional procedure. For purposes of code selection, the term "defect" includes the primary and secondary defects. The primary defect resulting from the excision and the secondary defect resulting from flap design to perform the reconstruction are measured together to determine the code.

14000	Adjacent tissue transfer or rearrangement, trunk; defect 10 sq cm or less	
14001	defect 10.1 sq cm to 30.0 sq cm	
14020	Adjacent tissue transfer or rearrangement, scalp, arms and/or legs; defect 10 sq cm or less	
14021	defect 10.1 sq cm to 30.0 sq cm	
14040	Adjacent tissue transfer or rearrangement, forehead, cheeks, chin, mouth, neck, axillae, genitalia, hands and/or feet; defect 10 sq cm or less	
14041	defect 10.1 sq cm to 30.0 sq cm	
14060	Adjacent tissue transfer or rearrangement, eyelids, nose, ears and/or lips; defect 10 sq cm or less	
14061	defect 10.1 sq cm to 30.0 sq cm	

(For eyelid, full thickness, see 67961 et seq)

14301	Adjacent tissue transfer or rearrangement, any area; defect 30.1 sq cm to 60.0 sq cm
+ **14302**	each additional 30.0 sq cm, or part thereof (List separately in addition to code for primary procedure)

(Use 14302 in conjunction with 14301)

14350	Filleted finger or toe flap, including preparation of recipient site

SKIN REPLACEMENT SURGERY

Skin replacement surgery consists of surgical preparation and topical placement of an autograft (including tissue cultured autograft) or skin substitute graft (ie, homograft, allograft, xenograft). The graft is anchored using the individual's choice of fixation. When services are performed in the office, routine dressing supplies are not reported separately.

The following definition should be applied to those codes that reference "100 sq cm or 1% of body area of infants and children" when determining the involvement of body size: The measurement of 100 sq cm is applicable to adults and children 10 years of age and older; and percentages of body surface area apply to infants and children younger than 10 years of age. The measurements apply to the size of the recipient area.

Procedures involving wrist and/or ankle are reported with codes that include arm or leg in the descriptor.

When a primary procedure requires a skin substitute or skin autograft for definitive skin closure (eg, orbitectomy, radical mastectomy, or deep tumor removal) use 15100-15278 in conjunction with primary procedure.

For biological implant for soft tissue reinforcement, use 15777 in conjunction with primary procedure.

The supply of skin substitute graft(s) should be reported separately in conjunction with 15271-15278.

Definitions

Surgical preparation codes 15002-15005 for skin replacement surgery describe the initial services related to preparing a clean and viable wound surface for placement of an autograft, flap, skin substitute graft or for negatie pressure wound therapy. In come cases, closure may be possible using adjacent tissue transfer (14000-14061) or complex repair (13100-13153). In add cases, appreciable nonviable tissue is removed to treat a burn, traumatic wound or a necrotizing infection. The clean wound bed may also be created by incisional release of a scar contracture resulting in a surface defect from separation of tissues. The intent is to heal the wound by primary intention, or by the use of negative pressure wound therapy. Patient conditions may require the closure or application of graft, flap, or skin substitute to be delayed, but in all cases the intent is to include these treatments or negative pressure wound therapy to heal the wound. Do not report 15002-15005 for removal of nonviable tissue/debris in a chronic wound (eg, venous or diabetic) when the wound is left to heal by secondary intention. See active wound management codes (97597, 97598) and debridement codes (11042-11047) for this service. For necrotizing soft tissue infections in specific anatomic locations, see 11004-11008.

Select the appropriate code from 15002-15005 based upon location and size of the resultant defect. For multiple wounds, sum the surface area of all wounds from all anatomic sites that are grouped together into the same code descriptor. For example, sum the surface area of all wounds on the trunk and arms. Do not sum wounds from different groupings of anatomic sites (eg, face and arms). Use 15002 or 15004, as appropriate, for excisions and incisional releases resulting in wounds up to and including 100 sq cm of surface area. Use 15003 or 15005 for each additional 100 sq cm or part thereof.

Autografts/tissue cultured autografts include the harvest and or application of an autologous skin graft. Repair of donor site requiring skin graft or local flaps is reported separately. Removal of current graft and/or simple cleansing of the wound is included, when performed. Do not report 97602. Debridement is considered a separate procedure only when gross contamination requires prolonged cleansing, when appreciable amounts of devialized or contaminated tissue ar removed, or when debridement is carried out separately without immediate primary closure.

Selecte the appropriate code from 15040-15261 based upon type of autograft and location and size of the defect. The measurements apply to the size of the recipient area. For multiple wounds, sum teh surface area of all wounds from all anatomic sites that are grouped together into the same code descriptor.

Skin substitute grafts include non-autologous human skin (dermal or epidermal, cellular and acellular) grafts (eg, homograft, allograft), non human skin substitute grafts (ie, xenograft), and biological products that form a sheet scaffolding for skin growth. These codes are not to be reported for application of non-graft wound dressings (eg, gel, ointment, foam, liquid) or injected skin substitutes. Removal of current graft and/or simple cleansing of the wound is included, when performed. Do not report 97602. Debridement is considered a separate procedure only when gross contamination requires prolonged cleansing, when appreciable amounts of devitalized or contaminated tissue are removed, or when debridement is carried out separately without immediate primary closure.

Select the appropriate code from 15271-15278 based upon location and size of the defect. For multiple wounds, sum the surface area of all wounds from all anatomic sites that are grouped together into the same code descriptor.

Surgical Preparation

 15002 Surgical preparation or creation of recipient site by excision of open wounds, burn eschar, or scar (including subcutaneous tissues), or incisional release of scar contracture, trunk, arms, legs; first 100 sq cm or 1% of body area of infants and children

(For linear scar revision, see 13100-13153)

+ **15003** each additional 100 sq cm, or part thereof, or each additional 1% of body area of infants and children (List separately in addition to code for primary procedure)

(Use 15003 in conjunction with 15002)

15004 Surgical preparation or creation of recipient site by excision of open wounds, burn eschar, or scar (including subcutaneous tissues), or incisional release of scar contracture, face, scalp, eyelids, mouth, neck, ears, orbits, genitalia, hands, feet and/or multiple digits; 1500405 first 100 sq cm or 1% of body area of infants and children

+ **15005** each additional 100 sq cm or part thereof, or each additional 1% of body area of infants and children (List separately in addition to code for primary procedure)

(Use 15005 in conjunction with 15004)

| � Separate Procedure | ▮ Unlisted Procedure | ▮ CCI Comp. Code | ▮ Non-specific Procedure | **221** |

Autografts/Tissue Cultured Autograft

15040 Harvest of skin for tissue cultured skin autograft, 100 sq cm or less

15050 Pinch graft, single or multiple, to cover small ulcer, tip of digit, or other minimal open area (except on face), up to defect size 2 cm diameter

15100 Split-thickness autograft, trunk, arms, legs; first 100 sq cm or less, or one percent of body area of infants and children (except 15050)

+ **15101** each additional 100 sq cm, or each additional one percent of body area of infants and children, or part thereof (List separately in addition to code for primary procedure)

(Use 15101 in conjunction with code 15100)

15110 Epidermal autograft, trunk, arms, legs; first 100 sq cm or less, or one percent of body area of infants and children

+ **15111** each additional 100 sq cm, or each additional one percent of body area of infants and children, or part thereof (List separately in addition to code for primary procedure)

(Use 15111 in conjunction with 15110)

15115 Epidermal autograft, face, scalp, eyelids, mouth, neck, ears, orbits, genitalia, hands, feet, and/or multiple digits; first 100 sq cm or less, or one percent of body area of infants and children

+ **15116** each additional 100 sq cm, or each additional one percent of body area of infants and children, or part thereof (List separately in addition to code for primary procedure)

(Use 15116 in conjunction with 15115)

15120 Split-thickness autograft, face, scalp, eyelids, mouth, neck, ears, orbits, genitalia, hands, feet, and/or multiple digits; first 100 sq cm or less, or one percent of body area of infants and children (except 15050)

+ **15121** each additional 100 sq cm, or each additional one percent of body area of infants and children, or part thereof (List separately in addition to code for primary procedure)

(Use 15121 in conjunction with code 15120)

(For eyelids, see also 67961-67975)

15130 Dermal autograft, trunk, arms, legs; first 100 sq cm or less, or one percent of body area of infants and children

+ **15131** each additional 100 sq cm, or each additional one percent of body area of infants and children, or part thereof (List separately in addition to code for primary procedure)

(Use 15131 in conjunction with 15130)

15135 Dermal autograft, face, scalp, eyelids, mouth, neck, ears, orbits, genitalia, hands, feet, and/or multiple digits; first 100 sq cm or less, or one percent of body area of infants and children

+ **15136** each additional 100 sq cm, or each additional one percent of body area of infants and children, or part thereof (List separately in addition to code for primary procedure)

(Use 15136 in conjunction with 15135)

15150 Tissue cultured skin autograft, trunk, arms, legs; first 25 sq cm or less

+ **15151** additional 1 sq cm to 75 sq cm (List separately in addition to code for primary procedure)

(Do not report 15151 more than once per session)

(Use 15151 in conjunction with 15150)

---

222 ● New Code ▲ Revised Code + Add-On Code ⊘ Modifier -51 Exempt ★ Telemedicine

+ 15152 each additional 100 sq cm, or each additional 1% of body area of infants and children, or part thereof (List separately in addition to code for primary procedure)

(Use 15152 in conjunction with 15151)

15155 Tissue cultured skin autograft, face, scalp, eyelids, mouth, neck, ears, orbits, genitalia, hands, feet, and/or multiple digits; first 25 sq cm or less

+ 15156 additional 1 sq cm to 75 sq cm (List separately in addition to code for primary procedure)

(Do not report 15156 more than once per session)

(Use 15156 in conjunction with 15155)

+ 15157 each additional 100 sq cm, or each additional 1% of body area of infants and children, or part thereof (List separately in addition to code for primary procedure)

(Use 15157 in conjunction with 15156)

15200 Full thickness graft, free, including direct closure of donor site, trunk; 20 sq cm or less

+ 15201 each additional 20 sq cm or part thereof (List separately in addition to code for primary procedure)

(Use 15201 in conjunction with 15200)

15220 Full thickness graft, free, including direct closure of donor site, scalp, arms, and/or legs; 20 sq cm or less

+ 15221 each additional 20 sq cm or part thereof (List separately in addition to code for primary procedure)

(Use 15221 in conjunction with 15220)

15240 Full thickness graft, free, including direct closure of donor site, forehead, cheeks, chin, mouth, neck, axillae, genitalia, hands, and/or feet; 20 sq cm or less

(For finger tip graft, use 15050)

(For repair of syndactyly, fingers, see 26560-26562)

+ 15241 each additional 20 sq cm or part thereof (List separately in addition to code for primary procedure)

(Use 15241 in conjunction with code 15240)

15260 Full thickness graft, free, including direct closure of donor site, nose, ears, eyelids, and/or lips; 20 sq cm or less

+ 15261 each additional 20 sq cm or part thereof (List separately in addition to code for primary procedure)

(Use 15261 in conjunction with code 15260)

(For eyelids, see also 67961-67975)

(Repair of donor site requiring skin graft or local flaps is considered a separate procedure)

Skin Substitute Grafts

The supply of skin substitute graft(s) should be reported separately in conjunction with 15271-15278. For biologic implant for soft tissue reinforcement, use 15777 in conjunction with code for primary procedure.

15271 Application of skin substitute graft to trunk, arms, legs, total wound surface area up to 100 sq cm; first 25 sq cm or less wound surface area

+ 15272 each additional 25 sq cm wound surface area, or part thereof (List separately in addition to code for primary procedure)

(Use 15272 in conjunction with 15271)

(For total wound surface area greater than or equal to 100 sq cm, see 15273, 15274)

(Do not report 15271, 15272 in conjunction with 15273, 15274)

15273   Application of skin substitute graft to trunk, arms, legs, total wound surface area greater than or equal to 100 sq cm; first 100 sq cm wound surface area, or 1% of body area of infants and children

+ **15274**   each additional 100 sq cm wound surface area, or part thereof, or each additional 1% of body area of infants and children, or part thereof (List separately in addition to code for primary procedure)

(Use 15274 in conjunction with 15273)

(For total wound surface area up to 100 sq cm, see 15271, 15272)

15275   Application of skin substitute graft to face, scalp, eyelids, mouth, neck, ears, orbits, genitalia, hands, feet, and/or multiple digits, total wound surface area up to 100 sq cm; first 25 sq cm or less wound surface area

+ **15276**   each additional 25 sq cm wound surface area, or part thereof (List separately in addition to code for primary procedure)

(Use 15276 in conjunction with 15275)

(For total wound surface area greater than or equal to 100 sq cm, see 15277, 15278)

(Do not report 15275, 15276 in conjunction with 15277, 15278)

15277   Application of skin substitute graft to face, scalp, eyelids, mouth, neck, ears, orbits, genitalia, hands, feet, and/or multiple digits, total wound surface area greater than or equal to 100 sq cm; first 100 sq cm wound surface area, or 1% of body area of infants and children

+ **15278**   each additional 100 sq cm wound surface area, or part thereof, or each additional 1% of body area of infants and children, or part thereof (List separately in addition to code for primary procedure)

(Use 15278 in conjunction with 15277)

(For total wound surface area up to 100 sq cm, see 15275, 15276)

(Do not report 15271-15278 in conjunction with 97602)

FLAPS (SKIN AND/OR DEEP TISSUES)

The regions listed refer to the recipient area (not the donor site) when a flap is being attached in a transfer or to a final site.

The regions listed refer to a donor site when a tube is formed for later transfer or when a "delay" of flap occurs prior to the transfer. Codes 15733-15738 are described by donor site of the muscle, myocutaneous, or fasciocutaneous flap.

Codes 15570-15738 do not include extensive immobilization (eg., large plaster casts and other immobilizing devices are considered additional separate procedures).

A repair of a donor site requiring a skin graft or local flaps is considered an additional separate procedure.

(For microvascular flaps, see 15756-15758)

(For flaps without inclusion of a vascular pedicle, see 15570-15576)

(For adjacent tissue transfer flaps, see 14000-14302)

15570   Formation of direct or tubed pedicle, with or without transfer; trunk

15572   scalp, arms, or legs

15574   forehead, cheeks, chin, mouth, neck, axillae, genitalia, hands or feet

15576   eyelids, nose, ears, lips, or intraoral

15600 Delay of flap or sectioning of flap (division and inset); at trunk

15610 at scalp, arms, or legs

15620 at forehead, cheeks, chin, neck, axillae, genitalia, hands, or feet

15630 at eyelids, nose, ears, or lips

15650 Transfer, intermediate, of any pedicle flap (eg, abdomen to wrist, Walking tube), any location

(For eyelids, nose, ears, or lips, see also anatomical area)

(For revision, defatting or rearranging of transferred pedicle flap or skin graft, see 13100-14302)

● **15730** Midface flap (ie, zygomaticofacial flap) with preservation of vascular pedicle(s)

15731 Forehead flap with preservation of vascular pedicle (eg, axial pattern flap, paramedian forehead flap)

(For muscle, myocutaneous, or fasciocutaneous flap of the head or neck, use 15733)

(**15732** deleted 2017 [2018 edition]. To report myocutaneous or fasciocutaneous flap, use 15733.)

● **15733** Muscle, myocutaneous, or fasciocutaneous flap; head and neck with named vascular pedicle (ie, buccinators, genioglossus, temporalis, masseter, sternocleidomastoid, levator scapulae)

(For forehead flap with preservation of vascular pedicle, use 15731)

(For anterior pericranial flap on named vascular pedicle, for repair of extracranial defect, use 15731)

(For repair of head and neck defects using non-axial pattern advancement flaps [including lesion] and/or repair by adjacent tissue transfer or rearrangement [eg, Z-plasty, W-plasty, V-Y plasty, rotation flap, random island flap, advancement flap], see 14040, 14041, 14060, 14061, 14301, 14302)

15734 trunk

15736 upper extremity

15738 lower extremity

OTHER FLAPS AND GRAFTS

Code 15740 describes a cutaneous flap, transposed into a nearby but not immediately adjacent defect, with a pedicle that incorporates an anatomically named axial vessel into its design. The flap is typically transferred through a tunnel underneath the skin and sutured into its new position. The donor site is closed directly.

Neurovascular pedicle procedures are reported with 15750. This code includes not only skin but also a functional motor or sensory nerve(s). The flap serves to reinnervate a damaged portion of the body dependent on touch or movement (eg, thumb).

Repair of donor site requiring skin graft or local flaps should be reported as an additional procedure.

For random island flaps, V-Y subcutaneous flaps, advancement flaps, and other flaps from adjacent areas without clearly defined anatomically named axial vessels, see 14000-14302.

15740 Flap; island pedicle requiring identification and dissection of an anatomically named axial vessel

15750 neurovascular pedicle

15756 Free muscle or myocutaneous flap with microvascular anastomosis

(Do not report code 69990 in addition to code 15756)

15757 Free skin flap with microvascular anastomosis

(Do not report code 69990 in addition to code 15757)

15758　Free fascial flap with microvascular anastomosis

(Do not report code 69990 in addition to code 15758)

15760　Graft; composite (eg, full thickness of external ear or nasal ala), including primary closure, donor area

15770　　derma-fat-fascia

15775　Punch graft for hair transplant; 1 to 15 punch grafts

15776　　more than 15 punch grafts

(For strip transplant, use 15220)

+ 15777　Implantation of biologic implant (eg, acellular dermal matrix) for soft tissue reinforcement (ie, breast, trunk) (List separately in addition to code for primary procedure)

(For implantation of biologic implants for soft tissue reinforcement in tissues other than breast and trunk, use 17999)

(For bilateral breast procedure, report 15777 with modifier 50)

(For implantation of mesh or other prosthesis for open incisional or ventral hernia repair, use 49568 in conjunction with 49560-49566)

(For insertion of mesh or other prosthesis for closure of a necrotizing soft tissue infectino wound, use 49568 in conjunction with 11004-11006)

(For topical application of skin substitute graft to a wound surface, see 15271-15278)

(For repair of anorectal fistula with plug (eg, porcine small intestine submucosa [SIS]), use 46707)

(For insertion of mesh or other prosthesis for repair of pelvic floor defect, use 57267)

(For implantation of non-biologic or synthetic implant for fascial reinforcement of the abdominal wall, use 0437T)

(The supply of biologic implant should be reported separately in conjunction with 15777)

OTHER PROCEDURES

15780　Dermabrasion; total face (eg, for acne scarring, fine wrinkling, rhytids, general keratosis)

15781　　segmental, face

15782　　regional, other than face

15783　　superficial, any site, (eg, tattoo removal)

15786　Abrasion; single lesion (eg, keratosis, scar)

+ 15787　　each additional 4 lesions or less (List separately in addition to code for primary procedure)

(Use 15787 in conjunction with code 15786)

15788　Chemical peel, facial; epidermal

15789　　dermal

15792　Chemical peel, nonfacial; epidermal

15793　　dermal

15819　Cervicoplasty

● New Code ▲ Revised Code + Add-On Code ⊘ Modifier -51 Exempt ★ Telemedicine

15820 Blepharoplasty, lower eyelid;

15821   with extensive herniated fat pad

15822 Blepharoplasty, upper eyelid;

15823   with excessive skin weighting down lid

(For bilateral blepharoplasty, add modifier -50)

15824 Rhytidectomy; forehead

(For repair of brow ptosis, use 67900)

15825   neck with platysmal tightening (platysmal flap, P-flap)

15826   glabellar frown lines

15828   cheek, chin, and neck

15829   superficial musculoaponeurotic system (SMAS) flap

(For bilateral rhytidectomy, add modifier -50)

15830 Excision, excessive skin and subcutaneous tissue (includes lipectomy); abdomen, infraumbilical panniculectomy

(Do not report 15830 in conjunction with 12031-12037, 13100-13102, 14000, 14001, 14302 for the same wound)

15832   thigh

15833   leg

15834   hip

15835   buttock

15836   arm

15837   forearm or hand

15838   submental fat pad

15839   other area

(For bilateral procedure, add modifier -50)

15840 Graft for facial nerve paralysis; free fascia graft (including obtaining fascia)

(For bilateral procedure, add modifier -50)

15841   free muscle graft (including obtaining graft)

15842   free muscle flap by microsurgical technique

(Do not report code 69990 in addition to code 15842)

15845   regional muscle transfer

(For intravenous fluorescein examination of blood flow in graft or flap, use 15860)

(For nerve transfers, decompression, or repair, see 64831-64876, 64905, 64907, 69720, 69725, 69740, 69745, 69955)

+ 15847   Excision, excessive skin and subcutaneous tissue (includes lipectomy), abdomen (eg, abdominoplasty) (includes umbilical transposition and fascial plication) (List separately in addition to code for primary procedure)

(Use 15847 in conjunction with 15830)

(For abdominal wall hernia repair, see 49491-49587)

(To report other abdominoplasty, use 17999)

15850   Removal of sutures under anesthesia (other than local), same surgeon

15851   Removal of sutures under anesthesia (other than local), other surgeon

15852   Dressing change (for other than burns) under anesthesia (other than local)

15860   Intravenous injection of agent (eg, fluorescein) to test vascular flow in flap or graft

15876   Suction assisted lipectomy; head and neck

15877   trunk

15878   upper extremity

15879   lower extremity

(Do not report 15876, 15877, 15878, 15879 in conjunction with 0489T, 0490T)

(For harvesting of adipose tissue for autologous adipose-derived regenerative cell therapy, see 0489T, 0490T)

PRESSURE ULCERS (DECUBITUS ULCERS)

15920   Excision, coccygeal pressure ulcer, with coccygectomy; with primary suture

15922   with flap closure

15931   Excision, sacral pressure ulcer, with primary suture;

15933   with ostectomy

15934   Excision, sacral pressure ulcer, with skin flap closure;

15935   with ostectomy

15936   Excision, sacral pressure ulcer, in preparation for muscle or myocutaneous flap or skin graft closure;

15937   with ostectomy

(For repair of defect using muscle or myocutaneous flap, use code(s) 15734 and/or 15738 in addition to 15936, 15937. For repair of defect using split skin graft, use codes 15100 and/or 15101 in addition to 15936, 15937)

15940   Excision, ischial pressure ulcer, with primary suture;

15941   with ostectomy (ischiectomy)

15944   Excision, ischial pressure ulcer, with skin flap closure;

   ● New Code   ▲ Revised Code   + Add-On Code   ⊘ Modifier -51 Exempt   ★ Telemedicine

| 15945 | with ostectomy |

| 15946 | Excision, ischial pressure ulcer, with ostectomy, in preparation for muscle or myocutaneous flap or skin graft closure |

(For repair of defect using muscle or myocutaneous flap, use code(s) 15734 and/or 15738 in addition to 15946. For repair of defect using split skin graft, use codes 15100 and/or 15101 in addition to 15946)

| 15950 | Excision, trochanteric pressure ulcer, with primary suture; |

| 15951 | with ostectomy |

| 15952 | Excision, trochanteric pressure ulcer, with skin flap closure; |

| 15953 | with ostectomy |

| 15956 | Excision, trochanteric pressure ulcer, in preparation for muscle or myocutaneous flap or skin graft closure; |

| 15958 | with ostectomy |

(For repair of defect using muscle or myocutaneous flap, use code(s) 15734 and/or 15738 in addition to 15956, 15958. For repair of defect using split skin graft, use codes 15100 and/or 15101 in addition to 15956, 15958)

| 15999 | Unlisted procedure, excision pressure ulcer |

(For free skin graft to close ulcer or donor site, see 15002 et seq)

BURNS, LOCAL TREATMENT

Procedures 16000-16036 refer to local treatment of burned surface only. Codes 16020-16030 include the application of materials (eg, dressings) not described in 15100-15278.

List percentage of body surface involved and depth of burn.

For necessary related medical services (eg., hospital visits, detention) in management of burned patients, see appropriate services in E/M and Medicine sections.

For the application of skin grafts or skin substitutes, see 15100-15777.

(For fractional ablative laser fenestration for functional improvement of traumatic or burn scars, see 0479T, 0480T)

| 16000 | Initial treatment, first degree burn, when no more than local treatment is required |

| 16020 | Dressings and/or debridement of partial-thickness burns, initial or subsequent; small (less than 5% total body surface area) |

| 16025 | medium (eg, whole face or whole extremity, or 5% to 10% total body surface area) |

| 16030 | large (eg, more than 1 extremity, or greater than 10% total body surface area) |

| 16035 | Escharotomy; initial incision |

| + 16036 | each additional incision (List separately in addition to code for primary procedure) |

(Use 16036 in conjunction with code 16035)

(For debridement, curettement of burn wound, see 16020-16030)

DESTRUCTION

Destruction means the ablation of benign, premalignant or malignant tissues by any method, with or without curetement, including local anesthesia, and not usually requiring closure.

Any method includes electrosurgery, cryosurgery, laser and chemical treatment. Lesions include condylomata, papillomata, molluscum contagiosum, herpetic lesions, warts (ie, common, plantar, flat), milia or other benign premalignant (eg., actinic keratoses), or malignant lesions.

(For destruction of lesion(s) in specific anatomic sites, see 40820, 46900-46917, 46924, 54050-54057, 54065, 56501, 56515, 57061, 57065, 67850, 68135)

(For laser treatment for inflammatory skin disease, see 96920-96922)

(For paring or cutting of benign hyperkeratotic lesions (eg, corns or calluses), see 11055-11057)

(For sharp removal or electrosurgical destruction of skin tags and fibrocutaneous tags, see 11200, 11201)

(For cryotherapy of acne, use 17340)

(For initiation or follow-up care of topical chemotherapy (eg, 5-FU or similar agents), see appropriate office visits)

(For shaving of epidermal or dermal lesions, see 11300-11313)

(For excision of cicatricial lesion[s] [eg, full thickness excision, through the dermis], see 11400-11446)

(For incisional removal of burn scar, see 16035, 16036)

(For fractional ablative laser fenestration for functional improvement of traumatic or burn scars, see 0479T, 0480T)

DESTRUCTION, BENIGN OR PREMALIGNANT LESIONS

17000 Destruction (eg, laser surgery, electrosurgery, cryosurgery, chemosurgery, surgical curettement), premalignant lesions (eg, actinic keratoses); first lesion

+ 17003 second through 14 lesions, each (List separately in addition to code for first lesion)

(Use 17003 in conjunction with 17000)

(For destruction of common or plantar warts, see 17110-17111)

⊘ **17004** Destruction (eg, laser surgery, electrosurgery, cryosurgery, chemosurgery, surgical curettement), premalignant lesions (eg, actinic keratoses), 15 or more lesions

(Do not report 17004 in conjunction with codes 17000-17003)

17106 Destruction of cutaneous vascular proliferative lesions (eg, laser technique); less than 10 sq cm

17107 10.0 to 50.0 sq cm

17108 over 50.0 sq cm

17110 Destruction (eg, laser surgery, electrosurgery, cryosurgery, chemosurgery, surgical curettement), of benign lesions other than skin tags or cutaneous vascular proliferative lesions; up to 14 lesions

17111 15 or more lesions

(For destruction of extensive cutaneous neurofibroma over 50-100 lesions, see 0419T, 0420T)

▲ **17250** Chemical cauterization of granulation tissue (ie, proud flesh)

(Do not report 17250 with removal or excision codes for the same lesion)

(Do not report 17250 when chemical cauterization is used to achieve wound hemostasis)

● New Code   ▲ Revised Code   ✛ Add-On Code   ⊘ Modifier -51 Exempt   ★ Telemedicine

(Do not report 17250 in conjunction with 97597, 97598, 97602 for the same lesion)

DESTRUCTION, MALIGNANT LESIONS, ANY METHOD

17260 Destruction, malignant lesion (eg, laser surgery, electrosurgery, cryosurgery, chemosurgery, surgical curettement), trunk, arms or legs; lesion diameter 0.5 cm or less

17261 lesion diameter 0.6 to 1.0 cm

17262 lesion diameter 1.1 to 2.0 cm

17263 lesion diameter 2.1 to 3.0 cm

17264 lesion diameter 3.1 to 4.0 cm

17266 lesion diameter over 4.0 cm

17270 Destruction, malignant lesion (eg, laser surgery, electrosurgery, cryosurgery, chemosurgery, surgical curettement), scalp, neck, hands, feet, genitalia; lesion diameter 0.5 cm or less

17271 lesion diameter 0.6 to 1.0 cm

17272 lesion diameter 1.1 to 2.0 cm

17273 lesion diameter 2.1 to 3.0 cm

17274 lesion diameter 3.1 to 4.0 cm

17276 lesion diameter over 4.0 cm

17280 Destruction, malignant lesion, (eg, laser surgery, electrosurgery, cryosurgery, chemosurgery, surgical curettement), face, ears, eyelids, nose, lips, mucous membrane; lesion diameter 0.5 cm or less

17281 lesion diameter 0.6 to 1.0 cm

17282 lesion diameter 1.1 to 2.0 cm

17283 lesion diameter 2.1 to 3.0 cm

17284 lesion diameter 3.1 to 4.0 cm

17286 lesion diameter over 4.0 cm

MOHS MICROGRAPHIC SURGERY

Mohs micrographic surgery is a technique for the removal of complex or ill-defined skin cancer with histologic examination of 100% of the surgical margins. It involves removing a skin cancer one layer at a time and examining these layers under a microscope immediately after they are removed. This procedure allows for a close examination of each layer of skin to detect cancer cells. It also allows a minimal amount of tissue to be removed while ensuring complete removal of all the cancer cells. A local anesthetic is injected into the skin before the surgery. The physician begins to remove the skin cancer and a small amount of healthy tissue, one layer of skin at a time. Each tissue layer is prepared and examined under the microscope for cancer cells. Surgery is complete when no more cancer cells are detected.

If repair is performed, use separate repair, flap, or graft codes. If a biopsy of a suspected skin cancer is performed on the same day as Mohs surgery because there was no prior pathology confirmation of a diagnosis, then report diagnostic skin biopsy (11100, 11101) and frozen section pathology (88331) with modifier 59 to distinguish from the subsequent definitive surgical procedure of Mohs surgery.

(If additional special pathology procedures, stains or immunostains are required, see 88311-88314, 88342)

(Do not report 88314 in conjunction with 17311-17315 for routine frozen section stain (eg., hematoxylin and eosin, toluidine blue) performed during Mohs surgery. When a nonroutine histochemical stain on frozen tissue is utilized, report 88314 with modifier -59)

(Do not report 88302-88309 on the same specimen as part of the Mohs surgery)

17311 Mohs micrographic technique, including removal of all gross tumor, surgical excision of tissue specimens, mapping, color coding of specimens, microscopic examination of specimens by the surgeon, and histopathologic preparation including routine stain(s) (eg, hematoxylin and eosin, toluidine blue), head, neck, hands, feet, genitalia, or any location with surgery directly involving muscle, cartilage, bone, tendon, major nerves, or vessels; first stage, up to 5 tissue blocks

+ **17312** each additional stage after the first stage, up to 5 tissue blocks (List separately in addition to code for primary procedure)

(Use 17312 in conjunction with 17311)

17313 Mohs micrographic technique, including removal of all gross tumor, surgical excision of tissue specimens, mapping, color coding of specimens, microscopic examination of specimens by the surgeon, and histopathologic preparation including routine stain(s) (eg, hematoxylin and eosin, toluidine blue), of the trunk, arms, or legs; first stage, up to 5 tissue blocks

+ **17314** each additional stage after the first stage, up to 5 tissue blocks (List separately in addition to code for primary procedure)

(Use 17314 in conjunction with 17313)

+ **17315** Mohs micrographic technique, including removal of all gross tumor, surgical excision of tissue specimens, mapping, color coding of specimens, microscopic examination of specimens by the surgeon, and histopathologic preparation including routine stain(s) (eg, hematoxylin and eosin, toluidine blue), each additional block after the first 5 tissue blocks, any stage (List separately in addition to code for primary procedure)

(Use 17315 in conjunction with 17311-17314)

OTHER PROCEDURES

17340 Cryotherapy (CO_2 slush, liquid N_2) for acne

17360 Chemical exfoliation for acne (eg, acne paste, acid)

17380 Electrolysis epilation, each 1/2 hour

(For actinotherapy, use 96900)

17999 Unlisted procedure, skin, mucous membrane and subcutaneous tissue

BREAST

Fine needle aspiration biopsies, core biopsies, open incisional or excisional biopsies, and related procedures performed to procure tissue from a lesion for which an established diagnosis exists are not to be reported separately at the time of a lesion excision unless performed on a different lesion or on the contralateral breast. However, if a diagnosis is not established, and the decision to perform the excision or mastectomy is dependent on the results of the biopsy, then the biopsy is separately reported. Modifier -58 may be used appropriately to indicate that the biopsy and the excision or mastectomy are staged or planned procedures.

Because excision of lesions occurs in the course of performing a mastectomy, breast excisions are not separately reported from a mastectomy unless performed to establish the malignant diagnosis before proceeding to the mastectomy. Specifically CPT codes 19110-19126 (breast excision) are in general included in all mastectomy CPT codes 19140-19240 of the same side. However, if the excision is performed to obtain tissue to determine pathologic diagnosis of malignancy prior to proceeding to a mastectomy, the excision is separately reportable with the mastectomy. Modifier -58 should be utilized in this situation.

Use of other integumentary codes for incision and closure are included in the codes describing various breast excision or mastectomy codes. Because of the frequent need to excise lymph node or muscle tissue in conjunction with mastectomies, these

● New Code   ▲ Revised Code   + Add-On Code   ⃠ Modifier -51 Exempt   ★ Telemedicine

procedures have been included in the CPT coding for mastectomy. It would be inappropriate to separately report ipsilateral lymph node excision in conjunction with the appropriate mastectomy codes. However, sentinel lymph node biopsy is separately reported when performed prior to a localized excision of breast or a mastectomy with or without lymphadenectomy.

Open biopsy or excision of sentinel lymph node(s) should be reported as follows: axillary (CPT codes 38500 or 38525), deep cervical (CPT code 38510), internal mammary (CPT code 38530). (CPT code 38740 (axillary lymphadenectomy; superficial) should not be reported for a sentinel lymph node biopsy. Sentinel lymph node biopsy of superficial axillary lymph node(s) is correctly reported as CPT code 38500 (biopsy or excision of lymph node(s), superficial) which includes the removal of one or more discretely identified superficial lymph nodes. By contrast a superficial axillary lymphadenectomy (CPT code 38740) requires removal of all superficial axillary adipose tissue with all lymph nodes in this adipose tissue.)

In the circumstance where a breast lesion is identified and it is determined to be medically necessary to biopsy or excise the contralateral lymph nodes, use of the biopsy or lymph node dissection codes (using the appropriate anatomic modifier, -LT or -RT for left or right) would be acceptable. Additionally, breast reconstruction codes that include the insertion of a prosthetic implant are not to be reported with CPT codes that describe the insertion of a breast prosthesis only.

The CPT coding for breast procedures generally refers to unilateral procedures; when performed bilaterally, modifier -50 would be appropriate. This is identified parenthetically, where appropriate, in the CPT narrative.

INCISION

19000   Puncture aspiration of cyst of breast;

+ **19001**   each additional cyst (List separately in addition to code for primary procedure)

(Use 19001 in conjunction with code 19000)

(If imaging guidance is performed, see 76942, 77021)

19020   Mastotomy with exploration or drainage of abscess, deep

19030   Injection procedure only for mammary ductogram or galactogram

(For radiological supervision and interpretation, see 77053, 77054)

EXCISION

Excisional breast surgery includes certain biopsy procedures, the removal of cysts or other benign or malignant tumors or lesions, and the surgical treatment of breast and chest wall malignancies. Biopsy procedures may be percutaneous or open, and they involve the removal of differing amounts of tissue for diagnosis.

Breast biopsies without image guidance are reported with 19100 and 19101. Image-guided breast biopsies, including the placement of localization devices when performed, are reported using codes 19081-19086. The image-guided placement of localization devices without biopsy are reported with 19281-19288. When more than one biopsy or localization device placement is performed using the same imaging modality, use an add-on code whether the additional service is on the same or contra-lateral breast. If additional biopsies or localization device placements are performed using different imaging modalities, report another primary code for each additional biopsy or localization device placement performed using a different image guidance modality. When an open incisional biopsy is performed after image-guided placement of a localization device, 19101 is reported and the appropriate image-guided localization device placement code is reported. The open excision of breast lesions (eg., lesions of the breast ducts, cysts, benign or malignant tumors), without specific attention to adequate surgical margins, with or without the preoperative placement of radiological markers, is reported using codes 19110-19126. Partial mastectomy procedures (eg., lumpectomy, tylectomy, quadrantectomy, or segmentectomy) describe open excisions of breast tissue with specific attention to adequate surgical margins.

Partial mastectomy procedures are reported using codes 19301 or 19302 as appropriate. Documentation for partial mastectomy procedures includes attention to the removal of adequate surgical margins surrounding the breast mass or lesion. Intraoperative placement of clip(s) is not separately reported.

Total mastectomy procedures include simple mastectomy, complete mastectomy, subcutaneous mastectomy, modified radical mastectomy, radical mastectomy, and more extended procedures (eg, Urban type operation). Total mastectomy procedures are reported using codes 19303-19307 as appropriate. Intraoperative placement of clip(s) is not separately reported.

Excisions or resections of chest wall tumors including ribs, with or without reconstruction, with or without mediastinal lymphadenectomy, are reported using codes 19260, 19271 or 19272. Codes 19260-19272 are not restricted to breast tumors and are used to report resections of chest wall tumors originating from any chest wall component. (For excision of lung or pleura, see 32310 et seq.)

When more than one breast biopsy is performed using the same imaging modality, use an add-on code whether the additional service(s) is on the same or contra-lateral breast. If additional biopsies are performed using different imaging modalities, report another primary code for each additional modality.

To report bilateral image-guided breast biopsies, report 19081, 19083, or 19085 for the initial biopsy. The contra-lateral and each additional breast image guided biopsy are then reported with code 19082, 19084, or 19086.

(To report bilateral procedures for codes 19100-19120, report modifier -50 with the procedure code)

19081 Biopsy, breast, with placement of breast localization device(s) (eg, clip, metallic pellet), when performed, and imaging of the biopsy specimen, when performed, percutaneous; first lesion, including stereotactic guidance

+ **19082** each additional lesion, including stereotactic guidance (List separately in addition to code for primary procedure)

(Use 19082 in conjunction with 19081)

19083 Biopsy, breast, with placement of breast localization device(s) (eg, clip, metallic pellet), when performed, and imaging of the biopsy specimen, when performed, percutaneous; first lesion, including ultrasound guidance

+ **19084** each additional lesion, including ultrasound guidance (List separately in addition to code for primary procedure)

(Use 19084 in conjunction with 19083)

19085 Biopsy, breast, with placement of breast localization device(s) (eg, clip, metallic pellet), when performed, and imaging of the biopsy specimen, when performed, percutaneous; first lesion, including magnetic resonance guidance

+ **19086** each additional lesion, including magnetic resonance guidance (List separately in addition to code for primary procedure)

(Use 19086 in conjunction with 19085)

(Do not report 19081-19086 in conjunction with 19281-19288, 76098, 76942, 77002, 77021 for same lesion)

19100 Biopsy of breast; percutaneous, needle core, not using imaging guidance (separate procedure)

(For fine needle aspiration, use 10021)

19101 open, incisional

(For placement of percutaneous localization clip with imaging guidance, see 19281-19288)

(**19102** deleted 2013 [2014 edition]. To report, see 19081-19086)

(**19103** deleted 2013 [2014 edition]. To report, see 19081-19086)

19105 Ablation, cryosurgical, of fibroadenoma, including ultrasound guidance, each fibroadenoma

(Do not report 19105 in conjunction with 76940, 76942)

(For adjacent lesions treated with one cryoprobe insertion, report once)

19110 Nipple exploration, with or without excision of a solitary lactiferous duct or a papilloma lactiferous duct

19112 Excision of lactiferous duct fistula

● New Code   ▲ Revised Code   + Add-On Code   ⊘ Modifier -51 Exempt   ★ Telemedicine

19120   Excision of cyst, fibroadenoma, or other benign or malignant tumor, aberrant breast tissue, duct lesion, nipple or areolar lesion (except 19300), open, male or female, 1 or more lesions

19125   Excision of breast lesion identified by preoperative placement of radiological marker, open; single lesion

+ **19126**   each additional lesion separately identified by a preoperative radiological marker (List separately in addition to code for primary procedure)

(Use 19126 in conjunction with code 19125)

(Intraoperative placement of clip[s] is not separately reported)

19260   Excision of chest wall tumor including ribs

19271   Excision of chest wall tumor involving ribs, with plastic reconstruction; without mediastinal lymphadenectomy

19272   with mediastinal lymphadenectomy

(Do not report 19260, 19271, 19272 in conjunction with 32100, 32503, 32504, 32551, 32554, 32555)

INTRODUCTION

Breast biopsies without image guidance are reported with 19100 and 19101. Image-guided breast biopsies, including the placement of localization devices when performed, are reported using 19081-19086. The image-guided placement of localization devices without image-guided biopsies are reported with 19281-19288. When more than one biopsy or localization device placement is performed using the same imaging modality, use an add-on code whether the additional service(s) is on the same or contra-lateral breast. If additional biopsies or localization device placements are performed using different imaging modalities, report another primary code for each additional biopsy or localization device placement performed using a different image guidance modality. When an open incisional biopsy is performed after image-guided placement of a localization device, 19101 is reported and the appropriate image-guided localization device placement code is reported.

When more than one breast localization device placement is performed using the same imaging modality, use an add-on code whether the additional service(s) is on the same or contra-lateral breast. If additional localization devices are placed using different imaging modalities, report another primary code for each additional modality. When an open incisional biopsy is performed after image-guided placement of a localization device, 19101 is reported and the appropriate image-guided localization device placement code is reported.

To report bilateral image-guided placement of localization devices, report 19281, 19283, 19285 or 19287 for the initial lesion localized. The contra-lateral and each additional breast image-guided localization device placement is reported with code 19282, 19284, 19286 or 19288.

Code 19294 is used to report the preparation of the tumor cavity with placement of an intraoperative radiation therapy applicator concurrent with partial mastectomy (19301, 19302).

19281   Placement of breast localization device(s) (eg, clip, metallic pellet, wire/needle, radioactive seeds), percutaneous; first lesion, including mammographic guidance

+ **19282**   each additional lesion, including mammographic guidance (List separately in addition to code for primary procedure)

(Use 19282 in conjunction with 19281)

19283   Placement of breast localization device(s) (eg, clip, metallic pellet, wire/needle, radioactive seeds), percutaneous; first lesion, including stereotactic guidance

+ **19284**   each additional lesion, including stereotactic guidance (List separately in addition to code for primary procedure)

(Use 19284 in conjunction with 19283)

19285   Placement of breast localization device(s) (eg, clip, metallic pellet, wire/needle, radioactive seeds), percutaneous; first lesion including ultrasound guidance

---

+ 19286   each additional lesion, including ultrasound guidance (List separately in addition to code for primary procedure)

(Use 19286 in conjunction with 19285)

19287   Placement of breast localization device(s) (eg, clip, metallic pellet, wire/needle, radioactive seeds), percutaneous; first lesion, including magnetic resonance guidance

+ 19288   each additional lesion, including magnetic resonance guidance (List separately in addition to code for primary procedure)

(Use 19288 in conjunction with 19287)

(Do not report 19281-19288 in conjunction with 19081-19086, 76942, 77002, 77021 for same lesion)

(For surgical specimen radiography, use 76098)

(To report image-guided placement of breast localization devices during image-guided biopsy, see 19081-19086. To report image-guided placement of breast localization devices without image-guided biopsy, see 19281-19288)

●+19294   Preparation of tumor cavity, with placement of a radiation therapy applicator for intraoperative radiation therapy (IORT) concurrent with partial mastectomy (List separately in addition to code for primary procedure)

(Use 19294 in conjunction with 19301, 19302)

19296   Placement of radiotherapy afterloading expandable catheter (single or multichannel) into the breast for interstitial radioelement application following partial mastectomy, includes imaging guidance; on date separate from partial mastectomy

+ 19297   concurrent with partial mastectomy (List separately in addition to code for primary procedure)

(Use 19297 in conjunction with 19160 or 19162)

19298   Placement of radiotherapy after loading brachytherapy catheters (multiple tube and button type) into the breast for interstitial radioelement application following (at the time of or subsequent to) partial mastectomy, includes imaging guidance

MASTECTOMY PROCEDURES

19300   Mastectomy for gynecomastia

19301   Mastectomy, partial (eg, lumpectomy, tylectomy, quadrantectomy, segmentectomy);

19302   with axillary lymphadenectomy

(For placement of radiotherapy afterloading balloon/brachytherapy catheters, see 19296-19298)

(Intraoperative placement of clip[s] is not separately reported)

(For the preparation of tumor cavity with placement of an intraoperative radiation therapy applicator concurrent with partial mastectomy, use 19294)

19303   Mastectomy, simple, complete

(Intraoperative placement of clip[s] is not separately reported)

(For immediate or delayed insertion of implant, see 19340, 19342)

(For gynecomastia, use 19300)

19304   Mastectomy, subcutaneous

(Intraoperative placement of clip[s] is not separately reported)

(For immediate or delayed insertion of implant, see 19340, 19342)

19305 Mastectomy, radical, including pectoral muscles, axillary lymph nodes

(Intraoperative placement of clip[s] is not separately reported)

(For immediate or delayed insertion of implant, see 19340, 19342)

19306 Mastectomy, radical, including pectoral muscles, axillary and internal mammary lymph nodes (Urban type operation)

(Intraoperative placement of clip[s] is not separately reported)

(For immediate or delayed insertion of implant, see 19340, 19342)

19307 Mastectomy, modified radical, including axillary lymph nodes, with or without pectoralis minor muscle, but excluding pectoralis major muscle

(Intraoperative placement of clip[s] is not separately reported)

(For immediate or delayed insertion of implant, see 19340, 19342)

REPAIR AND/OR RECONSTRUCTION

(To report bilateral procedures, report modifier -50 with the procedure code)

(For biologic implant for soft tissue reinforcement, use 15777 in conjunction with primary procedure)

19316 Mastopexy

19318 Reduction mammaplasty

19324 Mammaplasty, augmentation; without prosthetic implant

19325 with prosthetic implant

(For flap or graft, use also appropriate number)

19328 Removal of intact mammary implant

19330 Removal of mammary implant material

19340 Immediate insertion of breast prosthesis following mastopexy, mastectomy or in reconstruction

19342 Delayed insertion of breast prosthesis following mastopexy, mastectomy or in reconstruction

(For supply of implant, use 99070)

(For preparation of custom breast implant, use 19396)

19350 Nipple/areola reconstruction

19355 Correction of inverted nipples

19357 Breast reconstruction, immediate or delayed, with tissue expander, including subsequent expansion

19361 Breast reconstruction with latissimus dorsi flap, without prosthetic implant

(For insertion of prosthesis, use also 19340)

19364 Breast reconstruction with free flap

(Do not report code 69990 in addition to code 19364)

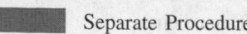 Separate Procedure   Unlisted Procedure   CCI Comp. Code   Non-specific Procedure   **237**

(19364 includes harvesting of the flap, microvascular transfer, closure of the donor site, and inset shaping the flap into a breast)

19366   Breast reconstruction with other technique

(For operating microscope, use 69990)

(For insertion of prosthesis, use also 19340 or 19342)

19367   Breast reconstruction with transverse rectus abdominis myocutaneous flap (TRAM), single pedicle, including closure of donor site;

19368   with microvascular anastomosis (supercharging)

(Do not report code 69990 in addition to code 19368)

19369   Breast reconstruction with transverse rectus abdominis myocutaneous flap (TRAM), double pedicle, including closure of donor site

19370   Open periprosthetic capsulotomy, breast

19371   Periprosthetic capsulectomy, breast

19380   Revision of reconstructed breast

19396   Preparation of moulage for custom breast implant

OTHER PROCEDURES

19499   Unlisted procedure, breast

● New Code   ▲ Revised Code   + Add-On Code   ⊘ Modifier -51 Exempt   ★ Telemedicine

MUSCULOSKELETAL SYSTEM

Musculoskeletal procedure codes include the application and removal of the initial cast or traction device. Use codes in range 29000 to 29999 to report subsequent cast or traction-device applications. Review the instructional notes under the "Application of Casts and Strapping" to identify other uses for these codes.

The procedures and services listed in this section of the CPT coding system include the application and removal of the first cast or traction device only. Subsequent replacement of the cast and/or traction device may be coded using the cast and strapping procedure CPT codes appearing at the end of the section.

MISCELLANEOUS CODING RULES

Most bone, cartilage and fascia graft procedures include obtaining of the graft by the operating surgeon. When a surgical associate obtains the graft for the operating surgeon, the additional service should be coded and coded separately using CPT codes from the 20900-20926 range. In addition, a surgical modifier for assistant surgeon or co-surgeon should be included when reporting the associates services.

CPT codes 20100-20103 relate to treatment of wounds resulting from penetrating trauma (e.g., gunshot, stab wound). Use these codes for wound explorations only if the procedure does not require a thoracotomy or laparotomy and/or repairs to major structure(s) or major blood vessels.

The term "complicated" appears in some narratives in the musculoskeletal subsection. This term implies that an infection occurred, treatment was delayed, or the surgery took longer than usual to perform. Send supporting documentation when the codes containing this descriptor are assigned.

An intermediate repair associated with a musculoskeletal surgery is an integral portion of the surgery and should not be coded separately.

Code the injection codes according to the location of the joint injected or aspirated. Example: small joint = fingers, toes; intermediate joint = wrist, elbow; and major joint = shoulder, hip, or knee.

When removing a foreign body or performing soft tissue biopsy, determine the site and whether or not the foreign body/biopsy is superficial or deep.

FRACTURES

Remember to differentiate between the type of fracture and the type of treatment when coding fractures. Review the meanings of open and closed treatment of fractures. Dislocations must also be coded with emphasis on whether the treatment is open or closed.

When coding the re-reduction of a fracture and/or dislocation performed by the primary physician, add modifier -76 to the procedure code. If the re-reduction were performed by another physician, then modifier -77 would be added to the procedure code.

DEFINITIONS

In orthopedic medicine, fractures are classified as closed or open (compound) and simple or multi-fragmentary (formerly comminuted).

Closed treatment

Closed fractures are those in which the skin is intact, i.e. not surgically open. A closed reduction re-aligns a bone by manipulation without surgery. Sometimes it is not possible for the physician to get the bones in the right position with a closed reduction. If this happens, traction can be put on the bones to gently pull them into position. Traction is usually used for a short period of time and before other forms of treatment are used.

Open treatment

Open (compound) fractures involve wounds that communicate with the fracture and may expose bone to contamination. Open injuries carry an elevated risk of infection; they require antibiotic treatment and usually urgent surgical treatment (debridement). This involves removal of all dirt, contamination, and dead tissue. An open reduction and internal fixation of the bone requires an orthopedic surgeon. The surgery requires cutting open the skin of the area over the fracture so bone fragments can be put back

MUSC-SKEL 20000

into place and the bone fixated or held in place. The bone fragments are held in place with special screws or by attaching metal plates to the bone. Pins that go through the bone or rods that go inside the length of the bone are used to keep the bone in place.

Percutaneous skeletal fixation

Percutaneous skeletal fixation defines fracture treatment which is neither open or closed. Prior to fixation a closed reduction may be performed if necessary for alignment of the broken bones. Pins or screws are then put through the skin and bone above and below the fracture, usually under x-ray guidance. The pins or screws are connected to metal bars on the outside of the skin to form a frame around the fracture. This frame keeps the bone pieces in place.

Simple fractures

Simple fractures are fractures that occur along one line, splitting the bone into two pieces, while multi-fragmentary fractures involve the bone splitting into multiple pieces. A simple, closed fracture is much easier to treat and has a much better prognosis than an open, contaminated fracture. Other considerations in fracture care are displacement (fracture gap) and angulation. If angulation or displacement is large, reduction (manipulation) of the bone may be required and, in adults, frequently requires surgical care. These injuries may take longer to heal than injuries without displacement or angulation

Additional coding rules

- *Codes for obtaining autogenous bone grafts, cartilage, tendon, fascia lata grafts or other tissues through separate incisions are to be used only when the graft is not already listed as part of the basic procedure.*

- *Re-reduction of a fracture and/or dislocation performed in the primary physician may be identified by the addition of modifier -76 to the usual procedure.*

- *Codes for external fixation are to be used only when external fixation is not already listed as part of the basic procedure.*

GENERAL

INCISION

(For incision and drainage procedures, cutaneous/subcutaneous, see 10060, 10061)

20005   Incision and drainage of soft tissue abscess, subfascial, (ie, involves the soft tissue below the deep fascia)

WOUND EXPLORATION—TRAUMA (EG, PENETRATING GUNSHOT, STAB WOUND)

20100-20103 relate to wound(s) resulting from penetrating trauma. These codes describe surgical exploration and enlargement of the wound, extension of dissection (to determine penetration), debridement, removal of foreign body(s), ligation or coagulation of minor subcutaneous and/or muscular blood vessel(s), of the subcutaneous tissue, muscle fascia, and/or muscle, not requiring thoracotomy or laparotomy. If a repair is done to major structure(s) or major blood vessel(s) requiring thoracotomy or laparotomy, then those specific code(s) would supersede the use of codes 20100-20103. To report simple, intermediate, or complex repair of wound(s) that do not require enlargement of the wound, extension of dissection, etc., as stated above, use specific Repair code(s) in the Integumentary System section.

20100   Exploration of penetrating wound (separate procedure); neck

20101   chest

20102   abdomen/flank/back

20103   extremity

EXCISION

20150   Excision of epiphyseal bar, with or without autogenous soft tissue graft obtained through same fascial incision

(For aspiration of bone marrow, use 38220)

20200   Biopsy, muscle; superficial

20205   deep

● New Code   ▲ Revised Code   ✛ Add-On Code   ⊘ Modifier -51 Exempt   ★ Telemedicine

20206 Biopsy, muscle, percutaneous needle

(If imaging guidance is performed, see 76942, 77002, 77012, 77021)

(For fine needle aspiration, use 10021 or 10022)

(For evaluation of fine needle aspirate, see 88172-88173)

(For excision of muscle tumor, deep, see specific anatomic section)

20220 Biopsy, bone, trocar, or needle; superficial (eg, ilium, sternum, spinous process, ribs)

20225 deep (eg, vertebral body, femur)

(Do not report 20225 in conjunction with 22510, 22511, 22512, 22513, 22514, 22515, 0200T, 0201T, when performed at the same level)

(For bone marrow biopsy[ies] and/or aspiration[s], see 38220, 38221, 38222)

(For radiologic supervision and interpretation, see 77002, 77012, 77021)

20240 Biopsy, bone, open; superficial (eg, sternum, spinous process, rib, patella, olecranon process, calcaneus, tarsal, metatarsal, carpal, metacarpal, phalanx)

20245 deep (eg, humeral shaft, ischium, femoral shaft)

20250 Biopsy, vertebral body, open; thoracic

20251 lumbar or cervical

(For sequestrectomy, osteomyelitis or drainage of bone abscess, see anatomical area)

INTRODUCTION OR REMOVAL

(For injection procedure for arthrography, see anatomical area)

(For injection of autologous adipose-derived regenerative cells, see 0489T, 0490T)

20500 Injection of sinus tract; therapeutic (separate procedure)

20501 diagnostic (sinogram)

(For radiological supervision and interpretation, use 76080)

(For contrast injection[s] and radiological assessment of gastrostomy, duodenostomy, jejunostomy, gastrojejunostomy, or cecostomy [or other colonic] tube including fluoroscopic imaging guidance, use 49465)

20520 Removal of foreign body in muscle or tendon sheath; simple

20525 deep or complicated

20526 Injection, therapeutic (eg, local anesthetic, corticosteroid), carpal tunnel

20527 Injection, enzyme (eg, collagenase), palmar fascial cord (ie, Dupuytren's contracture)

(For manipulation of palmar fascial cord (ie, Dupuytren's cord) post enzyme injection (eg, collagenase), use 26341)

20550 Injection(s); single tendon sheath, or ligament, aponeurosis (eg, plantar "fascia")

(For injection of Morton's neuroma, see 64455, 64632)

20551 single tendon origin/insertion

Separate Procedure ■ Unlisted Procedure ■ CCI Comp. Code ■ Non-specific Procedure **241**

(Do not report 20550, 20551 in conjunction with 0232T, 0481T)

(For harvesting, preparation, and injection[s] of platelet-rich plasma, use 0232T)

20552 Injection(s); single or multiple trigger point(s), 1 or 2 muscle(s)

20553 single or multiple trigger point(s), 3 or more muscle(s)

(If imaging guidance is performed, see 76942, 77002, 77021)

20555 Placement of needles or catheters into muscle and/or soft tissue for subsequent interstitial radioelement application (at the time of or subsequent to the procedure)

(For placement of devices into the breast for interstitial radioelement application, see 19296-19298)

(For placement of needles, catheters, or devices into muscle or soft tissue of the head and neck, for interstitial radioelement application, use 41019)

(For placement of needles or catheters for interstitial radioelement application into prostate, use 55875)

(For placement of needles or catheters into the pelvic organs or genitalia [except prostate] for interstitial radioelement application, use 55920)

(For interstitial radioelement application, see 77770, 77771, 77772, 77778)

(For imaging guidance, see 76942, 77002, 77012, 77021)

20600 Arthrocentesis, aspiration and/or injection, small joint or bursa (eg, fingers, toes); without ultrasound guidance

20604 with ultrasound guidance, with permanent recording and reporting

(Do not report 20600, 20604 in conjunction with 76942, 0489T, 0490T)

(If fluoroscopic, CT, or MRI guidance is performed, see 77002, 77012, 77021)

20605 Arthrocentesis, aspiration and/or injection, intermediate joint or bursa (eg, temporomandibular, acromioclavicular, wrist, elbow or ankle, olecranon bursa); without ultrasound guidance

20606 with ultrasound guidance, with permanent recording and reporting

(Do not report 20605, 20606 in conjunction with 76942)

(If fluoroscopic, CT, or MRI guidance is performed, see 77002, 77012, 77021)

20610 Arthrocentesis, aspiration and/or injection, major joint or bursa (eg, shoulder, hip, knee, subacromial bursa); without ultrasound guidance

20611 with ultrasound guidance, with permanent recording and reporting

(Do not report 20610, 20611 in conjunction with 27370, 76942)

(If fluoroscopic, CT, or MRI guidance is performed, see 77002, 77012, 77021)

20612 Aspiration and/or injection of ganglion cyst(s) any location

(To report multiple ganglion cyst aspirations/injections, use 20612 and append modifier -59)

20615 Aspiration and injection for treatment of bone cyst

20650 Insertion of wire or pin with application of skeletal traction, including removal (separate procedure)

20660 Application of cranial tongs, caliper, or stereotactic frame, including removal (separate procedure)

20661 Application of halo, including removal; cranial

● New Code ▲ Revised Code + Add-On Code ⊘ Modifier -51 Exempt ★ Telemedicine

20662   pelvic

20663   femoral

20664 Application of halo, including removal, cranial, 6 or more pins placed, for thin skull osteology (eg, pediatric patients, hydrocephalus, osteogenesis imperfecta)

20665 Removal of tongs or halo applied by another individual

20670 Removal of implant; superficial, (eg, buried wire, pin or rod) (separate procedure)

20680   deep (eg, buried wire, pin, screw, metal band, nail,rod or plate)

20690 Application of a uniplane (pins or wires in 1 plane), unilateral, external fixation system

20692 Application of a multiplane (pins or wires in more than 1 plane), unilateral, external fixation system (eg, Ilizarov, Monticelli type)

20693 Adjustment or revision of external fixation system requiring anesthesia (eg, new pin[s] or wire[s] and/or new ring[s] or bar[s])

20694 Removal, under anesthesia, of external fixation system

20696 Application of multiplane (pins or wires in more than 1 plane), unilateral, external fixation with stereotactic computer-assisted adjustment (eg, spatial frame), including imaging; initial and subsequent alignment(s), assessment(s), and computation(s) of adjustment schedule(s)

(Do not report 20696 in conjunction with 20692, 20697)

⊘ **20697**   exchange (ie, removal and replacement) of strut, each)

(Do not report 20697 in conjunction with 20692, 20696)

REPLANTATION

20802 Replantation, arm (includes surgical neck of humerus through elbow joint), complete amputation

(To report replantation of incomplete arm amputation, see specific code(s) for repair of bone(s), ligament(s), tendon(s), nerve(s), or blood vessel(s) with modifier -52)

20805 Replantation, forearm (includes radius and ulna to radial carpal joint), complete amputation

(To report replantation of incomplete forearm amputation, see specific code(s) for repair of bone(s), ligament(s), tendon(s), nerve(s), or blood vessel(s) with modifier -52)

20808 Replantation, hand (includes hand through metacarpophalangeal joints), complete amputation

(To report replantation of incomplete hand amputation, see specific code(s) for repair of bone(s), ligament(s), tendon(s), nerve(s), or blood vessel(s) with modifier -52)

20816 Replantation, digit, excluding thumb (includes metacarpophalangeal joint to insertion of flexor sublimis tendon), complete amputation

(To report replantation of incomplete digit amputation excluding thumb, see specific code(s) for repair of bone(s), ligament(s), tendon(s), nerve(s), or blood vessel(s) with modifier -52)

20822 Replantation, digit, excluding thumb (includes distal tip to sublimis tendon insertion), complete amputation

(To report replantation of incomplete digit amputation excluding thumb, see specific code(s) for repair of bone(s), ligament(s), tendon(s), nerve(s), or blood vessel(s) with modifier -52)

20824 Replantation, thumb (includes carpometacarpal joint to MP joint), complete amputation

(To report replantation of incomplete thumb amputation, see specific code(s) for repair of bone(s), ligament(s), tendon(s), nerve(s), or blood vessel(s) with modifier -52)

20827 Replantation, thumb (includes distal tip to MP joint), complete amputation

(To report replantation of incomplete thumb amputation, see specific code(s) for repair of bone(s), ligament(s), tendon(s), nerve(s), or blood vessel(s) with modifier -52)

(To report replantation of complete leg amputation see specific code(s) for repair of bone(s), ligament(s), tendon(s), nerve(s), or blood vessel(s) with modifier -52)

(To report replantation of incomplete leg amputation, see specific code(s) for repair of bone(s), ligament(s), tendon(s), nerve(s), or blood vessel(s) with modifier -52)

20838 Replantation, foot, complete amputation

(To report replantation of incomplete foot amputation, see specific code(s) for repair of bone(s), ligament(s), tendon(s), nerve(s), or blood vessel(s) with modifier -52)

GRAFTS (OR IMPLANTS)

Codes for obtaining autogenous bone, cartilage, tendon, fascia lata grafts, bone marrow, or other tissues through separate skin/fascial incisions should be reported separately, unless the code descriptor references the harvesting of the graft or implant (eg, includes obtaining graft).

Do not append modifier 62 to bone graft codes 20900-20938.

(For spinal surgery bone graft(s) see codes 20930-20938)

20900 Bone graft, any donor area; minor or small (eg, dowel or button)

20902   major or large

20910 Cartilage graft; costochondral

20912   nasal septum

(For ear cartilage, use 21235)

20920 Fascia lata graft; by stripper

20922   by incision and area exposure, complex or sheet

20924 Tendon graft, from a distance (eg, palmaris, toe extensor, plantaris)

20926 Tissue grafts, other (eg, paratenon, fat, dermis)

(Do not report 20926 in conjunction with 0489T, 0490T)

(For harvesting of adipose tissue for autologous adipose-derived regenerative cell therapy, see 0489T, 0490T)

(For injection of autologous adipose-derived regenerative cells, see 0489T, 0490T)

(For harvesting, preparation, and injection[s] of platelet-rich plasma, use 0232T)

+ **20930** Allograft, morselized, or placement of osteopromotive material, for spine surgery only (List separately in addition to code for primary procedure)

(Use 20930 in conjunction with 22319, 22532, 22533, 22548-22558, 22590-22612, 22630, 22633, 22634, 22800-22812)

+ **20931** Allograft, structural, for spine surgery only (List separately in addition to code for primary procedure)

● New Code   ▲ Revised Code   + Add-On Code   ⊘ Modifier -51 Exempt   ★ Telemedicine

(Use 20931 in conjunction with 22319, 22532-22533, 22548-22558, 22590-22612, 22630, 22633, 22634, 22800-22812)

+ 20936 Autograft for spine surgery only (includes harvesting the graft); local (eg, ribs, spinous process, or laminar fragments) obtained from same incision (List separately in addition to code for primary procedure)

(Use 20936 in conjunction with 22319, 22532, 22533, 22548-22558, 22590-22612, 22630, 22633, 22634, 22800-22812)

+ 20937 morselized (through separate skin or fascial incision) (List separately in addition to code for primary procedure)

(Use 20937 in conjunction with 22319, 22532, 22533, 22548-22558, 22590-22612, 22630, 22633, 22634, 22800-22812)

+ 20938 structural, bicortical or tricortical (through separate skin or fascial incision) (List separately in addition to code for primary procedure)

(Use 20938 in conjunction with 22319, 22532, 22533, 22548-22558, 22590-22612, 22630, 22633, 22634, 22800-22812)

(For aspiration of bone marrow for bone grafting, spine surgery only, use 20939)

●+20939 Bone marrow aspiration for bone grafting, spine surgery only, through separate skin or fascial incision (List separately in addition to code for primary procedure)

(Use 20939 in conjunction with 22319, 22532, 22533, 22534, 22548, 22551, 22552, 22554, 22556, 22558, 22590, 22595, 22600, 22610, 22612, 22630, 22633, 22634, 22800, 22802, 22804, 22808, 22810, 22812)

(For bilateral procedure, use 20939 with modifier 50)

(For aspiration of bone marrow for the purpose of bone grafting, other than spine surgery and other therapeutic musculoskeletal applications, use 20999)

(For bone marrow aspiration[s] for platelet-rich stem cell injection, use 0232T)

(For diagnostic bone marrow aspiration[s], see 38220, 38222)

OTHER PROCEDURES

20950 Monitoring of interstitial fluid pressure (includes insertion of device, eg, wick catheter technique, needle manometer technique) in detection of muscle compartment syndrome

20955 Bone graft with microvascular anastomosis; fibula

20956 iliac crest

20957 metatarsal

20962 other than fibula, iliac crest, or metatarsal

(Do not report code 69990 in addition to codes 20955-20962)

20969 Free osteocutaneous flap with microvascular anastomosis; other than iliac crest, metatarsal, or great toe

20970 iliac crest

20972 metatarsal

20973 great toe with web space

(Do not report code 69990 in addition to codes 20969-20973)

(For great toe, wrap-around procedure, use 26551)

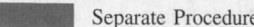

⊘ **20974** Electrical stimulation to aid bone healing; noninvasive (nonoperative)

⊘ **20975**   invasive (operative)

20979 Low intensity ultrasound stimulation to aid bone healing, noninvasive (nonoperative)

20982 Ablation therapy for reduction or eradication of 1 or more bone tumors (eg, metastasis) including adjacent soft tissue when involved by tumor extension, percutaneous, including imaging guidance when performed; radiofrequency

20983   cryoablation

(Do not report 20982, 20983 in conjunction with 76940, 77002, 77013, 77022)

+ **20985** Computer-assisted surgical navigational procedure for musculoskeletal procedures - image-less (List separately in addition to code for primary procedure)

(Do not report 20985 in conjunction with 61781-61783)

(**20986** deleted 2009 edition)

(**20987** deleted 2009 edition)

(For computer-assisted navigational procedures with image guidance based on pre-operative and intraoperatively obtained images, see 0054T, 0055T)

20999 Unlisted procedure, musculoskeletal system, general

HEAD

Skull, facial bones, and temporomandibular joint.

INCISION

(For incision and drainage of superficial abscess and hematoma, see 10060, 10061)

(For incision and drainage of soft tissue abscess, use 20005)

(For removal of embedded foreign body from dentoalveolar structure, see 41805, 41806)

21010 Arthrotomy, temporomandibular joint

(To report bilateral procedures, report 21010 with modifier -50)

EXCISION

21011 Excision, tumor, soft tissue of face or scalp, subcutaneous; less than 2 cm

21012   2 cm or greater

(For excision of benign lesions of cutaneous origin [eg, sebaceous cyst], see 11420-11426)

21013 Excision, tumor, soft tissue of face and scalp, subfascial (eg, subgaleal, intramuscular); less than 2 cm

21014   2 cm or greater

21015 Radical resection of tumor (eg, sarcoma), soft tissue of face or scalp; less than 2 cm

(To report excision of skull tumor for osteomyelitis, use 61501)

21016   2 cm or greater

(For radical resection of tumor[s] of cutaneous origin [eg, melanoma], see 11620-11646)

● New Code   ▲ Revised Code   + Add-On Code   ⊘ Modifier -51 Exempt   ★ Telemedicine

21025 Excision of bone (eg, for osteomyelitis or bone abscess); mandible

21026 facial bone(s)

21029 Removal by contouring of benign tumor of facial bone (eg, fibrous dysplasia)

21030 Excision of benign tumor or cyst of maxilla or zygoma by enucleation and curettage

21031 Excision of torus mandibularis

21032 Excision of maxillary torus palatinus

21034 Excision of malignant tumor of maxilla or zygoma

21040 Excision of benign tumor or cyst of mandible, by enucleation and/or curettage

(For enucleation and/or curettage of benign cysts or tumors of mandible not requiring osteotomy, use 21040)

(For excision of benign tumor or cyst of mandible requiring osteotomy, see 21046-21047)

21044 Excision of malignant tumor of mandible;

21045 radical resection

(For bone graft, use 21215)

21046 Excision of benign tumor or cyst of mandible; requiring intra-oral osteotomy (eg, locally aggressive or destructive lesion(s))

21047 requiring extra-oral osteotomy and partial mandibulectomy (eg, locally aggressive or destructive lesion(s))

21048 Excision of benign tumor or cyst of maxilla; requiring intra-oral osteotomy (eg, locally aggressive or destructive lesion(s))

21049 requiring extra-oral osteotomy and partial maxillectomy (eg, locally aggressive or destructive lesion(s))

21050 Condylectomy, temporomandibular joint (separate procedure)

(For bilateral procedures, report 21050 with modifier -50)

21060 Meniscectomy, partial or complete, temporomandibular joint (separate procedure)

(For bilateral procedures, report 21060 with modifier -50)

21070 Coronoidectomy (separate procedure)

(For bilateral procedures, report 21070 with modifier -50)

MANIPULATION

21073 Manipulation of temporomandibular joint(s) (TMJ), therapeutic, requiring an anesthesia service (ie, general or monitored anesthesia care)

(For TMJ manipulation without an anesthesia service [ie, general or monitored anesthesia care], see 97140, 98925-98929, 98943)

(For closed treatment of temporomandibular dislocation, see 21480, 21485)

| | Separate Procedure | | Unlisted Procedure | | CCI Comp. Code | | Non-specific Procedure | **247** |

HEAD PROSTHESIS

Codes 21076-21089 describe professional services for the rehabilitation of patients with oral, facial, or other anatomical deficiencies by means of prostheses, such as an artificial eye, ear, or nose or intraoral obturator to close a cleft. Codes 21076-21089 should only be used when the physician or other qualified health care professional actually designs and prepares the prosthesis (ie., not prepared by an outside laboratory).

(For application or removal of caliper or tongs, see 20660, 20665)

21076 Impression and custom preparation; surgical obturator prosthesis

21077 orbital prosthesis

21079 interim obturator prosthesis

21080 definitive obturator prosthesis

21081 mandibular resection prosthesis

21082 palatal augmentation prosthesis

21083 palatal lift prosthesis

21084 speech aid prosthesis

21085 oral surgical splint

21086 auricular prosthesis

21087 nasal prosthesis

21088 facial prosthesis

Other Procedures

21089 Unlisted maxillofacial prosthetic procedure

INTRODUCTION OR REMOVAL

21100 Application of halo type appliance for maxillofacial fixation, includes removal (separate procedure)

21110 Application of interdental fixation device for conditions other than fracture or dislocation, includes removal

(For removal of interdental fixation by another individual, see 20670-20680)

21116 Injection procedure for temporomandibular joint arthrography

(For radiological supervision and interpretation, use 70332. Do not report 77002 in addition to 70332)

REPAIR, REVISION AND/OR RECONSTRUCTION

(For cranioplasty, see 21179, 21180 and 62120, 62140-62147)

21120 Genioplasty; augmentation (autograft, allograft, prosthetic material)

21121 sliding osteotomy, single piece

21122 sliding osteotomies, 2 or more osteotomies (eg, wedge excision or bone wedge reversal for asymmetrical chin)

21123 sliding, augmentation with interpositional bone grafts (includes obtaining autografts)

---

248   ● New Code   ▲ Revised Code   ✛ Add-On Code   ⦸ Modifier -51 Exempt   ★ Telemedicine

21125 Augmentation, mandibular body or angle; prosthetic material

21127 with bone graft, onlay or interpositional (includes obtaining autograft)

21137 Reduction forehead; contouring only

21138 contouring and application of prosthetic material or bone graft (includes obtaining autograft)

21139 contouring and setback of anterior frontal sinus wall

21141 Reconstruction midface, LeFort I; single piece, segment movement in any direction (eg, for Long Face Syndrome), without bone graft

21142 2 pieces, segment movement in any direction, without bone graft

21143 3 or more pieces, segment movement in any direction, without bone graft

21145 single piece, segment movement in any direction, requiring bone grafts (includes obtaining autografts)

21146 2 pieces, segment movement in any direction, requiring bone grafts (includes obtaining autografts) (eg, ungrafted unilateral alveolar cleft)

21147 3 or more pieces, segment movement in any direction, requiring bone grafts (includes obtaining autografts) (eg, ungrafted bilateral alveolar cleft or multiple osteotomies)

21150 Reconstruction midface, LeFort II; anterior intrusion (eg, Treacher-Collins Syndrome)

21151 any direction, requiring bone grafts (includes obtaining autografts)

21154 Reconstruction midface, LeFort III (extracranial), any type, requiring bone grafts (includes obtaining autografts); without LeFort I

21155 with LeFort I

21159 Reconstruction midface, LeFort III (extra and intracranial) with forehead advancement (eg, mono bloc), requiring bone grafts (includes obtaining autografts); without LeFort I

21160 with LeFort I

21172 Reconstruction superior-lateral orbital rim and lower forehead, advancement or alteration, with or without grafts (includes obtaining autografts)

(For frontal or parietal craniotomy performed for craniosynostosis, use 61556)

21175 Reconstruction, bifrontal, superior-lateral orbital rims and lower forehead, advancement or alteration (eg, plagiocephaly, trigonocephaly, brachycephaly), with or without grafts (includes obtaining autografts)

(For bifrontal craniotomy performed for craniosynostosis, use 61557)

21179 Reconstruction, entire or majority of forehead and/or supraorbital rims; with grafts (allograft or prosthetic material)

21180 with autograft (includes obtaining grafts)

(For extensive craniectomy for multiple suture craniosynostosis, use only 61558 or 61559)

21181 Reconstruction by contouring of benign tumor of cranial bones (eg, fibrous dysplasia), extracranial

21182 Reconstruction of orbital walls, rims, forehead, nasoethmoid complex following intra- and extracranial excision of benign tumor of cranial bone (eg, fibrous dysplasia), with multiple autografts (includes obtaining grafts); total area of bone grafting less than 40 sq cm

---

21183	total area of bone grafting greater than 40 sq cm but less than 80 sq cm
21184	total area of bone grafting greater than 80 sq cm

(For excision of benign tumor of cranial bones, see 61563, 61564)

21188	Reconstruction midface, osteotomies (other than LeFort type) and bone grafts (includes obtaining autografts)
21193	Reconstruction of mandibular rami, horizontal, vertical, C, or L osteotomy; without bone graft
21194	with bone graft (includes obtaining graft)
21195	Reconstruction of mandibular rami and/or body, sagittal split; without internal rigid fixation
21196	with internal rigid fixation
21198	Osteotomy, mandible, segmental;
21199	with genioglossus advancement

(To report total osteotomy of the maxilla, see 21141-21160)

21206	Osteotomy, maxilla, segmental (eg, Wassmund or Schuchard)
21208	Osteoplasty, facial bones; augmentation (autograft, allograft, or prosthetic implant)
21209	reduction
21210	Graft, bone; nasal, maxillary or malar areas (includes obtaining graft)

(For cleft palate repair, see 42200-42225)

21215	mandible (includes obtaining graft)
21230	Graft; rib cartilage, autogenous, to face, chin, nose or ear (includes obtaining graft)
21235	ear cartilage, autogenous, to nose or ear (includes obtaining graft)

(To report graft augmentation of facial bones, use 21208)

21240	Arthroplasty, temporomandibular joint, with or without autograft (includes obtaining graft)
21242	Arthroplasty, temporomandibular joint, with allograft
21243	Arthroplasty, temporomandibular joint, with prosthetic joint replacement
21244	Reconstruction of mandible, extraoral, with transosteal bone plate (eg, mandibular staple bone plate)
21245	Reconstruction of mandible or maxilla, subperiosteal implant; partial
21246	complete
21247	Reconstruction of mandibular condyle with bone and cartilage autografts (includes obtaining grafts) (eg, for hemifacial microsomia)
21248	Reconstruction of mandible or maxilla, endosteal implant (eg, blade, cylinder); partial
21249	complete

(To report midface reconstruction, see 21141-21160)

21255 Reconstruction of zygomatic arch and glenoid fossa with bone and cartilage (includes obtaining autografts)

21256 Reconstruction of orbit with osteotomies (extracranial) and with bone grafts (includes obtaining autografts) (eg, micro-ophthalmia)

21260 Periorbital osteotomies for orbital hypertelorism, with bone grafts; extracranial approach

21261 combined intra- and extracranial approach

21263 with forehead advancement

21267 Orbital repositioning, periorbital osteotomies, unilateral, with bone grafts; extracranial approach

21268 combined intra- and extracranial approach

21270 Malar augmentation, prosthetic material

(For malar augmentation with bone graft, use 21210)

21275 Secondary revision of orbitocraniofacial reconstruction

21280 Medial canthopexy (separate procedure)

(For medial canthoplasty, use 67950)

21282 Lateral canthopexy

21295 Reduction of masseter muscle and bone (eg, for treatment of benign masseteric hypertrophy); extraoral approach

21296 intraoral approach

OTHER PROCEDURES

21299 Unlisted craniofacial and maxillofacial procedure

FRACTURE AND/OR DISLOCATION

(For operative repair of skull fracture, see 62000-62010)

(To report closed treatment of skull fracture, use the appropriate Evaluation and Management code)

21310 Closed treatment of nasal bone fracture without manipulation

21315 Closed treatment of nasal bone fracture; without stabilization

21320 with stabilization

21325 Open treatment of nasal fracture; uncomplicated

21330 complicated, with internal and/or external skeletal fixation

21335 with concomitant open treatment of fractured septum

21336 Open treatment of nasal septal fracture, with or without stabilization

21337 Closed treatment of nasal septal fracture, with or without stabilization

21338 Open treatment of nasoethmoid fracture; without external fixation

21339   with external fixation

21340   Percutaneous treatment of nasoethmoid complex fracture, with splint, wire or headcap fixation, including repair of canthal ligaments and/or the nasolacrimal apparatus

21343   Open treatment of depressed frontal sinus fracture

21344   Open treatment of complicated (eg, comminuted or involving posterior wall) frontal sinus fracture, via coronal or multiple approaches

21345   Closed treatment of nasomaxillary complex fracture (LeFort II type), with interdental wire fixation or fixation of denture or splint

21346   Open treatment of nasomaxillary complex fracture (LeFort II type); with wiring and/or local fixation

21347   requiring multiple open approaches

21348   with bone grafting (includes obtaining graft)

21355   Percutaneous treatment of fracture of malar area, including zygomatic arch and malar tripod, with manipulation

21356   Open treatment of depressed zygomatic arch fracture (eg, Gillies approach)

21360   Open treatment of depressed malar fracture, including zygomatic arch and malar tripod

21365   Open treatment of complicated (eg, comminuted or involving cranial nerve foramina) fracture(s) of malar area, including zygomatic arch and malar tripod; with internal fixation and multiple surgical approaches

21366   with bone grafting (includes obtaining graft)

21385   Open treatment of orbital floor blowout fracture; transantral approach (Caldwell-Luc type operation)

21386   periorbital approach

21387   combined approach

21390   periorbital approach, with alloplastic or other implant

21395   periorbital approach with bone graft (includes obtaining graft)

21400   Closed treatment of fracture of orbit, except blowout; without manipulation

21401   with manipulation

21406   Open treatment of fracture of orbit, except blowout; without implant

21407   with implant

21408   with bone grafting (includes obtaining graft)

21421   Closed treatment of palatal or maxillary fracture (LeFort I type), with interdental wire fixation or fixation of denture or splint

21422   Open treatment of palatal or maxillary fracture (LeFort I type);

21423   complicated (comminuted or involving cranial nerve foramina), multiple approaches

---

● New Code   ▲ Revised Code   + Add-On Code   ⊘ Modifier -51 Exempt   ★ Telemedicine

21431 Closed treatment of craniofacial separation (LeFort III type) using interdental wire fixation of denture or splint

21432 Open treatment of craniofacial separation (LeFort III type); with wiring and/or internal fixation

21433 complicated (eg, comminuted or involving cranial nerve foramina), multiple surgical approaches

21435 complicated, utilizing internal and/or external fixation techniques (eg, head cap, halo device, and/or intermaxillary fixation)

(For removal of internal or external fixation device, use 20670)

21436 complicated, multiple surgical approaches, internal fixation, with bone grafting (includes obtaining graft)

21440 Closed treatment of mandibular or maxillary alveolar ridge fracture (separate procedure)

21445 Open treatment of mandibular or maxillary alveolar ridge fracture (separate procedure)

21450 Closed treatment of mandibular fracture; without manipulation

21451 with manipulation

21452 Percutaneous treatment of mandibular fracture, with external fixation

21453 Closed treatment of mandibular fracture with interdental fixation

21454 Open treatment of mandibular fracture with external fixation

21461 Open treatment of mandibular fracture; without interdental fixation

21462 with interdental fixation

21465 Open treatment of mandibular condylar fracture

21470 Open treatment of complicated mandibular fracture by multiple surgical approaches including internal fixation, interdental fixation, and/or wiring of dentures or splints

21480 Closed treatment of temporomandibular dislocation; initial or subsequent

21485 complicated (eg, recurrent requiring intermaxillary fixation or splinting), initial or subsequent

21490 Open treatment of temporomandibular dislocation

(For interdental wire fixation, use 21497)

(**21495** deleted 2016 [2017 edition]. To report open treatment of hyoid fracture, use 31584)

(To report treatment of closed fracture of larynx, use the applicable Evaluation and Management codes)

21497 Interdental wiring, for condition other than fracture

OTHER PROCEDURES

21499 Unlisted musculoskeletal procedure, head

(For unlisted craniofacial or maxillofacial procedure, use 21299)

| | Separate Procedure | | Unlisted Procedure | | CCI Comp. Code | | Non-specific Procedure | **253** |

NECK (SOFT TISSUES) AND THORAX

(For cervical spine and back, see 21920 et seq)

(For injection of fracture site or trigger point, use 20550)

INCISION

(For incision and drainage of abscess or hematoma, superficial, see 10060, 10140)

21501 Incision and drainage, deep abscess or hematoma, soft tissues of neck or thorax;

(For posterior spine subfascial incision and drainage, see 22010-22015)

21502 with partial rib ostectomy

21510 Incision, deep, with opening of bone cortex (eg, for osteomyelitis or bone abscess), thorax

EXCISION

(For bone biopsy, see 20220-20251)

21550 Biopsy, soft tissue of neck or thorax

(For needle biopsy of soft tissue, use 20206)

21552 This code is out of order. See page 254.

21554 This code is out of order. See page 254.

21555 Excision, tumor, soft tissue of neck or anterior thorax, subcutaneous; less than 3 cm

21552 3 cm or greater

(For excision of benign lesions of cutaneous origin [eg, sebaceous cyst], see 11420-11426)

21556 Excision, tumor, soft tissue of neck or anterior thorax, subfascial (eg, intramuscular); less than 5 cm

21554 5 cm or greater

21557 Radical resection of tumor (eg, sarcoma), soft tissue of neck or anterior thorax; less than 5 cm

21558 5 cm or greater

(For radical resection of tumor[s] of cutaneous origin [eg, melanoma], see 11600-11620)

21600 Excision of rib, partial

(For radical resection of chest wall and rib cage for tumor, use 19260)

(For radical debridement of chest wall and rib cage for injury, see 11044, 11047)

21610 Costotransversectomy (separate procedure)

21615 Excision first and/or cervical rib;

21616 with sympathectomy

21620 Ostectomy of sternum, partial

21627 Sternal debridement

(For debridement and closure, use 21750)

● New Code ▲ Revised Code + Add-On Code ⊘ Modifier -51 Exempt ★ Telemedicine

21630   Radical resection of sternum;

21632   with mediastinal lymphadenectomy

REPAIR, REVISION, AND/OR RECONSTRUCTION

(For superficial wound, see Integumentary System section under Repair, Simple)

21685   Hyoid myotomy and suspension

21700   Division of scalenus anticus; without resection of cervical rib

21705   with resection of cervical rib

21720   Division of sternocleidomastoid for torticollis, open operation; without cast application

(For transection of spinal accessory and cervical nerves, see 63191, 64722)

21725   with cast application

21740   Reconstructive repair of pectus excavatum or carinatum; open

21742   minimally invasive approach (Nuss procedure), without thoracoscopy

21743   minimally invasive approach (Nuss procedure), with thoracoscopy

21750   Closure of median sternotomy separation with or without debridement (separate procedure)

FRACTURE AND/OR DISLOCATION

(21800   deleted 2014 [2015 edition])

(To report closed treatment of an uncomplicated rib fracture, use the Evaluation and Management codes)

(21805   deleted 2015 [2016 edition])

(21810   deleted 2014 [2015 edition]. For external rib fixation, use 21899)

21811   Open treatment of rib fracture(s) with internal fixation, includes thoracoscopic visualization when performed, unilateral; 1-3 ribs

(For bilateral procedure, report 21811 with modifier 50)

21812   4-6 ribs

(For bilateral procedure, report 21812 with modifier 50)

21813   7 or more ribs

(For bilateral procedure, report 21812 with modifier 50)

21820   Closed treatment of sternum fracture

21825   Open treatment of sternum fracture with or without skeletal fixation

(For sternoclavicular dislocation, see 23520-23532)

OTHER PROCEDURES

21899   Unlisted procedure, neck or thorax

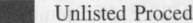

| Separate Procedure | Unlisted Procedure | CCI Comp. Code | Non-specific Procedure | **255** |

BACK AND FLANK

EXCISION

21920 Biopsy, soft tissue of back or flank; superficial

21925   deep

(For needle biopsy of soft tissue, use 20206)

21930 Excision, tumor, soft tissue of back or flank, subcutaneous; less than 3 cm

21931   3 cm or greater

(For excision of benign lesions of cutaneous origin [eg, sebaceous cyst], see 11400-11406)

21932 Excision, tumor, soft tissue of back or flank, subfascial (eg, intramuscular); less than 5 cm

21933   5 cm or greater

21935 Radical resection of tumor (eg, sarcoma), soft tissue of back or flank; less than 5 cm

21936   5 cm or greater

(For radical resection of tumor[s] of cutaneous origin [eg, melanoma], see 11600-11606)

SPINE (VERTEBRAL COLUMN)

Cervical, thoracic and lumbar spine.

Within the spine section, bone grafting procedures are reported separately and in addition to arthrodesis. For bone grafts in other Musculoskeletal sections, see specific code(s) descriptor(s) and/or accompanying guidelines.

To report bone grafts performed after arthrodesis, see 20930-20938. Do not append modifier 62 to bone graft codes 20900-20938.

For example, posterior arthrodesis of L5-S1 for degenerative disc disease utilizing morselized autogenous iliac bone graft harvested through a separate fascial incision. Report as 22612 and 20937.

Within the spine section, instrumentation is reported separately and in addition to arthrodesis. To report instrumentation procedures performed with definitive vertebral procedure(s), see 22840-22855, 22859. Instrumentation procedure codes 22840-22848, 22853, 22854, 22859 are reported in addition to the definitive procedure(s). Modifier 62 may not be appended to the definitive or add-on spinal instrumentation procedure code(s) 22840-22848, 22850, 22852, 22853, 22854, 22859.

For example, posterior arthrodesis of L4-S1 utilizing morselized autogenous iliac bone graft harvested through separate fascial incision, and pedicle screw fixation. Report as 22612, 22614, 22842 and 20937.

When arthrodesis is performed in addition to another procedure, the arthrodesis should be reported in addition to the original procedure with modifier 51 (multiple procedures). Examples are after osteotomy, fracture care, vertebral corpectomy, and laminectomy. Bone grafts and instrumentation are never performed without arthrodesis.

For example, treatment of a burst fracture of L2 by corpectomy followed by arthrodesis of L1-L3, utilizing anterior instrumentation L1-L3 and structural allograft. Report as 63090, 22558-51, 22585, 22845, and 20931.

When two surgeons work together as primary surgeons performing distinct part(s) of a single reportable procedure, each surgeon should report his/her distince operative work by appending modifier 62 to the single definitive procedure code. If additional procedure(s) (including add-on procedure[s]) are performed during the same surgical session, separate code(s) may be reported by each co-surgeon, with modifier 62 appended.

For example, a 42-year-old male with a history of posttraumatic degenerative disc disease at L3-4 and L4-5 (internal disc disruption) underwent surgical repair. Surgeon A performed an anterior exposure of the spine with mobilization of the great vessels. Surgeon B performed anterior (minimal) discectomy and fusion at L3-4 and L4-5 using anterior interbody technique.

Surgeon A report: 22558 append modifier 62, 22585 append modifier 62. Surgeon B report: 22558 append modifier 62, 22585 append modifier 62, 20931.

> (Do not append modifier -62 to bone graft code 20931)

> (For injection procedure for myelography, use 62284)

> (For injection procedure for discography, see 62290, 62291)

> (For injection procedure, chemonucleolysis, single or multiple leveles, use 62292)

> (For injection procedure for facet joints, see 64490-64495, 64633--22-64636)

> (For needle or trocar biopsy, see 20220-20225)

INCISION

22010 Incision and drainage, open, of deep abscess (subfascial), posterior spine; cervical, thoracic, or cervicothoracic

22015   lumbar, sacral, or lumbosacral

> (Do not report 22015 in conjunction with 22010)

> (Do not report 22015 in conjunction with instrumentation removal, 10180, 22850, 22852)

> (For incision and drainage of abscess or hematoma, superficial, see 10060, 10140)

EXCISION

For the following codes, when two surgeons work together as primary surgeons performing distinct part(s) of partial vertebral body excision, each surgeon should report his/her distinct operative work by appending modifier 62 to the procedure code. In this situation, modifier 62 may be appended to the procedure code(s) 22100-22102, 22110-22114 and, as appropriate, to the associated additional vertebral segment add-on code(s) 22103, 22116 as long as both surgeons continue to work together as primary surgeons.

> (For bone biopsy, see 20220-20251)

> (To report soft tissue biopsy of back or flank, see 21920-21925)

> (For needle biopsy of soft tissue, use 20206)

> (To report excision of soft tissue tumor of back or flank, use 21930)

22100 Partial excision of posterior vertebral component (eg, spinous process, lamina or facet) for intrinsic bony lesion, single vertebral segment; cervical

22101   thoracic

22102   lumbar

> (For insertion of posterior spinous process distraction devices, see 22867, 22868, 22869, 22870)

+ **22103**   each additional segment (List separately in addition to code for primary procedure)

> (Use 22103 in conjunction with codes 22100, 22101, 22102)

22110 Partial excision of vertebral body, for intrinsic bony lesion, without decompression of spinal cord or nerve root(s), single vertebral segment; cervical

22112   thoracic

22114   lumbar

+ **22116**   each additional vertebral segment (List separately in addition to code for primary procedure)

> (Use 22116 in conjunction with codes 22110, 22112, 22114)

(For complete or near complete resection of vertebral body, see vertebral corpectomy, 63081-63091)

(For spinal reconstruction with bone graft (autograft, allograft) and/or methacrylate of cervical vertebral body, use 63081 and 22554 and 20931 or 20938)

(For spinal reconstruction with bone graft (autograft, allograft) and/or methacrylate of thoracic vertebral body, use 63085 or 63087 and 22556 and 20931 or 20938)

(For spinal reconstruction with bone graft (autograft, allograft) and/or methacrylate of lumbar vertebral body, use 63087 or 63090 and 22558 and 20931 or 20938)

(For spinal reconstruction following vertebral body resection, use 63082 or 63086 or 63088 or 63091, and 22585)

(For harvest of bone autograft for vertebral reconstruction, see 20931 or 20938)

(For cervical spinal reconstruction with prosthetic replacement of resected vertebral bodies, see codes 63081 and 22554 and 20931 or 20938 and 22853, 22854, 22859)

(For thoracic spinal reconstruction with prosthetic replacement of resected vertebral bodies, see codes 63085 or 63087 and 22556 and 20931 or 20938 and 22853, 22854, 22859)

(For lumbar spinal reconstruction with prosthetic replacement of resected vertebral bodies, see codes 63087 or 63090 and 22558 and 20931 or 20938 and 22853, 22854, 22859)

(For osteotomy of spine, see 22210-22226)

OSTEOTOMY

To report arthrodesis, see codes 22590-22632. (Report in addition to code[s] for the definitive procedure with modifier -51.)

To report instrumentation procedures, see 22840- 22855, 22859. (Report in addition to code[s] for the definitive procedure[s].) Do not append modifier 62 to spinal instrumentation codes 22840-22848, 22850, 22852, 22853, 22854, 22859.

To report bone graft procedures, see 20930-20938. (Report in addition to code[s] for the definitive procedure[s].) Do not append modifier -62 to bone graft codes 20900-20938.

For the following codes, when two surgeons work together as primary surgeons performing distinct part(s) of an anterior spine osteotomy, each surgeon should report his/her distinct operative work by appending modifier 62 to the procedure code. In this situation, modifier 62 may be appended to the procedure code(s) 22210-22214, 22220-22224 and, as appropriate, to associated additional segment add-on code(s) 22216, 22226 as long as both surgeons continue to work together as primary surgeons.

Spinal osteotomy procedures are reported when a portion(s) of the vertebral segment(s) is cut and removed in preparation for re-aligning the spine as part of a spinal deformity correction. For excision of an intrinsic lesion of the vertebra without deformity correction, see 22100-22116. For decompression of the spinal cord and/or nerve roots, see 63001-63308.

The three columns are defined as anterior (anterior two-thirds of the vertabral body), middle (posterior third of the vertebral body and pedicle), and posterior (articular facets, lamina, and spinous process).

22206   Osteotomy of spine, posterior or posterolateral approach, 3 columns, 1 vertebral segment (eg, pedicle/vertebral body subtraction); thoracic

(Do not report 22206 in conjunction with 22207)

22207   lumbar

(Do not report 22207 in conjunction with 22206)

+ 22208   each additional vertebral segment (List separately in addition to code for primary procedure)

(Use 22208 in conjunction with 22206, 22207)

(Do not report 22206, 22207, 22208 in conjunction with 22210-22226, 22830, 63001-63048, 63055-63066, 63075-63091, 63101-63103, when performed at the same level)

22210   Osteotomy of spine, posterior or posterolateral approach, 1 vertebral segment; cervical

● New Code   ▲ Revised Code   + Add-On Code   ⊘ Modifier -51 Exempt   ★ Telemedicine

22212   thoracic

22214   lumbar

+ 22216   each additional vertebral segment (List separately in addition to primary procedure)

(Use 22216 in conjunction with codes 22210, 22212, 22214)

22220   Osteotomy of spine, including diskectomy, anterior approach, single vertebral segment; cervical

22222   thoracic

22224   lumbar

+ 22226   each additional vertebral segment (List separately in addition to code for primary procedure)

(Use 22226 in conjunction with codes 22220, 22222, 22224)

(For vertebral corpectomy, see 63081-63091)

FRACTURE AND/OR DISLOCATION

To report arthrodesis, see codes 22590-22632. (Report in addition to code[s] for the definitive procedure with modifier -51.)

To report instrumentation procedures, see 22840- 22855, 22859. (Report in addition to code[s] for the definitive procedure[s].) Do not append modifier 62 to spinal instrumentation codes 22840-22848, 22850, 22852, 22853, 22854, 22859.

To report bone graft procedures, see 20930-20938. (Report in addition to code[s] for the definitive procedure[s].) Do not append modifier -62 to bone graft codes 20900-20938.

For the following codes, when two surgeons work together as primary surgeons performing distinct part(s) of open fracture and/or dislocation procedure(s), each surgeon should report his/her distinct operative work by appending modifier 62 to the procedure code. In this situation, modifier 62 may be appended to the procedure code(s) 22318-22327 and, as appropriate, the associated additional fracture vertebrae or dislocated segment add-on code 22328 as long as both surgeons continue to work together as primary surgeons.

(22305   deleted 2016 [2017 edition]. To report, see the appropriate evaluation and management codes)

22310   Closed treatment of vertebral body fracture(s), without manipulation, requiring and including casting or bracing

(Do not report 22310 in conjunction with 22510, 22511, 22512, 22513, 22514, 22515, when performed at the same level)

22315   Closed treatment of vertebral fracture(s) and/or dislocation(s) requiring casting or bracing, with and including casting and/or bracing, by manipulation or traction

(Do not report 22315 in conjunction with 22510, 22511, 22512, 22513, 22514, 22515, when performed at the same level)

(For spinal subluxation, use 97140)

22318   Open treatment and/or reduction of odontoid fracture(s) and or dislocation(s) (including os odontoideum), anterior approach, including placement of internal fixation; without grafting

22319   with grafting

22325   Open treatment and/or reduction of vertebral fracture(s) and/or dislocation(s), posterior approach, 1 fractured vertebrae or dislocated segment; lumbar

(Do not report 22325 in conjunction with 22511, 22512, 22514, 22515, when performed at the same level)

22326   cervical

◼ Separate Procedure   ◼ Unlisted Procedure   ◼ CCI Comp. Code   ◼ Non-specific Procedure   **259**

(Do not report 22326 in conjunction with 22510, 22512, when performed at the same level)

22327   thoracic

(Do not report 22327 in conjunction with 22510, 22512, 22513, 22515, when performed at the same level)

+ 22328   each additional fractured vertebrae or dislocated segment (List separately in addition to code for primary procedure)

(Use 22328 in conjunction with codes 22325, 22326, 22327)

(For treatment of vertebral fracture by the anterior approach, see corpectomy 63081-63091, and appropriate arthrodesis, bone graft and instrument codes)

(For decompression of spine following fracture, see 63001-63091; for arthrodesis of spine following fracture, see 22548-22632)

MANIPULATION

(For spinal manipulation without anesthesia, use 97140)

22505   Manipulation of spine requiring anesthesia, any region

PERCUTANEOUS VERTEBROPLASTY AND VERTEBRAL AUGMENTATION

Codes 22510, 22511, 22512, 22513, 22514, 22515 describe procedures for percutaneous vertebral augmentation that include vertebroplasty of the cervical, thoracic, lumbar, and sacral spine and vertebral augmentation of the thoracic and lumbar spine.

For the purposes of reporting 22510, 22511, 22512, 22513, 22514, 22515, "vertebroplasty" is the process of injecting a material (cement) into the vertebral body to reinforce the structure of the body using image guidance. "Vertebral augmentation" is the process of cavity creation followed by the injection of a material (cement) under image guidance. For 0200T and 0201T, "sacral augmentation (sacroplasty)" refers to the creation of a cavity within a sacral vertebral body followed by injection of a material to fill that cavity.

The procedure codes are inclusive of bone biopsy, when performed, and imaging guidance necessary to perform the procedure. Use one primary procedure code and an add-on code for additional levels. When treating the sacrum, sacral procedures are reported only once per encounter.

22510   Percutaneous vertebroplasty (bone biopsy included when performed), 1 vertebral body, unilateral or bilateral injection, inclusive of all imaging guidance; cervicothoracic

22511   lumbosacral

+ 22512   each additional cervicothoracic or lumbosacral vertebral body (List separately in addition to code for primary procedure)

(Use 22512 in conjunction with 22510, 22511)

(Do not report 22510, 22511, 22512 in conjunction with 20225, 22310, 22315, 22325, 22327, when performed at the same level as 22510, 22511, 22512)

22513   Percutaneous vertebral augmentation, including cavity creation (fracture reduction and bone biopsy included when performed) using mechanical device (eg, kyphoplasty), 1 vertebral body, unilateral or bilateral cannulation, inclusive of all imaging guidance; thoracic

22514   lumbar

+ 22515   each additional thoracic or lumbar vertebral body (list separately in addition to code for primary procedure)

(Use 22515 in conjunction with 22513, 22514)

(Do not report 22513, 22514, 22515 in conjunction with 20225, 22310, 22315, 22325, 22327, when performed at the same level as 22513, 22514, 22515)

● New Code   ▲ Revised Code   + Add-On Code   ⊘ Modifier -51 Exempt   ★ Telemedicine

PERCUTANEOUS AUGMENTATION AND ANNULOPLASTY

22526 Percutaneous intradiscal electrothermal annuloplasty, unilateral or bilateral including fluoroscopic guidance; single level

+ 22527 1 or more additional levels (List separately in addition to code for primary procedure)

(Use 22527 in conjunction with 22526)

(Do not report codes 22526, 22527 in conjunction with 77002, 77003)

(For percutaneous intradiscal annuloplasty using method other than electrothermal, use 22899)

ARTHRODESIS

Arthrodesis may be performed in the absence of other procedures and therefore when it is combined with another definitive procedure (eg., osteotomy, fracture care, vertebral corpectomy, or laminectomy), modifier 51 is appropriate. However, arthrodesis codes 22585, 22614, and 22632 are considered add-on procedure codes and should not be used with modifier 51.

To report instrumentation procedures, see 22840- 22855, 22859. (Codes 22840-22848, 22853, 22854, 22859 are reported in conjunction with code[s] for the definitive procedure[s]. When instrumentation reinsertion or removal is reported in conjunction with other definitive procedures, including arthrodesis, decompression, and exploration of fusion, append modifier 51 to 22849, 22850, 22852, and 22855.) To report exploration of fusion, use 22830. (When exploration is reported in conjunction with other definitive procedures, including arthrodesis and decompression, append modifier 51 to 22830.) Do not append modifier 62 to spinal instrumentation codes 22840-22848, 22850, 22852, 22853, 22854, 22859.

To report bone graft procedures, see 20930-20938. (Report in addition to code[s] for the definitive procedure[s].) Do not append modifier -62 to bone graft codes 20900-20938.

Lateral Extracavitary Approach Technique

22532 Arthrodesis, lateral extracavitary technique, including minimal diskectomy to prepare interspace (other than for decompression); thoracic

22533 lumbar

+ 22534 thoracic or lumbar, each additional vertebral segment (List separately in addition to code for primary procedure)

(Use 22534 in conjunction with 22532 and 22533)

Anterior or Anterolateral Approach Technique

Procedure codes 22554-22558 are for SINGLE interspace; for additional interspaces, use 22585. A vertebral interspace is the non-bony compartment between two adjacent vertebral bodies, which contains the intervertebral disc, and includes the nucleus pulposus, annulus fibrosus, and two cartilagenous endplates.

For the following codes, when two surgeons work together as primary surgeons performing distinct part(s) of an anterior interbody arthrodesis, each surgeon should report his/her distinct operative work by appending modifier 62 to the procedure code. In this situation, modifier 62 may be appended to the procedure code(s) 22548-22558 and, as appropriate, to the associated additional interspace add-on code 22585 as long as both surgeons continue to work together as primary surgeons.

22548 Arthrodesis, anterior transoral or extraoral technique, clivus-C1-C2 (atlas-axis), with or without excision of odontoid process

(For intervertebral disc excision by laminotomy or laminectomy, see 63020-63042)

22551 Arthrodesis, anterior interbody, including disc space preparation, discectomy, osteophytectomy and decompression of spinal cord and/or nerve roots, cervical below C2;

+ 22552 each additional interspace (list separately in addition to code for separate procedure)

(Use 22552 in conjunction with 22551)

22554 Arthrodesis, anterior interbody technique, including minimal diskectomy to prepare interspace (other than for decompression); cervical below C2

(Do not report 22554 in conjunction with 63075, even if performed by a separate individual. To report anterior cervical discectomy and interbody fusion at the same level during the same session, use 22551)

22556 thoracic

22558 lumbar

(For arthrodesis using pre-sacral interbody technique, see 22586, 0195T)

+ 22585 each additional interspace (List separately in addition to code for primary procedure)

(Use 22585 in conjunction with codes 22554, 22556, 22558)

(Do not report 22585 in conjunction with 63075 even if performed by a separate individual. To report anterior cervical discectomy and interbody fusion at the same level during the same session, use 22552)

22586 Arthrodesis, pre-sacral interbody technique, including disc space preparation, discectomy, with posterior instrumentation, wiht image guidance, includes bone graft when performed, L5-S1 interspace

(Do not report 22586 in conjunction with 20930-20938, 22840, 22848, 72275, 77002, 77003, 77011, 77012)

Posterior, Posterolateral or Lateral Transverse Process Technique

To report instrumentation procedures, see 22840- 22855, 22859. (Report in addition to code[s] for the definitive procedure[s].) Do not append modifier 62 to spinal instrumentation codes 22840-22848, 22850, 22852, 22853, 22854, 22859

To report bone graft procedures, see 20930-20938. (Report in addition to code[s] for the definitive procedure[s].) Do not append modifier -62 to bone graft codes 20900-20938.

A vertebral segment describes the basic constituent part into which the spine may be divided. It represents a single complete vertebral bone with its associated articular processes and laminae. A vertebral interspace is the non-bony compartment between two adjacent vertebral bodies which contains the intervertebral disc, and includes the nucleus pulposus, annulus fibrosus, and two cartilagenous endplates.

22590 Arthrodesis, posterior technique, craniocervical (occiput-C2)

22595 Arthrodesis, posterior technique, atlas-axis (C1-C2)

22600 Arthrodesis, posterior or posterolateral technique, single level; cervical below C2 segment

22610 thoracic (with lateral transverse technique, when performed)

22612 lumbar (with lateral transverse technique, when performed)

(Do not report 22612 in conjunction with 22630 for the same interspace and segment, use 22633)

+ 22614 each additional vertebral segment (List separately in addition to code for primary procedure)

(Use 22614 in conjunction with 22600, 22610, 22612, 22630 or 22633 when performed at a different level. When performing a posterior or posterolateral technique for fusion/arthrodesis at an additional level, use 22614. When performing a posterior interbody fusion arthrodesis at an additional level, use 22632. When performing a combined posterior or posterolateral technique with posterior interbody arthrodesis at an additional level, use 22634)

(For facet joint fusion, see 0219T-0222T)

(For placement of a posterior intrafacet implant, see 0219T-0222T)

22630 Arthrodesis, posterior interbody technique, including laminectomy and/or diskectomy to prepare interspace (other than for decompression), single interspace; lumbar

---

● New Code   ▲ Revised Code   + Add-On Code   ⊘ Modifier -51 Exempt   ★ Telemedicine

(Do not report 22630 in conjunction with 22612 for the same interspace and segment, use 22633)

+ 22632   each additional interspace (List separately in addition to code for primary procedure)

(Use 22632 in conjunction with 22612, 22630, or 22633 when performed at a different level. When peforming a posterior interbody fusion arthrodesis at an additional level, use 22632. When performing a posterior or posterolateral technique for fusion/arthrodesis at an additional level, use 22614. When performing a combined posterior or posterolateral technique with posterior interbody arthrodesis at an additional level, use 22634)

22633   Arthrodesis, combined posterior or posterolateral technique with posterior interbody technique including laminectomy and/or discectomy sufficient to prepare interspace (other than for decompression), single interspace and segment; lumbar

(Do not report with 22612 or 22630 at the same level)

+ 22634   each additional interspace and segment (List separately in addition to code for primary procedure)

(Use 22634 in conjunction with 22633)

Spine Deformity (eg, Scoliosis, Kyphosis)

To report instrumentation procedures, see 22840- 22855, 22859. (Report in addition to code[s] for the definitive procedure[s].) Do not append modifier 62 to spinal instrumentation codes 22840-22848, 22850, 22852, 22853, 22854, 22859.

To report bone graft procedures, see 20930-20938. (Report in addition to code[s] for the definitive procedure[s].) Do not append modifier -62 to bone graft codes 20900-20938.

A vertebral segment describes the basic constituent part into which the spine may be divided. It represents a single complete vertebral bone with its associated articular processes and laminae.

For the following codes, when two surgeons work together as primary surgeons performing distinct part(s) of an arthrodesis for spinal deformity, each surgeon should report his/her distinct operative work by appending modifier 62 to the procedure code. In this situation, modifier 62 may be appended to procedure code(s) 22800-22819 as long as both surgeons continue to work together as primary surgeons.

22800   Arthrodesis, posterior, for spinal deformity, with or without cast; up to 6 vertebral segments

22802   7 to 12 vertebral segments

22804   13 or more vertebral segments

22808   Arthrodesis, anterior, for spinal deformity, with or without cast; 2 to 3 vertebral segments

22810   4 to 7 vertebral segments

22812   8 or more vertebral segments

22818   Kyphectomy, circumferential exposure of spine and resection of vertebral segment(s) (including body and posterior elements); single or 2 segments

22819   3 or more segments

(To report arthrodesis, see 22800-22804 and add modifier -51)

EXPLORATION

To report instrumentation procedures, see 22840- 22855, 22859. (Codes 22840-22848, 22853, 22854, 22859 are reported in conjunction with code[s] for the definitive procedure[s]. When instrumentation reinsertion or removal is reported in conjunction with other definitive procedures, including arthrodesis, decompression, and exploration of fusion, append modifier 51 to 22849, 22850, 22852, and 22855.) Code 22849 should not be reported with 22850, 22852, and 22855 at the same spinal levels. To report exploration of fusion, see 22830. (When exploration is reported in conjunction with other definitive procedures, including arthrodesis and decompression, append modifier 51 to 22830.)

(To report bone graft procedures, see 20930-20938)

22830 Exploration of spinal fusion

SPINAL INSTRUMENTATION

Segmental instrumentation is defined as fixation at each end of the construct and at least one additional interposed bony attachment.

Non-segmental instrumentation is defined as fixation at each end of the construct and may span several vertebral segments without attachment to the intervening segments.

Insertion of spinal instrumentation is reported separately and in addition to arthrodesis. Instrumentation procedure codes 22840-22848, 22853, 22854, 22859 are reported in addition to the definitive procedure(s). Do not append modifier 62 to spinal instrumentation codes 22840-22848, 22850, 22852, 22853, 22854, 22859.

To report bone graft procedures, see 20930-20938. (Report in addition to code[s] for definitive procedure[s].) Do not append modifier -62 to bone graft codes 20900-20938.

A vertebral segment describes the basic constituent part into which the spine may be divided. It represents a single complete vertebral bone with its associated articular processes and laminae. A vertebral interspace is the non-bony compartment between two adjacent vertebral bodies, which contains the intervertebral disc, and includes the nucleus pulposus, annulus fibrosus, and two cartilaginous endplates.

Codes 22849, 22850, 22852, and 22855 are subject to modifier 51 if reported with other definitive procedure(s), including arthrodesis, decompression, and exploration of fusion. Code 22849 should not be reported in conjincyion with 22850, 22852, and 22855 at the same spinal levels. Only the appropriate insertion code (22840-22848) should be reported when previously placed spinal instrumentation is being removed or revised during the same session where new instrumentation is inserted at levels including all or part of the previously instrumented segments. Do not report the reinsertion (22849) or removal (22850, 22852, 22855) procedures in addition to the insertion of the new instrumentation (22840-22848).

+ 22840 Posterior non-segmental instrumentation (eg, Harrington rod technique, pedicle fixation across 1 interspace, atlantoaxial transarticular screw fixation, sublaminar wiring at C1, facet screw fixation) (List separately in addition to code for primary procedure)

(Use 22840 in conjunction with 22100-22102, 22110- 22114, 22206, 22207, 22210-22214, 22220-22224, 22310- 22327, 22532, 22533, 22548-22558, 22590-22612, 22630, 22633, 22634, 22800-22812, 63001-63030, 63040-63042, 63045-63047, 63050-63056, 63064, 63075, 63077, 63081, 63085, 63087, 63090, 63101, 63102, 63170-63290, 63300-63307)

+ 22841 Internal spinal fixation by wiring of spinous processes (List separately in addition to code for primary procedure)

Use 22841 in conjunction with 22100-22102, 22110- 22114, 22206, 22207, 22210-22214, 22220-22224, 22310-22327, 22532, 22533, 22548-22558, 22590-22612, 22630, 22633, 22634, 22800-22812, 63001-63030, 63040-63042, 63045-63047, 63050-63056, 63064, 63075, 63077, 63081, 63085, 63087, 63090, 63101, 63102, 63170-63290, 63300-63307)

+ 22842 Posterior segmental instrumentation (eg, pedicle fixation, dual rods with multiple hooks and sublaminar wires); 3 to 6 vertebral segments (List separately in addition to code for primary procedure)

(Use 22842 in conjunction with 22100-22102, 22110- 22114, 22206, 22207, 22210-22214, 22220-22224, 22310-22327, 22532, 22533, 22548-22558, 22590-22612, 22630, 22633, 22634, 22800-22812, 63001-63030, 63040-63042, 63045-63047, 63050-63056, 63064, 63075, 63077, 63081, 63085, 63087, 63090, 63101, 63102, 63170-63290, 63300-63307)

+ 22843 7 to 12 vertebral segments (List separately in addition to code for primary procedure)

(Use 22843 in conjunction with 22100-22102, 22110-22114, 22206, 22207, 22210-22214, 22220-22224, 22310-22327, 22532, 22533, 22548-22558, 22590-22612, 22630, 22633, 22634, 22800-22812, 63001-63030, 63040-63042, 63045-63047, 63050-63056, 63064, 63075, 63077, 63081, 63085, 63087, 63090, 63101, 63102, 63170-63290, 63300-63307)

+ 22844 13 or more vertebral segments (List separately in addition to code for primary procedure)

● New Code ▲ Revised Code + Add-On Code ⊘ Modifier -51 Exempt ★ Telemedicine

(Use 22844 in conjunction with 22100-22102, 22110-22114, 22206, 22207, 22210-22214, 22220-22224, 22310-22327, 22532, 22533, 22548-22558, 22590-22612, 22630, 22633, 22634, 22800-22812, 63001-63030, 63040-63042, 63045-63047, 63050-63056, 63064, 63075, 63077, 63081, 63085, 63087, 63090, 63101, 63102, 63170-63290, 63300-63307)

+ **22845** Anterior instrumentation; 2 to 3 vertebral segments (List separately in addition to code for primary procedure)

(Use 22845 in conjunction with 22100-22102, 22110-22114, 22206, 22207, 22210-22214, 22220-22224, 22310-22327, 22532, 22533, 22548-22558, 22590-22612, 22630, 22633, 22634, 22800-22812, 63001-63030, 63040-63042, 63045-63047, 63050-63056, 63064, 63075, 63077, 63081, 63085, 63087, 63090, 63101, 63102, 63170-63290, 63300-63307)

+ **22846** 4 to 7 vertebral segments (List separately in addition to code for primary procedure)

(Use 22846 in conjunction with 22100-22102, 22110-22114, 22206, 22207, 22210-22214, 22220-22224, 22310-22327, 22532, 22533, 22548-22558, 22590-22612, 22630, 22633, 22634, 22800-22812, 63001-63030, 63040-63042, 63045-63047, 63050-63056, 63064, 63075, 63077, 63081, 63085, 63087, 63090, 63101, 63102, 63170-63290, 63300-63307)

+ **22847** 8 or more vertebral segments (List separately in addition to code for primary procedure)

(Use 22847 in conjunction with 22100-22102, 22110-22114, 22206, 22207, 22210-22214, 22220-22224, 22310-22327, 22532, 22533, 22548-22558, 22590-22612, 22630, 22633, 22634, 22800-22812, 63001-63030, 63040-63042, 63045-63047, 63050-63056, 63064, 63075, 63077, 63081, 63085, 63087, 63090, 63101, 63102, 63170-63290, 63300-63307)

+ **22848** Pelvic fixation (attachment of caudal end of instrumentation to pelvic bony structures) other than sacrum (List separately in addition to code for primary procedure)

(Use 22848 in conjunction with 22100-22102, 22110-22114, 22206, 22207, 22210-22214, 22220-22224, 22310-22327, 22532, 22533, 22548-22558, 22590-22612, 22630, 22633, 22634, 22800-22812, 63001-63030, 63040-63042, 63045-63047, 63050-63056, 63064, 63075, 63077, 63081, 63085, 63087, 63090, 63101, 63102, 63170-63290, 63300-63307)

22849 Reinsertion of spinal fixation device

22850 Removal of posterior nonsegmental instrumentation (eg, Harrington rod)

(**22851** deleted 2016 [2017 edition]. To report, see 22853, 22854, 22859)

22852 Removal of posterior segmental instrumentation

+ **22853** Insertion of interbody biomechanical device(s) (eg, synthetic cage, mesh) with integral anterior instrumentation for device anchoring (eg, screws, flanges), when performed, to intervertebral disc space in conjunction with interbody arthrodesis, each interspace (List separately in addition to code for primary procedure)

(Use 22853 in conjunction with 22100-22102, 22110-22114, 22206, 22207, 22210-22214, 22220-22224, 22310-22327, 22532, 22533, 22548-22558, 22590-22612, 22630, 22633, 22634, 22800-22812, 63001-63030, 63040-63042, 63045-63047, 63050-63056, 63064, 63075, 63077, 63081, 63085, 63087, 63090, 63101, 63102, 63170-63290, 63300-63307)

(Report 22853 for each treated intervertebral disc space)

+ **22854** Insertion of intervertebral biomechanical device(s) (eg, synthetic cage, mesh) with integral anterior instrumentation for device anchoring (eg, screws, flanges), when performed, to vertebral corpectomy(ies) (vertebral body resection, partial or complete) defect, in conjunction with interbody arthrodesis, each contiguous defect (List separately in addition to code for primary procedure)

(Use 22854 in conjunction with 22100-22102, 22110-22114, 22206, 22207, 22210-22214, 22220-22224, 22310-22327, 22532, 22533, 22548-22558, 22590-22612, 22630, 22633, 22634, 22800-22812, 63001-63030, 63040-63042, 63045-63047, 63050-63056, 63064, 63075, 63077, 63081, 63085, 63087, 63090, 63101, 63102, 63170-63290, 63300-63307)

+ 22859 Insertion of intervertebral biomechanical device(s) (eg, synthetic cage, mesh, methylmethacrylate) to intervertebral disc space or vertebral body defect without interbody arthrodesis, each contiguous defect (List separately in addition to code for primary procedure)

(Use 22859 in conjunction with 22100-22102, 22110- 22114, 22206, 22207, 22210-22214, 22220-22224, 22310-22327, 22532, 22533, 22548-22558, 22590-22612, 22630, 22633, 22634, 22800-22812, 63001-63030, 63040-63042, 63045-63047, 63050-63056, 63064, 63075, 63077, 63081, 63085, 63087, 63090, 63101, 63102, 63170-63290, 63300-63307)

(22853, 22854, 22859 may be reported more than once for noncontiguous defects)

(For application of an intervertebral bone device/graft, see 20930, 20931, 20936, 20937, 20938)

22855 Removal of anterior instrumentation

22856 Total disc arthroplasty (artificial disc), anterior approach, including discectomy with end plate preparation (includes osteophytectomy for nerve root or spinal cord decompression and microdissection); single interspace, cervical

(Do not report 22856 in conjunction with 22554, 22845, 22853, 22854, 22859, 63075, 0375T when performed at the same level)

(Do not report 22856 in conjunction with 69990)

(For additional interspace cervical total disc arthroplasty, see 22858, 0375T)

+ 22858 second level, cervical (List separately in addition to code for primary procedure)

(Use 22858 in conjunction with 22856)

(Do not report 22858 in conjunction with 0375T, when performed at the same level)

22857 Total disc arthroplasty (artificial disc), anterior approach, including discectomy to prepare interspace (other than for decompression), single interspace, lumbar

(Do not report 22857 in conjunction with 22558, 22845, 22853, 22854, 22859, 49010 when performed at the same level)

(For additional interspace, use Category III code 0163T)

22858 This code is out of order. See page 266.

22859 This code is out of order. See page 266.

22861 Revision including replacement of total disc arthroplasty (artificial disc), anterior approach, single interspace; cervical

(Do not report 22861 in conjunction with 22845, 22853, 22854, 22859, 22864, 63075 when performed at the same level)

(Do not report 22861 in conjunction with 69990)

(For additional interspace revision of cervical total disc arthroplasty, use 0098T)

22862 lumbar

(Do not report 22862 in conjunction with 22558, 22845, 22853, 22854, 22859, 22865, 49010 when performed at the same level)

(For additional interspace, use Category III code 0165T)

22864 Removal of total disc arthroplasty (artificial disc), anterior approach single interspace; cervical

(Do not report 22864 in conjunction with 22861, 69990)

(For additional interspace removal of cervical total disc arthroplasty, use 0095T)

● New Code   ▲ Revised Code   + Add-On Code   ⊘ Modifier -51 Exempt   ★ Telemedicine

22865   lumbar

(Do not report 22865 in conjunction with 49010)

(For additional interspace, use Category III code 0164T)

(22856-22865 include fluoroscopy when performed)

(For decompression, see 63001-63048)

22867 Insertion of interlaminar/interspinous process stabilization/distraction device, without fusion, including image guidance when performed, with open decompression, lumbar; single level

+ 22868   second level (List separately in addition to code for primary procedure)

(Use 22868 in conjunction with 22867)

(Do not report 22867, 22868 in conjunction with 22532, 22533, 22534, 22558, 22612, 22614, 22630, 22632, 22633, 22634, 22800, 22802, 22804, 22840, 22841, 22842, 22869, 22870, 63005, 63012, 63017, 63030, 63035, 63042, 63044, 63047, 63048, 77003 for the same level)

(For insertion of interlaminar/interspinous process stabilization/distraction device, without open decompression or fusion, see 22869, 22870)

22869   Insertion of interlaminar/interspinous process stabilization/distraction device, without open decompression or fusion, including image guidance when performed, lumbar; single level

+ 22870   second level (List separately in addition to code for primary procedure)

(Use 22870 in conjunction with 22869)

(Do not report 22869, 22870 in conjunction with 22532, 22533, 22534, 22558, 22612, 22614, 22630, 22632, 22633, 22634, 22800, 22802, 22804, 22840, 22841, 22842, 63005, 63012, 63017, 63030, 63035, 63042, 63044, 63047, 63048, 77003)

OTHER PROCEDURES

22899 Unlisted procedure, spine

ABDOMEN

EXCISION

22900 Excision, tumor, soft tissue of abdominal wall, subfascial (eg, intramuscular); less than 5 cm

22901   5 cm or greater

22902 Excision, tumor, soft tissue of abdominal wall, subcutaneous; less than 3 cm

22903   3 cm or greater

(For excision of benign lesions of cutaneous origin [eg, sebaceous cyst], see 11400-11406)

22904 Radical resection of tumor (eg, sarcoma), soft tissue of abdominal wall; less than 5 cm

22905   5 cm or greater

(For radical resection of tumor[s] of cutaneous origin [eg, melanoma], see 11600-11606)

OTHER PROCEDURES

22999 Unlisted procedure, abdomen, musculoskeletal system

SHOULDER

INCISION

23000   Removal of subdeltoid calcareous deposits, open

(For arthroscopic removal of bursal deposits, use 29999)

23020   Capsular contracture release (eg, Sever type procedure)

(For incision and drainage procedures, superficial, see 10040-10160)

23030   Incision and drainage, shoulder area; deep abscess or hematoma

23031   infected bursa

23035   Incision, bone cortex (eg, osteomyelitis or bone abscess), shoulder area

23040   Arthrotomy, glenohumeral joint, including exploration, drainage, or removal of foreign body

23044   Arthrotomy, acromioclavicular, sternoclavicular joint, including exploration, drainage, or removal of foreign body

EXCISION

23065   Biopsy, soft tissue of shoulder area; superficial

23066   deep

(For needle biopsy of soft tissue, use 20206)

23071   This code is out of order. See page 268.

23073   This code is out of order. See page 268.

23075   Excision, tumor, soft tissue of shoulder area, subcutaneous; less than 3 cm

23071   3 cm or greater

(For excision of benign lesions of cutaneous origin [eg, sebaceous cyst], see 11400-11406)

23076   Excision, tumor, soft tissue of shoulder area, subfascial (eg, intramuscular); less than 5 cm

23073   5 cm or greater

23077   Radical resection of tumor (eg, sarcoma), soft tissue of shoulder area; less than 5 cm

23078   5 cm or greater

(For radical resection of tumor[s] of cutaneous origin [eg, melanoma], see 11600-11606)

23100   Arthrotomy, glenohumeral joint, including biopsy

23101   Arthrotomy, acromioclavicular joint or sternoclavicular joint, including biopsy and/or excision of torn cartilage

23105   Arthrotomy; glenohumeral joint, with synovectomy, with or without biopsy

23106   sternoclavicular joint, with synovectomy, with or without biopsy

23107   Arthrotomy, glenohumeral joint, with joint exploration, with or without removal of loose or foreign body

---

   ● New Code   ▲ Revised Code   + Add-On Code   ⊘ Modifier -51 Exempt   ★ Telemedicine

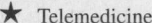

23120 Claviculectomy; partial

(For arthroscopic procedure, use 29824)

23125 total

23130 Acromioplasty or acromionectomy, partial, with or without coracoacromial ligament release

23140 Excision or curettage of bone cyst or benign tumor of clavicle or scapula;

23145 with autograft (includes obtaining graft)

23146 with allograft

23150 Excision or curettage of bone cyst or benign tumor of proximal humerus;

23155 with autograft (includes obtaining graft)

23156 with allograft

23170 Sequestrectomy (eg, for osteomyelitis or bone abscess), clavicle

23172 Sequestrectomy (eg, for osteomyelitis or bone abscess), scapula

23174 Sequestrectomy (eg, for osteomyelitis or bone abscess), humeral head to surgical neck

23180 Partial excision (craterization, saucerization, or diaphysectomy) bone (eg, osteomyelitis), clavicle

23182 Partial excision (craterization, saucerization, or diaphysectomy) bone (eg, osteomyelitis), scapula

23184 Partial excision (craterization, saucerization, or diaphysectomy) bone (eg, osteomyelitis), proximal humerus

23190 Ostectomy of scapula, partial (eg, superior medial angle)

23195 Resection, humeral head

(For replacement with implant, use 23470)

23200 Radical resection of tumor; clavicle

23210 scapula

23220 Radical resection of tumor, proximal humerus

(**23221** Deleted 2009 [2010 edition])

(**23222** Deleted 2009 [2010 edition])

INTRODUCTION OR REMOVAL

(For arthrocentesis or needling of bursa, use 20610)

(For K-wire or pin insertion or removal, see 20650, 20670, 20680)

23330 Removal of foreign body, shoulder; subcutaneous

(To report removal of foreign body, see 23330, 23333)

23333 deep (subfascial or intramuscular)

| Separate Procedure | Unlisted Procedure | CCI Comp. Code | Non-specific Procedure | **269** |

23334 Removal of prosthesis, includes debridement and synovectomy when performed; humeral or glenoid component

23335 humeral and glenoid components (eg, total shoulder)

(Do not report 23334, 23335 in conjunction with 23473, 23474 if a prosthesis [ie, humeral and/or glenoid component(s)] is being removed and replaced in the same shoulder during the same surgical session)

(To report removal of hardware, other than humeral and/or glenoid prosthesis, use 20680)

23350 Injection procedure for shoulder arthrography or enhanced CT/MRI shoulder arthrography

(For radiographic arthrography, radiological supervision and interpretation, use 73040. Fluoroscopy [77002] is inclusive of radiographic arthrography)

(When fluoroscopic guided injection is performed for enhanced CT arthrography, use 23350, 77002 and 73201 or 73202)

(When fluoroscopic guided injection is performed for enhanced MR arthrography, use codes 23350, 77002, and 73222 or 73223)

(For enhanced CT or enhanced MRI arthrography, use 77002 and either 73201, 73202, 73222 or 73223)

(To report biopsy of the shoulder and joint, see 29805-29826)

REPAIR, REVISION AND/OR RECONSTRUCTION

23395 Muscle transfer, any type, shoulder or upper arm; single

23397 multiple

23400 Scapulopexy (eg, Sprengels deformity or for paralysis)

23405 Tenotomy, shoulder area; single tendon

23406 multiple tendons through same incision

23410 Repair of ruptured musculotendinous cuff (eg, rotator cuff) open; acute

23412 chronic

(For arthroscopic procedure, use 29827)

23415 Coracoacromial ligament release, with or without acromioplasty

(For arthroscopic procedure, use 29826)

23420 Reconstruction of complete shoulder (rotator) cuff avulsion, chronic (includes acromioplasty)

23430 Tenodesis of long tendon of biceps

(For arthroscopic biceps tenodesis, use 29828)

23440 Resection or transplantation of long tendon of biceps

23450 Capsulorrhaphy, anterior; Putti-Platt procedure or Magnuson type operation

(To report arthroscopic thermal capsulorrhaphy, use 29999)

23455 with labral repair (eg, Bankart procedure)

(For arthroscopic procedure, use 29806)

23460 Capsulorrhaphy, anterior, any type; with bone block

● New Code ▲ Revised Code + Add-On Code ⊘ Modifier -51 Exempt ★ Telemedicine

23462   with coracoid process transfer

(To report open thermal capsulorrhaphy, use 23929)

23465   Capsulorrhaphy, glenohumeral joint, posterior, with or without bone block

(For sternoclavicular and acromioclavicular reconstruction, see 23530, 23550)

23466   Capsulorrhaphy, glenohumeral joint, any type multi-directional instability

23470   Arthroplasty, glenohumeral joint; hemiarthroplasty

23472   total shoulder (glenoid and proximal humeral replacement (eg, total shoulder))

(For removal of total shoulder implants, see 23334, 23335)

(For osteotomy, proximal humerus, use 24400)

23473   Revision of total shoulder arthroplasty, including allograft when performed; humeral **or** glenoid component

23474   humeral **and** glenoid component

(Do not report 23473, 23474 in conjunction with 23334, 23335 if a prosthesis [ie, humeral and/or glenoid component(s)] is being removed and replaced in the same shoulder during the same surgical session)

23480   Osteotomy, clavicle, with or without internal fixation;

23485   with bone graft for nonunion or malunion (includes obtaining graft and/or necessary fixation)

23490   Prophylactic treatment (nailing, pinning, plating or wiring) with or without methylmethacrylate; clavicle

23491   proximal humerus

FRACTURE AND/OR DISLOCATION

23500   Closed treatment of clavicular fracture; without manipulation

23505   with manipulation

23515   Open treatment of clavicular fracture, includes internal fixation, when performed

23520   Closed treatment of sternoclavicular dislocation; without manipulation

23525   with manipulation

23530   Open treatment of sternoclavicular dislocation, acute or chronic;

23532   with fascial graft (includes obtaining graft)

23540   Closed treatment of acromioclavicular dislocation; without manipulation

23545   with manipulation

23550   Open treatment of acromioclavicular dislocation, acute or chronic;

23552   with fascial graft (includes obtaining graft)

23570   Closed treatment of scapular fracture; without manipulation

23575   with manipulation, with or without skeletal traction (with or without shoulder joint involvement)

23585	Open treatment of scapular fracture (body, glenoid or acromion) includes internal fixation when performed
23600	Closed treatment of proximal humeral (surgical or anatomical neck) fracture; without manipulation
23605	with manipulation, with or without skeletal traction
23615	Open treatment of proximal humeral (surgical or anatomical neck) fracture, includes internal fixation, when performed includes repair of tuberosity(-ies) when performed;
23616	with proximal humeral prosthetic replacement
23620	Closed treatment of greater humeral tuberosity fracture; without manipulation
23625	with manipulation
23630	Open treatment of greater humeral tuberosity fracture, includes internal fixation, when performed
23650	Closed treatment of shoulder dislocation, with manipulation; without anesthesia
23655	requiring anesthesia
23660	Open treatment of acute shoulder dislocation

(Repairs for recurrent dislocations, see 23450-23466)

23665	Closed treatment of shoulder dislocation, with fracture of greater humeral tuberosity, with manipulation
23670	Open treatment of shoulder dislocation, with fracture of greater humeral tuberosity, includes internal fixation, when performed
23675	Closed treatment of shoulder dislocation, with surgical or anatomical neck fracture, with manipulation
23680	Open treatment of shoulder dislocation, with surgical or anatomical neck fracture, includes internal fixation, when performed

MANIPULATION

23700	Manipulation under anesthesia, shoulder joint, including application of fixation apparatus (dislocation excluded)

ARTHRODESIS

23800	Arthrodesis, glenohumeral joint;
23802	with autogenous graft (includes obtaining graft)

AMPUTATION

23900	Interthoracoscapular amputation (forequarter)
23920	Disarticulation of shoulder;
23921	secondary closure or scar revision

OTHER PROCEDURES

23929	Unlisted procedure, shoulder

● New Code   ▲ Revised Code   + Add-On Code   ⊘ Modifier -51 Exempt   ★ Telemedicine

HUMERUS (UPPER ARM) AND ELBOW

The elbow area includes the head and neck of the radius and olecranon process.

INCISION

(For incision and drainage procedures, superficial, see 10040-10160)

23930 Incision and drainage, upper arm or elbow area; deep abscess or hematoma

23931 bursa

23935 Incision, deep, with opening of bone cortex (eg, for osteomyelitis or bone abscess), humerus or elbow

24000 Arthrotomy, elbow, including exploration, drainage, or removal of foreign body

24006 Arthrotomy of the elbow, with capsular excision for capsular release (separate procedure)

EXCISION

24065 Biopsy, soft tissue of upper arm or elbow area; superficial

24066 deep (subfascial or intramuscular)

(For needle biopsy of soft tissue, use 20206)

24071 This code is out of order. See page 273.

24073 This code is out of order. See page 273.

24075 Excision, tumor, soft tissue of upper arm or elbow area, subcutaneous; less than 3 cm

24071 3 cm or greater

(For excision of benign lesions of cutaneous origin [eg, sebaceous cyst], see 11400-11406)

24076 Excision, tumor, soft tissue of upper arm or elbow area, subfascial (eg, intramuscular); less than 5 cm

24073 5 cm or greater

24077 Radical resection of tumor (eg, sarcoma), soft tissue of upper arm or elbow area; less than 5 cm

24079 5 cm or greater

(For radical resection of tumor[s] of cutaneous origin [eg, melanoma], see 11600-11606)

24100 Arthrotomy, elbow; with synovial biopsy only

24101 with joint exploration, with or without biopsy, with or without removal of loose or foreign body

24102 with synovectomy

24105 Excision, olecranon bursa

24110 Excision or curettage of bone cyst or benign tumor, humerus;

24115 with autograft (includes obtaining graft)

24116 with allograft

24120 Excision or curettage of bone cyst or benign tumor of head or neck of radius or olecranon process;

24125	with autograft (includes obtaining graft)
24126	with allograft
24130	Excision, radial head

(For replacement with implant, use 24366)

24134	Sequestrectomy (eg, for osteomyelitis or bone abscess), shaft or distal humerus
24136	Sequestrectomy (eg, for osteomyelitis or bone abscess), radial head or neck
24138	Sequestrectomy (eg, for osteomyelitis or bone abscess), olecranon process
24140	Partial excision (craterization, saucerization, or diaphysectomy) bone (eg, osteomyelitis), humerus
24145	Partial excision (craterization, saucerization, or diaphysectomy) bone (eg, osteomyelitis), radial head or neck
24147	Partial excision (craterization, saucerization, or diaphysectomy) bone (eg, osteomyelitis), olecranon process
24149	Radical resection of capsule, soft tissue, and heterotopic bone, elbow, with contracture release (separate procedure)

(For capsular and soft tissue release only, use 24006)

24150	Radical resection of tumor, shaft or distal humerus
24152	Radical resection of tumor, radial head or neck
24155	Resection of elbow joint (arthrectomy)

INTRODUCTION OR REMOVAL

(For K-wire or pin insertion or removal, see 20650, 20670, 20680)

(For arthrocentesis or needling of bursa or joint, use 20605)

24160	Removal of prosthesis, includes debridement and synovectomy when performed; humeral and ulnar components

(To report removal of foreign body, elbow, see 24200, 24201)

(To report removal of hardware from the distal humerus or proximal ulna, other than humeral and ulnar prosthesis, use 20680)

(Do not report 24160 in conjunction with 24370 or 24371 if a prosthesis [ie, humeral and/or ulnar component(s)] is being removed and replaced in the same elbow during the same surgical session)

24164	radial head

(To report removal of foreign body, elbow, see 24200, 24201)

(To report removal of hardware from proximal radius, other than radial head prosthesis, use 20680)

24200	Removal of foreign body, upper arm or elbow area; subcutaneous
24201	deep (subfascial or intramuscular)
24220	Injection procedure for elbow arthrography

(For radiological supervision and interpretation, use 73085. Do not report 77002 in addition to 73085)

(For injection of tennis elbow, use 20550)

● New Code ▲ Revised Code + Add-On Code ⊘ Modifier -51 Exempt ★ Telemedicine

REPAIR, REVISION, AND/OR RECONSTRUCTION

24300 Manipulation, elbow, under anesthesia

(For application of external fixation, see 20690 or 20692)

24301 Muscle or tendon transfer, any type, upper arm or elbow, single (excluding 24320-24331)

24305 Tendon lengthening, upper arm or elbow, each tendon

24310 Tenotomy, open, elbow to shoulder, each tendon

24320 Tenoplasty, with muscle transfer, with or without free graft, elbow to shoulder, single (Seddon-Brookes type procedure)

24330 Flexor-plasty, elbow (eg, Steindler type advancement);

24331 with extensor advancement

24332 Tenolysis, triceps

24340 Tenodesis of biceps tendon at elbow (separate procedure)

24341 Repair, tendon or muscle, upper arm or elbow, each tendon or muscle, primary or secondary (excludes rotator cuff)

24342 Reinsertion of ruptured biceps or triceps tendon, distal, with or without tendon graft

24343 Repair lateral collateral ligament, elbow, with local tissue

24344 Reconstruction lateral collateral ligament, elbow, with tendon graft (includes harvesting of graft)

24345 Repair medial collateral ligament, elbow, with local tissue

24346 Reconstruction medial collateral ligament, elbow, with tendon graft (includes harvesting of graft)

24357 Tenotomy, elbow, lateral or medial (eg, epicondylitis, tennis elbow, golfer's elbow); percutaneous

24358 debridement, soft tissue and/or bone, open

24359 debridement, soft tissue and/or bone, open with tendon repair or reattachment

(Do not report 24357-24359 in conjunction with 29837, 29838)

24360 Arthroplasty, elbow; with membrane (eg, fascial)

24361 with distal humeral prosthetic replacement

24362 with implant and fascia lata ligament reconstruction

24363 with distal humerus and proximal ulnar prosthetic replacement (eg, total elbow)

(For revision of total elbow implant, see 24370, 24371)

24365 Arthroplasty, radial head;

24366 with implant

24370 Revision of total elbow arthroplasty, including allograft when performed; humeral **or** ulnar component

---

24371   humeral **and** ulnar component

(Do not report 24370, 24371 in conjunction with 24160 if a prosthesis [ie, humeral and/or ulnar component(s)] is being removed and replaced in the same elbow)

24400   Osteotomy, humerus, with or without internal fixation

24410   Multiple osteotomies with realignment on intramedullary rod, humeral shaft (Sofield type procedure)

24420   Osteoplasty, humerus (eg, shortening or lengthening) (excluding 64876)

24430   Repair of nonunion or malunion, humerus; without graft (eg, compression technique)

24435   with iliac or other autograft (includes obtaining graft)

(For proximal radius and/or ulna, see 25400-25420)

24470   Hemiepiphyseal arrest (eg, cubitus varus or valgus, distal humerus)

24495   Decompression fasciotomy, forearm, with brachial artery exploration

24498   Prophylactic treatment (nailing, pinning, plating or wiring), with or without methylmethacrylate, humeral shaft

FRACTURE AND/OR DISLOCATION

24500   Closed treatment of humeral shaft fracture; without manipulation

24505   with manipulation, with or without skeletal traction

24515   Open treatment of humeral shaft fracture with plate/screws, with or without cerclage

24516   Treatment of humeral shaft fracture, with insertion of intramedullary implant, with or without cerclage and/or locking screws

24530   Closed treatment of supracondylar or transcondylar humeral fracture, with or without intercondylar extension; without manipulation

24535   with manipulation, with or without skin or skeletal traction

24538   Percutaneous skeletal fixation of supracondylar or transcondylar humeral fracture, with or without intercondylar extension

24545   Open treatment of humeral supracondylar or transcondylar fracture, includes internal fixation, when performed; without intercondylar extension

24546   with intercondylar extension

24560   Closed treatment of humeral epicondylar fracture, medial or lateral; without manipulation

24565   with manipulation

24566   Percutaneous skeletal fixation of humeral epicondylar fracture, medial or lateral, with manipulation

24575   Open treatment of humeral epicondylar fracture, medial or lateral, includes internal fixation, when performed

24576   Closed treatment of humeral condylar fracture, medial or lateral; without manipulation

24577   with manipulation

---

276   ● New Code   ▲ Revised Code   ✛ Add-On Code   ⊘ Modifier -51 Exempt   ★ Telemedicine

24579 Open treatment of humeral condylar fracture, medial or lateral, includes internal fixation, when performed

(To report closed treatment of fractures without manipulation, see 24530, 24560, 24576, 24650, 24670)

(To report closed treatment of fractures with manipulation, see 24535, 24565, 24577, 24675)

24582 Percutaneous skeletal fixation of humeral condylar fracture, medial or lateral, with manipulation

24586 Open treatment of periarticular fracture and/or dislocation of the elbow (fracture distal humerus and proximal ulna and/or proximal radius);

24587 with implant arthroplasty

(See also 24361)

24600 Treatment of closed elbow dislocation; without anesthesia

24605 requiring anesthesia

24615 Open treatment of acute or chronic elbow dislocation

24620 Closed treatment of Monteggia type of fracture dislocation at elbow (fracture proximal end of ulna with dislocation of radial head), with manipulation

24635 Open treatment of Monteggia type of fracture dislocation at elbow (fracture proximal end of ulna with dislocation of radial head), includes internal fixation, when performed

24640 Closed treatment of radial head subluxation in child, nursemaid elbow, with manipulation

24650 Closed treatment of radial head or neck fracture; without manipulation

24655 with manipulation

24665 Open treatment of radial head or neck fracture, includes internal fixation or radial head excision, when performed;

24666 with radial head prosthetic replacement

24670 Closed treatment of ulnar fracture, proximal end (eg, olecranon or coronoid process[es]); without manipulation

24675 with manipulation

24685 Open treatment of ulnar fracture proximal end (eg, olecranon or coronoid process[es]), includes internal fixation, when performed

(Do not report 24685 in conjunction with 24100-24102)

ARTHRODESIS

24800 Arthrodesis, elbow joint; local

24802 with autogenous graft (includes obtaining graft)

AMPUTATION

24900 Amputation, arm through humerus; with primary closure

24920 open, circular (guillotine)

24925 secondary closure or scar revision

| | Separate Procedure | | Unlisted Procedure | | CCI Comp. Code | | Non-specific Procedure | **277** |

24930   re-amputation

24931   with implant

24935   Stump elongation, upper extremity

24940   Cineplasty, upper extremity, complete procedure

OTHER PROCEDURES

24999   Unlisted procedure, humerus or elbow

FOREARM AND WRIST

INCISION

25000   Incision, extensor tendon sheath, wrist (eg, deQuervains disease)

     (For decompression median nerve or for carpal tunnel syndrome, use 64721)

25001   Incision, flexor tendon sheath, wrist (eg, flexor carpi radialis)

25020   Decompression fasciotomy, forearm and/or wrist, flexor OR extensor compartment; without debridement of nonviable muscle and/or nerve

25023   with debridement of nonviable muscle and/or nerve

     (For decompression fasciotomy with brachial artery exploration, use 24495)

     (For incision and drainage procedures, superficial, see 10040-10160)

     (For debridement, see also 11000-11044)

25024   Decompression fasciotomy, forearm and/or wrist, flexor AND extensor compartment; without debridement of nonviable muscle and/or nerve

25025   with debridement of nonviable muscle and/or nerve

25028   Incision and drainage, forearm and/or wrist; deep abscess or hematoma

25031   bursa

25035   Incision, deep, bone cortex, forearm and/or wrist (eg, osteomyelitis or bone abscess)

25040   Arthrotomy, radiocarpal or midcarpal joint, with exploration, drainage, or removal of foreign body

EXCISION

25065   Biopsy, soft tissue of forearm and/or wrist; superficial

25066   deep (subfascial or intramuscular)

     (For needle biopsy of soft tissue, use 20206)

25071   This code is out of order. See page 278.

25073   This code is out of order. See page 279.

25075   Excision, tumor, soft tissue of forearm and/or wrist area, subcutaneous; less than 3 cm

25071   3 cm or greater

   ●   New Code   ▲   Revised Code   +   Add-On Code   ⊘   Modifier -51 Exempt   ★   Telemedicine

(For excision of benign lesions of cutaneous origin [eg, sebaceous cyst], see 11400-11406)

25076 Excision, tumor, soft tissue of forearm and/or wrist area, subfascial (eg, intramuscular); less than 3 cm

25073   3 cm or greater

25077 Radical resection of tumor (eg, sarcoma), soft tissue of forearm and/or wrist area; less than 3 cm

25078   3 cm or greater

(For radical resection of tumor[s] of cutaneous origin [eg, melanoma], see 11600-11606)

25085 Capsulotomy, wrist (eg, contracture)

25100 Arthrotomy, wrist joint; with biopsy

25101   with joint exploration, with or without biopsy, with or without removal of loose or foreign body

25105   with synovectomy

25107 Arthrotomy, distal radioulnar joint including repair of triangular cartilage, complex

25109 Excision of tendon, forearm and/or wrist, flexor or extensor, each

25110 Excision, lesion of tendon sheath, forearm and/or wrist

25111 Excision of ganglion, wrist (dorsal or volar); primary

25112   recurrent

(For hand or finger, use 26160)

25115 Radical excision of bursa, synovia of wrist, or forearm tendon sheaths (eg, tenosynovitis, fungus, Tbc, or other granulomas, rheumatoid arthritis); flexors

25116   extensors, with or without transposition of dorsal retinaculum

(For finger synovectomies, use 26145)

25118 Synovectomy, extensor tendon sheath, wrist, single compartment;

25119   with resection of distal ulna

25120 Excision or curettage of bone cyst or benign tumor of radius or ulna (excluding head or neck of radius and olecranon process);

(For head or neck of radius or olecranon process, see 24120-24126)

25125   with autograft (includes obtaining graft)

25126   with allograft

25130 Excision or curettage of bone cyst or benign tumor of carpal bones;

25135   with autograft (includes obtaining graft)

25136   with allograft

25145 Sequestrectomy (eg, for osteomyelitis or bone abscess), forearm and/or wrist

---

25150   Partial excision (craterization, saucerization, or diaphysectomy) of bone (eg, for osteomyelitis); ulna

25151   radius

(For head or neck of radius or olecranon process, see 24145, 24147)

25170   Radical resection of tumor, radius or ulna

25210   Carpectomy; 1 bone

(For carpectomy with implant, see 25441-25445)

25215   all bones of proximal row

25230   Radial styloidectomy (separate procedure)

25240   Excision distal ulna partial or complete (eg, Darrach type or matched resection)

(For implant replacement, distal ulna, use 25442)

(For obtaining fascia for interposition, see 20920, 20922)

INTRODUCTION OR REMOVAL

(For K-wire, pin or rod insertion or removal, see 20650, 20670, 20680)

25246   Injection procedure for wrist arthrography

(For radiological supervision and interpretation, use 73115. Do not report 77002 in addition to 73115)

(For foreign body removal, superficial use 20520)

25248   Exploration with removal of deep foreign body, forearm or wrist

25250   Removal of wrist prosthesis; (separate procedure)

25251   complicated, including total wrist

25259   Manipulation, wrist, under anesthesia

(For application of external fixation, see 20690 or 20692)

REPAIR, REVISION, AND/OR RECONSTRUCTION

25260   Repair, tendon or muscle, flexor, forearm and/or wrist; primary, single, each tendon or muscle

25263   secondary, single, each tendon or muscle

25265   secondary, with free graft (includes obtaining graft), each tendon or muscle

25270   Repair, tendon or muscle, extensor, forearm and/or wrist; primary, single, each tendon or muscle

25272   secondary, single, each tendon or muscle

25274   secondary, with free graft (includes obtaining graft), each tendon or muscle

25275   Repair, tendon sheath, extensor, forearm and/or wrist, with free graft (includes obtaining graft) (eg, for extensor carpi ulnaris subluxation)

25280   Lengthening or shortening of flexor or extensor tendon, forearm and/or wrist, single, each tendon

25290   Tenotomy, open, flexor or extensor tendon, forearm and/or wrist, single, each tendon

---

25295 Tenolysis, flexor or extensor tendon, forearm and/or wrist, single, each tendon

25300 Tenodesis at wrist; flexors of fingers

25301 extensors of fingers

25310 Tendon transplantation or transfer, flexor or extensor, forearm and/or wrist, single; each tendon

25312 with tendon graft(s) (includes obtaining graft), each tendon

25315 Flexor origin slide (eg, for cerebral palsy, Volkmann contracture), forearm and/or wrist;

25316 with tendon(s) transfer

25320 Capsulorrhaphy or reconstruction, wrist, open (eg, capsulodesis, ligament repair, tendon transfer or graft) (includes synovectomy, capsulotomy and open reduction) for carpal instability

25332 Arthroplasty, wrist, with or without interposition, with or without external or internal fixation

(For obtaining fascia for interposition, see 20920, 20922)

(For prosthetic replacement arthroplasty, see 25441-25446)

25335 Centralization of wrist on ulna (eg, radial club hand)

25337 Reconstruction for stabilization of unstable distal ulna or distal radioulnar joint, secondary by soft tissue stabilization (eg, tendon transfer, tendon graft or weave, or tenodesis) with or without open reduction of distal radioulnar joint

(For harvesting of fascia lata graft, see 20920, 20922)

25350 Osteotomy, radius; distal third

25355 middle or proximal third

25360 Osteotomy; ulna

25365 radius AND ulna

25370 Multiple osteotomies, with realignment on intramedullary rod (Sofield type procedure); radius OR ulna

25375 radius AND ulna

25390 Osteoplasty, radius OR ulna; shortening

25391 lengthening with autograft

25392 Osteoplasty, radius AND ulna; shortening (excluding 64876)

25393 lengthening with autograft

25394 Osteoplasty, carpal bone, shortening

25400 Repair of nonunion or malunion, radius OR ulna; without graft (eg, compression technique)

25405 with autograft (includes obtaining graft)

25415 Repair of nonunion or malunion, radius AND ulna; without graft (eg, compression technique)

25420 with autograft (includes obtaining graft)

Separate Procedure   Unlisted Procedure   CCI Comp. Code   Non-specific Procedure   **281**

25425	Repair of defect with autograft; radius OR ulna
25426	radius AND ulna
25430	Insertion of vascular pedicle into carpal bone (eg, Hori procedure)
25431	Repair of nonunion of carpal bone (excluding carpal scaphoid (navicular) (includes obtaining graft and necessary fixation), each bone
25440	Repair of nonunion, scaphoid carpal (navicular) bone, with or without radial styloidectomy (includes obtaining graft and necessary fixation)
25441	Arthroplasty with prosthetic replacement; distal radius
25442	distal ulna
25443	scaphoid carpal (navicular)
25444	lunate
25445	trapezium
25446	distal radius and partial or entire carpus (total wrist)
25447	Arthroplasty, interposition, intercarpal or carpometacarpal joints
	(For wrist arthroplasty, use 25332)
25449	Revision of arthroplasty, including removal of implant, wrist joint
25450	Epiphyseal arrest by epiphysiodesis or stapling; distal radius OR ulna
25455	distal radius AND ulna
25490	Prophylactic treatment (nailing, pinning, plating or wiring) with or without methylmethacrylate; radius
25491	ulna
25492	radius AND ulna

FRACTURE AND/OR DISLOCATION

(For application of external fixation in addition to internal fixation, use 20690 and the appropriate internal fixation code)

25500	Closed treatment of radial shaft fracture; without manipulation
25505	with manipulation
25515	Open treatment of radial shaft fracture, includes internal fixation, when performed
25520	Closed treatment of radial shaft fracture and closed treatment of dislocation of distal radioulnar joint (Galeazzi fracture/dislocation)
25525	Open treatment of radial shaft fracture, includes internal fixation, when performed, and closed treatment of distal radioulnar joint dislocation (Galeazzi fracture/dislocation), includes percutaneous skeletal fixation, when performed

● New Code   ▲ Revised Code   + Add-On Code   ⊘ Modifier -51 Exempt   ★ Telemedicine

25526 Open treatment of radial shaft fracture, includes internal fixation, when performed, and open treatment, of distal radioulnar joint dislocation (Galeazzi fracture/dislocation), includes internal fixation, when performed, includes repair of triangular fibrocartilage complex

25530 Closed treatment of ulnar shaft fracture; without manipulation

25535   with manipulation

25545 Open treatment of ulnar shaft fracture, includes internal fixation, when performed

25560 Closed treatment of radial and ulnar shaft fractures; without manipulation

25565   with manipulation

25574 Open treatment of radial AND ulnar shaft fractures, with internal fixation, when performed; of radius OR ulna

25575   of radius AND ulna

25600 Closed treatment of distal radial fracture (eg, Colles or Smith type) or epiphyseal separation, includes closed treatment of fracture of ulnar styloid, when performed; without manipulation

25605   with manipulation

(Do not report 25600, 25605 in conjunction with 25650)

25606 Percutaneous skeletal fixation of distal radial fracture or epiphyseal separation

(Do not report 25606 in conjunction with 25650)

(For percutaneous treatment of ulnar styloid fracture, use 25651)

(For open treatment of ulnar styloid fracture, use 25652)

25607 Open treatment of distal radial extra-articular fracture or epiphyseal separation, with internal fixation

(Do not report 25607 in conjunction with 25650)

(For percutaneous treatment of ulnar styloid fracture, use 25651)

(For open treatment of ulnar styloid fracture, use 25652)

25608 Open treatment of distal radial intra-articular fracture or epiphyseal separation; with internal fixation of 2 fragments

(Do not report 25608 in conjunction with 25609)

25609   with internal fixation of 3 or more fragments

(Do not report 25608, 25609 in conjunction with 25650)

(For percutaneous treatment of ulnar styloid fracture, use 25651)

(For open treatment of ulnar styloid fracture, use 25652)

25622 Closed treatment of carpal scaphoid (navicular) fracture; without manipulation

25624   with manipulation

25628 Open treatment of carpal scaphoid (navicular) fracture, includes internal fixation, when performed

25630 Closed treatment of carpal bone fracture (excluding carpal scaphoid [navicular]); without manipulation, each bone

---

Separate Procedure   Unlisted Procedure   CCI Comp. Code   Non-specific Procedure   **283**

25635	with manipulation, each bone
25645	Open treatment of carpal bone fracture (other than carpal scaphoid [navicular]), each bone
25650	Closed treatment of ulnar styloid fracture

(Do not report 25650 in conjunction with 25600, 25605, 25607-25609)

25651	Percutaneous skeletal fixation of ulnar styloid fracture
25652	Open treatment of ulnar styloid fracture
25660	Closed treatment of radiocarpal or intercarpal dislocation, 1 or more bones, with manipulation
25670	Open treatment of radiocarpal or intercarpal dislocation, 1 or more bones
25671	Percutaneous skeletal fixation of distal radioulnar dislocation
25675	Closed treatment of distal radioulnar dislocation with manipulation
25676	Open treatment of distal radioulnar dislocation, acute or chronic
25680	Closed treatment of trans-scaphoperilunar type of fracture dislocation, with manipulation
25685	Open treatment of trans-scaphoperilunar type of fracture dislocation
25690	Closed treatment of lunate dislocation, with manipulation
25695	Open treatment of lunate dislocation

ARTHRODESIS

25800	Arthrodesis, wrist; complete, without bone graft (includes radiocarpal and/or intercarpal and/or carpometacarpal joints)
25805	with sliding graft
25810	with iliac or other autograft (includes obtaining graft)
25820	Arthrodesis, wrist; limited, without bone graft (eg, intercarpal or radiocarpal)
25825	with autograft (includes obtaining graft)
25830	Arthrodesis, distal radioulnar joint with segmental resection of ulna, with or without bone graft (eg, Sauve-Kapandji procedure)

AMPUTATION

25900	Amputation, forearm, through radius and ulna;
25905	open, circular (guillotine)
25907	secondary closure or scar revision
25909	re-amputation
25915	Krukenberg procedure
25920	Disarticulation through wrist;

● New Code   ▲ Revised Code   + Add-On Code   ⊘ Modifier -51 Exempt   ★ Telemedicine

25922   secondary closure or scar revision

25924   re-amputation

25927   Transmetacarpal amputation;

25929   secondary closure or scar revision

25931   re-amputation

OTHER PROCEDURES

25999   Unlisted procedure, forearm or wrist

HAND AND FINGERS

INCISION

26010   Drainage of finger abscess; simple

26011   complicated (eg, felon)

26020   Drainage of tendon sheath, digit and/or palm, each

26025   Drainage of palmar bursa; single, bursa

26030   multiple bursa

26034   Incision, bone cortex, hand or finger (eg, osteomyelitis or bone abscess)

26035   Decompression fingers and/or hand, injection injury (eg, grease gun)

26037   Decompressive fasciotomy, hand (excludes 26035)

(For injection injury, use 26035)

26040   Fasciotomy, palmar (eg, Dupuytren's contracture); percutaneous

26045   open, partial

(For palmar fasciotomy by enzyme injection (eg, collagenase), see 20527, 26341)

(For fasciectomy, see 26121-26125)

26055   Tendon sheath incision (eg, for trigger finger)

26060   Tenotomy, percutaneous, single, each digit

26070   Arthrotomy, with exploration, drainage, or removal of loose or foreign body; carpometacarpal joint

26075   metacarpophalangeal joint, each

26080   interphalangeal joint, each

EXCISION

26100   Arthrotomy with biopsy; carpometacarpal joint, each

26105   metacarpophalangeal joint, each

26110	interphalangeal joint, each

26111   This code is out of order. See page 286.

26113   This code is out of order. See page 286.

26115	Excision, tumor or vascular malformation, soft tissue of hand or finger, subcutaneous; less than 1.5 cm

26111	1.5 cm or greater

(For excision of benign lesions of cutaneous origin [eg, sebaceous cyst], see 11420-11426)

26116	Excision, tumor or vascular malformation, soft tissue of hand or finger, subfascial (eg, intramuscular); less than 1.5 cm

26113	1.5 cm or greater

26117	Radical resection of tumor (eg, sarcoma), soft tissue of hand or finger; less than 3 cm

26118	3 cm or greater

(For radical resection of tumor[s] of cutaneous origin [eg, melanoma], see 11620-11626)

26121	Fasciectomy, palm only, with or without Z-plasty, other local tissue rearrangement, or skin grafting (includes obtaining graft)

26123	Fasciectomy, partial palmar with release of single digit including proximal interphalangeal joint, with or without Z-plasty, other local tissue rearrangement, or skin grafting (includes obtaining graft);

+ 26125   each additional digit (List separately in addition to code for primary procedure)

(Use 26125 in conjunction with code 26123)

(For palmar fasciotomy by enzyme injection (eg, collagenase), see 20527, 26341)

(For fasciotomy, see 26040, 26045)

26130	Synovectomy, carpometacarpal joint

26135	Synovectomy, metacarpophalangeal joint including intrinsic release and extensor hood reconstruction, each digit

26140	Synovectomy, proximal interphalangeal joint, including extensor reconstruction, each interphalangeal joint

26145	Synovectomy, tendon sheath, radical (tenosynovectomy), flexor tendon, palm and/or finger, each tendon

(For tendon sheath synovectomies at wrist, see 25115, 25116)

26160	Excision of lesion of tendon sheath or joint capsule (eg, cyst, mucous cyst, or ganglion), hand or finger

(For wrist ganglion, see 25111, 25112)

(For trigger digit, use 26055)

26170	Excision of tendon, palm, flexor or extensor, single, each tendon

(Do not report 26170 in conjunction with 26390, 26415)

26180	Excision of tendon, finger, flexor or extensor, each tendon

(Do not report 26180 in conjunction with 26390, 26415)

26185	Sesamoidectomy, thumb or finger (separate procedure)

26200   Excision or curettage of bone cyst or benign tumor of metacarpal;

26205   with autograft (includes obtaining graft)

26210   Excision or curettage of bone cyst or benign tumor of proximal, middle, or distal phalanx of finger;

26215   with autograft (includes obtaining graft)

26230   Partial excision (craterization, saucerization, or diaphysectomy) bone (eg, osteomyelitis); metacarpal

26235   proximal or middle phalanx of finger

26236   distal phalanx of finger

26250   Radical resection of tumor, metacarpal

26260   Radical resection of tumor, proximal or middle phalanx of finger

26262   Radical resection of tumor, distal phalanx of finger

INTRODUCTION OR REMOVAL

26320   Removal of implant from finger or hand

(For removal of foreign body in hand or finger, see 20520, 20525)

REPAIR, REVISION, AND/OR RECONSTRUCTION

26340   Manipulation, finger joint, under anesthesia, each joint

(For application of external fixation, see 20690 or 20692)

26341   Manipulation, palmar fascial cord (ie, Dupuytren's cord), post enzyme injection (eg, collagenase), single cord

(For enzyme injection (eg, collagenase), palmar fascial cord (eg., Dupuytren's contracture), use 20527)

(Report custom orthotic fabrication/application separately)

26350   Repair or advancement, flexor tendon, not in zone 2 digital flexor tendon sheath (eg, no man's land); primary or secondary without free graft, each tendon

26352   secondary with free graft (includes obtaining graft), each tendon

26356   Repair or advancement, flexor tendon, in zone 2 digital flexor tendon sheath (eg, no man's land); primary, without free graft, each tendon

26357   secondary, without free graft, each tendon

26358   secondary with free graft (includes obtaining graft), each tendon

26370   Repair or advancement of profundus tendon, with intact superficialis tendon; primary, each tendon

26372   secondary with free graft (includes obtaining graft), each tendon

26373   secondary without free graft, each tendon

26390   Excision flexor tendon, with implantation of synthetic rod for delayed tendon graft, hand or finger, each rod

---

26392 Removal of synthetic rod and insertion of flexor tendon graft, hand or finger (includes obtaining graft), each rod

26410 Repair, extensor tendon, hand, primary or secondary; without free graft, each tendon

26412 with free graft (includes obtaining graft), each tendon

26415 Excision of extensor tendon, with implantation of synthetic rod for delayed tendon graft, hand or finger, each rod

26416 Removal of synthetic rod and insertion of extensor tendon graft (includes obtaining graft), hand or finger, each rod

26418 Repair, extensor tendon, finger, primary or secondary; without free graft, each tendon

26420 with free graft (includes obtaining graft) each tendon

26426 Repair of extensor tendon, central slip, secondary (eg, boutonniere deformity); using local tissue(s), including lateral band(s), each finger

26428 with free graft (includes obtaining graft), each finger

26432 Closed treatment of distal extensor tendon insertion, with or without percutaneous pinning (eg, mallet finger)

26433 Repair of extensor tendon, distal insertion, primary or secondary; without graft (eg, mallet finger)

26434 with free graft (includes obtaining graft)

(For tenovaginotomy for trigger finger, use 26055)

26437 Realignment of extensor tendon, hand, each tendon

26440 Tenolysis, flexor tendon; palm OR finger, each tendon

26442 palm AND finger, each tendon

26445 Tenolysis, extensor tendon, hand or finger; each tendon

26449 Tenolysis, complex, extensor tendon, finger, including forearm, each tendon

26450 Tenotomy, flexor, palm, open, each tendon

26455 Tenotomy, flexor, finger, open, each tendon

26460 Tenotomy, extensor, hand or finger, open, each tendon

26471 Tenodesis; of proximal interphalangeal joint, each joint

26474 of distal joint, each joint

26476 Lengthening of tendon, extensor, hand or finger, each tendon

26477 Shortening of tendon, extensor, hand or finger, each tendon

26478 Lengthening of tendon, flexor, hand or finger, each tendon

26479 Shortening of tendon, flexor, hand or finger, each tendon

---

● New Code   ▲ Revised Code   ✛ Add-On Code   ⊘ Modifier -51 Exempt   ★ Telemedicine

26480 Transfer or transplant of tendon, carpometacarpal area or dorsum of hand; without free graft, each tendon

26483   with free tendon graft (includes obtaining graft), each tendon

26485 Transfer or transplant of tendon, palmar; without free tendon graft, each tendon

26489   with free tendon graft (includes obtaining graft), each tendon

26490 Opponensplasty; superficialis tendon transfer type, each tendon

26492   tendon transfer with graft (includes obtaining graft), each tendon

26494   hypothenar muscle transfer

26496   other methods

(For thumb fusion in opposition, use 26820)

26497 Transfer of tendon to restore intrinsic function; ring and small finger

26498   all 4 fingers

26499 Correction claw finger, other methods

26500 Reconstruction of tendon pulley, each tendon; with local tissues (separate procedure)

26502   with tendon or fascial graft (includes obtaining graft) (separate procedure)

26508 Release of thenar muscle(s) (eg, thumb contracture)

26510 Cross intrinsic transfer, each tendon

26516 Capsulodesis, metacarpophalangeal joint; single digit

26517   2 digits

26518   3 or 4 digits

26520 Capsulectomy or capsulotomy; metacarpophalangeal joint, each joint

26525   interphalangeal joint, each joint

(To report carpometacarpal joint arthroplasty, use 25447)

26530 Arthroplasty, metacarpophalangeal joint; each joint

26531   with prosthetic implant, each joint

26535 Arthroplasty, interphalangeal joint; each joint

26536   with prosthetic implant, each joint

26540 Repair of collateral ligament, metacarpophalangeal or interphalangeal joint

26541 Reconstruction, collateral ligament, metacarpophalangeal joint, single; with tendon or fascial graft (includes obtaining graft)

26542   with local tissue (eg, adductor advancement)

 Separate Procedure   Unlisted Procedure   CCI Comp. Code   Non-specific Procedure   **289**

26545 Reconstruction, collateral ligament, interphalangeal joint, single, including graft, each joint

26546 Repair non-union, metacarpal or phalanx, (includes obtaining bone graft with or without external or internal fixation)

26548 Repair and reconstruction, finger, volar plate, interphalangeal joint

26550 Pollicization of a digit

26551 Transfer, toe-to-hand with microvascular anastomosis; great toe wrap-around with bone graft

(For great toe with web space, use 20973)

26553   other than great toe, single

26554   other than great toe, double

(Do not report code 69990 in addition to codes 26551-26554)

26555 Transfer, finger to another position without microvascular anastomosis

26556 Transfer, free toe joint, with microvascular anastomosis

(Do not report code 69990 in addition to code 26556)

(To report great toe-to-hand transfer, use 20973)

26560 Repair of syndactyly (web finger) each web space; with skin flaps

26561   with skin flaps and grafts

26562   complex (eg, involving bone, nails)

26565 Osteotomy; metacarpal, each

26567   phalanx of finger, each

26568 Osteoplasty, lengthening, metacarpal or phalanx

26580 Repair cleft hand

26587 Reconstruction of polydactylous digit, soft tissue and bone

(For excision of polydactylous digit, soft tissue only, use 11200)

26590 Repair macrodactylia, each digit

26591 Repair, intrinsic muscles of hand, each muscle

26593 Release, intrinsic muscles of hand, each muscle

26596 Excision of constricting ring of finger, with multiple Z-plasties

(To report release of scar contracture or graft repairs, see 11042, 14040-14041, or 15120, 15240)

FRACTURE AND/OR DISLOCATION

26600 Closed treatment of metacarpal fracture, single; without manipulation, each bone

26605   with manipulation, each bone

● New Code ▲ Revised Code + Add-On Code ⊘ Modifier -51 Exempt ★ Telemedicine

26607 Closed treatment of metacarpal fracture, with manipulation, with external fixation, each bone

26608 Percutaneous skeletal fixation of metacarpal fracture, each bone

26615 Open treatment of metacarpal fracture, single, includes internal fixation, when performed, each bone

26641 Closed treatment of carpometacarpal dislocation, thumb, with manipulation

26645 Closed treatment of carpometacarpal fracture dislocation, thumb (Bennett fracture), with manipulation

26650 Percutaneous skeletal fixation of carpometacarpal fracture dislocation, thumb (Bennett fracture), with manipulation

26665 Open treatment of carpometacarpal fracture dislocation, thumb (Bennett fracture), includes internal fixation, when performed

26670 Closed treatment of carpometacarpal dislocation, other than thumb, with manipulation, each joint; without anesthesia

26675   requiring anesthesia

26676 Percutaneous skeletal fixation of carpometacarpal dislocation, other than thumb, with manipulation, each joint

26685 Open treatment of carpometacarpal dislocation, other than thumb; includes internal fixation, when performed, each joint

26686   complex, multiple or delayed reduction

26700 Closed treatment of metacarpophalangeal dislocation, single, with manipulation; without anesthesia

26705   requiring anesthesia

26706 Percutaneous skeletal fixation of metacarpophalangeal dislocation, single, with manipulation

26715 Open treatment of metacarpophalangeal dislocation, single, includes internal fixation, when performed

26720 Closed treatment of phalangeal shaft fracture, proximal or middle phalanx, finger or thumb; without manipulation, each

26725   with manipulation, with or without skin or skeletal traction, each

26727 Percutaneous skeletal fixation of unstable phalangeal shaft fracture, proximal or middle phalanx, finger or thumb, with manipulation, each

26735 Open treatment of phalangeal shaft fracture, proximal or middle phalanx, finger or thumb, includes internal fixation, when performed, each

26740 Closed treatment of articular fracture, involving metacarpophalangeal or interphalangeal joint; without manipulation, each

26742   with manipulation, each

26746 Open treatment of articular fracture, involving metacarpophalangeal or interphalangeal joint, includes internal fixation, when performed, each

26750 Closed treatment of distal phalangeal fracture, finger or thumb; without manipulation, each

26755   with manipulation, each

■ Separate Procedure   ■ Unlisted Procedure   ■ CCI Comp. Code   ■ Non-specific Procedure   **291**

26756 Percutaneous skeletal fixation of distal phalangeal fracture, finger or thumb, each

26765 Open treatment of distal phalangeal fracture, finger or thumb, includes internal fixation, when performed, each

26770 Closed treatment of interphalangeal joint dislocation, single, with manipulation; without anesthesia

26775   requiring anesthesia

26776 Percutaneous skeletal fixation of interphalangeal joint dislocation, single, with manipulation

26785 Open treatment of interphalangeal joint dislocation, includes internal fixation, when performed, single

ARTHRODESIS

26820 Fusion in opposition, thumb, with autogenous graft (includes obtaining graft)

26841 Arthrodesis, carpometacarpal joint, thumb, with or without internal fixation;

26842   with autograft (includes obtaining graft)

26843 Arthrodesis, carpometacarpal joint, digit, other than thumb, each;

26844   with autograft (includes obtaining graft)

26850 Arthrodesis, metacarpophalangeal joint, with or without internal fixation;

26852   with autograft (includes obtaining graft)

26860 Arthrodesis, interphalangeal joint, with or without internal fixation;

\+ **26861**   each additional interphalangeal joint (List separately in addition to code for primary procedure)

     (Use 26861 in conjunction with code 26860)

26862   with autograft (includes obtaining graft)

\+ **26863**   with autograft (includes obtaining graft), each additional joint (List separately in addition to code for primary procedure)

     (Use 26863 in conjunction with code 26862)

AMPUTATION

     (For hand through metacarpal bones, use 25927)

26910 Amputation, metacarpal, with finger or thumb (ray amputation), single, with or without interosseous transfer

     (For repositioning see 26550, 26555)

26951 Amputation, finger or thumb, primary or secondary, any joint or phalanx, single, including neurectomies; with direct closure

26952   with local advancement flaps (V-Y, hood)

     (For repair of soft tissue defect requiring split or full thickness graft or other pedicle flaps, see 15050-15758)

OTHER PROCEDURES

26989 Unlisted procedure, hands or fingers

  ● New Code   ▲ Revised Code   ＋ Add-On Code   ⊘ Modifier -51 Exempt   ★ Telemedicine

PELVIS AND HIP JOINT

INCISION

(For incision and drainage procedures, superficial, see 10040-10160)

26990 Incision and drainage, pelvis or hip joint area; deep abscess or hematoma

26991   infected bursa

26992 Incision, bone cortex, pelvis and/or hip joint (eg, osteomyelitis or bone abscess)

27000 Tenotomy, adductor of hip, percutaneous (separate procedure)

27001 Tenotomy, adductor of hip, open

(To report bilateral procedures, report 27001 with modifier -50)

27003 Tenotomy, adductor, subcutaneous, open, with obturator neurectomy

(To report bilateral procedures, report 27003 with modifier -50)

27005 Tenotomy, hip flexor(s), open (separate procedure)

27006 Tenotomy, abductors and/or extensor(s) of hip, open (separate procedure)

27025 Fasciotomy, hip or thigh, any type

(To report bilateral procedures, report 27025 with modifier -50)

27027 Decompression fasciotomy(ies), pelvic (buttock) compartment(s) (eg, gluteus medius-minimus, gluteus maximus, iliopsoas, and/or tensor fascia lata muscle), unilateral

(To report bilateral procedure, report 27027 with modifier 50)

27030 Arthrotomy, hip, with drainage (eg, infection)

27033 Arthrotomy, hip, including exploration or removal of loose or foreign body

27035 Denervation, hip joint, intrapelvic or extrapelvic intra-articular branches of sciatic, femoral, or obturator nerves

(For obturator neurectomy, see 64763, 64766)

27036 Capsulectomy or capsulotomy, hip, with or without excision of heterotopic bone, with release of hip flexor muscles (ie, gluteus medius, gluteus minimus, tensor fascia latae, rectus femoris, sartorius, iliopsoas)

EXCISION

27040 Biopsy, soft tissue of pelvis and hip area; superficial

27041   deep, subfascial or intramuscular

(For needle biopsy of soft tissue, use 20206)

27043 This code is out of order. See page 293.

27045 This code is out of order. See page 294.

27047 Excision, tumor, soft tissue of pelvis and hip area, subcutaneous; less than 3 cm

27043   3 cm or greater

| Separate Procedure | Unlisted Procedure | CCI Comp. Code | Non-specific Procedure | **293** |

(For excision of benign lesions of cutaneous origin [eg, sebaceous cyst], see 11400-11406)

27048 Excision, tumor, soft tissue of pelvis and hip area, subfascial (eg, intramuscular); less than 5 cm

27045 5 cm or greater

27049 Radical resection of tumor (eg, sarcoma), soft tissue of pelvis and hip area; less than 5 cm

27059 5 cm or greater

(For radical resection of tumor[s] of cutaneous origin [eg, melanoma], see 11600-11606)

27050 Arthrotomy, with biopsy; sacroiliac joint

27052 hip joint

27054 Arthrotomy with synovectomy, hip joint

27057 Decompression fasciotomy(ies), pelvic (buttock) compartment(s) (eg, gluteus medius-minimus, gluteus maximus, iliopsoas, and/or tensor fascia lata muscle) with debridement of nonviable muscle, unilateral

(To report bilateral procedure, report 27057 with modifier 50)

27059 This code is out of order. See page 294.

27060 Excision; ischial bursa

27062 trochanteric bursa or calcification

(For arthrocentesis or needling of bursa, use 20610)

27065 Excision of bone cyst or benign tumor, wing of ilium, symphysis pubis, or greater trochanter of femur; superficial, includes autograft when performed

27066 deep (subfascial), includes autograft when performed

27067 with autograft requiring separate incision

27070 Partial excision, wing of ilium, symphysis pubis, or greater trochanter of femur, (craterization, saucerization) (eg, osteomyelitis or bone abscess); superficial

27071 deep (subfascial or intramuscular)

27075 Radical resection of tumor; wing of ilium, one pubic or ischial ramus or symphysis pubis

27076 ilium, including acetabulum, both pubic rami, or ischium and acetabulum

27077 innominate bone, total

27078 ischial tuberosity and greater trochanter of femur

27080 Coccygectomy, primary

(For pressure (decubitus) ulcer, see 15920, 15922 and 15931-15958)

INTRODUCTION OR REMOVAL

27086 Removal of foreign body, pelvis or hip; subcutaneous tissue

27087 deep (subfascial or intramuscular)

● New Code   ▲ Revised Code   + Add-On Code   ⊘ Modifier -51 Exempt   ★ Telemedicine

27090 Removal of hip prosthesis; (separate procedure)

27091   complicated, including total hip prosthesis, methylmethacrylate with or without insertion of spacer

27093 Injection procedure for hip arthrography; without anesthesia

(For radiological supervision and interpretation, use 73525. Do not report 77002 in conjunction with 73525)

27095   with anesthesia

(For radiological supervision and interpretation, use 73525. Do not report 77002 in conjunction with 73525)

27096 Injection procedure for sacroiliac joint, anesthetic/steroid, with image guidance (fluoroscopy or CT) including arthrography when performed

(27096 is to be used only with CT or fluoroscopic imaging confirmation of intra-articular needle positioning)

(If CT or fluoroscopic imaging is not performed, use 20552)

(Code 27096 is a unilateral procedure. For bilateral procedure, use modifier -50)

REPAIR, REVISION, AND/OR RECONSTRUCTION

27097 Release or recession, hamstring, proximal

27098 Transfer, adductor to ischium

27100 Transfer external oblique muscle to greater trochanter including fascial or tendon extension (graft)

27105 Transfer paraspinal muscle to hip (includes fascial or tendon extension graft)

27110 Transfer iliopsoas; to greater trochanter of femur

27111   to femoral neck

27120 Acetabuloplasty; (eg, Whitman, Colonna, Haygroves, or cup type)

27122   resection, femoral head (eg, Girdlestone procedure)

27125 Hemiarthroplasty, hip, partial (eg, femoral stem prosthesis, bipolar arthroplasty)

(For prosthetic replacement following fracture of the hip, use 27236)

27130 Arthroplasty, acetabular and proximal femoral prosthetic replacement (total hip arthroplasty), with or without autograft or allograft

27132 Conversion of previous hip surgery to total hip arthroplasty, with or without autograft or allograft

27134 Revision of total hip arthroplasty; both components, with or without autograft or allograft

27137   acetabular component only, with or without autograft or allograft

27138   femoral component only, with or without allograft

27140 Osteotomy and transfer of greater trochanter of femur (separate procedure)

27146 Osteotomy, iliac, acetabular or innominate bone;

27147   with open reduction of hip

27151	with femoral osteotomy
27156	with femoral osteotomy and with open reduction of hip
27158	Osteotomy, pelvis, bilateral (eg, congenital malformation)
27161	Osteotomy, femoral neck (separate procedure)
27165	Osteotomy, intertrochanteric or subtrochanteric including internal or external fixation and/or cast
27170	Bone graft, femoral head, neck, intertrochanteric or subtrochanteric area (includes obtaining bone graft)
27175	Treatment of slipped femoral epiphysis; by traction, without reduction
27176	by single or multiple pinning, in situ
27177	Open treatment of slipped femoral epiphysis; single or multiple pinning or bone graft (includes obtaining graft)
27178	closed manipulation with single or multiple pinning
27179	osteoplasty of femoral neck (Heyman type procedure)
27181	osteotomy and internal fixation
27185	Epiphyseal arrest by epiphysiodesis or stapling, greater trochanter of femur
27187	Prophylactic treatment (nailing, pinning, plating or wiring) with or without methylmethacrylate, femoral neck and proximal femur

FRACTURE AND/OR DISLOCATION

(27193	deleted 2016 [2017 edition]. To report, see 27197, 27198)
(27194	deleted 2016 [2017 edition]. To report, see 27197, 27198)
27197	Closed treatment of posterior pelvic ring fracture(s), dislocation(s), diastasis or subluxation of the ilium, sacroiliac joint, and/or sacrum, with or without anterior pelvic ring fracture(s) and/or dislocation(s) of the pubic symphysis and/or superior/inferior rami, unilateral or bilateral; without manipulation
27198	with manipulation, requiring more than local anesthesia (ie, general anesthesia, moderate sedation, spinal/epidural)

(To report closed treatment of only anterior pelvic ring fracture(s) and/or dislocation(s) of the pubic symphysis and/or superior/inferior rami, unilateral or bilateral, use the appropriate evaluation and management services codes)

27200	Closed treatment of coccygeal fracture
27202	Open treatment of coccygeal fracture
27215	Open treatment of iliac spine(s), tuberosity avulsion, or iliac wing fracture(s), unilateral for pelvic bone fracture patterns that do not disrupt the pelvic ring, includes internal fixation, when performed

(To report bilateral procedure, report 27215 with modifier 50)

27216	Percutaneous skeletal fixation of posterior pelvic bone fracture and/or dislocation, for fracture patterns that disrupt the pelvic ring, unilateral (includes ipsilateral ilium, sacroiliac joint and/or sacrum)

(To report bilateral procedure, report 27216 with modifier 50)

● New Code ▲ Revised Code ✛ Add-On Code ⊘ Modifier -51 Exempt ★ Telemedicine

(For percutaneous/minimally invasive arthrodesis of the sacroiliac joint without fracture and/or dislocation, use 27279)

27217 Open treatment of anterior pelvic bone fracture and/or dislocation for fracture patterns that disrupt the pelvic ring, unilateral, includes internal fixation, when performed (includes pubic symphysis and/or ipsilateral superior/inferior rami)

(To report bilateral procedure, report 27217 with modifier 50)

27218 Open treatment of posterior pelvic bone fracture and/or dislocation for fracture patterns that disrupt the pelvic ring, unilateral, includes internal fixation, when performed (includes ipsilateral ilium, sacroiliac joint and/or sacrum)

(To report bilateral procedure, report 27218 with modifier 50)

(For percutaneous/minimally invasive arthrodesis of the sacroiliac joint without fracture and/or dislocation, use 27279)

27220 Closed treatment of acetabulum (hip socket) fracture(s); without manipulation

27222 with manipulation, with or without skeletal traction

27226 Open treatment of posterior or anterior acetabular wall fracture, with internal fixation

27227 Open treatment of acetabular fracture(s) involving anterior or posterior (one) column, or a fracture running transversely across the acetabulum, with internal fixation

27228 Open treatment of acetabular fracture(s) involving anterior and posterior (two) columns, includes T-fracture and both column fracture with complete articular detachment, or single column or transverse fracture with associated acetabular wall fracture, with internal fixation

27230 Closed treatment of femoral fracture, proximal end, neck; without manipulation

27232 with manipulation, with or without skeletal traction

27235 Percutaneous skeletal fixation of femoral fracture, proximal end, neck

27236 Open treatment of femoral fracture, proximal end, neck, internal fixation or prosthetic replacement

27238 Closed treatment of intertrochanteric, pertrochanteric, or subtrochanteric femoral fracture; without manipulation

27240 with manipulation, with or without skin or skeletal traction

27244 Treatment of intertrochanteric, pertrochanteric or subtrochanteric femoral fracture; with plate/screw type implant, with or without cerclage

27245 with intramedullary implant, with or without interlocking screws and/or cerclage

27246 Closed treatment of greater trochanteric fracture, without manipulation

27248 Open treatment of greater trochanteric fracture, includes internal fixation, when performed

27250 Closed treatment of hip dislocation, traumatic; without anesthesia

27252 requiring anesthesia

27253 Open treatment of hip dislocation, traumatic, without internal fixation

27254 Open treatment of hip dislocation, traumatic, with acetabular wall and femoral head fracture, with or without internal or external fixation

---

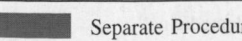 Separate Procedure   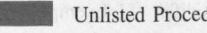 Unlisted Procedure   CCI Comp. Code   Non-specific Procedure   **297**

(For treatment of acetabular fracture with fixation, see 27226, 27227)

27256 Treatment of spontaneous hip dislocation (developmental, including congenital or pathological), by abduction, splint or traction; without anesthesia, without manipulation

27257 with manipulation, requiring anesthesia

27258 Open treatment of spontaneous hip dislocation (developmental, including congenital or pathological), replacement of femoral head in acetabulum (including tenotomy, etc);

27259 with femoral shaft shortening

27265 Closed treatment of post hip arthroplasty dislocation; without anesthesia

27266 requiring regional or general anesthesia

27267 Closed treatment of femoral fracture, proximal end, head; without manipulation

27268 with manipulation

27269 Open treatment of femoral fracture, proximal end, head, includes internal fixation, when performed

(Do not report 27269 in conjunction with 27033, 27253)

MANIPULATION

27275 Manipulation, hip joint, requiring general anesthesia

ARTHRODESIS

27279 Arthrodesis, sacroiliac joint, percutaneous or minimally invasive (indirect visualization), with image guidance, includes obtaining bone graft when performed, and placement of transfixing device

(For bilateral procedure, report 27279 with modifier 50)

27280 Arthrodesis, open, sacroiliac joint, including obtaining bone graft, including instrumentation, when performed

(To report bilateral procedures, report 27280 with modifier -50)

(For percutaneous/minimally invasive arthrodesis of the sacroiliac joint without fracture and/or disloation,, use 27279)

27282 Arthrodesis, symphysis pubis (including obtaining graft)

27284 Arthrodesis, hip joint (including obtaining graft);

27286 with subtrochanteric osteotomy

AMPUTATION

27290 Interpelviabdominal amputation (hindquarter amputation)

27295 Disarticulation of hip

OTHER PROCEDURES

27299 Unlisted procedure, pelvis or hip joint

● New Code ▲ Revised Code + Add-On Code ⊘ Modifier -51 Exempt ★ Telemedicine

FEMUR (THIGH REGION) AND KNEE JOINT

INCISION

(For incision and drainage of abscess or hematoma, superficial, see 10040-10160)

27301 Incision and drainage, deep abscess, bursa, or hematoma, thigh or knee region

27303 Incision, deep, with opening of bone cortex, femur or knee (eg, osteomyelitis or bone abscess)

27305 Fasciotomy, iliotibial (tenotomy), open

(For combined Ober-Yount fasciotomy, use 27025)

27306 Tenotomy, percutaneous, adductor or hamstring; single tendon (separate procedure)

27307 multiple tendons

27310 Arthrotomy, knee, with exploration, drainage, or removal of foreign body(eg, infection)

EXCISION

27323 Biopsy, soft tissue of thigh or knee area; superficial

27324 deep (subfascial or intramuscular)

(For needle biopsy of soft tissue, use 20206)

27325 Neurectomy, hamstring muscle

27326 Neurectomy, popliteal (gastrocnemius)

27327 Excision, tumor, soft tissue of thigh or knee area, subcutaneous; less than 3 cm

27337 3 cm or greater

(For excision of benign lesions of cutaneous origin [eg, sebaceous cyst], see 11400-11406))

27328 Excision, tumor, soft tissue of thigh or knee area, subfascial (eg, intramuscular); less than 5 cm

27339 5 cm or greater

27329 This code is out of order. See page 300.

27330 Arthrotomy, knee; with synovial biopsy only

27331 including joint exploration, biopsy, or removal of loose or foreign bodies

27332 Arthrotomy, with excision of semilunar cartilage (meniscectomy) knee; medial OR lateral

27333 medial AND lateral

27334 Arthrotomy, with synovectomy, knee; anterior OR posterior

27335 anterior AND posterior including popliteal area

27337 This code is out of order. See page 299.

27339 This code is out of order. See page 299.

27340 Excision, prepatellar bursa

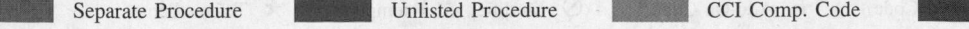

| Separate Procedure | Unlisted Procedure | CCI Comp. Code | Non-specific Procedure | **299** |

27345 Excision of synovial cyst of popliteal space (eg, Baker's cyst)

27347 Excision of lesion of meniscus or capsule (eg, cyst, ganglion), knee

27350 Patellectomy or hemipatellectomy

27355 Excision or curettage of bone cyst or benign tumor of femur;

27356   with allograft

27357   with autograft (includes obtaining graft)

+ **27358**   with internal fixation (List in addition to code for primary procedure)

(Use 27358 in conjunction with codes 27355, 27356 or 27357)

27360 Partial excision (craterization, saucerization, or diaphysectomy) bone, femur, proximal tibia and/or fibula (eg, osteomyelitis or bone abscess)

27329 Radical resection of tumor (eg, sarcoma), soft tissue of thigh or knee area; less than 5 cm

27364   5 cm or greater

(For radical resection of tumor[s] of cutaneous origin [eg, melanoma], see 11600-11606)

27365 Radical resection of tumor, femur or knee

(For radical resection of tumor, soft tissue of thigh or knee area, use 27329, 27364)

INTRODUCTION OR REMOVAL

27370 Injection of contrast for knee arthrography

(For radiological supervision and interpretation, use 73580. Do not report 77002 in conjunction with 73580)

(Do not report 27370 in conjunction with 20610, 20611, 29871)

(For arthrocentesis of the knee or injection other than contrast, see 20610, 20611)

(For arthroscopic lavage and drainage of the knee, use 29871)

27372 Removal of foreign body, deep, thigh region or knee area

(For removal of knee prosthesis including "total knee," use 27488)

(For surgical arthroscopic knee procedures, see 29870-29887)

REPAIR, REVISION, AND/OR RECONSTRUCTION

27380 Suture of infrapatellar tendon; primary

27381   secondary reconstruction, including fascial or tendon graft

27385 Suture of quadriceps or hamstring muscle rupture; primary

27386   secondary reconstruction, including fascial or tendon graft

27390 Tenotomy, open, hamstring, knee to hip; single tendon

27391   multiple tendons, 1 leg

27392   multiple tendons, bilateral

---

300   ● New Code   ▲ Revised Code   + Add-On Code   ⊘ Modifier -51 Exempt   ★ Telemedicine

27393 Lengthening of hamstring tendon; single tendon

27394   multiple tendons, 1 leg

27395   multiple tendons, bilateral

27396 Transplant or transfer (with muscle redirection or rerouting), thigh (eg., extensor to flexor); single tendon

27397   multiple tendons

27400 Transfer, tendon or muscle, hamstrings to femur (eg, Egger's type procedure)

27403 Arthrotomy with meniscus repair, knee

(For arthroscopic repair, use 29882)

27405 Repair, primary, torn ligament and/or capsule, knee; collateral

27407   cruciate

(For cruciate ligament reconstruction, use 27427)

27409   collateral and cruciate ligaments

(For ligament reconstruction, see 27427-27429)

27412 Autologous chondrocyte implantation, knee

(Do not report 27412 in conjunction with 20926, 27331, 27570)

(For harvesting of chondrocytes, use 29870)

27415 Osteochondral allograft, knee, open

(For arthroscopic implant of osteochondral allograft, use 29867)

(Do not report 27415 in conjunction with 27416)

27416 Osteochondral autograf(s), knee, open (eg, mosaicplasty) (includes harvesting of autograft[s])

(Do not report 27416 in conjunction with 27415, 29870, 29871, 29875, 29884 when performed at the same session and/or 29874, 29877, 29879, 29885-29887 when performed in the same compartment)

(For arthroscopic osteochondral autograft of knee, use 29866)

27418 Anterior tibial tubercleplasty (eg, Maquet type procedure)

27420 Reconstruction of dislocating patella; (eg, Hauser type procedure)

27422   with extensor realignment and/or muscle advancement or release (eg, Campbell, Goldwaite type procedure)

27424   with patellectomy

27425 Lateral retinacular release open

(For arthroscopic lateral release, use 29873)

27427 Ligamentous reconstruction (augmentation), knee; extra-articular

27428   intra-articular (open)

27429   intra-articular (open) and extra-articular

(For primary repair of ligament(s) performed in addition to reconstruction, report 27405, 27407 or 27409 in addition to code 27427, 27428 or 27429)

27430	Quadricepsplasty (eg, Bennett or Thompson type)
27435	Capsulotomy, posterior capsular release, knee
27437	Arthroplasty, patella; without prosthesis
27438	with prosthesis
27440	Arthroplasty, knee, tibial plateau;
27441	with debridement and partial synovectomy
27442	Arthroplasty, femoral condyles or tibial plateau(s), knee;
27443	with debridement and partial synovectomy
27445	Arthroplasty, knee, hinge prosthesis (eg, Walldius type)
27446	Arthroplasty, knee, condyle and plateau; medial OR lateral compartment
27447	medial AND lateral compartments with or without patella resurfacing (total knee arthroplasty)

(For revision of total knee arthroplasty, use 27487)

(For removal of total knee prosthesis, use 27488)

27448	Osteotomy, femur, shaft or supracondylar; without fixation

(To report bilateral procedures, report 27448 with modifier -50)

27450	with fixation

(To report bilateral procedures, report 27450 with modifier -50)

27454	Osteotomy, multiple, with realignment on intramedullary rod, femoral shaft (eg, Sofield type procedure)
27455	Osteotomy, proximal tibia, including fibular excision or osteotomy (includes correction of genu varus [bowleg] or genu valgus [knock-knee]); before epiphyseal closure

(To report bilateral procedures, report 27455 with modifier -50)

27457	after epiphyseal closure

(To report bilateral procedures, report 27457 with modifier -50)

27465	Osteoplasty, femur; shortening (excluding 64876)
27466	lengthening
27468	combined, lengthening and shortening with femoral segment transfer
27470	Repair, nonunion or malunion, femur, distal to head and neck; without graft (eg, compression technique)
27472	with iliac or other autogenous bone graft (includes obtaining graft)
27475	Arrest, epiphyseal, any method (eg, epiphysiodesis); distal femur
27477	tibia and fibula, proximal

● New Code ▲ Revised Code ＋ Add-On Code ⊘ Modifier -51 Exempt ★ Telemedicine

27479	combined distal femur, proximal tibia and fibula
27485	Arrest, hemiepiphyseal, distal femur or proximal tibia or fibula (eg, genu varus or valgus)
27486	Revision of total knee arthroplasty, with or without allograft; 1 component
27487	femoral and entire tibial component
27488	Removal of prosthesis, including total knee prosthesis, methylmethacrylate with or without insertion of spacer, knee
27495	Prophylactic treatment (nailing, pinning, plating or wiring) with or without methylmethacrylate, femur
27496	Decompression fasciotomy, thigh and/or knee, 1 compartment (flexor or extensor or adductor);
27497	with debridement of nonviable muscle and/or nerve
27498	Decompression fasciotomy, thigh and/or knee, multiple compartments;
27499	with debridement of nonviable muscle and/or nerve

FRACTURE AND/OR DISLOCATION

(For arthroscopic treatment of intercondylar spine(s) and tuberosity fracture(s) of the knee, see 29850, 29851)

(For arthroscopic treatment of tibial fracture, see 29855, 29856)

27500	Closed treatment of femoral shaft fracture, without manipulation
27501	Closed treatment of supracondylar or transcondylar femoral fracture with or without intercondylar extension, without manipulation
27502	Closed treatment of femoral shaft fracture, with manipulation, with or without skin or skeletal traction
27503	Closed treatment of supracondylar or transcondylar femoral fracture with or without intercondylar extension, with manipulation, with or without skin or skeletal traction
27506	Open treatment of femoral shaft fracture, with or without external fixation, with insertion of intramedullary implant, with or without cerclage and/or locking screws
27507	Open treatment of femoral shaft fracture with plate/screws, with or without cerclage
27508	Closed treatment of femoral fracture, distal end, medial or lateral condyle, without manipulation
27509	Percutaneous skeletal fixation of femoral fracture, distal end, medial or lateral condyle, or supracondylar or transcondylar, with or without intercondylar extension, or distal femoral epiphyseal separation
27510	Closed treatment of femoral fracture, distal end, medial or lateral condyle, with manipulation
27511	Open treatment of femoral supracondylar or transcondylar fracture without intercondylar extension, includes internal fixation, when performed
27513	Open treatment of femoral supracondylar or transcondylar fracture with intercondylar extension, includes internal fixation, when performed
27514	Open treatment of femoral fracture, distal end, medial or lateral condyle, includes internal fixation, when performed
27516	Closed treatment of distal femoral epiphyseal separation; without manipulation

27517   with manipulation, with or without skin or skeletal traction

27519   Open treatment of distal femoral epiphyseal separation, includes internal fixation, when performed

27520   Closed treatment of patellar fracture, without manipulation

27524   Open treatment of patellar fracture, with internal fixation and/or partial or complete patellectomy and soft tissue repair

27530   Closed treatment of tibial fracture, proximal (plateau); without manipulation

27532   with or without manipulation, with skeletal traction

(For arthroscopic treatment, see 29855, 29856)

27535   Open treatment of tibial fracture, proximal (plateau); unicondylar, includes internal fixation, when performed

27536   bicondylar, with or without internal fixation

(For arthroscopic treatment, see 29855, 29856)

27538   Closed treatment of intercondylar spine(s) and/or tuberosity fracture(s) of knee, with or without manipulation

(For arthroscopic treatment, see 29850, 29851)

27540   Open treatment of intercondylar spine(s) and/or tuberosity fracture(s) of the knee, includes internal fixation, when performed

27550   Closed treatment of knee dislocation; without anesthesia

27552   requiring anesthesia

27556   Open treatment of knee dislocation, includes internal fixation, when performed; without primary ligamentous repair or augmentation/reconstruction

27557   with primary ligamentous repair

27558   with primary ligamentous repair, with augmentation/ reconstruction

27560   Closed treatment of patellar dislocation; without anesthesia

(For recurrent dislocation, see 27420-27424)

27562   requiring anesthesia

27566   Open treatment of patellar dislocation, with or without partial or total patellectomy

MANIPULATION

27570   Manipulation of knee joint under general anesthesia (includes application of traction or other fixation devices)

ARTHRODESIS

27580   Arthrodesis, knee, any technique

AMPUTATION

27590   Amputation, thigh, through femur, any level;

● New Code   ▲ Revised Code   + Add-On Code   ⊘ Modifier -51 Exempt   ★ Telemedicine

27591	immediate fitting technique including first cast
27592	open, circular (guillotine)
27594	secondary closure or scar revision
27596	re-amputation
27598	Disarticulation at knee

OTHER PROCEDURES

| 27599 | Unlisted procedure, femur or knee |

LEG (TIBIA AND FIBULA) AND ANKLE JOINT

INCISION

27600	Decompression fasciotomy, leg; anterior and/or lateral compartments only
27601	posterior compartment(s) only
27602	anterior and/or lateral, and posterior compartment(s)

(For incision and drainage procedures, superficial, see 10040-10160)

(For decompression fasciotomy with debridement, see 27892-27894)

27603	Incision and drainage, leg or ankle; deep abscess or hematoma
27604	infected bursa
27605	Tenotomy, percutaneous, Achilles tendon (separate procedure); local anesthesia
27606	general anesthesia
27607	Incision (eg, osteomyelitis or bone abscess), leg or ankle
27610	Arthrotomy, ankle, including exploration, drainage, or removal of foreign body
27612	Arthrotomy, posterior capsular release, ankle, with or without Achilles tendon lengthening

(See also 27685)

EXCISION

| 27613 | Biopsy, soft tissue of leg or ankle area; superficial |
| 27614 | deep (subfascial or intramuscular) |

(For needle biopsy of soft tissue, use 20206)

| 27615 | Radical resection of tumor (eg, sarcoma), soft tissue of leg or ankle area; less than 5 cm |
| 27616 | 5 cm or greater |

(For radical resection of tumor[s] of cutaneous origin [eg, melanoma], see 11600-11606)

| 27618 | Excision, tumor, soft tissue of leg or ankle area, subcutaneous; less than 3 cm |
| 27632 | 3 cm or greater |

| | Separate Procedure | | Unlisted Procedure | | CCI Comp. Code | | Non-specific Procedure | **305** |

(For excision of benign lesions of cutaneous origin [eg, sebaceous cyst], see 11400-11406)

27619 Excision, tumor, soft tissue of leg or ankle area, subfascial (eg, intramuscular); less than 5 cm

27634   5 cm or greater

27620 Arthrotomy, ankle, with joint exploration, with or without biopsy, with or without removal of loose or foreign body

27625 Arthrotomy, with synovectomy, ankle;

27626   including tenosynovectomy

27630 Excision of lesion of tendon sheath or capsule (eg, cyst or ganglion), leg and/or ankle

27632 This code is out of order. See page 305.

27634 This code is out of order. See page 306.

27635 Excision or curettage of bone cyst or benign tumor, tibia or fibula;

27637   with autograft (includes obtaining graft)

27638   with allograft

27640 Partial excision (craterization, saucerization, or diaphysectomy) bone (eg, osteomyelitis); tibia

(For exostosis excision, use 27635)

27641   fibula

(For exostosis excision, use 27635)

27645 Radical resection of tumor; tibia

27646   fibula

27647   talus or calcaneus

INTRODUCTION OR REMOVAL

27648 Injection procedure for ankle arthrography

(For radiological supervision and interpretation use 73615. Do not report 77002 in addition to 73615)

(For ankle arthroscopy, see 29894-29898)

REPAIR, REVISION, AND/OR RECONSTRUCTION

27650 Repair, primary, open or percutaneous, ruptured Achilles tendon;

27652   with graft (includes obtaining graft)

27654 Repair, secondary, Achilles tendon, with or without graft

27656 Repair, fascial defect of leg

27658 Repair, flexor tendon, leg; primary, without graft, each tendon

27659   secondary, with or without graft, each tendon

● New Code   ▲ Revised Code   + Add-On Code   ⊘ Modifier -51 Exempt   ★ Telemedicine

27664   Repair, extensor tendon, leg; primary, without graft, each tendon

27665   secondary, with or without graft, each tendon

27675   Repair, dislocating peroneal tendons; without fibular osteotomy

27676   with fibular osteotomy

27680   Tenolysis, flexor or extensor tendon, leg and/or ankle; single, each tendon

27681   multiple tendons (through separate incision(s))

27685   Lengthening or shortening of tendon, leg or ankle; single tendon (separate procedure)

27686   multiple tendons (through same incision), each

27687   Gastrocnemius recession (eg, Strayer procedure)

(Toe extensors are considered as a group to be single tendon when transplanted into midfoot)

27690   Transfer or transplant of single tendon (with muscle redirection or rerouting); superficial (eg, anterior tibial extensors into midfoot)

27691   deep (eg, anterior tibial or posterior tibial through interosseous space, flexor digitorum longus, flexor hallucis longus, or peroneal tendon to midfoot or hind foot)

+ 27692   each additional tendon (List separately in addition to code for primary procedure)

(Use 27692 in conjunction with codes 27690, 27691)

27695   Repair, primary, disrupted ligament, ankle; collateral

27696   both collateral ligaments

27698   Repair, secondary disrupted ligament, ankle, collateral (eg, Watson-Jones procedure)

27700   Arthroplasty, ankle;

27702   with implant (total ankle)

27703   revision, total ankle

27704   Removal of ankle implant

27705   Osteotomy; tibia

27707   fibula

27709   tibia and fibula

27712   multiple, with realignment on intramedullary rod (eg, Sofield type procedure)

(For osteotomy to correct genu varus (bowleg) or genu valgus (knock-knee), see 27455-27457)

27715   Osteoplasty, tibia and fibula, lengthening or shortening

27720   Repair of nonunion or malunion, tibia; without graft, (eg, compression technique)

27722   with sliding graft

27724	with iliac or other autograft (includes obtaining graft)
27725	by synostosis, with fibula, any method
27726	Repair of fibula nonunion and/or malunion with internal fixation

(Do not reprt 27726 in conjunction with 27707)

27727	Repair of congenital pseudarthrosis, tibia
27730	Arrest, epiphyseal (epiphysiodesis), open; distal tibia
27732	distal fibula
27734	distal tibia and fibula
27740	Arrest, epiphyseal (epiphysiodesis), any method, combined, proximal and distal tibia and fibula;
27742	and distal femur

(For epiphyseal arrest of proximal tibia and fibula, use 27477)

27745	Prophylactic treatment (nailing, pinning, plating or wiring) with or without methylmethacrylate, tibia

FRACTURE AND/OR DISLOCATION

27750	Closed treatment of tibial shaft fracture (with or without fibular fracture); without manipulation
27752	with manipulation, with or without skeletal traction
27756	Percutaneous skeletal fixation of tibial shaft fracture (with or without fibular fracture) (eg, pins or screws)
27758	Open treatment of tibial shaft fracture, (with or without fibular fracture) with plate/screws, with or without cerclage
27759	Treatment of tibial shaft fracture (with or without fibular fracture) by intramedullary implant, with or without interlocking screws and/or cerclage
27760	Closed treatment of medial malleolus fracture; without manipulation
27762	with manipulation, with or without skin or skeletal traction
27766	Open treatment of medial malleolus fracture, includes internal fixation, when performed
27767	Closed treatment of posterior malleolus fracture; without manipulation
27768	with manipulation
27769	Open treatment of posterior malleolus fracture, includes internal fixation, when performed

(Do not report 27767-27769 in conjunction with 27808-27823)

27780	Closed treatment of proximal fibula or shaft fracture; without manipulation
27781	with manipulation
27784	Open treatment of proximal fibula or shaft fracture, includes internal fixation, when performed
27786	Closed treatment of distal fibular fracture (lateral malleolus); without manipulation

● New Code   ▲ Revised Code   + Add-On Code   ⊘ Modifier -51 Exempt   ★ Telemedicine

27788   with manipulation

27792   Open treatment of distal fibular fracture (lateral malleolus), includes internal fixation, when performed

(For treatment of tibia and fibula shaft fractures, see 27750-27759)

27808   Closed treatment of bimalleolar ankle fracture, (eg, lateral and medial malleoli, or lateral and posterior malleoli or medial and posterior malleoli); without manipulation

27810   with manipulation

27814   Open treatment of bimalleolar ankle fracture (eg, lateral and medial malleoli, or lateral and posterior malleoli, or medial and posterior malleoli), includes internal fixation, when performed

27816   Closed treatment of trimalleolar ankle fracture; without manipulation

27818   with manipulation

27822   Open treatment of trimalleolar ankle fracture, includes internal fixation, when performed, medial and/or lateral malleolus; without fixation of posterior lip

27823   with fixation of posterior lip

27824   Closed treatment of fracture of weight bearing articular portion of distal tibia (eg, pilon or tibial plafond), with or without anesthesia; without manipulation

27825   with skeletal traction and/or requiring manipulation

27826   Open treatment of fracture of weight bearing articular surface/portion of distal tibia (eg, pilon or tibial plafond), with internal fixation, when performed; of fibula only

27827   of tibia only

27828   of both tibia and fibula

27829   Open treatment of distal tibiofibular joint (syndesmosis) disruption, includes internal fixation, when performed

27830   Closed treatment of proximal tibiofibular joint dislocation; without anesthesia

27831   requiring anesthesia

27832   Open treatment of proximal tibiofibular joint dislocation, includes internal fixation, when performed, or with excision of proximal fibula

27840   Closed treatment of ankle dislocation; without anesthesia

27842   requiring anesthesia, with or without percutaneous skeletal fixation

27846   Open treatment of ankle dislocation, with or without percutaneous skeletal fixation; without repair or internal fixation

27848   with repair or internal or external fixation

(For surgical diagnostic arthroscopic procedures, see 29894-29898)

MANIPULATION

27860   Manipulation of ankle under general anesthesia (includes application of traction or other fixation apparatus)

ARTHRODESIS

27870   Arthrodesis, ankle, open

     (For arthroscopic ankle arthrodesis, use 29899)

27871   Arthrodesis, tibiofibular joint, proximal or distal

AMPUTATION

27880   Amputation, leg, through tibia and fibula;

27881   with immediate fitting technique including application of first cast

27882   open, circular (guillotine)

27884   secondary closure or scar revision

27886   re-amputation

27888   Amputation, ankle, through malleoli of tibia and fibula (eg, Syme, Pirogoff type procedures), with plastic closure and resection of nerves

27889   Ankle disarticulation

OTHER PROCEDURES

27892   Decompression fasciotomy, leg; anterior and/or lateral compartments only, with debridement of nonviable muscle and/or nerve

     (For decompression fasciotomy of the leg without debridement, use 27600)

27893   posterior compartment(s) only, with debridement of nonviable muscle and/or nerve

     (For decompession fasciotomy of the leg without debridement, use 27601)

27894   anterior and/or lateral, and posterior compartment(s), with debridement of nonviable muscle and/or nerve

     (For decompression fasciotomy of the leg without debridement, use 27602)

27899   Unlisted procedure, leg or ankle

FOOT AND TOES

INCISION

     (For incision and drainage procedures, superficial, see 10040-10160)

28001   Incision and drainage, bursa, foot

28002   Incision and drainage below fascia, with or without tendon sheath involvement, foot; single bursal space

28003   multiple areas

28005   Incision, bone cortex (eg, osteomyelitis or bone abscess), foot

28008   Fasciotomy, foot and/or toe

     (See also 28060, 28062, 28250)

28010   Tenotomy, percutaneous, toe; single tendon

28011   multiple tendons

(For open tenotomy, see 28230-28234)

28020 Arthrotomy, including exploration, drainage, or removal of loose or foreign body; intertarsal or tarsometatarsal joint

28022   metatarsophalangeal joint

28024   interphalangeal joint

28035 Release, tarsal tunnel (posterior tibial nerve decompression)

(For other nerve entrapments, see 64704, 64722)

EXCISION

28039 This code is out of order. See page 311.

28041 This code is out of order. See page 311.

28043 Excision, tumor, soft tissue of foot or toe, subcutaneous; less than 1.5 cm

28039   1.5 cm or greater

(For excision of benign lesions of cutaneous origin [eg, sebaceous cyst], see 11420-11426)

28045 Excision, tumor, soft tissue of foot or toe, subfascial (eg, intramuscular); less than 1.5 cm

28041   1.5 cm or greater

28046 Radical resection of tumor (eg, sarcoma), soft tissue of foot or toe; less than 3 cm

28047   3 cm or greater

(For radical resection of tumor[s] of cutaneous origin [eg, melanoma], see 11620-11626)

28050 Arthrotomy with biopsy; intertarsal or tarsometatarsal joint

28052   metatarsophalangeal joint

28054   interphalangeal joint

28055 Neurectomy, intrinsic musculature of foot

28060 Fasciectomy, plantar fascia; partial (separate procedure)

28062   radical (separate procedure)

(For plantar fasciotomy, see 28008, 28250)

28070 Synovectomy; intertarsal or tarsometatarsal joint, each

28072   metatarsophalangeal joint, each

28080 Excision, interdigital (Morton) neuroma, single, each

28086 Synovectomy, tendon sheath, foot; flexor

28088   extensor

28090	Excision of lesion, tendon, tendon sheath, or capsule (including synovectomy) (eg, cyst or ganglion); foot
28092	toe(s), each
28100	Excision or curettage of bone cyst or benign tumor, talus or calcaneus;
28102	with iliac or other autograft (includes obtaining graft)
28103	with allograft
28104	Excision or curettage of bone cyst or benign tumor, tarsal or metatarsal, except talus or calcaneus;
28106	with iliac or other autograft (includes obtaining graft)
28107	with allograft
28108	Excision or curettage of bone cyst or benign tumor, phalanges of foot

(For partial excision of bossing or exostosis for phalanx in the foot, use 28124)

28110	Ostectomy, partial excision, fifth metatarsal head (bunionette) (separate procedure)
28111	Ostectomy, complete excision; first metatarsal head
28112	other metatarsal head (second, third or fourth)
28113	fifth metatarsal head
28114	all metatarsal heads, with partial proximal phalangectomy, excluding first metatarsal (eg, Clayton type procedure)
28116	Ostectomy, excision of tarsal coalition
28118	Ostectomy, calcaneus;
28119	for spur, with or without plantar fascial release
28120	Partial excision (craterization, saucerization, sequestrectomy, or diaphysectomy) bone (eg, osteomyelitis or bossing); talus or calcaneus
28122	tarsal or metatarsal bone, except talus or calcaneus

(For partial excision of talus or calcaneus, use 28120)

(For cheilectomy for hallux rigidus, use 28289)

28124	phalanx of toe
28126	Resection, partial or complete, phalangeal base, each toe
28130	Talectomy (astragalectomy)

(For calcanectomy, use 28118)

28140	Metatarsectomy
28150	Phalangectomy, toe, each toe
28153	Resection, condyle(s), distal end of phalanx, each toe

28160   Hemiphalangectomy or interphalangeal joint excision, toe, proximal end of phalanx, each

28171   Radical resection of tumor; tarsal (except talus or calcaneus)

28173   metatarsal

28175   phalanx of toe

(For talus or calcaneus, use 27647)

INTRODUCTION OR REMOVAL

28190   Removal of foreign body, foot; subcutaneous

28192   deep

28193   complicated

REPAIR, REVISION, AND/OR RECONSTRUCTION

28200   Repair, tendon, flexor, foot; primary or secondary, without free graft, each tendon

28202   secondary with free graft, each tendon (includes obtaining graft)

28208   Repair, tendon, extensor, foot; primary or secondary, each tendon

28210   secondary with free graft, each tendon (includes obtaining graft)

28220   Tenolysis, flexor, foot; single tendon

28222   multiple tendons

28225   Tenolysis, extensor, foot; single tendon

28226   multiple tendons

28230   Tenotomy, open, tendon flexor; foot, single or multiple tendon(s) (separate procedure)

28232   toe, single tendon (separate procedure)

28234   Tenotomy, open, extensor, foot or toe, each tendon

(For tendon transfer to midfoot or hindfoot, see 27690, 27691)

28238   Reconstruction (advancement), posterior tibial tendon with excision of accessory tarsal navicular bone (eg, Kidner type procedure)

(For subcutaneous tenotomy, see 28010, 28011)

(For transfer or transplant of tendon with muscle redirection or rerouting, see 27690-27692)

(For extensor hallucis longus transfer with great toe IP fusion (Jones procedure), use 28760)

28240   Tenotomy, lengthening, or release, abductor hallucis muscle

28250   Division of plantar fascia and muscle (eg, Steindler stripping) (separate procedure)

28260   Capsulotomy, midfoot; medial release only (separate procedure)

28261   with tendon lengthening

Separate Procedure   Unlisted Procedure   CCI Comp. Code   Non-specific Procedure   **313**

28262   extensive, including posterior talotibial capsulotomy and tendon(s) lengthening (eg, resistant clubfoot deformity)

28264   Capsulotomy, midtarsal (eg, Heyman type procedure)

28270   Capsulotomy; metatarsophalangeal joint, with or without tenorrhaphy, each joint (separate procedure)

28272   interphalangeal joint, each joint (separate procedure)

28280   Syndactylization, toes (eg, webbing or Kelikian type procedure)

28285   Correction, hammertoe (eg, interphalangeal fusion, partial or total phalangectomy)

28286   Correction, cock-up fifth toe, with plastic skin closure (eg, Ruiz-Mora type procedure)

28288   Ostectomy, partial, exostectomy or condylectomy, metatarsal head, each metatarsal head

28289   Hallux rigidus correction with cheilectomy, debridement and capsular release of the first metatarsophalangeal joint; without implant

(28290   deleted 2016 [2017 edition]. See 28292)

28291   with implant

28292   Correction, hallux valgus (bunionectomy), with sesamoidectomy, when performed; with resection of proximal phalanx base, when performed, any method

(28293   deleted 2016 [2017 edition]. Use 28291)

(28294   deleted 2016 [2017 edition]. Use 28899)

28295   This code is out of order. See page 314.

28296   with distal metatarsal osteotomy, any method

28295   with proximal metatarsal osteotomy, any method

28297   with first metatarsal and medial cuneiform joint arthrodesis; any method

28298   with proximal phalanx osteotomy, any method

28299   with double osteotomy, any method

28300   Osteotomy; calcaneus (eg, Dwyer or Chambers type procedure), with or without internal fixation

28302   talus

28304   Osteotomy, tarsal bones, other than calcaneus or talus;

28305   with autograft (includes obtaining graft) (eg, Fowler type)

28306   Osteotomy, with or without lengthening, shortening or angular correction, metatarsal; first metatarsal

28307   first metatarsal with autograft (other than first toe)

28308   other than first metatarsal, each

28309   multiple (eg, Swanson type cavus foot procedure)

   ● New Code   ▲ Revised Code   + Add-On Code   ⊘ Modifier -51 Exempt   ★ Telemedicine

28310 Osteotomy, shortening, angular or rotational correction; proximal phalanx, first toe (separate procedure)

28312   other phalanges, any toe

28313 Reconstruction, angular deformity of toe, soft tissue procedures only (eg, overlapping second toe, fifth toe, curly toes)

28315 Sesamoidectomy, first toe (separate procedure)

28320 Repair, nonunion or malunion; tarsal bones

28322   metatarsal, with or without bone graft (includes obtaining graft)

28340 Reconstruction, toe, macrodactyly; soft tissue resection

28341   requiring bone resection

28344 Reconstruction, toe(s); polydactyly

28345   syndactyly, with or without skin graft(s), each web

28360 Reconstruction, cleft foot

FRACTURE AND/OR DISLOCATION

28400 Closed treatment of calcaneal fracture; without manipulation

28405   with manipulation

28406 Percutaneous skeletal fixation of calcaneal fracture, with manipulation

28415 Open treatment of calcaneal fracture, includes internal fixation, when performed;

28420   with primary iliac or other autogenous bone graft (includes obtaining graft)

28430 Closed treatment of talus fracture; without manipulation

28435   with manipulation

28436 Percutaneous skeletal fixation of talus fracture, with manipulation

28445 Open treatment of talus fracture, includes internal fixation, when performed

28446 Open osteochondral autograft, talus (includes obtaining graft[s])

(Do not report 28446 in conjunction with 27705, 27707)

(For arthroscopic osteochondral talus graft, use 29892)

(For open osteochondral allograft or repairs with industrial grafts, use 28899)

28450 Treatment of tarsal bone fracture (except talus and calcaneus); without manipulation, each

28455   with manipulation, each

28456 Percutaneous skeletal fixation of tarsal bone fracture (except talus and calcaneus), with manipulation, each

28465 Open treatment of tarsal bone fracture (except talus and calcaneus), includes internal fixation, when performed, each

---

28470	Closed treatment of metatarsal fracture; without manipulation, each
28475	with manipulation, each
28476	Percutaneous skeletal fixation of metatarsal fracture, with manipulation, each
28485	Open treatment of metatarsal fracture, includes internal fixation, when performed, each
28490	Closed treatment of fracture great toe, phalanx or phalanges; without manipulation
28495	with manipulation
28496	Percutaneous skeletal fixation of fracture great toe, phalanx or phalanges, with manipulation
28505	Open treatment of fracture great toe, phalanx or phalanges, includes internal fixation, when performed
28510	Closed treatment of fracture, phalanx or phalanges, other than great toe; without manipulation, each
28515	with manipulation, each
28525	Open treatment of fracture, phalanx or phalanges, other than great toe, includes internal fixation, when performed, each
28530	Closed treatment of sesamoid fracture
28531	Open treatment of sesamoid fracture, with or without internal fixation
28540	Closed treatment of tarsal bone dislocation, other than talotarsal; without anesthesia
28545	requiring anesthesia
28546	Percutaneous skeletal fixation of tarsal bone dislocation, other than talotarsal, with manipulation
28555	Open treatment of tarsal bone dislocation, includes internal fixation, when performed
28570	Closed treatment of talotarsal joint dislocation; without anesthesia
28575	requiring anesthesia
28576	Percutaneous skeletal fixation of talotarsal joint dislocation, with manipulation
28585	Open treatment of talotarsal joint dislocation, includes internal fixation, when performed
28600	Closed treatment of tarsometatarsal joint dislocation; without anesthesia
28605	requiring anesthesia
28606	Percutaneous skeletal fixation of tarsometatarsal joint dislocation, with manipulation
28615	Open treatment of tarsometatarsal joint dislocation, includes internal fixation, when performed
28630	Closed treatment of metatarsophalangeal joint dislocation; without anesthesia
28635	requiring anesthesia
28636	Percutaneous skeletal fixation of metatarsophalangeal joint dislocation, with manipulation
28645	Open treatment of metatarsophalangeal joint dislocation, includes internal fixation, when performed

● New Code   ▲ Revised Code   + Add-On Code   ⊘ Modifier -51 Exempt   ★ Telemedicine

28660	Closed treatment of interphalangeal joint dislocation; without anesthesia
28665	requiring anesthesia
28666	Percutaneous skeletal fixation of interphalangeal joint dislocation, with manipulation
28675	Open treatment of interphalangeal joint dislocation, includes internal fixation, when performed

ARTHRODESIS

28705	Arthrodesis; pantalar
28715	triple
28725	subtalar
28730	Arthrodesis, midtarsal or tarsometatarsal, multiple or transverse;
28735	with osteotomy (eg, flatfoot correction)
28737	Arthrodesis, with tendon lengthening and advancement, midtarsal, tarsal navicular-cuneiform (eg, Miller type procedure)
28740	Arthrodesis, midtarsal or tarsometatarsal, single joint
28750	Arthrodesis, great toe; metatarsophalangeal joint
28755	interphalangeal joint
28760	Arthrodesis, with extensor hallucis longus transfer to first metatarsal neck, great toe, interphalangeal joint (eg, Jones type procedure)

(For hammertoe operation or interphalangeal fusion, use 28285)

AMPUTATION

28800	Amputation, foot; midtarsal (eg, Chopart type procedure)
28805	transmetatarsal
28810	Amputation, metatarsal, with toe, single
28820	Amputation, toe; metatarsophalangeal joint
28825	interphalangeal joint

(For amputation of tuft of distal phalanx, use 11752)

OTHER PROCEDURES

| 28890 | Extracorporeal shock wave, high energy, performed by a physician or other qualified health care professional, requiring anesthesia other than local, including ultrasound guidance, involving the plantar fascia |

(For extracorporeal shock wave therapy involving musculoskeletal system not otherwise specified, see 0101T, 0102T)

(For extracorporeal shock wave therapy involving integumentary system not otherwise specified, see 0299T, 0300T)

(Do not report 28890 in conjunction with 0299T, 0300T when treating in the same area)

███ Separate Procedure ███ Unlisted Procedure ███ CCI Comp. Code ███ Non-specific Procedure **317**

28899   Unlisted procedure, foot or toes

APPLICATION OF CASTS AND STRAPPING

CPT codes in this section are used only when the cast application or strapping is a replacement procedure performed during or after the period of follow-up care. An additional evaluation and management service code, dependent on location, is reportable only if significant identifiable other services are provided at the time of the cast application or strapping.

For coding cast or strap application in situations not involving surgery, for example, casting of a sprained ankle or knee, use the appropriate level of evaluation and management services code plus code 99070 or equivalent HCPCS Level II code to report casting materials.

The listed procedures apply when the cast application or strapping is a replacement procedure used during or aftre the period of follow-up care, or when the cast application or strapping is an initial service performed without a restorative treatment or procedure(s) to stabilize or protect a fracture, injury, or dislocation and/or to afford comfort to a patient. Restorative treatment or procedure(s) rendered by another individual following the application of the initial cast/splint/strap may be reported with a treatment of fracture and/or dislocation code.

An individual who applies the initial cast, strap, or splint and also assumes all of the subsequent fracture, dislocation, or injury care cannot use the application of casts and strapping codes as an initial service, since the first cast/splint or strap application is included in the treatment of fracture and/or dislocation codes. (See notes under Musculoskeletal System.) A temporary cast/splint/strap is not considered to be part of the preoperative care, and the use of the modifier 56 is not applicable. Additional evaluation and management services are reportable only if significant identifiable further services are provided at the time of the cast application or strapping.

If a cast application or strapping is provided as an initial service (eg, casting of a sprained ankle or knee) in which no other procedure or treatment (eg, surgical repair, reduction of a fracture, or joint dislocation) is performed or is expected to be performed by an individual rendering the initial care only, use the casting, strapping, and/or supply code (99070) in addition to an evaluation and management code as appropriate.

Listed procedures include removal of cast or strapping.

(For orthotics management and training, see 97760, 97761, 97763)

BODY AND UPPER EXTREMITY

Casts

29000   Application of halo type body cast (see 20661-20663 for insertion)

29010   Application of Risser jacket, localizer, body; only

29015   including head

29035   Application of body cast, shoulder to hips;

29040   including head, Minerva type

29044   including 1 thigh

29046   including both thighs

29049   Application, cast; figure-of-eight

29055   shoulder spica

29058   plaster Velpeau

29065   shoulder to hand (long arm)

29075   elbow to finger (short arm)

  ●   New Code   ▲   Revised Code   +   Add-On Code   ⊘   Modifier -51 Exempt   ★   Telemedicine

29085   hand and lower forearm (gauntlet)

29086   finger (eg, contracture)

Splints

29105   Application of long arm splint (shoulder to hand)

29125   Application of short arm splint (forearm to hand); static

29126   dynamic

29130   Application of finger splint; static

29131   dynamic

Strapping - Any Age

29200   Strapping; thorax

(To report low back strapping, use 29799)

29240   shoulder (eg, Velpeau)

29260   elbow or wrist

29280   hand or finger

LOWER EXTREMITY

Casts

29305   Application of hip spica cast; 1 leg

29325   1 and one-half spica or both legs

(For hip spica (body) cast, including thighs only, use 29046)

29345   Application of long leg cast (thigh to toes);

29355   walker or ambulatory type

29358   Application of long leg cast brace

29365   Application of cylinder cast (thigh to ankle)

29405   Application of short leg cast (below knee to toes);

29425   walking or ambulatory type

29435   Application of patellar tendon bearing (PTB) cast

29440   Adding walker to previously applied cast

29445   Application of rigid total contact leg cast

29450   Application of clubfoot cast with molding or manipulation, long or short leg

(To report bilateral procedures, use 29450 with modifier -50)

Splints

29505	Application of long leg splint (thigh to ankle or toes)
29515	Application of short leg splint (calf to foot)

Strapping - Any Age

29520	Strapping; hip
29530	knee
29540	ankle and/or foot

(Do not report 29540 in conjunction with 29581)

29550	toes
29580	Unna boot

(Do not report 29580 in conjunction with 29581)

29581	Application of multi-layer compression system; leg (below knee), including ankle and foot

(Do not report 29581 in conjunction with 29540, 29580, 36468, 36470, 36471, 36475, 36476, 36478, 36479)

(**29582**	deleted 2017 [2018 edition].)
(**29583**	deleted 2017 [2018 edition].)
29584	upper arm, forearm, hand and fingers

(Do not report 29584 in conjunction with 29583)

REMOVAL OR REPAIR

29700	Removal or bivalving; gauntlet, boot or body cast
29705	full arm or full leg cast
29710	shoulder or hip spica, Minerva, or Risser jacket, etc.
(**29715**	deleted 2014 [2015 edition])
29720	Repair of spica, body cast or jacket
29730	Windowing of cast
29740	Wedging of cast (except clubfoot casts)
29750	Wedging of clubfoot cast

(To report bilateral procedures, use 29750 with modifier -50)

OTHER PROCEDURES

29799	Unlisted procedure, casting or strapping

ENDOSCOPY/ARTHROSCOPY

● New Code ▲ Revised Code + Add-On Code ⊘ Modifier -51 Exempt ★ Telemedicine

Surgical endoscopy/arthroscopy always includes a diagnostic endoscopy/ arthroscopy and is therefore never reported in addition to the surgical procedure. However, there are several arthroscopy procedures defined as separate procedures, indicating that the codes may be reported if the diagnostic arthroscopy is the only procedure performed.

When arthroscopy is performed in conjunction with arthrotomy, add modifier 51.

29800 Arthroscopy, temporomandibular joint, diagnostic, with or without synovial biopsy (separate procedure)

29804 Arthroscopy, temporomandibular joint, surgical

(For open procedure, use 21010)

29805 Arthroscopy, shoulder, diagnostic, with or without synovial biopsy (separate procedure)

(For open procedure, see 23065-23066, 23100-23101)

29806 Arthroscopy, shoulder, surgical; capsulorrhaphy

(For open procedure, see 23450-23466)

(To report thermal capsulorrhaphy, use 29999)

29807 repair of slap lesion

29819 with removal of loose body or foreign body

(For open procedure, see 23040-23044, 23107)

29820 synovectomy, partial

(For open procedure, see 23105)

29821 synovectomy, complete

(For open procedure, see 23105)

29822 debridement, limited

(For open procedure, see specific open shoulder procedure performed)

29823 debridement, extensive

(For open procedure, see specific open shoulder procedure performed)

29824 distal claviculectomy including distal articular surface (Mumford procedure)

(For open procedure, use 23120)

29825 with lysis and resection of adhesions, with or without manipulation

(For open procedure, see specific open shoulder procedure performed)

+ **29826** decompression of subacromial space with partial acromioplasty, with coracoacromial ligament (ie, arch) release, when performed (List separately in addition to code for primary procedure

(For open procedure, use 23130 or 23415)

(Use 29826 in conjunction with 29806-29825, 29827, 29828)

29827 with rotator cuff repair

(For open or mini-open rotator cuff repair, use 23412)

(When arthroscopic distal clavicle resection is performed at the same setting, use 29824 and append modifier '-51')

| | Separate Procedure | | Unlisted Procedure | | CCI Comp. Code | | Non-specific Procedure | **321** |

29828	biceps tenodesis

(Do not report 29828 in conjunction with 29805, 29820, 29822)

(For open biceps tenodesis, use 23430)

29830	Arthroscopy, elbow, diagnostic, with or without synovial biopsy (separate procedure)
29834	Arthroscopy, elbow, surgical; with removal of loose body or foreign body
29835	synovectomy, partial
29836	synovectomy, complete
29837	debridement, limited
29838	debridement, extensive
29840	Arthroscopy, wrist, diagnostic, with or without synovial biopsy (separate procedure)
29843	Arthroscopy, wrist, surgical; for infection, lavage and drainage
29844	synovectomy, partial
29845	synovectomy, complete
29846	excision and/or repair of triangular fibrocartilage and/or joint debridement
29847	internal fixation for fracture or instability
29848	Endoscopy, wrist, surgical, with release of transverse carpal ligament

(For open procedure, use 64721)

29850	Arthroscopically aided treatment of intercondylar spine(s) and/or tuberosity fracture(s) of the knee, with or without manipulation; without internal or external fixation (includes arthroscopy)
29851	with internal or external fixation (includes arthroscopy)

(For bone graft, use 20900, 20902)

29855	Arthroscopically aided treatment of tibial fracture, proximal (plateau); nicondylar, includes internal fixation, when performed (includes arthroscopy)
29856	bicondylar, includes internal fixation, when performed (includes arthroscopy)

(For bone graft, use 20900, 20902)

29860	Arthroscopy, hip, diagnostic with or without synovial biopsy (separate procedure)
29861	Arthroscopy, hip, surgical; with removal of loose body or foreign body
29862	with debridement/shaving of articular cartilage (chondroplasty), abrasion arthroplasty, and/or resection of labrum
29863	with synovectomy
29914	with femoroplasty (ie, treatment of cam lesion)
29915	with acetabuloplasty (ie, treatment of pincer lesion)

● New Code ▲ Revised Code + Add-On Code ⊘ Modifier -51 Exempt ★ Telemedicine

(Do not report 29914, 29915 in conjunction with 29862, 29863)

29916   with labral repair

(Do not report 29916 in conjunction with 29915, 29862, 29863)

29866   Arthroscopy, knee, surgical; osteochondral autograft(s) (eg, mosaicplasty) (includes harvesting of the autograft[s])

(Do not report 29866 in conjunction with 29870, 29871, 29875, 29884 when performed at the same session and/or 29874, 29877, 29879, 29885-29887 when performed in the same compartment)

(For open osteochondral autograft of knee, use 27416)

29867   osteochondral allograft (eg, mosaicplasty)

(Do not report 29867 in conjunction with 27570, 29870, 29871, 29875, 29884 when performed at the same session and/or 29874, 29877, 29879, 29885-29887 when performed in the same compartment)

(Do not report 29867 in conjunction with 27415)

29868   meniscal transplantation (includes arthrotomy for meniscal insertion), medial or lateral

(Do not report 29868 in conjunction with 29870, 29871, 29875, 29880, 29883, 29884 when performed at the same session or 29874, 29877, 29881, 29882 when performed in the same compartment)

29870   Arthroscopy, knee, diagnostic, with or without synovial biopsy (separate procedure)

(For open autologous chondrocyte implantation of the knee, use 27412)

29871   Arthroscopy, knee, surgical; for infection, lavage and drainage

(Do not report 29871 in conjunction with 27370)

(For implantation of osteochondral graft for treatment of articular surface defect, see 27412, 27415, 29866, 29867)

29873   with lateral release

(For open lateral release, use 27425)

29874   for removal of loose body or foreign body (eg, osteochondritis dissecans fragmentation, chondral fragmentation)

29875   synovectomy, limited (eg, plica or shelf resection) (separate procedure)

29876   synovectomy, major, 2 or more compartments (eg, medial or lateral)

29877   debridement/shaving of articular cartilage (chondroplasty)

(When performed with arthroscopic meniscectomy, see 29880 or 29881)

29879   abrasion arthroplasty (includes chondroplasty where necessary) or multiple drilling or microfracture

29880   with meniscectomy (medial AND lateral, including any meniscal shaving) including debridement/shaving of articular cartilage (chondroplasty), same or separate compartment(s), when performed

29881   with meniscectomy (medial OR lateral, including any meniscal shaving) including debridement/shaving of articular cartilage (chondroplasty), same or separate compartment(s), when performed

29882   with meniscus repair (medial OR lateral)

29883   with meniscus repair (medial AND lateral)

Separate Procedure   Unlisted Procedure   CCI Comp. Code   Non-specific Procedure   **323**

(For meniscal transplantation, medial or lateral, knee, use 29868)

29884   with lysis of adhesions, with or without manipulation (separate procedure)

29885   drilling for osteochondritis dissecans with bone grafting, with or without internal fixation (including debridement of base of lesion)

29886   drilling for intact osteochondritis dissecans lesion

29887   drilling for intact osteochondritis dissecans lesion with internal fixation

29888   Arthroscopically aided anterior cruciate ligament repair/augmentation or reconstruction

29889   Arthroscopically aided posterior cruciate ligament repair/augmentation or reconstruction

(Procedures 29888 and 29889 should not be used with reconstruction procedures 27427-27429)

29891   Arthroscopy, ankle, surgical, excision of osteochondral defect of talus and/or tibia, including drilling of the defect

29892   Arthroscopically aided repair of large osteochondritis dissecans lesion, talar dome fracture, or tibial plafond fracture, with or without internal fixation (includes arthroscopy)

29893   Endoscopic plantar fasciotomy

29894   Arthroscopy, ankle (tibiotalar and fibulotalar joints), surgical; with removal of loose body or foreign body

29895   synovectomy, partial

29897   debridement, limited

29898   debridement, extensive

29899   with ankle arthrodesis

(For open ankle arthrodesis, use 27870)

29900   Arthroscopy, metacarpophalangeal joint, diagnostic, includes synovial biopsy

(Do not report 29900 with 29901, 29902)

29901   Arthroscopy, metacarpophalangeal joint, surgical; with debridement

29902   with reduction of displaced ulnar collateral ligament (eg, Stenar lesion)

29904   Arthroscropy, subtalar joint, surgical; with removal of loose body or foreign body

29905   with synovectomy

29906   with debridement

29907   with subtalar arthrodesis

29914   This code is out of order. See page 322.

29915   This code is out of order. See page 322.

29916   This code is out of order. See page 323.

29999   Unlisted procedure, arthroscopy

---

324   ● New Code   ▲ Revised Code   + Add-On Code   ⊘ Modifier -51 Exempt   ★ Telemedicine

RESPIRATORY SYSTEM

CPT codes from this section of the CPT coding system are used to report invasive and surgical procedures performed on the nose, sinuses, larynx, trachea and bronchi, and the lungs and pleura.

MISCELLANEOUS CODING RULES

Functional Endoscopic Sinus Surgery (FESS) codes are coded based on the procedures described in the operative report or on the nasal sinus endoscopy report. Each FESS code represents a unilateral procedure. To express that a procedure was performed bilaterally requires the application of the modifier -50, bilateral procedure.

Indirect laryngoscopy involves the visualization of the larynx using a warm laryngeal mirror positioned at the back of the throat. Direct laryngoscopy involves the visualization using a rigid or fiberoptic endoscope. Operative direct laryngoscopy involves an endoscopic examination under general anesthesia.

To code nasal hemorrhages appropriately, documentation needs to substantiate whether the hemorrhage is anterior or posterior and how the hemorrhage is controlled. Control of anterior nasal hemorrhage typically involves the insertion of gauze packing, or anterior packing or performance of cauterization. Control of posterior nasal hemorrhage most likely requires the insertion of nasal stents, tampons, balloon catheters, or posterior packing.

NOSE

INCISION

30000   Drainage abscess or hematoma, nasal, internal approach

(For external approach, see 10060, 10140)

30020   Drainage abscess or hematoma, nasal septum

(For lateral rhinotomy, see specific application (eg, 30118, 30320))

EXCISION

30100   Biopsy, intranasal

(For biopsy skin of nose, see 11100, 11101)

30110   Excision, nasal polyp(s), simple

(30110 would normally be completed in an office setting)

(To report bilateral procedure, use 30110 with modifier -50)

30115   Excision, nasal polyp(s), extensive

(30115 would normally require the facilities available in a hospital setting)

(To report bilateral procedure, use 30115 with modifier -50)

30117   Excision or destruction (eg, laser), intranasal lesion; internal approach

30118   external approach (lateral rhinotomy)

30120   Excision or surgical planing of skin of nose for rhinophyma

30124   Excision dermoid cyst, nose; simple, skin, subcutaneous

30125   complex, under bone or cartilage

30130   Excision inferior turbinate, partial or complete, any method

RESP CVS 30000

| Separate Procedure | Unlisted Procedure | CCI Comp. Code | Non-specific Procedure | **325** |

(For excision of superior or middle turbinate, use 30999)

30140 Submucous resection inferior turbinate, partial or complete, any method

(Do not report 30130 or 30140 in conjunction with 30801, 30802, 30930)

(For submucous resection of superior or middle turbinate, use 30999)

(For endoscopic resection of concha bullosa of middle turbinate, use 31240)

(For submucous resection of nasal septum, use 30520)

30150 Rhinectomy; partial

30160 total

(For closure and/or reconstruction, primary or delayed, see Integumentary System, 13151-13160, 14060-14302, 15120, 15121, 15260, 15261, 15760, 20900-20912)

INTRODUCTION

30200 Injection into turbinate(s), therapeutic

30210 Displacement therapy (Proetz type)

30220 Insertion, nasal septal prosthesis (button)

REMOVAL OF FOREIGN BODY

30300 Removal foreign body, intranasal; office type procedure

30310 requiring general anesthesia

30320 by lateral rhinotomy

REPAIR

(For obtaining tissues for graft, see 20900-20926, 21210)

30400 Rhinoplasty, primary; lateral and alar cartilages and/or elevation of nasal tip

(For columellar reconstruction, see 13151 et seq)

30410 complete, external parts including bony pyramid, lateral and alar cartilages, and/or elevation of nasal tip

30420 including major septal repair

30430 Rhinoplasty, secondary; minor revision (small amount of nasal tip work)

30435 intermediate revision (bony work with osteotomies)

30450 major revision (nasal tip work and osteotomies)

30460 Rhinoplasty for nasal deformity secondary to congenital cleft lip and/or palate, including columellar lengthening; tip only

30462 tip, septum, osteotomies

30465 Repair of nasal vestibular stenosis (eg, spreader grafting, lateral nasal wall reconstruction)

(30465 excludes obtaining graft. For graft procedure, see 20900-20926, 21210)

● New Code   ▲ Revised Code   ✚ Add-On Code   ⦸ Modifier -51 Exempt   ★ Telemedicine

(30465 is used to report a bilateral procedure. For unilateral procedure, use modifier -52)

30520 Septoplasty or submucous resection, with or without cartilage scoring, contouring or replacement with graft

(For submucous resection of turbinates, use 30140)

30540 Repair choanal atresia; intranasal

30545   transpalatine

(Do not report modifier '-63' in conjunction with 30540, 30545)

30560 Lysis intranasal synechia

30580 Repair fistula; oromaxillary (combine with 31030 if antrotomy is included)

30600   oronasal

30620 Septal or other intranasal dermatoplasty (does not include obtaining graft)

30630 Repair nasal septal perforations

DESTRUCTION

30801 Ablation, soft tissue of inferior turbinates, unilateral or bilateral, any method (eg, electrocautery, radiofrequency ablation, or tissue volume reduction); superficial

(For ablation of superior or middle turbinates, use 30999)

30802   intramural (ie, submucosal)

(Do not report 30801 in conjunction with 30802)

(Do not report 30801, 30802, 30930 in conjunction with 30130 or 30140)

(For cautery performed for control of nasal hemorrhage, see 30901-30906)

OTHER PROCEDURES

30901 Control nasal hemorrhage, anterior, simple (limited cautery and/or packing) any method

(To report bilateral procedure, use 30901 with modifier -50)

30903 Control nasal hemorrhage, anterior, complex (extensive cautery and/or packing) any method

(To report bilateral procedure, use 30903 with modifier -50)

30905 Control nasal hemorrhage, posterior, with posterior nasal packs and/or cautery, any method; initial

30906   subsequent

30915 Ligation arteries; ethmoidal

30920   internal maxillary artery, transantral

(For ligation external carotid artery, use 37600)

30930 Fracture nasal inferior turbinate(s), therapeutic

(Do not report 30801, 30802, 30930 in conjunction with 30130 or 30140)

(For fracture of superior or middle turbinate(s), use 30999)

30999 Unlisted procedure, nose

▆▆▆ Separate Procedure   ▆▆▆ Unlisted Procedure   ▆▆▆ CCI Comp. Code   ▆▆▆ Non-specific Procedure   **327**

ACCESSORY SINUSES

INCISION

31000   Lavage by cannulation; maxillary sinus (antrum puncture or natural ostium)

(To report bilateral procedure, use 31000 with modifier -50)

31002   sphenoid sinus

31020   Sinusotomy, maxillary (antrotomy); intranasal

(To report bilateral procedure, use 31020 with modifier -50)

31030   radical (Caldwell-Luc) without removal of antrochoanal polyps

(To report bilateral procedure, use 31030 with modifier -50)

31032   radical (Caldwell-Luc) with removal of antrochoanal polyps

(To report bilateral procedure, use 31032 with modifier -50)

31040   Pterygomaxillary fossa surgery, any approach

(For transantral ligation of internal maxillary artery, use 30920)

31050   Sinusotomy, sphenoid, with or without biopsy;

31051   with mucosal stripping or removal of polyp(s)

31070   Sinusotomy frontal; external, simple (trephine operation)

(For frontal intranasal sinusotomy, use 31276)

31075   transorbital, unilateral (for mucocele or osteoma, Lynch type)

31080   obliterative without osteoplastic flap, brow incision (includes ablation)

31081   obliterative, without osteoplastic flap, coronal incision (includes ablation)

31084   obliterative, with osteoplastic flap, brow incision

31085   obliterative, with osteoplastic flap, coronal incision

31086   nonobliterative, with osteoplastic flap, brow incision

31087   nonobliterative, with osteoplastic flap, coronal incision

31090   Sinusotomy, unilateral, 3 or more paranasal sinuses (frontal, maxillary, ethmoid, sphenoid)

EXCISION

31200   Ethmoidectomy; intranasal, anterior

31201   intranasal, total

31205   extranasal, total

31225   Maxillectomy; without orbital exenteration

31230   with orbital exenteration (en bloc)

---

328   ● New Code   ▲ Revised Code   + Add-On Code   ⊘ Modifier -51 Exempt   ★ Telemedicine

(For orbital exenteration only, see 65110 et seq)

(For skin graft, see 15120 et seq)

ENDOSCOPY

A surgical sinus endoscopy includes a sinusotomy (when appropriate) and diagnostic endoscopy.

Codes 31295-31298 describe dilation of sinus ostia by displacement of tissue, any method, and include fluoroscopy if performed.

Stereotactic computer-assisted navigation may be used to facilitate the performance of endoscopic sinus surgery, and may be reported with 61782.

Codes 31233-31298 are used to report unilateral procedures unless otherwise specified.

Codes 31231-31235 for diagnostic evaluation refer to employing a nasal/sinus endoscope to inspect the interior of the nasal cavity and the middle and superior meatus, the turbinates, and the spheno-ethmoid recess. Any time a diagnostic evaluation is performed all these areas would be inspected and a separate code is not reported for each area. To report these services when all of the elements are not fully examined (eg, judged not clinically pertinent), or because the clinical situation precludes such exam (eg, technically unable, altered anatomy), append modifier 52 if repeat examination is not planned, or modifier 53 if repeat examination is planned.

31231   Nasal endoscopy, diagnostic, unilateral or bilateral (separate procedure)

31233   Nasal/sinus endoscopy, diagnostic with maxillary sinusoscopy (via inferior meatus or canine fossa puncture)

     (Do not report 31233 in conjunction with 31295 when performed on the same sinus)

31235   Nasal/sinus endoscopy, diagnostic with sphenoid sinusoscopy (via puncture of sphenoidal face or cannulation of ostium)

     (Do not report 31235 in conjunction with 31297 when performed on the same sinus)

31237   Nasal/sinus endoscopy, surgical; with biopsy, polypectomy or debridement (separate procedure)

31238   with control of nasal hemorrhage

     (Do not report 31238 in conjunction with 31241, when performed on the ipsilateral side)

31239   with dacryocystorhinostomy

31240   with concha bullosa resection

     (For endoscopic osteomeatal complex (OMC) resection with antrostomy and/or anterior ethmoidectomy, with or without removal of polyp(s), use 31254 and 31256)

     (For endoscopic osteomeatal complex (OMC) resection with antrostomy, removal of antral mucosal disease, and/or anterior ethmoidectomy, with or without removal of polyp(s), use 31254 and 31257)

     (For endoscopic frontal sinus exploration, osteomeatal complex (OMC) resection and./or anterior ethmoidecomy, with or without removal of polyp(s), use 31254 and 31276)

     (For endoscopic frontal sinus exploration, osteomeatal complex (OMC) resection, antrostomy, and./or anterior ethmoidecomy, with or without removal of polyp(s), use 31254, 31256 and 31276)

     (For endoscopic nasal diagnostic endoscopy, see 31231-31235)

     (For endoscopic osteomeatal complex (OMC) resection, frontal sinus exploration, antrostomy, removal of antral mucosal disease, and/or anterior ethmoidecomy, with or without removal of polyp(s), use 31254, 31267, and 31276)

● **31241**   with ligation of sphenopalatine artery

     (Do not report 31241 in conjunction with 31238, when performed on the ipsilateral side)

■ Separate Procedure   ■ Unlisted Procedure   ■ CCI Comp. Code   ■ Non-specific Procedure   **329**

31253 This code is out of order. See page 330.

▲ **31254** Nasal/sinus endoscopy, surgical with ethmoidectomy; partial (anterior)

(Do not report 31254 in conjunction with 31253, 31255, 31257, 31259, 0406T, 0407T, when performed on the ipsilateral side)

▲ **31255** total (anterior andposterior)

(Do not report 31255 in conjunction with 31253, 31254, 31257, 31259, 31276, 31287, 31288, 0406T, 0407T, when performed on the ipsilateral side)

● **31253** total (anterior and posterior), including frontal sinus exploration, with removal of tissue from frontal sinus, when performed

(Do not report 31253 in conjunction with 31237, 31254, 31255, 31276, 31296, 31298, 0406T, 0407T, when performed on the ipsilateral side)

● **31257** total (anterior and posterior), including sphenoidotomy

(Do not report 31257 in conjunction with 31235, 31237, 31254, 31255, 31259, 31287, 31288, 31297, 31298, 0406T, 0407T, when performed on the ipsilateral side)

● **31259** total (anterior and posterior), including sphenoidotomy, with removal of tissue from the sphenoid sinus

(Do not report 31259 in conjunction with 31235, 31237, 31254, 31255, 31257, 31287, 31288, 31297, 31298, 0406T, 0407T, when performed on the ipsilateral side)

31256 Nasal/sinus endoscopy, surgical, with maxillary antrostomy;

(For endoscopic anterior and posterior ethmoidectomy (APE) and antrostomy, with or without removal of polyp(s), use 31255 and 31256)

(For endoscopic anterior and posterior ethmoidectomy (APE), antrostomy and removal of antral mucosal disease, with or without removal of polyp(s), use 31255 and 31267)

(For endoscopic anterior and posterior ethmoidectomy (APE) and frontal sinus exploration, with or without removal of polyp(s), use 31255 and 31276)

31257 This code is out of order. See page 330.

31259 This code is out of order. See page 330.

31267 with removal of tissue from maxillary sinus

(Do not report 31256, 31267 in conjunction with 31295 when performed on the same sinus)

(For endoscopic anterior and posterior ethmoidectomy (APE) and frontal sinus exploration and antrostomy, with or without removal of polyp(s), use 31255, 31256, and 31276)

(For endoscopic anterior and posterior ethmoidectomy (APE), frontal sinus exploration, antrostomy, and removal of antral mucosal disease, with or without removal of polyp(s), use 31255, 31267, and 31276)

▲ **31276** Nasal/sinus endoscopy, surgical, with frontal sinus exploration, including removal of tissue from frontal sinus, when performed

(Do not report 31276 in conjunction with 31253, 31255, 31296, 31298, when performed on the ipsilateral side)

(For endoscopic anterior and posterior ethmoidectomy and sphenoidotomy (APS), with or without removal of polyp(s), use 31255, 31287 or 31288)

(For endoscopic anterior and posterior ethmoidectomy and sphenoidotomy (APS), and antrostomy, with or without removal of polyp(s), use 31255, 31256, and 31287 or 31288)

(For endoscopic anterior and posterior ethmoidectomy and sphenoidotomy (APS), antrostomy and removal of antral mucosal disease, with or without removal of polyp(s), use 31255, 31267, and 31287 or 31288)

● New Code ▲ Revised Code ＋ Add-On Code ⊘ Modifier -51 Exempt ★ Telemedicine

(For endoscopic anterior and posterior ethmoidectomy and sphenoidotomy (APS), and frontal sinus exploration, with or without removal of polyp(s), use 31255, 31287 or 31288, and 31276)

(For endoscopic anterior and posterior ethmoidectomy and sphenoidotomy (APS), with or without removal of polyp(s), with frontal sinus exploration and antrostomy, use 31255, 31256, 31287 or 31288, and 31276)

(For unilateral endoscopy of two or more sinuses, see 31231-31235)

(For endoscopic anterior and posterior ethmoidectomy and sphenoidotomy (APS), frontal sinus exploration, antrostomy and removal of antral mucosal disease, with or without the removal of polyp(s), see 31255, 31267, 31287 or 31288, and 31276)

31287　Nasal/sinus endoscopy, surgical, with sphenoidotomy;

(Do not report 31287 in conjunction with 31235, 31255, 31257, 31259, 31288, 31297, 31298, when performed on the ipsilateral side)

31288　　　with removal of tissue from the sphenoid sinus

(Do not report 31288 in conjunction with 31235, 31255, 31257, 31259, 31287, 31297, 31298, when performed on the ipsilateral side)

31290　Nasal/sinus endoscopy, surgical, with repair of cerebrospinal fluid leak; ethmoid region

31291　　　sphenoid region

31292　Nasal/sinus endoscopy, surgical; with medial or inferior orbital wall decompression

31293　　　with medial orbital wall and inferior orbital wall decompression

31294　　　with optic nerve decompression

31295　Nasal/sinus endoscopy, surgical; with dilation of maxillary sinus ostium (eg, balloon dilation), transnasal or via canine fossa

(Do not report 31295 in conjunction with 31233, 31256, 31267, when performed on the ipsilateral side)

31296　　　with dilation of frontal sinua ostium (eg, balloon dilation)

(Do not report 31296 in conjunction with 31253, 31276, 31297, 31298, when performed on the ipsilateral side)

31297　　　with dilation of sphenoid sinus ostium (eg, balloon dilation)

(Do not report 31297 in conjunction with 31235, 31257, 31259, 31287, 31288, 31296, 31298, when performed on the ipsilateral side)

● **31298**　　　with dilation of frontal and sphenoid sinus ostia (eg, balloon dilation)

(Do not report 31298 in conjunction with 31235, 31237, 31253, 31257, 31259, 31276, 31287, 31288, 31296, 31297, when performed on the ipsilateral side)

OTHER PROCEDURES

(For hypophysectomy, transantral or transeptal approach, use 61548)

(For transcranial hypophysectomy, use 61546)

31299　Unlisted procedure, accessory sinuses

LARYNX

EXCISION

31300　Laryngotomy (thyrotomy, laryngofissure); with removal of tumor or laryngocele, cordectomy

---

(**31320**   deleted 2017 [2018 edition].)

31360   Laryngectomy; total, without radical neck dissection

31365   total, with radical neck dissection

31367   subtotal supraglottic, without radical neck dissection

31368   subtotal supraglottic, with radical neck dissection

31370   Partial laryngectomy (hemilaryngectomy); horizontal

31375   laterovertical

31380   anterovertical

31382   antero-latero-vertical

31390   Pharyngolaryngectomy, with radical neck dissection; without reconstruction

31395   with reconstruction

31400   Arytenoidectomy or arytenoidopexy, external approach

         (For endoscopic arytenoidecomy, use 31560)

31420   Epiglottidectomy

INTRODUCTION

⊘ **31500**   Intubation, endotracheal, emergency procedure

31502   Tracheotomy tube change prior to establishment of fistula tract

ENDOSCOPY

For endoscopic procedures, report appropriate endoscopy of each anatomic site examined. Laryngoscopy includes examination of the tongue base, larynx, and hypopharynx. The anatomic structures examined with this procedure include both midline (single anatomic sites) and paired structures. Midline, single anatomic sites include tongue base, vallecula, epiglottis, subglottis, and posterior pharyngeal wall. Paired structures include true vocal cords, arytenoids, false vocal cords, ventricles, pyriform sinuses, and aryepiglottic folds. For the purposes of reporting therapeutic interventions, all paired structures contained within one side of the larynx/ pharynx are considered unilateral. If using operating microscope, telescope, or both, use the applicable code only once per operative session.

31505   Laryngoscopy, indirect; diagnostic (separate procedure)

31510   with biopsy

31511   with removal of foreign body

31512   with removal of lesion

31513   with vocal cord injection

31515   Laryngoscopy direct, with or without tracheoscopy; for aspiration

31520   diagnostic, newborn

         (Do not report modifier -63 in conjunction with 31520)

● New Code   ▲ Revised Code   + Add-On Code   ⊘ Modifier -51 Exempt   ★ Telemedicine

31525   diagnostic, except newborn

31526   diagnostic, with operating microscope or telescope

        (Do not report code 69990 in addition to code 31526)

31527   with insertion of obturator

31528   with dilation, initial

31529   with dilation, subsequent

31530 Laryngoscopy, direct, operative, with foreign body removal;

31531   with operating microscope or telescope

        (Do not report code 69990 in addition to code 31531)

31535 Laryngoscopy, direct, operative, with biopsy;

31536   with operating microscope or telescope

        (Do not report code 69990 in addition to code 31536)

31540 Laryngoscopy, direct, operative, with excision of tumor and/or stripping of vocal cords or epiglottis;

31541   with operating microscope or telescope

        (Do not report code 69990 in addition to code 31541)

31545 Laryngoscopy, direct, operative, with operating microscope or telescope, with submucosal removal of non-neoplastic lesion(s) of vocal cord; reconstruction with local tissue flap(s)

31546   reconstruction with graft(s) (includes obtaining autograft)

        (Do not report 31546 in addition to 20926 for graft harvest)

        (For reconstruction of vocal cord with allograft, use 31599)

        (Do not report 31545 or 31546 in conjunction with 31540, 31541, 69990)

31551 This code is out of order. See page 334.

31552 This code is out of order. See page 334.

31553 This code is out of order. See page 335.

31554 This code is out of order. See page 335.

31560 Laryngoscopy, direct, operative, with arytenoidectomy;

31561   with operating microscope or telescope

        (Do not report code 69990 in addition to code 31561)

31570 Laryngoscopy, direct, with injection into vocal cord(s), therapeutic;

31571   with operating microscope or telescope

        (Do not report code 69990 in addition to code 31571)

31572 This code is out of order. See page 334.

█ Separate Procedure   █ Unlisted Procedure   █ CCI Comp. Code   █ Non-specific Procedure   **333**

31573 This code is out of order. See page 334.

31574 This code is out of order. See page 334.

31575 Laryngoscopy, flexible; diagnostic

(Do not report 31575 in conjunction with 31231, unless performed for a separate condition using a separate endoscope)

(Do not report 31575 in conjunction with 31572, 31573, 31574, 31576, 31577, 31578, 43197, 43198, 92511, 92612, 92614, 92616)

31576   with biopsy(ies)

(Do not report 31576 in conjunction with 31572, 31578)

31577   with removal of foreign body(s)

31578   with removal of lesion(s), non-laser

31572   with ablation or destruction of lesion(s) with laser, unilateral

(Do not report 31572 in conjunction with 31576, 31578)

(To report flexible endoscopic evaluation of swallowing, see 92612-92613)

(To report flexible endoscopic evaluation with sensory testing, see 92614-92615)

(To report flexible endoscopic evaluation of swallowing with sensory testing, see 92616-92617)

(For flexible laryngoscopy as part of flexible endoscopic evaluation of swallowing and/or laryngeal sensory testing by cine or video recording, see 92612-92617)

31573   with therapeutic injection(s) (eg, chemodenervation agent or corticosteroid, injected percutaneous, transoral, or via endoscope channel), unilateral

31574   with injection(s) for augmentation (eg, percutaneous, transoral), unilateral

31579 Laryngoscopy, flexible or rigid telescopic, with stroboscopy

REPAIR

31580 Laryngoplasty; for laryngeal web, with indwelling keel or stent insertion

(Do not report 31580 in conjunction with 31551, 31552, 31553, 31554)

(To report tracheostomy, see 31600, 31601, 31603, 31605, 31610)

(To report removal of the keel or stent, use 31599)

(**31582** deleted 2016 [2017 edition]. To report, see 31551, 31552, 31553, 31554)

31551   for laryngeal stenosis, with graft, without indwelling stent placement, younger than 12 years of age

(Do not report graft separately if harvested through the laryngoplasty incision [eg, thyroid cartilage graft])

(Do not report 31551 in conjunction with 31552, 31553, 31554, 31580)

(To report tracheostomy, see 31600, 31601, 31603, 31605, 31610)

31552   for laryngeal stenosis, with graft, without indwelling stent placement, age 12 years or older

(Do not report graft separately if harvested through the laryngoplasty incision [eg, thyroid cartilage graft])

(Do not report 31552 in conjunction with 31551, 31553, 31554, 31580)

(To report tracheostomy, see 31600, 31601, 31603, 31605, 31610)

31553   for laryngeal stenosis, with graft, with indwelling stent placement, younger than 12 years of age

(Do not report graft separately if harvested through the laryngoplasty incision [eg, thyroid cartilage graft])

(Do not report 31553 in conjunction with 31551, 31552, 31554, 31580)

(To report tracheostomy, see 31600, 31601, 31603, 31605, 31610)

(To report removal of the stent, use 31599)

31554   for laryngeal stenosis, with graft, with indwelling stent placement, age 12 years or older

(Do not report graft separately if harvested through the laryngoplasty incision [eg, thyroid cartilage graft])

(Do not report 31554 in conjunction with 31551, 31552, 31553, 31580)

(To report tracheostomy, see 31600, 31601, 31603, 31605, 31610)

(To report removal of the stent, use 31599)

31584   with open reduction and fixation of (eg, plating) of fracture, includes tracheostomy, if performed

(Do not report graft separately if harvested through the laryngoplasty incision [eg, thyroid cartilage graft])

31587   Laryngoplasty, cricoid split, without graft placement

(To report tracheostomy, see 31600, 31601, 31603, 31605, 31610)

(**31588**   deleted 2016 [2017 edition]. To report laryngoplasty not otherwise specified, use 31599)

31590   Laryngeal reinnervation by neuromuscular pedicle

31591   Laryngoplasty, medialization, unilateral

31592   Cricotracheal resection

(Do not report graft separately if harvested through cricotracheal resection incision [eg, trachealis muscle])

(Do not report local advancement and rotational flaps separately if performed through the same incision)

(To report tracheostomy, see 31600, 31601, 31603, 31605, 31610)

(To report excision of tracheal stenosis and anastomosis, see 31780, 31781)

DESTRUCTION

31595   Section recurrent laryngeal nerve, therapeutic (separate procedure), unilateral

OTHER PROCEDURES

31599   Unlisted procedure, larynx

TRACHEA AND BRONCHI

INCISION

31600   Tracheostomy, planned (separate procedure);

31601   under 2 years

31603   Tracheostomy, emergency procedure; transtracheal

31605   cricothyroid membrane

| 31610 | Tracheostomy, fenestration procedure with skin flaps |

(For endotracheal intubation, use 31500)

(For tracheal aspiration under direct vision, use 31515)

| 31611 | Construction of tracheoesophageal fistula and subsequent insertion of an alaryngeal speech prosthesis (eg, voice button, Blom-Singer prosthesis) |

| 31612 | Tracheal puncture, percutaneous with transtracheal aspiration and/or injection |

| 31613 | Tracheostoma revision; simple, without flap rotation |

| 31614 | complex, with flap rotation |

ENDOSCOPY

For endoscopy procedures, code appropriate endoscopy of each anatomic site examined. Surgical bronchoscopy always includes diagnostic bronchoscopy when performed by the same physician. Codes 31622-31651, 31660, 31661 include fluoroscopic guidance, when performed.

Codes 31652 and 31653 are complete services used for sampling (eg, aspiration/biopsy) lymph node(s) or adjacent structure(s) utilizing endobronchial ultrasound (EBUS) and are reported separately. Code 31654 is an add-on code and should be reported for identifying one or more peripheral lesion(s) with transendoscopic ultrasound.

⊙ | 31615 | Tracheobronchoscopy through established tracheostomy incision |

(For tracheoscopy, see laryngoscopy codes 31515-31574)

(31620   deleted 2015 [2016 edition])

(For bronchoscopy with endobronchial ultrasound [EBUS] guided transtracheal/transbronchial sampling of mediastinal and/or hilar lymph node stations or structures, see 31652, 31653. For transendoscopic ultrasound during bronchoscopic diagnostic or therapeutic intervention[s] for peripheral lesions[s], use 31654)

| 31622 | Bronchoscopy, rigid or flexible, including fluoroscopic guidance, when performed; diagnostic, with cell washing, when performed (separate procedure) |

| 31623 | with brushing or protected brushings |

| 31624 | with bronchial alveolar lavage |

| 31625 | with bronchial or endobronchial biopsy(s), single or multiple sites |

| 31626 | with placement of fiducial markers, single or multiple |

(Report supply of device separately)

+ | 31627 | with computer-assisted, image-guided navigation (List separately in addition to code for primary procedure[s]) |

(31627 includes 3D reconstruction. Do not report 31627 in conjunction with 76376, 76377)

(Use 31627 in conjunction with 31615, 31622-31626, 31628-31631, 31635, 31636, 31638-31643)

| 31628 | with transbronchial lung biopsy(s), single lobe |

(31628 should be reported only once regardless of how many transbronchial lung biopsies are performed in a lobe)

(To report transbronchial lung biopsies performed on additional lobe, use 31632)

| 31629 | with transbronchial needle aspiration biopsy(s), trachea, main stem and/or lobar bronchus(i) |

● New Code   ▲ Revised Code   + Add-On Code   ⊘ Modifier -51 Exempt   ★ Telemedicine

(31629 should be reported only once for upper airway biopsies regardless of how many transbronchial needle aspiration biopsies are performed in the upper airway or in a lobe)

(To report transbronchial needle aspiration biopsies performed on additional lobe(s), use 31633)

31630   with tracheal/bronchial dilation or closed reduction of fracture

31631   with placement of tracheal stent(s) (includes tracheal/ bronchial dilation as required)

(For placement of bronchial stent, see 31636, 31637)

(For revision of tracheal/bronchial stent, use 31638)

+ 31632   with transbronchial lung biopsy(s), each additional lobe (List separately in addition to code for primary procedure)

(Use 31632 in conjunction with 31628)

(31632 should be reported only once regardless of how many transbronchial lung biopsies are performed in a lobe)

+ 31633   with transbronchial needle aspiration biopsy(s), each additional lobe (List separately in addition to code for primary procedure)

(Use 31633 in conjunction with 31629)

(31633 should be reported only once regardless of how many transbronchial needle aspiration biopsies are performed in the trachea or the additional lobe)

31634   with balloon occlusion, with assessment of air leak, with administration of occlusive substance (eg, fibrin glue), if performed

(Do not report 31534 in conjunction with 31647, 31651 at the same session)

31635   with removal of foreign body

(For removal of implanted bronchial valves, see 31648-31649)

31636   with placement of bronchial stent(s) (includes tracheal/bronchial dilation as required), initial bronchus

+ 31637   each additional major bronchus stented (List separately in addition to code for primary procedure)

(Use 31637 in conjunction with 31636)

31638   with revision of tracheal or bronchial stent inserted at previous session (includes tracheal/bronchial dilation as required)

31640   with excision of tumor

31641   with destruction of tumor or relief of stenosis by any method other than excision (eg, laser therapy, cryotherapy)

(For bronchoscopic photodynamic therapy, report 31641 in addition to 96570, 96571 as appropriate)

31643   with placement of catheter(s) for intracavitary radioelement application

(For intracavitary radioelement application, see 77761-77763, 77770, 77771, 77772)

▲ **31645**   with therapeutic aspiration of tracheobronchial tree, initial

▲ **31646**   with therapeutic aspiration of tracheobronchial tree, subsequent, same hospital stay

(For catheter aspiration of tracheobronchial tree with fiberscope at bedside, use 31725)

■ Separate Procedure   ■ Unlisted Procedure   ■ CCI Comp. Code   ■ Non-specific Procedure   **337**

31647   with balloon occlusion, when performed, assessment of air leak, airway sizing, and insertion of bronchial valve(s), initial lobe

+ 31651   with balloon occlusion, when performed, assessment of air leak, airway sizing, and insertion of bronchial valve(s), each additional lobe (List separately in addition to code for primary procedure[s])

(Use 31651 in conjunction with 31647)

31648   with removal of bronchial valve(s), initial lobe

(For removal and insertion of a bronchial valve at the same session, see 31647, 31648, and 31651)

+ 31649   with removal of bronchial valve(s), each additional lobe (List separately in addition to code for primary procedure)

(Use 31649 in conjunction with 31648)

31651 Code out of order. See page 338.

31652   with endobronchial ultrasound (EBUS) guided transtracheal and/or transbronchial sampling (eg, aspiration[s]/ biopsy[ies]), one or two mediastinal and/or hilar lymph node stations or structures

31653   with endobronchial ultrasound (EBUS) guided transtracheal and/or transbronchial sampling (eg, aspiration[s]/ biopsy[ies]), 3 or more mediastinal and/or hilar lymph node stations or structures

+ 31654   with transendoscopic endobronchial ultrasound (EBUS) during bronchoscopic diagnostic or therapeutic intervention(s) for peripheral lesion(s) (List separately in addition to code for primary procedure[s])

(Use 31654 in conjunction with 31622, 31623, 31624, 31625, 31626, 31628, 31629, 31640, 31643, 31645, 31646)

(For EBUS to access mediastinal or hilar lymph node station[s] or adjacent structure[s], see 31652, 31653)

(Report 31652, 31653, 31654 only once per session)

BRONCHIAL THERMOPLASTY

31660 Bronchoscopy, rigid or flexible, including fluoroscopic guidance, when performed; with bronchial thermoplasty, 1 lobe

31661   with bronchial thermoplasty, 2 or more lobes

INTRODUCTION

(For endotracheal intubation, use 31500)

(For tracheal aspiration under direct vision, see 31515)

31717 Catheterization with bronchial brush biopsy

31720 Catheter aspiration (separate procedure); nasotracheal

31725   tracheobronchial with fiberscope, bedside

31730 Transtracheal (percutaneous) introduction of needle wire dilator/stent or indwelling tube for oxygen therapy

EXCISION, REPAIR

31750 Tracheoplasty; cervical

31755   tracheopharyngeal fistulization, each stage

31760   intrathoracic

● New Code   ▲ Revised Code   + Add-On Code   ⊘ Modifier -51 Exempt   ★ Telemedicine

31766	Carinal reconstruction
31770	Bronchoplasty; graft repair
31775	excision stenosis and anastomosis

(For lobectomy and bronchoplasty, use 32501)

31780	Excision tracheal stenosis and anastomosis; cervical
31781	cervicothoracic
31785	Excision of tracheal tumor or carcinoma; cervical
31786	thoracic
31800	Suture of tracheal wound or injury; cervical
31805	intrathoracic
31820	Surgical closure tracheostomy or fistula; without plastic repair
31825	with plastic repair

(For repair tracheoesophageal fistula, see 43305, 43312)

31830	Revision of tracheostomy scar

OTHER PROCEDURES

31899	Unlisted procedure, trachea, bronchi

LUNGS AND PLEURA

Pleural cavity or lung biopsy procedures may be accomplished using a percutaneous, thorascopic (Video-Assisted Thoracoscopic Surgery [VATS]), or thoracotomy approach. They involve the removal of differing amounts of tissue for diagnosis. A biopsy may be performed using different techniques such as incision or wedge. Lung resection procedures include diagnostic and therapeutic procedures, including the removal of blebs, bullae, cysts, and benign or malignant tumors or lesions. These procedures may involve the removal of small portions of the lung or even an entire lung. Additionally, lung resection procedures may require the removal of adjacent structures. Both diagnostic lung biopsies and therapeutic lung resections can be performed utilizing a wedge technique. However, a diagnostic biopsy of a lung nodule using a wedge technique requires only that a tissue sample be obtained without particular attention to resection margins. A therapeutic wedge resection requires attention to margins and complete resection even when the wedge resection is ultimately followed by a more extensive resection. In the case of a wedge resection where intraoperative pathology consultation determines that a more extensive resection is required in the same anatomic location, it becomes classified as a diagnostic wedge resection (32507, 32668). When no more extensive resection is required, the same procedure is a therapeutic wedge resection (32505, 32666).

Pleural or lung biopsies or diagnostic wedge resections should be reported using codes 32096, 32097, 32098, 32400, 32405, 32507, 32607, 32608, 32609 or 32668. The open or thorasoscopic (VATS) therapeutic resection of lung mass or nodules via a wedge resection is reported using codes 32505, 32506, 32666 and 32667. More extensive anatomic lung resection procedures, which can be performed with either thoracotomy or thoracoscopic (VATS) approaches, include: segmentectomy, lobectomy, bilobectomy, and pneumonectomy.

When diagnostic biopsy(ies) of the lung are performed, regardless of the approach (ie, open or thoracoscopic [VATS]), or technique (eg, incisional resection, cautery resection, or stapled wedge), and the specimen is sent for intraoperative pathology consultation, and during that same operative session the surgeon uses these results to determine the extent of the necessary surgical resection that includes the anatomical location biopsied, only the most extensive procedure performed (eg, segmentectomy, lobectomy, thoracoscopic [VATS] lobectomy) should be reported.

The therapeutic wedge resection codes (32505, 32506, 32666, or 32667) should not be reported in addition to the more extensive lung procedure (eg, lobectomy) unless the therapeutic wedge resection was performed on a different lobe or on the contralateral lung, whether or not an intraoperative pathology consultation is used to determine the extent of lung resection. When a diagnostic wedge resection is followed by a more extensive procedure in the same anatomical location, report add-on codes 32507 or 32668 with the more extensive procedure(s). When a therapeutic wedge resection (32505, 32506, 32666 or 32667) is performed in a different lobe than the more extensive lung resection (eg, lobectomy), report the therapeutic wedge resection with modifier 59.

INCISION

32035 Thoracostomy; with rib resection for empyema

32036 with open flap drainage for empyema

(To report wound exploration due to penetrating trauma without thoracotomy, use 20101)

32096 Thoracotomy, with diagnostic biopsy(ies) of lung infiltrate(s) (eg, wedge, incisional), unilateral

(Do not report 32096 more than once per lung)

(Do not report 32096 in conjunction with 32440, 32442, 32445, 32488)

32097 Thoracotomy, with diagnostic biopsy(ies) of lung nodule(s) or mass(es) (eg, wedge, incisional), unilateral

(Do not report 32097 more than once per lung)

(Do not report 32097 in conjunction with 32440, 32442, 32445, 32488)

32098 Thoracotomy, with biopsy(ies) of pleura

32100 Thoracotomy; with exploration

(Do not report 32100 in conjunction with 19260, 19271, 19272, 32503, 32504, 33955, 33956, 33957, 33963, 33964)

32110 with control of traumatic hemorrhage and/or repair of lung tear

32120 for postoperative complications

32124 with open intrapleural pneumonolysis

32140 with cyst(s) removal, includes pleural procedure when performed

32141 with resection-plication of bullae, includes any pleural procedure when performed

(For lung volume reduction, use 32491)

32150 with removal of intrapleural foreign body or fibrin deposit

32151 with removal of intrapulmonary foreign body

32160 with cardiac massage

(For segmental or other resections of lung, see 32480-32504)

32200 Pneumonostomy; with open drainage of abscess or cyst

(For percutaneous image-guided drainage of abscess or cyst of lungs or mediastinum by catheter placement, use 49405)

32215 Pleural scarification for repeat pneumothorax

32220 Decortication, pulmonary (separate procedure); total

32225 partial

EXCISION/RESECTION

32310 Pleurectomy, parietal (separate procedure)

32320 Decortication and parietal pleurectomy

32400 Biopsy, pleura; percutaneous needle

(If imaging guidance is performed, see 76942, 77002, 77012, 77021)

(For fine needle aspiration, use 10021 or 10022)

32405 Biopsy, lung or mediastinum, percutaneous needle

(For open biopsy of lung, see 32096, 32097. For open biopsy of mediastinum, see 39000 or 39010. For thoracoscopic [VATS] biopsy of lung, pleura, pericardium or mediastinal space structure, see 32604, 32606, 32607, 32608, 32609)

(For radiological supervision and interpretation, see 76942, 77002, 77012, 77021)

(For fine needle aspiration, use 10022)

REMOVAL

32440 Removal of lung, pneumonectomy;

32442 with resection of segment of trachea followed by broncho-tracheal anastomosis (sleeve pneumonectomy)

32445 extrapleural

(For extrapleural pneumonectomy, with empyemectomy, use 32445 and 32540)

(If lung resection is performed with chest wall tumor resection, report the appropriate chest wall tumor resection 19260-19272, in addition to lung resection 32440-32445)

32480 Removal of lung, other than pneumonectomy; single lobe (lobectomy)

32482 2 lobes (bilobectomy)

32484 single segment (segmentectomy)

(For removal of lung with bronchoplasty, use 32501)

32486 with circumferential resection of segment of bronchus followed by broncho-bronchial anastomosis (sleeve lobectomy)

32488 with all remaining lung following previous removal of a portion of lung (completion pneumonectomy)

(For lobectomy or segmentectomy, with concomitant decortication, use 32320 and the appropriate removal of lung code)

32491 with resection-plication of emphysematous lung(s) (bullous or non-bullous) for lung volume reduction, sternal split or transthoracic approach, includes any pleural procedure, when performed

(If lung resection is performed with chest wall tumor resection, report the appropriate chest wall tumor resection 19260-19272, in addition to lung resection 32480, 32482, 32484, 32486, 32488, 32505, 32506, 32507)

+ **32501** Resection and repair of portion of bronchus (bronchoplasty) when performed at time of lobectomy or segmentectomy (List separately in addition to code for primary procedure)

(Use 32501 in conjunction with codes 32480, 32482, 32484)

| | Separate Procedure | | Unlisted Procedure | | CCI Comp. Code | | Non-specific Procedure | **341** |

(32501 is to be used when a portion of the bronchus to preserved lung is removed and requires plastic closure to preserve function of that preserved lung. It is not to be used for closure for the proximal end of a resected bronchus.)

32503   Resection of apical lung tumor (eg, Pancoast tumor), including chest wall resection, rib(s) resection(s), neurovascular dissection, when performed; without chest wall reconstruction(s)

32504   with chest wall reconstruction

(Do not report 32503, 32504 in conjunction with 19260, 19271, 19272, 32100, 32551, 32554, 32555)

32505   Thoracotomy; with therapeutic wedge resection (eg, mass, nodule), initial

(Do not report 32505 in conjunction with 32440, 32442, 32445, 32488)

+ **32506**   with therapeutic wedge resection (eg, mass or nodule), each additional resection, ipsilateral (List separately in addition to code for primary procedure)

(Report 32506 only in conjunction with 32505)

(If lung resection is performed with chest wall tumor resection, report the appropriate chest wall tumor resection 19260-19272, in addition to lung resection 32480, 32482, 32484, 32486, 32488, 32505, 32506, 32507)

+ **32507**   with diagnostic wedge resection followed by anatomic lung resection (List separately in addition to code for primary procedure)

(Report 32507 in conjunction with 32440, 32442, 32445, 32480, 32482, 32484, 32486, 32488, 32503, 32504)

32540   Extrapleural enucleation of empyema (empyemectomy)

(For extrapleural enucleation of empyema (empyemectomy) with lobectomy, use 32540 and the appropriate removal of lung code)

INTRODUCTION AND REMOVAL

32550   Insertion of indwelling tunneled pleural catheter with cuff

(Do not report 32550 in conjunction with 32554, 32555, 32556, 32557 when performed on the same side of the chest)

(If imaging guidance is performed, use 75989)

32551   Tube thoracostomy, includes connection to drainage system (eg, water seal), when performed, open (separate procedure)

32552   Removal of indwelling tunneled pleural catheter with cuff

32553   Placement of interstitial device(s) for radiation therapy guidance (eg, fiducial markers, dosimeter), percutaneous, intra thoracic, single or multiple

(Report supply of device separately)

(For imaging guidance, see 76942, 77002, 77012, 77021)

(For percutaneous placement of interstitial device[s] for intra-abdominal, intrapelvic, and/or retroperitoneal radiation therapy guidance, use 49411)

32554   Thoraqcentesis, needle or catheter, aspiration of the pleural space; without imaging guidance

32555   with imaging guidance

32556   Pleural drainage, percutaneous, with insertion of indwelling catheter; without imaging guidance

● New Code   ▲ Revised Code   + Add-On Code   ⊘ Modifier -51 Exempt   ★ Telemedicine

32557   with imaging guidance

(For insertion of indwelling tunneled pleural catheter with cuff, use 32550)

(For open procedure, use 32551)

(Do not report 32554-32557 in conjunction with 32550, 32551 when performed on the same side of the chest)

(Do not report 32554-32557 in conjunction with 75989, 76942, 77002, 77012, 77021)

DESTRUCTION

The instillation of a fibrinolytic agent may be performed multiple times per day over the course of several days. Code 32561 should be reported only once on the initial day treatment. Code 32562 should be reported only once on each subsequent day of treatment.

32560   Instillation, via chest tube/catheter, agent for pleurodesis (eg, talc for recurrent or persistent pneumothorax)

(For chest tube insertion, use 32551)

32561   Instillation(s), via chest tube/catheter, agent for fibrinolysis (eg, fibrinolytic agent for break up of multiloculated effusion); initial day

(For chest tube insertion, use 32551)

32562   subsequent day

(For chest tube insertion, use 32551)

THORACOSCOPY (VIDEO-ASSISTED THORACIC SURGERY [VATS])

Surgical thoracoscopy (video-assisted thoracic surgery [VATS]) always includes diagnostic thoracoscopy.

32601   Thoracoscopy, diagnostic (separate procedure); lungs, pericardial sac, mediastinal or pleural space, without biopsy

32604   pericardial sac, with biopsy

(For open pericardial biopsy, use 39010)

32606   mediastinal space, with biopsy

32607   Thoracoscopy; with diagnostic biopsy(ies) of lung infiltrate(s) (eg, wedge, incisional), unilateral

(Do not report 32607 more than once per lung)

(Do not report 32607 in conjunction with 32440, 32442, 32445, 32488, 32671)

32608   with diagnostic biopsy(ies) of lung nodule(s) or mass(es) (eg, wedge, incisional), unilateral

(Do not report 32608 more than once per lung)

(Do not report 32608 in conjunction with 32440, 32442, 32445, 32488, 32671)

32609   with biopsy(ies) of pleura

32650   Thoracoscopy, surgical; with pleurodesis (eg, mechanical or chemical)

32651   with partial pulmonary decortication

32652   with total pulmonary decortication, including intrapleural pneumonolysis

32653   with removal of intrapleural foreign body or fibrin deposit

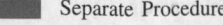

Separate Procedure   Unlisted Procedure   CCI Comp. Code   Non-specific Procedure   **343**

32654   with control of traumatic hemorrhage

32655   with resection-plication of bullae, including any pleural procedure when performed

(For thoracoscopic [VATS] lung volume reduction surgery, use 32672)

32656   with parietal pleurectomy

32658   with removal of clot or foreign body from pericardial sac

32659   with creation of pericardial window or partial resection of pericardial sac for drainage

32661   with excision of pericardial cyst, tumor, or mass

32662   with excision of mediastinal cyst, tumor, or mass

32663   with lobectomy (single lobe)

(For thoracoscopic [VATS] segmentectomy, use 32669)

32664   with thoracic sympathectomy

32665   with esophagomyotomy (Heller type)

(For exploratory thoracoscopy, and exploratory throacoscopy with biopsy, see 32601-32609)

32666   with therapeutic wedge resection (eg, mass, nodule), initial unilateral

(To report bilateral procedure, report 32666 with modifier 50)

(Do not report 32666 in conjunction with 32440, 32442, 32445, 32488, 32671)

+ 32667   with therapeutic wedge resection (eg, mass or nodule), each additional resection, ipsilateral (List separately in addition to code for primary procedure)

(Report 32667 only in conjunction with 32666)

(Do not report 32667 in conjunction with 32440, 32442, 32445, 32488, 32671)

+ 32668   with diagnostic wedge resection followed by anatomic lung resection (List separately in addition to code for primary procedure)

(Report 32668 in conjunction with 32440, 32442, 32445, 32480, 32482, 32484, 32486, 32488, 32503, 32504, 32663, 32669, 32670, 32671)

32669   with removal of a single lung segment (segmentectomy)

32670   with removal of two lobes (bilobectomy)

32671   with removal of lung (pneumonectomy)

32672   with resection-plication for emphysematous lung (bullous or non-bullous) for lung volume reduction (LVRS), unilateral includes any pleural procedure, when performed

32673   with resection of thymus, unilateral or bilateral

(For open thymectomy, see 60520, 60521, 60522)

(For open excision mediastinal cyst, see 39200. For open excision mediastinal tumor, use 39220)

(For exploratory thoracoscopy, and exploratory thoracoscopy with biopsy, see 32601-32609)

+ 32674   with mediastinal and regional lymphadenectomy (List separately in addition to code for primary procedure)

---

344   ● New Code   ▲ Revised Code   + Add-On Code   ⊘ Modifier -51 Exempt   ★ Telemedicine

(On the right, mediastinal lymph nodes include the paratracheal, subcarinal, paraesophageal, and inferior pulmonary ligament)

(On the left, mediastinal lymph nodes include the aortopulmonary window, subcarinal, paraesophageal, and inferior pulmonary ligament)

(Report 32674 in conjunction with 19260, 31760, 31766, 31786, 32096-32200, 32220-32320, 32440-32491, 32503-32505, 32601-32663, 32666, 32669-32673, 32815, 33025, 33030, 33050-33130, 39200-39220, 39560, 39561, 43101, 43112, 43117, 43118, 43122, 43123, 43287, 43288, 43351, 60270, 60505)

(To report mediastinal and regional lymphadenectomy via thoracotomy, use 38746)

STEREOTACTIC RADIATION THERAPY

Thoracic stereotactic body radiation therapy (SRS/SBRT) is a distinct procedure which may involve collaboration between a surgeon and radiation oncologist. The surgeon identifies and delineates the target for therapy. The radiation oncologist reports the appropriate code(s) for clinical treatment planning, physics and dosimetry, treatment delivery and management from the Radiation Oncology section (see 77295, 77331, 77370, 77373, 77435). The same physician should not report target delineation services with radiation treatment management codes (77427-77499).

Target delineation involves specific determination of tumor borders to identify tumor volume and relationship with adjacent structures (eg, chest wall, intraparenchymal vasculature and atelectatic lung) and previously placed fiducial markers, when present. Target delineation also includes availability to identify and validate the thoracic target prior to treatment delivery when a difucial-less tracking system is utilized.

Do not report target delineation more than once per entire course of treatment when the treatment requires greater than one session.

32701 Thoracic target(s) delineation for stereotactic body radiation therapy (SRS/SBRT), (photon or particle beam), entire course of treatment

((Do not report 32701 in conjunction with 77261-77799)

(For placement of fiducial markers, see 31626, 32553)

REPAIR

32800 Repair lung hernia through chest wall

32810 Closure of chest wall following open flap drainage for empyema (Clagett type procedure)

32815 Open closure of major bronchial fistula

32820 Major reconstruction, chest wall (posttraumatic)

LUNG TRANSPLANTATION

Lung allotransplantation involves three distinct components of physician work:

1) **Cadaver donor pneumonectomy(s)**, which include(s) harvesting the allograft and cold preservation of the allograft (perfusing with cold preservation solution and cold maintenance) (use 32850).

2) **Backbench work:**

Preparation of a cadaver donor single lung allograft prior to transplantation, including dissection of the allograft from surrounding soft tissues to prepare the pulmonary venous/atrial cuff, pulmonary artery, and bronchus unilaterally (use 32855).

Preparation of a cadaver donor double lung allograft prior to transplantation, including dissection of the allograft from surrounding soft tissues to prepare the pulmonary venous/atrial cuff, pulmonary artery, and bronchus bilaterally (use 32856).

3) **Recipient lung allotransplantation**, which includes transplantation of a single or double lung allograft and care of the recipient (see 32851-32854).

(For ex-vivo assessment of marginal donor lung transplant, see 0494T, 0495T, 0496T)

32850	Donor pneumonectomy (including cold preservation), from cadaver donor
32851	Lung transplant, single; without cardiopulmonary bypass
32852	with cardiopulmonary bypass
32853	Lung transplant, double (bilateral sequential or en bloc); without cardiopulmonary bypass
32854	with cardiopulmonary bypass
32855	Backbench standard preparation of cadaver donor lung allograft prior to transplantation, including dissection of allograft from surrounding soft tissues to prepare pulmonary venous/atrial cuff, pulmonary artery, and bronchus; unilateral
32856	bilateral

(For repair or resection procedures on the donor lung, see 32491, 32505, 32506, 32507, 35216, 35276)

SURGICAL COLLAPSE THERAPY; THORACOPLASTY

(See also 32503, 32504)

32900	Resection of ribs, extrapleural, all stages
32905	Thoracoplasty, Schede type or extrapleural (all stages);
32906	with closure of bronchopleural fistula

(For open closure of major bronchial fistula, use 32815)

(For resection of first rib for thoracic outlet compression, see 21615, 21616)

32940	Pneumonolysis, extraperiosteal, including filling or packing procedures
32960	Pneumothorax, therapeutic, intrapleural injection of air

OTHER PROCEDURES

32994	This code is out of order. See page 346.
32997	Total lung lavage (unilateral)

(For bronchoscopic bronchial alveolar lavage, use 31624)

▲ 32998	Ablation therapy for reduction or eradication of 1 or more pulmonary tumor(s) including pleura or chest wall when involved by tumor extension, percutaneous, including imaging guidance when performed, unilateral; radiofrequency
● 32994	cryoablation

(For bilateral procedure, report 32994, 32998 with modifier 50)

32999	Unlisted procedure, lungs and pleura

● New Code   ▲ Revised Code   + Add-On Code   ⊘ Modifier -51 Exempt   ★ Telemedicine

CARDIOVASCULAR SYSTEM

CPT codes from this section of the CPT coding system are used to report invasive and surgical procedures performed on the heart and pericardium, including pacemakers or defibrillators; cardiac valves; coronary arteries; aorta; and arteries and veins.

For coding services such as monitoring, operation of pump and other non-surgical services performed during cardiovascular surgery, see the Special Services CPT codes 99150, 99151, 99160-99162 or CPT codes 99291-99292 and 99190-99192 from the evaluation and management section of the CPT coding system.

MISCELLANEOUS CODING RULES

A pacemaker system includes a pulse generator containing electronics, a battery, and one or more electrodes (leads) inserted one of several ways. Pulse generators may be placed in a subcutaneous "pocket" created in either a subclavicular or intra-abdominal site. Electrodes may be inserted through a vein (transvenous) or on the surface of the heart (epicardial). A single chamber system includes a pulse generator, one electrode inserted into either the atrium or ventricle. A dual chamber system includes a pulse generator, one electrode inserted in the atrium, and one electrode inserted in the ventricle.

Assign two CPT codes when a pacemaker or cardioverter-defibrillator "battery"/pulse generator is replaced. One code should describe the removal of the old pulse generator and the other should describe the insertion of the new pulse generator.

Cardiac catheterization codes are classified in the Medicine Section of the CPT coding system. Insertion of a dilator into a vein prior to the placement of a catheter should not be separately coded.

Selective vascular catheterization should be coded to include introduction and all lesser order selective catheterization used in the approach (eg., the description for a selective right middle cerebral artery catheterization includes the introduction and placement catheterization of the right common and internal carotid arteries).

Additional second and/or third order arterial catheterizations within the same family of arteries supplied by a single first order artery should be expressed by 36218 or 36248. Additional first order or higher catheterizations in vascular families supplied by a first order vessel different from a previously selected and coded family should be separately coded using the conventions described above.

> (For monitoring, operation of pump and other nonsurgical services, see 99190-99192, 99291, 99292, 99354-99360)
>
> (For other medical or laboratory related services, see appropriate section)
>
> (For radiological supervision and interpretation, see 75600-75970)

HEART AND PERICARDIUM

PERICARDIUM

> (For thoracoscopic [VATS] pericardial procedures, see 32601, 32604, 32658, 32659, 32661)

33010 Pericardiocentesis; initial

> (For radiological supervision and interpretation, use 76930)

33011 subsequent

> (For radiological supervision and interpretation, use 76930)

33015 Tube pericardiostomy

33020 Pericardiotomy for removal of clot or foreign body (primary procedure)

33025 Creation of pericardial window or partial resection for drainage

> (For thoracoscopic [VATS] pericardial window, use 32659)

33030 Pericardiectomy, subtotal or complete; without cardiopulmonary bypass

---

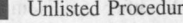

Separate Procedure   Unlisted Procedure   CCI Comp. Code   Non-specific Procedure   **347**

| 33031 | with cardiopulmonary bypass |

| 33050 | Resection of pericardial cyst or tumor electrode(s); atrial |

(For open pericardial biopsy, use 39010)

(For thoracoscopic [VATS] resection of pericardial cyst, tumor or mass, use 32661)

CARDIAC TUMOR

| 33120 | Excision of intracardiac tumor, resection with cardiopulmonary bypass |

| 33130 | Resection of external cardiac tumor |

TRANSMYOCARDIAL REVASCULARIZATION

| 33140 | Transmyocardial laser revascularization, by thoracotomy (separate procedure) |

+ 33141   performed at the time of other open cardiac procedure(s) (List separately in addition to code for primary procedure)

(Use 33141 in conjunction with codes 33390, 33391, 33404-33496, 33510-33536, 33542)

PACEMAKER OR IMPLANTABLE DEFIBRILLATOR

A pacemaker generally has two parts; a generator and the leads. The generator is where the battery and the information to regulate the heartbeat are stored. The leads are wires that go from the generator through a large vein to the heart, where the wires are anchored. The leads send the electrical impulses to the heart to tell it to beat. The battery can last anywhere from 7-8 years on average and will be routinely monitored by your health care professional and replaced when necessary.

A pacemaker can usually sense if the heartbeat is above a certain level, at which point it will automatically turn off. Likewise, the pacemaker can sense when the heartbeat slows down too much, and will automatically turn back on in order to start pacing again. A pacemaker is often the treatment of choice for bradycardia. Less commonly, pacemakers may also be used to terminate tachycardia. The pacemaker can sense the abnormally fast heart rate and take control of it by first speeding up, then slowing down to normal.

In most cases, the procedure for inserting a pacemaker takes about one hour. The patient is awake for the procedure, and pain medication is given throughout the procedure. A small incision is made traditionally in the left side of the chest, and a small "pocket" is created underneath the skin. After the leads have been positioned in the heart under X-ray guidance, they are then connected to the generator. The generator is then placed into the pocket, and the pocket is closed with sutures. Most patients are able to go home within 1 day of the procedure, if there are no other medical issues requiring further hospitalization.

A pacemaker system with lead(s) includes a pulse generator containing electronics, battery, and one or more leads. A lead consists of one or more electrodes as well as conductor wires, insulation, and a fixation mechanism. Pulse generators are placed in a subcutaneous "pocket" created in either a subclavicular site or just above the abdominal muscles just below the rib cage. Leads may be inserted through a vein (transvenous) or they may be placed on the surface of the heart (epicardial). The epicardial location of leads requires a thoracotomy for insertion.

A single chamber pacemaker system with lead includes a pulse generator and one electrode inserted in either the atrium or ventricle. A dual chamber pacemaker system with two leads includes a pulse generator and one lead inserted in the right atrium and one lead inserted in the right ventricle. In certain circumstances, an additional lead may be required to achieve pacing of the left ventricle (bi-ventricular pacing). In this event, transvenous (cardiac vein) placement of the lead should be separately reported using code 33224 or 33225. Epicardial placement of the lead should be separately reported using 33202-33203.

A leadless cardiac pacemaker system includes a pulse generator with built in battery and electrode for implantation in a cardiac chamber via a transcatheter approach. For these services, see codes 0387T, 0388T, 0389T, 0390T, 0391T.

Like a pacemaker system, an implantable defibrillator system includes a pulse generator and electrodes. Two general categories of implantable defibrillators exist: transvenous implantable pacing cardioverter-defibrillator (ICD) and subcutaneous implantable defibrillator (S-ICD). Implantable pacing cardioverter-defibrillator devices use a combination of antitachycardia pacing, low-energy cardioversion or defibrillating shocks to treat ventricular tachycardia or ventricular fibrillation. The subcutaneous implantable defibrillator uses a single subcutaneous electrode to treat ventricular tachyarrhythmias. Subcutaneous implantable

● New Code   ▲ Revised Code   + Add-On Code   ⊘ Modifier -51 Exempt   ★ Telemedicine

defibrillators differ from transvenous implantable pacing cardioverter-defibrillators in that subcutaneous defibrillators do not provide antitachycardia pacing or chronic pacing.

Implantable defibrillator pulse generators may be implanted in a subcutaneous infraclavicular, axillary, or abdominal pocket. Removal of an implantable defibrillator pulse generator requires opening of the existing subcutaneous pocket and disconnection of the pulse generator from its electrode(s). A thoracotomy (or laparotomy in the case of abdominally placed pulse generators).

The electrodes (leads) of an implantable defibrillator system may be positioned within the atrial and/or ventricular chambers of the heart via the venous system (transvenously), or placed on the surface of the heart (epicardial), or positioned under the skin overlying the heart (subcutaneous). Electrode positioning on the epicardial surface of the heart requires a thoracotomy or thoracoscopic placement of the leads. Epicardial placement of electrodes may be separately reported using 33202, 33203. The electrode (lead) of a subcutaneous implantable defibrillator system is tunneled under the skin to the left parasternal margin. Subcutaneous placement of electrode may be reported using 33270 or 33271. In certain sircumstances, an additional electrode may be required to achieve pacing of the left ventricle (bi-ventricular pacing). In this event, transvenous (cardiac vein) placement of the electrode may be separately reported using 33224 or 33225.

Removal of transvenous electrode(s) may first be attempted by transvenous extraction (33234, 33235, or 33244). However, if transvenous extraction is unsuccessful, a thoracotomy may be required to remove the electrodes (33238 or 33243). Use 33212, 33213, 33221, 33230, 33231, 33240 as appropriate in addition to the thoracotomy or endoscopic epicardial lead placement codes (33202 or 33203) to report the insertion of the generator if done by the same physician during the same session. Removal of a subcutaneous implantable defibrillator electrode may be separately reported using 33272. For removal of a leadless pacemaker system, use 0388T.

When the "battery" of a pacemaker system with lead(s) or implantable defibrillator is changed, it is actually the pulse generator that is changed. Removal of only the pacemaker or implantable defibrillator pulse generator is reported with 33233 or 33241. If only a pulse generator is inserted or replaced without any right atrial and/or right ventricular lead(s) inserted or replaced, report the appropriate code for only pulse generator insertion or replacement based on the number of final existing lead(s) (33227, 33228, 33229 and 33262, 33263, 33264). Do not report removal of a pulse generator (33233 or 33241) separately for this service. Insertion of a new pulse generator, when existing lead(s) are already in place and when no prior pulse generator is removed, is reported with 33212, 33213, 33221, 33230, 33231, 33240. When a pulse generator insertion involves the insertion or replacement of one or more right atrial and/or right ventricular lead(s) or subcutaneous lead(s), use system codes 33206, 33207, 33208 for pacemaker, 33249 for implantable pacing cardioverter-defibrillator, or 33270 for subcutaneous implantable defibrillator. When reporting the system insertion or replacement codes, removal of a pulse generator (33233 or 33241) may be reported separately, when performed. In addition, extraction of leads 33234, 33235 or 33244 for transvenous or 33272 for subcutaneous may be reported separately, when performed. An exception involves a pacemaker upgrade from single to dual system that includes removal of pulse generator, replacement of new pulse generator, and insertion of new lead, reported with 33214.

Revision of a skin pocket is included in 33206-33249, 33262, 33263, 33264, 33270, 33271, 33272, 33273. When revision of a skin pocket involves incision and drainage of a hematoma or complex wound infection, see 10140, 10180, 11042, 11043, 11044, 11045, 11046, 11047 as appropriate.

Relocation of a skin pocket for a pacemaker (33222) or implantable defibrillator (33223) is necessary for various clinical situations such as infection or erosion. Relocation of an existing pulse generator may be performed as a stand-alone procedure or at the time of a pulse generator or electrode insertion, replacement or repositioning. When skin pocket relocation is performed as part of an explant of an existing generator followed by replacement with a new generator, the pocket relocation is reported separately. Skin pocket relocation includes all work associated with the initial pocket (eg, opening the pocket, incision and drainage of hematoma or abscess if performed, and any closure performed) in addition to the creation of a new pocket for the new generator to be placed.

Repositioning of a pacemaker electrode, implantable defibrillator electrode(s), or a left ventricular pacing electrode is reported using 33215, 33226, or 33273 as appropriate.

Device evauation codes 93260, 93261, 93279-93299 for pacemaker system with lead(s) may not be reported in conjunction with pulse generator and lead insertion or revision codes 33206-33249, 33262, 33263, 33264, 33270, 33271, 33272, 33273. For leadless pacemaker systems, device evalution codes 0389T, 0390T, 0391T may not be reported in conjunction with leadless pacemaker insertion and removal codes 0387T, 0388T. Defibrillator threshold testing (DFT) during transvenous implantable defibrillator insertion or replacement may be separately reported using 93640, 93641. DFT testing during subcutaneous implantable defibrillator system insertion is not separately reportable. DFT testing for transvenous or subcutaneous implantable defibrillator in follow-up or at the time of replacement may be separately reported using 93642 or 93644.

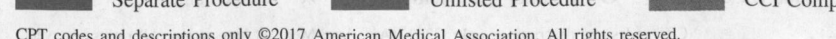

| | Separate Procedure | | Unlisted Procedure | | CCI Comp. Code | | Non-specific Procedure | **349** |

Radiological supervision and interpretation related to the pacemaker or implantable defibrillator procedure is included in 33206-33249, 33262, 33263, 33264, 33270, 33271, 33272, 33273, 0387T, 0388T. To report fluoroscopic guidance for diagnostic lead evaluation without lead insertion, replacement, or revision procedures, use 76000.

The following definitions apply to 33206-33249, 33262, 33263, 33264, 33270, 33271, 33272, 33273:

Single lead: a pacemaker or implantable defibrillator with pacing and sensing function in only one chamber of the heart or a subcutaneous electrode

Dual lead: a pacemaker or implantable defibrillator with pacing and sensing function in only two chambers of the heart.

Multiple lead: a pacemaker or implantable defibrillator with pacing and sensing function in three or more chambers of the heart.

Procedures	System	
	Pacemaker	**Implantable Defibrillator**
Insert transvenous single lead only without pulse generator	33216	33216
Insert transvenous dual leads without pulse generator	33217	33217
Insert transvenous multiple leads without pulse generator	33217 + 33224	33217 + 33224
Insert subcutaneous defibrillator electrode only without pulse generator	N/A	33271
Initial pulse generator insertion only with existing single lead, includes transvenous or subcutaneous defibrillator lead	33212	33240
Initial pulse generator insertion only with existing dual leads	33213	33230
Initial pulse generator insertion only with existing multiple leads	33221	33231
Initial pulse generator insertion or replacement plus insertion of transvenous single lead	33206 (atrial) or 33207 (ventricular)	33249
Initial pulse generator insertion or replacement plus insertion of transvenous dual leads	33208	33249
Initial pulse generator insertion or replacement plus insertion of transvenous multiple leads	33208 + 33225	33249 + 33225
Initial pulse generator insertion or replacement plus insertion of subcutaneous defibrillator electrode	N/A	33270
Upgrade single chamber system to dual chamber system	33214 (incl. removal of existing pulse generator)	33241 + 33249
Removal pulse generator only (without replacement)	33233	33241
Removal pulse generator with replacement pulse generator only single lead system, includes transvenous or subcutaneous defibrillator lead	33227	33262
Removal pulse generator with replacement pulse generator only dual lead system (transvenous)	33228	33263
Removal pulse generator with replacement pulse generator only multiple lead system (transvenous)	33229	33264
Removal transvenous electrode only single lead system	33234	33244
Removal transvenous electrode only dual lead system	33235	33244
Removal subcutaenous defibrillator lead only	N/A	33272
Removal and replacement of pulse generator and transvenous electrodes	33233 + (33234 or 33235) + (33206, 33207, or 33208) and 33225, when appropriate	33241 + 33244 + 33249 and 33225, when appropriate
Removal and replacement of implantable defibrillator pulse generator and subcutaneous electrode	N/A	33272 + 33241 + 33270
Conversion of existing system to bi-ventricular system (addition of LV lead and removal of current pulse generator with insertion of new pulse generator with bi-ventricular pacing capabilities)	33225 + 33228 or 33229	33225 + 33263 or 33264

● New Code ▲ Revised Code + Add-On Code ⊘ Modifier -51 Exempt ★ Telemedicine

33202 Insertion of epicardial electrode(s); open incision (eg, thoracotomy, median sternotomy, subxiphoid approach)

33203   endoscopic approach (eg, thoracoscopy, pericardioscopy)

(When epicardial lead placement is performed with insertion of the generator, report 33202, 33203 in conjunction with 33212, 33213, 33221, 33230, 33231, 33240)

33206 Insertion of new or replacement of permanent pacemaker with transvenous electrode(s); atrial

33207   ventricular

33208   atrial and ventricular

(Do not report 33206-33208 in conjunction with 33227-33229)

(Do not report 33206, 33207, 33208 in conjunction with 33216, 33217)

(Codes 33206-33208 include subcutaneous insertion of the pulse generator and transvenous placement of electrode[s])

(For removal and replacement of pacemaker pulse generator and transvenous electrode(s), use 33233 in conjunction with either 33234 or 33235 and 33206-33208)

33210 Insertion or replacement of temporary transvenous single chamber cardiac electrode or pacemaker catheter (separate procedure)

33211 Insertion or replacement of temporary transvenous dual chamber pacing electrodes (separate procedure)

33212 Insertion of pacemaker pulse generator only; with existing single lead

33213   with existing dual leads

33221   with existing multiple leads

(Do not report 33212, 33213, 33221 in conjunction with 33216, 33217)

(Do not report 33212, 33213, 33221 in conjunction with 33233 for removal and replacement of the pacemaker pulse generator. Use 33227-33229, as appropriate, when pulse generator replacment is indicated.)

(When epicardial lead placement is performed with insertion of generator, report 33202, 33203 in conjunction with 33212, 33213, 33221)

33214 Upgrade of implanted pacemaker system, conversion of single chamber system to dual chamber system (includes removal of previously placed pulse generator, testing of existing lead, insertion of new lead, insertion of new pulse generator)

(Do not report 33214 in conjunction with 33216, 33217, 33227, 33228, 33229)

33215 Repositioning of previously implanted transvenous pacemaker or implantable defibrillator (right atrial or right ventricular) electrode

33216 Insertion of a single transvenous electrode, permanent pacemaker or implantable defibrillator

(Do not report 33216 in conjunction with 33206, 33207, 33208, 33212, 33213, 33214, 33221, 33227, 33228, 33229, 33230, 33231, 33240, 33249, 33262, 33263, 33264)

33217 Insertion of 2 transvenous electrodes, permanent pacemaker or implantable defibrillator

(Do not report 33217 in conjunction with 33206, 33207, 33208, 33212, 33213, 33214, 33221, 33227, 33228, 33229, 33230, 33231, 33240, 33249, 33262, 33263, 33264)

(For insertion or replacement of cardiac venous system lead, see 33224, 33225)

Separate Procedure   Unlisted Procedure   CCI Comp. Code   Non-specific Procedure   **351**

33218 Repair of single transvenous electrode, permanent pacemaker or implantable defibrillator

(For repair of single permanent pacemaker or implantable defibrillator electrode with replacement of pulse generator, see 33227, 33228, 33229 or 33262, 33263, 33264 and 33218)

33220 Repair of 2 transvenous electrodes for permanent pacemaker or implantable defibrillator

(For repair of 2 tranvenous electrodes for permanent pacemaker or implantable defibrillator with replacement of pulse generator, use 33220 in conjunction with 33228, 33229, 33263, 33264)

33221 Code out of order. See page 351.

33222 Relocation of skin pocket for pacemaker

(Do not report 33222 in conjunction with 10140, 10180, 11042, 11043, 11044, 11045, 11046, 11047, 13100, 13101, 13102)

33223 Relocation of skin pocket for implantable defibrillator

(Do not report 33223 in conjunction with 10140, 10180, 11042, 11043, 11044, 11045, 11046, 11047, 13100, 13101, 13102)

33224 Insertion of pacing electrode, cardiac venous system, for left ventricular pacing, with attachment to previously placed pacemaker or implantable defibrillator pulse generator (including revision of pocket, removal, insertion and/or replacement of existing generator)

(When epicardial electrode placement is performed, report 33224 in conjunction with 33202, 33203)

+ **33225** Insertion of pacing electrode, cardiac venous system, for left ventricular pacing, at time of insertion of implantable defibrillator or pacemaker pulse generator (eg, for upgrade to dual chamber system) (List separately in addition to code for primary procedure)

(Use 33225 in conjunction with 33206, 33207, 33208, 33212, 33213, 33214, 33216, 33217, 33221, 33223, 33228, 33229, 33230, 33231, 33233, 33234, 33235, 33240, 33249, 33263, 33264)

(Use 33225 in conjunction with 33222 only with pacemaker pulse generator pocket relocation and with 33223 only with implantable defibrillator [ICD] pocket relocation)

33226 Repositioning of previously implanted cardiac venous system (left ventricular) electrode (including removal, insertion and/or replacement of existing generator)

33227 Code out of order. See page 352.

33228 Code out of order. See page 352.

33229 Code out of order. See page 352.

33230 Code out of order. See page 353.

33231 Code out of order. See page 353.

33233 Removal of permanent pacemaker pulse generator only

33227 Removal of permanent pacemaker pulse generator with replacement of pacemaker pulse generator; single lead system

33228 dual lead system

33229 multiple lead system

(Do not report 33227, 33228, 33229 in conjunction with 33214, 33216, 33217, 33233)

● New Code   ▲ Revised Code   + Add-On Code   ⊘ Modifier -51 Exempt   ★ Telemedicine

(For removal and replacement of pacemaker pulse generator and transvenous electrode[s], use 33233 in conjunction with either 33234 or 33235 and 33206-33208)

33234   Removal of transvenous pacemaker electrode(s); single lead system, atrial or ventricular

33235   dual lead system

33236   Removal of permanent epicardial pacemaker and electrodes by thoracotomy; single lead system, atrial or ventricular

33237   dual lead system

33238   Removal of permanent transvenous electrode(s) by thoracotomy

33240   Insertion of implantable defibrillator pulse generator only; with existing single lead

(Do not report 33240 in conjunction with 33271, 93260, 93261)

(Use 33240, as appropriate, in addition to the epicardial lead placement codes to report the insertion of the generator when done by the same physician during the same session)

33230   with existing dual leads

33231   with existing multiple leads

(Do not report 33230, 33231, 33240 in conjunction with 33216, 33217)

(Do not report 33230, 33231, 33240 in conjunction with 33241 for removal and replacement of the implantable defibrillator pulse generator. Use 33262, 33263, 33264, as appropriate, when pulse generator replacement is indicated)

(When epicardial lead placement if performed with insertion of generator, report 33202, 33203 in conjunction with 33230, 33231, 33240)

33241   Removal of implantable defibrillator pulse generator only

(Do not report 33241 in conjunction with 93260, 93261)

(Do not report 33241 in conjunction with 33230, 33231, 33240 for removal and replacement of the implantable defibrillator pulse generator. Use 33262, 33263, 33264, as appropriate, when pulse generator replacement is indicated)

(For removal and replacement of an implantable defibrillator pulse generator and electrode(s), use 33241 in conjunction with either 33243 or 33244 and 33249 for transvenous electrode[s] or 33270 and 33272 for subcutaneous electrode)

33262   Removal of implantable defibrillator pulse generator with replacement of implantable defibrillator pulse generator; single lead system

(Do not report 33262 in conjunction with 33271, 93260, 93261)

33263   dual lead system

33264   multiple lead system

(Do not report 33262, 33263, 33264 in conjunction with 33216, 33217, 33241)

(For removal of electrode[s] by thoracotomy in conjunction with pulse generator removal or replacement, use 33243 in conjunction with 33241 or 33262, 33263, 33264)

(For removal of electrode[s] by tranvenous extraction in conjunction with pulse generator removal or replacement, use 33244 in conjunction with 33241 or 33262, 33263, 33264)

(For repair of implantable defibrillator pulse generator and/or leads, see 33218, 33220)

Separate Procedure   Unlisted Procedure   CCI Comp. Code   Non-specific Procedure   **353**

(For removal of subcutaneous electrode in conjunction with implantable defibrillator pulse generator removal or replacement, use 33272 in conjunction with 33241 or 33262)

33243 Removal of single or dual chamber implantable defibrillator electrode(s); by thoracotomy

33244   by transvenous extraction

33249 Insertion or replacement of permanent implantable defibrillator system, with transvenous lead(s), single or dual chamber

(Do not report 33249 in conjunction with 33216, 33217)

(For removal and replacement of an implantable defibrillator pulse generator and transvenous electrode[s], use 33241 in conjunction with either 33243 or 33244 and 33249)

(For insertion of transvenous implantable defibrillator lead[s], without thoracotomy, use 33216 or 33217)

33270 Insertion or replacement of permanent subcutaneous implantable defibrillator system, with subcutaneous electrode, including defibrillation threshold evaluation, induction of arrhythmia, evaluation of sensing for arrhythmia termination, and programming or reprogramming of sensing or therapeutic parameters, when performed

(Do not report 33270 in conjunction with 33271, 93260, 93261, 93644)

(For removal and replacement of an implantable defibrillator pulse generator and subcutaneous electrode, use 33241 in conjunction with 33270 and 33272)

(For insertion of subcutaneous implantable defibrillator lead[s], use 33271)

33271 Insertion of subcutaneous implantable defibrillator electrode

(Do not report 33271 in conjunction with 33240, 33262, 33270, 93260, 93261)

(For insertion or replacement of a cardiac venous system lead, see 33224, 33225)

33272 Removal of subcutaneous implantable defibrillator electrode

33273 Repositioning of previously implanted subcutaneous implantable defibrillator electrode

(Do not report 33272, 33273 in conjunction with 93260, 93261)

ELECTROPHYSIOLOGIC OPERATIVE PROCEDURES

If excision or isolation of the left atrial appendage by any method, including stapling, oversewing, ligation, or plication, is performed in conjunction with any of the atrial tissue ablation and reconstruction (maze) procedures (33254-33259, 33265-33266), it is considered part of the procedure. Codes 33254-33256 are only to be reported when there is no concurrently performed procedure that requires median sternotomy or cardiopulmonary bypass. The appropriate atrial tissue ablation add-on code, 33257, 33258, 33259 should be reported in addition to an open cardiac procedure requiring sternotomy or cardiopulmonary bypass if performed concurrently.

Incision

33250 Operative ablation of supraventricular arrhythmogenic focus or pathway (eg, Wolff-Parkinson-White, atrioventricular node re-entry), tract(s) and/or focus (foci); without cardiopulmonary bypass

(For intraoperative pacing and mapping by a separate provider, use 93631)

33251   with cardiopulmonary bypass

33254 Operative tissue ablation and reconstruction of atria, limited (eg, modified maze procedure)

33255 Operative tissue ablation and reconstruction of atria, extensive (eg, maze procedure); without cardiopulmonary bypass

33256   with cardiopulmonary bypass

   ● New Code   ▲ Revised Code   + Add-On Code   ⊘ Modifier -51 Exempt   ★ Telemedicine

(Do not report 33254-33256 in conjunction with 32100, 32551, 33120, 33130, 33210, 33211, 33390, 33391, 33404-33507, 33510-33523, 33533-33548, 33600-33853, 33860-33864, 33910-33920)

+ 33257 Operative tissue ablation and reconstruction of atria, performed at the time of other cardiac procedure(s), limited (eg, modified maze procedure) (List separately in addition ot code for primary procedure)

(Use 33257 in conjunction with 33120-33130, 33250, 33251, 33261, 33300-33335, 33390, 33391, 33404-33496, 33500-33507, 33510-33516, 33533-33548, 33600-33619, 33641-33697, 33702-33732, 33735-33767, 33770-33814, 33840-33877, 33910-33922, 33925, 33926, 33935, 33945, 33975-33980)

+ 33258 Operative tissue ablation and reconstruction of atria, performed at the time of other cardiac procedure(s), extensive (eg, maze procedure), without cardiopulmonary bypass (List separately in addition to code for primary procedure)

(Use 33258 in conjunction with 33130, 33250, 33300, 33310, 33320, 33321, 33330, 33390, 33391, 33414-33417, 33420, 33470, 33471, 33501-33503, 33510-33516, 33533-33536, 33690, 33735, 33737, 33800-33813, 33840-33852, 33915, 33925, when the procedure is performed without cardiopulmonary bypass)

+ 33259 Operative tissue ablation and reconstruction of atria, performed at the time of other cardiac procedure(s), extensive (eg, maze procedure), with cardiopulmonary bypass (List separately in addition to code for primary procedure)

(Use 33259 in conjunction with 33120, 33251, 33261, 33305, 33315, 33322, 33335, 33390, 33391, 33404, 33405, 33406, 33410, 33411, 33412, 33413, 33422-33468, 33474-33478, 33496, 33500, 33504-33507, 33510-33516, 33533-33548, 33600-33688, 33692-33722, 33730, 33732, 33736, 33750-33767, 33770-33781, 33786-33788, 33814, 33853, 33860-33877, 33910, 33916-33922, 33926, 33935, 33945, 33975-33980 when the procedure is performed with cardiopulmonary bypass)

(Do not report 33257, 33258 and 33259 inconjunction with 32551, 33210, 33211, 33254-33256, 33265, 33266)

33261 Operative ablation of ventricular arrhythmogenic focus with cardiopulmonary bypass

33262 Code out of order. See page 353.

33263 Code out of order. See page 353.

33264 Code out of order. See page 353.

Endoscopy

33265 Endoscopy, surgical; operative tissue ablation and reconstruction of atria, limited (eg, modified maze procedure), without cardiopulmonary bypass

33266 operative tissue ablation and reconstruction of atria, extensive (eg, maze procedure), without cardiopulmonary bypass

(Do not report 33265-33266 in conjunction with 32551, 33210, 33211)

33270 This code is out of order. See page 354.

33271 This code is out of order. See page 354.

33272 This code is out of order. See page 354.

33273 This code is out of order. See page 354.

PATIENT-ACTIVATED EVENT RECORDER

33282 Implantation of patient-activated cardiac event recorder

(Initial implantation includes programming. For subsequent electronic analysis and/or reprogramming, use 93285, 93291, 93298, 93299)

33284   Removal of an implantable, patient-activated cardiac event recorder

HEART (INCLUDING VALVES) AND GREAT VESSELS

Patients receiving major cardiac procedures may require simultaneous cardiopulmonary bypass insertion of cannulae into the venous and arterial vasculatures with support of circulation and oxygenation by a heart-lung machine. Most services are described by codes in dyad arrangements to allow distinct reporting of procedures with or without cardiopulmonary bypass. Cardiopulmonary bypass is distinct from support of cardiac output using devices (eg, ventricular assist or intra-aortic balloon). For cardiac assist services see 33946, 33947, 33948, 33949, 33967-33983, 33990, 33991, 33992, 33993.

33300   Repair of cardiac wound; without bypass

33305   with cardiopulmonary bypass

33310   Cardiotomy, exploratory (includes removal of foreign body, atrial or ventricular thrombus); without bypass

33315   with cardiopulmonary bypass

(Do not report removal of thrombus (33310-33315) in conjunction with other cardiac procedures unless a separate incision in the heart is required to remove the atrial or ventricular thrombus)

(If removal of thrombus with coronary bypass (33315) is reported in conjunction with 33120, 33130, 33420-33430, 33460-33468, 33496, 33542, 33545, 33641-33647, 33670, 33681, 33975-33980 which requires a separate heart incision, report 33315 with modifier '-59')

33320   Suture repair of aorta or great vessels; without shunt or cardiopulmonary bypass

33321   with shunt bypass

33322   with cardiopulmonary bypass

33330   Insertion of graft, aorta or great vessels; without shunt, or cardiopulmonary bypass

(**33332**   deleted 2014 [2015 edition])

33335   with cardiopulmonary bypass

33340   Percutaneous transcatheter closure of the left atrial appendage with endocardial implant, including fluoroscopy, transseptal puncture, catheter placement(s), left atrial angiography, left atrial appendage angiography, when performed, and radiological supervision and interpretation

(Do not report 33340 in conjunction with 93462)

(Do not report 33340 in conjunction with 93452, 93453, 93458, 93459, 93460, 93461, 93531, 93532, 93533, unless catheterization of the left ventricle is performed by a non-transseptal approach for indications distinct from the left atrial appendage closure procedure)

(Do not report 33340 in conjunction with 93451, 93453, 93456, 93460, 93461, 93530, 93531, 93532, 93533, unless complete right heart catheterization is performed for indications distinct from the left atrial appendage closure procedure)

CARDIAC VALVES

(For multiple valve procedures, see 33390, 33391, 33404-33478 and add modifier 51 to the secondary valve procedure code)

Aortic Valve

Codes 33361, 33362, 33363, 33364, 33365, 33366 are used to report transcatheter aortic valve replacement (TAVR)/transcatheter aortic valve implantation (TAVI). TAVR/TAVI requires two physician operators and all components of the procedure are reported using modifier 62.

Codes 33361, 33362, 33363, 33364, 33365, 33366 include the work, when performed, of percutaneous access, placing the access sheath, balloon aortic valvuloplasty, advancing the valve delivery system into position, repositioning the valve as needed,

   ●   New Code   ▲   Revised Code   +   Add-On Code   ⊘   Modifier -51 Exempt   ★   Telemedicine

deploying the valve, temporary pacemaker insertion for rapid pacing (33210), and closure of the arteriotomy when performed. Codes 33361, 33362, 33363, 33364, 33365, 33366 include open arterial or cardiac approach.

Angiography, radiological supervision, and interpretation performed to guide TAVR/TAVI (eg, guiding valve placement, documenting completion of the intervention, assessing the vascular access site for closure) are included in these codes.

Diagnostic left heart catheterization codes (93452, 93453, 93458-93461) and the supravalvular aortography code (93567) should **not** be used with TAVR/TAVI services (33361, 33362, 33363, 33364, 33365, 33366) to report:

1. Contrast injections, angiography, roadmapping, and/or fluoroscopic guidance for the TAVR/TAVI,

2. Aorta/left ventricular outflow tract measurement for the TAVR/TAVI, or

3. Post-TAVR/TAVI aortic or left ventricular angiography, as this work is captured in the TAVR/TAVI services codes (33361, 33362, 33363, 33364, 33365, 33366).

Diagnostic coronary angiography performed at the time of TAVR/TAVI may be separately reportable if:

1. No prior catheter-based coronary angiography study is available and a full diagnostic study is performed, or

2. A prior study is available, but as documented in the medical record:

   a. The patient's condition with respect to the clinical indication has changed since the prior study, or

   b. There is inadequate visualization of the anatomy and/or pathology, or

   c There is a clinical change during the procedure that requires new evaluation.

   d. For same session/same day diagnostic coronary angiography services, report the appropriate diagnostic cardac catheterization code(s) appended with modifier 59 indicating separate and distance procedural service from TAVR/TAVI.

Diagnostic coronary angiography performed at a separate session from an interventional procedure may be separately reportable.

Other cardiac catheterization services may be reported separately when performed for diagnostic purposes not intrinsic to TAVR/TAVI.

Percutaneous coronary interventional procedures are reported separately, when performed.

When transcatheter ventricular support is required in conjunction with TAVR/TAVI, the appropriate code should be reported with the appropriate ventricular assist device (VAD) procedure code (33990-33993, 33975, 33976, 33999), or balloon pump insertion code (33967, 33970, 33973).

The TAVR/TAVI cardiovascular access and delivery procedures are reported with 33361, 33362, 33363, 33364, 33365, 33366. When cardiopulmonary bypass is performed in conjunction with TAVR/TAVI, codes 33361, 33362, 33363, 33364, 33365, 33366 should be reported with the appropriate add-on code for percutaneous peripheral bypass (33367), open peripheral bypass (33368), or central bypass (33369)

33361 Transcatheter aortic valve replacement (TAVR/TAVI) with prosthetic valve; percutaneous femoral artery approach

33362 open femoral artery approach

33363 open axillary artery approach

33364 open iliac artery approach

33365 transaortic approach (eg, median sternotomy, mediastinotomy)

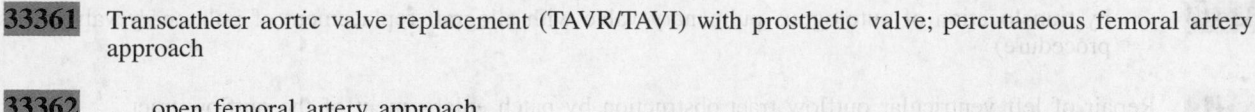

(Use 0318T for transapical approach [eg, left thoracotomy])

	33366	transapical exposure (eg, thoracotomy)
+	**33367**	cardiopulmonary bypass support with percutaneous peripheral arterial and venous cannulation (eg, femoral vessels) (List separately in addition to code for primary procedure)

(Use 33367 in conjunction with 33361, 33362, 33363, 33364, 33365, 33366, 33418, 33477, 0483T, 0484T)

(Do not report 33367 in conjunction with 33368, 33369)

+	**33368**	cardiopulmonary bypass support with open peripheral arterial and venous cannulation (eg, femoral, iliac, axillary vessels) (List separately in addition to code for primary procedure)

(Use 33368 in conjunction with 33361, 33362, 33363, 33364, 33365, 33366, 33418, 33477, 0483T, 0484T)

(Do not report 33368 in conjunction with 33367, 33369)

+	**33369**	cardiopulmonary bypass support with central arterial and venous cannulation (eg, aorta, right atrium, pulmonary artery) (List separately in addition to code for primary procedure)

(Use 33369 in conjunction with 33361, 33362, 33363, 33364, 33365, 33366, 33418, 33477, 0483T, 0484T)

(Do not report 33369 in conjunction with 33367, 33368)

33390 Valvuloplasty, aortic valve, open, with cardiopulmonary bypass; simple (ie, valvotomy, debridement, debulking, and/or simple commissural resuspension)

33391 complex (eg, leaflet extension, leaflet resection, leaflet reconstruction, or annuloplasty)

(Do not report 33391 in conjunction with 33390)

(33400, 33401, 33403 have been deleted.

(**33400** deleted 2016 [2017 edition]. To report, see 33390, 33391)

(**33401** deleted 2016 [2017 edition]. To report, see 33390, 33391)

(**33403** deleted 2016 [2017 edition]. To report, see 33390, 33391)

33404 Construction of apical-aortic conduit

33405 Replacement, aortic valve, open, with cardiopulmonary bypass; with prosthetic valve other than homograft or stentless valve

33406 with allograft valve (freehand)

33410 with stentless tissue valve

33411 Replacement, aortic valve; with aortic annulus enlargement, noncoronary sinus

33412 with transventricular aortic annulus enlargement (Konno procedure)

33413 by translocation of autologous pulmonary valve with allograft replacement of pulmonary valve (Ross procedure)

33414 Repair of left ventricular outflow tract obstruction by patch enlargement of the outflow tract

33415 Resection or incision of subvalvular tissue for discrete subvalvular aortic stenosis

33416 Ventriculomyotomy (-myectomy) for idiopathic hypertrophic subaortic stenosis (eg, asymmetric septal hypertrophy)

● New Code ▲ Revised Code + Add-On Code ⊘ Modifier -51 Exempt ★ Telemedicine

(For percutaneous transcatheter septal reduction therapy, use 93583)

33417   Aortoplasty (gusset) for supravalvular stenosis

Mitral Valve

Codes 33418 and 33419 are used to report transcatheter mitral valve repair TMVR. Code 33419 should only be reported once per session.

Codes 33418 and 33419 include the work, when performed, of percutaneous access, placing the access sheath, transseptal puncture, advancing the repair device delivery system into position, repositioning the device as needed, and deploying the devices.

Angiography, radiological supervision, and interpretation performed to guide TMVR (E.g., guiding device placement and documenting completion of the intervention) are included in these codes.

Diagnostic right and left heart catheterization codes (93451, 93452, 93453, 93456, 93457, 93458, 93459, 93460, 93461, 93530, 93531, 93532, 93533) should not be used with 33418, 33419 to report:

1.   Contrast injections, angiography, road-mapping, and/or fluoroscopic guidance for the transcatheter mitral valve repair (TMVR),

2.   Left ventricular angiography to assess mitral regurgitation for guidance of TMVR, or

3.   Right and left heart catheterization for hemodynamic measurements before, during, and after TMVR for guidance of TMVR.

Diagnostic right and left heart catheterization codes (93451, 93452, 93453, 93456, 93457, 93458, 93459, 93460, 93461, 93530, 93531, 93532, 93533) and diagnostic coronary angiography codes (93454, 93455, 93456, 93457, 93458, 93459, 93460, 93461, 93563, 93564) May be reported with 33418, 33419, representing separate and distinct services from TMVR, if:

1. No prior study is available and a full diagnostic study is performed, or

2. A prior study is available, but as documented in the medical record:

   a. There is inadequate visualization of the anatomy and/or pathology, or

   b. The patient's condition with respect to the clinical indication has changed since the prior study, or

   c. There is a clinical change during the procedure that requires new evaluation.

Other cardiac catheterization services may be reported separately when performed for diagnostic purposes not intrinsic to TMVR.

For same session/same day diagnostic cardiac catheterization services, report the appropriate diagnostic cardiac catheterization codes appended with modifier 59 indicating separate and distinct procedural service from TMVR.

Diagnostic coronary angiography performed at a separate session from an interventional procedure may be separately reportable.

Percutaneous coronary interventional procedures may be reported separately, when performed.

When transcatheter ventricular support is required in conjunction with TMVR, the appropriate code may be reported with the appropriate ventricular assist device (VAD) procedure code (33990, 33991, 33992, 33993) or balloon pump insertion code (33967, 33970, 33973).

When a cardiopulmonary bypass is performed in conjunction with TMVR, 33418, 33419 may be reported with the appropriate add-on code for percutaneous peripheral bypass (33367), open peripheral bypass (33368), or central bypass (33369).

33418   Transcatheter mitral valve repair, percutaneous approach, including transseptal puncture when performed; initial prosthesis

(Do not report 33418 in conjunction with 93462 unless transapical puncture is performed)

+ **33419**   additional prosthesis(es) during same session (list separately in addition to code for primary procedure)

(Use 33419 in conjunction with 33418)

(For transcatheter mitral valve repair, percutaneous approach via the coronary sinus, use 0345T)

(For transcatheter mitral valve implantation/ replacement [TMVI], see 0483T, 0484T)

33420 Valvotomy, mitral valve; closed heart

33422 open heart, with cardiopulmonary bypass

33425 Valvuloplasty, mitral valve, with cardiopulmonary bypass;

33426 with prosthetic ring

33427 radical reconstruction, with or without ring

33430 Replacement, mitral valve, with cardiopulmonary bypass

Tricuspid Valve

33460 Valvectomy, tricuspid valve, with cardiopulmonary bypass

33463 Valvuloplasty, tricuspid valve; without ring insertion

33464 with ring insertion

33465 Replacement, tricuspid valve, with cardiopulmonary bypass

33468 Tricuspid valve repositioning and plication for Ebstein anomaly

Pulmonary Valve

Code 33477 is used to report transcatheter pulmonary valve implantation (TPVI). code 33477 should only be reported once per session.

Code 33477 includes the work, when performed, of percutaneous access, placing the access sheath, advancing the repair device delivery system into position, repositioning the device as needed, and deploying the device(s). Angiography, radiological supervision, and interpretation performed to guide TPVI (eg, guiding device placement and documenting completion of the intervention) are included in the code.

Code 33477 includes all cardiac catheterization(s), intraprocedureal contrast injection(s), fluoroscopic radiological supervision and interpretation, and imaging guidance performed to complete the pulmonary valve procedure. Do not report 33477 in conjunction with 76000, 76001, 93451, 93453, 93454, 93455, 93456, 93457, 93458, 93459, 93460, 93461, 93530, 93531, 93532, 93533, 93563, 93566, 93567, 93568 for angiography intrinsic to the procedure.

Code 33477 includes percutaneous balloon angioplasty of the conduit/treatment zone, valvuloplasty of the pulmonaryt valve conduit, and stent deployment within the pulmonary conduit or an existing bioprosthetic pulmonary vavle, when performed. Do not report 33477 in conjunction with 37236, 37237, 92997, 92998 for pulmonary artery angioplasty/valvuloplasty or stenting within the prosthetic valve delivery site.

Codes 92997, 92998 may be reported separately when pulmonary artery angioplasty is performed at a site separate from the prosthetic valve delivery site. Codes 37236, 37237 may be reported separatey when pulmonary artery stenting is performed at a site separate from the prosthetic valve delivery site.

Diagnostic right heart catheterization and diagnostic coronary angiography codes (93451, 93453, 93454, 93455, 93456, 93457, 93458, 93459, 93460, 93461, 93530, 93531, 93532, 93533, 93563, 93566, 93567, 93568) should NOT be used with 33477 to report:

1. Contrast injections, angiography, roadmapping, and/or fluoroscopic guidance for the TPVI;

2. Pulmonary conduit angiography for guidance of TPVI; OR

3. Right heart catheterization for hemodynamic measurements before, during, and after TPVI for guidance of TPVI.

Diagnostic right and left heart catheterization codes (93451, 93452, 93453, 93456, 93457, 93458, 93459, 93460, 93461, 93530, 93531, 93532, 93533), diagnostic coronary angiography codes (93454, 93455, 93456, 93457, 93458, 93459, 93460, 93461, 93563, 93564), and diagnostic pulmonary angiography code (93568) may be reported with 33477, representing separate and distinct services from TPVI, if:

1. No prior study is available and a full diagnostic study is performed; OR

2. A prior study is available, but as documented in the medical record:

   a. There is inadequate visualization of the anatomy and or pathology; or

   b. The patient's condition with respect to the clinical indication has changed since the prior study; or

   c. There is a clinical change during the procedure that requires new evaluation.

Other cardiac catheterization services may be reported separately when performed for diagnostic purposes not intrinsic to TPVI.

For same session/same day diagnostic cardiac catheterization services, report the appropriate diagnostic cardiac catheterization code(s) appended with modifier 59 to indicate separate and distinct procedural services from TPVI.

Diagnostic coronary angiography peformed at a separate session from an interventional procedure may be separately reportable, when performed.

Percutaneous coronary interventional procedures may be reported separately, when performed.

Percutaneous pulmonary artery branch interventions may be reported separately, when performed.

When transcatheter ventricular support is required in conjunction with TPVI, the appropriate code may be reported with the appropriate percutaneous ventricular assist device (VAD) procedure codes (33990, 33991, 33992, 33993), extracorporeal membrane oxygenation (ECMO) or extracorporeal life support services (ECLS) procedure codes (33946-33989), or balloon pump insertion codes (33967, 33970, 33973).

When cardiopulmonary bypass is performed in conjunction with TPVI, code 33477 may be reported with the appropriate add-on code for percutaneous peripheral bypass (33367), open peripheral bypass (33368), or central bypass (33369).

33470 Valvotomy, pulmonary valve, closed heart; transventricular

(Do not report modifier '-63' in conjunction with 33470)

33471 via pulmonary artery

(To report percutaneous valvuloplasty of pulmonary valve, use 92990)

33474 with cardiopulmonary bypass

33475 Replacement, pulmonary valve

33476 Right ventricular resection for infundibular stenosis, with or without commissurotomy

33477 Transcatheter pulmonary valve implantation, percutaneous approach, including pre-stenting of the valve delivery site, when performed.

33478 Outflow tract augmentation (gusset), with or without commissurotomy or infundibular resection

(Use 33478 in conjunction with 33768 when a cavopulmonary anastomosis to a second superior vena cava is performed)

OTHER VALVULAR PROCEDURES

33496 Repair of non-structural prosthetic valve dysfunction with cardiopulmonary bypass (separate procedure)

(For reoperation, use 33530 in addition to 33496)

Separate Procedure   Unlisted Procedure   CCI Comp. Code   Non-specific Procedure   **361**

CORONARY ARTERY ANOMALIES

Basic procedures include endarterectomy or angioplasty.

33500 Repair of coronary arteriovenous or arteriocardiac chamber fistula; with cardiopulmonary bypass

33501 without cardiopulmonary bypass

33502 Repair of anomalous coronary artery from pulmonary artery origin; by ligation

33503 by graft, without cardiopulmonary bypass

(Do not report modifier '-63' in conjunction with 33502, 33503)

33504 by graft, with cardiopulmonary bypass

33505 with construction of intrapulmonary artery tunnel (Takeuchi procedure)

33506 by translocation from pulmonary artery to aorta

(Do not report modifier '-63' in conjunction with 33505, 33506)

33507 Repair of anomalous (eg, intramural) aortic origin of coronary artery by unroofing or translocation

ENDOSCOPY

Surgical vascular endoscopy always includes diagnostic endoscopy

+ 33508 Endoscopy, surgical, including video-assisted harvest of vein(s) for coronary artery bypass procedure (List separately in addition to code for primary procedure)

(Use 33508 in conjunction with code 33510-33523)

(For open harvest of upper extremity vein procedure, use 35500)

VENOUS GRAFTING ONLY FOR CORONARY ARTERY BYPASS

The following codes are used to report coronary artery bypass procedures using venous grafts only. These codes should NOT be used to report the performance of coronary artery bypass procedures using arterial grafts and venous grafts during the same procedure. See 33517-33523 and 33533-33536 for reporting combined arterial-venous grafts.

Procurement of the saphenous vein graft is included in the description of the work for 33510-33516 and should not be reported as a separate service or co-surgery. To report harvesting of an upper extremity vein, use 35500 in addition to the bypass procedure. To report harvesting of a femoropopliteal vein segment, report 35572 in addition to the bypass procedure. When surgical assistant performs graft procurement, add modifier 80 to 33510-33516. For percutaneous ventricular assist device insertion, removal, repositioning, see 33990-33993.

33510 Coronary artery bypass, vein only; single coronary venous graft

33511 2 coronary venous grafts

33512 3 coronary venous grafts

33513 4 coronary venous grafts

33514 5 coronary venous grafts

33516 6 or more coronary venous grafts

COMBINED ARTERIAL-VENOUS GRAFTING FOR CORONARY BYPASS

The following codes are used to report coronary artery bypass procedures using venous grafts and arterial grafts during the same procedure. These codes may NOT be reported alone.

● New Code   ▲ Revised Code   + Add-On Code   ⊘ Modifier -51 Exempt   ★ Telemedicine

To report combined arterial-venous grafts it is necessary to report two codes: 1) the appropriate combined arterial venous graft code (33517-33523); and 2) the appropriate arterial graft code (33533-33536).

Procurement of the saphenous vein graft is included in the description of the work for 33517-33523 and should not be reported as a separate service or co-surgery. Procurement of the artery for grafting is included in the description of the work for 33533-33536 and should not be reported as a separate service or co-surgery, except when an upper extremity artery (eg., radial artery) is procured. To report harvesting of an upper extremity artery, use 35600 in addition to the bypass procedure. To report harvesting of an upper extremity vein, use 35500 in addition to the bypass procedure. To report harvesting of a femoropopliteal vein segment, report 35572 in addition to the bypass procedure. When surgical assistant performs arterial and/or venous graft procurement, add modifier 80 to 33517-33523, 33533-33536 as appropriate. For percutaneous ventricular assist device insertion, removal, repositioning, see 33990-33993.

+ **33517**   Coronary artery bypass, using venous graft(s) and arterial graft(s); single vein graft (List separately in addition to code for primary procedure)

   (Use 33517 in conjunction with 33533-33536)

+ **33518**   2 venous grafts (List separately in addition to code for primary procedure)

   (Use 33518 in conjunction with 33533-33536)

+ **33519**   3 venous grafts (List separately in addition to code for primary procedure)

   (Use 33519 in conjunction with 33533-33536)

+ **33521**   4 venous grafts (List separately in addition to code for primary procedure)

   (Use 33521 in conjunction with 33533-33536)

+ **33522**   5 venous grafts (List separately in addition to code for primary procedure)

   (Use 33522 in conjunction with 33533-33536)

+ **33523**   6 or more venous grafts (List separately in addition to code for primary procedure)

   (Use 33523 in conjunction with 33533-33536)

+ **33530**   Reoperation, coronary artery bypass procedure or valve procedure, more than 1 month after original operation (List separately in addition to code for primary procedure)

   (Use 33530 in conjunction with 33390, 33391, 33404-33496; 33510-33536, 33863)

ARTERIAL GRAFTING FOR CORONARY ARTERY BYPASS

The following codes are used to report coronary artery bypass procedures using either arterial grafts only or a combination of arterial-venous grafts. The codes include the use of the internal mammary artery, gastroepiploic artery, epigastric artery, radial artery, and arterial conduits procured from other sites.

To report combined arterial-venous grafts it is necessary to report two codes: 1) the appropriate arterial graft code (33533-33536); and 2) the appropriate combined arterial-venous graft code (33517-33523).

Procurement of the artery for grafting is included in the description of the work for 33533-33536 and should not be reported as a separate service or co-surgery, except when an upper extremity artery (eg., radial artery) is procured. To report harvesting of upper extremity artery, report 35600 in addition to the bypass procedure. To report harvesting of a an upper extremity vein, report 35500 in addition to the bypass procedure. To report harvesting of a femoropopliteal vein segment, report 35572 in addition to the bypass procedure. When the surgical assistant performs arterial and/or venous graft procurement, add modifier -80 to 33517-33523, 33533-33536, as appropriate. For percutaneous ventricular assist device insertion, removal, repositioning, see 33990-33993.

33533   Coronary artery bypass, using arterial graft(s); single arterial graft

33534   2 coronary arterial grafts

33535   3 coronary arterial grafts

| ▮ Separate Procedure | ▮ Unlisted Procedure | ▮ CCI Comp. Code | ▮ Non-specific Procedure | **363** |

33536	4 or more coronary arterial grafts
33542	Myocardial resection (eg, ventricular aneurysmectomy)
33545	Repair of postinfarction ventricular septal defect, with or without myocardial resection
33548	Surgical ventricular restoration procedure, includes prosthetic patch, when performed (eg, ventricular remodeling, SVR, SAVER, DOR procedures)

(Do not report 33548 in conjunction with 32551, 33210, 33211, 33310, 33315)

(For Batista procedure or pachopexy, use 33999)

CORONARY ENDARTERECTOMY

+ **33572** Coronary endarterectomy, open, any method, of left anterior descending, circumflex, or right coronary artery performed in conjunction with coronary artery bypass graft procedure, each vessel (List separately in addition to primary procedure)

(Use 33572 in conjunction with 33510-33516, 33533-33536)

SINGLE VENTRICLE AND OTHER COMPLEX CARDIAC ANOMALIES

33600	Closure of atrioventricular valve (mitral or tricuspid) by suture or patch
33602	Closure of semilunar valve (aortic or pulmonary) by suture or patch
33606	Anastomosis of pulmonary artery to aorta (Damus-Kaye-Stansel procedure)
33608	Repair of complex cardiac anomaly other than pulmonary atresia with ventricular septal defect by construction or replacement of conduit from right or left ventricle to pulmonary artery

(For repair of pulmonary artery arborization anomalies by unifocalization, see 33925-33926)

33610	Repair of complex cardiac anomalies (eg, single ventricle with subaortic obstruction) by surgical enlargement of ventricular septal defect

(Do not report modifier '-63' in conjunction with 33610)

33611	Repair of double outlet right ventricle with intraventricular tunnel repair;

(Do not report modifier '-63' in conjunction with 33611)

33612	with repair of right ventricular outflow tract obstruction
33615	Repair of complex cardiac anomalies (eg, tricuspid atresia) by closure of atrial septal defect and anastomosis of atria or vena cava to pulmonary artery (simple Fontan procedure)
33617	Repair of complex cardiac anomalies (eg, single ventricle) by modified Fontan procedure

(Use 33617 in conjunction with 33768 when a cavopulmonary anastomosis to a second superior vena cava is performed)

33619	Repair of single ventricle with aortic outflow obstruction and aortic arch hypoplasia (hypoplastic left heart syndrome) (eg, Norwood procedure)

(Do not report modifier '-63' in conjunction with 33619)

33620	Application of right and left pulmonary artery bands (eg, hybrid approach stage 1)

(For banding of the main pulmonary artery related to septal defect, use 33690)

33621	Transthoracic insertion of catheter for stent placement with catheter removal and closure (eg, hybrid approach stage 1)

● New Code ▲ Revised Code + Add-On Code ⃠ Modifier -51 Exempt ★ Telemedicine

(For placement of stent, use 37236)

(Report both 33620, 33621 if performed in same session)

33622 Reconstruction of complex cardiac anomaly (eg, single ventricle or hypoplastic left heart) with palliation of single ventricle with aortic outflow obstruction and aortic arch hypoplasia, creation of cavopulmonary anastomosis, and removal of right and left pulmonary bands (eg, hybrid approach stage 2, Norwood, bidirectional Glenn, pulmonary artery debanding)

(Do not report 33622 in conjunction with 33619, 33767, 33822, 33840, 33845, 33851, 33853, 33917)

(For bilateral, bidirectional Glenn procedure, use 33622 in conjunction with 33768)

SEPTAL DEFECT

33641 Repair atrial septal defect, secundum, with cardiopulmonary bypass, with or without patch

33645 Direct or patch closure, sinus venosus, with or without anomalous pulmonary venous drainage

(Do not report 33645 in conjunction with 33724, 33726)

33647 Repair of atrial septal defect and ventricular septal defect, with direct or patch closure

(Do not report modifier -63 in conjunction with 33647)

(For repair of tricuspid atresia (eg., Fontan, Gago procedures), use 33615)

33660 Repair of incomplete or partial atrioventricular canal (ostium primum atrial septal defect), with or without atrioventricular valve repair

33665 Repair of intermediate or transitional atrioventricular canal, with or without atrioventricular valve repair

33670 Repair of complete atrioventricular canal, with or without prosthetic valve

(Do not report modifier -63 in conjunction with 33670)

33675 Closure of multiple ventricular septal defects;

33676 with pulmonary valvotomy or infundibular resection (acyanotic)

33677 with removal of pulmonary artery band, with or without gusset

(Do not report 33675-33677 in conjunction with 32100, 32551, 32554, 32555, 33210, 33681, 33684, 33688)

(For percutaneous closure, use 93581)

33681 Closure of single ventricular septal defect, with or without patch;

33684 with pulmonary valvotomy or infundibular resection (acyanotic)

33688 with removal of pulmonary artery band, with or without gusset

(For pulmonary vein repair requiring creation of atrial septal defect, use 33724)

33690 Banding of pulmonary artery

(For right and left pulmonary artery banding in a single ventricle [eg, hybrid approach stage 1], use 33620)

(Do not report modifier 63 in conjunction with 33690)

33692 Complete repair tetralogy of Fallot without pulmonary atresia;

33694   with transannular patch

(Do not report modifier 63 in conjunction with 33694)

(For ligation and takedown of a systematic-to-pulmonary artery shunt, performed in conjunction with a congenital heart procedure, see 33924)

33697   Complete repair tetralogy of Fallot with pulmonary atresia including construction of conduit from right ventricle to pulmonary artery and closure of ventricular septal defect

(For ligation and takedown of a systemic-to-pulmonary artery shunt, performed in conjunction with a congenital heart procedure, see 33924)

SINUS OF VALSALVA

33702   Repair sinus of Valsalva fistula, with cardiopulmonary bypass;

33710   with repair of ventricular septal defect

33720   Repair sinus of Valsalva aneurysm, with cardiopulmonary bypass

33722   Closure of aortico-left ventricular tunnel

VENOUS ANOMALIES

33724   Repair of isolated partial anomalous pulmonary venous return (eg, Scimitar Syndrome)

(Do not report 33724 in conjunction with 32551, 33210, 33211)

33726   Repair of pulmonary venous stenosis

(Do not report 33726 in conjunction with 32551, 33210, 33211)

33730   Complete repair of anomalous venous return (supracardiac, intracardiac, or infracardiac types)

(Do not report modifier '-63' in conjunction with 33730)

(For partial anomalous pulmonary venous return, use 33724; for repair of pulmonary venous stenosis, use 33726)

33732   Repair of cor triatriatum or supravalvular mitral ring by resection of left atrial membrane

(Do not report modifier -63 in conjunction with 33732)

SHUNTING PROCEDURES

33735   Atrial septectomy or septostomy; closed heart (Blalock-Hanlon type operation)

33736   open heart with cardiopulmonary bypass

(Do not report modifier '-63' in conjunction with 33735, 33736)

33737   open heart, with inflow occlusion

(For transvenous method cadiac catheterization balloon atrial septectomy or septostomy (Rashkind type), use 92992)

(For blade method cardiac catheterization atrial septectomy or septostomy (Sang-Park septostomy), use 92993)

33750   Shunt; subclavian to pulmonary artery (Blalock-Taussig type operation)

33755   ascending aorta to pulmonary artery (Waterston type operation)

● New Code   ▲ Revised Code   ✚ Add-On Code   ⊘ Modifier -51 Exempt   ★ Telemedicine

| 33762 | descending aorta to pulmonary artery (Potts-Smith type operation) |

(Do not report modifier -63 in conjunction with 33750, 33755, 33762)

| 33764 | central, with prosthetic graft |

| 33766 | superior vena cava to pulmonary artery for flow to 1 lung (classical Glenn procedure) |

| 33767 | superior vena cava to pulmonary artery for flow to both lungs (bidirectional Glenn procedure) |

| + 33768 | Anastomosis, cavopulmonary, second superior vena cava (List separately in addition to primary procedure) |

(Use 33768 in conjunction with 33478, 33617, 33622, 33767)

(Do not report 33768 in conjunction with 32551, 33210, 33211)

TRANSPOSITION OF THE GREAT VESSELS

| 33770 | Repair of transposition of the great arteries with ventricular septal defect and subpulmonary stenosis; without surgical enlargement of ventricular septal defect |

| 33771 | with surgical enlargement of ventricular septal defect |

| 33774 | Repair of transposition of the great arteries, atrial baffle procedure (eg, Mustard or Senning type) with cardiopulmonary bypass; |

| 33775 | with removal of pulmonary band |

| 33776 | with closure of ventricular septal defect |

| 33777 | with repair of subpulmonic obstruction |

| 33778 | Repair of transposition of the great arteries, aortic pulmonary artery reconstruction (eg, Jatene type); |

(Do not report modifier '-63' in conjunction with 33778)

| 33779 | with removal of pulmonary band |

| 33780 | with closure of ventricular septal defect |

| 33781 | with repair of subpulmonic obstruction |

| 33782 | Aortic root translocation with ventricular septal defect and pulmonary stenosis repair (ie, Nikaidoh procedure); without coronary ostium reimplantation |

(Do not report 33782 in conjunction with 33412, 33413, 33608, 33681, 33770, 33771, 33778, 33780, 33920)

| 33783 | with reimplantation of 1 or both coronary ostia |

TRUNCUS ARTERIOSUS

| 33786 | Total repair, truncus arteriosus (Rastelli type operation) |

(Do not report modifier '-63' in conjunction with 33786)

| 33788 | Reimplantation of an anomalous pulmonary artery |

(For pulmonary artery band, use 33690)

AORTIC ANOMALIES

| 33800 | Aortic suspension (aortopexy) for tracheal decompression (eg, for tracheomalacia) (separate procedure) |

| Separate Procedure | Unlisted Procedure | CCI Comp. Code | Non-specific Procedure | **367** |

33802 Division of aberrant vessel (vascular ring);

33803 with reanastomosis

33813 Obliteration of aortopulmonary septal defect; without cardiopulmonary bypass

33814 with cardiopulmonary bypass

33820 Repair of patent ductus arteriosus; by ligation

33822 by division, under 18 years

33824 by division, 18 years and older

(For percutaneous transcatheter closure of patent ductus arteriosus, use 93582)

33840 Excision of coarctation of aorta, with or without associated patent ductus arteriosus; with direct anastomosis

33845 with graft

33851 repair using either left subclavian artery or prosthetic material as gusset for enlargement

33852 Repair of hypoplastic or interrupted aortic arch using autogenous or prosthetic material; without cardiopulmonary bypass

33853 with cardiopulmonary bypass

(For repair of hypoplastic left heart syndrome (eg., Norwood type), via excision of coarctation of aorta, use 33619)

THORACIC AORTIC ANEURYSM

33860 Ascending aorta graft, with cardiopulmonary bypass, includes valve suspension when performed

33863 Ascending aorta graft, with cardiopulmonary bypass, with aortic root replacement using valved conduit and coronary reconstruction (eg., Bentall)

(Do not report 33863 in conjunction with 33405, 33406, 33410, 33411, 33412, 33413, 33860)

33864 Ascending aorta graft, with cardiopulmonary bypass with valve suspension, with coronary reconstruction and valve sparing aortic root remodeling (eg, David Procedure, Yacoub Procedure)

(Do not report 33864 in conjunction with 33860, 33863)

33870 Transverse arch graft, with cardiopulmonary bypass

33875 Descending thoracic aorta graft, with or without bypass

33877 Repair of thoracoabdominal aortic aneurysm with graft, with or without cardiopulmonary bypass

ENDOVASCULAR REPAIR OF DESCENDING THORACIC AORTA

Codes 33880-33891 represent a family of procedures to report placement of an endovascular graft for repair of the descending thoracic aorta. These codes include all device introduction, manipulation, positioning, and deployment. All balloon angioplasty and/or stent deployment within the target treatment zone for the endoprosthesis, either before or after endograft deployment, are not separately reportable. Open arterial exposure and associated closure of the arteriotomy sites (eg., 34812, 34820, 34833, 34834), introduction of guidewires and catheters (eg., 36140, 36200-36218), and extensive repair or replacement of an artery (eg., 35226, 35286) should be additionally reported. Transposition of subclavian artery to carotid, and carotid-carotid bypass performed in conjunction with endovascular repair of the descending thoracic aorta (eg., 33889, 33891)should be separately reported. The primary codes, 33880 and 33881, include placement of all distal extensions, if required, in the distal thoracic aorta, while proximal extensions, if needed, are reported separately.

---

368   ● New Code   ▲ Revised Code   + Add-On Code   ⊘ Modifier -51 Exempt   ★ Telemedicine

Open arterial exposure and associated closure of the arteriotomy sites (eg, 34714, 34715, 34716, 34812, 34820, 34833, 34834), introduction of guidewires and catheters (eg, 36140, 36200-36218), and extensive repair or replacement of an artery (eg, 35226, 35286) may be additionally reported. Transposition of subclavian artery to carotid, and carotid-carotid bypass performed in conjunction with endovascular repair of the descending thoracic aorta (eg, 33889, 33891) may be separately reported. The primary codes, 33880 and 33881, include placement of all distal extensions, if required, in the distal thoracic aorta, while proximal extensions, if needed, may be reported separately.

For fluoroscopic guidance in conjunction with endovascular repair of the thoracic aorta, see codes 75956-75959 as appropriate. Codes 75956 and 75957 include all angiography of the thoracic aorta and its branches for diagnostic imaging prior to deployment of the primary endovascular devices (including all routine components of modular devices), fluoroscopic guidance in the delivery of the endovascular components and intraprocedural arterial angiography (eg., confirm position, detect endoleak, evaluate runoff). Code 75958 includes the analogous services for placement of each proximal thoracic endovascular extension. Code 75959 includes the analogous services for placement of a distal thoracic endovascular extension(s) placed during a procedure after the primary repair.

Other interventional procedures performed at the time of endovascular repair of the descending thoracic aorta should be additionally reported (eg., innominate, carotid, subclavian, visceral, or iliac artery transluminal angioplasty or stenting, arterial embolization, intravascular ultrasound) when performed before or after deployment of the aortic prostheses.

33880 Endovascular repair of descending thoracic aorta (eg, aneurysm, pseudoaneurysm, dissection, penetrating ulcer, intramural hematoma, or traumatic disruption); involving coverage of left subclavian artery origin, initial endoprosthesis plus descending thoracic aortic extension(s), if required, to level of celiac artery origin

(For radiological supervision and interpretation, use 75956 in conjunction with 33880)

33881 not involving coverage of left subclavian artery origin, initial endoprosthesis plus descending thoracic aortic extension(s), if required, to level of celiac artery origin

(For radiological supervision and interpretation, use 75957 in conjunction with 33881)

33883 Placement of proximal extension prosthesis for endovascular repair of descending thoracic aorta (eg, aneurysm, pseudoaneurysm, dissection, penetrating ulcer, intramural hematoma, or traumatic disruption); initial extension

(For radiological supervision and interpretation, use 75958 in conjunction with 33883)

(Do not report 33881, 33883 when extension placement converts repair to cover left subclavian origin. Use only 33880)

+ 33884 each additional proximal extension (List separately in addition to code for primary procedure)

(Use 33884 in conjunction with 33883)

(For radiological supervision and interpretation, use 75958 in conjunction with 33884)

33886 Placement of distal extension prosthesis(es) delayed after endovascular repair of descending thoracic aorta

(Do not report 33886 in conjunction with 33880, 33881)

(Report 33886 once, regardless of number of modules deployed)

(For radiological supervision and interpretation, use 75959 in conjunction with 33886)

33889 Open subclavian to carotid artery transposition performed in conjunction with endovascular repair of descending thoracic aorta, by neck incision, unilateral

(Do not report 33889 in conjunction with 35694)

33891 Bypass graft, with other than vein, transcervical retropharyngeal carotid-carotid, performed in conjunction with endovascular repair of descending thoracic aorta, by neck incision

(Do not report 33891 in conjunction with 35509, 35601)

Separate Procedure   Unlisted Procedure   CCI Comp. Code   Non-specific Procedure   **369**

PULMONARY ARTERY

33910 Pulmonary artery embolectomy; with cardiopulmonary bypass

33915 without cardiopulmonary bypass

33916 Pulmonary endarterectomy, with or without embolectomy, with cardiopulmonary bypass

33917 Repair of pulmonary artery stenosis by reconstruction with patch or graft

33920 Repair of pulmonary atresia with ventricular septal defect, by construction or replacement of conduit from right or left ventricle to pulmonary artery

(For repair of other complex cardiac anomalies by construction or replacement of right or left ventricle to pulmonary artery conduit, use 33608)

33922 Transection of pulmonary artery with cardiopulmonary bypass

(Do not report modifier '-63' in conjunction with 33922)

+ **33924** Ligation and takedown of a systemic-to-pulmonary artery shunt, performed in conjunction with a congenital heart procedure (List separately in addition to code for primary procedure)

(Use 33924 in conjunction with 33470-33478, 33600-33617, 33622, 33684-33688, 33692-33697, 33735-33767, 33770-33783, 33786, 33917, 33920, 33922, 33925, 33926, 33935, 33945)

33925 Repair of pulmonary artery arborization anomalies by unifocalization; without cardiopulmonary bypass

33926 with cardiopulmonary bypass

HEART/LUNG TRANSPLANTATION

Heart with or without lung allotransplantation involves three distinct components of physician work:

1) **Cadaver donor cardiectomy with or without pneumonectomy**, which includes harvesting the allograft and cold preservation of the allograft (perfusing with cold preservation solution and cold maintenance) (see 33930, 33940).

2) **Backbench work**:

Preparation of a cadaver donor heart and lung allograft prior to transplantation, including dissection of the allograft from surrounding soft tissues to prepare the aorta, superior vena cava, inferior vena cava, and trachea for implantation (use 33933).

Preparation of a cadaver donor heart allograft prior to transplantation, including dissection of the allograft from surrounding soft tissues to prepare aorta, superior vena cava, inferior vena cava, pulmonary artery, and left atrium for implantation (use 33944).

3) **Recipient heart with or without lung allotransplantation**, which includes transplantation of allograft and care of the recipient (see 33935, 33945).

(For implantation of a total replacement heart system [artificial heart] with recipient cardiectomy, use 33927)

● **33927** Implantation of a total replacement heart system (artificial heart) with recipient cardiectomy

(For implantation of ventricular assist device, see 33975, 33976, 33979, 33990, 33991)

● **33928** Removal and replacement of total replacement heart system (artificial heart)

(For revision or replacement of components only of a replacement heart system [artificial heart], use 33999)

●+**33929** Removal of a total replacement heart system (artificial heart) for heart transplantation (List separately in addition to code for primary procedure)

(Use 33929 in conjunction with 33945)

● New Code   ▲ Revised Code   + Add-On Code   ⊘ Modifier -51 Exempt   ★ Telemedicine

33930 Donor cardiectomy-pneumonectomy (including cold preservation)

33933 Backbench standard preparation of cadaver donor heart/lung allograft prior to transplantation, including dissection of allograft from surrounding soft tissues to prepare aorta, superior vena cava, inferior vena cava, and trachea for implantation

33935 Heart-lung transplant with recipient cardiectomy-pneumonectomy

33940 Donor cardiectomy (including cold preservation)

33944 Backbench standard preparation of cadaver donor heart allograft prior to transplantation, including dissection of allograft from surrounding soft tissues to prepare aorta, superior vena cava, inferior vena cava, pulmonary artery, and left atrium for implantation

(For repair or resection procedures on the donor heart, see 33300, 33310, 33320, 33390, 33463, 33464, 33510, 33641, 35216, 35276, 35685)

33945 Heart transplant, with or without recipient cardiectomy

EXTRACORPOREAL MEMBRANE OXYGENATION OR EXTRACORPOREAL LIFE SUPPORT SERVICES

Prolonged extracorporeal membrane oxygenation capital (ECMO) or extracorporeal life-support (ECLS) is a procedure that provides cardiac and/or respiratory support to the heart and or lungs, which allows them to rest and recover when sick or injured. ECMO/ECLS supports the function of the heart and/or lungs by continuously pumping some of the patient's blood out of the body to an oxygenator (membrane lung) where oxygen is added to the blood, carbon dioxide (CO_2) is removed, and the blood is warmed before it is returned to the patient. There are two methods that can be used to accomplish ECMO/ ECLS. One method is veno-arterial extracorporeal life-support, which will support both the heart and lungs. Veno-arterial ECMO/ECLS requires that two cannula(e) are placed--one in a large vein and one in a large artery. The other method is veno-venous extracorporeal life support. Veno-venous ECMO/ECLS is used for lung support only and requires one or two cannula(e), which are placed in a vein.

Services directly related to the cannulation, initiation, management, and discontinuation of the ECMO/ECLS circuit and parameters (33946, 33947, 33948, 33949) are distinct from the daily overall management of the patient. The daily overall management of the patient is a factor that will vary greatly depending on the patient's age, disease process, and condition. Daily overall management of the patient may be separately reported using the relevant hospital observation services, hospital inpatient services, or critical care evaluation and management codes (99218, 99219, 99220, 99221, 99222, 99223, 99231, 99232, 99233, 99234, 99235, 99236, 99291, 99292, 99468, 99469, 99471, 99472, 99475, 99476, 99477, 99478, 99479, 99480).

Services directly related to the ECMO/ECLS involve the initial cannulation and repositioning, removing, or adding cannula(e) while the patient is being supported by the ECMO/ECLS. Initiation of the ECMO/ECLS circuit and setting parameters (33946, 33947) is performed by the physician and involves determining the necessary ECMO/ECLS device components, blood flow, gas exchange, and other necessary parameters to manage the circuit. The daily management of the ECMO/ECLS circuit and monitoring parameters, (33948, 33949), requires physician oversight to ensure that specific features of the interaction of the circuit with the patient are met. Daily management of the circuit and parameters includes management of blood flow, oxygenation, CO_2 clearance by the membrane lung, systemic response, anticoagulation and treatment of bleeding, and cannula(e) positioning, alarms and safety. Once the patient's heart and/or lung function has sufficiently recovered, the physician will wean the patient from the ECMO/ECLS circuit and finally decannulate the patient. The basic management of the ECMO/ECLS circuit and parameters are similar, regardless of the patient's condition.

ECMO/ECLS commonly involves multiple physicians and supporting nonphysician personnel to manage each patient. Different physicians may insert the cannula(e) and initiate ECMO/ECLS, manage the ECMO/ECLS circuit, and decannulate the patient. In addition, it would be common for one physician to manage the ECMO/ECLS circuit and patient-related issues (eg., anticoagulation, complications related to the ECMO/ECLS devices), while another physician manages the overall patient medical condition and underlying disorders, all on a daily basis. The physicians involved in the patient's care are commonly of different specialties, and significant physician team interaction may be required. Depending on the type of circuit and the patient's condition, there is substantial nonphysician work by ECMO/ECLS specialists, cardiac perfusionists, respiratory therapists, and specially trained nurses who provide long periods of constant attention.

If the same physician provides any or all of the services for placing a patient on an ECMO/ECLS circuit, they may report the appropriate codes for the services they performed, which may include codes for the cannula(e) insertion (33951, 33952, 33953, 33954, 33955, 33956), ECMO/ECLS initiation (33946 or 33947), and overall patient management (99218, 99219, 99220, 99221, 99222, 99223, 99231, 99232, 99233, 99234, 99235, 99236, 99291, 99292, 99468, 99469, 99471, 99472, 99475, 99476, 99477, 99478, 99479, 99480).

Separate Procedure　　Unlisted Procedure　　CCI Comp. Code　　Non-specific Procedure　　**371**

ECMO/ECLS daily management (33948, 33949), and repositioning services (33957, 33958, 33959, 33962, 33963, 33964), may not be reported on the same day as initiation services (33946, 33947) by the same or different individuals.

If different physicians provide parts of the service, each physician may report the correct code(s) for the service(s) they provided, except as noted.

Repositioning of the ECMO/ECLS cannula(e) (33957, 33958, 33959, 33962, 33963, 33964) at the same session as insertion (33951, 33952, 33953, 33954, 33955, 33956) is not separately reportable. Replacement of ECMO/ECLS cannula(e) in the same vessel should only be reported using the insertion code (33951, 33952, 33953, 33954, 33955, 33956). If cannula(e) are removed from one vessel and new cannula(e) are placed in a different vessel, report the appropriate cannula(e) removal (33965, 33966, 33969, 33984, 33985, 33986) and insertion (33951, 33952, 33953, 33954, 33955, 33956) codes. Expensive repair or replacement of an artery may be additionally reported (eg., 35266, 35286, 35371, and 35665). Fluoroscopic guidance used for cannula(e) repositioning (33957, 33958, 33959, 33962, 33963, 33964) is included in the procedure when performed and should not be separately reported.

Daily management codes (33948 and 33949) should not be reported on the same day as initiation of ECMO (33946 or 33947).

Initiation codes (33946 or 33947) should not be reported on the same day as repositioning codes (33957, 33958, 33959, 33962, 33963, 33964).

CPT CODES FOR ECMO/ECLS PROCEDURES						
INITIATION						
Management		Cannula insertion procedures				
Veno-venous 33946	Veno-arterial 33947	Percutaneous		Open		Sternotomy/thoracotomy	
		Birth-5 yrs 33951	≥ 6 yrs 33952	Birth-5 yrs 33953	≥ 6 yrs 33954	Birth-5 yrs 33955	≥ 6 yrs 33956

SUBSEQUENT						
Management		Cannula repositioning procedures				
Veno-venous 33948	Veno-arterial 33949	Percutaneous		Open		Sternotomy/thoracotomy	
		Birth-5 yrs 33957	≥ 6 yrs 33958	Birth-5 yrs 33959	≥ 6 yrs 33962	Birth-5 yrs 33963	≥ 6 yrs 33964

DECANNULATION						
Veno-venous and/or Veno-arterial →		Decannulation (removal) procedures				
		Percutaneous		Open		Sternotomy/thoracotomy	
		Birth-5 yrs 33965	≥ 6 yrs 33966	Birth-5 yrs 33969	≥ 6 yrs 33984	Birth-5 yrs 33985	≥ 6 yrs 33986

ADDITIONAL PROCEDURES			
Other cannula procedures			
Arterial exposure +33987	Insertion left heart vent 33988		Removal left heart vent 33989

33946 Extracorporeal membrane oxygenation (ECMO)/extracorporeal life support (ECLS) provided by physician; initiation, veno-venous

(Do not report modifier 63 in conjunction with 33946, 33947, 33948, 33949)

(For insertion of cannula[e] for extracorporeal circulation, see 33951, 33952, 33953, 33954, 33955, 33956)

33947 initiation, veno-arterial

(Do not report modifier 63 in conjunction with 33946, 33947, 33948, 33949)

(Do not report 33946, 33947 in conjunction with 33948, 33949, 33957, 33958, 33959, 33962, 33963, 33964)

33948 daily management, each day, veno-venous

(Do not report modifier 63 in conjunction with 33946, 33947, 33948, 33949)

33949 daily management, each day, veno-arterial

(Do not report modifier 63 in conjunction with 33946, 33947, 33948, 33949)

● New Code   ▲ Revised Code   + Add-On Code   ⊘ Modifier -51 Exempt   ★ Telemedicine

(Do not report 33948, 33949 in conjunction with 33946, 33947)

33951   insertion of peripheral (arterial and/or venous) cannula(e), percutaneous, birth through 5 years of age (includes fluoroscopic guidance, when performed)

(For initiation and daily management of extracorporeal circulation, see 33946, 33947, 33948, 33949)

33952   insertion of peripheral (arterial and/or venous) cannula(e), percutaneous, 6 years and older (includes fluoroscopic guidance, when performed)

(For maintenance of extracorporeal circulation, see 33946, 33947, 33948, 33949)

33953   insertion of peripheral (arterial and/or venous) cannula(e), open, birth through 5 years of age

(For maintenance of extracorporeal circulation, see 33946, 33947, 33948, 33949)

33954   insertion of peripheral (arterial and/or venous) cannula(e), open, 6 years and older

(Do not report 33953, 33954 in conjunction with 34714, 34715, 34716, 34812, 34820, 34833, 34834)

(For maintenance of extracorporeal circulation, see 33946, 33947, 33948, 33949)

33955   insertion of central cannula(e) by sternotomy or thoracotomy, birth through 5 years of age

(For maintenance of extracorporeal circulation, see 33946, 33947, 33948, 33949)

33956   insertion of central cannula(e) by sternotomy or thoracotomy, 6 years and older

(Do not report 33955, 33956 in conjunction with 32100, 39010)

(For maintenance of extracorporeal circulation, see 33946, 33947, 33948, 33949)

33957   reposition peripheral (arterial and/or venous) cannula(e), percutaneous, birth through 5 years of age (includes fluoroscopic guidance, when performed)

33958   reposition peripheral (arterial and/or venous) cannula(e), percutaneous, 6 years and older (includes fluoroscopic guidance, when performed)

(Do not report 33957, 33958 in conjunction with 34713)

33959   reposition peripheral (arterial and/or venous) cannula(e), open, birth through 5 years of age (includes fluoroscopic guidance, when performed)

33962   reposition peripheral (arterial and/or venous) cannula(e), open, 6 years and older (includes fluoroscopic guidance, when performed)

(Do not report 33959, 33962 in conjunction with 34714, 34715, 34716, 34812, 34820, 34834)

33963   reposition of central cannula(e) by sternotomy or thoracotomy, birth through 5 years of age (includes fluoroscopic guidance, when performed)

33964   reposition central cannula(e) by sternotomy or thoracotomy, 6 years and older (includes fluoroscopic guidance, when performed)

(Do not report 33963, 33964 in conjunction with 32100, 39010)

(Do not report 33957, 33958, 33959, 33962, 33963, 33964 in conjunction with 33946, 33947)

33965   removal of peripheral (arterial and/or venous) cannula(e), percutaneous, birth through 5 years of age

33966   removal of peripheral (arterial and/or venous) cannula(e), percutaneous, 6 years and older

33969   removal of peripheral (arterial and/or venous) cannula(e), open, birth through 5 years of age

---

(Do not report 33969 in conjunction with 34714, 34715, 34716, 34812, 34820, 34834, 35201, 35206, 35211, 35226)

33984   removal of peripheral (arterial and/or venous) cannula(e), open, 6 years and older

(Do not report 33984 in conjunction with 34714, 34715, 34716, 34812, 34820, 34834, 35201, 35206, 35211, 35226)

33985   removal of central cannula(e) by sternotomy or thoracotomy, birth through 5 years of age

(Do not report 33985 in conjunction with 35211)

33986   removal of central cannula(e) by sternotomy or thoracotomy, 6 years and older

(Do not report 33986 in conjunction with 35211)

+ **33987** Arterial exposure with creation of graft conduit (eg, chimney graft) to facilitate arterial perfusion for ECMO/ECLS (List separately in addition to code for primary procedure)

(Use 33987 in conjunction with 33953, 33954, 33955, 33956)

(Do not report 33987 in conjunction with 34714, 34716, 34833)

33988 Insertion of left heart vent by thoracic incision (eg, sternotomy, thoracotomy) for ECMO/ECLS

33989 Removal of left heart vent by thoracic incision (eg, sternotomy, thoracotomy) for ECMO/ECLS

CARDIAC ASSIST

The insertion of a ventricular assist device (VAD) can be performed via percutaneous (33990, 33991) or transthoracic (33975, 33976, 33979) approach. The location of the ventricular assist device may be intracorporeal or extracorporeal.

Open arterial exposure when necessary to facilitate percutaneous ventricular assist device insertion (33990, 33991), may be reported separately (34714, 34715, 34716, 34812, 34820, 34833, 34834). Extensive repair or replacement of an artery may be additionally reported (eg, 35226 or 35286).

Removal of a ventricular assist device (33977, 33978, 33980, 33992) includes removal of the entire device, including the cannulas. Removal of a percutaneous ventricular assist device at the same session as insertion is not separately reportable. For removal of a percutaneous ventricular assist device at a separate and distinct session, but on the same day as insertion, report 33992 appended with modifier 59 indicating a distinct procedural service.

Repositioning of a percutaneous ventricular assist device at the same session as insertion is not separately reportable. Repositioning of percutaneous ventricular assist device not necessitating imaging guidance is not a reportable service. For repositioning of a percutaneous ventricular assist device necessitating imaging guidance at a separate and distinct session, but on the same day as insertion, report 33993 with modifier 59 indicating a distinct procedural service.

Replacement of a ventricular assist device pump (ie, 33981-33983) includes the removal of the pump and insertion of a new pump, connection, de-airing, and initiation of the new pump.

Replacement of the entire implantable ventricular assist device system, ie., pump(s) and cannulas, is reported using the insertion codes (ie, 33975, 33976, 33979). Removal (ie, 33977, 33978, 33980) of the ventricular assist device system being replaced is not separately reported. Replacement of a percutaneous ventricular assist device is reported using implantation codes (ie, 33990, 33991). Removal (ie, 33992) is not reported separately.

33962 This codes is out of order. See page 373.

33963 This codes is out of order. See page 373.

33964 This codes is out of order. See page 373.

33965 This codes is out of order. See page 373.

33966 This codes is out of order. See page 373.

● New Code   ▲ Revised Code   + Add-On Code   ⊘ Modifier -51 Exempt   ★ Telemedicine

33967 Insertion of intra-aortic balloon assist device, percutaneous

33968 Removal of intra-aortic balloon assist device, percutaneous

(For removal of implantable aortic counterpulsation ventricular assist system, see 0455T, 0456T, 0457T, 0458T)

33969 This codes is out of order. See page 373.

33970 Insertion of intra-aortic balloon assist device through the femoral artery, open approach

(For insertion or replacement of implantable aortic counterpulsation ventricular assist system, see 0451T, 0452T, 0453T, 0454T)

33971 Removal of intra-aortic balloon assist device including repair of femoral artery, with or without graft

(For removal of implantable aortic counterpulsation ventricular assist system, see 0455T, 0456T, 0457T, 0458T)

33973 Insertion of intra-aortic balloon assist device through the ascending aorta

(For insertion or replacement of implantable aortic counterpulsation ventricular assist system, see 0451T, 0452T, 0453T, 0454T)

33974 Removal of intra-aortic balloon assist device from the ascending aorta, including repair of the ascending aorta, with or without graft

(For removal of implantable aortic counterpulsation ventricular assist system, see 0455T, 0456T, 0457T, 0458T)

33975 Insertion of ventricular assist device; extracorporeal, single ventricle

33976   extracorporeal, biventricular

33977 Removal of ventricular assist device; extracorporeal, single ventricle

33978   extracorporeal, biventricular

33979 Insertion of ventricular assist device, implantable intracorporeal, single ventricle

(For insertion or replacement of implantable aortic counterpulsation ventricular assist system, see 0451T, 0452T, 0453T, 0454T)

33980 Removal of ventricular assist device, implantable intracorporeal, single ventricle

(For removal of implantable aortic counterpulsation ventricular assist system, see 0455T, 0456T, 0457T, 0458T)

33981 Replacement of extracorporeal ventricular assist device, single or biventricular, pump(s), single or each pump

33982 Replacement of ventricular assist device pump(s); implantable intracorporeal, single ventricle, without cardiopulmonary bypass

33983   implantable intracorporeal, single ventricle, with cardiopulmonary bypass

(For insertion or replacement of implantable aortic counterpulsation ventricular assist system, see 0451T, 0452T, 0453T, 0454T)

33984 This codes is out of order. See page 374.

33985 This codes is out of order. See page 374.

Separate Procedure   Unlisted Procedure   CCI Comp. Code   Non-specific Procedure   **375**

33986 This codes is out of order. See page 374.

33987 This codes is out of order. See page 374.

33988 This codes is out of order. See page 374.

33989 This codes is out of order. See page 374.

33990 Insertion of ventricular assist device, percutaneous including radiological supervision and interpretation; arterial access only

33991 both arterial and venous access, with transseptal puncture

(For insertion or replacement of implantable aortic counterpulsation ventricular assist system, see 0451T, 0452T, 0453T, 0454T)

33992 Removal of percutaneous ventricular assist device at separate and distinct session from insertion

(For removal of implantable aortic counterpulsation ventricular assist system, see 0455T, 0456T, 0457T, 0458T)

33993 Repositioning of percutaneous ventricular assist device with imaging guidance at separate and distinct session from insertion

(For relocating and repositioning of implantable aortic counterpulsation ventricular assist system, see 0459T, 0460T, 0461T)

OTHER PROCEDURES, CARDIAC SURGERY

33999 Unlisted procedure, cardiac surgery

ARTERIES AND VEINS

Primary vascular procedure listings include establishing both inflow and outflow by whatever procedures necessary. Also included is that portion of the operative arteriogram performed by the surgeon, as indicated. Sympathectomy, when done, is included in the listed aortic procedures. For unlisted vascular procedures, use 37799.

EMBOLECTOMY/THROMBECTOMY

Arterial, With or Without Catheter

34001 Embolectomy or thrombectomy, with or without catheter; carotid, subclavian or innominate artery, by neck incision

34051 innominate, subclavian artery, by thoracic incision

34101 axillary, brachial, innominate, subclavian artery, by arm incision

34111 radial or ulnar artery, by arm incision

34151 renal, celiac, mesentery, aortoiliac artery, by abdominal incision

34201 femoropopliteal, aortoiliac artery, by leg incision

34203 popliteal-tibio-peroneal artery, by leg incision

Venous, Direct or With Catheter

34401 Thrombectomy, direct or with catheter; vena cava, iliac vein, by abdominal incision

34421 vena cava, iliac, femoropopliteal vein, by leg incision

---

● New Code ▲ Revised Code + Add-On Code ⊘ Modifier -51 Exempt ★ Telemedicine

| 34451 | vena cava, iliac, femoropopliteal vein, by abdominal and leg incision |

| 34471 | subclavian vein, by neck incision |

| 34490 | axillary and subclavian vein, by arm incision |

VENOUS RECONSTRUCTION

| 34501 | Valvuloplasty, femoral vein |

| 34502 | Reconstruction of vena cava, any method |

| 34510 | Venous valve transposition, any vein donor |

| 34520 | Cross-over vein graft to venous system |

| 34530 | Saphenopopliteal vein anastomosis |

ENDOVASCULAR REPAIR OF ABDOMINAL AORTA AND/OR ILIAC ARTERIES

Codes 34701, 34702, 34703, 34704, 34705, 34706 describe introduction, positioning, and deployment of an endograft for treatment of abdominal aortic pathology (with or without rupture), such as aneurysm, pseudoaneurysm, dissection, penetrating ulcer, or traumatic disruption in the infrarenal abdominal aorta with or without extension into the iliac artery(ies). The terms, endovascular graft, endoprosthesis, endograft, and stentgraft, refer to a covered stent. The infrarenal aortic endograft may be an aortic tube device, a bifurcated unibody device, a modular bifurcated docking system with docking limb(s), or an aorto-uni-iliac device. Codes 34707 and 34708 describe introduction, positioning, and deployment of an ilio-iliac endograft for treatment of isolated arterial pathology (with or without rupture), such as aneurysm, pseudoaneurysm, arteriovenous malformation, or trauma involving the iliac artery. For treatment of atherosclerotic occlusive disease in the iliac artery(ies) with a covered stent(s), see 37221, 37223. For covered stent placement for atherosclerotic occlusive disease in the aorta, see 37236, 37237.

Report 34705 or 34706 for simultaneous bilateral iliac artery aneurysm repairs with aorto-bi-iliac endograft.

For isolated bilateral iliac artery repair, report 34707 or 34708 with modifier 50 appended.

Decompressive laparotomy for abdominal compartment syndrome after ruptured abdominal aortic and/or iliac artery aneurysm repair may be separately reported with 49000 in addition to 34702, 34704, 34706, or 34708.

The treatment zone for endograft procedures is defined by those vessels that contain an endograft(s) (main body, docking limb[s], and/or extension[s]) deployed during that operative session. Adjunctive procedures outside the treatment zone may be separately reported (eg, angioplasty, endovascular stent placement, embolization). For example, when an endograft terminates in the common iliac artery, any additional treatment performed in the external and/or internal iliac artery may be separately reportable. Placement of a docking limb is inherent to a modular endograft(s), and, therefore, 34709 may not be reported separately if the docking limb extends into the external iliac artery. In addition, any interventions (eg, angioplasty, stenting, additional stent graft extension[s]) in the external iliac artery where the docking limb terminates may not be reported separately. Any catheterization or treatment of the internal iliac artery, such as embolization, may be separately reported. For 34701 and 34702, the abdominal aortic treatment zone is defined as the infrarenal aorta. For 34703 and 34704, the abdominal aortic treatment zone is typically defined as the infrarenal aorta and ipsilateral common iliac artery. For 34705 and 34706, the abdominal aortic treatment zone is typically defined as the infrarenal aorta and both common iliac arteries. For 34707 and 34708, the treatment zone is defined as the portion of the iliac artery(ies) (eg, common, internal, external iliac arteries) that contains the endograft. For a bifurcated iliac branch device, use 0254T.

Codes 34702, 34704, 34706, 34708 are reported when endovascular repair is performed on ruptured aneurysm in the aorta or iliac artery(ies). Rupture is defined as clinical and/or radiographic evidence of acute hemorrhage for purposes of reporting these codes. A chronic, contained rupture is considered a pseudoaneurysm, and endovascular treatment of a chronic, contained rupture is reported with 34701, 34703, 34705, or 34707.

Code 34709 is reported for placement of extension prosthesis(es) that terminate(s) either in the internal iliac, external iliac, or common femoral artery(ies) or in the abdominal aorta proximal to the renal artery(ies) in conjunction with 34701, 34702, 34703, 34704, 34705, 34706, 34707, 34708. Code 34709 may only be reported once per vessel treated (ie, multiple endograft extensions placed in a single vessel may only be reported once). Endograft extension(s) that terminate(s) in the common iliac arteries are included in 34703, 34704, 34705, 34706, 34707, 34708 and are not separately reported. Treatment zone angioplasty/stenting, when performed, is included in 34709. In addition, proximal infrarenal abdominal aortic extension prosthesis(es) that terminate(s)

| | Separate Procedure | | Unlisted Procedure | | CCI Comp. Code | | Non-specific Procedure | **377** |

in the aorta below the renal artery(ies) are also included in 34701, 34702, 34703, 34704, 34705, 34706 and are not separately reportable.

Codes 34710, 34711 are reported for delayed placement of distal or proximal extension prosthesis(es) for endovascular repair of infrarenal abdominal aortic or iliac aneurysm, false aneurysm, dissection, endoleak, or endograft migration. Pre-procedure sizing and device selection, all nonselective catheterization(s), all associated radiological supervision and interpretation, and treatment zone angioplasty/stenting, when performed, are included in 34710 and 34711. Codes 34710 and 34711 may only be reported once per vessel treated (ie, multiple endograft extensions placed in a single vessel may only be reported once).

Nonselective catheterization is included in 34701, 34702, 34703, 34704, 34705, 34706, 34707, 34708 and is not separately reported. However, selective catheterization of the hypogastric artery(ies), renal artery(ies), and/or arterial families outside the treatment zone of the endograft may be separately reported. Intravascular ultrasound (37252, 37253) performed during endovascular aneurysm repair may be separately reported. Balloon angioplasty and/or stenting within the treatment zone of the endograft, either before or after endograft deployment, is not separately reported. Fluoroscopic guidance and radiological supervision and interpretation in conjunction with endograft repair is not separately reported, and includes all intraprocedural imaging (eg, angiography, rotational CT) of the aorta and its branches prior to deployment of the endovascular device, fluoroscopic guidance and roadmapping used in the delivery of the endovascular components, and intraprocedural and completion angiography (eg, confirm position, detect endoleak, evaluate runoff) performed at the time of the endovascular infrarenal aorta and/or iliac repair.

Codes 34709, 34710, 34711 include nonselective introduction of guidewires and catheters into the treatment zone from peripheral artery access(es). However, selective catheterization of the hypogastric artery(ies), renal artery(ies), and/or arterial families outside the treatment zone may be separately reported. Codes 34709, 34710, 34711 also include balloon angioplasty and/or stenting within the treatment zone of the endograft extension, either before or after deployment of the endograft, fluoroscopic guidance, and all associated radiological supervision and interpretation performed in conjunction with endovascular endograft extension (eg, angiographic diagnostic imaging of the aorta and its branches prior to deployment of the endovascular device, fluoroscopic guidance in the delivery of the endovascular components, and intraprocedural and completion angiography to confirm endograft position, detect endoleak, and evaluate runoff).

Code 34712 describes transcatheter delivery of accessoryenhanced fixation devices to the endograft (eg, anchor, screw, tack), including all associated radiological supervision and interpretation. Code 34712 may only be reported once per operative session.

Vascular access requiring use of closure devices for large sheaths (ie, 12 French or larger) or access requiring open surgical arterial exposure may be separately reported (eg, 34713, 34714, 34715, 34716, 34812, 34820, 34833, 34834). Code 34713 describes percutaneous access and closure of a femoral arteriotomy for delivery of endovascular prosthesis through a large arterial sheath (ie, 12 French or larger). Ultrasound guidance (ie, 76937), when performed, is included in 34713. (Percutaneous access using a sheath smaller than 12 French is included in 34701-34712 and is not separately reported.)

Code 34812 describes open repair and closure of the femoral artery. Extensive repair of an artery (eg, 35226, 35286, 35371) may also be reported separately. Iliac exposure for device delivery through a retroperitoneal incision, open brachial exposure, or axillary or subclavian exposure through an infraclavicular, or supraclavicular or sternotomy incision during endovascular aneurysm repair may be separately reported (eg, 34715, 34812, 34820, 34834). Endovascular device delivery or establishment of cardiopulmonary bypass that requires creation of a prosthetic conduit utilizing a femoral artery, iliac artery with a retroperitoneal incision, or axillary or subclavian artery exposure through an infraclavicular, supraclavicular, or sternotomy incision (eg, 34714, 34716, 34833) and oversewing of the conduit at the time of procedure completion may be separately reported during endovascular aneurysm repair or cardiac procedures requiring cardiopulmonary bypass. If a conduit is converted to a bypass, report the bypass (eg, 35665) and not the arterial exposure with conduit (ie, 34714, 34716, 34833). Arterial embolization(s) of renal, lumbar, inferior mesenteric, hypogastric or external iliac arteries to facilitate complete endovascular aneurysm exclusion may be separately reported (eg, 37242).

Balloon angioplasty and/or stenting at the sealing zone(s) of an endograft is an integral part of the procedure and is not separately reported. However, balloon angioplasty and/or stent deployment in vessels that do not contain endograft (outside the treatment zone for the endograft), either before or after endograft deployment, may be separately reported (eg, 37220, 37221, 37222, 37223).

Other interventional procedures performed at the time of endovascular abdominal aortic aneurysm repair may be additionally reported (eg, renal transluminal angioplasty, arterial embolization, intravascular ultrasound, balloon angioplasty or stenting of native artery[s] outside the endograft treatment zone, when done before or after deployment of endograft).

(For fenestrated endovascular repair of the visceral aorta, see 34841-34844. For fenestrated endovascular repair of the visceral aorta and concomitant infrarenal abdominal aorta, see 34845-34848)

● **34701**   Endovascular repair of infrarenal aorta by deployment of an aorto-aortic tube endograft including pre-procedure sizing and device selection, all nonselective catheterization(s), all associated radiological supervision and interpretation, all endograft extension(s) placed in the aorta from the level of the renal arteries to the aortic bifurcation, and all angioplasty/stenting performed from the level of the renal arteries to the aortic bifurcation; for other than rupture (eg, for aneurysm, pseudoaneurysm, dissection, penetrating ulcer)

(For covered stent placement[s] for atherosclerotic occlusive disease isolated to the aorta, see 37236, 37237)

● **34702**   for rupture including temporary aortic and/or iliac balloon occlusion, when performed (eg, for aneurysm, pseudoaneurysm, dissection, penetrating ulcer, traumatic disruption)

● **34703**   Endovascular repair of infrarenal aorta and/or iliac artery(ies) by deployment of an aorto-uni-iliac endograft including pre-procedure sizing and device selection, all nonselective catheterization(s), all associated radiological supervision and interpretation, all endograft extension(s) placed in the aorta from the level of the renal arteries to the iliac bifurcation, and all angioplasty/stenting performed from the level of the renal arteries to the iliac bifurcation; for other than rupture (eg, for aneurysm, pseudoaneurysm, dissection, penetrating ulcer)

● **34704**   for rupture including temporary aortic and/or iliac balloon occlusion, when performed (eg, for aneurysm, pseudoaneurysm, dissection, penetrating ulcer, traumatic disruption)

● **34705**   Endovascular repair of infrarenal aorta and/or iliac artery(ies) by deployment of an aorto-bi-iliac endograft including pre-procedure sizing and device selection, all nonselective catheterization(s), all associated radiological supervision and interpretation, all endograft extension(s) placed in the aorta from the level of the renal arteries to the iliac bifurcation, and all angioplasty/stenting performed from the level of the renal arteries to the iliac bifurcation; for other than rupture (eg, for aneurysm, pseudoaneurysm, dissection, penetrating ulcer)

● **34706**   for rupture including temporary aortic and/or iliac balloon occlusion, when performed (eg, for aneurysm, pseudoaneurysm, dissection, penetrating ulcer, traumatic disruption)

● **34707**   Endovascular repair of iliac artery by deployment of an ilio-iliac tube endograft including pre-procedure sizing and device selection, all nonselective catheterization(s), all associated radiological supervision and interpretation, and all endograft extension(s) proximally to the aortic bifurcation and distally to the iliac bifurcation, and treatment zone angioplasty/stenting, when performed, unilateral; for other than rupture (eg, for aneurysm, pseudoaneurysm, dissection, arteriovenous malformation)

(For covered stent placement[s] for atherosclerotic occlusive disease of the abdominal aorta, see 37236, 37237)

(For covered stent placement[s] for atherosclerotic occlusive disease of the iliac artery, see 37221, 37223)

● **34708**   for rupture including temporary aortic and/or iliac balloon occlusion, when performed (eg, for aneurysm, pseudoaneurysm, dissection, arteriovenous malformation, traumatic disruption)

●+**34709**   Placement of extension prosthesis(es) distal to the common iliac artery(ies) or proximal to the renal artery(ies) for endovascular repair of infrarenal abdominal aortic or iliac aneurysm, false aneurysm, dissection, penetrating ulcer, including pre-procedure sizing and device selection, all nonselective catheterization(s), all associated radiological supervision and interpretation, and treatment zone angioplasty/stenting, when performed, per vessel treated (List separately in addition to code for primary procedure)

(Use 34709 in conjunction with 34701, 34702, 34703, 34704, 34705, 34706, 34707, 34708)

(34709 may only be reported once per vessel treated [ie, multiple endograft extensions placed in a single vessel may only be reported once])

(Do not report 34709 for placement of a docking limb that extends into the external iliac artery)

(For endograft placement into a renal artery that is being covered by a proximal extension, see 37236, 37237)

● **34710**   Delayed placement of distal or proximal extension prosthesis for endovascular repair of infrarenal abdominal aortic or iliac aneurysm, false aneurysm, dissection, endoleak, or endograft migration, including pre-procedure sizing and device selection, all nonselective catheterization(s), all associated radiological

| ▇ Separate Procedure | ▇ Unlisted Procedure | ▇ CCI Comp. Code | ▇ Non-specific Procedure | **379** |

supervision and interpretation, and treatment zone angioplasty/stenting, when performed; initial vessel treated

●+**34711**   each additional vessel treated (List separately in addition to code for primary procedure)

(Use 34711 in conjunction with 34710)

(34710, 34711 may each be reported only once per operative session [ie, multiple endograft extensions placed in a single vessel may only be reported with a single code])

(For decompressive laparotomy, use 49000 in conjunction with 34702, 34704, 34706, 34708, 34710)

(If the delayed revision is a transcatheter enhanced fixation device [eg, anchors, screws], report 34712)

(Do not report 34710, 34711 in conjunction with 34701, 34702, 34703, 34704, 34705, 34706, 34707, 34708, 34709)

(Do not report 34701-34711 in conjunction with 34841, 34842, 34843, 34844, 34845, 34846, 34847, 34848)

(For endovascular repair of iliac artery bifurcation [eg, aneurysm, pseudoaneurysm, arteriovenous malformation, trauma] using bifurcated endograft, use 0254T)

(Report 37252, 37253 for intravascular ultrasound when performed during endovascular aneurysm repair)

(For isolated bilateral iliac artery repair, report 34707 or 34708 with modifier 50)

(For open arterial exposure, report 34714, 34715, 34716, 34812, 34820, 34833, 34834 as appropriate, in conjunction with 34701, 34702, 34703, 34704, 34705, 34706, 34707, 34708, 34710)

(For percutaneous arterial closure, report 34713 as appropriate, in conjunction with 34701, 34702, 34703, 34704, 34705, 34706, 34707, 34708, 34710)

(For simultaneous bilateral iliac artery aneurysm repairs with aorto-biiliac endograft, see 34705, 34706, as appropriate)

● **34712**   Transcatheter delivery of enhanced fixation device(s) to the endograft (eg, anchor, screw, tack) and all associated radiological supervision and interpretation

(Report 34712 only once per operative session)

●+**34713**   Percutaneous access and closure of femoral artery for delivery of endograft through a large sheath (12 French or larger), including ultrasound guidance, when performed, unilateral (List separately in addition to code for primary procedure)

(Use 34713 in conjunction with 33880, 33881, 33883, 33884, 33886, 34701, 34702, 34703, 34704, 34705, 34706, 34707, 34708, 34841, 34842, 34843, 34844, 34845, 34846, 34847, 34848 as appropriate. However, do not report 34713 in conjunction with 33880, 33881, 33883, 33884, 33886, 34701, 34702, 34703, 34704, 34705, 34706, 34707, 34708, 34841, 34842, 34843, 34844, 34845, 34846, 34847, 34848 for percutaneous closure of femoral artery after delivery of endovascular prosthesis if a sheath smaller than 12 French was used)

(34713 may only be reported once per side. For bilateral procedure, report 34713 twice)

(Do not report ultrasound guidance [ie, 76937] for percutaneous vascular access in conjunction with 34713 for the same access)

(Do not report 34713 for percutaneous access and closure of the femoral artery in conjunction with 37221, 37223, 37236, 37237)

(Do not report 34713 in conjunction with 37221, 37223 for covered stent placement[s] for atherosclerotic occlusive disease of the iliac artery[ies])

▲+**34812**   Open femoral artery exposure for delivery of endovascular prosthesis, by groin incision, unilateral (List separately in addition to code for primary procedure)

(Use 34812 in conjunction with 33880, 33881, 33883, 33884, 33886, 33990, 33991, 34701, 34702, 34703, 34704, 34705, 34706, 34707, 34708, 34841, 34842, 34843, 34844, 34845, 34846, 34847, 34848, 0254T)

   ● New Code   ▲ Revised Code   + Add-On Code   ⊘ Modifier -51 Exempt   ★ Telemedicine

(34812 may only be reported once per side. For bilateral procedure, report 34812 twice)

(Do not report 34812 in conjunction with 33953, 33954, 33959, 33962, 33969, 33984, 33987)

●+**34714**   Open femoral artery exposure with creation of conduit for delivery of endovascular prosthesis or for establishment of cardiopulmonary bypass, by groin incision, unilateral (List separately in addition to code for primary procedure)

(Use 34714 in conjunction with 32852, 32854, 33031, 33120, 33251, 33256, 33259, 33261, 33305, 33315, 33322, 33335, 33390, 33391, 33404-33417, 33422, 33425, 33426, 33427, 33430, 33460, 33463, 33464, 33465, 33468, 33474, 33475, 33476, 33478, 33496, 33500, 33502, 33504, 33505, 33506, 33507, 33510, 33511, 33512, 33513, 33514, 33516, 33533, 33534, 33535, 33536, 33542, 33545, 33548, 33600-33688, 33692, 33694, 33697, 33702, 33710, 33720, 33722, 33724, 33726, 33730, 33732, 33736, 33750, 33755, 33762, 33764, 33766, 33767, 33770-33783, 33786, 33788, 33802, 33803, 33814, 33820, 33822, 33824, 33840, 33845, 33851, 33853, 33860, 33863, 33864, 33870, 33875, 33877, 33880, 33881, 33883, 33884, 33886, 33910, 33916, 33917, 33920, 33922, 33926, 33935, 33945, 33975, 33976, 33977, 33978, 33979, 33980, 33983, 33990, 33991, 34701, 34702, 34703, 34704, 34705, 34706, 34707, 34708, 34841, 34842, 34843, 34844, 34845, 34846, 34847, 34848, 0254T)

(34714 may only be reported once per side. For bilateral procedure, report 34714 twice)

(Do not report 34714 in conjunction with 33362, 33953, 33954, 33959, 33962, 33969, 33984, 34812 when performed on the same side)

▲+**34820**   Open iliac artery exposure for delivery of endovascular prosthesis or iliac occlusion during endovascular therapy, by abdominal or retroperitoneal incision, unilateral (List separately in addition to code for primary procedure)

(Use 34820 in conjunction with 33880, 33881, 33883, 33884, 33886, 33990, 33991, 34701, 34702, 34703, 34704, 34705, 34706, 34707, 34708, 34841, 34842, 34843, 34844, 34845, 34846, 34847, 34848, 0254T)

(34820 may only be reported once per side. For bilateral procedure, report 34820 twice)

(Do not report 34820 in conjunction with 33953, 33954, 33959, 33962, 33969, 33984)

▲+**34833**   Open iliac artery exposure with creation of conduit for delivery of endovascular prosthesis or for establishment of cardiopulmonary bypass, by abdominal or retroperitoneal incision, unilateral (List separately in addition to code for primary procedure)

(Use 34833 in conjunction with 32852, 32854, 33031, 33120, 33251, 33256, 33259, 33261, 33305, 33315, 33322, 33335, 33390, 33391, 33404-33417, 33422, 33425, 33426, 33427, 33430, 33460, 33463, 33464, 33465, 33468, 33474, 33475, 33476, 33478, 33496, 33500, 33502, 33504, 33505, 33506, 33507, 33510, 33511, 33512, 33513, 33514, 33516, 33533, 33534, 33535, 33536, 33542, 33545, 33548, 33600-33688, 33692, 33694, 33697, 33702, 33710, 33720, 33722, 33724, 33726, 33730, 33732, 33736, 33750, 33755, 33762, 33764, 33766, 33767, 33770-33783, 33786, 33788, 33802, 33803, 33814, 33820, 33822, 33824, 33840, 33845, 33851, 33853, 33860, 33863, 33864, 33870, 33875, 33877, 33880, 33881, 33883, 33884, 33886, 33910, 33916, 33917, 33920, 33922, 33926, 33935, 33945, 33975, 33976, 33977, 33978, 33979, 33980, 33983, 33990, 33991, 34701, 34702, 34703, 34704, 34705, 34706, 34707, 34708, 34841, 34842, 34843, 34844, 34845, 34846, 34847, 34848, 0254T)

(34833 may only be reported once per side. For bilateral procedure, report 34833 twice)

(Do not report 34833 in conjunction with 33364, 33953, 33954, 33959, 33962, 33969, 33984, 34820 when performed on the same side)

▲+**34834**   Open brachial artery exposure for delivery of endovascular prosthesis, unilateral (List separately in addition to code for primary procedure)

(Use 34834 in conjunction with 33880, 33881, 33883, 33884, 33886, 33990, 33991, 34701, 34702, 34703, 34704, 34705, 34706, 34707, 34708, 34841, 34842, 34843, 34844, 34845, 34846, 34847, 34848, 0254T)

(34834 may only be reported once per side. For bilateral procedure, report 34834 twice)

(Do not report 34834 in conjunction with 33953, 33954, 33959, 33962, 33969, 33984)

●+**34715**   Open axillary/subclavian artery exposure for delivery of endovascular prosthesis by infraclavicular or supraclavicular incision, unilateral (List separately in addition to code for primary procedure)

■ Separate Procedure   ★ ■ Unlisted Procedure   ■ CCI Comp. Code   ■ Non-specific Procedure   **381**

(Use 34715 in conjunction with 33880, 33881, 33883, 33884, 33886, 33990, 33991, 34701, 34702, 34703, 34704, 34705, 34706, 34707, 34708, 34841, 34842, 34843, 34844, 34845, 34846, 34847, 34848, 0254T)

(34715 may only be reported once per side. For bilateral procedure, report 34715 twice)

(Do not report 34715 in conjunction with 33363, 33953, 33954, 33959, 33962, 33969, 33984, 0451T, 0452T, 0455T, 0456T)

●+34716   Open axillary/subclavian artery exposure with creation of conduit for delivery of endovascular prosthesis or for establishment of cardiopulmonary bypass, by infraclavicular or supraclavicular incision, unilateral (List separately in addition to code for primary procedure)

(Use 34716 in conjunction with 32852, 32854, 33031, 33120, 33251, 33256, 33259-33261, 33305, 33315, 33322, 33335, 33390, 33391, 33404-33417, 33422, 33425, 33426, 33427, 33430, 33460, 33463, 33464, 33465, 33468, 33474, 33475, 33476, 33478, 33496, 33500, 33502, 33504, 33505, 33506, 33507, 33510, 33511, 33512, 33513, 33514, 33516, 33533, 33534, 33535, 33536, 33542, 33545, 33548, 33600-33688, 33692, 33694, 33697, 33702-33722, 33724, 33726, 33730, 33732, 33736, 33750, 33755, 33762, 33764, 33766, 33767, 33770-33783, 33786, 33788, 33802, 33803, 33814, 33820, 33822, 33824, 33840, 33845, 33851, 33853, 33860, 33863, 33864, 33870, 33875, 33877, 33880, 33881, 33883, 33884, 33886, 33910, 33916, 33917, 33920, 33922, 33926, 33935, 33945, 33975, 33976, 33977, 33978, 33979, 33980, 33983, 33990, 33991, 34701, 34702, 34703, 34704, 34705, 34706, 34707, 34708, 34841, 34842, 34843, 34844, 34845, 34846, 34847, 34848, 0254T)

(34716 may only be reported once per side. For bilateral procedure, report 34716 twice)

(Do not report 34716 in conjunction with 33953, 33954, 33959, 33962, 33969, 33984, 0451T, 0452T, 0455T, 0456T)

(34800   deleted 2017 [2018 edition]. To report, see 34701, 34702, 34703, 34704, 34705, 34706, 34707, 34708)

(34802   deleted 2017 [2018 edition]. To report, see 34701, 34702, 34703, 34704, 34705, 34706, 34707, 34708)

(34803   deleted 2017 [2018 edition]. To report, see 34701, 34702, 34703, 34704, 34705, 34706, 34707, 34708)

(34804   deleted 2017 [2018 edition]. To report, see 34701, 34702, 34703, 34704, 34705, 34706, 34707, 34708)

(34805   deleted 2017 [2018 edition]. To report, see 34701, 34702, 34703, 34704, 34705, 34706, 34707, 34708)

(34806   deleted 2017 [2018 edition]. To report, see 34701, 34702, 34703, 34704, 34705, 34706, 34707, 34708)

+ 34808   Endovascular placement of iliac artery occlusion device (List separately in addition to code for primary procedure)

(Use 34808 in conjunction with 34701, 34702, 34707, 34708, 34709, 34710, 34813, 34841, 34842, 34843, 34844)

34812   This code is out of order. See page 380.

+ 34813   Placement of femoral-femoral prosthetic graft during endovascular aortic aneurysm repair (List separately in addition to code for primary procedure)

(Use 34813 in conjunction with code 34812)

(For femoral artery grafting, see 35521, 35533, 35539, 35540, 35556, 35558, 35566, 35621, 35646, 35654-35661, 35666, 35700)

34820   This code is out of order. See page 381.

(34825   deleted 2017 [2018 edition]. To report, see 34709, 34710, 34711)

(34826   deleted 2017 [2018 edition]. To report, see 34709, 34710, 34711)

34830   Open repair of infrarenal aortic aneurysm or dissection, plus repair of associated arterial trauma, following unsuccessful endovascular repair; tube prosthesis

● New Code   ▲ Revised Code   + Add-On Code   ⊘ Modifier -51 Exempt   ★ Telemedicine

| 34831 | aorto-bi-iliac prosthesis |
| 34832 | aorto-bifemoral prosthesis |

34833 This code is out of order. See page 381.

34834 This code is out of order. See page 381.

FFENESTRATED ENDOVASCULAR REPAIR OF THE VISCERAL AND INFRARENAL AORTA

The upper abdominal aorta that contains the celiac, superior mesenteric, and renal arteries is termed the visceral aorta. For reporting purposes, the thoracic aorta extends from the aortic valve to the aortic segment just proximal to the celiac artery.

Code 34839 is used to report the physician planning and sizing for a patient-specific fenestrated visceral aortic endograft. The planning includes review of high-resolution cross-sectional images (eg, CT, CTA, MRI) and utilization of 3D software for iterative modeling of the aorta and device in multiplanar views and center line of flow analysis. Code 34839 may only be reported when the physician spends a minimum of 90 total minutes performing patient-specific fenestrated endograft planning. Physician planning time does not need to be continuous and should be clearly documented in the patient record. Code 34839 is reported on the date that planning work is complete and may not include time spent on the day before or the day of the fenestrated endovascular repair procedure (34841, 34842, 34843, 34844, 34845, 34846, 34847, 34848) nor be reported on the day before or the day of the fenestrated endovascular repair procedure.

Codes 34841, 34842, 34843, 34844, 34845, 34846, 34847, 34848 are used to report placement of a fenestrated endovascular graft in the visceral aorta, either alone or in combination with the infrarenal aorta for aneurysm, pseudoaneurysm, dissection, penetrating ulcer, intramural hematoma, or traumatic disruption. The fenestrated main body endoprosthesis is deployed within the visceral aorta. Fenestrations within the fabric allow for selective catheterization of the visceral and/or renal arteries and subsequent placement of an endoprosthesis (ie, bare metal or covered stent) to maintain flow to the visceral artery. Patient variation in the location and relative orientation of the renal and visceral artery origins requires use of a patient-specific fenestrated endograft for endovascular repair that preserves flow to essential visceral arteries and allows proximal seal and fixation to be achieved above the renal level as well as in the distal aorta or iliac vessel(s).

Fenestrated aortic repair is reported based on the extent of aorta treated. Codes 34841, 34842, 34843, 34844 describe repair using proximal endoprostheses that span from the visceral aortic component to one, two, three, or four visceral artery origins and distal extent limited to the infrarenal aorta. These devices do not extend into the common iliac arteries. Codes 34845, 34846, 34847, 34848 are used to report deployment of a fenestrated endograft that spans from the visceral aorta (including one, two, three, or four visceral artery origins) through the infrarenal aorta into the common iliac arteries. The infrarenal component may be a bifurcated unibody device, a modular bifurcated docking system with docking limb(s), or an aorto-uniiliac device. Codes 34845, 34846, 34847, 34848 include placement of unilateral or bilateral docking limbs (depending on the device). Any additional endograft extensions that terminate in the common iliac arteries are included in 34845, 34846, 34847, 34848. Codes 34709, 34710, 34711 may not be separately reported for proximal abdominal aortic extension prosthesis(es) or for distal extension prosthesis(es) that terminate(s) in the aorta or the common iliac arteries. However, 34709, 34710, 34711 may be reported for distal extension prosthesis(es) that terminate(s) in the internal iliac, external iliac, or common femoral artery(ies).

Codes 34841-34844 and 34845-34848 define the total number of visceral and/or renal arteries (ie, celiac, superior mesenteric, and/or unilateral or bilateral renal artery(s)) requiring placement of an endoprosthesis (ie, bare metal or covered stent) through an aortic endograft fenestration.

Introduction of guide wires and catheters in the aorta and visceral and/or renal arteries is included in the work of 34841-34848 and is not separately reportable. However, catheterization of the hypogastric artery(s) and/or arterial families outside the treatment zone of the graft may be separately reported. Balloon angioplasty within the target treatment zone of the endograft, either before or after endograft deployment, is not separately reportable. Fluoroscopic guidance and radiological supervision and interpretation in conjunction with fenestrated endovascular aortic repair is not separately reportable and includes angiographic diagnostic imaging of the aorta and its branches prior to deployment of the fenestrated endovascular device, fluoroscopic guidance in the delivery of the fenestrated endovascular components, and intraprocedural arterial angiography (eg, confirm position, detect endoleak, evaluate runoff) done at the time of the endovascular aortic repair.

Exposure of the access vessels (eg, 34713, 34714, 34715, 34716, 34812, 34820, 34833, 34834) may be reported separately. Extensive repair of an artery (eg, 35226, 35286) may be reported separately. For concomitant endovascular treatment of the descending thoracic aorta, 33880-33886 and 75956-75959 may be reported with 34841, 34842, 34843, 34844, 34845, 34846, 34847, 34848. For isolated endovascular infrarenal abdominal aortic aneurysm repair that does not require placement of a fenestrated graft to preserve flow to the visceral branch(es), see 34701, 34702, 34703, 34704, 34705, 34706.

| ■ Separate Procedure | ■ Unlisted Procedure | ■ CCI Comp. Code | ■ Non-specific Procedure | **383** |

Other interventional procedures performed at the time of fenestrated endovascular abdominal aortic aneurysm repair may be reported separately (eg, arterial embolization, intravascular ultrasound, balloon angioplasty or stenting of native artery(s) outside the endoprosthesis target zone, when done before or after deployment of endoprosthesis).

34839 Physician planning of a patient-specific fenestrated visceral aortic endograft requiring a minimum of 90 minutes of physician time

(Do not report 34839 in conjunction with 76376, 76377)

(Do not report 34839 in conjunction with 34841, 34842, 34843, 34844, 34845, 34846, 34847, 34848 when performed on the day before or the day of the fenestrated endovascular repair procedure)

34841 Endovascular repair of visceral aorta (eg, aneurysm, pseudoaneurysm, dissection, penetrating ulcer, intramural hematoma, or traumatic disruption) by deployment of a fenestrated visceral aortic endograft and all associated radiological supervision and interpretation, including target zone angioplasty, when performed; including one visceral artery endoprosthesis (superior mesenteric, celiac or renal artery)

34842 including two visceral artery endoprostheses (superior mesenteric, celiac and/or renal artery[s])

34843 including three visceral artery endoprostheses (superior mesenteric, celiac and/or renal artery[s])

34844 including four or more visceral artery endoprostheses (superior mesenteric, celiac and/or renal artery[s])

(Do not report 34841, 34842, 34843, 34844 in conjunction with 34701, 34702, 34703, 34704, 34705, 34706, 34845, 34846, 34847, 34848)

(Do not report 34841, 34842, 34843, 34844 in conjunction with 34839 when planning services are performed on the day before or the day of the fenestrated endovascular repair procedure)

34845 Endovascular repair of visceral aorta and infrarenal abdominal aorta (eg, aneurysm, pseudoaneurysm, dissection, penetrating ulcer, intramural hematoma, or traumatic disruption) with a fenestrated visceral aortic endograft and concomitant unibody or modular infrarenal aortic endograft and all associated radiological supervision and interpretation, including target zone angioplasty, when performed; including one visceral artery endoprosthesis (superior mesenteric, celiac or renal artery)

34846 including two visceral artery endoprostheses (superior mesenteric, celiac and/or renal artery[s])

34847 including three visceral artery endoprostheses (superior mesenteric, celiac and/or renal artery[s])

34848 including four or more visceral artery endoprostheses (superior mesenteric, celiac and/or renal artery[s])

(Do not report 34845, 34846, 34847, 34848 in conjunction with 34701, 34702, 34703, 34704, 34705, 34706, 34841, 34842, 34843, 34844, 35081, 35102)b

(Do not report 34845, 34846, 34847, 34848 in conjunction with 34839 when planning services are performed on the day before or the day of the fenestrated endovascular repair procedure)

(Do not report 34841-34848 in conjunction with 37236, 37237 for bare metal or covered stents placed into visceral branches within the endoprosthesis target zone)

(For placement of distal extension prosthesis[es] terminating in the internal iliac, external iliac, or common femoral artery[s], see 34709, 34710, 34711, 0254T)

(Use 34845, 34846, 34847, 34848 in conjunction with 37220, 37221, 37222, 37223 only when 37220, 37221, 37222, 37223 are performed outside the target treatment zone of the endoprosthesis)

ENDOVASCULAR REPAIR OF ILIAC ANEURYSM

(**34900** deleted 2017 [2018 edition]. To report, see 34707, 34708)

● New Code   ▲ Revised Code   + Add-On Code   ⊘ Modifier -51 Exempt   ★ Telemedicine

DIRECT REPAIR OF ANEURYSM OR EXCISION (PARTIAL OR TOTAL) AND GRAFT INSERTION FOR ANEURYSM, PSEUDOANEURYSM, RUPTURED ANEURYSM, AND ASSOCIATED OCCLUSIVE DISEASE

Procedures 35001-35152 include preparation of artery for anastomosis including endarterectomy.

(For direct repairs associated with occlusive disease only, see 35201-35286)

(For intracranial aneurysm, see 61700 et seq)

(For endovascular repair of abdominal aortic and/or iliac artery aneurysm, see 34701-34716)

(For thoracic aortic aneurysm, see 33860-33875)

(For endovascular repair of descending thoracic aorta, involving coverage of left subclavian artery origin, use 33880)

35001 Direct repair of aneurysm, pseudoaneurysm, or excision (partial or total) and graft insertion, with or without patch graft; for aneurysm and associated occlusive disease, carotid, subclavian artery, by neck incision

35002 for ruptured aneurysm, carotid, subclavian artery, by neck incision

35005 for aneurysm, pseudoaneurysm, and associated occlusive disease, vertebral artery

35011 for aneurysm and associated occlusive disease, axillary-brachial artery, by arm incision

35013 for ruptured aneurysm, axillary-brachial artery, by arm incision

35021 for aneurysm, pseudoaneurysm, and associated occlusive disease, innominate, subclavian artery, by thoracic incision

35022 for ruptured aneurysm, innominate, subclavian artery, by thoracic incision

35045 for aneurysm, pseudoaneurysm, and associated occlusive disease, radial or ulnar artery

35081 for aneurysm, pseudoaneurysm, and associated occlusive disease, abdominal aorta

35082 for ruptured aneurysm, abdominal aorta

35091 for aneurysm, pseudoaneurysm, and associated occlusive disease, abdominal aorta involving visceral vessels (mesenteric, celiac, renal)

35092 for ruptured aneurysm, abdominal aorta involving visceral vessels (mesenteric, celiac, renal)

35102 for aneurysm, pseudoaneurysm, and associated occlusive disease, abdominal aorta involving iliac vessels (common, hypogastric, external)

35103 for ruptured aneurysm, abdominal aorta involving iliac vessels (common, hypogastric, external)

35111 for aneurysm, pseudoaneurysm, and associated occlusive disease, splenic artery

35112 for ruptured aneurysm, splenic artery

35121 for aneurysm, pseudoaneurysm, and associated occlusive disease, hepatic, celiac, renal, or mesenteric artery

35122 for ruptured aneurysm, hepatic, celiac, renal, or mesenteric artery

35131 for aneurysm, pseudoaneurysm, and associated occlusive disease, iliac artery (common, hypogastric, external)

35132 for ruptured aneurysm, iliac artery (common, hypogastric, external)

■ Separate Procedure   ■ Unlisted Procedure   ■ CCI Comp. Code   ■ Non-specific Procedure   **385**

35141	for aneurysm, pseudoaneurysm, and associated occlusive disease, common femoral artery (profunda femoris, superficial femoral)
35142	for ruptured aneurysm, common femoral artery (profunda femoris, superficial femoral)
35151	for aneurysm, pseudoaneurysm, and associated occlusive disease, popliteal artery
35152	for ruptured aneurysm, popliteal artery

REPAIR ARTERIOVENOUS FISTULA

35180	Repair, congenital arteriovenous fistula; head and neck
35182	thorax and abdomen
35184	extremities
35188	Repair, acquired or traumatic arteriovenous fistula; head and neck
35189	thorax and abdomen
35190	extremities

REPAIR BLOOD VESSEL OTHER THAN FOR FISTULA, WITH OR WITHOUT PATCH ANGIOPLASTY

(For AV fistula repair, see 35180-35190)

35201	Repair blood vessel, direct; neck

(Do not report 35201 in conjunction with 33969, 33984, 33985, 33986)

35206	upper extremity

(Do not report 35206 in conjunction with 33969, 33984, 33985, 33986)

35207	hand, finger
35211	intrathoracic, with bypass

(Do not report 35211 in conjunction with 33969, 33984, 33985, 33986)

35216	intrathoracic, without bypass

(Do not report 35216 in conjunction with 33969, 33984, 33985, 33986)

35221	intra-abdominal
35226	lower extremity

(Do not report 35226 in conjunction with 33969, 33984, 33985, 33986)

35231	Repair blood vessel with vein graft; neck
35236	upper extremity
35241	intrathoracic, with bypass
35246	intrathoracic, without bypass
35251	intra-abdominal
35256	lower extremity

● New Code   ▲ Revised Code   ＋ Add-On Code   ⊘ Modifier -51 Exempt   ★ Telemedicine

35261	Repair blood vessel with graft other than vein; neck
35266	upper extremity
35271	intrathoracic, with bypass
35276	intrathoracic, without bypass
35281	intra-abdominal
35286	lower extremity

THROMBOENDARTERECTOMY

(For coronary artery, see 33510-33536 and 33572)

(35301-35372 include harvest of saphenous or upper extremity vein when performed)

35301	Thromboendarterectomy, including patch graft, if performed; carotid, vertebral, subclavian, by neck incision
35302	superficial femoral artery
35303	popliteal artery

(Do not report 35302, 35303 in conjunction with 37225, 37227 when performed in the same vessel)

35304	tibioperoneal trunk artery
35305	tibial or peroneal artery, initial vessel
+ 35306	each additional tibial or peroneal artery (List separately in addition to code for primary procedure)

(Use 35306 in conjunction with 35305)

(Do not report 35304, 35305, 35306 in conjunction with 37229, 37231, 37233, 37235 when performed in the same vessel)

35311	subclavian, innominate, by thoracic incision
35321	axillary-brachial
35331	abdominal aorta
35341	mesenteric, celiac, or renal
35351	iliac
35355	iliofemoral
35361	combined aortoiliac
35363	combined aortoiliofemoral
35371	common femoral
35372	deep (profunda) femoral
+ 35390	Reoperation, carotid, thromboendarterectomy, more than 1 month after original operation (List separately in addition to code for primary procedure)

(Use 35390 in conjunction with code 35301)

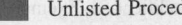

| Separate Procedure | Unlisted Procedure | CCI Comp. Code | Non-specific Procedure | **387** |

ANGIOSCOPY

+ **35400** Angioscopy (non-coronary vessels or grafts) during therapeutic intervention (List separately in addition to code for primary procedure)

TRANSLUMINAL ANGIOPLASTY

Open

(**35450** deleted 2016 [2017 edition]. To report, see 36902, 36905, 36907, 37246, 37247, 37248, 37249)

(**35452** deleted 2016 [2017 edition]. To report, see 36902, 36905, 36907, 37246, 37247, 37248, 37249)

(**35458** deleted 2016 [2017 edition]. To report, see 36902, 36905, 36907, 37246, 37247, 37248, 37249)

(**35460** deleted 2016 [2017 edition]. To report, see 36902, 36905, 36907, 37246, 37247, 37248, 37249)

Percutaneous

(**35471** deleted 2016 [2017 edition]. To report, see 36902, 36905, 36907, 37246, 37247, 37248, 37249)

(**35472** deleted 2016 [2017 edition]. To report, see 36902, 36905, 36907, 37246, 37247, 37248, 37249)

(**35475** deleted 2016 [2017 edition]. To report, see 36902, 36905, 36907, 37246, 37247, 37248, 37249)

(**35476** deleted 2016 [2017 edition]. To report, see 36902, 36905, 36907, 37246, 37247, 37248, 37249)

BYPASS GRAFT

Peripheral vascular bypass CPT codes describe bypass procedures using venous grafts (CPT codes 35500-35587) and using other types of bypass procedures (arterial reconstruction, composite). Because, at a given site of obstruction, only one type of bypass is performed, these groups of codes are mutually exclusive. When different sites are treated with different bypass procedures in the same operative session, the different bypass procedures may be separately reported, using an anatomic modifier or modifier -59.

Procurement of the saphenous vein graft is included in the description of the work for 35501-35587 and should not be reported as a separate service or co-surgery. To report harvesting of an upper extremity vein, use 35500 in addition to the bypass procedure. To report harvesting of a femoropopliteal vein segment, use 35572 in addition to the bypass procedure. To report harvesting and construction of an autogenous composite graft of two segments from two distant locations, report 35682 in addition to the bypass procedure, for autogenous composite of three or more segments from distant sites, report 35683.

Vein

+ **35500** Harvest of upper extremity vein, 1 segment, for lower extremity or coronary artery bypass procedure (List separately in addition to code for primary procedure)

(Use 35500 in conjunction with 33510-33536, 35556, 35566, 35570, 35571, 35583-35587)

(For harvest of more than one vein segment, see 35682, 35683)

(For endoscopic procedure, use 33508)

35501 Bypass graft, with vein; common carotid-ipsilateral internal carotid

35506 carotid-subclavian or subclavian-carotid

35508 carotid-vertebral

35509 carotid-contralateral carotid

35510 carotid-brachial

35511 subclavian-subclavian

● New Code   ▲ Revised Code   **+** Add-On Code   ⊘ Modifier -51 Exempt   ★ Telemedicine

35512	subclavian-brachial
35515	subclavian-vertebral
35516	subclavian-axillary
35518	axillary-axillary
35521	axillary-femoral

(For bypass graft performed with synthetic graft, use 35621)

35522	axillary-brachial
35523	brachial-ulnar or -radial

(Do not report 35523 in conjunction with 35206, 35500, 35525, 36838)

(For bypass graft performed with synthetic conduit, use 37799)

35525	brachial-brachial
35526	aortosubclavian, aortoinnominate, or aortocarotid

(For bypass graft performed with synthetic graft, use 35626)

35531	aortoceliac or aortomesenteric
35533	axillary-femoral-femoral

(For bypass graft performed with synthetic graft, use 35654)

35535	hepatorenal

(Do not report 35535 in conjunction with 35221, 35251, 35281, 35500, 35536, 35560, 35631, 35636)

35536	splenorenal
35537	aortoiliac

(For bypass graft performed with synthetic graft, use 35637)

(Do not report 35537 in conjunction with 35538)

35538	aortobi-iliac

(For bypass graft performed with synthetic graft, use 35638)

(Do not report 35538 in conjunction with 35537)

35539	aortofemoral

(For bypass graft performed with synthetic graft, use 35647)

(Do not report 35539 in conjunction with 35540)

35540	aortobifemoral

(For bypass graft performed with synthetic graft, use 35646)

(Do not report 35540 in conjunction with 35539)

35556	femoral-popliteal

	Separate Procedure		Unlisted Procedure		CCI Comp. Code		Non-specific Procedure	**389**

35558	femoral-femoral
35560	aortorenal
35563	ilioiliac
35565	iliofemoral
35566	femoral-anterior tibial, posterior tibial, peroneal artery or other distal vessels
35570	tibial-tibial, peroneal-tibial, or tibial/peroneal trunk-tibial

(Do not report 35570 in conjunction with 35256, 35286)

| 35571 | popliteal-tibial, -peroneal artery or other distal vessels |

+ 35572 Harvest of femoropopliteal vein, 1 segment, for vascular reconstruction procedure (eg, aortic, vena caval, coronary, peripheral artery) (List separately in addition to code for primary procedure)

(Use 35572 in conjunction with codes 33510-33516, 33517-33523, 33533-33536, 34502, 34520, 35001, 35002, 35011-35022, 35102, 35103, 35121-35152, 35231-35256, 35501-35587, 35879-35907)

(For bilateral procedure, use modifier '-50')

In-Situ Vein

(To report aortobifemoral bypass using synthetic conduit, and femoral-popliteal bypass with vein conduit in situ, use 35646 and 35583. To report aorto(uni)femoral bypass with synthetic conduit, and femoral-popliteal bypass with vein conduit in-situ, use 35647 and 35583. To report aortofemoral bypass using vein conduit, and femoral-popliteal bypass with vein conduit in situ, use 35539 and 35583)

35583	In-situ vein bypass; femoral-popliteal
35585	femoral-anterior tibial, posterior tibial, or peroneal artery
35587	popliteal-tibial, peroneal

Other Than Vein

(For aterial transposition and/or reimplantation, see 35691-35695)

+ 35600 Harvest of upper extremity artery, 1 segment, for coronary artery bypass procedure (List separately in addition to code for primary procedure)

(Use 35600 in conjunction with 33533-33536)

| 35601 | Bypass graft, with other than vein; common carotid-ipsilateral internal carotid |
| 35606 | carotid-subclavian |

(For open transcervical common carotid-common carotid bypass performed in conjunction with endovascular repair of descending thoracic aorta, use 33891)

(For open subclavian to carotid artery transposition performed in conjunction with endovascular thoracic aneurysm repair by neck incision, use 33889)

35612	subclavian-subclavian
35616	subclavian-axillary
35621	axillary-femoral
35623	axillary-popliteal or -tibial

● New Code   ▲ Revised Code   + Add-On Code   ⊘ Modifier -51 Exempt   ★ Telemedicine

35626   aortosubclavian, aortoinnominate, or aortocarotid

35631   aortoceliac, aortomesenteric, aortorenal

35632   ilio-celiac

(Do not report 35632 in conjunction with 35221, 35251, 35281, 35531, 35631)

35633   ilio-mesenteric

(Do not report 35633 in conjunction with 35221, 35251, 35281, 35531, 35631)

35634   iliorenal

(Do not report 35634 in conjunction with 35221, 35251, 35281, 35560, 35536, 35631)

35636   splenorenal (splenic to renal arterial anastomosis)

35637   aortoiliac

(Do not report 35637 in conjunction with 35638, 35646)

35638   aortobi-iliac

(Do not report 35638 in conjunction with 35637, 35646)

(For open placement of aorto-bi-iliac prosthesis following unsuccessful endovascular repair, use 34831)

35642   carotid-vertebral

35645   subclavian-vertebral

35646   aortobifemoral

(For bypass graft performed with vein graft, use 35540)

(For open placement of aortobifemoral prosthesis following unsuccessful endovascular repair, use 34832)

35647   aortofemoral

(For bypass graft performed with vein graft, use 35539)

35650   axillary-axillary

35654   axillary-femoral-femoral

35656   femoral-popliteal

35661   femoral-femoral

35663   ilioiliac

35665   iliofemoral

35666   femoral-anterior tibial, posterior tibial, or peroneal artery

35671   popliteal-tibial or -peroneal artery

| Separate Procedure | Unlisted Procedure | CCI Comp. Code | Non-specific Procedure | **391** |

COMPOSITE GRAFTS

Codes 35682, 35683 are used to report harvest and anastomosis of multiple vein segments from distant sites for use as arterial bypass graft conduits. These codes are intended for use when the two or more vein segments are harvested from a limb other than that undergoing bypass.

+ **35681** Bypass graft; composite, prosthetic and vein (List separately in addition to code for primary procedure)

(Do not report 35681 in addition to 35682, 35683)

+ **35682** autogenous composite, 2 segments of veins from 2 locations (List separately in addition to code for primary procedure)

(Use 35682 in conjunction with 35556, 35566, 35570, 35571, 35583-35587)

(Do not report 35682 in addition to 35681, 35683)

+ **35683** autogenous composite, 3 or more segments of vein from 2 or more locations (List separately in addition to code for primary procedure)

(Use 35683 in conjunction with 35556, 35566, 35570, 35571, 35583-35587)

(Do not report 35683 in addition to 35681, 35682)

ADJUVANT TECHNIQUES

Adjuvant (additional) technique(s) may be required at the time a bypass graft is created to improve patency of the lower extremity autogenous or synthetic bypass graft (eg., femoral-popliteal, femoral-tibial, or popliteal-tibial arteries). Code 35685 should be reported in addition to the primary synthetic bypass graft procedure, when an interposition of venous tissue (vein patch or cuff) is placed at the anastomosis between the synthetic bypass conduit and the involved artery (includes harvest).

Code 35686 should be reported in addition to the primary bypass graft procedure, when autogenous vein is used to create a fistula between the tibial or peroneal artery and vein at or beyond the distal bypass anastomosis site of the involved artery.

(For composite graft(s), see 35681-35683)

+ **35685** Placement of vein patch or cuff at distal anastomosis of bypass graft, synthetic conduit (List separately in addition to code for primary procedure)

(Use 35685 in conjunction with codes 35656, 35666 or 35671)

+ **35686** Creation of distal arteriovenous fistula during lower extremity bypass surgery (non-hemodialysis) (List separately in addition to code for primary procedure)

(Use 35686 in conjunction with 35556, 35566, 35570, 35571, 35583-35587, 35623, 35656, 35666, 35671)

ARTERIAL TRANSPOSITION

35691 Transposition and/or reimplantation; vertebral to carotid artery

35693 vertebral to subclavian artery

35694 subclavian to carotid artery

(For open subclavian to carotid artery transposition performed in conjunction with endovascular repair of descending thoracic aorta, use 33889)

35695 carotid to subclavian artery

+ **35697** Reimplantation, visceral artery to infrarenal aortic prosthesis, each artery (List separately in addition to code for primary procedure)

(Do not report 35697 in conjunction with 33877)

● New Code   ▲ Revised Code   + Add-On Code   ⊘ Modifier -51 Exempt   ★ Telemedicine

EXCISION, EXPLORATION, REPAIR, REVISION

+ 35700   Reoperation, femoral-popliteal or femoral (popliteal)-anterior tibial, posterior tibial, peroneal artery or other distal vessels, more than 1 month after original operation (List separately in addition to code for primary procedure)

     (Use 35700 in conjunction with codes 35556, 35566, 35570, 35571, 35583, 35585, 35587, 35656, 35666, 35671)

35701   Exploration (not followed by surgical repair), with or without lysis of artery; carotid artery

35721   femoral artery

35741   popliteal artery

35761   other vessels

35800   Exploration for postoperative hemorrhage, thrombosis or infection; neck

35820   chest

35840   abdomen

35860   extremity

35870   Repair of graft-enteric fistula

35875   Thrombectomy of arterial or venous graft (other than hemodialysis graft or fistula);

35876   with revision of arterial or venous graft

     (For thrombectomy of hemodialysis graft or fistula, see 36831, 36833)

Codes 35879 and 35881 describe open revision of graft-threatening stenoses of lower extremity arterial bypass graft(s) (previously constructed with autogenous vein conduit) using vein patch angioplasty or segmental vein interposition techniques. For thrombectomy with revision of any non-coronary arterial or venous graft, including those of the lower extremity, (other than hemodialysis graft or fistula), use 35876. For direct repair (other than for fistula) of a lower extremity blood vessel (with or without patch angioplasty), use 35226. For repair (other than for fistula) of a lower extremity blood vessel using a vein graft, use 35256.

35879   Revision, lower extremity arterial bypass, without thrombectomy, open; with vein patch angioplasty

35881   with segmental vein interposition

     (For revision or femoral anastomosis of sythetic arterial bypass graft, see 35883, 35884)

     (For excision of infected graft, see 35901-35907 and appropriate revascularization code)

35883   Revision, femoral anastomosis of synthetic arterial bypass graft in groin, open; with nonautogenous patch graft (eg, Dacron, ePTFE, bovine pericardium)

     (For bilateral procedure, use modifier 50)

     (Do not report 35883 in conjunction with 35700, 35875, 35876, 35884)

35884   with autogenous vein patch graft

     (For bilateral procedure, use modifier -50)

     (Do not report 35884 in conjunction with 35700, 35875, 35876, 35883)

35901   Excision of infected graft; neck

Separate Procedure   Unlisted Procedure   CCI Comp. Code   Non-specific Procedure   **393**

35903	extremity
35905	thorax
35907	abdomen

VASCULAR INJECTION PROCEDURES

Listed services for injection procedures include necessary local anesthesia, introduction of needles or catheter, injection of contrast media with or without automatic power injection, and/or necessary pre- and post-injection care specifically related to the injection procedure.

Catheters, drugs, and contrast media are not included in the listed service for the injection procedures.

Selective vascular catheterization should be coded to include introduction and all lesser order selective catheterization used in the approach (eg., the description for a selective right middle cerebral artery catheterization includes the introduction and placement catheterization of the right common and internal carotid arteries).

Additional second and/or third order arterial catheterization within the same family of arteries or veins supplied by a single first order vessel should be expressed by 36012, 36218, or 36248.

Additional first order or higher catheterization in vascular families supplied by a first order vessel different from a previously selected and coded family should be separately coded using the conventions described above.

(For radiological supervision and interpretation, see RADIOLOGY)

(For injection procedures in conjunction with cardiac catheterization, see 93452-93461, 93563-93568)

(For chemotherapy of malignant disease, see 96400-96549)

Intravenous

| 36000 | Introduction of needle or intracatheter, vein |

| 36002 | Injection procedures (eg, thrombin) for percutaneous treatment of extremity pseudoaneurysm |

(For imaging guidance, see 76942, 77002, 77012, 77021)

(For ultrasound guided compression repair of pseudoaneurysms, use 76936)

(Do not report 36002 for vascular sealant of an arteriotomy site)

| 36005 | Injection procedure for extremity venography (including introduction of needle or intracatheter) |

(For radiological supervision and interpretation, see 75820, 75822)

| 36010 | Introduction of catheter, superior or inferior vena cava |

| 36011 | Selective catheter placement, venous system; first order branch (eg, renal vein, jugular vein) |

| 36012 | second order, or more selective, branch (eg, left adrenal vein, petrosal sinus) |

| 36013 | Introduction of catheter, right heart or main pulmonary artery |

| 36014 | Selective catheter placement, left or right pulmonary artery |

| 36015 | Selective catheter placement, segmental or subsegmental pulmonary artery |

(For insertion of flow directed catheter (eg, Swan-Ganz), use 93503)

(For venous catheterization for selective organ blood sampling, use 36500)

● New Code   ▲ Revised Code   + Add-On Code   ⊘ Modifier -51 Exempt   ★ Telemedicine

Intra-Arterial/Intra-Aortic

> (For radiological supervision and interpretation, see RADIOLOGY)

36100 Introduction of needle or intracatheter, carotid or vertebral artery

> (For bilateral procedure, report 36100 with modifier -50)

(**36120** deleted 2017 [2018 edition])

▲ **36140** Introduction of needle or intracatheter, upper or lower extremity artery

> (For insertion of arteriovenous cannula, see 36810-36821)

(**36147** deleted 2016 [2017 edition]. To report, see 36901, 36902, 36903, 36904, 36905, 36906)

(**36148** deleted 2016 [2017 edition]. To report, see 36901, 36902, 36903, 36904, 36905, 36906)

36160 Introduction of needle or intracatheter, aortic, translumbar

Diagnostic Studies of Cervicocerebral Arteries

Codes 36221-36228 describe non-selective and selective arterial catheter placement and diagnostic imaging of the aortic arch, carotid, and vertebral arterial. Codes 36221-36226 include the work of accessing the vessel, placement of catheter(s), contrast injection(s), fluoroscopy, radiological supervision and interpretation, and closure of the arteriotomy by pressure, or application of an arterial closure device. Codes 36221-36228 describe arterial contrast injections with arterial, capillary, and venous phase imaging, when performed.

Code 36227 is an add-on code to report unilateral selective arterial catheter placement and diagnostic imaging of the ipsilateral external carotid circulation and includes all the work of accessing the additional vessel, placement of catheter(s), contrast injection(s), fluoroscopy, radiological supervision and interpretation. Code 36227 is reported in conjunction with 36222, 36223, or 36224.

Code 36228 is an add-on code to report unilateral selective arterial catheter placement and diagnostic imaging of the initial and each additional intracranial branch of the internal carotid or vertebral arteries. Code 36228 is reported in conjunction with 36223, 36224, 36225 or 36226. This includes any additional second or third order catheter selective placement in the same primary branch of the internal carotid, vertebral, or basilar artery and includes all the work of accessing the additional vessel, placement of catheter(s), contrast injection(s), fluoroscopy, radiological supervision and interpretation. It is not reported more than twice per side regardless of the number of additional branches selectively catheterized.

Codes 36221-36226 are built on progressive hierarchies with more intensive services inclusive of less intensive services. The code inclusive of all the services provided for that vessel should be reported (ie, use the code inclusive of the most intensive services provided). Only one code in the range 36222-36224 may be reported for each ipsilateral carotid territory. Only one code in the range 36225-36226 may be reported for each ipsilateral vertebral territory.

Code 36221 is reported for non-selective arterial catheter placement in the thoracic aorta and diagnostic imaging of the aortic arch and great vessel origins. Codes 36222-36228 are reported for unilateral artery catheterization. Do not report 36221 in conjunction with 36222-36226 as these selective codes include the work of 36221 when performed.

Do not report 36222, 36223, or 36224 together for ipsilateral angiography. Instead, select the code that represents the most comprehensive service using the following hierarchy of complexity (listed in descending order of complexity): 36224>36223>36222.

Do not report 36225 and 36226 together for ipsilateral angiography. Select the code that represents the more comprehensive service using the following hierarchy of complexity (listed in descending order of complexity): 36226>36225.

When bilateral carotid and/or vertebral arterial catheterization and imaging is performed, add modifier 50 to codes 36222-36228 if the same procedure is performed on both sides. For example, bilateral extracranial carotid angiography with selective catheterization of each common carotid artery would be reported with 36222 and modifier 50. However, when different territory(ies) is studied in the same session on both sides of the body, modifiers may be required to report the imaging performed. use modifier 59 to denote that different carotid and/or vertebral arteries are being studied. For example, when selective right internal carotid artery catheterization accompanied by right extracranial and intracranial carotid angiography is followed by

---

selective left common carotid artery catheterization with left extracranial carotid angiography, use 36224 to report the right side and 36222-59 to report the left side.

Diagnostic angiography of the cervicocerebral vessels may be followed by an interventional procedure at the same session. Interventional procedure may be separately reportable using standard coding conventions.

Do not report 36218 or 75774 as part of diagnostic angiography of the extracranial and intracranial cervicocerebral vessels. It may be appropriate to report 36218 or 75774 for diagnostic angiography of upper extremities and other vascular beds of the neck and/or shoulder girdle performed in the same session as vertibral angiography (eg, workup of a neck tumor that requires catheterization and angiography of the vertebral artery as well as other brachiocephalic arteries).

Report 76376 or 76377 for 3D rendering when performed in conjunction with 36221-36228.

Report 76937 for ultrasound guidance for vascular access, when performed in conjunction with 36221-36228.

36200 Introduction of catheter, aorta

(For non-selective angiography of the extracranial carotid and/or cerebral vessels adn cervicocerebral arch, when performed, use 36221)

36215 Selective catheter placement, arterial system; each first order thoracic or brachiocephalic branch, within a vascular family

(For catheter placement for coronary angiography, see 93454-93961)

36216 initial second order thoracic or brachiocephalic branch, within a vascular family

36217 initial third order or more selective thoracic or brachiocephalic branch, within a vascular family

+ 36218 additional second order, third order, and beyond, thoracic or brachiocephalic branch, within a vascular family (List in addition to code for initial second or third order vessel as appropriate)

(Use 36218 in conjunction with 36216, 36217, 36225, 36226)

(For angiography, see 36222-36228, 75600-75774)

(For transluminal balloon angioplasty [except lower extremity artery[ies] for occlusive disease, intracranial, coronary, pulmonary, or dialysis circuit], see 37246, 37247)

(For transcatheter therapies, see 37200, 37211, 37213, 37214, 37236, 37237, 37238, 37239, 37241, 37242, 37243, 37244, 61624, 61626)

(When coronary artery, arterial conduit [eg., internal mammary, inferior epigastric or free radical artery] or venous bypass graft angiography is performed in conjunction with cardiac catheterization, see the appropriate cardiac catheterization, injection procedure, and imaging supervision code(s) [93455, 93457, 93459, 93461, 93530-93533, 93564] in the **Medicine** section of CPT. When internal mammary artery angiography only is performed without a concomitant cardiac catheterization, use 36216 or 36217 as appropriate.)

36221 Non-selective catheter placement, thoracic aorta, with angiography of the extracranial carotid, vertebral, and/or intracranial vessels, unilateral or bilateral, and all associated radiological supervision and interpretation, includes angiography of the cervicocerebral arch, when performed

(Do not report 36221 with 36222-36226)

36222 Selective catheter placement, common carotid or innominate artery, unilateral, any approach, with angiography of the ipsilateral extracranial carotid circulation and all associated radiological supervision and interpretation, includes angiography of the cervicocerebral arch, when performed

(Do not report 36222 in conjunction with 37215, 37216, 37218 for the treated carotic artery)

36223 Selective catheter placement, common carotid or innominate artery, unilateral, any approach, with angiography of the ipsilateral intracranial carotid circulation and all associated radiological supervision and interpretation, includes angiography of the extracranial carotid and cervicocerebral arch, when performed

(Do not report 36223 in conjunction with 37215, 37216, 37218 for the treated carotic artery)

36224 Selective catheter placement, internal carotid artery, unilateral, with angiography of the ipsilateral intracranial carotid circulation and all associated radiological supervision and interpretation, includes angiography of the extracranial carotid and cervicocerebral arch, when performed

(Do not report 36224 in conjunction with 37215, 37216, 37218 for the treated carotic artery)

36225 Selective catheter placement, subclavian or innominate artery, unilateal with angiography of the ipsilateral vertebral circulation and allassociated radiological supervision and interpretation, includes angiography of the cervicocerebral arch, when performed

36226 Selective catheter placement, vertebral artery, unilateral, with angiography of the ipsilateral vertebral circulation and all associated radiological supervision and interpretation, includes angiography of the cervicocerebral arch, when performed

+ 36227 Selective catheter placement, external carotid artery, unilateral, with angiography of the ipsilateral external carotid circulation and all associated radiological supervision and interpretation (List separately in addition to code for primary procedure)

(Use 36227 in conjunction with 36222, 36223 or 36224)

(Do not report 36221-36227 in conjunction with 37217 for ipsilateral services)

+ 36228 Selective catheter placement, each intracranial branch of the internal carotid or vertebral arteries, unilateral, with angiography of the selected vessel circulation and all associated radiological supervision adn interpretation (eg, middle cerebral artery, posterior inferior cerebellar artery) (List separately in addition to code for primary procedure)

(Use 36228 in conjunction with 36223, 36224, 36225 or 36226)

(Do not report 36228 more than twice per side)

36245 Selective catheter placement, arterial system; each first order abdominal, pelvic, or lower extremity artery branch, within a vascular family

36246 initial second order abdominal, pelvic, or lower extremity artery branch, within a vascular family

36247 initial third order or more selective abdominal, pelvic, or lower extremity artery branch, within a vascular family

+ 36248 additional second order, third order, and beyond, abdominal, pelvic, or lower extremity artery branch, within a vascular family (List in addition to code for initial second or third order vessel as appropriate)

(Use 36248 in conjunction with codes 36246, 36247)

36251 Selective catheter placement (first-order), main renal artery and any accessory renal artery(s) for renal angiography, including arterial puncture and catheter placement(s), fluoroscopy, contrast injection(s), image postprocessing, permanent recording of images, and radiological supervision and interpretation, including pressure gradient measurements when performed, and flush aortogram when performed; unilateral

36252 bilateral

36253 Superselective catheter placement (one or more second order or higher renal artery branches) renal artery and any accessory renal artery(s) for renal angiography, including arterial puncture, catheterization, fluoroscopy, contrast injection(s), image postprocessing, permanent recording of images, and radiological supervision and interpretation, including pressure gradient measurements when performed, and flush aortogram when performed; unilateral

(Do not report 36253 in conjunction with 36251 when performed for the same kidney)

36254 bilateral

Separate Procedure   Unlisted Procedure   CCI Comp. Code   Non-specific Procedure   **397**

(Do not report 36254 in conjunction with 36252)

(Placement of closure device at the vascular access site is not separately reported with 36251-36254)

(Do not report 36251, 36252, 36253, 36254 in conjunction with 0338T, 0339T)

36260 Insertion of implantable intra-arterial infusion pump (eg, for chemotherapy of liver)

36261 Revision of implanted intra-arterial infusion pump

36262 Removal of implanted intra-arterial infusion pump

36299 Unlisted procedure, vascular injection

Venous

Venipuncture, needle or catheter for diagnostic study or intravenous therapy, percutaneous. These codes are also used to report the therapy as specified. For collection of a specimen from an established catheter, use 36592. For collection of a specimen from a completely implantable venous access device, use 36591.

36400 Venipuncture, younger than age 3 years, necessitating the skill of a physician or other qualified health care professional, not to be used for routine venipuncture; femoral or jugular vein

36405   scalp vein

36406   other vein

36410 Venipuncture, age 3 years or older, necessitating the skill of a physician or other qualified health care professional (separate procedure), for diagnostic or therapeutic purposes (not to be used for routine venipuncture)

36415 Collection of venous blood by venipuncture

(Do not report modifier 63 in conjunction with 36415)

36416 Collection of capillary blood specimen (eg, finger, heel, ear stick)

36420 Venipuncture, cutdown; under age 1 year

(Do not report modifier 63 in conjunction with 36420)

36425   age 1 or over

(Do not report 36425 in conjunction with 36475, 36476, 36478)

36430 Transfusion, blood or blood components

(When a partial exchange transfusion is performed in a newborn, use 36456)

36440 Push transfusion, blood, 2 years or under

(When a partial exchange transfusion is performed in a newborn, use 36456)

36450 Exchange transfusion, blood; newborn

(When a partial exchange transfusion is performed in a newborn, use 36456)

(Do not report modifier 63 in conjunction with 36450)

36455   other than newborn

36456 Partial exchange transfusion, blood, plasma or crystalloid necessitating the skill of a physician or other qualified health care professional, newborn

  ● New Code   ▲ Revised Code   + Add-On Code   ⊘ Modifier -51 Exempt   ★ Telemedicine

(Do not report 36456 in conjunction with 36430, 36440, 36450)

(Do not report modifier 63 in conjunction with 36456)

36460 Transfusion, intrauterine, fetal

(Do not report modifier 63 in conjunction with 36460)

(For radiological supervision and interpretation, use 76941)

Codes 36468, 36470, 36471 describe injection(s) of a sclerosant for sclerotherapy of telangiectasia and/or incompetent vein(s). Code 36468 may only be reported once per extremity per session, regardless of the number of needle injections performed. Codes 36466, 36471 may only be reported once per extremity, regardless of the number of veins treated. Ultrasound guidance (76942), when performed, is not included in 36468, 36470, 36471 and may be reported separately.

Codes 36465, 36466 describe injection(s) of a noncompounded foam sclerosant into an extremity truncal vein (eg, great saphenous vein, accessory saphenous vein) using ultrasound-guided compression of the junction of the central vein (saphenofemoral junction or saphenopopliteal junction) to limit the dispersion of injectate. Do not report 36465, 36466 for injection of compounded foam sclerosant(s).

Compounding is a practice in which a qualified health care professional (eg, pharmacist, physician) combines, mixes, or alters ingredients of a drug to create a medication tailored to the needs of an individual patient.

When performed in the office setting, all required supplies and equipment are included in 36465, 36466, 36468, 36470, 36471 and may not be separately reported. In addition, application of compression dressing(s) (eg, compression bandages/stockings) is included in 36465, 36466, 36468, 36470, 36471, when performed, and may not be reported separately.

36465 This code is out of order. See page 399.

36466 This code is out of order. See page 399.

▲ **36468** Injection(s) of sclerosant for spider veins (telangiectasia), limb or trunk

(For ultrasound imaging guidance performed in conjunction with 36468, use 76942)

(Do not report 36468 in conjunction with 29581)

(Do not report 36468 more than once per extremity)

(Do not report 36468 in conjunction with 37241 in the same surgical field)

(**36469** deleted 2014 [2015 edition])

▲ **36470** Injection of sclerosant; single incompetent vein (other than telangiectasia)

▲ **36471** multiple incompetent veins (other than telangiectasia), same leg

(For ultrasound imaging guidance performed in conjunction with 36470, 36471, use 76942)

(Do not report 36470, 36471 in conjunction with 29581)

(Do not report 36471 more than once per extremity)

(If the targeted vein is an extremity truncal vein and injection of non-compounded foam sclerosant with ultrasound guided compression maneuvers to guide dispersion of the injectate is performed, see 36465, 36466)

(Do not report 36470, 36471 in conjunction with 37241 in the same surgical field)

● **36465** Injection of non-compounded foam sclerosant with ultrasound compression maneuvers to guide dispersion of the injectate, inclusive of all imaging guidance and monitoring; single incompetent extremity truncal vein (eg, great saphenous vein, accessory saphenous vein)

● **36466** multiple incompetent truncal veins (eg, great saphenous vein, accessory saphenous vein), same leg

(Do not report 36465, 36466 in conjunction with 29581)

Separate Procedure   Unlisted Procedure   CCI Comp. Code   Non-specific Procedure   **399**

(Do not report 36465, 36466 in conjunction with 37241 in the same surgical field)

(For extremity truncal vein injection of compounded foam sclerosant[s], see 36470, 36471)

(For injection of a sclerosant into an incompetent vein without compression maneuvers to guide dispersion of the injectate, see 36470, 36471)

(For endovenous ablation therapy of incompetent vein[s] by transcatheter delivery of a chemical adhesive, see 36482, 36483)

(For vascular embolization and occlusion procedures, see 37241, 37242, 37243, 37244)

Codes 36473, 36474, 36475, 36476, 36478, 36479, 36482, 36483 describe endovascular ablation therapy of incompetent extremity vein(s), including all necessary imaging guidance and monitoring. Sclerosant injection(s) of vein(s) by needle or mini-catheter (36468, 36470, 36471) followed by a compression technique is not endovascular ablation therapy. Codes 36473, 36474, 36482, 36483 can be performed under local anesthesia without the need for tumescent (peri-saphenous) anesthesia. Codes 36475, 36476, 36478, 36479 are performed using adjunctive tumescent anesthesia.

Codes 36473, 36474 involve concomitant use of an intraluminal device that mechanically disrupts/abrades the venous intima and infusion of a physician-specified medication in the target vein(s).

Codes 36482, 36483 involve positioning an intravenous catheter the length of an incompetent vein, remote from the percutaneous access site, with subsequent delivery of a chemical adhesive to ablate the incompetent vein. This often includes ultrasound compression of the outflow vein to limit the dispersion of the injected solution.

Codes 36475, 36476 involve advancing a radiofrequency device the length of an incompetent vein, with subsequent delivery of radiofrequency energy to ablate the incompetent vein.

Codes 36478, 36479 involve advancing a laser device the length of an incompetent vein, with subsequent delivery of thermal energy to ablate the incompetent vein.

Codes 36474, 36476, 36479, 36483 for subsequent vein(s) treated in the same extremity may only be reported once per extremity, regardless of the number of additional vein(s) treated.

When performed in the office setting, all required supplies and equipment are included in 36473, 36474, 36475, 36476, 36478, 36479, 36482, 36483 and may not be separately reported. In addition, application of compression dressing(s) (eg, compression bandages/stockings) is included in 36473, 36474, 36475, 36476, 36478, 36479, 36482, 36483, when performed, and may not be reported separately.

36473 Endovenous ablation therapy of incompetent vein, extremity, inclusive of all imaging guidance and monitoring, percutaneous, mechanochemical; first vein treated

+ **36474** subsequent vein(s) treated in a single extremity, each through separate access sites (List separately in addition to code for primary procedure)

(Use 36474 in conjunction with 36473)

(Do not report 36474 more than once per extremity)

(Do not report 36473, 36474 in conjunction with 29581, 36000, 36002, 36005, 36410, 36425, 36475, 36476, 36478, 36479, 37241, 75894, 76000, 76001, 76937, 76942, 76998, 77022, 93970, 93971 in the same surgical field)

36475 Endovenous ablation therapy of incompetent vein, extremity, inclusive of all imaging guidance and monitoring, percutaneous, radiofrequency; first vein treated

+ **36476** subsequent vein(s) treated in a single extremity, each through separate access sites (list separately in addition to code for primary procedure)

(Use 36476 in conjunction with 36475)

(Do not report 36476 more than once per extremity)

(Do not report 36475, 36476 in conjunction with 29581, 36000, 36002, 36005, 36410, 36425, 36478, 36479, 36482, 36483, 37241-37244, 75894, 76000, 76001, 76937, 76942, 76998, 77022, 93970, 93971 in the same surgical field)

● New Code   ▲ Revised Code   + Add-On Code   ⊘ Modifier -51 Exempt   ★ Telemedicine

36478　Endovenous ablation therapy of incompetent vein, extremity, inclusive of all imaging guidance and monitoring, percutaneous, laser; first vein treated

+ 36479　　　subsequent vein(s) treated in a single extremity, each through separate access sites (List separately in addition to code for primary procedure)

(Use 36479 in conjunction with 36478)

(Do not report 36479 more than once per extremity)

(Do not report 36478, 36479 in conjunction with 29581, 36000, 36002, 36005, 36410, 36425, 36475, 36476, 36482, 36483, 37241, 75894, 76000, 76001, 76937, 76942, 76998, 77022, 93970, 93971 in the same surgical field)

● 36482　Endovenous ablation therapy of incompetent vein, extremity, by transcatheter delivery of a chemical adhesive (eg, cyanoacrylate) remote from the access site, inclusive of all imaging guidance and monitoring, percutaneous; first vein treated

●+36483　　　subsequent vein(s) treated in a single extremity, each through separate access sites (List separately in addition to code for primary procedure)

(Use 36483 in conjunction with 36482)

(Do not report 36483 more than once per extremity)

(Do not report 36482, 36483 in conjunction with 29581, 36000, 36002, 36005, 36410, 36425, 36475, 36476, 36478, 36479, 37241, 75894, 76000, 76001, 76937, 76942, 76998, 77022, 93970, 93971 in the same surgical field)

36481　Percutaneous portal vein catheterization by any method

36482　This code is out of order. See page 401.

36483　This code is out of order. See page 401.

(For radiological supervision and interpretation, see 75885, 75887)

36500　Venous catheterization for selective organ blood sampling

(For catheterization in superior or inferior vena cava, use 36010)

(For radiological supervision and interpretation, use 75893)

36510　Catheterization of umbilical vein for diagnosis or therapy, newborn

(Do not report modifier '-63' in conjunction with 36510)

36511　Therapeutic apheresis; for white blood cells

36512　　　for red blood cells

36513　　　for platelets

(Report 36513 only when platelets are removed by apheresis for treatment of the patient. Do not report 36513 for donor platelet collections)

36514　　　for plasma pheresis

(36515　deleted 2017 [2018 edition]. For therapeutic aphaeresis with extracorporeal immunoadsorption and plasma rein fusion, use 36516)

▲ 36516　　　with extracorporeal immunoadsorption, selective adsorption or selective filtration and plasma reinfusion

(For professional evaluation, use modifier -26)

■ Separate Procedure　　■ Unlisted Procedure　　■ CCI Comp. Code　　■ Non-specific Procedure　　**401**

36522   Photopheresis, extracorporeal

    (For dialysis services, see 90935-90999)

    (For ultrafiltration, use 90999)

    (For therapeutic apheresis for white blood cells, red blood cells, platelets and plasma pheresis, see 36511, 36512, 36513, 36514)

    (For therapeutic apheresis extracorporeal adsorption procedures, use 36516)

Central Venous Access Procedures

To qualify as a central venous access catheter or device, the tip of the catheter/device must terminate in the subclavian, brachiocephalic (innominate) or iliac veins, the superior or inferior vena cava, or the right atrium. The venous access device may be either centrally inserted (jugular, subclavian, femoral vein or inferior vena cava catheter entry site) or peripherally inserted (eg, basilic or cephalic vein). The device may be accessed for use either via exposed catheter (external to the skin), via a subcutaneous port or via a subcutaneous pump.

The procedures involving these types of devices fall into five categories:

1. **Insertion** (placement of catheter through a newly established venous access)

2. **Repair** (fixing device without replacement of either catheter or port/pump, other than pharmacologic or mechanical correction of intracatheter or pericatheter occlusion [see 36595 or 36596])

3. **Partial replacement** of only the catheter component associated with a port/pump device, but not entire device

4. **Complete replacement** of entire device via same venous access site (complete exchange)

5. **Removal** of entire device.

There is no coding distinction between venous access achieve percutaneously vrsus by cutdown or based on catheter size.

For the repair, partial (catheter only) replacement, complete replacement, or removal of both catheters (placed from separate venous access sites) of a multi-catheter device, with or without subcutaneous ports/pumps, use the appropriate code describing the service with a frequency of two.

If an existing central venous access device is removed and a new one placed via a separate venous access site, appropriate codes for both procedures (removal of old, if code exists, and insertion of new device) should be reported.

When imaging is used for these procedures, either for gaining access to the venous entry site or for manipulating the catheter into final central position, use 76937, 77001.

    (For refilling and maintenance of an implantable pump or reservoir for intravenous or intra-arterial drug delivery, use 96530)

Insertion of Central Venous Access Device

36555   Insertion of non-tunneled centrally inserted central venous catheter; under 5 years of age

    (For peripherally inserted non-tunneled central venous catheter, under 5 years of age, use 36568)

36556   age 5 years or older

    (For peripherally inserted non-tunneled central venous catheter, age 5 years or older, use 36569)

36557   Insertion of tunneled centrally inserted central venous catheter, without subcutaneous port or pump; under 5 years of age

36558   age 5 years or older

    (For peripherally inserted central venous catheter with port, age 5 years or older, use 36571)

   ● New Code   ▲ Revised Code   + Add-On Code   ⊘ Modifier -51 Exempt   ★ Telemedicine

The Central Venous Access Procedures Table								
Non-Tunneled	Tunneled w/o port or pump	Central Tunneled	Tunneled with port	Tunneled with pump	Peripheral	<5 years	≥5 years	Any Age
Insertion								
Catheter								
36555						36555		
36556							36556	
	36557	36557				36557		
	36558	36558					36558	
36568 (w/o port or pump)					36568 (w/o port or pump)	36568 (w/o port or pump)		
36569 (w/o port or pump)					36569 (w/o port or pump)		36569 (w/o port or pump)	
Device								
		36560	36560			36560		
		36561	36561				36561	
		36563		36563				36563
	36565	36565						36565
		36566	36566					
36570 (w port0)			36570 (w port)		36570 (w port)	36570 (w port)		
36571 (w port)			36571 (w port)		36571 (w port)		36571 (w port)	
Repair								
Catheter								
36575 (w/o port or pump)	36575 (w/o port or pump)	36575 (w/o port or pump)			36575 (w/o port or pump)			36575
Device								
36576 (w port or pump)					36576 (w port or pump)			36576
Partial Replacement - Central Venous Access Device (Catheter only)								
		36578	36578	36578	36578			36578
Complete Replacement - Central Venous Access Device (through same venous access site)								
Catheter								
36580 (w/o port or pump)								36580
	36581	36581						36581
36584 (w/o port or pump)					36584 (w/o port or pump)			36584
Device								
		36582	36582					36582
		36583		36583				36583
			36585 (w port)		36585 (w port)			36585
Removal								
Catheter								
	36589							36589
Device								
		36590	36590	36590	36590			36590
Removal of Obstructive Material from Device								
36595 peri-catheter	36595 peri-catheter	36595 peri-catheter	36595 peri-catheter	36595 peri-catheter	36595 peri-catheter			36595 peri-catheter
36596 intraluminal	36596 intraluminal	36596 intraluminal	36596 intraluminal	36596 intraluminal	36596 intraluminal			36596 intraluminal
Repositioning of Catheter								
36597	36597	36597	36597	36597	36597	36597	36597	36597

36560 Insertion of tunneled centrally inserted central venous access device, with subcutaneous port; under 5 years of age

(For peripherally inserted central venous access device with subcutaneous port, under 5 years of age, use 36570)

36561 age 5 years or older

(For peripherally inserted central venous catheter with subcutaneous port, 5 years or older, use 36571)

36563 Insertion of tunneled centrally inserted central venous access device with subcutaneous pump

36565 Insertion of tunneled centrally inserted central venous access device, requiring 2 catheters via 2 separate venous access sites; without subcutaneous port or pump (eg, Tesio type catheter)

36566 with subcutaneous port(s)

36568 Insertion of peripherally inserted central venous catheter (PICC), without subcutaneous port or pump; under 5 years of age

(For placement of centrally inserted non-tunneled central venous catheter, without subcutaneous port or pump, under 5 years of age, use 36555)

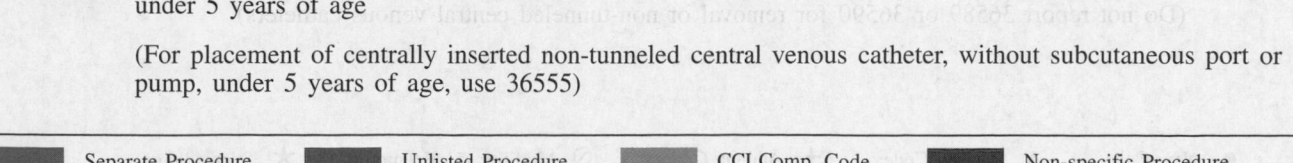

Separate Procedure   Unlisted Procedure   CCI Comp. Code   Non-specific Procedure   **403**

36569   age 5 years or older

(For placement of centrally inserted non-tunneled central venous catheter, without subcutaneous port or pump, age 5 years or older, use 36556)

36570   Insertion of peripherally inserted central venous access device, with subcutaneous port; under 5 years of age

(For insertion of tunneled centrally inserted central venous access device with subcutaneous port, under 5 years of age, use 36560)

36571   age 5 years or older

(For insertion of tunneled centrally inserted central venous access device with subcutaneous port, age 5 years or older, use 36561)

Repair of Central Venous Access Device

(For mechanical removal of pericatheter obstructive material, use 36595)

(For mechancial removal of intracatheter obstructive material, use 36596)

36575   Repair of tunneled or non-tunneled central venous access catheter, without subcutaneous port or pump, central or peripheral insertion site

36576   Repair of central venous access device, with subcutaneous port or pump, central or peripheral insertion site

Partial Replacement of Central Venous Access Device (Catheter Only)

36578   Replacement, catheter only, of central venous access device, with subcutaneous port or pump, central or peripheral insertion site

(For complete replacement of entire device through same venous access, use 36582 or 36583)

Complete Replacement of Central Venous Access Device Through Same Venous Access Site

36580   Replacement, complete, of a non-tunneled centrally inserted central venous catheter, without subcutaneous port or pump, through same venous access

36581   Replacement, complete, of a tunneled centrally inserted central venous catheter, without subcutaneous port or pump, through same venous access

36582   Replacement, complete, of a tunneled centrally inserted central venous access device, with subcutaneous port, through same venous access

36583   Replacement, complete, of a tunneled centrally inserted central venous access device, with subcutaneous pump, through same venous access

36584   Replacement, complete, of a peripherally inserted central venous catheter (PICC), without subcutaneous port or pump, through same venous access

36585   Replacement, complete, of a peripherally inserted central venous access device, with subcutaneous port, through same venous access

Removal of Central Venous Access Device

36589   Removal of tunneled central venous catheter, without subcutaneous port or pump

36590   Removal of tunneled central venous access device, with subcutaneous port or pump, central or peripheral insertion

(Do not report 36589 or 36590 for removal of non-tunneled central venous catheters)

● New Code   ▲ Revised Code   + Add-On Code   ⊘ Modifier -51 Exempt   ★ Telemedicine

Other Central Venous Access Procedures

36591   Collection of blood specimen from a completely implantable venous access device

(Do not report 36591 in conjunction with other service except a laboratory service)

(For collection of venous blood specimen by venipuncture, use 36415)

(For collection of capillary blood specimen, use 36416)

36592   Collection of blood specimen using established central or peripheral catheter, venous, not otherwise specified

(For blood collection from an established arterial catheter, use 37799)

(Do not report 36592 in conjunction with other services except a laboratory service)

36593   Declotting by thrombolytic agent of implanted vascular access device or catheter

36595   Mechanical removal of pericatheter obstructive material (eg, fibrin sheath) from central venous device via separate venous access

(Do not report 36595 in conjunction with 36593)

(For venous catheterization, see 36010-36012)

(For radiological supervision and interpretation, use 75901)

36596   Mechanical removal of intraluminal (intracatheter) obstructive material from central venous device through device lumen

(Do not report 365596 in conjunction with 36593)

(For venous catheterization, see 36010-36012)

(For radiological supervision and interpretation, use 75902)

36597   Repositioning of previously placed central venous catheter under fluoroscopic guidance

(For fluoroscopic guidance, use 76000)

36598   Contrast injection(s) for radiologic evaluation of existing central venous access device, including fluoroscopy, image documentation and report

(Do not report 36598 in conjunction with 76000)

(Do not report 36598 in conjunction with 36595, 36596)

(For complete diagnostic studies, see 75820, 75825, 75827)

ARTERIAL

36600   Arterial puncture, withdrawal of blood for diagnosis

⊘ **36620**   Arterial catheterization or cannulation for sampling, monitoring or transfusion (separate procedure); percutaneous

36625   cutdown

36640   Arterial catheterization for prolonged infusion therapy (chemotherapy), cutdown

(See also 96420-96425)

(For arterial catheterization for occlusion therapy, see 75894)

36660   Catheterization, umbilical artery, newborn, for diagnosis or therapy

(Do not report modifier '-63' in conjunction with 36660)

INTRAOSSEOUS

36680 Placement of needle for intraosseous infusion

HEMODIALYSIS ACCESS, INTERVASCULAR CANNULIZATION FOR EXTRACORPOREAL CIRCULATION, OR SHUNT INSERTION

36800 Insertion of cannula for hemodialysis, other purpose (separate procedure); vein to vein

36810 arteriovenous, external (Scribner type)

36815 arteriovenous, external revision, or closure

36818 Arteriovenous anastomosis, open; by upper arm cephalic vein transposition

(Do not report 36818 in conjunction with 36819, 36820, 36821, 36830 during a unilateral upper extremity procedure. For bilateral upper extremity open arteriovenous anastomoses performed at the same operative session, use modifier 50 or 59 as appropriate)

36819 by upper arm basilic vein transposition

(Do not report 36819 in conjunction with 36818, 36820, 36821, 36830 during a unilateral upper extremity procedure. For bilateral upper extremity open arteriovenous anastomoses performed at the same operative session, use modifier 50 or 59 as appropriate)

36820 by forearm vein transposition

36821 direct, any site (eg, Cimino type) (separate procedure)

(36822 deleted 2014 [2015 edition]. To report, see 33951, 33952, 33953, 33954, 33955, 33956)

36823 Insertion of arterial and venous cannula(s) for isolated extracorporeal circulation including regional chemotherapy perfusion to an extremity, with or without hyperthermia, with removal of cannula(s) and repair of arteriotomy and venotomy sites

(36823 includes chemotherapy perfusion supported by a membrane oxygenator/perfusion pump. Do not report 96408-96425 in conjunction with 36823)

36825 Creation of arteriovenous fistula by other than direct arteriovenous anastomosis (separate procedure); autogenous graft

(For direct arteriovenous anastomosis, use 36821)

36830 nonautogenous graft (eg, biological collagen, thermoplastic graft)

(For direct arteriovenous anastomosis, use 36821)

36831 Thrombectomy, open, arteriovenous fistula without revision, autogenous or nonautogenous dialysis graft (separate procedure)

36832 Revision, open, arteriovenous fistula; without thrombectomy, autogenous or nonautogenous dialysis graft (separate procedure)

36833 with thrombectomy, autogenous or nonautogenous dialysis graft (separate procedure)

(For percutaneous thrombectomy within the dialysis circuit, see 36904, 36905, 36906)

(For central dialysis segment angioplasty in conjunction with 36818-36833, use 36907)

(For central dialysis segment stent placement in conjunction with 36818-36833, use 36908)

● New Code   ▲ Revised Code   ✛ Add-On Code   ⊘ Modifier -51 Exempt   ★ Telemedicine

(Do not report 36832, 36833 in conjunction with 36901, 36902, 36903, 36904, 36905, 36906 for revision of the dialysis circuit)

36835 Insertion of Thomas shunt (separate procedure)

36838 Distal revascularization and interval ligation (DRIL), upper extremity hemodialysis access (steal syndrome)

(Do not report 36838 in conjunction with 35512, 35522, 35523, 36832, 37607, 37618)

36860 External cannula declotting (separate procedure); without balloon catheter

36861 with balloon catheter

(If imaging guidance is performed, use 76000)

(36870 deleted 2016 [2017 edition]. To report percutaneous transluminal mechanical thrombectomy and/or infusion for thrombolysis within the dialysis circuit, see 36904, 36905, 36906)

DIALYSIS CIRCUIT

Definitions:

Dialysis circuit: The arteriovenous (AV) dialysis circuit is designed for easy and repetitive access to perform hemodialysis. It begins at the arterial anastomosis and extends to the right atrium. The circuit may be created using either an arterial-venous anastomosis, known as an arteriovenous fistula (AVF), or a prosthetic graft placed between an artery and vein, known as an arteriovenous graft (AVG). The dialysis circuit is comprised of two segments, termed the (1) peripheral dialysis segment and (2) central dialysis segment. Both are defined below.

Peripheral dialysis segment: The peripheral dialysis segment is the portion of the dialysis circuit that begins at the arterial anastomosis and extends to the central dialysis segment. In the upper extremity, the peripheral dialysis segment extends through the axillary vein (or entire cephalic vein in the case of cephalic venous outflow). In the lower extremity, the peripheral dialysis segment extends through the common femoral vein. The peripheral dialysis segment includes the historic "perianastomotic region" (defined below).

Central dialysis segment: The central dialysis segment includes all draining veins central to the peripheral dialysis segment. In the upper extremity, the central dialysis segment includes the veins central to the axillary and cephalic veins, including the subclavian and innominate veins through the superior vena cava. In the lower extremity, the central dialysis segment includes the veins central to the common femoral vein, including the external iliac and common iliac veins through the inferior vena cava.

Peri-anastomotic region: A historic term referring to the region of a dialysis circuit near the arterial anastomosis encompassing a short segment of the parent artery, the anastomosis, and a short segment of the dialysis circuit immediately adjacent to the anastomosis. The perianastomotic region is included within the peripheral segment of the dialysis circuit.

Performed through dialysis circuit: Any diagnostic study or therapeutic intervention within the dialysis circuit that is performed through a direct percutaneous access to the dialysis circuit.

Code 36901 includes direct access and imaging of the entire dialysis circuit. Antegrade and/or retrograde punctures of the dialysis circuit are typically used for imaging, and contrast may be injected directly through a needle or through a catheter placed into the dialysis circuit. All dialysis circuit punctures required to perform the procedure are included in 36901. Occasionally, the catheter needs to be advanced further into the circuit to adequately visualize the arterial anastomosis or the central veins, or selective catheterization of a venous branch may be required. All manipulation(s) of the catheter for diagnostic imaging of the dialysis circuit is included in 36901. Advancement of the catheter to the vena cava to adequately image that segment of the dialysis circuit is included in 36901 and is not separately reported. Code 36901 also includes catheterization of additional venous side branches communicating with the dialysis circuit, known as accessory veins. Advancement of the catheter tip through the arterial anastomosis to adequately visualize the anastomosis is also included in the service described by 36901 and is not separately reported. Evaluation of the peri-anastomotic portion of the inflow is an integral part of the dialysis circuit angiogram and is included in 36901.

For the purposes of reporting dialysis access maintenance services, the arterial inflow to the dialysis circuit is considered a separate vessel. If a more proximal arterial inflow problem separate from the peripheral dialysis segment is suspected, additional catheter placement and imaging required for adequate evaluation of the artery may be separately reported. If a catheter is selectively advanced from the dialysis circuit puncture beyond the peri-anastomotic segment into the inflow artery, an additional catheterization code may be reported. For example, 36215 may be used to report image-guided retrograde catheter placement into the inflow artery and into the aorta, if necessary (36200 is not reported in addition to 36215 in this example). Note that 75710 may also be reported if contrast injection for diagnostic arteriography is performed through this catheter and radiological supervision and interpretation and imaging documentation is performed.

Ultrasound guidance for puncture of the dialysis circuit access is not typically performed and is not included in 36901, 36902, 36903, 36904, 36905, 36906. However, in the case of a new (immature) or failing AVF, ultrasound may be necessary to safely and effectively puncture the dialysis circuit for evaluation, and this may be reported separately with 76937, if all the appropriate elements for reporting 76937 are performed and documented.

For radiological supervision and interpretation of dialysis circuit angiography performed through existing access(es) or catheter-based arterial access, report 36901 with modifier 52.

Dialysis Circuit Interventions (AV Grafts and AV Fistulae): For the purposes of coding interventional procedures in the dialysis circuit (both AVF and AVG), the dialysis circuit is artificially divided into two distinct segments: peripheral dialysis segment and central dialysis segment (see definitions).

Codes 36901, 36902, 36903 and 36904, 36905, 36906 are built on progressive hierarchies that have more intensive services, which include less intensive services. Report only one code (36901, 36902, 36903, 36904, 36905, 36906) for services provided in a dialysis circuit.

Code 36901 describes the diagnostic evaluation of the dialysis circuit, and this service is included in the services described by 36901, 36902, 36903, 36904, 36905, 36906. All catheterizations required to perform diagnostic fistulography are included in 36901. All catheterizations required to perform additional interventional services are included in codes 36902, 36903, 36904, 36905, 36906, 36907, 36908, 36909 and not separately reported. All angiography, fluoroscopic image guidance, roadmapping, and radiological supervision and interpretation required to perform each service are included in each code. Closure of the puncture(s) by any method is included in the service of each individual code.

Code 36902 includes the services in 36901 plus transluminal balloon angioplasty in the peripheral segment of the dialysis circuit. Code 36902 would be reported only once per session to describe all angioplasty services performed in the peripheral segment of the dialysis circuit, regardless of the number of distinct lesions treated within that segment, the number of times the balloon is inflated, or the number of balloon catheters or sizes required to open all lesions, and includes angioplasty of the peri-anastomotic segment when performed. Code 36903 includes the services in 36902 plus transcatheter stent placement in the peripheral segment of the dialysis circuit. Code 36903 is reported only once per session to describe placing stent(s) within the peripheral segment, regardless of the number ofstent(s) placed or the number of discrete lesion(s) treated within the peripheral segment. If both angioplasty and stenting are performed in the peripheral segment, including treatment of separate lesions, report 36903 only once.

Code 36904 describes percutaneous transluminal mechanical thrombectomy and/or infusion for thrombolysis in the dialysis circuit (all thrombus treated in both the peripheral and central dialysis circuit segments) and includes diagnostic angiography (36901), fluoroscopic image guidance, catheter placement(s), and all maneuvers required to remove thrombus from the peripheral and/or central segments, including all intraprocedural pharmacological thrombolytic injection(s)/infusion(s). It is never appropriate to report removal of the arterial plug during a declot/thrombectomy procedure as an angioplasty (36905). Removal of the arterial plug is included in a fistula thrombectomy, even if a balloon catheter is used to mechanically dislodge the resistant thrombus. Codes 36905 (angioplasty) and 36906 (stent) describe services in the peripheral circuit when performed in conjunction with thrombolysis/thrombectomy. Code 36905 includes the services in 36904 plus transluminal balloon angioplasty in the peripheral segment of the dialysis circuit. Code 36905 may be reported only once per session to describe all angioplasty performed in the peripheral segment of the dialysis circuit, regardless of the number of distinct lesions treated within that segment, the number of times the balloon is inflated, or the number of balloon catheters required to open all lesions.

Code 36906 includes the services in 36905 plus transcatheter stent placement in the peripheral segment of the dialysis circuit. Code 36906 is reported only once per session to describe placing stent(s) within the peripheral segment, regardless of the number of stent(s) placed or the number of discrete lesion(s) treated within the peripheral segment.

Codes 36907 and 36908 describe procedures performed through puncture(s) in the dialysis circuit. Similar procedures performed from a different access (eg, common femoral vein) may be reported using 37248, 37249 or 37238, 37239. Code 36907 is an add-on code used in conjunction with 36901, 36902, 36903, 36904, 36905, 36906 to report angioplasty within the central dialysis segment when performed through puncture of the dialysis circuit, and is reported once per session independent of the number of discrete lesions treated, the number of balloon inflations, and number of balloon catheters or sizes required. These additional services should be clearly documented in the patient record, including the recorded images. Code 36907 may be reported only once per session with 36901, 36902, 36903, 36904, 36905, 36906, as appropriate. Report 36907 once for all angioplasty performed within the central dialysis segment.

Code 36908 is an add-on code used in conjunction with 36901, 36902, 36903, 36904, 36905, 36906 to report stenting lesion(s) in the central dialysis segment when performed through puncture of the dialysis circuit. It is reported once, regardless of the number of discrete lesions treated or the number of stents placed. Code 36908 includes the services in 36907; therefore, 36908 may not be reported with 36907 in the same session. Code 36908 may be reported only once per session with 36901, 36902, 36903, 36904, 36905, 36906, as appropriate.

Code 36909 is an add-on code used to report endovascular embolization or occlusion of the main vessel or side branches arising from (emptying into) the dialysis circuit. Code 36909 may only be reported once per therapeutic session, irrespective of the number of branches embolized or occluded. Embolization or occlusion of the main vessel or these side branches may not be reported with 37241.

If open dialysis circuit creation, revision, and/or thrombectomy (36818-36833) are performed, completion angiography is bundled, as is peripheral segment angioplasty and/or stent placement (36901, 36902, 36903) and, therefore, not separately reported. However, dialysis circuit central segment angioplasty and/or stent placement may be separately reported (36907, 36908)

36901 Introduction of needle(s) and/or catheter(s), dialysis circuit, with diagnostic angiography of the dialysis circuit, including all direct puncture(s) and catheter placement(s), injection(s) of contrast, all necessary imaging from the arterial anastomosis and adjacent artery through entire venous outflow including the inferior or superior vena cava, fluoroscopic guidance, radiological supervision and interpretation and image documentation and report;

(Do not report 36901 in conjunction with 36833, 36902, 36903, 36904, 36905, 36906)

36902 with transluminal balloon angioplasty, peripheral dialysis segment, including all imaging and radiological supervision and interpretation necessary to perform the angioplasty

(Do not report 36902 in conjunction with 36903)

36903 with transcatheter placement of intravascular stent(s), peripheral dialysis segment, including all imaging and radiological supervision and interpretation necessary to perform the stenting, and all angioplasty within the peripheral dialysis segment

(Do not report 36902, 36903 in conjunction with 36833, 36904, 36905, 36906)

(Do not report 36901, 36902, 36903 more than once per operative session)

(For transluminal balloon angioplasty within central vein(s) when performed through dialysis circuit, use 36907)

(For transcatheter placement of intravascular stent(s) within central vein(s) when performed through dialysis circuit, use 36908)

36904 Percutaneous transluminal mechanical thrombectomy and/or infusion for thrombolysis, dialysis circuit, any method, including all imaging and radiological supervision and interpretation, diagnostic angiography, fluoroscopic guidance, catheter placement(s), and intraprocedural pharmacological thrombolytic injection(s);

(For open thrombectomy within the dialysis circuit, see 36831, 36833)

36905 with transluminal balloon angioplasty, peripheral dialysis segment, including all imaging and radiological supervision and interpretation necessary to perform the angioplasty

(Do not report 36905 in conjunction with 36904)

36906 with transcatheter placement of intravascular stent(s), peripheral dialysis segment, including all imaging and radiological supervision and interpretation necessary to perform the stenting, and all angioplasty within the peripheral dialysis circuit

(Do not report 36906 in conjunction with 36901, 36902, 36903, 36904, 36905)

(Do not report 36904, 36905, 36906 more than once per operative session)

(For transluminal balloon angioplasty within central vein(s) when performed through dialysis circuit, use 36907)

(For transcatheter placement of intravascular stent(s) within central vein(s) when performed through dialysis circuit, use 36908)

Separate Procedure   Unlisted Procedure   CCI Comp. Code   Non-specific Procedure   **409**

+ 36907   Transluminal balloon angioplasty, central dialysis segment, performed through dialysis circuit, including all imaging and radiological supervision and interpretation required to perform the angioplasty (List separately in addition to code for primary procedure)

     (Use 36907 in conjunction with 36818-36833, 36901, 36902, 36903, 36904, 36905, 36906)

     (Do not report 36907 in conjunction with 36908)

     (Report 36907 once for all angioplasty performed within the central dialysis segment)

▲+36908   Transcatheter placement of intravascular stent(s), central dialysis segment, performed through dialysis circuit, including all imaging and radiological supervision and interpretation required to perform the stenting, and all angioplasty in the central dialysis segment (List separately in addition to code for primary procedure)

     (Use 36908 in conjunction with 36818-36833, 36901, 36902, 36903, 36904, 36905, 36906)

     (Do not report 36908 in conjunction with 36907)

     (Report 36908 once for all stenting performed within the central dialysis segment)

+ 36909   Dialysis circuit permanent vascular embolization or occlusion (including main circuit or any accessory veins), endovascular, including all imaging and radiological supervision and interpretation necessary to complete the intervention (List separately in addition to code for primary procedure)

     (36909 includes all permanent vascular occlusions within the dialysis circuit and may only be reported once per encounter per day)

     (Report 36909 in conjunction with 36901, 36902, 36903, 36904, 36905, 36906)

     (For open ligation/occlusion in dialysis access, use 37607)

PORTAL DECOMPRESSION PROCEDURES

37140   Venous anastomosis, open; portocaval

     (For peritoneal-venous shunt, use 49425)

37145   renoportal

37160   caval-mesenteric

37180   splenorenal, proximal

37181   splenorenal, distal (selective decompression of esophagogastric varices, any technique)

     (For percutaneous procedure, use 37182)

37182   Insertion of transvenous intrahepatic portosystemic shunt(s) (TIPS) (includes venous access, hepatic and portal vein catheterization, portography with hemodynamic evaluation, intrahepatic tract formation/dilatation, stent placement and all associated imaging guidance and documentation)

     (Do not report 75885 or 75887 in conjunction with code 37182)

     (For open procedure, use 37140)

37183   Revision of transvenous intrahepatic portosystemic shunt(s) (TIPS) (includes venous access, hepatic and portal vein catheterization, portography with hemodynamic evaluation, intrahepatic tract recanulization/dilatation, stent placement and all associated imaging guidance and documentation)

     (Do not report 75885 or 75887 in conjunction with code 37183)

     (For repair of arteriovenous aneurysm, use 36832)

  ● New Code   ▲ Revised Code   + Add-On Code   ⊘ Modifier -51 Exempt   ★ Telemedicine

TRANSCATHETER PROCEDURES

Codes for catheter placement and the radiologic supervision and interpretation should also be reported, in addition to the code(s) for the therapeutic aspect of the procedure.

Mechanical Thrombectomy

Code(s) for catheter placement(s), diagnostic studies, and other percutaneous interventions (eg., transluminal balloon angioplasty, stent placement) provided are separately reportable.

Codes 37184-37188 specifically include intraprocedural fluoroscopic radiological supervision and interpretation services for guidance of the procedure.

Intraprocedural injection(s) of a thrombolytic agent is an included service and not separately reportable in conjunction with mechanical thrombectomy. However, subsequent or prior continuous infusion of a thrombolytic is not an included service and is separately reportable (see 37211-37214).

For coronary mechanical thrombectomy, use 92973.

For intracranial arterial mechanical thrombectomy for dialysis fistula, use 61645.

For mechanical thrombectomy for dialysis fistula, use 36870.

Transcatheter Thrombolytic Infusion

Codes 37211 or 37212 are used to report the initial day of transcatheter thrombolytic infusion(s) including follow-up arteriography/venography, and catheter position change or exchange, when performed. To report bilateral thrombolytic infusion through a separate access site(s), use modifier 50 in conjunction with 37211, 37212. Code 37213 is used to report continued transcatheter thrombolytic infusion(s) on subsequent day(s), other than initial day and final day of treatment. Code 37214 is used to report final day of transcatheter thrombolytic infusion(s). When initiation and completion of thrombolysis occur on the same day, report only 37211 or 37212.

Code(s) for catheter placement(s), diagnostic studies, and other percutaneous interventions (eg, transluminal balloon angioplasty, stent placement) provided may be separately reportable.

Codes 37211-37214 include fluoroscopic guidance and associated radiological supervision and interpretation.

Ongoing E/M services on the day of the procedure related to thrombolysis are included in 37211-37214. If a significant, separately identifiable E/M service is performed by the same physician on the same day of the procedure, report the appropriate level of E/M service and append modifier 25.

Ultrasound guidance for vascular access is not included in 37211-37214. Code 76937 may be reported separately when performed if all the required elements are performed.

For intracranial arterial mechanical thrombectomy and/or infusion for thrombolysis, use 61645.

Arterial Mechanical Thrombectomy

Primary mechanical thrombectomy is reported per vascular family using 37184 for the initial vessel treated and 37185 for second or all subsequent vessel(s) within the same vascular family. To report mechanical thrombectomy of an additional vascular family treated through a separate access site, use modifier 51 in conjunction with 37184-37185.

Do NOT report 37184-37185 for mechanical thrombectomy performed for the retrieval of short segments of thrombus or embolus evident during other percutaneous interventional procedures. See 37186 for these procedures.

Secondary mechanical thrombectomy is reported using 37186. Do NOT report 37186 in conjunction with 37184-37185.

Venous Mechanical Thrombectomy

Use 37187 to report the initial application of venous mechanical thrombectomy. To report bilateral venous mechanical thrombectomy performed through a separate access site(s), use modifier 50 in conjunction with 37187. For repeat treatment on a subsequent day during a course of thrombolytic therapy, use 37188.

Arterial Mechanical Thrombectomy

37184 Primary percutaneous transluminal mechanical thrombectomy, noncoronary, nonintracranial, arterial or arterial bypass graft, including fluoroscopic guidance and intraprocedural pharmacological thrombolytic injection(s); initial vessel

(Do not report 37184 in conjunction with 61645, 76000, 76001, 96374, 99151, 99152, 99153, 99155, 99156, 99157)

+ 37185 second and all subsequent vessel(s) within the same vascular family (List separately in addition to code for primary mechanical thrombectomy procedure)

(Do not report 37185 in conjunction with 76000, 76001, 96375)

(Do not report 37185 in conjunction with 61645 for treatment of the same vascular territory. See Nervous System Endovascular Therapy)

+ 37186 Secondary percutaneous transluminal thrombectomy (eg, nonprimary mechanical, snare basket, suction technique), noncoronary, non-intracranial, arterial or arterial bypass graft, including fluoroscopic guidance and intraprocedural pharmacological thrombolytic injections, provided in conjunction with another percutaneous intervention other than primary mechanical thrombectomy (List separately in addition to code for primary procedure)

(Do not report 37186 in conjunction with 76000, 76001, 96375)

(Do not report 37186 in conjunction with 61645 for treatment of the same vascular territory. See Nervous System Endovascular Therapy)

Venous Mechanical Thrombectomy

37187 Percutaneous transluminal mechanical thrombectomy, vein(s), including intraprocedural pharmacological thrombolytic injections and fluoroscopic guidance

(Do not report 37187 in conjunction with 76000, 76001, 96375)

37188 Percutaneous transluminal mechanical thrombectomy, vein(s), including intraprocedural pharmacological thrombolytic injections and fluoroscopic guidance, repeat treatment on subsequent day during course of thrombolytic therapy

(Do not report 37188 in conjunction with 76000, 76001, 96375)

Other Procedures

37191 Insertion of intravascular vena cava filter, endovascular approach including vascular access, vessel selection, and radiological supervision and interpretation, intraprocedural roadmapping, and imaging guidance (ultrasound and fluoroscopy), when performed

(For open surgical interruption of the inferior vena cava through a laparotomy or retroperitoneal exposure, use 37619)

37192 Repositioning of intravascular vena cava filter, endovascular approach including vascular access, vessel selection, and radiological supervision and interpretation, intraprocedural roadmapping, and imaging guidance (ultrasound and fluoroscopy), when performed

(Do not report 37192 in conjunction with 37191)

37193 Retrieval (removal) of intravascular vena cava filter, endovascular approach including vascular access, vessel selection, and radiological supervision and interpretation, intraprocedural roadmapping, and imaging guidance (ultrasound and fluoroscopy), when performed

(Do not report 37193 in conjunction with 37197)

37195 Thrombolysis, cerebral, by intravenous infusion

● New Code   ▲ Revised Code   + Add-On Code   ⊘ Modifier -51 Exempt   ★ Telemedicine

37197 Transcatheter retrieval, percutaneous, of intravascular foreign body (eg, fractured venous or arterial catheter), includes radiological supervision and interpretation, and imaging guidance (ultrasound or fluoroscopy), when performed

(For percutaneous retrieval of a vena cava filter, use 37193)

(For transcatheter removal of permanent leadless pacemaker, use 0388T)

37200 Transcatheter biopsy

(For radiological supervision and interpretation, use 75970)

37211 Transcatheter therapy, arterial infusion for thrombolysis other than coronary or intracranial, any method, including radiological supervision and interpretation, initial treatment day

(For intracranial arterial mechanical thrombectomy and/or infujsion for thrombolysis, use 61645)

37212 Transcatheter therapy, venous infusion for thrombolysis, any method, including radiological supervision and interpretation, initial treatment day

37213 Transcatheter therapy, arterial or venous infusion for thrombolysis other than coronary, any method, including radiological supervision and interpretation, continued treatment on subsequent day during course of thrombolytic therapy, including follow-up catheter contrast injection, position change, or exchange, when performed;

37214 cessation of thrombolysis including removal of catheter and vessel closure by any method

(Report 37211-37214 once per date of treatment)

(For declotting by thrombolytic agent of implanted vascular access device or catheter, use 36593)

(Do not report 37211-37214 in conjunction with 75898)

(37202 deleted 2015 [2016 edition]. For intracranial arterial administration of pharmacological agent[s] other than for thrombolysis, see 616520, 61651)

37211 Code out of order. See page 413.

37212 Code out of order. See page 413.

37213 Code out of order. See page 413.

37214 Code out of order. See page 413.

37215 Transcatheter placement of intravascular stent(s), cervical carotid artery, open or percutaneous, including angioplasty, when performed, and radiological supervision and interpretation; with distal embolic protection

37216 without distal embolic protection

(37215 and 37216 include all ipsilateral selective carotid catheterization, all diagnostic imaging for ipsilateral, cervical and cerebral carotid arteriography, and all related radiological supervision and interpretation. When ipsilateral carotid arteriogram (including imaging and selective catheterization) confirms the need for carotid stenting, 37215 and 37216 are inclusive of these services. If carotid stenting is not indicated, then the appropriate codes for carotid catheterization and imaging should be reported in lieu of 37215 and 37216)

(Do not report 37215, 37216 in conjunction with 36222-36224 for the treated carotid artery)

(For open or percutaneous transcatheter placement of extracranial vertebral artery stent[s], see Category III codes 0075T, 0076T)

37217 Transcatheter placement of intravascular stent(s), intrathoracic common carotid artery or innominate artery by retrograde treatment, open ipsilateral cervical carotid artery exposure, including angioplasty, when performed, and radiological supervision and interpretation

Separate Procedure   Unlisted Procedure   CCI Comp. Code   Non-specific Procedure   **413**

(37217 includes open vessel exposure and vascular access closure, all access and selective catheterization of the vessel, traversing the lesion, and any radiological supervision and interpretation directly related to the intervention when performed, standard closure of arteriotomy by suture, and imaging performed to document completion of the intervention in addition to the intervention[s] performed. Carotid artery revascularization services [eg, 33891, 35301, 35509, 35510, 35601, 35606] performed during the same session may be reported separately, when performed)

(Do not report 37217 in conjunction with 35201, 36221-36227, 37246, 37247 for ipsilateral services)

(For open or percutaneous transcatheter placement of intravascular cervical carotid artery stent[s], see 37215, 37216)

(For open or percutaneous antegrade transcatheter placement of innominate and/or intrathoracic carotid artery stent[s], use 37218)

(For open or percutaneous transcatheter placement of extracranial vertebral artery stent[s], see 0075T, 0076T)

(For transcatheter placement of intracranial stent[s], use 61635)

37218   Transcatheter placement of intravascular stent(s), intrathoracic common carotid artery or innominate artery, open or percutaneous antegrade approach, including angioplasty, when performed, and radiological supervision and interpretation

(37218 includes all ipsilateral extracranial intrathoracic selective innominate and carotid catheterization, all diagnostic imaging for ipsilateral extracranial intrathoracic innominate and/or carotid artery stenting, and all related radiologic supervision and interpretation. Report 37218 when the ipsilateral extracranial intrathoracic carotid arteriogram (including imaging and selective catheterization) confirms the need for stenting. If stenting is not indicated, report the appropriate codes for selective catheterization and imaging)

(Do not report 37218 in conjunction with 36222, 36223, 36224 for the treated carotid artery)

(For open or percutaneous transcatheter placement of intravascular cervical carotid artery stent[s], see 37215, 37216)

(For open or percutaneous transcatheter placement of extracranial vertebral artery stent[s], see 0075T, 0076T)

(For transcatheter placement of intracranial stent[s], use 61635)

ENDOVASCULAR REVASCULARIZATION (OPEN OR PERCUTANEOUS, TRANSCATHETER)

Codes 37220-37235 are to be used to describe lower extremity endovascular revascularization services performed for occlusive disease. These lower extremity codes are built on progressive hierarchies with more intensive services inclusive of lesser intensive services. The code inclusive of all of the services provided for that vessel should be reported (ie, use the code inclusive of the most intensive services provided). Only one code from this family (37220-37235) should be reported for each lower extremity vessel treated.

These lower extremity endovascular revascularization codes all include the work of accessing and selectively catheterizing the vessel, traversing the lesion, radiological supervision and interpretation directly related to the intervention(s) performed, embolic protection if used, closure of the arteriotomy by pressure and application of an arterial closure device or standard closure of the puncture by suture, and imaging performed to document completion of the intervention in addition to the intervention(s) performed. Extensive repair or replacement of an artery may be additionally reported (eg, 35226, or 35286). These codes describe endovascular procedures performed percutaneously and/or through an open surgical exposure. These codes include balloon angioplasty (eg, low-profile, cutting balloon, cryoplasty), atherectomy (eg, directional, rotational, laser), and stentin (eg, balloon-expandable, self-expanding, bare metal, covered, drug-eluting). Each code in this family (37220-37235) includes balloon angioplasty, when performed.

These codes describe revascularization therapies (ie, transluminal angioplasty, atherectomy, and stent placement) provided in three arterial vascular territories: iliac, femoral/popliteal, and tibial/peroneal.

When treating multiple vessels within a territory, report each additional vessel using an add-on code, as applicable. Select the base code that represents the most complex service using the following hierarchy of complexity (in descending order of complexity): atherectomy and stent>atherectomy>stent>angioplasty. When treating multiple lesions within the same vessel, report one service that reflects the combined procedures, whether done on one lesion or different lesions, using the same hierarchy.

---

1. **Iliac Vascular Territor**y — The iliac territory is divided into 3 vessels: common iliac, internal iliac, and external iliac.

2. **Femoral/Popliteal Vascular Territory** — The entire femoral/popliteal territory of 1 lower extremity is considered a single vessel for CPT reporting specifically for the endovascular lower extremity revascularization codes 37224-37227.

3. **Tibial/Peroneal Territory** — The tibial/peroneal territory is divided into 3 vessels: anterior, tibial, posterial tibial, and peroneal arteries.

There are specific coding guidelines for each of the 3 vascular territories.

1. **Iliac Vascular Territory** — A single primary code is used for the initial iliac artery treated in each leg (37220 or 37221). If other iliac vessels are also treated in that leg, these interventions are reported with th appropriate add-on code(s) (37222, 37223). Up to 2 add-on codes can be used in a unilateral iliac vascular territory since there are 3 vessels which could be treated. Add-on codes are used for different vessels, not distinct lesions within the same vessel.

2. **Femoral/Popliteal Territory** — A single interventional code is used no matter what combination of angioplasty/stent/atherectomy is applied to all segments, including the common, deep and superficial femoral arteries as well as the popliteal artery (37224, 37225, 37226 or 37227). There are no add-on codes for additional vessels treated within the femoral/popliteal territory. Because only 1 service is reported when 2 lesions are treated in this territory, report the most complex service (eg, use 37227 if a stent is placed for 1 lesion and an atherectomy is performed on a second lesion).

3. **Tibial/Peroneal Territory** — A single primary code is used for the initial tibial/peroneal artery treated in each leg (37228, 37229, 37230, or 37231). If other tibial/peroneal vessels are also treated in the same leg, these interventions are reported with the appropriate add-on code(s) (37232-37235). Up to 2 add-on codes could be used to describe services provided in a single leg since there are 3 tibial/peroneal vessels which could be treated. Add-on codes are used for different vessels, not distinct lesions within the same vessel. The common tibio-peroneal trunk is considered part of the tibial/peroneal territory, but is not considered a separate, fourth segment of vessel in the tibio-peroneal family for CPT reporting of endovascular lower extremity interventions. For instance, if lesions in the common tibio-peroneal trunk are treated in conjunction with lesions in the posterior tibial artery, a single code would be reported for treatment of this segment.

When treating multiple territories in the same leg, one primary lower extremity revascularization code is used for each territory treated. When second or third vessel(s) are treated in the iliac and/or tibial/peroneal territories, add-on codes are used to report the additional services. When more than one stent is placed in the same vessel, the code should be reported only once.

When multiple vessels in multiple territories in a single leg are treated at the same setting, the primary code for the treatment in the initial vessel in each vascular territory is reported. Add-on code(s) are reported when second and third iliac or tibial/peroneal arteries are treated in addition to the initial vessel in that vascular territory.

If a lesion extends across the margins of one vessel vascular territory into another, but can be opened with a single therapy, this intervention should be reported with a single code despite treating more than one vessel and/or vascular territory. For instance, if a stenosis extends from the common iliac artery into the proximal external iliac artery, and a single stent is placed to open the entire lesion, this therapy should be coded as a single stent placement in the iliac artery (37221). In this example, a code for an additional vessel treatment would not be used (do not report both 37221 and 37223).

For bifurcation lesions distal to the common iliac origins which require therapy of 2 distinct branches of the iliac or tibial/peroneal vascular territories, a primary code and an add-on code would be used to describe the intervention. In the femoral/popliteal territory, all branches are included in the primary code, so treatment of a bifurcation lesion would be reported as a single code.

When the same territor(ies) of both legs are treated in the same session, modifiers may be required to describe the interventions. Use modifier 59 to denote that different legs are being treated, even if the mode of therapy is different.

Mechanical thrombectomy and/or thrombolysis in the lower extremity vessels are sometimes necessary to aid in restoring flow to areas of occlusive disease, and are reported separately.

37220 Revascularization, endovascular, open or percutaneous, iliac artery, unilateral, initial vessel, with transluminal angioplasty

37221 with transluminal stent placement(s), includes angioplasty within the same vessel, when performed

(Use 37220, 37221 in conjunction with 34701-34711, 34845, 34846, 34847, 34848, 0254T only when 37220 or 37221 are performed outside the treatment zone of the endograft)

| Separate Procedure | Unlisted Procedure | CCI Comp. Code | Non-specific Procedure | **415** |

+ 37222 Revascularization, endovascular, open or percutaneous, iliac artery, each additional ipsilateral iliac vessel, with transluminal angioplasty (list separately in addition to code for primary procedure)

(Use 37222 in conjunction with 37220, 37221)

+ 37223 with transluminal stent placement(s), includes angioplasty within the same vessel, when performed (list separately in addition to code for primary procedure)

(Use 37223 in conjunction with 37221)

(Use 37222, 37223 in conjunction with 34701-34711, 34845, 34846, 34847, 34848, 0254T only when 37222 or 37223 are performed outside the treatment zone of the endograft)

37224 Revascularization, endovascular, open or percutaneous, femoral, popliteal artery(s), unilateral, with transluminal angioplasty

37225 with atherectomy, includes angioplasty within the same vessel, when performed

37226 with transluminal stent placement(s), includes angioplasty within the same vessel, when performed

37227 with transluminal stent placement(s) and atherectomy, includes angioplasty within the same vessel when performed

37228 Revascularization, endovascular, open or percutaneous, tibial, peroneal artery, unilateral, initial vessel, with transluminal angioplasty

37229 with atherectomy, includes angioplasty within the same vessel, when performed

37230 with transluminal stent placement(s), includes angioplasty within the same vessel, when performed

37231 with transluminal stent placement(s) and atherectomy, includes angioplasty within the same vessel, when performed

+ 37232 Revascularization, endovascular, open or percutaneous, tibial/peroneal artery, unilateral, each additional vessel, with transluminal angioplasty (list separately in addition to code for primary procedure)

(Use 37232 in conjunction with 37228-37231)

+ 37233 with atherectomy, includes angioplasty within the same vessel, when performed (list separately in addition to code for primary procedure)

(Use 37233 in conjunction with 37229, 37231)

+ 37234 with transluminal stent placement(s), includes angioplasty within the same vessel, when performed (list separately in addition to code for primary procedure)

(Use 37234 in conjunction with 37229, 37230, 37231)

+ 37235 with transluminal stent placement(s) and atherectomy, includes angioplasty within the same vessel, when performed (list separately in addition to code for primary procedure)

(Use 37235 in conjunction with 37231)

Codes 37246, 37247, 37248, 37249 describe open or percutaneous transluminal balloon angioplasty (eg, conventional, low profile, cutting, drug-coated balloon). Codes 37246, 37247 describe transluminal balloon angioplasty in an artery excluding the central nervous system (61630, 61635), coronary (92920-92944), pulmonary (92997, 92998), and lower extremities for occlusive disease (37220-37235). Codes 37248 and 37249 describe transluminal balloon angioplasty in a vein excluding the dialysis circuit (36902, 36905, 36907) when approached through the ipsilateral dialysis access. Transluminal balloon angioplasty is inherent to stenting in the extracranial carotid and innominate arteries (37215, 37216, 37217, 37218), peripheral arteries (37220-37237), and in peripheral veins (37238, 37239) and, therefore, is not separately reportable. Multiple angioplasties performed in a single vessel, including treatment of separate and distinct lesions within a single vessel, are reported with a single code. If a lesion extends across the margins of one vessel into another, but can be treated with a single therapy, the intervention should be reported only once. When additional, separate and distinct ipsilateral or contralateral vessels are treated in the same session, 37247 and/or 37249 may be reported as appropriate.

● New Code   ▲ Revised Code   ＋ Add-On Code   ⊘ Modifier -51 Exempt   ★ Telemedicine

Non-selective and/or selective catheterization (eg, 36005, 36010, 36011, 36012, 36200, 36215, 36216, 36217, 36218, 36245, 36246, 36247, 36248) is reported separately. Codes 37246, 37247, 37248, 37249 include radiological supervision and interpretation directly related to the intervention performed and imaging performed to document completion of the intervention. Extensive repair or replacement of an artery may be reported separately (eg, 35226, 35286). Intravascular ultrasound may be reported separately (ie, 37252, 37253). Mechanical thrombectomy and/or thrombolytic therapy, when performed, may be reported separately (eg, 37184, 37185, 37186, 37187, 37188, 37211, 37212, 37213, 37214).

37246   Transluminal balloon angioplasty (except lower extremity artery(ies) for occlusive disease, intracranial, coronary, pulmonary, or dialysis circuit), open or percutaneous, including all imaging and radiological supervision and interpretation necessary to perform the angioplasty within the same artery; initial artery

+ 37247   each additional artery (List separately in addition to code for primary procedure)

(Use 37247 in conjunction with 37246)

(Do not report 37246, 37247 in conjunction with 37215, 37216, 37217, 37218, 37220-37237 when performed in the same artery during the same operative session)

(Do not report 37246, 37247 in conjunction with 34841, 34842, 34843, 34844, 34845, 34846, 34847, 34848 for angioplasty[ies] performed, when placing bare metal or covered stents into the visceral branches within the endoprosthesis target zone)

37248   Transluminal balloon angioplasty (except dialysis circuit), open or percutaneous, including all imaging and radiological supervision and interpretation necessary to perform the angioplasty within the same vein; initial vein

+ 37249   each additional vein (List separately in addition to code for primary procedure)

(Use 37249 in conjunction with 37248)

(Do not report 37248, 37249 in conjunction with 37238, 37239 when performed in the same vein during the same operative session)

(For transluminal balloon angioplasty in aorta/visceral artery[ies] in conjunction with fenestrated endovascular repair, see 34841, 34842, 34843, 34844, 34845, 34846, 34847, 34848)

(For transluminal balloon angioplasty in iliac, femoral, popliteal, or tibial/peroneal artery[ies] for occlusive disease, see 37220-37235)

(For transluminal balloon angioplasty in a dialysis circuit performed through the circuit, see 36902, 36903, 36904, 36905, 36906, 36907, 36908)

(For transluminal balloon angioplasty in an intracranial artery, see 61630, 61635)

(For transluminal balloon angioplasty in a coronary artery, see 92920-92944)

(For transluminal balloon angioplasty in a pulmonary artery, see 92997, 92998)

Codes 37236-37239 are used to report endovascular revascularization for vessels other than lower extremity artery(ies) for occlusive disease (ie, 37221, 37223, 37226, 37227, 37230, 37231, 37234, 37235), cervical carotid (ie, 37215, 37216), intracranial (ie, 61635), intracoronary (ie, 92928, 92929, 92933, 92934, 92937, 92938, 92941, 92943, 92944), innominate and/or intrathoracic carotid artery through an antegrade approach (37218), extracranial vertebral (ie, 0075T, 0076T) performed percutaneously and/or through an open surgical exposure, open retrograde intrathoracic common carotid or innominate (37217), or dialysis circuit when performed through the dialysis circuit (36903, 36905, 36908).

Codes 37236, 37237 describe transluminal intravascular stent insertion in an artery while 37238, 37239 describe transluminal intravascular stent insertion in a vein. Multiple stents placed in a single vessel may only be reported with a single code. If a lesion extends across the margins of one vessel into another, but can be treated with a single therapy, the intervention should be reported only once. When additional, different vessels are treated in the same session, report 37237 and/or 37239 as appropriate. Each coding in this family (37236-37239) includes any and all balloon angioplasty(s) performed in the treated vessel, including any pre-dilation (whether performed as a primary or secondary angioplasty), post-dilation following stent placement, treatment of a lesion outside the stented segment but in the same vessel, or use of larger/smaller balloon to achieve therapeutic result. Angioplasty in a separate and distinct vessel may be reported separately. Non-selective and/or selective catheterization(s) (eg, 36005, 36010-36015, 36200, 36215-36218, 36245-36248), is reported separately.

Codes 37236-37239 include radiological supervision and interpretation directly related to the intervention(s) performed, closure of the arteriotomy by pressure, application of an arterial closure device or standard closure of the puncture by suture, and imaging performed to document completion of the intervention in addition to the intervention(s) performed. Extensive repair or replacement of an artery may be reported separately (eg, 35226 or 35286). Report 76937 for ultrasound guidance for vascular access, when performed in conjunction with 37236-37239. Intravascular ultrasound may be reported separately (ie, 37252, 37253). For mechanical thrombectomy and/or thrombolytic therapy, when performed, see 37184-37188, 37211-37214.

Intravascular stents, both covered and uncovered, are a class of device that may be used as part of an embolization procedure. As such, there is the potential for overlap among codes used for placement of vascular stents and those use for embolization. When a stent is placed for the purpose of providing a latticework for deployment of embolization coils, such as for embolization of an aneurysm, the embolization code is reported and not the stent code. If a covered stent is deployed as the sole management of an aneurysm, pseudoaneurysm, or vascular extravasation, then the stent deployment code should be reported and not the embolization code.

37236 Transcatheter placement of an intravascular stent(s) (except lower extremity artery(s) for occlusie disease, cervical carotid, extracranial vertebral or intrathoracic carotid, intracranial, or coronary), open or percutaneous, including radiological supervision and interpretation and including all angioplasty within the same vessel, when performed; initial artery

+ 37237 each additional artery (List separately in addition to code for primary procedure)

(Use 37237 in conjunction with 37236)

(Do not report 37236, 37237 in conjunction with 34841-34848 for bare metal or covered stents placed into the visceral branches within the endoprosthesis target zone)

(For stent placement(s) in iliac, femoral, popliteal, or tibial/perineal artery(s) for occlusive disease, see 37221, 37223, 37226, 37227, 37230, 37231, 37234, 37235)

(For transcatheter placement of intravascular cervical carotid artery stent(s), see 37215, 37216)

(For transcatheter placement of intracranial stent(s), use 61635)

(For transcatheter placement of intracoronary stent(s), see 92928, 92929, 92933, 92934, 92937, 92938, 92941, 92943, 92944)

(For stenting of visceral arteries in conjunction with fenestrated endovascular repair, see 34841-34848)

(For open or percutaneous antegrade transcatheter placement of intrathoracic carotid/innominate artery stent[s], use 37218)

(For open or percutaneous transcatheter placement of extracranial vertebral artery stent[s], see Category III codes 0075T, 0076T)

(For open retrograde transcatheter placement of intrathoracic common carotid/innominate artery stent(s), use 37217)

(For placement of a stent at the arterial anastomosis of a dialysis circuit with or without transluminal mechanical thrombectomy and/or infusion for thrombolysis, see 36903, 36906)

37238 Transcatheter placement of an intravascular stent(s), open or percutaneous, including radiological supervision and interpretation and including angioplasty within the same vessel, when performed; initial vein

+ 37239 each additional vein (List separately in addition to code for primary procedure)

(Use 37239 in conjunction with 37238)

(For placement of a stent[s] within the peripheral segment of the dialysis circuit, see 36903, 36906)

(For transcatheter placement of an intravascular stent[s] within central dialysis segment when performed through the dialysis circuit, use 36908)

VASCULAR EMBOLIZATION AND OCCLUSION

Codes 37241-37244 are used to describe vascular embolization and occlusion procedures, excluding the central nervous system and the head and neck, which are reported using 61624, 61626, 61710, and 75894, and excluding the ablation/sclerotherapy procedures for venous insufficiency/telangiectasia of the extremities/skin, which are reported using 36468, 36470, and 36471. Embolization and occlusion procedures are performed for a wide variety of clinical indications and in a range of vascular territories. Arteries, veins, and lymphatics may all be the target of embolization.

The embolization codes include all associated radiological supervision and interpretation, intra-procedural guidance and road-mapping, and imaging necessary to document completion of the procedure. They do not include diagnostic angiography and all necessary catheter placement(s). Code(s) for catheter placement(s) may be separately reportable using selecrive catheter placement code(s), if used consistent with guidelines. Code(s) for diagnostic angiography may also be separately reported, when performed according to guidelines for diagnostic angiography during endovascular procedures. Report these services with an appropriate modifier (eg, modifier 59). Please see the guidelines on the reporting of diagnostic angiography preceding 75600 in the Vascular Procedures, Aorta and Arteries section.

Code 37241 is used to report endovascular embolization or occlusion procedures performed for venous conditions other than hemorrhage or hemodialysis access. Examples include embolization of venous malformations, capillary hemangiomas, varicoceles, and visceral varices. (For endovascular embolization or occlusion of side branch[es] of an outflow vein[s] from a hemodialysis access, use 36909.)

Code 37242 is used report vascular embolization or occlusion performed for arterial conditions other than hemorrhage or tumor such as arteriovenous malformations and arteriovenous fistulas whether congenital or acquired. Embolizations of aneurysms and pseudoaneurysms are also reported with 37242. Tumor embolization is reported with 37243. Note that injection to treat an extremity pseudoaneurysm is correctly reported with 36002. Sometimes, embolization and occlusion of an artery are performed prior to another planned interventional procedure; an example is embolization of the left gastric artery prior to planned implantation of a hepatic artery chemotherapy port. The artery embolization is reported with 37242.

Code 37243 is used report embolization for the purpose of tissue ablation and organ infarction and or ischemia. This can be performed in many clinical circumstances including embolization of benign or malignant tumors of the liver, kidney, uterus, or other organs. When chemotherapy is given as part of an embolization procedure, additional codes (eg, 96420), maybe separately reported. When a radioisotope (eg, Yttrium-90) is injected as part of an embolization, then additional codes (eg, 79445) may be separately reported. Uterine fibroid embolization is reported with 37243.

Code 37244 is used to report embolization for treatment of hemorrhage or vascular or lymphatic extravasation. Examples include embolization for management of gastrointestinal bleed, trauma-induced hemorrhage of the viscera or pelvis, embolization of the thoracic duct for chylous effusion and bronchial artery embolization for hemoptysis. Embolization of the uterine arteries for management of hemorrhage (eg, postpartum hemorrhage), is also reported with 37244.

Intravascular stents, both covered and uncovered, are a class of devices that may be used as part of an embolization procedure. As such, there is the potential for overlap among codes used for placement of vascular stents and those use for embolization. When a stent is placed for the purpose of providing a latticework for deployment of embolization coils, such as for embolization of an aneurysm, the embolization code is reported and not the stent code. If a stent is deployed as the sole management of an aneurysm pseudoaneurysm or vascular extravasation, then the stent deployment code should be reported and not the embolization code.

Only one embolization code should be reported for each surgical field (ie, the area immediately surrounding and directly involved in a treatment/procedure). Embolization procedures performed at a single setting and including multiple surgical fields (eg, a patient with multiple trauma and bleeding from the pelvis and the spleen) may be reported with multiple embolization codes with the appropriate modifier (eg, modifier 59).

There may be overlapping indications for an embolization procedure. The code for the immediate indication for the embolization should be used. For instance, if the immediate cause for embolization is bleeding in a patient with an aneurysm, report 37244.

37241 Vascular embolization or occlusion, inclusive of all radiological supervision and interpretation, intraprocedural roadmapping, and imaging guidance necessary to complete the intervention; venous, other than hemorrhage (eg, congenital or acquired venous malformations, venous and capillary hemangiomas, varices, varioceles)

(Do not report 37241 in conjunction with 36468, 36470, 36471, 36473, 36474, 36475-36479, 75894, 75898 in the same surgical field)

(For sclerosis of veins or endovenous ablation of incompetent extremity veins, see 36468-36479)

(For dialysis circuit permanent endovascular embolization or occlusion, use 36909)

37242 arterial, other than hemorrhage or tumor (eg, congenital or acquired arterial malformations, arteriovenous malformations, arteriovenous fistulas, aneurysms, pseudoaneurysms)

(For percutaneous treatment of extremity pseudoaneurysm, use 36002)

37243   for tumors, organ ischemia, or infarction

37244   for arterial or venous hemorrhage or lymphatic extravasation

(Do not report 37242-37244 in conjunction with 75894, 75898 in the same surgical field)

(For embolization procedures of the central nervous system or head and neck, see 61624, 61626, 61710)

37246   Code out of order. See page 417.

37247   Code out of order. See page 417.

37248   Code out of order. See page 417.

37249   Code out of order. See page 417.

INTRAVASCULAR ULTRASOUND SERVICES

Intravascular ultrasound (IVUS) services include all transducer manipulations and repositioning within the specific vessel being examined during a diagnostic procedure or before, during, and/or after therapeutic intervention (eg, stent or stent graft placement, angioplasty, atherectomy, embolization, thrombolysis, transcatheter biopsy).

IVUS is included in the work described by codes 37191, 37192, 37193, 37197 (intravascular vena cava [IVC] filter placement, repositioning and removal, and intravascular foreign body retrieval) and should not be separately reported with those procedures. If a lesion extends across the margins of one vessel into another, this should be reported with a single code despite imaging more than one vessel.

Non-selective and/or selective vascular catheterization may be separately reportable (eg, 36005-36248).

(37250, 37251 have been deleted. To report noncoronary intravascular ultrasound during diagnostic evaluation and/or therapeutic intervention, see 37252, 37253)

+ **37252**   Intravascular ultrasound (noncoronary vessel) during diagnostic evaluation and/or therapeutic intervention, including radiological supervision and interpretation; initial noncoronary vessel (List separately in addition to code for primary procedure)

+ **37253**   each additional noncoronary vessel (List separately in addition to code for primary procedure)

(Use 37253 in conjunction with 37252)

(Report 37252, 37253 in conjunction with 33361, 33362, 33363, 33364, 33365, 33366, 33367, 33368, 33369, 33477, 33880, 33881, 33883, 33884, 33886, 34701, 34702, 34703, 34704, 34705, 34706, 34707, 34708, 34709, 34710, 34711, 34841, 34842, 34843, 34844, 34845, 34846, 34847, 34848, 36010, 36011, 36012, 36013, 36014, 36015, 36100, 36140, 36160, 36200, 36215, 36216, 36217, 36218, 36221, 36222, 36223, 36224, 36225, 36226, 36227, 36228, 36245, 36246, 36247, 36248, 36251, 36252, 36253, 36254, 36481, 36555-36571, 36578, 36580, 36581, 36582, 36583, 36584, 36585, 36595, 36901, 36902, 36903, 36904, 36905, 36906, 36907, 36908, 36909, 37184, 37185, 37186, 37187, 37188, 37200, 37211, 37212, 37213, 37214, 37215, 37216, 37218, 37220, 37221, 37222, 37223, 37224, 37225, 37226, 37227, 37228, 37229, 37230, 37231, 37232, 37233, 37234, 37235, 37236, 37237, 37238, 37239, 37241, 37242, 37243, 37244, 37246, 37247, 37248, 37249, 61623, 75600, 75605, 75625, 75630, 75635, 75705, 75710, 75716, 75726, 75731, 75733, 75736, 75741, 75743, 75746, 75756, 75774, 75805, 75807, 75810, 75820, 75822, 75825, 75827, 75831, 75833, 75860, 75870, 75872, 75885, 75887, 75889, 75891, 75893, 75894, 75898, 75901, 75902, 75956, 75957, 75958, 75959, 75970, 76000, 77001, 0075T, 0076T, 0234T, 0235T, 0236T, 0237T, 0238T, 0254T, 0338T)

(Do not report 37252, 37253 in conjunction with 37191, 37192, 37193, 37197)

ENDOSCOPY

Surgical vascular endoscopy always includes diagnostic endoscopy.

37500   Vascular endoscopy, surgical, with ligation or perforator veins, subfascial (SEPS)

● New Code   ▲ Revised Code   + Add-On Code   ⊘ Modifier -51 Exempt   ★ Telemedicine

(For open procedure, use 37760)

| 37501 | Unlisted vascular endoscopy procedure |

LIGATION

(For phleborraphy and arteriorraphy, see 35201-35286)

| 37565 | Ligation, internal jugular vein |

| 37600 | Ligation; external carotid artery |

| 37605 | internal or common carotid artery |

| 37606 | internal or common carotid artery, with gradual occlusion, as with Selverstone or Crutchfield clamp |

(For transcatheter permanent arterial occlusion or embolization, see 61624-61626)

(For endovascular temporary arterial balloon occlusion, use 61623)

(For ligation treatment of intracranial aneurysm, use 61703)

| 37607 | Ligation or banding of angioaccess arteriovenous fistula |

| 37609 | Ligation or biopsy, temporal artery |

| 37615 | Ligation, major artery (eg, post-traumatic, rupture); neck |

| 37616 | chest |

| 37617 | abdomen |

| 37618 | extremity |

| 37619 | Ligation of inferior vena cava |

(For endovascular delivery of an inferior vena cava filter, use 37191)

| 37650 | Ligation of femoral vein |

(For bilateral procedure, report 37650 with modifier -50)

| 37660 | Ligation of common iliac vein |

| 37700 | Ligation and division of long saphenous vein at saphenofemoral junction, or distal interruptions |

(Do not report 37700 in conjunction with 37718, 37722)

(For bilateral procedure, report 37700 with modifier -50)

| 37718 | Ligation, division, and stripping, short saphenous vein |

(For bilateral procedure, use modifier 50)

(Do not report 37718 in conjunction with 37735, 37780)

| 37722 | Ligation, division, and stripping, long (greater) saphenous veins from saphenofemoral junction to knee or below |

(For ligation and stripping of the short saphenous vein, use 37718)

(For bilateral procedure, report 37722 with modifier 50)

(Do not report 37722 in conjunction with 37700, 37735)

Separate Procedure   Unlisted Procedure   CCI Comp. Code   Non-specific Procedure   **421**

(For ligation, division, and stripping of the greater saphenous vein, use 37722. For ligation, division, and stripping of the short saphenous vein, use 37718)

37735 Ligation and division and complete stripping of long or short saphenous veins with radical excision of ulcer and skin graft and/or interruption of communicating veins of lower leg, with excision of deep fascia

(Do not report 37735 in conjunction with 37700, 37718, 37722, 37780)

(For bilateral procedure, report 37735 with modifier -50)

37760 Ligation of perforator veins, subfascial, radical (Linton type), including skin graft, when performed, open, 1 leg

(For endoscopic procedure, use 37500)

37761 Ligation of perforator vein(s), subfascial, open, including ultrasound guidance, when performed, 1 leg

(For bilateral procedure, report 37761 with modifier -50)

(Do not report 37760, 37761 in conjunction with 76937, 76942, 76998, 93971)

(For endoscopic ligation of subfascial perforator veins, use 37500)

37765 Stab phlebectomy of varicose veins, 1 extremity; 10-20 stab incisions

(For less than 10 incisions, use 37799)

(For more than 20 incisions, use 37766)

37766 more than 20 incisions

37780 Ligation and division of short saphenous vein at saphenopopliteal junction (separate procedure)

(For bilateral procedure, report 37780 with modifier -50)

37785 Ligation, division, and/or excision of varicose vein cluster(s), 1 leg

(For bilateral procedure, report 37785 with modifier -50)

OTHER PROCEDURES

37788 Penile revascularization, artery, with or without vein graft

37790 Penile venous occlusive procedure

37799 Unlisted procedure, vascular surgery

HEMIC AND LYMPHATIC SYSTEMS

CPT codes from this section of CPT are used to report invasive and surgical procedures performed on the spleen and lymph nodes. Bone marrow transplants are reported using CPT codes 38230-38241 from this section.

When bone marrow aspiration is performed alone, the appropriate code to report is CPT code 38220. When a bone marrow biopsy is performed, the appropriate code is CPT code 38221 (bone marrow biopsy). This code cannot be reported with CPT code 20220 (bone biopsy). CPT codes 38220 and 38221 may only be reported together if the two procedures are performed at separate sites or at separate patient encounters. Separate sites include bone marrow aspiration and biopsy in different bones or two separate skin incisions over the same bone.

When both a bone marrow biopsy (CPT code 38221) and bone marrow aspiration (CPT code 38220) are performed at the same site through the same skin incision, do not report the bone marrow aspiration, CPT code 38220, in addition to the bone marrow biopsy (CPT code 38221). HCPCS/CPT code G0364 may be reported to describe the bone marrow aspiration performed with bone marrow biopsy through the same skin incision on the same date of service.

SPLEEN

EXCISION

38100   Splenectomy; total (separate procedure)

38101   partial (separate procedure)

+ **38102**   total, en bloc for extensive disease, in conjunction with other procedure (List in addition to code for primary procedure)

REPAIR

38115   Repair of ruptured spleen (splenorrhaphy) with or without partial splenectomy

LAPAROSCOPY

Surgical laparoscopy always includes diagnostic laparoscopy. To report a diagnostic laparoscopy (peritoneoscopy) (separate procedure), use 49320.

38120   Laparoscopy, surgical, splenectomy

38129   Unlisted laparoscopy procedure, spleen

INTRODUCTION

38200   Injection procedure for splenoportography

(For radiological supervision and interpretation, use 75810)

GENERAL

BONE MARROW OR STEM CELL SERVICES/PROCEDURES

Codes 38207-38215 describe various steps used to preserve, prepare and purify bone marrow/stem cells prior to transplantation or reinfusion. Each code may be reported only once per day regardless of the quantity of bone marrow/stem cells manipulated.

38204   Management of recipient hematopoietic progenitor cell donor search and cell acquisition

38205   Blood-derived hematopoietic progenitor cell harvesting for transplantation, per collection; allogeneic

38206   autologous

38207   Transplant preparation of hematopoietic progenitor cells; cryopreservation and storage

---

(For diagnostic cryopreservation and storage, see 88240)

38208   thawing of previously frozen harvest, without washing, per donor

(For diagnostic thawing and expansion of frozen cells, see 88241)

38209   thawing of previously frozen harvest, with washing, per donor

38210   specific cell depletion within harvest, T-cell depletion

38211   tumor cell depletion

38212   red blood cell removal

38213   platelet depletion

38214   plasma (volume) depletion

38215   cell concentration in plasma, mononuclear, or buffy coat layer

(Do not report 38207-38215 in conjunction with 88182, 88184-88189)

▲ **38220**   Diagnostic bone marrow; aspiration(s)

(Do not report 38220 in conjunction with 38221)

(For diagnostic bone marrow biopsy[ies] and aspiration[s] performed at the same session, use 38222)

(For aspiration of bone marrow for bone graft, spine surgery only, use 20939)

(For bone marrow aspiration[s] for platelet-rich stem cell injection, use 0232T)

▲ **38221**   biopsy (ies)

(Do not report 38221 in conjunction with 38220)

(For diagnostic bone marrow biopsy[ies] and aspiration[s] performed at the same session, use 38222)

● **38222**   biopsy(ies) and aspiration(s)

(Do not report 38222 in conjunction with 38220 and 38221)

(For bilateral procedure, report 38220, 38221, 38222 with modifier 50)

(For bone marrow biopsy interpretation, use 88305)

38230   Bone marrow harvesting for transplantation; allogenic

38232   autologous

(For autologous and allogeneic blood-derived peripheral stem cell harvesting for transplantation, see 38205, 38206)

(For diagnostic bone marrow aspiration[s], see 38220, 38222)

(For aspiration of bone marrow for bone graft, spine surgery only, use 20939)

(For bone marrow aspiration[s] for platelet-rich stem cell injection, use 0232T)

TRANSPLANTATION AND POST-TRANSPLANTATION CELLULAR INFUSIONS

Hematopoietic cell transplantation (HCT) refers to the infusion of hematopoietic progenitor cells (HPC) obtained from bone marrow, peripheral blood apheresis, and/or umbilical cord blood. These procedure codes (38240-38243) include physician monitoring of multiple physiologic parameters, physician verification of cell processing, evaluation of the patient during as well as immediately before and after the HPC/lymphocyte infusion, physician presence during the HPC/lymphocyte infusion with

● New Code   ▲ Revised Code   + Add-On Code   ⊘ Modifier -51 Exempt   ★ Telemedicine

associated direct physician supervision of clinical staff, and management of uncomplicated adverse events (eg, nausea, urticaria) during the infusion, which is not separately reportable.

HOT may be autologous (when the HPV donor and recipient are the same person) or allogenic (when the HPV donor and recipient are not the same person). Code 38241 is used to report any autologous transplant while 38240 is used to report an allogenic transplant. In some cases allogenic transplants involve more than one donor and cells from each donor are infused sequentially whereby one unit of 38240 is reported for each donor infused. code 38242 is used to report a donor lymphocyte infusion. Code 38243 is used to report a HPC boost from the original allogenic HPC donor. A lymphocyte infusion or HPC boost can occur days, months or even years after the initial hematopoietic cell transplant. The lymphocyte infusion is used to treat relapse, infection, or post-transplant lymphoproliferative syndrome. HPC boost represents an infusion of hematopoietic progenitor cells from the original donor that is being used to treat a relapse or or post-transplant cytopenia(s). Codes 38240, 38242, and 38243 should not be reported together on the same date of service.

If a separately identifiable E/M service is performed on the same date of service, the appropriate E/M service code, including office or other outpatient services, established (99211-99215), hospital observation services (99217-99220, 99224-99226), hospital inpatient services (99221-99223, 99231-99239), and inpatient neonatal and pediatric critical care (99471, 99472, 99475, 99476) may be reported, using modifier 25, in addition to 38240, 38242, or 38243. Post transplant infusion management of adverse reactions is reported separately using the appropriate E/M, prolonged service or critical care code(s). In accordance with place of service and facility reporting guideline, the fluid used to administer the cells and other infusions for incidental hydration (eg, 96360, 96361) are not separately reportable. Similarly, infusions of any medication(s) concurrently with the transplant infusion are not separately reportable. However, hydration or administration of medication (eg, antibiotics, narcotics) unrelated to the transplant are separately reportable using modifier 59.

38240	Hematopoietic progenitor cell (HPC); allogeneic transplantation per donor
38241	autologous transplantation
38243	HPC boost
38242	Allogeneic lymphocyte infusions

(For diagnostic bone marrow aspiration[s], see 38220, 38222)

(For aspiration of bone marrow for bone graft, spine surgery only, use 20939)

(For bone marrow aspiration[s] for platelet-rich stem cell injection, use 0232T)

(For modification, treatment, and processing of hematopoietic progenitor cell specimens for transplantation, see 38210-38215)

(For cryopreservation, freezing and storage of hematopoietic progenitor cells for transplantation, use 38207)

(For thawing and expansion of hematopoietic progenitor cells for transplantation, use 38208, 38209)

(For compatibility studies, see 81379-81383, 86812, 86813, 86816, 86817, 86821)

38243 Code out of order. See page 425.

LYMPH NODES AND LYMPHATIC CHANNELS

INCISION

38300	Drainage of lymph node abscess or lymphadenitis; simple
38305	extensive
38308	Lymphangiotomy or other operations on lymphatic channels
38380	Suture and/or ligation of thoracic duct; cervical approach
38381	thoracic approach
38382	abdominal approach

| ▬ Separate Procedure | ▬ Unlisted Procedure | ▬ CCI Comp. Code | ▬ Non-specific Procedure | **425** |

EXCISION

(For injection for sentinel node identification, use 38792)

38500 Biopsy or excision of lymph node(s); open, superficial

(Do not report 38500 with 38700-38780)

38505   by needle, superficial (eg, cervical, inguinal, axillary)

(If imaging guidance is performed, see 76942, 77002, 77012, 77021)

(For fine needle aspiration, use 10021 or 10022)

(For evaluation of fine needle aspirate, see 88172, 88173)

38510   open, deep cervical node(s)

38520   open, deep cervical node(s) with excision scalene fat pad

38525   open, deep axillary node(s)

38530   open, internal mammary node(s)

(Do not report 38530 with 38720-38746)

(For percutaneous needle biopsy, retroperitoneal lymph node or mass, use 49180. For fine needle aspiration, use 10022)

38542 Dissection, deep jugular node(s)

(For radical cervical neck dissection, use 38720)

38550 Excision of cystic hygroma, axillary or cervical; without deep neurovascular dissection

38555   with deep neurovascular dissection

LIMITED LYMPHADENECTOMY FOR STAGING

38562 Limited lymphadenectomy for staging (separate procedure); pelvic and para-aortic

(When combined with prostatectomy, use 55812 or 55842)

(When combined with insertion of radioactive substance into prostate, use 55862)

38564   retroperitoneal (aortic and/or splenic)

LAPAROSCOPY

Surgical laparoscopy always includes diagnostic laparoscopy. To report a diagnostic laparoscopy (peritoneoscopy), (separate procedure), use 49320.

38570 Laparoscopy, surgical; with retroperitoneal lymph node sampling (biopsy), single or multiple

38571   with bilateral total pelvic lymphadenectomy

38572   with bilateral total pelvic lymphadenectomy and peri-aortic lymph node sampling (biopsy), single or multiple

(For drainage of lymphocele to peritoneal cavity, use 49323)

● **38573**   with bilateral total pelvic lymphadenectomy and periaortic lymph node sampling, peritoneal washings, peritoneal biopsy(ies), omentectomy, and diaphragmatic washings, including diaphragmatic and other serosal biopsy(ies), when performed

---

426   ● New Code   ▲ Revised Code   + Add-On Code   ⊘ Modifier -51 Exempt   ★ Telemedicine

(Do not report 38573 in conjunction with 38562, 38564, 38570, 38571, 38572, 38589, 38770, 38780, 49255, 49320, 49326, 58541, 58542, 58543, 58544, 58548, 58550, 58552, 58553, 58554)

38589 Unlisted laparoscopy procedure, lymphatic system

RADICAL LYMPHADENECTOMY (RADICAL RESECTION OF LYMPH NODES)

(For limited pelvic and retroperitoneal lymphadenectomies, see 38562, 38564)

38700 Suprahyoid lymphadenectomy

(For bilateral procedure, report 38700 with modifier -50)

38720 Cervical lymphadenectomy (complete)

(For bilateral procedure, report 38720 with modifier -50)

38724 Cervical lymphadenectomy (modified radical neck dissection)

38740 Axillary lymphadenectomy; superficial

38745 complete

+ **38746** Thoracic lymphadenectomy by thoracotomy, mediastinal and regional lymphadenectomy (List separately in addition to code for primary procedure)

(On the right, mediastinal lymph nodes include the paratracheal, subcarinal, paraesophageal, and inferior pulmonary ligament)

(On the left, mediastinal lymph nodes include the aortopulmonary window, subcarinal, paraesophageal, and inferior pulmonary ligament)

(Report 38746 in conjunction with 19260, 31760, 31766, 31786, 32096-32200, 32220-32320, 32440-32491, 32503-32505, 33025, 33030, 33050-33130, 39200-39220, 39560, 39561, 43101, 43112, 43117, 43118, 43122, 43123, 43351, 60270, 60505)

(To report mediastinal and regional lymphadenectomy via thoracoscopy [VATS], see 32674)

+ **38747** Abdominal lymphadenectomy, regional, including celiac, gastric, portal, peripancreatic, with or without para-aortic and vena caval nodes (List separately in addition to code for primary procedure)

38760 Inguinofemoral lymphadenectomy, superficial, including Cloquets node (separate procedure)

(For bilateral procedure, report 38760 with modifier -50)

38765 Inguinofemoral lymphadenectomy, superficial, in continuity with pelvic lymphadenectomy, including external iliac, hypogastric, and obturator nodes (separate procedure)

(For bilateral procedure, report 38765 with modifier -50)

38770 Pelvic lymphadenectomy, including external iliac, hypogastric, and obturator nodes (separate procedure)

(For bilateral procedure, report 38770 with modifier -50)

38780 Retroperitoneal transabdominal lymphadenectomy, extensive, including pelvic, aortic, and renal nodes (separate procedure)

(For excision and repair of lymphedematous skin and subcutaneous tissue, see 15004-15005, 15570-15650)

INTRODUCTION

38790 Injection procedure; lymphangiography

(For bilateral procedure, report 38790 with modifier -50)

(For radiological supervision and interpretation, see 75801-75807)

Separate Procedure   Unlisted Procedure   CCI Comp. Code   Non-specific Procedure   **427**

38792   radioactive tracer for identification of sentinel node

(For excision of sentinel node, see 38500-38542)

(For nuclear medicine lymphatics and lymph gland imaging, use 78195)

(For intraoperative identification (eg, mapping) of sentinel lymph node(s) including injection of non-radioactive dye, see 38900)

38794   Cannulation, thoracic duct

OTHER PROCEDURES

+ **38900**   Intraoperative identification (eg, mapping) of sentinel lymph node(s) includes injection of non-radioactive dye, when performed (list separately in addition to code for primary procedure)

(Use 38900 in conjunction with 19302, 19307, 38500, 38510, 38520, 38525, 38530, 38542, 38740, 38745)

(For injection of radioactive tracer for identification of sentinel node, use 38792)

38999   Unlisted procedure, hemic or lymphatic system

● New Code   ▲ Revised Code   + Add-On Code   ⊘ Modifier -51 Exempt   ★ Telemedicine

MEDIASTINUM AND DIAPHRAGM

MEDIASTINUM

INCISION

39000 Mediastinotomy with exploration, drainage, removal of foreign body, or biopsy; cervical approach

39010 transthoracic approach, including either transthoracic or median sternotomy

(Do not report 39010 in conjunction with 33955, 33956, 33963, 33964)

(For VATS pericardial biopsy, use 32604)

EXCISION/RESECTION

39200 Resection of mediastinal cyst

39220 Resection of mediastinal tumor

(For substernal thyroidectomy, use 60270)

(For thymectomy, use 60520)

(For thoracoscopic [VATS] resection of mediastinal cyst, tumor or mass, use 32662)

ENDOSCOPY

(**39400** deleted 2015 [2016 edition]. To report mediastinoscopy with biopsy, see 39401, 39402)

39401 Mediastinoscopy; includes biopsy(ies) of mediastinal mass (eg, lymphoma), when performed

39402 with lymph node biopsy(ies) (eg, lung cancer staging

OTHER PROCEDURES

39499 Unlisted procedure, mediastinum

DIAPHRAGM

REPAIR

(For transabdominal repair of diaphragmatic [esophageal hiatal] hernia, use 43325)

(For laparoscopic repair of diaphragmatic [esophageal hiatal] hernias and fundoplication, see 43280, 43281, 43282)

39501 Repair, laceration of diaphragm, any approach

(For laparoscopic paraesophageal hernia repair, see 43281, 43282)

39503 Repair, neonatal diaphragmatic hernia, with or without chest tube insertion and with or without creation of ventral hernia

(Do not report modifier 63 in conjunction with 39503)

(For laparoscopic paraesophageal hernia repair, see 43281, 43282)

39540 Repair, diaphragmatic hernia (other than neonatal), traumatic; acute

39541 chronic

39545 Imbrication of diaphragm for eventration, transthoracic or transabdominal, paralytic or nonparalytic

---

Separate Procedure   Unlisted Procedure   CCI Comp. Code   Non-specific Procedure   **429**

39560   Resection, diaphragm; with simple repair (eg, primary suture)

39561   with complex repair (eg, prosthetic material, local muscle flap)

OTHER PROCEDURES

39599   Unlisted procedure, diaphragm

● New Code   ▲ Revised Code   + Add-On Code   ⊘ Modifier -51 Exempt   ★ Telemedicine

DIGESTIVE SYSTEM

MISCELLANEOUS CODING RULES

Gastrointestinal endoscopy codes should be assigned based on the extent of visualization performed. CMS's official guidelines for excision or destruction of a lesion are:

1. *use only the biopsy code if a single lesion is biopsied but not excised;*

2. *code only for the excision if a lesion is biopsied and the remaining portion is excised;*

3. *use the biopsy code once even if multiple biopsies are performed and none are excised; and*

4. *use both a biopsy and excision code if each lesion is taken from different sites.*

If the phrase "with or without biopsy" appears in the excision code's narrative, do not use a separate biopsy code. Diagnostic endoscopies are included in surgical endoscopies.

For upper gastrointestinal endoscopies, choose the appropriate code from documentation indicating whether the procedure was a simple exam, a diagnostic procedure or surgical procedure. Remember that code selection is based on the procedure(s) performed and the anatomical sites through which the scope passes. For example, if the scope is passed to the esophagus only, the code would be chosen from endoscopy codes beginning with 43200. If the scope is passed through the esophagus to the stomach, duodenum and/or the jejunum, the code selection would begin at 43235.

HERNIA REPAIR

Review the patient's age, the kind of hernia, the clinical presentation of the hernia, and method of repair documented in the medical record before assigning a hernia repair code.

APPENDECTOMY

To code appendectomies appropriately, review the documentation for an indicated purpose for the removal. If there is none, then it is probably incidental to a more serious surgery and should not be coded.

LIPS

(For procedures on skin of lips, see 10040 et seq)

EXCISION

40490	Biopsy of lip
40500	Vermilionectomy (lip shave), with mucosal advancement
40510	Excision of lip; transverse wedge excision with primary closure
40520	V-excision with primary direct linear closure

(For excision of mucous lesions, see 40810-40816)

40525	full thickness, reconstruction with local flap (eg, Estlander or fan)
40527	full thickness, reconstruction with cross lip flap (Abbe-Estlander)
40530	Resection of lip, more than one-fourth, without reconstruction

(For reconstruction, see 13131 et seq)

REPAIR (CHEILOPLASTY)

40650	Repair lip, full thickness; vermilion only

40652	up to half vertical height
40654	over one-half vertical height, or complex
40700	Plastic repair of cleft lip/nasal deformity; primary, partial or complete, unilateral
40701	primary bilateral, 1 stage procedure
40702	primary bilateral, 1 of 2 stages
40720	secondary, by recreation of defect and reclosure

(For bilateral procedure, report 40720 with modifier -50)

(To report rhinoplasty only for nasal deformity secondary to congenital cleft lip, see 30460, 30462)

(For repair of cleft lip, with cross lip pedicle flap (Abbe-Estlander type), use 40527)

| 40761 | with cross lip pedicle flap (Abbe-Estlander type), including sectioning and inserting of pedicle |

(For repair cleft palate, see 42200 et seq)

(For other reconstructive procedures, see 14060, 14061, 15120-15261, 15574, 15576, 15630)

OTHER PROCEDURES

| 40799 | Unlisted procedure, lips |

VESTIBULE OF MOUTH

INCISION

40800	Drainage of abscess, cyst, hematoma, vestibule of mouth; simple
40801	complicated
40804	Removal of embedded foreign body, vestibule of mouth; simple
40805	complicated
40806	Incision of labial frenum (frenotomy)

EXCISION, DESTRUCTION

40808	Biopsy, vestibule of mouth
40810	Excision of lesion of mucosa and submucosa, vestibule of mouth; without repair
40812	with simple repair
40814	with complex repair
40816	complex, with excision of underlying muscle
40818	Excision of mucosa of vestibule of mouth as donor graft
40819	Excision of frenum, labial or buccal (frenumectomy, frenulectomy, frenectomy)
40820	Destruction of lesion or scar of vestibule of mouth by physical methods (eg, laser, thermal, cryo, chemical)

● New Code ▲ Revised Code + Add-On Code ⊘ Modifier -51 Exempt ★ Telemedicine

REPAIR

40830 Closure of laceration, vestibule of mouth; 2.5 cm or less

40831 over 2.5 cm or complex

40840 Vestibuloplasty; anterior

40842 posterior, unilateral

40843 posterior, bilateral

40844 entire arch

40845 complex (including ridge extension, muscle repositioning)

(For skin grafts, see 15002 et seq)

OTHER PROCEDURES

40899 Unlisted procedure, vestibule of mouth

TONGUE AND FLOOR OF MOUTH

INCISION

41000 Intraoral incision and drainage of abscess, cyst, or hematoma of tongue or floor of mouth; lingual

41005 sublingual, superficial

41006 sublingual, deep, supramylohyoid

41007 submental space

41008 submandibular space

41009 masticator space

41010 Incision of lingual frenum (frenotomy)

41015 Extraoral incision and drainage of abscess, cyst, or hematoma of floor of mouth; sublingual

41016 submental

41017 submandibular

41018 masticator space

(For frenoplasty, use 41520)

41019 Placement of needles, catheters, or other device(s) into the head and/or neck region (percutaneous, transoral, or transnasal) for subsequent interstitial radioelement application

(For imaging guidance, see 76942, 77002, 77012, 77021)

(For stereotactic insertion of intracranial brachytherapy radiation sources, use 61770)

(For interstitial radioelement application, see 77770, 77771, 77772, 77778)

EXCISION

41100 Biopsy of tongue; anterior two-thirds

Separate Procedure   Unlisted Procedure   CCI Comp. Code   Non-specific Procedure   **433**

41105   posterior one-third

41108   Biopsy of floor of mouth

41110   Excision of lesion of tongue without closure

41112   Excision of lesion of tongue with closure; anterior two-thirds

41113   posterior one-third

41114   with local tongue flap

(Do not report 41114 in conjunction with 41112, 41113)

41115   Excision of lingual frenum (frenectomy)

41116   Excision, lesion of floor of mouth

41120   Glossectomy; less than one-half tongue

41130   hemiglossectomy

41135   partial, with unilateral radical neck dissection

41140   complete or total, with or without tracheostomy, without radical neck dissection

41145   complete or total, with or without tracheostomy, with unilateral radical neck dissection

41150   composite procedure with resection floor of mouth and mandibular resection, without radical neck dissection

41153   composite procedure with resection floor of mouth, with suprahyoid neck dissection

41155   composite procedure with resection floor of mouth, mandibular resection, and radical neck dissection (Commando type)

REPAIR

41250   Repair of laceration 2.5 cm or less; floor of mouth and/or anterior two-thirds of tongue

41251   posterior one-third of tongue

41252   Repair of laceration of tongue, floor of mouth, over 2.6 cm or complex

OTHER PROCEDURES

41500   Fixation of tongue, mechanical, other than suture (eg, K-wire)

41510   Suture of tongue to lip for micrognathia (Douglas type procedure)

41512   Tongue base suspension, permanent suture technique

(For fixation of tongue, mechanical, other than suture, use 41500)

(For suture of tongue to lip for micrognathia, use 41510)

41520   Frenoplasty (surgical revision of frenum, eg, with Z-plasty)

(For frenotomy, see 40806, 41010)

41530   Submucosal ablation of the tongue base, radiofrequency, 1 or more sites, per session

---

● New Code   ▲ Revised Code   ✛ Add-On Code   ⊘ Modifier -51 Exempt   ★ Telemedicine

41599   Unlisted procedure, tongue, floor of mouth

DENTOALVEOLAR STRUCTURES

INCISION

41800   Drainage of abscess, cyst, hematoma from dentoalveolar structures

41805   Removal of embedded foreign body from dentoalveolar structures; soft tissues

41806   bone

EXCISION, DESTRUCTION

41820   Gingivectomy, excision gingiva, each quadrant

41821   Operculectomy, excision pericoronal tissues

41822   Excision of fibrous tuberosities, dentoalveolar structures

41823   Excision of osseous tuberosities, dentoalveolar structures

41825   Excision of lesion or tumor (except listed above), dentoalveolar structures; without repair

41826   with simple repair

41827   with complex repair

(For nonexcisional destruction, use 41850)

41828   Excision of hyperplastic alveolar mucosa, each quadrant (specify)

41830   Alveolectomy, including curettage of osteitis or sequestrectomy

41850   Destruction of lesion (except excision), dentoalveolar structures

OTHER PROCEDURES

41870   Periodontal mucosal grafting

41872   Gingivoplasty, each quadrant (specify)

41874   Alveoloplasty, each quadrant (specify)

(For closure of lacerations, see 40830, 40831)

(For segmental osteotomy, use 21206)

(For reduction of fractures, see 21421-21490)

41899   Unlisted procedure, dentoalveolar structures

PALATE AND UVULA

INCISION

42000   Drainage of abscess of palate, uvula

EXCISION, DESTRUCTION

42100   Biopsy of palate, uvula

42104	Excision, lesion of palate, uvula; without closure
42106	with simple primary closure
42107	with local flap closure

(For skin graft, see 14040-14302)

(For mucosal graft, use 40818)

42120	Resection of palate or extensive resection of lesion

(For reconstruction of palate with extraoral tissue, see 14040-14302, 15050, 15120, 15240, 15576)

42140	Uvulectomy, excision of uvula
42145	Palatopharyngoplasty (eg, uvulopalatopharyngoplasty, uvulopharyngoplasty)

(For removal of exostosis of the bony palate, see 21031, 21032)

42160	Destruction of lesion, palate or uvula (thermal, cryo or chemical)

REPAIR

42180	Repair, laceration of palate; up to 2 cm
42182	over 2 cm or complex
42200	Palatoplasty for cleft palate, soft and/or hard palate only
42205	Palatoplasty for cleft palate, with closure of alveolar ridge; soft tissue only
42210	with bone graft to alveolar ridge (includes obtaining graft)
42215	Palatoplasty for cleft palate; major revision
42220	secondary lengthening procedure
42225	attachment pharyngeal flap
42226	Lengthening of palate, and pharyngeal flap
42227	Lengthening of palate, with island flap
42235	Repair of anterior palate, including vomer flap

(For repair of oronasal fistula, use 30600)

42260	Repair of nasolabial fistula

(For repair of cleft lip, see 40700 et seq)

42280	Maxillary impression for palatal prosthesis
42281	Insertion of pin-retained palatal prosthesis

OTHER PROCEDURES

42299	Unlisted procedure, palate, uvula

● New Code ▲ Revised Code ✚ Add-On Code ⊘ Modifier -51 Exempt ★ Telemedicine

SALIVARY GLAND AND DUCTS

INCISION

42300 Drainage of abscess; parotid, simple

42305 parotid, complicated

42310 submaxillary or sublingual, intraoral

42320 submaxillary, external

42330 Sialolithotomy; submandibular (submaxillary), sublingual or parotid, uncomplicated, intraoral

42335 submandibular (submaxillary), complicated, intraoral

42340 parotid, extraoral or complicated intraoral

EXCISION

42400 Biopsy of salivary gland; needle

(For fine needle aspiration, see 10021, 10022)

(For evaluation of fine needle aspirate, see 88172, 88173)

(If imaging guidance, is performed, see 76942, 77002, 77012, 77021)

42405 incisional

(If imaging guidance is performed, see 76942, 77002, 77012, 77021)

42408 Excision of sublingual salivary cyst (ranula)

42409 Marsupialization of sublingual salivary cyst (ranula)

42410 Excision of parotid tumor or parotid gland; lateral lobe, without nerve dissection

42415 lateral lobe, with dissection and preservation of facial nerve

42420 total, with dissection and preservation of facial nerve

42425 total, en bloc removal with sacrifice of facial nerve

42426 total, with unilateral radical neck dissection

(For suture or grafting of facial nerve, see 64864, 64865, 69740, 69745)

42440 Excision of submandibular (submaxillary) gland

42450 Excision of sublingual gland

REPAIR

42500 Plastic repair of salivary duct, sialodochoplasty; primary or simple

42505 secondary or complicated

42507 Parotid duct diversion, bilateral (Wilke type procedure);

(**42508** deleted 2014 [2015 edition])

| 42509 | with excision of both submandibular glands |
| 42510 | with ligation of both submandibular (Wharton's) ducts |

OTHER PROCEDURES

| 42550 | Injection procedure for sialography |

(For radiological supervision and interpretation, use 70390)

42600	Closure salivary fistula
42650	Dilation salivary duct
42660	Dilation and catheterization of salivary duct, with or without injection
42665	Ligation salivary duct, intraoral
42699	Unlisted procedure, salivary glands or ducts

PHARYNX, ADENOIDS, AND TONSILS

INCISION

42700	Incision and drainage abscess; peritonsillar
42720	retropharyngeal or parapharyngeal, intraoral approach
42725	retropharyngeal or parapharyngeal, external approach

EXCISION, DESTRUCTION

42800	Biopsy; oropharynx
42804	nasopharynx, visible lesion, simple
42806	nasopharynx, survey for unknown primary lesion

(For laryngoscopic biopsy, see 31510, 31535, 31536)

42808	Excision or destruction of lesion of pharynx, any method
42809	Removal of foreign body from pharynx
42810	Excision branchial cleft cyst or vestige, confined to skin and subcutaneous tissues
42815	Excision branchial cleft cyst, vestige, or fistula, extending beneath subcutaneous tissues and/or into pharynx
42820	Tonsillectomy and adenoidectomy; under age 12
42821	age 12 or over
42825	Tonsillectomy, primary or secondary; under age 12
42826	age 12 or over
42830	Adenoidectomy, primary; under age 12
42831	age 12 or over

---

438   ● New Code   ▲ Revised Code   + Add-On Code   ⊘ Modifier -51 Exempt   ★ Telemedicine

42835 Adenoidectomy, secondary; under age 12

42836 age 12 or over

42842 Radical resection of tonsil, tonsillar pillars, and/or retromolar trigone; without closure

42844 closure with local flap (eg, tongue, buccal)

42845 closure with other flap

(For closure with other flap(s), use appropriate number for flap(s))

(When combined with radical neck dissection, use also 38720)

42860 Excision of tonsil tags

42870 Excision or destruction lingual tonsil, any method (separate procedure)

(For resection of the nasopharynx (eg., juvenile angiofibroma) by bicoronal and/or transzygomatic approach, see 61586 and 61600)

42890 Limited pharyngectomy

42892 Resection of lateral pharyngeal wall or pyriform sinus, direct closure by advancement of lateral and posterior pharyngeal walls

(When combined with radical neck dissection, use also 38720)

42894 Resection of pharyngeal wall requiring closure with myocutaneous or fasciocutaneous flap or free muscle, skin, or fascial flap with microvascular anastamosis

(When combined with radical neck dissection, use also 38720)

(For limited pharyngectomy with radical neck dissection, use 38720 with 42890)

(For flap used for reconstruction, see 15730, 15733, 15734, 15756, 15757, 15758)

REPAIR

42900 Suture pharynx for wound or injury

42950 Pharyngoplasty (plastic or reconstructive operation on pharynx)

(For pharyngeal flap, use 42225)

42953 Pharyngoesophageal repair

(For closure with myocutaneous or other flap, use appropriate number in addition)

OTHER PROCEDURES

42955 Pharyngostomy (fistulization of pharynx, external for feeding)

42960 Control oropharyngeal hemorrhage, primary or secondary (eg, post-tonsillectomy); simple

42961 complicated, requiring hospitalization

42962 with secondary surgical intervention

42970 Control of nasopharyngeal hemorrhage, primary or secondary (eg, postadenoidectomy); simple, with posterior nasal packs, with or without anterior packs and/or cautery

42971 complicated, requiring hospitalization

| | Separate Procedure | | Unlisted Procedure | | CCI Comp. Code | | Non-specific Procedure | **439** |

42972   with secondary surgical intervention

42999   Unlisted procedure, pharynx, adenoids, or tonsils

ESOPHAGUS

INCISION

(For esophageal intubation with laparotomy, use 43510)

43020   Esophagotomy, cervical approach, with removal of foreign body

43030   Cricopharyngeal myotomy

43045   Esophagotomy, thoracic approach, with removal of foreign body

EXCISION

(For gastrointestinal reconstruction for previous esophagectomy, see 43360, 43361)

43100   Excision of lesion, esophagus, with primary repair; cervical approach

43101   thoracic or abdominal approach

(For wide excision of malignant lesion of cervical esophagus, with total laryngectomy without radical neck dissection, see 43107, 43116, 43124 and 31360)

(For wide excision of malignant lesion of cervical esophagus, with total laryngectomy with radical neck dissection, see 43107, 43116, 43124, and 31365)

43107   Total or near total esophagectomy, without thoracotomy; with pharyngogastrostomy or cervical esophagogastrostomy, with or without pyloroplasty (transhiatal)

43108   with colon interposition or small intestine reconstruction, including intestine mobilization, preparation and anastomosis(es)

▲ **43112**   Total or near total esophagectomy, with thoracotomy; with pharyngogastrostomy or cervical esophagogastrostomy, with or without pyloroplasty (ie, McKeown esophagectomy or tri-incisional esophagectomy)

43113   with colon interposition or small intestine reconstruction, including intestine mobilization, preparation, and anastomosis(es)

43116   Partial esophagectomy, cervical, with free intestinal graft, including microvascular anastomosis, obtaining the graft and intestinal reconstruction

(Do not report 43116 in conjunction with 69990)

(Report 43116 with the modifier -52 appended if intestinal or free jejunal graft with microvascular anastomosis is performed by another physician)

(For free jejunal graft with microvascular anastomosis performed by another physician, use 43496)

43117   Partial esophagectomy, distal two-thirds, with thoracotomy and separate abdominal incision, with or without proximal gastrectomy; with thoracic esophagogastrostomy, with or without pyloroplasty (Ivor Lewis)

43118   with colon interposition or small intestine reconstruction, including intestine mobilization, preparation, and anastomosis(es)

(For total esophagectomy with gastropharyngostomy, see 43107, 43124)

(For esophagogastrectomy (lower third) and vagotomy, use 43122)

● New Code   ▲ Revised Code   ＋ Add-On Code   ⊘ Modifier -51 Exempt   ★ Telemedicine

43121 Partial esophagectomy, distal two-thirds, with thoracotomy only, with or without proximal gastrectomy, with thoracic esophagogastrostomy, with or without pyloroplasty

43122 Partial esophagectomy, thoracoabdominal or abdominal approach, with or without proximal gastrectomy; with esophagogastrostomy, with or without pyloroplasty

43123 with colon interposition or small intestine reconstruction, including intestine mobilization, preparation, and anastomosis(es)

43124 Total or partial esophagectomy, without reconstruction (any approach), with cervical esophagostomy

43130 Diverticulectomy of hypopharynx or esophagus, with or without myotomy; cervical approach

43135 thoracic approach

(For endoscopic diverticulectomy of hypopharynx or cervical esophagus, use 43180)

ENDOSCOPY

When bleeding occurs as a result of an endoscopic procedure, control of bleeding is not reported separately during the same operative session.

Esophagoscopy includes examination from the cricopharyngeus muscle (upper esophageal sphincter) to and including the gastroesophageal junction. It may also include examination of the proximal region of the stomach via retroflexion when performed.

Esophagoscopy

43180 Esophagoscopy, rigid, transoral with diverticulectomy of hypopharynx or cervical esophagus (eg, Zenker's diverticulum), with cricopharyngeal myotomy, includes use of telescope or operating microscope and repair, when performed

(Do not report 43180 in conjunction with 43210, 69990)

(For diverticulectomy of hypopharynx or esophagus [open], see 43130, 43135)

43191 Esophagoscopy, rigid, transoral; diagnostic, including collection of specimen(s) by brushing or washing when performed (separate procedure)

(Do not report 43191 in conjunction with 43192, 43193, 43194, 43195, 43196, 43197, 43198, 43210)

(For diagnostic transnasal esophagoscopy, see 43197, 43198)

(For diagnostic flexible transoral esophagoscopy, use 43200)

43192 with directed submucosal injection(s), any substance

(Do not report 43192 in conjunction with 43191, 43197, 43198)

(For flexible transoral esophagoscopy with directed submucosal injection(s), use 43201)

(For flexible transoral esophagoscopy with injection sclerosis of esophageal varices, use 43204)

(For rigid transoral esophagoscopy with injection sclerosis of esophageal varices, use 43499)

43193 with biopsy, single or multiple

(Do not report 43193 in conjunction with 43191, 43197, 43198)

(For flexible transoral esophagoscopy with biopsy, use 43202)

43194 with removal of foreign body(s)

(Do not report 43194 in conjunction with 43191, 43197, 43198)

(If fluoroscopic guidance is performed, use 76000)

(For flexible transoral esophagoscopy with removal of foreign body(s), use 43215)

43195   with balloon dilation (less than 30 mm diameter)

(Do not report 43195 in conjunction with 43191, 43197, 43198)

(If fluoroscopic guidance is performed, use 74360)

(For esophageal dilation with balloon 30 mm diameter or larger, see 43214, 43233)

(For dilation without endoscopic visualization, see 43450, 43453)

(For flexible transoral esophagoscopy with balloon dilation [less than 30 mm diameter], use 43220)

43196   with insertion of guide wire followed by dilation over guide wire

(Do not report 43196 in conjunction with 43191, 43197, 43198)

(If fluoroscopic guidance is performed, use 74360)

(For flexible transoral esophagoscopy with insertion of guide wire followed by dilation over guide wire, use 43226)

43197   Esophagoscopy, flexible, transnasal; diagnostic, including collection of specimen(s) by brushing or washing, when performed (separate procedure)

(Do not report 43197 in conjunction with 31575, 43191, 43192, 43193, 43194, 43195, 43196, 43198, 43200-43232, 43235-43259, 43266, 43270, 92511)

(For transoral esophagoscopy, see 43191, 43200)

(Do not report 43197 in conjunction with 31231 unless separate type of endoscope [eg, rigid endoscope] is used)

43198   with biopsy, single or multiple

(Do not report 43198 in conjunction with 31575, 43191, 43192, 43193, 43194, 43195, 43196, 43197, 43200-43232, 43235-43259, 43266, 43270, 92511)

(For transoral esophagoscopy with biopsy, see 43193, 43202)

(Do not report 43198 in conjunction with 31231 unless separate type of endoscope [eg, rigid endoscope] is used)

43200   Esophagoscopy, flexible, transoral; diagnostic, including collection of specimen(s) by brushing or washing, when performed (separate procedure)

(Do not report 43200 in conjunction with 43197, 43198, 43201-43232)

(For diagnostic rigid transoral esophagoscopy, use 43191)

(For diagnostic flexible transnasal esophacoscopy, use 43197)

(For diagnostic flexible esophagogastroduodenoscopy, use 43235)

43201   with directed submucosal injection(s), any substance

(Do not report 43201 in conjunction with 43204, 43211, 43227 for the same lesion)

(Do not report 43201 in conjunction with 43197, 43198, 43200)

(For rigid transoral esophagoscopy with directed submucosal injection[s], use 43192)

(For flexible transoral esophagoscopy with injection sclerosis of esophageal varices, use 43204)

(For rigid transoral esophagoscopy with injection sclerosis of esophageal varices, use 43499)

43202   with biopsy, single or multiple

● New Code   ▲ Revised Code   + Add-On Code   ⊘ Modifier -51 Exempt   ★ Telemedicine

(Do not report 43202 in conjunction with 43211 for the same lesion)

(Do not report 43202 in conjunction with 43197, 43198, 43200)

(For rigid transoral esophagoscopy with biopsy, use 43193)

(For flexible transnasal esophagoscopy with biopsy, use 43198)

43204   with injection sclerosis of esophageal varices

(Do not report 43204 in conjunction with 43201, 43227 for the same lesion)

(Do not report 43204 in conjunction with 43197, 43198, 43200)

(For rigid transoral esophagoscopy with injection sclerosisk of esophageal varices, use 43499)

43205   with band ligation of esophageal varices

(Do not report 43205 in conjunction with 43227 for the same lesion)

(Do not report 43205 in conjunction with 43197, 43198, 43200)

(To report control of nonvariceal bleeding with band ligation, use 43227)

43206   with optial endomicroscopy

(Report supply of contrast agent separately)

(Do not report 43206 in conjunction with 43197, 43198, 43200, 88375)

43210 This code is out of order. See page 448.

43211 This code is out of order. See page 443.

43212 This code is out of order. See page 444.

43213 This code is out of order. See page 444.

43214 This code is out of order. See page 444.

43215   with removal of foreign body(s)

(Do not report 43215 in conjunction with 43197, 43198, 43200)

(If fluoroscopic guidance is performed, use 76000)

(For rigid transoral esophagoscopy with removal of foreign body(s), use 43194)

43216   with removal of tumor(s), polyp(s), or other lesion(s) by hot biopsy forceps or bipolar cautery

(Do not report 43216 in conjunction with 43197, 43198, 43200)

43217   with removal of tumor(s), polyp(s), or other lesion(s) by snare technique

(Do not report 43217 in conjunction with 43211 for the same lesion)

(Do not report 43217 in conjunction with 43197, 43198, 43200)

(For esophagogastroduodenoscopy with removal of tumor[s], polyp[s], or other lesion[s] by snare technique, use 43251)

(For endoscopic mucosal resection, use 43211)

43211   with endoscopic mucosal resection

(Do not report 43211 in conjunction with 43201, 43202, 43217 for the same lesion)

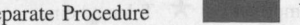

(Do not report 43211 in conjunction with 43197, 43198, 43200)

43212   with placement of endoscopic stent (includes pre- and post-dilation and guide wire passage, when performed)

(Do not report 43212 in conjunction with 43197, 43198, 43200, 43220, 43226, 43241)

(If fluoroscopic guidance is performed, use 74360)

43220   with transendoscopic balloon dilation (less than 30 mm diameter)

(Do not report 43220 in conjunction with 43197, 43198, 43200, 43212, 43226, 43229)

(If fluoroscopic guidance is performed, use 74360)

(For rigid transoral esophagoscopy with balloon dilation [less than 30 mm diameter], use 43195)

(For esophageal dilation with balloon 30 mm diameter or larger, use 43214)

(For dilation without endoscopic visualization, see 43450, 43453)

43213   with dilation of esophagus, by balloon or dilator, retrograde (includes fluoroscopic guidance, when performed)

(Do not report 43213 in conjunction with 43197, 43198, 43200, 74360, 76000, 76001)

(For transendoscopic balloon dilation of multiple strictures during the same session, report 43213 with modifier 59 for each additiional stricture dilated)

43214   with dilation of esophagus with balloon (30 mm diameter or larger) (includes fluoroscopic guidance, when performed)

(Do not report 43214 in conjunction with 43197, 43198, 43200, 74360, 76000, 76001)

43226   with insertion of guide wire followed by passage of dilator(s) over guide wire

(Do not report 43226 in conjunction with 43229 for the same lesion)

(Do not report 43226 in conjunction with 43197, 43198, 43200, 43212, 43220)

(If fluoroscopic guidance is performed, use 74360)

(For rigid transoral esophagoscopy wit insertion of guide wire followed by dilation over guide wire, use 43196)

43227   with control of bleeding, any method

(Do not report 43227 in conunction with 43201, 43204, 43205 for the same lesion)

(Do not report 43227 in conjunction with 43197, 43198, 43200)

43229   with ablation of tumor(s), polyp(s), or other lesion(s) (includes pre- and post-dilation and guide wire passage, when performed)

(Do not report 43229 in conjunction with 43220, 43226 for the same lesion)

(Do not report 43229 in conjunction with 43197, 43198, 43200)

(For esophagoscopic photodynamic therapy, report 43229 in conjunction with 96570, 96571 as appropriate)

43231   with endoscopic ultrasound examination

(Do not report 43231 in conjunction with 43197, 43198, 43200, 43232, 76975)

(Do not report 43231 more than once per session)

43232   with transendoscopic ultrasound-guided intramural or transmural fine needle aspiration/biopsy(s)

● New Code   ▲ Revised Code   + Add-On Code   ⊘ Modifier -51 Exempt   ★ Telemedicine

(Do not report 43232 in conjunction with 43197, 43198, 43200, 43231, 76942, 76975)

(Do not report 43232 more than once per session)

43233 This code is out of order. See page 447.

Esophagogastroduodenoscopy

(For examination of the esophagus from the cricopharyngeus muscle [upper esophageal sphincter] to and including the gastroesophageal junction, including examination of the proximal region of the stomach via retroflexion when perofrmed, see 43197, 43198, 43200, 43201, 43202, 43204, 43205, 43206, 43211, 43212, 43213, 43214, 43215, 43216, 43217, 43220, 43226, 43227, 43229, 43231, 43232)

(Use 43233, 43235-43259, 43266, 43270 for examination of a surgically altered stomach where the jejunum is examined distal to the anastomosis [eg, gastric bypass, gastroenterostomy{BillrothII}])

To report esophagogastroscopy where the duodenum is deliberately not examined (eg, judged clinically not pertinent), or because the clinical situation precludes such exam (eg, significant gastric retention precludes safe exam of duodenum], append modifier 52 if repeat examination is not planned, or modifier 53 if repeat examiniation is planned.

43235 Esophagogastroduodenoscopy, flexible, transoral; diagnostic, including collection of specimen(s) by brushing or washing, when performed (separate procedure)

(Do not report 43235 in conjunction with 43197, 43198, 43210, 43236-43259, 43266, 43270, 44360, 44361, 44363, 44364, 44365, 44366, 44369, 44370, 44372, 44373, 44376, 44377, 44378, 44379)

43236 with directed submucosal injection(s), any substance

(Do not report 43236 in conjunction with 43243, 43254, 43255 for the same lesion)

(Do not report 43236 in conjunction with 43197, 43198, 43235, 44360, 44361, 44363, 44364, 44365, 44366, 44369, 44370, 44372, 44373, 44376, 44377, 44378, 44379)

(For flexible, transoral esophagogastroduodenoscopy with injection sclerosis of esophageal and/or gastric varicies, use 43243)

43237 with endoscopic ultrasound examination limited to the esophagus, stomach or duodenum, and adjacent structures

(Do not report 43237 in conjunction with 43197, 43198, 43235, 43238, 43242, 43253, 43259, 44360, 44361, 44363, 44364, 44365, 44366, 44369, 44370, 44372, 44373, 44376, 44377, 44378, 44379, 76975)

(Do not report 43237 more than once per session)

43238 with transendoscopic ultrasound-guided intramural or transmural fine needle aspiration/biopsy(s), esophagus (includes endoscopic ultrasound examination limited to the esophagus, stomach or duodenum, and adjacent structures)

(Do not report 43238 in conjunction with 43197, 43198, 43235, 43237, 43242, 44360, 44361, 44363, 44364, 44365, 44366, 44369, 44370, 44372, 44373, 44376, 44377, 44378, 44379, 76942, 76975)

(Do not report 43238 more than once per session)

43239 with biopsy, single or multiple

(Do not report 43239 in conjunction with 43254 for the same lesion)

(Do not report 43238 in conjunction with 43197, 43198, 43235, 44360, 44361, 44363, 44364, 44365, 44366, 44369, 44370, 44372, 44373, 44376, 44377, 44378, 44379)

43240 with transmural drainage of pseudocyst (includes placement of transmural drainage catheter[s]/stent[s], when performed, and endoscopic ultrasound, when performed

(Do not report 43240 in conjunction with 43253 for the same lesion)

(Do not report 43240 in conjunction with 43197, 43198, 43235, 43242, 43259, 43266, 44360, 44361, 44363, 44364, 44365, 44366, 44369, 44370, 44372, 44373, 44376, 44377, 44378, 44379)

(Do not report 43240 more than once per session)

(For endoscopic pancreatic necrosectomy, use 48999)

43241   with insertion of intraluminal tube or catheter

(Do not report 43241 in conjunction with 43197, 43198, 43212, 43235, 43266, 44360, 44361, 44363, 44364, 44365, 44366, 44369, 44370, 44372, 44373, 44376, 44377, 44378, 44379)

(For naso- or oro-gastric tube placement requiring physician's or other qualified health care professional's skill and fluoroscopic guidance, use 43752)

(For nonendoscopic enteric tube placement, see 44500, 74340)

43242   with transendoscopic ultrasound-guided intramural or transmural fine needle aspiration/biopsy(s) (includes endoscopic ultrasound examination of the esophagus, stomach, and either the duodenum or a surgically latered stomach where the jejunum is examined distal to the anastomosis)

(Do not report 43242 in conjunction with 43197, 43198, 43235, 43237, 43238, 43240, 43259, 44360, 44361, 44363, 44364, 44365, 44366, 44369, 44370, 44372, 44373, 44376, 44377, 44378, 44379, 76942, 76975)

(Do not report 43242 more than once per session)

(For transendoscopic ultrasound-guided transmural fine needle aspiration/biopsy limited to the esophagus, stomach, duodenum, or adjacent structure, use 43238)

43243   with injection sclerosis of esophagea/gastric varices

(Do not report 43243 in conjunction with 43236, 43255 for the same lesion)

(Do not report 43243 in conjunction with 43197, 43198, 43235, 44360, 44361, 44363, 44364, 44365, 44366, 44369, 44370, 44372, 44373, 44376, 44377, 44378, 44379)

43244   with band ligation of esophageal/gastric varices

(Do not report 43244 in conjunction with 43197, 43198, 43235, 43255, 44360, 44361, 44363, 44364, 44365, 44366, 44369, 44370, 44372, 44373, 44376, 44377, 44378, 44379)

(To report control of noninvasive bleeding with band ligation, use 43255)

43245   with dilation of gastric/duodenal stricture(s) (eg, balloon, bougie)

(Do not report 43245 in conjunction with 43197, 43198, 43235, 43266, 44360, 44361, 44363, 44364, 44365, 44366, 44369, 44370, 44372, 44373, 44376, 44377, 44378, 44379)

(If fluoroscopic guidance is performed, use 74360)

43246   with directed placement of percutaneous gastrostomy tube

(Do not report 43246 in conjunction with 43197, 43198, 43235, 44360, 44361, 44363, 44364, 44365, 44366, 44369, 44370, 44372, 44376, 44377, 44378, 44379)

(For nonendoscopic percutaneous placement of gastrostomy tube, use 49440)

(For replacement of gastrostomy tube without imaging or endoscopy, use 43760)

43247   with removal of foreign body(s)

(Do not report 43247 in conjunction with 43197, 43198, 43235, 44360, 44361, 44363, 44364, 44365, 44366, 44369, 44370, 44372, 44373, 44376, 44377, 44378, 44379)

(If fluoroscopic guidance is performed, use 76000)

43248   with insertion of guide wire followed by passage of dilator(s) through esophagus over guide wire

(Do not report 43248 in conjunction with 43197, 43198, 43235, 43266, 43270, 44360, 44361, 44363, 44364, 44365, 44366, 44369, 44370, 44372, 44373, 44376, 44377, 44378, 44379)

  ● New Code ▲ Revised Code ✛ Add-On Code ⊘ Modifier -51 Exempt ★ Telemedicine

(If fluoroscopic guidance is performed, use 74360)

43249   with transendoscopic balloon dilation of esophagus (less than 30 mm diameter)

(Do not report 43249 in conjunction with 43197, 43198, 43235, 43266, 43270, 44360, 44361, 44363, 44364, 44365, 44366, 44369, 44370, 44372, 44373, 44376, 44377, 44378, 44379)

(If fluoroscopic guidance is performed, use 74360)

43233   with dilation of esophagus with balloon (30 mm diameter or larger) (includes fluoroscopic guidance, when performed)

(Do not report 43233 in conjunction with 43197, 43198, 43235, 44360, 44361, 44363, 44364, 44365, 44366, 44369, 44370, 44372, 44373, 44376, 44377, 44378, 44379, 74360, 76000, 76001)

43250   with removal of tumor(s), polyp(s), or other lesion(s) by hot biopsy forceps

(Do not report 43250 in conjunction with 43197, 43198, 43235, 44360, 44361, 44363, 44364, 44365, 44366, 44369, 44370, 44372, 44373, 44376, 44377, 44378, 44379)

43251   with removal of tumor(s), polyp(s), or other lesion(s) by snare technique

(Do not report 43251 in conjunction with 43254 for the same lesion)

(Do not report 43251 in conjunction with 43197, 43198, 43235, 44360, 44361, 44363, 44364, 44365, 44366, 44369, 44370, 44372, 44373, 44376, 44377, 44378, 44379)

(For endoscopic mucosal resection, use 43254)

43252   with optical endomicroscopy

(Report supply of contrast agent separately)

(Do not report 43252 in conjunction with 43197, 43198, 43235, 44360, 44361, 44363, 44364, 44365, 44366, 44369, 44370, 44372, 44373, 44376, 44377, 44378, 44379, 88375)

43253   with transendoscopic ultrasound-guided transmural injection of diagnostic or therapeutic substance(s) (eg, anesthetic, neurolytic agent) or fiducial marker(s) (includes endoscopic ultrasound examination of the esophagus, stomach, and either the duodenum or a surgically altered stomach where the jejunum is examined distal to the anastomosis)

(Do not report 43253 in conjunction with 43240 for the same lesion)

(Do not report 43253 in conjunction with 43197, 43198, 43235, 43237, 43259, 44360, 44361, 44363, 44364, 44365, 44366, 44369, 44370, 44372, 44373, 44376, 44377, 44378, 44379, 76942, 76975)

(Do not report 43253 more than once per session)

(For transendoscopic ultrasound-guided transmural fine needle aspiration/biopsy, see 43238, 43242)

43254   with endoscopic mucoal resection

(Do not report 43254 in conjunction with 43236, 43239, 43251 for the same lesion)

(Do not report 43254 in conjunction with 43197, 43198, 43235, 44360, 44361, 44363, 44364, 44365, 44366, 44369, 44370, 44372, 44373, 44376, 44377, 44378, 44379)

43255   with control of bleeding, any method

(Do not report 43255 in conjunction with 43236, 43243, 43244 for the same lesion)

(Do not report 43255 in conjunction with 43197, 43198, 43235, 44360, 44361, 44363, 44364, 44365, 44366, 44369, 44370, 44372, 44373, 44376, 44377, 44378, 44379)

43266   with placement of endoscopic stent (includes pre- and post-dilation and guide wire passage, when performed)

(Do not report 43266 in conjunction with 43197, 43198, 43235, 43240, 43241, 43245, 43248, 43249, 44360, 44361, 44363, 44364, 44365, 44366, 44369, 44370, 44372, 44373, 44376, 44377, 44378, 44379)

(If fluoroscopic guidance is performed, use 74360)

43257   with delivery of thermal energy to the muscle of lower esophageal sphincter and/or gastric cardia, for treatment of gastroesophageal reflux disease

(Do not report 43257 in conjunction with 43197, 43198, 43235, 44360, 44361, 44363, 44364, 44365, 44366, 44369, 44370, 44372, 44373, 44376, 44377, 44378, 44379)

(For ablation of metaplastic/dysplastic esophageal lesion [eg., Barrett's esophagus], see 43229, 43270)

43270   with ablation of tumor(s), polyp(s), or other lesion(s) (includes pre-and post-dilation and guide wire passage, when performed)

(Do not report 43270 in conjunction with 43248, 43249 for the same lesion)

(Do not report 43270 in conjunction with 43197, 43198, 43235, 44360, 44361, 44363, 44364, 44365, 44366, 44369, 44370, 44372, 44373, 44376, 44377, 44378, 44379)

(For esophagoscopic photodynamic therapy, use 43270 in conjunction with 96570, 96571 as appropriate)

43259   with endoscopic ultrasound examination, including the esophagus, stomach, and either the duodenum or a surgically altered stomach where the jejunum is examined distal to the anastomosis

(Do not report 43259 in conjunction with 43197, 43198, 43235, 43237, 43240, 43242, 43253, 44360, 44361, 44363, 44364, 44365, 44366, 44369, 44370, 44372, 44373, 44376, 44377, 44378, 44379, 76975)

(Do not report 43259 more than once per session)

43210   with esophagogastric fundoplasty, partial or complete, includes duodenoscopy when performed

(Do not report 43210 in conjunction with 43180, 43191, 43197, 43200, 43235)

Endoscopic Retrograde Cholangiopancreatography (ERCP)

Report the appropriate code(s) for each service performed. Therapeutic ERCP (43261, 43262, 43263, 43264, 43265, 43274, 43275, 43276, 43277, 43278) includes diagnostic ERCP (43260). ERCP includes guide wire passage when performed. An ERCP is considered complete if one or more of the ductal system(s), (pancreatic/biliary) is visualized. To report ERCP attempted but with unsuccessful cannulation of any ductal system, see 43235-43259, 43266, 43270.

(For percutaneous biliary catheter procedures, see 47490-47544)

Codes 43274, 43275, 43276 and 43277 describe ERCP with stent placement, removal or replacement (exchange) of stent(s), and balloon dilation within the pancreatico-biliary system. For reporting purposes, ducts that may be reported as stented or subject to stent repalcement (exchange) or to balloon dilation include:

Pancreas: major and minor ducts.

Biliary tree: common bile duct, right hepatic duct, left hepatic duct, cystic duct/gallbladder

ERCP with stent placement includes any balloon dilation performed in that duct. ERCP with more than one stent placement (eg, different ducts or side-by-side in the same duct) performed during the same day/session may be reported with 43274 more than once with modifier 59 appended to the subsequent procedure(s). For ERCP with more than one stent exchanged during the same day/session, 43276 may be reported for the initial stent exchange, and 43276 with modifier 59 for each additional stent exchange. ERCP with balloon dilation of more than one duct during the same day/session may be reported with modifier 59 appended to the subsequent procedure(s). Sphincteroplasty, which is balloon dilation of the ampulla (sphincter of Oddi), is reported with 43277, and includes sphincterotomy (43262) when performed.

To report ERCP via altered postoperative anatomy, see 43260, 43262, 43263, 43264, 43265, 43273, 43274, 43275, 43276, 43277, 43278, for Billroth II gastroenterostomy. See 47999 (Unlisted procedure, biliary tract), or 48999 (Unlisted procedure, pancreas) for ERCP via gastrostomy (laparoscopic or open) or via Roux-en-Y anatomy (eg, post-bariatric gastric bypass, post-total gastrectomy).

To report optical endomicroscopy of the biliary tract and pancreas, use 0397T. Do not report optical endomicroscopy more than once per session

Stone destruction includes any stone removal in the same ductal system (biliary/pancreatic). Code 43277 may be separately reported if sphincteroplasty or dilation of the ductal stricture is required before proceeding to remove stones/debris from the duct during the same session. Dilation that is incidental to the passage of an instrument to clear stones or debris is not separately reported.

(Do not report 43277 for use of a balloon catheter to clear stones/debris from a duct. Any dilation of the duct that may occur during this maneuver is considered inherent to the work of 43264 and 43265)

(If imaging of the ductal systems is performed, including images saved to the permanent record and report of the imaging, see 74328, 74329, 74330)

43260 Endoscopic retrograde cholangiopancreatography (ERCP); diagnostic, including collection of specimen(s) by brushing or washing, when performed (separate procedure)

(Do not report 43260 in conjunction with 43261, 43262, 43263, 43264, 43265, 43274, 43275, 43276, 43277, 43278)

43261 with biopsy, single or multiple

(Do not report 43261 in conjunction with 43260)

(For percutaneous endoluminal biopsy of biliary tree, use 47543)

43262 with sphincterotomy/papillotomy

(43262 may be reported when sphincterotomy is performed in addition to 43261, 43263, 43264, 43265, 43275, 43278)

(Do not report 43262 in conjunction with 43274 for stent placement or with 43276 for stent replacement [exchange] in the same location)

(Do not report 43262 in conjunction with 43260, 43277)

(For percutaneous balloon dilation of biliary duct(s) or of ampulla, use 47542)

43263 with pressure measurement of sphincter of Oddi

(Do not report 43263 in conjunction with 43260)

(Do not report 43263 more than once per session)

43264 with removal of calculi/debris from biliary/pancreatic duct(s)

(Do not report 43264 if no calculi or debris are found, even if balloon catheter is deployed)

(Do note report 43264 in conjunction with 43260, 43265)

(For percutaneous removal of calculi/debris, use 47544)

43265 with destruction of calculi, any method (eg, mechanical, electrohydraulic, lithotripsy)

(Do not report 43265 in conjunction with 43260, 43264)

(For percutaneous removal of calculi/debris, use 47544)

43266 This code is out of order. See page 447.

43270 This code is out of order. See page 448.

43274 with placement of endoscopic stent into biliary or pancreatic duct, including lpre- and post-dilation and guide wire passage, when performed, including sphincterotomy, when performed, each stent

(For stent placement in both the pancreatic duct and the common bile duct during the same operative session, placement of separate stents in both the right and left hepatic ducts, or placement of two

| Separate Procedure | | Unlisted Procedure | | CCI Comp. Code | | Non-specific Procedure | **449** |

side-by-side stents in the same duct 43274 may be reported for each additional stent placed, using modifier 59 with the subsequent procedure[s])

(To report naso-biliary or naso-pancreatic drainage tube placement, use 43274)

(Do not report 43274 in conjunction with 43262, 43275, 43276, 43277 for stent placement or replacement [exchange] in the same duct)

(For percutaneous placement of biliary stent(s), see 47538, 47539, 47540)

43275   with removal of foreign body(s) or stent(s) from biliary/pancreatic duct(s)

(Do not report 43275 in conjunction with 43260, 43274, 43276)

(For removal of stent from biliary or pancreatic duct without ERCP, use 43247)

(Report 43275 only once for removal of one or more stents or foreign bodies from biliary/pancreatic ducts during the same session)

(For percutaneous removal of calculi/debris, use 47544)

43276   with removal and exchange of stent(s), biliary or pancreatic duct, including pre- and post-dilation and guide wire passage, when performed, including sphincterotomy, when performed, each stent exchanged

(43276 includes removal and replacement [exchange] of one stent. For replacement [exchange] of additional stent[s] during the same session, report 43276 with modifier 59 for each additional replacement [exchange])

(Do not report 43276 in conjunction with 43260, 43275)

(Do not report 43276 in conjunction with 43262, 43274 for stent placement or exchange in the same duct)

43277   with trans-endoscopic balloon dilation of biliary/pancreatic duct(s) or of ampulla (sphincteroplasty), including sphincterotomy, when performed, each duct

(Do not report 43277 in conjunction with 43278 for the same lesion)

(Do not report 43277 in conjunction with 43260, 43262)

(Do not report 43277 for incidental dilation using balloon for stone/debris removal reported with 43264, 43265)

(If sphincterotomy without sphincteroplasty is performed on a separate pancreatic duct orifice during the same session [ie, pancreas divisum], report 43262 with modifier 59)

(Do not report 43277 in conjunction with 43274, 43276 for dilation and stent placement/replacement [exchange] in the same duct)

(For transendoscopic balloon dilation of multiple strictures during the same session, use 43277 with modifier 59 for each additional stricture dilated)

(For bilateral balloon dilation [both right and left hepatic ducts], 43277 may be reported twice with modifier 59 appended to the second procedure)

(For percutaneous balloon dilation of biliary duct(s) or of ampulla (sphincteroplasty), use 47542)

43278   with ablation of tumor(s), polyp(s), or other lesion(s), including pre- and post-dilation and guide wire passage, when performed

(Do not report 43278 in conjunction with 43277 for the same lesion)

(Do not report 43278 in conjunction with 43260)

(For ampullectomy, use 43254)

+ **43273**   Endoscopic cannulation of papilla with direct visualization of pancreatic/common bile duct(s) (List separately in addition to code(s) for primary procedure)

(Report 43273 once per procedure)

(Use 43273 in conjunction with 43260, 43261, 43262, 43263, 43264, 43265, 43274, 43275, 43276, 43277, 43278)

43274 This code is out of order. See page 449.

43275 This code is out of order. See page 450.

43276 This code is out of order. See page 450.

43277 This code is out of order. See page 450.

43278 This code is out of order. See page 450.

LAPAROSCOPY

Surgical laparoscopy always includes diagnostic laparoscopy. To report a diagnostic laparoscopy (peritoneoscopy) (separate procedure), use 49320.

43279 Laparoscopy, surgical, esophagomyotomy (Heller type), with fundoplasty, when performed

(For open approach, see 43330, 43331)

(Do not report 43279 in conjunction with 43280)

43280 Laparoscopy, surgical, esophagogastric fundoplasty (eg, Nissen, Toupet procedures)

(Do not report 43280 in conjunction with 43279, 43281, 43282)

(For open esophagogastric fundoplasty, see 43327, 43328)

(For laparoscopy, surgical, esophageal sphincter augmentation procedure, placement of sphincter augmentation device, see 43284, 43285)

(For esophagogastroduodenoscopy fundoplasty, partial or complete, transoral approach, use 43210)

43281 Laparoscopy, surgical, repair of paraesophageal hernia, includes fundoplasty, when performed; without implantation of mesh

43282   with implantation of mesh

(To report transabdominal paraesophageal hiatal hernia repair, see 43332, 43333)

(To report transthoracic diaphragmatic hernia repair, see 43334, 43335)

(Do not report 43281, 43282 in conjunction with 43280, 43450, 43453)

+ 43283 Laparoscopy, surgical, esophageal lengthening procedure (eg, Collis gastroplasty or wedge gastroplasty) (list separately in addition to code for primary procedure)

(Use 43283 in conjunction with 43280, 43281, 43282)

43284 Laparoscopy, surgical, esophageal sphincter augmentation procedure, placement of sphincter augmentation device (ie, magnetic band), including cruroplasty when performed

(Do not report 43284 in conjunction with 43279, 43280, 43281, 43282)

43285 Removal of esophageal sphincter augmentation device

● **43286** Esophagectomy, total or near total, with laparoscopic mobilization of the abdominal and mediastinal esophagus and proximal gastrectomy, with laparoscopic pyloric drainage procedure if performed, with open cervical pharyngogastrostomy or esophagogastrostomy (ie, laparoscopic transhiatal esophagectomy)

● **43287** Esophagectomy, distal two-thirds, with laparoscopic mobilization of the abdominal and lower mediastinal esophagus and proximal gastrectomy, with laparoscopic pyloric drainage procedure if performed, with

---

| | Separate Procedure | | Unlisted Procedure | | CCI Comp. Code | | Non-specific Procedure | **451** |

separate thoracoscopic mobilization of the middle and upper mediastinal esophagus and thoracic esophagogastrostomy (ie, laparoscopic thoracoscopic esophagectomy, Ivor Lewis esophagectomy)

(Do not report 43287 in conjunction with 32551 for right tube thoracostomy)

● **43288** Esophagectomy, total or near total, with thoracoscopic mobilization of the upper, middle, and lower mediastinal esophagus, with separate laparoscopic proximal gastrectomy, with laparoscopic pyloric drainage procedure if performed, with open cervical pharyngogastrostomy or esophagogastrostomy (ie, thoracoscopic, laparoscopic and cervical incision esophagectomy, McKeown esophagectomy, tri-incisional esophagectomy)

(Do not report 43288 in conjunction with 32551 for right tube thoracostomy)

43289 Unlisted laparoscopy procedure, esophagus

REPAIR

43300 Esophagoplasty, (plastic repair or reconstruction), cervical approach; without repair of tracheoesophageal fistula

43305 with repair of tracheoesophageal fistula

43310 Esophagoplasty, (plastic repair or reconstruction), thoracic approach; without repair of tracheoesophageal fistula

43312 with repair of tracheoesophageal fistula

43313 Esophagoplasty for congenital defect, (plastic repair or reconstruction), thoracic approach; without repair of congenital tracheoesophageal fistula

43314 with repair of congenital tracheoesophageal fistula

(Do not report modifier 63 in conjunction with 43313, 43314)

43320 Esophagogastrostomy (cardioplasty), with or without vagotomy and pyloroplasty, transabdominal or transthoracic approach

(For laparoscopic procedure, use 43280)

43325 Esophagogastric fundoplasty; with fundic patch (Thal-Nissen procedure)

(For cricopharyngeal myotomy, use 43030)

43327 Esophagogastric fundoplasty, partial or complete; laparotomy

43328 thoracotomy

(For esophagogastroduodenoscopy fundoplasty, partial or complete, transoral approach, use 43210)

43330 Esophagomyotomy (Heller type); abdominal approach

(For laparoscopic esophagomyotomy procedure, use 43279)

43331 thoracic approach

(For thoracoscopic esophagomyotomy, use 32665)

43332 Repair, paraesophageal hiatal hernia (including fundoplication), via laparotomy, except neonatal; without implantation of mesh or other prosthesis

43333 with implantation of mesh or other prosthesis

(For neonatal diaphragmatic hernia repair, use 39503)

● New Code ▲ Revised Code + Add-On Code ⊘ Modifier -51 Exempt ★ Telemedicine

43334   Repair, paraesophageal hiatal hernia (including fundoplication), via thoracotomy, except neonatal; without implantation of mesh or other prosthesis

43335   with implantation of mesh or other prosthesis

(For neonatal diaphragmatic hernia repair, use 39503)

43336   Repair, paraesophageal hiatal hernia (including fundoplication), via thoracoabdominal incision, except neonatal; without implantation of mesh or other prosthesis

43337   with implantation of mesh or other prosthesis

(For neonatal diaphragmatic hernia repair, use 39503)

+ 43338   Esophageal lengthening procedure (eg, Collis gastroplasty or wedge gastroplasty) (List separately in addition to code for primary procedure)

(Use 43338 in conjunction with 43280, 43327-43337)

43340   Esophagojejunostomy (without total gastrectomy); abdominal approach

43341   thoracic approach

(43350   deleted 2014 [2015 edition])

43351   Esophagostomy, fistulization of esophagus, external; thoracic approach

43352   cervical approach

43360   Gastrointestinal reconstruction for previous esophagectomy, for obstructing esophageal lesion or fistula, or for previous esophageal exclusion; with stomach, with or without pyloroplasty

43361   with colon interposition or small intestine reconstruction, including intestine mobilization, preparation, and anastomosis(es)

43400   Ligation, direct, esophageal varices

43401   Transection of esophagus with repair, for esophageal varices

43405   Ligation or stapling at gastroesophageal junction for pre-existing esophageal perforation

43410   Suture of esophageal wound or injury; cervical approach

43415   transthoracic or transabdominal approach

43420   Closure of esophagostomy or fistula; cervical approach

43425   transthoracic or transabdominal approach

(To report transabdominal paraesophageal hiatal hernia repair, see 43332, 43333. To report transthoracic diaphragmatic hernia repair, see 43334, 43335.)

MANIPULATION

(For associated esophagogram, use 74220)

43450   Dilation of esophagus, by unguided sound or bougie, single or multiple passes

(For radiological supervision and interpretation, use 74360)

43453   Dilation of esophagus, over guide wire

(For dilation with endoscopic visualization, see 43195, 43226)

(For dilation of esophagus, by balloon or dilator, see 43214, 43220, 43233, 43249)

(For radiological supervision and interpretation, use 74360)

(For endoscopic dilation of esophagus with balloon less than 30 mm diameter, see 43195, 43220, 43249)

(For endoscopic dilation of esophagus with balloon 30 mm diameter or larger, see 43214, 43233)

43460 Esophagogastric tamponade, with balloon (Sengstaken type)

(For removal of esophageal foreign body by balloon catheter, see 43499, 74235)

OTHER PROCEDURES

43496 Free jejunum transfer with microvascular anastomosis

(Do not report code 69990 in addition to code 43496)

43499 Unlisted procedure, esophagus

STOMACH

INCISION

43500 Gastrotomy; with exploration or foreign body removal

43501 with suture repair of bleeding ulcer

43502 with suture repair of pre-existing esophagogastric laceration (eg, Mallory-Weiss)

43510 with esophageal dilation and insertion of permanent intraluminal tube (eg, Celestin or Mousseaux-Barbin)

43520 Pyloromyotomy, cutting of pyloric muscle (Fredet-Ramstedt type operation)

(Do not report modifier '-63' in conjunction with 43520)

EXCISION

43605 Biopsy of stomach by laparotomy

43610 Excision, local; ulcer or benign tumor of stomach

43611 malignant tumor of stomach

43620 Gastrectomy, total; with esophagoenterostomy

43621 with Roux-en-Y reconstruction

43622 with formation of intestinal pouch, any type

43631 Gastrectomy, partial, distal; with gastroduodenostomy

43632 with gastrojejunostomy

43633 with Roux-en-Y reconstruction

43634 with formation of intestinal pouch

+ **43635** Vagotomy when performed with partial distal gastrectomy (List separately in addition to code(s) for primary procedure)

(Use 43635 in conjunction with codes 43631, 43632, 43633, 43634)

● New Code   ▲ Revised Code   + Add-On Code   ⊘ Modifier -51 Exempt   ★ Telemedicine

43640 Vagotomy including pyloroplasty, with or without gastrostomy; truncal or selective

(For pyloroplasty, use 43800)

(For vagotomy, see 64755, 64760)

43641 parietal cell (highly selective)

(For upper gastrointestinal endoscopy, see 43235-43259)

LAPAROSCOPY

Surgical laparoscopy always includes diagnostic laparoscopy. To report a diagnostic laparoscopy (peritoneoscopy) (separate procedure), use 49320.

(For upper gastrointestinal endoscopy including esophagus, stomach, and either the duodenum and/or jejunum, see 43235-43259)

43644 Laparoscopy, surgical, gastric restrictive procedure; with gastric bypass and Roux-en-Y gastroenterostomy (Roux limb 150 cm or less)

(Do not report 43644 in conjunction with 43846, 49320)

(Esophagogastroduodenoscopy (EGD) performed for a separate condition should be reported with modifier 59)

(For greater than 150 cm, use 43645)

(For open procedure, use 43846)

43645 with gastric bypass and small intestine reconstruction to limit absorption

(Do not report 43645 in conjunction with 49320, 43847)

43647 Laparoscopy, surgical; implantation or replacement of gastric neurostimulator electrodes, antrum

43648 revision or removal of gastric neurostimulator electrodes, antrum

(For open approach, see 43881, 43882)

(For insertion of gastric neruostimulator pulse generator, use 64590)

(For revision or removal of gastric neurostimulator pulse generator, use 64595)

(For electronic analaysis and programming of gastric neurostimulator pulse generator, see 95980-95982)

(For laparoscopic implantation, revision, or removal of gastric neurostimulator electrodes, lesser curvature [morbid obesity], use 43659)

(For laparoscopic implantation, revision, replacement, or removal of vagus nerve blocking neurostimulator electrode array and/or pulse generator at the esophagogastric junction, see 0312T-0317T)

43651 Laparoscopy, surgical; transection of vagus nerves, truncal

43652 transection of vagus nerves, selective or highly selective

43653 gastrostomy, without construction of gastric tube (eg, Stamm procedure) (separate procedure)

43659 Unlisted laparoscopy procedure, stomach

INTRODUCTION

43752 Naso- or oro-gastric tube placement, requiring physician's skill and fluoroscopic guidance (includes fluoroscopy, image documentation and report)

■ Separate Procedure   ■ Unlisted Procedure   ■ CCI Comp. Code   ■ Non-specific Procedure   **455**

(Do not report 43752 in conjunction with critical care codes 99291-99292, neonatal critical care codes 99468, pediatric critical care codes 99471, 99472 or low birth weight intensive care service codes 99478, 99479)

(For percutaneous placement of gastrostomy tube, use 49440)

(For enteric tube placement, see 44500, 74340)

43753 Gastric intubation and aspiration(s), therapeutic, necessitating physician's skill (eg, for gastrointestinal hemorrhage), including lavage if performed

43754 Gastric intubation and aspiration, diagnostic; single specimen (eg, acid analysis)

43755 collection of multiple fractional specimens with gastric stimulation, single or double lumen tube (gastric secretory study) (eg, histamine, insulin, pentagastrin, calcium, secretin), includes drug administration

(For gastric acid analysis, use 82930)

(For naso- or oro-gastric tube placement by physician with fluoroscopic guidance, use 43752)

(Report the drug(s) or substance(s) administered. The fluid used to administer the drug(s) is not separately reported)

43756 Duodenal intubation and aspiration, diagnostic, includes image guidance; single specimen (eg, bile study for crystals or afferent loop culture)

43757 collection of multiple fractional specimens with pancreatic or gallbladder stimulation, single or double lumen tube, includes drug administration

(For appropriate chemical analysis procedures, see 89049-89240)

(Report the substance(s) or drug(s) administered. The fluid used to administer the drug(s) is not separately reported)

43760 Change of gastrostomy tube, percutaneous, without imaging or endoscopic guidance

(To report fluoroscopically guided replacement of gastrostomy tube, use 49450)

(For endoscopic placement of gastrostomy tube, use 43246)

43761 Repositioning of a naso- or oro-gastric feeding tube, through the duodenum for enteric nutrition

(Do not report 43761 in conjunction with 44500, 49446)

(If imaging guidance is performed, use 76000)

(For endoscopic conversion of a gastrostomy tube to jejunostomy tube, use 44373)

(For placement of a long gastrointestinal tube into the duodenum, use 44500)

BARIATRIC SURGERY

Laparoscopy

Surgical laparoscopy always includes diagnostic laparoscopy. To report a diagnostic laparoscopy (separate procedure), use 49320.

43770 Laparoscopy, surgical, gastric restrictive procedure; placement of adjustable gastric restrictive device (eg, gastric band and subcutaneous port components)

(For individual component placement, report 43770 with modifier 52)

43771 revision of adjustable gastric restrictive device component only

43772 removal of adjustable gastric restrictive device component only

---

● New Code   ▲ Revised Code   + Add-On Code   ⊘ Modifier -51 Exempt   ★ Telemedicine

43773   removal and replacement of adjustable gastric restrictive device component only

(Do not report 43773 in conjunction with 43772)

43774   removal of adjustable gastric restrictive device and subcutaneous port components

(For removal and replacement of both gastric band and subcutaneous port components, use 43659)

43775   longitudinal gastrectomy (ie, sleeve gastrectomy)

(For open gastric restrictive procedure, without gastric bypass, for morbid obesity, other than vertical-banded gastroplasty, use 43843)

(For laparoscopic implantation, revision, replacement, removal or reprogramming of vagus nerve blocking neurostimulator electrode array and/or pulse generator at the esophagogastric junction, see 0312T-0317T)

OTHER PROCEDURES

43800 Pyloroplasty

(For pyloroplasty and vagotomy, use 43640)

43810 Gastroduodenostomy

43820 Gastrojejunostomy; without vagotomy

43825   with vagotomy, any type

43830 Gastrostomy, open; without construction of gastric tube (eg, Stamm procedure) (separate procedure)

43831   neonatal, for feeding

(For change of gastrostomy tube, use 43760)

(Do not report modifier '-63' in conjunction with 43831)

43832   with construction of gastric tube (eg, Janeway procedure)

(For percutaneous endoscopic gastrostomy, use 43246)

43840 Gastrorrhaphy, suture of perforated duodenal or gastric ulcer, wound, or injury

43842 Gastric restrictive procedure, without gastric bypass, for morbid obesity; vertical-banded gastroplasty

43843   other than vertical-banded gastroplasty

(For laparoscopic longitudinal gastrectomy [ie, sleeve gastrectomy], use 43775)

43845 Gastric restrictive procedure with partial gastrectomy, pylorus- preserving duodenoileostomy and ileoileostomy (50 to 100 cm common channel) to limit absorption (biliopancreatic diversion with duodenal switch)

(Do not report 43845 in conjunction with 43633, 43847, 44130, 49000)

43846 Gastric restrictive procedure, with gastric bypass for morbid obesity; with short limb (150 cm or less) Roux-en-Y gastroenterostomy

(For greater than 150 cm, use 43847)

(For laparoscopic procedure, use 43644)

43847   with small intestine reconstruction to limit absorption

---

| Separate Procedure | Unlisted Procedure | CCI Comp. Code | Non-specific Procedure | **457** |

43848 Revision, open, of gastric restrictive procedure for morbid obesity, other than adjustable gastric restrictive device (separate procedure)

(For laparoscopic adjustable gastric restrictive procedures, see 43770-43774)

(For gastric restrictive port procedures, see 43886-43888)

43850 Revision of gastroduodenal anastomosis (gastroduodenostomy) with reconstruction; without vagotomy

43855 with vagotomy

43860 Revision of gastrojejunal anastomosis (gastrojejunostomy) with reconstruction, with or without partial gastrectomy or intestine resection; without vagotomy

43865 with vagotomy

43870 Closure of gastrostomy, surgical

43880 Closure of gastrocolic fistula

43881 Implantation or replacement of gastric neurostimulator electrodes, antrum, open

43882 Revision or removal of gastric neurostimulator electrodes, antrum, open

(For laparoscopic approach, see 43647, 43648)

(For insertion of gastric neurostimulator pulse generator, use 64590)

(For revision or removal of gastric neurostimulator pulse generator, use 64595)

(For electronic analysis and programming of gastric neurostimulator pulse generator, use 95980-95982)

(For open implantation, revision, or removal of gastric neurostimulator electrodes, lesser curvature [morbid obesity], use 43999)

(For laparaoscopic implantation, revision, replacement, removal or reprogramming of vagus nerve blocking neurostimulator electrode array and/or pulse generator at the esophagogastric junction, see 0312T-0317T)

(For open implantation, revision, or removal of gastric lesser curvature or vagal trunk (EGJ) neurostimulator electrodes, [morbid obesity], use 43999)

43886 Gastric restrictive procedure, open; revision of subcutaneous port component only

43887 removal of subcutaneous port component only

43888 removal and replacement of subcutaneous port component only

(Do not report 43888 in conjunction with 43774, 43887)

(For laparoscopic removal of both gastric restrictive device and subcutaneous port components, use 43774)

(For removal and replacement of both gastric restrictive device and subcutaneous port components, use 43659)

43999 Unlisted procedure, stomach

INTESTINES (EXCEPT RECTUM)

INCISION

44005 Enterolysis (freeing of intestinal adhesion) (separate procedure)

(Do not report 44005 in addition to 45136)

(For laparoscopic approach, use 44180)

● New Code ▲ Revised Code ＋ Add-On Code ⊘ Modifier -51 Exempt ★ Telemedicine

44010 Duodenotomy, for exploration, biopsy(s), or foreign body removal

+ **44015** Tube or needle catheter jejunostomy for enteral alimentation, intraoperative, any method (List separately in addition to primary procedure)

44020 Enterotomy, small intestine, other than duodenum; for exploration, biopsy(s), or foreign body removal

44021   for decompression (eg, Baker tube)

44025 Colotomy, for exploration, biopsy(s), or foreign body removal

    (For exteriorization of intestine (Mikulicz resection with crushing of spur), see 44602-44605)

44050 Reduction of volvulus, intussusception, internal hernia, by laparotomy

44055 Correction of malrotation by lysis of duodenal bands and/or reduction of midgut volvulus (eg, Ladd procedure)

    (Do not report modifier '-63' in conjunction with 44055)

EXCISION

Intestinal allotransplantation involves three distinct components of physician work:

1) **Cadaver donor enterectomy**, which includes harvesting the intestine graft and cold preservation of the graft (perfusing with cold preservation solution and cold maintenance) (use 44132). **Living donor enterectomy**, which includes harvesting the intestine graft, cold preservation of the graft (perfusing with cold preservation solution and cold maintenance), and care of the donor (use 44133).

2) **Backbench work**:

Standard preparation of an intestine allograft prior to transplantation includes mobilization and fashioning of the superior mesenteric artery and vein (see 44715).

Additional reconstruction of an intestine allograft prior to transplantation may include venous and/or arterial anastomosis(es) (see 44720-44721).

3) **Recipient intestinal allotransplantation with or without recipient enterectomy**, which includes transplantation of allograft and care of the recipient (see 44135, 44136)

44100 Biopsy of intestine by capsule, tube, peroral (1 or more specimens)

44110 Excision of 1 or more lesions of small or large intestine not requiring anastomosis, exteriorization, or fistulization; single enterotomy

44111   multiple enterotomies

44120 Enterectomy, resection of small intestine; single resection and anastomosis

    (Do not report 44120 in addition to 45136)

+ **44121**   each additional resection and anastomosis (List separately in addition to code for primary procedure)

    (Use 44121 in conjunction with code 44120)

44125   with enterostomy

44126 Enterectomy, resection of small intestine for congenital atresia, single resection and anastomosis of proximal segment of intestine; without tapering

44127   with tapering

+ **44128** each additional resection and anastomosis (List separately in addition to code for primary procedure)

(Use 44128 in conjunction with codes 44126, 44127)

(Do not report modifier '-63' in conjunction with 44126, 44127, 44128)

44130 Enteroenterostomy, anastomosis of intestine, with or without cutaneous enterostomy (separate procedure)

44132 Donor enterectomy (including cold preservation), open; from cadaver donor

44133 partial, from living donor

(For backbench intestinal graft preparation or reconstruction, see 44715, 44720, 44721)

44135 Intestinal allotransplantation; from cadaver donor

44136 from living donor

44137 Removal of transplanted intestinal allograft, complete

(For partial removal of transplant allograft, see 44120, 44121, 44140)

+ **44139** Mobilization (take-down) of splenic flexure performed in conjunction with partial colectomy (List separately in addition to primary procedure)

(Use 44139 in conjunction with codes 44140-44147)

44140 Colectomy, partial; with anastomosis

(For laparoscopic procedure, use 44204)

44141 with skin level cecostomy or colostomy

44143 with end colostomy and closure of distal segment (Hartmann type procedure)

(For laparoscopic procedure, use 44206)

44144 with resection, with colostomy or ileostomy and creation of mucofistula

44145 with coloproctostomy (low pelvic anastomosis)

(For laparoscopic procedure, use 44207)

44146 with coloproctostomy (low pelvic anastomosis), with colostomy

(For laparoscopic procedure, use 44208)

44147 abdominal and transanal approach

44150 Colectomy, total, abdominal, without proctectomy; with ileostomy or ileoproctostomy

(For laparoscopic procedure, use 44210)

44151 with continent ileostomy

44155 Colectomy, total, abdominal, with proctectomy; with ileostomy

(For laparoscopic procedure, use 44212)

44156 with continent ileostomy

44157 with ileoanal anastomosis, includes loop ileostomy, and rectal mucosectomy, when performed

---

● New Code ▲ Revised Code + Add-On Code ⊘ Modifier -51 Exempt ★ Telemedicine

44158 with ileoanal anastomosis, creation of ileal reservoir (S or J), includes loop ileostomy, and rectal mucosectomy, when performed

(For laparoscopic procedure, use 44211)

44160 Colectomy, partial, with removal of terminal ileum and ileocolostomy

(For laparoscopic procedure, use 44205)

LAPAROSCOPY

Surgical laparoscopy always includes diagnostic laparoscopy. To report a diagnostic laparoscopy (peritoneoscopy) (separate procedure), use 49320.

Incision

44180 Laparoscopy, surgical, enterolysis (freeing of intestinal adhesion) (separate procedure)

(For laparoscopy with salpingolysis, ovariolysis, use 58660)

Enterostomy—External Fistulization of Intestines

44186 Laparoscopy, surgical; jejunostomy (eg, for decompression or feeding)

44187 ileostomy or jejunostomy, non-tube

(For open procedure, use 44310)

44188 Laparoscopy, surgical, colostomy or skin level cecostomy

(For open procedure, use 44320)

(Do not report 44188 in conjunction with 44970)

Excision

44202 Laparoscopy, surgical; enterectomy, resection of small intestine, single resection and anastomosis

+ **44203** each additional small intestine resection and anastomosis (List separately in addition to code for primary procedure)

(Use 44203 in conjunction with code 44202)

(For open procedure, see 44120, 44121)

44204 colectomy, partial, with anastomosis

(For open procedure, use 44140)

44205 colectomy, partial, with removal of terminal ileum with ileocolostomy

(For open procedure, use 44160)

44206 colectomy, partial, with end colostomy and closure of distal segment (Hartmann type procedure)

(For open procedure, use 44143)

44207 colectomy, partial, with anastomosis, with coloproctostomy (low pelvic anastomosis)

(For open procedure, use 44145)

44208 colectomy, partial, with anastomosis, with coloproctostomy (low pelvic anastomosis) with colostomy

(For open procedure, use 44146)

Separate Procedure ■ Unlisted Procedure ■ CCI Comp. Code ■ Non-specific Procedure **461**

44210 colectomy, total, abdominal, without proctectomy, with ileostomy or ileoproctostomy

(For open procedure, use 44150)

44211 colectomy, total, abdominal, with proctectomy, with ileoanal anastomosis, creation of ileal reservoir (S or J), with loop ileostomy, includes rectal mucosectomy, when performed

(For open procedure, see 44157, 44158)

44212 colectomy, total, abdominal, with proctectomy, with ileostomy

(For open procedure, use 44155)

+ **44213** Laparoscopy, surgical, mobilization (take-down) of splenic flexure performed in conjunction with partial colectomy (List separately in addition to primary procedure)

(Use 44213 in conjunction with 44204-44208)

(For open procedure, use 44139)

Repair

44227 Laparoscopy, surgical, closure of enterostomy, large or small intestine, with resection and anastomosis

(For open procedure, see 44625, 44626)

Other Procedures

44238 Unlisted laparoscopy procedure, intestine (except rectum)

ENTEROSTOMY—EXTERNAL FISTULIZATION OF INTESTINES

44300 Placement, enterostomy or cecostomy, tube open (eg, for feeding or decompression) (separate procedure)

(Do not report 44300 in conjunction with 44701 for cannulation of the colon for intraoperative colonic lavage)

(For percutaneous placement of duodenostomy, jejunostomy, gastro-jejunostomy or cecostomy [or other colonic] tube including fluoroscopic imaging guidance, see 49441-49442)

44310 Ileostomy or jejunostomy, non-tube

(For laparoscopic procedure, use 44187)

(Do not report 44310 in conjunction with 44144, 44150-44153, 44155, 44156, 45113, 45119, 45136)

44312 Revision of ileostomy; simple (release of superficial scar) (separate procedure)

44314 complicated (reconstruction in-depth) (separate procedure)

44316 Continent ileostomy (Kock procedure) (separate procedure)

(For fiberoptic evaluation, use 44385)

44320 Colostomy or skin level cecostomy

(For laparoscopic procedure, use 44188)

(Do not report 44320 in conjunction with 44141, 44144, 44146, 44605, 45110, 45119, 45126, 45563, 45805, 45825, 50810, 51597, 57307, or 58240)

44322 with multiple biopsies (eg, for congenital megacolon) (separate procedure)

44340 Revision of colostomy; simple (release of superficial scar) (separate procedure)

● New Code ▲ Revised Code + Add-On Code ⊘ Modifier -51 Exempt ★ Telemedicine

44345   complicated (reconstruction in-depth) (separate procedure)

44346   with repair of paracolostomy hernia (separate procedure)

ENDOSCOPY, SMALL INTESTINE AND STOMAL

When bleeding occurs as the result of an endoscopic procedure, control of bleeding is not reported separately during the same operative session.

Antegrade transoral small intestinal endoscopy (enteroscopy) is defined by the most distal segment of small intestine that is examined. Codes 44360, 44361, 44363, 44364, 44365, 44366, 44369, 44370, 44372, 44373 are endoscopic procedures to visualize the esophagus through the jejunum using an antegrade approach. Codes 44376, 44377, 44378, 44379 are endscopic procedures to visualize the esophagus through the ileum using an antegrade approach. If an endscope cannot be advanced at least 50cm beyond the pylorus, see 43233, 43235-43259, 43266, 43270; if an endoscope can be passed at least 50cm beyond pylorus but only into jejunum, see 44360, 44361, 44363, 44364, 44365, 44366, 44369, 44370, 44372, 44373.

To report retrograde examination of small intestine via anus or colon stoma, use 44799, unlisted procedure, intestine.

> (Do not report 44360, 44361, 44363, 44364, 44365, 44366, 44369, 44370, 44372, 44373 in conjunction with 43233, 43235-43259, 43266, 43270, 44376, 44377, 44378, 44379)

> (Do not report 44376, 44377, 44378, 44379 in conjunction with 43233, 43235-43259, 43266, 43270, 44360, 44361, 44363, 44364, 44365, 44366, 44369, 44370, 44372, 44373)

> (For esophagogastroduodenoscopy, see 43233, 43235-43259, 43266, 43270)

44360   Small intestinal endoscopy, enteroscopy beyond second portion of duodenum, not including ileum; diagnostic, including collection of specimen(s) by brushing or washing, when performed (separate procedure)

44361   with biopsy, single or multiple

44363   with removal of foreign body(s)

44364   with removal of tumor(s), polyp(s), or other lesion(s) by snare technique

44365   with removal of tumor(s), polyp(s), or other lesion(s) by hot biopsy forceps or bipolar cautery

44366   with control of bleeding (eg, injection, bipolar cautery, unipolar cautery, laser, heater probe, stapler, plasma coagulator)

44369   with ablation of tumor(s), polyp(s), or other lesion(s) not amenable to removal by hot biopsy forceps, bipolar cautery or snare technique

44370   with transendoscopic stent placement (includes predilation)

44372   with placement of percutaneous jejunostomy tube

44373   with conversion of percutaneous gastrostomy tube to percutaneous jejunostomy tube

> (For fiberoptic jejunostomy through stoma, use 43235)

44376   Small intestinal endoscopy, enteroscopy beyond second portion of duodenum, including ileum; diagnostic, with or without collection of specimen(s) by brushing or washing (separate procedure)

> (Do not report 44376 in conjunction with 44360, 44361, 44363, 44364, 44365, 44366, 44369, 44370, 44372, 44373)

44377   with biopsy, single or multiple

> (Do not report 44377 in conjunction with 44360, 44361, 44363, 44364, 44365, 44366, 44369, 44370, 44372, 44373)

■ Separate Procedure   ■ Unlisted Procedure   ■ CCI Comp. Code   ■ Non-specific Procedure   **463**

with control of bleeding (eg, injection, bipolar cautery, unipolar cautery, laser, heater probe, stapler, plasma coagulator)

(Do not report 44378 in conjunction with 44360, 44361, 44363, 44364, 44365, 44366, 44369, 44370, 44372, 44373)

 with transendoscopic stent placement (includes predilation)

(Do not report 44379 in conjunction with 44360, 44361, 44363, 44364, 44365, 44366, 44369, 44370, 44372, 44373)

ENDOSCOPY, STOMAL

Definitions:

Proctosigmoidoscopy is the examination of the rectum and may include examination of a portion of the sigmoid colon.

Sigmoidoscopy is the examination of the entire recturm, sigmoid colon and may include examination of a portion of the descending colon.

Colonoscopy is the examination of the entire colon, from the rectum to the cecum, and may include examination of the terminal ileum or small intestine proximal to an anastomosis.

Colonoscopy through stoma is the examination of the colon, from the colostomy stoma to the cecum or colon-small intestine anastomosis, and may include examination of the terminal ileum or small instestine proximal to an anastomosis.

When performing a disgnostic or screening endoscopic procedure on a patient who is scheduled and prepared for a total colonoscopy, if the physician is unable to advance the colonscope to the cecum or colon-small intestine anastomosis due to unforeseen circumstances, report 45378 (colonoscopy) or 44388 (colonoscopy through stoma) with modifier 53 and provide appropriate documentation.

If a therapeutic colonoscopy (44389-44407, 45379, 45380, 45381, 45382, 45384, 45388, 45398) is performed and does not reach the cecum or colon-small intestine anastomosis, report the approprite therapeutic colonoscopy code with modifier 52 and provide appropriate documentation.

Report ileoscopy through stoma (44380, 44381, 44382, 44384) for endoscopic examination of a patient who has an ileostomy.

Report colonoscopy through stoma (44388-44408) for endoscopic examination of a patient who has undergone segmental resection of the colon (eg, hemicolectomy, sigmoid colectomy, low anterior resection) and has a colostomy.

For colonoscopy per rectum, see 45378, 45390, 45392, 45393, 45398.

Report proctosigmoidoscopy (45300-45327), flexible sigmoidoscopy (45330- 45347), or anoscopy (46600, 46604, 46606, 46608, 46610, 46611, 46612, 46614, 46615), as appropriate for endoscopic examination of the defunctionalized rectum or distal colon in a patient who has undergone colectomy, in addition to colonoscopy through stoma (44388-44408) or ileoscopy through stoma (44380, 44381, 44382, 44384) if appropriate.

When bleeding occurs as the result of an endoscopic procedure, control of bleeding is not reported separately during the same operative session.

For computed tomographic colonography, see 74261, 74262, 74263.

COLONOSCOPY DECISION TREE					
Decision to Undergo Colonoscopy					
Diagnostic Procedure			Therapeutic Procedure		
Does not reach splenic flexure:	Beyond splenic flexure, but not to the cecum:	To cecum:	Does not reach splenic flexure:	Beyond splenic flexure, but not to the cecum:	To cecum:
Flexible Sigmoidoscopy (45330)	Colonoscopy (45378; modifer 53)	Colonoscopy (45378; no modifier)	Flexible Sigmoidoscopy (45331-45347)	Colonoscopy (45379-45398; modifier 52)	Colonoscopy (45379-45398; no modifier)

● New Code   ▲ Revised Code   + Add-On Code   ⊘ Modifier -51 Exempt   ★ Telemedicine

44380 Ileoscopy, through stoma; diagnostic, including collection of specimen(s) by brushing or washing, when performed (separate procedure)

(Do not report 44380 in conjunction with 44381, 44382, 44384)

44381 This code is out of order. See page 465.

44382 with biopsy, single or multiple

(Do not report 44382 in conjunction with 44380)

44381 with transendoscopic balloon dilation

(Do not report 44381 in conjunction with 44380, 44384)

(If fluoroscoic guidance is performed, use 74360)

(For transendoscopic balloon dilation of multiple strictures during the same session, report 44381 with modifier 59 for each additional stricture dilated)

44384 with placement of endoscopic stent (includes pre- and post-dilation and guide wire passage, when performed)

(Do not report 44384 in conjunction with 44380, 44381)

(If fluoroscopic guidance is performed, use 74360)

44385 Endoscopic evaluation of small intestinal pouch (eg, Kock pouch, ileal reservoir [S or J]); diagnostic, including collection of specimen(s) by brushing or washing, when performed (separate procedure)

(Do not report 44385 in conjunction with 44386)

44386 with biopsy, single or multiple

(Do not report 44386 in conjunction with 44385)

44388 Colonoscopy through stoma; diagnostic, including collection of specimen(s) by brushing or washing, when performed (separate procedure)

(Do not report 44388 in conjunction with 44389-44408)

44389 with biopsy, single or multiple

(Do not report 44389 in conjunction with 44403 for the same lesion)

(Do not report 44389 in conjunction with 44388)

44390 with removal of foreign body(s)

(Do not report 44390 in conjunction with 44388)

(If fluoroscopic guidance is performed, use 76000)

44391 with control of bleeding, any method

(Do not report 44391 in conjunction with 44404 for the same lesion)

(Do not report 44391 in conjunction with 44388)

44392 with removal of tumor(s), polyp(s), or other lesion(s) by hot biopsy forceps

(Do not report 44392 in conjunction with 44388)

44401 with ablation of tumor(s), polyp(s), or other lesion(s) (includes pre- and post-dilation and guide wire passage, when performed)

(Do not report 44401 in conjunction with 44405 for the same lesion)

(Do not report 44401 in conjunction with 44388)

44394   with removal of tumor(s), polyp(s), or other lesion(s) by snare technique

(Do not report 44394 in conjunction with 44403 for the same lesion)

(Do not report 44394 in conjunction with 44388)

(For endoscopic mucosal resection, use 44403)

44401   This code is out of order. See page 465.

44402   with endoscopic stent placement (including pre- and post-dilation and guide wire passage, when performed)

(Do not report 44402 in conjunction with 44388, 44405)

(If fluoroscopic guidance is performed, use 74360)

44403   with endoscopic mucosal resection

(Do not report 44403 in conjunction with 44389, 44394, 44404 for the same lesion)

(Do not report 44403 in conjunction with 44388)

44404   with directed submucosal injection(s), any substance

(Do not report 44404 in conjunction with 44391, 44403 for the same lesion)

(Do not report 44404 in conjunction with 44388)

44405   with transendoscopic balloon dilation

(Do not report 44405 in conjunction with 44388, 44401, 44402)

(If fluorscopic guidance is performed, use 74360)

(For transendoscopic balloon dilation of multiple strictures during the same session, report 44405 with modifier 59 for each additional stricture dilated)

44406   with endoscopic ultrasound examination, limited to the sigmoid, descending, transverse, or ascending colon and cecum and adjacent structures

(Do not report 44406 in conjunction with 44388, 44407, 76975)

(Do not report 44406 more than once per session)

44407   with transendoscopic ultrasound guided intramural or transmural fine needle aspiration/biopsy(s), includes endoscopic ultrasound examination limited to the sigmoid, descending, transverse, or ascending colon and cecum and adjacent structures

(Do not report 44407 in conjunction with 44388, 44406, 76942, 76975)

(Do not report 44407 more than once per session)

44408   with decompression (for pathologic distention) (eg, volvulus, megacolon), including placement of decompression tube, when performed

(Do not report 44408 in conjunction with 44388)

(Do not report 44408 more than once per session)

INTRODUCTION

⊘ **44500**   Introduction of long gastrointestinal tube (eg, Miller-Abbott) (separate procedure)

  ● New Code   ▲ Revised Code   ✛ Add-On Code   ⊘ Modifier -51 Exempt   ★ Telemedicine

(For radiological supervision and interpretation, use 74340)

(For naso- or oro-gastric tube placement, use 43752)

REPAIR

44602 Suture of small intestine (enterorrhaphy) for perforated ulcer, diverticulum, wound, injury or rupture; single perforation

44603 multiple perforations

44604 Suture of large intestine (colorrhaphy) for perforated ulcer, diverticulum, wound, injury, or rupture (single or multiple perforations); without colostomy

44605 with colostomy

44615 Intestinal stricturoplasty (enterotomy and enterorrhaphy) with or without dilation, for intestinal obstruction

44620 Closure of enterostomy, large or small intestine;

44625 with resection and anastomosis other than colorectal

44626 with resection and colorectal anastomosis (eg, closure of Hartmann type procedure)

(For laparoscopic procedure, use 44227)

44640 Closure of intestinal cutaneous fistula

44650 Closure of enteroenteric or enterocolic fistula

44660 Closure of enterovesical fistula; without intestinal or bladder resection

44661 with intestine and/or bladder resection

(For closure of renocolic fistula, see 50525, 50526)

(For closure of gastrocolic fistula, use 43880)

(For closure of rectovesical fistula, see 45800, 45805)

44680 Intestinal plication (separate procedure)

OTHER PROCEDURES

44700 Exclusion of small intestine from pelvis by mesh or other prosthesis, or native tissue (eg, bladder or omentum)

(For therapeutic radiation clinical treatment, see Radiation Oncology section)

+ **44701** Intraoperative colonic lavage (List separately in addition to code for primary procedure)

(Use 44701 in conjunction with codes 44140, 44145, 44150, or 44604 as appropriate)

(Do not report 44701 in conjunction with 44950- 44960)

44705 Preparation of fecal microbiota for instillation, including assessment of donor specimen

(Do not report 44705 in conjunction with 74283)

(For fecal instillation by oro-nasogastric tube or enema, use 44799)

44715 Backbench standard preparation of cadaver or living donor intestine allograft prior to transplantation, including mobilization and fashioning of the superior mesenteric artery and vein

---

Separate Procedure   Unlisted Procedure   CCI Comp. Code   Non-specific Procedure   **467**

| 44720 | Backbench reconstruction of cadaver or living donor intestine allograft prior to transplantation; venous anastomosis, each |

| 44721 | arterial anastomosis, each |

| 44799 | Unlisted procedure, small intestine |

(For unlisted laparoscopic procedure, intestine except rectum, use 44238)

(For unlisted procedure, colon, use 45399)

MECKEL'S DIVERTICULUM AND THE MESENTERY

EXCISION

| 44800 | Excision of Meckel's diverticulum (diverticulectomy) or omphalomesenteric duct |

| 44820 | Excision of lesion of mesentery (separate procedure) |

(With intestine resection, see 44120 or 44140 et seq)

SUTURE

| 44850 | Suture of mesentery (separate procedure) |

(For reduction and repair of internal hernia, use 44050)

OTHER PROCEDURES

| 44899 | Unlisted procedure, Meckel's diverticulum and the mesentery |

APPENDIX

INCISION

| 44900 | Incision and drainage of appendiceal abscess; open |

(For percutaneous image-guided drainage by catheter of appendiceal abscess, use 49406)

EXCISION

| 44950 | Appendectomy; |

(Incidental appendectomy during intra-abdominal surgery does not usually warrant a separate identification. If necessary to report, add modifier -52)

| + 44955 | when done for indicated purpose at time of other major procedure (not as separate procedure) (List separately in addition to code for primary procedure) |

| 44960 | for ruptured appendix with abscess or generalized peritonitis |

LAPAROSCOPY

Surgical laparoscopy always includes diagnostic laparoscopy. To report a diagnostic laparoscopy (peritoneoscopy) (separate procedure), use 49320.

| 44970 | Laparoscopy, surgical, appendectomy |

| 44979 | Unlisted laparoscopy procedure, appendix |

● New Code ▲ Revised Code + Add-On Code ⊘ Modifier -51 Exempt ★ Telemedicine

COLON AND RECTUM

INCISION

45000 Transrectal drainage of pelvic abscess

(For transrectal image-guided fluid collection drainage by catheter of pelvic abscess, use 49407)

45005 Incision and drainage of submucosal abscess, rectum

45020 Incision and drainage of deep supralevator, pelvirectal, or retrorectal abscess

(See also 46050, 46060)

EXCISION

45100 Biopsy of anorectal wall, anal approach (eg, congenital megacolon)

(For endoscopic biopsy, use 45305)

45108 Anorectal myomectomy

45110 Proctectomy; complete, combined abdominoperineal, with colostomy

(For laparoscopic procedure, use 45395)

45111 partial resection of rectum, transabdominal approach

45112 Proctectomy, combined abdominoperineal, pull-through procedure (eg, colo-anal anastomosis)

(For colo-anal anastomosis with colonic reservoir or pouch, use 45119)

45113 Proctectomy, partial, with rectal mucosectomy, ileoanal anastomosis, creation of ileal reservoir (S or J), with or without loop ileostomy

45114 Proctectomy, partial, with anastomosis; abdominal and transsacral approach

45116 transsacral approach only (Kraske type)

45119 Proctectomy, combined abdominoperineal pull-through procedure (eg, colo-anal anastomosis), with creation of colonic reservoir (eg, J-pouch), with diverting enterostomy when performed

(For laparoscopic procedure, use 45397)

45120 Proctectomy, complete (for congenital megacolon), abdominal and perineal approach; with pull-through procedure and anastomosis (eg, Swenson, Duhamel, or Soave type operation)

45121 with subtotal or total colectomy, with multiple biopsies

45123 Proctectomy, partial, without anastomosis, perineal approach

45126 Pelvic exenteration for colorectal malignancy, with proctectomy (with or without colostomy), with removal of bladder and ureteral transplantations, and/or hysterectomy, or cervicectomy, with or without removal of tube(s), with or without removal of ovary(s), or any combination thereof

45130 Excision of rectal procidentia, with anastomosis; perineal approach

45135 abdominal and perineal approach

45136 Excision of ileoanal reservoir with ileostomy

(Do not report 45136 in conjunction with 44005, 44310)

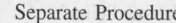 Separate Procedure   Unlisted Procedure   CCI Comp. Code    Non-specific Procedure   **469**

45150 Division of stricture of rectum

45160 Excision of rectal tumor by proctotomy, transsacral or transcoccygeal approach

45171 Excision of rectal tumor, transanal approach; not including muscularis propria (ie, partial thickness)

45172 including muscularis propria (ie, full thickness)

(For destruction of rectal tumor, transanal approach, use 45190)

(For transanal endoscopic microsurgical [ie, TEMS] excision of rectal tumor, including muscularis propria [ie., full thickness], use 0184T)

DESTRUCTION

45190 Destruction of rectal tumor (eg, electrodesiccation, electrosurgery, laser ablation, laser resection, cryosurgery) transanal approach

(For excision of rectal tumor, transanal approach, see 45171, 45172)

(For transanal endoscopic microsurgical [ie, TEMS] excision of rectal tumor, including muscularis propria [ie., full thickness], use 0184T)

ENDOSCOPY

When performing a diagnostic or screening endoscopic procedure on a patient who is scheduled and prepared for a total colonoscopy, if the physician is unable to advance the colonoscope to the cecum or colon-small intestine anastomosis due to unforseen circumstances, report 45378 (colonoscopy) or 44388 (colonoscopy through stoma) with modifier 53 and provide appropriate documentation.

If therapeutic colonoscopy (44389-44407, 45379, 45380, 45381, 45382, 45384, 45388, 45389) is performed and does not reach the cecum or colon-small intestine anastomosis, report the appropriate therapeutic colonoscopy code with modifier 52 and provide appropriate documentation.

Report flexible sigmoidoscopy (45330-45347) for endoscopic examination during which the endoscope is not advanced beyond the splenic flexure.

Report flexible sigmoidoscopy (45330-45347) for endoscopic examination of a patient who has undergone resection of the colon proximal to the sigmoid (eg, subtotal colectomy) and has an ileo-sigmoid or ileo-rectal anastomosis. Report pouch endoscopy codes (44385, 44386) for endoscopic examination of a patient who has undergone resection of colon with ileo-anal anastomosis (eg., J-pouch).

Report colonoscopy (45378-45398) for endoscopic examination of a patient who has undergone segmental resection of the colon (eg., hemicolectomy, sigmoid colectomy, low anterior resection).

For colonoscopy through stoma, see 44388-44408.

Report proctosigmoidoscopy (45300-45327), flexible sigmoidoscopy (45330- 45347), or anoscopy (46600, 46604, 46606, 46608, 46610, 46611, 46612, 46614, 46615) as appropriate for endoscopic examination of the defunctionalized rectum or distal colon in a patient who has undergone colectomy, in addition to colonoscopy through stoma (44388-44408) or ileoscopy through stoma (44380, 44381, 44382, 44384) if appropriate.

When bleeding occurs as a result of an endoscopic procedure, control of bleeding is not reported separately during the same operative session.

For computed tomographic colonography, see 74261-74263.

45300 Proctosigmoidoscopy, rigid; diagnostic, with or without collection of specimen(s) by brushing or washing (separate procedure)

45303 with dilation (eg, balloon, guide wire, bougie)

(For radiological supervision and interpretation, use 74360)

● New Code ▲ Revised Code ✛ Add-On Code ⊘ Modifier -51 Exempt ★ Telemedicine

45305   with biopsy, single or multiple

45307   with removal of foreign body

45308   with removal of single tumor, polyp, or other lesion by hot biopsy forceps or bipolar cautery

45309   with removal of single tumor, polyp, or other lesion by snare technique

45315   with removal of multiple tumors, polyps, or other lesions by hot biopsy forceps, bipolar cautery or snare technique

45317   with control of bleeding (eg, injection, bipolar cautery, unipolar cautery, laser, heater probe, stapler, plasma coagulator)

45320   with ablation of tumor(s), polyp(s), or other lesion(s) not amenable to removal by hot biopsy forceps, bipolar cautery or snare technique (eg, laser)

45321   with decompression of volvulus

45327   with transendoscopic stent placement (includes predilation)

45330   Sigmoidoscopy, flexible; diagnostic, including collection of specimen(s) by brushing or washing, when performed (separate procedure)

(Do not report 45330 in conjunction with 45331-45342, 45346, 45347, 45349, 45350)

45331   with biopsy, single or multiple

(Do not report 45331 in conjunction with 45349 for the same lesion)

45332   with removal of foreign body(s)

(Do not report 45332 in conjunction with 45330)

(If fluoroscopic guidance is performed, use 76000)

45333   with removal of tumor(s), polyp(s), or other lesion(s) by hot biopsy forceps

(Do not report 45333 in conjunction with 45330)

45334   with control of bleeding, any method

(Do not report 45334 in conjunction with 45335, 45350 for the same lesion)

(Do not report 45334 in conjunction with 45330)

45335   with directed submucosal injection(s), any substance

(Do not report 45335 in conjunction with 45334, 45349 for the same lesion)

(Do not report 45335 in conjunction with 45330)

45337   with decompression (for pathologic distention) (eg, volvulus, megacolon), including placement of decompression tube, when performed

(Do not report 45337 in conjunction with 45330)

(Do not report 45337 more than once per session)

45338   with removal of tumor(s), polyp(s), or other lesion(s) by snare technique

(Do not report 45338 in conjunction with 45349 for the same lesion)

(Do not report 45338 in conjunction with 45330)

(For endoscopic mucosal resection, use 45349)

45346   with ablation of tumor(s), polyp(s), or other lesion(s) (includes pre- and post-dilation and guide wire passage, when performed)

(Do not report 45346 in conjunction with 45330)

(Do not report 45346 in conjunction with 45340 for the same lesion)

45340   with transendoscopic balloon dilation

(Do not report 45340 in conjunction with 45330, 45346, 45347)

(If fluoroscopic guidance is performed, use 74360)

(For transendoscopic balloon dilation of multiple strictures during the same session, use 45340 with modifier 59 for each additional stricture dilated)

45341   with endoscopic ultrasound examination

(Do not report 45341 in conjunction with 45330, 45342, 76872, 76975)

(Do not report 45341 more than once per session)

45342   with transendoscopic ultrasound guided intramural or transmural fine needle aspiration/biopsy(s)

(Do not report 45342 in conjunction with 45330, 45341, 76872, 76942, 76975)

(Do not report 45342 more than once per session)

45346   This code is out of order. See page 472.

45347   with placement of endoscopic stent (includes pre- and post-dilation and guide wire passage, when performed)

(Do not report 45347 in conjunction with 45330, 45340)

(If fluoroscopic guidance is performed, use 74360)

45349   with endoscopic mucosal resection

(Do not report 45349 in conjunction with 45331, 45335, 45338, 45350 for the same lesion)

(Do not report 45349 in conjunction with 45330)

45350   with band ligation(s) (eg, hemorrhoids)

(Do not report 45350 in conjunction with 45334 for the same lesion)

(Do not report 45350 in conjunction with 45330, 45349, 46221)

(Do not report 45350 more than once per session)

(To report control of active bleeding with band ligation[s], use 45334)

45378   Colonoscopy, flexible; diagnostic, including collection of specimen(s) by brushing or washing, when performed (separate procedure)

(Do not report 45378 in conjunction with 45379-45393, 45398)

(For colonoscopy with decompression [pathologic distention], use 45393)

45379   with removal of foreign body(s)

(Do not report 45379 in conjunction with 45378)

(If fluoroscopic guidance is performed, use 76000)

● New Code   ▲ Revised Code   + Add-On Code   ⊘ Modifier -51 Exempt   ★ Telemedicine

45380   with biopsy, single or multiple

(Do not report 45380 in conjunction with 45390 for the same lesion)

(Do not report 45380 in conjunction with 45378)

45381   with directed submucosal injection(s), any substance

(Do not report 45381 in conjunction with 45382, 45390 for the same lesion)

(Do not report 45381 in conjunction with 45378)

45382   with control of bleeding, any method

(Do not report 45382 in conjunction with 45381, 45398 for the same lesion)

(Do not report 45382 in conjunction with 45378)

45388   with ablation of tumor(s), polyp(s), or other lesion(s) (includes pre- and post-dilation and guide wire passage, when performed)

(Do not report 45388 in conjunction with 45386 for the same lesion)

(Do not report 45388 in conjunction with 45378)

45384   with removal of tumor(s), polyp(s), or other lesion(s) by hot biopsy forceps

(Do not report 45384 in conjunction with 45378)

45385   with removal of tumor(s), polyp(s), or other lesion(s) by snare technique

(Do not report 45385 in conjunction with 45390 for the same lesion)

(Do not report 45385 in conjunction with 45378)

(For endoscopic mucosal resection, use 45390)

45386   with transendoscopic balloon dilation

(Do not report 45386 in conjunction with 45378, 45388, 45389)

(If fluoroscopic guidance is performed, use 74360)

(For transendoscopic balloon dilation of multiple strictures during the same session, report 45386 with modifier 59 for each additional stricture dilated)

45388 This code is out of order. See page 473.

45389   with endoscopic stent placement (includes pre- and post-dilation and guide wire passage, when performed)

(Do not report 45389 in conjunction with 45378, 45386)

(If fluoroscopic guidance is performed, use 74360)

45390 This code is out of order. See page 474.

45391   with endoscopic ultrasound examination limited to the rectum, sigmoid, descending, transverse, or ascending colon and cecum, and adjacent structures

(Do not report 45391 in conjunction with 45378, 45392, 76872, 76975)

(Do not report 45391 more than once per session)

45392   with transendoscopic ultrasound guided intramural or transmural fine needle aspiration/biopsy(s), includes endoscopic ultrasound examination limited to the rectum, sigmoid, descending, transverse, or ascending colon and cecum, and adjacent structures

Separate Procedure   Unlisted Procedure   CCI Comp. Code   Non-specific Procedure   **473**

(Do not report 45392 in conjunction with 45378, 45391, 76872, 76942, 76975)

(Do not report 45392 more than once per session)

45390   with endoscopic mucosal resection

(Do not report 45390 in conjunction with 45380, 45381, 45385, 45398 for the same lesion)

(Do not report 45390 in conjunction with 45378)

45393   with decompression (for pathologic distention) (eg, volvulus, megacolon), including placement of decompression tube, when performed

(Do not report 45393 in conjunction with 45378)

(Do not report 45393 more than once per session)

45398   with band ligation(s) (eg, hemorrhoids)

(Do not report 45398 in conjunction with 45382 for the same lesion)

(Do not report 45398 in conjunction with 45378, 45390, 46221)

(Do not report 45398 more than once per session)

(To report control of active bleeding with band ligation[s], use 45382)

LAPAROSCOPY

Surgical laparoscopy always includes diagnostic laparoscopy. To report a diagnostic laparoscopy (peritoneoscopy) (separate procedure), use 49320.

Excision

45395   Laparoscopy, surgical; proctectomy, complete, combined abdominoperineal, with colostomy

(For open procedure, use 45110)

45397   proctectomy, combined abdominoperineal pull-through procedure (eg, colo-anal anastomosis), with creation of colonic reservoir (eg, J-pouch), with diverting enterostomy, when performed

(For open procedure, use 45119)

45398   This code is out of order. See page 474.

45399   This code is out of order. See page 475.

Repair

45400   Laparoscopy, surgical; proctopexy (for prolapse)

(For open procedure, use 45540, 45541)

45402   proctopexy (for prolapse), with sigmoid resection

(For open procedure, use 45550)

45499   Unlisted laparoscopy procedure, rectum

REPAIR

45500   Proctoplasty; for stenosis

45505   for prolapse of mucous membrane

45520   Perirectal injection of sclerosing solution for prolapse

● New Code   ▲ Revised Code   ＋ Add-On Code   ⊘ Modifier -51 Exempt   ★ Telemedicine

45540 Proctopexy (eg, for prolapse); abdominal approach

(For laparoscopic procedure, use 45400)

45541 perineal approach

45550 with sigmoid resection, abdominal approach

(For laparoscopic procedure, use 45402)

45560 Repair of rectocele (separate procedure)

(For repair of rectocele with posterior colporrhaphy, use 57250)

45562 Exploration, repair, and presacral drainage for rectal injury;

45563 with colostomy

45800 Closure of rectovesical fistula;

45805 with colostomy

45820 Closure of rectourethral fistula;

45825 with colostomy

(For rectovaginal fistula closure, see 57300-57308)

MANIPULATION

45900 Reduction of procidentia (separate procedure) under anesthesia

45905 Dilation of anal sphincter (separate procedure) under anesthesia other than local

45910 Dilation of rectal stricture (separate procedure) under anesthesia other than local

45915 Removal of fecal impaction or foreign body (separate procedure) under anesthesia

OTHER PROCEDURES

Surgical diagnostic anorectal exam (45990) includes the following elements: external perineal exam, digital rectal exam, pelvic exam (when performed), diagnostic anoscopy, and diagnostic rigid proctoscopy.

45399 Unlisted procedure, colon

45990 Anorectal exam, surgical, requiring anesthesia (general, spinal, or epidural), diagnostic

(Do not report 45990 in conjunction with 45300-45327, 46600, 57410, 99170)

45999 Unlisted procedure, rectum

(For unlisted laparoscopic procedure, rectum, use 45499)

ANUS

For incision of thrombosed external hemorrhoid, use 46083. For ligation of internal hemorrhoid(s), see 46221, 46945, 46946. For excision of internal and/or external hemorrhoid(s), see 46250-46262, 46320. For injection of hemorrhoid(s), use 46500. For destruction of internal hemorrhoid(s) by thermal energy, use 46930. For destruction of hemorrhoid(s) by cryosurgery, use 46999. For hemorrhoidopexy, use 46947. Do not report 46600 in conjunction with 46020-46942, 0184T, 0249T, 0377T during the same operative session.

| | Separate Procedure | | Unlisted Procedure | | CCI Comp. Code | | Non-specific Procedure | **475** |

INCISION

(For subcutaneous fistulotomy, use 46270)

46020 Placement of seton

(Do not report 46020 in addition to 46060, 46280, 46600, 0249T)

46030 Removal of anal seton, other marker

46040 Incision and drainage of ischiorectal and/or perirectal abscess (separate procedure)

46045 Incision and drainage of intramural, intramuscular, or submucosal abscess, transanal, under anesthesia

46050 Incision and drainage, perianal abscess, superficial

(See also 45020, 46060)

46060 Incision and drainage of ischiorectal or intramural abscess, with fistulectomy or fistulotomy, submuscular, with or without placement of seton

(Do not report 46060 in addition to 46020)

(See also 45020)

46070 Incision, anal septum (infant)

(For anoplasty, see 46700-46705)

(Do not report modifier '-63' in conjunction with 46070)

46080 Sphincterotomy, anal, division of sphincter (separate procedure)

46083 Incision of thrombosed hemorrhoid, external

EXCISION

46200 Fissurectomy, including sphincterotomy when performed

(**46210** Deleted 2009 [2010 edition]; see 46999)

(**46211** Deleted 2009 [2010 edition]; see 46999)

46220 This code is out of order. See page 475.

46221 Hemorrhoidectomy, internal, by rubber band ligation(s)

(Do not report 46221 in conjunction with 45350, 45398)

(For ligation, hemorrhoidal vascular bundle(s), including ultrasound guidance, use 0249T)

46945 Hemorrhoidectomy, internal, by ligation other than rubber band; single hemorrhoid column/group

46946 2 or more hemorrhoid columns/groups

(Do not report 46221, 46945, and 46946 in conjunction with 0249T)

46220 Excision of single external papilla or tag, anus

46230 Excision of multiple external papillae or tags, anus

46320 Excision of thrombosed hemorrhoid, external

● New Code ▲ Revised Code + Add-On Code ⊘ Modifier -51 Exempt ★ Telemedicine

46250 Hemorrhoidectomy, external, 2 or more columns/groups

(For hemorrhoidectomy, external, single column/group, use 46999)

46255 Hemorrhoidectomy, internal and external, single column/group;

46257   with fissurectomy

46258   with fistulectomy, including fissurectomy, when performed

46260 Hemorrhoidectomy, internal and external, 2 or more columns/groups;

46261   with fissurectomy

46262   with fistulectomy, including fissurectomy, when performed

(Do not report 46250-46262 in conjunction with 0249T)

46270 Surgical treatment of anal fistula (fistulectomy/fistulotomy); subcutaneous

46275   intersphincteric

46280   transsphincteric, suprasphincteric, extrasphincteric or multiple, including placement of seton, when performed

(Do not report 46280 in addition to 46020)

46285   second stage

46288 Closure of anal fistula with rectal advancement flap

46320 This code is out of order. See page 476.

INTRODUCTION

46500 Injection of sclerosing solution, hemorrhoids

(For anoscopy with directed submucosal injection of bulking agent for fecal incontinence, use 0377T)

46505 Chemodenervation of internal anal sphincter

(For chemodenervation of other muscles, see 64612, 64616, 64617, 64642, 64643, 64644, 64645, 64646, 64647. For destruction of nerve by neurolytic agent, use 64630)

(Report the specific service in conjunction with the specific substance(s) or drug(s) provided)

ENDOSCOPY

Surgical endoscopy always includes diagnostic endoscopy.

(For anoscopy with directed submucosal injection of bulking agent for fecal incontinence, use 0377T)

46600 Anoscopy; diagnostic, including collection of specimen(s) by brushing or washing, when performed (separate procedure)

(Do not report 46600 in conjunction with 46020-46947, 0184T, 0249T, 0377T during the same operative session)

(For diagnostic high-resolution anoscopy [HRA], use 46601)

46601   diagnostic, with high-resolution magnification (hra) (eg, colposcope, operating microscope) and chemical agent enhancement, including collection of specimen(s) by brushing or washing, when performed

---

■ Separate Procedure   ■ Unlisted Procedure   ■ CCI Comp. Code   ■ Non-specific Procedure   **477**

(Do not report 46601 in conjunction with 69990)

46604   with dilation (eg, balloon, guide wire, bougie)

46606   with biopsy, single or multiple

(For high-resolution anoscopy [HRA] with biopsy, use 46607)

46607   with high-resolution magnification (hra) (eg, colposcope, operating microscope) and chemical agent enhancement, with biopsy, single or multiple

(Do not report 46607 in conjunction with 69990)

46608   with removal of foreign body

46610   with removal of single tumor, polyp, or other lesion by hot biopsy forceps or bipolar cautery

46611   with removal of single tumor, polyp, or other lesion by snare technique

46612   with removal of multiple tumors, polyps, or other lesions by hot biopsy forceps, bipolar cautery or snare technique

46614   with control of bleeding (eg, injection, bipolar cautery, unipolar cautery, laser, heater probe, stapler, plasma coagulator)

46615   with ablation of tumor(s), polyp(s), or other lesion(s) not amenable to removal by hot biopsy forceps, bipolar cautery or snare technique

(For delivery of thermal energy to the muscle of the anal canal, use 0288T)

REPAIR

46700   Anoplasty, plastic operation for stricture; adult

46705   infant

(Do not report modifier '-63' in conjunction with 46705)

(For simple incision of anal septum, use 46070)

46706   Repair of anal fistula with fibrin glue

46707   Repair of anorectal fistula with plug (eg, porcine small intestine submucosa [SIS])

46710   Repair of ileoanal pouch fistula/sinus (eg, perineal or vaginal), pouch advancement; transperineal approach

46712   combined transperineal and transabdominal approach

46715   Repair of low imperforate anus; with anoperineal fistula (cut-back procedure)

46716   with transposition of anoperineal or anovestibular fistula

(Do not report modifier 63 in conjunction with 46715, 46716)

46730   Repair of high imperforate anus without fistula; perineal or sacroperineal approach

46735   combined transabdominal and sacroperineal approaches

(Do not report modifier 63 in conjunction with 46730, 46735)

46740   Repair of high imperforate anus with rectourethral or rectovaginal fistula; perineal or sacroperineal approach

---

46742   combined transabdominal and sacroperineal approaches

(Do not report modifier 63 in conjunction with 46740, 46742)

46744   Repair of cloacal anomaly by anorectovaginoplasty and urethroplasty, sacroperineal approach

(Do not report modifier 63 in conjunction with 46744)

46746   Repair of cloacal anomaly by anorectovaginoplasty and urethroplasty, combined abdominal and sacroperineal approach;

46748   with vaginal lengthening by intestinal graft or pedicle flaps

46750   Sphincteroplasty, anal, for incontinence or prolapse; adult

46751   child

46753   Graft (Thiersch operation) for rectal incontinence and/or prolapse

46754   Removal of Thiersch wire or suture, anal canal

46760   Sphincteroplasty, anal, for incontinence, adult; muscle transplant

46761   levator muscle imbrication (Park posterior anal repair)

46762   implantation artificial sphincter

(For anoscopy with directed submucosal injection of bulking agent for fecal incontinence, use 0377T)

46947   Hemorrhoidopexy (eg, for prolapsing internal hemorrhoids) by stapling

DESTRUCTION

46900   Destruction of lesion(s), anus (eg, condyloma, papilloma, molluscum contagiosum, herpetic vesicle), simple; chemical

46910   electrodesiccation

46916   cryosurgery

46917   laser surgery

46922   surgical excision

46924   Destruction of lesion(s), anus (eg, condyloma, papilloma, molluscum contagiosum, herpetic vesicle), extensive (eg, laser surgery, electrosurgery, cryosurgery, chemosurgery)

46930   Destruction of internal hemorrhoid(s) by thermal energy (eg, infrared coagulation, cautery, radiofrequency)

(46937   Deleted 2009 [2010 edition]; use 45190)

(46938   Deleted 2009 [2010 edition]; use 45190)

46940   Curettage or cautery of anal fissure, including dilation of anal sphincter (separate procedure); initial

46942   subsequent

46945   This code is out of order. See page 476.

46946   This code is out of order. See page 476.

46947   This code is out of order. See page 479.

OTHER PROCEDURES

46999   Unlisted procedure, anus

LIVER

INCISION

47000   Biopsy of liver, needle; percutaneous

(If imaging guidance is performed, see 76942, 77002, 77012, 77021)

+ **47001**   when done for indicated purpose at time of other major procedure (List separately in addition to code for primary procedure)

(If imaging guidance is performed, see 76942, 77002)

(For fine needle aspiration in conjunction with 47000, 47001, see 10021, 10022)

(For evaluation of fine needle aspirate in conjunction with 47000, 47001, see 88172, 88173)

47010   Hepatotomy; for open drainage of abscess or cyst, 1 or 2 stages

(For percutaneous image-guided fluid collection drainage by catheter of hepatic abscess or cyst, use 49405)

47015   Laparotomy, with aspiration and/or injection of hepatic parasitic (eg, amoebic or echinococcal) cyst(s) or abscess(es)

EXCISION

47100   Biopsy of liver, wedge

47120   Hepatectomy, resection of liver; partial lobectomy

47122   trisegmentectomy

47125   total left lobectomy

47130   total right lobectomy

LIVER TRANSPLANTATION

Liver allotransplantation involves three distinct components of physician work:

1) **Cadaver donor hepatectomy**, which includes harvesting the graft and cold preservation of the graft (perfusing with cold preservation solution and cold maintenance) (use 47133). **Living donor hepatectomy**, which includes harvesting the graft, cold preservation of the graft (perfusing with cold preservation solution and cold maintenance), and care of the donor (see 47140-47142).

2) **Backbench work**:

Standard preparation of the whole liver graft will include one of the following:

Preparation of whole liver graft (including cholecystectomy, if necessary, and dissection and removal of surrounding soft tissues to prepare vena cava, portal vein, hepatic artery, and common bile duct for implantation) (use 47143).

Preparation as described for whole liver graft, plus trisegment split into two partial grafts (use 47144).

Preparation as described for whole liver graft, plus lobe split into two partial grafts (use 47145).

Additional reconstruction of the liver graft may include venous and/or arterial anastomosis(es) (see 47146, 47147).

● New Code   ▲ Revised Code   + Add-On Code   ⊘ Modifier -51 Exempt   ★ Telemedicine

3) **Recipient liver allotransplantation**, which includes recipient hepatectomy (partial or whole), transplantation of the allograft (partial or whole), and care of the recipient (see 47135).

47133 Donor hepatectomy (including cold preservation), from cadaver donor

47135 Liver allotransplantation; orthotopic, partial or whole, from cadaver or living donor, any age

(**47136** deleted 2015 [2016 edition]. To report, use 47399)

47140 Donor hepatectomy (including cold preservation), from living donor; left lateral segment only (segments II and III)

47141 total left lobectomy (segments II, III, and IV)

47142 total right lobectomy (segments V, VI, VII, and VIII)

47143 Backbench standard preparation of cadaver donor whole liver graft prior to allotransplantation, including cholecystectomy, if necessary, and dissection and removal of surrounding soft tissues to prepare the vena cava, portal vein, hepatic artery, and common bile duct for implantation; without trisegment or lobe split

47144 with trisegment split of whole liver graft into 2 partial liver grafts (ie, left lateral segment [segments II and III] and right trisegment [segments I and IV through VIII])

47145 with lobe split of whole liver graft into 2 partial liver grafts (ie, left lobe (segments II, III, and IV) and right lobe (segments I and V through VIII))

47146 Backbench reconstruction of cadaver or living donor liver graft prior to allotransplantation; venous anastomosis, each

47147 arterial anastomosis, each

(Do not report 47143-47147 in conjunction with 47120-47125, 47600, 47610)

REPAIR

47300 Marsupialization of cyst or abscess of liver

47350 Management of liver hemorrhage; simple suture of liver wound or injury

47360 complex suture of liver wound or injury, with or without hepatic artery ligation

47361 exploration of hepatic wound, extensive debridement, coagulation and/or suture, with or without packing of liver

47362 re-exploration of hepatic wound for removal of packing

LAPAROSCOPY

Surgical laparoscopy always include diagnostic laparoscopy. To report a diagnostic laparoscopy (peritneoscopy) (separate procedure), use 49320.

47370 Laparoscopy, surgical, ablation of 1 or more liver tumor(s); radiofrequency

(For imaging guidance, use 76490)

47371 cryosurgical

(For imaging guidance, use 76490)

47379 Unlisted laparoscopic procedure, liver

| | Separate Procedure | | Unlisted Procedure | | CCI Comp. Code | | Non-specific Procedure | **481** |

OTHER PROCEDURES

47380   Ablation, open, of 1 or more liver tumor(s); radiofrequency

(For imaging guidance, use 76490)

47381   cryosurgical

(For imaging guidance, use 76490)

47382   Ablation, 1 or more liver tumor(s), percutaneous, radiofrequency

(For imaging guidance and monitoring, see 76490, 77013, 77022)

47383   Ablation, 1 or more liver tumor[s], percutaneous, cryoablation

(For imaging guidance and monitoring, see 76940, 77013, 77022)

47399   Unlisted procedure, liver

BILIARY TRACT

INCISION

47400   Hepaticotomy or hepaticostomy with exploration, drainage, or removal of calculus

47420   Choledochotomy or choledochostomy with exploration, drainage, or removal of calculus, with or without cholecystotomy; without transduodenal sphincterotomy or sphincteroplasty

47425   with transduodenal sphincterotomy or sphincteroplasty

47460   Transduodenal sphincterotomy or sphincteroplasty, with or without transduodenal extraction of calculus (separate procedure)

47480   Cholecystotomy or cholecystostomy, open, with exploration, drainage, or removal of calculus (separate procedure)

(For percutaneous cholecystostomy, use 47490)

INTRODUCTION

Percutaneous biliary procedures (eg, transhepatic, transcholecystic) are described by 47490 and 47531-47544, and are performed with imaging guidance. They are differentiated from endoscopic procedures that utilize an access to the biliary tree from a hollow viscus for diagnosis and therapy. Diagnostic cholangiography is typically performed with percutaneous biliary procedures, and is included in 47490, 47533, 47534, 47535, 47536, 47537, 47538, 47539, 47540, and 47541.

Codes 47531 and 47532 describe percutaneous diagnostic cholangiography that includes injection(s) of contrast material, all associated radiological supervision and interpretation, and procedural imaging guidance (eg, ultrasound and/or fluoroscopy). Code 47532 also includes accessing the biliary system with a needle or catheter. Codes 47531 and 47532 may not be reported with codes 47533, 47534, 47535, 47536, 47537, 47538, 47539, 47540, and 47541.

An external biliary drainage catheter is a catheter placed into a bile duct that does not terminate in bowel, and that drains bile externally only. An internal-external biliary drainage catheter is a single, externally accessible catheter that terminates in the small intestine, and may drain bile into the small intestine and/or externally. A "stent," as used in this code set, is a percutaneously placed device (eg, self-expanding metallic mesh stent, plastic tube) that is positioned within the biliary tree and is completely internal, with no portion extending outside the patient.

Codes 47533, 47534, 47535, 47536, 47537, 47538, 47539, and 47540 describe percutaneous therapeutic biliary procedures that include catheter or stent placement, catheter removal and replacement (exchange), and/or catheter removal. These codes include the elements of access, drainage catheter manipulations, diagnostic cholangiography, imaging guidance (eg, ultrasonography and/or fluoroscopy), and all associated radiological supervision and interpretation. Codes 47533, 47534, 47538, 47539, 47540 may be reported once for each catheter or stent placed (eg, bilobar placement, multi-segmental placement). Codes 47535, 47536, and 47537 may be reported once for each catheter conversion, exchange, or removal (eg, bilobar, bisegmental).

Codes 47538, 47539, 47540 may be reported only once per session to describe one or more overlapping or serial stent(s) placed within a single bile duct, or bridging more than one ductal segment (eg, left hepatic duct and common bile duct) through a single percutaneous access. Codes 47538, 47539, 47540 may be reported more than once in the same session using modifier 59 for the additional procedures in the following circumstances: (i) placement of side-by-side (double-barrel) stents within a single bile duct; (ii) placement of two or more stents into separate bile ducts through a single percutaneous access; or (iii) placement of stents through two or more percutaneous access sites (eg, placement of one stent through the interstices of another stent). Code 47538 describes biliary stent placement through an existing access. Therefore, 47538 should not be reported together with 47536 if a biliary drainage catheter (eg, external or internal-external) is replaced after the biliary stent is placed. Code 47540 describes biliary stent placement with the additional service of placing a biliary drainage catheter (eg, external or internal-external). Therefore, 47540 should not be reported with 47533, 47534 for the same ductal system.

Code 47541 describes a procedure to assist with endoscopic procedures performed in conjunction with other physician specialists. Access placed may include wire and/or catheter. Code 47541 may not be reported if a wire is placed through existing percutaneous access.

Codes 47542, 47543, and 47544 describe procedures that may be performed in conjunction with other codes in this family, are add-on codes and do not include access, catheter placement, or diagnostic imaging. Do not report 47542 with 47538, 47539, 47540 because balloon dilation is included in 47538, 47539, and 47540. Code 47544 should not be reported with 47531-47543 for incidental removal of debris. Code 47542 should not be reported with 47544, if a balloon is used for removal of calculi or debris rather than for dilation.

EXCHANGES/CONVERSIONS				
(Existing Access)		**To**		
Do not report exchange with stent for same percutaneous access		**Internal-External**	**External**	**Stent**
From	External Drain	47535 Conversion	47536 Exchange	47538 Stent
	Internal-External Drain	47536 Exchange	47536 Exchange	47538 Stent

47490 Cholecystostomy, percutaneous, complete procedure, including imaging guidance, catheter placement, cholecystogram when performed, and radiological supervision and interpretation

(Do not report 47490 in conjunction with 47531, 47532, 75989, 76942, 77002, 77012, 77021)

(**47500** deleted 2015 [2016 edition]. To report, see 47531-47541)

(**47505** deleted 2015 [2016 edition]. To report, see 47531-47541)

(**47510** deleted 2015 [2016 edition]. To report, see 47531-47541)

(**47511** deleted 2015 [2016 edition]. To report, see 47531-47541)

(**47525** deleted 2015 [2016 edition]. To report, see 47531-47541)

(**47530** deleted 2015 [2016 edition]. To report, see 47531-47541)

47531 Injection procedure for cholangiography, percutaneous, complete diagnostic procedure including imaging guidance (eg, ultrasound and/or fluoroscopy) and all associated radiological supervision and interpretation; existing access

47532   new access (eg, percutaneous transhepatic cholangiogram)

(Do not report 47531, 47532 in conjunction with 47490, 47533, 47534, 47535, 47536, 47537, 47538, 47539, 47540, 47541 for procedures performed through the same percutaneous access)

(For intraoperative cholangiography, see 74300, 74301)

47533 Placement of biliary drainage catheter, percutaneous, including diagnostic cholangiography when performed, imaging guidance (eg, ultrasound and/or fluoroscopy), and all associated radiological supervision and interpretation; external

47534   internal-external

47535   Conversion of external biliary drainage catheter to internal-external biliary drainage catheter, percutaneous, including diagnostic cholangiography when performed, imaging guidance (eg, fluoroscopy), and all associated radiological supervision and interpretation

47536   Exchange of biliary drainage catheter (eg, external, internal-external, or conversion of internal-external to external only), percutaneous, including diagnostic cholangiography when performed, imaging guidance (eg, fluoroscopy), and all associated radiological supervision and interpretation

(Do not report 47536 in conjunction with 47538 for the same access)

(47536 includes exchange of one catheter. For exchange of additional catheter[s] during the same session, report 47536 with modifier 59 for each additional exchange)

47537   Removal of biliary drainage catheter, percutaneous, requiring fluoroscopic guidance (eg, with concurrent indwelling biliary stents), including diagnostic cholangiography when performed, imaging guidance (eg, fluoroscopy), and all associated radiological supervision and interpretation

(Do not report 47537 in conjunction with 47538 for the same access)

(For removal of biliary drainage catheter not requiring fluoroscopic guidance, see E/M services and report the appropriate level of service provided [eg 99201-99215, 99217, 99218, 99219, 99220, 99221, 99222, 99223, 99224, 99225, 99226, 99231, 99232, 99233])

47538   Placement of stent(s) into a bile duct, percutaneous, including diagnostic cholangiography, imaging guidance (eg, fluoroscopy and/or ultrasound), balloon dilation, catheter exchange(s) and catheter removal(s) when performed, and all associated radiological supervision and interpretation; existing access

(Do not report 47538 in conjunction with 47536, 47537 for the same percutaneous access)

47539   new access, without placement of separate biliary drainage catheter

47540   new access, with placement of separate biliary drainage catheter (eg, external or internal-external)

(Do not report 47538, 47539, 47540 in conjunction with 43277, 47542, 47555, 47556 for the same lesion in the same session)

(Do not report 47540 in conjunction with 47533, 47534 for the same percutaneous access)

(47538, 47539, 47540 may be reported more than once per session, when specific conditions described in the Introduction within the Biliary Tract subsection guidelines are met)

47541   Placement of access through the biliary tree and into small bowel to assist with an endoscopic biliary procedure (eg, rendezvous procedure), percutaneous, including diagnostic cholangiography when performed, imaging guidance (eg, ultrasound and/or fluoroscopy), and all associated radiological supervision and interpretation, new access

(Do not report 47541 in conjunction with 47531, 47532, 47533, 47534, 47535, 47536, 47537, 47538, 47539, 47540)

(Do not report 47541 when there is existing catheter access)

(For use of existing access through the biliary tree into small bowel to assist with an endoscopic biliary procedure, see 47535, 47536, 47537)

+ **47542**   Balloon dilation of biliary duct(s) or of ampulla (sphincteroplasty), percutaneous, including imaging guidance (eg, fluoroscopy), and all associated radiological supervision and interpretation, each duct (List separately in addition to code for primary procedure)

(Use 47542 in conjunction with 47531, 47532, 47533, 47534, 47535, 47536, 47537, 47541)

(Do not report 47542 in conjunction with 43262, 43277, 47538, 47539, 47540, 47555, 47556)

(Do not report 47542 in conjunction with 47544 if a balloon is used for removal of calculi, debris, and/or sludge rather than for dilation)

● New Code   ▲ Revised Code   + Add-On Code   ⊘ Modifier -51 Exempt   ★ Telemedicine

(For percutaneous balloon dilation of multiple ducts during the same session, report an additional dilation once with 47542 and modifier 59, regardless of the number of additional ducts dilated)

(For endoscopic balloon dilation, see 43277, 47555, 47556)

+ **47543** Endoluminal biopsy(ies) of biliary tree, percutaneous, any method(s) (eg, brush, forceps, and/or needle), including imaging guidance (eg, fluoroscopy), and all associated radiological supervision and interpretation, single or multiple (List separately in addition to code for primary procedure)

(Use 47543 in conjunction with 47531, 47532, 47533, 47534, 47535, 47536, 47537, 47538, 47539, 47540)

(Report 47543 once per session)

(For endoscopic brushings, see 43260, 47552)

(For endoscopic biopsy, see 43261, 47553)

+ **47544** Removal of calculi/debris from biliary duct(s) and/or gallbladder, percutaneous, including destruction of calculi by any method (eg, mechanical, electrohydraulic, lithotripsy) when performed, imaging guidance (eg, fluoroscopy), and all associated radiological supervision and interpretation (List separately in addition to code for primary procedure)

(Use 47544 in conjunction with 47531, 47532, 47533, 47534, 47535, 47536, 47537, 47538, 47539, 47540)

(Do not report 47544 if no calculi or debris are found, even if removal device is deployed)

(Do not report 47544 in conjunction with 43264, 47554)

(Do not report 47544 in conjunction with 47531-47543 for incidental removal of debris)

(For endoscopic removal of calculi, see 43264, 47554)

(For endoscopic destruction of calculi, use 43265)

ENDOSCOPY

Surgical endoscopy always includes diagnostic endoscopy.

+ **47550** Biliary endoscopy, intraoperative (choledochoscopy) (List separately in addition to code for primary procedure)

47552 Biliary endoscopy, percutaneous via T-tube or other tract; diagnostic, with collection of specimen(s) by brushing and/or washing, when performed (separate procedure)

47553   with biopsy, single or multiple

47554   with removal of calculus/calculi

47555   with dilation of biliary duct stricture(s) without stent

47556   with dilation of biliary duct stricture(s) with stent

(For ERCP, see 43260-43278, 74328, 74329, 74330, 74363)

(If imaging guidance is performed, see 74363)

LAPAROSCOPY

Surgical laparoscopy always include diagnostic laparoscopy. To report a diagnostic laparoscopy (peritneoscopy) (separate procedure), use 49320.

(**47560** deleted 2015 [2016 edition]. To report laparoscopically guided transhepatic cholangiography with biopsy, use 47579)

(**47561** deleted 2015 [2016 edition]. To report laparoscopically guided transhepatic cholangiography with biopsy, use 47579)

Separate Procedure   Unlisted Procedure   CCI Comp. Code   Non-specific Procedure   **485**

47562	Laparoscopy, surgical; cholecystectomy
47563	cholecystectomy with cholangiography

(For intraoperative cholangiography radiological supervision and interpretation, see 74300, 74301)

(For percutaneous cholangiography, see 47531, 47532)

47564	cholecystectomy with exploration of common duct
47570	cholecystoenterostomy
47579	Unlisted laparoscopy procedure, biliary tract

EXCISION

47600	Cholecystectomy;
47605	with cholangiography

(For laparoscopic approach, see 47562-47564)

47610	Cholecystectomy with exploration of common duct;

(For cholecystectomy with exploration of common duct with biliary endoscopy, use 47610 with 47550)

47612	with choledochoenterostomy
47620	with transduodenal sphincterotomy or sphincteroplasty, with or without cholangiography
(47630	deleted 2015 [2016 edition]. For percutaneous biliary duct stone extraction, use 47544)
47700	Exploration for congenital atresia of bile ducts, without repair, with or without liver biopsy, with or without cholangiography

(Do not report modifier 63 in conjunction with 47700)

47701	Portoenterostomy (eg, Kasai procedure)

(Do not report modifier 63 in conjunction with 47701)

47711	Excision of bile duct tumor, with or without primary repair of bile duct; extrahepatic
47712	intrahepatic

(For anastomosis, see 47760-47800)

47715	Excision of choledochal cyst

REPAIR

47720	Cholecystoenterostomy; direct

(For laparoscopic approach, use 47570)

47721	with gastroenterostomy
47740	Roux-en-Y
47741	Roux-en-Y with gastroenterostomy
47760	Anastomosis, of extrahepatic biliary ducts and gastrointestinal tract

---

● New Code ▲ Revised Code + Add-On Code ⊘ Modifier -51 Exempt ★ Telemedicine

| 47765 | Anastomosis, of intrahepatic ducts and gastrointestinal tract |

| 47780 | Anastomosis, Roux-en-Y, of extrahepatic biliary ducts and gastrointestinal tract |

| 47785 | Anastomosis, Roux-en-Y, of intrahepatic biliary ducts and gastrointestinal tract |

| 47800 | Reconstruction, plastic, of extrahepatic biliary ducts with end-to-end anastomosis |

| 47801 | Placement of choledochal stent |

| 47802 | U-tube hepaticoenterostomy |

| 47900 | Suture of extrahepatic biliary duct for pre-existing injury (separate procedure) |

OTHER PROCEDURES

| 47999 | Unlisted procedure, biliary tract |

PANCREAS

(For peroral pancreatic endoscopic procedures, see 43260-43265, 43274-43278)

INCISION

| 48000 | Placement of drains, peripancreatic, for acute pancreatitis; |

| 48001 | with cholecystostomy, gastrostomy, and jejunostomy |

| 48020 | Removal of pancreatic calculus |

EXCISION

| 48100 | Biopsy of pancreas, open (eg, fine needle aspiration, needle core biopsy, wedge biopsy) |

| 48102 | Biopsy of pancreas, percutaneous needle |

(For radiological supervision and interpretation, see 76942, 77002, 77012, 77021)

(For fine needle aspiration, use 10022)

(For evaluation of fine needle aspirate, see 88172, 88173)

| 48105 | Resection or debridement of pancreas and peripancreatic tissue for acute necrotizing pancreatitis |

| 48120 | Excision of lesion of pancreas (eg, cyst, adenoma) |

| 48140 | Pancreatectomy, distal subtotal, with or without splenectomy; without pancreaticojejunostomy |

| 48145 | with pancreaticojejunostomy |

| 48146 | Pancreatectomy, distal, near-total with preservation of duodenum (Child-type procedure) |

| 48148 | Excision of ampulla of Vater |

| 48150 | Pancreatectomy, proximal subtotal with total duodenectomy, partial gastrectomy, choledochoenterostomy and gastrojejunostomy (Whipple-type procedure); with pancreatojejunostomy |

| 48152 | without pancreatojejunostomy |

| 48153 | Pancreatectomy, proximal subtotal with near-total duodenectomy, choledochoenterostomy, and duodenojejunostomy (pylorus-sparing, whipple-type procedure); with pancreatojejunostomy |

| ▮ Separate Procedure | ▮ Unlisted Procedure | ▮ CCI Comp. Code | ▮ Non-specific Procedure | **487** |

48154	without pancreatojejunostomy
48155	Pancreatectomy, total
48160	Pancreatectomy, total or subtotal, with autologous transplantation of pancreas or pancreatic islet cells

INTRODUCTION

| + 48400 | Injection procedure for intraoperative pancreatography (List separately in addition to code for primary procedure) |

(For radiological supervision and interpretation, see 74300, 74301)

(For intraoperative pancreatography radiological supervision and interpretation, see 74300, 74301)

REPAIR

| 48500 | Marsupialization of pancreatic cyst |
| 48510 | External drainage, pseudocyst of pancreas; open |

(For percutaneous image-guided fluid collection drainage by catheter of pancreatic pseudocyst, use 49405)

48520	Internal anastomosis of pancreatic cyst to gastrointestinal tract; direct
48540	Roux-en-Y
48545	Pancreatorrhaphy for injury
48547	Duodenal exclusion with gastrojejunostomy for pancreatic injury
48548	Pancreaticojejunostomy, side-to-side anastomosis (Puestow-type operation)

PANCREAS TRANSPLANTATION

Pancreas allotransplantation involves three distinct components of physician work:

1) **Cadaver donor pancreatectomy**, which includes harvesting the pancreas graft, with or without duodenal segment, and cold preservation of the graft (perfusing with cold preservation solution and cold maintenance) (use 48550).

2) **Backbench work**:

Standard preparation of a cadaver donor pancreas allograft prior to transplantation includes dissection of the allograft from surrounding soft tissues, splenectomy, duodenotomy, ligation of bile duct, ligation of mesenteric vessels, and Y-graft arterial anastomoses from the iliac artery to the superior mesenteric artery and to the splenic artery (use 48551).

Additional reconstruction of a cadaver donor pancreas allograft prior to transplantation may include venous anastomosis(es) (use 48552).

3) **Recipient pancreas allotransplantation**, which includes transplantation of allograft, and care of the recipient (use 48554).

48550	Donor pancreatectomy (including cold preservation), with or without duodenal segment for transplantation
48551	Backbench standard preparation of cadaver donor pancreas allograft prior to transplantation, including dissection of allograft from surrounding soft tissues, splenectomy, duodenotomy, ligation of bile duct, ligation of mesenteric vessels, and Y-graft arterial anastomoses from iliac artery to superior mesenteric artery and to splenic artery
48552	Backbench reconstruction of cadaver donor pancreas allograft prior to transplantation, venous anastomosis, each

(Do not report 48551 and 48552 in conjunction with 35531, 35563, 35685, 38100-38102, 44010, 44820, 44850, 47460, 47550-47556, 48100-48120, 48545)

● New Code   ▲ Revised Code   + Add-On Code   ⊘ Modifier -51 Exempt   ★ Telemedicine

| 48554 | Transplantation of pancreatic allograft |
| 48556 | Removal of transplanted pancreatic allograft |

OTHER PROCEDURES

| 48999 | Unlisted procedure, pancreas |

ABDOMEN, PERITONEUM, AND OMENTUM

INCISION

49000 Exploratory laparotomy, exploratory celiotomy with or without biopsy(s) (separate procedure)

(To report wound exploration due to penetrating trauma without laparatomy, use 20102)

49002 Reopening of recent laparotomy

(To report re-exploration of hepatic wound for removal of packing, use 47362)

49010 Exploration, retroperitoneal area with or without biopsy(s) (separate procedure)

(To report wound exploration due to penetrating trauma without laparotomy, use 20102)

49020 Drainage of peritoneal abscess or localized peritonitis, exclusive of appendiceal abscess; open

(For appendiceal abscess, use 44900)

(For percutaneous image-guided drainage of peritoneal abscess or localized peritonitis by catheter, use 49406)

(For transrectal or transvaginal image-guided drainage of peritoneal abscess by catheter, use 49407)

49040 Drainage of subdiaphragmatic or subphrenic abscess; open

(For percutaneous image-guided drainage of subdiaphragmatic or subphrenic abscess by catheter, use 49406)

49060 Drainage of retroperitoneal abscess; open

(For percutaneous image-guided drainage of retroperitoneal abscess by catheter, use 49406)

(For transrectal or transvaginal image-guided drainage of retroperitoneal abscess by catheter, use 49407)

49062 Drainage of extraperitoneal lymphocele to peritoneal cavity, open

(For laparoscopic drainage of lymphocele to peritoneal cavity, use 49323)

(for percutaneous image-guided drainage of peritoneal or retroperitoneal lymphocele by catheter, use 49406)

49082 Abdominal paracentesis (diagnostic or therapeutic); without imaging guidance

49083 with imaging guidance

(Do not report 49083 in conjunction with 76942, 77002, 77012, 77021)

(For percutaneous image-guided drainage of retroperitoneal abscess by catheter, use 49406)

49084 Peritoneal lavage, including imaging guidance, when performed

(Do not report 49084 in conjunction with 76942, 77002, 77012, 77021)

(For percutaneous image-guided drainage of retroperitoneal abscess by cathete, use 49406)

■ Separate Procedure   ■ Unlisted Procedure   ■ CCI Comp. Code   ■ Non-specific Procedure   **489**

EXCISION, DESTRUCTION

Code 49185 describes sclerotherapy of a fluid collection (eg, lymphocele, cyst, or seroma) through a percutaneous access. It includes contrast injection(s), sclerosant injection(s), sclerosant dwell time, diagnostic study, imaging guidance (eg, ultrasound, fluoroscopy), and radiological supervision and interpretation, when performed. Code 49185 may be reported once per day for each lesion treated through a separate catheter. Do not report 49185 more than once if treating multiple lesions through the same catheter. Codes for access to and drainage of the collection may be separately reportable according to location (eg, 10030, 10160, 49405, 49406, 49407, 50390).

(For lysis of intestinal adhesions, use 44005)

49180 Biopsy, abdominal or retroperitoneal mass, percutaneous needle

(If imaging guidance is performed, see 76942, 77002, 77012, 77021)

(For fine needle aspiration, use 10021 or 10022)

(For evaluation of fine needle aspirate, see 88172, 88173)

49185 Sclerotherapy of a fluid collection (eg, lymphocele, cyst, or seroma), percutaneous, including contrast injection(s), sclerosant injection(s), diagnostic study, imaging guidance (eg, ultrasound, fluoroscopy) and radiological supervision and interpretation when performed

(For treatment of multiple lesions in a single day requiring separate access, use modifier 59 for each additional treated lesion)

(For treatment of multiple interconnected lesions treated through a single access, report 49185 once)

(For access/drainage with needle, see 10160, 50390)

(For access/drainage with catheter, see 10030, 49405, 49406, 49407, 50390)

(For exchange of existing catheter, before or after injection of sclerosant, see 49423, 75984)

(For sclerotherapy of a lymphatic/vascular malformation, use 37241)

(For sclerosis of veins or endovenous ablation of incompetent extremity veins, see 36468, 36470, 36471, 36475, 36476, 36478, 36479)

(For pleurodesis, use 32560)

(Do not report 49185 in conjunction with 49424, 76080)

49203 Excision or destruction, open, intra-abdominal tumors, cysts or endometriomas, 1 or more peritoneal, mesenteric, or retroperitoneal primary or secondary tumors; largest tumor 5 cm diameter or less

49204 largest tumor 5.1-10.0 cm diameter

49205 largest tumor greater than 10.0 cm diameter

(Do not report 49203-49205 in conjunction with 38770, 38780, 49000, 49010, 49215, 50010, 50205, 50225, 50236, 50250, 50290, 58920, 58925, 58940, 58943, 58951, 58952, 58953, 58954, 58956, 58957, 58958, 58960)

(For partial or total nephrectomy, use 50220 or 50240 in conjunction with 49203-49205)

(For colectomy, use 44140 in conjunction with 49203-49205)

(For small bowel resection, use 44120 in conjunction with 49203-49205)

(For vena caval resection with reconstruction, use 49203-49205 in conjunction with 37799)

(For resection of recurrent ovarian, tubal, primary peritoneal, or uterine malignancy, see 58957, 58958)

(For cryoablation of renal tumors, see 50250, 50593)

49215 Excision of presacral or sacrococcygeal tumor

● New Code   ▲ Revised Code   + Add-On Code   ⊘ Modifier -51 Exempt   ★ Telemedicine

(Do not report modifier 63 in conjunction with 49215)

49220 Staging laparotomy for Hodgkins disease or lymphoma (includes splenectomy, needle or open biopsies of both liver lobes, possibly also removal of abdominal nodes, abdominal node and/or bone marrow biopsies, ovarian repositioning)

49250 Umbilectomy, omphalectomy, excision of umbilicus (separate procedure)

49255 Omentectomy, epiploectomy, resection of omentum (separate procedure)

LAPAROSCOPY

Surgical laparoscopy always includes diagnostic laparoscopy. To report a diagnostic laparoscopy (peritneoscopy) (separate procedure), use 49320.

For laparoscopic fulguration or excision of lesions of the ovary, pelvic viscera, or peritoneal surface, use 58662.

49320 Laparoscopy, abdomen, peritoneum, and omentum; diagnostic, with or without collection of specimen(s) by brushing or washing (separate procedure)

49321 Laparoscopy, surgical; with biopsy (single or multiple)

49322   with aspiration of cavity or cyst (eg, ovarian cyst) (single or multiple)

49323   with drainage of lymphocele to peritoneal cavity

(For open drainage of lymphocele to peritoneal cavity, use 49062)

49324   with insertion of tunneled intraperitoneal catheter

(For subcutaneous extension of intraperitoneal catheter with remote chest exit site, use 49435 in conjunction with 49324)

(For open insertion of tunneled intraperitoneal catheter, use 49421)

49325   with revision of previously placed intraperitoneal cannula or catheter, with removal of intraluminal obstructive material if performed

+ 49326   with omentopexy (omental tacking procedure) (List separately in addition to code for primary procedure)

(Use 49326 in conjunction with 49324, 49325)

+ 49327   with placement of interstitial device(s) for radiation therapy guidance (eg, fiducial markers, dosimeter), intra-abdominal, intrapelvic, and/or retroperitoneum, including imaging guidance, if performed, single or multiple (List separately in addition to code for primary procedure)

(Use 49327 in conjunction with laparoscopic abdominal, pelvic, or retroperitoneal procedure[s] performed concurrently)

(For placement of interstitial device[s] for intra-abdominal, intrapelvic, and/or retroperitoneal radiation therapy guidance concurrent with open procedure, use 49412)

(For percutaneous placement of interstitial device[s] for intra-abdominal, intrapelvic, and/or retroperitoneal radiation therapy guidance, use 49411)

49329 Unlisted laparoscopy procedure, abdomen, peritoneum and omentum

INTRODUCTION, REVISION, REMOVAL

49400 Injection of air or contrast into peritoneal cavity (separate procedure)

(For radiological supervision and interpretation, use 74190)

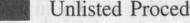

49402 Removal of peritoneal foreign body from peritoneal cavity

(For lysis of intestinal adhesions, use 44005)

(For open or percutaneous peritoneal drainage or lavage, see 49406, 49020, 49040, 49082-49084, as appropriate)

(For percutaneous insertion of a tunneled intraperitoneal catheter without subcutaneous port, use 49418)

49405 Image-guided fluid collection drainage by catheter (eg, abscess, hematoma, seroma, lymphocele, cyst); visceral (eg, kidney, liver, spleen, lung/mediastinum), percutaneous

(Do not report 49405 in conjunction with 75989, 76942, 77002, 77003, 77012, 77021)

(For percutaneous cholecystostomy, use 47490)

(For pneumonostomy, use 32200)

(For thoracentesis, see 32554, 32555)

(For pleural drainage, see 32556, 32557)

(For percutaneous pleural drainage, see 32556, 32557)

(For open visceral drainage, see 32200 [lung abscess or cyst], 47010 [liver abscess or cyst], 48510 [pseudocyst of pancreas], 50020 [perirenal or renal abscess])

49406 peritoneal or retroperitoneal, percutaneous

(Do not report 49406 in conjunction with 75989, 76942, 77002, 77003, 77012, 77021)

(For abdominal paracentesis [diagnostic or therapeutic], see 49082, 49083)

(For transrectal or transveginal image-guided peritoneal or retroperitoneal fluid collection drainage by catheter, use 49407)

(For open transrectal drainage of pelvic abscess, use 45000)

(For open peritoneal or retroperitoneal drainage, see 44900 [appendiceal abscess], 49020 [subdiaphragmatic or subphrenic abscess], 49060 [retroperitoneal abscess], 49062 [extraperitoneal lymphocele], 49084 [peritoneal lavage], 50020 [perirenal or renal abscess], 58805 [ovarian cyst], 58822 [ovarian abscess])

(For percutaneous paracentesis, see 49082, 49083)

(For percutaneous insertion of a tunneled intraperitoneal catheter without subcutaneous port, use 49418)

49407 peritoneal or retroperitoneal, transvaginal or transrectal

(Do not report 49407 in conjunction with 75989, 76942, 77002, 77003, 77012, 77021)

(Report 49405, 49406, 49407 separately for each individual collection drained with a separate catheter)

(For open transrectal or transvaginal drainage, see 45000 [pelvic abscess], 58800 [ovarian cyst], 58820 [ovarian abscess])

(For percutaneous image-guided fluid collection drainage by catheter [eg, abscess, hematoma, seroma, lymphocele, cyst] for soft tissue [eg, extremity, abdominal wall, neck], use 10030)

49411 Placement of interstitial device(s) for radiation therapy guidance (eg, fiducial markers, dosimeter), percutaneous, intra abdominal, intra-pelvic (except prostate), and/or retroperitoneum, single or multiple

(Report supply of device separately)

(For imaging guidance, see 76942, 77002, 77012, 77021)

(For percutaneous placement of interstitial device[s] for intra-thoracic radiation therapy guidance, use 32553)

● New Code   ▲ Revised Code   ＋ Add-On Code   ⊘ Modifier -51 Exempt   ★ Telemedicine

+ 49412 Placement of interstitial device(s) for radiation therapy guidance (eg, fiducial markers, dosimeter), open, intra-abdominal, intrapelvic and/or retroperitoneum, including imaging guidance, if performed, single or multiple (List separately in addition to code for primary procedure)

(Use 49412 in conjunction with open abdominal, pelvic, or retroperitoneal procedure[s] performed concurrently)

(For placement of interstitial device[s] for intra-abdominal, intrapelvic, and/or retroperitoneal radiation therapy guidance concurrent with laparoscopic procedure, use 49327)

(For percutaneous placement of interstitial device[s] for intra-abdominal, intrapelvic, and/or retroperitoneal radiation therapy guidance, use 49411)

49418 Insertion of tunneled intraperitoneal catheter (eg, dialysis, intraperitoneal chemotherapy instillation, management of ascites), complete procedure, including imaging guidance, catheter placement, contrast injection when performed, and radiological supervision and interpretation, percutaneous

49419 Insertion of tunneled intraperitoneal catheter, with subcutaneous port (ie, totally implantable)

(For removal, use 49422)

(49420 deleted 2010 [2011 edition]. To report open placement of a tunneled intraperitoneal catheter for dialysis, use 49421. To report open or percutaneous peritoneal drainage or lavage, see 49406, 49020, 49040, 49082-49084, as appropriate. To report percutaneous insertion of a tunneled intraperitoneal catheter without subcutaneous port, use 49418.)

49421 Insertion of tunneled intraperitoneal catheter for dialysis, open

(For laparoscopic insertion of tunneled intraperitoneal catheter, use 49324)

(For subcutaneous extension of intraperitoneal catheter with remote chest exit site, use 49435 in conjunction with 49421)

49422 Removal of tunneled intraperitoneal catheter

(For removal of a non-tunneled catheter, use appropriate E/M code)

49423 Exchange of previously placed abscess or cyst drainage catheter under radiological guidance (separate procedure)

(For radiological supervision and interpretation, use 75984)

49424 Contrast injection for assessment of abscess or cyst via previously placed drainage catheter or tube (separate procedure)

(For radiological supervision and interpretation, use 76080)

49425 Insertion of peritoneal-venous shunt

49426 Revision of peritoneal-venous shunt

(For shunt patency test, use 78291)

49427 Injection procedure (eg, contrast media) for evaluation of previously placed peritoneal-venous shunt

(For radiological supervision and interpretation, see 75809, 78291)

49428 Ligation of peritoneal-venous shunt

49429 Removal of peritoneal-venous shunt

+ 49435 Insertion of subcutaneous extension to intraperitoneal cannula or catheter with remote chest exit site (List separately in addition to code for primary procedure)

(Use 49435 in conjunction with 49324, 49421)

Separate Procedure   Unlisted Procedure   CCI Comp. Code   Non-specific Procedure   **493**

49436 Delayed creation of exit site from embedded subcutaneous segment of intraperitoneal cannula or catheter

Initial Placement

Do not additionally report 43752 for placement of a nasogastric (NG) or orogastric (OG) tube to insufflate the stomach prior to percutaneous gastrointestinal tube placement. NG or OG tube placement is considered part of the procedure in this family of codes.

49440 Insertion of gastrostomy tube, percutaneous, under fluoroscopic guidance including contrast injection(s), image documentation and report

(For conversion to a gastro-jejunostomy tube at the time of initial gastrostomy tube placement, use 49440 in conjunction with 49446)

49441 Insertion of duodenostomy or jejunostomy tube, percutaneous, under fluoroscopic guidance including contrast injection(s), image documentation and report

(For conversion of gastrostomy tube to gastro-jejunostomry tube, use 49446)

49442 Insertion of cecostomy or other colonic, tube, percutaneous, under fluoroscopic guidance including contrast injection(s), image documentation and report

Conversion

49446 Conversion of gastrostomy tube to gastro-jejunostomy tube, percutaneous, under fluoroscopic guidance including contrast injection(s), image documentation and report

(For conversion to a gastro-jejunostomy tube at the time of initial gastrostomy tube placement, use 49446 in conjunction with 49440)

Replacement

If an existing gastrostomy, duodenostomy, jejunostomy, gastro-jejunostomy, or cecostomy (or other colonic) tube is removed and a new tube is placed via a separate percutaneous access site, the placement of the new tube is not considered a replacement and would be reported using the appropriate initial placement codes 49440-49442.

49450 Replacement of gastrostomy or cecostomy (or other colonic) tube, percutaneous, under fluoroscopic guidance including contrast injection(s), image documentation and report

(To report a percutaneous change of a gastrostomy tube without imaging or endoscopic guidance, use 43760)

49451 Replacement of duodenostomy or jejunostormy tube, percutaneous, under fluoroscopic guidance including contrast injection(s), image documentation and report

49452 Replacement of gastro-jejunostomy tube, percutaneous, under fluoroscopic guidance including contrast injection(s), image documentation and report

Mechanical Removal Of Obstructive Material

49460 Mechanical removal of obstructive material from gastrostomy, duodenostomy, jejunostomy, gastro-jejunostomy, or cecostomy (or other colonic) tube, any method, under fluoroscopic guidance including contrast injection(s), if performed, image documentation and report

(Do not report 49460 in conjunction with 49450-49452, 49465)

Other

49465 Contrast injection(s) for radiological evaluation of existing gastrostomy, duodenostomy, jejunostomy, gastro-jejunostomy, or cecostomy (or other colonic) tube, from a percutaneous approach including image documentation and report

(Do not report 49465 in conjunction with 49450-49460)

● New Code ▲ Revised Code ＋ Add-On Code ⊘ Modifier -51 Exempt ★ Telemedicine

REPAIR

Hernioplasty, Herniorrhaphy, Herniotomy

The hernia repair codes in this section are categorized primarily by the type of hernia (inguinal, femoral, incisional, etc.).

Some types of herias are further categorized as initial or recurrent based on whether or not the hernia has required previous repairs.

Additional variables accounted for by some of the codes include patient age and clinical presentation (reducible vs. incarcerated or strangulated).

With the exception of the incisional hernia repairs (see 49560-49566) the use of mesh or other prostheses is not separately reported.

The excision/repair of strangulated organs or structures such as testicle(s), intestine, ovaries are reported by using the appropriate code for the excision/repair (eg., 44120, 54520, and 58940) in addition to the appropriate code for the repair of the strangulated hernia.

(For reduction and repair of intra-abdominal hernia, use 44050)

(For debridement of abdominal wall, see 11042, 11043)

(Codes 49491-49651 are unilateral procedures. To report bilateral procedures, report modifier -50 with the appropriate procedure code)

49491 Repair, initial inguinal hernia, preterm infant (less than 37 weeks gestation at birth), performed from birth up to 50 weeks postconception age, with or without hydrocelectomy; reducible

49492 incarcerated or strangulated

(Do not report modifier -63 in conjunction with 49491, 49492)

(Post-conception age equals gestational age at birth plus age of infant in weeks at the time of the hernia repair. Initial inguinal hernia repairs that are performed on preterm infants who are over 50 weeks postconceptual age and under age 6 months at the time of surgery, should be reported using codes 49495, 49496)

49495 Repair, initial inguinal hernia, full term infant under age 6 months, or preterm infant over 50 weeks postconception age and under age 6 months at the time of surgery, with or without hydrocelectomy; reducible

49496 incarcerated or strangulated

(Do not report modifier -63 in conjunction with 49491, 49492)

(Post-conception age equals gestational age at birth plus age in weeks at the time of the hernia repair. Initial inguinal hernia repairs that are performed on preterm infants who are under or up to 50 weeks postconceptual age but under 6 months of age since birth, should be reported using codes 49491, 49492. Inguinal hernia repairs on infants age 6 months to under 5 years should be reported using codes 49500-49501)

49500 Repair initial inguinal hernia, age 6 months to under 5 years, with or without hydrocelectomy; reducible

49501 incarcerated or strangulated

49505 Repair initial inguinal hernia, age 5 years or over; reducible

49507 incarcerated or strangulated

(For inguinal hernia repair, with simple orchiectomy, see 49505 or 49507 and 54520)

(For inguinal hernia repair, with excision of hydrocele or spermatocele, see 49505 or 49507 and 54840 or 55040)

49520 Repair recurrent inguinal hernia, any age; reducible

49521   incarcerated or strangulated

49525 Repair inguinal hernia, sliding, any age

    (For incarcerated or strangulated inguinal hernia repair, see 49496, 49501, 49507, 49521)

49540 Repair lumbar hernia

49550 Repair initial femoral hernia, any age; reducible

49553   incarcerated or strangulated

49555 Repair recurrent femoral hernia; reducible

49557   incarcerated or strangulated

49560 Repair initial incisional or ventral hernia; reducible

49561   incarcerated or strangulated

49565 Repair recurrent incisional or ventral hernia; reducible

49566   incarcerated or strangulated

+ 49568 Implantation of mesh or other prosthesis for open incisional or ventral hernia repair or mesh for closure of debridement for necrotizing soft tissue infection (List separately in addition to code for the incisional or ventral hernia repair)

    (Use 49568 in conjunction with 11004-11006, 49560-49566)

49570 Repair epigastric hernia (eg, preperitoneal fat); reducible (separate procedure)

49572   incarcerated or strangulated

49580 Repair umbilical hernia, under age 5 years; reducible

49582   incarcerated or strangulated

49585 Repair umbilical hernia, age 5 years or over; reducible

49587   incarcerated or strangulated

49590 Repair spigelian hernia

49600 Repair of small omphalocele, with primary closure

    (Do not report modifier -63 in conjunction with 49600)

49605 Repair of large omphalocele or gastroschisis; with or without prosthesis

49606   with removal of prosthesis, final reduction and closure, in operating room

    (Do not report modifier -63 in conjunction with 49605, 49606)

49610 Repair of omphalocele (Gross type operation); first stage

49611   second stage

    (Do not report modifier -63 in conjunction with 49610, 49611)

  ● New Code   ▲ Revised Code   + Add-On Code   ⊘ Modifier -51 Exempt   ★ Telemedicine

(For diaphragmatic or hiatal hernia repair, see 39503, 43332)

(For surgical repair of omentum, use 49999)

LAPAROSCOPY

Surgical laparoscopy always includes diagnostic laparoscopy. To report a diagnostic laparoscopy (peritoneoscopy) (separate procedure), use 49320.

49650 Laparoscopy, surgical; repair initial inguinal hernia

49651 repair recurrent inguinal hernia

49652 Laparoscopy, surgical, repair, ventral, umbilical, spigelian or epigastric hernia (includes mesh insertion, when performed); reducible

(Do not report 49652 in conjunction with 44180, 49568)

49653 incarcerated or strangulated

(Do not report 49653 in conjunction with 44180, 49568)

49654 Laparoscopy, surgical, repair, incisional hernia (includes mesh insertion, when performed); reducible

(Do not report 49654 in conjunction with 44180, 49568)

49655 incarcerated or strangulated

(Do not report 49655 in conjunction with 44180, 49568)

49656 Laparoscopy, surgical, repair, recurrent incisional hernia (includes mesh insertion, when performed); reducible

(Do not report 49656 in conjunction with 44180, 49568)

49657 incarcerated or strangulated

(Do not report 49657 in conjunction with 44180, 49568)

49659 Unlisted laparoscopy procedure, hernioplasty, herniorrhaphy, herniotomy

SUTURE

49900 Suture, secondary, of abdominal wall for evisceration or dehiscence

(For suture of ruptured diaphragm, see 39540, 39541)

(For debridement of abdominal wall, see 11042, 11043)

OTHER PROCEDURES

49904 Omental flap, extra-abdominal (eg, for reconstruction of sternal and chest wall defects)

(Code 49904 includes harvest and transfer. If a second surgeon harvests the omental flap, then the two surgeons should code 49904 as co-surgeons, using modifier -62)

+ **49905** Omental flap, intra-abdominal (List separately in addition to code for primary procedure)

(Do not report 49905 in conjunction with 44700)

49906 Free omental flap with microvascular anastomosis

(Do not report code 69990 in addition to code 49906)

49999 Unlisted procedure, abdomen, peritoneum and omentum

| Separate Procedure | Unlisted Procedure | CCI Comp. Code | Non-specific Procedure | **497** |

This page intentionally left blank.

● New Code   ▲ Revised Code   + Add-On Code   ⊘ Modifier -51 Exempt   ★ Telemedicine

URINARY SYSTEM

CPT codes from this section are used to report invasive and surgical procedures performed on the kidney; ureter; bladder; prostate (resection); and urethra.

URODYNAMICS

CPT codes in this section may be used separately or in various combinations.When multiple procedures are performed in the same session, modifier -51 should be added .to the second and all subsequent CPT codes. Procedures in this section are performed by, or under the direct supervision of, a physician.

In addition, all materials and supplies, used in the provision of these services, such as instruments, equipment, fluids, gases, probes, catheters, technician's fees, medications, gloves, trays, tubing and other sterile supplies are considered to be included in the base code. Use modifier -26 to code and report interpretation of results or operation of equipment only.

CYSTOSCOPY, URETHROSCOPY, and CYSTOURETHROSCOPY

The descriptions of CPT codes in this section are listed so that the main procedure can be identified without having to list all of the minor related procedures performed at the same time. For example:

52601 Transurethral electrosurgical resection of prostate, including control of postoperative bleeding, complete (vasectomy, meatotomy, cystourethroscopy, urethral calibration and/or dilation, and internal urethrotomy are included)

All of the secondary procedures are included in the single code 52601. If any of the secondary procedures requires significant additional time and effort, to the point of making the procedure "unusual", modifier -22 should be added with an appropriate increase in fee and a report explaining what made the procedure unusual.

(For provision of chemotherapeutic agents, report both the specific service in addition to code(s) for the specific substance(s) or drug(s) provided)

KIDNEY

INCISION

(For retroperitoneal exploration, abscess, tumor, or cyst, see 49010, 49060, 49203-49205)

50010 Renal exploration, not necessitating other specific procedures

(For laparoscopic ablation of renal mass lesion(s), use 50542)

50020 Drainage of perirenal or renal abscess; open

(For percutaneous image-guided fluid collection drainage by catheter of perirenal/renal abscess, use 49405)

50040 Nephrostomy, nephrotomy with drainage

50045 Nephrotomy, with exploration

(For renal endoscopy performed in conjunction with this procedure, see 50570-50580)

50060 Nephrolithotomy; removal of calculus

50065 secondary surgical operation for calculus

50070 complicated by congenital kidney abnormality

50075 removal of large staghorn calculus filling renal pelvis and calyces (including anatrophic pyelolithotomy)

50080 Percutaneous nephrostolithotomy or pyelostolithotomy, with or without dilation, endoscopy, lithotripsy, stenting, or basket extraction; up to 2 cm

---

Separate Procedure Unlisted Procedure CCI Comp. Code Non-specific Procedure **499**

50081 over 2cm

(For establishment of nephrostomy without nephrostolithotomy, see 50040, 50395, 52334)

(For fluoroscopic guidance, see 76000, 76001)

50100 Transection or repositioning of aberrant renal vessels (separate procedure)

50120 Pyelotomy; with exploration

(For renal endoscopy performed in conjunction with this procedure, see 50570-50580)

50125 with drainage, pyelostomy

50130 with removal of calculus (pyelolithotomy, pelviolithotomy, including coagulum pyelolithotomy)

50135 complicated (eg, secondary operation, congenital kidney abnormality)

(For supply of anticarcinogenic agents, use 99070 in addition to code for primary procedure)

EXCISION

(For excision of retroperitoneal tumor or cyst, see 49203-49205)

(For laparoscopic ablation of renal mass lesion(s), use 50542)

50200 Renal biopsy; percutaneous, by trocar or needle

(For radiological supervision and interpretation, see 76942, 77002, 77012, 77021)

(For fine needle aspiration, use 10022)

(For evaluation of fine needle aspirate, see 88172, 88173)

50205 by surgical exposure of kidney

50220 Nephrectomy, including partial ureterectomy, any open approach including rib resection;

50225 complicated because of previous surgery on same kidney

50230 radical, with regional lymphadenectomy and/or vena caval thrombectomy

(When vena caval resection with reconstruction is necessary, use 37799)

50234 Nephrectomy with total ureterectomy and bladder cuff; through same incision

50236 through separate incision

50240 Nephrectomy, partial

(For laparoscopic partial nephrectomy, use 50543)

50250 Ablation, open, 1 or more renal mass lesion(s), cryosurgical, including intraoperative ultrasound guidance and monitoring, if performed

(For laparoscopic ablation of renal mass lesions, use 50542)

(For percutaneous ablation of renal tumors, see 50592, 50593)

50280 Excision or unroofing of cyst(s) of kidney

(For laparoscopic ablation of renal cysts, use 50541)

50290 Excision of perinephric cyst

● New Code ▲ Revised Code + Add-On Code ⊘ Modifier -51 Exempt ★ Telemedicine

RENAL TRANSPLANTATION

Renal *auto*transplantation includes reimplantation of the autograft as the primary procedure, along with secondary extra-corporeal procedure(s) (eg., partial nephrectomy, nephrolithotomy) reported with modifier 51 (see 50380 and applicable secondary procedure[s]).

Renal *allo*transplantation involves three distinct components of physician work:

1. **Cadaver donor nephrectomy, unilateral or bilateral**, which includes harvesting the graft(s) and cols preservation of the graft(s) (perfusing with cold preservation solution and cold maintenance) (use 50300). **Living donor nephrectomy**, which includes harvesting the graft, cold preservation of the graft (perfusing with cold preservation solution and cold maintenance), and care of the donor (see 50320, 50547).

2. **Backbench work**:

Standard preparation of a cadaver donor renal allograft prior to transplantation including dissection and removal of perinephric fat, diaphragmatic and retroperitoneal attachments; excision of adrenal gland; and preparation of ureter(s), renal vein(s), and renal artery(s), ligating branches as necessary (use 50325).

Standard preparation of a living donor renal allograft (open or laparoscopic) prior to transplantation including dissection and removal of perinephric fat and preparation of ureter(s), renal vein(s), and renal artery(s), ligating branches as necessary (use 50325).

Additional reconstruction of a cadaver or living donor renal allograft prior to transplantation may include venous, arterial, and/or ureteral anastomosis(es) necessary for implantation (see 50327-50329)

3. **Recipient renal allotransplantation,** which includes transplantation of the allograft (with or without recipient nephrectomy) and care of the recipient (see 50360, 50365).

> (For dialysis, see 90935-90999)
>
> (For laparoscopic donor nephrectomy, use 50547)
>
> (For laparoscopic drainage of lymphocele to peritoneal cavity, use 49323)

50300 Donor nephrectomy (including cold preservation); from cadaver donor, unilateral or bilateral

50320 open, from living donor

50323 Backbench standard preparation of cadaver donor renal allograft prior to transplantation, including dissection and removal of perinephric fat, diaphragmatic and retroperitoneal attachments, excision of adrenal gland, and preparation of ureter(s), renal vein(s), and renal artery(s), ligating branches, as necessary

> (Do not report 50323 in conjunction with 60540, 60545)

50325 Backbench standard preparation of living donor renal allograft (open or laparoscopic) prior to transplantation, including dissection and removal of perinephric fat and preparation of ureter(s), renal vein(s), and renal artery(s), ligating branches, as necessary

50327 Backbench reconstruction of cadaver or living donor renal allograft prior to transplantation; venous anastomosis, each

50328 arterial anastomosis, each

50329 ureteral anastomosis, each

50340 Recipient nephrectomy (separate procedure)

> (For bilateral procedure, report 50340 with modifier -50)

50360 Renal allotransplantation, implantation of graft; without recipient nephrectomy

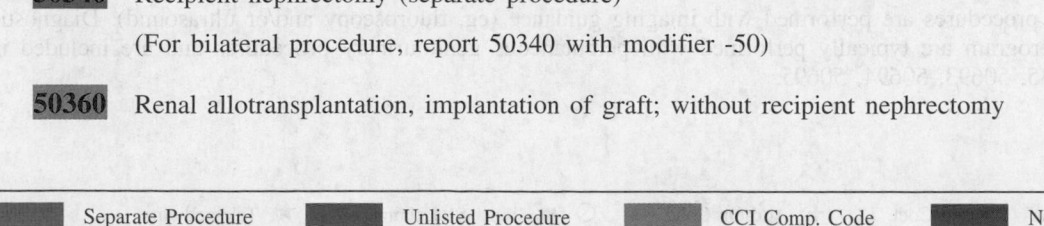

| | Separate Procedure | | Unlisted Procedure | | CCI Comp. Code | | Non-specific Procedure | **501** |

50365   with recipient nephrectomy

(For bilateral procedure, report 50365 with modifier -50)

50370   Removal of transplanted renal allograft

50380   Renal autotransplantation, reimplantation of kidney

(For renal autotransplantation extra-corporeal (bench) surgery, use autotransplantation as the primary procedure and report secondary procedure(s) (eg, partial nephrectomy, nephrolithotomy) with modifier -51)

INTRODUCTION

Renal Pelvis Catheter Procedures

Internally Dwelling

50382   Removal (via snare/capture) and replacement of internally dwelling ureteral stent via percutaneous approach, including radiological supervision and interpretation

(For bilateral procedure, use modifier -50)

(For removal and replacement of an internally dwelling ureteral stent via a transurethral approach, use 50385)

50384   Removal (via snare/capture) of internally dwelling ureteral stent via percutaneous approach, including radiological supervision and interpretation

(For bilateral procedure, use modifier 50)

(Do not report 50382, 50384 in conjunction with 50395)

(For removal of an internally dwelling ureteral stent via a transurethral approach, use 50386)

50385   Removal (via snare/capture) and replacement of internally dwelling ureteral stent via transurethral approach, without use of cystoscopy, including radiological supervision and interpretation

50386   Removal (via snare/capture) of internally dwelling ureteral stent via transurethral approach, without use of cystoscopy, including radiological supervision and interpretation

Externally Accessible

50387   Removal and replacement of externally accessible nephroureteral catheter (eg, external/internal stent) requiring fluoroscopic guidance, including radiological supervision and interpretation

(For bilateral procedure, use modifier 50)

(For removal and replacement of externally accessible ureteral stent via ureterostomy or ileal conduit, use 50688)

(For removal without replacement of an externally accessible ureteral stent not requiring fluoroscopic guidance, see Evaluation and Management services codes)

50389   Removal of nephrostomy tube, requiring fluoroscopic guidance (eg, with concurrent indwelling ureteral stent)

(Removal of nephrostomy tube not requiring fluoroscopic guidance is considered inherent to E/M services. Report the appropriate level of E/M service provided)

Other Introduction (Injection/Change/Removal) Procedures

Percutaneous genitourinary procedures are performed with imaging guidance (eg, fluoroscopy and/or ultrasound). Diagnostic nephrostogram and/or ureterogram are typically performed with percutaneous genitourinary procedures and are included in 50432, 50433, 50434, 50435, 50693, 50694, 50695.

Codes 50430 and 50431 are diagnostic procedure codes that include injection(s) of contrast material, all associated radiological supervision and interpretation, and procedural imaging guidance (eg, ultrasound and/or fluoroscopy). Code 50430 also includes accessing the collecting system and/or associated ureter with a needle and/or catheter. Code 50430 or 50431 may not be reported together with 50432, 50433, 50434, 50435, 50693, 50694, 50695.

Codes 50432, 50433, 50434, 50435 represent therapeutic procedures describing catheter placement or exchange, and include the elements of access, drainage catheter manipulations, and imaging guidance (eg, ultrasonography and/or fluoroscopy), as well as diagnostic imaging supervision and interpretation, when performed.

Code 50433 describes percutaneous nephrostomy with the additional accessing of the ureter/bladder to ultimately place a nephroureteral catheter (a single transnephric catheter with nephrostomy and ureteral components that allows drainage internally, externally, or both).

For codes 50430, 50431, 50432, 50433, 50434, 50435, 50606, 50693, 50694, 50695, 50705, and 50706, the renal pelvis and its associated ureter are considered a single entity for reporting purposes. Codes 50430, 50431, 50432, 50433, 50434, 50435, 50606, 50693, 50694, 50695, 50705, and 50706 may be reported once for each renal collecting system/ureter accessed (eg, two separate codes would be reported for bilateral nephrostomy tube placement or for unilateral duplicated collecting system/ureter requiring two separate procedures.

50390 Aspiration and/or injection of renal cyst or pelvis by needle, percutaneous

(For radiological supervision and interpretation, see 74425, 74470, 76942, 77002, 77012, 77021)

(For antegrade nephrostogram and/or antegrade pyelogram, see 50430, 50431)

50391 Instillation(s) of therapeutic agent into renal pelvis and/or ureter through established nephrostomy, pyelostomy or ureterostomy tube (eg, anticarcinogenic or antifungal agent)

(**50392** deleted 2015 [2016 edition]. To report nephrostomy tube placement, use 50432)

(**50393** deleted 2015 [2016 edition]. To report ureteral catheter placement, see 50693, 50694, 50695)

(**50394** deleted 2015 [2016 edition]. To report injection procedures for antegrade nephrostogram and/or antegrade pyelogram, see 50430, 50431)

50395 Introduction of guide into renal pelvis and/or ureter with dilation to establish nephrostomy tract, percutaneous

(For radiological supervision and interpretation, use 74485)

(For nephrostolithotomy, see 50080, 50081)

(For retrograde percutaneous nephrostomy, use 52334)

(For endoscopic surgery, see 50551-50561)

50396 Manometric studies through nephrostomy or pyelostomy tube, or indwelling ureteral catheter

(For radiological supervision and interpretation, use 74425)

(**50398** deleted 2015 [2016 edition]. To report exchange of a percutaneous nephrostomy catheter, use 50435)

50430 Injection procedure for antegrade nephrostogram and/or ureterogram, complete diagnostic procedure including imaging guidance (eg, ultrasound and fluoroscopy) and all associated radiological supervision and interpretation; new access

50431 existing access

(Do not report 50430, 50431 in conjunction with 50432, 50433, 50434, 50435, 50693, 50694, 50695, 74425 for the same renal collecting system and/or associated ureter)

50432 Placement of nephrostomy catheter, percutaneous, including diagnostic nephrostogram and/or ureterogram when performed, imaging guidance (eg, ultrasound and/or fluoroscopy) and all associated radiological supervision and interpretation

---

Separate Procedure   Unlisted Procedure   CCI Comp. Code   Non-specific Procedure   **503**

(Do not report 50432 in conjunction with 50430, 50431, 50433, 50694, 50695, 74425 for the same renal collecting system and/or associated ureter)

(Do not report 50432 in conjunction with 50395 for dilation of the nephrostomy tube tract)

50433 Placement of nephroureteral catheter, percutaneous, including diagnostic nephrostogram and/or ureterogram when performed, imaging guidance (eg, ultrasound and/or fluoroscopy) and all associated radiological supervision and interpretation, new access

(Do not report 50433 in conjunction with 50430, 50431, 50432, 50693, 50694, 50695, 74425 for the same renal collecting system and/or associated ureter)

(Do not report 50433 in conjunction with 50395 for dilation of the nephroureteral catheter tract)

(For nephroureteral catheter removal and replacement, use 50387)

50434 Convert nephrostomy catheter to nephroureteral catheter, percutaneous, including diagnostic nephrostogram and/or ureterogram when performed, imaging guidance (eg, ultrasound and/or fluoroscopy) and all associated radiological supervision and interpretation, via preexisting nephrostomy tract

(Do not report 50434 in conjunction with 50430, 50431, 50435, 50684, 50693, 74425 for the same renal collecting system and/or associated ureter)

50435 Exchange nephrostomy catheter, percutaneous, including diagnostic nephrostogram and/or ureterogram when performed, imaging guidance (eg, ultrasound and/or fluoroscopy) and all associated radiological supervision and interpretation

(Do not report 50435 in conjunction with 50430, 50431, 50434, 50693, 74425 for the same renal collecting system and/or associated ureter)

(For removal of nephrostomy catheter requiring fluoroscopic guidance, use 50389)

REPAIR

50400 Pyeloplasty (Foley Y-pyeloplasty), plastic operation on renal pelvis, with or without plastic operation on ureter, nephropexy, nephrostomy, pyelostomy, or ureteral splinting; simple

50405 complicated (congenital kidney abnormality, secondary pyeloplasty, solitary kidney, calycoplasty)

(For laparoscopic approach, use 50544)

50430 This code is out of order. See page 503.

50431 This code is out of order. See page 503.

50432 This code is out of order. See page 503.

50433 This code is out of order. See page 504.

50434 This code is out of order. See page 504.

50435 This code is out of order. See page 504.

50500 Nephrorrhaphy, suture of kidney wound or injury

50520 Closure of nephrocutaneous or pyelocutaneous fistula

50525 Closure of nephrovisceral fistula (eg, renocolic), including visceral repair; abdominal approach

50526 thoracic approach

50540 Symphysiotomy for horseshoe kidney with or without pyeloplasty and/or other plastic procedure, unilateral or bilateral (1 operation)

● New Code   ▲ Revised Code   + Add-On Code   ⊘ Modifier -51 Exempt   ★ Telemedicine

LAPAROSCOPY

Surgical laparoscopy always includes diagnostic laparoscopy. To report a diagnostic laparoscopy (peritoneoscopy) (separate procedure), use 49320.

50541 Laparoscopy, surgical; ablation of renal cysts

50542 ablation of renal mass lesion(s), including intraoperative ultrasound guidance and monitoring, when performed

(For open procedure, see 50250)

(For percutaneous ablation of renal tumors, see 50592, 50593)

50543 partial nephrectomy

(For open procedure, use 50240)

50544 pyeloplasty

50545 radical nephrectomy (includes removal of Gerota's fascia and surrounding fatty tissue, removal of regional lymph nodes, and adrenalectomy

(For open procedure, use 50230)

50546 nephrectomy including partial ureterectomy

50547 donor nephrectomy (including cold preservation), from living donor

(For open procedure, use 50320)

(For backbench renal allograft standard preparation prior to transplantation, use 50325)

(For backbench renal allograft reconstruction prior to transplantation, see 50327-50329)

50548 nephrectomy with total ureterectomy

(For open procedure, see 50234, 50236)

50549 Unlisted laparoscopy procedure, renal

(For laparoscopic drainage of lymphocele to peritoneal cavity, use 49323)

ENDOSCOPY

(For supplies and materials, use 99070)

50551 Renal endoscopy through established nephrostomy or pyelostomy, with or without irrigation, instillation, or ureteropyelography, exclusive of radiologic service;

50553 with ureteral catheterization, with or without dilation of ureter

(For image-guided dilation of ureter without endoscopic guidance, use 50706)

50555 with biopsy

(For image-guided biopsy of ureter and/or renal pelvis without endoscopic guidance, use 50606)

50557 with fulguration and/or incision, with or without biopsy

50561 with removal of foreign body or calculus

50562 with resection of tumor

(When procedures 50570-50580 provide a significant identifiable service, they may be added to 50045 and 50120)

50570 Renal endoscopy through nephrotomy or pyelotomy, with or without irrigation, instillation, or ureteropyelography, exclusive of radiologic service;

(For nephrotomy, use 50045)

(For pyelotomy, use 50120)

50572 with ureteral catheterization, with or without dilation of ureter

(For image-guided dilation of ureter without endoscopic guidance, use 50706)

50574 with biopsy

(For image-guided biopsy of ureter and/or renal pelvis without endoscopic guidance, use 50606)

50575 with endopyelotomy (includes cystoscopy, ureteroscopy, dilation of ureter and ureteral pelvic junction, incision of ureteral pelvic junction and insertion of endopyelotomy stent)

50576 with fulguration and/or incision, with or without biopsy

50580 with removal of foreign body or calculus

OTHER PROCEDURES

50590 Lithotripsy, extracorporeal shock wave

50592 Ablation, one or more renal tumor(s), percutaneous, unilateral, radiofrequency

(50592 is a unilateral procedure. For bilateral procedure, report 50592 with modifier 50)

(For imaging guidance and monitoring, see 76940, 77013, 77022)

50593 Ablation, renal tumor(s), unilateral, percutaneous, cryotherapy

(50593 is a unilatral procedure. For bilateral procedure, report 50593 with modifier -50)

(For imaging guidance and monitoring, see codes 76940, 77013, 77022)

URETER

INCISION/BIOPSY

Code 50606 is an add-on code describing endoluminal biopsy (eg, brush) using non-endoscopic imaging guidance, which may be reported once per ureter per day. This code includes the work of the biopsy and the imaging guidance and radiological supervision and interpretation required to accomplish the biopsy. The biopsy may be performed through de novo transrenal access, an existing renal/ureteral access, transurethral access, an ileal conduit, or ureterostomy. The service of gaining access may be reported separately. Diagnostic pyelography/ureterography is not included in the work of 50606 and may be reported separately. Other interventions or catheter placements performed at the same setting as the biopsy may be reported separately. For codes 50430, 50431, 50432, 50433, 50434, 50435, 50606, 50693, 50694, 50695, 50705, and 50706, the renal pelvis and its associated ureter are considered a single entity for reporting purposes. Codes 50430, 50431, 50432, 50433, 50434, 50435, 50606, 50693, 50694, 50695, 50705, and 50706 may be reported once for each renal collecting system/ureter accessed (eg, two separate codes would be reported for bilateral nephrostomy tube placement or for unilateral duplicated collecting system/ureter requiring two separate procedures.

50600 Ureterotomy with exploration or drainage (separate procedure)

(For ureteral endoscopy performed in conjunction with this procedure, see 50970-50980)

50605 Ureterotomy for insertion of indwelling stent, all types

+ **50606** Endoluminal biopsy of ureter and/or renal pelvis, nonendoscopic, including imaging guidance (eg, ultrasound and/or fluoroscopy) and all associated radiological supervision and interpretation (List separately in addition to code for primary procedure)

(Use 50606 in conjunction with 50382, 50384, 50385, 50386, 50387, 50389, 50430, 50431, 50432, 50433, 50434, 50435, 50684, 50688, 50690, 50693, 50694, 50695, 51610)

(Do not report 50606 in conjunction with 50555, 50574, 50955, 50974, 52007, 74425 for the same renal collecting system and/or associated ureter)

50610 Ureterolithotomy; upper one-third of ureter

50620 middle one-third of ureter

50630 lower one-third of ureter

(For laparoscopic approach, use 50945)

(For transvesical ureterolithotomy, use 51060)

(For cystotomy with stone basket extraction of ureteral calculus, use 51065)

(For endoscopic extraction or manipulation of ureteral calculus, see 50080, 50081, 50561, 50961, 50980, 52320-52330, 52352, 52353, 52356)

EXCISION

(For ureterocele, see 51535, 52300)

50650 Ureterectomy, with bladder cuff (separate procedure)

50660 Ureterectomy, total, ectopic ureter, combination abdominal, vaginal and/or perineal approach

INTRODUCTION

Other Introduction (Injection/Change/Removal) Procedures

Codes 50693, 50694, 50695 are therapeutic procedure codes describing percutaneous placement of ureteral stents. These codes include access, drainage, catheter manipulations, diagnostic nephrostogram and/or ureterogram, when performed, imaging guidance (eg, ultrasonography and/or fluoroscopy), and all associated radiological supervision and interpretation. When a separate ureteral stent and a nephrostomy catheter are placed into a ureter and its associated renal pelvis during the same session through a new percutaneous renal access, use 50695 to report the procedure.

50684 Injection procedure for ureterography or ureteropyelography through ureterostomy or indwelling ureteral catheter

(Do not report 50684 in conjunction with 50433, 50434, 50693, 50694, 50695)

(For radiological supervision and interpretation, use 74425)

50686 Manometric studies through ureterostomy or indwelling ureteral catheter

50688 Change of ureterostomy tube or externally accessible ureteral stent via ileal conduit

(If imaging guidance is performed, use 75984)

50690 Injection procedure for visualization of ileal conduit and/or ureteropyelography, exclusive of radiologic service

(For radiological supervision and interpretation, use 74425)

50693 Placement of ureteral stent, percutaneous, including diagnostic nephrostogram and/or ureterogram when performed, imaging guidance (eg, ultrasound and/or fluoroscopy), and all associated radiological supervision and interpretation; pre-existing nephrostomy tract

50694 new access, without separate nephrostomy catheter

50695 new access, with separate nephrostomy catheter

| | Separate Procedure | | Unlisted Procedure | | CCI Comp. Code | | Non-specific Procedure | **507** |

(Do not report 50693, 50694, 50695 in conjunction with 50430, 50431, 50432, 50433, 50434, 50435, 50684, 74425 for the same renal collecting system and/or associated ureter)

REPAIR

Codes 50705, 50706 are add-on codes describing embolization and balloon dilation of the ureter using non-endoscopic imaging guidance, and each may be reported once per ureter per day. These codes include embolization or dilation plus imaging guidance and radiological supervision and interpretation required to accomplish the embolization or dilation. These procedures may be performed through de novo transrenal access, an existing renal/ureteral access, transurethral access, an ileal conduit, or ureterostomy. The service of gaining access may be reported separately. Diagnostic pyelography/ureterography is not included in 50705 and 50706 and may be reported separately. Other interventions or catheter placements performed at the same setting as the embolization/dilation may be reported separately.

50700   Ureteroplasty, plastic operation on ureter (eg, stricture)

+ **50705**   Ureteral embolization or occlusion, including imaging guidance (eg, ultrasound and/or fluoroscopy) and all associated radiological supervision and interpretation (List separately in addition to code for primary procedure)

     (Use 50705 in conjunction with 50382, 50384, 50385, 50386, 50387, 50389, 50430, 50431, 50432, 50433, 50434, 50435, 50684, 50688, 50690, 50693, 50694, 50695, 51610)

+ **50706**   Balloon dilation, ureteral stricture, including imaging guidance (eg, ultrasound and/or fluoroscopy) and all associated radiological supervision and interpretation (List separately in addition to code for primary procedure)

     (Use 50706 in conjunction with 50382, 50384, 50385, 50386, 50387, 50389, 50430, 50431, 50432, 50433, 50434, 50435, 50684, 50688, 50690, 50693, 50694, 50695, 51610)

     (Do not report 50706 in conjunction with 50553, 50572, 50953, 50972, 52341, 52344, 52345, 74485)

     (For percutaneous nephrostomy, nephroureteral catheter, and/or ureteral catheter placement use 50385, 50387, 50432, 50433, 50434, 50435, 50693, 50694, 50695)

50715   Ureterolysis, with or without repositioning of ureter for retroperitoneal fibrosis

     (For bilateral procedure, report 50715 with modifier -50)

50722   Ureterolysis for ovarian vein syndrome

50725   Ureterolysis for retrocaval ureter, with reanastomosis of upper urinary tract or vena cava

50727   Revision of urinary-cutaneous anastomosis (any type urostomy);

50728   with repair of fascial defect and hernia

50740   Ureteropyelostomy, anastomosis of ureter and renal pelvis

50750   Ureterocalycostomy, anastomosis of ureter to renal calyx

50760   Ureteroureterostomy

50770   Transureteroureterostomy, anastomosis of ureter to contralateral ureter

     (Codes 50780-50785 include minor procedures to prevent vesicoureteral reflux)

50780   Ureteroneocystostomy; anastomosis of single ureter to bladder

     (For bilateral procedure, report 50780 with modifier -50)

     (When combined with cystourethroplasty or vesical neck revision, use 51820)

50782   anastomosis of duplicated ureter to bladder

50783   with extensive ureteral tailoring

50785   with vesico-psoas hitch or bladder flap

(For bilateral procedure, report 50785 with modifier -50)

50800   Ureteroenterostomy, direct anastomosis of ureter to intestine

(For bilateral procedure, report 50800 with modifier -50)

50810   Ureterosigmoidostomy, with creation of sigmoid bladder and establishment of abdominal or perineal colostomy, including intestine anastomosis

50815   Ureterocolon conduit, including intestine anastomosis

(For bilateral procedure, report 50815 with modifier -50)

50820   Ureteroileal conduit (ileal bladder), including intestine anastomosis (Bricker operation)

(For bilateral procedure, report 50820 with modifier -50)

(For combination of 50800-50820 with cystectomy, see 51580-51595)

50825   Continent diversion, including intestine anastomosis using any segment of small and/or large intestine (Kock pouch or Camey enterocystoplasty)

50830   Urinary undiversion (eg, taking down of ureteroileal conduit, ureterosigmoidostomy or ureteroenterostomy with ureteroureterostomy or ureteroneocystostomy)

50840   Replacement of all or part of ureter by intestine segment, including intestine anastomosis

(For bilateral procedure, report 50840 with modifier -50)

50845   Cutaneous appendico-vesicostomy

50860   Ureterostomy, transplantation of ureter to skin

(For bilateral procedure, report 50860 with modifier -50)

50900   Ureterorrhaphy, suture of ureter (separate procedure)

50920   Closure of ureterocutaneous fistula

50930   Closure of ureterovisceral fistula (including visceral repair)

50940   Deligation of ureter

(For ureteroplasty, ureterolysis, see 50700-50860)

LAPAROSCOPY

Surgical laparoscopy always includes diagnostic laparoscopy. To report a diagnostic laparoscopy (peritoneoscopy) (separate procedure), use 49320.

50945   Laparoscopy, surgical; ureterolithotomy

50947   ureteroneocystostomy with cystoscopy and ureteral stent placement

50948   ureteroneocystostomy without cystoscopy and ureteral stent placement

(For open ureteroneocystostomy, see 50780-50785)

50949   Unlisted laparoscopy procedure, ureter

■ Separate Procedure	■ Unlisted Procedure	■ CCI Comp. Code	■ Non-specific Procedure	**509**

ENDOSCOPY

50951 Ureteral endoscopy through established ureterostomy, with or without irrigation, instillation, or ureteropyelography, exclusive of radiologic service;

50953 with ureteral catheterization, with or without dilation of ureter

(For image-guided dilation of ureter without endoscopic guidance, use 50706)

50955 with biopsy

(For image-guided biopsy of ureter and/or renal pelvis without endoscopic guidance, use 50606)

50957 with fulguration and/or incision, with or without biopsy

50961 with removal of foreign body or calculus

50970 Ureteral endoscopy through ureterotomy, with or without irrigation, instillation, or ureteropyelography, exclusive of radiologic service;

(For ureterotomy, use 50600)

50972 with ureteral catheterization, with or without dilation of ureter

(For image-guided dilation of ureter without endoscopic guidance, use 50706)

50974 with biopsy

(For image-guided biopsy of ureter and/or renal pelvis without endoscopic guidance, use 50606)

50976 with fulguration and/or incision, with or without biopsy

50980 with removal of foreign body or calculus

BLADDER

INCISION

51020 Cystotomy or cystostomy; with fulguration and/or insertion of radioactive material

51030 with cryosurgical destruction of intravesical lesion

51040 Cystostomy, cystotomy with drainage

51045 Cystotomy, with insertion of ureteral catheter or stent (separate procedure)

51050 Cystolithotomy, cystotomy with removal of calculus, without vesical neck resection

51060 Transvesical ureterolithotomy

51065 Cystotomy, with calculus basket extraction and/or ultrasonic or electrohydraulic fragmentation of ureteral calculus

51080 Drainage of perivesical or prevesical space abscess

(For percutaneous image-guided fluid collection drainage by catheter of perivesicular or prevesicular space abscess, use 49406)

REMOVAL

51100 Aspiration of bladder; by needle

● New Code   ▲ Revised Code   + Add-On Code   ⊘ Modifier -51 Exempt   ★ Telemedicine

51101	by trocar or intracatheter
51102	with insertion of suprapubic catheter

(For imaging guidance, see 76942, 77002, 77012)

EXCISION

51500	Excision of urachal cyst or sinus, with or without umbilical hernia repair
51520	Cystotomy; for simple excision of vesical neck (separate procedure)
51525	for excision of bladder diverticulum, single or multiple (separate procedure)
51530	for excision of bladder tumor

(For transurethral resection, see 52234-52240, 52305)

51535	Cystotomy for excision, incision, or repair of ureterocele

(For bilateral procedure, report 51535 with modifier -50)

(For transurethral excision, use 52300)

51550	Cystectomy, partial; simple
51555	complicated (eg, postradiation, previous surgery, difficult location)
51565	Cystectomy, partial, with reimplantation of ureter(s) into bladder (ureteroneocystostomy)
51570	Cystectomy, complete; (separate procedure)
51575	with bilateral pelvic lymphadenectomy, including external iliac, hypogastric, and obturator nodes
51580	Cystectomy, complete, with ureterosigmoidostomy or ureterocutaneous transplantations;
51585	with bilateral pelvic lymphadenectomy, including external iliac, hypogastric, and obturator nodes
51590	Cystectomy, complete, with ureteroileal conduit or sigmoid bladder, including intestine anastomosis;
51595	with bilateral pelvic lymphadenectomy, including external iliac, hypogastric, and obturator nodes
51596	Cystectomy, complete, with continent diversion, any open technique, using any segment of small and/or large intestine to construct neobladder
51597	Pelvic exenteration, complete, for vesical, prostatic or urethral malignancy, with removal of bladder and ureteral transplantations, with or without hysterectomy and/or abdominoperineal resection of rectum and colon and colostomy, or any combination thereof

(For pelvic exenteration for gynecologic malignancy, use 58240)

INTRODUCTION

51600	Injection procedure for cystography or voiding urethrocystography

(For radiological supervision and interpretation, see 74430, 74455)

51605	Injection procedure and placement of chain for contrast and/or chain urethrocystography

(For radiological supervision and interpretation, use 74430)

51610	Injection procedure for retrograde urethrocystography

(For radiological supervision and interpretation, use 74450)

51700 Bladder irrigation, simple, lavage and/or instillation

(Codes 51701-51702 are reported only when performed independently. Do not report 51701-51702 when catheter insertion is an inclusive component of another procedure.)

51701 Insertion of non-indwelling bladder catheter (eg, straight catheterization of residual urine)

51702 Insertion of temporary indwelling bladder catheter; simple (eg, Foley)

(Do not report 51702 in conjunction with 0071T, 0072T)

51703 complicated (eg, altered anatomy, fractured catheter/balloon)

51705 Change of cystostomy tube; simple

51710 complicated

(If imaging guidance is performed, use 75984)

51715 Endoscopic injection of implant material into the submucosal tissues of the urethra and/or bladder neck

(For anoscopy with directed submucosal injection of bulking agent for fecal incontinence, use 0377T)

51720 Bladder instillation of anticarcinogenic agent (including retention time)

URODYNAMICS

The following section (51725-51798) lists procedures that may be used separately or in many and varied combinations.

When multiple procedures are performed in the same investigative session, modifier -51 should be employed.

All procedures in this section imply that these services are performed by, or are under the direct supervision of, a physician or other qualified health care professional and that all instruments, equipment, fluids, gases, probes, catheters, technician's fees, medications, gloves, trays, tubing and other sterile supplies be provided by that individual. When the individual only interprets the results and/or operates the equipment, a professional component, modifier -26 should be used to identify physcians' services.

51725 Simple cystometrogram (CMG) (eg, spinal manometer)

51726 Complex cystometrogram (ie, calibrated electronic equipment)

51727 with urethral pressure profile studies (ie, urethral closure pressure profile), any technique

51728 with voiding pressure studies (ie, bladder voiding pressure), any technique

51729 with voiding pressure studies (ie, bladder voiding pressure) and urethral pressure profile studies (ie, urethral closure pressure profile), any technique

+ 51797 Voiding pressure studies, intra-abdominal (ie, rectal, gastric, intraperitoneal) (List separately in addition to code for primary procedure)

(Use 51797 in conjunction with 51728, 51729)

51736 Simple uroflowmetry (UFR) (eg, stop-watch flow rate, mechanical uroflowmeter)

51741 Complex uroflowmetry (eg, calibrated electronic equipment)

51784 Electromyography studies (EMG) of anal or urethral sphincter, other than needle, any technique

(Do not report 51784 in conjunction with 51792)

• New Code ▲ Revised Code + Add-On Code ⊘ Modifier -51 Exempt ★ Telemedicine

51785   Needle electromyography studies (EMG) of anal or urethral sphincter, any technique

51792   Stimulus evoked response (eg, measurement of bulbocavernosus reflex latency time)

(Do not report 51792 in conjunction with 51784)

51797   This code is out of order. See page 512.

51798   Measurement of post-voiding residual urine and/or bladder capacity by ultrasound, non-imaging

REPAIR

51800   Cystoplasty or cystourethroplasty, plastic operation on bladder and/or vesical neck (anterior Y-plasty, vesical fundus resection), any procedure, with or without wedge resection of posterior vesical neck

51820   Cystourethroplasty with unilateral or bilateral ureteroneocystostomy

51840   Anterior vesicourethropexy, or urethropexy (eg, Marshall-Marchetti-Krantz, Burch); simple

51841   complicated (eg, secondary repair)

(For urethropexy (Pereyra type), use 57289)

51845   Abdomino-vaginal vesical neck suspension, with or without endoscopic control (eg, Stamey, Raz, modified Pereyra)

51860   Cystorrhaphy, suture of bladder wound, injury or rupture; simple

51865   complicated

51880   Closure of cystostomy (separate procedure)

51900   Closure of vesicovaginal fistula, abdominal approach

(For vaginal approach, see 57320-57330)

51920   Closure of vesicouterine fistula;

51925   with hysterectomy

(For closure of vesicoenteric fistula, see 44660, 44661)

(For closure of rectovesical fistula, see 45800-45805)

51940   Closure, exstrophy of bladder

(See also 54390)

51960   Enterocystoplasty, including intestinal anastomosis

51980   Cutaneous vesicostomy

LAPAROSCOPY

Surgical laparoscopy always includes diagnostic laparoscopy. To report a diagnostic laparoscopy (peritoneoscopy) (separate procedure), use 49320.

51990   Laparoscopy, surgical; urethral suspension for stress incontinence

51992   sling operation for stress incontinence (eg, fascia or synthetic)

(For open sling operation for stress incontinence, use 57288)

     Separate Procedure   Unlisted Procedure   CCI Comp. Code   Non-specific Procedure   **513**

(For reversal or removal of sling operation for stress incontinence, use 57287)

51999   Unlisted laparoscopy procedure, bladder

ENDOSCOPY—CYSTOSCOPY, URETHROSCOPY, CYSTOURETHROSCOPY

Endoscopic descriptions are listed so that the main procedure can be identified without having to list all the minor related functions performed at the same time. For example, meatotomy, urethral calibration and/or dilation, urethroscopy, and cystoscopy prior to a transurethral resection of prostate; ureteral catheterization following extraction of ureteral calculus; internal urethrotomy and bladder neck fulguration when performing a cystourethroscopy for the female urethral syndrome. When the secondary procedure requires significant additional time and effort, it may be identified by the addition of modifier 22.

For example, urethrotomy performed for a documented pre-existing stricture or bladder neck contracture.

Because cutaneous urinary diversions utilizing ileum or colon serve as functional replacements of a native bladder, endoscopy of such bowel segments, as well as performance of secondary procedures can be captured by using the cystourethroscopy codes. For example, endoscopy of an ileal loop with removal of ureteral calculus would be coded as cystourethroscopy (including ureteral catheterization); with removal of ureteral calculus (52320).

52000   Cystourethroscopy (separate procedure)

(Do not report 52000 in conjunction with 52001, 52320, 52325, 52327, 52330, 52332, 52334, 52341, 52342, 52343, 52356)

(Do not report 52000 in conjunction with 57240, 57260, 57265)

52001   Cystourethroscopy with irrigation and evacuation of multiple obstructing clots

(Do not report 52001 in addition to 52000)

52005   Cystourethroscopy, with ureteral catheterization, with or without irrigation, instillation, or ureteropyelography, exclusive of radiologic service;

52007   with brush biopsy of ureter and/or renal pelvis

(For image-guided biopsy of ureter and/or renal pelvis without endoscopic guidance, use 50606)

52010   Cystourethroscopy, with ejaculatory duct catheterization, with or without irrigation, instillation, or duct radiography, exclusive of radiologic service

(For radiological supervision and interpretation, use 74440)

TRANSURETHRAL SURGERY

Urethra and Bladder

52204   Cystourethroscopy, with biopsy(s)

52214   Cystourethroscopy, with fulguration (including cryosurgery or laser surgery) of trigone, bladder neck, prostatic fossa, urethra, or periurethral glands

(For transurethral fulguration of prostate tissue performed within the postoperative period of 52601 or 52630 performed by the same physician, append modifier 78)

(For transurethral fulguration of prostate tissue performed within the postoperative period of a related procedure performed by the same physician, append modifier 78)

(For transurethral fulguration of prostate for postoperative bleeding performed by the same physician, append modifier 78)

52224   Cystourethroscopy, with fulguration (including cryosurgery or laser surgery) or treatment of MINOR (less than 0.5 cm) lesion(s) with or without biopsy

52234   Cystourethroscopy, with fulguration (including cryosurgery or laser surgery) and/or resection of; SMALL bladder tumor(s) (0.5 up to 2.0 cm)

52235   MEDIUM bladder tumor(s) (2.0 to 5.0 cm)

52240   LARGE bladder tumor(s)

52250   Cystourethroscopy with insertion of radioactive substance, with or without biopsy or fulguration

52260   Cystourethroscopy, with dilation of bladder for interstitial cystitis; general or conduction (spinal) anesthesia

52265   local anesthesia

52270   Cystourethroscopy, with internal urethrotomy; female

52275   male

52276   Cystourethroscopy with direct vision internal urethrotomy

52277   Cystourethroscopy, with resection of external sphincter (sphincterotomy)

52281   Cystourethroscopy, with calibration and/or dilation of urethral stricture or stenosis, with or without meatotomy, with or without injection procedure for cystography, male or female

   (To report cystourethroscopy with urethral therapeutic drug delivery, use 0499T)

52282   Cystourethroscopy, with insertion of permanent urethral stent

   (For placement of temporary prostatic urethral stent, use 53855)

52283   Cystourethroscopy, with steroid injection into stricture

52285   Cystourethroscopy for treatment of the female urethral syndrome with any or all of the following: urethral meatotomy, urethral dilation, internal urethrotomy, lysis of urethrovaginal septal fibrosis, lateral incisions of the bladder neck, and fulguration of polyp(s) of urethra, bladder neck, and/or trigone

52287   Cystourethroscopy, with injection(s) for chemodenervation of the bladder

   (The suppy of the chemodenervation agent is reported separately)

52290   Cystourethroscopy; with ureteral meatotomy, unilateral or bilateral

52300   with resection or fulguration of orthotopic ureterocele(s), unilateral or bilateral

52301   with resection or fulguration of ectopic ureterocele(s), unilateral or bilateral

52305   with incision or resection of orifice of bladder diverticulum, single or multiple

52310   Cystourethroscopy, with removal of foreign body, calculus, or ureteral stent from urethra or bladder (separate procedure); simple

52315   complicated

52317   Litholapaxy: crushing or fragmentation of calculus by any means in bladder and removal of fragments; simple or small (less than 2.5 cm)

52318   complicated or large (over 2.5 cm)

URETER AND PELVIS

Therapeutic cystourethroscopy always includes diagnostic cystourethroscopy. To report diagnostic cystourethroscopy, use 52000. Therapeutic cystourethroscopy with ureteroscopy and/or pyeloscopy always includes diagnostic cystourethroscopy with ureteroscopy and/or pyeloscopy. To report a diagnostic cystourethroscopy with ureteroscopy and/or pyeloscopy, use 52351.

Separate Procedure   Unlisted Procedure   CCI Comp. Code   Non-specific Procedure   **515**

Do not report 52000 in conjunction with 52320-52343, 52356.

Do not report 52351 in conjunction with 52344-52346, 52352-52356.

The insertion and removal of a temporary ureteral catheter (52005) during diagnostic or therapeutic cystourethroscopy with ureteroscopy and/or pyeloscopy is included in 52320-52356 and should not be reported separately.

To report insertion of a self-retaining, indwelling stent performed during diagnostic or therapeutic cystourethroscopy with ureteroscopy and/or pyeloscopy, report 52332 in addition to primary procedure(s) performed (52320-52330, 52334-52352, 52354, 52355) and append modifier 51. Code 52332 is used to report a unilateral procedure unless otherwise specified.

For bilateral insertion of self-retaining, indwelling ureteral stents, use code 52332, and append modifier 50.

To report cystourethroscopic removal of a self-retaining indwelling ureteral stent, see 52310, 52315, and append modifier 58 if appropriate

52320   Cystourethroscopy (including ureteral catheterization); with removal of ureteral calculus

52325   with fragmentation of ureteral calculus (eg, ultrasonic or electro-hydraulic technique)

52327   with subureteric injection of implant material

52330   with manipulation, without removal of ureteral calculus

(Do not report 52320, 52325, 52327, 52330 in conjunction with 52000)

52332   Cystourethroscopy, with insertion of indwelling ureteral stent (eg, Gibbons or double-J type)

(Do not report 52332 in conjunction with 52000, 52353, 52356 when performed together on the same side)

52334   Cystourethroscopy with insertion of ureteral guide wire through kidney to establish a percutaneous nephrostomy, retrograde

(For percutaneous nephrostolithotomy, see 50080, 50081; for establishment of nephrostomy tract only, use 50395)

(For cystourethroscopy, with ureteroscopy and/or pyeloscopy, see 52351-52356)

(For cystourethroscopy with incision, fulguration, or resection of congential posterior urethral valves or obstructive hypertrophic mucosal folds, use 52400)

(Do not report 52334 in conjunction with 52000, 52351)

52341   Cystourethroscopy; with treatment of ureteral stricture (eg, balloon dilation, laser, electrocautery, and incision)

52342   with treatment of ureteropelvic junction stricture (eg, balloon dilation, laser, electrocautery, and incision)

52343   with treatment of intra-renal stricture (eg, balloon dilation, laser, electrocautery, and incision)

(Do note report 52341, 52342, 52343 in conjunction with 52000, 52351)

(For image-guided dilation of ureter, ureteropelvic junction stricture without endoscopic guidance, use 50706)

52344   Cystourethroscopy with ureteroscopy; with treatment of ureteral stricture (eg, balloon dilation, laser, electrocautery, and incision)

52345   with treatment of ureteropelvic junction stricture (eg, balloon dilation, laser, electrocautery, and incision)

52346   with treatment of intra-renal stricture (eg, balloon dilation, laser, electrocautery, and incision)

(For transurethral resection or incision of ejaculatory ducts, use 52402)

(Do not report 52344, 52345, 52346 in conjunction with 52351)

(For image-guided dilation of ureter, ureteropelvic junction stricture without endoscopic guidance, use 50706)

52351 Cystourethroscopy, with ureteroscopy and/or pyeloscopy; diagnostic

(For radiological supervision and interpretation, use 74485)

(Do not report 52351 in conjunction with 52341, 52342, 52343, 52344, 52345, 52346, 52352-52356)

52352 with removal or manipulation of calculus (ureteral catheterization is included)

52353 with lithotripsy (ureteral catheterization is included)

(Do not report 52353 in conjunction with 52332, 52356 when performed together on the same side)

52356 with lithotripsy including insertion of indwelling ureteral stent (eg, Gibbons or double-J type)

(Do not report 52356 in conjunction with 52332, 52353 when performed together on the same side)

52354 with biopsy and/or fulguration of ureteral or renal pelvic lesion

(For image-guided biopsy of ureter and/or renal pelvic without endoscopic guidance, use 50606)

52355 with resection of ureteral or renal pelvic tumor

52356 This code is out of order. See page 517.

VESICAL NECK AND PROSTATE

52400 Cystourethroscopy with incision, fulguration, or resection of congenital posterior urethral valves, or congenital obstructive hypertrophic mucosal folds

52402 Cystourethroscopy with transurethral resection or incision of ejaculatory ducts

52441 Cystourethroscopy, with insertion of permanent adjustable transprostatic implant; single implant

+ **52442** each additional permanent adjustable transprostatic implant (list separately in addition to code for primary procedure)

(Use 52442 in conjunction with 52441)

(To report removal of implant[s], use 52310)

(For insertion of a permanent urethral stent, use 52282. For insertion of a temporary prostatic urethral stent, use 53855)

52450 Transurethral incision of prostate

52500 Transurethral resection of bladder neck (separate procedure)

52601 Transurethral electrosurgical resection of prostate, including control of postoperative bleeding, complete (vasectomy, meatotomy, cystourethroscopy, urethral calibration and/or dilation, and internal urethrotomy are included)

(For transurethral waterjet ablation of prostate, use 0421T)

(For other approaches, see 55801-55845)

(**52612** deleted 2009 edition. For first stage transurethral partial resection of prostate, use 52601. For second stage partial resection of prostate, use 52601 with modifier -58. For transurethral resection of residual or regrowth of obstructive prostate tissue, use 52630)

Separate Procedure   Unlisted Procedure   CCI Comp. Code   Non-specific Procedure   **517**

(**52614** deleted 2009 edition. For first stage transurethral partial resection of prostate, use 52601. For second stage partial resection of prostate, use 52601 with modifier -58. For transurethral resection of residual or regrowth of obstructive prostate tissue, use 52630)

(**52620** deleted 2009 edition. For first stage transurethral partial resection of prostate, use 52601. For second stage partial resection of prostate, use 52601 with modifier -58. For transurethral resection of residual or regrowth of obstructive prostate tissue, use 52630)

52630 Transurethral resection; residual or regrowth of obstructive prostate tissue including control of postoperative bleeding, complete (vasectomy, meatotomy, cystourethroscopy, urethral calibration and/or dilation, and internal urethrotomy are included)

(For resection of residual prostate tissue performed within the postoperative period of a related procedure performed by the same physician, append modifier 78)

(For transurethral waterjet ablation of prostate, use 0421T)

52640 of postoperative bladder neck contracture

52647 Laser coagulation of prostate, including control of postoperative bleeding, complete (vasectomy, meatotomy, cystourethroscopy, urethral calibration and/or dilation, and internal urethrotomy are included if performed)

52648 Laser vaporization of prostate, including control of postoperative bleeding, complete (vasectomy, meatotomy, cystourethroscopy, urethral calibration and/or dilation, internal urethrotomy and transurethral resection of prostate are included if performed)

52649 Laser enucleation of the prostate with morcellation, including control of postoperative bleeding, complete (vasectomy, meatotomy, cystourethroscopy, urethral calibration and/or dilation, internal urethrotomy and transurethral resection of prostate are included if performed)

(Do not report 52649 in conjunction with 52000, 52276, 52281, 52601, 52647, 52648, 53020, 55250)

52700 Transurethral drainage of prostatic abscess

(For litholapaxy, use 52317, 52318)

URETHRA

(For endoscopy, see cystoscopy, urethroscopy, cystourethroscopy, 52000-52700)

(For injection procedure for urethrocystography, see 51600-51610)

INCISION

53000 Urethrotomy or urethrostomy, external (separate procedure); pendulous urethra

53010 perineal urethra, external

53020 Meatotomy, cutting of meatus (separate procedure); except infant

53025 infant

(Do not report modifier '-63' in conjunction with 53025)

53040 Drainage of deep periurethral abscess

(For subcutaneous abscess, see 10060, 10061)

53060 Drainage of Skene's gland abscess or cyst

53080 Drainage of perineal urinary extravasation; uncomplicated (separate procedure)

---

518 ● New Code ▲ Revised Code + Add-On Code ⊘ Modifier -51 Exempt ★ Telemedicine

53085	complicated

EXCISION

53200	Biopsy of urethra
53210	Urethrectomy, total, including cystostomy; female
53215	male
53220	Excision or fulguration of carcinoma of urethra
53230	Excision of urethral diverticulum (separate procedure); female
53235	male
53240	Marsupialization of urethral diverticulum, male or female
53250	Excision of bulbourethral gland (Cowper's gland)
53260	Excision or fulguration; urethral polyp(s), distal urethra
	(For endoscopic approach, see 52214, 52224)
53265	urethral caruncle
53270	Skene's glands
53275	urethral prolapse

REPAIR

	(For hypospadias, see 54300-54352)
53400	Urethroplasty; first stage, for fistula, diverticulum, or stricture (eg, Johannsen type)
53405	second stage (formation of urethra), including urinary diversion
53410	Urethroplasty, 1-stage reconstruction of male anterior urethra
53415	Urethroplasty, transpubic or perineal, one stage, for reconstruction or repair of prostatic or membranous urethra
53420	Urethroplasty, 2-stage reconstruction or repair of prostatic or membranous urethra; first stage
53425	second stage
53430	Urethroplasty, reconstruction of female urethra
53431	Urethroplasty with tubularization of posterior urethra and/or lower bladder for incontinence (eg, Tenago, Leadbetter procedure)
53440	Sling operation for correction of male urinary incontinence (eg, fascia or synthetic)
53442	Removal or revision of sling for male urinary incontinence (eg, fascia or synthetic)
53444	Insertion of tandem cuff (dual cuff)
53445	Insertion of inflatable urethral/bladder neck sphincter, including placement of pump, reservoir, and cuff

■	Separate Procedure	■	Unlisted Procedure	■	CCI Comp. Code	■	Non-specific Procedure	**519**

53446 Removal of inflatable urethral/bladder neck sphincter, including pump, reservoir, and cuff

53447 Removal and replacement of inflatable urethral/bladder neck sphincter including pump, reservoir, and cuff at the same operative session

53448 Removal and replacement of inflatable urethral/bladder neck sphincter including pump, reservoir, and cuff through an infected field at the same operative session including irrigation and debridement of infected tissue

(Do not report 11042, 11043 in addition to 53448)

53449 Repair of inflatable urethral/bladder neck sphincter, including pump, reservoir, and cuff

53450 Urethromeatoplasty, with mucosal advancement

(For meatotomy, see 53020, 53025)

53460 Urethromeatoplasty, with partial excision of distal urethral segment (Richardson type procedure)

53500 Urethrolysis, transvaginal, secondary, open, including cystourethroscopy (eg, postsurgical obstruction, scarring)

(For urethrolysis by retropubic approach, use 53899)

(Do not report 53500 in conjunction with 52000)

53502 Urethrorrhaphy, suture of urethral wound or injury; female

53505   penile

53510   perineal

53515   prostatomembranous

53520 Closure of urethrostomy or urethrocutaneous fistula, male (separate procedure)

(For closure of urethrovaginal fistula, use 57310)

(For closure of urethrorectal fistula, see 45820, 45825)

MANIPULATION

(For radiological supervision and interpretation, use 74485)

53600 Dilation of urethral stricture by passage of sound or urethral dilator, male; initial

53601   subsequent

53605 Dilation of urethral stricture or vesical neck by passage of sound or urethral dilator, male, general or conduction (spinal) anesthesia

(For dilation of urethral stricture, male, performed under local anesthesia, see 53600, 53601, 53620, 53621)

53620 Dilation of urethral stricture by passage of filiform and follower, male; initial

53621   subsequent

53660 Dilation of female urethra including suppository and/or instillation; initial

53661   subsequent

53665 Dilation of female urethra, general or conduction (spinal) anesthesia

● New Code   ▲ Revised Code   ✛ Add-On Code   ⊘ Modifier -51 Exempt   ★ Telemedicine

(For urethral catheterization, see 51701-51703)

(For dilation of urethra performed under local anesthesia, female, see 53660, 53661)

OTHER PROCEDURES

(For two or three glass urinalysis, use 81020)

53850　Transurethral destruction of prostate tissue; by microwave thermotherapy

53852　　by radiofrequency thermotherapy

53855　Insertion of a temporary prostatic urethral stent, including urethral measurement

(For insertion of permanent urethral stent, use 52282)

53860　Transurethral radiofrequency micro-remodeling of the female bladder neck and proximal urethra for stress urinary incontinence

53899　Unlisted procedure, urinary system

This page intentionally left blank

● New Code ▲ Revised Code ✚ Add-On Code ⊘ Modifier -51 Exempt ★ Telemedicine

MALE GENITAL SYSTEM

CPT codes from this section of CPT are used to report invasive and surgical procedures performed on the penis; testis; epididymis; scrotum; spermatic cord and prostate.

Transurethral drainage of a prostatic abscess (e.g. CPT code 52700) is included in male transurethral prostatic procedures and is not reported separately.

Urethral catheterization (e.g. CPT codes 51701, 51702, and 51703), when medically necessary to successfully accomplish a procedure, should not be separately reported.

The puncture aspiration of a hydrocele (e.g. CPT code 55000) is included in services involving the tunica vaginalis and proximate anatomy (scrotum, vas deferens) and in inguinal hernia repairs.

A number of codes describe surgical procedures of a progressively more comprehensive nature or with different approaches to accomplish similar services. In general, these groups of codes are not to be reported together (see mutually exclusive policy). While a number of these groups of codes exist in CPT, a specific example includes the series of codes describing prostate procedures (CPT codes 55801-55845). In addition, all prostatectomy procedures (e.g. CPT codes 52601-52648 and 55801-55845) are also mutually exclusive of one another.

PENIS

INCISION

(For abdominal perineal gangrene debridement, see 11004-11006)

54000   Slitting of prepuce, dorsal or lateral (separate procedure); newborn

(Do not report modifier '-63' in conjunction with 54000)

54001   except newborn

54015   Incision and drainage of penis, deep

(For skin and subcutaneous abscess, see 10060-10160)

DESTRUCTION

54050   Destruction of lesion(s), penis (eg, condyloma, papilloma, molluscum contagiosum, herpetic vesicle), simple; chemical

54055   electrodesiccation

54056   cryosurgery

54057   laser surgery

54060   surgical excision

54065   Destruction of lesion(s), penis (eg, condyloma, papilloma, molluscum contagiosum, herpetic vesicle), extensive (eg, laser surgery, electosurgery, cryosurgery, chemosurgery)

(For destruction or excision of other lesions, see Integumentary System)

EXCISION

54100   Biopsy of penis; (separate procedure)

54105   deep structures

54110   Excision of penile plaque (Peyronie disease);

■ Separate Procedure   ■ Unlisted Procedure   ■ CCI Comp. Code   ■ Non-specific Procedure   **523**

54111 with graft to 5 cm in length

54112 with graft greater than 5 cm in length

54115 Removal foreign body from deep penile tissue (eg, plastic implant)

54120 Amputation of penis; partial

54125 complete

54130 Amputation of penis, radical; with bilateral inguinofemoral lymphadenectomy

54135 in continuity with bilateral pelvic lymphadenectomy, including external iliac, hypogastric and obturator nodes

(For lymphadenectomy (separate procedure) see 38760-38770)

54150 Circumcision, using clamp or other device with regional dorsal penile or ring block

(Do not report modifier -63 in conjunction with 54150)

(Report 54150 with modifier 52 when performed without dorsal penile or ring block)

54160 Circumcision, surgical excision other than clamp, device or dorsal slit; neonate (28 days of age or less)

(Do not report modifier -63 in conjunction with 54160)

54161 older than 28 days of age

54162 Lysis or excision of penile post-circumcision adhesions

54163 Repair incomplete circumcision

54164 Frenulotomy of penis

(Do not report with circumcision codes 54150-54161, 54162, 54163)

INTRODUCTION

54200 Injection procedure for Peyronie disease;

54205 with surgical exposure of plaque

54220 Irrigation of corpora cavernosa for priapism

54230 Injection procedure for corpora cavernosography

(For radiological supervision and interpretation, use 74445)

54231 Dynamic cavernosometry, including intracavernosal injection of vasoactive drugs (eg, papaverine, phentolamine)

54235 Injection of corpora cavernosa with pharmacologic agent(s) (eg, papaverine, phentolamine)

54240 Penile plethysmography

54250 Nocturnal penile tumescence and/or rigidity test

REPAIR

(For other urethroplasties, see 53400-53430)

 ● New Code ▲ Revised Code + Add-On Code ⊘ Modifier -51 Exempt ★ Telemedicine

(For penile revascularization, use 37788)

54300 Plastic operation of penis for straightening of chordee (eg, hypospadias), with or without mobilization of urethra

54304 Plastic operation on penis for correction of chordee or for first stage hypospadias repair with or without transplantation of prepuce and/or skin flaps

54308 Urethroplasty for second stage hypospadias repair (including urinary diversion); less than 3 cm

54312 greater than 3 cm

54316 Urethroplasty for second stage hypospadias repair (including urinary diversion) with free skin graft obtained from site other than genitalia

54318 Urethroplasty for third stage hypospadias repair to release penis from scrotum (eg, third stage Cecil repair)

54322 1 stage distal hypospadias repair (with or without chordee or circumcision); with simple meatal advancement (eg, Magpi, V-flap)

54324 with urethroplasty by local skin flaps (eg, flip-flap, prepucial flap)

54326 with urethroplasty by local skin flaps and mobilization of urethra

54328 with extensive dissection to correct chordee and urethroplasty with local skin flaps, skin graft patch, and/or island flap

(For urethroplasty and straightening of chordee, use 54308)

54332 1 stage proximal penile or penoscrotal hypospadias repair requiring extensive dissection to correct chordee and urethroplasty by use of skin graft tube and/or island flap

54336 1 stage perineal hypospadias repair requiring extensive dissection to correct chordee and urethroplasty by use of skin graft tube and/or island flap

54340 Repair of hypospadias complications (ie, fistula, stricture, diverticula); by closure, incision, or excision, simple

54344 requiring mobilization of skin flaps and urethroplasty with flap or patch graft

54348 requiring extensive dissection and urethroplasty with flap, patch or tubed graft (includes urinary diversion)

54352 Repair of hypospadias cripple requiring extensive dissection and excision of previously constructed structures including re-release of chordee and reconstruction of urethra and penis by use of local skin as grafts and island flaps and skin brought in as flaps or grafts

54360 Plastic operation on penis to correct angulation

54380 Plastic operation on penis for epispadias distal to external sphincter;

54385 with incontinence

54390 with exstrophy of bladder

54400 Insertion of penile prosthesis; non-inflatable (semi-rigid)

54401 inflatable (self-contained)

(For removal or replacement of penile prosthesis, see 54415, 54416)

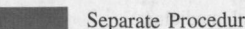

Separate Procedure   Unlisted Procedure   CCI Comp. Code   Non-specific Procedure   **525**

54405 Insertion of multi-component inflatable penile prosthesis, including placement of pump, cylinders, and reservoir

(For reduced services, report 54405 with modifier -52)

54406 Removal of all components of a multi-component inflatable penile prosthesis without replacement of prosthesis

(For reduced services, report 54406 with modifier -52)

54408 Repair of component(s) of a multi-component, inflatable penile prosthesis

54410 Removal and replacement of all component(s) of a multi-component inflatable penile prosthesis at the same operative session

54411 Removal and replacement of all components of a multi-component inflatable penile prosthesis through an infected field at the same operative session, including irrigation and debridement of infected tissue

(For reduced services, report 54411 with modifier -52)

(Do not report 11042, 11043 in addition to 54411)

54415 Removal of non-inflatable (semi-rigid) or inflatable (self-contained) penile prosthesis, without replacement of prosthesis

54416 Removal and replacement of non-inflatable (semi-rigid) or inflatable (self-contained) penile prosthesis at the same operative session

54417 Removal and replacement of non-inflatable (semi-rigid) or inflatable (self-contained) penile prosthesis through an infected field at the same operative session, including irrigation and debridement of infected tissue

(Do not report 11042, 11043 in addition to 54417)

54420 Corpora cavernosa-saphenous vein shunt (priapism operation), unilateral or bilateral

54430 Corpora cavernosa-corpus spongiosum shunt (priapism operation), unilateral or bilateral

54435 Corpora cavernosa-glans penis fistulization (eg, biopsy needle, Winter procedure, rongeur, or punch) for priapism

54437 Repair of traumatic corporeal tear(s)

(For repair of urethra, see 53410, 53415)

54438 Replantation, penis, complete amputation including urethral repair

(To report replantation of incomplete penile amputation, see 54437 for repair of corporeal tear[s], and 53410, 53415 for repair of the urethra)

54440 Plastic operation of penis for injury

MANIPULATION

54450 Foreskin manipulation including lysis of preputial adhesions and stretching

TESTIS

EXCISION

(For abdominal perineal gangrene debridement, see 11004-11006)

54500 Biopsy of testis, needle (separate procedure)

(For fine needle aspiration, see 10021, 10022)

(For evaluation of fine needle aspirate, see 88172, 88173)

54505 Biopsy of testis, incisional (separate procedure)

(For bilateral procedure, report 54505 with modifier -50)

(When combined with vasogram, seminal vesiculogram, or epididymogram, use 55300)

54512 Excision of extraparenchymal lesion of testis

54520 Orchiectomy, simple (including subcapsular), with or without testicular prosthesis, scrotal or inguinal approach

(For bilateral procedure, report 54520 with modifier -50)

54522 Orchiectomy, partial

54530 Orchiectomy, radical, for tumor; inguinal approach

54535   with abdominal exploration

(For orchiectomy with repair of hernia, see 49505 or 49507 and 54520)

(For radical retroperitoneal lymphadenectomy, use 38780)

EXPLORATION

54550 Exploration for undescended testis (inguinal or scrotal area)

(For bilateral procedure, report 54550 with modifier -50)

54560 Exploration for undescended testis with abdominal exploration

(For bilateral procedure, report 54560 with modifier -50)

REPAIR

54600 Reduction of torsion of testis, surgical, with or without fixation of contralateral testis

54620 Fixation of contralateral testis (separate procedure)

54640 Orchiopexy, inguinal approach, with or without hernia repair

(For bilateral procedure, report 54640 with modifier -50)

(For inguinal hernia repair performed in conjunction with inguinal orchiopexy, see 49495-49525)

54650 Orchiopexy, abdominal approach, for intra-abdominal testis (eg, Fowler-Stephens)

(For laparoscopic approach, use 54692)

54660 Insertion of testicular prosthesis (separate procedure)

(For bilateral procedure, report 54660 with modifier -50)

54670 Suture or repair of testicular injury

54680 Transplantation of testis(es) to thigh (because of scrotal destruction)

LAPAROSCOPY

Surgical laparoscopy always includes diagnostic laparoscopy. To report a diagnostic laparoscopy (peritoneoscopy) (separate procedure), use 49320.

54690 Laparoscopy, surgical; orchiectomy

54692   orchiopexy for intra-abdominal testis

54699 Unlisted laparoscopy procedure, testis

EPIDIDYMIS

INCISION

54700 Incision and drainage of epididymis, testis and/or scrotal space (eg, abscess or hematoma)

(For debridement of necrotizing soft tissue infection of external genitalia, see 11004-11006)

EXCISION

54800 Biopsy of epididymis, needle

(For fine needle aspiration, see 10021, 10022)

(For evaluation of fine needle aspirate, see 88172, 88173)

54830 Excision of local lesion of epididymis

54840 Excision of spermatocele, with or without epididymectomy

54860 Epididymectomy; unilateral

54861   bilateral

EXPLORATION

54865 Exploration of epididymis, with or without biopsy

REPAIR

54900 Epididymovasostomy, anastomosis of epididymis to vas deferens; unilateral

54901   bilateral

(For operating microscope, use 69990)

TUNICA VAGINALIS

INCISION

55000 Puncture aspiration of hydrocele, tunica vaginalis, with or without injection of medication

EXCISION

55040 Excision of hydrocele; unilateral

55041   bilateral

(With hernia repair, see 49495-49501)

REPAIR

55060 Repair of tunica vaginalis hydrocele (Bottle type)

● New Code   ▲ Revised Code   ✛ Add-On Code   ⊘ Modifier -51 Exempt   ★ Telemedicine

SCROTUM

INCISION

55100 Drainage of scrotal wall abscess

(See also 54700)

(For debridement of necrotizing soft tissue infection of external genitalia, see 11004-11006)

55110 Scrotal exploration

55120 Removal of foreign body in scrotum

EXCISION

(For excision of local lesion of skin of scrotum, see Integumentary System)

55150 Resection of scrotum

REPAIR

55175 Scrotoplasty; simple

55180   complicated

VAS DEFERENS

INCISION

55200 Vasotomy, cannulization with or without incision of vas, unilateral or bilateral (separate procedure)

EXCISION

55250 Vasectomy, unilateral or bilateral (separate procedure), including postoperative semen examination(s)

INTRODUCTION

55300 Vasotomy for vasograms, seminal vesiculograms, or epididymograms, unilateral or bilateral

(For radiological supervision and interpretation, use 74440)

(When combined with biopsy of testis, see 54505 and use modifier -51)

REPAIR

55400 Vasovasostomy, vasovasorrhaphy

(For bilateral procedure, report 55400 with modifier -50)

(For operating microscope, use 69990)

SUTURE

(**55450** deleted 2017 [2018 edition]. To report, use 55250)

SPERMATIC CORD

EXCISION

55500 Excision of hydrocele of spermatic cord, unilateral (separate procedure)

55520 Excision of lesion of spermatic cord (separate procedure)

55530 Excision of varicocele or ligation of spermatic veins for varicocele; (separate procedure)

55535   abdominal approach

55540   with hernia repair

LAPAROSCOPY

Surgical laparoscopy always includes diagnostic laparoscopy. To report a diagnostic laparoscopy (peritoneoscopy) (separate procedure), use 49320.

55550   Laparoscopy, surgical, with ligation of spermatic veins for varicocele

55559   Unlisted laparoscopy procedure, spermatic cord

SEMINAL VESICLES

INCISION

55600   Vesiculotomy;

(For bilateral procedure, report 55600 with modifier -50)

55605   complicated

EXCISION

55650   Vesiculectomy, any approach

(For bilateral procedure, report 55650 with modifier -50)

55680   Excision of Mullerian duct cyst
(For injection procedure, see 52010, 55300)

PROSTATE

INCISION

55700   Biopsy, prostate; needle or punch, single or multiple, any approach

(If imaging guidance is performed, see 76942, 77002, 77012, 77021)

(For fine needle aspiration, see 10021, 10022)

(For evaluation of fine needle aspirate, see 88172, 88173)

(For transperineal stereotactic template guided saturation prostate biopsies, use 55706)

55705   incisional, any approach

55706   Biopsies, prostate, needle, transperineal, stereotactic template guided saturation sampling, including imaging guidance

(Do not report 55706 in conjunction with 55700)

55720   Prostatotomy, external drainage of prostatic abscess, any approach; simple

55725   complicated

(For transurethral drainage, use 52700)

EXCISION

(For transurethral removal of prostate, see 52601-52640)

(For transurethral destruction of prostate, see 53850-53852)

● New Code   ▲ Revised Code   + Add-On Code   ⊘ Modifier -51 Exempt   ★ Telemedicine

(For limited pelvic lymphadenectomy for staging (separate procedure), use 38562)

(For independent node dissection, see 38770-38780)

55801 Prostatectomy, perineal, subtotal (including control of postoperative bleeding, vasectomy, meatotomy, urethral calibration and/or dilation, and internal urethrotomy)

55810 Prostatectomy, perineal radical;

55812   with lymph node biopsy(s) (limited pelvic lymphadenectomy)

55815   with bilateral pelvic lymphadenectomy, including external iliac, hypogastric and obturator nodes

(If 55815 is carried out on separate days, use 38770 with modifier -50 and 55810)

55821 Prostatectomy (including control of postoperative bleeding, vasectomy, meatotomy, urethral calibration and/or dilation, and internal urethrotomy); suprapubic, subtotal, one or two stages

55831   retropubic, subtotal

55840 Prostatectomy, retropubic radical, with or without nerve sparing;

55842   with lymph node biopsy(s) (limited pelvic lymphadenectomy)

55845   with bilateral pelvic lymphadenectomy, including external iliac, hypogastric, and obturator nodes

(If 55845 is carried out on separate days, use 38770 with modifier -50 and 55840)

(For laparoscopic retropubic radical prostatectomy, use 55866)

55860 Exposure of prostate, any approach, for insertion of radioactive substance;

(For application of interstitial radioelement, see 77770, 77771, 77772, 77778)

55862   with lymph node biopsy(s) (limited pelvic lymphadenectomy)

55865   with bilateral pelvic lymphadenectomy, including external iliac, hypogastric and obturator nodes

LAPAROSCOPY

Surgical laparoscopy always includes diagnostic laparoscopy. To report a diagnostic laparoscopy (peritoneoscopy) (separate procedure), use 49320.

55866 Laparoscopy, surgical prostatectomy, retropubic radical, including nerve sparing, includes robotic assistance, when performed

(For open procedure, use 55840)

OTHER PROCEDURES

(For artificial insemination, see 58321, 58322)

55870 Electroejaculation

55873 Cryosurgical ablation of the prostate (includes ultrasonic guidance and monitoring)

● **55874** Transperineal placement of biodegradable material, periprostatic, single or multiple injection(s), including image guidance, when performed

(Do not report 55874 in conjunction with 76942)

55875 Transperineal placement of needles or catheters into prostate for interstitial radioelement application, with or without cystoscopy

(For placement of needles or catheters into pelvic organs and/or genitalia [except prostate] for interstitial radioelement application, use 55920)

(For interstitial radioelement application, see 77770, 77771, 77772, 77778)

(For ultrasonic guidance for interstitial radioelement application, use 76965)

55876 Placement of interstitial device(s) for radiation therapy guidance (eg, fiducial markers, dosimeter), prostate (via needle, any approach), single or multiple

(Report supply of device separately)

(For imaging guidance, see 76942, 77002, 77012, 77021)

55899 Unlisted procedure, male genital system

● New Code   ▲ Revised Code   + Add-On Code   ⊘ Modifier -51 Exempt   ★ Telemedicine

REPRODUCTIVE SYSTEM PROCEDURES

 55920 Placement of needles or catheters into pelvic organs and/or genitalia (except prostate) for subsequent interstitial radioelement application

(For placement of needles or catheters into prostate, use 55875)

(For insertion of uterine tandems and/or vaginal ovoids for clinical brachytherapy, use 57155)

(For insertion of Heyman capsules for clinical brachytherapy, us 58346)

INTERSEX SURGERY

55970 Intersex surgery; male to female

55980 female to male

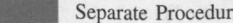 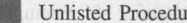

This page intentionally left blank.

● New Code ▲ Revised Code ＋ Add-On Code ⊘ Modifier -51 Exempt ★ Telemedicine

FEMALE GENITAL SYSTEM

When a pelvic examination is performed in conjunction with a gynecologic procedure, either as a necessary part of the procedure or as a confirmatory examination, the pelvic examination is not separately reported. A diagnostic pelvic examination may be performed for the purposes of deciding to perform a procedure; however, this examination is included in the evaluation and management service at the time the decision to perform the procedure is made.

All surgical laparoscopic, hysteroscopic or peritoneoscopic procedures include diagnostic procedures. Therefore, CPT code 49320 is included in 38120, 38570- 38572, 43280, 43651-43653, 44200- 44202, 44970, 47560-47570, 49321- 49323, 49650-49651, 54690-54692, 55550, 58545-58554, 58660-58673, 60650; and 58555 is included in 58558- 58563.

Lysis of adhesions (CPT code 58660) is not to be reported separately when done in conjunction with other surgical laparoscopic procedures.

Pelvic exam under anesthesia indicated by CPT code 57410, is included in all major and most minor gynecological procedures and is not to be reported separately. This procedure represents routine evaluation of the surgical field.

Dilation of vagina or cervix (CPT codes 57400 or 57800), when done in conjunction with vaginal approach procedures, is not to be reported separately unless the CPT code descriptor states "without cervical dilation." 6. Administration of anesthesia, when necessary, is included in every surgical procedure code, when performed by the surgeon.

Colposcopy (CPT codes 56820, 57420, 57452) should not be reported separately when performed as a "scout" procedure to confirm the lesion or to assess the surgical field prior to a surgical procedure. A diagnostic colposcopy resulting in the decision to perform a non-colposcopic procedure may be reported with modifier - 58. Diagnostic colposcopies (56820, 57420, 57452) are not separately reported with other colposcopic procedures.

(For pelvic laparotomy, use 49000)

(For excision or destruction of endometriomas, open method, see 49203-49205, 58957, 58958)

(For paracentesis, see 49082, 49083, 49084)

(For secondary closure of abdominal wall evisceration or disruption, use 49900)

(For fulguration or excision of lesions, laparoscopic approach, use 58662)

(For chemotherapy, see 96401-96549)

VULVA, PERINEUM AND INTROITUS

The following definitions apply to the vulvectomy codes (56620-56640):

A **simple** procedure is the removal of skin and superficial subcutaneous tissues.

A **radical** procedure is the removal of skin and deep subcutaneous tissues.

A **partial** procedure is the removal of less than 80% of the vulvar area.

A **complete** procedure is the removal of greater than 80% of the vulvar area.

INCISION

(For incision and drainage of sebaceous cyst, furuncle, or abscess, see 10040, 10060, 10061)

56405 Incision and drainage of vulva or perineal abscess

56420 Incision and drainage of Bartholin's gland abscess

(For incision and drainage of Skene's gland abscess or cyst, use 53060)

56440 Marsupialization of Bartholin's gland cyst

56441 Lysis of labial adhesions

56442   Hymenotomy, simple incision

DESTRUCTION

56501   Destruction of lesion(s), vulva; simple (eg, laser surgery, electrosurgery, cryosurgery, chemosurgery)

56515   extensive (eg, laser surgery, electrosurgery, cryosurgery, chemosurgery)

(For destruction of Skene's gland cyst or abscess, use 53270)

(For cautery destruction of urethral caruncle, use 53265)

EXCISION

56605   Biopsy of vulva or perineum (separate procedure); 1 lesion

+ 56606   each separate additional lesion (List separately in addition to code for primary procedure)

(Use 56606 in conjunction with code 56605)

(For excision of local lesion, see 11420-11426, 11620-11626)

56620   Vulvectomy simple; partial

56625   complete

(For skin graft, see 15002 et seq)

56630   Vulvectomy, radical, partial;

(For skin graft, if used, see 15004-15005, 15120, 15121, 15240, 15241)

56631   with unilateral inguinofemoral lymphadenectomy

56632   with bilateral inguinofemoral lymphadenectomy

56633   Vulvectomy, radical, complete;

56634   with unilateral inguinofemoral lymphadenectomy

56637   with bilateral inguinofemoral lymphadenectomy

56640   Vulvectomy, radical, complete, with inguinofemoral, iliac, and pelvic lymphadenectomy

(For bilateral procedure, report 56640 with modifier -50)

(For lymphadenectomy, see 38760-38780)

56700   Partial hymenectomy or revision of hymenal ring

56740   Excision of Bartholin's gland or cyst

(For excision of Skene's gland, use 53270)

(For excision of urethral caruncle, use 53265)

(For excision or fulguration of urethral carcinoma, use 53220)

(For excision or marsupialization of urethral diverticulum, see 53230, 53240)

REPAIR

(For repair of urethra for mucosal prolapse, use 53275)

56800   Plastic repair of introitus

● New Code   ▲ Revised Code   + Add-On Code   ⊘ Modifier -51 Exempt   ★ Telemedicine

56805 Clitoroplasty for intersex state

56810 Perineoplasty, repair of perineum, nonobstetrical (separate procedure)

(See also 56800)

(For repair of wounds to genitalia, see 12001-12007, 12041-12047, 13131-13133)

(For repair of recent injury of vagina and perineum, nonobstetrical, use 57210)

(For anal sphincteroplasty, see 46750, 46751)

(For episiorrhaphy, episioperineorrhaphy for recent injury of vulva and/or perineum, nonobstetrical, use 57210)

ENDOSCOPY

56820 Colposcopy of the vulva

56821 with biopsy(s)

(For colposcopic examinations/procedures involving the vagina, see 57420, 57421; cervix, see 57452-57461)

VAGINA

INCISION

57000 Colpotomy; with exploration

57010 with drainage of pelvic abscess

57020 Colpocentesis (separate procedure)

57022 Incision and drainage of vaginal hematoma; obstetrical/ postpartum

57023 non-obstetrical (eg, post-trauma, spontaneous bleeding)

DESTRUCTION

57061 Destruction of vaginal lesion(s); simple (eg, laser surgery, electrosurgery, cryosurgery, chemosurgery)

57065 extensive (eg, laser surgery, electrosurgery, cryosurgery, chemosurgery)

EXCISION

57100 Biopsy of vaginal mucosa; simple (separate procedure)

57105 extensive, requiring suture (including cysts)

57106 Vaginectomy, partial removal of vaginal wall;

57107 with removal of paravaginal tissue (radical vaginectomy)

57109 with removal of paravaginal tissue (radical vaginectomy) with bilateral total pelvic lymphadenectomy and para-aortic lymph node sampling (biopsy)

57110 Vaginectomy, complete removal of vaginal wall;

57111 with removal of paravaginal tissue (radical vaginectomy)

Separate Procedure   Unlisted Procedure   CCI Comp. Code   Non-specific Procedure

57112	with removal of paravaginal tissue (radical vaginectomy) with bilateral total pelvic lymphadenectomy and para-aortic lymph node sampling (biopsy)
57120	Colpocleisis (Le Fort type)
57130	Excision of vaginal septum
57135	Excision of vaginal cyst or tumor

INTRODUCTION

| 57150 | Irrigation of vagina and/or application of medicament for treatment of bacterial, parasitic, or fungoid disease |
| 57155 | Insertion of uterine tandem and/or vaginal ovoids for clinical brachytherapy |

(For placement of needles or catheters into pelvic organs and/or genitalia [except prostate] for interstitial radioelement application, use 55920)

(For insertion of radioelement sources or ribbons, see 77761-77763, 77770, 77771, 77772)

57156	Insertion of a vaginal radiation afterloading apparatus for clinical brachytherapy
57160	Fitting and insertion of pessary or other intravaginal support device
57170	Diaphragm or cervical cap fitting with instructions
57180	Introduction of any hemostatic agent or pack for spontaneous or traumatic nonobstetrical vaginal hemorrhage (separate procedure)

REPAIR

(For urethral suspension, Marshall-Marchetti-Krantz type, abdominal approach, see 51840, 51841)

(For laparoscopic suspension, use 51990)

57200	Colporrhaphy, suture of injury of vagina (nonobstetrical)
57210	Colpoperineorrhaphy, suture of injury of vagina and/or perineum (nonobstetrical)
57220	Plastic operation on urethral sphincter, vaginal approach (eg, Kelly urethral plication)
57230	Plastic repair of urethrocele
▲ 57240	Anterior colporrhaphy, repair of cystocele with or without repair of urethrocele, including cystourethroscopy, when performed

(Do not report 57240 in conjunction with 52000)

| 57250 | Posterior colporrhaphy, repair of rectocele with or without perineorrhaphy |

(For repair of rectocele (separate procedure) without posterior colporrhaphy, use 45560)

| ▲ 57260 | Combined anteroposterior colporrhaphy, including cystourethroscopy, when performed; |

(Do not report 57260 in conjunction with 52000)

| ▲ 57265 | with enterocele repair |

(Do not report 57265 in conjunction with 52000)

| + 57267 | Insertion of mesh or other prosthesis for repair of pelvic floor defect, each site (anterior, posterior compartment), vaginal approach (List separately in addition to code for primary procedure) |

● New Code   ▲ Revised Code   + Add-On Code   ⊘ Modifier -51 Exempt   ★ Telemedicine

(Use 57267 in addition to 45560, 57240-57265, 57285)

57268	Repair of enterocele, vaginal approach (separate procedure)
57270	Repair of enterocele, abdominal approach (separate procedure)
57280	Colpopexy, abdominal approach
57282	Colpopexy, vaginal; extra-peritoneal approach (sacrospinous, iliococcygeus)
57283	intra-peritoneal approach (uterosacral, levator myorrhaphy)

(Do not report 57283 in conjunction with 58263, 57556, 58270, 58280, 58292, 58294)

57284	Paravaginal defect repair (including repair of cystocele, if performed); open abdominal approach

(Do not report 57284 in conjunction with 51840, 51841, 51990, 57240, 57260, 57265, 58152, 58267)

57285	vaginal approach

(Do not report 57285 in conjunction with 51990, 57240, 57260, 57265, 58267)

57287	Removal or revision of sling for stress incontinence (eg, fascia or synthetic)
57288	Sling operation for stress incontinence (eg, fascia or synthetic)

(For laparoscopic approach, use 51992)

57289	Pereyra procedure, including anterior colporrhaphy
57291	Construction of artificial vagina; without graft
57292	with graft
57295	Revision (including removal) of prosthetic vaginal graft, vaginal approach
57296	open abdominal approach

(For laparoscopic approach, use 57426)

57300	Closure of rectovaginal fistula; vaginal or transanal approach
57305	abdominal approach
57307	abdominal approach, with concomitant colostomy
57308	transperineal approach, with perineal body reconstruction, with or without levator plication
57310	Closure of urethrovaginal fistula;
57311	with bulbocavernosus transplant
57320	Closure of vesicovaginal fistula; vaginal approach

(For concomitant cystostomy, see 51020-51040, 51101, 51102)

57330	transvesical and vaginal approach

(For abdominal approach, use 51900)

57335	Vaginoplasty for intersex state

Separate Procedure   Unlisted Procedure   CCI Comp. Code   Non-specific Procedure   **539**

MANIPULATION

57400 Dilation of vagina under anesthesia (other than local)

57410 Pelvic examination under anesthesia (other than local)

57415 Removal of impacted vaginal foreign body (separate procedure) under anesthesia (other than local)

(For removal without anesthesia of an impacted vaginal foreign body, use the appropriate E/M code)

ENDOSCOPY/LAPAROSCOPY

57420 Colposcopy of the entire vagina, with cervix if present;

57421 with biopsy(s) of vagina/cervix

(For colposcopic visualization of cervix and adjacent upper vagina, use 57452)

(When reporting colposcopies of multiple sites, use modifier -51 as appropriate. For colposcopic examinations/procedures involving the vulva, see 56820, 56821; cervix, see 57452-57461)

(For endometrial sampling (biopsy) performed in conjunction with colposcopy, use 58110)

57423 Paravaginal defect repair (including repair of cystocele, if performed), laparoscopic approach

(Do not report 57423 in conjunction with 49320, 51840, 51841, 51990, 57240, 57260, 58152, 58267)

57425 Laparoscopy, surgical, colpopexy (suspension of vaginal apex)

57426 Revision (including removal) of prosthetic vaginal graft, laparoscopic approach

(For vaginal approach, see 57295. For open abdominal approach, see 57296)

CERVIX UTERI

(For cervicography, see Category III code 0003T)

ENDOSCOPY

(For colposcopic examinations/procedures involving the vulva, see 56820, 56821; vagina, see 57420, 57421)

57452 Colposcopy of the cervix including upper/adjacent vagina

(Do not report 57452 in addition to 57454-57461)

57454 with biopsy(s) of the cervix and endocervical curettage

57455 with biopsy(s) of the cervix

57456 with endocervical curettage

57460 with loop electrode biopsy(s) of the cervix

57461 with loop electrode conization of the cervix

(Do not report 57456 in addition to 57461)

(For endometrial sampling (biopsy) performed in conjunction with colposcopy, use 58110)

EXCISION

(For radical surgical procedures, see 58200-58240)

● New Code ▲ Revised Code + Add-On Code ⊘ Modifier -51 Exempt ★ Telemedicine

57500   Biopsy of cervix, single or multiple, or local excision of lesion, with or without fulguration (separate procedure)

57505   Endocervical curettage (not done as part of a dilation and curettage)

57510   Cautery of cervix; electro or thermal

57511   cryocautery, initial or repeat

57513   laser ablation

57520   Conization of cervix, with or without fulguration, with or without dilation and curettage, with or without repair; cold knife or laser

(See also 58120)

57522   loop electrode excision

57530   Trachelectomy (cervicectomy), amputation of cervix (separate procedure)

57531   Radical trachelectomy, with bilateral total pelvic lymphadenectomy and para-aortic lymph node sampling biopsy, with or without removal of tube(s), with or without removal of ovary(s)

(For radical abdominal hysterectomy, use 58210)

57540   Excision of cervical stump, abdominal approach;

57545   with pelvic floor repair

57550   Excision of cervical stump, vaginal approach;

57555   with anterior and/or posterior repair

57556   with repair of enterocele

(For insertion of intrauterine device, use 58300)

(For insertion of any hemostatic agent or pack for control of spontaneous non-obstetrical hemorrhage, see 57180)

57558   Dilation and curettage of cervical stump

REPAIR

57700   Cerclage of uterine cervix, nonobstetrical

57720   Trachelorrhaphy, plastic repair of uterine cervix, vaginal approach

MANIPULATION

57800   Dilation of cervical canal, instrumental (separate procedure)

CORPUS UTERI

EXCISION

58100   Endometrial sampling (biopsy) with or without endocervical sampling (biopsy), without cervical dilation, any method (separate procedure)

(For endocervical curettage only, use 57505)

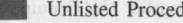

(For endometrial sampling (biopsy) performed in conjunction with colposcopy (57420, 57421, 57452-57461), use 58110)

+ 58110   Endometrial sampling (biopsy) performed in conjunction with colposcopy (List separately in addition to code for primary procedure)

(Use 58110 in conjunction with 57420, 57421, 57452-57461)

58120   Dilation and curettage, diagnostic and/or therapeutic (nonobstetrical)

(For postpartum hemorrhage, use 59160)

58140   Myomectomy, excision of fibroid tumor(s) of uterus, 1 to 4 intramural myoma(s) with total weight of 250 grams or less and/or removal of surface myomas; abdominal approach

58145   vaginal approach

58146   Myomectomy, excision of fibroid tumor(s) of uterus, 5 or more intramural myomas and/or intramural myomas with total weight greater than 250 grams, abdominal approach

(Do not report 58146 in addition to 58140-58145, 58150-58240)

Hysterectomy Procedures

58150   Total abdominal hysterectomy (corpus and cervix), with or without removal of tube(s), with or without removal of ovary(s);

58152   with colpo-urethrocystopexy (eg, Marshall-Marchetti-Krantz, Burch)

(For urethrocystopexy without hysterectomy, see 51840, 51841)

58180   Supracervical abdominal hysterectomy (subtotal hysterectomy), with or without removal of tube(s), with or without removal of ovary(s)

58200   Total abdominal hysterectomy, including partial vaginectomy, with para-aortic and pelvic lymph node sampling, with or without removal of tube(s), with or without removal of ovary(s)

58210   Radical abdominal hysterectomy, with bilateral total pelvic lymphadenectomy and para-aortic lymph node sampling (biopsy), with or without removal of tube(s), with or without removal of ovary(s)

(For radical hysterectomy with ovarian transposition, use also 58825)

58240   Pelvic exenteration for gynecologic malignancy, with total abdominal hysterectomy or cervicectomy, with or without removal of tube(s), with or without removal of ovary(s), with removal of bladder and ureteral transplantations, and/or abdominoperineal resection of rectum and colon and colostomy, or any combination thereof

(For pelvic exenteration for lower urinary tract or male genital malignancy, use 51597)

58260   Vaginal hysterectomy, for uterus 250 grams or less;

58262   with removal of tube(s), and/or ovary(s)

58263   with removal of tube(s), and/or ovary(s), with repair of enterocele

58267   with colpo-urethrocystopexy (Marshall-Marchetti-Krantz type, Pereyra type) with or without endoscopic control

58270   with repair of enterocele

(For repair of enterocele with removal of tubes and/or ovaries, use 58263)

58275   Vaginal hysterectomy, with total or partial vaginectomy;

58280   with repair of enterocele

58285 Vaginal hysterectomy, radical (Schauta type operation)

58290 Vaginal hysterectomy, for uterus greater than 250 grams;

58291   with removal of tube(s) and/or ovary(s)

58292   with removal of tube(s) and/or ovary(s), with repair of enterocele

58293   with colpo-urethrocystopexy (Marshall-Marchetti-Krantz type, Pereyra type) with or without endoscopic control

58294   with repair of enterocele

INTRODUCTION

(To report insertion of non-biodegradable drug delivery implant for contraception, use 11981. To report removal of implantable contraceptive capsules with subsequent insertion of non-biodegradable drug delivery implant, use 11976 and 11981)

58300 Insertion of intrauterine device (IUD)

58301 Removal of intrauterine device (IUD)

58321 Artificial insemination; intra-cervical

58322   intra-uterine

58323 Sperm washing for artificial insemination

58340 Catheterization and introduction of saline or contrast material for saline infusion sonohysterography (SIS) or hysterosalpingography

(For radiological supervision and interpretation of saline infusion sonohysterography, use 76831)

(For radiological supervision and interpretation of hysterosalpingography, use 74740)

58345 Transcervical introduction of fallopian tube catheter for diagnosis and/or re-establishing patency (any method), with or without hysterosalpingography

(For radiological supervision and interpretation, use 74742)

58346 Insertion of Heyman capsules for clinical brachytherapy

(For placement of needles or catheters into pelvic organs and/or genitalia [except prostate] for interstitial radioelement application, use 55920)

(For insertion of radioelement sources or ribbons, see 77761-77763, 77770, 77771, 77772)

58350 Chromotubation of oviduct, including materials

(To report the supply of any materials, use 99070)

58353 Endometrial ablation, thermal, without hysteroscopic guidance

(For hysteroscopic procedure, use 58563)

58356 Endometrial cryoablation with ultrasonic guidance, including endometrial curettage, when performed

(Do not report 58356 in conjunction with 58100, 58120, 58340, 76700, 76856)

REPAIR

58400 Uterine suspension, with or without shortening of round ligaments, with or without shortening of sacrouterine ligaments; (separate procedure)

58410 with presacral sympathectomy

(For anastomosis of tubes to uterus, use 58752)

58520 Hysterorrhaphy, repair of ruptured uterus (nonobstetrical)

58540 Hysteroplasty, repair of uterine anomaly (Strassman type)

(For closure of vesicouterine fistula, use 51920)

LAPAROSCOPY/HYSTEROSCOPY

Surgical laparoscopy always includes diagnostic laparoscopy. To report diagnostic laparoscopy (peritoneoscopy) (separate procedure), use 49320. To report a diagnostic hysteroscopy (separate procedure), use 58555.

58541 Laparoscopy, surgical, supracervical hysterectomy, for uterus 250 g or less;

58542 with removal of tube(s) and/or ovary(s)

(Do not report 58541-58542 in conjunction with 49320, 57000, 57180, 57410, 58140-58146, 58545, 58546, 58561, 58661, 58670, 58671)

58543 Laparoscopy, surgical, supracervical hysterectomy, for uterus greater than 250 g;

58544 with removal of tube(s) and/or ovary(s)

(Do not report 58543-58544 in conjunction with 49320, 57000, 57180, 57410, 58140-58146, 58545, 58546, 58561, 58661, 58670, 58671)

58545 Laparoscopy, surgical, myomectomy, excision; 1 to 4 intramural myomas with total weight of 250 g or less and/or removal of surface myomas

58546 5 or more intramural myomas and/or intramural myomas with total weight greater than 250 g

58548 Laparoscopy, surgical, with radical hysterectomy, with bilateral total pelvic lymphadenectomy and para-aortic lymph node sampling (biopsy), with removal of tube(s) and ovary(s), if performed

(Do not report 58548 in conjunction with 38570-38572, 58210 58285, 58550-58554)

58550 Laparoscopy, surgical with vaginal hysterectomy, for uterus 250 grams or less;

58552 with removal of tube(s) and/or ovary(s)

(Do not report 58550-58552 in conjunction with 49320, 57000, 57180, 57410, 58140-58146, 58545, 58546, 58561, 58661, 58670, 58671)

58553 Laparoscopy, surgical, with vaginal hysterectomy, for uterus greater than 250 grams;

58554 with removal of tube(s) and/or ovary(s)

(Do not report 58553-58554 in conjunction with 49320, 57000, 57180, 57410, 58140-58146, 58545, 58546, 58561, 58661, 58670, 58671)

58555 Hysteroscopy, diagnostic (separate procedure)

58558 Hysteroscopy, surgical; with sampling (biopsy) of endometrium and/or polypectomy, with or without D & C

● New Code   ▲ Revised Code   + Add-On Code   ⊘ Modifier -51 Exempt   ★ Telemedicine

58559	with lysis of intrauterine adhesions (any method)

58560	with division or resection of intrauterine septum (any method)

58561	with removal of leiomyomata

58562	with removal of impacted foreign body

58563	with endometrial ablation (eg, endometrial resection, electrosurgical ablation, thermoablation)

58565	with bilateral fallopian tube cannulation to induce occlusion by placement of permanent implants

(Do not report 58565 in conjunction with 58555 or 57800)

(For unilateral procedure, use modifier -52)

58570	Laparoscopy, surgical, with total hysterectomy, for uterus 250g or less;

58571	with removal of tube(s) and/or ovary(s)

58572	Laparoscopy, surgical, with total hysterectomy, for uterus greater than 250g;

58573	with removal of tube(s) and/or ovary(s)

(Do not report 58570-58573 in conjunction with 49320, 57000, 57180, 57410, 58140-58146, 58150, 58545, 58546, 58561, 58661, 58670, 58671)

● **58575** Laparoscopy, surgical, total hysterectomy for resection of malignancy (tumor debulking), with omentectomy including salpingo-oophorectomy, unilateral or bilateral, when performed

(Do not report 58575 in conjunction with 49255, 49320, 49321, 58570, 58571, 58572, 58573, 58661)

58578	Unlisted laparoscopy procedure, uterus

58579	Unlisted hysteroscopy procedure, uterus

OVIDUCT/OVARY

INCISION

58600	Ligation or transection of fallopian tube(s), abdominal or vaginal approach, unilateral or bilateral

58605	Ligation or transection of fallopian tube(s), abdominal or vaginal approach, postpartum, unilateral or bilateral, during same hospitalization (separate procedure)

(For laparoscopic procedures, use 58670, 58671)

+ **58611** Ligation or transection of fallopian tube(s) when done at the time of cesarean delivery or intra-abdominal surgery (not a separate procedure) (List separately in addition to code for primary procedure)

58615	Occlusion of fallopian tube(s) by device (eg, band, clip, Falope ring) vaginal or suprapubic approach

(For laparoscopic approach, use 58671)

(For lysis of adnexal adhesions, use 58740)

LAPAROSCOPY

Surgical laparoscopy always includes diagnostic laparoscopy. To report diagnostic laparoscopy (peritoneoscopy) (separate procedure), use 49320.

58660	Laparoscopy, surgical; with lysis of adhesions (salpingolysis, ovariolysis) (separate procedure)

	Separate Procedure		Unlisted Procedure		CCI Comp. Code		Non-specific Procedure	**545**

58661	with removal of adnexal structures (partial or total oophorectomy and/or salpingectomy)
58662	with fulguration or excision of lesions of the ovary, pelvic viscera, or peritoneal surface by any method
58670	with fulguration of oviducts (with or without transection)
58671	with occlusion of oviducts by device (eg, band, clip, or Falope ring)
58672	with fimbrioplasty
58673	with salpingostomy (salpingoneostomy)

(Codes 58672 and 58673 are used to report unilateral procedures. For bilateral procedure, use modifier -50)

58674	Laparoscopy, surgical, ablation of uterine fibroid(s) including intraoperative ultrasound guidance and monitoring, radiofrequency

(Do not report 58674 in conjunction with 49320, 58541- 58554, 58570, 58571, 58572, 58573, 76998)

58679	Unlisted laparoscopy procedure, oviduct, ovary

(For laparoscopic aspiration of ovarian cyst, use 49322)

(For laparoscopic biopsy of the ovary or fallopian tube, use 49321)

EXCISION

58700	Salpingectomy, complete or partial, unilateral or bilateral (separate procedure)
58720	Salpingo-oophorectomy, complete or partial, unilateral or bilateral (separate procedure)

REPAIR

58740	Lysis of adhesions (salpingolysis, ovariolysis)

(For laparoscopic approach, use 58660)

(For excision or destruction of endometriomas, open method, see 49203-49205, 58957, 58958)

(For fulguration or excision of lesions, laparscopic approach, use 58662)

58750	Tubotubal anastomosis
58752	Tubouterine implantation
58760	Fimbrioplasty

(For laparoscopic approach, use 58672)

58770	Salpingostomy (salpingoneostomy)

(For laparscopic approach, use 58673)

OVARY

INCISION

58800	Drainage of ovarian cyst(s), unilateral or bilateral, (separate procedure); vaginal approach
58805	abdominal approach

● New Code   ▲ Revised Code   + Add-On Code   ⊘ Modifier -51 Exempt   ★ Telemedicine

58820 Drainage of ovarian abscess; vaginal approach, open

58822   abdominal approach

(For transrectal image-guided fluid collection drainage by catheter of pelvic abscess, use 49407)

58825 Transposition, ovary(s)

EXCISION

58900 Biopsy of ovary, unilateral or bilateral (separate procedure)

(For laparoscopic biopsy of the ovary or fallopian tube, use 49321)

58920 Wedge resection or bisection of ovary, unilateral or bilateral

58925 Ovarian cystectomy, unilateral or bilateral

58940 Oophorectomy, partial or total, unilateral or bilateral;

(For oophorectomy with concomitant debulking for ovarian malignancy, use 58952)

58943   for ovarian, tubal or primary peritoneal malignancy, with para-aortic and pelvic lymph node biopsies, peritoneal washings, peritoneal biopsies, diaphragmatic assessments, with or without salpingectomy(s), with or without omentectomy

58950 Resection (initial) of ovarian, tubal or primary peritoneal malignancy with bilateral salpingo-oophorectomy and omentectomy;

58951   with total abdominal hysterectomy, pelvic and limited para-aortic lymphadenectomy

58952   with radical dissection for debulking (ie, radical excision or destruction, intra-abdominal or retroperitoneal tumors)

(For resection of recurrent ovarian, tubal, primary peritoneal, or uterine malignancy, see 58957, 58958)

58953 Bilateral salpingo-oophorectomy with omentectomy, total abdominal hysterectomy and radical dissection for debulking;

58954   with pelvic lymphadenectomy and limited para-aortic lymphadenectomy

58956 Bilateral salpingo-oophorectomy with total omentectomy, total abdominal hysterectomy for malignancy

(Do not report 58956 in conjunction with 49255, 58150, 58180, 58262, 58263, 58550, 58661, 58700, 58720, 58900, 58925, 58940, 58957, 58958)

58957 Resection (tumor debulking) of recurrent ovarian, tubal, primary peritoneal, uterine malignancy (intra-abdominal, retroperitoneal tumors), with omentectomy, if performed;

58958   with pelvic lymphadenectomy and limited para-aortic lymphadenectomy

(Do not report 58957, 58958 in conjunction with 38770, 38780, 44005, 49000, 49203-49215, 49255, 58900-58960)

58960 Laparotomy, for staging or restaging of ovarian, tubal or primary peritoneal malignancy (second look), with or without omentectomy, peritoneal washing, biopsy of abdominal and pelvic peritoneum, diaphragmatic assessment with pelvic and limited para-aortic lymphadenectomy

(Do not report 58960 in conjunction with 58957, 58958)

IN VITRO FERTILIZATION

58970 Follicle puncture for oocyte retrieval, any method

      Separate Procedure   Unlisted Procedure   CCI Comp. Code   Non-specific Procedure   **547**

(For radiological supervision and interpretation, use 76948)

58974 Embryo transfer, intrauterine

58976 Gamete, zygote, or embryo intrafallopian transfer, any method

(For laparoscopic adnexal procedures, see 58660-58673)

OTHER PROCEDURES

58999 Unlisted procedure, female genital system (nonobstetrical)

MATERNITY CARE AND DELIVERY

The services normally provided in uncomplicated maternity cases include antepartum care, delivery, and postpartum care. Pregnancy confirmation during a problem oriented or preventive visit is not considered a part of antepartum care and should be reported using the appropriate E/M service code for that visit.

ANTEPARTUM CARE

Antepartum care includes the initial prenatal history and physical examination; subsequent prenatal history and physical examination; recording of weight, blood pressures, fetal heart tones, routine chemical urinalysis, and routine visits:

- Monthly visits up to 28 weeks gestation

- Biweekly visits up to 36 weeks gestation, and

- Weekly visits until delivery

Any other visits or services within this time period should be coded separately.

DELIVERY

Delivery services include admission to the hospital, the admission history and physical examination, management of uncomplicated labor, vaginal delivery (with or without episiotomy, with or without forceps), or cesarean delivery. When reporting delivery only services (59409, 59514, 59612, 59620) report inpatient post delivery management and discharge services using Evaluation and Management Services codes (99217-99239). Delivery and postpartum services (59410, 59515, 59614, 59622) include delivery services and all inpatient and outpatient postpartum services. Medical complications of pregnancy (eg, cardiac problems, neurological problems, diabetes, hypertension, toxemia, hpyeremesis, preterm labor, premature rupture of membraines, trauma) and medical problems complicating labor and delivery management may require additional resources and may be reported separately.

POSTPARTUM CARE

Postpartum care only services (59430) include office or other outpatient visits following vaginal or cesarean section delivery.

COMPLICATIONS OF PREGNANCY

The services defined previously are for normal, uncomplicated maternity care. For medical complications of pregnancy, for example, cardiac problems, neurological problems, diabetes, hypertension, toxemia, hyperemesis, pre-term labor and premature rupture of membranes, use evaluation and management service codes.

For surgical complications of pregnancy (eg., appendectomy, hernia, ovarian cyst, Bartholin cyst), see services in the Surgery section.

If all or part of the antepartum and/or postpartum patient care is provided except delivery due to termination of pregnancy by abortion or referral to another physician or other qualified health care professional for delivery, see the antepartum and postpartum care codes 59425, 59426 and 59430.

(For circumcision of newborn, see 54150, 54160)

ANTEPARTUM AND FETAL INVASIVE SERVICES

(For fetal intrauterine transfusion, use 36460)

(For unlisted fetal invasive procedure, use 59897)

59000 Amniocentesis, diagnostic

(For radiological supervision and interpretation, use 76946)

59001 therapeutic amniotic fluid reduction (includes ultrasound guidance)

59012 Cordocentesis (intrauterine), any method

(For radiological supervision and interpretation, use 76941)

■ Separate Procedure	■ Unlisted Procedure	■ CCI Comp. Code	■ Non-specific Procedure

549

59015 Chorionic villus sampling, any method

(For radiological supervision and interpretation, use 76945)

59020 Fetal contraction stress test

59025 Fetal non-stress test

59030 Fetal scalp blood sampling

(For repeat fetal scalp blood sampling, use 59030 and see modifiers -76 and -77)

59050 Fetal monitoring during labor by consulting physician (ie, non-attending physician) with written report; supervision and interpretation

59051 interpretation only

59070 Transabdominal amnioinfusion, including ultrasound guidance

59072 Fetal umbilical cord occlusion, including ultrasound guidance

59074 Fetal fluid drainage (eg, vesicocentesis, thoracocentesis, paracentesis), including ultrasound guidance

59076 Fetal shunt placement, including ultrasound guidance

EXCISION

59100 Hysterotomy, abdominal (eg, for hydatidiform mole, abortion)

(When tubal ligation is performed at the same time as hysterotomy, use 58611 in addition to 59100)

59120 Surgical treatment of ectopic pregnancy; tubal or ovarian, requiring salpingectomy and/or oophorectomy, abdominal or vaginal approach

59121 tubal or ovarian, without salpingectomy and/or oophorectomy

59130 abdominal pregnancy

59135 interstitial, uterine pregnancy requiring total hysterectomy

59136 interstitial, uterine pregnancy with partial resection of uterus

59140 cervical, with evacuation

59150 Laparoscopic treatment of ectopic pregnancy; without salpingectomy and/or oophorectomy

59151 with salpingectomy and/or oophorectomy

59160 Curettage, postpartum

INTRODUCTION

(For intrauterine fetal transfusion, use 36460)

(For introduction of hypertonic solution and/or prostaglandins to initiate labor, see 59850-59857)

59200 Insertion of cervical dilator (eg, laminaria, prostaglandin) (separate procedure)

● New Code   ▲ Revised Code   + Add-On Code   ⊘ Modifier -51 Exempt   ★ Telemedicine

REPAIR

(For tracheoplasty, use 57700)

59300 Episiotomy or vaginal repair, by other than attending

59320 Cerclage of cervix, during pregnancy; vaginal

59325 abdominal

59350 Hysterorrhaphy of ruptured uterus

VAGINAL DELIVERY, ANTEPARTUM AND POSTPARTUM CARE

59400 Routine obstetric care including antepartum care, vaginal delivery (with or without episiotomy, and/or forceps) and postpartum care

59409 Vaginal delivery only (with or without episiotomy and/or forceps);

59410 including postpartum care

59412 External cephalic version, with or without tocolysis

(Use 59412 in addition to code(s) for delivery)

59414 Delivery of placenta (separate procedure)

(For antepartum care only, see 59425, 59426 or appropriate E/M code(s))

(For 1-3 antepartum care visits, see appropriate E/M code(s))

59425 Antepartum care only; 4-6 visits

59426 7 or more visits

59430 Postpartum care only (separate procedure)

CESAREAN DELIVERY

(For standby attendance for infant, use 99360)

(For low cervical cesarean section, see 59510, 59515, 59525)

59510 Routine obstetric care including antepartum care, cesarean delivery, and postpartum care

59514 Cesarean delivery only;

59515 including postpartum care

(For classic cesarean section, see 59510, 59515, 59525)

+ **59525** Subtotal or total hysterectomy after cesarean delivery (List separately in addition to code for primary procedure)

(Use 59525 in conjunction with codes 59510, 59514, 59515, 59618, 59620, 59622)

(For extraperitoneal cesarean section, or cesarean section with subtotal or total hysterectomy, see 59510, 59515, 59525)

DELIVERY AFTER PREVIOUS CESAREAN DELIVERY

Patients who have had a previous cesarean delivery and now present with the expectation of a vaginal delivery are coded using codes 59610-59622. If the patient has a successful vaginal delivery after a previous cesarean delivery (VBAC), use codes

| Separate Procedure | Unlisted Procedure | CCI Comp. Code | Non-specific Procedure | **551** |

59610-59614. If the attempt is unsuccessful and another cesarean delivery is carried out, use codes 59618-59622. To report elective cesarean deliveries use code 59510, 59514 or 59515.

59610 Routine obstetric care including antepartum care, vaginal delivery (with or without episiotomy, and/or forceps) and postpartum care, after previous cesarean delivery

59612 Vaginal delivery only, after previous cesarean delivery (with or without episiotomy and/or forceps);

59614 including postpartum care

59618 Routine obstetric care including antepartum care, cesarean delivery, and postpartum care, following attempted vaginal delivery after previous cesarean delivery

59620 Cesarean delivery only, following attempted vaginal delivery after previous cesarean delivery;

59622 including postpartum care

ABORTION

(For medical treatment of spontaneous complete abortion, any trimester, use E/M codes 99201-99233)

(For surgical treatment of spontaneous abortion, use 59812)

59812 Treatment of incomplete abortion, any trimester, completed surgically

59820 Treatment of missed abortion, completed surgically; first trimester

59821 second trimester

59830 Treatment of septic abortion, completed surgically

59840 Induced abortion, by dilation and curettage

59841 Induced abortion, by dilation and evacuation

59850 Induced abortion, by 1 or more intra-amniotic injections (amniocentesis-injections), including hospital admission and visits, delivery of fetus and secundines;

59851 with dilation and curettage and/or evacuation

59852 with hysterotomy (failed intra-amniotic injection)

(For insertion of cervical dilator, use 59200)

59855 Induced abortion, by 1 or more vaginal suppositories (eg, prostaglandin) with or without cervical dilation (eg, laminaria), including hospital admission and visits, delivery of fetus and secundines;

59856 with dilation and curettage and/or evacuation

59857 with hysterotomy (failed medical evacuation)

OTHER PROCEDURES

59866 Multifetal pregnancy reduction(s) (MPR)

59870 Uterine evacuation and curettage for hydatidiform mole

59871 Removal of cerclage suture under anesthesia (other than local)

59897 Unlisted fetal invasive procedure, including ultrasound guidance, when performed

---

● New Code   ▲ Revised Code   + Add-On Code   ⊘ Modifier -51 Exempt   ★ Telemedicine

59898 Unlisted laparoscopy procedure, maternity care and delivery

59899 Unlisted procedure, maternity care and delivery

This page intentionally left blank.

● New Code   ▲ Revised Code   ✚ Add-On Code   ⊘ Modifier -51 Exempt   ★ Telemedicine

ENDOCRINE SYSTEM

(For pituitary and pineal surgery, see Nervous System)

THYROID GLAND

INCISION

60000 Incision and drainage of thyroglossal duct cyst, infected

EXCISION

60100 Biopsy thyroid, percutaneous core needle

(If imaging guidance is performed, see 76942, 77002, 77012, 77021)

(For fine needle aspiration, use 10021 or 10022)

(For evaluation of fine needle aspirate, see 88172, 88173)

60200 Excision of cyst or adenoma of thyroid, or transection of isthmus

60210 Partial thyroid lobectomy, unilateral; with or without isthmusectomy

60212   with contralateral subtotal lobectomy, including isthmusectomy

60220 Total thyroid lobectomy, unilateral; with or without isthmusectomy

60225   with contralateral subtotal lobectomy, including isthmusectomy

60240 Thyroidectomy, total or complete

(For thyroidectomy, subtotal or partial, use 60271)

60252 Thyroidectomy, total or subtotal for malignancy; with limited neck dissection

60254   with radical neck dissection

60260 Thyroidectomy, removal of all remaining thyroid tissue following previous removal of a portion of thyroid

(For bilateral procedure, report 60260 with modifier -50)

60270 Thyroidectomy, including substernal thyroid; sternal split or transthoracic approach

60271   cervical approach

60280 Excision of thyroglossal duct cyst or sinus;

60281   recurrent

(For thyroid ultrasonography, use 76536)

REMOVAL

60300 Aspiration and/or injection, thyroid cyst

(For fine needle aspiration, see 10021, 10022)

(If imaging guidance is performed, see 76942, 77012)

PARATHYROID, THYMUS, ADRENAL GLANDS, PANCREAS, AND CAROTID BODY

EXCISION

(For pituitary and pineal surgery, see Nervous System)

60500   Parathyroidectomy or exploration of parathyroid(s);

60502   re-exploration

60505   with mediastinal exploration, sternal split or transthoracic approach

+ 60512   Parathyroid autotransplantation (List separately in addition to code for primary procedure)

(Use 60512 in conjunction with codes 60500, 60502, 60505, 60212, 60225, 60240, 60252, 60254, 60260, 60270, 60271)

60520   Thymectomy, partial or total; transcervical approach (separate procedure)

60521   sternal split or transthoracic approach, without radical mediastinal dissection (separate procedure)

60522   sternal split or transthoracic approach, with radical mediastinal dissection (separate procedure)

(For thoracoscopic [VATS] thymectomy, see 32673)

60540   Adrenalectomy, partial or complete, or exploration of adrenal gland with or without biopsy, transabdominal, lumbar or dorsal (separate procedure);

60545   with excision of adjacent retroperitoneal tumor

(Do not report 60540, 60545 in conjunction with 50323)

(For bilateral procedure, report 60540 with modifier 50)

(For excision of remote or disseminated pheochromocytoma, see 49203-49205)

(For laparoscopic approach, use 56321)

60600   Excision of carotid body tumor; without excision of carotid artery

60605   with excision of carotid artery

LAPAROSCOPY

Surgical laparoscopy always includes diagnostic laparoscopy. To report a diagnostic laparoscopy (peritoneoscopy) (separate procedure), use 49320.

60650   Laparoscopy, surgical, with adrenalectomy, partial or complete, or exploration of adrenal gland with or without biopsy, transabdominal, lumbar or dorsal

60659   Unlisted laparoscopy procedure, endocrine system

OTHER PROCEDURES

60699   Unlisted procedure, endocrine system

   ● New Code   ▲ Revised Code   + Add-On Code   ⊘ Modifier -51 Exempt   ★ Telemedicine

NERVOUS SYSTEM

There are numerous codes for spinal injections found in this section. Review documentation for whether the injection is a single one, differential one or continuous. Also determine the number of levels involved when a regional block is administered.

SKULL, MENINGES, AND BRAIN

(For injection procedure for cerebral angiography, see 36100-36218)

(For injection procedure for ventriculography, see 61026, 61120, 61130)

(For injection procedure for pneumoencephalography, use 61055)

INJECTION, DRAINAGE OR ASPIRATION

61000 Subdural tap through fontanelle, or suture, infant, unilateral or bilateral; initial

61001 subsequent taps

61020 Ventricular puncture through previous burr hole, fontanelle, suture, or implanted ventricular catheter/reservoir; without injection

61026 with injection of medication or other substance for diagnosis or treatment

61050 Cisternal or lateral cervical (C1-C2) puncture; without injection (separate procedure)

61055 with injection of medication or other substance for diagnosis or treatment

(Do not report 61055 in conjunction with 62302, 62303, 62304, 62305)

(For radiological supervision and interpretation by a different physician or qualified health care professional, see Radiology)

61070 Puncture of shunt tubing or reservoir for aspiration or injection procedure

(For radiological supervision and interpretation, use 75809)

TWIST DRILL, BURR HOLE(S), OR TREPHINE

61105 Twist drill hole(s) for subdural or ventricular puncture;

⊘ **61107** Twist drill hole(s) for subdural, intracerebral or ventricular puncture; for implanting ventricular catheter, pressure recording device, or other intracerebral monitoring device

(For intracranial neuroendoscopic ventricular catheter placement, use 62160)

61108 for evacuation and/or drainage of subdural hematoma

61120 Burr hole(s) for ventricular puncture (including injection of gas, contrast media, dye, or radioactive material)

61140 Burr hole(s) or trephine; with biopsy of brain or intracranial lesion

61150 with drainage of brain abscess or cyst

61151 with subsequent tapping (aspiration) of intracranial abscess or cyst

61154 Burr hole(s) with evacuation and/or drainage of hematoma, extradural or subdural

(For bilateral procedure, report 61154 with modifier -50)

61156 Burr hole(s); with aspiration of hematoma or cyst, intracerebral

---

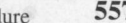

■ Separate Procedure   ■ Unlisted Procedure   ■ CCI Comp. Code   ■ Non-specific Procedure   **557**

61210   for implanting ventricular catheter, reservoir, EEG electrode(s), pressure recording device, or other cerebral monitoring device (separate procedure)

(For intracranial neuroendoscopic ventricular catheter placement, use 62160)

61215   Insertion of subcutaneous reservoir, pump or continuous infusion system for connection to ventricular catheter

(For refilling and maintenance of an implantable infusion pump for spinal or brain drug therapy, use 95990)

(For chemotherapy, use 96450)

61250   Burr hole(s) or trephine, supratentorial, exploratory, not followed by other surgery

(For bilateral procedure, report 61250 with modifier -50)

61253   Burr hole(s) or trephine, infratentorial, unilateral or bilateral

(If burr hole(s) or trephine are followed by craniotomy at same operative session, use 61304-61321; do not use 61250 or 61253)

CRANIECTOMY OR CRANIOTOMY

61304   Craniectomy or craniotomy, exploratory; supratentorial

61305   infratentorial (posterior fossa)

61312   Craniectomy or craniotomy for evacuation of hematoma, supratentorial; extradural or subdural

61313   intracerebral

61314   Craniectomy or craniotomy for evacuation of hematoma, infratentorial; extradural or subdural

61315   intracerebellar

+ **61316**   Incision and subcutaneous placement of cranial bone graft (List separately in addition to code for primary procedure)

(Use 61316 in conjunction with codes 61304, 61312, 61313, 61322, 61323, 61340, 61570, 61571, 61680-61705)

61320   Craniectomy or craniotomy, drainage of intracranial abscess; supratentorial

61321   infratentorial

61322   Craniectomy or craniotomy, decompressive, with or without duraplasty, for treatment of intracranial hypertension, without evacuation of associated intraparenchymal hematoma; without lobectomy

(Do not report 61313 in addition to 61322)

(For subtemporal decompression, use 61340)

61323   with lobectomy

(Do not report 61313 in addition to 61323)

(For subtemporal decompression, use 61340)

61330   Decompression of orbit only, transcranial approach

(For bilateral procedure, report 61330 with modifier -50)

61332   Exploration of orbit (transcranial approach); with biopsy

● New Code   ▲ Revised Code   + Add-On Code   ⊘ Modifier -51 Exempt   ★ Telemedicine

61333   with removal of lesion

(**61334**   deleted 2014 [2015 edition].)

61340   Subtemporal cranial decompression (pseudotumor cerebri, slit ventricle syndrome)

(For bilateral procedure, report 61340 with modifier -50)

(For decompressive craniotomy or craniectomy for intracranial hypertension, without hematoma evacuation, see 61322, 61323)

61343   Craniectomy, suboccipital with cervical laminectomy for decompression of medulla and spinal cord, with or without dural graft (eg, Arnold-Chiari malformation)

61345   Other cranial decompression, posterior fossa

(For orbital decompression by lateral wall approach, Kroenlein type, use 67445)

(**61440**   deleted 2014 [2015 edition].)

61450   Craniectomy, subtemporal, for section, compression, or decompression of sensory root of gasserian ganglion

61458   Craniectomy, suboccipital; for exploration or decompression of cranial nerves

61460   for section of 1 or more cranial nerves

(**61470**   deleted 2014 [2015 edition].)

61480   for mesencephalic tractotomy or pedunculotomy

(**61490**   deleted 2014 [2015 edition].)

61500   Craniectomy; with excision of tumor or other bone lesion of skull

61501   for osteomyelitis

61510   Craniectomy, trephination, bone flap craniotomy; for excision of brain tumor, supratentorial, except meningioma

61512   for excision of meningioma, supratentorial

61514   for excision of brain abscess, supratentorial

61516   for excision or fenestration of cyst, supratentorial

(For excision of pituitary tumor or craniopharyngioma, see 61545, 61546, 61548)

+ **61517**   Implantation of brain intracavitary chemotherapy agent (List separately in addition to code for primary procedure)

(Use 61517 only in conjunction with codes 61510 or 61518)

(Do not report 61517 for brachytherapy insertion. For intracavitary insertion of radioelement sources or ribbons, see 77770, 77771, 77772)

61518   Craniectomy for excision of brain tumor, infratentorial or posterior fossa; except meningioma, cerebellopontine angle tumor, or midline tumor at base of skull

61519   meningioma

61520   cerebellopontine angle tumor

61521 midline tumor at base of skull

61522 Craniectomy, infratentorial or posterior fossa; for excision of brain abscess

61524 for excision or fenestration of cyst

61526 Craniectomy, bone flap craniotomy, transtemporal (mastoid) for excision of cerebellopontine angle tumor;

61530 combined with middle/posterior fossa craniotomy/ craniectomy

61531 Subdural implantation of strip electrodes through 1 or more burr or trephine hole(s) for long term seizure monitoring

(For stereotactic implantation of electrodes, use 61760)

(For craniotomy for excision of intracranial arteriovenous malformation, see 61680-61692)

61533 Craniotomy with elevation of bone flap; for subdural implantation of an electrode array, for long term seizure monitoring

(For continuous EEG monitoring, see 95950-95954)

61534 for excision of epileptogenic focus without electrocorticography during surgery

61535 for removal of epidural or subdural electrode array, without excision of cerebral tissue (separate procedure)

61536 for excision of cerebral epileptogenic focus, with electrocorticography during surgery (includes removal of electrode array)

61537 for lobectomy, temporal lobe, without electrocorticography during surgery

61538 for lobectomy, temporal lobe, with electrocorticography during surgery

61539 for lobectomy, other than temporal lobe, partial or total, with electrocorticography during surgery

61540 for lobectomy, other than temporal lobe, partial or total, without electrocorticography during surgery

61541 for transection of corpus callosum

(**61542** deleted 2014 [2015 edition].)

61543 for partial or subtotal (functional) hemispherectomy

61544 for excision or coagulation of choroid plexus

61545 for excision of craniopharyngioma

(For craniotomy for selective amygdalohippocampectomy, use 61566)

(For craniotomy for multiple subpial transections during surgery, use 61567)

61546 Craniotomy for hypophysectomy or excision of pituitary tumor, intracranial approach

61548 Hypophysectomy or excision of pituitary tumor, transnasal or transseptal approach, nonstereotactic

(Do not report code 69990 in addition to code 61548)

61550 Craniectomy for craniosynostosis; single cranial suture

61552 multiple cranial sutures

● New Code ▲ Revised Code + Add-On Code ⊘ Modifier -51 Exempt ★ Telemedicine

(For cranial reconstruction for orbital hypertelorism, see 21260-21263)

(For reconstruction, see 21172-21180)

61556 Craniotomy for craniosynostosis; frontal or parietal bone flap

61557 bifrontal bone flap

61558 Extensive craniectomy for multiple cranial suture craniosynostosis (eg, cloverleaf skull); not requiring bone grafts

61559 recontouring with multiple osteotomies and bone autografts (eg, barrel-stave procedure) (includes obtaining grafts)

(For reconstruction, see 21172-21180)

61563 Excision, intra and extracranial, benign tumor of cranial bone (eg, fibrous dysplasia); without optic nerve decompression

61564 with optic nerve decompression

(For reconstruction, see 21181-21183)

61566 Craniotomy with elevation of bone flap; for selective amygdalohippocampectomy

61567 for multiple subpial transections, with electrocorticography during surgery

61570 Craniectomy or craniotomy; with excision of foreign body from brain

61571 with treatment of penetrating wound of brain

(For sequestrectomy for osteomyelitis, use 61501)

61575 Transoral approach to skull base, brain stem or upper spinal cord for biopsy, decompression or excision of lesion;

61576 requiring splitting of tongue and/or mandible (including tracheostomy)

(For arthrodesis, use 22548)

SURGERY OF SKULL BASE

The surgical management of lesions involving the skull base (base of anterior, middle, and posterior cranial fossae) often requires the skills of several surgeons of different surgical specialties working together or in tandem during the operative session. These operations are usually not staged because of the need for definitive closure of dura, subcutaneous tissues, and skin to avoid serious infections such as osteomyelitis and/or meningitis.

For primary closure, see the appropriate codes (ie, 15730, 15733, 15756, 15757, 15758).

When one surgeon performs the approach procedure, another surgeon performs the definitive procedure, and another surgeon performs the repair/reconstruction procedure, each surgeon reports only the code for the specific procedure performed.

If one surgeon performs more than one procedure (ie, approach procedure and definitive procedure), then both codes are reported, adding modifier -51 to the seondary, additional procedure(s).

APPROACH PROCEDURES

Anterior Cranial Fossa

61580 Craniofacial approach to anterior cranial fossa; extradural, including lateral rhinotomy, ethmoidectomy, sphenoidectomy, without maxillectomy or orbital exenteration

---

Separate Procedure   Unlisted Procedure   CCI Comp. Code   Non-specific Procedure   **561**

61581 extradural, including lateral rhinotomy, orbital exenteration, ethmoidectomy, sphenoidectomy and/or maxillectomy

61582 extradural, including unilateral or bifrontal craniotomy, elevation of frontal lobe(s), osteotomy of base of anterior cranial fossa

61583 intradural, including unilateral or bifrontal craniotomy, elevation or resection of frontal lobe, osteotomy of base of anterior cranial fossa

61584 Orbitocranial approach to anterior cranial fossa, extradural, including supraorbital ridge osteotomy and elevation of frontal and/or temporal lobe(s); without orbital exenteration

61585 with orbital exenteration

61586 Bicoronal, transzygomatic and/or LeFort I osteotomy approach to anterior cranial fossa with or without internal fixation, without bone graft

Middle Cranial Fossa

61590 Infratemporal pre-auricular approach to middle cranial fossa (parapharyngeal space, infratemporal and midline skull base, nasopharynx), with or without disarticulation of the mandible, including parotidectomy, craniotomy, decompression and/or mobilization of the facial nerve and/or petrous carotid artery

61591 Infratemporal post-auricular approach to middle cranial fossa (internal auditory meatus, petrous apex, tentorium, cavernous sinus, parasellar area, infratemporal fossa) including mastoidectomy, resection of sigmoid sinus, with or without decompression and/or mobilization of contents of auditory canal or petrous carotid artery

61592 Orbitocranial zygomatic approach to middle cranial fossa (cavernous sinus and carotid artery, clivus, basilar artery or petrous apex) including osteotomy of zygoma, craniotomy, extra- or intradural elevation of temporal lobe

Posterior Cranial Fossa

61595 Transtemporal approach to posterior cranial fossa, jugular foramen or midline skull base, including mastoidectomy, decompression of sigmoid sinus and/or facial nerve, with or without mobilization

61596 Transcochlear approach to posterior cranial fossa, jugular foramen or midline skull base, including labyrinthectomy, decompression, with or without mobilization of facial nerve and/or petrous carotid artery

61597 Transcondylar (far lateral) approach to posterior cranial fossa, jugular foramen or midline skull base, including occipital condylectomy, mastoidectomy, resection of C1-C3 vertebral body(s), decompression of vertebral artery, with or without mobilization

61598 Transpetrosal approach to posterior cranial fossa, clivus or foramen magnum, including ligation of superior petrosal sinus and/or sigmoid sinus

DEFINITIVE PROCEDURES

Base of Anterior Cranial Fossa

61600 Resection or excision of neoplastic, vascular or infectious lesion of base of anterior cranial fossa; extradural

61601 intradural, including dural repair, with or without graft

Base of Middle Cranial Fossa

61605 Resection or excision of neoplastic, vascular or infectious lesion of infratemporal fossa, parapharyngeal space, petrous apex; extradural

61606 intradural, including dural repair, with or without graft

---

● New Code ▲ Revised Code ＋ Add-On Code ⊘ Modifier -51 Exempt ★ Telemedicine

61607 Resection or excision of neoplastic, vascular or infectious lesion of parasellar area, cavernous sinus, clivus or midline skull base; extradural

61608 intradural, including dural repair, with or without graft

Codes 61610, 61611, 61612 are reported in addition to code(s) for primary procedure(s) 61605-61608. Report only one transection or ligation of carotid artery code per operative session.

+ **61610** Transection or ligation, carotid artery in cavernous sinus, with repair by anastomosis or graft (List separately in addition to code for primary procedure)

+ **61611** Transection or ligation, carotid artery in petrous canal; without repair (List separately in addition to code for primary procedure)

+ **61612** with repair by anastomosis or graft (List separately in addition to code for primary procedure)

61613 Obliteration of carotid aneurysm, arteriovenous malformation, or carotid-cavernous fistula by dissection within cavernous sinus

Base of Posterior Cranial Fossa

61615 Resection or excision of neoplastic, vascular or infectious lesion of base of posterior cranial fossa, jugular foramen, foramen magnum, or C1-C3 vertebral bodies; extradural

61616 intradural, including dural repair, with or without graft

REPAIR AND/OR RECONSTRUCTION OF SURGICAL DEFECTS OF SKULL BASE

61618 Secondary repair of dura for cerebrospinal fluid leak, anterior, middle or posterior cranial fossa following surgery of the skull base; by free tissue graft (eg, pericranium, fascia, tensor fascia lata, adipose tissue, homologous or synthetic grafts)

61619 by local or regionalized vascularized pedicle flap or myocutaneous flap (including galea, temporalis, frontalis or occipitalis muscle)

ENDOVASCULAR THERAPY

61623 Endovascular temporary balloon arterial occlusion, head or neck (extracranial/intracranial) including selective catheterization of vessel to be occluded, positioning and inflation of occlusion balloon, concomitant neurological monitoring, and radiologic supervision and interpretation of all angiography required for balloon occlusion and to exclude vascular injury post occlusion

(If selective catheterization and angiography of arteries other than artery to be occluded is performed, use appropriate catheterization and radiologic supervision and interpretation codes)

(If complete diagnostic angiography of the artery to be occluded is performed immediately prior to temporary occlusion, use appropriate radiologic supervision and interpretation codes only)

61624 Transcatheter permanent occlusion or embolization (eg, for tumor destruction, to achieve hemostasis, to occlude a vascular malformation), percutaneous, any method; central nervous system (intracranial, spinal cord)

(For non-central nervous system and non-head or neck embolization, see 37241-37244)

(For radiological supervision and interpretation, use 75894)

61626 non-central nervous system, head or neck (extracranial, brachiocephalic branch)

(For non-central nervous system and non-head or neck embolization, see 37241-37244)

(For radiological supervision and interpretation, use 75894)

61630 Balloon angioplasty, intracranial (eg, atherosclerotic stenosis), percutaneous

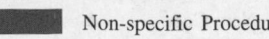

Separate Procedure   Unlisted Procedure   CCI Comp. Code   Non-specific Procedure   **563**

61635 Transcatheter placement of intravascular stent(s), intracranial (eg, atherosclerotic stenosis), including balloon angioplasty, if performed

(61630 and 61635 include all selective vascular catheterization of the target vascular family, all diagnostic imaging for arteriography of the target vascular family, and all related radiological supervision and interpretation. When diagnostic arteriogram (including imaging and selective catheterization) confirms the need for angioplasty or stent placement, 61630 and 61635 are inclusive of these services. If angioplasty or stenting are not indicated, then the appropriate codes for selective catheterization and imaging should be reported in lieu of 61630 and 61635)

(Do not report 61630 or 61635 in conjunction with 61645 for the same vascular territory)

(For definition of vascular territory, see the Nervous System Endovascular Therapy guidelines)

61640 Balloon dilatation of intracranial vasospasm, percutaneous; initial vessel

+ 61641 each additional vessel in same vascular family (List separately in addition to code for primary procedure)

+ 61642 each additional vessel in different vascular family (List separately in addition to code for primary procedure)

(Use 61641 and 61642 in conjunction with 61640)

(61640, 61641, 61642 include all selective vascular catheterization of the target vessel, contrast injection(s), vessel measurement, roadmapping, postdilatation angiography, and fluoroscopic guidance for the balloon dilatation)

(Do not report 61640, 61642 in conjunction with 61650 ir 61651 for the same vascular territory)

(For definition of vascular territory, see the Nervous System Endovascular Therapy guidelines)

Codes 61645, 61650, 61651 describe cerebral endovascular therapeutic interventions in any intracranial artery. They include selective catheterization, diagnostic angiographpy, and all subsequent angiography including associated radiological supervision and interpretation within the treated vascular territory, fluoroscopic guidance, neurologic and hemodynamic monitoring of the patient, and closure of the arteriotomy by manual pressure, an arterial closure device, or suture.

For purposes of reporting services described by 61645, 61650, 61651, the intracranial arteries are divided into three vascular territories: 1) right carotid circulation; 2) left carotid circulation; 3) vertebro basilar circulation. Code 61645 may be reported once for each intracranial vascular territory treated. Code 61650 is reported once for the first intracranial vascular territory treated with intra-arterial prolonged administration of pharmacologic agent(s). If additional intracranial vascular territory(ies) is also treated with intra-arterial prolonged administration of pharmacologic agent(s) during the same session, the treatment of each additional vascular territory(ies) is reported using 61651 (may be reported maximally two times per day).

Code 61645 describes endovascular revascularization of thrombotic/embolic occlusion of intracranial arterial vessel(s) via any method, including mechanical thrombectomy (eg, mechanical retrieval device, aspiration catheter) and/or the administration of any agent(s) for the purpose of revascularization, such as thrombolytics or IIB/IIIA inhibitors.

Code 61650, 61651 describe the cerebral endovascular continuous or intermittent therapeutic prolonged administration of any non-thrombolytic agent(s) (eg, spasmolytics or chemotherapy) into an artery to treat non-iatrogenic central nervous system diseases or sequelae thereof. These code should not be used to report administration of agents (eg, heparin, nitroglycerin, saline) usually administered during endovascular interventions. These codes are used for prolonged administrations, ie, of at least 10 minutes continuous or intermittent duration.

Do not report 61645, 61650, or 61651 in conjunction with 36221, 36226, 36228, 37184, or 37186 for the treated vascular territory. Do not report 61645 in conjunction with 61650 or 61651 for the same vascular distribution. Diagnostic angiography of a non-treated vascular territory may be reported separately. For example, angiography of the left carotid and/or the vertebral circulations may be reported if the intervention is performed in the right carotid circulation.

 61645 Percutaneous arterial transluminal mechanical thrombectomy and/or infusion for thrombolysis, intracranial, any method, including diagnostic angiography, fluoroscopic guidance, catheter placement, and intraprocedural pharmacological thrombolytic injection(s)

(Do not report 61645 in conjunction with, 37184, 61630, 61635, 61650, 61651 for the same vascular territory)

● New Code   ▲ Revised Code   + Add-On Code   ⊘ Modifier -51 Exempt   ★ Telemedicine

(To report venous mechanical thrombectomy and/or thrombolysis, see 37187, 37188, 37212, 37214)

61650 Endovascular intracranial prolonged administration of pharmacologic agent(s) other than for thrombolysis, arterial, including catheter placement, diagnostic angiography, and imaging guidance; initial vascular territory

+ 61651 each additional vascular territory (List separately in addition to code for primary procedure)

(Use 61651 in conjunction with 61650)

(Do not report 61650 or 61651 in conjunction with 36221, 36222, 36223, 36224, 36225, 36226, 61640, 61641, 61642, 61645 for the same vascular territory)

(Do not report 61650 or 61651 in conjunction with 96420, 96422, 96423, 96425 for the same vascular territory)

SURGERY FOR ANEURYSM, ARTERIOVENOUS MALFORMATION OR VASCULAR DISEASE

Includes craniotomy when appropriate for procedure.

61680 Surgery of intracranial arteriovenous malformation; supratentorial, simple

61682 supratentorial, complex

61684 infratentorial, simple

61686 infratentorial, complex

61690 dural, simple

61692 dural, complex

61697 Surgery of complex intracranial aneurysm, intracranial approach; carotid circulation

61698 vertebrobasilar circulation

(61697, 61698 involve aneurysms that are larger than 15 mm or with calcification of the aneurysm neck, or with incorporation of normal vessels into the aneurysm neck, or a procedure requiring temporary vessel occlusion, trapping or cardiopulmonary bypass to successfully treat the aneurysm)

61700 Surgery of simple intracranial aneurysm, intracranial approach; carotid circulation

61702 vertebrobasilar circulation

61703 Surgery of intracranial aneurysm, cervical approach by application of occluding clamp to cervical carotid artery (Selverstone-Crutchfield type)

(For cervical approach for direct ligation of carotid artery, see 37600-37606)

61705 Surgery of aneurysm, vascular malformation or carotid-cavernous fistula; by intracranial and cervical occlusion of carotid artery

61708 by intracranial electrothrombosis

(For ligation or gradual occlusion of internal/common carotid artery, see 37605, 37606)

61710 by intra-arterial embolization, injection procedure, or balloon catheter

61711 Anastomosis, arterial, extracranial-intracranial (eg, middle cerebral/cortical) arteries

(For carotid or vertebral thromboendarterectomy, use 35301)

(Use 69990 when the surgical microscope is employed for the microsurgical procedure. Do not use 69990 for visualization with magnifying loupes or corrected vision)

STEREOTAXIS

61720 Creation of lesion by stereotactic method, including burr hole(s) and localizing and recording techniques, single or multiple stages; globus pallidus or thalamus

61735 subcortical structure(s) other than globus pallidus or thalamus

61750 Stereotactic biopsy, aspiration, or excision, including burr hole(s), for intracranial lesion;

61751 with computed tomography and/or magnetic resonance guidance

(For radiological supervision and interpretation of computerized tomography, see 70450, 70460, or 70470 as appropriate)

(For radiological supervision and interpretation of magnetic resonance imaging, see 70551, 70552, or 70553 as appropriate)

61760 Stereotactic implantation of depth electrodes into the cerebrum for long term seizure monitoring

61770 Stereotactic localization, including burr hole(s), with insertion of catheter(s) or probe(s) for placement of radiation source

+ 61781 Stereotactic computer-assisted (navigational) procedure; cranial, intradural (list separately in addition to code for primary procedure)

(Do not report 61781 in conjunction with 61720-61791, 61796-61799, 61863-61868, 62201, 77371-77373, 77432)

+ 61782 cranial, extradural (list separately in addition to code for primary procedure)

(Do not report 61781, 61782 by the same individual during the same surgical session)

+ 61783 spinal (list separately in addition to code for primary procedure)

(Do not report 61783 in conjunction with 63620, 63621)

61790 Creation of lesion by stereotactic method, percutaneous, by neurolytic agent (eg, alcohol, thermal, electrical, radiofrequency); gasserian ganglion

61791 trigeminal medullary tract

STEREOTACTIC RADIOSURGERY (CRANIAL)

Cranial stereotactic radiosurgery is a distinct procedure that utilizes externally generated ionizing radiation to inactivate or eradicate defined target(s) in the head without the need to make an incision. The target is defined by and the treatment is delivered using high-resolution stereotactic imaging. Stereotactic radiosurgery codes and headframe application procedures are reported by the neurosurgeon. The radiation oncologist reports the appropriate code(s) for clinical treatment planning, physics and dosimetry, treatment delivery, and management from the Radiation Oncology section (77261-77790). Any necessary planning, dosimetry, targeting, positioning, or blocking by the neurosurgeon is included in the stereotactic radiation surgery services. The same individual should not report stereotactic radiosurgery services with radiation treatment management codes (77427-77435).

Do not report stereotactic radiosurgery more than once per lesion per course of treatment when the treatment requires more than one session.

Codes 61796 and 61797 involve stereotactic radiosurgery for simple cranial lesions. Simple cranial lesions are lesions less than 3.5 cm in maximum dimension that do not meet the definition of a complex lesion provided below. Report code 61796 when all lesions are simple.

Codes 61798 and 61799 involve stereotactic radiosurgery for complex cranial lesions and procedures that create therapeutic lesions (eg., thalamotomy or pallidotomy). All lesions 3.5 cm in maximum dimension or greater are complex. When performing

● New Code   ▲ Revised Code   + Add-On Code   ⊘ Modifier -51 Exempt   ★ Telemedicine

therapeutic lesion creation procedures, report code 61798 only once regardless of the number of lesions created. Schwannomas, arterio-venous malformations, pituitary tumors, glomus tumors, pineal region tumors and cavernous sinus/parasellar/petroclival tumors are complex. Any lesion that is adjacent (5 mm or less) to the optic nerve/optic chasm/optic tract or within the brainstem is complex. If treating multiple lesions, and any single lesion treated is complex, use 61798.

Do not report 61796-61800 in conjunction with code 20660.

Codes 61796-61799 include computer-assisted planning. Do not report codes 61796-61799 in conjunction with 61795.

> (For intensity modulated beam delivery plan and treatment, see 77301, 77385, 77386. For stereotactic body radiation therapy, see 77373, 77435)

61796 Stereotactic radiosurgery (particle beam, gamma ray, or linear accelerator); 1 simple cranial lesion

> (Do not report 61796 more than once per course of treatment)

> (Do not report 61796 in conjunction with 61798)

+ 61797 each additional cranial lesion, simple (list separately in addition to code for primary procedure)

> (Use 61797 in conjunction with 61796, 61798)

> (For each course of treatment, 61797 and 61799 may be reported no more than once per lesion. Do not report any combination of 61797 and 61799 more than 4 times for entire course of treatment regardless of number of lesions treated)

61798 1 complex cranial lesion

> (Do not report 61798 more than once per course of treatment)

> (Do not report 61798 in conjunction with 61796)

+ 61799 each additional cranial lesion, complex (list separately in addition to code for primary procedure)

> (Use 61799 in conjunction with 61798)

> (For each course of treatment, 61797 and 61799 may be reported no more than once per lesion. Do not report any combination of 61797 and 61799 more than 4 times for entire course of treatment regardless of number of lesions treated)

+ 61800 Application of stereotactic headframe for stereotactic radiosurgery (list separately in addition to code for primary procedure)

> (Use 61800 in conjunction with 61796, 61798)

NEUROSTIMULATORS (INTRACRANIAL)

Codes 61850-61888 apply to both simple and complex neurostimulators. For initial or subsequent electronic analysis and programming of neurostimulator pulse generators, see codes 95970-95975.

Microelectrode recording, when performed by the operating surgeon in association with implantation of neurostimulator electrode arrays, is an inclusive service and should not be reported separately. If another individual participates in neurophysiological mapping during a deep brain stimulator implantation procedure, this service may be reported by the second individual with codes 95961-95962.

61850 Twist drill or burr hole(s) for implantation of neurostimulator electrodes, cortical

61860 Craniectomy or craniotomy for implantation of neurostimulator electrodes, cerebral, cortical

61863 Twist drill, burr hole, craniotomy, or craniectomy with stereotactic implantation of neurostimulator electrode array in subcortical site (eg, thalamus, globus pallidus, subthalamic nucleus, periventricular, periaqueductal gray), without use of intraoperative microelectrode recording; first array

+ 61864 each additional array (List separately in addition to primary procedure)

(Use 61864 in conjunction with 61863)

61867 Twist drill, burr hole, craniotomy, or craniectomy with stereotactic implantation of neurostimulator electrode array in subcortical site (eg, thalamus, globus pallidus, subthalamic nucleus, periventricular, periaqueductal gray), with use of intraoperative microelectrode recording; first array

+ **61868** each additional array (List separately in addition to primary procedure)

(Use 61868 in conjunction with 61867)

61870 Craniectomy for implantation of neurostimulator electrodes, cerebellar; cortical

(**61875** deleted 2014 [2015 edition])

61880 Revision or removal of intracranial neurostimulator electrodes

61885 Insertion or replacement of cranial neurostimulator pulse generator or receiver, direct or inductive coupling; with connection to a single electrode array

61886 with connection to 2 or more electrode arrays

(For percutaneous placement of cranial nerve (eg, vagus, trigeminal) neurostimulator electrode(s), use 64553)

(For revision or removal of cranial nerve (eg, vagus, trigeminal) neurostimulator electrode array, use 64569)

61888 Revision or removal of cranial neurostimulator pulse generator or receiver

(Do not report 61888 in conjunction with 61885 or 61886 for the same pulse generator)

REPAIR

62000 Elevation of depressed skull fracture; simple, extradural

62005 compound or comminuted, extradural

62010 with repair of dura and/or debridement of brain

62100 Craniotomy for repair of dural/cerebrospinal fluid leak, including surgery for rhinorrhea/otorrhea

(For repair of spinal dural/CSF leak, see 63707, 63709)

62115 Reduction of craniomegalic skull (eg, treated hydrocephalus); not requiring bone grafts or cranioplasty

62117 requiring craniotomy and reconstruction with or without bone graft (includes obtaining grafts)

62120 Repair of encephalocele, skull vault, including cranioplasty

62121 Craniotomy for repair of encephalocele, skull base

62140 Cranioplasty for skull defect; up to 5 cm diameter

62141 larger than 5 cm diameter

62142 Removal of bone flap or prosthetic plate of skull

62143 Replacement of bone flap or prosthetic plate of skull

62145 Cranioplasty for skull defect with reparative brain surgery

62146 Cranioplasty with autograft (includes obtaining bone grafts); up to 5 cm diameter

62147	larger than 5 cm diameter

+ **62148** Incision and retrieval of subcutaneous cranial bone graft for cranioplasty (List separately in addition to code for primary procedure)

(Use 62148 in conjunction with codes 62140-62147)

NEUROENDOSCOPY

Surgical endoscopy always includes diagnostic endoscopy

+ **62160** Neuroendoscopy, intracranial, for placement or replacement of ventricular catheter and attachment to shunt system or external drainage (List separately in addition to code for primary procedure)

(Use 62160 only in conjunction with codes 61107, 61210, 62220-62230, 62258)

62161 Neuroendoscopy, intracranial; with dissection of adhesions, fenestration of septum pellucidum or intraventricular cysts (including placement, replacement, or removal of ventricular catheter)

62162 with fenestration or excision of colloid cyst, including placement of external ventricular catheter for drainage

62163 with retrieval of foreign body

62164 with excision of brain tumor, including placement of external ventricular catheter for drainage

62165 with excision of pituitary tumor, transnasal or transsphenoidal approach

CEREBROSPINAL FLUID (CSF) SHUNT

62180 Ventriculocisternostomy (Torkildsen type operation)

62190 Creation of shunt; subarachnoid/subdural-atrial, -jugular, -auricular

62192 subarachnoid/subdural-peritoneal, -pleural, other terminus

62194 Replacement or irrigation, subarachnoid/subdural catheter

62200 Ventriculocisternostomy, third ventricle;

62201 stereotactic, neuroendoscopic method

(For intracranial neuroendoscopic procedures, see 62161-62165)

62220 Creation of shunt; ventriculo-atrial, -jugular, -auricular

(For intracranial neuroendoscopic ventricular catheter placement, use 62160)

62223 ventriculo-peritoneal, -pleural, other terminus

(For intracranial neuroendoscopic ventricular catheter placement, use 62160)

62225 Replacement or irrigation, ventricular catheter

(For intracranial neuroendoscopic ventricular catheter placement, use 62160)

62230 Replacement or revision of cerebrospinal fluid shunt, obstructed valve, or distal catheter in shunt system

(For intracranial neuroendoscopic ventricular catheter placement, use 62160)

(For replacement of **only** the valve and proximal catheter, use 62230 in conjunction with 62225)

62252 Reprogramming of programmable cerebrospinal shunt

▮ Separate Procedure	▮ Unlisted Procedure	▮ CCI Comp. Code	▮ Non-specific Procedure

569

62256 Removal of complete cerebrospinal fluid shunt system; without replacement

62258   with replacement by similar or other shunt at same operation

(For percutaneous irrigation or aspiration of shunt reservoir, use 61070)

(For reprogramming of programmable CSF shunt, use 62252)

(For intracranial neuroendoscopic ventricular catheter placement, use 62160)

SPINE AND SPINAL CORD

(For application of caliper or tongs, use 20660)

(For treatment of fracture or dislocation of spine, see 22310-22327)

INJECTION, DRAINAGE, OR ASPIRATION

Injection of contrast during fluoroscopic guidance and localization is an inclusive component of 62263, 62264, 62267, 62270, 62272, 62273, 62280, 62281, 62282, 62302, 62303, 62304, 62305, 62321, 62323, 62325, 62327. Fluoroscopic guidance and localization is reported with 77003, unless a formal contrast study (myelography, epidurography, or arthrography) is performed, in which case the use of fluoroscopy is included in the supervision and interpretation codes or the myelography via lumbar injection code. Image guidance and the injection of contrast are inclusive components and are required for the performance of myelography, as described by codes 62302, 62303, 62304, 62305.

For radiologic supervision and interpretation of epidurography, use 72275. Code 72275 is only to be used when an epidurogram is performed, images documented, and a formal radiologic report is issued.

Code 62263 describes a catheter-based treatment involving targeted injection of various substances (eg., hypertonic saline, steroid, anesthetic) via an indwelling epidural catheter. Code 62263 includes percutaneous insertion and removal of an epidural catheter (remaining in place over a several-day period), for the administration of multiple injections of a neurolytic agent(s) performed during serial treatment sessions (ie., spanning two or more treatment days). If required, adhesions or scarring may also be lysed by mechanical means. Code 62263 is NOT reported for each adhesiolysis treatment, but should be reported ONCE to describe the entire series of injections/infusions spanning two or more treatment days.

Code 62264 describes multiple adhesiolysis treatment sessions performed on the same day. Adhesions or scarring may be lysed by injections of neurolytic agent(s). If required, adhesions or scarring may also be lysed mechanically using a percutaneously-deployed catheter.

Codes 62263 and 62264 include the procedure of injections of contrast for epidurography (72275) and fluoroscopic guidance and localization (77003) during initial or subsequent sessions.

Fluoroscopy or CT and any injection of contrast are inclusive components of 62321, 62323, 62325, 62327. For epidurography, use 72275.

The placement and use of a catheter to administer one or more epidural or subarachnoid injections on a single calendar day should be reported in the same manner as if a needle had been used, ie, as a single injection using either 62320, 62321, 62322, or 62323. Such injections should not be reported with 62324, 62325, 62326, or 62327.

Threading a catheter into the epidural space, injecting substances at one or more levels and then removing the catheter should be treated as a single injection (62320, 62321, 62322, 62323). If the catheter is left in place to deliver substance(s) over a prolonged period (ie, more than a single calendar day) either continuously or via intermittent bolus, use 62324, 62325, 62326, 62327 as appropriate.

When reporting 62320, 62321, 62322, 62323, 62324, 62325, 62326, 62327 code choice is based on the region at which the needle or catheter entered the body (eg, lumbar). Codes 62320, 62321, 62322, 62323, 62324, 62325, 62326, 62327 should be reported only once, when the substance injected spreads or catheter tip insertion moves into another spinal region (eg, 62322 is reported only once for injection or catheter insertion at L3-4 with spread of the substance or placement of the catheter tip to the thoracic region).

Percutaneous spinal procedures are done with indirect visualization (eg, image guidance) (eg, 62287). Endoscopic assistance during an open procedure with continuous and direct visualization (light-based) is reported using excision codes (eg, 63020-63035).

(For transforaminal epidural injection, see 64479- 64484)

(Report 01996 for daily hospital management of continuous epidural or subarachnoid drug administration performed in conjunction with 62324, 62325, 62326, 62327)

Definitions

For purposes of CPT coding, the following definitions of approach and visualization apply. The primary approach and visualization define the service, whether another method is incidentally applied. Surgical services are presumed open, unless otherwise specified.

Percutaneous: Image-guided procedures (eg, computer tomography [CT] or fluoroscopy) performed with indirect visualization of the spine without the use of any device that allows visualization through a surgical incision.

Endoscopic: Spinal procedures performed with continuous direct visualization of the spine through an endoscope.

Open: Spinal procedures performed with continuous direct visualization of the spine through a surgical opening.

Indirect visualization: Image-guided (eg, CT or fluoroscopy), not light-based visualization.

Direct visualization: Light-based visualization; can be performed by eye, or with surgical loupes, microscope, or endoscope.

(For the techniques of microsurgery and/or use of microscope, use 69990)

62263 Percutaneous lysis of epidural adhesions using solution injection (eg, hypertonic saline, enzyme) or mechanical means (eg, catheter) including radiologic localization (includes contrast when administered), multiple adhesiolysis sessions; 2 or more days

(62263 includes codes 72275 and 77003)

62264 1 day

(Do not report 62264 with 62263)

(62264 includes codes 72275 and 77003)

62267 Percutaneous aspiration within the nucleus pulposus, intervertebral, disc, or paravertebral tissue for diagnostic purposes

(For imaging, use 77003)

(Do not report 62267 in conjunction with 10022, 20225, 62287, 62290, 62291)

62268 Percutaneous aspiration, spinal cord cyst or syrinx

(For radiological supervision and interpretation, see 76942, 77002, 77012)

62269 Biopsy of spinal cord, percutaneous needle

(For radiological supervision and interpretation, see 76942, 77002, 77012)

(For fine needle aspiration, see 10021, 10022)

(For evaluation of fine needle aspirate, see 88172, 88173)

62270 Spinal puncture, lumbar, diagnostic

62272 Spinal puncture, therapeutic, for drainage of cerebrospinal fluid (by needle or catheter)

62273 Injection, epidural, of blood or clot patch

(For injection of diagnostic or therapeutic substance[s], see 62320, 62321, 62322, 62323, 62324, 62325, 62326, 62327)

62280   Injection/infusion of neurolytic substance (eg, alcohol, phenol, iced saline solutions), with or without other therapeutic substance; subarachnoid

62281   epidural, cervical or thoracic

62282   epidural, lumbar, sacral (caudal)

62284   Injection procedure for myelography and/or computed tomography, lumbar

(Do not report 62284 in conjunction with 62302, 62303, 62304, 62305, 72240, 72255, 72265, 72270)

(When both 62284 and 72240, 72255, 72265, 72270 are performed by the same physician or other qualified health care professional for myelography, see 62302, 62303, 62304, 62305)

(For injection procedure at C1-C2, use 61055)

(For radiological supervision and interpretation, see Radiology)

62287   Decompression procedure, percutaneous, of nucleus pulposus of intervertebral disc, any method utilizing needle based technique to remove disc material under fluoroscopic imaging or other form of indirect visualization, with discography and/or epidural injection(s) at the treated level(s), when performed, single or multiple levels, lumbar

(Do not report 62287 in conjunction with 62267, 62290, 62322, 77003, 77012, 72295, when performed at same level)

(For non-needle based technique for percutaneous decompression of nucleus pulposus of intervertebral disc, see codes 0274T, 0275T)

62290   Injection procedure for diskography, each level; lumbar

62291   cervical or thoracic

(For radiological supervision or interpretation, see 72285, 72295)

62292   Injection procedure for chemonucleolysis, including diskography, intervertebral disk, single or multiple levels, lumbar

62294   Injection procedure, arterial, for occlusion of arteriovenous malformation, spinal

62302   Myelography via lumbar injection, including radiological supervision and interpretation; cervical

(Do not report 62302 in conjunction with 62284, 62303, 62304, 62305, 72240, 72255, 72265, 72270)

62303   thoracic

(Do not report 62303 in conjunction with 62284, 62302, 62304, 62305, 72240, 72255, 72265, 72270)

62304   lumbosacral

(Do not report 62304 in conjunction with 62284, 62302, 62303, 62305, 72240, 72255, 72265, 72270)

62305   2 or more regions (eg, lumbar/thoracic, cervical/thoracic, lumbar/cervical, lumbar/thoracic/cervical)

(Do not report 62305 in conjunction with 62284, 62302, 62303, 62304, 72240, 72255, 72265, 72270)

(For myelography lumbar injection and imaging performed by different physicians or other qualified health care professionals, see 62284 or 72240, 72255, 72265, 72270)

(For injection procedure at C1-C2, use 61055)

(62310   deleted 2016 [2017 edition]. To report, use 62320)

(62311   deleted 2016 [2017 edition]. To report, use 62322)

(**62318** deleted 2016 [2017 edition]. To report, use 62324)

(**62319** deleted 2016 [2017 edition]. To report, use 62326)

62320 Injection(s), of diagnostic or therapeutic substance(s) (eg, anesthetic, antispasmodic, opioid, steroid, other solution), not including neurolytic substances, including needle or catheter placement, interlaminar epidural or subarachnoid, cervical or thoracic; without imaging guidance

62321 with imaging guidance (ie, fluoroscopy or CT)

(Do not report 62321 in conjunction with 77003, 77012, 76942)

62322 Injection(s), of diagnostic or therapeutic substance(s) (eg, anesthetic, antispasmodic, opioid, steroid, other solution), not including neurolytic substances, including needle or catheter placement, interlaminar epidural or subarachnoid, lumbar or sacral (caudal); without imaging guidance

62323 with imaging guidance (ie, fluoroscopy or CT)

(Do not report 62323 in conjunction with 77003, 77012, 76942)

62324 Injection(s), including indwelling catheter placement, continuous infusion or intermittent bolus, of diagnostic or therapeutic substance(s) (eg, anesthetic, antispasmodic, opioid, steroid, other solution), not including neurolytic substances, interlaminar epidural or subarachnoid, cervical or thoracic; without imaging guidance

62325 with imaging guidance (ie, fluoroscopy or CT)

(Do not report 62325 in conjunction with 77003, 77012, 76942)

62326 Injection(s), including indwelling catheter placement, continuous infusion or intermittent bolus, of diagnostic or therapeutic substance(s) (eg, anesthetic, antispasmodic, opioid, steroid, other solution), not including neurolytic substances, interlaminar epidural or subarachnoid, lumbar or sacral (caudal); without imaging guidance

62327 with imaging guidance (ie, fluoroscopy or CT)

(Do not report 62327 in conjunction with 77003, 77012, 76942)

(Report 01996 for daily hospital management of continuous epidural or subarachnoid drug administration performed in conjunction with 62324, 62325, 62326, 62327)

CATHETER IMPLANTATION

(For percutaneous placement of intrathecal or epidural catheter, see 62270, 62272, 62273, 62280, 62281, 62282, 62284, 62320, 62321, 62322, 62323, 62324, 62325, 62326, 62327)

62350 Implantation, revision or repositioning of tunneled intrathecal or epidural catheter, for long-term medication administration via an external pump or implantable reservoir/infusion pump; without laminectomy

62351 with laminectomy

(For refilling and maintenance of an implantable infusion pump for spinal or brain drug therapy, use 95990)

62355 Removal of previously implanted intrathecal or epidural catheter

RESERVOIR/PUMP IMPLANTATION

62360 Implantation or replacement of device for intrathecal or epidural drug infusion; subcutaneous reservoir

62361 non-programmable pump

62362 programmable pump, including preparation of pump, with or without programming

---

| 62365 | Removal of subcutaneous reservoir or pump, previously implanted for intrathecal or epidural infusion |

| 62367 | Electronic analysis of programmable, implanted pump for intrathecal or epidural drug infusion (includes evaluation of reservoir status, alarm status, drug prescription status); without reprogramming or refill |

| 62368 | with reprogramming |

(For refilling and maintenance of an implantable infusion pump for spinal or brain drug therapy, use 95990)

| 62369 | with reprogramming and refill |

| 62370 | with reprogramming and refill (requiring skill of a physician or other qualified health care professional) |

(Do not report 62367-62370 in conjunction with 95990, 95991. For refilling and maintenance of a reservoir or an implantable infusion pump for spinal or brain drug delivery without reprogramming, see 95990, 95991)

Endoscopic Decompression of Neural Elements and/or Excision of Herniated Intervertebral Discs

Definitions

For purposes of CPT coding, the following definitions of approach and visualization apply. The primary approach and visualization define the service, whether another method is incidentally applied. Surgical services are presumed open, unless otherwise specified. Percutaneous: Image-guided procedures (eg, computer tomography [CT] or fluoroscopy) performed with indirect visualization of the spine without the use of any device that allows visualization through a surgical incision.

Endoscopic: Spinal procedures performed with continuous direct visualization of the spine through an endoscope.

Open: Spinal procedures performed with continuous direct visualization of the spine through a surgical opening.

Indirect visualization: Image-guided (eg, CT or fluoroscopy), not light-based visualization.

Direct visualization: Light-based visualization; can be performed by eye, or with surgical loupes, microscope, or endoscope.

(For the techniques of microsurgery and/or use of microscope, use 69990)

(For percutaneous decompression, see 62287, 0274T, 0275T)

| 62380 | Endoscopic decompression of spinal cord, nerve root(s), including laminotomy, partial facetectomy, foraminotomy, discectomy and/or excision of herniated intervertebral disc, 1 interspace, lumbar |

(For open procedures, see 63030, 63056)

(For bilateral procedure, report 62380 with modifier 50)

POSTERIOR EXTRADURAL LAMINOTOMY OR LAMINECTOMY FOR EXPLORATION/DECOMPRESSION OF NEURAL ELEMENTS OR EXCISION OF HERNIATED INTERVERTEBRAL DISKS

Definitions

For purposes of CPT coding, the following definitions of approach and visualization apply. The primary approach and visualization define the service, whether another method is incidentally applied. Surgical services are presumed open, unless otherwise specified. Percutaneous: Image-guided procedures (eg, computer tomography [CT] or fluoroscopy) performed with indirect visualization of the spine without the use of any device that allows visualization through a surgical incision.

Endoscopic: Spinal procedures performed with continuous direct visualization of the spine through an endoscope.

Open: Spinal procedures performed with continuous direct visualization of the spine through a surgical opening.

Indirect visualization: Image-guided (eg, CT or fluoroscopy), not light-based visualization.

Direct visualization: Light-based visualization; can be performed by eye, or with surgical loupes, microscope, or endoscope.

(When 63001-63048 are followed by arthrodesis, see 22590-22614)

(For open procedures, see 63030, 63056)

(For bilateral procedure, report 62380 with modifier 50)

63001 Laminectomy with exploration and/or decompression of spinal cord and/or cauda equina, without facetectomy, foraminotomy or diskectomy, (eg, spinal stenosis), one or two vertebral segments; cervical

63003 thoracic

63005 lumbar, except for spondylolisthesis

63011 sacral

63012 Laminectomy with removal of abnormal facets and/or pars inter-articularis with decompression of cauda equina and nerve roots for spondylolisthesis, lumbar (Gill type procedure)

63015 Laminectomy with exploration and/or decompression of spinal cord and/or cauda equina, without facetectomy, foraminotomy or diskectomy, (eg, spinal stenosis), more than 2 vertebral segments; cervical

63016 thoracic

63017 lumbar

63020 Laminotomy (hemilaminectomy), with decompression of nerve root(s), including partial facetectomy, foraminotomy and/or excision of herniated intervertebral disc; 1 interspace, cervical

(For bilateral procedure, report 63020 with modifier -50)

63030 1 interspace, lumbar

(For bilateral procedure, report 63030 with modifier -50)

+ 63035 each additional interspace, cervical or lumbar (List separately in addition to code for primary procedure)

(Use 63035 in conjunction with codes 63020-63030)

(For bilateral procedures, report 63035 with modifier -50)

(For percutaneous endoscopic approach, see 0274T, 0275T)

63040 Laminotomy (hemilaminectomy), with decompression of nerve root(s), including partial facetectomy, foraminotomy and/or excision of herniated intervertebral disk, reexploration, single interspace; cervical

(For bilateral procedure, report 63040 with modifier -50)

63042 lumbar

(For bilateral procedure, report 63042 with modifier -50)

+ 63043 each additional cervical interspace (List separately in addition to code for primary procedure)

(Use 63043 in conjunction with code 63040)

(For bilateral procedure, report 63043 with modifier -50)

+ 63044 each additional lumbar interspace (List separately in addition to code for primary procedure)

(Use 63044 in conjunction with code 63042)

(For bilateral procedure, report 63044 with modifier -50)

Separate Procedure ■ Unlisted Procedure ■ CCI Comp. Code ■ Non-specific Procedure **575**

63045 Laminectomy, facetectomy and foraminotomy (unilateral or bilateral with decompression of spinal cord, cauda equina and/or nerve root(s), (eg, spinal or lateral recess stenosis)), single vertebral segment; cervical

63046 thoracic

63047 lumbar

+ 63048 each additional segment, cervical, thoracic, or lumbar (List separately in addition to code for primary procedure)

(Use 63048 in conjunction with codes 63045-63047)

63050 Laminoplasty, cervical, with decompression of the spinal cord, 2 or more vertebral segments;

63051 with reconstruction of the posterior bony elements (including the application of bridging bone graft and non-segmental fixation devices (eg, wire, suture, mini-plates), when performed)

(Do not report 63050 or 63051 in conjunction with 22600, 22614, 22840-22842, 63001, 63015, 63045, 63048, 63295 for the same vertebral segment(s))

TRANSPEDICULAR OR COSTOVERTEBRAL APPROACH FOR POSTEROLATERAL EXTRADURAL EXPLORATION/ DECOMPRESSION

63055 Transpedicular approach with decompression of spinal cord, equina and/or nerve root(s) (eg, herniated intervertebral disk), single segment; thoracic

63056 lumbar (including transfacet, or lateral extraforaminal approach) (eg, far lateral herniated intervertebral disk)

+ 63057 each additional segment, thoracic or lumbar (List separately in addition to code for primary procedure)

(Use 63057 in conjunction with codes 63055, 63056)

63064 Costovertebral approach with decompression of spinal cord or nerve root(s), (eg, herniated intervertebral disk), thoracic; single segment

+ 63066 each additional segment (List separately in addition to code for primary procedure)

(Use 63066 in conjunction with code 63064)

(For excision of thoracic intraspinal lesions by laminectomy, see 63266, 63271, 63276, 63281, 63286)

ANTERIOR OR ANTEROLATERAL APPROACH FOR EXTRADURAL EXPLORATION/DECOMPRESSION

For the following codes, when two surgeons work together as primary surgeons performing distinct part(s) of spinal cord exploration/decompression operation, each surgeon should report his/her distinct operative work by appending modifier 62 to the procedure code (and any associated add-on codes for that procedure code as long as both surgeons continue to work together as primary surgeons). In this situation, modifier 62 may be appended to the definitive procedure code(s) 63075, 63077, 63081, 63085, 63087, 63090 and, as appropriate, to associated additional interspace add-on code(s) 63076, 63078 or additional segment add-on codes 63082, 63086, 63088, 63091 as long as both surgeons continue to work together as primary surgeons.

For vertebral corpectomy, the term **partial** is used to describe removal of a substantial portion of the body of the vertebra. In the cervical spine, the amount of bone removed is defined as at least one-half of the vertebral body. In the thoracic and lumbar spine, the amount of bone removed is defined as at least one-third of the vertebral body.

63075 Diskectomy, anterior, with decompression of spinal cord and/or nerve root(s), including osteophytectomy; cervical, single interspace

(Do not report 63075 in conjunction with 22554, even if performed by separate individuals. To report anterior cervical discectomy and interbody fusion at the same level during the same session, use 22551)

+ 63076 cervical, each additional interspace (List separately in addition to code for primary procedure)

(Do not report 63076 in conjunction with 22554, even if performed by separate individuals. To report anterior cervical discectomy and interbody fusion at the same level during the same session, use 22552)

(Use 63076 in conjunction with code 63075)

63077 thoracic, single interspace

+ 63078 thoracic, each additional interspace (List separately in addition to code for primary procedure)

(Use 63078 in conjunction with code 63077)

(Do not report code 69990 in addition to codes 63075-63078)

63081 Vertebral corpectomy (vertebral body resection), partial or complete, anterior approach with decompression of spinal cord and/or nerve root(s); cervical, single segment

+ 63082 cervical, each additional segment (List separately in addition to code for primary procedure)

(Use 63082 in conjunction with code 63081)

(For transoral approach, see 61575, 61576)

63085 Vertebral corpectomy (vertebral body resection), partial or complete, transthoracic approach with decompression of spinal cord and/or nerve root(s); thoracic, single segment

+ 63086 thoracic, each additional segment (List separately in addition to code for primary procedure)

(Use 63086 in conjunction with code 63085)

63087 Vertebral corpectomy (vertebral body resection), partial or complete, combined thoracolumbar approach with decompression of spinal cord, cauda equina or nerve root(s), lower thoracic or lumbar; single segment

+ 63088 each additional segment (List separately in addition to code for primary procedure)

(Use 63088 in conjunction with code 63087)

63090 Vertebral corpectomy (vertebral body resection), partial or complete, transperitoneal or retroperitoneal approach with decompression of spinal cord, cauda equina or nerve root(s), lower thoracic, lumbar, or sacral; single segment

+ 63091 each additional segment (List separately in addition to code for primary procedure)

(Use 63091 in conjunction with code 63090)

(Procedures 63081-63091 include diskectomy above and/or below vertebral segment)

(If followed by arthrodesis, see 22548-22812)

(For reconstruction of spine, use appropriate vertebral corpectomy codes 63081-63091, bone graft codes 20930-20938, arthrodesis codes 22548-22812, and spinal instrumentation codes 22840-22855, 22859)

LATERAL EXTRACAVITARY APPROACH FOR EXTRADURAL EXPLORATION/DECOMPRESSION

For vertebral corpectomy, the term partial is used to describe removal of a substantial portion of the body of the vertebra. In the cervical spine, the amount of bone removed is defined as at least one-half of the vertebral body. In the thoracic and lumbar spine, the amount of bone removed is defined as at least one-third of the vertebral body

63101 Vertebral corpectomy (vertebral body resection), partial or complete, lateral extracavitary approach with decompression of spinal cord and/or nerve root(s) (eg, for tumor or retropulsed bone fragments); thoracic, single segment

63102 lumbar, single segment

+ 63103 thoracic or lumbar, each additional segment (List separately in addition to code for primary procedure)

(Use 63103 in conjunction with 63101 and 63102)

INCISION

63170	Laminectomy with myelotomy (eg, Bischof or DREZ type), cervical, thoracic, or thoracolumbar
63172	Laminectomy with drainage of intramedullary cyst/syrinx; to subarachnoid space
63173	to peritoneal or pleural space
63180	Laminectomy and section of dentate ligaments, with or without dural graft, cervical; 1 or 2 segments
63182	more than 2 segments
63185	Laminectomy with rhizotomy; 1 or 2 segments
63190	more than 2 segments
63191	Laminectomy with section of spinal accessory nerve

(For bilateral procedure, report 63191 with modifier -50)

(For resection of sternocleidomastoid muscle, use 21720)

63194	Laminectomy with cordotomy, with section of one spinothalamic tract, 1 stage; cervical
63195	thoracic
63196	Laminectomy with cordotomy, with section of both spinothalamic tracts, 1 stage; cervical
63197	thoracic
63198	Laminectomy with cordotomy with section of both spinothalamic tracts, 2 stages within 14 days; cervical
63199	thoracic
63200	Laminectomy, with release of tethered spinal cord, lumbar

EXCISION BY LAMINECTOMY OF LESION OTHER THAN HERNIATED DISC

63250	Laminectomy for excision or occlusion of arteriovenous malformation of spinal cord; cervical
63251	thoracic
63252	thoracolumbar
63265	Laminectomy for excision or evacuation of intraspinal lesion other than neoplasm, extradural; cervical
63266	thoracic
63267	lumbar
63268	sacral
63270	Laminectomy for excision of intraspinal lesion other than neoplasm, intradural; cervical
63271	thoracic
63272	lumbar
63273	sacral

● New Code   ▲ Revised Code   + Add-On Code   ⊘ Modifier -51 Exempt   ★ Telemedicine

63275 Laminectomy for biopsy/excision of intraspinal neoplasm; extradural, cervical

63276 extradural, thoracic

63277 extradural, lumbar

63278 extradural, sacral

63280 intradural, extramedullary, cervical

63281 intradural, extramedullary, thoracic

63282 intradural, extramedullary, lumbar

63283 intradural, sacral

63285 intradural, intramedullary, cervical

63286 intradural, intramedullary, thoracic

63287 intradural, intramedullary, thoracolumbar

63290 combined extradural-intradural lesion, any level

(For drainage of intramedullary cyst/syrinx, use 63172, 63173)

+ 63295 Osteoplastic reconstruction of dorsal spinal elements, following primary intraspinal procedure (List separately in addition to code for primary procedure)

(Use 63295 in conjunction with 63172, 63173, 63185, 63190, 63200-63290)

(Do not report 63295 in conjunction with 22590-22614, 22840-22844, 63050, 63051 for the same vertebral segment(s))

EXCISION, ANTERIOR OR ANTEROLATERAL APPROACH, INTRASPINAL LESION

For the following codes, when two surgeons work together as primary surgeons performing distinct part(s) of an anterior approach for an intraspinal excision, each surgeon should report his/her distinct operative work by appending modifier 62 to the single definitive procedure code. In this situation, modifier 62 may be appended to the definitive procedure code(s) 63300-63307 and, as appropriate, to the associated additional segment add-on code 63308 as long as both surgeons continue to work together as primary surgeons.

For vertebral corpectomy, the term partial is used to describe removal of a substantial portion of the body of the vertebra. In the cervical spine, the amount of bone removed is defined as at least one-half of the vertebral body. In the thoracic and lumbar spine, the amount of bone removed is defined as at least one-third of the vertebral body.

(For arthrodesis, see 22548-22585)

(For reconstruction of spine, see 20930-20938)

63300 Vertebral corpectomy (vertebral body resection), partial or complete, for excision of intraspinal lesion, single segment; extradural, cervical

63301 extradural, thoracic by transthoracic approach

63302 extradural, thoracic by thoracolumbar approach

63303 extradural, lumbar or sacral by transperitoneal or retroperitoneal approach

63304 intradural, cervical

63305 intradural, thoracic by transthoracic approach

Separate Procedure　Unlisted Procedure　CCI Comp. Code　Non-specific Procedure　**579**

63306	intradural, thoracic by thoracolumbar approach
63307	intradural, lumbar or sacral by transperitoneal or retroperitoneal approach
+ 63308	each additional segment (List separately in addition to codes for single segment)

(Use 63308 in conjunction with codes 63300-63307)

STEREOTAXIS

63600	Creation of lesion of spinal cord by stereotactic method, percutaneous, any modality (including stimulation and/or recording)
63610	Stereotactic stimulation of spinal cord, percutaneous, separate procedure not followed by other surgery
63615	Stereotactic biopsy, aspiration, or excision of lesion, spinal cord

STEREOTACTIC RADIOSURGERY (SPINAL)

Spinal stereotactic radiosurgery is a distinct procedure that utilizes externally generated ionizing radiation to inactivate or eradicate defined target(s) in the spine without the need to make an incision. The target is defined by and the treatment is delivered using high-resolution stereotactic imaging. These codes are reported by the surgeon. The radiation oncologist reports the appropriate code(s) for clinical treatment planning, physics and dosimetry, treatment delivery and management from the Radiation Oncology section (77261-77790). Any necessary planning, dosimetry, targeting, positioning, or blocking by the neurosurgeon is included in the stereotactic radiation surgery services. The same individual should not report stereotactic radiosurgery services with radiation treatment management codes (77427-77432).

Spinal stereotactic radiosurgery is typically performed in a single planning and treatment session using a stereotactic image-guidance system, but can be performed with a planning session and in a limited number of treatment sessions, up to a maximum of five sessions. Do not report stereotactic radiosurgery more than once per lesion per course of treatment when the treatment requires greater than one session.

Stereotactic spinal surgery is only used when the tumor being treated affects spinal neural tissue or abuts the dura mater. Arteriovenous malformations must be subdural. For other radiation services of the spine, see Radiation Oncology Services.

Codes 63620, 63621 include computer-assisted planning. Do not report 63620, 63621 in conjunction with 61781-61783.

(For intensity modulated beam delivery plan and treatment, see 77301, 77385, 77386. For stereotactic body radiation therapy, see 77373, 77435)

| 63620 | Stereotactic radiosurgery (particle beam, gamma ray, or linear accelerator); 1 spinal lesion |

(Do not report 63620 more than once per course of treatment)

| + 63621 | each additional spinal lesion (list separately in addition to code for primary procedure) |

(Report 63621 in conjunction with 63620)

(For each course of treatment, 63621 may be reported no more than once per lesion. Do not report 63621 more than 2 times for entire course of treatment regardless of number of lesions treated)

NEUROSTIMULATORS (SPINAL)

Codes 63650-63688 apply to both simple and complex neurostimulators. For initial or subsequent electronic analysis and programming of neurostimulator pulse generators, see codes 95970-95975.

Codes 63650, 63655, and 63661-63664 describe the operative placement, revision, replacement, or removal of the spinal neurostimulator system components to provide spinal electrical stimulation. A neurostimulator system includes an implanted neurostimulator, external controller, extension, and collection of contacts. Multiple contacts or electrodes (4 or more) provide the actual electrical stimulation in the epidural space.

For percutaneously placed neurostimulator systems (63650, 63661, 63663), the contacts are on a catheter-like lead. An array defines the collection of contacts that are on one catheter.

● New Code   ▲ Revised Code   + Add-On Code   ⊘ Modifier -51 Exempt   ★ Telemedicine

For systems placed via an open surgical exposure (63655, 63662, 63664), the contacts are on a plate or paddle-shaped surface.

Do not report 63661 or 63663 when removing or replacing a temporary percutaneously placed array for an external generator.

63650 Percutaneous implantation of neurostimulator electrode array, epidural

63655 Laminectomy for implantation of neurostimulator electrodes, plate/paddle, epidural

63661 Removal of spinal neurostimulator electrode percutaneous array(s), including fluoroscopy, when performed

63662 Removal of spinal neurostimulator electrode plate/paddle(s) placed via laminotomy or laminectomy, including fluoroscopy, when performed

63663 Revision including replacement, when performed, of spinal neurostimulator electrode percutaneous array(s), including fluoroscopy, when performed

(Do not report 63663 in conjunction with 63661, 63662 for the same spinal level)

63664 Revision including replacement, when performed, of spinal neurostimulator electrode plate/paddle(s) placed via laminotomy or laminectomy, including fluoroscopy, when performed

(Do not report 63664 in conjunction with 63661, 63662 for the same spinal level)

63685 Insertion or replacement of spinal neurostimulator pulse generator or receiver, direct or inductive coupling

(Do not report 63685 in conjunction with 63688 for the same pulse generator or receiver)

63688 Revision or removal of implanted spinal neurostimulator pulse generator or receiver

(For electronic analysis of implanted neurostimulator pulse generator system, see 95970-95975)

REPAIR

63700 Repair of meningocele; less than 5 cm diameter

63702 larger than 5 cm diameter

(Do not use modifier -63 in conjunction with 63700, 63702)

63704 Repair of myelomeningocele; less than 5 cm diameter

63706 larger than 5 cm diameter

(Do not use modifier -63 in conjunction with 63704, 63706)

(For complex skin closure, see Integumentary System)

63707 Repair of dural/cerebrospinal fluid leak, not requiring laminectomy

63709 Repair of dural/cerebrospinal fluid leak or pseudomeningocele, with laminectomy

63710 Dural graft, spinal

(For laminectomy and section of dentate ligaments, with or without dural graft, cervical, see 63180, 63182)

SHUNT, SPINAL CSF

63740 Creation of shunt, lumbar, subarachnoid-peritoneal, -pleural, or other; including laminectomy

63741 percutaneous, not requiring laminectomy

63744 Replacement, irrigation or revision of lumbosubarachnoid shunt

---

Separate Procedure   Unlisted Procedure   CCI Comp. Code   Non-specific Procedure   **581**

| 63746 | Removal of entire lumbosubarachnoid shunt system without replacement |

(For insertion of subarachnoid catheter with reservoir and/or pump for intermittent or continuous infusion of drug including laminectomy, see 62351 and 62360, 62361 or 62362)

(For insertion or replacement of subarachnoid or epidural catheter, with reservoir and/or pump for drug infusion without laminectomy, see 62350 and 62360, 62361 or 62362)

EXTRACRANIAL NERVES, PERIPHERAL NERVES, AND AUTONOMIC NERVOUS SYSTEM

(For intracranial surgery on cranial nerves, see 61450, 61460, 61790)

INTRODUCTION/INJECTION OF ANESTHETIC AGENT (NERVE BLOCK), DIAGNOSTIC OR THERAPEUTIC

(For destruction by neurolytic agent or chemodenervation, see 62280-62282, 64600-64681)

(For epidural or subarachnoid injection, see 62320, 62321, 62322, 62323, 62324, 62325, 62326, 62327)

(64479-64495 are unilateral procedures. For bilateral procedures, use modifier -50)

Somatic Nerves

64400	Injection, anesthetic agent; trigeminal nerve, any division or branch
64402	facial nerve
64405	greater occipital nerve
64408	vagus nerve
64410	phrenic nerve
(64412	deleted 2015 [2016 edition]. To report, use 64999)
64413	cervical plexus
64415	brachial plexus, single
64416	brachial plexus, continuous infusion by catheter (including catheter placement)

(Do not report 64416 in conjunction with 01996)

64417	axillary nerve
64418	suprascapular nerve
64420	intercostal nerve, single
64421	intercostal nerves, multiple, regional block
64425	ilioinguinal, iliohypogastric nerves
64430	pudendal nerve
64435	paracervical (uterine) nerve
64445	sciatic nerve, single
64446	sciatic nerve, continuous infusion by catheter, (including catheter placement)

● New Code   ▲ Revised Code   + Add-On Code   ⊘ Modifier -51 Exempt   ★ Telemedicine

(Do not report 64446 in conjuction with 01996)

64447   femoral nerve, single

(Do not report 64447 in conjunction with 01996)

64448   femoral nerve, continuous infusion by catheter (including catheter placement)

(Do not report 64448 in conjunction with 01996)

64449   lumbar plexus, posterior approach, continuous infusion by catheter (including catheter placement)

(Do not report 64449 in conjunction with 01996)

64450   other peripheral nerve or branch

64455   Injection(s), anesthetic agent and/or steroid, plantar common digital nerve(s) (eg, morton's neuroma)

(Do note report 64455 in conjunction with 64632)

(Imaging guidance (fluoroscopy or CT) and any injection of contrast are inclusive components of 64479-64484. Imaging guidance and localization are required for the performance of 64479-64484.)

(Codes 64470-64476 have been deleted. To report, see 64490-64495)

64461   Code is out of order. See page 583.

64462   Code is out of order. See page 583.

64463   Code is out of order. See page 584.

64479   Injection(s), anesthetic agent and/or steroid, transforaminal epidural, with imaging guidance (fluoroscopy or CT); cervical or thoracic, single level

(For transforaminal epidural injection under ultrasound guidance, use 0228T)

+ 64480   cervical or thoracic, each additional level (List separately in addition to code for primary procedure)

(Use 64480 in conjunction with code 64479)

(For transforaminal epidural injection under ultrasound guidance, use 0229T)

(For transforaminal epidural injection at the T12-L1 level, use 64479)

64483   lumbar or sacral, single level

(For transforaminal epidural injection under ultrasound guidance, use 0230T)

+ 64484   lumbar or sacral, each additional level (List separately in addition to code for primary procedure)

(Use 64484 in conjunction with code 64483)

(For transforaminal epidural injection under ultrasound guidance, use 0231T)

(64479-64484 are unilateral procedures. For bilateral procedures, use modifier 50.)

64461   Paravertebral block (PVB) (paraspinous block), thoracic; single injection site (includes imaging guidance, when performed)

+ 64462   second and any additional injection site(s) (includes imaging guidance, when performed) (List separately in addition to code for primary procedure)

(Use 64462 in conjunction with 64461)

(Do not report 64462 more than once per day)

64463   thoracic; continuous infusion by catheter (includes imaging guidance, when performed)

(Do not report 64461, 64462, 64463 in conjunction with 62320, 62324, 64420, 64421, 64479, 64480, 64490, 64491, 64492, 76942, 77002, 77003)

64486   Transversus abdominis plane (tap) block (abdominal plane block, rectus sheath block) unilateral; by injection(s) (includes imaging guidance, when performed)

64487   by continuous infusion(s) (includes imaging guidance, when performed)

64488   Transversus abdominis plane (tap) block (abdominal plane block, rectus sheath block) bilateral; by injections (includes imaging guidance, when performed)

64489   by continuous infusions (includes imaging guidance, when performed)

Paravertebral Spinal Nerves and Branches

(Image guidance [fluoroscopy or CT] and any injection of contrast are inclusive components of 64490-64495. Imaging guidance and localization are required for the performance of paravertebral facet joint injections described by codes 64490-64495. If imaging is not used, report 20552-20553. If ultrasound guidance is used, report 0213T-0218T)

(For bilateral paravertebral facet injection procedure, use modifier 50)

(For paravertebral facet injection of the T12-L1 joint, or nerves innervating that joint, use 64490)

64490   Injection(s), diagnostic or therapeutic agent, paravertebral facet (zygapophyseal) joint (or nerves innervating that joint) with image guidance (fluoroscopy or CT), cervical or thoracic; single level

+ **64491**   second level (List separately in addition to code for primary procedure)

(Use 64491 in conjunction with 64490)

+ **64492**   third and any additional level(s) (List separately in addition to code for primary procedure)

(Do not report 64492 more than once per day)

(Use 64492 in conjunction with 64490, 64491)

64493   Injection(s), diagnostic or therapeutic agent, paravertebral facet (zygapophyseal) joint (or nerves innervating that joint) with image guidance (fluoroscopy or CT), lumbar or sacral; single level

+ **64494**   second level (List separately in addition to code for primary procedure)

(Use 64494 in conjunction with 64493)

+ **64495**   third and any additional level(s) (List separately in addition to code for primary procedure)

(Do not report 64495 more than once per day)

(Use 64495 in conjunction with 64493, 64494)

Autonomic Nerves

64505   Injection, anesthetic agent; sphenopalatine ganglion

64508   carotid sinus (separate procedure)

64510   stellate ganglion (cervical sympathetic)

64517   superior hypogastric plexus

64520   lumbar or thoracic (paravertebral sympathetic)

64530   celiac plexus, with or without radiologic monitoring

(For transendoscopic ultrasound-guided transmural injection, anesthetic, celiac plexus, use 43253)

NEUROSTIMULATORS (PERIPHERAL NERVE)

Codes 64553-64595 apply to both simple and complex neurostimulators. For initial or subsequent electronic analysis and programming of neurostimulator pulse generators, see codes 95970-95975. An electrode array is a catheter or other device with more than one contact. The function of each contact may be capable of being adjusted during programming services.

Codes 64553, 64555, and 64561 may be used to report both temporary and permanent placement of percutaneous electrode arrays. Code 64550 describes application of surface (transcutaneous) neurostimulator (eg, TENS unit) at any anatomical site.

▲ **64550**   Application of surface (transcutaneous) neurostimulator (eg, TENS unit)

64553   Percutaneous implantation of neurostimulator electrode array; cranial nerve

(For percutaneous electrical stimulation of a cranial nerve using needle[s] or needle electrode[s] [eg, PENS, PNT], use 64999)

(For open placement of cranial nerve (eg, vagus, trigeminal) neurostimulator pulse generator or receiver, see 61885, 61886, as appropriate)

64555   peripheral nerve (excludes sacral nerve)

(Do not report 64555 in conjunction with 64566)

(For percutaneous electrical stimulation of a peripheral nerve using needle[s] or needle electrode[s] [eg, PENS, PNT], use 64999)

64561   sacral nerve (transforaminal placement) including image guidance, if performed

(**64565**   deleted 2017 [2018 edition.)

(For percutaneous electrical neuromuscular stimulation or neuromodulation using needle[s] or needle electrode[s] [eg, PENS, PNT], use 64999)

64566   Posterior tibial neurostimulation, percutaneous needle electrode, single treatment, includes programming

(Do not report 64566 in conjunction with 64555, 95970-95972)

64568   Incision for implantation of cranial nerve (eg, vagus nerve) neurostimulator electrode array and pulse generator

(Do not report 64568 in conjunction with 61885, 61886, 64570)

(For insertion of chest wall respiratory sensor electrode or electrode array, including connection to pulse generator, use 0466T)

64569   Revision or replacement of cranial nerve (eg, vagus nerve) neurostimulator electrode array, including connection to existing pulse generator

(Do not report 64569 in conjunction with 64570 or 61888)

(For replacement of pulse generator, use 61885)

(For revision or replacement of chest wall respiratory sensor electrode or electrode array, including connection to existing pulse generator, use 0467T)

64570   Removal of cranial nerve (eg, vagus nerve) neurostimulator electrode array and pulse generator

(Do not report 64570 in conjunction with 61888)

(For laparoscopic implantation, revision, replacement, or removal of vagus nerve blocking neurostimulator electrode array and/or pulse generator at the esophagogastric junction, see 0312T-0317T)

■ Separate Procedure   ■ Unlisted Procedure   ■ CCI Comp. Code   ■ Non-specific Procedure   **585**

(For removal of chest wall respiratory sensor electrode or electrode array, use 0468T)

64575 Incision for implantation of neurostimulator electrode array; peripheral nerve (excludes sacral nerve)

64580 neuromuscular

64581 sacral nerve (transforaminal placement)

64585 Revision or removal of peripheral neurostimulator electrode array

64590 Insertion or replacement of peripheral or gastric neurostimulator pulse generator or receiver, direct or inductive coupling

(Do not report 64590 in conjunction with 64595)

64595 Revision or removal of peripheral or gastric neurostimulator pulse generator or receiver

DESTRUCTION BY NEUROLYTIC AGENT (eg, CHEMICAL, THERMAL, ELECTRICAL, OR RADIOFREQUENCY), CHEMODENERVATION

Codes 64600-64681 include the injection of other therapeutic agents (eg., corticosteroids). Do not report diagnostic/therapeutic injections separately. Do not report a code labeled as destruction when using theraies that are not destructive of the target nerve (eg, pulsed radiofrequency), use 64999. For codes labeled as chemodenervation, the supply of the chemodenervation agent is reported separately.

(For chemodenervation of internal anal sphincter, use 46505)

(For chemodenervation of the bladder, use 52287)

(For chemodenervation for strabismus involving the extraocular muscles, use 67345)

(For chemodenervation guided by needle electromyography or muscle electrical stimulation, see 95873, 95874)

Somatic Nerves

64600 Destruction by neurolytic agent, trigeminal nerve; supraorbital, infraorbital, mental, or inferior alveolar branch

64605 second and third division branches at foramen ovale

64610 second and third division branches at foramen ovale under radiologic monitoring

64611 Chemodenervation of parotid and submandibular salivary glands, bilateral

(Report 64611 with modifier 52 if fewer than four salivary glands are injected)

64612 Chemodenervation of muscle(s); muscle(s) innervated by facial nerve, unilateral (eg, for blepharospasm, hemifacial spasm)

(For bilateral procedure, report 64612 with modifier 50)

64615 muscle(s) innervated by facial, trigeminal, cervical spinal and accessory nerves, bilateral (eg, for chronic migraine)

(Report 64615 only once per session)

(Do not report 64615 in conjunction with 64612, 64616, 64617, 64642, 64643, 64644, 64645, 64646, 64647)

(For guidance see 95873, 95874. Do not report more than one guidance code for 64615)

64616 neck muscle(s), excluding muscles of the larynx, unilateral (eg, for cervical dystonia, spasmodic torticollis)

(For bilateral procedure, report 64616 with modifier 50)

(For chemodenervation guided by needle electromyography or muscle electrical stimulation, see 95873, 95874. Do not report more than one guidance code for any unit of 64616)

64617   larynx, unilateral, percutaneous (eg, for spasmodic dysphonia), includes guidance by needle electromyography, when performed

(For bilateral procedure, report 64617 with modifier 50)

(Do not report 64617 in conjunction with 95873, 95874)

(For diagnostic needle electromyography of the larynx, use 95865)

(For chemodenervation of the larynx performed with direct laryngoscopy, see 31570, 31571)

64620 Destruction by neurolytic agent, intercostal nerve

(Imaging guidance [fluoroscopy, CT] are inclusive components of 64633-64636)

(Imaging guidance [fluoroscopy, CT] and any injection of contrast are inclusive components of 64633-64636. Image guidance and localization are required for the performance of paravertebral facet joint nerve destruction by neurolytic agent described by 64633-64636. If CT or fluoroscopic imaging is not used, report 64999)

Report 64633, 64634, 64635, 64636 per joint, not per nerve. Although two nerves innervate each facet joint, only one code may be reported for each joint denervated, regardless of the number of nerves treated. Use 64634 or 64636 to report each additional facet joint at a different vertebral level in the same spinal region.

For neurolytic destruction of the nerves innervating the T12-L1 paravertebral facet joint, use 64633.

Do not report 64633, 64634, 64635, 64636 for non-thermal facet joint denervation including chemical, low-grade thermal energy (<80 degrees Celsius), or any form of pulsed radiofrequency. To appropriately report any of these modalities, use 64999.

64633 Destruction by neurolytic agent, paravertebral facet joint nerve(s), with imaging guidance (fluoroscopy or CT); cervical or thoracic, single facet joint

(For bilateral procedure, report 64633 with modifier 50)

+ 64634   cervical or thoracic, each additional facet joint (List separately in addition to code for primary procedure)

(Use 64634 in conjunction with 64633)

(For bilateral procedure, report 64634 with modifier 50)

64635   lumbar or sacral, single facet joint

(For bilateral procedure, report 64635 with modifier 50)

+ 64636   lumbar or sacral, each additional facet joint (List separately in addition to code for primary procedure)

(Use 64636 in conjunction with 64635)

(For bilateral procedure, report 64636 with modifier 50)

(Do not report 64633-64636 in conjunction with 77003, 77012)

(For destruction by neurolytic agent, individual nerves, sacroiliac joint, use 64640)

64630 Destruction by neurolytic agent; pudendal nerve

64632   plantar common digital nerve

(Do not report 64632 in conjunction with 64455)

64633 Code out of order. See page 587.

64634   Code out of order. See page 587.

64635   Code out of order. See page 587.

64636   Code out of order. See page 587.

64640   other peripheral nerve or branch

Report 64642, 64643, 64644, 64645 once per extremity. Codes 64642, 64643, 64644, 64645 can be reported together up to a combined total of four units of service per patient when all four extremities are injected. Report only one base code (64642 or 64644) per session. Report one or more units of additional extremity code(s) (64643 or 64645) for each additional extremity injected.

Report 64646 or 64647 for chemodenervation of muscles of the trunk.

Trunk muscles include the erector spinae and paraspinal muscles, rectus abdominus and obliques. All other somatic muscles are extremity muscles, head muscles, or neck muscles.

   (For chemodenervation guided by needle electromyography or muscle electrical stimulation, see 95873, 95874. Do not report more than one guidance code for each corresponding chemodenervation of extremity or trunk code)

   (Do not report modifier 50 in conjunction with 64642, 64643, 64644, 64645, 64646, 64647)

64642   Chemodenervation of one extremity; 1-4 muscle(s)

+ **64643**   each additional extremity, 1-4 muscle(s) (List separately in addition to code for primary procedure)

   (Use 64643 in conjunction with 64642, 64644)

64644   Chemodenercvation of one extremity; 5 or more muscles

+ **64645**   each additional extremity, 5 or more muscles (List separately in addition to code for primary procedure)

   (Use 64645 in conjunction with 64644)

64646   Chemodenervation of trunk muscle(s); 1-5 muscle(s)

64647   6 or more muscles

   (Report either 64646 or 64647 only once per session)

Sympathetic Nerves

64650   Chemodenervation of eccrine glands; both axillae

64653   other area(s) (eg, scalp, face, neck), per day

   (Report the specific service in conjunction with code(s) for the specific substance(s) or drug(s) provided)

   (For chemodenervation of extremities (eg, hands or feet), use 64999)

   (For chemodenervation of bladder, use 52287)

64680   Destruction by neurolytic agent, with or without radiologic monitoring; celiac plexus

   (For transendoscopic ultrasound-guided transmural injection, neurolytic agent, celiac plexus, use 43253)

64681   superior hypogastric plexus

NEUROPLASTY (EXPLORATION, NEUROLYSIS OR NERVE DECOMPRESSION)

Neuroplasty is the surgical decompression or freeing of intact nerve from scar tissue, including extrenal neurolysis and/or transposition to repair or restore the nerve.

      (For percutaneous neurolysis, see 62263, 62264, 62280-62282)

      (For internal neurolysis requiring use of operating microscope, use 64727)

      (For facial nerve decompression, use 69720)

      (For neuroplasty with nerve wrapping, see 64702-64727, 64999)

64702   Neuroplasty; digital, 1 or both, same digit

64704   nerve of hand or foot

64708   Neuroplasty, major peripheral nerve, arm or leg, open; other than specified

64712   sciatic nerve

64713   brachial plexus

64714   lumbar plexus

64716   Neuroplasty and/or transposition; cranial nerve (specify)

64718   ulnar nerve at elbow

64719   ulnar nerve at wrist

64721   median nerve at carpal tunnel

      (For arthroscopic procedure, use 29848)

64722   Decompression; unspecified nerve(s) (specify)

64726   plantar digital nerve

+ 64727   Internal neurolysis, requiring use of operating microscope (List separately in addition to code for neuroplasty) (Neuroplasty includes external neurolysis)

      (Do not report code 69990 in addition to code 64727)

TRANSECTION OR AVULSION

      (For stereotactic lesion of gasserian ganglion, use 61790)

64732   Transection or avulsion of; supraorbital nerve

64734   infraorbital nerve

64736   mental nerve

64738   inferior alveolar nerve by osteotomy

64740   lingual nerve

64742   facial nerve, differential or complete

64744   greater occipital nerve

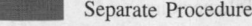 Separate Procedure   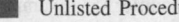 Unlisted Procedure   CCI Comp. Code   Non-specific Procedure   **589**

64746	phrenic nerve

(For section of recurrent laryngeal nerve, use 31595)

(64752	deleted 2014 [2015 edition])

64755	vagus nerves limited to proximal stomach (selective proximal vagotomy, proximal gastric vagotomy, parietal cell vagotomy, supra- or highly selective vagotomy)

(For laparoscopic approach, use 43652)

64760	vagus nerve (vagotomy), abdominal

(For laparoscopic approach, use 43651)

(64761	deleted 2014 [2015 edition])

(For bilateral procedure, report 64761 with modifier -50)

64763	Transection or avulsion of obturator nerve, extrapelvic, with or without adductor tenotomy

(For bilateral procedure, report 64763 with modifier -50)

64766	Transection or avulsion of obturator nerve, intrapelvic, with or without adductor tenotomy

(For bilateral procedure, report 64766 with modifier -50)

64771	Transection or avulsion of other cranial nerve, extradural

64772	Transection or avulsion of other spinal nerve, extradural

(For excision of tender scar, skin and subcutaneous tissue, with or without tiny neuroma, see 11400-11446, 13100-13153)

EXCISION

Somatic Nerves

(For Morton neurectomy, use 28080)

64774	Excision of neuroma; cutaneous nerve, surgically identifiable
64776	digital nerve, 1 or both, same digit
+ 64778	digital nerve, each additional digit (List separately in addition to code for primary procedure)

(Use 64778 in conjunction with code 64776)

64782	hand or foot, except digital nerve
+ 64783	hand or foot, each additional nerve, except same digit (List separately in addition to code for primary procedure)

(Use 64783 in conjunction with code 64782)

64784	major peripheral nerve, except sciatic
64786	sciatic nerve
+ 64787	Implantation of nerve end into bone or muscle (List separately in addition to neuroma excision)

(Use 64787 in conjunction with codes 64774-64786)

64788	Excision of neurofibroma or neurolemmoma; cutaneous nerve

---

● New Code ▲ Revised Code + Add-On Code ⊘ Modifier -51 Exempt ★ Telemedicine

64790	major peripheral nerve
64792	extensive (including malignant type)

(For destruction of extensive cutaneous neurofibroma, see 0419T, 0420T)

64795	Biopsy of nerve

Sympathetic Nerves

64802	Sympathectomy, cervical

(For bilateral procedure, report 64802 with modifier -50)

64804	Sympathectomy, cervicothoracic

(For bilateral procedure, report 64804 with modifier -50)

64809	Sympathectomy, thoracolumbar

(For bilateral procedure, report 64809 with modifier -50)

64818	Sympathectomy, lumbar

(For bilateral procedure, report 64818 with modifier -50)

64820	Sympathectomy; digital arteries, each digit

(Do not report 69990 in addition to code 64820)

64821	radial artery

(Do not report 69990 in addition to code 64821)

64822	ulnar artery

(Do not report 69990 in addition to code 64822)

64823	superficial palmar arch

(Do not report 69990 in addition to code 64823)

NEURORRHAPHY

64831	Suture of digital nerve, hand or foot; 1 nerve
+ 64832	each additional digital nerve (List separately in addition to code for primary procedure)

(Use 64832 in conjunction with code 64831)

64834	Suture of 1 nerve; hand or foot, common sensory nerve
64835	median motor thenar
64836	ulnar motor
+ 64837	Suture of each additional nerve, hand or foot (List separately in addition to code for primary procedure)

(Use 64837 in conjunction with codes 64834-64836)

64840	Suture of posterior tibial nerve
64856	Suture of major peripheral nerve, arm or leg, except sciatic; including transposition

▣ Separate Procedure	▣ Unlisted Procedure	▣ CCI Comp. Code	▣ Non-specific Procedure	**591**

64857	without transposition
64858	Suture of sciatic nerve
+ 64859	Suture of each additional major peripheral nerve (List separately in addition to code for primary procedure)

(Use 64859 in conjunction with codes 64856, 64857)

64861	Suture of; brachial plexus
64862	lumbar plexus
64864	Suture of facial nerve; extracranial
64865	infratemporal, with or without grafting
64866	Anastomosis; facial-spinal accessory
64868	facial-hypoglossal
(64870	deleted 2014 [2015 edition])
+ 64872	Suture of nerve; requiring secondary or delayed suture (List separately in addition to code for primary neurorrhaphy)

(Use 64872 in conjunction with codes 64831-64865)

| + 64874 | requiring extensive mobilization, or transposition of nerve (List separately in addition to code for nerve suture) |

(Use 64874 in conjunction with codes 64831-64865)

| + 64876 | requiring shortening of bone of extremity (List separately in addition to code for nerve suture) |

(Use 64876 in conjunction with codes 64831-64865)

NEURORRHAPHY WITH NERVE GRAFT, VEIN GRAFT, OR CONDUIT

64885	Nerve graft (includes obtaining graft), head or neck; up to 4 cm in length
64886	more than 4 cm length
64890	Nerve graft (includes obtaining graft), single strand, hand or foot; up to 4 cm length
64891	more than 4 cm length
64892	Nerve graft (includes obtaining graft), single strand, arm or leg; up to 4 cm length
64893	more than 4 cm length
64895	Nerve graft (includes obtaining graft), multiple strands (cable), hand or foot; up to 4 cm length
64896	more than 4 cm length
64897	Nerve graft (includes obtaining graft), multiple strands (cable), arm or leg; up to 4 cm length
64898	more than 4 cm length
+ 64901	Nerve graft, each additional nerve; single strand (List separately in addition to code for primary procedure)

(Use 64901 in conjunction with codes 64885-64893)

● New Code   ▲ Revised Code   + Add-On Code   ⊘ Modifier -51 Exempt   ★ Telemedicine

+ **64902**   multiple strands (cable) (List separately in addition to code for primary procedure)

(Use 64902 in conjunction with codes 64885, 64886, 64895-64898)

64905   Nerve pedicle transfer; first stage

64907   second stage

64910   Nerve repair; with synthetic conduit or vein allograft (eg, nerve tube), each nerve

64911   with autogenous vein graft (includes harvest of vein graft), each nerve

(Do not report 69990 in addition to 64910, 64911)

● **64912**   with nerve allograft, each nerve, first strand (cable)

●+**64913**   with nerve allograft, each additional strand (List separately in addition to code for primary procedure)

(Use 64913 in conjunction with 64912)

(Do not report 64912, 64913 in conjunction with 69990)

OTHER PROCEDURES

64999   Unlisted procedure, nervous system

■ Separate Procedure   ■ Unlisted Procedure   ■ CCI Comp. Code   ■ Non-specific Procedure   **593**

This page intentionally left blank.

● New Code ▲ Revised Code + Add-On Code ⊘ Modifier -51 Exempt ★ Telemedicine

EYE AND OCULAR ADNEXA

CPT codes from this section of the CPT coding system are used to report surgical procedures on the eye and ocular adnexa. Diagnostic services and medical treatment of the eye are defined in the Medicine Section of the CPT manual.

If surgical procedures are performed only on the eyelid, code from the Integumentary System subsection of the CPT coding system. Cataract codes are selected on the type of procedure performed. Whenever injections are performed during cataract surgery, do not report them separately.

When a subconjunctival injection (e.g. CPT code 68200) with a local anesthetic is performed as part of a more extensive anesthetic procedure (e.g. peribulbar or retrobulbar block), a separate service for this procedure is not to be reported. This is a routine part of the anesthetic procedure and does not represent a separate service.

Iridectomy, trabeculectomy, and anterior vitrectomy may be performed in conjunction with cataract removal. When an iridectomy is performed in order to accomplish the cataract extraction, it is an integral part of the procedure; it does not represent a separate service, and is not separately reported. Similarly, the minimal vitreous loss occurring during routine cataract extraction does not represent a vitrectomy and is not to be separately reported unless it is medically necessary for a different diagnosis.

While a trabeculectomy is not performed as a part of a cataract extraction, it may be performed to control glaucoma at the same time as a cataract extraction. If the procedure is medically necessary at the same time as a cataract extraction, it can be reported under a different diagnosis (e.g. glaucoma). The codes describing iridectomies, trabeculectomies, and anterior vitrectomies, when performed with a cataract extraction under a separate diagnosis, must be reported with modifier - 59. This indicates that the procedure was performed as a different service for a separate situation. The medical record should reflect the medical necessity of the service if separately reported.

For example, if a patient presents with a cataract and has evidence of glaucoma, (i.e. elevated intraocular pressure preoperatively) and a trabeculectomy represents the appropriate treatment for the glaucoma, a separate service for the trabeculectomy would be separately reported. Performance of a trabeculectomy as a preventative service for an expected transient increase in intraocular pressure postoperatively, without other evidence for glaucoma, is not to be separately reported.

The various approaches to removing a cataract are mutually exclusive of one another when performed on the same eye.

Some retinal detachment repair procedures include some vitreous procedures (e.g. CPT code 67108 includes 67015, 67025, 67028, 67031, 67036, 67039, and 67040). Certain retinal detachment repairs are mutually exclusive to anterior procedures such as focal endolaser photocoagulation (e.g. CPT codes 67110 and 67112 are mutually exclusive to CPT code 67108).

CPT codes 68020-68200 (incision, drainage, excision of the conjunctiva) are included in all conjunctivoplasties (CPT codes 68320-68362).

CPT code 67950 (canthoplasty) is included in repair procedures such as blepharoplasties (CPT codes 67917, 67924, 67961, 67966).

Correction of lid retraction (CPT code 67911) includes full thickness graft (e.g. CPT code 15260) as part of the total service performed.

In the circumstance that it is medically necessary and reasonable to inject sclerosing agents in the same session as surgery to correct glaucoma, the service is included in the glaucoma surgery. Accordingly, codes such as CPT codes 67500, 67515, and 68200 for injection of sclerosing agents (e.g. 5-FU, HCPCS/CPT code J9190) should not be reported with other pressure-reducing or glaucoma procedures.

(For diagnostic and treatment ophthalmological services, see Medicine, Ophthalmology, and 92002 et seq)

(Do not report code 69990 in addition to codes 65091-68850)

EYEBALL

REMOVAL OF EYE

65091   Evisceration of ocular contents; without implant

65093   with implant

Separate Procedure   Unlisted Procedure   CCI Comp. Code   Non-specific Procedure   **595**

65101   Enucleation of eye; without implant

65103   with implant, muscles not attached to implant

65105   with implant, muscles attached to implant

(For conjunctivoplasty after enucleation, see 68320 et seq)

65110   Exenteration of orbit (does not include skin graft), removal of orbital contents; only

65112   with therapeutic removal of bone

65114   with muscle or myocutaneous flap

(For skin graft to orbit (split skin), see 15120, 15121; free, full thickness, see 15260, 15261)

(For eyelid repair involving more than skin, see 67930 et seq)

SECONDARY IMPLANT(S) PROCEDURES

65125   Modification of ocular implant with placement or replacement of pegs (eg, drilling receptacle for prosthesis appendage) (separate procedure)

65130   Insertion of ocular implant secondary; after evisceration, in scleral shell

65135   after enucleation, muscles not attached to implant

65140   after enucleation, muscles attached to implant

65150   Reinsertion of ocular implant; with or without conjunctival graft

65155   with use of foreign material for reinforcement and/or attachment of muscles to implant

65175   Removal of ocular implant

(For orbital implant (implant outside muscle cone) insertion, use 67550; removal, use 67560)

REMOVAL OF FOREIGN BODY

(For removal of implanted material: ocular implant, use 65175; anterior segment implant, use 65920; posterior segment implant, use 67120; orbital implant, use 67560)

(For diagnostic x-ray for foreign body, use 70030)

(For diagnostic echography for foreign body, use 76529)

(For removal of foreign body from orbit: frontal approach, use 67413; lateral approach, use 67430)

(For removal of foreign body from eyelid, embedded, use 67938)

(For removal of foreign body from lacrimal system, use 68530)

65205   Removal of foreign body, external eye; conjunctival superficial

65210   conjunctival embedded (includes concretions), subconjunctival, or scleral nonperforating

65220   corneal, without slit lamp

65222   corneal, with slit lamp

(For repair of corneal laceration with foreign body, use 65275)

65235   Removal of foreign body, intraocular; from anterior chamber of eye or lens

---

(For removal of implanted material from anterior segment, use 65920)

65260   from posterior segment, magnetic extraction, anterior or posterior route

65265   from posterior segment, nonmagnetic extraction

(For removal of implanted material from posterior segment, use 67120)

REPAIR OF LACERATION

(For fracture of orbit, see 21385 et seq)

(For repair of wound of eyelid, skin, linear, simple, see 12011-12018; intermediate, layered closure, see 12051-12057; linear, complex, see 13151-13160; other, see 67930, 67935)

(For repair of wound of lacrimal system, use 68700)

(For repair of operative wound, use 66250)

65270 Repair of laceration; conjunctiva, with or without nonperforating laceration sclera, direct closure

65272   conjunctiva, by mobilization and rearrangement, without hospitalization

65273   conjunctiva, by mobilization and rearrangement, with hospitalization

65275   cornea, nonperforating, with or without removal foreign body

65280   cornea and/or sclera, perforating, not involving uveal tissue

65285   cornea and/or sclera, perforating, with reposition or resection of uveal tissue

(65280 amd 65285 are not used for repair of a surgical wound)

65286   application of tissue glue, wounds of cornea and/or sclera

(Repair of laceration includes use of conjunctival flap and restoration of anterior chamber, by air or saline injection when indicated)

(For repair of iris or ciliary body, use 66680)

65290 Repair of wound, extraocular muscle, tendon and/or Tenon's capsule

ANTERIOR SEGMENT

CORNEA

Excision

65400 Excision of lesion, cornea (keratectomy, lamellar, partial), except pterygium

65410 Biopsy of cornea

65420 Excision or transposition of pterygium; without graft

65426   with graft

Removal or Destruction

65430 Scraping of cornea, diagnostic, for smear and/or culture

65435 Removal of corneal epithelium; with or without chemocauterization (abrasion, curettage)

(Do not report 65435 in conjunction with 0402T)

| 65436 | with application of chelating agent (eg, EDTA) |

| 65450 | Destruction of lesion of cornea by cryotherapy, photocoagulation or thermocauterization |

| 65600 | Multiple punctures of anterior cornea (eg, for corneal erosion, tattoo) |

Keratoplasty

Corneal transplant includes use of fresh or preserved grafts. The preparation of donor material is included for penetrating or anterior lamellar keratoplasty, but reported separately for endothelial keratoplasty. Do not report 65710-65757 in conjunction with 92025.

(Keratoplasty excludes refractive keratoplasty procedures, 65760, 65765, and 65767)

| 65710 | Keratoplasty (corneal transplant); anterior lamellar |

| 65730 | penetrating (except in aphakia or pseudoaphakia) |

| 65750 | penetrating (in aphakia) |

| 65755 | penetrating (in pseudophakia) |

| 65756 | endothelial |

+ 65757 Backbench preparation of corneal endothelial allograft prior to transplantation (list separately in addition to code for primary procedure)

(Use 65757 in conjunction with 65756)

Other Procedures

Do not report 65760-65771 in conjunction with 92025.

| 65760 | Keratomileusis |

| 65765 | Keratophakia |

| 65767 | Epikeratoplasty |

| 65770 | Keratoprosthesis |

| 65771 | Radial keratotomy |

| 65772 | Corneal relaxing incision for correction of surgically induced astigmatism |

| 65775 | Corneal wedge resection for correction of surgically induced astigmatism |

(For fitting of contact lens for treatment of disease, use 92071, 92072)

(For unlisted procedures on cornea, use 66999)

| 65778 | Placement of amniotic membrane on the ocular surface; without sutures |

| 65779 | single layer, sutured |

(Do not report 65778, 65779 in conjunction with 65430, 65435, 65780)

(For placement of amniotic membrane using tissue glue, use 66999)

| 65780 | Ocular surface reconstruction; amniotic membrane transplantation, multiple layers |

(For placement of amniotic membrane without reconstruction using no sutures or single layer suture technique, see 65778, 65779)

● New Code ▲ Revised Code + Add-On Code ⊘ Modifier -51 Exempt ★ Telemedicine

65781   limbal stem cell allograft (eg, cadaveric or living donor)

65782   limbal conjunctival autograft (includes obtaining graft)

(For harvesting conjunctival allograft, living donor, use 68371)

65785   Implantation of intrastromal corneal ring segments

ANTERIOR CHAMBER

Incision

65800   Paracentesis of anterior chamber of eye (separate procedure); with removal of aqueous

65810   with removal of vitreous and/or discission of anterior hyaloid membrane, with or without air injection

65815   with removal of blood, with or without irrigation and/or air injection

(For injection, see 66020-66030)

(For removal of blood clot, use 65930)

65820   Goniotomy

(Do not report modifier -63 in conjunction with 65820)

(For use of ophthalmic endoscope with 65820, use 66990)

65850   Trabeculotomy ab externo

65855   Trabeculoplasty by laser surgery

(Do not report 65855 in conjunction with 65860, 65865, 65870, 65875, 65880)

(For trabeculectomy, use 66170)

65860   Severing adhesions of anterior segment, laser technique (separate procedure)

65865   Severing adhesions of anterior segment of eye, incisional technique (with or without injection of air or liquid) (separate procedure); goniosynechiae

(For trabeculoplasty by laser surgery, use 65855)

65870   anterior synechiae, except goniosynechiae

65875   posterior synechiae

(For use of ophthalmic endoscope with 65875, use 66990)

65880   corneovitreal adhesions

(For laser surgery, use 66821)

Removal

65900   Removal of epithelial downgrowth, anterior chamber of eye

65920   Removal of implanted material, anterior segment of eye

(For use of ophthalmic endoscope with 65920, use 66990)

65930   Removal of blood clot, anterior segment of eye

Introduction

66020   Injection, anterior chamber of eye (separate procedure); air or liquid

66030   medication

         (For unlisted procedures on anterior segment, use 66999)

ANTERIOR SCLERA

Excision

         (For removal of intraocular foreign body, use 65235)

         (For operations on posterior sclera, use 67250, 67255)

66130   Excision of lesion, sclera

66150   Fistulization of sclera for glaucoma; trephination with iridectomy

66155   thermocauterization with iridectomy

66160   sclerectomy with punch or scissors, with iridectomy

(**66165**   deleted 2014 [2015 edition])

66170   trabeculectomy ab externo in absence of previous surgery

         (For trabeculotomy ab externo, use 65850)

         (For repair of operative wound, use 66250)

66172   trabeculectomy ab externo with scarring from previous ocular surgery or trauma (includes injection of antifibrotic agents)

66174   Transluminal dilation of aqueous outflow canal; without retention of device or stent

66175   with retention of device or stent

Aqueous Shunt

66179   Aqueous shunt to extraocular equatorial plate reservois, external approach; without graft

66180   with graft

         (Do not report 66180 in conjunction with 67255)

66183   Insertion of anterior segment aqueous drainage device, without extraocular reservoir, external approach

66184   Revision of aqueous shunt to extraocular equatorial plate reservoir; without graft

66185   with graft

         (Do not report 66185 in conjunction with 67255)

         (For removal of implanted shunt, use 67120)

Repair or Revision

         (For scleral procedures in retinal surgery, see 67101 et seq)

66220   Repair of scleral staphyloma; without graft

66225   with graft

   ● New Code   ▲ Revised Code   + Add-On Code   ⊘ Modifier -51 Exempt   ★ Telemedicine

(For scleral reinforcement, see 67250, 67255)

66250 Revision or repair of operative wound of anterior segment, any type, early or late, major or minor procedure

(For unlisted procedures on anterior sclera, use 66999)

IRIS, CILIARY BODY

Incision

66500 Iridotomy by stab incision (separate procedure); except transfixion

66505 with transfixion as for iris bombe

(For iridotomy by photocoagulation, use 66761)

Excision

66600 Iridectomy, with corneoscleral or corneal section; for removal of lesion

66605 with cyclectomy

66625 peripheral for glaucoma (separate procedure)

66630 sector for glaucoma (separate procedure)

66635 optical (separate procedure)

(For coreoplasty by photocoagulation, use 66762)

Repair

66680 Repair of iris, ciliary body (as for iridodialysis)

(For reposition or resection of uveal tissue with perforating wound of cornea or sclera, use 65285)

66682 Suture of iris, ciliary body (separate procedure) with retrieval of suture through small incision (eg, McCannel suture)

Destruction

66700 Ciliary body destruction; diathermy

66710 cyclophotocoagulation, transscleral

66711 cyclophotocoagulation, endoscopic

(Do not report 66711 in conjunction with 66990)

66720 cryotherapy

66740 cyclodialysis

66761 Iridotomy/iridectomy by laser surgery (eg, for glaucoma) (per session)

66762 Iridoplasty by photocoagulation (1 or more sessions) (eg, for improvement of vision, for widening of anterior chamber angle)

66770 Destruction of cyst or lesion iris or ciliary body (nonexcisional procedure)

(For excision lesion iris, ciliary body, see 66600, 66605; for removal of epithelial downgrowth, use 65900)

Separate Procedure   Unlisted Procedure   CCI Comp. Code   Non-specific Procedure   **601**

(For unlisted procedures on iris, ciliary body, use 66999)

LENS

Incision

66820   Discission of secondary membranous cataract (opacified posterior lens capsule and/or anterior hyaloid); stab incision technique (Ziegler or Wheeler knife)

66821   laser surgery (eg, YAG laser) (1 or more stages)

66825   Repositioning of intraocular lens prosthesis, requiring an incision (separate procedure)

Removal

Lateral canthotomy, iridectomy, iridotomy, anterior capsulotomy, posterior capsulotomy, the use of viscoelastic agents, enzymatic zonulysis, use of other pharmacologic agents, and subconjunctival or sub-tenon injections are included as part of the code for the extraction of lens.

66830   Removal of secondary membranous cataract (opacified posterior lens capsule and/or anterior hyaloid) with corneo-scleral section, with or without iridectomy (iridocapsulotomy, iridocapsulectomy)

66840   Removal of lens material; aspiration technique, 1 or more stages

66850   phacofragmentation technique (mechanical or ultrasonic) (eg, phacoemulsification), with aspiration

66852   pars plana approach, with or without vitrectomy

66920   intracapsular

66930   intracapsular, for dislocated lens

66940   extracapsular (other than 66840, 66850, 66852)

(For removal of intralenticular foreign body without lens extraction, use 65235)

(For repair of operative wound, use 66250)

INTRAOCULAR LENS PROCEDURES

66982   Extracapsular cataract removal with insertion of intraocular lens prosthesis (1 stage procedure), manual or mechanical technique (eg, irrigation and aspiration or phacoemulsification), complex, requiring devices or techniques not generally used in routine cataract surgery (eg, iris expansion device, suture support for intraocular lens, or primary posterior capsulorrhexis) or performed on patients in the amblyogenic developmental stage

(For insertion of ocular telescope prosthesis including removal of crystalline lens, use 0308T)

66983   Intracapsular cataract extraction with insertion of intraocular lens prosthesis (1 stage procedure)

(Do not report 66983 in conjunction with 0308T)

66984   Extracapsular cataract removal with insertion of intraocular lens prosthesis (1 stage procedure), manual or mechanical technique (eg, irrigation and aspiration or phacoemulsification)

(For complex extracapsular cataract removal, use 66982)

(For insertion of ocular telescope prosthesis including removal of crystalline lens, use 0308T)

66985   Insertion of intraocular lens prosthesis (secondary implant), not associated with concurrent cataract removal

(To code implant at time of concurrent cataract surgery, see 66982, 66983, 66984)

(To report supply of intraocular lens prosthesis, use 99070)

● New Code   ▲ Revised Code   + Add-On Code   ⊘ Modifier -51 Exempt   ★ Telemedicine

(For ultrasonic determination of intraocular lens power, use 76519)

(For removal of implanted material from anterior segment, use 65920)

(For secondary fixation (separate procedure), use 66682)

(For use of ophthalmic endoscope with 66985, use 66990)

66986 Exchange of intraocular lens

(For use of ophthalmic endoscope with 66986, use 66990)

OTHER PROCEDURES

+ **66990** Use of ophthalmic endoscope (List separately in addition to code for primary procedure)

(66990 may be used only with codes 65820, 65875, 65920, 66985, 66986, 67036, 67039, 67040, 67041, 67042, 67043, 67113)

66999 Unlisted procedure, anterior segment of eye

POSTERIOR SEGMENT

VITREOUS

67005 Removal of vitreous, anterior approach (open sky technique or limbal incision); partial removal

67010 subtotal removal with mechanical vitrectomy

(For removal of vitreous by paracentesis of anterior chamber, use 65810)

(For removal of corneovitreal adhesions, use 65880)

67015 Aspiration or release of vitreous, subretinal or choroidal fluid, pars plana approach (posterior sclerotomy)

67025 Injection of vitreous substitute, pars plana or limbal approach, (fluid-gas exchange), with or without aspiration (separate procedure)

67027 Implantation of intravitreal drug delivery system (eg, ganciclovir implant), includes concomitant removal of vitreous

(For removal, use 67121)

67028 Intravitreal injection of a pharmacologic agent (separate procedure)

67030 Discission of vitreous strands (without removal), pars plana approach

67031 Severing of vitreous strands, vitreous face adhesions, sheets, membranes or opacities, laser surgery (1 or more stages)

67036 Vitrectomy, mechanical, pars plana approach;

(For application of intraocular epiretinal radiation with 67036, use 0190T)

67039 with focal endolaser photocoagulation

67040 with endolaser panretinal photocoagulation

67041 with removal of preretinal cellular membrane (eg, macular pucker)

67042 with removal of internal limiting membrane of retina (eg, for repair of macular hole, diabetic macular edema), includes, if performed, intraocular tamponade (ie, air, gas or silicone oil)

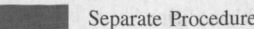 Separate Procedure   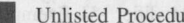 Unlisted Procedure   CCI Comp. Code   Non-specific Procedure   **603**

67043   with removal of subretinal membrane (eg, choroidal neovascularization), includes, if performed, intraocular tamponade (ie, air, gas or silicone oil) and laser photocoagulation

(For use of ophthalmic endoscope with 67036, 67039, 67040-67043, use 66990)

(For associated lensectomy, use 66850)

(For use of vitrectomy in retinal detachment surgery, see 67108, 67113)

(For associated removal of foreign body, see 65260, 65265)

(For unlisted procedures on vitreous, use 67299)

RETINA OR CHOROID

Repair

(If diathermy, cryotherapy and/or photocoagulation are combined, report under principal modality used)

67101   Repair of retinal detachment, including drainage of subretinal fluid when performed; cryotherapy

67105   photocoagulation

67107   Repair of retinal detachment; scleral buckling (such as lamellar scleral dissection, imbrication or encircling procedure), including, when performed, implant, cryotherapy, photocoagulation, and drainage of subretinal fluid

67108   with vitrectomy, any method, including, when performed, air or gas tamponade, focal endolaser photocoagulation, cryotherapy, drainage of subretinal fluid, scleral buckling, and/or removal of lens by same technique

67110   by injection of air or other gas (eg, pneumatic retinopexy)

(67112   deleted 2015 [2016 edition]. To report, see 67107, 67108, 67110, 67113)

(For aspiration of drainage of subretinal or subchoroidal fluid, use 67015)

67113   Repair of complex retinal detachment (eg, proliferative vitreoretinopathy, stage C-1 or greater, diabetic traction retinal detachment, retinopathy of prematurity, retinal tear of greater than 90 degrees), with vitrectomy and membrane peeling, including, when performed, air, gas, or silicone oil tamponade, cryotherapy, endolaser photocoagulation, drainage of subretinal fluid, scleral buckling, and/or removal of lens

(To report vitrectomy, pars plana approach, other than in retinal detachment surgery, see 67036-67043)

(For use of ophthalmic endoscope with 67113, use 66990)

67115   Release of encircling material (posterior segment)

67120   Removal of implanted material, posterior segment; extraocular

67121   intraocular

(For removal from anterior segment, use 65920)

(For removal of foreign body, see 65260, 65265)

Prophylaxis

Codes 67141, 67145 include treatment at one or more sessions that may occur at different encounters. These codes should be reported once during a defined treatment period.

Repetitive services. The services listed below are often performed in multiple sessions or groups of sessions. The methods of reporting vary. The following descriptors are intended to include all sessions in a defined treatment period.

67141 Prophylaxis of retinal detachment (eg, retinal break, lattice degeneration) without drainage, 1 or more sessions; cryotherapy, diathermy

67145   photocoagulation (laser or xenon arc)

Destruction

Codes 67208, 67210, 67218, 67220, 67229 include treatment at one or more sessions that may occur at different encounters. These codes should be reported once during a defined treatment period.

67208 Destruction of localized lesion of retina (eg, macular edema, tumors), 1 or more sessions; cryotherapy, diathermy

67210   photocoagulation

67218   radiation by implantation of source (includes removal of source)

67220 Destruction of localized lesion of choroid (eg, choroidal neovascularization); photocoagulation (eg, laser), 1 or more sessions

67221   photodynamic therapy (includes intravenous infusion)

+ **67225**   photodynamic therapy, second eye, at single session (List separately in addition to code for primary eye treatment)

(Use 67225 in conjunction with code 67221)

67227 Destruction of extensive or progressive retinopathy (eg, diabetic retinopathy), cryotherapy, diathermy

67228 Treatment of extensive or progressive retinopathy (eg, diabetic retinopathy), photocoagulation

67229   preterm infant (less than 37 weeks gestation at birth), performed from birth up to 1 year of age (eg, retinopathy of prematurity), photocoagulation or cryotherapy

(For bilateral procedure, use modifier 50 with 67208, 67210, 67218, 67220, 67227, 67228, 67229)

(For unlisted procedures on retina, use 67299)

POSTERIOR SCLERA

Repair

(For excision lesion sclera, use 66130)

67250 Scleral reinforcement (separate procedure); without graft

67255   with graft

(Do not report 67255 in conjunction with 66180, 66185)

(For repair scleral staphyloma, see 66220, 66225)

OTHER PROCEDURES

67299 Unlisted procedure, posterior segment

OCULAR ADNEXA

EXTRAOCULAR MUSCLES

67311 Strabismus surgery, recession or resection procedure; 1 horizontal muscle

67312   2 horizontal muscles

67314	1 vertical muscle (excluding superior oblique)
67316	2 or more vertical muscles (excluding superior oblique)

(For adjustable sutures, use 67335 in addition to codes 67311-67334 for primary procedure reflecting number of muscles operated on)

67318	Strabismus surgery, any procedure, superior oblique muscle
+ 67320	Transposition procedure (eg, for paretic extraocular muscle), any extraocular muscle (specify) (List separately in addition to code for primary procedure)

(Use 67320 in conjunction with codes 67311-67318)

+ 67331	Strabismus surgery on patient with previous eye surgery or injury that did not involve the extraocular muscles (List separately in addition to code for primary procedure)

(Use 67331 in conjunction with codes 67311-67318)

+ 67332	Strabismus surgery on patient with scarring of extraocular muscles (eg, prior ocular injury, strabismus or retinal detachment surgery) or restrictive myopathy (eg, dysthyroid ophthalmopathy) (List separately in addition to code for primary procedure)

(Use 67332 in conjunction with codes 67311-67318)

+ 67334	Strabismus surgery by posterior fixation suture technique, with or without muscle recession (List separately in addition to code for primary procedure)

(Use 67334 in conjunction with codes 67311-67318)

+ 67335	Placement of adjustable suture(s) during strabismus surgery, including postoperative adjustment(s) of suture(s) (List separately in addition to code for specific strabismus surgery)

(Use 67335 in conjunction with codes 67311-67334)

+ 67340	Strabismus surgery involving exploration and/or repair of detached extraocular muscle(s) (List separately in addition to code for primary procedure)

(Use 67340 in conjunction with codes 67311-67334)

67343	Release of extensive scar tissue without detaching extraocular muscle (separate procedure)

(Use 67343 in conjunction with codes 67311-67340, when such procedures are performed other than on the affected muscle)

67345	Chemodenervation of extraocular muscle

(For chemodenervation for blepharospasm and other neurological disorders, see 64612 and 64616)

67346	Biopsy of extraocular muscle

(For repair of wound, extraocular muscle, tendon or Tenon's capsule, use 65290)

Other Procedures

67399	Unlisted procedure, extraocular muscle

ORBIT

Exploration, Excision, Decompression

67400	Orbitotomy without bone flap (frontal or transconjunctival approach); for exploration, with or without biopsy
67405	with drainage only

● New Code   ▲ Revised Code   + Add-On Code   ⊘ Modifier -51 Exempt   ★ Telemedicine

67412	with removal of lesion
67413	with removal of foreign body
67414	with removal of bone for decompression
67415	Fine needle aspiration of orbital contents

(For exenteration, enucleation, and repair, see 65101 et seq; for optic nerve decompression, use 67570)

67420	Orbitotomy with bone flap or window, lateral approach (eg, Kroenlein); with removal of lesion
67430	with removal of foreign body
67440	with drainage
67445	with removal of bone for decompression

(For optic nerve sheath decompression, use 67570)

67450	for exploration, with or without biopsy

(For orbitotomy, transcranial approach, see 61330, 61332, 61333)

(For orbital implant, see 67550, 67560)

(For removal of eyeball or for repair after removal, see 65091-65175)

Other Procedures

67500	Retrobulbar injection; medication (separate procedure, does not include supply of medication)
67505	alcohol
67515	Injection of medication or other substance into Tenon's capsule

(For subconjunctival injection, use 68200)

67550	Orbital implant (implant outside muscle cone); insertion
67560	removal or revision

(For ocular implant (implant inside muscle cone), see 65093-65105, 65130-65175)

(For treatment of fractures of malar area, orbit, see 21355 et seq)

67570	Optic nerve decompression (eg, incision or fenestration of optic nerve sheath)
67599	Unlisted procedure, orbit

EYELIDS

Incision

67700	Blepharotomy, drainage of abscess, eyelid
67710	Severing of tarsorrhaphy
67715	Canthotomy (separate procedure)

(For canthoplasty, use 67950)

(For division of symblepharon, use 68340)

67810   Incisional biopsy of eyelid skin includnig lid margin

      (For biopsy of skin of eyelid, see 11100, 11101, 11310-11313)

Excision, Destruction

Codes for removal of lesions include more than skin (ie., involving lid margin, tarsus, and/or palpebral conjunctiva).

      (For removal of lesion, involving mainly skin of eyelid, see 11310-11313; 11440-11446, 11640-11646; 17000-17004)

      (For repair of wounds, blepharoplasty, grafts, reconstructive surgery, see 67930-67975)

67800   Excision of chalazion; single

67801   multiple, same lid

67805   multiple, different lids

67808   under general anesthesia and/or requiring hospitalization, single or multiple

67810   Code out of order. See page 608.

67820   Correction of trichiasis; epilation, by forceps only

67825   epilation by other than forceps (eg, by electrosurgery, cryotherapy, laser surgery)

67830   incision of lid margin

67835   incision of lid margin, with free mucous membrane graft

67840   Excision of lesion of eyelid (except chalazion) without closure or with simple direct closure

      (For excision and repair of eyelid by reconstructive surgery, see 67961, 67966)

67850   Destruction of lesion of lid margin (up to 1 cm)

      (For Mohs micrographic surgery, see 17311-17315)

      (For initiation or follow-up care of topical chemotherapy (eg, 5-FU or similar agents), see appropriate office visits)

Tarsorrhaphy

67875   Temporary closure of eyelids by suture (eg, Frost suture)

67880   Construction of intermarginal adhesions, median tarsorrhaphy, or canthorrhaphy;

67882   with transposition of tarsal plate

      (For severing of tarsorrhaphy, use 67710)

      (For canthoplasty, reconstruction canthus, use 67950)

      (For canthotomy, use 67715)

Repair (Brow Ptosis, Blepharoptosis, Lid Retraction, Ectropion, Entropion)

67900   Repair of brow ptosis (supraciliary, mid-forehead or coronal approach)

      (For forehead rhytidectomy, use 15824)

67901   Repair of blepharoptosis; frontalis muscle technique with suture or other material (eg, banked fascia)

67902   frontalis muscle technique with autologous fascial sling (includes obtaining fascia)

67903   (tarso) levator resection or advancement, internal approach

67904   (tarso) levator resection or advancement, external approach

67906   superior rectus technique with fascial sling (includes obtaining fascia)

67908   conjunctivo-tarso-Muller's muscle-levator resection (eg, Fasanella-Servat type)

67909   Reduction of overcorrection of ptosis

67911   Correction of lid retraction

(For obtaining autogenous graft materials, see 20920, 20922, or 20926)

(For correction of trichiasis by mucous membrane graft, use 67835)

67912   Correction of lagophthalmos, with implantation of upper eyelid load (eg, gold weight)

67914   Repair of ectropion; suture

67915   thermocauterization

67916   excision tarsal wedge

67917   extensive (eg, tarsal strip operations)

(For correction of everted punctum, use 68705)

67921   Repair of entropion; suture

67922   thermocauterization

67923   excision tarsal wedge

67924   extensive (eg, tarsal strip or capsulopalpebral fascia repairs operation)

(For repair of cicatricial ectropion or entropion requiring scar excision or skin graft, see also 67961 et seq)

Reconstruction

Codes for blepharoplasty involve more than skin (ie., involving lid margin, tarsus, and/or palpebral conjunctiva).

67930   Suture of recent wound, eyelid, involving lid margin, tarsus, and/or palpebral conjunctiva direct closure; partial thickness

67935   full thickness

67938   Removal of embedded foreign body, eyelid

(For repair of skin of eyelid, see 12011-12018; 12051-12057; 13151-13153)

(For tarsorrhaphy, canthorrhaphy, see 67880, 67882)

(For repair of blepharoptosis and lid retraction, see 67901-67911)

(For blepharoplasty for entropion, ectropion, see 67916, 67917, 67923, 67924)

(For correction of blepharochalasis (blepharorhytidectomy), see 15820-15823)

(For repair of skin of eyelid, adjacent tissue transfer, see 14060, 14061; preparation for graft, use 15004; free graft, see 15120, 15121, 15260, 15261)

(For excision of lesion of eyelid, use 67800 et seq)

(For repair of lacrimal canaliculi, use 68700)

67950 Canthoplasty (reconstruction of canthus)

67961 Excision and repair of eyelid, involving lid margin, tarsus, conjunctiva, canthus, or full thickness, may include preparation for skin graft or pedicle flap with adjacent tissue transfer or rearrangement; up to one-fourth of lid margin

67966 over one-fourth of lid margin

(For canthoplasty, use 67950)

(For free skin grafts, see 15120, 15121, 15260, 15261)

(For tubed pedicle flap preparation, use 15576; for delay, use 15630; for attachment, use 15650)

67971 Reconstruction of eyelid, full thickness by transfer of tarsoconjunctival flap from opposing eyelid; up to two-thirds of eyelid, 1 stage or first stage

67973 total eyelid, lower, 1 stage or first stage

67974 total eyelid, upper, 1 stage or first stage

67975 second stage

Other Procedures

67999 Unlisted procedure, eyelids

CONJUNCTIVA

(For removal of foreign body, see 65205 et seq)

INCISION AND DRAINAGE

68020 Incision of conjunctiva, drainage of cyst

68040 Expression of conjunctival follicles (eg, for trachoma)

(To report automated evacuation of Meibomian glands, use 0207T)

EXCISION AND/OR DESTRUCTION

68100 Biopsy of conjunctiva

68110 Excision of lesion, conjunctiva; up to 1 cm

68115 over 1 cm

68130 with adjacent sclera

68135 Destruction of lesion, conjunctiva

INJECTION

(For injection into Tenon's capsule or retrobulbar injection, see 67500-67515)

68200 Subconjunctival injection

● New Code ▲ Revised Code ＋ Add-On Code ⊘ Modifier -51 Exempt ★ Telemedicine

CONJUNCTIVOPLASTY

(For wound repair, see 65270-65273)

68320 Conjunctivoplasty; with conjunctival graft or extensive rearrangement

68325 with buccal mucous membrane graft (includes obtaining graft)

68326 Conjunctivoplasty, reconstruction cul-de-sac; with conjunctival graft or extensive rearrangement

68328 with buccal mucous membrane graft (includes obtaining graft)

68330 Repair of symblepharon; conjunctivoplasty, without graft

68335 with free graft conjunctiva or buccal mucous membrane (includes obtaining graft)

68340 division of symblepharon, with or without insertion of conformer or contact lens

OTHER PROCEDURES

68360 Conjunctival flap; bridge or partial (separate procedure)

68362 total (such as Gunderson thin flap or purse string flap)

(For conjunctival flap for perforating injury, see 65280, 65285)

(For repair of operative wound, use 66250)

(For removal of conjunctival foreign body, see 65205, 65210)

68371 Harvesting conjunctival allograft, living donor

68399 Unlisted procedure, conjunctiva

LACRIMAL SYSTEM

Incision

68400 Incision, drainage of lacrimal gland

68420 Incision, drainage of lacrimal sac (dacryocystotomy or dacryocystostomy)

68440 Snip incision of lacrimal punctum

Excision

68500 Excision of lacrimal gland (dacryoadenectomy), except for tumor; total

68505 partial

68510 Biopsy of lacrimal gland

68520 Excision of lacrimal sac (dacryocystectomy)

68525 Biopsy of lacrimal sac

68530 Removal of foreign body or dacryolith, lacrimal passages

68540 Excision of lacrimal gland tumor; frontal approach

68550 involving osteotomy

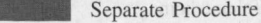 Separate Procedure ▮ Unlisted Procedure ▮ CCI Comp. Code ▮ Non-specific Procedure **611**

Repair

68700   Plastic repair of canaliculi

68705   Correction of everted punctum, cautery

68720   Dacryocystorhinostomy (fistulization of lacrimal sac to nasal cavity)

68745   Conjunctivorhinostomy (fistulization of conjunctiva to nasal cavity); without tube

68750   with insertion of tube or stent

68760   Closure of the lacrimal punctum; by thermocauterization, ligation, or laser surgery

68761   by plug, each

(For insertion and removal of drug-eluting implant into lacrimal canaliculus for intra-ocular pressure, use 0356T)

(For placement of drug-eluting insert under the eyelid[s], see 0444T, 0445T)

68770   Closure of lacrimal fistula (separate procedure)

Probing and/or Related Procedures

68801   Dilation of lacrimal punctum, with or without irrigation

(To report a bilateral procedure, use 68801 with modifier -50)

68810   Probing of nasolacrimal duct, with or without irrigation;

(For bilateral procedure, report 68810 with modifier -50)

68811   requiring general anesthesia

(For bilateral procedure, report 68811 with modifier -50)

68815   with insertion of tube or stent

(See also 92018)

(For bilateral procedure, report 68815 with modifier -50)

(For insertion and removal of drug-eluting implant into lacrimal canaliculus for intra-ocular pressure, use 0356T)

(For placement of drug-eluting insert under the eyelid[s], see 0444T, 0445T)

68816   with transluminal balloon catheter dilation

(Do not report 68816 in conjunction with 68810, 68811, 68815)

(For bilateral procedure, report 68816 with modifier -50)

68840   Probing of lacrimal canaliculi, with or without irrigation

68850   Injection of contrast medium for dacryocystography

(For radiological supervision and interpretation, see 70170, 78660)

Other Procedures

68899   Unlisted procedure, lacrimal system

---

612   ● New Code   ▲ Revised Code   + Add-On Code   ⊘ Modifier -51 Exempt   ★ Telemedicine

AUDITORY SYSTEM

CPT codes from this subsection of the CPT coding system are used to report invasive and surgical procedures performed on the external ear; middle ear; inner ear and temporal bone. Includes procedures performed on the inner, outer and middle ear and to the temporal bone.

Diagnostic services, such as otoscopy under general anesthesia, audiometry and vestibular tests, are defined in the Medicine Section of the CPT manual.

Wound repairs to the external ear are located in the Integumentary Subsection of the CPT coding system.

When a mastoidectomy is included in the description of an auditory procedure (e.g. CPT codes 69530, 69910), separate codes describing mastoidectomy are not reported.

Myringotomies (e.g. CPT codes 69420 and 69421) are included in tympanoplasties and tympanostomies.

(For diagnostic services (eg, audiometry, vestibular tests), see 92502 et seq)

EXTERNAL EAR
INCISION

69000 Drainage external ear, abscess or hematoma; simple

69005   complicated

69020 Drainage external auditory canal, abscess

69090 Ear piercing

EXCISION

69100 Biopsy external ear

69105 Biopsy external auditory canal

69110 Excision external ear; partial, simple repair

69120   complete amputation

(For reconstruction of ear, see 15120 et seq)

69140 Excision exostosis(es), external auditory canal

69145 Excision soft tissue lesion, external auditory canal

69150 Radical excision external auditory canal lesion; without neck dissection

69155   with neck dissection

(For resection of temporal bone, use 69535)

(For skin grafting, see 15004-15261)

REMOVAL

69200 Removal foreign body from external auditory canal; without general anesthesia

69205   with general anesthesia

69209 Removal impacted cerumen using irrigation/lavage, unilateral

(Do not report 69209 in conjunction with 69210 when performed on the same ear)

(For bilateral procedure, report 69209 with modifier 50)

(For removal of impacted cerumen requiring instrumentation, use 69210)

(For cerumen removal that is not impacted, see E/M service code, which may include new or established patient office or other outpatient services [99201-99215], hospital observation services [99217-99220, 99224-99226], hospital care [99221-99223, 99231-99233], consultations [99241-99255], emergency department services [99281-99285], nursing facility services [99304-99318], domiciliary, rest home or custodial care services [99324-99337], home services [99341-99350])

69210 Removal impacted cerumen requiring instrumentation, unilateral

(Do not report 69210 in conjunction with 69209 when performed on the same ear)

(For bilateral procedure, report 69210 with modifier 50)

(For removal of impacted cerumen achieved with irrigation and/or lavage but without instrumentation, use 69209)

(For cerumen removal that is not impacted, see E/M service code, which may include new or established patient office or other outpatient services [99201-99215], hospital observation services [99217-99220, 99224-99226], hospital care [99221-99223, 99231-99233], consultations [99241-99255], emergency department services [99281-99285], nursing facility services [99304-99318], domiciliary, rest home or custodial care services [99324-99337], home services [99341-99350])

69220 Debridement, mastoidectomy cavity, simple (eg, routine cleaning)

(For bilateral procedure, report 9220 with modifier -50)

69222 Debridement, mastoidectomy cavity, complex (eg, with anesthesia or more than routine cleaning)

(For bilateral procedure, report 69222 with modifier -50)

REPAIR

(For suture of wound or injury of external ear, see 12011-14302)

69300 Otoplasty, protruding ear, with or without size reduction

(For bilateral procedure, report 69300 with modifier -50)

69310 Reconstruction of external auditory canal (meatoplasty) (eg, for stenosis due to injury, infection) (separate procedure)

69320 Reconstruction external auditory canal for congenital atresia, single stage

(For combination with middle ear reconstruction, see 69631, 69641)

(For other reconstructive procedures with grafts (eg, skin, cartilage, bone), see 13151-15760, 21230-21235)

OTHER PROCEDURES

(For otoscopy under general anesthesia, use 92502)

69399 Unlisted procedure, external ear

MIDDLE EAR

INTRODUCTION

(**69400** deleted 2014 [2015 edition]. To report, use 69799)

(**69401** deleted 2014 [2015 edition]. To report, see the appropriate E/M code 99201, 99202, 99203, 99204, 99205, 99211, 99212, 99213, 99214, 99215)

● New Code   ▲ Revised Code   ✛ Add-On Code   ⊘ Modifier -51 Exempt   ★ Telemedicine

(**69405**   deleted 2014 [2015 edition]. To report, use 69799)

INCISION

69420   Myringotomy including aspiration and/or eustachian tube inflation

69421   Myringotomy including aspiration and/or eustachian tube inflation requiring general anesthesia

69424   Ventilating tube removal requiring general anesthesia

(For bilateral procedure, report 69424 with modifier -50)

(Do not report code 69424 in conjunction with codes 69205, 69210, 69420, 69421, 69433-69676, 69710-69745, 69801-69930)

69433   Tympanostomy (requiring insertion of ventilating tube), local or topical anesthesia

(For bilateral procedure, report 69433 with modifier -50)

69436   Tympanostomy (requiring insertion of ventilating tube), general anesthesia

(For bilateral procedure, report 69436 with modifier -50)

69440   Middle ear exploration through postauricular or ear canal incision

(For atticotomy, see 69601 et seq)

69450   Tympanolysis, transcanal

EXCISION

69501   Transmastoid antrotomy (simple mastoidectomy)

69502   Mastoidectomy; complete

69505   modified radical

69511   radical

(For skin graft, see 15004 et seq)

(For mastoidectomy cavity debridement, see 69220, 69222)

69530   Petrous apicectomy including radical mastoidectomy

69535   Resection temporal bone, external approach

(For middle fossa approach, see 69950-69970)

69540   Excision aural polyp

69550   Excision aural glomus tumor; transcanal

69552   transmastoid

69554   extended (extratemporal)

REPAIR

69601   Revision mastoidectomy; resulting in complete mastoidectomy

69602   resulting in modified radical mastoidectomy

   Separate Procedure   Unlisted Procedure   CCI Comp. Code   Non-specific Procedure   **615**

| 69603 | resulting in radical mastoidectomy |
| 69604 | resulting in tympanoplasty |

(For planned secondary tympanoplasty after mastoidectomy, see 69631, 69632)

| 69605 | with apicectomy |

(For skin graft, see 15120, 15121, 15260, 15261)

69610	Tympanic membrane repair, with or without site preparation or perforation for closure, with or without patch
69620	Myringoplasty (surgery confined to drumhead and donor area)
69631	Tympanoplasty without mastoidectomy (including canalplasty, atticotomy and/or middle ear surgery), initial or revision; without ossicular chain reconstruction
69632	with ossicular chain reconstruction (eg, postfenestration)
69633	with ossicular chain reconstruction and synthetic prosthesis (eg, partial ossicular replacement prosthesis [PORP], total ossicular replacement prosthesis [TORP])
69635	Tympanoplasty with antrotomy or mastoidotomy (including canalplasty, atticotomy, middle ear surgery, and/or tympanic membrane repair); without ossicular chain reconstruction
69636	with ossicular chain reconstruction
69637	with ossicular chain reconstruction and synthetic prosthesis (eg, partial ossicular replacement prosthesis [PORP], total ossicular replacement prosthesis [TORP])
69641	Tympanoplasty with mastoidectomy (including canalplasty, middle ear surgery, tympanic membrane repair); without ossicular chain reconstruction
69642	with ossicular chain reconstruction
69643	with intact or reconstructed wall, without ossicular chain reconstruction
69644	with intact or reconstructed canal wall, with ossicular chain reconstruction
69645	radical or complete, without ossicular chain reconstruction
69646	radical or complete, with ossicular chain reconstruction
69650	Stapes mobilization
69660	Stapedectomy or stapedotomy with reestablishment of ossicular continuity, with or without use of foreign material;
69661	with footplate drill out
69662	Revision of stapedectomy or stapedotomy
69666	Repair oval window fistula
69667	Repair round window fistula
69670	Mastoid obliteration (separate procedure)
69676	Tympanic neurectomy

● New Code   ▲ Revised Code   ✚ Add-On Code   ⊘ Modifier -51 Exempt   ★ Telemedicine

(For bilateral procedure, report 69676 with modifier -50)

OTHER PROCEDURES

69700 Closure postauricular fistula, mastoid (separate procedure)

69710 Implantation or replacement of electromagnetic bone conduction hearing device in temporal bone

(Replacement procedure includes removal of old device)

69711 Removal or repair of electromagnetic bone conduction hearing device in temporal bone

69714 Implantation, osseointegrated implant, temporal bone, with percutaneous attachment to external speech processor/cochlear stimulator; without mastoidectomy

69715 with mastoidectomy

69717 Replacement (including removal of existing device), osseointegrated implant, temporal bone, with percutaneous attachment to external speech processor/cochlear stimulator; without mastoidectomy

69718 with mastoidectomy

69720 Decompression facial nerve, intratemporal; lateral to geniculate ganglion

69725 including medial to geniculate ganglion

69740 Suture facial nerve, intratemporal, with or without graft or decompression; lateral to geniculate ganglion

69745 including medial to geniculate ganglion

(For extracranial suture of facial nerve, use 64864)

69799 Unlisted procedure, middle ear

INNER EAR

INCISION AND/OR DESTRUCTION

69801 Labyrinthotomy, with perfusion of vestibuloactive drug(s); transcanal

(Do not report 69801 more than once per day)

(Do not report 69801 in conjunction with 69420, 69421, 69433, 69436 when performed on the same ear)

69805 Endolymphatic sac operation; without shunt

69806 with shunt

(**69820** deleted 2017 [2018 edition])

(**69840** deleted 2017 [2018 edition])

EXCISION

69905 Labyrinthectomy; transcanal

69910 with mastoidectomy

69915 Vestibular nerve section, translabyrinthine approach

(For transcranial approach, use 69950)

| Separate Procedure | Unlisted Procedure | CCI Comp. Code | Non-specific Procedure | **617** |

INTRODUCTION

69930 Cochlear device implantation, with or without mastoidectomy

OTHER PROCEDURES

69949 Unlisted procedure, inner ear

TEMPORAL BONE, MIDDLE FOSSA APPROACH

(For external approach, use 69535)

69950 Vestibular nerve section, transcranial approach

69955 Total facial nerve decompression and/or repair (may include graft)

69960 Decompression internal auditory canal

69970 Removal of tumor, temporal bone

OTHER PROCEDURES

69979 Unlisted procedure, temporal bone, middle fossa approach

● New Code   ▲ Revised Code   ✛ Add-On Code   ⊘ Modifier -51 Exempt   ★ Telemedicine

OPERATING MICROSCOPE

The surgical microscope is employed when the surgical services are performed using the techniques of microsurgery. Code 69990 should be reported (without modifier 51 appended) in addition to the code for the primary procedure performed. Do not use 69990 for visualization with magnifying loupes or corrected vision. Do not report 69990 in addition to procedures where use of the operating microscope is an inclusive component (15756-15758, 15842, 19364, 19368, 20955-20962, 20969-20973, 22551, 22552, 22856-22861, 26551-26554, 26556, 31526, 31531, 31536, 31541, 31545, 31546, 31561, 31571, 43116, 43180, 43496, 46601, 46607, 49906, 61548, 63075-63078, 64727, 64820-64823, 64912, 64913, 65091-68850, 0184T, 0308T, 0402T).

+ **69990** Microsurgical techniques, requiring use of operating microscope (List separately in addition to code for primary procedure)

This page intentionally left blank.

● New Code ▲ Revised Code ✚ Add-On Code ⊘ Modifier -51 Exempt ★ Telemedicine

RADIOLOGY

RADIOLOGY SECTION OVERVIEW

The fourth section of the CPT coding system is the radiology section, which includes diagnostic and therapeutic radiology, nuclear medicine and diagnostic ultrasound services. Within each subsection, the CPT codes are arranged by anatomical site.

Diagnostic radiology uses all modalities of radiant energy in medical diagnosis and therapeutic procedures requiring radiologic guidance. This includes imaging techniques and methodologies using radiation emitted by x-ray tubes, radionuclides, ultrasonographic devices, and radiofrequency electromagnetic radiation.

RADIOLOGY SUBSECTIONS

The RADIOLOGY section of the CPT coding system is divided into 7 subsections; namely:

Diagnostic Radiology (Diagnostic Imaging)	70010-76499
Diagnostic Ultrasound	76506-76999
Radiologic Guidance	77001-77022
Breast, Mammography	77051-77059
Bone/Joint Studies	77071-77084
Radiation Oncology	77261-77799
Nuclear Medicine	78012-79999

COMPLETE PROCEDURES

Interventional radiologic procedures or diagnostic studies involving injection of contrast media include all usual preinjection and postinjection services, for example, necessary local anesthesia, placement of needle or catheter, injection of contrast media, supervision of the study, and interpretation of results. When one of these procedures is performed in full by a single physician, it is designated as a "complete procedure."

SUPERVISION AND INTERPRETATION ONLY

When a procedure is performed by a radiologist-clinician team, it is designated as "supervision and interpretation only" and the separate injection procedure is listed in the appropriate section of the SURGERY section of the CPT coding system. These CPT codes are used only when a procedure is performed by more than one physician, for example, a radiologist-clinician team.

RADIOLOGY SERVICE MODIFIERS

Listed surgical services and procedures may be modified under certain circumstances. When applicable, the modifying circumstance is identified by adding the appropriate two digit modifier to the base procedure code(s). Modifiers commonly used to report RADIOLOGY services include:

-22   Unusual services

-26   Professional component

-32   Mandated services

-51   Multiple procedures

-52   Reduced services

-62   Two surgeons

-66   Surgical team

-76   Repeat procedure by same physician

-77   Repeat procedure by another physician

Separate Procedure   Unlisted Procedure   CCI Comp. Code   Non-specific Procedure   **621**

-78 Return to the operating room for a related procedure during the postoperative period

-79 Unrelated procedure or service by the same physician during the postoperative period

-80 Assistant surgeon

-90 Reference (outside) laboratory

-99 Multiple modifiers

-LT Left side of body

-RT Right side of body

BILATERAL PROCEDURE CODES

The RADIOLOGY section includes some CPT codes which include the term "bilateral" in the definition. When reporting these services, do not add the modifier -50, because the procedure is already defined as "bilateral."

RADIOLOGY SERVICES MEDICARE CONSIDERATIONS

Most of the CPT codes in this section are subject to Medicare Purchased Diagnostic Services guidelines. Coding and reporting should be as instructed by your local Medicare carrier.

● New Code ▲ Revised Code + Add-On Code ⊘ Modifier -51 Exempt ★ Telemedicine

RADIOLOGY CODES

DIAGNOSTIC RADIOLOGY (DIAGNOSTIC IMAGING)

HEAD AND NECK

70010   Myelography, posterior fossa, radiological supervision and interpretation

70015   Cisternography, positive contrast, radiological supervision and interpretation

70030   Radiologic examination, eye, for detection of foreign body

70100   Radiologic examination, mandible; partial, less than 4 views

70110   complete, minimum of 4 views

70120   Radiologic examination, mastoids; less than 3 views per side

70130   complete, minimum of 3 views per side

70134   Radiologic examination, internal auditory meati, complete

70140   Radiologic examination, facial bones; less than3e views

70150   complete, minimum of 3 views

70160   Radiologic examination, nasal bones, complete, minimum of 3 views

70170   Dacryocystography, nasolacrimal duct, radiological supervision and interpretation

70190   Radiologic examination; optic foramina

70200   orbits, complete, minimum of 4 views

70210   Radiologic examination, sinuses, paranasal, less than 3 views

70220   Radiologic examination, sinuses, paranasal, complete, minimum of 3 views

70240   Radiologic examination, sella turcica

70250   Radiologic examination, skull; less than 4 views

70260   complete, minimum of 4 views

70300   Radiologic examination, teeth; single view

70310   partial examination, less than full mouth

70320   complete, full mouth

70328   Radiologic examination, temporomandibular joint, open and closed mouth; unilateral

70330   bilateral

70332   Temporomandibular joint arthrography, radiological supervision and interpretation

      (Do not report 70332 in conjunction with 77002)

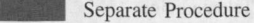 Separate Procedure   Unlisted Procedure   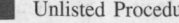 CCI Comp. Code   Non-specific Procedure   **623**

70336 Magnetic resonance (eg, proton) imaging, temporomandibular joint(s)

70350 Cephalogram, orthodontic

70355 Orthopantogram (eg, panoramic x-ray)

70360 Radiologic examination; neck, soft tissue

70370 pharynx or larynx, including fluoroscopy and/or magnification technique

70371 Complex dynamic pharyngeal and speech evaluation by cine or video recording

(**70373** deleted 2015 [2016 edition]. For contrast laryngography, use 76499)

(For laryngeal computed tomography, see 70490, 70491, 70492)

70380 Radiologic examination, salivary gland for calculus

70390 Sialography, radiological supervision and interpretation

70450 Computed tomography, head or brain; without contrast material

70460 with contrast material(s)

70470 without contrast material, followed by contrast material(s) and further sections

(To report 3D rendering, see 76376, 76377)

70480 Computed tomography, orbit, sella, or posterior fossa or outer, middle, or inner ear; without contrast material

70481 with contrast material(s)

70482 without contrast material, followed by contrast material(s) and further sections

(To report 3D rendering, see 76376, 76377)

70486 Computed tomography, maxillofacial area; without contrast material

70487 with contrast material(s)

70488 without contrast material, followed by contrast material(s) and further sections

(To report 3D rendering, see 76376, 76377)

70490 Computed tomography, soft tissue neck; without contrast material

70491 with contrast material(s)

70492 without contrast material followed by contrast material(s) and further sections

(To report 3D rendering, see 76376, 76377)

(For cervical spine, see 72125, 72126)

70496 Computed tomographic angiography, head, with contrast material(s), including noncontrast images, if performed, and image post-processing

70498 Computed tomographic angiography, neck, with contrast material(s), including noncontrast images, if performed, and image post-processing

---

● New Code   ▲ Revised Code   ✛ Add-On Code   ⊘ Modifier -51 Exempt   ★ Telemedicine

70540 Magnetic resonance (eg, proton) imaging, orbit, face, and/or neck; without contrast material(s)

(For head or neck magnetic resonance angiography studies, see 70544-70546, 70547-70549)

70542 with contrast material(s)

70543 without contrast material(s), followed by contrast material(s) and further sequences

(Report 70540-70543 once per imaging session)

70544 Magnetic resonance angiography, head; without contrast materials

70545 with contrast materials

70546 without contrast material(s), followed by contrast material(s) and further sequences

70547 Magnetic resonance angiography, neck; without contrast materials

70548 with contrast materials

70549 without contrast material(s), followed by contrast material(s) and further sequences

70551 Magnetic resonance (eg, proton) imaging, brain (including brain stem); without contrast material

70552 with contrast material(s)

70553 without contrast material, followed by contrast material(s) and further sequences

(For magnetic spectroscopy, use 76390)

Functional MRI involves identification and mapping of stimulation of brain function. When neurofunctional tests are administered by a technologist or other non-physician or non-physiologist, use 70554. When neurofunctional tests are entirely administered by a physician or psychologist, use 70555.

70554 Magnetic resonance imaging, brain, functional MRI; including test selection and administration of repetitive body part movement and/or visual stimulation, not requiring physician or psychologist administration

(Do not report 70554 in conjunction with 96020)

70555 requiring physician or psychologist administration of entire neurofunctional testing

(Do not report 70555 unless 96020 is performed)

(Do not report 70554, 70555 in conjunction with 70551-70553 unless a separate diagnostic MRI is performed)

70557 Magnetic resonance (eg, proton) imaging, brain (including brain stem and skull base), during open intracranial procedure (eg, to assess for residual tumor or residual vascular malformation); without contrast material

70558 with contrast material(s)

70559 without contrast material(s), followed by contrast material(s) and further sequences

(For stereotactic biopsy of intracranial lesion with magnetic resonance guidance, use 61751. 70557, 70558 or 70559 may be reported only if a separate report is generated. Report only one of the above codes once per operative session. Do not use these codes in conjunction with 61751, 77021, 77022)

CHEST

(For fluoroscopic or ultrasonic guidance for needle placement procedures (eg., biopsy, aspiration, injection, localization device) of the thorax, see 76942, 77002)

(**71010**   deleted 2017 [2018 edition]. To report, use 71045)

(**71015**   deleted 2017 [2018 edition]. To report, use 71045)

(**71020**   deleted 2017 [2018 edition]. To report, use 71046)

(**71021**   deleted 2017 [2018 edition]. To report, use 71047)

(**71022**   deleted 2017 [2018 edition]. To report, see 71047, 71048)

(**71023**   deleted 2017 [2018 edition]. To report, see 71046, 76000, 76001)

(**71030**   deleted 2017 [2018 edition]. To report, use 71048)

(**71034**   deleted 2017 [2018 edition]. To report, see 71048, 76000, 76001)

(**71035**   deleted 2017 [2018 edition]. To report, see 71046, 71047, 71048)

● **71045**   Radiologic examination, chest; single view

● **71046**   2 views

● **71047**   3 views

● **71048**   4 or more views

(For acute abdomen series that includes a single view of the chest and one or more views of the abdomen, use 74022)

(For concurrent computer-aided detection [CAD] performed in addition to 71045, 71046, 71047, 71048, use 0174T)

(Do not report 71045, 71046, 71047, 71048 in conjunction with 0175T for computer-aided detection [CAD] performed remotely from the primary interpretation)

71100   Radiologic examination, ribs, unilateral; 2 views

71101   including posteroanterior chest, minimum of 3 views

71110   Radiologic examination, ribs, bilateral; 3 views

71111   including posteroanterior chest, minimum of 4 views

71120   Radiologic examination; sternum, minimum of 2 views

71130   sternoclavicular joint or joints, minimum of 3 views

71250   Computed tomography, thorax; without contrast material

71260   with contrast material(s)

71270   without contrast material, followed by contrast material(s) and further sections

(For cardiac computed tomography of the heart, see 75571-75574)

(To report 3D rendering, see 76376, 76377)

71275   Computed tomographic angiography, chest (noncoronary), with contrast material(s), including noncontrast images, if performed, and image post-processing

(For coronary artery computed tomographic angiography including calcification score and/or cardiac morphology, use 75574)

   ● New Code   ▲ Revised Code   + Add-On Code   ⊘ Modifier -51 Exempt   ★ Telemedicine

71550 Magnetic resonance (eg, proton) imaging, chest (eg, for evaluation of hilar and mediastinal lymphadenopathy); without contrast material(s)

71551   with contrast material(s)

71552   without contrast material(s), followed by contrast material(s) and further sequences

(For breast MRI, see 77058, 77059)

71555 Magnetic resonance angiography, chest (excluding myocardium), with or without contrast material(s)

SPINE AND PELVIS

(**72010** deleted 2015 [2016 edition]. To report, use 72082)

72020 Radiologic examination, spine, single view, specify level

(For a single view that includes the entire thoracic and lumbar spine, use 72081)

72040 Radiologic examination, spine, cervical; 2 or 3 views

72050   of 4 or 5 views

72052   6 or more views

(**72069** deleted 2015 [2016 edition]. To report, see 72081, 72082, 72083, 72084)

72070 Radiologic examination, spine; thoracic, 2 views

72072   thoracic, 3 views

72074   thoracic, minimum of 4 views

72080   thoracolumbar, junction, minimum of 2 views

(For a single view examination of the thoracolumbar junction, use 72020)

72081 Radiologic examination, spine, entire thoracic and lumbar, including skull, cervical and sacral spine if performed (eg, scoliosis evaluation); one view

72082   2 or 3 views

72083   4 or 5 views

72084   minimum of 6 views

(**72090** deleted 2015 [2016 edition]. To report, see 72081, 72082, 72083, 72084)

72100 Radiologic examination, spine, lumbosacral; 2 or 3 views

72110   minimum of 4 views

72114   complete, including bending views, minimum of 6 views

72120   bending views only, 2 or 3 views

(Contrast material in CT of spine is either by intrathecal or intravenous injection. For intrathecal injection, use also 61055 or 62284. IV injection of contrast material is part of the CT procedure)

72125 Computed tomography, cervical spine; without contrast material

---

■ Separate Procedure   ■ Unlisted Procedure   ■ CCI Comp. Code   ■ Non-specific Procedure   **627**

72126 with contrast material

72127 without contrast material, followed by contrast material(s) and further sections

(For intrathecal injection procedure, see 61055, 62284)

72128 Computed tomography, thoracic spine; without contrast material

72129 with contrast material

(For intrathecal injection procedure, see 61055, 62284)

72130 without contrast material, followed by contrast material(s) and further sections

(For intrathecal injection procedure, see 61055, 62284)

72131 Computed tomography, lumbar spine; without contrast material

72132 with contrast material

72133 without contrast material, followed by contrast material(s) and further sections

(For intrathecal injection procedure, see 61055, 62284)

(To report 3D rendering, see 76376, 76377)

72141 Magnetic resonance (eg, proton) imaging, spinal canal and contents, cervical; without contrast material

72142 with contrast material(s)

(For cervical spinal canal imaging without contrast material followed by contrast material, use 72156)

72146 Magnetic resonance (eg, proton) imaging, spinal canal and contents, thoracic; without contrast material

72147 with contrast material(s)

(For thoracic spinal canal imaging without contrast material followed by contrast material, use 72157)

72148 Magnetic resonance (eg, proton) imaging, spinal canal and contents, lumbar; without contrast material

72149 with contrast material(s)

(For lumbar spinal canal imaging without contrast material followed by contrast material, use 72158)

72156 Magnetic resonance (eg, proton) imaging, spinal canal and contents, without contrast material, followed by contrast material(s) and further sequences; cervical

72157 thoracic

72158 lumbar

72159 Magnetic resonance angiography, spinal canal and contents, with or without contrast material(s)

72170 Radiologic examination, pelvis; 1 or 2 views

72190 complete, minimum of 3 views

(For pelvimetry, use 74710)

(For a combined computed tomography (CT) or computed tomographic angiography abdomen and pelvis study, see 74174, 74176-74178)

● New Code ▲ Revised Code ✛ Add-On Code ⊘ Modifier -51 Exempt ★ Telemedicine

72191 Computed tomographic angiography, pelvis; with contrast material(s), including noncontrast images, if performed, and image post-processing

(Do not report 72191 in conjunction with 73706 or 75635. For CTA aorto-iliofemoral runoff, use 75635)

(Do not report 72191 in conjunction with 74175. For a combined computed tomographic angiography abdomen and pelvis study, use 74174)

72192 Computed tomography, pelvis; without contrast material

72193   with contrast material(s)

72194   without contrast material, followed by contrast material(s) and further sections

(For a combined CT abdomen and pelvis study, see 74176-74178)

(To report 3D rendering, see 76376, 76377)

(For computed tomographic colonography, diagnostic, see 74261-74262. For computed tomographic colonography, screening, use 74263)

(Do not report 72192-72194 in conjunction with 74261-74263)

72195 Magnetic resonance (eg, proton) imaging, pelvis; without contrast material(s)

72196   with contrast material(s)

72197   without contrast material(s), followed by contrast material(s) and further sequences

(Do not report 72195, 72196, 72197 in conjunction with 74712, 74713)

(For magnetic resonance imaging of a fetus[es], see 74712, 74713)

72198 Magnetic resonance angiography, pelvis, with or without contrast material(s)

72200 Radiologic examination, sacroiliac joints; less than 3e views

72202   3 or more views

72220 Radiologic examination, sacrum and coccyx, minimum of 2 views

72240 Myelography, cervical, radiological supervision and interpretation

(Do not report 72240 in conjunction with 62284, 62302, 62303, 62304, 62305)

(When both 62284 and 72240 are performed by the same physician or other qualified health care professional for cervical myelography, use 62302)

(For complete cervical myelography via injection procedure at C1-C2, see 61055, 72240)

72255 Myelography, thoracic, radiological supervision and interpretation

(Do not report 72255 in conjunction with 62284, 62302, 62303, 62304, 62305)

(When both 62284 and 72255 are performed by the same physician or other qualified health care professional for cervical myelography, use 62303)

(For complete thoracic myelography via injection procedure at C1-C2, see 61055, 72255)

72265 Myelography, lumbosacral, radiological supervision and interpretation

(Do not report 72265 in conjunction with 62284, 62302, 62303, 62304, 62305)

(When both 62284 and 72265 are performed by the same physician or other qualified health care professional for cervical myelography, use 62304)

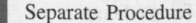 Separate Procedure   Unlisted Procedure   CCI Comp. Code   Non-specific Procedure   **629**

(For complete lumbosacral myelography via injection procedure at C1-C2, see 61055, 72265)

72270 Myelography, 2 or more regions (eg, lumbar/thoracic, cervical/thoracic, lumbar/cervical, lumbar/thoracic/cervical), radiological supervision and interpretation

(Do not report 72270 in conjunction with 62284, 62302, 62303, 62304, 62305)

(When both 62284 and 72270 are performed by the same physician or other qualified health care professional for cervical myelography, use 62305)

(For complete myelography of 2 or more regions via injection procedure at C1-C2, see 61055, 72270)

72275 Epidurography, radiological supervision and interpretation

(72275 includes 77003)

(For injection procedure, see 62280, 62281, 62282, 62320, 62321, 62322, 62323, 62324, 62325, 62326, 62327, 64479, 64480, 64483, 64484)

(Use 72275 only when an epidurogram is performed, images documented, and a formal radiologic report is issued)

(Do not report 72275 in conjunction with 22586, 0195T, 0196T)

72285 Discography, cervical or thoracic, radiological supervision and interpretation

72295 Discography, lumbar, radiological supervision and interpretation

UPPER EXTREMITIES

(For stress views, any joint, use 77071)

73000 Radiologic examination; clavicle, complete

73010   scapula, complete

73020 Radiologic examination, shoulder; 1 view

73030   complete, minimum of 2 views

73040 Radiologic examination, shoulder, arthrography, radiological supervision and interpretation

(Do not report 77002 in conjunction with 73040)

73050 Radiologic examination; acromioclavicular joints, bilateral, with or without weighted distraction

73060   humerus, minimum of 2 views

73070 Radiologic examination, elbow; 2 views

73080   complete, minimum of 3 views

73085 Radiologic examination, elbow, arthrography, radiological supervision and interpretation

(Do not report 77002 in conjunction with 73085)

73090 Radiologic examination; forearm, 2 views

73092   upper extremity, infant, minimum of 2 views

73100 Radiologic examination, wrist; 2 views

73110   complete, minimum of 3 views

● New Code   ▲ Revised Code   + Add-On Code   ⊘ Modifier -51 Exempt   ★ Telemedicine

73115 Radiologic examination, wrist, arthrography, radiological supervision and interpretation

(Do not report 77002 in conjunction with 73115)

73120 Radiologic examination, hand; 2 views

73130   minimum of 3 views

73140 Radiologic examination, finger(s), minimum of 2 views

73200 Computed tomography, upper extremity; without contrast material

73201   with contrast material(s)

73202   without contrast material, followed by contrast material(s) and further sections

(To report 3D rendering, see 76376, 76377)

73206 Computed tomographic angiography, upper extremity, with contrast material(s), including noncontrast images, if performed, and image post-processing

73218 Magnetic resonance (eg, proton) imaging, upper extremity, other than joint; without contrast material(s)

73219   with contrast material(s)

73220   without contrast material(s), followed by contrast material(s) and further sequences

73221 Magnetic resonance (eg, proton) imaging, any joint of upper extremity; without contrast material(s)

73222   with contrast material(s)

73223   without contrast material(s), followed by contrast material(s) and further sequences

73225 Magnetic resonance angiography, upper extremity, with or without contrast material(s)

LOWER EXTREMITIES

(For stress views, any joint, use 77071)

(**73500** deleted 2015 [2016 edition]. To report, use 73501)

73501 Radiologic examination, hip, unilateral, with pelvis when performed; 1 view

73502   2-3 views

73503   minimum of 4 views

(**73510** deleted 2015 [2016 edition]. To report, see 73502, 73503)

(**73520** deleted 2015 [2016 edition]. To report, see 73521, 73522, 73523)

73521 Radiologic examination, hips, bilateral, with pelvis when performed; 2 views

73522   3-4 views

73523   minimum of 5 views

73525 Radiologic examination, hip, arthrography, radiological supervision and interpretation

(Do not report 73525 in conjunction with 77002)

(**73530**   deleted 2015 [2016 edition]. To report, see 73501, 73502, 73503)

(**73540**   deleted 2015 [2016 edition]. To report, see 73501, 73502, 73503)

(**73550**   deleted 2015 [2016 edition]. To report, see 73551, 73552)

73551   Radiologic examination, femur; 1 view

73552   minimum 2 views

73560   Radiologic examination, knee; 1 or 2 views

73562   3 views

73564   complete, 4 or more views

73565   both knees, standing, anteroposterior

73580   Radiologic examination, knee, arthrography, radiological supervision and interpretation

       (Do not report 73580 in conjunction with 77002)

73590   Radiologic examination; tibia and fibula, 2 views

73592   lower extremity, infant, minimum of 2 views

73600   Radiologic examination, ankle; 2 views

73610   complete, minimum of 3 views

73615   Radiologic examination, ankle, arthrography, radiological supervision and interpretation

       (Do not report 73615 in conjunction with 77002)

73620   Radiologic examination, foot; 2 views

73630   complete, minimum of 3 views

73650   Radiologic examination; calcaneus, minimum of 2 views

73660   toe(s), minimum of 2 views

73700   Computed tomography, lower extremity; without contrast material

73701   with contrast material(s)

73702   without contrast material, followed by contrast material(s) and further sections

       (To report 3D rendering, see 76376, 76377)

73706   Computed tomographic angiography, lower extremity, with contrast material(s), including noncontrast images, if performed, and image post-processing

       (For CTA aorto-iliofemoral runoff, use 75635)

73718   Magnetic resonance (eg, proton) imaging, lower extremity, other than joint; without contrast material(s)

73719   with contrast material(s)

73720   without contrast material(s), followed by contrast material(s) and further sequences

---

632   ● New Code   ▲ Revised Code   ✛ Add-On Code   ⊘ Modifier -51 Exempt   ★ Telemedicine

73721	Magnetic resonance (eg, proton) imaging, any joint of lower extremity; without contrast material	
73722	with contrast material	
73723	without contrast material followed by contrast material(s) and further sequences	
73725	Magnetic resonance angiography, lower extremity, with or without contrast material(s)	

ABDOMEN

(**74000**   deleted 2017 [2018 edition]. To report, use 74018)

(**74010**   deleted 2017 [2018 edition]. To report, see 74019, 74021)

(**74020**   deleted 2017 [2018 edition]. To report, see 74019, 74021)

● **74018**   Radiologic examination, abdomen; 1 view

● **74019**   2 views

● **74021**   3 or more views

74022   complete acute abdomen series, including supine, erect, and/or decubitus views, single view chest

For combinations of CT of the abdomen with CT of the pelvis performed at the same session, use the following table. Do not report more than one CT of the abdomen or CT of the pelvis for any session.

Stand Alone Code	**74150** CT Abdomen WO Contrast	**74160** CT Abdomen W Contrast	**74170** CT Abdomen WO/W Contrast
72192 CT Pelvis WO Contrast	74176	74178	74178
72193 CT Pelvis W Contrast	74178	74177	74178
72194 CT Pelvis WO/W Contrast	74178	74178	74178

74150   Computed tomography, abdomen; without contrast material

74160   with contrast material(s)

74170   without contrast material, followed by contrast material(s) and further sections

(For a combined CT abdomen and pelvis study, see 74176-74178)

(To report 3D rendering, see 76376, 76377)

(For computed tomographic colonography, diagnostic, see 74261-74262. For computed tomographic colonography, screening, use 74263)

(Do not report 74150-74170 in conjunction with 74261-74263)

74174   Computed tomographic angiography, abdomen and pelvis, with contrast material(s), including noncontrast images, if performed, and image postprocessing

(Do not report 74174 in conjunction with 72191, 73706, 74175, 75635, 76376, 76377)

(For CTA aorto-iliofemoral runoff, use 75635)

Separate Procedure	Unlisted Procedure	CCI Comp. Code	Non-specific Procedure	**633**

74175 Computed tomographic angiography, abdomen, with contrast material(s), including noncontrast images, if performed, and image post-processing

(Do not report 74175 in conjunction with 73706 or 75635. For CTA aorto-iliofemoral runoff, use 75635)

(Do not report 74175 in conjunction with 72191. For a combined computed tomographic angiography abdomen and pelvis study, use 74174)

74176 Computed tomography, abdomen and pelvis; without contrast material

74177   with contrast material(s)

74178   without contrast material in one or both body regions, followed by contrast material(s) and further sections in one or both body regions

(Do not report 74176-74178 in conjunction with 72192-72194, 74150-74170)

(Report 74176, 74177, or 74178 only once per CT abdomen and pelvis examination)

74181 Magnetic resonance (eg, proton) imaging, abdomen; without contrast material(s)

74182   with contrast material(s)

74183   without contrast material, followed by contrast material(s) and further sequences

74185 Magnetic resonance angiography, abdomen, with or without contrast material(s)

74190 Peritoneogram (eg, after injection of air or contrast), radiological supervision and interpretation

(For procedure, use 49400)

(For computerized axial tomography, see 72192 or 74150)

GASTROINTESTINAL TRACT

(For percutaneous placement of gastrostomy tube, use 43246)

74210 Radiologic examination; pharynx and/or cervical esophagus

74220   esophagus

74230 Swallowing function, with cineradiography/videoradiography

74235 Removal of foreign body(s), esophageal, with use of balloon catheter, radiological supervision and interpretation

(For procedure, see 43499)

74240 Radiologic examination, gastrointestinal tract, upper; with or without delayed images, without KUB

74241   with or without delayed images, with KUB

74245   with small intestine, includes multiple serial images

74246 Radiological examination, gastrointestinal tract, upper, air contrast, with specific high density barium, effervescent agent, with or without glucagon; with or without delayed images, without KUB

74247   with or without delayed images, with KUB

74249   with small intestine follow-through

74250 Radiologic examination, small intestine, includes multiple serial images;

  ● New Code   ▲ Revised Code   + Add-On Code   ⊘ Modifier -51 Exempt   ★ Telemedicine

74251   via enteroclysis tube

74260 Duodenography, hypotonic

74261 Computed tomographic (CT) colonography, diagnostic, including image postprocessing; without contrast material

74262   with contrast material(s) including non contrast images, if performed

(Do not report 74261, 74262 in conjunction with 72192-72194, 74150-74170, 74263, 76376, 76377)

74263 Computed tomographic (CT) colonography, screening, including image postprocessing

(Do not report 74263 in conjunction with 72192-72194, 74150-74170, 74261, 74262, 76376, 76377)

74270 Radiologic examination, colon; contrast (eg., barium) enema, with or without KUB

74280   air contrast with specific high density barium, with or without glucagon

74283 Therapeutic enema, contrast or air, for reduction of intussusception or other intraluminal obstruction (eg, meconium ileus)

74290 Cholecystography, oral contrast

(**74291** deleted 2014 [2015 edition].)

74300 Cholangiography and/or pancreatography; intraoperative, radiological supervision and interpretation

+ **74301**   additional set intraoperative, radiological supervision and interpretation (List separately in addition to code for primary procedure)

(Use 74301 in conjunction with code 74300)

(**74305** deleted 2015 [2016 edition]. To report, use 47531)

(**74320** deleted 2015 [2016 edition]. To report, use 47532)

(**74327** deleted 2015 [2016 edition]. For percutaneous biliary stone extraction, use 47544)

74328 Endoscopic catheterization of the biliary ductal system, radiological supervision and interpretation

(For procedure, see 43260-43278 as appropriate)

74329 Endoscopic catheterization of the pancreatic ductal system, radiological supervision and interpretation

(For procedure, see 43260-43278 as appropriate)

74330 Combined endoscopic catheterization of the biliary and pancreatic ductal systems, radiological supervision and interpretation

(For procedure, see 43260-43278 as appropriate)

74340 Introduction of long gastrointestinal tube (eg, Miller-Abbott), including multiple fluoroscopies and images, radiological supervision and interpretation

(For tube placement, use 44500)

74355 Percutaneous placement of enteroclysis tube, radiological supervision and interpretation

74360 Intraluminal dilation of strictures and/or obstructions (eg, esophagus), radiological supervision and interpretation

(For procedure, see 43195, 43196, 43220, 43226, 43453)

(Do not report 74360 in conjunction with 43213, 43214, 43233)

74363 Percutaneous transhepatic dilation of biliary duct stricture with or without placement of stent, radiological supervision and interpretation

(For procedure, see 47555, 47556)

URINARY TRACT

74400 Urography (pyelography), intravenous, with or without KUB, with or without tomography

74410 Urography, infusion, drip technique and/or bolus technique;

74415   with nephrotomography

74420 Urography, retrograde, with or without KUB

74425 Urography, antegrade, (pyelostogram, nephrostogram, loopogram), radiological supervision and interpretation

(Do not report 74425 in conjunction with 50430, 50431, 50432, 50433, 50434, 50435, 50693, 50694, 50695)

74430 Cystography, minimum of three views, radiological supervision and interpretation

74440 Vasography, vesiculography, or epididymography, radiological supervision and interpretation

74445 Corpora cavernosography, radiological supervision and interpretation

74450 Urethrocystography, retrograde, radiological supervision and interpretation

74455 Urethrocystography, voiding, radiological supervision and interpretation

74470 Radiologic examination, renal cyst study, translumbar, contrast visualization, radiological supervision and interpretation

(**74475** deleted 2015 [2016 edition]. To report, see 50432, 50433, 50434, 50435, 50606, 50693, 50694, 50695)

(**74480** deleted 2015 [2016 edition]. To report, see 50432, 50433, 50434, 50435, 50606, 50693, 50694, 50695)

74485 Dilation of nephrostomy, ureters, or urethra, radiological supervision and interpretation

(For dilation of ureter without radiologic guidance, use 52341, 52344)

(For change of nephrostomy or pyelostomy tube, use 50435)

GYNECOLOGICAL AND OBSTETRICAL

(For abdomen and pelvis, see 72170-72190, 74018, 74019, 74021, 74022, 74150, 74160, 74170)

74710 Pelvimetry, with or without placental localization

74712 Magnetic resonance (eg, proton) imaging, fetal, including placental and maternal pelvic imaging when performed; single or first gestation

+ **74713**   each additional gestation (List separately in adddition to code for primary procedure)

(Use 74713 in conjunction with 74712)

(Do not report 74712, 74713 in conjunction with 72195, 72196, 72197)

(If only placenta or maternal pelvis is imaged without fetal imaging, see 72195, 72196, 72197)

74740 Hysterosalpingography, radiological supervision and interpretation

(For introduction of saline or contrast for hysterosalpingography, see 58340)

74742 Transcervical catheterization of fallopian tube, radiological supervision and interpretation

(For procedure, use 58345)

74775 Perineogram (eg, vaginogram, for sex determination or extent of anomalies)

HEART

Cardiac magnetic imaging differs from traditional magnetic resonance imaging (MRI) in its ability to provide a physiologic evaluation of cardiac function. Traditional MRI relies on static images to obtain clinical diagnoses based upon anatomic information. Improvement in spatial and temporal resolution has expanded the application from an anatomic test and includes physiologic evaluation of cardiac function. Flow and velocity assessment for valves and intracardiac shunts is performed in addition to a function and morphologic evaluation. Use 75559 with 75565 to report flow with pharmacologic wall motion stress evaluation without contrast. Use 75563 with 75565 to report flow with pharmacologic perfusion stress with contrast.

Cardiac MRI for velocity flow mapping can be reported in conjunction with 75557, 75559, 75561, or 75563.

Listed procedures may be performed independently or in the course of overall medical care. If the individual providing these services is also responsible for diagnostic workup and/or follow-up care of the patient, see appropriate sections also. Only one procedure in the series 75557-75563 is appropriately reported per session. Only one add-on code for flow velocity can be reported per session.

Cardiac MRI studies may be performed at rest and/or during pharmacologic stress. Therefore, the appropriate stress testing code from the 93015-93018 series should be reported in addition to 75559 or 75563.

Cardiac computed tomography (CT) and coronary computed tomographic angiography (CTA) include the axial source images of the pre-contrast, arterial phase sequence, and venous phase sequence (if performed(, as well as the two-dimensional and three-dimensional reformatted images resulting from the study, including cine review. Contrast enhanced cardiac CT and coronary CTA codes 75571-75574 include any quantitative assessment when performed as part of the same encounter. Report only one computed tomography heart service per encounter.

(For separate injection procedures for vascular radiology, see Surgery section, 36000-36299)

(For cardiac catheterization procedures, see 93451-93572)

(75552-75556 have been deleted. To report, see 75557, 75559, 75561, 75563, 75565)

75557 Cardiac magnetic resonance imaging for morphology and function without contrast material;

75559 with stress imaging

75561 Cardiac magnetic resonance imaging for morphology and function without contrast material(s), followed by contrast material(s) and further sequences;

75563 with stress imaging

(75558, 75560, 75562, 75564 have been deleted. To report flow velocity, use 75565)

+ 75565 Cardiac magnetic resonance imaging for velocity flow mapping (List separately in addition to code for primary procedure)

(Use 75565 in conjunction with 75557, 75559, 75561, 75563)

(Do not report 75557, 75559, 75561, 75563, 75565 in conjunction with 76376, 76377)

75571 Computed tomography, heart, without contrast material, with quantitative evaluation of coronary calcium

75572 Computed tomography, heart, with contrast material, for evaluation of cardiac structure and morphology (including 3D image postprocessing, assessment of cardiac function, and evaluation of venous structures, if performed)

75573 Computed tomography, heart, with contrast material, for evaluation of cardiac structure and morphology in the setting of congenital heart disease (including 3D image postprocessing, assessment of LV cardiac function, RV structure and function and evaluation of venous structures, if performed)

 75574 Computed tomographic angiography, heart, coronary arteries and bypass grafts (when present), with contrast material, including 3D image postprocessing (including evaluation of cardiac structure and morphology, assessment of cardiac function, and evaluation of venous structures, if performed)

VASCULAR PROCEDURES

AORTA AND ARTERIES

Selective vascular catheterizations should be coded to include introduction and all lesser order selective catheterizations used in the approach (eg., the description for a selective right middle cerebral artery catheterization includes the introduction and placement catheterization of the right common and internal carotid arteries).

Additional second and/or third order arterial catheterizations within the same family of arteries supplied by a single first order artery should be expressed by 36218 or 36248. Additional first order or higher catheterizations in vascular families supplied by a first order vessel different from a previously selected and coded family should be separately coded using the conventions described above.

The lower extremity endovascular revascularization codes describing services performed for occlusive disease (37220-37235) include catheterization (36200, 36240, 36245-36248) in the work described by the codes. Catheterization codes are not additionally reported for diagnostic lower extremity angiography when performed through the same access site as the therapy (37220-37235) performed in the same session. However, catheterization for the diagnostic lower extremity angiogram may be reported separately if a different arterial puncture site is necessary.

For angiography performed in conjunction with therapeutic transcatheter radiological supervision and interpretation services, see the Radiology Transcatheter Procedures guidelines.

Diagnostic angiography (radiological supervision and interpretation) codes should NOT be used with interventional procedures for:

1. Contrast injections, angiography, roadmapping, and/or fluoroscopic guidance for the intervention;

2. Vessel measurement; AND

3. Post-angioplasty/stent/atherectomy angiography, as this work is captured in the radiological supervision and interpretation code(s). In those therapeutic codes that include radiological supervision and interpretation, this work is captured in the therapeutic code.

Diagnostic angiography performed at the time of an interventional procedure is separately reportable if:

1. No prior catheter-based angiographic study is available and a full diagnostic study is performed, and the decision to intervene is based on the diagnostic study, OR

2. A prior study is available, but as documented in the medical record:

   a. The patient's condition with respect to the clinical indication has changed since the prior study; OR

   b. There is inadequate visualization of the anatomy and/or pathology; OR

   c. There is a clinical change during the procedure that requires new evaluation outside the target area of intervention.

Diagnostic angiography performed at a separate session from an interventional procedure is separately reported.

If diagnostic angiography is necessary, is performed at the same session as the interventional procedure, and meets the above criteria, modifier 59 must be appended to the diagnostic radiological supervision and interpretation code(s) to denote that diagnostic work has been done following these guidelines.

Diagnostic angiography performed at the time of an interventional procedure is NOT separately reportable if it is specifically included in the interventional code descriptor.

(For intravenous procedure, see 36000, 36005-36015, and for intra-arterial procedure, see 36100-36248)

(For radiological supervision and interpretation, see 75600-75893)

75600   Aortography, thoracic, without serialography, radiological supervision and interpretation

(For isupravalvular aortography performed at the time of cardiac catheterization, use 93567, which includes imaging supervision, interpretation and report)

75605   Aortography, thoracic, by serialography, radiological supervision and interpretation

(For supravalvular aortography performed at the time of cardiac catheterization, use 93567, which includes imaging supervision, interpretation and report)

75625   Aortography, abdominal, by serialography, radiological supervision and interpretation

75630   Aortography, abdominal plus bilateral iliofemoral lower extremity, catheter, by serialography, radiological supervision and interpretation

75635   Computed tomographic angiography, abdominal aorta and bilateral iliofemoral lower extremity runoff, with contrast material(s), including noncontrast images, if performed, and image post-processing

(Do not report 75635 in conjunction with 72191, 73706, 74175, or 74174)

(**75658**   deleted 2017 [2018 edition]. To report, use 75710)

75705   Angiography, spinal, selective, radiological supervision and interpretation

75710   Angiography, extremity, unilateral, radiological supervision and interpretation

75716   Angiography, extremity, bilateral, radiological supervision and interpretation

75726   Angiography, visceral, selective or supraselective, (with or without flush aortogram), radiological supervision and interpretation

(For selective angiography, each additional visceral vessel studied after basic examination, use 75774)

75731   Angiography, adrenal, unilateral, selective, radiological supervision and interpretation

75733   Angiography, adrenal, bilateral, selective, radiological supervision and interpretation

75736   Angiography, pelvic, selective or supraselective, radiological supervision and interpretation

75741   Angiography, pulmonary, unilateral, selective, radiological supervision and interpretation

75743   Angiography, pulmonary, bilateral, selective, radiological supervision and interpretation

75746   Angiography, pulmonary, by nonselective catheter or venous injection, radiological supervision and interpretation

(For pulmonary angiography by nonselective catheter or venous injuection performed at the time of cardiac catheterization, use 93568, which includes imaging supervision, interpretation and report)

75756   Angiography, internal mammary, radiological supervision and interpretation

(For internal mammary angiography performed at the time of cardiac catheterization, see 93455, 93457, 93459, 93461, 93564 which include imaging supervision, interpretation and report)

+ **75774**   Angiography, selective, each additional vessel studied after basic examination, radiological supervision and interpretation (List separately in addition to code for primary procedure)

(Use 75774 in addition to code for specific initial vessel studied)

| | Separate Procedure | | Unlisted Procedure | | CCI Comp. Code | | Non-specific Procedure | **639** |

(Do not report 75774 as part of diagnostic angiography of the extracranial and intracranial cervicocerebral vessels. It may be appropriate to reort 75774 for diagnostic angiography of upper extremities and other vascular beds performed in the same session)

(For angiography, see 75600-75756)

(For catheterizations, see codes 36215-36248)

(For cardiac catheterization procedures, see 93452-93462, 93531-93533, 93563-93568)

(75791   deleted 2016 [2017 edition]. To report, see 36901, 36902, 36903, 36904, 36905, 36906)

(For radiological supervision and interpretation of dialysis circuit angiography performed through existing access[es] or catheter-based arterial access, use 36901 with modifier 52)

VEINS AND LYMPHATICS

For venography performed in conjunction with therapeutic transcatheter radiological supervision and interpretation services, see the Radiology Transcatheter Procedures guidelines.

Diagnostic venography (radiological supervision and interpretation) codes should NOT be used with interventional procedures for:

(1) Contrast injections, venography, roadmapping, and/or fluoroscopic guidance for intervention;

(2) Vessel measurement; and

(3) Post-angioplasty/stent venography, as this work is captured in the radiological supervision and interpretation code(s).

Diagnostic venography performed at the time of an interventional procedure is separately reportable if:

1. No prior catheter-based venographic study is available and a full diagnostic study is performed, and decision to intervene is based on the diagnostic study, OR

2. A prior study is available, but as documented in the medical record:

a. The patient's condition with respect to the clinical indication has changed since the prior study, OR

b. There is inadequate visualization of the anatomy and/or pathology, OR

c. There is a clinical change during the procedure that requires new evaluation outside the target area of intervention.

Diagnostic venography performed at a separate setting from an interventional procedure is separately reported.

Diagnostic venography performed at the time of an interventional procedure is NOT separately reportable if it is specifically included in the interventional code descriptor.

(For injection procedure for venous system, see 36000-36015, 36400-36510)

(For injection procedure for lymphatic system, use 38790)

75801   Lymphangiography, extremity only, unilateral, radiological supervision and interpretation

75803   Lymphangiography, extremity only, bilateral, radiological supervision and interpretation

75805   Lymphangiography, pelvic/abdominal, unilateral, radiological supervision and interpretation

75807   Lymphangiography, pelvic/abdominal, bilateral, radiological supervision and interpretation

75809   Shuntogram for investigation of previously placed indwelling nonvascular shunt (eg, LeVeen shunt, ventriculoperitoneal shunt, indwelling infusion pump), radiological supervision and interpretation

(For procedure, see 49427 or 61070)

75810   Splenoportography, radiological supervision and interpretation

---

● New Code   ▲ Revised Code   + Add-On Code   ⊘ Modifier -51 Exempt   ★ Telemedicine

75820	Venography, extremity, unilateral, radiological supervision and interpretation
75822	Venography, extremity, bilateral, radiological supervision and interpretation
75825	Venography, caval, inferior, with serialography, radiological supervision and interpretation
75827	Venography, caval, superior, with serialography, radiological supervision and interpretation
75831	Venography, renal, unilateral, selective, radiological supervision and interpretation
75833	Venography, renal, bilateral, selective, radiological supervision and interpretation
75840	Venography, adrenal, unilateral, selective, radiological supervision and interpretation
75842	Venography, adrenal, bilateral, selective, radiological supervision and interpretation
75860	Venography, venous sinus (eg, petrosal and inferior sagittal) or jugular, catheter, radiological supervision and interpretation
75870	Venography, superior sagittal sinus, radiological supervision and interpretation
75872	Venography, epidural, radiological supervision and interpretation
75880	Venography, orbital, radiological supervision and interpretation
75885	Percutaneous transhepatic portography with hemodynamic evaluation, radiological supervision and interpretation
75887	Percutaneous transhepatic portography without hemodynamic evaluation, radiological supervision and interpretation
75889	Hepatic venography, wedged or free, with hemodynamic evaluation, radiological supervision and interpretation
75891	Hepatic venography, wedged or free, without hemodynamic evaluation, radiological supervision and interpretation
75893	Venous sampling through catheter, with or without angiography (eg, for parathyroid hormone, renin), radiological supervision and interpretation

(For procedure, use 36500)

TRANSCATHETER PROCEDURES

Therapeutic transcatheter radiological supervision and interpretation code(s) include the following services associated with that intervention:

1. Contrast injections, angiography/venography, roadmapping, and fluoroscopic guidance for the intervention;

2. Vessel measurement; and

3. Completion angiography/venography (except for those uses permitted by 75898).

Unless specifically included in the code descriptor, diagnostic angiography/venography performed at the time of transcatheter service(s) is separately reportable (eg., no prior catheter-based diagnostic angiography/ venography study of the target vessel is available, prior diagnostic study is inadequate, patient's condition with respect to the clinical indication has changed since the prior study or during the intervention). See 75600-75893.

Codes 75956 and 75957 include all angiography of the thoracic aorta and its branches for diagnostic imaging prior to deployment of the primary endovascular devices (including all routine components of modular devices), fluoroscopic guidance in the delivery of the endovascular components, and intraprocedural arterial angiography (eg, confirm position, detect endoleak, evaluate runoff).

Separate Procedure   Unlisted Procedure   CCI Comp. Code   Non-specific Procedure   **641**

Code 75958 includes the analogous services for placement of each proximal thoracic endovascular extension. Code 75959 includes the analogous services for placement of a distal thoracic endovascular extension(s) placed during a procedure after the primary repair.

75894 Transcatheter therapy, embolization, any method, radiological supervision and interpretation

(Do not report 75894 in conunction with 36475, 36476, 36478, 36479, 37241-37244)

(**75896** deleted 2015 [2016 edition]. For radiological supervision and interpretation for thrombolysis other than coronary, see 37211, 37212, 37213, 37214. For radiological supervision and interpretation for intracranial arterial administration of pharmacological agent(s) other than for thrombolysis, see 61650, 61651)

75898 Angiography through existing catheter for follow-up study for transcatheter therapy, embolization or infusion, other than for thrombolysis

(For thrombolysis infusion management other than coronary, see 37211-37214, 61645)

(For non-thrombolysis infusion management other than coronary, see 61650, 61651)

(Do not report 75898 in conjunction with 37211-37214, 37241-37244, 61645, 61650, 61651)

75901 Mechanical removal of pericatheter obstructive material (eg., fibrin sheath) from central venous device via separate venous access, radiologic supervision and interpretation

(For procedure, use 36595)

(For venous catheterization, see 36010-36012)

75902 Mechanical removal of intraluminal (intracatheter) obstructive material from central venous device through device lumen, radiologic supervision and interpretation

(For procedure, use 36596)

(For venous catheterization, see 36010-36012)

(**75945** deleted 2015 [2016 edition]. To report noncoronary intravascular ultrasound during diagnostic evaluation and/or therapeutic intervention, see 37252, 37253)

(**75946** deleted 2015 [2016 edition]. To report noncoronary intravascular ultrasound during diagnostic evaluation and/or therapeutic intervention, see 37252, 37253)

(**75952** deleted 2017 [2018 edition]. To report, see 34701-34711, 0254T)

(**75953** deleted 2017 [2018 edition]. To report, see 34701-34711, 0254T)

(**75954** deleted 2017 [2018 edition]. To report, see 34701-34711, 0254T)

75956 Endovascular repair of descending thoracic aorta (eg, aneurysm, pseudoaneurysm, dissection, penetrating ulcer, intramural hematoma, or traumatic disruption); involving coverage of left subclavian artery origin, initial endoprosthesis plus descending thoracic aortic extension(s), if required, to level of celiac artery origin, radiological supervision and interpretation

(For implantation of endovascular graft, use 33880)

75957 not involving coverage of left subclavian artery origin, initial endoprosthesis plus descending thoracic aortic extension(s), if required, to level of celiac artery origin, radiological supervision and interpretation

(For implantation of endovascular graft, use 33881)

75958 Placement of proximal extension prosthesis for endovascular repair of descending thoracic aorta (eg, aneurysm, pseudoaneurysm, dissection, penetrating ulcer, intramural hematoma, or traumatic disruption), radiological supervision and interpretation

(Report 75958 for each proximal extension)

● New Code   ▲ Revised Code   + Add-On Code   ⊘ Modifier -51 Exempt   ★ Telemedicine

(For implantation of proximal endovascular extension, see 33883, 33884)

75959 Placement of distal extension prosthesis(es) (delayed) after endovascular repair of descending thoracic aorta, as needed, to level of celiac origin, radiological supervision and interpretation

(Do not report 75959 in conjunction with 75956, 75957)

(Report 75959 once, regardless of number of modules deployed)

(For implantation of distal endovascular extension, use 33886)

(**75960** deleted 2013 [2014 edition])

(Radiologic supervision for transcatheter placement of stent(s) is included in the therapeutic service codes)

(For removal of a vena cava filter, use 37193)

(**75962** deleted 2016 [2017 edition]. To report, see 36902, 36905, 37246, 37247)

(**75964** deleted 2016 [2017 edition]. To report, see 36902, 36905, 37246, 37247)

(**75966** deleted 2016 [2017 edition]. To report, see 36902, 36905, 37246, 37247)

(**75968** deleted 2016 [2017 edition]. To report, see 36902, 36905, 37246, 37247)

75970 Transcatheter biopsy, radiological supervision and interpretation

(For injection procedure only for transcatheter therapy or biopsy, see 36100-36299)

(For transcatheter renal and ureteral biopsy, use 52007)

(For percutaneous needle biopsy of pancreas, use 48102; of retroperitoneal lymph node or mass, use 49180)

(**75978** deleted 2016 [2017 edition]. To report, see 36902, 36905, 36907, 37248, 37249)

(For radiological supervision and interpretation of transluminal balloon angioplasty within the peripheral and/or central segments of a dialysis circuit performed through the dialysis circuit, see 36902, 36905, 36907)

(**75980** deleted 2015 [2016 edition]. To report, see 47533, 47534, 47535, 47536, 47537)

(**75982** deleted 2015 [2016 edition]. To report, see 47533, 47534, 47535, 47536, 47537, 47538, 47539, 47540)

75984 Change of percutaneous tube or drainage catheter with contrast monitoring (eg, genitourinary system, abscess), radiological supervision and interpretation

(For percutaneous replacement of gastrostomy, duodenostomy, jejunostomy, gastro-jejunostomy, or cecostomy [or other colonic] tube including fluoroscopic imaging guidance, see 49450-49452)

(To report exchange of a percutaneous nephrostomy catheter, use 50435)

(For percutaneous choloecystostomy, use 47490)

(For percutaneous biliary procedures, including radiological supervision and interpretation, see 47531-47544)

(For percutaneous nephrostolithotomy or pyelostolithotomy, see 50080, 50081)

(For removal and/or replacement of an internally dwelling ureteral stent via a transurethral approach, see 50385-50386)

75989 Radiological guidance (ie, fluoroscopy, ultrasound, or computed tomography), for percutaneous drainage (eg., abscess, specimen collection), with placement of catheter, radiological supervision and interpretation

(Do not report 75989 in conjunction with 10030, 32554, 32555, 32556, 32557, 47490, 49405, 49406, 49407)

OTHER PROCEDURES

(For computed tomography cerebral perfusion analysis, see Category III code 0042T)

(For arthrography of shoulder, use 73040; elbow, use 73085; wrist, use 73115; hip, use 73525; knee, use 73580; ankle, use 73615)

▲ **76000** Fluoroscopy (separate procedure), up to 1 hour physician or other qualified health care professional time

(Do not report 76000 in conjunction with 33957, 33958, 33959, 33962, 33963, 33964)

76001 Fluoroscopy, physician or other qualified health care professional time more than 1 hour, assisting a non-radiologic physician or other qualified health care professional (eg, nephrostolithotomy, ERCP, bronchoscopy, transbronchial biopsy)

(Do not report 76001 in conjunction with 33957, 33958, 33959, 33962, 33963, 33964)

76010 Radiologic examination from nose to rectum for foreign body, single view, child

76080 Radiologic examination, abscess, fistula or sinus tract study, radiological supervision and interpretation

(For contrast injection[s] and radiological assessment of gastrostomy, duodenostomy, jejunostomy, gastro-jejunostomy, or cecostomy [or other colonic] tube including fluoroscopic imaging guidance, use 49465)

76098 Radiological examination, surgical specimen

(Do not report 76098 in conjunction with 19081-19086)

76100 Radiologic examination, single plane body section (eg, tomography), other than with urography

76101 Radiologic examination, complex motion (ie, hypercycloidal) body section (eg, mastoid polytomography), other than with urography; unilateral

76102 bilateral

(Do not report 76101, 76102 more than once per day)

(For panoramic X-ray, use 70355)

(For nephrotomography, use 74415)

76120 Cineradiography/videoradiography, except where specifically included

+ **76125** Cineradiography/videoradiography to complement routine examination (List separately in addition to code for primary procedure)

76140 Consultation on x-ray examination made elsewhere, written report

(2D reformatting is no longer separately reported. To report 3D rendering, see 76376, 76377)

76376 3D rendering with interpretation and reporting of computed tomography, magnetic resonance imaging, ultrasound, or other tomographic modality with image post processing under concurrent supervision; not requiring image postprocessing on an independent workstation

(Use 76376 in conjunction with code(s) for base imaging procedure(s))

(Do not report 76376 in conjunction with 31627, 34839, 70496, 70498, 70544, 70545, 70546, 70547, 70548, 70549, 71275, 71555, 72159, 72191, 72198, 73206, 73225, 73706, 73725, 74174, 74175, 74185, 74261, 74262, 74263, 75557, 75559, 75561, 75563, 75565, 75571, 75572, 75573, 75574, 75635, 76377, 77061, 77062, 77063, 78012-78999, 93355, 0159T)

76377 requiring image postprocessing on an independent workstation

(Use 76377 in conjunction with code(s) for base imaging procedure(s))

● New Code ▲ Revised Code + Add-On Code ⊘ Modifier -51 Exempt ★ Telemedicine

(Do not report 76377 in conjunction with 34839, 70496, 70498, 70544, 70545, 70546, 70547, 70548, 70549, 71275, 71555, 72159, 72191, 72198, 73206, 73225, 73706, 73725, 74174, 74175, 74185, 74261, 74262, 74263, 75557, 75559, 75561, 75563, 75565, 75571, 75572, 75573, 75574, 75635, 76376, 77061, 77062, 77063, 78012-78999, 93355, 0159T)

(To report computer-aided detection, including computer algorithm analysis of MRI data for lesion detection/ characterization, pharmacokinetic analysis, breast MRI, use Category III code 0159T)

(76376, 76377 require concurrent supervision of image post processing 3D manipulation of volumetric data set and image rendering)

76380 Computed tomography, limited or localized follow-up study

76390 Magnetic resonance spectroscopy

(For magnetic resonance imaging, use appropriate MRI body site code)

76496 Unlisted fluoroscopic procedure (eg., diagnostic, interventional)

76497 Unlisted computed tomography procedure (eg., diagnostic, interventional)

76498 Unlisted magnetic resonance procedure (eg., diagnostic, interventional)

76499 Unlisted diagnostic radiographic procedure

DIAGNOSTIC ULTRASOUND

Diagnostic ultrasound is a non-invasive medical imaging technology that uses high frequency sound waves to form an image of body tissues. Ultrasound, when compared to other imaging modalities like MRI (Magnetic Resonance Imaging) and CT (Computed Tomography), is a relatively low cost non-invasive procedure that does not utilize either magnetic fields or ionizing radiation (x-rays).

All diagnostic ultrasound examinations require permanently recorded images with measurements, when such measurements are clinically indicated. For those codes whose sole diagnostic goal is a biometric measure (ie., 76514, 76516, 76519), permanently recorded images are not required. A final, written report should be issued for inclusion in the patient's medical record. The prescription form for the intraocular lens satisfies the written report requirement for 76519. For those anatomic regions that have "complete" and "limited" ultrasound codes, note the elements that comprise a "complete"exam. The report should contain a description of these elements or the reason that an element could not be visualized (eg., obscured by bowel gas, surgically absent).

If less than the required elements for a "complete" exam are reported (eg., limited number of organs or limited portion of region evaluated), the "limited" code for that anatomic region should be used once per patient exam session. A "limited" exam of an anatomic region should not be reported for the same exam session as a "complete" exam of the same region.

Evaluation of vascular structures using both color and spectral Doppler is separately reportable. To report, see Noninvasive Vascular Diagnostic Studies (93875-93990). However, color Doppler alone, when performed for anatomic structure identification in conjunction with a real-time ultrasound examination, is not reported separately.

Ultrasound guidance procedures also require permanently recorded images of the site to be localized, as well as a documented description of the localization process, either separately or within the report of the procedure for which the guidance is utilized.

Use of ultrasound, without thorough evaluation of organ(s) or anatomic region, image documentation, and final written report, is not separately reportable.

Ultrasound Modes

A-mode   *Now obsolete in medical imaging. Wave spikes are represented when a single beam passes through objects of different consistency and hardness. The distance between these spikes (for example A and B) can be measured accurately by dividing the speed of sound in tissue (1540 m/sec) by half the sound travel time.*

B-mode   *Same as A-mode, but one-dimensional graphical display, with brightness corresponding to amplitude of reflected sound.*

M-mode   *A single beam in an ultrasound scan can be used to produce an M-mode picture, where movement of a structure such as a heart valve can be depicted in a wave-like manner. Because of its high sampling frequency (up to 1000 pulses per second), this is useful in assessing rates and motion and is still used extensively in cardiac and fetal cardiac imaging.*

Real time   *Most modern ultrasound devices are 2D-real time imaging systems. Multiple crystals (linear, curved or phased-array) or moving crystal. Sequential B-mode pulses sweeping across a plane to display the image in either a linear or 'sector' format. Displayed as real time imaging with up to 100 images per second.*

(To report diagnostic vascular ultrasound studies, see 93880-93990)

(For focused ultrasound ablation treatment of uterine leiomyomata, see Category III codes 0071T, 0072T)

HEAD AND NECK

76506   Echoencephalography, real time with image documentation (gray scale) (for determination of ventricular size, delineation of cerebral contents and detection of fluid masses or other intracranial abnormalities), including A-mode encephalography as secondary component where indicated

76510   Ophthalmic ultrasound, diagnostic; B-scan and quantitative A-scan performed during the same patient encounter

76511   quantitative A-scan only

76512   B-scan (with or without superimposed non-quantitative A-scan)

76513   anterior segment ultrasound, immersion (water bath) B-scan or high resolution biomicroscopy

(For scanning computerized ophthalmic diagnostic imaging of the anterior and posterior segments using technology other than ultrasound, see 92132, 92133, 92134)

76514   corneal pachymetry, unilateral or bilateral (determination of corneal thickness)

(Do not report 76514 in conjunction with 0402T)

76516   Ophthalmic biometry by ultrasound echography, A-scan;

76519   with intraocular lens power calculation

(For partial coherence interferometry, use 92136)

76529   Ophthalmic ultrasonic foreign body localization

76536   Ultrasound, soft tissues of head and neck (eg, thyroid, parathyroid, parotid), real time with image documentation

CHEST

Code 76641 represents a complete ultrasound examination of the breast. Code 76641 consists of an ultrasound examination of all four quadrants of the breast and the retroareolar region. It also includes ultrasound examination of the axilla, if performed.

Code 76642 consists of a focused ultrasound examination of the breast limited to the assessment of one or more, but not all of the elements listed in code 76641. It also includes ultrasound examination of the axilla, if performed.

Use of ultrasound, without thorough evaluation of organ(s) or anatomic region, image documentation, and final written report, is not separately reportable.

76604   Ultrasound, chest, (includes mediastinum) real time with image documentation

76641   Ultrasound, breast, unilateral, real time with image documentation, including axilla when performed; complete

76642   limited

(Report 76641, 76442 only once per breast, per session)

(For axillary ultrasound only, use 76882)

(**76645**   deleted 2014 [2015 edition]. To report, see 76641, 76642)

ABDOMEN AND PERITONEUM

A complete ultrasound examination of the abdomen (76700) consists of real-time scans of the liver, gall bladder, common bile duct, pancreas, spleen, kidneys, and the upper abdominal aorta and inferior vena cava including any demonstrated abdominal abnormality.

A complete ultrasound examination of the retroperitoneum (76770) consists of real-time scans of the kidneys, abdominal aorta, common iliac artery origins, and inferior vena cava, including any demonstrated retroperitoneal abnormality. Alternatively, if clinical history suggests urinary tract pathology, complete evaluation of the kidneys and urinary bladder also comprises a complete retroperitoneal ultrasound.

Use of ultrasound, without thorough evaluation of organ(s) or anatomic region, image documentation and final, written report, is not separately reportable.

76700   Ultrasound, abdominal, real time with image documentation; complete

76705   limited (eg, single organ, quadrant, follow-up)

76706   Ultrasound, abdominal aorta, real time with image documentation, screening study for abdominal aortic aneurysm (AAA)

(For ultrasound or duplex ultrasound of the abdominal aorta other than screening, see 76770, 76775, 93978, 93979)

76770   Ultrasound, retroperitoneal (eg, renal, aorta, nodes), real time with image documentation; complete

76775   limited

76776   Ultrasound, transplanted kidney, real time and duplex Doppler with image documentation

(For ultrasound or transplanted kidney without duplex Doppler, use 76775)

(For ultrasound and duplex Doppler of a transplanted kidney, do not report 76776 in conjunction with 93975, 93976)

SPINAL CANAL

76800   Ultrasound, spinal canal and contents

PELVIS

OBSTETRICAL

Codes 76801 and 76802 include determination of the number of gestational sacs and fetuses, gestational sac/fetal measurements appropriate for gestation (younger than 14 weeks 0 days), survey of visible fetal and placental anatomic structure, qualitative assessment of amniotic fluid volume/gestational sac shape and examination of the maternal uterus and adnexa.

Codes 76805 and 76810 include determination of number of fetuses and amniotic/chorionic sacs, measurements appropriate for gestational age (older than or equal to 14 weeks 0 days), survey of intracranial/spinal/abdominal anatomy, 4 chambered heart, umbilical cord insertion site, placenta location and amniotic fluid assessment, and when visible, examination of maternal adnexa.

Codes 76811 and 76812 include all elements of codes 76805 and 76810 plus detailed anatomic evaluation of the fetal brain/ventricles, face, heart/outflow tracts and chest anatomy, abdominal organ specific anatomy, number/length/architecture of limbs and detailed evaluation of the umbilical cord and placenta and other fetal anatomy as clinically indicated.

Report should document the results of the evaluation of each element described above or the reason for non-visualization.

Code 76815 represents a focused "quick look" exam limited to the assessment of one or more of the elements listed in code 76815.

Code 76816 describes an examination designed to reassess fetal size and interval growth or reevaluate one or more anatomic abnormalities of a fetus previously demonstrated on ultrasound, and should be coded once for each fetus requiring reevaluation using modifier 59 for each fetus after the first.

Code 76817 describes a transvaginal obstetric ultrasound performed separately or in addition to one of the transabdominal examinations described above. For transvaginal examinations performed for non-obstetrical purposes, use code 76830

76801 Ultrasound, pregnant uterus, real time with image documentation, fetal and maternal evaluation, first trimester (>14 weeks 0 days), transabdominal approach; single or first gestation

(To report first trimester fetal nuchal translucency measurement, use 76813)

+ 76802 each additional gestation (List separately in addition to code for primary procedure)

(Use 76802 in conjunction with code 76801)

(To report first trimester fetal nuchal translucency measurement, use 76814)

76805 Ultrasound, pregnant uterus, real time with image documentation, fetal and maternal evaluation, after first trimester (>or = 14 weeks 0 days), transabdominal approach; single or first gestation

+ 76810 each additional gestation (List separately in addition to code for primary procedure)

(Use 76810 in conjunction with code 76805)

76811 Ultrasound, pregnant uterus, real time with image documentation, fetal and maternal evaluation plus detailed fetal anatomic examination, transabdominal approach; single or first gestation

+ 76812 each additional gestation (List separately in addition to code for primary procedure)

(Use 76812 in conjunction with code 76811)

76813 Ultrasound, pregnant uterus, real time with image documentation, first trimester fetal nuchal translucency measurement, transabdominal or transvaginal approach; single or first gestation

+ 76814 each additional gestation (List separately in addition to code for primary procedure)

(Use 76814 in conjunction with 76813)

76815 Ultrasound, pregnant uterus, real time with image documentation, limited (eg., fetal heart beat, placental location, fetal position, and/or qualitative amniotic fluid volume), 1 or more fetuses

(Use 76815 only once per exam and not per element)

(To report first trimester fetal nuchal translucency measurement, see 76813, 76814)

76816 Ultrasound, pregnant uterus, real time with image documentation, follow-up (eg., re-evaluation of fetal size by measuring standard growth parameters and amniotic fluid volume, re-evaluation of organ system(s) suspected or confirmed to be abnormal on a previous scan), transabdominal approach, per fetus

(Report 76816 with modifier -59 for each additional fetus examined in a multiple pregnancy)

76817 Ultrasound, pregnant uterus, real time with image documentation, transvaginal

(For non-obstetrical transvaginal ultrasound, use 76830)

(If transvaginal examination is done in addition to transabdominal obstetrical ultrasound exam, use 76817 in addition to appropriate transabdominal exam code)

76818 Fetal biophysical profile; with non-stress testing

76819 without non-stress testing

● New Code ▲ Revised Code + Add-On Code ⊘ Modifier -51 Exempt ★ Telemedicine

(Fetal biophysical profile assessments for the second and any additional fetuses, should be reported separately by code 76818 or 76819 with the modifier -59 appended)

(For amniotic fluid index without non-stress test, use 76815)

76820 Doppler velocimetry, fetal; umbilical artery

76821 middle cerebral artery

76825 Echocardiography, fetal, cardiovascular system, real time with image documentation (2D), with or without M-mode recording;

76826 follow-up or repeat study

76827 Doppler echocardiography, fetal, pulsed wave and/or continuous wave with spectral display; complete

76828 follow-up or repeat study

(To report the use of color mapping, use 93325)

NON-OBSTETRICAL

Code 76856 includes the complete evaluation of the female pelvic anatomy. Elements of this examination include a description and measurements of the uterus and adnexal structures, measurement of the endometrium, measurement of the bladder (when applicable) and a description of any pelvic pathology (eg., ovarian cysts, uterine leiomyomata, free pelvic fluid).

Code 76856 is also applicable to a complete evaluation of the male pelvis. Elements of the examination include evaluation and measurement (when applicable) of the urinary bladder, evaluation of the prostate and seminal vesicles to the extent that they are visualized transabdominally, and any pelvic pathology (eg., bladder tumor, enlarged prostate, free pelvic fluid, pelvic abscess).

Code 76857 represents a focused examination limited to the assessment of one or more elements listed in code 76856 and/or the reevaluation of one or more pelvic abnormalities previously demonstrated on ultrasound. Code 76857, rather than 76770, should be utilized if the urinary bladder alone (ie., not including the kidneys) is imaged, whereas code 51798 should be utilized if a bladder volume or post-void residual measurement is obtained without imaging the bladder.

Use of ultrasound, without thorough evaluation of organ(s) or anatomic region, image documentation, and final, written report, is not separately reportable.

76830 Ultrasound, transvaginal

(For obstetrical transvaginal ultrasound, use 76817)

(If transvaginal examination is done in addition to transabdominal non-obstetrical ultrasound exam, use 76830 in addition to appropriate transabdominal exam code)

76831 Saline infusion sonohysterography (SIS), including color flow Doppler, when performed

(For introduction of saline for saline infusion sonohysterography, use 58340)

76856 Ultrasound, pelvic (nonobstetric), real time with image documentation; complete

76857 limited or follow-up (eg, for follicles)

GENITALIA

76870 Ultrasound, scrotum and contents

76872 Ultrasound, transrectal;

(Do not report 76872 in conjunction with 45341, 45342, 45391, 45392, 0249T, 0421T)

76873 prostate volume study for brachytherapy treatment planning (separate procedure)

EXTREMITIES

Code 76881 represents a complete evaluation of a specific joint in an extremity. Code 76881 requires ultrasound examination of all of the following joint elements: joint space (eg, effusion), peri-articular softtissue structures that surround the joint (ie, muscles, tendons, other soft-tissue structures), and any identifiable abnormality. In some circumstances, additional evaluations such as dynamic imaging or stress maneuvers may be performed as part of the complete evaluation. Code 76881 also requires permanently recorded images and a written report containing a description of each of the required elements or reason that an element(s) could not be visualized (eg, absent secondary to surgery or trauma).

When fewer than all of the required elements for a "complete" exam (76881) are performed, report the "limited" code (76882).

Code 76882 represents a limited evaluation of a joint or an evaluation of a structure(s) in an extremity other than a joint (eg, soft-tissue mass, fluid collection, or nerve[s]). Limited evaluation of a joint includes assessment of a specific anatomic structure(s) (eg, joint space only [effusion] or tendon, muscle, and/or other soft-tissue structure[s] that surround the joint) that does not assess all of the required elements included in 76881. Code 76882 also requires permanently recorded images and a written report containing a description of each of the elements evaluated.

For spectral and color Doppler evaluation of the extremities, use 93925, 93926, 93930, 93931, 93970, or 93971 as appropriate.

▲ **76881** Ultrasound, complete joint (ie, joint space and periarticular soft-tissue structures), real-time with image documentation

▲ **76882** Ultrasound, limited, joint or other nonvascular extremity structure(s) (eg, joint space, peri-articular tendon[s], muscle[s], nerve[s], other soft-tissue structure[s], or softtissue mass[es]), real-time with image documentation

76885 Ultrasound, infant hips, real time with imaging documentation; dynamic (requiring physician or other qualified health care professional manipulation)

76886 limited, static (not requiring physician or other qualified health care professional manipulation)

ULTRASONIC GUIDANCE PROCEDURES

76930 Ultrasonic guidance for pericardiocentesis, imaging supervision and interpretation

76932 Ultrasonic guidance for endomyocardial biopsy, imaging supervision and interpretation

76936 Ultrasound guided compression repair of arterial pseudoaneurysm or arteriovenous fistulae (includes diagnostic ultrasound evaluation, compression of lesion and imaging)

+ **76937** Ultrasound guidance for vascular access requiring ultrasound evaluation of potential access sites, documentation of selected vessel patency, concurrent realtime ultrasound visualization of vascular needle entry, with permanent recording and reporting (List separately in addition to code for primary procedure)

(Do not report 76937 in conjunction with 37191, 37192, 37193, 37760, 37761, 76942)

(If extremity venous non-invasive vascular diagnostic study is performed separate from venous access guidance, see 93970, 93971)

76940 Ultrasound guidance for, and monitoring of, parenchymal tissue ablation

(Do not report 76940 in conjunction with 20982, 20983, 32994, 32998, 50250, 50542, 76942, 76998)

(For ablation, see 47370-47382, 47383, 50592, 50593)

76941 Ultrasonic guidance for intrauterine fetal transfusion or cordocentesis, imaging supervision and interpretation

(For procedure, see 36460, 59012)

76942 Ultrasonic guidance for needle placement (eg, biopsy, aspiration, injection, localization device) imaging supervision and interpretation

---

● New Code   ▲ Revised Code   + Add-On Code   ⊘ Modifier -51 Exempt   ★ Telemedicine

(Do not report 76942 in conjunction with 10030, 19083, 19285, 20604, 20606, 20611, 27096, 32554, 32555, 32556, 32557, 37760, 37761, 43232, 43237, 43242, 45341, 45342, 55874, 64479, 64480, 64483, 64484, 64490, 64491, 64493, 64494, 64495, 76975, 0213T, 0214T, 0215T, 0216T, 0217T, 0218T, 0228T, 0229T, 0230T, 0231T, 0232T, 0249T, 0481T)

(For harvesting, preparation, and injection[s] of platelet-rich plasma, use 0232T)

76945   Ultrasonic guidance for chorionic villus sampling, imaging supervision and interpretation

(For procedure, use 59015)

76946   Ultrasonic guidance for amniocentesis, imaging supervision and interpretation

76948   Ultrasonic guidance for aspiration of ova, imaging supervision and interpretation

(76950   deleted 2014 [2015 edition]. To report, use 77387)

(For placement of interstitial device[s] for radiation therapy guidance, see 31627, 32553, 49411, 55876)

76965   Ultrasonic guidance for interstitial radioelement application

OTHER PROCEDURES

76970   Ultrasound study follow-up (specify)

76975   Gastrointestinal endoscopic ultrasound, imaging supervision and interpretation

(Do not report 76975 in conjunction with 43231, 43232, 43237, 43238, 43240, 43242, 43259, 44406, 44407, 45341, 45342, 45391, 45392, 76942)

76977   Ultrasound bone density measurement and interpretation, peripheral site(s), any method

76998   Ultrasonic guidance, intraoperative

(Do not report 76998 in conjunction with 36475, 36479, 37760, 37761, 47370, 47371, 47380, 47381, 47382, 0249T)

(For ultrasound guidance for open and laparoscopic radiofrequency tissue ablation, use 76940)

76999   Unlisted ultrasound procedure (eg., diagnostic, interventional)

RADIOLOGIC GUIDANCE

FLUOROSCOPIC GUIDANCE

(Do not report guidance codes 77001, 77002, 77003 for services in which fluoroscopic guidance is included in the descriptor)

+ 77001   Fluoroscopic guidance for central venous access device placement, replacement (catheter only or complete), or removal (includes fluoroscopic guidance for vascular access and catheter manipulation, any necessary contrast injections through access site or catheter with related venography radiologic supervision and interpretation, and radiographic documentation of final catheter position) (List separately in addition to code for primary procedure)

(Do not use 77001 in conjunction with 33957, 33958, 33959, 33962, 33963, 33964, 77002)

(If formal extremity venography is performed from separate venous access and separately interpreted, use 36005 and 75820, 75822, 75825 or 75827)

+ 77002   Fluoroscopic guidance for needle placement (eg, biopsy, aspiration, injection, localization device) (List separately in addition to code for primary procedure)

(See appropriate surgical code for procedure and anatomic location)

(Use 77002 in conjunction with 10022, 10160, 20206, 20220, 20225, 20520, 20525, 20526, 20550, 20551, 20552, 20553, 20555, 20600, 20605, 20610, 20612, 20615, 21116, 21550, 23350, 24220, 25246, 27093, 27095, 27370, 27648, 32400, 32405, 32553, 36002, 38220, 38221, 38505, 38794, 41019, 42400, 42405, 47000, 47001, 48102, 49180, 49411, 50200, 50390, 51100, 51101, 51102, 55700, 55876, 60100, 62268, 62269, 64505, 64508, 64600, 64605)

(77002 is included in allarthrography radiological supervision and interpretation codes. See Administration of Contrast Material[s] introductory guidelines for reporting of arthrography procedures)

+ 77003   Fluoroscopic guidance and localization of needle or catheter tip for spine or paraspinous diagnostic or therapeutic injection procedures (epidural or subarachnoid) (List separately in addition to code for primary procedure)

(Use 77003 in conjunction with 61050, 61055, 62267, 62270, 62272, 62273, 62280, 62281, 62282, 62284, 64510, 64517, 64520, 64610)

(Do not report 77003 in conjunction with 62320, 62321, 62322, 62323, 62324, 62325, 62326, 62327)

COMPUTED TOMOGRAPHY GUIDANCE

77011   Computed tomography guidance for stereotactic localization

77012   Computed tomography guidance for needle placement (eg, biopsy, aspiration, injection, localization device), radiological supervision and interpretation

(Do not report 77011, 77012 in conjunction with 22586, 0195T, 0196T)

(Do not report 77012 in conjunction with 10030, 27096, 32554, 32555, 32556, 32557, 64479, 64480, 64483, 64484, 64490, 64491, 64492, 64493, 64494, 64495, 64633, 64634, 64635, 64636, 0232T, 0481T)

(For harvesting, preparation, and injection[s] of platelet-rich plasma, use 0232T)

77013   Computerized tomography guidance for, and monitoring of, parenchymal tissue ablation

(Do not report 77013 in conjunction with 20982, 20983, 32994, 32998)

(For percutaneous ablation, see 47382, 47383, 50592, 50593)

77014   Computed tomography guidance for placement of radiation therapy fields

(For placement of interstitial device(s) for radiation therapy guidance, see 31627, 32553, 49411, 55876)

MAGNETIC RESONANCE GUIDANCE

77021   Magnetic resonance guidance for needle placement (eg, for biopsy, needle aspiration, injection, or placement of localization device) radiological supervision and interpretation

(For procedure, see appropriate organ or site)

(Do not report 77021 in conjunction with 10030, 19085, 19287, 32554, 32555, 32556, 32557, 0232T, 0481T)

(For harvesting, preparation, and injection[s] of platelet-rich plasma, use 0232T)

77022   Magnetic resonance guidance for, and monitoring of, parenchymal tissue ablation

(Do not report 77022 in conjunction with 20982, 20983, 32994, 32998, 0071T, 0072T)

(For percutaneous ablation, see 47382, 47383, 50592, 50593)

(For focused ultrasound ablation treatment of uterine leiomyomata, see Category III codes 0071T, 0072T)

(To report stereotactic localization guidance for breast biopsy or for placement of breast localization device[s], see 19081, 19283)

(To report mammographic guidance for placement of breast localization device[s], use 19281)

   ● New Code   ▲ Revised Code   + Add-On Code   ⊘ Modifier -51 Exempt   ★ Telemedicine

BREAST, MAMMOGRAPHY

(For mammographic guidance for needle placement of breast lesion, use 77032)

(77051 deleted 2016 [2017 edition]. To report, see 77065, 77066)

(77052 deleted 2016 [2017 edition]. To report, see 77067)

77053 Mammary ductogram or galactogram, single duct, radiological supervision and interpretation

   (For mammary ductogram or galactogram injection, use 19030)

77054 Mammary ductogram or galactogram, multiple ducts, radiological supervision and interpretation

(77055 deleted 2016 [2017 edition]. To report, use 77065)

(77056 deleted 2016 [2017 edition]. To report, use 77066)

(77057 deleted 2016 [2017 edition]. To report, use 77067)

77058 Magnetic resonance imaging, breast, without and/or with contrast material(s); unilateral

77059   bilateral

77061 Digital breast tomosynthesis; unilateral

77062   bilateral

   (Do not report 77061, 77062 in conjunction with 76376, 76377, 77067)

+ 77063 Screening digital breast tomosynthesis, bilateral (list separately in addition to code for primary procedure)
   (Do not report 77063 in conjunction with 76376, 76377, 77065, 77066)
   (Use 77063 in conjunction with 77067)

77065 Diagnostic mammography, including computer-aided detection (CAD) when performed; unilateral

77066   bilateral

77067 Screening mammography, bilateral (2-view study of each breast), including computer-aided detection (CAD) when performed

   (For electrical impedance breast scan, use 76499)

BONE/JOINT STUDIES

77071 Manual application of stress performed by physician or other qualified health care professional for joint radiography, including contralateral joint if indicated

   (For radiographic interpretation of stressed images, see appropriate anatomic site and number of views)

77072 Bone age studies

77073 Bone length studies (orthoroentgenogram, scanogram)

77074 Radiologic examination, osseous survey; limited (eg, for metastases)

77075   complete (axial and appendicular skeleton)

77076 Radiologic examination, osseous survey, infant

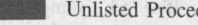 Separate Procedure Unlisted Procedure CCI Comp. Code Non-specific Procedure **653**

77077   Joint survey, single view, 2 or more joints (specify)

77078   Computed tomography, bone mineral density study, 1 or more sites; axial skeleton (eg, hips, pelvis, spine)

77080   Dual-energy X-ray absorptiometry (DXA), bone density study, 1 or more sites; axial skeleton (eg, hips, pelvis, spine)

(Do not report 77080 in conjunction with 77085, 77086)

77081   appendicular skeleton (peripheral) (eg, radius, wrist, heel)

(77082   deleted 2014 [2015 edition]. To report, use 77086)

(For dual-energy X-ray absorptiometry [DEXA] body composition study, use 76499)

77085   axial skeleton (eg, hips, pelvis, spine), including vertebral fracture assessment

(Do not report 77085 in conjunction with 77080, 77086)

77086   Vertebral fracture assessment via dual-energy X-ray absorptiometry (DXA)

(Do not report 77086 in conjunction with 77080, 77085)

77084   Magnetic resonance (eg, proton) imaging, bone marrow blood supply

77085   This code is out of order. See page 654.

77086   This code is out of order. See page 654.

RADIATION ONCOLOGY

Listings for Radiation Oncology provide for teletherapy and brachytherapy to include initial consultation, clinical treatment planning, simulation, medical radiation physics, dosimetry, treatment devices, special services, and clinical treatment management procedures. They include normal follow-up care during course of treatment and for three months following its completion.

When a service or procedure is provided that is not listed in this edition of CPT, it should be identified by a Special Report and one of the following unlisted procedure codes: **77299** Unlisted procedure, therapeutic radiology clinical treatment planning; or **77399** Unlisted procedure, medical radiation physics, dosimetry and treatment devices, and special services; or **77499** Unlisted procedure, therapeutic radiology treatment management; or **77799** Unlisted procedure, clinical brachytherapy.

For treatment by injectable or ingestible isotopes, see subsection Nuclear Medicine.

CONSULTATION: CLINICAL MANAGEMENT

Preliminary consultation, evaluation of patient prior to decision to treat, or full medical care (in addition to treatment management) when provided by the therapeutic radiologist may be identified by the appropriate procedure codes from Evaluation and Management, Medicine, or Surgery sections.

CLINICAL TREATMENT PLANNING (EXTERNAL AND INTERNAL SOURCES)

The clinical treatment planning process is a complex service including interpretation of special testing, tumor localization, treatment volume determination, treatment time/dosage determination, choice of treatment modality, determination of number and size of treatment ports, selection of appropriate treatment devices, and other procedures.

Definitions

Simple planning requires a single treatment area of interest encompassed in a single port or simple parallel opposed ports with simple or no blocking.

Intermediate planning requires 3 or more converging ports, 2 separate treatment areas, multiple blocks, or special time dose constraints.

● New Code   ▲ Revised Code   + Add-On Code   ⊘ Modifier -51 Exempt   ★ Telemedicine

Complex planning requires highly complex blocking, custom shielding blocks, tangential ports, special wedges or compensators, 3 or more separate treatment areas, rotational or special beam considerations, combination of therapeutic modalities.

77261 Therapeutic radiology treatment planning; simple

77262 intermediate

77263 complex

Simulation is the process of defining relevant normal and abnormal target anatomy, and acquiring the images and data necessary to develop the optimal radiation treatment process for the patient. A simulation is defined as complex if any of these criteria are met: particle, rotation or arc therapy, complex or custom blocking, brachytherapy simulation, hyperthermia probe verification, or any use of contrast material. If a simulation does not meet any of these criteria, the complexity is defined by the number of treatment areas: one treatment area is simple, two treatment areas are intermediate, and three or more treatment areas are complex.

A treatment area is a contiguous anatomic location that will be treated with radiation therapy. Generally, this includes the primary tumor organ or the resection bed and the draining lymph node chains, if indicated. An example is a breast cancer patient for whom a single treatment area could be the breast alone or the breast, adjacent supraclavicular fossa, and internal mammary nodes. In some cases, a patient might receive radiation therapy to more than one discontinuous anatomic location. An example would be a patient with multiple bone metastases in separate sites (eg, femur and cervical spine); in this case, each distinct and separate anatomic site to be irradiated is a separate treatment area.

Definitions.

Simple: simulation of a single treatment area.

Intermediate: two separate treatment areas.

Complex: three or more treatment areas, or any number of treatment areas if any of the following are involved: particle, rotation or arc therapy, complex blocking, custom shielding blocks, brachytherapy simulation, hyperthermia probe verification, any use of contrast materials.

77280 Therapeutic radiology simulation-aided field setting; simple

77285 intermediate

77290 complex

+ 77293 Respiratory motion management simulation (List separately in addition to code for primary procedure)

(Use 77293 in conjunction with 77295, 77301)

77295 This code is out of order. See page 655.

77299 Unlisted procedure, therapeutic radiology clinical treatment planning

MEDICAL RADIATION PHYSICS, DOSIMETRY, TREATMENT DEVICES, AND SPECIAL SERVICES

77295 3-dimensional radiotherapy plan, including dose-volume histograms

77300 Basic radiation dosimetry calculation, central axis depth dose calculation, TDF, NSD, gap calculation, off axis factor, tissue inhomogeneity factors, calculation of non-ionizing radiation surface and depth dose, as required during course of treatment, only when prescribed by the treating physician

(Do not report 77300 in conjunction with 77306, 77307, 77316, 77317, 77318, 77321, 77767, 77768, 77770, 77771, 77772, 0394T, 0395T)

77301 Intensity modulated radiotherapy plan, including dose-volume histograms for target and critical structure partial tolerance specifications

(Dose plan is optimized using inverse or forward planning technique for modulated beam delivery (eg, binary, dynamic MLC) to create highly conformal dose distribution. Computer plan distribution must be verified for positional accuracy based on dosimetric verification of the intensity map with verification of treatment set up and interpretation of verification methodology)

(**77305** deleted 2014 [2015 edition]. To report, use 77306)

77306 Teletherapy isodose plan; simple (1 or 2 unmodified ports directed to a single area of interest), includes basic dosimetry calculation(s)

77307 complex (multiple treatment areas, tangential ports, the use of wedges, blocking, rotational beam, or special beam considerations), includes basic dosimetry calculation(s)

(Only one teletherapy isodose plan may be reported for a given course of therapy to a specific treatment area)

(Do not report 77306, 77307 in conjunction with 77300)

(**77310** deleted 2014 [2015 edition]. To report, use 77306, 77307)

(**77315** deleted 2014 [2015 edition]. To report, use 77307)

77316 Brachytherapy isodose plan; simple (calculation[s] made from 1 to 4 sources, or remote afterloading brachytherapy, 1 channel), includes basic dosimetry calculation(s)

(For definition of source, see clinical brachytherapy introductory guidelines)

77317 intermediate (calculation[s] made from 5 to 10 sources, or remote afterloading brachytherapy, 2-12 channels), includes basic dosimetry calculation(s)

77318 complex (calculation[s] made from over 10 sources, or remote afterloading brachytherapy, over 12 channels), includes basic dosimetry calculation(s)

(Do not report 77316, 77317, 77318 in conjunction with 77300)

77321 Special teletherapy port plan, particles, hemibody, total body

(**77326** deleted 2014 [2015 edition]. To report, use 77316)

(**77327** deleted 2014 [2015 edition]. To report, use 77317)

(**77328** deleted 2014 [2015 edition]. To report, use 77318)

77331 Special dosimetry (eg, TLD, microdosimetry) (specify), only when prescribed by the treating physician

77332 Treatment devices, design and construction; simple (simple block, simple bolus)

77333 intermediate (multiple blocks, stents, bite blocks, special bolus)

77334 complex (irregular blocks, special shields, compensators, wedges, molds or casts)

77336 Continuing medical physics consultation, including assessment of treatment parameters, quality assurance of dose delivery, and review of patient treatment documentation in support of the radiation oncologist, reported per week of therapy

77338 Multi leaf collimator (MLC) device(s) for intensity modulated radiation therapy (IMRT), design and construction per IMRT plan

(Do not report 77338 in conjunction with 77385 for compensator based IMRT)

(Do not report 77338 more than once per IMRT plan)

(For immobilization in IMRT treatment, see 77332-77334)

77370   Special medical radiation physics consultation

STEREOTACTIC RADIATION TREATMENT DELIVERY

77371   Radiation treatment delivery, stereotactic radiosurgery (SRS), complete course of treatment of cranial lesion(s) consisting of 1 session; multi-source Cobalt 60 based

77372   linear accelerator based

(For radiation treatment management, use 77432)

77373   Stereotactic body radiation therapy, treatment delivery, per fraction to 1 or more lesions, including image guidance, entire course not to exceed 5 fractions

(Do not report 77373 in conjunction with 77385, 77386, 77401, 77402, 77407, 77412)

(For single fraction cranial lesions(s), see 77371, 77372)

77385   This code is out of order. See page 658.

77386   This code is out of order. See page 658.

77387   This code is out of order. See page .

OTHER PROCEDURES

77399   Unlisted procedure, medical radiation physics, dosimetry and treatment devices, and special services

RADIATION TREATMENT DELIVERY

Following dosimetry calculations, there are a number of alternative methods to deliver external radiation treatments, which are described with specific CPT codes:

X-ray (photon), including conventional and intensity modulated radiation therapy IMRT beams;

Electron beams;

Neutron beams;

Proton beams.

All treatment delivery codes are reported once per treatment session. The treatment delivery codes recognize technical-only services and contain no physician work (the professional component). In contrast, the treatment management codes contain only the professional component.

Radiation treatment delivery with conventional X-ray or electron beams is assigned levels of complexity based on the number of treatment sites and complexity of the treatment fields, blocking, wedges, and physical or virtual tissue compensators. A simple block is straight-edged or an approximation of a straight edge created by a multileaf collimator (MLC). Energy of the megavoltage less than or equal to 1MEV beam does not contribute to complexity. Techniques such as treating a field-in-field to ensure dose homogeneity reflect added complexity.

Energies below the megavoltage range maybe used in the treatment of skin lesions. Superficial radiation energies (up to 200 kV) may be generated by a variety of technologies and should not be reported with megavoltage (77402, 77407, 77412) for surface application. Do not report clinical treatment planning (77261, 77262, 77263), treatment devices (77332, 77333, 77334), isodose planning (77306, 77307, 77316, 77317, 77318), physics consultation (77336), or radiation treatment management (77427, 77431, 77432, 77435, 77469, 77470, 77499), with 77401, 0394T, or 0395T. When reporting 77401 alone, evaluation and management, when performed, may be reported with the appropriate E/M codes.

Intensity modulated radiation therapy (IMRT) uses computer-based optimization techniques with non-uniform radiation beam intensities to create highly conformal dose distributions that can be delivered by a radiotherapy treatment machine. A number of technologies, including spatially and temporally modulated beams, cylindrical beamlets, dynamic MLC, single or multiple fields or arcs, or compensators, may be used to generate IMRT. The complexity of IMRT may vary depending on the area being treated or the technique being used.

Image guided radiation therapy (IGRT) may be used to direct the radiation beam and to reflect motion during treatment. A variety of techniques may be used to perform this guidance including imaging (eg., ultrasound, CT, MRI, stereoscopic imaging) and non-imaging (eg., electromagnetic or infrared) techniques. Guidance may be used with any radiation treatment delivery technique and is typically used with IMRT delivery. IMRT delivery codes include the technical component of guidance or tracking, if performed. Because only the technical portion of IGRT is bundled into IMRT, the physician involvement in guidance or tracking may be reported separately. When guidance is required with conventional radiation treatment delivery, both the professional and technical components are reported because neither component of guidance is bundled into conventional radiation treatment delivery services.

The technical and professional components of guidance are handled differently with each radiation delivery code depending on the type of radiation being administered. The Radiation Management and Treatment Table is provided for clarity.

Definitions

Radiation Treatment Delivery, megavoltage (less than or equal to 1MeV, any energy.

Simple: all of the following criteria are met and none of the complex or intermediate criteria are met: single treatment area, one or two ports, and two or fewer simple blocks.

Intermediate: any of the following criteria are met and none of the complex criteria are met: two separate treatment areas, three or more ports on a single treatment area, or three or more simple blocks.

Complex: any of the following criteria are met: three or more separate treatment areas, custom blocking, tangential ports, wedges, rotational beam, field-in-field or other tissue compensation that does not meet IMRT guidelines, or electron beam.

Intensity Modulated Radiation Therapy (IMRT), any energy, includes the technical services for guidance

Simple: any of the following: prostate, breast, and all sites using physical compensator based IMRT.

Complex: includes all other sites if not using physical compensator based IMRT

77401   Radiation treatment delivery, superficial and/or ortho voltage, per day

(Do not report 77401 in conjunction with 77373)

77402   Radiation treatment delivery, ≥ 1 MeV; simple

(Do not report 77402 in conjunction with 77373)

77407   intermediate

(Do not report 77407 in conjunction with 77373)

77412   complex

(Do not report 77412 in conjunction with 77373)

77417   Therapeutic radiology port image(s)

(**77418**   deleted 2014 [2015 edition])

(For intensity modulated treatment planning, use 77301)

77385   Intensity modulated radiation treatment delivery (IMRT), includes guidance and tracking, when performed; simple

(To report professional component [PC] of guidance and tracking, use 77387 with modifier 26)

77386   complex

(To report professional component [PC] of guidance and tracking, use 77387 with modifier 26)

(Do not report 77385, 77386 in conjunction with 77371, 77372, 77373)

77387   Guidance for localization of target volume for delivery of radiation treatment delivery, includes intrafraction tracking, when performed

(Do not report technical component [TC] with 77385, 77386, 77371, 77372, 77373)

(**77421**   deleted 2014 [2015 edition]. To report, use 77387)

(For placement of interstitial device(s) for radiation therapy guidance, see 31627, 32553, 49411, 55876)

77424   Intraoperative radiation treatment delivery, x-ray, single treatment session

77425   Intraoperative radiation treatment delivery, electrons, single treatment session

NEUTRON BEAM TREATMENT DELIVERY

(**77422**   deleted 2017 [2018 edition])

77423   High energy neutron radiation treatment delivery, 1 or more isocenter(s) with coplanar or non-coplanar geometry with blocking and/or wedge, and/or compensator(s)

77424   Code out of order. See page 659.

77425   Code out of order. See page 659.

RADIATION TREATMENT MANAGEMENT

CPT codes in this section presume treatment on a daily basis (4 or 5 fractions per week) with the use of megavoltage photon or high energy particle sources. Daily and weekly clinical treatment management are mutually exclusive for the same dates. CPT defines three distinct levels of clinical treatment management: simple, intermediate and complex. Review this section of CPT for detailed definitions of these levels of service.

Radiation treatment management is reported in units of five fractions or treatment sessions, regardless of the actual time period in which the services are furnished. The services need not be furnished on consecutive days. Multiple fractions representing two or more treatment sessions furnished on the same day may be counted separately as long as there has been a distinct break in therapy sessions, and the fractions are of the character usually furnished on different days. Code 77427 is also reported if there are three or four fractions beyond a multiple of five at the end of a course of treatment; one or two fractions beyond a multiple of five at the end of a course of treatment are not reported separately.

Radiation treatment management requires **and includes** a minimum of one examination of the patient by the physician for medical evaluation and management (eg., assessment of the patient's response to treatment, coordination of care and treatment, review of imaging and/or lab test results with doumentation) for each reporting of the radiation treatment management service. Code 77469 represents only the intraoperative session management and does not include medical evaluation and management outside of that session. The professional services furnished during treatment management typically include:

- Review of port images;

- Review of dosimetry, dose delivery, and treatment parameters;

- Review of patient treatment set-up.

Stereotactic radiosurgery (SRS [77432]) and stereotactic body radiation treatment (SBRT [77435]) management also include the professional component of guidance for localization of target volume for the delivery of radiation therapy (77387). See also the Radiation Management and Treatment Table.

77427   Radiation treatment management, 5 treatments

77431   Radiation therapy management with complete course of therapy consisting of 1 or 2 fractions only

(77431 is not to be used to fill in the last week of a long course of therapy)

77432   Stereotactic radiation treatment management of cranial lesion(s) (complete course of treatment consisting of 1 session)

| ■ Separate Procedure | ■ Unlisted Procedure | ■ CCI Comp. Code | ■ Non-specific Procedure | **659** |

(The same physician should not report both stereotactic radiosurgery services [61796-61800] and radiation treatment management [77432 or 77435] for cranial lesions)

(For stereotactic body radiation therapy treatment, use 77435)

(To report the technical component of guidance for localization of target volume, use 77387 with a technical component modifier [TC])

77435 Stereotactic body radiation therapy, treatment management, per treatment course, to 1 or more lesions, including image guidance, entire course not to exceed 5 fractions

(Do not report 77435 in conjunction with 77427-77432)

(The same physician should not report both stereotactic radiosurgery services [32701, 63620, 63621] and radiation treatment management [77435])

(To report the technical component of guidance for localization of target volume, use 77387 with a technical component modifier [TC])

77469 Intraoperative radiation treatment management

RADIATION MANAGEMENT AND TREATMENT TABLE

Category	Code	Descriptor	IGRT TC (77387-TC) Bundled into code?	IGRT PC (77387-PC) Bundled into code?	Code Type (Technical/ Professional)
Radiation Treatment Management	77427	Treatment management, 1-5 treatments	N	N	Professional
	77431	Treatment management, 1-2 fractions	N	N	Professional
	77432	SRS management, cranial lesion(s)	N	Y	Professional
	77435	SBRT management	N	Y	Professional
SRS Treatment Delivery	77371	SRS Multisource 60 Based	Y	N	Technical
	77372	SRS Linear Based	Y	N	Technical
SBRT Treatment Delivery	77373	SBRT, 1 or more lesions, 1-5 fractions	Y	N	Technical
Radiation Treatment Delivery	77401	Superficial and/or Ortho Voltage	N	N	Technical
	77402	Radiation treatment delivery, simple	N	N	Technical
	77407	Radiation treatment delivery, intermediate	N	N	Technical
	77412	Radiation treatment delivery, complex	N	N	Technical
IMRT Treatment Delivery	77385	IMRT treatment delivery, simple	Y	N	Technical
	77386	IMRT treatment delivery, complex	Y	N	Technical
Neutron Beam Treatment Delivery	77423	Neutron beam treatment, complex	N	N	Technical
Proton Treatment Delivery	77520	Proton treatment, simple	N	N	Technical
	77522	Proton treatment, simple	N	N	Technical
	77523	Proton treatment, intermediate	N	N	Technical
	77525	Proton treatment, complex	N	N	Technical

KEY:
SRS - Stereotactic radiosurgery
SBRT - Stereotactic body radiation therapy
IMRT - Intensity modulated radiation therapy
IGRT - Image guided radiation therapy
TC - Technical component
PC - Professional component

● New Code   ▲ Revised Code   + Add-On Code   ⊘ Modifier -51 Exempt   ★ Telemedicine

77470 Special treatment procedure (eg, total body irradiation, hemibody irradiation, per oral or endocavitary irradiation)

(77470 assumes that the procedure is performed one or more times during the course of therapy, in addition to daily or weekly patient management)

(For intraoperative radiation treatment delivery and management, see 77424, 77425, 77469)

77499 Unlisted procedure, therapeutic radiology treatment management

PROTON BEAM TREATMENT DELIVERY

Definitions

Simple proton treatment delivery to a single treatment area utilizing a single non-tangential/oblique port, custom block with compensation (77522) and without compensation (77520).

Intermediate proton treatment delivery to one or more treatment areas utilizing two or more ports or one or more tangential/oblique ports, with custom blocks and compensators.

Complex proton treatment delivery to one or more treatment areas utilizing two or more ports per treatment area with matching or patching fields and/or multiple isocenters, with custom blocks and compensators.

77520 Proton treatment delivery; simple, without compensation

77522   simple, with compensation

77523   intermediate

77525   complex

HYPERTHERMIA

Hyperthermia treatments as listed in this section include external (superficial and deep), interstitial, and intracavitary. Radiation therapy when given concurrently is listed separately.

Hyperthermia is used only as an adjunct to radiation therapy or chemotherapy. It may be induced by a variety of sources (eg., microwave, ultrasound, low energy radiofrequency conduction, or by probe).

The listed treatments include management during the course of therapy and follow-up care for three months after completion.

Preliminary consultation is not included (see Evaluation and Management 99241-99255). Physics planning and interstitial insertion of temperature sensors, and use of external or interstitial heat generating sources are included.

The following descriptors are included in the treatment schedule:

77600 Hyperthermia, externally generated; superficial (ie, heating to a depth of 4 cm or less)

77605   deep (ie, heating to depths greater than 4 cm)

(For focused microwave thermotherapy of the breast, use 0301T)

77610 Hyperthermia generated by interstitial probe(s); 5 or fewer interstitial applicators

77615   more than 5 interstitial applicators

CLINICAL INTRACAVITARY HYPERTHERMIA

77620 Hyperthermia generated by intracavitary probe(s)

CLINICAL BRACHYTHERAPY

Services 77750-77799 include admission to the hospital and daily visits.

For insertion of ovoids and tandems, use 57155.

For insertion of Heyman capsules, use 58346.

Definitions

A *simple* application has 1 to 4 sources/ribbons.

An *intermediate* application has 5 to 10 sources/ribbons.

A *complex* application has greater than 10 sources/ribbons.

High dose-rate brachytherapy involves treatment with radiation sources that cannot safely be handled manually. These systems are remotely controlled and place a radionuclide source (radioelement or radioisotope) within an applicator placed in or near the target. These applicators may be placed in the body or on the skin surface.

Small electronic X-ray sources placed into an applicator within or close to the target may also be used to generate radiation at high-dose rates. This is referred to as high dose-rate electronic brachytherapy.

To report high dose-rate electronic brachytherapy, see 0394T, 0395T.

77750   Infusion or instillation of radioelement solution (includes 3 months follow-up care)

(For administration of radiolabeled monoclonal antibodies, use 79403)

(For non-antibody radiopharmaceutical therapy by intravenous administration only, not including three month follow-up care, use 79101)

77761   Intracavitary radiation source application; simple

77762   intermediate

77763   complex

(Do not report 77761-77763 in conjunction with Category III codes 0394T, 0395T)

77767   Remote afterloading high dose rate radionuclide skin surface brachytherapy, includes basic dosimetry, when performed; lesion diameter up to 2.0 cm or 1 channel

77768   lesion diameter over 2.0 cm and 2 or more channels, or multiple lesions

77770   Remote afterloading high dose rate radionuclide interstitial or intracavitary brachytherapy, includes basic dosimetry, when performed; 1 channel

77771   2-12 channels

77772   over 12 channels

(Do not report 77767, 77768, 77770, 77771, 77772 in conjunction with 77300, 0394T, 0395T)

(For non-brachytherapy superficial [eg, ≤200kV] radiation treatment delivery, use 77401)

(**77776**   deleted 2015 [2016 edition]. To report, use 77799)

(**77777**   deleted 2015 [2016 edition]. To report, use 77799)

77778   Interstitial radiation source application, complex, includes supervision, handling, loading of radiation source, when performed

---

(Do not report 77778 in conjunction with Category III codes 0394T, 0395T)

(Do not report 77778 in conjunction with 77790)

(77782   deleted 2009 edition; see 77767, 77768, 77770, 77771, 77772)

(77783   deleted 2009 edition; see 77767, 77768, 77770, 77771, 77772)

(77784   deleted 2009 edition; see 77767, 77768, 77770, 77771, 77772)

(77785   deleted 2015 [2016 edition]. To report, see 77770, 77771, 77772)

(77786   deleted 2015 [2016 edition]. To report, see 77770, 77771, 77772)

(77787   deleted 2015 [2016 edition]. To report, see 77770, 77771, 77772)

77789   Surface application of low dose rate radionuclide source

(Do not report 77789 in conjunction with 77401, 77767, 77768, 0394T, 0395T)

77790   Supervision, handling, loading of radiation source

(Do not report 77790 in conjunction with 77778)

77799   Unlisted procedure, clinical brachytherapy

NUCLEAR MEDICINE

Introduction

Nuclear medicine is used in the diagnosis, management, treatment, and prevention of serious disease. Nuclear medicine imaging procedures often identify abnormalities very early in the progression of a disease. This early detection allows a disease to be treated early in its course when there may be a more successful prognosis.

Nuclear medicine uses very small amounts of radioactive materials or radiopharmaceuticals to diagnose and treat disease. Radiopharmaceuticals are substances that are attracted to specific organs, bones, or tissues. The radiopharmaceuticals used in nuclear medicine emit gamma rays that can be detected externally by special types of cameras: gamma or PET cameras. These cameras work in conjunction with computers used to form images that provide data and information about the area of body being imaged. The amount of radiation from a nuclear medicine procedure is comparable to that received during a diagnostic x-ray.

Nuclear medicine procedures may be performed independently or in the course of overall medical care. If the physician providing nuclear medicine services is also responsible for the diagnostic work-up and/or follow-up care of the patient, evaluation and management service codes should be coded in addition to the nuclear medicine procedures.

Radioimmunoassay tests are located in the Clinical Pathology section (codes 82000-84999). These CPT codes can be appropriately used by any specialist performing such tests in a laboratory licensed and/or certified for radioimmunoassays. The reporting of these tests is not confined to clinical pathology laboratories alone.

The injection of a radiopharmaceutical is included as an inherent component of the procedure. Separate vascular access and injection codes (e.g. 36000, 90783 (90773 in 2006), G0345-G0354 (90760-90772, 90774-90775 in 2006) should not be reported. However, the services do not include the actual radiopharmaceutical or drug used. Diagnostic and therapeutic radiopharmaceuticals and drugs supplied by the physician should be reported separately using the appropriate supply code(s), in addition to the procedure code.

Single photon emission computed tomography (SPECT) studies represent an enhanced methodology over standard planar nuclear imaging. When a limited anatomic area is studied, there is no additional information procured by obtaining both planar and SPECT studies. While both represent medically acceptable imaging studies, when a SPECT study of a limited area is performed, a planar study is not to be separately reported. When vascular flow studies are obtained using planar technology in addition to SPECT studies, the appropriate CPT code for the vascular flow study should be reported, not the flow, planar and SPECT studies. In cases where planar images must be procured because of the extent of the scanned area (e.g. bone imaging), both planar and SPECT scans may be necessary and reported separately.

Separate Procedure   Unlisted Procedure   CCI Comp. Code   Non-specific Procedure   **663**

Myocardial perfusion imaging (CPT codes 78451-78454) are not reportable with cardiac blood pool imaging by gated equilibrium (CPT codes 78472-78473) because the two types of tests utilize different radiopharmaceuticals.

CPT codes 76376, 76377 (3-D rendering) are not separately reportable for nuclear medicine procedures (CPT codes 78000-78999). However, they may be separately reported with modifier - 59 on the same date of service as a nuclear medicine procedure if the 3D rendering procedure is performed in association with a third procedure (other than nuclear medicine) for which 3D rendering is appropriately reported.

Nuclear Medicine Notes

Listed procedures may be performed independently or in the course of overall medical care. If the individual providing these services is also responsible for diagnostic work-up and/or follow-up care of patient, see appropriate sections also.

Radioimmunoassay tests are found in the Clinical Pathology section (codes 82009-84999). These codes can be appropriately used by any specialist performing such tests in a laboratory licensed and/or certified for radioimmunoassays. The reporting of these tests is not confined to clinical pathology laboratories alone.

The services listed do not include the radiopharmaceutical or drug. To separately report supply of diagnostic and therapeutic radiopharmaceuticals and drugs, use the appropriate supply code(s), in addition to the procedure code..

DIAGNOSTIC NUCLEAR MEDICINE

ENDOCRINE SYSTEM

78012 Thyroid uptake, single or multiple quantitative measurement(s) (including stimulation, suppression, or discharge, when performed)

78013 Thyroid imaging (including vascular flow, when performed);

78014 with single or multiple uptake(s) quantitative measurement(s) (including stimulation, suppression, or discharge, when performed)

78015 Thyroid carcinoma metastases imaging; limited area (eg, neck and chest only)

78016 with additional studies (eg, urinary recovery)

78018 whole body

+ **78020** Thyroid carcinoma metastases uptake (List separately in addition to code for primary procedure)

(Use 78020 in conjunction with code 78018 only)

78070 Parathyroid planar imaging (including subtraction, when performed);

78071 with tomographic (SPECT)

78072 with tomographic (SPECT), and concurrently acquired computed tomography (CT) for anatomical localization

78075 Adrenal imaging, cortex and/or medulla

78099 Unlisted endocrine procedure, diagnostic nuclear medicine

(For chemical analysis, see Chemistry section)

HEMATOPOIETIC, RETICULOENDOTHELIAL AND LYMPHATIC SYSTEM

78102 Bone marrow imaging; limited area

78103 multiple areas

78104 whole body

● New Code ▲ Revised Code + Add-On Code ⊘ Modifier -51 Exempt ★ Telemedicine

78110   Plasma volume, radiopharmaceutical volume-dilution technique (separate procedure); single sampling

78111   multiple samplings

78120   Red cell volume determination (separate procedure); single sampling

78121   multiple samplings

78122   Whole blood volume determination, including separate measurement of plasma volume and red cell volume (radiopharmaceutical volume-dilution technique)

78130   Red cell survival study;

78135   differential organ/tissue kinetics, (eg, splenic and/or hepatic sequestration)

78140   Labeled red cell sequestration, differential organ/tissue, (eg, splenic and/or hepatic)

78185   Spleen imaging only, with or without vascular flow

      (If combined with liver study, use procedures 78215 and 78216)

(78190   deleted 2017 [2018 edition])

78191   Platelet survival study

78195   Lymphatics and lymph nodes imaging

      (For sentinel node identification without scintigraphy imaging, use 38792)

      (For sentinal node excision, see 38500-38542)

78199   Unlisted hematopoietic, reticuloendothelial and lymphatic procedure, diagnostic nuclear medicine

      (For chemical analysis, see Chemistry section)

GASTROINTESTINAL SYSTEM

78201   Liver imaging; static only

78202   with vascular flow

      (For spleen imaging only, use 78185)

78205   Liver imaging (SPECT);

78206   with vascular flow

78215   Liver and spleen imaging; static only

78216   with vascular flow

78226   Hepatobiliary system imaging, including gallbladder when present;

78227   with pharmacologic intervention, including quantitative measurement(s) when performed.=

78230   Salivary gland imaging;

78231   with serial images

78232   Salivary gland function study

78258 Esophageal motility

78261 Gastric mucosa imaging

78262 Gastroesophageal reflux study

78264 Gastric emptying imaging study (eg, solid, liquid, or both);

78265 with small bowel transit

78266 with small bowel and colon transit, multiple days

(Report 78264, 78265, or 78266 only once per imaging study)

78267 Urea breath test, C-14 (isotopic); acquisition for analysis

78268 analysis

(For breath hydrogen or methane testing and analysis, use 91065)

78270 Vitamin B-12 absorption study (eg, Schilling test); without intrinsic factor

78271 with intrinsic factor

78272 Vitamin B-12 absorption studies combined, with and without intrinsic factor

78278 Acute gastrointestinal blood loss imaging

78282 Gastrointestinal protein loss

78290 Intestine imaging (eg, ectopic gastric mucosa, Meckels localization, volvulus)

78291 Peritoneal-venous shunt patency test (eg, for LeVeen, Denver shunt)

(For injection procedure, use 49427)

78299 Unlisted gastrointestinal procedure, diagnostic nuclear medicine

MUSCULOSKELETAL SYSTEM

78300 Bone and/or joint imaging; limited area

78305 multiple areas

78306 whole body

78315 3 phase study

78320 tomographic (SPECT)

78350 Bone density (bone mineral content) study, 1 or more sites; single photon absorptiometry

78351 dual photon absorptiometry, 1 or more sites

(For radiographic bone density (photodensitometry), use 77083)

78399 Unlisted musculoskeletal procedure, diagnostic nuclear medicine

● New Code   ▲ Revised Code   + Add-On Code   ⊘ Modifier -51 Exempt   ★ Telemedicine

CARDIOVASCULAR SYSTEM

Myocardial perfusion and cardiac blood pool imaging studies may be performed at rest and/or during stress. When performed during exercise and/or pharmacologic stress, the appropriate stress testing code from the 93015-93018 series should be reported in addition to 78451-78454, 78472-78492.

78414 Determination of central c-v hemodynamics (non-imaging) (eg, ejection fraction with probe technique) with or without pharmacologic intervention or exercise, single or multiple determinations

78428 Cardiac shunt detection

78445 Non-cardiac vascular flow imaging (ie, angiography, venography)

78451 Myocardial perfusion imaging, tomographic (SPECT) (including attenuation correction, qualitative or quantitative wall motion, ejection fraction by first pass or gated technique, additional quantification, when performed); single study, at rest or stress (exercise or pharmacologic)

78452 multiple studies, at rest and/or stress (exercise or pharmacologic) and/or redistribution and/or rest reinjection

78453 Myocardial perfusion imaging, planar (including qualitative or quantitative wall motion, ejection fraction by first pass or gated technique, additional quantification, when performed); single study, at rest or stress (exercise or pharmacologic)

78454 multiple studies, at rest and/or stress (exercise or pharmacologic) and/or redistribution and/or rest reinjection

78456 Acute venous thrombosis imaging, peptide

78457 Venous thrombosis imaging, venogram; unilateral

78458 bilateral

78459 Myocardial imaging, positron emission tomography (PET), metabolic evaluation

(For myocardial perfusion study, see 78491-78492)

78466 Myocardial imaging, infarct avid, planar; qualitative or quantitative

78468 with ejection fraction by first pass technique

78469 tomographic SPECT with or without quantification

(For myocardial sympathetic innervation imaging, see 0331T, 0332T)

78472 Cardiac blood pool imaging, gated equilibrium; planar, single study at rest or stress (exercise and/or pharmacologic), wall motion study plus ejection fraction, with or without additional quantitative processing

(For assessment of right ventricular ejection fraction by first pass technique, use 78496)

78473 multiple studies, wall motion study plus ejection fraction, at rest and stress (exercise and/or pharmacologic), with or without additional quantification

(Do not report 78472, 78473 in conjunction with 78451-78454, 78481, 78483, 78494)

78481 Cardiac blood pool imaging, (planar), first pass technique; single study, at rest or with stress (exercise and/or pharmacologic), wall motion study plus ejection fraction, with or without quantification

78483 multiple studies, at rest and with stress (exercise and/or pharmacologic), wall motion study plus ejection fraction, with or without quantification

(For cerebral blood flow study, use 78610)

| ▰ Separate Procedure | ▰ Unlisted Procedure | ▰ CCI Comp. Code | ▰ Non-specific Procedure | **667** |

(Do not report 78481-78483 in conjunction with 78451-78454)

78491   Myocardial imaging, positron emission tomography (PET), perfusion; single study at rest or stress

78492   multiple studies at rest and/or stress

78494   Cardiac blood pool imaging, gated equilibrium, SPECT, at rest, wall motion study plus ejection fraction, with or without quantitative processing

+ **78496**   Cardiac blood pool imaging, gated equilibrium, single study, at rest, with right ventricular ejection fraction by first pass technique (List separately in addition to code for primary procedure)

     (Use 78496 in conjunction with code 78472)

78499   Unlisted cardiovascular procedure, diagnostic nuclear medicine

RESPIRATORY SYSTEM

78579   Pulmonary ventilation imaging (eg, aerosol or gas)

78580   Pulmonary perfusion imaging (eg, particulate)

78582   Pulmonary ventilation (eg, aerosol or gas) and perfusion imaging

78597   Quantitative differential pulmonary perfusion, including imaging when performed

78598   Quantitative differential pulmonary perfusion and ventilation (eg, aerosol or gas), including imaging when performed

     (Report 78579, 78580, 78582-78598 only once per imaging session)

     (Do not report 78580, 78582-78598 in conjunction with 78451-78454)

78599   Unlisted respiratory procedure, diagnostic nuclear medicine

NERVOUS SYSTEM

78600   Brain imaging, less than 4 static views;

78601   with vascular flow

78605   Brain imaging, minimum 4 static views;

78606   with vascular flow

78607   Brain imaging, tomographic (SPECT)

78608   Brain imaging, positron emission tomography (PET); metabolic evaluation

78609   perfusion evaluation

78610   Brain imaging, vascular flow only

78630   Cerebrospinal fluid flow, imaging (not including introduction of material); cisternography

     (For injection procedure, see 61000-61070, 62270-62319)

78635   ventriculography

     (For injection procedure, see 61000-61070, 62270-62294)

78645   shunt evaluation

(For injection procedure, see 61000-61070, 62270-62294)

78647   tomographic (SPECT)

78650   Cerebrospinal fluid leakage detection and localization

(For injection procedure, see 61000-61070, 62270-62294)

78660   Radiopharmaceutical dacryocystography

78699   Unlisted nervous system procedure, diagnostic nuclear medicine

GENITOURINARY SYSTEM

78700   Kidney imaging morphology;

78701   with vascular flow

78707   with vascular flow and function, single study without pharmacological intervention

78708   with vascular flow and function, single study, with pharmacological intervention (eg, angiotensin converting enzyme inhibitor and/or diuretic)

78709   with vascular flow and function, multiple studies, with and without pharmacological intervention (eg, angiotensin converting enzyme inhibitor and/or diuretic)

(For introduction of radioactive substance in association with renal endoscopy, see 77778)

78710   tomographic (SPECT)

78725   Kidney function study, non-imaging radioisotopic study

\+ **78730**   Urinary bladder residual study (List separately in addition to code for primary procedure)

(Use 78730 in conjunction with 78740)

(For measurement of postvoid residual urine and/or bladder capacity by ultrasound, nonimaging, use 51798)

(For ultrasound imaging of the bladder only, with measurement of postvoid residual urine when performed, use 76857)

78740   Ureteral reflux study (radiopharmaceutical voiding cystogram)

(Use 78740 in conjunction with 78730 for urinary bladder residual study)

(For catheterization, see 51701-51703)

78761   Testicular imaging with vascular flow

78799   Unlisted genitourinary procedure, diagnostic nuclear medicine

(For chemical analysis, see Chemistry section)

OTHER PROCEDURES

(For specific organ, see appropriate heading)

(For radiophosphorus tumor identification, ocular, see 78800)

78800   Radiopharmaceutical localization of tumor or distribution of radiopharmaceutical agent(s); limited area

(For specific organ, see appropriate heading)

78801	multiple areas
78802	whole body, single day imaging
78803	tomographic (SPECT)
78804	whole body, requiring 2 or more days imaging
78805	Radiopharmaceutical localization of inflammatory process; limited area
78806	whole body
78807	tomographic (SPECT)

(For imaging bone infectious or inflammatory disease with a bone imaging radiopharmaceutical, see 78300, 78305, 78306)

78808   Injection procedure for radiopharmaceutical localization by non-imaging probe study, intravenous (eg, parathyroid adenoma)

(For sentinel lymph node identification, use 38792)

(For PET of brain, see 78608, 78609)

(For PET myocardial imaging, see 78459, 78491, 78492)

78811   Positron emission tomography (PET) imaging; limited area (eg, chest, head/neck)

78812	skull base to mid-thigh
78813	whole body

78814   Positron emission tomography (PET) with concurrently acquired computed tomography (CT) for attenuation correction and anatomical localization imaging; limited area (eg, chest, head/neck)

78815	skull base to mid-thigh
78816	whole body

(Report 78811-78816 only once per imaging session)

(Computed tomography (CT) performed for other than attenuation correction and anatomical localization is reported using the appropriate site specific CT code with modifier 59)

78999   Unlisted miscellaneous procedure, diagnostic nuclear medicine

THERAPEUTIC

The oral and intravenous administration codes in this section are inclusive of the mode of administration. For intra-arterial, intra-cavitary, and intra-articular administration, also use the appropriate injection and/or procedure code, as well as imaging guidance and radiological supervision and interpretation codes, when appropriate.

79005   Radiopharmaceutical therapy, by oral administration

(For monoclonal antibody therapy, use 79403)

79101   Radiopharmaceutical therapy, by intravenous administration

(Do not report 79101 in conjunction with 36400, 36410, 79403, 96360, 96374 or 96375, 96409)

(For radiolabeled monoclonal antibody by intravenous infusion, use 79403)

(For infusion or instillation of non-antibody radioelement solution that includes three months follow-up care, use 77750)

79200   Radiopharmaceutical therapy, by intracavitary administration

79300   Radiopharmaceutical therapy, by interstitial radioactive colloid administration

79403   Radiopharmaceutical therapy, radiolabeled monoclonal antibody by intravenous infusion

(For pre-treatment imaging, see 78802, 78804)

(Do not report 79403 in conjunction with 79101)

79440   Radiopharmaceutical therapy, by intra-articular administration

79445   Radiopharmaceutical therapy, by intra-arterial particulate administration

(Do not report 79445 in conjunction with 96373, 96420)

(Use appropriate procedural and radiological supervision and interpretation codes for the angiographic and interventional procedures provided pre-requisite to intra-arterial radiopharmaceutical therapy)

79999   Radiopharmaceutical therapy, unlisted procedure

This page intentionally left blank.

● New Code   ▲ Revised Code   + Add-On Code   ⃠ Modifier -51 Exempt   ★ Telemedicine

PATHOLOGY/ LABORATORY

LABORATORY SECTION OVERVIEW

The fifth section of the CPT coding system is the laboratory section, which includes codes for pathology and laboratory services. Within each subsection, the CPT codes are arranged by the type of testing or service.

LABORATORY SUBSECTIONS

The PATHOLOGY AND LABORATORY section of CPT is divided into the following subsections:

Organ or Disease Oriented Panels	80047-80081
Drug Assay	80305-80377
Therapeutic Drug Assays	80150-80299
Evocative/Suppression Testing	80400-80439
Consultations (Clinical Pathology)	80500-80502
Urinalysis	81000-81099
Molecular Pathology	81161-81479
Genomic Sequencing Procedures and Other Molecular Mutlianalyte Assays	81410-81471
Multianalyte Assays with Algorithmic Assays	81490-81599
Chemistry	82009-84999
Hematology and Coagulation	85002-85999
Immunology	86000-86849
Transfusion Medicine	86850-86999
Microbiology	87003-87999
Anatomic Pathology	88000-88099
Cytopathology	88104-88199
Cytogenetic Studies	88230-88299
Surgical Pathology	88300-88399
In Vivo (eg. Transcutaneous) Laboratory Procedures	88720-88749
Other Procedures	89049-89240
Reproductive Medicine Procedures	89250-89398
Proprietary Laboratory Analyses	0001U-0017U

LABORATORY SERVICE MODIFIERS

Pathology and laboratory services and procedures may be modified under certain circumstances. When applicable, the modifying circumstances should be identified by adding the appropriate modifier to the basic service code. The addition of modifier -22 requires a special report. Modifiers commonly used to report PATHOLOGY and LABORATORY procedures include:

-22 unusual services

-26 professional component

-32 mandated services

-52 reduced services

-90 reference (outside) laboratory

PATHOLOGY

Pathology is that discipline of the practice of medicine that deals with the causes and nature of disease. It contributes to diagnosis, prognosis, and treatment through knowledge gained by the laboratory application of the biologic, chemical, and physical sciences to man, or materials obtained from man. Pathologists diagnose, exclude, and monitor disease by means of information gathered from the microscopic examination of tissue specimens, cells, and body fluids, and from clinical laboratory tests on body fluids and secretions. Pathologists are involved with the management of laboratories and in data processing and with new developments in high technology.

LAB
80000

CLINICAL PATHOLOGY

Clinical Pathology focuses on microbiology (including bacteriology, mycology, parasitology, and virology), immunopathology, blood banking/transfusion medicine, chemical pathology, cytogenetics, hematology, coagulation, toxicology, medical microscopy (including urinalysis), molecular biologic techniques, and other advanced diagnostic techniques as they become available.

MOLECULAR PATHOLOGY GENE TABLE

Claim Designation	Abbreviated Gene Name	Full Gene Name	Commonly Associated Proteins/Disease	CPT Code(s)
ABCA4	ABCA4	ATP-binding cassette, sub-family A [ABC1], member 4	Stargardt disease, age-related macular degeneration, hereditary retinal disorders	81408, 81434
ABCC8	ABCC8	ATP-binding cassette, sub-family C [CFTR/MRP], member 8	Familial hyperinsulinism	81401, 81407
ABCD1	ABCD1	ATP-binding cassette, sub-family D [ALD], member 1	Adrenoleukodystrophy	81405
	ABL1	ABL proto-oncogene 1, non-receptor tyrosine kinase	Acquired imatinib tyrosine kinase inhibitor resistance	81170
ABL1	ABL1	ABL proto-oncogene 1, non-receptor tyrosine kinase	Acquired imatinib resistance	81401
ACADM	ACADM	Acyl-CoA dehydrogenase, C-4 to C-12 straight chain, MCAD	Medium chain acyl dehydrogenase deficiency	81400, 81401
ACADS	ACADS	Acyl-CoA dehydrogenase, C-2 to C-3 short chain	Short chain acyl-CoA dehydrogenase deficiency	81404, 81405
ACADVL	ACADVL	Acyl-CoA dehydrogenase, very long chain	Very long chain acyl-coenzyme A dehydrogenase deficiency	81406
ACE	ACE	Angiotensin converting enzyme	Hereditary blood pressure regulation	81400
ACTA2	ACTA2	Actin, alpha 2, smooth muscle, aorta	Thoracic aortic aneurysms and aortic dissections, aortic dysfunction or dilation	81405, 81410
ACTC1	ACTC1	Actin, alpha, cardiac muscle 1	Familial hypertrophic cardiomyopathy	81405
ACTN4	ACTN4	Actinin, alpha 4	Focal segmental glomerulosclerosis	81406
ADRB2	ADRB2	Adrenergic beta-2 receptor surface	Drug metabolism	81401
AFF2	AFF2	AF4/FMR2 family, member 2 [FMR2]	Fragile X mental retardation 2 [FRAXE]	81401, 81404
AFG3L2	AFG3L2	AFG3 ATPase family gene 3-like 2 [S. cerevisiae]	Spinocerebellar ataxia	81406
AGL	AGL	Amylo-alpha-1, 6-glucosidase, 4-alpha-glucanotransferase	Glycogen storage disease type III	81407
AGTR1	AGTR1	Angiotensin II receptor, type 1	Essential hypertension	81400
AH1	AHI1	Abelson helper integration site 1	Joubert syndrome	81407
AIRE	AIRE	Autoimmune regulator	Autoimmune polyendocrinopathy syndrome type 1	81406
ALDH7A1	ALDH7A1	Aldehyde dehydrogenase 7 family, member A1	Pyridoxine-dependent epilepsy	81406
ALK	ALK	Anaplastic lymphoma receptor tyrosine kinase	Solid organ neoplasm or hematolymphoid neoplasm	81445, 81455
ANG	ANG	Angiogenin, ribonuclease, RNase A family, 5	Amyotrophic lateral sclerosis	81403
ANK2	ANK2	Ankyrin-2	Cardiac ion channelopathies	81413
ANKRD1	ANKRD1	Ankyrin repeat domain 1	Dilated cardiomyopathy	81405
ANO5	ANO5	Anoctamin 5	Limb-girdle muscular dystrophy	81406
ANOS1	ANOS1	Anosmin-1	Kallman syndrome 1	81406
	APC	Adenomatous polyposis coli	Familial adenomatosis polyposis [FAP], attenuated FAP, hereditary colon cancer disorders	81201, 81202, 81203, 81435
APOB	APOB	Apolipoprotein B	Familial hypercholesterolemia type B	81401
APOE	APOE	Apolipoprotein E	Hyperlipoproteinemia type III, cardiovascular disease, Alzheimer disease	81401
APP	APP	Amyloid beta [A4] precursor protein	Alzheimer disease	81406
APTX	APTX	Aprataxin	Ataxia with oculomotor apraxia 1	81405
AQP2	AQP2	Aquaporin 2 [collecting duct]	Nephrogenic diabetes insipidus	81404
AR	AR	Androgen receptor	Spinal and bulbar muscular atrophy, Kennedy disease, X chromosome inactivation, androgen insensitivity syndrome	81401,81405

● New Code ▲ Revised Code ✛ Add-On Code ⊘ Modifier -51 Exempt ★ Telemedicine

MOLECULAR PATHOLOGY GENE TABLE

Claim Designation	Abbreviated Gene Name	Full Gene Name	Commonly Associated Proteins/Disease	CPT Code(s)
ARSA	ARSA	Arylsulfatase A	Arylsulfatase A deficiency	81405
ARX	ARX	Aristaless related homeobox	X-linked lissencephaly with ambiguous genitalia, X-linked mental retardation, X-linked intellectual disability (XLID)	81403, 81404, 81470, 81471
	ASPA	Aspartoacylase	Canavan disease, Ashkenazi Jewish-associated disorders	81200, 81412
ASPM	ASPM	Asp [abnormal spindle] homolog, microcephaly associated [Drosophila]	Primary microcephaly	81407
ASS1	ASS1	Argininosuccinate synthase 1	Citrullinemia type I	81406
ASXL1	ASXL1	Additional sex combs like 1, transcriptional regulator	Myelodysplastic syndrome, myeloproliferative neoplasms, chronic myelomonocytic leukemia	81175, 81176
ATL1	ATL1	Atlastin GTPase 1	Spastic paraplegia	81406
ATM	ATM	Ataxia telangiectasia mutated	Ataxia telangiectasia	81408
ATN1	ATN1	Atrophin 1	Dentatorubral-pallidoluysian atrophy	81401
ATP1A2	ATP1A2	ATPase, Na+/K+ transporting, alpha 2 polypeptide	Familial hemiplegic migraine	81406
ATP7B	ATP7B	ATPase, Cu++ transporting, beta polypeptide	Wilson disease	81406
ATRX	ATRX	Alpha thalassemia/mental retardation syndrome X-linked	X-linnked intellectual disability (XLID)	81470, 81471
ATXN1	ATXN1	Ataxin 1	Spinocerebellar ataxia	81401
ATXN2	ATXN2	Ataxin 2	Spinocerebellar ataxia	81401
ATXN3	ATXN3	Ataxin 3	Spinocerebellar ataxia, Machado-Joseph disease	81401
ATXN7	ATXN7	Ataxin 7	Spinocerebellar ataxia	81401
ATXN8OS	ATXN8OS	ATXN8 opposite strand [non-protein coding]	Spinocerebellar ataxia	81401
ATXN10	ATXN10	Ataxin 10	Spinocerebellar ataxia	81401
AVPR2	AVPR2	Arginine vasopressin receptor 2	Nephrogenic diabetes insipidus	81404
BBS1	BBS1	Bardet-Biedl syndrome 1	Bardet-Biedl syndrome	81406
BBS2	BBS2	Bardet-Biedl syndrome 2	Bardet-Biedl syndrome	81406
BBS10	BBS10	Bardet-Biedl syndrome 10	Bardet-Biedl syndrome	81404
BCKDHA	BCKDHA	Branched chain keto acid dehydrogenase E1, alpha polypeptide	Maple syrup urine disease, type 1A	81400, 81405
	BCKDHB	Branched-chain keto acid dehydrogenase E1, beta polypeptide	Maple syrup urine disease	81205
BCKDHB	BCKDHB	Branched-chain keto acid dehydrogenase E1,beta polypeptide	Maple syrup urine disease, type 1B	81406
	BCR/ABL1	t(9;22)	Chronic myelogenous leukemia	81206, 81207, 81208
BCS1L	BCS1L	BCS1-like [S. cerevisiae]	Leigh syndrome, mitochondrial complex III deficiency, GRACILE syndrome, mitochondrial disorders	81405, 81440
BEST1	BEST1	Bestrophin 1	Vitelliform macular dystrophy	81406
	BLM	Bloom syndrome, RecQ helicase-like	Bloom syndrome, Ashkenazi Jewish-associated disorders	81209, 81412
BMPR1A	BMPR1A	Bone morphogenetic protein receptor, type 1A	Hereditary colon cancer disorders	81435
BMPR2	BMPR2	Bone morphogenetic protein receptor, type II [serine/threonine kinase]	Heritable pulmonary arterial hypertension	81405, 81406
	BRAF	V-raf murine sarcoma viral oncogene homolog B1	Colon cancer	81210
BRAF	BRAF	B-Raf proto-oncogene, serine/threonine kinase	Noonan syndrome, Noonan spectrum disorders, solid organ neoplasm, hematolymphoid neoplasm or disorder	81406, 81442, 81445, 81450, 81455
	BRCA1	Breast cancer 1	Hereditary breast and ovarian cancer, hereditary breast cancer-related disorders	81214, 81215, 81432, 81433
	BRCA2	Breast cancer 2	Hereditary breast and ovarian cancer, hereditary breast cancer-related disorders	81216, 81217, 81432, 81433
	BRCA1 & BRCA2	Breast cancer 1 and 2	Hereditary breast and ovarian cancer	81162, 81211, 81212, 81213
BRIP1	BRIP1	BRCA1 interacting protein C-terminal helicase 1	Mitochondrial disorders	81440
BSCL2	BSCL2	Berardinelli-Seip congenital lipodystrophy 2 [seipin]	Berardinelli-Seip congenital lipodystrophy, hereditary peripheral neuropathies	81406, 81448

| | Separate Procedure | | Unlisted Procedure | | CCI Comp. Code | | Non-specific Procedure | **675** |

MOLECULAR PATHOLOGY GENE TABLE

Claim Designation	Abbreviated Gene Name	Full Gene Name	Commonly Associated Proteins/Disease	CPT Code(s)
BTD	BTD	Biotinidase	Biotinidase deficiency	81404
BTK	BTK	Bruton agammaglobulinemia tyrosine kinase	X-linked agammaglobulinemia	81406
C10ORF2	C10ORF2	Chromosome 10 open reading frame 2	Mitochondrial DNA depletion syndrome, mitochondrial disorders	81404, 81440
CACNA1A	CACNA1A	Calcium channel, voltage-dependent, P/Q type, alpha 1A subunit	Spinocerebellar ataxia	81401, 81407
CACNB2	CACNB2	Calcium channel, voltage-dependent, beta 2 subunit	Brugada syndrome	81406
	CALR	Calreticulin	Myeloproliferative disorders	81219
CAPN3	CAPN3	Calpain 3	Limb-girdle muscular dystrophy [LGMD] type 2A, calpainopathy	81406
CASR	CASR	Calcium-sensing receptor	Hypocalcemia	81405
CASQ2	CASQ2	Calsequestrin 2 [cardiac muscle]	Catecholaminergic polymorphic ventricular tachycardia, cardiac ion channelopathies	81405, 81413
CAV3	CAV3	Caveolin 3	CAV3-related distal myopathy, limb-girdle muscular dystrophy type 1C, cardiac ion channelopathies	81404, 81413
CBFBMYH11	CBFB/MYH11	Inv(16)	Acute myeloid leukemia	81401
CBL	CBL	Cbl proto-oncogene, E3 ubiquitin protein ligase	Noonan spectrum disorders	81442
CBS	CBS	Cystathionine-beta-synthase	Homocystinuria, cystathionine beta-synthase deficiency	81401, 81406
CCND1/GH	CCND1/IGH	BCL1/IgH, t(11;14)	Mantle cell lymphoma	81401
CCR5	CCR5	Chemokine C-C motif receptor 5	HIV resistance	81400
CD40LG	CD40LG	CD40 ligand	X-linked hyper IgM syndrome	81404
CDH1	CDH1	Cadherin 1, type 1, E-Cadherin [epithelial]	Hereditary diffuse gastric cancer, herditary breast cancer-related disorders, hereditary colon cancer disorders	81406, 81432, 81435
CHD23	CDH23	Cadherin-related 23	Usher syndrome, type 1, hearing loss	81408, 81430
CDKL5	CDKL5	Cyclin-dependent kinase-like 5	Early infantile epileptic encephalopathy, X-linked intellectual disability (XLID)	81405, 81406, 81470, 81471
CDKN2A	CDKN2A	Cyclin-dependent kinase inhibitor 2A	CDKN2A-related cutaneous malignant melanoma, solid organ neoplasm or hematolymphoid neoplasm	81404, 81445, 81455
	CEBPA	CCAAT/enhancer binding protein [C/EBP], alpha	Acute myeloid leukemia, hematolymphoid neoplasm or disorder, solid organ neoplasm	81218, 81450, 81455
CEL	CEL	Carboxyl ester lipase [bile salt-stimulated lipase]	Maturity-onset diabetes of the young [MODY]	81403
CEP290	CEP290	Centrosomal protein 290kDa	Joubert syndrome	81408
CFHARMS2	CFH/ARMS2	Complement factor H/age-related maculopathy susceptibility 2	Macular degeneration	81401
	CFTR	Cystic fibrosis transmembrane conductance regulator	Cystic fibrosis, Ashkenazi Jewish-associated disorders	81220, 81221, 81222, 81223, 81224, 81412
CHD7	CHD7	Chromodomain helicase DNA binding protein 7	CHARGE syndrome	81407
	Chimerism engraftment analysis	N/A	Post-transplantation specimen (eg, hematopoietic stem cell)	81267, 81268
CHRNA4	CHRNA4	Cholinergic receptor, nicotinic, alpha 4	Nocturnal frontal lobe epilepsy	81405
CHRNB2	CHRNB2	Cholinergic receptor, nicotinic, beta 2 [neuronal]	Nocturnal frontal lobe epilepsy	81405
C1P19Q	Chromosome 1p-/19q- deletion analysis	N/A	Glial tumors	81402
CHROM18Q	Chromosome 18q-		Colon cancer	81402
CLCN1	CLCN1	Chloride channel 1, skeletal muscle	Myotonia congenita	81406
CLCNKB	CLCNKB	Chloride channel, voltage-sensitive Kb	Bartter syndrome 3 and 4b	81406
CLRN1	CLRN1	Clarin 1	Usher syndrome, type 3, hearing loss	81400, 81404, 81430
CNBP	CNBP	CCHC-type zinc finger, nucleic acid binding protein	Myotonic dystrophy type 2	81401
CNGA1	CNGA1	Cyclic nucleotide gated channel alpha 1	Hereditary retinal disorders	81434
CNTNAP2	CNTNAP2	Contactin associated protein-like 2	Pitt-Hopkins-like syndrome 1	81406

● New Code   ▲ Revised Code   + Add-On Code   ⊘ Modifier -51 Exempt   ★ Telemedicine

MOLECULAR PATHOLOGY GENE TABLE

Claim Designation	Abbreviated Gene Name	Full Gene Name	Commonly Associated Proteins/Disease	CPT Code(s)
COL1A1	COL1A1	Collagen, type I, alpha 1	Osteogenesis imperfecta, type I	81408
COL1A1PDGFB	COL1A1/PDGFB	t(17;22)	Dermatofibrosarcoma protuberans	81402
COL1A2	COL1A2	Collagen, type I, alpha 2	Osteogenesis imperfecta, type I	81408
COL3A1	COL3A1	Collagen, type III, alpha 1	Aortic dysfunction or dilation	81410, 81411
COL4A1	COL4A1	Collagen, type IV, alpha 1	Brain small-vessel disease with hemorrhage	81408
COL4A3	COL4A3	Collagen, type IV, alpha 3 [Goodpasture antigen]	Alport syndrome	81408
COL4A4	COL4A4	Collagen, type IV, alpha 4	Alport syndrome	81407
COL4A5	COL4A5	Collagen, type IV, alpha 5	Alport syndrome	81407, 81408
COL6A1	COL6A1	Collagen, type VI, alpha 1	Collagen type VI-related disorders	81407
COL6A2	COL6A2	Collagen, type VI, alpha 2	Collagen type VI-related disorders	81406, 81407
COL6A3	COL6A3	Collagen, type VI, alpha 3	Collagen type VI-related disorders	81407
COQ2	COQ2	Coenzyme Q2, prolyprenyltransferase	Mitochondrial disorders	81440
COX10	COX10	COX10 homolog, cytochrome c oxidase assembly protein	Mitochondrial respiratory chain complex IV deficiency, mitochoncrial disorders	81405, 81440
COX15	COX15	COX15 homolog, cytochrome c oxidase assembly protein	Mitochondrial respiratory chain complex IV deficiency	81405
COX6B1	COX6B1	Cytochrome c oxidase subunit VIb polypeptide 1	Mitochondrial respiratory chain complex IV deficiency	81404
CPOX	CPOX	Coproporphyrlnogen oxidase	Hereditary coproporphyria	81405
CPT1A	CPT1A	Carnitine palmitoyltransferase 1A [liver]	Carnitine palmitoyltransferase 1A [CPT1A] deficiency	81406
CPT2	CPT2	Carnitine palmitoyltransferase 2	Carnitine palmitoyltransferase II deficiency	81404
CRB1	CRB1	Crumbs homolog 1 [Drosophila]	Leber congenital amaurosis, hereditary retinal disorders	81406, 81434
CREBBP	CREBBP	CREB binding protein	Rubinstein-Taybi syndrome	81406, 81407
CRX	CRX	Cone-rod homeobox	Cone-rod dystrophy 2, Leber congenital amaurosis	81404
CSTB	CSTB	Cystatin B [stefin B]	Unverricht-Lundborg disease	81401, 81404
CTNNB1	CTNNB1	Catenin [cadherin- associated protein], beta 1, 88kDa	Desmoid tumors	81403
CTRC	CTRC	Chymotrypsin C	Hereditary pancreatitis	81405
CYP11B1	CYP11B1	Cytochrome P450, family 11, subfamily B, polypeptide 1	Congenital adrenal hyperplasia	81405
CYP17A1	CYP17A1	Cytochrome P450, family 17, subfamily A, polypeptide 1	Congenital adrenal hyperplasia	81405
CYP1B1	CYP1B1	Cytochrome P450, family 1, subfamily B, polypeptide 1	Primary congenital glaucoma	81404
CYP21A2	CYP21A2	Cytochrome P450, family 21, subfamily A, polypeptide 2	Congenital adrenal hyperplasia, 21-hydroxylase deficiency, steroid 21-hydroxylase isoform	81402, 81405
	CYP2C9	Cytochrome P450, family 2, subfamily C, polypeptide 9	Drug metabolism	81227
	CYP2C19	Cytochrome P450, family 2, subfamily C, polypeptide 19	Drug metabolism	81225
	CYP2D6	Cytochrome P450, family 2, subfamily D, polypeptide 6	Drug metabolism	81226
CYP3A4	CYP3A4	Cytochrome P450 family 3, subfamily A, member 4	Drug metabolism	81230
CYP3A5	CYP3A5	Cytochrome P450, family 3, subfamily A, member 5	Drug metabolism	81231
	Cytogenomic constitutional (genome-wide) microarray analysis	N/A	N/A	81228, 81229

MOLECULAR PATHOLOGY GENE TABLE

Claim Designation	Abbreviated Gene Name	Full Gene Name	Commonly Associated Proteins/Disease	CPT Code(s)
Ch22Q13	Cytogenomic constitutional targeted microarray analysis of chromosome 22q13 by interrogation of genomic regions for copy number and single nucleotide polymorphism (SNP) variants	N/A	N/A	81405
CGHSNP	Cytogenomic microarray analysis neoplasia	N/A	N/A	81406
DAZSRY	DAZ/SRY	Deleted in azoospermia and sex determining region Y	Male infertility	81403
DBT	DBT	Dihydrolipoamide branched chain transacylase E2	Maple syrup urine disease, type 2	81405, 81406
DCX	DCX	Doublecortin	X-linked lissencephaly	81405
DEKNUP214	DEK/NUP214	t(6;9)	Acute myeloid leukemia	81401
DES	DES	Desmin	Myofibrillar myopathy	81405
DFNB1	DFNB1	N/A	Hearing loss	81431
DFNB59	DFNB59	Deafness, autosomal recessive 59	Autosomal recessive nonsyndromic hearing impairment	81405
DGUOK	DGUOK	Deoxyguanosine kinase	Hepatocerebral mitochondrial DNA depletion syndrome, mitochondrial disorders	81405, 81440
DHCR7	DHCR7	7-dehydrocholesterol reductase	Smith-Lemli-Opitz syndrome	81405
DLAT	DLAT	Dihydrolipoamide S-acetyltransferase	Pyruvate dehydrogenase E2 deficiency	81406
DLD	DLD	Dihydrolipoamide dehydrogenase	Maple syrup urine disease, type III	81406
	DMD	Dystrophin	Duchenne/Becker muscular dystrophy	81161
DMD	DMD	Dystrophin	Duchenne/Becker muscular dystrophy	81408
DMPK	DMPK	Dystrophia myotonica-protein kinase	Myotonic dystrophy, type 1	81401, 81404
DNMT3A	DNMT3A	DNA [cytosine-5-]- methyltransferase 3 alpha	Acute myeloid leukemia, hematolymphoid neoplasm or disorder, solid organ neoplasm	81403, 81450, 81455
DPYD	DPYD	Dihydropyrimidine dehydrogenase	5-fluorouracil/5-FU and capecitabine drug metabolism	81232
DSC2	DSC2	Desmocollin	Arrhythmogenic right ventricular dysplasia/ cardiomyopathy 11	81406
DSG2	DSG2	Desmoglein 2	Arrhythmogenic right ventricular dysplasia/ cardiomyopathy 10, hereditary cardiomyopathy	81406, 81439
DSP	DSP	Desmoplakin	Arrhythmogenic right ventricular dysplasia/ cardiomyopathy 8	81406
DYSF	DYSF	Dysferlin, limb girdle muscular dystrophy 2B [autosomal recessive]	Limb-girdle muscular dystrophy	81408
E2APBX1	E2A/PBX1	t(1;19)	Acute lymphocytic leukemia	81401
EFHC1	EFHC1	EF-hand domain [C-terminal] containing 1	Juvenile myoclonic epilepsy	81406
	EGFR	Epidermal growth factor receptor	Non-small cell lung cancer, solid organ neoplasm or hematolymphoid neoplasm	81235, 81445, 81455
EGR2	EGR2	Early growth response 2	Charcot-Marie-Tooth	81404
EIF2B2	EIF2B2	Eukaryotic translation initiation factor 2B, subunit 2 beta, 39kDa	Leukoencephalopathy with vanishing white matter	81405
EIF2B3	EIF2B3	Eukaryotic translation initiation factor 2B, subunit 3 gamma, 58kDa	Leukoencephalopathy with vanishing white matter	81406
EIF2B4	EIF2B4	Eukaryotic translation initiation factor 2B, subunit 4 delta, 67kDa	Leukoencephalopathy with vanishing white matter	81406
EIF2B5	EIF2B5	Eukaryotic translation initiation factor 2B, subunit 5 epsilon, 82kDa	Childhood ataxia with central nervous system hypomyelination/ vanishing white matter	81406
EMD	EMD	Emerin	Emery-Dreifuss muscular dystrophy	81404, 81405
EML4ALK	EML4/ALK	inv(2)	Non-small cell lung cancer	81401
ENG	ENG	Endoglin	Hereditary hemorrhagic telangiectasia, type 1	81405, 81406

● New Code   ▲ Revised Code   + Add-On Code   ⊘ Modifier -51 Exempt   ★ Telemedicine

MOLECULAR PATHOLOGY GENE TABLE

Claim Designation	Abbreviated Gene Name	Full Gene Name	Commonly Associated Proteins/Disease	CPT Code(s)
EPCAM	EPCAM	Epithelial cell adhesion molecule	Lynch syndrome, hereditary colon cancer disorders	81403, 81436
EPM2A	EPM2A	Epilepsy, progressive myoclonus type 2A, Lafora disease [laforin]	Progressive myoclonus epilepsy	81404
ERBB2	ERBB2	V-Erb-B2 avian erythroblastic leukemia viral oncogene homolog 2	Solid organ neoplasm or hematolymphoid neoplasm	81445, 81455
ESR1PGR	ESR1/PGR	Receptor 1/progesterone receptor ratio	Breast cancer	81402
ETV6NTRK3	ETV6/NTRK3	t(12;15)	Congenital/infantile fibrosarcoma	81401
ETV6RUNX1	ETV6/RUNX1	t(12;21)	acute lymphocytic Aeukemia	81401
EWSR1ATF1	EWSR1/ATF1	t(12;22)	Clear cell sarcoma	81401
EWSR1ERG	EWSR1/ERG	t(21;22)	Ewing sarcoma/ peripheral neuroectodermal tumor	81401
EWSR1FL1	EWSR1/FLI1	t(11;22)	Ewing sarcoma/ peripheral neuroectodermal tumor	81401
EWSR1WT1	EWSR1/WT1	t(11;22)	Desmoplastic small round cell tumor	81401
EYA1	EYA1	Eyes absent homolog 1 [Drosophila]	Bbranchio-oto-renal [BOR] spectrum disorders	81405, 81406
EYS	EYS	Eyes shut homolog (Drosophila)	Hereditary retinal disorders	81434
EZH2	EZH2	Enhancer of zeste homolog 2 (Drosophila)	Hematolymphoid neoplasm or disorder or solid organ neoplasm	81450, 81455
	F2	Prothrombin, coagulation factor II	Hereditary hypercoagulability	81240
F2	F2	Prothrombin, coagulation factor II	Hereditary hypercoagulability	81400
	F5	Coagulation Factor V	Hereditary hypercoagulability	81241
F5	F5	Coagulation Factor V	Hereditary hypercoagulability	81400
F7	F7	Coagulation factor VII [serum prothrombin conversion accelerator]	Hereditary hypercoagulability	81400
F8	F8	Coagulation factor VIII	Hemophilia A	81403, 81406, 81407
F9	F9	Coagulation factor IX	Hemophilia B	81238
F11	F11	Coagulation factor XI	Coagulation disorder	81401
F12	F12	Coagulation factor XII [Hageman factor]	Angioedema, hereditary, type III; factor XII deficiency	81403
F13B	F13B	Coagulation factor XIII, B polypeptide	Hereditary hypercoagulability	81400
FAH	FAH	Fumarylacetoacetate hydrolase [fumarylaceto- acetase]	Tyrosinemia, type 1	81406
	FANCC	Fanconi anemia, complementation group C	Fanconi anemia, type C, Ashkenazi Jewish-associated disorders	81242, 81412
FASTKD2	FASTKD2	FAST kinase domains 2	Mitochondrial respiratory chain complex IV deficiency	81406
FBN1	FBN1	Fibrillin 1	Marfan syndrome, aortic dysfunction or dilation	81408, 81410
FGB	FGB	Fibrinogen beta chain	Hereditary ischemic heart disease	81400
FGD1	FGD1	FYVE, RhoGEF and PH domain containing 1	X-linked intellectual disability (XLID)	81470, 81471
FGF23	FGF23	Fibroblast growth factor 23	Hypophosphatemic rickets	81404
FGFR1	FGFR1	Fibroblast growth factor receptor 1	Pfeiffer syndrome type 1, craniosynostosis	81400, 81405
FGFR2	FGFR2	Fibroblast growth factor receptor 2	Craniosynostosis, Apert syndrome, Crouzon syndrome	81404
FGFR3	FGFR3	Fibroblast growth factor receptor 3	Muenke syndrome	81400, 81401, 81403, 81404
FH	FH	Fumarate hydratase	Fumarate hydratase deficiency, hereditary leiomyomatosis with renal cell cancer	81405
FHL1	FHL1	Four and a half LIM domains 1	Emery-Dreifuss muscular dystrophy	81404
FIG4	FIG4	FIG4 homolog, SAC1 lipid phosphatase domain containing [S. cerevisiae]	Charcot-Marie-Tooth disease	81406
FIP1L1PDGFRA	FIP1L1/ PDGFRA	Del[4q12]	Imatinib-sensitive chronic eosinophilic leukemia	81401
FKRP	FKRP	Fukutin related protein	Congenital muscular dystrophy type 1C [MDC1C], limb-girdle muscular dystrophy [LGMD] type 2l	81404
FKTN	FKTN	Fukutin	Fukuyama congenital muscular dystrophy	81400, 81405
FLG	FLG	Filaggrin	Ichthyosis vulgaris	81401
	FLT3	FMS-related tyrosine kinase 3	Acute myeloid leukemia, hematolymphoid neoplasm or disorder, solid organ neoplasm	81245, 81426, 81450, 81455

| ▮ Separate Procedure | ▮ Unlisted Procedure | ▮ CCI Comp. Code | ▮ Non-specific Procedure | **679** |

MOLECULAR PATHOLOGY GENE TABLE

Claim Designation	Abbreviated Gene Name	Full Gene Name	Commonly Associated Proteins/Disease	CPT Code(s)
	FMR1	Fragile X mental retardation 1	Fragile X mental retardation, X-linked intellectual disability (XLID)	81243, 81244, 81470, 81471
FOXG1	FOXG1	Forkhead box G1	Rett syndrome	81404
FOXO1PAX3	FOXO1/PAX3	t(12;13)	Ewing sarcoma/peripheral neuroectodermal tumor	81401
FOXO1PAX7	FOXO1/PAX7	t(2;13)	Ewing sarcoma/peripheral neuroectodermal tumor translocation analysis	81401
FSHMD1A	FSHMD1A	Facioscapulohumeral muscular dystrophy 1A	Facioscapulohumeral muscular dystrophy	81404
FTSJ1	FTSJ1	FtsJ RNA methyltransferase homolog 1 [E. coli]	X-linked mental retardation 9	81405, 81406
FUS	FUS	Fused in sarcoma	Amyotrophic lateral sclerosis	81406
FUSDDIT3	FUS/DDIT3	t(12;16)	Myxoid liposarcoma	81401
FXN	FXN	Frataxin	Friedreich ataxia	81401, 81404
	G6PC	Glucose-6-phosphatase, catalytic subunit	Glycogen storage disease, Type 1a, von Gierke disease	81250
G6PD	G6PD	Glucose-6-phosphatase dehydrogenase	Hemolytic anemia, jaundice	81247, 81248, 81249
GAA	GAA	Glucosidase, alpha; acid	Glycogen storage disease type II [Pompe disease]	81406
GABRG2	GABRG2	Gamma-aminobutyric acid [GABA] A receptor, gamma 2	Generalized epilepsy with febrile seizures	81405
GALC	GALC	Galactosyl- ceramidase	Krabbe disease	81401, 81406
GALT	GALT	Galactose-1- phosphate uridylyltransferase	Galactosemia	81401, 81406
GARS	GARS	Glycyl-tRNA synthetase	Charcot-Marie-Tooth disease	81406
	GBA	Glucosidase, beta, acid	Gaucher disease, Ashkenazi Jewish-associated disorders	81251, 81412
GCDH	GCDH	Glutaryl-CoA dehydrogenase	Glutaricacidemia type 1	81406
GCH1	GCH1	GTP cyclohydrolase 1	Autosomal dominant dopa-responsive dystonia	81405
GCK	GCK	Glucokinase [hexokinase 4]	Maturity-onset diabetes of the young [MODY]	81406
GDAP1	GDAP1	Ganglioside-induced differentiation-associated protein 1	Charcot-Marie-Tooth disease	81405
GFAP	GFAP	Glial fibrillary acidic protein	Alexander disease	81405
GH1	GH1	Growth hormone 1	Growth hormone deficiency	81404
GHR	GHR	Growth hormone receptor	Laron syndrome	81405
GHRHR	GHRHR	Growth hormone releasing hormone receptor	Growth hormone deficiency	81405
GJB1	GJB1	Gap junction protein, beta 1	Charcot-Marie-Tooth X-linked, hereditary peripheral neuropathies	81403, 81448
	GJB2	Gap junction protein, beta 2, 26kDa, connexin 26	Nonsyndromic hearing loss	81252, 81253, 81430, 81431
	GJB6	Gap junction protein, beta 6, 30kDa, connexin 30	Nonsyndromic hearing loss	81254, 81431
GLA	GLA	Galactosidase, alpha	Fabry disease	81405
GLUD1	GLUD1	Glutamate dehydrogenase 1	Familial hyperinsulinism	81406
GNAQ	GNAQ	Guanine nucleotide- binding protein G[q] subunit alpha	Uveal melanoma	81403
GNE	GNE	Glucosamine [UDP-N-acetyl]-2-epimerase/N-acetylmanno samine kinase	Inclusion body myopathy 2 [IBM2], Nonaka myopathy	81400, 81406
GP1BB	GP1BB	Glycoprotein Ib [platelet], beta polypeptide	Bernard-Soulier syndrome type B	81404
GPR98	GPR98	G-protein couple receptor 98	Hearing loss	81430
GRN	GRN	Granulin	Frontotemporal dementia	81406
H19	H19	Imprinted maternally expressed transcript [non-protein coding]	Beckwith-Wiedemann syndrome	81401
HADHA	HADHA	Hydroxyacyl-CoA dehydrogenase/3-ketoacyl-CoA thiolase/enoyl-CoA hydratase [trifunctional protein] alpha subunit	Long chain acyl-coenzyme A dehydrogenase deficiency	81406
HADHB	HADHB	Hydroxyacyl-CoA dehydrogenase/3-ketoacyl-CoA thiolase/enoyl-CoA hydratase [trifunctional protein], beta subunit	Trifunctional protein deficiency	81406

---

680   ● New Code   ▲ Revised Code   + Add-On Code   ⊘ Modifier -51 Exempt   ★ Telemedicine

MOLECULAR PATHOLOGY GENE TABLE

Claim Designation	Abbreviated Gene Name	Full Gene Name	Commonly Associated Proteins/Disease	CPT Code(s)
HBA1/HBA2	HBA1/HBA2	Alpha globin 1 and alpha globin 2	Alpha thalassemia, thalassemia, Hb Bart hyrdrops fetalis syndrme, HbH disease	81257, 81258, 81259, 81269
HBB	HBB	Hemoglobin, subunit beta	Sickle cell anemia, beta thalassemia, hemoglobinopathy	81361, 81362, 81363, 81364
HEA	HEA	Human erythrocyte antigen	Sickle cell disease, thalassemia, hemolytic transfusion reactions, hemolytic disease of fetus/newborn	81403
		Hexosaminidase A [alpha polypeptide]	Tay-Sachs disease	81255
HEXA	HEXA	Hexosaminidase A [alpha polypeptide]	Tay-Sachs disease, Ashkenazi Jewish-associated disorders	81406, 81412
	HFE	Hemochromatosis	Hereditary hemochromatosis	81256
	HLA	Human leukocyte antigene genes	Pretransplant and drug therapy testing	81370-81383
HLCS	HLCS	HLCS holocarboxylase synthetase	Holocarboxylase synthetase deficiency	81406
HMBS	HMBS	Hydroxymethylbilane synthetase	Acute intermittent porphyria	81406
HNF1A	HNF1A	HNF1 homeobox A	Maturity-onset diabetes of the young [MODY]	81405
HNF1B	HNF1B	HNF1 homeobox B	Maturity-onset diabetes of the young [MODY]	81404, 81405
HNF4A	HNF4A	Hepatocyte nuclear factor 4, alpha	Maturity-onset diabetes of the young [MODY]	81406
HPA1	Human platelet antigen 1 genotyping (HPA-1), ITGB3	Integrin, beta 3 [platelet glycoprotein IIIa], antigen CD61 [GPIIIa]	Neonatal alloimmune thrombocytopenia [NAIT], post-transfusion purpura	81105
HPA2	Human platelet antigen 2 genotyping (HPA-2), GP1BA	Glycoprotein Ib [platelet], alpha polypeptide [GPIba]	Neonatal alloimmune thrombocytopenia [NAIT], post-transfusion purpura	81106
HPA3	Human platelet antigen 3 genotyping (HPA-3), ITGA2B	Integrin, alpha 2b [platelet glycoprotein IIb of IIb/IIIa complex], antigen CD41 [GPIIb]	Neonatal alloimmune thrombocytopenia [NAIT], post-transfusion purpura	81107
HPA4	Human platelet antigen 4 genotyping (HPA-4), ITGB3	Integrin, beta 3 [platelet glycoprotein IIIa], antigen CD61 [GPIIIa]	Neonatal alloimmune thrombocytopenia [NAIT], post-transfusion purpura	81108
HPA5	Human platelet antigen 5 genotyping (HPA-5), ITGA2	Integrin, alpha 2 [CD49B, alpha 2 subunit of VLA-2 receptor] [GPIa]	Neonatal alloimmune thrombocytopenia [NAIT], post-transfusion purpura	81109
HPA6	Human platelet antigen 6 genotyping (HPA-6w), ITGB3	Integrin, beta 3 [platelet glycoprotein IIIa, antigen CD61] [GPIIIa]	Neonatal alloimmune thrombocytopenia [NAIT], post-transfusion purpura	81110
HPA9	Human platelet antigen 9 genotyping (HPA-9w), ITGA2B	Integrin, alpha 2b [platelet glycoprotein IIb of IIb/IIIa complex, antigen CD41] [GPIIb]	Neonatal alloimmune thrombocytopenia [NAIT], post-transfusion purpura	81111
HPA15	Human platelet antigen 15 genotyping (HPA-15), CD109	CD109 molecule	Neonatal alloimmune thrombocytopenia [NAIT], post-transfusion purpura	81112
HRAS	HRAS	v-Ha-ras Harvey rat sarcoma viral oncogene homolog	Costello syndrome, Noonan spectrum disorders	81403, 81404, 81442
HSD3B2	HSD3B2	Hydroxy-delta-5-steroid dehydrogenase, 3 beta- and steroid delta-isomerase 2	3-beta-hydroxysteroid dehydrogenase type II deficiency	81404
HSD11B2	HSD11B2	Hydroxysteroid [11-beta] dehydrogenase 2	Mineralocorticoid excess syndrome	81404
HSPB1	HSPB1	Heat shock 27kDa protein 1	Charcot-Marie-Tooth disease	81404
HTRA1	HTRA1	HtrA serine peptidase 1	Macular degeneration	81400
HTT	HTT	Huntingtin	Huntington disease	81401
HUWE1	HUWE1	HECT, UBA and WWE domain containing 1, E3 ubiquitin protein ligase	X-linked intellectual disability (XLID)	81470, 81471
IDH1	IDH1	Isocitrate dehydrogenase 1 [NADP+], soluble	Glioma, hematolymphoid neoplasm or disorder, solid organ neoplasm	81120, 81450, 81455
IDH2	IDH2	Isocitrate dehydrogenase 2 [NADP+], mitochondrial	Glioma, hematolymphoid neoplasm or disorder, solid organ neoplasm	81121, 81450, 81455
IDS	IDS	Iduronate 2-sulfatase	Mucopolysaccharidosis type II	81405

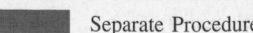 Separate Procedure   Unlisted Procedure   CCI Comp. Code   Non-specific Procedure   **681**

MOLECULAR PATHOLOGY GENE TABLE

Claim Designation	Abbreviated Gene Name	Full Gene Name	Commonly Associated Proteins/Disease	CPT Code(s)
IDUA	IDUA	Iduronidase, alpha-L-	Mucopolysaccharidosis type I	81406
IFNL3	IFNL3	Interferon, lambda 3	Drug response	81283
	IGH@	Immunoglobulin heavy chain locus	Leukemias and lymphomas, B-cell	81261, 81262, 81263
IGHBCL2	IGH@/BCL2	t(14;18)	Follicular lymphoma	81401, 81402
	IGK@	Immunoglobulin kappa light chain locus	Leukemia and lymphoma, B-cell	81264
	IKBKAP	Inhibitor of kappa light polypeptide gene enhancer in B-cells, kinase complex-associated protein	Familial dysautonomia, Ashkenazi Jewish-associated disorders	81260, 81412
IL1RAPL	IL1RAPL	Interleukin 1 receptor accessory protein	X-linked intellectual disability (XLID)	81470, 81471
IL2RG	IL2RG	Interleukin 2 receptor, gamma	X-linked severe combined immunodeficiency	81405
INF2	INF2	Inverted formin, FH2 and WH2 domain containing	Focal segmental glomerulosclerosis	81406
INS	INS	Insulin	Diabetes mellitus	81404
ISPD	ISPD	Isoprenoid synthase domain containing	Muscle-eye-brain disease, Walker-Warburg syndrome	81405
ITPR1	ITPR1	Inositol 1,4,5-trisphosphate receptor, type 1	Spinocerebellar ataxia	81408
IVD	IVD	Isovaleryl-CoA dehydrogenase	Isovaleric acidemia	81400, 81406
JAG1	JAG1	Jagged 1	Alagille syndrome	81406, 81407
	JAK2	Janus kinase 2	Myeloproliferative disorder	81270
JAK2	JAK2	Janus kinase 2	Myeloproliferative disorder, hematolymphoid neoplasm or disorder, solid organ neoplasm	81403, 81450, 81455
JUP	JUP	Junction plakoglobin	Arrhythmogenic right ventricular dysplasia/ cardiomyopathy 11	81406
KCNC3	KCNC3	Potassium voltage-gated channel, Shaw-related subfamily, member 3	Spinocerebellar ataxia	81403
KCNE1	KCNE1	Potassium voltage-gated channel, subfamily E, member 1	Cardiac ion channelopathies	81413
KCNE2	KCNE2	Potassium voltage-gated channel, subfamily E, member 2	Cardiac ion channelopathies	81413
KCNH2	KCNH2	Potassium voltage- gated channel, subfamily H [eag-related], member 2	Short QT syndrome, long QT syndrome, cardiac ion channelopathies	81406, 81413, 81414
KCNJ1	KCNJ1	Potassium inwardly-rectifying channel, subfamily J, member 1	Bartter syndrome	81404
KCNJ2	KCNJ2	Potassium inwardly-rectifying channel, subfamily J, member 2	Andersen-Tawil syndrome, cardiac ion channelopathies	81403, 81413
KCNJ10	KCNJ10	Potassium inwardly-rectifying channel, subfamily J, member 10	SeSAME syndrome, EAST syndrome, sensorineural hearing loss	81404
KCNJ11	KCNJ11	Potassium inwardly-rectifying channel, subfamily J, member 11	Familial hyperinsulinism	81403
KCNQ1	KCNQ1	Potassium voltage-gated channel, KQT-like subfamily, member 1	Short QT syndrome, long QT syndrome, cardiac ion channelopathies	81406, 81413, 81414
KCNQ1OT1	KCNQ1OT1	KCNQ1 overlapping transcript 1 [non-protein coding]	Beckwith-Wiedemann syndrome	81401
KCNQ2	KCNQ2	Potassium voltage-gated channel, KQT-like subfamily, member 2	Epileptic encephalopathy	81406
KDM5C	KDM5C	Lysine [K]-specific demethylase 5C	X-linked mental retardation, X-linked intellectual disability (XLID)	81407, 81470, 81471
KIAA0196	KIAA0196	KIAA0196	Spastic paraplegia	81407
KIR	KIR	Killer cell immunoglobulin-like receptor	Hematopoietic stem cell transplantation	81403
	KIT	v-kit Hardy- Zuckerman 4 feline sarcoma viral oncogene homolog	Gstrointestinal stromal tumor, acute myeloid leukemia, melanoma, solid organ neoplasm, hematolymphoid neoplasm or disorder	81272, 81273, 81445, 81450, 81455
NOS	Known familial variant NOS	N/A	N/A	81403
	KRAS	v-Ki-ras2 Kirsten rat sarcoma viral oncogene homolog	Carcinoma, Noonan syndrome	81275, 81276
KRAS	KRAS	Kirsten rat sarcoma viral oncogene homolog	Noonam syndrome, Noonam spectrum disorders, solid organ neoplasm, hematolymphoid neoplasm or disorder	81405, 81442, 81445, 81450, 81455
L1CAM	L1CAM	L1 cell adhesion molecule	MASA syndrome, X-linked hydrocephaly, X-linked intellectual disability (XLID)	81407, 81470, 81471
LAMA2	LAMA2	Laminin, alpha 2	Congenital muscular dystrophy	81408

● New Code ▲ Revised Code + Add-On Code ⊘ Modifier -51 Exempt ★ Telemedicine

MOLECULAR PATHOLOGY GENE TABLE

Claim Designation	Abbreviated Gene Name	Full Gene Name	Commonly Associated Proteins/Disease	CPT Code(s)
LAMB2	LAMB2	Laminin, beta 2 [laminin S]	Pierson syndrome	81407
LAMP2	LAMP2	Lysosomal- associated membrane protein 2	Danon disease	81405
LCT	LCT	Lactase-phlorizin hydrolase	Lactose intolerance	81400
LDB3	LDB3	LIM domain binding 3	Familial dilated cardiomyopathy, myofibrillar myopathy	81406
LDLR	LDLR	Low density lipoprotein receptor	Familial hypercholesterolemia	81405, 81406
LEPR	LEPR	Leptin receptor	Obesity with hypogonadism	81406
LHCGR	LHCGR	Luteinizing hormone/ choriogonadotropin receptor	Precocious male puberty	81406
LINC00518	LINC00518	Long intergenic non-protein coding RNA 518	Melanoma	81401
LITAF	LITAF	Lipopolysaccharide- induced TNF factor	Charcot-Marie-Tooth	81404
LMNA	LMNA	Lamin A/C	Emery-Dreifuss muscular dystrophy [EDMD1, 2 and 3] limb-girdle muscular dystrophy [LGMD] type 1B, dilated cardio-myopathy [CMD1A], familiar portal lipodystrophy [FPLD2]	81406
LRP5	LRP5	Low density lipoprotein receptor-related protein 5	Osteopetrosis	81406
LRRK2	LRRK2	Leucine-rich repeat kinase 2	Parkinson disease	81401, 81408
MAP2K1	MAP2K1	Mitogen-activated protein kinase 1	Cardiofaciocutaneous syndrome, Noonan spectrum disorders	81406, 81442
MAP2K2	MAP2K2	Mitogen-activated protein kinase 2	Cardiofaciocutaneous syndrome, Noonan spectrum disorders	81406, 81442
MAPT	MAPT	Microtubule- associated protein tau	Frontotemporal dementia	81406
MAX	MAX	MYC-associated factor X	Hereditary neuroendocrine tumor disorders	81437
MC4R	MC4R	Melanocortin 4 receptor	Obesity	81403
MCCC1	MCCC1	Methylcrotonyl-CoA carboxylase 1 [alpha]	3-methylcrotonyl-CoA carboxylase deficiency	81406
MCCC2	MCCC2	Methylcrotonyl-CoA carboxylase 2 [beta]	3-methylcrotonyl carboxylase deficiency	81406
	MCOLN1	Mucolipin 1	Mucolipidosis, type IV, Ashkenazi Jewish-associated disorders	81290, 81412
	MECP2	Methyl CpG binding protein 2	Rett syndrome, X-linked intellectual disability (XLID)	81302, 81303, 81304, 81470, 81471
MED12	MED12	Mediator complex subunit 12	FG syndrome type 1, Lujan syndrome, X-linked intellectual disability (XLID)	81401, 81470, 81471
MEFV	MEFV	Mediterranean fever	Familial Mediterranean fever	81402, 81404
MEG3DLK1	MEG3/DLK1	Maternally expressed 3 [non-protein coding]/delta-like 1 homolog [Drosophila]	Intrauterine growth retardation	81401
MEN1	MEN1	Multiple endocrine neoplasia I	Multiple endocrine neoplasia type 1, Wermer syndrome	81404, 81405
MET	MET	Met proto-oncogene	Solid organ neoplasm or hematolymphoid neoplasm	81445, 81455
MFN2	MFN2	Mitofusin 2	Charcot-Marie-Tooth disease, hereditary peripheral neuropathies	81406, 81448
	MGMT	0-6-methylguanine- DNA methyltransferase	Glioblastoma multiforme	81287
MICA	MICA	MHC class I polypeptide-related sequence A	Solid organ transplantation	81403
	Micro-satellite instability analysis	N/A	Hereditary nonpolyposis colorectal cancer, Lynch syndrome	81301
MID1	MID1	Midline 1	X-linked intellectual disability (XLID)	81470, 81471
	MLH1	mutL homolog 1, colon cancer, nonpolyposis type 2	Hereditary non-polyposis colorectal cancer, Lynch syndrome, hereditary breast cancer-related disorders, hereditary colon cancer disorders	81288, 81292, 81293, 81294, 81432, 81433, 81435, 81436
MLL	MLL	N/A	Hematolymphoid neoplasm or disorder, solid organ neoplasm	81450, 81455
MLLAFF1	MLL/AFF1	t(4;11)	Acute lymphoblastic leukemia	81401
MLLMLLT3	MLL/MLLT3	t(9;11)	Acute myeloid leukemia	81401
MMAA	MMAA	Methylmalonic aciduria [cobalamine deficiency] type A	MMAA-related methylmalonic acidemia	81405

| � | Separate Procedure | ▪ Unlisted Procedure | ▪ CCI Comp. Code | ▪ Non-specific Procedure | **683** |

MOLECULAR PATHOLOGY GENE TABLE

Claim Designation	Abbreviated Gene Name	Full Gene Name	Commonly Associated Proteins/Disease	CPT Code(s)
MMB	MMAB	Methylmalonic aciduria [cobalamine deficiency] type B	MMAA-related methylmalonic acidemia	81405
MMACHC	MMACHC	Methylmalonic aciduria [cobalamin deficiency] cblC type, with homocystinuria	Methylmalonic acidemia and homocystinuria	81404
MPI	MPI	Mannose phosphate isomerase	Congenital disorder of glycosylation 1b	81405
MPL	MPL	Myeloproliferative leukemia virus oncogene, thrombopoietin receptor, TPOR	Myeloproliferative disorder	81402, 81403
MPV17	MPV17	MpV17 mitochondrial inner membrane protein	Mitochondrial DNA depletion syndrome, mitochondrial disorders	81404, 81405, 81440
MPZ	MPZ	Myelin protein zero	Charcot-Marie-Tooth disease, hereditary peripheral neuropathies	81405, 81448
	MSH2	mutS homolog 2, colon cancer, nonpolyposis type 1	Hereditary non-polyposis colorectal cancer, Lynch syndrome, hereditary breast cancer-related disorders, hereditary colon cancer disorders	81295, 81296, 81297, 81432, 81433, 81435, 81436
	MSH6	mutS homolog 6 [E. coli]	Hereditary nonpolyposis colorectal cancer, Lynch syndrome, hereditary breast cancer-related disorders, hereditary colon cancer disorders	81298, 81299, 81300, 81432, 81435
MTATP6	MT-ATP6	Mitochondrially encoded ATP synthase 6	Neuropathy with ataxia and retinitis pigmentosa [NARP], Leigh syndrome	81401
	MTHFR	5,10-methylenetetrahydrofolate reductase	Hereditary hypercoagulability	81291
MTM1	MTM1	Myotubularin 1	X-linked centronuclear myopathy	81405, 81406
MTND4ND6	MT-ND4, MT-ND6	Mitochondrially encoded NADH dehydrogenase 4, mitochondrially encoded NADH dehydrogenase 6	Leber hereditary optic neuropathy [LHON]	81401
MTND5	MT-ND5	Mitochondrially encoded tRNA leucine 1 [UUA/G], mitochondrially encoded NADH dehydrogenase 5	Mitochondrial encephalopathy with lactic acidosis and stroke-like episodes [MELAS]	81401
MTRNR1	MT-RNR1	Mitochondrially encoded 12S RNA	Nonsyndromic hearing loss	81401, 81403, 81430
MTTK	MT-TK	Mitochondrially encoded tRNA lysine	Myoclonic epilepsy with ragged-red fibers [MERRF]	81401
MTTL1	MT-TL1	Mitochondrially encoded tRNA leucine 1 [UUA/G]	Diabetes and hearing loss	81401
MTTS1	MT-TS1	Mitochondrially encoded tRNA serine 1	Nonsyndromic hearing loss	81403
MTTS1RNR1	MT-TS1, MT-RNR1	Mitochondrially encoded tRNA serine 1 [UCN], mitochondrially encoded 12S RNA	Nonsyndromic sensori-neural deafness [including aminoglycoside-induced nonsyndromic deafness]	81401
MUT	MUT	Methylmalonyl CoA mutase	Methylmalonic acidemia	81406
MUTYH	MUTYH	mutY homolog [E. coli]	MYH-associated polyposis, hereditary colon cancer disorders	81401, 81406, 81435
MYBPC3	MYBPC3	Myosin binding protein C, cardiac	Familial hypertrophic cardiomyopathy, hereditary cardiomyopathy	81407, 81439
MYH6	MYH6	Myosin , heavy chain 6, cardiac muscle, alpha	Familial dilated cardiomyopathy	81407
MYH7	MYH7	Myosin, heavy chain 7, cardiac muscle, beta	Familial hypertrophic cardiomyopathy, Liang distal myopathy, hereditary cardiomyopathy	81407, 81439
MYH11	MYH11	Myosin, heavy chain 11, smooth muscle	Thoracic aortic aneurysms and aortic dissections, aortic dysfunction or dilation	81408, 81410, 81411
MYL2	MYL2	Myosin, light chain 2, regulatory, cardiac, slow	Familial hypertrophic cardiomyopathy	81405
MYL3	MYL3	Myosin, light chain 3, alkali, ventricular, skeletal, slow	Familial hypertrophic cardiomyopathy	81405
MYLK	MYLK	Myosin light chain kinase	Aortic dysfunction or dilation	81410
MYO7A	MYO7A	Myosin VIIA	Usher syndrome, type 1, hearing loss	81407, 81430
MYO15A	MYO15A	Myosin XVA	Hearing loss	81430
MYOT	MYOT	Myotilin	Limb-girdle muscular dystrophy	81405
NBN	NBN	Nibrin	Hereditary breast cancer-related disorders	81432
NDP	NDP	Norrie disease [pseudoglioma]	Norrie disease	81403, 81404
NDUFA1	NDUFA1	NADH dehydrogenase [ubiquinone] 1 alpha subcomplex, 1, 7.5kDa	Leigh syndrome, mitochondrial complex I deficiency	81404
NDUFAF2	NDUFAF2	NADH dehydrogenase [ubiquinone] 1 alpha subcomplex, assembly factor 2	Leigh syndrome, mitochondrial complex I deficiency	81404

● New Code   ▲ Revised Code   + Add-On Code   ⊘ Modifier -51 Exempt   ★ Telemedicine

MOLECULAR PATHOLOGY GENE TABLE

Claim Designation	Abbreviated Gene Name	Full Gene Name	Commonly Associated Proteins/Disease	CPT Code(s)
NDUFS1	NDUFS1	NADH dehydrogenase [ubiquinone] Fe-S protein 1, 75kDa [NADH-coenzyme Q reductase]	Leigh syndrome, mitochondrial complex I deficiency	81406
NDUFS4	NDUFS4	NADH dehydrogenase [ubiquinone] Fe-S protein 4, 18kDa [NADH-coenzyme Q reductase]	Leigh syndrome, mitochondrial complex I deficiency	81404
NDUFS7	NDUFS7	NADH dehydrogenase [ubiquinone] Fe-S protein 7, 20kDa [NADH-coenzyme Q reductase]	Leigh syndrome, mitochondrial complex I deficiency	81405
NDUFS8	NDUFS8	NADH dehydrogenase [ubiquinone] Fe-S protein 8, 23kDa [NADH-coenzyme Q reductase]	Leigh syndrome, mitochondrial complex I deficiency	81405
NDUFV1	NDUFV1	NADH dehydrogenase [ubiquinone] flavoprotein 1, 51kDa	Leigh syndrome, mitochondrial complex I deficiency	81405
NEB	NEB	Nebulin	Nemaline myopathy 2	81400, 81408
NEFL	NEFL	Neurofilament, light polypeptide	Charcot-Marie-Tooth	81405
NF1	NF1	Neurofibromin 1	Neurofibromatosis, type 1	81408
NF2	NF2	Neurofibromin 2 [merlin]	Neurofibromatosis, type 2	81405, 81406
NHLRC1	NHLRC1	NHL repeat containing 1	Progressive myoclonus epilepsy	81403
NIPA1	NIPA1	Non-imprinted in Prader-Willi/ Angelman syndrome 1	Spastic paraplegia	81404
NLGN3	NLGN3	Neuroligin 3	Autism spectrum disorders	81405
NLGN4X	NLGN4X	Neuroligin 4, X-linked	Autism spectrum disorders	81404, 81405
NOD2	NOD2	Nucleotide-binding oligomerization domain containing 2	Crohn's disease, Blau syndrome	81401
NOTCH1	NOTCH1	Notch 1	Aortic valve disease, hematolymphoid neoplasm or disorder, solid organ neoplasm	81407, 81450, 81455
NOTCH3	NOTCH3	Notch 3	Cerebral autosomal dominant arteriopathy with subcortical infarcts and leukoencephalopathy [CADASIL]	81406
NPC1	NPC1	Niemann-Pick disease, type C1	Niemann-Pick disease	81406
NPC2	NPC2	Niemann-Pick disease, type C2 [epididymal secretory protein E1]	Niemann-Pick disease type C2	81404
NPHP1	NPHP1	Nephronophthisis 1 [juvenile]	Joubert syndrome	81405, 81406
NPHS1	NPHS1	Nephrosis 1, congenital, Finnish type [nephrin]	Congenital Finnish nephrosis	81407
NPHS2	NPHS2	Nephrosis 2, idiopathic, steroid-resistant [podocin]	Steroid-resistant nephrotic syndrome	81405
	NPM1	Nucleophosmin	Acute myeloid leukemia, hematolymphoid neoplasm or disorder, solid organ neoplasm	81310, 81450, 81455
NPM1ALK	NPM1/ALK	t(2;5)	Anaplastic large cell lymphoma	81401
NR0B1	NR0B1	Nuclear receptor subfamily 0, group B, member 1	Congenital adrenal hypoplasia	81404
	NRAS	Neuroblastoma RAS viral [V-RAS] oncogene homolog	Colorectal carcinoma, Noonan spectrum disorders, solid organ neoplasm, hematolymphoid neoplasm or disorder	81311, 81442, 81445, 81450, 81455
NSD1	NSD1	Nuclear receptor binding SET domain protein 1	Sotos syndrome	81405, 81406
OCRL	OCRL	Oculocerebrorenal syndrome of Lowe	X-linked intellectual disability (XLID)	81470, 81471
OPA1	OPA1	Optic atrophy 1	Optic atrophy, mitochondrial disorders	81406, 81407, 81440
OPTN	OPTN	Optineurin	Amyotrophic lateral sclerosis	81406
OTC	OTC	Ornithine carbamoyltransferase	Ornithine transcarbamylase deficiency	81405
OTOF	OTOF	Otoferlin	Hearing loss	81430
PABPN1	PABPN1	Poly[A] binding protein, nuclear 1	Oculopharyngeal muscular dystrophy	81401
PAFAH1B1	PAFAH1B1	Platelet-activating factor acetylhydrolase 1b, regulatory subunit 1 [45kDa]	Lissencephaly, Miller-Dieker syndrome	81405, 81406
PAH	PAH	Phenylalanine hydroxylase	Phenylketonuria	81406
PALB2	PALB2	Partner and localizer of BRCA2	Breast and pancreatic cancer, hereditary breast cancer-related disorders	81406, 81432

■	Separate Procedure	■	Unlisted Procedure	■	CCI Comp. Code	■	Non-specific Procedure	**685**

MOLECULAR PATHOLOGY GENE TABLE

Claim Designation	Abbreviated Gene Name	Full Gene Name	Commonly Associated Proteins/Disease	CPT Code(s)
PARK2	PARK2	Parkinson protein 2, E3 ubiquitin protein ligase [parkin]	Parkinson disease	81405, 81406
PAX2	PAX2	Paired box 2	Renal coloboma syndrome	81406
PAX8PPARG	PAX8/PPARG	t(2;3) (q13;p25)	Follicular thyroid carcinoma	81401
PC	PC	Pyruvate carboxylase	Pyruvate carboxylase deficiency	81406
	PCA3/KLK3	Prostate cancer antigen 3/kallikrein-related peptidase 3	Prostate cancer	81313
PCCA	PCCA	Propionyl CoA carboxylase, alpha polypeptide	Propionic acidemia, type 1	81405, 81406
PCCB	PCCB	Propionyl CoA carboxylase, beta polypeptide	Propionic acidemia	81406
PCDH15	PCDH15	Protocadherin-related 15	Usher syndrome type 1F, Usher syndrome type 1, hearing loss	81400, 81406, 81407, 81430
PCDH19	PCDH19	Protocadherin 19	Epileptic encephalopathy	81405
PCSK9	PCSK9	Proprotein convertase subtilisin/ kexin type 9	Familial hypercholesterolemia	81406
	PDGFRA	Platelet-derived growth factor receptor alpha polypeptide	Gastrointestinal stromal tumor, solid organ neoplasm or hematolymphoid neoplasm	81314, 81445, 81455
	PDGFRB	Platelet-derived growth factor receptor beta polypeptide	Solid organ neoplasm or hematolymphoid neoplasm	81445, 81455
PDE6A	PDE6A	Phosphodiesterase 6A, CGMP-specific, rod, alpha	Hereditary retinal disorders	81434
PDE6B	PDE6B	Phosphodiesterase 6B, CGMP-specific, rod, beta	Hereditary retinal disorders	81434
PDHA1	PDHA1	Pyruvate dehydrogenase [lipoamide] alpha 1	Lactic acidosis	81405, 81406
PDHB	PDHB	Pyruvate dehydrogenase [lipoamide] beta	Lactic acidosis	81405
PDHX	PDHX	Pyruvate dehydrogenase complex, component X	Lactic acidosis	81406
PDSS2	PDSS2	Decaprenyl diphosphate synthase subunit 2	Mitochondrial disorders	81440
PDX1	PDX1	Pancreatic and duodenal homeobox 1	Maturity-onset diabetes of the young [MODY]	81404
PGR	PGR	Progesterone receptor	Solid organ or hematolymphoid neoplasm	81445, 81455
PHEX	PHEX	Phosphate regulating endopeptidase homolog, X-linked	Hypophosphatemic rickets	81406
PHOX2B	PHOX2B	Paired-like homeobox 2b	Congenital central hypoventilation syndrome	81403, 81404
PIK3CA	PIK3CA	Phosphatidylinositol-4, 5-bisphosphate 3-kinase, catalytic subunit alpha	Colorectal cancer, solid organ neoplasm or hematolymphoid neoplasm	81404, 81445, 81455
PINK1	PINK1	PTEN induced putative kinase 1	Parkinson disease	81405
PKD1	PKD1	Polycystic kidney disease 1 [autosomal dominant]	Polycystic kidney disease	81407
PKD2	PKD2	Polycystic kidney disease 2 [autosomal dominant]	Polycystic kidney disease	81406
PKHD1	PKHD1	Polycystic kidney and hepatic disease 1	Autosomal recessive polycystic kidney disease	81408
PKLR	PKLR	Pyruvate kinase, liver and RBC	Pyruvate kinase deficiency	81405
PKP2	PKP2	Plakophilin 2	Arrhythmogenic right ventricular dysplasia/ cardiomyopathy 9, hereditary cardiomyopathy	81406, 81439
PLCE1	PLCE1	Phospholipase C, epsilon 1	Nephrotic syndrome type 3	81407
PLN	PLN	Phospholamban	Dilated cardiomyopathy, hypertrophic cardiomyopathy	81403
PLP1	PLP1	Proteolipid protein 1	Pelizaeus-Merzbacher disease, spastic paraplegia	81404, 81405
	PML/RARalpha	t(15;17) promyelocytic leukemia/retinoic acid receptor alpha	Promyelocytic leukemia	81315, 81316
	PMP22	Peripheral myelin protein 22	Charcot-Marie-Tooth, hereditary neuropathy with liability to pressure palsies	81324, 81325, 81326
	PMS2	Postmeiotic segregation increased 2 [S. cerevisiae]	Hereditary non-polyposis colorectal cancer, Lynch syndrome	81317, 81318, 81319
PNKD	PNKD	Paroxysmal nonkinesigenic dyskinesia	Paroxysmal nonkinesigenic dyskinesia, mitochondrial disorders	81406, 81440

● New Code   ▲ Revised Code   + Add-On Code   ⊘ Modifier -51 Exempt   ★ Telemedicine

MOLECULAR PATHOLOGY GENE TABLE

Claim Designation	Abbreviated Gene Name	Full Gene Name	Commonly Associated Proteins/Disease	CPT Code(s)
POLG	POLG	Polymerase [DNA directed], gamma	Alpers-Huttenlocher syndrome, autosomal dominant progressive external ophthalmoplegia, mitochondrial disorders	81406, 81440
POLG2	POLG2	Polymerase [DNA directed], gamma 2	Mitochondrial disorders	81440
POMGNT1	POMGNT1	Protein O-linked mannose beta1,2-N acetylglucosaminyltransferase	Muscle-eye-brain disease, Walker-Warburg syndrome	81406
POMT1	POMT1	Protein-O-mannosyltransferase 1	Limb-girdle muscular dystrophy [LGMD] type 2K, Walker-Warburg syndrome	81406
POMT2	POMT2	Protein-O-mannosyltransferase 2	Limb-girdle muscular dystrophy [LGMD] type 2N, Walker-Warburg syndrome	81406
POU1F1	POU1F1	POU class 1 homeobox 1	Combined pituitary hormone deficiency	81405
PPOX	PPOX	Protoporphyrinogen oxidase	Variegate porphyria	81406
PPP2R2B	PPP2R2B	Protein phosphatase 2, regulatory subunit B, beta	Spinocerebellar ataxia	81401
PQBP1	PQBP1	Polyglutamine binding protein 1	Renpenning syndrome	81404, 81405
PRAME	PRAME	Preferentially expressed antigen in melanoma	Melanoma	81401
PRKAG2	PRKAG2	Protein kinase, AMP-activated, gamma 2 non-catalytic subunit	Familial hypertrophic cardiomyopathy with Wolff-Parkinson-White syndrome, lethal congenital glycogen storage disease of heart	81406
PRKCG	PRKCG	Protein kinase C, gamma	Spinocerebellar ataxia, hyperkalemic periodic paralysis	81406
PRNP	PRNP	Prion protein	Genetic prion disease	81404
PROP1	PROP1	PROP paired-like homeobox 1	Combined pituitary hormone deficiency	81404
PRPF31	PRPF31	Pre-MRNA processing factor 31	Hereditary retinal disorders	81434
PRPH2	PRPH2	Peripherin 2 [retinal degeneration, slow]	Retinitis pigmentosa, hereditary retinal disorders	81404, 81434
PRSS1	PRSS1	Protease, serine, 1 [trypsin 1]	Hereditary pancreatitis	81401, 81404
PRX	PRX	Periaxin	Charcot-Marie-Tooth disease	81405
PSEN1	PSEN1	Presenilin 1	Alzheimer disease	81405
PSEN2	PSEN2	Presenilin 2 [Alzheimer disease 4]	Alzheimer disease	81406
	PTEN	Phosphatase and tensin homolog	Cowden syndrome, PTEN hamartoma tumor syndrome, hereditary breast cancer-related disorders, hereditary colon cancer disorders, solid organ neoplasm or hematolymphoid neoplasm	81321, 81322, 81323, 81432, 81435, 81445, 81455
PTPN11	PTPN11	Protein tyrosine phosphatase, non-receptor type 11	Noonan syndrome, LEOPARD syndrome, Noonan spectrum disorders	81406, 81442
PYGM	PYGM	Phosphorylase, glycogen, muscle	Glycogen storage disease type V, McArdle disease	81401, 81406
RAB7A	RAB7A	RAB7A, member RAS oncogene family	Charcot-Marie-Tooth disease	81405
RAF1	RAF1	v-raf-1 murine leukemia viral oncogene homolog 1	LEOPARD syndrome, Noonan spectrum disorder	81404, 81406, 81442
RAI1	RAI1	Retinoic acid induced 1	Smith-Magenis syndrome	81405
RDH12	RDH12	Retinol dehydrogenase 12 (All-Trans/9-Cis/11-Cis)	Hereditary retinal disorders	81434
REEP1	REEP1	Receptor accessory protein 1	Spastic paraplegia, hereditary peripheral neuropathies	81405, 81448
RET	RET	Ret proto-oncogene	Multiple endocrine neoplasia, type 2B and familial medullary thyroid carcinoma, Hirschsprung disease, solid organ neoplasm or hematolymphoid neoplasm	81404, 81405, 81406, 81445, 81455
RHDDA	RHD, deletion analysis	Rh blood group, D antigen	Hemolytic disease of fetus/newborn, Rh maternal/fetal compatibility	81403
RHDDAMB	RHD, deletion analysis, cell-free fetal DNA in maternal blood	Rh bood group D, antigen	Hemolytic disease of fetus/newborn, Rh maternal/fetal compatibility	81403
RHO	RHO	Rhodopsin	Retinitis pigmentosa, hereditary retinal disorders	81404, 81434
RIT1	RIT1	Ras-like without CAAX 1	Noonan spectrum disorders	81442
RP1	RP1	Retinitis pigmentosa 1	Retinitis pigmentosa, hereditary retinal disorders	81404, 81434
RP2	RP2	Retinitis pigmentosa 2	Hereditary retinal disorders	81434
RPE65	RPE65	Retinal pigment epithelium-specific protein 65kDa	Retinitis pigmentosa, Leber congenital amaurosis, hereditary retinal disorders	81406, 81434
RPGR	RPGR	Retinitis pigmentosa GTPase regulator	Hereditary retinal disorders	81434

MOLECULAR PATHOLOGY GENE TABLE

Claim Designation	Abbreviated Gene Name	Full Gene Name	Commonly Associated Proteins/Disease	CPT Code(s)
RPS19	RPS19	Ribosomal protein S19	Diamond-Blackfan anemia	81405
RPS6KA3	RPS6KA3	Ribosomal protein S6 kinase, 90kDa, polypeptide3	X-linked intellectual disability (XLID)	81470, 81471
RRM2B	RRM2B	Ribonucleotide reductase M2 B [TP53 inducible]	Mitochondrial DNA depletion, mitochondrial disorders	81405, 81440
RUNX1	RUNX1	Runt related transcription factor 1	Acute myeloid leukemia, familial platelet disorder with associated myeloid malignancy	81334
RUNX1RUNX1T1	RUNX1/RUNX1T1	t(8;21)	Acute myeloid leukemia	81401
RYR1	RYR1	Ryanodine receptor 1, skeletal	Malignant hyperthermia	81406, 81408
RYR2	RYR2	Ryanodine receptor 2 [cardiac]	Catecholaminergic polymorphic ventricular tachycardia, arrhythmogenic right ventricular dysplasia, cardiac ion channelopathies	81408, 81413
scn1a	SCN1A	Sodium channel, voltage-gated, type 1, alpha subunit	Generalized epilepsy with febrile seizures	81407
SCN1B	SCN1B	Sodium channel, voltage-gated, type I, beta	Brugada syndrome	81404
SCN4A	SCN4A	Sodium channel, voltage-gated, type IV, alpha subunit	Hyperkalemic periodic paralysis	81406
SCN5A	SCN5A	Sodium channel, voltage-gated, type V, alpha subunit	Familial dilated cardiomyopathy, cardiac ion channelopathies	81407, 81413
SCNN1A	SCNN1A	Sodium channel, nonvoltage-gated 1 alpha	Pseudohypoaldo- steronism	81406
SCNN1B	SCNN1B	Sodium channel, nonvoltage-gated 1, beta	Liddle syndrome, pseudohypoaldo- steronism	81406
SCNN1G	SCNN1G	Sodium channel, nonvoltage-gated 1, gamma	Liddle syndrome, pseudohypoaldo- steronism	81406
SCO1	SCO1	SCO cytochrome oxidase deficient homolog 1	Mitochondrial respiratory chain complex IV deficiency, mitochondrial disorders	81405, 81440
SCO2	SCO2	SCO cytochrome oxidase deficient homolog 2 [SCO1L]	Mitochondrial respiratory chain complex IV deficiency, mitochondrial disorders	81404, 81440
SDHA	SDHA	Succinate dehydrogenase complex, subunit A, flavoprotein [Fp]	Leigh syndrome, mitochondrial complex II deficiency	81406
SDHB	SDHB	Succinate dehydrogenase complex, subunit B, iron sulfur	Hereditary paraganglioma, hereditary neuroendocrine tumor disorders	81405, 81437, 81438
SDHC	SDHC	Succinate dehydrogenase complex, subunit C, integral membrane protein, 15kDa	Hereditary paraganglioma- pheochromocytoma syndrome, hereditary neuroendocrine tumor disorders	81404, 81405, 81437, 81438
SDHD	SDHD	Succinate dehydrogenase complex, subunit D, integral membrane protein	Hereditary paraganglioma, hereditary neuroendocrine tumor disorders	81327, 81404, 81437, 81438
SEPT9	SEPT9	Septin 9	Colorectal cancer	81327
	SERPINA1	Serpin peptidase inhibitor, clade A, alpha-1 antiproteinase, antitrypsin, member 1	Alpha-1-antitrypsin deficiency	81332
SERPINE1	SERPINE1	Serpine peptidase inhibitor clade E, member 1, plasminogen activator inhibitor -1, PAI-1	Thrombophilia	81400
SETX	SETX	Senataxin	Ataxia	81406
SGCA	SGCA	Sarcoglycan, alpha [50kDa dystrophin-associated glycoprotein]	Limb-girdle muscular dystrophy	81405
SGCB	SGCB	Sarcoglycan, beta [43kDa dystrophin-associated glycoprotein]	Limb-girdle muscular dystrophy	81405
SGCD	SGCD	Sarcoglycan, delta [35kDa dystrophin-associated glycoprotein]	Limb-girdle muscular dystrophy	81405
SGCE	SGCE	Sarcoglycan, epsilon	Myoclonic dystonia	81405, 81406
SGCG	SGCG	Sarcoglycan, gamma [35kDa dystrophin-associated glycoprotein]	Limb-girdle muscular dystrophy	81404, 81405
SH2D1A	SH2D1A	SH2 domain containing 1A	X-linked lymphoproliferative syndrome	81403, 81404
SH3TC2	SH3TC2	SH3 domain and tetratricopeptide repeats 2	Charcot-Marie-Tooth disease	81406
SHOC2	SHOC2	Soc-2 suppressor of clear homolog	Noonan-like syndrome with loose anagen hair, Noonan spectrum disorders	81400, 81405, 81442
	Short tandem repeat (STR)	N/A	Pretransplant recipient, donor germline testing, post-transplant recipient	81265, 81266
SHOX	SHOX	Short stature homeobox	Langer mesomelic dysplasia	81405
SIL1	SIL1	SIL1 homolog, endoplasmic reticulum chaperone [S. cerevisiae]	Ataxia	81405

● New Code   ▲ Revised Code   + Add-On Code   ⊘ Modifier -51 Exempt   ★ Telemedicine

MOLECULAR PATHOLOGY GENE TABLE

Claim Designation	Abbreviated Gene Name	Full Gene Name	Commonly Associated Proteins/Disease	CPT Code(s)
SLC2A1	SLC2A1	Solute carrier family 2 [facilitated glucose transporter], member 1	Glucose transporter type 1 [GLUT 1] deficiency syndrome	81405
SLC2A10	SLC2A10	Solute carrier family 2 [facilitated glucose transporter], member 10	Aortic dysfunction or dilation	81410
SLC9A6	SLC9A6	Solute carrier family 9 [sodium/hydrogen exchanger], member 6	Christianson syndrome	81406
SLC12A1	SLC12A1	Solute carrier family 12 [sodium/potassium/chloride transporters], member 1	Bartter syndrome	81407
SLC12A3	SLC12A3	Solute carrier family 12 [sodium/chloride transporters], member 3	Gitelman syndrome	81407
SLC16A2	SLC16A2	Solute carrier family 16, member 2 [thyroid hormone transporter]	Specific thyroid hormone cell transporter deficiency, Allan-Herndon-Dudley syndrome, X-linked intellectual disability (XLID)	81404, 81405, 81470, 81471
SLC22A5	SLC22A5	Solute carrier family 22 [organic cation/carnitine transporter], member 5	Systemic primary carnitine deficiency	81405
SLC25A20	SLC25A20	Solute carrier family 25 [carnitine/acylcarnitine translocase], member 20	Carnitine-acylcarnitine translocase deficiency	81404, 81405
SLC25A4	SLC25A4	Solute carrier family 25 [mitochondrial carrier; adenine nucleotide translocator], member 4	Progressive external ophthalmoplegia, mitochondrial disorders	81404, 81440
SLC26A4	SLC26A4	Solute carrier family 26, member 4	Pendred syndrome, hearing loss	81406, 81430
SLC37A4	SLC37A4	Solute carrier family 37 [glucose-6-phosphate transporter], member 4	Glycogen storage disease type Ib	81406
SLCO1B1	SLCO1B1	Solute carrier organic anion transporter family, member 1B1	Adverse drug reaction	81328
SMAD3	SMAD3	SMAD family member 3	Aortic dysfunction or dilation	81410
SMAD4	SMAD4	SMAD family member 4	Hemorrhagic telangiectasia syndrome, juvenile polyposis, hereditary colon cancer disorders	81405, 81406, 81435, 81436
SMN1	SMN1	Survival of motor neuron 1, telomeric	Spinal muscular atrophy	81400, 81403. 81405
SMN1SMN2	SMN1/SMN2	Survival of motor neuron 1, telomeric/survival of motor neuron 2, centromeric	Spinal muscular atrophy	81401
	SMPD1	Sphingomyelin phospho-diesterase 1, acid lysosomal	Niemann-Pick disease, type A, Ashkenazi Jewish-associated disorders	81330, 81412
	SNRPN/ UBE3A	Small nuclear ribonucleoprotein polypeptide N and ubiquitin protein ligase E3A	Prader-Willi syndrome and/or Angelman syndrome	81331
SOD1	SOD1	Superoxide dismutase 1, soluble	Amyotrophic lateral sclerosis	81404
SOS1	SOS1	Son of sevenless homolog 1	Noonan syndrome, gingival fibromatosis, Noonan spectrum disorders	81406, 81442
SPAST	SPAST	Spastin	Spastic paraplegia, hereditary peripheral neuropathies	81405, 81406, 81448
SPG11	SPG11	Spastic paraplegia 11 [autosomal recessive]	Spastic paraplegia, hereditary peripheral neuropathies	81407, 81448
SPG7	SPG7	Spastic paraplegia 7 [pure and complicated autosomal recessive]	Spastic paraplegia	81405, 81406
SPINK1	SPINK1	Serine peptidase inhibitor, Kazal type 1	Hereditary pancreatitis	81404
SPRED1	SPRED1	Sprouty-related, EVH1 domain containing 1	Legius syndrome	81405
SPTBN2	SPTBN2	Spectrin, beta, non-erythrocytic 2	Spinocerebellar ataxia	81407
SPTLC1	SPTLC1	Serine palmitoyltransferase, long chain base subunit 1	Hereditary peripheral neuopathies	81448
SRY	SRY	Sex determining region Y	46,XX testicular disorder of sex development, gonadal dysgenesis	81400
SS18SSX1	SS18/SSX1	t(X;18)	Synovial sarcoma	81401
SS18SSX2	SS18/SSX2	t(X;18)	Synovial sarcoma	81401
STAT3	STAT3	Signal transducer and activator of transcription 3 [acute-phase response factor]	Autosomal dominant hyper-IgE syndrome	81405
STK11	STK11	Serine/threonine kinase 11	Peutz-Jeghers syndrome, hereditary breast cancer-related disordres, hereditary colon cancer disorders	81404, 81405, 81432, 81433, 81435, 81436
STRC	STRC	Stereocilin	Hearing loss	81431

MOLECULAR PATHOLOGY GENE TABLE

Claim Designation	Abbreviated Gene Name	Full Gene Name	Commonly Associated Proteins/Disease	CPT Code(s)
STXBP1	STXBP1	Syntaxin binding protein 1	Epileptic encephalopathy	81406
SUCLA2	SUCLA2	Succinate-CoA ligase ADP-forming beta subunit	Mitochondrial disorders	81440
SUCLG1	SUCLG1	Succinate-CoA ligase alpha subunit	Mitochondrial disordres	81440
SURF1	SURF1	Surfeit 1	Mitochondrial respiratory chain complex IV deficiency	81405
TACO1	TACO1	Translational activator of mitochondrial encoded cytochrome c oxidase I	Mitochondrial respiratory chain complex IV deficiency	81404
TARDBP	TARDBP	TAR DNA binding protein	Amyotrophic lateral sclerosis	81405
TAZ	TAZ	Tafazzin	Methylglutaconic aciduria type 2, Barth syndrome, mitochondrial disordres	81406, 81440
TBP	TBP	TATA box binding protein	Spinocerebellar ataxia	81401
TBX5	TBX5	T-box 5	Holt-Oram syndrome	81405
TCF4	TCF4	Transcription factor 4	Pitt-Hopkins syndrome	81405, 81406
TGFBR1	TGFBR1	Transforming growth factor, beta receptor 1	Marfan syndrome, aortic dysfunction or dilation	81405, 81410, 81411
TGFBR2	TGFBR2	Transforming growth factor, beta receptor 2	Marfan syndrome, aortic dysfunction or dilation	81405, 81410, 81411
TH	TH	Tyrosine hydroxylase	Segawa syndrome	81406
THAP1	THAP1	THAP domain containing, apoptosis associated protein 1	Torsion dystonia	81404
THRB	THRB	Thyroid hormone receptor, beta	Thyroid hormone resistance, thyroid hormone beta receptor deficiency	81405
TK2	TK2	Thymidine kinase 2, mitochondrial	Mitochondrial DNA depletion syndrome, mitochondrial disorders	81405, 81440
TMC1	TMC1	Transmembrane channel-like 1	Hearing loss	81430
TMEM43	TMEM43	Transmembrane protein 43	Arrhythmogenic right ventricular cardiomyopathy	81406
TMEM67	TMEM67	Transmembrane protein 67	Joubert syndrome	81407
TMEM127	TMEM127	Transmembrane protein 127	Hereditary neuroendocrine tumor disorders	81437
TMPRSS3	TMPRSS3	Transmembrane protease, serine 3	Hearing loss	81430
TNNC1	TNNC1	Troponin C type 1 [slow]	Hypertrophic cardiomyopathy or dilated cardiomyopathy	81405
TNNI3	TNNI3	Troponin I, type 3 [cardiac]	Familial hypertrophic cardiomyopathy	81405
TNNT2	TNNT2	Troponin T, type 2 [cardiac]	Familial hypertrophic cardiomyopathy	81406
TOR1A	TOR1A	Torsin family 1, member A [torsin A]	Early-onset primary dystonia [DYT1], torsion dystonia	81400, 81404
TP53	TP53	Tumor protein 53	Tumor samples, Li-Fraumeni syndrome, hereditary breast cancer-related disorders	81404, 81405, 81432
TPM1	TPM1	Tropomyosin 1 [alpha]	Familial hypertrophic cardiomyopathy	81405
TPMT	TPMT	Thiopurine S-methyltransferase	Drug metabolism	81335
	TRB@	T cell antigen receptor, beta	Leukemia and lymphoma	81340, 81341
TRD	TRD@	T cell antigen receptor, delta	Leukemia and lymphoma	81402
	TRG@	T cell antigen receptor, gamma	Leukemia and lymphoma	81342
TRPC6	TRPC6	Transient receptor potential cation channel, subfamily C, member 6	Focal segmental glomerulosclerosis	81406
TSC1	TSC1	Tuberous sclerosis 1	Tuberous sclerosis	81405, 81406
TSC2	TSC2	Tuberous sclerosis 2	Tuberous sclerosis	81406, 81407
TTN	TTN	Titin	Hereditary cardiomyopathy	81439
TTPA	TTPA	Tocopherol [alpha] transfer protein	Ataxia	81404
TTR	TTR	Transthyretin	Familial transthyretin amyloidosis	81404
TWIST1	TWIST1	Twist homolog 1 [Drosophila]	Saethre-Chotzen syndrome	81403, 81404
TYMP	TYMP	Thymidine phosphorylase	Mitochondrial DNA depletion syndrome, mitochondrial disorders	81405, 81440
TYMS	TYMS	Thymidylate synthetase	5-fluorouracil/5-FU drug metabolism	81346
TYR	TYR	Tyrosinase [oculocutaneous albinism IA]	Oculocutaneous albinism IA	81404
UBA1	UBA1	Ubiquitin-like modifier activating enzyme 1	Spinal muscular atrophy, X-linked	81403
UBE3A	UBE3A	Ubiquitin protein ligase E3A	Angelman syndrome	81406

● New Code ▲ Revised Code ✛ Add-On Code ⊘ Modifier -51 Exempt ★ Telemedicine

MOLECULAR PATHOLOGY GENE TABLE

Claim Designation	Abbreviated Gene Name	Full Gene Name	Commonly Associated Proteins/Disease	CPT Code(s)
	UGT1A1	UDP glucurono- syltransferase 1 family, polypeptide A1	Irinotecan metabolism	81350
UMOD	UMOD	Uromodulin	Glomerulocystic kidney disease with hyperuricemia and isosthenuria	81406
UPD	Uniparental disomy	UPD	Russell-Silver syndrome, Prader-Willi/Angelman syndrome	81402
USH1C	USH1C	Usher syndrome 1C [autosomal recessive, severe]	Usher syndrome, type 1, hearing loss	81407, 81430
USH1G	USH1G	Usher syndrome 1G [autosomal recessive]	Usher syndrome, type 1, hearing loss	81404, 81430
USH2A	USH2A	Usher syndrome 2A [autosomal recessive, mild]	Usher syndrome, type 2, hearing loss, hereditary retinal disorders	81408, 81430, 81434
VHL	VHL	Von Hippel-Lindau tumor suppressor	Von Hippel-Lindau familial cancer syndrome, hereditary nueroendocrine tumor disorders	81403, 81404, 81437, 81438
	VKORC1	Vitamin K epoxide reductase complex, subunit 1	Warfarin metabolism	81355
VPS13B	VPS13B	Vacuolar protein sorting 13 homolog B [yeast]	Cohen syndrome	81407, 81408
VWF	VWF	Von Willebrand factor	Von Willebrand disease types 1, 1C, 2A, 2B, 2M, 2N, 3	81401, 81403, 81404 81405, 81406, 81408
WAS	WAS	Wiskott-Aldrich syndrome [eczema-thrombocytopenia]	Wiskott-Aldrich syndrome	81406
WDR62	WDR62	WD repeat domain 62	Primary autosomal recessive microcephaly	81407
WFS1	WFS1	Wolfram syndrome 1	Hearing loss	81430
WT1	WT1	Wilms tumor 1	Denys-Drash syndrome, familial Wilms tumor	81405
ZEB2	ZEB2	Zinc finger E-box binding homeobox 2	Mowat-Wilson syndrome	81404, 81405
ZNF41	ZNF41	Zinc finger protein 41	X-linked mental retardation 89	81404

PATHOLOGY AND LABORATORY CODES

ORGAN OR DISEASE ORIENTED PANELS

CPT codes for organ or disease oriented panels were included in CPT due to the increased use of general screening programs by physicians, clinics, hospitals, and other health care facilities. Other codes in this section define profiles that combine laboratory tests together under a problem oriented classification. There is a list of specific laboratory tests under each of the panel CPT codes which define the components of each panel. However, each laboratory typically establishes its own profile and provides a listing of the components of that panel performed by the laboratory with test results.

The CPT coding system assigns CPT codes to organ or disease oriented panels consisting of a group of specified tests. If all tests of a CPT defined panel are performed, the provider may bill the panel code or the individual component test codes. The panel codes may be used when the tests are ordered as that panel or if the individual component tests of a panel are ordered separately. For example, if the individually ordered tests are cholesterol (CPT code 82465), triglycerides (CPT code 84478), and HDL cholesterol (CPT code 83718), the service could be billed as a lipid panel (CPT code 80061).

These panels were developed for coding purposes only and should not be interpreted as clinical parameters. The tests listed with each panel identify the defined components of that panel.

These panel components are not intended to limit the performance of other tests. If one performs tests in addition to those specifically indicated for a particular panel, those tests should be reported separately in addition to the panel code.

Do not report two or more panel codes that include any of the same constituent tests performed from the same patient collection. If a group of tests overlaps two or more panels, report the panel that incorporates the greater number of tests to fulfill the code definition and report the remaining tests using individual test codes (eg., do not report 80047 in conjunction with 80054).

80047   Basic metabolic panel (Calcium, ionized)

This panel must include the following:
Calcium, ionized (82330)
Carbon dioxide (82374)
Chloride (82435)

Separate Procedure   Unlisted Procedure   CCI Comp. Code   Non-specific Procedure   **691**

Creatinine (82565)
Glucose (82947)
Potassium (84132)
Sodium (84295)
Urea Nitrogen (BUN) (84520)

80048   Basic metabolic panel (Calcium, total)

This panel must include the following:
Calcium, total (82310)
Carbon dioxide (82374)
Chloride (82435)
Creatinine (82565)
Glucose (82947)
Potassium (84132)
Sodium (84295)
Urea Nitrogen (BUN) (84520)

80050   General health panel

This panel must include the following:
Comprehensive metabolic panel (80053)
Blood count, complete (CBC), automated and automated differential WBC count (85025 or 85027 and
    85004)
OR
Blood count, complete (CBC), automated (85027) and appropriate manual differential WBC count (85007
    or 85009)
Thyroid stimulating hormone (TSH) (84443)

80051   Electrolyte panel

This panel must include the following:
Carbon dioxide (82374)
Chloride (82435)
Potassium (84132)
Sodium (84295)

80053   Comprehensive metabolic panel

This panel must include the following:
Albumin (82040)
Bilirubin, total (82247)
Calcium, total (82310)
Carbon dioxide (bicarbonate) (82374)
Chloride (82435)
Creatinine (82565)
Glucose (82947)
Phosphatase, alkaline (84075)
Potassium (84132)
Protein, total (84155)
Sodium (84295)
Transferase, alanine amino (ALT) (SGPT) (84460)
Transferase, aspartate amino (AST) (SGOT) (84450)
Urea Nitrogen (BUN) (84520)

80055   Obstetric panel

This panel must include the following:
Blood count, complete (CBC), automated and automated differential WBC count (85025 or 85027 and
    85004)
OR
Blood count, complete (CBC), automated (85027) and appropriate manual differential WBC count (85007
    or 85009)
Hepatitis B surface antigen (HBsAg) (87340)
Antibody, rubella (86762)

Syphilis test, non-treponemal antibody; qualitative (eg, VDRL, RPR, ART) (86592)
Antibody screen, RBC, each serum technique (86850)
Blood typing, ABO (86900) AND
Blood typing, Rh (D) (86901)

(When syphilis screening is performed using a treponemal antibody approach [86780], do not use 80055. Use the individual codes for the tests performed in the obstetric panel)

80081 Obstetric panel (includes HIV testing)

This panel must include the following:
Blood count, complete (CBC), and automated differential WBC count (85025 or 85207 and 85004)
OR
Blood count, complete (CBC), automated (85027) and appropriate manual differential WBC count (85007 or 85009)
Hepatitis B surface antigen (HBsAg) (87340)
HIV-1 antigen(s), with HIV-1 and HIV-2 antibodies, single result (87389)
Antibody, rubella (86762)
Syphilis test, non-treponemal antibody; qualitative (eg, VDRL, RPR, ART) (86592)
Antibody screen, RBC, each serum technique (86850)
Blood typing, ABO (86900) AND
Blood typing, Rh (D) (86901)

(When syphilis screening is performed using a treponemal antibody approach [86780], do not use 80081. Use the individual codes for the tests performed in the obstetric panel)

80061 Lipid panel

This panel must include the following:
Cholesterol, serum, total (82465)
Lipoprotein, direct measurement, high density cholesterol (HDL cholesterol) (83718)
Triglycerides (84478)

80069 Renal function panel

This panel must include the following:
Albumin (82040)
Calcium, total (82310)
Carbon dioxide (bicarbonate) (82374)
Chloride (82435)
Creatinine (82565)
Glucose (82947)
Phosphorus inorganic (phosphate) (84100)
Potassium (84132)
Sodium (84295)
Urea nitrogen (BUN) (84520)

80074 Acute hepatitis panel

This panel must include the following:
Hepatitis A antibody (HAAb), IgM antibody (86709)
Hepatitis B core antibody (HbcAb), IgM antibody (86705)
Hepatitis B surface antigen (HbsAg) (87340)
Hepatitis C antibody (86803)

80076 Hepatic function panel

This panel must include the following:
Albumin (82040)
Bilirubin, total (82247)
Bilirubin, direct (82248)
Phosphatase, alkaline (84075)
Protein, total (84155)
Transferase, alanine amino (ALT) (SGPT) (84460)
Transferase, aspartate amino (AST) (SGOT) (84450)

80081   Code out of order. See page 693.

DRUG ASSAY

Drug procedures are divided into three subsections: Therapeutic Drug Assay, Drug Assay, and Chemistry – with code selection dependent on the purpose and type of patient results obtained. Therapeutic Drug Assays are performed to monitor clinical response to a known, prescribed medication. The two major categories for drug testing in the drug assay subsection are:

1. **Presumptive drug class** procedures are used to identify possible use or non-use of a drug or drug class. A presumptive test may be followed by a definitive test in order to specifically identify drugs or metabolites.

2. **Definitive drug class** procedures are qualitative or quantitative tests to identify possible use or nonuse of a drug. These tests identify specific drugs and associated metabolites, if performed. A presumptive test is not required prior to a definitive drug test.

The material for drug class procedures may be any specimen type unless otherwise specified in the code descriptor (eg., urine, blood, oral fluid, meconium, hair). Procedures can be qualitative (eg., positive/negative or present/absent), semi quantitative, or quantitative (measured) depending on the purpose of the testing. Therapeutic drug assay (TDA) procedures are typically quantitative tests and the specimen type is whole blood, serum, plasma, and or cerebrospinal fluid.

DEFINITIONS AND ACRONYM CONVERSION LISTING	
Drug Testing Term/Acronym	**Definition**
6-MAM	Acronym for the heroin drug metabolite 6-monacetylmorphine
Acid	Descriptor for classifying drug/drug metabolite molecules based upon chemical ionization properties. Laboratory procedures for drug isolation and identification may include acid, base, or neutral groupings.
AM	A category of synthetic marijuana drugs discovered by and named after Alexandros Makriyannis at Northeastern Univ.
Analog	A structural derivative of a parent chemical compound that often differs from it by a single element.
Analyte	The substance or chemical constituent that is of interest in an analytical procedure.
Base	Descriptor for classifying drug/drug metabolite molecules based upon chemical ionization properties. Laboratory procedures for drug isolation and identification may include acid, base, or neutral groupings.
Card(s)	Multiplexed presumptive drug class(es) immunoassay product that is read by visual observation, including instrumented when performed
Cassette(s)	Multiplexed presumptive drug class immunoassay product(s) that is read by visual observation, including instrumented when performed
CEDIA	Acronym for Cloned-Enzyme-Donor-Immuno-Assay. CEDIA immunoassay is a competitive antibody binding procedure that utilizes enzyme donor fragment-labeled antigens (drugs) to compete for antigens (drugs) contained in the patient sample. Recombination of enzyme donor fragment and enzyme acceptor fragment produces a functional enzyme. CEDIA immunoassay enzyme activity is proportional to concentration of drug(s) detected.
Chromatograpy	An analytical technique used to separate components of a mixture. See thin layer chromatography, gas chromatography, and high performance chromatography.
Confirmatory	Term used to describe definitive identification/quantitation procedures that are secondary to presumptive screening methods.
DART	Acronym for Direct-Analysis-in-Real-Time. DART is an atmospheric pressure ionization method for mass spectrometry analysis.
Definitive Drug Procedure	A procedure that provides specific identification of individual drugs and drug metabolites.
DESI	Acronym for Desorption-ElectroSpray-Ionization. DESI is a combination of electrospray ionization and desorption ionization methods for mass spectrometry analysis.
Dipstick	A multiplexed presumptive drug class immunoassay product that is read by visual observation, including instrumented when performed.
Drug test cup	A multiplexed presumptive drug class immunoassay product that is read by visual observation, including instrumented when performed.
EDDP	Acronum for the methadone drug metabolite 2-ethylidene-1, 5-dimethyl-3, 3-diphenylpyrrolidine
EIA	Acronym for Enzyme-Immuno-Assay. Enzyme immunoassay is a competitive antibody binding procedure that utilizes enzyme-labeled antigens (drugs) to compete for antigens (drugs) contained in the patient sample. Enzyme immunoassay enzyme activity is proportional to concentration of drug(s) detected.
ELISA	Acronym for Enzyme-Linked Immunosorbent Assay. ELISA is a competitive binding immunoassay that is designed to measure antigens (drugs) or antibodies. ELISA immunoassay results are proportional to concentration of drug(s) detected.
EMIT	Acronym for Enzyme-Multiplied-Immunoassay-Test. EMIT is a trade name for a type of enzyme immunoassay (EIA).

● New Code   ▲ Revised Code   ✛ Add-On Code   ⊘ Modifier -51 Exempt   ★ Telemedicine

DEFINITIONS AND ACRONYM CONVERSION LISTING

Drug Testing Term/Acronym	Definition
FPIA	Acronym for Fluorescence-Polarization-Immuno-Assay. FPIA is a competitive binding immunoassay that utilizes fluorexcein-labeled antigens (drugs) to compete for antigens (drugs) contained in the patient sample. The measure of polarized light emission is inversely proportional to the concentration of drug(s) detected.
Gas chromatography	Gas chromatography is a chromatography technique in which patient sample preparations are vaporized into a gas (mobile phase) which flows through a tubular column (containing a stational phase) and into a detector. The retention time of a drug on the column is determined by partitioning characteristics of the drug into the mobile and stationary phases. Chromatography column detectors may be non-specific (eg, flame ionization) or specific (eg, mass spectrometry). The combination of column retention time and specific detector response provides a definitive identification of the drug or drug metabolite.
GC	Acronym for gas chromatography.
GC-MS	Acronym for gas chromatography mass spectrometry.
GC-MS/MS	Acronym for gas chromatography mass spectrometry/mass spectrometry.
High performance liquid chromatography	High performance liquid chromatography is a chromatography technique in which patient sample preparations are injected into a liquid (mobile phase) which flows through a tubular column (containing a stationary phase) and into a detector. The retention time of a drug on the column is determined by partitioning characteristics of the drug into the mobile and stationary phases. Chromatography column detectors may be non-specific (eg, ultra-violet spectrophotometry) or specific (eg, mass spectrometry). The combination of column retention time and specific detector response provides a definitive identification of the drug or drug metabolite. High performance liquid chromatography is also called high pressure liquid chromatography.
HPLC	Acronym for high performance liquid chromatography
HU	A category of synthetic marijuana drugs discovered by and named after Raphael Mechoulam at Hebrew University.
IA	Acronym of immunoassay.
Immunoassay	Antigen-antibody binding procedures utilized to detect antigens (eg, drugs and/or drug metabolites) in patient samples. Immunoassay designs include competitive or non-competitive with various mechanisms for detection.
Isobaric	In mass spectrometry, ions with the same mass
Isomers	Compounds that have the same molecular formula but differ in structural formula
JWH	A category of synthetic marijuana drugs discovered by and named after John W. Huffman at Clemson University.
KIMS	Acronym for kinetic interaction of microparticles in solution. KIMS immunoassay is a competitive antibody binding procedure that utilizes microparticle-labeled antigens (drugs) to compete for antigens (drugs) contained in the patient sample. Microparticle immunoassay absorbance increase is inversely proportional to concentration of drug(s) detected.
LC-MS	Acronym for liquid chromatography mass spectrometry
LC-MS/MS	Acronym for liquid chromatography mass spectrometry/mass spectrometry
LDTD	Acronym for laser diode thermal desorption. LDTD is a combination of atmospheric pressure chemical ionization and laser diode thermal desorption methods for mass spectrometry analysis.
MALDI	Acronym for matrix assisted laser desorption/Ionization mass spectrometry. MALDI is a soft ionization technique that reduces molecular fragmentation.
MDA	Acronym for the drug 3,4-methylenedioxyamphetamine. MDA is also a drug metabolite of MDMA.
MDEA	Acronym for the drug 3,4-methylenedioxy-N-ethylamphetamine
MDMA	Acronym for the drug 3,4-methylenedioxy-N-methylamphetamine
MDPV	Acronym for the drug methylenedioxypyrovalerone
MS	Acronym for mass spectrometry. MS is an identification technique that measures the charge-to-mass ratio of charged particles. There are several types of mass spectrometry instruments, such as magnetic sectoring, time of flight, quadrapole mass filter, ion traps, and Fourier transformation. Mass spectrometry is used as part of the process to assign definitive identification of drugs and drug metabolites.
MS/MS	Acronym for mass spectrometry/mass spectrometry. MS/MS instruments combine multiple units of mass spectrometry filters into a single instrument. MS/MS is also called tandem mass spectrometry.
MS-TOF	Acronym for mass spectrometry time of flight. Time of flight is a mass spectrometry identification technique that utilizes ion velocity to determine the mass-to-charge ratio.
Multiplexed	Descriptor for a multiple component test device that simultaneously measures multiple analytes (drug classes) in a single analysis.
Neutral	Descriptor for classifying drug/drug metabolite molecules based upon chemical ionization properties. Laboratory procedures for drug isolation and identification may include acid, base, or neutral groupings.
ng/mL	Unit of measure for weight per volume calculated as nanograms per milliliter. The ng/mL unit of measure is equivalent to the ug/L unit of measure.
Optical observation	Optical observation refers to procedure results that are interpreted visually with or without instrumentation assistance.

DEFINITIONS AND ACRONYM CONVERSION LISTING

Drug Testing Term/Acronym	Definition
Opiate	Medicinal category of narcotic alkaloid drugs that are natural products in the opium poppy plant Papaver somniferum. This immunoassay class of drugs typically includes detection of codeine, dihydrocodeine, hydrocodone, hydromorphone, and morphine.
Opioids	A category of medicinal synthetic or semi-synthetic narcotic alkaloid opioid receptor stimulating drugs including butorphanol, desomorphine, dextromethorphan, dextrorphan, levorphanol, meperidine, naloxone, naltrexone, normeperidine, and pentazocine.
Presumptive	Drug test results that indicate possible, but not definitive, presence of drugs and or drug metabolites.
QTOF	Acronym for Quadrapole-Time-Of-Flight mass spectrometry. QTOF is a hybrid mass spectrometry identification technique that combines ion velocity with tandem quadrapole mass spectrometry (MS or MS/MS) to determine the mass-to-charge ratio.
RCS	A category of synthetic marijuana drugs that are analogs of JHW compounds. See JWH
RIA	Acronym for radio-immuno-assay. Radioimmunoassay is a competitive antibody binding procedure that utilizes radioactive-labeled antigens (drugs) to compete for antigens (drugs) contained in the patient sample. The measure of radioactivity is inversely proportional to concentration of drug(s) detected.
Stereoisomers	Isomeric molecules that have the same molecular formula and sequence of bonded atoms (constitution), but that differ only in the three-dimensional orientations of their atoms in space.
Substance	A substance is a drug that does not have an established therapeutic use as distinguished from other analytes listed in the Chemistry section (82000-84999)
TDM	Acronym for Therapeutic Drug Monitoring
THC	Acronym for marijuana active drug ingredient tetrahydrocannabinol
Therapeutic Drug Monitoring	Analysis of blood (serum, plasma) drug concentration to monitor clinical response to therapy.
Time of Flight	A mass spectrometry technique that utilizes ion velocity to determine the mass-to-charge ratio.
TLC	Acronym for Thin Layer Chromatography
TOF	Acronym for Time Of Flight
ug/L	Unit of measure for mass per volume calculated as micrograms per liter. The ug/L unit of measure is equivalent to the ng/mL unit of measure.

When the same procedure(s) is performed on more than one specimen type (eg., blood and urine), the appropriate code is reported separately for each specimen type using modifier 59. Drugs or classes of drugs maybe commonly assayed first by a presumptive screening method followed by a definitive drug identification method. Presumptive methods include, but are not limited to, immunoassays (IA, EIA, ELISA, RIA, EMIT, FPIA, etc.), enzymatic methods (alcohol dehydrogenase, etc.), chromatographic methods without mass spectrometry (TLC, HPLC, GC, etc.), or mass spectrometry without adequate drug resolution by chromatography (MS-TOF, DART, DESI, LDTD, MALDI). LC-MS, LC-MS/MS, or mass spectrometry without adequate drug resolution by chromatography may also be used for presumptive testing if the chromatographic phase is not adequate to identify individual drugs and distinguish between structural isomers or isobaric compounds. All drug class immunoassays are considered presumptive, whether qualitative, semi-quantitative, or quantitative. Methods that cannot distinguish between structural isomers (such as morphine and hydromorephone or methamphetamine and phentermine) are also considered presumptive.

Definitive drug identification methods are able to identify individual drugs and distinguish between structural isomers but not necessarily stereoisomers. Definitive methods include, but are not limited to, gas chromatography with mass spectrometry (any type, single or tandem) and liquid chromatography mass spectrometry (any type, single or tandem) and exclude immunoassays (eg., IA, EIA, ELISA, RIA, EMIT, FPIA), and enzymatic methods (eg., alcohol dehydrogenase).

For chromatography, each combination of stationary and mobile phase is to be counted as one procedure.

PRESUMPTIVE DRUG CLASS SCREENING

Drugs or classes of drugs may be commonly assayed first by a presumptive screening method followed by a definitive drug identification method. The methodology is considered when coding presumptive procedures. Each code (80305, 80306, 80307) represents all drugs and drug classes performed by the respective methodology per date of service. Each code also includes all sample validation procedures performed. Examples of sample validation procedures may include, but are not limited to, pH, specific gravity, and nitrite. The codes (80305, 80306, 80307) represent three different method categories:

1. Code 80305 is used to report procedures in which the results are read by direct optical observation. The results are visually read. Examples of these procedures are dipsticks, cups, cards, and cartridges. Report 80305 once, irrespective of the number of direct observation drug class procedures performed or results on any date of service.

2. Code 80306 is used to report procedures when an instrument is used to assist in determining the result of a direct optical observation methodology. Examples of these procedures are dipsticks, cards, and cartridges inserted into an instrument

that determines the final result of an optical observation methodology. Report 80306 once, irrespective of the number of drug class procedures or results on any date of service.

3. Code 80307 is used to report any number of devices or procedures by instrumented chemistry analyzers. There are many different instrumented methodologies available to perform presumptive drug assays. Examples include immunoassay (eg, EIA, ELISA, EMIT, FPIA, IA, KIMS, RIA), chromatography (eg, GC, HPLC), and mass spectrometry, either with or without chromatography (eg, DART, DESI, GC-MS, GC-MS/MS, LC-MS, LC-MS/MS, LDTD, MALDI, TOF). Some of these methodologies may be used for definitive drug testing also, but, for the purpose of presumptive drug testing, the presumptive method is insufficient to provide definitive drug identification. Report 80307 once, irrespective of the number of drug class procedures or results on any date of service.

(**80300** deleted 2016 [2017 edition]. To report, see 80305, 80306, 80307)

(**80301** deleted 2016 [2017 edition]. To report, see 80305, 80306, 80307)

(**80302** deleted 2016 [2017 edition]. To report, see 80305, 80306, 80307)

(**80303** deleted 2016 [2017 edition]. To report, see 80305, 80306, 80307)

(**80304** deleted 2016 [2017 edition]. To report, see 80305, 80306, 80307)

▲ **80305** Drug test(s), presumptive, any number of drug classes, any number of devices or procedures; capable of being read by direct optical observation only (eg, utilizing immunoassay [eg, dipsticks, cups, cards, or cartridges]), includes sample validation when performed, per date of service

▲ **80306** read by instrument assisted direct optical observation (eg, utilizing immunoassay [eg, dipsticks, cups, cards, or cartridges]), includes sample validation when performed, per date of service

▲ **80307** by instrument chemistry analyzers (eg, utilizing immunoassay [eg, EIA, ELISA, EMIT, FPIA, IA, KIMS, RIA]), chromatography (eg, GC, HPLC), and mass spectrometry either with or without chromatography, (eg, DART, DESI, GC-MS, GC-MS/MS, LC-MS, LC-MS/MS, LDTD, MALDI, TOF) includes sample validation when performed, per date of service

DEFINITIVE DRUG TESTING

Definitive drug identification methods are able to identify individual drugs and distinguish between structural isomers but not necessarily stereoisomers. Definitive methods include, but are not limited to, gas chromatography with mass spectrometry, any type, single or tandem and liquid chromatography mass spectrometry, any type, single or tandem, exclude immunoassays (eg., IA, EIA, ELISA, RIA, EMIT, FPIA), and enzymatic methods (e.g. alcohol dehydrogenase).

Use 80320-80377 to eport definitive drug class procedures. Definitive testing maybe qualitative, quantitative, or a combination of qualitative and quantitative for the same patient on the same date of service.

The Definitive Drug Classes Listing provides the drug classes, their associated CPT codes, and the drugs included in each class. Each category of a drug class, including metabolites if performed (except stereoisomers), is reported once per date of service. Metabolites not listed in the table may be reported using the code for the parent drug. Drug class metabolite(s) is not reported separately unless the metabolite(s) is listed as a separate category in Definitive Drug Classes Listing (e.g. heroin metabolite).

Drug classes may contain one or more codes based on the number of analytes. For example, an analysis in which five or more amphetamines and/or amphetamine metabolites would be reported with 80326. The code is based on the number of reported analytes and not the capacity of the analysis.

Definitive drug procedures that are not specified in 80320–80373 should be reported using the unlisted definitive procedure codes 80375, 80376, 80377, unless the specific analyte is listed in the Therapeutic Drug Assays (80150–80203), or Chemistry (82009–84830) sections.

See the Definitive Drug Classes Listing for a listing of the more common analytes within each drug class.

80320 Alcohols

80321 Alcohol biomarkers; 1 or 2

Separate Procedure   Unlisted Procedure   CCI Comp. Code   Non-specific Procedure   **697**

80322	3 or more
80323	Alkaloids, not otherwise specified
80324	Amphetamines; 1 or 2
80325	3 or 4
80326	5 or more
80327	Anabolic steroids; 1 or 2
80328	3 or more
80329	Analgesics, non-opiod; 1 or 2
80330	3-5
80331	6 or more
80332	Antidepressants, serotonergic class; 1 or 2
80333	3-5
80334	6 or more
80335	Antidepressants, tricyclic and other cyclicals; 1 or 2
80336	3-5
80337	6 or more
80338	Antidepressants, not otherwise specified
80339	Antiepileptics, not otherwsie specified; 1-3
80340	4-6
80341	7 or more

(To report definitive drug testing for antihistamines, see 80375, 80376, 80377)

80342	Antipsychotics, not otherwise specified; 1-3
80343	4-6
80344	7 or more
80345	Barbiturates
80346	Benzodiazepines; 1-12
80347	13 or more
80348	Buprenorphine
80349	Cannabinoids, natural
80350	Cannabinoids, synthetic; 1-3

● New Code   ▲ Revised Code   + Add-On Code   ⊘ Modifier -51 Exempt   ★ Telemedicine

80351	4-6
80352	7 or more
80353	Cocaine
80354	Fentanyl
80355	Gabapentin, non-blood
	(For therapeutic drug assay, use 80171)
80356	Heroin metabolite
80357	Ketamine and norketamine
80358	Methadone
80359	Methylenedioxyamphetamines (MDA, MDEA, MDMA)
80360	Methylphenidate
80361	Opiates, 1 or more
80362	Opioids and opiate analogs; 1 or 2
80363	3 or 4
80364	5 or more
80365	Oxycodone
83992	Phencyclidine (PCP)
	(Phenobarbital, use 80345)
80366	Pregabalin
80367	Propoxyphene
80368	Sedative hypnotics (non-benzodiazepines)
80369	Skeletal muscle relaxants; 1 or 2
80370	3 or more
80371	Stimulants, synthetic
80372	Tapentadol
80373	Tramadol
80374	Stereoisomer (enantiomer) analysis; single drug class
	(Use 80374 in conjunction with an index drug analysis when performed)
80375	Drug(s) or substance(s), definitive, qualitative or quantitative, not otherwise specified; 1-3
80376	4-6

| ▇ Separate Procedure | ▇ Unlisted Procedure | ▇ CCI Comp. Code | ▇ Non-specific Procedure | **699** |

80377   7 or more

(To report definitive drug testing for antihistamines, see 80375, 80376, 80377)

For Example:

To report amphetamine and methamphetamine using any number of definitive procedures, report 80324 once per facility per date of service.

To report codeine, hydrocodone, hydromorphone, morphine using any number of definitive procedures, report 80361 once per facility per date of service.

To report codeine, hydrocodone, hydromorphone, morphine, oxycodone, oxymorphone, naloxone, naltrexone performed using any number of definitive procedures, report 80361 x 1, 80362 x 1, and 80365 x 1 per facility per date of service.

DEFINITIVE DRUG CLASSES LISTING

Drugs and metabolites included in each definitive drug class are listed in the Definitive Drug Class Listing. This is not a comprehensive list. FDA classifications of drugs not listed should be used where possible within the defined drug classes. Any metabolites that are not listed should be categorized with the parent drug. Drugs and metabolites not listed may be reported using codes from the Therapeutic Drug Assay (80150-80299) or Chemistry (82009-84999) sections.

DEFINITIVE DRUG CLASSES LISTING		
Codes	**Classes**	**Drugs**
80320	Alcohol(s)	Acetone, ethanol, ethchlorvynol, ethylene glycol, isopropanol, isopropyl alcohol, methanol
80321-80322	Alcohol Biomarker	Ethanol conjugates (ethyl glucuronid [ETG], ethyl sulfate [ETS], fatty acid ethyl esters, phosphatidylethanol)
80323	Alkaloids, not otherwise specified	7-Hydroxymitragynine, atropine, cotinine, lysergic acid diethylamoide
80324-80326	Amphetamines	Amphetamine, ephedrinelisdexamphetamine, methamphetamine, phentermine, phenylpropanolamine, pseudoephedrine
80327-80328	Anabolic steroids	1-Androstenediol, 1-androstenedione, 1-testosterone, 4-hydroxy-testosterone, 6-oxo, 19-norandrostenedione, androstenedione, androstanolone, bolandiol, bolasterone, boldenone, boldione, calusterone, clostebol, danazol, dehydrochlormethyltestosterone, dihydrotestosterone, drostanolone, epiandrosterone, epitestosterone, fluoxymesterone, furazabol, mestanolone, mesterolone, methandienone, methandriol, methenolone, methydienolone, methyl-1-testosterone, methylnortestosterone, methyltestosterone, mibolerone, nandrolone, norbolethone, norclostebol, norethandrolone, norethindrone, oxabolone, oxandrolone, oxymesterone, oxymetholone, stanozolol, stenbolone, tibolone, trenbolone, zeranol
80329-80331	Analgesics, non-opioid	Acetaminophen, diclofenac ibuprofen, ketoprofen, naproxen, oxaprozin, salicylate
80332-80334	Antidepressants, serotonergic class	Citalopram, duloxetine, escitalopram, fluoxetine, fluvoxamine, paroxetine, sertraline
80335-80337	Antidepressants, tricyclic and other cyclicals	Amitriptyline, amoxapine, clomipramine, demexiptiline, desipramine, doxepin, imipramine, maprotiline, mirtazpine, nortriptyline, protriptyline
80338	Antidepressants, not otherwise specified	Bupropion, desyenlafaxine, isocarboxazid, nefazodone, phenelzine, selegiline, tranylcypromine, trazodone, venlafaxine
80339-80341	Antiepileptics, not otherwise specified	Carbamazepine, clobazam, diamethadione, ethosuximide, ezogabine, lamotrigine, levetiracetam, methsuximide, oxcarbazepine, phenytoin, primidone, rufinamide, tiagabine, topiramate, trimethadione, valproic acid, zonisamide
80342-80344	Antipsychotics, not otherwise specified	Aripiprazole, chlorpromazine, clozapine, fluphenazine, haloperidol, loxapine, mesoridazine, molindone, olanzapine, paliperidone, perphenazine, phenothiazine, pimozide, prochlorperazine, quetiapine, risperidone, trifluoperazine, thiothixene, thoridazine, ziprasidone
80345	Barbiturates	Amobarbital, aprobarbital, butalbital, cyclobarbital, mephobarbital, pentobarbital, phenobarbital, secobarbital, talbutal, thiopental
80346, 80347	Benzodiazepines	Alprazolam, chlordiazepoxide, clonazepam, clorazepate, diazepam, estazolam, flunitrazepam, flurazepam, halazepamlorazepammidazolam, nitrazepam, nordazepam, oxazepam, prazepam, quazepam, temazepam
80348	Buprenorphine	Buprenorphine
80349	Cannabinoids, natural	Marijuana, dronabinol carboxy-THC

● New Code   ▲ Revised Code   ✚ Add-On Code   ⊘ Modifier -51 Exempt   ★ Telemedicine

DEFINITIVE DRUG CLASSES LISTING

Codes	Classes	Drugs
80350-80352	Cannabinoids, synth.	CP-47, 497, CP497 C8-homolog, JWH-018 and AM678, JWH-073, JWH-019, JWH-200, JWH-210, JWH-250, JWH-081, JWH-122, HWH-398, AM-2201, AM-694, SR-19 and RCS-4, SR-18 and RCS-8, JWH-203, UR-144, XLR-11, MAM-2201, AKB-48
80353	Cocaine	Benzoylecgonine, cocaethylene, cocaine, ecgonine methyl ester, norcocaine
80354	Fentanyls	Acetylfentanyl, alfentanil, fentanyl, remifentanil, sufentanil
80355	Gabapentin, non-blood	Gabapentin
80356	Heroin metabolite	6-acetylmorphine, acetylcodeine, diacetylmorphine
80368	Hypnotics, sedative (non-benzodiazepine)	See Sedative Hypnotics
80357	Ketamine and Norketamine	Ketamine, norketamine
80358	Methadone	Methadone and EDDP
80359	Methylenedioxy-amphetamines	MDA, MDEA, MDMA
80360	Methylphenidate	Methylphenidate, ritalinic acid
80357	Norketamine	See Ketamine
80368	Non-Benzodiazepine	See Hypnotics, sedative
80361	Opiates	Codeine, dihydrocodeine, hydrocodone, hydromorphone, morphine
80362-80364	Opiods and opiate analogs	Butorphanol, desomorphine, dextromethorphan, dextrorphan, levorphanol, meperidine, naloxone, naltrexone, normeperidine, pentazocine
80365	Oxycodone	Oxycodone, oxymorphone
83992	Phencyclidine	Phencyclidine
80366	Pregabalin	Pregabalin
80367	Propoxyphene	Norpropoxyphene, propoxyphene
80368	Sedative hypnotics (non-benzodiazepine)	Eszopiclone, zaleplon, zolpidem
80369, 80370	Skeletal muscle relaxants	Baclofen, carisoprodol, cyclobenzaprine, meprobamate, metaxalone, methocarbamol, orphenadrine, tizanidide
80371	Stimulants, synthetic	2C-B, 2C-E, 2C-I, 2C-H, 3TFMPP, 4-methylethcathinone, alpha-PVP, benzylpiperazine, bromodragonfly, cathinone, m-CPP, MDPBP, MDPPP, MDPV, mephedrone, methcathinone, methylone, phenethylamines, salvinorin, tryptamines
80372	Tapentadol	Tapentadol
80373	Tramadol	Tramadol

THERAPEUTIC DRUG ASSAYS

Therapeutic Drug Assays are performed to monitor clinical response to a known, prescribed medication. The material for examination is whole blood, serum, plasma, or cerebrospinal fluid. Examination is quantitative. Coding is by parent drug; measured metabolites of the drug are included in the code, if performed..

80150   Amikacin

(**80152**   deleted 2014 [2015 edition]. To report definitive drug testing for amitryptyline, see 80335, 80336, 80337)

(**80154**   deleted 2014 [2015 edition]. To report definitive drug testing for benzodiazepines, see 80346, 80347)

80155   Caffeine

80156   Carbamazepine; total

80157   free

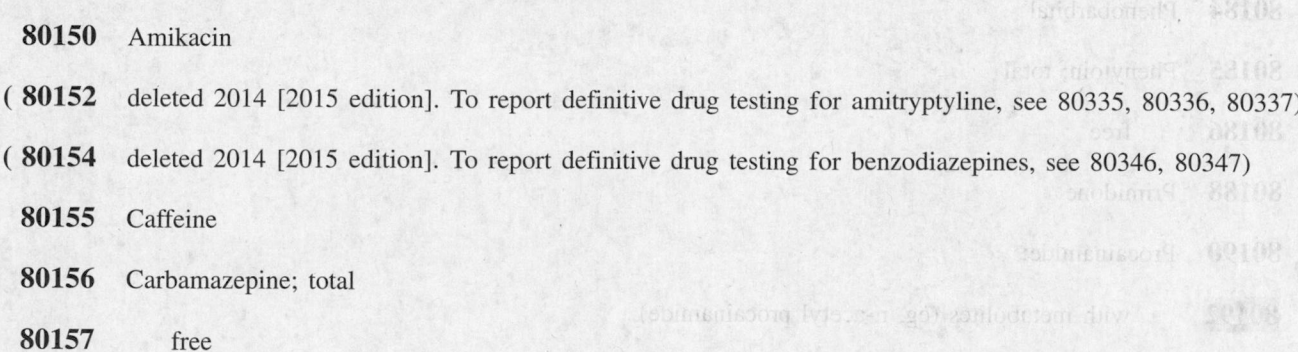

80158	Cyclosporine
80159	Clozapine
(80160	deleted 2014 [2015 edition]. To report definitive drug testing for desipramine, see 80335, 80336, 80337)
80162	Digoxin; total
80163	free
80164	This code is out of order. See page 703.
80165	This code is out of order. See page 703.
(80166	deleted 2014 [2015 edition]. To report definitive drug testing for doxepin, see 80335, 80336, 80337)
80168	Ethosuximide
80169	Everolimus
80171	Gabapentin, whole blood, serum, or plasma
80170	Gentamicin
80171	This code is out of order. See page 702.
(80172	deleted 2014 [2015 edition]. To report definitive drug testing for gold, use 80375)
80173	Haloperidol
(80174	deleted 2014 [2015 edition]. To report testing for imipramine, use 80335, 80336, 80337)
80175	Lamotrigine
80176	Lidocaine
80177	Levetiracetam
80178	Lithium
80180	Mycophenolate (mycophenolic acid)
(80182	deleted 2014 [2015 edition]. To report definitive drug testing for nortriptyline, use 80335, 80336, 80337)
80183	Oxcarbazepine
80184	Phenobarbital
80185	Phenytoin; total
80186	free
80188	Primidone
80190	Procainamide;
80192	with metabolites (eg, n-acetyl procainamide)
80194	Quinidine

● New Code   ▲ Revised Code   ✛ Add-On Code   ⊘ Modifier -51 Exempt   ★ Telemedicine

80195 Sirolimus

(80196 deleted 2014 [2015 edition]. To report definitive drug testing for salicylate, use 80329, 80330, 80331)

80197 Tacrolimus

80198 Theophylline

80199 Tiagabine

80200 Tobramycin

80201 Topiramate

80164 Valproic acid (dipropylacetic acid); total

80165   free

80202 Vancomycin

80203 Zonisamide

80299 Quantitation of therapeutic drug, not elsewhere specified

80305 This code is out of order. See Drug Assay, page 697.

80306 This code is out of order. See Drug Assay, page 697.

80307 This code is out of order. See Drug Assay, page 697.

80320 This code is out of order. See Drug Assay, page 697.

80321 This code is out of order. See Drug Assay, page 697.

80322 This code is out of order. See Drug Assay, page 698.

80323 This code is out of order. See Drug Assay, page 698.

80324 This code is out of order. See Drug Assay, page 698.

80325 This code is out of order. See Drug Assay, page 698.

80326 This code is out of order. See Drug Assay, page 698.

80327 This code is out of order. See Drug Assay, page 698.

80328 This code is out of order. See Drug Assay, page 698.

80329 This code is out of order. See Drug Assay, page 698.

80330 This code is out of order. See Drug Assay, page 698.

80331 This code is out of order. See Drug Assay, page 698.

80332 This code is out of order. See Drug Assay, page 698.

80333 This code is out of order. See Drug Assay, page 698.

80334   This code is out of order. See Drug Assay, page 698.

80335   This code is out of order. See Drug Assay, page 698.

80336   This code is out of order. See Drug Assay, page 698.

80337   This code is out of order. See Drug Assay, page 698..

80338   This code is out of order. See Drug Assay, page 698..

80339   This code is out of order. See Drug Assay, page 698..

80340   This code is out of order. See Drug Assay, page 698.

80341   This code is out of order. See Drug Assay, page 698..

80342   This code is out of order. See Drug Assay, page 698..

80343   This code is out of order. See Drug Assay, page 698..

80344   This code is out of order. See Drug Assay, page 698.

80345   This code is out of order. See Drug Assay, page 698.

80346   This code is out of order. See Drug Assay, page 698.

80347   This code is out of order. See Drug Assay, page 698.

80348   This code is out of order. See Drug Assay, page 698.

80349   This code is out of order. See Drug Assay, page 698.

80350   This code is out of order. See Drug Assay, page 698.

80351   This code is out of order. See Drug Assay, page 699.

80352   This code is out of order. See Drug Assay, page 699.

80353   This code is out of order. See Drug Assay, page 699.

80354   This code is out of order. See Drug Assay, page 699.

80355   This code is out of order. See Drug Assay, page 699.

80356   This code is out of order. See Drug Assay, page 699.

80357   This code is out of order. See Drug Assay, page 699.

80358   This code is out of order. See Drug Assay, page 699.

80359   This code is out of order. See Drug Assay, page 699.

80360   This code is out of order. See Drug Assay, page 699.

80361   This code is out of order. See Drug Assay, page 699.

80362   This code is out of order. See Drug Assay, page 699.

80363 This code is out of order. See Drug Assay, page 699.

80364 This code is out of order. See Drug Assay, page 699.

80365 This code is out of order. See Drug Assay, page 699.

80366 This code is out of order. See Drug Assay, page 699.

80367 This code is out of order. See Drug Assay, page 699.

80368 This code is out of order. See Drug Assay, page 699.

80369 This code is out of order. See Drug Assay, page 699.

80370 This code is out of order. See Drug Assay, page 699.

80371 This code is out of order. See Drug Assay, page 699.

80372 This code is out of order. See Drug Assay, page 699.

80373 This code is out of order. See Drug Assay, page 699.

80374 This code is out of order. See Drug Assay, page 699.

80375 This code is out of order. See Drug Assay, page 699.

80376 This code is out of order. See Drug Assay, page 699.

80377 This code is out of order. See Drug Assay, page 700.

EVOCATIVE/SUPPRESSION TESTING

Evocative/suppression testing involves administration of agents to determine a patient's response to those agents. CPT codes 80400-80440 are to be used for reporting the laboratory components of the testing. When the test requires physician administration of the evocative/suppression agent, see codes 96390, 96361, 96372-96374, 96375. However, when physician attendance is not required, and the agent is administered by ancillary personnel, these codes are not to be separately reported.

In the inpatient setting, these codes are only reported if the physician performs the service personally. In the office setting, the service can be reported when performed by office personnel if the physician is directly supervising the service. While supplies necessary to perform the testing are included in the testing, the appropriate HCPCS J codes for the drugs can be separately reported for the diagnostic agents. Separate evaluation and management services are not to be reported, including prolonged services (in the case of prolonged infusions) unless a significant, separately identifiable service is provided and documented.

The following test panels involve the administration of evocative or suppressive agents, and the baseline and subsequent measurement of their effects on chemical constituents. These codes are to be used for the reporting of the laboratory component of the overall testing protocol. For the administration of the evocative or suppressive agents, see Hydration, Therapeutic, Prophylactic, Diagnostic Injections and Infusions, and Chemotherapy and Other Highly Complex drug or Highly Complex Biologic Agent Administration (eg, 96365, 96366, 96367, 96368, 96372, 96374, 96375, 96376). In the code descriptors where reference is made to a particular analyte (eg., Cortisol: 82533 x 2) the "x 2" refers to the number of times the test for that particular analyte is performed.

80400 ACTH stimulation panel; for adrenal insufficiency

This panel must include the following:
Cortisol (82533 x 2)

80402 for 21 hydroxylase deficiency

This panel must include the following:
Cortisol (82533 x 2)

---

17 hydroxyprogesterone (83498 x 2)

80406   for 3 beta-hydroxydehydrogenase deficiency

This panel must include the following:
Cortisol (82533 x 2)
17 hydroxypregnenolone (84143 x 2)

80408 Aldosterone suppression evaluation panel (eg, saline infusion)

This panel must include the following:
Aldosterone (82088 x 2)
Renin (84244 x 2)

80410 Calcitonin stimulation panel (eg, calcium, pentagastrin)

This panel must include the following:
Calcitonin (82308 x 3)

80412 Corticotropic releasing hormone (CRH) stimulation panel

This panel must include the following:
Cortisol (82533 x 6)
Adrenocorticotropic hormone (ACTH) (82024 x 6)

80414 Chorionic gonadotropin stimulation panel; testosterone response.

This panel must include the following:
Testosterone (84403 x 2 on three pooled blood samples)

80415   estradiol response.

This panel must include the following:
Estradiol (82670 x 2 on three pooled blood samples)

80416 Renal vein renin stimulation panel (eg, captopril)

This panel must include the following:
Renin (84244 x 6)

80417 Peripheral vein renin stimulation panel (eg, captopril)

This panel must include the following:
Renin (84244 x 2)

80418 Combined rapid anterior pituitary evaluation panel

This panel must include the following:
Adrenocorticotropic hormone (ACTH) (82024 x 4)
Luteinizing hormone (LH) (83002 x 4)
Follicle stimulating hormone (FSH) (83001 x 4)
Prolactin (84146 x 4)
Human growth hormone (HGH)(83003 x 4)
Cortisol (82533 x 4)
Thyroid stimulating hormone (TSH) (84443 x 4)

80420 Dexamethasone suppression panel, 48 hour

This panel must include the following:
Free cortisol, urine (82530 x 2)
Cortisol (82533 x 2)
Volume measurement for timed collection (81050 x 2)

(For single dose dexamethasone, use 82533)

80422 Glucagon tolerance panel; for insulinoma

This panel must include the following:
Glucose (82947 x 3)
Insulin (83525 x 3)

80424 for pheochromocytoma.

This panel must include the following:
Catecholamines, fractionated (82384 x 2)

80426 Gonadotropin releasing hormone stimulation panel

This panel must include the following:
Follicle stimulating hormone (FSH) (83001 x 4)
Luteinizing hormone (LH)(83002 x 4)

80428 Growth hormone stimulation panel (eg, arginine infusion, l-dopa administration)

This panel must include the following:
Human growth hormone (HGH)(83003 x 4)

80430 Growth hormone suppression panel (glucose administration)

This panel must include the following:
Glucose (82947 x 3)
Human growth hormone (HGH)(83003 x 4)

80432 Insulin-induced C-peptide suppression panel

This panel must include the following:
Insulin (83525)
C-peptide (84681 x 5)
Glucose (82947 x 5)

80434 Insulin tolerance panel; for ACTH insufficiency

This panel must include the following:
Cortisol (82533 x 5)
Glucose (82947 x 5)

80435 for growth hormone deficiency

This panel must include the following:
Glucose (82947 x 5)
Human growth hormone (HGH) (83003 x 5)

80436 Metyrapone panel

This panel must include the following:
Cortisol (82533 x 2)
11 deoxycortisol (82634 x 2)

80438 Thyrotropin releasing hormone (TRH) stimulation panel; 1 hour

This panel must include the following:
Thyroid stimulating hormone (TSH) (84443 x 3)

80439 2 hour

This panel must include the following:
Thyroid stimulating hormone (TSH) (84443 x 4)

(**80440** deleted 2014 [2015 edition]. For prolactin, use 84146)

Separate Procedure   Unlisted Procedure   CCI Comp. Code   Non-specific Procedure   **707**

CONSULTATIONS (CLINICAL PATHOLOGY)

A clinical pathology consultation is a service, including a written report, rendered by the pathologist in response to a request from a physicia nor qualified health care professional in relation to a test result(s) requiring additional medical interpretive judgment. Reporting of a test result(s) without medical interpretive judgment is not considered a clinical pathology consultation.

80500 Clinical pathology consultation; limited, without review of patients history and medical records

80502 comprehensive, for a complex diagnostic problem, with review of patients history and medical records

(These codes may also be used for pharmacokinetic consultations)

(For consultations involving the examination and evaluation of the patient, see 99241-99275)

URINALYSIS

For specific analyses, see appropriate section.

81000 Urinalysis, by dip stick or tablet reagent for bilirubin, glucose, hemoglobin, ketones, leukocytes, nitrite, pH, protein, specific gravity,urobilinogen, any number of these constituents; non-automated, with microscopy

81001 automated, with microscopy

81002 non-automated, without microscopy

81003 automated, without microscopy

81005 Urinalysis; qualitative or semiquantitative, except immunoassays

(For non-immunoassay reagent strip urinalysis, see 81000, 81002)

(For immunoassay, qualitative or semiquantitative, use 83518)

(For microalbumin, see 82043, 82044)

81007 bacteriuria screen, except by culture or dipstick

(For culture, see 87086-87088)

(For dipstick, use 81000 or 81002)

81015 microscopic only

(For sperm evaluation for retrograde ejaculation, use 89331)

81020 2 or 3 glass test

81025 Urine pregnancy test, by visual color comparison methods

81050 Volume measurement for timed collection, each

81099 Unlisted urinalysis procedure

MOLECULAR PATHOLOGY

Molecular pathology procedures are medical laboratory procedures involving the analyses of nucleic acid (ie, DNA, RNA) to detect variants in genes that may be indicative of germline (eg, constitutional disorders) or somatic (eg, neoplasia) conditions, or to test for histocompatibility antigens (eg, HLA). Code selection is typically based on the specific gene(s) that is being analyzed. Genes are described using Human Genome Organization (HUGO) approved gene names and are italicized in the code descriptors. Gene names were taken from tables of the HUGO Gene Nomenclature Committee (HGNC) at the time the CPT

● New Code   ▲ Revised Code   + Add-On Code   ⊘ Modifier -51 Exempt   ★ Telemedicine

codes were developed. For the most part, Human Genome Variation Society (HGVS) recommendations were followed for the names of specific molecular variants. The familiar name is used for some variants because defined criteria were not in place when the variant was first described or because HGVS recommendations were changed over time (eg, intronic variants, processed proteins). When the gene name is represented by an abbreviation, the abbreviation is listed first, followed by the full gene name italicized in parentheses (eg, "F5 [coagulation Factor V]"), except for the HLA series of codes. Proteins or diseases commonly associated with the genes are listed as examples in the code descriptors. The examples do not represent all conditions in which testing of the gene may be indicated

Codes that describe tests to assess for the presence of gene variants use common gene variant names. Typically, all of the listed variants would be tested. However, these lists are not exclusive. If other variants are also tested in the analysis, they would be included in the procedure and not reported separately. Full gene sequencing should not be reported using codes that assess for the presence of gene variants unless specifically stated in the code descriptor.

The molecular pathology codes include all analytical services performed in the test (eg, cell lysis, nucleic acid stabilization, extraction, digestion, amplification, and detection). Any procedures required prior to cell lysis (eg, microdissection, codes 88380 and 88381) should be reported separately.

The results of the procedure may require interpretation by a physician or other qualified health care professional. When only the interpretation and report are performed, modifier 26 may be appended to the specific molecular pathology code.

All analyses are qualitative unless otherwise noted.

For microbial identification, see 87149-87153 and 87471-87801, and 87900-87904. For in situ hybridization analyses, see 88271-88275 and 88365-88368.

Molecular pathology procedures that are not specified in 81200-81383 should be reported using either the appropriate Tier 2 code (81400-81408) or the unlisted molecular pathology procedure code, 81479.

TIER 1 MOLECULAR PATHOLOGY PROCEDURES

The following codes represent gene-specific and genomic procedures.

81105 This code is out of order. See page 713.

81106 This code is out of order. See page 713.

81107 This code is out of order. See page 713.

81108 This code is out of order. See page 713.

81109 This code is out of order. See page 713.

81110 This code is out of order. See page 713.

81111 This code is out of order. See page 713.

81112 This code is out of order. See page 713.

81120 This code is out of order. See page 713.

81121 This code is out of order. See page 713.

81161 This code is out of order. See page 711.

81162 This code is out of order. See page 710.

81170 ABL1 (ABL proto-oncogene 1, non-receptor tyrosine kinase) (eg, acquired imatinib tyrosine kinase inhibitor resistance), gene analysis, variants in the kinase domain

● **81175** ASXL1 (additional sex combs like 1, transcriptional regulator) (eg, myelodysplastic syndrome, myeloproliferative neoplasms, chronic myelomonocytic leukemia), gene analysis; full gene sequence

| Separate Procedure | Unlisted Procedure | CCI Comp. Code | Non-specific Procedure | **709** |

● **81176**   targeted sequence analysis (eg, exon 12)

81200   *ASPA (aspartoacylase)* (eg, Canavan disease) gene analysis, common variants (eg, E285A, Y231X)

81201   *APC (adenomatous polyposis coli)* (eg, familial adenomatosis polyposis [FAP], attenuated FAP) gene analysis; full gene sequence

81202   known familiar variants

81203   duplication/deletion variants

81205   *BCKDHB (branched-chain keto acid dehydrogenase E1, beta polypeptide)* (eg, Maple syrup urine disease) gene analysis, common variants (eg, R183P, G278S, E422X)

81206   *BCR/ABL1 (t(9;22))* (eg, chronic myelogenous leukemia) translocation analysis; major breakpoint, qualitative or quantitative

81207   minor breakpoint, qualitative or quantitative

81208   other breakpoint, qualitative or quantitative

81209   *BLM (Bloom syndrome, RecQ helicase-like)* (eg, Bloom syndrome) gene analysis, 2281del6ins7 variant

81210   *BRAF (B-Raf proto-oncogene, serine/threonine kinase)* (eg, colon cancer), gene analysis, V600 variant*(s)*

81211   *BRCA1, BRCA2 (breast cancer 1 and 2)* (eg, hereditary breast and ovarian cancer) gene analysis; full sequence analysis and common duplication/deletion variants in BRCA1 (ie, exon 13 del 3.835kb, exon 13 dup 6kb, exon 14-20 del 26kb, exon 22 del 510bp, exon 8-9 del 7.1kb)

(Do not report 81211 in conjunction with 81162)

81162   full sequence analysis and full duplication/deletion analysis

(Do not report 81162 in conjunction with 81211, 81213, 81214, 81216)

81212   185delAG, 5385insC, 6174delT variants

81213   uncommon duplication/deletion variants

(Do not report 81213 in conjunction with 81162)

81214   *BRCA1 (breast cancer 1)* (eg, hereditary breast and ovarian cancer) gene analysis; full sequence analysis and common duplication/deletion variants (ie, exon 13 del 3.835kb, exon 13 dup 6kb, exon 14-20 del 26kb, exon 22 del 510bp, exon 8-9 del 7.1kb)

(When performing *BRCA1* full sequence analysis with *BRCA2* full sequence analysis, see 81162, 81211)

(Do not report 81214 in conjunction with 81162)

81215   known familial variant

81216   *BRCA2 (breast cancer 2)* (eg, hereditary breast and ovarian cancer) gene analysis; full sequence analysis

(When performing *BRCA2* full sequence analysis with *BRCA1* full sequence analysis, see 81162, 81211)

(Do not report 81216 in conjunction with 81162)

81217   known familial variant

81218   *CEBPA (CCAAT/enhancer binding protein [C/EBP], alpha)* (eg, acute myeloid leukemia), gene analysis, full gene sequence

81219   *CALR (calreticulin)* (eg, myeloproliferative disorders), gene analysis, common variants in exon 9

● New Code   ▲ Revised Code   ✛ Add-On Code   ⊘ Modifier -51 Exempt   ★ Telemedicine

81220   CFTR (cystic fibrosis transmembrane conductance regulator) (eg, cystic fibrosis) gene analysis; common variants (eg, ACMG/ACOG guidelines)

(When Intron 8 poly-T analysis is performed in conjunction with 81220 in a R117H positive patient, do not report 81224)

81221   known familial variants

81222   duplication/deletion variants

81223   full gene sequence

81224   intron 8 poly-T analysis (eg, male infertility)

81225   *CYP2C19 (cytochrome P450, family 2, subfamily C, polypeptide 19)* (eg, drug metabolism), gene analysis, common variants (eg, *2, *3, *4, *8, *17)

81226   *CYP2D6 (cytochrome P450, family 2, subfamily D, polypeptide 6)* (eg, drug metabolism), gene analysis, common variants (eg, *2, *3, *4, *5, *6, *9, *10, *17, *19, *29, *35, *41, *1XN, *2XN, *4XN)

81227   *CYP2C9 (cytochrome P450, family 2, subfamily C, polypeptide 9)* (eg, drug metabolism), gene analysis, common variants (eg, *2, *3, *5, *6)

● **81230**   *CYP3A4 (cytochrome P450 family 3 subfamily A member 4)* (eg, drug metabolism), gene analysis, common variant(s) (eg, *2, *22)

● **81231**   *CYP3A5 (cytochrome P450 family 3 subfamily A member 5)* (eg, drug metabolism), gene analysis, common variants (eg, *2, *3, *4, *5, *6, *7)

81228   Cytogenomic constitutional (genome-wide) microarray analysis; interrogation of genomic regions for copy number variants (eg, Bacterial Artificial Chromosome [BAC] or oligo-based comparative genomic hybridization [CGH] microarray analysis)

81229   interrogation of genomic regions for copy number and single nucleotide polymorphism (SNP) variants for chromosomal abnormalities

(Do not report 81228 in conjunction with 81229)

(When performing cytogenomic constitutional microarray analysis that is not genome-wide [ie, regionally targeted], report the specific code for the targeted analysis if available [eg, 81405] or the unlisted molecular pathology code [81479])

(Do not report analyte-specific molecular pathology procedures separately in conjunction with 81228, 81229 when the specific analytes are included as part of the microarray analysis)

(Do not report 88271 when performing cytogenomic microarray analysis)

(For genomic sequencing procedures or other molecular multianalyte assays for copy number analysis using circulating cell-free fetal DNA in maternal blood, see 81420, 81422, 81479)

81230   This code is out of order. See page 711.

81231   This code is out of order. See page 711.

81161   *DMD (dystrophin)* (eg, Duchene/Becker muscular dystrophy) deletion analysis, and duplication analysis, if performed

● **81232**   *DPYD (dihydropyrimidine dehydrogenase)* (eg, 5-fluorouracil/5-FU and capecitabine drug metabolism), gene analysis, common variant(s) (eg, *2A, *4, *5, *6)

81235   *EGFR (epidermal growth factor receptor)* (eg, non-small cell lunch cancer) gene analysis, common variants (eg, exon 19 LREA deletion, L858R, T790M, G719A, G719S, L861Q)

81238   This code is out of order. See page 712.

■ Separate Procedure   ■ Unlisted Procedure   ■ CCI Comp. Code   ■ Non-specific Procedure   **711**

81240   *F2 (prothrombin, coagulation factor II)* (eg, hereditary hypercoagulability) gene analysis, 20210G>A variant

81241   *F5 (coagulation Factor V)* (eg, hereditary hypercoagulability) gene analysis, Leiden variant

● **81238**   *F9 (coagulation factor IX)* (eg, hemophilia B), full gene sequence

81242   *FANCC (Fanconi anemia, complementation group C)* (eg, Fanconi anemia, type C) gene analysis, common variant (eg, IVS4+4A>T)

81243   *FMR1 (Fragile X mental retardation 1)* (eg, fragile X mental retardation) gene analysis; evaluation to detect abnormal (eg, expanded) alleles

       (For evaluation to detect and characterize abnormal alleles, see 81243, 81244)

       (For evaluation to detect and characterize abnormal alleles using a single assay [eg, PCR], use 81243)

81244   characterization of alleles (eg, expanded size and methylation status)

81245   *FLT3 (fms-related tyrosine kinase 3)* (eg, acute myeloid leukemia), gene analysis; internal tandem duplication (ITD) variants (ie, exons 14, 15)

81246   tyrosine kinase domain (TKD) variants (eg., D835, I836)

● **81247**   *G6PD (glucose-6-phosphate dehydrogenase)* (eg, hemolytic anemia, jaundice), gene analysis; common variant(s) (eg, A, A-)

● **81248**   known familial variant(s)

● **81249**   full gene sequence

81250   *G6PC (glucose-6-phosphatase, catalytic subunit)* (eg, Glycogen storage disease, Type 1a, von Gierke disease) gene analysis, common variants (eg, R83C, Q347X)

81251   *GBA (glucosidase, beta, acid)* (eg, Gaucher disease) gene analysis, common variants (eg, N370S, 84GG, L444P, IVS2+1G>A)

81252   *GJB2 (gap junction protein, beta 2, 26kDa; connexin 26)* (eg, nonsyndromic hearing loss) gene analysis; full gene sequence

81253   known familial variants

81254   *GJB6 (gap junction protein, beta 6, 30kDa, connexin 30)* (eg, nonsyndromic hearing loss) gene analysis, common variants (eg, 309kb [del(GJB6-D13S1830)] and 232kb [del(GJB6-D13S1854)])

81255   *HEXA (hexosaminidase A [alpha polypeptide])* (eg, Tay-Sachs disease) gene analysis, common variants (eg, 1278insTATC, 1421+1G>C, G269S)

81256   *HFE (hemochromatosis)* (eg, hereditary hemochromatosis) gene analysis, common variants (eg, C282Y, H63D)

▲ **81257**   *HBA1/HBA2 (alpha globin 1 and alpha globin 2)* (eg, alpha thalassemia, Hb Bart hydrops fetalis syndrome, HbH disease), gene analysis; common deletions or variant (eg, Southeast Asian, Thai, Filipino, Mediterranean, alpha3.7, alpha4.2, alpha20.5, Constant Spring)

● **81258**   known familial variant

● **81259**   full gene sequence

● **81269**   duplication/deletion variants

   ● New Code   ▲ Revised Code   ✛ Add-On Code   ⊘ Modifier -51 Exempt   ★ Telemedicine

● **81105**   *Human Platelet Antigen 1 genotyping (HPA-1), ITGB3(integrin, beta 3 [platelet glycoprotein IIIa], antigen CD61 [GPIIIa])* (eg, neonatal alloimmune thrombocytopenia [NAIT], post-transfusion purpura), gene analysis, common variant, HPA-1a/b (L33P)

● **81106**   *Human Platelet Antigen 2 genotyping (HPA-2), GP1BA (glycoprotein Ib [platelet], alpha polypeptide [GPIba])* (eg, neonatal alloimmune thrombocytopenia [NAIT], posttransfusion purpura), gene analysis, common variant, HPA-2a/b (T145M)

● **81107**   *Human Platelet Antigen 3 genotyping (HPA-3), ITGA2B (integrin, alpha 2b [platelet glycoprotein IIb of IIb/IIIa complex], antigen CD41 [GPIIb])* (eg, neonatal alloimmune thrombocytopenia [NAIT], post-transfusion purpura), gene analysis, common variant, HPA-3a/b (I843S)

● **81108**   *Human Platelet Antigen 4 genotyping (HPA-4), ITGB3 (integrin, beta 3 [platelet glycoprotein IIIa], antigen CD61 [GPIIIa])* (eg, neonatal alloimmune thrombocytopenia [NAIT], post-transfusion purpura), gene analysis, common variant, HPA-4a/b (R143Q)

● **81109**   *Human Platelet Antigen 5 genotyping (HPA-5), ITGA2 (integrin, alpha 2 [CD49B, alpha 2 subunit of VLA-2 receptor] [GPIa])* (eg, neonatal alloimmune thrombocytopenia [NAIT], post-transfusion purpura), gene analysis, common variant (eg, HPA-5a/b (K505E))

● **81110**   *Human Platelet Antigen 6 genotyping (HPA-6w), ITGB3 (integrin, beta 3 [platelet glycoprotein IIIa, antigen CD61] [GPIIIa])* (eg, neonatal alloimmune thrombocytopenia [NAIT], post-transfusion purpura), gene analysis, common variant, HPA-6a/b (R489Q)

● **81111**   *Human Platelet Antigen 9 genotyping (HPA-9w), ITGA2B (integrin, alpha 2b [platelet glycoprotein IIb of IIb/IIIa complex, antigen CD41] [GPIIb])* (eg, neonatal alloimmune thrombocytopenia [NAIT], post-transfusion purpura), gene analysis, common variant, HPA-9a/b (V837M)

● **81112**   *Human Platelet Antigen 15 genotyping (HPA-15), CD109 (CD109 molecule)* (eg, neonatal alloimmune thrombocytopenia [NAIT], post-transfusion purpura), gene analysis, common variant, HPA-15a/b (S682Y)

● **81120**   *IDH1 (isocitrate dehydrogenase 1 [NADP+], soluble)* (eg, glioma), common variants (eg, R132H, R132C)

● **81121**   *IDH2 (isocitrate dehydrogenase 2 [NADP+], mitochondrial)* (eg, glioma), common variants (eg, R140W, R172M)

● **81283**   *IFNL3 (interferon, lambda 3)* (eg, drug response), gene analysis, rs12979860 variant

81260   *IKBKAP (inhibitor of kappa light polypeptide gene enhancer in B-cells, kinase complex-associated protein)* (eg, familial dysautonomia) gene analysis, common variants (eg, 2507+6T>C, R696P)

81261   *IGH@ (Immunoglobulin heavy chain locus)* (eg, leukemias and lymphomas, B-cell), gene rearrangement analysis to detect abnormal clonal population(s); amplified methodology (eg, polymerase chain reaction)

81262   direct probe methodology (eg, Southern blot)

81263   *IGH@ (Immunoglobulin heavy chain locus)* (eg, leukemia and lymphoma, B-cell), variable region somatic mutation analysis

81264   *IGK@ (Immunoglobulin kappa light chain locus)* (eg, leukemia and lymphoma, B-cell), gene rearrangement analysis, evaluation to detect abnormal clonal population(s)

(For immunoglobulin lambda gene [*IGL@*] rearrangement or immunoglobulin kappa deleting element, [*IGKDEL*] analysis, use 81479)

81265   Comparative analysis using Short Tandem Repeat (STR) markers; patient and comparative specimen (eg, pre-transplant recipient and donor germline testing, post-transplant non-hematopoietic recipient germline [eg, buccal swab or other germline tissue sample] and donor testing, twin zygosity testing, or maternal cell contamination of fetal cells)

+ **81266**   each additional specimen (eg, additional cord blood donor, additional fetal samples from different cultures, or additional zygosity in multiple birth pregnancies) (List separately in addition to code for primary procedure)

(Use 81266 in conjunction with 81265)

81267 Chimerism (engraftment) analysis, post transplantation specimen (eg, hematopoietic stem cell), includes comparison to previously performed baseline analyses; without cell selection

81268 with cell selection (eg, CD3, CD33), each cell type

(If comparative STR analysis of recipient [using buccal swab or other germline tissue sample] and donor are performed after hematopoietic stem cell transplantation, report 81265, 81266 in conjunction with 81267, 81268 for chimerism testing)

81269 This code is out of order. See page 712.

81270 *JAK2 (Janus kinase 2)* (eg, myeloproliferative disorder) gene analysis, p.Val617Phe (V617F) variant

81272 *KIT (v-kit-Hardy-Zuckerman 4 feline sarcoma viral oncogene homolog)* (eg, gastrointestinal stromal tumor [GIST], acute myeloid leukemia, melanoma), gene analysis, targeted sequence analysis (eg, exons 8, 11, 13, 17, 18)

81273 *KIT (v-kit-Hardy-Zuckerman 4 feline sarcoma viral oncogene homolog)* (eg, mastocytosis), gene analysis, D816 variant(s)

81275 *KRAS (Kirsten rat sarcoma viral oncogene homolog)* (eg, carcinoma) gene analysis, variants in exon 2 (eg, codons 12 and 13)

81276 additional variant(s) (eg, codon 61, codon 146)

(81280 deleted 2016 [2017 edition])

(81281 deleted 2016 [2017 edition])

(81282 deleted 2016 [2017 edition])

81283 This code is out of order. See page 713.

81287 This code is out of order. See page 714.

81288 This code is out of order. See page 714.

81290 *MCOLN1 (mucolipin 1)* (eg, Mucolipidosis, type IV) gene analysis, common variants (eg, IVS3-2A>G, del6.4kb)

81287 *MGMT (0-6 methylguanin-DNA methyltransferase)* (eg, glioblastoma multiforme), methylation analysis

81291 *MTHFR (5,10-methylenetetrahydrofolate reductase)* (eg, hereditary hypercoagulability) gene analysis, common variants (eg, 677T, 1298C)

81292 *MLH1 (mutL homolog 1, colon cancer, nonpolyposis type 2)* (eg, hereditary non-polyposis colorectal cancer, Lynch syndrome) gene analysis; full sequence analysis

81288 promoter methylation analysis

81293 known familial variants

81294 duplication/deletion variants

81295 *MSH2 (mutS homolog 2, colon cancer, nonpolyposis type 1)* (eg, hereditary non-polyposis colorectal cancer, Lynch syndrome) gene analysis; full sequence analysis

81296 known familial variants

81297 duplication/deletion variants

● New Code   ▲ Revised Code   ✛ Add-On Code   ⊘ Modifier -51 Exempt   ★ Telemedicine

81298   *MSH6 (mutS homolog 6 [E. coli])* (eg, hereditary non-polyposis colorectal cancer, Lynch syndrome) gene analysis; full sequence analysis

81299   known familial variants

81300   duplication/deletion variants

81301   Microsatellite instability analysis (eg, hereditary non-polyposis colorectal cancer, Lynch syndrome) of markers for mismatch repair deficiency (eg, BAT25, BAT26), includes comparison of neoplastic and normal tissue, if performed

81302   *MECP2 (methyl CpG binding protein 2)* (eg, Rett syndrome) gene analysis; full sequence analysis

81303   known familial variant

81304   duplication/deletion variants

81310   *NPM1 (nucleophosmin)* (eg, acute myeloid leukemia) gene analysis, exon 12 variants

81311   *NRAS (neuroblastoma RAS viral [v-ras] oncogene homolog)* (eg, colorectal carcinoma), gene analysis, variants in exon 2 (eg, codons 12 and 13) and exon 3 (eg, codon 61)

81313   *PCA3/KLK3 (prostate cancer antigen 3 [non-protein coding]/kallikrein-related peptidase 3 [prostate specific antigen])* ratio (eg, prostate cancer)

81314   *PDGFRA (platelet-derived growth factor receptor, alpha polypeptide)* (eg, gastrointestinal stromal tumor [GIST]), gene analysis, targeted sequence analysis (eg, exons 12,18)

81315   *PML/RAR-alpha, (t(15;17)),* (promyelocytic leukemia/retinoic acid receptor alpha) (eg, promyelocytic leukemia) translocation analysis; common breakpoints (eg, intron 3 and intron 6), qualitative or quantitative

81316   single breakpoint (eg, intron 3, intron 6 or exon 6), qualitative or quantitative

       (For intron 3 and intron 6 [including exon 6 if performed] analysis, use 81315)

       (If both intron 6 and exon 6 are analyzed, without intron 3, use one unit of 81316)

81317   *PMS2 (postmeiotic segregation increased 2 [S. cerevisiae])* (eg, hereditary non-polyposis colorectal cancer, Lynch syndrome) gene analysis; full sequence analysis

81318   known familial variants

81319   duplication/deletion variants

81321   *PTEN (phosphatase and tensin homolog)* (eg, Cowden syndrome, *PTEN* hamartoma tumor syndrome) gene analysis; full sequence analysis

81322   known familial variant

81323   duplication/deletion variant

81324   *PMP22 (peripheral myelin protein 22)* (eg, Charcot-Marie-Tooth, hereditary neuropathy with liability to pressure palsies) gene analysis; duplication/deletion analysis

81325   full sequence analysis

81326   known familial variant

● **81334**   *RUNX1 (runt related transcription factor 1)* (eg, acute myeloid leukemia, familial platelet disorder with associated myeloid malignancy), gene analysis, targeted sequence analysis (eg, exons 3-8)

     ▨ Separate Procedure   ▨ Unlisted Procedure   ▨ CCI Comp. Code   ▨ Non-specific Procedure   **715**

● 81327   *SEPT9 (Septin9)* (eg, colorectal cancer) methylation analysis

● 81328   *SLCO1B1 (solute carrier organic anion transporter family, member 1B1)* (eg, adverse drug reaction), gene analysis, common variant(s) (eg, *5)

81330   *SMPD1(sphingomyelin phosphodiesterase 1, acid lysosomal)* (eg, Niemann-Pick disease, Type A) gene analysis, common variants (eg, R496L, L302P, fsP330)

81331   *SNRPN/UBE3A (small nuclear ribonucleoprotein polypeptide N and ubiquitin protein ligase E3A)* (eg, Prader-Willi syndrome and/or Angelman syndrome), methylation analysis

81332   *SERPINA1 (serpin peptidase inhibitor, clade A, alpha-1 antiproteinase, antitrypsin, member 1)* (eg, alpha-1-antitrypsin deficiency), gene analysis, common variants (eg, *S and *Z)

81334   This code is out of order. See page 715.

● 81335   TPMT (thiopurine S-methyltransferase) (eg, drug metabolism), gene analysis, common variants (eg, *2, *3)

81340   *TRB@ (T cell antigen receptor, beta)* (eg, leukemia and lymphoma), gene rearrangement analysis to detect abnormal clonal population(s); using amplification methodology (eg, polymerase chain reaction)

81341   using direct probe methodology (eg, Southern blot)

81342   *TRG@ (T cell antigen receptor, gamma)* (eg, leukemia and lymphoma), gene rearrangement analysis, evaluation to detect abnormal clonal population(s)

        (For T cell antigen alpha [*TRA@*] gene rearrangement analysis, use 81479)

        (For T cell antigen delta [*TRD@*] gene rearrangement analysis, report 81402)

● 81346   TYMS (thymidylate synthetase) (eg, 5-fluorouracil/5-FU drug metabolism), gene analysis, common variant(s) (eg, tandem repeat variant)

81350   *UGT1A1 (UDP glucuronosyltransferase 1 family, polypeptide A1)* (eg, irinotecan metabolism), gene analysis, common variants (eg, *28, *36, *37)

81355   *VKORC1 (vitamin K epoxide reductase complex, subunit 1)* (eg, warfarin metabolism), gene analysis, common variant(s) (eg, -1639G>A, c.173+1000C>T)

● 81361   *HBB (hemoglobin, subunit beta)* (eg, sickle cell anemia, beta thalassemia, hemoglobinopathy); common variant(s) (eg, HbS, HbC, HbE)

● 81362   known familial variant(s)

● 81363   duplication/deletion variant(s)

● 81364   full gene sequence

HUMAN LEUKOCYTE ANTIGEN (HLA) TYPING

Human Leukocyte Antigen (HLA) typing is performed to assess compatibility of recipients and potential donors as a part of solid organ and hematopoietic stem cell pre-transplant testing. HLA testing is also performed to identify HLA alleles and allele groups (antigen equivalents) associated with specific diseases and individualized responses to drug therapy (eg, HLA-B*27 and ankylosing spondylitis and HLA0B*57:01 and abacavir hypersensitivity). as well as other clinical uses. One of more HLA genes may be tested in specific clinical situations (eg, HLA-DQB1 for narcolepsy and HLA-A, -B, -C, -DRB1 and -DQB1 for kidney transplantation). Each HLA gene typically has multiple variant alleles or allele groups that can be identified by typing. For HLA result reporting, a low resolution HLA type is denoted by a two digit HLA name (eg, A*02) and intermediate resolution typing by a string of alleles or an NMDP (National Marrow Donor Program) code (eg, B*14:01/07N/08/12/14, B*39CKGN). Both low and intermediate resolution are considered low resolution for code assignment. High resolution typing resolves the common well defined (CWD) alleles and is usually denoted by at least 4 digits (eg, A*02:02, *03:01:01:01, A*26:01:01G, and C*03:04P), however, high resolution typing may include some ambiguities for rare alleles, which may be reported as a string of alleles or an NMDP code.

If additional testing is required to resolve ambiguous allele combinations for high resolution typing, this is included in the base HLA typing codes below. The gene names have been italicized similar to other molecular pathology codes.

(For HLA antigen typing by non-molecular pathology techniques, see 86812, 86813, 86816, 86817, 86821)

81370 HLA Class I and II typing, low resolution (eg, antigen equivalents); *HLA-A, -B, -C, -DRB1/3/4/5*, and *-DQB1*

81371 *HLA-A, -B,* and *-DRB1* (eg, verification typing)

(When HLA typing includes a determination of the presence or absence of the DRB3/4/5 genes, that service is included in the typing and is not separately reported)

81372 HLA Class I typing, low resolution (eg, antigen equivalents); complete (ie, *HLA-A, -B,* and *-C*)

(When performing both Class I and II low resolution HLA typing for *HLA-A, -B, -C, -DRB1/3/4/5*, and *-DQB1*, use 81370)

81373 one locus (eg, *HLA-A, -B,* or *-C*), each

(When performing a complete Class I [*HLA-A, -B* and *-C*] low resolution HLA typing, use 81372)

(When the presence or absence of a single antigen equivalent is reported using low resolution testing, use 81374)

81374 one antigen equivalent (eg, *B*27*), each

(When testing for presence or absence of more than 2 antigen equivalents at a locus, use 81373 for each locus tested)

81375 HLA Class II typing, low resolution (eg, antigen equivalents); *HLA-DRB1/3/4/5* and *-DQB1*

(When performing both Class I and II low resolution HLA typing for *HLA-A, -B, -C, -DRB1/3/4/5* and *-DQB1*, use 81370)

81376 one locus (eg, *HLA-DRB1, -DRB3/4/5, -DQB1, -DQA1, -DPB1,* or *-DPA1*), each

(When low resolution typing is performed for *HLA-DRG1/3/4/5* and *-DQB1*, use 81375)

(When HLA typing includes a determination of the presence or absence of the DRB3/4/5 genes, that service is included in the typing and is not separately reported. When low or intermediate resolution typing of any or all of the DRB3/4/5 genes is performed, treat as one locus)

81377 one antigen equivalent, each

(When testing for presence of absence of more than 2 antigen equivalents at a locus, use 81376 for each locus)

81378 HLA Class I and II typing, high resolution (ie, alleles or allele groups), *HLA-A, -B, -C,* and *-DRB1*

81379 HLA Class I typing, high resolution (ie, alleles or allele groups); complete (ie, *HLA-A, -B,* and *-C*)

81380 one locus (eg, *HLA-A, -B,* or *-C*), each

(When a complete Class I high resolution typing for *HLA-A, -B,* and *-C* is performed, use 81379)

(When the presence of absence of a single allele or allele group is reported using high resolution testing, use 81381)

81381 one allele or allele group (eg, *B*57:01P*), each

(When testing for the presence or absence of more than 2 alleles or allele groups at a locus, use 81380 for each locus)

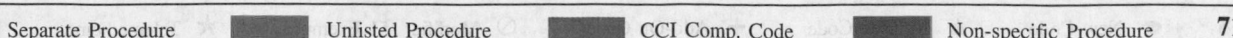

Separate Procedure   Unlisted Procedure   CCI Comp. Code   Non-specific Procedure   **717**

81382   HLA Class II typing, high resolution (ie, alleles or allele groups); one locus (eg, *HLA-DRB1*, *-DRB3/4/5*, *-DQB1*, *-DQA1*, *-DPB1*, or *-DPA1*), each

(When only the presence or absence of a single allele or allele group is reported using high resolution testing, use 81383)

(When high resolution typing of any or all of the DRB3/4/5 genes is performed, treat as one locus)

81383   one allele or allele group (eg, *HLA-DQB1*06:02P*), each

(When testing for the presence or absence of more than 2 alleles or allele groups at a locus, use 81382 for each locus)

TIER 2 MOLECULAR PATHOLOGY PROCEDURES

The following molecular pathology procedures (Tier 2) codes are used to report procedures not listed in the Tier 1 molecular pathology codes (81200-81383). They represent medically useful procedures that are generally performed in lower volumes than Tier 1 procedures (eg, the incidence of the disease being tested is rare). They are arranged by level of technical resources and interpretive work by the physician or other qualified health care professional. The individual analyses listed under each code (ie, level of procedure) utilize the definitions and coding principles as described in the introduction preceding the Tier 1 molecular pathology codes. The parenthetical examples of methodologies presented near the beginning of each code provide general guidelines used to group procedures for a given level and are not all-inclusive.

Use the appropriate molecular pathology procedure level code that includes the specific analyte listed after the code descriptor. If the analyte tested is not listed under one of the Tier 2 codes or is not represented by a Tier 1 code, use the unlisted molecular pathology procedure code, 81479.

▲ **81400**   Molecular pathology procedure, Level 1 *(eg, identification of single germline variant [eg, SNP] by techniques such as restriction enzyme digestion or melt curve analysis)*

ACADM (acyl-CoA dehydrogenase, C-4 to C-12 straight chain, MCAD) (eg, medium chain acyl dehydrogenase deficiency), K304E variant

ACE (angiotensin converting enzyme) (eg, hereditary blood pressure regulation), insertion/deletion variant

AGTR1 (angiotensin II receptor, type 1) (eg, essential hypertension), 1166A>C variant

BCKDHA (branched chain keto acid dehydrogenase E1, alpha polypeptide) (eg, maple syrup urine disease, type 1A), Y438N variant

CCR5 (chemokine C-C motif receptor 5) (eg, HIV resistance), 32-bp deletion mutation/794 825del32 deletion

CLRN1 (clarin1) (eg, Usher syndrome, type3), N48K variant

F2 (coagulation factor 2) (eg, hereditary hypercoagulability), 1199G>A variant

F5 (coagulation factor V) (eg, hereditary hypercoagulability), HR2 variant

F7 (coagulation factor VII [serum prothrombin conversion accelerator]) (eg, hereditary hypercoagulability), R353Q variant

F13B (coagulation factor XIII, B polypeptide) (eg, hereditary hypercoagulability), V34L variant

FGB (fibrinogen beta chain) (eg, hereditary ischemic heart disease), -455G>A variant

FGFR1 (fibroblast growth factor receptor 1) (eg, Pfeiffer syndrome type 1, craniosynostosis), P252R variant

FGFR3 (fibroblast growth factor receptor 3) (eg, Muenke syndrome), P250R variant

FKTN (fukutin) (eg, Fukuyama congenital muscular dystrophy), retrotransposon insertion variant

GNE (glucosamine [UDP-N-acetyl]-2-epimerase/ N-acetylmannosamine kinase) (eg, inclusion body myopathy 2 [IBM2], Nonaka myopathy), M712T variant

IVD (isovaleryl-CoA dehydrogenase) (eg, isovaleric acidemia), A282V variant

LCT (lactase-phlorizin hydrolase) (eg, lactose intolerance), 13910 C>T variant

NEB (nebulin) (eg, nemaline myopathy 2), exon 55 deletion variant

PCDH15 (protocadherin-related 15) (eg, Usher syndrome type 1F), R245X variant

SERPINE1 (serpine peptidase inhibitor clade E, member 1, plasminogen activator inhibitor -1, PAI-1) (eg, thrombophilia), 4G variant

SHOC2 (soc-2 suppressor of clear homolog) (eg, Noonan-like syndrome with loose anagen hair), S2G variant

SMN1 (survival of motor neuron 1, telomeric) (eg, spinal muscular atrophy), exon 7 deletion

SRY (sex determining region Y) (eg, 46,XX testicular disorder of sex development, gonadal dysgenesis), gene analysis

TOR1A (torsin family 1, member A [torsin A]) (eg, early-onset primary dystonia [DYT1]), 907_909delGAG (904_906delGAG) variant

▲ **81401**　Molecular pathology procedure, Level 2 (eg, 2-10 SNPs, 1 methylated variant, or 1 somatic variant [typically using nonsequencing target variant analysis], or detection of a dynamic mutation disorder/triplet repeat)

ABCC8 (ATP-binding cassette, sub-family C [CFTR/MRP], member 8) (eg, familial hyperinsulinism), common variants (eg, c.3898-9G>A [c.3992-9G>A], F1388del)

ABL1 (ABL proto-oncogene 1, non-receptor tyrosine kinase) (eg, acquired imatinib resistance), T315I variant

ACADM (acyl-CoA dehydrogenase, C-4 to C-12 straight chain, MCAD) (eg, medium chain acyl dehydrogenase deficiency), commons variants (eg, K304E, Y42H)

ADRB2 (adrenergic beta-2 receptor surface) (eg, drug metabolism), common variants (eg, G16R, Q27E)

AFF2 (AF4/FMR2 family, member 2[FMR2]) (eg, fragile X mental retardation 2 [FRAXE]), evaluation to detect abnormal (eg, expanded) alleles

APOB (apolipoprotein B) (eg, familial hypercholesterolemia type B), common variants (eg, R3500Q, R3500W)

APOE (apolipoprotein E) (eg, hyperlipoproteinemia type III, cardiovascular disease, Alzheimer disease), common variants (eg, *2, *3, *4)

AR (androgen receptor) (eg, spinal and bulbar muscular atrophy, Kennedy disease, X chromosome inactivation), characterization of alleles (eg, expanded size or methylation status)

ATN1 (atrophin 1) (eg, dentatorubral-pallidoluysian atrophy), evaluation to detect abnormal (eg, expanded alleles)

ATXN1 (ataxin 1) (eg, spinocerebellar ataxia), evaluation to detect abnormal (eg, expanded) alleles

ATXN2 (ataxin 2) (eg, spinocerebellar ataxia) evaluation to detect abnormal (eg, expanded) alleles

ATXN3 (ataxin 3) (eg, spinocerebellar ataxia, Machado-Joseph disease), evaluation to detect abnormal (eg, expanded) alleles

ATXN7 (ataxin 7) (eg, spinocerebellar ataxia), evaluation to detect abnormal (eg, expanded) alleles

ATXN8OS (ATXN8 opposite strand [non-protein coding]) (eg, spinocerebellar ataxia), evaluation to detect abnormal (eg, expanded) alleles

ATXN10 (ataxin 10) (eg, spinocerebellar ataxia), evaluation to detect abnormal (eg, expanded) alleles

CACNA1A (calcium channel, voltage-dependent, P?Q type, alpha 1A subunit) (eg, spinocerebellar ataxia), evaluation to detect abnormal (eg, expanded) alleles

CBFB/MYH11 (inv(16)) (eg, acute myeloid leukemia), qualitative, and quantitative, if performed

CBS (cystathionine-beta-synthase) (eg, homocystinuria, cystathionin beta-synthase deficiency), common variants (eg, I278T, G307S)

CCND1/IGH (BCL1/IgH, t(11;14)) (eg, mantle cell lymphoma) translocation analysis, major breakpoint, qualitative, and quantitative, if performed

CFH/ARMS2 (complement factor H/age-related maculopathy susceptibility 2) (eg, macular degeneration), common variants (eg, Y402H [CFH], A69S [ARMS2])

CNBP (CCHC-type zinc finger, nucleic acid binding protein) (eg, myotonic dystrophy type 2), evaluation to detect abnormal (eg, expanded) alleles

CSTB (cystatin B [stefin B]) (eg, Unverricht-Lundborg disease), evaluation to detect abnormal (eg, expanded) alleles

DEK/NUP214 (t(6;9)) (eg, acute myeloid leukemia), translocation analsysis, qualitative, and quantitative, if performed

DMPK (dystrophia myotonica-protein kinase) (eg, myotonic dystrophy, type 1), evaluation to detect abnormal (eg, expanded) alleles

E2A/PBX1 (t(1;19)) (eg, acute lymphocytic leukemia), translocation analysis, qualitative and quantitative, if performed

EML4/ALK (inv(2)) (eg, non-small cell lunch cancer), translocation or inversion analysis

ETV6/NTRK3 (t(12;15)) (eg, congenital/infantile fibrosarcoma), translocation analysis, qualitative, and quantitative, if performed

ETV6/RUNX1 (t(12;21)) (eg, acute lymphocytic leukemia), translocation analysis, qualitative, and quantitative if performed

EWSR1/ATF1 (t(12;22)) (eg, clear cell sarcoma), translocation analysis, qualitative, and quantitative, if performed

EWSR1/ERG (t(21;22)) (eg, Ewing sarcoma/peripheral neuroectodermal tumor), translocation analysis, qualitative, and quantitative, if performed

EWSR1/FLI1 (t(11;22)) (eg, Ewing sarcoma/peripheral neuroectodermal tumor), translocation analysis, qualitative, and quantitative, if performed

EWSR1/WT1 (t(11;22)) (eg, desmoplastic small round cell tumor), translocation analysis, qualitative, and quantitative, if performed

F11 (coagulation factor XI) (eg, coagulation disorder), common variants (eg, E117X [Type II], F283L [Type III], IVS14del14, and IVS14+1G>A [Type I])

FGFR3 (fibroblast growth factor receptor 3) (eg, achondroplasia), common variants (eg, 1138G>A, 1138G>C)

FIP1L1/PDGFRA (del[4q12]) (eg, imatinib-sensitive chronic eosinophilic leukemia), qualitative, and quantitative, if performed

FLG (filaggrin) (eg, icthyosis vulgaris), common variants (eg, R501X, 2282del4, R2447X, S3247X, 3702delG)

FOXO1/PAX3 (t(2;13)) (eg, alveolar rhabdomyosarcoma), translocation analysis, qualitative, and quantitative, if performed

FOXO1/PAX7 (t(1;13)) (eg, alveolar rhabdymyocarcoma), translocation analysis, qualitative, and quantitative, if performed

FUS/DDIT3 (t(12;16)) (eg, myxoid liposarcoma), translocation analysis, qualitative, and quantitative, if performed

FXN (frataxin) (eg, Friedreich ataxia), evaluation to detect abnormal (expanded) alleles

GALC (galactosylceramidase) (eg, Krabbe disease), common variants (eg, c.857G>A, 30-kb deletion)

GALT (galactose-1-phosphate uridylyltransferase) (eg, galactosemia), common variants (eg, Q188R, S135L, K285N, T138M, L195P, Y209C, IVS2-2A>G, P171S, del5kb, N314D, L218L/N314D)

H19 (imprinted maternally expressed transcript [non-protein coding]) (eg, Beckwith-Wiedemann syndrome), methylation analysis

HTT (huntingtin) (eg, Huntington disease), evaluation to detect abnormal (eg, expanded) alleles

---

● New Code ▲ Revised Code ✛ Add-On Code ⊘ Modifier -51 Exempt ★ Telemedicine

IGH@/BCL2 (t(14;18)) (eg, follicular lymphoma), translocation analysis; single breakpoint (eg, major breakpoint region [MBR] or minor cluster region [mcr]), qualitative or quantitative

(When both MBR and mcr breakpoints are performed, use 81402)

KCNQ10T1 (KCNQ1 overlapping transcript 1 [non-protein coding]) (eg, Beckwith-Wiedemann syndrome), methylation analysis

LINC00518 (long intergenic non-protein coding RNA 518) (eg, melanoma), expression analysis

LRRK2 (leucine-rich repeat kinase 2) (eg, Parkinson disease), common variants (eg, R1441G, G2019S, I2020T)

MED12 (mediator complex subunit 12) (eg, FG syndrome type 1, Lujan syndrome), common variants (eg, R961W, N1007S)

MEG3/DLK1 (maternally expressed 3 [non-protein coding]/delta-like 1 homolog [Drosophila]) (eg, intrauterine growth retardation), methylation analysis

MLL/AFF1 (t(4;11)) (eg, acute lymphoblastic leukemia), translocation analysis, qualitative, and quantitative if performed

MLL/MLLT3 (t(9;11)) (eg, acute myeloid leukemia), translocation analysis, qualitative, and quantitative, if performed

MT-ATP6 (mitochondrially encoded ATP synthase 6) (eg, neuropathy with ataxia and retinitis pigmentosa [NARP], Leigh syndrome), common variants (eg, m.8993T>G, m.8993T>C)

MT-ND4, MT-ND6 (mitochondrially encoded NADH dehydrogenase 4, mitochondrially encoded NADH dehydrogenase 6) (eg, Leber hereditary optic neuropathy [LHON]), common variants (eg, m.11778G>A, M.3460G>A, m.14484T>C)

MT-ND5 (mitochondrially encoded tRNA leucine 1 [UUA/G], mitochondrially encoded NADH dehydrogenase 5) (eg, mitochondrial encephalopathy with lactic acidosis and stroke-like episodes [MELAS]), common variants (eg, m.3243A>G, m.3271T>C, m.3252A>G, m.13513G>A)

MT-RNR1 (mitochondrially encoded 12S RNA) (eg, nonsyndromic hearing loss), common variants (eg, m.1555A>G, m.1494C>T)

MT-TK (mitochondrially encoded tRNA lysine) (eg, myoclonic epilepsy with ragged-red fibers [MERRF]), common variants (eg, m.8344A>G, m.8356T>C)

MT-TL1 (mitochondrially encoded tRNA leucine 1 [UUA/G]) (eg, diabetes and hearing loss), common variants (eg, M3243A>G, M.14709T>C) MT-TL1,

MT-TS1, MT-RNR1 (mitochondrially encoded tRNA serine 1 [UCN], mitochondrially encoded 12S RNA) (eg, nonsyndromic sensorineural deafness [including aminoglycoside-induced nonsyndromic deafness]), common variants (eg, m.7445A>G, m.1555A>G)

MUTYH (mutY homolog [E.coli]) (eg, MYH-associated polyposis), common variants (eg, Y165C, G382D)

NOD2 (nucleotide-binding oligomerization domain containing 2) (eg, Crohn's disease, Blau syndrome), common variants (eg, SNP8, SNP 12, SNP 13)

NPM1/ALK (t(2;5)) (eg, anaplastic large cell lymphoma), transloation analysis

PABPN1 (poly[A] binding protein, nuclear 1) (eg, oculopharyngeal muscular dystrophy), evaluation to detect abnormal (eg, expanded) alleles

PAX8/PPARG (t(2;3) (q13;p25)) (eg, follicular thyroid carcinoma), translocation analysis

PPP2R2B (protein phosphatase 2, regulatory subunit B, beta) (eg, spinocerebellar ataxia), evaluation to detect abnormal (eg, expanded) alleles

PRAME (preferentially expressed antigen in melanoma) (eg, melanoma), expression analysis

PRSS1 (protease, serine, 1 [trypsin1]) (eg, hereditary pancreatitis), common variants (eg, N29I, A16V, R122H)

PYGM (phosphorylase, glycogen, muscle) (eg, glycogen storage disease type V, McArdle disease), common variants (eg, R50X, G205S)

RUNX1/RUNX1T1 (t(8;21)) (eg, acute myeloid leukemia) translocation analysis, qualitative, and quantitative, if performed

SMN1/SMN2 (survival of motor neuron 1, telomeric/survival of motor neuron 2, centromeric), (eg, spinal muscular atrophy), dosage analysis (eg, carrier testing)

(For duplication/deletion analysis of SMN1/SMN2, use 81401)

SS18/SSX1 (t(X;18)) (eg, synovial sarcoma), translocation analysis, qualitative, and quantitative, if performed

SS18/SSX2 (t(X;18)) (eg, synovial sarcoma), translocation analysis, qualitative and quantitative if performed

TBP (TATA box binding protein) (eg, spinocerebellar ataxia), evaluation to detect abnormal (eg, expanded) alleles

VWF (von Willebrand factor) (eg, von Willebrand disease type 2N), common variants (eg, T791M, R816W, R854Q)

81402 Molecular pathology procedure, Level 3 (eg, >10 SNPs, 2-10 methylated variants, or 2-10 somatic variants [typically using non-sequencing target variant analysis], immunoglobulin and T-cell receptor gene rearrangements, duplication/deletion variants of 1 exon, loss of heterozygosity [LOH], uniparental disomy [UPD])

Chromosome 1p-/19q- (eg., glial tumors), deletion analysis

Chromosome 18q- (eg, D18S55, D18S58, D18S61, D18S64, and D18S69) (eg, colon cancer), allelic imbalance assessment (ie, loss of heterozygosity)

COL1A1/PDGFB (t(17;22)) (eg, dermatofibrosarcoma protuberans), translocation analysis, mutiple breakpoints, qualitative, and quantitative, if performed

CYP21A2 (cytochrome P450, family 21, subfamily A, polypeptide 2) (eg, congenital adrenal hyperplasia, 21-hydroxylase deficiency), common variants (eg, IVS2-13G, P30L, I172N, exon 6 mutation cluster [I235N, V236E, M238K], V281L, L307FfsX6, Q318X, R356W, P453S, G110VfsX21, 30-kb deletion variant)

ESR1/PGR (receptor 1/progesterone receptor) ratio (eg, breast cancer)

IGH@/BCL2 (t(14;18)) (eg, follicular lymphoma), translocation analysis; major breakpoint region (MBR), and minor cluster region (mcr) breakpoints, qualitative or quantitative

MEFV (Mediterranean fever) (eg, familial Mediterranean fever), common variants (eg, E148Q, P369S, F479L, M680I, I692del, M694V, M694I, K695R, V726A, A744S, R761H)

MPL (myeloproliferative leukemia virus oncogene, thrombopoietin receptor, TPOR) (eg, myeloproliferative disorder), common variants (eg, W515A, W515K, W515L, W515R)

TRD@ (T cell antigen receptor, delta) (eg, leukemia and lymphoma), gene rearrangement analysis, evaluation to detect abnormal clonal population

Uniparental disomy (UPD) (eg, Russell-Silver syndrome, Prader-Willi/Angelman syndrome), short tandem repeat (STR) analysis

▲ **81403** Molecular pathology procedure, Level 4 (eg, analysis of single exon by DNA sequence analysis, analysis of >10 amplicons using multiplex PCR in 2 or more independent reactions, mutation scanning or duplication/deletion variants of 2-5 exons)

ANG (angiogenin, ribonuclease, RNase A family, 5) (eg, amyotrophic lateral sclerosis), full gene sequence

ARX (aristaless-related homeobox) (eg, X-linked lissencephaly with ambiguous genitalia, X-linked mental retardation), duplication/deletion analysis

CEL (carboxyl ester lipase [bile salt-stimulated lipase]) (eg, maturity-onset diabetes of the young [MODY]), targeted sequence analysis of exon 11 (eg, c.1785delC, c.1686delT)

CTNNB1 (catenin [cadherin-associated protein], beta 1, 88kDa) (eg, desmoid tumors) targeted sequence analysis (ex, exon 3)

DAZ/SRY (deleted in azoospermia and sex determining region Y) (eg, male infertility), common deletions (eg, AZFa, AZFb, AZFc, AZFd)

DNMT3A (DNA [cytosine-5-]-methyltransferase 3 alpha) (eg, acute myeloid leukemia), targeted sequence analysis (eg, exon 23)

EPCAM (epithelial cell adhesion molecule) (eg, Lynch syndrome), duplication/deletion analysis

F8 (coagulation factor VIII) (eg, hemophilia A), inversion analysis, intron 1 and intron 22A

F12 (coagulation factor XII [Hageman factor]) (eg, angioedema, hereditary, type III, factor XII deficiency), targeted sequence analysis of exon 9

FGFR3 (fibroblast growth factor receptor 3) (eg, isolated craniosynostosis), targeted sequence analysis (ex, exon 7)

(For targeted sequence analysis of multiple FGFR3 exons, use 81404)

GJB1 (gap junction protein, beta 1) (eg, Charcot-Marie-Tooth X-linked), full gene sequence

GNAQ (guanine nucleotide-binding protein G[q] subunit alpha) (eg, uveal melanoma), common variants (eg, R183, Q209)

Human erythrocyte antigen gene analyses (eg., SLC14A1 [Kidd blood group], BCAM [Lutheran blood group], ICAM4 [Landsteiner-Wiener blood group], SLC4A1 [Diego blood group], AQP1 [Colton blood group], ERMAP [Scianna blood group], RHCE [Rh blood group, CcEe antigens], KEL [Kell blood group], DARC [Duffy blood group], GYPA, GYPB, GYPE [MNS blood group], ART4 {Dombrock blood group],) e(eg., sickle cell disease, thalassemia, hemolytic transfusion reactions, hemolytic disease of the fetus or newborn), common variants

HRAS (v-Ha-ras Harvey rat sarcoma viral oncogene homolog) (eg, Costello syndrome), exon 2 sequence

JAK2 (Janus kinase 2) (eg, myeloproliferative disorder), exon 12 sequence and exon 13 sequence, if performed

KCNC3 (potassium voltage-gated channel, Shaw-related subfamily, member 3) (eg, spinocerebellar ataxia), targeted sequence analysis (eg, exon 2)

KCNJ2 (potassium inwardly-rectifying channel, subfamily J, member 2) (eg, Andersen-Tawil syndrome), full gene sequence

KCNJ11 (potassium inwardly-rectifying channel, subfamily J, member 11) (eg, familial hyperinsulinism), full gene sequence

Killer cell immunoglobulin-like receptor (KIR) gene family (eg, hematopoietic stem cell transplantation), genotyping of KIR family genes

Known familial variant not otherwise specified, for gene listed in Tier 1 or Tier 2, or identified during a genomic sequencing procedure, DNA sequence analysis, each variant exon
(For a known familial variant that is considered a common variant, use specific common variant Tier 1 or Tier 2 code)

MC4R (melanocortin 4 receptor) (eg, obesity), full gene sequence

MICA (MHC class I polypeptide-related sequence A) (eg, solid organ transplantation), common varients (eg, *001, *002)

MPL (myeloproliferative leukemia virus oncogene, thrombopoietin receptor, TPOR) (eg, myeloproliferative disorder), exon 10 sequence

MT-RNR1 (mitochondrially encoded 12S RNA) (eg, nonsyndromic hearing loss), full gene sequence

MT-TS1 (mitochondrially encoded tRNA serine 1) (eg, nonsyndromic hearing loss), full gene sequence

NDP (Norrie disease [pseydoglioma]) (eg, Norrie disease), duplication/deletion analysis

NHLRC1 (NHL repeat containing 1) (eg, progressive myoclonus epilepsy), full gene sequence

PHOX2B (paired-like homeobox 2b) (eg, congenital central hypoventilation syndrome), duplication/deletion analysis

---

Separate Procedure   Unlisted Procedure   CCI Comp. Code   Non-specific Procedure   **723**

PLN (phospholamban) (eg, dilated cardiomyopathy, hypertrophic cardiomyopathy), full gene sequence

RHD (Rh blood group, D antigen) (eg., hemolytic disease of the fetus and newborn, Rh maternal/fetal compatibility), deletion analsysis (eg., exons 4, 5, and 7, pseudogene)

RHD (Rh blood group, D antigen) (eg., hemolytic disease of the fetus and newborn, Rh maternal/fetal compatibility), deletion analsysis (eg., exons 4, 5, and 7, pseudogene) performed on cell-free fetal DNA in maternal blood

(For human erythrocyte gene analysis of RHD, use a separate unit of 81403)

SH2D1A (SH2 domain containing 1A) (eg, X-linked ymphoproliferative syndrome), duplication/deletion analysis

SMN1 (survival of motor neuron 1, telomeric) (eg, spinal muscular atrophy), known familial sequence variants

TWIST1 (twist homolog 1 [Drosophila]) (eg, Saethre-Chotzen syndrome), duplication/deletion analysis

UBA1 (ubiquitin-like modifier activating enzyme 1) (eg, spinal muscular atrophy, X-linked), target sequence analysis (eg, exon 15)

VHL (von Hippel-Lindau tumor suppressor) (eg, von Hippel-Lindau familial cancer syndrome), deletion/duplication analysis

VWF (von Willebrand factor) (eg, von Willebrand disease types 2A, 2B, 2M), targeted sequence analysis (eg, exon 28)

▲ **81404** Molecular pathology procedure, Level 5 (eg, analysis of 2-5 exons by DNA sequence analysis, mutation scanning or duplication/deletion variants of 6-10 exons, or characterization of a dynamic mutation disorder/triplet repeat by Southern blot analysis)

ACADS (acyl-CoA dehydrogenase, C-2 to C-3 short chain) (eg, short chain acyl-CoA dehydrogenase deficiency), targeted sequence analysis (eg, exons 5 and 6)

AFF2 (AF4/FMR2 family, member 2 [FMR2]) (eg, fragile X mental retardation 2 [FRAXE]), characterization of alleles (eg, expanded size and methylation status)

AQP2 (aquaporin 2 [collecting duct]) (eg, nephrogenic diabetes insipidus), full gene sequence

ARX (aristaless related homeobox) (eg, X-linked lissencephaly with ambiguous genitalia, X-linked mental retardation) full gene sequence

AVPR2 (arginine vasopressin receptor 2) (eg, nephrogenic diabetes insipidus), full gene sequence

BBS10 (Bardet-Biedl syndrome 10) (eg, Bardet-Biedl syndrome), full gene sequence

BTD (biotinidase) (eg, biotinidase deficiency), full gene sequence

C10orf2 (chromosome 10 open reading frame 2) (eg, mitochondrial DNA depletion syndrome), full gene sequence

CAV3 (caveolin 3) (eg, CAV3-related distal myopathy, limb-girdle muscular dystrophy type 1C), full gene sequence

CD4OLG (CD40 ligand) (eg, X-linked hyper IgM syndrome), full gene sequence

CDKN2A (cyclin-dependent kinase inhibitor 2A) (eg, CDKN2A-related cutaneous malignant melanoma, familiarl atypical mole-malignant melanoma syndrome), full gene sequence

CLRN1 (clarin 1) (eg, Usher syndrome, type 3), full gene sequence

COX6B1 (cytochrome c oxidase subunit VIb polypeptide 1) (eg, mitochondrial respiratory chain complex IV deficiency), full gene sequence

CPT2 (carnitine palmitoyltransferase 2) (eg, carnitine palmitoyltransferase II deficiency), full gene sequence

CRX (cone-rod homeobox) (eg, cone-rod dystrophy 2, Leber congenital amaurosis), full gene sequence

CSTB (cystatin B [stefin B]) (eg, Unverricht-Lundborg disease), full gene sequence

CYP1B1 (cytochrome P450, family 1, subfamily B, polypeptide 1) (eg, primary congenital glaucoma), full gene sequence

DMPK (dystrophia myotonica-protein kinase) (eg, myotonic dystrophy type 1), characterization of abnormal (eg, expanded) alleles

EGR2 (early growth response 2) (eg, Charcot-Marie-Tooth), full gene sequence

EMD (emerin) (eg, Emery-Dreifuss muscular dystrophy), duplication/deletion analysis

EPM2A (epilepsy, progressive myoclonus type 2A, Lafora disease [laforin]) (eg, progressive myoclonus epilepsy), full gene sequence

FGF23 (fibroblast growth factor 23) (eg, hypophosphatemic rickets), full gene sequence

FGFR2 (fibroblast growth factor receptor 2) (eg, craniosynostosis, Apert syndrome, Crouzon syndrome), targeted sequence analysis (eg, exons 8,10)

FGFR3 (fibroblast growth factor receptor 3) (eg, achondroplasia, hypochondroplasia), targeted sequence analysis (eg, exons 8, 11,12,13)

FHL1 (four and a half LIM domains 1) (eg, Emery-Dreifuss muscular dystrophy), full gene sequence

FKRP (Fukutin related protein) (eg, congenital muscular dystrophy type 1C [MDC1C], limb-girdle muscular dystrophy [LGMD] type 2I), full gene sequence

FOXG1 (forkhead box G1) (eg, Rett syndrome), full gene sequence

FSHMD1A (facioscapulohumeral muscular dystrophy 1A) (eg, facioscapulohumeral muscular dystrophy), evaluation to detect abnormal (eg, deleted) alleles

FSHMD1A (facioscapulohumeral muscular dystrophy 1A) (eg, facioscapulohumeral muscular dystrophy), characterization of haplotype(s) (ie, chromosome 4A and 4B haplotypes)

FXN (frataxin) (eg, Friedreich ataxia), full gene sequence

GH1 (growth hormone 1) (eg, growth hormone deficiency), full gene sequence

GP1BB (glycoprotein 1b [platelet], beta polypeptide) (eg, Bernard-Soulier syndrome type B), full gene sequence

(For common deletion variants of alpha globin 1 and alpha globin 2 genes, use 81257)

HNF1B (HNF1 homeobox B) (eg, maturity-onset diabetes of the young [MODY]), duplication/deletion analysis

HRAS (v-Ha-ras Harvey rat sarcoma viral oncogene homolog) (eg, Costello syndrome), full gene sequence

HSD3B2 (hydroxy-delta-5-steroid dehydrogenase, 3 beta- and steroid delta-isomerase 2) (eg, 3-beta-hydroxysteroid dehydrogenase type II deficiency), full gene sequence

HSD11B2 (hydroxysteroid [11-beta] dehydrogenase 2) (eg, mineralocorticoid excess syndrome), full gene sequence

HSPB1 (heat shock 27kDa protein 1) (eg, Charcot-Marie-Tooth disease), full gene sequence

INS (insulin) (eg, diabetes mellitus), full gene sequence

KCNJ1 (potassium inwardly-rectifying channel, subfamily J, member 1) (eg, Bartter syndrome), full gene sequence

KCNJ10 (potassium inwardly-rectifying channel, subfamily J, member 10) (eg, SeSAME syndrome, EAST syndrome, sensorineural hearing loss), full gene sequence

LITAF (lipopolysaccharide-induced TNF factor) (eg, Charcot-Marie-Tooth), full gene sequence

MEFV (Mediterranean fever) (eg, familial Mediterranean fever), full gene sequence

MEN1 (multiple endocrine neoplasia 1) (eg, multiple endocrine neoplasia type 1, Wermer syndrome), duplication/deletion analysis

---

■ Separate Procedure   ■ Unlisted Procedure   ■ CCI Comp. Code   ■ Non-specific Procedure   **725**

MMACHC (methylmalonic aciduria [cobalamin deficiency] cblC type, with homocystinuria) (eg, methylmalonic acidemia and homocystinuria), full gene sequence

MPV17 (MpV17 mitochrondrial inner membrane protein) (eg., mitochondrial DNA depletion syndrome), duplication/deletion analysis

NDP (Norrie disease [pseudoglioma]) (eg, Norrie disease}, full gene sequence

NDUFA1 (NADH dehydrogenase [ubiquinone] 1 alpha subcomplex, 1, 7.5kDa) (eg, Leigh syndrome, mitochondrial complex 1 deficiency), full gene sequence

NDUFAF2 (NADH dehydrogenase [ubiquinone] 1 alpha subcomplex, assembly factor 2) (eg, Leigh syndrome, mitochondrial complex 1 deficiency), full gene sequence

NDUFS4 (NADH dehydrogenase [ubiquinone] Fe-S protein 4, 18kDa [NADH-coenzyme Q reductase]) (eg, Leigh syndrome, mitochondrial complex 1 deficiency), full gene sequence

NIPA1 (non-imprinted in Prader-Willi/Angelman syndrome 1) (eg, spastic paraplegia), full gene sequence

NLGN4X (neuroligin 4, X-linked) (eg, autism spectrum disorders), duplication/deletion analysis

NPC2 (Niemann-Pick disease, type C2 [epididymal secretory protein E1]) (eg, Niemann-Pick disease type C2), full gene sequence

NR0B1 (nuclear receptor subfamily 0, group B, member 1) (eg, congenital adrenal hypoplasia), full gene sequence

PDX1 (pancreatic and duodenal homeobox 1) (eg, maturity-onset diabetes of the young [MODY]), full gene sequence

PHOX2B (paired-like homeobox 2b) (eg, congenital central hypoventilation syndrome), full gene sequence

PIK3CA (phosphatidylinositol-4, 5-bisphosphate 3-kinase, catalytic subunit alpha) (eg., colorectal cancer), targeted sequence alaysis (eg., exons 9 and 20)

PLP1 (proteolipid protein 1) (eg, Pelizaeus-Merzbacher disease, spastic paraplegia), duplication/deletion analysis

PQBP1 (polyglutamine binding protein 1) (eg, Renpenning syndrome), duplication/deletion analysis

PRNP (prion protein) (eg, genetic prion disease), full gene sequence

PROP1 (PROP paired-like homeobox 1) (eg, combined pituitary hormone deficiency), full gene sequence

PRPH2 (peripherin 2[retinal degeneration, slow]) (eg, retinitis pigmentosa), full gene sequence

PRSS1 (protease, serine, 1[trypsin1]) (eg, hereditary pancreatitis), full gene sequence

RAF1 (v-raf-1 murine leukemia viral oncogene homolog 1) (eg, LEOPARD syndrome), targeted sequence analysis (eg, exons 7, 12, 14, 17)

RET (ret proto-oncogene) (eg, multiple endocrine neoplasia, type 2B and familial medullary thyroid carcinoma), common variants (eg, M918T, 2647_2648delinsTT, A883F)

RHO (rhodopsin) (eg, retinitis pigmentosa), full gene sequence

RP1 (retinitis pigmentosa 1) (eg, retinitis pigmentosa), full gene sequence

SCN!B (sodium channel, voltage-gated, type I, beta) (eg, Brugada syndrome), full gene sequence

SCO2 (SCO cytochrome oxidase deficient homolog 2 [SCO1L]) (eg, mitochondrial respiratory chain complex IV deficiency), full gene sequence

SDHC (succinate dehydrogenase complex, subunit C, integral membrane protein, 15kDa) (eg, hereditary paraganglioma-pheochromocytoma syndrome), duplication/deletion analysis

SDHD (succinate dehydrogenase complex, subunit D, integral membrane protein) (eg, hereditary paraganglioma), full gene sequence

SCGC (sarcoglycan, gamma [35kDa dystrophin-associated glycoprotein]) (eg, limb-girdle muscular dystrophy), duplication/deletion analysis

SH2D1A (SH2 domain containing 1A) (eg, X-linked lymphoproliferative syndrome), full gene sequence

SLC16A2 (solute carrier family 16, member 2 [thyroid hormone transporter]) (eg, specific thyroid hormone cell transporter deficiency, Allan-Herndon-Dudley syndrome), duplication/deletion analysis

SLC25A20 (solute carrier family 25 [carnitine/acylcarnitine translocase], member 20) (eg, carnitine-acylcarnitine translocase deficiency), duplication/deletion analysis

SLC25A4 (solute carrier family 25 [mitochondrial carrier; adenine nucleotide translocator], member 4) (eg, progressive external ophthalmoplegia), full gene sequence

SOD1 (superoxide dismutase 1, soluble) (eg, amyotrophic lateral sclerosis), full gene sequence

SPINK1 (serine peptidase inhibitor, Kazal type 1) (eg, hereditary pancreatitis), full gene sequence

STK11 (werine/threonine kinase 11) (eg, Peutz-Jeghers syndrome), duplication/deletion analysis

TACO1 (translational activator of mitochondrial encoded cytochrome c oxidase I) (eg, mitochondrial respiratory chain complex IV deficiency), full gene sequence

THAP1 (THAP domain continaing, apoptosis associated protein 1) (eg, torsion dystonia), full gene sequence

TOR1A (torsin family 1, member A [torsin A]) (eg, torsion dystonia), full gene sequence

TP53 (tumor protein 53) (eg, tumor samples), targeted s equence analysis of 2-5 exons

TTPA (tocopherol [alpha] transfer protein) (eg, ataxia), full gene sequence

TTR (transthyretin) (eg, familial transthyretin amyloidosis), full gene sequence

TWIST1 (twist homolog 1 [Drosophila]) (eg, Saethre-Chotzen syndrome), full gene sequence

TYR (tyrosinase [oculocutaneous albinism IA]) (eg, oculocutaneous albinism IA), full gene sequence

USH1G (Usher syndrome 1G [autosomal recessive]) (eg, Usher syndrome type 1), full gene sequence

VHL (von Hippel-Lindau tumor suppressor) (eg, von Hippel-Lindau familial cancer syndrome), full gene sequence

VWF (von Willebrand factor) (eg, von Willebrand disease type 1C), targeted sequence analysis (eg, exons 26, 27, 37)

ZEB2 (zinc finger E-box binding homeobox 2) (eg, Mowat-Wilson syndrome), duplication/deletion analysis

ZNF41 (zinc finger protein 41) (eg, X-linked mental retardation 89), full gene sequence

▲ **81405**   Molecular pathology procedure, Level 6 (eg, analysis of 6-10 exons by DNA sequence analysis, mutation scanning or duplication/deletion variants of 11-25 exons, regionally targeted cytogenomic array analysis)

ABCD1 (ATP-binding cassette, sub-family D [ALD], member 1) (eg, adrenoleukodystrophy), full gene sequence

ACADS (acyl-CoA dehydrogenase, C-2 to C-3 short chain) (eg, short chain acyl-CoA dehydrogenase deficiency) full gene sequence

ACTA2 (actin, alpha 2, smooth muscle, aorta) (eg, thoracic aortic aneurysms and aortic dissections), full gene sequence

ACTC1 (actin, alpha, cardiac muscle 1) (eg, familial hypertrophic cardiomyopathy), full gene sequence

ANKRD1 (ankyrin repeat domain 1) (eg, dilated cardiomyopathy), full gene sequence

APTX (aprataxin) (eg, ataxia with oculomotor apraxia 1), full gene sequence

AR (androgen receptor) (eg, androgen insensitivity syndrome), full gene sequence

ARSA (arylsulfatase A) (eg, arylsulfatase A deficiency), full gene sequence

BCKDHA (branched chain keto acid dehydrogenase E1, alpha polypeptide) (eg, maple syrup urine disease, type 1A), full gene sequence

---

BCS1L (BCS1-like [S. cerevisiae]) (eg, Leigh syndrome, mitochondrial complex III deficiency, GRACILE syndrome), full gene sequence

BMPR2 (bone morphogenetic protein receptor, typye II [serine/threonine kinase]) (eg, heritable pulmonary arterial hypertension), duplication/deletioin analsyis

CASQ2 (calsequestrin 2 [cardiac muscle]) (eg, catecholaminergic polymorphic ventricular tachycardia), full gene sequence

CASR (calcium-sensing receptor) (eg, hypocalcemia), full gene sequence

CDKL5 (cyclin-dependent kinase-like 5) (eg, early infantile epileptic encephalopathy), duplication/deletion analysis

CHRNA4 (cholinergic receptor, nicotinic, alpha 4) (eg, nocturnal frontal lobe epilepsy), full gene sequence

CHRNB2 (cholinergic receptor, nicotinic, beta 2 [neuronal]) (eg, nocturnal frontal lobe epilepsy), full gene sequence

COX10 (COX10 homolog, cytochrome c oxidase assembly protein) (eg, mitochondrial respiratory chain complex IV deficiency), full gene sequence

COX15 (COX15 homolog, cytochrome c oxidase assembly protein) (eg, mitochondrial respiratory chain complex IV deficiency), full gene sequence

CPOX (coproporphyrinogen oxidase) (eg, hereditary coproporphyria), full gene sequence

CTRC (chymotrypsin C) (eg, hereditary pancreatitis), full gene sequence

CYP11B1 (cytochrome P450, family 11, subfamily B, polypeptide 1) (eg, congenital adrenal hyperplasia), full gene sequence

CYP17A1 (cytochrome P450, family 17, subfamily A, polypeptide 1) (eg, congenital adrenal hyperplasia), full gene sequence

CYP21A2 (cytochrome P450, family 21, subfamily A, polypeptide2) (eg, steroid 21-hydroxylase isoform, congenital adrenal hyperplasia), full gene sequence

Cytogenomic constitutional targeted microarray analysis of chromosome 22q13 by interrogation of genomic regions for copy number and single nucleotide polymorphism (SNP) variants for chromosomal abnormalities

(When performing genome-wide cystogenomic constitutional microarray analysis, see 81228, 81229)

(Do not report analyte-specific molecular pathology procedures separately when the specific analytes are included as part of the microarray analysis of chromosome 22q13)

(Do not report 88271 when performing cytogenomic microarray analysis)

DBT (dihydrolipoamide branched chain transacylase E2) (eg, maple syrup urine disease, type 2), duplication/deletion analysis

DCX (doublecortin) (eg, X-linked lissencephaly), full gene sequence

DES (desmin) (eg, myofibrillar myopathy), full gene sequence

DFNB59 (deafness, autosomal recessive 59) (eg, autosomal recessive nonsyndromic hearing impairment), full gene sequence

DGUOK (deoxyguanosine kinase) (eg, hepatocerebral mitochondrial DNA depletion syndrome), full gene sequence

DHCR7 (7-dehydrocholesterol reductase) (eg, Smith-Lemli-Opitz syndrome), full gene sequence

EIF2B2 (eukaryotic translation initiation factor 2B, subunit 2 beta, 39kDa) (eg, leukoencephalopathy with vanishing white matter), full gene sequence

EMD (emerin) (eg, Emery-Dreifuss muscular dystrophy), full gene sequence

ENG (endoglin) (eg, hereditary hemorrhagic telangiectasia, type 1), duplication/deletion analysis

● New Code　　▲ Revised Code　　+ Add-On Code　　⊘ Modifier -51 Exempt　　★ Telemedicine

EYA1 (eyes absent homolog 1 [Drosophila]) (eg, branchio-oto- renal [BOR] spectrum disorders), duplication/deletion analysis

FGFR1 (fibrobast growth factor receptor 1) (eg, Kallmann syndrome 2), full gene sequence

FH (fumarate hydratase) (eg, fumarate hydratase deficiency, hereditary leiomyomatosis with renal cell cancer), full gene sequence

FKTN (fukutin) (eg, limb-girdle muscular dystrophy [LGMD] type 2M or 2L), full gene sequence

FTSJ1 (FtsJ RNA methyltransferase homolog 1 [E. coli]) (eg, X-linked mental retardation 9), duplication/deletion analysis

GABRG2 (gamma-aminobutyric acid [GABA] A receptor, gamma 2) (eg, generalized epilepsy with febrile seizures), full gene sequence

GCH1 (GTP cyclohydrolase 1) (eg, autosomal dominant dopa-responsive dystonia), full gene sequence

GDAP1 (ganglioside-induced differentiation-associated protein 1) (eg, Charcot-Marie-Tooth disease), full gene sequence

GFAP (glial fibrillary acidic protein) (eg, Alexander disease), full gene sequence

GHR (growth hormone receptor) (eg, Laron syndrome), full gene sequence

GHRHR (growth hormone releasing hormone receptor) (eg, growth hormone deficiency), full gene sequence

GLA (galactosidase, alpha) (eg, Fabry disease), full gene sequence

HNF1A (HNF1 homeobox A) (eg, maturity-onset diabetes of the young [MODY]), full gene sequence

HNF1B (HNF1 homeobox B) (eg, maturity-onset diabetes of the yound [MODY]), full gene sequence

HTRA1 (HtrA serine peptidase 1) (eg, macular degeneration), full gene sequence

IDS (iduronate 2-sulfatase) (eg, mucopolysacchridosis, type II), full gene sequence

IL2RG (interleukin 2 receptor, gamma) (eg, X-linked severe combined immunodeficiency), full gene sequence

ISPD (isoprenoid synthase domain containing) (eg, muscle-eye-brain disease, Walker-Warburg syndrome), full gene sequence

KRAS (Kirsten rat sarcoma viral oncogene homolog) (eg, Noonan syndrome), full gene sequence

LAMP2 (lysosomal-associated membrane protein 2) (eg, Danon disease), full gene sequence

LDLR (low density lipoprotein receptor) (eg, familial hypercholesterolemia), duplication/deletion analysis

MEN1 (multiple endocrine neoplasia 1) (eg, multiple endocrine neoplasia type 1, Wermer syndrome), full gene sequence

MMAA (methylmalonic aciduria [cobalamine deficiency] type A) (eg, MMAA-related methylmalonic acidemia), full gene sequence

MMAB (methylmalonic aciduria [cobalamine deficiency] type B) (eg, MMAB-related methylmalonic acidemia), full gene sequence

MPI (mannose phosphate isomerase) (eg, congenital disorder of slycosylation 1b), full gene sequence

MPV17 (MpV17 mitochondrial inner membrane protein) (eg, mitochondrial DNA depletion syndrome), full gene sequence

MPZ (myelin protein zero) (eg, Charcot-Marie-Tooth), full gene sequence

MTM1 (myotubularin 1) (eg, X-linked centronuclear myopathy), duplication/deletion analysis

MYL2 (myosin, light chain 2, regulatory, cardiac, slow) (eg, familial hypertrophic cardiomyopathy), full gene sequence

---

Separate Procedure   Unlisted Procedure   CCI Comp. Code   Non-specific Procedure   **729**

MYL3 (myosin, light chain 3, alkali, ventricular, skeletal, slow) (eg, familial hypertrophic cardiomyopathy), full gene sequence

MYOT (myotilin) (eg, limb-girdle muscular dystrophy), full gene sequence

NDUFS7 (NADH dehydrogenase [ubiquinone] Fe-S protein 7, 20kDa [NADH-coenzyme Q reductase]) (eg, Leigh syndrome, mitochondrial complex I deficiency), full gene sequence

NDUFS8 (NADH dehydrogenase [ubiquinone] Fe-S protein 8, 23kDa [NADH-coenzyme Q reductase]) (eg, Leigh syndrome, mitochondrial complex I deficiency), full gene sequence

NDUFV1 (NADH dehydrogenase [ubiquinone] flavoprotein 1, 51kDa) (eg, Leigh syndrome, mitochondrial complex I deficiency), full gene sequence

NEFL (neurofilament, light polypeptide) (eg, Charcot-Marie- Tooth), full gene sequence

NF2 (neurofibromin 2 [merlin]) (eg, neurofibromatosis, type 2), duplication/deletion analysis

NLGN3 (neuroligin 3) (eg, autism spectrum disorders), full gene sequence

NLGN4X (neuroligin 4, X-linked) (eg, autism spectrum disorders), full gene sequence

NPHP1 (nephronophthisis 1 [juvenile]) (eg, Joubert syndrome), deletion analysis, and duplication analysis if performed

NPHS2 (nephrosis 2, idiopathic, steroid-resistant [podocin]) (eg, steroid-resistant nephrotic syndrome), full gene sequence

NSD1 (nuclear receptor binding SET domain protein 1) (eg, Sotos syndrome), duplication/deletion analysis

OTC (ornithine carbamoyltransferase) (eg, ornithine transcarbamylase deficiency), full gene sequence

PAFAH1B1 (platelet-activating factor acetylhydrolase 1b, regulatory subunit 1 [45kDa]) (eg, lissencephaly, Miller-Dieker syndrome), duplication/deletion analysis

PARK2 (Parkinson protein 2, E3 ubiquitin protein ligase [parkin]) (eg, Parkinson disease), duplication/deletion anaysis

PCCA (propionyl CoA carboxylase, alpha polypeptide) (eg, propionic acidemia, type 1) duplication/deletion analysis

PCDH19 (protocadherin 19) (eg, epileptic encephalopathy), full gene sequence

PDHA1 (pyruvate dehydrogenase [lipoamide] alpha 1) (eg, lactic acidosis), duplication/deletion analysis

PDHB (pyruvate dehydrogenase [lipoamide] beta) (eg, lactic acidosis), full gene sequence

PINK1 (PTEN induced putative kinase 1) (eg, Parkinson disease), full gene sequence

PKLR (pyruvate kinase, liver and RBC) (eg, pyruvate kinase deficiency), full gene sequence

PLP1 (proteolipid protein 1) (eg, Pelizaeus-Merzbacher disease, spastic paraplegia), full gene sequence

POU1F1 (POU class 1 homeobox 1) (eg, combined pituitary hormone deficiency), full gene sequence

PRX (periaxin) (eg, Charcot-Marie-Tooth disease), full gene sequence

PQBP1 (polyglutamine binding protein 1) (eg, Renpenning syndrome), full gene sequence

PSEN1 (presenilin 1) (eg, Alzheimer disease), full gene sequence

RAB7A (RAB7A, member RAS oncogene family) (eg, Charcot-Marie-Toothe disease), full gene sequence

RAI1 (retinoic acid induced 1) (eg, Smith-Magenis syndrome), full gene sequence

REEP1 (receptor accessory protein 1) (eg, spastic paraplegia), full gene sequence

RET (ret proto-oncogene) (eg, multiple endocrine neoplasia, type 2A and familial medullary thyroid carcinoma), targeted sequence analysis (eg, exons 10, 11, 13-16)

RPS19 (ribosomal protein S19) (eg, Diamond-Blackfan anemia), full gene sequence

RRM2B (ribonucleotide reductase M2 B[TP53 inducible]) (eg, mitochondrial DNA depletion), full gene sequence

SCO1 (SCO cytochrome oxidase deficient homolog 1) (eg, mitochondrial respiratory chain complex IV deficiency), full gene sequence

SDHB (succinate dehydrogenase complex, subunit B, iron sulfur) (eg, hereditary paraganglioma), full gene sequence

SDHC (succinate dehydrogenase complex, submit C, integral membrane protein, 15kDa) (eg, hereditary paraganglioma-pheochromocytoma syndrome), full gene sequence

SGCA (sarcoglycan, alpha [50kDa dystrophin-associated glycoprotein]) (eg, limb-girdle muscular dystrophy), full gene sequence

SGCB (sarcoglycan, beta [43kDa dystrophin-associated glycoprotein]) (eg, limb-girdle muscular dystrophy), full gene sequence

SGCD (sarcoglycanm delta [35kDa dystrophin-associated glycoprotein]) (eg, limb-girdle muscular dystrophy), full gene sequence

SGCE (sarcoglycan, epsilon) (eg, myoclonic dystonia), duplication/deletion analysis

SGCG (sarcoglycan, gamma [35kDa dystrophin-associated glycoprotein]) (eg, limb-girdle muscular dystrophy), full gene sequence

SHOC2 (soc-2 suppressor of clear homolog) (eg, Noonan-like syndrome with loose anagen hair), full gene sequence

SHOX (short stature homeobox) (eg, Langer mesomelic dysplasia), full gene sequence

SIL1 (SIL 1 homolog, endoplasmic reticulum chaperone [S. cerevisiae]) (eg, ataxia), full gene sequence

SLC2A1 (solute carrier family 2 [facilitated glucose transporter], member 1) (eg, glucose transporter type 1 [GLUT 1] deficiency syndrome), full gene sequence

SLC16A2 (solute carrier family 16, member 2 [thyroid hormone transporter]) (eg, specific thyroid hormone cell transporter deficiency, Allan-Herndon-Dudley syndrome), full gene sequence

SLC22A5 (solute carrier family 22 [organic cation/carnitine transporter], member 5) (eg, systemic primary carnitine deficiency),, full gene sequence

SLC25A20 (solute carrier family 25 [carnitine/acylcarnitine translocase], member 20) (eg, carnitine-acylcarnitine translocase deficiency), full gene sequence

SMAD4 (SMAD family member 4) (eg, hemorrhagic telangiectasia syndrome, juvenile polyposis), duplication/deletion analsysi

SMN1 (survival of motor neuron 1, telomeric) (eg, spinal muscular atrophy), full gene sequence

SPAST (spastin) (eg, spastic paraplegia), duplication/deletion analsysis

SPG7 (spastic paraplegia 7 [pure and complicated autosomal recessive]) (eg, spastic paraplegia), duplication/deletion analysis

SPRED1 (sprouty-related, EVH1 domain containing 1) (eg, Legius syndrome), full gene sequence

STAT3 (signal transducer and activator of transcription 3 [acute-phase response factor]) (eg, autosomal dominant hyper-Ig-E syndrome), targeted sequence analysis (eg, exons 12, 13, 14, 16, 17, 20, 21)

STK11 (serine/threonine kinase 11) (eg, Peutz-Jeghers syndrome), full gene sequence

SURF1 (surfeit 1) (eg, mitochondrial respiratory chain complex IV deficiency), full gene sequence

TARDBP (TAR DNA binding protein) (eg, amyotrophic lateral sclerosis), full gene sequence

TBX5 (T-box 5) (eg, Holt-Oram syndrome), full gene sequence

TCF4 (transcription factor 4) (eg, Pitt-Hopkins syndrome), duplication/deletion analysis

TGFBR1 (transforming growth factor, beta receptor 1) (eg, Marfan syndrome), full gene sequence

---

| Separate Procedure | Unlisted Procedure | CCI Comp. Code | Non-specific Procedure | **731** |

TGFBR2 (transforming growth factor, beta receptor 2) (eg, Marfan syndrome), full gene sequence

THRB (thyroid hormone receptor, beta) (eg, thyroid hormone resistance, thyroid hormone beta receptor deficiency), full gene sequence or targeted sequence analysis of >5 exons

TK2 (thymidine kinase 2, mitochondrial) (eg, mitochondrial DNA depletion syndrome), full gene sequence

TNNC1 (troponin C type 1 [slow]) (eg, hypertrophic cardiomyopathy or dilated cardiomyopathy), full gene sequence

TNNI3 (troponin I, type 3 [cardiac]) (eg, familial hypertrophic cardiomyopathy), full gene sequence

TP53 (tumor protein 53) (eg, Li-Fraumeni syndrome, tumor samples), full gene sequence or targeted sequence analysis of >5 exons

TPM1 (tropomyosin 1 [alpha]) (eg, familial hypertrophic cardiomyopathy), full gene sequence

TSC1 (tuberous sclerosis 1) (eg, tuberous sclerosis), duplication/ deletion analysis

TYMP (thymidine phosphorylase) (eg, mitochondrial DNA depletion syndrome), full gene sequence

VWF (von Willebrand factor) (eg, von Willebrand disease type 2N), targeted sequence analysis (eg, exons 18-20, 23-25)

WT1 (Wilms tumor 1) (eg, Denys-Drash syndrome, familial Wilms tumor), full gene sequence

ZEB2 (zinc finger E-box binding homeobox 2) (eg, Mowat-Wilson syndrome), full gene sequence

▲ **81406**   Molecular pathology procedure, Level 7 (eg, analysis of 11-25 exons by DNA sequence analysis, mutation scanning or duplication/deletion variants of 26-50 exons, cytogenomic array analysis for neoplasia)

ACADVL (acyl-CoA dehydrogenase, very long chain) (eg, very long chain acyl-coenzyme A dehydrogenase deficiency), full gene sequence

ACTN4 (actinin, alpha 4) (eg, focal segmental glomerulosclerosis), full gene sequence

AFG3L2 (AFG3 ATPase family gene 3-like 2 [S. cerevisiae]) (eg, spinocerebellar ataxia), full gene sequence

AIRE (autoimmune regulator) (eg, autoimmune polyendocrinopathy syndrome type 1), full gene sequence

ALDH7A1 (aldehyde dehydrogenase 7 family, member A1) (eg, pyridoxine-dependent epilepsy), full gene sequence

ANO5 (anoctamin 5) (eg, limb-girdle muscular dystrophy), full gene sequence

ANOS1 (anosmin-1) (eg, Kallmann syndrome 1), full gene sequence

APP (amyloid beta [A4] precursor protein) (eg, Alzheimer disease), full gene sequence

ASS1 (argininosuccinate synthase 1) (eg, citrullinemia type I), full gene sequence

ATL1 (atlastin GTPase 1) (eg, spastic paraplegia), full gene sequence

ATP1A2 (ATPase, Na+/K+ transporting, alpha 2 polypeptide) (eg, familial hemiplegic migraine), full gene sequence

ATP7B (ATPase, Cu++ transporting, beta polypeptide) (eg, Wilson disease), full gene sequence

BBS1 (Bardet-Biedl syndrome 1) (eg, Bardet-Biedl syndrome), full gene sequence

BBS2 (Bardet-Biedl syndrome 2) (eg, Bardet-Biedl syndrome), full gene sequence

BCKDHB (branched-chain keto acid dehydrogenase E1, beta polypeptide) (eg, maple syrup urine disease, type 1B), full gene sequence

BEST1 (bestrophin 1) (eg, vitelliform macular dystrophy), full gene sequence

BMPR2 (bone morphogenetic protein receptor, type II [serine/threonine kinase]) (eg, heritable pulmonary arterial hypertension), full gene sequence

BRAF (B-raf proto-oncogene, serine/threonine kinase) (eg, Noonan syndrome), full gene sequence

● New Code   ▲ Revised Code   ✛ Add-On Code   ⊘ Modifier -51 Exempt   ★ Telemedicine

BSCL2 (Berardinelli-Seip congenital lipodystrophy 2 [seipin]) (eg, Berardinelli-Seip congenital lipodystrophy), full gene sequence

BTK (Bruton agammaglobulinemia tyrosine kinase) (eg, X-linked agammaglobulinemia), full gene sequence

CACNB2 (calcium channel, voltage-dependent beta 2 subunit) (eg, Brugada syndrome), full gene sequence

CAPN3 (Calpain 3) (eg, limb-girdle muscular dystrophy [LGMD] type 2A, calpainopathy), full gene sequence

CBS (cystathionine-beta-synthase) (eg, homocystinuria, cystathionine beta-synthase deficiency), full gene sequence

CDH1 (cadherin 1, type 1, E-cadherin [epithelial]) (eg, hereditary diffuse gastric cancer), full gene sequence

CDKL5 (cyclin-dependent kinase-like 5) (eg, early infantile epileptic encephalopathy), full gene sequence

CLCN1 (chloride channel 1, skeletal muscle) (eg, myotonia congenita), full gene sequence

CLCNKB (chlorid channel, voltage-sensitive Kb) (eg, Bartter syndrome 3 and 4b), full gene sequence

CNTNAP2 (contactin-associated protein-like 2) (eg, Pitt-Hopkins-like syndrome 1), full gene sequence

COL6A2 (collagen, type VI, alpha 2) (eg, collagen type VI-related disorders), duplication/deletion analysis

CPT1A (carnitine palmitoyltransferase 1A [liver]) (eg, carnitine palmitoyltransferase 1A[CPT1A] deficiency), full gene sequence

CRB1 (crumbs homolog 1 [Drosophila]) (eg, Leber congenital amaurosis), full gene sequence

CREBBP (CREB binding protein) (eg, Rubinstein-Taybi syndrome), duplication/deletion analisys

Cytogenomic microarray analysis, neoplasia (eg, interrogation of copy number, and loss-of-heterozygosity via single nucleotide polymorphism [SNP]-based comparative genomic hybridization [CGH] microarray analysis)

(Do not report analyte-specific molecular pathology procedures separately when the specific analytes are included as part of the cytogenomic microarray analysis for neoplasia)

(Do not report 88271 when performing cytogenomic microarray analysis)

DBT (dihydrolipoamide branched chain transacylase E2) (eg, maple syrup urine disease, type 2), full gene sequence

DLAT (dihydrolipoamide S-acetyltransferase) (eg, pyruvate dehydrogenase E2 deficiency), full gene sequence

DLD (dihydrolipoamide dehydrogenase) (eg, maple syrup urine disease, type III), full gene sequence

DSC2 (desmocollin) (eg, arrhythmogenic right ventricular dysplasia/cardiomyopathy 11), full gene sequence

DSG2 (dismoglein 2) (eg, arrhythmogenic right ventricular dysplasia/cardiomyopathy 10), full gene sequence

DSP (desmoplakin) (eg, arrhythmogenic right ventricular dysplasia/cadiomyopathy 8), full gene sequence

EFHC1 (EG-hand domain [C-terminal] containing 1) (eg, juvenile myoclonic epilepsy), full gene sequence

EIF2B3 (eukaryotic translation initiation factor 2B, subunit 3 gamma, 58kDa) (eg, leukoencephalopathy with vanishing white matter), full gene sequence

EIF2B4 (eukaryotic translation initiation factor 2B, subunit 4 delta, 67kDa) (eg, leukoencephalopathy with vanishing white matter), full gene sequence

EIF2B5 (eukaryotic translation initiation factor 2B, subunit 5 epsilon, 82kDa) (eg, childhood ataxia with central nervous system hypomyelination/vanishing white matter), full gene sequence

ENG (endoglin) (eg, hereditary hemorrhagic telangiectasia, type 1), full gene sequence

---

EYA1 (eyes absent homolog 1 [Drosophila]) (eg, branchio-otorenal [BOR] spectrum disorders), full gene sequence

F8 (coagulation factor VIII) (eg, hemophilia A), duplication/ deletion analysis

FAH (fumarylacetoacetate hydrolase [fumarylacetoacetase]) (eg, tyrosinemia, type 1), full gene sequence

FASTKD2 (FAST kinase domains2) (eg, mitochrondrial respiratory chain complex IV deficiency), full gene sequence

FIG4 (FIG4 homolog, SAC1 lipid phosphatase domain containing [S. cerevisiae]) (eg, Charcot-Marie-Tooth disease), full gene sequence

FTSJ1 (FtsJ RNA methyltransferase homolog 1 [E. coli]) (eg, X-linked mental retardation 9), full gene sequence

FUS (fused in sarcoma) (eg, amyotrophic lateral sclerosis), full gene sequence

GAA (glucosidase, alpha; acid) (eg, glycogen storage disease type II [Pompe disease]), full gene sequence

GALC (galactosylceramidase) (eg, Krabbe disease), full gene sequence

GALT (galactose-1-phosphate uridylyltransferase) (eg, galactosemia), full gene sequence

GARS (glycyl-tRNA synthetase) (eg, Charcot-Marie-Tooth disease), full gene sequence

GCDH (glutaryl-CoA dehydrogenase) (eg, glutaricacidemia type 1), full gene sequence

GCK (glucokinase [hexokinase 4]) (eg, maturity-onset diabetes of the young [MODY]), full gene sequence

GLUD1 (glutamate dehydrogenase 1) (eg, familial hyperinsulinism), full gene sequence

GNE (glucosamine [UDP-N-acetyl]-2-epimerase/N- acetylmannosamine kinase) (eg, inclusion body myopathy 2 [EBM2], Nonaka myopathy), full gene sequence

GRN (granulin) (eg, frontotemporal dementia), full gene sequence

HADHA (hydroxyacyl-CoA dehydrogenase/3-ketoacyl-CoA thiolase/enoyl-CoA hydratase [trifunctional protein] alpha subunit) (eg, long chain acyl-coenzyme A dehydrogenase deficiency), full gene sequence

HADHB (hydroxyacyl-CoA dehydrogenase/3-ketoacyl-CoA thiolase/enoyl-CoA hydratase [trifunctional protein], beta subunit) (eg, trifunctional protein deficiency), full gene sequence

HEXA (hexosaminidase A, alpha polypeptide) (eg, Tay-Sachs disease), full gene sequence

HLCS (HLCS holocarboxylase synthetase) (eg, holocarboxylase synthetase deficiency), full gene sequence

HMBS (hydroxymethylbilane synthase) (eg, acute intermittent porphyria), full gene sequence

HNF4A (hepatocyte nuclear factor 4, alpha) (eg, maturity-onset diabetes of the young [MODY]), full gene sequence

IDUA (iduronidase, alpha-L-) (eg, mucopolysaccharidosis type I), full gene sequence

INF2 (inverted formin, FH2 and WH2 domain containing) (eg, focal segmental glomerulosclerosis), full gene sequence

IVD (isovaleryl-CoA dehydrogenase) (eg, isovaleric acidemia), full gene sequence

JAG1 (jagged 1) (eg, Alagille syndrome), duplication/deletion analysis

JUP (junction plakoglobin) (eg, arrhythmogenic right ventricular dysplasia/cardiomyopathy 11), full gene sequence

KCNH2 (potassium voltage-gated channel, subfamily H [eag-related], member 2) (eg, short QT syndrome, long QT syndrome), full gene sequence

KCNQ1 (potassium voltage-gated channel, KQT-like subfamily, member 1) (eg, short QT syndrome, long QT syndrome), full gene sequence

KCNQ2 (potassium voltage-gated channel, KQT-like subfamily, member 2) (eg, epileptic encephalopathy), full gene sequence

● New Code   ▲ Revised Code   ✛ Add-On Code   ⊘ Modifier -51 Exempt   ★ Telemedicine

LDB3 (LIM domain binding 3) (eg, familial dilated cardiomyopathy, myofibrillar myopathy), full gene sequence

LDLR (low density lipoprotein receptor) (eg, familial hypercholesterolemia), full gene sequence

LEPR (leptin receptor) (eg, obesity with hypogonadism), full gene sequence

LHCGR (luteinizing hormone/choriogonadotropin receptor) (eg, precocious male puberty), full gene sequence

LMNA (lamin A/C) (eg, Emery-Dreifuss muscular dystrophy [EDMD1, 2 and 3] limb-girdle muscular dystrophy [LGMD] type 1B, dilated cardiomyopathy [CMD1A], familial partial lipodystrophy [FPLD2]), full gene sequence

LRP5 (low density lipoprotein receptor-related protein 5) (eg, osteopetrosis), full gene sequence

MAP2K1 (mitogen-activated protein kinase 1) (eg, cardiofaciocutaneous syndrome), full gene sequence

MAP2K2 (mitogen-activated protein kinase 2) (eg, cardiofaciocutaneous syndrome), full gene sequence

MAPT (microtubule-associated protein tau) (eg, frontotemporal dementia), full gene sequence

MCCC1 (methylcrotonoyl-CoA carboxylase 1 [alpha]) (eg, 3-methylcrotonyl-CoA-carboxylase deficiency), full gene sequence

MCCC2 (methylcrotonoyl-CoA carboxylase 2 [beta]) (eg, 3-methylcrotonyl carboxylase deficiency), full gene sequence

MFN2 (mitofusin 1) (eg, Charcot-Marie-Tooth disease), full gene sequence

MTM1 (myotubularin 1) (eg, X-linked centronuclear myopathy), full gene sequence

MUT 9methylmalonyl CoA mutase) (eg, methylmalonic acidemia), full gene sequence

MUTYH (mutY homolog [E. coli]) (eg, MYH-associated polyposis), full gene sequence

NDUFS1 (NADH dehydrogenase [ubiquinone] Fe-S protein 1, 75kDa [NADH-coenzyme Q reductase]) (eg, Leigh syndrome, mitochondrial complex I deficiency), full gene sequence

NF2 (neurofibromin 2 [merlin]) (eg, neurofibromatosis, type 2), full gene sequence

NOTCH3 (notch 3) (eg, cerebral autosomal dominant arteriopathy with subcortical infarcts and leukoencephalopathy [CADASIL]), targeted sequence analysis (eg, exons 1-23)

NPC1 (Niemann-Pick disease, type C1) (eg, Niemann-Pick disease), full gene sequence

NPHP1 (nephronophthisis 1 [juvenile]) (eg, Joubert syndrome), full gene sequence

NSD1 (nuclear receptor binding SET domain protein 1) (eg, Sotos syndrome), full gene sequence

OPA1 (optic atrophy 1) (eg, optic atrophy), duplication/deletion analysis

OPTN (optineurin) (eg, amyotrophic lateral sclerosis), full gene sequence

PAFAH1B1 (platelet-activating factor acetylhydrolase 1b, regulatory subunit 1 [45kDa]) (eg, lissencephaly, Miller-Dieker syndrome), full gene sequence

PAH (phenylalanine hydroxylase) (eg, phenylketonuria), full gene sequence

PALB2 (partner and localizer of BRCA2) (eg, breast and pancreatic cancer), full gene sequence

PARK2 (Parkinson protein 2, E3 ubiquitin protein ligase [parkin]) (eg, Parkinson disease), full gene sequence

PAX2 (paired box 2) (eg, renal coloboma syndrome), full gene sequence

PC (pyruvate carboxylase) (eg, pyruvate carboxylase deficiency), full gene sequence

PCCA (propionyl CoA-carboxylase, alpha polypeptide) (eg, propionic acidemia, type 1

PCCB (propionyl CoA carboxylase, beta polypeptide) (eg, propionic acidemia), full

735

PCDH15 (protocadherin-related 15) (eg, Usher syndrome type 1F), duplication/deletion analysis

PCSK9 (proprotein convertase subtilisin/kexin type 9) (eg, familial hypercholesterolemia), full gene sequence

PDHA1 (pyruvate dehydrogenase [lipoamide] alpha 1) (eg, lactic acidosis), full gene sequence

PDHX (pyruvate dehydrogenase complex, component X) (eg, lactic acidosis), full gene sequence

PHEX (phosphate-regulating endopeptidase homolog, X-linked) (eg, hypophosphatemic rickets), full gene sequence

PKD2 (polycystic kidney disease 2 [autosomal dominant]) (eg, polycystic kidney disease), full gene sequence

PKP2 (plakophilin 2) (eg, arrhythmogenic right ventricular dysplasia/cardiomyopathy 9), full gene sequence

PNKD (eg, paroxysmal nonkinesigenic dyskinesia) (eg, paroxysmal nonkinesigenic dyskinesia), full gene sequence

POLG (polymerase [DNA directed], gamma) (eg, Alpers-Huttenlocher syndrome, autosomal dominant progressive external ophthalmoplegia), full gene sequence

POMGNT1 (protein O-linked mannose beta1,2-N acetylglucosaminyltransferase) (eg, muscle-eye-brain disease, Walker-Warburg syndrome), full gene sequence

POMT1 (protein-O-mannosyltransferase 1) (eg, limb-girdle muscular dystrophy [LGMD] type 2K, Walker-Warburg syndrome), full gene sequence

POMT2 (protein-O-mannosyltransferase 2) (eg, limb-girdle muscular dystrophy [LGMD] type 2N, Walker-Warburg syndrome), full gene sequence

PPOX (protoporphyrinogen oxidase) (eg, variegate porphyria), full gene sequence

PRKAG2 (protein kinase, AMP-activated, gamma 2 non-catalytic subunit) (eg, familial hypertrophic cardiomyopathy with Wolff-Parkinson-White syndrome, lethal congenital glycogen storagedisease of heart), full gene sequence

PRKCG (protein kinase C, gamma) (eg, spinocerebellar ataxia), full gene sequence

PSEN2 (presenilin 2 [Alzheimer disease 4]) (eg, Alzheimer disease), full gene sequence

PTPN11 (protein tyrosine phosphatase, non-receptor type 11) (eg, Noonan syndrome, LEOPARD syndrome), full gene sequence

PYGM (phosphorylase, glycogen, muscle) (eg, glycogen storage disease type V, McArdle disease), full gene sequence

RAF1 (v-raf-1 murine leukemia viral oncogene homolog 1) (eg, LEOPARD syndrome), full gene sequence

RET (ret proto-oncogene) (eg, Hirschsprung disease), full gene sequence

RPE65 (retinal pigment epithelium-specific protein 65kDa) (eg, retinitis pigmentosa, Leber congenital amaurosis), full gene sequence

RYR1 (ryanodine receptor 1, skeletal) (eg, malignant hyperthermia), targeted sequence analysis of exons with functionally-confirmed mutations

SCN4A (sodium channel, voltage-gated, type IV, alpha subunit) (eg, hyperkalemic periodic paralysis), full gene sequence

SCNN1A (sodium channel, nonvoltage-gated 1 alpha) (eg, pseudohypoaldosteronism), full gene sequence

SCNN1B (sodium channel, nonvoltage-gated 2, beta) (eg, Liddle syndrome, pseudohypoaldosteronism), full gene sequence

SCNN1G (sodium channel, nonvoltage-gated 1, gamma) (eg, Liddle syndrome, pseudohypoaldosteronism), full gene sequence

SDHA (succinate dehydrogenase complex, subunit A, flavoprotein [Fp]) (eg, Leigh syndrome, mitochondrial complex II deficiency), full gene sequence

---

SETX (senataxin) (eg, ataxia), full gene sequence

SGCE (sarcoglycan, epsilon) (eg, myoclonic dystonia), full gene sequence

SH3TC2 (SH3 domain and tetratricopeptide repeats 2) (eg, Charcot-Marie-Tooth disease), full gene sequence

SLC9A6 (solute carrier family 9 [sodium/hydrogen exchanger], member 6) (eg, Christianson syndrome), full gene sequence

SLC26A4 (solute carrier family 26, member 4) (eg, Pendred syndrome), full gene sequence

SLC37A4 (solute carrier family 37 [glucose-6-phosphate transporter], member 4) (eg, glycogen storage disease type Ib), full gene sequence

SMAD4 (SMAD family member 4) (eg, hemorrhagic telangiectasia syndrome, juvenile polyposis), full gene sequence

SOS1 (son of sevenless homolog 1) (eg, Noonan syndrome, gingival fibromatosis), full gene sequence

SPAST (spastin) (eg, spastic paraplegia), full gene sequence

SPG7 (spastic paraplegia 7 [pure and complicated autosomal recessive]) (eg, spastic paraplegia), full gene sequence

STXBP1 (syntaxin-binding protein 1) (eg, epileptic encephalopathy), full gene sequence

TAZ (tafazzin) (eg, methylglutaconic aciduria type 2, Barth syndrome), full gene sequence

TCF4 (transcription factor 4) (eg, Pitt-Hopkins syndrome), full gene sequence

TH (tyrosine hydroxylase) (eg, Segawa syndrome), full gene sequence

TMEM43 (transmembrane protein 43) (eg, arrhythmogenic right ventricular cardiomyopathy), full gene sequence

TNNT2 (troponin T, type 2 [cardiac]) (eg, familial hypertrophic cardiomyopathy), full gene sequence

TRPC6 (transient receptor potential cation channel, subfamily C, member 6) (eg, focal segmental glomerulosclerosis), full gene sequence

TSC1 (tuberous sclerosis 1) (eg, tuberous sclerosis), full gene sequence

TSC2 (tuberous sclerosis 2) (eg, tuberous sclerosis), duplication/deletion analysis

UBE3A (ubiquitin protein ligase E3A) (eg, Angelman syndrome), full gene sequence

UMOD (uromodulin) (eg, glomerulocystic kidney disease with hyperuricemia and isosthenuria), full gene sequence

VWF (von Willebrand factor) (von Willebrand disease type 2A), extended targeted sequence analysis (eg, exons 11-16, 24-26, 51, 52)

WAS (Wiskott-Aldrich syndrome [eczema-thrombocytopenia]) (eg, Wiskott-Aldrich syndrome), full gene sequence

81407 Molecular pathology procedure, Level 8 (eg, analysis of 26-50 exons by DNA sequence analysis, mutation scanning or duplication/deletion variants of >50 exons, sequence analysis of multiple genes on one platform)

ABCC8 (ATP-binding cassette, sub-family C [CFTR/MRP], member 8) (eg, familial hyperinsulinism), full gene sequence

AGL (amylo-alpha-1, 6-glucosidase, 4-alpha-glucanotransferase) (eg, glycogen storage disease type III), full gene sequence

AHI1 (Abelson helper integration site 1) (eg, Joubert syndrome), full gene sequence

ASPM (asp [abnormal spindle] homolog, microcephaly associated [Drosophila]) (eg, primary microcephaly), full gene sequence

---

| | Separate Procedure | | Unlisted Procedure | | CCI Comp. Code | | Non-specific Procedure | **737** |

CACNA1A (calcium channel, voltage-dependent, P/Q type, alpha 1A subunit) (eg, familial hemiplegic migraine), full gene sequence

CHD7 (chromodomain helicase DNA binding protein 7) (eg, CHARGE syndrome), full gene sequence

COL4A4 (collagen, type IV, alpha 4) (eg, Alport syndrome), full gene sequence

COL4A5 (collagen, type IV, alpha 5) (eg, Alport syndrome), duplication/deletion analysis

COL6A1 (collagen, type VI, alpha 1) (eg, collagen type VI-related disorders), full gene sequence

COL6A2 (collagen, type VI, alpha 2) (eg, collagen type VI-related disorders), full gene sequence

COL6A3 (collagen, type VI, alpha 3) (eg, collagen type VI-related disorders), full gene sequence

CREBBP (CREB binding protein) (eg, Rubinstein-Taybi syndrome), full gene sequence

F8 (coagulation factor VIII) (eg, hemophilia A), full gene sequence

JAG1 (jagged 1) (eg, Alagille syndrome), full gene sequence

KDM5C (lysine [K]-specific demethylase 5C) (eg, X-linked mental retardation), full gene sequence

KIAA0196 (KIAA0196) (eg, spastic paraplegia), full gene sequence

L1CAM (L1 cell adhesion molecule) (eg, MASA syndrome, X-linked hydrocephaly), full gene sequence

LAMB2 (laminin, beta 2 [laminin S]) (eg, Pierson syndrome), full gene sequence

MYBPC3 (myosin binding protein C, cardiac) (eg, familial hypertrophic cardiomyopathy), full gene sequence

MYH6 (myosin, heavy chain 6, cardiac muscle, alpha) (eg, familial dilated cardiomyopathy), full gene sequence

MYH7 (myosin, heavy chain 7, cardiac muscle, beta) (eg, familial hypertrophic cardiomyopathy, Liang distal myopathy), full gene sequence

MYO7A (myosin VIIA) (eg, Usher syndrome, type 1), full gene sequence

NOTCH1 (notch 1) (eg, aortic valve disease), full gene sequence

NPHS1 (nephrosis 1, congenital, Finnish type [nephrin]) (eg, congenital Finnish nephrosis), full gene sequence

OPA1 (optic atrophy 1) (eg, optic atrophy), full gene sequence

PCDH15 (protocadherin-related 15) (eg, Usher syndrome, type 1), full gene sequence

PKD1 (polycystic kidney disease 1 [autosomal dominant]) (eg, polycystic kidney disease), full gene sequence

PLCE1 (phospholipase C, epsilon 1) (eg, nephrotic syndrome type 3), full gene sequence

SCN1A (sodium channel, voltage-gated, type 1, alpha subunit) (eg, generalized epilepsy with febrile seizures), full gene sequence

SCN5A (sodium channel, voltage-gated, type V, alpha subunit) (eg, familial dilated cardiomyopathy), full gene sequence

SLC12A1 (solute carrier family 12 [sodium/potassium/chloride transporters], member 1) (eg, Bartter syndrome), full gene sequence

SLC12A3 (solute carrier family 12 [sodium/chloride transporters], member 3) (eg, Gitelman syndrome), full gene sequence

SPG11 (spastic paraplegia 11 [autosomal recessive]) (eg, spastic paraplegia), full gene sequence

SPTBN2 (spectrin, beta, non-erythrocytic 2) (eg, spinocerebellar ataxia), full gene sequence

TMEM67 (transmembrane protein 67) (eg, Joubert syndrome), full gene sequence

---

● New Code   ▲ Revised Code   ✚ Add-On Code   ⊘ Modifier -51 Exempt   ★ Telemedicine

TSC2 (tuberous sclerosis 2) (eg, tuberous sclerosis), full gene sequence

USH1C (Usher syndrome 1C [autosomal recessive, severe]) (eg, Usher syndrome, type 1), full gene sequence

VPS13B (vacuolar protein sorting 13 homolog B [yeast]) (eg, Cohen syndrome), duplication/deletion analysis

WDR62 (WD repeat domain 62) (eg, primary autosomal recessive microcephaly), full gene sequence

81408 Molecular pathology procedure, Level 9 (eg, analysis of >50 exons in a single gene by DNA sequence analysis)

ABCA4 (ATP-binding cassette, sub-family A [ABC1], member 4) (eg, Stargardt disease, age-related macular degeneration), full gene sequence

ATM (ataxia telangiectasia mutated) (eg, ataxia telangiectasia),full gene sequence

CDH23 (cadherin-related 23) (eg, Usher syndrome, type 1), full gene sequence

CEP290 (centrosomal protein 290kDa) (eg, Joubert syndrome), full gene sequence

COL1A1 (collagen, type I, alpha 1) (eg, osteogenesis imperfecta, type I), full gene sequence

COL1A2 (collagen, type I, alpha 2) (eg, osteogenesis imperfecta, type I), full gene sequence

COL4A1 (collagen, type IV, alpha 1) (eg, brain small-vessel disease with hemorrhage), full gene sequence

COL4A3 (collagen, type IV, alpha 3 [Goodpasture antigen]) (eg, Alport syndrome), full gene sequence

COL4A5 (collagen, type IV, alpha 5) (eg, Alport syndrome), full gene sequence

DMD (dystrophin) (eg, Duchenne/Becker muscular dystrophy), full gene sequence

DYSF (dysferlin, limb girdle muscular dystrophy 2B [autosomal recessive]) (eg, limb-girdle muscular dystrophy), full gene sequence

FBN1 (fibrillin 1) (eg, Marfan syndrome), full gene sequence

ITPR1 (inositol 1, 4, 5-trisphosphate receptor, type 1) (eg, spinocerebellar ataxia), full gene sequence

LAMA2 (laminin, alpha 2) (eg, congenital muscular dystrophy), full gene sequence

LRRK2 (leucine-rich repeat kinase 2) (eg, Parkinson disease), full gene sequence

MYH11 (myosin, heavy chain 11, smooth muscle) (eg, thoracic aortic aneurysms and aortic dissections), full gene sequence

NEB (nebulin) (eg, nemaline myopathy 2), full gene sequence

NF1 (neurofibromin 1) (eg, neurofibromatosis, type 1), full gene sequence

PKHD1 (polycystic kidney and hepatic disease 1) (eg, autosomal recessive polycystic kidney disease), full gene sequence

RYR1 (ryanodine receptor 1, skeletal) (eg, malignant hyperthermia), full gene sequence

RYR2 (ryanodine receptor 2 [cardiac]) (eg, catecholaminergic polymorphic ventricular tachycardia, arrhythmogenic right ventricular dysplasia), full gene sequence or targeted sequence analysis of > 50 exons

USH2A (Usher syndrome 2A [autosomal recessive, mild]) (eg, Usher syndrome, type 2), full gene sequence

VPS13B (vacuolar protein sorting 13 homolog B [yeast]) (eg, Cohen syndrome), full gene sequence

VWF (von Willebrand factor) (eg, von Willebrand disease types 1 and 3), full gene sequence

81479 Unlisted molecular pathology procedure

GENOMIC SEQUENCING PROCEDURES AND OTHER MOLECULAR MULTIANALYTE ASSAYS

Genomic sequencing procedures (GSPs) and other molecular multianalyte assays GSPs are DNA or RNA sequence analysis methods that simultaneously assay multiple genes or genetic regions relevant to a clinical situation. They may target specific combinations of genes or genetic material, or assay the exome or genome. The technology used for genomic sequencing is commonly referred to as next generation sequencing (NGS) or massively parallel sequencing (MPS). GSPs are performed on nucleic acids from germline or neoplastic samples. Examples of applications include aneuploidy analysis of cell-free circulating fetal DNA, gene panels for somatic alterations in neoplasms, and sequence analysis of the exome or genome to determine the cause of developmental delay. The exome and genome procedures are designed to evaluate the genetic material in totality or near totality. Although commonly used to identify sequence (base) changes, they can also be used to identify copy number, structural changes, and abnormal zygosity patterns. Another unique feature of GSPs is the ability to "re-query" or re-evaluate the sequence data (eg, complex phenotype such as developmental delay is reassessed when new genetic knowledge is attained, or for a separate unrelated clinical indication). The analyses listed below represent groups of genes that are often performed by GSPs; however, the analyses may also be performed by other molecular techniques (polymerase chain reaction [PCR] methods and microarrays). These codes should be used when the components of the descriptor(s) are fulfilled regardless of the technique used to provide the analysis, unless specifically noted in the code descriptor. When a GSP assay includes gene(s) that is listed in more than one code descriptor, the code for the most specific test for the primary disorder sought should be reported, rather than reporting multiple codes for the same gene(s). When all of the components of the descriptor are not performed, use individual Tier 1 codes, Tier 2 codes, or 81479 (Unlisted molecular pathology procedure).

The assays in this section represent distinct discrete genetic values, properties, or characteristics in which the measurement or analysis of each analyte is potentially of independent medical significance or useful in medical management. In contrast to multianalyte assays with algorithmic analyses (MAAAs), the assays in this section do not represent algorithmically combined results to obtain a risk score or other value, which in itself represents a new and distinct medical property that is of independent medical significance relevant to the individual, component test results.

(For cytogenetic MicroArray analyses, see 81228, 81229, 81405, 81406)

(For long QT syndrome gene analyses, see 81280, 81282)

81410 Aortic dysfunction or dilation (eg, Marfan syndrome, Loeys Dietz syndrome, Ehler Danlos syndrome type IV, arterial tortuosity syndrome); genomic sequence analysis panel, must include sequencing of at least 9 genes, including *FBN1, TGFBR1, TGFBR2, COL3A1, MYH11, ACTA2, SLC2A10, SMAD3,* and *MYLK*

81411 duplication/deletion analysis panel, must include analyses for *TGFBR1, TGFBR2, MYH11,* and *COL3A1*

81412 Ashkenazi Jewish associated disorders (eg, Bloom syndrome, Canavan disease, cystic fibrosis, familial dysautonomia, Fanconi anemia group C, Gaucher disease, Tay-Sachs disease), genomic sequence analysis panel, must include sequencing of at least 9 genes, including *ASPA, BLM, CFTR, FANCC,GBA, HEXA, IKBKAP, MCOLN1,* and *SMPD1*

81413 Cardiac ion channelopathies (eg, Brugada syndrome, long QT syndrome, short QT syndrome, catecholaminergic polymorphic ventricular tachycardia); genomic sequence analysis panel, must include sequencing of at least 10 genes, including ANK2, CASQ2, CAV3, KCNE1, KCNE2, KCNH2, KCNJ2, KCNQ1, RYR2, and SCN5A

81414 duplication/deletion gene analysis panel, must include analysis of at least 2 genes, including KCNH2 and KCNQ1

(For genomic sequencing panel testing for cardiomyopathies, use 81439)

(Do not report 81413, 81414 in conjunction with 81439 when performed on the same date of service)

81415 Exome (eg, unexplained constitutional or heritable disorder or syndrome); sequence analysis

+ 81416 sequence analysis, each comparator exome (eg, parents, siblings) (List separately in addition to code for primary procedure)

(Use 81416 in conjunction with 81415)

● New Code ▲ Revised Code + Add-On Code ⊘ Modifier -51 Exempt ★ Telemedicine

81417 re-evaluation of previously obtained exome sequence (eg, updated knowledge or unrelated condition/syndrome)

(Do not report 81417 for incidental findings)

(For exome-wide copy number assessment by microarray, see 81228, 81229)

81420 Fetal chromosomal aneuploidy (eg, trisomy 21, monosomy X) genomic sequence analysis panel, circulating cell-free fetal DNA in maternal blood, must include analysis of chromosomes 13, 18, and 21

(Do not report 81228, 81229, 88271 when performing genomic sequencing procedures or other molecular multianalyte assays for copy number analysis)

81422 Fetal chromosomal microdeletion(s) genomic sequence analysis (eg, DiGeorge syndrome, Cri-du-chat syndrome), circulating cell-free fetal DNA in maternal blood

(Do not report 81228, 81229, 88271 when performing genomic sequencing procedures or other molecular multianalyte assays for copy number analysis)

81425 Genome (eg, unexplained constitutional or heritable disorder or syndrome); sequence analysis

81426 sequence analysis, each comparator genome (eg, parents, siblings) (List separately in addition to code for primary procedure)

(Use 81426 in conjunction with 81425)

81427 re-evaluation of previously obtained genome sequence (eg, updated knowledge or unrelated condition/syndrome)

(Do not report 81427 for incidental findings)

(For genome-wide copy number assessment by microarray, see 81228, 81229)

81430 Hearing loss (eg, nonsyndromic hearing loss, Usher syndrome, Pendred syndrome); genomic sequence analysis panel, must include sequencing of at least 60 genes, including *CDH23, CLRN1, GJB2, GPR98, MTRNR1, MYO7A, MYO15A, PCDH15, OTOF, SLC26A4, TMC1, TMPRSS3, USH1C, USH1G, USH2A, and WFS1*

81431 duplication/deletion analysis panel, must include copy number analyses for *STRC* and *DFNB1* deletions in *GJB2* and *GJB6* genes

▲ **81432** Hereditary breast cancer-related disorders (eg, hereditary breast cancer, hereditary ovarian cancer, hereditary endometrial cancer); genomic sequence analysis panel, must include sequencing of at least 10 genes, always including *BRCA1, BRCA2, CDH1, MLH1, MSH2, MSH6, PALB2, PTEN, STK11, and TP53*

81433 duplication/deletion analysis panel, must include analyses for *BRCA1, BRCA2, MLH1, MSH2, and STK11*

81434 Hereditary retinal disorders (eg, retinitis pigmentosa, Leber congenital amaurosis, cone-rod dystrophy), genomic sequence analysis panel, must include sequencing of at least 15 genes, including *ABCA4, CNGA1, CRB1, EYS, PDE6A, PDE6B, PRPF31, PRPH2, RDH12, RHO, RP1, RP2, RPE65, RPGR, and USH2A*

81435 Hereditary colon cancer disorders (eg, Lynch syndrome, PTEN hamartoma syndrome, Cowden syndrome, familial adenomatosis polyposis); genomic sequence analysis panel, must include sequencing of at least 10 genes, including *APC, BMPR1A, CDH1, MLH1, MSH2, MSH6, MUTYH, PTEN, SMAD4, and STK11*

81436 duplication/deletion analysis panel, must include analysis of at least 5 genes, including *MLH1, MSH2, EPCAM, SMAD4, and STK11*

81437 Hereditary neuroendocrine tumor disorders (eg, medullary thyroid carcinoma, parathyroid carcinoma, malignant pheochromocytoma or paraganglioma); genomic sequence analysis panel, must include sequencing of at least 6 genes, including *MAX, SDHB, SDHC, SDHD, TMEM127, and VHL*

▮ Separate Procedure	▮ Unlisted Procedure	▮ CCI Comp. Code	▮ Non-specific Procedure	**741**

81438   Hereditary neuroendocrine tumor disorders (eg, medullary thyroid carcinoma, parathyroid carcinoma, malignant pheochromocytoma or paraganglioma); duplication/deletion analysis panel, must include analyses for *SDHB, SDHC, SDHD,* and *VHL*

● **81448**   Hereditary peripheral neuropathies (eg, Charcot-Marie- Tooth, spastic paraplegia), genomic sequence analysis panel, must include sequencing of at least 5 peripheral neuropathy-related genes (eg, *BSCL2, GJB1, MFN2, MPZ, REEP1, SPAST, SPG11, SPTLC1*)

▲ **81439**   Hereditary cardiomyopathy (eg, hypertrophic cardiomyopathy, dilated cardiomyopathy, arrhythmogenic right ventricular cardiomyopathy), genomic sequence analysis panel, must include sequencing of at least 5 cardiomyopathy-related genes (eg, *DSG2, MYBPC3, MYH7, PKP2, TTN*)

(Do not report 81439 in conjunction with 81413, 81414 when performed on the same date of service)

(For genomic sequencing panel testing for cardiac ion channelopathies, see 81413, 81414)

81440   Nuclear encoded mitochondrial genes (eg, neurologic or myopathic phenotypes), genomic sequence panel, must include analysis of at least 100 genes, including *BCS1L, C10orf2, COQ2, COX10, DGUOK, MPV, OPA1, PDSS2, POLG, POLG2, RRM2B, SCO1, SCO2, SLC25A4, SUCLA2, SUCLG1, TAZ, TK2,* and *TYMP*

81442   Noonan spectrum disorders (eg, Noonan syndrome, cardio-facio-cutaneous syndrome, Costello syndrome, LEOPARD syndrome, Noonan-like syndrome), genomic sequence analysis panel, must include sequencing of at least 12 genes, including *BRAF, CBL, HRAS, KRAS, MAP2K1, MAP2K2, NRAS, PTPN11, RAF1, RIT1, SHOC2,* and *SOS1*

81445   Targeted genomic sequence analysis panel, solid organ neoplasm, DNA analysis, and RNA analysis when performed, 5-50 genes (eg, *ALK, BRAF, CDKN2A, EGFR, ERBB2, KIT, KRAS, NRAS, MET, PDGFRA, PDGFRB, PGR, PIK3CA, PTEN, RET*), interrogation for sequence variants and copy number variants or rearrangements, if performed

(For copy number assessment by microarray, use 81406)

81448   This code is out of order. See page 742.

81450   Targeted genomic sequence analysis panel, hematolymphoid neoplasm or disorder, DNA analysis, and RNA analysis when performed, 5-50 genes (eg, *BRAF, CEBPA, DNMT3A, EZH2, FLT3, IDH1, IDH2, JAK2, KRAS, KIT, MLL, NRAS, NPM1, NOTCH1*), interrogation for sequence variants, and copy number variants or rearrangements, or isoform expression or mRNA expression levels, if performed

(For copy number assessment by microarray, use 81406)

81455   Targeted genomic sequence analysis panel, solid organ or hematolymphoid neoplasm, DNA analysis, and RNA analysis when performed, 51 or greater genes (eg, *ALK, BRAF, CDKN2A, CEBPA, DNMT3A, EGFR, ERBB2, EZH2, FLT3, IDH1, IDH2, JAK2, KIT, KRAS, MLL, NPM1, NRAS, MET, NOTCH1, PDGFRA, PDGFRB, PGR, PIK3CA, PTEN, RET*), interrogation for sequence variants and copy number variants or rearrangements, if performed

(For copy number assessment by microarray, use 81406)

81460   Whole mitochondrial genome (eg, Leigh syndrome, mitochondrial encephalomyopathy, lactic acidosis, and stroke-like episodes [MELAS], myoclonic epilepsy with ragged-red fibers [MERFF], neuropathy, ataxia, and retinitis pigmentosa [NARP], leber hereditary optic neuropathy [LHON]), genomic sequence, must include sequence analysis of entire mitochondrial genome with heteroplasmy detection

81465   Whole mitochondrial genome large deletion analysis panel (eg, Kearns-Sayre syndrome, chronic progressive external ophthalmoplegia), including heteroplasmy detection, if performed

81470   X-linked intellectual disability (XLID) (eg, syndromic and non-syndromic XLID); genomic sequence analysis panel, must include sequencing of at least 60 genes, including *ARX, ATRX, CDKL5, FGD1, FMR1, HUWE1, IL1RAPL, KDM5C, L1CAM, MECP2, MED12, MID1, OCRL, RPS6KA3,* and *SLC16A2*

81471   duplication/deletion gene analysis, must include analysis of at least 60 genes, including *ARX, ATRX, CDKL5, FGD1, FMR1, HUWE1, IL1RAPL, KDM5C, l1CAM, MECP2, MED12, MID1, OCRL, RPS6KA3*, and *SLC16a2*

81479   This code is out of order. See page 739.

MULTIANALYTE ASSAYS WITH ALGORITHMIC ANALYSES

Multianalyte Assays with Algorithmic Analyses (MAAAs) are procedures that utilize multiple results derived from panels of analyses of various types, including molecular pathology assays, fluorescent in situ hybridization assays and non-nucleic acid based assays (eg, proteins, polypeptides, lipids, carbohydrates). Algorithmic analysis using the results of these assays as well as other patient information (if used) is then performed, and typically reported as a numeric score(s) or as a probability. MAAAs are typically unique to a single clinical laboratory or manufacturer. The results of individual component procedure(s) that are inputs to the MAAAs may be provided on the associated laboratory report; however these assays are not separately reported using additional codes.

The format for the code descriptors of MAAAs usually include (in order):

Disease type (eg, oncology, autoimmune, tissue rejection),

Material(s) analyzed (eg, DNA, RNA, protein, antibody),

Number of markers (eg, number of genes, number of proteins),

Methodology(ies) (eg, microarray, real-time [RT]-PCR, in situ hybridization [ISH], enzyme linked immunosorbent assays [ELISA],

Number of functional domains (if indicated),

Specimen type (eg, blood, fresh tissue, formalin-fixed paraffin embedded),

Algorithm result type (eg, prognostic, diagnostic),

Report (eg, probability index, risk score)

In contrast to GSPs and other molecular multianalyte assays, the assays in this section represent alorithmically combined results of analyses of multiple analytes to obtain a risk score or other value which in itself represents a new and distinct medical property that is of independent medical significance relative to the individual component test results in clinical context in which the assay is performed.

MAAAs, including those that do not have a Category I code, may be found in Appendix O. MAAAs that do not have a Category I code are identified in Appendix O by a four-digit number followed by the letter "M." The Category 1 MAAA codes that are included in this subsection are also included in Appendix O. All MAAA codes are listed in Appendix O along with the procedure's proprietary name. In order to report a MAAA code, the analysis performed must fulfill the code descriptor AND, if proprietary, must be the test represented by the proprietary name listed in Appendix O.

When a specific MAAA procedure is not listed below or in Appendix O, the procedure must be reported using the Category 1 MAAA unlisted code (81599).

These codes encompass all analytical services required (eg, cell lysis, nucleic acid stabilization, extraction, digestion, amplification, hybridization, adn detection) in addition to the algorithmic analysis itself. Procedures that are required prior to cell lysis (eg, microdissection, codes 88380 and 88381) should be reported separately.

81490   Autoimmune (rheumatoid arthritis), analysis of 12 biomarkers using immunoassays, utilizing serum, prognostic algorithm reported as a disease activity score

         (Do not report 81490 in conjunction with 86140)

81493   Coronary artery disease, mRNA, gene expression profiling by real-time RT-PCR of 23 genes, utilizing whole peripheral blood, algorithm reported as a risk score

81500   Oncology (ovarian), biochemical assays of two proteins (CA-125 adn HE4), utilizing serum, with menopausal status, algorithm reported as a risk score

---

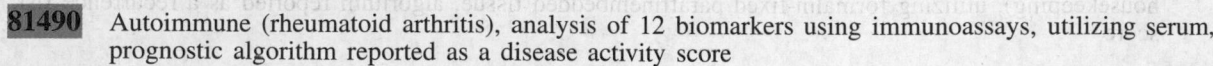 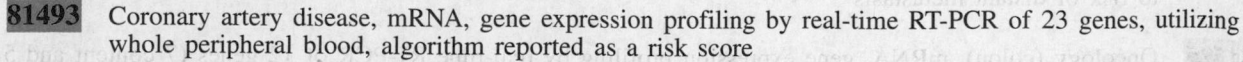

(Do note report 81500 in conjunction with 86304, 86305)

81503 Oncology (ovarian), biochemical assays of five proteins (CA-125, apolipoprotein A1, beta-2 microglobulin, transferrin, and pre-albumin), utilizing serum, algorithm reported as a risk score

(Do not report 81503 in conjunction with 82172, 82232, 84134, 84466, 86304)

81504 Oncology (tissue of origin), microarray gene expression profiling of > 2000 genes, utilizing formalin-fixed paraffin-embedded tissue, algorithm reported as tissue similarity scores

81506 Endocrinology (type 2 diabetes), biochemical assays of seven analytes (glucose, HbA1c, insulin, hs-CRP, adoponectin, ferritin, interleukin 2-receptor alpha), utilizing serum or plasma, algorithm reporting a risk score

(Do not report 81506 in conjunction with constituent components [ie, 82728, 82947, 83036, 83525, 86141], 84999 [for adopectin], and 83520 [for interleukin 2-receptor alpha])

81507 Fetal aneuploidy (trisomy 21, 18, and 13) DNA sequence analysis of selected regions using maternal plasma, algorithm reported as a risk score for each trisomy

(Do not report 81228, 81229, 88271 when performing genomic sequencing procedures or other molecular multianalyte assays for copy number analysis)

81508 Fetal congenital abnormalities, biochemical assays of two proteins (PAPP-A, hCG [any form]), utilizing maternal serum, algorithm reported as a risk score

(Do not report 81508 in conjunction with 84163, 84702)

81509 Fetal congenital abnormalities, biochemical assays of three proteins (PAPP-A, hCG [any form], DIA), utilizing maternal serum, algorithm reported as a risk score

(Do not report 81509 in conjunction with 84163, 84702, 86336)

81510 Fetal congenital abnormalities, biochemical assays of three analytes (AFP, uE3, hCG [any form]), utilizing maternal serum, algorithm reported as a risk score

(Do note report 81510 in conjunction with 82105, 82677, 84702)

81511 Fetal congenital abnormalities, biochemical assays of four analytes (AFP, uE3, hCG [any form], DIA) utilizing maternal serum, algorithm reported as a risk score (may include additional results from previous biochemical testing)

(Do not report 81511 in conjunction with 82105, 82677, 84702,. 86336)

81512 Fetal congenital abnormalities, biochemical assays of five analytes (AFP, uE3, total hCG, hyperglycosylated hCG, DIA) utilizing maternal serum, algorithm reported as a risk score

(Do not report 81512 in conjunction with 82105, 82677, 84702, 86336)

81519 Oncology (breast), mRNA, gene expression profiling by real-time RT-PCR of 21 genes, utilizing formalin-fixed paraffin embedded tissue, algorithm reported as recurrence score

● **81520** Oncology (breast), mRNA gene expression profiling by hybrid capture of 58 genes (50 content and 8 housekeeping), utilizing formalin-fixed paraffinembedded tissue, algorithm reported as a recurrence risk score

● **81521** Oncology (breast), mRNA, microarray gene expression profiling of 70 content genes and 465 housekeeping genes, utilizing fresh frozen or formalin-fixed paraffinembedded tissue, algorithm reported as index related to risk of distant metastasis

81525 Oncology (colon), mRNA, gene expression profiling by real-time RT-PCR of 12 genes (7 content and 5 housekeeping), utilizing formalin-fixed paraffin-embedded tissue, algorithm reported as a recurrence score

---

● New Code ▲ Revised Code + Add-On Code ⊘ Modifier -51 Exempt ★ Telemedicine

81528 Oncology (colorectal) screening, quantitative real-time target and signal amplification of 10 DNA markers (KRAS mutations, promoter methylation of NDRG4 and BMP3) and fecal hemoglobin, utilizing stool, algorithm reported as a positive or negative result

(Do not report 81528 in conjunction with 81275, 82274)

81535 Oncology (gynecologic), live tumor cell culture and chemotherapeutic response by DAPI stain and morphology, predictive algorithm reported as a drug response score; first single drug or drug combination

+ **81536** each additional single drug or drug combination (List separately in addition to code for primary procedure)

(Use 81536 in conjunction with 81535)

81538 Oncology (lung), mass spectrometric 8-protein signature, including amyloid A, utilizing serum, prognostic and predictive algorithm reported as good versus poor overall survival

81539 Oncology (high-grade prostate cancer), biochemical assay of four proteins (Total PSA, Free PSA, Intact PSA, and human kallikrein-2 [hK2]), utilizing plasma or serum, prognostic algorithm reported as a probability score

81540 Oncology (tumor of unknown origin), mRNA, gene expression profiling by real-time RT-PCR of 92 genes (87 content and 5 housekeeping) to classify tumor into main cancer type and subtype, utilizing formalin-fixed paraffin-embedded tissue, algorithm reported as a probability of a predicted main cancer type and subtype

● **81541** Oncology (prostate), mRNA gene expression profiling by real-time RT-PCR of 46 genes (31 content and 15 housekeeping), utilizing formalin-fixed paraffinembedded tissue, algorithm reported as a diseasespecific mortality risk score

81545 Oncology (thyroid), gene expression analysis of 142 genes, utilizing fine needle aspirate, algorithm reported as a categorical result (eg, benign or suspicious)

● **81551** Oncology (prostate), promoter methylation profiling by real-time PCR of 3 genes (GSTP1, APC, RASSF1), utilizing formalin-fixed paraffin-embedded tissue, algorithm reported as a likelihood of prostate cancer detection on repeat biopsy

81595 Cardiology (heart transplant), mRNA, gene expression profiling by real-time quantitative PCR of 20 genes (11 content and 9 housekeeping), utilizing subfraction of peripheral blood, algorithm reported as a rejection risk score

81599 Unlisted multianalyte assay with algorithmic analysis

(Do not report 81599 for multianalyte assays with algorithmic analyses listed in Appendix O)

CHEMISTRY

The material for examination may be from any source unless otherwise specified in the code descriptor. When an analyte is measured in multiple specimens from different sources, or in specimens that are obtained at different times, the analyte is reported separately for each source and for each specimen. The examination is quantitative unless specified. To report an organ or disease oriented panel, see codes 80048-80076.

When a code describes a method where measurement of multiple analytes may require one or several procedures, each procedure is coded separately (eg., 82491-82492, 82541-82544). For example, if two analytes are measured using column chromatography using a single stationary or mobile phase, use 82492. If the same two analytes are measured using different stationary or mobile phase conditions, 82491 would be used twice. If a total of four analytes are measured where two analytes are measured with a single stationary and mobile phase, and the other two analytes are measured using a different stationary and mobile phase, use 82492 twice. If a total of three analytes are measured where two analytes are measured using a single stationary or mobile phase condition, and the third analyte is measured separately using a different stationary or mobile phase procedure, use 82492 once for the two analytes measured under the same condition, and use 82491 once for the third analyte measured separately.

Clinical information or mathematically calculated values, which are not specifically requested by the ordering physician and are derived from the results of other ordered or performed laboratory tests, are considered part of the ordered test procedure(s) and therefore are not separately reportable service(s).

When the requested analyte result is derived using a calculation that requires values from nonrequested laboratory analyses, only the requested analyte code should be reported.

When the calculated analyte determination requires values derived from other requested and nonrequested laboratory analyses, the requested analyte codes (including those calculated) should be reported.

An exception to the above is when an analyte (eg, urinary creatinine) is performed to compensate for variations in urine concentration (eg, microalbumin, thromboxane metabolites) in random urine samples; the appropriate CPT code is reported for both the ordered analyte and the additional required analyte. When the calculated result(s) represent an algorithmically derived numeric score or probability, see the appropriate multianalyte assay with algorithmic analyses (MAAA) code or the MAAA unlisted code (81599).

(82000   deleted 2014 [2015 edition])

(82003   deleted 2014 [2015 edition]. For acetaminophen, see 80329, 80330, 80331)

82009   Ketone body(s) (eg, acetone, acetoacetic acid, beta-hydroxybutyrate); qualitative

82010   quantitative

82013   Acetylcholinesterase

(For gastric acid analysis, use 82930)

(Acid phosphatase, see 84060-84066)

82016   Acylcarnitines; qualitative, each specimen

82017   quantitative, each specimen

(For carnitine, use 82379)

82024   Adrenocorticotropic hormone (ACTH)

82030   Adenosine, 5-monophosphate, cyclic (cyclic AMP)

82040   Albumin; serum, plasma or whole blood

82042   This code is out of order. See page 746.

▲ 82043   urine (eg, microalbumin), quantitative

▲ 82044   urine (eg, microalbumin), semiquantitative (eg, reagent strip assay)

(For prealbumin, use 84134)

82045   ischemia modified

▲ 82042   other source, quantitative, each specimen

(For total protein, see 84155, 84156, 84157, 84160)

(82055   deleted 2014 [2015 edition]. For alcohol, any specimen except breath, see 80320, 80321, 80322)

82075   Alcohol (ethanol), breath

82085   Aldolase

● New Code   ▲ Revised Code   + Add-On Code   ⊘ Modifier -51 Exempt   ★ Telemedicine

82088   Aldosterone

(Alkaline phosphatase, see 84075, 84080)

(**82101**   deleted 2014 [2015 edition]. For alkaloids, use 80323)

(Alphaketoglutarate, see 82009, 82010)

(Alpha tocopherol (Vitamin E), use 84446)

82103   Alpha-1-antitrypsin; total

82104   phenotype

82105   Alpha-fetoprotein; serum

82106   amniotic fluid

82107   AFP-L3 fraction isoform and total AFP (including ratio)

82108   Aluminum

82120   Amines, vaginal fluid, qualitative

(For combined pH and amines test for vaginitis, use 82120 and 83986)

82127   Amino acids; single, qualitative, each specimen

82128   multiple, qualitative, each specimen

82131   single, quantitative, each specimen

82135   Aminolevulinic acid, delta (ALA)

82136   Amino acids, 2 to 5 amino acids, quantitative, each specimen

82139   Amino acids, 6 or more amino acids, quantitative, each specimen

82140   Ammonia

82143   Amniotic fluid scan (spectrophotometric)

(For L/S ratio, use 83661)

(Amobarbital, use 80345)

(**82145**   deleted 2014 [2015 edition]. For amphetamine or methamphetamine, see 80324, 80325, 80326)

82150   Amylase

82154   Androstanediol glucuronide

82157   Androstenedione

82160   Androsterone

82163   Angiotensin II

82164   Angiotensin I - converting enzyme (ACE)

(Antidiuretic hormone (ADH), use 84588)

(Antimony, use 83015)

(Antitrypsin, alph-1-, see 82103, 82104)

82172 Apolipoprotein, each

82175 Arsenic

(For heavy metal screening, use 83015)

82180 Ascorbic acid (Vitamin C), blood

(Aspirin, see acetylsalicylic acid, 80329, 80330, 80331)

(Atherogenic index, blood, ultracentrifugation, quantitative, use 83717)

82190 Atomic absorption spectroscopy, each analyte

(**82205** deleted 2014 [2015 edition]. For barbiturates not elsewhere specified, see 80345)

82232 Beta-2 microglobulin

(Bicarbonate, use 82374)

82239 Bile acids; total

82240 cholylglycine

(For bile pigments, urine, see 81000-81005)

82247 Bilirubin; total

82248 direct

82252 feces, qualitative

82261 Biotinidase, each specimen

82270 Blood, occult, by peroxidase activity (eg, guaiac), qualitative; feces, consecutive collected specimens with single determination, for colorectal neoplasm screening (ie, patient was provided three cards or single triple card for consecutive collection)

82271 other sources

82272 Blood, occult, by peroxidase activity (eg, guaiac), qualitative, feces, 1-3 simultaneous determinations, performed for other than colorectal neoplasm screening

(Blood urea nitrogen (BUN), see 84520, 84525)

82274 Blood, occult, by fecal hemoglobin determination by immunoassay, qualitative, feces, 1-3 simultaneous determinations

82286 Bradykinin

82300 Cadmium

82306 Vitamin D; 25 hydroxy, includes fraction(s), if performed

82652 1, 25-dihydroxy, includes fraction(s), if performed

82308 Calcitonin

82310 Calcium; total

82330   ionized

82331   after calcium infusion test

82340   urine quantitative, timed specimen

82355 Calculus; qualitative analysis

82360   quantitative analysis, chemical

82365   infrared spectroscopy

82370   x-ray diffraction

(Carbamates, see individual listings)

82373 Carbohydrate deficient transferrin

82374 Carbon dioxide (bicarbonate)

(See also 82803)

82375 Carboxyhemoglobin; quantitative

82376   qualitative

(For transcutaneous measurement of carboxyhemoglobin, use 88740)

82378 Carcinoembryonic antigen (CEA)

82379 Carnitine (total and free), quantitative, each specimen

(For acylcarnitine, see 82016, 82017)

82380 Carotene

82382 Catecholamines; total urine

82383   blood

82384   fractionated

(For urine metabolites, see 83835, 84585)

82387 Cathepsin-D

82390 Ceruloplasmin

82397 Chemiluminescent assay

82415 Chloramphenicol

82435 Chloride; blood

82436   urine

82438   other source

(For sweat collection by iontophoresis, use 89230)

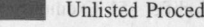

■ Separate Procedure   ✱ ■ Unlisted Procedure   ■ CCI Comp. Code   ■ Non-specific Procedure   **749**

82441 Chlorinated hydrocarbons, screen

(Chlorpromazine, use 84022)

(Cholecalciferol [Vitamin D], use 82306)

82465 Cholesterol, serum or whole blood, total

(For high density lipoprotein (HDL), use 83718)

82480 Cholinesterase; serum

82482   RBC

82485 Chondroitin B sulfate, quantitative

(Chorionic gonadotropin, see gonadotropin, 84702, 84703)

(**82486** deleted 2015 [2016 edition]. For a qualitative column chromatography procedure, use the appropriate specific analyte code, if available, or 82542)

(**82487** deleted 2015 [2016 edition]. For a paper chromatography procedure, use the appropriate specific analyte code, if available, or 84999)

(**82488** deleted 2015 [2016 edition]. For a paper chromatography procedure, use the appropriate specific analyte code, if available, or 84999)

(**82489** deleted 2015 [2016 edition]. For a thin layer chromatography procedure, use the appropriate specific analyte code, if available, or 84999)

(**82491** deleted 2015 [2016 edition]. For a quantitative column chromatography procedure, use the appropriate specific analyte code, if available, or 82542)

(**82492** deleted 2015 [2016 edition]. For a quantitative column chromatography procedure that detects more than one analyte, use a single specific code that represents all of the analytes, if available, or one unit of 82542 for all of the analytes)

82495 Chromium

82507 Citrate

(**82520** deleted 2014 [2015 edition]. For cocaine or metabolite, see 80353)

(Cocaine, qualitative analysis, use 80353)

(Codeine, qualitative analysis, see 80361)

(Complement, see 86160-86162)

82523 Collagen cross links, any method

82525 Copper

(Coproporphyrin, see 84119, 84120)

(Corticosteroids, use 83491)

82528 Corticosterone

82530 Cortisol; free

82533   total

(C-peptide, use 84681)

---

750 ● New Code ▲ Revised Code ✛ Add-On Code ⊘ Modifier -51 Exempt ★ Telemedicine

82540 Creatine

(82541 deleted 2015 [2016 edition]. For a quantitative chromatography procedure with mass spectrometry that only detects a single specific analyte, use the appropriate specific analyte code, if available, or 82542)

82542 Column chromatography, includes mass spectrometry, if performed (eg, HPLC, LC, LC/MS, LC/MS-MS, GC, GC/MS-MS, GC/MS, HPLC/MS), non-drug analyte(s) not elsewhere specified, qualitative or quantitative, each specimen

(Do not report more than one unit of 82542 for each specimen)

(82543 deleted 2015 [2016 edition]. For a quantitative chromatography procedure with mass spectrometry that only detects a single specific analyte, use the appropriate specific analyte code, if available, or 82542)

(82544 deleted 2015 [2016 edition]. For a quantitative chromatography procedure with mass spectrometry that detects more than one analyte, use a single specific code that represents all of the analytes, if available, or one unit of 82542 for all of the analytes)

(For column chromatography/mass spectrometry of drugs or substances, see 80305, 80306, 80307, 80320-80377, or specific analyte code[s] in Chemistry section)

82550 Creatine kinase (CK), (CPK); total

82552 isoenzymes

82553 MB fraction only

82554 isoforms

82565 Creatinine; blood

82570 other source

82575 clearance

82585 Cryofibrinogen

82595 Cryoglobulin, qualitative or semi-quantitative (eg,cryocrit)

(For quantitative, cryoglobulin, see 82784, 82785)

(Crystals, pyrophosphate vs. urate, use 89060)

82600 Cyanide

82607 Cyanocobalamin (Vitamin B-12);

82608 unsaturated binding capacity

(Cyclic AMP, use 82030)

(Cyclosporine, use 80158)

82610 Cystatin C

82615 Cystine and homocystine, urine, qualitative

82626 Dehydroepiandrosterone (DHEA)

(Do not report 82626 in conjunction with 80327, 80328 to identify anabolic steroid testing for testosterone)

| Separate Procedure | Unlisted Procedure | CCI Comp. Code | Non-specific Procedure | **751** |

82627   Dehydroepiandrosterone-sulfate (DHEA-S)

(Delta-aminolevulinic acid (ALA), use 82135)

82633   Desoxycorticosterone, 11-

82634   Deoxycortisol, 11-

(Dexamethasone suppression test, use 80420)

(Diastase, urine, use 82150)

82638   Dibucaine number

(Dichloroethane, use 82441)

(Dichloromethane, use 82441)

(Diethylether, use 84600)

(**82646**   deleted 2014 [2015 edition]. For dihydrocodeinone, use 80361)

(**82649**   deleted 2014 [2015 edition]. For opiates, use 80361)

(**82651**   deleted 2014 [2015 edition]. For anabolic steroids, see 80327, 80328)

82652   This code is out of order. See page 748.

(**82654**   deleted 2014 [2015 edition]. For dimethadione, see 80339, 80340, 80341)

(Dipropylacetic acid, use 80164)

(Dopamine, see 82382-82384)

(Duodenal contents, see individual enzymes; for intubation and collection, see 43756, 43757)

82656   Elastase, pancreatic (EL-1), fecal, qualitative or semi-quantitative

82657   Enzyme activity in blood cells, cultured cells, or tissue, not elsewhere specified; nonradioactive substrate, each specimen

82658   radioactive substrate, each specimen

82664   Electrophoretic technique, not elsewhere specified

(Endocrine receptor assays, see 84233-84235

(**82666**   deleted 2014 [2015 edition]. For epiandrosterone, see 80327, 80328)

82668   Erythropoietin

82670   Estradiol

82671   Estrogens; fractionated

82672   total

(Estrogen receptor assay, use 84233)

82677   Estriol

82679   Estrone

(Ethanol, use 80320)

● New Code   ▲ Revised Code   ✛ Add-On Code   ⊘ Modifier -51 Exempt   ★ Telemedicine

(82690   deleted 2014 [2015 edition]. For ethchlorvynol, ethyl alcohol, use 80320)

82693   Ethylene glycol

82696   Etiocholanolone

(For fractionation of ketosteroids, use 83593)

82705   Fat or lipids, feces; qualitative

82710   quantitative

82715   Fat differential, feces, quantitative

82725   Fatty acids, nonesterified

82726   Very long chain fatty acids

(For long-chain (C20-22) omega-3 fatty acids in red blood cell (RBC) membranes, use Category III code 0111T)

82728   Ferritin

(Fetal hemoglobin, see hemoglobin 83030, 83033, and 85460)

(Fetoprotein, alpha-1, see 82105, 82106)

82731   Fetal fibronectin, cervicovaginal secretions, semi-quantitative

82735   Fluoride

(82742   deleted 2014 [2015 edition]. For flurazepam, see 80346, 80347)

(Foam stability test, use 83662)

82746   Folic acid; serum

82747   RBC

(Follicle stimulating hormone (FSH), use 83001)

82757   Fructose, semen

(Fructosamine, use 82985)

(Fructose, TLC screen, use 84375)

82759   Galactokinase, RBC

82760   Galactose

82775   Galactose-1-phosphate uridyl transferase; quantitative

82776   screen

82777   Galectin-3

82784   Gammaglobulin (immunoglobulin); IgA, IgD, IgG, IgM, each

82785   IgE

(For allergen specific IgE, see 86003, 86005)

82787   immunoglobulin subclasses (eg, IgG1, 2, 3, or 4), each

(Gamma-glutamyltransferase (GGT), use 82977)

82800   Gases, blood, pH only

82803   Gases, blood, any combination of pH, pCO_2, pO_2, CO_2, HCO_3 (including calculated O_2 saturation);

(Use 82803 for two or more of the above listed analytes)

82805   with O_2 saturation, by direct measurement, except pulse oximetry

82810   Gases, blood, O_2 saturation only, by direct measurement, except pulse oximetry

(For pulse oximetry, use 94760)

82820   Hemoglobin-oxygen affinity (pO_2 for 50% hemoglobin saturation with oxygen)

(**82926**   deleted 2010 [2011 edition])

(**82928**   deleted 2010 [2011 edition])

(For gastric acid analysis, use 82930)

82930   Gastric acid analysis, includes pH if performed, each specimen

82938   Gastrin after secretin stimulation

82941   Gastrin

(Gentamicin, use 80170)

(GGT, use 82977)

(For a qualitative column chromatography procedure [eg, gas liquid chromatography], use the appropriate specific analyte code, if available, or 82542)

82943   Glucagon

82945   Glucose, body fluid, other than blood

82946   Glucagon tolerance test

82947   Glucose; quantitative, blood, (except reagent strip)

82948   blood, reagent strip

82950   post glucose dose (includes glucose)

82951   tolerance test (GTT), 3 specimens (includes glucose)

+ **82952**   tolerance test, each additional beyond 3 specimens (List separately in addition to code for primary procedure)

(Use 82952 in conjunction with 82951)

(**82953**   deleted 2014 [2015 edition].)

(For insulin tolerance test, see 80434, 80435)

(For leucine tolerance test, use 80428)

(For semiquantitative urine glucose, see 81000, 81002, 81005, 81099)

   ●   New Code   ▲   Revised Code   +   Add-On Code   ⊘   Modifier -51 Exempt   ★   Telemedicine

82955   Glucose-6-phosphate dehydrogenase (G6PD); quantitative

82960   screen

     (For glucose tolerance test with medication, use 96374 in addition)

82962   Glucose, blood by glucose monitoring device(s) cleared by the FDA specifically for home use

82963   Glucosidase, beta

82965   Glutamate dehydrogenase

(82975   deleted 2014 [2015 edition]. For glutamine [glutamic acid amide], see 82127, 82128, 82131)

82977   Glutamyltransferase, gamma (GGT)

82978   Glutathione

82979   Glutathione reductase, RBC

(82980   deleted 2014 [2015 edition])

     (Glycohemoglobin, use 83036)

82985   Glycated protein

     (Gonadotropin, chorionic, see 84702, 84703)

83001   Gonadotropin; follicle stimulating hormone (FSH)

83002   luteinizing hormone (LH)

     (For luteinizing releasing factor (LRH), use 83727)

83003   Growth hormone, human (HGH) (somatotropin)

     (For antibody to human growth hormone, use 86277)

83006   Growth stimulation expressed gene 2 (ST2, Interleukin 1 receptor like1)

(83008   deleted 2014 [2015 edition])

83009   Helicobacter pylori, blood test analysis for urease activity, non-radioactive isotope (eg, C-13)

     (For H. pylori, breath test analysis for urease activity, see 83013, 83014)

83010   Haptoglobin; quantitative

83012   phenotypes

83013   Helicobacter pylori; breath test analysis for urease activity, non-radioactive isotope (eg, C-13)

83014   drug administration

     (For H. pylori, stool, use 87338. For H. pylori, liquid scintillation counter, see 78267, 78268. For H. pylori immunoassay, use 87339)

     (For H. pylori, blood test analysis for urease activity, use 83009)

83015   Heavy metal (eg, arsenic, barium, beryllium, bismuth, antimony, mercury); qualitative, any number of analytes

---

▬ Separate Procedure   ▬ Unlisted Procedure   ▬ CCI Comp. Code   ▬ Non-specific Procedure   **755**

83018   quantitative, each, not elsewhere specified

(Use an analyte-specific heavy metal quantitative code, instead of 83018, when available)

83020   Hemoglobin fractionation and quantitation; electrophoresis (eg, A2, S, C, and/or F)

83021   chromotography (eg, A2, S, C,and/or F)

(For glycosylated [A1c] hemoglobin analysis, by electrophoresis or chromatography, in the absence of an identified hemoglobin variant, use 83036)

83026   Hemoglobin; by copper sulfate method, non-automated

83030   F (fetal), chemical

83033   F (fetal), qualitative

83036   glycosylated (A1C)

(For glycosylated [A1C] hemoglobin analysis, by electrophoresis or chromatography, in the setting of an identified hemoglobin variant, use 83020, 83021)

(For fecal hemoglobin detection by immunoassay, use 82274)

83037   glycosylated (A1C) by device cleared by FDA for home use

83045   methemoglobin, qualitative

83050   methemoglobin, quantitative

(For transcutaneous quantitative methemoglobin determination, use 88741)

83051   plasma

(83055   deleted 2014 [2015 edition])

83060   sulfhemoglobin, quantitative

83065   thermolabile

83068   unstable, screen

83069   urine

83070   Hemosiderin; qualitative

(83071   deleted 2014 [2015 edition])

(Heroin, see 80100-80103)

(HIAA, use 83497)

(For a qualitative column chromatography procedure [eg, high performance liquid chromatography], use the appropriate specific analyte code, if available, or 82542)

83080   b-Hexosaminidase, each assay

83088   Histamine

(Hollander test, see 43754, 43755)

83090   Homocystine

● New Code   ▲ Revised Code   + Add-On Code   ⊘ Modifier -51 Exempt   ★ Telemedicine

83150 Homovanillic acid (HVA)

(Hormones, see individual alphabetic listings in Chemistry section)

(For hydrogen/methane breath test, use 91065)

83491 Hydroxycorticosteroids, 17- (17-OHCS)

(For cortisol, see 82530, 82533. For deoxycortisol, use 82634)

83497 Hydroxyindolacetic acid, 5-(HIAA)

(For urine qualitative test, use 81005)

(5-Hydroxytryptamine, use 84260)

83498 Hydroxyprogesterone, 17-d

(**83499** deleted 2017 [2018 edition])

83500 Hydroxyproline; free

83505 total

83516 Immunoassay for analyte other than infectious agent antibody or infectious agent antigen; qualitative or semiquantitative, multiple step method

83518 qualitative or semiquantitative, single step method (eg, reagent strip)

83519 quantitative, by radioimmunoassay (eg, RIA)

83520 quantitative, not otherwise specified

(For immunoassays for antibodies to infectious agent antigens, see analyte and method specific codes in the Immunology section)

(For immunoassay of tumor antigen not elsewhere specified, use 86316)

(Immunoglobulins, see 82784, 82785)

83525 Insulin; total

(For proinsulin, use 84206)

83527 free

83528 Intrinsic factor

(For intrinsic factor antibodies, use 86340)

83540 Iron

83550 Iron binding capacity

83570 Isocitric dehydrogenase (IDH)

(Isonicotinic acid hydrazide, INH, see code for specific method)

(Isopropyl alcohol, use 80320)

83582 Ketogenic steroids, fractionation

(Ketone bodies, for serum, see 82009, 82010; for urine, see 81000-81003)

▮ Separate Procedure   ▮ Unlisted Procedure   ▮ CCI Comp. Code   ▮ Non-specific Procedure   **757**

83586	Ketosteroids, 17- (17-KS); total
83593	fractionation
83605	Lactate (lactic acid)
83615	Lactate dehydrogenase (LD), (LDH);
83625	isoenzymes, separation and quantitation
83630	Lactoferrin, fecal; qualitative
83631	quantitative
83632	Lactogen, human placental (HPL) human chorionic somatomammotropin
83633	Lactose, urine; qualitative
(83634	deleted 2014 [2015 edition]1)

(For tolerance, see 82951, 82952)

(For breath hydrogen/methane test for lactase deficiency, use 91065)

83655	Lead
83661	Fetal lung maturity assessment; lecithin-sphingomyelin ratio (L/S ratio)
83662	foam stability test
83663	fluorescence polarization
83664	lamellar body density

(For phosphatidylglycerol, use 84081)

83670	Leucine aminopeptidase (LAP)
83690	Lipase
83695	Lipoprotein (a)
83698	Lipoprotein-associated phospholipase A2, (Lp-PLA2)

(For secretory type II phospholipase A2 [sPLA2-IIA], use 0423T)

83700	Lipoprotein, blood; electrophoretic separation and quantitation
83701	high resolution fractionation and quantitation of lipoproteins including lipoprotein subclasses when performed (eg, electrophoresis, ultracentrifugation)
83704	quantitation of lipoprotein particle number(s) (eg, by nuclear magnetic resonance spectroscopy), includes lipoprotein particle subclass(es), when performed
83718	Lipoprotein, direct measurement; high density cholesterol (HDL cholesterol)
83719	VLDL cholesterol
83721	LDL cholesterol

(For fractionation by high resolution electrophoresis or ultracentrifugation, use 83701)

---

758 ● New Code   ▲ Revised Code   + Add-On Code   ⊘ Modifier -51 Exempt   ★ Telemedicine

(For lipoprotein particle numbers and subclasses analysis by nuclear magnetic resonance spectroscopy, use 83695)

83727 Luteinizing releasing factor (LRH)

(Luteinizing hormone (LH), use 83002)

(For qualitative analysis, see 80100-80103)

(Macroglobulins, alpha-2, use 86329)

83735 Magnesium

83775 Malate dehydrogenase

(Maltose tolerance, see 82951, 82952)

(Mammotropin, use 84146)

83785 Manganese

(Marijuana, see 80100-80103)

(83788 deleted 2015 [2016 edition]. For a qualitative mass spectrometry or tandem mass spectrometry procedure, use the specific analyte code, if available, or 83789)

83789 Mass spectrometry and tandem mass spectrometry (eg, MS, MS/MS, MALDI, MS-TOF, QTOF), non-drug analyte(s) not elsewhere specified, qualitative or quantitative, each specimen

(Do not report more than one unit of 83789 for each specimen)

(For column chromatography/mass spectrometry of drugs or substances, see 80305, 80306, 80307, 80320-80377, or specific analyte code[s] in the Chemistry section)

(83805 deleted 2014 [2015 edition]. For quantitative testing for meprobamate, see 80369, 80370)

83825 Mercury, quantitative

(Mercury screen, use 83015)

83835 Metanephrines

(For catecholamines, see 82382-82384)

(83840 deleted 2014 [2015 edition]. For methadone, use 80358)

(Methamphetamine, see 80324, 80325, 80326)

(Methane breath test, use 91065)

83857 Methemalbumin

(Methemoglobin, see hemoglobin 83045, 83050)

(83858 deleted 2014 [2015 edition]. For methsuximide, see 80339, 80340, 80341)

(Methyl alcohol, use 80320)

(Microalbumin, see 82043 for quantitative, see 82044 for semiquantitative)

83861 Microfluidic analysis utilizing an integrated collection and analysis device, tear osmolarity

(Microglobulin, beta-2, use 82232)

(For microfluidic tear osmolarity of both eyes, report 83861 twice)

Separate Procedure ▮ Unlisted Procedure ▮ CCI Comp. Code ▮ Non-specific Procedure **759**

83864 Mucopolysaccharides, acid; quantitative

(83866 deleted 2014 [2015 edition])

83872 Mucin, synovial fluid (Ropes test)

83873 Myelin basic protein, cerebrospinal fluid

(For oligoclonal bands, use 83916)

83874 Myoglobin

(Nalorphine, use 83925)

83876 Myeloperoxidase (MPO)

83880 Natriuretic peptide

83883 Nephelometry, each analyte not elsewhere specified

83885 Nickel

(83887 deleted 2014 [2015 edition]. For nicotine, use 80323)

83915 Nucleotidase 5-

83916 Oligoclonal immune (oligoclonal bands)

83918 Organic acids; total, quantitative, each specimen

83919 qualitative, each specimen

83921 Organic acid, single; quantitative

(83925 deleted 2014 [2015 edition]. For opiates, see 80361, 80362, 80363, 80364, or the specific drug [eg, fentanyls, oxycodone])

83930 Osmolality; blood

83935 urine

(For tear osmolarity using microfluidic analysis, use 83861)

83937 Osteocalcin (bone g1a protein)

83945 Oxalate

83950 Oncoprotein; HER-2/neu

(For tissue, see 88342, 88365)

83951 des-gamma-carboxy-prothrombin (DCP)

83970 Parathormone (parathyroid hormone)

(Pesticide, quantitative, see code for specific method. For screen for chlorinated hydrocarbons, use 82441)

83986 pH; body fluid, not otherwise specified

83987 exhaled breath condensate

● New Code   ▲ Revised Code   ✛ Add-On Code   ⊘ Modifier -51 Exempt   ★ Telemedicine

(For blood pH, see 82800, 82803)

83992 This code is out of order. See page 699.

(Phenobarbital, use 80345)

83993 Calprotectin, fecal

(84022 deleted 2014 [2015 edition]. For phenothiazine, see 80342, 80343, 80344)

84030 Phenylalanine (PKU), blood

(Phenylalanine-tyrosine ratio, see 84030, 84510)

84035 Phenylketones, qualitative

84060 Phosphatase, acid; total

(84061 deleted 2017 [2018 edition])

84066 prostatic

84075 Phosphatase, alkaline;

84078 heat stable (total not included)

84080 isoenzymes

84081 Phosphatidylglycerol

(Phosphates inorganic, use 84100)

(Phosphates, organic, see code for specific method. For cholinesterase, see 82480, 82482)

84085 Phosphogluconate, 6-, dehydrogenase, RBC

84087 Phosphohexose isomerase

84100 Phosphorus inorganic (phosphate);

84105 urine

(Pituitary gonadotropins, see 83001-83002)

(PKU, see 84030, 84035)

84106 Porphobilinogen, urine; qualitative

84110 quantitative

84112 Evaluation of cervicovaginal fluid for specific amniotic fluid protein(s) (eg, placental alpha microglobulin-1 [PAMG-1], placental protein 12 [PP12], alpha-fetoprotein), qualitative, each specimen

84119 Porphyrins, urine; qualitative

84120 quantitation and fractionation

84126 Porphyrins, feces; quantitative

(84127 deleted 2014 [2015 edition])

(Porphyrin precursors, see 82135, 84106, 84110)

■ Separate Procedure ■ Unlisted Procedure ■ CCI Comp. Code ■ Non-specific Procedure **761**

(For protoporphyrin, RBC, see 84202, 84203)

84132 Potassium; serum, plasma or whole blood

84133 urine

84134 Prealbumin

(For microalbumin, see 82043, 82044)

84135 Pregnanediol

84138 Pregnanetriol

84140 Pregnenolone

84143 17-hydroxypregnenolone

84144 Progesterone

(Progesterone receptor assay, use 84234)

(For proinsulin, use 84206)

84145 Procalcitonin (PCT)

84146 Prolactin

84150 Prostaglandin, each

84152 Prostate specific antigen (PSA); complexed (direct measurement)

84153 total

84154 free

84155 Protein, total, except by refractometry; serum, plasma or whole blood

84156 urine

84157 other source (eg, synovial fluid, cerebrospinal fluid)

84160 Protein, total, by refractometry, any source

(For urine total protein by dipstick method, use 81000-81003)

84163 Pregnancy-associated plasma protein-A (PAPP-A)

84165 Protein; electrophoretic fractionation and quantitation, serum

84166 electrophoretic fractionation and quantitation, other fluids with concentration (eg, urine, CSF)

84181 Western Blot, with interpretation and report, blood or other body fluid

84182 Western Blot, with interpretation and report, blood or other body fluid, immunological probe for band identification, each

(For Western Blot tissue analysis, use 88371)

84202 Protoporphyrin, RBC; quantitative

● New Code   ▲ Revised Code   + Add-On Code   ⊘ Modifier -51 Exempt   ★ Telemedicine

84203	screen
84206	Proinsulin
	(Pseudocholinesterase, use 82480)
84207	Pyridoxal phosphate (Vitamin B-6)
84210	Pyruvate
84220	Pyruvate kinase
84228	Quinine
84233	Receptor assay; estrogen
84234	progesterone
84235	endocrine, other than estrogen or progesterone (specify hormone)
84238	non-endocrine (specify receptor)
84244	Renin
84252	Riboflavin (Vitamin B-2)
	(Salicylates, see 80329, 80330, 80331)
	(Secretin test, see 99070, 43756, 43757 and appropriate analyses)
84255	Selenium
84260	Serotonin
	(For urine metabolites (HIAA), use 83497)
84270	Sex hormone binding globulin (SHBG)
84275	Sialic acid
	(Sickle hemoglobin, use 85660)
84285	Silica
84295	Sodium; serum, plasma or whole blood
84300	urine
84302	other source
	(Somatomammotropin, use 83632)
	(Somatotropin, use 83003)
84305	Somatomedin
84307	Somatostatin
84311	Spectrophotometry, analyte not elsewhere specified
84315	Specific gravity (except urine)

| Separate Procedure | Unlisted Procedure | CCI Comp. Code | Non-specific Procedure | **763** |

(For specific gravity, urine, see 81000-81003)

(Stone analysis, see 82355-82370)

(For suppression of growth stimulation expressed gene 2 [ST2] testing, use 83006)

84375   Sugars, chromatographic, TLC or paper chromatography

84376   Sugars (mono, di, and oligosaccharides); single qualitative, each specimen

84377   multiple qualitative, each specimen

84378   single quantitative, each specimen

84379   multiple quantitative, each specimen

84392   Sulfate, urine

(Sulfhemoglobin, use hemoglobin, 83060)

(T-3, see 84479-84481)

(T-4, see 84436-84439)

84402   Testosterone; free

84403   total

84410   bioavailable, direct measurement (eg, differential precipitation)

(Do not report 84402, 84403 in conjunction with 80327, 80328 to identify anabolic steroid testing for testosterone)

84425   Thiamine (Vitamin B-1)

84430   Thiocyanate

84431   Thromboxane metabolite(s), including thromboxane if performed, urine

(For concurrent urine creatinine determination, use 84431 in conjunction with 82470)

84432   Thyroglobulin

(Thyroglobulin, antibody, use 86800)

(Thyrotropin releasing hormone (TRH) test, see 80438, 80439)

84436   Thyroxine; total

84437   requiring elution (eg, neonatal)

84439   free

84442   Thyroxine binding globulin (TBG)

84443   Thyroid stimulating hormone (TSH)

84445   Thyroid stimulating immune globulins (TSI)

(Tobramycin, use 80200)

84446   Tocopherol alpha (Vitamin E)

● New Code   ▲ Revised Code   ✛ Add-On Code   ⊘ Modifier -51 Exempt   ★ Telemedicine

(Tolbutamide tolerance, use 82953)

84449 Transcortin (cortisol binding globulin)

84450 Transferase; aspartate amino (AST) (SGOT)

84460 alanine amino (ALT) (SGPT)

84466 Transferrin

(Iron binding capacity, use 83550)

84478 Triglycerides

84479 Thyroid hormone (T3 or T4) uptake or thyroid hormone binding ratio (THBR)

84480 Triiodothyronine T3; total (TT-3)

84481 free

84482 reverse

84484 Troponin, quantitative

(For Troponin, qualitative assay, use 84512)

84485 Trypsin; duodenal fluid

84488 feces, qualitative

84490 feces, quantitative, 24-hour collection

84510 Tyrosine

(Urate crystal identification, use 89060)

84512 Troponin, qualitative

(For Troponin, quantitative assay, use 84484)

84520 Urea nitrogen; quantitative

84525 semiquantitative (eg, reagent strip test)

84540 Urea nitrogen, urine

84545 Urea nitrogen, clearance

84550 Uric acid; blood

84560 other source

84577 Urobilinogen, feces, quantitative

84578 Urobilinogen, urine; qualitative

84580 quantitative, timed specimen

84583 semiquantitative

(Uroporphyrins, use 84120)

| | Separate Procedure | | Unlisted Procedure | | CCI Comp. Code | | Non-specific Procedure |

(Valproic acid (dipropylacetic acid), ues 80164)

84585   Vanillylmandelic acid (VMA), urine

84586   Vasoactive intestinal peptide (VIP)

84588   Vasopressin (antidiuretic hormone, ADH)

84590   Vitamin A

(Vitamin B-1, use 84425)

(Vitamin B-2, use 84252)

(Vitamin B-6, use 84207)

(Vitamin B-12, use 82607)

(Vitamin B-12, absorption (Schilling), see 78270, 78271)

(Vitamin C, use 82180)

(Vitamin D, see 82306, 82652)

(Vitamin E, use 84446)

84591   Vitamin, not otherwise specified

84597   Vitamin K

(VMA, use 84585)

84600   Volatiles (eg, acetic anhydride, diethylether)

(For carbon tetrachloride, dichloroethane, dichloromethane, use 82441)

(For isopropyl alcohol and methanol, use 80320)

(Volume, blood, RISA or Cr-51, see 78110, 78111)

84620   Xylose absorption test, blood and/or urine

(For administration, use 99070)

84630   Zinc

84681   C-peptide

84702   Gonadotropin, chorionic (hCG); quantitative

84703   qualitative

(For urine pregnancy test by visual color comparison, use 81025)

84704   free beta chain

84830   Ovulation tests, by visual color comparison methods for human luteinizing hormone

84999   Unlisted chemistry procedure

(For definitive testing of a drug, not otherwise specified, see 80299, 80375, 80376, 80377)

HEMATOLOGY AND COAGULATION

(For blood banking procedures, see Transfusion Medicine)

(Agglutinins, see Immunology)

(Antiplasmin, use 85410)

(Antithrombin III, see 85300, 85301)

85002 Bleeding time

85004 Blood count; automated differential WBC count

85007 blood smear, microscopic examination with manual differential WBC count

85008 blood smear, microscopic examination without manual differential WBC count

(For other fluids (eg, CSF), see 89050, 89051)

85009 manual differential WBC count, buffy coat

(Eosinophils, nasal smear, use 89190)

85013 spun microhematocrit

85014 hematocrit (Hct)

85018 hemoglobin (Hgb)

(For other hemoglobin determination, see 83020-83069)

(For immunoassay, hemoglobin, fecal, use 82274)

(For transcutaneous hemoglobin measurement, use 88738)

85025 complete (CBC), automated (Hgb, Hct, RBC, WBC and platelet count) and automated differential WBC count

85027 complete (CBC), automated (Hgb, Hct, RBC, WBC and platelet count)

85032 manual cell count (erythrocyte, leukocyte, or platelet) each

85041 red blood cell (RBC), automated

(Do not report code 85041 in conjunction with 85025 or 85027)

85044 reticulocyte, manual

85045 reticulocyte, automated

85046 reticulocytes, automated, including 1 or more cellular parameters (eg, reticulocyte hemoglobin content [CHr], immature reticulocyte fraction [IRF], reticulocyte volume [mrv], RNA content), direct measurement

85048 leukocyte (WBC), automated

85049 platelet, automated

85055 Reticulated platelet assay

85060 Blood smear, peripheral, interpretation by physician with written report

| Separate Procedure | Unlisted Procedure | CCI Comp. Code | Non-specific Procedure | 767 |

85097   Bone marrow, smear interpretation

(For special stains, see 85540, 88312, 88313)

(For bone biopsy, see 20220, 20225, 20240, 20245, 20250, 20251)

85130   Chromogenic substrate assay

(Circulating anti-coagulant screen (mixing studies), see 85611, 85732)

85170   Clot retraction

85175   Clot lysis time, whole blood dilution

(Clotting factor I (fibrinogen), see 85384, 85385)

85210   Clotting; factor II, prothrombin, specific

(See also 85610-85613)

85220   factor V (AcG or proaccelerin), labile factor

85230   factor VII (proconvertin, stable factor)

85240   factor VIII (AHG), 1 stage

85244   factor VIII related antigen

85245   factor VIII, VW factor, ristocetin cofactor

85246   factor VIII, VW factor antigen

85247   factor VIII, von Willebrands factor, multimetric analysis

85250   factor IX (PTC or Christmas)

85260   factor X (Stuart-Prower)

85270   factor XI (PTA)

85280   factor XII (Hageman)

85290   factor XIII (fibrin stabilizing)

85291   factor XIII (fibrin stabilizing), screen solubility

85292   prekallikrein assay (Fletcher factor assay)

85293   high molecular weight kininogen assay (Fitzgerald factor assay)

85300   Clotting inhibitors or anticoagulants; antithrombin III, activity

85301   antithrombin III, antigen assay

85302   protein C, antigen

85303   protein C, activity

85305   protein S, total

85306   protein S, free

● New Code   ▲ Revised Code   ✛ Add-On Code   ⊘ Modifier -51 Exempt   ★ Telemedicine

85307 Activated Protein C (APC) resistance assay

85335 Factor inhibitor test

85337 Thrombomodulin

(For mixing studies for inhibitors, use 85732)

85345 Coagulation time; Lee and White

85347   activated

85348   other methods

(Differential count, see 85007 et seq)

(Duke bleeding time, use 85002)

(Eosinophils, nasal smear, use 89190)

85360 Euglobulin lysis

(Fetal hemoglobin, see 83030, 83033, 85460)

85362 Fibrin(ogen) degradation (split) products (FDP)(FSP); agglutination slide, semiquantitative

(Immunoelectrophoresis, use 86320)

85366   paracoagulation

85370   quantitative

85378 Fibrin degradation products, D-dimer; qualitative or semiquantitative

85379   quantitative

(For ultrasensitive and standard sensitivity quantitative D-dimer, use 85379)

85380   ultrasensitive (eg., for evaluation for venous thromboembolism), qualitative or semiquantitative

85384 Fibrinogen; activity

85385   antigen

85390 Fibrinolysins or coagulopathy screen, interpretation and report

85396 Coagulation/fibrinolysis assay, whole blood (eg, viscoelastic clot assessment), including use of any pharmacologic additive(s), as indicated, including interpretation and written report, per day

85397 Coagulation and fibrinolysis, functional activity, not otherwise specified (eg, adamts-13), each analyte

85400 Fibrinolytic factors and inhibitors; plasmin

85410   alpha-2 antiplasmin

85415   plasminogen activator

85420   plasminogen, except antigenic assay

85421   plasminogen, antigenic assay

(Fragility, red blood cell, see 85547, 85555-85557)

    Separate Procedure   Unlisted Procedure   CCI Comp. Code   Non-specific Procedure   **769**

85441   Heinz bodies; direct

85445   induced, acetyl phenylhydrazine

     (Hematocrit (PCV), see 85014)

     (Hemoglobin, see 83020-83068, 85018-85027)

85460   Hemoglobin or RBCs, fetal, for fetomaternal hemorrhage; differential lysis (Kleihauer-Betke)

     (See also 83030, 83033)

     (Hemolysins, see 86940, 86941)

85461   rosette

85475   Hemolysin, acid

     (See also 86940, 86941)

85520   Heparin assay

85525   Heparin neutralization

85530   Heparin-protamine tolerance test

85536   Iron stain, peripheral blood

     (For iron stains on bone marrow or other tissues with physician evaluation, use 88313)

85540   Leukocyte alkaline phosphatase with count

85547   Mechanical fragility, RBC

85549   Muramidase

     (Nitroblue tetrazolium dye test, use 86384)

85555   Osmotic fragility, RBC; unincubated

85557   incubated

     (Packed cell volume, use 85013)

     (Partial thromboplastin time, see 85730, 85732)

     (Parasites, blood (eg, malaria smears), use 87207)

     (Plasmin, use 85400)

     (Plasminogen, use 85420)

     (Plasminogen activator, use 85415)

85576   Platelet; aggregation (in vitro), each agent

     (For thromboxane metabolite[s], including thromboxane, if performed, measurement[s] in urine, use 84431)

85597   Phospholipid neutralization; platelet

85598   hexagonal phospholipid

85610   Prothrombin time;

85611   substitution, plasma fractions, each

85612   Russell viper venom time (includes venom); undiluted

85613   diluted

(Red blood cell count, see 85025, 85027, 85041)

85635   Reptilase test

(Reticulocyte count, see 85044, 85045)

85651   Sedimentation rate, erythrocyte; non-automated

85652   automated

85660   Sickling of RBC, reduction

(Hemoglobin electrophoresis, use 83020)

(Smears (eg, for parasites, malaria), use 87207)

85670   Thrombin time; plasma

85675   titer

85705   Thromboplastin inhibition, tissue

(For individual clotting factors, see 85245-85247)

85730   Thromboplastin time, partial (PTT); plasma or whole blood

85732   substitution, plasma fractions, each

85810   Viscosity

(von Willebrand factor assay, see 85245-85247)

(WBC count, see 85025-85031, 85048, 89050)

85999   Unlisted hematology and coagulation procedure

IMMUNOLOGY

(Acetylcholine receptor antibody, see 83519, 86255, 86256)

(Actinomyces, antibodies to, use 86602)

(Adrenal cortex antibodies, see 86255, 86256)

86000   Agglutinins, febrile (eg, Brucella, Francisella, Murine typhus, Q fever, Rocky Mountain spotted fever, scrub typhus), each antigen

(For antibodies to infectious agents, see 86602-86804)

86001   Allergen specific IgG quantitative or semiquantitative, each allergen

(Agglutinins and autohemolysins, see 86940, 86941)

▲ **86003**   Allergen specific IgE; quantitative or semiquantitative, crude allergen extract, each

(For total quantitative IgE, use 82785)

▲ **86005**   qualitative, multiallergen screen (eg, disk, sponge, card)

■ Separate Procedure   ■ Unlisted Procedure   ■ CCI Comp. Code   ■ Non-specific Procedure   **771**

● **86008**   quantitative or semiquantitative, recombinant or purified component, each

(For total qualitative IgE, use 83518)

(Alpha-1 antitrypsin, see 82103, 82104)

(Alpha-1 feto-protein, see 82105, 82106)

(Anti-AChR (acetylcholine receptor) antibody titer, see 86255, 86256)

(Anticardiolipin antibody, use 86147)

(Anti-DNA, use 86225)

(Anti-deoxyribonuclease titer, use 86215)

86021   Antibody identification; leukocyte antibodies

86022   platelet antibodies

86023   platelet associated immunoglobulin assay

86038   Antinuclear antibodies (ANA);

86039   titer

(Antistreptococcal antibody, ie, anti-DNAse, use 86215)

(Antistreptokinase titer, use 86590)

86060   Antistreptolysin 0; titer

(For antibodies to infectious agents, see 86602-86804)

86063   screen

(For antibodies to infectious agents, see 86602-86804)

(Blastomyces, antibodies to, use 86612)

86077   Blood bank physician services; difficult cross match and/or evaluation of irregular antibody(s), interpretation and written report

86078   investigation of transfusion reaction including suspicion of transmissible disease, interpretation and written report

86079   authorization for deviation from standard blood banking procedures (eg, use of outdated blood, transfusion of Rh incompatible units), with written report

(Brucella, antibodies to, use 86622)

(Candida, antibodies to, use 86628. For skin testing, use 86485)

86140   C-reactive protein;

(Candidiasis, use 86628)

86141   high sensitivity (hsCRP)

86146   Beta 2 Glycoprotein 1 antibody, each

86147   Cardiolipin (phospholipid) antibody, each lg class

86152   Cell enumeration using immunologic selection and identification in fluid specimen (eg, circulating tumor cells in blood);

(For physician interpretation and report, use 86153. For cell enumeration with interpretation and report, use 86152 and 86153)

86153   physician interpretation and report, when required

(For cell enumeration, use 86152. For cell enumeration with interpretation and report, use 86152 and 86153)

(For flow cytometric immunophenotyping, see 88184-88189)

(For flow cytometric quantitation, see 86355, 86356, 86357, 86359, 86360, 86361, 86367)

86148   Anti-phosphatidylserine (phospholipid) antibody

(To report antiprothrombin (phospholipid cofactor) antibody, use 86849)

(For cell enumeration using immunologic selection and identification in fluid specimen [eg, circulating tumor cells in blood], see 0279T, 0280T)

86152   Code out of order. See page 772.

86153   Code out of order. See page 773.

86155   Chemotaxis assay, specify method

(Clostridium difficile toxin, use 87230)

(Coccidioides, antibodies, to, see 86635. For skin testing, use 86490)

86156   Cold agglutinin; screen

86157   titer

86160   Complement; antigen, each component

86161   functional activity, each component

86162   total hemolytic (CH50)

86171   Complement fixation tests, each antigen

(Coombs test, see 86880-86886)

(86185   deleted 2017 [2018 edition])

86200   Cyclic citrullinated peptide (CCP), antibody

86215   Deoxyribonuclease, antibody

86225   Deoxyribonucleic acid (DNA) antibody; native or double stranded

(Echinococcus, antibodies to, see code for specific method)

(For HIV antibody tests, see 86701-86703)

86226   single stranded

(Anti D.S., DNA, IFA, eg, using C.Lucilae, see 86255 and 86256)

86235   Extractable nuclear antigen, antibody to, any method (eg, nRNP, SS-A, SS-B, Sm, RNP, Sc170, J01), each antibody

(86243   deleted 2017 [2018 edition])

■ Separate Procedure   ■ Unlisted Procedure   ■ CCI Comp. Code   ■ Non-specific Procedure   **773**

86255 Fluorescent noninfectious agent antibody; screen, each antibody

86256 titer, each antibody

(Fluorescent technique for antigen identification in tissue, use 88346; for indirect fluorescence, see 88346, 88350)

(FTA, use 86780)

(Gel (agar) diffusion tests, use 86331)

86277 Growth hormone, human (HGH), antibody

86280 Hemagglutination inhibition test (HAI)

(For rubella, use 86762)

(For antibodies to infectious agents, see 86602-86804)

86294 Immunoassay for tumor antigen, qualitative or semiquantitative (eg, bladder tumor antigen)

(for qualitative NMP22 protein, use 86386)

86300 Immunoassay for tumor antigen, quantitative; CA 15-3 (27.29)

86301 CA 19-9

86304 CA 125

(For measurement of serum HER-2/neu oncoprotein, see 83950)

(For hepatitis delta agent, antibody, use 86692)

86305 Human epididymis protein 4 (HE4)

86308 Heterophile antibodies; screening

(For antibodies to infectious agents, see 86602-86804)

86309 titer

(For antibodies to infectious agents, see 86602-86804)

86310 titers after absorption with beef cells and guinea pig kidney

(Histoplasma, antibodies to, use 86698. For skin testing, use 86510)

(For antibodies to infectious agents, see 86602-86804)

(Human growth hormone antibody, use 86277)

86316 Immunoassay for tumor antigen, other antigen, quantitative (eg, CA 50, 72-4, 549), each

86317 Immunoassay for infectious agent antibody, quantitative, not otherwise specified

(For immunoassay techniques for antigens, see 83516, 83518, 83519, 83520, 87301-87450, 87810-87899)

(For particle agglutination procedures, use 86403)

86318 Immunoassay for infectious agent antibody, qualitative or semiquantitative, single step method (eg, reagent strip)

86320 Immunoelectrophoresis; serum

86325 other fluids (eg, urine, cerebrospinal fluid) with concentration

● New Code   ▲ Revised Code   + Add-On Code   ⊘ Modifier -51 Exempt   ★ Telemedicine

86327	crossed (2-dimensional assay)
86329	Immunodiffusion; not elsewhere specified
86331	gel diffusion, qualitative (Ouchterlony), each antigen or antibody
86332	Immune complex assay
86334	Immunofixation electrophoresis; serum
86335	other fluids with concentration (eg, urine, CSF)
86336	Inhibin A
86337	Insulin antibodies
86340	Intrinsic factor antibodies

(Leptospira, antibodies to, use 86720)

(Leukoagglutinins, use 86021)

86341	Islet cell antibody
86343	Leukocyte histamine release test (LHR)
86344	Leukocyte phagocytosis
86352	Cellular function assay involving stimulation (eg, mitogen or antigen) and detection of biomarker (eg, ATP)
86353	Lymphocyte transformation, mitogen (phytomitogen) or antigen induced blastogenesis

(Malaria antibodies, use 86750)

(For cellular function assay involving stimulation and detection of biomarker, use 86352)

86355	B cells, total count
86356	Mononuclear cell antigen, quantitive (eg, flow cytometry), not otherwise specified, each antigen

(Do not report 88187-88189 for interpretation of 86355, 86356, 86357, 86359, 86360, 86361, 86367)

86357	Natural killer (NK) cells, total count
86359	T cells; total count
86360	absolute CD4 and CD8 count, including ratio
86361	absolute CD4 count
86367	Stem cells (ie, CD34), total count

(For flow cytometric immunophenotyping for the assessment of potential hematolymphoid neoplasia, see 88184-88189)

86376	Microsomal antibodies (eg, thyroid or liver-kidney), each
(86378	deleted 2017 [2018 edition])
86382	Neutralization test, viral

■ Separate Procedure	■ Unlisted Procedure	■ CCI Comp. Code	■ Non-specific Procedure	**775**

86384   Nitroblue tetrazolium dye test (NTD)

86386   Nuclear Matrix Protein 22 (NMP22), qualitative

     (Ouchterlony diffusion, use 86331)

     (Platelet antibodies, see 86022, 86023)

86403   Particle agglutination; screen, each antibody

86406   titer, each antibody

     (Pregnancy test, see 84702, 84703)

     (Rapid plasma reagin test (RPR), see 86592, 86593)

86430   Rheumatoid factor; qualitative

86431   quantitative

     (Serologic test for syphilis, see 86592, 86593)

86480   Tuberculosis test, cell mediated immunity antigen response measurement; gamma interferon

86481   enumeration of gamma interferon-producing T-cells in cell suspension

86485   Skin test; candida

     (For antibody, candida, use 86628)

86486   unlisted antigen, each

86490   coccidioidomycosis

86510   histoplasmosis

     (For histoplasma, antibody, use 86698)

86580   tuberculosis, intradermal

     (For tuberculosis test, cell mediated immunity measurement of gamma interferon antigen response, use 86480)

     (For skin tests for allergy, see 95012-95199)

     (Smooth muscle antibody, see 86255, 86256)

     (Sporothrix, antibodies to, see code for specific method)

86590   Streptokinase, antibody

     (For antibodies to infectious agents, see 86602-86804)

     (Streptolysin O antibody, see antistreptolysin O, 86060, 86063)

86592   Syphilis test, non-treponemal antibody; qualitative (eg, VDRL, RPR, ART)

     (For antibodies to infectious agents, see 86602-86804)

86593   quantitative

     (For antibodies to infectious agents, see 86602-86804)

     (Tetanus antibody, use 86774)

     (Thyroglobulin antibody, use 86800)

(Thyroglobulin, use 84432)

(Thyroid microsomal antibody, use 86376)

(For toxoplasma antibody, see 86777-86778)

The following codes (86602-86804) are qualitative or semiquantitative immunoassays performed by multiple-step methods for the detection of antibodies to infectious agents. For immunoassays by single-step method (eg., reagent strips), use code 86318. Procedures for the identification of antibodies should be coded as precisely as possible. For example, an antibody to a virus could be coded with increasing specificity for virus, family, genus, species or type. In some cases, further precision may be added to codes by specifying the class of immunoglobulin being detected. When multiple tests are done to detect antibodies to organisms classified more precisely than the specificity allowed by available codes, it is appropriate to code each as a separate service. For example, a test for antibody to an enterovirus is coded as 86658. Coxsackie viruses are enteroviruses, but there are no codes for the individual species of enterovirus. If assays are performed for antibodies to coxsackie A and B species, each assay should be separately coded. Similarly, if multiple assays are performed for antibodies of different immunoglobulin classes, each assay should be coded separately. When a coding option exists for reporting IgM specific antibodies (eg., 86632), the corresponding nonspecific code (eg., 86631) may be reported for performance of either an antibody analysis not specific for a particular immunoglobulin class or for an IgG analysis.

(For the detection of antibodies other than those to infectious agents, see specific antibody [eg, 86021, 86022, 86023, 86376, 86800, 86850-86870] or specific method [eg, 83516, 86255, 86256])

(For infectious agent/antigen detection, see 87260-87899)

86602	Antibody; actinomyces
86603	adenovirus
86606	Aspergillus
86609	bacterium, not elsewhere specified
86611	Bartonella
86612	Blastomyces
86615	Bordetella
86617	Borrelia burgdorferi (Lyme disease) confirmatory test (eg, Western blot or immunoblot)
86618	Borrelia burgdorferi (Lyme disease)
86619	Borrelia (relapsing fever)
86622	Brucella
86625	Campylobacter
86628	Candida

(For skin test, candida, use 86485)

86631	Chlamydia
86632	Chlamydia, IgM

(For chlamydia antigen, see 87270, 87320. For fluorescent antibody technique, see 86255, 86256)

86635	Coccidioides
86638	Coxiella Brunetii (Q fever)

86641	Cryptococcus
86644	cytomegalovirus (CMV)
86645	cytomegalovirus (CMV), IgM
86648	Diphtheria
86651	encephalitis, California (La Crosse)
86652	encephalitis, Eastern equine
86653	encephalitis, St. Louis
86654	encephalitis, Western equine
86658	enterovirus (eg, coxsackie, echo, polio)

(Trichinella, antibodies to, use 86784)

(Trypanosoma, antibodies to, see code for specific method)

(Tuberculosis, use 86580 for skin testing)

(Viral antibodies, see code for specific method)

86663	Epstein-Barr (EB) virus, early antigen (EA)
86664	Epstein-Barr (EB) virus, nuclear antigen (EBNA)
86665	Epstein-Barr (EB) virus, viral capsid (VCA)
86666	Ehrlichia
86668	Francisella Tularensis
86671	fungus, not elsewhere specified
86674	Giardia Lamblia
86677	Helicobacter Pylori
86682	helminth, not elsewhere specified
86684	Hemophilus influenza
86687	HTLV-I
86688	HTLV-II
86689	HTLV or HIV antibody, confirmatory test (eg, Western Blot)
86692	hepatitis, delta agent

(For hepatitis delta agent, antigen, use 87380)

86694	herpes simplex, non-specific type test
86695	herpes simplex, type 1
86696	herpes simplex, type 2

● New Code ▲ Revised Code + Add-On Code ⊘ Modifier -51 Exempt ★ Telemedicine

86698	histoplasma
86701	HIV-1
86702	HIV-2
86703	HIV-1 and HIV-2, single result

(For HIV-1 antigen(s) with HIV-1 and HIV-2 antibodies, single result, use 87389)

(When HIV immunoassay [HIV testing 86701-86703 or 87389] is performed using a kit or transportable instrument that wholly or in part consists of a single use, disposable analytical chamber, the service may be identified by adding modifier 92 to the usual code)

(For HIV-1 antigen, use 87390)

(For HIV-2 antigen, use 87391)

(For confirmatory test for HIV antibody (eg, Western Blot), use 86689)

86704	Hepatitis B core antibody (HBcAb); total
86705	IgM antibody
86706	Hepatitis B surface antibody (HBsAb)
86707	Hepatitis Be antibody (HBeAb)
86708	Hepatitis A antibody (HAAb)
86709	Hepatitis A antibody (HAAb), IgM antibody
86710	Antibody; influenza virus
86711	JC (John Cunningham) virus
86713	Legionella
86717	Leishmania
86720	Leptospira
86723	Listeria monocytogenes
86727	lymphocytic choriomeningitis
(86729	deleted 2017 [2018 edition])
86732	mucormycosis
86735	mumps
86738	Mycoplasma
86741	Neisseria meningitidis
86744	Nocardia
86747	parvovirus
86750	Plasmodium (malaria)

86753	protozoa, not elsewhere specified
86756	respiratory syncytial virus
86757	Rickettsia
86759	rotavirus
86762	rubella
86765	rubeola
86768	Salmonella
86771	Shigella
86774	tetanus
86777	Toxoplasma
86778	Toxoplasma, IgM
86780	Treponema pallidum

(For syphilis testing by non-treponemal antibody analysis, see 86592-86593)

86784	Trichinella
86787	varicella-zoster
86788	West Nile virus, IgM
86789	West Nile virus
86790	virus, not elsewhere specified
86793	Yersinia
● 86794	Zika virus, IgM
86800	Thyroglobulin antibody

(For thyroglobulin, use 84432)

86803	Hepatitis C antibody;
86804	confirmatory test (eg, immunoblot)

TISSUE TYPING

86805	Lymphocytotoxicity assay, visual crossmatch; with titration
86806	without titration
86807	Serum screening for cytotoxic percent reactive antibody (PRA); standard method
86808	quick method
86812	HLA typing; A, B, or C (eg, A10, B7, B27), single antigen

● New Code ▲ Revised Code ✚ Add-On Code ⃠ Modifier -51 Exempt ★ Telemedicine

86813	A, B, or C, multiple antigens
86816	DR/DQ, single antigen
86817	DR/DQ, multiple antigens
86821	lymphocyte culture, mixed (MLC)
(86822	deleted 2017 [2018 edition])
86825	Human leukocyte antigen (HLA) crossmatch, non cytotoxic (eg, using flow cytometry); first serum sample or dilution
+ 86826	each additional serum sample or sample dilution (List separately in addition to primary procedure)

(Use 86826 in conjunction with 86825)

(Do not report 86825, 86826 in conjunction with 86355, 86359, 88184-88189 for antibody surface markers integral to crossmatch testing)

(For autologous HLA crossmatch, see 86825, 86826)

(For lymphocytotoxicity visual crossmatch, see 86805, 86806)

86828	Antibody to human leukocyte antigens (HLA), solid phase assays (eg, microspheres or beads, ELISA, flow cytometry); qualitative assessment of the presence of absence of antibody(ies) to HLA Class I and Class II HLA antigens
86829	qualitative assessment of the presence or absence of antibody(ies) to HLA Class I or Class II HLA antigens

(If solid phase testing is performed to assess presence or absence of antibody to both HLA classes, use 86828)

86830	antibody identification by qualitative panel using complete HLA phenotypes, HLA Class I
86831	antibody identification by qualitative panel using complete HLA phenotypes, HLA Class II
86832	high definition qualitative panel for identification of antibody sepcificities (eg, individual antigen per bead methodology), HLA Class I
86833	high definition qualitative panel for identification of antibody specificities (eg, individual antigen per bead methodology), HLA Class II

(If solid phase testing is performed to test for HLA Class I or II antibody after treatment [eg, to remove IgM antibodies or other interfering substances], report 86828-86833 once for each panel with the untreated serum and once for each panel with the treated serum)

86834	semi-quantitative panel (eg, titer), HLA Class I
86835	semi-quantiative panel (eg, titer), HLA Class II
86849	Unlisted immunology procedure

TRANSFUSION MEDICINE

(For apheresis, see 36511-36512)

(For therapeutic phlebotomy, use 99195)

86850	Antibody screen, RBC, each serum technique

86860   Antibody elution (RBC), each elution

86870   Antibody identification, RBC antibodies, each panel for each serum technique

86880   Antihuman globulin test (Coombs test); direct, each antiserum

86885   indirect, qualitative, each reagent red cell

86886   indirect, each antibody titer

(For indirect antihuman globulin [Coombs] test for RBC antibody screening, use 86850)

(For indirect antihuman globulin [Coombs] test for RBC antibody identification using reagent red cell panels, use 86870)

86890   Autologous blood or component, collection processing and storage; predeposited

86891   intra-or postoperative salvage

86900   Blood typing, serologic; ABO

86901   Rh (D)

86902   antigen testing of donor blood using reagent serum, each antigen test

(If multiple blood units are tested for the same antigen, 86902 should be reported once for each antigen for each unit tested.)

86904   antigen screening for compatible unit using patient serum, per unit screened

86905   RBC antigens, other than ABO or Rh (D), each

86906   Rh phenotyping, complete

(For human erythrocyte antigen typing by molecular pathology techniques, use 81403)

86910   Blood typing, for paternity testing, per individual; ABO, Rh and MN

86911   each additional antigen system

86920   Compatibility test each unit; immediate spin technique

86921   incubation technique

86922   antiglobulin technique

86923   electronic

(Do not use 86923 in conjunction with 86920-86922 for same unit crossmatch)

86927   Fresh frozen plasma, thawing, each unit

86930   Frozen blood, each unit; freezing (includes preparation)

86931   thawing

86932   freezing (includes preparation) and thawing

86940   Hemolysins and agglutinins; auto, screen, each

● New Code   ▲ Revised Code   + Add-On Code   ⊘ Modifier -51 Exempt   ★ Telemedicine

86941   incubated

86945   Irradiation of blood product, each unit

86950   Leukocyte transfusion

     (For allogenic lymphocyte infusion, use 38242)

     (For leukapheresis, use 36511)

86960   Volume reduction of blood or blood product (eg, red blood cells or platelets), each unit

86965   Pooling of platelets or other blood products

     (For harvesting, preparation, and injection[s] of platelet rich plasma, use 0232T)

     (For harvesting, preparation, and injection[s] of autologous white blood cell/autologous protein solution, use 0481T)

86970   Pretreatment of RBCs for use in RBC antibody detection, identification, and/or compatibility testing; incubation with chemical agents or drugs, each

86971   incubation with enzymes, each

86972   by density gradient separation

86975   Pretreatment of serum for use in RBC antibody identification; incubation with drugs, each

86976   by dilution

86977   incubation with inhibitors, each

86978   by differential red cell absorption using patient RBCs or RBCs of known phenotype, each absorption

86985   Splitting of blood or blood products, each unit

86999   Unlisted transfusion medicine procedure

MICROBIOLOGY

Includes bacteriology, mycology, parasitology, and virology.

Presumptive identification of microorganisms is defined as identification by colony morphology, growth on selective media, Gram stains, or up to three tests (eg., catalase, oxidase, indole, urease). Definitive identification of microorganisms is defined as an identification to the genus or species level that requires additional tests (eg., biochemical panels, slide cultures). If additional studies involve molecular probes, nucleic acid sequencing, chromatography, or immunologic techniques, these should be separately coded using 87140-87158, in addition to definitive identification codes. The molecular diagnostic codes (eg., 81200-81408) are not to be used in combination with or instead of the procedures represented by 87140-87158. For multiple specimens/sites, used modifier 59. For repeat laboratory tests performed on the same day, use modifier 91.

    (**87001**   deleted 2014 [2015 edition])

87003   with observation and dissection

87015   Concentration (any type), for infectious agents

     (Do not report 87015 in conjunction with 87177)

87040   Culture, bacterial; blood, aerobic, with isolation and presumptive identification of isolates (includes anaerobic culture, if appropriate)

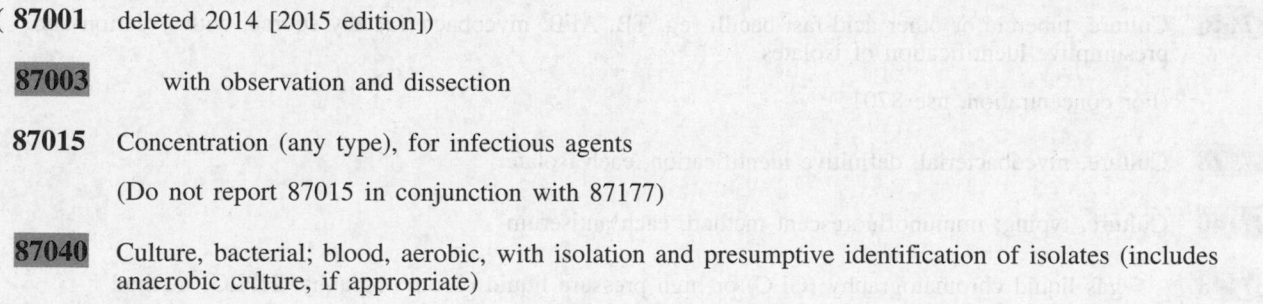

87045	stool, aerobic, with isolation and preliminary examination (eg, KIA, LIA), Salmonella and Shigella species
87046	stool, aerobic, additional pathogens, isolation and presumptive identification of isolates, each plate
87070	any other source except urine, blood or stool, aerobic, with isolation and presumptive identification of isolates

(For urine, use 87088)

87071	quantitative, aerobic with isolation and presumptive identification of isolates, any source except urine, blood or stool

(For urine, use 87088)

87073	quantitative, anaerobic with isolation and presumptive identification of isolates, any source except urine, blood or stool

(For definitive identification of isolates, use 87076 or 87077. for typing of isolates see 87140-87158)

87075	any source, except blood, anaerobic with isolation and presumptive identification of isolates
87076	anaerobic isolate, additional methods required for definitive identification, each isolate
87077	aerobic isolate, additional methods required for definitive identification, each isolate
87081	Culture, presumptive, pathogenic organisms, screening only;
87084	with colony estimation from density chart
87086	Culture, bacterial; quantitative colony count, urine
87088	with isolation and presumptive identification of each isolate, urine
87101	Culture, fungi (mold or yeast) isolation, with presumptive identification of isolates; skin, hair, or nail
87102	other source (except blood)
87103	blood
87106	Culture, fungi, definitive identification, each organism; yeast
87107	mold
87109	Culture, mycoplasma, any source
87110	Culture, chlamydia, any source

(For immunofluorescence staining of shell vials, use 87140)

87116	Culture, tubercle or other acid-fast bacilli (eg, TB, AFB, mycobacteria) any source, with isolation and presumptive identification of isolates

(For concentration, use 87015)

87118	Culture, mycobacterial, definitive identification, each isolate
87140	Culture, typing; immunofluorescent method, each antiserum
87143	gas liquid chromatography (GLC) or high pressure liquid chromotography (HPLC) method

---

● New Code   ▲ Revised Code   ✛ Add-On Code   ⊘ Modifier -51 Exempt   ★ Telemedicine

| **87147** | immunologic method, other than immunofluorescence (eg, agglutination grouping), per antiserum |

| **87149** | identification by nucleic acid (DNA or RNA) probe, direct probe technique, per culture or isolate, each organism probed |

(Do not report 87149 in conjunction with 81200-81408)

| **87150** | identification by nucleic acid (DNA or RNA) probe, amplified probe technique, per culture or isolate, each organism probed |

(Do not report 87150 in conjunction with 81200-81408)

| **87152** | identification by pulse field gel typing |

(Do not report 87152 in conjunction with 81200-81408)

| **87153** | identification by nucleic acid sequencing method, each isolate (eg, sequencing of the 16S rRNA gene) |

| **87158** | other methods |

| **87164** | Dark field examination, any source (eg, penile, vaginal, oral, skin); includes specimen collection |

| **87166** | without collection |

| **87168** | Macroscopic examination; arthropod |

| **87169** | parasite |

| **87172** | Pinworm exam (eg, cellophane tape prep) |

| **87176** | Homogenization, tissue, for culture |

| **87177** | Ova and parasites, direct smears, concentration and identification |

(Do not report 87177 in conjunction with 87015)

(For direct smears from a primary source, use 87207)

(For coccidia or microsporidia exam, use 87207)

(For complex special stain (trichrome, iron hematoxylin), use 87209)

(For nucleic acid probes in cytologic material, use 88365)

| **87181** | Susceptibility studies, antimicrobial agent; agar diffusion method, per agent (eg, antibiotic gradient strip) |

| **87184** | disk method, per plate (12 or fewer disks) |

| **87185** | enzyme detection (eg, beta lactamase), per enzyme |

| **87186** | microdilution or agar dilution (minimum inhibitory concentration [MIC] or breakpoint), each multi-antimicrobial, per plate |

| + **87187** | microdilution or agar dilution, minimum lethal concentration (MLC), each plate ((List separately in addition to code for primary procedure) |

(Use 87187 in conjunction with 87186 or 87188)

| **87188** | macrobroth dilution method, each agent |

| **87190** | mycobacteria, proportion method, each agent |

(For other mycobacterial susceptibility studies, see 87181, 87184, 87186, or 87188)

Separate Procedure   Unlisted Procedure   CCI Comp. Code   Non-specific Procedure   **785**

87197   Serum bactericidal titer (Schlicter test)

87205   Smear, primary source with interpretation; Gram or Giemsa stain for bacteria, fungi, or cell types

87206   fluorescent and/or acid fast stain for bacteria, fungi, or cell types

87207   special stain for inclusion bodies or parasites (eg, malaria, coccidia, microsporidia, trypanosomes, herpes viruses)

(For direct smears with concentration and identification, use 87177)

(For thick smear preparation, use 87015)

(For fat, meat, fibers, nasal eosinophils, and starch, see miscellaneous section)

87209   complex special stain (eg, trichrome, iron hemotoxylin) for ova and parasites

87210   wet mount for infectious agents (eg, saline, India ink, KOH preps)

(For KOH examination of skin, hair or nails, see 87220)

87220   Tissue examination by KOH slide of samples from skin, hair, or nails for fungi or ectoparasite ova or mites (eg, scabies)

87230   Toxin or antitoxin assay, tissue culture (eg, Clostridium difficile toxin)

87250   Virus isolation; inoculation of embryonated eggs, or small animal, includes observation and dissection

87252   tissue culture inoculation, observation, and presumptive identification by cytopathic effect

87253   tissue culture, additional studies or definitive identification (eg, hemabsorption, neutralization, immunofluorescence stain) each isolate

(Electron microscopy, use 88348)

(Inclusion bodies in tissue sections, see 88304-88309; in smears, see 87207-87210; in fluids, use 88106)

87254   centrifuge enhanced (shell vial) technique, includes identification with immunofluorescence stain, each virus

(Report 87254 in addition to 87252 as appropriate)

87255   including identification by non-immunologic method, other than by cytopathic effect (eg., virus specific enzymatic activity)

These codes are intended for primary source only. For similar studies on culture material, refer to codes 87140-87158. Infectious agents by antigen detection, immunofluorescence microscopy, or nucleic acid probe techniques should be reported as precisely as possible. The molecular pathology procedures codes (81161, 81200-81408) are not to be used in combination with or instead of the procedures represented by 87471-87801. The most specific code possible should be reported. If there is no specific agent code, the general methodology code (eg, 87299, 87449, 87450, 87797, 87798, 87799, 87899) should be used. For identification of antibodies to many of the listed infectious agents, see 86602-86804. When separate results are reported for different species or strain of organisms, each result should be coded separately. Use modifier 59 when separate results are reported for different species or strains that are described by the same code.

87260   Infectious agent antigen detection by immunofluorescent technique; adenovirus

87265   Bordetella pertussis/parapertussis

87267   Enterovirus, direct fluorescent antibody (DFA)

87269   giardia

● New Code   ▲ Revised Code   + Add-On Code   ⊘ Modifier -51 Exempt   ★ Telemedicine

87270	Chlamydia trachomatis
87271	Cytomegalovirus, direct fluorescent antibody (DFA)
87272	cryptosporidium
87273	Herpes simplex virus type 2
87274	Herpes simplex virus 1
87275	Influenza B virus
87276	influenza A virus

(87277   deleted 2017 [2018 edition])

87278	Legionella pneumophila
87279	Parainfluenza virus, each type
87280	respiratory syncytial virus
87281	Pneumocystis carinii
87283	Rubeola
87285	Treponema pallidum
87290	Varicella zoster virus
87299	not otherwise specified, each organism

87300   Infectious agent antigen detection by immunofluorescent technique, polyvalent for multiple organisms, each polyvalent antiserum

(For physican evaluation of infectious disease agents by immunofluorescence, use 88346)

87301   Infectious agent antigen detection by immunoassay technique, (eg, enzyme immunoassay [EIA], enzyme-linked immunosorbent assay [ELISA], immunochemiluminometric assay [IMCA]) qualitative or semiquantitative, multiple-step method; adenovirus enteric types 40/41

87305	Aspergillus
87320	Chlamydia trachomatis
87324	Clostridium difficile toxin(s)
87327	Cryptococcus neoformans

(For Cryptococcus latex agglutination, use 86403)

87328	cryptosporidium
87329	giardia
87332	cytomegalovirus
87335	Escherichia coli 0157

(For giardia antigen, use 87329)

87336	Entamoeba histolytica dispar group
87337	Entamoeba histolytica group
87338	Helicobacter pylori, stool
87339	Helicobacter pylori

(For H. pylori, stool, use 87338. For H. pylori, breath and blood by mass spectrometry, see 83013, 83014. For H. pylori, liquid scintillation counter, see 78267, 78268)

87340	hepatitis B surface antigen (HBsAg)
87341	hepatitis B surface antigen (HBsAg) neutralization
87350	hepatitis Be antigen (HBeAg)
87380	hepatitis, delta agent
87385	Histoplasma capsulatum
87389	HIV-1 antigen(s), with HIV-1 and HIV-2 antibodies, single result
87390	HIV-1
87391	HIV-2
87400	Influenza, A or B, each
87420	respiratory syncytial virus
87425	rotavirus
87427	Shiga-like toxin
87430	Streptococcus, group A
87449	Infectious agent antigen detection by immunoassay technique, (eg, enzyme immunoassay [EIA], enzyme-linked immunosorbent assay [ELISA], immunochemiluminometric assay [IMCA]), qualitative or semiquantitative; multiple-step method, not otherwise specified, each organism
87450	single step method, not otherwise specified, each organism
87451	multiple step method, polyvalent for multiple organisms, each polyvalent antiserum
(87470	deleted 2017 [2018 edition])
87471	Infectious agent detection by nucleic acid (DNA or RNA); Bartonella henselae and Bartonella quintana, amplified probe technique
87472	Bartonella henselae and Bartonella quintana, quantification
87475	Borrelia burgdorferi, direct probe technique
87476	Borrelia burgdorferi, amplified probe technique
(87477	deleted 2017 [2018 edition])
87480	Candida species, direct probe technique

● New Code ▲ Revised Code + Add-On Code ⊘ Modifier -51 Exempt ★ Telemedicine

87481	Candida species, amplified probe technique
87482	Candida species, quantification
87483	Central nervous system pathogen (eg, Neisseria meningitidis, Streptococcus pneumoniae, Listeria, Haemophilus influenzae, E. coli, Streptococcus agalactiae, enterovirus, human parechovirus, herpes simplex virus type 1 and 2, human herpesvirus 6, cytomegalovirus, varicella zoster virus, Cryptococcus), includes multiplex reverse transcription, when performed, and multiplex amplified probe technique, multiple types or subtypes, 12-25 targets
87485	Chlamydia pneumoniae, direct probe technique
87486	Chlamydia pneumoniae, amplified probe technique
87487	Chlamydia pneumoniae, quantification
87490	Chlamydia trachomatis, direct probe technique
87491	Chlamydia trachomatis, amplified probe technique
87492	Chlamydia trachomatis, quantification
87493	Clostridium difficile, toxin gene(s), amplified probe technique
87495	cytomegalovirus, direct probe technique
87496	cytomegalovirus, amplified probe technique
87497	cytomegalovirus, quantification
87498	enterovirus, amplified probe technique, includes reverse transcription when performed
87500	vancomycin resistance (eg, enterococcus species van A, van B), amplified probe technique
87501	influenza virus, includes reverse transcription, when performed, and amplified probe technique, each type or subtype
87502	influenza virus, for multiple types or sub-types, includes multiplex reverse transcription, when performed, and multiplex amplified probe technique, first 2 types or sub-types
+ 87503	influenza virus, for multiple types or sub-types, includes multiplex reverse transcription, when performed, and multiplex amplified probe technique, each additional influenza virus type or sub-type beyond 2 (List separately in addition to code for primary procedure)

(Use 87503 in conjunction with 87502)

87505	gastrointestinal pathogen (eg, Clostridium difficile, E. coli, Salmonella, Shigella, norovirus, Giardia), includes multiplex reverse transcription, when performed, and multiplex amplified probe technique, multiple types or subtypes, 3-5 targets
87506	gastrointestinal pathogen (eg, Clostridium difficile, E.coli, Salmonella, Shigella, norovirus, Giardia), includes multiplex reverse transcription, when performed, and multiplex amplified probe technique, multiple types or subtypes, 6-11 targets
87507	gastrointestinal pathogen (eg, Clostridium difficile, E. coli, Salmonella, Shigella, norovirus, Giardia), includes multiplex reverse transcription, when performed, and multiplex amplified probe technique, multiple types or subtypes, 12-25 targets
87510	Gardnerella vaginalis, direct probe technique

87511	Gardnerella vaginalis, amplified probe technique
87512	Gardnerella vaginalis, quantification
(87515	deleted 2017 [2018 edition])
87516	hepatitis B virus, amplified probe technique
87517	hepatitis B virus, quantification
87520	hepatitis C, direct probe technique
87521	hepatitis C, amplified probe technique, includes reverse transcription when performed
87522	hepatitis C, quantification, includes reverse transcription when performed
87525	hepatitis G, direct probe technique
87526	hepatitis G, amplified probe technique
87527	hepatitis G, quantification
87528	Herpes simplex virus, direct probe technique
87529	Herpes simplex virus, amplified probe technique
87530	Herpes simplex virus, quantification
87531	Herpes virus-6, direct probe technique
87532	Herpes virus-6, amplified probe technique
87533	Herpes virus-6, quantification
87534	HIV-1, direct probe technique
87535	HIV-1, amplified probe technique, includes reverse transcription when performed
87536	HIV-1, quantification, includes reverse transcription when performed
87537	HIV-2, direct probe technique
87538	HIV-2, amplified probe technique, includes reverse transcription when performed
87539	HIV-2, quantification, includes reverse transcription when performed
87623	Human Papillomavirus (HPV), low-risk types (eg., 6, 11, 42, 43, 44)
87624	Human Papillomavirus (HPV), high-risk types (eg., 16, 18, 31, 33, 35, 39, 45, 51, 56, 58, 59, 68)

(When both low-risk and high-risk HPV types are performed in a single assay, use only 87624)

87625	Human Papillomavirus (HPV), types 16 and 18 only, includes type 45, if performed

(For Human Papillomavirus [HPV] detection of five or greater separately reported high-risk HPV types [ie, genotyping], use 0500T)

87540	Legionella pneumophila, direct probe technique

87541	Legionella pneumophila, amplified probe technique
87542	Legionella pneumophila, quantification
87550	Mycobacteria species, direct probe technique
87551	Mycobacteria species, amplified probe technique
87552	Mycobacteria species, quantification
87555	Mycobacteria tuberculosis, direct probe technique
87556	Mycobacteria tuberculosis, amplified probe technique
87557	Mycobacteria tuberculosis, quantification
87560	Mycobacteria avium-intracellulare, direct probe technique
87561	Mycobacteria avium-intracellulare, amplified probe technique
87562	Mycobacteria avium-intracellulare, quantification
87580	Mycoplasma pneumoniae, direct probe technique
87581	Mycoplasma pneumoniae, amplified probe technique
87582	Mycoplasma pneumoniae, quantification
87590	Neisseria gonorrhoeae, direct probe technique
87591	Neisseria gonorrhoeae, amplified probe technique
87592	Neisseria gonorrhoeae, quantification

(**87620** deleted 2014 [2015 edition]. To report, see 87623, 87624, 87625)

(**87621** deleted 2014 [2015 edition]. To report, see 87623, 87624, 87625)

(**87622** deleted 2014 [2015 edition]. To report, see 87623, 87624, 87625)

87623 This code is out of order. See page 790.

87624 This code is out of order. See page 790.

87625 This code is out of order. See page 790.

87631 respiratory virus (eg, adenovirus, influenza virus, coronavirus, metapneumovirus, parainfluenza virus, respiratory syncytial virus, rhinovirus), includes multiplex reverse transcription, when performed, and multiplex amplified probe technique, multiple types or subtypes, 3-5 targets

87632 respiratory virus (eg, adenovirus, influenza virus, coronavirus, metapneumovirus, parainfluenza virus, respiratory syncytial virus, rhinovirus), includes multiplex reverse transcription, when performed, and multiplex amplified probe technique, multiple types or subtypes, 6-11 targets

87633 respiratory virus (eg, adenovirus, influenza virus, coronavirus, metapneumovirus, parainfluenza virus, respiratory syncytial virus, rhinovirus), includes multiplex reverse transcription, when performed, and multiplex amplified probe technique, multiple types or subtypes, 12-25 targets

(Use 87631-87633 for nucleic acid assays which detect multiple respiratory viruses in a multiplex reaction [ie, single procedure with multiple results])

| | Separate Procedure | | Unlisted Procedure | | CCI Comp. Code | | Non-specific Procedure | **791** |

(For assays that are used to type or subtype influenza viruses only, see 87501-87503)

(For assays that include influenza viruses with additional respiratory viruses, see 87631-87633)

(For detection of multiple infectious agents not otherwise specified which report a single result, see 87800, 87801)

● **87634** respiratory syncytial virus, amplified probe technique

(For assays that include respiratory syncytial virus with additional respiratory viruses, see 87631, 87632, 87633)

87640 Staphylococcus aureus, amplified probe technique

87641 Staphylococcus aureus, methicillin resistant, amplified probe technique

(For assays that detect methicillin resistance and identify Staphylococcus aureus using a single nucleic acid sequenc, use 87641)

87650 Streptococcus, group A, direct probe technique

87651 Streptococcus, group A, amplified probe technique

87652 Streptococcus, group A, quantification

87653 Streptococcus, group B, amplified probe technique

87660 Trichomonas vaginalis, direct probe technique

87661 Trichomonas vaginalis, amplified probe technique

● **87662** Zika virus, amplified probe technique

87797 Infectious agent detection by nucleic acid (DNA or RNA), not otherwise specified; direct probe technique, each organism

87798 amplified probe technique, each organism

87799 quantification, each organism

87800 Infectious agent detection by nucleic acid (DNA or RNA), multiple organisms; direct probe(s) technique

87801 amplified probe(s) technique

(For each specific organism nucleic acid detection from a primary source, see 87471-87660. For detection of specific infectious agents not otherwise specified, see 87797, 87798, or 87799 1 time for each agent)

(For detection of multiple infectious agents not otherwise specified which report a single result, see 87800, 87801)

(Do not use 87801 for nucleic acid assays that detect multiple respiratory viruses in a multiplex reaction [ie, single procedure with multiple results], see 87631-87633)

87802 Infectious agent antigen detection by immunoassay with direct optical observation; Streptococcus, group B

87803 Clostridium difficile toxin A

87806 HIV-1 antigen(s), with HIV-1 and HIV-2 antibodies

87804 Influenza

87806 This code is out of order. See page 792.

● New Code   ▲ Revised Code   ✛ Add-On Code   ⊘ Modifier -51 Exempt   ★ Telemedicine

87807	respiratory syncytial virus
87808	Trichomonas vaginalis
87809	adenovirus
87810	Chlamydia trachomatis
87850	Neisseria gonorrhoeae
87880	Streptococcus, group A
87899	not otherwise specified
87900	Infectious agent drug susceptibility phenotype prediction using regularly updated genotypic bioinformatics
87910	Infectious agent genotype analysis by nucleic acid (DNA or RNA); cytomegalovirus

(For infectious agent drug susceptibility phenotype prediction for HIV-1, use 87900)

(For Human Papillomavirus [HPV] for high-risk types (ie, genotyping), of five or greater separately reported HPV types, use 0500T)

87901	HIV-1, reverse transciptase and protease regions
87906	HIV-1, other region (eg, integrase, fusion)

(For infectious agent drug susceptibility phenotype prediction for HIV-1, use 87900)

87912	Hepatitis B virus
87902	Hepatitis C virus
87903	Infectious agent phenotype analysis by nucleic acid (DNA or RNA) with drug resistance tissue culture analysis, HIV 1; first through 10 drugs tested
+ 87904	each additional drug tested (List separately in addition to code for primary procedure)

(Use 87904 in conjunction with code 87903)

87905	Infectious agent enzymatic activity other than virus (eg, sialidase activity in vaginal fluid)

(For virus isolation including identification by non-immunologic method, other than by cytopathic effect, use 87255)

87906	This code is out of order. See page 793.
87910	This code is out of order. See page 793.
87912	This code is out of order. See page .793
87999	Unlisted microbiology procedure

ANATOMIC PATHOLOGY

POSTMORTEM EXAMINATION

Procedures 88000 through 88099 represent physician services only. Use modifier 90 for outside laboratory services.

88000	Necropsy (autopsy), gross examination only; without CNS

■	Separate Procedure	■	Unlisted Procedure	■	CCI Comp. Code	■ Non-specific Procedure **793**

88005	with brain
88007	with brain and spinal cord
88012	infant with brain
88014	stillborn or newborn with brain
88016	macerated stillborn
88020	Necropsy (autopsy), gross and microscopic; without CNS
88025	with brain
88027	with brain and spinal cord
88028	infant with brain
88029	stillborn or newborn with brain
88036	Necropsy (autopsy), limited, gross and/or microscopic; regional
88037	single organ
88040	Necropsy (autopsy); forensic examination
88045	coroner's call
88099	Unlisted necropsy (autopsy) procedure

CYTOPATHOLOGY

When cytopathology codes are reported, the appropriate CPT code to bill is that which describes, to the highest level of specificity, what services were rendered. Accordingly, for a given specimen, only one code from a group of related codes describing a group of services that could be performed on a specimen with the same end result (e.g. 88104-88112, 88142- 88143, 88150-88154, 88164-88167, etc.) is to be reported.

If multiple services (i.e., separate specimens from different anatomic sites) are reported, modifier -59 should be used to indicate that different levels of service were provided for different specimens from different anatomic sites. This should be reflected in the cytopathologic reports. A cytopathology preparation from a fluid, washing, or brushing is to be reported using one code from the range of CPT codes 88104-88112. It is inappropriate to additionally use CPT codes 88160-88162 because the smears are included in the codes referable to fluids (or washings or brushings) and 88160-88162 references any other source which would exclude fluids, washings, or brushings.

88104	Cytopathology, fluids, washings or brushings, except cervical or vaginal; smears with interpretation
88106	simple filter method with interpretation

(Do not report 88106 in conjunction with 88104)

(For nongynecological selective cellular enhancement including filter transfer techniques, use 88112)

88108	Cytopathology, concentration technique, smears and interpretation (eg, Saccomanno technique)

(For cervical or vaginal smears, see 88150-88155)

(For gastric intubation with lavage, see 43754, 43755)

(For x-ray localization, use 74340)

● New Code ▲ Revised Code + Add-On Code ⊘ Modifier -51 Exempt ★ Telemedicine

88112 Cytopathology, selective cellular enhancement technique with interpretation (eg, liquid based slide preparation method), except cervical or vaginal

(Do not report 88112 with 88108)

88120 Cytopathology, in situ hybridization (eg, fish), urinary tract specimen with morphometric analysis, 3-5 molecular probes, each specimen; manual

88121   using computer-assisted technology

(For morphometric in situ hybridization on cytologic specimens other than urinary tract, see 88367, 88368)

(For more than 5 probes, use 88399)

88125 Cytopathology, forensic (eg, sperm)

88130 Sex chromatin identification; Barr bodies

88140   peripheral blood smear, polymorphonuclear drumsticks

(For Guard stain, use 88313)

Codes 88141-88155, 88164-88167, 88174-88175 are used to report cervical or vaginal screening by various methods and to report physician interpretation services. Use codes 88150, 88152, 88153 to report conventional Pap smears that are examined using non-Bethesda reporting. Use codes 88164-88167 to report conventional Pap smears that are examined using the Bethesda System of reporting. Use codes 88142-88143 to report liquidbased specimens processed as thin-layer preparations that are examined using any system of reporting (Bethesda or non-Bethesda). Use codes 88174-88175 to report automated screening of liquid-based specimens that are examined using any system of reporting (Bethesda or non-Bethesda).Within each of these three code families choose the one code that describes the screening method(s) used. Codes 88141 and 88155 should be reported in addition to the screening code chosen when the additional services are provided. Manual rescreening requires a complete visual reassessment of the entire slide initially screened by either an automated or manual process. Manual review represents an assessment of selected cells or regions of a slide identified by initial automated review.

88141 Cytopathology, cervical or vaginal (any reporting system), requiring interpretation by physician

(Use 88141 in conjunction with 88142, 88143, 88147, 88148, 88150, 88152, 88153, 88164-88167, 88174-88175)

88142 Cytopathology, cervical or vaginal (any reporting system), collected in preservative fluid, automated thin layer preparation; manual screening under physician supervision

88143   with manual screening and rescreening under physician supervision

(For automated screening of automated thin layer preparation, see 88174, 88175)

88147 Cytopathology smears, cervical or vaginal; screening by automated system under physician supervision

88148   screening by automated system with manual rescreening under physician supervision

88150 Cytopathology, slides, cervical or vaginal; manual screening under physician supervision

88152   with manual screening and computer-assisted rescreening under physician supervision

88153   with manual screening and rescreening under physician supervision

(**88154** deleted 2017 [2018 edition])

+ **88155** Cytopathology, slides, cervical or vaginal, definitive hormonal evaluation (eg, maturation index, karyopyknotic index, estrogenic index) (List separately in addition to code[s] for other technical and interpretation services)

(Use 88155 in conjunction with 88142, 88143, 88147, 88148, 88150, 88152, 88153, 88164-88167, 88174-88175)

■ Separate Procedure   ■ Unlisted Procedure   ■ CCI Comp. Code   ■ Non-specific Procedure   **795**

88160   Cytopathology, smears, any other source; screening and interpretation

88161   preparation, screening and interpretation

88162   extended study involving over 5 slides and/or multiple stains

(For aerosol collection of sputum, use 89350)

(For special stains, see 88312-88314)

88164   Cytopathology, slides, cervical or vaginal (the Bethesda System); manual screening under physician supervision

88165   with manual screening and rescreening under physician supervision

88166   with manual screening and computer-assisted rescreening under physician supervision

88167   with manual screening and computer-assisted rescreening using cell selection and review under physician supervision

(To report collection of specimen via fine needle aspiration, see 10021, 10022)

88172   Cytopathology, evaluation of fine needle aspirate; immediate cytohistologic study to determine adequacy for diagnosis, first evaluation episode, each site

(The evaluation episode represents a complete set of cytologic material submitted for evaluation and is independent of the number of needle passes or slides prepared. A separate evaluation episode occurs if the proceduralist provider obtains additional material from the same site, based on the prior immediate adequacy assessment, or a separate lesion is aspirated.)

88173   interpretation and report

(Report one unit of 88173 for the interpretation and report from each anatomic site, regardless of the number of passes or evaluation episodes performed during the aspiration procedure)

(For fine needle aspirate, see 10021, 10022)

(Do not report 88172, 88173 in conjunction with 88333 and 88334 for the same specimen)

+ 88177   immediate cytohistologic study to determine adequacy for diagnosis, each separate additional evaluation episode, same site (List separately in addition to code for primary procedure)

(When repeat immediate evaluation episode(s) is required on subsequent cytologic material from the same site, eg, following determination the prior sampling that was not adequate for diagnosis, use 1 unit of 88177 for each additional evaluation episode)

(Use 88177 in conjunction with 88172)

88174   Cytopathology, cervical or vaginal (any reporting system), collected in preservative fluid, automated thin layer preparation; screening by automated system, under physician supervision

88175   with screening by automated system and manual rescreening or review, under physician supervision

(For manual screening, see 88142, 88143)

88177   This code is out of order. See page 796.

88182   Flow cytometry; cell cycle or DNA analysis

(For DNA ploidy analysis by morphometric techniques, use 88358)

88184   Flow cytometry, cell surface, cytoplasmic, or nuclear marker, technical component only; first marker

+ 88185   each additional marker (List separately in addition to code for first marker)

(Report 88185 in conjunction with 88184)

88187   Flow cytometry, interpretation; 2 to 8 markers

88188   9 to 15 markers

88189   16 or more markers

(Do not report 88187-88189 for interpretation of 86355, 86356, 86357, 86359, 86360, 86361, 86367)

(For assessment of circulating antibodies by flow cytometric techniques, see analyte and method-specific codes in the Chemistry section [83516-83520] or Immunology section [86000-86849])

(For cell enumeration using immunologic selection and identification in fluid specimen [eg, circulating tumor cells in blood], see 0279T, 0280T)

88199   Unlisted cytopathology procedure

(For electron microscopy, see 88348)

CYTOGENETIC STUDIES

Molecular pathology procedures should be reported using the appropriate code from Tier 1 (81161, 81200-81383), Tier 2 (81400-81408), Genomic Sequencing Procedures and Other Molecular Multianalyte Assays (81410-81471), or Multianalyte Assays wit Algorithmic Analyses (81500-81512) sections. If no specific code exists, one of the unlisted codes (81479 or 81599) should be used.

(For acetylcholinesterase, use 82013)

(For alpha-fetoprotein, serum or amniotic fluid, see 82105, 82106)

(For laser microdissection of cells from tissue sample, see 88380)

88230   Tissue culture for non-neoplastic disorders; lymphocyte

88233   skin or other solid tissue biopsy

88235   amniotic fluid or chorionic villus cells

88237   Tissue culture for neoplastic disorders; bone marrow, blood cells

88239   solid tumor

88240   Cryopreservation, freezing and storage of cells, each cell line

(For therapeutic cryopreservation and storage, use 38207)

88241   Thawing and expansion of frozen cells, each aliquot

(For therapeutic thawing of previous harvest, use 38208)

88245   Chromosome analysis for breakage syndromes; baseline Sister Chromatid Exchange (SCE), 20-25 cells

88248   baseline breakage, score 50-100 cells, count 20 cells, 2 karyotypes (eg, for ataxia telangiectasia, Fanconi anemia, fragile X)

88249   score 100 cells, clastogen stress (eg, diepoxybutane, mitomycin C, ionizing radiation, UV radiation)

88261   Chromosome analysis; count 5 cells, 1 karyotype, with banding

88262   count 15-20 cells, 2 karyotypes, with banding

Separate Procedure   Unlisted Procedure   CCI Comp. Code   Non-specific Procedure   **797**

88263	count 45 cells for mosaicism, 2 karyotypes, with banding

88264	analyze 20-25 cells

88267	Chromosome analysis, amniotic fluid or chorionic villus, count 15 cells, 1 karyotype, with banding

88269	Chromosome analysis, in situ for amniotic fluid cells, count cells from 6-12 colonies, 1 karyotype, with banding

88271	Molecular cytogenetics; DNA probe, each (eg, FISH)

(For cytogenomic microarray analysis, see 81228, 81229, 81405, 81406, 81479)

(For genomic sequencing procedures or other molecular multianalyte assays for copy number analysis using circulating cell-free fetal DNA in maternal blood, see 81420, 81422, 81479)

88272	chromosomal in situ hybridization, analyze 3-5 cells (eg, for derivatives and markers)

88273	chromosomal in situ hybridization, analyze 10-30 cells (eg, for microdeletions)

88274	interphase in situ hybridization, analyze 25-99 cells

88275	interphase in situ hybridization, analyze 100-300 cells

88280	Chromosome analysis; additional karyotypes, each study

88283	additional specialized banding technique (eg, NOR, C-banding)

88285	additional cells counted, each study

88289	additional high resolution study

88291	Cytogenetics and molecular cytogenetics, interpretation and report

88299	Unlisted cytogenetic study

SURGICAL PATHOLOGY

The CPT codes 88321-88325 are to be used to review slides, tissues, or other material obtained and prepared at a different location and referred to a pathologist for a second opinion. (These codes should not be reported by pathologists reporting a second opinion on slides, tissue, or material also examined and reported by another pathologist in the same provider group. Medicare generally does not pay twice for an interpretation of a given technical service (e.g., EKGs, radiographs, etc.).

CPT codes 88321- 88325 are reported with one unit of service regardless of the number of specimens, paraffin blocks, stained slides, etc. When reporting CPT codes 88321-88325, providers should not report other pathology CPT codes such as 88312, 88313, 88342, 88187, 88188, 88189, etc., for interpretation of stains, slides or material previously interpreted by another pathologist. CPT codes 88312, 88313 and 88342 may be reported with CPT code 88323 if provider performs and interprets these stains de novo.

CPT codes 88321-88325 are not to be used for a face-to-face evaluation of a patient. In the event that a physician provides an evaluation and management service to a patient and, in the course of this service, specimens obtained elsewhere are reviewed as well, this is part of the evaluation and management service and is not to be reported separately. Only the evaluation and management service would be reported.

Medicare does not pay for duplicate testing. CPT codes 88342 (immuno-cytochemistry, each antibody) and 88184, 88187, 88188, 88189 (flow cytometry) should not in general be reported for the same or similar specimens. The diagnosis should be established using one of these methods. The provider may report both CPT codes if both methods are required because the initial method is nondiagnostic or does not explain all the light microscopic findings. The provider can report both methods utilizing modifier -59 and document the need for both methods in the medical record.

If the abnormal cells in two or more specimens are morphologically similar and testing on one specimen by one method (88342 or 88184, 88187, 88188, 88189) establishes the diagnosis, the same or other method should not be reported on the same or similar specimen. Similar specimens would include, but are not limited to: (1) blood and bone marrow; (2) bone marrow aspiration and bone marrow biopsy; (3) two separate lymph nodes; or (4) lymph node and other tissue with lymphoid infiltrate.

Services 88300 through 88309 include accession, examination, and reporting. They do not include the services designated in codes 88311 through 88365 and 88399, which are coded in addition when provided.

The unit of service for codes 88300 through 88309 is the specimen.

A specimen is defined as tissue or tissues that is (are) submitted for individual and separate attention, requiring individual examination and pathologic diagnosis. Two or more such specimens from the same patient (eg., separately identified endoscopic biopsies, skin lesions), are each appropriately assigned an individual code reflective of its proper level of service.

Service code 88300 is used for any specimen that in the opinion of the examining pathologist can be accurately diagnosed without microscopic examination. Service code 88302 is used when gross and microscopic examination is performed on a specimen to confirm identification and the absence of disease. Service codes 88304 through 88309 describe all other specimens requiring gross and microscopic examination, and represent additional ascending levels of physician work. Levels 88302 through 88309 are specifically defined by the assigned specimens.

Any unlisted specimen should be assigned to the code which most closely reflects the physician work involved when compared to other specimens assigned to that code.

(Do not report 88302-88309 on the same specimen as part of Mohs surgery)

88300   Level I - Surgical pathology, gross examination only

88302   Level II - Surgical pathology, gross and microscopic examination

> Appendix, Incidental
> Fallopian Tube, Sterilization
> Fingers/Toes, Amputation, Traumatic
> Foreskin, Newborn
> Hernia Sac, Any Location
> Hydrocele Sac
> Nerve
> Skin, Plastic Repair
> Sympathetic Ganglion
> Testis, Castration
> Vaginal Mucosa, Incidental
> Vas Deferens, Sterilization

88304   Level III - Surgical pathology, gross and microscopic examination

> Abortion, Induced
> Abscess
> Aneurysm - Arterial/Ventricular
> Anus, Tag
> Appendix, Other than Incidental
> Artery, Atheromatous Plaque
> Bartholin's Gland Cyst
> Bone Fragment(s), Other than Pathologic Fracture
> Bursa/Synovial Cyst
> Carpal Tunnel Tissue
> Cartilage, Shavings
> Cholesteatoma
> Colon, Colostomy Stoma
> Conjunctiva - Biopsy/Pterygium
> Cornea
> Diverticulum - Esophagus/Small Intestine
> Dupuytren's Contracture Tissue
> Femoral Head, Other than Fracture
> Fissue/Fistula
> Foreskin, Other than Newborn

Gallbladder
Ganglion Cyst
Hematoma
Hemorrhoids
Hydatid of Morgagni
Intervertebral Disc
Joint, Loose Body
Meniscus
Mucocele, Salivary
Neuroma - Morton's/Traumatic
Pilonidal Cyst/Sinus
Polyps, Inflammatory - Nasal/Sinusoidal
Skin - Cyst/Tag/Debridement
Soft Tissue, Debridement
Soft Tissue, Lipoma
Spermatocele
Tendon/Tendon Sheath
Testicular Appendage
Thrombus or Embolus
Tonsil and/or Adenoids
Varicocele
Vas Deferens, Other than Sterilizaton
Vein, Varicosity

88305 Level IV - Surgical pathology, gross and microscopic examination

Abortion - Spontaneous/Missed
Artery, Biopsy
Bone Marrow, Biopsy
Bone Exostosis
Brain/Meninges, Other than for Tumor Resection
Breast Biopsy, Not Requiring Microscopic Evaluation of Surgical Margins
Breast, Reduction Mammoplasty
Bronchus, Biopsy
Cell Block, Any Source
Cervix, Biopsy
Colon, Biopsy
Duodenum, Biopsy
Endocervix, Curettings/Biopsy
Endometrium, Currettings/Biopsy
Esophagus, Biopsy
Extremity, Amputation, Traumatic
Fallopian Tube, Biopsy
Fallopian Tube, Ectopic Pregnancy
Femoral Head, Fracture
Fingers/Toes, Amputation, Non-Traumatic
Gingiva/Oral Mucosa, Biopsy
Heart Valve
Joint, Resection
Kidney, Biopsy
Larynx, Biopsy
Leiomyoma(s), Uterine Myomectomy - without Uterus
Lip, Biopsy/Wedge Resection
Lung, Transbronchial Biopsy
Lymph Node, Biopsy
Muscle, Biopsy
Nasal Mucosa, Biopsy
Nasopharynx/Oropharynx, Biopsy
Nerve, Biopsy
Odontogenic/Dental Cyst
Omentum, Biopsy
Ovary with or without Tube, Non-neoplastic
Ovary, Biopsy/Wedge Resection
Parathyroid Gland
Peritoneum, Biopsy

● New Code   ▲ Revised Code   ✛ Add-On Code   ⊘ Modifier -51 Exempt   ★ Telemedicine

Pituitary Tumor
Placenta, Other than Third Trimester
Pleura/Pericardium - Biopsy/Tissue
Polyp, Cervical/Endometrial
Polyp, Colorectal
Polyp, Stomach/Small Intestine
Prostate, Needle Biopsy
Prostate, TUR
Salivary Gland, Biopsy
Sinus, Paranasal Biopsy
Skin, Other than Cyst/Tag/Debridement/Plastic Repair
Small Intestine, Biopsy
Soft Tissue, Other than Tumor/Mass/Lipoma/Debridement
Spleen
Stomach, Biopsy
Synovium
Testis, Other than Tumor/Biopsy/Castration
Thyroglossal Duct/Brachial Cleft Cyst
Tongue, Biopsy
Tonsil, Biopsy
Trachea, Biopsy
Ureter, Biopsy
Urethra, Biopsy
Urinary Bladder, Biopsy
Uterus, with or without Tubes and Ovaries, for Prolapse
Vagina, Biopsy
Vulva/Labia, Biopsy

88307 Level V - Surgical pathology, gross and microscopic examination

Adrenal, Resection
Bone - Biopsy/Curettings
Bone Fragment(s), Pathologic Fracture
Brain, Biopsy
Brain/Meninges, Tumor Resection
Breast, Excision of Lesion, Requiring Microscopic Evaluation of Surgical Margins
Breast, Mastectomy - Partial/Simple
Cervix, Conization
Colon, Segmental Resection, Other than for Tumor
Extremity, Amputation, Non-traumatic
Eye, Enucleation
Kidney, Partial/Total Nephrectomy
Larynx, Partial/Total Resection
Liver, Biopsy - Needle/Wedge
Lung, Wedge Biopsy
Lymph Nodes, Regional Resection
Mediastinum, Mass
Myocardium, Biopsy
Odontogenic Tumor
Ovary with or without Tube, Neoplastic
Pancreas, Biopsy
Placenta, Third Trimester
Prostate, Except Radical Resection
Salivary Gland
Sentinel Lymph Node
Small Intestine, Resection, Other Than for Tumor
Soft Tissue Mass (except Lipoma) - Biopsy/Simple Excision
Stomach - Subtotal/Total Resection, Other than for Tumor
Testis, Biopsy
Thymus, Biopsy
Thyroid, Total/Lobe
Ureter, Resection
Urinary Bladder, TUR
Uterus, with or without Tubes and Ovaries, Other than Neoplastic/Prolapse

88309   Level VI - Surgical pathology, gross and microscopic examination

Bone Resection
Breast, Mastectomy - with Regional Lymph Nodes
Colon, Segmental Resection for Tumor
Colon, Total Resection
Esophagus, Partial/Total Resection
Extremity, Disarticulation
Fetus, with Dissection
Larynx, Partial/Total Resection - with Regional Lymph Nodes
Lung - Total/Lobe/Segment Resection
Pancreas, Total/Subtotal Resection
Prostate, Radical Resection
Small Intestine, Resection for Tumor
Soft Tissue Tumor, Extensive Resection
Stomach - Subtotal/Total Resection for Tumor
Testis, Tumor
Tongue/Tonsil - Resection for Tumor
Urinary Bladder, Partial/Total Resection
Uterus, with or without Tubes and Ovaries, Neoplastic
Vulva, Total/Subtotal Resection

(For fine needle aspiration, see 10021, 10022)

(For evaluation of fine needle aspirate, see 88172-88173)

(Do not report 88302-88309 on the same specimen as part of Mohs surgery)

+ 88311   Decalcification procedure (List separately in addition to code for surgical pathology examination)

88312   Special stain including interpretation and report; Group I for microorganisms (eg, acid fast, methenamine silver)

(Report one unit of 88312 for each special stain, on each surgical pathology block, cytologic specimen, or hematologic smear)

(For immunocytochemistry and immunohistochemistry, use 88342)

88313   Group II, all other, (eg, iron, trichrome), except stain for microorganisms, stains for enzyme constituents, or immunocytochemistry and immunohistochemistry

(Report one unit of 88313 for each special stain, on each surgical pathology block, cytologic specimen, or hematologic smear)

(For immunocytochemistry and immunohistochemistry, see 88342, 88343)

+ 88314   histochemical stain on frozen tissue block (List separately in addition to code for primary procedure)

(Use 88314 in conjunction with 17311-17315, 88302-88309, 88331, 88332)

(Do not report 88314 with 17311-17315 for routine frozen section stain [eg., hematoxylin and eosin, toluidine blue], performed during Mohs surgery. When a nonroutine histochemical stain on frozen tissue during Mohs surgery is utilized, report 88314 with modifier 59)

(Report one unit of 88314 for each special stain on each frozen surgical pathology block)

(For a special stain performed on frozen tissue section material to identify enzyme constituents, use 88319)

(For determinative histochemistry to identify chemical components, use 88313)

88319   Group III, for enzyme constituents

(For each stain on each surgical pathology block, cytologic specimen, or hematologic smear, use one unit of 88319)

(For detection of enzyme constituents by immunohistochemical or immunocytochemical technique, see 88342)

   ● New Code   ▲ Revised Code   ✛ Add-On Code   ⊘ Modifier -51 Exempt   ★ Telemedicine

| 88321 | Consultation and report on referred slides prepared elsewhere |

| 88323 | Consultation and report on referred material requiring preparation of slides |

| 88325 | Consultation, comprehensive, with review of records and specimens, with report on referred material |

| 88329 | Pathology consultation during surgery; |

| 88331 | first tissue block, with frozen section(s), single specimen |

+ | 88332 | each additional tissue block with frozen section(s) (List separately in addition to code for primary procedure) |

(Use 88332 in conjunction with 88331)

| 88333 | cytologic examination (eg, touch prep, squash prep), initial site |

+ | 88334 | cytologic examination (eg, touch prep, squash prep), each additional site (List separately in addition to code for primary procedure) |

(Use 88334 in conjunction with 88331, 88333)

(For intraoperative consultation on a specimen requiring both frozen section and cytologic evaluation, use 88331 and 88334)

(For percutaneous needle biopsy requiring intraprocedural cytologic examination, use 88333)

(Do not report 88333 and 88334 for non-intraoperative cytologic examination, see 88160-88162)

(Do not report 88333 and 88334 for intraprocedural cytologic evaluation of fine needle aspirate, see 88172).

| 88341 | This code is out of order. See page 803. |

| 88342 | Immunohistochemistry or immunocytochemistry, per specimen; initial single antibody stain procedure |

(For quantitative or semiquantitative immunohistochemistry, see 88360, 88361)

+ | 88341 | each additional single antibody stain procedure (List separately in addition to code for primary procedure) |

(Use 88341 in conjunction with 88342)

(For multiplex antibody stain procedure, use 88344)

| 88344 | each multiplex antibody stain procedure |

(Do not use more than one unit of 88341, 88342, or 88344 for the same separately identifiable antibody per specimen)

(Do not report 88341, 88342, 88344 in conjunction with 88360, 88361 unless each procedure is for a different antibody)

(When multiple separately identifiable antibodies are applied to the same specimen [ie, multiplex antibody stain procedure], use one unit of 88344)

(When multiple antibodies are applied to the same slide that are not separately identifiable [eg, antibody cocktails], use 88342, unless an additional separately identiable antibody is also used, then use 88344)

| 88346 | Immunofluorescence, per specimen; initial single antibody stain procedure |

(| 88347 | deleted 2015 [2016 edition]. To report, see 88346, 88350) |

+ | 88350 | each additional single antibody stain procedure (List separately in addition to code for primary procedure) |

(Report 88350 in conjunction with 88346)

(Do not report 88346 and 88350 for fluorescent in situ hybridization studies, see 88364, 88365, 88366, 88367, 88368, 88369, 88373, 88374, and 88377)

(Do not report 88346 and 88350 for multiplex immunofluorescence analysis, use 88399)

88348   Electron microscopy; diagnostic

(88349   deleted 2014 [2015 edition]. To report, use 88348)

88350   This code is out of order. See page 803.

88355   Morphometric analysis; skeletal muscle

88356   nerve

88358   tumor (eg, DNA ploidy)

(Do not report 88358 with 88313 unless each procedure is for a different special stain)

88360   Morphometric analysis, tumor immunohistochemistry (eg, Her-2/neu, estrogen receptor/progesterone receptor), quantitative or semiquantitative, per specimen, each single antibody stain procedure; manual

88361   using computer-assisted technology

(Do not report 88360, 88361 in conjunction with 88341, 88342, or 88344 unless each procedure is for a different antibody)

(Morphometric analysis of a multiplex antibody stain should be reported with one unit of 88360 or 88361, per specimen)

(For morphometric analysis using in situ hyvridization techniques, see 88367, 88368)

(When semi-thin plastic-embedded sections are performed in conjunction with morphometric analysis, only the morphometric analysis should be coded; if performed as an independent procedure, see codes 88300-88309 for surgical pathology)

88362   Nerve teasing preparations

88363   Examination and selection of retrieved archival (ie, previously diagnosed) tissue(s) for molecular analysis (eg, Kras mutational analysis)

88364   This code is out of order. See page 804.

88365   In situ hybridization (eg, FISH), per specimen; initial single probe stain procedure

+ 88364   each additional single probe stain procedure (List separately in addition to code for primary procedure)

(Use 88364 in conjunction with 88365)

88366   each multiplex probe stain procedure

(Do not report 88365, 88366 in conjunction with 88367, 88368, 88374, 88377 for the same probe)

88367   Morphometric analysis, in situ hybridization, (quantitative or semi-quantitative), using computer-assisted technology, per specimen; initial single probe stain procedure

+ 88373   each additional single probe stain procedure (List separately in addition to code for primary procedure)

(Use 88373 in conjunction with 88367)

88374   each multiplex probe stain procedure

● New Code   ▲ Revised Code   ✛ Add-On Code   ⊘ Modifier -51 Exempt   ★ Telemedicine

(Do not report 88367, 88374 in conjunction with 88365, 88366, 88368, 88377 for the same probe)

88368 Morphometric analysis, in situ hybridization (quantitative or semi-quantitative), manual, per specimen; initial single probe stain procedure

+ 88369   each additional single probe stain procedure (List separately in addition to code for primary procedure)

(Use 88369 in conjunction with 88368)

88377   each multiplex probe stain procedure

(Do not report 88368 or 88377 in conjunction with 88365, 88366, 88367, 88374 for the same probe)

(For morphometric in situ hybridization evaluation of urinary tract cytologic specimens, see 88120, 88121)

88371 Protein analysis of tissue by Western Blot, with interpretation and report;

88372   immunological probe for band identification, each

88373 This code is out of order. See page 804.

88374 This code is out of order. See page 804.

88375 Optical endomicroscopic image(s), interpretation and report, real-time or referred, each endoscopic session

(Do not report 88375 in conjunction with 43206, 43252, 0397T)

88377 This code is out of order. See page 805.

88380 Microdissection (ie, sample preparation of microscopically identified target); laser capture

88381   manual

(Do not report 88380 in conjunction with 88381)

88387 Macroscopic examination, dissection, and preparation of tissue for non microscopic analytical studies (eg, nucleic acid based molecular studies); each tissue preparation (eg, a single lymph node)

(Do not report 88387 for tissue preparation for microbiologic cultures or flow cytometric studies)

(Do not report 88387 in conjunction with 88388, 88329-88334)

+ 88388   in conjunction with a touch imprint, intraoperative consultation, or frozen section, each tissue preparation (eg, a single lymph node) (List separately in addition to code for primary procedure)

(Use 88388 in conjunction with 88329-88334)

(Do not report 88387 or 88388 for tissue preparation for microbiologic cultures or flow cytometric studies)

88399 Unlisted surgical pathology procedure

IN VIVO (eg, TRANSCUTANEOUS) LABORATORY PROCEDURES

(For all in vivo measurements not specifically listed, use 88749)

(For wavelength fluorescent spectroscopy of advanced glycation end products [skin], use 88749)

(For transcutaneous oxyhemoglobin measurement in a lower extremity wound by near infrared spectroscopy, use 0493T)

88720 Bilirubin, total, transcutaneous

(For transdermal oxygen saturation, see 94760-94762)

| | Separate Procedure | | Unlisted Procedure | | CCI Comp. Code | | Non-specific Procedure | **805** |

88738 Hemoglobin (Hgb), quantitative, transcutaneous

(For in vitro hemoglobin measurement, use 85018)

88740 Hemoglobin, quantitative, transcutaneous, per day; carboxyhemoglobin

(For in vitro carboxyhemoglobin measurement, use 82375)

88741 methemoglobin

(For in vitro quantitative methemoglobin determination, use 83050)

88749 Unlisted in vivo (eg, transcutaneous) laboratory service

OTHER PROCEDURES

89049 Caffeine halothane contracture test (CHCT) for malignant hyperthermia susceptibility, including interpretation and report

89050 Cell count, miscellaneous body fluids (eg, cerebrospinal fluid, joint fluid), except blood;

89051 with differential count

89055 Leukocyte assessment, fecal, qualitative or semiquantitative

89060 Crystal identification by light microscopy with or without polarizing lens analysis, tissue or any body fluid (except urine)

(Do not report 89060 for crystal identification on paraffin-embedded tissue)

89125 Fat stain, feces, urine, or respiratory secretions

89160 Meat fibers, feces

89190 Nasal smear for eosinophils

(Occult blood, feces, use 82270)

(Paternity tests, use 86910)

89220 Sputum, obtaining specimen, aerosol induced technique (separate procedure)

89230 Sweat collection by iontophoresis

89240 Unlisted miscellaneous pathology test

REPRODUCTIVE MEDICINE PROCEDURES

89250 Culture of oocyte(s)/embryo(s), less than 4 days;

89251 with co-culture of oocyte(s)/embryo(s)

(For extended culture of oocyte(s)/embryo(s), see 89272)

89253 Assisted embryo hatching, microtechniques (any method)

89254 Oocyte identification from follicular fluid

89255 Preparation of embryo for transfer (any method)

89257 Sperm identification from aspiration (other than seminal fluid)

● New Code ▲ Revised Code + Add-On Code ⊘ Modifier -51 Exempt ★ Telemedicine

(For semen analysis, see 89300-89320)

(For sperm identification from testis tissue, use 89264)

89258 Cryopreservation; embryo(s)

89259 sperm

(For cryopreservation of reproductive tissue, testicular, use 89335)

89260 Sperm isolation; simple prep (eg, sperm wash and swim-up) for insemination or diagnosis with semen analysis

89261 complex prep (eg, Percoll gradient, albumin gradient) for insemination or diagnosis with semen analysis

(For semen analysis without sperm wash or swim-up, use 89320)

89264 Sperm identification from testis tissue, fresh or cryopreserved

(For biopsy of testis, see 54500, 54505)

(For sperm identification from aspiration, use 89257)

(For semen analysis, see 89300-89320)

89268 Insemination of oocytes

89272 Extended culture of oocyte(s)/embryo(s), 4-7 days

89280 Assisted oocyte fertiliation, microtechnique; less than or equal to 10 oocytes

89281 greater than 10 oocytes

89290 Biopsy, oocyte polar body or embryo blastomere, microtechnique (for pre-implantation genetic diagnosis); less than or equal to 5 embryos

89291 greater than 5 embryos

89300 Semen analysis; presence and/or motility of sperm including Huhner test (post coital)

89310 motility and count (not including Huhner test)

89320 volume, count, motility, and differential

(Skin tests, see 86485-86580 and 95012-95199)

89321 sperm presence and motility of sperm, if performed

(To report Hyaluronan binding assay [HBA], use 89398)

89322 volume, count, motility, and differential using strict morphologic criteria (eg, Kruger)

89325 Sperm antibodies

(For medicolegal identification of sperm, use 88125)

89329 Sperm evaluation; hamster penetration test

89330 cervical mucus penetration test, with or without spinnbarkeit test

89331 Sperm evaluation, for retrograde ejaculation, urine (sperm concentration, motility, and morphology, as indicated)

(For semen analysis on concurrent semen specimen, see 89300-89322 in conjunction with 89331)

(For detection of sperm in urine, use 81015)

89335 Cryopreservation, reproductive tissue, testicular

(For cryopreservation of embryo(s), use 89258. For cryopreservation of sperm, use 89259)

(For cryopreservation, ovarian tissue, oocytes, use 0058T; for mature oocytes, use 89337; for immature oocytes, use 0357T)

89337 Cryopreservation, mature oocyte(s)

(For cryopreservation of immature oocyte(s), use 0357T)

89342 Storage, (per year); embryo(s)

89343 sperm/semen

89344 reproductive tissue, testicular/ovarian

89346 oocyte(s)

89352 Thawing of cryopreserved; embryo(s)

89353 sperm/semen, each aliquot

89354 reproductive tissue, testicular/ovarian

89356 oocytes, each aliquot

89398 Unlisted reproductive medicine laboratory procedure

PROPRIETARY LABORATORY ANALYSES

Proprietary laboratory analyses (PLA) codes describe proprietary clinical laboratory analyses and can be provided either by a single ("sole-source") laboratory or licensed or marketed to multiple providing laboratories (eg, cleared or approved by the Food and Drug Administration [FDA]).

These codes include advanced diagnostic laboratory tests (ADLTs) and clinical diagnostic laboratory tests (CDLTs) as defined under the Protecting Access to Medicare Act (PAMA) of 2014.

● **0001U** Red blood cell antigen typing, DNA, human erythrocyte antigen gene analysis of 35 antigens from 11 blood groups, utilizing whole blood, common RBC alleles reported

● **0002U** Oncology (colorectal), quantitative assessment of three urine metabolites (ascorbic acid, succinic acid and carnitine) by liquid chromatography with tandem mass spectrometry (LC-MS/MS) using multiple reaction monitoring acquisition, algorithm reported as likelihood of adenomatous polyps

● **0003U** Oncology (ovarian) biochemical assays of five proteins (apolipoprotein A-1, CA 125 II, follicle stimulating hormone, human epididymis protein 4, transferrin), utilizing serum, algorithm reported as a likelihood score

● **0004U** Infectious disease (bacterial), DNA, 27 resistance genes, PCR amplification and probe hybridization in microarray format (molecular detection and identification of AmpC, carbapenemase and ESBL coding genes), bacterial culture colonies, report of genes detected or not detected, per isolate

● **0005U** Oncology (prostate) gene expression profile by real-time RT-PCR of 3 genes (ERG, PCA3, and SPDEF), urine, algorithm reported as risk score

● **0006U** Prescription drug monitoring, 120 or more drugs and substances, definitive tandem mass spectrometry with chromatography, urine, qualitative report of presence (including quantitative levels, when detected) or

---

● New Code ▲ Revised Code ＋ Add-On Code ⊘ Modifier -51 Exempt ★ Telemedicine

absence of each drug or substance with description and severity of potential interactions, with identified substances, per date of service

● **0007U** Drug test(s), presumptive, with definitive confirmation of positive results, any number of drug classes, urine, includes specimen verification including DNA authentication in comparison to buccal DNA, per date of service

● **0008U** Helicobacter pylori detection and antibiotic resistance, DNA, 16S and 23S rRNA, gyrA, pbp1, rdxA and rpoB, next generation sequencing, formalin-fixed paraffin-embedded or fresh tissue, predictive, reported as positive or negative for resistance to clarithromycin, fluoroquinolones, metronidazole, amoxicillin, tetracycline and rifabutin

● **0009U** Oncology (breast cancer), ERBB2 (HER2) copy number by FISH, tumor cells from formalin-fixed paraffin-embedded tissue isolated using image-based dielectrophoresis (DEP) sorting, reported as ERBB2 gene amplified or nonamplified

● **0010U** Infectious disease (bacterial), strain typing by whole genome sequencing, phylogenetic-based report of strain relatedness, per submitted isolate

● **0011U** Prescription drug monitoring, evaluation of drugs present by LC-MS/MS, using oral fluid, reported as a comparison to an estimated steady-state range, per date of service including all drug compounds and metabolites

● **0012U** Germline disorders, gene rearrangement detection by whole genome next-generation sequencing, DNA, whole blood, report of specific gene rearrangement(s)

● **0013U** Oncology (solid organ neoplasia), gene rearrangement detection by whole genome next-generation sequencing, DNA, fresh or frozen tissue or cells, report of specific gene rearrangement(s)

● **0014U** Hematology (hematolymphoid neoplasia), gene rearrangement detection by whole genome nextgeneration sequencing, DNA, whole blood or bone marrow, report of specific gene rearrangement(s)

● **0015U** Drug metabolism (adverse drug reactions), DNA, 22 drug metabolism and transporter genes, real-time PCR, blood or buccal swab, genotype and metabolizer status for therapeutic decision support

● **0016U** Oncology (hematolymphoid neoplasia), RNA, BCR/ABL1 major and minor breakpoint fusion transcripts, quantitative PCR amplification, blood or bone marrow, report of fusion not detected or detected with quantitation

● **0017U** Oncology (hematolymphoid neoplasia), JAK2 mutation, DNA, PCR amplification of exons 12-14 and sequence analysis, blood or bone marrow, report of JAK2 mutation not detected or detected

This page intentionally left blank.

● New Code ▲ Revised Code ✛ Add-On Code ⊘ Modifier -51 Exempt ★ Telemedicine

MEDICINE SECTION OVERVIEW

The sixth section of the CPT coding system is the medicine section, which includes codes for immunizations, therapeutic or diagnostic injections, psychiatric services, dialysis, ophthalmology services, specialty specific diagnostic services, chemotherapy administration, physical medicine and rehabilitation services, osteopathic and chiropractic services. Within each subsection, the CPT codes are arranged by the type of service provided.

MEDICINE SUBSECTIONS

The MEDICINE section of CPT is divided into the following subsections:

Immune Globulins	90281-90399
Immunization Administration for Vaccines/Toxoids	90460-90474
Vaccines, Toxoids	90476-90756
Psychiatry	90785-90899
Biofeedback	90901-90911
Dialysis	90935-90999
Gastroenterology	91010-91299
Ophthalmology	92002-92499
Special Otorhinolaryngologic Services	92502-92700
Cardiovascular	92920-93799
Noninvasive Vascular Diagnostic Studies	93880-93998
Pulmonary	94002-94799
Allergy and Clinical Immunology	95004-95199
Endocrinology	95249-95251
Neurology and Neuromuscular Procedures	95782-96020
Medical Genetics and Genetic Counseling Services	96040
Central Nervous System Assessments/Tests	96101-96127
Health and Behavior Assessment/Intervention	96150-96161
Hydration, Therapeutic, Prophylactic, Diagnostic Injections and Infusions, and Chemotherapy	96360-96549
Photodynamic Therapy	96567-96574
Special Dermatological Procedures	96900-96999
Physical Medicine and Rehabilitation	97010-97799
Medical Nutrition Therapy	97802-97804
Acupuncture	97810-97814
Osteopathic Manipulative Treatment	98925-98929
Chiropractic Manipulative Tretment	98940-98943
Education and Training for Patient Self-Management	98960-98962
Non-Face-to-Face Non-Physician Services	98966-98969
Special Services, Procedures and Reports	99000-99091
Qualifying Circumstances for Anesthesia	99100-99140
Moderate (Conscious) Sedation	99151-99157
Other Services and Procedures	99170-99199
Home Health Procedures/Services	99500-99602
Medication Therapy Management	99605-99607

Most of the subsections have special needs or instructions unique to that section which should be reviewed carefully before reporting.

MEDICINE SERVICES MODIFIERS

MEDICINE services and procedures may be modified under certain circumstances. When applicable, the modifying circumstance is identified by the addition of the appropriate modifier code. The following modifiers are frequently used with MEDICINE services.

-22   Unusual services

-26   Professional component

-51   Multiple procedures

This modifier may be used to report multiple medical procedures performed at the same session, as well as a combination of medical and surgical procedures.

-52   Reduced services

-76   Repeat procedure by same physician

-77   Repeat procedure by another physician

-90   Reference (outside) laboratory

-99   Multiple modifiers

● New Code   ▲ Revised Code   + Add-On Code   ⊘ Modifier -51 Exempt   ★ Telemedicine

MEDICINE CODES

IMMUNE GLOBULINS, SERUM OR RECOMBINANT PRODUCTS

Codes 90281-90399 identify the serum globulins, extracted from human blood; or recombinant immune globulin products created in a laboratory through genetic modification of human and/or animal proteins. Both are reported in addition to the administration codes 96365, 96366, 96367, 96368, 96369, 96370, 96371, 96372, 96374, 96375, as appropriate. Modifier 51 should not be reported with this section of products codes when performed with another procedure. The serum or recombinant globulin products listed here include broadspectrum anti-infective immune globulins, antitoxins, various isoantibodies, and monoclonal antibodies.

90281	Immune globulin (Ig), human, for intramuscular use
90283	Immune globulin (IgIV), human, for intravenous use
90284	Immune globulin (SCIg), human, for use in subcutaneous infusions, 100 mg, each
90287	Botulinum antitoxin, equine, any route
90288	Botulism immune globulin, human, for intravenous use
90291	Cytomegalovirus immune globulin (CMV-IgIV), human, for intravenous use
90296	Diphtheria antitoxin, equine, any route
90371	Hepatitis B immune globulin (HBIg), human, for intramuscular use
90375	Rabies immune globulin (RIg), human, for intramuscular and/or subcutaneous use
90376	Rabies immune globulin, heat-treated (RIg-HT), human, for intramuscular and/or subcutaneous use
90378	Respiratory syncytial virus monoclonal antibody, recombinant, for intramuscular use, 50 mg, each
90384	Rho(D) immune globulin (RhIg), human, full-dose, for intramuscular use
90385	Rho(D) immune globulin (RhIg), human, mini-dose, for intramuscular use
90386	Rho(D) immune globulin (RhIgIV), human, for intravenous use
90389	Tetanus immune globulin (TIg), human, for intramuscular use
90393	Vaccinia immune globulin, human, for intramuscular use
90396	Varicella-zoster immune globulin, human, for intramuscular use
90399	Unlisted immune globulin

IMMUNIZATION ADMINISTRATION FOR VACCINES/TOXOIDS

Immunization is the administration of a vaccine or toxoid to stimulate the immune system to provide protection against disease. Immunizations are usually given in conjunction with an evaluation and management service. When an immunization is the only service performed, a minimal evaluation and management service code may be listed in addition to the injection code.

Coding Rules

1. *When an immunization is the only service provided, evaluation and management service code 99211, Minimal service, may be reported in addition to the immunization.*

▇ Separate Procedure	▇ Unlisted Procedure	▇ CCI Comp. Code	▇ Non-specific Procedure	**813**

2. *Immunization administration CPT codes must be reported in addition to the vaccine and toxoid CPT codes.*

3. *Supplies or equipment used to inject the vaccine or toxoid are not reported separately.*

Report vaccine immunization administration codes 90460, 90461, 90471-90474 in addition to the vaccine and toxoid code(s) 90476-90749.

Report codes 90460 and 90461 only when the physician or qualified health care professional provides face-to-face counseling of the patient/family during the administration of a vaccine. For immunization administration of any vaccine that is not accompanied by face-to-face physician or qualified health care professional counseling to the patient/family, or for administration of vaccines to patients over 18 years of age, report codes 90471-90474.

If a significant separately identifiable Evaluation and Management service (eg., new or established patient office or other outpatient services [99201-99215], office or other outpatient consultations [99241-99245], emergency department services [99281-99285], preventive medicine services[99381-99429]) is performed, the appropriate E/M service code should be reported in addition to the vaccine and toxoid administration codes.

A component refers to all antigen in a vaccine that prevent disease(s) caused by one organism (90460 and 90461). Multi-valent antigens or multiple serotypes of antigens against a single organism are considered a single component of vaccines. Combination vaccines are those vaccines that contain multiple vaccine components. Conjugates or adjuvants contained in vaccines are not considered to be component parts of the vaccine as defined above.

IMMUNIZATION ADMINISTRATION

(For allergy testing, see 95004 et seq)

(For skin testing of bacterial, viral, fungal extracts, see 86485-86580)

(For therapeutic or diagnostic injections, see 96372-96379)

90460 Immunization administration through 18 years of age via any route of administration, with counseling by physician or other qualified health care professional; first or only component of each vaccine or toxoid administered

+ **90461** each additional vaccine or toxoid component administered (List separately in addition to code for primary procedure)

(Use 90460 for each vaccine administered. For vaccines with multiple components [combination vaccines], report 90460 in conjunction with 90461 for each additional component in a given vaccine)

90471 Immunization administration (includes percutaneous, intradermal, subcutaneous, or intramuscular injections); 1 vaccine (single or combination vaccine/toxoid)

(Do not report 90471 in conjunction with 90473)

+ **90472** each additional vaccine (single or combination vaccine/toxoid) (List separately in addition to code for primary procedure)

(Use 90472 in conjunction with 90460, 90471, 90473)

(For immune globulins, see 90281-90399. For administration of immune globulins, see 96365, 96366, 96367, 96368, 96369, 96370, 96371; 96374)

(For intravesical administration of BCG vaccine, use 51720, and see 90586)

90473 Immunization administration by intranasal or oral route; 1 vaccine (single or combination vaccine/toxoid)

(Do not report 90473 in conjunction with 90471)

+ **90474** each additional vaccine (single or combination vaccine/toxoid) (List separately in addition to code for primary procedure)

(Use 90474 in conjunction with 90460, 90471, 90473)

● New Code ▲ Revised Code + Add-On Code ⊘ Modifier -51 Exempt ★ Telemedicine

VACCINES, TOXOIDS

Vaccines and toxoids are administered to provide protection from hepatitis, influenza, typhoid, measles, mumps, polio, and other diseases. Vaccine and toxoid CPT codes 90476-90749 identify the vaccine or toxoid only and must be reported in addition to immunization administration CPT codes.

Codes 90476-90749 identify the vaccine product **only**. To report the administration of a vaccine/toxoid, the vaccine/toxoid product codes 90476-90749 must be used in addition to an immunization administration code(s) 90460, 90461, 90471, 90472, 90473, 90474. Modifier -51 should not be reported with vaccine/toxoid codes 90476-90479, when reported in conjunction with administratino codes 90460, 90461, 90471-90474.

If a significant separately identifiable E/M service (eg., office or other outpatient services, preventive medicine services) is performed, the appropriate E/M service code should be reported in addition to the vaccine and toxoid administration codes.

To meet the reporting requirements of immunization registries, vaccine distribution programs, and reporting systems (eg., Vaccine Adverse Event Reporting System) the exact vaccine product administered needs to be reported. Multiple codes for a particular vaccine are provided in the CPT codebook when the schedule (number of doses or timing) differs for two or more products of the same vaccine type (eg., hepatitis A, Hib) or the vaccine product is available in more than one chemical formulation, dosage, or route of administration.

The "when administered to" age descriptions included in CPT vaccine codes are not intended to identify a product's licensed age indication. The term "preservative free" includes use for vaccines that contain no preservative and vaccines that contain trace amounts of preservative agents that are not present in a sufficient concentration for the purpose of preserving the final vaccine formulation. The absence of a designation regarding a preservative does not necessarily indicate the presence or absence of preservative in the vaccine. Refer to the product's prescribing information (PI) for the licensed age indication before administering vaccine to a patient.

Separate codes are available for combination vaccines (eg., DTP-Hib, DTaP-Hib, HepB-Hib). It is inappropriate to code each component of a combination vaccine separately. If a specific vaccine code is not available, the unlisted procedure code should be reported, until a new code becomes available.

(For immune globulins, see 90281-90399. For administration of immune globulins, see 96365-96375)

90476 Adenovirus vaccine, type 4, live, for oral use

90477 Adenovirus vaccine, type 7, live, for oral use

90581 Anthrax vaccine, for subcutaneous or intramuscular use

90585 Bacillus Calmette-Guerin vaccine (BCG) for tuberculosis, live, for percutaneous use

90586 Bacillus Calmette-Guerin vaccine (BCG) for bladder cancer, live, for intravesical use

● **90587** Dengue vaccine, quadrivalent, live, 3 dose schedule, for subcutaneous use

(FDA approval pending)

90620 This code is out of order .See page 819.

90621 This code is out of order. See page 819.

90625 This code is out of order. See page 818.

90630 This code is out of order. See page 816.

90632 Hepatitis A vaccine (HepA), adult dosage, for intramuscular use

90633 Hepatitis A vaccine (HepA), pediatric/adolescent dosage-2 dose schedule, for intramuscular use

90634 Hepatitis A vaccine (HepA), pediatric/adolescent dosage-3 dose schedule, for intramuscular use

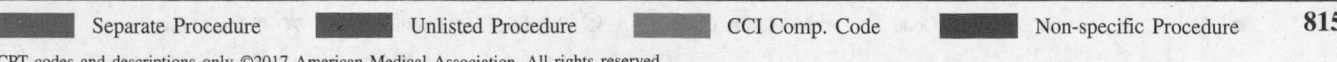

Separate Procedure   Unlisted Procedure   CCI Comp. Code   Non-specific Procedure   **815**

90636 Hepatitis A and hepatitis B vaccine (HepA-HepB), adult dosage, for intramuscular use

90644 This code is out of order. See page 818.

(**90645** deleted 2015 [2016 edition])

(**90646** deleted 2015 [2016 edition])

90647 Hemophilus influenza tybe b vaccine (Hib), PRP-OMP conjugate 3 dose schedule, for intramuscular use

90648 Hemophilus influenza type b vaccine (Hib), PRP-T conjugate, 4 dose schedule, for intramuscular use

90649 Human Papillomavirus (HPV) vaccine, types 6, 11, 16, 18, quadrivalent (4vHPV), 3 dose schedule, for intramuscular use

90650 Human Papillomavirus (HPV) vaccine, types 16, 18, bivalent (2vHPV), 3 dose schedule, for intramuscular use

▲ **90651** Human Papillomavirus vaccine types 6, 11, 16, 18, 31, 33, 45, 52, 58, nonavalent (9vHPV), 2 or 3 dose schedule, for intramuscular use

90653 Influenza vaccine, inactivated (IIV), subunit, adjuvanted, for intramuscular use

90654 Influenza virus vaccine, trivalent (IIV3), split virus, preservative-free, for intradermal use

90630 Influenza virus vaccine, quadrivalent (IIV4), split virus, preservative free, for intradermal use

90655 Influenza virus vaccine, trivalent (IIV3), split virus, preservative free, 0.25 mL dosage, for intramuscular use

90656 Influenza virus vaccine, trivalent (IIV3), split virus, preservative free, 0.5 mL dosage, for intramuscular use

90657 Influenza virus vaccine, trivalent (IIV3), split virus, 0.25 mL dosage, for intramuscular use

90658 Influenza virus vaccine, trivalent (IIV3), split virus, 0.5 mL dosage, for intramuscular use

90660 Influenza virus vaccine, trivalent, live (LAIV3), for intranasal use

90672 Influenza virus vaccine, quadrivalent, live (LAIV4), for intranasal use

90661 Influenza virus vaccine, trivalent (ccIIV3), derived from cell cultures, subunit, preservative and antibiotic free, 0.5 mL dosage, for intramuscular use

90674 Influenza virus vaccine, quadrivalent (ccIIV4), derived from cell cultures, subunit, preservative and antibiotic free, 0.5 mL dosage, for intramuscular use

● **90756** Influenza virus vaccine, quadrivalent (ccIIV4), derived from cell cultures, subunit, antibiotic free, 0.5 mL dosage, for intramuscular use

90673 Influenza virus vaccine, trivalent (RIV3), derived from recombinant DNA, hemagglutinin (HA) protein only, preservative and antibiotic free, for intramuscular use

90662 Influenza virus vaccine (IIV), split virus, preservative free, enhanced immunogenicity via increased antigen content, for intramuscular use

90664 Influenza virus vaccine, live (LAIV), pandemic formulation, for intranasal use

90666 Influenza virus vaccine (IIV), pandemic formulation, split virus, preservative free, for intramuscular use

(FDA approval pending)

---

816 ● New Code ▲ Revised Code ＋ Add-On Code ⊘ Modifier -51 Exempt ★ Telemedicine

90667   Influenza virus vaccine (IIV), pandemic formulation, split virus, adjuvanted, for intramuscular use

(FDA approval pending)

90668   Influenza virus vaccine (IIV), pandemic formulation, split virus, for intramuscular use

(FDA approval pending)

(**90669**   deleted 2015 [2016 edition])

90670   Pneumococcal conjugate vaccine, 13 valent (PCV13), for intramuscular use

90672   This code is out of order. See page 816.

90673   This code is out of order. See page 816.

90674   This code is out of order. See page816

90675   Rabies vaccine, for intramuscular use

90676   Rabies vaccine, for intradermal use

90680   Rotavirus vaccine, pentavalent (RV5), 3 dose schedule, live, for oral use

90681   Rotavirus vaccine, human, attenuated (RV1), 2 dose schedule, live, for oral use

● **90682**   Influenza virus vaccine, quadrivalent (RIV4), derived from recombinant DNA, hemagglutinin (HA) protein only, preservative and antibiotic free, for intramuscular use

90685   Influenza virus vaccine, quadrivalent (IIV4), split virus, preservative free, 0.25 mL dosage, for intramuscular use

90686   Influenza virus vaccine, quadrivalent (IIV4), split virus, preservative free, 0.5 mL dosage, for intramuscular use

90687   Influenza virus vaccine, quadrivalent (IIV4), split virus, 0.25 mL dosage, for intramuscular use

90688   Influenza virus vaccine, quadrivalent (IIV4), split virus, 0.5 mL dosage, for intramuscular use

90690   Typhoid vaccine, live, oral

90691   Typhoid vaccine, Vi capsular polysaccharide (ViCPs), for intramuscular use

(**90692**   deleted 2015 [2016 edition])

(**90693**   deleted 2015 [2016 edition])

90696   Diphtheria, tetanus toxoids, acellular pertussis vaccine and inactivated poliovirus vaccine (DTaP-IPV), when administered to children 4 through 6 years of age, for intramuscular use

90697   Diphtheria, tetanus toxoids, acellular pertussis vaccine, inactivated poliovirus vaccine, Haemophilus influenzae type b PRP-OMP conjugate vaccine, and hepatitis B vaccine (DTaP-IPV-Hib-HepB), for intramuscular use

(FDA approval pending)

90698   Diphtheria, tetanus toxoids, acellular pertussis vaccine, Haemophilus influenza type b, and inactivated poliovirus vaccine (DTaP-IPV/Hib), for intramuscular use

90700   Diphtheria, tetanus toxoids, and acellular pertussis vaccine (DTaP), when administered to individuals younger than 7 years, for intramuscular use

| ■ Separate Procedure | ■ Unlisted Procedure | ■ CCI Comp. Code | ■ Non-specific Procedure | **817** |

90702 Diphtheria and tetanus toxoids adsorbed (DT), when administered to individuals younger than 7 years, for intramuscular use

(**90703** deleted 2015 [2016 edition])

(**90704** deleted 2015 [2016 edition])

(**90705** deleted 2015 [2016 edition])

(**90706** deleted 2015 [2016 edition])

90707 Measles, mumps and rubella virus vaccine (MMR), live, for subcutaneous use

(**90708** deleted 2015 [2016 edition])

90710 Measles, mumps, rubella, and varicella vaccine (MMRV), live, for subcutaneous use

(**90712** deleted 2015 [2016 edition])

90713 Poliovirus vaccine, inactivated, (IPV), for subcutaneous or intramuscular use

90714 Tetanus and diphtheria toxoids adsorbed (Td), preservative free, when administered to individuals 7 years or older, for intramuscular use

90715 Tetanus, diphtheria toxoids and acellular pertussis vaccine (Tdap), when administered to individuals 7 years or older, for intramuscular use

90716 Varicella virus vaccine (VAR), live, for subcutaneous use

90717 Yellow fever vaccine, live, for subcutaneous use

(**90719** deleted 2015 [2016 edition])

(**90720** deleted 2015 [2016 edition])

(**90721** deleted 2015 [2016 edition])

90723 Diphtheria, tetanus toxoids, acellular pertussis vaccine, hepatitis B, and inactivated poliovirus vaccine (DTaP-HepB-IPV), for intramuscular use

(**90725** deleted 2015 [2016 edition])

90625 Cholera vaccine, live, adult dosage, 1 dose schedule, for oral use

(FDA approval pending)

(**90727** deleted 2015 [2016 edition])

90732 Pneumococcal polysaccharide vaccine, 23-valent (PPSV23), adult or immunosuppressed patient dosage, when administered to individuals 2 years or older, for subcutaneous or intramuscular use

90644 Meningococcal conjugate vaccine, serogroups C & Y and Haemophilus influenzae type b vaccine (Hib-MenCY), 4 dose schedule, when administered to children 6 weeks-18 months of age, for intramuscular use

90733 Meningococcal polysaccharide vaccine, serogroups A, C, Y, W-135, quadrivalent (MPSV4), for subcutaneous use

90734 Meningococcal conjugate vaccine, serogroups A, C, Y and W-135, quadrivalent (MCV4 or MenACWY), for intramuscular use

---

● New Code ▲ Revised Code + Add-On Code ⊘ Modifier -51 Exempt ★ Telemedicine

▲ 90620 Meningococcal recombinant protein and outer membrane vesicle vaccine, serogroup B (MenB-4C), 2 dose schedule, for intramuscular use

▲ 90621 Meningococcal recombinant lipoprotein vaccine, serogroup B (MenB-FHbp), 2 or 3 dose schedule, for intramuscular use

(90735 deleted 2015 [2016 edition])

90736 Zoster (shingles) vaccine (HZV), live, for subcutaneous injection

● 90750 Zoster (shingles) vaccine (HZV), recombinant, subunit, adjuvanted, for intramuscular use

(FDA approval pending)

90738 Japanese encephalitis virus vaccine, inactivated, for intramuscular use

90739 Hepatitis B vaccine (HepB), adult dosage, 2 dose schedule, for intramuscular use

(FDA approval pending)

90740 Hepatitis B vaccine (HepB), dialysis or immunosuppressed patient dosage, 3 dose schedule, for intramuscular use

90743 Hepatitis B vaccine (HepB), adolescent, 2 dose schedule, for intramuscular use

90744 Hepatitis B vaccine (HepB), pediatric/adolescent dosage, 3 dose schedule, for intramuscular use

90746 Hepatitis B vaccine (HepB), adult dosage, 3 dose schedule, for intramuscular use

90747 Hepatitis B vaccine (HepB), dialysis or immunosuppressed patient dosage, 4 dose schedule, for intramuscular use

90748 Hepatitis B and Haemophilus influenza type b vaccine (Hib-HepB), for intramuscular use

90749 Unlisted vaccine/toxoid

90750 This code is out of order. See page 819.

90756 This code is out of order. See page 816

PSYCHIATRY

Patient condition, characteristics, or situational factors may require services described as being with interactive complexity. Services may be provided to a patient in crisis. Services are provided in all settings of care and psychiatry services codes are reported without regard to setting. Services may be provided by a physician or other qualified health care professional. Some psychiatry services may be reported with E/M services (99201-99255, 99281-99285, 99304-99337, 99341-99350) or other services when performed. Evaluation and Management Services (99201-99285, 99304-99337, 99341-99350) may be reported for treatment of psychiatric conditions rather than using Psychiatry Services codes, when appropriate.

Hospital care in treating a psychiatric inpatient or partial hospitalization may be initial or subsequent in nature (see 99221-99233).

Some patients receive hospital evaluation and management services only and others receive evaluation and management services and other procedures. If other procedures such as electroconvulsive therapy or psychotherapy are rendered in addition to hospital evaluation and management services, these should be listed separately (ie., hospital care services [99221-99223, 99231-99233] plus electroconvulsive therapy [90870] or when psychotherapy is done, with appropriate code(s) defining psychotherapy services.

Consultation for psychiatric evaluation of a patient includes examination of a patient and exchange of information with the primary physician and other informants, such as nurses or family members, and preparation of a report. These services may be reported usin consultation codes.

(Do not report 90785-90899 in conjunction wtih 90839, 90840, 0364T, 0365T, 0366T, 0367T, 0373T, 0374T)

INTERACTIVE COMPLEXITY

Code 90785 is an add-on code for interactive complexity to be reported in conjunction with codes for diagnostic psychiatric evaluation (90791, 90792), psychotherapy (90832, 90834, 90837), psychotherapy when performed with an E/M service (90833, 90836, 90838, 99201-99255, 99304-99337, 99341-99350), and group psychotherapy (90853).

Interactive complexity refers to specific communication factors that complicate the delivery of a psychiatric procedure. Common factors include more difficult communication with discordant or emotional family members and engagement of young and verbally undeveloped or impaired patients. Typical patients are those who have third parties, such as parents, guardians, other family members, interpreters, language translators, agencies, court officers, or schools involved in their psychaitric care.

Psychiatric procedures may be reported "with interactive complexity" when at least one of the following is present:

1. The need to manage maladaptive communication (related to, eg, high anxiety, high reactivity, repeated questions, or disagreement) among participants that complicates delivery of care.

2. Caregiver emotions or behavior that interferes with the caregiver's understanding and ability to assist in the implementation of the treatment plan.

3. Evidence or disclosure of a sentinel event and mandated report to third party (eg, abuse or neglect with report to state agency) with initiation of discussion of the sentinel event and/or report with patient and other visit participants.

4. Use of play equipment, other physical devices, interpreter or translator to communicate with the patient to overcome barriers to therapeutic or diagnostic interaction between the physician or other qualified health care professional and a patient who:

* is not fluent in the same language as the physician or other qualified health care professional, or

* has not developed or has lost either the expressive language communication skills to explain his/her symptoms and response to treatment, or the receptive communication skills to understand the physician or other qualified health care professional if he/she were to use typical language for communication.

When provided in conjunction with the psychotherapy services (90832-90838), the amount of time spent by a physician or other qualified health care professional providing interactive complexity services should be reflected in the timed service code for psychotherapy (90832, 90834, 90837) or the psychotherapy add-on code performed with an evaluation and management service (90833, 90836, 90838) and must relate to the psychotherapy service only. Interactive complexity is not a factor for E/M services selection (99201-99255, 99281-99285, 99304-99337, 99341-99350), except as it directly affects key components as defined in the E/M services guidelines (ie, history, examination, and medical decision making).

+ **90785**   Interactive complexity (List separately in addition to the code for primary procedure)

(Use 90785 in conjunction with codes for diagnostic psychiatric evaluation [90791, 90792], psychotherapy [90832, 90834, 90837], psychotherapy when performed with an evaluation and management service [90833, 90836, 90838, 99201-99255, 99304-99337, 99341-99350], and group psychotherapy [90853])

(Do not report 90785 in conjunction with 90839, 90840, 0364T, 0365T, 0366T, 0367T, 0373T, 0374T)

PSYCHIATRIC DIAGNOSTIC PROCEDURES

Psychiatric diagnostic evaluation is an integrated biopsychosocial assessment, including history, mental status and recommendations. The evaluation may include communication with family or other sources and review and ordering of diagnostic services.

Psychiatric diagnostic evaluation with medical services is an integrated biopsychosocial and medical assessment, including history, mental status, other physical examination elements as indicated, and recommendations. The evaluation may include communication with family or other sources, prescription of medications, and review and ordering of laboratory or other diagnostic studies.

In certain circumstances one or more other informants (family members, guardians, or significant others) may be seen in lieu of the patient. Codes 90791, 90792 may be reported more than once for the patient when separate diagnostic evaluations are conducted with the patient and other informants. Report services as being provided to the patient and not the informant or other party in such circumstances. Codes 90791, 90792 may be reported once per day and not on the same day as an evaluation and management service performed by the same individual for the same patient.

The psychiatric diagnostic evaluation may include interactive complexity services when factors exist that complicate the delivery of the psychiatric procedure. These services should be reported with add-on code 90785 used in conjunction with the diagnostic psychiatric evaluation codes 90791, 90792.

Codes 90791, 90792 are used for the diagnostic assessment(s) or reassessment(s) if required, and do not include psychotherapeutic services. Psychotherapy services, including for crisis, may not be reported on the same day.

> (Do not report 90791-90899 in conjunction with 90839, 90840, 0364T, 0365T, 0366T, 0367T, 0373T, 0374T)

★ **90791**   Psychiatric diagnostic evaluation

★ **90792**   Psychiatric diagnostic evaluation with medical services

> (Do not report 90791 or 90792 in conjunction with 99201-99337, 99341-99350, 99366-99368, 99401-99444, 0368T, 0369T, 0370T, 0371T)

> (Use 90785 in conjunction with 90791, 90792 when the diagnostic evaluation includes interactive complxity services)

PSYCHOTHERAPY

Psychotherapy is the treatment of menal illness and behavioral disturbances in which the physician or other qualified health care professional, through definitive therapeutic communication, attempts to alleviate the emotional disturbances, reverse or change maladaptive patterns of behavior, and encourage personality growth and development.

The psychotherapy service codes 90832-90838 include ongoing assessment and adjustment of psychotherapeutic interventions, and may include involvement of informants in the treatment process.

Codes 90832, 90833, 90834, 90836, 90837, 90838 describe psychotherapy for the individual patient, although times are for face-to-face services with patient and may include informant(s). The patient must be present for all or a majority of the service.

See codes 90846, 90847 when utilizing family psychotherapy techniques, such as focusing on family dynamics. Do not report 90846, 90847 for family psychotherapy services less than 26 minutes. Codes 90832, 90833, 90834, 90836, 90837, 90838 may be reported on the same day as codes 90846, 90847, when the services are separate and distinct.

In reporting, choose the code closest to the actual time (ie, 16-37 minutes for 90832 and 90833, 38-52 minutes for 90834 and 90836, and 53 or more minutes for 90837 and 90838). Do not report psychotherapy of less than 16 minutes duration. (See instructions for the usage of time in the Introduction of the CPT code set.)

Psychotherapy provided to a patient in a crisis state is reported with codes 90839 and 90840 and cannot be reported in addition to the psychotherapy codes 90832-90838. For psychotherapy for crisis, see "Other Psychotherapy."

Code 90785 is an add-on code to report interactive complexity services when provided in conjunction with the psychotherapy codes 90832-90838. For family psychotherapy, see 90846, 90847. The amount of time spent by a physician or other qualified health care professional providing interactive complexity services should be reflected in the timed service code for psychotherapy (90832, 90834, 90837) or the psychotherapy add-on code performed with an evaluation and management service (90833, 90836, 90838)

Some psychiatric patients receive a medical evaluation and management (E/M) service on the same day as the psychotherapy service by the same physician or other qualified health care professional. To report both E/M and psychotherapy, the two services must be significant and separately identifiable. These services are reported by using codes specific for psychotherapy when performed with evaluation and managment services (90833, 90836, 90838) as add-on codes to the evaluation and management service.

Medical symptoms and disorders inform treatment choices of psychotherapeutic interventions, and data from therapeutic communications are used to evaluate the presence, type, and severity of medical symptoms and disorders. For the purposes of reporting, the medical and psychotherapeutic components of the service may be separately identified as follows:

1. The type and level of E/M service is selected first based upon the key components of history, examination and medical decision making

---

2. Time associated with activities used to meet criteria for the E/M service is not included in the time used for reporting the psychotherapy service (ie, time spent on history, examination and medical decision making **when used for the E/M service** is not psychotherapy time). Time may not be used as the basis of E/M code selection and Prolonged Services may not be reported when psychotherapy with E/M (90833, 90836, 90838) are reported.

3. A separate diagnosis is not required for the reportin of E/M and psychotherapy on the same date of service.

★ **90832**   Psychotherapy, 30 minutes with patient

★+**90833**   Psychotherapy, 30 minutes with patient when performed with an evaluation and management service (List separately in addition to the code for primary procedure)

       (Use 90833 in conjunction with 99201-99255, 99304-99337, 99341-99350)

★ **90834**   Psychotherapy, 45 minutes with patient

★+**90836**   Psychotherapy, 45 minutes with patient when performed with an evaluation and management service (List separately in addition to the code for primary procedure)

       (Use 90836 in conjunction with 99201-99255, 99304-99337, 99341-99350)

★ **90837**   Psychotherapy, 60 minutes with patient

       (Use the appropriate prolonged service code [99354, 99355, 99356, 99357] for psychotherapy services not performed with an E/M service of 90 minutes or longer face-to-face with the patient)

★+**90838**   Psychotherapy, 60 minutes with patientn when performed with an evaluation and management service (List separately in addition to the code for primary procedure)

       (Use 90838 in conjunction with 99201-99255, 99304-99337, 99341-99350)

       (Use 90785 in conjunction with 90832, 90833, 90834, 90836, 90837, 90838 when psychotherapy includes interactive complexity services)

PSYCHOTHERAPY FOR CRISIS

Psychotherapy for crisis is an urgent assessment and history of a crisis state, a mental status exam, and a disposition. The treatment includes psychotherapy, mobilization of resources to defuse the crisis and restore safety, and implementation of psychotherapeutic interventions to minimize the potential for psychological trauma. The presenting problem is typically life threatening or complex and requires immediate attention to a patient in high distress.

Codes 90839, 90840 are used to report the total duration of time face-to-face with the patient and/or family spent by the physician or other qualified health care professional providing psychotherapy for crisis, even if the time spent on that date is not continuous. For any given period of time spent providing psychotherapy for crisis state, the physician or other qualified health care professional must devote his or her full attention to the patient and, therefore, cannot provide services to any other patients during the same time period. The patient must be present for all or some of the service. Do not report with 90791 or 90792.

Code 90839 is used to report the first 30-74 minutes of psychotherapy for crisis on a given date. It should be used only once per date if the time spent by the physician or other qualified health care professional is not continuous on that date. Psychotherapy for crisis of less than 30 minutes total duration on a given date should be reported with 90832 or 90833 (when provided with evaluation and management services). Code 90840 is used to report additional block(s) of time, up to 30 minutes each beyond the first 74 minutes.

90839   Psychotherapy for crisis; first 60 minutes

+ **90840**   each additional 30 minutes (List separately in addition to code for primary service)

       (Use 90840 in conjunction with 90839)

       (Do not report 90839, 90840 in conjunction with 90791, 90792, psychotherapy codes 90832-90838 or other psychiatric services, or 90785-90899)

OTHER PSYCHOTHERAPY

★ **90845**   Psychoanalysis

★ **90846** Family psychotherapy (without the patient present), 50 minutes

★ **90847** Family psychotherapy (conjoint psychotherapy) (with patient present), 50 minutes

(Do not report 90846, 90847 for family psychotherapy services less than 26 minutes)

(Do not report 90846, 90847 in conjunction with 0368T, 0369T, 0370T, 0371T)

90849 Multiple-family group psychotherapy

90853 Group psychotherapy (other than of a multiple-family group)

(Use 90853 in conjunction with 90785 for the specified patient when group psychotherapy includes interactive complexity)

(Do not report 90853 in conjunction with 0372T)

OTHER PSYCHIATRIC SERVICES OR PROCEDURES

(For analysis / programming of neurostimulators used for vagus nerve stimulation therapy, see 95970, 95974, 95975)

★+**90863** Pharmacologic management, including prescription and review of medication, when performed with psythotherapy services (List separately in addition to the code for primary procedure)

(Use 90863 in conjunction with 90832, 90834, 90837)

(For pharmacologic management with psychotherapy services performed by a physician or other qualified health care professional who may report evaluation adn management codes, use the appropriate evaluation and management codes 99201-99255, 99281-99285, 99304-99337, 99341-99350 and the appropriate psychotherapy with evaluation and management service 90833, 90836, 90838)

(Do not count time spent on providing pharmacologic management services in the time used for selection of the psychotherapy service)

90865 Narcosynthesis for psychiatric diagnostic and therapeutic purposes (eg, sodium amobarbital (Amytal) interview)

90867 Therapeutic repetitive transcranial magnetic stimulation (TMS) treatment; initial, including cortical mapping, motor threshold determination, delivery and management

(Report only once per course of treatment)

(Do not report 90867 in conjunction with 90868, 90869, 95860-95870, 95928, 95929, 95939)

90868   subsequent delivery and management, per session

90869   subsequent motor threshold re-determination with delivery and management

(Do not report 90869 in conjunction with 90867, 90868, 95860-95870, 95928, 95929, 95939)

(If a significant, separately identifiableevaluation and management, medication management, or psychotherapy service is performed, the appropriate E/M or psychotherapy code may be reported in addition to 90867-90869. Evaluation and management activities directly related to cortical mapping, motor threshold determination, delivery and management of TMS are not separately reported)

(For transcranial magnetic stimulation motor function mapping for therapeutic planning other than for repetitive transcranial magnetic stimulation, use 0310T)

(Do not count time spent on providing pharmacologic management services in the time used for selection of the psychotherapy service)

90870 Electroconvulsive therapy (includes necessary monitoring)

90875 Individual psychophysiological therapy incorporating biofeedback training by any modality (face-to-face with the patient), with psychotherapy (eg, insight oriented, behavior modifying or supportive psychotherapy); 30 minutes

90876 45 minutes

90880 Hypnotherapy

90882 Environmental intervention for medical management purposes on a psychiatric patients behalf with agencies, employers, or institutions

90885 Psychiatric evaluation of hospital records, other psychiatric reports, psychometric and/or projective tests, and other accumulated data for medical diagnostic purposes

90887 Interpretation or explanation of results of psychiatric, other medical examinations and procedures, or other accumulated data to family or other responsible persons, or advising them how to assist patient

(Do not report 90887 in conjunction with 0368T, 0369T, 0370T, 0371T)

90889 Preparation of report of patient's psychiatric status, history, treatment, or progress (other than for legal or consultative purposes) for other individuals, agencies, or insurance carriers

90899 Unlisted psychiatric service or procedure

BIOFEEDBACK

Biofeedback is the process of detecting information about a patient's biological functions, eg. heart rate, breathing rate, skin temperature, and amount of muscle tension, picked up by surface electrodes (sensors) and electronically amplified to provide feedback, usually in the form of an audio-tone and/or visual read-out to the patient. Biofeedback training uses the information that has been monitored from the sensors attached to a muscle on the skin's surface, or to the skin only for thermal or other readings. With the help of a trained clinician, the patient can learn how to make voluntary changes in those biological functions and bring them under control.

Biofeedback services involve the use of electromyographic techniques to detect and record muscle activity. The CPT codes 95860-95872 (EMG) should not be reported with biofeedback services based on the use of electromyography during a biofeedback session. If an EMG is performed as a separate medically necessary service for diagnosis or follow-up of organic muscle dysfunction, the appropriate EMG codes (e.g. CPT codes 95860-95872) may be reported.

Modifier -59 should be added to indicate that the service performed was a separately identifiable diagnostic service. Reporting only an objective electromyographic response to biofeedback is not sufficient to bill the codes referable to diagnostic EMG.

(For psychophysiological therapy incorporating biofeedback training, see 90875, 90876)

90901 Biofeedback training by any modality

90911 Biofeedback training, perineal muscles, anorectal or urethral sphincter, including EMG and/or manometry

(For testing of rectal sensation, tone and compliance, use 91120)

(For incontinence treatment by pulsed magnetic neuromodulation, use 53899)

DIALYSIS

(For therapeutic apheresis for white blood cells, red blood cells, platelets and plasma pheresis, see 36511, 36512, 36513, 36514)

(For therapeutic apheresis extracorporeal adsorption procedures, use 36516)

(90918 deleted 2009 edition. To report ESRD-related services for patients younger than 2 years of age, see 90951-90953, 90963, 90967)

● New Code   ▲ Revised Code   ✛ Add-On Code   ⊘ Modifier -51 Exempt   ★ Telemedicine

(**90919**   deleted 2009 edition. To report ESRD-related services for patients between 2 and 11 years of age, see 90954-90956, 90964, 90968)

(**90920**   deleted 2009 edition. To report ESRD-related services for patients between 12 and 19 years of age, see 90957-90959, 90965, 90969)

(**90921**   deleted 2009 edition. To report ESRD-related services for patients 20 years of age and older, see 90960-90962, 90966, 90970)

(**90922**   deleted 2009 edition. To report ESRD-related services for patients younger than 2 years of age, see 90951-90953, 90963, 90967)

(**90923**   deleted 2009 edition. To report ESRD-related services for patients between 2 and 11 years of age, see 90954-90956, 90964, 90968)

(**90924**   deleted 2009 edition. To report ESRD-related services for patients between 12 and 19 years of age, see 90957-90959, 90965, 90969)

(**90925**   deleted 2009 edition. To report ESRD-related services for patients 20 years of age and older, see 90960-90962, 90966, 90970)

HEMODIALYSIS

Codes 90935, 90937 are reported to describe the hemodialysis procedure with all evaluation and management services related to the patient's renal disease on the day of the hemodialysis procedure. These codes are used for inpatient ESRD and non-ESRD procedures or for outpatient non-ESRD dialysis services. Code 90935 is reported if only one evaluation of the patient is required related to that hemodialysis procedure. Code 90937 is reported when patient re-evaluation(s) is required during a hemodialysis procedure. Use modifier 25 with E/M codes, including new or established patient office or other outpatient services (99201-99215), office or other outpatient consultations (99241-99245), observation care (99217-99220, 99224-99226), observation or inpatient care including admission and discharge (99234-99236), initial hospital care (99221-99226, 99231-99239), new or established patient emergency department services (99281-99285), critical care services (99291, 99292), inpatient neonatal intensive care services and pediatric and neonatal critical care services (99466-99480), nursing facility services (99304-99318), domiciliary, rest home services, or custodial care (99324-99337), and home services (99341-99350), for separately identifiable services unrelated to the dialysis procedure or renal failure which cannot be rendered during the dialysis session.

> (For home visit hemodialysis services performed by a non-physician health care professional, use 99512)
>
> (For cannula declotting, see 36831, 36833, 36860, 36861)
>
> (For declotting of implanted vascular access device or catheter by thrombolytic agent, use 36593)
>
> (For collection of blood specimen from a partially or completely implantable venous access device, use 36591)
>
> (For prolonged attendance by a physician or other qualified health care professional, see 99354-99360)

90935   Hemodialysis procedure with single evaluation by a physician or other qualified health care professional

90937   Hemodialysis procedure requiring repeated evaluation(s) with or without substantial revision of dialysis prescription

90940   Hemodialysis access flow study to determine blood flow in grafts and arteriovenous fistulae by an indicator method

> (For duplex scan of hemodialysis access, use 93990)

MISCELLANEOUS DIALYSIS PROCEDURES

Codes 90945, 90947 describe dialysis procedures other than hemodialysis (eg., peritoneal dialysis, hemofiltration or continuous renal replacement therapies), and all evaluation and management services related to the patient's renal disease on the day of the procedure. Code 90945 is reported if only one evaluation of the patient is required related to that procedure. Code 90947 is reported when patient re-evaluation(s) is required during a procedure. Use modifier 25 with E/M codes, including new or established patient office or other outpatient services (99201-99215), office or other outpatient consultations (99241-99245), observation care (99217-99220, 99224-99226), observation or inpatient care including admission and discharge (99234-99239), hospital care (99221-99226, 99231-99239), new or established patient emergency department services (99281-99285), critical care services (99291, 99292), inpatient neonatal intensive care services and pediatric and neonatal critical care services (99466-99480), nursing facility services (99304-99318), domiciliary, rest home or custodial care (99324-99337), and home services (99341-99350) for separately identifiable services unrelated to the procedure or the renal failure which cannot be rendered during the dialysis session.

> (For percutaneous insertion of intraperitoneal tunneled catheter, use 49418. For open insertion of tunneled intraperitoneal catheter, use 49421.)

> (For prolonged attendance by a physician or other qualified heatlh care professional, see 99354-99360)

90945　Dialysis procedure other than hemodialysis (eg, peritoneal dialysis, hemofiltration or other continuous renal replacement therapies), with single evaluation by a physician or other qualified health care professional

> (For home infusion of peritoneal dialysis, use 99559)

90947　Dialysis procedure other than hemodialysis (eg, peritoneal dialysis, hemofiltration, or other continuous renal replacement therapies) requiring repeated evaluation by a physician or other qualified health care professional, with or without substantial revision of dialysis prescription

END-STAGE RENAL DISEASE SERVICES

Codes 90951-90962 are reported **once** per month to distinguish age-specific services related to the patient's end-stage renal disease (ESRD) performed in an outpatient setting with three levels of service based on the number of face-to-face visits. ESRD-related services by a physician or other qualified health care professional include establishment of a dialyzing cycle, outpatient evaluation and management of the dialysis visits, telephone calls, and patient management during the dialysis provided during a full month. In circumstances in which the patient has had a complete assessment visit during the month and services are provided over a period of less than a month, 90951-90962 may be used according to the number of visits performed.

Codes 90963-90966 are reported once per month for a full month of service to distinguish age-specific services for end-stage renal disease (ESRD) services for home dialysis patients.

For ESRD and non-ESRD dialysis services performed in an inpatient setting, and for non-ESRD dialysis services performed in an outpatient setting, see 90935-90937 and 90945-90947.

Evaluation and Management services unrelated to ESRD services that cannot be performed during the dialysis session may be reported separately.

Codes 90967-90970 are reported to distinguish age-specific services for end-stage renal disease (ESRD) services for less than a full month of service, per day, for services provided under the following circumstances: transient patients, partial month where there was one or more face-to-face visits without the complete assessment, the patient was hospitalized before a complete assessment was furnished, dialysis was stopped due to recovery or death, or the patient received a kidney transplant. For reporting purposes, each month is considered 30 days.

> (Do not report 90951-90970 during the same month in conjunction with 99487-99489)

> (Do not report 90951-90970 during the service time of 99495-99496)

★ **90951**　End-stage renal disease (ESRD) related services monthly, for patients younger than 2 years of age to include monitoring for the adequacy of nutrition, assessment of growth and development, and counseling of parents; with 4 or more face-to-face visits by a physician or other qualified health care professional, per month

★ **90952**　with 2-3 face-to-face visits by a physician or other qualified health care professional, per month

90953　with 1 face-to-face visit by a physician or other qualified health care professional per month

★ **90954**　End-stage renal disease (ESRD) related services monthly, for patients 2-11 years of age to include monitoring for the adequacy of nutrition, assessment of growth and development, and counseling of parents; with 4 or more face-to-face visits by a physician or other qualified health care professional per month

---

★ **90955**   with 2-3 face-to-face visits by a physician or other qualified health care professional per month

90956   with 1 face-to-face visits by a physician or other qualified health care professional per month

★ **90957**   End-stage renal disease (ESRD) related services monthly, for patients 12-19 years of age to include monitoring for the adequacy of nutrition, assessment of growth and development, and counseling of parents; with 4 or more face-to-face visits by a physician or other qualified health care professional per month

★ **90958**   with 2-3 face-to-face visits by a physician or other qualified health care professional per month

90959   with 1 face-to-face visit by a physician or other qualified health care professional per month

★ **90960**   End-stage renal disease (ESRD) related services monthly, for patients 20 years of age and older; with 4 or more face-to-face visits by a physician or other qualified health care professional per month

★ **90961**   with 2-3 face-to-face visits by a physician or other qualified health care professional per month

90962   with 1 face-to-face visit by a physician or other qualified health care professional per month

90963   End-stage renal disease (ESRD) related services for home dialysis per full month, for patients younger than 2 years of age to include monitoring for the adequacy of nutrition, assessment of growth and development, and counseling of parents

90964   End-stage renal disease (ESRD) related services for home dialysis per full month, for patients 2-11 years of age to include monitoring for the adequacy of nutrition, assessment of growth and development, and counseling of parents

90965   End-stage renal disease (ESRD) related services for home dialysis per full month, for patients 12-19 years of age to include monitoring for the adequacy of nutrition, assessment of growth and development, and counseling of parents

90966   End-stage renal disease (ESRD) related services for home dialysis per full month, for patients 20 years of age and older

90967   End-stage renal disease (ESRD) related services for dialysis less than a full month of service, per day; for patients younger than 2 years of age

90968   for patients 2-11 years of age

90969   for patients 12-19 years of age

90970   for patients 20 years of age and older

OTHER DIALYSIS PROCEDURES

90989   Dialysis training, patient, including helper where applicable, any mode, completed course

90993   Dialysis training, patient, including helper where applicable, any mode, course not completed, per training session

90997   Hemoperfusion (eg, with activated charcoal or resin)

90999   Unlisted dialysis procedure, inpatient or outpatient

GASTROENTEROLOGY

91010   Esophageal motility (manometric study of the esophagus and/or gastroesophageal junction) study with interpretation and report;

+ 91013   with stimulation or perfusion (eg, stimulant, acid or alkali perfusion) (List separately in addition to code for primary procedure)

(Use 91013 in conjunction with 91010)

(Do not report 91013 more than once per session)

(To report esophageal motility studies with high resolution esophageal pressure topography, use 91299)

91020   Gastric motility (manometric) studies

91022   Duodenal motility (manometric) study

(If gastrointestinal endoscopy is performed, use 43235)

(If fluoroscopy is performed, use 76000)

(If gastric motility study is performed, use 91020)

(Do not report 91020, 91022 in conjunction with 91112)

91030   Esophagus, acid perfusion (Bernstein) test for esophagitis

91034   Esophagus, gastroesophageal reflux test; with nasal catheter pH electrode(s) placement, recording, analysis and interpretation

91035   with mucosal attached telemetry pH electrode placement, recording, analysis and interpretation

91037   Esophageal function test, gastroesophageal reflux test with nasal catheter intraluminal impedance electrode(s) placement, recording, analysis and interpretation;

91038   prolonged (greater than 1 hour, up to 24 hours)

91040   Esophageal balloon distension provocation study, diagnostic, with provocation when performed

(Do not report 91040 more than once per session)

91065   Breath hydrogen or methane test (eg, for detection of lactase deficiency, fructose intolerance, bacterial overgrowth, or oro-cecal gastrointestinal transit)

(Report 91065 once for each administered challenge)

(For H. pylori breath test analysis, use 83013 for non-radioactive (C-13) isotope or 78268 for radioactive (C-14) isotope)

(To report placement of an esophageal tamponade tube for management of variceal bleeding, use 43460. To report placement of a long intestinal Miller-Abbott tube, use 44500)

(For abdominal paracentesis, see 49082, 49083, 49084; with instillation of medication, see 96440, 96446)

(For peritoneoscopy, use 49320; with biopsy, use 49321)

(For splenoportography, see 38200, 75810)

91110   Gastrointestinal tract imaging, intraluminal (eg, capsule endoscopy), esophagus through ileum, with interpretation and report

(Do not report 91110 in conjunction with 91111, 0355T)

(Visualization of the colon is not reported separately)

(Append modifier -52 if the ileum is not visualized)

91111   Gastrointestinal tract imaging, intraluminal (eg, capsule endoscopy), esophagus with interpretation and report

(Do not report 91111 in conjunction with 91110, 0355T)

  ●   New Code   ▲   Revised Code   +   Add-On Code   ⊘   Modifier -51 Exempt   ★   Telemedicine

(For measurement of gastrointestinal tract transit times or pressure using wireless capsule, use 91112)

91112 Gastrointestinal transit and pressure measurement, stomach through colon, wireless capsule, with interpretation and report

(Do not report 91112 in conjunction with 83986, 91020, 91022, 91117)

91117 Colon motility (manometric) study, minimum 6 hours continuous recording (including provocation tests, eg, meal, intracolonic balloon distension, pharmacologic agents, if performed), with interpretation and report

(For wireless capsule pressure measurements, use 91112)

(Do not report 91117 in conjunction with 91120, 91122)

91120 Rectal sensation, tone, and compliance test (ie, response to graded balloon distention)

(For biofeedback training, use 90911)

(For anorectal manometry, use 91122)

91122 Anorectal manometry

(Do not report 91120, 91122 in conjunction with 91117)

GASTRIC PHYSIOLOGY

91132 Electrogastrography, diagnostic, transcutaneous;

91133   with provocative testing

OTHER PROCEDURES

91200 Liver elastography, mechanically induced shear wave (eg, vibration), without imaging, with interpretation and report

91299 Unlisted diagnostic gastroenterology procedure

OPHTHALMOLOGY

(For surgical procedures, see Surgery, Eye and Ocular Adnexa, 65091 et seq)

Ophthalmology is the study and treatment of diseases of the eye. Ophthalmological diagnostic and treatment services are reported using CPT Medicine codes 92002-92499.

Coding Rules

1. *Minimal, brief and limited office services, and hospital, home, extended care, emergency department and consultations are reported using appropriate evaluation and management service codes.*

2. *Surgical procedures on the eye(s) are reported using CPT codes from the Eye and Ocular Adnexa subsection of the SURGERY section of CPT.*

3. *To report intermediate ophthalmological services, the following must be performed and documented: a) evaluation of new or existing condition, b) complications of new diagnostic or management problems (not necessarily related to the primary diagnosis), c) history, d) general medical observation e) external ocular and adnexal examination, f) other diagnostic procedures as indicated, and g) may include the use of mydriasis. Intermediate ophthalmological services do not usually include determination of refractive state but may in an established patient under continuing active treatment.*

4. *To report comprehensive ophthalmological services the following must be performed and documented: a) reported as a single service but may be performed at more than one session, b) history, c) general medical observation, d) external and ophthalmoscopic examination, e) gross visual fields, f) basic sensorimotor examination, g. may include, as indicated; biomicroscopy, examination with cycloplegia or mydriasis and tonometry, h) always includes initiation of diagnostic and treatment programs.*

5.   *For both intermediate and comprehensive ophthalmological services, service components, such as slip lamp examination, keratomy, ophthalmoscopy, retinoscopy, tonometry and motor evaluation are not reported separately.*

For procedures requiring intravenous injection of dye or other diagnostic agent, insertion of an intravenous catheter and dye injection are necessary to accomplish the procedure and are included in the procedure. Accordingly, HCPCS/CPT codes 36000 (introduction of a needle or catheter), 36410 (venipuncture), G0345-G0350 (90760-90768 in 2006)(IV infusion), and G0353-G0354 (90774-90775 in 2006)(IV injection)as well as selective vascular catheterization codes are not to be separately reported with services requiring intravenous injection (e.g. CPT codes 92230, 92235, 92240, 92287, for angioscopy and angiography).

Fundus photography (CPT code 92250) and scanning ophthalmic computerized diagnostic imaging (CPT code 92135) are generally mutually exclusive of one another in that a provider would use one technique or the other to evaluate fundal disease. However, there are a limited number of clinical conditions where both techniques are medically reasonable and necessary on the ipsilateral eye. In these situations, both CPT codes may be reported appending modifier -59 to CPT code 92250.

GENERAL OPHTHALMOLOGICAL SERVICES

General ophthalmological services (e.g. CPT codes 92002-92014) describe components of the ophthalmologic examination. When evaluation and management codes are reported, these general ophthalmological service codes (e.g. CPT codes 92002-92014) are not to be reported; the same services would be represented by both series of codes.

NEW PATIENT

(For distinguishing between new and established patients, see E/M guidelines)

92002 Ophthalmological services: medical examination and evaluation with initiation of diagnostic and treatment program; intermediate, new patient

(Do not report 92002 in conjunction with 99173, 99174, 99177, 0469T)

92004   comprehensive, new patient, 1 or more visits

(Do not report 92004 in conjunction with 99173, 99174, 99177, 0469T)

ESTABLISHED PATIENT

(For distinguishing between new and established patients, see E/M guidelines)

92012 Ophthalmological services: medical examination and evaluation, with initiation or continuation of diagnostic and treatment program; intermediate, established patient

(Do not report 92012 in conjunction with 99173, 99174, 99177, 0469T)

92014   comprehensive, established patient, 1 or more visits

(Do not report 92014 in conjunction with 99173, 99174, 99177, 0469T)

(For surgical procedures, see Surgery, Eye and Ocular Adnexa, 65091 et seq)

SPECIAL OPHTHALMOLOGICAL SERVICES

Special ophthalmological services are defined as a level of service in which a special evaluation of part of the visual system is made which goes beyond the services usually included under general ophthalmological services, or in which special treatment is given. Fluorescein angioscopy, quantitative visual field examination, or extended color vision examination should be specifically reported as special ophthalmological services.

Special ophthalmologic services represent specific services not described as part of a general or routine ophthalmological examination. Special ophthalmological services are recognized as significant, separately identifiable services.

92015 Determination of refractive state

(Do not report 92015 in conjunction with 99173, 99174, 99177)

(For instrument-based ocular screening, use 99174, 99177)

92018 Ophthalmological examination and evaluation, under general anesthesia, with or without manipulation of globe for passive range of motion or other manipulation to facilitate diagnostic examination; complete

92019 limited

92020 Gonioscopy (separate procedure)

(For gonioscopy under general anesthesia, use 92018)

92025 Computerized corneal topography, unilateral or bilateral, with interpretation and report

(Do not report 92025 in conjunction with 65710-65771)

(92025 is not used for manual keratoscopy, which is part of a single system of E/M or ophthalmological service)

92060 Sensorimotor examination with multiple measurements of ocular deviation (eg, restrictive or paretic muscle with diplopia) with interpretation and report (separate procedure)

92065 Orthoptic and/or pleoptic training, with continuing medical direction and evaluation

92071 Fitting of contact lens for treatment of ocular surface disease

(Do not report 92071 in conjunction with 92072)

(Report supply of lens separately with 99070 or appropriate supply codes)

92072 Fitting of contact lens for management of keratoconus, initial fitting

(For subsequent fittings, report using E/M services or General Ophthalmological services)

(Do not report 92072 in conjunction with 92071)

(Report supply of lens separately with 99070 or appropriate supply code)

92081 Visual field examination, unilateral or bilateral, with interpretation and report; limited examination (eg, tangent screen, Autoplot, arc perimeter, or single stimulus level automated test, such as Octopus 3 or 7 equivalent)

92082 intermediate examination (eg, at least 2 isopters on Goldmann perimeter, or semiquantitative, automated suprathreshold screening program, Humphrey suprathreshold automatic diagnostic test, Octopus program 33)

92083 extended examination (eg, Goldmann visual fields with at least 3 isopters plotted and static determination within the central 30 degrees, or quantitative, automated threshold perimetry, Octopus programs G-1, 32 or 42, Humphrey visual field analyzer full threshold programs 30-2, 24-2, or 30/60-2)

(Gross visual field testing (eg, confrontation testing) is a part of general ophthalmological services and is not reported separately)

(For visual field assessment by patient activated data transmission to a remote surveillance center, see 0378T, 0379T)

92100 Serial tonometry (separate procedure) with multiple measurements of intraocular pressure over an extended time period with interpretation and report, same day (eg, diurnal curve or medical treatment of acute elevation of intraocular pressure)

(For monitoring of intraocular pressure for 24 hours or longer, use 0329T)

(Ocular blood flow measurements are reported with 0198T. Single-episode tonomemtry is a component of general ophthalmological service or E/M service)

92132 Scanning computerized ophthalmic diagnostic imaging, anterior segment, with interpretation and report, unilateral or bilateral

---

Separate Procedure   Unlisted Procedure   CCI Comp. Code   Non-specific Procedure   **831**

(For spectral microscopy and endothelial cell analysis, use 92286)

(For tear film imaging, use 0330T)

92133 Scanning computerized ophthalmic diagnostic imaging, posterior segment, with interpretation and report, unilateral or bilateral; optic nerve

92134 retina

(Do not report 92133 and 92134 at the same patient encounter)

(For scanning computerized ophthalmic diagnostic imaging of the optic nerve and retina, see 92133, 92134)

92136 Ophthalmic biometry by partial coherence interferometry with intraocular lens power calculation

(For tear film imaging, use 0330T)

(**92140** deleted 2016 [2017 edition]).

92145 Corneal hysteresis determination, by air impulse stimulation, unilateral or bilateral, with interpretation and report

OPHTHALMOSCOPY

Routine ophthalmoscopy is part of general and special ophthalmologic services whenever indicated. It is a non-itemized service and is not reported separately.

92225 Ophthalmoscopy, extended, with retinal drawing (eg, for retinal detachment, melanoma), with interpretation and report; initial

92226 subsequent

★ **92227** Remote imaging for detection of retinal disease (eg, retinopathy in a patient with diabetes) with analysis and report under physician supervision, unilateral or bilateral

(Do not report 92227 in conjunction with 92002-92014, 92133, 92134, 92250, 92228 or with the evaluation and management of the single organ system, the eye, 99201-99350)

★ **92228** Remote imaging for monitoring and management of active retinal disease (eg, diabetic retinopathy) with physician review, interpretation and report, unilateral or bilateral

(Do not report 92228 in conjunction with 92002-92014, 92133, 92134, 92250, 92227 or with the evaluation and management of the single organ system, the eye, 99201-99350)

92230 Fluorescein angioscopy with interpretation and report

92235 Fluorescein angiography (includes multiframe imaging) with interpretation and report, unilateral or bilateral

(When fluorescein and indocyanine-green angiography are performed at the same patient encounter, use 92242)

92240 Indocyanine-green angiography (includes multiframe imaging) with interpretation and report, unilateral or bilateral

(When indocyanine-green and fluorescein angiography are performed at the same patient encounter, use 92242)

92242 Fluorescein angiography and indocyanine-green angiography (includes multiframe imaging) performed at the same patient encounter with interpretation and report, unilateral or bilateral

(To report fluorescein angiography and indocyaninegreen angiography not performed at the same patient encounter, see 92235, 92240)

● New Code ▲ Revised Code + Add-On Code ⊘ Modifier -51 Exempt ★ Telemedicine

| 92250 | Fundus photography with interpretation and report |

| 92260 | Ophthalmodynamometry |

(For opthalmoscopy under general anesthesia, use 92018)

OTHER SPECIALIZED SERVICES

For prescription, fitting, and/or medical supervision of ocular prosthetic (artificial eye) adaptation by a physician, see E/M services including Office or Other Outpatient services (99201-99215), Office or Other Outpatient Consultations (99241-99245) or General Ophthalmological service codes (92002-92014)

| 92265 | Needle oculoelectromyography, 1 or more extraocular muscles, one or both eyes, with interpretation and report |

| 92270 | Electro-oculography with interpretation and report |

(For vestibular function tests with recording, see 92537, 92538, 92540, 92541, 92542, 92544, 92545, 92546, 92547, 92548)

(Do not report 92270 in conjunction with 92537, 92538, 92540, 92541, 92542, 92544, 92545, 92546, 92547, 92548)

(To report saccadic eye movement testing with recording, use 92700)

| 92275 | Electroretinography with interpretation and report |

(For electronystagmography for vestibular function studies, see 92541 et seq)

(For ophthalmic echography (diagnostic ultrasound), see 76511-76529)

| 92283 | Color vision examination, extended, eg, anomaloscope or equivalent |

(Color vision testing with pseudoisochromatic plates (such as HRR or Ishihara) is not reported separately. It is included in the appropriate general or ophthalmological service, or 99172)

| 92284 | Dark adaptation examination with interpretation and report |

| 92285 | External ocular photography with interpretation and report for documentation of medical progress (eg, close-up photography, slit lamp photography, goniophotography, stereo-photography) |

(For tear film imaging, use 0330T)

| 92286 | Anterior segment imaging with interpretation and report; with specular microscopy and endothelial cell analysis |

| 92287 | with fluorescein angiography |

CONTACT LENS SERVICES

Follow-up of successfully fitted extended wear lenses is reported as part of a general ophthalmological service (92012 et seq).

The supply of contact lenses may be reported as part of the service of fitting. It may also be reported separately by using the appropriate supply codes.

(For therapeutic or surgical use of contact lens, see 68340, 92071, 92072)

| 92310 | Prescription of optical and physical characteristics of and fitting of contact lens, with medical supervision of adaptation; corneal lens, both eyes, except for aphakia |

(For prescription and fitting of one eye, add modifier -52)

| 92311 | corneal lens for aphakia, 1 eye |

92312   corneal lens for aphakia, both eyes

92313   corneoscleral lens

92314   Prescription of optical and physical characteristics of contact lens, with medical supervision of adaptation and direction of fitting by independent technician; corneal lens, both eyes except for aphakia

(For prescription and fitting of one eye, add modifier -52)

92315   corneal lens for aphakia, 1 eye

92316   corneal lens for aphakia, both eyes

92317   corneoscleral lens

92325   Modification of contact lens (separate procedure), with medical supervision of adaptation

92326   Replacement of contact lens

(For prescription, fitting, and/or medical supervision of ocular prosthetic adaptation by a physician, see Evaluation and Management services or General Ophthalmological service codes 92002-92014)

SPECTACLE SERVICES (INCLUDING PROSTHESIS FOR APHAKIA)

Prescription of lenses, when required, is included in 92015, Determination of refractive state. It includes specification of lens type (monofocal, bifocal, other), lens power, axis, prism, absorptive factor, impact resistance, and other factors.

When provided, fitting of spectacles is a separate service and is reported as indicated by 92340-92371.

Fitting includes measurement of anatomical facial characteristics, the writing of laboratory specifications, and the final adjustment of the spectacles to the visual axes and anatomical topography. Presence of the physician or other qualified health care professional is not required.

Supply of materials is a separate service component; it is not part of the service of fitting spectacles.

92340   Fitting of spectacles, except for aphakia; monofocal

92341   bifocal

92342   multifocal, other than bifocal

92352   Fitting of spectacle prosthesis for aphakia; monofocal

92353   multifocal

92354   Fitting of spectacle mounted low vision aid; single element system

92355   telescopic or other compound lens system

92358   Prosthesis service for aphakia, temporary (disposable or loan, including materials)

92370   Repair and refitting spectacles; except for aphakia

92371   spectacle prosthesis for aphakia

OTHER PROCEDURES

92499   Unlisted ophthalmological service or procedure

   ● New Code   ▲ Revised Code   + Add-On Code   ⊘ Modifier -51 Exempt   ★ Telemedicine

SPECIAL OTORHINOLARYNGOLOGIC SERVICES

Otorhinolaryngology is the study and treatment of diseases of the head and neck, including the ears, nose and throat.

Diagnostic or treatment procedures that are reported as evaluation and management services (eg, otoscopy, anterior rhinoscopy, tuning fork test, removal of non-impacted cerumen) are not reported separately.

Special otorhinolaryngologic services are those diagnostic and treatment services not included in an evaluation and management service, including office or other outpatient services (99201-99215), or office or other outpatient consultations (99241-99245).

Codes 92507, 92508, 92520, 92521, 92522, 92523, 92524, and 92526 are used to report evaluation and treatment of speech sound production, receptive language, and expressive language abilities, voice and resonance production, speech fluency, and swallowing. Evaluations may include examination of speech sound production, articulatory movements of oral musculature, oral-pharyngeal swallowing function, qualitative analysis of voice and resonance, and measures of frequency, type, and duration of stuttering. Evaluations may also include the patient's ability to understand the meaning and intent of written and verbal expressions, as well as the appropriate formulation and utterance of expressive thought. In contrast, 92626 and 92627 are reported for an evaluation of auditory rehabilitation status determining the patient's ability to use residual hearing in order to identify the acoustic characteristics of sounds associated with speech communication.

(For laryngoscopy with stroboscopy, use 31579)

92502 Otolaryngologic examination under general anesthesia

92504 Binocular microscopy (separate diagnostic procedure)

92507 Treatment of speech, language, voice, communication, and/or auditory processing disorder; individual

(Do not report 92507 in conjunction with 0364T, 0365T, 0368T, 0369T)

92508 group, two or more individuals

(Do not report 92508 in conjunction with 0366T, 0367T, 0372T)

(For auditory rehabilitation, prelingual hearing loss, use 92630)

(For auditory rehabilitation, postlingual hearing loss, use 92633)

(For cochlear implant programming, see 92601-92604)

92511 Nasopharyngoscopy with endoscope (separate procedure)

(Do not report 92511 in conjunction with 31575, 43197, 43198)

92512 Nasal function studies (eg, rhinomanometry)

92516 Facial nerve function studies (eg, electroneuronography)

92520 Laryngeal function studies (ie, aerodynamic testing and acoustic testing)

(For performance of a single test, use modifier 52)

(To report flexible fiberoptic laryngeal evaluation of swallowing and laryngeal sensory testing, see 92611-92617)

(To report other testing of laryngeal function (eg, electroglottography), use 92700)

92521 Evaluation of speech fluency (eg, stuttering, cluttering)

92522 Evaluation of speech sound production (eg, articulation, phonological process, apraxia, dysarthria);

92523 with evaluation of language comprehension and expression (eg, receptive and expressive language)

92524 Behavioral and qualitative analysis of voice and resonance

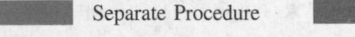

Separate Procedure   Unlisted Procedure   CCI Comp. Code   Non-specific Procedure   **835**

92526 Treatment of swallowing dysfunction and/or oral function for feeding

VESTIBULAR FUNCTION TESTS, WITHOUT ELECTRICAL RECORDING

92531 Spontaneous nystagmus, including gaze

92532 Positional nystagmus test

(Do not report 92531, 92532 with evaluation and management services including office or other outpatient services [99201-99215], observation care [99218-99220, 99224-99226], observation of inpatient care including admission and discharge [99234-99236], hospital care [99221-99223, 99231-99233], office or other outpatient consultations [99241-99245], nursing facility services [99304-99318], and domiciliary, rest home or custodial care services [99324-99337])

92533 Caloric vestibular test, each irrigation (binaural, bithermal stimulation constitutes 4 tests)

92534 Optokinetic nystagmus test

VESTIBULAR FUNCTION TESTS, WITH RECORDING (eg, ENG)

92537 Caloric vestibular test with recording, bilateral; bithermal (ie, one warm and one cool irrigation in each ear for a total of four irrigations)

(Do not report 92537 in conjunction with 92270, 92538)

(For three irrigations, use modifier 52)

(For monothermal caloric vestibular testing, use 92538)

92538   monothermal (ie, one irrigation in each ear for a total of two irrigations)

(Do not report 92538 in conjunction with 92270, 92537)

(For one irrigation, use modifier 52)

(For bilateral, bithermal caloric vestibular testing, use 92537)

92540 Basic vestibular evaluation, includes spontaneous nystagmus test with eccentric gaze fixation nystagmus, with recording, positional nystagmus test, minimum of 4 positions, with recording, optokinetic nystagmus test, bidirectional foveal and peripheral stimulation, with recording, and oscillating tracking test, with recording

(Do not report 92540 in conjunction with 92270, 92541, 92542, 92544, 92545)

92541 Spontaneous nystagmus test, including gaze and fixation nystagmus, with recording

(Do not report 92541 in conjunction with 92270, 92540 or the set of 92542, 92544, and 92545)

92542 Positional nystagmus test, minimum of 4 positions, with recording

(Do not report 92542 in conjunction with 92270, 92540 or the set of 92541, 92544, and 92545)

(**92543** deleted 2015 [2016 edition]. To report caloric vestibular testing, see 92537, 92538)

92544 Optokinetic nystagmus test, bidirectional, foveal or peripheral stimulation, with recording

(Do not report 92544 in conjunction with 92270, 92540 or the set of 92541, 92542, and 92545)

92545 Oscillating tracking test, with recording

(Do not report 92545 in conjunction with 92270, 92540 or the set of 92541, 92542, and 92544)

92546 Sinusoidal vertical axis rotational testing

(Do not report 92546 in conjunction with 92270)

+ 92547 Use of vertical electrodes (List separately in addition to code for primary procedure)

(Use 92547 in conjunction with codes 92540-92546)

(For unlisted vestibular tests, use 92700)

(Do not report 92547 in conjunction with 92270)

92548 Computerized dynamic posturography

(Do not report 92548 in conjunction with 92270)

AUDIOLOGIC FUNCTION TESTS

The audiometric tests listed below require the use of calibrated electronic equipment, recording of results and a report with interpretation. Hearing tests (such as whispered voice, tuning fork) that are otorhinolaryngologic E/M services are not reported separately. All services include testing of both ears. Use modifier 52 if a test is applied to one ear instead of two ears. All codes (except 92559) apply to testing of individuals. For testing of groups, use 92559 and specify test(s) used.

(For evaluation of speech, language and/or hearing problems through observation and assessment of performance, see 92521, 92522, 92523, 92524)

92550 Tympanometry and reflex threshold measurements

(Do not report 92550 in conjunction with 92567, 92568)

92551 Screening test, pure tone, air only

92552 Pure tone audiometry (threshold); air only

92553 air and bone

92555 Speech audiometry threshold;

92556 with speech recognition

92557 Comprehensive audiometry threshold evaluation and speech recognition (92553 and 92556 combined)

(For hearing aid evaluation and selection, see 92590-92595)

(For automated audiometry, see 0208T-0212T)

92558 Code out of order. See page 838.

92559 Audiometric testing of groups

92560 Bekesy audiometry; screening

92561 diagnostic

92562 Loudness balance test, alternate binaural or monaural

92563 Tone decay test

92564 Short increment sensitivity index (SISI)

92565 Stenger test, pure tone

92567 Tympanometry (impedance testing)

92568 Acoustic reflex testing; threshold

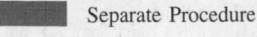

| 92570 | Acoustic immittance testing, includes tympanometry (impedance testing), acoustic reflex threshold testing, and acoustic reflex decay testing |

(Do not report 92570 in conjunction with 92567, 92568)

| 92571 | Filtered speech test |

| 92572 | Staggered spondaic word test |

| 92575 | Sensorineural acuity level test |

| 92576 | Synthetic sentence identification test |

| 92577 | Stenger test, speech |

| 92579 | Visual reinforcement audiometry (VRA) |

| 92582 | Conditioning play audiometry |

| 92583 | Select picture audiometry |

| 92584 | Electrocochleography |

| 92585 | Auditory evoked potentials for evoked response audiometry and/or testing of the central nervous system; comprehensive |

| 92586 | limited |

| 92558 | Evoked otoacoustic emissions, screening (qualitative measurement of distortion product or transient evoked otoacoustic emissions), automated analysis |

| 92587 | Distortion product evoked otoacoustic emissions; limited evaluation (to confirm the presence or absence of hearing disorder, 3-6 frequencies) or transient evoked otoacoustic emissions, with interpretation and report |

| 92588 | comprehensive diagnostic evaluation (quantitative analysis of outer hair cell function by cochlear mapping, minimum of 12 frequencies), with interpretation and report |

(For central auditory function evaluation, see 92620, 92621)

| 92590 | Hearing aid examination and selection; monaural |

| 92591 | binaural |

| 92592 | Hearing aid check; monaural |

| 92593 | binaural |

| 92594 | Electroacoustic evaluation for hearing aid; monaural |

| 92595 | binaural |

| 92596 | Ear protector attenuation measurements |

| 92597 | This code is out of order. See page 839. |

EVALUATIVE AND THERAPEUTIC SERVICES

Codes 92601 and 92603 describe post-operative analysis and fitting of previously placed external devices, connection to the cochlear implant, and programming of the stimulator. Codes 92602 and 92604 describe subsequent sessions for measurements and adjustments of the external transmitter and re-programming of the internal stimulator.

● New Code ▲ Revised Code + Add-On Code ⊘ Modifier -51 Exempt ★ Telemedicine

(For placement of cochlear implant, use 69930)

92601 Diagnostic analysis of cochlear implant, patient under 7 years of age; with programming

92602   subsequent reprogramming

(Do not report 92602 in addition to 92601)

(For aural rehabilitation services following cochlear implant, including evaluation of rehabilitation status, see 92626-92627, 92630-92633)

92603 Diagnostic analysis of cochlear implant, age 7 years or older; with programming

92604   subsequent reprogramming

(Do not report 92604 in addition to 92603)

92597 Evaluation for use and/or fitting of voice prosthetic device to supplement oral speech

(To report augmentative and alternative communication device services, see 92605, 92607, 92608, 92618)

92605 Evaluation for prescription of non-speech-generating augmentative and alternative communication device, face-to-face with the patient; first hour

(To report evaluation for use and/or fitting of voice prosthetic device, use 92597)

+ **92618**   each additional 30 minutes (List separately in addition to code for primary procedure)

(Use 92618 in conjunction with 92605)

92606 Therapeutic service(s) for the use of non-speech-generating device, including programming and modification

92607 Evaluation for prescription for speech-generating augmentative and alternative communication device, face-to-face with the patient; first hour

(To report evaluation for use and/or fitting of voice prosthetic device, use 92597)

(For evaluation for prescription of a non-speech-generating device, use 92605)

+ **92608**   each additional 30 minutes (List separately in addition to code for primary procedure)

(Use 92608 in conjunction with 92607)

92609 Therapeutic services for the use of speech-generating device, including programming and modification

(For therapeutic service(s) for the use of a non-speech-generating device, use 92606)

92610 Evaluation of oral and pharyngeal swallowing function

(For motion fluoroscopic evaluation of swallowing function, use 92611)

(For flexible endoscopic examination, use 92612-92617)

92611 Motion fluoroscopic evaluation of swallowing function by cine or video recording

(For radiological supervision and interpretation, use 74230)

(For evaluation of oral and pharyngeal swallowing function, use 92610)

(For flexible diagnostic laryngoscopy, use 31575.)

92612 Flexible endoscopic evaluation of swallowing by cine or video recording;

(If flexible or endoscopic evaluation of swallowing is performed without cine or video recording, use 92700)

(Do not report 92612 in conjunction with 31575)

92613   interpretation and report only

(To report an evaluation of oral and pharyngeal swallowing function, use 92610)

(To report motion fluoroscopic evaluation of swallowing function, use 92611)

92614   Flexible endoscopic evaluation, laryngeal sensory testing by cine or video recording;

(If flexible endoscopic evaluation of swallowing is performed without cine or video recording, use 92700)

(Do not report 92614 in conjunction with 31575)

92615   interpretation and report only

92616   Flexible endoscopic evaluation of swallowing and laryngeal sensory testing by cine or video recording;

(If flexible endoscopic evaluation of swallowing is performed without cine or video recording, use 92700)

(Do not report 92616 in conjunction with 31575)

92617   interpretation and report only

92618   Code out of order. See page 839.

92620   Evaluation of central auditory function, with report; initial 60 minutes

+ 92621   each additional 15 minutes (List separately in addition to code for primary procedure)

(Use 92621 in conjunction with 92620)

(Do not report 92620, 92621 in conjunction with 92521, 92522, 92523, 92524)

92625   Assessment of tinnitus (includes pitch, loudness matching, and masking)

(Do not report 92625 in conjunction with 92562)

(For unilateral assessment, use modifier 52)

92626   Evaluation of auditory rehabilitation status; first hour

+ 92627   each additional 15 minutes (List separately in addition to code for primary procedure)

(Use 92627 in conjunction with 92626)

(When reporting 92626, 92627, use the face-to-face time with the patient or family)

92630   Auditory rehabilitation; pre-lingual hearing loss

92633   post-lingual hearing loss

SPECIAL DIAGNOSTIC PROCEDURES

92640   Diagnostic analysis with programming of auditory brainstem implant, per hour

(Report nonprogramming services separately [eg., cardiac monitoring])

OTHER PROCEDURES

92700   Unlisted otorhinolaryngological service or procedure

   ●   New Code   ▲   Revised Code   +   Add-On Code   ⊘   Modifier -51 Exempt   ★   Telemedicine

CARDIOVASCULAR

Cardiovascular services refers to the study and treatment of diseases of the heart and vascular (arteries and veins) system. Cardiovascular services CPT codes are used to report therapeutic services such as cardiopulmonary resuscitation (CPR), cardioversion and percutaneous transluminal coronary angioplasty (PTCA) and diagnostic procedures such as electrocardiography, echocardiography and cardiac catheterization.

Cardiovascular medicine services include non-invasive and invasive diagnostic testing (including intracardiac testing) as well as therapeutic services (e.g. electrophysiological procedures).

When cardiopulmonary resuscitation is performed without other evaluation and management services (e.g. a physician responds to a "code blue" and directs cardiopulmonary resuscitation with the patient's attending physician then resuming the care of the patient after the patient has been revived), only the CPT code 92950 for CPR should be reported. Levels of critical care services and prolonged management services are determined by time; when CPT code 92950 is reported, the time required to perform CPR is not included in critical care or other timed evaluation and management services.

In keeping with the policies outlined previously, procedures routinely performed as part of a comprehensive service are included in the comprehensive service and not separately reported. A number of therapeutic and diagnostic cardiovascular procedures (e.g. CPT codes 92950-92998, 93501-93545, 93600-93624, 93640- 93652) routinely utilize intravenous or intra-arterial vascular access, routinely require electrocardiographic monitoring, and frequently require agents administered by injection or infusion techniques; accordingly, separate codes for routine access, monitoring, injection or infusion services are not to be reported.

Fluoroscopic guidance procedures are integral to invasive intravascular procedures and are included in those services. In unique circumstances, where these services are performed, not as an integral part of the procedure, the appropriate code can be separately reported with modifier -59. When supervision and interpretation codes are identified in the CPT code book for a given procedure, these can be separately reported.

Cardiac output measurement (e.g. CPT codes 93561-93562) is routinely performed during cardiac catheterization procedures per CPT definition and, therefore, CPT codes 93561-93562 are not to be reported with cardiac catheterization codes.

THERAPEUTIC SERVICES AND PROCEDURES

92920 This code is out of order. See page 844.

92921 This code is out of order. See page 844.

92924 This code is out of order. See page 844.

92925 This code is out of order. See page 844.

92928 This code is out of order. See page 844.

92929 This code is out of order. See page 844.

92933 This code is out of order. See page 844.

92934 This code is out of order. See page 844.

92937 This code is out of order. See page 845.

92938 This code is out of order. See page 845.

92941 This code is out of order. See page 845.

92943 This code is out of order. See page 845.

92944 This code is out of order. See page 845.

OTHER THERAPEUTIC SERVICES AND PROCEDURES

(For nonsurgical septal reduction therapy [eg, alcohol ablation], use 93799)

92950 Cardiopulmonary resuscitation (eg, in cardiac arrest)

(See also critical care services, 99291, 99292)

92953 Temporary transcutaneous pacing

(For direction of ambulance or rescue personnel outside the hospital by a physician or other qualified health care professional, use 99288)

92960 Cardioversion, elective, electrical conversion of arrhythmia; external

92961   internal (separate procedure)

(Do not report 92961 in conjunction with 93282-93284, 93287, 93289, 93295, 93296, 93618-93624, 93631, 93640-93642, 93650, 93653-93657, 93662)

92970 Cardioassist-method of circulatory assist; internal

92971   external

(For balloon atrial-septostomy, use 92992)

(For placement of catheters for use in circulatory assist devices such as intra-aortic balloon pump, use 33970)

92973 This code is out of order. See page 845.

92974 This code is out of order. See page 845.

92975 This code is out of order. See page 845.

92977 This code is out of order. See page 845.

92978 This code is out of order. See page 845.

92979 This code is out of order. See page 845.

92986 Percutaneous balloon valvuloplasty; aortic valve

92987   mitral valve

92990   pulmonary valve

92992 Atrial septectomy or septostomy; transvenous method, balloon (eg, Rashkind type) (includes cardiac catheterization)

92993   blade method (Park septostomy) (includes cardiac catheterization)

92997 Percutaneous transluminal pulmonary artery balloon angioplasty; single vessel

+ 92998   each additional vessel (List separately in addition to code for primary procedure)

(Use 92998 in conjunction with code 92997)

CORONARY THERAPEUTIC SERVICES AND PROCEDURES

Codes 92920-92944 describe percutaneous revascularization services performed for occlusive disease of the coronary vessels (major coronary arteries, coronary artery branches, or coronary artery bypass grafts). These percutaneous coronary intervention (PCI) codes are built on progressive hierarchies with more intensive services inclusive of lesser intensive services. These PCI codes all include the work of accessing and selectively catheterizing the vessel, traversing the lesion, radiological supervision and interpretation directly related to the intervention(s) performed, closure of the arteriotomy when performed through the access sheath, and imaging performed to document completion of the intervention in addition to the intervention(s) performed. These

● New Code   ▲ Revised Code   + Add-On Code   ⊘ Modifier -51 Exempt   ★ Telemedicine

codes include angioplasty (eg, balloon, cutting balloon, wired balloons, cryoplasty), atherectomy (eg, directional, rotational, laser), and stenting (eg, balloon expandable, self-expanding, bare metal, drug eluting, covered). Each code in this family includes balloon angioplasty, when performed. Diagnostic coronary angiography may be reported separately under specific circumstances.

Diagnostic coronary angiography codes (93454-93461) and injection procedure codes (93563-93564) should not be used with percutaneous coronary revascularization services (92920-92944) to report:

1. Contrast injections, angiography, roadmapping, and/or fluoroscopic guidance for the coronary intervention,

2. Vessel measurement for the coronary intervention, or

3. Post-coronary angioplasty/stent/atherectomy angiography, as this work is captured in the percutaneous coronary revascularization services codes (92920-92944).

Diagnostic angiography performed at the time of a coronary interventional procedure may be separately reportable if:

1. No prior catheter-based coronary angiography study is available, and a full diagnostic study is performed, and a decision to intervene is based on the diagnostic angiography, OR

2. A prior study is available, but as documented in the medical record:

    a. The patient's condition with respect to the clinical indication has changed since the prior study, OR

    b. There is inadequate visualization of the anatomy and/or pathology, OR

    c. There is a clinical change during the procedure that requires a new evaluation outside the target area of intervention.

Diagnostic coronary angiography performed at a separate session from an interventional procedure is separately reportable.

Major coronary arteries: The major coronary arteries are the left main, left anterior descending, left circumflex, right, and ramus intermediate arteries. All PCI procedures performed in all segments (proximal, mid, distal) of a single major coronary artery through the native coronary circulation are reported with one code. When one segment of a major coronary artery is treated through the native circulation and treatment of another segment of the same artery requires access through a coronary artery bypass graft, the intervention through the bypass graft is reported separately.

Coronary artery branches: Up to two coronary artery branches of the left anterior descending (diagonals), left circumflex (marginals), and right (posterior descending, posterolaterals) coronary arteries are recognized. The left main and ramus intermedius coronary arteries do not have recognized branches for reporting purposes. All PCI(s) performed in any segment (proximal, mid, distal) of a coronary of artery branch is reported with one code. PCI is reported for up to two branches of a major coronary artery. Additional PCI in a third branch of the same major coronary artery is not separately reportable.

Coronary artery bypass grafts: Each coronary artery bypass graft represents a coronary vessel. A sequential bypass graft with more than one distal anastomosis represents only one graft. A branching bypass graft (eg, Y graft) represents a coronary vessel for the main graft, and each branch off the main graft constitutes an additional coronary vessel. PCI performed on major coronary arteries or coronary artery branches by access through a bypass graft is reported using the bypass graft PCI codes. All bypass graft PCI codes include the use of coronary artery embolic protection devices when performed.

Only one base code from this family may be reported for revascularization of a major coronary artery and its recognized branches. Only one base code should be reported for revascularization of a coronary artery bypass graft, its subtended coronary artery, and recognized branches of the subtended coronary artery. If one segment of a major coronary artery and its recognized branches is treated through the native circulation, and treatment of another segment of the same vessel requires access through a coronary artery bypass graft, an additional base code is reported to describe the intervention performed through the bypass graft. The PCI base codes are 92920, 92924, 92928, 92933, 92937, 92941, and 92943. The PCI base code that includes the most intensive service provided for the target vessel should be reported. The hierarchy of these services is built on an intensity of service ranked from highest to lowest as 92943 = 92941 = 92933 > 92924 > 92937 = 92928 > 92920.

PCI performed during the same session in additional recognized branches of the target vessel should be reported using the applicable add-on code(s). The add-on codes are 92921, 92925, 92929, 92934, 92938, and 92944 and follow the same principle in regard to reporting the most intensive service provided. The intensity of service is ranked from highest to lowest as 92944 = 92938 > 92934 > 92925 > 92929 > 92921.

PCI performed during the same session in additional major coronary or in additional coronary artery bypass grafts should be reported using the applicable additional base code(s). PCI performed during the same session in additional coronary artery branches should be reported using the applicable additional add-on code(s).

If a single lesion extends from one target vessel (major coronary artery, coronary artery bypass graft, or coronary artery branch) into another target vessel, but can be revascularized with a single intervention bridging the two vessels, this PCI should be reported with a single code despite treating more than one vessel. For example, if a left main coronary lesion extends into the proximal left circumflex coronary artery and a single stent is placed to treat the entire lesion, this PCI should be reported as a single vessel stent (92928). In this example, a code for additional vessel treatment (92929) would not be additionally reported.

When bifurcation lesions are treated, PCI is reported for both vessels treated. For example, when a bifurcation lesion involving the left anterior descending artery and the first diagonal artery is treated by stenting both vessels, 92928 and 92929 are both reported.

Target vessel PCI for acute myocardial infarction is inclusive of all balloon angioplasty, atherectomy, stenting, manual aspiration thrombectomy, distal protection, and intracoronary rheolytic agent administration performed. Mechanical thrombectomy is reported separately.

Chronic total occlusion of a coronary vessel is present when there is no antegrade flow through the true lumen, accompanied by suggestive angiographic and clinical criteria (eg, antegrade "bridging" collaterals present, calcification at the occlusion site, no current presentation with ST elevation or Q wave acute myocardial infarction attributable to the occluded target lesion). Current presentation with ST elevation or Q wave acute myocardial infarction attributable to the occluded target lesion, subtotal occlusion, and occlusion with dye staining at the site consistent with fresh thrombus are not considered chronic total occlusion.

Codes 92973 (percutaneous transluminal coronary thrombectomy, mechanical), 92974 (coronary brachytherapy), 92978 and 92979 (intravascular ultrasound/optical coherence tomography), and 93571 and 93572 (intravascular Doppler velocity and/or pressure [fractional flow reserve (FFR) or coronary flow reserve (CFR)]) are add-on codes for reporting procedures performed in addition to coronary and bypass graft diagnostic and interventional services, unless included in the base code. Non-mechanical, aspiration thrombectomy is not reported with 92973, and is included in the PCI code for acute myocardial infarction (92941), when performed

> (To report transcatheter placement of radiation delivery device for coronary intravascular brachytherapy, use 92974)
>
> (For intravascular radioelement application, see 77770, 77771, 77772)
>
> (For nonsurgical septal reduction therapy [eg, alcohol ablation], use 93799)

92920   Percutaneous transluminal coronary angioplasty; single major coronary artery or branch

+ **92921**   each additional branch of a major coronary artery (List separately in addition to code for primary procedure)

> (Use 92921 in conjunction with 92920, 92924, 92928, 92933, 92937, 92941, 92943)

92924   Percutaneous transluminal coronary atherectomy, with coronary angioplasty when performed; single major coronary artery or branch

+ **92925**   each additional branch of a major coronary artery (List separately in addition to code for primary procedure)

> (Use 92925 in conjunction with 92924, 92928, 92933, 92937, 92941, 92943)

92928   Percutaneous transcatheter placement of intracoronary stent(s), with coronary angioplasty when performed; single majore coronary artery or branch

+ **92929**   each additional branch of a major coronary artery (List separately in addition to code for primary procedure)

> (Use 92929 in conjunction with 92928, 92933, 92937, 92941, 92943)

92933   Percutaneous transluminal coronary atherectomy, with intracoronary stent, with coronary angioplasty when performed; single major coronary artery or branch

+ **92934**   each additional branch of a major coronary artery (List separately in addition to code for primary procedure)

> (Use 92934 in conjunction with 92933, 92937, 92941, 92943)

● New Code   ▲ Revised Code   + Add-On Code   ⊘ Modifier -51 Exempt   ★ Telemedicine

92937 Percutaneous transluminal revascularization of or through coronary artery bypass graft (internal mammary, free arterial, venous), any combination of intracoronary stent, atherectomy and angioplasty, including distal protection when performed; single vessel

+ 92938 each additional branch subtended by the bypass graft (List separately in addition to code for primary procedure)

(Use 92938 in conjunction with 92937)

92941 Percutaneous transluminal revascularization of acute total/subtotal occlusion during acute myocardial infarction, coronary artery or coronary artery bypass graft, any combination of intracoronary stent, atherectomy and angioplasty, including aspiration thrombectomy when performed; single vessel

(For additional vessels treated, see 92920-92938, 92943, 92944)

92943 Percutaneous transluminal revascularization of chronic total occlusion, coronary artery, coronary artery branch, or coronary artery bypass graft, any combination of intracoronary stent, atherectomy and angioplasty; single vessel

+ 92944 each additional coronary artery, coronary artery branch, or bypass graft (List separately in addition to code for primary procedure)

(Use 92944 in conjunction with 92924, 92928, 92933, 92937, 92941, 92943)

(To report transcatheter placement of radiation delivery device for coronary intravascular brachytherapy, use 92974)

(For intravascular radioelement application, see 77770, 77771, 77772)

+ 92973 Percutaneous transluminal coronary thrombectomy, mechanical (List separately in addition to code for primary procedure)

(Use 92973 in conjunction with codes 92920, 92924, 92928, 92933, 92937, 92941, 92943, 92975, 93454-93461, 93563, 93564)

(Do not report 92973 for aspiration thrombectomy)

+ 92974 Transcatheter placement of radiation delivery device for subsequent coronary intravascular brachytherapy (List separately in addition to code for primary procedure)

(Use 92974 in conjunction with 92920, 92924, 92928, 92933, 92937, 92941, 92943, 93454-93461)

(For intravascular radioelement application, see 77770, 77771, 77772)

92975 Thrombolysis, coronary; by intracoronary infusion, including selective coronary angiography

92977 by intravenous infusion

(For thrombolysis of vessels other than coronary, see 37211-37214)

(For cerebral thrombolysis, use 37195)

+ 92978 Endoluminal imaging of coronary vessel or graft using intravascular ultrasound (IVUS) or optical coherence tomography (OCT) during diagnostic evaluation and/or therapeutic intervention including imaging supervision, interpretation and report; initial vessel (List separately in addition to code for primary procedure)

(Report 92978 once per session)

(Use 92978 in conjunction with 92975, 92920, 92924, 92928, 92933, 92937, 92941, 92943, 93454-93461, 93563, 93564)

+ 92979 each additional vessel (List separately in addition to code for primary procedure)

(Report 92979 once per additional vessel)

(Use 92979 in conjunction with code 92978)

(Intravascular ultrasound and optical coherence tomography services include all transducer manipulations and repositioning within the specific vessel being examined, both before and after therapeutic intervention [eg, stent placement])

(For intravascular spectroscopy, use 0205T)

CARDIOGRAPHY

Routine monitoring of EKG rhythm and review of daily hemodynamics, including cardiac outputs, is a part of critical care evaluation and management. Separate billing for review of EKG rhythm strips and cardiac output measurements (e.g. CPT codes 93040-93042, 93561, 93562) and critical care services is inappropriate.

An exception to this may include a sudden change in patient status associated with a change in cardiac rhythm requiring a return to the ICU or telephonic transmission to review a rhythm strip. If reported separately, time included for this service is not included in the critical care time calculated for the critical care service.

Codes 93040-93042 are appropriate when an order for the test is triggered by an event, the rhythm strip is used to help diagnose the presence or absence of an arrhythmia, and a report is generated.

(For echocardiography, see 93303-93350)

(For electrocardiogram, 64 leads or greater, with graphic presentation and analysis, see 0178T-0180T)

(For acoustic cardiography services, use 93799)

93000   Electrocardiogram, routine ECG with at least 12 leads; with interpretation and report

93005   tracing only, without interpretation and report

93010   interpretation and report only

(For ECG monitoring, see 99354-99360)

93015   Cardiovascular stress test using maximal or submaximal treadmill or bicycle exercise, continuous electrocardiographic monitoring, and/or pharmacological stress; with supervision, with interpretation and report

93016   supervision only, without interpretation and report

93017   tracing only, without interpretation and report

93018   interpretation and report only

93024   Ergonovine provocation test

93025   Microvolt T-wave alternans for assessment of ventricular arrhythmias

93040   Rhythm ECG, 1 to 3 leads; with interpretation and report

93041   tracing only without interpretation and report

93042   interpretation and report only

93050   Arterial pressure waveform analysis for assessment of central arterial pressures, includes obtaining waveform(s), digitization and application of nonlinear mathematical transformations to determine central arterial pressures and augmentation index, with interpretation and report, upper extremity artery, non-invasive

(Do not report 93050 in conjunction with diagnostic or interventional intra-arterial procedures)

CARDIOVASCULAR MONITORING SERVICES

Cardiovascular monitoring services are diagnostic medical procedures using in-person and remote technology to assess cardiovascular rhythm (ECG) data. Holter monitors (93224-93227) include up to 48 hours of continuous recording. Mobile cardiac telemetry monitors (93228, 93229) have the capability of transmitting a tracing at any time, always have internal ECG analysis algorithms designed to detect major arrhythmias, and transmit to an attended surveillance center. Event monitors (93268-93272) record segments of ECGs with recording initiation triggered either by patient activation or by an internal automatic, pre-programmed detection algorithm (or both) and transmit the recorded electrocardiographic data when requested (but cannot transmit immediately based upon the patient or algorighmic activation rhythm) and require attended surveillance.

93224 External electrocardiographic recording up to 48 hours by continuous rhythm recording and storage; includes recording, scanning analysis with report, review and interpretation

93225 recording (includes connection, recording, and disconnection)

93226 scanning analysis with report

93227 review and interpretation by a physician or other qualified health care professional

(For less than 12 hours of continuous recording, use modifier 52)

(For greater than 48 hours of monitoring, see 0295T-0298T0

★ **93228** External mobile cardiovascular telemetry with electrocardiographic recording, concurrent computerized real time data analysis and greater than 24 hours of accessible ECG data storage (retrievable with query) with ECG triggered and patient selected events transmitted to a remote attended surveillance center for up to 30 days; review and interpretation with report by a physician or other qualified health care professional

(Report 93228 only once per 30 days)

(Do not report 93228 in conjunction with 93224, 93227)

★ **93229** technical support for connection and patient instructions for use, attended surveillance, analysis and transmission of daily and emergent data reports as prescribed by a physician or other qualified health care professional

(Report 93229 only once per 30 days)

(Do not report 93229 in conjunction with 93224, 93226)

(For external cardiovascular monitors that do not perform automatic ECG triggered transmissions to an attended surveillance center, see 93224-93227, 932268-93272)

93260 This code is out of order. See page 851.

93261 This code is out of order. See page 851.

★ **93268** External patient and, when performed, auto activated electrocardiographic rhythm derived event recording with symptom-related memory loop with remote download capability up to 30 days, 24-hour attended monitoring; includes transmission, review and interpretation by a physician or other qualified health care professional

★ **93270** recording (includes connection, recording, and disconnection)

★ **93271** transmission download and analysis

★ **93272** review and interpretation by a physician or other qualified health care professional

(For implanted patient activated cardiac event recording, see 33282, 93285, 93291, 93298)

93278 Signal-averaged electrocardiography (SAECG), with or without ECG

(For interpretation and report only, use 93278 with modifier -26)

(For unlisted cardiographic procedure, use 93799)

| | Separate Procedure | | Unlisted Procedure | | CCI Comp. Code | | Non-specific Procedure | **847** |

IMPLANTABLE AND WEARABLE CARDIAC DEVICE EVALUATIONS

Cardiac device evaluation services are diagnostic medical procedures using in-person and remote technology to assess device therapy and cardiovascular physiologic data. Codes 93260, 93261, 93279-93299 describe this technology and technical/professional and service center practice. Codes 93260, 93261, 93279-93292 are reported per procedure. Codes 93293, 93294, 93295, 93296 are reported no more than **once** every 90 days. Do not report 93293, 93294, 93295, 93296 if the monitoring period is less than 30 days. Codes 93297, 93298 are reported no more than **once** up to every 30 days. Do not report 93297-93299 if the monitoring period is less than 10 days.

A service center may report 93296 or 93299 during a period in which a physician or other qualified health care professional performs an in-person interrogation device evaluation. The same individual may not report an in-person and remote interrogation of the same device during the same period. Report only remote services when an in-person interrogation device evaluation is performed during a period of remote interrogation device evaluation. A period is established by the initiation of the remote monitoring or the 91st day of a pacemaker or implantable defibrillator monitoring or the 31st day of an implantable loop recorder (ILR) or implantable cardiovascular monitor (ICM) monitorin,g and extends for the subsequent 90 or 30 days respectively, for which remote monitoring is occurring. Programming device evaluations and in-person interrogation device evaluations may not be reported on the same date by the same individual. Programming device evaluations and remote interrogation device evaluations may both be reported during the remote interrogation device evaluation period.

For monitoring by wearable devices, see 93224-93272.

ECG rhythm derived elements are distinct from physiologic data, even when the same device is capable of producing both. ICM device services are always separately reported from implantable defibrillator services. When ILR data is derived from an implantable defibrillator or pacemaker, do not report ILR services with pacemaker or implantable defibrillator services.

Do not report 93268-93272 when performing 93260, 93261, 93279-93289, 93291-93296 or 93298-93299. Do not report 93040, 93041, 93042 when performing 93260, 93261, 93279-93289, 93291-93296, or 93298-93299.

The pacemaker and implantable defibrillator interrogation device evaluations, peri-procedural device evaluations and programming, and programming device evaluations may not be reported in conjunction with pacemaker or implantable defibrillator device and/or lead insertion or revision services by the same individual.

The following definitions and instructions apply to codes 93260, 93261, 93279-93299:

Attended surveillance: the immediate availability of a remote technician to respond to rhythm or device alert transmissions from a patient, either from an implanted or wearable monitoring or therapy device, as they are generated and transmitted to the remote surveillance location or center.

Device, single lead: a pacemaker or implantable defibrillator with pacing and sensing function in only one chamber of the heart or a subcutaneous electrode..

Device, dual lead: a pacemaker or implantable defibrillator with pacing and sensing function in only two chambers of the heart.

Device, multiple lead: a pacemaker or implantable defibrillator with pacing and sensing function in three or more chambers of the heart.

Electrocardiographic rhythm derived elements: elements derived from recordings of the electrical activation of the heart including, but not limited to heart rhythm, rate, ST analysis, heart rate variability, T-wave alternans.

Implantable cardiovascular monitor (ICM): an implantable cardiovascular device used to assist the physician in the management of non-rhythm related cardiac conditions such as heart failure. The device collects longitudinal physiologic cardiovascular data elements from one or more internal sensors (such as right ventricular pressure, left atrial pressure or an index of lung water) and/or external sensors (such as blood pressure or body weight) for patient assessment and management. The data are stored and transmitted by either local telemetry or remotely to an Internet-based file server or surveillance technician. The function of the ICM may be an additional function of an implantable cardiac device (eg., implantable defibrillator) or a function of a stand-alone device. When ICM functionality is included in an implantable defibrillator device or pacemaker, the ICM data and the implantable defibrillator or pacemaker, heart rhythm data such as sensing, pacing and tachycardia detection therapy are distinct and therefore, the monitoring processes are distinct.

Implantable defibrillator: two general categories of implantable defibrillators exist: transvenous implantable pacing cardioverter-defibrillator (ICD), and subcutaneous implantable defibrillator (SICD). An implantable pacing cardioverter-defibrillator device provides high-energy and low-energy stimulation to one or more chambers of the heart to terminate rapid heart rhythms called tachycardia or fibrillation. Implantable pacing cardioverter-defibrillators also have

● New Code ▲ Revised Code + Add-On Code ⊘ Modifier -51 Exempt ★ Telemedicine

pacemaker functions to treat slow heart rhythms called bradycardia. In addition to the tachycardia and bradycardia functions, the implantable pacing cardioverter-defibrillator may or may not include the functionality of an implantable cardiovascular monitor or an implantable loop recorder. The subcutaneous implantable defibrillator uses a single subcutaneous electrode to treat ventricular tachyarrhythmias. Subcutaneous implantable defibrillators differ from transvenous implantable pacing cardioverter-defibrillators in that subcutaneous implantable defibrillators do not provide antitachycardia pacing or chronic pacing. For subcutaneous implantable defibrillator device evaluations, see 93260, 93261.

Implantable loop recorder (ILR): an implantable device that continuously records the electrocardiographic rhythm triggered automatically by rapid and slow heart rates or by the patient during a symptomatic episode. The ILR function may be the only function of the device or it may be part of a pacemaker or implantable defibrillator device. The data are stored and transmitted either local telemetry or remotely to an Internet based file server or surveillance technician. Extraction of data and compilation or report for physician or qualified health care profesional interpretation is usually performed in the office setting.

Interrogation device evaluation: an evaluation of an implantable device such as a cardiac pacemaker, implantable defibrillator, implantable cardiovascular monitor, or implantable loop recorder. Using an office, hospital, or emergency room instrument or via a remote interrogation system, stored and measured information about the lead(s) when present, sensor(s) when present, battery and the implanted device function, as well as data collected about the patient's heart rhythm and heart rate is retrieved. The retrieved information is evaluated to determine the current programming of the device and to evaluate certain aspects of the device function such as battery voltage, lead impedance, tachycardia detection settings, and rhythm treatment settings.

The components that must be evaluated for the various types of implantable cardiac devices are listed below. (The required components for both remote and in-person interrogations are the same.)

Pacemaker: Programmed parameters, lead(s), battery, capture and sensing function and heart rhythm.

Implantable defibrillator: Programmed parameters, lead(s), battery, capture and sensing function, presence or absence of therapy for ventricular tachyarrhythmias and underlying heart rhythms.

Implantable cardiovascular monitor: Programmed parameters and analysis of at least one recorded physiologic cardiovascular data element from either internal or external sensors.

Implantable loop recorder: Programmed parameters and the heart rate and rhythm during recorded episodes from both patient initiated and device algorithm detected events, when present.

Interrogation device evaluation (remote): a procedure performed for patients with pacemakers, implantable defibrillators or implantable loop recorders using data obtained remotely. All device functions, including the programmed parameters, lead(s), battery, capture and sensing function, presence or absence of therapy for ventricular tachyarrhythmias (for implantable defibrillators) and underlying heart rhythm are evaluated.

The components that must be evaluated for the various types of implantable cardiac devices are listed below. (The required components for both remote and in person interrogations are the same.)

Pacemaker: Programmed parameters, lead(s), battery, capture and sensing function and heart rhythm.

Implantable defibrillator: Programmed parameters, lead(s), battery, capture and sensing function, presence or absence of therapy for ventricular tachyarrhythmias and underlying heart rhythms.

Implantable cardiovascular monitor: Programmed parameters and analysis of at least one recorded physiologic cardiovascular data element from either internal or external sensors.

Implantable loop recorder: Programmed parameters and the heart rate and rhythm during recorded episodes from both patient initiated and device algorithm detected events, when present.

Pacemaker: an implantable device that provides low energy localized stimulation to one or more chambers of the heart to initiate contraction in that chamber.

Peri-procedural device evaluation and programming: an evaluation of an implantable device system (either a pacemaker or implantable defibrillator) to adjust the device to settings appropriate for the patient prior to a surgery, procedure, or test. The device system data are interrogated to evaluate the lead(s), sensor(s), and battery in addition to review of stored information including patient and system measurements. The device is programmed to settings appropriate for the surgery, procedure, or test, as required. A second evaluation and programming are performed after the surgery, procedure, or test to provide settings appropriate to the post procedural situation, as required. If one performs both the pre- and post-evaluation and programming service, the appropriate code, either 93286 or 93287, would be reported two times. If one performs the pre-surgical service and a separate provider performs the post-surgical service, each reports either 93286 or 93287 only one time.

Physiologic cardiovascular data elements: data elements from one or more internal sensors (such as right ventricular pressure, left atrial pressure, or an index of lung water) and/or external sensors (such as blood pressure or body weight) for patient assessment and management. It does not include ECG rhythm derived data elements.

Programming device evaluations (in person): a procedure performed for patients with a pacemaker, implantable defibrillator, or implantable loop recorder. All device functions, including the battery, programmable settings and lead(s), when present, are evaluated. To assess capture thresholds, iterative adjustments (eg., progressive changes in pacing output of a pacing lead) of the programmable parameters are conducted. The iterative adjustments provide information that permits the operator to assess and select the most appropriate final program parameters to provide for consistent delivery of the appropriate therapy and to verify the function of the device. The final program parameters may or may not change after evaluation.

The programming device evaluation includes all of the components of the interrogation device evaluation (remote) or the interrogation device evaluation (in person), and it includes the selection of patient specific programmed parameters depending on the type of device.

The components that must be evaluated for the various types of programming device evaluations are listed below. (See also required interrogation device evaluation [remote and in person] components above.)

Pacemaker: Programmed parameters, lead(s), battery, capture and sensing function and heart rhythm. Often, but not always, the sensor rate response, lower and upper heart rates, AV intervals, pacing voltage and pulse duration, sensing value, and diagnostics will be adjusted during a programming evaluation.

Implantable defibrillator: Programmed parameters, lead(s), battery, capture and sensing function, presence or absence of therapy for ventricular tachyarrhythmias and underlying heart rhythms. Often, but not always, the sensor rate response, lower and upper heart rates, AV intervals, pacing voltage and pulse duration, sensing value, and diagnostics will be adjusted during a programming evaluation. In addition, ventricular tachycardia detection and therapies are sometimes altered depending on the interrogated data, patient's rhythm, symptoms, and condition.

Implantable loop recorder: Programmed parameters and the heart rhythm during recorded episodes from both patient initiated and device algorithm detected events. Often, but not always, the tachycardia and bradycardia detection criteria will be adjusted during a programming evaluation.

Transtelephonic rhythm strip pacemaker evaluation: service of transmission of an electrocardiographic rhythm strip over the telephone by the patient using a transmitter and recorded by a receiving location using a receiver/recorder (also commonly known as transtelephonic pacemaker monitoring). The electrocardiographic rhythm strip is recorded both with and without a magnet applied over the pacemaker. The rhythm strip is evaluated for heart rate and rhythm, atrial and ventricular capture (if observed) and atrial and ventricular sensing (if observed). In addition, the battery status of the pacemaker is determined by measurement of the paced rate on the electrocardiographic rhythm strip recorded with the magnet applied.

93279 Programming device evaluation (in person) with iterative adjustment of the implantable device to test the function of the device and select optimal permanent programmed values with analysis, review and report by a physician or other qualified health care professional; single lead pacemaker system

(Do not report 93279 in conjunction with 93286, 93288)

93280 dual lead pacemaker system

(Do not report 93280 in conjunction with 93286, 93288)

93281 multiple lead pacemaker system

(Do not report 93281 in conjunction with 93286, 93288)

93282 single lead transvenous implantable defibrillator system

(Do not report 93282 in conjunction with 93260, 93287, 93289, 93745)

93283 dual lead transvenous implantable defibrillator system

(Do not report 93283 in conjunction with 93287, 93289)

93284 multiple lead transvenous implantable defibrillator system

(Do not report 93284 in conjunction with 93287, 93289)

93260   implantable subcutaneous lead defibrillator system

(Do not report 93260 in conjunction with 93261, 93282, 93287)

(Do not report 93260 in conjunction with pulse generator and lead insertion or repositioning codes 33240, 33241, 33262, 33270, 33271, 33272, 33273)

93285   implantable loop recorder system

(Do not report 93285 in conjunction with 33282, 93279-93284, 93291)

93286   Peri-procedural device evaluation (in person) and programming of device system parameters before or after a surgery, procedure, or test with analysis, review and report by a physician or other qualified health care professional; single, dual, or multiple lead pacemaker system

(Report 93286 once before and once after surgery, procedure, or test, when device evaluation and programming is performed before and after surgery, procedure, or test)

(Do not report 93286 in conjunction with 93279-93281, 93288, 0408T, 0409T, 0410T, 0411T, 0414T, 0415T)

93287   single, dual, or multiple lead implantable defibrillator system

(Report 93287 once before and once after surgery, procedure, or test, when device evaluation and programming is performed before and after surgery, procedure, or test)

(Do not report 93287 in conjunction with 93260, 93261, 93282, 93283, 93284, 93289, 0408T, 0409T, 0410T, 0411T, 0414T, 0415T)

93288   Interrogation device evaluation (in person) with analysis, review and report by a physician or other qualified health care professional, includes connection, recording and disconnection per patient encounter; single, dual, or multiple lead pacemaker system

(Do not report 93288 in conjunction with 93279-93281, 93286, 93294, 93296)

93289   single, dual, or multiple lead transvenous implantable defibrillator system, including analysis of heart rhythm derived data elements

(For monitoring physiologic cardiovascular data elements derived froman implantable defibrillator, use 93290)

(Do not report 93289 in conjunction with 93261, 93282, 93283, 93284, 93287, 93295, 93296)

93261   implantable subcutaneous lead defibrillator system

(Do not report 93261 in conjunction with 93260, 93287, 93289)

(Do not report 93261 in conjunction with pulse generator and lead insertion or repositioning codes 33240, 33241, 33262, 33270, 33271, 33272, 33273)

93290   implantable cardiovascular monitor system, including analysis of 1 or more recorded physiologic cardiovascular data elements from all internal and external sensors

(For heart rhythm derived data elements, use 93289)

(Do not report 93290 in conjunction with 93297, 93299)

93291   implantable loop recorder system, including heart rhythm derived data analysis

(Do not report 93291 in conjunction with 93282, 93288-93290, 93298, 93299)

93292   wearable defibrillator system

(Do not report 93292 in conjunction with 93745)

93293 Transtelephonic rhythm strip pacemaker evaluation(s) single, dual, or multiple lead pacemaker system, includes recording with and without magnet application with analysis, review and report(s) by a physician or other qualified health care professional, up to 90 days

(Do not report 93293 in conjunction with 93294)

(For in person evaluation, see 93040, 93041, 93042)

(Report 93293 only once per 90 days)

93294 Interrogation device evaluation(s) (remote), up to 90 days; single, dual, or multiple lead pacemaker system with interim analysis, review(s) and report(s) by a physician or other qualified health care professional

(Do not report 93294 in conjunction with 93288, 93293)

(Report 93294 only once per 90 days)

93295   single, dual, or multiple lead implantable defibrillator system with interim analysis, review(s) and report(s) by a physician or other qualified health care professional

(For remote monitoring of physiologic cardiovascular data elements derived from an ICD, use 93297)

(Do not report 93295 in conjunction with 93289)

(Report 93295 only once per 90 days)

93296   single, dual, or multiple lead pacemaker system or implantable defibrillator system, remote data acquisition(s), receipt of transmissions and technician review, technical support and distribution of results

(Do not report 93296 in conjunction with 93288, 93289, 93299)

(Report 93296 only once per 90 days)

93297 Interrogation device evaluation(s), (remote) up to 30 days; implantable cardiovascular monitor system, including analysis of 1 or more recorded physiologic cardiovascular data elements from all internal and external sensors, analysis, review(s) and report(s) by a physician or other qualified health care professional

(For heart rhythm derived data elements, use 93295)

(Do not report 93297 in conjunction with 93290, 93298)

(Report 93297 only once per 30 days)

93298   implantable loop recorder system, including analysis of recorded heart rhythm data, analysis, review(s) and report(s) by a physician or other qualified health care professional

(Do not report 93298 in conjunction with 33282, 93291, 93297)

(Report 93298 only once per 30 days)

93299   implantable cardiovascular monitor system or implantable loop recorder system, remote data acquisition(s), receipt of transmissions and technician review, technical support and distribution of results

(Do not report 93299 in conjunction with 93290, 93291, 93296)

(Report 93299 only once per 30 days)

ECHOCARDIOGRAPHY

An echocardiogram is an ultrasound of the heart. Using standard ultrasound techniques, two-dimensional slices of the heart can be imaged. The latest ultrasound systems employ 3D real-time imaging. The standard echocardiogram is also known as a transthoracic echocardiogram, or TTE. In this case, the echocardiography transducer (or probe) is placed on the chest wall (or thorax) of the subject, and images are taken through the chest wall. This is a non-invasive, highly accurate and quick assessment of the overall health of the heart.

● New Code   ▲ Revised Code   + Add-On Code   ⊘ Modifier -51 Exempt   ★ Telemedicine

Another method to perform an echocardiogram is to insert a specialized scope containing an echocardiography transducer (TOE probe) into the patient's esophagus and record pictures from there. This is known as a transesophageal echocardiogram, or TEE. The advantages of TEE over TTE are clearer images, since the transducer is closer to the heart. Some structures are better imaged with the TEE. These structures include the aorta, the pulmonary artery, the valves of the heart, and the left and right atria. While TTE can be performed easily and without pain for the patient, TEE may require light sedation and a local anesthetic lubricant for the esophagus. Unlike the TTE, the TEE is considered an invasive procedure.

In addition to creating two-dimensional pictures of the cardiovascular system, the echocardiogram can also produce accurate assessment of the direction of blood flow and the velocity of blood and cardiac tissue at any arbitrary point using Doppler ultrasound. This allows assessment of cardiac valve areas and function, any abnormal communications between the left and right side of the heart, any leaking of blood through the valves (valvular regurgitation), and calculation of the cardiac output as well as the ejection fraction.

Echocardiography includes obtaining ultrasonic signals from the heart and great vessels, with real time image and/or Doppler ultrasonic signal documentation, with interpretation and report. When interpretation is performed separately, use modifier 26.

A complete transthoracic echocardiogram without spectral or color flow Doppler (93307) is a comprehensive procedure that includes 2-dimensional and, when performed, selected M-mode examination of: the left and right atria; left and right ventricles; the aortic, mitral, and tricuspid valves; the pericardium; and adjacent portions of the aorta. Multiple views are required to obtain a complete functional and anatomic evaluation, and appropriate measurements are obtained and recorded. Despite significant effort, identification and measurement of some structures may not always be possible. In such instances, the reason that an element could not be visualized must be documented. Additional structures that may be visualized (eg., pulmonary veins, pulmonary artery, pulmonic valve, inferior vena cava) would be included as part of the service.

A complete transthoracic echocardiogram with spectral and color flow Doppler (93306) is a comprehensive procedure that includes spectral Doppler and color flow Doppler in addition to the 2-dimensional and selected M-mode examinations, when performed. Spectral Doppler (93320, 93321) and color flow Doppler (93325) provide information regarding intracardiac blood flow and hemodynamics.

A follow-up or limited echocardiographic study (93308) is an examination that does not evaluate or document the attempt to evaluate all the structures that comprise the complete echocardiographic exam. This is typically limited to, or performed in follow-up of a focused clinical concern.

When a stress echocardiogram is performed with a complete cardiovascular stress test (continuous electrocardiographic monitoring, supervision, interpretation and report by a physician or other qualified health care professional), use 93351. When only the professional components of a complete stress test and a stress echocardiogram are provided (eg, in a facility setting) by the same physician, use 93351 with modifier 26. When all professional services of a stress test are not performed by the same physician performing the stress echocardiogram, use 93350 in conjunction with the appropriate codes (93016-93018) for the components of the cardiovascular stress test that are provided.

When left ventricular endocardial borders cannot be adequately identified by standard echocardiographic imaging, echocardiographic contrast may be infused intravenously both at rest and with stress to achieve that purpose. Code 93352 is used to report the administration of echocardiographic contrast agent in conjunction with the stress echocardiography codes (93350 or 93351). Supply of contrast agent and/or drugs used for pharmacological stress is reported separately in addition to the procedure code.

Code 93355 is used to report transesophageal echocardiography (TEE) services during transcatheter intracardiac therapies. Code 93355 is reported once per interventin and only by an individual who is not performing the interventional procedure. Code 93355 includes the work of passing the endoscopic ultrasound transducer through the mouth into the esophagus, when performed by the individual performing the TEE, diagnostic transesophageal echocardiography adn ongoing manipulation of the transducer to guide sizing and/or placement of implants, determination of adequacy of the intervention, and assessment for potential complications. Real-time image acquisition, measurements, and interpretation of image(s), documentation of completion of the intervention, and final written report are included in this code.

A range of intracardiac therapies may be performed with TEE guidance. Code 93355 describes TEE during advanced transcatheter structural heart procedures (eg., transcatheter aortic valve replacement [TAVE], left atrial appendage closure [LAA], or percutaneous mitral valve repair).

See 93313 for separate reporting of the probe insertion by a physician other than the physician performing the TEE.

Report of an echocardiographic study, whether complete or limited, includes an interpretation of all obtained information, documentation of all clinically relevant findings including quantitative measurements obtained, plus a description of any recognized abnormalities. Pertinent images, videotape, and/or digital data are archived for permanent storage and are available for subsequent review. Use of echocardiography not meeting these criteria is not separately reportable.

Use of ultrasound, without thorough evaluation of organ(s) or anatomic region, image documentation and final, written report, is not separately reportable.

(For fetal echocardiography, see 76825-76828)

93303 Transthoracic echocardiography for congenital cardiac anomalies; complete

93304 follow-up or limited study

93306 Echocardiography, transthoracic, real-time with image documentation (2D), includes M-mode recording, when performed, complete, with spectral doppler echocardiography, and with color flow doppler echocardiography

(For transthoracic echocardiography without spectral and color Doppler, use 93307)

93307 Echocardiography, transthoracic, real-time with image documentation (2D) includes M-mode recording, when performed, complete, without spectral or color Doppler echocardiography

(Do not report 93307 in conjunction with 93320, 93321, 93325)

93308 Echocardiography, transthoracic, real-time with image documentation (2D), includes M-mode recording, when performed, follow-up or limited study

93312 Echocardiography, transesophageal, real-time with image documentation (2D) (with or without M-mode recording); including probe placement, image acquisition, interpretation and report

(Do not report 93312 in conjunction with 93355)

93313 placement of transesophageal probe only

(The same individual may not report 93313 in conjunction with 93355)

93314 image acquisition, interpretation and report only

(Do not report 93314 in conjunction with 93355)

93315 Transesophageal echocardiography for congenital cardiac anomalies; including probe placement, image acquisition, interpretation and report

(Do not report 93315 in conjunction with 93355)

93316 placement of transesophageal probe only

(Do not report 93316 in conjunction with 93355)

93317 image acquisition, interpretation and report only

(Do not report 93317 in conjunction with 93355)

93318 Echocardiography, transesophageal (TEE) for monitoring purposes, including probe placement, real time 2-dimensional image acquisition and interpretation leading to ongoing (continuous) assessment of (dynamically changing) cardiac pumping function and to therapeutic measures on an immediate time basis

(Do not report 93318 in conjunction with 93355)

+ **93320** Doppler echocardiography, pulsed wave and/or continuous wave with spectral display (List separately in addition to codes for echocardiographic imaging); complete

(Use 93320 in conjunction with 93303, 93304, 93312, 93314, 93315, 93317, 93350, 93351)

(Do not report 93320 in conjunction with 93355)

+ 93321   follow-up or limited study (List separately in addition to codes for echocardiographic imaging)

(Use 93321 in conjunction with 93303, 93304, 93308, 93312, 93314, 93315, 93317, 93350, 93351)

(Do not report 93321 in conjunction with 93355)

+ 93325   Doppler echocardiography color flow velocity mapping (List separately in addition to codes for echocardiography)

(Use 93325 in conjunction with 76825, 76826, 76827, 76828, 93303, 93304, 93308, 93312, 93314, 93315, 93317, 93350, 93351)

(Do not report 93325 in conjunction with 93355)

93350   Echocardiography, transthoracic, real-time with image documentation (2D), includes M-mode recording, when performed, during rest and cardiovascular stress test using treadmill, bicycle exercise and/or pharmacologically induced stress, with interpretation and report

(Stress testing codes 93016-93018 should be reported, when appropriate, in conjunction with 93350 to capture the cardiovascular stress portion of the study)

(Do not report 93350 in conjunction with 93015)

93351   including performance of continuous electrocardiographic monitoring, with supervision by a physician or other qualified health care professional

(Do not report 93351 in conjunction with 93015-93018, 93350. Do not report 93351-26 in conjunction with 93016, 93018, 93350-26))

+ 93352   Use of echocardiographic contrast agent during stress echocardiography (list separately in addition to code for primary procedure)

(Do not report 93352 more than once per stress echocardiogram)

(Use 93352 in conjunction with 93350, 93351)

93355   Echocardiography, transesophageal (TEE) for guidance of a transcatheter intracardiac or great vessel(s) structural intervention(s) (eg, TAVR, transcathether pulmonary valve replacement, mitral valve repair, paravalvular regurgitation repair, left atrial appendage occlusion/closure, ventricular septal defect closure) (peri-and intra-procedural), real-time image acquisition and documentation, guidance with quantitative measurements, probe manipulation, interpretation, and report, including diagnostic transesophageal echocardiography and, when performed, administration of ultrasound contrast, Doppler, color flow, and 3D

(To report placement of transesophageal probe by separate physician, use 93313)

(Do not report 93355 in conjunction with 76376, 76377, 93312, 93313, 93314, 93315, 93316, 93317, 93318, 93320, 93321, 93325)

CARDIAC CATHETERIZATION

A coronary catheterization is a minimally invasive procedure to access the coronary circulation and blood filled chambers of the heart using a catheter. It is performed for both diagnostic and interventional (treatment) purposes.

Specifically, coronary catheterization is a visually interpreted test performed to recognize occlusion, stenosis, restenosis, thrombosis or aneurysmal enlargement of the coronary artery lumens, heart chamber size, heart muscle contraction performance and some aspects of heart valve function. Important internal heart and lung blood pressures, not measurable from outside the body, can be accurately measured during the test. The relevant problems that the test deals with most commonly occur as a result of advanced atherosclerosis, atheroma activity within the wall of the coronary arteries. Less frequently, other issues, valvular, heart muscle or arrhythmia issues are the primary focus of the test.

Coronary artery luminal narrowing reduces the flow reserve for oxygenated blood to the heart, typically producing intermittent angina if very advanced; luminal occlusion usually produces a heart attack. However, it has been increasingly recognized, since the late 1980s, that coronary catheterization does not allow the recognition of the presence or absence of coronary atherosclerosis itself, only significant luminal changes which have occurred as a result of end stage complications of the atherosclerotic process. See IVUS and atheroma for a better understanding of this issue.

Separate Procedure   Unlisted Procedure   CCI Comp. Code   Non-specific Procedure   **855**

Coronary catheterization is performed in a cardiac catheterization lab, usually located within a hospital.

Catheterization to treat luminal disease

By changing the diagnostic catheter to a guiding catheter, physicians can also pass a variety of instruments through the catheter and into the artery to a lesion site. The most commonly used are guide wires and the balloon dilation catheters.

By injecting radiocontrast agent through a tiny passage extending down the balloon catheter and into the balloon, the balloon is progressively expanded. The hydraulic pressures are chosen and applied by the physician, according to how the balloon within the stenosis responds. The radiocontrast filled balloon is watched under fluoroscopy (it typically assumes a "dog bone" shape imposed on the outside of the balloon by the stenosis as the balloon is expanded), as it opens. As much hydraulic brute force is applied as judged needed and visualized to be effective to make the stenosis of the artery lumen visibly enlarge.

Additionally, several other devices can be advanced into the artery via a guiding catheter. These include laser catheters, stent catheters, IVUS catheters, Doppler catheter, pressure or temperature measurement catheter and various clot and grinding or removal devices. Most of these devices have turned out to be niche devices, only useful in a small percentage of situations or for research.

Stents, specially manufactured expandable stainless steel mesh tubes, mounted on a balloon catheter, are the most commonly used device beyond the balloon catheter. When the stent/balloon device is positioned within the stenosis, the balloon is inflated which, in turn, expands the stent and the artery. The balloon is removed and the stent remains in place, supporting the inner artery walls in the more open, dilated position.

There are two code families for cardiac catheterization: one for congenital heart disease, and one for all other conditions. Anomalous coronary arteries, patent foramen ovale, mitral valve prolapse, and bicuspid aortic valve are to be reported with 93451-93464, 93566-93568.

Right heart catheterization includes catheter placement in one or more right-sided cardiac chamber(s) or structures (ie, the right atrium, right ventricle, pulmonary artery, pulmonary wedge), obtaining blood samples for measurement of blood gases, and cardiac output measurements (Fick or other method), when performed. Left heart catheterization involves catheter placement in a left-sided (systemic) cardiac chamber(s) (left ventricle or left atrium) and includes left ventricular injection(s) when performed. Do not report code 93503 in conjunction with other diagnostic cardiac catheterization codes. When right heart catheterization is performed in conjunction with other cardiac catheterization services, report 93453, 93456, 93457, 93460 or 93461. For placement of a flow directed catheter (eg, Swan-Ganz) performed for hemodynamic monitoring purposes not in conjunction with other catheterization services, use 93503. Right heart catheterization does not include right ventricular or right atrial angiography (93566). When left heart catheterization if performed using either transapical puncture of the left ventricle or transseptal puncture of an intact septum, report 93462 in conjunction with 93452, 93453, 93458-93461, 93653, 93654. Catheter placement(s) in coronary artery(ies) involves selective engagement of the origins of the native coronary artery(ies) for the purpose of coronary angiography. Catheter placement(s) in bypass graft(s) (venous, internal mammary, free arterial graft[s]) involve selective engagement of the origins of the graft(s) for the purpose of bypass angiography. It is typically performed only in conjunction with coronary angiography of native vessels.

The cardiac catheterization codes (93452-93462), other than those for congenital heart disease, include contrast injection(s), imaging supervision, interpretation, and report for imaging typically performed. Codes for left heart catheterization (93452, 93453, 93458-93461) other than those for congenital heart disease, include intraprocedural injection(s) for left ventricular/left atrial angiography, imaging supervision, and interpretation, when performed. Codes for coronary catheter placement(s) (93454-93461), other than those for congenital heart disease, include intraprocedural injection(s) for coronary angiography, imaging supervision, and interpretation. Codes for catheter placement(s) in bypass graft(s) (93455, 93457, 93459, 93461) other than those for congenital heart disease, include intraprocedural injection(s) for bypass graft angiography, imaging supervision, and interpretation. Do not report 93563-93565 in conjunction with 93452-93461.

For cardiac catheterization for congenital cardiac anomalies, see 93530-93533. When contrast injection(s) are performed in conjunction with cardiac catheterization for congenital anomalies, see 93563-93568.

Cardiac catheterization (93451-93461) includes all roadmapping angiography in order to place the catheters, including any injections and imaging supervision, interpretation, and report. It does not include contrast injection(s) and imaging supervision, interpretation, and report for imaging that is separately identified by specific procedure code(s). For right ventricular or right atrial angiography performed in conjunction with cardiac catheterization for congenital or noncongenital heart disease (93451-93461, 93530-93533), use 93566. For aortography, use 93567. For pulmonary angiography, use 93568. For angiography of noncoronary arteries and veins, performed as a distinct service, use appropriate codes from the Radiology section and the Vascular Injection Procedures section.

● New Code   ▲ Revised Code   + Add-On Code   ⦸ Modifier -51 Exempt   ★ Telemedicine

When cardiac catheterization is combined with pharmacologic agent administration with the specific purpose of repeating hemodynamic measurements to evaluate hemodynamic response, use 93463 in conjunction with 93451-93453 and 93456-93461. Do not report 93463 for intracoronary administration of pharmacologic agents during percutaneous coronary interventional procedures, during intracoronary assessment of coronary pressure, flow or resistance, or during intracoronary imaging procedures. Do not report 93463 in conjunction with 92920-92944, 92975, 92977.

When cardiac catheterization is combined with exercise (eg, walking or arm or leg ergometry protocol) with the specific purpose of repeating hemodynamic measurements to evaluate hemodynamic response, report 93464 in conjunction with 93451-93453, 93456-93461, and 93530-93533.

Contrast injection to image the access site(s) for the specific purpose of placing a closure device is inherent to the catheterization procedure and not separately reportable. Closure device placement at the vascular access site is inherent to the catheterization procedure and not separately reportable.

Modifier 51 should not be appended to 93451, 93456, 93503.

Please see the cardiac catheterization table, located following 93572.

⊘ **93451** Right heart catheterization including measurement(s) of oxygen saturation and cardiac output, when performed

(Do not report 93451 in conjunction with 93453, 93456, 93457, 93460, 93461)

(Do not report 93451 in conjunction with 0345T for diagnostic left and right heart catheterization procedures intrinsic to the valve repair procedure)

93452 Left heart catheterization including intraprocedural injection(s) for left ventriculography, imaging supervision and interpretation, when performed

(Do not report 93452 in conjunction with 93453, 93458- 93461, 0408T, 0409T, 0410T, 0411T, 0414T, 0415T)

93453 Combined right and left heart catheterization including intraprocedural injection(s) for left ventriculography, imaging supervision and interpretation, when performed

(Do not report 93453 in conjunction with 93451, 93452, 93456-93461, 0408T, 0409T, 0410T, 0411T, 0414T, 0415T)

(Do not report 93453 in conjunction with 0345T for diagnostic left and right heart catheterization procedures intrinsic to the valve repair procedure)

93454 Catheter placement in coronary artery(s) for coronary angiography, including intraprocedural injection(s) for coronary angiography, imaging supervision and interpretation

(Do not report 93453, 93454 in conjunction with 0345T for coronary angiography intrinsic to the valve repair procedure)

93455 with catheter placement(s) in bypass graft(s) (internal mammary, free arterial venous grafts) including intraprocedural injection(s) for bypass graft angiography

⊘ **93456** with right heart catheterization

(Do not report 93456 in conjunction with 0345T for diagnostic left and right heart catheterization procedures intrinsic to the valve repair procedure)

93457 with catheter placement(s) in bypass graft(s) (internal mammary, free arterial, venous grafts) including intraprocedural injection(s) for bypass graft angiography and right heart catheterization

93458 with left heart catheterization including intraprocedural injection(s) for left ventriculography, when performed

(Do not report 93458 in conjunction with 0408T, 0409T, 0410T, 0411T, 0414T, 0415T)

| | Separate Procedure | | Unlisted Procedure | | CCI Comp. Code | | Non-specific Procedure | **857** |

93459   with left heart catheterization including intraprocedural injection(s) for left ventriculography, when performed, catheter placement(s) in bypass graft(s) (internal mammary, free arterial, venous grafts) with bypass graft angiography

(Do not report 93459 in conjunction with 0408T, 0409T, 0410T, 0411T, 0414T, 0415T)

93460   with right and left heart catheterization including intraprocedural injection(s) for left ventriculography, when performed

(Do not report 93460 in conjunction with 0408T, 0409T, 0410T, 0411T, 0414T, 0415T)

93461   with right and left heart catheterization including intraprocedural injection(s) for left ventriculography, when performed, catheter placement(s) in bypass graft(s) (internal mammary, free arterial, venous grafts) with bypass graft angiography

(Do not report 93461 in conjunction with 0345T for diagnostic left and right heart catheterization procedures intrinsic to the valve repair procedure)

(Do not report 93461 in conjunction with 0408T, 0409T, 0410T, 0411T, 0414T, 0415T)

+ **93462**   Left heart catheterization by transseptal puncture through intact septum or by transapical puncture (List separately in addition to code for primary procedure)

(Use 93462 in conjunction with 33477, 93452, 93453, 93458, 93459, 93460, 93461, 93582, 93653, 93654)

(Use 93462 in conjunction with 93590, 93591 for transapical puncture performed for left heart catheterization and percutaneous transcatheter closure of paravalvular leak)

(Do not report 93462 in conjunction with 93590 for transeptal puncture through intact septum performed for left heart catheterization and percutaneous transcatheter closure of paravalvular leak)

(Do not report 93462 in conjunction with 93656)

(Do not report 93462 in conjunction with 0345T unless transapical puncture is performed)

+ **93463**   Pharmacologic agent administration (eg, inhaled nitric oxide, intravenous infusion of nitroprusside, dobutamine, milrinone, or other agent) including assessing hemodynamic measurements before, during, after and repeat pharmacologic agent administration, when performed (List separately in addition to code for primary procedure)

(Use 93463 in conjunction with 33477, 93451-93453, 93456-93461, 93530, 93531, 93532, 93533, 93580, 93581)

(Report 93463 only once per catheterization procedure)

(Do not report 93463 for pharmacologic agent administration in conjunction with coronary interventional procedure codes 92920-92944, 92975, 92977)

+ **93464**   Physiologic exercise study (eg, bicycle or arm ergometry) including assessing hemodynamic measurements before and after (List separately in addition to code for primary procedure)

(Use 93464 in conjunction with 33477, 93451-93453, 93456-93461, 93530-93533)

(Report 93464 only once per catheterization procedure)

(For pharmacologic agent administration, use 93463)

(For bundle of His recording, use 93600)

⃠ **93503**   Insertion and placement of flow directed catheter (eg, Swan-Ganz) for monitoring purposes

(For subsequent monitoring, see 99356-99357)

93505   Endomyocardial biopsy

(To report transcatheter placement of radiation delivery device for coronary intravascular brachytherapy, use 92974)

● New Code   ▲ Revised Code   + Add-On Code   ⃠ Modifier -51 Exempt   ★ Telemedicine

Table of Catheterization Codes

CPT Code	Catheter Placement Type				Add-On Procedures (Can be reported separately)					
	RHC	LHC	Coronary Artery Placement	Bypass Graft(s)	With Transseptal or Transapical Puncture 93462	With Pharmacological Study 93463	With Exercise Study 93464	Injection Procedure for Selective Rt Ventricular or Rt Atrial Angiography 93566	Injection Procedure for Supravalvular Aortography 93567	Injection Procedure for Pulmonary Angiography 93568
93451	•					•	•	•		•
93452		•			•	•	•		•	
93453	•	•			•	•	•	•	•	•
93454			•						•	
93455			•	•					•	
93456	•		•			•	•	•	•	•
93457	•		•	•		•	•	•	•	•
93458		•	•		•	•	•		•	
93459		•	•	•	•	•	•		•	
93460	•	•	•		•	•	•	•	•	•
93461	•	•	•	•	•	•	•	•	•	•

(For intravascular radioelement application, see 77770, 77771, 77772)

93530 Right heart catheterization, for congenital cardiac anomalies

93531 Combined right heart catheterization and retrograde left heart catheterization, for congenital cardiac anomalies

93532 Combined right heart catheterization and transseptal left heart catheterization through intact septum with or without retrograde left heart catheterization, for congenital cardiac anomalies

93533 Combined right heart catheterization and transseptal left heart catheterization through existing septal opening, with or without retrograde left heart catheterization, for congenital cardiac anomalies

INJECTION PROCEDURES

All injection codes include radiological supervision, interpretation, and report. Cardiac catheterization codes (93452-93461), other than those for congenital heart disease, include contrast injection(s) for imaging typically performed during these procedures (see Cardiac Catheterization above.) Do not report 93563-93565 in conjunction with 93452-93461. When injection procedures for right ventricular, right atrial, aortic, or pulmonary angiography are performed in conjunction with cardiac catheterization, these services are reported separately (93566-93568). When right ventricular or right atrial angiography is performed at the time of heart catheterization, use 93566 with the appropriate catheterization code ((93451, 93453, 93456, 93457, 93460, or 93461). Use 93567 when supravalvular ascending aortography is performed at the t ime of heart catheterization. Use 93568 with the appropriate right heart catheterization code when pulmonary angiography is preformed. Separately reported injection procedures do not include introduction of catheters but do include repositioning of catheters when necessary and use of automatic power injectors, when performed.

When contrast injection(s) are performed in conjunction with cardiac catheterization for congenital cardiac anomalies (93530-93533), see 93563-93568. Injection procedure codes 93563-93568 include imaging supervision, interpretation, and report.

Injection procedures 93563-93568 represent separate identifiable services and may be coded in conjunction with one another when appropriate. The technical details of angiography, supervision of imaging and processing, interpretation, and report are included.

93561 Indicator dilution studies such as dye or thermodilution, including arterial and/or venous catheterization; with cardiac output measurement (separate procedure)

93562 subsequent measurement of cardiac output

(Do not report 93561, 93562 in conjunction with 93451-93462, 93582)

(For radioisotope method of cardiac output, see 78472, 78473 or 78481)

+ **93563**   Injection procedure during cardiac catheterization including imaging supervision, interpretation, and report; for selective coronary angiography during congenital heart catheterization (List separately in addition to code for primary procedure)

+ **93564**   for selective opacification of aortocoronary venous or arterial bypass graft(s) (eg, aortocoronary saphenous vein, free radial artery, or free mammary artery graft) to one or more coronary arteries and in situ arterial conduits (eg, internal mammary), whether native or used for bypass to one or more coronary arteries during congenital heart catheterization, when performed (List separately in addition to code for primary procedure)

          (Do not report 93563, 93564 in conjunction with 0345T for coronary angiography intrinsic to the valve repair procedure)

+ **93565**   for selective left ventricular or left atrial angiography (List separately in addition to code for primary procedure)

          (Do not report 93563-93565 in conjunction with 93452-93461)

          (Use 93563-93565 in conjunction with 93530-93533)

+ **93566**   for selective right ventricular or right atrial angiography (List separately in addition to code for primary procedure)

          (Use 93566 in conjunction with 93451, 93453, 93456, 93457, 93460, 93461, 93530-93533)

          (Do not report 93566 in conjunction with 0387T for right ventriculography performed during leadless pacemaker insertion)

+ **93567**   for supravalvular aortography (List separately in addition to code for primary procedure)

          (Use 93567 in conjunction with 93451-93461, 93530-93533)

          (For non-supravalvular thoracic aortography or abdominal aortography performed at the time of cardiac catheterization, use the appropriate radiological supervision and interpretation codes [36221, 75600-75630])

+ **93568**   for pulmonary angiography (List separately in addition to code for primary procedure)

          (Use 93568 in conjunction with 93451, 93453, 93456, 93457, 93460, 93461, 93530-93533)

+ **93571**   Intravascular Doppler velocity and/or pressure derived coronary flow reserve measurement (coronary vessel or graft) during coronary angiography including pharmacologically induced stress; initial vessel (List separately in addition to code for primary procedure)

          (Use 93571 in conjunction with 92920, 92924, 92928, 92933, 92937, 92941, 92943, 92975, 93454-93461, 93563, 93564)

+ **93572**   each additional vessel (List separately in addition to code for primary procedure)

          (Use 93572 in conjunction with 93571)

          (Intravascular distal coronary blood flow velocity measurements include all Doppler transducer manipulations and repositioning within the specific vessel being examined, during coronary angiography or therapeutic intervention (eg, angioplasty))

          (For unlisted cardiac catheterization procedure, use 93799)

REPAIR OF SEPTAL HEART DEFECT

93580   Percutaneous transcatheter closure of congenital interatrial communication (i.e., fontan fenestration, atrial septal defect) with implant

          (Percutaneous transcatheter closure of atrial septal defect includes a right heart catheterization procedure. Code 93580 includes injection of contrast for atrial and ventricular angiograms. Codes 93451-93453, 93455-93461, 93530-93533, 93564-93566 should not be reported separately in addition to code 93580)

93581   Percutaneous transcatheter closure of a congenital ventricular septal defect with implant

   ● New Code   ▲ Revised Code   + Add-On Code   ⊘ Modifier -51 Exempt   ★ Telemedicine

(Percutaneous transcatheter closure of ventricular septal defect includes a right heart catheterization procedure. Code 93581 includes injection of contrast for atrial and ventricular angiograms. Codes 93451-93453, 93455-93461, 93530-93533, 93564-93566 should not be reported separately in addition to 93581)

(For echocardiographic services performed in addition to 93580, 93581, see 93303-93317 as appropriate)

93582 Percutaneous transcatheter closure of patent ductus arteriosus

(93582 includes congenital right and left heart catheterization, catheter placement in the aorta, and aortic arch angiography, when performed)

(Do not report 93582 in conjunction with 36013, 36014, 36200, 75600, 75605, 93451-93461, 93530, 93531, 93532, 93533, 93567)

(For other cardiac angiographic procedures performed at the time of transcatheter PDA closure, see 93563, 93564, 93565, 93566, 93568 as appropriate)

(For left heart catheterization by transseptal puncture through intact septum or by transapical puncture performed at the time of transcatheter PDA closure, use 93462)

(For repair of patent ductus arteriosus by ligation, see 33820, 33822, 33824)

(For intracardiac echocardiographic services performed at the time of transcatheter PDA closure, use 93662. Other echocardiographic services provided by a separate individual are reported using the appropriate echocardiography service codes, 93315, 93316, 93317)

93583 Percutaneous transcatheter septal reduction therapy (eg, alcohol septal ablation) including temporary pacemaker insertion when performed

(93583 includes insertion of temporary pacemaker, when performed, and left heart catheterization)

(Do not report 93583 in conjunction with 33210, 93452, 93453, 93458, 93459, 93460, 93461, 93531, 93532, 93533, 93565)

(93583 includes left anterior descending coronary angiography for the purpose of roadmapping to guide the intervention. Do not report 93454, 93455, 93456, 93457, 93458, 93459, 93460, 93461, 93563 for coronary angiography performed during alcohol septal ablation for the purpose of roadmapping, guidance of the intervention, vessel measurement, and completion angiography)

(Diagnostic cardiac catheterization procedures may be separately reportable when no prior catheter-based diagnostic study of the treatment zone is available, the prior diagnostic study is inadequate, or the patient's condition with respect to the clinical indication has changed since the prior study or during the intervention. Use the appropriate codes from 93451, 93454, 93455, 93456, 93457, 93530, 93563, 93564, 93566, 93567, 93568)

(Do not report 93583 in conjunction with 33210, 33211)

(Do not report 93463 for the injection of alcohol for this procedure)

(For intracardiac echocardiographic services performed at the time of alcohol septal ablation, use 93662)

(Other echocardiographic services provided by a separate physician are reported using the appropriate echocardiography services codes, 93312, 93313, 93314, 93315, 93316, 93317)

(For surgical ventriculomyotomy [–mectomy] for idiopathic hypertrophic subaortic stenosis, use 33416)

Transcatheter Closure of Paravalvular Leak

Codes 93590, 93591, 93592 are used to report transcatheter closure of paravalvular leak (PVL). Codes 93590 and 93591 include, when performed, percutaneous access, placing the access sheath(s), advancing the delivery system to the paravalvular leak, positioning the closure device, repositioning the closure device as needed, and deploying the device.

Codes 93590 and 93591 include, when performed, fluoroscopy (76000), angiography, radiological supervision and interpretation services performed to guide the PVL closure (eg, guiding the device placement and documenting completion of the intervention).

Code 93590 includes transseptal puncture, and left heart catheterization/left ventriculography (93452, 93453, 93458, 93459, 93460, 93461, 93531, 93532, 93533, 93565), when performed. Transapical left heart catheterization (93462) may be reported separately, when performed.

Code 93591 includes, when performed, supravalvular aortography (93567), left heart catheterization/left ventriculography (93452, 93453, 93458, 93459, 93460, 93461, 93531, 93532, 93533, 93565). Transapical left heart catheterization (93462) may be reported separately, when performed.

Diagnostic right heart catheterization codes (93451, 93456, 93457, 93530) and diagnostic coronary angiography codes (93454, 93455, 93456, 93457, 93563, 93564) may be reported with 93590, 93591, representing separate and distinct services from PVL closure, if:

1. No prior study is available and a full diagnostic study is performed, or

2. A prior study is available, but as documented in the medical record:

a. there is inadequate visualization of the anatomy and/or pathology, or

b. the patient's condition with respect to the clinical indication has changed since the prior study, or

c. there is a clinical change during the procedure that requires new evaluation.

Other cardiac catheterization services may be reported separately, when performed for diagnostic purposes not intrinsic to PVL closure.

For same session/same day diagnostic cardiac catheterization services, report the appropriate diagnostic cardiac catheterization code(s) appended with modifier 59 indicating separate and distinct procedural service from PVL closure.

93590   Percutaneous transcatheter closure of paravalvular leak; initial occlusion device, mitral valve

(Do not report 93590 in conjunction with 93462 for transseptal puncture)

(For transapical puncture performed in conjunction with 93590, use 93462)

93591   initial occlusion device, aortic valve

(For transseptal or transapical puncture performed in conjunction with 93591, use 93462)

+ 93592   each additional occlusion device (List separately in addition to code for primary procedure)

(Use 93592 in conjunction with 93590, 93591)

INTRACARDIAC ELECTROPHYSIOLOGICAL PROCEDURES/STUDIES

Intracardiac electrophysiology study (EPS) involves placing wire electrodes within the heart to determine the characteristics of heart arrhythmias. Before performing EPS, which is invasive, the cardiologist will try to identify a suspected arrhythmia using other, less invasive tests like ambulatory cardiac monitoring. If the abnormal rhythm is not detected by these other methods and symptoms suggest an arrhythmia, EPS may be recommended. Additional reasons that EPS may be considered include:

- *To find the location of a known arrhythmia and determine the best therapy*

- *To assess the severity of the arrhythmia and determine if the patient is at risk for future cardiac events, especially sudden cardiac death*

- *To evaluate the effectiveness of medication in controlling an arrhythmia*

- *To determine if the focus (the place where the arrhythmia is coming from) should be ablated*

- *To evaluate the need for a permanent pacemaker or an implantable cardioverter-defibrillator (ICD)*

During EPS, the cardiologist inserts a catheter through a small incision in a groin vein after cleansing the site and numbing it with a local anesthetic. This catheter is equipped with an electrode connected to electrocardiographic monitors. The catheter is then carefully threaded into the heart using an x-ray imaging technique called fluoroscopy to guide the insertion. Electrodes are placed in the heart to measure electrical activity along the heart's conduction system and within heart muscle cells themselves.

Normal electrical activity is signaled from the heart's natural pacemaker known as the sinoatrial (SA) node. It then travels through the atria, the atrioventricular (AV) node, and the ventricles. Abnormal electrical activity can occur anywhere along this conduction system, including in the muscle cells of either the atria or ventricles. The electrodes inserted during EPS will map the type of arrhythmia the patient has and where the problem arises in the heart.

If ablation is thought to be the appropriate therapy, it is performed at the time of EPS.

Definitions

Arrhythmia Induction: In most electrophysiologic studies, an attempt is made to induce arrhythmia(s) from single or multiple sites within the heart. Arrhythmia induction may be achieved by multiple techniques, eg. by performing pacing at different rates or programmed stimulation (introduction of critically timed electrical impulses). Because arrhythmia induction occurs via the same catheter(s) inserted for the electrophysiologic study(ies), catheter insertion and temporary pacemaker codes are not additionally reported. Codes 93600-93603, 93610-93612 and 93618 are used to describe unusual situations where there may be recording, pacing or an attempt at arrhythmia induction from only one site in the heart. Code 93619 describes only evaluation of the sinus node, atrioventricular node, and His-Purkinje conduction system, without arrhythmia induction. Codes 93620-93624, 93640-93642, 93653, 93654 and 93656 all include recording, pacing and attempted arrhythmia induction from one or more site(s) in the heart.

Mapping: When a tachycardia is induced, the site of tachycardia origination or its electrical path through the heart is often defined by mapping. Mapping creates a multidimensional depiction of a tachycardia by recording multiple electrograms obtained sequentially or simultaneously from multiple catheter sites in the heart. Depending upon the technique, certain types of mapping catheters may be repositioned from point-to-point within the heart, allowing sequential recording from the various sites to construct maps. Other types of mapping catheters allow mapping without a point-to-point technique by allowing simultaneous recording from many electrodes on the same catheter and computer-assisted three-dimensional reconstruction of the tachycardia activation sequence.

Mapping is a distinct procedure performed in addition to a diagnostic electrophysiologic study or ablation procedure and may be separately reported using 93609 or 93613. Do not report standard mapping (93609) in addition to 3-dimensional mapping (93613).

Ablation: Once the part of the heart involved in the tachycardia is localized, the tachycardia may be treated by ablation (the delivery of a radiofrequency or cryo-energy to the area to selectively destroy cardiac tissue). Ablation procedures (93653-93657) are performed at the same session as electrophysiology studies and therefore represent a combined code description. When reporting ablation therapy codes (93653-93657), the single site electrophysiology studies (93600-93603, 93610, 93612, 93618) and the comprehensive electrophysiology studies (93619, 93620) may not be reported separately. Code 93622 may be reported separately with 93653 and 93656. Code 93623 may be reported separately with 93653, 93654, and 93656. However, 93621 for left atrial pacing and recording from coronary sinus or left atrium should not be reported in conjunction with 93656 as this procedure is a component of 93656. Codes 93653 and 93654 include right ventricular pacing and recording and His bundle recording when clinically indicated. When performance of one or more components is not possible or indicated, document the reason for not performing. Code 93656 includes each of left atrial pacing/recording, right ventricular pacing/recording, and His bundle recording when clinically indicated. When performance of one or more components is not possible or indicated, document the reason for not performing.

The differences in the techniques involved for ablation of supraventricular arrhythmias, ventricular arrhythmias, and atrial fibrillation are reflected within the descriptions for 93653-93657. Code 93653 is a primary code for catheter ablation for treatment of supraventricular tachycardia caused by dual atrioventricular nodal pathways, accessory atrioventricular connections, or other atrial foci. Code 93654 describes catheter ablation for treatment of ventricular tachycardia or focus of ventricular ectopy. Code 93656 is a primary code for reporting treatment of atrial fibrillation by ablation to achieve complete pulmonary vein electrical isolation. Codes 93653, 93654 and 93656 are distinct primary procedure codes and may not be reported together.

Codes 93655 and 93657 are add-on codes listed in addition to the primary ablation code to report ablation of sites distinct from the primary ablation site. After ablation of the primary target site, post-ablation electrophysiologic evaluation is performed as part of those ablation services (93653, 93654, 93656) and additional mechanisms of tachycardia may be identified. For example, if the primary tachycardia ablated was atrioventricular nodal reentrant tachycardia and during post-ablation testing an atrial tachycardia, atrial flutter, or accessory pathway with orthodromic reentry tachycardia was identified, this would be considered a separate mechanism of tachycardia. Pacing maneuvers are performed to define the mechanism(s) of the new tachycardia(s). Catheter ablation of this distinct mechanism of tachycardia is then performed at the newly discovered atrial or ventricular origin. Appropriate post-ablation attempts at re-induction and observation are again performed. Code 93655 is listed in conjunction with 93653 when repeat ablation is for treatment of an additional supraventricular tachycardia mechanism and with 93654 when the repeat ablation is for treatment of an additional ventricular tachycardia mechanism. Code 93655 may be reported with 93656 when an additional non-atrial fibrillation tachycardia is separately diagnosed after pulmonary vein isolation. Code 93657 is

---

reported in conjunction with 93656 when successful pulmonary vein isolation is achieved, attempts at re-induction of atrial fibrillation identify an additional left or right atrial focus for atrial fibrillation, and further ablation of this new focus is performed.

In certain circumstances, depending on the chamber of origin, a catheter or catheters may be maneuvered into the left ventricle to facilitate arrhythmia diagnosis. This may be accomplished via a retrograde aortic approach by means of the arterial access or through a transseptal puncutre. For ablation treatment of supraventricular tachycardia (93653) and ventricular tachycardia (93654), the left heart catheterization by transseptal puncture through intact septum (93462) may be reported separately as an add-on code. However, for ablation treatment of atrial fibrillation (93656), the transseptal puncture (93462) is a standard component of the procedure and may not be reported separately. Do not report 93462 in conjunction with 93656.

Modifier 51 should not be appended to 93600-93603, 93610, 93612, 93615-93618, 93631.

⊘ **93600**   Bundle of His recording

(Do not report 93600 in conjunction with 93619, 93620, 93653, 93654, 93656)

⊘ **93602**   Intra-atrial recording

(Do not report 93602 in conjunction with 93619, 93620, 93653, 93654, 93656)

⊘ **93603**   Right ventricular recording

(Do not report 93603 in conjunction with 93619, 93620, 93653, 93654, 93656)

+ **93609**   Intraventricular and/or intra-atrial mapping of tachycardia site(s) with catheter manipulation to record from multiple sites to identify origin of tachycardia (List separately in addition to code for primary procedure)

(Use 93609 in conjunction with 93620, 93653, 93656)

(Do not report 93609 in conjunction with 93613, 93654)

⊘ **93610**   Intra-atrial pacing

(Do not report 93610 in conjunction with 93619, 93620, 93653, 93654, 93656)

⊘ **93612**   Intraventricular pacing

(Do not report 93612 in conjunction with 93619, 93620, 93621, 93622, 93653, 93654, 93656)

+ **93613**   Intracardiac electrophysiologic 3-dimensional mapping (List separately in addition to code for primary procedure)

(Use 93613 in conjunction with 93620, 93653, 93656)

(Do not report 93613 in addition to 93609, 93654)

⊘ **93615**   Esophageal recording of atrial electrogram with or without ventricular electrogram(s);

⊘ **93616**   with pacing

⊘ **93618**   Induction of arrhythmia by electrical pacing

(Do not report 93618 in conjunction with 93619, 93620, 93621, 93622, 93653, 93654, 93656)

(For intracardiac phonocardiogram, use 93799)

93619   Comprehensive electrophysiologic evaluation with right atrial pacing and recording, right ventricular pacing and recording, His bundle recording, including insertion and repositioning of multiple electrode catheters without induction or attempted induction of arrhythmia

(Do not report 93619 in conjunction with 93600, 93602, 93603, 93610, 93612, 93618, 93620, 93621, 93622, 93653, 93654, 93655, 93656, 93657)

93620   Comprehensive electrophysiologic evaluation including insertion and repositioning of multiple electrode catheters with induction or attempted induction of arrhythmia; with right atrial pacing and recording, right ventricular pacing and recording, His bundle recording

---

● New Code   ▲ Revised Code   + Add-On Code   ⊘ Modifier -51 Exempt   ★ Telemedicine

(Do not report 93620 in conjunction with 93600, 93602, 93603, 93610, 93612, 93618, 93619, 93653, 93654, 93655, 93656, 93657)

+ 93621   with left atrial pacing and recording from coronary sinus or left atrium (List separately in addition to code for primary procedure)

(Use 93621 in conjunction with 93620, 93653, 93654)

(Do not report 93621 in conjunction with 93656)

+ 93622   with left ventricular pacing and recording (List separately in addition to code for primary procedure)

(Use 93622 in conjunction with 93620, 93653, 93654)

(Do not report 93622 in conjunction with 93654)

+ 93623 Programmed stimulation and pacing after intravenous drug infusion (List separately in addition to code for primary procedure)

(Use 93623 in conjunction with 93610, 93612, 93619, 93620, 93653, 93654, 93656)

93624 Electrophysiologic follow-up study with pacing and recording to test effectiveness of therapy, including induction or attempted induction of arrhythmia

⊘ 93631 Intra-operative epicardial and endocardial pacing and mapping to localize the site of tachycardia or zone of slow conduction for surgical correction

(For operative ablation of an arrhythmogenic focus or pathway by a separate individual, see 33250-33261)

93640 Electrophysiologic evaluation of single or dual chamber pacing cardioverter-defibrillator leads including defibrillation threshold evaluation (induction of arrhythmia, evaluation of sensing and pacing for arrhythmia termination) at time of initial implantation or replacement;

93641   with testing of single or dual chamber pacing cardioverter-defibrillator pulse generator

(For subsequent or periodic electronic analysis and/or reprogramming of single or dual chamber pacing cardioverter-defibrillators, see 93282, 93283, 93289, 93292, 93295, 93642)

(For electrophysiologic evaluation of a subcutaneous implantable defibrillator device evaluation, use 0326T)

93642 Electrophysiologic evaluation of single or dual chamber transvenous pacing defibrillator (includes defibrillation threshold evaluation, induction of arrhythmia, evaluation of sensing and pacing for arrhythmia termination, and programming or reprogramming of sensing or therapeutic parameters)

93644 Electrophysiologic evaluation of subcutaneous implantable defibrillator (includes defibrillation threshold evaluation, induction of arrhythmia, evaluation of sensing for arrhythmia termination, and programming or reprogramming of sensing or therapeutic parameters)

(Do not report 93644 in conjunction with 33270 at the time of subcutaneous implantable defibrillator device insertion)

(For subsequent electrophysiologic evaluation of a subcutaneous implantable defibrillator device, see 93260, 93261)

93650 Intracardiac catheter ablation of atrioventricular node function, atrioventricular conduction for creation of complete heart block, with or without temporary pacemaker placement

93653 Comprehensive electrophysiologic evaluation including insertion and repositioning of multiple electrode catheters with induction or attempted induction of an arrhythmia with right atrial pacing and recording, right ventricular pacing and recording (when necessary), and His recording (when necessary) with intracardiac catheter ablation of arrhythmogenic focus; with treatment of supraventricular tachycardia by ablation of fast or slow atrioventricular pathway, accessory atrioventricular connection, cavo-tricuspid isthmus or other single atrial focus or source of atrial re-entry.

(Do not report 93653 in conjunction with 93600-93603, 93610, 93612, 93618-93620, 93642, 93654, 93656)

▮ Separate Procedure	▮ Unlisted Procedure	▮ CCI Comp. Code	▮ Non-specific Procedure	**865**

93654 with treatment of ventricular tachycardia or focus of ventricular ectopy including intracardiac electrophysiologic 3D mapping, when performed, and left ventricular pacing and recording, when performed

(Do not report 93654 in conjunction with 93279-93284, 93286-93289, 93600-93603, 93609, 93610, 93612, 93613, 93618-93620, 93622, 93642, 93653, 93656)

+ 93655 Intracardiac catheter ablation of a discrete mechanism of arrhythmia which is distinct from the primary ablated mechanism, including repeat diagnostic maneuvers, to treat a spontaneous or induced arrhythmia (List separately in addition to code for primary procedure)

(Use 93655 in conjunction with 93653, 93654, 93656)

93656 Comprehensive electrophysiologic evaluation including transseptal catheterizations, insertion and repositioning of multiple electrode catheters with induction or attempted induction of an arrhythmia including left or right atrial pacing/recording when necessary, right ventricular pacing/recording when necessary, and His bundle recording when necessary with intracardiac catheter ablation of atrial fibrillation by pulmonary vein isolation

(Do not report 93656 in conjunction with 93279-93284, 93286-93289, 93462, 93600, 93602, 93603, 93610, 93612, 93618, 93619, 93620, 93621, 93653, 93654)

+ 93657 Additional linear or focal intracardiac catheter ablation of the left or right atrium for treatment of atrial fibrillation remaining after completion of pulmonary vein isolation (List separately in addition to code for primary procedure)

(Use 93657 in conjunction with 93656)

93660 Evaluation of cardiovascular function with tilt table evaluation, with continuous ECG monitoring and intermittent blood pressure monitoring, with or without pharmacological intervention

(For testing of autonomic nervous system function, see 95921, 95924, 95943)

+ 93662 Intracardiac echocardiography during therapeutic/diagnostic intervention, including imaging supervision and interpretation (List separately in addition to code for primary procedure)

(Use 93662 in conjunction with 92987, 93453, 93460-93462, 93532, 93580, 93581, 93620, 93621, 93622, 93653, 93654, 93656 as appropriate)

(Do not report 92961 in addition to 93662)

PERIPHERAL ARTERIAL DISEASE REHABILITATION

Peripheral Arterial Disease (PAD) rehabilitation is an outpatient service for patients diagnosed with peripheral artery disease—a disorder of the vessels of the legs or arms resulting in pain. PAD rehabilitation requires a physician's referral. The referring physician receives progress notes about his or her patient's progress in the program.

ehabilitation consists of a series of sessions involving physical exercise, using a motorized treadmill and various other pieces of exercise equipment to permit each patient to achieve symptom-limited claudication. Claudication is taken from the Latin word 'to limp' and refers to the pain that occurs in PAD patients when they exercise. A medically supervised walking program can improve the symptoms of claudication and lead to an enhanced quality of life. Each rehabilitation session lasts about 45 to 60 minutes and is supervised by an exercise physiologist or nurse. A patient's claudication threshold and other cardiovascular limitations are monitored and adjustments are made to the workload during the exercises.

During this supervised rehabilitation program, the development of new arrhythmias, symptoms that might suggest angina or the continued inability of the patient to progress to an adequate level of exercise may require review and examination of the patient by a physician or other qualified health care professional. These services would be separately reported with an appropriate E/M service code including office or other outpatient services (99201-99215), initial hospital care (99221-99223), subsequent hospital care (99231-99233), or crirical care services (99291-99292).

93668 Peripheral arterial disease (PAD) rehabilitation, per session

---

● New Code ▲ Revised Code + Add-On Code ⊘ Modifier -51 Exempt ★ Telemedicine

NONINVASIVE PHYSIOLOGIC STUDIES AND PROCEDURES

(For arterial cannulization and recording of direct arterial pressure, use 36620)

(For radiographic injection procedures, see 36000-36299)

(For vascular cannulization for hemodialysis, see 36800-36821)

(For chemotherapy for malignant disease, see 96409-96549)

(For penile plethysmography, use 54240)

93701 Bioimpedance-derived physiologic cardiovascular analysis

(For bioelectrical impedance analysis whole body composition, use 0358T. For left ventricular filling pressure indirect measurement by computerized calibration of the arterial waveform response to Valsalva, use 93799)

93702 Bioimpedance spectroscopy (BIS), extracellular fluid analysis for lymphedema assessment(s)

(For bioelectrical impedance analysis whole body composition, use 0358T)

(For bioimpedance-derived physiological cardiovascular analysis, use 93701)

93724 Electronic analysis of antitachycardia pacemaker system (includes electrocardiographic recording, programming of device, induction and termination of tachycardia via implanted pacemaker, and interpretation of recordings)

(For interrogation of dual lead pacemaker, see 93288, 93294. For programming of dual chamber pacemaker, use 93280)

(For interrogation of single lead pacemaker, see 93288, 93294. For programming of single lead pacemaker, use 93279)

93740 Temperature gradient studies

(For interrogation of single implantable defibrillator, see 93289, 93295. For programming of single implantable defibrillator, use 93282. For interrogation of wearable defibrillator, use 93292)

(For interrogation of dual implantable defibrillator, see 93289, 93295. For programming of dual implantable defibrillator, use 93283)

93745 Initial set-up and programming by a physician or other qualified health care professional of wearable cardioverter-defibrillator includes initial programming of system, establishing baseline electronic ECG, transmission of data to data repository, patient instruction in wearing system and patient reporting of problems or events

(Do not report 93745 in conjunction with 93282, 93292)

93750 Interrogation of ventricular assist device (VAD), in person, with physician or other qualified health care professional analysis of device parameters (eg, drivelines, alarms, power surges), review of device function (eg, flow and volume status, septum status, recovery), with programming, if performed, and report

(Do not report 93750 in conjunction with 33975, 33976, 33979, 33981-33983)

93770 Determination of venous pressure

(For central venous cannulization see 36555-36556, 36500)

93784 Ambulatory blood pressure monitoring, utilizing a system such as magnetic tape and/or computer disk, for 24 hours or longer; including recording, scanning analysis, interpretation and report

93786 recording only

93788 scanning analysis with report

93790   review with interpretation and report

HOME AND OUTPATIENT INTERNATIONAL NORMALIZED RATIO (INR) MONITORING SERVICES

Home and outpatient international normalized ratio (INR) monitoring services describe the management of warfarin therapy, including ordering, review, and interpretation of new INR test result(s), patient instructions, and dosage adjustments as needed.

If a significantly, separately identifiable evaluation and management (E/M) service is performed on the same day as 93792, the appropriate E/M service may be reported using modifier 25.

Do not report 93793 on the same day as an E/M service.

Do not report 93792, 93793 in conjunction with 98966, 98967, 98968, 98969, 99441, 99442, 99443, 99444, when telephone or online services address home and outpatient INR monitoring.

Do not report 93792, 93793 when performed during the service time of 99487, 99489, 99490, 99495, 99496.

● **93792**   Patient/caregiver training for initiation of home international normalized ratio (INR) monitoring under the direction of a physician or other qualified health care professional, face-to-face, including use and care of the INR monitor, obtaining blood sample, instructions for reporting home INR test results, and documentation of patient's/caregiver's ability to perform testing and report results

   (For provision of test materials and equipment for home INR monitoring, see 99070 or the appropriate supply code)

● **93793**   Anticoagulant management for a patient taking warfarin, must include review and interpretation of a new home, office, or lab international normalized ratio (INR) test result, patient instructions, dosage adjustment (as needed), and scheduling of additional test(s), when performed

   (Do not report 93793 in conjunction with 99201, 99202, 99203, 99204, 99205, 99211, 99212, 99213, 99214, 99215, 99241, 99242, 99243, 99244, 99245)

   (Report 93793 no more than once per day, regardless of the number of tests reviewed)

OTHER PROCEDURES

93797   Physician or other qualified health care professional services for outpatient cardiac rehabilitation; without continuous ECG monitoring (per session)

93798   with continuous ECG monitoring (per session)

93799   Unlisted cardiovascular service or procedure

NON-INVASIVE VASCULAR DIAGNOSTIC STUDIES

Vascular studies refers to diagnostic procedures performed to determine blood flow and/or the condition of arteries and/or veins. Vascular studies include patient care required to perform the studies, supervision of the studies and interpretation of the study results with copies for patient records of hard copy output with analysis of all data, including bi-directional vascular flow or imaging when provided.

The use of a simple hand-held or other Doppler device that does not produce hard copy output, or that produces a record that does not permit analysis of bi-directional vascular flow, is considered to be part of the physical examination of the vascular system and is not reported separately. To report unilateral non-invasive diagnostic studies, add modifier -52 to the basic code.

Coding Rules

1.   *Non-invasive vascular studies are usually performed in addition to evaluation and management service, such as a consultation or visit, and should be reported separately in addition to the evaluation and management service.*

2.   *All of the non-invasive vascular services fall under the Medicare Purchased Diagnostic Services guidelines; therefore, reporting should be as instructed by your local Medicare carrier.*

● New Code   ▲ Revised Code   ✛ Add-On Code   ⊘ Modifier -51 Exempt   ★ Telemedicine

The use of a simple hand-held or other Doppler device that does not produce hard copy output, or that produces a record that does not permit analysis of bidirectional vascular flow, is considered to be part of the physical examination of the vascular system and is not separately reported. The Ankle-Brachial Index (or ABI) is reportable with 93922 or 93923 as logn as simultaneous Doppler recording and analysis of bidirectional blood flow, volume plethysmography, or transcutaneous oxygen tension measurements are also performed.

Duplex scan (eg., 93880, 93882) describes an ultrasonic scanning procedure for characterizing the pattern and direction of blood flow in arteries or veins with the production of real-time images integrating B-mode two-dimensional vascular structure, Doppler spectral analysis and color flow Doppler imaging.

Physiologic studies: Noninvasive physiologic studies are performed using equipment separate and distinct from the duplex ultrasound imager. Codes 93922, 93923, 93924 describe the evaluation of non-imaging physiologic recordings of pressures with Doppler analysis of bi-directional blood flow, plethysmography, and/or oxygen tension measurements appropriate for the anatomic area studied.

CEREBROVASCULAR ARTERIAL STUDIES

A complete transcranial Doppler (TCD) study (93886) includes ultrasound evaluation of the right and left anterior circulation territories and the posterior circulation territory (to include vertebral arteries and basilar artery). In a limited TCD study (93888) there is ultrasound evaluation of two or fewer of these territories. For TCD, ultrasound evaluation is a reasonable and concerted attempt to identify arterial signals through an acoustic window.

Code 93895 includes the acquisition and storage of images of the common carotid arteries, carotid bulbs, and internal carotid arteries bilaterally with quantification of intima media thickness (common carotid artery mean and maximal values) and determination of presence of atherosclerotic plaque. When any of these elements are not obtained, use 0126T.

93880   Duplex scan of extracranial arteries; complete bilateral study

     (Do not report 93880 in conjunction with 93895, 0126T)

93882   unilateral or limited study

     (Do not report 93882 in conjunction with 93895, 0126T)

     (To report common carotid intima-media thickness (IMT) study for evaluation of atherosclerotic burden or coronary heart disease risk factor assessment, use Category III code 0126T)

93886   Transcranial Doppler study of the intracranial arteries; complete study

93888   limited study

93890   vasoreactivity study

93892   emboli detection without intravenous microbubble injection

93893   emboli detection with intravenous microbubble injection

93895   Quantitative carotid intima media thickness and carotid atheroma evaluation, bilateral

     (Do not report 93895 in conjunction with 93880, 93882, 0126T)

     (Do not report 93890-93893 in conjunction with 93888)

EXTREMITY ARTERIAL STUDIES (INCLUDING DIGITS)

93922   Limited bilateral non-invasive physiologic studies of upper or lower extremity arteries, (eg, for lower extremity: ankle/brachial indices at distal posterior tibial and anterior tibial/dorsalis pedis arteries plus bidirectional, Doppler waveform recording and analysis at 1-2 levels, or ankle/brachial indices at distal posterior tibial and anterior tibial/dorsalis pedis arteries plus volume plethysmography at 1-2 levels, or ankle/brachial indices at distal posterior tibial and anterior tibial/dorsalis pedis arteries with transcutaneous oxygen tension measurements at 1-2 levels)

(When only 1 arm or leg is available for study, report 93922 with modifier 52 for a unilateal study when recording 1-2 levels. Report 93922 when recording 3 or more levels or performing provocative functional maneuvers.)

(Report 93922 only once in the upper extremity(s) and/or once in the lower extremity(s). When both the upper and lower extremities are evaluated in the same setting, 93922 may be reported twice by adding modifier 59 to the second procedure)

(For transcutaneous oxyhemoglobin measurement in a lower extremity wound by near infrared spectroscopy, use 0493T)

(Do not report 93922 in conjunction with 0337T)

93923 Complete bilateral non-invasive physiologic studies of upper or lower extremity arteries, 3 or more levels (eg, for lower extremity: ankle/brachial indices at distal posterior tibial and anterior tibial/dorsalis pedis arteries plus segmental blood pressure measurements with bidirectional Doppler waveform recording and analysis, at 3 or more levels, or ankle/brachial indices at distal posterior tibial and anterior tibial/dorsalis pedis arteries plus segmental volume plethysmography at 3 or more levels, or ankle/brachial indices at distal posterior tibial and anterior tibial/dorsalis pedis arteries plus segmental transcutaneous oxygen tension measurements at 3 or more levels), or single level study—with provocative functional maneuvers (eg, measurements with postural provocative tests or measurements with reactive hyperemia)

(When only 1 arm or leg is available for study, report 93922 for a unilateral study when recording 3 or more levels or when performing provocative functional maneuvers.)

(Report 93923 only once in the upper extremity(s) and/or once in the lower extremity(s). When both the upper and lower extremities are evaluated in the same setting, 93923 may be reported twice by adding modifier 59 to the second procedure.)

(For transcutaneous oxyhemoglobin measurement in a lower extremity wound by near infrared spectroscopy, use 0286T)

(Do not report 93923 in conjunction with 0337T)

93924 Non-invasive physiologic studies of lower extremity arteries, at rest and following treadmill stress testing, (ie, bidirectional Doppler waveform or volume plethysmography recording and analysis at rest with ankle/brachial indices immediately after and at timed intervals following performance of a standardized protocol on a motorized treadmill plus recording of time of onset of claudication or other symptoms, maximal walking time, and time to recovery) complete bilateral study

(Do not report 93924 in conjunction with 93922, 93923)

93925 Duplex scan of lower extremity arteries or arterial bypass grafts; complete bilateral study

93926 unilateral or limited study

93930 Duplex scan of upper extremity arteries or arterial bypass grafts; complete bilateral study

93931 unilateral or limited study

EXTREMITY VENOUS STUDIES (INCLUDING DIGITS)

(93965 deketed 2016 [2017 edition]).

93970 Duplex scan of extremity veins including responses to compression and other maneuvers; complete bilateral study

93971 unilateral or limited study

(Do not report 93970, 93971 in conjunction with 36475, 37476, 36478, 36479)

● New Code ▲ Revised Code ✛ Add-On Code ⊘ Modifier -51 Exempt ★ Telemedicine

VISCERAL AND PENILE VASCULAR STUDIES

93975 Duplex scan of arterial inflow and venous outflow of abdominal, pelvic, scrotal contents and/or retroperitoneal organs; complete study

93976 limited study

93978 Duplex scan of aorta, inferior vena cava, iliac vasculature, or bypass grafts; complete study

93979 unilateral or limited study

(For ultrasound screening study for abdominal aortic aneurysm [AAA], real time with image documentation, use 76706)

93980 Duplex scan of arterial inflow and venous outflow of penile vessels; complete study

93981 follow-up or limited study

(**93982** deleted 2017 [2018 edition])

EXTREMITY ARTERIAL-VENOUS STUDIES

93990 Duplex scan of hemodialysis access (including arterial inflow, body of access and venous outflow)

(For measurement of hemodialysis access flow using indicator dilution methods, use 90940)

OTHER NONINVASIVE VASCULAR DIAGNOSTIC STUDIES

93998 Unlisted noninvasive vascular diagnostic study

PULMONARY

Pulmonary disease is concerned with diseases of the lungs and airways. The Pulmonologist diagnoses and treats pneumonia, cancer, pleurisy, asthma, occupational diseases, bronchitis, sleep disorders, emphysema, and other complex disorders of the lungs. Pulmonologists test lung functions in many ways, endoscope the bronchial airways and prescribe and monitor mechanical assistance to ventilation. Many pulmonary disease physicians are also expert in critical care.

Pulmonary services refer to diagnostic procedures performed to determine air flow, blood gases, and the condition of the lungs and respiratory system. Pulmonary services include the laboratory procedure(s), interpretation, and physician's services (except surgical and anesthesia services) unless otherwise stated. It is common for pulmonologists to provide interpretation services only, under contract to medical facilities.

CPT coding for pulmonary function tests includes both comprehensive and component codes to accommodate variation among pulmonary function laboratories. As a result of these code combinations, several issues are addressed in this policy section.

Alternate methods of reporting data obtained during a spirometry or other pulmonary function session cannot be separately reported. Specifically, the flow volume loop is an alternative method of calculating a standard spirometric parameter. The CPT code 94375 is included in standard spirometry (rest and exercise) studies.

When a physician who is in attendance for a pulmonary function study, obtains a limited history, and performs a limited examination referable specifically to the pulmonary function testing, separately coding for an evaluation and management service is not appropriate. If a significant, separately identifiable service is performed unrelated to the technical performance of the pulmonary function test, an evaluation and management service may be reported.

When multiple spirometric determinations are necessary (e.g. CPT code 94070) to complete the service described in the CPT code, only one unit of service is reported.

Complex pulmonary stress testing (e.g. CPT code 94621) is a comprehensive stress test with a number of component tests separately defined in the CPT code book. It is inappropriate to separately code venous access, EKG monitoring, spirometric parameters performed before, during and after exercise, oximetry, O2 consumption, CO2 production, rebreathing cardiac output calculations, etc., when performed as part of a complex pulmonary stress test. It is also inappropriate to bill for a cardiac stress test and the component codes used to perform a simple pulmonary stress test (CPT code 94620), when a complex pulmonary stress test is performed. If using a standard exercise protocol, serial electrocardiograms are obtained, and a separate report describing a cardiac stress test (professional component) is included in the medical record, the professional components for both a cardiac and pulmonary stress test may be reported. Modifier -59 should be reported with the secondary procedure. Both tests must satisfy the requirement for medical necessity. (Since a complex pulmonary stress test includes electrocardiographic recordings, the technical components for both the cardiac stress test and the pulmonary stress test should not be reported separately.)

VENTILATOR MANAGEMENT

94002   Ventilation assist and management, initiation of pressure or volume preset ventilators for assisted or controlled breathing; hospital inpatient/observation, initial day

94003   hospital inpatient/observation, each subsequent day

94004   nursing facility, per day

(Do not report 94002-94004 in conjunction with E/M services 99201-99499)

94005   Home ventilator management care plan oversight of a patient (patient not present) in home, domiciliary or rest home (eg, assisted living) requiring review of status, review of laboratories and other studies and revision of orders and respiratory care plan (as appropriate),within a calendar month, 30 min. or more

(Do not report 94005 in conjunction with 99339-99340, 99374-99378)

(Ventilator management care plan oversight is reported separately from home or domiciliary, rest home [eg., assisted living] services. A physician or other qualified health care professional may report 94005, when performed, including when a different Individual reports 99339, 99340, 99374-99378 for the same 30 days)

PULMONARY DIAGNOSTIC TESTING AND THERAPIES

Codes 94010-94799 include laboratory procedure(s) and interpretation of test results. If a separate identifiable E/M service is performed, the appropriate E/M service code (including new or established patient office or other outpatient services [99201-99215], office or other outpatient consultations [99241-99245], emergency department services [99281-99285], nursing facility services [99304-99318], domiciliary, rest home or custodial care services [99324-99337] and home services [99341-99350]) may be reported in addition to 94010-94799.

Spirometry (94010) measures expiratory airflow and volumes and forms the basis of most pulmonary function testing. When spirometry is performed before and after administration of a bronchodilator, report 94060. Measurement of vital capacity (94150) is a component of spirometry and is only reported when performed alone. The flow-volume loop (94375) is used to identify patterns of inspiratory and/or expiratory obstruction in central or peripheral airways. Spirometry (94010, 94060) includes maximal breathing capacity (94200) and flow-volume loop (94375), when performed.

Measurement of lung volumes may be performed using plethysmography, helium dilution, or nitrogen washout. Plethysmyography (94726) is utilized to determine total lung capacity, residual volume, functional residual capacity, and airway resistance. Nitrogen washout or heliu dilution (94727) may be used to measure lung volumes, distribution of ventilation and closing volume. Impulse oscillometry (94728) assesses airway resistance and may be reported in addition to gas dilution techniques. Spirometry (94010, 94060) and bronchial provocation (94070) are not included in 94726 and 94727 and may be reported separately.

Diffusing capacity (94729) is most commonly performed in conjunction with lung volumes or spirometry and is an add-on code to 94726-94728, 94010, 94060, 94070, and 94375.

Pulmonary function tests (94011-94013) are reported for measurements in infants and young children though 2 years of age.

Pulmonary function testing measurements are reported as actual values and as a percent of predicted values by age, gender, height and race.

Chest wall manipulation for the mobilization of secretions and improvement in lung function can be performed using manual (94667, 94668) or mechanical (94669) methods. Manual techniiques include cupping, percussing, and use of a hand-held vibration device. A mechanical technique is the application of an external vest or wrap that delivers mechanical oscillation.

● New Code   ▲ Revised Code   ✛ Add-On Code   ⊘ Modifier -51 Exempt   ★ Telemedicine

94010 Spirometry, including graphic record, total and timed vital capacity, expiratory flow rate measurement(s), with or without maximal voluntary ventilation

(Do not report 94010 in conjunction with 94150, 94200, 94375, 94728)

94011 Measurement of spirometric forced expiratory flows in an infant or child through 2 years of age

94012 Measurement of spirometric forced expiratory flows, before and after bronchodilator, in an infant or child through 2 years of age

94013 Measurement of lung volumes (ie, functional residual capacity [FRC], forced vital capacity [FVC], and expiratory reserve volume [ERV]) in an infant or child through 2 years of age

94014 Patient-initiated spirometric recording per 30-day period of time; includes reinforced education, transmission of spirometric tracing, data capture, analysis of transmitted data, periodic recalibration, and review and interpretation by a physician or other qualified health care professional

94015 recording (includes hook-up, reinforced education, data transmission, data capture, trend analysis, and periodic recalibration)

94016 review and interpretation only by a physician or other qualified health care professional

94060 Bronchodilation responsiveness, spirometry as in 94010, pre- and post-bronchodilator administration

(Do not report 94060 in conjunction with 94150, 94200, 94375, 94640, 94728)

(Report bronchodilator supply separately with 99070 or appropriate supply code)

(For exercise test for bronchospasm with pre- and postspirometry, use 94617)

94070 Bronchospasm provocation evaluation, multiple spirometric determinations as in 94010, with administered agents (eg, antigen(s), cold air, methacholine)

(Do not report 94070 in conjunction with 94640)

(Report antigen(s) administration separately with 99070 or appropriate supply code)

94150 Vital capacity, total (separate procedure)

(Do not report 94150 in conjunction with 94010, 94060, 94728. To report thoracic gas volumes, see 94726, 94727)

94200 Maximum breathing capacity, maximal voluntary ventilation

(Do not report 94200 in conjunction with 94010, 94060)

94250 Expired gas collection, quantitative, single procedure (separate procedure)

(Do not report 94250 in conjunction with 94621)

94375 Respiratory flow volume loop

(Do not report 94375 in conjunction with 94010, 94060)

94400 Breathing response to CO2 (CO2 response curve)

(Do not report 94400 in conjunction with 94640)

94450 Breathing response to hypoxia (hypoxia response curve)

(For high altitude simulation test (HAST), see 94452, 94453)

94452 High altitude simulation test (HAST), with interpretation and report by a physician or other qualified health care professional;

(For obtaining arterial blood gases, use 36600)

(Do not report 94452 in conjunction with 94453, 94760, 94761)

94453   with supplemental oxygen titration

(For obtaining arterial blood gases, use 36600)

(Do not report 94453 in conjunction with 94452, 94760, 94761)

⊘ **94610**   Intrapulmonary surfactant administration by a physician or other qualified health care professional through endotracheal tube

(Do not report 94610 in conjunction with 99468-99472)

(For endotracheal intubation, use 31500)

(Report 94610 once per dosing episode)

● **94617**   Exercise test for bronchospasm, including pre- and postspirometry, electrocardiographic recording(s), and pulse oximetry

● **94618**   Pulmonary stress testing (eg, 6-minute walk test), including measurement of heart rate, oximetry, and oxygen titration, when performed

(**94620**   deleted 2017 [2018 edition]. To report pulmonary stress testing, use 94618)

▲ **94621**   Cardiopulmonary exercise testing, including measurements of minute ventilation, CO2 production, O2 uptake, and electrocardiographic recordings

(Do not report 94617, 94621 in conjunction with 93000, 93005, 93010, 93040, 93041, 93042 for ECG monitoring performed during the same session)

(Do not report 94617, 94621 in conjunction with 93015, 93016, 93017, 93018)

(Do not report 94621 in conjunction with 94250, 94680, 94681, 94690)

(Do not report 94617, 94618, 94621 in conjunction with 94760, 94761)

94640   Pressurized or nonpressurized inhalation treatment for acute airway obstruction for therapeutic purposes and/or for diagnostic purposes such as sputum induction with an aerosol generator, nebulizer, metered dose inhaler or intermittent positive pressure breathing (IPPB) device

(Do not report 94640 in conjunction with 94060, 94070, or 94400)

(For more than one inhalation treatment performed on the same date, append modifier -76)

(For continuous inhalation treatment of 1 hour or more, see 94644, 94645)

94642   Aerosol inhalation of pentamidine for pneumocystis carinii pneumonia treatment or prophylaxis

94644   Continuous inhalation treatment with aerosol medication for acute airway obstruction; first hour

(For services of less than 1 hour, use 94640)

+ **94645**   each additional hour (List separately in addition to code for primary procedure)

(Use 94645 in conjunction with 94644)

94660   Continuous positive airway pressure ventilation (CPAP), initiation and management

94662   Continuous negative pressure ventilation (CNP), initiation and management

94664   Demonstration and/or evaluation of patient utilization of an aerosol generator, nebulizer, metered dose inhaler or IPPB device

(94664 can be reported one time only per day of service)

---

874   ● New Code   ▲ Revised Code   + Add-On Code   ⊘ Modifier -51 Exempt   ★ Telemedicine

94667 Manipulation chest wall, such as cupping, percussing, and vibration to facilitate lung function; initial demonstration and/or evaluation

94668 subsequent

94669 Mechanical chest wall oscillation to facilitate lung function, per session

94680 Oxygen uptake, expired gas analysis; rest and exercise, direct, simple

94681 including CO2 output, percentage oxygen extracted

94690 rest, indirect (separate procedure)

(For single arterial puncture, use 36600)

(Do not report 94680, 94681, 94690 in conjunction with 94621)

94726 Plethysmography for determination of lung volumes and, when performed, airway resistance

(Do not report 94726 in conjunction with 94727, 94728)

94727 Gas dilution or washout for determination of lung volumes and, when performed, distribution of ventilation and closing volumes

(Do not report 94727 in conjunction with 94726)

94728 Airway resistance by impulse oscillometry

(Do not report 94728 in conjunction with 94010, 94060, 94070, 94375, 94726)

+ **94729** Diffusing capacity (eg, carbon monoxide, membrane) (List separately in addition to code for primary procedure)

(Report 94729 in conjunction with 94010, 94060, 94070, 94375, 94726-94728)

94750 Pulmonary compliance study (eg, plethysmography, volume and pressure measurements)

94760 Noninvasive ear or pulse oximetry for oxygen saturation; single determination

(For blood gases, see 82803-82810)

94761 multiple determinations (eg, during exercise)

(Do not report 94760, 94761 in conjunction with 94617, 94618, 94621)

94762 by continuous overnight monitoring (separate procedure)

(For other in vivo laboratory procedures, see 88720-88741)

94770 Carbon dioxide, expired gas determination by infrared analyzer

(For bronchoscopy, see 31622-31654)

(For placement of flow directed catheter, use 93503)

(For venipuncture, use 36410)

(For central venous catheter placement, see 36555-36556)

(For arterial puncture, use 36600)

(For arterial catheterization, use 36620)

(For thoracentesis, use 32554, 32555)

(For phlebotomy, therapeutic, use 99195)

Separate Procedure   Unlisted Procedure   CCI Comp. Code   Non-specific Procedure   **875**

(For lung biopsy, needle, use 32405)

(For intubation, orotracheal or nasotracheal, use 31500)

94772   Circadian respiratory pattern recording (pediatric pneumogram), 12 to 24 hour continuous recording, infant

(Separate procedure codes for electromyograms, EEG, ECG, and recordings of respiration are excluded when 94772 is reported)

94774   Pediatric home apnea monitoring event recording including respiratory rate, pattern and heart rate per 30-day period of time; includes monitor attachment, download of data, review, interpretation, and preparation of a report by a physician or other qualified health care professional

(Do not report 94774 in conjunction with 94775-94777 during the same reporting period)

94775   monitor attachment only (includes hook-up, initiation of recording and disconnection)

94776   monitoring, download of information, receipt of transmission(s) and analyses by computer only

94777   review, interpretation and preparation of report only by a physician or other qualified health care professional

(When oxygen saturation monitoring is used in addition to heart rate and respiratory monitoring, it is not reported separately)

(Do not report 94774-94777 in conjunction with 93224-93272)

(Do not report apnea recording device separately)

(For sleep study, see 95805-95811)

94780   Car seat/bed testin for airway integrity, neonate, with continual nursing observation and continuous recording of pulse oximetry, heart rate and respiratory rate, with interpretation and report; 60 minutes

(Do not report 94780 for less than 60 minutes)

(Do not report 94780 in conjunction with 93040-93042, 94760, 94761, 99468-99472, 99477-99480)

+ **94781**   each additional full 30 minutes (List separately in addition to code for primary procedure)

(Use 94781 in conjunction with 94780)

94799   Unlisted pulmonary service or procedure

ALLERGY AND CLINICAL IMMUNOLOGY

Allergy and Immunology refers to diagnostic services performed to determine a patient's sensitivity to specific substances, the treatment of patients with allergens by the administration or allergenic extracts, and/or medical conference services.

The CPT coding system divides allergy and clinical immunology into testing and immunotherapy. Immunotherapy is divided into codes that include preparation of the antigen when it is administered at the same session and when it is prepared but delivered for immunotherapy by a different physician. Several specific issues are identified regarding allergy testing and immunotherapy.

If percutaneous or intracutaneous (intradermal)single test (CPT codes 95004 or 95024) and "sequential and incremental" tests (CPT codes 95010, 95015, or 95027) are performed on the same date of service, both the "sequential and incremental" test and single test codes may be reported if the tests are for different allergens or different dilutions of the same allergen. The unit of service to report is the number of separate tests. Do not report both a single test and a sequential and incremental test for the same dilution of an allergen. For example, if the single test for an antigen is positive and the provider proceeds to sequential and incremental tests with three additional different dilutions of the same antigen, the provider may report one unit of service for the single test code and three units of service for the sequential and incremental test code.

When photo patch tests (e.g. CPT code 95052) are performed (same antigen/same session) with patch or application tests, only the photo patch testing should be reported. Additionally, if photo testing is performed including application or patch testing, the

● New Code   ▲ Revised Code   + Add-On Code   ⊘ Modifier -51 Exempt   ★ Telemedicine

code for photo patch testing (CPT code 95052) is to be reported, not CPT code 95044 (patch or application tests) and CPT code 95056 (photo tests).

Evaluation and management codes reported with allergy testing or allergy immunotherapy are appropriate only if a significant, separately identifiable service is administered. Obtaining informed consent, is included in the immunotherapy. If E & M services are reported, medical documentation of the separately identifiable service should be in the medical record.

Allergy testing is not performed on the same day as allergy immunotherapy in standard medical practice. These codes should, therefore, not be reported together. Additionally, the testing becomes an integral part to rapid desensitization kits (CPT code 95180) and would therefore not be reported separately.

Do not report Evaluation and Management (E/M) services for test interpretation and report.

If a significant separately identifiable E/M service is performed, the appropriate E/M service code should be reported using modifier -25.

ALLERGY TESTING

(For allergy laboratory tests, see 86000-86999)

(For administration of medications [eg, epinephrine, steroidal agents, antihistamines] for therapy for severe or intractable allergic reaction, use 96372)

95004 Percutaneous tests (scratch, puncture, prick) with allergenic extracts, immediate type reaction, including test interpretation and report, specify number of tests

95012 Nitric oxide expired gas determination

95017 Allergy testing, any combination of percutaneous (scratch, puncture, prick) and intracutaneous (intradermal), sequential and incremental, with venoms, immediate type reaction, including test interpretation and report, specify number of tests

95018 Allergy testing, any combination of percutaneous (scratch, puncture, prick) and intracutaneous (intradermal), sequential and incremental, with drugs or biologicals, immediate type reaction, including test interpretation and report, specify number of tests

95024 Intracutaneous (intradermal) tests with allergenic extracts, immediate type reaction, including test interpretation and report, specify number of tests

95027 Intracutaneous (intradermal) tests, sequential and incremental, with allergenic extracts for airborne allergens, immediate type reaction, including test interpretation and report, specify number of tests

95028 Intracutaneous (intradermal) tests with allergenic extracts, delayed type reaction, including reading, specify number of tests

95044 Patch or application test(s) (specify number of tests)

95052 Photo patch test(s) (specify number of tests)

95056 Photo tests

95060 Ophthalmic mucous membrane tests

95065 Direct nasal mucous membrane test

95070 Inhalation bronchial challenge testing (not including necessary pulmonary function tests); with histamine, methacholine, or similar compounds

95071 with antigens or gases, specify

(For pulmonary function tests, see 94060, 94070)

INGESTION CHALLENGE TESTING

Codes 95076 and 95079 re used to report ingestion challenge testing. Report 95076 for initial 120 minutes of testing time (ie, not physician face-to-face time). Report 95079 for each additional 60 minutes of testing time (ie, not physician face-to-face time). For total testing time less than 61 minutes (eg, positive challenge resulting in cessation of testing), report and evaluation and management service, if appropriate. Patient assessment/monitoring activities for allergic reactin (eg, blood pressure testing, peak flow meter testing) are not separately reported. Intervention therapy (eg, injection of steroid or epinephrine) may be reported separately as appropriate.

For purposes of reporting testing times, if an E/M service is required, then testing time ends.

95076 Ingestion challenge test (sequential and incremental ingestion of test items, eg. food, drug or other substance); initial 120 minutes of testing

+ 95079 each additional 60 minutes of testing (List separately in addition to code for primary procedure

(Use 95079 in conjunction with 95076)

ALLERGEN IMMUNOTHERAPY

Allergen immunotherapy CPT codes include the professional services necessary for allergen immunotherapy. Evaluation and management service codes may be reported in addition to allergen immunotherapy if other identifiable services are provided at the same time.

Codes 95115-95199 include the professional services necessary for allergen immunotherapy. Office visit codes may be used in addition to allergen immunotherapy if other identifiable services are provided at that time.

95115 Professional services for allergen immunotherapy not including provision of allergenic extracts; single injection

95117 2 or more injections

95120 Professional services for allergen immunotherapy in the office or institution of the prescribing physician or other qualified health care professional, including provision of allergenic extract; single injection

95125 2 or more injections

95130 single stinging insect venom

95131 2 stinging insect venoms

95132 3 stinging insect venoms

95133 4 stinging insect venoms

95134 5 stinging insect venoms

95144 Professional services for the supervision of preparation and provision of antigens for allergen immunotherapy; single dose vials(s) (specify number of vials)

(A single dose vial contains a single dose of antigen administered in one injection)

95145 Professional services for the supervision of preparation and provision of antigens for allergen immunotherapy (specify number of doses); single stinging insect venom

95146 2 single stinging insect venoms

95147 3 single stinging insect venoms

95148 4 single stinging insect venoms

95149   5 single stinging insect venoms

95165   Professional services for the supervision of preparation and provision of antigens for allergen immunotherapy; single or multiple antigens (specify number of doses)

95170   whole body extract of biting insect or other arthropod (specify number of doses)

(For allergy immunotherapy reporting, a dose is the amount of antigen(s) administered in a single injection from a multiple dose vial)

95180   Rapid desensitization procedure, each hour (eg, insulin, penicillin, equine serum)

95199   Unlisted allergy/clinical immunologic service or procedure

(For skin testing of bacterial, viral, fungal extracts, see 86485-86580, 95028)

(For special reports on allergy patients, use 99080)

(For testing procedures such as radioallergosorbent testing (RAST), rat mast cell technique (RMCT), mast cell degranulation test (MCDT), lymphocytic transformation test (LTT), leukocyte histamine release (LHR), migration inhibitory factor test (MIF), transfer factor test (TFT), nitroblue tetrazolium dye test (NTD), see Immunology section in Pathology or use 95199)

ENDOCRINOLOGY

Codes 95249 and 95250 are used to report the service for subcutaneous interstitial sensor placement, hook-up of the sensor to the transmitter, calibration of continuous glucose monitoring (CGM) device, patient training on CGM device functions and management, removal of the interstitial sensor, and the print-out of captured data recordings. For the CGM device owned by the physician's or other qualified health care professional's office, use 95250 for the data capture occurring over a minimum period of 72 hours.

Code 95249 may be reported only once during the time that a patient owns a given data receiver, including the initial episode of data collection.

Code 95249 may not be reported for subsequent episodes of data collection, unless the patient obtains a new and/or different model of data receiver. Obtaining a new sensor and/or transmitter without a change in receiver may not be reported with 95249.

Code 95249 may not be reported unless the patient brings the data receiver in to the physician's or other qualified health care professional's office with the entire initial data collection procedure conducted in the physician's or other qualified health care professional's office.

95249   This code is out of order. See page 879.

▲ 95250   Ambulatory continuous glucose monitoring of interstitial tissue fluid via a subcutaneous sensor for a minimum of 72 hours; physician or other qualified health care professional (office) provided equipment, sensor placement, hook-up, calibration of monitor, patient training, removal of sensor, and printout of recording

(Do not report 95250 more than once per month)

(Do not report 95250 in conjunction with 99091, 0446T)

● 95249   patient-provided equipment, sensor placement, hookup, calibration of monitor, patient training, and printout of recording

(Do not report 95249 more than once for the duration that the patient owns the data receiver)

(Do not report 95249 in conjunction with 99091, 0446T)

▲ 95251   analysis, interpretation and report

(Do not report 95251 more than once per month)

(Do not report 95251 in conjunction with 99091)

NEUROLOGY AND NEUROMUSCULAR PROCEDURES

Neurology refers to the study and treatment of the nervous system. Neurology services are usually performed in conjunction with a medical consultation. The consultation should be reported separately using the appropriate evaluation and management consultation code.

Neurologic services are typically consultative, and any of the levels of consultation (99241-99255) may be appropriate.

The EEG, autonomic function, evoked potential, reflex tests, EMG, NCV, and MEG services (95812-95829 and 95860-95967) include recording, interpretation by a physician, and report. For interpretation only, use modifier 26. For EMG guidance, see 95873, 95874.

The CPT coding system defines codes for neuromuscular diagnostic or therapeutic services not requiring surgical procedures. Sleep testing, nerve and muscle testing and electroencephalographic procedures are included. The CPT code book guidelines regarding sleep testing are very precise and should be reviewed carefully before billing for these services.

Sleep testing differs from polysomnography in that the latter requires the presence of sleep staging. Sleep staging includes a qualitative and quantitative assessment of sleep as determined by standard sleep scoring techniques. Accordingly, at the same session, a "sleep study" and "polysomnography" are not reported together.

Polysomnography requires at least one central and usually several other EEG electrodes. EEG procurement for polysomnography (sleep staging) differs greatly from that required for diagnostic EEG testing (i.e. speed of paper, number of channels, etc.). Accordingly, EEG testing is not to be reported with polysomnography unless performed separately; the EEG tests, if rendered with a separate report, are to be reported with modifier -59, indicating that this represents a different session from the sleep study.

Continuous electroencephalographic monitoring services (CPT codes 95950- 95962) represent different services than those provided during sleep testing; accordingly these codes are only to be reported when a separately identifiable service is performed and documented. Additionally, billing standard EEG services would only be appropriate if a significant, separately identifiable service is provided. These codes are to be reported with modifier -59 to indicate that a different service is clearly documented.

When nerve testing (EMG, nerve conduction velocity, etc.) is performed to assess the level of paralysis during anesthesia or during mechanical ventilation, the series of CPT codes 95851-95937 are not to be separately reported; these codes reflect significant, separately identifiable diagnostic services requiring a formal report in the medical record. Additionally, electrical stimulation used to identify or locate nerves as part of a procedure involving treatment of a cranial or peripheral nerve (e.g. nerve block, nerve destruction, neuroplasty, transection, excision, repair, etc.) is part of the primary procedure.

Intraoperative neurophysiology testing (CPT code 95920) should not be reported by the physician performing an operative procedure since it is included in the global package. However, when performed by a different physician during the procedure, it is separately reportable by the second physician. The physician performing an operative procedure should not bill other 90000 neurophysiology testing codes for intraoperative neurophysiology testing since they are also included in the global package.

The NCCI edit with column one CPT code 95903 (Motor nerve conduction studies with F-wave study, each nerve) and column two CPT code 95900 (Motor nerve conduction studies without F-wave study, each nerve) is often bypassed by utilizing modifier -59. Use of modifier -59 with the column two CPT code 95900 of this NCCI edit is only appropriate if the two procedures are performed on different nerves or in separate patient encounters.

Neurologic services are typically consultative, and any of the levels of consultation (99241-99255) may be appropriate. In addition, services and skills outlined under Evaluation and Management levels of service appropriate to neurologic illnesses should be reported similarly.

The EEG, autonomic function, evoked potential, reflex tests, EMG, NCV, and MEG services (95812-95829 and 95860-95967) include recording, interpretation and report by a physician or other qualified health care professional. For interpretation only, use modifier 26. For EMG guidelines, see 95873, 95874.

Codes 95812-95822, 95950-95953 and 95956 use recording time as a basis for code use. Recording time is when the recording is underway and data is being collected. Recording time excludes set up and take down time. Codes 95961-95962 use physician or other qualified health care professional attendance time as a basis for code use.

(Do not report codes 95860-95875 in addition to 96000-96004)

● New Code   ▲ Revised Code   + Add-On Code   ⊘ Modifier -51 Exempt   ★ Telemedicine

SLEEP MEDICINE TESTING

Polysomnography includes sleep staging that is refined to include a 1-4 lead electroencephalogram (EEG), an electro-oculogram (EOG), and a submental electromyogram (EMG). For a study to be reported as polysomnography, sleep must be recorded and staged. Additional parameters of sleep include:

    Electrocardiogram (ECG)

    airflow

    ventilation and respiratory effort

    gas exchange by oximetry, transcutaneous monitoring, or end tidal gas analysis

    extremity muscle activity, motor activity-movement

    extended EEG monitoring

    penile tumescence

    gastroesophageal reflux

    continuous blood pressure monitoring

    snoring

    body positions, etc.

For a study to be reported as a polysomnogram:

    studies must be performed for 6 hours

    sleep must be recorded and staged

    an attendant must be present throughout the course of the study

Diagnostic testing is covered when a patient has the symptoms or complaints of one of the following conditions:

Narcolepsy - Narcolepsy is a neurologic disorder of unknown etiology characterized predominantly by abnormalities of REM, some abnormalities of NREM sleep and the presence of excessive daytime sleepiness often with involuntary daytime sleep episodes (e.g., while driving, in the middle of a meal, amnesiac episodes).

Sleep Apnea - Sleep Apnea is defined as a cessation of airflow for at least 10 seconds. These cessations of breathing may be due to either an occlusion of the airway (obstructive sleep apnea), absence of respiratory effort (central sleep apnea), or a combination of these factors (mixed sleep apnea).

Parasomnias - Parasomnias are a group of behavioral disorders during sleep that are associated with brief or partial arousals but not with marked sleep disruption or impaired daytime alertness. The presenting complaint is usually related to the behavior itself.

All sleep services (95800-95811) include recording, interpretation and report. (Report with modifier 52 if less than 6 hours of recording for 95800, 95801 and 95806, 95807, 95810, 95811; if less than 7 hours of recording for 95782, 95783, or if less than 4 nap opportunities are recorded for 95805).

    (Report with modifier 52 if less than 6 hours of recording or in other cases of reduced services as appropriate)

    (For unattended sleep study, use 95806)

95782   This code is out of order. See page 882.

95783   This code is out of order. See page 882.

95800   This code is out of order. See page 882.

95801   This code is out of order. See page 882.

95803   Actigraphy testing, recording, analysis, interpretation, and report (minimum of 72 hours to 14 consecutive days of recording)

    (Do not report 95803 more than once in any 14 day period)

    (Do not report 95803 in conjunction with 95806-95811)

95805   Multiple sleep latency or maintenance of wakefulness testing, recording, analysis and interpretation of physiological measurements of sleep during multiple trials to assess sleepiness

95806   Sleep study, unattended, simultaneous recording of heart rate, oxygen saturation, respiratory airflow and respiratory effort (eg, thoracoabdominal movement)

    (Do not report 95806 in conjunction with 93041-93227, 93228, 93229, 93268-93272, 95800, 95801)

    (For unattended sleep study that measures heart rate, oxygen saturation, respiratory analysis, and sleep time, use 95800)

    (For unattended sleep study that measures a minimum heart rate, oxygen saturation, and respiratory analysis, use 95801)

95800   Sleep study, unattended, simultaneous recording; heart rate, oxygen saturation, respiratory analysis (eg, by airflow or peripheral arterial tone), and sleep time

    (Do not report 95800 in conjunction with 93041-93227, 93228, 93229, 93268-93272, 95803, 95806, 95801)

    (For unattended sleep study that measures a minimum of heart rate, oxygen saturation, and respiratory analysis, use 95801)

95801   minimum of heart rate, oxygen saturation, and respiratory analysis (eg, by airflow or peripheral arterial tone)

    (Do not report 95801 in conjunction with 93041-93227, 93228, 93229, 93268-93272, 95806, 95800)

    (For unattended sleep study that measures heart rate, oxygen saturation, respiratory analysis, and sleep time, use 95800)

95807   Sleep study, simultaneous recording of ventilation, respiratory effort, ECG or heart rate, and oxygen saturation, attended by a technologist

95808   Polysomnography; any age, sleep staging with 1-3 additional parameters of sleep, attended by a technologist

95810   age 6 years or older, sleep staging with 4 or more additional parameters of sleep, attended by a technologist

95811   age 6 years or older, sleep staging with 4 or more additional parameters of sleep, with initiation of continuous positive airway pressure therapy or bilevel ventilation, attended by a technologist

95782   younger than 6 years, sleep staging with 4 or more additional parameters of sleep, attended by a technolgist

95783   younger than 6 years, sleep staging with 4 or more additional parameters of sleep, with initiation of continuous positive airway pressure therapy or bi-level ventilation, attended by a technologist

ROUTINE ELECTROENCEPHALOGRAPHY (EEG)

EEG codes 95812-95822 include hyperventilation and/or photic stimulation when appropriate. Routine EEG codes 95816-95822 include 20 to 40 minutes of recording. Extended EEG codes 95812-95813 include reporting times longer than 40 minutes.

95812   Electroencephalogram (EEG) extended monitoring; 41-60 minutes

    ● New Code   ▲ Revised Code   + Add-On Code   ⊘ Modifier -51 Exempt   ★ Telemedicine

95813   greater than 1 hour

95816   Electroencephalogram (EEG) including recording awake and drowsy

95819   including recording awake and asleep

95822   recording in coma or sleep only

95824   cerebral death evaluation only

95827   all night recording

       (For 24-hour EEG monitoring, see 95950-95953 or 95956)

       (For EEG during nonintracranial surgery, use 95955)

       (For Wada test, use 95958)

       (For digital analysis of EEG, use 95957)

95829   Electrocorticogram at surgery (separate procedure)

95830   Insertion by physician or other qualified health care professional of sphenoidal electrodes for electroencephalographic (EEG) recording

MUSCLE AND RANGE OF MOTION TESTING

95831   Muscle testing, manual (separate procedure) with report; extremity (excluding hand) or trunk

95832   hand, with or without comparison with normal side

95833   total evaluation of body, excluding hands

95834   total evaluation of body, including hands

95851   Range of motion measurements and report (separate procedure); each extremity (excluding hand) or each trunk section (spine)

95852   hand, with or without comparison with normal side

95857   Cholinesterase inhibitor challenge test for myasthenia gravis

ELECTROMYOGRAPHY

Needle electromyographic (EMG) procedures include the interpretation of electrical waveforms measured by equipment that produces both visible and audible components of electrical signals recorded from the muscle(s) studied by the needle electrode.

Use 95870 or 95885 when four or fewer muscles are tested in an extremity. Use 95860-95864 or 95886 when five or more muscles are tested in an extremity.

Use EMG codes (95860-95864 and 95867-95870) when no nerve conduction studies (95907-95913) are performed on that day. Use 95885, 95886 and 95887 for EMG services when nerve conduction studies (95907-95913) are performed in conjunction with EMG on the same day.

Report either 95885 or 95886 once per extremity. Codes 95885 and 95886 can be reported together up to a combined total of four units of service per patient when all four extremities are tested.

Report 95887 once per anatomic site (ie, cervical paraspinal muscle[s], thoracic paraspinal muscle[s], lumbar paraspinal muscle[s], chest wall muscle[s], and abdominal wall muscle[s]). Use 95887 for a unilateral study of the cranial nerve innervated muscles (excluding extra-ocular and larynx); when performed bilaterally, 95887 may be reported twice.

     ■ Separate Procedure   ■ Unlisted Procedure   ■ CCI Comp. Code   ■ Non-specific Procedure   **883**

Use 95887 when a study of the cervical paraspinal muscle(s) or the lumbar paraspinal muscle(s) is performed with no corresponding limb study (95885 or 95886) on the same day.

(For needle electromyography of anal or urethral sphincter, use 51785)

(For non-needle electromyography of anal or urethral sphincter, use 51784)

(For needle electromyography of larynx, use 95865)

(For needle electromyography of hemidiaphram, use 95866)

(For needle electromyography of extra-ocular muscles, use 92265)

95860 Needle electromyography; 1 extremity with or without related paraspinal areas

95861 2 extremities with or without related paraspinal areas

(For dynamic electromyography performed during motion analysis studies, see 96002-96003)

95863 3 extremities with or without related paraspinal areas

95864 4 extremities with or without related paraspinal areas

95865 larynx

(Do not report modifier 50 in conjunction with 95865)

(For unilateral procedure, report modifier 52 in conjunction with 95865)

95866 hemidiaphragm

95867 cranial nerve supplied muscle(s), unilateral

95868 cranial nerve supplied muscles, bilateral

95869 thoracic paraspinal muscles (excluding T1 or T12)

95870 limited study of muscles in 1 extremity or non-limb (axial) muscles (unilateral or bilateral), other than thoracic paraspinal, cranial nerve supplied muscles, or sphincters

(To report a complete study of the extremities, see 95860-95864)

(For anal or urethral sphincter, detrusor, urethra, perineum musculature, see 51785-51792)

(For eye muscles, use 92265)

95872 Needle electromyography using single fiber electrode, with quantitative measurement of jitter, blocking and/or fiber density, any/all sites of each muscle studied

+ **95885** Needle electromyography, each extremity, with related paraspinal areas, when performed, done with nerve conduction, amplitude and latency/velocity study; limited (List separately in addition to code for primary procedure)

+ **95886** complete, five or muscles studied, innervated by three or more nerves or four or more spinal levels (List separately in addition to code for primary procedure)

(Use 95885, 95886 in conjunction with 95907-95913)

(Do not report 95885, 95886 in conjunction with 95860-95864, 95870, 95905)

+ **95887** Needle electromyography, non-extremity (cranial nerve supplied or axial) muscle(s) done with nerve conduction, amplitude and latency/velocity study (List separately in addition to code for primary procedure)

(Use 95887 in conjunction with 95907-95913)

● New Code   ▲ Revised Code   ✛ Add-On Code   ⊘ Modifier -51 Exempt   ★ Telemedicine

(Do not report 95887 in conjunction with 95867-95870, 95905)

ISCHEMIC MUSCLE TESTING AND GUIDANCE FOR CHEMODENERVATION

+ **95873**   Electrical stimulation for guidance in conjunction with chemodenervation (List separately in addition to code for primary procedure)

(Do not report 95873 in conjunction with 64617, 95860-95870, 95874)

+ **95874**   Needle electromyography for guidance in conjunction with chemodenervation (List separately in addition to code for primary procedure)

(Use 95873, 95874 in conjunction with 64612, 64615, 64616, 64642, 64643, 64644, 64645, 64646, 64647)

(Do not report more than one guidance code for each corresponding chemodenervation code)

(Do not report 95874 in conjunction with 64617, 95860-95870, 95873)

95875   Ischemic limb exercise test with serial specimen(s) acquisition for muscle(s) metabolite(s)

95885   Code out of order. See page 884.

95886   Code out of order. See page 884.

95887   Code out of order. See page 884.

NERVE CONDUCTION TESTS

Codes 95907-95913 describe nerve conduction tests when performed with individually placed stimulating, recording, and ground electrodes.

For the purposes of coding, a single conduction study is defined as a sensory conduction test, a motor conduction test with or without a F wave test, or an H-reflex test. Each type of study (sensory, motor with or without F wave, or H-reflex) for each nerve includes all orthodromic and antidromic impulses associated with that nerve and constitutes a distinct study when determining the number of studies in each grouping (eg. 1-2 or 3-4 nerve conduction studies). Each type of nerve conduction study is counted only once when multiple sites on the same nerve are stimulated or recorded. The numbers of these separate tests should be added to determine which code to use. Use 95885-95887 in conjunction with 95907-95913 when performing eletromyography with nerve conduction studies.

Code 95905 describes nerve conduction tests when performed with preconfigured electrodes customized to a specific anatomic site.

⊘ **95905**   Motor and/or sensory nerve conduction, using preconfigured electrode array(s), amplitude and latency/velocity study, each limb, includes F wave study when performed, with interpretation and report

(Report 95905 only once per limb studied)

(Do not report 95905 in conjunction with 95885, 95886, 95907-95913)

95907   Nerve conduction studies; 1-2 studies

95908   3-4 studies

95909   5-6 studies

95910   7-8 studies

95911   9-10 studies

95912   11-12 studies

95913   13 or more studies

| | Separate Procedure | | Unlisted Procedure | | CCI Comp. Code | | Non-specific Procedure | **885** |

INTRAOPERATIVE NEUROPHYSIOLOGY

Codes 95940, 95941 describe ongoing neurophysiologic monitoring, testing, and data interpretation distinct from performance of specific type(s) of baseline neurophysiologic study(s) performed during surgical procedures. When the service is performed by a surgeon or anesthesiologist, the professional services are included in the surgeon's or anesthesiologist's primary service code(s) for the procedure and are not reported separately. Do not report these codes for automated monitoring devices that do not require continuous attendance by a professional qualified to interpret the testing and monitoring.

Recording and testing are performed either personally or by a technologist who is physically present with the patient during the service. Supervision is performed either in the operating room or by real time connection outside the operating room. The monitoring professional must be solely dedicated to performing the intraoperative neurophysiologic monitoring and must be available to intervene at all times during the service as necessary, for the reported time period(s). For any given period of time spent providing these services, the service takes full attention and therefore other clinical activities beyond providing and interpreting of monitoring cannot be provided during the same period.

Throughout the monitoring, there must be provisions for continuous and immediate communication directly with the operating room team in the surgical suite. One or more simultaneous cases may be reported (95941). When monitoring more than one procedure, there must be the immediate ability to transfer patient monitoring to another monitoring professional during the surgical procedure should that individual's exclusive attention be required for another procedure. Report 95941 for all remote or non-one-on-one monitoring time connected to each case regardless of overlap with other cases.

Codes 95940, 95941 include only the ongoing neurophysiologic monitoring time distinct from performance of specific type(s) of baseline neurophysiologic study(s) or other services such as intraoperative functional cortical or subcortical mapping. Codes 95940 and 95941 are reported based upon the time spent monitoring only, and not the number of baseline tests performed or parameters monitored. The time spent performing or interpreting the baseline neurophysiologic study(ies) should not be counted as intraoperative monitoring, but represents separately reportable procedures. When reporting 95940 and 95941, the same neurophysiologic study(ies) performed at baseline should be reported not more than once per operative session. Baseline study reporting is based upon the total unique studies performed. For example, if during the course of baseline testing and one-on-one monitoring, two separate nerves have motor testing performed in conjunction with limited single extremity EMG, then 95885 and 95907 would be reported in addition to 95940. Time spent monitoring (95940, 95941) excludes time to set up, record, and interpret the baseline studies, and to remove electrodes at the end of the procedure. To report time spent waiting on standby for a case to start, use 99360. For procedures that last beyond midnight, report services using the day on which the monitoring began and using the total time monitored.

Code 95940 is reported per 15 minutes of service. Code 95940 requires reporting only the portion of time the monitoring professional was physically present in the operating room providing one-on-one patient monitoring, and no other cases may be monitored at the same time. Time spent in the operating room is cumulative. To dtermine units of service of 95940, use the total minutes monitoring in the operating room one-on-one. Monitoring may begin prior to incision (eg, when positioning on the table is a time of risk). Report continuous intraoperative neurophysiologic monitoring in the operating room (95940) in addition to the services related to monitoring from outside the operating room (95941).

Code 95941 should be used once per hour even if multiple methods of neurophysiologic monitoring are used during the time. Code 95941 requires the monitoring of neurophysiological data that is collected from the operating room continuously on-line in real time via a secure data link. When reporting 95941, real-time ability must be available through sufficient data bandwidth transfer rates to view and interrogate the neurophysiologic data contemporaneously.

Report 95941 for all cases in which there was no physical presence by the monitoring professional in the operating room during the monitoring time or when monitoring more than one case in an operating room. It is also used to report the time of monitoring physically performed outside of the operating room in those cases where monitoring occurred both within and outside the operating room. Do not report 95941 if monitoring lasts 30 minutes or less.

Intraoperative neurophysiology monitoring codes 95940 and 95941 are each used to report the total duration of respective time spent providing each service, even if that time is not in a single continuous block.

+ 95940   Continuous intraoperative neurophysiology monitoring in the operating room, one on one monitoring requiring personal attendance, each 15 minutes (List separately in addition to code for primary procedure)

     (Use 95940 in conjunction with the study performed, 92585, 95822, 95860-95870, 95907-95913, 95925, 95926, 95927, 95928, 95929, 95930-95937, 95938, 95939)

+ 95941   Continuous intraoperative neurophysiology monitoring, from outside the operating room (remote or nearby) or for monitoring of more than one case while in the operating room, per hour (List separately in addition to code for primary procedure)

(Use 95941 in conjunction with the study performed, 92585, 95822, 95860-95870, 95907-95913, 95925, 95926, 95927, 95928, 95929, 95930-95937, 95938, 95939)

(For time spent waiting on standby before monitoring, use 99360)

(For electrocorticography, use 95829)

(For intraoperative EEG during nonintracranial surgery, use 95955)

(For intraoperative functional cortical or subcortical mapping, see 95961-95962)

(For intraoperative neurostimulator programming and analysis, see 95970-95975)

AUTONOMIC FUNCTION TESTS

The purpose of autonomic nervous sytem function testing is to determine the presence of autonomic dysfunction, the site of autonomic dysfunction, and the various autonomic subsystems that may be disordered.

Code 95921 should be reported only when electrocardiographic monitoring of heart rate derived from the time elapsing between two consecutive R waves in the electrocardiogram, or the R-R interval, is displayed on a monitor and stored for subsequent analysis of waveforms. Testing is typically performed in the prone position. A tilt table may be used, but is not required equipment for testing of the parasympathetic function. At least two of the following components need to be included in testing:

1. Heart rate response to deep breathing derived from a visual quantitative analysis of recording with subject breathing at a rate of 5-6 breaths per minute

2. Valsalva ratio determined by dividing the maximum heart rate by the lowest heart rate. The initial heart rate responses to sustained oral pressure (blowing into a tube with an open glottis) consist of tachycardia followed by a bradycardia at 15-45 seconds after the Valsalva pressure has been released. A minimum of two Valsalva maneuvers are to be performed. The initial cardioacceleration is an exercise reflex while the subsequent tachycardia and bradycardia are baroreflex-mediated.

3. A 30:15 ratio (R-R interval at beat 30)/(R-R interval at beat 15) used as an index of cardiovascular function.

Code 95922 should be reported only when all of the following components are included in testing:

1. Continuous recording of beat-to-beat BP and heart rate. The heart rate needs to be derived from an electrocardiogram (ECG) unit such that an accurate quantitative graphical measurement of the R-R interval is obtained.

2. A period of supine rest of at least 20 minutes prior to testing.

3. The performance and recording of beat-to-beat blood pressure and heart rate during a minimum of two (2) Valsalva maneuvers.

4. The performance of passive head-up tilt with continuous recording of beat-to-beat blood pressure and heart rate for a minimum of five minutes, followed by passive tilt-back to the supine position. This must be performed using a tilt table.

Code 95924 should be reported only when both the parasympathetic function and the adrenergic function are tested together with the use of a tilt table.

(To report autonomic function testing that does not include beat-to-beat recording or for testing without use of a tilt table, use 95943)

95921 Testing of autonomic nervous system function; cardiovagal innervation (parasympathetic function), including 2 or more of the following: heart rate response to deep breathing with recorded R-R interval, Valsalva ratio, and 30:15 ratio

95922 vasomotor adrenergic innervation (sympathetic adrenergic function), including beat-to-beat blood pressure and R-R interval changes during Valsalva maneuver and at least 5 minutes of passive tilt

(Do not report 95922 in conjunction with 95921)

95923 sudomotor, including 1 or more of the following: quantitative sudomotor axon reflex test (QSART), silastic sweat imprint, thermoregulatory sweat test, and changes in sympathetic skin potential

95924   combined parasympathetic and sympathetic adrenergic function testing with at least 5 minutes of passive tilt

(Do not report 95924 in conjunction with 95921 or 95922)

95943   Simultaneous, independent, quantitative measures of both parasympathetic function and sympathetic function, based on time-frequency analysis of heart rate variability concurrent with time-frequency analysis of continuous respiratory activity, with mean heart rate and blood pressure measures, during rest, paced (deep) breathing, Valsalva maneuvers, and head-up postural change

(Do not report 95943 in conjunction with 93040, 95921, 95922, 95924)

EVOKED POTENTIALS AND REFLEX TESTS

95925   Short-latency somatosensory evoked potential study, stimulation of any/all peripheral nerves or skin sites, recording from the central nervous system; in upper limbs

(Do not report 95925 in conjunction with 95926)

95926   in lower limbs

(Do not report 95926 in conjunction with 95925)

95938   in upper and lower limbs

(Do not report 95938 in conjunction with 95925, 95926)

95927   in the trunk or head

(To report a unilateral study, use modifier -52)

(For auditory evoked potentials, use 92585)

95928   Central motor evoked potential study (transcranial motor stimulation); upper limbs

(Do not report 95928 in conjunction with 95929)

95929   lower limbs

(Do not report 95929 in conjunction with 95928)

95939   in upper and lower limbs

(Do not report 95939 in conjunction with 95928, 95929)

▲ **95930**   Visual evoked potential (VEP) checkerboard or flash testing, central nervous system except glaucoma, with interpretation and report

(For visual evoked potential testing for glaucoma, use 0464T)

(For screening of visual acuity using automated visual evoked potential devices, use 0333T)

95933   Orbicularis oculi (blink) reflex, by electrodiagnostic testing

95937   Neuromuscular junction testing (repetitive stimulation, paired stimuli), each nerve, any 1 method

95938   Code out of order, See page 888.

95939   Code out of order. See page 888.

95940   Code out of order. See page 886.

95941   Code out of order. See page 886.

● New Code   ▲ Revised Code   + Add-On Code   ⊘ Modifier -51 Exempt   ★ Telemedicine

95943   Code out of order. See page 888.

SPECIAL EEG TESTS

Codes 95950-95953 and 95956 are used per 24 hours of recording. For recording more than 12 hours, do not use modifier 52. For recording 12 hours or less, use modifier 52. Codes 95951 and 95956 are used for recording in which interpretations can be made throughout the recording time, with interventions to alter or end the recording or to alter the patient care during the recordings as needed.

Codes 95961 and 95962 use physician or other qualified health care professional time as a basis for unit of service. Report 95961 for the first hour of attendance. Use modifier 52 with 95961 for 30 minutes or less. Report 95962 for each additional hour of attendance.

95950   Monitoring for identification and lateralization of cerebral seizure focus, electroencephalographic (eg, 8 channel EEG) recording and interpretation, each 24 hours

95951   Monitoring for localization of cerebral seizure focus by cable or radio, 16 or more channel telemetry, combined electroencephalographic (EEG) and video recording and interpretation (eg, for presurgical localization), each 24 hours

95953   Monitoring for localization of cerebral seizure focus by computerized portable 16 or more channel EEG, electroencephalographic (EEG) recording and interpretation, each 24 hours, unattended

95954   Pharmacological or physical activation requiring physician or other qualified health care professional attendance during EEG recording of activation phase (eg, thiopental activation test)

95955   Electroencephalogram (EEG) during nonintracranial surgery (eg, carotid surgery)

95956   Monitoring for localization of cerebral seizure focus by cable or radio,16 or more channel telemetry, electroencephalographic (EEG) recording and interpretation, each 24 hours, attended by a technologist or nurse

95957   Digital analysis of electroencephalogram (EEG) (eg, for epileptic spike analysis)

95958   Wada activation test for hemispheric function, including electroencephalographic (EEG) monitoring

95961   Functional cortical and subcortical mapping by stimulation and/or recording of electrodes on brain surface, or of depth electrodes, to provoke seizures or identify vital brain structures; initial hour of attendance by a physician or other qualified health care professional

+ **95962**   each additional hour of attendance by a physician or other qualified health care professional (List separately in addition to code for primary procedure)

(Use 95962 in conjunction with code 95961)

95965   Magnetoencephalography (MEG), recording and analysis; for spontaneous brain magnetic activity (eg, epileptic cerebral cortex localization)

95966   for evoked magnetic fields, single modality (eg, sensory, motor, language, or visual cortex localization)

+ **95967**   for evoked magnetic fields, each additional modality (eg, sensory, motor, language, or visual cortex localization) (List separately in addition to code for primary procedure)

(Use 95967 in conjunction with code 95966)

(For electroencephalography performed in addition to magnetoencephalography, see 95812-95827)

(For somatosensory evoked potentials, auditory evoked potentials, and visual evoked potentials performed in addition to magnetic evoked field responses, see 92585, 95925, 95926, and/or 95930)

(For computerized tomography performed in addition to magnetoencephalography, see 70450-70470, 70496)

(For magnetic resonance imaging performed in addition to magnetoencephalography, see 70551-70553)

NEUROSTIMULATORS, ANALYSIS-PROGRAMMING

Simple intraoperative or subsequent programming of the neurostimulator pulse generator/transmitter (95971) includes changes to three or fewer of the following parameters: rate, pulse amplitude, pulse duration, pulse frequency, eight or more electrode contacts, cycling, stimulation train duration, train spacing, number of programs, number of channels, alternating electrode polarities, dose time (stimulation parameters changing in time periods of minutes including dose lockout times), more than one clinical feature (eg., rigidity, dyskinesia, tremor). Complex intraoperative or subsequent programming (95972-95979) includes changes to more than three of the above.

Code 95970 describes subsequent electronic analysis of a previously implanted simple or complex brain, spinal cord, or peripheral neurostimulator pulse generator system, without reprogramming. Code 95971 describes intraoperative or subsequent electronic analysis of an implanted simple spinal cord, or peripheral (ie, peripheral nerve, autonomic nerve, neuromuscular) neurostimulator pulse generator system, with programming. Code 95972 describes intraoperative (at initial insertion/revision) or subsequent electronic analysis of an implanted complex spinal cord or peripheral (except cranial nerve) neurostimulator pulse generator system, with programming. Codes 95974 and 95975 describe intraoperative (at initial insertion/revision) or subsequent electronic analysis of an implanted complex cranial nerve neurostimulator pulse generator system, with programming. Codes 95978 and 95979 describe initial or subsequent electronic analysis of an implanted brain neurostimulator pulse generator system, with programming

Code 95980 describes intraoperative electronic analysis of an implanted gastric neurostimulator pulse generator system, with programming. Code 95981 describes subsequent analysis of the device; code 95982 describes subsequent analysis and re-programming. For electronic analysis and reprogramming of gastric neurostimulator, lesser curvature, see 95980-95982.

For 95974 and 95978, use modifier 52 if less than 31 minutes in duration.

> (For electronic analysis and reprogramming of a peripheral subcutaneous field stimulation pulse generator, use 0285T)
>
> (For insertion of neurostimulator pulse generator, see 61885, 63685, 64590)
>
> (For revision or removal of neurostimulator pulse generator or receiver, see 61888, 63688, 64595)
>
> (For implantation of neurostimulator electrodes, see 43647, 43881, 61850-61870, 63650-63655, 64553-64580. For revision or removal of neurostimulator electrodes, see 43648, 43882, 61880, 63661-63664, 64585)

95970 Electronic analysis of implanted neurostimulator pulse generator system (eg, rate, pulse amplitude, pulse duration, configuration of wave form, battery status, electrode selectability, output modulation, cycling, impedance and patient compliance measurements); simple or complex brain, spinal cord, or peripheral (ie, cranial nerve, peripheral nerve, sacral nerve, neuromuscular) neurostimulator pulse generator/transmitter, without reprogramming

95971 simple spinal cord, or peripheral (ie, peripheral nerve, sacral nerve, neuromuscular) neurostimulator pulse generator/transmitter, with intraoperative or subsequent programming

95972 complex spinal cord, or peripheral (ie, peripheral nerve, sacral nerve, neuromuscular) (except cranial nerve) neurostimulator pulse generator/transmitter, with intraoperative or subsequent programming

(**95973** deleted 2015 [2016 edition])

95974 complex cranial nerve neurostimulator pulse generator/transmitter, with intraoperative or subsequent programming, with or without nerve interface testing, first hour

+ **95975** complex cranial nerve neurostimulator pulse generator/transmitter, with intraoperative or subsequent programming, each additional 30 minutes after first hour (List separately in addition to code for primary procedure)

> (Use 95975 in conjunction with code 95974)

95978 Electronic analysis of implanted neurostimulator pulse generator system (eg, rate, pulse amplitude and duration, battery status, electrode selectability and polarity, impedance and patient compliance

---

● New Code ▲ Revised Code + Add-On Code ⊘ Modifier -51 Exempt ★ Telemedicine

measurements), complex deep brain neurostimulator pulse generator/transmitter, with initial or subsequent programming; first hour

+ **95979**   each additional 30 minutes after first hour (List separately in addition to code for primary procedure)

(Use 95979 in conjunction with 95978)

95980   Electronic analysis of implanted neurostimulator pulse generator system (eg, rate, pulse amplitude and duration, configuration of wave form, battery status, electrode selectability, output modulation, cycling, impedance and patient measurement(s) gastric neurostimulator pulse generator/transmitter; intraoperative, with programming

95981   subsequent, without reprogramming

95982   subsequent, with reprogramming

(For intraoperative or subsequent analysis, with programming, when performed, of vagus nerve trunk stimulator used for blocking therapy [morbid obesity], see 0312T, 0317T)

OTHER PROCEDURES

95990   Refilling and maintenance of implantable pump or reservoir for drug delivery, spinal (intrathecal, epidural) or brain (intraventricular), includes electronic analysis of pump, when performed;

95991   requiring skill of a physician or other qualified health care professional

(Do not report 95990, 95991 in conjunction with 62367-62370. For analysis and/or reprogramming of implantable infusion pump, see 62367-62370)

(For refill and maintenance of implanted infusion pump or reservoir for systemic drug therapy [eg, chemotherapy] use 96522)

⊘ **95992**   Canalith repositioning procedure(s) (eg, Epley maneuver, Semont maneuver), per day

(Do not report 95992 in conjunction with 92531, 92532)

95999   Unlisted neurological or neuromuscular diagnostic procedure

MOTION ANALYSIS

Codes 96000-96004 describe services performed as part of a major therapeutic or diagnostic decision making process. Motion analysis is performed in a dedicated motion analysis laboratory (ie., facility capable of performing videotaping from the front, back and both sides, computerized 3D kinematics, 3D kinetics, and dynamic electromyography). Code 96000 may include 3D kinetics and stride characteristics. Codes 96002-96003 describe dynamic electromyography.

Code 96004 should only be reported once regardless of the number of studies reviewed/interpreted.

(For performance of needle electromyography procedures, see 95860-95870, 95872, 95885-95887)

(For gait training, use 97116)

96000   Comprehensive computer-based motion analysis by video-taping and 3-D kinematics;

96001   with dynamic plantar pressure measurements during walking

96002   Dynamic surface electromyography, during walking or other functional activities, 1-12 muscles

96003   Dynamic fine wire electromyography, during walking or other functional activities, 1 muscle

(Do not report 96002, 96003 in conjunction with 95860-95866, 95869-95872, 95885-95887)

96004   Review and interpretation by physician or other qualified health care professional of comprehensive computer-based motion analysis, dynamic plantar pressure measurements, dynamic surface

---

     Separate Procedure   Unlisted Procedure   CCI Comp. Code   Non-specific Procedure   **891**

electromyography during walking or other functional activities, and dynamic fine wire electromyography, with written report

FUNCTIONAL BRAIN MAPPING

Code 96020 includes selection and administration of testing of language, memory, cognition, movement, sensation, and other neurological functions when conducted in association with functional neuroimaging, monitoring of performance of this testing, and determination of validity of neurofunctional testing relative to separately interpreted functional magnetic resonance images.

96020 Neurofunctional testing selection and administration during noninvasive imaging functional brain mapping, with test administered entirely by a physician or other qualified health care professional (ie, psychologist), with review of test results and report

(For functional magnetic resonance imaging [fMRI], brain, use 70555)

(Do not report 96020 in conjunction with 96101-96103, 96116-96120)

(Do not report 96020 in conjunction with 70554)

(Evaluation and Management services codes should not be reported on the same day as 96020)

MEDICAL GENETICS AND GENETIC COUNSELING SERVICES

These sevices are provided by trained genetic counselors and may include obtaining a structured family genetic history, pedigree construction, analysis for genetic risk assessment, and counseling of the patient and family. These activities may be provided during one or more sessions and may include review of medical data and family information, face-to-face interviews, and counseling services.

Code 96040 is reported for each 30-minute increment of face-to-face time. Do not report 96040 for 15 minutes or less of face-to-face time. Report 96040 once for 16 to 30 minutes of face-to-face time.

★ **96040** Medical genetics and genetic counseling services, each 30 minutes face-to-face with patient/family

(For genetic counseling and education provided to an individual by a physician or other qualified health care professional who may report E/M services, see the appropriate E/M codes)

(For genetic counseling and education provided to a group by a physician or other qualified health care professional, use 99078)

(For education regarding genetic risks by a nonphysician to a group, see 98961, 98962)

(For genetic counseling and/or risk factor reduction intervention provided to patient(s) without symptoms or established disease, by a physician or other qualified health care professional who may report evaluation and management services, see 99401-99412)

CENTRAL NERVOUS SYSTEM ASSESSMENTS/TESTS (eg, NEURO-COGNITIVE, MENTAL STATUS, SPEECH TESTING)

The following codes are used to report the services provided during testing of the cognitive function of the central nervous system. The testing of cognitive processes, visual motor responses, and abstractive abilities is accomplished by the combination of several types of testing procedures. It is expected that the administration of these tests will generate material that will be formulated into a report. A minimum of 31 minutes must be provided to report any per hour code. Services 96101, 96116, 96118, and 96125 report time as face-to-face time with the patient and the time spent interpreting and preparing the report.

(For development of cognitive skills, see 97127, 97533)

(For dementia screens, [eg, Folstein Mini-Mental State Examination, by a physician or other qualified health care professional], see Evaluation and Management services codes)

(Do not report 96101-96125 in conjunction with 0364T, 0365T, 0366T, 0367T, 0373T, 0374T)

96101 Psychological testing (includes psychodiagnostic assessment of emotionality, intellectual abilities, personality and psychopathology, eg, MMPI, Rorschach, WAIS), per hour of the psychologist's or physician's time, both face-to-face time administering tests to the patient and time interpreting test results and preparing the report

(96101 is also used in those circumstances when additional time is necessary to integrate other sources of clinical data, including previously completed and reported technician- and computer-administered tests)

(Do not report 96101 for the interpretation and report of 96102, 96103)

96102 Psychological testing (includes psychodiagnostic assessment of emotionality, intellectual abilities, personality and psychopathology, eg, MMPI and WAIS), with qualified health care professional interpretation and report, administered by technician, per hour of technician time, face-to-face

96103 Psychological testing (includes psychodiagnostic assessment of emotionality, intellectual abilities, personality and psychopathology, eg, MMPI), administered by a computer, with qualified health care professional interpretation and report

96105 Assessment of aphasia (includes assessment of expressive and receptive speech and language function, language comprehension, speech production ability, reading, spelling, writing, eg, by Boston Diagnostic Aphasia Examination) with interpretation and report, per hour

96110 Developmental screening (eg., developmental milestone survey, speech and language delay screen), with scoring adn documentation, per standardized instrument

(For an emotional/behavioral assessment, use 96127)

96111 Developmental testing, (includes assessment of motor, language, social, adaptive and/or cognitive functioning by standardized developmental instruments) with interpretation and report

★ **96116** Neurobehavioral status exam (clinical assessment of thinking, reasoning and judgment, eg, acquired knowledge, attention, language, memory, planning and problem solving, and visual spatial abilities), per hour of the psychologist's or physician's time, both face-to-face time with the patient and time interpreting test results and preparing the report

96118 Neuropsychological testing (eg, Halstead-Reitan Neuropsychological Battery, Wechsler Memory Scales and Wisconsin Card Sorting Test), per hour of the psychologist's or physician's time, both face-to-face time administering tests to the patient and time interpreting these test results and preparing the report

(96118 is also used in those circumstances when additional time is necessary to integrate other sources of clinical data, including previously completed and reported technician- and computer-administered tests)

(Do not report 96118 for the interpretation and report of 96119 or 96120)

96119 Neuropsychological testing (eg, Halstead-Reitan Neuropsychological Battery, Wechsler Memory Scales and Wisconsin Card Sorting Test), with qualified health care professional interpretation and report, administered by technician, per hour of technician time, face-to-face

96120 Neuropsychological testing (eg, Wisconsin Card Sorting Test), administered by a computer, with qualified health care professional interpretation and report

96125 Standardized cognitive performance testing (eg, Ross Information Processing Assessment) per hour of a qualified health care professional's time, both face-to-face time administering tests to the patient and time interpreting these test results and preparing the report

(For psychological and neuropsychological testing by a physician or psychologist, see 96101-96103, 96118-96120)

96127 Brief emotional/behavioral assessment (eg, depression inventory, attention-deficit/hyperactivity disorder [adhd] scale), with scoring and documentation, per standardized instrument

(For developmental screening, use 96110)

HEALTH AND BEHAVIOR ASSESSMENT/ INTERVENTION

Codes 96150-96155 describe services offered to patients who present with primary physical illnesses, diagnoses, or symptoms and may benefit from assessments and interventions that focus on the biopsychosocial factors related to the patient's health status. These services do not represent preventive medicine counseling and risk factor reduction interventions.

For patients that require psychiatric services (90801-90899) as well as health and behavior assessment/intervention (96150-96155), report the predominant service performed. Do not report 96150-96155 in conjunction with 90801-90899 on the same date.

Evaluation and Management services codes (including Counseling Risk Factor Reduction and Behavior Change Intervention [99401-99412]), should not be reported on the same day.

> (For health and behavior assessment and/or intervention performed by a physician or other qualified health care professional who may report evaluation and management services, see Evaluation and Management or Preventive Medicine services codes)

> (Do not report 96150, 96151, 96152, 96153, 96154, 96155 in conjunction with 0364T, 0365T, 0366T, 0367T, 0373T, 0374T)

★ **96150** Health and behavior assessment (eg, health-focused clinical interview, behavioral observations, psychophysicological monitoring, health-oriented questionnaires), each 15 minutes face-to-face with the patient; intial assessment

★ **96151** re-assessment

★ **96152** Health and behavior intervention, each 15 minutes, face-to-face; individual

★ **96153** group (2 or more patients)

★ **96154** family (with the patient present)

96155 family (without the patient present)

96160 Administration of patient-focused health risk assessment instrument (eg, health hazard appraisal) with scoring and documentation, per standardized instrument

96161 Administration of caregiver-focused health risk assessment instrument (eg, depression inventory) for the benefit of the patient, with scoring and documentation, per standardized instrument

HYDRATION, THERAPEUTIC, PROPHYLACTIC, DIAGNOSTIC INJECTIONS AND INFUSIONS, AND CHEMOTHERAPY AND OTHER HIGHLY COMPLEX DRUG OR HIGHLY COMPLEX BIOLOGIC ADMINISTRATION

Coding Rules

1. *If a significant E/M service is performed, report the E/M service code with modifier -25 in addition to the infusion/injection codes.*

2. *Local anesthesia, IV start, access to indwelling IV, subcutaneous catheter or port, fFlush at the conclusion of infusion and standard tubing, syringes and supplies are included and not reported separately if performed to facilitate the infusion/injection.*

3. *When multiple drugs are administered, the service(s) and specific drugs or materials for each are reported.*

4. *When administering multiple infusions, injections or combinations, report only one "initial" service code unless two IV sites must be used.*

5. *When reported by the physician, report the "initial" code that best describes the primary reason for the encounter regardless of the order in which the infusions or injections are administered.*

6. *When reported by the facility, the "initial" code should reported in the order of chemotherapy services, followed by therapeutic/prophylactic/diagnostic services, followed by hydrationi services, followed by infusions, followed by pushes, and finally injections.*

Physician or other qualified health care professional work related to hydration, injection, and infusion services predominantly involves affirmation of treatment plan and direct supervision of staff.

Codes 96360-96379, 96401, 96402, 96409-96425, 96521-96523 are not intended to be reported by the physician in the facility setting. If a significant, separately identifiable office or other outpatient E/M service is performed, the appropriate E/M service (99201-99215, 99241-99245, 99354-99355) should be reported using modifier 25 in addition to 96360-96549. For same day E/M service, a different diagnosis is not required.

If performed to facilitate the infusion or injection, the following services are included and are not reported separately:

a. Use of local anesthesia

b. IV start

c. Access to indwelling IV, subcutaneous catheter or port

d. Flush at conclusion of infusion

e. Standard tubing, syringes, and supplies

   (For declotting a catheter or port, use 36593)

When multiple drugs are administered, report the service(s) and the specific materials or drugs for each.

When administering multiple infusions, injections or combinations, only one "initial" service code should be reported for a given date, unless protocol requires that two separate IV sites must be used. Do not report a second initial service on the same date due to an intravenous line requiring a re-start, an IV rate not being able to be reached without two lines, or for accessing a port of a nulti-lumen catheter. If an injection or infusion is of a subsequent or concurrent nature, even if it is the first such service within that group of services, then a subsequent or concurrent code from the appropriate section should be reported (eg., the first IV push given subsequent to an initial one-hour infusion is reported using a subsequent IV push code).

In order to determine which service should be reported as the initial service when there is more than one type of service, hierarchies have been created. These vary by whether they physician or other qualified health care professional or a facility is reporting. The order of selection for reporting is based upon the physician's or other qualified health care professional's knowledge of the clinical condition(s) and treatment(s). The hierarchy that facilities are to use is based upon a structural algorithm. When these codes are reported by the physician or other qualified health care professional, the "initial" code that best describes the key or primary reason for the encounter should always be reported irrespective of the order in which the infusions or injections occur.

When these codes are reported *by the facility,* the following instructions apply: The initial code should be selected using a hierarchy whereby chemotherapy services are primary to therapeutic, prophylactic, and diagnostic services which are primary to hydration services. Infusions are primary to pushes, which are primary to injections. This hierarchy is to be followed by facilities and supersedes parenthetical instructions for add-on codes that suggest an add-on of a higher hierarchical position may be reported in conjunction with a base code of a lower position. (For example, the hierarchy would not permit reporting 96376 with 96360, as 96376 is a higher order code. IV push is primary to hydration.)

When reporting multiple infusions of the same drug/substance on the same date of service, the initial code should be selected. The second and subsequent infusion(s) should be reported based on the individual time(s) of each additional infusion(s) of the same drug/substances using the appropriate add-on code.

When reporting codes for which infusion time is a factor, use the actual time over which the infusion is administered. Intravenous or intra-arterial push is defined as: (a) an injection in which the individual who administers the drug/substance is continuously present to administer the injection and observe the patient; or (b) an infusion of 15 minutes or less. If intravenous hydration (96360, 96361) is given from 11 p.m. to 2 a.m., 96360 would be reported once and 96361 twice. For continuous services that last beyond midnight, use the date in which the service began and report the total units of time provided continuously. However, if instead of a continuous infusion, a medication was given by intravenous push at 10 pm and 2 am, as the service was not continuous, the two administrations would be reported as an initial service (96374) and sequential (96376) as: (1) no other infusion services were performed; and (2) the push of the same drug was performed more than 30 minutes beyond the initial administration. A "keep open" infusion of any type is not separately reported.

| | Separate Procedure | | Unlisted Procedure | | CCI Comp. Code | | Non-specific Procedure | **895** |

HYDRATION

Codes 96360-96361 are intended to report a hydration IV infusion to consist of a pre-packaged fluid and electrolytes (eg., normal saline, D5-1/2 normal saline + 30mEq KCl/liter), but are not used to report infusion of drugs or other substances. Hydration IV infusions typically require direct supervision for purposes of consent, safety oversight, or intraservice supervision of staff. Typically, such infusions require little special handling to prepare or dispose of, and staff that administer these do not typically require advanced practice training. After initial set-up, infusion typically entails little patient risk and thus little monitoring. These codes are not intended to be reported by the physician or other qualified health care profesional in the facility setting.

Some chemotherapeutic agents and other therapeutic agents require pre- and/or post-hydration to be given in order to avoid specific toxicities. A minimum time duration of 31 minutes of hydration infusion is required to report the service. However, the hydration codes 96360 or 96361 are not used when the purpose of the intravenous fluid is to "keep open" and IV line prior or subsequent to a therapeutic infusion, or as a free-flowing IV during chemotherapy or other therapeutic infusion.

96360 Intravenous infusion, hydration; initial, 31 minutes to 1 hour

(Do not report 96360 if performed as a concurrent infusion service)

(Do not report intravenous infusion for hydration of 30 minutes or less)

+ 96361   each additional hour (list separately in addition to code for primary procedure)

(Use 96361 in conjunction with 96360)

(Report 96361 for hydration infusion intervals of greater than 30 minutes beyond 1 hour increments)

(Report 96361 to identify hydration if provided as a secondary or subsequent service after a different initial service [96360, 96365, 96374, 96409, 96413] is administered through the same IV access)

THERAPEUTIC, PROPHYLACTIC, AND DIAGNOSTIC INJECTIONS AND INFUSIONS (EXCLUDES CHEMOTHERAPY AND OTHER HIGHLY COMPLEX DRUG OR HIGHLY COMPLEX BIOLOGIC AGENT ADMINISTRATION)

A therapeutic, prophylactic or diagnostic IV infusion or injection (other than hydration) is for the administration of substances/drugs. When fluids are used to administer the drug(s), the administration of the fluid is considered incidental hydration and is not separately reportable. These services typically require direct supervision for any or all purposes of patient assessment, provision of consent, safety oversight, and intra-service supervision of staff. Typically, such infusions require special consideration to prepare, dose or dispose of, require practice training and competency for staff who administer the infusions, and require periodic patient assessment with vital sign monitoring during the infusion. These codes are not intended to be reported by the physician or other qualified health care professional in the facility setting.

See codes 96401-96549 for the administration of chemotherapy or other highly complex drug or highly complex biologic agent services. These highly complex services require advanced practice training and competency for staff who provide these services; special considerations for preparation, dosage or disposal; and commonly, these services entail significant patient risk and frequent monitoring. Examples are frequent changes in the infusion rate, prolonged presence of nurse administering the solution for patient monitoring and infusion adjustments, and frequent conferring with the physician or other qualified health care profesisonal about these issues.

(Do not report 96365-96379 with codes for which IV push or infusion is an inherent part of the procedure [eg, administration of contrast material for a diagnostic imaging study])

96365 Intravenous infusion, for therapy, prophylaxis, or diagnosis (specify substance or drug); initial, up to 1 hour

+ 96366   each additional hour (list separately in addition to code for primary procedure)

(Report 96366 in conjunction with 96365, 96367)

(Report 96366 for additional hour[s] of sequential infusion)

(Report 96366 for infusion intervals of greater than 30 minutes beyond 1 hour increments)

(Report 96366 in conjunction with 96365 to identify each second and subsequent infusions of the same drug/substance)

● New Code   ▲ Revised Code   + Add-On Code   ⊘ Modifier -51 Exempt   ★ Telemedicine

+ **96367** additional sequential infusion of a new drug/substance, up to 1 hour (list separately in addition to code for primary procedure)

(Report 96367 in conjunction with 96365, 96374, 96409, 96413 to identify the infusion of a new drug/substance provided as a secondary or subsequent service after a different initial service is administered through the same IV access. Report 96367 only once per sequential infusion of same infusate mix)

+ **96368** concurrent infusion (list separately in addition to code for primary procedure)

(Report 96368 only once per date of service)

(Report 96368 in conjunction with 96365, 96366, 96413, 96415, 96416)

96369 Subcutaneous infusion for therapy or prophylaxis (specify substance or drug); initial, up to 1 hour, including pump set-up and establishment of subcutaneous infusion site(s)

(For infusions of 15 minutes or less, use 96372)

+ **96370** each additional hour (list separately in addition to code for primary procedure)

(Use 96370 in conjunction with 96369)

(Use 96370 for infusion intervals of greater than 30 minutes beyond 1 hour increments)

+ **96371** additional pump set-up with establishment of new subcutaneous infusion site(s) (list separately in addition to code for primary procedure)

(Use 96371 in conjunction with 96369)

(Use 96369, 96371 only once per encounter)

96372 Therapeutic, prophylactic, or diagnostic injection (specify substance or drug); subcutaneous or intramuscular

(For administration of vaccines/toxoids, see 90460, 90461, 90471, 90472)

(Report 96372 for non-antineoplastic hormonal therapy injections)

(Report 96401 for antineoplastic nonhormonal injection therapy)

(Report 96402 for antineoplastic hormonal injection therapy)

(Do not report 96372 for injections given without direct physician or other qualified health care professional supervision. To report, use 99211. Hospitals may report 96372 when the physician or other qualified health care professional is not present)

(96372 does not include injections for allergen immunotherapy. For allergen immunotherapy injections, see 95115-95117)

96373 intra-arterial

96374 intravenous push, single or initial substance/drug

+ **96375** each additional sequential intravenous push of a new substance/drug (list separately in addition to code for primary procedure)

(Use 96375 in conjunction with 96365, 96374, 96409, 96413)

(Report 96375 to identify intravenous push of a new substance/drug if provided as a secondary or subsequent service after a different initial sevice is administered through the same IV access)

+ **96376** each additional sequential intravenous push of the same substance/drug provided in a facility (list separately in addition to code for primary procedure)

(Do not report 96376 for a push performed within 30 minutes of a reported push of the same substance or drug)

(96376 may be reported by facilities only)

(Report 96376 in conjunction with 96365, 96374, 96409, 96413)

96377 Application of on-body injector (includes cannula insertion) for timed subcutaneous injection

96379 Unlisted therapeutic, prophylactic, or diagnostic intravenous or intra-arterial injection or infusion

(For allergy immunology, see 95004 et seq)

CHEMOTHERAPY AND OTHER HIGHLY COMPLEX DRUG OR HIGHLY COMPLEX BIOLOGIC AGENT ADMINISTRATION

Chemotherapy administration codes 96401-96549 apply to parenteral administration of non-radionuclide anti-neoplastic drugs; and also to anti-neoplastic agents provided for treatment of noncancer diagnoses (eg, cyclophosphamide for auto-immune conditions) or to substances such as certain monoclonal antibody agents, and other biologic response modifiers. The highly complex infusion of chemotherapy or other drug or biologic agents requires physician or other qualified health care professional work and/or clinical staff monitoring well beyond that of therapeutic drug agents (96360-96379) because the incidence of severe adverse patient reactions are typically greater. These services can be provided by any physician or other qualified health care professional. Chemotherapy services are typically highly complex and require direct supervision for any or all purposes of patient assessment, provision of consent, safety oversight, and intra-service supervision of staff. Typically, such chemotherapy services require advanced practice training and competency for staff who provide these services; special considerations for preparation, dosage, or disposal; and commonly, these services entail significant patient risk and frequent monitoring. Examples are frequent changes in the infusion rate, prolonged presence of the nurse administering the solution for patient monitoring and infusion adjustments, and frequent conferring with the physician or other qualified health care professional about these issues. When performed to facilitate the infusion of injection, preparation of chemotherapy agent(s), highly complex agent(s), or other highly complex drug is included and is not reported separately. To report infusions that do not require this level of complexity, see 96360-96379. Codes 96401-96402, 96409-96425, 96521-96523 are not intended to be reported by the physician or other qualified health care professional in the facility setting.

The term "chemotherapy" in 96401-96549 includes other highly complex drugs or highly complex biologic agents.

Report separate codes for each parenteral method of administration employed when chemotherapy is administered by different techniques. The administration of medications (eg., antibiotics, steroidal agents, antiemetics, narcotics, analgesics) administered independently or sequentially as supportive management of chemotherapy administration, should be separately reported using 96360, 96361, 96365, 96379 as appropriate.

Report both the specific service as well as code(s) for the specific substance(s) or drug(s) provided. The fluid used to administer the drug(s) is considered incidental hydration and is not separately reportable.

Regional (isolation) chemotherapy perfusion should be reported using the codes for arterial infusion (96420-96425). Placement of the intra-arterial catheter should be reported using the appropriate code from the Cardiovascular Surgery section. Placement of arterial and venous cannula(s) for extracorporeal circulation via a membrane oxygenator perfusion pump should be reported using 36823. Code 36823 includes dose calculation and administration of the chemotherapy agent by injection into the perfusate. Do not report 96409-96425 in conjunction with 36823.

(For home infusion services, see 99601-99602)

INJECTION AND INTRAVENOUS INFUSION CHEMOTHERAPY AND OTHER HIGHLY COMPLEX DRUG OR HIGHLY COMPLEX BIOLOGIC AGENT ADMINISTRATION

Intravenous or intra-arterial push is defined as: (a) an injection in which the healthcare professional who administers the substance/drug is continuously present to administer the injection and observe the patient, or (b) an infusion of 15 minutes or less.

96401 Chemotherapy administration, subcutaneous or intramuscular; non-hormonal anti-neoplastic

96402 hormonal anti-neoplastic

96405 Chemotherapy administration; intralesional, up to and including 7 lesions

96406 intralesional, more than 7 lesions

96409 intravenous, push technique, single or initial substance/drug

● New Code   ▲ Revised Code   + Add-On Code   ⊘ Modifier -51 Exempt   ★ Telemedicine

+ 96411   intravenous, push technique, each additional substance/drug (List separately in addition to code for primary procedure)

(Use 96411 in conjunction with 96409, 96413)

96413   Chemotherapy administration, intravenous infusion technique; up to 1 hour, single or initial substance/drug

(Report 96361 to identify hydration if administered as a secondary or subsequent service in association with 96413 through the same IV access)

(Report 96366, 96367, 96375 to identify therapeutic, prophylactic, or diagnostic drug infusion or injection, if administered as a secondary or subsequent service in association with 96413 through the same IV access)

+ 96415   each additional hour (List separately in addition to code for primary procedure)

(Use 96415 in conjunction with 96413)

(Report 96415 for infusion intervals of greater than 30 minutes beyond 1-hour increments)

96416   initiation of prolonged chemotherapy infusion (more than 8 hours), requiring use of a portable or implantable pump

(For refilling and maintenance of a portable pump or an implantable infusion pump or reservoir for drug delivery, see 96521-96523)

+ 96417   each additional sequential infusion (different substance/drug), up to 1 hour (List separately in addition to code for primary procedure)

(Use 96417 in conjunction with 96413)

(Report only once per sequential infusion. Report 96415 for additional hour(s) of sequential infusion)

INTRA-ARTERIAL CHEMOTHERAPY AND OTHER HIGHLY COMPLEX DRUG OR HIGHLY COMPLEX BIOLOGIC AGENT ADMINISTRATION

96420   Chemotherapy administration, intra-arterial; push technique

96422   infusion technique, up to 1 hour

+ 96423   infusion technique, each additional hour (List separately in addition to code for primary procedure)

(Use 96423 in conjunction with code 96422)

(Report 96423 for infusion intervals of greater than 30 minutes beyond 1-hour increments)

(For regional chemotherapy perfusion via membrane oxygenator perfusion pump to an extremity, use 36823)

96425   infusion technique, initiation of prolonged infusion (more than 8 hours), requiring the use of a portable or implantable pump

(For refilling and maintenance of a portable pump or an implantable infusion pump or reservoir for drug delivery, see 96521-96523)

OTHER INJECTION AND INFUSION SERVICES

Code 96523 does not require direct supervision. Codes 96521-96523 may be reported when these devices are used for therapeutic drugs other than chemotherapy.

(For collection of blood specimen from a completely implantable venous access device, use 36591)

96440   Chemotherapy administration into pleural cavity, requiring and including thoracentesis

96446   Chemotherapy administration into the peritoneal cavity via indwelling port or catheter

---

▮ Separate Procedure	▮ Unlisted Procedure	▮ CCI Comp. Code	▮ Non-specific Procedure **899**

96450   Chemotherapy administration, into CNS (eg, intrathecal), requiring and including spinal puncture

(For intravesical (bladder) chemotherapy administration, use 51720)

(For insertion of subarachnoid catheter and reservoir for infusion of drug, see 62350, 62351, 62360, 62361, 62362; for insertion of intraventricular catherter and reservoir, see 61210, 61215)

96521   Refilling and maintenance of portable pump

96522   Refilling and maintenance of implantable pump or reservoir for drug delivery, systemic (eg, intravenous, intra-arterial)

(For refilling and maintenance of an implantable infusion pump for spinal or brain drug infusion, use 95990-95991)

96523   Irrigation of implanted venous access device for drug delivery systems

(Do not report 96523 in conjunction with other services. To report collection of blood specimen, use 36591)

96542   Chemotherapy injection, subarachnoid or intraventricular via subcutaneous reservoir, single or multiple agents

(For radioactive isotope therapy, use 79005)

96549   Unlisted chemotherapy procedure

PHOTODYNAMIC THERAPY

Codes 96573, 96574 should be used to report nonsurgical treatment of cutaneous lesions using photodynamic therapy by external application of light to destroy premalignant lesion(s) of the skin and adjacent mucosa (eg, face, scalp) by activation of photosensitizing drug(s).

A treatment session is defined as an application of photosensitizer to all lesions within an anatomic area (eg, face, scalp), with or without debridement of all premalignant hyperkeratotic lesions in that area, followed by illumination/activation with an appropriate light source to the same area.

Do not report codes for debridement (11000, 11001, 11004, 11005), lesion shaving (11300-11313), biopsy (11100, 11101), or lesion excision (11400-11471) within the treatment area(s) on the same day as photodynamic therapy (96573, 96574).

(To report ocular photodynamic therapy, use 67221)

▲ 96567   Photodynamic therapy by external application of light to destroy premalignant lesions of the skin and adjacent mucosa with application and illumination/activation of photosensitive drug(s), per day

(Use 96567 for reporting photodynamic therapy when physician or other qualified health care professional is not directly involved in the delivery of the photodynamic therapy service)

+ 96570   Photodynamic therapy by endoscopic application of light to ablate abnormal tissue via activation of photosensitive drug(s); first 30 minutes (List separately in addition to code for endoscopy or bronchoscopy procedures of lung and gastrointestinal tract)

(Report 96570 with modifier 52 for service of less than 23 minutes with report)

+ 96571   each additional 15 minutes (List separately in addition to code for endoscopy or bronchoscopy procedures of lung and gastrointestinal tract)

(For 23-27 minutes of service, use 96570. For 38-52 minutes of service, use 96570 in conjunction with 96571)

(96570, 96571 are to be used in addition to bronchoscopy, endoscopy codes)

(Use 96570, 96571 in conjunction with 31641, 43229 as appropriate)

   ● New Code   ▲ Revised Code   + Add-On Code   ⊘ Modifier -51 Exempt   ★ Telemedicine

- **96573** Photodynamic therapy by external application of light to destroy premalignant lesions of the skin and adjacent mucosa with application and illumination/activation of photosensitizing drug(s) provided by a physician or other qualified health care professional, per day

  (Do not report 96573 in conjunction with 96567, 96574 for the same anatomic area)

- **96574** Debridement of premalignant hyperkeratotic lesion(s) (ie, targeted curettage, abrasion) followed with photodynamic therapy by external application of light to destroy premalignant lesions of the skin and adjacent mucosa with application and illumination/activation of photosensitizing drug(s) provided by a physician or other qualified health care professional, per day

  (Do not report 96574 in conjunction with 96567, 96573 for the same anatomic area)

SPECIAL DERMATOLOGICAL PROCEDURES

See the **Evaluation and Management coding guidelines** for further instructions on reporting that is appropriate for management of dermatologic illnesses.

(For intralesional injections, see 11900, 11901)

(For Tzanck smear, see 88160-88161)

96900 Actinotherapy (ultraviolet light)

(For rhinophototherapy, intranasal application of ultraviolet and visible light, use 30999)

96902 Microscopic examination of hairs plucked or clipped by the examiner (excluding hair collected by the patient) to determine telogen and anagen counts, or structural hair shaft abnormality

96904 Whole body integumentary photography, for monitoring of high risk patients with dysplastic nevus syndrome or a history of dysplastic nevi, or patients with a personal or familial history of melanoma

96910 Photochemotherapy; tar and ultraviolet B (Goeckerman treatment) or petrolatum and ultraviolet B

96912 psoralens and ultraviolet A (PUVA)

96913 Photochemotherapy (Goeckerman and/or PUVA) for severe photoresponsive dermatoses requiring at least 4 to 8 hours of care under direct supervision of the physician (includes application of medication and dressings)

96920 Laser treatment for inflammatory skin disease (psoriasis); total area less than 250 sq cm

96921 250 sq cm to 500 sq cm

96922 over 500 sq cm

(For laser destruction of premalignant lesions, see 17000-17004)

(For laser destruction of cutaneous vascular proliferative lesions, see 17106-17108)

(For laser destruction of benign lesions, see 17110-17111)

(For laser destruction of malignant lesions, see 17260-17286)

Codes 96931, 96932, 96933, 96934, 96935, 96936 describe the acquisition and/or diagnostic interpretation of the device generated stitched image mosaics related to a single lesion. Do not report 96931, 96932, 96933, 96934, 96935, 96936 for a reflectance confocal microscopy examination that does not produce mosaic images. For services rendered using reflectance confocal microscopy not generating mosaic images, use 96999.

(For optical coherence tomography [OCT] for microstructural and morphological imaging of skin, see 0470T, 0471T)

96931 Reflectance confocal microscopy (RCM) for cellular and sub-cellular imaging of skin; image acquisition and interpretation and report, first lesion

---

Separate Procedure   Unlisted Procedure   CCI Comp. Code   Non-specific Procedure   **901**

| 96932 | image acquisition only, first lesion |
| 96933 | interpretation and report only, first lesion |

+ 96934   image acquisition and interpretation and report, each additional lesion (List separately in addition to code for primary procedure)

(Use 96934 in conjunction with 96931)

+ 96935   image acquisition only, each additional lesion (List separately in addition to code for primary procedure)

(Use 96935 in conjunction with 96932)

+ 96936   interpretation and report only, each additional lesion (List separately in addition to code for primary procedure)

(Use 96936 in conjunction with 96933)

96999   Unlisted special dermatological service or procedure

PHYSICAL MEDICINE AND REHABILITATION

Codes 97010-97763 should be used to report each distinct procedure performed. Do not append modifier 51 to 97010-97763.

The work of the physician or other qualified health care professional consists of face-to-face time with the patient (and caregiver, if applicable) delivering skilled services. For the purpose of determining the total time of a service, incremental intervals of treatment at the same visit may be accumulated.

The meanings of terms in the Physical Medicine and Rehabilitation section are not the same as those in the Evaluation and Management Services section (99201-99350). Do not use the Definitions of Commonly Used Terms in the Evaluation and Management (E/M) Guidelines for Physical Medicine and Rehabilitation services.

(For muscle testing, range of joint motion, electromyography, see 95831 et seq)

(For biofeedback training by EMG, use 90901)

(For transcutaneous nerve stimulation (TNS), use 64550)

Physical Therapy Evaluations

Physical therapy evaluations include a patient history and an examination with development of a plan of care, conducted by the physician or other qualified health care professional, which is based on the composite of the patient's presentation.

Coordination, consultation, and collaboration of care with physicians, other qualified health care professionals, or agencies is provided consistent with the nature of the problem(s) and the needs of the patient, family, and/or other caregivers.

At a minimum, each of the following components noted in the code descriptors must be documented, in order to report the selected level of physical therapy evaluation. Physical therapy evaluations include the following components:

- History
- Examination
- Clinical decision making
- Development of plan of care

Report 97164 for performance of patient re-evaluation that is based on an established and ongoing plan of care.

Definitions

The level of the physical therapy evaluation performed is dependent on clinical decision making and on the nature of the patient's condition (severity). For the purpose of reporting physical therapy evaluations, the body regions and body systems are defined as follows:

● New Code   ▲ Revised Code   + Add-On Code   ⊘ Modifier -51 Exempt   ★ Telemedicine

Body regions: head, neck, back, lower extremities, upper extremities, and trunk.

Body systems: musculoskeletal, neuromuscular, cardiovascular pulmonary, and integumentary.

A *review of body systems* include the following:

- For the musculoskeletal system: the assessment of gross symmetry, gross range of motion, gross strength, height, and weight

- For the neuromuscular system: a general assessment of gross coordinated movement (eg, balance, gait, locomotion, transfers, and transitions) and motor function (motor control and motor learning)

- For the cardiovascular pulmonary system: the assessment of heart rate, respiratory rate, blood pressure, and edema

- For the integumentary system: the assessment of pliability (texture), presence of scar formation, skin color, and skin integrity

A review of any of the body systems also includes the assessment of the ability to make needs known, consciousness, orientation (person, place, and time), expected emotional/behavioral responses, and learning preferences (eg, learning barriers, education needs)

Body structures: The structural or anatomical parts of the body, such as organs, limbs, and their components, classified according to body systems.

Personal factors: Factors that include sex, age, coping styles, social background, education, profession, past and current experience, overall behavior pattern, character, and other factors that influence how disability is experienced by the individual. Personal factors that exist but do not impact the physical therapy plan of care are not to be considered, when selecting a level of service.

97161 Physical therapy evaluation: low complexity, requiring these components:

—A history with no personal factors and/or comorbidities that impact the plan of care;

—An examination of body system(s) using standardized tests and measures addressing 1-2 elements from any of the following: body structures and functions, activity limitations, and/or participation restrictions;

—A clinical presentation with stable and/or uncomplicated characteristics; and

—Clinical decision making of low complexity using standardized patient assessment instrument and/or measurable assessment of functional outcome. Typically, 20 minutes are spent face-to-face with the patient and/or family.

97162 Physical therapy evaluation: moderate complexity, requiring these components:

—A history of present problem with 1-2 personal factors and/or comorbidities that impact the plan of care;

—An examination of body systems using standardized tests and measures in addressing a total of 3 or more elements from any of the following: body structures and functions, activity limitations, and/or participation restrictions;

—An evolving clinical presentation with changing characteristics; and

—Clinical decision making of moderate complexity using standardized patient assessment instrument and/or measurable assessment of functional outcome.

Typically, 30 minutes are spent face-to-face with the patient and/or family.

97163 Physical therapy evaluation: high complexity, requiring these components:

—A history of present problem with 3 or more personal factors and/or comorbidities that impact the plan of care;

—An examination of body systems using standardized tests and measures addressing a total of 4 or more elements from any of the following: body structures and functions, activity limitations, and/or participation restrictions;

—A clinical presentation with unstable and unpredictable characteristics; and

—Clinical decision making of high complexity using standardized patient assessment instrument and/or measurable assessment of functional outcome.

Typically, 45 minutes are spent face-to-face with the patient and/or family.

 97164 Re-evaluation of physical therapy established plan of care, requiring these components:

—An examination including a review of history and use of standardized tests and measures is required; and

—Revised plan of care using a standardized patient assessment instrument and/or measurable assessment of functional outcome

Typically, 20 minutes are spent face-to-face with the patient and/or family.

Occupational Therapy Evaluations

Occupational therapy evaluations include an occupational profile, medical and therapy history, relevant assessments, and development of a plan of care, which reflects the therapist's clinical reasoning and interpretation of the data.

Coordination, consultation, and collaboration of care with physicians, other qualified health care professionals, or agencies is provided consistent with the nature of the problem(s) and the needs of the patient, family and/or other caregivers.

At a minimum, each of the following components noted in the code descriptors must be documented, in order to report the selected level of occupational therapy evaluation.

Occupational therapy evaluations include the following components:

● Occupational profile and client history (medical and therapy)

● Assessments of occupational performance

● Clinical decision making

● Development of plan of care

Report 97168 for performance of a re-evaluation that is based on an established and ongoing plan of care.

Definitions

The level of the occupational therapy evaluation performed is determined by patient condition, complexity of clinical decision making, and the scope and nature of the patient's performance deficits relating to physical, cognitive, or psychosocial skills to be assessed. The patient's plan of treatment should reflect assessment of each of the identified performance deficits.

Performance deficits: performance deficits refer to the inability to complete activities due to the lack of skills in one or more of the categories below (ie, relating to physical, cognitive, or psychosocial skills):

Physical skills: Physical skills refer to impairments of body structure or body function (eg, balance, mobility, strength, endurance, fine or gross motor coordination, sensation, dexterity).

Cognitive skills: Cognitive skills refer to the ability to attend, perceive, think, understand, problem solve, mentally sequence, learn, and remember resulting in the ability to organize occupational performance in a timely and safe manner. These skills are observed when: (1) a person attends to and selects, interacts with, and uses task tools and materials; (2) carries out individual actions and steps; and (3) modifies performance when problems are encountered.

Psychosocial skills: Psychosocial skills refer to interpersonal interactions, habits, routines and behaviors, active use of coping strategies, and/or environmental adaptations to develop skills necessary to successfully and appropriately participate in everyday tasks and social situations.b

 97165 Occupational therapy evaluation, low complexity, requiring these components:

—An occupational profile and medical and therapy history, which includes a brief history including review of medical and/or therapy records relating to the presenting problem;

—An assessment(s) that identifies 1-3 performance deficits (ie, relating to physical, cognitive, or psychosocial skills) that result in activity limitations and/or participation restrictions; and

—Clinical decision making of low complexity, which includes an analysis of the occupational profile, analysis of data from problem-focused assessment(s), and consideration of a limited number of treatment options. Patient presents with no comorbidities that affect occupational performance. Modification of tasks or assistance (eg, physical or verbal) with assessment(s) is not necessary to enable completion of evaluation component.

Typically, 30 minutes are spent face-to-face with the patient and/or family.

97166 Occupational therapy evaluation, moderate complexity, requiring these components:

—An occupational profile and medical and therapy history, which includes an expanded review of medical and/or therapy records and additional review of physical, cognitive, or psychosocial history related to current functional performance;

—An assessment(s) that identifies 3-5 performance deficits (ie, relating to physical, cognitive, or psychosocial skills) that result in activity limitations and/or participation restrictions; and

—Clinical decision making of moderate analytic complexity, which includes an analysis of the occupational profile, analysis of data from detailed assessment(s), and consideration of several treatment options. Patient may present with comorbidities that affect occupational performance. Minimal to moderate modification of tasks or assistance (eg, physical or verbal) with assessment(s) is necessary to enable patient to complete evaluation component.

Typically, 45 minutes are spent face-to-face with the patient and/or family.

97167 Occupational therapy evaluation, high complexity, requiring these components:

—An occupational profile and medical and therapy history, which includes review of medical and/or therapy records and extensive additional review of physical, cognitive, or psychosocial history related to current functional performance;

—An assessment(s) that identifies 5 or more performance deficits (ie, relating to physical, cognitive, or psychosocial skills) that result in activity limitations and/or participation restrictions; and

—Clinical decision making of high analytic complexity, which includes an analysis of the patient profile, analysis of data from comprehensive assessment(s), and consideration of multiple treatment options. Patient presents with comorbidities that affect occupational performance. Significant modification of tasks or assistance (eg, physical or verbal) with assessment(s) is necessary to enable patient to complete evaluation component.

Typically, 60 minutes are spent face-to-face with the patient and/or family.

97168 Re-evaluation of occupational therapy established plan of care, requiring these components:

—An assessment of changes in patient functional or medical status with revised plan of care;

—An update to the initial occupational profile to reflect changes in condition or environment that affect future interventions and/or goals; and

—A revised plan of care. A formal reevaluation is performed when there is a documented change in functional status or a significant change to the plan of care is required.

Typically, 30 minutes are spent face-to-face with the patient and/or family.

Athletic Training Evaluations

Athletic training evaluations include a patient history and an examination with development of a plan of care, conducted by the physician or other qualified health care professional.

Coordination, consultation, and collaboration of care with physicians, other qualified health care professionals, or agencies is provided consistent with the nature of the problem(s) and the needs of the patient, family, and/or other caregivers.

At a minimum, each of the following components noted in the code descriptors must be documented, in order to report the selected level of athletic training evaluation.

Athletic training evaluations include the following components:

- History and physical activity profile
- Examination

- Clinical decision making

- Development of plan of care

Report 97172 for performance of patient re-evaluation that is based on an established and ongoing plan of care.

Definitions

For the purpose of reporting athletic training evaluations, the body areas and body systems are defined as follows:

Body areas: head, neck, back, lower extremities, upper extremities, and trunk

Body systems: musculoskeletal, neuromuscular, cardiovascular pulmonary, and integumentary.

The body systems review includes the following:

For the musculoskeletal system: the assessment of gross symmetry, gross range of motion, gross strength, height, and weight

For the neuromuscular system: a general assessment of gross coordinated movement (eg, balance, gait, locomotion, transfers, and transitions) and motor function (motor control and motor learning)

For the cardiovascular pulmonary system: the assessment of heart rate, respiratory rate, blood pressure, and edema

For the integumentary system: the assessment of pliability (texture), presence of scar formation, skin color, and skin integrity

97169 Athletic training evaluation, low complexity, requiring these components:

—A history and physical activity profile with no comorbidities that affect physical activity;

—An examination of affected body area and other symptomatic or related systems addressing 1-2 elements from any of the following: body structures, physical activity, and/or participation deficiencies; and

—Clinical decision making of low complexity using standardized patient assessment instrument and/or measurable assessment of functional outcome.

Typically, 15 minutes are spent face-to-face with the patient and/or family.

97170 Athletic training evaluation, moderate complexity, requiring these components:

—A medical history and physical activity profile with 1-2 comorbidities that affect physical activity;

—An examination of affected body area and other symptomatic or related systems addressing a total of 3 or more elements from any of the following: body structures, physical activity, and/or participation deficiencies; and

—Clinical decision making of moderate complexity using standardized patient assessment instrument and/or measurable assessment of functional outcome.

Typically, 30 minutes are spent face-to-face with the patient and/or family.

97171 Athletic training evaluation, high complexity, requiring these components:

—A medical history and physical activity profile, with 3 or more comorbidities that affect physical activity;

—A comprehensive examination of body systems using standardized tests and measures addressing a total of 4 or more elements from any of the following: body structures, physical activity, and/or participation deficiencies;

—Clinical presentation with unstable and unpredictable characteristics; and

—Clinical decision making of high complexity using standardized patient assessment instrument and/or measurable assessment of functional outcome.

Typically, 45 minutes are spent face-to-face with the patient and/or family.

● New Code   ▲ Revised Code   + Add-On Code   ⊘ Modifier -51 Exempt   ★ Telemedicine

97172 Re-evaluation of athletic training established plan of care requiring these components:

—An assessment of patient's current functional status when there is a documented change; and

—A revised plan of care using a standardized patient assessment instrument and/or measurable assessment of functional outcome with an update in management options, goals, and interventions.

Typically, 20 minutes are spent face-to-face with the patient and/or family

(**97001** deleted 2016 [2017 edition]. To report, see 97161-97172)

(**97002** deleted 2016 [2017 edition]. To report, see 97161-97172)

(**97003** deleted 2016 [2017 edition]. To report, see 97161-97172)

(**97004** deleted 2016 [2017 edition]. To report, see 97161-97172)

(**97005** deleted 2016 [2017 edition]. To report, see 97161-97172)

(**97006** deleted 2016 [2017 edition]. To report, see 97161-97172)

MODALITIES

SUPERVISED

The application of a modality that does not require direct (one-on-one) patient contact.

97010 Application of a modality to 1 or more areas; hot or cold packs

97012 traction, mechanical

97014 electrical stimulation (unattended)

(For acupuncture with electrical stimulation, see 97813, 97814)

97016 vasopneumatic devices

97018 paraffin bath

97022 whirlpool

97024 diathermy (eg, microwave)

97026 infrared

97028 ultraviolet

CONSTANT ATTENDANCE

The application of a modality that requires direct (one-on-one) patient contact.

97032 Application of a modality to 1 or more areas; electrical stimulation (manual), each 15 minutes

(For transcutaneous electrical modulation pain reprocessing (TEMPR/scrambler therapy], use 0278T)

97033 iontophoresis, each 15 minutes

97034 contrast baths, each 15 minutes

97035 ultrasound, each 15 minutes

97036 Hubbard tank, each 15 minutes

■ Separate Procedure   ■ Unlisted Procedure   ■ CCI Comp. Code   ■ Non-specific Procedure   **907**

97039   Unlisted modality (specify type and time if constant attendance)

THERAPEUTIC PROCEDURES

A manner of effecting change through the application of clinical skills and/or services that attempt to improve function. Physician or other qualified health care professional (ie, therapist) required to have direct (one-on-one) patient contact.

97110   Therapeutic procedure, 1 or more areas, each 15 minutes; therapeutic exercises to develop strength and endurance, range of motion and flexibility

97112   neuromuscular reeducation of movement, balance, coordination, kinesthetic sense, posture, and/or proprioception for sitting and/or standing activities

97113   aquatic therapy with therapeutic exercises

97116   gait training (includes stair climbing)

(Use 96000-96003 to report comprehensive gait and motion analysis procedures)

97124   massage, including effleurage, petrissage and/or tapotement (stroking, compression, percussion)

(For myofascial release, use 97140)

● 97127   Therapeutic interventions that focus on cognitive function (eg, attention, memory, reasoning, executive function, problem solving, and/or pragmatic functioning) and compensatory strategies to manage the performance of an activity (eg, managing time or schedules, initiating, organizing and sequencing tasks), direct (one-on-one) patient contact

(Report 97127 only once per day)

(Do not report 97127 in conjunction with 0364T, 0365T, 0368T, 0369T)

97139   Unlisted therapeutic procedure (specify)

97140   Manual therapy techniques (eg, mobilization/ manipulation, manual lymphatic drainage, manual traction), 1 or more regions, each 15 minutes

97150   Therapeutic procedure(s), group (2 or more individuals)

(Report 97150 for each member of group)

(Group therapy procedures involve constant attendance of the physician or other qualified health care professional [ie, therapist], but by definition do not require one-on-one patient contact by the same physician or other qualified health care professional)

(For manipulation under general anesthesia, see appropriate anatomic section in Musculoskeletal System)

(For osteopathic manipulative treatment (OMT), see 98925-98929)

(Do not report 97150 in conjunction with 0366T, 0376T, 0372T)

97161   This code is out of order. See page 903.

97162   This code is out of order. See page 903.

97163   This code is out of order. See page 903.

97164   This code is out of order. See page 904.

97165   This code is out of order. See page 904.

97166   This code is out of order. See page 905.

● New Code   ▲ Revised Code   ✛ Add-On Code   ⊘ Modifier -51 Exempt   ★ Telemedicine

97167 This code is out of order. See page 905.

97168 This code is out of order. See page 905.

97169 This code is out of order. See page 906.

97170 This code is out of order. See page 906.

97171 This code is out of order. See page 906.

97172 This code is out of order. See page 907.

97530 Therapeutic activities, direct (one-on-one) patient contact (use of dynamic activities to improve functional performance), each 15 minutes

(**97532** deleted 2017 [2018 edition]. To report, use 97127)

97533 Sensory integrative techniques to enhance sensory processing and promote adaptive responses to environmental demands, direct (one-on-one) patient contact, each 15 minutes

97535 Self-care/home management training (eg, activities of daily living (ADL) and compensatory training, meal preparation, safety procedures, and instructions in use of assistive technology devices/adaptive equipment) direct one-on-one contact, each 15 minutes

97537 Community/work reintegration training (eg, shopping, transportation, money management, avocational activities and/or work environment/modification analysis, work task analysis, use of assistive technology device/adaptive equipment), direct one-on-one contact, each 15 minutes

(For wheelchair management/propulsion training, use 97542)

97542 Wheelchair management (eg, assessment, fitting, training), each 15 minutes

97545 Work hardening/conditioning; initial 2 hours

+ 97546 each additional hour (List separately in addition to code for primary procedure)

(Use 97546 in conjunction with code 97545)

ACTIVE WOUND CARE MANAGEMENT

Active wound care procedures are performed to remove devitalized and/or necrotic tissue and promote healing. Chemical cauterization (17250) to achieve wound hemostasis is included in active wound care procedures (97597, 97598, 97602) and should not be separately reported for the same lesion. Services require direct (one-on-one) contact with the patient.

(Do not report 97597-97602 in conjunction with 11042-11047 for the same wound)

(For debridement of burn wounds, see 16020-16030)

97597 Debridement (eg, high pressure waterjet with/without suction, sharp selective debridement with scissors, scalpel and forceps), open wound, (eg, fibrin, devitalized epidermis and/or dermis, exudate, debris, biofilm) including topical application(s), wound assessment, use of a whirlpool, when performed, and instruction(s) for ongoing care, per session, total wound(s) surface area; first 20 square centimeters or less

+ 97598 each additional 20 square centimeters or part thereof (List separately in addition to code for primary procedure)

(Use 97598 in conjunction with 97597)

97602 Removal of devitalized tissue from wound(s), nonselective debridement, without anesthesia (eg, wet-to-moist dressings, enzymatic, abrasion, larval therapy), including topical application(s), wound assessment, and instruction(s) for ongoing care, per session

97605 Negative pressure wound therapy (eg, vacuum assisted drainage collection), utilizing durable medical equipment (DME), including topical application(s), wound assessment, and instruction(s) for ongoing care, per session; total wound(s) surface area less than or equal to 50 square centimeters

97606 total wound(s) surface area greater than 50 square centimeters

97607 Negative pressure wound therapy, (eg, vacuum assisted drainage collection), utilizing disposable, non-durable medical equipment including provision of exudate management collection system, topical application(s), wound assessment, and instructions for ongoing care, per session; total wound(s) surface area less than or equal to 50 square centimeters

97608 total wound(s) surface area less than or equal to 50 square centimeters

(Do not report 97607, 97608 in conjunction with 97605, 97606)

97610 Low frequency, non-contact, non-thermal ultrasound, including topical application(s), when performed, wound assessment, and instruction(s) for ongoing care, per day

TESTS AND MEASUREMENTS

(For muscle testing, manual or electrical, joint range of motion, electromyography or nerve velocity determination, see 95831-95857, 95860-95872, 95885-95887, 95907-95913)

97750 Physical performance test or measurement (eg, musculo-skeletal, functional capacity), with written report, each 15 minutes

97755 Assistive technology assessment (eg, to restore, augment or compensate for existing function, optimize functional tasks and/or maximize environmental accessibility), direct one-on-one contact, with written report, each 15 minutes

(To report augmentative and alternative communication devices, use 92605 or 92607)

ORTHOTIC MANAGEMENT AND TRAINING AND PROSTHETIC TRAINING

▲ **97760** Orthotic(s) management and training (including assessment and fitting when not otherwise reported), upper extremity(ies), lower extremity(ies) and/or trunk, initial orthotic(s) encounter, each 15 minutes

(Code 97760 should not be reported with 97116 for the same extremity[ies])

▲ **97761** Prosthetic(s) training, upper and/or lower extremity(ies), initial prosthetic(s) encounter, each 15 minutes

(**97762** deleted 2017 [2018 edition]. To report, use 97763)

● **97763** Orthotic(s)/prosthetic(s) management and/or training, upper extremity(ies), lower extremity(ies), and/or trunk, subsequent orthotic(s)/prosthetic(s) encounter, each 15 minutes

(Do not report 97763 in conjunction with 97760, 97761)

OTHER PROCEDURES

(For extracorporeal shock wave musculoskeletaltherapy, see 0101T, 0102T)

97799 Unlisted physical medicine/rehabilitation service or procedure

● New Code   ▲ Revised Code   + Add-On Code   ⊘ Modifier -51 Exempt   ★ Telemedicine

MEDICAL NUTRITION THERAPY

Medical nutrition therapy (MNT) is the assessment of nutritional status followed by nutritional therapy. The nutrition assessment includes review and analysis of 1) medical, nutrition and medication histories, 2) physical examination, 3) anthropometric measurements, and 4) laboratory test values. Nutrition therapy may include 1) diet modification, 2) counseling and education, 3) disease self-management skills training, and 4) administration of specialized therapies such as medical foods, intravenous or tube feedings.

★ **97802**   Medical nutrition therapy; initial assessment and intervention, individual, face-to-face with the patient, each 15 minutes

★ **97803**   re-assessment and intervention, individual, face-to-face with the patient, each 15 minutes

★ 97804   group (2 or more individual(s)), each 30 minutes

   (Physicians and other qualified health care professional who may report evaluation and management services should use the appropriate E/M codes)

ACUPUNCTURE

Acupuncture refers to the insertion of thin needles through the skin at specific points on the body to control pain and other symptoms. It is a type of complementary and alternative medicine. The acupuncture needle is a stainless steel needle that is slightly thicker than a human hair. The specific spot on the body where a acupuncture needle may be inserted is call an acupuncture point or acupoint.

Acupuncture is reported based on 15-minute increments of personal (face-to-face) contact with the patient, not the duration of acupuncture needle(s) placement.

If no electrical stimulation is used during a 15-minute increment, use 97810, 97811. If electrical stimulation of any needle is used during a 15-minute increment, use 97813, 97814.

Only one code may be reported for each 15-minute increment. Use either 97810 or 97813 for the initial 15-minute increment. Only one initial code is reported per day.

Evaluation and Management services may be reported in addition to acupuncture procedures when performed by physicians or other qualified health care professionals who may report E/M services, including new or established patient office or other outpatient services (99201-99215), hospital observation care (99217-99220, 99224-99226), hospital care (99221-99223, 99231-99233), office or other outpatient consultations (99241-99245), inpatient consultations (99251-99255), critical care services (99291, 99292), inpatient neonatal intensive care services and pediatric and neonatal critical care services (99466-99480), emergency department service (99281-99285), nursing facility services (99304-99318), domiciliary, rest home, or custodial care services (99324-99337), and home services (99341-99350) may be reported separately, using modifier -25, if the patient's condition requires a significant separately identifiable E/M service above and beyond the usual preservice and postservice work associated with the acupuncture services. The time of the E/M service is not included in the time of the acupuncture service.

   97810   Acupuncture, one or more needles; without electrical stimulation, initial 15 minutes of personal one-on-one contact with the patient

     (Do not report 97810 in conjunction with 97813)

+ 97811   without electrical stimulation, each additional 15 minutes of personal one-on-one contact with the patient, with re-insertion of needle(s) (List separately in addition to code for primary procedure)

     (Use 97811 in conjunction with 97810, 97813)

   97813   with electrical stimulation, initial 15 minutes of personal one-on-one contact with the patient

     (Do not report 97813 in conjunction with 97810)

+ 97814   with electrical stimulation, each additional 15 minutes of personal one-on-one contact with the patient, with re-insertion of needle(s) (List separately in addition to code for primary procedure)

     (Use 97814 in conjunction with 97810, 97813)

| ▮ Separate Procedure | ▮ Unlisted Procedure | ▮ CCI Comp. Code | ▮ Non-specific Procedure | **911** |

OSTEOPATHIC MANIPULATIVE TREATMENT

Osteopathic medicine is a system of therapy based on the theory that the body is capable of making its own remedies against disease and other toxic conditions when it is in normal structural relationship and has favorable environmental conditions and adequate nutrition. Osteopathic manipulative treatment (OMT) is a form of manual treatment applied by a physician to eliminate or alleviate somatic dysfunction and related disorders. This treatment may be accomplished by a variety of techniques.

Osteopathic Manipulative Treatment (OMT) is subject to Global Surgery Rules. Per Medicare Anesthesia Rules a provider performing OMT cannot separately report anesthesia services such as nerve blocks or epidural injections for OMT. In addition, per Medicare Global Surgery Rules, postoperative pain management after OMT (e.g., nerve block, epidural injection) is not separately reportable. Epidural or nerve block injections performed on the same date of service as OMT and unrelated to the MT may be reported with OMT using modifier -59.

Coding Rules

1. *Evaluation and management services may be reported separately, if, and only if the patient's condition requires a significant separately identifiable evaluation and management service, above and beyond the usual pre-service and post service work associated with the osteopathic manipulation.*

2. *CPT codes in this section are used to report OMT services provided in any location.*

Evaluation and Management services including new or established patient office or other outpatient services (99201-99215), hospital observation care (99217-99220, 99224-99226), hospital care (99221-99223, 99231-99233), office or other outpatient consultations (99241-99245), observation or inpatient care services (99234-99236), critical care services (99291, 99292), emergency department service (99281-99285), nursing facility services (99304-99318), domiciliary, rest home, or custodial care services (99324-99337), and home services (99341-99350) may be reported separately using modifier 25 if the patient's condition requires a significant separately identifiable E/M service, above and beyond the usual pre-service and post service work associated with the procedure. The E/M service may be caused or prompted by the same symptoms or condition for which the OMT service was provided. As such, different diagnoses are not required for the reporting of the OMT and E/M service on the same date.

98925	Osteopathic manipulative treatment (OMT); 1-2 body regions involved
98926	3-4 body regions involved
98927	5-6 body regions involved
98928	7-8 body regions involved
98929	9-10 body regions involved

CHIROPRACTIC MANIPULATIVE TREATMENT

Chiropractic medicine is a system of diagnosis and treatment based on the theory that irritation of the nervous system by mechanical, chemical or psychic factors is the cause of disease. Chiropractic services may include office visits, diagnostic tests, physical therapy, and/or chiropractic manipulation. Chiropractic manipulation treatment (CMT) is a form of manual treatment applied by a chiropractic physician to eliminate or alleviate somatic dysfunction and related disorders.

Coding Rules

1. *Chiropractic manipulation treatment includes a pre-manipulation patient assessment.*

2. *Evaluation and management services provided in conjunction with CMT may be reported separately with the addition of CPT modifier -25, along with any diagnostic tests or other therapy provided.*

REPORTING CHIROPRACTIC MANIPULATION TO MEDICARE

Medicare restricts the number of times the CMT code may be reported, provides a maximum reimbursement amount per year, and requires extensive supporting documentation as described below:

● New Code   ▲ Revised Code   + Add-On Code   ⊘ Modifier -51 Exempt   ★ Telemedicine

Documentation of Treatment Phase

Proper documentation of the treatment phase is extremely important when submitting claims for chiropractic services to Medicare. The treatment phase consists of the date the course of treatment was initiated and the number of treatments rendered to date. Proper documentation enables Medicare to process your claims quickly and accurately. For payment of chiropractic claims, the following information must be on the CMS1500 claim form:

1. *The service must be manual manipulation of the spine. This service is reported by CPT codes 98940-98943.*

2. *The primary diagnosis must be subluxation of the spine, either so stated or identified by a term descriptive of the subluxation. The following diagnoses are acceptable because they would always involve a subluxation:*

Intervertebral disc disorders	722.0-722.9
Curvatures of the spine	737.0-737.9
Spondylolisthesis	738.4,756.12
Nonallopathic lesions	739.1-739.4
Spondylolysis	756.11

3. *The level of subluxation must be stated.*

4. *The symptoms related to the level of subluxation must be given.*

5. *The date of the confirming x-ray must be on the claim. Note that the x-ray must have been taken within 12 months prior to or 3 months after the course of treatment was initiated.*

6. *The date this course of treatment was initiated and the number of treatments rendered since the start of this course must be on the claim.*

Special Situations

If a patient returns with a new condition or injury, this represents a new treatment phase. The treatment phase information should reflect when you first saw the patient for this condition. Do not use the date you first saw the patient for an earlier course of treatment. Note on your CMS1500 claim form that this is a new condition. Remember that a new documenting x-ray may be required.

In the case of chronic conditions, an x-ray older than 12 months may be acceptable. For coverage of chronic conditions such as scoliosis, spondylolysis, and spondylolisthesis, there must be a reasonable expectation that there is a restorative potential. Remember that maintenance care is not covered by Medicare.

Chiropractic Manipulative Treatment Medicare covers chiropractic manipulative treatment (CMT) of five spinal regions. Physical therapy services described by CPT codes 97112, 97124 and 97140 are not separately reportable when performed in a spinal region undergoing CMT. If these physical therapy services are performed in a different region than CMT and the provider is eligible to report physical therapy codes under the Medicare program, the provider may report CMT and the above physical therapy codes using modifier -59.

The chiropractic manipulative treatment codes include a pre-manipulative patient assessment. Additional E/M services including office or other outpatient services (99201-99215), subsequent observation care (99224-99226), subsequent hospital care (99231-99233), office or other outpatient consultations (99241-99245), subsequent nursing facility services (99307-99310), domiciliary, rest home, or custodial care services (99324-99337), and home services (99341-99350) may be reported separately using modifier 25 if the patient's condition requires a significant separately identifiable E/M service, above and beyond the usual pre-service and postservice work associated with the procedure. The E/M service may be caused or prompted by the same symptoms or condition for which the CMT service was provided. As such, different diagnoses are not required for the reporting of the CMT and E/M service on the same date.

For purposes of CMT, the five spinal regions referred to are: cervical region (includes atlanto-occipital joint); thoracic region (includes costovertebral and costotransverse joints); lumbar region; sacral region; and pelvic (sacro-iliac joint) region. The five extraspinal regions referred to are: head (including temporomandibular joint, excluding atlanto-occipital) region; lower extremities; upper extremities; rib cage (excluding costotransverse and costovertebral joints) and abdomen.

98940   Chiropractic manipulative treatment (CMT); spinal, 1-2 regions

98941   spinal, 3-4 regions

98942	spinal, 5 regions
98943	extraspinal, 1 or more regions

EDUCATION AND TRAINING FOR PATIENT SELF-MANAGEMENT

The following codes are used to report educational and training services prescribed by a physician or other qualified health care professional and provided by a qualified, nonphysician health care professional using a standardized curriculum to an individual or group of patients for the treatment of established illness/disease(s) or to delay comorbidity(s). Education and training for patient self-management may be reported with these codes only when using a standardized curriculum as described below. This curriculum may be modified as necessary for the clinical needs, cultural norms and health literacy of the patient(s).

(For counseling and education provided by a physician to an individual, see the appropriate E/M codes, including office or other outpatient services [99201-99215], hospital observation care [99217-99220, 99224-99226], hospital care [99221-99223, 99231-99233], office or other outpatient consultations [99241-99245], inpatient consultations [99251-99255], emergency department services [99281-99285], nursing facility services [99304-99318], domiciliary, rest home, or custodial care services [99324-99337], home services [99341-99350], and counseling risk factor reduction and behavior change intervention [99401-99429].)

(For counseling and education provided by a physician to a group, use 99078)

(For counseling and/or risk factor reduction intervention provided by a physician to patient(s) without symptoms or established disease, see 99401-99412)

(For medical nutrition therapy, see 97802-97804)

(For health and behavior assessment/intervention that is not part of a standardized curriculum, see 96150-96155)

(For education provided as genetic counseling services, use 96040. For education to a group regarding genetic risks, see 98961, 98962)

★ 98960   Education and training for patient self-management by a qualified, nonphysician health care professional using a standardized curriculum, face-to-face with the patient (could include caregiver/family) each 30 minutes; individual patient

★ 98961   2-4 patients

★ 98962   5-8 patients

NON-FACE-TO-FACE NONPHYSICIAN SERVICES

TELEPHONE SERVICES

Telephone services are non-face-to-face assessment and management services provided by a qualified health care professional to a patient via telephone. If the telephone call results in a decision to see the patient within 24 hours, the telephone call is not reported.

These codes are used to report episodes of care by the qualified health care professional initiated by an established patient or guardian of an established patient. If the telephone service ends with a decision to see the patient within 24 hours or the next available urgent visit appointment, the code is not reported; rather the encounter is considered part of the preservice work of the subsequent assessment and management service, procedure and visit. Likewise, if the telephone call refers to a service performed and reported by the qualified health care professional within the previous seven days (either qualified health care professional requested or unsolicited patient follow-up) or within the postoperative period of the previously completed procedure, then the service(s) are considered part of that previous service or procedure. (Do not report 98966-98969 if reporting 98966-98969 performed in the previous seven days.)

(For telephone services provided by a physician, see 99441-99443)

98966   Telephone assessment and management service provided by a qualified nonphysician health care professional to an established patient, parent, or guardian not originating from a related assessment and management service provided within the previous 7 days nor leading to an assessment and management

   ● New Code   ▲ Revised Code   + Add-On Code   ⊘ Modifier -51 Exempt   ★ Telemedicine

service or procedure within the next 24 hours or soonest available appointment; 5-10 minutes of medical discussion

98967   11-20 minutes of medical discussion

98968   21-30 minutes of medical discussion

(Do not report 98966-98968 during the same month with 99487-99489)

(Do not report 98966-98968 when performed during the service time of codes 99495, 99496)

(Do not report 98966, 98967, 98968 in conjunction with 93792, 93793)

ONLINE MEDICAL EVALUATION

An on-line electronic medical evaluation consists of non-face-to-face assessment and management services provided by a qualified health care professional to a patient via the internet in response to an on-line inquiry. To qualify for reporting, the service must include:

- *Timely response to the patient's inquiry by the health care professional*

- *Permanent storage of the on-line encounter (electronic or print copy is acceptable)*

- *The service may be reported only once per seven-day period for the same episode of care*

- *The reported service incorporates all related telephone calls, prescriptions, laboratory orders, etc. related to the on-line encounter.*

Reportable services involve the qualified health care professional's personal timely response to the patient's inquiry and must involve permanent storage (electronic or hard copy) of the encounter. This service is reported only once for the same episode of care during a seven-day period, although multiple qualified healthcare professionals could report their exchange with the same patient. If the on-line medical evaluation refers to an assessment and management service previously performed and reported by the qualified health care professional within the previous seven days (either qualified health care professional requested or unsolicited patient follow-up) or within the postoperative period of the previously completed procedure, then the service(s) are considered covered by the previous assessment and management office service or procedure. A reportable service encompasses the sum of communication (eg, related telephone calls, prescription provision, laboratory orders) pertaining to the on-line patient encounter.

(For an on-line medical evaluation provided by a physician, use 99444)

98969   Online assessment and management service provided by a qualified nonphysician health care profesional to an established patient or guardian, not originating from a related assessment and management service provided within the previous 7 days, using the internet or similar electronic communications network

(Do not report 98969 when using 99339-99340, 99374-99380 for the same communication[s])

(Do not report 98969 for home and outpatient INR monitoring when reporting 93792, 93793)

(Do not report 98969 during the same month with 99487-99489)

(Do not report 98969 when performed during the service time of codes 99495, 99496)

SPECIAL SERVICES, PROCEDURES AND REPORTS

The MEDICINE section of CPT includes a subsection Special Services and Reports, with CPT codes 99000-99090 which provides the reporting physician with a means of identifying the completion of special reports and services that are an adjunct to the basic services rendered. The specific special services code reported indicates the special circumstances under which a basic procedure is performed.

The proper use of Special Services CPT codes can result in a significant increase in reimbursement. Most codes in this section are "add on" codes which means that they are used in addition to whatever other CPT codes describe the procedures or services performed.

The procedures with code numbers 99000 through 99091 provide the reporting physician or other qualified health care professional with the means of identifying the completion of special reports and services that are an adjunct to the basic services rendered. The specific number assigned indicates the special circumstances under which a basic procedure is performed.

Separate Procedure   Unlisted Procedure   CCI Comp. Code   Non-specific Procedure   **915**

Code 99091 should be reported no more than once in a 30-day period to include the physician or other qualified health care professional time involved with data accession, review and interpretation, modification of care plan as necessary (including communication to patient and/or caregiver), and associated documentation.

If the services described by 99091 are provided on the same day the patient presents for an E/M service, these services should be considered part of the E/M service and not separately reported.

Do not report 99091 if it occurs within 30 days of care plan oversight services 99374-99380. Do not report 99091 if other more specific CPT codes exist (eg, 93227, 93272 for cardiographic services; 95250 for continuous glucose monitoring). Do not report 99091 for transfer and interpretation of data from hospital or clinical laboratory computers.

Codes 99050-99060 are reported in addition to an associated basic service. Do not append modifier 51 to 99050-99060. Typically, only a single adjunct code from among 99050-99060 would be reported per patient encounter. However, there may be circumstances in which reporting multiple adjunct codes per patient encounter may be appropriate.

MISCELLANEOUS SERVICES

99000 Handling and/or conveyance of specimen for transfer from the office to a laboratory

99001 Handling and/or conveyance of specimen for transfer from the patient in other than an office to a laboratory (distance may be indicated)

99002 Handling, conveyance, and/or any other service in connection with the implementation of an order involving devices (eg, designing, fitting, packaging, handling, delivery or mailing) when devices such as orthotics, protectives, prosthetics are fabricated by an outside laboratory or shop but which items have been designed, and are to be fitted and adjusted by the attending physician or other qualified health care professional

(For routine collection of venous blood, use 36415)

99024 Postoperative follow-up visit, normally included in the surgical package, to indicate that an evaluation and management service was performed during a postoperative period for a reason(s) related to the origianl procedure

(As a component of a surgical "package," see Surgery guidelines)

99026 Hospital mandated on call service; in-hospital, each hour

99027   out-of-hospital, each hour

(For standby services requiring prolonged attendance, use 99360, as appropriate. Time spent performing separately reportable procedure(s) or service(s) should not be included in the time reported as mandated on call service)

99050 Services provided in the office at times other than regularly scheduled office hours, or days when the office is normally closed (eg, holidays, Saturday or Sunday), in addition to basic service

99051 Service(s) provided in the office during regularly scheduled evening, weekend, or holiday office hours, in addition to basic service

99053 Service(s) provided between 10:00 PM and 8:00 AM at 24-hour facility, in addition to basic service

99056 Service(s) typically provided in the office, provided out of the office at request of patient, in addition to basic service

99058 Service(s) provided on an emergency basis in the office, which disrupts other scheduled office services, in addition to basic service

99060 Service(s) provided on an emergency basis, out of the office, which disrupts other scheduled office services, in addition to basic service

99070 Supplies and materials (except spectacles), provided by the physician or other qualified health care professional over and above those usually included with the office visit or other services rendered (list drugs, trays, supplies, or materials provided)

(For supply of spectacles, use the appropriate supply codes)

99071 Educational supplies, such as books, tapes, and pamphlets, for the patient's education at cost to physician or other qualified health care professional

99075 Medical testimony

99078 Physician or other qualified health care professional qualified by education, training, licensure/regulation (when applicable) educational services rendered to patients in a group setting (eg, prenatal, obesity, or diabetic instructions)

99080 Special reports such as insurance forms, more than the information conveyed in the usual medical communications or standard reporting form

(Do not report 99080 in conjunction with 99455, 99456 for the completion of Workmen's Compensation forms)

99082 Unusual travel (eg, transportation and escort of patient)

99090 Analysis of clinical data stored in computers (eg, ECGs, blood pressures, hematologic data)

(For physician or other qualified health care professional qualified by education, training, licensure/regulatin [when applicable] collection and interpretation of physiologic data stored/transmitted by patient/caregiver, see 99091)

(Do not report 99090 if other more specific CPT codes exist, eg, 93227, 93272, 0206T for cardiographic services; 95250 for continuous glucose monitoring; 97750 for musculoskeletal function testing)

99091 Collection and interpretation of physiologic data (eg, ECG, blood pressure, glucose monitoring) digitally stored and/or transmitted by the patient and/or caregiver to the physician or other qualified health care professional, qualified by education, training, licensure/regulation (when applicable) requiring a minimum of 30 minutes of time

QUALIFYING CIRCUMSTANCES FOR ANESTHESIA

(For explanation of these services, see Anesthesia guidelines)

+ 99100 Anesthesia for patient of extreme age, younger than 1 year and older than 70 (List separately in addition to code for primary anesthesia procedure)

(For procedure performed on infants less than 1 year of age at time of surgery, see 00326, 00561, 00834, 00836)

+ 99116 Anesthesia complicated by utilization of total body hypothermia (List separately in addition to code for primary anesthesia procedure)

+ 99135 Anesthesia complicated by utilization of controlled hypotension (List separately in addition to code for primary anesthesia procedure)

+ 99140 Anesthesia complicated by emergency conditions (specify) (List separately in addition to code for primary anesthesia procedure)

(An emergency is defined as existing when delay in treatment of the patient would lead to a significant increase in the threat to life or body part)

MODERATE (CONSCIOUS) SEDATION

Moderate (also known as conscious) sedation is a drug induced depression of consciousness during which patients respond purposefully to verbal commands, either alone or accompanied by light tactile stimulation. No interventions are required to maintain cardiovascular function or a patent airway, and spontaneous ventilation is adequate.

Moderate sedation codes 99151, 99152, 99153, 99155, 99156, 99157 are not used to report administration of medications for pain control, minimal sedation (anxiolysis), deep sedation, or monitored anesthesia care (00100-01999).

For purposes of reporting, intraservice time of moderate sedation is used to select the appropriate code(s). The following definitions are used to determine intraservice time (compared to pre- and postservice time). An independent trained observer is an individual who is qualified to monitor the patient during the procedure, who has no other duties (eg, assisting at surgery) during the procedure.

Preservice Work

The preservice activities required for moderate sedation are included in the work described by each of these codes (99151, 99152, 99153, 99155, 99156, 99157) and are not reported separately. The following preservice work components are not included when determining intraservice time for reporting:

- Assessment of the patient's past medical and surgical history with particular emphasis on cardiovascular, pulmonary, airway, or neurological conditions;

- Review of the patient's previous experiences with anesthesia and/or sedation;

- Family history of sedation complications;

- Summary of the patient's present medication list;

- Drug allergy and intolerance history;

- Focused physical examination of the patient with emphasis on:

  —Mouth, jaw, oropharynx, neck and airway for Mallampati score assessment;

  —Chest and lungs;

  —Heart and circulation;

- Vital signs, including heart rate, respiratory rate, blood pressure, and oxygenation with end tidal CO_2 when indicated;

- Review of any pre-sedation diagnostic tests;

- Completion of a pre-sedation assessment form (with an American Society of Anesthesiologists [ASA] Physical Status classification);

- Patient informed consent;

- Immediate pre-sedation assessment prior to first sedating doses; and

- Initiation of IV access and fluids to maintain patency.

Intraservice Work

Intraservice time is used to determine the appropriate CPT code to report moderate sedation services:

- Begins with the administration of the sedating agent(s);

- Ends when the procedure is completed, the patient is stable for recovery status, and the physician or other qualified health care professional providing the sedation ends personal continuous face-to-face time with the patient;

- Includes ordering and/or administering the initial and subsequent doses of sedating agents;

- Requires continuous face-to-face attendance of the physician or other qualified health care professional;

- Requires monitoring patient response to the sedating agents, including:

  —Periodic assessment of the patient;

  —Further administration of agent(s) as needed to maintain sedation; and

● New Code ▲ Revised Code ＋ Add-On Code ⊘ Modifier -51 Exempt ★ Telemedicine

—Monitoring of oxygen saturation, heart rate, and blood pressure.

If the physician or other qualified health care professional who provides the sedation services also performs the procedure supported by sedation (99151, 99152, 99153), the physician or other qualified health care professional will supervise and direct an independent trained observer who will assist in monitoring the patient's level of consciousness and physiological status throughout the procedure.

Postservice Work

The postservice activities required for moderate sedation are included in the work described by each of these codes (99151, 99152, 99153, 99155, 99156, 99157) and are not reported separately. Once continuous face-to-face time with the patient has ended, additional face-to-face time with the patient is not added to the intraservice time, however, it is considered as part of the postservice work. The following postservice work components are not included, when determining intraservice time for reporting:

● Assessment of the patient's vital signs, level of consciousness, neurological, cardiovascular, and pulmonary stability in the post-sedation recovery period;

● Assessment of the patient's readiness for discharge following the procedure;

● Preparation of documentation regarding sedation service; and

● Communication with family/caregiver regarding sedation service.

Postservice work/times are not used to select the appropriate code.

Do not report 99151, 99152, 99153, 99155, 99156, 99157 in conjunction with 94760, 94761, 94762.

Codes 99151, 99152, 99155, 99156 are reported for the first 15 minutes of intraservice time providing moderate sedation. Codes 99153, 99157 are reported for each additional 15 minutes, in addition to the code for the primary service.

(99143, 99144, 99145 have been deleted. To report moderate sedation services provided by the same physician or other qualified health care professional performing the diagnostic or therapeutic service that the sedation supports, see 99151, 99152, 99153)

(99148, 99149, 99150 have been deleted. To report moderate sedation services provided by a physician or other qualified health care professional other than the physician or other qualified health care professional performing the diagnostic or therapeutic service that the sedation supports, see 99155, 99156, 99157)

		Moderate sedation (MS) provided by physician or other qualified health care professional (same physician or qualified health care professional also performing the procedure MS is supporting)	MS provided by different physician or other qualified health care professional (not the physician or qualified health care professional who is performing the procedure MS is supporting)
Total Intraservice Time for MS	**Patient Age**	**Code(s)**	**Code(s)**
Less than 10 minutes	Any age	Not reported separately	Not reported separately
10-22 minutes	< 5 years	99151	99155
10-22 minutes	5 years or older	99152	99156
23-37 minutes	< 5 years	99151 + 99153 x 1	99155 + 99157 x 1
23-37 minutes	5 years or older	99152 + 99153 x 1	99156 + 99157 x 1
38-52 minutes	< 5 years	99151 + 99153 x 2	99155 + 99157 x 2
38-52 minutes	5 years or older	99152 + 99153 x 2	99156 + 99157 x 2
53-67 minutes (53 min. to 1 hr. 7 min.)	< 5 years	99151 + 99153 x 3	99155 + 99157 x 3
53-67 minutes (53 min. to 1 hr. 7 min.)	5 years or older	99152 + 99153 x 3	99156 + 99157 x 3
68-82 minutes (1 hr. 8 min. to 1 hr. 22 min.)	< 5 years	99151 + 99153 x 4	99155 + 99157 x 4
68-82 minutes (1 hr. 8 min. to 1 hr. 22 min.)	5 years or older	99152 + 99153 x 4	99156 + 99157 x 4
83 minutes or longer	< 5 years	99153	Add 99157
83 minutes or longer	5 years or older	Add 99153	Add 99157

⊘ **99151** Moderate sedation services provided by the same physician or other qualified health care professional performing the diagnostic or therapeutic service that the sedation supports, requiring the presence of an independent trained observer to assist in the monitoring of the patient's level of consciousness and physiological status; initial 15 minutes of intraservice time, patient younger than 5 years of age

⊘ **99152** initial 15 minutes of intraservice time, patient age 5 years or older

+ **99153** each additional 15 minutes intraservice time (List separately in addition to code for primary service)

(Use 99153 in conjunction with 99151, 99152)

(Do not report 99153 in conjunction with 99155, 99156)

99155 Moderate sedation services provided by a physician or other qualified health care professional other than the physician or other qualified health care professional performing the diagnostic or therapeutic service that the sedation supports; initial 15 minutes of intraservice time, patient younger than 5 years of age

99156 initial 15 minutes of intraservice time, patient age 5 years or older

+ **99157** each additional 15 minutes intraservice time (List separately in addition to code for primary service)

(Use 99157 in conjunction with 99155, 99156)

(Do not report 99157 in conjunction with 99151, 99152)

OTHER SERVICES AND PROCEDURES

99170 Anogenital examination, magnified, in childhood for suspected trauma, including image recording when performed

(For moderate sedation, see 99151, 99152, 99153, 99155, 99156, 99157)

99172 Visual function screening, automated or semi-automated bilateral quantitative determination of visual acuity, ocular alignment, color vision by pseudoisochromatic plates, and field of vision (may include all or some screening of the determination(s) for contrast sensitivity, vision under glare)

(This service must employ graduated visual acuity stimuli that allow a quantitative determination of visual acuity (eg, Snellen chart). This service may not be used in addition to a gernal ophthalmological service or an E/M service)

(Do not report 99172 in conjunction with 99173, 99174, 99177, 0469T)

99173 Screening test of visual acuity, quantitative, bilateral

(The screening test used must employ graduated visual acuity stimuli that allow a quantitative estimate of visual acuity (eg, Snellen chart). Other identifiable services unrelated to this screening test provided at the same time may be reported separately (eg, preventive medicine services). When acuity is measured as part of a general ophthalmological service or of an E/M service of the eye, it is a diagnostic examination and not a screening test.)

(Do not report 99173 in conjunction with code 99172, 99174, 99177)

99174 Instrument-based ocular screening (eg, photoscreening, automated-refraction), bilateral; with remote analysis and report

(Do not report 99174 in conjunction with 92002-92014, 99172, 99173, 99177)

99177 with on-site analysis

(Do not report 99177 in conjunction with 92002-92014, 99172, 99173, 99174)

(For retinal polarization scan, use 0469T)

99175 Ipecac or similar administration for individual emesis and continued observation until stomach adequately emptied of poison

---

920 ● New Code ▲ Revised Code + Add-On Code ⊘ Modifier -51 Exempt ★ Telemedicine

(For diagnostic intubation, see 43754, 43755)

(For gastric lavage for diagnostic purposes, see 43754, 43755)

99177   This code is out of order. See page 920.

99183   Physician or other qualified health care professional attendance and supervision of hyperbaric oxygen therapy, per session

(Evaluation and Management services and/or procedures [eg, wound debridement] provided in a hyperbaric oxygen treatment facility in conjunction with a hyperbaric oxygen therapy session should be reported separately)

99184   Initiation of selective head or total body hypothermia in the critically ill neonate, includes appropriate patient selection by review of clinical, imaging and laboratory data, confirmation of esophageal temperature probe location, evaluation of amplitude EEG, supervision of controlled hypothermia, and assessment of patient tolerance of cooling

(Do not report 99184 more than once per hospital stay)

99188   Application of topical fluoride varnish by a physician or other qualified health care professional

99190   Assembly and operation of pump with oxygenator or heat exchanger (with or without ECG and/or pressure monitoring); each hour

99191   45 minutes

99192   30 minutes

99195   Phlebotomy, therapeutic (separate procedure)

99199   Unlisted special service, procedure or report

HOME HEALTH PROCEDURES/SERVICES

Home health procedures/services codes are used by non-physician health care professionals to report services provided in the patient's residence.

Physicians should utilize the home visit codes 99341-99350 and utilize CPT codes other than 99500-99600 for any additional procedure/service provided to a patient living in a residence.

The following codes are used to report services provided in a patient's residence (including assisted living apartments, group homes, nontraditional private homes, custodial care facilities, or schools).

Health care professionals who are authorized to use Evaluation and Management (E/M) Home Visit codes (99341-99350) may report 99500-99600 in addition to 99341-99350 if both services are performed. E/M services may be reported separately, using modifier 25, if the patient's condition requires a significant separately identifiable E/M service, above and beyond the home health service(s)/procedure(s) codes 99500-99600.

99500   Home visit for prenatal monitoring and assessment to include fetal heart rate, non-stress test, uterine monitoring, and gestational diabetes monitoring

99501   Home visit for postnatal assessment and follow-up care

99502   Home visit for newborn care and assessment

99503   Home visit for respiratory therapy care (eg, bronchodilator, oxygen therapy, respiratory assessment, apnea evaluation)

99504   Home visit for mechanical ventilation care

99505   Home visit for stoma care and maintenance including colostomy and cystostomy

99506   Home visit for intramuscular injections

99507   Home visit for care and maintenance of catheter(s) (eg, urinary, drainage, and enteral)

99509   Home visit for assistance with activities of daily living and personal care

   (To report self-care/home management training, see 97535)

   (To report home medical nutrition assessment and intervention services, see 97802-97804)

   (To report home speech therapy services, see 92507-92508)

99510   Home visit for individual, family, or marriage counseling

99511   Home visit for fecal impaction management and enema administration

99512   Home visit for hemodialysis

   (For home infusion of peritoneal dialysis, use 99601, 99602)

99600   Unlisted home visit service or procedure

HOME INFUSION PROCEDURES/SERVICES

Home infusion procedures codes are used to report per diem home visits for the purpose of administering infusions. With the exception of the infusion drug; all materials, equipments and supplies are included in the basic code. Drugs used for the infusion are coded separately.

99601   Home infusion/specialty drug administration, per visit (up to 2 hours)

+ 99602   each additional hour (List separately in addition to code for primary procedure)

   (Use 99602 in conjunction with 99601)

MEDICATION THERAPY MANAGEMENT SERVICES

Medication Therapy Management Services or MTMS describes in-person patient assessment and intervention as appropriate by a pharmacist. The purpose of MTMS is to maximize medication response and/or managed medication interactions or complications. MTMS includes review of history, medication profile, and recommendations regarding outcomes and compliance. MTMS codes are not used to report product information at the point of dispensing or other routine activities related to dispensing.

These codes are not to be used to describe the provision of product-specific information at the point of dispensing or any other routine dispensing-related activities.

99605   Medication therapy management service(s) provided by a pharmacist, individual, face-to-face with patient, with assessment and intervention if provided; initial 15 minutes, new patient

99606   initial 15 minutes, established patient

+ 99607   each additional 15 minutes (List separately in addition to code for primary service)

   (Use 99607 in conjunction with 99605, 99606)

● New Code   ▲ Revised Code   + Add-On Code   ⊘ Modifier -51 Exempt   ★ Telemedicine

This section of the CPT coding system is the Category II Performance Measurement section. The primary purpose of this section is to provide classification codes which will allow the collection of data for performance measurement.

The assignment of a Category II code to a given service or procedure does not mean that the particular service or procedure is endorsed, approved, safe or has applicability to clinical practice. The Category II code simply provides a mechanism to identify and review performance measurements.

The most current codes and their implementation dates can be found on the Web at http://www.ama-assn.org/go/cpt.

CPT Category II codes are arranged according to the following categories:

Composite Codes	0001F-0015F
Patient Management	0500F-0584F
Patient History	1000F-1505F
Physical Examination	2000F-2060F
Diagnostic/Screening Processes or Results	3006F-3776F
Therapeutic, Preventive or Other Interventions	4000F-4563F
Follow-up or Other Outcomes	5005F-5250F
Patient Safety	6005F-6150F
Structural Measures	7010F-7025F
Nonmeasure Code Listing	9001F-9007F

MODIFIERS

The following performance measurement modifiers may be used for Category II codes to indicate that a service specified in the associate measure(s) was considered but, due to either medical, patient or system circumstance(s) documented in the medical record, the service was not provided. These modifiers serve as denominator exclusions from the performance measure.

Category II modifiers should only be reported with Category II codes; they should not be reported with Category I or Category III codes. In addition, the modifiers in the Category II section should only be used where specified in the guidelines, reporting instructions, parenthetic notes, or code descriptor language listed in the Cateogry II section.

1P Performance Measure Exclusion Modifier due to Medical Reasons:

Reasons include:
- Not indicated (absence of organ/limb, already received/performed, other)
- Contraindicated (patient allergic history, potential adverse drug interaction, other)
- Other medical reason

2P Performance Measure Exclusion Modifier due to Patient Reason:

Reasons include:
- Patient declined
- Economic, social or religious reasons
- Other patient reasons

3P Performance Measure Exclusion Modifier due to System Reason:

Reasons include:
- Resources to perform the services not available
- Insurance coverage/payor-related limitations
- Other reasons attributable to health care delivery system

Modifier 8P is intended to be used as a "reporting modifier" to allow the reporting of circumstances when an action described in a measure's numerator is not performed and the reason is not otherwise specified.

8P Performance measure reporting modifier—action not performed, reason not otherwise specified

---

■ Separate Procedure	■ Unlisted Procedure	■ CCI Comp. Code	■ Non-specific Procedure

923

COMPOSITE CODES

Composite codes combine several measures grouped within a single code descriptor to facilitate reporting for a clinical condition when all components are met. If only some of the components are met, or if services are provided in addition to those included in the composite code, they may be reported individually using the corresponding CPT Category II codes for those services.

0001F Heart failure assessed (includes assessment of all the following components) (CAD)[1]:

Blood pressure measured (2000F)[1]
Level of activity assessed (1003F)[1]
Clinical symptoms of volume overload (excess) assessed (1004F)[1]
Weight, recorded (2001F)[1]
Clinical signs of volume overload (excess) assessed (2002F)[1]

(To report blood pressure measured, use 2000F)

0005F Osteoarthritis assessed (OA)[1]

Includes assessment of all the following components:
Osteoarthritis symptoms and functional status assessed (1006F)[1]
Use of anti-inflammatory or over-the-counter (OTC) analgesic medications assessed (1007F)[1]
Initial examination of the involved joint(s) (includes visual inspection, palpation, range of motion) (2004F)[1]

(To report tobacco use cessation intervention, use 4001F)

0012F Community-acquired bacterial pneumonia assessment (includes all of the following components) (CAP)[1]:

Co-morbid conditions assessed (1026F)[1]
Vital signs recorded (2010F)[1]
Mental status assessed (2014F)[1]
Hydration status assessed (2018F)[1]

0014F Comprehensive preoperative assessment performed for cataract surgery with intraocular lens (IOL) placement (includes assessment of all of the following components) (EC)[5]:

Dilated fundus evaluation performed within 12 months prior to cataract surgery (2020F)[5]
Pre-surgical (cataract) axial length, corneal power measurement and method of intraocular lens power calculation documented (must be performed within 12 months prior to surgery) (3073F)[5]
Preoperative assessment of functional or medical indication(s) for surgery prior to the cataract surgery with intraocular lens placement (must be performed within 12 months prior to cataract surgery) (3325F)[5]

0015F Melanoma follow up completed (includes assessment of all of the following components) (ML)[5]:

History obtained regarding new or changing moles (1050F)[5]
Complete physical skin exam performed (2029F)[5]
Patient counseled to perform a monthly self skin examination (5005F)[5]

PATIENT MANAGEMENT

Patient management codes describe utilization measures or measures of patient care provided for specific clinical purposes (eg, prenatal care, pre- and post-surgical care).

0500F Initial prenatal care visit (report at first prenatal encounter with health care professional providing obstetrical care. Report also date of visit and, in a separate field, the date of the last menstrual period [LMP]) (Prenatal)[2]

0501F Prenatal flow sheet documented in medical record by first prenatal visit (documentation includes at minimum blood pressure, weight, urine protein, uterine size, fetal heart tones, and estimated date of delivery). Report also: date of visit and, in a separate field, the date of the last menstrual period [LMP] (Note: if reporting 0501F prenatal flow sheet, it is not necessary to report 0500F initial prenatal care visit) (Prenatal)[1]

0502F Subsequent prenatal care visit (Prenatal)[2]

● New Code ▲ Revised Code + Add-On Code ⊘ Modifier -51 Exempt ★ Telemedicine

[Excludes: patients who are seen for a condition unrelated to pregnancy or prenatal care (eg, an upper respiratory infection; patients seen for consultation only, not for continuing care)]

0503F Postpartum care visit(Prenatal)[2]

0505F Hemodialysis plan of care documented (ESRD, P-ESRD)[1]

0507F Peritoneal dialysis plan of care documented (ESRD)[1]

0509F Urinary incontinence plan of care documented (GER)[5]

0513F Elevated blood pressure plan of care documented (CKD)[1]

0514F Plan of care for elevated hemoglobin level documented for patient receiving Erythropoiesis-Stimulating Agent therapy (ESA) (CKD)[1]

0516F Anemia plan of care documented (ESRD)[1]

0517F Glaucoma plan of care documented (EC)[5]

0518F Falls plan of care documented (GER)[5]

0519F Planned chemotherapy regimen, including at a minimum: drug(s) prescribed, dose, and duration, documented prior to initiation of a new treatment regimen (ONC)[1]

0520F Radiation dose limits to normal tissues established prior to the initiation of a course of 3D conformal radiation for a minimum of 2 tissue/organ (ONC)[1]

0521F Plan of care to address pain documented (COA)[2] (ONC)[1]

0525F Initial visit for episode (BkP)[2]

0526F Subsequent visit for episode (BkP)[2]

0528F Recommended follow up interval for repeat colonoscopy of at least 10 years documented in colonoscopy report (End/Polyp)[5]

0529F Interval of 3 or more years since patient's last colonoscopy, documented (End/Polyp)[5]

0535F Dyspnea management plan of care, documented (Pall Cr)[5]

0540F Glucorticoid Management Plan Documented (RA)[5]

0545F Plan for follow-up care for major depressive disorder, documented (MDD ADOL)[1]

Footnotes

1-Physician Consortium for Performance Improvement (PCPI), www.physicianconsortium.org

2-National Committee on Quality Assurance (NCQA), Health Employer Data Information Set (HEDIS®), www.ncqa.org

3-The Joint Commission (TJC), ORYX Initiative Performance Measures, http://www.jointcommission.org/performancemeasurement.aspx

4-National Diabetes Quality Improvement Alliance (NDQIA), http://www.nationaldiabetesalliance.org

5-Joint measure from The Physician Consortium for Performance Improvement, www.physicianconsortium.org and National Committee on Quality Assurance (NCQA), www.ncqa.org

6-The Society of Thoracic Surgeons, http://www.sts.org, and National Quality Forum, http://www.qualityforum.org

7-Optum, www.optum.com

8-American Academy of Neurology, www.aan.com/go/practice/quality/measurements or quality@aan.com

9-College of American Pathologists (CAP), www.cap.org/apps/docs/advocacy/pathology_performance_measurement.pdf

10-American Gastroenterological Association (AGA), www.gastro.org/quality

11-American Society of Anesthesiologists (ASA), http://www.asahq.org

12-American College of Gastroenterology (ACG), www.gi.org; American Gastroenterology Association (AGA), www.gastro.org; and American Society for Gastrointestinal Endoscopy (ASGE), www. asge.org

---

Separate Procedure   Unlisted Procedure   CCI Comp. Code   Non-specific Procedure   **925**

0550F Cytopathology report on routine nongynecologic specimen finalized within two working days of accession date (PATH)[9]

0551F Cytopathology report on nongynecologic specimen with documentation that the specimen was non-routine (PATH)[9]

0555F Symptom management plan of care documented (HF)[1]

0556F Plan of care to achieve lipid control documented (CAD)[1]

0557F Plan of care to manage anginal symptoms documented (CAD)[1]

0575F HIV RNA control plan of care, documented (HIV)[5]

0580F Multidisciplinary care plan developed or updated (ALS)[8]

0581F Patient transferred directly from anesthetizing location to critical care unit (Peri2)[11]

0582F Patient not transferred directly from anesthetizing location to critical care unit (Peri2)[11]

0583F Transfer of care checklist used (Peri2)[11]

0584F Transfer of care checklist not used (Peri2)[11]

PATIENT HISTORY

Patient history codes describe measures for select aspects of patient history or review of systems.

1000F Tobacco use assessed (CAD, CAP, COPD, PV)[1] (DM)[4]

1002F Anginal symptoms and level of activity, assessed(NMA- No Measure Associated)

1003F Level of activity assessed (NMA-No Measure Associated)

1004F Clinical symptoms of volume overload (excess) assessed (NMA-No Measure Associated)

1005F Asthma symptoms evaluated (includes documentation of numeric frequency of symptoms or patient completion of an asthma assessment tool/survey/questionnaire) (NMA-No Measure Associated)

1006F Osteoarthritis symptoms and functional status assessed (may include the use of a standardized scale or the completion of an assessment questionnaire, such as the SF-36, AAOS Hip & Knee Questionnaire) (OA)[1]

[Instructions: report when osteoarthritis is addressed during the patient encounter]

1007F Use of anti-inflammatory or analgesic over-the-counter (OTC) medications for symptom relief assessed (OA)[1]

1008F Gastrointestinal and renal risk factors assessed for patients on prescribed or OTC non-steroidal anti-inflammatory drug (NSAID) (OA)[1]

1010F Severity of angina assessed by level of activity (CAD)[1]

1011F Angina present (CAD)[1]

1012F Angina absent (CAD)[1]

1015F Chronic obstructive pulmonary disease (COPD) symptoms assessed (Includes assessment of at least one of the following: dyspnea, cough/sputum, wheezing), or respiratory symptom assessment tool completed (COPD)[1]

● New Code ▲ Revised Code + Add-On Code ⊘ Modifier -51 Exempt ★ Telemedicine

1018F Dyspnea assessed, not present (COPD)[1]

1019F Dyspnea assessed, present (COPD)[1]

1022F Pneumococcus immunization status assessed (CAP, COPD)[1]

1026F Co-morbid conditions assessed (eg, includes assessment for presence or absence of: malignancy, liver disease, congestive heart failure, cerebrovascular disease, renal disease, chronic obstructive pulmonary disease, asthma, diabetes, other co-morbid conditions) (CAP)[1]

1030F Influenza immunization status assessed (CAP)[1]

1031F Smoking status and exposure to second hand smoke in the home assessed (Asthma)[1]

1032F Current tobacco smoker OR currently exposed to secondhand smoke (Asthma)[1]

1033F Current tobacco non-smoker AND not currently exposed to secondhand smoke (Asthma)[1]

1034F Current tobacco smoker (CAD, CAP, COPD, PV)[1] (DM)[4]

1035F Current smokeless tobacco user (eg, chew, snuff) (PV)[1]

1036F Current tobacco non-user (CAD, CAP, COPD, PV)[1] (DM)[4] (IBD)[10]

1038F Persistent asthma (mild, moderate or severe) (Asthma)[1]

1039F Intermittent asthma (Asthma)[1]

1040F DSM-5™ criteria for major depressive disorder documented at the initial evaluation (MDD, MDD ADOL)[1]

1050F History obtained regarding new or changing moles (ML)[5]

1052F Type, anatomic location, and activity all assessed (IBD)[10]

1055F Visual functional status assessed (EC)[5]

1060F Documentation of permanent OR persistent OR paroxysmal atrial fibrillation (STR)[5]

1061F Documentation of absence of permanent AND persistent AND paroxysmal atrial fibrillation (STR)[5]

1065F Ischemic stroke symptom onset of less than 3 hours prior to arrival (STR)[5]

1066F Ischemic stroke symptom onset greater than or equal to 3 hours prior to arrival (STR)[5]

1070F Alarm symptoms (involuntary weight loss, dysphagia, or gastrointestinal bleeding) assessed; none present (GERD)[5]

1071F one or more present (GERD)[5]

(1080F deleted. To report surrogate decision maker or advance care plan documented in the medical record, report 1123F or 1124F)

1090F Presence or absence or urinary incontinence assessed (GER)[5]

1091F Urinary incontinence characterized (eg, frequency, volume, timing, type of symptoms, how bothersome) (GER)[5]

1100F Patient screened for future fall risk; documentation of two or more falls in the past year or any fall with injury in the past year (GER)[5]

| Separate Procedure | Unlisted Procedure | CCI Comp. Code | Non-specific Procedure | **927** |

1101F   documentation of no falls in the past year or only one fall without injury in the past year (GER)[5]

1110F   Patient discharged from an inpatient facility (eg hospital, skilled nursing facility, or rehabilitation facility) within the last 60 days (GER)[5]

1111F   Discharge medications reconciled with the current medication list in outpatient medical record (COA)[2] (GER)[5]

1116F   Auricular or periauricular pain assessed (AOE)[1]

1118F   Gerd symptoms assessed after 12 months of therapy (GERD)[5]

1119F   Initial evaluation for condition (HEP C)[1] (EPI, DSP)[8]

1121F   Subsequent evaluation for condition (HEP C)[1] (EPI)[8]

1123F   Advance care planning discussed and documented advance care plan or surrogate decision maker documented in the medical record (DEM)[1] (GER, PallCr)[5]

1124F   Advance care planning discussed and documented in the medical record patient did not wish or was not able to name a surrogate decision maker or provide an advance care plan (DEM)[1] (GER, PallCr)[5]

1125F   Pain severity quantified; pain present (COA)[2] (ONC)[1]

1126F   no pain present (COA)[2] (ONC)[1]

1127F   New episode for condition (NMA-No Measure Associated)

1128F   Subsequent episode for condition (NMA-No Measure Associated)

1130F   Back pain and function assessed, including all of the following: Pain assessment AND functional status AND patient history, including notation of presence or absence of "red flags" (warning signs) AND assessment of prior treatment and response, AND employment status (BkP)[2]

1134F   Episode of back pain lasting 6 weeks or less (BkP)[2]

1135F   Episode of back pain lasting longer than 6 weeks (BkP)[2]

1136F   Episode of back pain lasting 12 weeks or less (BkP)[2]

1137F   Episode of back pain lasting longer than 12 weeks (BkP)[2]

1150F   Documentation that a patient has a substantial risk of death within 1 year (Pall Cr)[5]

1151F   Documentation that a patient does not have a substantial risk of death within one year (Pall Cr)[5]

1152F   Documentation of advanced disease diagnosis, goals of care prioritize comfort (Pall Cr)[5]

1153F   Documentation of advanced disease diagnosis, goals of care do not prioritize comfort (Pall Cr)[5]

1157F   Advance care plan or similar legal document present in the medical record (COA)[2]

1158F   Advance care planning discussion documented in the medical record (COA)[2]

1159F   Medication list documented in medical record (COA)[2]

1160F   Review of all medications by a prescribing practitioner or clinical pharmacist (such as, prescriptions, OTCs, herbal therapies and supplements) documented in the medical record (COA)[2]

1170F   Functional status assessed (COA)[2] (RA)[5]

1175F Functional status for dementia assessed and results reviewed (DEM)[1]

1180F All specified thromboembolic risk factors assessed (AFIB)[1]

1181F Neuropsychiatric symptoms assessed and results reviewed (DEM)[1]

1182F Neuropsychiatric symptoms, one or more present (DEM)[1]

1183F Neuropsychiatric symptoms, absent (DEM)[1]

1200F Seizure type(s) and current seizure frequency(ies) documented (EPI)[8]

1205F Etiology of epilepsy or epilepsy syndrome(s) reviewed and documented (EPI)[8]

1220F Patient screened for depression (SUD)[5]

1400F Parkinson's disease diagnosis reviewed (PRKNS)[8]

1450F Symptoms improved or remained consistent with treatment goals since last assessment (HF)[1]

1451F Symptoms demonstrated clinically important deterioration since last assessment (HF)[1]

1460F Qualifying cardiac event/diagnosis in previous 12 months (CAD)[1]

1461F No qualifying cardiac event/diagnosis in previous 12 months (CAD)[1]

1490F Dementia severity classified, mild (DEM)[1]

1491F Dementia severity classified, moderate (DEM)[1]

1493F Dementia severity classified, severe (DEM)[1]

1494F Cognition assessed and reviewed (DEM)[1]

1500F Symptoms and signs of distal symmetric polyneuropathy reviewed and documented (DSP)[8]

1501F Not initial evaluation for condition (DSP)[8]

1502F Patient queried about pain and pain interference with function using a valid and reliable instrument (DSP)[8]

1503F Patient queried about symptoms of respiratory insufficiency (ALS)[8]

1504F Patient has respiratory insufficiency (ALS)[8]

Footnotes

1-Physician Consortium for Performance Improvement (PCPI), www.physicianconsortium.org

2-National Committee on Quality Assurance (NCQA), Health Employer Data Information Set (HEDIS®), www.ncqa.org

3-The Joint Commission (TJC), ORYX Initiative Performance Measures, http://www.jointcommission.org/performancemeasurement.aspx

4-National Diabetes Quality Improvement Alliance (NDQIA), http://www.nationaldiabetesalliance.org

5-Joint measure from The Physician Consortium for Performance Improvement, www.physicianconsortium.org and National Committee on Quality Assurance (NCQA), www.ncqa.org

6-The Society of Thoracic Surgeons, http://www.sts.org, and National Quality Forum, http://www.qualityforum.org

7-Optum, www.optum.com

8-American Academy of Neurology, www.aan.com/go/practice/quality/measurements or quality@aan.com

9-College of American Pathologists (CAP), www.cap.org/apps/docs/ advocacy/pathology_performance_measurement.pdf

10-American Gastroenterological Association (AGA), www.gastro.org/quality

11-American Society of Anesthesiologists (ASA), http://www.asahq.org

12-American College of Gastroenterology (ACG), www.gi.org; American Gastroenterology Association (AGA), www.gastro.org; and American Society for Gastrointestinal Endoscopy (ASGE), www. asge.org

---

Separate Procedure   Unlisted Procedure   CCI Comp. Code   Non-specific Procedure   **929**

1505F   Patient does not have respiratory insufficiency (ALS)[8]

PHYSICAL EXAMINATION

Physical examination codes describe aspects of physical examination or clinical assessment.

2000F   Blood pressure measured (CKD)[1] (DM)[2,4]

2001F   Weight recorded(PAG)[1]

2002F   Clinical signs of volume overload (excess) assessed (NMA-No Measure Associated)

2004F   Initial examination of the involved joint(s) (includes visual inspection, palpation, range of motion) (OA)[1]

       [Instructions: report only for initial osteoarthritis visit or for visits for new joint involvement]

2010F   Vital signs (temperature, pulse, respiratory rate, and blood pressure) documented and reviewed (CAP)[1](EM)[5]

2014F   Mental status assessed (CAP)[1](EM)[5]

2015F   Asthma impairment assessed (Asthma)[1]

2016F   Asthma risk assessed (Asthma)[1]

2018F   Hydration status assessed (normal/mildly dehydrated/severely dehydrated) (CAP)[1]

2019F   Dilated macular exam performed, including documentation of the presence or absence of macular thickening or hemorrhage AND the level of macular degeneration severity (EC)[5]

2020F   Dilated fundus evaluation performed within 12 months prior to cataract surgery (EC)[5]

2021F   Dilated macular or fundus exam performed, including documentation of the presence or absence of macular edema AND level of severity of retinopathy (EC)[5]

2022F   Dilated retinal eye exam with interpretation by an ophthalmologist or optometrist documented and reviewed (DM)[2,4]

2024F   7 standard field stereoscopic photos with interpretation by an ophthalmologist or optometrist documented and reviewed (DM)[2,4]

2026F   Eye imaging validated to match diagnosis from 7 standard field stereoscopic photos results documented and reviewed (DM)[2,4]

2027F   Optic nerve head evaluation performed (EC)[5]

2028F   Foot examination performed (includes examination through visual inspection, sensory exam with monofilament, and pulse exam — report when any of the 3 components are completed) (DM)[4]

2029F   Complete physical skin exam performed (ML)[5]

2030F   Hydration status documented, normally hydrated (PAG)[1]

2031F   Hydration status documented, dehydrated (PAG)[1]

2035F   Tympanic membrane mobility assessed with pneumatic otoscoopy or tympanometry (OME)[1]

2040F   Physical examination on the date of the initial visit for low back pain performed, in accordance with specifications (BkP)[2]

2044F Documentation of mental health assessment prior to intervention (back surgery or epidural steroid injection) or for back pain episode lasting longer than 6 weeks (BkP)[2]

2050F Wound characteristics including size AND nature of wound base tissue AND amount of drainage prior to debridement documented (CWC)[5]

2060F Patient interviewed directly on or before date of diagnosis of major depressive disorder (MDD ADOL)[1]

DIAGNOSTIC/SCREENING PROCESSES OR RESULTS

Diagnostic/screening processes or results codes describe results of tests ordered (clinical laboratory tests, radiological or other procedural examinations and conclusions of medical decision-making).

(To report blood pressure, use the corresponding systolic codes [3074F, 3075F, 3077F] and diastolic codes [3078F, 3079F, 3080F])

3006F Chest X-ray results documented and reviewed (CAP)[1]

3008F Body mass index (BMI), documented (PV)[1]

3011F Lipid panel results documented and reviewed (must include total cholesterol, HDL-C, triglycerides and calculated LDL-C) (CAD)[1]

3014F Screening mammography results documented and reviewed (PV)[1,2]

3015F Cervical cancer screening results documented and reviewed (PV)[1]

3016F Patient screened for unhealthy alcohol use using a systematic screening method (PV)[1](DSP)[8]

3017F Colorectal cancer screening results documented and reviewed (PV) [1,2]

3018F Pre procedure risk assessment AND depth of insertion AND quality of the bowel prep AND complete description of polyp(s) found, including location of each polyp, size, number and gross morphology AND recommendations for follow up in final colonoscopy report documented (End/Polyp)[5]

3019F Left ventricular ejection fracrtion (LVEF) assessment planned post discharge (HF)[1]

3020F Left ventricular function (LVF) assessment (eg, echocardiography, nuclear test, or ventriculography) documented in the medical record (Includes quantitative or qualitative assessment results) (NMA-No Measure Associated)

3021F Left ventricular ejection fraction (LVEF) 40% or documentation of moderately or severely depressed left ventricular systolic function (CAD, HF)[1]

3022F Left ventricular ejection fraction (LVEF) 40% or documentation as normal or mildly depressed left ventricular systolic function (CAD, HF)[1]

3023F Spirometry results documented and reviewed (COPD)[1]

3025F Spirometry test results demonstrate FEV1/FVC70% with COPD symptoms (eg, dyspnea, cough/sputum, wheezing) (CAP, COPD)[1]

3027F Spirometry test results demonstrate FEV1/FVC greater than or equal to 70% or patient does not have COPD symptoms (COPD)[1]

3028F Oxygen saturation results documented and reviewed (Includes assessment through pulse oximetry or arterial blood gas measurement) (CAP, COPD)[1] (EM)[5]

3035F Oxygen saturation less than or equal to 88 % or a PaO_2 less than or equal to 55 mm Hg (COPD)[1]

■ Separate Procedure   ■ Unlisted Procedure   ■ CCI Comp. Code   ■ Non-specific Procedure   **931**

3037F Oxygen saturation greater than 88% or PaO_2 greater than 55 mmHg (COPD)[1]

3038F Pulmonary function test performed within 12 months prior to surgery (Lung/Esop Cx)[6]

3040F Functional expiratory volume (FEV_1) < 40% of predicted value (COPD)[1]

3042F Functional expiratory volume (FEV_1) greater than or equal to 40% of predicted value (COPD)[1]

3044F Most recent hemoglobin A1c (HbA1c) level < 7.0% (DM)[2,4]

3045F Most recent hemoglobin A1c (HbA1c) level 7.0 - 9.0% (DM)[2,4]

3046F Most recent hemoglobin A1c level greater than 9.0% (DM)[4]

(To report most recent hemoglobin A1c level ≤ 9.0%, see codes 3044F-3045F)

3048F Most recent LDL-C < 100 mg/dL (CAD)[1] (DM)[4]

3049F Most recent LDL-C 100-129 mg/dL (CAD)[1] (DM)[4]

3050F Most recent LDL-C≥ 130 mg/dL (CAD)[1] (DM)[4]

3055F Left ventricular ejection fraction (LVEF) less than or equal to 35% (HF)[1]

3056F Left ventricular ejection fraction (LVEF) greater than 35% or no LVEF result available (HF)[1]

3060F Positive microalbuminuria test result documented and reviewed (DM)[2,4]

3061F Negative microalbuminuria test result documented and reviewed (DM)[2,4]

3062F Positive macroalbuminuria test result documented and reviewed (DM)[2,4]

3066F Documentation of treatment for nephropathy (eg, patient receiving dialysis, patient being treated for ESRD, CRF, ARF, or renal insufficiency, any visit to a nephrologist) (DM)[2,4]

3072F Low risk for retinopathy (no evidence of retinopathy in the prior year) (DM)[2,4]

3073F Pre-surgical (cataract) axial length, corneal power measurement and method of intraocular lens power calculation documented within 12 months prior to surgery (EC)[5]

3074F Most recent systolic blood pressure less than 130mm Hg (DM)[2,4](HTN,CKD, CAD)[1]

3075F Most recent systolic blood pressure 130-139 mm Hg (DM)[2,4](HTN,CKD, CAD)[1]

(To report most recent systolic blood pressure less than 140 mm Hg, see codes 3047F-3075F)

3077F Most recent systolic blood pressure greater than or equal to 140 mmHg (HTN,CKD, CAD)[1] (DM)[2,4]

3078F Most recent diastolic blood pressure less than 80 mm Hg (HTN,CKD, CAD)[1] (DM)[2,4]

3079F Most recent diastolic blood pressure 80-89 mm Hg (HTN,CKD, CAD)[1] (DM)[2,4]

3080F Most recent diastolic blood pressuregreater than or equal to 90 mmHg (HTN,CKD, CAD)[1] (DM)[2,4]

3082F Kt/V less than 1.2 (Clearance of urea [Kt]/volume [V]) (ESRD, P-ESRD)[1]

3083F Kt/V equal to or greater than 1.2 and less than 1.7 (Clearance of urea [Kt]/volume [V]) (ESRD, P-ESRD)[1]

3084F Kt/V greater than or equal to 1.7 (Clearance of urea [Kt]/volume [V]) (ESRD, P-ESRD)[1]

3085F Suicide risk assessed (MDD, MDD ADOL)[1]

3088F Major depressive disorder, mild (MDD)[1]

3089F Major depressive disorder, moderate (MDD)[1]

3090F Major depressive disorder, severe without psychotic features (MDD)[1]

3091F Major depressive disorder, severe with psychotic features (MDD)[1]

3092F Major depressive disorder, in remission (MDD)[1]

3093F Documentation of new diagnosis of initial or recurrent episode of major depressive disorder (MDD)[1]

3095F Dual-energy X-ray Absorptiometry (DXA) results documented (OP)[5](IBD)[10]

3096F Central dual-energy X-ray Absorptiometry (DXA) ordered (OP)[5](IBD)[10]

3100F Carotid imaging study report (includes direct or indirect reference to measurements of distal internal carotid diameter as the denominator for stenosis measurement) (STR, RAD)[5]

3110F Documentation in final CT or MRI report of presence or absence of hemorrhage and mass lesion and acute infarction (STR)[5]

3111F CT or MRI of the brain performed in the hospital within 24 hours of arrival OR performed in an outpatient imaging center, to confirm initial diagnosis of stroke, TIA, or intracranial hemorrhage (STR)[5]

3112F CT or MRI of the brain performed greater than 24 hours after arrival to the hospital OR performed in an outpatient imaging center for purpose other than confirmation of initial diagnosis of stroke, TIA, or intracranial hemorrhage (STR)[5]

3115F Quantitative results of an evaluation of current level of activity and clinical symptoms (HF)[1]

3117F Heart Failure disease specific structured assessment tool completed (HF)[1]

3118F New York Heart Association (NYHA) Class documented (HF)[1]

3119F No Evaluation of level of activity or clinical symptoms (HF)[1]

3120F 12-Lead ECG Performed (EM)[5]

(**3125F** deleted 2014 [2014 edition])

Footnotes

1-Physician Consortium for Performance Improvement (PCPI), www.physicianconsortium.org

2-National Committee on Quality Assurance (NCQA), Health Employer Data Information Set (HEDIS®), www.ncqa.org

3-The Joint Commission (TJC), ORYX Initiative Performance Measures, http://www.jointcommission.org/performancemeasurement.aspx

4-National Diabetes Quality Improvement Alliance (NDQIA), http://www.nationaldiabetesalliance.org

5-Joint measure from The Physician Consortium for Performance Improvement, www.physicianconsortium.org and National Committee on Quality Assurance (NCQA), www.ncqa.org

6-The Society of Thoracic Surgeons, http://www.sts.org, and National Quality Forum, http://www.qualityforum.org

7-Optum, www.optum.com

8-American Academy of Neurology, www.aan.com/go/practice/quality/measurements or quality@aan.com

9-College of American Pathologists (CAP), www.cap.org/apps/docs/ advocacy/pathology_performance_measurement.pdf

10-American Gastroenterological Association (AGA), www.gastro.org/quality

11-American Society of Anesthesiologists (ASA), http://www.asahq.org

12-American College of Gastroenterology (ACG), www.gi.org; American Gastroenterology Association (AGA), www.gastro.org; and American Society for Gastrointestinal Endoscopy (ASGE), www. asge.org

---

3126F Esophageal bipsy report with a statement about dysplasia (present, absent, or indefinite, and if present, contains appropriate grading) (PATH)[9]

3130F Upper gastrointestinal endoscopy performed (GERD)[5]

3132F Documentation of referral for upper gastrointestinal endoscopy (GERD)[5]

3140F Upper gastrointestinal endoscopy report indicates suspicion of Barrett's esophagus (GERD)[5]

3141F Upper gastrointestinal endoscopy report indicates no suspicion of Barrett's esophagus (GERD)[5]

3142F Barium swallow test ordered (GERD)[1]

(To report documentation of barium swallow study, use code 3142F)

3150F Forceps esophageal biopsy performed (GERD)[5]

3155F Cytogenetic testing performed on bone marrow at time of diagnosis or prior to initiating treatment (HEM)[1]

3160F Documentation of iron stores prior to initiating erythropoietin therapy (HEM)[1]

3170F Flow cytometry studies performed at time of diagnosis or prior to initiating treatment (HEM)[1]

3200F Barium swallow test not ordered (GERD)[5]

3210F Group A Strep Test Performed (PHAR)[2]

3215F Patient has documented immunity to Hepatitis A (HEP-C)[1]

3216F Patient has documented immunity to Hepatitis B (HEP-C)[1] (IBD)[10]

3218F RNA testing for Hepatitis C documented as performed within 6 months prior to initiation of antiviral treatment for Hepatitis C (HEP-C)[1]

3220F Hepatitis C quantitative RNA testing documented as performed at 12 weeks from initiation of antiviral treatment (HEP-C)[1]

3230F Documentation that hearing test was performed within 6 months prior to tympanostomy tube insertion (OME)[1]

3250F Specimen site other than anatomic location of primary tumor (PATH)[1]

3260F pT category (primary tumor), pN category (regional lymph nodes), and histologic grade documented in pathology report (PATH)[1]

3265F Ribonucleic acid (RNA) testing for Hepatitis C viremia ordered or results documented (HEP C)[1]

3266F Hepatitis C genotype testing documented as performed prior to initiation of antiviral treatment for Hepatitis C (HEP C)[1]

3267F Pathology report includes pT category, pN category, Gleason score, and statement about margin status (PATH)[9]

3268F Prostate-specific antigen (PSA), AND primary tumor (T) stage, AND Gleason score documented prior to initiation of treatment (PRCA)[1]

3269F Bone scan performed prior to initiation of treatment or at any time since diagnosis of prostate cancer (PRCA)[1]

3270F Bone scan not performed prior to initiation of treatment nor at any time since diagnosis of prostate cancer (PRCA)[1]

● New Code   ▲ Revised Code   ✛ Add-On Code   ⊘ Modifier -51 Exempt   ★ Telemedicine

3271F   Low risk of recurrence, prostate cancer (PRCA)[1]

3272F   Intermediate risk of recurrence, prostate cancer (PRCA)[1]

3273F   High risk of recurrence, prostate cancer (PRCA)[1]

3274F   Prostate cancer risk of recurrence not determined or neither low, intermediate nor high (PRCA)[1]

3278F   Serum levels of calcium, phosphorus, intact parathyroid hormone (PTH) and lipid profile ordered (CKD)[1]

3279F   Hemoglobin level greater than or equal to 13 g/dl (CKD, ESRD)[1]

3280F   Hemoglobin level 11 g/dl to 12.9 g/dl (CKD, ESRD)[1]

3281F   Hemoglobin level less than 11 g/dl (CKD, ESRD)[1]

3284F   Intraocular pressure (IOP) reduced by a value of greater than or equal to 15% from the pre-intervention level (EC)[5]

3285F   Intraocular pressure (IOP) reduced by a value less than 15% from the pre-intervention level (EC)[5]

3288F   Falls risk assessment documented (GER)[5]

3290F   Patient is D (Rh) negative and unsensitized (Pre-Cr)[1]

3291F   Patient is D (Rh) positive or sensitized (Pre-Cr)[1]

3292F   HIV testing ordered or documented and reviewed during the first or second prenatal visit (Pre-Cr)[1]

3293F   ABO and Rh blood typing documented as performed (Pre-Cr)[7]

3294F   Group B streptococcus (GBS) screening documented as performed during week 35-37 gestation (Pre-Cr)[7]

3300F   American Joint Committee on Cancer (AJCC) stage documented and reviewed (ONC)[1]

3301F   Cancer stage documented in medical record as metastatic and reviewed (ONC)[1]

       (To report measures for cancer staging, see 3321F-3390F)

3315F   Estrogen receptor (ER) or progesterone receptor (PR) positive breast cancer (ONC)[1]

3316F   Estrogen receptor (ER) and progesterone receptor (PR) negative breast cancer (ONC)[1]

3317F   Pathology report confirming malignancy documented in the medical record and reviewed prior to the initiation of chemotherapy (ONC)[1]

3318F   Pathology report confirming malignancy documented in the medical record and reviewed prior to the initiation of radiation therapy (ONC)[1]

3319F   1 of the following diagnostic imaging studies ordered: chest X-ray, CT, ultrasound, MRI, PET, or nuclear medicine scans (ML)[5]

3320F   None of the following diagnostic imaging studies ordered: chest X-ray, CT, ultrasound, MRI, PET, or nuclear medicine scans (ML)[5]

3321F   AJCC Cancer Stage 0 or IA Melanoma, documented (ML)[5]

3322F   Melanoma greater than AJCC Stage 0 or IA (ML)[5]

3323F Clinical tumor, node and metastases (TNM) staging documented and reviewed prior to surgery (Lung/Esop Cx)[6]

3324F MRI or CT scan ordered, reviewed or requested (EPI)[8]

3325F Preoperative assessment of functional or medical indication(s) for surgery prior to the cataract surgery with intraocular lens placement (must be performed within twelve months prior to cataract surgery) (EC)[5]

3328F Performance status documented and reviewed within 2 weeks prior to surgery (Lung/Esop Cx)[6]

3330F Imaging study ordered (BkP)[2]

3331F Imaging study not ordered (BkP)[2]

3340F Mammogram assessment category of "incomplete: need additional imaging evaluation", documented (RAD)[5]

3341F Mammogram assessment category of "negative", documented (RAD)[5]

3342F Mammogram assessment category of "benign", documented (RAD)[5]

3343F Mammogram assessment category of "probably benign", documented (RAD)[5]

3344F Mammogram assessment category of "suspicious", documented (RAD)[5]

3345F Mammogram assessment category of "highly suggestive of malignancy", documented (RAD)[5]

3350F Mammogram assessment category of "known biopsy proven malignancy", documented (RAD)[5]

3351F Negative screen for depressive symptoms as categorized by using a standardized depression screening/assessment tool (MDD)[2]

3352F No significant depressive symptoms as categorized by using a standardized depression assessment tool (MDD)[2]

3353F Mild to moderate depressive symptoms as categorized by using a standardized depression screening/assessment tool (MDD)[2]

3354F Clinically significant depressive symptoms as categorized by using a standardized depression screening/assessment tool (MDD)[2]

3370F AJCC Breast Cancer Stage 0 documented (ONC)[1]

3372F AJCC Breast Cancer Stage I: T1mic, T1a or T1b (tumor size <= 1 cm) documented (ONC)[1]

3374F AJCC Breast Cancer Stage I: T1c (tumor size > 1 cm to 2 cm) documented (ONC)[1]

3376F AJCC Breast Cancer Stage II documented (ONC)[1]

3378F AJCC Breast Cancer Stage III documented (ONC)[1]

3380F AJCC Breast Cancer Stage IV documented (ONC)[1]

3382F AJCC colon cancer, Stage 0 documented (ONC)[1]

3384F AJCC colon cancer, Stage I documented (ONC)[1]

3386F AJCC colon cancer, Stage II documented (ONC)[1]

3388F AJCC colon cancer, Stage III documented (ONC)[1]

● New Code ▲ Revised Code + Add-On Code ⊘ Modifier -51 Exempt ★ Telemedicine

3390F AJCC colon cancer, Stage IV documented (ONC)[1]

3394F Quantitative HER2 immunohistochemistry (IHC) evaluation of breast cancer consistent with the scoring system defined in the ASCO/CAP guidelines (PATH)[9]

3395F Quantitative non-HER2 immunohistochemistry (IHC) evaluation of breast cancer (eg, testing for estrogen or progesterone receptors [ER/PR]) performed (PATH)[9]

3450F Dyspnea screened, no dyspnea or mild dyspnea (Pall Cr)[5]

3451F Dyspnea screened, moderate or severe dyspnea (Pall Cr)[5]

3452F Dyspnea not screened (Pall Cr)[5]

3455F TB screening performed and results interpreted within six months prior to initiation of first time biologic disease modifying anti rheumatic drug therapy for RA (RA)[5]

3470F Rheumatoid arthritis (RA) disease activity, low (RA)[5]

3471F Rheumatoid arthritis (RA) disease activity, moderate (RA)[5]

3472F Rheumatoid arthritis (RA) disease activity, high (RA)[5]

3475F Disease prognosis for rheumatoid arthritis assessed, poor prognosis documented (RA)[5]

3476F Disease prognosis for rheumatoid arthritis assessed, good prognosis documented (RA)[5]

3490F History of AIDS defining condition (HIV)[5]

3491F HIV indeterminate (infants of undetermined HIV status born of HIV infected mothers) (HIV)[5]

3492F History of nadir CD4+ cell count <350 cells/mm (HIV)[5]

3493F No history of nadir CD4+ cell count <350 cells/mm AND no history of AIDS defining condition (HIV)[5]

3494F CD4+ cell count <200 cells/mm (HIV)[5]

3495F CD4+ cell count 200 - 499 cells/mm (HIV)[5]

3496F CD4+ cell count >=500 cells/mm (HIV)[5]

3497F CD4+ cell percentage <15% (HIV)[5]

3498F CD4+ cell percentage >=15% (HIV)[5]

Footnotes

1-Physician Consortium for Performance Improvement (PCPI), www.physicianconsortium.org

2-National Committee on Quality Assurance (NCQA), Health Employer Data Information Set (HEDIS®), www.ncqa.org

3-The Joint Commission (TJC), ORYX Initiative Performance Measures, http://www.jointcommission.org/performancemeasurement.aspx

4-National Diabetes Quality Improvement Alliance (NDQIA), http://www.nationaldiabetesalliance.org

5-Joint measure from The Physician Consortium for Performance Improvement, www.physicianconsortium.org and National Committee on Quality Assurance (NCQA), www.ncqa.org

6-The Society of Thoracic Surgeons, http://www.sts.org, and National Quality Forum, http://www.qualityforum.org

7-Optum, www.optum.com

8-American Academy of Neurology, www.aan.com/go/practice/quality/measurements or quality@aan.com

9-College of American Pathologists (CAP), www.cap.org/apps/docs/ advocacy/pathology_performance_measurement.pdf

10-American Gastroenterological Association (AGA), www.gastro.org/quality

11-American Society of Anesthesiologists (ASA), http://www.asahq.org

12-American College of Gastroenterology (ACG), www.gi.org; American Gastroenterology Association (AGA), www.gastro.org; and American Society for Gastrointestinal Endoscopy (ASGE), www. asge.org

| ▮ Separate Procedure | ▮ Unlisted Procedure | ▮ CCI Comp. Code | ▮ Non-specific Procedure | **937** |

3500F CD4+ cell count or CD4+ cell percentage documented as performed (HIV)[5]

3502F HIV RNA viral load below limits of quantification (HIV)[5]

3503F HIV RNA viral load not below limits of quantification (HIV)[5]

3510F Documentation that tuberculosis (TB) screening test performed and results interpreted (HIV)[5] (IBD)[10]

3511F Chlamydia and gonorrhea screenings documented as performed (HIV)[5]

3512F Syphilis screening documented as performed (HIV)[5]

3513F Hepatitis B screening documented as performed (HIV)[5]

3514F Hepatitis C screening documented as performed (HIV)[5]

3515F Patient has documented immunity to Hepatitis C (HIV)[5]

3517F Hepatitis B Virus (HBV) status assessed and results interpreted within one year prior to receiving a first course of anti-TNF (tumor necrosis factor) therapy (IBD)[10]

3520F Clostridium difficile testing performed (IBD)[10]

3550F Low risk for thromboembolism (AFIB)[1]

3551F Intermediate risk for thromboembolism (AFIB)[1]

3552F High risk for thromboembolism (AFIB)[1]

3555F Patient had International Normalized Ratio (INR) measurement performed (AFIB)[1]

3570F Final report for bone scintigraphy study includes correlation with existing relevant imaging studies (eg, x ray, MRI, CT) corresponding to the same anatomical region in question (NUC_MED)[1]

3572F Patient considered to be potentially at risk for fracture in a weight bearing site (NUC_MED)[1]

3573F Patient not considered to be potentially at risk for fracture in a weight bearing site (NUC_MED)[1]

3650F Electroencephalogram (EEG) ordered, reviewed or requested (EPI)[8]

3700F Psychiatric disorders or disturbances assessed (Prkns)[8]

3702F Cognitive impairment or dysfunction assessed (Prkns)[8]

3725F Screening for depression performed (DEM)[1]

3750F Patient not receiving dose of corticosteroids greater than or equal to 10 mg/day for 60 or greater consecutive days (IBD)[10]

3751F Electrodiagnostic studies for distal symmetric polyneuropathy conducted (or requested), documented, and reviewed within 6 months of initial evaluation for condition (DSP)[8]

3752F Electrodiagnostic studies for distal symmetric polyneuropathy **not** conducted (or requested), documented, or reviewed within 6 months of initial evaluation for condition (DSP)[8]

3753F Patient has clear clinical symptoms and signs that are highly suggestive of neuropathy AND cannot be attributed to another condition, AND has an obvious cause for the neuropathy (DSP)[8]

3754F Screening tests for diabetes mellitus reviewed, requested, or ordered (DSP)[8]

● New Code ▲ Revised Code + Add-On Code ⊘ Modifier -51 Exempt ★ Telemedicine

3755F Cognitive and behavioral impairment screening performed (ALS)[8]

3756F Patient has pseudobulbar affect, sialorrhea, or ALS-related symptoms (ALS)[8]

3757F Patient does not have pseudobulbar affect, sialorrhea, or ALS-related symptoms (ALS)[8]

3758F Patient referred for pulmonary function testing or peak cough expiratory flow (ALS)[8]

3759F Patient screened for dysphagia, weight loss, and impaired nutrition, and results documented (ALS)[8]

3760F Patient exhibits dysphagia, weight loss, or impaired nutrition (ALS)[8]

3761F Patient does not exhibit dysphagia, weight loss, or impaired nutrition (ALS)[8]

3762F Patient is dysarthric (ALS)[8]

3763F Patient is not dysarthric (ALS)[8]

3775F Adenoma(s) or other neoplasm detected during screening colonoscopy (SCADR)[12]

3776F Adenoma(s) or other neoplasm not detected during screening colonoscopy (SCADR)[12]

THERAPEUTIC, PREVENTIVE OR OTHER INTERVENTIONS

Therapeutic, preventive or other interventions codes describe pharmacologic, procedural, or behavioral therapies, including preventive services such as patient education and counseling.

4000F Tobacco use cessation intervention, counseling (COPD, CAP, CAD, Asthma)[1](DM)[4](PV)[2]

4001F Tobacco use cessation intervention, pharmacologic therapy (COPD, CAD, CAP, PV, Asthma)[1] (DM)[4] (PV)[2]

4003F Patient education, written/oral, appropriate for patients with heart failure performed (NMA-No Measure Associated)

4004F Patient screened for tobacco use AND received tobacco cessation intervention (counseling, pharmacotherapy, or both), if identified as a tobacco user (PV, CAD)[1]

4005F Pharmacologic therapy (other than minerals/vitamins) for osteoporosis prescribed (OP)[5] (IBD)[10]

4008F Beta-blocker therapy prescribed or currently being taken (CAD,HF)[1]

4010F Angiotensin converting enzyme (ACE) inhibitor or angiotensin receptor blocker (ARB) therapy prescribed or currently being taken (CAD, CKD, HF)[1] (DM)[2]

4011F Oral antiplatelet therapy prescribed (CAD)[1]

4012F Warfarin therapy prescribed (NMA-No Measure Associated)

4013F Statin therapy prescrived or currently being taken (CAD)[1]

4014F Written discharge instructions provided to heart failure patients discharged home. (Instructions include all of the following components: activity level, diet, discharge medications, follow-up appointment, weight monitoring, what to do if symptoms worsen) (NMA-No Measure Associated)

4015F Persistent asthma, preferred long term control medication or an acceptable alternative treatment, prescribed (NMA-No Meausre Associated)

(Note: There are no medical exclusion criteria)

(Do not report modifier 1P with 4015F)

■ Separate Procedure ■ Unlisted Procedure ■ CCI Comp. Code ■ Non-specific Procedure **939**

(To report patient reasons for not prescribing, use modifier 2P)

4016F Anti-inflammatory/analgesic agent prescribed (OA)[1]

(Use for prescribed or continued medication(s), including over-the-counter medication[s])

4017F Gastrointestinal prophylaxis for NSAID use prescribed (OA)[1]

4018F Therapeutic exercise for the involved joint(s) instructed or physical or occupational therapy prescribed (OA)[1]

4019F Documentation of receipt of counseling on exercise AND either both calcium and vitamin D use or counseling regarding both calcium and vitamin D use (OP)[5]

4025F Inhaled bronchodilator prescribed (COPD)[1]

4030F Long term oxygen therapy prescribed (more than fifteen hours per day) (COPD)[1]

4033F Pulmonary rehabilitation exercise training recommended (COPD)[1]

(Report 4033F with 1019F)

4035F Influenza immunization recommended (COPD)[1](IBD)[10]

4037F Influenza immunization ordered or administered (COPD, PV, CKD, ESRD)[1](IBD)[10]

4040F Pneumococcal vaccine administered or previously received (COPD)[1] (IBD)[10](PV)[1,2]

4041F Documentation of order for cefazolin OR cefurozime for antimicrobial prophylaxis (PERI 2)[5]

4042F Documentation that prophylactic antibiotics were neither given within 4 hours prior to surgical incision nor given intraoperatively (PERI 2)[5]

4043F Documentation that an order was given to discontinue prophylactic antibiotics within 48 hours of surgical end time, cardiac procedures (PERI 2)[5]

4044F Documentation that an order was given for venous thromboembolism (VTE) prophylaxis to be given within 24 hours prior to incision time or 24 hours after surgery end time (PERI 2)[5]

4045F Appropriate empiric antibiotic prescribed (CAP)[1] (EM)[5]

4046F Documentation that prophylactic antibiotics were given within 4 hours prior to surgical incision or given intraoperatively (PERI 2)[5]

4047F Documentation of order for prophylactic parenteral antibiotics to be given within 1 hour (if fluoroquinolone or vancomycin, 2 hours) prior to surgical incision (or start of procedure when no incision is required) (PERI 2)[5]

4048F Documentation that administration of prophylactic parenteral antibiotic was initiated within 1 hour (if fluoroquinolone or vancomycin, 2 hours) prior to surgical incision (or start of procedure when no incision is required), as ordered (PERI 2)[5]

4049F Documentation that order was given to discontinue prophylactic antibiotics within 24 hours of surgical end time, non-cardiac procedure (PERI 2)[5]

4050F Hypertension plan of care documented as appropriate (NMA-No Measure Associated)

4051F Referred for an arterio-venous (AV) fistula (ESRD, CKD)[1]

4052F Hemodialysis via functioning arteriovenous (AV) fistula (ESRD)[1]

● New Code   ▲ Revised Code   + Add-On Code   ⊘ Modifier -51 Exempt   ★ Telemedicine

4053F   Hemodialysis via functioning arteriovenous (AV) graft (ESRD)[1]

4054F   Hemodialysis via catheter (ESRD)[1]

4055F   Patient receiving peritoneal dialysis (ESRD)[1]

4056F   Appropriate oral rehydration solution recommended (PAG)[1]

4058F   Pediatric gastroenteritis education provided to caregiver (PAG)[1]

4060F   Psychotherapy services provided (MDD, MDD ADOL)[1]

4062F   Patient referral for psychotherapy documented (MDD, MDD ADOL)[1]

4063F   Antidepressant pharmacotherapy considered and not prescribed (MDD ADOL)[1]

4064F   Antidepressant pharmacotherapy prescribed (MDD, MDD ADOL)[1]

4065F   Antipsychotic pharmacotherapy prescribed (MDD)[1]

4066F   Electroconvulsive therapy (ECT) provided (MDD)[1]

4067F   Patient referral for electroconvulsive therapy (ECT) documented (MDD)[1]

4069F   Venous thromboembolism (VTE) prophylaxis received (IBD)[10]

4070F   Deep vein thrombosis (DVT) prophylaxis received by end of hospital day 2 (STR)[5]

4073F   Oral antiplatelet therapy prescribed at discharge (STR)[5]

4075F   Anticoagulant therapy prescribed at discharge (STR)[5]

4077F   Documentation that tissue plasminogen activator (t-PA) administration was considered (STR)[5]

4079F   Documentation that rehabilitation services were considered (STR)[5]

4084F   Aspirin received within 24 hours before emergency department arrival or during emergency department stay (EM)[5]

4086F   Aspirin or clopidogrel prescribed or currently being taken (CAD)[1]

4090F   Patient receiving erythropoietin therapy (HEM)[1]

4095F   Patient not receiving erythropoietin therapy (HEM)[1]

Footnotes

1-Physician Consortium for Performance Improvement (PCPI), www.physicianconsortium.org

2-National Committee on Quality Assurance (NCQA), Health Employer Data Information Set (HEDIS®), www.ncqa.org

3-The Joint Commission (TJC), ORYX Initiative Performance Measures, http://www.jointcommission.org/performancemeasurement.aspx

4-National Diabetes Quality Improvement Alliance (NDQIA), http://www.nationaldiabetesalliance.org

5-Joint measure from The Physician Consortium for Performance Improvement, www.physicianconsortium.org and National Committee on Quality Assurance (NCQA), www.ncqa.org

6-The Society of Thoracic Surgeons, http://www.sts.org, and National Quality Forum, http://www.qualityforum.org

7-Optum, www.optum.com

8-American Academy of Neurology, www.aan.com/go/practice/quality/measurements or quality@aan.com

9-College of American Pathologists (CAP), www.cap.org/apps/docs/ advocacy/pathology_performance_measurement.pdf

10-American Gastroenterological Association (AGA), www.gastro.org/quality

11-American Society of Anesthesiologists (ASA), http://www.asahq.org

12-American College of Gastroenterology (ACG), www.gi.org; American Gastroenterology Association (AGA), www.gastro.org; and American Society for Gastrointestinal Endoscopy (ASGE), www. asge.org

---

4100F Bisphosphonate therapy, intravenous, ordered or received (HEM)[1]

4110F Internal mammary artery graft performed for primary, isolated coronary artery bypass graft procedure (CABG)[6]

4115F Beta blocker administered within 24 hours prior to surgical incision (CABG)[6]

4120F Antibiotic prescribed or dispensed (URI, PHAR)[2] , (A-BRONCH)[2]

4124F Antibiotic neither prescribed nor dispensed (URI, PHAR)[2] , (A-BRONCH)[2]

4130F Topical preparations (including OTC) prescribed for acute otitis externa (AOE)[1]

4131F Systemic antimicrobial therapy prescribed (AOE)[1]

4132F Systemic antimicrobial therapy not prescribed (AOE)[1]

4133F Antihistamines or decongestants prescribed or recommended (OME)[1]

4134F Antihistamines or decongestants neither prescribed nor recommended (OME)[1]

4135F Systemic corticosteroids prescribed (OME)[1]

4136F Sysemic corticosteroids not prescribed (OME)[1]

4140F Inhalded corticosteroids prescribed (Asthma)[1]

4142F Corticosteroid sparing therapy prescribed (IBD)[10]

4144F Alternative long-term control medication prescribed (Asthma)[1]

4145F Two or more anti-hypertensive agents prescribed or currently being taken (CAD, HTN)[1]

4148F Hepatitis A vaccine injection administered or previously received (Hep-C)[1]

4149F Hepatitis B vaccine injection administered or previously received (Hep-C, HIV)[1] (IBD)[10]

4150F Patient receiving antiviral treatment for Hepatitis C (Hep-C)[1]

4151F Patient did not start or is not receiving antiviral treatment for Hepatitis C during the measurement period (Hep-C)[1]

4153F Combination peginterferon and ribavirin therapy prescribed (HEP-C)[1]

4155F Hepatitis A vaccine series previously received (Hep-C)[1]

4157F Hepatitis B vaccine series previously received (Hep-C)[1]

4158F Patient counseled about risk of alcohol use (Hep-C)[1]

4159F Counseling regarding contraception received prior to initiation of antiviral treatment (Hep-C)[1]

4163F Patient counseling at a minimum on all of the following treatment options for clinically localized prostate cancer: active surveillance, AND interstitial prostate brachytherapy, AND external beam radiotherapy, AND radical prostatectomy, provided prior to initiation of treatment (PRCA)[1]

4164F Adjuvant (ie, in combination with external beam radiotherapy to the prostate for prostate cancer) hormonal therapy (gonadotropin-releasing hormone [GNRH] agonist or antagonist) prescribed/administered (PRCA)[1]

● New Code ▲ Revised Code + Add-On Code ⊘ Modifier -51 Exempt ★ Telemedicine

4165F Three-dimensional conformal radiotherapy (3D-CRT) or intensity modulated radiation therapy (IMRT) received (PRCA)[1]

4167F Head of bed elevation (30-45 degrees) on first ventilator day ordered (CRIT)[1]

4168F Patient receiving care in the intensive care unit (ICU) and receiving mechanical ventilation, 24 hours or less (CRIT)[1]

4169F Patient either not receiving care in the intensive care unit (ICU) OR not receiving mechanical ventilation OR receiving mechanical ventilation greater than 24 hours (CRIT)[1]

4171F patient receiving erythropoiesis-stimulating agents (ESA) therapy (CKD)[1]

4172F Patient not receiving erythropoiesis-stimulating agents (ESA) therapy (CKD)[1]

4174F Counseling about the potential impact of glaucoma on visual functioning and quality of life, and importance of treatment adherence provided to patient and/or caregiver(s) (EC)[5]

4175F Best-corrected visual acuity of 20/40 or better (distance or near) achieved within the 90 days following cataract surgery (EC)[5]

4176F Counseling about value of protection from UV light and lack of proven efficacy of nutritional supplements in prevention or progression of cataract development provided to patient and/or caregiver(s) (NMA-No Measure Associated)

4177F Counseling about the benefits and/or risks of the age-related eye disease study (AREDS) formulation for preventing progression of age-related macular degeneration (AMD) provided to patient and/or caregiver(s) (EC)[5]

4178F Anti-D immune globulin received between 26 and 30 weeks gestation (Pre-Cr)[1]

4179F Tamoxifen or aromatase inhibitor (AI) prescribed (ONC)[1]

4180F Adjuvant chemotherapy referred, prescribed or previously received for Stage III colon cancer (ONC)[1]

4181F Conformal radiation therapy received (NMA-No Measure Assoc.)

4182F Conformal radiation therapy not received (NMA-No Measure Assoc.)

4185F Continuous (12-months) therapy with proton pump inhibitor (PPI) or histamine H2 receptor antagonist (H2RA) received (GERD)[5]

4186F no continuous (12-months) therapy with either proton pump inhibitor (PPI) or histamine H2 receptor antagonist (H2RA) received (GERD)[5]

4187F Disease modifying anti-rheumatic drug therapy prescribed or dispensed (RA)[2]

4188F Appropriate angiotensin converting enzyme (ACE)/angiotensin receptor blockers (ARB) therapeutic monitoring test ordered or performed (AM)[2]

4189F Appropriate digoxin therapeutic monitoring test ordered or performed (AM)[2]

4190F Appropriate diuretic therapeutic monitoring test ordered or performed (AM)[2]

4191F Appropriate anticonvulsant therapeutic monitoring test ordered or performed (AM)[2]

4192F Patient not receiving glucocorticoid therapy (RA)[5]

4193F Patient receiving <10 mg daily prednisone (or equivalent), or RA activity is worsening, or glucocorticoid use is for less than 6 months (RA)[5]

4194F Patient receiving >=10 mg daily prednisone (or equivalent) for longer than 6 months, and improvement or no change in disease activity (RA)[5]

4195F Patient receiving first time biologic disease modifying anti rheumatic drug therapy for rheumatoid arthritis (RA)[5]

4196F Patient not receiving first time biologic disease modifying anti rheumatic drug therapy for rheumatoid arthritis (RA)[5]

4200F External beam radiotherapy as primary therapy to prostate with or without nodal irradiation (PRCA)[1]

4201F External beam radiotherapy with or without nodal irradiation as adjuvant or salvage therapy for prostate cancer patient (PRCA)[1]

4210F Angiotensin converting enzyme (ACE) or angiotensin receptor blockers (ARB) medication therapy for 6 months or more (MM)[2]

4220F Digoxin medication therapy for 6 months or more (MM)[2]

4221F Diuretic medication therapy for 6 months or more (MM)[2]

4230F Anticonvulsant medication therapy for 6 months or more (MM)[2]

4240F Instruction in therapeutic exercise with follow-up provided to patients during episode of back pain lasting longer than 12 weeks (BkP)[2]

4242F Counseling for supervised exercise program provided to patients during episode of back pain lasting longer than 12 weeks (BkP)[2]

4245F Patient counseled during the initial visit to maintain or resume normal activities (BkP)[2]

4248F Patient counseled during the initial visit for an episode of back pain against bed rest lasting 4 days or longer (BkP)[2]

4250F Active warming used intraoperatively for the purpose of maintaining normothermia, OR at least one body temperature equal to or greater than 36 degrees Centigrade (or 96.8 degrees Fahrenheit) recorded within the 30 minutes immediately before or the 15 minutes immediately after anesthesia end time (CRIT)[1]

4255F Duration of general or neuraxial anesthesia 60 minutes or longer, as documented in the anesthesia record (CRIT)[5] (Peri2)[11]

4256F Duration of general or neuraxial anesthesia less than 60 minutes, as documented in the anesthesia record (CRIT)[5] (Peri2)[11]

4260F Wound surface culture technique used (CWC)[5]

4261F Technique other than surface culture of the wound exudate used (eg, Levine/deep swab technique, semi quantitative or quantitative swab technique) OR wound surface culture technique not used (CWC)[5]

4265F Use of wet to dry dressings prescribed or recommended (CWC)[5]

4266F Use of wet to dry dressings neither prescribed nor recommended (CWC)[5]

4267F Compression therapy prescribed (CWC)[5]

4268F Patient education regarding the need for long term compression therapy including interval replacement of compression stockings received (CWC)[5]

4269F Appropriate method of offloading (pressure relief) prescribed (CWC)[5]

4270F Patient receiving potent antiretroviral therapy for 6 months or longer (HIV)[5]

---

944 ● New Code ▲ Revised Code ✛ Add-On Code ⊘ Modifier -51 Exempt ★ Telemedicine

4271F Patient receiving potent antiretroviral therapy for less than 6 months or not receiving potent antiretroviral therapy (HIV)[5]

4274F Influenza immunization administered or previously received (HIV)[5] (P ESRD)[1]

4276F Potent antiretroviral therapy prescribed (HIV)[5]

4279F Pneumocystis jiroveci pneumonia prophylaxis prescribed (HIV)[5]

4280F Pneumocystis jiroveci pneumonia prophylaxis prescribed within 3 months of low CD4+ cell count or percentage (HIV)[5]

4290F Patient screened for injection drug use (HIV)[5]

4293F Patient screened for high risk sexual behavior (HIV)[5]

4300F Patient receiving warfarin therapy for nonvalvular atrial fibrillation or atrial flutter (AFIB)[1]

4301F Patient not receiving warfarin therapy for nonvalvular atrial fibrillation or atrial flutter (AFIB)[1]

4305F Patient education regarding appropriate foot care AND daily inspection of the feet received (CWC)[5]

4306F Patient counseled regarding psychosocial AND pharmacologic treatment options for opioid addiction (SUD)[1]

4320F Patient counseled regarding psychosocial AND pharmacologic treatment options for alcohol dependence (SUD)[5]

4322F Caregiver provided with education and referred to additional resources for support (DEM)[1]

4324F Patient (or caregiver) queried about parkinson's disease medication related motor complications (Prkns)[8]

4325F Medical and surgical treatment options reviewed with patient (or caregiver) (Prkns)[8]

4326F Patient (or caregiver) queried about symptoms of autonomic dysfunction (Prkns)[8]

4328F Patient (or caregiver) queried about sleep disturbances (Prkns)[8]

4330F Counseling about epilepsy specific safety issues provided to patient (or caregiver(s)) (EPI)[8]

4340F Counseling for women of childbearing potential with epilepsy (EPI)[8]

4350F Counseling provided on symptom management, end of life decisions, and palliation (DEM)[1]

Footnotes

1-Physician Consortium for Performance Improvement (PCPI), www.physicianconsortium.org

2-National Committee on Quality Assurance (NCQA), Health Employer Data Information Set (HEDIS®), www.ncqa.org

3-The Joint Commission (TJC), ORYX Initiative Performance Measures, http://www.jointcommission.org/performancemeasurement.aspx

4-National Diabetes Quality Improvement Alliance (NDQIA), http://www.nationaldiabetesalliance.org

5-Joint measure from The Physician Consortium for Performance Improvement, www.physicianconsortium.org and National Committee on Quality Assurance (NCQA), www.ncqa.org

6-The Society of Thoracic Surgeons, http://www.sts.org, and National Quality Forum, http://www.qualityforum.org

7-Optum, www.optum.com

8-American Academy of Neurology, www.aan.com/go/practice/quality/measurements or quality@aan.com

9-College of American Pathologists (CAP), www.cap.org/apps/docs/ advocacy/pathology_performance_measurement.pdf

10-American Gastroenterological Association (AGA), www.gastro.org/quality

11-American Society of Anesthesiologists (ASA), http://www.asahq.org

12-American College of Gastroenterology (ACG), www.gi.org; American Gastroenterology Association (AGA), www.gastro.org; and American Society for Gastrointestinal Endoscopy (ASGE), www. asge.org

---

4400F   Rehabilitative therapy options discussed with patient (or caregiver) (Prkns)[8]

4450F   Self-care education provided to patient (HF)[1]

4470F   Implantable cardioverter-defibrillator (ICD) counseling provided (HF)[1]

4480F   Patient receiving ACE inhibitor/ARB therapy and beta-blocker therapy for 3 months or longer (HF)[1]

4481F   Patient receiving ACE inhibitor/ARB therapy and beta-blocker therapy for less than 3 months or patient not receiving ACE inhibitor/ARB therapy and beta blocker therapy (HF)[1]

4500F   Referred to an outpatient cardiac rehabilitation program (CAD)[1]

4510F   Previous cardiac rehabilitation for qualifying cardiac event completed (CAD)[1]

4525F   Neuropsychiatric intervention ordered (DEM)[1]

4526F   Neuropsychiatric intervention received (DEM)[1]

4540F   Disease modifying pharmacotherapy discussed (ALS)[8]

4541F   Patient offered treatment for pseudobulbar affect, sialorrhea, or ALS-related symptoms (ALS)[8]

4550F   Options for noninvasive respiratory support discussed with patient (ALS)[8]

4551F   Nutritional support offered (ALS)[8]

4552F   Patient offered referral to a speech language pathologist (ALS)[8]

4553F   Patient offered assistance in planning for end of life issues (ALS)[8]

4554F   Patient received inhalational anesthetic agent (Peri2)[11]

4555F   Patient did not receive inhalational anesthetic agent (Peri2)[11]

4556F   Patient exhibits 3 or more risk factors for post-operative nausea and vomiting (Peri2)[11]

4557F   Patient does not exhibit 3 or more risk factors for post-operative nausea and vomiting (Peri2)[11]

4558F   Patient received at least 2 prophylactic pharmacologic anti-emetic agents of different classes preoperatively and intraoperatively (Peri2)[11]

4559F   At least 1 body temperature measurement equal to or greater than 35.5 degrees Celsius (or 95.9 degrees Fahrenheit) recorded within the 30 minutes immediately before or the 15 minutes immediately after anesthesia end time (Peri2)[11]

4560F   Anesthesia technique did not involve general or neuraxial anesthesia (Peri2)[11]

4561F   Patient has a coronary artery stent (Peri2)[11]

4562F   Patient does not have a coronary artery stent (Peri2)[11]

4563F   Patient received aspirin within 24 hours prior to anesthesia start time (Peri2)[11]

FOLLOW-UP OR OTHER OUTCOMES

Follow-up or other outcomes codes describe review and communication of test results to patients, patient satisfaction or experience with care, patient functional status, and patient morbidity and mortality.

5005F   Patient counseled on self-examination for new or changing moles (ML)[5]

5010F   Findings of dilated macular or fundus exam communicated to the physician or other qualified health care professional managing the diabetes care (EC)[5]

5015F   Documentation of communication that a fracture occurred and that the patient was or should be tested or treated for osteoporosis (OP)[5]

5020F   Treatment summary report communicated to physician(s) or other qualified health care professional(s) managing continuing care and to the patient within 1 month of completing treatment (ONC)[1]

5050F   Treatment plan communicated to provider(s) managing continuing care within 1 month of diagnosis (ML)[5]

5060F   Findings from diagnostic mammogram communicated to practice managing patient's ongoing care within 3 business daysof exam interpretation(RAD)[5]

5062F   Findings from diagnostic mammogram communicated to practic managingthe patient's on-going care within 5 business days of exam interpretation (RAD)[5]

5100F   Potential risk for fracture communicated to the referring physician or other qualified health care professional within 24 hours of completion of the imaging study (NUC_MED)[1]

5200F   Consideration of referral for a neurological evaluation of appropriateness for surgical therapy for intractable epilepsy within the past 3 years (EPI)[8]

5250F   Asthma discharge plan provided to patient (Asthma)[1]

PATIENT SAFETY

Patient safety codes that describe patient safety practices.

6005F   Rationale (eg, severity of illness and safety) for level of care (eg, home, hospital) documented (CAP)[1]

6010F   Dysphagia screening conducted prior to order for or receipt of any foods, fluids or medication by mouth (STR)[5]

6015F   Patient receiving or eligible to receive foods, fluids or medication by mouth (STR)[5]

6020F   NPO (nothing by mouth) ordered (STR)[5]

6030F   All elements of maximal sterile barrier technique followed including: cap AND mask AND sterile gown AND sterile gloves AND a large sterile sheet AND hand hygiene AND 2% chlorhexidine for cutaneous antisepsis (or acceptable alternative antiseptics, per current guideline) (CRIT)[1]

6040F   Use of appropriate radiation dose reduction devices or manual techniques for appropriate moderation of exposure, documented (RAD)[5]

6045F   Radiation exposure or exposure time in final report for procedure using fluoroscopy, documented (RAD)[5]

6070F   Patient queried and counseled about anti-epileptic drug (AED) side effects (EPI)[8]

6080F   Patient (or caregiver) queried about falls (Prkns, DSP)[8]

6090F   Patient (or caregiver) counseled about safety issues appropriate to patient's stage of disease (Prkns)[8]

6100F   Timeout to verify correct patient, correct site, and correct procedure, documented (PATH)[9]

6101F   Safety counseling for dementia provided (DEM)[1]

6102F   Safety counseling for dementia ordered (DEM)[1]

▆ Separate Procedure   ▆ Unlisted Procedure   ▆ CCI Comp. Code   ▆ Non-specific Procedure   **947**

6110F Counseling provided regarding risks of driving and the alternatives to driving (DEM)[1]

6150F Patient not receiving a first course of anti-TNF (tumor necrosis factor) therapy (IBD)[10]

STRUCTURAL MEASURES

Structural measures codes are used to identify measures that address the setting or system of the delivered care. These codes also address aspects of the capabilities of the organization or health care professional providing the care.

7010F Patient information entered into a recall system that includes: target date for the next exam specified AND a process to follow up with patients regarding missed or unscheduled appointments (ML)[5]

7020F Mammogram assessment category [eg, Mammography Quality Standards Act (MQSA), Breast Imaging Reporting and Data System (BI-RADS®), or FDA approved equivalent categories] entered into an internal database to allow for analysis of abnormal interpretation (recall) rate (RAD)5

7025F Patient information entered into a reminder system with a target due date for the next mammogram (RAD)[5]

NONMEASURE CODE LISTING

The following codes are included for reporting of certain aspects of care. These factors are not represented by measures developed by existing measures organizations or recognized measures-development processes at the time they are placed in the CPT code set, but may ultimately be associated with measures approved by an appropriate quality improvement organization.

9001F Aortic aneurysm less than 5.0 cm maximum diameter on centerline formatted CT or minor diameter on axial formatted CT (NMA-No Measure Associated)

9002F Aortic aneurysm 5.0-5.4 cm maximum diameter on centerline formatted CT or minor diameter on axial formatted CT (NMA-No Measure Associated)

9003F Aortic aneurysm 5.5-5.9 cm maximum diameter on centerline formatted CT or minor diameter on axial formatted CT (NMA-No Measure Associated)

9004F Aortic aneurysm 6.0 cm or greater maximum diameter on centerline formatted CT or minor diameter on axial formatted CT (NMA-No Measure Associated)

9005F Asymptomatic carotid stenosis: No history of any transient ischemic attack or stroke in any carotid or vertebrobasilar territory (NMA-No Measure Associated)

9006F Symptomatic carotid stenosis: Ipsilateral carotid territory TIA or stroke less than 120 days prior to procedure (NMA-No Measure Associated)

9007F Other carotid stenosis: Ipsilateral TIA or stroke 120 days or greater prior to procedure or any prior contralateral carotid territory or vertebrobasilar TIA or stroke (NMA-No Measure Associated)

● New Code   ▲ Revised Code   + Add-On Code   ⊘ Modifier -51 Exempt   ★ Telemedicine

CATEGORY III CODES

CATEGORY III SECTION OVERVIEW

The following section contains a set of temporary codes for emerging technology, services, procedures, and service paradigms. Category III codes allow data collection for these services/procedures. Use of unlisted codes does not offer the opportunity for the collection of specific data. If a Category III code is available, this code must be reported instead of a Category I unlisted code. This is an activity that is critically important in the evaluation of health care delivery and the formation of public and private policy. The use of the codes in this section allows physicians and other qualified health care professionals, insurers, health services researchers, and health policy experts to identify emerging technology, services, procedures, and service paradigms for clinical efficacy, utilization and outcomes.

The inclusion of a service or procedure in this section does not constitute a finding of support, or lack thereof, with regard to clinical efficacy, safety, applicability to clinical practice, or payer coverage. The codes in this section may not conform to the usual requirements for CPT Category I codes established by the Editorial Panel. For Category I codes, the Panel requires that the service/procedure be performed by many health care professionals in clinical practice in multiple locations and that FDA approval, as appropriate, has already been received. The nature of emerging technology, services, procedures, and service paradigms is such that these requirements may not be met. For these reasons, temporary codes for emerging technology, services, procedures, and service paradigms have been placed in a separate section of the CPT code set and the codes are differentiated from Category I CPT codes by the use of alphanumeric characters.

Services and procedures described in this section make use of alphanumeric characters. These codes have an alpha character as the 5th character in the string (ie, four digits followed by the letter T). The digits are not intended to reflect the placement of the code in the Category I section of CPT nomenclature. Codes in this section may or may not eventually receive a Category I CPT code. In either case, in general, a given Category III code will be archived five years from the date of initial publication or extension unless a modification of the archival date is specifically noted at the time of a revision or change to a code (eg, addition of parenthetical instructions, reinstatement). Services and procedures described by Category III codes which have been archived after five years, without conversion, must be reported using the Category I unlisted code unless another specific cross-reference is established at the time of archiving. New codes or revised codes in this section are released semi-annually via the AMA CPT website to expedite dissemination for reporting. The full set of temporary codes for emerging technology, services, procedures, and service paradigms are published annually in the CPT code set. Go to www.ama-assn.org/go/cpt for the most current listing

CATEGORY III CODES

(For destruction of localized lesion of choroid by transpupillary thermotherapy, use 67299)

(For destruction of macular drusen, photocoagulation, use 67299)

(**0019T** deleted 2016 [2017 edition])

(For extracorporeal shock wave involving musculoskeletal system, not otherwise specified, low energy, use 20999)

(For application of high energy extracorporeal shock wave involving musculoskeletal system not otherwise specified, use 0101T)

(For application of high energy extracorporeal shock wave involving lateral humeral epicondyle, use 0102T)

(For non-surgical reduction therapy, use 93799)

(For lipoprotein, direct measurement, intermediate density lipoproteins [IDL] [remnant lipoprotein], use 84999)

(For endoscopic lysis of epidural adhesions with direct visualization using mechanical means or solution injection [eg, normal saline], use 64999)

(For dual x-ray absorptiometry [DEXA] body composition study, use 76499)

(For pulsed magnetic neuromodulation incontinence treatment, use 53899)

(To report antiprothrombin [phospholipid cofactor] antibody, use 86849)

(0031T, 0032T have been deleted)

(For speculoscopy, including sampling, use 58999)

(For urinalysis infectious agent detection, semi-quantitative analysis of volatile compounds, use 81099)

0042T   Cerebral perfusion analysis using computed tomography with contrast administration, including post-processing of parametric maps with determination of cerebral blood flow, cerebral blood volume, and mean transit time (Sunset January 2019)

(For carbon monoxide, expired gas analysis [eg, ETC0/hemolysis greath test], use 84999)

(0046T, 0047T have been deleted)

(For mammary duct[s] catheter lavage, use 19499)

(**0051T**   deleted 2017 [2018 edition]. To report, see 33927, 33928, 33929)

(**0052T**   deleted 2017 [2018 edition]. To report, see 33927, 33928, 33929)

(**0053T**   deleted 2017 [2018 edition]. To report, see 33927, 33928, 33929)

+ **0054T**   Computer-assisted musculoskeletal surgical navigational orthopedic procedure, with image-guidance based on fluoroscopic images (list separately in addition to code for primary procedure) (Sunset January 2019)

+ **0055T**   Computer-assisted musculoskeletal surgical navigational orthopedic procedure, with image-guidance based on ct/mri images (list separately in addition to code for primary procedure) (Sunset January 2019)

(When CT and MRI are both performed, report 0055T only once)

0058T   Cryopreservation; reproductive tissue, ovarian (Sunset January 2016)

(**0059T**   deleted 2014 [2015 edition])

(For cryopreservation of mature oocytes, use 89337. For cryopreservation of immature oocytes, use 0357T)

0357T   immature oocyte(s) (Sunset January 2020)

(For cryopreservation of mature oocyte(s), use 89337)

(For cryopreservation of embryos, sperm and testicular reproductive tissue, see 89258, 89259, 89335)

(For electrical impedance breast scan, use 76499)

(For destruction/reduction of malignant breast tumor, microwave phased array thermotherapy, use 19499)

(0062T, 0063T have been deleted)

(For percutaneous intradiscal annuloplasty, any method other than electrothermal, use 22899)

(For intradiscal electrothermal annuloplasty, see 22526-22527)

(To report CT colon, screening, use 74263)

(To report CT colon, diagnostic, use 74261-74262)

(0068T-0070T have been deleted)

(For acoustic heart sound recording and computer analysis, use 93799)

0071T   Focused ultrasound ablation of uterine leiomyomata, including MR guidance; total leiomyomata volume less than 200 cc of tissue (Sunset January 2020)

0072T   total leiomyomata volume greater or equal to 200 cc of tissue (Sunset January 2020)

(Do not report 0071T, 0072T in conjunction with 51702 or 77022)

● New Code   ▲ Revised Code   + Add-On Code   ⊘ Modifier -51 Exempt   ★ Telemedicine

(**0073T** deleted 2014 [2015 edition]. To report, use 77385)

0075T Transcatheter placement of extracranial vertebral arteru stemt(s). including radiologic supervision and interpretation, open or percutaneous; initial vessel (Sunset January 2020)

+ **0076T** each additional vessel (List separately in addition to code for primary procedure) (Sunset January 2020)

(Use 0076T in conjunction with 0075T)

(When the ipsilateral extracranial vertebral arteriogram (including imaging and selective catheterization) confirms the need for stenting, then 0075T and 0076T include all ipsilateral extracranial vertebral catheterization, all diagnostic imaging for ipsilateral extracranial vertebral artery stenting, and all related radiologic supervision and interpretation. If stenting is not indicated, then the appropriate codes for selective catheterization and imaging should be reported in lieu of code 0075T or 0076T.)

0085T Breath test for heart transplant rejection (Sunset January 2016)

(To report total disc lumbar arthroplasty, use 22857)

(For cervical arthroplasty procedure on three or more levels, use 0375T)

+ **0095T** Removal of total disc arthroplasty (artificial disc), anterior approach, each additional interspace, cervical (List separately in addition to code for primary procedure) (Sunset January 2019)

(Use 0095T in conjunction with 22864)

(To report revision of total disc lumbar arthroplasty, use 22862)

+ **0098T** Revision including replacement of total disc arhtroplasty (artificial disc), anterior approach, each additional interspace, cervical (List separately in addition to code for primary procedure) (Sunset January 2019)

(Use 0098T in conjunction with 22861)

(Do not report 0098T in conjunction with 0095T)

(Do not report 0098T in conjunction with 22853, 22854, 22859 when performed at the same level)

(For decompression, see 63001-63048)

(**0099T** deleted 2015 [2016 edition]. To report, use 65785)

0100T Placement of a subconjunctival retinal prosthesis receiver and pulse generator, and implantation of intra-ocular retinal electrode array, with vitrectomy (Sunset January 2016)

(For initial programming of implantable intraocular retinal electrode array device, use 0472T)

0101T Extracorporeal shock wave involving musculoskeletal system, not otherwise specified, high energy (Sunset January 2016)

0102T Extracorporeal shock wave, high energy, performed by a physician, requiring anesthesia other than local, involving lateral humeral epicondyle (Sunset January 2016)

(**0103T** deleted 2015 [2016 edition].)

(For holotranscobalamin, quantitative, use 84999)

(For inert gas rebreathing for cardiac output measurement during rest, use 93799)

(For intert gas rebreathing for cardiac output measurement during exercise, use 93799)

0106T Quantitative sensory testing (QST), testing and interpretation per extremity; using touch pressure stimuli to assess large diameter sensation (Sunset January 2016)

0107T using vibration stimuli to assess large diameter fiber sensation (Sunset January 2016)

Separate Procedure   Unlisted Procedure   CCI Comp. Code   Non-specific Procedure   **951**

0108T   using cooling stimuli to assess small nerve fiber sensation and hyperalgesia (Sunset January 2016)

0109T   using heat-pain stimuli to assess small nerve fiber sensation and hyperalgesia (Sunset January 2016)

0110T   using other stimuli to assess sensation (Sunset January 2016)

0111T   Long-chain (C20-22) omega-3 fatty acids in red blood cell (RBC) membranes (Sunset January 2016)

(For very long chain fatty acids, use 82726)

(0123T   deleted 2015 [2016 edition].)

(For fistulization of sclera for glaucoma, through ciliary body, use 66999)

(For conjunctival incision with posterior extrascleral placement of pharmacological agent, use 68399)

0126T   Common carotid intima-media thickness (IMT) study for evaluation of atherosclerotic burden or coronary heart disease risk factor assessment (Sunset January 2016)

(Do not report 0126T in conjunction with 93880, 93882, 93895)

(For bilateral quantitative carotid intima media thickness and carotid atheroma evaluation that includes all required elements, use 93895)

(For validated, statistically reliable, randomized, controlled, single-patient clinical investigation of FDA approved chronic care drugs, provided by a pharmacist, interpretation and report to the prescribing health care professional, use 99199)

(To report pancreatic islet cell transplantation, use 48999)

(0144T   Deleted 2009 [2010 edition]. To report, see 75571-75574.)

(0145T   Deleted 2009 [2010 edition]. To report, see 75571-75574.)

(0146T   Deleted 2009 [2010 edition]. To report, see 75571-75574.)

(0147T   Deleted 2009 [2010 edition]. To report, see 75571-75574.)

(0148T   Deleted 2009 [2010 edition]. To report, see 75571-75574.)

(0149T   Deleted 2009 [2010 edition]. To report, see 75571-75574.)

(0150T   Deleted 2009 [2010 edition]. To report, see 75571-75574.)

(0151T   Deleted 2009 [2010 edition]. To report, see 75571-75574.)

(For laparoscopic implantation, replacement, revision or removal of gastric stimulation electrodes, lesser curvature, use 43659)

(For open implantation, replacement, revision, or removal of gastric stimulation electrodes, lesser curvature, use 43999)

+ 0159T   Computer-aided detection, including computer algorithm analysis of MRI image data for lesion detection/characterization, pharmacokinetic analysis, with further physician review for interpretation, breast MRI (List separately in addition to code for primary procedure) (Sunset January 2017)

(Use 0159T in conjunction with 77058, 77059)

(Do not report 0159T in conjunction with 76376, 76377)

+ 0163T   Total disc arthroplasty (artificial disc), anterior approach, including discectomy to prepare interspace (other than for decompression), each additional interspace, lumbar (List separately in addition to code for primary procedure) (Sunset January 2019)

(Use 0163T in conjunction with 22857)

● New Code   ▲ Revised Code   ＋ Add-On Code   ⊘ Modifier -51 Exempt   ★ Telemedicine

+ 0164T Removal of total disc arthroplasty, (artificial disc), anterior approach, each additional interspace, lumbar (List separately in addition to code for primary procedure) (Sunset January 2019)

(Use 0164T in conjunction with 22865)

+ 0165T Revision including replacement of total disc arthroplasty, (artificial disc), anterior approach, each additional interspace, lumbar (List separately in addition to code for primary procedure) (Sunset January 2019)

(Use 0165T in conjunction with 22862)

(Do not report 0163T, 0164T, 0165T in conjunction with 22853, 22854, 22859, 49010, when performed at the same level)

(For decompression, see 63001-63048)

(For transmyocardial transcatheter closure of ventricular septal defect, with implant, including cadiopulmonary bypass if performed, use 33999)

(For rhinophototherapy, intranasal application of ultraviolet and visible light, use 30999)

(0169T deleted 2016 [2017 edition])

(For stereotactic placement of infusion catheter[s] in the brain for delivery of therapeutic agent[s], use 64999)

(0171T deleted 2016 [2017 edition])

(To report insertion of interlaminar/interspinous process stabilization/distraction device, without fusion, including image guidance when performed, with openm decompression, lumbar, single level, use 22867. To report insertion of interlaminar/interspinous process stabilization/distraction device, without open decompression or fusion, including image guidance when performed, lumbar, single level, use 22869)

(0172T deleted 2016 [2017 edition])

(To report insertion of interlaminar/interspinous process stabilization/distraction device, without fusion, including image guidance when performed, with open decompression, lumbar, second level, use 22868. To report insertion of interlaminar/interspinous process stabilization/distraction device, without open decompression or fusion, including image guidance when performed, lumbar, second level use, 22870)

+ 0174T Computer-aided detection (CAD) (computer algorithm analysis of digital image data for lesion detection) with further physician review for interpretation and report, with or without digitization of film radiographic images, chest radiograph(s), performed concurrent with primary interpretation (List separately in addition to code for primary procedure) (Sunset January 2017)

(Use 0174T in conjunction with 71045, 71046, 71047, 71048)

0175T Computer-aided detection (CAD) (computer algorithm analysis of digital image data for lesion detection) with further physician review for interpretation and report, with or without digitization of film radiographic images, chest radiograph(s), performed remote from primary interpretation (Sunset January 2017)

(Do not report 0175T in conjunction with 71045, 71046, 71047, 71048)

(0178T deleted 2017 [2018 edition])

(0179T deleted 2017 [2018 edition])

(0180T deleted 2017 [2018 edition])

(For electrocardiogram, 64 leads or greater, with graphic presentation and analysis, use 93799)

(For electrocardiogram, routine, with at least 12 leads separately performed, see 93000-93010)

(0182T deleted 2015 [2016 edition]. To report, see 0394T, 0395T)

0184T Excision of rectal tumor, transanal endoscopic microsurgical approach (ie, TEMS), including muscularis propria (ie, full thickness) (Sunset January 2019)

(For non-endoscopic excision of rectal tumor, see 45160, 45171, 45172)

(Do not report 0184T in conjunction with 45300, 45308, 45309, 45315, 45317, 45320, 69990)

(For multivariate analysis of patient-specific findings with quantifiable computer probability assessment, including report, use 99199)

(For suprachoroidal delivery of pharmacologic agent, use 67299)

Remote Real-Time Interactive Videoconferenced Critical Care Service

In order to report remote real-time interactive video conferenced critical care, the physician(s) or other qualified health care professionals in the remote location must have real-time access to the patient's medical record including progress notes, nursing notes, current medications, vital signs, clinical laboratory test results, other diagnostic test results, and radiographic images. The remote physician or other qualified health care professional must have real-time capability to enter electronic orders; document the remote care services provided in the hospital medical record; videoconference with the on-site health care team in the patient room; assess patients in their individual rooms, using high fidelity audio and video capabilities, including clear observation of the patient, monitors, ventilators, and infusion pumps; and speak to patients and family members.

The review and/or interpretation of all diagnostic information is included in reporting remote real-time interactive video-conferenced critical care when performed during the critical period by the individual(s) providing remote real-time interactive video-conferenced critical care and should not be reported separately.

The remote real-time interactive video conferenced critical care codes 0188T and 0189T are used to report the total duration of time spent by the individual providing remote real-time interactive video conferenced critical care services to a critically ill or critically injured patient, even if the time spent by the physician on that date is not continuous. For any given period of time spent providing remote real-time interactive video-conferenced critical care services, the physician or other qualified health care professional must devote his or her full attention to the patient and, therefore, cannot provide services to any other patient during the same period of time.

Only one physician or other qualified health care professional may report either Critical Care Services (99291, 99292) or remote real-time interactive video-conferenced Critical Care for the same period of time. Do not report remote real-time interactive video-conferenced critical care if another individual reports Pediatric or Neonatal Critical Care or Intensive Care services (99468-99476).

Code 0188T is used to report the first 30 to 74 minutes of remote real-time interactive video-conferenced critical care on a given date. It should be used only once per date even if the time spent by the physician or other qualified health care professional is not continuous on that date. Remote real-time interactive video-conferenced critical care of less than 30 minutes total duration on a given date should not be reported.

Code 0189T is used to report additional block(s) of time, of up to 30 minutes each, beyond the first 74 minutes (see table below).

The following examples illustrate the correct reporting of remote critical care services:

Total Duration of Critical Care	Code(s)
less than 30 minutes (less than 1/2 hour)	Do not report
30-74 minutes (1/2 hr. - 1 hr. 14 min.)	0188T
75-104 minutes (1 hr. 15 min. - 1 hr. 44 min.)	0188T once AND 0189T once
105-134 minutes (1 hr. 45 min. - 2 hr. 14 min.)	0188T once AND 0189 twice

★ **0188T** Remote real-time interactive video-conferenced critical care, evaluation and management of the critically ill or critically injured patient; first 30- 74 minutes (Sunset January 2019)

★+**0189T** each additional 30 minutes (List separately in addition to code for primary service) (Sunset January 2019)

(Use 0189T in conjunction with 0188T)

+ **0190T** Placement of intraocular radiation source applicator (list separately in addition to primary procedure) (Sunset January 2019)

(Use 0190T in conjunction with 67036)

(For application of the source by radiation oncologist, see Clinical Brachytherapy section)

0191T Insertion of anterior segment aqueous drainage device, without extraocular resevoir; internal approach, into the trabecular meshwork; initial insertion (Sunset January 2019)

+ 0376T each additional device insertion {List separately in addition to code for primary procedure) (Sunset January 2020)

(Use 0376T in conjunction with 0191T)

0253T Insertion of anterior segment aqueous drainage device, without extraocular resevoir; internal approach, into the suprachoroidal space (Sunset January 2019)

(To report insertion of drainage device by external approach, use 66183)

0195T Arthrodesis, pre-sacral interbody technique, disc space preparation, discectomy, without instrumentation, with image guidance, includes bone graft when performed; L5-S1 interspace (Sunset January 2019)

+ 0196T L4-L5 interspace (List separately in addition to code for primary procedure) (Sunset January 2019)

(Use 0196T in conjunction with 0195T)

(Do not report 0195T, 0196T in conjunction with 20930-20938, 22558, 22840, 22845, 22848, 22853, 22854, 22859, 72275, 76000, 76380, 76496, 76497, 77002, 77003, 77011, 77012)

(0197T deleted 2014 [2015 edition]. To report, use 77387)

0198T Measurement of ocular blood flow by repetitive intraocular pressure sampling, with interpretation and report (Sunset January 2020)

(0199T deleted 2014 [2015 edition])

(For tremor measurement with accelerometer(s) and/or gyroscope(s), use 95999)

0200T Percutaneous sacral augmentation (sacroplasty), unilateral injection(s), including the use of a balloon or mechanical device, when used, 1 or more needles, includes imaging guidance and bone biopsy, when performed (Sunset January 2020)

0201T Percutaneous sacral augmentation (sacroplasty), bilateral injections, including the use of a balloon or mechanical device, when used, 2 or more needles includes imaging guidance and bone biopsy, when performed (Sunset January 2020)

(Do not report 0200T, 0201T in conjunction with 20225 when performed at the same level)

0202T Posterior vertebral joint(s) arthroplasty (eg, facet joint[s] replacement), including facetectomy, laminectomy, foraminotomy, and vertebral column fixation, injection of bone cement, when performed, including fluoroscopy, single level, lumbar spine (Sunset January 2020)

(Do not report 0202T in conjunction with 22511, 22514, 22840, 22853, 22854, 22857, 22859, 63005, 63012, 63017, 63030, 63042, 63047, 63056 at the same level)

+ 0205T Intravascular catheter based coronary vessel or graft spectroscopy (eg, infrared) during diagnostic evaluation and/or therapeutic intervention including imaging supervision, interpretation, and report, each vessel (List separately in addition to code for primary procedure) (Sunset January 2020)

(Use 0205T in conjunction with 92920, 92924, 92928, 92933, 92937, 92941, 92943, 92975, 93454-93461, 93563, 93564)

0206T Computerized database analysis of multiple cycles of digitized cardiac electrical data from two or more ECG leads, including transmission to a remote center, application of multiple nonlinear mathematical transormations, with coronary artery obstruction severity assessment (Sunset January 2020)

(When a 12-lead ECG is performed, 93000-93010 may be reported, as appropriate)

0207T Evacuation of meibomian glands, automated, using heat and intermittent pressure, unilateral (Sunset January 2020)

0208T Pure tone audiometry (threshold), automated; air only (Sunset January 2016)

0209T   air and bone (Sunset January 2016)

0210T Speech audiometry threshold, automated; (Sunset January 2016)

0211T   with speech recognition (Sunset January 2016)

0212T Comprehensive audiometry threshold evaluation and speech recognition (0209T, 0211T combined), automated (Sunset January 2016)

(For audiometric testing using audiometers performed manually by a qualified health care professional, see 92551-92557)

0213T Injection(s), diagnostic or therapeutic agent, paravertebral facet (zygapophyseal) joint (or nerves innervating that joint) with ultrasound guidance, cervical or thoracic; single level (Sunset January 2016)

(To report bilateral procedure, use 0213T with modifier 50)

+ 0214T   second level (list separately in addition to code for primary procedure) (Sunset January 2016)

(Use 0214T in conjunction with 0213T)

(To report bilateral procedure, use 0214T with modifier 50)

+ 0215T   third and any additional level(s) (list separately in addition to code for primary procedure) (Sunset January 2016)

(Do not report 0215T more than once per day)

(Use 0215T in conjunction with 0214T)

(To report bilateral procedure, use 0215T with modifier 50)

0216T Injection(s), diagnostic or therapeutic agent, paravertebral facet (zygapophyseal) joint (or nerves innervating that joint) with ultrasound guidance, lumbar or sacral; single level (Sunset January 2016)

(To report bilateral procedure, use 0216T with modifier 50)

+ 0217T   second level (list separately in addition to code for primary procedure) (Sunset January 2016)

(Use 0217T in conjunction with 0216T)

(To report bilateral procedure, use 0217T with modifier 50)

+ 0218T   third and any additional level(s) (list separately in addition to code for primary procedure) (Sunset January 2016)

(Do not report 0218T more than once per day)

(Use 0218T in conjunction with 0216T, 0217T)

(If injection(s) are performed using fluoroscopy or CT, see 64490-64495)

(To report bilateral procedure, use 0218T with modifier 50)

0219T Placement of a posterior intrafacet implant(s), unilateral or bilateral, including imaging and placement of bone graft(s) or synthetic device(s), single level; cervical (Sunset January 2016)

0220T   thoracic (Sunset January 2016)

0221T   lumbar (Sunset January 2016)

   ● New Code   ▲ Revised Code   + Add-On Code   ⊘ Modifier -51 Exempt   ★ Telemedicine

(Do not report 0219T-0221T in conjunction with any radiological service)

(Do not report 0219T, 0220T, 0221T in conjunction with 20930, 20931, 22600-22614, 22840, 22853, 22854, 22859 at the same level)

+ 0222T   each additional vertebral segment (list separately in addition to code for primary procedure) (Sunset January 2016)

(Use 0222T in conjunction with 0219T-0221T)

(For posterior or posterolateral arthrodesis technique, see 22600-22614)

(0223T   deleted 2015 [2016 edition]. To report acoustic cardiography, use 93799)

(0224T   deleted 2015 [2016 edition]. To report acoustic cardiography, use 93799)

(0225T   deleted 2015 [2016 edition]. To report acoustic cardiography, use 93799)

(0226T   deleted 2014 [2015 edition]. To report, use 46601)

(0227T   deleted 2014 [2015 edition]. To report, use 46607)

0228T   Injection(s), anesthetic agent and/or steroid, transforaminal epidural, with ultrasound guidance, cervical or thoracic; single level (Sunset January 2016)

+ 0229T   each additional level (list separately in addition to code for primary procedure) (Sunset January 2016)

(Use 0229T in conjunction with 0228T)

0230T   Injection(s), anesthetic agent and/or steroid, transforaminal epidural, with ultrasound guidance, lumbar or sacral; single level (Sunset January 2016)

+ 0231T   each additional level (list separately in addition to code for primary procedure) (Sunset January 2016)

(Use 0231T in conjunction with 0230T)

(For transforaminal epidural injections performed under fluoroscopy or CT, see 64479-64484)

(Do not report 0228T-0231T in conjunction with 76942, 76998, 76999)

0232T   Injection(s), platelet rich plasma, any site, including image guidance, harvesting and preparation when performed (Sunset January 2016)

(Do not report 0232T in conjunction with 20550, 20551, 20600, 20604, 20605, 20606, 20610, 20611, 20926, 36415, 36592, 76942, 77002, 77012, 77021, 86965, 0481T)

(Do not report 38220-38230 for bone marrow aspiration for platelet rich stem cell injection. For bone marrow aspiration for platelet rich stem cell injection, use 0232T)

(0233T   deleted 2015 [2016 edition]. To report skin advanced glycation endproducts measurement by multi-wavelength fluorescent spectroscopy, use 88749)

Atherectomy (Open or Percutaneous) for Supra-Inguinal Arteries

Codes 0234T-0238T describe atherectomy performed by any method (eg, directional, rotational, laser) in arteries above the inguinal ligaments. These codes are structured differently than the codes describing atherectomy performed below the inguinal legaments (37225, 37227, 37229, 37231, 37233, 37235).

0234T   Transluminal peripheral atherectomy, open or percutaneous, including radiological supervision and interpretation; renal artery (Sunset January 2016)

0235T   visceral artery (except renal), each vessel (Sunset January 2016)

0236T   abdominal aorta (Sunset January 2016)

0237T   brachiocephalic trunk and branches, each vessel (Sunset January 2016)

0238T   iliac artery, each vessel (Sunset January 2016)

(0239T   deleted 2014 [2015 edition]. To report, use 93702)

(0240T   deleted 2015 [2016 edition].)

(0241T   deleted 2015 [2016 edition])

(To report esophageal motility studies without high-resolution esophageal pressure topography, use 91010 and with stimulant or perfusion, use 91013)

(0243T   deleted 2015 [2016 edition]. To report intermittent measurement of wheeze rate for bronchodilator or bronchial challenge diagnostic evaluation, use 94799)

(0244T   deleted 2015 [2016 edition]. To report intermittent measurement of wheeze rate for bronchodilator or bronchial challenge diagnostic evaluation, use 94799)

0249T   Ligation, hemorrhoidal vascular bundle(s), including ultrasound guidance (Sunset January 2016)

(Do not report 0249T in conjunction with 46020, 46221, 46250-46262, 46600, 46945, 46946, 76872, 76942, 76998)

0253T   This code is out of order. See page 953.

▲ **0254T**   Endovascular repair of iliac artery bifurcation (eg, aneurysm, pseudoaneurysm, arteriovenous malformation, trauma, dissection) using bifurcated endograft from the common iliac artery into both the external and internal iliac artery, including all selective and/or nonselective catheterization(s) required for device placement and all associated radiological supervision and interpretation, unilateral (Sunset January 2021)

(0255T   deleted 2017 [2018 edition]. To report, use 0254T)

(0262T   deleted. To report transcatheter pulmonary valve implantation, use 33477)

0263T   Intramuscular autologous bone marrow cell therapy, with preparation of harvested cells, multiple injections, one leg, including ultrasound guidance, if performed; complete procedure including unilateral or bilateral bone marrow harvest (Sunset January 2017)

(Do not report 0263T in conjunction with 38204-38242, 76942, 93925, 93926)

0264T   complete procedure excluding bone marrow harvest (Sunset January 2017)

(Do not report 0264T in conjunction with 38204-38242, 76942, 93925, 93926, 0265T)

0265T   unilateral or bilateral bone marrow harvest only for intramuscular autologous bone marrow cell therapy (Sunset January 2017)

(Do not report 0265T in conjunction with 38204-38242, 0264T. For complete procedure, use 0263T)

0266T   Implantation or replacement of carotid sinus baroreflex activation device; total system (includes generator placement, unilateral or bilateral lead placement, intra-operative interrogation, programming, and repositioning, when performed) (Sunset January 2017)

0267T   lead only, unilateral (includes intra-operative interrogation, programming, and repositioning, when performed) (Sunset January 2017)

(For bilateral lead implantation or replacement, use 0267T with modifier 50)

0268T   pulse generator only (includes intra-operative interrogation, programming, and repositioning, when performed) (Sunset January 2017)

(Do not report 0267T, 0268T in conjunction with 0266T, 0269T-0273T)

0269T Revision or removal of carotid sinus baroreflex activation device; total system (includes generator placement, unilateral or bilateral lead placement, intra-operative interrogation, programming, and repositioning, when performed) (Sunset January 2017)

(Do not report 0269T in conjunction with 0266T-0268T, 0270T-0273T)

0270T lead only, unilateral (includes intra-operative interrogation, programming, and repositioning, when performed) (Sunset January 2017)

(Do not report 0270T in conjunction with 0266T-0269T, 0271T-0273T)

(For bilateral lead removal, use 0270T with modifier 50)

(For removal of total carotic sinus baroreflex activation device, use 0269T)

0271T pulse generator only (includes intra-operative interrogation, programming, and repositioning, when performed) (Sunset January 2017)

(Do not report 0271T in conjunction with 0266T-0270T, 0272T, 0273T)

(For removal and replacement, see 0266T, 0267T, 0268T)

0272T Interrogation device evaluation (in person), carotid sinus baroreflex activation system, including telemetric ineractive communication with the implantable device to monitor device diagnostics and programmed therapy values, with interpretation and report (eg, battery status, lead impedance, pulse amplitude, pulse width, therapy frequency, pathway mode, burst mode, therapy start/stop times each day); (Sunset January 2017)

(Do not report 0272T in conjunction with 0266T-0271T, 0273T)

0273T with programming (Sunset January 2017)

(Do not report 0273T in conjunction with 0266T-0272T)

0274T Percutaneous laminotomy/laminectomy (interlaminar approach) for decompression of neural elements, (with or without ligamentous resection, discectomy, facetectomy and/or foraminotomy), any method, under indirect image guidance (eg, fluoroscopic, CT), single or multiple levels, unilateral or bilateral; cervical or thoracic

0275T lumbar

(For percutaneous decompression of the nucleus pulposus of intervertebral disc utilizing needle based technique, use 62287)

0278T Transcutaneous electrical modulation pain reprocessing (eg, scrambler therapy), each treatment session (includes placement of electrodes) (Sunset January 2017)

(**0281T** deleted 2016 [2017 edition]. To report, use 33340)

(**0282T** deleted 2016 [2017 edition].)

(**0283T** deleted 2016 [2017 edition].)

(**0284T** deleted 2016 [2017 edition].)

(**0285T** deleted 2016 [2017 edition].)

(For implantation of trial or permanent electrode arrays or pulse generators for peripheral subcutaneous field stimulation, use 64999)

(**0286T** deleted 2016 [2017 edition].)

(**0287T** deleted 2016 [2017 edition].)

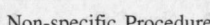

959

(**0288T**   deleted 2016 [2017 edition].)

(For delivery of thermal energy to the muscle of the anal canal, use 46999)

(**0289T**   deleted 2016 [2017 edition].)

+ **0290T**   Corneal incisions in the recipient cornea created using a laser, in preparation for penetrating or lamellar keratoplasty (List separately in addition to code for primary procedure) (Sunset January 2017)

(Use 0290T in conjunction with 65710, 65730, 65750, 65755)

(**0291T**   deleted 2016 [2017 edition]. To report, see 92978, 92979)

(**0292T**   deleted 2016 [2017 edition]. To report, see 92978, 92979)

(**0293T**   deleted 2017 [2018 edition])

(**0294T**   deleted 2017 [2018 edition])

0295T   External electrocardiographic recording for more than 48 hours up to 21 days by continuous rhythm recording and storage; includes recording, scanning analysis with report, review and interpretation (Sunset January 2018)

0296T   recording (includes connection and initial recording) (Sunset January 2018)

0297T   scanning analysis with report (Sunset January 2018)

0298T   review and interpretation (Sunset January 2018)

(Do not report 0295T-0298T in conjunction with 93224-93272 for same monitoring period)

(**0299T**   deleted 2017 [2018 edition])

(**0300T**   deleted 2017 [2018 edition])

(For extracorporeal shock wave for integumentary wound healing, high energy, use 28899)

(**0301T**   deleted 2017 [2018 edition])

(For focused microwave thermotherapy of the breast, use 19499)

(**0302T**   deleted 2017 [2018 edition])

(**0303T**   deleted 2017 [2018 edition])

(**0304T**   deleted 2017 [2018 edition])

(**0305T**   deleted 2017 [2018 edition])

(**0306T**   deleted 2017 [2018 edition])

(**0307T**   deleted 2017 [2018 edition])

0308T   Insertion of ocular telescope prosthesis including removal of crystalline lens or intraocular lens prosthesis (Sunset January 2021)

(Do not report 0308T in conjunction with 65800-65815, 66020, 66030, 66600-66635, 66761, 66825, 66982-66986, 69990)

(**0309T**   deleted 2017 [2018 edition])

---

960   ● New Code   ▲ Revised Code   + Add-On Code   ⊘ Modifier -51 Exempt   ★ Telemedicine

(For arthrodesis, pre-sacral interbody technique, including disc space preparation, discectomy, with posterior instrumentation, with image guidance, including bone graft, when performed, lumbar, L4-L5 interspace, use 22899)

(**0310T** deleted 2017 [2018 edition])

(For motor function mapping using non-invasive navigated transcranial magnetic stimulation [nTMS] for therapeutic treatment planning, upper and lower extremity, use 64999)

(**0311T** deleted 2015 [2016 edition]. To report, use 93050)

0312T Vagus nerve blocking therapy (morbid obesity); laparoscopic implantation of neurostimulator electrode array, anterior and posterior vagal trunks adjacent to esophagogastric junction (EGJ), with implantation of pulse generator, includes programming (Sunset January 2018)

0313T laparoscopic revision or replacement of vagal trunk neurostimulator electrode array, including connection to existing pulse generator (Sunset January 2018)

0314T laparascopic removal of vagal trunk neurostimulator (Sunset January 2018)

0315T removal of pulse generator (Sunset January 2018)

0316T replacement of pulse generator (Sunset January 2018)

(Do not report 0315T in conjunction with 0316T)

0317T neurostimulator pulse generator electronic analysis, includes reprogramming when performed (Sunset January 2018)

(For implantation, revision, replacement, and/or removal of vagus [cranial] nerve neurostimulator electrode array and/or pulse generator for vagus nerve stimulation performed other than at the ECJ [eg, epilepsy], see 64568-64570)

(For analsysis and/or [re]programming for vagus nerve stimulator, see 95970, 95974, 95975)

0329T Monitoring of intraocular pressure 24 hours or longer, unilateral or bilateral, with interpretation and report (Sunset January 2019)

0330T Tear film imaging, unilateral or bilateral, with interpretation adn report (Sunset January 2019)

0331T Myocardial sympathetic innervation imaging, planar qualitative and quantitative assessment; (Sunset January 2019)

0332T with tomographic SPECT (Sunset January 2019)

(For myocardial infarct avid imaging, see 78466, 78468, 78469)

▲ **0333T** Visual evoked potential, screening of visual acuity, automated, with report (Sunset January 2019)

(For visual evoked potential testing for glaucoma, use 0464T)

● **0464T** Visual evoked potential, testing for glaucoma, with interpretation and report (Sunset January 2023)

(**0334T** deleted 2014 [2015 edition])

(To report percutaneous/minimally invasive [indirect visualization] arthrodesis of the sacroiliac joint with image guidance, use 27279)

(For visual evoked potential screening of visual acuity, use 0333T)

0335T Extra-osseous subtalar joint implant for talotarsal stabilazation (Sunset January 2019)

(**0336T** deleted 2016 [2017 edition]. To report laparoscopy, surgical, ablation of uterine fibroid[s], use 58674)

Separate Procedure   Unlisted Procedure   CCI Comp. Code   Non-specific Procedure   **961**

0337T Endothelial function assessment, using peripheral vascular response to reactive hyperemia, non-invasive (eg, brachial artery ultrasound, peripheral artery tonometry), unilateral or bilateral (Sunset January 2019)

(Do not report 0337T in conjunction with 93922, 93923)

0338T Transcatheter renal sympathetic denervation, percutaneous approach including arterial puncture, selective catheter placement(s) renal artery(ies), fluoroscopy, contrast injection(s), intraprocedural roadmapping and radiological supervision and interpretation, including pressure gradient measurements, flush aortogram and diagnostic renal angiography when performed; unilateral (Sunset January 2019)

0339T bilateral (Sunset January 2019)

(Do not report 0338T, 0339T in conjunction with 36251, 36252, 36253, 36254)

(**0340T** deleted 2017 [2018 edition]. To report, use 32994)

0341T Quantitative pupillometry with interpretation and report, unilateral or bilateral (Sunset January 2020)

0342T Therapeutic apheresis with selective HDL delipidation and plasma reinfusion (Sunset January 2020)

Fluoroscopy (76000, 76001) and radiologic supervision and interpretation are inherent to the transcatheter mitral valve repair (TMVR) procedure and are not separately reportable. Diagnostic cardiac catheterization (93451, 93452, 93453, 93454, 93455, 93456, 93457, 93458, 93459, 93460, 93461, 93530, 93531, 93532, 93533) should **not** be reported with transcatheter mitral valve repair 0345T for:

- Contrast injections, angiography, roadmapping, and/or fluoroscopic guidance for the transcatheter mitral valve repair (TMVR),
- Left ventricular angiography to assess mitral regurgitation, for guidance of TMVR, or
- Right and left heart catheterization for hemodynamic measurements before, during, and after TMVR for guidance of TMVR.

Diagnostic right and left heart catheterization, (93451, 93452, 93453, 93456, 93457, 93458, 93459, 93460, 93461, 93530, 93531, 93532, 93533) and diagnostic coronary angiography (93454, 93455, 93456, 93457, 93458, 93459, 93460, 93461, 93563, 93564) not inherent to the TMVR, may be reported with 0345T, appended with modifier 59 if:

1. No prior study is available and a full diagnostic study is performed, or

2. A prior study is available, but as documented in the medical record:

   a. There is inadequate visualization of the anatomy and/or pathology, or

   b. The patient's condition with respect to the clinical indication has changed since the prior study, or

   c. There is a clinical change during the procedure that requires new evaluation.

Percutaneous coronary interventional procedures may be reported separately, when performed.

Other cardiac catheterization services may be reported separately, when performed for diagnostic purposes not intrinsic to the TMVR.

When transcatheter ventricular support is required, the appropriate code may be reported with the appropriate ventricular assist device (VAD) procedure (33990, 33991, 33992, 33993) or balloon pump insertion (33967, 33970, 33973).

(**0343T** deleted 2014 [2015 edition]. To report, use 33418)

(**0344T** deleted 2014 [2015 edition]. To report, use 33419)

0345T Transcatheter mitral valve repair percutaneous approach via the coronary sinus (Sunset January 2020)

(For transcatheter mitral valve repair percutaneous approach including transseptal puncture when performed, see 33418, 33419)

(Do not report 0345T in conjunction with 93451, 93452, 93453, 93456, 93457, 93458, 93459, 93460, 93461 for diagnostic left and right heart catheterization procedures intrinsic to the valve repair procedure)

● New Code   ▲ Revised Code   + Add-On Code   ⊘ Modifier -51 Exempt   ★ Telemedicine

(Do not report 0345T in conjunction with 93453, 93454, 93563, 93564 for coronary angiography intrinsic to the valve repair procedure)

(For transcatheter mitral valve implantation/ replacement [TMVI], see 0483T, 0484T)

+ **0346T** Ultrasound, elastography (List separately in addition to code for primary procedure) (Sunset January 2020)

(Use 0346T in conjunction with 76536, 76604, 76641, 76642, 76700, 76705, 76770, 76775, 76830, 76856, 76857, 76870, 76872, 76881, 76882)

0347T Placement of interstitial device(s) in bone for radiostereometric analysis (RSA) (Sunset January 2020)

0348T Radiologic examination, radiostereometric analysis (RSA); spine, (includes cervical, thoracic and lumbosacral, when performed) (Sunset January 2020)

0349T upper extremity(ies), (includes shoulder, elbow, and wrist, when performed) (Sunset January 2020)

0350T lower extremity(ies), (includes hip, proximal femur, knee, and ankle, when performed) (Sunset January 2020)

0351T Optical coherence tomography of breast or axillary lymph node, excised tissue, each specimen; real-time intraoperative (Sunset January 2020)

0352T interpretation and report, real-time or referred (Sunset January 2020)

(Do not report 0352T in conjunction with 0351T, when performed by the same physician)

0353T Optical coherence tomography of breast, surgical cavity; real-time intraoperative (Sunset January 2020)

(Report 0353T once per session)

0354T interpretation and report, real-time or referred (Sunset January 2020)

(Do not report 0354T in conjunction with 0353T, when performed by the same physician)

0355T Gastrointestinal tract imaging, intraluminal (e.g. capsule endoscopy), colon, with interpretation and report (Sunset January 2020)

(Use 0355T for imaging of distal ileum, when performed)

(Do not report 0355T in conjunction with 91110, 91111)

0356T Insertion of drug-eluting implant (including punctal dilation and implant removal when performed) into lacrimal canaliculus, each (Sunset January 2020)

(For placement of drug-eluting insert under the eyelid[s], see 0444T, 0445T)

0357T This code is out of order. See page 950.

0358T Bioelectrical impedance analysis whole body composition assessment, with interpretation and report (Sunset January 2020)

(For bioimpedance-derived physiological cardiovascular analysis, use 93701)

(For bioimpedance spectroscopy use 93702)

ADAPTIVE BEHAVIOR ASSESSMENT

Behavior identification assessment (0359T) conducted by the physician or other qualified health care professional includes a detailed behavioral history, patient observation, administration of standardized and non-standardized tests, and structured guardian/caregiver interview to identify and describe deficient adaptive or maladaptive behaviors (eg., impaired social skills and communication deficits, destructive behaviors, and additional functional limitations secondary to maladaptive behaviors). Code 0359T also includes the physician's or other qualified health care professional's interpretation of results and development of plan of care, which may include further observational or exposure behavioral follow-up assessment(s) (0360T, 0361T, 0362T, 0363T), discussion of findings and recommendations with the primary guardian(s)/caregiver(s), and preparation of report.

Observational behavioral follow-up assessment (0360T, 0361T) is administered by a technician under the direction of a physician or other qualified health care professional. The physician or other qualified health care professional may or may not be on site during the face-to-face assessment process. Codes 0360T and 0361T include the physician's or other qualified health care professional's interpretation of results, discussion of findings and recommendations with the primary caregiver(s), and preparation of report.

Codes 0360T and 0361T describe services provided to patients who present with specific destructive behaviors (eg., self-injurious behavior, aggression, property destruction) or behavioral problems secondary to repetitive behaviors or deficits in communication or social relatedness. These assessments include use of structured observation and/or standardized and non-standardized tests to determine levels of adaptive behavior. Areas assessed may include cooperation, motivation, visual understanding, receptive and expressive language, imitation, requests, labeling, play and leisure, and social interactions. Specific destructive behavior(s) assessments include structured observational testing to examine events, cues, responses, and consequences associated with the behaviors.

Exposure behavioral follow-up assessment (0362T, 0363T) is administered by the physician or other qualified health care professional with the assistance of one or more technicians. Code 0362T and 0363T include the physician's or other qualified health care professional's interpretation of results, discussion of findings and recommendations with the primary caregiver(s), and preparation of report.

The typical patients for 0362T and 0363T include patients with one or more specific severe destructive behavior(s) (eg., self-injurious behavior, aggression, property destruction). Specific severe destructive behaviors are assessed using structured testing to examine events, cues, responses, and consequences associated with the behavior(s).

Codes 0362T and 0363T include exposing the patient to a series of social and environmental conditions associated with the destructive behavior(s). Assessment methods include using testing methods designed to examine triggers, events, cues, responses, and consequences associated with the aforementioned maladaptive behaviors. This assessment is completed in a structured, safe environment.

Codes 0360T, 0361T, 0362T, and 0363T are reported following 0359T based on the time that the patient is face-to-face with one or more technician(s). Only count the time of one technician when two or more are present. Codes 0360T, 0361T, 0362T, and 0363T, are reported per the CPT Time-Rule (eg, a unit of time is attained when the mid-point is passed). See table below. The time reported with 0360T, 0361T, 0362T, and 0363T is over a single day and is not cumulative over a longer period.

(Do not report 0359T, 0360T, 0361T, 0362T, 0363T in conjunction with 90785–90899, 96101–96125, 96150, 96151, 96152, 96153, 96154, 96155 on the same date)

(For psychiatric diagnostic evaluation, see 90791, 90792)

For speech evaluations, see 92521, 92522, 92523, 92524)

(For occupational therapy evaluation, see 97165, 97166, 97167, 97168)

(For medical team conference, see 99366, 99367, 99368)

(For health and behavior assessment/intervention, see 96150, 96151, 96152, 96153, 96154, 96155)

(For neurobehavioral status exam, use 96116)

(For neuropsychological testing, use 96118)

CPT Time-Rule for Face-to-Face Technician time: Codes 0360T, 0361T, 0362T, 0363T	
TIME	**CPT Code(s)**
Less than 16 minutes	Not reportable
16 - 45 minutes	0360T or 0362T
46 - 75 minutes	0360T and 0361T or 0362T and 0363T
Each additional increment, up to 30 minutes	Additional 0361T or 0363T

0359T   Behavior identification assessment, by the physician or other qualified health care professional, face-to-face with patient and caregiver(s), includes administration of standardized and non-standardized tests, detailed behavioral history, patient observation and caregiver interview, interpretation of test results, discussion of findings and recommendations with the primary guardian(s)/caregiver(s), and preparation of report (Sunset January 2020)

0360T Observational behavioral follow-up assessment, includes physician or other qualified health care professional direction with interpretation and report, administered by one technician; first 30 minutes of technician time, face-to-face with the patient (Sunset January 2020)

+ 0361T each additional 30 minutes of technician time, face-to-face with the patient (List separately in addition to code for primary service) (Sunset January 2020)

(Use 0361T in conjunction with 0360T)

0362T Exposure behavioral follow-up assessment, includes physician or other qualified health care professional direction with interpretation and report, administered by physician or other qualified health care professional with the assistance of one or more technicians; first 30 minutes of technician(s) time, face-to-face with the patient (Sunset January 2020)

+ 0363T each additional 30 minutes of technician(s) time, face-to-face with the patient (List separately in addition to code for primary procedure) (Sunset January 2020)

(Use 0363T in conjunction with 0362T)

(0362T, 0363T are reported based on a single technician's face to face time with the patient and not the combined time of multiple technicians)

(Do not report 0359T, 0360T, 0361T, 0362T, 0363T in conjunction with 90785–90899, 96101–96125, 96150, 96151, 96152, 96153, 96154, 96155)

ADAPTIVE BEHAVIOR TREATMENT

Adaptive behavior treatment codes 0364T, 0365T, 0366T, 0367T, 0368T, 0369T, 0370T, 0371T, 0372T, 0373T, 0374T describe services provided to patients who present with deficient adaptive or maladaptive behaviors (eg, impaired social skills and communication, destructive behaviors, or additional functional limitations secondary to maladaptive behaviors). Specific target problems and treatment goals are based on results of previous assessments (see 0359T, 0360T, 0361T, 0362T, 0363T).

Adaptive behavior treatment by protocol and group adaptive behavior treatment by protocol are administered by a technician face-to-face with one patient (0364T and 0365T), or two or more patients (0366T, 0367T) under the direction of a physician or other qualified health care professional, utilizing a behavioral intervention protocol designed in advance by the physician or other qualified health care professional, who may or may not provide direct supervision during the face-to-face therapy. Do not report 0366T, 0367T if the group is larger than eight patients.

Adaptive behavior treatment with protocol modification (0368T, 0369T) is administered by a physician or other qualified health care professional face-to-face with a single patient. The physician or other qualified health care professional resolves one or more problems with the protocol and may simultaneously instruct a technician and/or guardian(s)/caregiver(s) in administering the modified protocol. Physician or other qualified health care professional instruction to the technician without the patient present is not reported separately.

Family adaptive behavior treatment guidance and multiple family group adaptive behavior treatment guidance are administered by a physician or other qualified health care professional face-to-face with guardian(s)/caregiver(s), without the presence of a patient, and involves identifying problem behaviors and deficits and teaching guardian(s)/caregiver(s) of one patient (0370T) or multiple patients (0371T) to utilize treatment protocols designed to reduce maladaptive behaviors and/or skill deficits. Do not report 0371T if the group is larger than eight patients.

Adaptive behavior treatment social skills group (0372T)is administered by a physician or other qualified health care professional face-to-face with multiple patients, focusing on social skills training, and identifying and targeting individual patient social deficits and problem behaviors. The physician or other qualified health care professional monitors the needs of individual patients and adjust the therapeutic techniques during the group, as needed. Services to increase target social skills may include modeling, rehearsing, corrective feedback, and homework assignments. In contrast to adaptive behavior treatment by protocol techniques (0364T, 0365T, 0366T, 0367T), adjustments required in social skills group setting are made in real time rather than for a subsequent service. Do not report 0372T if the group is larger than eight patients.

Codes 0364T, 0365T, 0366T, 0367T, 0368T, 0369T, 0372T may include services involving patient interaction with other individuals, including other patients. Report group services (0366T, 0367T, 0372T) only for patients who are participating in the interaction in order to meet their own individual treatment goals.

0364T Adaptive behavior treatment by protocol, administered by technician, face-to-face with one patient; first 30 minutes of technician time (Sunset January 2020)

+ 0365T   each additional 30 minutes of technician time (List separately in addition to code for primary procedure) (Sunset January 2020)

(Use 0365T in conjunction with 0364T)

(Do not report 0364T, 0365T in conjunction with 90785- 90899, 92507, 96101-96155, 97127)

0366T   Group adaptive behavior treatment by protocol, administered by technician, face-to-face with two or more patients; first 30 minutes of technician time (Sunset January 2020)

+ 0367T   each additional 30 minutes of technician time (List separately in addition to code for primary procedure) (Sunset January 2020)

(Use 0367T in conjunction with 0366T)

(Do not report 0366T, 0367T if the group is larger than 8 patients)

(Do not report 0366T, 0367T in conjunction with 90785-90899, 92508, 96101-96155, 97150)

0368T   Adaptive behavior treatment with protocol modification administered by physician or other qualified health care professional with one patient; first 30 minutes of patient face-to-face time (Sunset January 2020)

+ 0369T   each additional 30 minutes of patient face-to-face time (List separately in addition to code for primary procedure) (Sunset January 2020)

(Use 0369T in conjunction with 0368T)

(Do not report 0368T, 0369T in conjunction with 90791, 90792, 90846, 90847, 90887, 92507, 97127)

0370T   Family adaptive behavior treatment guidance, administered by physician or other qualified health care professional (without the patient present) (Sunset January 2020)

0371T   Multiple-family group adaptive behavior treatment guidance, administered by physician or other qualified health care professional (without the patient present) (Sunset January 2020)

(Do not report 0371T when the families of more than 8 patients are participants)

(Do not report 0370T, 0371T in conjunction with 90791, 90792, 90846, 90847, 90887)

0372T   Adaptive behavior treatment social skills group, administered by physician or other qualified health care professional face-to-face with multiple patients (Sunset January 2020)

(Do not report 0372T if the group is larger than 8 patients)

(Do not report 0372T in conjunction with 90853, 92508, 97150)

EXPOSURE ADAPTIVE BEHAVIOR TREATMENT WITH PROTOCOL MODIFICATION

Codes 0373T and 0374T describe services provided to patients with one or more specific severe destructive behaviors (eg., self-injurious behavior, aggression, property destruction), with direct supervision by a physician or other qualified health care professional that requires two or more technicians face-to-face with the patient for safe treatment. Technicians elicit behavioral effects of exposing the patient to specific environmental conditions and treatments. Technicians record all occurrences of targeted behaviors. The physician or other qualified health care professional reviews and analyzes data and refines the therapy using single-case designs; ineffective components are modified or replaced until discharge goals are achieved (eg., reducing destructive behavior by at least 90%, generalizing the treatment effects across caregivers and settings, or maintaining the treatment effects over time). The therapy is conducted in a structured, safe, environment. Precautions may include environmental modifications and/or protective equipment for the safety of the patient or the technicians.

0373T   Exposure adaptive behavior treatment with protocol modification requiring two or more technicians for severe maladaptive behavior(s); first 60 minutes of technicians' time, face-to-face with patient (Sunset January 2020)

+ 0374T   each additional 30 minutes of technicians' time face-to-face with patient (List separately in addition to code for primary procedure) (Sunset January 2020)

(Use 0374T in conjunction with 0373T)

---

966   ● New Code   ▲ Revised Code   + Add-On Code   ⊘ Modifier -51 Exempt   ★ Telemedicine

(0373T, 0374T are reported based on a single technician's face-to-face time with the patient and not the combined time of multiple technicians)

(Do not report 0373T, 0374T in conjunction with 90785-90899, 96101-96155)

0375T Total disc arthroplasty (artificial disc), anterior approach, including discectomy with end plate preparation (includes osteophytectomy for nerve root or spinal cord decompression and microdissection), cervical, three or more levels (Sunset January 2020)

(Do not report 0375T in conjunction with 22853, 22854, 22856, 22858, 22859 when performed at the same level)

0376T This code is out of order. See page 955.

0377T Anoscopy with directed submucosal injection of bulking agent for fecal incontinence (Sunset January 2020)

(Do not report 0377T in conjunction with 46600)

0378T Visual field assessment, with concurrent real time data analysis and accessible data storage with patient initiated data transmitted to a remote surveillance center for up to 30 days; review and interpretation with report by a physician or other qualified health care professional (Sunset January 2020)

0379T   technical support and patient instructions, surveillance, analysis, and transmission of daily and emergent data reports as prescribed by a physician or other qualified health care professional (Sunset January 2020)

0380T Computer-aided animation and analysis of time series retinal images for the monitoring of disease progression, unilateral or bilateral, with interpretation and report (Sunset January 2020)

0381T External heart rate and 3-axis accelerometer data recording up to 14 days to assess changes in heart rate and to monitor motion analysis for the purposes of diagnosing nocturnal epilepsy seizure events; includes report, scanning analysis with report, review and interpretation by a physician or other qualified health care professional (Sunset January 2021)

0382T   review and interpretation only (Sunset January 2021)

(Do not report 0381T, 0382T in conjunction with 0383T, 0384T, 0385T, 0386T)

0383T External heart rate and 3-axis accelerometer data recording from 15 to 30 days to assess changes in heart rate and to monitor motion analysis for the purposes of diagnosing nocturnal epilepsy seizure events; includes report, scanning analysis with report, review and interpretation by a physician or other qualified health care professional (Sunset January 2021)

0384T   review and interpretation only (Sunset January 2021)

(Do not report 0383T, 0384T in conjunction with 0381T, 0382T, 0385T, 0386T)

0385T External heart rate and 3-axis accelerometer data recording more than 30 days to assess changes in heart rate and to monitor motion analysis for the purposes of diagnosing nocturnal epilepsy seizure events; includes report, scanning analysis with report, review and interpretation by a physician or other qualified health care professional (Sunset January 2021)

0386T   review and interpretation only (Sunset January 2021)

(Do not report 0385T, 0386T in conjunction with 0381T, 0382T, 0383T, 0384T)

PACEMAKER—LEADLESS AND POCKETLESS SYSTEM

A leadless cardiac pacemaker system is a pulse generator with built-in battery and electrode for implantation in a cardiac chamber via a transfemoral catheter approach. For these services, see 0387T, 0388T, 0389T, 0390T, 0391T. Codes 0387T, 0388T include fluoroscopy (76000), right ventriculography (93566), and femoral venography (75820) intrinsic to procedure, when performed.

0387T Transcatheter insertion or replacement of permanent leadless pacemaker, ventricular (Sunset January 2021)

| | Separate Procedure | | Unlisted Procedure | | CCI Comp. Code | | Non-specific Procedure | **967** |

(For insertion, repositioning, or replacement of pacemaker systems with lead[s], use the appropriate epicardial [33202, 33203] or transvenous codes [33206-33222, 33224, 33225, 33226])

(Do not report 0387T in conjunction with 0388T, 0389T, 0390T, 0391T)

(Do not report 0387T in conjunction with 93566 for right ventriculography performed during leadless pacemaker insertion)

0388T Transcatheter removal of permanent leadless pacemaker, ventricular (Sunset January 2021)

(For removal of pacemaker systems with lead[s], see the appropriate transvenous [33227, 33228, 33229, 33233, 33234, 33235] or thoracotomy codes [33236, 33237, 33238])

(Do not report 0388T in conjunction with 0387T)

0389T Programming device evaluation (in person) with iterative adjustment of the implantable device to test the function of the device and select optimal permanent programmed values with analysis, review and report, leadless pacemaker system (Sunset January 2021)

(Do not report 0389T in conjunction with 0387T, 0390T, 0391T)

(For programming device evaluations of pacemaker systems with lead[s], see 93279, 93280, 93281)

0390T Peri-procedural device evaluation (in person) and programming of device system parameters before or after a surgery, procedure or test with analysis, review and report, leadless pacemaker system (Sunset January 2021)

(Do not report 0390T in conjunction with 0387T, 0389T, 0391T)

(For peri-procedural device evaluation of systems with lead[s], see 93286, 93287)

0391T Interrogation device evaluation (in person) with analysis, review and report, includes connection, recording and disconnection per patient encounter, leadless pacemaker system (Sunset January 2021)

(Do not report 0391T in conjunction with 0387T, 0389T, 0390T)

(For interrogation device evaluation of systems with lead[s], see 93288, 93289)

(**0392T** deleted 2016 [2017 edition]. To report, use 43284)

(**0393T** deleted 2016 [2017 edition]. To report, use 43285)

(Electronic brachytherapy is a form of radiation therapy in which an electrically generated X-ray source of ionizing radiation is placed inside or in close proximity to the tumor or target tissue to deliver therapeutic radiation dosage)

0394T High dose rate electronic brachytherapy, skin surface application, per fraction, includes basic dosimetry, when performed (Sunset January 2021)

(Do not report 0394T in conjunction with 77261, 77262, 77263, 77300, 77306, 77307, 77316, 77317, 77318, 77332, 77333, 77334, 77336, 77427, 77431, 77432, 77435, 77469, 77470, 77499, 77761, 77762, 77763, 77767, 77768, 77770, 77771, 77772, 77778, 77789)

(For high dose rate radionuclide surface brachytherapy, see 77767, 77768)

(For non-brachytherapy superficial [eg, =200 kV] radiation treatment delivery, use 77401)

0395T High dose rate electronic brachytherapy, interstitial or intracavitary treatment, per fraction, includes basic dosimetry, when performed (Sunset January 2021)

(Do not report 0395T in conjunction with 77261, 77262, 77263, 77300, 77306, 77307, 77316, 77317, 77318, 77332, 77333, 77334, 77336, 77427, 77431, 77432, 77435, 77469, 77470, 77499, 77761, 77762, 77763, 77767, 77768, 77770, 77771, 77772, 77778, 77789)

(For skin surface application of high dose rate electronic brachytherapy, use 0394T)

● New Code   ▲ Revised Code   + Add-On Code   ⊘ Modifier -51 Exempt   ★ Telemedicine

+ ▨ **0396T** Intra-operative use of kinetic balance sensor for implant stability during knee replacement arthroplasty (List separately in addition to code for primary procedure) (Sunset January 2021)

(Use 0396T in conjunction with 27445, 27446, 27447, 27486, 27487, 27488)

+ ▨ **0397T** Endoscopic retrograde cholangiopancreatography (ERCP), with optical endomicroscopy (List separately in addition to code for primary procedure) (Sunset January 2021)

(Use 0397T in conjunction with 43260, 43261, 43262, 43263, 43264, 43265, 43274, 43275, 43276, 43277, 43278)

(Do not report 0397T in conjunction with 88375)

(Do not report optical endomicroscopy more than once per session)

▨ **0398T** Magnetic resonance image guided high intensity focused ultrasound (MRgFUS), stereotactic ablation lesion, intracranial for movement disorder including stereotactic navigation and frame placement when performed (Sunset January 2021)

(Do not report 0398T in conjunction with 61781, 61800)

+ **0399T** Myocardial strain imaging (quantitative assessment of myocardial mechanics using image-based analysis of local myocardial dynamics) (List separately in addition to code for primary procedure) (Sunset January 2021)

(Use 0399T in conjunction with 93303, 93304, 93306, 93307, 93308, 93312, 93314, 93315, 93317, 93350, 93351, 93355)

(Report 0399T once per session)

0400T Multi-spectral digital skin lesion analysis of clinically atypical cutaneous pigmented lesions for detection of melanomas and high risk melanocytic atypia; one to five lesions (Sunset January 2021)

▨ **0401T** six or more lesions (Sunset January 2021)

(Do not report 0401T in conjunction with 0400T)

▨ **0402T** Collagen cross-linking of cornea (including removal of the corneal epithelium and intraoperative pachymetry when performed) (Sunset January 2021)

(Do not report 0402T in conjunction with 65435, 69990, 76514)

A diabetes prevention program consists of intensive behavioral counseling that is provided in person, online, or via electronic technology, or a combination of both modalities.

Intensive behavioral counseling consists of care management, lifestyle coaching, facilitation of a peersupport group, and provision of clinically validated educational lessons based on a standardized curriculum that is focused on nutrition, exercise, stress, and weight management. Lifestyle coaches must complete a nationally recognized training program. The lifestyle coach is available to interact with the participants.

Codes 0403T and 0488T describe diabetes prevention programs that use a standardized diabetes prevention curriculum. For educational services that use a standardized curriculum provided to patients with an established illness/disease, see 98960, 98961, 98962. Use 0403T for diabetes prevention programs that are provided only in person. Use 0488T for programs that are provided online or via electronic technology. Code 0488T includes in-person components, if provided.

0403T Preventive behavior change, intensive program of prevention of diabetes using a standardized diabetes prevention program curriculum, provided to individuals in a group setting, minimum 60 minutes, per day (Sunset January 2021)

(Do not report 0403T in conjunction with 98960, 98961, 98962, 0488T)

● **0488T** Preventive behavior change, online/electronic structured intensive program for prevention of diabetes using a standardized diabetes prevention program curriculum, provided to an individual, per 30 days

(Do not report 0488T in conjunction with 98960, 98961, 98962, 0403T)

| ▨ Separate Procedure | ▨ Unlisted Procedure | ▨ CCI Comp. Code | ▨ Non-specific Procedure | **969** |

0404T Transcervical uterine fibroid(s) ablation with ultrasound guidance, radiofrequency (Sunset January 2021)

0405T Oversight of the care of an extracorporeal liver assist system patient requiring review of status, review of laboratories and other studies, and revision of orders and liver assist care plan (as appropriate), within a calendar month, 30 minutes or more of non-face-to-face time (Sunset January 2021)

0406T Nasal endoscopy, surgical, ethmoid sinus, placement of drug eluting implant; (Sunset January 2021)

0407T   with biopsy, polypectomy or debridement (Sunset January 2021)

(Do not report 0406T, 0407T in conjunction with 31200, 31201, 31205, 31231, 31237, 31240, 31254, 31255, 31288, 31290 when performed on the same side)

(Do not report 0407T in conjunction with 0406T if performed on the same side)

Codes 0408T-0418T describe procedures related to cardiac contractility modulation systems (CCM). These systems consist of a pulse generator plus one atrial and two ventricular pacemaker electrodes (leads). In contrast to a pacemaker or a defibrillator, which modulate the heart's rhythm, the CCM systems' impulses are designed to modulate the strength of contraction of the heart muscle. Unlike pacemakers, these systems stimulate for specific time intervals in order to improve myocardial function.

All catheterization and imaging guidance required to complete a CCM procedure are included in the work of each code. Left heart catheterization with a high fidelity transducer is intrinsic to the CCM procedure. Left heart catheterization codes (93452, 93453, 93458, 93459, 93460, 93461) at the time of CCM placement, replacement, or revision may not be reported separately. Removal of only the CCM pulse generator is reported with 0412T. If only the pulse generator is removed and replaced at the same session without any right atrial and/or right ventricular lead(s) inserted or replaced, report 0414T. For removal and replacement of the pulse generator and leads, individual codes for removal of the generator (0412T) and removal of the leads (0413T for each lead removed) are used in conjunction with the insertion/replacement system code (0408T). When individual transvenous electrodes are inserted or replaced, report using 0410T and 0411T, as appropriate. When the entire system is inserted or replaced, report with 0408T.

Revision of the CCM generator skin pocket is included in 0408T, 0412T, 0414T. Relocation of a skin pocket for a CCM may be necessary for various clinical situations such as infection or erosion. Relocation is reported with 0416T, and follows conventions for pacemaker skin pocket relocation.

Repositioning of a CCM electrode is reported using 0415T.

CCM device evaluation codes 0417T, 0418T may not be reported in conjunction with pulse generator and lead insertion or revision codes.

0408T Insertion or replacement of permanent cardiac contractility modulation system, including contractility evaluation when performed, and programming of sensing and therapeutic parameters; pulse generator with transvenous electrodes

0409T   pulse generator only

0410T   atrial electrode only

0411T   ventricular electrode only

(Report 0410T, 0411T once for each transvenous electrode inserted or replaced)

(If the entire system is inserted or replaced, report 0408T)

0412T Removal of permanent cardiac contractility modulation system; pulse generator only

0413T   transvenous electrode (atrial or ventricular)

(Report 0413T once for each transvenous electrode removed)

(For removal of the pulse generator and all 3 leads, use 0412T plus 0413T once for each electrode removed)

(If transvenous electrodes are removed and replaced, report 0413T once for each electrode removed in conjunction with 0410T, 0411T, as appropriate)

● New Code   ▲ Revised Code   + Add-On Code   ⊘ Modifier -51 Exempt   ★ Telemedicine

0414T Removal and replacement of permanent cardiac contractility modulation system pulse generator only

(For removal and replacement of the pulse generator plus all three electrodes, report 0408T in conjunction with 0412T, 0413T once for each transvenous electrode removed)

0415T Repositioning of previously implanted cardiac contractility modulation transvenous electrode (atrial or ventricular lead)

(Do not report 0408T, 0409T, 0410T, 0411T, 0414T, 0415T in conjunction with 93286, 93287, 93452, 93453, 93458, 93459, 93460, 93461)

(Do not report 0415T in conjunction with 0408T, 0410T, 0411T)

0416T Relocation of skin pocket for implanted cardiac contractility modulation pulse generator

0417T Programming device evaluation (in person) with iterative adjustment of the implantable device to test the function of the device and select optimal permanent programmed values with analysis, including review and report, implantable cardiac contractility modulation system

(Do not report 0417T in conjunction with 0408T, 0409T, 0410T, 0411T, 0412T, 0413T, 0414T, 0415T, 0418T)

0418T Interrogation device evaluation (in person) with analysis, review and report, includes connection, recording and disconnection per patient encounter, implantable cardiac contractility modulation system

(Do not report 0418T in conjunction with 0408T, 0409T, 0410T, 0411T, 0412T, 0413T, 0414T, 0415T, 0417T)

0419T Destruction of neurofibroma, extensive (cutaneous, dermal extending into subcutaneous); face, head and neck, greater than 50 neurofibromas

(For excision of neurofibroma, use 64792)

(Report 0419T once per session regardless of the number of lesions treated)

0420T trunk and extremities, extensive, greater than 100 neurofibromas

(For excision of neurofibroma, use 64792)

(Report 0420T once per session regardless of the number of lesions treated)

0421T Transurethral waterjet ablation of prostate, including control of post-operative bleeding, including ultrasound guidance, complete (vasectomy, meatotomy, cystourethroscopy, urethral calibration and/or dilation, and internal urethrotomy are included when performed)

(Do not report 0421T in conjunction with 52500, 52630, 76872)

0422T Tactile breast imaging by computer-aided tactile sensors, unilateral or bilateral

0423T Secretory type II phospholipase A2 (sPLA2-IIA)

(For lipoprotein-associated phospholipase A2 [Lp-PLA2], use 83698)

Phrenic Nerve Stimulation System

A phrenic nerve stimulation system includes a pulse generator (containing electronics and a battery), one stimulation lead (electrode), and one sensing lead (electrode). Pulse generators are placed in a submuscular or subcutaneous "pocket" in the pectoral region. The stimulation lead is placed transvenously into the right brachiocephalic vein or left pericardiophrenic vein. The sensing lead is placed transvenously into the azygos vein.

If replacing less than a complete system, report 0425T, 0426T, and/or 0427T (for sensing lead, stimulation lead or pulse generator respectively). If all three components are replaced, report only 0424T in conjunction with codes for removal of each of the components (0428T, 0429T, 0430T).

Codes 0424T-0433T include vessel catheterization, all image guidance required for the procedure, and interrogation and programming, when performed. Interrogation device evaluation and programming device evaluation include parameters of rate, pulse amplitude, pulse duration, configuration of waveform, battery status, electrode selectability, output modulation, cycling, impedance, and patient compliance measurements. For patients that require programming during an overnight sleep study, report 0436T once, regardless of how many programming changes are made during the sleep study.

0424T   Insertion or replacement of neurostimulator system for treatment of central sleep apnea; complete system (transvenous placement of right or left stimulation lead, sensing lead, implantable pulse generator)

0425T   sensing lead only

0426T   stimulation lead only

0427T   pulse generator only

(Do not report 0425T, 0426T, 0427T in conjunction with 0424T)

0428T   Removal of neurostimulator system for treatment of central sleep apnea; pulse generator only

0429T   sensing lead only

0430T   stimulation lead only

(Report 0429T, 0430T once for each transvenous sensing or stimulation lead removed)

(For removal of the entire system, report 0428T for pulse generator removal plus 0429T or 0430T for each transvenous lead removal)

0431T   Removal and replacement of neurostimulator system for treatment of central sleep apnea, pulse generator only

(For removal and replacement of the pulse generator plus all three leads, report 0424T in conjunction with 0428T, 0429T, 0430T)

0432T   Repositioning of neurostimulator system for treatment of central sleep apnea; stimulation lead only

0433T   sensing lead only

(Do not report 0432T, 0433T in conjunction with 0424T, 0425T, 0426T, 0427T)

0434T   Interrogation device evaluation implanted neurostimulator pulse generator system for central sleep apnea

0435T   Programming device evaluation of implanted neurostimulator pulse generator system for central sleep apnea; single session

0436T   during sleep study

(Do not report 0434T, 0435T, 0436T in conjunction with 0424T, 0425T, 0426T, 0427T, 0428T, 0429T, 0430T, 0431T, 0432T, 0433T)

(Do not report 0436T in conjunction with 0435T)

(Report 0436T once per sleep study)

+ 0437T   Implantation of non-biologic or synthetic implant (eg, polypropylene) for fascial reinforcement of the abdominal wall (List separately in addition to code for primary procedure)

(For implantation of mesh or other prosthesis for open incisional or ventral hernia repair, use 49568 in conjunction with 49560, 49561, 49565, 49566)

(For insertion of mesh or other prosthesis for closure of a necrotizing soft tissue infection wound, use 49568 in conjunction with 11004, 11005, 11006)

(**0438T**   deleted 2017 [2018 edition]. To report, use 55874)

+ **0439T** Myocardial contrast perfusion echocardiography, at rest or with stress, for assessment of myocardial ischemia or viability (List separately in addition to code for primary procedure)

(Use 0439T in conjunction with 93306, 93307, 93308, 93350, 93351)

0440T Ablation, percutaneous, cryoablation, includes imaging guidance; upper extremity distal/peripheral nerve

0441T lower extremity distal/peripheral nerve

0442T nerve plexus or other truncal nerve (eg, brachial plexus, pudendal nerve)

+ **0443T** Real-time spectral analysis of prostate tissue by fluorescence spectroscopy, including imaging guidance (List separately in addition to code for primary procedure)

(Use 0443T in conjunction with 55700)

(Report 0443T only once per session)

0444T Initial placement of a drug-eluting ocular insert under one or more eyelids, including fitting, training, and insertion, unilateral or bilateral

0445T Subsequent placement of a drug-eluting ocular insert under one or more eyelids, including re-training, and removal of existing insert, unilateral or bilateral

(For insertion and removal of drug-eluting implant into lacrimal canaliculus, use 0356T)

0446T Creation of subcutaneous pocket with insertion of implantable interstitial glucose sensor, including system activation and patient training

(Do not report 0446T in conjunction with 95251, 0447T, 0448T)

0447T Removal of implantable interstitial glucose sensor from subcutaneous pocket via incision

0448T Removal of implantable interstitial glucose sensor with creation of subcutaneous pocket at different anatomic site and insertion of new implantable sensor, including system activation

(Do not report 0448T in conjunction with 0446T, 0447T)

(For placement of non-implantable interstitial glucose sensor without pocket, use 95250)

0449T Insertion of aqueous drainage device, without extraocular reservoir, internal approach, into the subconjunctival space; initial device

+ **0450T** each additional device (List separately in addition to code for primary procedure)

(Use 0450T in conjunction with 0449T)

(For removal of aqueous drainage device without extraocular reservoir, placed into the subconjunctival space via internal approach, use 92499)

Codes 0451T-0463T describe a family of services related to the placement and maintenance of permanent aortic counterpulsation ventricular assistance devices. These devices are used to treat congestive heart failure, and they employ a counterpulsation device that is implanted in the aorta, which inflates during diastole to reduce end diastolic ventricular pressure on a long-term basis without rerouting blood flow. The counterpulsation assistance device implantation is achieved by surgically placing a subclavian arterial graft and creating of a subcutaneous pocket to implant a mechano-electrical interface, without requiring access to the heart. The counterpulsation device's mechano-electrical skin interface receives ECG signals from the subcutaneous electrodes and digitizes and transmits a signal through an external driveline to an external "driver," which is carried by the patient. The "driver" receives the ECG signal and determines the location of the dichrotic notch. The "driver" then activates a bellows, which sends compressed air through the external driveline to the mechanoelectrical skin interface in which the compressed air enters the internal driveline and inflates the balloon. After diastole, the bellows creates suction that deflates the balloon through the same pathway.

These services differ from those performed for the implantation, revision, and removal of existing aortic balloon pumps in several ways in that they: (1) use a permanently implanted balloon that is intended for longterm use; (2) require surgical placement of a vascular graft; (3) use a vascular hemostatic seal; (4) implant a mechano-electrical skin interface that contains a programmable processor; and (5) implant subcutaneous electrodes. In addition, they also differ from procedures to insert, revise, and remove extracorporeal and intracorporeal ventricular assist devices because these procedures require access to the heart and include inflow or outflow grafts into the heart, which divert blood flow from either the left and/or right cardiac chambers into a pump that then pumps blood directly into the corresponding artery (either aorta and/or pulmonary artery).

Codes 0451T-0463T are inclusive of all vessel catheterization, diagnostic angiography, radiological supervision and interpretation, and imaging guidance. Removal of a counterpulsation assistance device at the same session as insertion is not separately reportable.

0451T Insertion or replacement of a permanently implantable aortic counterpulsation ventricular assist system, endovascular approach, and programming of sensing and therapeutic parameters; complete system (counterpulsation device, vascular graft, implantable vascular hemostatic seal, mechano-electrical skin interface and subcutaneous electrodes)

Do not report 0451T in conjunction with 33973, 33979, 33990, 33991, 0452T, 0453T, 0454T, 0455T, 0456T, 0457T, 0458T)

(For insertion of intra-aortic balloon assist device, see 33967, 33970, 33973)

(For insertion or replacement of extracorporeal ventricular assist device, see 33975, 33976, 33981)

(For insertion or replacement of intracorporeal ventricular assist device, see 33979, 33982, 33983)

(For percutaneous insertion of ventricular assist device, see 33990, 33991)

0452T aortic counterpulsation device and vascular hemostatic seal

(Do not report 0452T in conjunction with 33973, 33979, 33990, 33991, 0451T, 0455T, 0456T)

(For insertion or replacement of intracorporeal ventricular assist device, see 33979, 33982, 33983)

0453T mechano-electrical skin interface

(Do not report 0453T in conjunction with 33973, 33979, 33990, 33991, 0451T, 0455T, 0457T)

(For insertion or replacement of intracorporeal ventricular assist device, see 33979, 33982, 33983)

0454T subcutaneous electrode

(Report 0454T once for each subcutaneous electrode inserted or replaced)

(If the entire system is inserted or replaced, use 0451T)

(Do not report 0454T in conjunction with 33973, 33979, 33990, 33991, 0451T, 0455T, 0458T)

(For insertion or replacement of intracorporeal ventricular assist device, see 33979, 33982, 33983)

0455T Removal of permanently implantable aortic counterpulsation ventricular assist system; complete system (aortic counterpulsation device, vascular hemostatic seal, mechano-electrical skin interface and electrodes)

(Do not report 0455T in conjunction with 33974, 33980, 33992, 0451T, 0452T, 0453T, 0454T, 0456T, 0457T, 0458T)

(For removal of intra-aortic balloon assist device, see 33968, 33971, 33974)

(For removal of extracorporeal ventricular assist device, see 33977, 33978)

(For removal of intracorporeal ventricular assist device, use 33980)

(For removal of percutaneous ventricular assist device, use 33992)

0456T aortic counterpulsation device and vascular hemostatic seal

(Do not report 0456T in conjunction with 33974, 33980, 33992, 0451T, 0452T, 0455T)

0457T mechano-electrical skin interface

(Do not report 0457T in conjunction with 33974, 33980, 33992, 0451T, 0453T, 0455T)

0458T   subcutaneous electrode

(Report 0458T once for each subcutaneous electrode removed)

(Do not report 0458T in conjunction with 33974, 33980, 33992, 0451T, 0454T, 0455T)

0459T Relocation of skin pocket with replacement of implanted aortic counterpulsation ventricular assist device, mechano-electrical skin interface and electrodes

(Do not report 0459T in conjunction with 33993)

(For repositioning of percutaneous ventricular assist device, use 33993)

0460T Repositioning of previously implanted aortic counterpulsation ventricular assist device; subcutaneous electrode

(Report 0460T once for each subcutaneous electrode repositioned)

(Do not report 0460T in conjunction with 33993, 0451T, 0454T)

(For repositioning of percutaneous ventricular assist device, use 33993)

0461T   aortic counterpulsation device

(Do not report 0461T in conjunction with 33993)

(For repositioning of percutaneous ventricular assist device, use 33993)

0462T Programming device evaluation (in person) with iterative adjustment of the implantable mechano-electrical skin interface and/or external driver to test the function of the device and select optimal permanent programmed values with analysis, including review and report, implantable aortic counterpulsation ventricular assist system, per day

(Do not report 0462T in conjunction with 0451T-0461T, 0463T)

0463T Interrogation device evaluation (in person) with analysis, review and report, includes connection, recording and disconnection per patient encounter, implantable aortic counterpulsation ventricular assist system, per day

(Do not report 0463T in conjunction with 0451T-0462T)

(Do not report 0451T-0463T with 36000, 36002, 36005, 36010, 36200-36228, 75600-75791, 76000, 76001, 76936, 76937, 77001, 77002, 77011, 77012, 77021, 93451-93533, 93561-93572)

0464T This code is out of order. See page 961.

● **0465T** Suprachoroidal injection of a pharmacologic agent (does not include supply of medication) (Sunset January 2023)

(To report intravitreal injection/implantation, see 67025, 67027, 67028)

●+**0466T** Insertion of chest wall respiratory sensor electrode or electrode array, including connection to pulse generator (List separately in addition to code for primary procedure) (Sunset January 2023)

(Use 0466T in conjunction with 64568)

● **0467T** Revision or replacement of chest wall respiratory sensor electrode or electrode array, including connection to existing pulse generator (Sunset January 2023)

(Do not report 0467T in conjunction with 0466T, 0468T)

(For revision or replacement of cranial nerve [eg, vagus nerve] neurostimulator electrode array, including connection to existing pulse generator, use 64569)

● **0468T** Removal of chest wall respiratory sensor electrode or electrode array (Sunset January 2023)

(Do not report 0468T in conjunction with 0466T, 0467T)

(For removal of cranial nerve [eg, vagus nerve] neurostimulator electrode array and pulse generator, use 64570)

● **0469T**   Retinal polarization scan, ocular screening with on-site automated results, bilateral   (Sunset January 2023)

(Do not report 0469T in conjunction with 92002, 92004, 92012, 92014)

(For ocular photoscreening, see 99174, 99177)

● **0470T**   Optical coherence tomography (OCT) for microstructural and morphological imaging of skin, image acquisition, interpretation, and report; first lesion   (Sunset January 2023)

●+**0471T**   each additional lesion (List separately in addition to code for primary procedure)   (Sunset January 2023)

(Use 0471T in conjunction with 0470T)

(For optical coherence tomography for coronary vessel or graft, see 92978, 92979)

(For reflectance confocal microscopy [RCM] of the skin, see 96931, 96932, 96933, 96934, 96935, 96936)

● **0472T**   Device evaluation, interrogation, and initial programming of intraocular retinal electrode array (eg, retinal prosthesis), in person, with iterative adjustment of the implantable device to test functionality, select optimal permanent programmed values with analysis, including visual training, with review and report by a qualified health care professional   (Sunset January 2023)

● **0473T**   Device evaluation and interrogation of intraocular retinal electrode array (eg, retinal prosthesis), in person, including reprogramming and visual training, when performed, with review and report by a qualified health care professional   (Sunset January 2023)

(For implantation of intraocular electrode array, use 0100T)

(For reprogramming of implantable intraocular retinal electrode array device, use 0473T)

● **0474T**   Insertion of anterior segment aqueous drainage device, with creation of intraocular reservoir, internal approach, into the supraciliary space   (Sunset January 2023)

● **0475T**   Recording of fetal magnetic cardiac signal using at least 3 channels; patient recording and storage, data scanning with signal extraction, technical analysis and result, as well as supervision, review, and interpretation of report by a physician or other qualified health care professional   (Sunset January 2023)

● **0476T**   patient recording, data scanning, with raw electronic signal transfer of data and storage   (Sunset January 2023)

● **0477T**   signal extraction, technical analysis, and result   (Sunset January 2023)

● **0478T**   review, interpretation, report by physician or other qualified health care professional   (Sunset January 2023)

● **0479T**   Fractional ablative laser fenestration of burn and traumatic scars for functional improvement; first 100 cm2 or part thereof, or 1% of body surface area of infants and children   (Sunset January 2023)

●+**0480T**   each additional 100 cm2, or each additional 1% of body surface area of infants and children, or part thereof (List separately in addition to code for primary procedure)   (Sunset January 2023)

(Use 0480T in conjunction with 0479T)

(Report 0479T, 0480T only once per day)

(Do not report 0479T, 0480T in conjunction with 0492T)

(For excision of cicatricial lesion[s] [eg, full thickness excision, through the dermis], see 11400-11446)

● **0481T**   Injection(s), autologous white blood cell concentrate (autologous protein solution), any site, including image guidance, harvesting and preparation when performed   (Sunset January 2023)

● New Code   ▲ Revised Code   + Add-On Code   ⊘ Modifier -51 Exempt   ★ Telemedicine

(Do not report 0481T in conjunction with 20550, 20551, 20600, 20604, 20605, 20606, 20610, 20611, 20926, 36415, 36592, 76942, 77002, 77012, 77021, 86965, 0232T)

(Do not report 38220, 38221, 38222, 38230 for bone marrow aspiration for autologous white blood cell concentrate [autologous protein solution] injection. For bone marrow aspiration for autologous white blood cell concentrate [autologous protein solution] injection, use 0481T)

●+**0482T**　Absolute quantitation of myocardial blood flow, positron emission tomography (PET), rest and stress (List separately in addition to code for primary procedure) (Sunset January 2023)

(Use 0482T in conjunction with 78491, 78492)

(For myocardial imaging metabolic evaluation, use 78459)

(For positron emission tomography [PET] myocardial perfusion study, see 78491, 78492)

Codes 0483T, 0484T include vascular access, catheterization, balloon valvuloplasty, deploying the valve, repositioning the valve as needed, temporary pacemaker insertion for rapid pacing, and access site closure, when performed.

Angiography, radiological supervision and interpretation, intraprocedural roadmapping (eg, contrast injections, fluoroscopy) to guide the TMVI, left ventriculography (eg, to assess mitral regurgitation for guidance of TMVI), and completion angiography are included in codes 0483T, 0484T.

Diagnostic right and left heart catheterization codes (93451, 93452, 93453, 93456, 93457, 93458, 93459, 93460, 93461, 93530, 93531, 93532, 93533) should not be used with 0483T, 0484T to report:

　1. contrast injections, angiography, road-mapping, and/or fluoroscopic guidance for the transcatheter mitral valve implantation (TMVI),

　2. left ventricular angiography to assess or confirm valve positioning and function,

　3. right and left heart catheterization for hemodynamic measurements before, during, and after TMVI for guidance of TMVI.

Diagnostic right and left heart catheterization codes (93451, 93452, 93453, 93456, 93457, 93458, 93459, 93460, 93461, 93530, 93531, 93532, 93533) and diagnostic coronary angiography codes (93454, 93455, 93456, 93457, 93458, 93459, 93460, 93461, 93563, 93564) performed at the time of TMVI may be separately reportable, if:

　1. no prior study is available and a full diagnostic study is performed, or

　2. a prior study is available, but as documented in the medical record:

　　a. there is inadequate visualization of the anatomy and/or pathology, or

　　b. the patient's condition with respect to the clinical indication has changed since the prior study, or

　　c. there is a clinical change during the procedure that requires new evaluation.

For same session/same day diagnostic cardiac catheterization services, report the appropriate diagnostic cardiac catheterization code(s) appended with modifier 59, indicating separate and distinct procedural service from TMVI.

When cardiopulmonary bypass is performed in conjunction with TMVI, 0483T, 0484T may be reported with the appropriate add-on code for percutaneous peripheral bypass (33367), open peripheral bypass (33368), or central bypass (33369).

●　**0483T**　Transcatheter mitral valve implantation/replacement (TMVI) with prosthetic valve; percutaneous approach, including transseptal puncture, when performed (Sunset January 2023)

●　**0484T**　　　transthoracic exposure (eg, thoracotomy, transapical) (Sunset January 2023)

●　**0485T**　Optical coherence tomography (OCT) of middle ear, with interpretation and report; unilateral (Sunset January 2023)

●　**0486T**　　　bilateral (Sunset January 2023)

●　**0487T**　Biomechanical mapping, transvaginal, with report (Sunset January 2023)

　　0488T　This code is out of order. See page 969.

██ Separate Procedure　　██ Unlisted Procedure　　░░ CCI Comp. Code　　██ Non-specific Procedure　　**977**

CPT codes and descriptions only ©2017 American Medical Association. All rights reserved.

● **0489T** Autologous adipose-derived regenerative cell therapy for scleroderma in the hands; adipose tissue harvesting, isolation and preparation of harvested cells including incubation with cell dissociation enzymes, removal of non-viable cells and debris, determination of concentration and dilution of regenerative cells (Sunset January 2023)

(Do not report 0489T in conjunction with 15876, 15877, 15878, 15879, 20600, 20604, 20926)

● **0490T** multiple injections in one or both hands (Sunset January 2023)

(Do not report 0490T in conjunction with 15876, 15877, 15878, 15879, 20600, 20604, 20926)

(Do not report 0490T for a single injection)

(For complete procedure, use 0490T in conjunction with 0489T)

● **0491T** Ablative laser treatment, non-contact, full field and fractional ablation, open wound, per day, total treatment surface area; first 20 sq cm or less (Sunset January 2023)

●+**0492T** each additional 20 sq cm, or part thereof (List separately in addition to code for primary procedure) (Sunset January 2023)

(Use 0492T in conjunction with 0491T)

(Do not report 0492T in conjunction with 0479T, 0480T)

● **0493T** Near-infrared spectroscopy studies of lower extremity wounds (eg, for oxyhemoglobin measurement) (Sunset January 2023)

● **0494T** Surgical preparation and cannulation of marginal (extended) cadaver donor lung(s) to ex vivo organ perfusion system, including decannulation, separation from the perfusion system, and cold preservation of the allograft prior to implantation, when performed (Sunset January 2023)

● **0495T** Initiation and monitoring marginal (extended) cadaver donor lung(s) organ perfusion system by physician or qualified health care professional, including physiological and laboratory assessment (eg, pulmonary artery flow, pulmonary artery pressure, left atrial pressure, pulmonary vascular resistance, mean/peak and plateau airway pressure, dynamic compliance and perfusate gas analysis), including bronchoscopy and X ray when performed; first two hours in sterile field (Sunset January 2023)

●+**0496T** each additional hour (List separately in addition to code for primary procedure) (Sunset January 2023)

(Report 0496T in conjunction with 0495T

● **0497T** External patient-activated, physician- or other qualified health care professional-prescribed, electrocardiographic rhythm derived event recorder without 24 hour attended monitoring; in-office connection (Sunset January 2023)

● **0498T** review and interpretation by a physician or other qualified health care professional per 30 days with at least one patient-generated triggered event (Sunset January 2023)

(Do not report 0497T, 0498T in conjunction with 93040, 93041, 93042, 93228, 93229, 93268, 93271, 93272, 0295T, 0296T, 0297T, 0298T)

● **0499T** Cystourethroscopy, with mechanical dilation and urethral therapeutic drug delivery for urethral stricture or stenosis, including fluoroscopy, when performed (Sunset January 2023)

(Do not report 0499T in conjunction with 52281, 52283)

● **0500T** Infectious agent detection by nucleic acid (DNA or RNA), human papillomavirus (HPV) for five or more separately reported high-risk HPV types (eg, 16, 18, 31, 33, 35, 39, 45, 51, 52, 56, 58, 59, 68) (ie, genotyping) (Sunset January 2023)

(For reporting four or fewer separately reported highrisk HPV types, see 87624, 87625)

(For reporting of separately reported high-risk HPV types 16, 18 and 45, if performed, use 87625)

(Do not report 0500T in conjunction with 87624 or 87625 for the same procedure)

● New Code   ▲ Revised Code   ✚ Add-On Code   ⦸ Modifier -51 Exempt   ★ Telemedicine

● **0501T** Noninvasive estimated coronary fractional flow reserve (FFR) derived from coronary computed tomography angiography data using computation fluid dynamics physiologic simulation software analysis of functional data to assess the severity of coronary artery disease; data preparation and transmission, analysis of fluid dynamics and simulated maximal coronary hyperemia, generation of estimated FFR model, with anatomical data review in comparison with estimated FFR model to reconcile discordant data, interpretation and report (Sunset January 2023)

● **0502T** data preparation and transmission (Sunset January 2023)

● **0503T** analysis of fluid dynamics and simulated maximal coronary hyperemia, and generation of estimated FFR model (Sunset January 2023)

● **0504T** anatomical data review in comparison with estimated FFR model to reconcile discordant data, interpretation and report (Sunset January 2023)

(Report 0501T, 0502T, 0503T, 0504T one time per coronary CT angiogram)

(Do not report 0501T in conjunction with 0502T, 0503T, 0504T)

■ Separate Procedure   ■ Unlisted Procedure   ■ CCI Comp. Code   ■ Non-specific Procedure   **979**

This page intentionally left blank.

● New Code ▲ Revised Code ✚ Add-On Code ⊘ Modifier -51 Exempt ★ Telemedicine

ALPHABETICAL INDEX

The alphabetical index includes listings by procedure, CPT® headings and sub-headings and anatomic site. Procedures and services commonly known by their acronyms, eponyms, homonyms or other designations are also included. The alphabetical index of CPT® PLUS is unique in that both indexes to specific page numbers and indexes to CPT code numbers are included.

HOW TO USE THE ALPHABETICAL INDEX

When using the alphabetical index to locate CPT codes, use the following search sequence:

- Look for the CPT HEADING for the general category of surgical procedure(s) or medical service(s) or TOPIC for instructional and/or explanatory information.

- Look for the CPT Sub-heading for the organ system(s) involved or service(s) performed or the TOPIC sub-heading for the instructional or explanatory issue. Scan the index listings to determine if the specific procedure or service or topic is listed.

- For CPT codes, use the thumb-tab indexes to locate the appropriate CPT code section. If the specific procedure or service was listed in the index, locate the procedure or service in the CPT code section and verify the full description of the CPT code before using. If the specific procedure or service was not listed in the index, first locate the organ system and/or medical service sub-heading and then review the CPT code section until you locate the specific procedure and/or service.

- For instructional and/or explanatory topics, turn to the page number specified in the alphabetical index.

- Alternately, look for SYNONYMS, HOMONYMS, EPONYMS or ACRONYMS.

The alphabetic index is NOT a substitute for the main text of CPT. Even if codes are found in the index, the user must refer to the main text to ensure that the code selection is accurate.

This page intentionally left blank.

A

Abbe-Estlander procedure ~ 40527, 40761
Abdomen
  abdonminal aorta, angiography ~ 75635
  abdominal wall
    debridement, infected~ 11005, 11006
    fascial reinforcement with implant ~ 0437T
    implantation, non-biologic or synthetic implant ~ 0437T
    removal, mesh/prosthesis ~ 11008
    repair hernia ~ 49491-49496, 49501, 49507, 49521, 49590
    tumor, excision ~ 22900-22905
      radical resection ~ 22904, 22905
    unlisted services and procedures ~ 22999
  abscess
    incision and drainage ~ 49020, 49040
  angiography ~ 74174, 74175, 75635
  artery ligation ~ 37617
  biopsy ~ 49000
  bypass graft ~ 35907
  catheter removal ~ 49422
  celiotomy for staging ~ 49220
  CT scan ~ 74150-74178, 75635
  cyst destruction/excision ~ 49203-49205
  drainage fluid ~ 49082-49083
  ectopic pregnancy ~ 59130
  endometrioma destruction/excision ~ 49203-49205
  exploration ~ 49000-49002
    blood vessel ~ 35840
    staging ~ 58960
  incision ~ 49000-49084
    staging ~ 58960
  incision and drainage pancreatitis ~ 48000
  infraumbilical panniculectomy ~ 15830
  injection
    air ~ 49400
    contrast material ~ 49400
  insertion
    catheter ~ 49324, 49418-49419, 49421
    venous shunt ~ 49425
  intraperitoneal
    catheter exit site ~ 49436
    catheter insertion ~ 49418-49421, 49435
    catheter removal ~ 49422
    catheter revision ~ 49325
    shunt
      insertion ~ 49425
      ligation ~ 49428
      removal ~ 49429
      revision ~ 49426
  laparoscopy ~ 49320-49327, 49329
  laparotomy
    reopening ~ 49002
    staging ~ 49220, 58960
  magnetic resonance imaging (MRI) ~ 74181-74183
  needle biopsy, mass ~ 49180
  paracentesis ~ 49082-49083
  peritoneal lavage ~ 49084
  radical resection ~ 51597
  radiation therapy, guidance ~ 49411-49412
  repair
    blood vessel ~ 35221
      with other graft ~ 35281
      with vein graft ~ 35251
    hernia ~ 49491-49525, 49560-49587
    suture ~ 49900
  revision venous shunt ~ 49426
  suture ~ 49900
  tumor destruction/excision ~ 49203-49205
  ultrasound ~ 76700-76705
  unlisted services and procedures ~ 49999
  wound exploration penetrating ~ 20102
  X-ray ~ 74018, 74019, 74021, 74022
Abdominal aorta ~ *see* aorta, abdominal
Abdominal deliveries ~ *see* cesarean delivery
Abdominal hysterectomy ~ *see* hysterectomy, abdominal
Abdominal lymphangiogram ~ 75805, 75807
Abdominal paracentesis ~ *see* abdomen, drainage

Abdominal wall
  debridement, infected ~ 11005-11006
  reconstruction ~ 49905
  removal
    mesh ~ 11008
    prosthesis ~ 11008
  surgery ~ 22999
  tumor excision ~ 22900-22905
Abdominopelvic amputation ~ 27290
Abdominoplasty
  excision ~ 15847
Ablation
  anal polyp or tumor ~ 46615
  bone tumor ~ 20982, 20983
  colon tumor ~ 44401, 45346, 45388
  cryosurgical
    fibroadenoma ~ 19105
    liver tumor ~ 47381
    renal mass ~ 50250
    renal tumor, percutaneous ~ 50593
  CT scan guidance ~ 77013
  endometrial ~ 58353, 58356, 58563
    with ultrasound guidance ~ 58356
  heart
    arrhythmogenic focus ~ 33250-33251, 33261, 93653, 93654, 93655
    atrioventricular ~ 93650, 93653, 93654
  larynx, lesion ~ 31572
  laser, wound ~ 0491T, 0492T
  liver tumor
    cryosurgical ~ 47381, 47383
    laparoscopic ~ 47370, 47371
    radiofrequency ~ 47380-47382
  lung tumor
    radiofrequency ~ 32998
  nerve, percutaneous ~ 0440T-0442T
  parenchymal tissue
    CT scan guidance ~ 77013
    magnetic resonance guidance ~ 77022
    ultrasound guidance ~ 76940
  prostate ~ 55873
  pulmonry tumor ~ 32994, 32998
  radiofrequency
    liver tumor ~ 47382
    lung tumor ~ 32998
    renal tumor ~ 50592
    tongue base ~ 41530
    uterine fibroid ~ 0404T
  rectum, polyp or tumor ~ 45346
  renal
    cyst ~ 50541
    mass ~ 50542
    tumor, percutaneous cryotherapy ~ 50593
  stereotactic, intracranial lesion, MRI-guided intensity focused ultrasound ~ 0398T
  tongue base, radiofrequency ~ 41530
  turbinate mucosa ~ 30801-30802
  uterine fibroids
    laparoscpic ~ 58674
    radiofrequency ~ 0404T
  uterine tumor, ultrasound, focused ~ 0071T-0072T
  vein, endovenous
    chemical adhesive ~ 36482, 36483
    laser ~ 36478, 36479
    mechanochemical ~ 36473, 36474
    radiofrequency ~ 36475, 36476
Abortion
  incomplete ~ 59812
  induced by
    dilation and curettage ~ 59840
    dilation and evacuation ~ 59841
    saline ~ 59850-59851
    vaginal suppositories ~ 59855-59856
  missed
    first trimester ~ 59820
    second trimester ~ 59821
  septic ~ 59830
  spontaneous ~ 59812
  therapeutic, by saline ~ 59850
    with dilation and curettage ~ 59851
    with hysterectomy ~ 59852
  with hysterectomy ~ 59100, 59852, 59857

Abrasion (skin)
chemical peel ~ 15788-15793
dermabrasion ~ 15780-15783
lesion ~ 15786-15787
salabrasion ~ 15810-15811
Abscess
abdomen ~ 49040
  incision and drainage ~ 49040
anal, incision and drainage ~ 46045-46050
ankle ~ 27603, 27607
appendix, incision and drainage ~ 44900
  open ~ 44900
arm, lower ~ 25028
  excision ~ 25145
  incision and drainage ~ 25035
arm, upper, incision and drainage ~ 23930-23935
auditory canal, external ~ 69020
Bartholin's gland, incision and drainage ~ 56420
bladder, incision and drainage ~ 51080
brain
  drainage ~ 61150-61151
  excision ~ 61514, 61522
  incision and drainage ~ 61320-61321
breast, incision and drainage ~ 19020
carpals, incision, deep ~ 25035
clavicle sequestrectomy ~ 23170
drainage, with X-ray ~ 75989
ear, external
  complicated ~ 69005
  simple ~ 69000
elbow, incision and drainage ~ 23930-23935
epididymis, incision and drainage ~ 54700
excision
  olecranon process ~ 24138
  radius ~ 24136
  ulna ~ 24138
eyelid, incision and drainage ~ 67700
facial bones, excision ~ 21026
femur ~ 27303
finger ~ 26010-26011
  incision and drainage ~ 26034
foot, incision ~ 28005
gums, incision and drainage ~ 41800
hand, incision and drainage ~ 26034
hematoma, incision and drainage ~ 27603
hip, incision and drainage ~ 26990-26992
humeral head ~ 23174
humerus
  excision ~ 24134
  incision and drainage ~ 23935
kidney incision and drainage ~ 50020
leg, lower, incision and drainage ~ 27603
liver ~ 47010
  drainage, open ~ 47010
  injection ~ 47015
  repair ~ 47300
localization, nuclear medicine ~ 78806-78807
lung, percutaneous drainage ~ 32200
lymph node, incision and drainage ~ 38300-38305
lymphocele drainage ~ 49062
mandible, excision ~ 21025
mouth, incision and drainage ~ 40800-40801, 41005-41009, 41015-41018
nasal septum, incision and drainage ~ 30020
neck, incision and drainage ~ 21501-21502
ovarian incision and drainage ~ 58820-58822
  abdominal approach ~ 58822
  vaginal approach ~ 58820
palate, incision and drainage ~ 42000
paraurethral gland, incision and drainage ~ 53060
parotid gland drainage ~ 42300-42305
pelvis, incision and drainage ~ 26990-26992, 45000
perineum, incision and drainage ~ 56405
perirenal or renal
  drainage ~ 50020
peritoneum
  incision and drainage ~ 49020
prostate
  incision and drainage ~ 55720-55725
  transurethral drainage ~ 52700
radius, incision, deep ~ 25035

Abscess ~ continued
rectum, incision and drainage ~ 45005-45020, 46040, 46060
retroperitoneal ~ 49060
  drainage ~ 49060
salivary gland, drainage ~ 42300-42320
scapula, sequestrectomy ~ 23172
scrotum, incision & drainage ~ 54700, 55100
shoulder, drainage ~ 23030
Skene's gland, incision and drainage ~ 53060
skin
  incision and drainage ~ 10060-10061
  puncture aspiration ~ 10160
soft tissue, incision ~ 20005
subdiaphragmatic ~ 49040
sublingual gland, drainage ~ 42310-42320
submaxillary gland, drainage ~ 42310-42320
subphrenic ~ 49040
testis, incision and drainage ~ 54700
thoracostomy ~ 32551
thorax, incision and drainage ~ 21501-21502
throat, incision and drainage ~ 42700-42725
tongue, incision and drainage ~ 41000-41006
tonsil, incision and drainage ~ 42700
ulna, incision, deep ~ 25035
urethra, incision and drainage ~ 53040
uvula, incision and drainage ~ 42000
vagina, incision and drainage ~ 57010
vulva, incision and drainage ~ 56405
wrist
  excision ~ 25145
  incision and drainage ~ 25028, 25035
X-ray ~ 76080
Absorptiometry
dual energy ~ 3095F-3096F
  bone
    appendicular ~ 77081
    axial skeleton ~ 77080
    vertebral ~ 77086
dual photon, bone ~ 78351
single photon, bone ~ 78350
Absorption spectrophotometry, atomic ~ 82190
Accessory nerve, spinal ~ 63191
Accessory, toes ~ 28344
ACE (angiotensin converting enzyme) ~ 82164
Acetabuloplasty ~ 27120-27122
Acetabulum
fracture
  closed treatment ~ 27220-27222
  open treatment ~ 27226-27228
  with manipulation ~ 27222
  without manipulation ~ 27220
reconstruction ~ 27120
  with resection, femoral head ~ 27122
tumor, excision ~ 27076
Acetaminophen, urine ~ 80329-80331
Acetic anhydrides ~ 84600
Acetone, blood or urine ~ 82009-82010
Acetone body ~ 82009-82010
Acetylcholinesterase, blood or urine ~ 82013
AcG ~ 85220
Achilles tendon
incision ~ 27605-27606
lengthening ~ 27612
repair ~ 27650-27654
Achillotomy ~ 27605-27606
Acid(s)
adenylic ~ 82030
amino ~ 82127-82139
aminolevulinic ~ see aminolevulinic acid (ALA)
ascorbic ~ 82180
bile ~ 82239
deoxyribonucleic ~ 86225-86226
fatty ~ see fatty acid
folic ~ 82747
glycocholic ~ 82240
lactic ~ 83605
n-acetylneuraminic ~ 84275
n-acetylneuraminic ~ 84275
phenylethylbarbituric ~ 80345
uric ~ see uric acid
Acidity/alkalinity ~ see pH

Acid fast bacilli (AFB), culture ~ 87116
Acid fast stain ~ 88312
Acid perfusion test, esophagus ~ 91030
Acid phosphatase ~ 84060-84066
Acid probes, nucleic ~ *see* nucleic acid probes
Acid reflux test, esophagus ~ 91034-91038
Acne surgery
  incision and drainage
    abscess ~ 10060-10061
    comedones ~ 10040
    cyst ~ 10040
    milia, multiple ~ 10040
    pustules ~ 10040
Acne treatment
  abrasion ~ 15786-15787
  chemical peel ~ 15788-15793
  cryotherapy ~ 17340
  dermabrasion ~ 15780-15783
  exfoliation, chemical ~ 17360
  salabrasion ~ 15810-15811
Acoustic evoked brain stem potential ~ 92585-92586
Acoustic neuroma (*see also* brainstem, skull base surgery) ~ 61510,
  61518, 61520-61521, 61526-61530, 61545, 62164
Acoustic recording, heart sounds, with computer analysis ~ 93799
Acromioclavicular joint, arthrocentesis ~ 20605
  arthrotomy ~ 23044
    with biopsy ~ 23101
  dislocation ~ 23540-23552
  open treatment ~ 23550-23552
  X-ray ~ 73050
Acromion, excision, shoulder ~ 23130
Acromionectomy, partial ~ 23130
Acromioplasty ~ 23415-23420
  partial ~ 23130
ACTH releasing factor ~ 80412
Actigraphy, sleep study ~ 95803
Actinomyces, antibody ~ 86602
Actinomycosis ~ 86000
Actinomycotic infection ~ 86000
Actinotherapy ~ see dermatology ~ 96900
Activated factor X ~ 85260
Activated partial thromboplastin time ~ 85730-85732
Activation, lymphocyte ~ 86353
Activities of daily living ~ *see* physical medicine/therapy/occupational
  therapy
Activity, glomerular procoagulant ~ *see* thromboplastin
Acupuncture
  with electrical stimulation ~ 97813-97814
  without electrical stimulation ~ 97810-97811
Acute poliomyelitis ~ *see* polio
Acylcarnitines ~ 82016-82017
Adamantinoma, pituitary ~ *see* craniopharyngioma
Addam operation ~ 26040-26045
Adductor tenotomy of hip ~ 27000-27003
Adenoidectomy ~ 42820-42821, 42830-42836
Adenoids
  excision ~ 42830-42836
    with tonsils ~ 42820-42821
  unlisted services and procedures ~ 42999
Adenoma
  pancreas, excision ~ 48120
  thyroid gland excision ~ 60200
Adenosine 3'5' monophosphate ~ 82030
Adenosine diphosphate, blood ~ 82030
Adenosine monophosphate (AMP), blood ~ 82030
Adenovirus
  antibody ~ 86603
  antigen detection
    enzyme immunoassay ~ 87301
    immunofluorescense ~ 87260
Adenovirus vaccine ~ *see* vaccines
Adenylic acid ~ *see* adenosine monophosphate (AMP)
ADH (antidiuretic hormone) ~ 84588
Adhesions
  epidural ~ , 62263-62264
  eye
    corneovitreal ~ 65880
    incision
      anterior segment ~ 65860-65870
      posterior segment ~ 65875

Adhesions ~ *continued*
  intermarginal, construction ~ 67880
    transposition of tarsal plate ~ 67882
  intestinal, enterolysis ~ 44005
    laparoscopic ~ 44180
  intracranial, dissection ~ 62161
  intrauterine, lysis ~ 58559
  labial, lysis ~ 56441
  liver, lysis ~ 58660
  lungs, pneumolysis ~ 32124, 32940
  nose, lysis ~ 30560
  pelvic, lysis ~ 58660, 58740
  penile, lysis, post-circumcision ~ 54162
  preputial, lysis ~ 54450
  urethral, lysis ~ 53500
Adipectomy ~ *see* lipectomy
ADL ~ *see* activities of daily living
Administration
  immunization
    each additional vaccine/toxoid ~ 90472, 90474
      with counseling ~ 90461
    one vaccine/toxoid ~ 90471, 90473
      with counseling ~ 90460
  occlusive substance ~ 31634
  pharmacologic agent ~ 93463
ADP ~ *see* adenosine diphosphate
ADP phosphocreatine phosphotransferase ~ *see* CPK
Adrenal cortex hormone ~ *see* corticosteroids
Adrenal gland
  biopsy ~ 60540-60545
  excision ~ 60540
    laparoscopy ~ 60650
    retroperitoneal tumor ~ 60545
  exploration ~ 60540-60545
  nuclear medicine, imaging ~ 78075
Adrenal medulla ~ *see* medulla
Adrenalectomy ~ 60540
  anesthesia ~ 00866
  laparoscopic ~ 50545
Adrenalin ~ 80424, 82382-82384
  blood ~ 82383
  urine ~ 82382, 82384
Adrenaline-noradrenaline
  testing ~ 82382-82384
Adrenocorticotropic hormone (ACTH) ~ 80400-80406, 80412, 80418,
  82024
  blood or urine ~ 82024
  stimulation panel ~ 80400-80406
Adrenogenital syndrome ~ 56805, 57335
Adult T cell leukemia lymphoma virus I ~ *see* HTLV I
Advanced life support ~ 99281-99288
  physician direction ~ 99288
Advancement
  genioglossus ~ 21199
  tendon foot ~ 28238
Advancement flap ~ 14000-14350
Aerosol inhalation ~ *see* pulmonology, therapeutic
  pentamidine ~ 94642
AFB ~ *see* acid fast bacilli
Afferent nerve ~ *see* sensory nerve
AFP ~ *see* alpha-fetoprotein
After hours medical services ~ 99050
Agents, anticoagulant ~ 85300-85305, 85307
Agglutinin
  cold ~ 86156-86157
  febrile ~ 86000
Aggregation, platelet ~ 85576
AHG ~ 85210-85293
AICD (pacing cardioverter-defibrillator) ~ *see* defibrillator, heart;
  pacemaker, heart
Aid, hearing ~ *see* hearing aid
AIDS antibodies ~ 86689, 86701-86703
AIDS virus ~ *see* HIV-1
Akin operation ~ 28296-28299
ALA ~ *see* aminolevulinic acid
Alanine 2 oxoglutarate aminotransferase ~ 84460
Alanine amino (ALT) ~ 84460
Alanine transaminase ~ 84460

Albumin
ischemia modified ~ 82045
serum ~ 82040
urine ~ 82042-82044
Alcohol
breath ~ 82075
ethyl
blood ~ 80321-80322
urine ~ 80321-80322
ethylene glycol ~ 82693
dehydrogenase ~ 84588
isopropyl ~ 84600
methyl ~ 84600
Aldolase, blood ~ 82085
Aldosterone
blood ~ 82088
suppression evaluation ~ 80408
urine ~ 82088
Alimentary canal ~ *see* gastrointestinal tract
Alkaline phosphatase ~ 84075-84080
leukocyte ~ 85540
WBC ~ 85540
Alkaloids ~ *see* specific drug
urine ~ 80323
Allergen bronchial provocation tests ~ 95070-95071
Allergen challenge, endobronchial ~ 95070-95071
Allergen immunotherapy
allergen
IgE ~ 86003, 86005, 86008
IgG ~ 86001
multiallergen screen ~ 86005
allergenic extracts
injection ~ 95115, 95117
injection and provision ~ 95120-95134
insect venom ~ 95130-95134
antigens ~ 95144-95165
insect venom ~ 95145-95149
insect, whole body extract ~ 95170
rapid desensitization ~ 95180
Allergy services/procedures ~ 95004-95199
education and counseling ~ 99201-99215
unlisted services and procedures ~ 95199
Allergy tests
challenge test
bronchial ~ 95070-95071
ingestion ~ 95076, 95079
eye allergy ~ 95060
food allergy ~ 95076, 95079
intradermal
allergen extract ~ 95024-95028
biologicals ~ 95018
drugs ~ 95018
incremental ~ 95027
venoms ~ 95017
nasal mucous membrane test ~ 95065
nose allergy ~ 95065
patch
application tests ~ 95044
photo patch ~ 95052
photosensitivity ~ 95056
skin tests
allergen extract ~ 95004, 95024, 95027
biologicals ~ 95018
drugs ~ 95018
venoms ~ 95017
Allogeneic donor, lymphocyte infusion ~ 38242
Allogeneic transplantation ~ *see* homograft
Allograft
aortic valve ~ 33406, 33413
bone
elbow joint ~ 24370, 24371
shoulder joint ~ 23473-23474
spine surgery
morselized ~ 20930
structural ~ 20931
cartilage, knee ~ 27415
cornea
amniotic membrane ~65780
endothelial ~ 65756
lamellar ~ 65710
penetrating ~ 65730, 65750, 65755

Allograft ~ *continued*
for Aphakia ~ 65750
lung transplant ~ 32850
nerve ~ 64910, 64912, 64913
skin ~ 15350-15351
skin substitute graft ~ 15271-15278
spine surgery
morselized ~ 20930
structural ~ 20931
Allograft preparation
cornea ~ 65757
heart ~ 33933, 33944
intestines ~ 44715-44721
kidney ~ 50323-50329
liver ~ 47143-47147
lung ~ 32855-32856, 33933
pancrease ~ 48551-48552
renal ~ 50323-50329
Allotransplantation
intestines ~ 44135-44137
renal ~ 50360-50365
removal ~ 50370
Almen test ~ 82270
Alpha-1 antitrypsin ~ 82103-82104
Alpha-2 antiplasmin ~ 85410
Alpha-fetoprotein
amniotic fluid ~ 82106
serum ~ 82105, 82107
Alphatocopherol ~ 84446
ALT ~ 84460
Altemeier procedure ~ (*see* anus) 45130-45135
Aluminum, blood ~ 82108
Alveolafracture
closed treatment ~ 21421
open treatment ~ 21422-21423
Alveolar cleft
ungrafted bilateral ~ 21147
ungrafted unilateral ~ 21146
Alveolar nerve
avulsion ~ 64738
incision ~ 64738
transection ~ 64738
Alveolar ridge fracture
closed treatment ~ 21440
open treatment ~ 21445
Alveolectomy ~ 41830
Alveoloplasty ~ 41874
Alveolus, excision ~ 41830
Amide, procaine ~ *see* procainamide
Amikacin, assay ~ 80150
Amine, vaginal fluid ~ 82120
Amino acids ~ 82127-82139
Aminolevulinic acid (ALA), blood or urine ~ 82135
Aminotransferase ~ *see* transaminase
Aminotransferase, alanine ~ 84460
Aminotransferase, aspartate ~ 84450
Amitriptyline, assay ~ 80335, 80336, 80337
Ammonia
blood ~ 82140
urine ~ 82140
Amniocenteses ~ 59000
with amniotic fluid reduction ~ 59001
induced abortion ~ 59850
with dilation and curettage ~ 59851
with dilation and evacuation ~ 59851
with hysterectomy ~ 59852
Amnioinfusion, transabdominal ~ 59070
Amnion ~ 59001
amniocentesis ~ 59000
with amniotic fluid reduction ~ 59001
amnioinfusion, transabdominal ~ 59070
Amniotic fluid
alpha-fetoprotein ~ 82106
scan ~ 82143
testing ~ 83661, 83663-83664
Amniotic membrane ~ 59001
ocular wound healing ~ 65778-65779
Amobarbital ~ 80345
AMP ~ 82030
AMP, cyclic ~ 82030
Amphetamine, blood or urine ~ 80324-80326

Amputation ~ *see* radical resection; replantation
  ankle ~ 27888
  arm, lower ~ 25900-25905, 25915
    revision ~ 25907-25909
  arm, upper ~ 24900-24920
    and shoulder ~ 23900-23921
    revision ~ 24925-24930
    with implant ~ 24931-24935
  cervix, total ~ 57530
  ear
    partial ~ 69110
    total ~ 69120
  finger ~ 26910-26952
  foot ~ 28800-28805
  hand at metacarpal ~ 25927
    at wrist ~ 25920
      revision ~ 25922
    revision ~ 25924, 25929-25931
  interpelviabdominal ~ 27290
  interthoracoscapular ~ 23900
  leg, lower ~ 27598, 27880-27882
    revision ~ 27884-27886
  leg, upper ~ 27590-27592
    at hip ~ 27290-27295
    revision ~ 27594-27596
  metacarpal ~ 26910
  metatarsal ~ 28810
  nose ~ *see* resection, nose
  penis
    partial ~ 54120
    radical ~ 54130-54135
    total ~ 54125
  thumb ~ 26910-26952
  toe ~ 28810-28825
  upper extremity ~ 24900-24940
    cineplasty ~ 24940
    revision ~ 24925, 24930, 24935
    with implant ~ 24931-24935
Amylase
  blood ~ 82150
  urine ~ 82150
ANA ~ 86038-86039
Anabolic steroid ~ *see* androstenedione
Anal abscess ~ *see* abscess, anal
Anal bleeding ~ *see* anus, hemorrhage
Anal fistula ~ *see* fistula, anal
Anal fistulectomy ~ 46288, 46706
Anal fistulotomy ~ 46270, 46280
Anal sphincter
  dilation ~ 45905
  incision ~ 46080
Anal ulceration ~ *see* anus, fissure
Analgesia ~ *see* anesthesia; sedation 99141-99142
Analgesic cutaneous electrostimulation ~ 64550
Analysis
  computer data ~ 99090
    cardiovascular monitoring ~ 93290, 93297, 93299
    implantable defibrillator ~ 93260, 93261, 93282-93284, 93287, 93289, 93295, 93296, 93640, 93641
    leadless pacemaker system ~ 0388T-0391T
    loop recorder ~ 93285, 93291, 93298-93299
    pacemaker ~ 93279-93281, 93288, 93293-93294
  electroencephalogram, digital ~ 95957
  electronic
    drug infusion pump ~ 62367-62368
    pacing cardioverter-defibrillator
      data analysis ~ 93289, 93295-93296
      evaluation of programming ~ 93282-93284, 93287, 93641-93642
      initial evaluation ~ 93640, 93641
    pulse generator ~ 95970-95971, 95980-95982
  multianalyte assays with algorithmic analysis (MAAA)
    endocrinology analytes ~ 81506
    fetal aneuploidy DNA sequence ~ 81507
    fetal congenital abnormal ~ 81508-81512
    gene expression for oncology ~ 81504
    ovarian oncology proteins ~ 81500, 81503
    unlisted assay ~ 81599
  physiologic data, remote ~ 99091
    proprietary laboratory ~ 0001U-0017U

Analysis ~ *continued*
  protein, tissue western blot ~ 88372
  semen ~ 89320-89322
    sperm isolation ~ 89260-89261
  spectrum ~ *see* spectrophotometry
  waveform, central arterial pressure ~ 93050
Anaspadias ~ *see* epispadias
Anastomosis
  aorta-pulmonary artery ~ 33606
  arteriovenous fistula
    direct ~ 36821
    with bypass graft ~ 35686
    with graft ~ 36825-36830, 36832
  artery
    to aorta ~ 33606
    to artery, cranial ~ 61711
  bile duct
    to bile duct ~ 47800
    to intestines ~ 47760, 47780
  bile duct to gastrointestinal ~ 47785
  bladder, to intestine ~ 51960
  broncho-bronchial ~ 32486
  caval to mesenteric ~ 37160
  colorectal ~ 44620
  epididymis
    to vas deferens
      bilateral ~ 54901
      unilateral ~ 54900
  excision trachea ~ 31780-31781
  fallopian tube ~ 58750
  gallbladder to intestines ~ 47720-47740
  hepatic duct ~ *see* hepatic duct, anastomosis
Anastomosis ~ *continued*
  hepatic duct to intestines ~ 47765, 47802
  ileo-anal ~ 45113
  intestines
    colo-anal ~ 45119
    cystectomy ~ 51590
    enterocystoplasty ~ 51960
    resection, laparoscopic ~ 44202-44205
  intestine to intestine ~ 44130
  intrahepatic portosystemic ~ 37182-37183
  jejunum ~ 43825
  lacrimal sac to conjunctival sac ~ see conjunctivorhinostomy
  microvascular, free transfer, jejunum ~ 43496
  nerve
    facial to hypoglossal ~ 64868
  oviduct ~ 58750
  pancreas ~ see pancreas, anastomosis
  pancreas to intestines ~ 48520-48540, 48548
  portocaval ~ 37140
  pulmonary ~ 33606
  renoportal ~ 37145
  splenorenal ~ 37180-37181
  stomach ~ 43825
    to duodenum ~ 43810, 43855
      revision ~ 43850
    to jejunum ~ 43820, 43860-43865
  tubotubal ~ 58750
  ureter
    to bladder ~ 50780-50785
    to colon ~ 50810-50815
      removal ~ 50830
    to intestine ~ 50800, 50820-50825
      removal ~ 50830
    to kidney ~ 50727-50750
    to ureter ~ 50727, 50760-50770
  vein, saphenopopliteal ~ 34530
  vein to vein ~ 37140-37160, 37182-37183
Anatomic pathology services ~ 88000-88099
Anderson tibial lengthening ~ *see* ankle 27715
Androstanediol glucuronide ~ 82154
Androstanolone ~ 80327, 80328
Androstenedione, blood or urine ~ 82157
Androstenolone ~ 82626
Androsterone, blood or urine ~ 82160

Anesthesia ~ 00100-01999
  Abbe-Estlander procedure ~ 00102
  abdomen
    abdominal wall ~ 00700, 00730, 00800-00802, 00820, 00836
      Halsted repair ~ 00750-00756
    blood vessels ~ 00770, 00880-00882
    endoscopy ~ 00731, 00732, 00811-00813
    extraperitoneal ~ 00860-00870
    hernia repair ~ 00830-00836
      Halsted repair ~ 00750-00756
    intraperitoneal ~ 00790-00797, 00840-00851
  abdominoperineal resection ~ 00844
  abortion, induced ~ 01964
  Achilles tendon repair ~ 01472
  acromioclavicular joint ~ 01620
  adrenalectomy ~ 00866
  amniocentesis ~ 00842
  aneurysm
    axillary-brachial ~ 01652
    knee ~ 01444
    popliteal artery ~ 01444
  angiography ~ 01920
  ankle ~ 00400, 01462-01522
  anorectal procedure ~ 00902
  anus ~ 00902
  arm
    lower ~ 00400, 01810-01820, 01830-01860
    upper ~ 00400, 01710-01782
  arrhythmias ~ 00410
  arteriography ~ 01916
  arteriovenous fistula ~ 01432, 01784
  arthroplasty
    hip ~ 01214-01215
    knee ~ 01402
  arthroscopic procedures
    ankle ~ 01464
    elbow ~ 01732-01740
    foot ~ 01464
    hip ~ 01202
    knee ~ 01382, 01400
    shoulder ~ 01622-01630
    wrist ~ 01829-01830
  auditory canal, external, removal foreign body ~ 69205
  axilla ~ 00400, 01610, 01650, 01652, 01654, 01656, 01670
  back skin ~ 00300
  Batch-Spittler-McFaddin operation ~ 01404
  biopsy ~ 00100
    liver ~ 00702
  bladder ~ 00870, 00912
  brain ~ 00210-00218, 00220-00222
  breast ~ 00402-00406
  bronchi ~ 00542
    intrathoracic repair of trauma ~ 00548
    reconstruction ~ 00539
  bronchoscopy ~ 00520
  burns
    debridement and/or excision ~ 01951-01953
    dressings and/or debridement ~ 16010-16015
  burr hole ~ 00214
  bypass graft
    leg, lower ~ 01500
    leg, upper ~ 01270
    shoulder, axillary ~ 01654-01656
  cardiac catheterization ~ 01920
  cast, knee ~ 01420
  cast application
    forearm, wrist and hand ~ 01860
    leg ~ 01490
    pelvis ~ 01130
    shoulder ~ 01680
  central venous circulation ~ 00532
  cervical cerclage ~ 00948
  cervix ~ 00948
  cesarean delivery ~ 01961, 01963

Anesthesia ~ *continued*
  chest ~ 00400-00406, 00410, 00470-00474, 00522, 00530-00539, 00542, 00546-00550
  chest skin ~ 00400
  childbirth
    cesarean delivery ~ 01961, 01963, 01968-01969
    external cephalic version ~ 01958
    vaginal delivery ~ 01960, 01967
  clavicle ~ 00450-00454
  cleft lip repair ~ 00102
  cleft palate repair ~ 00172
  colonoscopy, screening ~ 00812
  colpectomy ~ 00942
  colporrhaphy ~ 00942
  colpotomy ~ 00942
  corneal transplant ~ 00144
  cranioplasty ~ 00215
  culdoscopy ~ 00950
  cystectomy ~ 00864
  cystolithotomy ~ 00870
  cystourethroscopy
    local ~ 52265
    spinal ~ 52260
  decortication ~ 00542
  defibrillator ~ 00534, 00560
  diaphragm ~ 00540-00541
  disarticulation
    hip ~ 01212
    knee ~ 01404
    shoulder ~ 01634
  diskography ~ 01935, 01936
  dressing change ~ 15852
  drug administration, epidural or subarachnoid ~ 01996
  ear ~ 00120-00126
  elbow ~ 00400, 01710-01782
  electrocoagulation, intracranial nerve ~ 00222
  electroconvulsive therapy ~ 00104
  embolectomy
    arm, upper ~ 01772
    femoral ~ 01274
    femoral artery ~ 01274
    forearm, wrist and hand ~ 01842
    leg, lower ~ 01502
  endoscopy
    arm, lower ~ 01830
    gastrointestinal ~ 00731, 00732, 00813
    intestines ~ 00811-00812
    uterus ~ 00952
    vagina ~ 00950
  esophagus ~ 00320, 00500
  external cephalic version ~ 01958
  external fixation system
    adjustment/revision ~ 20693
    removal ~ 20694
  eye ~ 00140-00148
    cornea ~ 00144
    iridectomy ~ 00147
    iris ~ 00147
  eyelid ~ 00103
  facial bones ~ 00190-00192
  fallopian tube, ligation ~ 00851
  femoral artery, ligation ~ 01272
  femur ~ 01220-01234, 01340-01360
  fibula ~ 01390-01392
  foot ~ 00400, 01462-01522
  forearm ~ 00400, 01810-01820, 01830-01860
  Fowler-Stephens orchiopexy ~ 00930
  gastrocnemius recession ~ 01474
  gastrointestinal endoscopy ~ 00731, 00732, 00813
  genitalia
    female ~ 00940-00952, 01958-01969
    male ~ 00920-00938
  great vessels of chest ~ 00560-00563
  hand ~ 00400, 01810-01820, 01830-01860
  Harrington rod technique ~ 00670
  head ~ 00222, 00300
    muscles ~ 00300
    nerves ~ 00300

Anesthesia ~ *continued*
  heart ~ 00560-00567, 00580
    coronary artery bypass grafting ~ 00566-00567
    electrophysiology/ablation ~ 00537
    transplant ~ 00580
  hepatectomy, partial ~ 00792
  hernia repair, abdomen
    lower ~ 00830-00836
    upper ~ 00750-00752, 00756
  hip ~ 01200-01215
  humerus ~ 01620, 01730, 01742-01744, 01758
  hysterectomy ~ 01962
    cesarean ~ 01963, 01969
    radical ~ 00846
    vaginal ~ 00944
  hysterosalpingography ~ 00952
  hysteroscopy ~ 00952
  induced abortion ~ 01964
  inferior vena cava ligation ~ 00882
  injections, nerve ~ 01991-01992
  integumentary system
    anterior trunk ~ 00400
    arm, upper ~ 00400
    axilla ~ 00400
    elbow ~ 00400
    extremity ~ 00400
    forearm ~ 00400
    hand ~ 00400
    head ~ 00300
    knee ~ 00400
    leg, lower ~ 00400
    leg, upper ~ 00400
    neck ~ 00300
    perineum ~ 00400
    popliteal area ~ 00400
    posterior pelvis ~ 00300
    posterior trunk ~ 00300
    shoulder ~ 00400
    wrist ~ 00400
  intestines, endoscopy ~ 00811-00813
  intracranial procedures ~ 00210-00218, 00220-00222
  intraoral procedures ~ 00170-00176
  intrathoracic procedures
    bronchi ~ 00539, 00548
    trachea ~ 00539, 00548
  intrathoracic system ~ 00500, 00520-00529, 00530-00539, 00540-00548, 00550, 00560-00567, 00580
  iridectomy ~ 00147
  Keen operation ~ 00604
  kidney ~ 00862, 00868, 00872-00873
  knee ~ 00400, 01320-01444
  knee skin ~ 00400
  laminectomy ~ 00604
  laparoscopy ~ 00790-00792, 00840
  larynx ~ 00320, 00326
  leg
    lower ~ 00400, 01462-01522
    upper ~ 01200-01274
  lens ~ 00142
  life support for organ donor ~ 01990
  ligation, fallopian tube ~ 00851
  lithotripsy ~ 00872-00873
  liver ~ 00702, 00796
    transplant ~ 00796
  liver hemorrhage ~ 00792
  lumbar puncture ~ 00635
  lungs ~ 00522, 00539, 00540-00548
    transplant ~ 00580
  lymphadenectomy ~ 00934-00936
  lymphatic system ~ 00320
  mammoplasty ~ 00402
  marcellation operation ~ 00944
  mediastinoscopy ~ 00528-00529
  mediastinum ~ 00528-00529, 00540-00541
  mouth ~ 00170-00172
  myelography ~ 01935, 01936

Anesthesia ~ *continued*
  myringotomy ~ 69421
  neck ~ 00300, 00320-00322, 00350-00352
  nephrectomy ~ 00862
  neuraxial
    cesarean delivery ~ 01968-01969
    labor ~ 01967-01969
    vaginal delivery ~ 01967
  nose ~ 00160-00164
    removal, foreign body ~ 30310
  omphalocele ~ 00754
  ophthalmoscopy ~ 00148
  orchiectomy ~ 00926-00928
  orchiopexy ~ 00930
    Torek procedure ~ 00930
  organ harvesting, brain dead patient ~ 01990
  osteoplasty, tibia/fibula ~ 01484
  osteotomy
    humerus ~ 01742
    tibia/fibula ~ 01484
  other procedures ~ 01990, 01996-01999
  otoscopy ~ 00124
  pacemaker insertion ~ 00530
  pacing cardioverter/defibrillator ~ 00534
  pancreas ~ 00794
  pancreatectomy ~ 00794
  panniculectomy ~ 00802
  patella ~ 01390-01392
  pectus excavatum ~ 00474
  pelvic exenteration ~ 00848
  pelvis ~ 00400, 00865, 01112
    amputation ~ 01140
    bone ~ 01120
    bone marrow ~ 01112
    examination ~ 57400
    extraperitoneal ~ 00864
    intraperitoneal ~ 00844-00848
    repair ~ 01173
    skin ~ 00300, 00400
  penis ~ 00932-00938
  pericardial sac ~ 00560-00563
  perineum ~ 00904-00908
  pharynx ~ 00174-00176
  phleborrhaphy
    arm, upper ~ 01782
    forearm, wrist, and hand ~ 01852
  pleura ~ 00540-00541
    needle biopsy ~ 00522
  pneumocentesis ~ 00524
  popliteal area ~ 00400, 01320, 01430-01444
  prognathism ~ 00192
  prostate ~ 00865, 00908, 00914
  prostatectomy
    perineal ~ 00908
    radical ~ 00865
    Walsh modified radical ~ 00865
  radiologic procedures ~ 01916-01936
    arterial, therapeutic ~ 01924-01926
    venous/lymphatic, therapeutic ~ 01930-01933
  renal procedures ~ 00862
  repair of skull ~ 00215
  replacement
    ankle ~ 01486
    elbow ~ 01760
    hip ~ 01212-01215
    knee ~ 01402
    shoulder ~ 01638
    wrist ~ 01832
  restriction, gastric
    for obesity ~ 00797
  retropharyngeal tumor excision ~ 00174
  rib resection ~ 00470-00474
  sacroiliac joint ~ 01160-01170, 27096
  salivary glands ~ 00100
  Scheie procedure ~ 00147
  sedation, moderate ~ 99151-99153, 99155-99157
    with independent observation ~ 99151-99153

Anesthesia ~ *continued*
  seminal vesicles ~ 00922
  shoulder ~ 00400, 00450-00454, 01610, 01620, 01622, 01630, 01634, 01636, 01638
    dislocation, closed treatment ~ 23655
  shunt, spinal fluid ~ 00220
  sinuses, accessory ~ 00160-00164
  skull ~ 00190
  skull fracture, elevation ~ 00215
  special circumstances
    emergency ~ 99140
    extreme age ~ 99100
    hypotension ~ 99135
    hypothermia ~ 99116
  spinal instrumentation ~ 00670
  spinal manipulation ~ 00640
  spine and spinal cord ~ 00600-00604, 00620, 00670
    cervical ~ 00600-00604, 00640, 00670
    injection ~ 62320-62327
    lumbar ~ 00630-00635, 00640, 00670
    percutaneous image guided ~ 01935, 01936
    thoracic ~ 00620-00626, 00640, 00670
    vascular ~ 00670
  sternoclavicular joint ~ 01620
  sternum ~ 00550
  stomach, restriction, for obesity ~ 00797
  Strayer procedure ~ 01474
  subdural taps ~ 00212
  suture removal ~ 15850-15851
  sympathectomy
    lumbar ~ 00632
  symphysis pubis ~ 01160-01170
  tenodesis ~ 01716
  tenoplasty ~ 01714
  tenotomy ~ 01712
  testis ~ 00924-00930
  thoracoplasty ~ 00472
  thoracoscopy ~ 00528-00529, 00540-00541
  thoracotomy ~ 00540-00541
  thorax ~ 00400-00406, 00410, 00450-00454, 00470-00474
  thromboendarterectomy ~ 01442
  thyroid ~ 00320-00322
  tibia ~ 01390-01392, 01484
  trachea ~ 00320, 00326, 00542
    reconstruction ~ 00539
  transplantation
    cornea ~ 00144
    heart ~ 00580
    kidney ~ 00868
    liver ~ 00796, 01990
    lungs ~ 00580
    organ harvesting ~ 01990
  transurethral procedures ~ 00910-00918
  tubal ligation ~ 00851
  tuffier vaginal hysterectomy ~ 00944
  TURP ~ 00914
  tympanostomy ~ 00120
  tympanotomy ~ 00126
  unlisted services and procedures ~ 01999
  urethra ~ 00910, 00918-00920, 00942
  urethrocystoscopy ~ 00910
  urinary bladder ~ 00864, 00870, 00912
  urinary tract ~ 00860
  uterus ~ 00952
  vagina ~ 00940-00942, 00950
    dilation ~ 57400
    removal, foreign body ~ 57415
  vaginal delivery ~ 01960
  vas deferens, excision ~ 00921
  vascular access ~ 00532
  vascular shunt ~ 01844
  vascular surgery
    abdomen, lower ~ 00880-00882
    abdomen, upper ~ 00770
    arm, lower ~ 01840-01852
    arm, upper ~ 01770-01782
    brain ~ 00216
    elbow ~ 01770-01782
    hand ~ 01840-01852

Anesthesia ~ *continued*
  knee ~ 01430-01444
  leg, lower ~ 01500-01522
  leg, upper ~ 01260-01274
  neck ~ 00350-00352
  shoulder ~ 01650-01670
  wrist ~ 01840-01852
  vasectomy ~ 00921
  venography ~ 01916
  ventriculography ~ 00214, 01920
  vertebral process, fracture/dislocation, closed treatment ~ 22315
  vertebroplasty ~ 01935, 01936
  vitrectomy ~ 00145
  vitreoretinal surgery ~ 00145
  vitreous body ~ 00145
  vulva ~ 00906
  vulvectomy ~ 00906
  Wertheim operation ~ 00846
  wrist ~ 00400, 01810-01860

Aneurysm repair
  abdominal aorta ~ 34830-34832, 34845-34848, 35081-35103
  axillary artery ~ 35011-35013
  basilar artery ~ 61698, 61702
  brachial artery ~ 35011-35013
  carotid artery ~ 35001-35002, 61613, 61697, 61700, 61703
  celiac artery ~ 35121-35122
  femoral artery ~ 35141-35142
  hepatic artery ~ 35121-35122
  iliac artery ~ 34703-34708, 35131, 35132
  infrarenal artery ~ 34701-34706, 34709-34711
  innominate artery ~ 35021, 35022
  intracranial artery ~ 61705-61708
  mesenteric artery ~ 35121-35122
  popliteal artery ~ 35151-35152
  radial artery ~ 35045
  renal artery ~ 35121-35122
  splenic artery ~ 35111-35112
  subclavian artery ~ 35001-35002, 35021-35022
  thoracoabdominal aorta ~ 33877
  ulnar artery ~ 35045
  vascular malformation or carotid-cavernous fistula ~ 61710
  vertebral artery ~ 61698, 61702

Angel dust ~ 83992
Angina assessment ~ *see* performance measure
Angiocardiographies ~ *see* heart, angiography
Angiography
  abdomen ~ 74174-74175, 74185, 75635, 75726
  adrenal ~ 75731-75733
  arm artery ~ 73206, 75710, 75716
  brain ~ 70496
  bypass graft ~ 93455, 93457, 93459-93461
  carotid artery ~ 36221-36228
  cervicocerebral arch ~ 36221-36226
  chest ~ 71275, 71555
  congenital heart ~ 93563-93564
  common carotid, selective catheterization ~ 36222, 36223
  endovascular repair ~ 75956, 75957
  extracranial carotid
    non-selective ~ 36221
    selective ~ 36222-36224
  extremity, lower ~ 73725
  extremity, upper ~ 73225
  fluorescein ~ 92235, 92242
  head ~ 70496, 70544-70546
  heart
    abdominal aorta ~ 75635
    aorta, injection ~ 93567
    atrial ~ 93565, 93566
    congenital heart ~ 93563, 93564
    coronary artery ~ 93454-93461, 93563
      flow velocity measurement ~ 93571, 93572
    left heart injection ~ 93565
    right heart injection ~ 93566
    injection ~ 93454-93461, 93563, 93565, 93566
  indocyanine-green ~ 92240, 92242
  innominate artery ~ 36222, 36223, 36225
  intracranial ~ 36221, 36223, 36224
    with endovascular infusion ~ 61640, 61650, 61651
    with thrombectomy ~ 61645

Angiography~*continued*
left heart, injection ~ 93565
leg artery ~ 73706, 75635, 75710-75716
lung, injection ~ 93568
mammary artery ~ 75756
neck ~ 70498, 70547-70549
   artery ~ 36221-36226
nuclear medicine ~ 78445
other artery ~ 75774
pelvic artery ~ 72198, 75736
pelvis ~ 72191, 74174
pulmonary ~ 75741-75746, 93568
renal artery ~ 36251-36254
right heart, injection ~ 93566
spinal artery ~ 75705
spinal canal ~ 72159
thorax ~ 71275
transcatheter therapy
   embolization ~ 75894, 75898
   infusion ~ 75894, 75898
ventricular ~ 93565-93566
vertebral ~ 36211, 36225-36226, 36228
Angioma ~ see lesion, skin
Angioplasties, coronary balloon ~ see percutaneous transluminal angioplasty
Angioplasty
aorta
   intraoperative ~ 37246, 37247
   percutaneous ~ 37246, 37247
axillary artery, intraoperative ~ 37246, 37247
brachiocephalic artery
   intraoperative ~ 37246, 37247
   percutaneous ~ 37246, 37247
coronary artery
   percutaneous transluminal ~ 92920, 92921
   with atherectomy ~ 92937, 92938, 92941, 92943, 92944
   with stent placement ~ 92928, 92929, 92937, 92938, 92941, 92943, 92944
femoral artery, intraoperative ~ 37224
iliac artery, intraoperative ~ 37220, 37222
intracranial, percutaneous ~ 61630
patch
   blood vessel ~ 35201-35286
   vein ~ 35879
percutaneous transluminal angioplasty ~ see percutaneous transluminal angioplasty
perineal artery ~ 37228
popliteal artery, intraoperative ~ 37224
pulmonary artery, percutaneous transluminal ~ 92997, 92998
renal artery
   open ~ 37246-37249
   percutaneous ~ 37246-37249
subclavian artery, intraoperative ~ 37246, 37247
tibioperoneal artery, intraoperative ~ 37228
   balloon ~ 37246-37249
   dialysis circuit ~ 36902, 36907
   venous ~ 37248, 37249
venous
   open ~ 37248, 37249
   percutaneous ~ 37248, 37249
visceral artery
   open ~ 37246, 37247
   percutaneous ~ 37246, 37247
with endovascular repair ~ 34841-34848
with intravascular stent placement ~ 37215-37218, 37236-37239
Angioscopy, non-coronary vessels ~ 35400
Angiotensin converting enzyme (ACE) ~ 82164
Angiotensin forming enzyme ~ 80408, 80416, 84244
Angiotensin I ~ 84244
riboflavin ~ 84252
Angiotensin II, blood or urine ~ 82163
Angle deformity, reconstruction toe ~ 28313
Anhydride, carbonic ~ 82374
Anhydrides, acetic ~ 84600
Animal inoculation ~ 87003, 87250

Ankle
(see also fibula; leg, lower; tibia; tibiofibular joint)
abscess, incision and drainage ~ 27603
amputation ~ 27888
arthrocentesis ~ 20605
arthrodesis ~ 27870
arthrography ~ 73615
arthroplasty ~ 27700-27703
arthroscopy, surgical ~ 29891-29899
arthrotomy ~ 27610-27612, 27620-27626
biopsy ~ 27613-27614, 27620
bursa, incision and drainage ~ 27604
disarticulation ~ 27889
dislocation
   closed treatment ~ 27840-27842
   open treatment ~ 27846-27848
exploration ~ 27610, 27620
fracture
   bimalleolar ~ 27808-27814
   lateral ~ 27786-27814, 27792
   medial ~ 27760-27766, 27808-27814
   posterior ~ 27767-27769, 27808-27814
   trimalleolar ~ 27816-27823
fusion ~ 27870
hematoma, incision and drainage ~ 27603
incision ~ 27607
injection, radiologic ~ 27648
lesion excision ~ 27630
magnetic resonance imaging (MRI) ~ 73721-73723
manipulation ~ 27860
removal
   foreign body ~ 27610, 27620
   implant ~ 27704
   loose body ~ 27620
repair
   Achilles tendon ~ 27650-27654
   ligament ~ 27695-27698
   tendon ~ 27612, 27680-27687
strapping ~ 29540
synovium, excision ~ 27625-27626
tenotomy ~ 27605-27606
tumor, excision ~ 27615-27619, 27632, 27634
unlisted services and procedures ~ 27899
X-ray ~ 73600-73610
   with contrast ~ 73615
Ankylosis (surgical) ~ see arthrodesis
Annuloplasty
percutaneous, intradiscal ~ 22526-22527
Anogenital region ~ see perineum
Anoplasty, stricture ~ 46700-46705
Anorectal myectomy ~ 45108
Anorectal procedure, biofeedback ~ 90911
Anorectovaginoplasty ~ 46744-46746
Anoscopy
ablation, polyp/tumor ~ 46615
biopsy ~ 46606
collection of specimen ~ 46600, 46601
dilation ~ 46604
exploration ~ 46600
hemorrhage ~ 46614
high resolution anoscopy (HRA)
   diagnostic ~ 46601
   with biopsies ~ 46607
injection, bulking agent ~ 0377T
removal
   foreign body ~ 46608
   polyp/tumor ~ 46610-46612
Antebrachium ~ 20805
Antecedent, plasma thromboplastin ~ 85270
Antepartum care
vaginal delivery ~ 59400, 59425-59426
with cesarean delivery ~ 59510
   previous ~ 59610, 59618
Anterior ramus of thoracic nerve ~ see intercostal nerve
Anthrax vaccine ~ 90476-90749
Anthrogon ~ 80418, 80426, 83001
Anti Australia antigens ~ see antibody, hepatitis B
Anti D immunoglobulin ~ 90384-90386

Anti-human globulin consumption test ~ 86880
Anti-phospholipid antibody ~ 86147
Antiactivator, plasmin ~ 85410
Antibiotic administration
  injection ~ 96372
  prescribed or dispensed ~ 4120F-4124F
Antibiotic sensitivity ~ 87181-87184, 87188
  enzyme detection ~ 87185
  minimum bactericidal concentration ~ 87187
  minimum inhibitory concentration ~ 87186
Antibody detection
  actinomyces ~ 86602
  adenovirus ~ 86603
  antinuclear ~ 86038-86039
  antiphosphatidylserine (phospholipid) ~ 86148
  antistreptolysin O ~ 86060-86063
  aspergillus ~ 86606
  bacterium ~ 86609
  bartonella ~ 86611
  beta 2 glycoprotein 1 ~ 86146
  blastomyces ~ 86612
  blood crossmatch ~ 86920-86923
  bordetella ~ 86615
  borrelia ~ 86618-86619
  brucella ~ 86622
  campylobacter ~ 86625
  candida ~ 86628
  cardiolipin ~ 86147
  chlamydia ~ 86631-86632
  coccidioides ~ 86635
  coxiella burnetii ~ 86638
  c-reactive protein (CRP) ~ 86140-86141
  cryptococcus ~ 86641
  cyclic citrullinated peptide (CCP)~ 86200
  cytomegalovirus ~ 86644-86645
  cytotoxic screen ~ 86807-86808
  deoxyribonuclease ~ 86215
  deoxyribonucleic acid (DNA) ~ 86225-86226
  diphtheria ~ 86648
  ehrlichia ~ 86666
  encephalitis ~ 86651-86654
  enterovirus ~ 86658
  Epstein-Barr virus ~ 86663-86665
  fluorescent ~ 86255-86256
  francisella tularensis ~ 86668
  fungus ~ 86671
  giardia lamblia ~ 86674
  growth hormone ~ 86277
  helicobacter pylori ~ 86677
  helminth ~ 86682
  hemophilus influenza ~ 86684
  hepatitis, delta agent ~ 86692
  hepatitis A ~ 86708-86709
  hepatitis B
    core ~ 86704
    IgM ~ 86705
    surface ~ 86706
  hepatitis Be ~ 86707
  hepatitis C ~ 86803-86804
  herpes simplex ~ 86694-86696
  heterophile ~ 86308-86310
  histoplasma ~ 86698
  HIV ~ 86689, 86701-86703
  HIV 1 ~ 86701, 86703
  HIV 2 ~ 86702-86703
  HTLV I ~ 86687, 86689
  HTLV II ~ 86688
  human leukocyte antigens (HLA) ~ 86828-86835
  infectious agent, other ~ 86317
  influenza virus ~ 86710
  insulin ~ 86337
  intrinsic factor ~ 86340
  islet cell ~ 86341
  JC (John Cunningham) virus ~ 86711
  legionella ~ 86713
  leishmania ~ 86717
  leptospira ~ 86720
  listeria monocytogenes ~ 86723

Antibody detection ~ *continued*
  Lyme disease ~ 86617
  lymphocytic choriomeningitis ~ 86727
  malaria ~ 86750
  microsomal ~ 86376
  mucormycosis ~ 86732
  mumps ~ 86735
  mycoplasma ~ 86738
  neisseria meningitidis ~ 86741
  nocardia ~ 86744
  nuclear antigen ~ 86235
  parvovirus ~ 86747
  phospholipid ~ 85597, 85598, 86147
  plasmodium ~ 86750
  platelet ~ 85597-85598, 86022-86023
  protozoa ~ 86753
  red blood cell ~ 86850, 86860, 86870
  respiratory syncytial virus (RSV) ~ 86756
  rickettsia ~ 86757
  rotavirus ~ 86759
  rubella ~ 86762
  rubeola ~ 86765
  salmonella ~ 86768
  shigella ~ 86771
  sperm ~ 89325
  streptokinase ~ 86590
  tetanus ~ 86774
  thyroglobulin ~ 86800
  toxoplasma ~ 86777-86778
  treponema pallidum ~ 86780
  trichinella ~ 86784
  varicella-zoster ~ 86787
  virus, other ~ 86790
  West Nile virus ~ 86788-86789
  white blood cell ~ 86021
  yersinia ~ 86793
  Zika virus, IgM ~ 86794
Antibody identification
  fluorescent ~ 86255-86256
  immunoassay ~ 83516, 83518-83520
  immunocytochemistry ~ 88342, 88344
  immunoelectrophoresis ~ 86320, 86325, 86327, 86334-86335
  leukocyte antibodies ~ 86021, 86828-86835
  platelet ~ 86022-86023
  red blood cell ~ 86850, 86860, 86870
    pretreatment ~ 86970-86972, 86975-86978
  solid phase assay ~ 86828-86835
Antibody neutralization test ~ 86382
Antibody screening
  fluorescent noninfectious ~ 86255
  cytotoxic percent reactive antibody (PRA) ~ 86807-86808
Anticoagulant ~ 85300-85305, 85307
Antidiabetic hormone ~ 82943
Antidiuretic hormone measurement~ 84588
AntiDNA autoantibody ~ 86038-86039
Antigen(s)
  allergen immunotherapy ~ 95144-95149, 95165, 95170
  carcinoembryonic ~ 82378
  prostate specific ~ 84152-84153
Antigen detection
  direct fluorescence ~ 87265-87272, 87276, 87278, 87280, 87285-87290
    bordetella ~ 87265
    chlamydia trachomatis ~ 87270
    cryptosporidium ~ 87272
    cytomegalovirus ~ 87271
    enterovirus ~ 87267
    giardia ~ 87269
    influenza A ~ 87276
    legionella pneumophila ~ 87278
    not otherwise specified ~ 87299
    respiratory syncytial virus ~ 87280
    treponema pallidum ~ 87285
    varicella-zoster ~ 87290

Antigen detection ~ *continued*
  enzyme immunoassay ~ 87301-87451
    adenovirus ~ 87301
    aspergillus ~ 87305
    chlamydia trachomatis ~ 87320
    clostridium difficile ~ 87324
    cryptococcus neoformans ~ 87327
    cryptosporidium ~ 87328
    cytomegalovirus ~ 87332
    entomoeba histolytica dispar group ~ 87336
    entomoeba histolytica group ~ 87337
    escherichia coli 0157 ~ 87335
    giardia ~ 87329
    helicobacter pylori ~ 87338-87339
    hepatitis Be antigen (HBeAg) ~ 87350
    hepatitis B surface antigen (HBsAg) ~ 87340
    hepatitis B surface antigen (HBsAg) neutralization ~ 87341
    hepatitis delta agent ~ 87380
    histoplasma capsulatum ~ 87385
    HIV 1 ~ 87389-87390
    HIV 2 ~ 87391
    infectious agent, otherwise ~ 87449, 87451
    influenza A ~ 87400
    influenza B ~ 87400
    multiple step method ~ 87301-87449
      polyvalent ~ 87451
    not otherwise specified ~ 87449, 87451
    respiratory syncytial virus ~ 87420
    rotavirus ~ 87425
    shigella-like toxin ~ 87427
    single step method ~ 87450
    streptococcus, group A ~ 87430
  immunoassay, direct optical
    clostridium difficile toxin A ~ 87803
    influenza ~ 87804
    respiratory syncytial virus ~ 87807
    streptococcus, group B ~ 87802
    trichomonas vaginalis ~ 87808
  immunofluorescence ~ 87260-87300
    adenovirus ~ 87260
    bordetella pertussis ~ 87265
    chlamydia trachomatis ~ 87270
    cryptosporidium ~ 87272
    giardia ~ 87269
    herpes simplex ~ 87273-87274
    influenza A ~ 87276
    influenza B ~ 87275
    legionella pneumophila ~ 87278
    not otherwise specified ~ 87299
    parainfluenza virus ~ 87279
    pneumocystis carinii ~ 87281
    polyvalent ~ 87300
    rubeola ~ 87283
    treponema pallidum ~ 87285
    varicella zoster ~ 87290

Antihemophilic factor B ~ 85250
Antihemophilic factor C ~ 85270
Antihemophilic globulin (AHG) ~ 85240
Antihuman globulin ~ 86880-86886
Antimony ~ 83015
Antinuclear antibodies (ANA) ~ 86038-86039
Antiplasmin, alpha 2 ~ Antigen detection
Antiplatelet therapy ~ see performance measures
Antiprotease, alpha 1 ~ 82103-82104, 99565
Antistreptococcal antibody ~ 86215
Antistreptokinase titer ~ 86590
Antistreptolysin O ~ 86060-86063
Antithrombin III ~ 85300-85301
Antithrombin VI (six) ~ 85362-85380
Antitoxin assay ~ 87230
Antiviral antibody ~ 86280
Antrostomy, sinus, maxillary ~ 31256-31267
Antrotomy, sinus
  maxillary ~ 31020-31032
  transmastoid ~ 69501
Antrum puncture, sinus
  maxillary ~ 31000
  sphenoid ~ 31002

Anus ~ see also hemorrhoids; rectum
  ablation ~ 46615
  abscess, incision and drainage ~ 46045-46050
  biofeedback ~ 90911
  biopsy, endoscopy ~ 46606
  crypt, excision ~ 46999
  dilation, endoscopy ~ 46604
  endoscopy
    biopsy ~ 46606
    dilation ~ 46604
    exploration ~ 46600
    hemorrhage ~ 46614
    removal
      foreign body ~ 46608
      polyp ~ 46610, 46612
      tumor ~ 46610, 46612
  excision, tag ~ 46220, 46230
  exploration, endoscopy ~ 46600
  fissure
    destruction ~ 46940-46942
    excision ~ 46200
  fistula
    excision ~ 46270-46285
    repair ~ 46706
  hemorrhage, endoscopic control ~ 46614
  hemorrhoids
    clot excision ~ 46320
    destruction ~ 46930
    excision ~ 46250-46262
    injection ~ 46500
    ligation ~ 46221, 46945-46946
    stapling ~ 46947
    suture ~ 46945-46946
  imperforated, repair ~ 46715-46742
  incision, septum ~ 46070
  lesion
    destruction ~ 46900-46917, 46924
    excision ~ 45108, 46922
  manometry ~ 91122
  placement, seton ~ 46020
  reconstruction ~ 46742
    congenital absence ~ 46730-46740
    sphincter ~ 46750-46751, 46760-46762
    with graft ~ 46753
    with implant ~ 46762
  removal
    foreign body ~ 46608
    seton ~ 46030
    suture ~ 46754
    wire ~ 46754
  repair
    anovaginal fistula ~ 46715-46716
    cloacal anomaly ~ 46748
    fistula ~ 46706
    stricture ~ 46700-46705
  sphincter
    electromyography ~ 51784-51785
    needle ~ 51785
  unlisted services and procedures ~ 46999
Aorta
  abdominal
    aneurysm
      endovascular repair ~ 34845-34848
      screening ~ 76706
    angiography ~ 75635
    thromboendarterectomy ~ 35331
  anastomosis, to pulmonary artery ~ 33606
  angiogram, radiologic injection ~ 93567
  angioplasty ~ 37246, 37247
  aortography ~ 75600-75630
  ascending, graft ~ 33864
  balloon ~ 33967, 33970
  catheterization
    catheter ~ 36200
    intracatheter/needle ~ 36160
  circulation assist
    insertion ~ 33967, 33970, 33973
    removal ~ 33968, 33971, 33974

Aorta~continued
  conduit to heart ~ 33404
  endograft, fenestrated ~ 34839, 34841-34848
  excision, coarctation ~ 33840-33851
  implantable counterpulsation ventricular assist system
    insertion ~ 0451T-0454T
    interrogation device evaluation ~ 0463T
    programming device evaluation ~ 0462T
    relocation ~ 0459T
    removal ~ 0455T-0458T
    replacement ~ 0451T-0454T
    repositioning ~ 0460T, 0461T
  infrarenal abdominal repair
    endovascular ~ 34701-34706, 34709-34711, 34845-34848
  insertion
    balloon device ~ 33967, 33970, 33973
    catheter ~ 36200
    graft ~ 33330-33335, 33864
    intracatheter/needle ~ 36160
  removal, balloon assist device ~ 33968, 33971, 33974
  repair ~ 33320-33322, 33802, 33803
    aneurysm
      ascending ~ 33860, 33863, 33864
      sinus of valsalva ~ 33720
      thoracic ~ 33875, 33877
      transverse arch ~ 33870
    coarctation ~ 33840-33851
    hypoplastic or interrupted aortic arch
      with cardiopulmonary bypass ~ 33853
      without cardiopulmonary bypass ~ 33852
    sinus of Valsalva ~ 33702-33720
  suspension ~ 33800
  suture ~ 33320-33322
  thoracic repair ~ 75956-75959
    endovascular ~ 33880-33891
  translocation, aortic root ~ 33782-33783
  valve
    implantation ~ 33361-33369
    incision ~ 33415
    repair ~ 33390, 33391
      left ventricle ~ 33414
      supravalvular stenosis ~ 33417
  X-ray with contrast ~ 75600-75630
Aortic sinus ~ 33702-33720
Aortic stenosis
  repair ~ 33415
  supravalvular ~ 33417
Aortic valve
  closure, paravalvular leak ~ 93591, 93592
  construction, apical-aortic conduit ~ 33404
  implantation, transcatheter ~ 33361-33369
  occlusion, paravalvular leak ~ 93591, 93592
  repair
    Gusset aortoplasty ~ 33417
    outflow tract obstruction, left ventricle ~ 33414
    stenosis
      idiopathic hypertrophic ~ 33416
      subvalvular ~ 33415
      supravalvular ~ 33417
    valvuloplasty
      open with cardiopulmonary bypass ~ 33390, 33391
Aortic valve replacement
  open
    with allograft valve ~ 33406
    with cardiopulmonary bypass ~ 33405, 33406, 33410
    with prosthesis ~ 33405
    with stentless tissue valve ~ 33410
  Ross procedure ~ 33413
  transcatheter ~ see transcatheter aortic valve replacement
  with allograft valve ~ 33406
  with aortic annulus enlargement ~ 33411, 33412
  with cardiopulmonary bypass ~ 33367-33369, 33405, 33406, 33410
  with prosthesis ~ 33405, 33361-33369
  with stentless tissue valve ~ 33410
  with translocation, pulmonary valve ~ 33413
Aortocoronary bypass ~ 33503-33505, 33510-33516
Aortography ~ (see angiography) 75600-75605, 75630, 93567
  serial ~ 75625
  with iliofemoral artery ~ 75630

Aortoiliac
  embolectomy ~ 34151-34201
  thrombectomy ~ 34151-34201
Aortopexy ~ 33800
Aortoplasty, supravalvular stenosis ~ 33417
AP ~ see voiding pressure studies
Apert-Gallais syndrome ~ see adrenogenital syndrome
Aphasia testing ~ (see neurology, diagnostic) 96105
Apheresis, therapeutic ~ 36511-36516
Apical-aortic conduit ~ 33404
Apicectomy
  with mastoidectomy ~ 69605
  petrous ~ 69530
Apoaminotransferase, aspartate ~ see transaminase, glutamic oxaloacetic
Apolipoprotein, blood or urine ~ 82172
Appendectomy ~ 44950-44960
  laparoscopic ~ 44970
Appendiceal abscess ~ see abscess, appendix
Appendico-vesicostomy, cutaneous ~ 50845
Appendix
  abscess
    incision and drainage
      open ~ 44900
  excision ~ 44950, 44955, 44960, 44970
Application
  allergy tests ~ 95044
  bone fixation device
    multiplane ~ 20692
      stereotactic computer assisted ~ 20696-20697
    uniplane ~ 20690
  caliper ~ 20660
  cranial tongs ~ 20660
  fixation device, shoulder ~ 23700
  halo
    cranial ~ 20661
      thin skull osteology ~ 20664
    femoral ~ 20663
    maxillofacial fixation ~ 21100
    pelvic ~ 20662
  injector device for timed subcutaneous injection ~ 96377
  interdental fixation device ~ 21110
  neurostimulation ~ 64550, 64566
  radioelement
    infusion or instillation ~ 77750
    interstitial ~ 77770-77772, 77778
    intracavitary ~ 77761-77763, 77770-77772, 77790, 77799
    surface ~ 77767, 7776877789
    with ultrasound ~ 76965
  stereotactic frame ~ 20660
    headframe ~ 61800
  strapping, multi-layer compression system
    arm ~ 29584
    leg ~ 29581
Application of external fixation device ~ see fixation device, application, external
APPT ~ see thromboplastin, partial, time
Aquatic therapy ~ 97113
Aqueous shunt
  to extraocular reservoir ~ 66180
  revision ~ 66185
Arch, zygomatic ~ see zygomatic arch
Arm
  see also radius; ulna; wrist
  lower
    abscess ~ 25028
      excision ~ 25145
      incision and drainage, bone ~ 25035
    amputation ~ 24900-24920, 25900-25905, 25915
      cineplasty ~ 24940
      revision ~ 25907-25909
    angiography ~ 73206
    artery ligation ~ 37618
    biopsy ~ 25065-25066
    bursa, incision and drainage ~ 25031
    bypass graft ~ 35903
    cast ~ 29075
    CT scan ~ 73200-73206
    decompression ~ 25020-25025
    exploration, blood vessel ~ 35860
    fasciotomy ~ 24495, 25020-25025

Arm ~ *continued*
  hematoma ~ 25028
  lesion, tendon sheath, excision ~ 25110
  magnetic resonance imaging (MRI) ~ 73218-73220, 73223
  reconstruction, ulna ~ 25337
  removal, foreign body ~ 25248
  repair
    blood vessel with other graft ~ 35266
    blood vessel with vein graft ~ 35236
    decompression ~ 24495
    muscle ~ 25260-25263, 25270
    secondary muscle or tendon ~ 25272-25274
    tendon ~ 25260-25263, 25270, 25280-25295, 25310-25316
      secondary ~ 25265
    tendon sheath ~ 25275
  replantation ~ 20805
  splint ~ 29125-29126
  tenotomy ~ 25290
  tumor, excision ~ 25071-25078
  unlisted services and procedures ~ 25999
  X-ray ~ 73090
    with upper arm ~ 73092
  removal, foreign body, forearm or wrist ~ 25248
  repair
    muscle ~ 24341
    tendon ~ 24341
  upper
    abscess, incision and drainage ~ see elbow; humerus ~ 23930
    amputation ~ 23900-23921, 24900-24920
      cineplasty ~ 24940
      revision ~ 24925-24930
      with implant ~ 24931-24935
    anesthesia ~ 00400, 01710-01782
    angiography ~ 73206
    artery, ligation ~ 37618
    biopsy ~ 24065-24066
    bypass graft ~ 35903
    cast ~ 29065
    CT scan ~ 73200-73206
    exploration, blood vessel ~ 35860
    hematoma, incision and drainage ~ 23930
    magnetic resonance imaging (MRI) ~ 73218-73220, 73223
    muscle revision ~ 24330-24331
    removal
      cast ~ 29705
      foreign body ~ 24200-24201
    repair
      blood vessel with other graft ~ 35266
      blood vessel with vein graft ~ 35236
      muscle transfer ~ 24301, 24320
      tendon ~ 24332
      tendon lengthening ~ 24305
      tendon revision ~ 24320
      tendon transfer ~ 24301
      tenotomy ~ 24310
    replantation ~ 20802
    splint ~ 29105
    tumor, excision ~ 24071-24079
    unlisted services and procedures ~ 24999
    wound exploration, penetrating ~ 20103
    X-ray, with lower arm, infant ~ 73092
Arnold-Chiari malformation repair ~ 61343
Arrest, epiphyseal ~ see epiphyseal arrest
Arrhythmogenic focus, heart
  ablation ~ 33250-33251, 33261, 93653-93654, 93656
    catheter ~ 93655
Arsenic
  blood or urine ~ 82175
  detection ~ 83015
  measurement ~ 82175, 83018
ART (syphilis test) ~ 86592, 86593
Arterial
  catheterization ~ see cannulation, arterial
  dilation, transluminal ~ see angioplasty, transluminal
  grafting for coronary artery bypass ~ see bypass graft, coronary artery, arterial
  pressure ~ see also blood pressure
    noninvasive waveform analysis ~ 93050
  puncture ~ 36600
Arteriography, aorta ~ see aortography
Arteriosus, ductus ~ see ductus arteriosus

Arteriosus, truncus ~ see truncus arteriosus
Arteriotomy ~ see incision, artery; transection, artery
Arteriovenous anastomosis ~ 36818-36820
Arteriovenous fistula
  cannulization vein ~ 36815
  creation ~ 36825-36830
  hemodialysis via fistula ~ 4052F
  referral ~ 4051F
  repair
    abdomen ~ 35182
      acquired or traumatic ~ 35189
    head ~ 35180
      acquired or traumatic ~ 35188
    lower extremity ~ 35184
      acquired or traumatic ~ 35190
    neck ~ 35180
      acquired or traumatic ~ 35188
    thorax ~ 35182
      acquired or traumatic ~ 35189
    upper extremity ~ 35184
      acquired or traumatic ~ 35190
  revision
    with thrombectomy ~ 36833
    without thrombectomy ~ 36832
  thrombectomy
    dialysis graft, without revision ~ 36831
    graft ~ 36830-36833
Arteriovenous malformation
  carotid
    obliteration ~ 61613
    occlusion ~ 61705
  cranial, repair
    carotid artery occlusion ~ 61705
    dural ~ 61690, 61692
    electrothrombosis ~ 61708
    infratentorial ~ 61684, 61686
    supratentorial ~ 61680, 61682
  iliac artery repair ~ 0254T, 34707, 34708
  spinal
    excision ~ 63250-63252
    injection ~ 62294
    repair ~ 63250-63252
Arteriovenous shunt
  aorta to pulmonary artery ~ 33755, 33762
  Blalock-Taussig shunt ~ 33750
  intrahepatic portosystemic ~ 37182, 37183
  patency ~ 78291
  peritoneal venous
    evaluation ~ 49427
    insertion ~ 49425
    ligation ~ 49428
    removal ~ 49429
    revision ~ 49426
  Potts-Smith shunt ~ 33762
  subclavian to pulmonary artery ~ 33750
  Thomas shunt ~ 36835
  Waterston shunt ~ 33755
Artery
  abdomen
    angiography ~ 75726
    catheterization ~ 36245-36248
    ligation ~ 37617
  adrenal, angiography ~ 75731-75733
  anastomosis, cranial ~ 61711
  angioplasty ~ see angioplasty
  aorta
    angioplasty ~ 37246, 37247
    aortobi-iliac bypass graft ~ 35538, 35638
    aortobifemoral bypass graft ~ 35540
    aortocarotid bypass graft ~ 35526, 35626
    aortofemoral bypass graft ~ 35539
    aortoiliac
      bypass graft ~ 35537, 35637
      embolectomy/thrombectomy ~ 34151-34201
    aortoiliofemoral ~ 35363
    aortoinnominate bypass graft ~ 35526, 35626
    aortosubclavian bypass graft ~ 35526, 35626
  arm
    angiography ~ 75710-75716
    harvest of artery for coronary artery bypass graft ~ 35600

Artery ~ *continued*
 atherectomy
  brachiocephalic ~ 0237T
  coronary ~ 92924-92925, 92933-92934, 92937-92938, 92941,
   92943-92944
  femoral ~ 37225, 37227
  iliac ~ 0238T
  peroneal ~ 37229, 37231, 37333, 37335
  popliteal ~ 37225, 37227
  renal ~ 0234T
  tibial ~ 37229, 37231, 37333, 37335
  visceral ~ 0235T
  transluminal ~ 0234T-0238T, 92924-92925, 92933-92934, 92937-92938,
   92941, 92943-92944
 axillary
  aneurysm ~ 35011-35013
  angioplasty ~ 37246, 37247
  bypass graft ~ 35518, 35521-35522, 35533, 35623, 35650, 35654
  embolectomy/thrombectomy ~ 34101
  thromboendarterectomy ~ 35321
 basilar, aneurysm ~ 61698, 61702
 biopsy, transcatheter ~ 75970
 brachial
  aneurysm ~ 35011-35013
  bypass graft ~ 35510, 35512, 35522-35525
  embolectomy ~ 34101
  exploration ~ 24495
  exposure ~ 34834
  thrombectomy ~ 34101
  thromboendarterectomy ~ 35321
 brachiocephalic
  angioplasty ~ 37246, 37247
  catheterization ~ 36215-36218
 bypass graft, with composite graft ~ 35681-35683
 cannulization
  for extra corporeal circulation ~ 36823
  to vein ~ 36810-36815
 carotid
  aneurysm ~ 35001-35002, 61697, 61700, 61703, 61705, 61708, 61710
  bypass graft ~ 33891, 35501-35510, 35601-35606, 35642
  carotid-cavernous fistula ~ 61705, 61708, 61710
  catheterization ~ 36100, 36221-36224, 36227-36228
  decompression ~ 61590-61591, 61596
  embolectomy ~ 34001
  exploration ~ 35701
  ligation ~ 37600-37606, 61611-61612
  reimplantation ~ 35691, 35694-35695
  stenosis, imaging study measurement ~ 3100F
  stent placement, transcatheter ~ 37217
  thrombectomy ~ 34001
  thromboendarterectomy ~ 35301, 35390
  transection ~ 61611-61612
  transposition ~ 33889, 35691, 35694-35695
  vascular malformation ~ 61705, 61708, 61710
 celiac
  aneurysm ~ 35121-35122
  bypass graft ~ 35531, 35631
  embolectomy ~ 34151
  endoprosthesis ~ 34841-34848
  thrombectomy ~ 34151
  thromboendarterectomy ~ 35341
 chest, ligation ~ 37616
 coronary
  angiography ~ 93454-93461, 9292492925, 92933-92934
  atherectomy ~ 92924-92925, 92933-92934
  bypass ~ 33510-33536
   internal mammary artery graft ~ 4110F
  fractional flow reserve ~ 0501T-0504T
  graft ~ 33503-33504
  ligation ~ 33502
  repair ~ 33500-33507
  thrombectomy, percutaneous ~ 92973
  thrombolysis ~ 92975, 92977
  translocation ~ 33506-33507
  unroofing ~ 33507
 digital, sympathectomy ~ 64820
 ethmoidal, ligation ~ 30915
 extracorporeal circulation, for regional chemotherapy of extremity ~
  36823

Artery ~ *continued*
 extracranial anastomosis ~ 61711
 extremities
  vascular studies ~ 93922-93931
   bypass grafts ~ 93925-93931
  bypass graft revision ~ 35879-35884
  catheterization ~ 36140, 36245-36248
  ligation ~ 37618
 femoral
  aneurysm ~ 35141-35142
  angiography ~ 73706
  angioplasty ~ 37224
  approach
   transcatheter aortic valve replacement ~ 33361-33366
  bypass graft ~ 35521, 35533, 35556-35558, 35566, 35621,
   35646-35647, 35654-35661, 35666, 35700
  bypass graft revision ~ 35883-35884
  bypass in-situ ~ 35583-35585
  embolectomy ~ 34201
  exploration ~ 35721
  exposure ~ 34812
  thrombectomy ~ 34201
  thromboendarterectomy ~ 35371-35372
 great vessel, repair ~ 33770-33781
 hepatic
  aneurysm ~ 35121-35122
  bypass graft ~ 35535
 iliac
  aneurysm
   direct repair ~ 35001, 35131, 35132
   endovascular repair ~ 34703-34711
  angioplasty ~ 37220, 37222
  atherectomy ~ 0238T
  bypass graft ~ 35563, 35632-35634, 35637, 35663
  embolectomy ~ 34151-34201
  endograft ~ 0254T
  exposure ~ 34820, 34833
  occlusion device ~ 34808
  revascularization ~ 37220-37222
  thrombectomy ~ 34151-34201
  thromboendarterectomy ~ 35351, 35361-35363
 ilio-celiac bypass graft ~ 35632
 iliofemoral
  bypass graft ~ 35565
  thromboendarterectomy ~ 35355, 35363
  X-ray with contrast ~ 75630
 ilio-mesenteric bypass graft ~ 35633
 iliorenal bypass graft ~ 35634
 innominate
  aneurysm ~ 35021-35022
  catheterization ~ 36222-36223, 36225
  embolectomy ~ 34001-34101
  stent placement, trasncatheter ~ 37217
  thrombectomy ~ 34001-34101
  thromboendarterectomy ~ 35311
 intracranial
  anastomosis ~ 33606
  aneurysm ~ 61705, 61708
  angiography, with thrombectomy ~ 61645
  angioplasty ~ 61630
  infusion
   for other than thrombolysis ~ 61650, 61651
   for thrombolysis ~ 61645
  thrombectomy ~ 61645
 leg
  angiography ~ 73706, 75710-75716
  catheterization ~ 36245-36248
 mammary, angiography ~ 75756
 maxillary, ligation ~ 30920
 mesenteric
  aneurysm ~ 35121-35122
  bypass graft ~ 35531, 35631
  embolectomy ~ 34151
  thrombectomy ~ 34151
  thromboendarterectomy ~ 35341
 middle cerebral artery
  fetal, vascular studies ~ 76821
  ligation ~ 37615

Artery ~ *continued*
- neck
  - angiography ~ 36221-36226
  - ligation ~ 37615
- nose, incision ~ 30915-30920
- other angiography ~ 75774
- other artery
  - angiography ~ 75774
  - exploration ~ 35761
- pelvic
  - angiography ~ 72198, 75736
  - catheterization ~ 36245-36248
- peripheral arterial rehabilitation ~ 93668
- peroneal
  - angioplasty ~ 37228-37235
  - atherectomy ~ 37229, 37231, 37333, 37335
  - bypass graft ~ 35566-35571, 35666-35671
  - bypass in-situ ~ 35585-35587
  - embolectomy ~ 34203
  - thrombectomy ~ 34203
  - thromboendarterectomy ~ 35305-35306
- popliteal
  - aneurysm ~ 35151-35152
  - angioplasty ~ 37224
  - atherectomy ~ 37225, 37227
  - bypass graft ~ 35556, 35571, 35623, 35656, 35671, 35700
  - bypass in-situ ~ 35583, 35587
  - embolectomy ~ 34203
  - exploration ~ 35741
  - thrombectomy ~ 34201-34203
  - thromboendarterectomy ~ 35303
- pressure
  - waveform analysis ~ 93050
- pulmonary
  - anastomosis ~ 33606
  - angiography ~ 75741-75746
  - angioplasty ~ 92997-92998
  - banding ~ 33620, 33622, 33690
  - embolectomy ~ 33910, 33915-33916
  - endarterectomy ~ 33916
  - ligation ~ 33924
  - repair ~ 33917, 33920, 33925-33926
- radial
  - aneurysm ~ 35045
  - bypass graft ~ 35523
  - embolectomy ~ 34111
  - sympathectomy ~ 64821
  - thrombectomy ~ 34111
- rehabilitation ~ 93668
- reimplantation
  - carotid ~ 35691, 35694-35695
  - subclavian ~ 35693-35695
  - vertebral ~ 35691-35693
  - visceral ~ 35697
- renal
  - aneurysm ~ 35121-35122
  - angiography ~ 36251-36254
  - angioplasty ~ 37246, 37247
  - atherectomy ~ 0234T
  - bypass graft ~ 35631, 35634, 35636
  - catheterization ~ 36251-36254
  - embolectomy ~ 34151
  - endoprosthesis ~ 34841-34848
  - fluoroscopy ~ 36251-36254
  - thrombectomy ~ 34151
  - thromboendarterectomy ~ 35341
- repair
  - aneurysm ~ 61697-61708
  - angioplasty
    - radiological supervision ~ 37246, 37247
  - revision
    - hemodialysis graft or fistula~ 36831-36833
  - spine, angiography ~ 75705
- splenic
  - aneurysm ~ 35111-35112
  - bypass graft ~ 35536, 35636

Artery ~ *continued*
- subclavian
  - aneurysm ~ 35001-35002, 35021-35022
  - angioplasty ~ 37246, 37247
  - bypass graft ~ 35506, 35511-35516, 35606-35616, 35626, 35645
  - catheterization ~ 36225
  - embolectomy ~ 34001-34101
  - reimplantation ~ 35693-35695
  - thrombectomy ~ 34001-34101
  - thromboendarterectomy ~ 35301, 35311
  - transposition ~ 33889, 35693-35695
  - unlisted services and procedures ~ 37799
- superficial palmar arch, sympathectomy ~ 64823
- temporal biopsy/ligation ~ 37609
- thoracic, catheterization ~ 33621, 36215-36218
- thrombectomy
  - coronary ~ 92973
  - dialysis circuit ~ 36904-36906
  - intracranial ~ 61645
  - noncoronary ~ 37184-37186
  - hemodialysis graft or fistula ~ 36831
  - other than hemodialysis graft or fistula ~ 35875, 36830-36833
- thrombolysis
  - intracranial ~ 61645
  - non-coronary ~ 37211, 37213, 37214
- tibial
  - angiography ~ 73706
  - angioplasty ~ 37228
  - atherectomy ~ 37229, 37231, 37333, 37335
  - bypass graft ~ 35566-35571, 35623, 35666-35671
  - bypass in-situ ~ 35585-35587
  - embolectomy ~ 34203
  - thrombectomy ~ 34203
  - thromboendarterectomy ~ 35305-35306
- transcatheter therapy, with angiography ~ 75894-75898
- transposition
  - carotid ~ 33889, 35691, 35694-35695
  - subclavian ~ 33889, 35693-35695
  - vertebral ~ 35691-35693
- ulnar
  - aneurysm ~ 35045
  - bypass graft ~ 35523
  - embolectomy ~ 34111
  - sympathectomy ~ 64822
  - thrombectomy ~ 34111
- umbilical vascular study ~ 76820
- unlisted services and procedures ~ 37799
- vertebral
  - aneurysm ~ 35005, 61698, 61702
  - bypass graft ~ 35508, 35515, 35642-35645
  - catheterization ~ 36100, 36221, 36225-36226, 36228
  - decompression ~ 61597
  - reimplantation ~ 35691-35693
  - thromboendarterectomy ~ 35301
  - transposition ~ 35691-35693
- visceral
  - angioplasty ~ 37246, 37247
  - atherectomy ~ 0235T
  - reimplantation ~ 35697

Artery catheterization, pulmonary ~ see catheterization, pulmonary artery
Arthrectomy, elbow ~ 24155
Arthrocentesis
- intermediate joint ~ 20605
- large joint ~ 20610
- small joint ~ 20600

Arthrodesis
- ankle ~ 27870
  - tibiotalar and fibulotalar joints ~ 29899
- anterior interbody ~ 22551-22552
- carpometacarpal joint
  - hand ~ 26843-26844
  - thumb ~ 26841-26842
- cervical anterior, with discectomy ~ 22554
- elbow ~ 24800-24802
- finger joint ~ 26852
  - interphalangeal ~ 26860-26863
  - metacarpophalangeal ~ 26850

Arthrotomy~*continued*
finger joint ~ 26075
  interphalangeal
    with synovial biopsy ~ 26110
  metacarpophalangeal
    with biopsy, synovium ~ 26105
glenohumeral joint ~ 23040
hip ~ 27033
  for infection
    with drainage ~ 27030
  with synovectomy ~ 27054
interphalangeal joint ~ 26080, 26110
  toe ~ 28024, 28054
intertarsal joint ~ 28020, 28050
knee ~ 27310, 27330-27335, 27403, 29868
metacarpophalangeal joint ~ 26075, 26105
metatarsophalangeal joint ~ 28022, 28052
shoulder ~ 23044, 23105-23107
shoulder joint ~ 23100-23101
  exploration and/or removal of loose or foreign body ~ 23107
sternoclavicular joint ~ 23044
tarsometatarsal joint ~ 28020, 28050
temporomandibular joint ~ 21010
with biopsy
  acromioclavicular joint ~ 23101
  glenohumeral joint ~ 23100
  hip joint ~ 27052
  knee joint ~ 27330
  sacroiliac joint
    hip joint ~ 27050
  sternoclavicular joint ~ 23101
with synovectomy
  glenohumeral joint ~ 23105
  sternoclavicular joint ~ 23106
wrist ~ 25040, 25100-25107
Articular ligament ~ see ligament
Artificial abortion ~ see abortion
Artificial cardiac pacemaker ~ see heart, pacemaker
Artificial eye ~ see prosthesis
Artificial genitourinary sphincter ~ see prosthesis, urethral sphincter
Artificial insemination ~ 58976
intra-cervical ~ 58321
intra-uterine ~ 58322
sperm washing ~ 58323
Artificial knee joints ~ 27438, 27445
Artificial penis ~ see penile prosthesis
Artificial pneumothorax ~ 32960
Arytenoid, excision, endoscopic ~ 31560-31561
Arytenoid cartilage
excision ~ 31400
repair ~ 31400
Arytenoidectomy ~ 31400
endoscopic ~ 31560
Arytenoidopexy ~ 31400
Ascorbic acid, blood ~ 82180
Aspartate aminotransferase ~ 84450
Aspergillus
antibody ~ 86606
antigen detection
  enzyme immunoassay ~ 87305
Aspiration ~ see puncture aspiration
abdomen ~ 49322
amniotic fluid
  diagnostic ~ 59000
  therapeutic ~ 59001
bladder ~ 51100-51102
bone marrow ~ 38220, 38222
  spine surgery ~ 20939
brain lesion ~ 61750-61751
bronchi ~ 31629, 31633, 31645, 31646, 31725
bursa ~ 20600-20611
catheter
  nasotracheal ~ 31720
  tracheobronchial ~ 31725
chest ~ 32554-32555
cyst
  bone ~ 20615
  ganglion ~ 20612
  kidney ~ 50390
  pelvis ~ 50390

Aspiration ~ *continued*
spinal cord ~ 62268
thyroid ~ 60300
disc ~ 62267
duodenal ~ 43756-43757
evaluation ~ 88172, 88173, 88177
fetal fluid ~ 59074
ganglion cyst ~ 20612
gastric ~ 43753-43755
hydrocele, tunica vaginalis ~ 55000
joint ~ 20600-20610
laryngoscopy
  direct ~ 31515
lens material ~ 66840
liver ~ 47015
lung ~ 32405
lung puncture ~ 32405
nail ~ 11740
nucleus of disk, lumbar ~ 62287
orbital contents ~ 67415
pelvis, endoscopy ~ 49322
pericardium ~ 33010-33011
pleural cavity ~ 32554-32555
puncture, cyst, breast ~ 19000-19001
spinal cord, stereotaxis ~ 63615
spinal puncture ~ see spinal tap
syrinx, spinal cord ~ 62268
thyroid ~ 60300
trachea
  nasotracheal ~ 31720
  puncture ~ 31612
tunica vaginalis, hydrocele ~ 55000
vitreous ~ 67015
Aspiration lipectomies ~ 15876-15879
Aspiration of bone marrow from donor for transplant ~ 38230
Assay, very long chain fatty acids ~ 82726
Assay tobramycin ~ 80200
Assisted circulation ~ see circulation assist
AST ~ 84450
Astragalectomy ~ 28130
Astragalus ~ see talus
Asymmetry, face ~ 21247
Ataxia telangiectasia, chromosome analysis ~ 88248
Ataxy, telangiectasia ~ 88248
Atherectomy
abdominal aorta ~ 0236T
brachiocephalic ~ 0237T
coronary ~ 92924-92925, 92937-92938, 92941, 92943-92944
femoral ~ 37225, 37227
iliac ~ 0238T
peroneal ~ 37229, 37231, 37333, 37335
popliteal ~ 37225, 37227
renal ~ 0234T
tibial ~ 37229, 37231, 37333, 37335
visceral ~ 0235T
Athletic training
evaluation ~ 97169-97171
re-evaluation ~ 97172
ATLV ~ see HTLV I
ATLV antibodies ~ 86688
Atomic absorption spectroscopy ~ 82190
ATP creatine phosphotranferase ~ 82550-82552
Atresia
choanal ~ 30540-30545
congenital
  auditory canal, external ~ 69320
  bile duct ~ 47700
  small intestine ~ 44126-44127
pulmonary artery ~ 33920
tetralogy of fallot ~ 33697
tricuspid ~ 33615
Atria
ablation ~ 33254-33256, 33265-33266
Baffle procedure ~ 33774
Blalock-Hanlon operation ~ 33735
cor triatriatum repair ~ 33732
cuff preparation ~ 32855-32856
electrogram ~ 93615-93616
endoscopy, surgical ~ 33265-33266
left atrial appendage closure ~ 33340

999

Atria ~ *continued*
membrane resection ~ 33732
pacemaker
electrode removal ~ 33229, 33236
electrode repositioning ~ 33215
insertion ~33206, 33208
Rashkind procedure ~ 92992
reconstruction ~ 33254-33256, 33265-33266
septectomy ~ 33735, 92992-92993
shunt ~ 62190, 62220
thrombus ~ 33310
Atrial electrogram ~ see cardiology, diagnostic
esophageal recording ~ 93615-93616
Atrial fibrillation ~ see fibrillation, atrial
Atrioseptopexy ~ see heart, repair, atrial septum
Atrioseptoplasty ~ see heart, repair, atrial septum
Attachment ~ see fixation
Atticotomy ~ 69631, 69635
Audiologic function tests ~ 92590-92595
acoustic reflex ~ 92568
acoustic reflex decay ~ 92570
audiometry
Bekesy ~ 92560-92561
comprehensive ~ 0212T, 92557
conditioning play ~ 92582
groups ~ 92559
pure tone ~ 0208T-0209T, 92552-92553
select picture ~ 92583
speech ~ 0210T-0211T, 92555-92556
visual reinforcement ~ 92579
auditory brainstem implant ~ 92640
auditory processing treatment ~ 92507-92508
central auditory function ~ 92620-92621
ear protector attenuation ~ 92596
electrocochleography ~ 92584
evoked otoacoustic emission ~ 92558, 92587-92588
filtered speech ~ 92571
hearing aid evaluation ~ 92590-92595
loudness balance ~ 92562
screening ~ 92551
sensorineural acuity ~ 92575
short increment sensitivity index ~ 92564
staggered spondaic word test ~ 92572
Stenger test ~ 92565, 92577
synthetic sentence test ~ 92576
tinnitus assessment ~ 92625
tone decay ~ 92563
tympanometry ~ 92550, 92567, 92570
Audiometry
Bekesy ~ 92560-92561
brainstem evoked response ~ 92585-92586
comprehensive ~ 0212T, 92557
conditioning play ~ 92582
groups ~ 92559
pure tone ~ 92552-92553
automated 0208T-0209T
select picture ~ 92583
speech ~ 0210T-0211T, 92555-92556
tympanometry ~ 92550, 92567, 92570
Auditory brain stem evoked response ~ 92585-92586
Auditory canal
decompression ~ 61591
external
abscess, incision and drainage ~ 69020
biopsy ~ 69105
lesion, excision ~ 69140-69155
reconstruction
for congenital atresia ~ 69320
for stenosis ~ 69310
removal
cerumen ~ 69209, 69210
ear wax ~ 69209, 69210
foreign body ~ 69200-69205
internal, decompression ~ 69960
Auditory atresia, external ~ 69320
Auditory evoked otoacoustic emission ~ 92587-92588
Auditory evoked potentials ~ 92585-92586, 92590-92595
Auditory labyrinth ~ see ear, inner
Auditory meatus, X-ray ~ 70134
Auditory system surgical procedures ~ 69000-69990

Auditory tube ~ see eustachian tube
Augmentation
chin ~ 21120, 21123
cruciate ligament ~ 29888, 29889
facial bones ~ 21208
knee ligament ~ 27427, 27556-27558
larynx ~ 31574
malar ~ 21210, 21270
mandibular body
with bone graft ~ 21127
with prosthesis ~ 21125
palate ~ 21082
pulmonary valve outflow ~ 33478
spine
lumbar ~ 22514, 22515
thoracic ~ 22513, 22515
Aural rehabilitation ~ 92510
Auricle (heart) ~ see atria
Auricular fibrillation ~ fibrillation, atria
Auricular prosthesis ~ 21086
Australia antigen ~ 87340-87341
Autograft
bone ~ 20936-20938
bone marrow ~ 20939
chondrocytes, knee ~ 27412
osteochondral
knee ~ 27416
talus ~ 28446
skin
dermal ~ 15130-15136
epidermal ~ 15110-15116
tissue culture ~ 15150-15157
harvesting ~ 15040
spine ~ 20936-20939
Autologous blood transfusion ~ 86890-86891
Autologous transplantation ~ see autograft
Autonomic nervous system function ~ see neurology, diagnostic;
neurophysiologic testing
Autoprothrombin
C ~ 85260
I ~ 85230
II ~ 85250
III ~ 85260
Autopsy
coroner's exam ~ 88045
forensic exam ~ 88040
gross and micro exam ~ 88020-88029
gross exam ~ 88000-88016
organ ~ 88037
regional ~ 88036
unlisted services and procedures ~ 88099
Autotransfusion, blood ~ 86890-86891
Autotransplant ~ see autograft
Autotransplantation, renal ~ 50380
Avulsion
nails ~ 11730-11732
nerve ~ 64732-64772
AV fistula ~ see arteriovenous fistula
AV shunt ~ see arteriovenous shunt
Axillary arteries ~ see artery, axillary
Axillary nerve, injection, anesthetic ~ 64417
Axis, dens ~ 22548

B

B antibodies, hepatitis ~ see antibody, hepatitis B
B antigens, hepatitis ~ 87516, 87517
B complex vitamins, B12 absorption ~ 78270-78272
B-DNA ~ 86225-86226
B-hexosaminidase ~ 83080
B1 vitamin ~ see 84425
B6 vitamin ~ 84207
B12 vitamin ~ 82607-82608
Babcock operation ~ 37700-37735, 37780
Bacillus Calmette Guerin vaccine ~ see BCG vaccine

Back/ flank
  biopsy ~ 21920-21925
  repair, hernia ~ 49540
  strapping ~ 29799
  tumor
    excision ~ 21930-21936
    radical resection ~ 21935, 21936
  wound exploration
    penetrating ~ 20102
Backbone ~ see spine
Bacteria culture
  additional methods ~ 87077
  aerobic ~ 87040-87071
  anaerobic ~ 87073-87076
  blood ~ 87040
  other source ~ 87070-87075
  screening ~ 87081
  stool ~ 87045-87046
  typing ~ 87140, 87143, 87147, 87149-87150, 87152-87153, 87158
  urine ~ 87086-87088
Bacterial endotoxins ~ 87176, 87205
Bacterial overgrowth breath test ~ 91065
Bactericidal titer, serum ~ 87197
Bacterium, antibody ~ 86609
Baer ~ 92585-92586
Baker's cyst ~ 27345
Baker tube, intestine decompression ~ 44021
Balanoplasty ~ see penis, repair
Baldy-Webster operation ~ 58400
Balkan grippe ~ 86000, 86638
Balloon
  angioplasty ~ *see* angioplasty
  assisted device
    aorta ~ 33967-33974
    bronchoscopy ~ 31647-31649, 31651
Band, pulmonary artery ~ 33690
Banding, artery
  fistula ~ 37607
  pulmonary ~ 33610, 33620, 33690
Bank, blood ~ see blood banking
Bankart procedure ~ 23450-23462
Barany caloric test ~ 92533
Barbiturates, blood or urine ~ 80345
Bardenheurer operation ~ 37616
Bariatric surgery
  gastric bypass ~ 43644-43645, 43846-43847
  gastric restriction ~ 43644-43645, 43842-43843, 43845-43846, 43847-43848
    device placement ~ 43770
    device removal ~ 43772-43774
    device replacement ~ 43773
    device revision ~ 43771
    port component ~ 43886-43888
  sleeve gastrectomy ~ 43775
  surgically altered stomach ultrasound examination ~ 43242
Barium ~ 83015
Barium enema ~ 74270-74280
Barker operation ~ 28120, 28130
Barr bodies ~ 88130
Barr procedure ~ 27690-27692
Bartholin's gland
  abscess, incision and drainage ~ 56420
  cyst, repair ~ 56440
  excision ~ 56740
  marsupialization ~ 56440
Bartonella
  antibody ~ 86611
  detection ~ 87472
Basic life services ~ 99450
Basic proteins, myelin ~ 83873
Basilar arteries ~ 61698, 61702
Batch-Spittler-McFaddin operation ~ 27598
BCG vaccine ~ 90585, 90586
Be antigens, hepatitis ~ 87350
Bed sores ~ see debridement; skin graft and flap; 15920-15999
Bed testing ~ 94780, 94781
Bekesy audiometry ~ 92560-92561
Belsey IV procedure ~ see fundoplasty
Bender-Gestalt test ~ 96100
Benedict test for urea ~ 81005
Benign cystic mucinous tumour ~ see ganglion

Benign neoplasm of cranial nerves ~ see cranial nerve
Bennett fracture ~ see phalanx, finger; 26720-26727
Bennett procedure ~ see revision; 27385-27386, 27400, 27430
Benzidine test ~ 82270, 82272
Benzodiazepine, assay ~ 80346, 80347
Benzoyl cholinesterase ~ 82480-82482
Bernstein test ~ 91030
Beryllium ~ 83015
Beta-2 -microglobulin
  blood ~ 82232
  urine ~ 82232
Beta-hydroxydehydrogenase ~ 80406
Beta 2 glycoprotein 1 antibody ~ 86146
Beta blocker therapy ~ see performance measures
Beta glucosidase ~ 82963
Beta hypophamine ~ 84588
Beta lipoproteins ~ 83700-83704, 83721
Beta test ~ see psychiatric diagnosis ~ 96100
Bethesda system ~ 88164-88167
Bicarbonate ~ 82374
Biceps tendon, insertlon ~ 24342
Bichloride, methylene ~ 84600
Bicuspid valve ~ see mitral valve
Bifrontal craniotomy ~ 61557
Bilaminate skin substitute/ neodermis ~ see tissue
  repair ~ see tissue, culture; 15100-15101, 15120-15121
Bile acids ~ 82239
  blood ~ 82240
Bile duct ~ see gallbladder
  anastomosis
    with intestines ~ 47760, 47780-47785
  biopsy
    endoluminal ~ 47543
    endoscopy ~ 47553
  cholangiography
    injection ~ 47531, 47532
    with catheterization ~ 47533-47537
    with placement of access to small bowel ~ 47541
    with stent placement ~ 47538-47540
  cyst, excision ~ 47715
  destruction
    calculi (stone) ~ 43265, 47544
  dilation
    endoscopy ~ 43277, 47555, 47556
    percutaneous ~ 47542
    X-ray ~ 74360
  drainage
    catheter
      change ~ 75984
      conversion of external to internal-external ~ 47535
      exchange ~ 47536
      placement ~ 47533, 47534
      removal ~ 47537
  endoscopic retrograde cholangiopancreatography (ERCP) with optical
    endomicroscopy ~ 0397T
  endoscopy
    biopsy ~ 47553
    cannulation ~ 43273
    destruction, calculi (stone) ~ 43265
    dilation ~ 43277, 47555-47556
    exploration ~ 47552
    intraoperative ~ 47550
    placement, stent ~ 43274
    removal
      calculi (stone) ~ 43264, 47554
      foreign body ~ 43275
    specimen collection ~ 43260
    sphincterotomy ~ 43262, 43274
    sphincter pressure ~ 43263
  exploration
    atresia ~ 47700
    endoscopy ~ 47552
  incision, sphincter ~ 43262, 47460
  incision and drainage ~ 47420-47425
  insertion
    stent ~ 47801
  nuclear medicine, imaging ~ 78226-78227

Biopsy ~ continued
- nail ~ 11755
- nasopharynx ~ 42804-42806
- neck ~ 21550
- nerve ~ 64795
- nose
  - endoscopic ~ 31237
  - intranasal ~ 30100
- oocyte polar body ~ 89290-89291
- orbit ~ 61332
  - exploration ~ 67400, 67450
  - fine needle aspiration ~ 67415
- oropharynx ~ 42800
- ovary ~ 58900
- palate ~ 42100
- pancreas ~ 48100
- pelvis ~ 27040-27041
- penis ~ 54100
  - deep structures ~ 54105
- percutaneous needle, spinal cord ~ 62269
- perineum ~ 56605-56606
- pharynx ~ 42800-42806
- pleura
  - needle ~ 32400
  - thoracoscopy ~ 32609
  - thoracotomy ~ 32098, 32400
- prostate
  - incisional ~ 55705
  - needle or punch ~ 55700, 55706
  - stereotactic ~ 55706
- lymph nodes ~ 55812, 55842, 55862
- rectum ~ 45100, 45305, 45331
- renal pelvis ~ 50606
- retroperitoneal area ~ 49010
- sacroiliac joint ~ 27050
- salivary gland ~ 42405
- shoulder
  - deep ~ 23066
  - soft tissue ~ 23065
- shoulder joint ~ 23100-23101
- sinus, sphenoid ~ 31050-31051
- skin ~ see skin, biopsy
- skin lesion ~ 11100-11101
- spinal cord ~ 63275-63290
  - percutaneous ~ 62269
  - stereotaxis ~ 63615
- stomach ~ 43605
- tarsometatarsal joint, synovial ~ 28050
- testis ~ 54500-54505
- thorax ~ 21550
- throat ~ 42800-42806
- tongue ~ 41100-41105
- transcatheter ~ 37200
- ureter ~ 52354
  - endoluminal, non-endoscopic ~ 50606
  - endoscopic ~ 50955-50957, 50974-50976
- urethra ~ 52204, 52354, 53200
- uterus
  - endometrial ~ 58100
  - endoscopic ~ 58558
- uvula ~ 42100
- vagina ~ 57100-57105, 57421
- vein ~ 75970
- vertebral body ~ 20250-20251
- vulva ~ 56605-56606, 56821
- with arthrotomy
  - acromioclavicular joint ~ 23101
  - glenohumeral joint ~ 23100
  - sternoclavicular joint ~ 23101
- with cystourethroscopy ~ 52354
- wrist ~ 25065-25066, 25100-25101

Biostatistics ~ 76516-76519, 92136
Biosterol ~ 84590
Biotinidase ~ 82261
Birthing room, newborn care ~ 99465
Bischof procedure ~ 63170-63172
Bismuth ~ 83015
Bizzozero's corpuscle/cell ~ see blood, platelet

Bladder
- abscess, incision and drainage ~ 51080
- anastomosis ~ 51960
- aspiration ~ 51100-51102
- biopsy ~ 52204
- catheterization ~ 51045, 51701-51703
- change tube ~ 51705-51710
- creation, stoma ~ 51980
- cyst, urachal, excision ~ 51500
- destruction, endoscopic ~ 52214-52224, 52354
- dilation, ureter ~ 52260-52265, 52341-52342, 52344-52345
- diverticulum
  - excision ~ 51525
  - incision ~ 52305
  - resection ~ 52305
- endoscopy ~ 52000
  - biopsy ~ 52204, 52354
  - catheterization ~ 52005, 52010
  - destruction ~ 52214-52224, 52400
  - dilation ~ 52260-52265
  - diverticulum ~ 52305
  - evacuation, clot ~ 52001
  - excision, tumor ~ 52234-52240, 52355
  - exploration ~ 52351
  - injection ~ 52283
  - lithotripsy ~ 52353
  - radiotracer ~ 52250
  - removal
    - calculus ~ 52310-52315, 52352
    - foreign body ~ 52310-52315
  - sphincter surgery ~ 52277
  - tumor, excision ~ 52355
  - ureter surgery ~ 52290-52300
  - urethral syndrome ~ 52285
  - with urethrotomy ~ 52270-52276
- excision
  - partial ~ 51550-51565
  - total ~ 51570, 51580, 51590-51597
    - with nodes ~ 51575, 51585, 51595
  - transurethral ~ 52640
  - tumor ~ 52234-52240
- incision
  - catheter ~ 51045
  - with destruction ~ 51020-51030
  - with radiotracer ~ 51020
- incision and drainage ~ 51040
- injection, radiologic ~ 51600-51610
- insertion, stent ~ 51045, 52334
- instillation, drugs ~ 51720
- irrigation ~ 51700
- lesion, destruction ~ 51030
- neck, endoscopy, injection of implant material ~ 51715
  - excision ~ 51520
  - micro-remodeling ~ 53860
- nuclear medicine, residual study ~ 78730
- radiotracer ~ 52250
- reconstruction, and urethra ~ 51800-51820
  - with intestines ~ 51960
- removal
  - calculus ~ 51050, 52310-52315
  - foreign body ~ 52310-52315
  - urethral stent ~ 52310-52315
- repair
  - diverticulum ~ 52305
  - exstrophy ~ 51940
  - fistula ~ 44660-44661, 45800-45805, 51880-51925
  - neck ~ 51845
  - wound ~ 51860-51865
- resection ~ 52500
- sphincter surgery ~ 52277
- suspension ~ 51990
- suture
  - fistula ~ 44660-44661, 45800-45805, 51880-51925
  - wound ~ 51860-51865
- tumor, excision ~ 51530

Bladder ~ *continued*
iunlisted services and procedures ~ 53899
urethrocystography ~ 74450-74455
urethrotomy ~ 52270-52276
urinary incontinence procedures
laparoscopy ~ 51990-51992
plan of care documented ~ 0509F
X-ray ~ 74430
with contrast ~ 74450-74455
Bladder voiding pressure studies ~ 51728-51729
Blalock-Hanlon procedure ~ 33735-33737
Blalock-Taussig procedure ~ see shunt, great vessel
Blastocyst implantation ~ see implantation
Blastocyst transfer ~ see embryo transfer
Blastogenesis ~ 86353
Blastomyces, antibody ~ 86612
Blastomycosis, european ~ see cryptococcus
Blast cells ~ see stem cell
Blast transformation ~ 86353
Bleeding ~ see also hemorrhage
anal ~ 46614
disorder ~ 85390
time ~ 85002
tube, passage and placement ~ 43460
uterine ~ 59160
vaginal ~ 57180
Blepharoplasty ~ 15820-15823, 67950
anesthesia ~ 00103
Blepharoptosis
repair ~ 67901-67909
frontalis muscle technique ~ 67901
with fascial sling ~ 67902
superior rectus technique with fascial sling ~ 67906
tarso levator resection/advancement
external approach ~ 67904
internal approach ~ 67903
Blepharorrhaphy ~ 67875
Blepharospasm, chemodenervation ~ 64612
Blepharotomy ~ 67700
Blister ~ see bulla
Blom-Singer prosthesis ~ 31611
Blood ~ 85025-85027
bleeding time ~ 85002
collection, for autotransfusion
intraoperative ~ 86891
preoperative ~ 86890
feces ~ 82270
by hemoglobin immunoassay ~ 82274
hemoglobin A1c (HbA1c) level ~ 3044F-3045F
hemoglobin concentration ~ 85046
nuclear medicine
flow imaging ~ 78445
plasma iron ~ 78160
red cell ~ 78140
red cell survival ~ 78130-78135
osmolality ~ 83930
plasma, exchange ~ 36514-36516
platelet
aggregation ~ 85576
automated count ~ 85049
count ~ 85008
manual count ~ 85032
stem cell
count ~ 86587
donor search ~ 38204
erythropoietin therapy ~ 3160F, 4090F-4095F
harvesting ~ 38205-38206
transplantation ~ 38240-38242
cell concentration ~ 38215
cryopreservation ~ 38207, 88240
plasma depletion ~ 38214
platelet depletion ~ 38213
red blood cell depletion ~ 38212
T-cell depletion ~ 38210
thawing ~ 38208-38209, 88241
tumor cell depletion ~ 38211
washing ~ 38209

Blood ~ *continued*
transfusion ~ 36430
exchange ~ 36455
newborn ~ 36450, 36456
fetal ~ 36460
push, infant ~ 36440
unlisted services and procedures ~ 85999
urine ~ 83491
viscosity ~ 85810
Blood, occult ~ 82270-82272
Blood banking
frozen blood preparation ~ 86930-86932
frozen plasma preparation ~ 86927
physician services ~ 86077-86079
Blood cell
CD4 and CD8, including ratio ~ 86360
enzyme activity ~ 82657
exchange ~ 36511-36513
red ~ see red blood cell (RBC)
sedimentation rate
automated ~ 85652
manual ~ 85651
white ~ see leukocyte
Blood cell count
automated ~ 85049
B-cells ~ 86064
blood smear ~ 85007-85008
differential WBC count ~ 85004-85007, 85009
hematocrit ~ 85014
hemoglobin ~ 85018
hemogram
added indices ~ 85025-85027
automated ~ 85025-85027
manual ~ 85032
microhematocrit ~ 85013
natural killer (NK) cells ~ 86379
red ~ 85032-85041
red blood cells ~ 85032-85041
reticulocyte ~ 85044-85046
stem cells ~ 86587
T-cells ~ 86359-86361
white ~ 85032, 85048, 89055
white blood cells ~ 85032, 85048, 89055
Blood clot
assay ~ 85396
clotting factor ~ 85250-85293
clotting factor test ~ 85210-85244
clotting inhibitors ~ 85300-85302, 85305, 85307
clot lysis time ~ 85175
clot retraction ~ 85170
coagulation time ~ 85345-85348
thrombolytic agent(s), tissue plasminogen activator (tPA) ~ 4077F
Blood coagulation
defect ~ 85390
disorders ~ 34401-34490, 35875-35876, 50230
factor ~ 85210-85293
factor I ~ 85384-85385
factor II ~ 85210
factor III ~ see thromboplastin
factor IV ~ see calcium
factor VII ~ 85230
factor VIII ~ 85210-85293
factor IX ~ 85250
factor X ~ 85260
factor X, activated ~ 85260
factor XI ~ 85270
factor XIII ~ 85290-85291
test ~ 85999
Blood component removal ~ 36511-36516
Blood count, complete ~ 85025-85027
Blood flow
graft check ~ 15860, 90940
myocardial, absolute quantitation ~ 0482T
Blood gases
CO_2 ~ 82803
HCO_3 ~ 82803
O_2 saturation ~ 82805-82810
pCO_2 ~ 82803
pH ~ 82800-82803
pO_2 ~ 82803

Blood letting ~ 99195
Blood lipoprotein ~ see lipoprotein
Blood pool imaging ~ 78472-78473, 78481-78483, 78494-78496
Blood pressure
  baroreflex activation device ~ 0266T-0273T
  central arterial noninvasive waveform analysis ~ 93050
  monitoring, 24 hour ~ 93784, 93786, 93788, 93790
  ocular
    measurement ~ 0198T
    monitoring ~ 0329T
  performance measures
    chronic kidney disease ~ 0513F, 2000F, 3074F, 3075F, 3077F-3080F
    coronary artery disease ~ 0001F, 3074F
    hypertension ~ 3074F, 3075F, 3077F-3080F
  venous ~ 93770
Blood products
  irradiation ~ 86945
  pooling ~ 86965
  splitting ~ 86985
Blood sample, fetal ~ 59030
Blood serum ~ see serum
Blood smear ~ 85060
Blood syndrome, chromosome analysis ~ 88245-88248
Blood tests
  iron stores ~ 3160F
  Kt/V ~ 3082F-3084F
  nuclear medicine
    iron, chelatable ~ 78172
    iron absorption ~ 78162
    iron utilization ~ 78170
    plasma volume ~ 78110-78111
    platelet survival ~ 78191
    red cell volume ~ 78120-78121
    whole blood volume ~ 78122
  panels
    acute hepatitis ~ 80074
    electrolyte ~ 80051
    general health panel ~ 80050
    hepatic function ~ 80076
    hepatitis, acute ~ 80074
    lipid panel ~ 80061
    metabolic
      basic, total calcium ~ 80048
      basic, ionized calcium ~ 80047
      comprehensive ~ 80053
    obstetric panel ~ 80055, 80081
    renal function ~ 80069
  volume determination ~ 78122
Blood transfusion, autologous ~ 86890-86891
Blood typing, serologic
  ABO only ~ 86900
  antigen screen ~ 86904
  antigen testing, donor blood ~ 86902
  compatibility ~ 86920-86923
  crossmatch ~ 86920-86923
  other RBC antigens ~ 86905
  paternity testing ~ 86910-86911
  Rh (D) ~ 86901
  Rh phenotype ~ 86906
Blood urea nitrogen ~ 84520-84525
Blood vessels ~ see also artery; vein
  angioscopy, non-coronary ~ 35400
  endoscopy, surgical ~ 37500
  excision, arteriovenous malformation ~ 63250-63252
  exploration
    abdomen ~ 35840
    chest ~ 35820
    extremity ~ 35860
    neck ~ 35800
  great, suture ~ 33320-33322
  harvest
    endoscopic ~ 33508
    lower extremity vein ~ 35572
    upper extremity artery ~ 35600
    upper extremity vein ~ 35500
  kidney, repair ~ 50100

Blood vessels ~ *continued*
  repair
    abdomen ~ see aneurysm repair; fistula, repair
      with composite graft ~ 35681-35683
      with other graft ~ 35281
      with vein graft ~ 35251
    aneurysm ~ 61705-61708
    arteriovenous malformation ~ 61680-61692, 61705-61710, 63250-63252
    chest
      with composite graft ~ 35681-35683
      with other graft ~ 35271-35276
      with vein graft ~ 35241-35246
    direct ~ 35201-35226
    finger ~ 35207
    graft defect ~ 35870
    hand ~ 35207
    lower extremity ~ 35226
      with composite graft ~ 35681-35683
      with other graft ~ 35281
      with vein graft ~ 35251
    neck
      with composite graft ~ 35681-35683
      with other graft ~ 35261
      with vein graft ~ 35231
    upper extremity ~ 35206
      with composite graft ~ 35681-35683
      with other graft ~ 35266
      with vein graft ~ 35236
  shunt creation, direct ~ 36818, 36821
    thomas shunt ~ 36835
    with bypass graft ~ 35686
    with graft ~ 36825-36830
  shunt revision, with graft ~ 36832
Blood, occult ~ see occult blood
Bloom syndrome, chromosome analysis ~ 88245
Blotting, western ~ see western blot
Blot test, ink ~ 96100
Blow-out fracture, orbital floor ~ 21385-21395
Blue, dome cyst ~ 19000-19001
BMT ~ 38240-38242
Boarding home care ~ 99321-99333
Bodies
  acetone ~ 82009-82010
  Barr ~ 88130
  carotid ~ see carotid body
  ciliary ~ see ciliary body
  Heinz ~ 85441-85445
  inclusion ~ see inclusion bodies
  ketone ~ 82009-82010
Body cast
  halo ~ 29000
  removal ~ 29700, 29710
  repair ~ 29720
  Risser jacket ~ 29010-29015
  upper body and head ~ 29040
  upper body and legs ~ 29046
  upper body and one leg ~ 29044
  upper body only ~ 29035
Body fluid, crystal identification ~ 89060
Body of vertebra ~ see vertebral, body
Body section
  X-ray ~ 76100
    motion ~ 76101-76102
Body system, neurologic ~ *78699*
Boil ~ 10060-10061
Boil, vulva ~ 56405
Bone ~ see also specific bone***
  ablation, tumor ~ 20982
  biopsy ~ 20220-20245
  carpal ~ see carpal bone
  cheek ~ see cheekbone
  CT scan, density study ~ 77078
  cyst
    drainage ~ 20615
    injection ~ 20615
  dual energy X-ray absorptiometry ~ 77080-77081

1005

Bone ~ *continued*
excision
  epiphyseal bar ~ 20150
  facial bones ~ 21026
  mandible ~ 21025
facial ~ see facial bone
fixation
  caliper ~ 20660
  cranial tong ~ 20660
  halo ~ 20661-20663, 21100
  interdental ~ 21110
  multiplane ~ 20692
    stereotactic computer assisted ~ 20696-20697
  pin/wire ~ 20650
  skeletal, humeral epicondyle, percutaneous ~ 24566
  stereotactic frame ~ 20660
  uniplane ~ 20690
fracture, osteoporosis screening ~ 5015F
insertion
  needle ~ 36680
  osseointegrated implant, for external speech processor/cochlear
    stimulator ~ 69714-69718
marrow, cytogenic testing ~ 3155F
metatarsal ~ see metatarsal
nasal ~ see nasal bone
navicular ~ see navicular
nuclear medicine
  density study ~ 78350-78351
  imaging ~ 78300-78320
  spect ~ 78320
  unlisted services and procedures ~ 78399
osetoporosis, pharmacologic therapy ~ 4005F
protein ~ 83937
removal, fixation device ~ 20670-20680
replacement, osseointegrated implant, for external speech
  processor/cochlear stimulator ~ 69717-69718
scan ~ see bone, nuclear medicine; nuclear medicine
semilunar ~ see lunate
sesamoid ~ see sesamoid bone
tarsal ~ see ankle
temporal ~ see temporal bone
X-ray
  age study ~ 77072
  dual energy absorptiometry ~ 77080-77081
  length study ~ 77073
  osseous survey ~ 77074-77077
Bone 4-carboxyglutamic protein ~ 83937
Bone conduction hearing device, electromagnetic
implantation/replacement ~ 69710
removal/repair ~ 69711
Bone density study
appendicular skeleton ~ 77081
axial skeleton ~ 77078, 77080
ultrasound ~ 76977
vertebral fracture assessment ~ 77085, 77086
Bone graft
any donor area ~ 20900, 20902
clavicle ~ 23485
craniofacial separation ~ 21436
cranium ~ 61316, 61559, 62146-62148
femur ~ 27170, 27177, 27470
harvesting ~ 20900-20902
knee drilling ~ 29885
malar area ~ 21210, 21366
mandible ~ 21127, 21194, 21215
mandibular ramus ~ 21194
maxilla ~ 21210
metacarpal nonunion ~ 26546
metatarsal nonunion ~ 28322
microvascular anastomosis
  fibula ~ 20955
  iliac crest ~ 20956
  metatarsal ~ 20957
  other ~ 20962
nasal area ~ 21210
nasomaxillary complex fracture ~ 21348
osteocutaneous flap ~ 20969-20973
palate, cleft ~ 42210

Bone graft ~ *continued*
spine surgery ~ 0195T, 0196T, 20930, 20931, 22586, 22899
  bone marrow aspiration ~ 20939
toe transfer ~ 26551
ulna ~ 25830
vertebra ~ 0222T
  cervical ~ 0219T, 63051
  lumbar ~ 0221T
  thoracic ~ 0220T
wrist ~ 25810, 25825
Bone healing
electrical stimulation
  invasive ~ 20975
  noninvasive ~ 20974
ultrasound stimulation ~ 20979
Bone infection ~ 20005
Bone marrow
aspiration ~ 38220, 38222
biopsy ~ 38221, 38222, 88305
cell therapy ~ 0263T-0265T
harvesting
  allogenic ~ 38230
  autologous ~ 38232
magnetic resonance imaging (MRI) ~ 77084
needle biopsy ~ 38221
nuclear medicine, imaging ~ 78102-78104
smear ~ 85097
T-cell transplantation ~ 38240-38242
trocar biopsy ~ 38221
Bone plate, mandible ~ 21244
Bone scan ~ see bone, nuclear medicine; nuclear medicine
Bone spur ~ 69140
Bone wedge reversal, osteotomy ~ 21122
Bordetella
antibody ~ 86615
antigen detection, direct fluorescence ~ 87265
Borrelia, antibody ~ 86618-86619
Borrelia burgdorferi ab ~ 86617
Borreliosis, Lyme ~ 86617-86618
Bost fusion ~ 25800
Bosworth operation ~ see arthrodesis, vertebrae; fasciotomy; 23540-23552
Bottle type procedure ~ 55060
Botulinum toxin ~ see chemodenervation
Boutonniere deformity ~ 26426-26428
Bowel ~ see intestine
Bowleg repair ~ 27455-27457
Boyce operation ~ 50040-50045
Boyd hip disarticulation ~ see radical resection; replantation; 27590-27592
Brace ~ see cast for leg cast ~ 29358
Brachial arteries ~ see artery, brachial
Brachial plexus
decompression ~ 64713
injection anesthetic ~ 64415-64416
neuroplasty ~ 64713
release ~ 64713
repair/suture ~ 64861
Brachiocephalic artery ~ see artery, brachiocephalic
Brachycephaly ~ 21175
Brachytherapy
device placement
  breast ~ 19296-19298
  genitalia ~ 55920
  head~ 41019
  intraocular ~ 0190T
  neck ~ 41019
  pelvis ~ 55920
  uterus ~ 57155
  vagina ~ 57155, 57156
dose plan ~ 77316-77318
high dose electronic ~ 0394T, 0395T
interstitial application ~ 0395T, 77778
planning
  isodose plan ~ 77316-77318
  prostate volume study ~ 76873
radioelement solution ~ 77750

Brachytherapy ~ *continued*
  remote afterloading
    interstitial ~ 77770-77772
    intracavitary ~ 77770-77772
    surface ~ 77767, 77768
  surface application ~ 0394T, 77789
  remote afterloading ~ 77767, 77768
  unlisted clinical procedures ~ 77799
Bradykinin, blood or urine ~ 82286
Brain ~ see also brainstem; skull base surgery; 61480
  abscess
    drainage ~ 61150-61151
    excision ~ 61514, 61522
    incision and drainage ~ 61320-61321
  adhesions, lysis ~ 62161
  anesthesia ~ 00210-00218, 00220-00222
  angiography ~ 70496
  biopsy ~ 61140
    stereotactic ~ 61750-61751
  catheter
    irrigation ~ 62194, 62225
    replacement ~ 62160, 62194, 62225
  cisternography ~ 70015
  cortex, magnetic stimulation ~ 90867-90868
  craniopharyngioma, excision ~ 61545
  CT scan ~ 0042T, 70450-70470, 70496
  cyst
    drainage ~ 61150-61151, 62161-62162
    excision ~ 61516, 61524, 62162
  Doppler, transcranial ~ 93886-93893
  epileptogenic focus, excision ~ 61534, 61536
  excision
    amygdala ~ 61566
    choroid plexus ~ 61544
    hemisphere ~ 61543
    hippocampus ~ 61566
    other lobe ~ 61323, 61539-61540
    temporal lobe ~ 61537-61538
  exploration
    infratentorial ~ 61305
    supratentorial ~ 61304
  hematoma
    drainage ~ 61154
    incision and drainage ~ 61312-61315
  implantation
    chemotherapy agent ~ 61517
    electrode ~ 61210, 61533, 61850, 61860, 61863-61864, 61867, 61868, 61870
    pulse generator ~ 61885-61886
    reservoir ~ 61210, 61215
  incision
    corpus callosum ~ 61541
    mesencephalic tract ~ 61480
    subpial ~ 61567
  insertion, catheter ~ 61210
    electrode ~ 61531-61533, 61850
    pulse generator ~ 61885-61886
    receiver ~ 61885-61886
    reservoir ~ 61210-61215
  lesion
    aspiration stereotactic ~ 61750-61751
    excision ~ 61600, 61601, 61605-61608, 61615, 61616
  meningioma, excision ~ 61512, 61519
  myelography ~ 70010
  nuclear medicine
    blood flow ~ 78610
    cerebrospinal fluid ~ 78630-78650
    imaging ~ 78600-78607
    vascular flow ~ 78610
  positron emission tomography ~ 78608-78609
  removal
    electrode ~ 61535, 61880
    foreign body ~ 61570, 62163
    pulse generator ~ 61888
    receiver ~ 61888
    shunt ~ 62256-62258

Brain ~ *continued*
  repair
    dura ~ 61618
    wound ~ 61571
  shunt
    creation ~ 62180-62192, 62200-62223
    removal ~ 62256-62258
    replacement ~ 62160, 62194, 62225-62230, 62256-62258
    reprogramming ~ 62252
  skull
    transcochlear approach ~ 61596
  transcondylar approach ~ 61597
  transpetrosal approach ~ 61598
  transtemporal approach ~ 61595
  skull base
    craniofacial approach ~ 61580-61585
    infratemporal approach ~ 61590-61591
    orbitocranial-zygomatic approach ~ 61592
  stereotaxis-aided procedures
    aspiration ~ 61750-61751
    biopsy ~ 61750-61751
    catheter placement ~ 61770
    create lesion ~ 61720-61735, 61790-61791
    localization for placement of therapy fields ~ 61770
    navigation ~ 61781, 61782
    procedure ~ 61781, 61782
    radiation treatment ~ 77432
    radiosurgery ~ 61796-61800, 77371-77373
    trigeminal tract ~ 61791
  transection, subpial ~ 61567
  tumor, excision ~ 61510, 61518, 61520-61521, 61526-61530, 61545, 62164
  X-ray, with contrast ~ 70010-70015
Brainstem ~ see also brain
  auditory evoked potential ~ 92585-92586
  biopsy ~ 61575-61576
  decompression ~ 61575-61576
  evoked potentials ~ 92585-92586
  lesion, excision ~ 61575-61576
Brain coverings ~ 61512, 61519
Brain death, determination ~ 95824
Brain surface electrode, stimulation ~ 95961-95962
Brain tumor
  acoustic neuroma ~ 61510, 61518, 61520-61521, 61526-61530, 61545, 62164
  craniopharyngioma ~ 61545
  meningioma ~ 61512, 61519
Brain ventriculography ~ see ventriculography
Branchial cleft cyst excision ~ 42810-42815
Branchioma ~ 42810-42815
BRCA gene alaysis
  BRCA1 ~ 81214, 81215
  BRCA2 ~ 81216, 81217
  BRCA1 and BRCA2 ~ 81211-81213
Breast
  ablation
    cryosurgical, fibroadenoma ~ 19105
  abscess
    incision and drainage ~ 19020
  augmentation ~ 19324-19325
  biopsy ~ 19100-19101
    with imaging of specimen ~ 19081-19086
    with localization device palcement
      magnetic resonance guided ~ 19085-19086
      stereotactic guidance ~ 19081-19082
      ultrasound guided ~ 19083-19084
  cancer gene analysis ~ 81162, 81211-81217
  cyst
    excision ~ 19120
    puncture aspiration ~ 19000-19001
  diagnostic imaging
    ductogram ~ 19030, 77053, 77054
    galactobram ~ 77053, 77054
    injection ~ 19030
    MRI ~ 0159T, 77058, 77059
    mammography, diagnostic ~ 77065, 77066
    mammogram, screening ~ 3014F, 77067
    ultrasound ~ 76641, 76642

Breast ~ *continued*
excision
  biopsy ~ 19100-19101
  capsules ~ 19371
  chest wall tumor ~ 19260-19272
  cyst ~ 19120
  lactiferous duct fistula ~ 19110, 19112
  lesion ~ 19120, 19125-19126, 19301
    by needle localization ~ 19125-19126
  mastectomy ~ 19300-19307
  tumor ~ 19120, 19260, 19271-19272
exploration
  abscess ~ 19020
  nipple ~ 19110
implants
  insertion ~ 19325, 19340, 19342
  preparation of moulage ~ 19396
  removal ~ 19328, 19330
  supply ~ 19396
lesion, localizatiion device placement
  with magetnic resonance guidance ~ 19287-19288
  with mammographic guidance ~ 19281-19282
  with stereotactic guidance ~ 19283-19284
  with ultrasound guidance ~ 19285-19286
magnetic resonance imaging (MRI) ~ 77058-77059
mammogram screening ~ 3014F, 77067
mammoplasty
  augmentation ~ 19324-19325
  reduction ~ 19318
mastectomy
  complete ~ 19303
  gynecomastia ~ 19300
  modified radical ~ 19307
  partial ` 19301-19302
  radical ~ 19303-19306
  subcutaneous ~ 19304
  with axillary lymphadenectomy ~ 19302
mastopexy ~ 19316
periprosthetic capsulectomy ~ 19371
periprosthetic capsulotomy ~ 19370
radiation therapy
  catheter placement, for interstitial radioelement application ~
    19296-19298
  preparation of tumor cavity ~ 19294
reconstruction
  augmentation ~ 19324-19325
  mammoplasty ~ 19318-19325
  nipple ~ 19350, 19355
    areola ~ 19350
  revision ~ 19380
  with free flap ~ 19364
  with latissimus dorsi flap ~ 19361
  with other techniques ~ 19366
  with tissue expander ~ 19357
  with transverse rectus abdominis myocutaneous flap ~ 19367-19369
reduction ~ 19318
removal
  capsules ~ 19371
  modified radical ~ 19307
  partial ~ 19300-19302
  radical ~ 19305-19306
  simple, complete ~ 19303
  subcutaneous ~ 19304
repair, suspension ~ 19316
unlisted services and procedures ~ 19499
Breath odor alcohol ~ 82075
Breath test
alcohol, ethyl ~ 82075
heart transplant rejection detection ~ 0085T
helicobacter pylori ~ 78267-78268, 83013-83014
hydrogen ~ 91065
Bricker procedure, intestines anastomosis ~ 50820
Bristow procedure ~ 23450-23462
Brock operation ~ 33470-33474
Broken, nose ~ see fracture, nasal bone

Bronchi
allograft preparation ~ 32855, 32856
aspiration
  catheter ~ 31720, 31725
  endoscopic ~ 31629, 31633, 31645, 31646
biopsy ~ 31625-31629, 31632, 31633
bronchial valve
  insertion ~ 31647, 31651
  removal ~ 31648, 31649
bronchodilator
  home care ~ 99503
  spirometry ~ 94012, 94060
bronchoscopy
  alveolar lavage ~ 31624
  aspiration ~ 31629, 31633, 31645, 31646
  biopsy ~ 31625-31629, 31632, 31633
  catheter placement for radiotherapy ~ 31643
  cell brushing ~ 31623
  cell washing ~ 31622
  computer assisted/image guided navigation ~ 31627
  dilation ~ 31630, 31631, 31636, 31638
  endobronchial ultrasound (EBUS) ~ 31652-31654
  exploration ~ 31622
    with balloon occlusion ~ 31634, 31647, 31651
  foreign body removal ~ 31635
  stenosis relief ~ 31641
  stent placement ~ 31631, 31636-31638
  thermoplasty ~ 31660, 31661
  tumor destruction ~ 31641
  tumor excision ~ 31640
catheterization
  aspiration ~ 31725
  bronchial brush biopsy ~ 31717
endoscopy
  ablation, photodynamic therapy ~ 96570, 96571
exploration ~ 31622, 31634, 31647, 31651
fracture reduction ~ 31630
insertion, bronchial valve ~ 31647, 31651
needle biopsy ~ 31629, 31633
reconstruction
  anastomosis ~ 31775, 32486
  graft repair ~ 31770
  stenosis ~ 31775
removal, foreign body ~ 31635
repair ~ 32501
  fistula ~ 32815, 32906
stenosis ~ 31641, 96570, 96571
stent
  placement ~ 31636, 31637
  revision ~ 31638
tests
  air leak assessment ~ 31647, 31651
  bronchospasm evaluation ~ 94070, 94617
  wheeze rate ~ 94799
thermoplasty ~ 31660, 31661
tumor
  destruction ~ 31641
  excision ~ 31640
unlisted services and procedures ~ 31899
Bronchial
alveolar lavage ~ 31624
brushings/protected brushing ~ 31623
brush biopsy, with catheterization ~ 31717
challenge test
  bronchospasm evaluation ~ 94070, 94617
  for wheeze rate ~ 94799
  with antigens ~ 95071
  with chemicals ~ 95070
  with gases ~ 95071
  with histamine ~ 95070
  with methacholine ~ 95070
lavage ~ 31624
Broncho-bronchial anastomosis ~ 32486
Bronchoalveolar lavage ~ 31624
Bronchography ~ 76499
injection, transtracheal ~ 31899
segmental, injection ~ 31899
Bronchoplasty ~ 32501
excision stenosis and anastomosis ~ 31775
graft repair ~ 31770
Bronchopneumonia, hiberno-vernal ~ 86000, 86638

Bronchopulmonary lavage ~ 31624
Bronchoscopy
  ablation ~ 96570, 96571
  alveolar lavage ~ 31624
  aspiration ~ 31629, 31633, 31645, 31646
  balloon occlusion ~ 31634, 31647, 31651
  biopsy ~ 31625-31629, 31632, 31633
  brushing/protected brushing ~ 31623
  catheter placement
    aspiration ~ 31725
    intracavitary radioelement ~ 31643
  computer assisted navigation ~ 31627
  dilation ~ 31630-31631, 31636-31638
  exploration ~ 31622, 31634, 31647, 31651
  fiducial marker placement ~ 31626
  fracture ~ 31630
  insertion of bronchial valve(s) ~ 31647, 31651
  needle biopsy ~ 31629, 31633
  removal
    bronchial valve ~ 31648, 31649
    foreign body ~ 31635
    tumor ~ 31640-31641
  stenosis ~ 31641
  stent placement ~ 31631, 31636-31637
  stent revision ~ 31638
  with airway resizing ~ 31647, 31648, 31649
  with assessment of airway leak ` 31647, 31648, 31649
  with balloon occlusion ~ 31647, 31648, 31649
  with bronchial thermoplasty ~ 31660, 31661
  with endobronchial ultrasound (EBUS) ~ 31652-31654
Bronchospasm evaluation ~ 94010-94070
Bronkodyl ~ 80198
Brow ptosis, repair ~ 67900
Brucella ~ 86000
  antibody ~ 86622
Bruise ~ see hematoma
Brunschwig operation ~ see hip ~ 45126, 58240
Brush biopsy ~ see biopsy; needle biopsy
  bronchi ~ 31717
Brush border ab ~ 86308-86310
Bucca ~ see cheek
Buccal mucosa ~ 40818
Bulbourethral gland, excision ~ 53250
Bulla
  incision and drainage
    puncture aspiration ~ 10160
  lung
    excision-plication ~ 32141
      endoscopic ~ 32655
Bun ~ see urea nitrogen ~ 84520-84525
Bunion repair
  bunionectomy ~ 28292
  by phalanx osteotomy ~ 28298, 28299
  Chevron procedure ~ 28296
  concentric procedure ~ 28296
  Keller procedure ~ 28292
  Lapidus procedure ~ 28297
  Mayo procedure ~ 28292
  McBride procedure ~ 28292
  Mitchell procedure ~ 28296
  with metatarsal osteotomy ~ 28295, 28296
  with sesamoidectomy ~ 28292
Burgess amputation ~ 27889
Burhenne procedure ~ see gallbladder ~ 43264, 47420-47425
Burkitt herpesvirus ~ 86663-86665
Burns
  debridement ~ 15002-15005, 16020-16030
  dressings ~ 16020-16030
  escharotomy ~ 15002-15005, 16035, 16036
  fenestration, body surface ~ 0479T, 0480T
  first degree, initial treatment ~ 16000
  tissue cultured skin grafts ~ 15150-15152, 15155-15157
  total body surface area (TBSA) calculation ~ 16000
Burrow's operation ~ 14000-14350

Burr hole
  anesthesia ~ 00214
  skull
    biopsy brain ~ 61140
    catheterization ~ 61210
    drainage
      abscess ~ 61150-61151
      cyst ~ 61150-61151
      hematoma ~ 61154-61156
    exploration
      infratentorial ~ 61253
      supratentorial ~ 61250
    for implant of neurostimulator array ~ 61863-61868
    injection, contrast media ~ 61120
    insertion, catheter ~ 61210
      reservoir ~ 61210
Bursa
  ankle ~ 27604
  arm, lower ~ 25031
  elbow
    excision ~ 24105
    incision and drainage ~ 23931
  femur, excision ~ 27062
  foot, incision and drainage ~ 28001
  hip, incision and drainage ~ 26991
  injection ~ 20600-20610
  ischial, excision ~ 27060
  joint
    aspiration ~ 20600-20610
    drainage ~ 20600-20610
    injection ~ 20600-20610
  knee, excision ~ 27340
  leg, lower ~ 27604
  palm, incision and drainage ~ 26025-26030
  pelvis, incision and drainage ~ 26991
  shoulder, drainage ~ 23031
  wrist ~ 25031
    excision ~ 25115-25116
Bursectomy ~ see excision, bursa
Bursitis, radiohumeral ~ 24357-24359
Bursocentesis ~ 20600-20610
Button, nasal septal prosthesis, insertion ~ 30220
Butyrylcholine esterase ~ 82480-82482
Bypass, cardiopulmonary ~ 33926
Bypass graft
  arterial, coronary ~ 33533-33536, 35600
  arterial-venous coronary ~ 33517-33519, 33521-33523, 33530
  harvest
    artery ~ 35600
    endoscopic ~ 33508
    vein ~ 35500, 35572
  reoperation ~ 35700
  repair
    abdomen ~ 35907
    extremity ~ 35903
    lower extremity with composite graft ~ 356j81-35683
    neck·~ 35901
    thorax ~ 35905
  revascularization
    extremity ~ 35903
    neck ~ 35901
    thorax ~ 35905
  revision
    lower extremity
      femoral artery ~ 35883-35884
      with angioplasty ~ 35879
      with vein interposition ~ 35881
  secondary repair ~ 35870
  thrombectomy ~ 37184-37186
    other than hemodialysis graft or fistula ~ 35875-35876

Bypass graft ~ continued
  venous
    aortobi-iliac ~ 35538, 35638
    aortobifemoral ~ 35540, 35646
    aortocarotid ~ 35526, 35626
    aortoceliac ~ 35531, 35631
    aortofemoral ~ 35539, 35647
    aortoiliac ~ 35537, 35637
    aortoinnominate ~ 35526, 35626
    aortomesenteric ~ 35531, 35631
    aortorenal ~ 35560, 35631
    aortosubclavian ~ 35526, 35626
    axillary-axillary ~ 35518, 35650
    axillary-brachial ~ 35522
    axillary-femoral ~ 35521, 35621
    axillary-femoral-femoral ~ 35533, 35654
    axillary-popliteal ~ 35623
    axillary-tibial ~ 35623
    brachial-brachial ~ 35525
    brachial-radial ~ 35523
    brachial-ulnar ~ 35523
    carotid-brachial ~ 35510
    carotid-contralateral carotid ~ 35509
    carotid-subclavian ~ 35506, 35606
    carotid-vertebral ~ 35508, 35642
    common carotid-ipsilateral internal carotid ~ 35501, 35601
    coronary ~ 33510-33514, 33516
    femoral-popliteal ~ 35556, 35572, 35656
    femoral-femoral ~ 35558, 35661
    femoral-tibial ~ 35566, 35666
    femoral-peroneal ~ 35566
    hepatorenal ~ 35535
    ilioceliac ~ 35632
    iliofemoral ~ 35565, 35665
    ilioiliac ~ 35563, 35663
    ilimesenteric ~ 35633
    iliorenal ~ 35634
    mesenteric ~ 35531, 35631
    peroneal ~ 35566-35571, 35666-35671
    peroneal-tibial ~ 35570
    popliteal-peroneal ~ 35571, 35671
    popliteal-tibial ~ 35571, 35671
    splenorenal ~ 35536, 35636
    subclavian-axillary ~ 35516, 35616
    subclavian-brachial ~ 35512
    subclavian-carotid ~ 35506
    subclavian-subclavian ~ 35511, 35612
    subclavian-vertebral ~ 35515, 35645
    tibial/peroneal trunk-tibial ~ 35570
    tibial-tibial ~ 35570
  with composite graft ~ 35681
Bypass in-situ
  femoral artery ~ 35583-35585
  peroneal artery ~ 35585-35587
  popliteal artery ~ 35583, 35587
  tibial artery ~ 35585-35587
  ventricular restoration ~ 33548

C

C vitamin ~ 82180
C-13
  urea breath test ~ 83013-83014
  urease activity ~ 83013-83014
C-14
  urea breath test ~ 78267-78268
  urease activity ~ 83013-83014
C-peptide ~ 80432, 84681
C-reactive protein ~ 86140-86141
C-section ~ see cesarean delivery
CABG ~ see coronary artery bypass graft (CABG) ~ 33503-33505, 33510-33516
Cadmium, urine ~ 82300
Calcaneal spur ~ 28119

Calcaneus
  craterization ~ 28120
  cyst, excision ~ 28100-28103
  diaphysectomy ~ 28120
  excision ~ 28118-28120
  fracture
    open treatment ~ 28415-28420
    percutaneous fixation ~ 28406
    without manipulation ~ 28400
    with manipulation ~ 28405-28406
  repair, osteotomy ~ 28300
  saucerization ~ 28120
  tumor, excision ~ 27647, 28100-28103
  X-ray ~ 73650
Calcareous deposits, subdeltoid, removal ~ 23000
Calcifediol, blood or urine ~ 82306
Calciferol, blood or urine ~ 82306
Calcification ~ see calcium, deposits
Calciol ~ 82306
Calcitonin
  blood or urine ~ 82308
  stimulation panel ~ 80410
Calcium, blood, infusion test ~ 82331
  deposits ~ see removal, calculi (stone) ~ 65205-65265
  ionized ~ 82330
  total ~ 82310
  urine ~ 82340
Calcium-binding protein, vitamin K-dependent ~ 83937
Calcium-pentagastrin stimulation ~ 80410
Calculus
  analysis ~ 82355-82370
  destruction
    bile duct ~ 43265, 47544
    extracorporeal shock wave lithotripsy ~ 50590
    gallbaldder ~ 47544
    pancreatic duct ~ 43265
  removal
    bile duct ~ 43264, 47544, 47554
    biliary tract ~ 47400, 47420, 47425, 47480
    bladder ~ 51050, 52310, 52315, 52352
    gallbladder ~ 74544
    kidney ~ 50060-50081, 50130, 50561, 50580, 52352
    liver ~ 47400
    pancreatic duct ~ 43264, 48020
    renal pelvis ~ 50075, 50080, 50081, 50130
    ureter ~ 50610-50630, 50945, 50961, 50980, 52310, 52315, 52320, 52352
Calculus of kidney ~ 50060-50081, 50130, 50561, 50580, 52352
Caldwell-Luc procedure ~ 21385
  sinusotomy ~ 31030-31032
Caliper, application/removal ~ 20660
Callander knee disarticulation ~ 27598
Callosum, corpus ~ 61541
Calmette Guerin Bacillus vaccine ~ see BCG vaccine
Caloric vestibular test ~ 92533
Calprotectin, fecal ~ 83993
Calycoplasty ~ 50405
Camey enterocystoplasty ~ 50825
Campbell procedure ~ 27422
Campylobacter, antibody ~ 86625
Campylobacter pylori ~ see helicobacter pylori
Canal, ear ~ see auditory canal
Canalith repositioning ~ 95992
Canaloplasty ~ 69631, 69635
Candida
  antibody ~ 86628
  skin test ~ 86485
Cannulation ~ 36821
  arterial ~ 36620-36625
  sinus
    maxillary ~ 31000
    sphenoid ~ 31002
  thoracic duct ~ 38794
Cannulation, renoportal ~ 37145

Cannulization ~ see catheterization
  arteriovenous ~ 36810-36815
  declotting ~ 36593, 36860-36861
  diaysis circuit ~ 36901-36903
  external, declotting ~ 36860, 36861
  vas deferens ~ 55200
  vein to vein ~ 36800
Canthocystostomy ~ 68745, 68750
Canthopexy
  lateral ~ 21282
  medial ~ 21280
Canthoplasty ~ 67950
Canthorrhaphy ~ 67880-67882
Canthotomy ~ 67715
Canthus, reconstruction ~ 67950
Cap, cervical ~ 57170
Capsule ~ 26516-26518
  ankle ~ 27612, 27630
  elbow ~ 24006, 24149
  eye ~ 66830
  finger ~ 26160, 26520
  foot ~ 28090, 28264, 28289, 28291
  hand ~ 26160, 26520
  heyman ~ 58346
  hip ~ 27036
  interphalangeal joint ~ 26525, 28272
  knee ~ 27347, 27405, 27435
  leg ~ 27630
  shoulder ~ 23020
  Tenon's ~ 67515
  toe ~ 28270, 28272
  wrist, excision ~ 25320
Capsulectomy, breast, periprosthetic ~ 19371
Capsulodesis
  metacarpophalangeal joint ~ 26516-26518
  wrist ~ 25320
Capsulorrhaphy
  anterior ~ 23450-23462
  glenohumeral joint ~ 23465-23466
  multi-directional instability ~ 23466
  posterior ~ 23465
  shoulder ~ 29806
  wrist ~ 25320
Capsulotomy
  breast, periprosthetic ~ 19370
  eye ~ 66830
  foot ~ 28260-28262, 28264
  hip, with release, flexor muscles ~ 27036
  interphalangeal joint ~ 28272
  knee ~ 27435
  leg ~ 27630
  metacarpophalangeal joint ~ 26520
  metatarsophalangeal joint ~ 28270
  shoulde ~ 23020
  toe ~ 28270-28272
  wrist ~ 25085, 25320
Captopril ~ 80416-80417
Car seat testing ~ 94780, 94781
Carbamazepine, assay ~ 80156-80157
Carbazepin ~ 80156-80157
Carbinol ~ 84600
Carbohydrate deficient transferrin ~ 82373
Carbon dioxide, blood or urine ~ 82374
Carbon monoxide, blood ~ 82375-82376
Carbon tetrachloride ~ 84600
Carboxycathepsin ~ 82164
Carboxyhemoglobin ~ 82375-82376, 88740
Carbuncle, incision and drainage ~ 10060-10061
Carcinoembryonal antigen ~ 82378
Carcinoembryonic antigen ~ 82378
Cardiac ~ *see* coronary
Cardiac anomoly, reconstruction ~ 33622
Cardiac arrhythmia, tachycardia ~ 93609
Cardiac atria ~ see atria

Cardiac catheterization
  combined left and right heart ~ 93460, 93461
    with left ventriculography ~ 93453, 93460, 93461
  combined right and retrograde left congenital cardiac anomalies ~ 93531
  combined right and transseptal left congenital cardiac anomalies ~ 93532, 93533
  congenital cardiac anomalies ~ 93530-93533
  for angiography
    bypass graft(s) ~ 93455, 93457, 93459, 93461
    congenital heart ~ 93563, 93564
    coronary ~ 93454-93461, 93563, 93571
    left atrial ~ 93565
    left ventricular ~ 93565
    pulmonary ~ 93568
    right atrial ~ 93566
    right ventricular ~ 93566
  for biopsy ~ 93505
  for congenital prosthetic valve implantation ~ 33477
  for dilution studies ~ 93561, 93562
  for flow measurement ~ 93571, 93572
  for measurement of O2, cardiac output ~ 93451
  for supravalvular aortography ~ 93567
  imaging ~ 93452-93461, 93563-93568
  injection ~ 93454-93461, 93563-93568
  left heart
    by transapical puncture ~ 93462
    with ventriculography ~ 93452, 93458, 93459, 93565
  pacemaker ~ 33210
  right heart ~ 93451, 93456, 93503
    congenital cardiac anomalies ~ 93530
Cardiac electroversion ~ 92960-92961
Cardiac event recorder
  implantation ~ 33282
  removal ~ 33284
Cardiac magnetic resonance imaging (CMRI) ~ 75557-75563, 75565
Cardiac massage, thoracotomy ~ 32160
Cardiac muscle ~ see myocardium
Cardiac neoplasm ~ 33120-33130
Cardiac output, indicator dilution ~ 93561-93562
Cardiac pacemaker ~ see heart, pacemaker
Cardiac rehabilitation ~ 93797-93798
Cardiac septal defect ~ 33813-33814
Cardiac transplantation ~ 33935, 33945
Cardiectomy, donor ~ 33930, 33940
Cardioassist ~ 92970-92971
Cariography
  acoustic ~ 93799
  arterial pressure waveform analysis ~ 93050
Cardiolipin antibody ~ 86147
Cardiology
  diagnostic
    acoustic cardiography ~ 93799
    arrhythmia induction ~ 93618-93624, 93640, 93641, 93653-93656
    arterial pressure waveform analysis ~ 93050
    atrial electrogram ~ 93615, 93616
      esophageal recording ~ 93615, 93616
    bioimpedence derived analysis ~ 93701
    echocardiography
      Doppler ~ 76827-76828, 93306-93308, 93320-93350
        intracardiac ~ 93662
        transesophageal ~ 93318
        transthoracic ~ 93303-93317
      congenital cardiac anomoly
        fetal ~ 76825, 76826
        doppler, fetal ~ 76827, 76828
        transesophageal ~ 93315-93317
        transthoracic ~ 93303, 93304
    ergonovine provocation test ~ 93024
    external heart rate data recording
      for nocturnal epilepsy seizure ~ 0381T-0386T
    intracardiac pacing and mapping
      3-D mapping ~ 93613, 93654
      follow-up study ~ 93624
      localization ~ 93631
      stimulation and pacing ~ 93623

Cardiology ~ *continued*

   intracardiac pacing and recording
      arrhythmia induction ~ 93618-93624, 93653-93654, 93656
      bundle of His ~ 93600, 93619-93620, 93653-93654, 93656
      comprehensive ~ 93619-93622
      intra-atrial ~ 93602, 93610, 93616, 93656
      left ventricular ~ 93654
      right ventricle ~ 93603, 93653, 93656
      tachycardia sites ~ 93609
      ventricular ~ 93612
   intravascular ultrasound ~ 92978-92979
   perfusion imaging ~ see nuclear medicine ~ 78460-78461
   stress tests
      cardiovascular ~ 93015-93018
      drug induced ~ 93024
      multiple gated acquisition (MUGA) ~ 78473
   temperature gradient studies ~ 93740
   tilt table evaluation ~ 93660
   venous pressure determination ~ 93784, 93786, 93788, 93790
   therapeutic
      ablation ~ 93650, 93653-93656
      cardioassist ~ 92970-92971
      cardioversion ~ 92960-92961
      intravascular ultrasound ~ 92978-92979
      pacing, transcutaneous, temporary ~ 92953
      rehabilitation ~ 93668, 93797-93798
      thrombolysis ~ 92975-92977
      thrombolysis, coronary ~ 92977
      valvuloplasty, percutaneous ~ 92986-92990

Cardiomyotomy ~ 32665, 43330-43331

Cardioplasty ~ 43320

Cardiopulmonary bypass
   establishment ~ 34714, 34716, 34833
   with transcatheter aortic valve replacement ~ 33367-33369

Cardiopulmonary resuscitation ~ 92950

Cardiotomy ~ 33310-33315

Cardiovascular stress test ~ 93015-93018

Cardiovascular system
   medical services ~ 92950-93799
   surgical procedures ~ 33000-39599

Cardioversion ~ 92960-92961

Care, custodial ~ see nursing facility services

Care, neonatal intensive ~ see intensive care, neonatal

Care, self ~ see self care

Care plan oversight services ~ 99339-99340, 99374-99380

Carneous mole ~ see abortion

Carnitine ~ 82379

Carotene ~ 82380

Caroticum, glomus ~ 60605, 60600

Carotid artery
   aneurysm repair
      vascular malformation or carotid-cavernous fistula ~ 61710
   bypass graft ~ 33891, 35501-35510, 35601-35606, 35642
   catheterization ~ 36100, 36221-36224, 36227-36228
   decompression ~ 61590-61591, 61596
   embolectomy ~ 34001
   evauation ~ 93895
   excision ~ 60605
   ligation ~ 37600-37606, 61611-61612
   stenosis imaging ~ 3100F
   stent placement ~ 37217, 37218
   thrombectomy ~ 34001
   thromboendarterectomy ~ 35301, 35390
   transection ~ 61611-61612
   transposition ~ 33889, 35691, 35694-35695

Carotid body
   lesion
      carotid artery ~ 60605
      excision ~ 60600

Carotid, common
   intima-media thickness (IMT) study ~ 0126T

Carpals, incision and drainage ~ 25035

Carpal bone ~ see wrist
   arthroplasty, with implant ~ 25443
   cyst, excision ~ 25130-25136
   dislocation
      closed treatment ~ 25690
      open treatment ~ 25695
   excision ~ 25210-25215
      partial ~ 25145

Carpal bone ~ *continued*
   fracture
      closed treatment ~ 25622, 25630
      open treatment ~ 25628, 25645
      without manipulation ~ 25630
      with manipulation ~ 25624, 25635
   incision and drainage ~ 26034
   insertion, vascular pedicle ~ 25430
   osteoplasty ~ 25394
   repair ~ 25431-25440
   sequestrectomy ~ 25145
   tumor, excision ~ 25130-25136

Carpal tunnel, injection, therapeutic ~ 20526

Carpal tunnel syndrome, decompression ~ 64721

Carpectomy ~ 25210-25215

Carpometacarpal joint
   arthrodesis
      hand ~ 26843-26844
      thumb ~ 26841-26842
   arthrotomy ~ 26070
   biopsy, synovium ~ 26100
   dislocation
      closed treatment ~ 26670
         with manipulation ~ 26675-26676
      open treatment ~ 26685-26686
   exploration ~ 26070
   fusion
      hand ~ 26843-26844
      thumb ~ 26841-26842
   removal, foreign body ~ 26070
   repair ~ 25447
   synovectomy ~ 26130

Cartilage, arytenoid ~ 31560-31561

Cartilage, ear ~ 21235

Cartilage graft
   ear to face ~ 21235
   harvesting ~ 20910-20912
   rib to face ~ 21230

Cartilaginous exostoses ~ 69140

Case management services
   On-line ~ 98969, 99444
   team conferences ~ 99366-99368
   telephone calls ~ 98966-98968, 99441-99443

Cast ~ see also splint ~ 29358
   body, Risser jacket ~ 29010-29015
   body cast
      halo ~ 29000
      upper body and head ~ 29040
      upper body and legs ~ 29046
      upper body and one leg ~ 29044
      upper body only ~ 29035
   clubfoot ~ 29450
   cylinder ~ 29365
   finger ~ 29086
   hand ~ 29085
   hip ~ 29305-29325
   leg, rigid total contact ~ 29445
   long arm ~ 29065
   long leg ~ 29345-29355, 29365, 29450
   long leg brace ~ 29358
   patellar tendon bearing (PTB) ~ 29435
   removal ~ 29700
   repair ~ 29720
   short arm ~ 29075
   short leg ~ 29405-29435, 29450
   shoulder ~ 29049-29058
   walking ~ 29355, 29425
      revision ~ 29440
   wedging ~ 29740-29750
   windowing ~ 29730
   wrist ~ 29085

Casting, unlisted services and procedures ~ 29799

Castration ~ see orchiectomy

Castration, female ~ 58262-58263, 58291-58292, 58552, 58554, 58661, 58940-58943

Cat scan ~ see CT scan

Cataract
- discission ~ 66820-66821
- excision ~ 66830
  - dilated fundus evaluation ~ 2021F
- incision ~ 66820-66821
  - laser ~ 66821
  - stab incision ~ 66820
- removal/extraction
  - extracapsular ~ 66982, 66984
  - intracapsular ~ 66983
  - presurgical measurement/calculation ~ 3073F

Catecholamines ~ 80424, 82382-82384
- blood ~ 82383
- urine ~ 82382

Cathepsin-D ~ 82387

Catheter ~ see also cannulization; venipuncture
- aspiration
  - nasotracheal ~ 31720
  - tracheobronchial ~ 31725
- bladder ~ 51701-51703
  - irrigation ~ 51700
- blood specimen collection ~ 36592, 37799
- conversion
  - biliary drainage, external to internal- external~ 47535
  - nephrostomy to nephroureteral ~ 50434
- declotting ~ 36593, 36861
- drainage
  - biliary
    - conversion ~ 47535
    - exchange ~ 47536
    - placement ~ 47533, 47534
    - removal ~ 47537
  - peritoneal ~ 49406, 49407
  - pleural ~ 32556, 32557
  - retroperitoneal ~ 49406, 49407
  - spinal ~ 62272
  - ureteral ~ 50693
  - ventricular ~ 62162, 62164
  - visceral ~ 49405
- electrode array ~ 63650
- embolization ~ 61624, 61626
  - peritoneal ~ 49423
- exchange
  - nephrostomy ~ 50435
  - with biliary stent placement ~ 47538-47540
- flow directed ~ 93503
- for cystourethroscopy ~ 52320-52356
- for embolectomy ~ 34001, 34051, 34101-34111, 34151, 34201, 34203
- intraperitoneal, tunneled
  - insertion
    - laparoscopic ~ 49324
    - open ~ 49421
    - percutaneous ~ 49418-49419
- obstruction clearance ~ 36595-36596
- occlusion ~ 61624, 61626
- removal
  - central venous ~ 36589
  - foreign body ~ 37197
  - peritoneal ~ 49422
  - spinal cord ~ 62355
  - with biliary stent placement ~ 47538-47540
- repair
  - central venous ~ 36575
  - intraperitoneal ~ 49325
- replacement
  - central venous ~ 36580-36581, 36584
  - shunt system ~ 62230
  - subarachnoid ~ 62194
  - subdural ~ 62194
  - ventricular ~ 62225
- repositioning ~ 36597
- transcatheter therapy
  - arterial for chemotherapy ~ 36640
  - arterial, intracranial ~ 61650, 61651
  - epidural or subarachnoid ~ 62320-62327
  - newborn ~ 36660
  - thrombolysis ~ 37211-37214
- ureteral
  - manometric studies ~ 50396, 50686
  - ureterography ~ 50684

Catheterization ~ see also catheter
- abdomen ~ 49421
- abdominal artery ~ 36245-36248
- aorta ~ 36160, 36200
- arterial system ~ 36215, 36245-36248
  - cutdown ~ 36625
  - intracatheter/needle ~ 36100-36140
  - percutaneous ~ 36620
- bile duct, percutaneous
  - conversion ~ 47535
  - exchange ~ 47536
  - placement ~ 47533, 47534
  - removal ~ 47537
- bladder ~ 51045, 51102, 51702-51703
- brachiocephalic artery ~ 36215-36218
- brain ~ 61210
  - replacement ~ 62160, 62194, 62225
- breast ~ 19296-19298, 20555, 41019
- bronchus ~ 31643, 31710
- cardiac ~ see cardiac catheteriztaion
- carotid artery ~ 36100, 36221-36224, 36227-36228
- cerebral artery ~ 36215
- cholecystostomy ~ 47490
- coronary artery ~ 93455
- cystourethroscopy, ejaculatory duct ~ 52010
  - ureteral ~ 52005
- dialysis ~ 36901-36903, 49418, 49419, 49421
- ear, middle ~ 69799
- electrode array ~ 63650
- eustachian tube ~ 69799
- extremity, artery ~ 36140
- fallopian tube ~ 58345, 74742
- gastrointestinal ~ 43241
- hepatic vein ~ 37182-37183
- innominate artery ~ 36222-36223, 36225
- intracardiac, ablation ~ 93650, 93653-93657
- intraperitoneal, tunneled ~ 49324, 49421
- jejunum, for enteral ~ 44015
- kidney, percutaneous
  - for nephrostomy ~ 50432
  - nephroureteral ~ 50433
- legs ~ 36245-36248
- nasotracheal ~ 31720
- newborn, umbilical vein ~ 36510
- pelvic artery ~ 36245-36248
- peripheral ~ 36568-36571
- pleural cavity ~ 32550-32552
- portal vein ~ 36481, 37182-37183
- pulmonary artery ~ 36013-36015
- radioelement application ~ 519296-19297, 20555, 31643, 41019, 55875, 55920
- removal
  - fractured catheter ~ 37197
  - obstructive material
    - intracatheter ~ 36596
    - pericatheter ~ 36595
- renal artery ~ 36251-36254
- salivary duct ~ 42660
- skull ~ 61107
- spinal cord ~ 62350-62351
- subclavian artery ~ 36225
- thoracic artery ~ 36215-36218
- tracheobronchi ~ 31725
- umbilical artery ~ 36660
- umbilical vein ~ 36510
- ureter
  - endoscopic ~ 50553, 50572, 50953, 50972, 52005
  - injection ~ 50684
  - manometric studies ~ 50396, 50686
  - via kidney ~ 50693
- uterus, radiology ~ 58340
- vena cava ~ 36010
- venous
  - central line ~ see Central venous catheter
  - first order ~ 36011
  - intracatheter/needle ~ 36000
  - organ blood ~ 36500
  - second order ~ 36012
  - umbilical vein ~ 36510

Catheterization ~ continued
  vertebral artery ~ 36100, 36221, 36225-36226, 36228
  ventricular ~ 61020-61026, 61210-61215, 62160-62162, 62164, 62225
Cauda equina ~ see spinal cord
  decompression ~ 63005-63011, 63017, 63047-63048, 63055-63057,
    63087-63091
  exploration ~ 63005-63011, 63017
Cauterization
  anal fissure ~ 46940-46942
  cervix ~ 57522
    cryocautery ~ 57511
    electro or thermal ~ 57510
    laser ablation ~ 57513
  chemical, granulation tissue ~ 17250
  everted punctum ~ 68705
  lower esophageal sphincter, thermal, via endoscopy ~ 0057T
  nasopharyngeal hemorrhage ~ 42970
  nose, hemorrhage ~ 30901-30906
  skin lesion ~ 11055-11057, 17000-17004
  skin tags ~ 11200-11201
  turbinate mucosa ~ 30801-30802
Cavernitides, fibrous ~ see Peyronie disease
Cavernosography, corpora ~ 54230
Cavernosometry ~ 54231
Cavities, pleural ~ see pleural cavity
Cavus foot correction ~ 28309
CBC ~ see blood cell count ~ 85025-85027
CCL4 ~ 84600
CCU visit ~ see Critical Care Services
CD142 antigens ~ see thromboplastin
CD143 antigens ~ 82164
CD4 ~ 86360
CD8 ~ 86360
CEA ~ 82378
Cecil repair ~ 46744-46746
Cecostomy ~ 44300
  contrast ~ 49465
  insertion of tube ~ 49442
  laparoscopic ~ 44188
  obstructive material removal ~ 49460
  radiological evaluation of tube ~ 49465
  tube replacement ~ 49450
Celiac plexus
  destruction ~ 64680
  injection
    anesthetic ~ 64530
    neurolytic ~ 64680
Celiac trunk artery ~ see artery, celiac
Celioscopy ~ see endoscopy, peritoneum
Celiotomy ~ 49000
  abdomen, for staging ~ 49220
Cell count, body fluid ~ 89050-89051
Cell, blood ~ see blood cell
Cell, islet ~ 86341
Cell, mother ~ see stem cell
Cell-stimulating hormone, interstitial ~ 80418, 80426, 83002
Cellobiase ~ 82963
Cellular function assay ~ 86352
Cellular inclusion ~ see inclusion bodies
Central shunt ~ 33764
Central nervous system assessments or tests ~ 96101-96120
Central venous catheter placement
  insertion
    central ~ 36555-36558
    peripheral ~ 36568-36569
  repair ~ 36575
  replacement ~ 36580-36585
  repositioning ~ 36597
Central venous catheter removal ~ 36589
Cephalic version, of fetus, external ~ 59412
Cephalocele ~ 62120-62121
Cephalogram, orthodontic ~ 70350
Cerclage, cervix ~ 57700
  abdominal ~ 59325
  removal under anesthesia ~ 59871
  vaginal ~ 59320
Cerebellopontine angle tumor ~ see brainstem; skull base surgery ~
  61480, 61510, 61518, 61520-61521, 61526-61530, 61545, 62164
Cerebral cortex decortication ~ see decortication
Cerebral death ~ 95824
Cerebral hernia ~ 62120-62121

Cerebral perfusion analysis ~ 0042T
Cerebral ventriculographies ~ see ventriculography
Cerebral vessels, occlusion ~ 61623
Cerebrose ~ 82760
Cerebrospinal fluid ~ 86325
  nuclear imaging ~ 78630-78650
Cerebrospinal fluid leak ~ 63744
  brain, repair ~ 61618-61619, 62100
  nasal/sinus endoscopy, repair ~ 31290-31291
  spinal cord, repair ~ 63707-63709
Cerebrospinal fluid shunt ~ 63740, 63746
  creation ~ 62180-62192, 62200-62223
  irrigation ~ 62194
  removal ~ 62256-62258
  replacement ~ 62160, 62194, 62225-62230
  reprogramming ~ 62252
Ceruloplasmin ~ 82390
Cerumen
  removal
    with instrumentation ~ 69210
    with irrigation/lavage ~ 69209
Cervical cap ~ 57170
Cervical lymphadenectomy ~ 38720-38724
Cervical mucus penetration test ~ 89330
Cervical plexus, injection, anesthetic ~ 64413
Cervical pregnancy ~ 59140
Cervical puncture ~ 61050-61055
Cervical smears ~ 88141, 88155, 88164-88167, 88174-88175
Cervical spine ~ see vertebra, cervical
Cervical sympathectomy ~ 64802
Cervicectomy ~ 57530
Cervicography ~ 0003T
Cervicoplasty ~ 15819
Cervicothoracic ganglia ~ 64510
Cervix ~ see cytopathology
  amputation, total ~ 57530
  biopsy ~ 57500, 57520
    colposcopy ~ 57454-57455, 57460
  cauterization ~ 57522
    cryocautery ~ 57511
    electro or thermal ~ 57510
    laser ablation ~ 57513
  cerclage ~ 57700
    abdominal ~ 59325
    removal under anesthesia ~ 59871
    vaginal ~ 59320
  cervicography ~ 0003T
  colposcopy ~ 57452-57461
  conization ~ 57461, 57520-57522
  curettage, endocervical ~ 57454, 57456, 57505
  dilation
    canal ~ 57800
    stump ~ 57558
  dilation and curettage ~ 57558
  ectopic pregnancy ~ 59140
  excision
    radical ~ 57531
    stump
      abdominal approach ~ 57540-57545
      vaginal approach ~ 57550-57556
    total ~ 57530
  exploration, endoscopy ~ 57452
  insertion
    dilation ~ 59200
    laminaria ~ 59200
    prostaglandin ~ 59200
    sensor, fetal oximetry ~ 0021T
  repair, cerclage ~ 57700
    abdominal ~ 59325
    suture ~ 57720
    vaginal ~ 59320
  unlisted services and procedures ~ 58999
Cesarean delivery
  antepartum care ~ 59610, 59618
  delivery
    after attempted vaginal delivery ~ 59618
      delivery only ~ 59620
      postpartum care ~ 59622
      routine care ~ 59610, 59618
  delivery only ~ 59514

Cesarean delivery ~ *continued*
  postpartum care ~ 59515
  routine care ~ 59510
  tubal ligation at time of ~ 58611
  with hysterectomy ~ 59525
Chalazion, excision ~ 67805
  multiple
    different lids ~ 67805
    same lid ~ 67801
  single ~ 67800
  under anesthesia ~ 67808
Challenge tests, bronchial/ingestion ~ 95070-95071, 95076-95079
Chambers procedure ~ 28300
Change
  catheter
    bile duct ~ 75984
  fetal position
    by manipulation ~ 59412
  tube or stent
    endoscopic
      bile or pancreatic duct ~ 43275-43276
Change, gastrostomy tube ~ 43760
Change of, dressing ~ 15852
Cheek
  bone
    excision ~ 21030, 21034
    fracture
      closed treatment with manipulation ~ 21355
      open treatment ~ 21360-21366
    reconstruction ~ 21270
  fascia graft ~ 15840
  muscle graft ~ 15841-15845
  muscle transfer ~ 15845
Cheilectomy, metatarsophalangeal joint release ~ 28289, 28291
Cheiloplasty ~ 40650-40654
Cheiloschisis ~ 30460-30462, 40700-40761
Cheilotomy ~ 40806
Chemical cauterization, granulation tissue ~ 17250
Chemical exfoliation ~ 17360
Chemical peel ~ 15788-15793
Chemiluminescent assay ~ 82397
Chemistry tests ~ 84999
Chemocauterization
  corneal epithelium ~ 65435
    with chelating agent ~ 65436
Chemodenervation
  anal sphincter ~ 46505
  bladder ~ 52287
  eccrine glands
    axillae ~ 64650
    other area ~ 64653
  extraocular muscle ~ 67345
  extremity muscle ~ 64642-64645
  facial muscle ~ 64612, 64615
  guidance
    electrical stimulation ~ 95873
    needle electromyography ~ 64617, 95874
  neck muscle ~ 64615, 64616
  salivary gland ~ 64611
  trunk muscle ~ 64646-64647
Chemonucleolysis ~ 62292
Chemosurgery
  destruction of benign lesion ~ 17110-17111
  skin lesion ~ 17000-17004, 17110-17111, 17270, 17280
Chemotaxis assay ~ 86155
Chemotherapy
  administration ~ 96401-96549
  arterial catheterization ~ 36640
  bladder instillation ~ 51720
  brain ~ 61517
  CNS ~ 61517, 96450
  extracorporeal circulation, extremity ~ 36823
  home infusion procedures ~ 99601-99602
  intra-arterial ~ 96420-96425
  intralesional ~ 96405-96406
  intramuscular ~ 96401-96402
  intravenous ~ 96409-96417
  kidney instillation ~ 50391
  peritoneal cavity ~ 96446
    catheterization ~ 49418

Chemotherapy ~ *continued*
  pleural cavity ~ 96440
  pump services
    implantable ~ 96530
    maintenance ~ 95990-95991
    portable ~ 96520
  reservoir filling ~ 96542
  subcutaneous ~ 96400
  supply of agent ~ 96545
  unlisted services and procedures ~ 96549
  ureteral instillation ~ 50391
  venous cannulation ~ 36823
Chest ~ see mediastinum; thorax
  angiography ~ 71275
  artery, ligation ~ 37616
  CT scan ~ 71250-71275
  exploration, blood vessel ~ 35820
  magnetic resonance imaging (MRI) ~ 71550-71552
  repair, blood vessel ~ 35211-35216
    with other graft ~ 35271-35276
    with vein graft ~ 35241-35246
  ultrasound ~ 76604
  wound exploration, penetrating ~ 20101
  X-ray ~ 71045-71048
    with computer-aided detection ~ 0174T, 0175T
Chest, funnel ~ 21740, 21742-21743
Chest cavity, bypass graft ~ 35905
  endoscopy
    exploration ~ 32601-32606
    surgical ~ 32650-32665
Chest wall
  debridement ~ 11044, 11047
  manipulation ~ 94667, 94668
  mechanical oscillation ~ 94669
  reconstruction ~ 49904
    with lung tumor resection ~ 32504
    trauma ~ 32820
  repair ~ 32905
    closure ~ 32810
    fistula ~ 32906
    lung hernia ~ 32800
  resection ~ 32503
  tumor
    cryoablation ~ 32994
    excision ~ 19260, 19271, 19272
  unlisted services and procedures ~ 32999
Chest wall fistula ~ 32906
Chevron procedure ~ 28296
Chiari osteotomy of the pelvis ~ 27158
Chicken pox vaccine ~ 90716
Child procedure ~ 48140-48146, 48150, 48153-48154, 48160
Chin
  repair
    augmentation ~ 21120
    osteotomy ~ 21121-21123
Chinidin ~ 80194
Chiropractic manipulation (CMT) ~ 98940-98943
Chiropractic treatment
  spinal
    extraspinal ~ 98940-98943
Chlamydia
  antibody ~ 86631-86632
  antigen detection
    amplified nucleic acid probe ~ 87486, 87491
    direct nucleic acid probe ~ 87485, 87490
    direct optical ~ 87810
    enzyme immunoassay ~ 87320
    immunofluorescence ~ 87270
    nucleic acid quantification ~ 87487, 87492
  culture ~ 87110
Chloramphenicol ~ 82415
Chloride
  blood ~ 82435
  other source ~ 82438
  spinal fluid ~ 82438
  urine ~ 82436
Chloride, methylene ~ 84600
Chlorinated hydrocarbons ~ 82441
Chlorohydrocarbon ~ 82441
Chlorpromazine ~ 80342-80344
Choanal atresia, repair ~ 30540-30545

Cholangiography
  injection ~ 47531, 47532
  intraoperative ~ 74300-74301
  postoperative ~ 47531
  repair
    with bile duct exploration ~ 47700
    with cholecystectomy ~ 47563, 47605, 47620
  transhepatic, laparoscopically guided ~ 47579
  with
    conversion of drainage catheter ~ 47535
    exchange of drainage catheter ~ 47536
    placement
      of access to small bowel ~ 47541
      of drainage catheter ~ 47533, 47534
      of stent ~ 47538-47540
    removal of drainage catheter ~ 47537
Cholangiopancreatography ~ see bile duct; pancreatic duct
  endoscopic retrograde (ERCP)
    with ablation
      lesion/polyp/tumor ~ 43278
    with biopsy ~ 43261
    with collection of specimen(s) ~ 43260
    with exchange stent ~ 43276
    with optical endomciroscopy ~ 0397T
    with papillotomy ~ 43262
    with placement stent ~ 43274
    with pressure measurement, sphincter of Oddi ~ 43263
    with removal, foreign body ~ 43275
    with removal, stent ~ 43275, 43276
    with removal/destruction of calculus ~ 43264-43265
    with sphincterotomy ~ 43262, 43274, 43276, 43277
    with transendoscopic balloon dilation ~ 43277
  intraoperative ~ 74300, 74301
  postoperative ~ 47531
Cholangiostomy ~ 47400
Cholangiotomy ~ 47400
Cholecalciferol ~ 82306
Cholecystectomy
  any method
    with cholangiography ~ 47563, 47605, 47620
    with choledochoenterostomy ~ 47612
    with exploration common duct ~ 47564, 47610
  donor liver ~ 47143
  excision ~ 47600-47620
  laparoscopic ~ 47562-47564
Cholecystenterostomy
  direct ~ 47720
    with gastroenterostomy ~ 47721, 47741
  laparoscopic ~ 47570
  Roux-en-Y ~ 47740-47741
Cholecystography ~ 47490, 74290-74291
Cholecystostomy
  open ~ 47480
  percutaneous ~ 47490
  with peripancreatic drain placement ~ 48000
Choledochoplasty ~ 47701
Choledochoscopy ~ 47550
Choledochostomy ~ 47420-47425
Choledochotomy ~ 47420-47425
Choledochus, cyst ~ see cyst, choledochal
Cholera vaccine
  live, for oral use ~ 90625
Cholesterol
  measurement ~ 83721
  serum ~ 82465
  testing ~ 83718-83719
Cholinesterase, blood ~ 82480-82482
Choline esterase I ~ 82013
Choline esterase II ~ 82480-82482
Cholylglycine, blood ~ 82240
Chondroitin sulfate ~ 82485
Chondromalacia patella, repair ~ 27418
Chondropathia patellae ~ 27418
Chondrosteoma ~ 69140
Chopart procedure ~ see radical resection; replantation ~ 28800-28805
Chordotomies ~ 63194-63199
Chorioangioma ~ see lesion, skin
Choriogonadotropin ~ 80414-80415, 84702-84703
Choriomeningitides, lymphocytic ~ 86727
Chorionic gonadotropin ~ 80414, 84702-84704
  stimulation ~ 80414-80415

Chorionic growth hormone ~ 83632
Chorionic tumor ~ 59100, 59870
Chorionic villi ~ 59015
Chorionic villus, biopsy ~ 59015
Choroid, destruction, lesion ~ 67220-67225
Choroid plexus, excision ~ 61544
Christmas factor ~ 85250
Chromaffinoma, medullary ~ 80424
Chromatin, sex ~ 88130
Chromatography
  column ~ see specific analyte in Drug Assay, Pathology and Laboratory
    unspecified non-drug analyte(s) ~ 82542
  column/mass spectrometry ~ see specific analyte in Drug Assay, Pathology and Laborary
    unspecified non-drug analyte(s) ~ 82542
  drug screen ~ 80305-80307, 80320-80377
  gas liquid or HPLC
    typing ~ 87143
    unspecified non-drug analyte(s) ~ 82542
  hemoglobin ~ 83021, 83036
  paper
    sugars ~ 84375
    unlisted chemistruy procedure ~ 84999
  thin layer
    unlisted chemistry procedure ~ 84999
Chromium ~ 82495
Chromogenic substrate assay ~ 85130
Chromosome analysis
  added study ~ 88280-88289
  amniotic fluid ~ 88267, 88269
    culture ~ 88235
  biopsy culture, tissue ~ 88233
  bone marrow culture ~ 88237
  chorionic villus ~ 88267
    5 cells ~ 88261
    15-20 cells ~ 88262
    20-25 cells ~ 88264
    45 cells ~ 88263
    culture ~ 88235
  for breakage syndromes ~ 88245-88249
  fragile-X ~ 88248
  lymphocyte culture ~ 88230
  pregnancy associated plasma protein-A ~ 84163
  skin culture, tissue ~ 88233
  tissue culture ~ 88239
  unlisted services and procedures ~ 88299
Chromotubation ~ 58350
  oviduct ~ 58350
Chronic erection ~ see priapism
Chronic interstitial cystitides ~ 52260-52265
Ciliary body
  cyst
    destruction
      cryotherapy ~ 66720
      cyclodialysis ~ 66740
      cyclophotocoagulation ~ 66710, 66711
      diathermy ~ 66700
      nonexcisional ~ 66770
  destruction ~ 66770
    cyclophotocoagulation ~ 66710, 66711
    endoscopic ~ 66711
  lesion, destruction ~ 66770
  repair ~ 66680
Cimino type procedure ~ 36821
Cinefluorographies ~ see cineradiography
Cineplasty, arm, lower or upper ~ 24940
Cineradiography
  esophagus ~ 74230
  pharynx ~ 70371, 74230
  speech evaluation ~ 70371
  swallowing evaluation ~ 74230
  unlisted services and procedures ~ 76120-76125
Circulation, extracorporeal ~ 33946-33949
Circulation assist
  aortic ~ 33967, 33970
  balloon ~ 33967, 33970
  external ~ 33946-33949
Circulatory assist ~ see circulation assist

Circumcision
  repair ~ 54163
  surgical excision ~ 54161
    newborn ~ 54160
  with clamp or other device ~ 54150
    newborn ~ 54150
Cisternal puncture ~ 61050-61055
Cisternography ~ 70015
  nuclear ~ 78630
Citrate, blood or urine ~ 82507
Clagett procedure ~ 32810
Clavicle
  craterization ~ 23180
  cyst
    excision ~ 23140
      with allograft ~ 23146
      with autograft ~ 23145
  diaphysectomy ~ 23180
  dislocation
    acromioclavicular joint
      closed treatment ~ 23540-23545
      open treatment ~ 23550-23552
    sternoclavicular joint
      closed treatment ~ 23520-23525
      open treatment ~ 23530-23532
    without manipulation ~ 23540
  excision ~ 23170
    partial ~ 23120, 23180
    total ~ 23125
  fracture
    closed treatment
      without manipulation ~ 23500
      with manipulation ~ 23505
    open treatment ~ 23515
  pinning, wiring ~ 23490
  prophylactic treatment ~ 23490
  repair osteotomy ~ 23480-23485
  saucerization ~ 23180
  sequestrectomy ~ 23170
  tumor, excision ~ 23140, 23146, 23200
    with autograft ~ 23145
    radical resection ~ 23200
  X-ray ~ 73000
Clavicula ~ see clavicle
Claviculectomy
  partial ~ 23120
  total ~ 23125
Claw finger repair ~ 26499
Cleft, branchial ~ see branchial cleft
Cleft cyst, branchial ~ 42810-42815
Cleft foot, reconstruction ~ 28360
Cleft hand, repair ~ 26580
Cleft lip
  repair ~ 40700-40761
  rhinoplasty ~ 30460-30462
Cleft palate
  repair ~ 42200-42225
  rhinoplasty ~ 30460-30462
Clinical act of insertion ~ see insertion
Clinical chemistry test ~ 84999
Clinical pathology ~ 80500-80502
Clitoroplasty, intersex state ~ 56805
Closed [transurethral] biopsy of bladder ~ 52224, 52250
Clostridial tetanus ~ 86280
Clostridium botulinum toxin ~ see chemodenervation
Clostridium difficile
  antigen detection
    enzyme immunoassay ~ 87324
  by immunoassay
    with direct optical observation ~ 87803
Clostridium tetani AB ~ 86774

Closure
  anal fistula ~ 46288
  atrioventricular valve ~ 33600
  cystostomy ~ 51880
  enterostomy ~ 44227, 44620, 44625, 44626
    laparoscopic ~ 44227
  lacrimal fistula ~ 68770
  lacrimal punctum
    plug ~ 68761
    thermocauterization, ligation or laser surgery ~ 68760
  left atrial appendage, with implant ~ 33340
  paravalvular leak, percutaneous transcatheter
    aortic valve ~ 93591, 93592
    mitral valve ~ 93590, 93592
  rectovaginal fistula ~ 57300-57308
  semilunar valve ~ 33602
  septal defect
    ventricular ~ 33776, 33780, 93581
  ventricular tunnel ~ 33722
Clot ~ 34401-34490, 35875, 35876, 50230
Clotting disorder ~ 85390
Clotting factor
  factor I (fibrinogen) ~ 85384, 85385
  factor II (prothrombin) ~ 85210
  factor III (thromboplastin) ~ 85730, 85732
  factor IV (calcium) ~ 82310
  factor VII (proconvertin) ~ 85230
  factor VIII (AHG) ~ 85240-85247
    AHG ~ 85240
    related antigen ~ 85244
    von Willebrand factor ~ 85247
    VW factor ~ 85245, 85246
  factor IX (Christmas factor) ~ 85250
  factor X (thrombokinase) (Stuart-Prower factor) ~ 85260
  factor XI (plasma thromboplastin, antecedent [PTA]) ~ 85270
  factor XII (Hageman factor) ~ 85280
  factor XIII (fibrin stabilizing) ~ 85290, 85291
  inhibition ~ 85705
  inhibition test ~ 85347
  partial time ~ 85730-85732
Clotting operation ~ 11765
Clotting test
  protein C ~ 85303, 85307
  protein S ~ 85306
Clotting time ~ 85345-85348
Clot lysis time ~ 85175
Clot retraction ~ 85170
Clubfoot cast ~ 29450
  wedging ~ 29750
CMG ~ 51725-51726
CMRI ~ see cardiac magnetic resonance imaging
CMV ~ see cytomegalovirus
CNPB (continuous negative pressure breathing) ~ 94662
Co-factor I , heparin ~ 85300-85301
CO2 ~ 82374
Coagulation
  blood ~ see blood clot
  defect ~ 85390
  light ~ see photocoagulation
  time ~ 85345-85348
  unlisted services and procedures ~ 85999
Coagulin ~ see thromboplastin
Coagulopathy ~ 85390
  assay ~ 85130
Cocaine
  blood or urine ~ 80353
Coccidioides, antibody ~ 86635
Coccidioidin test ~ 86590
Coccidioidomycosis, skin test ~ 86490
Coccygeal spine fracture ~ 27200, 27202
Coccygectomy ~ 15920-15922, 27080
Coccyx
  excision ~ 27080
  fracture
    closed treatment ~ 27200
    open treatment ~ 27202
  tumor, excision ~ 49215
  X-ray ~ 72220
Cochlear device
  insertion ~ 69930
  programming ~ 92601-92604

Codeine, alkaloid screening ~ 80323
Cofactor protein S ~ 85305, 85306
Coffey operation ~ 58400
Cognitive function tests ~ 96101-96125 (see also neurology, diagnostic)
Cognitive skills development
one-on-one patient contact ~ 97127
Cold agglutinin ~ 86156-86157
Cold pack treatment ~ 97010
Cold preservation ~ see cryopreservation
Colectomy
partial ~ 44140
  laparoscopic ~ 44213
  with anastomosis ~ 44140
    laparoscopic ~ 44204, 44207-44208
  with coloproctostomy ~ 44145-44146
  with colostomy ~ 44141-44144
    laparoscopic ~ 44206, 44208
  with ileocolostomy, laparoscopic ~ 44205
  with ileostomy ~ 44144
  with ileum removal ~ 44160
  with splenic flexure mobilization ~ 44139
    laparoscopic ~ 44213
  with transcanal approach ~ 44147
total
  laparoscopic ~ 44210-44212
    with creation of ileal reservoir ~ 44211
    with ileoanal anastomosis ~ 44211
    with ileoproctostomy ~ 44210
    with ileostomy ~ 44210-44212
    with protectomy ~ 44211--44212
    with rectal mucosectomy ~ 44211
    without protectomy ~ 44210
  open
    with complete proctectomy ~ 45121
    with ileoproctostomy ~ 44150
    with ileostomy ~ 44150-44151
    with protectomy ~ 44155-44158
Collagen cross links
any method ~ 82523
cornea ~ 0402T
Collagen injection ~ 11950-11954
Collar bone ~ see clavicle
Collateral ligament
ankle repair ~ 27695-27698
interphalangeal joint ~ 26545
knee
  joint repair ~ 27409
  repair ~ 27405
metacarpophalangeal joint ~ 26540-26542
Collection and processing
allogeneic blood harvesting of stem cells ~ 38205
autologous blood
  harvesting of stem cells ~ 38206
  intraoperative ~ 86891
  preoperative ~ 86890
brushings and washings
  abdomen ~ 49320
  anus ~ 46600, 46601
  biliary tract ~ 47552
  colon ~ 44388, 45300, 45330, 45378
  duodenum ~ 43235, 44360, 44376
  esophagus ~ 43197, 43200, 43235
  hepatobiliary system ~ 43260
  ileum ~ 44376, 44380
  jejunum ~ 43235
  omentum ~ 49320
  peritoneum ~ 49320
  rectum ~ 45300, 45330
  small intestine ~ 44385
  stomach ~ 43235
radiologic guidance ~ 75989
specimen
  capillary blood ~ 36416
  duodenum ~ 43756-43757
  for dark field examination ~ 87164
  ear ~ 36416
  hematoma ~ 10140
  sputum ~ 89220
  stomach ~ 43754
  sweat ~ 89230

Collection and processing ~ *continued*
tears ~ 83861
venous blood ~ 36415, 36591-36592
venous catheter ~ 36592
stem cells
  harvesting
    allogenic blood ~ 38205
    autologous blood ~ 38206, 86890-86891
  processing ~ 38210-38215
Colles fracture ~ 25600-25605
Colles fracture reversed ~ see Smith fracture
Collins syndrome, Treacher ~ 21150-21151
Collis procedure ~ 43283, 43842-43843
Colon ~ see also colon-sigmoid
biopsy ~ 44025, 44100, 44322
  endoscopic ~ 44389, 45380, 45391, 45392
colostomy, revision ~ 44340-44346
colotomy ~ 44322
  colostomy ~ 44320
CT scan
  colonography ~ 74261-74263
destruction
  lesion ~ 44401, 45383
  tumor ~ 44401, 45383
endoscopy
  biopsy ~ 44389, 45380, 45391, 45392
  destruction
    lesion ~ 44401
    tumor ~ 44401, 45383
  dilation ~ 45386
  exploration ~ 44388, 45378, 45381, 45386
  hemorrhage ~ 44391, 45382
  injection, submucosal ~ 45381
  placement, stent ~ 45389
  removal
    foreign body ~ 44390, 45379
    polyp ~ 44392, 45384-45385
    tumor ~ 45384-45385
  specimen collection ~ 44388, 45380
  ultrasound ~ 45391-45392
  via colotomy ~ 45399
  via stoma ~ 44402
excision
  partial ~ 44140-44141, 44143-44147, 44160
    laparoscopic ~ 44204-44208
  total ~ 44150-44151, 44155-44158
    laparoscopic ~ 44210-44212
exploration ~ 44025
  endoscopic ~ 44388, 45378, 45381, 45386
hemorrhage, endoscopic control ~ 44391, 45382
hernia ~ 44050
incision
  creation, stoma ~ 44320-44322
  exploration ~ 44025
  revision, stoma ~ 44340-44346
lavage, intraoperative ~ 44701
lesion
  destruction ~ 45383
  excision ~ 44110-44111
lysis, adhesions ~ 44005
obstruction ~ 44025-44050
reconstruction, bladder from ~ 50810
removal
  foreign body ~ 44025, 44390, 45379
  polyp ~ 44392
repair
  diverticula ~ 44605
  fistula ~ 44650-44661
  hernia ~ 44050
  malrotation ~ 44055
  obstruction ~ 44050
  ulcer ~ 44605
  volvulus ~ 44050
  wound ~ 44605
stoma closure ~ 44620-44625
suture
  diverticula ~ 44605
  fistula ~ 44650-44661
  plication ~ 44680
  stoma ~ 44620-44625

Colon ~ continued
  ulcer ~ 44605
  wound ~ 44605
  tumor, destruction ~ 45383
  ultrasound, endoscopic ~ 45391-45392
  X-ray with contrast, barium enema ~ 74270-74280
Colon-sigmoid ~ see also colon
  biopsy, endoscopy ~ 45331
  dilation, endoscopy ~ 45340
  endoscopy
    ablation
      polyp ~ 45346
      tumor ~ 45346
    biopsy ~ 45331
    dilation ~ 45340
    exploration ~ 45330, 45335
    hemorrhage ~ 45334
    needle biopsy ~ 45342
    placement, stent ~ 45327, 45347
    removal
      foreign body ~ 45332
      polyp ~ 45333, 45338
      tumor ~ 45333, 45338
    ultrasound ~ 45341-45342
    volvulus ~ 45337
  exploration, endoscopy ~ 45330, 45335
  hemorrhage, endoscopy ~ 45334
  needle biopsy, endoscopy ~ 45342
  removal, foreign body ~ 45332
  repair, volvulus, endoscopy ~ 45337
  ultrasound, endoscopy ~ 45341-45342
Colonna procedure ~ 27120
Colonography, CT scan
  diagnostic ~ 74261-74262
  screening ~ 74263
Colonoscopy
  biopsy ~ 45380, 45392
  collection specimen ~ 45380
    via colotomy ~ 45399
  destruction, lesion or tumor ~ 45383
  dilation ~ 45386
  follow-up interval ~ 0528F-0529F
  hemorrhage control ~ 45382
  injection, submucosal ~ 45381
  placement, stent ~ 45389
  removal
    foreign body ~ 45379
    polyp ~ 45384-45385
    tumor ~ 45384-45385
  surveillance intervals ~ 0528F-0529F
  ultrasound ~ 45391-45392
  via stoma ~ 44388-44390
    biopsy ~ 44389
    destruction
      of lesion ~ 44401
      of tumor ~ 44401
    exploration ~ 44388
    hemorrhage ~ 44391
    placement, stent ~ 44402
    removal
      foreign body ~ 44390
      polyp ~ 44392, 44394
      tumor ~ 44392, 44394
Colorrhaphy ~ 44604
Color vision examination ~ 92283
Colostomy ~ 44320, 45563
  abdominal, establishment ~ 50810
  home visit ~ 99505
  intestine, large, with suture ~ 44605
  perineal, establishment ~ 50810
  revision ~ 44340
    paracolostomy hernia ~ 44345-44346
Colotomy ~ 44025
Colpectomy
  partial ~ 57106
  total ~ 57110
  with hysterectomy ~ 58275-58280
    with repair of enterocele ~ 58280
Colpo-urethrocystopexy ~ 58152, 58267, 58293
  Marshall-Marchetti-Krantz procedure ~ 58152, 58267, 58293
  Pereyra procedure ~ 58267, 58293

Colpoceliocentesis ~ 57020
Colpocentesis ~ 57020
Colpocleisis ~ 57120
Colpohysterectomies ~ 58260, 58290-58294, 58550, 58553
Colpoperineorrhaphy ~ 57210
Colpopexy
  extra-peritoneal ~ 57282
  intra-peritoneal ~ 57283
  laparoscopic ~ 57425
  open ~ 57280
Colpoplasty ~ see repair, vagina
Colporrhaphy
  anterior ~ 57240, 57289
    with insertion of mesh ~ 57267
    with insertion of prosthesis ~ 57267
  anteroposterior ~ 57260-57265
    with enterocele repair ~ 57265
    with insertion of mesh ~ 57267
    with insertion of prosthesis ~ 57267
  nonobstetrical ~ 57200
  posterior ~ 57250
    with insertion of mesh ~ 57267
    with insertion of prosthesis ~ 57267
Colposcopy
  biopsy ~ 56821, 57421, 57454-57455, 57460
  cervix ~ 57421, 57452-57461
  exploration ~ 57452
  loop electrode excision ~ 57460
  loop electrode conization ~ 57461
  perineum ~ 99170
  vagina ~ 57420-57421
  vulva ~ 56820
    biopsy ~ 56821
Colpotomy
  drainage, abscess ~ 57010
  exploration ~ 57000
Colprosterone ~ 84144
Columna vertebralis ~ see spine
Combined heart-lung transplantation ~ 33935
Combined right and left heart cardiac catheterization ~ 93453
Comedones, removal ~ 10040
Commissurotomy, right ventricle ~ 33476-33478
Common sensory nerve, repair/suture ~ 64834
Common truncus ~ 33786
Communication device
  non-speech-generating ~ 92605-92606
  speech-generating ~ 92606-92609
Community/work reintegration training ~ 97537
Compatibility test, blood ~ 86920
Complement
  antigen ~ 86160
  fixation test ~ 86171
  functional activity ~ 86161
  hemolytic, total ~ 86162
  total ~ 86162
Complete blood count (CBC) ~ see also blood cell count ~ 85025-85027
Complete colectomy ~ see colectomy, total
Complete pneumonectomy ~ 32488
Complete transposition of great vessels ~ 33770-33781
Complex, factor IX ~ 85250
Complex, vitamin B ~ 78270-78272
Component removal, blood ~ 36511-36516
Composite graft ~ 15760-15770, 35681-35683
Compound B ~ 82528
Compound F ~ 80400-80406, 80418-80420, 80436, 82530
Compression, nerve, median ~ 64721
Computed tomographic scintigraphy ~ 78607
Computed tomography (CT) ~ see CT scan; specific anatomic site
Computer assisted navigation, orthopedic surgery ~ 0054T-0055T, 20985
Computer analysis
  acoustic recording, heart sounds ~ 93799
  digital image data, mammography ~ 77065-77067
  electrocardiographic data ~ 93228
  motion analysis ~ 96000-96004
  pediatric home apnea monitor ~ 94776
Computer-aided detection
  lesion, chest radiograph ~ 0174T, 0175T
  mammography ~ 77065-77067
    MRI ~ 0159T
Computerized emission tomography ~ 78607
Concentration, hydrogen ion ~ see pH

Concentration, minimum inhibitory ~ 87186
Concentration of specimen ~ 87015
Concentric procedure ~ 28296
Conchae nasale ~ 30930
Concha Bullosa resection
  with nasal/sinus endoscopy ~ 31240
Conduction, nerve ~ see nerve conduction
Conduit, ileal ~ 50690
Condyle
  humerus, fracture
    closed treatment ~ 24576-24577
    open treatment ~ 24579
    percutaneous ~ 24582
  mandibular ~ 21247, 21465
  metatarsal, excision ~ 28288
  phalanges, toe, excision ~ 28126
Condylectomy
  temporomandibular joint ~ 21050
  with skull base surgery ~ 61596-61597
Condyloma, destruction ~ 54050-54065
Conference, medical, with interdisciplinary team ~ 99366-99368
Congenital arteriovenous malformation ~ see arteriovenous malformation
Congenital elevation of scapula ~ 23400
Congenital heart septum defect ~ 33813-33814
Congenital kidney abnormality
  nephrolithotomy ~ 50070
  pyeloplasty ~ 50405
  pyelotomy ~ 50135
Congenital laryngocele ~ 31300
Congenital vascular anomaly ~ see vascular malformation
Conisation ~ 57461, 57520-57522
Conization, cervix ~ 57461, 57520-57522
Conjoint psychotherapy ~ 90846-90849, 99510
Conjunctiva
  biopsy ~ 68100
  cyst, incision and drainage ~ 68020
  fistulize for drainage, with tube ~ 68750
    without tube ~ 68745
  follicle expression ~ 68040
  graft ~ 65150, 65782
    harvesting ~ 68371
  injection ~ 68200
  insertion
    aqueous drainage device ~ 0449T, 0450T, 0474T
    stent ~ 68750
  lesion
    destruction ~ 68135
    excision ~ 68110, 68115
      with adjacent sclera ~ 68130
  reconstruction ~ 68320, 68325, 68326, 68328
    with flap ~ 67971, 68360, 68362
  removal, foreign body ~ 65205, 65210
  repair
    eyelid wound ~ 67961, 67966
      direct closure ~ 65270, 67930, 67935
      mobilization and rearrangement ~ 65272, 65273
    symblepharon
      division ~ 68340
      with graft ~ 68335
      without graft ~ 68330
  unlisted services and procedures ~ 68399
Conjunctivo-tarso-Muller resection ~ 67908
Conjunctivocystorhinostomy ~ 68745-68750
Conjunctivodacryocystostomy ~ 68745-68750
Conjunctivoplasty ~ 68320-68330
  reconstruction cul de sac, with extensive rearrangement ~ 68326
    with graft ~ 68326
      buccal mucous membrane ~ 68328
  with extensive rearrangement ~ 68320
    with graft ~ 68320
      buccal mucous membrane ~ 68325
Conjunctivorhinostomy
  with tube ~ 68750
  without tube ~ 68745
Conscious sedation ~ see sedation
Construction
  finger, toe to hand transfer ~ 26551-26556
  neobladder ~ 51596
  vagina
    with graft ~ 57292
    without graft ~ 57291

Consultation(s) ~ 99241-99255
  clinical pathology ~ 80500-80502
  initial inpatient ~ 99251-99255
    new or established patient ~ 99251-99255
  office and/or other outpatient ~ 99241-99245
    new or established patient ~ 99241-99245
  psychiatric, with family ~ 90887
  radiation therapy, radiation physics ~ 77336-77370
  surgical pathology ~ 88321-88325
    intraoperation ~ 88329-88332
  X-ray ~ 76140
Consumption test, antiglobulin ~ 86880
Contact lens services
  fittings and prescription ~ 92071-92072, 92310-92313
  modification ~ 92325
  prescription ~ 92314-92317
  replacement ~ 92326
Continuous negative pressure breathing (CNPD) ~ 94662
Continuous positive airway pressure (CPAP) ~ 94660
Contouring
  silicone injections ~ 11950-11954
  tumor, facial bone ~ 21029
Contraception
  cervical cap
    fitting ~ 57170
  diaphragm
    fitting ~ 57170
  intrauterine device (IUD)
    insertion ~ 58300
    removal ~ 58301
Contraceptive capsules, implantable
  removal ~ 11976
Contraceptive device, intrauterine ~ 58300-58301
Contracture
  elbow, release
    with radical resection of capsule ~ 24149
  palm, release ~ 26121-26125
  thumb, release ~ 26508
Contracture of palmar fascia ~ 26040-26045
Contralateral ligament repair, knee ~ 27405
Contrast aortogram ~ 75600-75605, 75630, 93567
Contrast bath therapy ~ see also physical medicine/therapy/occupational therapy ~ 97034
Contrast material
  injection via peritoneal catheter ~ 49424
Contrast phlebogram ~ see venography
Contusion ~ see hematoma
Converting enzyme, angiotensin ~ 82164
Coombs test ~ 86880
Copper ~ 82525
Coprobilinogen, feces ~ 84577
Coproporphyrin ~ 84120
Coracoacromial ligament release ~ 23415
Coracoid process transfer ~ 23462
Cord
  spermatic ~ see spermatic cord
  spinal ~ see spinal cord
  vocal ~ see vocal cords
Cordectomy ~ 31300
Cordocentesis ~ 59012
Cordotomy ~ 63194-63199
Corectomy ~ see excision, iris
Coreoplasty ~ 66762
Cornea
  astigmatism
    relaxing incision ~ 65772
    wedge resection ~ 65775
  biopsy ~ 65410
  collagen cross links ~ 0402T
  curettage ~ 65435-65436
    with chelating agent ~ 65436
  epithelium, excision ~ 65435-65436
    with chelating agent ~ 65436
  hysteresis determination ~ 92145
  implantation, corneal ring segments ~ 65785
  incision
    for astigmatism correction ~ 65772

Cornea ~ continued
  lesion
    destruction ~ 65450
    excision ~ 65400
      with graft ~ 65426
      without graft ~ 65420
  pachymetry ~ 76514
  prosthesis ~ 65770
  pterygium, excision ~ 65420
  puncture ~ 65600
  relaxing incisions ~ 65772-65775
  repair
    astigmatism ~ 65772-65775
    wedge resection ~ 65775
    with glue ~ 65286
    wound
      nonperforating ~ 65275
      perforating ~ 65280-65285
      tissue glue ~ 65286
  reshape
    epikeratoplasty ~ 65765
    keratomileusis ~ 65760
    keratoprosthesis ~ 65767
  scraping, smear ~ 65430
  tattoo ~ 65600
  thickness measurement ~ 76514
  transplantation
    amniotic membrane ~ 65780
    autograft or homograft
      allograft preparation ~ 0290T, 65757
      endothelial ~ 65756
      lamellar ~ 65710
      penetrating ~ 65730-65755
    for aphakia ~ 65750
  unlisted procedure ~ 66999
Coronary
  atherectomy, percutaneous ~ 92995-92996
  thrombectomy, percutaneous ~ 92973
Coronary angioplasty, transluminal balloon ~ see percutaneous
  transluminal angioplasty
Coronary artery
  angiography ~ 93454-93461
  angioplasty ~ 92920, 92921
    with atherectomy ~ 92933, 92934, 92937, 92938, 92941, 92943, 92944
    with stent placement ~ 92928, 92929, 92933, 92934, 92937, 92938, 92941, 92943, 92944
  atherectomy ~ 92924-92295
    with angioplasty ~ 92933, 92934, 92937, 92938, 92941, 92943, 92944
    with stent ~ 92933, 92934, 92937, 92938, 92941, 92943, 92944
  endarterectomy ~ 33572
  fractional flow reserve ~ 0501T-0504T
  graft
    anomaly ~ 33503, 33504
    arterial bypass ~ 33533-33536
      harvest ~ 35600
    arterial-venous bypass ~ 33517-33519, 33521-33523
    internal mammary artery graft ~ 4110F
    venous bypass ~ 33510-33516
      harvest ~ 35500
  insertion, stent ~ 92928, 92929
  ligation ~ 33502
  obstruction severity assessment ~ 0206T
  placement, radiation delivery device ~ 92974
  reconstruction ~ 33863, 33864
  repair, anomaly ~ 33500-33507
  revascularization ~ 92937, 92938, 92941, 92943, 92944
  thrombectomy ~ 92973
  thrombolysis ~ 92975, 92977
  translocation ~ 33506, 33507
  ventricular restoration ~ 33548
Coronary artery bypass graft (CABG) ~ 33503-33505, 33510-33516
  arterial ~ 33533-33536
  arterial-venous ~ 33517-33523
  beta-blocker administration ~ 4115F
  harvest, upper extremity artery ~ 35600
  internal mammary artery graft ~ 4110F
  reoperation ~ 33530
  venous ~ 33510-33516
Coronary endarterectomy ~ 33572
Coroner's exam ~ 88045
Coronoidectomy, temporomandibular joint ~ 21070

Corpectomy ~ 63101-63103
Corpora cavernosa
  corpus spongiosum shunt ~ 54430
  glans penis fistulization ~ 54435
  injection ~ 54235
  irrigation, priapism ~ 54220
  saphenous vein shunt ~ 54420
  X-ray with contrast ~ 74445
Corpora cavernosography ~ 74445
Corpus callosum, transection ~ 61541
Corpus vertebrae (vertebrale) ~ see vertebral body
Correction (of)
  cleft palate ~ 42200-42225
  lid retraction ~ 67911
  malrotation of duodenum ~ 44055
  syndactyly ~ 26560-26562
  ureteropelvic junction ~ 50400-50405, 50544
Cortex decortication, cerebral ~ see decortication
Cortical mapping
  transection, by electric stimulation ~ 95961-95962
Corticoids ~ 83491
Corticoliberin ~ 80412
Corticosteroids
  blood ~ 83491
  urine ~ 83491
Corticosteroid-binding globulin ~ 84449
Corticosteroid-binding protein ~ 84449
Corticosterone, blood or urine ~ 82528
Corticotropic releasing hormone (CRH) ~ 80412
Cortisol ~ 80400-80406, 80418-80420, 80436, 82530
  stimulation ~ 80412
  total ~ 82533
Cortisol binding globulin ~ 84449
Costectomy ~ 19260-19272, 32900
Costen syndrome ~ see temporomandibular joint (TMJ)
Costotransversectomy ~ 21610
Cothromboplastin ~ 85230
Cotte operation ~ see revision ~ 58400-58410
Cotton procedure, Bohler procedure ~ 28405
Counseling and/or risk factor reduction intervention ~ 99401-99429
  alcohol and/or substance abuse ~ 99408-99409
  behavior change ~ 99406-99409
  smoking and tobacco use ~ 99406-99407
Count
  blood cell ~ see blood cell count
  blood platelet ~ 85008
  cell ~ 89050-89051
  complete blood ~ 85025-85027
  erythrocyte ~ 85032-85041
  leukocyte ~ 85032, 85048, 89055
  reticulocyte ~ 85044-85045
Counters, cell ~ 89050-89051
Countershock, electric ~ 92960-92961
Coventry tibial wedge osteotomy ~ 27455-27457, 27705, 27709-27712
Cowper's gland, excision ~ 53250
Coxiella burnetii, antibody ~ 86638
Coxsackie, antibody ~ 86658
CPAP ~ 94660
CPK, blood ~ 82550-82552
CPR (cardiopulmonary resuscitation) ~ 92950
Cranial bone
  halo, thin skull osteology ~ 20664
  reconstruction, extracranial ~ 21181-21184
  tumor, excision ~ 61563-61564
Cranial halo ~ 20661
Cranial nerve ~ see specific nerve
  avulsion ~ 64732-64760, 64771
  decompression ~ 61458, 61460, 64716
  implantation ~ 64568-64569
    electrode ~ 64553
  injection
    anesthetic ~ 64400, 64408
    neurolytic ~ 64600, 64605, 64610
  insertion, electrode ~ 64553
  neuroplasty ~ 64716
  release ~ 64716
  removal, neurostimulator ~ 64570
  repair, suture, with or without graft ~ 64864-64865
  section ~ 61460
  transection ~ 64732-64760, 64771
  transposition ~ 64716

Cranial nerve II ~ see optic nerve
Cranial nerve V (five) ~ see trigeminal nerve
Cranial nerve VII (seven) ~ see facial nerve
Cranial nerve X (ten) ~ see vagus nerve
Cranial nerve XI ~ see accessory nerve
Cranial nerve XII (twelve) ~ 64868
Cranial tongs
  application/removal ~ 20660
  removal ~ 20665
Craniectomy ~ see also craniotomy ~ 61501
  abscess drainage ~ 61320-61321
  anesthesia ~ 00211
  decompression ~ 61322-61323, 61340, 61343
  drainage ~ 61320-61321
  evacuation of hematoma ~ 61312-61315
  excision
    abscess ~ 61514, 61522
    bone lesion ~ 61500
    fenestration of cyst ~ 61516, 61524
    meningioma ~ 60512, 61519
    tumor ~ 61500, 61510, 61518, 61520, 61521
  exploratory ~ 61304-61305, 61458
  extensive, for multiple suture craniosynostosis ~ 61558, 61559
  for electrode ~ 61860-61870
  release stenosis ~ 61550-61552
  section ~ 61450, 61460
  with craniotomy ~ 61316, 61530
  wound treatment ~ 61571
Craniofacial, unlisted procedures ~ 21299
Craniofacial separation
  closed treatment ~ 21431
  open treatment ~ 21432-21436
  wire fixation ~ 21431
Craniomegalic skull, reduction ~ 62115-62117
Craniopharyngioma, excision ~ 61545
Cranioplasty ~ 62120
  autograft ~ 62146-62147
  bone graft ~ 61316, 62146-62147
  bone graft retrieval ~ 62148
  encephalocele repair ~ 62120
  skull defect ~ 62140-62141, 62145
Craniostenosis ~ see craniosynostosis
Craniosynostosis
  bifrontal craniotomy ~ 61557
  extensive craniectomy ~ 61558-61559
Craniotomy ~ see burr hole; drill hole; puncture ~ 61501
  bifrontal ~ 61557
  decompression ~ 61322-61323
  exploratory ~ 61304-61305
  for craniosynostosis ~ 61556-61557
  for encephalocele ~ 62121
  for implant of neurostimulators ~ 61850
  frontal ~ 61556
  parietal ~ 61556
  surgery ~ 61312-61315, 61320-61323, 61546, 61570-61571, 61582-61583, 61590, 61592, 61760, 62120
  with bone flap ~ 61510-61516, 61526-61530, 61533-61545, 61566-61567
Cranium ~ see skull
Craterization
  calcaneus ~ 28120
  clavicle ~ 23180
  femur ~ 27070-27071, 27360
  fibula ~ 27360, 27641
  hip ~ 27070
  humerus ~ 23184, 24140
  ileum ~ 27070
  metacarpal ~ 26230
  metatarsal ~ 28122
  olecranon process ~ 24147
  phalanges
    finger ~ 26235-26236
    toe ~ 28124
  pubis ~ 27070
  radius ~ 24145, 25151
  scapula ~ 23182
  talus ~ 28120
  tarsal ~ 28122
  tibia ~ 27360, 27640
  ulna ~ 24147, 25150

Creatine ~ 82553-82554
  blood or urine ~ 82540
Creatine kinase, total ~ 82550
Creatine phosphokinase
  blood ~ 82552
  total ~ 82550
Creatinine
  blood ~ 82565
  clearance ~ 82575
  other source ~ 82570
  urine ~ 82570-82575
Creation
  arteriovenous fistula ~ 35686, 36825, 36830
  catheter exit site ~ 49436
  cavopulmonary anastomosis ~ 33622
  colonic reservoir ~ 45119, 45397
  complete heart block ~ 93650
  defect ~ 40720
  ileal reservoir ~ 44158, 44211, 45113
  iliac artery conduit ~ 34833
  lesion ~ 61720, 61735, 61790, 63600
  mucofistula ~ 44144
  pericardial window ~ 32659, 33025
  recipient site ~ 15002-15005
  shunt
    cerebrospinal fluid ~ 62200
    subarachnoid, lumbar-peritoneal ~ 63740
    subarachnoid-subdural ~ 62190
    ventriculo ~ 62200
  sigmoid bladder ~ 50810
  speech prosthesis ~ 31611
  stoma
    bladder ~ 51980
    kidney ~ 50395
    renal pelvis ~ 50395
    tympanic membrane ~ 69433, 69436
    ureter ~ 50860
  subcutaneous pocket with glucose sensor insertion ~ 0446T, 0448T
  ventral hernia ~ 39503
  vertebral cavity ~ 22513-22515
CRH ~ see corticotropic releasing hormone (CRH)
Cricoid cartilage split, larynx ~ 31587
Cricothyroid membrane, incision ~ 31605
Cristobalite ~ 84285
Critical care services
  cardiopulmonary resuscitation ~ 92950
  evaluation and management ~ 99291-99292
  interfacility transport ~ 99466-99467
  ipecac administration for poison ~ 99175
  neonatal
    initial ~ 99468
    intensive ~ 99477
    low birth weight infant ~ 99478-99479
    subsequent ~ 99469
  pediatric
    initial ~ 99471, 99475
    interfacility transport ~ 99466-99467
      supervision ~ 99485-99486
    subsequent ~ 99472, 99476
  remote ~ 0188T-0189T
Cross finger flap ~ 15574
Crossmatch ~ 86920-86922
Crossmatching, tissue ~ 86812-86817, 86821
Cruciate ligament
  arthroscopic repair ~ 29888-29889
  repair ~ 27407-27409
    knee, with collateral ligament ~ 27409
Cryoablation
  nerve, percutaneous ~ 0440T-0442T
Cryofibrinogen ~ 82585
Cryofixation ~ see cryopreservation
Cryoglobulin ~ 82595
Cryopreservation
  cells ~ 38207-38209, 88240-88241
  embryo ~ 89258
  for transplantation ~ 32850, 33930, 33940, 44132, 47133, 47140, 48550, 50300-50320, 50547
  freezing and storage ~ 38207, 88240
  sperm ~ 89259
  testes ~ 89335

Cryopreservation ~ *continued*
  thawing
    embryo ~ 89352
    oocytes ~ 89353
    reproductive tissue ~ 89354
    sperm ~ 89356
Cryosurgery ~ 17000-17286, 47371, 47381
  ablation
    fibroadenoma, breast ~ 19105
    lesion/tumor
      chest wall ~ 32994
      liver ~ 47371, 47381, 47383, 50250
      pleura ~ 32994
  bladder ~ 52214
    tumor ~ 52234, 52235, 52240
  hemorrhoids ~ 46999
  lesion
    anus ~ 46916, 46924
    bladder ~ 51030, 52224
    ear ~ 17280-17284, 17286
    eyelid ~ 17280-17284, 17286
    face ~ 17280-17284, 17286
    lips ~ 17280-17284, 17286
    kidney ~ 50250
    mouth ~ 17280-17284, 17286, 40820
    nose ~ 17280-17284, 17286
    penis ~ 54056, 54065
    skin ~ 17000, 17003, 17004, 17106-17108, 17110, 17111
    urethra ~ 52224
    vagina ~ 57061, 57065
    vulva ~ 56501, 56515
  prostate ~ 52214, 55873
  trichiasis ~ 67825
  urethra ~ 52214
Cryotherapy
  ablation, renal tumor ~ 50593
  acne ~ 17340
  bronchial stenosis ~ 31641
  destruction
    bronchial tumor ~ 31641
    ciliary body ~ 66720
    retinopathy ~ 67227
  lesion
    cornea ~ 65450
    retina ~ 67208
  retinal detachment
    prophylaxis ~ 67141
    repair ~ 67101, 67107, 67108, 67113
  trichiasis, correction ~ 67825
Cryptectomy ~ 46999
Cryptococcus
  antibody ~ 86641
  antigen detection, enzyme immunoassay ~ 87327
Cryptococcus neoformans, antigen detection, enzyme immunoassay ~ 87327
Cryptorchism ~ 54550-54560
Cryptosporidium
  antigen detection
    direct fluorescence ~ 87272
    enzyme immunoassay ~ 87328
Crystal identification, any body fluid ~ 89060
CSF ~ see cerebrospinal fluid leak
CT angiography ~ 75574
CT scan
  3-D rendering ~ 76376-76377
  abdomen ~ 74150-74178, 75635
  arm ~ 73200-73206
  bone, density study ~ 77078
  brain ~ 3111F-3112F
  drainage ~ 75989
  follow-up study ~ 76380
  guidance
    localization ~ 77011
    needle placement ~ 77012
    parenchymal tissue ablation ~ 77013
    radiation therapy ~ 77014
    vertebroplasty ~ 72292
    visceral tissue ablation ~ 77013

CT scan ~ *continued*
  heart ~ 75571-75574
    hemorrhage documented ~ 3110F
    infarction documented ~ 3110F
    lesion documented ~ 3110F
  unlisted services and procedures ~ 76497
  with contrast ~ 70460
    abdomen ~ 74160, 74177
    arm ~ 73201
    brain ~ 0042T, 70460
    cerebral blood flow/volume ~ 0042T
    ear ~ 70481
    face ~ 70487
    head ~ 70460
    leg ~ 73701
    maxilla ~ 70487
    neck ~ 70491
    orbit ~ 70481
    pelvis ~ 72193, 74177
    sella tucica ~ 70481
    spine
      cervical ~ 72126
      lumbar ~ 72132
      thoracic ~ 72129
    thorax ~ 71260
  without and with contrast
    abdomen ~ 74170, 74174-74175, 74178, 75635
    arm ~ 73202
    brain ~ 70470, 70496
    chest ~ 71275
    ear ~ 70482
    face ~ 70488
    head ~ 70470, 70496
    leg ~ 73702-73706, 75635
    maxilla ~ 70488
    neck ~ 70492, 70498
    orbit ~ 70482
    pelvis ~ 72194, 74174, 74178
    sella tucica ~ 70482
    spine, cervical ~ 72127
      lumbar ~ 72133
      thoracic ~ 72130
    thorax ~ 71270
  without contrast ~ 70450
    abdomen ~ 74150, 74176, 74178
    arm ~ 73200
    brain ~ 70450
    colonography ~ 74261-74263
    ear ~ 70480
    face ~ 70486
    head ~ 70450
    leg ~ 73700
    maxilla ~ 70486
    neck ~ 70490
    orbit ~ 70480
    pelvis ~ 72192, 74176, 74178
    sella tucica ~ 70480
    spine
      cervical ~ 72125
      lumbar ~ 72131
      thoracic ~ 72128
    thorax ~ 71250
CT scan, radionuclide ~ 78607
Cuff, rotator ~ 23410-23420
Culdocentesis ~ 57020
Culture
  acid fast bacilli ~ 87116
  amniotic fluid, chromosome analysis ~ 88235
  bacteria
    aerobic ~ 87040-87071, 87077
    anaerobic ~ 87073-87076
    blood ~ 87040
    other ~ 87070-87075
    screening ~ 87081
    stool ~ 87045-87046
    urine ~ 87086-87088
  bone marrow, chromosome analysis ~ 88237
  chlamydia ~ 87110
  chorionic villus, chromosome analysis ~ 88235

Culture ~ *continued*
  fertilized oocyte for in vitro fertilization ~ 89250
    co-culture of embryo ~ 89251
  fungus
    blood ~ 87103
    hair ~ 87101
    identification ~ 87106
    nail ~ 87101
    other ~ 87102
    skin ~ 87101
  lymphocyte
    chromosome analysis ~ 88230
    HLA typing ~ 86821
  mold ~ 87107
  mycobacteria ~ 87118
  mycoplasma ~ 87109
  oocyte/embryo ~ 89250
    co-culture of oocyte/embryo ~ 89251
    extended culture ~ 89272
  pathogen ~ 87081-87084
  skin, chromosome analysis ~ 88233
  tissue
    homogenization ~ 87176
    infectious agent drug resistance ~ 87903-87904
    toxin/antitoxin ~ 87230
    virus ~ 87252-87253
  tubercle bacilli ~ 87116
  typing ~ 87140-87158
  unlisted services and procedures ~ 87999
  yeast ~ 87106
Curettage ~ 59840
  cervix, endocervical ~ 57454, 57456, 57505
  cornea ~ 65435-65436
    chelating agent ~ 65436
  hydatidiform mole ~ 59870
  postpartum ~ 59160
  uterus ~ 58356
Curettage and dilatation ~ 59840
Curettement, skin lesion ~ 11055-11057, 17004, 17110, 17270, 17280
Curietherapy ~ 77761-77778, 77789
Custodial care ~ see domiciliary services; nursing facility services
Cutaneolipectomy ~ *see* lipectomy
Cutaneous-vesicostomy ~ 51980
Cutaneous electrostimulation, analgesic ~ 64550
Cutaneous tag ~ 11200-11201
Cutaneous tissue ~ see integumentary system
CVS ~ 59015
Cyanacobalamin ~ 82607-82608
Cyanide
  blood ~ 82600
  tissue ~ 82600
Cyanocobalamin ~ 82607-82608
Cyclic AMP ~ 82030
Cyclic somatostatin ~ 84307
Cyclocryotherapy ~ 66720
Cyclodialysis, destruction ciliary body ~ 66740
Cyclophotocoagulation, destruction ciliary body ~ 66710
Cyclosporine, assay ~ 80158
Cyst
  abdomen, destruction/excision ~ 49203-49205
  ankle
    capsule ~ 27630
    tendon sheath ~ 27630
  Bartholin's gland excision ~ 56740
    repair ~ 56440
  bile duct ~ 47715
  bladder, excision ~ 51500
  bone
    drainage ~ 20615
    injection ~ 20615
  brain
    drainage ~ 61150-61151, 61156, 62161-62162
    excision ~ 61516, 61524, 62162
  branchial cleft, excision ~ 42810-42815
  breast
    incision and drainage ~ 19020
    puncture aspiration ~ 19000-19001
  calcaneus ~ 28100-28103
  carpal ~ 25130-25136
  choledochal ~ 47715

Cyst ~ *continued*
  ciliary body, destruction ~ 66770
  clavicle, excision ~ 23140-23146
  conjunctiva ~ 68020
  dermoid, nose, excision ~ 30124-30125
  drainage
    contrast injection ~ 49424
    with X-ray ~ 76080
  excision
    cheekbone ~ 21030
    clavicle ~ 23140
      with allograft ~ 23146
      with autograft ~ 23145
    femur ~ 27355-27358
    ganglion ~ see ganglion
    humerus
      with allograft ~ 23156
      with autograft ~ 23155
    hydatid ~ 86171, 86280
    lymphatic ~ 49062, 49323
    maxilla ~ 21030
    mediastinum ~ 32662
    olecranon process
      with allograft ~ 24126
      with autograft ~ 24125
    pericardial ~ 32661
    pilonidal ~ 11770-11772
    radius
      with allograft ~ 24126
      with autograft ~ 24125
    scapula ~ 23140
      with allograft ~ 23146
      with autograft ~ 23145
    ulna
      with allograft ~ 24126
      with autograft ~ 24125
    zygoma ~ 21030
  facial bones
    excision ~ 21030
  femur ~ 27065-27067
  fibula ~ 27635-27638
  ganglion, aspiration/injection ~ 20612
  gums, incision and drainage ~ 41800
  hip ~ 27065-27067
  humerus
    excision ~ 23150-23156, 24110
      with allograft ~ 24116
      with autograft ~ 24115
  ileum ~ 27065-27067
  incision and drainage ~ 10060-10061
    pilonidal ~ 10080-10081
  iris, destruction ~ 66770
  kidney
    ablation ~ 50541
    aspiration ~ 50390
    excision ~ 50280-50290
    injection ~ 50390
    X-ray ~ 74470
  knee
    Baker's ~ 27345
    excision ~ 27347
  leg, lower
    capsule ~ 27630
    tendon sheath ~ 27630
  liver ~ 47010
    drainage ~ 47010
      open ~ 47010
    repair ~ 47300
  lung
    incision and drainage ~ 32200
    removal ~ 32140
  lymph node
    axillary/cervical
      excision ~ 38550-38555
  mandible, excision ~ 21040, 21046-21047
  maxilla, excision ~ 21030, 21048-21049
  mediastinal, excision ~ 39200
  metacarpal ~ 26200-26205
  metatarsal ~ 28104-28107

Cyst ~ *continued*
mouth ~ 41005-41009, 41015-41018
    incision and drainage ~ 40800-40801
mullerian duct, excision ~ 55680
nose, excision ~ 30124-30125
olecranon ~ 24120
ovarian
    excision ~ 58925
    incision and drainage ~ 58800-58805
pancreas ~ 48500
    anastomosis ~ 48520-48540
    excision ~ 48120
pelvis
    aspiration ~ 50390
    injection ~ 50390
pericardial, excision ~ 33050
phalanges
    finger ~ 26210-26215
    toe ~ 28108
pilonidal
    excision ~ 11770-11772
    incision and drainage ~ 10080-10081
pubis ~ 27065-27067
radius ~ 24120, 25120-25126
Rathke's pouch ~ 61545
removal, skin ~ 10040
retroperitoneal, destruction/excision ~ 49203-49205, 58957, 58958
salivary gland creation
    destruction/excision, fistula ~ 42325-42326
    drainage ~ 42409
    excision ~ 42408
scapula, excision ~ 23140-23146
seminal vesicle, excision ~ 55680
skin, puncture aspiration ~ 10160
spinal cord
    aspiration ~ 62268
    incision and drainage ~ 63172-63173
sublingual gland drainage ~ 42409
    excision ~ 42408
talus ~ 28100-28103
tarsal ~ 28104-28107
thyroglossal duct
    excision ~ 60280-60281
    incision and drainage ~ 60000
thyroid gland aspiration ~ 60300
    excision ~ 60200
    injection ~ 60300
tibia ~ 27635-27638
tongue ~ 41000-41006, 41015
ulna ~ 24120, 25120-25126
urachal, bladder, excision ~ 51500
vaginal, excision ~ 57135
wrist ~ 25130-25136
    excision ~ 25111-25112
zygoma
    excision ~ 21030
Cyst ovary ~ see ovary, cyst
Cystatin C ~ 82610
Cystatins, kininogen ~ 85293
Cystectomy
complete ~ 51570
    with bilateral pelvic lymphadenectomy ~ 51575, 51585, 51595
    with continent diversion ~ 51596
    with ureteroileal conduit ~ 51590
    with ureterosigmoidostomy ~ 51580
ovarian ~ 58925
    laparoscopic ~ 58661
partial
    complicated ~ 51555
    reimplantation of ureters ~ 51565
    simple ~ 51550
Cystic hygroma ~ 38550-38555
Cystine, urine ~ 82615
Cystitis, interstitial ~ 52260-52265
Cystography ~ 74430
injection ~ 52281
radiologic ~ 51600
Cystolithotomy ~ 51050
Cystometrogram ~ 51725-51726
Cystoplasty ~ 51800
Cystorrhaphy ~ 51860-51865

Cystoscopy ~ 52000
Cystoscopy, with biopsy ~ 52224, 52250
Cystostomy
change tube ~ 51705-51710
closure ~ 51880
home visit ~ 99505
with fulguration ~ 51020
with insertion radioactive material ~ 51020
with urethrectomy
    female ~ 53210
    male ~ 53215
Cystotomy
excision
    bladder diverticulum ~ 51525
    bladder tumor ~ 51530
    repair of ureterocele ~ 51535
    vesical neck ~ 51520
repair of ureterocele ~ 51535
with calculus basket extraction ~ 51065
with destruction intravesical lesion ~ 51030
with drainage ~ 51040
with fulguration ~ 51020
with insertion
    radioactive material ~ 51020
    ureteral catheter ~ 51045
with removal calculus ~ 51050, 51065
Cystourethrogram, retrograde ~ 51610
Cystourethropexy ~ 51840-51841
Cystourethroplasty ~ 51800-51820
Cystourethroscopy
biopsy ~ 52204, 52224, 52250, 52354
    brush ~ 52007
calibration and/or dilation
    urethral stricture or stenosis ~ 52281, 52630, 52647-52649
catheterization
    ejaculatory duct ~ 52010
    ureteral ~ 52005, 52320
chemodenervation, bladder ~ 52287
dilation
    bladder ~ 52260, 52265
    intra-renal stricture ~ 52343, 52346
    ureter ~ 52341-52342, 52344-52345
    urethra ~ 52281, 52285, 0499T
drug delivery, urethra ~ 0499T
evacuation, clot ~ 52001
examination ~ 52000
female urethral syndrome ~ 52285
incision, ejaculatory duct ~ 52402
injection of implant material ~ 52327
insertion
indwelling ureteral stent ~ 50947, 52332
    radioactive substance ~ 52250
    ureteral guide wire ~ 52334
    urethral stent ~ 52282
lithotripsy ~ 52353
manipulation of ureteral calculus ~ 52330
meatotomy, ureteral ~ 52290-52305
removal
    calculus ~ 52310-52315, 52320-52325, 52352
    foreign body ~ 52310-52315
    urethral stent ~ 52310-52315
resection
    ejaculatory duct ~ 52402
    external sphincter ~ 52277
    tumor ~ 52355
urethral syndrome ~ 52285
vasectomy, transurethral ~ 52402
vasotomy
    transurethral ~ 52402
with direct vision internal urethromtomy ~ 52276
with ejaculatory duct catheterization ~ 52010
with fulguration ~ 52214, 52354
    lesion ~ 52224
    tumor ~ 52234-52240
with internal urethrotomy
    female ~ 52270
    male ~ 52275
with steroid injection ~ 52283
with ureteral catheterization ~ 52005
with ureteral meatotomy ~ 52290-52305
Cytochrome reductase, lactic ~ 83615-83625

Cytogenetic studies
bone marrow ~ 3155F
molecular, DNA probe ~ 88271-88275, 88291, 88365
unlisted services and procedures ~ 88299
Cytomegalovirus
antibody ~ 86644-86645
antigen detection
direct fluorescence ~ 87271
enzyme immunoassay ~ 87332
nucleic acid ~ 87495-87497
Cytometries, flow ~ 88184-88189
Cytopathology
cervical or vaginal
definitive hormone evaluationi ~ 88155
Pap ~ 88164-88167
requiring interpretation by physician ~ 88141
thin layer prep ~ 88142-88143, 88174-88175
evaluation ~ 88172, 88177
fluids, washings, brushings ~ 88104, 88106
forensic ~ 88125
other source ~ 88160-88162
sex chromatin identification ~ 88130, 88140
selective cellular enhancement technique ~ 88112
smears
any other source ~ 88160-88162
brushings ~ 88104
cervical or vaginal
automated screen ~ 88174
hormone evaluation ~ 88155
manual screen ~ 88150, 88153, 88164-88165
washings ~ 88104
unlisted services and procedures ~ 88199
urinary tract specimen ~ 88120-88121
Cytoscopy ~ 52000
Cytosol aminopeptidase ~ 83670
Cytotoxic screen
lymphocyte ~ 86805-86806
percent reactive antibody (PRA) ~ 86807-86808
serum antibodies ~ 86807-86808

D

D and C ~ 59840
D and E ~ 59841
D-xylose absorption test ~ 84620
Dacryoadenectomy
partial ~ 68505
total ~ 68500
Dacryocystectomy ~ 68520
Dacryocystogram ~ 68850, 70170
Dacryocystography ~ 68850, 70170
nuclear imaging ~ 78660
Dacryocystorhinostomy ~ 68720
total, with nasal/sinus endoscopy ~ 31239
Dacryocystostomies ~ 68420
Dacryocystotomy ~ 68420
Daily living activities ~ 97535, 99509
Damus-Kaye-Stansel procedure ~ 33606
Dana operation ~ 63185-63190
Dandy operation ~ 62180, 62200-62201
Dark adaptation examination ~ 92284
Dark field examination ~ 87164-87166
Darrach procedure ~ 25150-25151, 25240
Day test ~ 82270, 82272
De Quervain's disease treatment ~ 25000
Death, brain ~ 95824
Debridement
ankle ~ 29897, 29898
bone ~ 11044, 11047
with open fracture or dislocation ~ 11012
brain ~ 62010
burns ~ 01951-01953, 16010-16030
cartilage ~ 29862, 29877, 29880, 29881, 29885
elbow ~ 29837, 29838
with prosthesis removal ~ 24160, 24164
forearm ~ 25023, 25025

Debridement ~ continued
knee ~ 27441, 27443, 27497, 27499
leg ~ 27892, 27894
lesion, premalignant ~ 96574
liver ~ 47361
mastoid cavity
complex ~ 69222
simple ~ 69220
metatarsophalangeal joint ~ 28289, 28291, 29901, 29902
muscle ~ 11043, 11044, 11046, 11047
infected ~ 11004-11006, 11008
nails ~ 11720, 11721
nonviable tissue ~ 25023, 25025, 27497, 27892-27894
nose
endoscopic ~ 31237
pancreatic tissue ~ 48105
shoulder ~ 29822, 29823
with prosthesis removal ~ 23334, 23335
skin
eczematous ~ 11000, 11001
excision ~ 15920-15999
infected ~ 11000-11006
with open fracture and/or dislocation ~ 11010-11012
subcutaneous tissue ~ 11042-11047
infected ~ 11004-11006
sternum ~ 21627, 21750
wound
non-selective ~ 97602
selective ~ 97597, 97598
wrist joint ~ 29846
nonviable tissue ~ 25023, 25025
Debulking procedure
ovary/pelvis ~ 58952-58954
Decompression ~ see section
arm, lower ~ 24495, 25020-25025
auditory canal, internal ~ 69960
brainstem ~ 61575-61576
cauda equina ~ 63011, 63017, 63047-63048, 63056-63057, 63087-63091
cranial nerve ~ 61458
esophagogastric varices ~ 37181
facial nerve ~ 61590
intratemporal
lateral to geniculate ganglion ~ 69720, 69740
medial to geniculate ganglion ~ 69725, 69745
total ~ 69955
finger ~ 26035
gasserian ganglion
sensory root ~ 61450
hand ~ 26035-26037
intestines
small ~ 44021
jejunostomy
laparoscopic ~ 44201
leg, fasciotomy ~ 27600-27602
nerve ~ 64702-64727
root ~ 63020-63048, 63055-63103
nucleus of disk
lumbar ~ 62287
optic nerve ~ 67570
orbit ~ 61330
removal of bone ~ 67414, 67445
skull ~ 61322-61323, 61340-61345
spinal cord ~ 0375T, 22856, 22858, 62287, 62380, 63001-63017, 63045-63103
cauda equina ~ 63005
tarsal tunnel release ~ 28035
volvulus ~ 45321, 45337
with nasal/sinus endoscopy
optic nerve ~ 31294
orbit wall ~ 31292-31293
wrist ~ 25020-25025
Decortication
lung
endoscopic ~ 32651-32652
with parietal pleurectomy ~ 32320
partial ~ 32225
total ~ 32220
Decubiti ~ see pressure ulcer (decubitus)
Decubitus ulcers ~ see debridement; pressure ulcer (decubitus); skin graft and flap
Deetjeen's body ~ see blood, platelet

Defect, coagulation ~ 85390
Defect, heart septal ~ 33813-33814
Defect, septal closure, atrial ~ see heart, repair, atrial septum
Deferens, ductus ~ see vas deferens
Defibrillation ~ 92960-92961
Defibrillator, implantable
  device evaluation
    electrophysiologic ~ 93644
    interrogation
      in-person
        subcutaneous ~ 93261
        transvenous ~ 93289
      remote ~ 93295, 93296
      peri-procedural ~ 93287
    programming device evaluation
      subcutaneous ~ 93260
      transvenous ~ 93282-93284
  insertion
    electrodes ~ 33202, 33203, 33216, 33217, 33224, 33225, 33271
    pulse generator ~ 33230, 33231, 33240
    system ~ 33249, 33270
  removal
    electrodes ~ 33238, 33243, 33244, 33272
    pulse generator ~ 33241, 33262-33264
  repair, electrodes ~ 33218, 33220
  replacement
    pulse generator ~ 33224, 33262-33264
    system ~ 33249, 33270
  repositioning, electrode ~ 33215, 33273
  wearable device ~ 93745
    data analysis ~ 93292
Deformity, boutonniere ~ 26426-26428
Deformity, Sprengel's ~ 23400
Degenerative, articular cartilage, patella ~ 27418
Degradation products, fibrin ~ 85362-85380
Dehydroepiandrosterone ~ 82626
Dehydroepiandrosterone sulfate ~ 82627
Dehydrogenase, 6-phosphogluconate ~ 84085
Dehydrogenase, alcohol ~ 84588
Dehydrogenase, glucose-6-phosphate ~ 82955-82960
Dehydrogenase, glutamate ~ 82965
Dehydrogenase, isocitrate ~ 83570
Dehydrogenase, lactate ~ 83615-83625
Dehydrogenase, malate ~ 83775
Dehydroisoandrosterone sulfate ~ 82626
Delay of flap, skin graft ~ 15600-15630
Deligation, ureter ~ 50940
Deliveries, abdominal ~ see cesarean delivery
Delivery ~ see cesarean delivery; vaginal delivery
Delorme operation ~ see pericardiectomy
Denervation
  hip
    femoral ~ 27035
    obturator ~ 27035
    sciatic ~ 27035
Denervation, sympathetic ~ 64802-64818
Dens axis ~ 22548
Denver developmental screening test ~ 96100
  Denver shuntpatency test ~ 78291
Denver Krupic procedure ~ 66180
Denver-Krupin procedure ~ 66180
Deoxycorticosterone ~ 82633
Deoxycortisol ~ 80436, 82634
Deoxyephedrine ~ 80324-80326
Deoxyribonuclease antibody ~ 86215
Deoxyribonuclease I ~ 86215
Deoxyribonucleic acid antibody ~ 86225-86226
Depilation ~ see removal, hair
Depletion
  plasma ~ 38214
  platelet ~ 38213
  T-cell ~ 38210
  tumor cell ~ 38211
Deposit calcium ~ 82310, 82330, 82340
Depth electrode
  insertion ~ 61760
Derma-fat-fascia graft ~ 15770
Dermabrasion ~ 15780-15783

Dermatology
  actinotherapy ~ 96900
  microscopic examination of hair ~ 96902
  photochemotherapy
    ultraviolet A treatment ~ 96912, 96913
    ultraviolet B treatment ~ 96910, 96913
  psoriasis laser treatment ~ 96920-96922
  reflectance confocal microscopy (RCM) skin imaging ~ 96931-96936
  unlisted services and procedures ~ 96999
  whole body photography ~ 96904
Dermatoplasty, septal ~ 30620
Dermoid ~ 30124-30125
Derrick-Burnet disease ~ 86000, 86638
Descending abdominal aorta ~ see aorta, abdominal
Desipramine, assay ~ 80335-80337
Desmotomy ~ 23415, 29848
Desoxycorticosterone ~ 82633
Desoxycortone ~ 82633
Desoxyephedrine ~ 80324-80326
Desoxynorephedrin ~ 80324-80326
Desoxyphenobarbital ~ 80188
Desquamation ~ 17360
Destruction
  acne ~ 17340-17360
    cryotherapy ~ 17340
  arrhythmogenic focus, heart ~ 33250-33251, 33261
  bladder ~ 51020, 52214-52224, 52354
  calculus
    bile duct ~ 43265
    kidney ~ 50590
    pancreatic duct ~ 43265
  chemical cauterization, granulation tissue ~ 17250
  chemosurgery ~ 17110-17111
  ciliary body
    cryotherapy ~ 66720
    cyclodialysis ~ 66740
    cyclophotocoagulation ~ 66710-66711
    diathermy ~ 66700
    endoscopic ~ 66711
  cryosurgery ~ 17110-17111
  cyst
    abdomen ~ 49203-49205
    ciliary body ~ 66770
    iris ~ 66770
  endometrial ablation ~ 58356
  endometriomas
    abdomen ~ 49203-49205
  fissure, anal ~ 46940-46942
  hemorrhoids, thermal ~ 46930
  kidney ~ 52354
    endoscopic ~ 50557, 50576
  laser surgery ~ 17110-17111
  lesion
    anal ~ 46900-46917, 46924
    bladder ~ 51030
    choroid ~ 67220-67225
    ciliary body ~ 66770
    conjunctiva ~ 68135
    cornea ~ 65450
    eyelid ~ 67850
    facial ~ 17000-17004, 17280-17286
    gums ~ 41850
    iris ~ 66770
    larynx ~ 31572
    mouth ~ 40820
    nerve plantar ~ 64632
    nose, intranasal ~ 30117-30118
    palate ~ 42160
    penis
      cryosurgery ~ 54056
      electrodesiccation ~ 54055
      extensive ~ 54065
      laser surgery ~ 54057
      simple ~ 54050-54060
      surgical excision ~ 54060
    pharynx ~ 42808
    prostrate ~ 45320
      thermotherapy ~ 53850-53852
        microwave ~ 53850
        radio frequency ~ 53852

1027

Destruction ~ *continued*
  retina
    cryotherapy, diathermy ~ 67208-67218, 67227
    photocoagulation ~ 67210, 67228-67229
    radiation by implantation of source ~ 67218
  skin
    benign ~ 17110-17111
    malignant ~ 17260-17286, 96567
    premalignant ~ 17000-17004, 96567
  spinal cord ~ 62280-62282
  ureter ~ 52341-52342, 52344-52345
  urethra ~ 52400, 53265
  uvula ~ 42160
  vagina
    extensive ~ 57065
    simple ~ 57061
  vascular, cutaneous ~ 17106-17108
  vulva
    extensive ~ 56515
    simple ~ 56501
  nerve ~ 64600-64610, 64620-64640, 64680-64681
    laryngeal, recurrent ~ 31595
  neurofibroma, extensive ~ 0419T, 0420T
  polyp
    aural ~ 69540
    nose ~ 30110-30115
    urethra ~ 53260
  prostate ~ 55873
  prostate tissue, transurethral thermotherapy ~ 53850-53852
  sinus, frontal ~ 31080-31085
  Skene's gland ~ 53270
  skin lesion
    benign ~ 17110, 17111
    malignant ~ 17260-17286
      by photodynamic therapy ~ 96567
    premalignant ~ 17000-17004, 96567, 96573, 96574
  tonsil, lingual ~ 42870
  tumor
    abdomen ~ 49203-49205
    breast, microwave thermotherapy ~ 19499
    colon ~ 45383
    intestines
      large ~ 44401
      small ~ 44369
    mesentery ~ 49203-49205
    pancreatic duct ~ 43272
    rectum ~ 45190, 46937-46938
    retroperitoneal ~ 49203-49205
    urethra ~ 53220
  tumor or polyp, rectum ~ 45320
  turbinate mucosa ~ 30801-30802
  ureter ~ 52354
    endoscopic ~ 50957, 50976
  urethra ~ 52214-52224, 52354
    prolapse ~ 53275
  warts, flat ~ 17110-17111
  with cystourethroscopy ~ 52354
Determination, blood pressure ~ see blood pressure
Developmental testing ~ 96110-96111
Device
  iliac artery occlusion device insertion ~ 34808
  venous access
    collection of blood specimen ~ 36591
    fluoroscopic guidance ~ 36598, 77001
    insertion
      central ~ 36560-36566
      peripheral ~ 36570-36571
    obstruction clearance ~ 36595-36596
      imaging ~ 75901-75902
    removal ~ 36590
    repair ~ 36576
    replacement ~ 36582-36583, 36585
      catheter ~ 36578
  ventricular assist
    extracorporeal
      removal ~ 33990-33993
      replacement ~ 33981
    implantable
      removal ~ 33980
      replacement ~ 33982-33983
Device, intrauterine ~ 58300-58301

Device, orthotic ~ 97760
Device handling ~ 99002
Dexamethasone suppression test ~ 80420
DHA sulfate ~ 82627
Dhea ~ 82626
Dhea sulfate ~ 82627
Diagnosis, psychiatric ~ see psychiatric diagnosis
Diagnostic amniocentesis ~ 59000
Diagnostic aspiration of anterior chamber of eye ~ 65800
Diagnostic radiology ~ 70010-76499
Diagnostic skin and sensitization tests ~ see allergy tests
Diagnostic ultrasound ~ 76506-76999
Diagnostic ultrasound of heart ~ see echocardiography
Dialysis
  anesthesia ~ 01844
  arteriovenous fistula ~ 36831-36833
  end stage renal disease ~ 90951-90970
  hemodialysis ~ 90935-90937, 4051F-4054F
    blood flow study ~ 90940
    plan of care documented ~ 0505F
  hemoperfusion ~ 90997
  hepatitis B vaccine (HepB) ~ 90740, 90747
  introduction
    dialysis circuit ~ 36901-36903
      with transcatheter placement of stent ~ 36906
  Kt/V level ~ 3082F-3084F
  patient training
    completed course ~ 90989
    per session ~ 90993
  peritoneal ~ 90945, 90947, 4055F
    catheter insertion ~ 49418, 49419, 49421
    catheter removal ~ 49422
    home infusion ~ 99601, 99602
    plan of care documented ~ 0507F
  thrombectomy
    dialysis circuit ~ 36904-36906
  with transcatheter stent placemehnt via dialysis circuit ~ 36908
  with transluminal balloon angioplasty via dialysis circuit ~ 36907
  with vascular embolization/occlusion ~ 36909
  unlisted services and procedures ~ 90999
Dialysis, extracorporeal ~ 90935-90937
Diaphragm
  repair
    for eventration ~ 39545
    hernia ~ 39503-39541
    laceration ~ 39501
  resection ~ 39560-39561
  unlisted procedures ~ 39599
  vagina
    fitting ~ 57170
Diaphragm contraception ~ 57170
Diaphysectomy
  calcaneus ~ 28120
  clavicle ~ 23180
  femur ~ 27360
  fibula ~ 27360, 27641
  humerus ~ 23184, 24140
  metacarpal ~ 26230
  metatarsal ~ 28122
  olecranon process ~ 24147
  phalanges
    finger ~ 26235-26236
    toe ~ 28124
  radius ~ 24145, 25151
  scapula ~ 23182
  talus ~ 28120
  tarsal ~ 28122
  tibia ~ 27360, 27640
  ulna ~ 24147, 25150
Diastase ~ 82150
Diastasis ~ see separation
  pelvic ring, closed treatment ~ 27197, 27198
Diathermy ~ 97024
  destruction ciliary body ~ 66700
  lesion retina ~ 67208, 67227
  retinal detachment
    prophylaxis ~ 67141
    repair ~ 67101
  surgical ~ 17000-17286
Dibucaine number ~ 82638
Dichloride, methylene ~ 84600

Dichlorides, ethylene ~ 84600
Dichloroethane ~ 84600
Dichloromethane ~ 84600
Diethylether ~ 84600
Differential count ~ 85032, 85048, 89055
Differentiation reversal factor ~ 85210
Diffusion test, gel ~ 86329-86331
Digestive system, surgical procedures ~ 40490-49999
Digestive tract ~ see gastrointestinal tract
Digit replantation ~ 20816-20822
Digital artery sympathectomy ~ 64820
Digital slit-beam radiograph ~ see scanogram
Digits pinch graft ~ 15050
Digoxin assay ~ 80162
Dihydrocodeinone ~ 80361
Dihydroepitestosterone ~ 80327, 80328
Dihydromorphinone ~ 80361
Dihydrotestosterone ~ 80327, 80328
Dihydroxyethanes ~ 82693
Dihydroxyvitamin D ~ 82652
Dilation ~ 59840
  anal
    endoscopy ~ 46604
    sphincter ~ 45905, 46940
  aortic valve ~ 33930, 33931
  bile duct
    balloon ~ 47542
    endoscopy ~ 43277, 47555, 47556
    stricture ~ 74363
    with stent placement ~ 47538-47540
  biliary ampulla, balloon ~ 47542
  bladder, cystourethroscopy ~ 52260, 52265
  bronchi, endoscopy ~ 31630, 31636
  cerebral vessels ~ 61640-61642
  cervix
    canal ~ 57800
    stump ~ 57558
  colon endoscopy ~ 45386
  colon-sigmoid endoscopy ~ 45340
  esophagus ~ 43450, 43453
    balloon ~ 43195, 43213-43214, 43220, 43233, 43249
    endoscopy ~ 43195-43196, 43212-43213, 43220, 43226, 43229, 43233, 43453
  gastric/duodenol stricture ~ 43245
    surgical ~ 43510
  intestines~ 44615
    endoscopy ~ 44370
    stent placement ~ 44379, 44384, 44402
  kidney ~ 50080-50081, 50395
    intra-renal stricture ~ 52343, 52346
  lacrimal punctum ~ 68801
  larynx
    endoscopy ~ 31528-31529
  nasal/sinus endoscopy ~ 31295-31297
  nasolacrimal duct ~ 68816
  pancreatic duct
    endoscopy ~ 43277
  rectum
    endoscopy ~ 45303, 45327, 45340, 45347, 45386-45389
    sphincter ~ 45910
  salivary duct ~ 42650, 42660
  sclera, aqueous outflow canal ~ 66174-66175
  sinus ostium ~ 31295-31297
  sphincter of Oddi, balloon ~ 47542
  trachea
    endoscopy ~ 31630, 31631, 31636, 31638
  ureter
    balloon ~ 50706
    endoscopy ~ 50553, 50572, 50575, 50953, 50972
    percutaneous ~ 50395
    with cystourethroscopy ~ 52341-52343
      with ureteroscopy ~ 52344-52346
  urethra ~ 52285, 52601, 52630, 52647-52649, 53660, 53661, 53665, 55801, 55821
    stenosis ~ 52281
    stricture ~ 52281, 53600-53601, 53605, 53620-53621, 53655
  vagina ~ 57400

Dilation and curettage ~ 59840
  cervix ~ 57558, 57800
  corpus uteri ~ 58120
  hysteroscopy ~ 58558
  postpartum ~ 59160
  with amniotic injections ~ 59851
  with vaginal suppositories ~ 59856
Dilation and evacuation ~ 59841
  with amniotic injections ~ 59851
Dimethadione ~ 80339-80341
Dioxide, carbon ~ 82374
Dioxide, silicon ~ 84285
Dipeptidyl peptidase A ~ 82164
Diphenylhydantoin ~ 80185-80186
Diphosphate, adenosine ~ 82030
Diphtheria ~ 86648
Dipropylacetic acid assay ~ 80164
Direct pedicle flap formation ~ 15570-15576
Disability evaluation services
  basic life and/or disability evaluation ~ 99450
  work-related or medical disability evaluation ~ 99455-99456
Disarticulation
  ankle ~ 27889
  hip ~ 27295
  knee ~ 27598
  shoulder ~ 23920-23921
  wrist ~ 25920, 25924
    revision ~ 25922
Disc, intervertebral ~ see intervertebral disk
Discectomies ~ 63075-63078
  percutaneous ~ 62287
Discectomy
  additional segment ~ 22226
  arthrodesis
    additional interspace ~ 22534, 22585, 22634
    cervical ~ 22551, 22552, 22554, 22585
    lumbar ~ 0195T, 0196T, 22533, 22534, 22558, 22585, 22630, 62380
    sacral ~ 0195T, 22586
    thoracic ~ 22532, 22534, 22556, 22585, 63077, 63078
  cervical ~ 0375T, 22220, 22551, 22552, 22554, 22856-22858, 63075, 63076
  lumbar ~ 0163T, 0164T, 0195T, 0196T, 22224, 22630, 22633, 22634, 22857
  percutaneous ~ 0274T, 0275T
  sacral ~ 0195T, 22586
  thoracic ~ 22222
  with end plate preparation ~ 22856, 22858
Discharge services
  hospital ~ 99238, 99239
  newborn ~ 99463
  nursing facility ~ 99315, 99316
  observation care ~ 99217, 99234, 99236
Discission
  cataract
    laser surgery ~ 66821
    stab incision ~ 66820
  vitreous strands ~ 67030
Discography
  cervical disk ~ 72285
  injection ~ 62290-62291
  lumbar disk ~ 62287, 72295
  thoracic ~ 72285
Discolysis ~ 62292
Disease
  Erb-Goldflam ~ 95857
  Heine-Medin ~ see polio
  hydatid ~ see echinococcosis
  Lyme ~ see Lyme disease
  Ormond ~ see retroperitoneal fibrosis
  Peyronie ~ see Peyronie disease
  Posada-Wernicke ~ 86490
Disease/organ panel ~ see organ or disease oriented panel
Disk chemolyses, intervertebral ~ 62292
Dislocated joint ~ see dislocation
Dislocation
  acromioclavicular joint, open treatment ~ 23550-23552
  ankle
    closed treatment ~ 27840-27842
    open treatment ~ 27846-27848

Dislocation ~ *continued*
carpal
  closed treatment ~ 25690
  open treatment ~ 25695
carpometacarpal joint ~ 26670
  closed treatment
    with manipulation ~ 26675-26676
  open treatment ~ 26685-26686
  percutaneous fixation ~ 26676
clavicle
  closed treatment ~ 23540-23545
  open treatment ~ 23550-23552
  without manipulation ~ 23540
  with manipulation ~ 23545
closed treatment
  carpometacarpal joint ~ 26670-26675
  metacarpophalangeal ~ 26700-26706
  thumb ~ 26641
elbow
  closed treatment ~ 24600-24605, 24640
  open treatment ~ 24615
hip joint
  closed treatment ~ 27250-27252, 27265-27266
  congenital ~ 27256-27259
  open treatment ~ 27253-27254, 27258-27259
  without trauma ~ 27265-27266
interphalangeal joint
  closed treatment ~ 26770-26775
  open treatment ~ 26785
  percutaneous fixation ~ 26776
  toe
    closed treatment ~ 28660-28665
    open treatment ~ 28675
    percutaneous fixation ~ 26770-26776, 28666
  with manipulation ~ 26770
knee ~ 27560-27562
  closed treatment ~ 27550-27552, 27560-27562
  open treatment ~ 27556-27558, 27566, 27730
  recurrent ~ 27420-27424
lunate
  closed treatment ~ 25690
  open treatment ~ 25695
  with manipulation ~ 25690, 26670-26676, 26700-26706
metacarpophalangeal joint
  closed treatment ~ 26700-26706
  open treatment ~ 26715
metatarsophalangeal joint
  closed treatment ~ 28630-28635
  open treatment ~ 28645
  percutaneous fixation ~ 28636
open treatment ~ 26685-26686
patella
  closed treatment ~ 27560-27562
  open treatment ~ 27566
recurrent ~ 27420-27424
pelvic ring
  closed treatment ~ 27197, 27198
  open treatment ~ 27217, 27218
  percutaneous fixation ~ 27216
  with manipulation ~ 27198
  without manipulation ~ 27197
percutaneous fixation
  metacarpophalangeal ~ 26705
peroneal tendons ~ 27675-27676
radiocarpal joint ~ 25660
radio-ulnar joint ~ 25520-25526
radius
  closed treatment ~ 24640
  with fracture
    closed treatment ~ 24620
    open treatment ~ 24635
shoulder
  closed treatment with manipulation ~ 23650-23655
  open treatment ~ 23660
  with greater tuberosity fracture
    closed treatment ~ 23665
    open treatment ~ 23670
  with surgical or anatomical neck fracture
    closed treatment ~ 23675
    open treatment ~ 23680

Dislocation ~ *continued*
skin debridement ~ 11010-11012
sternoclavicular joint
  closed treatment
    without manipulation ~ 23520
    with manipulation ~ 23525
  open treatment ~ 23530-23532
talotarsal joint
  closed treatment ~ 28570-28575
  open treatment ~ 28546
  percutaneous fixation ~ 28576
tarsal
  closed treatment ~ 28540-28545
  open treatment ~ 28555
  percutaneous fixation ~ 28546
tarsometatarsal joint
  closed treatment ~ 28600-28605
  open treatment ~ 28615
  percutaneous fixation ~ 28606
temporomandibular joint
  closed treatment ~ 21480-21485
  open treatment ~ 21490
thumb
  closed treatment ~ 26641-26645
  open treatment ~ 26665
  percutaneous fixation ~ 26650
  with fracture ~ 26645
    open treatment ~ 26665
    percutaneous fixation ~ 26650-26665
  with manipulation ~ 26641-26650
tibiofibular joint
  closed treatment ~ 27830-27831
  open treatment ~ 27832
vertebra
  additional segment, open treatment ~ 22328
  cervical, open treatment ~ 22318, 22319, 22326
  closed, with manipulation, casting and/or bracing ~ 22315
  lumbar, open treatment ~ 22325
  thoracic, open treatment ~ 22327
wrist
  closed treatment ~ 25660, 25675, 25680
  intercarpal ~ 25660
    open treatment ~ 25670
  open treatment ~ 25670, 25685
  percutaneous fixation ~ 25671
  radiocarpal ~ 25660
    open treatment ~ 25670
  radioulnar
    closed treatment ~ 25675
    open treatment ~ 25676
    percutaneous fixation ~ 25671
  with fracture
    closed treatment ~ 25680
    open treatment ~ 25685
  with manipulation ~ 25660, 25675, 25680

Disorder
blood coagulation ~ 85390
penis ~ see penis
retinal ~ see retina

Displacement therapy
nose ~ 30210

Dissection
cavernous sinus ~ 61613
cranial adhesions ~ 62161
donor organ
  heart ~ 33944
  heart/lung ~ 33933
  kidney ~ 50323, 50325
  liver ~ 47143
  lung ~ 32855
  pancreas ~ 48551
facial nerve ~ 42420
hygroma, cystic
  axillary/cervical ~ 38550-38555
infrarenal aneurysm ~ 34701-34706, 34709-34711, 34830-34832
lymph nodes ~ 38542
mediastinal ~ 60521, 60522
neurovascular ~ 32503
sclera ~ 67107
urethra ~ 54328, 54332, 54336, 54348, 54352

Distention ~ see dilation
Diverticula, Meckel's ~ 44800
Diverticulectomy ~ 44800
  esophagus ~ 43130-43135
  Meckel's ~ 44800
Diverticulum
  bladder ~ see bladder, diverticulum
  Meckel's, excision ~ 44800
  repair, urethra ~ 53400-53405
Division
  isthmus, horseshoe kidney ~ 50540
  muscle, foot ~ 28250
  plantar fascia, foot ~ 28250
Division, scalenus anticus muscle ~ 21700-21705
Di-amphetamine ~ 80324-80326
DMO ~ 80339-80341
DNA antibody ~ 86225-86226
  endonuclease ~ 86215
DNAse antibody ~ 86215
Domiciliary services ~ 99324-99340
  discharge services ~ 99315-99316
  established patient ~ 99331-99333
  new patient ~ 99321-99323
Donor procedures
  conjunctival graft ~ 68371
  heart/lung excision ~ 33930
  heart excision ~ 33940
  liver segment ~ 47140-47142
  stem cells
    donor search ~ 38204
Dopamine ~ 80424, 82382-82384
  blood ~ 82383-82384
  urine ~ 82382, 82384
Doppler echocardiography ~ 76827-76828, 93306-93308, 93320-93350
  intracardiac ~ 93662
  transesophageal ~ 93318
  transthoracic ~ 93303-93317
Doppler scan
  arterial studies
    coronary flow reserve ~ 93571, 93572
    extremities ~ 93922-93924
    fetal
      middle cerebral artery ~ 76821
      umbilical artery ~ 76820
  duplex, transplanted kidney ~ 76776
  intracranial arteries
    complete study ~ 93886
    emboli detection ~ 93892, 93893
    limited study ~ 93888
    vasoreactivity study ~ 93890
  saline infusion sonohysterography (SIS) ~ 76831
  transplanted kidney ~ 76776
Dorsal vertebra ~ 22101, 22112
Dosimetry
  radiation therapy ~ 77300, 77331
    brachytherapy ~ 77316-77318
    intensity modulation IMRT ~ 77301, 77338, 77385, 77386
    special ~ 77331
    teletherapy ~ 77306, 77307, 77321
  Unlisted procedure ~ 77399
Double-stranded DNA ~ 86225-86226
Doxepin
  assay ~ 80335-80337
DPH ~ 80185-80186
Drainage ~ see also excision; incision; incision and drainage
  abdomen
    abdomen fluid ~ 49082-49083
  abscess
    appendix ~ 44900
    brain ~ 61150, 61151, 61320, 61321
    breast ~ 19020
    elbow ~ 23930
    eyelid ~ 67700
    knee ~ 27301
    lef ~ 27603
    liver ~ 47010
    lung ~ 31645, 31646, 32200
    lymph node ~ 38300, 38305

Drainage ~ *continued*
  mouth
    lingual ~ 41000
    masticator space ~ 41009, 41018
    sublingual ~ 41005, 41006, 41015, 42310
    submandibular space ~ 41008, 41017
    submaxillary ~ 42310, 42320
    submental space ~ 41007, 41016
  neck ~ 21501, 21502
  nasal ~ 30000
  nasal septum ~ 30020
  ovary ~ 58820, 58822
  palate ~ 42000
  parotid ~ 42300, 42305
  pelvic ~ 45000, 45020
  perineal ~ 56405
  peri-renal or renal ~ 50020
  peritoneal ~ 49020
  peritonsillar ~ 42700
  pharyngeal ~ 42720, 42725
  prostate ~ 52700, 55720, 55725
  rectum ~ 45005, 45020, 46040
  retroperitoneal ~ 49060, 49323
  shoulder ~ 23030
  skene's gland ~ 53060
  soft tissue
    percutaneous ~ 10030
    subfascial ~ 20005, 22010, 22015
  subdiaphragmatic or subphrenic ~ 49040
  urethra ~ 53040
  uvula ~ 42000
  vestible of mouth ~ 40800, 40801
  with X-ray ~ 75989
  wrist ~ 25028
  amniotic fluid
    diagnostic aspiration ~ 59000
    therapeutic aspiration ~ 59001
  bile duct ~ 47533-47540
  biliary tract ~ 47400, 47420, 47425, 47480
    catheterization ~ 47533, 47534
  bladder ~ 51040, 51080
  brain ~ 62160, 62162, 62164
  bursa
    arm, upper ~ 23930
    foot ~ 28001-28003
    forearm ~ 25028
    hip ~ 26990
    knee ~ 27301
    leg ~ 27604
    palm ~ 26025, 26030
    pelvis ~ 26990
    shoulder ~ 23031
    thigh ~ 27301
    wrist ~ 25028
  cerebrospinal fluid ~ 62272
  cyst
    brain ~ 61150, 61151, 62162
    breast ~ 19000, 19001
    conjunctiva ~ 68020
    dentoalveolar structures ~ 41800
    intramedullary ~ 63172
    liver ~ 47010
    lung ~ 32200
    ovary ~ 58800, 58805
    pilondial ~ 10080, 10081
    skene's gland ~ 53060
    vestible of mouth ~ 40800, 40801
  empyema, chest ~ 32036, 32810
  elbow ~ 23930
  eye ~ 0191T, 0253T, 0376T, 66183
    lacrimal gland ~ 68400
    lacrimal sac ~ 68420
  fetal fluid ~ 59074
  ganglion cyst ~ 20612
  hematoma
    brain ~ 61108, 61154, 61156
    subungual ~ 11740
    superficial ~ 10140
    vagina ~ 57022, 57023

Drainage ~ *continued*
joint
  ankle ~ 27610
  carpometacarpal ~ 26070
  hip ~ 26990, 27030
  interphalangeal ~ 26080, 28024
  intertarsal ~ 28022
  knee ~ 29871
  metacarpophalangeal ~ 26075
  metatarsophalangeal ~ 28022
  midcarpal ~ 25040
  pelvis ~ 26990
  radiocarpal ~ 25040
  sternoclavicular ~ 23044
  thigh ~ 27301
  wrist ~ 29843
liver
  abscess or cyst ~ 47010
lymphocele, endoscopic ~ 49323
onychia ~ 10060-10061
orbit ~ 67405, 67440
pancreas
  pseudocyst ~ 48510
paronychia ~ 10060-10061
pericardial sac ~ 32659
pericardium ~ 33010-33011
pseudocyst
  gastrointestinal, upper
    transmural endoscopic ~ 43240
  pancreas ~ 48510
puncture
  chest ~ 32554-32555
skin ~ 10040-10180
spinal cord
  cerebrospinal fluid ~ 62272
subdural fluid ~ 61000-61001
urethra
  extravasation ~ 53080-53085
ventricular fluid ~ 61020
Drainage implant, glaucoma ~ 66180, 66185
Dressings
burns ~ 16010-16030
change
  anesthesia ~ 15852
Drez procedure ~ see incision, spinal cord ~ 63200
Dril ~ 36838
Drill hole, skull
catheter ~ 61107
drain hematoma ~ 61108
exploration ~ 61105
implant electrode ~ 61850, 61863-61868
Drug ~ see drug assay; specific drug
aspirin ~ 4084F
infusion ~ 62360-62362
Drugs, anticoagulant ~ 85300-85305, 85307
Drug assay (testing)
Presumptive Drug Class ~ 80305-80307
Definitive Drug Class
  alcohols ~ 80320
  alcohol biomarkers ~ 80321, 80322
  alkaloids, NOS ~ 80323
  amphetamines ~ 80324-80326
  anabolic steroids ~ 80327, 80328
  analgesics, non-opioid ~ 80329-80331
  antidepressants
    not otherwise specified ~ 80338
    serotonergic class ~ 80332-80334
    tricyclic and other cyclicals ~ 80335-80337
  antiepileptics ~ 80339-80341
  antipsychotics, NOS ` 80342-80344
  barbiturates ~ 80345
  benzodiazepines ~ 80346, 80347
  buprenorphine ~ 80348
  cannabinoids ~ 80349, 80350-80352
  cocaine ~ 80353
  codeine ~ 80361
  fentanyl ~ 80354
  gabapentin, non-blood ~ 80355
  heroin metabolite ~ 80356
  ketamine and norketamine ~ 80357

Drug Assay ~ *continued*
methadone ~ 80358
methylenedioxyamphetamines (MDMA) ~ 80359
methylphenidate ~ 80360
opiates ~ 80361
opioids and other analogs ~ 80362-80364
oxycodone ~ 80365
pregabalin ~ 80366
propoxyphene ~ 80367
sedative hypnotics ~ 80368
skeletal muscle relaxants ~ 80369, 80370
stimulants ~ 80371
tapentadol ~ 80372
tramadol ~ 80373
Therapeutic Drug Assay
  amikacin ~ 80150
  amitriptyline ~ 80335-80337
  benzodiazepine ~ 80346, 80347
  caffeine ~ 80155
  carbamazepine ~ 80156-80157
  clozapine ~ 80159
  cyclosporine ~ 80158
  desipramine ~ 80335-80337
  digoxin ~ 80162, 80163
  dipropylacetic acid ~ 80164, 80165
  doxepin ~ 80335-80337
  ethosuximide ~ 80168
  everolimus ~ 80169
  gabapentin ~ 80171
  gentamicin ~ 80170
  gold ~ 80375
  haloperidol ~ 80173
  imipramine ~ 80335-80337
  lamotrigine ~ 80175
  levetiracetam ~ 80177
  lidocaine ~ 80176
  lithium ~ 80178
  nortriptyline ~ 80335-80337
  oxcarbazepine ~ 80183
  phenobarbital ~ 80184
  phenytoin ~ 80185-80186
  primidone ~ 80188
  procainamide ~ 80190-80192
  quantitative, other ~ 80299
  quinidine ~ 80194
  salicylate ~ 80329-80331
  sirolimus ~ 80195
  tacrolimus ~ 80197
  theophylline ~ 80198
  tiagabine ~ 80199
  tobramycin ~ 80200
  topiramate ~ 80201
  vancomycin ~ 80202
  zonisamide ~ 80203
Drug delivery implant
insertion ~ 11981
maintenance and refill
  brain ~ 95990-95991
  epidural ~ 95990-95991
  intra-arterial ~ 96522
  intrathecal ~ 95990-95991
  intravenous ~ 96522
  intraventricular ~ 95990-95991
removal ~ 11982-11983
  with reinsertion ~ 11983
Drug instillation ~ see instillation, drugs
Drug management
by pharmacist ~ 99605-99607
psychiatric ~ 90863
Drug screen ~ *see* Drug assay
Drug testing ~ *see* Drug assay
DST ~ 80420
DT shots
diphtheria and tetanus toxoids (DT) ~ 90702
diphtheria and tetanus toxoids, acellular pertussis, haemophilus influenzae type b, and inactivated poliovirus (DTaP-IPV/Hib) ~ 90698
diphtheria and tetanus toxoids, acellular pertussis, inactivated poliovirus, haemophilus influenzae type b PRP-OMP conjugate, an Hepatitis B (DTaP-IPV-Hib- HepB) ~ 60697
DTaP-HepB-IPV immunization ~ 90723
DTaP immunization ~ 90700

Dual X-ray absorptiometry (DXA) ~ 3095F-3096F
  appendicular ~ 77081
  axial skeleton ~ 77080
  vertebral fracture ~ 77086
Dual photon absorptiomety ~ 78351
Duct
  bile ~ see bile duct
  hepatic ~ see hepatic duct
  nasolacrimal ~ see nasolacrimal duct
  omphalomesenteric ~ 44800
  pancreatic ~ see pancreatic duct
  salivary ~ see salivary duct
  Stensen's ~ see parotid duct
  thoracic ~ see thoracic duct
Ductogram, mammary ~ galactogram
Ductus arteriosus repair ~ 33820-33824
Ductus deferens ~ see vas deferens
Duhamel procedure ~ 45110, 45112, 45119-45120
Dunn operation ~ 28730-28735, 28740
Duodenostomy
  contrast ~ 49465
  insertion ~ 49441
  obstructive material removal ~ 49460
  radiological evaluation ~ 49465
  replacement ~ 49451
Duodenotomy ~ 44010
Duodenum
  biopsy ~ 44010
  exclusion ~ 48547
  exploration ~ 44010
  incision ~ 44010
  intubation and aspiration ~ 43756-43757
  removal, foreign body ~ 44010
  X-ray ~ 74260
Duplex scan ~ see vascular studies
  arterial studies
    aorta ~ 93978-93979
    extracranial ~ 93880-93882
    lower extremity ~ 93925-93926
    penile ~ 93980-93981
    upper extremity ~ 93930-93931
    visceral ~ 93975-93979
  hemodialysis access ~ 93990
  venous studies
    extremity ~ 93970-93971
    penile ~ 93980-93981
Dupuy-Dutemp operation ~ see reconstruction, eyelid; revision
Dupuytren's contracture
  fasciotomy ~ 26040-26045
  injection, enzyme ~ 20527
  manipulation ~ 26341
Dust, Angel ~ 83992
Duvries operation ~ 01714
Dwyer procedure ~ 28300
DXA ~ see dual X-ray absorptiometry (DXA)
Dynamometry ~ 28300
  venous studies ~ 28300
    with ophthalmoscopy ~ 92260
D & C yellow no. 7 (seven) ~ see fluorescein
D 2, vitamin ~ 82306
D galactose ~ 82760
D glucose ~ 80422-80424, 80430-80435, 95250-95251
D vitamin ~ 82306, 82652

E

E1 ~ 82679
E2 ~ 82670
E3 ~ 82677

Ear
  collection of blood ~ 36415-36416
  drum ~ 69420-69421, 69433-69436, 69450, 69610-69620
  external
    abscess incision and drainage
      complicated ~ 69005
      simple ~ 69000
    biopsy ~ 69100
    excision
      partial ~ 69110
      total ~ 69120
    hematoma, incision and drainage ~ 69000-69005
    reconstruction ~ 69300
    removal
      foreign body ~ 69200, 69205
      impacted cerumen ~ 69209, 69210
    unlisted services and procedures ~ 69399
  inner
    CT scan ~ 70480-70482
    endolymphatic sac ~ 69805-69806
    insertion cochlear device ~ 69930
    labyrinth
      excision ~ 69905, 69910
      incision for perfusion ~ 69801
    unlisted services and procedures ~ 69949
  meatoplasty ~ 69310
    for congenital atresia ~ 69320
  middle
    CT scan ~ 70480-70482
    exploration ~ 69440
    excision
      polyp ~ 69540
      glomus tumor ~ 69550, 69552, 69554
    facial nerve decompression ~69720, 69725
    facial nerve suture ~ 69740, 69745
    optical coherence tomography ~ 0485T, 0486T
    repair, fistula ~ 69666, 69667
    stapedectomy ~ 69660-69662
    tumor excision ~ 69550-69554
  temporal bone
    bone conduction hearing device ~ 69710, 69711
    osseointegrated implant ~ 69714, 69715, 69717
    resection ~ 69535
    unlisted services and procedures ~ 69799
Ear canal ~ see auditory canal
Ear cartilage graft to face ~ 21235
Ear lobes, pierce ~ 69090
Ear, nose, and throat ~ see also hearing aid services ~ 92700
  audiologic function tests
    acoustic reflex ~ 92568
    acoustic reflex decay ~ 92570
    audiometry
      Bekesy ~ 92560-92561
      comprehensive ~ 92557
      conditioning play ~ 92582
      evoked response ~ 92585-92586
      groups ~ 92559
      pure tone ~ 92552-92553
      select picture ~ 92583
      speech ~ 92555-92556
    brainstem evoked response ~ 92585-92586
    central auditory function ~ 92620-92621
    ear protector evaluation ~ 92596
    electrocochleography ~ 92584
    filtered speech ~ 92571
    hearing aid evaluation ~ 92590-92595
    Lombard test ~ 92700
    loudness balance ~ 92562
    screening test ~ 92551
    sensorineural acuity ~ 92575
    short increment sensitivity index (SISI) ~ 92564
    staggered spondaic word test ~ 92572
    Stenger test ~ 92565, 92577
    synthetic sentence test ~ 92576
    tone decay ~ 92563
    tympanometry ~ 92567
  audiometry
    evoked otoacoustic emissions ~ 92587-92588
    visual reinforcement ~ 92579

Ear, nose and throat ~ *continued*
binocular microscopy ~ 92504
diagnostic analysis
  auditory brainstem implant ~ 92640
  cochlear implant ~ 92601-92604
evaluation
  auditory rehabilitation status ~ 92626-92627, 92630, 92633
  language comprehension/expression ~ 92523
  laryngeal sensory testing ~ 92614-92617
  prescription of communication device
    non-speech generating ~ 92605, 92618
    speech generating ~ 92607-92608
  speech fluency ~ 92521
  speech sound production ~ 92522
  swallowing ~ 92610-92613, 92616
  voice resonance analysis ~ 92524
examination under anesthesia ~ 92502
facial nerve function study ~ 92516
laryngeal function study ~ 92520
nasal function study ~ 92512
nasopharyngoscopy ~ 92511
treatment
  hearing, language and speech disorder ~ 92507-92508
  oral function for feeding ~ 92526
  swallowing dysfunction ~ 92526
vestibular function tests
  additional electrodes ~ 92547
  basic ~ 92540
  caloric tests ~ 92533
  nystagmus
    optokinetic ~ 92534, 92544
    positional ~ 92532, 92542
    spontaneous ~ 92531, 92541
  posturography ~ 92548
  torsion swing test ~ 92546
  tracking tests ~ 92545

Ear protector attenuation ~ see also hearing aid services ~ 92596
Ear wax ~ 69210
Ebstein anomaly repair ~ 33468
ECG ~ see electrocardiography
Echinococcosis ~ 86171, 86280
Echocardiography
cardiac ~ 93320-93350
  intracardiac ~ 93662
  transesophageal ~ 93318
  transthoracic ~ 93303-93317
    with stress test ~ 93350-93352
Doppler ~ 93303-93317, 93320-93321, 93662
fetal heart ~ 76825-76826
  Doppler
    complete ~ 76827
    follow-up or repeat study ~ 76828
for congenital anomalies
  transesophageal ~ 93315-93317
  transthoracic ~ 93303-93304
intracardiac ~ 93662
myocardial, contrast perfusion ~ 0439T
transesophageal ~ 93318
  for congenital anomalies ~ 93315-93317
transthoracic ~ 93303-93318, 93350
  for congenital anomalies ~ 93303-93304
  with stress test ~ 93350-93352
Echoencephalography ~ 76506
Echography
abdomen ~ 76700-76705
arm ~ 76881, 76882
breast ~ 76641, 76642
cardiac ~ 93303-93317, 93320-93321, 93350-93352, 93662
  guidance ~ 76932
chest ~ 76604
extracranial arteries ~ 93880-93882
eyes ~ 76510-76529
follow-up ~ 76970
head ~ 76536
heart imaging guidance ~ 76932
hip infant ~ 76885-76886
intracranial arteries ~ 93886-93893
intraoperative ~ 76998
kidney transplant ~ 76776
leg ~ 76881, 76882

Echography ~ *continued*
neck ~ 76536
pelvis ~ 76856-76857
placement therapy fields ~ 77387
pregnant uterus ~ 76801-76828
prostate ~ 76872-76873
retroperitoneal ~ 76770-76775
scrotum ~ 76870
spine ~ 76800
transvaginal ~ 76817, 76830
unlisted services and procedures ~ 76999
vagina ~ 76817, 76830
Echotomography ~ see echography
ECMO ~ see extracorporeal membrane oxygenation
ECS ~ see emission computerized tomography
ECSF (erythrocyte colony stimulating factor) ~ 82668
ECT ~ see emission computerized tomography
Ectasia ~ see dilation
Ectopic pregnancy ~ see obstetrical care
abdominal ~ 59130
cervix ~ 59140
interstitial
  partial resection uterus ~ 59136
  total hysterectomy ~ 59135
laparoscopy ~ 59150
  with salpingectomy and/or oophorectomy ~ 59151
tubal ~ 59121
  with salpingectomy and/or oophorectomy ~ 59120
Ectropion, repair
excision tarsal wedge ~ 67916
extensive ~ 67917
suture ~ 67914
thermocauterization ~ 67915
Education services
group ~ 98961-98962, 99078
individual, pediatric gastroenteritis ~ 4058F
Education supplies ~ 99071
EEG ~ see electroencephalography (EEG)
Egg (ova) ~ 87177
Ehrlichia antibody ~ 86666
EKG ~ see electrocardiogram
Elastase ~ 82656
Elbow ~ see also humerus; radius; ulna
abscess, incision and drainage ~ 23930, 23935
anesthesia ~ 00400, 01710-01782
arthrectomy ~ 24155
arthrocentesis ~ 20605
arthrodesis ~ 24800-24802
arthroplasty ~ 24360
  with implant ~ 24361-24362
  prosthesis removal ~ 24160, 24164
  revision ~ 24370-24371
  total replacement ~ 24361-24363, 24365-24366
arthroscopy
  diagnostic ~ 29830
  surgical ~ 29834-29838
arthrotomy ~ 24000
  capsular release ~ 24006
  removal of foreign body ~ 24000
  with joint exploration ~ 24000, 24101
  with synovectomy ~ 24102
biopsy ~ 24065-24066, 24101
bursa, incision and drainage ~ 23931
dislocation
  closed treatment ~ 24600-24605, 24640
  open treatment ~ 24615
  subluxate ~ 24640
excision ~ 24155
  bursa ~ 24105
  synovium ~ 24102, 29835-29836
exploration ~ 24000, 24101
fracture
  Monteggia ~ 24620-24635
    open treatment ~ 24586-24587
hematoma, incision and drainage ~ 23930
implant, removal ~ 24164
incision and drainage ~ 24000
injection, arthrography, radiologic ~ 24220
magnetic resonance imaging (MRI) ~ 73221
manipulation ~ 24300

Elbow ~ continued
  radical resection, capsule, soft tissue and bone with contracture release ~
    24149
  removal
    foreign body ~ 24000, 24101, 24200-24201, 29834
    implant ~ 24160
    loose body ~ 24101, 29834
  repair
    epicondylitis ~ 24357-24359
    flexorplasty ~ 24330
    graft ~ 24320
    hemiepiphyseal arrest ~ 24470
    ligament ~ 24343-24346
    muscle ~ 24341
    muscle transfer ~ 24301
    tendon ~ 24340-24342, 24357-24359
      lengthening ~ 24305
      transfer ~ 24301
    tennis elbow ~ 24357-24359
    Steindler advancement ~ 24330
  strapping ~ 29260
  tumor excision ~ 24071-24079
  unlisted services and procedures ~ 24999
  X-ray ~ 73070-73080
    with contrast ~ 73085
Elbow, golfer ~ 24357-24359
Elbows, tennis ~ 24357-24359
Electrical stimulation
  bone healing
    invasive ~ 20975
    noninvasive ~ 20974
  brain surface ~ 95961-95962
  physical therapy
    attended, manual ~ 97032
    unattended ~ 97014
Electric countershock ~ 92960-92961
Electric stimulation, transcutaneous ~ 64550
Electro-hydraulic procedure ~ 52325
Electro-oculography ~ 92270
Electroanalgesia ~ 64550
Electrocardiography
  12-lead ~ 3120F, 93000
  evaluation ~ 93000, 93010, 93660
  external recording
    auto-activated ~ 93268, 93270-93272
    Holter monitor, up to 48 hours continuous monitoring ~ 93224-93227
    interpretation ~ 93272, 0295T, 0298T
    mobile
      more than 24 hours ~ 93228, 93229
      more than 48 hours up to 21 days ~ 0295T-0298T
    patient-activated ~ 0497T, 0498T, 93268, 93270-93272
    transmission and evaluation ~ 93268, 93270-93272
    up to 30 days ~ 93268, 93270-93272
    up to 48 hours duration ~ 93224-93229
  rhythm
    evaluation ~ 93042
    microvolt T-wave alternans ~ 93025
    recording ~ 0295T, 0296T
    tracing ~ 93041
    tracing and evaluation ~ 93040
  signal averaged ~ 93278
  symptom-activated memory loop ~ 93268, 93270-93272
Electrocautery ~ see also destruction ~ 17000-17285
  inferior turbinates soft tissue ~ 30801-30802
  prostate resection ~ 52601
  ureteral stricture ~ 52341-52346
Electrochemistry ~ 17380
Electroconvulsive therapy ~ 90870-90871
Electrocortiogram, intraoperative ~ 95829
Electrode, depth ~ 61760
Electrodesiccation ~ 17000-17286
  lesion, penis ~ 54055
Electroejaculation ~ 55870
Electroencephalography (EEG) ~ 95816
  brain death ~ 95824
  coma ~ 95822
  digital analysis ~ 95957
  electrode placement ~ 95830
  intraoperative ~ 95955

Electroencephalography (EEG) ~ continued
  monitoring ~ 95812-95813, 95950-95953, 95956
    with drug activation ~ 95954
    with physical activation ~ 95954
    with wada activation ~ 95958
  sleep ~ 95822, 95827
  standard ~ 95819
Electrogastrography ~ 91132-91133
Electrogram, atrial esophageal recording ~ 93615-93616
Electrolysis ~ 17380
Electromyography
  anorectal with biofeedback ~ 90911
  fine wire dynamic ~ 96004
  needle
    extremities ~ 95860-95864
    extremity ~ 95860, 95885-95886
    face and neck muscles ~ 95867-95868
    ocular ~ 92265
    other than thoracic paraspinal ~ 95870
    single fiber electrode ~ 95872
    thoracic paraspinal muscles ~ 95869
  sphincter muscles
    anus ~ 51784-51785
      needle ~ 51785
    urethra ~ 51784-51785
      needle ~ 51785
  surface dynamic ~ 96002-96004
Electron microscopy ~ 88348
Electronic analysis
  cardioverter-defibrillator, implantable
    data analysis ~ 93289, 93295-93296
    evaluation of programming ~ 93282-94284, 93287, 93640, 93642
  drug infusion pump ~ 62367-62368
  loop recorder, implantable
    data analysis ~ 93291, 93298-93299
    evaluation of programming ~ 93285
  neurostimulator pulse generator ~ 95970-95982
Electrophoresis
  hemoglobin ~ 83020
  hight resolution ~ 83701
  immuno- ~ 86320, 86325, 86327
  immunofixation ~ 86334-86335
  protein ~ 84165-84166
  unlisted services and procedures ~ 82664
Electrophysiology procedure ~ 93600-93660
Electroretinogram ~ 92275
Electroretinography ~ 92275
Electrostimulation, analgesic cutaneous ~ 64550
Electrosurgery, trichiasis correction ~ 67825
Electroversion, cardiac ~ 92960-92961
Elevation, scapula, congenital ~ 23400
Elliot operation ~ 66130
Eloesser procedure ~ 32035-32036
Eloesser thoracoplasty ~ 32905
Embolectomy
  aortoiliac artery ~ 34151, 34201
  axillary artery ~ 34101
  brachial artery ~ 34101
  carotid artery ~ 34001
  celiac artery ~ 34151
  femoral ~ 34201
  iliac ~ 34151, 34201
  innominate artery ~ 34001-34101
  mesentery artery ~ 34151
  peroneal artery ~ 34203
  popliteal artery ~ 34201, 34203
  pulmonary artery ~ 33910, 33915-33916
  radial artery ~ 34111
  renal artery ~ 34151
  subclavian artery ~ 34001, 34101
  tibial artery ~ 34203
  ulnar artery ~ 34111
Embolization
  central nervous system ~ 61624
  non-central nervous system, head or neck ~ 61626
  intra-arterial
    for aneurysm ~ 61710
    for carotid-cavernous fistula ~ 61710
    for vascular malformation ~ 61710
  ureteral ~ 50705

Embolization ~ *continued*
  vascular
    arterial ~ 37242
    dialysis circuit ~ 36909
    for hemorrhage ~ 37244
    for infarction ~ 37243
    for lymphatic extravasation ~ 37244
    for organ ischemia ~ 37243
    for tumors ~ 37243
    venous ~ 37241
Embryo
  biopsy ~ 89290-89291
  cryopreservation ~ 89258
  cryopreserved preparation thawing ~ 89352
  culture ~ 89250
    with co-culture oocyte ~ 89251
  hatching assisted microtechnique ~ 89253
  preparation for transfer ~ 89255
  storage ~ 89342
Embryonated eggs inoculation ~ 87250
Embryo/fetus monitoring ~ 59050-59051, 99500
Embryo transfer
  in vitro fertilization ~ 58974-58976
    intrafallopian transfer ~ 58976
    intrauterine transfer ~ 58974
Emergency department services ~ 99281-99288
  anesthesia ~ 99140
  physician direction of advanced life support ~ 99288
Emesis induction ~ 99175
EMG ~ see electromyography, needle
Emission-computed tomography, single-photon ~ 78607
Emission computerized tomography ~ 78607
EMI scan ~ see CAT scan
Emmet operation ~ 59300
Empyema
  closure, chest wall ~ 32810
  lung ~ 21501-21502
  thoracostomy ~ 32035-32036, 32551
Empyemectomy ~ 32540
Encephalitis
  antibody ~ 86651-86654
Encephalocele
  repair ~ 62120
    craniotomy ~ 62121
Encephalon ~ see brain
End stage renal disease services ~ 90951-90970
End-expiratory pressure, positive ~ 94660
Endarterectomy
  coronary artery ~ 33572
  pulmonary ~ 33916
Endemic flea-borne typhus ~ 86000
Endobronchial challenge tests ~ 95070-95071
Endobronchial Ultrasound (EBUS)
  with bronchoscopy ~ 31652-31654
Endocavitary fulguration ~ 17000-17286
Endocrine, pancreas ~ 86341
Endocrine system surgical procedures 60000-60699
Endolymphatic sac
  exploration
    with shunt ~ 69806
    without shunt ~ 69805
Endometrial ablation ~ 0009T, 58353
  exploration via hysteroscopy ~ 58563
Endometrioma
  abdomen
    destruction/excision ~ 49203-49205, 58957, 58958
  retroperitoneal
    destruction/excision ~ 49203-49205, 58957, 58958
Endometriosis, adhesive ~ 58559
Endometrium
  ablation ~ 58356
  biopsy ~ 58100, 58558
Endonuclease, DNA ~ 86215
Endoscopic retrograde cannulation of pancreatic duct (ERCP) ~ 43260
Endoscopies, pleural ~ see thoracoscopy

Endoscopy ~ see arthroscopy; thoracoscopy
  adrenal gland
    biopsy ~ 60650
    excision ~ 60650
  anus
    biopsy ~ 46606
    dilation ~ 46604
    exploration ~ 46600
    hemorrhage ~ 46614
    removal
      foreign body ~ 46608
      polyp ~ 46610, 46612
      tumor ~ 46610, 46612
  atria ~ 33265-33266
  bile duct ~ 43273
    biopsy ~ 47553
    cannulation ~ 43273
    catheterization ~ 47533-47537, 74328, 74330
    destruction, calculi (stone) ~ 43265
    dilation ~ 43277, 47555-47556
    exploration ~ 47552
    intraoperative ~ 47550
    percutaneous ~ 47552-47556
    placement, stent ~ 43274
    removal
      calculi (stone) ~ 43264, 47554
      foreign body ~ 43275
      stent ~ 43275
    specimen collection ~ 43260
    sphincter pressure ~ 43263
    sphincterotomy ~ 43262
    tube placement ~ 43274
  bladder ~ 52000
    biopsy ~ 52204, 52354
    catheterization ~ 52005, 52010
    destruction ~ 52354
      lesion ~ 52400
    evacuation clot ~ 52001
    excision tumor ~ 52355
    exploration ~ 52351
    lithotripsy ~ 52353
    removal calculus ~ 52352
    urethral stent ~ 52282
  bladder neck
    injection of implant material ~ 51715
  brain shunt creation ~ 62201
  bronchi
    aspiration ~ 31645-31646
    biopsy ~ 31625-31629, 31632-31633
    destruction
      lesion ~ 31641
      tumor ~ 31641
    dilation ~ 31630-31631, 31636-31638
    exploration ~ 31622
    injection ~ 31899
    lesion destruction ~ 31641
    needle biopsy ~ 31629, 31633
    placement stent ~ 31631, 31636-31637
    revision stent ~ 31638
    specimen collection ~ 31623-61324
    stenosis ~ 31641
    tumor destruction ~ 31641
    with endobronchial ultrasound (EBUS) ~ 31652, 31653
  cervix
    biopsy ~ 57454-57455, 57460
    curettage ~ 57454, 57456
    exploration ~ 57452
    loop electrode biopsy ~ 57460
    loop electrode conization ~ 57461
  chest cavity
    exploration ~ 32601-32606
    surgical ~ 32650-32665
  colon
    biopsy ~ 44389, 45380, 45392
    destruction
      lesion ~ 44401, 45383
      tumor ~ 44401, 45383

Endoscopy ~ *continued*

    exploration ~ 45378

    hemorrhage ~ 44391, 45382

    injection ~ 45381

    placement stent ~ 45389

    removal

        foreign body ~ 44390, 45379

        polyp ~ 44392, 45384-45385

        tumor ~ 44392, 45384-45385

    specimen collection ~ 45380

    ultrasound ~ 45391-45392

    via colotomy ~ 45399

    via stoma ~ 44401, 44402

  colon-sigmoid

    ablation

        polyp ~ 45346

        tumor ~ 45346

    biopsy ~ 45331

    dilation ~ 45340

    exploration ~ 45330, 45335

    hemorrhage ~ 45334

    needle biopsy ~ 45342

    placement stent ~ 45327, 45347

    removal

        foreign body ~ 45332

        polyp ~ 45333, 45338

        tumor ~ 45333, 45338

    specimen collection ~ 45331

    ultrasound ~ 45341-45342

    volvulus ~ 45337

  esophagus

    biopsy ~ 43202

    dilation ~ 43220-43226

    exploration ~ 43200

    hemorrhage ~ 43227

    injection ~ 43201, 43204

    insertion stent ~ 43212

    needle biopsy ~ 43232

    removal

        foreign body ~ 43215

        polyp ~ 43216-43217, 43229

        tumor ~ 43216, 43229

    ultrasound ~ 43231-43232

    vein ligation ~ 43205

  eye ~ 66990

  foot, plantar fasciotomy ~ 29893

  gastrointestinal, upper ~ 3130F-3132F, 3140F-3141F

    biopsy ~ 43239

    catheterization ~ 43241

    destruction of lesion ~ 43270

    dilation ~ 43245, 43248-43249

    drainage of pseudocyst ~ 43240

    exploration ~ -43235

    foreign body ~ 43247

    gastric bypass ~ 43644-43645

    gastroenterostomy ~ 43644-43645

    hemorrhage ~ 43255

    inject varices ~ 43243

    injection ~ 43236

    needle biopsy ~ 43238, 43242

    referral ~ 3132F

    removal ~ 43247, 43250-43251

    roux-en-y ~ 43644

    stent placement ~ 43266

    thermal radiation ~ 43257

    tube placement ~ 43246

    ultrasound ~ 43237-43242, 43259, 76975

    vein ligation ~ 43244

  ileum via stoma ~ 44384

  intestines, small

    biopsy ~ 44361, 44377

    destruction

        lesion ~ 44369

        tumor ~ 44369

    diagnostic ~ 44376

    exploration ~ 44360

    hemorrhage ~ 44366, 44378

    insertion

        stent ~ 44370, 44379

        tube ~ 44379

Endoscopy ~ *continued*

  pelvic pouch ~ 44385-44386

  removal

    foreign body ~ 44363

    lesion ~ 44365

    polyp ~ 44364-44365

  tube placement ~ 44372

  tube revision ~ 44373

  via stoma ~ 44380-44384

    tumor ~ 44364-44365

  intracranial ~ 62160-62165

  kidney

    biopsy ~ 50555, 50574-50576, 52354

    catheterization ~ 50553, 50572

    destruction ~ 50557, 50576, 52354

    dilation of ureter ~ 50553

    excision tumor ~ 52355

    exploration ~ 52351

    lithotripsy ~ 52353

    removal

        calculus ~ 50561, 50580, 52352

        foreign body ~ 50561, 50580

    via incision ~ 50562-50580

    via stoma ~ 50551-50561

  larynx

    ablation, lesion ~ 31572

    aspiration ~ 31515

    biopsy ~ 31510, 31535-31536

    dilation ~ 31528, 31529

    direct ~ 31515, 31520, 31525-31529

        diagnostic ~ 31520, 31525, 31526

        operative ~ 31530, 31531, 31535, 31536, 31540, 31541, 31545,

          31546, 31560, 31561

    epiglottis stripping ~ 31540, 31541

    excision, tumor ~ 31540

    flexible ~ 31575-31579

    indirect ~ 31505-31513

    laser destruction, lesion ~ 31572

    operative ~ 31530-31561

    reconstruction ~ 31545, 31546

    removal

        foreign body ~ 31511, 31530-31531

        lesion ~ see endoscopic ~ 31512, 31545-31546

  mediastinoscopy

    biopsy ~ 39401, 39402

  nose

    diagnostic ~ 31231-31235

    surgical ~ 31237-31241, 31253-31257, 31259, 31267, 31276, 31287,

       31288, 31290-31298

    unlisted services and procedures ~ 31299

  pancreatic duct

    cannulation ~ 43273

    destruction

        calculi (stone) ~ 43265

        tumor ~ 43272

    dilation ~ 43277

    removal

        calculi (stone) ~ 43264

        foreign body ~ 43275-43276

        stent ~ 43275-43276

    specimen collection ~ 43260

    sphincter pressure ~ 43263

    sphincterotomy ~ 43262

    tube placement ~ 43274

  pelvis

    aspiration ~ 49322

    destruction of lesion ~ 58662

    lysis of adhesions ~ 58660

    oviduct surgery ~ 58670-58671

    removal of adnexal structures ~ 58661

  peritoneum

    drainage lymphocele ~ 49323, 54690

  rectum

    biopsy ~ 45305

    destruction tumor ~ 45320

    dilation ~ 45303

    exploration ~ 45300

    hemorrhage ~ 45317

Endoscopy ~ continued
removal
foreign body ~ 45307
polyp ~ 45308-45315
tumor ~ 45308-45315
volvulus ~ 45321
spinal cord, nerve root decompression ~ 62380
spleen, removal ~ 38120
testis, removal ~ 54690
trachea
dilation ~ 31630-31631, 31636-31638
via tracheostomy ~ 31615
ureter
biopsy ~ 50955-50957, 50974-50976, 52354
catheterize ~ 50953, 50972
destruction ~ 50957, 50976, 52354
excision tumor ~ 52355
exploration ~ 52351
injection of implant material ~ 52327
lithotripsy ~ 52353
manipulation of ureteral calculus ~ 52330
placement stent ~ 50947
removal
calculus ~ 50961, 50980, 52352
foreign body ~ 50961, 50980
resection ~ 52355
via incision ~ 50970-50980
via stoma ~ 50951-50961
ureteral
biopsy ~ 52007
catheterization ~ 52005
urethra ~ 52000
biopsy ~ 52204, 52354
catheterization ~ 52010
destruction ~ 52354
lesion ~ 52400
evacuation clot ~ 52001
excision tumor ~ 52355
exploration ~ 52351
incision ejaculatory duct ~ 52402
injection of implant material ~ 51715
lithotripsy ~ 52353
removal calculus ~ 52352
resection ejaculatory duct ~ 52402
vasectomy ~ 52402
vasotomy ~ 52402
uterus
anesthesia ~ 00952
hysteroscopy
diagnostic ~ 58555
with division/resection intrauterine septum ~ 58560
with lysis of intrauterine adhesions ~ 58559
placement fallopian tube ~ 58565
removal
endometrial ~ 58563
impacted foreign body ~ 58562
leiomyomata ~ 58561
surgical with biopsy ~ 58558
vagina ~ 57420
anesthesia ~ 00950
biopsy ~ 57421, 57454
exploration ~ 57452
vascular, surgical ~ 33508, 37500-37501
vulva ~ 56820
biopsy ~ 56821
Endosteal implant
reconstruction
mandible ~ 21248-21249
maxilla ~ 21248-21249
Endothelioma, dural ~ 61512, 61519
Endotracheal intubation ~ 31500
Endotracheal tube
intubation ~ 31500
Endovascular repair
angiography ~ 75956-75959
delivery of endograft ~ 34712, 34713
delivery of endovascular prosthesis ~ 34714-34716
iliac artery
with endograft ~ 0254T, 34703-34708
with prosthesis ~ 34709-34711

Endovascular repair ~ continued
infrarenal abdominal aorta
with endograft ~ 34701-34706, 34845-34848
vena cava ~ 37191-37193
visceral aorta, with fenestrated endograft ~ 34839, 34841-34848
Endovascular revascularization ~ 37220-37235
Endovascular therapy
ablation, vein ~ 36473-36479, 36482, 36483
balloon angioplasty ~ 61630
intracranial
dilatation ~ 61640-61642
infusion
for other than thrombolysis ~ 61650, 61651
for thrombolysis ~ 61645
injection ~ 61645
thrombectomy ~ 61645
occlusion
arterial balloon ~ 61623
transcatheter ~ 61624, 61626
vascular catheterization ~ 61630, 61635
Enema
home visit for fecal impaction ~ 99511
intussusception ~ 74283
therapeutic, for intussusception ~ 74283
Energies, electromagnetic ~ 86945
ENT ~ see ear nose and throat ~ 92700
Entamoeba histolytica
antigen detection
enzyme immunoassay ~ 87336-87337
Enterectomy ~ 44120-44121, 44126-44128, 44137, 44202
donor ~ 44132-44133
with enterostomy ~ 44125
Enterocele
repair ~ 57556
hysterectomy
with colpectomy ~ 58280
Enterocystoplasty ~ 51960
Camey ~ 50825
Enteroenterostomy ~ see anastomosis, intestines
Enterolysis ~ 44005
laparoscopic ~ 44200
Enteropancreatostomy ~ see anastomosis, pancreas to intestines
Enterorrhaphy ~ 44602-44603, 44615
Enterostomy ~ 44300
closure ~ 44625-44626
with enterectomy
intestine, small ~ 44125
Enterotomy ~ 44615
Enterovirus
antibody ~ 86658
Entropion
repair ~ 67921-67924
excision tarsal wedge ~ 67923
suture ~ 67921
thermocauterization ~ 67922
Enucleation
eye
with implant ~ 65103
muscles attached ~ 65105
without implant ~ 65101
pleural ~ 32540
Enucleation, cyst, ovarian ~ 58925
Environmental intervention
for psychiatric patients ~ 90882
Enzyme
angiotensin converting ~ 82164
angiotensin-forming ~ 80408, 80416, 84244
Enzyme activity ~ 82657
radioactive substrate ~ 82658
EOG ~ 92700
Eosinocyte ~ 89190
Eosinophils
nasal smear ~ 89190
Epiandrosterone ~ 80327, 80328
Epicondylitides, lateral humeral ~ 24357-24359
Epicondylitis, radiohumeral ~ 24357-24359
Epidemic parotitis ~ see mumps
Epididymectomy
bilateral ~ 54861
unilateral ~ 54860

Epididymis
- abscess, incision and drainage ~ 54700
- anastomosis
  - to vas deferens
    - bilateral ~ 54901
    - unilateral ~ 54900
- biopsy ~ 54800, 54865
- epididymography ~ 74440
- excision
  - bilateral ~ 54861
  - unilateral ~ 54860
- exploration biopsy ~ 54865
- hematoma, incision and drainage ~ 54700
- lesion
  - excision
    - local ~ 54830
    - spermatocele ~ 54840
- needle biopsy ~ 54800
- spermatocele excision ~ 54840
- unlisted services and procedures ~ 55899
- X-ray with contrast ~ 74440

Epididymograms ~ 55300
Epididymography ~ 74440
Epididymoplasty ~ 54900-54901
Epididymovasostomy
- bilateral ~ 54901
- unilateral ~ 54900

Epidural
- administration
  - device ~ 62360-62362, 62365
    - analysis ~ 62367
  - drug ~ 62320-62327
    - hospital management ~ 01996
- catheterization ~ 62350, 62351
  - removal ~ 62355
- electrode
  - insertion ~ 61531, 63650, 63655
  - removal ~ 61535
- injection ~ 62281, 62282, 62320-62327
  - blood or clot patch ~ 62273
  - neurolytic substance ~ 62281, 62282
  - transforaminal ~ 64479, 64480, 64483, 64484
    - ultrasound guidance ~ 0228T-0231T
  - with disc decompression ~ 62287
- lysis ~ 62263-62264

Epidural anesthesia
- Infusion
  - with imaging guidance ~ 62325, 62327
  - without imaging guidance ~ 62324, 62326
- Injection
  - with imaging guidance ~ 62321, 62323
  - without imaging guidance ~ 62320, 62322

Epidurography ~ 72275
Epigastric hernia repair ~ 49572
Epiglottidectomy ~ 31420
Epiglottis excision ~ 31420
Epikeratoplasty ~ 65767
Epilation ~ 17380
Epinephrine ~ 80424, 82382-82384
- blood ~ 82383-82384
- urine ~ 82384
Epiphysis ~ see bone; specific bone
Epiphyseal arrest
- femur ~ 20150, 27185, 27475, 27479-27485, 27742
- fibula ~ 20150, 27477-27485, 27730-27742
- radius ~ 20150, 25450-25455
- tibia ~ 20150, 27477-27485, 27730, 27734-27742
- ulna ~ 20150, 25450-25455
Epiphyseal separation
- radius
  - closed treatment ~ 25600
  - open treatment ~ 25607-25609
Epiphysiodesis ~ see epiphyseal arrest
Epiploectomy ~ 49255
Episiotomy ~ 59300
Epispadias
- penis reconstruction ~ 54385
- repair ~ 54380-54390
  - with extrophy of bladder ~ 54390
  - with incontinence ~ 54380-54390

Epistaxis ~ 30901-30906
- with nasal/sinus endoscopy ~ 31238
EPO ~ see erythropoietin
Epstein-Barr virus
- antibody ~ 86663-86665
Equina, cauda ~ see cauda equina
ERCP ~ see bile duct; pancreatic duct ~ 43260
ERG ~ 92275
Ergocalciferol ~ 82306
Ergocalciferols ~ 82306
Ergonovine provocation test ~ 93024
Erythrocyte ~ see red blood cell (RBC)
Erythrocyte AB ~ see antibody, red blood cell
Erythrocyte count ~ 85032-85041
Erythropoietin ~ 82668
Escharotomy, burns ~ 16035-16036
Escherichia coli 0157
- antigen detection, enzyme immunoassay ~ 87335
ESD ~ see endoscopy, gastrointestinal, upper
Esophageal
- acid infusion test ~ 91030
- lengthening ~ 43283, 43338
- polyp ~ 43229
- tumor ~ 43229
- varices
  - decompression ~ 37181
  - ligation ~ 43205, 43244, 43400
  - sclerosis injection ~ 43204, 43243
  - transection/repair ~ 43401
Esophagectomy
- Ivor Lewis ~ 43287
- laparoscopic thoracoscopic ~ 43287
- McKeown ~ 43112, 43288
- partial ~ 43116-43118, 43121-43124, 43287
- total ~ 43107, 43108, 43112, 43113, 43124, 43286, 43288
- tri-incisional ~ 43112, 43288
Esophagoenterostomy with total gastrectomy ~ 43620
Esophagogastroduodenoscopy
- flexible transoral
  - ablation ~ 43270
  - band ligation ~ 43244
  - biopsy ~ 43239
  - collection of specimen ~ 43235
  - control of bleeding ~ 43255
  - delivery of thermal energy ~ 43257
  - dilation of esophagus ~ 43233, 43249
  - dilation of gastric/duodenal stricture ~ 43245
  - drainage of pseudocyst ~ 43240
  - esophagogastric fundoplasty ~ 43210
  - examination, ultrasound guided ~ 43237, 43238, 43253, 43259
  - injection ~ 43236, 43243, 43253
  - insertion
    - catheter or tube ~ 43241
    - guide wire ~ 43248
  - needle aspiration/biopsy ~ 43238, 43242
  - placement
    - gastrostomy tube ~ 43246
    - stent ~ 43266
  - removal
    - foreign body ~ 43247
    - lesion/polyp/tumor ~ 43250, 43251
  - resection, mucosal ~ 43254
  - with optical endomicroscopy ~ 43252
Esophagogastromyotomy ~ 32665, 43330-43331
Esophagogastrostomy ~ 43320
Esophagojejunostomy ~ 43340-43341
Esophagomyotomy ~ 32665, 43330-43331
- with fundoplasty ~ 43279
Esophagorrhaphy ~ 43405
Esophagoscopies ~ see endoscopy, esophagus
Esophagostomy ~ 43352
- closure ~ 43420-43425
Esophagotomy ~ 43020, 43045
Esophagotracheal fistula ~ see fistula, tracheoesophageal
Esophagus
- ablation ~ 43229
- acid perfusion test ~ 91030
- acid reflux tests ~ 91034-91035, 91037-91038
- balloon distention provocation study ~ 91040

Esophagus ~ continued
biopsy
  endoscopy ~ 43198, 43202
  forceps ~ 3150F
cricopharyngeal myotomy ~ 43030
dilation ~ 43450, 43453
  endoscopic ~ 43195-43196, 43212-43214, 43220, 43226, 43229, 43233, 43248-43249
  surgical ~ 43510
excision
  diverticula ~ 43130, 43135
  Ivor Lewis ~ 43287
  laparascopic Thoracoscopic ~ 43287
  laparascopic Transhiatal ~ 43286
  McKeown ~ 43112, 43288
  partial ~ 43116-43118, 43121-43124, 432
  total ~ 43107, 43108, 43112, 43113, 43124, 43286, 43288
  tri-incisional ~ 43112, 43288
exploration endoscopy ~ 43200
hemorrhage ~ 43227
incision ~ 43020, 43045
  muscle ~ 43030
imaging studies ~ 91110-91111
  motility ~ 78258
  obstructions ~ 74360
  reflux ~ 78262
  removal of foreign body ~ 74235
  strictures ~ 74360
  swallowing cineradiography ~ 74230
  X-ray ~ 74210, 74220
injection
  sclerosing agent ~ 43204
  submucosal ~ 43192, 43201
insertion
  stent ~ 43212
  tamponade ~ 43460
  tube ~ 43510
lengthening ~ 43283, 43338
lesion excision ~ 43100-43101
ligation ~ 43405
motility study ~ 78258, 91010, 91013
mucosal resection ~ 43211
needle biopsy endoscopy ~ 43232
nuclear medicine
  imaging (motility) ~ 78258
  reflux study ~ 78262
reconstruction ~ 43300, 43310, 43313
  creation stoma ~ 43352
  esophagostomy ~ 43352
  fistula ~ 43305, 43312, 43314
  gastrointestinal ~ 43360-43361
removal
  foreign bodies ~ 43020, 43045, 43194, 43215, 74235
  lesion ~ 43216
  polyp ~ 43216-43217
repair ~ 43300, 43310, 43313
  esophagogastroduodenoscopy ~ 43235-43239
  esophagogastric fundoplasty ~ 43325, 43327-43328
    esophagogastroduodenoscopic ~ 43210
    laparoscopic ~ 43280
  esophagogastrostomy ~ 43320
  esophagojejunostomy ~ 43340, 43341
  esophagomyotomy ~ 43279
  esophagoplasty ~ 43300, 43305, 43310, 43312
  fistula ~ 43305, 43312, 43314, 43420-43425
  Heller esophagomyotomy ~ 32665
  muscle ~ 43330-43331
  Nissen procedure ~ 43280
  paraesophageal hernia
    laparoscopic ~ 43281-43282
    via laparotomy ~ 43332-43333
    via thoracoabdominal incision ~ 43336-43337
    via thoracotomy ~ 43334-43335
  pre-existing perforation ~ 43405
  Thal-Nissen procedure ~ 43325
  Toupet procedure ~ 43280
  varices ~ 43401
  wound ~ 43410, 43415

Esophagus ~ continued
sphincter augmentation
  device placement ~ 43284
  device removal ~ 43285
suture ~ 43405
  wound ~ 43410, 43415
ultrasound endoscopy ~ 43231-43232
unlisted services and procedures ~ 43289, 43499
vein ligation ~ 43205, 43400
Esophagus, varix ~ 43205, 43400-43401
Esophagus neoplasm ~ 43229
Established patient
critical care ~ 99291, 99292
domiciliary or rest home visit ~ 99334-99337, 99339, 99340
emergency department services ~ 99281-99285
evaluation services
  basic life and/or disability ~ 99450
  work-related or medical disability ~ 99455
home services ~ 99347-99350, 99606
hospital inpatient services ~ 99221-99239
hospital observation services ~ 99217-99220, 99224-99226, 99235, 99236
initial inpatient consultations ~ 99251-99255
nursing facility ~ 99304-99310, 99315, 99316, 99318
office and/or other outpatient consultations ~ 99241-99245
office visit ~ 99211-99215
online medical evaluation ~ 98969, 99444
ophthalmological services ~ 92012, 92014
outpatient visit ~ 99211-99215
preventive medicine ~ 99391-99397
prolonged services
  with patient contact ~ 99354-99357
    with physician supervision ~ 99415, 99416
  without patient contact ~ 99358, 99359
telephone services ~ 98966-98968, 99441-99443
Establishment
colostomy
  abdominal ~ 50810
  perineal ~ 50810
Estes operation ~ 58825
Estlander procedure ~ 40525
Estradiol ~ 82670
response ~ 80414
Estriol
blood or urine ~ 82677
Estrogen
blood or urine ~ 82671-82672
receptor ~ 84233
Estrone blood or urine ~ 82679
Ethanediols ~ 82693
Ethanol
blood ~ 80321-80322
breath ~ 82075
urine ~ 80321-80322
Ethchlorovynol ~ 80320
Ethchlorvinol ~ 80320
Ethchlorvynol
blood ~ 80320
urine ~ 80320
Ethmoid fracture with fixation ~ 21340
Ethmoid, sinus ~ see sinus, ethmoid
Ethmoidectomy ~ 31200-31205
endoscopic ~ 31254-31255
skull base surgery ~ 61580-61581
with nasal/sinus endoscopy ~ 31254-31255
Ethosuccimid ~ 80168
Ethosuximide ~ 80168
assay ~ 80168
Ethylene dichlorides ~ 84600
Ethyl alcohol ~ 80321-80322, 82075
Ethylene glycol ~ 82693
Ethylmethylsuccimide ~ 80168
Etiocholanolone ~ 82696
Etiocholanolone measurement ~ 82696
ETOH ~ 80321-80322
Euglobulin lysis ~ 85360
Eustachian tube
catheterization ~ 69799
inflation
  myringotomy ~ 69420
    anesthesia ~ 69421
insertion, catheter ~ 69799

Eutelegenesis ~ 58976
Evacuation
cervical pregnancy ~ 59140
hematoma
brain ~ 61312-61315
subungual ~ 11740
hydatidiform mole ~ 59870
Evaluation
athletic training ~ 97169-97172
evaluation ~ 97169-97171
re-evaluation ~ 97172
carotid artery
atheroma ~ 93895
intima media thickness ~ 93895
cine ~ 74230
electrophysiologic ~ 93653, 93654, 93656
implantable defibrillator device ~ 93287, 93289, 93295, 93296
physical therapy ~ 97161-97164
treatment ~ 92526
video ~ 74230
Evaluation and management services
advance care planning ~ 99497, 99498
assistive technology, assessment ~ 97755
basic life and/or disability evaluation services ~ 99450
care management
behavioral health conditions ~ 99484
psychiatric collaborative care ~ 99492-99494
care plan oversight services ~ 0405T, 99339, 99340, 99374-99380
home health agency care ~ 99374-99375
home or rest home ~ 99339-99340
hospice ~ 99377-99378
nursing facility ~ 99379-99380
care planning, cognitive impairment ~ 99483
case management services ~ 99366-99368
consultation ~ 99241-99255
interprofessional ~ 99446-99449
critical care ~ 99291-99292
interfacility pediatric transport ~ 99466-99467, 99485-99486
domiciliary or rest home
established patient ~ 99334-99337
new patient ~ 99324-99328
emergency department ~ 99281-99288
health behavior
assessment ~ 96150
family intervention ~ 96154-96155
group intervention ~ 96153
individual intervention ~ 96152
re-assessment ~ 96151
home services ~ 99341-99350
hospital ~ 99221-99233
discharge ~ 99238-99239
observation care ~ 99217-99220, 99224-99226, 99234-99236
hyperbaric oxygen treatment facility ~ 99183
insurance exam ~ 99455-99456
internet communication ~ 98969, 99444
low birthweight infant ~ 99478-99479
medical team conferences ~ 99366-99368
neonatal critical care ~ 99468-99469
newborn care ~ 99460-99465
nursing facility ~ see nursing facility services ~ 99304-99318
occupation therapy evaluation ~ 97166, 97167
re-evaluation ~ 97168
office and other outpatient ~ 99201-99215
online ~ 98969, 99444
pediatric critical care ~ 99471-99476
pediatric interfacility transport ~ 99466-99467, 99485-99486
physician standby services ~ 99360
post-discharge transitional care ~ 99495-99496
preventive services ~ 99381-99429
prolonged services ~ 99354-99360, 99415, 99416
standby services ~ 99360
team conferences ~ 99366-99368
telephone services ~ 98966-98968, 99441-99443
unlisted services and procedures ~ 99499
with psychotherapy ~ 90833, 90836, 90838
work-related and/or medical disability evaluation ~ 99455
Evisceration
ocular contents
with implant ~ 65093
without implant ~ 65091
pelvic ~ 45126, 58240

Evocative/suppression testing ~ 80400-80439, 84146
stimulation panel ~ 80410
Evoked potential ~ see audiologic function tests
auditory brainstem ~ 92585-92586
central nervous system
somatosensory testing ~ 95925-95927, 95938
transcranial motor stimulation ~ 95928, 95929, 95939
visual ~ 95930
visual
acuity ~ 0333T
central nervous system ~ 95930
glaucoma test ~ 0464T
Ewart procedure ~ 42226-42227
Excavatum, pectus ~ 21740-21743
Exchange
arterial catheter ~ 37211-37214
drainage catheter
under radiologic guidance ~ 49423
intraocular lens ~ 66986
transfusion ~ 36455
Excision ~ see debridement; destruction
abscess
brain ~ 61514, 61522
olecranon process ~ 24138
radius ~ 24136
ulna ~ 24138
acromion
shoulder ~ 23130
adenoids ~ 42830-42836
adenoma thyroid gland ~ 60200
adrenal gland ~ 60540
with excision retroperitoneal tumor ~ 60545
laparoscopic ~ 60650
alveolus ~ 41830
anal crypt ~ 46999
anal fissure ~ 46200
anal tag ~ 46220, 46230
aorta coarctation ~ 33840-33851
appendix ~ 44950-44960
arteriovenous malformation
spinal ~ 63250-63252
arytenoid cartilage ~ 31400
endoscopic ~ 31560-31561
atrial septum ~ 33735-33737
Bartholin's gland ~ 56740
bladder
diverticulum ~ 51525
neck ~ 51520
partial ~ 51550-51565
total ~ 51570, 51580, 51590-51597
with nodes ~ 51575, 51585, 51595
transurethral ~ 52640
tumor ~ 51530
bladder neck contracture, postoperative ~ 52640
bone
facial ~ 21026
mandible ~ 21025
postoperative
femur ~ 20150
fibula ~ 20150
radius ~ 20150
tibia ~ 20150
ulna ~ 20150
bone abscess
facial ~ 21026
mandible ~ 21025
brain
amygdala ~ 61566
epileptogenic focus ~ 61536
hemisphere ~ 61543
hippocampus ~ 61566
other lobe ~ 61323, 61539-61540
temporal lobe ~ 61537-61538
brain lobe ~ 61323, 61537-61540

1041

Excision ~ *continued*
  breast
    biopsy ~ 19100-19101
    chest wall tumor ~ 19260-19272
    cyst ~ 19120-19126
    lactiferous duct fistula ~ 19112
    lesion ~ 19120-19126
      by needle localization ~ 19125-19126
    mastectomy ~ 19300-19307
    nipple exploration ~ 19110
  bulbourethral gland ~ 53250
  bullae
    lung ~ 32141
      endoscopic ~ 32655
  burns ~ 01951-01953, 15002-15005
  bursa
    elbow ~ 24105
    femur ~ 27062
    ischial ~ 27060
    knee ~ 27340
    wrist ~ 25115-25116
  bypass graft ~ 35901-35907
  calcaneus ~ 28118-28120
  calculi (stone)
    parotid gland ~ 42330, 42340
    salivary gland ~ 42330-42340
    sublingual gland ~ 42330
    submandibular gland ~ 42330-42335
  carotid artery ~ 60605
  carpal ~ 25145, 25210-25215
  cartilage
    knee joint ~ 27332-27333
    shoulder joint ~ 23101
    temporomandibular joint ~ 21060
    wrist ~ 25107
  caruncle
    urethra ~ 53265
  cataract
    secondary ~ 66830
  cervix
    radical ~ 57531
    stump
      abdominal approach ~ 57540-57545
      vaginal approach ~ 57550-57556
    total ~ 57530
  chalazion
    multiple
      different lids ~ 67805
      same lid ~ 67801
    single ~ 67800
    with anesthesia ~ 67808
  chest wall tumor ~ 19260-19272
  choroid plexus ~ 61544
  clavicle
    partial ~ 23120, 23180
    sequestrectomy ~ 23170
    total ~ 23125
    tumor
      radical resection ~ 23200
  coccyx ~ 27080
  colon
    excision
      partial ~ 44140-44147, 44160
        with anastomosis ~ 44140
      total ~ 44150-44158
    laparoscopic
      with anastomosis ~ 44204, 44207-44208
      with colostomy ~ 44206, 44208
        with ileocolostomy ~ 44205
  condyle, temporomandibular joint ~ 21050
  constricting ring
    finger ~ 26596
  cornea
    epithelium ~ 65435
      with chelating agent ~ 65436
    scraping ~ 65430
  coronoidectomy ~ 21070
  Cowper's gland ~ 53250
  cranial bone tumor ~ 61563-61564

Excision ~ *continued*
  cyst ~ see also ganglion cyst
    bile duct ~ 47715
    bladder ~ 51500
    brain ~ 61516, 61524, 62162
    branchial ~ 42810-42815
    calcaneus ~ 28100-28103
    carpal ~ 25130-25136
    cheekbone ~ 21030
    clavicle ~ 23140
      with allograft ~ 23146
      with autograft ~ 23145
    facial bone ~ 21030
    femur ~ 27065-27067, 27355-27358
    fibula ~ 27635-27638
    finger ~ 26160
    foot ~ 28090
    hand ~ 26160
    hip ~ 27065-27067
    humerus ~ 23150, 24110
      with allograft ~ 23156, 24116
      with autograft ~ 23155, 24115
    ileum ~ 27065-27067
    kidney ~ 50280-50290
    knee ~ 27345-27347
    lung ~ 32140
    mandible ~ 21040, 21046-21047
    maxilla ~ 21030, 21048-21049
    mediastinal ~ 39200
    mediastinum ~ 32662
    metacarpal ~ 26200-26205
    metatarsal ~ 28104-28107
    mullerian duct ~ 55680
    nose ~ 30124-30125
    olecranon ~ 24120
    olecranon process
      with allograft ~ 24126
      with autograft ~ 24125
    ovarian ~ 58925
    pericardial ~ 33050
      endoscopic ~ 32661
    phalanges ~ 26210-26215
      toe ~ 28108
    pilonidal ~ 11770-11772
    pubis ~ 27066-27067
    radius ~ 24120, 25120-25126
      with allograft ~ 24126
      with autograft ~ 24125
    salivary gland ~ 42408
    scapula ~ 23140
      with allograft ~ 23146
      with autograft ~ 23145
    seminal vesicle ~ 55680
    sublingual gland ~ 42408
    talus ~ 28100-28103
    tarsal ~ 28104-28107
    thyroglossal duct ~ 60280-60281
    thyroid gland ~ 60200
    tibia ~ 27635-27638
    toe ~ 28092
    ulna ~ 24120, 25120-25126
      with allograft ~ 24126
      with autograft ~ 24125
    urachalbladder ~ 51500
    vaginal ~ 57135
  destruction of the vestibule of the mouth ~ 40808-40820
  diverticulum, Meckel's ~ 44800
  ear, external
    partial ~ 69110
    total ~ 69120
  elbow joint ~ 24155
  electrode ~ 57522

Excision ~ *continued*
  embolectomy/thrombectomy
    aortoiliac artery ~ 34151-34201
    axillary artery ~ 34101
    brachial artery ~ 34101
    carotid artery ~ 34001
    celiac artery ~ 34151
    femoral artery ~ 34201
    heart ~ 33310-33315
    iliac artery ~ 34151-34201
    innominate artery ~ 34001-34101
    mesentery artery ~ 34151
    peroneal artery ~ 34203
    popliteal artery ~ 34203
    radial artery ~ 34111
    renal artery ~ 34151
    subclavian artery ~ 34001-34101
    tibial artery ~ 34203
    ulnar artery ~ 34111
  embolism, pulmonary artery ~ 33910-33916
  empyema
    lung ~ 32540
    pleural ~ 32540
  epididymis
    bilateral ~ 54861
    unilateral ~ 54860
  epiglottis ~ 31420
  esophagus
    diverticula ~ 43130-43135
    partial ~ 43116-43124
    total ~ 43107-43113, 43124
  eye ~ 65101, 65103, 65109
  fallopian tube
    salpingectomy ~ 58700
    salpingo-oophorectomy ~ 58720
  fascia ~ see fasciectomy
  femur ~ 27360
    partial ~ 27070-27071
  fibula ~ 27360, 27455-27457, 27641
  fistula
    anal ~ 46270-46285
  foot
    fasciectomy ~ 28060
      radical ~ 28060-28062
  gallbladder ~ 47600-47620
    cholecystectomy ~ 47562-47564
      with cholangiography ~ 47563
      with exploration common duct ~ 47564
  ganglion cyst
    knee ~ 27347
    wrist ~ 25111-25112
  gingiva ~ 41820
  gums ~ 41820
    alveolus ~ 41830
    operculum ~ 41821
  heart
    donor ~ 33940
  heart/lung
    donor ~ 33930
  hemangioma ~ 11400-11446
  hemorrhoids ~ 46221, 46250
    clot ~ 46320
    complex ~ 46260-46262
    with fissurectomy ~ 46257-46258
    simple ~ 46255
  hip, partial ~ 27070-27071
  hippocampus ~ 61566
  humeral head
    resection ~ 23195
    sequestrectomy ~ 23174
  humerus ~ 23184, 23220, 24134, 24140, 24150
  hydrocele
    spermatic cord ~ 55500
    tunica vaginalis ~ 55040-55041
      bilateral ~ 55041
      unilateral ~ 55040
  hygroma, cystic, axillary/cervical ~ 38550-38555
  hymenotomy ~ 56700

Excision ~ *continued*
  ileum
    ileoanal reservoir ~ 45136
    partial ~ 27070-27071
  inner ear ~ 69905-69910
  interphalangeal joint
    toe ~ 28160
  intervertebral disk
    decompression ~ 63075-63078
    hemilaminectomy ~ 63040, 63043-63044
    herniated ~ 63020-63044, 63055-63066
  intestine
    laparoscopic
      with anastomosis ~ 44202-44203
  intestines
    donor ~ 44132-44133
  intestines, small ~ 44120-44128
    transplantation ~ 44137
  iris
    iridectomy
      with corneoscleral or corneal section ~ 66600
      with cyclectomy ~ 66605
      optical ~ 66635
      peripheral ~ 66625
      sector ~ 66630
  kidney
    donor ~ 50300-50320, 50547
    partial ~ 50240
    recipient ~ 50340
    transplantation ~ 50370
    with ureters ~ 50220-50236
  kneecap ~ 27350
  labyrinth
    with mastoidectomy ~ 69910
    transcanal ~ 69905
  lacrimal gland
    partial ~ 68505
    total ~ 68500
  lacrimal sac ~ 68520
  larynx
    partial ~ 31367-31382
    with pharynx ~ 31390-31395
    total ~ 31360-31365
  lesion
    anal ~ 45108, 46922
    ankle ~ 27630
      arthroscopic ~ 29891
    auditory canal, external
      exostosis ~ 69140
      radical with neck dissection ~ 69155
      radical without neck dissection ~ 69150
      soft tissue ~ 69145
    bladder ~ 52224
    brain ~ 61534, 61536-61540
    brainstem ~ 61575-61576
    carotid body ~ 60600-60605
    colon ~ 44110-44111
    conjunctiva ~ 68110-68130
      over 1cm ~ 68115
      with adjacent sclera ~ 68130
    cornea ~ 65400
      without graft ~ 65420
    ear, middle ~ 69540
    epididymis
      local ~ 54830
      spermatocele ~ 54840
    esophagus ~ 43100-43101
    eye ~ 65900
    eyelid
      multiple, different lids ~ 67805
      multiple, same lid ~ 67801
      single ~ 67800
      under anesthesia ~ 67808
      without closure ~ 67840
    femur ~ 27062
    finger ~ 26160
    foot ~ 28080, 28090
    gums ~ 41822-41828
    hand ~ 26160

Excision ~ *continued*

intestines ~ 44110
  small ~ 43250, 44111
intraspinal ~ 63265-63273
knee ~ 27347
larynx, endoscopic ~ 31545-31546
leg, lower ~ 27630
meniscus ~ 27347
mesentery ~ 44820
mouth ~ 40810-40816, 41116
nerve ~ 64774-64792
neuroma ~ 64778
nose, intranasal ~ 30117-30118
orbit ~ 61333
  lateral approach ~ 67420
palate ~ 42104-42120
pancreas ~ 48120
penis ~ 54060
  surgical excision penile plaque ~ 54110-54112
pharynx ~ 42808
rectum ~ 45108
sclera ~ 66130
skin
  benign ~ 11400-11471
  malignant ~ 11600-11646
skull ~ 61500, 61615-61616
spermatic cord ~ 55520
spinal cord ~ 63300-63308
stomach ~ 43611
talus, arthroscopic ~ 29891
testis ~ 54512
tibia, arthroscopic ~ 29891
toe ~ 28092
tongue ~ 41110-41114
urethra ~ 52224, 53265
uterus ~ 59100
  leiomyomata ~ 58140, 58545-58546, 58561
uvula ~ 42104-42107
wrist tendon ~ 25110
lesion, arthroscopic
  ankle ~ 29891
  talus ~ 29891
  tibia ~ 29891
lesion, tendon sheath
  arm, lower ~ 25110
lip ~ 40500-40530
  frenum ~ 40819
liver
  extensive ~ 47122
  lobectomy ~ 47125-47130
  partial ~ 47120, 47125-47130, 47140-47142
  total ~ 47133
lung
  bronchus resection ~ 32486
  bullae, completion ~ 32488
  lobe ~ 32480-32482
  pleurectomy ~ 32310, 32320
  pneumonectomy 32440-32445
  segment ~ 32484
  tumor, apical ~ 32503-32504
lung/heart donor ~ 33930
lymph nodes ~ 38500, 38510-38530
  abdominal ~ 38747
  inguinofemoral ~ 38760-38765
  limited, for staging
    para-aortic ~ 38562
    pelvic ~ 38562
    retroperitoneal ~ 38564
  pelvic ~ 38770
  radical
    axillary ~ 38740-38745
    cervical ~ 38720-38724
    suprahyoid ~ 38700
  retroperitoneal transabdominal ~ 38780
  thoracic ~ 38746
mandibular exostosis ~ 21031

Excision ~ *continued*

mastoid
  complete ~ 69502
  radical ~ 69511
    modified ~ 69505
    petrous apicectomy ~ 69530
  simple ~ 69501
maxilla exotosis ~ 21032
maxillary torus palatinus ~ 21032
meningioma, brain ~ 61512, 61519
meniscectomy, temporomandibular joint ~ 21060
metacarpal ~ 26230
metatarsal ~ 28110-28114, 28122, 28140
  condyle ~ 28288
mouth, frenum ~ 40819
mucosa
  gums ~ 41828
  mouth ~ 40818
nail fold ~ 11765
nails ~ 11750
nerve
  foot ~ 28055
  leg, upper ~ 27325
  sympathetic ~ 64802-64818
neurofibroma ~ 64788-64790
neurolemmoma ~ 64788-64792
neuroma ~ 64774-64786
nose
  cyst ~ 30124-30125
  lesion ~ 30117-30118
  polyp ~ 30110-30115
  rhinectomy ~ 30150, 30160
  skin ~ 30120
  turbinate ~ 30130, 30140
odontoid process ~ 22548
olecranon process ~ 24147
omentum ~ 49255
ovary ~ 58720
  cystectomy ~ 58925
  oophorectomy ~ 58940, 58943
  salpingo-oophorectomy ~ 58720
  wedge resection/bisection ~ 58920
oviduct ~ 58700, 58720
palate ~ 42120, 42145
  lesion ~ 42104, 42106-42107
pancreas
  ampulla of Vater ~ 48148
  duct ~ 48148
  partial ~ 48140-48146, 48150, 48153-48154, 48160
  peripancreatic tissue ~ 48105
  total ~ 48155-48160
parathyroid gland ~ 60500-60502
parotid gland ~ 42340
  partial ~ 42410-42415
  total ~ 42420-42426
patella ~ 27350, 27424
penile adhesions, post-circumcision ~ 54162
penis
  amputation ~ 54120, 54125, 54130, 54135
  circumcision ~ 54150, 54160-54161, 54163
  frenulum ~ 54164
  partial ~ 54120
  post circumcision adhesion ~ 54162
  prepuce ~ 54150-54161, 54163
  radical ~ 54130-54135
  total ~ 54125
pericardium ~ 33030-33031
  endoscopic ~ 32659
petrous temporal
  apex ~ 69530
phalanges
  fingers ~ 26235-26236
  toe ~ 28124-28126, 28150-28160
pharynx ~ 42145
  with larynx ~ 31390-31395
  partial ~ 42890
  resection ~ 42892-42894

Excision ~ *continued*
  pituitary gland ~ 61546-61548
  pleura ~ 32310-32320
    endoscopic ~ 32656
  polyp
    nose
      endoscopic ~ 31237
      extensive ~ 30115
      simple ~ 30110
    urethra ~ 53260, 53265
  pressure ulcers ~ see also skin graft and flap ~ 15920-15999
  prostate
    abdominoperineal ~ 45119
    partial ~ 55801, 55821-55831
    perineal ~ 55801-55815
    radical ~ 55810-55815, 55840-55845
    regrowth ~ 52630
    residual obstructive tissue ~ 52630
    retropubic ~ 55831-55845
    suprapubic ~ 55821
    transurethral ~ 52601, 52630
  pterygium, with graft ~ 65426
  pubis, partial ~ 27070-27071
  radical synovium wrist ~ 25115-25116
  radius ~ 24130, 24136, 24145, 24152, 25145
    styloid process ~ 25230
  rectum
    with colon ~ 45121
    partial ~ 45111, 45113-45116, 45123
    prolapse ~ 45130-45135
    stricture ~ 45150
    total ~ 45119-45120
  redundant skin of eyelid ~ 15820-15823
  ribs ~ 21600-21616, 32900
  scapula
    ostectomy ~ 23190
    partial ~ 23182
    sequestrectomy ~ 23172
    tumor/cyst ~ 23140, 23145, 23146
  sclera ~ 66150, 66155, 66160, 66170
  scrotum ~ 55150
  semilunar cartilage of knee ~ 27332-27333
  seminal vesicle ~ 55650
  sesamoid bone
    foot ~ 28315
  sinus
    ethmoid ~ 31200-31205
    maxillary ~ 31225-31230
  Skene's gland ~ 53270
  skin
    excess ~ 15830-15839, 15847
    lesion
      benign ~ 11400-11471
      malignant ~ 11600-11646
    nose ~ 30120
  skin graft, preparation of site ~ 15000
  skull ~ 61501
  spermatic veins ~ 55530-55540
    abdominal approach ~ 55535
    hernia repair ~ 55540
  spleen ~ 38100-38102
    laparoscopic ~ 38120
  stapes
    with footplate drill out ~ 69661
    without foreign material ~ 69660
  sternum ~ 21620, 21630-21632
  stomach
    partial ~ 43631-43639, 43845
    total ~ 43620-43622
  sublingual gland ~ 42450
  submandibular gland ~ 42440
  sweat glands
    axillary ~ 11450-11451
    inguinal ~ 11462-11463
    perianal ~ 11470-11471
    perineal ~ 11470-11471
    umbilical ~ 11470-11471

Excision ~ *continued*
  synovium
    ankle ~ 27625-27626
    carpometacarpal joint ~ 26130
    elbow ~ 24102
    hip joint ~ 27054
    interphalangeal joint ~ 26140
    intertarsal joint ~ 28070
    knee joint ~ 27334-27335
    metacarpophalangeal joint ~ 26135
    metatarsophalangeal joint ~ 28072
    shoulder ~ 23105-23106
    tarsometatarsal joint ~ 28070
    wrist ~ 25105, 25118-25119
  talus ~ 28120, 28130
  tarsal ~ 28116, 28122
  temporal bone ~ 69535
  temporal, petrous apex ~ 69530
  tendon
    arm
      lower ~ 25109
    finger ~ 26180, 26390, 26415
    hand ~ 26390, 26415
    palm ~ 26170
  tendon sheath
    finger ~ 26145
    foot ~ 28086-28088
    palm ~ 26145
    wrist ~ 25115-25116
  testis
    laparoscopic ~ 54690
    partial ~ 54522
    radical ~ 54530-54535
    simple ~ 54520
    tumor ~ 54530-54535
  thrombectomy
    axillary vein ~ 34490
    bypass graft ~ 35875-35876
    femoropopliteal vein ~ 34401-34451
    iliac vein ~ 34401-34451
    subclavian vein ~ 34471-34490
    vena cava ~ 34401-34451
  thromboendarterectomy
    aorta, abdominal ~ 35331
    aortoiliofemoral ~ 35363
    axillary artery ~ 35321
    brachial artery ~ 35321
    carotid artery ~ 35301, 35390
    celiac artery ~ 35341
    femoral artery ~ 35371-35372
    iliac ~ 35361-35363
    iliac artery ~ 35351
    iliofemoral artery ~ 35355, 35363
    innominate artery ~ 35311
    mesenteric artery ~ 35341
    peroneal artery ~ 35305-35306
    popliteal artery ~ 35303
    renal artery ~ 35341
    subclavian artery ~ 35301-35311
    tibial artery ~ 35305-35306
    vertebral artery ~ 35301
  thymus gland ~ 60521
  thyroid gland for malignancy
    partial ~ 60210-60225
    removal all thyroid tissue ~ 60260
    secondary ~ 60260
    total ~ 60240
      cervical approach ~ 60271
      sternal split/transthoracic approach ~ 60270
        limited neck dissection ~ 60252
        radical neck dissection ~ 60254
  tibia ~ 27360, 27640
  tongue
    complete ~ 41140-41155
    frenum ~ 41115
      with mouth resection ~ 41150-41153
    partial ~ 41120-41135
    with radical neck ~ 41135, 41145-41155

Excision ~ *continued*
tonsils ~ 42825-42826
  lingual ~ 42870
  radical ~ 42842-42845
  tag ~ 42860
  with adenoids ~ 42820-42821
torus mandibularis ~ 21031
trachea stenosis ~ 31780-31781
transcervical approach ~ 60520
tricuspid valve ~ 33460
tumor
  abdominal wall ~ 22900-22905
  acetabulum ~ 27076
  ankle ~ 27615-27619, 27632, 27634
  arm, lower ~ 25071-25078
  arm, upper ~ 24071-24079
  back/flank ~ 21930
  bile duct ~ 47711-47712
  bladder ~ 51530, 52234-52240, 52355
  brain ~ 61510, 61518, 61520-61521, 61526-61530, 61545, 62164
  bronchi ~ 31640
  calcaneus ~ 27647, 28100-28103
  carpal ~ 25130-25136
  cheekbone ~ 21030, 21034, 21048-21049
  clavicle ~ 23140
    with allograft ~ 23146
    with autograft ~ 23145
  ear, middle
    extended ~ 69554
    transcanal ~ 69550
    transmastoid ~ 69552
  elbow ~ 24071-24079
  esophagus endoscopic ablation ~ 43229
  facial bones ~ 21029-21030, 21034-21040, 21046-21049
  facial tissue ~ 21011-21016
  femur ~ 27065-27067, 27355-27358, 27365
  fibula ~ 27635-27638, 27646
  finger ~ 26111-26118
  foot ~ 28039-28047
  gums ~ 41825-41827
  hand ~ 26111-26118
  heart ~ 33120-33130
  hip ~ 27043-27045, 27049, 27059, 27065-27067
    radical ~ 27075-27076
  humerus ~ 23150, 23220, 24110-24115
    with allograft ~ 23156, 24116
    with autograft ~ 23155, 24116
    radial head or neck ~ 24152
  ileum ~ 27065-27067
  innominate ~ 27077
  intestines, small ~ 43250
  ischial ~ 27078
  kidney ~ 52355
  knee ~ 27327-27328, 27337-27339, 27365
  lacrimal gland
    frontal approach ~ 68540
    involving osteotomy ~ 68550
  larynx ~ 31300
    endoscopic ~ 31540-31541, 31578
  leg, lower ~ 27615-27619, 27632, 27634
  leg, upper ~ 27327-27329, 27337-27339, 27365
  mandible ~ 21040-21047
  maxilla ~ 21030, 21034, 21048-21049
  mediastinal ~ 39220
  mediastinum ~ 32662
  metacarpal ~ 26200-26205, 26250
  metatarsal ~ 28104-28107, 28173
  neck ~ 21552-21558
  olecranon process ~ 24120
    with allograft ~ 24126
    with autograft ~ 24125
  parotid gland ~ 42410-42426
  pelvis ~ 27043-27045, 27049, 27059
  pericardial ~ 33050
  pericardium ~ 32661
  phalanges ~ 26210-26215, 26260-26262
    toe ~ 26215, 28108, 28175
  pituitary gland ~ 61546-61548, 62165

Excision ~ *continued*
  presacral ~ 49215
  pubis ~ 27065-27067
  radius ~ 24120-24125, 25120-25126, 25170
  rectum ~ 45160-45172
  sacrococcygeal ~ 49215
  scapula ~ 23140
    with allograft ~ 23146
    with autograft ~ 23145
  shoulder ~ 23071-23078
  skull ~ 61500
  spermatocele ~ 54840
  spinal cord ~ 63275-63290
  spleen, total ~ 38100
  sternum ~ 21630
  stomach ~ 43610
  talus ~ 27647, 28100-28103
  tarsal ~ 28104-28107, 28171
  thorax ~ 21552-21558
  thyroid ~ 60200
  tibia ~ 27635-27638, 27645-27646
  trachea
    cervical ~ 31785
    thoracic ~ 31786
  ulna ~ 24120-24125, 25120-25126, 25170
  ureter ~ 52355
  urethra ~ 52234-52240, 52355, 53220
  uterus
    abdominal approach ~ 58140, 58146
    vaginal approach ~ 58145
  vagina ~ 57135
  vertebra, lumbar ~ 22102
  vertebra, thoracic ~ 22101
  wrist ~ 25071-25078
  zygoma ~ 21030, 21034
turbinate ~ 30130-30140
tympanic nerve ~ 69676
ulcer
  stomach ~ 43610
ulna ~ 24147, 25145
  complete ~ 25240
  partial ~ 25150-25151, 25240
umbilicus ~ 49250
ureter ~ 50650-50660
ureterocele ~ 51535
urethra
  diverticulum ~ 53230-53235
  prolapse ~ 53275
  total
    female ~ 53210
    male ~ 53215
uterus
  laparoscopic ~ 58550
  leiomyomata ~ 58546
  partial ~ 58180
  radical ~ 58210, 58285
  removal tubes and/ or ovaries ~ 58262-58263, 58291, 58552, 58554
  total ~ 58150-58152, 58200
  vaginal ~ 58260, 58290-58294, 58550, 58553
    with colpectomy ~ 58275-58280
    with colpo-urethrocystopexy ~ 58267, 58293
    with repair of enterocele ~ 58270, 58292, 58294
uvula ~ 42140-42145
vagina
  cyst ~ 57135
  lumen ~ 57120
  repair of enterocele ~ 58280
  septum ~ 57130
  total ~ 57110-57112
    with hysterectomy ~ 58275-58280
varicocele
  spermatic cord ~ 55530-55540
    abdominal approach ~ 55535
    hernia repair ~ 55540
vas deferens ~ 55250
vascular malformation
  finger ~ 26115
  hand ~ 26115
vein, varicose ~ 37765-37766

Excision ~ *continued*
  vertebra
    additional segment ~ 22103, 22116
    cervical ~ 22110
    for tumor ~ 22100, 22110
    lumbar ~ 22102
      for tumor ~ 22114
    thoracic ~ 22112
      for tumor ~ 22101
  vertebral body
    decompression ~ 63081-63103
    lesion ~ 63300-63308
  vitreous ~ 67039
    with retinal surgery ~ 67041-67043
    total
      pars plana approach ~ 67036
      with epiretinal membrane stripping ~ 67041-67043
  vulva
    radical
      complete ~ 56633-56640
      partial ~ 56630-56632
    simple
      complete ~ 56625
      partial ~ 56620

Exclusion
  duodenum ~ 48547
  small intestine ~ 44700

Exenteration
  eye
    removal orbital contents ~ 65110
    therapeutic removal of bone ~ 65112
    with muscle or myocutaneous flap ~ 65114
  pelvis ~ 45126, 58240

Exercise stress tests
  cardiovascular ~ 93015-93018, 93464
  pulmonary ~ 94617, 94618

Exercise test ~ see also electromyography, needle
  cardiopulmonary ~ 94621
  ischemic limb ~ 95875

Exercise therapy ~ 97110-97113
Exfoliation, chemical ~ 17360
Exocrine, pancreas ~ see pancreas
Exomphalos ~ 49600-49611
Exostectomy ~ 28288
Exostoses ~ 69140
Exostoses, cartilaginous ~ 69140
Exostosis excision ~ 69140
Expander, skin, inflatable ~ see tissue, expander
Expired gas analysis ~ 94680-94690, 94770
  nitric oxide ~ 95012
  spectroscopic ~ 94799

Exploration
  abdomen ~ 49000-49002
    penetrating wound ~ 20102
    staging ~ 58960
  adrenal gland ~ 60540-60545
  anal endoscopy ~ 46600
  ankle ~ 27610, 27620
  arm, lower ~ 25248
  artery
    brachial ~ 24495
    carotid ~ 35701
    femoral ~ 35721
    other ~ 35761
    popliteal ~ 35741
  back, penetrating wound ~ 20102
  bile duct
    atresia ~ 47700
    endoscopy ~ 47552-47553
  blood vessel
    abdomen ~ 35840
    chest ~ 35820
    extremity ~ 35860
    neck ~ 35800
  brain
    via burr hole
      infratentorial ~ 61253
      supratentorial ~ 61250
    infratentorial ~ 61305
    supratentorial ~ 61304

Exploration ~ *continued*
  breast ~ 19020
  bronchi endoscopy ~ 31622
  bronchoscopy ~ 31622
  cauda equina ~ 63005-63011, 63017
  chest penetrating wound ~ 20101
  colon endoscopic ~ 44388, 45378
  colon-sigmoid endoscopic ~ 45330, 45335
  common bile duct with cholecystectomy ~ 47610
  duodenum ~ 44010
  ear, inner
    endolymphatic sac
      with shunt ~ 69806
      without shunt ~ 69805
  ear, middle ~ 69440
  elbow ~ 24000, 24101
  epididymis ~ 54865
  esophagus endoscopy ~ 43200
  extremity penetrating wound ~ 20103
  finger joint ~ 26075-26080
  flank penetrating wound ~ 20102
  gallbladder ~ 47480
  gastrointestinal tract, upper endoscopy ~ 43235-43236
  hand joint ~ 26070
  heart ~ 33310-33315
  hepatic duct ~ 47400
  hip ~ 27033
  interphalangeal joint toe ~ 28024
  intertarsal joint ~ 28020
  intestines, small
  endoscopy ~ 44360
  enterotomy ~ 44020
  kidney ~ 50010, 50045, 50120
  knee ~ 27310, 27331
  lacrimal duct ~ 68810
    canaliculi ~ 68840
    with anesthesia ~ 68811
    with insertion tube or stent ~ 68815
  liver wound ~ 47361-47362
  mediastinum ~ 39000-39010
  metatarsophalangeal joint ~ 28022
  nasolacrimal duct ~ 68810
    with anesthesia ~ 68811
    with insertion tube or stent ~ 68815
  neck
    lymph nodes ~ 38542
    penetrating wound ~ 20100
  nipple ~ 19110
  nose endoscopy ~ 31231-31235
  orbit ~ 61332, 61333
    with/without biopsy ~ 67450
    without bone flap ~ 67400
  parathyroid gland ~ 60500-60505
  pelvis ~ 49320
  prostate ~ 55860
    with nodes ~ 55862-55865
  rectum
    endoscopic ~ 45300
    injury ~ 45562-45563
  retroperitoneal area ~ 49010
  scrotum ~ 55110
  shoulder joint ~ 23040-23044, 23107
  sinus
    frontal ~ 31070-31075
    maxillary ~ 31020-31030
  skull ~ 61105
  spinal cord ~ 63001-63011, 63015-63017, 63040-63044
  spine fusion ~ 22830
  stomach ~ 43500
  tarsometatarsal joint ~ 28020
  testis, undescended ~ 54550-54560
  toe joint ~ 28024
  ureter ~ 50600
  vagina ~ 57000
    endocervical ~ 57452
  wrist ~ 25101, 25248
    joint ~ 25040
Exploratory laparotomy ~ 49000-49002
Expression lesion, conjunctiva ~ 68040
Exteriorization, small intestine ~ 44300
External cephalic version ~ 59412

External ear ~ see ear, external
External extoses ~ 69140
External fixation
  adjustment/revision ~ 20693
  application ~ 20690-20692
    stereotactic computer assisted ~ 20696-20697
  mandibular fracture
    open treatment ~ 21454
    percutaneous treatment ~ 21452
    removal ~ 20694
Extirpation, lacrimal sac ~ 68520
Extracorporeal circulation
  cannulation
    chemotherapy perfusion ~ 36823
Extracorporeal dialyses ~ 90935-90937
Extracorporeal membrane oxygenation cannulization (ECMO)
  arterial exposure with graft creation ~ 33987
  insertion of cannula(e)
    open ~ 33953, 33954
    percutaneous ~ 33951, 33952
    sternotomy/thoracotomy ~ 33955, 33956
  daily management
    veno-arterial ~ 33947
    veno-venous ~ 33946
  left heart valve
    insertion ~ 33988
    removal ~ 33989
  removal of cannula(e)
    open ~ 33969, 33984
    percutaneous ~ 33965, 33966
    sternotomy/thoracotomy ~ 33985, 33986
  repositioning of cannula(e)
    open ~ 33959, 33962
    percutaneous ~ 33957, 33958
    sternotomy/thoracotomy ~ 33963, 33964
Extracorporeal photochemotherapies ~ 36522
Extracorporeal shock wave therapy ~ see lithotripsy
  plantar fascia ~ 0020T
Extracranial intracranial ~ 61623
Extraction lens
  extracapsular ~ 66940
  intracapsular ~ 66920
    for dislocated lens ~ 66930
Extraction, cataract ~ 66830
Extradural injection
  Infusion
    with imaging guidance ~ 62325, 62327
    without imaging guidance ~ 62324, 62326
  Injection
    with imaging guidance ~ 62321, 62323
    without imaging guidance ~ 62320, 62322
Extraocular muscle ~ 67340
Extrauterine pregnancy ~ see ectopic pregnancy
Extravasation blood ~ see hemorrhage
Extremity
  lower
    harvest of vein for bypass graft ~ 35500
    harvest of vein for vascular reconstruction ~ 35572
    revision ~ 35879-35881
    ultrasound ~ 76881-76882
  upper
    harvest of artery for coronary artery bypass graft ~ 35600
    harvest of vein for bypass graft ~ 35500
    repair blood vessel ~ 35206
  wound exploration penetrating wound ~ 20103
Eye
  age-related eye disease study (AREDS) ~ 4177F
  biometry ~ 76516-76519, 92136
  computerized corneal topography ~ 92025
  dilation outflow canal ~ 66174-66175
  discission of anterior hyaloid membrane ~ 65810
  drainage, anterior chamber
    with diagnostic aqueous aspiration ~ 65800
    with removal of blood ~ 65815
    with removal of vitreous ~ 65810
    with therapeutic aqueous release ~ 65800
  endoscopy ~ 66990
  evaluation
    dilated fundus ~ 2020F-2021F
    dilated macular ~ 2019F

Eye ~ *continued*
  goniotomy ~ 65820
  incision
    adhesions
      anterior synechiae ~ 65860, 65870
      corneovitreal adhesions ~ 65880
      goniosynechiae ~ 65865
      posterior synechiae ~ 65875
    anterior chamber ~ 65820
    trabeculae ~ 65850
  injection
    air ~ 66020
    medication ~ 66030, 67500
    pharmacologic agent ~ 0465T, 67028
  insertion
    aqueous drainage device ~ 66179, 66180
    drug eluting ocular inseert, eyelid ~ 0444T, 0445T
  implantation
    corneal ring segments ~ 65785
    drainage device ~ 0191T, 0253T
    drug delivery system ~ 67027
    electrode array ~ 0100T
    foreign material for reinforcement ~ 65155
    muscles attached ~ 65140
    muscles, not attached ~ 65135
    reinsertion ~ 65150
    scleral shell ~ 65130
  interferometry biometry ~ 92136
  lesion excision ~ 65900
  nerve
    destruction ~ 67345
    optic, head evaluation ~ 2027F
  paracentesis anterior chamber
    with diagnostic aspiration of aqueous ~ 65800
    removal of blood ~ 65815
    removal of vitreous and/or discission anterior hyaloid membrane ~ 65810
    with therapeutic release of aqueous ~ 65800
  radial keratotomy ~ 65771
  reconstruction
    graft
      conjunctiva ~ 65782
      stem cell ~ 65781
      transplantation
        amniotic membrane ~ 65780
  removal
    blood clot ~ 65930
    bone ~ 65112
    foreign body
      conjunctival embedded ~ 65210
      conjunctival superficial ~ 65205
      corneal with slit lamp ~ 65222
      corneal without slit lamp ~ 65220
      intraocular ~ 65235-65265
    implant ~ 65175
      anterior segment ~ 65920
      muscles, not attached ~ 65103
      posterior segment ~ 67120-67121
  repair
    amniotic membrane ~ 65778-65779
    conjunctiva
      by mobilization and rearrangement without hospitalization ~ 65272
      by mobilization and rearrangement with hospitalization ~ 65273
      direct closure ~ 65270
    cornea
      nonperforating ~ 65275
      perforating ~ 65280-65285
    muscles ~ 65290
    sclera
      anterior segment ~ 66250
      with graft ~ 66225
      without graft ~ 66220
      with tissue glue ~ 65286
    trabeculae ~ 65855
    wound
      by mobilization and rearrangement ~ 65272-65273
      direct closure ~ 65270
  shunt, aqueous to extraocular reservoir ~ 66180
  transluminal dilation, aqueous outflow canal ~ 66174-66175

Eye ~ *continued*
  ultrasound ~ 76510-76514
    biometry ~ 76516-76519
    foreign body ~ 76529
  unlisted services and procedures
    anterior segment ~ 66999
    posterior segment ~ 67299
  with muscle or myocutaneous flap ~ 65114
    muscles attached ~ 65105
    ocular contents
      without implant ~ 65091
      with implant ~ 65093
    orbital contents ~ 65110
      without implant ~ 65101
  X-ray ~ 70030
Eye and ocular adnexa, surgical procedures 65091-68899
Eyebrow repair
  ptosis ~ 67900
Eyeglasses ~ 92340-92342
Eyelashes
  repair trichiasis
    epilation
      by forceps only ~ 67820
      by other than forceps ~ 67825
    incision of lid margin ~ 67830
      with free mucous membrane graft ~ 67835
Eyelid
  abscess, incision and drainage ~ 67700
  biopsy ~ 67810
  blepharoplasty ~ 15820-15823
  chalazion
    excision ~ 67805
      with anesthesia ~ 67808
      multiple ~ 67801-67805
      single ~ 67800
  closure by suture ~ 67875
  incision
    canthus ~ 67715
    sutures ~ 67710
  injection, subconjunctival ~ 68200
  lesion
    destruction ~ 67850
    excision
      with anesthesia ~ 67808
      without closure ~ 67840
      multiple ~ 67801-67805
      single ~ 67800
  placement, drug-eluting ocular insert ~ 0444T, 0445T
  reconstruction
    canthus ~ 67950
    total ~ 67973-67975
    total eyelid
      lower ~ 67973-67975
      second stage ~ 67975
      upper ~ 67974
    transfer of tarsoconjunctival flap from opposing eyelid ~ 67971
  removal foreign body ~ 67938
  repair ~ 21280-21282
    blepharoptosis
      conjunctivo-tarso-muller's muscle-levator resection ~ 67908
      frontalis muscle technique ~ 67901-67094
      reduction overcorrection of ptosis ~ 67909
      superior rectus technique with fascial sling ~ 67906
    ectropion
      blepharoplasty ~ 67914
      suture ~ 67914
    entropion
      excision tarsal wedge ~ 67923
      extensive ~ 67924
      suture ~ 67921
      thermocauterization ~ 67922
    excisional ~ 67961
      over one-fourth of lid margin ~ 67966
    lagophthalmos ~ 67912
    lashes
      epilation, by forceps only ~ 67820
      epilation, by other than forceps ~ 67825
      lid margin ~ 67830-67835
    wound
      full thickness ~ 67935
      partial thickness ~ 67930

Eyelid ~ *continued*
  repair with graft retraction ~ 67911
  skin graft
    full thickness ~ 67961
    split ~ 67961
  suture ~ 67880
    with transposition of tarsal plate ~ 67882
  tissue transfer, adjacent ~ 67961
  unlisted services and procedures ~ 67999
Eyelid ptoses ~ see blepharoptosis
Eye allergy test ~ 95060
Eye evisceration ~ 65091, 65093
Eye exam
  established patient ~ 92012-92014
  new patient ~ 92002-92004
  with anesthesia ~ 92018-92019
Eye exercises, training ~ 92065
Eye muscles
  biopsy ~ 67346
  repair
    strabismus
      adjustable sutures ~ 67335
      exploration and/or repair detached extraocular muscle ~ 67340
      one vertical muscle ~ 67314
      on patient with previous surgery ~ 67331
      posterior fixation suture ~ 67334
      recession or resection ~ 67311-67312
      release of scar tissue without detaching extraocular muscle ~ 67343
      two or more vertical muscles ~ 67316
      with scarring extraocular muscles ~ 67332
      with superior oblique muscle ~ 67318
    transposition ~ 67320
  unlisted services and procedures ~ 67399
Eye prosthesis ~ see prosthesis
Eye socket ~ see orbit ~ 21385-21395, 21260-21263, 21267-21268, 67415
E antigens ~ 87350
E B virus ~ 86663-86665
E vitamin ~ 84446

F

Face
  CT scan ~ 70486-70488
  lesion
    destruction ~ 17000-17004, 17280-17286
  lift ~ 15824-15828
  magnetic resonance imaging (MRI) ~ 70540-70543
  tumor resection ~ 21015
Facial asymmetries ~ 21247
Facial bones ~ see also mandible; maxilla
  abscess excision ~ 21026
  reconstruction
    secondary ~ 21275
  repair ~ 21208-21209
  tumor
    excision ~ 21029-21034
    resection
      radical ~ 21015
  X-ray ~ 70140-70150
Facial nerve
  anastomosis
    to hypoglossal ~ 64868
    to spinal accessory ~ 64866
  avulsion ~ 64742
  chemodenervation, muscles ~ 64615
  decompression ~ 61590, 61596
    intratemporal
      lateral to geniculate ganglion ~ 69720, 69740
      medial to geniculate ganglion ~ 69725, 69745
      total ~ 69955
  function study ~ 92516
  incision ~ 64742
  injection, anesthetic ~ 64402
  mobilization ~ 61590

Facial nerve ~ continued
repair
lateral to geniculate ganglion ~ 69740
medial to geniculate ganglion ~ 69745
repair/suture
with or without graft ~ 64864-64865
suture
lateral to geniculate ganglion ~ 69740
medial to geniculate ganglion ~ 69745
transection ~ 64742
Facial nerve paralysis
graft ~ 15840-15845
repair ~ 15840-15845
Facial prosthesis impression ~ 21088
Facial rhytidectomy ~ 15824-15828
Factor
ACTH-releasing ~ 80412
antinuclear ~ 86038-86039
blood coagulation ~ 85210-85293
Factor I ~ 85384-85385
Factor II ~ 85210
Factor III ~ see thromboplastin
Factor inhibitor test ~ 85335
Factor IV ~ see calcium
Factor IXix ~ 85250
Factor rheumatoid ~ 86430-86431
Factor VII ~ 85230
Factor VIII ~ 85210-85293
Factor X ~ 85260
Factor X, activated ~ 85260
Factor XA inhibitor ~ 85300-85301
Factor XI ~ 85270
Factor XII ~ 85280
Factor XIII ~ 85290-85291
Fitzgerald ~ 85293
Fletcher ~ 85293
hyperglycemic-glycogenolytic ~ 82943
intrinsic ~ 83528
sulfation ~ 84305
Fallopian tube
anastomosis ~ 58750
catheterization ~ 58345, 74742
destruction endoscopy ~ 58670
ectopic pregnancy ~ 59121
with salpingectomy and/or oophorectomy ~ 59120
excision ~ 58700-58720
ligation ~ 58600-58611
lysis adhesions ~ 58740
occlusion ~ 58615
endoscopy ~ 58671
placement, implant for occlusion ~ 58568
pregnancy ~ 59121
repair ~ 58752
anastomosis ~ 58750
create stoma ~ 58770
tumor resection ~ 58950, 58952-58956
unlisted services and procedures ~ 58999
X-ray ~ 74742
Fallot, tetralogy of ~ 33692-33697, 33924
Family psychotherapy ~ 90846-90849, 99510
Fanconi anemia chromosome analysis ~ 88248
Farnsworth-Munsell color test ~ 92283
Farr test ~ 82784-82787
Fasanella-Servat procedure ~ 67908
Fascia graft ~ 15840
Fascia lata graft harvesting ~ 20920-20922
Fascial defect
leg ~ 27656
urostomy ~ 50728
Fascial graft
cheek ~ 15840
fascia and skin flap ~ 15733, 15734, 15736, 15738
free microvascular anastomosis ~ 15758
harvest ~ 20920, 20922
reconstruction
collateral ligament ~ 26541
hamstring muscle ~ 27386
infrapatellar tendon ~ 27381
quadriceps muscle ~ 27386
tendon pulley ~ 26502
sternoclavicular dislocation ~ 23532

Fasciectomy
foot ~ 28060
radical ~ 28060-28062
palm ~ 26121-26125
Fasciocutaneous flaps ~ 15733-15738
Fasciotomy
arm, lower ~ 24495, 25020-25025
buttock, decompression ~ 27027
with debridement ~ 27057
foot ~ 28008
hand decompression ~ 26037
hip ~ 27025
knee ~ 27305, 27496-27499
leg, lower ~ 27600-27602, 27892-27894
leg, upper ~ 27305, 27496-27499, 27892-27894
palm ~ 26040-26045
pelvis, decompression ~ 27027
with debridement ~ 27057
plantar endoscopic ~ 29893
thigh ~ 27025
toe ~ 28008
wrist ~ 25020-25023
FAST ~ see allergen immunotherapy
Fat
feces ~ 82705-82715
removal, lipectomy ~ 15876-15879
Fatty acid
blood ~ 82725
very long chain ~ 82726
Fat stain
feces ~ 89125
respiratory secretions ~ 89125
sputum ~ 89125
urine ~ 89125
FDP ~ 85362-85380
Fe (iron) ~ 83540
Feedback, psychophysiologic (see biofeedback) ~ 90901-90911
Female castration ~ 58262-58263, 58291-58292, 58552, 58554, 58661, 58940-58943
Female genital system, surgical procedures ~ 56405-58999
Female gonad ~ see ovary
Femoral arteries ~ see artery, femoral
Femoral nerve
injection, anesthetic ~ 64447-64448
Femoral stem prosthesis ~ 27132
Femoral vein ~ 34501
Femur ~ see hip; knee; leg, upper
abscess, incision ~ 27303
bursa, excision ~ 27062
craterization ~ 27070, 27360
cyst, excision ~ 27065-27067, 27355-27358
diaphysectomy ~ 27360
drainage ~ 27303
excision ~ 27070, 27360
epiphyseal bar ~ 20150
fracture ~ 27244
closed treatment ~ 27501-27503
distal ~ 27508, 27510, 27514
distal, medial or lateral condyle ~ 27509
epiphysis ~ 27516-27519
intertrochanteric ~ 27244
intertrochanteric
closed treatment ~ 27238
treatment with implant ~ 27244
with implant ~ 27245
with manipulation ~ 27240
neck
closed treatment ~ 27230-27232
open treatment ~ 27236
percutaneous fixation ~ 27235
open treatment ~ 27245, 27269, 27506-27507, 27511-27513
percutaneous fixation ~ 27509
pertrochanteric ~ 27244
pertrochanteric
closed treatment ~ 27238
treatment with implant ~ 27244
with implant ~ 27245
with manipulation ~ 27240
proximal end, head
closed treatment ~ 27267-27268
open treatment ~ 27269

Femur ~ *continued*
  shaft ~ 27500, 27502, 27506-27507
  subtrochanteric ~ 27244
  subtrochanteric
    closed treatment ~ 27238
    treatment with implant ~ 27244
    with implant ~ 27245
    with manipulation ~ 27240
  supracondylar ~ 27501-27503, 27509, 27511-27513
  transcondylar ~ 27501-27503, 27509, 27511-27513
  trochanteric
    closed treatment ~ 27246
    open treatment ~ 27248
    without manipulation ~ 27501
    with manipulation ~ 27503
  halo ~ 20663
  lesion excision ~ 27062
  osteoplasty
    lengthening ~ 27466-27468
    shortening ~ 27465, 27468
  osteotomywithout fixation ~ 27448
  prophylactic treatment ~ 27187, 27495
  realignment ~ 27454
  reconstruction ~ 27468
    at knee ~ 27442-27443, 27446
    lengthening ~ 27466-27468
    shortening ~ 27465, 27468
  repair ~ 27470-27472
    epiphysis ~ 27181, 27475, 27742
      arrest ~ 27185
    muscle transfer ~ 27110
    osteotomy ~ 27140, 27151-27156, 27161-27165, 27450-27454
    with graft ~ 27170
  saucerization ~ 27070, 27360
  tumor excision ~ 27065-27067, 27355-27358, 27365
  X-ray ~ 7355, 73552
Fenestration, pericardium ~ 33015
Fenestration procedure
  skin, laser ~ 0479T, 0480T
  tracheostomy ~ 31610
Fern test ~ 87210
Ferric chloride, urine ~ 81005
Ferrihemoglobin ~ 83045-83050
Ferritin, blood or urine ~ 82728
Ferroxidase ~ (ceruloplasmin) 82390
Fertility control ~ see contraception
Fertility test
  semen analysis ~ 89300-89321
  sperm analysis
    cervical mucus penetration test ~ 89330
    hamster penetration ~ 89329
Fertilization, assisted
  oocyte ~ 89250, 89251
    microtechnique ~ 89280-89281
    with co-culture ~ 89251
Fertilization in vitro ~ 58321-58322
Fetal biophysical profile ~ 76818-76819
Fetal contraction stress test ~ 59020
Fetal hemoglobin ~ 85461
Fetal lung maturity assessment; lecithin sphingomyelin ratio ~ 83661
Fetal monitoring ~ 59050-59051, 99500
Fetal non-stress test ~ 59025
  ultrasound ~ 76818
Fetal procedure
  amniocentesis ~ 59000
  amnioinfusion ~ 59070
  amniotic fluid reduction ~ 59001
  cord occlusion ~ 59072
  cordocentesis ~ 59012
    ultrasound guidance ~ 76941
  fluid drainage ~ 59074
  intrauterine transfusion ~ 36460
    ultrasound guidance ~ 76941
  magnetic cardiac signal recording ~ 0475T-0478T
  MRI ~ 74712, 74713
  non-stress test ~ 59025
  shunt placement ~ 59076
  stress test ~ 59020
  unlisted fetal invasive procedure ~ 59897
  unlisted laparoscopy procedure ~ 59898
  unlisted procedure, maternity care and delivery ~ 59899

Fetal testing
  amniocentesis ~ 59000
  amniotic fluid lung maturity ~ 83661, 83663-83664
  heart ~ 76825-76826
    Doppler
      complete ~ 76827
      follow-up or repeat study ~ 76828
  hemoglobin ~ 83030-83033, 85460
  MRI ~ 74712, 74713
  non-stess test ~ 59025
    ultrasound ~ 76815-76818
  ultrasound ~ 76801-76828
    biophysical profile ~ 76818, 76819
    fetal ~ 76813-76816
    fetal and maternal ~ 76801, 76802, 76805, 76810-76812, 76817
    heart ~ 76825-76828
    middle cerebral artery ~ 76821
    umbilical artery ~ 76820
Fetuin ~ 82105-82106
Fever, Australian Q ~ 86000, 86638
  documentation ~ 1060F-1061F
Fever, Japanese river ~ 86000
Fibrillation, atrial ~ 33254-33256, 33265-33266
  documentation ~ 1060F-1061F
Fibrillation, heart ~ see heart, fibrillation
Fibrin
  degradation products ~ 85362-85380
  deposit removal ~ 32150
  stabilizing factor ~ 85290-85291
Fibrinase ~ 85400
Fibrinogen ~ 85384-85385
Fibrinolysin ~ 85400
Fibrinolysins ~ 85390
Fibrinolysis
  alpha-2 antiplasmin ~ 85410
  assay ~ 85396
    activity ~ 85397
  plasmin ~ 85400
  plasminogen ~ 85420-85421
  plasminogen activator ~ 85415
  pleural cavity, instillation of agent ~ 32561, 32562
Fibroadenoma, excision ~ 19120-19126
  ablation
    cryosurgical ~ 19105
Fibroblastoma, arachnoidal ~ 61512, 61519
Fibrocutaneous tags ~ 11200-11201
Fibromatosis, Dupuytren's ~ 26040-26045
Fibromatosis, penile ~ see Peyronie disease
Fibromyoma ~ 58140, 58545-58546, 58561
Fibronectin, fetal ~ 82731
Fibrosis, penile ~ see Peyronie disease
Fibrosis, retroperitoneal ~ 50715
Fibrous cavernitides ~ see Peyronie disease
Fibrous dysplasia ~ 21029, 21181-21184
Fibula ~ see ankle; knee; tibia
  bone graft with microvascular anastomosis ~ 20955
  craterization ~ 27360, 27641
  cyst excision ~ 27635-27638
  diaphysectomy ~ 27360, 27641
  excision ~ 27360, 27641
    epiphyseal bar ~ 20150
  fracture
    malleolus ~ 27786-27814
    shaft ~ 27780-27784
  incision ~ 27607
  osteoplasty lengthening ~ 27715
  repair
    epiphysis ~ 27477-27485, 27730-27742
    nonunion or malunion ~ 27726
    osteotomy ~ 27707-27712
  saucerization ~ 27360, 27641
  tumor excision ~ 27635-27638, 27646
  X-ray ~ 73590
Figure of eight cast ~ 29049
Filariasis ~ 86280
Filtering operation ~ see incision, sclera, fistulization
Filtration implant, glaucoma ~ 66180, 66185
Fimbrioplasty ~ 58760
  laparoscopic ~ 58672
Fine needle aspiration ~ 10021-10022
  evaluation ~ 88172-88173

Finger ~ see phalanx, finger
  abscess
    bone, incision and drainage ~ 26034
    incision and drainage ~ 26010-26011
  amputation ~ 26951-26952
    with exploration or removal ~ 26910
  arthrocentesis ~ 20600
  arthrodesis
    interphalangeal joint ~ 26860-26863
    metacarpophalangeal joint ~ 26850-26852
  bone, incision and drainage ~ 26034
  cast ~ 29086
  collection of blood ~ 36415-36416
  decompression ~ 26035
  excision
    constricting ring ~ 26596
    tendon ~ 26180, 26390, 26415
  insertion, tendon graft ~ 26392
  magnetic resonance imaging (MRI) ~ 73221
  reconstruction
    extra digit ~ 26587
    toe to hand transfer ~ 26551-26556
  removal
    implantation ~ 26320
    tube ~ 26392, 26416
  repair
    blood vessel ~ 35207
    claw finger ~ 26499
    extra digit ~ 26587
    macrodactylia ~ 26590
    tendon
      extensor ~ 26415-26434, 26445-26449, 26460
      flexor ~ 26356-26358, 26440-26442, 26455
    volar plate ~ 26548
    web finger ~ 26560-26562
  replantation ~ 20816-20822
  reposition ~ 26555
  sesamoidectomy ~ 26185
  splint ~ 29130-29131
  strapping ~ 29280
  tendon sheath
    excision ~ 26145
    incision ~ 26055
    incision and drainage ~ 26020
  tenotomy ~ 26060, 26460
    flexor ~ 26455
  tumor excision ~ 26111-26118
  unlisted services and procedures ~ 26989
  X-ray ~ 73140
Finger flap, tissue transfer ~ 14350
Finger joint ~ see intercarpal joint
Finney operation ~ 43810, 43850-43855
FISH ~ 88365
Fissurectomy, anal ~ 46200
Fissure in ano ~ 46200, 46949-46942
Fistula
  anal, repair ~ 46288, 46706
  autogenous graft ~ 36825
  bronchi, repair ~ 32815
  carotid-cavernous, repair ~ 61710
  chest wall, repair ~ 32906
  conjunctiva
    without tube ~ 68745
    with tube or stent ~ 68750
  enterovesical
    closure ~ 44660-44661
  kidney ~ 50520-50526
  lacrimal gland closure ~ 68770
    dacryocystorhinostomy ~ 68720
  nose repair ~ 30580-30600
  oval window ~ 69666
  postauricular ~ 69700
  rectovaginal
    abdominal approach ~ 57305
    transperineal approach ~ 57308
    with concomitant colostomy ~ 57307
  round window ~ 69667

Fistula ~ *continued*
  sclera
    sclerectomy with punch or scissors with iridectomy ~ 66160
    thermocauterization with iridectomy ~ 66155
    trabeculectomy ab externo in absence previous surgery ~ 66170
    trabeculectomy ab externo with scarring ~ 66172
    trephination with iridectomy ~ 66150
  suture
    kidney ~ 50520-50526
    ureter ~ 50920-50930
  trachea ~ 31755
  tracheoesophageal
    repair ~ 43305, 43312, 43314
    speech prothesis ~ 31611
  ureter ~ 50920-50930
  urethra ~ 53400-53405
  urethrovaginal ~ 57310
    with bulbocavernosus transplant ~ 57311
  vesicouterine closure ~ 51920-51925
  vesicovaginal
    closure ~ 51900
    transvesical and vaginal approach ~ 57330
    vaginal approach ~ 57320
  X-ray ~ 76080
Fistulectomy, anal ~ 46060, 46270-46285
Fistulization
  conjunction to nasal cavity ~ 68745
  esophagus ~ 43352
  intestines ~ 44300-44346
  lacrimal sac to nasal cavity ~ 68720
  penis ~ 54435
  pharynx ~ 42955
  repair salivary cyst, sublingual ~ 42325-42326
  tracheopharyngeal ~ 31755
Fistulization, interatrial ~ 33735-33737
Fistulotomy, anal ~ 46270, 46280
Fitting
  cervical cap ~ 57170
  contact lens ~ 92071-92072, 92310-92313
  diaphragm ~ 57170
  low vision aid ~ 92354-92355
  ocular prosthesis ~ 92330
  spectacles ~ 92340-92342
  spectacle prosthesis ~ 92352-92353
Fitzgerald factor ~ 85293
Fixation, interdental without fracture ~ 21497
Fixation, external ~ see external fixation
Fixation, kidney ~ see nephropexy
Fixation, rectum ~ see proctopexy
Fixation, tongue ~ see tongue, fixation
Fixation (device) ~ see application; bone, fixation; spinal instrumentation
  application, external ~ 20690-20692, 20696-20697
  pelvic, insertion ~ 22848
  removal
    external ~ 20694
    internal ~ 20670-20680
  sacrospinous ligament, vaginal prolapse ~ 57282
  shoulder ~ 23700
  skeletal, humeral epycondyle, percutaneous ~ 24566
  spinal ~ see spinal instrumentation
Fixation test, complement ~ 86171
Flank ~ see back/flank
Flap ~ see skin graft and flap
  free, breast reconstruction ~ 19364
  grafts ~ 15570-15738, 15842
  latissimus dorsi breast reconstruction ~ 19361
  omentum ~ 49905
  omentum, free, with microvascular anastomosis ~ 49906
  transverse rectus abdominis myocutaneous breast reconstruction ~ 19367-19369
Flatfoot correction ~ 28735
Flea typhus ~ 86000
Fletcher factor ~ 85292
Flow cytometry ~ 88182-88189
  diagnostic/pre-treatment ~ 3170F
Flow-volume loop, pulmonary ~ 94375
Fluid
  amniotic ~ see amniotic fluid
  body ~ 89060
  cerebrospinal ~ 86325
  collection, incision and drainage, skin ~ 10140

Fluorescein
  angiography, ocular ~ 92287
  intravenous injection
    vascular flow check, graft ~ 15860
Fluorescein angiography ~ 92235
Fluorescent in situ hybridization ~ 88365
Fluoride
  blood ~ 82735
  urine ~ 82735
Fluoroscopy
  examination
    angiography ~ 36901, 36902, 36903
    central venous access device~ 36598
    GI tract~ 74340
    larynx ~ 70370
    pharynx ~ 70370
  guidance
    abscess drainage~ 75989
    bile duct
      calculus removal~ 47544
      guide catheter~ 74328, 74330
    catheterization
      central venous~ 36597
      dialysis circuit ~ 36901, 36902, 36903
      renal artery~ 36251-36254
      spine/paraspinous~ 77003
    chest
      bronchoscopy~ 31622-31638, 31640, 31641, 31643, 31645, 31646,
        31647-31649, 31651, 31660, 31661
    disc decompression~ 62287
    electrothermal annuloplasty~ 22526, 22527
    esophagoscopy~ 43213, 43214
    intubation
      colonic~ 49442, 49450
      duodenostomy~ 49441, 49451
      gastro-jejunostomy~ 49446, 49452
      gastrostomy~ 49440, 49446, 49450
      GI tract~ 74340
      jejunostomy~ 49441, 49446, 49451
      nasogastric~ 43752
      nephrostomy~ 50389
      orogastric~ 43752
    nephroureteral catheter
      replacement~ 50387
    spinal neurostimulator electrode
      removal~ 63661, 63662
      revision/replacement~ 63663, 63664
    stoma
      creation~ 49465
      removal of foreign body~ 49460
    thrombectomy
      arterial
        coronary ~ 92973
        intracranial ~ 61645
        noncoronary ~ 37184-37186
      venous ~ 37187, 37188
    vena cava filter
      insertion ~ 37191
      removal ~ 37193
      repositioning ~ 37192
    venous access device ~ 36598, 77001
  hourly ~ 76000, 76001
  needle biopsy ~ 77002
  unlisted services and procedures ~ 76496
Flurazepam, blood or urine ~ 80346, 80347
Flush aortogram ~ 36251-36254
FNA ~ see fine needle aspiration
Foam stability test ~ 83662
Fold, vocal ~ see vocal cords
Foley operation pyeloplasty ~ 50400-50405, 50544
Foley Y-pyeloplasty ~ 50400-50405
Folic acid ~ 82747
  blood ~ 82746
Follicle stimulating hormone (FSH) ~ 80418, 80426, 83001
Folliculin ~ 82679
Follitropin ~ 80418, 80426, 83001
Follow-up inpatient consultations ~ 99251-99255
Follow-up services
  post-op ~ 99024
Fontan procedure ~ 33600-33617

Food allergy test
  allergen-specific IgE ~ 86003, 86005, 86008
  challenge test ~ 95076, 95079
Foot ~ see metatarsal ~ 28456
  amputation ~ 28800-28805
  bursa incision and drainage ~ 28001
  capsulotomy ~ 28260-28264
  cast ~ 29450
  fasciectomy ~ 28060
    radical ~ 28060-28062
  fasciotomy ~ 28008
    endoscopic ~ 29893
  incision ~ 28002-28005
  joint ~ see tarsometatarsal joint ~ 28570-28576, 28585
    magnetic resonance imaging (MRI) ~ 73721-73723
  lesion excision ~ 28080, 28090
  magnetic resonance imaging (MRI) ~ 73718-73720
  nerve
    excision ~ 28055
    incision ~ 28035
  neuroma excision ~ 28080
  reconstruction cleft foot ~ 28360
  removal foreign body ~ 28190-28193
  repair
    muscle ~ 28250
    tendon ~ 28200-28230, 28234-28238
  replantation ~ 20838
  sesamoid excision ~ 28315
  strapping ~ 29540
  suture tendon ~ 28200-28210
  tendon sheath excision ~ 28086-28088
  tenotomy ~ 28230, 28234
  tumor excision ~ 28039-28047
  unlisted services and procedures ~ 28899
  X-ray ~ 73620-73630
Foot abscess ~ 28005
Forearm ~ see arm, lower ~ 20805
Forehead
  flap ~ 15731
  reconstruction ~ 21179, 21180, 21182-21184
    midface ~ 15730, 21159, 21160
  reduction ~ 21137-21139
Forehead and orbital rim
  reconstruction ~ 21172-21180
Foreign body removal
  anal ~ 46608
  arm
    lower ~ 25248
    upper ~ 24200, 24201
  auditory canal, external ~ 69200
    with anesthesia ~ 69205
  bronchi ~ 31635
  colon ~ 44025, 44390, 45332, 45379
  conjunctival, embedded ~ 65210
  cornea ~ 65220, 65222
  duodenum ~ 44010
  external eye ~ 65205
  eyelid ~ 67938
  finger ~ 26075, 26080
  foot ~ 28190, 28193
  gum ~ 41805
  hand ~ 26070
  hip ~ 27033, 27086, 27087
  intraocular ~ 65235
  knee joint ~ 27310, 27331, 27372
  lacrimal duct/gland ~ 68530
  larynx ~ 31511, 31530, 31531, 31577
  leg, upper ~ 27372
  lung ~ 32151
  mandible ~ 41806
  maxillary sinus ~ 31299
  mediastinum ~ 39000, 39010
  mouth ~ 40804, 40805
  nose ~ 30300
    with anesthesia ~ 30310
    lateral rhinotomy ~ 30320
  orbit ~ 67413, 67430
  pancreatic duct ~ 43275-43276
  pelvis ~ 27086, 27087
  penis ~ 54115

Foreign body removal ~ *continued*
pericardium ~ 33020
  endoscopic ~ 32658
pharynx ~ 42809
pleura ~ 32150, 32151
  endoscopic ~ 32653
rectum ~ 45307, 45915
scrotum ~ 55120
shoulder ~ 23040, 23044
  complicated ~ 23335
  deep ~ 23334
subcutaneous 23330
skin with debridement ~ 11010-11012
subcutaneous ~ 10120, 10121
  with debridement ~ 11010-11012
ureter ~ 50961, 50980
urethra ~ 52310, 52315
uterus ~ 58562
vagina ~ 57415
Forensic exam
autopsy ~ 88040
cytopathology ~ 88125
Foreskin of penis ~ 54450
Formycin diphosphate ~ 85362-85380
Fournier's gangrene ~ 11004-11006
Fowler-Stephens orchiopexy ~ 54640, 54650, 54692
Fowler-Stephens procedure ~ 54650
Fox operation ~ 67921-67924
Fraction, factor IX (nine) ~ 85250
Fracture
acetabulum
  closed treatment ~ 27220-27222
    with manipulation ~ 27222
    without manipulation ~ 27220
  open treatment ~ 27226-27228
alveola
  closed treatment ~ 21421
  open treatment ~ 21422-21423
alveolar ridge
  closed treatment ~ 21440
  open treatment ~ 21445
ankle
  bimalleolar ~ 27808-27814
  closed treatment ~ 27816-27818
  lateral ~ 27786-27814, 27792
  medial ~ 27760-27766, 27808-27814
  posterior ~ 27767-27769, 27808-27814
  trimalleolar ~ 27816-27823
ankle bone
  medial ~ 27760-27762
Bennett's thumb fracture
  with dislocation ~ 26645, 26650
  open treatment ~ 26665
bronchi endoscopy ~ 31630
calcaneus
  closed treatment ~ 28400-28405
    with manipulation ~ 28405-28406
    without manipulation ~ 28400
  open treatment ~ 28415-28420
  percutaneous fixation ~ 28436
carpal
  closed treatment
    with manipulation ~ 25624, 25635
    without manipulation ~ 25622, 25630
  open treatment ~ 25628, 25645
carpal scaphoid, closed treatment ~ 25622
cheekbone
  with manipulation ~ 21355
  open treatment ~ 21360-21366
clavicle
  closed treatment
    with manipulation ~ 23505
    without manipulation ~ 23500
  open treatment ~ 23515
closed treatment ~ 27520
coccyx
  closed treatment ~ 27200
  open treatment ~ 27202
Colles ~ see Colles fracture
Colles-reversed ~ see Smith fracture

Fracture ~ *continued*
elbow
  Monteggia
    closed treatment ~ 24620
    open treatment ~ 24635
  open treatment ~ 24586-24587
femur ~ 27244
  closed treatment ~ 27230, 27238-27240, 27246, 27500-27503, 27508, 27510, 27516-27517
    with manipulation ~ 27232
  distal ~ 27508, 27510, 27514
  epiphysis ~ 27516-27519
  intertrochanteric ~ 27244
    closed treatment ~ 27238
    intramedullary implant ~ 27245
    open treatment ~ 27244
      with implant ~ 27245
    with manipulation ~ 27240
  neck
    closed treatment ~ 27230
      with manipulation ~ 27232
    open treatment ~ 27236
    percutaneous fixation ~ 27235
  open treatment ~ 27245, 27248, 27506-27507, 27511-27514, 27519
  percutaneous fixation ~ 27235, 27509
  pertrochanteric
    closed treatment ~ 27238
      with manipulation ~ 27240
    intramedullary implant shaft ~ 27245, 27500, 27502, 27506-27507
    open treatment ~ 27245, 27245
  subtrochanteric
    closed treatment ~ 27238
      with manipulation ~ 27240
    intramedullary implant ~ 27245
    open treatment ~ 27245
  supracondylar ~ 27501-27503, 27509, 27511-27513
  transcondylar ~ 27501-27503, 27509, 27511-27513
  trochanteric
    closed treatment ~ 27246
    open treatment ~ 27248
  with manipulation ~ 27232, 27502-27503, 27510
  without manipulation ~ 27230, 27238, 27246, 27500-27501, 27508, 27516-27517, 27520
fibula
  closed treatment ~ 27780-27781, 27786-27788, 27808-27810
  malleolus ~ 27786-27814
  open treatment ~ 27784, 27792, 27814
  shaft ~ 27780-27786, 27808
  with manipulation ~ 27788, 27810
  without manipulation ~ 27780-27781
frontal sinus, open treatment ~ 21343-21344
great toe
  closed treatment ~ 28490
  without manipulation ~ 28490
heel
  closed treatment
    with manipulation ~ 28405-28406
    without manipulation ~ 28400
  open treatment ~ 28415-28420
humerus
  closed treatment ~ 24500-24505
    with manipulation ~ 23605
    without manipulation ~ 23600
  condyle
    closed treatment ~ 24576-24577
    open treatment ~ 24579
    percutaneous ~ 24582
  epicondyle
    closed treatment ~ 24560-24565
    open treatment ~ 24575
    skeletal fixation, percutaneous ~ 24566
  greater tuberosity fracture
    closed treatment with manipulation ~ 23625
    closed treatment without manipulation ~ 23620
    open treatment ~ 23630
  open treatment ~ 23615-23616
  shaft ~ 24500-24505, 24516
    open treatment ~ 24515

Fracture ~ *continued*

  supracondylar
    closed treatment ~ 24530-24535
    open treatment ~ 24545-24546
    percutaneous fixation ~ 24538
  transcondylar
    closed treatment ~ 24530-24535
    open treatment ~ 24545-24546
    percutaneous fixation ~ 24538
  with dislocation
    closed treatment ~ 23665
    open treatment ~ 23670
  with shoulder dislocation
    closed treatment ~ 23675
    open treatment ~ 23680
  hyoid bone
    closed treatment
      manipulation ~ 21494
      without manipulation ~ 21493
  ilium
    open treatment ~ 27215, 27218
    percutaneous fixation ~ 27216
  knee ~ 27520
    arthroscopic treatment ~ 29850-29851
    open treatment ~ 27524
  larynx
    closed treatment
      with manipulation ~ 31586
      without manipulation ~ 31585
    open treatment ~ 31584
  malar area
    open treatment ~ 21360-21366
    with bone graft ~ 21366
    with manipulation ~ 21355
  mandible
    closed treatment
      interdental fixation ~ 21453
      with manipulation ~ 21451
      without manipulation ~ 21450
    open treatment ~ 21454-21470
      external fixation ~ 21454
      with interdental fixation ~ 21462
      without interdental fixation ~ 21461
    percutaneous treatment ~ 21452
  maxilla
    closed treatment ~ 21421
    open treatment ~ 21422-21423
  metacarpal
    closed treatment ~ 26600-26605
      with fixation ~ 26607
      with manipulation ~ 26605-26607
      without manipulation ~ 26600
    open treatment ~ 26615
    percutaneous fixation ~ 26608
  metatarsal
    closed treatment ~ 28470-28475
      with manipulation ~ 28475-28476
      without manipulation ~ 28450, 28470
    open treatment ~ 28485
    percutaneous fixation ~ 28476
  Monteggia ~ see fracture, ulna ~ 24620-24635
  nasal bone
    closed treatment ~ 21310-21320
      with manipulation ~ 21315-21320
      without manipulation ~ 21310
    open treatment ~ 21325-21335
  nasal septum
    closed treatment ~ 21337
    open treatment ~ 21336
  nasal turbinate therapeutic ~ 30930
  nasoethmoid
    open treatment ~ 21338-21339
    percutaneous treatment ~ 21340
    with fixation ~ 21340
  nasomaxillary
    closed treatment ~ 21345
    open treatment ~ 21346-21348
    with bone grafting ~ 21348
    with fixation ~ 21345-21347

Fracture ~ *continued*

  navicular
    closed treatment ~ 25622
    open treatment ~ 25628
    with manipulation ~ 25624
  odontoid
    open treatment
      with graft ~ 22319
      without graft ~ 22318
  orbit
    closed treatment
      with manipulation ~ 21401
      without manipulation ~ 21400
    open treatment ~ 21406-21408
      blowout fracture ~ 21385-21395
  orbital floor
    blow out ~ 21385-21395
  palate
    closed treatment ~ 21421
    open treatment ~ 21422-21423
  patella
    closed treatment, without manipulation ~ 27520
    open treatment ~ 27524
  pelvic ring
    closed treatment ~ 27197, 27198
    open treatment
      anterior ~ 27217
      posterior ~ 27218
    percutaneous fixation ~ 27216
    with manipulation ~ 27198
    without manipulation ~ 27197
  phalanges
    articular
      closed treatment ~ 26740
      open treatment ~ 26746
      with manipulation ~ 26742
    closed treatment ~ 26742, 28510
      articular ~ 26740
      distal ~ 26750
      with manipulation ~ 26755
    distal ~ 26755-26756
      closed treatment ~ 26750
      open treatment ~ 26765
      percutaneous fixation ~ 26756
    finger/thumb
      closed treatment ~ 26720-26725
        with manipulation ~ 26725-26727
      shaft ~ 26720, 26727
    great toe ~ 28490
      closed treatment ~ 28495
        with manipulation ~ 28495-28496
      open treatment ~ 28505
      percutaneous fixation ~ 28496
    open treatment ~ 26735, 26746
      distal ~ 26765
    shaft
      closed treatment ~ 26725
      open treatment ~ 26735
      percutaneous fixation ~ 26727
    toe
      closed treatment ~ 28515
        with manipulation ~ 28515
        without manipulation ~ 28510
      open treatment ~ 28525
    with manipulation ~ 26742, 26755
    without manipulation ~ 26740, 26750

Fracture ~ *continued*
radius
  closed treatment ~ 25560-25565
  Colles ~ 25600-25605
  distal ~ 25600-25606
    open treatment ~ 25607-25609
    Smith ~ 25600-25605
  head/neck
    closed treatment ~ 24650-24655
    open treatment ~ 24665-24666
  open treatment ~ 25515, 25607-25609
  percutaneous fixation ~ 25606
  shaft ~ 25500, 25525-25526
    closed treatment ~ 25500-25505, 25520
    open treatment ~ 25515, 25525-25526, 25574
  with manipulation ~ 25565, 25605
  without manipulation ~ 25560, 25600
  with ulna ~ 25560-25565
    open treatment ~ 25575
rib
  with internal fixation ~ 21811-21813
scaphoid
  closed treatment ~ 25622
  open treatment ~ 25628
  with dislocation
    closed treatment ~ 25680
    open treatment ~ 25685
  with manipulation ~ 25624
scapula
  closed treatment
    with manipulation ~ 23575
    without manipulation ~ 23570
  open treatment ~ 23585
sesamoid
  closed treatment ~ 28530
  foot ~ 28530-28531
  open treatment ~ 28531
skin debridement ~ 11010-11012
skull ~ 62000-62010
sternum
  closed treatment ~ 21820
  open treatment ~ 21825
talus
  closed treatment ~ 28430-28435
  open treatment ~ 28445
  with manipulation ~ 28435-28436
  without manipulation ~ 28430
tarsal
  open treatment ~ 28465
  percutaneous fixation ~ 28456
  with manipulation ~ 28455-28456
thumb
  open treatment ~ 26665
  with dislocation ~ 26645-26650
tibia ~ 27759
  arthroscopic treatment ~ 29855-29856
  closed treatment ~ 27530-27532, 27538, 27750-27752, 27760-27762, 27808-27810, 27824-27825
  distal ~ 27824-27828
  intercondylar ~ 27538-27540
  malleolus ~ 27760-27766, 27808-27814
  open treatment ~ 27535-27536, 27540, 27758, 27766, 27814, 27826-27828
  percutaneous fixation ~ 27756
  plateau ~ 27530-27536, 29855-29856
  shaft ~ 27750-27759
  with manipulation ~ 27752, 27760-27762, 27810
  without manipulation ~ 27530, 27750, 27760-27762, 27808, 27825
trachea, endoscopy ~ 31630

Fracture ~ *continued*
ulna
  closed treatment ~ 25560-25565
  olecranon
    closed treatment ~ 24670-24675
    open treatment ~ 24685
  open treatment ~ 25574-25575
  shaft
    closed treatment ~ 25530-25535
    open treatment ~ 25545, 25574
  styloid process
    closed treatment ~ 25650
    open treatment ~ 25652
    percutaneous fixation ~ 25651
  with dislocation ~ 24620, 24635
    closed treatment ~ 24620
    Monteggia ~ 24620-24635
    open treatment ~ 24635
  with manipulation ~ 25535, 25565
  with radius ~ 25560-25565
    open treatment ~ 25575
  without manipulation ~ 25530, 25560
vertebra
  additional segment, open treatment ~ 22328
  cervical, open treatment ~ 22326
  closed treatment
    with manipulation, casting and/or bracing ~ 22315
    without manipulation ~ 22310
  lumbar, open treatment ~ 22325
  posterior, open treatment ~ 22325-22327
  thoracic, open treatment ~ 22327
  with shoulder dislocation
    closed treatment ~ 23675
    open treatment ~ 23680
wrist, with dislocation
  closed treatment ~ 25680
  open treatment ~ 25685
zygomatic arch
  open treatment ~ 21356-21366
  with manipulation ~ 21355
Fragile-X chromosome analysis ~ 88248
Fragility
red blood cell
  mechanical ~ 85547
  osmotic ~ 85555-85557
Frames, stereotactic ~ 20660
Francisella ~ 86000
  antibody ~ 86668
Fredet-Ramstedt procedure ~ 43520
Free E3 ~ 82677
Free skin graft ~ 15050-15157, 15200-15261, 15271-15278, 15757
Free T4 (four) ~ 84439
Frenectomy ~ 40819, 41115
Frenectomy, lingual ~ 41115
Frenotomy ~ 40806, 41010
Frenulectomy ~ 40819
Frenuloplasty ~ 41520
Frenum lip, incision ~ 40806
Frenumectomy ~ 40819
Frickman operation ~ see proctopexy
Frontal craniotomy ~ 61556
Frontal sinus ~ see sinus, frontal
Frontal sinusotomy ~ 31070-31075
Frost suture ~ 67875
Frozen blood preparation ~ 86930-86932
Fructose ~ 84375
  semen ~ 82757
Fructose intolerance breath test ~ 91065
Fruit sugar ~ 84375
FSF ~ 85290-85291
FSH ~ 80418, 80426, 83001
FT-4 ~ 84439

Fulguration ~ see destruction
  bladder ~ 51020
  cystourethroscopy with ~ 52214
    lesion ~ 52224
    tumor ~ 52234-52240
  ureter ~ 50957-50959, 50976-50978
  ureterocele
    ectopic ~ 52301
    orthotopic ~ 52300
Fulguration, endocavitary ~ 17000-17286
Full thickness graft ~ 15200-15261
Function, study, nasal ~ 92512
Function test, lung ~ see pulmonology, diagnostic
Function test, vestibular ~ see vestibular function tests
Fundoplasty
  esophagogastric ~ 43325
  esophagogastroduodenoscopic ~ 43210
    laparoscopic ~ 43279, 43280, 43282
    laparotomy ~ 43327
    via thoracotomy ~ 43328
  esophagomyotomy, laparoscopic ~ 43279
  paraesophageal hiatal hernia repair
    laparoscopic ~ 43281, 43282
    with fundoplication
      laparotomy ~ 43332, 43333
      thoracoabdominal incision ~ 43336, 43337
      thoractomy ~ 43334, 43335
Fundoplication ~ 43325
Fungus
  antibody ~ 86671
  culture
    blood ~ 87103
    hair ~ 87101
    identification ~ 87106
    nail ~ 87101
    other ~ 87102
    skin ~ 87101
  tissue exam ~ 87220
Funnel chest ~ 21740-21743
Furuncle
  incision and drainage ~ 10060-10061
  vulva ~ 56405
Fusion ~ see arthrodesis
  pleural cavity ~ 32560
  thumb in opposition ~ 26820
Fusion, epiphyseal-diaphyseal ~ see epiphyseal arrest
Fusion, joint ~ see arthrodesis
Fusion, joint, interphalangeal, finger ~ 26860-26863

G

Gabapentin assay ~ 80171
Gago procedure ~ 33463-33465
Gait training ~ 97116
Galactogram ~ 77053-77054
  injection ~ 19030
Galactokinase, blood ~ 82759
Galactose
  blood ~ 82760
  urine ~ 82760
Galactose-1-phosphate
  uridyl transferase ~ 82775-82776
Gallbladder ~ see also bile duct
  anastomosis with intestines ~ 47720-47741
  biopsy ~ 43261
  diagnostic imaging
    nuclear medicine ~ 78223, 78227
    X-ray with conrast ~ 74290
  destruction, calculi (stone) ~ 47544
  excision ~ 47562-47564, 47600-47620
  exploration ~ 47480
    endoscopic retrograde cholangio- pancreatography (ERCP)~ 43260
  fistulization ~ 47480, 47490
  incision ~ 47490
  incision and drainage ~ 47480

Gallbladder ~ *continued*
  removal, calculi (stone) ~ 47480, 47544
  repair
    with gastroenterostomy ~ 47741
    with intestines ~ 47720-47740
  unlisted services and procedures ~ 47999
  X-ray with contrast ~ 74290
Galvanocautery ~ 17000-17286
Galvanoionization ~ 97033
Gamete intrafallopian transfer ~ see GIFT
Gamete transfer, in vitro fertilization ~ 58976
Gamma camera imaging ~ see nuclear medicine
Gamma glutamyl transferase ~ 82977
Gamma seminoprotein ~ 84152-84153
Gammacorten ~ 80420
Gammaglobulin, blood ~ 82784-82787
Gamulin Rh ~ 90384-90386
Ganglia, trigeminal ~ 61450, 61790
Ganglion cyst ~ 61450, 61790
  aspiration/injection ~ 20612
  drainage ~ 20612
  injection, anesthetic ~ 64505, 64510
  wrist excision ~ 25111-25112
Ganglion, Gasser's ~ 61450, 61790
Ganglion cervicothoracicum ~ 64510
Ganglion pterygopalatinum ~ 64505
Gardner operation ~ 63700-63702
Gardnerella vaginalis detection ~ 87510-87512
Gasserian ganglion
  sensory root
    decompression ~ 61450
    section ~ 61450
    stereotactic ~ 61790
Gasser ganglion ~ 61450, 61790
Gastrectomy
  longitudinal ~ 43775
  partial ~ 43631-43635, 43845, 48150-48152
    with gastrojejunostomy ~ 43632
  proximal ~ 43117-43118, 43121-43123
  sleeve ~ 43775
  total ~ 43620-43622
    with esophagoenterostomy ~ 43620
  with gastroduodenostomy ~ 43631
Gastric acid ~ 82930
Gastric analysis test
  secretory study ~ 43755-43757, 89135
Gastric electrodes
  implantation
    laparoscopic, neurostimulator ~ 43647
    open. neurostimulator ~ 43881
  removal
    laparoscopic, neurostimulator ~ 43648
    open, neurostimulator ~ 43882
  replacement
    laparoscopic, neurostimulator ~ 43647
    open, neurostimulator ~ 43881
  revision
    laparoscopic, neurostimulator ~ 43648
    open, neurostimulator ~ 43882
Gastric intubation
  diagnostic ~ 43754-43757
  therapeutic ~ 43753
Gastric lavage, therapeutic ~ 43753
Gastric tests
  acid reflux ~ 91034, 91035, 91037, 91038
  manometry ~ 91020
  motility ~ 91020
Gastric ulcer disease ~ 43610
Gastrin ~ 82938-82941
Gastrocnemius recession, leg, lower ~ 27687
Gastroduodenostomy ~ 43810, 43850-43855, 43631
Gastroenterology
  B-12 absorption study ~ 78270-78272
  breath test
    hydrogen ~ 91065
    urea ~ 78267, 78268
  diagnostic services ~ 91010-91299

Gastroenterology ~ continued
  esophagus tests
    acid perfusion ~ 91030
    acid reflux ~ 91032-91033
    balloon distension provocation study ~ 91040
    motility study ~ 91010
  gastroesophageal reflux test ~ 91034-91038
  gastric tests
    emptying ~ 78264
      with small bowel transit ~ 78265
      with small bowel and colon transit ~ 78266
    motility ~ 91020
  manometry ~ 91010, 91013, 91020, 91022
  rectum sensation, tone, compliance ~ 91120
  rectum/anus manometry ~ 91122
  stomach stimulation of secretion ~ 43755
  unlisted services and procedures ~ 91299
Gastroenterostomy
  for obesity ~ 43644-43645, 43842-43848
Gastroesophageal reflux test ~ 91034-91038
Gastrointestinal exam
  CT scan, colon ~ 74261-74263
  endoscopic imaging ~ 91110-91111
  radiologic imaging
    bile ducts ~ 47531, 47532, 74300, 74301
    colon ~ 74270, 74280
    duodenum ~ 74260
    esophagus ~ 74210, 74220, 73230
    gallbladder ~ 74290-74291, 78226
    pharynx ~ 74210
    protein loss ~ 78282
    small intestine ~ 74249, 74250-74251
  nuclear medicine
    blood loss study ~ 78278
    esophageal motility ~ 78258
    gastric emptying study ~ 78264
      with small bowel transit ~ 78265
      with small bowel and colon transit ~ 78266
    gastric mucosa imaging ~ 78261
    gastroesophageal reflux study ~ 78262
    hepatobiliary ~ 78226-78227
    liver ~ 78201, 78215-78216
      SPECT ~ 78205
      with vascular flow ~ 78202, 78206
    peritoneal-venous shunt patency ~ 78291
    protein loss study ~ 78282
    salivary gland ~ 78230-78232
    spleen ~ 78215
    unlisted services and procedures ~ 78299
Gastrointestinal tract
  imaging intraluminal ~ 91110-91111
  reconstruction ~ 43360-43361
  upper dilation ~ 43249
  X-ray ~ 74240-74245
    with contrast ~ 74246-74249
    guide dilator ~ 74360
    guide intubation ~ 74340
Gastrointestinal, upper
  biopsy, endoscopy ~ 43239
  dilation
    endoscopy ~ 43245
    esophagus ~ 43248
  endoscopy
    catheterization ~ 43241
    destruction lesion ~ 43270
    dilation ~ 43245
    drainage pseudocyst ~ 43240
    exploration ~ 43235
    hemorrhage ~ 43255
    inject varices ~ 43243
    injection ~ 43236
    needle biopsy ~ 43242, 43238
    removal
      foreign body ~ 43247
      lesion ~ 43251
      polyp ~ 43251
      tumor ~ 43251
    stent placement ~ 43266
    thermal radiation ~ 43257
    tube placement ~ 43246
    ultrasound ~ 43237-43238, 43242, 43259, 76975

Gastrointestinal, upper ~ continued
  exploration endoscopy ~ 43235
  hemorrhage endoscopic control ~ 43255
  injection
    submucosal ~ 43236
    varices ~ 43243
  lesion destruction ~ 43270
  ligation of vein ~ 43244
  needle biopsy, endoscopy ~ 43238, 43242
  removal
    foreign body ~ 43247
    lesion ~ 43250
    polyp ~ 43250-43251
    tumor ~ 43250
  tube placement, endoscopy ~ 43246
  ultrasound endoscopy ~ 43237-43238, 43242, 43259, 76975
Gastrojejunostomy ~ 43860-43865
  conversion from gastostomy tube ~ 49446
  contrast injection ~ 49465
  removal of obstructive material ~ 49460
  replacement of tube ~ 49452
  with duodenal exclusion ~ 48547
  with partial gastrectomy ~ 43632
  with vagotomy ~ 43825
  without vagotomy ~ 43820
Gastroplasty
  Collis ~ 43283, 43338
  evision for obesity ~ 43644-43645, 43842-43848
  wedge gastroplasty ~ 43283, 43338
  with esophagogastric fundoplasty ~ 43842-43843
Gastrorrhaphy ~ 43840
Gastroschises ~ 49605
Gastrostomy
  closure ~ 43870
  laparoscopic, temporary ~ 43653
  temporary ~ 43830
    laparoscopic ~ 43653
    neonatal ~ 43831
  with pancreatic drain ~ 48001
  with pyloroplasty ~ 43640
  with vagotomy ~ 43640
Gastrostomy tube
  change of ~ 43760
  contrast injection ~ 49465
  conversion to gastro-jejunostomy tube ~ 49446
  directed placement, endoscopic ~ 43246
  insertion ~ 49440
  obstructive material removal ~ 49460
  placement, percutaneous
    endoscopic ~ 43246
    nonendoscopic ~ 49440
  replacement ~ 49450
  repositioning ~ 43761
Gastrotomy ~ 43500-43501, 43510
GDH ~ 82965
Gel diffusion ~ 86331
Gel diffusion test ~ 86329-86331
Gene Analysis
  Analytes
    ABCA4 (ATP-binding cassette, sub-family A [ABC1], member 4) ~ 81408
    ABCC8 (ATP-binding cassette, sub-family C [CFTR/MRP], member 8) ~ 81400, 81401, 81407
    ABCD1 (ATP-binding cassette, sub-family D [ALD], member 1) ~ 81405
    ABL1 (ABL proto-oncogene 1, non-receptor tyrosine kinase) ~ 81170, 81401
    ACADM (acyl-CoA dehydrogenase, C4 to C12 straight chain) ~ 81400, 81401
    ACADS (acyl-CoA dehydrogenase, C2 to C3 short chain) ~ 81404, 81405
    ACADVL (acyl-CoA dehydrogenase, very long chain) ~ 81406
    ACE (angiotensin I converting enzyme [peptidyl-dipeptidase A] 1) ~ 81400
    ACTA2 (actin, alpha 2, smooth muscle, aorta) ~ 81405
    ACTC1 (actin, alpha, cardiac muscle 1) ~ 81405
    ACTN4 (actinin, alpha 4) ~ 81406
    ADRB2 (adrenergic, beta-2-, receptor, surface) ~ 81401
    AFF2 (AF4/FMR2 family, member 2 [FMR2]) ~ 81401, 81404
    AFG3L2 (AFG3 ATPase family gene 3 like 2 [S. cerevisiae]) ~ 81406

Gene Analysis ~ *continued*

AGL (amylo-alpha-1, 6-glucosidase, 4-alpha-glucanotransferase) ~ 81407

AHI1 (Abelson helper integration site 1) ~ 81407

AIRE (autoimmune regulator) ~ 81406

ALDH7A1 (aldehyde dehydrogenase 7 family, member A1) ~ 81406

ANG (angiogenin, ribonuclease, RNase A family, 5) ~ 81403

ANKRD1 (ankyrin repeat domain 1) ~ 81405

ANO5 (anoctamin 5) ~ 81406

ANOS1 (anosmin-1) ~ 81406

APOB (apolipoprotein B) ~ 81401

APOE (apolipoprotein E) ~ 81401

APP (amyloid beta [A4] precursor protein) ~ 81406

AGTR1 (angiotensin II receptor, type 1) ~ 81400

APC (adenomatous polyposis coli) ~ 81201, 81202

APTX (aprataxin) ~ 81405

AQP2 (aquaporin 2 [collecting duct]) ~ 81404

AR (androgen receptor) ~ 81401, 81405

ARSA (arylsulfatase A) ~ 81405

ARX (aristaless related homeobox) ~ 81403, 81404

ASPA (aspartoacylase) ~ 81200

ASPM (asp [abnormal spindle] homolog, microcephaly associated [Drosophila]) ~ 81407

ASS1 (argininosuccinate synthase 1) ~ 81406

ASXL1 (additional sex combs like 1, transcriptional regulator) ~ 81175, 81176

ATL1 (atlastin GTPase 1) ~ 81406

ATM (ataxia telangiectasia mutated) ~ 81408

ATN1 (atrophin 1) ~ 81401

ATP1A2 (ATPase, Na+/K+ transporting, alpha 2 polypeptide) ~ 81406

ATP7B (ATPase, Cu++ transporting, beta polypeptide) ~ 81406

ATXN1 (ataxin 1) ~ 81401

ATXN2 (ataxin 2) ~ 81401

ATXN3 (ataxin 3) ~ 81401

ATXN7 (ataxin 7) ~ 81401

ATXN8OS (ATXN8 opposite strand [non-protein coding]) ~ 81401

ATXN10 (ataxin 10) ~ 81401

AVPR2 (arginine vasopressin receptor 2) ~ 81404

BBS1 (Bardet-Biedl syndrome 1) ~ 81406

BBS2 (Bardet-Biedl syndrome 2) ~ 81406

BBS10 (Bardet-Biedl syndrome 10) ~ 81404

BCKDHA (branched chain keto acid dehydrogenase E1, alpha polypeptide) ~ 81400, 81405

BCKDHB (branched chain keto acid dehydrogenase E1, beta polypeptide) ~ 81205, 81406

BCL1/IgH, t(11;14) ~ 81401

BCR/ABL1 (chronic myelogenous leukemia) Translocation ~ 81206-81208

BCS1L (BCS1-like [S. cerevisiae]) ~ 81405

BEST1 (bestrophin 1) ~ 81406

BLM (Bloom syndrome, RecQ helicase-like) ~ 81209

BMPR2 (bone morphogenetic protein receptor, type II [serine/threonine kinase]) ~ 81405, 81406

BRAF (B-Raf proto-oncogene , serine/threonine kinase) ~ 81210, 81406

BRCA1, BRCA2 (breast cancer 1 and 2) ~ 81162, 81211-81213

BRCA1 (breast cancer 1) ~ 81214, 81215

BRCA2 (breast cancer 2) ~ 81216, 81217

BSCL2 (Berardinelli-Seip congenital lipodystrophy 2 [seipin]) ~ 81406

BTD (biotinidase) ~ 81404

BTK (Bruton agammaglobulinemia tyrosine kinase) ~ 81406

C10orf2 (chromosome 10 open reading frame 2) ~ 81404

CACNA1A (calcium channel, voltagedependent, P/Q type, alpha 1A subunit) ~ 81401, 81407

CACNB2 (calcium channel, voltage-dependent, beta 2 subunit) ~ 81406

CALR (calreticulin) (eg, myeloproliferative disorders) ~ 81219

CAPN3 (calpain 3) ~ 81406

CASQ2 (calsequestrin 2 [cardiac muscle]) ~ 81405

CASR (calcium-sensing receptor) ~ 81405

CAV3 (caveolin 3) ~ 81404

CBFB/MYH11 (inv (16)) ~ 81401

CBS (cystathionine-beta-synthase) ~ 81401, 81406

CD40LG (CD40 ligand) ~ 81404

CCND1/IGH (BCL1/IgH, t(11;14)) ~ 81401

CCR5 (chemokine C-C motif receptor 5) ~ 81400

CDH1 (cadherin 1, type 1, E-cadherin [epithelial]) ~ 81406

CDH23 (cadherin-related 23) ~ 81408

CDKL5 (cyclin-dependent kinase-like 5) ~ 81405, 81406

CDKN2A (cyclin-dependent kinase inhibitor 2A) ~ 81404

CEBPA (CCAAT/enhancer binding protein [C/EBP], alpha) ~ 81218

Gene Analysis ~ *continued*

CEL (carboxyl ester lipase [bile salt stimulated lipase]) ~ 81403

CEP290 (centrosomal protein 290kDa) ~ 81408

CFH/ARMS2 (complement factor H/age-related maculopathy susceptibility 2) ~ 81401

CFTR (cystic fibrosis transmembrane conductance regulator) ~ 81220-81224

CHD7 (chromodomain helicase DNA binding protein 7) ~ 81407

CHRNA4 (cholinergic receptor, nicotinic, alpha 4) ~ 81405

CHRNB2 (cholinergic receptor, nicotinic, beta 2 [neuronal]) ~ 81405

Chromosome 1p-/19q- ~ 81402

Chromosome 18q- ~ 81402

CLCN1 (chloride channel 1, skeletal muscle) ~ 81406

CLCNKB (chloride channel, voltage-sensitive Kb) ~ 81406

CLRN1 (clarin 1) ~ 81400, 81404

CNBP (CCHC-type zinc finger, nucleic acid binding protein) ~ 81401

CNTNAP2 (contactin associated protein-like 2) ~ 81406

COL1A1 (collagen, type I, alpha 1) ~ 81408

COL1A1/PDGFB (t(17;22)) ~ 81402

COL1A2 (collagen, type I, alpha 2) ~ 81408

COL4A1 (collagen, type IV, alpha 1) ~ 81408

COL4A3 (collagen, type IV, alpha 3 [Goodpasture antigen]) ~ 81408

COL4A4 (collagen, type IV, alpha 4) ~ 81407

COL4A5 (collagen, type IV, alpha 5) ~ 81407, 81408

COL6A1 (collagen, type VI, alpha 1) ~ 81407

COL6A2 (collagen, type VI, alpha 2) ~ 81406, 81407

COL6A3 (collagen, type VI, alpha 3) ~ 81407

COX6B1 (cytochrome c oxidase subunit VIb polypeptide 1) ~ 81404

COX10 (COX10 homolog, cytochrome c oxidase assembly protein) ~ 81405

COX15 (COX15 homolog, cytochrome c oxidase assembly protein) ~ 81405

CPOX (coproporphyrinogen oxidase) ~ 81405

CPT1A (carnitine palmitoyltransferase 1A [liver]) ~81406

CPT2 (carnitine palmitoyltransferase 2) ~ 81404

CRB1 (crumbs homolog 1 [Drosophila]) ~ 81406

CREBBP (CREB binding protein) ~ 81406, 81407

CRX (cone-rod homeobox) ~ 81404

CSTB (cystatin B [stefin B]) ~ 81401, 81404

CTNNB1 (catenin [cadherin-associated protein], beta 1, 88kDa) ~ 81403

CTRC (chymotrypsin C) (eg, hereditary pancreatitis) ~ 81405

CYP1B1 (cytochrome P450, family 1, subfamily B, polypeptide 1) ~ 81404

CYP21A2 (cytochrome P450, family 21, subfamily A, polypeptide 2) ~ 81402, 81405

CYP2C19 (cytochrome P450, family 2, subfamily C, polypeptide 19) ~ 81225

CYP2C9 (cytochrome P450, family 2, subfamily C, polypeptide 9) ~ 81227

CYP2D6 (cytochrome P450, family 2, subfamily D, polypeptide 6) ~ 81226

CYP3A4 (cytochrome P450, family 3, subfamily A member 4) ~ 81230

CYP3A5 (cytochrome P450, family 3, subfamily A member 5) ~ 81231

CYP11B1 (cytochrome P450, family 11, subfamily B, polypeptide 1) ~ 81405

CYP17A1 (cytochrome P450, family 17, subfamily A, polypeptide 1) ~ 81405

CYP21A2 (cytochrome P450, family 21, subfamily A, polypeptide2) ~ 81402, 81405

Constitution ~ 81228, 81229

Neoplasia. ~ 81406

DAZ/SRY (deleted in azoospermia and sex determining region Y) ~ 81403

DBT (dihydrolipoamide branched chain transacylase E2) ~ 81405, 81406

DCX (doublecortin) ~ 81405

DEK/NUP214 (t(6;9)) ~ 81401

DES (desmin) ~ 81405

DFNB59 (deafness, autosomal recessive 59) ~ 81405

DGUOK (deoxyguanosine kinase) ~ 81405

DHCR7 (7-dehydrocholesterol reductase) ~ 81405

DLAT (dihydrolipoamide S-acetyltransferase) ~ 81406

DLD (dihydrolipoamide dehydrogenase) ~ 81406

DMD (dystrophin) ~ 81161, 81408

DMPK (dystrophia myotonica-protein kinase) ~ 81401, 81404

DNMT3A (DNA [cytosine-5-]-methyltransferase 3 alpha) ~ 81403

DPYD (dihydropyrimidine dehydrogenase) ~ 81232

DSC2 (desmocollin) ~ 81406

DSG2 (desmoglein 2) ~ 81406

Gene Analysis ~ *continued*

DSP (desmoplakin) ~ 81406

DYSF (dysferlin, limb girdle muscular dystrophy 2B [autosomal recessive]) ~ 81408

E2A/PBX1 (t(1;19)) ~ 81401

EFHC1 (EF-hand domain [C terminal] containing 1) ~ 81406

EGFR (epidermal growth factor receptor) 81235

EGR2 (early growth response 2) ~ 81404

EIF2B2 (eukaryotic translation initiation factor 2B, subunit 2 beta, 39kDa) ~ 81405

EIF2B3 (eukaryotic translation initiation factor 2B, subunit 3 gamma, 58kDa) ~ 81406

EIF2B4 (eukaryotic translation initiation factor 2B, subunit 4 delta, 67kDa) ~ 81406

EIF2B5 (eukaryotic translation initiation factor 2B, subunit 5 epsilon, 82kDa) ~ 81406

EMD (emerin) ~ 81404, 81405

EML4/ALK (inv(2)) ~ 81401

ENG (endoglin) ~ 81405, 81406

EPCAM (epithelial cell adhesion molecule) ~ 81403

EPM2A (epilepsy, progressive myoclonus type 2A, Lafora disease [laforin]) ~ 81404

ESR1/PGR (receptor 1/progesterone receptor) ~ 81402

ETV6/NTRK3 (t(12;15)) ~ 81401

ETV6/RUNX1 (t(12;21)) ~ 81401

EWSR1/ATF1 (t1(2;22)) ~ 81401

EWSR1/ERG (t(21;22)) ~ 81401

EWSR1/FLI1 (t(11;22)) ~ 81401

EWSR1/WT1 (t(11;22)) ~ 81401

EYA1 (eyes absent homolog 1 [Drosophila]) ~ 81405, 81406

F2 (prothrombin, coagulation factor II) ~ 81240, 81400

F5 (coagulation factor V) ~ 81241, 81400

F7 (coagulation factor VII [serum prothrombin conversion accelerator]) ~ 81400

F8 (coagulation factor VIII) ~ 81403, 81406, 81407

F9 (coagulation factor IX) ~ 81238

F11 (coagulation factor XI) ~ 81401

F12 (coagulation factor XII [Hageman factor]) ~ 81403

F13B (coagulation factor XIII, B polypeptide) ~ 81400

FAH (fumarylacetoacetate hydrolase [fumarylacetoacetase]) ~ 81406

FANCC (Fanconi anemia, complementation group C) ~ 81242

FASTKD2 (FAST kinase domains 2) ~ 81406

FBN1 (fibrillin 1) ~ 81408

FGB (fibrinogen beta chain) ~ 81400

FGF23 (fibroblast growth factor 23) ~ 81404

FGFR1 (fibroblast growth factor receptor 1) ~ 81400, 81405

FGFR2 (fibroblast growth factor receptor 2) ~ 81404

FGFR3 (fibroblast growth factor receptor 3) ~ 81400, 81401, 81403, 81404

FH (fumarate hydratase) ~ 81405

FHL1 (four and a half LIM domains 1) ~ 81404

FIG4 (FIG4 homolog, SAC1 lipid phosphatase domain containing [S. cerevisiae]) ~ 81406

FIP1L1/PDGFRA (del(4q12)) ~ 81401

FKRP (fukutin related protein) ~ 81404

FKTN (fukutin) ~ 81400, 81405

FLG (filaggrin) ~ 81401

FLT3 (fms-related tyrosine kinase 3) ~ 81245, 81246

FMR1 (fragile X mental retardation 1) ~ 81243, 81244

FOXG1 (forkhead box G1) ~ 81404

FOXO1/PAX3 (t(2;13)) ~ 81401

FOXO1/PAX7 (t(1;13)) ~ 81401

FSHMD1A (facioscapulohumeral muscular dystrophy 1A) ~ 81404

FTSJ1 (FtsJ RNA methyltransferase homolog 1 [E. coli]) ~ 81405, 81406

FUS (fused in sarcoma) ~ 81406

FUS/DDIT3 (t(12;16)) ~ 81401

FXN (frataxin) ~ 81401, 81404

G6PC (glucose-6-phosphatase, catalytic subunit) ~ 81250

G6PD (glucose-6-phosphate dehydrogenase) ~ 81247-81249

GAA (glucosidase, alpha; acid) ~ 81406

GABRG2 (gamma-aminobutyric acid [GABA] A receptor, gamma 2) ~ 81405

GALC (galactosylceramidase) ~ 81401, 81406

GALT (galactose-1-phosphate uridylyltransferase) ~ 81401, 81406

GARS (glycyl-tRNA synthetase) ~ 81406

GBA (glucosidase, beta, acid) ~ 81251

GCDH (glutaryl-CoA dehydrogenase) ~ 81406

Gene Analysis ~ *continued*

GCH1 (GTP cyclohydrolase 1) ~ 81405

GCK (glucokinase [hexokinase 4]) ~ 81406

GDAP1 (ganglioside-induced differentiationassociated protein 1) ~ 81405

GFAP (glial fibrillary acidic protein) ~ 81405

GH1 (growth hormone 1) ~ 81404

GHR (growth hormone receptor) ~ 81405

GHRHR (growth hormone releasing hormone receptor) ~ 81405

GJB1 (gap junction protein, beta 1) ~ 81403

GJB2 (gap junction protein, beta 2, 26kDa, connexin 26) ~ 81252, 81253

GJB6 (gap junction protein, beta 6, 30kDa, connexin 30) ~ 81254

GLA (galactosidase, alpha) ~ 81405

GLUD1 (glutamate dehydrogenase 1) ~ 81406

GNAQ (guanine nucleotide-binding protein G[q] subunit alpha) ~ 81403

GNE (glucosamine [UDP-N-acetyl]-2-epimerase/N-acetylmannosamine kinase) ~ 81400, 81406

GP1BB (glycoprotein Ib [platelet], beta polypeptide) ~ 81404

GRN (granulin) ~ 81406

H19 (imprinted maternally expressed transcript [non-protein coding]) ~ 81401

HADHA (hydroxyacyl-CoA dehydrogenase/3-ketoacyl-CoA thiolase/enoyl-CoA hydratase [trifunctional protein] alpha subunit) ~ 81406

HADHB (hydroxyacyl-CoA dehydrogenase/ 3 ketoacyl-CoA thiolase/enoyl-CoA hydratase [trifunctional protein], beta subunit) ~ 81406

HBA1/HBA2 (alpha globin 1 and alpha globin 2) ~ 81257-81259, 81269

HBB (hemoglobin, beta, beta-Globin) ~ 81361-81364

HEXA (hexosaminidase A [alpha polypeptide]) ~ 81255, 81406

HFE (hemochromatosis) ~ 81256

HLA Class I and II Typing, Low Resolution ~ 81370, 81371

HLA Class I Typing, Low Resolution ~ 81372-81374

HLA Class II Typing, Low Resolution ~ 81375-81377

HLA Class I and II Typing, High Resolution ~ 81378

HLA Class I Typing, High Resolution ~ 81379-81381

HLA Class II Typing,High Resolution ~ 81382, 81383

HLCS (HLCS holocarboxylase synthetase) ~ 81406

HMBS (hydroxymethylbilane synthase) ~ 81406

HNF1A (HNF1 homeobox A) ~ 81405

HPA (Human Platelet Antigen) ~ 81105-81112

HNF1B (HNF1 homeobox B) ~ 81404, 81405

HNF4A (hepatocyte nuclear factor 4, alpha) ~ 81406

HRAS (v-Ha-ras Harvey rat sarcoma viral oncogene homolog) ~ 81403, 81404

HSD3B2 (hydroxyl-delta-5-steroid dehydrogenase, 3 beta- and steroid-delta isomerase 2) ~ 81404

HSD11B2 (hydroxysteroid [11-beta] dehydrogenase 2) ~ 81404

HSPB1 (heat shock 27kDa protein 1) ~ 81404

HTRA1 (HtrA serine peptidase 1) ~ 81405

HTT (huntingtin) ~ 81401

Human Erythrocyte Antigen. ~ 81403

Human Platelet Antigen 1 (HPA-1) ~ 81105

Human Platelet Antigen 2 (HPA-2) ~ 81106

Human Platelet Antigen 3 (HPA-3) ~ 81107

Human Platelet Antigen 4 (HPA-4) ~ 81108

Human Platelet Antigen 5 (HPA-5) ~ 81109

Human Platelet Antigen 6 (HPA-6w) ~ 81110

Human Platelet Antigen 9 (HPA-9w) ~ 81111

Human Platelet Antigen 15 (HPA-15) ~ 81112

IDH1 (isocitrate dehydrogenase 1 [NADP+], soluble) ~ 81120

IDH2 (isocitrate dehydrogenase 2 [NADP+], mitochondrial) ~ 81121

IDS (iduronate 2-sulfatase) ~ 81405

IDUA (iduronidase, alpha L-) ~ 81406

IFNL3 (interferon, lambda 3) ~ 81283

IGH@ (immunoglobulin heavy chain locus) ~ 81261-81263

IGH@/BCL2 (t(14;18)) ~ 81401, 81402

IGK@ (immunoglobulin kappa light chain locus) ~ 81264

IKBKAP (inhibitor of kappa light polypeptide gene enhancer in B-cells, kinase complex-associated protein) ~ 81260

IL2RG (interleukin 2 receptor, gamma) ~ 81405

INF2 (inverted formin, FH2 and WH2 domain containing) ~ 81406

INS (insulin) ~ 81404

ISPD (isoprenoid synthase domain containing) ~ 81405

ITPR1 (inositol 1,4,5-trisphosphate receptor, type 1) ~ 81408

IVD (isovaleryl-CoA dehydrogenase) ~ 81400, 81406

JAG1 (jagged 1) ~ 81406, 81407

Gene Analysis ~ continued

JAK2 (Janus kinase 2) ~ 81270, 81403

JUP (junction plakoglobin) ~ 81406

KCNC3 (potassium voltage-gated channel, Shaw-related subfamily, member 3) ~ 81403

KCNH2 (potassium voltage-gated channel, subfamily H [eag-related], member 2) ~ 81406

KCNJ2 (potassium inwardly-rectifying chanel, subfamily J, member 2) ~ 81403

KCNJ1 (potassium inwardly-rectifying channel, subfamily J, member 1) ~ 81404

KCNJ10 (potassium inwardly-rectifying channel, subfamily J, member 10) ~ 81404

KCNJ11 (potassium inwardly-rectifying channel, subfamily J, member 11) ~ 81403

KCNQ1 (potassium voltage-gated channel, KQT-like subfamily, member 1) ~ 81406

KCNQ1OT1 (KCNQ1 overlapping transcript 1 [non-protein coding]) ~ 81401

KCNQ2 (potassium voltage-gated channel, KQT-like subfamily, member 2) ~ 81406

KDM5C (lysine [K]-specific demethylase 5C) ~ 81407

KIAA0196 (KIAA0196) ~ 81407

Killer cell immunoglobulin-like receptor (KIR) gene family ~ 81403

KIT (v-kit Hardy-Zuckerman 4 feline sarcoma viral oncogene homolog) ~ 81272, 81273

Known familial variant not otherwise specified. ~ 81403

KRAS (Kirsten rat sarcoma viral oncogene homolog) ~ 81275, 81276, 81405

L1CAM (L1 cell adhesion molecule) ~ 81407

LAMA2 (laminin, alpha 2) ~ 81408

LAMB2 (laminin, beta 2 [laminin S]) ~ 81407

LAMP2 (lysosomal-associated membrane protein 2) ~ 81405

LCT (lactase-phlorizin hydrolase) ~ 81400

LDB3 (LIM domain binding 3) ~ 81406

LDLR (low density lipoprotein receptor) ~ 81405, 81406

LEPR (leptin receptor) ~ 81406

LHCGR (luteinizing hormone/ choriogonadotropin receptor) ~ 81406

LINC00518 (long intergenic non-protein coding RNA 518) ~ 81401

LITAF (lipopolysaccharide-induced TNF factor) ~ 81404

LMNA (lamin A/C) ~ 81406

LRP5 (low density lipoprotein receptor-related protein 5) ~ 81406

LRRK2 (leucine-rich repeat kinase 2) ~ 81401, 81408

MAP2K1 (mitogen-activated protein kinase 1) ~ 81406

MAP2K2 (mitogen-activated protein kinase 2) ~ 81406

MAPT (microtubule-associated protein tau) ~ 81406

MC4R (melanocortin 4 receptor) ~ 81403

MCCC1 (methylcrotonoyl-CoA carboxylase 1 [alpha]) ~ 81406

MCCC2 (methylcrotonoyl-CoA carboxylase 2 [beta]) ~ 81406

MCOLN1 (mucolipin 1) ~ 81290

MECP2 (methyl CpG binding protein 2 [Rett syndrome]) ~ 81302-81304

MED12 (mediator complex subunit 12) ~ 81401

MEFV (Mediterranean fever) ~ 81402, 81404

MEG3/DLK1 (maternally expressed 3 [non-protein coding]/delta-like 1 homolog [Drosophila]) ~ 81401

MEN1 (multiple endocrine neoplasia I) ~ 81404, 81405

MFN2 (mitofusin 2) ~ 81406

MGMT (O-6-methylguanine DNA methyltransferase) ~ 81287

MICA (MHC class I polypeptide-related sequence A) ~ 81403

MLH1 (mutL homolog 1, colon cancer, nonpolyposis type 2) ~ 81288, 81292-81294

MLL/AFF1 (t(4;11)) ~ 81401

MLL/MLLT3 (t(9;11)) ~ 81401

MMAA (methylmalonic aciduria [cobalamine deficiency] type A) ~ 81405

MMAB (methylmalonic aciduria [cobalamine deficiency] type B) ~ 81405

MMACHC (methylmalonic aciduria [cobalamin deficiency] cblC type, with

homocystinuria) ~ 81404

MPI (mannose phosphate isomerase) ~ 81405

MPL (myeloproliferative leukemia virus oncogene, thrombopoietin receptor, TPOR) ~ 81402, 81403

MPV17 (MpV17 mitochondrial inner membrane protein) ~ 81404, 81405

MPZ (myelin protein zero) ~ 81405

MSH2 (mutS homolog 2, colon cancer, nonpolyposis type 1) ~ 81295-81297

MSH6 (mutS homolog 6 [E. coli]) ~ 81298-81300

Gene Analysis ~ continued

MT-ATP6 (mitochondrially encoded ATP synthase 6) ~ 81401

MT-ND4, MT-ND6 (mitochondrially encoded NADH dehydrogenase 4, mitochondrially encoded NADH dehydrogenase 6) ~ 81401

MT-RNR1 (mitochondrially encoded 12S RNA) ~ 81401, 81403

MT-TK (mitochondrially encoded tRNA lysine) ~ 81401

MT-TL1 (mitochondrially encoded tRNA leucine 1 [UUA/G]) ~ 81401

MT-TL1, MT-ND5 (mitochondrially encoded tRNA leucine 1 [UUA/G], tochondrially encoded NADH dehydrogenase 5) ~ 81401

MT-TS1 (mitochondrially encoded tRNA serine 1) ~ 81403

MT-TS1, MT-RNR1 (mitochondrially encoded tRNA serine 1 [UCN], mitochondrially encoded 12S RNA) ~ 81401

MTM1 (myotubularin 1) ~ 81405, 81406

MTHFR (5, 10-methylenetetrahydrofolate reductase) ~ 81291

MUT (methylmalonyl CoA mutase) ~ 81406

MUTYH (mutY homolog [E. coli]) ~ 81401, 81406

MYBPC3 (myosin binding protein C, cardiac) ~ 81407

MYH6 (myosin, heavy chain 6, cardiac muscle, alpha) ~ 81407

MYH7 (myosin, heavy chain 7, cardiac muscle, beta) ~ ~ 81407

MYH11 (myosin, heavy chain 11, smooth muscle) ~ 81408

MYL2 (myosin, light chain 2, regulatory, cardiac, slow) ~ 81405

MYL3 (myosin, light chain 3, alkali, ventrcular, skeletal, slow) ~ 81405

MYO7A (myosin VIIA) ~ 81407

MYOT (myotilin) ~ 81405

NDP (Norrie disease [pseudoglioma]) ~ 81403, 81404

NDUFA1 (NADH dehydrogenase [ubiquinone] 1 alpha subcomplex, 1, 7.5kDa) ~ 81404

NDUFAF2 (NADH dehydrogenase [ubiquinone] 1 alpha subcomplex, assembly factor 2) ~ 81404

NDUFS1 (NADH dehydrogenase [ubiquinone] Fe-S protein 1, 75kDa [NADH-coenzyme Q reductase]) ~ 81406

NDUFS4 (NADH dehydrogenase [ubiquinone] Fe-S protein 4, 18kDa [NADH-coenzyme Q reductase]) ~ 81404

NDUFS7 (NADH dehydrogenase [ubiquinone] Fe-S protein 7, 20kDa [NADH-coenzyme Q reductase]) ~ 81405

NDUFS8 (NADH dehydrogenase [ubiquinone] Fe-S protein 8, 23kDa [NADH-coenzyme Q reductase]) ~ 81405

NDUFV1 (NADH dehydrogenase [ubiquinone] flavoprotein 1, 51kDa) ~ 81405

NEB (nebulin) ~ 81400, 81408

NEFL (neurofilament, light polypeptide) 81405

NF1 (neurofibromin 1) ~ 81408

NF2 (neurofibromin 2 [merlin]) ~ 81405, 81406

NHLRC1 (NHL repeat containing 1) ~ 81403

NIPA1 (non-imprinted in Prader-Willi/ Angelman syndrome 1) ~ 81404

NLGN3 (neuroligin 3) ~ 81405

NLGN4X (neuroligin 4, X-linked) ~ 81404, 81405

NOD2 (nucleotide-binding oligomerization domain containing 2) ~ 81401

NOTCH1 (notch 1) ~ 81407

NOTCH3 (notch 3) ~ 81406

NPC1 (Niemann-Pick disease, type C1) ~ 81406

NPC2 (Niemann-Pick disease, type C2 [epididymal secretory protein E1]) ~ 81404

NPHP1 (nephronophthisis 1 [juvenile]) ~ 81405, 81406

NPHS1 (nephrosis 1, congenital, Finnish type [nephrin]) ~ 81407

NPHS2 (nephrosis 2, idiopathic, steroid resistant [podocin]) ~ 81405

NPM1 (nucleophosmin [nucleolar phosphoprotein B23, numatrin]) ~ 81310

NPM1/ALK (t(2;5)) ~ 81401

NRAS (neuroblastoma RAS viral [v-ras] oncogene homolog) ~ 81311

NR0B1 (nuclear receptor subfamily 0, group B, member 1) ~ 81404

NSD1 (nuclear receptor binding SET domain protein 1) ~ 81405, 81406

OPA1 (optic atrophy 1) ~ 81406, 81407

OPTN (optineurin) ~ 81406

OTC (ornithine carbamoyltransferase) ~ 81405

PABPN1 (poly[A] binding protein, nuclear 1) ~ 81401

PAFAH1B1 (platelet-activating factor acetylhydrolase 1b, regulatory subunit 1 [45kDa]) ~ 81405, 81406

PAH (phenylalanine hydroxylase) ~ 81406

PALB2 (partner and localizer of BRCA2) 81406

PARK2 (Parkinson protein 2, E3 ubiquitin protein ligase [parkin]) ~ 81405, 81406

PAX2 (paired box 2) ~ 81406

PAX8/PPARG (t(2;3) (q13;p25)) ~ 81401

PC (pyruvate carboxylase) ~ 81406

PCA3/KLK3 (prostate cancer antigen 3 [non protein coding]/kallikrein related peptidase 3 [prostate specific antigen]) ~ 81313

PCCA (propionyl CoA carboxylase, alpha polypeptide) ~ 81405, 81406

PCCB (propionyl CoA carboxylase, beta polypeptide) ~ 81406

1061

Gene Analysis ~ *continued*

PCDH15 (protocadherin-related 15) ~ 81400, 81406, 81407
PCDH19 (protocadherin 19) ~ 81405
PCSK9 (proprotein convertase subtilisin/kevin type 9) ~ 81406
PDGFRA (platelet-derived growth factor receptor, alpha polypeptide) ~ 81314
PDHA1 (pyruvate dehydrogenase [lipoamide] alpha 1) ~ 81405, 81406
PDHB (pyruvate dehydrogenase [lipoamide] beta) ~ ~ 81405
PDHX (pyruvate dehydrogenase complex, component X) ~ 81406
PDX1 (pancreatic and duodenal homeobox 1) ~ 81404
PHEX (phosphate regulating endopeptidase homolog, X-linked) ~ 81406
PHOX2B (paired-like homeobox 2b) ~ 81403, 81404
PIK3CA (phosphatidylinositol-4,5-bisphosphate 3-kinase, catalytic subunit alpha) ~ 81404
PINK1 (PTEN induced putative kinase 1) ~ 81405
PKD1 (polycystic kidney disease1 [autosomal dominant]) ~ 81407
PKD2 (polycystic kidney disease 2 [autosomal dominant]) ~ 81406
PKHD1 (polycystic kidney and hepatic disease 1) ~ 81408
PKLR (pyruvate kinase, liver and RBC) (eg, pyruvate kinase deficiency) ~ 81405
PKP2 (plakophilin 2) ~ 81406
PLCE1 (phospholipase C, epsilon 1) ~ 81407
PLN (phospholamban) ~ 81403
PLP1 (proteolipid protein 1) ~ 81404, 81405
PML/RARalpha, (t(15;17)) (promyelocytic leukemia/retinoic acid receptor alpha) ~ 81315, 81316
PMP22 (peripheral myelin protein 22) ~ 81324-81326
PMS2 (PMS2 postmeiotic segregation increased 2 [S. cerevisiae]) ~ 81317-81319
PNKD (paroxysmal nonkinesigenic dyskinesia) ~ 81406
POLG (polymerase [DNA directed], gamma) ~ 81406
POMGNT1 (protein O-linked mannose beta1, 2-N-cetylglucosaminyltransferase) ~ 81406
POMT1 (protein-O-mannosyltransferase 1) ~ 81406
POMT2 (protein-O-mannosyltransferase 2) ~ 81406
POU1F1 (POU class 1 homeobox 1) ~ 81405
PPOX (protoporphyrinogen oxidase) ~ 81406
PPP2R2B (protein phosphatase 2, regulatory subunit B, beta) ~ 81401
PQBP1 (polyglutamine binding protein 1) ~ 81404, 81405
PRAME (preferentially expressed antigen in melanoma) ~ 81401
PRKAG2 (protein kinase, AMP-activated, gamma 2 non-catalytic subunit) ~ 81406
PRKCG (protein kinase C, gamma) ~ 81406
PRNP (prion protein) ~ 81404
PROP1 (PROP paired-like homeobox 1) ~ 81404
PRPH2 (peripherin 2 [retinal degeneration slow]) ~ 81404
PRSS1 (protease, serine, 1 [trypsin 1]) ~ 81401, 81404
PRX (periaxin) ~ 81405
PSEN1 (presenilin 1) ~ 81405
PSEN2 (presenilin 2 [Alzheimer disease 4]) ~ 81406
PTEN (phosphatase and tensin homolog) ~ 81321-81323
PTPN11 (protein tyrosine phosphatase, non-receptor type 11) ~ 81406
PYGM (phosphorylase, glycogen, muscle) ~ 81401, 81406
RAB7A (RAB7A, member RAS oncogene family) ~ 81405
RAF1 (v-raf-1 murine leukemia viral oncogene homolog 1) ~ 81404, 81406
RAI1 (retinoic acid induced 1) ~ 81405
REEP1 (receptor accessory protein 1) ~ 81405
RET (ret proto-oncogene) ~ 81404-81406
RHD (Rh blood group, D antigen) ~ 81403
RHO (rhodopsin) ~ 81404
RP1 (retinitis pigmentosa 1) ~ 81404
RPE65 (retinal pigment epithelium specific protein 65kDa) ~ 81406
RPS19 (ribosomal protein S19) ~ 81405
RRM2B (ribonucleotide reductase M2 B [TP53 inducible]) ~ 81405
RUNX1 (runt related transcription factor 1) ~ 81334
RUNX1/RUNX1T1(t(8;21)) ~ 81401
RYR1 (ryanodine receptor 1, skeletal) ~ 81406, 81408
RYR2 (ryanodine receptor 2 [cardiac]) ~ 81408
SCN1A (sodium channel, voltage-gated, type I, alpha subunit) ~ 81407
SCN1B (sodium channel, voltage-gated, type I, beta) ~ ~ 81404
SCN4A (sodium channel, voltage-gated, type IV, alpha subunit) ~ 81406
SCN5A (sodium channel, voltage-gated, type V, alpha subunit) ~ 81407
SCNN1A (sodium channel, nonvoltage-gated 1 alpha) ~ 81406
SCNN1B (sodium channel, nonvoltage-gated 1, beta) ~ ~ 81406
SCNN1G (sodium channel, nonvoltage-gated 1, gamma) ~ 81406
SCO1 (SCO cytochrome oxidase deficient homolog 1) ~ 81405
SCO2 (SCO cytochrome oxidase deficient homolog 2 [SCO1L]) ~ 81404

Gene Analysis ~ *continued*

SDHA (succinate dehydrogenase complex, subunit A, flavoprotein [Fp]) ~ 81406
SDHB (succinate dehydrogenase complex, subunit B, iron sulfur) ~ 81405
SDHC (succinate dehydrogenase complex, subunit C, integral membrane protein, 15kDa) ~ 81404, 81405
SDHD (succinate dehydrogenase complex, subunit D, integral membrane protein) ~ 81404
SEPT9 (septin 9) ~ 81327
SERPINA1 (serpin peptidase inhibitor, clade A [alpha-1 antiproteinase, antitrypsin], member 1) ~ 81332
SERPINE1 (serpine peptidase inhibitor clade E, member 1, plasminogen activator inhibitor 1, PAI 1) ~ 81400
SETX (senataxin) ~ 81406
SGCA (sarcoglycan, alpha [50kDa dystrophin-associated glycoprotein]) ~ 81405
SGCB (sarcoglycan, beta [43kDa dystrophinassociated glycoprotein]) ~ 81405
SGCD (sarcoglycan, delta [35kDa dystrophinassociated glycoprotein]) ~ 81405
SGCE (sarcoglycan, epsilon) ~ 81405, 81406
SGCG (sarcoglycan, gamma [35kDa dystrophinassociated glycoprotein]) ~ 81404, 81405
SH2D1A (SH2 domain containing 1A) ~ 81403, 81404
SH3TC2 (SH3 domain and tetratricopeptide repeats 2) ~ 81406
SHOC2 (soc-2 suppressor of clear homolog) ~ 81400, 81405
SHOX (short stature homeobox) ~ 81405
SIL1 (SIL1 homolog, endoplasmic reticulum chaperone [S. cerevisiae]) ~ 81405
SLC9A6 (solute carrier family 9 [sodium/ hydrogen exchanger], member 6) ~ 8406
SLC2A1 (solute carrier family 2 [facilitated glucose transporter], member 1) ~ 81405
SLC12A1 (solute carrier family 12 [sodium/potassium/chloride transporters], member 1) ~ 81407
SLC12A3 (solute carrier family 12 [sodium/ chloride transporters], member 3) ~ 81407
SLC16A2 (solute carrier family 16, member 2 [thyroid hormone transporter]) ~ 81404, 81405
SLC22A5 (solute carrier family 22 organic cation/carnitine transporter], member 5) ~ 81405
SLC25A4 (solute carrier family 25 [mitochondrial carrier; adenine nucleotide translocator], member 4) ~ 81404
SLC25A20 (solute carrier family 25 [carnitine/acylcarnitine translocase], member 20) ~ 81404, 81405
SLC26A4 (solute carrier family 26, member 4) ~ 81406
SLC37A4 (solute carrier family 37 [glucose-6- phosphate transporter], member 4) ~ 81406
SLCO1B1 (solute carrier organic anion transporter family, member 1B1) ~ 81328
SMAD4 (SMAD family member 4) ~ 81405, 81406
SMN1 (survival of motor neuron 1, telomeric) ~ 81400, 81403, 81405
SMN1/SMN2 (survival of motor neuron 1, telomeric/survival of motor neuron 2, centromeric) ~ 81401
SMPD1 (sphingomyelin phosphodiesterase 1, acid lysosomal) ~ 81330
SNRPN/UBE3A (small nuclear ribonucleoprotein polypeptide N/ubiquitin protein ligase E3A) ~ 81331
SOD1 (superoxide dismutase 1, soluble) 81404
SOS1 (son of sevenless homolog 1) ~ 81406
SPAST (spastin) ~ 81405, 81406
SPG7 (spastic paraplegia 7 [pure and complicated autosomal recessive]) ~ 81405, 81406
SPG11 (spastic paraplegia 11 [autosomal recessive]) ~ 81407
SPINK1 (serine peptidase inhibitor, Kazal type 1) ~ 81404
SPRED1 (sprouty-related, EVH1 domain containing 1) ~ 81405
SPTBN2 (spectrin, beta, non-erythrocytic 2) ~ 81407
SRY (sex determining region Y) ~ 81400
SS18/SSX1 (t(X;18)) ~ 81401
SS18/SSX2 (t(X;18)) ~ 81401
STAT3 (signal transduce and activator of transcription 3 [acute-phase response factor]) ~ 81405
STK11 (serine/threonine kinase 11) ~ 81404, 81405
STXBP1 (syntaxin binding protein 1) ~ 81406
SURF1 (surfeit 1) ~ 81405
TACO1 (translational activator of mitochondrial encoded cytochrome c oxidase ~ 81404
TARDBP (TAR DNA binding protein) ~ 81405
TAZ (tafazzin) ~ 81406
TBP (TATA box binding protein) ~ 81401

Gene Analysis ~ *continued*

TBX5 (T-box 5) ~ 81405
TCF4 (transcription factor 4) ~ 81405, 81406
TGFBR1 (transforming growth factor, beta receptor 1) ~ 81405
TGFBR2 (transforming growth factor, beta receptor 2) ~ 81405
TH (tyrosine hydroxylase) ~ 81406
THAP1 (THAP domain containing, apoptosis associated protein 1) ~ 81404
THRB (thyroid hormone receptor, beta) ~ 81405
TK2 (thymidine kinase 2, mitochondrial) 81405
TMEM43 (transmembrane protein 43) ~ 81406
TMEM67 (transmembrane protein 67) ~ 81407
TNNC1 (troponin C type 1 [slow]) ~ 81405
TNNI3 (troponin I, type 3 [cardiac]) ~ 81405
TNNT2 (troponin T, type 2 [cardiac]) ~ 81406
TOR1A (torsin family 1, member A [torsin A]) ~ 81400, 81404
TP53 (tumor protein 53) ~ 81404, 81405
TPM1 (tropomyosin 1 [alpha]) ~ 81405
TPMT (thiopurine S-methyltransferase) 81335
TRB@ (T cell receptor beta locus) 81340, 81341
TRD@ (T cell antigen receptor, delta) Rearrangement ~ 81402
TRG@ (T cell receptor gamma locus) ~ 81342
TRPC6 (transient receptor potential cation channel, subfamily C, member 6) ~ 81406
TSC1 (tuberous sclerosis 1) ~ 81405, 81406
TSC2 (tuberous sclerosis 2) ~ 81406, 81407
TTPA (tocopherol [alpha] transfer protein) ~ 81404
TTR (transthyretin) ~ 81404
TWIST1 (twist homolog 1 [Drosophila]) ~ 81403, 81404
TYMP (thymidine phosphorylase) ~ 81405
TYMS (thymidylate synthetase) ~ 81346
TYR (tyrosinase [oculocutaneous albinism IA]) ~ 81404
UBA1 (ubiquitin-like modifier activating enzyme 1) ~ 81403
UBE3A (ubiquitin protein ligase E3A) ~ 81406
UGT1A1 (UDP glucuronosyltransferase 1 family, polypeptide A1) ~ 81350
UMOD (uromodulin) ~ 81406
Uniparental disomy (UPD) ~ 81402
USH1C (Usher syndrome 1C [autosomal recessive, severe]) ~ 81407
USH1G (Usher syndrome 1G [autosomal recessive]) ~ 81404
USH2A (Usher syndrome 2A [autosomal recessive, mild]) ~ 81408
VHL (von Hippel-Lindau tumor suppressor) ~ 81403, 81404
VKORC1 (vitamin K epoxide reductase complex, subunit 1) ~ 81355
VPS13B (vacuolar protein sorting 13 homolog B [yeast]) ~ 81407, 81408
VWF (von Willebrand factor) ~ 81401, 81403-81406, 81408
WAS (Wiskott-Aldrich syndrome [eczemathrombocytopenia]) ~ 81406
WDR62 (WD repeat domain 62) ~ 81407
WT1 (Wilms tumor 1) ~ 81404
ZEB2 (zinc finger E-box binding homeobox 2) ~ 81404, 81405
ZNF41 (zinc finger protein 41) ~ 81404
chimerism Analysis ~ 81267, 81268
comparative Analysis Using Short Tandem Repeat (STR) Markers ~ 81265, 81266
cytogenomic Constitutional Targeted Microarray Analysis, Chromosome 22q13 ~ 81405
cytogenomic Microarray Analysis, Neoplasia ~ 81406
HLA Class I and II Typing, Low Resolution. ~ 81370, 81371
HLA Class I Typing, Low Resolution ~ 81372-81374
HLA Class II Typing, Low Resolution ~ 81375-81377
HLA Class I and II Typing, High Resolution ~ 81378
HLA Class I Typing, High Resolution. ~ 81379-81381
HLA Class II Typing, High Resolution. ~ 81382, 81383
human Platelet Antigen Genotyping ~ 81105-81112
microsatellite Instability Analysis ~ 81301
short Tandem Repeat (STR) Analysis. ~ 81265, 81266, 81402
translocation Analysis
BCR/ABL1 (t(9;22)) ~ 81206-81208
CCND1/IGH (BCL1/IgH, t(11;14)) ~ 81401
COL1A1/PDGFB (t(17;22)) ~ 81402
E2A/PBX1 (t(1;19)) ~ 81401
EML4/ALK (inv(2)) ~ 81401
ETV6/NTRK3 (t(12;15)) ~ 81401
ETV6/RUNX1 (t(12;21)) ~ 81401
EWSR1/ATF1 (t(12;22)) ~ 81401
EWSR1/ERG (t(21;22) ~ 81401
EWSR1/FLI1 (t(11;22)) ~ 81401
EWSR1/WT1 (t(11;22)) ~ 81401
FOXO1/PAX3 (t(2;13)) ~ 81401
FOXO1/PAX7 (t(1;13)) ~ 81401

Gene Analysis ~ *continued*

FUS/DDIT3 (t(12;16)) ~ 81401
IGH@/BCL2 (t(14;18) ~ 81402
MLL/AFF1 (t(4;11)) ~ 81401
MLL/MLLT3 (t(9;11)) ~ 81401
NPM1/ALK (t(2;5)) ~ 81401
PAX8/PPARG (t(2;3)) (q13;p25)) ~ 81401
PML/RARalpha (t(15;17)) ~ 81315, 81316
RUNX1/RUNX1T1 (t(8;21)) ~ 81401
SS18/SSX1 (t(X;18)) ~ 81401
SS18/SSX2 (t(X;18)) ~ 81401
Gene product ~ see protein
Genioplasty ~ 21120-21123
augmentation ~ 21120, 21123
osteotomy ~ 21121-21123
Genitourinary sphincter, artificial ~ 53444-53449
Genomic sequencing procedures (GSPs)
aortic Dysfunction or Dilation ~ 81410, 81411
Ashkenazi Jewish Associated Disorders ~ 81412
cardiac Ion Channelopathies ~ 81413, 81414
exome ~ 81415-81417
fetal Chromosomal Aneuploidy ~ 81420
fetal Chromosomal Microdeletion(s) ~ 81422
genome ~ 81425-81427
germline Disorders ~ 0012U
hearing Loss ~ 81430, 81431
helicobacter Pylori Detection and Antibiotic Resistance. ~ 0008U
hematolymphoid Neoplasia ~ 0014U, 0016U, 0017U
hereditary Breast Cancer-Related Disorders. ~ 81432, 81433
hereditary Cardiomyopathy ~ 81439
hereditary Colon Cancer Disorders ~ 81435, 81436
hereditary Neuroendocrine Tumor Disorders. ~ 81437, 81438
hereditary Peripheral Neuropathies. ~ 81448
hereditary Retinal Disorders ~ 81434
infectious Disease (Bacterial) ~ 0004U, 0010U
Noonan Spectrum Disorders. ~ 81442
nuclear Encoded Mitochondrial Genes ~ 81440
proprietary Laboratory Analysis ~ 0001U, 0004U, 0008U-0010U, 0012U-0017U
red Blood Cell Antigen Typing ~ 0001U
solid Organ Neoplasia ~ 0013U
targeted Genomic Sequence Analysis Panel ~ 81445, 81450, 81455
whole Mitochondrial Genome ~ 81460, 81465
X-linked Intellectual Disability (XLID) ~ 81470, 81471
Genotype analysis
by Nucleic Acid
hepatitis C Virus ~ 87902
high-risk HPV Types. ~ 0500T
HIV-1 ~ 87901, 87906
protease/Reverse Transcriptase Regions. ~ 87901
vancomycin Resistance ~ 87500
human Platelet Antigen ~ 81105-81112human platelet antigen ~ 81400
Gentamicin ~ 80170
assay ~ 80170
Gentamycin level ~ 80170
Gentiobiase ~ 82963
GERD ~ 91034-91038
German measles ~ 86762
Gestational trophoblastic tumor ~ 59100, 59870
GGT ~ 82977
GI tract ~ see gastrointestinal tract
Giardia
antigen detection
immunofluorescence ~ 87269
enzyme immunoassay ~ 87329
Giardia lamblia
antibody ~ 86674
Gibbons stent ~ 52332
GIF ~ 84307
GIFT (gamete intrafallopian transfer) ~ 58976
Gillies approach
fracture, zygomatic arch ~ 21356
Gill operation ~ 63012
Gingiva ~ see gums
Gingiva, abscess ~ see abscess
fracture ~ see 41800 ~ gums
zygomatic arch ~ 41800
Gingivectomy ~ 41820
Gingivoplasty ~ 41872
Girdlestone laminectomy ~ see laminectomy
Girdlestone procedure ~ 27120

G1A protein (bone) ~ 83937
Gland ~ see specific gland
Glasses ~ see spectacle services
Glaucoma
  counseling ~ 4174F
  cryotherapy ~ 66720
  cyclophotocoagulation ~ 66710, 66711
  diathermy ~ 66700
  fistulization of sclera ~ 66150
    through ciliary body ~ 66999
  iridectomy ~ 66625, 66630
  plan of care ~ 0517F
Glaucoma drainage implant ~ 66180, 66185
Glenn procedure ~ 33766-33767
  bidirectional ~ 33622
Glenohumeral joint
  arthrotomy ~ 23040
    with biopsy ~ 23100
    with synovectomy ~ 23105
  exploration ~ 23107
  removalforeign or loose body ~ 23107
Glenoid Fossa reconstruction ~ 21255
GLN ~ 82127, 82128, 82131
Globulin
  antihuman ~ 86880-86886
  corticosteroid-binding ~ 84449
  immune
    administration ~ 96365-96368
    product
      botulinum antitoxin ~ 90288
      botulism ~ 90288
      cytomegalovirus (CMV-IgIV) ~ 90291
      diphtheria antitoxin ~ 90296
      gammaglobulin ~ 82784-82785
      hepatitis B (HBIg) ~ 90371
      Ig ~ 90281
      IgIV ~ 90281
      rabies (RIg/Rig-HT) ~ 90375-90376
      respiratory syncytial virus ~ 90378
      Rho(D) (RhIg/RhIgV) ~ 90384-90386
      SCIg ~ 90284
      tetanus (TIg) ~ 90389
      unlisted ~ 90399
      vaccinia ~ 90393
      varicella-zoster ~ 90396
  sex hormone binding ~ 84270
  thyroxine-binding ~ 84442
Glomerular procoagulant activity ~ see thromboplastin
Glomus caroticum ~ 60600, 60605
Glossectomies ~ see excision, tongue
Glossopexy ~ 41500
Glossorrhaphy ~ see suture, tongue
Glucagon ~ 82943
  tolerance panel ~ 80422-80424
  tolerance test ~ 82946
Glucose
  blood test ~ 82947, 82948, 82950
    home test ~ 82962
  body fluid ~ 82945
  interstitial fluid
    continuous monitoring ~ 95249-95251
    data interpretation ~ 99091
  panel
    basic metabolic ~ 80047, 80048
    comprehensive metabolic ~ 80053
    glucagon tolerance ~ 80422, 80424
    growth hormone suppression ~ 80430
    insulin tolerance ~ 80434, 80435
    insulin-induced C-peptide suppression ~ 80432
    renal function ~ 80069
  sensor
    insertion, subcutaneous pocket ~ 0446T, 0448T
    removal ~ 0447T, 0448T
  tolerance test ~ 82951, 82952
    intravenous push ~ 96374
  urinalysis ~ 81000-81003, 81005
Glucose-6-phosphate dehydrogenase ~ 82955-82960
Glucose phosphate isomerase ~ 84087
Glucosidase ~ 82963
Glucuronide androstanediol ~ 82154

Glue
  cornea wound ~ 65286
  sclera wound ~ 65286
Glukagon ~ see glucagon
Glutamate dehydrogenase, blood ~ 82965
Glutamate pyruvate transaminase ~ 84460
Glutamic
  alanine transaminase ~ 84460
  aspartic transaminase ~ 84450
  dehydrogenase ~ 82965
Glutamine ~ 82127, 82128, 82131
Glutamyltransferase, gamma ~ 82977
Glutathione ~ 82978
Glutathione reductase ~ 82979
Glycanhydrolase, N-acetylmuramide ~ 85549
Glycated hemoglobins ~ 83036
Glycated protein ~ 82985
Glycerol, phosphatidyl ~ 84081
Glycerol, phosphoglycerides ~ 84081
Glycerophosphatase ~ 84075-84080
Glycinate, theophylline sodium ~ 80198
Glycocholic acid ~ 82240
Glycohemoglobin ~ 83036
Glycol, ethylene ~ 82693
Glycosaminoglycan ~ 83864
Goeckerman treatment ~ 96910-96913
Gol-Vernet operation
  pyelotomy, exploration 50120
Gold assay ~ 80375
Goldwaite procedure ~ 27422
Golfer's elbow ~ 24357-24359
Gonadectomy, female ~ 58262-58263, 58291-58292, 58552, 58554, 58661, 58940-58943
Gonadectomy, male ~ 54520, 54522, 54530-54535, 54690
Gonadotropin
  chorionic ~ 84702-84704
  FSH ~ 83001
  ICSH ~ 83002
  LH ~ 83002
  panel ~ 80426
Gonioscopy ~ 92020
Goniotomy ~ 65820
Gonococcus ~ 87590-87592, 87850
Goodenough Harris drawing test ~ 96100
GOTT ~ 84450
GPUT ~ 82775-82776
Graft ~ see bone graft; bypass graft
  anal ~ 46753
  aorta ~ 33840-33851, 33860-33877
  artery
    coronary ~ 33503-33505
  bone ~ 38240-38242
    harvesting ~ 20900-20902
    microvascular anastomosis ~ 20955-20962
    osteocutaneous flap with microvascular anastomosis ~ 20969-20973
    vascular pedicle ~ 25430
  bone marrow, aspiration ~ 20939
  bone and skin ~ 20969-20973
  cartilage
    ear to face ~ 21235
    harvesting ~ 20910-20912
    rib to face ~ 21230
  conjunctiva ~ 65782
    harvesting ~ 68371
  cornea, with lesion excision ~ 65426
  cornea transplant
    allograft preparation ~ 65757
    endothelial ~ 65756
    in aphakia ~ 65750
    lamellar ~ 65710
    penetrating ~ 65730
    in pseudophakia ~ 65755
  dura, spinal cord ~ 63710
  eye
    amniotic membrane ~ 65780
    conjunctiva ~ 65782
    stem cell ~ 65781
  facial nerve paralysis ~ 15840-15845
  fascia, cheek ~ 15840
  fascia lata, harvesting ~ 20920-20922

Graft ~ continued
gum mucosa ~ 41870
heart ~ 33935, 33945
heart lung ~ 33935
kidney ~ see kidney, transplantation
liver ~ 47135
lung ~ 32851-32854, 33935
muscle, cheek ~ 15841-15845
nail bed reconstruction ~ 11762
nerve ~ 64885-64907
oral mucosa ~ 40818
organ ~ see transplantation
pancreas ~ 48160, 48550, 48554-48556
skin
  biological—see Allograft, skin substitute
  blood flow check, graft ~ 15860
tendon
  finger ~ 26392
  hand ~ 26392
  harvesting ~ 20924
tissue harvesting ~ 20926
vein cross-over ~ 34520
Grain alcohol ~ see alcohol, ethyl
Granulation tissue cauterization, chemical ~ 17250
Great toe
flap ~ 20973
fracture ~ 28490, 28496, 28505
Great vessels
graft insertion ~ 33330, 33335
shunt
  aorta to pulmonary artery
    ascending ~ 33755
    descending ~ 33762
  central ~ 33764
  subclavian to pulmonary artery ~ 33750
  vena cava to pulmonary artery ~ 33766-33767
unlisted services and procedures ~ 33999
Great vessels transposition ~ 33770-33781
Greater tuberosity fracture
with shoulder dislocation
  closed treatment ~ 23665
  open treatment ~ 23670
Greater vestibular gland ~ see Bartholin's gland
Green operation ~ (scapulopexy) 23400
Gridley stain ~ 88312
Grippe, Balkan ~ 86000, 86638
Gritti operation ~ 27590-27592
Groin repair, hernia ~ 49550-49557
Group health education ~ 99078
Grouping, blood ~ see blood typing
Growth factors, insulin-like ~ 84305
Growth hormone ~ 83003
human ~ 80418, 80428-80430, 86277
Growth hormone release inhibiting factor ~ 84307
GTT (hydatidiform mole) ~ 82951, 82952
Guaiac test, blood in feces ~ 82270
Guard stain ~ 88313
Gullett ~ see esophagus
Gums
abscess, incision and drainage ~ 41800
alveolus, excision ~ 41830
cyst, incision and drainage ~ 41800
excision
  gingiva ~ 41820
  operculum ~ 41821
graft, mucosa ~ 41870
hematoma, incision and drainage ~ 41800
lesion
  destruction ~ 41850
  excision ~ 41822-41828
mucosa, excision ~ 41828
reconstruction
  alveolus ~ 41874
  gingiva ~ 41872
removal, foreign body ~ 41805
tumor, excision ~ 41825-41827
unlisted services and procedures ~ 41899
Gunning-Lieben test ~ 82009-82010
Guthrie test ~ 84030

H

H flu ~ see Hemophilus influenza
HAAb (antibody, hepatitis) ~ 86708, 86709
HAA (hepatitis associated antigen) ~ 87340-87380, 87516-87527
Haemoglobin F ~ see fetal hemoglobin
Haemorrhage ~ see hemorrhage
Haemorrhage rectum ~ see hemorrhage, rectum
Hageman factor ~ 85280
Hair
electrolysis ~ 17380
KOH examination ~ 87220
microscopic evaluation ~ 96902
removal ~ see removal, hair
transplant
  punch graft ~ 15775-15776
  strip graft ~ 15220-15221
HAI test ~ see hemagglutination inhibition test
Hallux ~ see great toe
Halo
body cast ~ 29000
cranial ~ 20661
  for thin skull osteology ~ 20664
femur ~ 20663
maxillofacial ~ 21100
pelvic ~ 20662
removal ~ 20665
Haloperidol assay ~ 80173
Halsted mastectomy ~ see mastectomy, radical
Halsted hernia repair ~ 49495
Ham test ~ 85475
Hammertoe repair ~ 28285-28286
Hamster penetration test ~ 89329
Hand ~ see also carpometacarpal joint; intercarpal joint
amputation
  at metacarpal ~ 25927
  revision ~ 25924, 25929-25931
  at wrist ~ 25920
    revision ~ 25922
arthrodesis
  carpometacarpal joint ~ 26843-26844
  intercarpal joint ~ 25820-25825
bone, incision and drainage ~ 26034
cast ~ 29085
decompression ~ 26035-26037
fracture metacarpal
  carpometacarpal ~ 26645, 26650
  metacarpal
    closed treatment ~ 26600, 26605, 26607
    open treatment ~ 26615
    skeletal fixation ~ 26608
  metacarpophalangeal ~ 26740-26746
  phalangeal ~ 26720-26735, 26750-26765
injection, cell therapy for scleroderma ~ 0490T
insertion tendon graft ~ 26392
magnetic resonance imaging (MRI) ~ 73218-73223
reconstruction tendon pulley ~ 26500-26502
removal
  implantation ~ 26320
    tube/rod ~ 26390-26392, 26416
repair
  blood vessel ~ 35207
  cleft hand ~ 26580
  muscle ~ 26591-26593
  tendon
    extensor ~ 26410-26416, 26426-26428, 26433-26437
    flexor ~ 26350-26358, 26440
    profundus ~ 26370-26373
replantation ~ 20808
strapping ~ 29280
tendon excision ~ 26390
  extensor ~ 26415
tenotomy ~ 26450, 26460
tumor excision ~ 26111-26118
unlisted services and procedures ~ 26989
X-ray ~ 73120-73130

Handling
  device ~ 99002
  radioelement ~ 77790
  specimen ~ 99000-99001
Hand abscess ~ see abscess, hand
Hand phalange ~ see finger, bone
Hanganutziu Deicher antibodies ~ see antibody, heterophile
Haptoglobin ~ 83010-83012
Hard palate ~ see palate
Harelip operation ~ see cleft lip, repair
Harii procedure ~ 25430
Harrington rod
  insertion ~ 22840
  removal ~ 22850
Hartmann procedure
  open ~ 44143
  laparoscopic ~ 44206
Harvesting
  adipose tissue cells
    cell therapy for scleroderma ~ 0489T
  bone graft ~ 20900-20902
  bone marrow
    allogenic ~ 38230
    autograft ~ 0265T, 20939, 38232
  cartilage graft ~ 20910-20912
  conjunctival graft ~ 68371
  eggs, in vitro fertilization ~ 58970
  endoscopic, vein for bypass graft ~ 33508
  fascia lata graft ~ 20920-20922
  intestines ~ 44132-44133
  kidney ~ 50300-50320, 50547
  liver ~ 47133, 47140-47142
  lower extremity vein for vascular reconstruction ~ 35572
  stem cell ~ 38205-38206
  tendon graft ~ 20924
  tissue grafts ~ 20926
  upper extremity
    artery for coronary artery bypass graft ~ 35600
    vein for bypass graft ~ 35500
Hauser procedure ~ 27420
Haygroves procedure ~ 27120, 27122
HBcAb ~ 86704, 86705
HBeAb ~ 86707
HBeAg ~ 87350
HBsAb ~ 86706
HBsAg (hepatitis B surface antigen) ~ 87340
HCG ~ 84702, 84703
HCO3 ~ see bicarbonate
Hct (hematocrit) ~ 85014
HCV antibodies ~ see antibody, hepatitis C
HDL (high density lipoprotein) ~ 83718
Head
  angiography ~ 70496, 70544-70546
  CT scan ~ 70450-70470, 70496
  excision ~ 21015-21070
  fracture and/or dislocation ~ 21310-21497
  incision ~ 21010, 61316, 62148
  introduction or removal ~ 21076-21116
  lipectomy, suction assisted ~ 15876
  magnetic resonance angiography (MRA) ~ 70544-70546
  nerve graft ~ 64885-64886
  other procedures ~ 21299, 21499
  repair/revision and/or reconstruction ~ 21120-21296
  ultrasound exam ~ 76506, 76536
  unlisted services and procedures ~ 21499
  X-ray ~ 70350
Head rings, stereotactic ~ see stereotactic frame
Headbrace
  application ~ 21100
  application/removal ~ 20661
Heaf TB test ~ 86580
Health and behavior assessment ~ 96150-96155
Health risk assessment instrument
  administration
    caregiver-focused ~ 96160
    patient-focused ~ 96161
Hearing aid
  bone conduction
    implantation ~ 69710
    removal ~ 69711
    repair ~ 69711

Hearing aid ~ *continued*
  replacement ~ 69710
  check ~ 92592-92593
  services
    electroacoustic test ~ 92594-92595
    examination ~ 92590-92591
Hearing evaluation ~ 92510
Hearing tests ~ see audiologic function tests; hearing evaluation
Hearing therapy ~ 92507-92510, 92601-92604
Heart
  ablation
    arrhythmogenic focus ~ 33250-33251, 33261
    atrial tissue ~ 33254-33259
      endoscopic ~ 33265-33266
  anomoly repair ~ 33615, 33617
  artificial heart
    implantation ~ 33927
    removal ~ 33929
    replacement ~ 33928
  atria ~ see atria
  balloon device ~ 33973-33974
  biopsy ~ 93505
    ultrasound imaging guidance ~ 76932
  blood vessel repair ~ 33320-33322
  cardiac contractility modulation
    electrode reposition ~ 0415T
  cardiac event recorder ~ 33282, 33284
  cardiac output measurements ~ 93451, 93561-93562
  cardiac rehabilitation ~ 93797-93798
  cardioassist ~ 92970-92971
  cardiopulmonary bypass
    with aortic aneurysm repair ~ 33877
    with ascending aorta graft ~ 33860, 33863-33864
    with atrial septectomy/septostomy ~ 33736
    with chamber fistula repair ~ 33500
    with descending thoracic aorta graft ~ 33875
    with lung transplant ~ 32852, 32854
    with operative ablation ~ 33251, 33256, 33259, 33261
    with pericardiectomy ~ 33031
    with pulmonary artery repair ~ 33910, 33916, 33922, 33926
    with replacement of ventricular assist ~ 33983
    with sinus of valsalva repair ~ 33702, 33720
    with transcatheter aortic valve replacement (TAVR/TAVI) ~
      33367-33369
    with transverse arch graft ~ 33870
    with tumor excision ~ 33120
    with wound repair ~ 33305
  cardioversion ~ 92960-92961
  catheterization ~ see Cardiac catheterization
  cor triatriatum repair ~ 33732
  CT scan ~ 75571-75573
    angiography ~ 75574
  cyst, pericardial, resection ~ 33050
  diagnostic imaging
    blood pool ~ 78472-78473, 78481, 78483, 78496
      SPECT ~ 78494
    CT scan ~ 75571-75573
      angiography ~ 75574
    myocardial imaging
      infarct avid ~ 78466, 78468-78469
      perfusion ~ 78451-78454
      perfusion study ~ 78491-78492
      PETMetabolic evaluation ~ 78459
    quantitative assessment of mechanics ~ 0399T
    shunt detection ~ 78428
    unlisted cardiovascular diagnostic nuclear medicine procedure ~ 78499
  electrophysiologic procedure ~ 93600-93660
  electrode
    insertion ~ 33202-33203, 33210-33211, 33216-33217, 33224-33225
    removal ~ 33238
      single/dual chamber ~ 33243-33244
  exploration ~ 33310-33315
  external heart rate data for nocturnal epilepsy seizure ~ 0381T-0386T
  foreign body removal ~ 33310
  great vessels ~ see great vessels
  heart-lung bypass ~ see cardiopulmonary bypass
  heart-lung transplantation ~ see transplantation, heart-lung

Heart ~ *continued*
  hemodynamic monitoring
    non-invasive ~ 93880, 93882, 93922-93931, 93970-93990, 93998
    with pharmacologic agent ~ 93463
    with physiologic exercise study ~ 93464
  implantation
    artificial heart, intracorporeal ~ 33927
    total replacement heart system, intracorporeal ~ 33928
    ventricular assist device ~ 33975-33976, 33979
  infundibular stenosis ~ 33476-33478
  intraoperative pacing and mapping ~ 93631
  ligation, fistula ~ 37607
  magnetic resonance imaging (MRI) ~ 75557-75565
  mitral valve ~ see mitral valve
  muscle ~ see myocardial
  myocardial infarction
    revascularization ~ 92941, 92943-92944
    tissue plasminogen activator (tPA) ~ 4077F
  myocardium
    imaging ~ 78466-78469
    quantitative assessment of mechanics ~ 0399T
    perfusion study ~ 78451-78454
    revascularization ~ 33140-33141
  open chest massage ~ 32160
  output ~ see cardiac output
  pacemaker ~ see also Pacemaker, heart
    conversion ~ 33214
    insertion ~ 33206-33208
    pulse generator ~ 33212-33213, 33221
    removal ~ 33233-33237
    replacement
      catheter ~ 33210
      electrode ~ 33210-33211
      insertion ~ 33206-33208
      pulse generator ~ 33227-33229
  pacing
    arrhythmia induction ~ 93618
    atria ~ 93610
    transcutaneous, temporary ~ 92953
    ventricular ~ 33224-33226, 93612
  pacing cardioverter-defibrillator ~ see Cardioverter-defibrillator
  pericardium
    drainage ~ 33025
    pericardiectomy ~ 33030, 33031
    pericardiocentesis ~ 33010-33011
  reconstruction
    atrial septum ~ 33735-33737
    vena cava ~ 34502
  removal
    balloon device ~ 33974
    electrode ~ 33238
    ventricular assist device ~ 33977-33978
      extracorporeal ~ 33990-33993
      intracorporeal ~ 33980
  removal single/dual chamber
    electrodes ~ 33243-33244
    pulse generator ~ 33241
    repair ~ 33218-33220
  repair
    anomaly ~ 33615-33617
    aortic sinus ~ 33702-33722
    atrial septum ~ 33641, 33647
    atrioventricular canal ~ 33660-33665
      complete ~ 33670
      prosthetic valve ~ 33670
    atrioventricular valve ~ 33660-33665
    cor triatriatum ~ 33732
    electrode ~ 33218
    fenestration ~ 93580
    infundibular ~ 33476-33478
    mitral valve ~ 33420-33430
    myocardium ~ 33542
    outflow tract ~ 33476-33478
    postinfarction ~ 33542-33545
    prosthetic valve dysfunction ~ 33496
    septal defect ~ 33608-33610, 33660, 33813-33814, 93581
    sinus of valsalva ~ 33702-33722
    sinus venosus ~ 33645
    tetralogy of Fallot ~ 33692-33697, 33924

Heart ~ *continued*
  total replacement heart system
    implantation ~ 33927
    removal ~ 33929
    replacement ~ 33928
  tricuspid valve ~ 33463-33468
  ventricle ~ 33611-33612
    obstruction ~ 33619
  ventricular septum ~ 33545, 33647, 33681-33688, 33692-33697, 93581
  ventricular tunnel ~ 33722
  wound ~ 33300-33305
  replacement
    electrode ~ 33210-33211, 33217
    mitral valve ~ 33430
    total replacement heart system ~ 33928
    tricuspid valve ~ 33465
    ventricular assist device ~ 33981-33983
  repositioning
    electrode ~ 33215, 33217, 33226
    tricuspid valve ~ 33468
  resuscitation ~ 92950
  septal defect ~ see septal defect
  sinus of valsalvus repair ~ 33702-33722
  sinus venosus repair ~ 33645
  tetralogy of fallot repair ~ 33692-33697, 33924
  thrombectomy ~ see thrombectomy
  transplantation ~ 33935, 33945
    allograft preparation ~ 33933, 33944
  tumor excision ~ 33120-33130
  unlisted services and procedures ~ 33999
  valve closure ~ 33600, 33602
  vena cava reconstruction ~ 34502
  ventricle
    commissurotomy, right ventricle ~ 33476-33478
    leadless pacemaker system
      device evaluation, in person
        interrogation ~ 0391T
        peri-procedural ~ 0390T
        programming ~ 0389T
      transcatheter insertion ~ 0387T
      transcatheter removal ~ 0388T
      transcatheter replacement ~ 0387T
    obstruction removal ~ 33619
    pacing ~ 33224-33226, 93612
    repair ~ 33548, 33611-33612
    tunnel repair ~ 33722
    ventriculomyectomy ~ 33416
  wound repair ~ 33300-33305
Heart sounds, acoustic recording, with computer analysis ~ 93799
Heart vessels
  angioplasty, percutaneous ~ 92982-92984
  insertion graft ~ 33330-33335
  thrombolysis ~ 92975-92977
  valvuloplasty, percutaneous ~ 92986-92990
Heat unstable haemoglobin ~ see hemoglobin, thermolabile
Heavy lipoproteins ~ see lipoprotein
Heavy metal ~ 83015-83018
Heel ~ 36415-36416
  X-ray ~ 73650
Heel bone ~ see calcaneus
Heel fracture ~ see calcaneus, fracture
Heel spur excision ~ 28119
Heine-Medin disease ~ see polio
Heine operation ~ see cyclodialysis
Heinz bodies ~ 85441-85445
Helicobacter pylori
  antibody ~ 86677
  antigen detection enzyme immunoassay ~ 87338-87339
  blood test ~ 83009
  breath test ~ 78267-78268, 83013-83014
  stool ~ 87338
  urease activity ~ 83009, 83013-83014
Heller procedure ~ 32665, 43330-43331
Helminth antibody ~ 86682
Hemagglutination inhibition test ~ 86280
Hemangioma ~ 17106-17108
Hemapheresis ~ 36511-36516
Hematochezia ~ 82270, 82274
Hematologic test ~ see blood tests
Hematology and coagulation ~ 85002-85999

Hematoma
- ankle ~ 27603
- arm, lower ~ 25028
- arm, upper, incision and drainage ~ 23930
- brain
  - drainage ~ 61154-61156
  - evacuation ~ 61312-61315
  - incision and drainage ~ 61312-61315
- drain ~ 61108
- ear, external
  - complicated ~ 69005
  - simple ~ 69000
- elbow, incision and drainage ~ 23930
- epididymis, incision and drainage ~ 54700
- gums, incision and drainage ~ 41800
- hip ~ 26990
- incision and drainage
  - neck ~ 21501-21502
  - skin ~ 10140
  - thorax ~ 21501-21502
- knee ~ 27301
- leg, lower ~ 27603
- leg, upper ~ 27301
- mouth ~ 41005-41009, 41015-41018
  - incision and drainage ~ 40800-40801
- nasal septum, incision and drainage ~ 30020
- nose, incision and drainage ~ 30000-30020
- pelvis ~ 26990
- scrotum, incision and drainage ~ 54700
- shoulder, drainage ~ 23030
- skin
  - incision and drainage ~ 10140
  - puncture aspiration ~ 10160
- subdural ~ 61108
- subungual, evacuation ~ 11740
- testis, incision and drainage ~ 54700
- tongue ~ 41000-41006, 41015
- vagina, incision and drainage ~ 57022-57023
- wrist ~ 25028

Hematopoietic stem cell transplantation ~ see stem cell, transplantation
Hematopoietin ~ see erythropoietin
Hematuria ~ see blood, urine
Hemic and lymphatic systems, surgical procedures ~ 38100-38999
Hemiepiphyseal arrest, elbow ~ 24470
Hemifacial microsomia, reconstruction, mandibular condyle ~ 21247
Hemilaminectomy ~ 63020-63044
Hemilaryngectomy ~ 31370-31382
Hemipelvectomies ~ see amputation, interpelviabdominal
Hemiphalangectomy, toe ~ 28160
Hemispherectomy
- partial ~ 61543

Hemocytoblast ~ see stem cell
Hemodialysis ~ 90935-90937
- blood flow study ~ 90940
- duplex scan of access ~ 93990
- Kt/V level ~ 3082F-3084F
- plan of care documented ~ 0505F
- via catheter ~ 4054F
- via functioning arteriovenous
  - fistula 4052F
  - graft 4053F

Hemodynamic monitoring, non-invasive left ventricular ~ 93799
Hemofiltration ~ 90945-90947
Hemoglobin
- A1c (HbA1c) level ~ 3044F-3045F
- analysis, O2 affinity ~ 82820
- carboxyhemoglobin ~ 82375-82376, 88740
- chromatography ~ 83021
- concentration ~ 85046
- electrophoresis ~ 83020
- fetal ~ 83030-83033, 85460-85461
- fractionation and quantitation ~ 83020
- glycosated (A1C) ~ 83036-83037
- methemoglobin ~ 83045-83050
  - transcutaneous ~ 88741
- non-automated ~ 83026
- plasma ~ 83051
- sulfhemoglobin ~ 83060
- thermolabile ~ 83065-83068
- transcutaneous ~ 88738, 88740
- urine ~ 83069

Hemoglobin, glycosylated ~ see glycohemoglobin
Hemoglobin F (fetal)
- chemical ~ 83030
- qualitative ~ 83033
Hemogram
- added indices ~ 85025-85027
- automated ~ 85025-85027
- manual ~ 85014-85018, 85032
Hemolysins ~ 85475
- with agglutinins ~ 86940-86941
Hemolytic complement ~ see complement, hemolytic
Hemolytic complement, total ~ see complement, hemolytic, total
Hemoperfusion ~ 90997
Hemophil ~ see clotting factor
Hemophilus influenza
- antibody ~ 86684
- vaccines ~ 90644-90648, 90748
Hemorrhage
- abdomen ~ 49002
- anal, endoscopic control ~ 46614
- chest cavity, endoscopic control ~ 32654
- colon, endoscopic control ~ 44391, 45382
- colon-sigmoid, endoscopic control ~ 45334
- esophagus, endoscopic control ~ 43227
- gastrointestinal, upper, endoscopic control ~ 43255
- intestines, small, endoscopic control ~ 44366, 44378
- liver, control ~ 47350
- lung ~ 32110
- nasal
  - cauterization ~ 30901-30906
  - endoscopic control ~ 31238
- nasopharynx ~ 42970-42972
- oropharynx ~ 42960-42962
- rectum, endoscopic control ~ 45317
- throat ~ 42960-42962
- uterus, postpartum ~ 59160
- vagina ~ 57180
Hemorrhoidectomy
- complex ~ 46260
  - with fissurectomy ~ 46261-46262
- external complete ~ 46250
- ligature ~ 46221
- simple ~ 46255
  - with fissurectomy ~ 46257-46258
Hemorrhoidopexy ~ 46947
Hemorrhoids
- destruction ~ 46930
- excision ~ 46250-46262, 46320
- incision, external ~ 46083
- injection, sclerosing solution ~ 46500
- ligation ~ 46945-46946
- stapling ~ 46947
- suture ~ 46945-46946
Hemosiderin ~ 83070
Hemothorax, thoracostomy ~ 32551
Heparin ~ see clotting inhibitors ~ 85520
- neutralization ~ 85525
- protamine tolerance test ~ 85530
Heparin cofactor I ~ see antithrombin III
Hepatectomy
- extensive ~ 47122
- left lobe ~ 47125
- partial
  - donor ~ 47140-47142
  - lobe ~ 47120
- right lobe ~ 47130
- total
  - donor ~ 47133
Hepaticodochotomy ~ see hepaticostomy
Hepaticoenterostomy ~ 47802
Hepaticostomy ~ 47400
Hepaticotomy ~ 47400
Hepatic arteries ~ see artery, hepatic
Hepatic artery aneurysm ~ see artery, hepatic, aneurysm
Hepatic duct
- anastomosis, with intestines ~ 47765, 47802
- exploration ~ 47400
- incision and drainage ~ 47400
- removalcalculi (stone) ~ 47400
- repair, with intestines ~ 47765, 47802
- unlisted services and procedures ~ 47999

Hepatic haemorrhage ~ see hemorrhage, liver
Hepatic portal vein ~ see vein, hepatic portal
Hepatic portoenterostomies ~ see hepaticoenterostomy
Hepatic transplantation ~ see liver, transplantation
Hepatitis A and hepatitis B ~ 90636
Hepatitis antibody
  A ~ 86708-86709
  B core ~ 86704-86705
  B surface ~ 86706
  Be ~ 86707
  C ~ 86803-86804
  delta agent ~ 86692
  IgG ~ 86704, 86708
  IgM ~ 86704, 86705, 86709
  Panel
    acute hepatitis ~ 80074
    obstetric ~ 80055, 80081
Hepatitis antigen
  B ~ 87516, 87517
  B surface ~ 87340-87341
  Be ~ 87350
  C ~ 87520-87522
  delta agent ~ 87380
  G ~ 87525-87527
Hepatitis A vaccine
  adolescent/pediatric
    2 dose schedule ~ 90633
    3 dose schedule ~ 90634
  adult dosage ~ 90632
Hepatitis B and Hib ~ 90748
Hepatitis B vaccine dosage
  adolescent ~ 90743
  adult ~ 90746
  immunosuppressed ~ 90740, 90747
  pediatric/adolescent ~ 90744
Hepatitis B virus e antibody ~ see antibody, hepatitis
Hepatitis B virus surface ab ~ see antibody, hepatitis B, surface
Hepatorrhaphy ~ see liver, repair
Hepatotomy
  abscess ~ 47010
  cyst ~ 47010
Hernia repair
  abdominal ~ 49590
    incisional ~ 49560
    recurrent ~ 49565
  diaphragmatic ~ 39503, 39540--39541
  epigastric ~ 49570
    incarcerated ~ 49572
    laparoscopic ~ 49652-49653
  femoral ~ 49550
    incarcerated ~ 49553
    recurrent ~ 49555
    recurrent incarcerated ~ 49557
  incisional
    incarcerated ~ 49561
    laparoscopic ~ 49654-49657
    thoracoabdominal 43336-43337
  inguinal ~ 49491, 49495-49500, 49505
    incarcerated ~ 49492, 49496, 49501, 49507, 49521
    laparoscopic ~ 49650-49651
    recurrent ~ 49520
    sliding ~ 49525
    strangulated ~ 49492
  lumbar ~ 49540
  lung ~ 32800
  orchiopexy ~ 54640
  paraesophageal hiatal
    via
      laparotomy ~ 43332-43333
      thoracoabdominal incision ~ 43336-43337
      thoractomy ~ 43334-43335
  recurrent incisional
    incarcerated ~ 49566
    reducible ~ 49565
  umbilicus
    incarcerated ~ 49582, 49587
    laparoscopic ~ 49652-49653
    reducible ~ 49580, 49585
  with spermatic cord ~ 55540
    spigelian ~ 49590
  ventral, laparoscopic ~ 49652-49653

Hernia, cerebral ~ see encephalocele
Hernia, rectovaginal ~ see rectocele
Hernia, umbilical ~ see omphalocele
Heroin screening ~ see Drug assay
Herpes simplex
  antibody ~ 86696
  antigen detection
    immunofluorescence ~ 87273-87274
    nucleic acid ~ 87528-87530
  identification smear and stain ~ 87207
Herpes smear and stain ~ 87207
Herpes virus-4 (gamma), human ~ see Epstein-Barr virus
Herpes virus-6 (six) detection ~ 87531-87533
Herpetic vesicle destruction ~ 54050-54065
Heteroantibodies ~ see antibody, heterophile
Heterologous transplant ~ see xenograft
Heterologous transplantation ~ see heterograft
Heterophile antibody ~ 86308-86310
Heterotropia ~ see strabismus
Hex b ~ see b-hexosaminidase
Hexadecadrol ~ see dexamethasone
Hexosephosphate isomerase ~ see phosphohexose isomerase
Heyman procedure ~ 27179, 28264
Hgb (hemoglobin) ~ 85018
HGH (human growth hormone) ~ 80418, 80428, 80430, 83003, 86277
Hg factor ~ see glucagon
HHV-4 ~ see Epstein-Barr virus
HIAA (hydroxyindolacetic acid, urine) 83497
Hibb operation ~ 22841
Hib vaccine
  4 dose schedule
    PRP-T ~ 90648
  PRP-OMP
    3 dose schedule ~ 90647
Hickmann catheterization ~ see cannulization; catheterization, venous, central line; venipuncture
Hidradenitis (see also sweat gland)
  excision ~ 11450-11471
  suppurative, incision and drainage ~ 10060-10061
Highly selective vagotomy ~ see vagotomy, highly selective
Highmore antrum ~ see sinuses, maxillary
High altitude simulation test ~ 94452-94453
High density lipoprotein ~ 83718
High molecular weight kininogen ~ 85293
Hill procedure
  laparoscopic ~ 43280
Hinton positive ~ 86592, 86593
Hip joint
  arthroplasty ~ 27132
    revision ~ 27134-27138
  arthrotomy ~ 27052
  biopsy ~ 27052
  capsulotomy, with release, flexor muscles ~ 27036
    dislocation ~ 27250-27252
    congenital ~ 27256-27259
    open treatment ~ 27253-27254
    without trauma ~ 27265-27266
  manipulation ~ 27275
  reconstruction, revision ~ 27134-27138
  synovium
    excision ~ 27054
    arthroscopic ~ 29863
  total replacement ~ 27132
Hip ~ see also femur; pelvis
  abscess, incision and drainage ~ 26990
  arthrocentesis ~ 20610
  arthrodesis ~ 27284-27286
  arthrography ~ 73525
  arthroplasty ~ 27130-27132
  arthroscopy ~ 29860-29863, 29914
  arthrotomy ~ 27030-27033
  biopsy ~ 27040-27041
  bone, drainage ~ 26992
  bursa, incision and drainage ~ 26991
  capsulectomy with release, flexor muscles ~ 27036
  cast ~ 29305-29325
  craterization ~ 27070
  cyst, excision ~ 27065-27067
  denervation ~ 27035
  echography, infant ~ 76885-76886

Hip ~ *continued*
 endoprosthesis ~ see prosthesis, hip
 excision ~ 27070
 exploration ~ 27033
 fasciotomy ~ 27025
 fusion ~ 27284-27286
 hematoma, incision and drainage ~ 26990
 injectio, radiologic ~ 27093-27096
 reconstruction, total replacement ~ 27130
 removal
  cast ~ 29710
  foreign body ~ 27033, 27086-27087
   arthroscopic ~ 29861
  loose body
   arthroscopic ~ 29861
  prosthesis ~ 27090-27091
 repair
  muscle transfer ~ 27100-27105, 27111
  osteotomy ~ 27146-27156
  tendon ~ 27097
 saucerization ~ 27070
 stem prosthesis ~ see arthroplasty, hip
 strapping ~ 29520
 tenotomy
  abductor tendon ~ 27006
  adductor tendon ~ 27000-27003
  iliopsoas ~ 27005
 total replacement ~ 27130-27132
 tumor
  excision ~ 27043-27045, 27049, 27059, 27065-27067
   radical ~ 27075-27076
 ultrasound, infant ~ 76885-76886
 X-ray
  bilateral ~ 73521-73523
  unilateral ~ 73501-73503
  with contrast ~ 73525
Hip stem prostheses ~ see arthroplasty, hip
Hippocampus excision ~ 61566
Histamine ~ 83088
Histamine release test ~ 86343
Histochemistry ~ 88319
Histocompatibility testing ~ see tissue typing
Histoplasma
 antibody ~ 86698
 antigen ~ 87385
Histoplasma capsulatum, antigen detection, enzyme immunoassay ~ 87385
Histoplasmin test ~ see histoplasmosis, skin test
Histoplasmoses ~ see histoplasmosis
Histoplasmosis skin test ~ 86510
History and physical ~ 57410
HIV
 antibody ~ 86701-86703
 confirmation test ~ 86689
HIV-1
 antibody detection, enzyme immunoassay ~ 86701, 86703, 87389
 antigen detection, enzyme immunoassay ~ 87389-87390
 genotype analysis ~ 87901, 87906
 infectious agent detection
  amplified probe ~ 87535
  direct probe ~ 87534
  quantification ~ 87536
HIV-2
 antibody detection, enzyme immunoassay ~ 86702-86703, 87389
 antigen detection
  enzyme immunoassay ~ 87389, 87391
 infectious agent detection
  amplified probe ~ 87538
  direct probe ~ 87537
  quantification ~ 87539
HK3 kallikrein ~ see prostate specific antigen
HLA
 crossmatch ~ 86825, 86826
 molecular pathology ~ 81370-81383
 typing ~ 86812-868122
HMRK ~ see Fitzgerald factor
HMW kininogen ~ see Fitzgerald factor
Hoffman apparatus ~ 20690
Hofmeister operation (gastrectomy, total) ~ 43632
Holographic imaging ~ 76375
Holten test ~ 82575

Home health services
 activities of daily living ~ 99509
 anticoagulant management ~ 93793
 apnea monitoring ~ 94774-94777
 catheter care ~ 99507
 enema administration ~ 99511
 established patient ~ 99347-99350
 hemodialysis ~ 99512
 home infusion procedures ~ 99601, 99602
 individual or family counseling ~ 99510
 intramuscular injections ~ 99506
 mechanical ventilation ~ 99504
 newborn care ~ 99502
 new patient ~ 99341-99345
 postnatal assessment ~ 99501
 prenatal monitoring ~ 99500
 respiratory therapy ~ 99503
 sleep studies ~ 95805-95811
 stoma care ~ 99505
 unlisted services and procedures ~ 99600
 ventilation assist ~ 94005
Home visits ~ 99341-99350
Homocystine ~ 83090
 urine ~ 82615
Homogenization, tissue ~ 87176
Homograft, skin ~ 15350
Homologous grafts ~ see graft
Homologous transplantation ~ see homograft
Homovanillic acid, urine ~ 83150
Hormone adrenocorticotrophic (ACTH) ~ 80400-80406, 80412, 80418, 82024
 corticotropic-releasing ~ 80412
 growth ~ see human growth hormone
 human growth ~ 80418, 80428, 80430, 86277, 83003
 interstitial cell-stimulating ~ see luteinizing hormone (LH)
 luteinizing hormone (LH) ~ 80418, 80426, 83002
 parathyroid ~ 83970
 pituitary lactogenic (prolactin) ~ 80418, 84146
 placental lactogen ~ 83632
 somatotropin release-inhibiting (somatostatin) ~ 84307
 thyroid-stimulating (TSH) ~ 80418, 80438-80439, 80443, 84146
Hormone-binding globulin, sex ~ see globulin, sex hormone binding
Hormones, adrenal cortex ~ see corticosteroids
Hormones, antidiuretic ~ see antidiuretic hormone
Hormone assay
 ACTH ~ 82024
 aldosterone, blood or urine ~ 82088
 androstenedione, blood or urine ~ 82157
 androsterone, blood or urine ~ 82160
 angiotensin II ~ 82163
 corticosterone ~ 82528
 cortisol, total ~ 82533
 dehydroepiandrosterone ~ 82626
 dihydroelestosterone ~ 80327, 80328
 dihydrotestosterone ~ 80327, 80328
 epiandrosterone ~ 80327, 80328
 estradiol ~ 82670
 estriol ~ 82677
 estrogen ~ 82671-82672
 estrone ~ 82679
 follicle stimulating hormone (FSH) ~ 83001
 growth hormone, human ~ 83003
 hydroxyprogesterone ~ 83498
 luteinizing hormone ~ 83002
 somatotropin ~ 83003
 testosterone
  bioavailable ~ 84410
  free ~ 84402
  total ~ 84403
 vasopressin ~ 84588
Hormone pellet implantation ~ 11980
Hospital discharge services ~ 99238-99239
Hospital services
 inpatient services ~ 99238-99239
  discharge services ~ 99238-99239, 1110F-1111F
  initial care, new or established patient ~ 99221-99223
  initial hospital care ~ 99221-99223
  newborn ~ 99460-99462, 99477
  prolonged services ~ 99356-99357
  subsequent hospital care ~ 99231-99233

Hospital services ~ *continued*
  observation
    discharge services ~ 99234-99236
    initial care ~ 99218-99220
      new or established patient ~ 99218-99220
    subsequent ~ 99224-99226
    same day admission, discharges services ~ 99234-99236
    subsequent newborn care ~ 99462
    subsequent observation care ~ 99224-99226
Hot pack treatment ~ 97010
House calls ~ 99341-99350
Howard test ~ 52005
HPL ~ (lactogen, human placental) 83632
HTLV I antibody
  confirmatory test ~ 86689
  detection ~ 86687
HTLV II antibody ~ 86688
HTLV III ~ see HIV
HTLV III antibodies ~ see antibody, HIV
HTLV IV ~ see HIV-2
Hubbard tank therapy ~ 97036
Hue test ~ 92283
Huggin operation ~ 54520
Huhner test ~ 89300, 89320
Human chorionic gonadotropin ~ see chorionic gonadotropin
Human chorionic somatomammotropin ~ see lactogen, human placental
Human epididymus protein ~ 86305
Human growth hormone(HGH) ~ 80418, 80428-80430
Human herpes virus 4 ~ see Epstein-Barr virus
Human immunodeficiency virus ~ see HIV
Human immunodeficiency virus 1 ~ see HIV-1
Human immunodeficiency virus 2 ~ see HIV-2
Human papillomavirus detection
  nucleic acid probe ~ 0500T, 87623-87625
Human placental lactogen ~ 83632
Human T cell leukemia virus I ~ see HTLV I
Human T cell leukemia virus II ~ see HTLV II
Human T cell leukemia virus I antibodies ~ see antibody, HTLV
  I**Human T cell** leukemia virus II antibodies ~ see antibody, HTLV II
Humeral epicondylitides, lateral (tennis elbow) ~ 24357-24359
Humeral fracture ~ see fracture, humerus
Humerus ~ see arm, upper; shoulder
  abscess
    incision and drainage ~ 23935
  craterization ~ 23184, 24140
  cyst
    excision ~ 23150, 24110
      with allograft ~ 23156, 24116
      with autograft ~ 23155, 24115
  diaphysectomy ~ 23184, 24140
  excision ~ 23174, 23184, 23195, 24134, 24140, 24150
  fracture
    closed treatment ~ 24500-24505
      with manipulation ~ 23605
      without manipulation ~ 23600
    condyle
      closed treatment ~ 24576-24577
      open treatment ~ 24579
      percutaneous fixation ~ 24582
    epicondyle
      closed treatment ~ 24560-24565
      open treatment ~ 24575
      skeletal fixation, percutaneous ~ 24566
    greater tuberosity fracture
      closed treatment with manipulation ~ 23625
      closed treatment without manipulation ~ 23620
      open treatment ~ 23630
    open treatment ~ 23615-23616
    shaft ~ 24500-24505, 24516
      open treatment ~ 24515
    supracondylar
      closed treatment ~ 24530-24535
      open treatment ~ 24545-24546
      percutaneous fixation ~ 24538
    transcondylar
      closed treatment ~ 24530-24535
      open treatment ~ 24545-24546
      percutaneous fixation ~ 24538
    with dislocation ~ 23665-23670
  osteomyelitis ~ 24134

Humerus ~ *continued*
  pinning, wiring ~ 23491, 24498
  prophylactic treatment ~ 23491, 24498
  radical resection ~ 23220
  repair ~ 24430
    with graft ~ 24435
    nonunion, malunion ~ 24430-24435
    osteoplasty ~ 24420
    osteotomy ~ 24400-24410
    resection head ~ 23195
  saucerization ~ 23184, 24140
  sequestrectomy ~ 23174, 24134
  tumor
    excision ~ 23150, 23220, 24110
      with allograft ~ 23156, 24116
      with autograft ~ 23155, 24115
      radial head or neck ~ 24152
  X-ray ~ 73060
Hummelshein operation ~ see strabismus, repair
Humor shunt, aqueous ~ 66180, 66185
HVA (homovanillic acid) ~ 83150
Hyaluron binding assay ~ 89398
Hybrid approach
  stage 1 ~ 33620-33621
  stage 2 ~ 33622
Hybridization probes, DNA ~ see nucleic acid probe
Hydatid disease ~ see echinococcosis
Hydatidiform mole
  evacuation and curettage ~ 59870
  excision ~ 59100
Hydration ~ 96360-96361
  rehydration oral solution ~ 4056F
  status ~ 2030F-2031F
Hydrocarbons, chlorinated ~ 82441
Hydrocele
  aspiration ~ 55000
  excision
    bilateral, tunica vaginalis ~ 55041
    unilateral
      spermatic cord ~ 55500
      tunica vaginalis ~ 55040
  repair ~ 55060
Hydrochloric acid, gastric ~ see acid, gastric
Hydrochloride, vancomycin ~ see vancomycin
Hydrocodon ~ see dihydrocodeinone
Hydrogen ion concentration ~ see pH
Hydrolase, acetylcholine ~ see acetylcholinesterase
Hydrolase, triacylglycerol ~ see lipase
Hydrolases, phosphoric monoester ~ see phosphatase
Hydrotherapy (Hubbard tank) ~ 97036, 97113
Hydrotubation ~ 58350
Hydroxyacetanilide ~ see acetaminophen
Hydroxycorticosteroid ~ 83491
Hydroxyindolacetic acid ~ 83497
  urine ~ 83497
Hydroxypregnenolone ~ 80406, 84143
Hydroxyprogesterone ~ 80402-80406, 83498
Hydroxyproline ~ 83500-83505
Hydroxytyramine ~ see dopamine
Hygroma, cystic, axillary/cervical, excision ~ 38550-38555
Hymen
  excision ~ 56700
  incision ~ 56442
Hymenal ring, revision ~ 56700
Hymenectomy ~ 56700
Hymenotomy ~ 56442
Hyoid
  bone, fracture
    closed treatment
      with manipulation ~ 21494
      without manipulation ~ 21493
  muscle, incision and suspension ~ 21685
Hyperbaric oxygen pressurization ~ 99183
Hypercycloidal X-ray ~ 76101-76102
Hyperdactylies ~ see supernumerary digit
Hyperglycemic glycogenolytic factor ~ see glucagon
Hypertelorism of orbit ~ see orbital hypertelorism
Hyperthermia therapy ~ see thermotherapy
Hyperthermia treatment ~ 77600-77620
Hypnotherapy ~ 90880
Hypodermis ~ see subcutaneous tissue

Hypogastric plexus
destruction ~ 64681
injection
anesthetic ~ 64517
neurolytic ~ 64681
Hypoglossal-facial anastomosis ~ see anastomosis, nerve, facial to
hypoglossal
Hypoglossal nerve
anastomosis, to facial nerve ~ 64868
Hypopharynges ~ see hypopharynx
Hypopharynx, biopsy ~ 31510, 31535, 31536, 31576
Hypophysectomy ~ 61546-61548, 62165
Hypophysis ~ see pituitary gland
Hypopyrexia ~ see hypothermia
Hypospadias repair ~ 54300, 54352
complications ~ 54340-54348
first stage ~ 54304
proximal penile or penoscrotal ~ 54332
one stage
meatal advancement ~ 54322
perineal ~ 54336
urethroplasty
local skin flaps ~ 54324
local skin flaps and mobilization of urethra ~ 54326
local skin flaps, skin graft patch and/or island flap ~ 54328
urethroplasty for second stage ~ 54308-54316
free skin graft ~ 54316
urethroplasty for third stage ~ 54318
Hypoxia
breathing response ~ 94450
high altitude simulation test ~ 94452-94453
Hysterectomy
abdominal
radical ~ 58210
resection of ovarian malignancy ~ 58951, 58953-58956
supracervical ~ 58180
total ~ 58150, 58200, 58956
with colpo-urethrocystopexy ~ 58152
with partial vaginectomy ~ 58200
with omentectomy ~ 58956
cesarean
after cesarean delivery ~ 59525
with closure of vesicouterine fistula ~ 51925
laparoscopic ~ 58541-58544
radical ~ 58548
total ~ 58570-58573, 58575
removal lesion ~ 59100
supracervical
laparoscopic ~ 58541-58544
vaginal ~ 58260-58270, 58290-58294, 58550-58554
with colpectomy ~ 58275-58280
with colpo-urethrocystopexy ~ 58267, 58293
laparoscopic ~ 58550, 58570-58573, 58575
radical ~ 58285
removal tubes/ovaries ~ 58262-58263, 58291-58292, 58552, 58554
repair of enterocele ~ 58263, 58292, 58294
Hysterolysis ~ 58559
Hysteroplasty ~ 58540
Hysterorrhaphy ~ 58520, 59350
Hysterosalpingography ~ 74740
catheterization ~ 58345
injection procedure ~ 58340
Hysterosalpingostomy ~ see implantation, tubouterine
Hysteroscopy
ablation, endometrial ~ 58563
diagnostic ~ 58555
lysis adhesions ~ 58559
placement fallopian tube implants ~ 58565
removal
impacted foreign body ~ 58562
leiomyomata ~ 58561
resection of intrauterine septum ~ 58560
surgical with biopsy ~ 58558
unlisted services and procedures ~ 58579
Hysterosonography ~ 76831
Hysterotomy ~ 59100
induced abortion
with amniotic injections ~ 59852
with vaginal suppositories ~ 59857
Hysterotrachelectomy ~ 57530

I

I, angiotensin ~ see angiotensin I
1 antibodies, HTLV ~ see antibody, HTLV-1
I, coagulation factor ~ see fibrinogenI, heparin cofactor ~ see antithrombin
IIIICCE ~ see extraction, lens, intracapsular
Ichthyosis, sex linked ~ see syphilis test
ICSH ~ see luteinizing hormone (LH)
Identification
oocyte, from follicular fluid ~ 89254
sex chromatin ~ 88130, 88140
sperm
from aspiration ~ 89257
from tissue ~ 89264
medicolegal ~ 88125
urate crystal ~ 89060
IDH (isocitric dehydrogenase, blood) ~ 83570
Ig ~ see immune globulins
IgA ~ 82784
IgD ~ 82784
IgE ~ 82785, 86003, 86005, 86008
IgG ~ 82784, 82787, 86001
IgM ~ 82784
II, coagulation factor ~ see prothrombin
II, cranial nerve ~ see optic nerve
Ileal conduit visualization ~ 50690
Ileoscopy via stoma ~ 44384
Ileostomy ~ 44310, 45136
continent (Kock procedure) ~ 44316
revision ~ 44312-44314
Iliac arteries ~ see artery, iliac
Iliac crest (free osteocutaneous flap with microvascular anastomosis) ~
20970
Iliohypogastric nerve, injection anesthetic ~ 64425
Ilioinguinal nerve, injection anesthetic ~ 64425
Ilium
craterization ~ 27070
cyst excision ~ 27065-27067
excision ~ 27070
fracture, open treatment ~ 27215, 27218
saucerization ~ 27070
tumor excision ~ 27065-27067
Ilizarov procedure, Monticelli type ~ (see also application, bone fixation
device) 20692
Imaging ~ see vascular studies
Imaging, gamma camera ~ see nuclear medicine
Imaging, magnetic resonance ~ see magnetic resonance imaging (MRI)
Imaging, ultrasonic ~ see echography
Imbrication, diaphragm ~ 39545
Imidobenzyle ~ 80335-80337
Imipramine assay ~ 80335-80337
Immune complex assay ~ 86332
Immune globulins
antitoxin
botulinum ~ 90287
diphtheria ~ 90296
botulism ~ 90288
cytomegalovirus ~ 90291
hepatitis B ~ 90371
human ~ 90281, 90283-90284
rabies ~ 90375-90376
respiratory syncytial virus ~ 90378
Rho (D) ~ 90384-90386
tetanus ~ 90389
unlisted immune globulin ~ 90399
vaccinia ~ 90393
varicella-zoster ~ 90396
Immune globulin administration ~ 96365-96368, 96372, 96374-96375
Immune globulin E ~ 82785, 86003-86005
Immunization administration
one vaccine/toxoid ~ 90471, 90473
with counseling ~ 90460
each additional vaccine/toxoid ~ 90472, 90474
with counseling ~ 90461

Immunizations
active
acellular pertussis ~ 90700, 90723
BCG ~ 90585, 90586
diphtheria ~ 90700-90702, 90723
diphtheria, tetanus, acellular influenza B and poliovirus inactivated ~ 90698
hemophilus influenza B ~ 90648, 90748
hepatitis A ~ 90632-90636
hepatitis B ~ 90740-90748
influenza ~ 90655-90660
influenza B ~ 90647, 90648
measles, mumps, rubella (MMR) ~ 90707
measles, mumps, rubella, varicella ~ 90710
meingococcal ~ 90733, 90734
pneumococcal ~ 90732
poliomyelitis ~ 90713
rabies ~ 90675, 90676
rotavirus vaccine ~ 90680
tetanus ~ 90700-90702, 90715, 90723
typhoid ~ 90690
varicella (chicken pox) ~ 90716
yellow fever ~ 90717
passive
hyperimmune serum globulin ~ 90287-90399
immune serum globulin ~ 90281, 90283
unlisted services and procedures ~ 90749
Immunoassay
amniotic fluid protein ~ 84112
analyte ~ 83516, 83518-83520
calprotectin, fecal ~ 83993
hemoglobin, fecal ~ 82274
cellular function, detection of biomarker ~ 86352
infectious agent ~ 86317-86318, 87449-87451
nonantibody ~ 83516-83519
tumor antigen
human epididymis protein 4 (HE4) ~ 86305
qualitative/semiqualitative ~ 86294
quantitative
CA-125 ~ 86304
CA 15-3 ~ 86300
CA 19-9 ~ 86301
other antigen ~ 86316
Immunoblotting, Western ~ see Western Blot
Immunochemical, lysozyme (muramidase) ~ see lysozyme
Immunocytochemistry ~ 88342, 88344
Immunodeficiency virus, human ~ see HIV
Immunodeficiency virus type 1 , human ~ see HIV 1
Immunodeficiency virus type 2 , human ~ see HIV 2
Immunodiffusion ~ 86329-86331
Immunoelectrophoresis ~ 86320-86327, 86334-86335
Immunofixation electrophoresis ~ 86334-86335
Immunofluorexcence microscopy
antibody stain procedure ~ 88346, 88350
antiserum culture typing ~ 87140
Immunofluorescent study ~ 87140, 88346
Immunogen ~ see antigen
Immunoglobulin ~ 82784-82787
platelet associated ~ 86023
thyroid stimulating ~ 84445
Immunoglobulin E ~ 86003-86005
Immunologic skin test ~ see skin, tests
Immunology ~ 86000-86849
Immunotherapies, allergen ~ see allergen immunotherapy
Impedance testing ~ (see also audiologic function tests) 92567
Imperfectly descended testis ~ 54550, 54560
Implantable defibrillator
device evaluation
electrophysiologic ~ 93644
interrogation
in-person
subcutaneous ~ 93261
transvenous ~ 93289
remote ~ 93295, 93296
peri-procedural ~ 93287
programming device evaluation
subcutaneous ~ 93260
transvenous ~ 93282-93284

Implantable defibrillator ~ *continued*
insertion
electrodes ~ 33202, 33203, 33216, 33217, 33224, 33225, 33271
pulse generator ~ 33230, 33231, 33240
system ~ 33249, 33270
removal
electrodes ~ 33238, 33243, 33244, 33272
pulse generator ~ 33241, 33262-33264
repair, electrodes ~ 33218, 33220
replacement
pulse generator ~ 33224, 33262-33264
system ~ 33249, 33270
repositioning, electrode ~ 33215, 33273
wearable device ~ 93745
data analysis ~ 93292
Implantation
abdominal wall, non-biologic or synthetic implant ~ 0437T
aortic valve
transcatheter ~ 33361-33369
artificial heart, ~ 33927
artificial sphincter ~ 46762
baroreflex activation device ~ 0266T-0268T
biologic, soft tissue reinforcement ~ 15777
bone, for external speech processor/cochlear stimulator ~ 69714-69718
brain, chemotherapy ~ 61517
cardiac event recorder ~ 33282
drug delivery device ~ 11981, 11983, 61517
electrode(s)
brain ~ 61531, 61863, 61864, 61867, 61868
gastric ~ 43647-43648
nerve ~ 0312T, 64553-64581
spinal cord ~ 63650-63655
ethmoid sinus drug-eluting impllant ~ 0406T, 0407T
eye
anterior segment ~ 65920
aqueous shunt to extraocular placement or replacement of pegs ~ 65125
corneal ring segments ~ 65785
posterior segment
extraocular ~ 67120
intraocular ~ 67121
reservoir ~ 66180
vitreous, drug delivery system ~ 67027
fallopian tube ~ 58565
hearing aid hormone pellet(s)
bone conduction ~ 69710
hip prosthesis ~ see arthroplasty, hip
hormone pellet ~ 11980
joint ~ see arthroplasty
left atrial appendage ~ 33340
mesh ~ 49568
hernia repair ~ 43333, 43335, 43337, 49568, 49652-49657
vaginal repair ~ 57267
nerve
into bone ~ 64787
into muscle ~ 64787
neurostimulators
gastric ~ 95980-95982
pulse generator ~ 61885
receiver ~ 61886
ovum ~ 58976
pulmonary valve transcatheter percutaneous ~ 33477
pulse generator
brain ~ 61885, 61886
spinal cord electrode array ~ 63685
receiver
brain ~ 61885-61886
spinal cord ~ 63685
removal ~ 20670-20680
elbow/radius ~ 24164
reservoir vascular access device
declotting ~ 36593
retinal electrode array ~ 0100T
total replacement heart system ~ 33927
tubouterine ~ 58752
ventricular assist device ~ 33975-33979
percutaneousl ~ 33990-33991
Implant removal ~ see specific anatomical site

Impression, maxillofacial
  auricular prosthesis ~ 21086
  definitive obturator prosthesis ~ 21080
  facial prosthesis ~ 21088
  interim obturator ~ 21079
  mandibular resection prosthesis ~ 21081
  nasal prosthesis ~ 21087
  oral surgical splint ~ 21085
  orbital prosthesis ~ 21077
  palatal augmentation prosthesis ~ 21082
  palatal lift prosthesis ~ 21083
  speech aid prosthesis ~ 21084
  surgical obturator ~ 21076
In situ hybridization ~ see nucleic acid probe, cytogenetic studies,
  morphometric analysis
IM injection ~ see injection, intramuscular
In vitro fertilization ~ 58321-58322
In vivo NMR spectroscopy ~ see magnetic resonance spectroscopy
Incision ~ see also incision and drainage
  abdomen ~ 49000
    exploration ~ 58960
  abscess, soft tissue ~ 20005
  accessory nerve ~ 63191
  anal
    fistula ~ 46270, 46280
    septum ~ 46070
    sphincter ~ 46080
  ankle ~ 27607
    tendon ~ 27605-27606
  anus ~ see anus, incision
  aortic valve for stenosis ~ 33415
  artery, nose ~ 30915-30920
  atrial septum ~ 33735-33737
  bile duct sphincter ~ 43262, 47460
  bladder
    catheterization ~ 51045
    with destruction ~ 51020-51030
    with radiotracer ~ 51020
  bladder diverticulum ~ 52305
  brachial artery exposure ~ 34834
  brain
    amygdalohippocampectomy ~ 61566
    subpial ~ 61567
  breast capsules ~ 19370
  burn scab ~ 16035-16036
  cataract, secondary
    laser surgery ~ 66821
    stab incision technique ~ 66820
  chest, biopsy ~ 32096-32098
  colon
    exploration ~ 44025
    stoma
      creation ~ 44320-44322
      revision ~ 44340-44346
  cornea, for astigmatism ~ 65772
  corpus callosum ~ 61541
  cricothyroid membrane ~ 31605
  dentate ligament ~ 63180-63182
  duodenum ~ 44010
  ear, inner labyrinth
    transcanal ~ 69801
  elbow ~ 24000
  esophagus ~ 43020, 43045
    muscle ~ 43030
  exploration
    heart ~ 33310-33315
    kidney ~ 50010
  eye
    adhesions ~ 65880
      anterior segment ~ 65860-65865
      anterior synechiae ~ 65870
      corneovitreal ~ 65880
      posterior ~ 65875
    anterior chamber ~ 65820
    trabeculae ~ 65850
  eyelid
    canthus ~ 67715
    sutures ~ 67710
  femoral artery
    exposure ~ 34812-34813

Incision ~ *continued*
  fibula ~ 27607
  finger
    decompression ~ 26035
    tendon ~ 26060, 26455-26460
    tendon sheath ~ 26055
  foot ~ 28005
    capsule ~ 28260-28264
    fasciotomy ~ 28008
    for infection ~ 28002-28003
    tendon ~ 28230, 28234
  gallbladder ~ 47490
  hand decompression ~ 26035-26037
    tendon ~ 26450, 26460
  heartexploration ~ 33310-33315
  hemorrhoids, external ~ 46083
  hepatic ducts ~ see hepaticostomy
  hip
    denervation ~ 27035
    exploration ~ 27033
    fasciotomy ~ 27025
    joint capsule
      for flexor release ~ 27036
    tendon
      abductor ~ 27006
      adductor ~ 27000-27003
      iliopsoas ~ 27005
  hymen ~ see hymen, incision
  hymenotomy ~ 56442
  hyoid muscle ~ 21685
  iliac artery exposure ~ 34820, 34833
  intercarpal joint dislocation ~ 25670
  interphalangeal joint capsule ~ 26525
  intestines, small ~ 44010
    biopsy ~ 44020
    creation
      pouch ~ 44316
      stoma ~ 44300-44310, 44314
    decompression ~ 44021
    exploration ~ 44020
    incision ~ 44020
    removal foreign body ~ 44020
    revision stoma ~ 44312
  iris ~ 66500-66505
  kidney ~ 50010, 50045
  knee
    capsule ~ 27435
    exploration ~ 27310
    fasciotomy ~ 27305
    removal of foreign body ~ 27310
  lacrimal punctum ~ 68440
  lacrimal sac ~ see dacryocystotomy
  leg, lower fasciotomy ~ 27600-27602
  leg, upper fasciotomy ~ 27305
    tenotomy ~ 27306-27307, 27390-27392
  lip, frenum ~ 40806
  liver ~ see hepatotomy
  lung
    biopsy ~ 32096-32097
    decortication
      partial ~ 32225
      total ~ 32220
  lymphatic channels ~ 38308
  mastoid ~ see mastoidotomy
  mesencephalic tract ~ 61480
  metacarpophalangeal joint capsule ~ 26520
  mitral valve ~ 33420-33422
  muscle ~ see myotomy
  nerve ~ 64575-64580, 64585, 64595, 64702-64772
    foot ~ 28035
    root ~ 63185-63190
    sacral ~ 64581
    vagus ~ 43640-43641
  nose ~ see rhinotomy
  orbit ~ see orbitotomy
  palm fasciotomy ~ 26040-26045
  pancreas sphincter ~ 43262
  penis
    prepuce ~ 54000-54001
      newborn ~ 54000

Incision ~ continued

pericardium
    with clot removal ~ 33020
    with foreign body removal ~ 33020
    with tube ~ 33015
pharynx stoma ~ 42955
pleura biopsy ~ 32098
pleural cavity
    empyema ~ 32035-32036
    pneumothorax ~ 32551
prostate
    exposure
        bilateral pelvic lymphadenectomy ~ 55865
        insertion radioactive substance ~ 55860
        lymph node biopsy ~ 55862
    transurethral ~ 52450
pterygomaxillary fossa ~ 31040
pulmonary valve ~ 33470-33474
pyloric sphincter ~ 43520
retina, encircling material ~ 67115
sclera
    fistulization
        sclerectomy with punch or scissors with iridectomy ~ 66160
        thermocauterization with iridectomy ~ 66155
        trabeculectomy ab externo in absence previous surgery ~ 66170
        trephination with iridectomy ~ 66150
seminal vesicle ~ 55600-55605
    complicated ~ 55605
shoulder
    bone ~ 23035
    capsular contracture release ~ 23020
    removal, calcareous deposits ~ 23000
    tenomyotomy ~ 23405-23406
shoulder joint ~ 23040-23044
sinus
    frontal ~ 31070-31087
    maxillary ~ 31020-31032
        endoscopic ~ 31256-31267
    multiple ~ 31090
    sphenoid
        sinusotomy ~ 31050-31051
skin ~ 10040-10180
skull ~ 61316, 62148
    suture ~ 61550-61552
spinal cord ~ 63200
    tract ~ 63170, 63194-63199
stomach
    creation, stoma ~ 43830-43832
    exploration ~ 43500
    pyloric sphincter ~ 43520
synovectomy ~ 26140
temporomandibular joint ~ 21010
tendon, arm, upper ~ 24310
thigh, fasciotomy ~ 27025
thorax
    empyema ~ 32035-32036
    pneumothorax ~ 32551
thyroid gland ~ see thyrotomy
tibia ~ 27607
toe
    capsule ~ 28270-28272
    fasciotomy ~ 28008
    tendon ~ 28232-28234
    tenotomy ~ 28010-28011
tongue, frenum ~ 41010
trachea
    emergency ~ 31603-31605
    planned ~ 31600-31601
    with flaps ~ 31610
tympanic membrane ~ 69420
    with anesthesia ~ 69421
ureter ~ 50600
ureterocele ~ 51535
urethra ~ 53000-53010
    meatus ~ 53020-53025
uterus, remove lesion ~ 59100
vagina, exploration ~ 57000
vas deferens ~ 55200
    for X-ray ~ 55300
vestibule of the mouth ~ see mouth, vestibule

Incision ~ continued

vitreous strands
    laser surgery ~ 67031
    pars plana approach ~ 67030
wrist ~ 25100-25105
    capsule ~ 25085
    decompression ~ 25020-25025
    tendon sheath ~ 25000-25001
Incisional hernia repair ~ see hernia, repair, incisional
Incision and drainage ~ see also drainage; incision
abdomen
    fluid ~ 49082-49083
    pancreatitis ~ 48000
abscess
    abdomen ~ 49020, 49040
    anal ~ 46045-46050
    ankle ~ 27603
    appendix ~ 44900
    arm, lower ~ 25028
    arm, upper ~ 23930-23931
    auditory canal, external ~ 69020
    Bartholin's gland ~ 56420
    bladder ~ 51080
    brain ~ 61320-61321
    breast ~ 19020
    ear, external
        complicated ~ 69005
        simple ~ 69000
    elbow ~ 23930
    epididymis ~ 54700
    eyelid ~ 67700
    finger ~ 26010-26011
    gums ~ 41800
    hip ~ 26990
    kidney ~ 50020
    knee ~ 27301
    leg, lower ~ 27603
    leg, upper ~ 27301
    liver ~ 47010
    lung ~ 32200
    lymph node ~ 38300-38305
    mouth ~ 40800-40801, 41005-41009, 41015-41018
    nasal septum ~ 30020
    neck ~ 21501-21502
    nose ~ 30000-30020
    ovary ~ 58820-58822
        abdominal approach ~ 58822
    palate ~ 42000
    paraurethral gland ~ 53060
    parotid gland ~ 42300-42305
    pelvis ~ 26990, 45000
    perineum ~ 56405
    peritoneum ~ 49020
    prostrate ~ 55720-55725
    rectum ~ 45005-45020, 46040, 46050-46060
    retroperitoneal ~ 49060
        open ~ 49060
    salivary gland ~ 42300-42320
    scrotum ~ 54700, 55100
    Skene's gland ~ 53060
    skin ~ 10060-10061
    subdiaphragmatic, percutaneous ~ 49040
    sublingual gland ~ 42310-42320
    submaxillary gland ~ 42310-42320
    subphrenic, percutaneous ~ 49040
    testis ~ 54700
    thorax ~ 21501-21502
    throat ~ 42700-42725
    tongue ~ 41000-41006, 41015
    tonsil ~ 42700
    urethra ~ 53040
    uvula ~ 42000
    vagina ~ 57010
    vulva ~ 56405
    wrist ~ 25028
ankle ~ 27610
bile duct ~ 47420-47425
bladder ~ 51040
bulla, skin, puncture aspiration ~ 10160

Incision and drainage ~ *continued*
  bursa
    ankle ~ 27604
    arm, lower ~ 25031
    elbow ~ 23931
    foot ~ 28001
    hip ~ 26991
    knee ~ 27301
    leg, lower ~ 27604
    leg, upper ~ 27301
    palm ~ 26025-26030
    pelvis ~ 26991
    wrist ~ 25031
  carbuncle
    skin ~ 10060-10061
  carpals ~ 25035, 26034
  comedones
    skin ~ 10040
  cyst
    conjunctiva ~ 68020
    gums ~ 41800
    liver ~ 47010
    lung ~ 32200
    mouth ~ 40800-40801, 41005-41009, 41015-41018
    ovarian ~ 58800-58805
    skin ~ 10040-10061
      pilonidal ~ 10080-10081
      puncture aspiration ~ 10160
      spinal cord ~ 63172-63173
    thyroid gland ~ 60000
    tongue ~ 41000-41006, 41015, 60000
  elbow
    abscess ~ 23935
    arthrotomy ~ 24000
  femur ~ 27303
  fluid collection
    skin ~ 10140
  foreign body, skin ~ 10120-10121
  furuncle ~ 10060-10061
  gallbladder ~ 47480
  hematoma
    ankle ~ 27603
    arm, lower ~ 25028
    arm, upper ~ 23930
    brain ~ 61312-61315
    ear, external
      complicated ~ 69005
      simple ~ 69000
    elbow ~ 23930
    epididymis ~ 54700
    gums ~ 41800
    hip ~ 26990
    knee ~ 27301
    leg, lower ~ 27603
    leg, upper ~ 27301
    mouth ~ 40800-40801, 41005-41009, 41015-41018
    nasal septum ~ 30020
    neck ~ 21501-21502
    nose ~ 30000-30020
    pelvis ~ 26990
    scrotum ~ 54700
    skin ~ 10140
      puncture aspiration ~ 10160
    skull ~ 61312-61315
    testis ~ 54700
    thorax ~ 21501-21502
    tongue ~ 41000-41006, 41015
    vagina ~ 57022-57023
    wrist ~ 25028
  hepatic duct ~ 47400
  hip bone ~ 26992, 27030
  humerus abscess ~ 23935
  interphalangeal joint
    toe ~ 28024
  intertarsal joint ~ 28020
  kidney ~ 50040, 50125
  knee ~ 27303, 27310
  lacrimal gland ~ 68400
  lacrimal sac ~ 68420

Incision and drainage ~ *continued*
  liver
    abscess or cyst ~ 47010
  mediastinum ~ 39000-39010
  metatarsophalangeal joint ~ 28022
  milia, multiple ~ 10040
  onychia ~ 10060-10061
  orbit ~ 67405, 67440
  paronychia ~ 10060-10061
  pelvic bone ~ 26992
  penis ~ 54015
  pericardium ~ 33025
  phalanges, finger ~ 26034
  pilonidal cyst ~ 10080-10081
  pustules, skin ~ 10040
  radius ~ 25035
  seroma, skin ~ 10140
  shoulder
    abscess ~ 23030
    arthrotomy
      acromioclavicular joint ~ 23044
      sternoclavicular joint ~ 23044
    bursa ~ 23031
    hematoma ~ 23030
  shoulder joint, arthrotomy, glenohumeral joint ~ 23040
  tarsometatarsal joint ~ 28020
  tendon sheath
    finger ~ 26020
    palm ~ 26020
  thorax
    deep ~ 21510
  toe ~ 28024
  ulna ~ 25035
  ureter ~ 50600
  vagina ~ 57020
  wound infection, skin ~ 10180
  wrist ~ 25028, 25040
Inclusion bodies
  fluid ~ 88106
  smear ~ 87207-87210
Incomplete abortion ~ see abortion, incomplete
Indicator dilution studies ~ 93561-93562
Induced abortion ~ see abortion
Induced hyperthermia ~ see thermotherapy
Induced hypothermia ~ see hypothermia
Induratio penis plastica ~ see Peyronie disease
Infant, newborn, intensive care ~ see intensive care, neonatal
Infantile paralysis ~ see polio
Infection
  actinomyces ~ see actinomycosis
  bone ~ see osteomyelitis
  diagnosis, group A strep test ~ 3210F
  filarioidea ~ see filariasis
  immunoassay ~ 86317-86318
  postoperative wound ~ see postoperative wound infection
  rapid test ~ 86403-86406
  treatment, antibiotic prescribed ~ 4045F
  wound ~ see wound, infection
Infectious agent
  antigen detection
    direct fluorescence
      bordetella ~ 87265
      chlamydia trachomatis ~ 87270
      cryptosporidium ~ 87272
      cytomegalovirus ~ 87271
      enterovirus ~ 87267
      giardia ~ 87269
      influenza A ~ 87276
      legionella pneumophila ~ 87278
      respiratory syncytial virus ~ 87280
      treponema pallidum ~ 87285
      varicella-zoster ~ 87290
    immunoassay
      adenovirus ~ 87301, 87809
      aspergillus ~ 87305
      chlamydia trachomatis ~ 87320
      clostridium difficile ~ 87324
      cryptococcus neoformans ~ 87327
      cryptosporidium ~ 87328
      cytomegalovirus ~ 87332

Infectious agent ~ *continued*

    entamoeba histolytica dispar group ~ 87336
    entamoeba histolytica group ~ 87337
    escherichia coli 0157 ~ 87335
    giardia ~ 87329
    helicobacter pylori ~ 87338-87339
    hepatitis B surface antigen (HBsAg) ~ 87340
    hepatitis B surface antigen (HBsAg) neutralization ~ 87341
    hepatitis Be antigen (HBeAg) ~ 87350
    hepatitis, delta agent ~ 87380
    histoplasma capsulatum ~ 87385
    HIV-1 ~ 87390
    HIV-2 ~ 87391
    influenza A ~ 87400
    influenza B ~ 87400
    multiple step method ~ 87301-87449, 87451
    not otherwise specified ~ 87449, 87451
    respiratory syncytial virus ~ 87420
    rotavirus ~ 87425
    shiga-like toxin ~ 87427
    single step method ~ 87450
    streptococcus, group A ~ 87430
  immunofluorescence ~ 87260, 87273-87275, 87279, 87281-87283, 87299-87300
    adenovirus ~ 87260
    herpes simplex ~ 87273-.87274
    influenza B ~ 87275
    not otherwise specified ~ 87299
    parainfluenza virus ~ 87279
    pneumocystis carinii ~ 87281
    polyvalent ~ 87300
    rubeola ~ 87283
  concentration ~ 87015
  detection
    by immunoassay
      adenovirus ~ 87809
      chlamydia trachomatis ~ 87810
      clostridium difficile ~ 87803
      influenza ~ 87804
      neisseria gonorrheae ~ 87850
      not otherwise specified ~ 87899
      respiratory syncytial virus ~ 87807
      streptococcus, group A ~ 87880
      streptococcus, group B ~ 87802
      trichomonas vaginalis ~ 87808
      with direct optical observation ~ 87802-87899
    by nucleic acid probe
      bartonella henselae ~ 87472
      bartonella quintana ~ 87472
      borrelia burgdorferi ~ 87475, 87476
      candida species ~ 87480-87482
      chlamydia pneumoniae ~ 87485-87487
      chlamydia trachomatis ~ 87490-87492
      clostridium difficile ~ 87493
      cytomegalovirus ~ 87495-87497
      enterovirus ~ 87498
      gardnerella vaginalis ~ 87510-87512
      hepatitis B virus ~ 87516, 87517
      hepatitis B ~ 87520-87522
      hepatitis G ~ 87525-87527
      herpes simplex virus ~ 87528-87530
      herpes virus-6 (six) ~ 87531-87533
      HIV-1 ~ 87534-87536
      HIV-2 ~ 87537-87539
      influenza ~ 87501-87503
      legionella pneumophila ~ 87540-87542
      multiple organisms ~ 87800-87801
      mycobacteria avium-intracellulare ~ 87560-87562
      mycobacteria species ~ 87550-87552
      mycobacteria tuberculosis ~ 87555-87557
      mycoplasma pneumoniae ~ 87580-87582
      neisseria gonorrheae ~ 87590-87592
      not otherwise specified ~ 87797-87799
      papillomavirus, human ~ 0500T, 87623-87625
      respiratory virus ~ 87631-87634
      staphylococcus aureus ~ 87640-87641
      streptococcus, group A ~ 87650-87652
      streptococcus, group B ~ 87653
      trichomonas vaginalis ~ 87660
      vancomycin resistance ~ 87500
      Zika virus ~ 87662

Infectious agent ~ *continued*

  enzymatic activity ~ 87905
  genotype analysis by nucleic acid
    cytomegalovirus ~ 87910
    hepatitis B virus ~ 87912
    hepatitis C virus ~ 87902
    high-risk HPV types ~ 0500T
    HIV-1 regions ~ 87901, 87906
  phenotype analysis
    by nucleic acid
      HIV-1 drug resistance ~ 87903-87904
  phenotype prediction
    by genetic database ~ 87900

Infectious mononucleosis virus ~ see Epstein-Barr virus

Inflammatory process
  localization
    nuclear medicine ~ 78805-78807

Inflation
  ear, middle
    eustachian tube ~ 69799
  eustachian tube
    myringotomy ~ 69420
      anesthesia ~ 69424

Influenza A
  antigen detection
    direct fluorescence ~ 87276
    enzyme immunoassay ~ 87400

Influenza B
  antigen detection
    enzyme immunoassay ~ 87400
    immunofluorescence ~ 87275

Influenza vaccine ~ see vaccines

Influenza virus
  antibody ~ 86710
  by immunoassay
    with direct optical observation ~ 87804
  by nucleic acid ~ 87501-87503

Infraorbital nerve
  avulsion ~ 64734
  incision ~ 64734
  transection ~ 64734

Infrared light treatment ~ 97026

Infratentorial craniectomy ~ 61520-61521

Infusion
  amnion, transabdominal ~ 59070
  anesthetic
    paravertebral block (PVB) ~ 64463
  cerebral
    for other than thrombolysis ~ 61650, 61651
    for thrombolysis
      intravenous ~ 37195
      percutaneous ~ 61645

  for thrombolysis
    percutaneous transluminal ~ 61645
    transcatheter therapy ~ 37211-37214
  hydration ~ 96360, 96361
    status documented ~ 2030F, 2031F
  intraosseous ~ 36680
  intravenous, unlisted ~ 96379
    diagnostic/prophylactic/therapeutic ~ 96365-96368, 96379
    hydration ~ 96360, 96361
  radioelement ~ 77750
  subcutaneous ~ 96369-96371
  spinal
    device implantation/replacement ~ 62360-62362
    diagnostic/therapeutic ~ 62324-62327
  transcatheter therapy ~ 37211-37214

Infusion pump
  electronic analysis, spinal cord ~ 62367-62368
  insertion, intra-arterial ~ 36260
  intra-arterial
    removal ~ 36262
    revision ~ 36261
  intravenous
    insertion ~ 36563
    repair ~ 36576
    replacement ~ 36583
  maintenance ~ 95990-95991, 96520-96530
  spinal cord ~ 62361-62362
  ventricular catheter ~ 61215

1077

Infusion therapy ~ 62350-62351, 62360-62362
  arterial catheterization ~ 36640
  chemotherapy ~ 96410-96414, 96422-96425
  home infusion procedures ~ 99601-99602
  intravenous ~ 90780-90781
  pain ~ 62360-62362, 62367-62368
  subcutaneous ~ 96369-96371
Ingestion challenge test ~ 95076, 95079
Inguinal hernia repair ~ see hernia, repair, inguinal
INH ~ see drug assay
Inhalation pentamidine ~ 94642
Inhalation provocation tests ~ see bronchial challenge test
Inhalation treatment ~ (see also pulmonology, therapeutic) 94640,
  94644-94645, 94664, 99503
Inhibin A ~ 86336
Inhibition test, hemagglutination ~ see hemagglutination inhibition test
Inhibition, fertilization ~ see contraception
Inhibitor, alpha 1-protease ~ see alpha-1 antitrypsin
Inhibitor, alpha 2-plasmin ~ see alpha-2 antiplasmin
Inhibitory concentration, minimum ~ see minimum inhibitory
  concentration
Initial inpatient consultations ~ see consultation, initial inpatient
Injection ~ see allergen immunotherapy; infusion
  abdomen
    air ~ 49400
    contrast material ~ 49400
  anesthetic agent
    paravertebral block (PVB) ~ 64461, 64462
    sacroiliac joint ~ 27096
    spine
      cervical ~ 0228T, 0229T, 62320, 62321, 62324, 62325
      lumbar ~ 0230T, 0231T, 62322, 62323, 62326, 62327
      sacral ~ 0230T, 0231T, 62322, 62323, 62326, 62327
      thoracic ~ 0228T, 0229T, 62320, 62321, 62324, 62325
  angiography, pulmonary ~ 75746
  ankle, radial ~ 27648
  antibiotic ~ see antibiotic administration
  antigen (allergen) ~ 95115-95125
  aorta (aortography), radiologic ~ 93567
  aponeurosis ~ 20550
  bile duct, cholangiography ~ 47531, 47532
  bladder, radiologic ~ 51600-51610
  brain canal ~ 61070
  bronchography, segmental ~ 31899
  bursa ~ 20600-20610
  cardiac catheterization ~ 93563-93568
  carpal tunnel, therapeutic ~ 20526
  chemotherapy ~ 96400-96450, 96542
  cistern, medication or other ~ 61055
  contrast, via catheter ~ 49424
  corpora cavernosa ~ 54235
  cyst
    bone ~ 20615
    kidney ~ 50390
    pelvis ~ 50390
    thyroid ~ 60300
  diagnostic, additional sequential, each push ~ 96376
  elbow, arthrography, radiologic ~ 24220
  epidural ~ see epidural, injection
  esophageal varices, endoscopy ~ 43243
  esophagus
    sclerosing agent ~ 43204
    submucosal ~ 43201
  extremity, pseudoaneurysm ~ 36002
  eye
    anterior segment
      air ~ 66020
      medication ~ 66030
    pharmacologic agent ~ 0465T, 67028
    posterior segment
      intravitreal ~ 67028
      suprachoroidal ~ 0465T
  eyelid, subconjunctional ~ 68200
  fluid collection, sclerosant ~ 49185
  foot, nerve ~ 64455
  ganglion, anesthetic ~ 64505, 64510
  ganglion cyst ~ 20612
  gastric varices, endoscopy ~ 43243
  hand, cell therapy for scleroderma ~ 0490T

Injection ~ _continued_
  heart vessels
    cardiac catheterization ~ 93563-93568
    radiologic ~ 93563
  hemorrhoids, sclerosing solution ~ 46500
  hip, radiologic ~ 27093-27095
  insect venom ~ 95130-95134
  intervertebral disk
    chemonucleolysis agent ~ 62292
    radiological ~ 62290-62291
  intraamniotic ~ 59852
  intra-arterial ~ 96373, 96379
    thrombolytic ~ 37184-37186, 61645
  intradermal, for tattooing ~ 11920-11922
  intralesional, skin ~ 11900-11901
  intramuscular ~ 96372
    therapeutic ~ 96372, 99506
  intravenous ~ 96379
    nuclear diagnostic localization ~ 78808
    thrombolytic ~ 37187-37188
    unlisted ~ 96379
    vascular flow check, graft ~ 15860
  intravenous push ~ 96374-96376
  joint ~ 20600-20610
  kidney
    drugs ~ 50391
    for nephrostogram ~ 50430, 50431
  knee, radiologic ~ 27370
  lacrimal gland, radiologic ~ 68850
  larynx, endoscopic ~ 31570, 31573, 31574
  left heart, radiologic ~ 93565
  lesion, skin ~ 11900-11901
  ligament ~ 20550
  liver ~ 47015
  mammary ductogram/galactogram ~ 19030
  muscle endplate
    facial ~ 64612
  nerve
    anesthetic ~ 01991-01992, 64400-64530
    neurolytic agent ~ 64600-64640, 64680-64681
  orbit
    retrobulbar
      alcohol ~ 67505
      medication ~ 67500
    tenon's capsule ~ 67515
  pancreatography ~ 48400
  paraveretebral facet joint/nerve ~ 64490-64495
  penis
    for erection ~ 54235
    Peyronie disease ~ 54200
      with surgical exposure of plague ~ 54205
    radiology ~ 54230
    vasoactive drugs ~ 54231
  peritoneal cavity air ~ see pneumoperitoneum
  prophylactic, additional sequential, each push ~ 96376
  radiologic
    breast ~ 19030
    cholangiography ~ 47531, 47532
  rectum, sclerosing solution ~ 45520
  right heart ~ see cardiac catheterization, injection
    radiologic ~ 93566
  sacroiliac joint, for arthrography ~ 27096
  salivary duct ~ 42660
  salivary gland, radiologic ~ 42550
  sclerosing agent
    esophagus ~ 43204
    intravenous ~ 36465, 36466, 36468, 36470, 36471
  sentinel node identification ~ 38792
  shoulder, arthrography, radiologic ~ 23350
  shunt, peritoneal, venous ~ 49427
  sinus tract ~ 20500
    diagnostic ~ 20501
  spider veins, telangiectasia ~ 36468
  spinal artery ~ 62294
  spinal cord
    anesthetic ~ 62320-62327
    blood ~ 62273
    neurolytic agent ~ 62280-62282
    other ~ 62320-62327
    radiological ~ 62284

Injection ~ *continued*
  steroids
    spine
      cervial ~ 0228T, 0229T, 62320, 62321, 62324, 62325
      lumbar ~ 0230T, 0231T, 62322, 62323, 62326, 62327
      sacral ~ 0230T, 0231T, 62322, 62323, 62326, 62327
      thoracic ~ 0228T, 0229T, 62320, 62321, 62324, 62325
    urethral stricture ~ 52283
  subcutaneous ~ 96372
    silicone ~ 11950-11954
    therapeutic ~ 96372
    timed application of on-body injection device ~ 96377
  temporomandibular joint, arthrography ~ 21116
  tendon origin, insertion ~ 20551
  tendon sheath ~ 20550
  therapeutic
    extremity pseudoaneurysm ~ 36002
    lung ~ 32960
    thyroid ~ 60300
    turbinate ~ 30200
  thoracic cavity ~ see pleurodesis, chemical
  trachea ~ 31612
    puncture ~ 31612
  transtracheal, bronchography ~ 31899
  trigger point(s)
    one or two muscles ~ 20552
    two or more muscles ~ 20553
  turbinate ~ 30200
  unlisted services and procedures ~ 90799
  ureter
    drugs ~ 50391
    for ureterogram ~ 50430, 50431
    radiologic ~ 50684
  veins
    sclerosant ~ 36465, 36466, 36468, 36470, 36471
  venography ~ 36005
  ventricle
    dye ~ 61120
    medication or other ~ 61026
  vitreous ~ 67028
    fluid substitute ~ 67025
  vocal cords, therapeutic ~ 31513, 31570-31571
  white blood cells, autologous concentrate ~ 0481T
  wrist
    carpal tunnel, therapeutic ~ 20526
    radiologic ~ 25246
Inkblot test ~ 96101-96103
Inner ear ~ see ear, inner
Innominate arteries ~ see artery, brachiocephalic
Innominate tumor excision ~ 27077
Inorganic sulfates ~ see sulfate
Insemination, artificial ~ 58321-58322, 89268
Insertion ~ see also implantation; intubation; transplantation
  aqueous drainage device
    to extraocular reservoir ~ 66179, 66180
    without extraocular reservoir ~ 0376T, 0449T, 0450T, 66183
  balloon, intra-aortic ~ 33967, 33973
  breast implants ~ 19340-19342
  bronchial valve ~ 31647, 31651
  cannula
    arteriovenous ~ 36810-36815
    extra corporeal circulation for regional chemotherapy of extremity ~ 36823
    for on-body injector ~ 96377
    thoracic duct ~ 38794
    vein to vein ~ 36800
  catheter
    abdomen ~ 49324, 49419-49421, 49435
    abdominal artery ~ 36245-36248
    aorta ~ 36200
    bladder ~ 51045, 51701-51703
    brachiocephalic artery ~ 36215-36218
    brain ~ 61210, 61770
    breast, for interstitial radioelement application ~ 19296-19298
    bronchi ~ 31717
    bronchus, for intracavitary radioelement application ~ 31643
    cardiac ~ see catheterization, cardiac
      flow directed ~ 93503
    ear, middle ~ 69799
    eustachian tube ~ 69799

Insertion ~ *continued*
    gastrointestinal, upper ~ 43241
    intraperitoneal ~ 49418-49419
    jejunum ~ 44015
    lower extremity artery ~ 36245-36248
    nasotracheal ~ 31720
    pelvic artery ~ 36245-36248
    pleural cavity ~ 32550
    portal vein ~ 36481
    prostate ~ 55875
    pulmonary artery ~ 36013-36015
    right heart ~ 36013, 93451
    skull ~ 61107
    spinal cord ~ 62350-62351
    suprapubic ~ 51102, 51045
    thoracic artery ~ 36215-36218
    tracheobronchial ~ 31725
    urethra ~ 51701-51703
    vena cava ~ 36010
    venous ~ 36011-36012, 36400-36410, 36420-36425, 36500-36510, 36555-36558, 36568-36569
  cecostomy tube ~ 49442
  cervical dilation ~ 59200
  cochlear device ~ 69930
  colonic tube ~ 49442
  defibrillator system, subcutaneous ~ 33270
  distraction device
    interlaminar/interspinous process, lumbar ~ 22867-22870
  drug delivery implant ~ 11981, 11983
  duodenostomy tube ~ 49441
  electrode
    brain ~ 61531-61533, 61760, 61863, 61864, 61867, 61868
    chest wall, respiratory sensor ~ 0466T
    heart ~ 33202-33203, 33210-33211, 33216-33217, 33224-33225, 33271, 93620-93622
    nerve ~ 64553-64581
    retina ~ 0100T
    sphenoidal ~ 95830
    spinal cord ~ 63650-63655
    stomach
      laparoscopic, neurostimulator ~ 43647
      open, neurostimulator ~ 43881
  endotracheal tube ~ 31500
  gastrostomy tube
    laparoscopic ~ 43653
    percutaneous ~ 43246, 49440
  glucose sensor~ 0446T, 0448T
  graft
    aorta ~ 33330-33335
    heart vessel ~ 33330-33335
  guide, kidney pelvis ~ 50395
  guide wire
    endoscopy ~ 43248
    esophagoscopy ~ 43248
    with dilation ~ 43226
  Heyman capsule, uterus
    for brachytherapy ~ 58346
  iliac artery occlusion device ~ 34808
  implant, bone
    for external speech processor/cochlear stimulator ~ 69714-69718
  infusion pump
    intra-arterial ~ 36260
    intravenous ~ 36563
    spinal cord ~ 62361-62362
  intracatheter/needle
    aorta ~ 36160
    dialysis circuit ~ 36901-36903
    intra-arterial ~ 36100-36140
    intravenous ~ 36000
  intraocular lens ~ 66983
    manual or mechanical technique ~ 66982, 66984
    not associated with concurrent cataract removal ~ 66985
  intrauterine device (IUD) ~ 58300
  jejunostomy tube
    endoscopy ~ 44372
    percutaneous ~ 49441
  keel, laryngoplasty ~ 31580
  laminaria ~ 59200
  mesh, pelvic floor ~ 57267
  nasobiliary tube, endoscopy ~ 43274

1079

Insertion ~ *continued*
  nasopancreatic tube, endoscopy ~ 43274
  needle
    bone ~ 36680
    intraosseous ~ 36680
    prostate ~ 55875-55876
  needle wire, trachea ~ 31730
  neurostimulator
    pulse generator ~ 64590
    receiver ~ 64590
  nose, septal prosthesis ~ 30220
  obturator, larynx ~ 31527
  ocular implant
    with/without conjunctival graft ~ 65150
    with foreign material ~ 65155
    muscles attached ~ 65140
    muscles, not attached ~ 65135
    in scleral shell ~ 65130
  orbital transplant ~ 67550
  oviduct
    chromotubation ~ 58350
    hydrotubation ~ 58350
  ovoid, vagina, for brachytherapy ~ 57155
  pacemaker, heart ~ 33206-33208
    pulse generator only ~ 33212-33213, 33221
  pacemaker or implantable defibrillator
    leads ~ 33216, 33217, 33224, 33225, 33230, 33231,33243, 33244, 33249
    pulse generator only ~ 33240
  packing, vagina ~ 57180
  penile prosthesis, inflatable ~ see penile prosthesis, insertion, inflatable
  pessary, vagina ~ 57160
  pin, skeletal traction ~ 20650
  probe, brain ~ 61770
  prostaglandin ~ 59200
  prostate, radioactive substance ~ 55860
  prosthesis
    knee ~ 27438, 27445
    nasal septal ~ 30220
    palate ~ 42281
    pelvic floor ~ 57267
    penis
      inflatable ~ 54401-54405
      noninflatable ~ 54400
    speech ~ 31611
    testis ~ 54660
    urethral sphincter ~ 53444-53445
  pulse generator
    brain ~ 61885-61886
    heart ~ 33212-33213
    spinal cord ~ 63685
  radioactive material
    bladder ~ 51020
    cystourethroscopy ~ 52250
  receiver
    brain ~ 61885-61886
    spinal cord ~ 63685
  reservoir
    brain ~ 61210-61215
    spinal cord ~ 62360
    subcutaneous ~ 49419
  sensor, fetal oximetry
    cervix ~ 0021T
    vagina ~ 0021T
  shunt ~ 36835
    abdomen
      vein ~ 49425
      venous ~ 49426
    intrahepatic portosystemic ~ 37182
  spinal instrument ~ 22849
    spinous process ~ 22841
  spinal instrumentation
    anterior ~ 22845-22847
    biomechanical device ~ 22853, 22854, 22859
    internal spinal fixation ~ 22841
    pelvic fixation ~ 22848
    posterior nonsegmental
      Harrington rod technique ~ 22840
    posterior segmental ~ 22842-22844
    stabilization/distraction device ~ 22869, 22870

Insertion ~ *continued*
  stent
    bile duct ~ 43274, 47801
    bladder ~ 51045
    conjunctiva ~ 68750
    coronary ~ 92928, 92929
    esophagus ~ 43212
    gastrointestinal, upper ~ 43266
    ileum ~ 44384
    indwelling ~ 50605
    lacrimal duct ~ 68815
    pancreatic duct ~ 43274
    small intestines ~ 44370, 44379
    ureter ~ 50688
    ureter via kidney ~ 50693
    ureteral ~ 50947, 52332
    urethral ~ 52282
  tamponade, esophagus ~ 43460
  tandem uterus for brachytherapy ~ 57155
  tendon graft
    finger ~ 26392
    hand ~ 26392
  testicular prosthesis ~ see prosthesis, testicular, insertion
  tissue expanders, skin ~ 11960-11971
  tube
    bile duct ~ 43268
    esophagus ~ 43510
    gastrointestinal, upper ~ 43241
    ileum ~ 44384
    pancreatic duct ~ 43268
    small intestines ~ 44379
    trachea ~ 31730
    ureter ~ 50688
  ureteral guide wire ~ 52334
  vascular pedicle, carpal bone ~ 25430
  venous access device
    central ~ 36560-36566
    peripheral ~ 36570-36571
  ventilating tube ~ 69433
  ventricular assist device ~ 33975
  wire, skeletal traction ~ 20650
Inspiratory positive pressure breathing ~ see intermittent positive pressure breathing (IPPB)
Instillation
  agent for fibrinolysis ~ 32561-32562
  agent for pleurodesis ~ 32560
  bladder ~ see bladder, instillation
  drugs
    bladder ~ 51720
    kidney ~ 50391
    ureter ~ 50391
Instrumentation ~ see application; bone, fixation; spinal instrumentation
  spinal
    insertion ~ 22840-22848, 22853, 22854, 22859, 22869, 22870
    reinsertion ~ 22849
    removal ~ 22850, 22852-22855
    with arthrodesis ~ 22586
Insufflation, eustachian tube ~ see eustachian tube, inflation
Insulin ~ 80422, 80432-80435
  antibody ~ 86337
  blood ~ 83525
  free ~ 83527
Insulin C-peptide measurement ~ see C-peptide
Insulin like growth factors ~ see somatomedin
Insurance
  basic life and/or disability evaluation services ~ 99450
  examination ~ 99450-99456
Integumentary system
  ablation
    breast ~ 19105
    photodynamic therapy ~ 96570-96571
  biopsy ~ 11100-11101
    with imaging of specimen ~ 19081-19086
  breast ~ see Breast
  burns ~ 15002-15005, 15100-15121, 16000-16036
  debridement ~ 11000-11006, 11010-11047
  destruction ~ see also dermatology
    actinotherapy ~ 96900
    benign lesion ~ 17000, 17003-17004, 17110-17111
    chemical exfoliation ~ 17360

Integumentary system ~ *continued*
    cutaneous vascular proliferative ~ 17106-17108
    cryotherapy ~ 17340
    electrolysis epilation ~ 17380
    malignant lesion ~ 17260-17286
      by photodynamic therapy ~ 96567
    Mohs micrographic surgery ~ 17311-17315
    premalignant lesion ~ 17000, 17003, 17004
      by photodynamic therapy ~ 96567, 96573, 96574
    unlisted services and procedures ~ 17999
  drainage, image guided ~ 10030
  dressing change, with anesthesia ~ 15851
  excision
    benign lesion ~ 11400-11404, 11406, 11420-11424, 11426,
      11440-11444, 11446
    nail ~ 11750
    malignant lesion ~ 11600-11604, 11606, 11620-11624, 11626,
      11640-11644, 11646
  incision ~ 10040-10181
  introduction
    drug delivery implant ~ 11981, 11983
  nails ~ 11720-11765
  paring ~ 11055-11057
  photography ~ 96904
  pilonidal cyst ~ 10080-10081, 11770-11772
  pressure ulcers ~ 15920-15999
  removal
    contraceptive capsule implant ~ 11976
    drug delivery implant ~ 11982-11983
    foreign body ~ 10120-10121
    sutures with anesthesia ~ 15850-15852
    tissue expander ~ 11970-11971
  repair
    adjacent tissue transfer/rearrangement ~ 14000-14350
    complex ~ 13100-13160
    flaps, other ~ 15740-15776
    free skin grafts ~ 15050-15136, 15200-15261, 15271-15278
    intermediate ~ 12031-12057
    other procedures ~ 15780-15879
    simple ~ 12001-12021
    skin and/or deep tissue ~ 15570-15738
  shaving of epidermal or dermal lesion ~ 11300-11313
  skin replacement surgery and skin substitute grafts
    autograft/tissue cultured autograft ~ 15040-15157
    skin substitute graft ~ 15271-15278
    surgical preparation ~ 15002-15005
  skin tags, removal ~ 11200-11201
Intelligence test ~ 96100
Intensive care
  low birthweight infant, subsequent care ~ 99478-99480
  neonatal, initial ~ 99477
Intercarpal joint
  arthrodesis ~ 25820-25825
  dislocation, closed treatment ~ 25660
  repair ~ 25447
Intercostal nerve
  destruction ~ 64620
  injection
    anesthetic ~ 64420-64421
    neurolytic ~ 64620
Interdental fixation
  device application ~ 21110
  without fracture ~ 21497
  mandibular fracture
    closed treatment ~ 21453
    open treatment ~ 21462
Interdental papilla ~ see gums
Interdental wire fixation
  closed treatment craniofacial separation ~ 21431
Interferometry eye, biometry ~ 92136
Intermediate care facility (ICF) visits ~ 99304-99318
Intermittent positive pressure breathing (IPPB) ~ see continuous positive
  airway pressure (CPAP); continuous negative pressure breathing (CNPB)
Internal breast prostheses ~ see breast, implants
Internal ear ~ see ear, inner
Internal rigid fixation, reconstruction, mandibular rami ~ 21196
International Normalized Ratio
  patient/caregiver training ~ 93792
  test review ~ 93793
Internet E/M service ~ 98969, 99444

Interphalangeal joint
  arthrodesis ~ 26860-26863
  arthroplasty ~ 26535-26536
  arthrotomy ~ 26080, 28054
  biopsy, synovium ~ 26110
  capsule
    excision ~ 26525
    incision ~ 26525
  dislocation
    closed treatment ~ 26770
    with manipulation ~ 26340
    open treatment ~ 26785
    percutaneous fixation ~ 26776
  exploration ~ 26080
  fracture
    closed treatment ~ 26740
    with manipulation ~ 26742
    open treatment ~ 26746
  fusion ~ 26860-26863
  great toe
    arthrodesis ~ 28755
      with tendon transfer ~ 28760
    fusion ~ 28755
      with tendon transfer ~ 28760
  removal of foreign body ~ 26080
  repair
    collateral ligament ~ 26545
    volar plate ~ 26548
  synovectomy ~ 26140
  toe ~ 28272
    arthrotomy ~ 28024
    dislocation ~ 28660-28665, 28675
      percutaneous fixation ~ 28666
    excision ~ 28160
    exploration ~ 28024
    removal
      foreign body ~ 28024
      loose body ~ 28024
    synovial biopsy ~ 28054
Intersex state
  clitoroplasty ~ 56805
  vaginoplasty ~ 57335
Intersex surgery
  female to male ~ 55980
  male to female ~ 55970
Interstitial cell stimulating hormone ~ see luteinizing hormone (LH)
Interstitial cystitides, chronic ~ see cystitis, interstitial
Interstitial cystitis ~ see cystitis, interstitial
Interstitial fluid pressure monitoring ~ 20950
Interstitial cell stimulating hormone ~ see luteinizing hormone (LH)
Interstitial radiation therapy
  radioelement application ~ 77778
    device placement
      breast ~ 19296-19298
      genitalia ~ 55920
      head/neck ~ 41019
      pelvis ~ 55920
      uterus ~ 57155
      vagina ~ 57155, 57156
    heyman capsules insertion ~ 58346
    ultrasonic guidance ~ 76965
Intertarsal joint
  arthrotomy ~ 28020, 28050
  biopsy ~ 28050
  drainage ~ 28020
  exploration ~ 28020
  removal
    foreign body ~ 28020
    loose body ~ 28020
  synovial
    biopsy ~ 28050
    excision ~ 28070
Interthoracoscapular amputation ~ see amputation, interthoracoscapular
Intertrochanteric femur fracture ~ see femur, fracture, intertrochanteric
Intervertebral chemonucleolysis ~ see chemonucleolysis

Intervertebral disc
  annuloplasty ~ 22526-22527
  arthroplasty
    artificial disc ~ 0163T, 0375T, 22856-22858
      removal ~ 0095T, 0164T, 22864, 22865
      revision ~ 0098T, 0165T, 22861, 22862
  aspiration ~ 62267
  biopsy ~ 62267
  decompression ~ 63075-63078
    by needle ~ 62287
  diskography
    cervical ~ 62291, 72285
    lumbar ~ 62290, 62292, 72295
    thoracic ~ 62291, 72285
  herniated
    excision
      cervical ~ 63020, 63035, 63040, 63043
      lumbar ~ 62380, 63030, 63035, 63042-63044, 63056, 63057
      thoracic ~ 63055, 63057, 63064, 63066
  injection
    chemonucleolysis agent ~ 62292
    X-ray ~ 62290-62291
  insertion
    biomechanical device ~ 22853, 22854, 22859
  removal
    artificial disc ~ 0095T, 0164T, 22864, 22865
    by needle ~ 62287
  revision ~ 0098T, 0165T, 22861, 22862
Intestinal anastomosis ~ see anastomosis, intestines
Intestinal invagination ~ see intussusception
Intestinal peptide, vasoactive ~ see vasoactive intestinal peptide
Intestine(s)
  allotransplantation ~ 44135-44136
    removal ~ 44137
  anastomosis ~ 44625-44626
  biopsy ~ 44100
  bleeding tube ~ 43460
  closure
    enterostomy, large or small ~ 44625-44626
    stoma ~ 44620-44625
  excision, donor ~ 44132-44133
  exclusion ~ 44700
  laparoscopic resection, with anastomosis ~ 44202-44208
  lesion excision ~ 44110, 44111
  lysis of adhesions, laparoscopic ~ 44200
  nuclear medicine imaging ~ 78290
  reconstruction
    bladder ~ 50820
    colonic reservoir ~ 45119
  repair
    diverticula ~ 44605
    obstruction ~ 44615
    ulcer ~ 44605
    wound ~ 44605
  suture
    diverticula ~ 44605
    stoma ~ 44620-44625
    ulcer ~ 44605
    wound ~ 44605
  transplantation
    allograft preparation ~ 44715-44721
    donor enterectomy ~ 44132-44133
    removal of allograft ~ 44137
  unlisted services and procedures ~ 44238, 44799
Intestines, large ~ see anus; cecum; colon; rectum
Intestines, small
  anastomosis ~ 43845, 44130
  biopsy ~ 44020
    endoscopy ~ 44361
  catheterization jejunum ~ 44015
  decompression ~ 44021
  destruction lesion ~ 44369
    tumor ~ 44369
  endoscopy ~ 44364
    biopsy ~ 44361, 44377
    control of bleeding ~ 44366, 44378
      via stoma ~ 44382
    destruction
      lesion ~ 44369
      tumor ~ 44369

Intestine, small ~ continued
  diagnostic ~ 44376
  exploration ~ 44360
  hemorrhage ~ 44366
  insertion
    stent ~ 44370, 44379
    tube ~ 44379
  pelvic pouch ~ 44385-44386
  removal
    foreign body ~ 44363
    lesion ~ 44365
    polyp ~ 44364-44365
    tumor ~ 44364-44365
    via stoma ~ 44380
    tube placement ~ 44372
    tube revision ~ 44373
  enterostomy ~ 44300
  excision ~ 44120-44128
    partial with anastomosis ~ 44140
  exclusion ~ 44700
  exploration ~ 44020
  gastrostomy tube ~ 44373
  hemorrhage ~ 44378
  hemorrhage control ~ 44366
  ileostomy ~ 44310-44314, 45136
    continent ~ 44316
  incision ~ 44020
    creation
      pouch ~ 44316
      stoma ~ 44300-44310, 44314
    decompression ~ 44021
    exploration ~ 44020
    revision
      stoma ~ 44312
      stoma closure ~ 44620-44626
  insertion
    catheter ~ 44015
    jejunostomy tube ~ 44372
  jejunostomy ~ 44310
    laparoscopic ~ 44201
  lysis adhesions ~ 44005
  removal foreign body ~ 44020, 44363
  repair
    diverticula ~ 44602-44603
    enterocele
      abdominal approach ~ 57270
      vaginal approach ~ 57268
    fistula ~ 44640-44661
    hernia ~ 44050
    malrotation ~ 44055
    obstruction ~ 44050
    ulcer ~ 44602-44603
    volvulus ~ 44050
    wound ~ 44602-44603
  revision jejunostomy tube ~ 44373
  suture
    diverticula ~ 44602-44603
    fistula ~ 44640-44661
    plication ~ 44680
    ulcer ~ 44602-44603
    wound ~ 44602-44603
  X-ray ~ 74245, 74249-74251
    guide intubation ~ 74355
Intestinovesical fistula ~ see fistula, enterovesical
Intimectomy ~ see endarterectomy
Intra arterial injections ~ see injection, intra-arterial
Intra-abdominal voiding pressure studies ~ 51797
Intra-osseous infusion ~ see infusion, intraosseous
Intracapsular extraction of lens ~ see extraction, lens, intracapsular
Intracardiac echocardiography ~ 93662
Intracranial arterial perfusion, thrombolysis ~ 61624
  biopsy ~ 61140
  extracranial ~ 61623
  microdissection ~ 69990
  neoplasm
    acoustic neuroma ~ see brain, tumor, excision
    craniopharyngioma ~ see craniopharyngioma
    meningioma ~ see meningioma
Intrafallopian transfer, gamete ~ see GIFT
Intraluminal angioplasty ~ see angioplasty
Intramuscular injection ~ see injection, intramuscular

Intraocular lens
  exchange ~ 66986
  insertion ~ 66983
    not associated with concurrent cataract removal ~ 66985
    manual or mechanical technique ~ 66982, 66984
Intratracheal intubation ~ see insertion, endotracheal tube
Intrauterine contraceptive device ~ see intrauterine device (IUD)
Intrauterine device (IUD)
  insertion ~ 58300
  removal ~ 58301
Intravascular stent ~ *see* transcatheter, placement, intravascular stents
Intravascular ultrasound
  intraoperative, noncoronary ~ 37252, 37253
Intravenous infusion
  diagnosis ~ 96365-96368
  hydration ~ 96360-96361
    status documented ~ 2030F-2031F
Intravenous injection ~ see injection, intravenous
Intravenous pyelogram ~ see urography, intravenous
Intravenous therapy ~ (see also injection, chemotherapy) 90780-90781
  pain management ~ 90783-90784
Intravesical instillation ~ see bladder, instillation
Intravitreal injection pharmacologic agent ~ 67028
Intrinsic factor ~ 83528
  antibody ~ 86340
Introduction
  breast
    localization device placement ~ 19081-19086
  drug delivery implant ~ 11981, 11983
  gastrointestinal tube ~ 44500
    with fluoroscopic guidance ~ 74340
  tissue expanders, skin ~ 11960-11971
Intubation ~ *see also* insertion
  duodenal, with aspiration ~ 43756-43757
  endotracheal tube ~ 31500
  eustachian tube ~ see catheterization, eustachian tube
  gastric, with aspiration ~ 43753-43755
Intubation tube ~ see endotracheal tube
Intussusception
  barium enema ~ 74283
  reduction
    laparotomy ~ 44050
Invagination, intestinal ~ see intussusception
Inversion, nipple ~ see nipples, inverted
Iodide test ~ see nuclear medicine, thyroid, uptake
Iodine test ~ see starch granules, feces
Ionization, medical ~ see iontophoresis
Iontophoreses ~ see iontophoresis
Iontophoresis ~ 97033
  sweat collection ~ 89230
IP ~ see allergen immunotherapy
Ipecac administration ~ 99175
IPPB ~ see intermittent positive pressure breathing; pulmonology,
  therapeutic
Iridectomy
  with corneoscleral or corneal section ~ 66600
  by laser surgery ~ 66761
  peripheral for glaucoma ~ 66625
  with sclerectomy with punch or scissors ~ 66160
  with thermocauterization ~ 66155
  with transfixion as for iris bombe ~ 66605
  with trephination ~ 66150
Iridodialysis ~ 66680
Iridoplasty ~ 66762
Iridotomy
  excision
    with corneoscleral or corneal section ~ 66600
    with cyclectomy ~ 66605
    optical ~ 66635
    peripheral ~ 66625
  incision
    stab ~ 66500
    with transfixion as for iris bombe ~ 66505
  by laser surgery ~ 66761
  optical ~ 66635
  peripheral ~ 66625
  sector ~ 66630
    by stab incision ~ 66500

Iris
  cyst, destruction ~ 66770
  excision
    iridectomy
      with corneoscleral or corneal section ~ 66600
      with cyclectomy ~ 66605
      optical ~ 66635
      peripheral ~ 66625
      sector ~ 66630
  incision
    iridotomy
      stab ~ 66500
      with transfixion as for iris bombe ~ 66505
  lesion, destruction ~ 66770
  repair
    with ciliary body ~ 66680
    suture ~ 66682
  revision
    laser surgery ~ 66761
    photocoagulation ~ 66762
  suture, with ciliary body ~ 66682
Iron ~ 83540
  absorption ~ 78162
  chelatable total body iron ~ 78172
  turnover rate ~ 78160
  utilization ~ 78170
Iron binding capacity ~ 83550
Iron hematoxylin stain ~ 88312
Iron stain ~ 85536, 88313
Irradiation blood products ~ 86945
Irrigation
  bladder ~ 51700, 52005, 52010, 53448
  bronchus ~ 31624
  caloric vestibular test ~ 92537, 92538
  catheter, brain ~ 62194, 62225
  corpora cavernosa, priapism ~ 54220
  eye ~ 65815, 68801, 68810
  lung ~ 32997
  penis ~ 54411, 54417
    for priapism ~ 54220
  peritoneal ~ see peritoneal lavage
  shunt
    cerebrospinal fluid ~ 61070
    spinal cord ~ 63744
  sinus
    maxillary ~ 31000
    sphenoid ~ 31002
  ureter, endoscopic ~ 50951, 50970
  vagina ~ 57150
  venous access device ~ 96523
  ventricular catheter ~ 62225
  wrist, arthroscopy ~ 29843
Irving sterilization (ligation, fallopian tube, oviduct) ~ 58600-58611,
  58670
Ischemic stroke
  onset ~ 1065F-1066F
  tissue plasminogen activator (tPA)
    documentation that administration was considered ~ 4077F
Ischial
  bursa excision ~ 27060
  tumor excision ~ 27075, 27078
Ischiectomy ~ 15941
Islands of Langerhans ~ see Islet cell
Island pedicle flaps ~ 15740
Islet cell
  antibody ~ 86341
Isocitrate dehydrogenase ~ see isocitric dehydrogenase
Isocitric dehydrogenase blood ~ 83570
Isolation sperm ~ 89260-89261
Isomerase, glucose 6 (six) phosphate ~ see phosphohexose isomerase
Isopropanol ~ see isopropyl alcohol
Isopropyl alcohol ~ 84600
Isthmusectomy, thyroid gland ~ 60210-60225
IUD ~ see intrauterine device (IUD)
IV infusion therapy ~ see allergen immunotherapy; chemotherapy;
  infusion; injection, chemotherapy
IV ~ see injection, chemotherapy; intravenous therapy
IVF ~ see artificial insemination; in vitro fertilization
Ivy bleeding time ~ 85002

IV injection ~ see injection, intravenous
IV, coagulation factor ~ see calcium
IX complex, factor ~ see Christmas factor

J

Jaboulay operation ~ 43810, 43850, 43855
Jannetta procedure ~ 61458
Japanese, river fever ~ see scrub typhus
Jatene type procedure~ 33770-33781
Jaw joint ~ see facial bones; mandible; maxilla
jaws
  muscle reduction ~ 21295-21296
  X-ray for orthodontics ~ 70355
Jejunostomy
  catheterization ~ 44015
  contrast ~ 49465
  insertion
    catheter ~ 44015
    percutaneous ~ 49441
  laparoscopic ~ 44186-44187
  non-tube ~ 44187, 44310
  obstructive material removal ~ 49460
  replacement ~ 49451
  with pancreatic drain ~ 48001
Jejunum
  creation, stoma
    laparoscopic ~ 44201
  transfer
    with microvascular anastomosis free ~ 43496
Johannsen procedure ~ 53400
Johanson operation ~ see reconstruction, urethra
Joint ~ see specific joint
  arthrocentesis ~ 20600-20610
  aspiration ~ 20600-20610
  dislocation ~ see dislocation
  drainage ~ 20600-20610
  finger ~ see intercarpal joint
    fixation (surgical) ~ see arthrodesis
  injection ~ 20600-20610
  nuclear medicine imaging ~ 78300, 78315
  radiology stress views ~ 77071
  replacement
    temporomandibular ~ 21243
    vertebral ~ 0202T, 20931, 20938, 22554, 22556, 22854, 63081, 63085, 63087, 63090
  shoulder ~ see glenohumeral joint
  survey ~ 77077
  wrist ~ see radiocarpal joint
Joint syndrome, temporomandibular ~ see temporomandibular joint (TMJ)
Jones and Cantarow test ~ see blood urea nitrogen; urea nitrogen, clearance
Jones procedure ~ 28760
Jugal bone ~ see cheek bone
Jugular vein ~ see vein, jugular

K

K-wire fixation, tongue ~ 41500
Kader operation ~ see incision, stomach, creation, stoma; incision and drainage
Kala Azar smear ~ 87207
Kallidin I /Kallidin 9 ~ see Bradykinin
Kallikreinogen ~ see Fletcher factor
Kallikrein HK3 ~ see antigen, prostate specific
Kasai procedure ~ 47701
Kedani fever ~ see scrub typhus
Keel, insertion/removal, laryngoplasty ~ 31580
Keen operation (laminectomy) ~ 63600
Kelikian procedure ~ 28280
Keller procedure ~ 28292
Kelly urethral plication ~ 57220
Keratectomy, partial, for lesion ~ 65400

Keratomileusis ~ 65760
Keratophakia ~ 65765
Keratoplasty
  endothelial ~ 65756
    allograft preparation ~ 65757
  lamellar ~ 65710
  penetrating ~ 65730
    in aphakia ~ 65750
    in pseudophakia ~ 65755
Keratoprosthesis ~ 65770
Keratotomy, radial ~ 65771
Ketogenic steroids ~ 83582
Ketone body, acetone ~ 82009-82010
Ketosteroids ~ 83586-83593
Kidner procedure ~ 28238
Kidney
  abscess
    incision and drainage ~ 50020
  anesthesia ~ 00862
  biopsy ~ 50200-50205
    endoscopic ~ 50555-50559, 52354
  catheterization, endoscopic ~ 50572
  cyst
    ablation ~ 50541
    aspiration ~ 50390
    excision ~ 50280-50290
    injection ~ 50390
    X-ray ~ 74470
  destruction
    calculus ~ 50590
    endoscopic ~ 50557, 50576, 52354
  dilation ~ 50395
  endoscopy
    biopsy ~ 50555, 50574-50576, 52354
    catheterization ~ 50553, 50572
    destruction ~ 50557, 50576, 52354
    dilation
      intra-renal stricture ~ 52343, 52346
      ureter ~ 50553
    excision tumor ~ 52355
    exploration ~ 52351
    lithotripsy ~ 52353
    removal
      calculus ~ 50561, 50580, 52352
      foreign body ~ 50561, 50580
    via incision ~ 50562-50580
    via stoma ~ 50551-50561
  excision
    donor ~ 50300-50320, 50547
    partial ~ 50240
    recipient ~ 50340
    transplantation ~ 50370
    with ureters ~ 50220-50236
  exploration ~ 50010, 50045, 50120
  incision ~ 50010, 50045
  incision and drainage ~ 50040, 50125
  injection
    drugs ~ 50391
    for nephrostogram ~ 50430, 50431
  insertion, guide ~ 50395
  instillation drugs ~ 50391
  lithotripsy ~ 50590
  manometry pressure ~ 50396
  mass ablation ~ 50542
  needle biopsy ~ 50200
  nuclear medicine
    function study ~ 78725
    imaging ~ 78700-78710
    unlisted services and procedures ~ 78799
  placement, catheter
    nephrostomy ~ 50432
    nephroureteral ~ 50433
  removal
    calculus ~ 50060-50081, 50130, 50561
    foreign body ~ 50561, 50580
  repair
    blood vessels ~ 50100
    fistula ~ 50520-50526
    horseshoe kidney ~ 50540
    renal pelvis ~ 50400-50405
    wound ~ 50500

Kidney ~ *continued*
solitary ~ 50405
suture
  fistula ~ 50520-50526
  horseshoe kidney ~ 50540
transplantation
  anesthesia
    donor ~ 00862
    recipient ~ 00868
  allograft preparation ~ 50323-50329
  donor ~ 00862
  donor nephrectomy ~ 50300-50320, 50547
  implantation of graft ~ 50360
  recipient nephrectomy ~ 50340, 50365
  reimplantation kidney ~ 50380
  removal transplant renal autograft ~ 50370
ultrasound ~ 76770-76776
Kidney stone ~ see calculus, removal, kidney
Killian operation ~ see sinusotomy, frontal
Kinase, creatine ~ see CPK
Kineplasty ~ see cineplasty
Kinetic therapy ~ 97530
Kininase A ~ see angiotensin converting enzyme (ACE)
Kininogen ~ 85293
Kininogen, high molecular weight ~ see Fitzgerald factor
Kleihauer-Betke test ~ 85460
Kloramfenikol ~ see chloramphenicol
Knee ~ see femur; fibula; patella; tibia
abscess ~ 27301
arthrocentesis ~ 20610
arthrodesis ~ 27580
arthroplasty ~ 27440-27445, 27447
  revision ~ 27486-27487
arthroscopy
  diagnostic ~ 29870
  surgical ~ 29866-29868, 29871-29889
arthrotomy ~ 27310, 27330-27335, 27403
autograft, osteochondral, open ~ 27416
biopsy ~ 27323-27324, 27330-27331
  synovium ~ 27330
bone, drainage ~ 27303
bursa ~ 27301
  excision ~ 27340
cyst, excision ~ 27345-27347
disarticulation ~ 27598
dislocation ~ 27550-27552, 27560-27562
  open treatment ~ 27556-27558, 27566
drainage ~ 27310
excision
  cartilage ~ 27332-27333
  ganglion ~ 27347
  lesion ~ 27347
  synovial lung ~ 27334-27335
exploration ~ 27310, 27331
fasciotomy ~ 27305, 27496-27499
fracture ~ 27520-27524
  arthroscopic treatment ~ 29850-29851
fusion ~ 27580
hematoma ~ 27301
incision, capsule ~ 27435
injection, X-ray ~ 27370
magnetic resonance (MRI) ~ 73721-73723
manipulation ~ 27570
meniscectomy ~ 27332-27333
reconstruction ~ 27437-27438
  ligament ~ 27427-27429
  with prosthesis ~ 27445
removal
  foreign body ~ 27310, 27331, 27372
  loose body ~ 27331
  prosthesis ~ 27488
repair
  ligament ~ 27405-27409
    collateral ~ 27405
    collateral and cruciate ~ 27409
    cruciate ~ 27407-27409
    meniscus ~ 27403
    tendon ~ 27380-27381
replacement ~ 27447
  sensor ~ 0396T

Knee ~ *continued*
retinacular release ~ 27425
strapping ~ 29530
suture tendon ~ 27380-27381
transplantation
  chondrocytes ~ 27412
  meniscus ~ 29868
  osteochondral
    allograft ~ 27415-29867
    autograft ~ 27412-29866
tumor excision ~ 27327-27329, 27337-27339, 27365
unlisted services and procedures ~ 27599
X-ray ~ 73560-73564
  arthrography ~ 73580
  bilateral ~ 73565
X-ray with contrast arthrography ~ 73580
Knee cap
excision ~ 27350
repair, instability ~ 27420-27424
Knee joint arthroplasty ~ 27446
Knee prosthesis ~ see prosthesis, knee
Knock-knee repair ~ 27455-27457
Kocher operation ~ 23650-23680
Kocher pylorectomy ~ see gastrectomy, partial
Kock pouch ~ 44316
formation ~ 50825
Kock procedure ~ 44316
Kraske procedure ~ 45116
Krause operation ~ see gasserian ganglion, sensory root, decompression
Kroenlein procedure ~ 67420
Krukenberg procedure ~ 25915
Kuhlmann test ~ 96100
Kyphectomy
more than two segments ~ 22819
up to two segments ~ 22818

L

L-alanine ~ see aminolevulinic acid (ALA)
L ascorbic acid ~ see ascorbic acid
L aspartate 2 oxoglutarate aminotransferase ~ see transaminase, glutamic oxaloacetic
L glutamine ~ see glutamine
L-leucylnaphthylamidase ~ see leucine aminopeptidase
L/S ratio, amniotic fluid ~ 83661
Labial adhesions, lysis ~ 56441
Laboratory panel
ACTH stimulation panel ~ 80400
acute hepatitis panel ~ 80074
basic metabolic panel ~ 80048
comprehensive metabolic panel ~ 80053
corticotropic releasing hormone (CRH) stimulation panel ~ 80412
electrolyte panel ~ 80051
general health panel ~ 80050
glucagon tolerance panel ~ 80422-80424
gonadotropin releasing hormone stimulation panel ~ 80426
growth hormone
  stimulation panel ~ 80428
  suppression panel ~ 80430
hepatic function panel ~ 80076
insulin
  tolerance panel ~ 80434-80435
  induced C-peptide suppression panel ~ 80432
lipid panel ~ 80061
metyrapone panel ~ 80436
obstetric panel ~ 80055
renal function ~ 80069
thyrotropin releasing hormone (TRH) stimulation panel ~ 80438-80439, 84146
Laboratory services ~ 8000-8999
anatomic pathology ~ 88000-88999
chemistry, unlisted ~ 84999
consultations, clinical pathology ~ 80500-80502
cytogenetic studies ~ 88230-88299
cytopathology ~ 88104-88199
evocative/suppression testing ~ 80400-80439, 84146
hematology and coagulation ~ 85002-85999

Laboratory services ~ *continued*
immunology ~ 86000-86849
microbiology ~ 87999
organ or disease oriented panels ~ 80048-80076
other pathology and laboratory procedures ~ 89050-89240
reproductive medicine procedures ~ 89250-89356
surgical pathology ~ 88300-88399
therapeutic drug assays ~ 80150-80299
transcutaneous procedures ~ 88720
transfusion medicine ~ 86850-86999
urinalysis ~ 81000-81099
Labyrinth ~ see ear, inner
Labyrinthectomy ~ 69905
with mastoidectomy ~ 69910
with skull base surgery ~ 61596
Labyrinthotomy
transcanal ~ 69801
Laceration repair ~ see specific site **
Lacrimal duct
canaliculi, repair ~ 68700
exploration ~ 68810
with anesthesia ~ 68811
canaliculi ~ 68840
stent ~ 68815
insertion, stent ~ 68815
removal
dacryolith ~ 68530
foreign body ~ 68530
X-ray with contrast ~ 70170
Lacrimal gland
biopsy ~ 68510
close fistula ~ 68770
excision
partial ~ 68505
total ~ 68500
fistulization ~ 68720
incision and drainage ~ 68400
injection, X-ray ~ 68850
nuclear medicine, tear flow ~ 78660
removal
dacryolith ~ 68530
foreign body ~ 68530
repair, fistula ~ 68770
tumor, excision
without closure ~ 68540
with osteotomy ~ 68550
Lacrimal punctum
closure
by plug ~ 68761
by thermocauterization, ligation or laser surgery ~ 68760
dilation ~ 68801
incision ~ 68440
repair ~ 68705
Lacrimal sac
biopsy ~ 68525
excision ~ 68520
incision and drainage ~ 68420
Lacrimal system, unlisted services and procedures ~ 68899
Lactase deficiency breath test ~ 91065
Lactate ~ 83605
Lactate dehydrogenase ~ see lactic dehydrogenase
Lactic acid ~ 83605
Lactic acid measurement ~83605
Lactic cytochrome reductase ~ see lactic dehydrogenase
Lactic dehydrogenase ~ 83615-83625
Lactiferous duct
excision ~ 19112
exploration ~ 19110
Lactoferrin, fecal ~ 83630
Lactogen, human placental ~ 83632
Lactogenic hormone ~ see prolactin
Lactose, urine ~ 83633
Ladd procedure ~ 44055
Lagophthalmos, repair ~ 67912
Laki Lorand factor ~ see fibrin stabilizing factor
Lamblia intestinalis ~ see giardia lamblia
Lambrinudi operation ~ see arthrodesis, foot joint
Lamellar keratoplasties ~ see keratoplasty, lamellar
Laminaria, insertion ~ 59200

Laminectomy ~ 62351, 63001, 63005-63011, 63015-63044, 63180-63200, 63265-63290, 63300-63655
with facetectomy ~ 63045-63048
lumbar ~ 22630, 63012
surgical ~ 63170-63172
Laminoplasty, cervical ~ 63050-63051
Langerhans islands ~ see islet cell
Language evaluation
comprehension and expression ~ 92523
speech fluency ~ 92521
speech sound production ~ 92522
voice resonance ~ 92524
Language therapy ~ 92507-92508
LAP ~ 83670
Laparoscopic appendectomy ~ see appendectomy, laparoscopic
Laparoscopic biopsy of ovary ~ see biopsy, ovary, laparoscopic
Laparoscopy
abdominal ~ 49320-49327, 49329
adrenalectomy ~ 50545
adrenal gland, biopsy or excision ~ 60650
appendectomy ~ 44970
aspiration ~ 49322
biopsy ~ 49321
lymph nodes ~ 38570
bladder repair ~ 51990, 51992, 51999
cecostomy ~ 44188
cholecystectomy ~ 47562-47564
cholecystenterostomy ~ 47570
colectomy
laparoscopic ~ 44213
partial ~ 44204-44208, 44213
total ~ 44210-44212
colostomy ~ 44188
destruction, lesion ~ 58662
ectopic pregnancy ~ 59150
with salpingectomy and/or oophorectomy ~ 59151
enterectomy ~ 44202
enterolysis ~ 44180
enterostomy, closure ~ 44227
esophageal lengthening ~ 43283
esophagus
esophagogastric fundoplasty ~ 43280
esophagomyotomy fundoplasty ~ 43279
hernia repair ~ 43281, 43282
lengthening ~ 43283
sphincter augmentation
device placement ~ 43284
device removal ~ 43285
fimbrioplasty ~ 58672
gastrectomy, longitudinal/sleeve ~ 43775
gastric
electrode
implantation ~ 43647, 43648
removal ~ 43648
replacement ~ 43647
gastric ~ 43648
restrictive procedures ~ 43644-43645, 43770-43775
gastrostomy, temporary ~ 43653
hernia repair
epigastric
incarcerated or strangulated ~ 49653
reducible ~ 49652
incisional
incarcerated or strangulated ~ 49655
reducible ~ 49654
incisional recurrent
incarcerated or strangulated ~ 49657
reducible ~ 49656
inguinal
initial ~ 49650
recurrent ~ 49651
paraesophageal ~ 43281-43282
spigelian
incarcerated or strangulated ~ 49653
reducible ~ 49652
umbilical
incarcerated or strangulated ~ 49653
reducible ~ 49652
ventral
incarcerated or strangulated ~ 49653
reducible ~ 49652

Laparoscopy ~ continued
  hysterectomy ~ 58541-58544
    radical ~ 58548
    total ~ 58570-58573, 58575
  ileostomy ~ 44187
  incontinence repair ~ 51990-51992
  in vitro fertilization ~ 58976
    retrieve oocyte ~ 58970
    transfer embryo ~ 58974
    transfer gamete ~ 58976
  jejunostomy ~ 44186-44187
  kidney, ablation ~ 50541-50542
  ligation, veins, spermatic ~ 55550
  liver ablation, tumor ~ 47370-47371
  lymph system
    biopsy ~ 38570
    lymphadenectomy ~ 38571-38573
  lysis of adhesions ~ 58660
  lysis of intestinal adhesions ~ 44180
  nephrectomy ~ 50545-50548
    partial ~ 50543
  omentopexy ~ 49326
  orchiectomy ~ 54690
  orchiopexy ~ 54692
  oviduct surgery ~ 58670-58671, 58679
  pelvis ~ 49320
  proctectomy
    complete ~ 45395
    with creation of colonic reservoir ~ 45397
  proctopexy, for prolapse ~ 45400-45402
  prostatectomy ~ 55866
  pyeloplasty ~ 50544
  rectum, resection ~ 45395-45397
    unlisted ~ 45499
  removal
    fallopian tubes ~ 58661
    leiomyomata ~ 58545-58546
    ovaries ~ 58661
    spleen ~ 38120
    testis ~ 54690
  resection, intestines, with anastomosis ~ 44202-44203
  salpingostomy ~ 58673
  splenectomy ~ 38120-38129
  splenic flexure, mobilization ~ 44213
  stomach ~ 43647-43659
    gastric bypass ~ 43644-63645
    gastric restrictive ~ 43770-43775, 43848, 43886-43888
    gastroenterostomy ~ 43644-43645
    gastrostomy, temporary ~ 43653
    neurostimulator electrode
      implantation ~ 0312T, 43647
      removal ~ 0314T, 43648
      replacement ~ 0313T, 43647
      revision ~ 0313T, 43648
    Roux-en-Y ~ 43644
  testis
    orchiectomy ~ 54690
    orchiopexy ~ 54692
    unlisted procedure ~ 54699
  transplantation, donor allograft preparation, kidney ~ 50325
  uterus
    ablation, fibroids ~ 58674
    hysterectomy ~ 58541-58544
      radical ~ 58548
      total ~ 58570-58573, 58575
  unlisted services and procedures ~ 38129, 38589, 43289, 43659,
    44238-44239, 44979, 47379, 47579, 49329, 49659, 50549, 50949,
    54699, 55559, 58578-58579, 58679, 59898
  ureterolithotomy ~ 50945
  ureteroneocystostomy ~ 50947-50948
  urethral suspension ~ 51990
  vaginal hysterectomy ~ 58550-58554
  vaginal suspension ~ 57425
  vagus nerves, transection ~ 43651-43652
Laparotomy
  with biopsy ~ 49000
  exploration ~ 47015, 49000-49002, 58960
  hemorrhage control ~ 49002
  second look ~ 58960
  staging ~ 58960
  for staging ~ 49220

Laparotomy, exploratory ~ see abdomen, exploration
Lapidus procedure ~ 28297
Large bowel ~ see anus; cecum; rectum
Laroyenne operation ~ see vagina, abscess, incision and drainage, 57010
Laryngeal function study ~ 92520
Laryngeal sensory testing ~ 92614-92617
Laryngectomy ~ 31360-31382
  partial ~ 31367-31382
  subtotal ~ 31367-31368
Laryngocele, removal ~ 31300
Laryngofissure ~ 31300
Laryngopharyngectomy ~ see excision, larynx, with pharynx, 31390, 31395
Laryngopharynx ~ see hypopharynx
Laryngoplasty
  cricoid split ~ 31587
  for fracture
    fixation ~ 31584
    open reduction ~ 31584
  for laryngeal stenosis ~ 31551-31554
  laryngeal web ~ 31580
  medialization ~ 31591
Laryngoscopy
  direct ~ 31515-31571
    aspiration ~ 31515
    biopsy ~ 31535, 31536
    diagnostic ~ 31525, 31526
    dilation ~ 31528, 31529
    exploration ~ 31520-31526, 31575
    newborn ~ 31520
  flexible ~ 31575-31579
    ablation, lesion ~ 31572
    biopsy ~ 31576
    diagnostic ~ 31575
    injection, vocal cord ~ 31570, 31571, 31573, 31574
    laser destruction, lesion ~ 31572
    removal
      foreign body ~ 31577
      lesion ~ 31578
  indirect ~ 31505-31513
    biopsy ~ 31510
    diagnostic ~ 31505
    exploration ~ 31505
    injection, vocal cord ~ 31513
  insertion
    obturator ~ 31527
  newborn ~ 31520
  with stroboscopy ~ 31579
Laryngotomy ~ 31300
Larynx
  aspiration, endoscopy ~ 31515
  biopsy, endoscopy ~ 31510, 31535-31536, 31576
  dilation, endoscopic ~ 31528-31529
  endoscopy
    ablation, lesion ~ 31572
    direct ~ 31515-31571
    excision ~ 31545-31546
    exploration ~ 31505, 31520-31526, 31575
    flexible ~ 31575-31579
      with stroboscopy ~ 31579
    indirect ~ 31505-31513
    laser destruction, lesion ~ 31572
    operative ~ 31530-31561
  excision
    lesion ~ 31512, 31578
      endoscopic ~ 31545-31546
    partial ~ 31367-31382
    with pharynx ~ 31390-31395
    total ~ 31360-31365
  exploration, endoscopic ~ 31505, 31520-31526, 31575
  fracture, closed treatment
    with manipulation ~ 31586
    without manipulation ~ 31585
    open treatment ~ 31584
  insertion, obturator ~ 31527
  lesion
    ablation ~ 31572
    laser destruction ~ 31572
    removal ~ 31512, 31578
  medialization ~ 31591

1087

Larynx ~ *continued*
nerve, destruction ~ 31595
reconstruction
  cricoid split ~ 31587
  stenosis ~ 31551-31554
  web ~ 31580
removal
  foreign body, endoscopic ~ 31511, 31530-31531, 31577
  lesion, endoscopic ~ 31512, 31545-31546, 31578
repair, reinnervation neuromuscular pedicle ~ 31590
stroboscopy ~ 31579
tumor excision ~ 31300
  endoscopic ~ 31540-31541
unlisted services and procedures ~ 31599
vocal cord(s)
  injection ~ 31513, 31570, 31571, 31573, 31574
  stripping ~ 31540, 31541
X-ray ~ 70370
Laser surgery
anal ~ , 46614, 46917
cautery, esophagus ~ 43227
fenestration, body surface ~ 0479T, 0480T
lacrimal punctum ~ 68760
lens, posterior ~ 66821
lesion
  larynx ~ 31572
  mouth ~ 40820
  nose ~ 30117-30118
  penis ~ 54057
  skin ~ 17000-17111, 17260-17286
myocardium ~ 33140-33141
prostate ~ 52647-52649
spine, diskectomy ~ 62287
tumors, urethra and bladder ~ 52234
urethra and bladder ~ 52214
Laser treatment ~ see destruction ~ 17000-17286, 96920-96922
Lateral epicondylitis ~ see tennis elbow
Latex fixation ~ 86403-86406
LATS ~ see thyrotropin releasing hormone (TRH)
Latzko operation ~ see repair, vagina, fistula; revision
LAV ~ see HIV
LAV-2 (two) ~ see HIV-2 (two)
LAV antibodies ~ see antibody, HIV
Lavage
colon ~ 44701
lung
  bronchial ~ 31624
  total ~ 32997
peritoneal ~ 49084
stomach ~ 43753
LCM ~ see lymphocytic choriomeningitis
LD ~ lactic dehydrogenase, 83615
LDH ~ 83615-83625
LDL ~ 83721
Lead ~ 83655
Leadbetter procedure ~ 53431
Lecithin-sphingomyelin ratio ~ 83661
Lecithinase C ~ see tissue typing
Lee and White test ~ 85345
Leep procedure ~ 57460
Lefort procedure, vagina ~ 57120
Lefort I procedure
midface reconstruction ~ 21141-21147, 21155, 21160
palatal of maxillary fracture ~ 21421-21423
Lefort II procedure
midface reconstruction ~ 21150-21151
nasomaxillary complex fracture ~ 21345-21348
Lefort III procedure
craniofacial separation ~ 21431-21436
midface reconstruction ~ 21154-21159
Left atrioventricular valve ~ see mitral valve
Left heart cardiac catheterization ~ see cardiac catheterization, left heart
Leg
cast
  full let ~ 29705
  rigid total contact ~ 29445
incision
  embolectomy ~ 34201, 34203
  thrombectomy ~ 34201, 34203, 34421, 34451
injection, sclerosant ~ 36465, 36466, 36468, 36470, 36471

Leg ~ *continued*
lower ~ see also ankle; fibula; knee; tibia
  abscess, incision and drainage ~ 27603
  amputation ~ 27598, 27880-27882
    revision ~ 27884-27886
  angiography ~ 73706
  artery, ligation ~ 37618
  biopsy ~ 27613-27614
  bursa, incision and drainage ~ 27604
  bypass graft ~ 35903
  cast ~ 29405-29435, 29450
  CAT scan ~ 73700-73706
  decompression ~ 27600-27602
  exploration, blood vessel ~ 35860
  fasciotomy ~ 27600-27602, 27892-27894
  hematoma, incision and drainage ~ 27603
  lesion, excision ~ 27630
  magnetic resonance imaging (MRI) ~ 73718-73720
  repair
    blood vessel ~ 35226
      with other graft ~ 35286
      with vein graft ~ 35256
    fascia ~ 27656
    tendon ~ 27658-27692
  splint ~ 29515
  strapping ~ 29580
  suture, tendon ~ 27658-27665
  tumor, excision ~ 27615-27619, 27632, 27634
  unlisted services and procedures ~ 27899
  Unna boot ~ 29580
  X-ray ~ 73592
upper ~ see femur
  abscess ~ 27301
  amputation ~ 27590-27592
    at hip ~ 27290-27295
    revision ~ 27594-27596
  angiography ~ 73706, 75635
  artery, ligation ~ 37618
  biopsy ~ 27323-27324
  bursa ~ 27301
  bypass graft ~ 35903
  cast ~ 29345-29355, 29365, 29450
  cast brace ~ 29358
  CT scan ~ 73700-73706, 75635
  exploration, blood vessel ~ 35860
  fasciotomy ~ 27305, 27496-27499, 27892-27894
  halo application ~ 20663
  hematoma ~ 27301
  magnetic resonance imaging (MRI) ~ 73718-73720
  neurectomy ~ 27325-27326
  removal
    cast ~ 29705
    foreign body ~ 27372
  repair
    blood vessel with other graft ~ 35286
    blood vessel with vein graft ~ 35256
    muscle ~ 27385-27386, 27400, 27430
    tendon ~ 27393-27400
  splint ~ 29505
  strapping ~ 29580
  suture, muscle ~ 27385-27386
  tenotomy ~ 27306-27307, 27390-27392
  tumor, excision ~ 27327-27329, 27337-27339, 27365
  unlisted services and procedures ~ 27599
  Unna boot ~ 29580
  X-ray ~ 73592
wound exploration, penetrating ~ 20103
Legionella
antibody ~ 86713
antigen ~ 87278, 87540-87542
Legionella pneumophila antigen detection, direct fluorescence ~ 87278
Leg length measurement X-ray ~ see scanogram
Leiomyomata, removal ~ 58140, 58545-58546, 58561
Leishmania, antibody ~ 86717
Lengthening, tendon ~ see tendon, lengthening
Lens
extracapsular ~ 66940
intracapsular ~ 66920
  dislocated ~ 66930

Lens ~ *continued*
  intraocular
    exchange ~ 66986
    reposition ~ 66825
    prosthesis, insertion ~ 66983
      manual or mechanical technique ~ 66982, 66984
      not associated with concurrent cataract removal ~ 66985
    removal, lens material
      aspiration technique ~ 66840
      extracapsular ~ 66940
      intracapsular ~ 66920-66930
      pars plana approach ~ 66852
      phacofragmentation technique ~ 66850
Lens material
  aspiration technique ~ 66840
  pars plana approach ~ 66852
  phacofragmentation technique ~ 66850
Leptomeningioma ~ see meningioma
Leptospira, antibody ~ 86720
Leriche operation ~ (thoracolumbar sympathectomy) 64809
Lesion ~ see tumor
  ablation
    endoscopic retrograde cholangio- pancreatography (ERCP) ~ 43278
    stereotactic MRI guided high intensity focused ultrasound (MRgFUS) ~ 0398T
  anal
    destruction ~ 46900-46917, 46924
    excision ~ 45108, 46922
  ankle, tendon sheath ~ 27630
  arm, lower
    tendon sheath
      excision ~ 25110
  auditory canal, external
    excision
      exostosis ~ 69140
      radical with neck dissection ~ 69155
      radical without neck dissection ~ 69150
      soft tissue ~ 69145
  bladder, destruction ~ 51030
  brain
    excision ~ 61534, 61536, 61600-61608, 61615-61616
    radiation treatment ~ 77432
  brainstem, excision ~ 61575-61576
  breast
    detection, mammography ~ 77065-77067
    excision ~ 19120-19126
  carotid body, excision ~ 60600-60605
  chemotherapy ~ 96405-96406
    destruction ~ 67220-67225
  ciliary body, destruction ~ 66770
  colon
    destruction ~ 44401, 45383
    excision ~ 44110-44111
  conjunctiva
    destruction ~ 68135
    excision ~ 68110-68130
      over 1cm ~ 68115
      with adjacent sclera ~ 68130
    expression ~ 68040
  cornea
    destruction ~ 65450
    excision ~ 65400
      of pterygium ~ 65420-65426
  destruction, ureter ~ 52341-52342, 52344-52345, 52354
  ear, middle, excision ~ 69540
  epididymis, excision ~ 54830
  esophagus
    ablation ~ 43229
    excision ~ 43100-43101
    removal ~ 43216
  excision ~ 59100
    bladder ~ 52224
    urethra ~ 52224, 53265
  eye, excision ~ 65900
  eyelid
    destruction ~ 67850
    excision
      under anesthesia ~ 67808
      without closure ~ 67840
    multiple, different lids ~ 67805

Lesion ~ *continued*
    multiple, same lid ~ 67801
    single ~ 67800
  facial, destruction ~ 17000-17004, 17280-17286
  femur, excision ~ 27062
  finger, tendon sheath ~ 26160
  foot, excision ~ 28080, 28090
  gums
    destruction ~ 41850
    excision ~ 41822-41828
  hand tendon sheath ~ 26160
  intestines, excision ~ 44110
  intestines, small
    destruction ~ 44369
    excision ~ 44111
  iris, destruction ~ 66770
  larynx
    ablation ~ 31572
    laser destruction ~ 31572
    removal ~ 31512, 31545, 31546, 31578
  leg, lower, tendon sheath ~ 27630
  lymph node, incision and drainage ~ 38300-38305
  mesentery, excision ~ 44820
  mouth
    destruction ~ 40820
    excision ~ 40810-40816, 41116
    vestibule
      destruction ~ 40820
      repair ~ 40830
  nerve, excision ~ 64774-64792
  nose, intranasal
    external approach ~ 30118
    internal approach ~ 30117
  orbit, excision ~ 61333, 67412
  palate
    destruction ~ 42160
    excision ~ 42104-42120
  pancreas, excision ~ 48120
  pelvis, destruction ~ 58662
  penis
    destruction
      cryosurgery ~ 54056
      electrodesiccation ~ 54055
      extensive ~ 54065
      laser surgery ~ 54057
      simple ~ 54050-54060
      surgical excision ~ 54060
    excision ~ 54060
      penile plague ~ 54110-54112
  pharynx
    destruction ~ 42808
    excision ~ 42808
  rectum, excision ~ 45108
  removal, larynx ~ 31512, 31578
  resection ~ 52354
  retina
    destruction
      extensive ~ 67227-67228
      localized ~ 67208-67210
    radiation by implantation of source ~ 67218
  sclera, excision ~ 66130
  skin
    abrasion ~ 15786, 15787
    biopsy ~ 11100, 11101
    destruction
      benign ~ 17110, 17111, 17250
      malignant ~ 17260-17286
      premalignant ~ 17000-17004
    excision
      benign ~ 11400-11471
      malignant ~ 11600-11646
    injection ~ 11900-11901
    multi-spectral analysis ~ 0400T, 0401T
    paring or curettement ~ 11055-11057
    reflectance confocal microscopic imaging ~ 96931
    shaving ~ 11300-11313
  skin tags, removal ~ 11200, 11201
  skull, excision ~ 61500, 61600-61608, 61615-61616
  spermatic cord, excision ~ 55520

Lesion ~ *continued*
  spinal cord
    destruction ~ 62280-62282
    excision ~ 63265-63273
  stomach, excision ~ 43611
  testis, excision ~ 54512
  toe, excision ~ 28092
  tongue, excision ~ 41110-41114
  uvula
    destruction ~ 42145
    excision ~ 42104-42107
  vagina, destruction ~ 57061-57065
  vulva
    destruction
      extensive ~ 56515
      simple ~ 56501
  wrist tendon, excision ~ 25110
Lesion of sciatic nerve ~ see sciatic nerve, lesion
Leucine aminopeptidase ~ 83670
Leukemia lymphoma virus I (one), adult T cell ~ see HTLV I (one)
Leukemia lymphoma virus II (two) antibodies, human T cell ~ see antibody, HTLV-II (two)
Leukemia lymphoma virus I (one) antibodies, human T cell ~ see antibody, HTLV I (one)
Leukemia virus II (two), hairy cell associated, human T cell ~ see HTLV II (two)
Leukoagglutinins ~ 86021
Leukocyte ~ see also white blood cell
  alkaline phosphatase ~ 85540
  antibody ~ 86021
  count ~ 85032, 85048, 89055
  histamine release test ~ 86343
  phagocytosis ~ 86344
  transfusion ~ 86950
Leu 2 antigens ~ see CD8
Levarterenol ~ see noradrenalin
Levator muscle rep ~ (blepharoptosis, repair) 67901-67909
Leveen shunt
  insertion ~ 49425
  patency test ~ 78291
  revision ~ 49426
Levulose ~ see fructose
LH ~ (luteinizing hormone) 80418, 80426, 83002
LHR ~ (leukocyte histamine release test) 86343
Lid suture ~ (blepharoptosis, repair) 67901-67909
Lidocaine, assay ~ 80176
Lift, face ~ see face lift
Ligament ~ see specific site
  collateral repair, knee with cruciate ligament ~ 27409
  dentate
    incision ~ 63180-63182
    section ~ 63180-63182
  injection ~ 20550
  release
    coracoacromial ~ 23415
    transverse carpal ~ 29848
  repair
    elbow ~ 24343-24346
    knee joint ~ 27405-27409
Ligation
  artery
    abdomen ~ 37617
    carotid ~ 37600-37606
    chest ~ 37616
    coronary ~ 33502
    coronary artery ~ 33502
    ethmoidal ~ 30915
    extremity ~ 37618
    fistula ~ 37607
    maxillary ~ 30920
    neck ~ 37615
    temporal ~ 37609
  esophageal varices ~ 43204, 43400
  fallopian tube, oviduct ~ 58600-58611, 58670
  gastroesophageal ~ 43405
  hemorrhoids ~ 46945-46946
  oviducts ~ 59100
  salivary duct ~ 42665

Ligation ~ *continued*
  shunt
    aorta, pulmonary ~ 33924
    peritoneal, venous ~ 49428
  thoracic duct ~ 38380
    abdominal approach ~ 38382
    thoracic approach ~ 38381
  vein
    clusters ~ 37785
    esophagus ~ 43205, 43244, 43400
    femoral ~ 37650
    gastric ~ 43244
    iliac ~ 37660
    jugular, internal ~ 37565
    perforate ~ 37500, 37760, 37761
    saphenous ~ 37700-37735, 37780
    spermatic ~ 55530, 55535, 55540, 55550
    vena cava ~ 37619
Ligature strangulation, skin tags ~ 11200-11201
Light coagulation ~ see photocoagulation
Light scattering measurement ~ see nephelometry
Light therapy, UV ~ see actinotherapy
Limb ~ see extremity
Limited lymphadenectomy for staging ~ see lymphadenectomy, limited, for staging
Limited neck dissection, with thyroidectomy ~ 60252
Limited resection mastectomies ~ see breast, excision, lesion
Lindholm operation ~ see tenoplasty
Lingual bone ~ see hyoid bone
Lingual frenectomy ~ see excision, tongue, frenum
Lingual nerve
  avulsion ~ 64740
  incision ~ 64740
  transection ~ 64740
Lingual tonsil ~ see tonsils, lingual
Linton procedure ~ 37760-37761
Lip
  biopsy ~ 40490
  excision ~ 40500-40530
    frenum ~ 40819
  incision, frenum ~ 40806
  reconstruction ~ 40525-40527
  repair ~ 40650-40654
    cleft lip ~ 40700-40761
    fistula ~ 42260
  unlisted services and procedures ~ 40799
Lip, cleft ~ see cleft lip
Lipase ~ 83690
Lipectomies, aspiration ~ see liposuction
Lipectomy ~ 15830-15839
  suction assisted ~ 15876-15879
Lipids, feces ~ 82705-82710
Lipo-lutin ~ see progesterone
Lipolysis, aspiration ~ see liposuction
Lipophosphodiesterase I (one) ~ see tissue typing
Lipoprotein
  (a) ~ 83695
  blood ~ 83695, 83700-83721
  LDL ~ 83700-83704-, 83721
  phospholipase A2 ~ 83698
Lipoprotein, alpha ~ see lipoprotein
Lipoprotein, pre-beta ~ see lipoprotein, blood
Liposuction ~ 15876-15879
Lisfranc operation ~ see amputation, foot; radical resection; replantation
Listeria monocytogenes, antibody ~ 86723
Lithium, assay ~ 80178
Litholapaxy ~ 52317-52318
Lithotripsy ~ see extracorporeal shock wave therapy
  bile duct calculi (stone), endoscopy ~ 43265
  bladder ~ 52353
  kidney ~ 50590, 52353
  pancreatic duct calculi (stone), endoscopy ~ 43265
  ureter ~ 52353
  urethra ~ 52353
  with cystourethroscopy ~ 52353
Lithotrity ~ see litholapaxy

Lung ~ *continued*
  removal ~ 32440-32445
    bilobectomy ~ thoracoscopic ~ 32670
    bronchial valve ~ 31648-31649
    bronchoplasty ~ 32501
    completion pneumonectomy ~ 32488
    extrapleural ~ 32445
    pneumonectomy 32440-32445
      thoracoscopic ~ 32671
    segmentectomy, thoracoscopic ~ 32669
    single lobe ~ 32480
    single segment ~ 32484
    sleeve lobectomy ~ 32486
    sleeve pneumonectomy ~ 32442
    two lobes ~ 32482
    volume reduction ~ 32491
  repair, hernia ~ 32800
  segmentectomy ~ 32484
  tear, repair ~ 32110
  thoracotomy
    biopsy ~ 32096-32097
    cardiac massage ~ 32160
    for post-op complications ~ 32120
    removal
      bullae ~ 32141
      cyst ~ 32140
      intrapleural foreign body ~ 32150
      intrapulmonary foreign body ~ 32151
    repair ~ 32110
  transplantation ~ 32851-32854, 33935
    allograft preparation
      heart/lung ~ 33933
      lung ~ 32855, 32856
      marginal (extended) lung ~ 0494T-0496T
    donor pneumonectomy
      heart-lung ~ 33930
      lung ~ 32850
  unlisted services and procedures ~ 32999
Lung function tests ~ see pulmonology, diagnostic
Lung volume reduction, emphysematous ~ 32491
Lupus anticoagulant assay ~ 85705
Lupus band test ~ see immunofluorescent study
Luteinizing hormone (LH) ~ 80418, 80426, 83002
Luteinizing releasing factor ~ 83727
Luteotropic hormone ~ see prolactin
Luteotropin ~ see prolactin
Luteotropin, placental ~ see lactogen, human placental
Lyme disease ~ 86617-86618
Lyme disease ab ~ see antibody, Lyme disease
Lyme disease vaccine ~ see vaccination
Lymph duct, injection ~ 38790
Lymph nodes
  abscess, incision and drainage ~ 38300-38305
  biopsy ~ 38500, 38510-38530, 38570
    needle ~ 38505
  dissection ~ 38542
  excision ~ 38500, 38510-38530
    abdominal ~ 38747
    aortic ~ 38780
    gastric ~ 38747
    hypogastric ~ 38770, 55845, 55865
    inguinofemoral ~ 38760-38765
    laparoscopic ~ 38571-38573
    limited, for staging
      para-aortic ~ 38562, 38747
    mediastinal ~ 21632, 32674, 38746
    obturator ~ 38770, 55845, 55865
      pelvic ~ 38562
      retroperitoneal ~ 38564
    pelvic ~ 38562, 38770, 38780, 57531
    radical
      axillary ~ 19305-19307, 38740-38745
      cervical ~ 38720-38724
      suprahyoid ~ 38700
    renal ~ 38780
    retroperitoneal transabdominal ~ 38780
    thoracic ~ 38746
  exploration ~ 38542
  gastric, excision ~ 38747

Lymph nodes ~ *continued*
  hilar, sampling
    endobrachial ultrasound (EBUS) guided ~ 31652, 31653
  hygroma, cystic
    axillary/cervical excision ~ 38550-38555
  hypogastric, excision ~ 38770, 55845, 55865
  mediastinal
    excision ~ 21632
      thoracoscopic ~ 32674
      by thoracotomy ~ 38746
  mediastinoscopy ~ 39402
    sampling, endobronchial ultrasound (EBUS) guided ~ 31652, 31653
  nuclear medicine, imaging ~ 78195
  removal
    abdominal ~ 38747
    inguinofemoral ~ 38760-38765
    pelvic ~ 38770
    retroperitoneal transabdominal ~ 38780
    thoracic ~ 38746
  sentinel, mapping ~ 38900
Lymph vessels
  abdomen, lymphangiography ~ 75805-75807
  arm, lymphangiography ~ 75801-75803
  leg, lymphangiography ~ 75801-75803
  nuclear medicine, imaging ~ 78195
  pelvis, lymphangiography ~ 75805-75807
Lymphadenectomy
  abdominal ~ 38747
  bilateral inguinofemoral ~ 54130, 56632, 56637
  bilateral pelvic ~ 51575, 51585, 51595, 54135, 55845, 55865
    total ~ 38571-38573, 57531, 58210
  diaphragmatic assessment ~ 58960
  gastric ~ 38747
  inguinofemoral ~ 38760-38765
  inguinofemoral, iliac and pelvic ~ 56640
  injection, sentinel node ~ 38792
  limited para-aortic, resection of ovarian malignancy ~ 58951, 58954
  limited pelvic ~ 55842, 55862, 58954
  limited, for staging
    para-aortic ~ 38562
    pelvic ~ 38562
    retroperitoneal ~ 38564
  mediastinal ~ 21632
  para-aortic ~ 58958
  pelvic ~ 58958
  peripancreatic ~ 38747
  portal ~ 38747
  radical
    axillary ~ 38740-38745
    cervical ~ 38720-38724
    pelvic ~ 54135, 55845, 58548
    suprahyoid ~ 38700
  regional ~ 50230
  retroperitoneal transabdominal ~ 38780
  thoracic ~ 38746
  unilateral inguinofemoral ~ 56631, 56634
Lymphadenitis, incision and drainage ~ 38300-38305
Lymphadenopathy associated antibodies ~ see antibody, HIV
Lymphadenopathy associated virus ~ see HIV
Lymphangiogram, abdominal ~ see lymphangiography, abdomen
Lymphangiography
  abdomen ~ 75805-75807
  arm ~ 75801-75803
  injection ~ 38790
  leg ~ 75801-75803
  pelvis ~ 75805-75807
Lymphangioma, cystic ~ see hygroma
Lymphangiotomy ~ 38308
Lymphatic channels, incision ~ 38308
Lymphatic cyst ~ see lymphocele
Lymphatic system, unlisted procedure ~ 38999
Lymphatics ~ see specific procedure
Lymphoblast transformation ~ see blastogenesis
Lymphocele
  drainage, laparoscopic ~ 49323
  extraperitoneal, open drainage ~ 49062
Lymphocoele ~ see lymphocele
Lymphocyte
  culture ~ 86821
  toxicity assay ~ 86805-86806
  transformation ~ 86353

Lymphocyte, thymus-dependent ~ see T cells
Lymphocytes, CD4 ~ see CD4
Lymphocytes, CD8 ~ see CD8
Lymphocytic choriomeningitis, antibody ~ 86727
Lymphocytotoxicity ~ 86805-86806
Lymphoma virus, Burkitt ~ see Epstein-Barr virus
Lynch procedure ~ 31075
Lysergide ~ see lysergic acid diethylamide
Lysis
  adhesions
    epidural ~ 62263-62264
    fallopian tube ~ 58740
    foreskin ~ 54450
    intestinal ~ 44005
    labial ~ 56441
    lung ~ 32124
    nose ~ 30560
    ovary ~ 58740
    oviduct ~ 58740
    penile, post-circumcision ~ 54162
    ureter ~ 50715-50725
    urethra ~ 53500
    uterus ~ 58559
  euglobulin ~ 85360
  labial, adhesions ~ 56441
  nose, intranasal synechia ~ 30560
Lysozyme ~ 85549

M

Macewen operation ~ see hernia, repair, inguinal
Machado test ~ (complement, fixation test) 86171
Maclean-De Wesselow test ~ see blood urea nitrogen; urea nitrogen, clearance
Macrodactylia, repair ~ 26590
Madlener operation ~ (tubal ligation) 58600
Magnesium ~ 83735
Magnet operation ~ see eye, removal of foreign body
Magnetic resonance, unlisted services and procedures ~ 76498
Magnetic resonance angiography (MRA)
  abdomen ~ 74185
  arm ~ 73225
  chest ~ 71555
  head ~ 70544-70546
  leg ~ 73725
  neck ~ 70547-70549
  pelvis ~ 72198
  spine ~ 72159
Magnetic resonance imaging (MRI)
  diagnostic
    3-D rendering ~ 76376, 76377
    abdomen ~ 74181-74183
    ankle ~ 73721-73723
    arm ~ 73218-73220, 73221-73223
    bone marrow study ~ 77084
    brain ~ 70551-70555
      intraoperative ~ 70557-70559
    chest ~ 71550-71552
    elbow ~ 73221
    face ~ 70540-70543
    fetal ~ 74712, 74713
    finger joint ~ 73221-73223
    foot ~ 73718-73719
    foot joints ~ 73721-73723
    hand ~ 73218-73220, 73223
    heart ~ 75557-75565
    joint
      lower extremity ~ 73721-73723
      upper extremity ~ 73221-73223
    knee ~ 73721-73723
    leg ~ 73718-73720
    neck ~ 70540-70543
    obstetrical, maternal pelvis ~ 74712, 74713
    pelvis ~ 72195-72197
    spectroscopy ~ 76390

Magnetic resonance imaging (MRI) ~ *continued*
  spine
    cervical ~ 72141, 72142, 72156
    lumbar ~ 72148, 72149, 72158
    thoracic ~ 72146, 72147, 72157
  temporomandibular joint (TMJ) ~ 70336
  toe ~ 73721-73723
  wrist ~ 73221
  guidance
    brain
      stereotactic lesion ablation
        MRgFUS ~ 0398T
      stereotactic lesion biopsy ~ 61751
    breast ~ 77058, 77059
      biopsy ~ 19085, 19086
      lesion localization device placement ~ 19085, 19086, 19287, 19288
      with computer-aided detection ~ 0159T
    needle placement ~ 77021
    parenchymal tissue ablation ~ 77022
  unlisted procedure ~ 76498
Magnetic resonance spectroscopy ~ 76390
Magnetic stimulation, transcranial ~ 90867-90868
Magnetoencephalography (MEG) ~ 95965-95967
Magnuson procedure ~ 23450
Magpi operation ~ (hypospadias, repair) 54322
Major vestibular gland ~ see Bartholin's gland
Malar area
  augmentation ~ 21270
  bone graft ~ 21210
  fracture
    with bone graft ~ 21366
    with manipulation ~ 21355
    open treatment ~ 21360-21366
  reconstruction ~ 21270
Malar bone ~ see cheekbone
Malaria antibody ~ 86750
Malaria smear ~ 87207
Malate dehydrogenase ~ 83775
Maldescent, testis ~ see testis, undescended
Male circumcision ~ see circumcision
Male genital system, surgical procedures ~ 54000-55899
Malformation, arteriovenous ~ see arteriovenous malformation
Malic dehydrogenase ~ (malate dehydrogenase) 83775
Malleolus ~ see ankle; fibula; leg, lower; tibia; tibiofibular joint
  metatarsophalangeal joint ~ 27889
Mallet finger repair ~ 26432
Maltose, tolerance test ~ 82951-82952
Malunion repair
  femur
    with graft ~ 27472
    without graft ~ 27470
  metatarsal ~ 28322
  tarsal joint ~ 28320
Mammalian oviduct ~ see fallopian tube
Mammaplasties ~ see breast, reconstruction
Mammary abscess ~ see abscess, breast
Mammary arteries ~ see artery, mammary
Mammary duct
  X-ray with contrast ~ 77053-77054
Mammary ductogram, injection ~ 19030
Mammary stimulating hormone ~ see prolactin
Mammilliplasty ~ see nipples, reconstruction
Mammography ~ 77065-77067
  localization, lesion, device placement ~ 19281, 19282
  magnetic resonance imaging (MRI) ~ 77058, 77059
    with computer aided detection ~ 0159T
  screening mammography ~ 77067
  tomosynthesis ~ 77061-77063
  with computer-aided detection ~ 77065-77067
Mammoplasty
  augmentation ~ 19324-19325
  reduction ~ 19318
Mammotomy ~ see mastotomy
Mammotropic hormone, pituitary ~ see prolactin
Mammotropic hormone, placental ~ see lactogen, human placental
Mammotropin ~ see prolactin
Mandated services, on call services ~ 99027

Mandible ~ see facial bones; maxilla; temporomandibular joint (TMJ)
  abscess, excision ~ 21025
  bone graft ~ 21215
  cyst, excision ~ 21040, 21046-21047
  fracture
    closed treatment
      with interdental fixation ~ 21453
      with manipulation ~ 21451
      without manipulation ~ 21450
    open treatment ~ 21454-21470
      external fixation ~ 21454
      with interdental fixation ~ 21462
      without interdental fixation ~ 21461
    percutaneous treatment ~ 21452
  osteotomy ~ 21198-21199
  reconstruction, with implant ~ 21244-21246, 21248-21249
  removal, foreign body ~ 41806
  torus mandibularis, excision ~ 21031
  tumor, excision ~ 21040-21047
  X-ray ~ 70100-70110
Mandibular body
  augmentation
    with bone graft ~ 21127
    with prosthesis ~ 21125
Mandibular condyle, fracture, open treatment ~ 21465
  reconstruction ~ 21247
Mandibular condylectomy ~ see condylectomy
Mandibular fracture ~ see fracture, mandible
Mandibular rami
  reconstruction
    with bone graft ~ 21194
    without bone graft ~ 21193
    with internal rigid fixation ~ 21196
    without internal rigid fixation ~ 21195
Mandibular resection prosthesis ~ 21081
Mandibular staple bone plate, reconstruction, mandible ~ 21244
Manganese ~ 83785
Manipulation
  chest wall ~ 94667-94668
  chiropractic ~ 98940-98943
  dislocation and/or fracture ~ 25535
    acetabulum ~ 27222
    acromioclavicular ~ 23545
    ankle ~ 27810, 27818, 27860
    carpometacarpal ~ 26670-26676
    clavicular ~ 23505
    elbow ~ 24300, 24640
    femoral ~ 27232, 27502, 27510, 27517
      pertrochanteric ~ 27240
    fibula ~ 27781, 27788
    finger ~ 26725-26727, 26742, 26755
    greater tuberosity, humeral ~ 23625
    hand ~ 26670-26676
    heel ~ 28405-28406
    hip ~ 27257
    hip socket ~ 27222
    humeral ~ 23605, 24505, 24535, 24577
      epicondyle ~ 24565
    hyoid ~ 21494
    intercarpal ~ 25660
    interphalangeal joint ~ 26340, 26770-26776
    larynx ~ 31586
    lunate ~ 25690
    malar area ~ 21355
    mandibular ~ 21451
    metacarpal ~ 26605-26607
    metacarpophalangeal ~ 26700-26706, 26742
    metacarpophlangeal joint ~ 26340
    metatarsal ~ 28475-28476
    nasal bone ~ 21315-21320
    orbit ~ 21401
    phalangeal shaft ~ 26727
      distal, finger or thumb ~ 26755
      phalanges, finger/thumb ~ 26725
    phalanges
      finger ~ 26742, 26755, 26770-26776
      finger/thumb ~ 26727
      great toe ~ 28495-28496
      toes ~ 28515
    radial ~ 24655, 25565

Manipulation ~ *continued*
  radial shaft ~ 25505
  radiocarpal ~ 25660
  radioulnar ~ 25675
  scapular ~ 23575
  shoulder ~ 23650-23655
    with greater tuberosity ~ 23665
  shoulder dislocation sternoclavicular ~ 23525
    with surgical or anatomical neck fracture ~ 23675
  talus ~ 28435-28436
  tarsal ~ 28455-28456
  thumb ~ 26641-26650
  tibial ~ 27532, 27752
  trans-scaphoperilunar ~ 25680
  ulnar ~ 24675, 25535, 25565
  vertebral ~ 22315
  wrist ~ 25259, 25624, 25635, 25660, 25675, 25680, 25690
  foreskin ~ 54450
  globe ~ 92018-92019
  hip ~ 27275
  interphalangeal joint, proximal ~ 26742
  knee ~ 27570
  osteopathic ~ 98925-98929
  shoulder, application of fixation apparatus ~ 23700
  spine, with anesthesia ~ 22505
  tibial, distal ~ 27762
Manometric studies
  kidney, pressure ~ 50396
  rectum/anus ~ 91122
  ureter, pressure ~ 50686
  ureterostomy ~ 50686
Manometry, rectum ~ 90911
Mantoux test ~ (TB skin test) 86580
Manual therapy ~ 97140
Maquet procedure ~ 27418
Marcellation operation ~ (vaginal hysterectomy) 58260-58270, 58550
Marrow, bone ~ see bone marrow
Marshall-Marchetti-Krantz procedure ~ 51840-51841, 58152, 58267, 58293
Marsupialization ~ 10040
  Bartholin's gland cyst ~ 56440
  cyst, sublingual salivary ~ 42409
  liver, cyst or abscess ~ 47300
  pancreatic cyst ~ 48500
  urethral diverticulum ~ 53240
Mass, kidney, ablation ~ 50542
Massage, cardiac ~ 32160
  therapy ~ 97124
Masseter muscle/bone, reduction ~ 21295-21296
  muscle flap ~ 15733
Mass spectrometry and tandem mass spectrometry
  analyte ~ 83789
Mastectomy
  gynecomastia ~ 19300
  modified radical ~ 19307
  partial ~ 19301-19302
  radical ~ 19305-19306
  simple, complete ~ 19303
  subcutaneous ~ 19304
Mastectomy, Halsted ~ see radical mastectomy
Mastoid
  excision
    complete ~ 69502
    radical ~ 69511
      modified ~ 69505
      petrous apicectomy ~ 69530
    simple ~ 69501
  obliteration ~ 69670
  repair
    with apicectomy ~ 69605
    by excision ~ 69601-69603
    fistula ~ 69700
    with tympanoplasty ~ 69604
Mastoid cavity, debridement ~ 69220-69222
Mastoidectomy
  cochlear device implantation ~ 69930
  complete ~ 69502
    revision ~ 69601
  ossicular chain reconstruction ~ 69605

Mastoidectomy ~ *continued*
  radical ~ 69511
    modified ~ 69505
    revision ~ 69602-69603
  simple ~ 69501
  with apicectomy ~ 69605
  with labyrinthectomy ~ 69910
  with petrous apicectomy ~ 69530
  with skull base surgery ~ 61590, 61597
    decompression ~ 61595
    facial nerve ~ 61595
  with tympanoplasty ~ 69604, 69641-69646
Mastoidotomy ~ 69635-69637
  with tympanoplasty ~ 69635
    ossicular chain reconstruction ~ 69636
      and synthetic prosthesis ~ 69636
Mastoids
  polytomography ~ 76101-76102
  X-ray ~ 70120-70130
Mastopexy ~ 19316
Mastotomy ~ 19020
Maternity care and delivery ~ see abortion; cesarean delivery; ectopic
  pregnancy; obstetrical care
Maxilla ~ see facial bones; mandible
  bone graft ~ 21210
  CT scan ~ 70486-70488
  cyst, excision ~ 21048-21049
  excision ~ 21030, 21032-21034
  fracture
    closed treatment ~ 21345, 21421
    open treatment ~ 21346-21348, 21422-21423
    with fixation ~ 21345-21347
  osteotomy ~ 21206
  reconstruction, with implant ~ 21245-21246, 21248-21249
  tumor, excision ~ 21048-21049
Maxillary arteries ~ see artery, maxillary
Maxillary sinus ~ see sinus, maxillary
Maxillary torus palatinus, tumor excision ~ 21032
Maxillectomy ~ 31225-31230
Maxillofacial fixation, application, halo type appliance ~ 21100
Maxillofacial impressions
  auricular prosthesis ~ 21086
  definitive obturator prosthesis ~ 21080
  facial prosthesis ~ 21088
  interim obturator prosthesis ~ 21079
  mandibular resection prosthesis ~ 21081
  nasal prosthesis ~ 21087
  oral surgical splint ~ 21085
  orbital prosthesis ~ 21077
  palatal augmentation prosthesis ~ 21082
  palatal lift prosthesis ~ 21083
  speech aid prosthesis ~ 21084
  surgical obturator prosthesis ~ 21076
Maxillofacial procedures, unlisted services and procedures ~ 21299
Maxillofacial prosthesis ~ 21076-21089
  unlisted services and procedures ~ 21089
Maydl operation ~ (colostomy) 45563, 50810
Mayo hernia repair ~ 49580-49587
Mayo operation ~ (varicose vein removal) 37700-37735, 37780, 37785
Mayo procedure ~ 28292
MBC ~ (minimum bactericidal concentration) 87181-87190
McBride procedure ~ 28292
McBurney operation ~ (see also hernia, repair, inguinal) 49495-49500,
  49505
McCannel procedure ~ 66682
McDonald operation ~ (repair, cervix, cerclage, abdominal; revision)
  57700
McIndoe procedure ~ (vagina, construction) 57291
McKissock surgery ~ (breast, reduction) 19318
McVay operation ~ (hernia, repair, inguinal) 49495-49500, 49505
Measles, German ~ see rubella
Measles uncomplicated ~ see rubeola
Measles vaccine ~ see vaccines
Meat fibers, feces ~ 89160
Meatoplasty ~ 69310
Meatotomy ~ 53020-53025
  contact laser vaporization with/without transurethral resection of prostate
    ~ 52648
  with cystourethroscopy ~ 52281
  infant ~ 53025

Meatotomy ~ *continued*
  non-contact laser coagulation prostate ~ 52647
  transurethral electrosurgical resection, prostate ~ 52601
  ureter ~ 52290
  ureteral, cystourethroscopy ~ 52290-52305
Meckel's diverticulum, excision ~ 44800
  unlisted services and procedures ~ 44899
Median nerve
  decompression ~ 64721
  neuroplasty ~ 64721
  release ~ 64721
  repair/suture, motor ~ 64835
  transposition ~ 64721
Median nerve compression ~ see carpal tunnel syndrome
Mediastinal cyst ~ see cyst, mediastinal
Mediastinoscopy ~ 39401, 39402
Mediastinotomy
  cervical approach ~ 39000
  transthoracic approach ~ 39010
Mediastinum ~ see chest; thorax
  cyst,
    excision ~ 32662
    resection ~ 39200
  drainage, image guided fluid collection ~ 49405
  endoscopy, biopsy ~ 39401, 39402
  excision
    cyst/mass/tumor ~ 32662
    lymph node ~ 19272, 21632, 32674, 38746
  exploration ~ 39000-39010, 60505
  incision and drainage ~ 39000-39010
  lymph node
    biopsy ~ 39402
    lymphadenectomy ~ 19272, 21632, 32674, 38746
    sampling, EBUS guided ~ 31652, 31653
  mass
    biopsy ~ 32405, 39401
    excision ~ 32662
  needle biopsy ~ 32405
  radical dissection ~ 60522
  removal, foreign body ~ 39000-39010
  resection
    cyst ~ 39200
    tumor ~ 39220
  thoracoscopy
    biopsy ~ 32606
    diagnostic ~ 32601
    excision, cyst/mass/tumor ~ 32662
  tumor, excision ~ 32662, 39220
  unlisted procedures ~ 39499
Mediastinum and diaphragm, surgical procedures ~ 39000-39599
Medical disability evaluation services ~ 99455-99456
Medical genetics ~ 96040
Medical nutrition therapy ~ 97802-97804
Medical testimony ~ 99075
Medication management therapy ~ 99605-99607
Medicine, preventive ~ see preventive medicine
Medicine, pulmonary ~ see pulmonology
Medicine services ~ 90281-99602
Meibomian cyst ~ see chalazion
Membrane, mucous ~ see mucosa
Membrane, tympanic ~ see ear, drum
Membrane oxygenation, extracorporeal ~ see extracorporeal membrane
  oxygenation
Meninges
  excision, tumor ~ 61512, 61519
  meningitis, meningococcal
    antibody ~ 86741
    vaccine ~ 90620, 90621, 90644, 90733, 90734
  repair
    meningocele ~ 63700, 63702
    myelomeningocele ~ 63704, 63706
    pseudomeningocele ~ 63709
Meningioma, excision ~ 61512, 61519
  tumor, excision ~ 61512, 61519
Meningitis, lymphocytic benign ~ see lymphocytic choriomeningitis
Meningocele repair
  meningocele ~ 63700, 63702
  myelomeningocele ~ 63704, 63706
  pseudomeningocele ~ 63709
Meningococcal vaccine ~ see vaccines
Meningococcus ~ see neisseria meningitidis

Meningomyelocele ~ see myelomeningocele
Meniscectomy
  knee joint ~ 27332-27333
  temporomandibular joint ~ 21060
Meniscus
  knee
    excision ~ 27332-27333
    repair ~ 27403
    transplantation ~ 29868
Mental nerve
  avulsion ~ 64736
  incision ~ 64736
  transection ~ 64736
Mercury ~ 83015, 83825
Merskey test ~ see fibrin degradation products
Mesencephalic tract
  incision ~ 61480
  section ~ 61480
Mesencephalon, tractotomy ~ 61480
Mesenteric arteries ~ see artery, mesenteric
Mesentery
  lesion, excision ~ 44820
  repair ~ 44850
  suture ~ 44850
  unlisted services and procedures ~ 44899
Mesh
  implantation, hernia ~ 49568
  insertion, pelvic floor ~ 57267
  removal, abdominal infected ~ 11008
Metabisulfite test ~ (red blood cell (RBC), sickling) 85660
Metabolite ~ 80353
  thromboxane ~ 84431
Metacarpal
  amputation ~ 26910
  craterization ~ 26230
  cyst, excision ~ 26200-26205
  diaphysectomy ~ 26230
  fracture
    closed treatment ~ 26605
      with fixation ~ 26607
    open treatment ~ 26615
    percutaneous fixation ~ 26608
    with manipulation ~ 26605-26607
    without manipulation ~ 26600
  ostectomy ~ 26250
  repair
    lengthening ~ 26568
    nonunion ~ 26546
    osteotomy ~ 26565
  saucerization ~ 26230
  tumor
    excision ~ 26200-26205
    radical resection ~ 26250
Metacarpophalangeal joint
  arthrodesis ~ 26850-26852
  arthroplasty ~ 26530-26531
  arthroscopy
    diagnostic ~ 29900
    surgical ~ 29901-29902
  arthrotomy ~ 26075
  biopsy, synovium ~ 26105
  capsule
    excision ~ 26520
    incision ~ 26520
  capsulodesis ~ 26516-26518
  dislocation
    closed treatment ~ 26700
    open treatment ~ 26715
    percutaneous fixation ~ 26705-26706
    with manipulation ~ 26340
  exploration ~ 26075
  fracture
    closed treatment ~ 26740
    open treatment ~ 26746
    with manipulation ~ 26742
  fusion ~ 26516-26518, 26850-26852
  removal of foreign body ~ 26075
  repair, collateral ligament ~ 26540-26542
  synovectomy ~ 26135

Metadrenaline ~ see metanephrines
Metals, heavy ~ see heavy metal
Metamfetamine ~ see methamphetamine
Metanephrines ~ 83835
Metatarsal ~ see foot
  amputation ~ 28810
  condyle, excision ~ 28288
  craterization ~ 28122
  cyst, excision ~ 28104-28107
  diaphysectomy ~ 28122
  excision ~ 28110-28114, 28122, 28140
  fracture
    closed treatment
      with manipulation ~ 28475-28476
      without manipulation ~ 28470
    open treatment ~ 28485
    percutaneous fixation ~ 28476
  free osteocutaneous flap with microvascular anastomosis ~ 20972
  repair ~ 28322
    lengthening ~ 28306-28307
    osteotomy ~ 28306-28309
  saucerization ~ 28122
  tumor, excision ~ 28104-28107, 28173
Metatarsectomy ~ 28140
Metatarsophalangeal joint
  amputation ~ 28820
  arthrotomy ~ 28022, 28052
  biopsy ~ 28052
  capsulotomy ~ 28270
  cheilectomy ~ 28289, 28291
  dislocation
    closed treatment ~ 28630-28635
    open treatment ~ 28645
    percutaneous fixation ~ 28636
  drainage ~ 28022
  exploration ~ 28022
  great toe
    arthrodesis ~ 28750
    fusion ~ 28750
  removal
    of foreign body ~ 28022
    of loose body ~ 28022
  repair, hallux rigidus ~ 28289, 28291
  synovial
    biopsy ~ 28052
    excision ~ 28072
  toe ~ 28270
Methaemoglobin ~ see methemoglobin
Methamphetamine, blood or urine ~ 80324-80326
Methanol ~ 84600
Methbipyranone ~ see metyrapone
Methemalbumin ~ 83857
Methemoglobin ~ 83045-83050, 88741
Methenamine silver stain ~ 88312
Methopyrapone ~ see metyrapone
Methoxyhydroxymandelic acid ~ see vanillylmandelic acid
Methylamphetamine ~ see methamphetamine
Methylene bichloride ~ see dichloromethane
Methylfluorprednisolone ~ see dexamethasone
Methylmorphine ~ see codeine
Methyl alcohol ~ (methanol) 84600
Metroplasty ~ see hysteroplasty
Metyrapone ~ 80436
MIC ~ (minimum inhibitory concentration) 87186
Micro-ophthalmia, orbit reconstruction ~ 21256
Microalbumin, urine ~ 82043-82044
Microbiology ~ 0023T, 87999
Microdissection ~ 88380-88381
Microfluorometries, flow ~ see flow cytometry
Microdissection ~ 88380
Microglobulin, beta 2
  blood ~ 82232
  urine ~ 82232
Micrographic surgery, Mohs technique ~ 17311-17315
Micropigmentation, correction ~ 11920-11922
Microscope, surgical ~ see operating microscope
Microscopic evaluation, hair ~ 96902
Microscopies, electron ~ see electron microscopy

Microscopy
binocular ear exam ~ 92504
reflectance confocal microscoopy (RCM)
skin imaging ~ 96931-96936
lesion ~ 96932
specular, endothelial cell analysis ~ 92286
Microsomal antibody ~ 86376
Microsomia, hemifacial ~ see hemifacial microsomia
Microsurgery, operating microscope ~ 69990
Microvascular anastomosis
bone graft
fibula ~ 20955
other ~ 20962
fascial flap, free ~ 15758
muscle flap, free ~ 15756
osteocutaneous flap with, ~ 20969-20973
skin flap, free ~ 15757
Microvite A ~ see vitamin A
Microwave therapy ~ (see also physical medicine/therapy/occupational therapy) 97020
Midbrain ~ see brain; brainstem; mesencephalon; skull base surgery
Midcarpal medioccipital joint, arthrotomy ~ 25040
Middle cerebral artery velocimetry ~ 76821
Middle ear ~ see ear, middle
Midface
reconstruction
with bone graft ~ 21145-21160, 21188
without bone graft ~ 21141-21143
forehead advancement ~ 21159-21160
Mile operation ~ see colectomy, total, with proctectomy
Milia, multiple, removal ~ 10040
Miller procedure ~ 28737
Miller-Abbott intubation ~ 44500, 74340
Minerva cast ~ 29035
removal ~ 29710
Minimum inhibitory concentration (MIC) ~ 87186
Minimum lethal concentration ~ 87187
Minnesota multiphasic personality inventory ~ see MMPI
Miscarriage
incomplete abortion ~ 59812
missed abortion
first trimester ~ 59820
second trimester ~ 59821
septic abortion ~ 59830
Missed abortion ~ see abortion; miscarriage, missed abortion
Mitchell procedure ~ 28296
Mitogen blastogenesis ~ 86353
Mitral valve
closure, paravalvular leak ~ 93590, 93592
incision ~ 33420-33422
occlusion, paravalvular leak ~ 93590, 93592
repair ~ 33420-33427
transcatheter ~ 0345T, 33418, 33419
replacement ~ 33430
transcatheter mitral valve implantation/replacement (TMVI) ~ 0483T, 0484T
Mitrofanoff operation ~ (appendico-vesicostomy) 50845
MMPI ~ (Minnesota multiphasic personality inventory) 96100
MMR shots ~ (measles, mumps and rubella vaccines) 90707
Mobilization
splenic flexure ~ 44139
stapes ~ 69650
Modified radical mastectomy ~ see mastectomy, modified radical
Mohs micrographic surgery ~ 17311-17315
Molar pregnancy ~ see hydatidiform mole
Mold, culture ~ 87107
Mole, carneous ~ see abortion
Mole, hydatid ~ see hydatidiform mole
Molecular cytogenetics ~ 88271-88275
interpretation and report ~ 88291
Molecular diagnostics
reverse transcription and amplified probe
central nervous system pathogen ~ 87483
enterovirus ~ 87498
hepatitis C ~ 87521
HIV-1 ~ 87535
HIV-2 ~ 87538
reverse transcription and quantification
hepatitis C ~ 87522
HIV-1 ~ 87536
HIV-2 ~ 87539

Molecular oxygen saturation ~ see oxygen saturation
Molecular pathology
~ (see also Gene analysis) 81200-81383, 81400-81408
Molluscum contagiosum
destruction ~ 17110-17111, 46900, 46910, 46916-46917, 54050-54065
excision
anus ~ 46922
penis ~ 54060
Molteno procedure ~ 66180
Monilia ~ see candida
Monitoring
ablation therapy
incompetent vein ~ 36473-36476, 36478, 36479, 36482, 36483
parenchymal tissue ~ 76940, 77013, 77022
renal mass ~ 50250, 50542
ACE/ARB therapy ~ 4188F
blood pressure, 24 hour ~ 93784-93790
electrocardiogram ~ (see also electrocardiography) 93224-93229
electroencephalogram ~ 95812-95813, 95950-95953, 95956
with drug activation ~ 95954
with physical activation ~ 95954
with WADA activation ~ 95958
fetal
during labor ~ 59050-59051, 99500
interpretation only ~ 59051
magnetic cardiac signal ~ 0475T-0478T
glucose
home device ~ 82962
interstitial fluid ~ 95249-95251
tolerance test ~ 82951, 82952
interstitial fluid pressure ~ 20950
pediatric apnea ~ 94774-94777
retinal disease ~ 92228
seizure ~ 0381T-0386T, 61531-61533, 61760
with contrast
biliary drainage ~ 47533-47540
catheter ~ 75984, 93503
Monitoring, sleep ~ see polysomnography
Monoethylene glycol ~ see ethylene glycol
Mononuclear cell antigen ~ 86356
Mononucleosis virus, infectious ~ see Epstein-Barr virus
Monophosphate
adenosine ~ (adenosine monophosphate (AMP)) 82030
adenosine cyclic ~ (cyclic AMP) 82030
Monospot test ~ (rapid test for infection) 86308
Monoxide, carbon ~ see carbon monoxide
Monteggia fracture ~ 24620-24635
Monticelli procedure ~ (application, bone fixation device) 20690, 20692
Morbilli ~ see rubeola
Morphine methyl ether ~ see codeine
Morphometric analysis
nerve ~ 88356
skeletal muscle ~ 88355
tumor ~ 88358-88361, 88367-88368
Morton's neuroma, excision ~ 28080
Moschcowitz operation ~ see repair, hernia, femoral; revision
Mosenthal test ~ (urinalysis, routine) 81002
Mother cell ~ see stem cell
Motility study, esophagus ~ 91010
Motion analysis
by video and 3-D kinematics ~ 96000, 96004
computer-based ~ 96000, 96004
Mouth
abscess, incision and drainage ~ 40800-40801, 41005-41009, 41015-41018
biopsy ~ 40808, 41108
cyst, incision and drainage ~ 40800-40801, 41005-41009, 41015-41018
excision, frenum ~ 40819
hematoma, incision and drainage ~ 40800-40801, 41005-41009, 41015-41018
lesion
destruction ~ 40820
excision ~ 40810-40816, 41116
vestibule of
destruction ~ 40820
repair ~ 40830
mucosa, excision ~ 40818
reconstruction ~ 40840-40845
removal, foreign body ~ 40804-40805
repair, laceration ~ 40830-40831
unlisted services, procedures ~ 40899, 41599

Mouth ~ *continued*
vestibule of
  excision, destruction ~ 40808-40820
  incision ~ 40800-40806
  other procedures ~ 40899
  removal, foreign body ~ 40804
  repair ~ 40830-40845
Move ~ see transfer
finger ~ 26555
toe joint ~ 26556
toe to hand ~ 26551-26554
Moynihan test ~ (gastrointestinal tract, X-ray, with contrast) 74246-74249
MPR ~ (multifetal pregnancy reduction) 59866
MRA ~ see magnetic resonance angiography
MRI ~ see magnetic resonance imaging
MSLT ~ (multiple sleep latency testing) 95805
Mucin, synovial fluid ~ 83872
Mucocele sinusotomy, frontal ~ 31075
Mucopolysaccharides ~ 83864
Mucormycoses ~ see mucormycosis
Mucormycosis, antibody ~ 86732
Mucosa
ablation, turbinates ~ 30801, 30802
ectopic gastric imaging ~ 78290
excision of lesion
  alveolar, hyperplastic ~ 41828
  vestibule of mouth ~ 40810-40818
  via esophagoscopy ~ 43229
  via small intestinal endoscopy ~ 44369
  via upper gi endoscopy ~ 43270
lesion
  ablation, vestibule of mouth ~ 40810-40818
  phtodynamic therapy ~ 96567, 96573, 96574
periodontal grafting ~ 41870
urethra, mucosal advancement ~ 53450
vaginal biopsy ~ 57100-57105
Mucosa, buccal ~ see mouth, mucosa
Mucous cyst antibody, hand or finger ~ 26160
Mucous membrane ~ see mouth, mucosa
cutaneous
  biopsy ~ 11100-11101
  excision
    benign lesion ~ 11440-11446
    malignant lesion ~ 11640-11646
  layer closure, wounds ~ 12051-12057
  simple repair, wounds ~ 12011-12018
excision, sphenoid sinus ~ 31288
lid margin
  correction of trichiasis ~ 67835
  nasal test ~ 95065
  ophthalmic test ~ 95060
rectum
  proctoplasty for prolapse ~ 45505
MUGA (multiple gated acquisition) ~ 78452, 78454, 78473, 78483
Muller procedure ~ see sleep study
Multianalyte Assays
with Algorithmic Analyses ~ 81500-81599
autoimmune, rheumatoid arthritis ~ 81490
cardiology, heart transplant ~ 81595
coronary artery disease ~ 81493
endocrinology ~ 81506
fetal
  congenital abnormalities ~ 81508-81512
  fetal aneuploidy ~ 81507
oncology
  breast ~ 0009U, 81519-81521
  colon ~ 81525
  colorectal ~ 0002U, 81528
  gynecologioc ~ 81535, 81536
  hematolymphoid neoplasia ~ 0016U, 0017U
  lung ~ 81538
  ovarian ~ 0003U, 81500, 81503
  prostate ~ 0005U, 81539, 81541, 81551
  solid organ neoplasia ~ 0013U
  thyroid ~ 81545
  tissue of origin ~ 81504
  tumor of unknown origin ~ 81540
prescription drug monitoring ~ 0006U, 0011U
unlisted multianalyte assay with algorithmic analysis ~ 81599

Multifetal pregnancy reduction ~ 59866
Multi-leaf collimator (MLC) device ~ 77338
Multiple sleep latency testing (MSLT) ~ 95805
Multiple valve procedures ~ see valvuloplasty
Mumford operation ~ (partial claviculectomy, arthroscopic) 29824
Mumps
antibody ~ 86735
immunization ~ 90707, 90710
vaccine
  MMR ~ 90707
  MMRV ~ 90710
Muramidase ~ 85549
Murine typhus ~ 86000
Muscle ~ see specific muscle
abdomen ~ see abdominal wall
biopsy ~ 20200-20206
debridement ~ 11043, 11046
  infected ~ 11004-11006
flaps
  fasciocutaneous ~ 15733, 15734, 15736, 15738
  muscle, free ~ 15842
  myocutaneous ~ 15733, 15734, 15736, 15738, 61619
grafts
  muscle, free ~ 15841, 25265, 25274
heart ~ see myocardium
neck ~ see neck muscle
incision
  esophagus ~ 32665, 43130, 43279, 43330, 43331
  hyoid ~ 21685
  pharynx ~ 43030, 43130
  pylorus ~ 43520
injection ~ 20552, 20553
oculomotor ~ see eye muscles
removal, foreign body ~ 20520-20525
repair
  extraocular ~ 65290
  forearm ~ 25260-25274
  wrist ~ 25260-25274
revision, arm, upper ~ 24330-24331
transfer
  arm, upper ~ 24301, 24320
  elbow ~ 24301
  femur ~ 27110
  hand ~ 26494
  hip ~ 27100-27105, 27111
  rotator cuff ~ 23410, 23412
  shoulder ~ 23395-23397, 24301, 24320, 23410, 23412
  thigh ~ 27400
unlisted extraocular muscle procedure ~ 67399
Muscle compartment syndrome, detection ~ 20950
Muscle denervation ~ see denervation
Muscle division
scalenus anticus ~ 21700-21705
sternocleidomastoid ~ 21720-21725
Muscle flaps ~ 15731-15738
Muscle grafts ~ 15841-15845
Muscle testing
dynamometry, eye ~ 92260
extraocular multiple muscles ~ 92265
manual ~ 95831-95834
Musculoplasty ~ see muscle, repair
Musculoskeletal system, surgical procedures ~ 20005-29999
Musculotendinous (rotator) cuff, repair ~ 23410-23412
Mustard procedure ~ (repair, great arteries; revision) 33774-33777
Myasthenia gravis, tensilon test ~ 95857-95858
Mycobacteria
culture ~ 87116
  identification ~ 87118
detection ~ 87550-87562
sensitivity studies ~ 87190
Mycoplasma
antibody ~ 86738
culture ~ 87109
detection ~ 87580-87582
Mycota ~ see fungus
Myectomy, anorectal ~ see myomectomy, anorectal
Myelencephalon ~ see medulla
Myelin basic protein, cerebrospinal fluid ~ 83873

Myelography
 brain ~ 70010
 spine
  cervical ~ 72240
  lumbosacral ~ 72265
  thoracic ~ 72255
  total ~ 72270
Myelomeningocele, repair ~ 63704-63706
Myeloperoxidase (MPO) ~ 83876
Myelotomy ~ 63170
Myocardial, perfusion imaging ~ 78451-78454
 positron emission tomography (PET) ~ 78459
Myocardial imaging ~ 78466-78469
 blood flow, absolute quantitation ~ 0482T
 echocardiography, contrast perfusion ~ 0439T
 infarct avid ~ 78466-78469
 metabolic evaluation, PET ~ 78459
 perfusion study
  planar ~ 78453, 78454
  positron emission tomography (PET) ~ 78491-78492
  single photon emission computed tomography (SPECT) ~ 78451-78452
 quantitative assessment of myocardial mechanics ~ 0399T
 repair, postinfarction ~ 33542
 sympathetic innervation ~ 0331T, 0332T
Myocardium
 ischemia assessment
  echocardiography ~ 0439T
 perfusion imaging ~ 78451-78454
  echocardiography ~ 0439T
 positron emissin tomography (PET) ~ 78459
 resection ~ 33542
 revascularization ~ 33140, 33141
Myocutaneous flaps ~ 15731, 15733-15738, 15756
Myofascial pain dysfunction syndrome ~ see temporomandibular joint (TMJ)
Myofibroma ~ see leiomyomata
Myoglobin ~ 83874
Myomectomy
 anorectal ~ 45108
 uterus ~ 58140-58146, 58545-58546
Myoplasty ~ see muscle, repair
Myotomy
 esophagus ~ 43030
 hyoid ~ 21685
Myringoplasty ~ 69620
Myringostomy ~ see myringostomy
Myringotomy ~ 69420-69421
Myxoid cyst ~ see ganglion

N

N. meningitidis ~ see Neisseria meningitidis
Naffziger operation ~ (decompression, orbit; section) 61330
Nagel test ~ (color vision examination) 92283
Nail(s)
 avulsion ~ 11730-11732
 biopsy ~ 11755
 debridement ~ 11720-11721
 drainage ~ 10060, 10061
 evacuation, hematoma, subungual ~ 11740
 excision ~ 11750
  cyst, pilonidal ~ 11770-11772
 KOH examination ~ 87220
 reconstruction ~ 11762
 removal ~ 11730-11732, 11750
 trimming ~ 11719
Nail bed, reconstruction ~ 11762
 repair ~ 11760
Nail fold, excision wedge ~ 11765
Nail plate separation ~ see onychia
Narcosynthesis, diagnostic and therapeutic ~ 90865
Nasal abscess ~ see nose, abscess
Nasal area, bone graft ~ 21210
Nasal bleeding ~ see epistaxis

Nasal bone
 fracture
  closed treatment ~ 21310-21320
  open treatment ~ 21325-21335
  with manipulation ~ 21315-21320
  without manipulation ~ 21310
 X-ray ~ 70160
Nasal deformity, repair ~ 40700-40761
Nasal function study ~ 92512
Nasal polyp ~ see nose, polyp
Nasal prosthesis, impression ~ 21087
Nasal septum
 abscess, incision and drainage ~ 30020
 fracture
  closed treatment ~ 21337
  open treatment ~ 21336
 hematoma, incision and drainage ~ 30020
 repair ~ 30630
 submucous resection ~ 30520
Nasal sinuses ~ see sinus; sinuses
Nasal smear, eosinophils ~ 89190
Nasal turbinate fracture, therapeutic ~ 30930
Nasoethmoid complex
 fracture
  open treatment ~ 21338-21339
  percutaneous treatment ~ 21340
 reconstruction ~ 21182-21184
Nasogastric tube, placement ~ 43752
Nasolacrimal duct
 exploration ~ 68810
  with anesthesia ~ 68811
 insertion
  catheter dilation 68816
  stent ~ 68815
 X-ray, with contrast ~ 70170
Nasomaxillary fracture
 closed treatment ~ 21345
 open treatment ~ 21346-21348
 with bone grafting ~ 21348
Nasopharynges ~ see nasopharynx
Nasopharyngoscopy ~ 92511
Nasopharynx ~ see also pharynx
 biopsy ~ 42804-42806
 hemorrhage ~ 42970-42972
 unlisted services and procedures ~ 42999
Natriuretic peptide ~ 83880
Natural ostium sinus
 maxillary ~ 31000
 sphenoid ~ 31002
Navicular
 arthroplasty, with implant ~ 25443
 fracture
  closed treatment ~ 25622
  open treatment ~ 25628
  with manipulation ~ 25624
 repair ~ 25440
Navigation, computer assisted ~ 0054T-0055T, 20985
 repair ~ 25440
Neck
 angiography ~ 70498, 70547-70549
 artery, ligation ~ 37615
 biopsy ~ 21550
 bypass graft ~ 35901
 CT scan ~ 70490-70492, 70498
 dissection, radical ~ see radical neck dissection
 exploration
  blood vessel ~ 35800
  lymph nodes ~ 38542
 incision and drainage
  abscess ~ 21501-21502
  hematoma ~ 21501-21502
 lipectomy, suction assisted ~ 15876
 magnetic resonance angiography (MRA) ~ 70547-70549
 magnetic resonance imaging(MRI) ~ 70540-70543
 nerve, graft ~ 64885-64886
 repair, blood vessel ~ 35201
  with other graft ~ 35261
  with vein graft ~ 35231
 skin, revision ~ 15819

Neck ~ *continued*
tumor
excision ~ 21552-21558
excision/resection ~ 21557-21558
ultrasound exam ~ 76536
unlisted services and procedures, surgery ~ 21899
wound exploration, penetrating ~ 20100
X-ray ~ 70360
Neck muscle
division
scalenus anticus ~ 21700-21705
sternocleidomastoid ~ 21720-21725
Necropsy
coroner's exam ~ 88045
forensic exam ~ 88040
gross and micro exam ~ 88020-88029
gross exam ~ 88000-88016
organ ~ 88037
regional ~ 88036
unlisted services and procedures ~ 88099
Needle biopsy ~ see also biopsy
abdomen mass ~ 49180
bone ~ 20220-20225
bone marrow ~ 38221, 38222
breast ~ 19100
colon, endoscopy ~ 45392
colon-sigmoid, endoscopy ~ 45342
CT scan guidance ~ 77012
epididymis ~ 54800
esophagus, endoscopy ~ 43232
fluoroscopic guidance ~ 77002
gastrointestinal, upper, endoscopy ~ 43238, 43242
kidney ~ 50200
liver ~ 47000-47001
lung ~ 32405
lymph nodes ~ 38505
mediastinum ~ 32405
muscle ~ 20206
pancreas ~ 48102
pleura ~ 32400
prostate ~ 55700
transperineal ~ 55706
retroperitoneal mass ~ 49180
salivary gland ~ 42400
spinal cord ~ 62269
testis ~ 54500
thyroid gland ~ 60100
transbronchial ~ 31629, 31633
Needle localization
breast
with lesion excision ~ 19125-19126
CT guidance ~ 77012
fluoroscopic guidance ~ 77002
spine ~ 77003
magnetic resonance guidance ~ 77021
ultrasonic guidance ~ 76942
Needle manometer technique ~ 20950
Needle wire
introduction, trachea ~ 31730
Neer procedure ~ 23470
Neisseria gonorrheae ~ 87590-87592, 87850
Neisseria meningitidis, antibody ~ 86741
Neobladder, construction ~ 51596
Neonatal critical care ~ see also newborn care
initial ~ 99468
subsequent ~ 99469
Neoplasm
cancer photoradiation therapy ~ see photochemotherapy
cardiac ~ see heart, tumor
colon ~ see colon, tumor
esophageal ~ see tumor, esophagus
spinal cord ~ see spinal cord, neoplasm
unspecified nature of brain ~ see brain, tumor
Neoplastic growth ~ see tumor
Nephelometry ~ 83883
Nephrectomy
donor ~ 50300-50320, 50547
laparoscopic ~ 50545-50548
partial ~ 50240
laparoscopic ~ 50543

Nephrectomy ~ *continued*
recipient ~ 50340
with ureters ~ 50220-50236, 50546, 50548
Nephrolith ~ see calculus, removal, kidney
Nephrolithotomy ~ 50060-50075
Nephropexy ~ 50400-50405
Nephroplasty ~ see kidney, repair
Nephropyeloplasty ~ see pyeloplasty
Nephrorrhaphy ~ 50500
Nephroscopy ~ see endoscopy, kidney
Nephrostogram
injection procedure ~ 50430, 50431
with catheter conversion, nephrostomy to nephroureteral ~ 50434
with nephrostomy catheter exchange ~ 50435
with placement of ureteral shunt ~ 50693-50695
Nephrostolithotomy, percutaneous ~ 50080-50081
Nephrostomy ~ 50040
endoscopic ~ 50562-50570
percutaneous ~ 52334
with drainage ~ 50040
X-ray with contrast, guide dilation ~ 74485
Nephrostomy tract, establishment ~ 50395
Nephrotomogram ~ see nephrotomography
Nephrotomography ~ 74415
Nephrotomy ~ 50040-50045
with exploration ~ 50045
Nerve
see also nerves
biopsy ~ 64795
neuroma, excision
cutaneous ~ 64774
digital ~ 64776, 64778
foot, other than digital ~ 64782, 64783
hand, other than digital ~ 64782, 64783
peripheral ~ 64784
sciatic ~ 64786
Nerve conduction
motor nerve ~ 95905, 95907-95913
preconfigured electrode array ~ 77387
Nerve graft
additional nerve ~ 64901-64902
arm or leg ~ 64892-64893, 64897-64898
foot or hand ~ 64890-64891, 64895-64896
head or neck ~ 64885-64886
neurovascular pedicle ~ 15750
pedicle ~ 64905, 64907
Nerve root ~ see also cauda equina; spinal cord
decompression ~ 22856, 63020-63048, 63055-63103
incision ~ 63185-63190
section ~ 63185-63190
Nerve stimulation, transcutaneous ~ see application, neurostimulation
Nerve teasing ~ 88362
Nerves
anastomosis
facial to hypoglossal ~ 64868
facial to spinal accessory ~ 64866
avulsion ~ 64732-64772
biopsy ~ 64795
cryoablation, percutaneous ~ 0440T-0442T
decompression ~ 64702-64727
cranial ~ 61458, 61460
laminotomy/laminectomy ~ 0274T-0275T
denervation ~ 27035
destruction ~ 64600-64681
laryngeal, recurrent ~ 31595
graft ~ 64885-64907
implantation, electrode ~ 64553-64581
to bone ~ 64787
to muscle ~ 64787
incision ~ 28035, 43640-43641, 64732-64772
injection
anesthetic ~ 01991-01992, 64400-64530
diagnostic agent ~ 0213T, 64493-64495
neurolytic agent ~ 64600-64681
therapeutic agent ~ 0213T, 64490-64495
insertion, electrode ~ 64553-64581
lesion, excision ~ 64774-64792
neurofibroma, excision ~ 64788-64792
neurolemmoma, excision ~ 64788-64792
neurolytic, internal ~ 64727

Nerves ~ *continued*
neuroma
destruction ~ 64632
excision ~ 64774-64786
injection ~ 64455
neuroplasty ~ 64702-64721
removal, electrode ~ 64585
repair
allograft ~ 64910, 64912, 64913
autogenous graft ~ 64911
microdissection ~ 69990
suture ~ 64831-64876
spinal accessory
incision ~ 63191
section ~ 63191
suture ~ 64831-64876
sympathectomy, excision ~ 64802-64818
transection ~ 64732-64772
transposition ~ 64718-64721
unlisted services and procedures ~ 64999
Nerve V, cranial ~ see trigeminal nerve
Nerve VII, cranial ~ see facial nerve
Nerve X, cranial ~ see vagus nerve
Nerve XI, cranial ~ see accessory nerve
Nerve XII, cranial ~ see hypoglossal nerve
Nervous system
central nervous system pathogen
nucleic acid detection ~ 87483
extracranial, peripheral nerves and autonomic nervous system
avulsion ~ 64732-64772
destruction ~ 64600-64681
excision ~ 64774-64823
injection ~ 64400-64530
neurorrhaphy ~ 64831-64911
neuroplasty ~ 64702-64727
neurostimulation ~ 64550-64595
transection ~ 64732-64772
nuclear medicine
unlisted services and procedures ~ 78699
skull, meninges and brain ~ 61000-62258
spine and spinal cord ~ 62263-63746
unlisted procedure ~ 64999
Nesidioblast ~ see islet cell
Neural conduction ~ see nerve conduction
Neural ganglion ~ see ganglion
Neurectomy
foot ~ 28055
gastrocnemius ~ 27326
hamstring muscle ~ 27325
leg, upper ~ 27325
popliteal ~ 27326
tympanic ~ 69676
Neuroendoscopy, intracranial ~ 62160-62165
Neurofibroma
cutaneous nerve, excision ~ 64788
extensive, excision ~ 64792
peripheral nerve, excision ~ 64790
Neurolemmoma
destruction, extensive ~ 0419T, 0420T
excision
cutaneous nerve ~ 64788
extensive ~ 64792
peripheral nerve ~ 64790
Neurologic system ~ see nervous system
Neurology procedures
brain cortex magnetic stimulation ~ 90867-90868
brain mapping ~ 90867, 96020
brain surface electrode stimulation ~ 95961-95962
central motor function mapping ~ 64999
cognitive performance ~ 96125
diagnostic
anal sphincter ~ 51785
autonomic function tests
heart rate response ~ 95921, 95943
parasympathetic ~ 95943
pseudomotor response ~ 95921-95924
sympathetic function ~ 95921-95924, 95943
valsalva maneuver ~ 95922, 95943
brain surface electrode stimulation ~ 95961-95962
central motor transcranial motor stimulation ~ 95928-95929

Neurology procedures ~ *continued*
electrocorticogram, intraoperative ~ 95829
electroencephalogram (EEG) ~ 95812-95827, 95955
brain death ~ 95824
electrode placement ~ 95830
intraoperative ~ 95955
monitoring ~ 95812-95813, 95950-95953, 95956
physical or drug activation ~ 95954
sleep ~ 95800-95801, 95822, 95827
standard ~ 95819
WADA activation ~ 95958
electroencephalography (EEG), digital analysis ~ 95957
electromyography
fine wire dynamic ~ 96004
ischemic limb exercise test ~ 95875
needle ~ 51785, 95860-95872
surface dynamic ~ 96002-96004
evoked potentials
auditory ~ 92585, 92586
central motor ~ 95928, 95929, 95939
somatosensory testing ~ 95925-95927, 95938
visual ~ 0333T, 0464T, 95930
higher cerebral function
aphasia test ~ 96105
cognitive function tests ~ 96116
developmental tests ~ 96110-96111
neurobehavioral status ~ 96116
neuropsychological testing ~ 96118-96120
magnetoencephalography (MEG) ~ 95965-95967
motion analysis
by video and 3-D kinematics ~ 96000, 96004
computer-based ~ 96000, 96004
muscle testing, manual ~ 95831-95834
nerve conduction
motor and sensory ~ 95905-95913
neurofunctional testing ~ 96020
neuromuscular junction tests ~ 95937
neurophysiological monitoring, intraoperative ~ 95940-95941
neuropsychological testing ~ 96118-96120
cognitive performance ~ 96125
computer assisted ~ 96120
plantar pressure measurements, dynamic ~ 96001, 96004
polysomnography ~ 95782-95783, 95808-95811
range of motion ~ 95851-95852
reflex
blink reflex ~ 95933
sleep study ~ 96800-95801, 95803-95811
somatosensory testing ~ 95925-95927, 95938-95939
tensilon test ~ 95857
unlisted services and procedures ~ 95999
urethral sphincter ~ 51785
visual evoked potential, CNS ~ 95930
Neurolysis
nerve ~ 64704-64708
internal ~ 64727
Neuroma
acoustic ~ see brain, tumor, excision
excision
cutaneous nerve ~ 64774
digital nerve ~ 64776-64778
foot ~ 28080
foot nerve ~ 64782-64783
hand nerve ~ 64782-64783
interdigital (Morton's) ~ 28080
peripheral nerve ~ 64784
sciatic nerve ~ 64786
injection, anesthetic or steroid ~ 64455
Neuromuscular junction tests ~ 95937
Neuromuscular pedicle reinnervation larynx ~ 31590
Neuromuscular reeducation ~ 97112
Neurophysiologic testing
autonomic nervous function
heart rate response ~ 95921-95924
pseudomotor response ~ 95921-95924
sympathetic function ~ 95921-95924
intraoperative ~ 95940-95941
Neuroplasty
cranial nerve ~ 64716
digital nerve ~ 64702-64704

Neuroplasty ~ *continued*
peripheral nerve
  arm ~ 64708
  brachial plexus ~ 64713
  cranial ~ 64716
  lrh ~ 64708
  lumbar plexus ~ 64714
  median at carpal tunnel ~ 64721
  sciatic ~ 64712
  ulnar at elbow ~ 64718
  ulnar at wrist ~ 64719
Neuropsychological testing ~ 96117
Neurorrhaphy ~ 64831-64876
peripheral nerve
  conduit ~ 64910-64911
  with graft ~ 64885-64907
Neurostimulation, application ~ 64550, 64566
Neurostimulators
analysis ~ 95970-95982
application ~ 64550, 64566
implantation
  electrode array ~ 64553, 64555, 64561
  by Burr hole ~ 61863, 61864
  by craniectomy ~ 61863, 61864, 61867, 61868
  vagus nerve ~ 0312T
  with image guidance ~ 64561
  electrodes ~ 43647, 43881, 64568
  by Burr hole ~ 61850
  by craniectomy ~ 61860
  pulse generator, vagus nerve ~ 0312T
insertion
  pulse generator ~ 0424T, 0427T, 61885, 61886, 64568, 64590
  receiver ~ 61885-61886, 64590
removal
  electrodes ~ 43648, 43882, 61880
  pulse generator ~ 61888, 64595
  receiver ~ 61888, 64595
  replacement ~ 61885
  electrodes ~ 43647, 43881
Neurotomy, sympathetic ~ see gasserian ganglion, sensory root, decompression
Neurovascular pedicle flaps ~ 15750
Neutralization test, virus ~ 86382
New patient
domiciliary or rest home visit ~ 99324-99328
emergency department services ~ 99281-99288
home services ~ 99341-99345
hospital inpatient services ~ 99221-99239
hospital observation services ~ 99217-99220
initial office visit ~ 99201-99205
inpatient consultations ~ 99251-99255
office and/or other outpatient consultations ~ 99241-99245
Newborn care ~ 99460-99465, 99502
attendance at delivery ~ 99464
blood transfusion
  exchange ~ 36450, 36456
  push ~ 36440
circumcision
  clamp or other device ~ 54150
  surgical excision ~ 54160
history and examination ~ 99460, 99463
laryngoscopy ~ 31520
normal ~ 99460-99463
prepuce slitting ~ 54000
preventive, office ~ 99461
resuscitation ~ 99465
standby for cesarean delivery ~ 99360
subsequent hospital care ~ 99462
umbilical artery catheterization ~ 36660
Next Generation Screening (NGS) and other molecular multianalyte assays
aortic dysfunction or dilation ~ 81410, 81411
exome ~ 81415-81417
fetal chromosoma aneuploidy ~ 81420
genome ~ 81425-81427
hearing loss ~ 81430, 81431

Next Generation Screening (NGS) ~ *continued*
hereditary
  breast cancer related disorders ~ 81432, 81433
  colon cancer disorders ~ 81435, 81436
  neuroendoscrine tymor disorders ~ 81437, 81438
  retinal disorders ~ 81434
noonan spectral disorders ~ 81442
nuclear encoded mitochondrial genes ~ 81440
targeted genomic sequence panel ~ 81445, 81450, 81455
whole mitochondrial genome ~ 81460, 81465
x-linked intellectual disability (XLID) ~ 81470, 81471
Nickel ~ 83885
Nicolas-Durand-Favre disease ~ see lymphogranuloma venereum
Nicotine ~ 83887
Nidation ~ see implantation
Nipples ~ see breast
inverted ~ 19355
reconstruction ~ 19350
Nissen operation ~ see fundoplasty, esophagogastric
Nissen procedure
laparoscopic ~ 43280
Nitrate reduction test ~ see urinalysis
Nitric Oxide ~ 95012
Nitroblue tetrazolium dye test ~ 86384
Nitrogen, blood urea ~ see blood urea nitrogen
NMR imaging ~ see magnetic resonance imaging (MRI)
NMR spectroscopies ~ see magnetic resonance spectroscopy
No man's land, tendon repair ~ 26356-26358
Noble procedure ~ see repair; suture
Nocardia, antibody ~ 86744
Nocturnal penile rigidity test ~ 54250
Nocturnal penile tumescence test ~ 54250
Node, lymph ~ see lymph nodes
Nodes ~ see lymph nodes
Node dissection, lymph ~ see dissection, lymph nodes
Non-office medical services ~ 99056
Non-stress test, fetal ~ 59025
Nonunion repairS
femur
  with graft ~ 27472
  without graft ~ 27470
metatarsal ~ 28322
tarsal joint ~ 28320
Noradrenalin
blood ~ 82383-82384
urine ~ 82384
Norchlorimipramine ~ see imipramine
Norepinephrine ~ see catecholamines
blood ~ 82383-82384
urine ~ 82384
Nortriptyline, assay ~ 80335-80337
Norwood procedure ~ 33611-33612, 33619, 33622
Nose
abscess, incision and drainage ~ 30000-30020
artery, incision ~ 30915-30920
biopsy, intranasal ~ 30100
dermoid cyst, excision
  complex ~ 30125
  simple ~ 30124
displacement therapy ~ 30210
endoscopy
  diagnostic ~ 31231-31235
  surgical ~ 31237-31241, 31253-31257, 31259, 31267, 31276, 31287, 31288, 31290-31298
excision
  rhinectomy ~ 30150-30160
  turbinate ~ 30140
fracture
  closed treatment ~ 21345
  open treatment ~ 21325-21336, 21338-21339, 21346-21347
  percutaneous treatment ~ 21340
  with fixation ~ 21330, 21340, 21345-21347
hematoma, incision and drainage ~ 30000-30020
hemorrhage, cauterization ~ 30901-30906
insertion, septal prosthesis ~ 30220
intranasal lesion
  external approach ~ 30118
  internal approach ~ 30117

Nose ~ *continued*
lysis of adhesions ~ 30560
polyp, excision
  extensive ~ 30115
  simple ~ 30110
reconstruction
  cleft lip/cleft palate ~ 30460-30462
  dermatoplasty ~ 30620
  primary ~ 30400-30420
  secondary ~ 30430-30450
  septum ~ 30520
removal
  foreign body ~ 30300
  anesthesia ~ 30310
  lateral rhinotomy ~ 30320
repair
  adhesions ~ 30560
  cleft lip ~ 40700-40761
  fistula ~ 30580-30600, 42260
  rhinophyma ~ 30120
  septum ~ 30540-30545, 30630
  synechia ~ 30560
  vestibular stenosis ~ 30465
skin
  excision ~ 30120
  surgical planing ~ 30120
submucous resection turbinate
  excision ~ 30140
turbinate
  excision ~ 30130-30140
  fracture ~ 30930
  injection ~ 30200
turbinate mucosa, cauterization ~ 30801-30802
unlisted services and procedures ~ 30999
Nose bleed ~ (hemorrhage, nasal) 30901-30906
NTD ~ (nitroblue tetrazolium dye test) 86384
Nuclear antigen, antibody ~ 86235
Nuclear imaging ~ see nuclear medicine
Nuclear magnetic resonance imaging ~ see magnetic resonance imaging (MRI)
Nuclear magnetic resonance spectroscopy ~ see magnetic resonance spectroscopy
Nuclear medicine ~ 78012-79999
adrenal gland imaging ~ 78075
bladder, residual study ~ 78730
blood
  flow imaging ~ 78445
  iron
    absorption ~ 78162
    chelatable ~ 78172
    plasma ~ 78160
    red cells ~ 78140
    utilization ~ 78170
  platelet survival ~ 78191
  red cells ~ 78120-78121
  red cells survival ~ 78130-78135
  unlisted services and procedures ~ 78199
  whole blood volume ~ 78122
bone
  density study ~ 78350-78351
  imaging ~ 78300-78320
  SPECT ~ 78320
  ultrasound ~ 76977
  ultrasound services and procedures ~ 78399
bone marrow imaging ~ 78102-78104
brain
  blood flow ~ 78610
  cerebrospinal flow ~ 78630-78650
  imaging ~ 78600-78609
  vascular flow ~ 78610
endocrine system, unlisted services and procedures ~ 78099
esophagus
  imaging (motility) ~ 78258
  reflux study ~ 78262
gastric mucosa imaging ~ 78261
gastrointestinal
  blood loss study ~ 78278
  protein loss study ~ 78282
  shunt testing ~ 78291
  unlisted services and procedures ~ 78299

Nuclear medicine ~ *continued*
genitourinary system, unlisted services and procedures ~ 78799
heart
  blood flow ~ 78414
  blood pool imaging ~ 78472-78473, 78481-78483, 78494-78496
  myocardial imaging ~ 78459, 78466-78469
  myocardial perfusion ~ 78451-78454
  shunt detection ~ 78428
  unlisted services and procedures ~ 78499
inflammatory process ~ 78805-78807
intestines imaging ~ 78290
kidney
  function study ~ 78725
  imaging ~ 78700-78707, 78710
lacrimal gland, tear flow ~ 78660
liver
  imaging ~ 78201-78216
  vascular flow ~ 78206
lung
  imaging perfusion ~ 78580, 78597, 78598
  imaging ventilation ~ 78579, 78582, 78598
  unlisted services and procedures ~ 78599
lymph nodes ~ 78195
lymphatics ~ 78195
  unlisted services and procedures ~ 78199
musculoskeletal system, unlisted services and procedures ~ 78399
nervous system, unlisted services and procedures ~ 78699
parathyroid gland imaging ~ 78070
pulmonary perfusion ~ 78580, 78597-78598
pulmonary ventilation ~ 78579, 78582, 78598
salivary gland function study ~ 78232
  imaging ~ 78230-78231
spleen
  imaging ~ 78185, 78215-78216
  unlisted services and procedures ~ 78199
stomach
  blood loss study ~ 78278
  emptying study ~ 78264
  protein loss study ~ 78282
  reflux study ~ 78262
  vitamin B-12 absorption ~ 78270-78272
testes imaging ~ 78761
therapeutic
  heart ~ 79440
  interstitial ~ 79300
  intra-arterial ~ 79445
  intra-articular ~ 79440
  intracavitary ~ 79200
  intravenous ~ 79101
  intravenous infusion ~ 79403
  oral ~ 79005
  thyroid ~ 79200-79300
  unlisted services and procedures ~ 79999
thyroid
  imaging for metastases ~ 78015-78018
  imaging with flow ~ 78013
  metastases uptake ~ 78020
  uptake ~ 78012, 78014
tumor imaging
  positron emission tomography (PET) ~ 78811-78816
    with computed tomography ~ 78814-78816
tumor localization ~ 78800-78804
unlisted services and procedures ~ 78999
urea breath test ~ 78267-78268
ureter, reflux study ~ 78740
vein thrombosis imaging ~ 78455-78458
Nucleases, DNA ~ see DNAse
Nucleic acid probe
amplified probe detection, infectious agent
  bartonella henselae ~ 87471
  bartonella quintana ~ 87471
  borrelia burgdorferi ~ 87476
  candida species ~ 87481
  central nervous system pathogen ~ 87483
  chlamydia pneumoniae ~ 87486
  chlamydia trachomatis ~ 87491
  cytomegalovirus ~ 87496
  enterovirus ~ 87498, 87500
  gardnerella vaginalis ~ 87511
  hepatitis B virus ~ 87516

1103

Nucleic acid probe ~ continued
    hepatitis C ~ 87521
    hepatitis G ~ 87526
    herpes simplex virus ~ 87529
    herpes virus-6 ~ 87532
    HIV-1 ~ 87535
    HIV-2 ~ 87538
    legionella pneumophila ~ 87541
    multiple organisms ~ 87801
    mycobacteria avium-intracellulare ~ 87561
    mycobacteria species ~ 87551
    mycobacteria tuberculosis ~ 87556
    mycoplasma pneumoniae ~ 87581
    neisseria gonorrheae ~ 87591
    not otherwise specified ~ 87798, 87801
    papillomavirus, human ~ 87623-87625
    staphylococcus aureus ~ 87640-87641
    streptococcus, group A ~ 87651
    streptococcus, group B ~ 87653
    Zika virus ~ 87662
  direct probe detection, infectious agent
    borrelia burgdorferi ~ 87475
    candida species ~ 87480
    chlamydia pneumoniae ~ 87485
    chlamydia trachomatis ~ 87490
    clostridium difficile ~ 87493
    cytomegalovirus ~ 87495
    gardnerella vaginalis ~ 87510
    hepatitis C ~ 87520
    hepatitis G ~ 87525
    herpes simplex virus ~ 87528
    herpes virus-6 ~ 87531
    HIV-1 ~ 87534
    HIV-2 ~ 87537
    legionella pneumophila ~ 87540
    multiple organisms ~ 87800
    mycobacteria avium-intracellulare ~ 87560
    mycobacteria species ~ 87550
    mycobacteria tuberculosis ~ 87555
    mycoplasma pneumoniae ~ 87580
    neisseria gonorrheae ~ 87590
    not otherwise specified ~ 87797
    papillomavirus, human ~ 0500T, 87623-87625
    streptococcus, group A ~ 87650
    trichomonas vaginalis ~ 87660
  genotype analysis, infectious agent
    HIV-1. ~ 87901, 87906
    hepatitis C virus ~ 87902
  in situ hybridization ~ 88120-88121, 88365-88368
  phenotype analysis, infectious agent
    HIV-1 drug resistance ~ 87903-87904
  quantification, infectious agent
    bartonella henselae ~ 87472
    bartonella quintana ~ 87472
    candida species ~ 87482
    chlamydia pneumoniae ~ 87487
    chlamydia trachomatis ~ 87492
    cytomegalovirus ~ 87497
    gardnerella vaginalis ~ 87512
    hepatitis B virus ~ 87517
    hepatitis C ~ 87522
    hepatitis G ~ 87527
    herpes simplex virus ~ 87530
    herpes virus-6 ~ 87533
    HIV-1 ~ 87536
    HIV-2 ~ 87539
    legionella pneumophila ~ 87542
    mycobacteria avium-intracellulare ~ 87562
    mycobacteria species ~ 87552
    mycobacteria tuberculosis ~ 87557
    mycoplasma pneumoniae ~ 87582
    neisseria gonorrheae ~ 87592
    not otherwise specified ~ 87799
    papillomavirus, human ~ 87623-87625
    streptococcus, group A ~ 87652
Nucleolysis, intervertebral disk ~ see chemonucleolysis
Nucleotidase ~ 83915
Nursemaid elbow ~ 24640
Nursing facility discharge services ~ see discharge services, nursing
    facility

Nursing facility services ~ 99304-99318
  annual assessment ~ 99318
  care plan oversight services ~ 99379-99380
  comprehensive assessments
    new or established patient ~ 99301-99303
  discharge services ~ 99315-99316, 1110F-1111F
  subsequent care ~ 99307-99310
Nuss procedure
  with thoracoscopy ~ 21743
  without thoracoscopy ~ 21742
Nutrition therapy
  group ~ 97804
  home infusion ~ 99601-99602
  initial assessment ~ 97802
  reassessment ~ 97803
Nystagmus tests ~ see vestibular function tests
  optokinetic ~ 92534, 92544
  positional ~ 92532, 92542
  spontaneous ~ 92531, 92540-92541

O

O2 (two) saturation ~ see oxygen saturation
Ober-Yount procedure ~ (fasciotomy, hip) 27025
Obliteration
  mastoid ~ 69670
  vagina
    total ~ 57110-57112
    vault ~ 57120
Oblongata, medulla ~ see medulla
Observation ~ (see Evaluation and Management; Hospital Services)
  99217-99220, 99224-99225, 99234-99236
Obstetrical care
  abortion
    induced
      by amniocentesis injection ~ 59850-59852
      by dilation and curettage ~ 59840
      by dilation and evaluation ~ 59841
    missed
      first trimester ~ 59820
      second trimester ~ 59821
    spontaneous ~ 59812
    therapeutic ~ 59840-59852
  antepartum care ~ 59425-59426
  cesarean delivery ~ 59618-59622
    only ~ 59514
    postpartum care ~ 59515
    routine ~ 59510
    with hysterectomy ~ 59525
  curettage, hydatidiform mole ~ 59870
  evacuation, hydatidiform mole ~ 59870
  external cephalic version ~ 59412
  miscarriage, surgical completion ~ 59812-59821
  placenta delivery ~ 59414
  postpartum care ~ 59430, 59514
  septic abortion ~ 59830
  total (global) ~ 59400, 59610, 59618
  unlisted services and procedures ~ 59898-59899
  vaginal, after cesarean ~ 59610-59614
  vaginal delivery ~ 59409-59410
    delivery after cesarean ~ 59610-59614
Obstruction ~ see occlusion
Obstruction clearance, venous access device ~ 36595-36596
Obstruction colon ~ see colon, obstruction
Obturator nerve
  avulsion ~ 64763-64766
  incision ~ 64763-64766
  transection ~ 64763-64766
Obturator prosthesis ~ 21076
  definitive ~ 21080
  insertion, larynx ~ 31527
  interim ~ 21079
Occipital nerve, greater
  avulsion ~ 64744
  incision ~ 64744
  injection, anesthetic ~ 64405
  transection ~ 64744

Occlusion
bronchi, balloon ~ 31634, 31647, 31651
fallopian tube, oviduct ~ 58565, 58615, 58671
paravalvular leak
  aortic valve ~ 93591, 93592
  mitral valve ~ 93590, 93592
penis, vein ~ 37790
umbilical cord ~ 59072
ureteral ~ 50705
vascular
  arterial, other than hemorrhage or tumor ~ 37242
  carotid artery ~ 37605, 61705
  dialysis circuit ~ 36909
  during endovascular therapy ~ 34820
  for hemorrhage ~ 37244
  for infarction ~ 37243
  for lymphatic extravasation ~ 37244
  for organ ischemia ~ 37243
  for tumors ~ 37243
  nervous system
    cranial ~ 61623, 61624, 61626
    spinal ~ 61624, 61626, 62294, 63250-63252
  placement of occlusive device ~ 34808
  venous, other than hemorrhage ~ 37241
  with ligation ~ 37606
Occlusive disease of artery ~ see repair, artery; revision
Occult blood ~ 82270
penis, by hemoglobin immunoassay ~ 82274
Occupational therapy
evaluation ~ 97165, 97166, 97167
re-evaluation ~ 97168
Ocular implant ~ see orbital implant
insertion
  drug-eluting insert, eyelid ~ 0444T, 0445T
  in scleral shell ~ 65130
  muscles attached ~ 65140
  muscles, not attached ~ 65135
modification ~ 65125
reinsertion ~ 65150
  with foreign material ~ 65155
removal ~ 65175
Ocular muscle ~ see eye muscles
Ocular orbit ~ see orbit
Ocular prostheses ~ see prosthesis, ocular
Ocular screening ~ 99174, 99177
retinal polarization scan ~ 0469T
Oculomotor muscle ~ see eye muscles
Oddi sphincter ~ see sphincter of Oddi
Odontoid dislocation
open treatment/reduction ~ 22318
  with grafting ~ 22319
Odontoid fracture
open treatment/reduction ~ 22318
  with grafting ~ 22319
Odontoid process, excision ~ 22548
Oesophageal neoplasm ~ see tumor, esophagus
Oesophageal varices ~ see esophageal varices
Oesophagus ~ see esophagus
Oestradiol ~ see estradiol
Office and/or other outpatient services
established patient ~ 99211-99215
new patient ~ 99201-99205
normal newborn ~ 99461
office visit
  established patient ~ 99211-99215
  new patient ~ 99201-99205
outpatient visit
  established patient ~ 99211-99215
  new patient ~ 99201-99205
  prolonged services ~ 99354, 99355, 99415, 99416
Office medical services
after hours ~ 99050
emergency care ~ 99058
extended hours ~ 99051
Office or other outpatient consultations ~ 99241-99245
Olecranon ~ see elbow; humerus; radius; ulna
bursa, arthrocentesis ~ 20605
cyst, excision ~ 24125-24126
tumor
  cyst ~ 24120
  excision ~ 24125-24126

Olecranon process
craterization ~ 24147
diaphysectomy ~ 24147
excision ~ 24147
  abscess ~ 24138
fracture ~ see elbow; humerus; radius
  closed treatment ~ 24670-24675
  open treatment ~ 24685
osteomyelitis ~ 24138, 24147
saucerization ~ 24147
sequestrectomy ~ 24138
Oligoclonal immunoglobulins ~ 83916
Omentectomy
separate procedure ~ 49255
with laparotomy ~ 58960
with lymph node laparoscopy ~ 38573
with oophorectomy ~ 58943
with tumor debulking ~ 58575, 58950-58954, 58956-58958, 58960
Omentum
excision ~ 49255, 58950-58958
flap ~ 49904-49905
  free, with microvascular anastomosis ~ 49906
unlisted services and procedures ~ 49999
Omphalectomy ~ 49250
Omphalocele, repair ~ 49600-49611
Omphalomesenteric duct, excision ~ 44800
Omphalomesenteric duct, persistent ~ see diverticulum, Meckel's
Oncoprotein
des-gamma-carboxyprothrombin (DCP) ~ 83951
HER-2/neu ~ 83950
One stage prothrombin time ~ (see also prothrombin time) 85610-85611
Online medical evaluation ~ 99444
Onychectomy ~ see excision, nails
Onychia, drainage ~ 10060-10061
Oocyte
assisted fertilization, microtechnique ~ 89280-89281
biopsy ~ 89290-89291
culture
  extended ~ 89272
  less than 4 (four) days ~ 89250
  with co-culture ~ 89251
identification, follicular fluid ~ 89254
insemination ~ 89268
retrieval, for in vitro fertilization ~ 58970
storage ~ 89346
thawing ~ 89356
Oophorectomy ~ 58262-58263, 58291-58292, 58552, 58554, 58661, 58940-58943
ectopic pregnancy
  laparoscopic treatment ~ 59120
  surgical treatment ~ 59120
Oophorectomy, partial ~ see excision, ovary, partial
Oophorocystectomy ~ see cystectomy, ovarian
Open biopsy, adrenal gland ~ see adrenal gland, biopsy
Operating microscope ~ 69990
Operation
Abbe-Estlander ~ 00102, 40527, 40761
Bischof ~ 63170
Blalock-Hanlon ~ 33735-33737
Blalock-Taussig ~ 33750
Bristow ~ 23460
Campbell ~ 27422
Chevron ~ 28296
Cotte ~ 58400-58410
Dunn ~ see arthrodesis, foot joint
Duvries ~ see tenoplasty
Estes ~ see ovary, transposition
Foley y-pyeloplasty ~ 50400-50405
Fontan ~ see repair, heart, anomaly
Gill ~ 63012
Green ~ see scapulopexy
Halsted ~ 49491
Heller ~ 32665
Hibb ~ 22610, 22612, 22614
Jaboulay gastroduodenostomy ~ 43810
Keller ~ 28292
Leriche ~ 64809
Mumford ~ 29824
Nissen ~ 43324
Norwood ~ 33611-33612, 33619

Operation ~ *continued*
Potts-Smith ~ 33762
Ramstedt ~ see pyloromyotomy
Raskind ~ 33735-33737
Raz ~ 51845
Richardson hysterectomy ~ 53460
Schlatter total gastrectomy ~ 43620-43622
Swanson ~ 28309
Swenson ~ 45120
Takeuchi ~ 33505
Thiersch ~ 15050
Winiwarter ~ 47720-47740
Winter ~ 54435
Operation microscopes ~ see operating microscope
Operculectomy ~ 41821
Operculum ~ see gums
Ophthalmic mucous membrane test ~ (see also allergy tests) 95060
Ophthalmology services ~ 92002-92499
Ophthalmology, diagnostic
color vision exam ~ 92283
computerized scanning ~ 92132-92134
computerized screening ~ 99172, 99174
dark adaptation ~ 92284
electro-oculography ~ 92270
electromyography, needle ~ 92265
electroretinography ~ 92275
endoscopy ~ 66990
evoked potentials
acuity ~ 0333T
central nervous system ~ 95930
glaucoma test ~ 0464T
eye exam
established patient ~ 92012-92014
new patient ~ 92002-92004
with anesthesia ~ 92018-92019
gonioscopy ~ 92020
ocular photography
external ~ 92285
internal ~ 92286-92287
ophthalmoscopy ~ 92225-92226
with dynamometry ~ 92260
with fluorescein angiography ~ 92235
with fluorescein angioscopy ~ 92230
with fundus photography ~ 92250
with indocyanine-green angiography ~ 92240
remote imaging ~ 92227-92228
photoscreening ~ 99174
refractive determination ~ 92015
sensorimotor exam ~ 92060
tonometry, serial ~ 92100
ultrasound ~ 76511-76529
visual acuity screen ~ 99172-99173
visual field exam ~ 92081-92083
visual function screen ~ 99172, 99174, 99177
Ophthalmoscopy ~ 92225-92226
Opiates ~ 80361-80364
Opinion, second ~ see confirmatory consultations
Optic nerve
decompression ~ 67570
with nasal/sinus endoscopy ~ 31294
head evaluation ~ 2027F
Optical coherence tomography (OCT)
axillary lymphy node ~ 0351T, 0352T
breast ~ 0351T-0354T
intravascular ~ 92978, 92979
middle ear ~ 0485T, 0486T
skin lesion ~ 0470T, 0471T
Optical endomicroscopy
esophageal ~ 43206
gastrointestinal ~ 43252
with endoscopic retrograde cholangio- pancreatopgraphy (ERCP) ~ 0397T
Optokinetic nystagmus test ~ see nystagmus tests, optokinetic
Oral lactose tolerance test ~ see glucose, tolerance test ~ 82951
Oral mucosa ~ see mouth, mucosa
Oral surgical splint ~ 21085
Orbit ~ see orbital contents; orbital floor; periorbital region
biopsy ~ 61332
exploration ~ 67450
fine needle aspiration or orbital contents ~ 67415
orbitotomy without bone flap ~ 67400

Orbit ~ *continued*
CT scan ~ 70480-70482
decompression ~ 61330
bone removal ~ 67414, 67445
exploration ~ 61332, 67400, 67450
lesion, excision ~ 61333
fracture
closed treatment
with manipulation ~ 21401
without manipulation ~ 21400
open treatment ~ 21406-21408
blowout fracture ~ 21385-21395
incision and drainage ~ 67405, 67440
injection
retrobulbar ~ 67500-67505
tenon's capsule ~ 67515
insertion, implant ~ 67550
lesion, excision ~ 67412, 67420
magnetic resonance imaging (MRI) ~ 70540-70543
removal
decompression ~ 67445
foreign body ~ 67413, 67430
implant ~ 67560
sella turcica ~ 70482
unlisted services and procedures ~ 67599
X-ray ~ 70190-70200
Orbital contents, aspiration ~ 67415
Orbital floor ~ see orbit; periorbital region
fracture, blow out ~ 21385-21395
Orbital hypertelorism, osteotomy
periorbital ~ 21260-21263
Orbital implant ~ see ocular implant
insertion ~ 67550
removal ~ 67560
Orbital prosthesis ~ 21077
Orbital rims, reconstruction ~ 21182-21184
Orbital rim and forehead, reconstruction ~ 21172-21180
Orbital transplant ~ 67560
Orbital walls, reconstruction ~ 21182-21184
Orbitocraniofacial reconstruction, secondary ~ 21275
Orbitotomy
with bone flap
for exploration ~ 67450
lateral approach ~ 67420
with drainage ~ 67440
with removal foreign body ~ 67430
with removal of bone for decompression ~ 67445
without bone flap
for exploration ~ 67400
with drainage only ~ 67405
with removal lesion ~ 67412
with removal foreign body ~ 67413
with removal of bone for decompression ~ 67414
Orbit area reconstruction, secondary ~ 21275
Orbit wall decompression with nasal/sinus endoscopy ~ 31292-31293
Orchidectomies ~ see excision, testis
Orchidopexy ~ see orchiopexy
Orchidoplasty ~ see repair, testis
Orchiectomy
laparoscopic ~ 54690
partial ~ 54522
radical
abdominal exploration ~ 54535
inguinal approach ~ 54530
simple ~ 54520
Orchiopexy
abdominal approach ~ 54650
inguinal approach ~ 54640
intra-abdominal testis ~ 54692
Orchioplasty ~ see repair, testis
Organ or disease oriented panels ~ 80048-80076
electrolyte ~ 80051
general health panel ~ 80050
hepatic function panel ~ 80076
hepatitis panel ~ 80074
lipid panel ~ 80061
metabolic
basic ~ 80047, 80048
comprehensive ~ 80053
obstetric panel ~ 80055, 80081
renal function ~ 80069

Organic acids ~ 83918-83921
Organ grafting ~ see transplantation
Organ system, neurologic ~ see nervous system
Ormond disease ~ see retroperitoneal fibrosis
Orogastric tube placement ~ 43752
Oropharynx, biopsy ~ 42800
Orthodontic cephalogram ~ 70350
Orthomyxoviridae ~ see influenza virus
Orthomyxovirus ~ see influenza virus
Orthopantogram ~ 70355
Orthopedic cast ~ see cast
Orthopedic surgery
  computer assisted navigation ~ 0054T-0055T, 20985
  stereotaxis, computer assisted ~ 20985
Orthoptic training ~ 92065
Orthoroentgenogram ~ 77073
Orthosis ~ see orthotics
Orthotics
  fitting ~ 97760
  management and training ~ 97760, 97763
Osmolality
  blood ~ 83930
  urine ~ 83935
Osseous survey ~ 77074-77076
Osseous tissue ~ see bone
Ossicles
  excision stapes
    with footplate drill out ~ 69661
    without foreign material ~ 69660-69661
  reconstruction ossicular chain
    tympanoplasty with antrotomy or mastoidotomy ~ 69636-69637
    tympanoplasty with mastoidectomy ~ 69642, 69644, 69646
    tympanoplasty without mastoidectomy ~ 69632-69633
  release, stapes ~ 69650
  replacement, with prosthesis ~ 69633, 69637
Ostectomy
  metacarpal ~ 26250
  metatarsal ~ 28288
  phalanges, finger ~ 26260-26262
  pressure ulcer
    ischial ~ 15941, 15945
    sacral ~ 15933, 15935, 15937
    trochanteric ~ 15951, 15953, 15958
  scapula ~ 23190
  sternum ~ 21620
Osteocalcin ~ 83937
Osteocartilaginous exostoses ~ see exostosis
Osteochondroma ~ see exostosis
Osteocutaneous flap, with microvascular anastomosis ~ 20969-20973
Osteoma sinusotomy, frontal ~ 31075
Osteomyelitis ~ 20005
  elbow, incision and drainage ~ 23935
  excision
    clavicle ~ 23180
    facial ~ 21026
    humerus, proximal ~ 23184
    mandible ~ 21025
    scapula ~ 23182
  femur/knee, incision and drainage ~ 27303
  finger incision ~ 26034
  hand incision ~ 26034
  hip incision, deep ~ 26992
  humerus ~ 24134
    incision and drainage ~ 23935
  incision
    foot ~ 28005
    shoulder ~ 23035
    thorax ~ 21510
  olecranon process ~ 24138, 24147
  pelvis incision, deep ~ 26992
  radius ~ 24136, 24145
  sequestrectomy
    clavicle ~ 23170
    humeral head ~ 23174
    scapula ~ 23172
    skull ~ 61501
Osteopathic manipulation ~ 98925-98929

Osteoplasty
  carpal bone ~ 25394
  facial bones
    augmentation ~ 21208
    reduction ~ 21209
  femoral neck ~ 27179
  femur ~ 27179
    lengthening ~ 27466-27468
    shortening ~ 27465, 27468
  fibula, lengthening ~ 27715
  humerus ~ 24420
  metacarpal ~ 26568
  phalanges, finger ~ 26568
  radius ~ 25390-25393
  tibia, lengthening ~ 27715
  ulna ~ 25390-25393
  vertebra ~ 72291-72292
    lumbar ~ 22521-22522
    thoracic ~ 22520-22522
Osteotomy
  calcaneus ~ 28300
  chin ~ 21121-21123
  clavicle ~ 23480-23485
  femur ~ 27140, 27151
    femoral neck ~ 27161
    for slipped epiphysis ~ 27181
    with fixation ~ 27165
    without fixation ~ 27448-27450
    with open reduction of hip ~ 27156
    with realignment ~ 27454
  fibula ~ 27707-27712
  hip ~ 27146-27151
    femoral, with open reduction ~ 27156
    femur ~ 27151
  humerus ~ 24400-24410
  mandible ~ 21198-21199
    extra-oral ~ 21047
    intra-oral ~ 21046
  maxilla ~ 21206
    extra-oral ~ 21049
    intra-oral ~ 21048
  metacarpal ~ 26565
  metatarsal ~ 28306-28309
    with bunionectomy ~ 28295, 28296
  orbit reconstruction ~ 21256
  pelvis ~ 27158
  periorbital
    orbital hypertelorism ~ 21260-21263
    osteotomy with graft ~ 21267-21268
  phalanges
    finger ~ 26567
    toe ~ 28299, 28310-28312
  radius
    and ulna ~ 25365, 25375
    distal third ~ 25350
    middle or proximal third ~ 25355
    multiple ~ 25370
  skull base ~ 61582-61585, 61592
  spine
    anterior ~ 22220-22226
    posterior, posterolateral ~ 22206-22208, 22210-22214
  talus ~ 28302
  tarsal ~ 28304-28305
  tibia ~ 27455-27457, 27705, 27709-27712
  ulna ~ 25360
    multiple ~ 25370
    and radius ~ 25365, 25375
  vertebra
    additional segment, anterior approach ~ 22226
      posterior/posterolateral approach ~ 22216
    cervical
      anterior approach ~ 22220
      posterior/posterolateral approach ~ 22210
    lumbar
      anterior approach ~ 22224
      posterior/posterolateral approach ~ 22214
    thoracic
      anterior approach ~ 22222
      posterior/posterolateral approach ~ 22212
  with graft reconstruction periorbital region ~ 21267-21268

Osteotomy ~ continued
  with bunionectomy ~ 28295, 28296, 28298, 28299
  with graft
    reconstruction, periorbital region ~ 21267, 21268
Os calcis fracture ~ see calcaneus, fracture
Otolaryngology, diagnostic exam under anesthesia ~ 92502
Otomy ~ see incision
Otoplasty ~ 69300
Otorhinolaryngology services ~ 92502-92597
Ouchterlony immunodiffusion ~ 86331
Outer ear ~ see ear, outer
Outpatient visit ~ see history and physical; office and/or other outpatient
  services
Output, cardiac ~ see cardiac output
Ova, smear ~ 87177
Oval window, repair fistula ~ 69666
Oval window fistula ~ see fistula, oval window
Ovarian cyst ~ see cyst, ovarian; ovary, cyst
Ovarian vein syndrome, ureterolysis ~ 50722
Ovariectomies ~ see oophorectomy
Ovariolysis ~ 58740
Ovary
  abscess, incision and drainage ~ 58820-58822
    abdominal approach ~ 58822
  biopsy ~ 49321, 58900
  cryopreservation ~ 0058T
  cyst
    excision ~ 58925
    incision and drainage ~ 58800-58805
  excision ~ 58662, 58720
    cyst ~ 58925
    partial
      oophorectomy ~ 58661, 58940
      ovarian malignancy ~ 58943
      peritoneal malignancy ~ 58943
      tubal malignancy ~ 58943
      wedge resection ~ 58920
    total ~ 58940-58943
  laparoscopy ~ 58660-58662, 58679
  lysis, adhesions ~ 58660, 58740
  malignancy
    resection ~ 58950-58952, 58957, 58958
    staging laparotomy ~ 58960
  oncology
    biochemical assay
      apolipoprotein A1 ~ 81503
      beta-2 microglobulin ~ 81503
      CA-125 ~ 81500, 81503
      HE4 ~ 81500
      menopausal status ~ 81500
      pre-albumin ~ 81503
      transferrin ~ 81503
    radical resection ~ 58950-58952
  removal
    with pelvic exenteration ~ 45126, 58240
    with radical trachelectomy ~ 58531
    with hysterectmy ~ 58150, 58152, 58180, 58200, 58210
    laparoscopic ~ 58542, 58544, 58548, 58554, 58552, 58571, 58573,
      58575
    vaginal ~ 58262, 58263, 58291, 58292
  transposition ~ 58825
  tumor, resection ~ 58950-58958
  unlisted services and procedures ~ 58679, 58999
  wedge resection ~ 58920
Oviduct
  anastomosis ~ 58750
  chromotubation ~ 58350
  ectopic pregnancy ~ 59120-59121
  excision ~ 58700-58720
  fulguration, laparoscopic ~ 58670
  hysterosalpingography ~ 74740
  laparoscopy ~ 58679
  ligation ~ 58600-58611
  lysis, adhesions ~ 58740
  occlusion ~ 58615
    laparoscopic ~ 58671
  repair ~ 58752
    anastomosis ~ 58750
    create stoma ~ 58770
  unlisted services and procedures ~ 58679, 58999
  X-ray with contrast ~ 74740

Ovocyte ~ see oocyte
Ovulation tests ~ 84830
Ovum implantation ~ see implantation
Ovum transfer surgery ~ see gamete intrafallopian transfer (GIT)
Oxalate ~ 83945
Oxidase, ceruloplasmin ~ see ceruloplasmin
Oxidoreductase, alcohol-nad+ ~ see antidiuretic hormone
Oximetry (noninvasive) ~ see pulmonology, diagnostic
  blood O2 saturation, ear or pulse ~ 94760-94762
  pulse, recording
    car seat/bed testing ~ 94780, 94781
  with pulmonary stess testing ~ 94618
Oxoisomerase ~ see phosphohexose isomerase
Oxosteroids ~ see ketosteroids
Oxygenation, extracorporeal membrane ~ see extracorporeal membrane
  oxygenation
Oxygen saturation ~ 82805-82810
Oxyproline ~ see hydroxyproline
Oxytocin stress test, fetal ~ 59020

P

P & P ~ (proconvertin) 85230
P-acetamidophenol ~ see acetaminophen
Pacemaker, heart
  conversion ~ 33214
  data analysis ~ 93288, 93293-93294
  electronic analysis ~ 93288
    antitachycardia system ~ 93724
  evaluation and programming
    dual lead ~ 93280, 93286, 93288, 93289
    implantable subcutaneou lead ~ 93260, 93261
    in person ~ 93261, 93279-93281, 93286, 93288, 93289
    multiple lead ~ 93281, 93286, 93288, 93289
    remote ~ 93293-93294, 93296
    single lead ~ 93279, 93286, 93288, 93289
  insertion ~ 33206-33208
    electrode ~ 33202-33203, 33216-33217, 33224-33225
    temporary ~ 33210-33211, 93583
    pulse generator only ~ 33212-33213, 33221
  lead placement ~ 33202-33203
  leadless system
    device evaluation, in person
      interrogation ~ 0391T
      peri-procedural ~ 0390T
      programming ~ 0389T
    transcatheter insertion ~ 0387T
    transcatheter removal ~ 0388T
    transcatheter replacement ~ 0387T
  relocate, skin pocket
    for pacemaker ~ 33222
  removal
    pulse generator only ~ 33233
    transvenous electrodes ~ 33234-33235
    via thoracotomy ~ 33236-33237
  repair, electrode ~ 33218-33220
  replacement
    catheter ~ 33210
    electrode ~ 33210-33211
    insertion ~ 33206-33208
    pulse generator ~ 33227-33229
  repositioning, electrode ~ 33215, 33226
  revise pocket, chest ~ 33222
  telephonic analysis ~ 93293
  upgrade ~ 33214
Pachymetry, eye ~ 76514
  with collagen cross-linking ~ 0402T
Packing, nasal hemorrhage ~ 30901-30906
Pain management
  epidural/intrathecal ~ 62350-62351, 62360-62362, 99601-99602
  intravenous therapy ~ 90783-90784
Palatal augmentation prosthesis ~ 21082
Palatal lift prosthesis ~ 21083

Palate
- abscess, incision and drainage ~ 42000
- biopsy ~ 42100
- excision ~ 42120, 42145
- fracture
  - closed treatment ~ 21421
  - open treatment ~ 21422-21423
- lesion
  - destruction ~ 42160
  - excision ~ 42104-42120
- prosthesis ~ 42280-42281
- reconstruction, lengthening ~ 42226-42227
- repair
  - cleft palate ~ 42200-42225
  - laceration ~ 42180-42182
  - Vomer flap ~ 42235
- unlisted services and procedures ~ 42299

Palate, cleft ~ see cleft palate
Palatoplasty ~ 42200-42225
Palatoschisis ~ see cleft palate
Palm
- bursa, incision and drainage ~ 26025-26030
- fasciectomy ~ 26121-26125
- fasciotomy ~ 26040-26045
- tendon, excision ~ 26170
- tendon sheath
  - excision ~ 26145
  - incision and drainage ~ 26020

Palsy, seventh nerve ~ see facial nerve paralysis
Pancreas
- anastomosis, with intestines ~ 48520-48540
- anesthesia ~ 00794
- biopsy ~ 48100
  - needle biopsy ~ 48102
- cyst
  - anastomosis ~ 48520-48540
  - repair ~ 48500
- debridement, peripancreatic tissue ~ 48105
- dilation, ampulla of vater ~ 47542, 43277
- excision
  - ampulla of vater ~ 48148
  - duct ~ 48148
  - partial ~ 48140-48146, 48150, 48154, 48160
  - peripancreatic tissue ~ 48105
  - total ~ 48155-48160
- lesion, excision ~ 48120
- needle biopsy ~ 48102
- placement, drainage ~ 48000-48001
- pseudocyst
  - drainage ~ 48510
- removal, calculi (stone) ~ 48020
- removal transplanted allograft ~ 48556
- repair, cyst ~ 48500
- suture ~ 48545
- transplantation ~ 48160, 48550, 48554-48556
  - allograft preparation ~ 48550-48552
- unlisted services and procedures ~ 48999
- X-ray with contrast ~ 74300
  - injection procedure ~ 48400

Pancreas, endocrine only ~ see islet cell
Pancreatectomy
- donor ~ 48550
- partial ~ 48140-48146, 48150-48154, 48160
- total ~ 48155-48160
- with transplantation ~ 48160

Pancreaticojejunostomy ~ 48548
Pancreatic DNAse ~ see DNAse
Pancreatic duct
- destruction, calculi (stone) ~ 43265
- dilation, endoscopy ~ 43277
- endoscopic retrograde cholangiopancreatography (ERCP) with optical endomicroscope ~ 0397T
- endoscopy ~ 43273
  - collection, specimen ~ 43260
  - destruction
    - calculi (stone) ~ 43265
    - tumor ~ 43272
  - dilation ~ 43277
  - removal (endoscopic)
    - calculi (stone) ~ 43264

Pancreatic duct ~ *continued*
  - foreign body ~ 43275-43276
    - stent ~ 43275-43276
  - sphincter pressure ~ 43263
  - sphincterotomy ~ 43262
  - tube placement ~ 43274
- incision, sphincter ~ 43262
- removal
  - calculi (stone) ~ 43264
  - foreign body ~ 43275-43276
  - stent ~ 43275-43276
- tube placement
  - nasopancreatic ~ 43274
  - stent ~ 43268
- tumor, destruction ~ 43272
- X-ray
  - guide catheter ~ 74329-74330
  - injection procedure ~ 47531, 47532, 48400
  - intra-operative ~ 74300, 74301

Pancreatic elastase 1 (PEL1) ~ 82656
Pancreatic islet cell ab ~ see antibody, islet cell
Pancreatitis, incision and drainage ~ 48000
Pancreatography
- injection procedure ~ 48400
- intraoperative ~ 74300-74301
- postoperative ~ 47531, 47532

Pancreatojejunostomies ~ see pancreaticojejunostomy
Pancreatorrhaphy ~ 48545
Pancreatotomy ~ see incision, pancreas
Pancreozymin-secretin test ~ 82938
Panel ~ see organ or disease oriented panel
Panniculectomy ~ see lipectomy
Paper chromatographies ~ see chromatography, paper
Papilla, interdental ~ see gums
Pap smears ~ 88141-88155, 88164-88167, 88174-88175
Papillectomy ~ 46220
Papilloma
- destruction ~ 54050-54065
  - anus ~ 46900-46924
  - penis ~ 54050-54065

PAPP D ~ see lactogen, human placental
Para-tyrosine ~ see tyrosine
Paracentesis
- abdomen ~ 49082-49083
- eye
  - with aqueous aspiration ~ 65800
  - with aqueous release ~ 65800
  - with discission of anterior hyaloid membrane ~ 65810
  - with removal
    - blood ~ 65815
    - vitreous ~ 65810
- thorax ~ 32554-32555

Paracervical nerve
- injection, anesthetic ~ 64435

Paraesophageal hiatal hernia
- repair via
  - laparotomy ~ 43332-43333
  - thoracoabdominal incision ~ 43336-43337
  - thoracotomy ~ 43334-43335

Paraffin bath therapy ~ 97018
Paraganglioma, medullary ~ see pheochromocytoma
Parainfluenza virus antigen detection, immunofluorescence ~ 87279
Paralysis, facial nerve ~ see facial nerve paralysis
Paralysis, infantile ~ see polio
Paranasal sinuses ~ see sinus; sinuses
Parasites
- blood ~ 87207
- examination ~ 87169
- smear ~ 87177

Parasitic worms ~ see helminth
Parathormone ~ 83970
Parathyrin ~ see parathormone
Parathyroidectomy ~ 60500-60505
Parathyroid autotransplantation ~ 60512
Parathyroid gland
- autotransplant ~ 60512
- excision ~ 60500-60502
- exploration ~ 60500-60505
- nuclear medicine, imaging ~ 78070

Parathyroid hormone ~ 83970
Parathyroid hormone measurement ~ see parathormone

1109

Parathyroid transplantation ~ see transplantation, parathyroid
Paraurethral gland
 abscess, incision and drainage ~ 53060
Paravertebral nerve
 destruction ~ 64633-64636
 injection
  anesthetic ~ 64461, 64462, 64490-64495
  neurolytic ~ 64633-64636
 infusion, anesthetic ~ 64463
Parietal cell vagotomies ~ see vagotomy, highly selective
Parietal craniotomy ~ 61556
Paring
 skin lesion, benign hyperkeratotic
  more than four lesions ~ 11057
  single lesion ~ 11055
  two to four lesions ~ 11056
Paronychia, incision and drainage ~ 10060-10061
Parotid duct
 diversion ~ 42507-42510
 reconstruction ~ 42507-42510
Parotid gland
 abscess, incision and drainage ~ 42300-42305
 calculi (stone), excision ~ 42330, 42340
 excision
  partial ~ 42410-42415
  total ~ 42420-42426
 tumor, excision ~ 42410-42426
Parotitides, epidemic ~ see mumps
Pars abdominalis aortae ~ see aorta, abdominal
Partial
 colectomy ~ see colectomy, partial
 cystectomy ~ see cystectomy, partial
 esophagectomy ~ see esophagectomy, partial
 gastrectomy ~ see excision, stomach, partial
 glossectomy ~ see excision, tongue, partial
 hepatectomy ~ see excision, liver, partial
 mastectomies ~ see breast, excision, lesion
 nephrectomy ~ see excision, kidney, partial
 pancreatectomy ~ see pancreatectomy, partial
 splenectomy ~ see splenectomy, partial
 thromboplastin time ~ see thromboplastin, partial, time
 ureterectomy ~ see ureterectomy, partial
Particle agglutination ~ 86403-86406
Parvovirus antibody ~ 86747
Patch allergy tests ~ 95044
Patella
 dislocation ~ 27560-27566
 excision ~ 27350
  with reconstruction ~ 27424
 fracture ~ 27520-27524
 reconstruction ~ 27437-27438
 repair
  chondromalacia ~ 27418
  instability ~ 27420-27424
Patella, chondromalacia ~ see chondromalacia patella
Patellar tendon bearing (PTB) cast ~ 29435
Patellectomy with reconstruction ~ 27424
Paternity testing ~ 86910-86911
Patey's operation ~ see mastectomy, radical
Pathologic dilatation ~ see dilation
Pathology and laboratory
 atomic absorption spectroscopy ~ 82190
 breath test
  alcohol, ethyl ~ 82075
  heart transplant rejection detection ~ 0085T
  Helicobacter pylori ~ 78267-78268, 83013-83014
  urea ~ 78267-78268
 caffeine ~ 89049
 cell count
  body fluid ~ 86152-86153, 89050-89051
   crystal identification ~ 89060
   with immunologic selection ~ 86152-86153
 cerebrospinal fluid
  cell count ~ 89050
  immunoelectrophoresis ~ 86325
  myelin basic protein ~ 83873
  protein, total ~ 84157
 chemiluminescent assay ~ 82397

Pathology and laboratory ~ *continued*
 chemistry ~ 82009-84999
  cocaine, screen ~ 80305-80307
  gammaglobulin IgA ~ 82784, 82787
  gammaglobulin IgE ~ 82785, 82787
   allergen specific ~ 86003, 86005, 86008
  gammaglobulin IgG ~ 82784, 82787
  gammaglobulin IgM ~ 82784, 82787
  heroin ~ 80305-80307, 80356
  marijuana ~ 80305-80307
  testosterone ~ 84402, 84403, 84410
 cholesterol
  HDL ~ 83718
  LDL ~ 83721
  lipid panel ~ 80061
  serum ~ 82465
  VLDL ~ 83719
 chronic gonadotropin ~ 84702-84704
  stimulation panel ~ 80414-80415
 clinical consultation ~ 80500-80502
 cytogenic studies ~ 88230-88299
 cytopathology ~ 88104-88140
 hematology and coagulation ~ 85002-85999
  blood typing ~ 86920-86923
 infectious agent
  immunoassay detection ~ 86317, 86318, 87449-87451, 87802-87804,
   87806-87810, 87850, 87880, 87899
 in vivo procedures ~ 88720-88749
 microbiology ~ 87003-87999
 molecular pathology ~ 81200-81099
 multianalyte assays with algorithmic analyses
  adoponectin ~ 81506
  apolipoprotein A1 ~ 81503
  AFP ~ 81510-81512
  beta-2 microglobulin ~ 81503
  CA-125 ~ 81500, 81503
  DIA ~ 81509, 81511, 81512
  ferritin ~ 81506
  glucose ~ 81506
  HbA1c ~ 81506
  hCG ~ 81508-81512
  HE4 ~ 81500
  hs-CRP ~ 81506
  insulin ~ 81506
  interleukin 2-receptor alpha ~ 81506
  mRNA ~ 81519-81521
  oncological gene profiling ~ 81504
  PAPP-A ~ 81508, 81509
  prealbumin ~ 81503
  trisomy 21, 18, and 13 ~ 81507
  transferrin ~ 81503
  uE3 ~ 81510-81512
  unlisted ~ 81599
 optical endomicroscopy ~ 88375
 ovulation tests ~ 84830
 particle agglutination ~ 86403-86406
 paternity testing ~ 86910-86911
 postmortem ~ 88000-88099
 radioimmunoassay ~ 82009-84999
 reproductive medicine ~ 89250-89398
 surgical pathology ~ 88300-88399
  antibody stain procedure immunofluorescence ~ 88346, 88350
  archived tissue examination ~ 88363
  consultation ~ 88321-88325
   intraoperative ~ 88329-88334
  decalcification procedure ~ 88311
  electron microscopy ~ 88348
  gross and micro exam
   level II ~ 88302
   level III ~ 88304
   level IV (four) ~ 88305
   level V (five) ~ 88307
   level VI (six) ~ 88309
  gross exam, level I ~ 88300
  histochemistry ~ 88313-88319
  immunocytochemistry ~ 88313, 88342
  immunofluorescent study ~ 88346, 88350
  nerve teasing ~ 88362
  special stain ~ 88312-88314, 88319
  tissue hybridization ~ 88365
  unlisted procedures ~ 88399, 89240

Pathology and laboratory ~ *continued*
toxicology screen ~ 80305-80307
transfusion medicine
  antibody ~ 86850, 86860, 86870
  blood processing
    autologous ~ 86890-86891
    frozen ~ 86927, 86930-86932
    irradiation ~ 86945
    pooling ~ 86965
    pretreatment ~ 86970-86972, 86975-86978
    splitting ~ 86985
    volume reduction ~ 86960
  leukocyte transfusion ~ 86950
  unlisted procedure ~ 86999
Western blot
  HIV ~ 86689
  protein ~ 84181-84182
  tissue analysis ~ 88371-88372
white blood cell
  alkaline phosphatase ~ 85540
  antibody ~ 86021
  count ~ 85032, 85048, 89055
  differential ~ 85004-85007, 85009
  histamine release test ~ 86343
  phagocytosis ~ 86344
  transfusion ~ 86950
Patterson's test ~ see blood urea nitrogen
Paul-Bunnell test ~ see antibody; antibody identification; microsomal antibody
P B antibodies ~ see antibody, heterophile
PBG ~ see porphobilinogen
PCP ~ (phencyclidine) 83992
Pean's operation ~ (amputation, upper leg, at hip) 27290
Pectoral cavity ~ see chest cavity
Pectus carinatum
reconstructive repair ~ 21740-21742
  with thoracoscopy ~ 21743
Pectus excavatum
reconstructive repair ~ 21740-21742
  with thoracoscopy ~ 21743
Pediatric critical care ~ 99471-99472
Pediatric intensive care ~ 99478
Pedicle fixation insertion ~ 22842-22844
Pedicle flap
abbe-estlander type ~ 40761
for breast reconstrucion
  double ~ 19369
  sincle ~ 19367
for cerebrospinal fluid leak ~ 61619
for eyelid repair ~ 67961
for lip repair ~ 40761
for vaginal lengthening ~ 46748
formation ~ 15570-15576
island ~ 15740
neurovascular ~ 15750
transfer ~ 15650
vascular ~ 15730, 15731, 15733
sygomaticofacial flap ~ 15730
PEEP ~ see pressure breathing, positive
Peet operation ~ see nerves, sympathectomy, excision
Pelvi-ureteroplasty ~ see pyeloplasty
Pelvic adhesions ~ see adhesions, pelvic
Pelvic exam ~ 57410
Pelvic exenteration ~ 51597
Pelvic fixation insertion ~ 22848
Pelvic lymphadenectomy ~ 58240
Pelvimetry ~ 74710
Pelviolithotomy ~ 50130
Pelvis ~ see also hip
abscess, incision and drainage ~ 26990, 45000
angiography ~ 72191
biopsy ~ 27040-27041
bone, drainage ~ 26992
brace application ~ 20662
bursa, incision and drainage ~ 26991
CT scan ~ 72191-72194, 74176-74178
cyst
  aspiration ~ 50390
  injection ~ 50390
destruction, lesion ~ 58662

Pelvis ~ *continued*
endoscopy
  destruction of lesion ~ 58662
  lysis of adhesions ~ 58660
  oviduct surgery ~ 58670-58671
exclusion, small intestine ~ 44700
exenteration ~ 45126, 58240
fasciotomy, decompression ~ 27027
  with debridement ~ 27057
halo ~ 20662
hematoma, incision and drainage ~ 26990
lysis, adhesions ~ 58660
magnetic resonance angiography ~ 72198
magnetic resonance imaging (MRI) ~ 72195-72197
  obstetric MRI ~ 74712, 74713
removal, foreign body ~ 27086-27087
repair
  osteotomy ~ 27158
  tendon ~ 27098
ring dislocation/fracture
  closed treatment ~ 27197, 27198
    with manipulation ~ 27198
    without manipulation ~ 27197
  open treatment ~ 27217, 27218
    with internal fixation ~ 27217, 27218
  percutaneous skeletal fixation ~ 27216
tumor
  excision ~ 27043-27048
  radical resectin ~ 27049, 27059
ultrasound ~ 76856, 76857
unlisted services and procedures for hips and hip joint ~ 27299
X-ray ~ 72170-72190
  with hip(s) ~ 73501-73503, 73521-73523
  manometry ~ 74710
Pemberton osteotomy of pelvis ~ see osteotomy, pelvis
Penectomy ~ see amputation, penis
Penetration keratoplasties ~ see keratoplasty, penetrating
Penile induration ~ see Peyronie disease
Penile prosthesis
insertion
  inflatable ~ 54401-54405
  noninflatable ~ 54400
removal
  inflatable ~ 54406, 54410-54417
  semi-rigid ~ 54415-54417
repair, inflatable ~ 54408
replacement
  inflatable ~ 54410-54411, 54416-54417
  semi-rigid ~ 54416-54417
Penile rigidity test ~ 54250
Penile tumescence test ~ 54250
Penis
amputation
  partial ~ 54120
  radical ~ 54130-54135
  replanted ~ 54438
  total ~ 54125
biopsy ~ 54100-54105
circumcision
  with clamp or other device ~ 54150
    newborn ~ 54150
  repair ~ 54163
  surgical excision, newborn ~ 54160
excision
  partial ~ 54120
  prepuce ~ 54150-54161, 54163
  total ~ 54125-54135
frenulum, excision ~ 54164
incision, prepuce ~ 54000-54001
incision and drainage ~ 54015
injection
  for erection ~ 54235
  peyronie disease ~ 54200
    surgical exposure plague ~ 54205
  vasoactive drugs ~ 54231
  X-ray ~ 54230
insertion, prosthesis
  inflatable ~ 54401-54405
  noninflatable ~ 54400
irrigation, priapism ~ 54220

Penis ~ *continued*
  lesion
    destruction
      cryosurgery ~ 54056
      electrodesiccation ~ 54055
      extensive ~ 54065
      laser surgery ~ 54057
      simple ~ 54050-54060
      surgical excision ~ 54060
    excision ~ 54060
      penile plague ~ 54110-54112
  nocturnal penile tumescence test ~ 54250
  occlusion, vein ~ 37790
  plaque, excision ~ 54110-54112
  plethysmography ~ 54240
  prepuce, stretch ~ 54450
  reconstruction
    angulation ~ 54360
    chordee ~ 54300-54304, 54328
    complications ~ 54340-54348
    epispadias ~ 54380-54390
    hypospadias ~ 54328-54352
    injury ~ 54440
  removal
    foreign body ~ 54115
    prosthesis
      inflatable ~ 54406, 54410-54417
      semi-rigid ~ 54415-54417
  repair
    corporeal tear(s) ~ 54437
    fistulization ~ 54435
    priapism with shunt ~ 54420-54430
    prosthesis, inflatable ~ 54408
  replacement, prosthesis
    inflatable ~ 54410-54411, 54416-54417
    semi-rigid ~ 54416-54417
  replantation ~ 54438
  revascularization ~ 37788
  rigidity test ~ 54250
  test erection ~ 54250
  unlisted services and procedures ~ 55899
  venous studies ~ 93980-93981
Penis adhesions
  lysis, post-circumcision ~ 54162
Penis prostheses ~ see penile prosthesis
Pentagastrin test ~ see gastric analysis test
Pentamidine ~ see inhalation treatment
Peptidase P ~ see angiotensin converting enzyme (ACE)
Peptidase S ~ see leucine aminopeptidase
Peptide, connecting ~ see C-peptide
Peptide, vasoactive intestinal ~ see vasoactive intestinal peptide
Peptidyl dipeptidase A ~ see angiotensin converting enzyme (ACE)
Percutaneous abdominal paracentesis ~ see abdomen, drainage
Percutaneous atherectomies ~ see artery, atherectomy
Percutaneous biopsy, gallbladder/bile ducts ~ see bile duct, biopsy
Percutaneous discectomies ~ see diskectomy, percutaneous
Percutaneous electric nerve stimulation ~ see application, neurostimulation
Percutaneous fixation ~ 25671
Percutaneous lumbar diskectomy ~ see aspiration, nucleus of disk, lumbar
Percutaneous lysis ~ 62263-62264
Percutaneous nephrostomies ~ see nephrostomy, percutaneous
Percutaneous transluminal angioplasty
  artery
    aortic ~ 37246, 37247
    brachiocephalic ~ 37246, 37247
    coronary ~ 92920, 92921
    pulmonary ~ 92997, 92998
    renal ~ 37246, 37247
    visceral ~ 37246, 37247
  vein ~ 36902, 36905, 36907, 37248, 37249
Percutaneous transluminal coronary angioplasty ~ see percutaneous transluminal angioplasty
Pereyra procedure ~ 51845, 57289, 58267

Performance measures
  acute bronchitis, interventions
    antibiotics prescribed ~ 4120F-4124F
  acute otitis externa/media with effusion
    hearing test ~ 3230F
    history auricular/periauricular pain ~ 1116F
    interventions
      antimicrobial therapy ~ 4131F-4132F
      effusion antihistamines/decongestants ~ 4133F-4134F
      systemic steroids ~ 4135F-4136F
      topical therapy ~ 4130F
    physical exam, membrane motility ~ 2035F
  advance care plan ~ 1157F-1158F
  age-related eye disease study (AREDS) ~ 4177F
  anginal symptom assessment ~ 1002F
  aortic aneurysm ~ 9001F-9004F
  antiplatelet therapy ~ 4011F
  asthma
    followup, discharge plan ~ 5250F
    history
      intermittent ~ 1039F
      persistent ~ 1038F
    interventions ~ 4140F, 4144F
    pharmacologic therapy ~ 4015F
  atrial fibrillation/flutter
    diagnostic screening processes ~ 3555F
    thromboembolism risk ~ 1180F, 3550F-3552F
    warfarin therapy ~ 4300F-4301F
  back pain ~ 3330F, 3331F
  care for older adults
    advance care plan ~ 1157F-1158F
    function status assessment ~ 1170F
    medication review ~ 1111F, 1159F-1160F
  carotid stenosis ~ 9005F-9007F
  chronic kidney disease
    diagnostic screening processes
      blood pressure, diastolic ~ 3078F-3080F
      blood pressure, systolic ~ 3074F-3079F
      hemoglobin ~ 3279F-3281F
      serum levels ~ 3278F
    interventions
      ESA therapy ~ 4171F-4172F
    patient management ~ 0513F, 0514F
  chronic obstructive pulmonary disease
    diagnostic screening processes
      functional expiratory volume ~ 3040F-3042F
      oxygen saturation ~ 3035F
      spirometry ~ 3023F, 3025F
    history
      dyspnea ~ 0535F, 1018F-1019F
      pneumococcus immunization ~ 1022F
      smokeless tobacco use ~ 1035F
      symptom assessment ~ 1015F
      tobacco use ~ 1000F
      tobacco smoker ~ 1034F
      tobacco non-use ~ 1036F
    intervention
      bronchodilator prescription ~ 4025F
      counseling ~ 4000F
      influenza immunization ~ 4035, 4037F
      oxygen therapy ~ 4030F
      pharmacologic therapy ~ 4001F
      pneumococcus immunization ~ 4040F
      pulmonary rehabilitation ~ 4033F
    test results
      chest X-ray ~ 3006F
      functional expiratory volume ~ 3040F
      oxygen saturation ~ 3035F
      spirometry ~ 3023F, 3025F
  community acquired bacterial pneumonia
    care level ~ 6005F
    examination
      hydration status ~ 2018F
      mental status ~ 2014F
      vital signs ~ 2010F

Performance measures ~ *continued*

patient management
  urinary incontinence plan ~ 0509F
heart failure
  assessment ~ 0001F
  examination ~ 2000F-2002F
  history ~ 1003F-1004F
  intervention
    ACE/ARB ~ 4010F, 4480F-4481F
    beta-blocker ~ 4008F
  test results ~ 3020F-3022F
hematology
  intervention ~ 4090F, 4095F, 4100F
  test results ~ 3155F, 3160F, 3170F
hepatitis
  intervention
    antiviral therapy ~ 4150F, 4153F
    counseling ~ 4158F, 4159F
    education, alcohol ~ 4158F
    education, contraception ~ 4159F
    hepatitis A vaccination ~ 4148F, 4155F
    hepatitis B vaccination ~ 4149F, 4157F
    peginterferon & ribavirin therapy ~ 4153F
    RNA testing ~ 4150F-4151F
  test results
    genotype testing ~ 3266F
    hepatitis A immunity ~ 3215F
    hepatitis B immunity ~ 3216F
    RNA testing ~ 3218F, 3220F, 3265F
hydration ~ 2030F-2031F
hypertension
  blood pressure measurement ~ 2000F
  intervention plan of care ~ 4050F
  test results, plan of care ~ 3074F-3075F, 3077F-3080F
major despressive disorder
  diagnostic/screening
    depression ~ 3351F-3354F
    severity classification ~ 3088F-3093F
    suicide risk ~ 3085F, 3092F
  history, diagnostic status ~ 1040F
  intervention
    counseling ~ 4000F
    electroconvulsive therapy ~ 4066F-4067F
    medication management ~ 4064F-4065F
    pharmacologic ~ 4001F
    psychotherapy ~ 4060F-4062F
  patient management, follow-up care documented ~ 0545F
  severity classification ~ 3088F-3093F
  suicide risk assessment ~ 3085F
melanoma
  diagnostic/screening processes
    cancer stage ~ 3321F-3322F
    imaging studies ~ 3319F, 3320F
  history, moles ~ 1050F
  outcomes, counseling ~ 5005F
  skin exam ~ 2029F
osteoarthritis
  assessment ~ 0005F
  examination, involved joint ~ 2004F
  history
    anti-inflammatory risk ~ 1008F
    assessment ~ 1006F
    medication use ~ 1007F
  intervention
    anti-inflammatory/analgesic ~ 4016F
    GI prophylaxis ~ 4017F
    therapeutic exercise ~ 4018F
osteoporosis
  care coordination ~ 5015F
  counseling ~ 4019F
  fracture management/scrreening ~ 3095F-3096F
  pharmacologic intervention ~ 4005F
Parkinson's disease
  diagnosis/screening
    cognitive impairment assessed ~ 3720F
    psychiatric disorders assessed ~ 3700F
  interventions
    autonomic dysfunction symptoms ~ 4326F
    medication-related complications ~ 4324F
    rehabilitation options discussed with patient ~ 4400F

Performance measures ~ *continued*

  sleep disturbances ~ 4328F
  treatment options reviewed ~ 4325F
patient history
  diagnosis reviewed ~ 1400F
patient safety
  falls incidence ~ 6080F
  stage-specific safety counseling ~ 6090F
patient history
  activity level assessment ~ 1003F
  advance care plan ~ 1123F, 1124F
  anti-inflammatory or analgesic ~ 1007F
  atrial fibrillation ~ 1060F-1061F
  asthma assessment ~ 1005F
  COPD assessment ~ 1015F
  co-morbid conditions assessment ~ 1026F
  community-acquired bacterial pneumonia assessment ~ 0012F
  current smokeless tobacco user ~ 1035F
  current tobacco non-user ~ 1036F
  dyspnea assessment ~ 1018F-1019F
  fall history ~ 1100F-1101F
  facility discharge ~ 1110F
  functional status assessed ~ 1170F
  gastroesophageal reflux ~ 1070F-1071F
  influenza immunization status ~ 1030F
  intermittent asthma ~ 1039F
  major depresive disorder ~ 1040F
  medication reconsiliation ~ 1111F
  moles ~ 1050F
  non-steroidal anti-inflammatory drug (NSAID) ~ 1008F
  osteoarthritis ~ 1006F
  persistent asthma ~ 1038F
  pneumococcus immunization assessment ~ 1022F
  risk of death ~ 1150F-1151F
  seizure type/frequency documented ~ 1200F
  stroke symptom ~ 1065F-1066F
  urinary incontinence ~ 1090F-1091F
  visual function ~ 1055F
patient management
  colonoscopy follow-up ~ 0528F-0529F
  dyspnea management plan ~ 0535F
  glucorticoid management plan ~ 0540F
  HIV RNA control plan ~ 0575F
  major depressive disorder plan of follow-up care ~ 0545F
  postpartum care visit ~ 0503F
  prenatal care visit, initial ~ 0500F
  prenatal care visit, subsequent ~ 0502F
  prenatal flow sheet ~ 0501F
  urinary incontinence plan of care ~ 0509F
patient safety
  anti-epileptic drug counseling ~ 6070F
  dysphagea screening ~ 6010F
  falls incidence queried with patient ~ 6080F
  level of care rationale ~ 6005F
  Parkinson's disease stage-specific safety counseling ~ 6090F
pediatric
  acute gastroenteritis
    examination
      hydration status ~ 2030F-2031F
      oral rehydration ~ 2030F-2031F
      weight measurement ~ 2001F
    intervention
      education ~ 4058F
      oral rehydration ~ 4056F
  pharyngitis
    intervention, testing ~ 4120F, 4124F
    test results, appropriate testing ~ 3210F
perioperative care, intervention
  discontinuation, prophylactics ~ 4042F-4043F, 4046F, 4049F
  selection, prophylactics ~ 4041F
  timing, prophylactics ~ 4047F-4048F
  venous thromboembolism ~ 4044F
physical examination
  dilated retinal eye exam ~ 2022F
  eye imaging ~ 2026F
  field stereoscopic photos ~ 2024F
  foot ~ 2028F
  fundus ~ 2020F-2021F
  hydration status ~ 2018F, 2030F-2031F
  macular ~ 2019F, 2021F

Performance measures ~ *continued*
   major depressive disorder clinical interview ~ 2060F
   mental status ~ 2014F, 2044F
   optic nerve ~ 2027F
   osteoarthritis assessment ~ 2004F
   skin ~ 2029F
   vital signs ~ 2010F
   volume overload assessment ~ 2002F
   weight ~ 2001F
  prenatal-postpartum care
   diagnosis/screening
    ABO and Rh typing ~ 3293F
    D Rh typing ~ 3290F-3291F
    HIV status ~ 3292F
   patient management ~ 0500F-0503F
  preventive care & screening
   history
    tobacco use ~ 1000F, 1034F-1036F
   intervention
    pharmacologic therapy ~ 4001F
    influenza immunization ~ 4037F
    tobacco use counseling ~ 4000F, 4004F
   test results
    screening mammography ~ 3014F
    colorectal screening ~ 3017F
  statin therapy ~ 4013F
  stroke and stroke rehabilitation
   history
    anticoagulant therapy ~ 1060F-1061F
    tissue plasminogen ~ 1065F-1066F
   intervention
    anticoagulant therapy ~ 4075F
    antiplatelet therapy ~ 4073F
    rehabilitation services ~ 4079F
    thrombosis prophylaxis ~ 4070F
    tissue plasminogen ~ 4077F
   test results
    carotid imaging ~ 3100F
    lesion screening ~ 3110F-3112F
   patient safety
    dysphagia screening ~ 6010F
    swallowing eligibility ~ 6015F
    NPO order ~ 6020F
  therapeutic, preventive or other interventions
   anesthesia ~ 4255F-4256F
   anti-inflammatory/analgesic ~ 4016F
   antibiotic agent ~ 4045F, 4048F. 4049F. 4120F. 4124F
   anticoagulant therapy ~ 4075F
   antiplatelet therapy ~ 4073F
   arterio-venous fistula ~ 4051F
   aspirin ~ 4084F
   asthma medication ~ 4015F
   beta blocker ~ 4115F
   bisphosphonate therapy ~ 4100F
   dialysis ~ 4052F-4055F
   electroconvulsive therapy ~ 4066F-4067F
   erythropoietin therapy ~ 4090F-4095F
   gastroenteritis education ~ 4058F
   gastrointestinal prophylaxis for NSAID use ~ 4017F
   heart failure education ~ 4003F
   hepatitis vaccination ~ 4148F-4149F, 4275F
   hypertension care plan ~ 4050F
   influenza immunization ~ 4035F-4037F
   inhaled bronchodilator ~ 4025F
   internal mammary artery graft ~ 4110F
   oxygen therapy, long term ~ 4030F
   pharmacologic therapy ~ 4005F, 4063F-4065F
   pneumococcal immunization ~ 4040F
   psychotherapy services ~ 4060F, 4062F
   pulmonary rehabilitation ~ 4033F
   rehabilitation services ~ 4089F
   rehydration solution ~ 4056F
   statin therapy ~ 4013F
   therapeutic exercise ~ 4018F
   thrombosis prophylaxis ~ 4070F
   tissue plasminogen administration ~ 4077F
   warfarin therapy ~ 4012F

Performance measures ~ *continued*
  tobacco use
   assessment ~ 1000F
   counseling ~ 4000F
   pharmacologic therapy ~ 4001
  vital signs, documented and reviewed ~ 2010F
Performance test ~ see physical medicine/therapy/occupational therapy
  performance test, physical therapy ~ 97750
  psychological test ~ 96100
Perfusion
  imaging
   brain
    CT Scan ~ 0042T
    PET Scan ~ 78609
   myocardial ~ 78451-78454
    PET Scan ~ 78491, 78492
   pulmonary ~ 78580, 78582, 78597, 78598
  for esophageal motility study ~ 91013
  test, esophageal acid 91030
  therapeutic
   hemoperfusion, dialysis ~ 90997
   vestibuloactive drugs ~ 69801
Perfusion, intracranial arterial thrombolysis ~ 61624
Perfusion pump ~ see infusion pump
Pericardectomies ~ see excision, pericardium
Pericardial cyst ~ see cyst, pericardial
Pericardial sac drainage ~ 32659
Pericardial window for drainage ~ 33025
Pericardial window technic ~ see pericardiostomy
Pericardiectomy
  complete ~ 33030-33031
  subtotal ~ 33030-33031
Pericardiocentesis ~ 33010-33011
  ultrasound guidance ~ 76930
Pericardiostomy tube ~ 33015
Pericardiotomy
  removal
   clot ~ 33020
   foreign body ~ 33020
Pericardium
  biopsy, endoscopic ~ 32604
  cyst, excision/resection ~ 32661, 33050
  diagnostic thoracoscopy ~ 32601
  excision ~ 32659, 33025, 33030-33031
  incision
   removal
    clot ~ 33020
    foreign body ~ 33020
   with tube ~ 33015
  incision and drainage ~ 33025
  puncture aspiration ~ 33010-33011
  removal
   clot, endoscopic ~ 32658
   foreign body, endoscopic ~ 32658
  tumor, excision ~ 32661, 33050
Peridural anesthesia
  infusion ~ 62324-62327
  injection ~ 62320-62323
Peridural injection ~ see epidural, injection
Perineal prostatectomy ~ see prostatectomy, perineal
Perineoplasty ~ 56810
Perineorrhaphy
  repair, rectocele ~ 57250
Perineum
  abscess, incision and drainage ~ 56405
  colposcopy ~ 99170
  debridement, infected ~ 11004, 11006
  removal, prosthesis ~ 53442
  repair ~ 56810
  X-ray with contrast ~ 74775
Perionychia ~ see paronychia
Periorbital region
  reconstruction, osteotomy with graft ~ 21267-21268
  repair, osteotomy ~ 21260-21263
Peripheral artery disease (PAD) rehabilitation ~ 93668
Peripheral nerve repair/suture, major ~ 64856, 64859
Periprosthetic capsulectomy breast ~ 19371
Peristaltic pumps ~ see infusion pump
Peritoneal dialysis ~ 90945-90947, 4055F
  Kt/V level ~ 3082F-3084F
Peritoneal free air ~ see pneumoperitoneum

Peritoneal lavage ~ 49084
Peritoneoscopy ~ see endoscopy, peritoneum
Peritoneum
  abscess, incision and drainage ~ 49020
  endoscopy
    drainage, lymphocele ~ 49323
  exchange, drainage catheter ~ 49423
  injection, contrast, via catheter ~ 49424
  ligation, shunt ~ 49428
  removal
    cannula/catheter ~ 49422
    foreign body ~ 49402
    shunt ~ 49429
  tumor, resection ~ 58950-58956
  unlisted services and procedures ~ 49999
  venous shunt, injection ~ 49427
  X-ray ~ 74190
Persistent, omphalomesenteric duct ~ see diverticulum, Meckel's
Persistent truncus arteriosus ~ see truncus arteriosus
Personal care ~ see self care
Pessary insertion ~ 57160
Pesticides chlorinated hydrocarbons ~ 82441
PET ~ see positron emission tomography
Petrous temporal excision, Apex ~ 69530
Peyronie disease
  with graft ~ 54110-54112
  injection ~ 54200
  surgical exposure ~ 54205
pH ~ *see also* blood
  exhaled breath ~ 83987
  other fluid ~ 83986
  urine ~ 83986
Phacoemulsification
  removal
    extracapsular cataract ~ 66982, 66984
    secondary membranous cataract ~ 66850
Phagocytosis, white blood cells ~ 86344
Phalangectomy
  toe ~ 28150
    partial ~ 28160
Phalanges (hand)) ~ see finger, bone
Phalanx, finger
  craterization ~ 26235-26236
  cyst, excision ~ 26210-26215
  diaphysectomy ~ 26235-26236
  excision ~ 26235-26236
    radical, for tumor ~ 26260-26262
  fracture
    articular
      closed treatment ~ 26740
      with manipulation ~ 26742
      open treatment ~ 26746
    distal ~ 26755-26756
      closed treatment ~ 26750
      open treatment ~ 26765
      percutaneous fixation ~ 26756
    open treatment ~ 26735
      distal ~ 26765
    shaft ~ 26720-26727
      open treatment ~ 26735
  incision and drainage ~ 26034
  ostectomy, radical, for tumor ~ 26260-26262
  repair
    lengthening ~ 26568
    nonunion ~ 26546
    osteotomy ~ 26567
  saucerization ~ 26235-26236
  thumb fracture, shaft ~ 26720-26727
  tumor, excision ~ 26210-26215
Phalanx, great toe ~ see also phalanx, toe
  fracture ~ 28490
    with manipulation ~ 28495-28496
    open treatment ~ 28505
  without manipulation ~ 28490
  percutaneous fixation ~ 28496
Phalanx, toe
  condyle, excision ~ 28126
  craterization ~ 28124
  cyst, excision ~ 28108
  diaphysectomy ~ 28124

Phalanx, toe ~ *continued*
  excision ~ 28124, 28150-28160
  fracture
    with manipulation ~ 28515
    without manipulation ~ 28510
    open treatment ~ 28525
  repair, osteotomy ~ 28310-28312
  saucerization ~ 28124
  tumor, excision ~ 28108, 28175
Pharmaceutic preparations ~ see drug
Pharmacotherapies ~ see chemotherapy
Pharyngeal tonsil ~ see adenoids
Pharyngectomy partial ~ 42890
Pharyngolaryngectomy ~ 31390-31395
Pharyngoplasty ~ 42950
Pharyngorrhaphy ~ see suture, pharynx
Pharyngostomy ~ 42955
Pharyngotomy ~ see incision, pharynx
Pharyngotympanic tube ~ see eustachian tube
Pharynx ~ see also nasopharynx; throat
  biopsy ~ 42800-42806
  cineradiography ~ 70371, 74230
  creation, stoma ~ 42955
  excision ~ 42145
    with larynx ~ 31390-31395
    partial ~ 42890
    resection ~ 42892-42894
  hemorrhage ~ 42960-42962
  lesion
    destruction ~ 42808
    excision ~ 42808
  reconstruction ~ 42950
  removal, foreign body ~ 42809
  repair, with esophagus ~ 42953
  unlisted services and procedures ~ 42999
  video study ~ 70371, 74230
  X-ray ~ 70370, 74210
Phencyclidine ~ 80305-80307, 83992
Phenobarbital ~ 80345
  assay ~ 80184
Phenothiazine ~ 80342-80344
Phenotype
Phenotype Analysis
  Alpha-1-antitrypsin ~ 82104
  by Genotypic Bioinformatics ~ 87900
  by Nucleic Acid ~ 87901-87904, 87906
    Infectious Agent
      HIV-1 Drug Resistance ~ 87903, 87904, 87906
Phenotype Prediction
  by Genetic Database
    HIV-1 Drug Susceptibility ~ 87900
Phenylalanine ~ 84030
Phenylalanine-tyrosine ratio ~ 84030
Phenylketones ~ 84035
Phenylketonuria ~ see phenylalanine
Phenytoin assay ~ 80185-80186
Pheochromocytoma ~ 80424
Pheresis ~ see apheresis
Phlebectasia ~ see varicose vein
Phlebectomy varicose veins ~ 37765-37766
Phlebographies ~ see venography
Phleborrhaphy ~ see suture, vein
Phlebotomy therapeutic ~ 99195
Phoria ~ see strabismus
Phosphatase
  alkaline ~ 84075, 84080
    blood ~ 84078
Phosphatase acid ~ 84060
  blood ~ 84066
Phosphate, pyridoxal ~ see pyridoxal phosphate
Phosphatidylcholine cholinephosphohydrolase ~ see tissue typing
Phosphatidylglycerol ~ 84081
Phosphatidyl glycerol ~ see phosphatidylglycerol
Phosphocreatine phosphotransferase, ADP ~ see CPK
Phosphogluconate-6 dehydrogenase ~ 84085
Phosphoglycerides, glycerol ~ see phosphatidylglycerol
Phosphohexose isomerase ~ 84087
Phosphohydrolases ~ see phosphatase
Phosphokinase, creatine ~ see CPK
Phospholipase C ~ see tissue typing
Phospholipid antibody ~ 86147

Phosphomonoesterase ~ see phosphatase
Phosphoric monoester hydrolases ~ see phosphatase
Phosphorus ~ 84100
   urine ~ 84105
Phosphotransferase, ADP phosphocreatine ~ see CPK
Photo patch allergy test ~ see allergy tests ~ 95052
Photochemotherapies, extracorporeal ~ see photopheresis
Photochemotherapy ~ see dermatology ~ 96910-96913
   endoscopic light ~ 96570-96571
Photocoagulation
   endolaser panretinal, vitrectomy ~ 67040
   focal endolaser, vitrectomy ~ 67040
   iridoplasty ~ 66762
   lesion
     cornea ~ 65450
     retina ~ 67210, 67227-67228
   retinal detachment
     prophylaxis ~ 67145
     repair ~ 67105
Photodynamic therapy
   for lesion ~ 67221, 67225, 96567, 96573, 96574
   for tissue ablation ~ 96570, 96571
Photography skin, diagnostic ~ 96904
Photography, ocular ~ see ophthalmoscopy, diagnostic
Photopheresis extracorporeal ~ 36522
Photophoresis ~ see actinotherapy; photochemotherapy
Photoradiation therapies ~ see actinotherapy
Photoscreen ocular ~ 99174
Photosensitivity testing ~ see allergy tests ~ 95056
Phototherapies ~ see actinotherapy
Phototherapy, ultraviolet ~ see actinotherapy
Phrenic nerve
   avulsion ~ 64746
   incision ~ 64746
   injection, anesthetic ~ 64410
   transection ~ 64746
Physical medicine/therapy/occupational therapy
   activities of daily living ~ 97535, 99509
   aquatic therapy, with exercises ~ 97113
   athletic training
     evaluation ~ 97169-97171
     re-evaluation ~ 97172
     orthotic/prosthetic ~ 97763
   cognitive skills development ~ 97127
   community/work reintegration ~ 97537
   evaluation
     athletic training ~ 97169-97171
       re-evaluation ~ 97172
     occupational therapy ~ 97165-97167
       re-evaluation ~ 97168
     physical therapy ~ 97161-97163
       re-evaluation ~ 97164
   kinetic therapy ~ 97530
   manual therapy ~ 97140
   modalities
     contrast baths ~ 97034
     diathermy treatment ~ 97024
     electric simulation
       unattended ~ 97014
       attended, manual ~ 97032
     hot or cold pack ~ 97010
     hydrotherapy (Hubbard tank) ~ 97036
     infrared light treatment ~ 97026
     iontophoresis ~ 97033
     microwave therapy ~ 97024
     paraffin bath ~ 97018
     traction ~ 97012
     ultrasound ~ 97035
     ultraviolet light ~ 97028
     unlisted services and procedures ~ 97039
     vasopneumatic device ~ 97016
     whirlpool therapy ~ 97022
   orthotics training ~ 97760, 97763
   osteopathic manipulation ~ 98925-98929
   procedures
     aquatic therapy ~ 97113
     gait training ~ 97116
     group therapeutic ~ 97150
     massage therapy ~ 97124
     neuromuscular reeducation ~ 97112

Physical medicine/therapy/occupational therapy ~ *continued*
   physical performance test ~ 97750
   therapeutic exercises ~ 97110
   traction therapy ~ 97140
   work hardening ~ 97545-97546
   prosthetic training ~ 97761
   sensory integration ~ 97533
   therapeutic activities ~ 97530
   unlisted services and procedures ~ 97139, 97799
   wheelchair management/propulsion ~ 97542
   work reintegration ~ 97537
Physical therapy
   evaluation ~ 97161-97163
   re-evaluation ~ 97164
Physician services
   care management
     behavioral health conditions ~ 99484
     psychiatric collaborative care ~ 99492-99494
   care planning
     cognitive impairment ~ 99483
   care plan oversight services
     domiciliary facility ~ 99339, 99340
     home health agency care ~ 99374, 99375
     home or rest home care ~ 99339, 99340
     hospice ~ 99377, 99378
     liver assiste patient oversight ~ 0405T
     nursing facility ~ 99379, 99380
   case management services ~ 99366-99368
   consultation, interprofessional telephone/ internet discussion ~ 99446-99449
   direction, advanced life support ~ 99288
   online ~ 99444
   prolonged
     with direct patient contact ~ 99354-99357
       inpatient ~ 99356, 99357
       outpatient/office ~ 99354, 99355, 99415, 99416
     without direct patient contact ~ 99358, 99359
   standby ~ 99360
   supervision, care plan oversight services ~ 99339, 99340, 99374-99380
   team conference ~ 99367
   telephone ~ 99441-99443
Piercing of ear lobe ~ 69090
Piles ~ see hemorrhoids
Pilonidal cyst
   excision ~ 11770-11772
   incision and drainage ~ 10080-10081
Pin ~ see also wire
   insertion/removal, skeletal traction ~ 20650
   prophylactic treatment
     femur ~ 27187
     humerus ~ 24498
     shoulder ~ 23490-23491
Pinch graft ~ 15050
Pinna ~ see ear, external
Pinworms examination ~ 87172
Pirogoff procedure ~ 27888
Pituitary epidermoid tumor ~ see craniopharyngioma
Pituitary gland
   excision ~ 61546-61548
   tumor, excision ~ 61546-61548, 62165
Pituitary growth hormone ~ see growth hormone
Pituitary lactogenic hormone ~ see prolactin
Pituitectomy ~ see excision, pituitary gland
PKU ~ see phenylalanine
Placement
   adjustable gastric restrictive device ~ 43770
   biodegradable material, peri-prostatic ~ 55874
   catheter
     breast, for interstitial radioelement application ~ 19296-19298
     bronchus, for intracavitary radioelement application (see also catheterization) ~ 31643
     kidney
       nephrostomy ~ 50432
       Nephroureteral ~ 50433
     prostate ~ 55875
     renal artery
       selective ~ 36251, 36252
       superselective ~ 36253, 36254
     reter via kidney ~ 50695
   catheter, cardiac (see also catheterization, cardiac) ~ 93503

Placement ~ *continued*
  dosimeter, prostate ~ 55876
  drainage, pancreas ~ 48001
  drug-eluting ocular insert, eyelid ~ 0444T, 0445T
  duodenostomy tube ~ 49441
  endovascular prosthesis
    aorta ~ 33883-33886, 34709-34711
    iliac artery ~ 34709-34711
  enterostomy tube ~ 44300
  esophageal sphincter augmentation device ~ 43284
  guidance
    catheter
      abscess ~ 75989
      specimen ~ 75989
    prosthesis
      thoracic aorta ~ 75958-75959
  interstitial device
    abdomen ~ 49411-49412
    lungs ~ 32553
    omentum ~ 49411-49412
    pelvis ~ 49411-49412
    pleura ~ 32553
    peritoneum ~ 49411-49412
    prostate ~ 55876
    retroperitoneum ~ 49411-49412
  intravascular stent
    coronary ~ 92980-92981
    intracranial ~ 61635
  jejunostomy tube
    endoscopic ~ 44372
    percutaneous ~ 49441
  lesion localization device, soft tissue ~ 10035, 10036
  nasogastric tube ~ 43752
  needle
    bone ~ 36680
    interstitial radioelement application
      genitalia ~ 55920
      head ~ 41019
      muscle ~ 20555
      neck ~ 41019
      pelvic organs ~ 55920
      soft tissue ~ 20555
      prostate ~ 55875
  orogastric tube ~ 43752
  radiation delivery device
    intracoronary artery ~ 92974
    pleural cavity ~ 32553
  radiation therapy applicator, breast ~ 19294
  seton, anal ~ 46020
  stent
    biliary ~ 47538-47540
    bronchial ~ 31636, 31637
    cardiac ~ 33621
    colonic ~ 44402, 45327, 45347, 45389
    intravascular
      coronary ~ 92928, 92929
      intracranial ~ 61635
    tracheal ~ 31631
    ureteral ~ 50947
  subconjunctival retinal prosthesis ~ 0100T
  synthetic device, vertebra ~ 0220T-0222T
Placenta delivery ~ 59414
Placental lactogen ~ see lactogen, human placental
Placental villi ~ see chorionic villus
Plagiocephaly ~ 21175
Planing nose, skin ~ 30120
Plantar common digital nerve
  destruction, neurolytic ~ 64632
Plantar digital nerve decompression ~ 64726
Plantar pressure measurements dynamic ~ 96001, 96004
Plasma frozen preparation ~ 86927
Plasma prokallikrein ~ see Fletcher factor
Plasma protein-A, pregnancy-associated (PAPP-A) ~ 84163
Plasma test volume determination ~ 78110-78111
Plasma thromboplastin
  antecedent ~ 85270
  component ~ 85250
Plasmin ~ 85400
Plasmin antiactivator ~ see alpha-2 antiplasmin
Plasminogen ~ 85420-85421
Plasmodium antibody ~ 86750

Plastic repair of mouth ~ see mouth, repair
Plate, bone ~ see bone plate
Platelet ~ see also blood cell count, complete blood count
  aggregation ~ 85576
  antibody ~ 86022-86023
  assay ~ 85055
  blood ~ 85025
  count ~ 85032, 85049
  neutralization ~ 85597
Platelet cofactor I ~ see clotting factor
Platelet test survival test ~ 78191
Platysmal flap ~ 15825
PLC ~ see tissue typing
Pleoptic training ~ 92065
Plethysmography ~ see also vascular studies
  extremities ~ 93922, 93923
  penis ~ 54240
  pulmonary ~ 94726, 94750
Pleura
  biopsy ~ 32098, 32400, 32609
  decortication ~ 32320
  empyema, excision ~ 32540
  excision ~ 32310-32320
    endoscopic ~ 32656
  foreign body, removal ~ 32150-32151
  needle biopsy ~ 32400
  placement, interstitial device ~ 32553
  pleurodesis
    by agent ~ 32560
    thoracoscopic ~ 32650
  removal
    catheter ~ 32552
    fibrin deposit ~ 32653
    foreign body ~ 32653
  repair ~ 32215
  thoracotomy ~ 32098, 32100
  tumor, cryoablation ~ 32994
  unlisted services and procedures ~ 32999
Pleural cavity
  aspiration ~ 32554-32555
  catheterization ~ 32550, 32552
  chemotherapy administration ~ see also chemotherapy ~ 96440
  incision
    empyema ~ 32035-32036
    pneumothorax ~ 32551
  instillation of agent for
    fibrinolysis ~ 32561-32562
    pleurodesis ~ 32560
  puncture and drainage ~ 32554-32555
  thoracostomy ~ 32035-32036
Pleural endoscopies ~ see thoracoscopy
Pleural scarification for repeat pneumothorax ~ 32215
Pleural tap ~ see thoracentesis
Pleurectomy
  anesthesia ~ 00542
  parietal ~ 32310-32320
    endoscopic ~ 32656
Pleuritis, purulent ~ see abscess, thorax
Pleurocentesis ~ see thoracentesis
Pleurodesis
  chemical ~ 32560
  endoscopic ~ 32650
Pleurosclerosis ~ see pleurodesis
Plexectomy, choroid ~ see choroid plexus, excision
Plexus, choroid ~ see choroid plexus
Plexus brachialis ~ see brachial plexus
Plexus cervicalis ~ see cervical plexus
Plexus coeliacus ~ see celiac plexus
Plexus lumbalis ~ see lumbar plexus
PLGN ~ see plasminogen
Plication, sphincter, urinary bladder ~ see bladder, repair, neck
Pneumocentesis lung ~ 32405
Pneumocisternogram ~ see cisternography
Pneumococcal vaccine ~ 90670, 90732
Pneumocystis carinii antigen detection, immunofluorescence ~ 87281
Pneumogastric nerve ~ see vagus nerve
Pneumogram pediatric ~ 94772
Pneumolysis ~ 32940

Pneumonectomy ~ 32440-325445
  completion ~ 32488
  donor ~ 32850, 33930
  sleeve ~ 32442
  thoracoscopic ~ 32671
Pneumonology ~ see pulmonology
Pneumonolysis ~ 32940
  intrapleural ~ 32652
  open intrapleural ~ 32124
Pneumonostomy ~ 32200
Pneumonotomy ~ see incision, lung
Pneumoperitoneum ~ 49400
Pneumothorax
  chemical pleurodesis ~ 32560
  pleural scarification for repeat ~ 32215
  therapeutic, injection intrapleural air ~ 32960
  thoracentesis with tube insertion ~ 32555
Polio
  antibody ~ 86658
  vaccine ~ 90713
Poliovirus vaccine, inactivated ~ see vaccines
Pollicization digit ~ 26550
Polya gastrectomy ~ see gastrectomy, partial
Polydactylism ~ see supernumerary digit
Polydactylous digit
  reconstruction ~ 26587
  repair ~ 26587
Polydactyly, toes ~ 28344
Polyp
  antrochoanal, removal ~ 31032
  esophagus, ablation ~ 43229
  nose, excision
    endoscopic ~ 31237-31240
    extensive ~ 30115
    simple ~ 30110
  sphenoid sinus, removal ~ 31051
  urethra, excision ~ 53260
Polypectomy
  nose, endoscopic ~ 31237
  uterus ~ 58558
Polypeptide, vasoactive intestinal ~ see vasoactive intestinal peptide
Polysomnography ~ 95808-95811
Polyuria test ~ see water load test
Pomeroy's operation ~ (tubal ligation) 58600
Pooling blood products ~ 86965
Popliteal arteries ~ see artery, popliteal
Popliteal synovial cyst ~ see Baker's cyst
Poradenitistras ~ see lymphogranuloma venereum
PORP (partial ossicular replacement prosthesis) ~ 69633, 69637
Porphobilinogen urine ~ 84106-84110
Porphyrin precursors ~ 82135
Porphyrins
  feces ~ 84126
  urine ~ 84119-84120
Portal vein ~ see vein, hepatic portal
Porter-Silber test ~ see corticosteroid, blood
Portoenterostomies, hepatic ~ see hepaticoenterostomy
Port film ~ 77417
Portoenterostomy ~ 47701
Posadas-Wernicke disease ~ see coccidioidomycosis
Positional nystagmus test ~ see nystagmus tests, positional
Positive-pressure breathing, inspiratory ~ see intermittent positive pressure breathing (IPPB)
Positive end expiratory pressure ~ see pressure breathing, positive
Positron emission tomography (PET)
  brain ~ 78608, 78609
  chest ~ 78811
  heart ~ 78459
  myocardial imaging
    blood flow absolute quantitation ~ 0482T
    perfusion study ~ 78491-78492
  whole body ~ 78813
  with computed tomography (CT) ~ 78814, 78815
Post-op visit ~ 99024
Postauricular fistula ~ see fistula, postauricular
Postcaval ureter ~ see retrocaval ureter
Postmortem ~ see autopsy
Postoperative wound infection incision and drainage ~ 10180
Postop vas reconstruction ~ see vasovasorrhaphy

Postpartum care
  cesarean delivery ~ 59515
    after attempted vaginal delivery ~ 59622
    previous ~ 59610, 59614-59618, 59622
  vaginal delivery ~ 59430
    after previous cesarean delivery ~ 59614
Potassium ~ 84132
  urine ~ 84133
Potential, auditory evoked ~ see auditory evoked potentials
Potential, evoked ~ see evoked potential
Potts-Smith procedure ~ 33762
Pouch, Kock ~ see Kock pouch
PPP ~ see fibrin degradation products
PRA ~ see cytotoxic screen
Prealbumin ~ 84134
Prebeta lipoproteins ~ see lipoprotein, blood
Pregl's test ~ (cystourethroscopy, catheterization, urethral) 52005
Pregnancy
  abortion
    induced ~ 59855-59857
      by amniocentesis injection ~ 59850-59852
      by dilation and curettage ~ 59840
      by dilation and evaluation ~ 59841
    septic ~ 59830
    therapeutic
      by dilation and curettage ~ 59851
      by hysterectomy ~ 59852
      by saline ~ 59850
  cesarean delivery ~ 59618-59622
    with hysterectomy ~ 59525
    only ~ 59514
    postpartum care ~ 59514-59515
    routine care ~ 59510
    vaginal birth after ~ 59610-59614
  ectopic
    abdominal ~ 59130
    cervix ~ 59140
    interstitial
      partial resection uterus ~ 59136
      total hysterectomy ~ 59135
    laparoscopy
      with salpingectomy and/or oophorectomy ~ 59151
      without salpingectomy and/or oophorectomy ~ 59150
    tubal ~ 59121
      with salpingectomy and/or oophorectomy ~ 59120
  miscarriage
    surgical completion
      any trimester ~ 59812
      first trimester ~ 59820
      second trimester ~ 59821
  molar ~ see also hydatidiform mole
  multifetal reduction ~ 59866
  placenta delivery ~ 59414
  test ~ 84702-84703
    urinalysis ~ 81025
  vaginal delivery ~ 59409-59410
    antepartum care ~ 59425-59426
    after cesarean delivery ~ 59610-59614
    postpartum care ~ 59430
    total obstetrical care ~ 59400, 59610, 59618
Pregnanediol ~ 84135
Pregnanetriol ~ 84138
Pregnenolone ~ 84140
Prekallikrein ~ see Fletcher factor
Prekallikrein factor ~ 85292
Premature, closure, cranial suture ~ see craniosynostosis
Prenatal procedure ~ 59897
  amnioinfusion, transabdominal ~ 59070
  drainage, fluid ~ 59074
  occlusion, umbilical cord ~ 59072
  stunt ~ 59076
Prenatal testing
  amniocentesis ~ 59000
    with amniotic fluid reduction ~ 59001
  chorionic villus sampling ~ 59015
  cordocentesis ~ 59012
  fetal blood sample ~ 59030
  fetal monitoring ~ 59050
    interpretation only ~ 59051

1119

Prenatal testing ~ *continued*
  magnetic resonance imaging (MRI) ~ 74712, 74713
  non-stress test, fetal ~ 59025, 99500
  oxytocin stress test ~ 59020
  stress test, oxytocin ~ 59020
  ultrasound ~ 76801-76817
    fetal biophysical profile ~ 76818-76819
    fetal heart ~ 76825
Prentiss operation ~ see orchiopexy, inguinal approach
Preparation
  for transfer, embryo ~ 89255
  thawing
    embryo, cryopreserved ~ 89352
    oocytes, cryopreserved ~ 89356
    reproductive tissue, cryopreserved ~ 89354
    sperm, cryopreserved ~ 89353
Presacral sympathectomy ~ see sympathectomy, presacral
Prescription
  contact lens (see also contact lens services) ~ 92310-92317
  ocular prosthesis (see also prosthesis, ocular) ~ 92330-92335
Pressure, blood ~ see blood pressure
Pressure, venous ~ see blood pressure, venous
Pressure breathing ~ (see also pulmonology, therapeutic)
  negative, continuous (CNP) ~ 94660
  positive, continuous (CPAP) ~ 94660
Pressure measurement of sphincter of Oddi ~ see sphincter of Oddi, pressure measurement
Pressure ulcer (decubitus) ~ see debridement; skin graft and flap
Pressure ulcers excision ~ 15920-15999
Pretreatment
  red blood cell
    antibody identification ~ 86970-86972
  serum
    antibody identification ~ 86975-86978
Prevention & control ~ see prophylaxis
Preventive medicine
  behavior change intervention
    group
      diabetes prevention ~ 0403T
      risk factor reduction ~ 99411, 99412
    individual
      diabetes prevention ~ 0488T
      substance abuse other than tobacco ~ 99408, 99409
      tobacco use cessation ~ 99406, 99407
  comprehensive
    established patient ~ 99382-99397
    new patient ~ 99381-99387
  counseling
    behavior change, individual ~ 99406-99408
    exercise ~ 4019F
    group ~ 99411, 99412
    self exam for moles ~ 5005F
  fluoride varnish application ~ 99188
  health risk assessment ~ 96160, 96161
  newborn care ~ 99461
  self-exam for moles ~ 5005F
  unlisted services and procedures ~ 99429
Priapism
  repair
    fistulization ~ 54435
    with shunt ~ 54420-54430
Primidone assay ~ 80188
PRL ~ see prolactin
Pro-insulin C peptide ~ see C-peptide
Proalbumin ~ see prealbumin
Probes, DNA ~ see nucleic acid probe
Probes, nucleic acid ~ see nucleic acid probe
Procainamide assay ~ 80190-80192
Procalcitonin (PCT) ~ 84145
Procedure, Fontan ~ see repair, heart, anomaly
Procedure, maxillofacial ~ see maxillofacial procedures
Process, odontoid ~ see odontoid process
Procidentia
  rectum
    excision ~ 45130-45135
    repair ~ 45900
Procoagulant activity, glomerular ~ see thromboplastin
Proconvertin ~ 85230
Proctectasis ~ see dilation, rectum

Proctectomy
  partial ~ 45111, 45113-45116, 45123
  total ~ 45110, 45112, 45119-45120
    with colon ~ 45121
  with colectomy ~ 44157-44158
  with ileostomy ~ 44212
Proctocele ~ see rectocele
Proctopexy ~ 45540-45541
  with sigmoid excision ~ 45550
Proctoplasty ~ 45500-45505
Proctorrhaphy ~ see rectum, suture
Proctoscopies ~ see anoscopy
Proctosigmoidoscopy
  ablation, polyp or lesion ~ 45320
  biopsy ~ 45305
  destruction, tumor ~ 45320
  dilation ~ 45303
  exploration ~ 45300
  hemorrhage control ~ 45317
  placement, stent ~ 45327
  removal
    foreign body ~ 45307
    polyp ~ 45308-45315
    tumor ~ 45315
  volvulus repair ~ 45321
Products, gene ~ see protein
Proetz therapy nose ~ 30210
Profibrinolysin ~ see plasminogen
Progenitor cell ~ see stem cell
Progesterone ~ 84144
Progesterone receptors ~ 84234
Progestin receptors ~ see progesterone receptors
Proinsulin ~ 84206
Projective test ~ 96100
Prokallikrein ~ see Fletcher factor
Prokallikrein, plasma ~ see Fletcher factor
Prokinogenase ~ see Fletcher factor
Prolactin ~ 80418, 84146
Prolapse ~ see procidentia
Prolapse, rectal ~ see procidentia, rectum
Prolastin ~ see alpha-1 antitrypsin
Prolonged services ~ 99354-99360
  with direct patient contact ~ 99354-99357
    inpatient ~ 99356, 99357
    outpatient/office ~ 99354, 99355
      clinical staff with physician supervision ~ 99415, 99416
  without direct patient contact ~ 99358-99359
Prophylactic treatment
  antibiotic ~ 4045F, 4047F-4049F
  antimicrobial ~ 4046F
    cefazolin or cefuroxime ~ 4041F-4043F
  femoral neck or proximal femur
    nailing, pinning or wiring ~ 27187
  femur
    nailing, pinning or wiring ~ 27495
  humerus
    pinning, wiring ~ 24498
  radius
    nailing, pinning, plating or wiring ~ 25490, 25492
  shoulder
    clavicle ~ 23490
    humerus ~ 23491
  tibia ~ 27745
  ulna
    nailing, pinning, plating or wiring ~ 25491-25492
  venous thromboembolism (VTE) ~ 4044F
Prophylaxis
  anticoagulant therapy ~ 4075F
  deep vein thrombosis (DVT) ~ 4070F
  retina detachment
    cryotherapy, diathermy ~ 67141
    photocoagulation ~ 67145
Prostaglandin ~ 84150
  insertion ~ 59200
Prostanoids ~ see prostaglandin
Prostate
  ablation, cryosurgery ~ 55873
  abscess, drainage ~ 52700
    incision and drainage ~ 55720-55725

Prostate ~ continued
  biopsy ~ 55700-55706
    transperineal ~ 55706
  brachytherapy, needle insertion ~ 55875-55976
  coagulation, laser ~ 52647
  destruction
    cryosurgery ~ 55873
    thermotherapy ~ 53850-53852
      microwave ~ 53850
      radio frequency ~ 53852
  enucleation, laser ~ 52649
  excision
    partial ~ 55801, 55821-55831
    perineal ~ 55801-55815
    radical ~ 55810-55815, 55840-55845
    retropubic ~ 55831-55845
    suprapubic ~ 55821
    transurethral ~ 52402, 52601, 52630
  exploration, exposure ~ 55860
    with nodes ~ 55862-55865
  incision
    exposure ~ 55860-55865
    transurethral ~ 52450
  insertion
    catheter or needle ~ 55875
    radioactive substance ~ 55860
  needle biopsy ~ 55700
    transperineal ~ 55706
  placement
    biodegradable material, transperineal ~ 55874
    catheter ~ 55875
    dosimeter ~ 55876
    fiducial marker ~ 55876
    interstitial device ~ 55876
    needle ~ 55875
  resection, transurethral ~ 52601, 52630
  spectral analysis, real-time ~ 0443T
  thermotherapy, transurethral ~ 53850-53852
  ultrasound ~ 76872-76873
  unlisted services and procedures ~ 55899
    urinary system ~ 53899
  urethra, stent insertion ~ 52282, 53855
  vaporization, laser ~ 52648
Prostate specific antigen ~ 84152-84154
Prostatectomy ~ 52601
  laparoscopic ~ 55866
  perineal
    partial ~ 55801
    radical ~ 55810-55815
  retropubic
    partial ~ 55831
    radical ~ 55840-55845, 55866
  suprapubic, partial ~ 55821
  transurethral ~ 52630
Prostatic abscess ~ see abscess, prostate
Prostatotomy ~ 55720-55725
Prosthesis
  arm, removal ~ 24160, 24164
  augmentation, mandibular body ~ 21125
  auricular ~ 21086
  breast
    insertion ~ 19325, 19340-19342
      with tissue expander ~ 19357
    removal ~ 19328-19330
    supply ~ 19396
  button
    bone graft ~ 20900
    nasal septum ~ 30220
    voice ~ 31611
  cheekbone, malar augmentation ~ 21270
  chin ~ 21120
  cornea ~ 65770
  diaphram, complex repair ~ 39561
  ear
    ossicle reconstruction ~ 69633, 69637
  elbow
    removal
      humeral and ulnar components ~ 24160
      radial head ~ 24164

Prosthesis ~ continued
  endovascular
    bypass, composite, with vein ~ 35681
    endoprosthesis
      abdominal aortic ~ 34845-34848
      aorto-bi-iliac ~ 34831
      aorto-bifemoral ~ 34832
      brachial ~ 34834
      celiac artery ~ 34841-34848
      femoral ~ 34812, 34813
      iliac ~ 0254T, 34709, 34710, 34711, 34820, 34833
      illio-iliac ~ 34707, 34708
      infrarenal abdominal aortic ~ 34709, 34710, 34711, 34845-34848
      infrarenal aortic ~ 34830, 35697
      mesenteric ~ 34841-34848
      renal artery ~ 34841-34848
      visceral aortic ~ 34841-34848
      visceral artery ~ 34841-34848
      thoracic aorta ~ 33883-33886
  facial, osteoplasty ~ 21208
  femur ~ 27236
  heart
    aortic arch repair ~ 33852
    aortic enlargement ~ 33851
    aortic valve ~ 33361-33365, 33367-33369, 33405
    atioventricular valve ~ 33670
    mitral valve ~ 33426
      repair ~ 0345T, 33418, 33419
    pulmonary valve ~ 33475, 33477
    shunt ~ 33764
    valve prosthesis repair ~ 33496
    ventricular patch ~ 33548
  hernia
    gastroschisis ~ 49605, 49606
    hiatal ~ 43333, 43335, 43337
    omphalocele ~ 49605, 49606
    ventral ~ 49568, 49652-49657
  hip
    insertion ~ 27125, 27130, 27236
    removal ~ 27090, 27091
  intestines ~ 44700
  knee
    insertion ~ 27438, 27445
    intraoperative use, kinetic balance sensor ~ 0396T
    removal ~ 27488
  lens
    insertion ~ 66982-66985
    without cataract removal ~ 66985
  mandibular resection ~ 21081
  nasal ~ 21087
  nasal septum, insertion ~ 30220
  obturator ~ 21076
    definitive ~ 21080
    interim ~ 21079
  ocular ~ 21077, 65770, 66982-66985, 92330-92335, 92358, 92393
    fitting and prescription ~ 92330
    loan ~ 92358
    prescription ~ 92335
    supply ~ 92393
  orbital ~ 21077
    partial or total ~ 69633, 69637
  ossicle reconstruction, chain ~ 69633
  palatal augmentation ~ 21082
  palatal lift ~ 21083
  palate ~ 42280-42281
  penile
    insertion ~ 54400-54405
    removal ~ 54406, 54410-54417
    repair ~ 54408
    replacement ~ 54410-54411, 54416-54417
  perineum, removal ~ 53442
  skull plate
    removal ~ 62142
    replacement ~ 62143
  spectacle ~ continued
    fitting ~ 92352-92353
    repair ~ 92371
  speech aid ~ 21084
  spine, insertion ~ 22853, 22854, 22859
  synthetic ~ 69633, 69637

Prosthesis ~ *continued*
  temporomandibular joint, arthroplasty ~ 21243
  testicular, insertion ~ 54660
  training ~ 97520
  urethral sphincter
    insertion ~ 53444-53445
    removal ~ 53446-53447
    repair ~ 53449
    replacement ~ 53448
  wrist, removal ~ 25250-25251
Protease F ~ see plasmin
Protein
  C-reactive ~ 86140-86141
  glycated ~ 82985
  myelin basic ~ 83873
  osteocalcin ~ 83937
  prealbumin ~ 84134
  serum ~ 84155, 84165
  total ~ 84155-84160
  urine ~ 84156
  western blot ~ 84181-84182, 88372
Protein analysis, tissue western blot ~ 88371
Protein C activator ~ 85337
Protein C antigen ~ 85302
Protein C assay ~ 85303
Protein C resistance assay ~ 85307
Protein S
  assay ~ 85306
  total ~ 85305
Prothrombase ~ see thrombokinase
Prothrombin ~ 85210
Prothrombinase ~ see thromboplastin
Prothrombin time ~ 85610-85611
Prothrombokinase ~ 85230
Protime ~ see prothrombin time
Proton treatment delivery
  complex ~ 77525
  intermediate ~ 77523
  simple ~ 77520-77522
Protoporphyrin ~ 84202-84203
Protozoa antibody ~ 86753
Provitamin A ~ see vitamin, A
Prower factor ~ see Stuart-Prower factor
PSA ~ see prostate specific antigen
Pseudocyst, pancreas ~ see pancreas, pseudocyst
PSG ~ see polysomnography
Psoriasis treatment ~ (see also dermatology; photochemotherapy)
  96910-96922
Psychiatric diagnosis
  evaluation of records or reports ~ 90885
  evaluation ~ 90791
    with medical services ~ 90792
  interactive complexity ~ 90785
  major depressive disorder (MDD) ~ 3088F-3093F
  psychological testing ~ 96101-96103, 96125
    computer assisted ~ 96103
  suicide risk assessment ~ 3085F
  unlisted services and procedures ~ 90899
Psychiatric treatment
  biofeedback training ~ 90875-90876
  consultation with family ~ 90887
  drug management ~ 90863
  electroconvulsive therapy ~ 90870, 4066F
    referral documented ~ 4067F
  environmental intervention ~ 90882
  family ~ 90846-90849, 99510
  group ~ 90853
  hypnotherapy ~ 90880
  narcosynthesis analysis ~ 90865
  pharmacotherapy
    antidepressant ~ 4063F-4064F
    antipsychotic ~ 4065F
    drug management ~ 90863
  psychoanalysis ~ 90845
  report preparation ~ 90889
  suicide risk assessment ~ 3085F
  transcranial magnetic stimulation ~ 90867-90869
  unlisted services and procedures ~ 90899

Psychoanalysis ~ 90845
Psychophysiologic feedback ~ see biofeedback
Psychotherapy
  family of patient ~ 90846-90847
  for crisis ~ 90839-90840
  group other than multifamily ~ 90853
  individual patient/family member ~ 90832-90834, 90836-90838
  interactive complexity ~ 90785
  major depressive disorder ~ 4060F-4062F
  multifamily ~ 90849
  referral, documented ~ 4062F
  with pharmacologic management ~ 90863
PTA (clotting factor XI (eleven)) ~ 85270
PTB (patellar tendon bearing) cast ~ 29435
PTC (clotting factor IX (nine); Christmas factor) ~ 85250
PTC ~ see percutaneous transluminal coronary angioplasty
Pteroylglutamic acid ~ see folic acid
Pterygium
  excision ~ 65420
    with graft ~ 65426
Pterygomaxillary fossa incision ~ 31040
Pterygopalatine ganglion ~ see sphenopalatine ganglion
PTH ~ see parathormone
Ptosis ~ see blepharoptosis; procidentia
PTT ~ see thromboplastin, partial, time
Ptyalectasis ~ see dilation, salivary duct
Pubic symphysis ~ 27282
Pubis
  craterization ~ 27070
  cyst, excision ~ 27065-27067
  excision ~ 27070
  saucerization ~ 27070
  tumor, excision ~ 27065-27067
Pudendal nerve
  destruction ~ 64630
  injection
    anesthetic ~ 64430
    neurolytic ~ 64630
Puestow procedure ~ 48548
Pulled elbow ~ see nursemaid elbow
Pulmonary artery ~ 33690
  banding ~ 33620
  catheterization ~ see also catheterization, pulmonary artery
  embolism ~ 33910-33916
  excision ~ 33910-33916
  percutaneous transluminal angioplasty ~ 92997-92998
  reimplantation ~ 33788
  repair ~ 33620, 33690, 33917-33920
    reimplantation ~ 33788
  shunt
    from aorta ~ 33755-33762, 33924
    subclavian ~ 33750
    from vena cava ~ 33766-33767
  transection ~ 33922
Pulmonary function test ~ see pulmonology, diagnostic
Pulmonary hemorrhage ~ see hemorrhage, lung
Pulmonary medical services ~ 94010-94799
Pulmonary perfusion imaging ~ 78580, 78597, 78598
Pulmonary valve
  implantation, prosthesis, transcatheter ~ 33477
  incision ~ 33470, 33471, 33474
  repair ~ 33470, 33471, 33474
  replacement ~ 33475
Pulmonary vein
  repair
    complete ~ 33730
    partial ~ 33724
    stenosis ~ 33726
  stenosis
    repair ~ 33726
Pulmonology
  diagnostic
    airway closing volume ~ 94727
    apnea monitoring, pediatric ~ 94774-94777
    bronchodilation ~ 94664
    bed testing, neonate ~ 94780-94781
    car seat testing, neonate ~ 94780-94781
    carbon dioxide response curve ~ 94400
    carbon monoxide diffusion capacity ~ 94729

Pulmonology ~ *continued*
  expired gas analysis
    CO2 ~ 94770
    NO ~ 95012
    O2 and CO2 ~ 94681
    O2 update, direct ~ 94680
    O2 uptake, indirect ~ 94690
    quantitative ~ 94250
  flow-volume loop ~ 94375
  hemoglobin O2 affinity ~ 82820
  high altitutde simulation test (HAST) ~ 94452-9444-53
  hypoxia response curve ~ 94450
  inhalation treatment ~ 94640
  maximum breathing capacity ~ 94200
  maximal voluntary ventilation ~ 94200
  membrane compliance ~ 94750
  membrane diffusion capacity ~ 94729
  oximetry, ear or pulse ~ 94760-94762
  resistance to airflow ~ 94726, 94728
  spirometry ~ 94010-94070
    evaluation ~ 94010-94070
    patient initiated with bronchospasm ~ 94014-94016
  sputum mobilization with inhalants ~ 94664
  stress test, pulmonary ~ 94618
  vital capacity ~ 94150
  wheeze rate ~ 94799
  therapeutic
    expired gas analysis ~ 94250
    inhalation, pentamidine ~ 94642
    inhalation treatment ~ 94640, 94644-94645, 94664, 99503
    intrapulmonary surfactant admin ~ 94610
    manipulation of chest wall ~ 94667-94668
    pressure ventilation
      negative CNPB ~ 94662
      positive CPAP ~ 94660
    unlisted services and procedures ~ 94799
    ventilation assist ~ 94002-94005, 99504
  unlisted services and procedures ~ 94799
Pulse generator
  baroreflex activation device
    implantation/replacement ~ 0268T
    revision/removal ~ 0271T
  implantable defibrillator
    insertion ~ 33230, 33231, 33240
    removal ~ 33241
    removal with replacement ~ 33262-33264
  pacemaker
    insertion ~ 33212, 33213, 33221
    removal ~ 33233
    replacement ~ 33227-33229
  neurostimulator
    insertion ~ 61885, 61886, 64568, 64590
    removal/revision ~ 61888, 64595, 64570
  respiratory Sensor Electrode/Electrode Array
    insertion ~ 0466T
    removal ~ 0468T
    replacement ~ 0467T
    revision ~ 0467T
Pulse rate increased ~ see tachycardia
Pump ~ see chemotherapy, pump services; infusion pump
Pump, infusion ~ see infusion pump
Pump services oxygenator/heat exchanger ~ 99190-99192
Punch graft ~ 15775-15776
Puncture
  artery ~ 36600
  chest, drainage ~ 32554-32555
  cisternal ~ see cisternal puncture
  lumbar ~ see spinal tap
  lung ~ 32405
  pericardium ~ 33010-33011
  pleural cavity, drainage ~ 32554-32555
  skull, drain fluid ~ 61000-61020
    cistern ~ 61050
    inject cistern ~ 61055
    inject ventricle ~ 61026
    shunt
      drain fluid ~ 61070
      injection ~ 61070

Puncture ~ *continued*
  spinal cord
    diagnostic ~ 62270
    drain fluid ~ 62272
    lumbar ~ 62270
  tracheal, aspiration and/or injection ~ 31612
Puncture aspiration
  abscess, skin ~ 10160
  bulla ~ 10160
  cyst
    breast ~ 19000-19001
    skin ~ 10160
  hematoma ~ 10160
Pure-tone audiometry ~ 92552, 92553
Pustules removal ~ 10040
PUVA ~ (dermatology; photochemotherapy; ultraviolet light therapy) 96912
Pyelogram ~ see urography, intravenous; urography, retrograde
Pyelography ~ 74400, 74425
Pyelolithotomy ~ 50130
  anatrophic ~ 50075
  coagulum ~ 50130
Pyeloplasty ~ 50400-50405, 50544
  repair, horseshoe kidney ~ 50540
  secondary ~ 50405
Pyeloscopy
  with cystourethroscopy ~ 52351
    biopsy ~ 52354
    destruction ~ 52354
    lithotripsy ~ 52353
    removal, calculus ~ 52352
    tumor excision ~ 52355
Pyelostolithotomy percutaneous ~ 50080-50081
Pyelostomy
  with drainage ~ 50125
  with pyeloplasty ~ 50400, 50405
  change tube ~ 50435
Pyelotomy
  complicated ~ 50135
  with drainage ~ 50125
  endoscopic ~ 50570
  exploration ~ 50120
  with removal calculus ~ 50130
Pyeloureteroplasty ~ see pyeloplasty
Pyloric sphincter
  incision ~ 43520
  reconstruction ~ 43800
Pyloromyotomy ~ 43520
  with gastrectomy ~ 43639
Pyloroplasty ~ 43800
  with gastrectomy ~ 43639
  with vagotomy ~ 43640
Pyothorax ~ see abscess, thorax
Pyridoxal phosphate ~ 84207
Pyrophosphate, adenosine ~ see adenosine diphosphate
Pyrophosphorylase, Udp galactose ~ (galactose-one-phosphate, uridyl transferase) 82775, 82776
Pyruvate ~ 84210-84220

Q

Q fever ~ 86000, 86638
Q fever ab ~ see antibody, coxiella burnetii
Quadriceps repair ~ 27430
Quantitative sudomotor axon reflex test (QSART) ~ 95923
Quick test ~ prothrombin time 85610, 85611
Quinidine assay ~ 80194
Quinine ~ 84228

R

Rabies vaccine ~ 90675-90676
Rachicentesis ~ see spinal tap
Radial head, subluxation ~ see nursemaid elbow
Radial keratotomy ~ 65771

Radiation ~ see irradiation
Radiation physics
  consultation ~ 77336-77370
  unlisted services and procedures ~ 77399
Radiation therapy
  CT scan guidance ~ 77014
  consultation, radiation physics ~ 77336-77370
  dose plan ~ 77300, 77301, 77306, 77307, 77331
    brachytherapy ~ 0394T, 0395T, 77316-77318
    intensity modulation IMRT ~ 77338
    teletherapy ~ 77306, 77307, 77321
  field set-up ~ 77280, 77285, 77290
  guidance
    CT ~ 77014
    for localization of target volume ~ 77387
    interstitial device placement ~ 49411-49412
  intraoperative radiation therapy
    breast, preparation of tumor cavity ~ 19294
  planning ~ 77261-77263, 77299
  port image(s) ~ 77417
  radiosurgery ~ 77317-77373
  special ~ 77470
  stereotactic
    body ~ 77373
    cerebral lesions ~ 77371-77372
  treatment delivery ~ 77401, 77402, 77407, 77412
    high energy neutron radiation ~ 77423
    intensity modulation ~ 77385, 77386
    intraoperative ~ 77424, 77425
    localization ~ 77387
    proton beam ~ 77520-77525
    stereotactic ~ 77371-77373
    superficial ~ 77401
    tracking ~ 77387
  treatment device ~ 77332-77334
  treatment management
    1 or 2 fractions only ~ 77431
    intraoperative ~ 77469
    unlisted services and procedures ~ 77499
    weekly ~ 77427
Radical excision of lymph nodes ~ see excision, lymph nodes, radical
Radical mastectomies, modified ~ see mastectomy, modified radical
Radical neck dissection
  with auditory canal surgery ~ 69155
  laryngectomy ~ 31365-31368
  pharyngolaryngectomy ~ 31390-31395
  with thyroidectomy ~ 60254
  with tongue excision ~ 41135, 41145, 41153-41155
Radical resection ~ see also resection, radical
  abdomen ~ 51597
  acetabulum ~ 27076
  ankle ~ 27615, 27616
  arm, lower ~ 25077
  calcaneus ~ 27647
  elbow, capsule, soft tissue,
    bone with contracture release ~ 24149
  face ~ 21015
  fibula ~ 27646
  finger ~ 26117
  foot ~ 28046, 28047
  forearm ~ 25077
  hand ~ 26115
  hip
    soft tissue ~ 27049
    tumor or infection ~ 27075-27076
  humerus ~ 23220
  innominate ~ 27077
  ischial ~ 27078
  knee ~ 27329
  leg
    lower ~ 27615
    upper ~ 27329
  metacarpal ~ 26250
  metatarsal ~ 28173
  mouth, with tongue excision ~ 41150, 41155
  ovarian tumor
    bilateral
      salpingo-oophorectomy-omentectomy ~ 58950-58954
      with radical dissection for debulking ~ 58952-58954
      with total abdominal hysterectomy ~ 58951, 58953-58954

Radical resection ~ *continued*
  pelvis, soft tissue ~ 27049
  peritoneal tumor
    bilateral
      salpingo-oophorectomy-omentectomy ~ 58952-58954
      with radical dissection for debulking ~ 58952-58954
  phalanges
    fingers ~ 26260-26262
    toe ~ 28175
  radius ~ 25170
  scalp ~ 21015
  scapula ~ 23210
  shoulder ~ 23077
  sternum ~ 21630-21632
  talus, tumor ~ 27647
  tarsal ~ 28171
  tibia ~ 27645
  tonsil ~ 42842-42845
  tumor
    back/flank ~ 21935, 21936
    femur ~ 27365
    knee ~ 27329, 27365
    leg, upper ~ 27329
    neck ~ 21557, 21558
    thorax ~ 21557, 21558
  ulna ~ 25170
  wrist ~ 25077
Radical vulvectomy ~ see vulvectomy, radical
Radio-cobalt B12 Schilling test ~ see vitamin, B-12, absorption study
Radioactive colloid therapy ~ 79200-79300
Radioactive substance
  insertion
    kidney ~ 50578
    prostate ~ 55860
    ureteral endoscopic ~ 50978
    urethral endoscopic ~ 50959
Radiocarpal joint
  arthrotomy ~ 25040
  dislocation, closed treatment ~ 25660
Radiocinematographies ~ see cineradiography
Radioelement
  application ~ 77761-77763, 77767, 77768, 77770-77772, 77778, 77789
  handling ~ 77790
  infusion ~ 77750
Radioelement device placement
  breast ~ 19296-19298
  genitalia ~ 55920
  head ~ 41019
  intracavitary ~ 31643
  muscle ~ 20555
  neck ~ 41019
  pelvis ~ 55920
  prostate ~ 55875
  soft tissue ~ 20555
  ultrasound guidance ~ 76965
  uterus ~ 57155
  vagina ~ 57155, 57156
Radioelement substance
  catheter placement
    breast ~ 19296-19298
    bronchus ~ 31643
    muscle or soft tissue ~ 20555
    pelvic organ ~ 55920
    prostate ~ 55875
    soft tissue ~ 20555
  needle placement
    head/neck ~ 41019
    muscle ~ 20555
    prostate ~ 55875-55876
    soft tissue ~ 20555
Radiography ~ see radiology, diagnostic; X-ray
Radioimmunosorbent test ~ see gammaglobulin, blood
Radioisotope brachytherapy ~ see brachytherapy
Radioisotope scan ~ see nuclear medicine
Radiological marker, preoperative placement, excision of breast lesion ~ 19125-19126
Radiology
  bone/joint studies
    computed tomography ~ 77078
    dual energy X-ray absorptiometry (DXA) ~ 77080, 77081, 77085, 77086

Radiology ~ *continued*
  radiography ~ 77071-77077
  diagnostic imaging
    abdomen ~ 74018, 74019, 74021
    abscess, fistula or sinus tract, study ~ 76080
    chest ~ 71045-71048
    computed tomography follow-up study ~ 76380
    fluoroscopy ~ 76000, 76001, 76496
    gastrointestinal tract ~ 74210-74363
    gynecological and obstetrical ~ 74710-74775
    head and neck ~ 70010-70559
    lower extremities ~ 73501-73725
    magnetic resonance spectroscopy ~ 76390
    spine and pelvis ~ 72020-72295
    3D rendering, tomographic ~ 76376, 76377
    upper extremities ~ 73000-73225
    urinary tract ~ 74018-74485
    vascular procedures
      aorta and arteries ~ 36901-36906, 75600-75774
      transcatheter procedures ~ 75894-75989
      veins and lymphatics ~ 75801-75893
  radiologic guidance
    computed tomography ~ 77011-77014
    fluoroscopy ~ 77001-77003
    magnetic resonance ~ 77021, 77022
Radionuclide CT scan ~ see emission computerized tomography
Radionuclide imaging ~ see nuclear medicine
Radionuclide therapy
  intra-articular ~ 79440
  intravascular ~ 79420
  intravenous infusion ~ 79403
  leukemia ~ 79100
  other ~ 79400
  polycythemia vera ~ 79100
  thyroid gland ~ 79000-79035
  unlisted services and procedures ~ 79999
Radionuclide tomography, single photon emission- computed ~ see SPECT
Radiopharmaceutical localization
  inflammatory process ~ 78805
  injection ~ 78808
Radiopharmaceutical therapy
  heart ~ 79440
  interstitial ~ 79300
  intra-arterial ~ 79445
  intra-articular ~ 79440
  intracavitary ~ 79200
  intravenous ~ 79101, 79403
  leukemia ~ 79100
  oral ~ 79005
  other ~ 79400
  polycythemia vera ~ 79100
  thyroid gland ~ 79020-79035
  unlisted services and procedures ~ 79999
Radiotherapeutic ~ see radiation therapy
Radiotherapies ~ see irradiation
Radiotherapy, surface ~ see application, radioelement, surface
Radioulnar joint
  arthrodesis, with resection of ulna ~ 25830
  dislocation
    closed treatment ~ 25675
    open treatment ~ 25676
Radius ~ see also also arm, lower; elbow; ulna
  arthroplasty ~ 24365
    with implant ~ 24366, 25441
  craterization ~ 24145, 25151
  cyst, excision ~ 24125-24126, 25120-25126
  diaphysectomy ~ 24145, 25151
  dislocation
    with fracture
      closed treatment ~ 24620
      open treatment ~ 24635
    partial ~ 24640
    subluxate ~ 24640
  excision ~ 24130, 24136, 24145, 24152
    epiphyseal bar ~ 20150
    partial ~ 25145
    styloid process ~ 25230

Radius ~ *continued*
  fracture ~ 25605
    closed treatment ~ 25500-25505, 25520, 25600-25605
      with manipulation ~ 25605
      without manipulation ~ 25600
    distal ~ 25600-25609
      open treatment ~ 25607-25609
    head/neck
      closed treatment ~ 24650-24655
      open treatment ~ 24665-24666
    open treatment ~ 25515, 25525-25526, 25574
    percutaneous fixation ~ 25606
    shaft ~ 25500-25526
      open treatment ~ 25574
    with ulna ~ 25560-25565
      open treatment ~ 25575
  implant, removal ~ 24164
  incision and drainage ~ 25035
  osteomyelitis ~ 24136, 24145
  osteoplasty ~ 25390-25393
  prophylactic treatment ~ 25490, 25492
  repair
    epiphyseal arrest ~ 25450-25455
    epiphyseal separation
      closed ~ 25600
      closed with manipulation ~ 25605
      open treatment ~ 25607-25609
      percutaneous fixation ~ 25606
    with graft ~ 25405, 25420-25426
    malunion or nonunion ~ 25400, 25415
    osteotomy ~ 25350-25355, 25370-25375
      and ulna ~ 25365
  saucerization ~ 24145, 25151
  sequestrectomy ~ 24136, 25145
  tumor, cyst ~ 24120
    excision ~ 24125-24126, 25120-25126, 25170
Ramstedt operation ~ see pyloromyotomy
Ramus anterior, nervus thoracicus ~ see intercostal nerve
Range of motion test
  extremities or trunk ~ 95851
  eye ~ 92018-92019
  hand ~ 95852
Rapid heart rate ~ see tachycardia
Rapid plasma reagin test ~ 86592-86593
Rapid test for infection ~ 86308, 86403-86406
  monospot test ~ 86308
Rapoport test ~ 52005
Raskind procedure ~ 33735-33737
Rathke pouch tumor ~ see craniopharyngioma
Rat typhus ~ (Murine typhus) 86000
Rays, roentgen ~ see X-ray
Raz procedure ~ (repair, bladder, neck) 51845
RBC ~ see red blood cell (RBC)
RBC ab ~ see antibody, red blood cell
Reaction lip without reconstruction ~ 40530
Reaction, polymerase chain ~ see polymerase chain reaction (PCR)
Realignment
  femur with osteotomy ~ 27454
  knee extensor ~ 27422
Receptor ~ see CD4; estrogen, receptor; FC receptor; progesterone receptors
Receptor assay
  hormone ~ 84233-84235
  non hormone ~ 84238
Recession gastrocnemius leg, lower ~ 27687
Reconstruction ~ see revision
  abdominal wall
    omental flap ~ 49905
  acetabulum ~ 27120-27122
  anal
    congenital absence ~ 46730-46740
    fistula ~ 46742
    graft ~ 46753
    with implant ~ 46762
    sphincter ~ 46750-46751, 46760-46762
  ankle ~ 27700-27703
  apical-aortic conduit ~ 33404
  atrial
    endoscopic ~ 33265-33266
    open ~ 33254-33256

Reconstruction ~ continued

auditory canal, external ~ 69310-69320
bile duct, anastomosis ~ 47800
bladder
 from colon ~ 50810
 from intestines ~ 50820, 51960
 and urethra ~ 51800-51820
breast ~ 19357-19369
 augmentation ~ 19324-19325
 with free flap ~ 19364
 with latissimus dorsi flap ~ 19361
 mammoplasty ~ 19318-19325
 nipple ~ 19350-19355
 with other techniques ~ 19366
 revision ~ 19380
 with tissue expander ~ 19357
 transverse rectus abdominis myocutaneous flap ~ 19367-19369
bronchi ~ 32501
 graft repair ~ 31770
 stenosis ~ 31775
canthus ~ 67950
cardiac anomoly, complex ~ 33622
carpal ~ 25443
carpal bone ~ 25394, 25430
cheekbone ~ 21270
chest wall, omental flap ~ 49904
 trauma ~ 32820
cleft palate ~ 42200-42225
conduit, apical-aortic ~ 33404
conjunctiva ~ 68320-68335
 with flap
  bridge or partial ~ 68360
  total ~ 68362
cranial bone, extracranial ~ 21181-21184
ear, middle
 tympanoplasty with antrotomy or mastoidotomy
  with ossicular chain reconstruction ~ 69636-69637
 tympanoplasty with mastoidectomy ~ 69641
  with intact or reconstructed wall ~ 69643-69644
  with ossicular chain reconstruction ~ 69642
  radical or complete ~ 69644-69645
 tympanoplasty without mastoidectomy ~ 69631
  with ossicular chain reconstruction ~ 69632-69633
elbow ~ 24360
 with implant ~ 24361-24362
 total replacement ~ 24363
esophagus ~ 43300, 43310, 43313
 creation, stoma ~ 43352
 esophagostomy ~ 43351, 43352
 fistula ~ 43305, 43312, 43314
 gastrointestinal ~ 43360-43361
eye
 graft
  conjunctiva ~ 65782
  stem cell ~ 65781
 transplantation
  amniotic membrane ~ 65780
eyelid
 canthus ~ 67950
 second stage ~ 67975
 total ~ 67973-67975
 total eyelid
  lower, one stage ~ 67973
  upper, one stage ~ 67974
 transfer tarsoconjunctival flap from opposing eyelid ~ 67971
facial bones, secondary ~ 21275
fallopian tube ~ see repair
femur
 lengthening ~ 27466-27468
 shortening ~ 27465, 27468
fibula, lengthening ~ 27715
finger, polydactylous ~ 26587
foot, cleft ~ 28360
forehead ~ 21172-21180, 21182-21184
glenoid fossa ~ 21255
gums
 alveolus ~ 41874
 gingiva ~ 41872

Reconstruction ~ continued

hand
 tendon pulley ~ 26390, 26500-26502
 toe to finger transfer ~ 26551-26556
heart
 atrial ~ 33253
  endoscopic ~ 33265-33266
  open ~ 33254-33256
 atrial septum ~ 33735-33737
 pulmonary artery shunt ~ 33924
 vena cava ~ 34502
hip
 replacement ~ 27130-27132
 secondary ~ 27134-27138
hip joint, with prosthesis ~ 27125
interphalangeal joint ~ 26535-26536
 collateral ligament ~ 26545
intestines, small, anastomosis ~ 44130
knee ~ 27437-27438
 femur ~ 27442-27443, 27446
 ligament ~ 27427-27429
 prosthesis ~ 27438, 27445
 replacement ~ 27447
 revision ~ 27486-27487
 tibia ~ 27440-27443, 27446
kneecap, instability ~ 27420-27424
larynx
 cricoid split ~ 31587
 medialization ~ 31591
 stenosis ~ 31551-31554
 web ~ 31580
lip ~ 40525-40527, 40761
lunate ~ 25444
malar augmentation,
 prosthetic material ~ 21270
 with bone graft ~ 21210
mandible, with implant ~ 21244-21246, 21248-21249
mandibular condyle ~ 21247
mandibular rami
 with bone graft ~ 21194
 without bone graft ~ 21193
 with internal rigid fixation ~ 21196
 without internal rigid fixation ~ 21195
maxilla, with implant ~ 21245-21246, 21248-21249
metacarpophalangeal joint ~ 26530-26531
midface
 with bone graft ~ 21145-21160, 21188
 without bone graft ~ 21141-21143
 forehead advancement ~ 21159-21160
mouth ~ 40840-40845
nail bed ~ 11762
nasoethmoid complex ~ 21182-21184
navicular ~ 25443
nose
 cleft lip/cleft palate ~ 30460-30462
 dermatoplasty ~ 30620
 primary ~ 30400-30420
 secondary ~ 30430-30450
 septum ~ 30520
orbit ~ 21256
orbit area, secondary ~ 21275
orbit with bone grafting ~ 21182-21184
orbital rim ~ 21172-21180
orbital rims ~ 21182-21184
orbital walls ~ 21182-21184
orbitocraniofacial, secondary revision ~ 21275
oviduct, fimbrioplasty ~ 58760
palate
 cleft palate ~ 42200-42225
 lengthening ~ 42226-42227
parotid duct, diversion ~ 42507-42510
patella ~ 27437-27438
 instability ~ 27420-27424
penis
 angulation ~ 54360
 chordee ~ 54300-54304
 complications ~ 54340-54348
 epispadias ~ 54380-54390

Reconstruction ~ *continued*
 hypospadias ~ 54332, 54352
  one stage distal with urethroplasty ~ 54324-54328
  one stage perineal ~ 54336
 periorbital region, osteotomy with graft ~ 21267-21268
 pharynx ~ 42950
 pyloric sphincter ~ 43800
 radius ~ 24365, 25390-25393, 25441
  arthroplasty, with implant ~ 24366
 shoulder joint, with implant ~ 23470-23472
 skull ~ 21172-21180
  defect ~ 62140-62141, 62145
 sternum ~ 21740-21742
  with thoracoscopy ~ 21743
 stomach
  with duodenum ~ 43810, 43850-43855, 43865
  gastric bypass ~ 43846
  with jejunum ~ 43820-43825, 43860
  for obesity ~ 43846-43848
  Roux-en-Y ~ 43846
 superior-lateral orbital rim and forehead ~ 21172-21175
 supraorbital rim and forehead ~ 21179-21180
 symblepharon ~ 68335
 temporomandibular joint, arthroplasty ~ 21240-21243
 throat ~ 42950
 thumb
  from finger ~ 26550
  opponensplasty ~ 26490-26496
 tibia
  lengthening ~ 27715
  tubercle ~ 27418
 toe
  angle deformity ~ 28313
  extra toes ~ 28344
  hammertoe ~ 28285-28286
  macrodactyly ~ 28340-28341
  polydactylous ~ 26587
  syndactyly ~ 28345
  webbed toe ~ 28345
 tongue, frenum ~ 41520
 trachea
  carina ~ 31766
  cervical ~ 31750
  fistula ~ 31755
  intrathoracic ~ 31760
 trapezium ~ 25445
 tympanic membrane ~ 69620
 ulna ~ 25390-25393, 25442
  radioulnar ~ 25337
 ureter ~ 50700
  with intestines ~ 50840
 urethra ~ 53410-53440, 53445
  complications ~ 54340-54348
  hypospadias
   one stage distal with meatal advancement ~ 54322
   one stage distal with urethroplasty ~ 54324-54328
   suture to bladder ~ 51840-51841
   urethroplasty for second stage ~ 54308-54316
   urethroplasty for third stage ~ 54318
 uterus ~ 58540
 vas deferens ~ see vasovasorrhaphy
 vena cava ~ 34502
  with resection ~ 37799
 wound repair ~ 13100-13160
 wrist ~ 25332
  capsulectomy ~ 25320
  capsulorrhaphy ~ 25320
  realign ~ 25335
 zygomatic arch ~ 21255
Rectal bleeding ~ see hemorrhage, rectum
Rectal prolapse ~ see procidentia, rectum
Rectal sphincter dilation ~ 45910
Rectocele repair ~ 45560
Rectopexy ~ see proctopexy
Rectoplasty ~ see proctoplasty
Rectorrhaphy ~ see rectum, suture
Rectovaginal fistula ~ see fistula, rectovaginal
Rectovaginal hernia ~ see rectocele

Rectum ~ see also anus
 abscess, incision and drainage ~ 45005-45020, 46040, 46060
 advancement flap ~ 46288
 biopsy ~ 45100
 dilation, endoscopy ~ 45303
 endoscopy
  biopsy ~ 45305
  destruction, tumor ~ 45320
  dilation ~ 45303, 45910
  exploration ~ 45300
  hemorrhage ~ 45317
  removal
   foreign body ~ 45307
   polyp ~ 45308-45315
   tumor ~ 45308-45315
  volvulus ~ 45321
 excision
  with colon ~ 45121
  partial ~ 45111, 45113-45116, 45123
  total ~ 45110, 45112, 45119-45120
 exploration, endoscopic ~ 45300
 hemorrhage, endoscopic ~ 45317
 incontinence, graft ~ 46753
 injection, sclerosing solution ~ 45520
 laparoscopy ~ 45499
 lesion, excision ~ 45108
 manometry ~ 91122
 mucosectomy ~ 44157-44158, 44211, 45113
 prolapse, excision ~ 45130-45135
 removal
  fecal impaction ~ 45915
  foreign body ~ 45307, 45915
 repair
  fistula ~ 45800-45825, 46707
  incontinence ~ 46753
  injury ~ 45562-45563
  prolapse ~ 45505-45541, 45900
  rectocele ~ 45560
  stenosis ~ 45500
  with sigmoid excision ~ 45550
 sensation, tone and compliance test ~ 91120
 stricture, excision ~ 45150
 suture
  fistula ~ 45800-45825
  prolapse ~ 45540-45541
 tumor
  destruction ~ 45190, 45320
  excision ~ 45160-45172
  transanal endoscopic ~ 0184T
 unlisted services and procedures ~ 45999
Reductase, glutathione ~ see glutathione reductase
Reductase, lactic cytochrome ~ see lactic dehydrogenase
Reduction
 amniotic fluid ~ 59001
 collateral ligament, ulnar ~ 29902
 craniomegalic skull ~ 62115, 62117
 ear, protruding ~ 69300
 for fracture
  laryngeal ~ 31584
  odontoid ~ 22318, 22319
  tracheal ~ 31630
  vertebral ~ 22325-22328
 internal hernia, mesentary ~ 44050
 mammaplasty ~ 19318
 overcorrection of ptosis ~ 67909
 pregnancy, multi-fetal ~ 59866
 tissue ~ 30801
 torsion, testis ~ 54600
 tumor
  bone, ablation therapy ~ 20982, 20983
  pulmonary ~ 32994, 32998
 volume
  blood products ~ 86960
  lung ~ 32491
 volvulus ~ 44050, 44055
 with reconstruction
  hip ~ 27147, 27156
  radioulnar joint ~ 25337
  wrist ~ 25230

1127

Red blood cell (RBC)
  antibody ~ 86850-86870
    pretreatment ~ 86970-86972
  count ~ 85032-85041
  fragility
    mechanical ~ 85547
    osmotic ~ 85555-85557
  hematocrit ~ 85014
  iron utilization ~ 78170
  morphology ~ 85007
  platelet estimation ~ 85007
  sedimentation rate
    automated ~ 85652
    manual ~ 85651
  sequestration ~ 78140
  sickling ~ 85660
  survival test ~ 78130-78135
  volume determination ~ 78120-78121
Red blood cell ab ~ see antibody, red blood cell
Reduction
  forehead ~ 21137-21139
  lung volume ~ 32491
  mammoplasty ~ 19318
  masseter muscle/bone ~ 21295-21296
  osteoplasty, facial bones ~ 21209
  pregnancy, multifetal ~ 59866
  skull, craniomegalic ~ 62115-62117
Reflex test
  blink reflex ~ 95933
Reflux study ~ 78262
Refraction ~ 92015
Rehabilitation
  artery, occlusive disease ~ 93668
  auditory
    post-lingual hearing loss ~ 92633
    pre-lingual hearing loss ~ 92630
    status evaluation ~ 92626-92627
  cardiac ~ 93797-93798
  services considered, documentation ~ 4079F
Rehabilitative ~ see rehabilitation
Rehfuss test ~ see gastroenterology diagnostic, stomach
Reichstein's substances ~ see deoxycortisol
Reimplantation
  arteries
    aorta prosthesis ~ 35697
    carotid ~ 35691, 35694-35695
    subclavian ~ 35693-35695
    vertebral ~ 35691-35693
    visceral ~ 35697
  kidney ~ 50380
  ovary ~ 58825
  pulmonary artery ~ 33788
  ureters ~ 51565
  ureter, to bladder ~ 50780-50785
Reinnervation larynx, neuromuscular pedicle ~ 31590
Reinsch test ~ 83015
Reinsertion
  drug delivery implant ~ 11983
  spinal fixation device ~ 22849
Relative density ~ see specific gravity
Release
  capsule
    ankle ~ 27612
    elbow ~ 24149
    foot ~ 28260
    knee ~ 27435
    metatarsophalangeal joint ~ 28289, 28291
    shoulder ~ 23020
  carpal tunnel ~ 64721
  elbow contracture, with radical release of capsule ~ 24149
  flexor muscles, hip ~ 27036
  muscle, knee ~ 27422
  nerve ~ 64702-64726
    neurolytic ~ 64727
  retina, encircling material ~ 67115
  spinal cord ~ 63200
  stapes ~ 69650
  tarsal tunnel ~ 28035
  tendon ~ 24332, 25295
Release-Inhibiting hormone, somatotropin ~ see somatostatin

Removal
  adjustable gastric restrictive device ~ 43772-43774
  allograft, intestinal ~ 44137
  artificial heart ~ 33929
  artificial intervertebral disc
    cervical interspace ~ 0095T, 22864
    lumbar interspace ~ 22865, 0164T
  balloon, intra-aortic ~ 33974
  balloon assist device, intra-aortic ~ 33968, 33971
  blood clot, eye ~ 65930
  blood component, apheresis ~ 36511-36516
  breast
    capsules ~ 19371
    implants ~ 19328-19330
    modified radical ~ 19307
    partial ~ 19300-19302
    radical ~ 19305-19306
    simple, complete ~ 19303
    subcutaneous ~ 19304
  calcareous deposit, subdeltoid ~ 23000
  calculi (stone)
    bile duct ~ 43264, 47420-47425
      percutaneous ~ 47554
    bladder ~ 51050, 52310-52318, 52352
    gallbladder ~ 47480
    hepatic duct ~ 47400
    kidney ~ 50060-50081, 50130, 50561, 50580, 52352
    pancreas ~ 48020
    pancreatic duct ~ 43264
    salivary gland ~ 42330-42340
    ureter ~ 50610-50630, 50961, 50980, 51060-51065, 52320-52330, 52352
    urethra ~ 52310-52315, 52352
  cardiac event recorder ~ 33284
  cast ~ 29700
  cataract
    dilated fundus evaluation ~ 2021F
    with replacement
      not associated with concurrent ~ 66983
      extracapsular ~ 66982, 66984
      intracapsular ~ 66983
  catheter
    central venous ~ 36589
    fractured ~ 37197
    peritoneum ~ 49422
    pleural cavity ~ 32552
    spinal cord ~ 62355
  cerclage, cervix ~ 59871
  cerumen, auditory canal, external ~ 69209, 69210
  clot pericardium ~ 33020
    endoscopic ~ 32658
  comedones ~ 10040
  contraceptive capsules ~ 11976
  cranial tongs ~ 20665
  cyst ~ 10040
  dacryolith
    lacrimal duct ~ 68530
    lacrimal gland ~ 68530
  defibrillator
    heart ~ 33244
      pulse generator only ~ 33241
      via thoracotomy ~ 33243
  drug delivery implant ~ 11982-11983
  ear wax, auditory canal, external ~ 69209, 69210
  electrode
    brain ~ 61535, 61880
    chest wall, respiratory sensor ~ 0468T
    heart ~ 33238
    nerve ~ 64585
    spinal cord ~ 63661-63664
    stomach ~ 43648, 43882
  esophageal sphincter augmentation device ~ 43285
  external fixation system ~ 20694
  eye
    bone ~ 67414, 67445
    with bone ~ 65112
    with implant
      muscles attached ~ 65105
      muscles, not attached ~ 65103
    without implant ~ 65101
    with muscle or myocutaneous flap ~ 65114

Removal ~ *continued*

   ocular contents
     with implant ~ 65093
     without implant ~ 65091
     orbital contents only ~ 65110
   fallopian tube, laparoscopy ~ 58661
   fat, lipectomy ~ 15876-15879
   fecal impaction, rectum ~ 45915
   fibrin deposit ~ 32150
   fixation device ~ 20670-20680
   foreign bodies ~ 65205-65265
    anal ~ 46608
    ankle joint ~ 27610, 27620
    arm
     lower ~ 25248
     upper ~ 24200-24201
    auditory canal, external ~ 69200
     with anesthesia ~ 69205
    bile duct ~ 43275-43276
    bladder ~ 52310-52315
    brain ~ 61570, 62163
    bronchi ~ 31635
    colon ~ 44025, 44390, 45379
    colon-sigmoid ~ 45332
    conjunctival embedded ~ 65210
    cornea
     with slit lamp ~ 65222
     without slit lamp ~ 65220
    duodenum ~ 44010
    elbow ~ 24000, 24101, 24200-24201
    esophagus ~ 43020, 43045, 43215, 74235
    external eye ~ 65205
    eyelid ~ 67938
    finger ~ 26075-26080
    foot ~ 28190-28193
    gastrointestinal, upper ~ 43247
    gum ~ 41805
    hand ~ 26070
    hip ~ 27033, 27086-27087
    hysteroscopy ~ 58562
    interphalangeal joint, toe ~ 28024
    intertarsal joint ~ 28020
    intestines, small ~ 44020, 44363
    intraocular ~ 65235
    kidney ~ 50561, 50580
    knee joint ~ 27310, 27331, 27372
    lacrimal duct ~ 68530
    lacrimal gland ~ 68530
    larynx ~ 31511, 31530-31531, 31577
    leg, upper ~ 27372
    lung ~ 32151
    mandible ~ 41806
    mediastinum ~ 39000-39010
    metatarsophalangeal joint ~ 28022
    mouth ~ 40804-40805
    muscle ~ 20520-20525
    nose ~ 30300
     anesthesia ~ 30310
     lateral rhinotomy ~ 30320
    orbit ~ 67413, 67430
     with bone flap ~ 67430
     without bone flap ~ 67413
    pancreatic duct ~ 43275-43276
    patella ~ see patellectomy
    pelvis ~ 27086-27087
    penile tissue ~ 54115
    penis ~ 54115
    pericardium ~ 33020
     endoscopic ~ 32658
    peritoneum ~ 49402
    pharynx ~ 42809
    pleura ~ 32150-32151
     endoscopic ~ 32653
    posterior segment
     magnetic extraction ~ 65260
     nonmagnetic extraction ~ 65265
    rectum ~ 45307, 45915
    scrotum ~ 55120

Removal ~ *continued*

   shoulder ~ 23040-23044
    complicated ~ 23335
    deep ~ 23334
    subcutaneous ~ 23330
   skin, with debridement ~ 11010-11012
   stomach ~ 43500
   subcutaneous tissue ~ 10120-10121
    with debridement ~ 11010-11012
   tarsometatarsal joint ~ 28020
   tendon sheath ~ 20520-20525
   toe ~ 28022
   ureter ~ 50961, 50980
   urethra ~ 52310-52315
   uterus ~ 58562
   vagina ~ 57415
   wrist ~ 25040, 25101, 25248
   foreign body, elbow ~ 24101
   hair, electrolysis ~ 17380
   halo ~ 20665
   hearing aid, bone conduction ~ 69711
   hematoma, brain ~ 61312-61315
   implantation ~ 20670-20680
    ankle ~ 27704
    contraceptive capsules ~ 11976
    elbow ~ 24160
    eye ~ 67120-67121
    finger ~ 26320
    hand ~ 26320
    radius ~ 24164
    wrist ~ 25449
   infusion pump
    intra-arterial ~ 36262
    intravenous ~ 36590
    spinal cord ~ 62365
   intra-aortic balloon ~ 33974
    assist device ~ 33968, 33971
   intrauterine device (IUD) ~ 58301
   keel, laryngoplasty ~ 31580
   lacrimal gland
    partial ~ 68505
    total ~ 68500
   lacrimal sac, excision/(optional) ~ 68520
   laryngocele ~ 31300
   leiomyomata ~ 58545-58546, 58561
   lens ~ 66920-66940
   lens material ~ 66840-66852
   lesion
    conjunctiva ~ 68040
    larynx ~ 31512, 31578
     endoscopic ~ 31545-31546
   loose body
    ankle ~ 27620
    carpometacarpal joint ~ 26070
    elbow ~ 24101
    interphalangeal joint, toe ~ 28024
    intertarsal joint ~ 28020
    knee joint ~ 27331
    metatarsophalangeal joint ~ 28022
    tarsometatarsal joint ~ 28020
    toe ~ 28022
    wrist ~ 25101
   lung
    apical tumor ~ 32503-32504
    bronchial valve ~ 31648-31649
    bronchoplasty ~ 32501
    completion pneumonectomy ~ 32488
    cyst ~ 32140
    extrapleural ~ 32445
    pneumonectomy ~ 32440-32445
    single lobe ~ 32480
    single segment ~ 32484
    sleeve lobectomy ~ 32486
    sleeve pneumonectomy ~ 32442
    two lobes ~ 32482
    volume reduction ~ 32491

Removal ~ *continued*
lymph nodes
  abdominal ~ 38747
  inguinofemoral ~ 38760-38765
  pelvic ~ 38770
  retroperitoneal, transabdominal ~ 38780
  thoracic ~ 38746
mammary implant ~ 19328-19330
mastoid, air cells ~ 69670
mesh, abdominal wall ~ 11008
milia, multiple ~ 10040
nails ~ 11730-11732, 11750
neurostimulators
  pulse generator ~ 64595
  receiver ~ 64595
ocular implant ~ 65175, 65920
orbital implant ~ 67560
ovaries, laparoscopy ~ 58661
pacemaker, heart ~ 33233-33237
patella, complete ~ 27424
plate, skull ~ 62142
polyp
  anal ~ 46610, 46612
  antrochoanal ~ 31032
  colon ~ 44392, 45385
  colon-sigmoid ~ 45333
  endoscopy ~ 44364-44365, 44394
  esophagus ~ 43217, 43250
  gastrointestinal, upper ~ 43250-43251
  rectum ~ 45315
  sphenoid sinus ~ 31051
prosthesis
  abdomen ~ 49606
  abdominal wall ~ 11008
  hip ~ 27090-27091
  knee ~ 27488
  penis ~ 54406, 54410-54417
  perineum ~ 53442
  skull ~ 62142
  urethral sphincter ~ 53446-53447
  wrist ~ 25250-25251
pulse generator
  brain ~ 61888
  spinal cord ~ 63688
pustules ~ 10040
receiver, brain ~ 61888
  spinal cord ~ 63688
reservoir, spinal cord ~ 62365
seton, anal ~ 46030
shoulder joint, foreign or loose body ~ 23107
shunt
  brain ~ 62256-62258
  heart ~ 33924
  peritoneum ~ 49429
  spinal cord ~ 63746
skin tags ~ 11200-11201
sling
  urethra ~ 53442
  vagina ~ 57287
spinal instrumentation
  anterior ~ 22855
  posterior nonsegmental
    Harrington rod ~ 22850
  posterior segmental ~ 22852
stent
  bile duct ~ 43275-43276
  pancreatic duct ~ 43275-43276
suture
  anal ~ 46754
  anesthesia ~ 15850-15851
thrombus ~ see thrombectomy
tissue expanders, skin ~ 11971
total replacement heart system ~ 33929
transplant intestines ~ 44137
transplant kidney ~ 50370
tube
  ear, middle ~ 69424
  finger ~ 26392, 26416
  hand ~ 26392, 26416

Removal ~ *continued*
tumor
  larynx ~ 31578
  small intestine ~ 43250
  temporal bone ~ 69970
ureter, ligature ~ 50940
urethral stent
  bladder ~ 52310-52315
  urethra ~ 52310-52315
vein
  clusters ~ 37785
  perforation ~ 37760-37761
  saphenous ~ 37720-37735, 37780
  varicose ~ 37765-37766
venous access device ~ 36590
  obstruction ~ 75901-75902
ventilating tube, ear, middle ~ 69424
ventricular assist device ~ 33977-33978
  extracorporeal ~ 33990-33993
  intracorporeal ~ 33980
vitreous, anterior approach ~ 67005-67010
wire, anal ~ 46754
Renal ~ (see also kidney)
abscess ~ see abscess, kidney
arteries ~ see artery, renal
autotransplantation ~ see autotransplantation, renal
calculus ~ see calculus, removal, kidney
cyst ~ see cyst, kidney
dialyses ~ see hemodialysis
disease services ~ see dialysis
transplantation ~ see kidney, transplantation
Renin ~ 80408, 80416, 84244
peripheral vein ~ 80417
Renin-converting enzyme ~ 82164
Reoperation
carotid thromboendarterectomy ~ 35390
coronary artery bypass
  valve procedure ~ 33530
distal vessel bypass ~ 35700
Repair ~ see also revision
abdomen ~ 49900
  hernia ~ 49491-49525, 49565, 49570, 49582-49590
  omphalocele ~ 49600-49611
  suture ~ 49900
abdominal wall ~ 15830, 15847
anal
  anomaly ~ 46744-46748
  fistula ~ 46288, 46706, 46715-46716
  stricture ~ 46700-46705
aneurysm
  aorta
    abdominal ~ 34845-34848
    infrarenal ~ 34830-34832
    thoracic ~ 33877-33886
  intracranial artery ~ 61697-61708
ankle
  ligament ~ 27695-27698
  tendon ~ 27612, 27650-27654, 27680-27687
aorta ~ 33320-33322, 33802-33803
  coarctation ~ 33840-33851
  graft ~ 33860-33877
  infrarenal abdominal endovascular ~ 34701-34706, 34845-34848
  sinus of valsalva ~ 33702-33720
  thoracic ~ 75956-75959
    endovascular ~ 33880-33891
  visceral
    endovascular ~ 34841-34848
    physician planning ~ 34839
anorectum fistula ~ 46707
aortic arch
  with cardiopulmonary bypass ~ 33853
  without cardiopulmonary bypass ~ 33852
aortic valve ~ 33390, 33391
  obstruction, outflow tract ~ 33414
  septic hypertrophy ~ 33416
  stenosis ~ 33415

Repair ~ *continued*
arm
  lower ~ 25260-25263, 25270
    fasciotomy ~ 24495
    secondary ~ 25265, 25272-25274
    tendon ~ 25290
    tendon sheath ~ 25275
  muscle ~ 24341
  tendon ~ 24332, 24341, 25280, 25295, 25310-25316
  upper
    muscle revision ~ 24330-24331
    muscle transfer ~ 24301, 24320
    tendon lengthening ~ 24305
    tendon revision ~ 24320
    tendon transfer ~ 24301
    tenotomy ~ 24310
arteriovenous aneurysm ~ 36832
arteriovenous fistula
  abdomen ~ 35182
    acquired or traumatic ~ 35189
  head ~ 35180
    acquired or traumatic ~ 35188
  lower extremity ~ 35184
    acquired or traumatic ~ 35190
  neck ~ 35180
    acquired or traumatic ~ 35188
  thorax ~ 35182
    acquired or traumatic ~ 35189
  upper extremity ~ 35184
    acquired or traumatic ~ 35190
arteriovenous malformation
  intracranial ~ 61680-61692
  intracranial artery ~ 61705-61708
  spinal artery ~ 62294
  spinal cord ~ 63250-63252
artery
  angioplasty
    aorta ~ 37246-37247
    axillary ~ 37246-37247
    brachiocephalic ~ 37246-37247
  bypass graft ~ 35501-35571, 35601-35683, 35691-35695, 35700
  bypass in-situ ~ 35582-35587
  bypass venous graft ~ 33510-33516, 35510-35525
  femoral ~ 35456
  iliac ~ 37220-37222, 37227
  occlusive disease ~ 35001, 35005-35021, 35045-35081, 35091, 35102,
    35111, 35121, 35131, 35141, 35151, 35161
  popliteal ~ 37224
  pulmonary ~ 33690
  renal ~ 37246, 37247
  renal or visceral ~ 37246, 37247
  subclavian ~ 37246-37247
  thromboendarterectomy ~ 35301-35321, 35341-35390
  tibioperoneal ~ 37228-37235
  viscera ~ 37246, 37247
arytenoid cartilage ~ 31400
bile duct ~ 47701
  with intestines ~ 47760, 47780-47785
  wound ~ 47900
bladder
  exstrophy ~ 51940
  fistula ~ 44660-44661, 45800-45805, 51880-51925
  neck ~ 51845
  resection ~ 52500
  wound ~ 51860-51865
blepharoptosis, frontalis muscle technique with fascial sling ~ 67902
blood vessel
  abdomen ~ 35221
    with other graft ~ 35281
    with vein graft ~ 35251
  chest ~ 35211-35216
    with other graft ~ 35271-35276
    with vein graft ~ 35241-35246
  finger ~ 35207
  graft defect ~ 35870
  hand ~ 35207
  kidney ~ 50100

Repair ~ *continued*
  lower extremity ~ 35226
    with other graft ~ 35286
    with vein graft ~ 35256
  neck ~ 35201
    with other graft ~ 35261
    with vein graft ~ 35231
  upper extremity ~ 35206
    with other graft ~ 35266
    with vein graft ~ 35236
body cast ~ 29720
brain, wound ~ 61571
breast, suspension ~ 19316
bronchi, fistula ~ 32815
brow pyrosis ~ 67900
bunion ~ 28292, 28295-28299
bypass graft ~ 35901-35907
  fistula ~ 35870
calcaneus, osteotomy ~ 28300
cannula ~ 36860-36861
carpal ~ 25440
carpal bone ~ 25431
cervix
  cerclage ~ 57700
    abdominal ~ 59320-59325
  suture ~ 57720
chest wall ~ 32905
  closure ~ 32810
  fistula ~ 32906
chin
  augmentation ~ 21120, 21123
  osteotomy ~ 21121-21123
clavicle, osteotomy ~ 23480-23485
cleft hand ~ 26580
cleft lip ~ 40525-40527, 40700-40761
  nasal deformity ~ 40700-40701, 40720-40761
cleft palate ~ see cleft palate, repair
colon
  fistula ~ 44650-44661
  hernia ~ 44050
  malrotation ~ 44055
  obstruction ~ 44050
cornea ~ see cornea, repair
coronary chamber fistula ~ 33500-33501
cyst
  Bartholin's gland ~ 56440
  liver ~ 47300
diaphragm
  for eventration ~ 39545
  hernia ~ 39503-39541
  laceration ~ 39501
ductus arteriosus ~ 33820-33824
ear, middle
  oval window fistula ~ 69666
  round window fistula ~ 69667
elbow
  hemiepiphyseal arrest ~ 24470
  ligament ~ 24343-24346
  muscle ~ 24341
  muscle transfer ~ 24301
  tendon ~ 24340-24342
    each ~ 24341
  tendon lengthening ~ 24305
  tendon transfer ~ 24301
  tennis elbow ~ 24357-24359
encephalocele ~ 62121
enterocele
  hysterectomy ~ 58270, 58294
epididymis ~ 54900-54901
epispadias ~ 54380-54390
esophagus ~ 43300, 43310, 43313
  esophagogastrostomy ~ 43320
  esophagojejunostomy ~ 43340-43341
  fistula ~ 43305, 43312, 43314, 43420-43425
  fundoplasty ~ 43210, 43325
  muscles ~ 43330-43331
  pre-existing perforation ~ 43405
  varices ~ 43401
  wound ~ 43410-43415

Repair ~ *continued*
eye
  ciliary body ~ 66680
    suture ~ 66682
  conjunctiva ~ 65270-65273
    wound ~ 65270-65273
  cornea ~ 65275
    astigmatism ~ 65772-65775
    with glue ~ 65286
    wound ~ 65275-65285
  fistula, lacrimal gland ~ 68770
  iris
    with ciliary body ~ 66680
    suture ~ 66682
  lacrimal duct, canaliculi ~ 68700
  lacrimal punctum ~ 68705
  retina, detachment ~ 67101-67113
  sclera
    with glue ~ 65286
    with graft ~ 66225
    reinforcement ~ 67250-67255
    staphyloma ~ 66220-66225
    wound ~ 65286, 66250
  strabismus, chemodenervation ~ 67345
  symblepharon
    division ~ 68340
    with graft ~ 68335
    without graft ~ 68330
  trabeculae ~ 65855
eye muscles
  strabismus
    adjustable sutures ~ 67335
    one horizontal muscle ~ 67311
    one vertical muscle ~ 67314
    posterior fixation suture technique ~ 67334-67335
    previous surgery, not involving extraocular muscles ~ 67331
    release extensive scar tissue ~ 67343
    superior oblique muscle ~ 67318
    two horizontal muscles ~ 67312
    two or more vertical muscles ~ 67316
  wound, extraocular muscle ~ 65290
eyebrow, ptosis ~ 67900
eyelashes
  epilation
    by forceps ~ 67820
    by other than forceps ~ 67825
    incision of lid margin ~ 67830
      with free mucous membrane graft ~ 67835
eyelid ~ 21280-21282
  ectropion ~ 67916-67917
    suture ~ 67914
    thermocauterization ~ 67915
  entropion ~ 67924
    excision tarsal wedge ~ 67923
    suture ~ 67921-67924
    thermocauterization ~ 67922
  excisional ~ 67961-67966
  lagophthalmos ~ 67912
  ptosis, conjunctivo-tarso-Muller's muscle-levator resection ~ 67908
    frontalis muscle technique ~ 67901-67902
    levator resection ~ 67903-67904
  reduction of overcorrection ~ 67909
    superior rectus technique ~ 67906
  retraction ~ 67911
  wound, suture ~ 67930-67935
facial bones ~ 21208-21209
facial nerve
  paralysis ~ 15840-15845
  suture, intratemporal, lateral to geniculate ganglion ~ 69740
    intratemporal, medial to geniculate ganglion ~ 69745
fallopian tube ~ 58752
  anastomosis ~ 58750
  create stoma ~ 58770
fascial defect ~ 50728
femur ~ 27470-27472
  epiphysis ~ 27475-27485, 27742
    arrest ~ 27185
    open treatment ~ 27177-27178
    osteoplasty ~ 27179
    osteotomy ~ 27181

Repair ~ *continued*
    by pinning ~ 27176
    by traction ~ 27175
    with graft ~ 27170
    muscle transfer ~ 27110
    osteotomy ~ 27140, 27151, 27450-27454
    femoral neck ~ 27161
      with fixation ~ 27165
      with open reduction ~ 27156
fibula
  epiphysis ~ 27477-27485, 27730-27742
  nonunion or malunion ~ 27726
  osteotomy ~ 27707-27712
finger
  claw finger ~ 26499
  macrodactylia ~ 26590
  polydactylous ~ 26587
  syndactyly ~ 26560-26562
  tendon
    extensor ~ 26415-26434, 26445-26449
    flexor ~ 26356-26358, 26440-26442
    joint stabilization ~ 26474
    pip joint ~ 26471
    toe transfer ~ 26551-26556
    trigger ~ 26055
    volar plate ~ 26548
    web finger ~ 26560-26562
fistula
  carotid-cavernous ~ 61710
  mastoid ~ 69700
  rectovaginal ~ 57308
foot
  fascia ~ 28250
  muscle ~ 28250
  tendon ~ 28200-28226, 28238
gallbladder
  with gastroenterostomy ~ 47741
  with intestines ~ 47720-47740
great arteries ~ 33770-33781
great vessel ~ 33320-33322
hallux valgus ~ 28292, 28295-28299
hamstring ~ 27097
hand
  cleft hand ~ 26580
  muscle ~ 26591-26593
  tendon
    extensor ~ 26410-26416, 26426-26428, 26433-26437
    flexor ~ 26350-26358, 26440
    profundus ~ 26370-26373
hearing aid, bone conduction ~ 69711
heart
  anomaly ~ 33600-33617
  aortic sinus ~ 33702-33722
  artificial heart ~ 33928
  atrioventricular canal ~ 33660-33665
    complete ~ 33670
  atrioventricular valve ~ 33660-33665
  blood vessel ~ 33320-33322
  cor triatriatum ~ 33732
  infundibular ~ 33476-33478
  mitral valve ~ 33420-33427
  myocardium ~ 33542
  outflow tract ~ 33476-33478
  postinfarction ~ 33542-33545
  prosthetic valve ~ 33670, 33852-33853
  prosthetic valve dysfunction ~ 33496
  pulmonary artery shunt ~ 33924
  pulmonary valve ~ 33470-33474
  septal defect ~ 33545, 33608-33610, 33681-33688, 33692-33697
    atrial and ventricular ~ 33647
    atrium ~ 33641
  sinus of valsalva ~ 33702-33722
  sinus venosus ~ 33645
  tetralogy of Fallot ~ 33692-33697
  total replacement heart system ~ 33927-33929
  tricuspid valve ~ 33465
  ventricle ~ 33611-33612
    obstruction ~ 33619
  ventricular tunnel ~ 33722
  wound ~ 33300-33305
hepatic duct, with intestines ~ 47765, 47802

Repair ~ *continued*
hernia
  abdomen ~ 49565, 49590
    incisional ~ 49560
  epigastric ~ 49570
    incarcerated ~ 49572
  epigelian
    incarcerated or strangulated ~ 49653
    reducible ~ 49652
  femoral ~ 49550
    incarcerated ~ 49553
    recurrent ~ 49555
    recurrent incarcerated ~ 49557
    reducible recurrent ~ 49555
  hiatal ~ 43332-43337
  incisional
    incarcerated or strangulated ~ 49561, 49655
    recurrent incarcerated ~ 49566, 49657
    recurrent reducible ~ 49656
    reducible ~ 49564
  inguinal ~ 49491-49521
    initial ~ 49650
    recurrent ~ 49651
    sliding ~ 49525
  intestinal ~ 44025-44050
  lumbar ~ 49540
  lung ~ 32800
  orchiopexy ~ 54640
  paraesophageal ~ 43332-43337
  reducible ~ 49565, 49570
    femoral ~ 49550
    incisional ~ 49560
    inguinal ~ 49500, 49505
    recurrent ~ 49520
  sliding ~ 49525
  spigelian ~ 49590
    incarcerated or strangulated ~ 49653
    reducible ~ 49652
  umbilical ~ 49580, 49585
    incarcerated ~ 49582, 49587, 49653
    reducible ~ 49580, 49652
  ventral
    incarcerated or strangulated ~ 49653
    reducible ~ 49652
  with spermatic cord ~ 54640
hip
  muscle transfer ~ 27100-27105, 27111
  osteotomy ~ 27146-27156
  tendon ~ 27097
humerus ~ 24420-24430
  with graft ~ 24435
  osteotomy ~ 24400-24410
ileostomy ~ see ileostomy, repair
interphalangeal joint, volar plate ~ 26548
intestines
  enterocele
    abdominal approach ~ 57270
    vaginal approach ~ 57268
  obstruction ~ 44615
intestines, large
  closure enterostomy ~ 44620-44626
  diverticula ~ 44605
  ulcer ~ 44605
  wound ~ 44605
intestines, small
  closure enterostomy ~ 44620-44626
  diverticula ~ 44602-44603
  fistula ~ 44640-44661
  hernia ~ 44050
  malrotation ~ 44055
  obstruction ~ 44025-44050
  ulcer ~ 44602-44603
  wound ~ 44602-44603
introitus, vagina ~ 56800
iris, ciliary body ~ 66680
jejunum
  free transfer, with microvascular anastomosis ~ 43496

Repair ~ *continued*
kidney
  fistula ~ 50520-50526
  horseshoe ~ 50540
  renal pelvis ~ 50400-50405
  wound ~ 50500
knee
  cartilage ~ 27403
  instability ~ 27420
  ligament ~ 27405-27409
    collateral ~ 27405
    collateral and cruciate ~ 27409
    cruciate ~ 27407-27409
  meniscus ~ 27403
  tendon ~ 27380-27381
larynx
  fracture ~ 31584-31586
  reinnervation, neuromuscular pedicle ~ 31590
leg
  lower
    fascia ~ 27656
    tendon ~ 27658-27692
  upper
    muscle ~ 27385-27386, 27400, 27430
    tendon ~ 27393-27400
ligament ~ see ligament, repair
lip ~ 40650-40654
  cleft lip ~ 40700-40761
  fistula ~ 42260
liver, abscess ~ 47300
  cyst ~ 47300
  wound ~ 47350-47361
lung
  hernia ~ 32800
  pneumolysis ~ 32940
  tear ~ 32110
mastoidectomy
  complete ~ 69601
  modified radical ~ 69602
  radical ~ 69603
  with apicectomy ~ 69605
  with tympanoplasty ~ 69604
maxilla, osteotomy ~ 21206
mesentery ~ 44850
metacarpal
  lengthening ~ 26568
  nonunion ~ 26546
  osteotomy ~ 26565
metacarpophalangeal joint
  capsulodesis ~ 26516-26518
  collateral ligament ~ 26540-26542
  fusion ~ 26516-26518
metatarsal ~ 28322
  osteotomy ~ 28306-28309
microsurgery ~ 69990
mitral valve ~ 33420-33427
mouth
  laceration ~ 40830-40831
  vestibule of ~ 40830-40845
musculotendinous cuff ~ 23410-23412
nail bed ~ 11760
nasal deformity, cleft lip ~ 40700-40761
nasal septum ~ 30630
navicular ~ 25440
neck muscles
  scalenus anticus ~ 21700-21705
  sternocleidomastoid ~ 21720-21725
nerve ~ 64876
  graft ~ 64885-64907
  microrepair ~ 69990
  suture ~ 64831-64876
nose
  adhesions ~ 30560
  fistula ~ 30580-30600, 42260
  rhinophyma ~ 30120
  septum ~ 30540-30545, 30630
  synechia ~ 30560
  vestibular stenosis ~ 30465
omphalocele ~ 49600-49611

Repair ~ continued
  osteotomy
    femoral neck ~ 27161
    radius, and ulna ~ 25365
    ulna, and radius ~ 25365
    vertebra
      additional segment ~ 22216, 22226
      cervical ~ 22210, 22220
      lumbar ~ 22214, 22224
      thoracic ~ 22212, 22222
  oviduct ~ 58752
    create stoma ~ 58770
  pacemaker, heart
    electrode ~ 33218-33220
  palate
    laceration ~ 42180-42182
    vomer flap ~ 42235
  pancreas
    cyst ~ 48500
    pseudocyst ~ 48510
  paravaginal defect ~ 57284-57285, 57423
  pectus carinatum ~ 21740-21742
    with thoracoscopy ~ 21743
  pectus excavatum ~ 21740-21742
    with thoracoscopy ~ 21743
  pelvic floor, prosthetic insertion ~ 57267
  pelvis
    osteotomy ~ 27158
    tendon ~ 27098
  penis
    corporeal tear ~ 54437
    fistulization ~ 54435
    injury ~ 54440
    priapism ~ 54420-54435
    shunt ~ 54420-54430
  perineum ~ 56810
  periorbital region, osteotomy ~ 21260-21263
  phalanx
    finger
      lengthening ~ 26568
      osteotomy ~ 26567
    nonunion ~ 26546
    toe, osteotomy ~ 28310-28312
  pharynx, with esophagus ~ 42953
  pleura ~ 32215
  prosthesis, penis ~ 54408
  pulmonary artery ~ 33917-33920
    reimplantation ~ 33788
  pulmonary valve ~ 33470-33474
  quadriceps ~ see quadriceps, repair
  radius
    epiphyseal ~ 25450-25455
    malunion or nonunion ~ 25400, 25415
    osteotomy ~ 25350-25355, 25370-25375
    with graft ~ 25405, 25420-25426
  rectocele ~ see rectocele, repair
  rectovaginal fistula ~ 57308
  rectum
    fistula ~ 45800-45825
    injury ~ 45562-45563
    prolapse ~ 45505-45541, 45900
    rectocele ~ 45560
    stenosis ~ 45500
    with sigmoid excision ~ 45550
  retinal detachment with diathermy ~ see diathermy, retinal detachment, repair
  rotator cuff ~ see rotator cuff, repair
  salivary duct ~ 42500-42505
    fistula ~ 42600
  scapula
    fixation ~ 23400
    scapulopexy ~ 23400
  sclera ~ see sclera, repair
  scrotum ~ 55175-55180
  septal defect ~ 33813-33814

Repair ~ continued
  shoulder, capsule ~ 23450-23466
    cuff ~ 23410-23412
    ligament release ~ 23415
    muscle transfer ~ 23395-23397
    musculotendinous rotator cuff ~ 23415-23420
    tendon ~ 23410-23412, 23430-23440
    tenomyotomy ~ 23405-23406
  simple, integumentary system ~ see integumentary system, repair, simple
  sinus
    ethmoid, cerebrospinal fluid leak ~ 31290
    sphenoid, cerebrospinal fluid leak ~ 31291
  sinus of valsalva ~ 33702-33722
  skin, wound
    complex ~ 13100-13160
    intermediate ~ 12031-12057
    simple ~ 12020-12021
  skull
    cerebrospinal fluid leak ~ 62100
    encephalocele ~ 62120
  spica cast ~ 29720
  spinal cord ~ 63700
    cerebrospinal fluid leak ~ 63707-63709
    meningocele ~ 63700-63702
    myelomeningocele ~ 63704-63706
  spinal meningocele ~ see meningocele, repair
  spine, osteotomy ~ 22210-22226
  spleen ~ 38115
  stomach
    esophagogastrostomy ~ 43320
    fistula ~ 43880
    fundoplasty ~ 43325, 43327-43328
    laceration ~ 43501-43502
    stoma ~ 43870
    ulcer ~ 43501
  talus, osteotomy ~ 28302
  tarsal ~ 28320
    osteotomy ~ 28304-28305
  testis
    injury ~ 54670
    suspension ~ 54620-54640
    torsion ~ 54600
  throat
    pharyngoesophageal ~ 42953
    wound ~ 42900
  thumb
    muscle ~ 26508
    tendon ~ 26510
  tibia ~ 27720-27725
    epiphysis ~ 27477-27485, 27730-27742
    osteotomy ~ 27455-27457, 27705, 27709-27712
    pseudoarthrosis ~ 27727
  toe
    bunion ~ 28292, 28295-28299
    muscle ~ 28240
    tendon ~ 28240
    webbing ~ 28280, 28345
  toes
    macrodactylia ~ 26590
    polydactylous ~ 26587
  tongue ~ 41250-41252
    fixation ~ 41500
    laceration ~ 41250-41252
    mechanical ~ 41500
    suture ~ 41510
  trachea, fistula ~ 31755
    stenosis ~ 31780-31781
    stoma ~ 31613-31614
      scar ~ 31830
      with plastic repair ~ 31825
      without plastic repair ~ 31820
    with plastic repair ~ 31825
    without plastic repair ~ 31820
    wound
      cervical ~ 31800
      intrathoracic ~ 31805
  tricuspid valve ~ 33463-33465
  truncus arteriosus, Rastelli type ~ 33786
  tunica vaginalis, hydrocele ~ 55060

Repair ~ *continued*
tympanic membrane ~ 69450, 69610
ulna
   epiphyseal ~ 25450-25455
   malunion or nonunion ~ 25400, 25415
   osteotomy ~ 25360, 25370-25375, 25425-25426
   with graft ~ 25405, 25420
umbilicus, omphalocele ~ 49600-49611
ureter
   anastomosis ~ 50740-50825
   continent diversion ~ 50825
   deligation ~ 50940
   fistula ~ 50920-50930
   lysis adhesions ~ 50715-50725
   suture ~ 50900
   urinary undiversion ~ 50830
ureterocele ~ 51535
urethra
   artificial sphincter ~ 53449
   diverticulum ~ 53240, 53400-53405
   fistula ~ 45820-45825, 53400-53405, 53520
   stoma ~ 53520
   stricture ~ 53400-53405
   urethrocele ~ 57230
   with replantation of penis ~ 54438
   wound ~ 53502-53515
urethral sphincter ~ 57220
urinary incontinence ~ 53431-53440, 57284
uterus
   fistula ~ 51920-51925
   rupture ~ 58520, 59350
   suspension ~ 58400-58410
vagina
   anterior ~ see colporrhaphy, anterior
   cystocele ~ 57240, 57260
   enterocele ~ 57265
   fistula ~ 46715-46716, 51900
      rectovaginal ~ 57300-57307
      transvesical and vaginal approach ~ 57330
      urethrovaginal ~ 57310-57311
      vesicovaginal ~ 57320-57330
   hysterectomy ~ 58267, 58293
   incontinence ~ 57284, 57288
   pereyra procedure ~ 57289
   postpartum ~ 59300
   prolapse ~ 57282-57284
   rectocele ~ 57250-57260
   suspension ~ 57280, 57284
      laparoscopic ~ 57425
   wound ~ 57200-57210
vaginal wall prolapse ~ see colporrhaphy
vas deferens, suture ~ 55400
vein
   angioplasty ~ 37248, 37249
   femoral ~ 34501
   graft ~ 34520
   pulmonary ~ 33730
   transposition ~ 34510
vulva, postpartum ~ 59300
wound
   complex ~ 13100-13160
   intermediate ~ 12031-12057
   simple ~ 12001-12021
wound dehiscence
   complex ~ 13160
   simple ~ 12020-12021
wrist ~ 25260-25263, 25270, 25447
   bone ~ 25440
   carpal bone ~ 25431
   cartilage ~ 25107
   removal, implant ~ 25449
   secondary ~ 25265, 25272-25274
   tendon ~ 25280-25316
   tendon sheath ~ 25275
   total replacement ~ 25446
Repeat surgeries ~ see reoperation

Replacement
aortic valve ~ 33405-33413
arthroplasties, hip ~ see arthroplasty, hip
artificial heart, intracorporeal ~ 33928
cerebrospinal fluid shunt ~ 62160, 62194, 62225-62230
contact lens ~ see contact lens services
elbow, total ~ 24363
electrode
   heart ~ 33210-33211, 33216-33217
   stomach ~ 43647
eye, drug delivery system ~ 67121
gastrostomy tube ~ 43760
hearing aid, bone conduction ~ 69710
hip ~ 27130-27132
   revision ~ 27134-27138
implant, bone, for external speech processor/cochlear stimulator ~
   69717-69718
knee, total ~ 27447
   intraoperative balance sensor ~ 0396T
mitral valve ~ 33430
nerve ~ 64726
neurostimulator
   pulse generator/receiver
      intracranial ~ 61885
      peripheral nerve ~ 64590
      spinal ~ 63685
ossicles, with prosthesis ~ 69633, 69637
ossicular replacement ~ see TORP (total ossicular replacement prosthesis)
pacemaker ~ 33206-33208
   catheter ~ 33210
   electrode ~ 33210-33211, 33216-33217
pacing cardioverter-defibrillator
   leads ~ 33243-33244
   pulse generator only ~ 33241
penile, prosthesis ~ 54410-54411, 54416-54417
prosthesis, skull ~ 62143
   urethral sphincter ~ 53448
pulmonary valve ~ 33475
pulse generator
   brain ~ 61885
   peripheral nerve ~ 64590
   spinal cord ~ 63685
receiver
   brain ~ 61885
   peripheral nerve ~ 64590
   spinal cord ~ 63685
skull plate ~ 62143
spinal cord, reservoir ~ 62360
tissue expanders, skin ~ 11970
total replacement ~ see hip, total replacement
total replacement heart system, intracorporeal ~ 33928
tricuspid valve ~ 33465
ureter, with intestines ~ 50840
venous access device ~ 36582-36583, 36585
   catheter ~ 36578
venous catheter, central ~ 36580-36581, 36584
ventricular assist device ~ 33981-33983
Replantation
arm, upper ~ 20802
digit ~ 20816-20822
foot ~ 20838
forearm ~ 20805
hand ~ 20808
penis ~ 54438
thumb ~ 20824-20827
Report preparation
extended, medical ~ 99080
psychiatric ~ 90889
Reposition toe to hand ~ 26551-26556
Repositioning
baroreflex activation device ~ 0266T-0271T
central venous catheter ~ 36597
electrode
   cardiac contractility modulation ~ 0415T
   heart ~ 33215, 33226
gastrostomy tube ~ 43761
heart, defibrillator leads ~ 33215-33216, 33226, 33249
intraocular lens ~ 66825
tricuspid valve ~ 33468

Reproductive tissue
  cryopreservation
    embryo(s) ~ 89258
    sperm ~ 89259
    testicular tissue ~ 89335
  thawing of cryopreserved
    embryo(s) ~ 89352
    oocytes, each aliquot ~ 89356
    sperm/semen ~ 89353
    testicular/ovarian tissue ~ 89354
  storage
    oocyte(s) ~ 89346
    sperm/semen ~ 89343
    testicular/ovarian ~ 89344
Reprogramming, shunt, brain ~ 62252
Reptilase test ~ 85635
Repilase time ~ see thrombin time
Resection
  aortic valve, stenosis ~ 33415
  bladder diverticulum ~ 52305
  bladder neck, transurethral ~ 52500
  brain lobe ~ see lobectomy, brain
  chest wall ~ 19260-19272
  clavicle, tumor ~ 23200
  cricotracheal ~ 31592
  diaphragm ~ 39560-39561
  endaural ~ see ear, inner, excision
  humeral head ~ 23195
  intestines, small, laparoscopic ~ 44202-44203
  lung ~ 32520-32525
  mouth, with tongue excision ~ 41153
  myocardium
    aneurysm ~ 33542
    septal defect ~ 33545
  nasal septum submucous ~ see nasal septum, submucous resection
  nose
    septum ~ 30520
  ovary, wedge ~ see ovary, wedge resection
  palate ~ 42120
  phalangeal head, toe ~ 28153
  prostate transurethral ~ see prostatectomy, transurethral
  radical
    arm, upper ~ 24077, 24079
    elbow ~ 24077, 24079
      with contracture release ~ 24149
    foot ~ 28046-28047
    humerus ~ 24150
    radius ~ 24152
    tumor
      ankle ~ 27615-27616
      calcaneus or talus ~ 27647
      clavicle ~ 23200
      femur ~ 27329, 27364-27365
      fibula ~ 27646
      humerus ~ 23220
      knee ~ 27329, 27364-27365
      leg, lower ~ 27615-27616
      leg, upper ~ 27329, 27364-27365
      metatarsal ~ 28173
      scapula ~ 23210
      shoulder 23077-23078
      tarsal ~ 28171
      tibia ~ 27645
      wrist ~ 25077-25078
  ribs ~ 19260-19272, 32900
  synovial membrane ~ see synovectomy
  temporal bone ~ 69535
  trachea, cricotracheal ~ 31592
  tumor
    fallopian tube ~ 58957-58958
    ovary ~ 58957-58958
    peritoneum ~ 58957-58958
  ulna, arthrodesis radioulnar joint ~ 25830
  ureterocele
    ectopic ~ 52301
    orthotopic ~ 52300
  vena cava, with reconstruction ~ 37799
Resonance spectroscopy, magnetic ~ see magnetic resonance spectroscopy
Respiration, positive-pressure ~ see pressure breathing, positive
Respiratory pattern recording, preventive, infant ~ 94772
Respiratory system, surgical procedures ~ 30000-32999

Respiratory syncytial virus (RSV)
  antibody ~ 86756
  antigen detection
    direct fluorescence ~ 87280
    direct optical observation ~ 87807
    enzyme immunoassay ~ 87420
    nucleic acid ~ 87631-87634
Response, auditory evoked ~ see auditory evoked potentials
Rest home visit ~ see domiciliary services
Resuscitation
  cardiac ~ see cardiac massage
  cardio-pulmonary ~ see cardio-pulmonary resuscitation (CPR)
  newborn ~ 99465
Reticulocyte count ~ 85044-85045
Retina
  diagnostic imaging
    computerized scanning ~ 92134
    electroretinography ~ 92275
    fluorescein angiography ~ 92235, 92242
    ophthalmoscopy ~ 92225, 92226
    remote ~ 92227, 92228
  incision, encircling material ~ 67115
  intr-ocular retinal electrode array
    device evaluation ~ 0472T, 0473T
    initial programming ~ 0472T
    interrogation ~ 0472T, 0473T
  lesion
    extensive, destruction ~ 67227-67228
    localized, destruction ~ 67208-67218
  macular/fundus exam, dilated ~ 2019F-2021F
    findings communicated for diabetes management ~ 5010F
  repair
    detachment ~ 67113
      cryotherapy or diathermy ~ 67101
      injection of air ~ 67110
      photocoagulation ~ 67105
      scleral dissection ~ 67107
      with vitrectomy ~ 67108
    prophylaxis, detachment ~ 67141-67145
  retinopathy
    destruction
      cryotherapy, diathermy ~ 67227
    treatment
      photocoagulation ~ 67228, 67229
Retinacular knee release ~ 27425
Retinopathy
  destruction
    cryotherapy, diathermy ~ 67227
  treatment
    photocoagulation, cryotherapy ~ 67228, 67229
Retraction, clot ~ see clot retraction
Retrieval transcatheter foreign body ~ 37197
Retrocaval ureter ureterolysis ~ 50725
Retrograde cholangiopancreatographies, endoscopic ~ see cholangiopancreatography
Retrograde cystourethrogram ~ see urethrocystography, retrograde
Retrograde pyelogram ~ see urography, retrograde
Retroperitoneal area
  abscess, incision and drainage ~ 49060
  biopsy ~ 49010
  cyst, destruction/excision ~ 49203-49205, 58957, 58958
  endometriomas, destruction/excision ~ 49203-49205, 58957, 58958
  exploration ~ 49010
  needle biopsy, mass ~ 49180
  tumor, destruction/excision ~ 49203-49205, 58957, 58958
Retroperitoneal fibrosis ureterolysis ~ 50715
Retropubic prostatectomies ~ see prostatectomy, retropubic
Revascularization
  distal upper extremity with interval ligation ~ 36838
  endovascular
    femoral ~ 37224-37227
    iliac ~ 37220-37223
    peroneal ~ 37228-37235
    popliteal ~ 37224-37227
    tibeal ~ 37228-37235
  interval ligation distal upper extremity ~ 36838
  penis ~ 37788
  transmyocardial ~ 33140-33141
Reversal, vasectomy ~ see vasovasorrhaphy
Reverse T3 ~ see triiodothyronine, reverse
Reverse triiodothyronine ~ see triiodothyronine, reverse

Revision ~ see reconstruction
  aorta ~ 33404
  blepharoplasty ~ 15820-15823
  bronchial stent ~ 31638
  bronchus ~ 32501
  bypass graft, vein patch ~ 35685
  cervicoplasty ~ 15819
  colostomy ~ see colostomy, revision
  cornea
    prosthesis ~ 65770
    reshaping
      epikeratoplasty ~ 65767
      keratomileusis ~ 65760
      keratophakia ~ 65765
  defibrillator site, chest ~ 33223
  ear, middle ~ 69662
  external fixation system ~ 20693
  eye, aqueous shunt ~ 66185
  gastrostomy tube ~ 44373
  hip replacement ~ see replacement, hip, revision
  hymenal ring ~ 56700
  ileostomy ~ see ileostomy, revision
  infusion pump
    intra-arterial ~ 36261
    intravenous ~ 36576-36578, 36582-36583
  iris
    iridoplasty ~ 66762
    iridotomy ~ 66761
  jejunostomy tube ~ 44373
  lower extremity arterial bypass ~ 35879-35881
  pacemaker site, chest ~ 33222
  rhytidectomy ~ 15824-15829
  semicircular canal, fenestration ~ 69840
  shunt, intrahepatic portosystemic ~ 37183
  sling ~ 53442
  stapedectomy ~ see stapedectomy, revision
  stomach, for obesity ~ 43848
  tracheostomy, scar ~ 31830
  urinary-cutaneous anastomosis ~ 50727-50728
  vagina
    prosthetic graft ~ 57295-57296
    sling
      stress incontinence ~ 57287
  venous access device ~ 36576-36578, 36582-36583, 36585
  ventricle
    ventriculomyectomy ~ 33416
    ventriculomyotomy ~ 33416
Rheumatoid factor ~ 86430-86431
Rhinectomy
  partial ~ 30150
  total ~ 30160
Rhinomanometry ~ 92512
Rhinopharynx ~ see nasopharynx
Rhinophyma repair ~ 30120
Rhinoplasty
  cleft lip/cleft palate ~ 30460-30462
  primary ~ 30400-30420
  secondary ~ 30430-30450
Rhinoscopy ~ see endoscopy, nose
Rhinotomy lateral ~ 30118, 30320
Rhizotomy ~ 63185-63190
Rho variant du ~ 86905
Rhytidectomy ~ 15824-15829
Rhytidoplasties ~ see face lift
Rh (D) ~ see blood typing
Rh immune globulin ~ see immune globulins, Rho (D)
Rib
  cartilage, graft to face ~ 21230
  excision ~ 21600-21616, 32900
  fracture
    with internal fixation ~ 21811-21813
  resection ~ 19260-19272, 32900
  X-ray ~ 71100-71111
Riboflavin ~ 84252
Richardson operation hysterectomy ~ see hysterectomy, abdominal, total
Richardson procedure ~ 53460
Rickettsia antibody ~ 86757

Ridell operation ~ see sinusotomy, frontal
Ridge, alveolar ~ see alveolar ridge
Right atrioventricular valve ~ see tricuspid valve
Right heart cardiac catheterization ~ see cardiac catheterization, right heart
Ripstein operation ~ see proctopexy
Risk factor reduction intervention
  group ~ 99411, 99412
    diabetes prevention ~ 0403T
  individual ~ 99401-99404
    diabetes prevention ~ 0488T
Risser jacket ~ 29010-29015
  removal ~ 29710
Rocky mountain spotted fever ~ 86000
Roentgenographic ~ see X-ray
Roentgenography ~ see radiology, diagnostic
Roentgen rays ~ see X-ray
Ropes test ~ 83872
Rorschach test ~ 96100
Ross procedure ~ 33413
Rotation flap ~ see skin, adjacent tissue transfer
Rotator cuff repair ~ 23410-23420
Rotavirus
  antibody ~ 86759
  antigen detection, enzyme immunoassay ~ 87425
Rotavirus vaccine ~ 90680
Round window repair fistula ~ 69667
Round window fistula ~ see fistula, round window
Roux-en-y procedure ~ 43621, 43633-43634, 43644, 43846, 47740-47741, 47780-47785, 48540
Rpr ~ 86592-86593
RSV (respiratory syncytial virus)
  antibody ~ 86756
  antigen detection
    by direct fluorescence ~ 87280
    by direct optical observation ~ 87807
    by enzyme immunoassay ~ 87420
  immune globulins ~ 90378
RT3 ~ see triiodothyronine, reverse
Rubbing alcohol ~ see isopropyl alcohol
Rubella
  antibody ~ 86762
Rubella/mumps ~ see vaccines
Rubella HI test ~ see hemagglutination inhibition test
Rubeola
  antibody ~ 86765
  antigen detection, immunofluorescence ~ 87283
Rubeolla ~ see rubeola
Russell viper venom time ~ 85612-85613

S

Sac, endolymphatic ~ see endolymphatic sac
Saccomanno technique ~ 88108
Sacral nerve
  implantation, electrode ~ 64561, 64581
  insertion, electrode ~ 64561, 64581
Sacroiliac joint
  arthrodesis ~ 27280
  arthrotomy ~ 27050
  biopsy ~ 27050
  dislocation, open treatment ~ 27218
  fusion ~ 27280
  injection for arthrography ~ 27096
  X-ray ~ 72200-72202
Sacrum
  augmentation
    percutaneous ~ 0200T-0201T
    with CT guidance ~ 72292
    with fluoroscopic guidance ~ 72291
  sacroplasty, percutaneous ~ 0200T-0201T
  tumor, excision ~ 49215
  X-ray ~ 72220
Salabrasion ~ 15810-15811
Salicylate assay ~ 80329-80331
Saline-solution abortion ~ see abortion, induced, by saline

Salivary duct
  catheterization ~ 42660
  dilation ~ 42650-42660
  ligation ~ 42665
  repair ~ 42500-42505
    fistula ~ 42600
Salivary gland virus ~ see Cytomegalovirus
Salivary glands
  abscess, incision and drainage ~ 42310-42320
  biopsy ~ 42405
  calculi (stone), excision ~ 42330-42340
  cyst
    creation, fistula ~ 42325-42326
    drainage ~ 42409
    excision ~ 42408
  injection, X-ray ~ 42550
  needle biopsy ~ 42400
  nuclear medicine
    function study ~ 78232
    imaging ~ 78230-78231
  parotid, abscess ~ 42300-42305
  unlisted services and procedures ~ 42699
  X-ray ~ 70380-70390
    with contrast ~ 70390
Salmonella antibody ~ 86768
Salpingectomy ~ 58262-58263, 58291-58292, 58552, 58554, 58661, 58700
  ectopic pregnancy
    laparoscopic treatment ~ 59151
    surgical treatment ~ 59120
  oophorectomy ~ 58943
Salpingo-oophorectomy ~ 58720
  laparoscopic ~ 58571, 58573, 58575
  resection ovarian malignancy ~ 58950-58956
  resection peritoneal malignancy ~ 58950-58956
  resection tubal malignancy ~ 58950-58956
Salpingohysterostomy ~ see implantation, tubouterine
Salpingolysis ~ 58740
Salpingoneostomy ~ 58673, 58770
Salplingoplasty ~ see fallopian tube, repair
Salpingostomy ~ 58673, 58770
  laparoscopic ~ 58673
Salter osteotomy of the pelvis ~ see osteotomy, pelvis
Sampling ~ see also biopsy; brush biopsy; needle biopsy
  blood
    arteial ~ 36620
    fetal scalp ~ 59030
    ocular ~ 0198T
    organ ~ 36500
    plasma ~ 78110, 78111
    red cell ~ 78120, 78121
    venous ~ 75893
  chorionic villus ~ 59015, 76945
  endometrium ~ 58100, 58558
  lymph node
    EBUS guided hilar ~ 31652, 31653
    para-aortic ~ 57109, 57112, 57531, 58200, 58210, 58548
    pelvic ~ 58200
    periaortic ~ 38572, 38573
    retroperitoneal ~ 38570
  stereotactic template guided ~ 55706
Sang-Park procedure ~ 33735-33737
Sao Paulo typhus ~ see Rocky Mountain spotted fever
Saucerization
  calcaneus ~ 28120
  clavicle ~ 23180
  femur ~ 27070, 27360
  fibula ~ 27360, 27641
  hip ~ 27070
  humerus ~ 23184, 24140
  ileum ~ 27070
  metacarpal ~ 26230
  metatarsal ~ 28122
  olecranon process ~ 24147
  phalanges, finger ~ 26235-26236
    toe ~ 28124
  pubis ~ 27070
  radius ~ 24145, 25151
  scapula ~ 23182
  talus ~ 28120

Saucerization ~ *continued*
  tarsal ~ 28122
  tibia ~ 27360, 27640
  ulna ~ 24147, 25150
Saundby test ~ see blood, feces
Scabies ~ see tissue, examination for ectoparasites
Scalenotomy ~ see muscle division, scalenus anticus
Scalenus anticus division ~ 21700-21705
Scaling ~ see exfoliation
Scalp tumor resection, radical ~ 21015
Scalp blood sampling ~ 59030
Scan ~ see specific site, nuclear medicine
  abdomen ~ see abdomen, CT scan
  CT ~ see CT scan
  MRI ~ see magnetic resonance imaging
  PET ~ see positron emission tomography
  radionuclide ~ see emission computerized tomography
Scanning, radioisotope ~ see nuclear medicine
Scanogram ~ 77073
Scaphoid fracture
  closed treatment ~ 25622
  open treatment ~ 25628
  with manipulation ~ 25624
Scapula
  craterization ~ 23182
  cyst excision ~ 23140
    with allograft ~ 23146
    with autograft ~ 23145
  diaphysectomy ~ 23182
  excision ~ 23172, 23190
    partial ~ 23182
  fracture
    closed treatment
      with manipulation ~ 23575
      without manipulation ~ 23570
    open treatment ~ 23585
  ostectomy ~ 23190
  repair
    fixation ~ 23400
    scapulopexy ~ 23400
  saucerization ~ 23182
  sequestrectomy ~ 23172
  tumor
    excision ~ 23140, 23210
      with allograft ~ 23146
      with autograft ~ 23145
      radical resection ~ 23210
  X-ray ~ 73010
Scapulopexy ~ 23400
Scarification pleural ~ 32215
Scarification of pleura ~ see pleurodesis
Schanz operation ~ see femur, osteotomy
Schauta operation ~ see hysterectomy, vaginal, radical
Schede procedure ~ 32905-32906
Scheie procedure ~ see iridectomy
Schilling test ~ see vitamin B-12 absorption study ~ 78270
Schlatter operation total gastrectomy ~ see excision, stomach, total
Schlicter test ~ (bactericidal titer, serum) 87197
Schocket procedure ~ (aqueous shunt) 66180
Schonbein test ~ see blood, feces
Schuchard procedure osteotomy, maxilla ~ 21206
Schwannoma, acoustic ~ see brain, tumor, excision
Sciatic nerve
  decompression ~ 64712
  injection, anesthetic ~ 64445-64446
  lesion, excision ~ 64786
  neuroma, excision ~ 64786
  neuroplasty ~ 64712
  release ~ 64712
  repair/suture ~ 64858
Scintigraphy ~ see nuclear medicine
  computed tomographic ~ see emission computerized tomography
Scissoring skin tags ~ 11200-11201
Sclera
  excision, sclerectomy with punch or scissors ~ 66160
  fistulization
    sclerectomy with punch or scissors with iridectomy ~ 66160
    thermocauterization with iridectomy ~ 66155
    trabeculectomy ab externo in absence of previous surgery ~ 66170
    trephination with iridectomy ~ 66150

Sclera ~ *continued*
  incision, fistulization
    sclerectomy with punch or scissors with iridectomy ~ 66160
    thermocauterization with iridectomy ~ 66155
    trabeculectomy ab externo in absence of previous surgery ~ 66170
    trephination with iridectomy ~ 66150
  lesion, excision ~ 66130
  repair
    reinforcement
      with graft ~ 67255
      without graft ~ 67250
    staphyloma
      with graft ~ 66225
      without graft ~ 66220
    with glue ~ 65286
    wound
      operative ~ 66250
      tissue glue ~ 65286
Scleral buckling operation ~ see retina, repair, detachment
Scleral ectasia ~ see staphyloma, sclera
Sclerectomy ~ 66160
Sclerotherapy
  esophageal varices ~ 43204, 43243
  fluid collection ~ 49185
  gastric varices ~ 43243
  hemorrhoids ~ 46500
  perirectal ~ 45520
  venous ~ 36465, 36466, 36468, 36470, 36471
Sclerotomy ~ see incision, sclera
Screening, drug ~ see drug screen
Scribner cannulization ~ 36810
Scrotal varices ~ see varicocele
Scrotoplasty ~ 55175-55180
Scrotum
  abscess, incision and drainage ~ 54700, 55100
  excision ~ 55150
  exploration ~ 55110
  hematoma, incision and drainage ~ 54700
  removal, foreign body ~ 55120
  repair ~ 55175-55180
  ultrasound ~ 76870
  unlisted services and procedures ~ 55899
Scrub typhus ~ 86000
Second look surgery ~ see reoperation
Second opinion ~ see confirmatory consultations
Section ~ see also decompression
  cesarean ~ see cesarean delivery
  cranial nerve ~ 61460
    spinal access ~ 63191
  dentate ligament ~ 63180-63182
  gasserian ganglion, sensory root ~ 61450
  medullary tract ~ 61470
  mesencephalic tract ~ 61480
  nerve root ~ 63185-63190
  spinal accessory nerve ~ 63191
  spinal cord tract ~ 63194-63199
  vestibular nerve
    transcranial approach ~ 69950
    translabyrinthine approach ~ 69915
Sedation
  moderate ~ 99151-99153, 99155-99157
    with independent observation ~ 99151-99153
Seddon-Brookes procedure ~ 24320
Sedimentation rate
  blood cell
    automated ~ 85652
    manual ~ 85651
Segmentectomy
  breast ~ 19301-19302
  lung ~ 32484
Seidlitz powder test ~ see X-ray, with contrast
Selective cellular enhancement technique ~ 88112
Selenium ~ 84255
Self care ~ see physical medicine/therapy/occupational therapy
  training ~ 97535, 99509
Sella turcica
  CT scan ~ 70480-70482
  X-ray ~ 70240
Semen ~ see sperm

Semen analysis ~ 89300-89322
  sperm analysis ~ 89331
    antibodies ~ 89325
  with sperm isolation ~ 89260-89261
Semenogelase ~ see antigen, prostate specific
Semilunar bone ~ see lunate
  ganglion ~ see gasserian ganglion
Seminal vesicle(s)
  cyst, excision ~ 55680
  excision ~ 55650
  incision ~ 55600-55605
  mullerian duct, excision ~ 55680
  unlisted services and procedures ~ 55899
  vesiculography ~ 74440
  X-ray with contrast ~ 74440
Seminin ~ see antigen, prostate specific
Semiquantitative ~ 81005
Sengstaaken tamponade esophagus ~ 43460
Senning procedure ~ (repair/revision, great arteries) 33774-33777
Senning type ~ 33774-33777
Sensitivity study
  antibiotic
    agar ~ 87181
    disc ~ 87184
    enzyme detection ~ 87185
    macrobroth ~ 87188
    MIC (minimum inhibitory concentration) ~ 87186
    microtiter ~ 87186
    MLC (minimum lethal concentration) ~ 87187
    mycobacteria ~ 87190
  antiviral drugs, HIV-1, tissue culture ~ 87904
Sensor, fetal oximetry
  cervix ~ 0021T
  vagina ~ 0021T
Sensorimotor exam ~ 92060
Sensory nerve common, repair/suture ~ 64834
Sentinel node injection procedure ~ 38792
Separation, craniofacial
  closed treatment ~ 21431
  open treatment ~ 21432-21436
Septal defect
  repair ~ 33813-33814
  ventricular
    closure ~ 33675-33688
    open ~ 33675-33688
Septectomy
  atrial ~ 33735-33737
    balloon (Rashkind type) ~ 92992
    blade method (Park) ~ 92993
    closed ~ see septostomy, atrial
  submucous nasal ~ see nasal septum, submucous resection
Septic abortion ~ see abortion, septic
Septoplasty ~ 30520
Septostomy, atrial ~ 33735-33737
  balloon (Rashkind type) ~ 92992
  blade method (Park) ~ 92993
Septum, nasal ~ see nasal septum
Sequestrectomy
  carpal ~ 25145
  clavicle ~ 23170
  humeral head ~ 23174
  humerus ~ 24134
  olecranon process ~ 24138
  radius ~ 24136, 25145
  scapula ~ 23172
  skull ~ 61501
  ulna ~ 24138, 25145
Serialography aorta ~ 75625
Serodiagnosis, syphilis ~ see serologic test for syphilis
Serologic test for syphilis ~ 86592-86593
Seroma incision and drainage, skin ~ 10140
Serotonin ~ 84260
Serum
  albumin ~ see albumin, serum
  antibody identification, pretreatment ~ 86975-86978
  CPK ~ see creatine kinase, total
  serum immune globulin ~ 90281-90283

Sesamoid bone
finger, excision ~ 26185
foot
  excision ~ 28292, 28295-28299
  fracture ~ 28530-28531
thumb, excision ~ 26185
toe, excision ~ 28315
Sesamoidectomy
finger ~ 26185
foot ~ 28292, 28295-28299
thumb ~ 26185
toe ~ 28315
Sever procedure ~ see contracture, palm, release
Severing of blepharorrhaphy ~ see tarsorrhaphy, severing
Sex change operation
female to male ~ 55980
male to female ~ 55970
Sex chromatin identification ~ 88130-88140
Sex hormone binding globulin ~ 84270
Sex-linked ichthyoses ~ see syphilis test
SGOT ~ 84450
SGPT ~ 84460
Shaving skin lesion ~ 11300-11313
SHBG (sex hormone binding globulin) ~ 84270
Shelf procedure ~ (see also osteotomy, hip) 27146-27151
Shiga-like toxin antigen detection, enzyme immunoassay ~ 87427
Shigella antibody ~ 86771
Shirodkar operation ~ (repair, cervix, cerclage, abdominal) 57700
Shock wave (extracorporeal) therapy ~ 0020T
Shock wave, lithotripsy ~ 50590
Shock wave, ultrasonic ~ see ultrasound
Shop typhus of Malaya ~ see Murine typhus
Shoulder ~ see also clavicle; scapula
abscess, drainage ~ 23030
amputation ~ 23900-23921
arthrocentesis ~ 20610
arthrodesis ~ 23800
  with autogenous graft ~ 23802
arthrography, injection, radiologic ~ 23350
arthroscopy
  diagnostic ~ 29805
  surgical ~ 29806-29828
    biceps tenodesis ~ 29828
arthrotomy, with removal loose or foreign body ~ 23107
biopsy
  deep ~ 23066
  soft tissue ~ 23065
blade ~ see scapula
bone
  excision
    acromion ~ 23130
    clavicle ~ 23120-23125
  incision ~ 23035
  tumor, excision ~ 23140-23146
bursa, drainage ~ 23031
capsular contracture release ~ 23020
cast
  figure eight ~ 29049
  removal ~ 29710
  spica ~ 29055
  velpeau ~ 29058
disarticulation ~ 23920-23921
dislocation, closed treatment, with manipulation ~ 23650-23655
exploration ~ 23107
hematoma, drainage ~ 23030
manipulation, application of fixation apparatus ~ 23700
prophylactic treatment ~ 23490-23491
radical resection ~ 23077
removal
  calcareous deposits ~ 23000
  cast ~ 29710
  foreign body
    intramuscular ~ 23333
    subcutaneous ~ 23330
  foreign or loose body ~ 23107

Shoulder ~ *continued*
repair
  capsule ~ 23450-23466
  ligament release ~ 23415
  muscle transfer ~ 23395-23397
  rotator cuff ~ 23410-23420
  tendon ~ 23410-23412, 23430-23440
  tenomyotomy ~ 23405-23406
strapping ~ 29240
surgery, unlisted services and procedures ~ 23929
tumor, excision ~ 23071-23078
unlisted services and procedures ~ 23929
X-ray ~ 73020-73030
X-ray with contrast ~ 73040
Shoulder joint ~ see also clavicle; scapula
arthroplasty, with implant ~ 23470-23472
arthrotomy
  with biopsy ~ 23100-23101
  with synovectomy ~ 23105-23106
dislocation
  with greater tuberosity fracture
    closed treatment ~ 23665
    open treatment ~ 23670
  open treatment ~ 23660
  with surgical or anatomical neck fracture
    closed treatment with manipulation ~ 23675
dislocation ~ *continued*
  open treatment ~ 23680
excision, torn cartilage ~ 23101
exploration ~ 23040-23044
incision and drainage ~ 23040-23044
removal, foreign body ~ 23040-23044
X-ray ~ 73050
Shunt(s)
aqueous
  to extraocular reservoir ~ 66180
    revision ~ 66185
arteriovenous ~ see arteriovenous shunt
brain
  creation ~ 62180-62223
  removal ~ 62256-62258
  replacement ~ 62160, 62194, 62225-62230, 62258
  reprogramming ~ 62252
cerebrospinal fluid ~ see cerebrospinal fluid shunt
creation
  arteriovenous
    direct ~ 36821
    Thomas shunt ~ 36835
    transposition ~ 36818-36820
    with bypass graft ~ 35686
    with graft ~ 36825-36830
  cerebrospinal fluid ~ 62200
  Thomas shunt ~ 36835
fetal ~ 59076
great vessel
  aorta to pulmonary artery, ascending ~ 33755
    descending ~ 33762
  central ~ 33764
  subclavian pulmonary artery ~ 33750
  systemic to pulmonary ~ 33924
  vena cava to pulmonary artery ~ 33766-33767
intra-atrial ~ 33735-33737
Levenn
  insertion ~ 49425
  patency test ~ 78291
  revision ~ 49426
nonvascular, X-ray ~ 75809
peritoneal, venous
  injection ~ 49427
  ligation ~ 49428
  removal ~ 49429
peritoneal X-ray ~ 75809
pulmonary artery
  from aorta ~ 33755-33762, 33924
  subclavian ~ 33750
  from vena cava ~ 33766-33767
revision, arteriovenous ~ 36832

Shunt(s) ~ *continued*
spinal cord
creation ~ 63740-63741
irrigation ~ 63744
removal ~ 63746
replacement ~ 63744
superior mesenteric-caval ~ see anastomosis, caval to mesenteric
ureter to colon ~ 50815
ventriculocisternal with valve ~ (ventriculocisternostomy) 62180, 62200, 62201
Shuntogram ~ 75809
Sialic acid ~ 84275
Sialodochoplasty ~ 42500-42505
Sialogram ~ see sialography
Sialography ~ 70390
Sickling electrophoresis ~ 83020
Siderocytes ~ 85536
Siderophilin ~ see transferrin
Sigmoid ~ see colon-sigmoid
Sigmoid bladder cystectomy ~ 51590
Sigmoidoscopy
ablation
polyp ~ 45346
tumor ~ 45346
biopsy ~ 45331
collection, specimen ~ 45331
exploration ~ 45330, 45335
hemorrhage control ~ 45334
injection, submucosal ~ 45335
needle biopsy ~ 45342
placement, stent ~ 45347
removal
foreign body ~ 45332
polyp ~ 45333, 45338
tumor ~ 45333, 45338
repair, volvulus ~ 45337
ultrasound ~ 45341-45342
Signal-averaged electrocardiography ~ see electrocardiogram
Silica ~ 84285
Silicon dioxide ~ see silica
Silicone contouring injections ~ 11950-11954
Silver operation ~ see Keller procedure
Simple mastectomies ~ see mastectomy
Single photon absorptiometry ~ see absorptiometry, single photon
Single photon emission computed tomography (SPECT) ~ *see also* emission computed tomography
abscess localization ~ 78807
bone ~ 78320
cerebrospinal fluid ~ 78647
heart ~ 78451-78454
kidney ~ 78710
liver ~ 78205
tumor localization ~ 78803
Sinus
ethmoidectomy, excision ~ 31254
pilonidal ~ see cyst, pilonidal
Sinus of valsalva repair ~ 33702-33722
Sinus venosus repair ~ 33645
Sinusectomy, ethmoid ~ see ethmoidectomy
Sinuses
cranial
decompression ~ 61595
excision of lesion ~ 61607
ligation ~ 61598
resection ~ 61591
dilation ~ 31295-31297
endoscopy, nasal
biopsy ~ 31237
debridement ~ 31237
decompression ~ 31292-31294
diagnostic ~ 31231, 31233, 31235
dilation ~ 31295-31297
exploration ~ 31276
hemorrhage control ~ 31238
polypectomy ~ 31237
surgical ~ 31237-31241, 31253-31257, 31259, 31267, 31276, 31287, 31288, 31290-31298

Sinuses ~ *continued*
ethmoid
drug-eluting implant placement ~ 0406T, 0407T
excision ~ 31200-31205
with nasal/sinus endoscopy ~ 31254-31255
repair of cerebrospinal leak ~ 31290
frontal
destruction ~ 31080-31085
exploration ~ 31070-31075
with nasal/sinus endoscopy ~ 31276
fracture, open treatment ~ 21343-21344
incision ~ 31070-31087
injection ~ 20500
diagnostic ~ 20501
maxillary
antrostomy ~ 31256-31267
excision ~ 31225-31230
exploration ~ 31020-31032
with nasal/sinus endoscopy ~ 31233
incision ~ 31020-31032, 31256-31267
irrigation ~ 31000
skull base ~ 61581
surgery ~ 61581
multiple
incision ~ 31090
paranasal, incision ~ 31090
nasal endoscopy
diagnostic ~ 31231, 31233, 31235
surgical ~ 31237-31241, 31253-31257, 31259, 31267, 31276, 31287, 31288, 31290-31298
sphenoid
biopsy ~ 31050, 31051
dilation ~ 31295-31298
exploration ~ 31050, 31051
with nasal/sinus endoscopy ~ 31235, 31253
incision ~ 31050, 31051
with nasal/sinus endoscopy ~ 31257, 31259, 31287, 31288
irrigation ~ 31002
repair of cerebrospinal leak ~ 31291
sinusotomy ~ 31050-31051
skull base surgery ~ 61580-61581
unlisted services and procedures ~ 31299
X-ray ~ 70210-70220
Sinusoidal rotational testing ~ see ear, nose and throat
Sinusoscopy
maxillary sinus ~ 31233
sphenoid sinus ~ 31235
Sinusotomy ~ see also sinus, multiple
combined ~ 31090
frontal sinus
exploratory ~ 31070-31075
nonobliterative ~ 31086-31087
obliterative ~ 31080-31085
maxillary ~ 31020-31032
multiple, paranasal ~ 31090
sphenoid sinus ~ 31050-31051
Sisi test ~ 92564
Sistrunk operation ~ see cyst, thyroid gland, excision
Six-minute walk test ~ 94618
Size reduction, breast ~ see breast, reduction
Skeletal fixation humeral epicondyle, percutaneous ~ 24566
Skeletal traction, insertion/removal pin/wire ~ 20650
Skene's gland abscess
destruction ~ 53270
excision ~ 53270
incision and drainage ~ 53060
Skilled nursing facilities (SNF) services
initial care ~ 99304-99306
discharge services ~ 99315-99316
other services ~ 99318
subsequent care ~ 99307-99310
Skin
abrasion ~ 15786-15787
chemical peel ~ 15788-15793
dermabrasion ~ 15780-15783
salabrasion ~ 15810-15811
abscess ~ see abscess, skin
adjacent tissue transfer ~ 14000-14350
autograft ~ see autograft, skin
biopsy ~ 11100-11101

Skin ~ continued

chemical exfoliation ~ 17360
complete physical examination ~ 2029F
cyst ~ see cyst, skin
debridement ~ 11000-11006, 11010-11047
  eczematous ~ 11000-11001
  infected ~ 11000-11006
  subcutaneous tissue ~ 11042, 11045
    infected ~ 11004-11006
  with open fracture and/or dislocation ~ 11010-11012
decubitus ulcer(s) ~ see pressure ulcer (decubitus)
desquamation ~ see exfoliation
destruction
  benign lesions
    fifteen or more lesions ~ 17004
    first lesion ~ 17000
    two-fourteen lesions ~ 17003
  flat warts ~ 17110-17111
  lesions ~ 17106-17108
  malignant lesions ~ 17260-17286
    by photodynamic therapy ~ 96567
  premalignant lesions
    by photodynamic therapy ~ 96567, 96573, 96574
    fifteen or more lesions ~ 17004
    first lesion ~ 17000
    two-fourteen lesions ~ 17003
excision
  debridement ~ 11000-11006, 11010-11047
  excess skin ~ 15830-15839, 15847
  hemangioma ~ 11400-11446
  lesion
    benign ~ 11400-11446
    malignant ~ 11600-11646
expanders ~ see tissue, expander
fasciocutaneous flaps ~ 15730, 15731, 15733, 15734, 15736, 15738
grafts
  free ~ 15050-15157, 15200-15261, 15757
  harvesting, for tissue culture ~ 15040
  skin substitute graft ~ 15271-15278
homografts ~ see homograft, skin
incision and drainage ~ see incision, skin ~ 10040-10180
lesion ~ see lesion; tumor
  multi-spectral analysis ~ 0400T, 0401T
  verrucous ~ see warts
muscle flaps ~ 15731-15738
myocutaneous flaps ~ 15731-15738
nevi
  history ~ 1050F
  patient self-examination counseling ~ 5005F
nose, surgical planing ~ 30120
paring ~ 11055-11057
photography, diagnostic ~ 96904
removal, skin tags ~ 11200-11201
revision
  blepharoplasty ~ 15820-15823
  cervicoplasty ~ 15819
  rhytidectomy ~ 15824-15829
shaving ~ 11300-11313
tags, removal ~ 11200-11201
tests ~ see allergy tests
  candida ~ 86485
  coccidioidomycosis ~ 86490
  histoplasmosis ~ 86510
  other antigen ~ 86486
  tuberculosis ~ 86580
unlisted services and procedures ~ 17999
wound repair
  complex ~ 13100-13160
  intermediate ~ 12031-12057
  simple ~ 12001-12021

Skin graft and flap

composite graft ~ 15760-15770
cross finger flap ~ 15574
delay ~ 15600-15630
delay of flap ~ 15600-15630
derma-fat-fascia ~ 15570
dermal autograft ~ 15130-15136
epidermal autograft ~ 15110-15116
fascial, free ~ 15758

Skin graft and flap ~ continued

fasciocutaneous ~ 15733, 15734, 15736, 15738
fillet flap, finger or toe ~ 14350
formation ~ 15570-15576
free, microvascular anastomosis ~ 15756-15758
free skin graft, full thickness ~ 15200-15261
island pedicle flap ~ 15740
muscle ~ 15733, 15734, 15736, 15738, 15842
  free ~ 15756
myocutaneous ~ 15731, 15733, 15734, 15736, 15756
pedicle flap
  formation ~ 15570-15576
  island ~ 15740
  neurovascular ~ 15750
  transfer ~ 15650
pinch graft ~ 15050
platysmal ~ 15825
punch graft ~ 15775-15776
punch graft for hair transplant ~ 15775-15776
recipient site preparation ~ 15002-15005
skin, free ~ 15757
skin substitute graft ~ 15271-15278
split graft ~ 15100-15101, 15120-15121
superficial musculoaponeurotic system ~ 15829
tissue transfer ~ 14000-14350
tissue-cultured ~ 15040, 15150-15157
transfer ~ 15650
vascular flow check ~ 15860
zygomaticofacial flap ~ 15730

Skull

burr hole
  biopsy brain ~ 61140
  drainage
    abscess ~ 61150-61151
    cyst ~ 61150-61151
    hematoma ~ 61154-61156
  exploration
    infratentorial ~ 61253
    supratentorial ~ 61250
  insertion
    catheter ~ 61210
    EEG electrode ~ 61210
    reservoir ~ 61210
  intracranial, biopsy ~ 61140
  with injection ~ 61120
decompression ~ 61322-61323, 61340-61345
  orbit ~ 61330
drill hole
  catheter ~ 61107
  drainage hematoma ~ 61108
  exploration ~ 61105
excision ~ 61501
exploration, drill hole ~ 61105
fracture ~ 62000-62010
ematoma, drainage ~ 61108
incision, suture ~ 61550-61552
insertion, catheter ~ 61107
lesion, excision ~ 61500, 61600-61608, 61615-61616
orbit
  biopsy ~ 61332
  excision, lesion ~ 61333
  exploration ~ 61332
puncture
  cervical ~ 61050
  cisternal ~ 61050
  drain fluid ~ 61070
  injection ~ 61070
  subdural ~ 61000-61001
  ventricular fluid ~ 61020
reconstruction ~ 21172-21180
  defect ~ 62140-62141, 62145
reduction, craniomegalic ~ 62115-62117
removal
  plate ~ 62142
  prosthesis ~ 62142
repair
  cerebrospinal fluid leak ~ 62100
  encephalocele ~ 62120

Skull ~ *continued*
replacement
plate ~ 62143
prosthesis ~ 62143
stereotactic navigational procedure ~ 61781-61783
tumor, excision ~ 61500
X-ray ~ 70250-70260
Skull base surgery
anterior cranial fossa
bicoronal approach ~ 61586
craniofacial approach ~ 61580-61583
extradural ~ 61600-61601
Lefort 1 osteotomy approach ~ 61586
orbitocranial approach ~ 61584-61585
transzygomatic approach ~ 61586
carotid aneurysm ~ 61613
carotid artery ~ 61610
transection/ligation ~ 61610-61612
craniotomy ~ 62121
dura, repair of cerebrospinal fluid leak ~ 61618-61619
middle cranial fossa
extradural ~ 61605, 61607
infratemporal approach ~ 61590-61591
intradural ~ 61606, 61608
orbitocranial zygomatic approach ~ 61592
posterior cranial fossa
extradural ~ 61615
intradural ~ 61616
transcondylar approach ~ 61596-61597
transpetrosal approach ~ 61598
transtemporal approach ~ 61595
Sleep study ~ 95800-95801, 95806-95807
actigraphy ~ 95803
latency testing ~ 95805
polysomnography ~ 95808-95811
Sliding inlay graft, tibia ~ see ankle; tibia, repair
Sling operation
incontinence ~ 53440
removal ~ 53442
stress incontinence ~ 51992, 57287
vagina ~ 57287-57288
Small bowel ~ see intestines, small
neoplasm ~ see tumor, intestines, small
Smas flap ~ 15829
Smear cervical ~ see cervical smears
Papanicolaou ~ see Pap smears
Smear and stain ~ see also cytopathology, smears
cornea ~ 65430
fluorescent ~ 87206
gram or giesma ~ 87205
ova, parasites ~ 87177
parasites ~ 87207
wet mount ~ 87210
Smith fracture ~ 25600-25605
Smith-Robinson operation ~ see arthrodesis, vertebra
Smithwick operation ~ see excision, nerve, sympathetic
SO4 ~ see sulfate
Soave procedure ~ 45120
Sodium ~ 84295, 84302
urine ~ 84300
Sodium glycinate, theophylline ~ see theophylline
Sofield procedure ~ 24410
Soft tissue ~ see tissue, soft
Solar plexus ~ see celiac plexus
Solitary cyst ~ see bone, cyst
Somatomammotropin, chorionic ~ 83632
Somatomedin ~ 84305
Somatosensory testing
lower limbs ~ 95926
trunk or head ~ 95927
upper limbs ~ 95925
Somatostatin ~ 84307
Somatotropin ~ 83003
Somatotropin release inhibiting hormone ~ see somatostatin
Somatropin ~ see growth hormone, human
Somnographies ~ see polysomnography
Somophyllin T ~ see theophylline
Sonography ~ see echography
Sonohysterography ~ 76831
saline infusion, injection procedure ~ 58340

Sore, bed ~ see pressure ulcer (decubitus)
Spasm eyelid ~ see blepharospasm
Special services, procedures and reports ~ 99000-99091
after hours medical services ~ 99050
analysis, remote physiologic data ~ 99091
computer data analysis ~ 99090, 0206T
device handling ~ 99002
emergency care in office ~ 99058
emergency care out of office ~ 99060
extended hours, medical services ~ 99051-99053
group education ~ 99078
self-management ~ 98961-98962
hyperbaric oxygen ~ 99183
individual education, self management ~ 98960
medical testimony ~ 99075
non-office medical services ~ 99056
on call services ~ 99026-99027
phlebotomy ~ 99199
post-op visit ~ 99024
pump services ~ 99190-99192
reports and forms
medical, extended ~ 99080
psychiatric ~ 90889
specimen handling ~ 99000-99001
supply of materials ~ 99070
educational ~ 99071
unlisted services and procedures ~ 99199
unusual travel ~ 99082
Specific gravity body fluid ~ 84315
Specimen concentration ~ 87015
Specimen handling ~ 99000-99001
SPECT
abscess localization ~ 78807
bone ~ 78320
brain imaging ~ 78607
cerebrospinal fluid ~ 78647
heart ~ 78451-78454, 78469, 78494
kidney ~ 78710
liver ~ 78205
parathyroid gland ~ 78071-78072
tumor localization ~ 78803
Spectacle services
fitting
low vision aid ~ 92354-92355
spectacle prosthesis ~ 92352-92353
spectacles ~ 92340-92342
repair ~ 92370-92371
Spectrometry, mass
analyte ~ 83789
Spectrophotometry ~ 84311
atomic absorption ~ see atomic absorption spectroscopy
Spectroscopy
atomic absorption ~ 82190
bioimpedance spectroscopy (BIS) ~ 93702
fluorescent
advanced glycation endproducts (AGE) ~ 88749
real-time spectral analysis, prostate tissue ~ 0443T
infrared ~ 82365
intravascular ~ 0205T
magnetic resonance ~ 76390
lipoprotein ~ 83704
near infrared wound study ~ 0493T
Spectrum analyses ~ see spectrophotometry
digital multi-spectral skin lesion ~ 0400T, 0401T
Speech evaluation
behavioral and qualitative analysis ~ 92524
cine ~ 70371
comprehension ~ 92523
expression ~ 92523
fluency ~ 92521
for prosthesis ~ 92597, 92607-92608
sound production ~ 92522, 92523
video ~ 70371
Speech prosthesis ~ 21084, 92609
creation ~ 31611
evaluation for speech ~ 92597, 92607-92608
insertion ~ 31611
Speech therapy ~ 92507-92508

1143

Sperm
cryopreservation ~ 89259
evaluation ~ 89329-89331
storage ~ 89343
thawing ~ 89353
washing ~ 58323
Sperm analysis
antibodies ~ 89325
cervical mucus penetration test ~ 89330
count ~ 89310, 89320, 89322
forensic ~ 88125
hamster penetration test ~ 89329
hyaluron binding assay ~ 89398
identification, aspiration ~ 89257
from testis tissue ~ 89264
isolation ~ 89260-89261
motility ~ 89300, 89310, 89320-89322
Sperm evaluation, cervical mucus penetration test ~ see Huhner test
Spermatic cord
hydrocele, excision ~ 55500
laparoscopy ~ 55559
lesion, excision ~ 55520
repair, veins ~ 55530-55540
abdominal approach ~ 55535
with hernia repair ~ 55540
varicocele, excision ~ 55530-55540
Spermatic veins
excision ~ 55530-55540
ligation ~ 55550
Spermatocele excision ~ 54840
Spermatocystectomy ~ (spermatocele excision) 54840
Sphenoid sinus ~ see sinuses, sphenoid
Sphenoidotomy excision, with nasal/sinus endoscopy ~ 31287-31288
Sphenopalatine ganglion injection, anesthetic ~ 64505
Sphincter ~ see specific sphincter
anal ~ see anal sphincter
artificial genitourinary ~ see prosthesis, urethral sphincter
pyloric ~ see pyloric sphincter
Sphincter of Oddi
dilation ~ 47542
excision ~ 43262
pressure measurement, endoscopy ~ 43263
Sphincteroplasty
ampulla of vater ~ 47542
anal ~ 46750-46751, 46760-46761
with implant ~ 46762
bile duct ~ 47460
bladder neck ~ see bladder, repair, neck
Sphincterotomy ~ 52277
anal ~ 46080
bile duct ~ 47460
Spica cast
hip ~ 29305-29325
repair ~ 29720
shoulder ~ 29055
Spinal accessory nerve
anastomosis to facial nerve ~ 64866
incision ~ 63191
section ~ 63191
Spinal column ~ see spine
Spinal cord ~ see also cauda equina; nerve root
biopsy ~ 63275-63290
cyst
aspiration ~ 62268
incision and drainage ~ 63172-63173
decompression ~ 63001-63003, 63055-63057, 63064, 63066, 63101-63103, 62380, 0274T, 0275T
with cervical laminoplasty ~ 63050, 63051
with craniectomy ~ 61343
with discectomy ~ 62380
with facetectomy ~ 62380
with foreaminotomy ~ 0202T, 62380
with laminotomy ~ 62380
drain fluid ~ 62272
exploration ~ 63001-63044
graft, dura ~ 63710
implantation
electrode ~ 63650-63655
pulse generator ~ 63685
receiver ~ 63685

Spinal cord ~ *continued*
incision ~ 63200
dentate ligament ~ 63180-63182
tract ~ 63170, 63194-63199
injection
anesthetic ~ 62320-62327
blood ~ 62273
CT scan ~ 62284
neurolytic agent ~ 62280-62282
other ~ 62320-62327
X-ray ~ 62284
insertion
electrode ~ 63650-63655
pulse generator ~ 63685
receiver ~ 63685
lesion
destruction ~ 62280-62282
excision ~ 63265-63273, 63300-63308
needle biopsy ~ 62269
neoplasm, excision ~ 63275-63290
puncture (tap) ~ *continued*
diagnostic ~ 62270
drain fluid ~ 62272
lumbar ~ 62270
release ~ 63200
reconstruction, dorsal spine elements ~ 63295
removal
catheter ~ 62355
electrode ~ 63661-63664
pulse generator ~ 63688
pump ~ 62365
receiver ~ 63688
reservoir ~ 62365
repair
cerebrospinal fluid leak ~ 63707-63709
meningocele ~ 63700-63702
myelomeningocele ~ 63704-63706
section
dentate ligament ~ 63180-63182
tract ~ 63194-63199
shunt
create ~ 63740-63741
irrigation ~ 63744
removal ~ 63746
replacement ~ 63744
stereotaxis
aspiration ~ 63615
biopsy ~ 63615
creation lesion ~ 63600
excision lesion ~ 63615
stimulation ~ 63610
syrinx, aspiration ~ 62268
tumor, excision ~ 63275-63290
Spinal fluid ~ see cerebrospinal fluid
Spinal fracture ~ see fracture, vertebra
Spinal instrumentation
anterior ~ 22845-22847
removal ~ 22855
biomechanical device ~ 22853, 22854, 22859
Harrington rod technique ~ 22840, 22850
internal fixation ~ 22841
pelvic fixation ~ 22848
posterior nonsegmental ~ 22840
removal ~ 22850
posterior segmental ~ 22842-22844
removal ~ 22852
reinsertion of spinal fixation device ~ 22849
Spinal manipulation ~ see manipulation, chiropractic
Spinal nerve
avulsion ~ 64772
decompression, root ~ 62380
transection ~ 64772
Spinal tap ~ see cervical puncture; cisternal puncture; subdural tap; ventricular puncture
drainage fluid ~ 62272
lumbar ~ 62270
Spine ~ see also spinal cord; vertebra; vertebral body; vertebral process
allograft
morselized ~ 20930
structural ~ 20931

Spine ~ continued
  arthroplasty, lumbar ~ 22856-22865
  aspiration ~ 62267
  autograft
    bone marrow aspiration ~ 20939
    local ~ 20936
    morselized ~ 20937
    structural ~ 20938
  biopsy ~ 20250-20251
  chemotherapy administration ~ (see also chemotherapy) 96450
  CT scan
    cervical ~ 72125-72127
    lumbar ~ 72131-72133
    thoracic ~ 72128-72130
  decompression ~ 62287, 62380, 0274T, 0275T
  deformity
    arthrodesis ~ 22800-22812
    exposure ~ 22818, 22819
    scoliosis x-ray study ~ 72081-72084
  fixation ~ 22842
  fusion
    anterior ~ 22808-22812
    anterior approach ~ 22548-22585, 22812
    exploration ~ 22830
    lateral extracavitary ~ 22532-22534
    posterior approach ~ 22590-22802
  injection
    cervical ~ 0228T, 0229T, 62320, 62321, 62324, 62325
    lumbar ~ 0230T, 0231T, 62322, 62323, 62326, 62327
    sacral ~ 0230T, 0231T, 62322, 62323, 62326, 62327
    thoracic ~ 0228T, 0229T, 62320, 62321, 62324, 62325
    with fluoroscopic guidance ~ 77003
  insertion, instrumentation ~ 22840-22848, 22853, 22854, 22859
  kyphectomy ~ 22818-22819
  magnetic resonance angiography ~ 72159
  magnetic resonance imaging
    cervical ~ 72141-72142, 72156-72158
    lumbar ~ 72148-72158
    thoracic ~ 72146-72147, 72156-72158
  manipulation, with anesthesia ~ 22505
  myelography
    cervical ~ 72240
    lumbosacral ~ 72265
    thoracic ~ 72255
    total ~ 72270
  reconstruction, dorsal spine elements ~ 63295
  reinsertion, instrumentation ~ 22849
  removal, instrumentation ~ 22850, 22852-22855
  repair, osteotomy
    anterior ~ 22220-22226
    posterior ~ 22210-22214
      cervical laminoplasty ~ 63050-63051
      posterolateral ~ 22216
  ultrasound ~ 76800
  unlisted services and procedures, surgery ~ 22899
  X-ray ~ 72020
    absorptiometry ~ 77080, 77081, 77085, 77086
    cervical ~ 72040, 72050, 72052
    lumbosacral ~ 72100, 72110, 72114, 72120
    scoliosis study ~ 72081-72084
    thoracic ~ 72070, 72072, 72074
    thoracolumbar ~ 72080
    total ~ 72081-72084
    with contrast
      cervical ~ 72240
      lumbosacral ~ 72265
      thoracic ~ 72255
      total ~ 72270
Spirometry ~ (see also pulmonology, diagnostic) 94010-94070
  patient initiated ~ 94014-94016
Splanchnicectomy ~ see nerves, sympathectomy, excision
Spleen
  excision ~ 38100-38102
    laparoscopic ~ 38120
  injection, radiologic ~ 38200
  nuclear medicine, imaging ~ 78185, 78215-78216
  repair ~ 38115

Splenectomy
  laparoscopic ~ 38120
  partial ~ 38101
  partial with repair, ruptured spleen ~ 38115
  total ~ 38100
    en bloc ~ 38102
Splenoplasty ~ see repair, spleen
Splenoportography ~ 75810
  injection procedures ~ 38200
Splenorrhaphy ~ 38115
Splint ~ see casting; strapping
  arm
    long ~ 29105
    short ~ 29125-29126
  finger ~ 29130-29131
  leg
    long ~ 29505
    short ~ 29515
  oral surgical ~ 21085
  ureteral ~ see ureteral splinting
Split grafts ~ 15100-15121
Split renal function test ~ see cystourethroscopy, catheterization, ureteral
Splitting blood products ~ 86985
Spontaneous abortion ~ see abortion
Sprengel's deformity ~ 23400
Spring water cyst ~ see cyst, pericardial
Spur, bone ~ see exostosis
  calcaneal ~ see heel spur
Sputum analysis ~ 89220
SRH ~ (somatostatin) 84307
Ssabanejew-Frank operation ~ (incision, stomach, creation, stoma) 43830-43832
Stabilizing factor, fibrin ~ see fibrin stabilizing factor
Stable factor ~ 85230
Stallard procedure ~ see conjunctivorhinostomy
Stamey procedure ~ (repair, bladder, neck) 51845
Standby services physician ~ 99360
Stanford-Binet test ~ see psychiatric diagnosis
Stanftan ~ (Binet test) 96101-96103
Stapedectomy
  revision ~ 69662
  with footplate drill out ~ 69661
  without foreign material ~ 69660
Stapedotomy
  revision ~ 69662
  with footplate drill out ~ 69661
  without foreign material ~ 69660
Stapes
  excision
    with footplate drill out ~ 69661
    without foreign material ~ 69660
  release ~ 69650
  revision ~ 69662
Staphyloma
  sclera repair
    with graft ~ 66225
    without graft ~ 66220
State operation ~ see proctectomy
Statin therapy ~ see performance measures
Statistics/biometry ~ see biometry
Steindler stripping ~ 28250
Stellate ganglion injection, anesthetic ~ 64510
Stem cell
  concentration ~ 38215
  count ~ 86587
  cryopreservation ~ 38207, 88240
  donor search ~ 38204
  harvesting ~ 38205-38206
  limbal, allograft ~ 65781
  plasma depletion ~ 38214
  platelet depletion ~ 38213
  red blood cell depletion ~ 38212
  T-cell depletion ~ 38210
  thawing ~ 38208-38209, 88241
  transplantation ~ 38240-38242
  tumor cell depletion ~ 38211
  washing ~ 38209
Stem, brain ~ see brainstem
Stenger test ~ (audiologic function test; ear, nose and throat) ~ 92565, 92577

Stenosis
aortic ~ see aortic stenosis
auditory canal, external reconstruction ~ 69310
bronchi ~ 96570, 96571
  reconstruction ~ 31775
  relief ~ 31641
laryngeal repair ~ 31551-31554
nasal repair ~ 30465
pulmonary artery repair ~ 33782, 33917
pulmonary vein repair ~ 33726
reconstruction, auditory canal, external ~ 69310
tracheal excision ~ 31780, 31781
urethral ~ see urethral stenosis
ventricular resection ~ 33476
Stensen duct ~ see parotid duct
Stent
exchange
  biliary duct ~ 43276
  pancreatic duct ~ 43276
for revascularization, intracoronary ~ 92937-92938, 92941, 92943-92944
indwelling insertion, ureter ~ 50605, 52282, 52356, 53855
placement
  bronchoscopy ~ 31631, 31636-31637
  cardiac ~ 33621
  colonoscopy ~ 45397
  endoscopy
    bile duct ~ 43274
    gastrointestinal, upper ~ 43266
    intestinal ~ 44379
    pancreatic ~ 43274
  enteroscopy ~ 44370
  esophagoscopy ~ 43212
  ileoscopy ~ 44384
  larynx ~ 31553, 31554, 31580
  proctosigmoidoscopy ~ 45327
  sigmoidoscopy ~ 45347
  tracheal ~ 31631
  transcatheter
    intracoronary ~ 92928-92928
    intravascular ~ 37215-37217, 37236-37239
    extracranial ~ 0075T-0076T
  ureteroneocystomy ~ 50947-50948
removal/replacement, ureteral ~ 50382-50387
revision, bronchoscopy ~ 31638
transcatheter, intravascular, intracranial ~ 61635
transluminal placement, arterial ~ 37221, 37223, 37226-37227, 37230-37231, 37234-37235
urethra ~ 52282
Stent, intravascular ~ see transcatheter, placement, intravascular stents
Stents, tracheal ~ see tracheal stent
Stereotactic frame application/removal ~ 20660
Stereotaxis
aspiration
  brain lesion ~ 61750
    with CT scan and/or MRI ~ 61751
  spinal cord ~ 63615
biopsy
  aspiration, brain lesion ~ 61750
  brain ~ 61750
    with CT scan and/or MRI ~ 61751
  prostate ~ 55706
  spinal cord ~ 63615
catheter placement, brain
  radiation source ~ 61770
computer assisted
  cranial ~ 61781-61782
  orthopedic surgery ~ 0054T-0055T, 20985
  spinal ~ 61783
creation lesion
  brain
    deep ~ 61720-61735
    percutaneous ~ 61790
  gasserian ganglion ~ 61790
  spinal cord ~ 63600
  trigeminal tract ~ 61791
CT scan
  aspiration ~ 61751
  biopsy ~ 61751

Stereotaxis ~ *continued*
excision lesion
  brain ~ 61750
  spinal cord ~ 63615
focus beam, radiosurgery ~ 77371-77373
  cranial ~ 61796-61799
  spinal ~ 63620-63621
  stereotactic frame application ~ 20660, 61800
lesion ablation, intracranial
  MRgFUS-guided ~ 0398T
radiation therapy ~ 77421, 77432-77435
stimulation, spinal cord ~ 63610
target volume guidance ~ 77421
Sterile coverings ~ see dressings
Sternal fracture ~ see fracture, sternum
Sternoclavicular joint
arthrotomy ~ 23044
  with biopsy ~ 23101
  with synovectomy ~ 23106
dislocation
  closed treatment
    with manipulation ~ 23525
    without manipulation ~ 23520
  open treatment ~ 23530-23532
    with fascial graft ~ 23532
Sternocleidomastoid division ~ 21720-21725
Sternotomy closure ~ 21750
Sternum
debridement ~ 21627
excision ~ 21620, 21630-21632
fracture
  closed treatment ~ 21820
  open treatment ~ 21825
ostectomy ~ 21620
radical resection ~ 21630-21632
reconstruction ~ 21740-21742, 21750
  with thoracoscopy ~ 21743
X-ray ~ 71120-71130
Steroid-binding protein, sex ~ see globulin, sex hormone binding
Steroids
anabolic ~ see androstenedione
injection, urethral stricture ~ 52283
ketogenic, urine ~ 83582
STH (somatotropic hormone) ~ see growth hormone
Stimulating antibody, thyroid ~ see immunoglobulin, thyroid stimulating
Stimulation
electric ~ see electrical stimulation
lymphocyte ~ see blastogenesis
spinal cord, stereotaxis ~ 63610
transcutaneous electric ~ see application, neurostimulation
Stimulator, long-acting thyroid ~ see thyrotropin releasing hormone (TRH)
Stimulators, cardiac ~ see heart, pacemaker
Stimulus evoked response ~ 51792
Stoffel operation ~ (rhizotomy) 63185, 63190
Stoma
creation
  bladder ~ 51980
  kidney ~ 50551-50561
  stomach, neonatal ~ 43831
    temporary ~ 43830-43831
  ureter ~ 50860
ureter, endoscopy via ~ 50951-50961
Stomach
anastomosis
  with duodenum ~ 43810, 43850-43855
  with jejunum ~ 43820-43825, 43860-43865
biopsy ~ 43605
creation
  stoma
    temporary ~ 43830-43831
    laparoscopic ~ 43653
electrogastrography ~ 91132-91133
excision
  partial ~ 43631-43639, 43845
  total ~ 43620-43622
exploration ~ 43500
gastric bypass ~ 43644-43645, 43846
  revision ~ 43848

Stomach ~ _continued_
  incision ~ 43830-43832
    exploration ~ 43500
    pyloric sphincter ~ 43520
    removal, foreign body ~ 43500
  nuclear medicine
    blood loss study ~ 78278
    emptying study ~ 78264
      with small bowel transit ~ 78265
      with small bowel and colon transit ~ 78266
    imaging ~ 78261
    protein loss study ~ 78282
    reflux study ~ 78262
    vitamin B-12 absorption ~ 78270-78272
  reconstruction
    for obesity ~ 43644-43645, 43842-43847
    Roux-en-Y ~ 43644, 43846
  removal, foreign body ~ 43500
  repair ~ 48547
    fistula ~ 43880
    fundoplasty ~ 43325
      laparoscopic ~ 43279-43282
    laceration ~ 43501-43502
    stoma ~ 43870
    ulcer ~ 43501
  suture
    fistula ~ 43880
    for obesity ~ 43842-43843
    stoma ~ 43870
    ulcer ~ 43840
    wound ~ 43840
  tumor, excision ~ 43610-43611
  ulcer, excision ~ 43610
  unlisted services and procedures ~ 43659, 43999
Stomatoplasty ~ see mouth, repair
Stone, kidney ~ see calculus, removal, kidney
Stookey-Scarff procedure ~ (ventriculocisternostomy) 62200
Stool blood ~ see blood, feces
Storage
  embryo ~ 89342
  oocyte ~ 89346
  reproductive tissue ~ 89344
  sperm ~ 89343
Strabismus
  chemodenervation ~ 67345
  repair
    adjustable sutures ~ 67335
    extraocular muscles ~ 67340
    one horizontal muscle ~ 67311
    one vertical muscle ~ 67314
    posterior fixation suture technique ~ 67334-67335
    previous surgery, not involving extraocular muscles ~ 67331
    release extensive scar tissue ~ 67343
    superior oblique muscle ~ 67318
    transposition ~ 67320
    two horizontal muscles ~ 67312
    two or more vertical muscles ~ 67316
Strapping ~ see cast; splint
  ankle ~ 29540
  back ~ 29799
  chest ~ 29200
  elbow ~ 29260
  finger ~ 29280
  foot ~ 29540
  hand ~ 29280
  hip ~ 29520
  knee ~ 29530
  shoulder ~ 29240
  thorax ~ 29200
  toes ~ 29550
  unlisted services and procedures ~ 29799
  Unna boot ~ 29580
  wrist ~ 29260
Strassman procedure ~ 58540
Strayer procedure leg, lower ~ 27687
Streptococcus pneumoniae vaccine ~ see vaccines

Streptococcus
  group A
    antigen detection
      enzyme immunoassay ~ 87430
      nucleic acid ~ 87650-87652
    direct optical observation ~ 87880
  group B
    antigen detection by immunoassay with direct optical observation ~ 87802
    prenatal screening ~ 3294F
Streptokinase, antibody ~ 86590
Stress tests
  cardiovascular ~ 93015-93024
  multiple gated acquisition (MUGA) ~ 78472-78473
  myocardial perfusion imaging ~ 78451-78454
  pulmonary ~ 94618
Stricture
  dilation
    gastric/duodenal ~ 43245
    ureteral
      balloon ~ 50706
      endoscopy ~ 50553, 50572, 50575, 50953, 50972
      with cystourethroscopy ~ 52341-52343
      with ureteroscopy ~ 52344-52346
  repair, urethra ~ 53400-53405
Stricturoplasty intestines ~ 44615
Stroboscopy larynx ~ 31579
STS ~ (syphilis test) 86592-86593
Stuart-Prower factor ~ 85260
Study, color vision ~ see color vision examination
Sturmdorf procedure ~ 57520
Styloid process radial, excision ~ 25230
Styloidectomy radial ~ 25230
Stypven time ~ see Russell viper venom time
Subacromial bursa arthrocentesis ~ 20610
Subclavian arteries ~ see artery, subclavian
Subcutaneous injection ~ see injection, subcutaneous
Subcutaneous mastectomies ~ see mastectomy, subcutaneous
Subcutaneous tissue excision ~ 15830-15839, 15847
Subdiaphragmatic abscess ~ see abscess, subdiaphragmatic
Subdural electrode
  insertion ~ 61531-61533
  removal ~ 61535
Subdural hematoma ~ see hematoma, subdural
Subdural puncture ~ 61105-61108
Subdural tap ~ 61000-61001
Sublingual gland
  abscess, incision and drainage ~ 42310-42320
  calculi (stone), excision ~ 42330
  cyst
    drainage ~ 42409
    excision ~ 42408
  excision ~ 42450
Subluxation elbow ~ 24640
Submandibular gland
  calculi (stone), excision ~ 42330-42335
  excision ~ 42440
Submaxillary gland abscess, incision and drainage ~ 42310-42320
Submucous resection of nasal septum ~ see nasal septum, submucous resection
Subperiosteal implant reconstruction
  mandible ~ 21245-21246
  maxilla ~ 21245-21246
Subphrenic abscess ~ see abscess, subdiaphragmatic
Substance S, Reichstein's ~ see deoxycortisol
Subtrochanteric fracture ~ see femur, fracture, subtrochanteric
Sucrose hemolysis test ~ see red blood cell (RBC), fragility, osmotic
Suction lipectomies ~ see liposuction
Sudiferous gland ~ see sweat gland
Sugar water test ~ see red blood cell (RBC), fragility, osmotic
Sugars ~ 84375-84379
Sugiura procedure ~ see esophagus, repair, varices
Sulfate
  chondroitin ~ see chondroitin sulfate
  DHA ~ see dehydroepiandrosterone sulfate
  urine ~ 84392
Sulfation factor ~ see somatomedin
Sulphates ~ see sulfate
Sumatran mite fever ~ see scrub typhus
Superficial musculoaponeurotic system (SMAS) flap rhytidectomy ~ 15829

Supernumerary digit
reconstruction ~ 26587
repair ~ 26587

Supply
chemotherapeutic agent ~ (see also chemotherapy) 96545
contact lenses ~ 92391, 92396
educational materials ~ 99071
low vision aids ~ (see also spectacle services) 92392
materials ~ 99070
ocular prosthesis ~ 92393
prosthesis, breast ~ 19396
spectacle prosthesis ~ 92395
spectacles ~ 92390

Suppositories, vaginal ~ see pessary
Suppression ~ 80400-80408
Suppression/testing ~ see evocative/suppression test
Suppressor T lymphocyte marker ~ see CD8
Suppurative hidradenitides ~ see hidradenitis, suppurative
Suprahyoid lymphadenectomy ~ 38700
Supraorbital nerve
avulsion ~ 64732
incision ~ 64732
transection ~ 64732

Supraorbital rim and forehead reconstruction ~ 21179-21180
Suprapubic prostatectomies ~ see prostatectomy, suprapubic
Suprarenal
gland ~ see adrenal gland
vein ~ see vein, adrenal

Suprascapular nerve injection, anesthetic ~ 64418
Suprasellar cyst ~ see craniopharyngioma
Surface CD4 receptor ~ see CD4
Surface radiotherapy ~ see application, radioelement, surface
Surgeries
breast-conserving ~ see breast, excision, lesion
conventional ~ see celiotomy
laser ~ see laser surgery
Mohs ~ see Mohs micrographic surgery
repeat ~ see reoperation

Surgery services ~ 10000-69999
auditory system ~ 69000-69979
cardiovascular system ~ 33000-37799
digestive system ~ 40490-49999
endocrine system ~ 60000-60699
eye and ocular adnexa ~ 65091-68899
female genital system ~ 56405-58999
hemic and lymphatic systems ~ 38100-38999
integumentary system ~ 10000-19999
intersex surgery ~ 55970-55980
male genital system ~ 54000-55899
maternity care and delivery ~ 59000-59899
mediastinum and diaphragm ~ 39000-39599
musculoskeletal system ~ 20005-29999
nervous system ~ 61000-64999
respiratory system ~ 30000-32999
urinary system ~ 50010-53899

Surgical
avulsion ~ see avulsion
cataract removal ~ see cataract, excision
collapse therapy; thoracoplasty ~ see thoracoplasty
diathermy ~ see electrocautery
galvanism ~ see electrolysis
incision ~ see incision
microscopes ~ see operating microscope
pathology ~ 88300-88309
planing, nose, skin ~ 30120
pneumoperitoneum ~ see pneumoperitoneum
removal, eye ~ see enucleation, eye
revision ~ see reoperation
services, post-op visit ~ 99024

Surveillance ~ see monitoring
Suspension
aorta ~ 33800
kidney ~ see nephropexy
muscle, hyoid ~ 21865
vagina ~ see colpopexy

Suture ~ see repair
abdomen ~ 49900
aorta ~ 33320-33322
bile duct, wound ~ 47900

Suture ~ *continued*
bladder
fistulization ~ 44660-44661, 45800-45805, 51880-51925
vesicouterine ~ 51920-51925
vesicovaginal ~ 51900
wound ~ 51860-51865
cervix ~ 57720
colon
diverticula ~ 44604-44605
fistula ~ 44650-44661
plication ~ 44680
stoma ~ 44620-44625
ulcer ~ 44604-44605
wound ~ 44604-44605
esophagus, wound ~ 43410-43415
eyelid ~ 67880
closure of ~ 67875
with transposition of tarsal plate ~ 67882
wound
full thickness ~ 67935
partial thickness ~ 67930
facial nerve, intratemporal
lateral to geniculate ganglion ~ 69740
medial to geniculate ganglion ~ 69745
foot, tendon ~ 28200-28210
gastroesophageal ~ 43405
great vessel ~ 33320-33322
hemorrhoids ~ 46945-46946
hepatic duct ~ see hepatic duct, repair
intestine, large
diverticula ~ 44605
ulcer ~ 44605
wound ~ 44605
intestines
large
diverticula ~ 44604
ulcer ~ 44604
wound ~ 44604
small
diverticula ~ 44602-44603
fistula ~ 44640-44661
plication ~ 44680
ulcer ~ 44602-44603
wound ~ 44602-44603
stoma ~ 44620-44625
iris, with ciliary body ~ 66682
kidney
fistula ~ 50520-50526
horseshoe ~ 50540
wound ~ 50500
leg, lower, tendon ~ 27658-27665
leg, upper, muscle ~ 27385-27386
liver, wound ~ 47350-47361
mesentery ~ 44850
nerve ~ 64831-64876
pancreas ~ 48545
pharynx, wound ~ 42900
rectum
fistula ~ 45800-45825
prolapse ~ 45540-45541
removal, anesthesia ~ 15850-15851
spleen ~ see splenorrhaphy
stomach
fistula ~ 43880
laceration ~ 43501-43502
stoma ~ 43870
ulcer ~ 43501, 43840
wound ~ 43840
tendon
foot ~ 28200-28210
knee ~ 27380-27381
testis
injury ~ 54670
suspension ~ 54620-54640
thoracic duct
abdominal approach ~ 38382
cervical approach ~ 38380
thoracic approach ~ 38381
throat, wound ~ 42900

Suture ~ *continued*
  tongue
    base suspension ~ 41512
    to lip ~ 41510
  trachea
    fistula
      with plastic repair ~ 31825
      without plastic repair ~ 31820
    stoma
      with plastic repair ~ 31825
      without plastic repair ~ 31820
    wound
      cervical ~ 31800
      intrathoracic ~ 31805
  ulcer ~ 44604-44605
  ureter ~ 50900
    deligation ~ 50940
    fistula ~ 50920-50930
  urethra
    fistula ~ 45820-45825, 53520
    stoma ~ 53520
    to bladder ~ 51840-51841
    wound ~ 53502-53515
  uterus
    fistula ~ 51920-51925
    rupture ~ 58520, 59350
    suspension ~ 58400-58410
  vagina
    cystocele ~ 57240, 57260
    enterocele ~ 57265
    fistula
      rectovaginal ~ 57300-57307
      transvesical and vaginal approach ~ 57330
      urethrovaginal ~ 57310-57311
      vesicovaginal ~ 51900, 57320-57330
    rectocele ~ 57250-57260
    suspension ~ 57280, 57283
    wound ~ 57200-57210
  vas deferens ~ 55400
  vein, femoral ~ 37650
    iliac ~ 37660
  wound ~ 44604-44605
Swallowing evaluation ~ 92526, 92610-92613, 92616-92617
  cine ~ 74230
  treatment ~ 92526
  video ~ 74230
Swanson procedure ~ 28309
Sweat collection iontophoresis ~ 89230
Sweat glands, excision
  axillary ~ 11450-11451
  inguinal ~ 11462-11463
  perianal ~ 11470-11471
  perineal ~ 11470-11471
  umbilical ~ 11470-11471
Sweat test ~ (chloride, blood) 82435
Swenson procedure ~ 45120
Syme procedure ~ 27888
Sympathectomy
  artery
    digital ~ 64820
    radial ~ 64821
    superficial palmar arch ~ 64823
    ulnar ~ 64822
  cervical ~ 64802
  cervicothoracic ~ 64804
  digital artery, with magnification ~ 64820
  lumbar ~ 64818
  presacral ~ 58410
  thoracic ~ 32664
  thoracolumbar ~ 64809
  with rib excision ~ 21616
Sympathetic nerve
  excision ~ 64802-64818
  injection, anesthetic ~ 64508, 64520-64530
Sympathins ~ see catecholamines
Symphysiotomy horseshoe kidney ~ 50540
Symphysis, pubic ~ see pubic symphysis
Syncytial virus, respiratory ~ see respiratory syncytial virus
Syndactylism, toes ~ see webbed, toe
Syndactyly repair ~ 26560-26562
Syndesmotomy ~ see ligament, release

Syndrome
  andrenogenital ~ see adrenogenital syndrome
  ataxia-telangiectasia ~ see ataxia telangiectasia
  Bloom ~ see Bloom syndrome
  carpal tunnel ~ see carpal tunnel syndrome
  Costen's ~ see temporomandibular joint (TMJ)
  Eerb-Goldflam ~ see myasthenia gravis
  ovarian vein ~ see ovarian vein syndrome
  synechiae, intrauterine ~ see adhesions, intrauterine
  Treacher Collins ~ see Treacher-Collins syndrome
  urethral ~ see urethral syndrome
Syngesterone ~ see progesterone
Synostosis (cranial) ~ see craniosynostosis
Synovectomy
  arthrotomy with, glenohumeral joint ~ 23105
    sternoclavicular joint ~ 23106
  elbow ~ 24102
  excision
    carpometacarpal joint ~ 26130
    finger joint ~ 26135-26140
    hip joint ~ 27054
    interphalangeal joint ~ 26140
    knee joint ~ 27334-27335
    metacarpophalangeal joint ~ 26135
    palm ~ 26145
  wrist ~ 25105, 25118-25119
    radical ~ 25115-25116
Synovial
  bursa ~ see bursa
  cyst ~ see ganglion
  membrane ~ see synovium
  popliteal space ~ see baker's cyst
Synovium
  biopsy
    carpometacarpal joint ~ 26100
    interphalangeal joint ~ 26110
    knee joint ~ 27330
    metacarpophalangeal joint, with synovial biopsy ~ 26105
  excision
    carpometacarpal joint ~ 26130
    finger joint ~ 26135-26140
    hip joint ~ 27054
    interphalangeal joint ~ 26140
    knee joint ~ 27334-27335
Syphilis ab ~ see antibody, Treponema pallidum
Syphilis test ~ 86592-86593
Syrinx spinal cord, aspiration ~ 62268
System
  endocrine ~ see endocrine system
  hemic ~ see hemic system
  lymphatic ~ see lymphatic system
  musculoskeletal ~ see musculoskeletal system
  nervous ~ see nervous system

T

T cell leukemia virus I antibodies, adult ~ 86687, 86689
T cell leukemia virus, I, human ~ 86687, 86689
T cell leukemia virus II antibodies, human ~ 86688
T cell leukemia virus II , human ~ 86688
T cells
  CD4, absolute ~ 86361
  count ~ 86359
  gene rearrangement ~ 81340-81342
  ratio ~ 86360
T lymphotropic virus type III antibodies, human ~ 86689, 86701-86703
T-3 ~ see triiodothyronine
T-4 ~ 84436-84439, 86360
T-7 index ~ 84436
T-8 ~ 86360
T-cells CD4, absolute ~ 86361
  count ~ 86359
  ratio ~ 86360
T- cell T8 antigens ~ 86360
T- phyl ~ 80198
T3 free ~ 84481
T4 molecule ~ 86360

T4 total ~ 84436
Taarnhoj Procedure ~ see section ~ 61450
Tachycardia heart, recording ~ 93609
Tacrolimus drug assay ~ 80197
Tag, skin ~ see skin, tags
Tail bone
  excision ~ 27080
  fracture ~ 27200-27202
Takeuchi Procedure ~ 33505
Talectomy ~ see astragalectomy
Talotarsal joint dislocation ~ 28570-28575, 28585
  percutaneous fixation ~ 28576
Talus
  arthrodesis
    pantalar ~ 28705
    subtalar ~ 28725
    triple ~ 28715
  arthroscopy
    surgical ~ 29891-29892
    subtalar ~ 29904-29907, 29915-29916
  autograft, osteochondral ~ 28446
  craterization ~ 28120
  cyst, excision ~ 28100-28103
  diaphysectomy ~ 28120
  excision ~ 28120, 28130
  fracture
    open treatment ~ 28445
    percutaneous fixation ~ 28436
    with manipulation ~ 28435-28436
    without manipulation ~ 28430
  repair
    osteochondritis dissecans ~ 29892
    osteotomy ~ 28302
  saucerization ~ 28120
  tumor, excision ~ 27647, 28100-28103
Tap
  cisternal ~ see cisternal puncture
  lumbar diagnostic ~ see spinal tap
Tarsal fracture
  percutaneous fixation ~ 28456
Tarsal bone ~ see ankle bone
Tarsal joint ~ see foot
  arthrodesis ~ 28730-28735, 28740
    with advancement ~ 28737
    with lengthening ~ 28737
  craterization ~ 28122
  cyst, excision ~ 28104-28107
  diaphysectomy ~ 28122
  dislocation ~ 28540-28545, 28555
    percutaneous fixation ~ 28545-28546
  excision ~ 28116, 28122
  fracture
    open treatment ~ 28465
    with manipulation ~ 28455-28456
    without manipulation ~ 28450
  fusion ~ 28730-28735, 28740
    with advancement ~ 28737
    with lengthening ~ 28737
  repair ~ 28320
    osteotomy ~ 28304-28305
  saucerization ~ 28122
  tumor, excision ~ 28104-28107, 28171
Tarsal strip procedure ~ 67917-67924
Tarsal tunnel release ~ 28035
Tarsal wedge procedure ~ 67916-67923
Tarsometatarsal joint
  arthrodesis ~ 28730-28735, 28740
  arthrotomy ~ 28020, 28050
  dislocation ~ 28600-28605, 28615
    percutaneous fixation ~ 28606
  exploration ~ 28020
  fusion ~ 28730-28735, 28740
  removal
    foreign body ~ 28020
    loose body ~ 28020
  synovial
    biopsy ~ 28050
    excision ~ 28070

Tarsorrhaphy ~ 67875
  median ~ 67880
  severing ~ 67710
    with transposition of tarsal plate ~ 67882
Tattoo
  cornea ~ 65600
  skin ~ 11920-11922
TB test, antigen response ~ 0010T
  skin test ~ 86580-86585
TBG ~ see thyroxine binding globulin
TBS ~ see Bethesda system
TCT ~ see thrombin time
TD shots ~ see tetanus immunization; vaccines
Team conference case management services ~ 99366-99368
Tear duct ~ see lacrimal duct
Tear gland ~ see lacrimal gland
Technique
  pericardial window ~ see pericardiostomy
  projective ~ see projective test
Teeth X-ray ~ 70300-70320
Telangiectasia
  chromosome analysis ~ 88248
  injection ~ 36468
Telangiectasia
  chromosome analysis ~ 88248
  sclerotherapy ~ 36465, 36466, 36468, 36470, 36471
Telephone
  evaluation and management services
    non-physician ~ 98966-98968
    physician ~ 99441-99443
  pacemaker analysis ~ 93293
Teletherapy dose plan ~ 77306, 77307
Temperature gradient studies ~ 93740
Temporal arteries ~ 37609
Temporal bone
  electromagnetic bone conduction hearing device
    implantation/replacement ~ 69710
    removal/repair ~ 69711
  excision ~ 69535
  resection ~ 69535
  tumor, removal ~ 69970
  unlisted services and procedures ~ 69979
Temporal, petrous
  excision, apex ~ 69530
Temporomandibular joint (TMJ)
  arthrocentesis ~ 20605
  arthrography ~ 70328-70332
    injection ~ 21116
  arthroplasty ~ 21240-21243
  arthroscopy
    diagnostic ~ 29800
    surgical ~ 29804
  arthrotomy ~ 21010
  cartilage, excision ~ 21060
  condylectomy ~ 21050
  coronoidectomy ~ 21070
  dislocation
    closed treatment ~ 21480-21485
    open treatment ~ 21490
  injection, radiologic ~ 21116
  magnetic resonance imaging (MRI) ~ 70336
  manipulation ~ 21073
  meniscectomy ~ 21060
  prostheses ~ see prosthesis, temporomandibular joint
  reconstruction ~ see reconstruction, temporomandibular joint
  X-ray with contrast ~ 70328-70332
Tenago Procedure ~ 53431
Tendinosuture ~ see suture, tendon
Tendon
  Achilles ~ see Achilles tendon
  arm, upper, revision ~ 24320
  excision
    forearm ~ 25109
  finger, excision ~ 26180
  forearm, repair ~ 25260-25274
  graft, harvesting ~ 20924
  insertion, biceps tendon ~ 24342

Tendon ~ *continued*
lengthening
  ankle ~ 27685-27686
  arm, upper ~ 24305
  elbow ~ 24305
  finger ~ 26476, 26478
  forearm ~ 25280
  hand ~ 26476, 26478
  leg, lower ~ 27685-27686
  leg, upper ~ 27393-27395
  toe ~ 28240
  wrist ~ 25280
palm, excision ~ 26170
release
  arm, lower ~ 25295
  arm, upper ~ 24332
  wrist ~ 25295
shortening
  ankle ~ 27685-27686
  finger ~ 26477, 26479
  hand ~ 26477, 26479
  leg, lower ~ 27685-27686
transfer
  arm, lower ~ 25310-25312, 25316
  arm, upper ~ 24301
  elbow ~ 24301
  finger ~ 26497-26498
  hand ~ 26480-26489
  leg, lower ~ 27690-27692
  leg, upper ~ 27400
  pelvis ~ 27098
  thumb ~ 26490-26492, 26510
  wrist ~ 25310-25312, 25316
transplant, leg, upper ~ 27396-27397
wrist, repair ~ 25260-25274
Tendon origin insertion, injection ~ 20551
Tendon pulley reconstruction of hand ~ see hand, reconstruction, tendon pulley
Tendon sheath
arm, lower, repair ~ 25275
finger
  incision ~ 26055
  incision and drainage ~ 26020
  lesion ~ 26160
foot, excision ~ 28086-28088
hand lesion ~ 26160
injection ~ 20550
palm, incision and drainage ~ 26020
removal, foreign body ~ 20520-20525
wrist
  excision, radical ~ 25115-25116
  incision ~ 25000-25001
  repair ~ 25275
Tenectomy, tendon sheath ~ 25110
Tennis elbow repair ~ 24357-24359
Tenodesis
biceps tendon
  arthroscopic ~ 29828
  at elbow ~ 24340
  shoulder ~ 23430
finger ~ 26471-26474
wrist ~ 25300-25301
Tenolysis
ankle ~ 27680-27681
arm, lower ~ 25295
arm, upper ~ 24332
finger
  extensor ~ 26445-26449
  flexor ~ 26440-26442
foot ~ 28220-28226
hand extensor ~ 26445-26449
  flexor ~ 26440-26442
leg, lower ~ 27680-27681
wrist ~ 25295
Tenomyotomy, shoulder ~ 23405-23406
Tenon's capsule injection ~ 67515
Tenoplasty anesthesia ~ 01714
Tenorrhaphy ~ see suture, tendon
Tenosuspension ~ see tenodesis
Tenosuture ~ see suture, tendon

Tenotomy
Achilles tendon ~ 27605-27606
ankle ~ 27605-27606
arm, lower ~ 25290
arm, upper ~ 24310
finger ~ 26060, 26455-26460
foot ~ 28230, 28234
hand ~ 26450, 26460
hip, iliopsoas tendon ~ 27005
hip, abductor ~ 27006
hip, adductor ~ 27000-27003
leg, upper ~ 27306-27307, 27390-27392
toe ~ 28010-28011, 28232-28234, 28240
wrist ~ 25290
TENS ~ see physical medicine/therapy/ occupational therapy ~ 64550
Tensilon test ~ 95857-95858
Tension, ocular ~ see glaucoma
Terman-Merrill test ~ 96100
Termination, pregnancy ~ see abortion
Test
antiglobulin ~ 86880
aphasia ~ 96105
Bender visual-motor Gestalt ~ 96101-96103
Binet ~ 96101-96103
blood ~ see blood tests
blood coagulation ~ see coagulation
breath ~ see breath test
cervical mucus penetration ~ 89330
clinical chemistry ~ 84999
complement fixation ~ 86171
exercise ~ 93015-93018
fern ~ 87210
fetal, nonstress ~ 59025
function, vestibular ~ see vestibular function tests
gel diffusion ~ 86329-86331
glucose tolerance ~ 82951-82952
hearing ~ see audiologic function tests
hemagglutination inhibition ~ 86280
ink blot ~ see inkblot test
intelligence ~ 96101-96102
lung function ~ see pulmonology, diagnostic
neutralization ~ 86382
Papanicolaou ~ 88141-88155, 88164-88167, 88174-88175
pregnancy ~ 84702-84703
quick ~ 85610-85611
radioimmunosorbent ~ 82784-82787
Rorschach ~ 96101
Schilling ~ 78270
skin ~ see skin, tests
Stanford-Binet ~ see psychiatric diagnosis
tuberculin ~ 86580
Test tube fertilization ~ 58321-58322
Tester, color vision ~ 92283
Testes
cryopreservation ~ 89335
nuclear medicine
  imaging ~ 78761
undescended ~ 54550-54560
Testicular vein ~ 55530-55540
Testimony, medical ~ 99075
Testing, histocompatibility ~ see tissue typing
Testing, neurophysiologic intraoperative ~ 95940-95941
Testing, neuropsychological ~ 96117
Testing, range of motion ~ see range of motion test
Testis
abscess, incision and drainage ~ 54700
biopsy ~ 54500-54505
excision
  laparoscopic ~ 54690
  partial ~ 54522
  radical ~ 54530-54535
  simple ~ 54520
hematoma, incision and drainage ~ 54700
insertion, prosthesis ~ 54660
lesion, excision ~ 54512
needle biopsy ~ 54500
repair
  injury ~ 54670
  suspension ~ 54620-54640
  torsion ~ 54600

Testis ~ *continued*
suture
  injury ~ 54670
  suspension ~ 54620-54640
transplantation, to thigh ~ 54680
tumor, excision ~ 54530-54535
undescended, exploration ~ 54550-54560
unlisted services and procedures ~ 54699, 55899
Testosterone ~ 84402
response ~ 80414
  stimulation ~ 80414-80415
total ~ 84403
Testosterone estradiol binding globulin ~ 84270
Tetanus ~ 86280
antibody ~ 86774
immunoglobulin ~ 90389
Tetrachloride, carbon ~ 84600
Tetralogy of Fallot ~ 33692-33697, 33924
Thal-Nissen Procedure ~ 43325
Thawing ~ 86930-86932
cryopreserved
  embryo ~ 89352
  oocytes ~ 89356
  reproductive tissue ~ 89354
  sperm ~ 89353
previously frozen cells ~ 38208-38209
Thawing and expansion of frozen cell ~ 88241
THBR ~ 84479
Theleplasty ~ 19350
Theophylline assay ~ 80198
Therapeutic
abortion ~ 59850-59852
apheresis ~ 36511-36516
mobilization ~ see mobilization
photopheresis ~ 36522
radiology ~ see radiology, therapeutic
Therapeutic Drug Assays
amikacin ~ 80150
amitriptyline ~ 80335-80337
benzodiazepine ~ 80346, 80347
caffeine ~ 80155
carbamazepine ~ 80156-80157
clozapine ~ 80159
cyclosporine ~ 80158
desipramine ~ 80335-80337
digoxin ~ 80162, 80163
dipropylacetic acid ~ 80164, 80165
doxepin ~ 80335-80337
ethosuximide ~ 80168
everolimus ~ 80169
gabapentin ~ 80171
gentamicin ~ 80170
gold ~ 80375
haloperidol ~ 80173
imipramine ~ 80335-80337
lamotrigine ~ 80175
levetiracetam ~ 80177
lidocaine ~ 80176
lithium ~ 80178
nortriptyline ~ 80335-80337
oxcarbazepine ~ 80183
phenobarbital ~ 80184
phenytoin ~ 80185-80186
primidone ~ 80188
procainamide ~ 80190-80192
quantitative, other ~ 80299
quinidine ~ 80194
salicylate ~ 80329-80331
sirolimus ~ 80195
tacrolimus ~ 80197
theophylline ~ 80198
tiagabine ~ 80199
tobramycin ~ 80200
topiramate ~ 80201
vancomycin ~ 80202
zonisamide ~ 8020

Therapies
cold ~ see cryotherapy
exercise ~ 97110-97113
family ~ 90846-90849, 99510
language ~ 92507-92508
milieu ~ 90882
occupational ~ 97165-97168
photodynamic ~ 96910-96913
photoradiation ~ 96900
physical ~ see physical medicine/therapy/occupational therapy
speech ~ 92507-92508
tocolytic ~ 59412
ultraviolet ~ 96900
Therapy
radiation, brachytherapy ~ 77767, 77768, 77770-77772, 0394T, 0395T
Thermocauterization
ectropion, repair ~ 67922
lesion, cornea ~ 65450
Thermocoagulation ~ 17000-17286
Thermotherapy
prostate ~ 53850-53852
  microwave ~ 53850
  radiofrequency ~ 53852
Thiamine ~ 84425
Thiersch Operation ~ 15050
Thiersch Procedure ~ 46753
Thigh fasciotomy ~ see femur; leg, upper ~ 27025
Thiocyanate ~ 84430
Third disease ~ 86762
Third opinion ~ see confirmatory consultations
Thompson Procedure ~ 27430
Thompson test ~ see smear and stain, routine
Thoracectomy ~ 32905
Thoracentesis ~ 32554-32555
Thoracic
anterior ramus ~ see intercostal nerve
arteries ~ 36215-36218
cavity ~ see chest cavity
duct ~ see lymphatics
  cannulation ~ 38794
  ligation ~ 38380
    abdominal approach ~ 38382
    thoracic approach ~ 38381
  suture
    abdominal approach ~ 38382
    cervical approach ~ 38380
    thoracic approach ~ 38381
empyema ~ 21501-21502
surgery, video-assisted ~ see thoracoscopy
vertebra ~ 22101, 22112
wall ~ see chest wall
Thoracocentesis ~ 32554-32555
Thoracoplasty ~ 32905
with closure bronchopleural fistula ~ 32906
Thoracoscopy
diagnostic
  with biopsy ~ 32604, 32606, 32607-32609
  without biopsy ~ 32601
surgical ~ 32650-32674
  with control traumatic hemorrhage ~ 32654
  with creation pericardial window ~ 32659
  with diagnostic wedge resection ~ 32668
  with esophagomyotomy ~ 32665
  with excision mediastinal cyst, tumor and/or mass ~ 32662
  with excision pericardial cyst, tumor and/or mass ~ 32661
  with lobectomy ~ 32663
  with mediastinal lymphadenectomy ~ 32674
  with parietal pleurectomy ~ 32656
  with partial pulmonary decortication ~ 32651
  with pleurodesis ~ 32650
  with regional lymphadenectomy ~ 32674
  with removal intrapleural foreign body ~ 32653
  with removal of clot/foreign body ~ 32658
  with resection of thymus ~ 32673
  with resection/plication of bullae ~ 32655
  with sternum reconstruction ~ 21743
  with therapeutic wedge resection ~ 32666, 32667
  with thoracic sympathectomy ~ 32664
  with total pulmonary decortication ~ 32652

Thoracostomy empyema ~ 32035-32036
  tube, with/without water seal ~ 32551
Thoracotomy
  cardiac massage ~ 32160
  for post-op complications ~ 32120
  hemorrhage ~ 32110
  lymphadenectomy, thoracic ~ 38746
  removal
    bullae ~ 32141
    cyst ~ 32140
    defibrillator ~ 33243
    electrodes ~ 33238
    foreign body
      intrapleural ~ 32150
      intrapulmonary ~ 32151
    pacemaker ~ 33236-33237
  resection
    diagnostic wedge ~ 32507
    therapeutic wedge ~ 32505-32506
  revascularization ~ 33140-33141
  transmyocardial laser
    with biopsy ~ 32096-32097
    with lung repair ~ 32110
    with open intrapleural pneumolysis ~ 32124
    with resection-plication of bullae ~ 32141
Thorax ~ see chest; chest cavity; mediastinum
  angiography ~ 71275
  bioimpedance ~ 93701
  biopsy ~ 21550
  CT scan ~ 71250-71275
  incision, empyema ~ 32035-32036
    pneumothorax ~ 32551
  incision and drainage
    abscess ~ 21501-21502
    deep ~ 21510
    hematoma ~ 21501-21502
  strapping ~ 29200
  tumor
    excision ~ 21552-21558
    excision/resection ~ 21557, 21558
  unlisted services and procedures, surgery ~ 21899
Three glass test ~ 81020
Three-day measles ~ 86762
Throat ~ see pharynx
  abscess, incision and drainage ~ 42700-42725
  biopsy ~ 42800-42806
  hemorrhage ~ 42960-42962
  reconstruction ~ 42950
  removal, foreign body ~ 42809
  repair
    pharyngoesophageal ~ 42953
    wound ~ 42900
  suture, wound ~ 42900
  unlisted services and procedures ~ 42999
Thrombectomy
  aortoiliac artery ~ 34151-34201
  arteriovenous fistula, graft ~ 36830-36833
  axillary artery ~ 34101
  axillary vein ~ 34490
  brachial artery ~ 34101
  bypass graft, other than hemodialysis graft or fistula ~ 35875-35876
  carotid artery ~ 34001
  celiac artery ~ 34151
  dialysis graft ~ 36831, 36833
  femoral ~ 34201
  femoropopliteal vein ~ 34421-34451
  iliac ~ 34151-34201
  iliac vein ~ 34401-34451
  innominate artery ~ 34001-34101
  mesenteric artery ~ 34151
  percutaneous
    coronary artery ~ 92973
    dialysis circuit ~ 36904-36906
    intracranial artery ~ 61645
    mechanical arterial ~ 37184-37186
    mechanical venous ~ 37187-37188
  peroneal artery ~ 34203
  popliteal artery ~ 34201-34203
  radial artery ~ 34111
  renal artery ~ 34151

Thrombectomy ~ *continued*
  subclavian artery ~ 34001-34101
  subclavian vein ~ 34471-34490
  tibial artery ~ 34203
  ulnar artery ~ 34111
  vena cava ~ 34401-34451
  vena caval ~ 50230
Thrombin inhibitor I ~ 85300-85301
Thrombin time ~ 85670-85675
Thrombocyte (platelet) ~ see blood, platelet
Thrombocyte AB ~ 86022-86023
Thromboendarterectomy ~ see thrombectomy
  aorta, abdominal ~ 35331
  aortoiliofemoral artery ~ 35363
  axillary artery ~ 35321
  brachial artery ~ 35321
  carotid artery ~ 35301, 35390
  celiac artery ~ 35341
  femoral artery ~ 35302, 35371-35372
  iliac artery ~ 35351, 35361-35363
  iliofemoral artery ~ 35355, 35363
  innominate artery ~ 35311
  mesenteric artery ~ 35341
  peroneal artery ~ 35305-35306
  popliteal artery ~ 35303
  renal artery ~ 35341
  subclavian artery ~ 35301-35311
  superficial femoral artery ~ 35302
  tibial artery ~ 35305-35306
  tibioperoneal trunk artery ~ 35304
  vertebral artery ~ 35301
Thrombokinase ~ 85260
Thrombolysin ~ 85400
Thrombolysis
  arterial
    intracranial
      transcatheter infusion ~ 37211, 37195
      percutaneous ~ 61645
    other than coronary
      transcatheter infusion ~ 37211, 37213
  cerebral, intravenous infusion ~ 37195
  coronary vessels ~ 92975, 92977
  cranial vessels ~ 37195
  infusion, arterial ~ 37211-37214, 37195
  transcatheter therapy ~ 37211-37214
Thrombolysis biopsy intracranial arterial perfusion ~ 61624
Thrombolysis intracranial ~ see ciliary body; cornea; eye, removal, foreign body; iris; lens; retina; sclera; vitreous ~ 65205
Thrombomodulin ~ 85337
Thromboplastin
  inhibition ~ 85705
  inhibition test ~ 85347
  partial time ~ 85730-85732
Thromboplastin antecedent, plasma ~ 85270
Thromboplastinogen ~ 85210-85293
Thromboplastinogen B ~ 85250
Thromboxane, urine ~ 84431
Thumb ~ 26720-26727
  amputation ~ 26910, 26952
  arthrodesis, carpometacarpal joint ~ 26841-26842
  dislocation
    with fracture ~ 26645-26650
      open treatment ~ 26665
    with manipulation ~ 26641
  fracture
    with dislocation ~ 26645-26650
      open treatment ~ 26665
  fusion, in opposition ~ 26820
  reconstruction
    from finger ~ 26550
    opponensplasty ~ 26490-26496
  repair
    muscle ~ 26508
    muscle transfer ~ 26494
    tendon transfer ~ 26510
  replantation ~ 20824-20827
  sesamoidectomy ~ 26185
  unlisted services and procedures ~ 26989

Thymectomy ~ 60520-60521
  sternal split/transthoracic approach ~ 60521-60522
  transcervical approach ~ 60520
Thymotaxin ~ 82232
Thymus gland ~ 60520
  excision ~ 60520-60521
Thyramine ~ 80324-80326
Thyrocalcitonin ~ 80410, 82308
Thyroglobulin ~ 84432
  antibody ~ 86800
Thyroglossal duct cyst, excision ~ 60280-60281
Thyroid gland
  cyst
    aspiration ~ 60300
    excision ~ 60200
    incision and drainage ~ 60000
    injection ~ 60300
  excision
    for malignancy
      limited neck dissection ~ 60252
      radical neck dissection ~ 60254
    partial ~ 60210-60225
    secondary ~ 60260
    total ~ 60240, 60271
      cervical approach ~ 60271
      removal all thyroid tissue ~ 60260
      sternal split/transthoracic approach ~ 60270
      transcervical approach ~ 60520
  metastatic cancer, nuclear imaging ~ 78015-78018
  needle biopsy ~ 60100
  nuclear medicine
    imaging for metastases ~ 78015-78018
    imaging with flow ~ 78013
    metastases uptake ~ 78020
    uptake ~ 78012, 78014
  tumor, excision ~ 60200
Thyroid hormone binding ratio ~ 84479
Thyroid hormone uptake ~ 84479
Thyroid stimulating hormone (TSH) ~ 80418, 80438-80439, 84443
Thyroid stimulating hormone receptor AB ~ 80438-80439
Thyroid stimulating immune globulins ~ 84445
Thyroid stimulator, long acting ~ 80438-80439
Thyroid suppression test ~ 78012, 78014
Thyroidectomy
  partial ~ 60210-60225
  secondary ~ 60260
  total ~ 60240, 60271
    cervical approach ~ 60271
    for malignancy
      limited neck dissection ~ 60252
      radical neck dissection ~ 60254
    removal all thyroid tissue ~ 60260
    sternal split/transthoracic approach ~ 60270
Thyrolingual cyst ~ 60000, 60280-60281
Thyrotomy ~ 31300
Thyrotropin receptor AB ~ 80438-80439
Thyrotropin releasing hormone (TRH) ~ 80438-80439
Thyroxine
  free ~ 84439
  neonatal ~ 84437
  total ~ 84436
  true ~ 84436
Thyroxine binding globulin ~ 84442
Tibia ~ see ankle
  arthroscopy surgical ~ 29891-29892
  craterization ~ 27360, 27640
  cyst, excision ~ 27635-27638
  diaphysectomy ~ 27360, 27640
  excision ~ 27360, 27640
    epiphyseal bar ~ 20150
  fracture ~ 27759
  fracture
    arthroscopic treatment ~ 29855-29856
      plafond ~ 29892
    closed treatment ~ 27824-27825
    distal ~ 27824-27828
    intercondylar ~ 27538-27540
    malleolus ~ 27760-27766, 27808-27814

Tibia ~ *continued*
  open treatment ~ 27535-27536, 27758-27759, 27826-27828
  plateau ~ 29855-29856
    closed treatment ~ 27530-27536
  shaft ~ 27752-27759
  with manipulation ~ 27825
  without manipulation ~ 27824
  incision ~ 27607
  osteoplasty, lengthening ~ 27715
  prophylactic treatment ~ 27745
  reconstruction ~ 27418
    at knee ~ 27440-27443, 27446
  repair ~ 27720-27725
    epiphysis ~ 27477-27485, 27730-27742
    osteochondritis dissecans arthroscopy ~ 29892
    osteotomy ~ 27455-27457, 27705, 27709-27712
    pseudoarthrosis ~ 27727
  saucerization ~ 27360, 27640
  tumor, excision ~ 27635-27638, 27645
  X-ray ~ 73590
Tibial
  arteries ~ see artery, tibial
  nerve
    neurostimulation ~ 64566
    repair/suture, posterior ~ 64840
Tibiofibular joint
  arthrodesis ~ 27871
  dislocation ~ 27830-27832
  disruption, open treatment ~ 27829
  fusion ~ 27871
TIG ~ see immune globulins, tetanus
Time
  bleeding ~ 85002
  prothrombin ~ 85610-85611
  reptilase ~ 85670-85675
Tinnitus assessment ~ 92625
Tissue
  culture
    chromosome analysis ~ 88230-88239
    homogenization ~ 87176
    non-neoplastic disorder ~ 88230, 88237
    skin grafts ~ 15100-15121, 15342-15343
    solid tumor ~ 88239
    toxin/antitoxin ~ 87230
    virus ~ 87252-87253
  dissection, macroscopic ~ 88387-88388
  enzyme activity ~ 82657
  examination
    for ectoparasites ~ 87220
    for fungi ~ 87220
    macroscopic ~ 88387-88388
  expander
    breast reconstruction with ~ 19357
    insertion, skin ~ 11960
    removal, skin ~ 11971
    replacement, skin ~ 11970
  grafts, harvesting ~ 20926
  granulation ~ 17250
  homogenization ~ 87176
  hybridization in situ ~ 88365-88368
  mucosal ~ see mucosa
  preparation
    macroscopic ~ 88387-88388
  skin harvest for culture ~ 15040
  soft, abscess ~ 20005
  transfer
    adjacent
      eyelids ~ 67961
      skin ~ 14000-14350
    facial muscles ~ 15845
    finger flap ~ 14350
    toe flap ~ 14350
  typing
    culture ~ 87140-87158
    HLA antibodies ~ 86812-86817
    HLA crossmatch ~ 86825-86826
    lymphocyte culture ~ 86821
Tissue factor ~ see thromboplastin
TLC
  screen ~ 84375

TMJ ~ see temporomandibular joint (TMJ)
  prostheses ~ 21243
Tobramycin assay ~ 80200
Tocolysis ~ 59412
Tocopherol ~ 84446
Toe ~ see phalanx ~ 28270, 28272
  amputation ~ 28810-28825
  capsulotomy ~ 28270-28272
  fasciotomy ~ 28008
  fracture ~ see fracture, phalanges, toe
  lesion, excision ~ 28092
  reconstruction
    angle deformity ~ 28313
    extra toes ~ 28344
    hammer toe ~ 28285-28286
    macrodactyly ~ 28340-28341
    syndactyly ~ 28345
    webbed toe ~ 28345
  repair
    bunion ~ 28292, 28295-28299
    muscle ~ 28240
    tendon ~ 28232-28234, 28240
    webbed ~ 28280
    webbed toe ~ 28345
  tenotomy ~ 28010-28011, 28232-28234
  unlisted services and procedures ~ 28899
Toe flap tissue transfer ~ 14350
Toes
  arthrocentesis ~ 20600
  dislocation ~ see specific joint**
  magnetic resonance imaging (MRI) ~ 73721-73723
  reconstruction, extra digit ~ 26587
  repair
    extra digit ~ 26587
    macrodactylia ~ 26590
  reposition to hand ~ 26551-26556
  strapping ~ 29550
  X-ray ~ 73660
Tolerance test
  glucagon ~ 82946
  glucose ~ 82951-82952
  heparin-protamine ~ 85530
  insulin ~ 80434-80435
  maltose ~ 82951-82952
Tomodensitometries ~ see CT scan
Tomographic scintigraphy, computed ~ 78607
Tomographic spect myocardial imaging ~ 78469
Tomographies, computed X-ray ~ see CT scan
Tomography, computerized axial abdomen ~ 74150-74175, 75635
  head ~ 70450-70470, 70496
Tomography, emission computed ~ see positron emission tomography
  single photon ~ 78607
Tompkins metroplasty ~ 58540
Tongue
  ablation, submucosal tongue base ~ 41530
  abscess, incision and drainage ~ 41000-41006, 41015
  base suspension ~ 41512
  biopsy ~ 41100-41105
  cyst, incision and drainage ~ 41000-41006, 41015, 60000
  excision
    complete ~ 41140-41155
    frenum ~ 41115
    partial ~ 41120-41135
    with mouth resection ~ 41150-41153
    with radical neck ~ 41135, 41145, 41153-41155
  fixation ~ 41500
  hematoma, incision and drainage ~ 41000-41006, 41015
  incision, frenum ~ 41010
  lesion, excision ~ 41110-41114
  reconstruction, frenum ~ 41520
  repair ~ 41250-41252
    laceration ~ 41250-41252
    suture ~ 41510
  suture ~ 41510
  unlisted services and procedures ~ 41599
Tonometry, serial ~ 92100
Tonsil, pharyngeal ~ see adenoids
Tonsillectomy ~ 42820-42826

Tonsils
  abscess, incision and drainage ~ 42700
  excision ~ 42825-42826
    lingual ~ 42870
    radical ~ 42842-42845
    tag ~ 42860
    with adenoids ~ 42820-42821
  lingual, destruction ~ 42870
  unlisted services and procedures ~ 42999
Topiramate assay ~ 80201
Torek Procedure ~ see orchiopexy
Torkildsen Procedure ~ 62180
TORP (total ossicular replacement prosthesis) ~ 69633, 69637
Torsion swing test ~ 92546
Torula ~ see cryptococcus
Torus mandibularis tumor excision ~ 21031
Total
  abdominal hysterectomy ~ 58150, 58200, 58956
  bilirubin level ~ 82247-82248, 88720
  catecholamines ~ 82382
  cystectomy ~ 51570, 51580, 51590-51597
  dacryoadenectomy ~ 68500
  elbow replacement ~ 24363
  esophagectomy ~ 43107-43113, 43124
  gastrectomy ~ 43620-43622
  hemolytic complement ~ 86162
  hip arthroplasty ~ 27130-27132
  knee arthroplasty ~ 27438, 27445
  mastectomies ~ see mastectomy
  ostectomy of patella ~ 27424
  splenectomy ~ 38100
Touroff Operation ~ 37615
Toxicology screen ~ 80305-80307
Toxin assay ~ 87230
Toxin, botulinum ~ see chemodenervation
Toxoplasma antibody ~ 86777-86778
Trabeculectomies ~ 65855
Trabeculectomy ab externo
  in absence of previous surgery ~ 66170
  with scarring previous surgery ~ 66172
Trabeculoplasty by laser surgery ~ 65855
Trabeculotomy AB externo eye ~ 65850
Trachea
  aspiration ~ 31720
  catheter ~ 31720-31725
  dilation ~ 31630-31631, 31636-31638
  endoscopy, via tracheostomy ~ 31615
  excision, stenosis ~ 31780-31781
  fistula
    with plastic repair ~ 31825
    without plastic repair ~ 31820
  fracture, endoscopy ~ 31630
  incision
    emergency ~ 31603-31605
    planned ~ 31600-31601
    with flaps ~ 31610
  introduction, needle wire ~ 31730
  puncture, aspiration and/or injection ~ 31612
  reconstruction
    carina ~ 31766
    cervical ~ 31750
    fistula ~ 31755
    intrathoracic ~ 31760
  repair
    cervical ~ 31750
    fistula ~ 31755
    intrathoracic ~ 31760
    stoma ~ 31613-31614
  resection, cricotracheal ~ 31592
  revision, stoma, scars ~ 31830
  scar, revision ~ 31830
  stenosis
    excision ~ 31780-31781
    repair ~ 31780-31781
  stoma
    repair
      with plastic repair ~ 31825
      without plastic repair ~ 31820
    revision, scars ~ 31830

Trachea ~ continued
tumor
  excision
    cervical ~ 31785
    thoracic ~ 31786
unlisted services and procedures, bronchi ~ 31899
wound, suture
  cervical ~ 31800
  intrathoracic ~ 31805
Tracheal stent, placement ~ 31631
tubes ~ 31500
Trachelectomy ~ 57530
radical ~ 57531
Tracheloplasty ~ 15819
Trachelorrhaphy ~ 57720
Tracheo-esophageal fistula ~ see fistula, tracheoesophageal
Tracheobronchoscopy through tracheostomy ~ 31615
Tracheoplasty
cervical ~ 31750
intrathoracic ~ 31760
tracheopharyngeal fistulization ~ 31755
Tracheostoma revision ~ 31613-31614
Tracheostomy
emergency ~ 31603-31605
planned ~ 31600-31601
revision, scar ~ 31830
surgical closure
  with plastic repair ~ 31825
  without plastic repair ~ 31820
tracheobronchoscopy through ~ 31615
with flaps ~ 31610
Tracheotomy tube change ~ 31502
Tracking tests (ocular) ~ 92545
Tract, urinary ~ 74400-74425
Traction therapy ~ 97140
manual ~ 97140
mechanical ~ 97012
Tractotomy
mesencephalon ~ 61480
Training
activities of daily living ~ 97535, 99509
biofeedback ~ 90875, 90901-90911
cognitive skills ~ 97127
community/work reintegration ~ 97537
compensatory ~ 97127, 97535
home management ~ 97535, 99509
orthoptic/pleoptic ~ 92065
orthotics ~ 97760, 97763
prosthetics ~ 97761
self care ~ 97535, 98960-98962, 99509
sensory integration ~ 97533
walking (physical therapy) ~ 97116
wheelchair management ~ 97542
Tram flap
breast reconstruction ~ 19367-19369
Trans-scaphoperilunar fracture/dislocation
closed treatment ~ 25680
open treatment ~ 25685
Transaminase
glutamic oxaloacetic ~ 84450
glutamic pyruvic ~ 84460
Transcatheter
aortic valve replacement
  open axillary artery approach ~ 33363
  open femoral artery approach ~ 33362
  open iliac artery approach ~ 33364
  percutaneous femoral artery approach ~ 33361
  transaortic approach ~ 33365
  transapical approach ~ 33366
  with cardiopulmonary bypass support ~ 33367-33369
biopsy ~ 37200
closure
  percutaneous
    ductus arteriosus ~ 93582
    heart ~ 93580-93582
  transmyocardial
    cranial ~ 61624-61626
denervation, renal sympathetic ~ 0338T, 0339T
embolization
  cranial ~ 61624-61626
  vascular ~ 37241-37244

Transcatheter ~ continued
insertion, leadless pacemaker system ~ 0387T
mitral valve implantation/replacement (TMVI) ~ 0483T, 0484T
mitral valve repair ~ 33418, 33419, 0345T
occlusion, cranial ~ 61624-61626
paravalvular leak
  aortic valve ~ 93591, 93592
  mitral valve ~ 93590, 93592
  vascular ~ 37241-37244
placement, intravascular stent ~ 0075T, 0076T, 37215-37218, 37236-37239, 92928, 92929
  central dialysis segment ~ 36908
  peripheral dialysis segment ~ 36906
removal, leadless pacemaker system ~ 0388T
replacement, leadless pacemaker system ~ 0387T
therapy
  embolization ~ 75894, 75898
  infusion (arterial or venous) ~ 37211-37214, 61650, 61651
  perfusion, cranial ~ 61624-61626
  septal reduction ~ 93583
Transcatheter Aortic Valve Replacement (TAVR/TAVI)
axillary artery approach ~ 33363
femoral artery approach ~ 33361-33362
iliac artery approach ~ 33364
transaortic approach ~ 33365
transapical approach ~ 33366
with cardiopulmonary bypass support ~ 33367-33369
with arterial./venous cannulation ~ 33367-33369
Transcatheter foreign body retrieval ~ 37197
Transcortin ~ 84449
Transcranial Doppler study (TCP) ~ 93886-93893
stimulation, motor ~ 95928-95929
Transcutaneous electric nerve stimulation ~ 64550
Transdermal electrostimulation ~ 64550
Transection
artery, carotid ~ 61610, 61612
blood vessel, kidney ~ 50100
brain, subpial ~ 61567
nerve ~ 64732-64772
  vagus ~ 43640-43641
pulmonary artery ~ 33922
Transesophageal Doppler echocardiography ~ 93312-93318
Transfer
blastocyst ~ 58974-58976
gamete intrafallopian ~ see GIFT
jejunum, with microvascular anastomosis, free ~ 43496
preparation, embryo ~ 89255
  cryopreserved ~ 89352
surgical ~ see transposition
tendon ~ see tendon, transfer
toe to hand ~ 26551-26556
Transferase
aspartate amino ~ 84450
glutamic oxaloacetic ~ 84450
Transferrin ~ 84466
Transformation lymphocyte ~ 86353
Transfusion
blood ~ 36430
  exchange ~ 36455
    newborn ~ 36450, 36456
  fetal ~ 36460
  push, infant ~ 36440
blood parts, exchange ~ 36511-36516
unlisted services and procedures ~ 86999
white blood cells ~ 86950
Transfusion medicine ~ 86850-86999
Transluminal
angioplasty, arterial
  radiological supervision ~ 37246, 37247
Transmyocardial laser revascularization ~ 33140-33141
Transosteal bone plate reconstruction, mandible ~ 21244
Transpeptidase, gamma-glutamyl ~ 82977
Transplant ~ see graft
bone ~ see bone graft
hair ~ see hair, transplant

Transplantation ~ see graft
  autologous ~ see autograft
  bone marrow ~ 38240-38242
  cartilage, knee
    allograft ~ 27415, 29867
    autograft ~ 27412, 29866
  chondrocytes, knee ~ 27412
  conjunctiva ~ 65782
  cornea
    autograft/homograft
      allograft preparation ~ 65757
      endothelials ~ 65756
      lamellar ~ 65710
      penetrating ~ 65730-65755
    for aphakia ~ 65750
  eye
    amniotic membrane ~ 65780
    conjunctiva ~ 65782
    stem cell ~ 65781
  hair
    punch graft ~ 15775-15776
    strip ~ 15220-15221
  heart ~ 33945
    allograft preparation ~ 33933, 33944
  heart-lung ~ 33935
  intestines
    allograft preparation ~ 44715-44721
    allotransplantation ~ 44135-44136
    donor enterectomy ~ 44132-44133
    removal of allograft ~ 44137
  liver ~ 47135
    allograft preparation ~ 47143-47147
  lung
    allograft preparation ~ 0494T, 32855-32856, 33933
    anesthesia ~ 00580
    donor pneumonectomy ~ 32850
    double, with cardiopulmonary bypass ~ 32854
    double, without cardiopulmonary bypass ~ 32853
    initiation and monitoring, cadaver ~ 0495T-0496T
    single, with cardiopulmonary bypass ~ 32852
    single, without cardiopulmonary bypass ~ 32851
  meniscus, knee ~ 29868
  pancreas ~ 48160, 48550, 48554-48556
    allograft preparation ~ 48551-48552
  parathyroid ~ 60512
  renal
    allograft preparation ~ 50323-50329
    allotransplantation ~ 50360
      with recipient nephrectomy ~ 50365
    autotransplantation ~ 50380
    donor nephrectomy ~ 50300-50320, 50547
    recipient nephrectomy ~ 50340
    removal transplanted renal allograft ~ 50370
  skin ~ see dermatology
  stem cells ~ 38240-38241
    cell concentration ~ 38215
    cryopreservation ~ 38207
    harvesting ~ 38205-38206
    plasma depletion ~ 38214
    platelet depletion ~ 38213
    red blood cell depletion ~ 38212
    T-cell depletion ~ 38210
    thawing ~ 38208
    tumor cell depletion ~ 38211
    washing ~ 38209
  testis ~ 38208
    to thigh ~ 54680
  tissue, harvesting ~ 20926
Transposition
  arteries
    carotid ~ 0037T, 35691, 35694-35695
    subclavian ~ 0037T, 35693-35695
    vertebral ~ 35691-35693
  cranial nerve ~ 64716
  eye muscles ~ 67320
  great arteries, repair ~ 33770-33781
  nerve ~ 64718-64721
  ovary ~ 58825
  peripheral nerve
    major ~ 64856
  vein valve ~ 34510

Transthoracic echocardiography ~ 93303-93318, 93350
Transthyretin ~ 84134
Transureteroureterostomy ~ 50770
Transurethral procedure ~ see specific procedure**
  prostate
    incision ~ 52450
    resection ~ 52630
    thermotherapy ~ 53850-53852
      microwave ~ 53850
      radiofrequency ~ 53852
Trapezium arthroplasty with implant ~ 25445
Travel, unusual ~ 99082
Treacher-Collins syndrome midface reconstruction ~ 21150-21151
Treatment, tocolytic ~ 59412
Trendelenburg Operation ~ 37785
Trephine procedure sinusotomy, frontal ~ 31070
Treponema pallidum
  antibody, confirmation test ~ 86780
  antigen detection, direct fluorescence ~ 87285
TRH ~ see thyrotropin releasing hormone (TRH)
Triacylglycerol ~ 84478
Triacylglycerol hydrolase ~ 83690
Tributyrinase ~ 83690
Trichiasis repair ~ 67825
  epilation, by forceps ~ 67820
  epilation, by other than forceps ~ 67825
  incision of lid margin ~ 67830
    with free mucous membrane graft ~ 67835
Trichina ~ 86784, 96902
Trichinella
  antibody ~ 86784
  trichogram ~ 96902
Trichomonas vaginalis
  antigen detection
    nucleic acid ~ 87660
    by immunoassay with direct optical observation ~ 87808
Trichrome stain ~ 88313
Tricuspid valve
  excision ~ 33460
  repair ~ 33463-33465
  replacement ~ 33465
  repositioning ~ 33468
Tridymite ~ 84285
Trigeminal ganglia ~ see Gasserian ganglion
Trigeminal nerve
  destruction ~ 64600-64610
  injection
    anesthetic ~ 64400
    neurolytic ~ 64600-64610
Trigeminal tract stereotactic, create lesion ~ 61791
Trigger finger repair ~ 26055
Trigger point injection
  one or two muscles ~ 20552
  two or more muscles ~ 20553
Triglyceridase ~ 83690
Triglyceride lipase ~ 83690
Triglycerides ~ 84478
Trigonocephaly ~ 21175
Triiodothyronine
  free ~ 84481
  reverse ~ 84482
  total ~ 84480
  true ~ 84480
Triolean hydrolase ~ 83690
Trioxopurine ~ 84550, 84560
Tripcellim ~ 84485, 84488-84490
Trisegmentectomy ~ 47122
Trocar biopsy bone marrow ~ 38221
Trochanteric femur fracture ~ 27246, 27248
Trophoblastic tumor GTT ~ 59100, 59870
Troponin ~ 84484
  qualitative ~ 84512
  quantitative ~ 84484
Truncal vagotomies ~ 43640
Truncus arteriosus repair ~ 33786
Truncus brachiocephalicus ~ see artery, brachiocephalic
Trunk, brachiocephalic ~ see artery, brachiocephalic
Trypanosomiases ~ 86171, 86280
Trypanosomiasis ~ 86171, 86280

Trypsin
   duodenum ~ 84485
   feces ~ 84488-84490
Trypsin inhibitor, alpha 1-antirypsin ~ see alpha-1 antitrypsin
Trypure ~ 84485, 84488-84490
Tsalicylate intoxication ~ 80329-80331
TSH ~ see thyroid stimulating hormone
TSI ~ see thyroid stimulating immunoglobulin
Tsutsugamushi disease ~ 86000
TT ~ see thrombin time
TT-3 ~ see triiodothyronine, true
TT-4 ~ see thyroxine, true
Tuba auditoria (auditiva) ~ see eustachian tube
Tubal embryo stage transfer ~ see embryo transfer
Tubal ligation ~ 58600
   laparoscopic ~ 58670
   with cesarean section ~ 58611
Tubal occlusion ~ 58615
   with cesarean delivery ~ see occlusion ~ 58615
      creat lesion ~ 58565, 58615
Tubal pregnancy ~ 59121
   with salpingectomy and/or oophorectomy ~ 59120
Tube change
   colonic ~ 49450
   duodenostomy ~ 49451
   gastro-jejunostomy ~ 49452
   gastrostomy ~ 43760, 49446
   jejunostomy ~ 49451
   tracheotomy ~ 31502
Tube placement
   cecostomy tube ~ 44300, 49442
   duodenostomy tube ~ 49441
   endoscopic
      bile duct, pancreatic duct ~ 43268
      jejunostomy tube, percutaneous ~ 49441
      nasobiliary, nasopancreatic
         for drainage ~ 43274
   enterostomy tube ~ 44300
   gastrostomy tube ~ 43246, 49440
   nasogastric tube ~ 43752
   orogastric tube ~ 43752
Tube, fallopian ~ see fallopian tube
Tubectomy ~ 58700, 58720
Tubed pedicle flap formation ~ 15570-15576
Tubercle bacilli culture ~ 87116
Tubercleplasty tibia, anterior ~ 27418
Tuberculin test ~ 85480
Tuberculosis
   antigen response test ~ 86480
   culture ~ 87116
   skin test ~ 86580
Tuberculosis vaccine (BCG) ~ 90585-90586
Tubes
   endotracheal ~ 31500
   gastrostomy ~ 43246, 43760-43761
Tudor "rabbit ear" ~ see urethra, repair
Tuffier vaginal hysterectomy ~ 58260-58270, 58290-58294, 58550-58554
Tumor
   abdomen, destruction/excision ~ 49203-49205, 58957, 58958
   abdominal wall, excision ~ 22900-22905
   acetabulum, excision ~ 27076
   ankle ~ 27615-27619, 27632, 27634
   arm, lower ~ 25071-25078
   arm, upper, excision ~ 24071-24079
   back/flank
      excision ~ 21930-21936
      radical resection ~ 21935, 21936
   bile duct
      destruction ~ 43272
      extrahepatic ~ 47711
      intrahepatic ~ 47712
   bladder ~ 52234-52240
      excision ~ 51530, 52355
   bone, ablation ~ 20982
   brain ~ 61510
      excision ~ 61518, 61520-61521, 61526-61530, 61545, 62164
   breast
      excision ~ 19120-19126
      intraoperative radiation therapy (IORT), preparation of tumor cavity ~ 19294

Tumor ~ *continued*
   bronchi, excision ~ 31640
   calcaneus ~ 28100-28103
      excision ~ 27647
   carpal ~ 25130-25136
   cheekbone ~ 21030, 21034
   chest wall
      cryoablation ~ 32994
      excision ~ 19260-19272
   clavicle   excision ~ 23140, 23200
      with allograft ~ 23146
      with autograft ~ 23145
   coccyx ~ 49215
   colon, destruction ~ 44401, 45383
   cranial bone, reconstruction ~ 21181-21184
   destruction
      chemosurgery ~ 17311-17315
      urethra ~ 53220
   ear, middle
      extended ~ 69554
      transcanal ~ 69550
      transmastoid ~ 69552
   elbow, excision ~ 24071-24079
   esophagus, ablation ~ 43229
   excision, femur ~ 27355-27358
   face or scalp
      excision ~ 21011-21014
      radical resection ~ 21015-21016
   facial bone ~ 21029-21030, 21034
   fallopian tube, resection ~ 58950, 58952-58958
   femoral ~ 27355-27358
   femur ~ 27065-27067
      excision ~ 27365
   fibroid ~ 58140, 58545-58546, 58561
   fibula ~ 27635-27638
      excision ~ 27646
   finger, excision ~ 26111-26118
   foot ~ 28039-28047
   forearm, radical resection ~ 25077
   gastrostomy ~ see lesion
   gums, excision ~ 41825-41827
   hand, excision ~ 26111-26118
   heart, excision ~ 33120-33130
   hip ~ 27043-27045, 27049, 27059, 27065-27067
      excision ~ 27075-27076
   humerus excision ~ 23150, 23220, 24110
      with allograft ~ 23156, 24116
      with autograft ~ 23155, 24115
   ileum ~ 27065-27067
   immunoassay for antigen ~ 86294, 86316
      CA 125 ~ 86304
      CA 15-3 ~ 86300
      CA 19-9 ~ 86301
   innominate, excision ~ 27077
   intestines, small, destruction ~ 44369
   ischial, excision ~ 27078
   kidney, excision ~ 50562, 52355
   knee, excision ~ 27327-27329, 27337-27339, 27365
   lacrimal gland, excision
      frontal approach ~ 68540
      with osteotomy ~ 68550
   larynx
      excision ~ 31300
         endoscopic ~ 31540-31541, 31578
      incision ~ 31300
   leg, lower ~ 27615-27619, 27632, 27634
   leg, upper, excision ~ 27327-27329, 27337-27339, 27365
   localization, nuclear medicine ~ 78800-78804
   mandible ~ 21044-21047
   maxilla ~ 21030, 21034, 21048-21049
   maxillary torus palatinus ~ 21032
   mediastinal, excision ~ 39220
   mediastinum ~ 32662
   meningioma ~ 61512
      excision ~ 61519
   metacarpal ~ 26200-26205, 26250
   metatarsal ~ 28104-28107
      excision ~ 28173
   neck
      excision ~ 21552-21558
      radical resection ~ 21557, 21558

Tumor ~ *continued*
olecranon, excision ~ 24120
olecranon process
   with allograft, excision ~ 24126
   with autograft, excision ~ 24125
ovary, resection ~ 58950-58958
pancreatic duct, destruction ~ 43272
parotid gland, excision ~ 42410-42426
pelvis ~ 27043-27045, 27049, 27059
pericardial
   endoscopic ~ 32661
   excision ~ 33050
peritoneum
   excision ~ 49203-49205
   debulking ~ 58575, 58950-58958
phalanges
   finger ~ 26210-26215, 26260-26262
   toe ~ 28108
     excision ~ 28175
pituitary gland, excision ~ 61546-61548, 62165
pleura, cryoablation ~ 32994
positron emission tomography (PET) ~ 78811-78816
pubis ~ 27065-27067
pulmonary ablation
   cryoablation ~ 32994
   radiofrequency ~ 32998
radiation therapy ~ 77295
radius ~ 25120-25126, 25170
   excision ~ 24120
   with allograft, excision ~ 24126
   with autograft, excision ~ 24125
rectum
   destruction ~ 45190, 45320, 46937-46938
   excision ~ 45160-45172
resection
   face ~ 21015
   scalp ~ 21015
   with cystourethroscopy ~ 52355
retroperitoneal, destruction/excision ~ 49203-49205, 58957, 58958
sacrum ~ 49215
scapula
   excision ~ 23140, 23210
     with allograft ~ 23146
     with autograft ~ 23145
shoulder, excision ~ 23071-23078
skull, excision ~ 61500
soft tissue
   elbow, excision ~ 24071-24079
   finger, excision ~ 26115
   forearm, radical resection ~ 25077
   hand, excision ~ 26115
   wrist
     excision ~ 25071-25078
     radical resection ~ 25077, 25078
spinal cord, excision ~ 63275-63290
stomach, excision ~ 43610-43611
talus ~ 28100-28103
   excision ~ 27647
tarsal ~ 28104-28107
   excision ~ 28171
temporal bone, removal ~ 69970
testis, excision ~ 54530-54535
thorax
   excision ~ 21552-21558
   radical resection ~ 21557, 21558
thyroid, excision ~ 60200
tibia ~ 27365, 27635-27638
   excision ~ 27645
torus mandibularis ~ 21031
trachea, excision
   cervical ~ 31785
   thoracic ~ 31786
ulna ~ 25120-25126, 25170
   excision ~ 24120
   with allograft, excision ~ 24126
   with autograft, excision ~ 24125
ureter, excision ~ 52355
urethra ~ 52234-52240, 53220
   excision ~ 52355

Tumor ~ *continued*
uterus
   excision ~ 58140-58146
   resection ~ 58950-58958
vagina, excision ~ 57135
vertebra, additional segment
   excision ~ 22116
   cervical, excision ~ 22100
   lumbar ~ 22102
   thoracic, excision ~ 22101
wrist ~ 25071-25078, 25135-25136
   radical resection ~ 25077
Tunica vaginalis hydrocele
aspiration ~ 55000
excision ~ 55040-55041
repair ~ 55060
Turbinate
excision ~ 30130-30140
fracture, therapeutic ~ 30930
injection ~ 30200
submucous resection, nose excision ~ 30140
Turbinate mucosa cauterization ~ 30801-30802
Turcica, sella ~ 70240, 70480-70482
TURP ~ 52630
Tylectomy ~ *see* breast, excision, lesion
Tylenol urine ~ 80329-80331
Tympanic membrane
create stoma ~ 69433-69436
incision ~ 69420-69421
Tympanic membrane ~ *continued*
reconstruction ~ 69620
repair ~ 69450, 69610
Tympanic nerve excision ~ 69676
Tympanolysis ~ 69450
Tympanomastoidectomy ~ see tympanoplasty
Tympanometry ~ see audiologic function tests ~ 92550, 92567, 92570
Tympanoplasty ~ 69620
radical or complete ~ 69645
   with ossicular chain reconstruction ~ 69646
with antrotomy or mastoidotomy ~ 69635
   with ossicular chain reconstruction ~ 69636
     and synthetic prosthesis ~ 69637
with mastoidectomy ~ 69641
   with intact or reconstructed wall ~ 69643
     and ossicular chain reconstruction ~ 69644
   with ossicular chain reconstruction ~ 69642
without mastoidectomy ~ 69631
   with ossicular chain reconstruction ~ 69632
     and synthetic prosthesis ~ 69633
Tympanostomy ~ 69433-69436
Tympanotomy ~ 69420-69421
Typhoid vaccine ~ 90690
oral ~ 90690
polysaccharide ~ 90691
Typhus
endemic ~ 86000
mite-bone ~ 86000
Sno Paulo ~ 86000
tropical ~ 86000
Typing, blood ~ see blood typing
Typing, HLA ~ 86812-86817
Typing, tissue ~ see tissue typing
Tyrosine ~ 84510
Tzank smear ~ 87207

U

Uchida Procedure ~ 58600
UDP galactose pyrophosphorylase ~ 82775-82776
UFR ~ 51736-51741
Ulcer
anal ~ 46200, 46940-46942
decubitus ~ see debridement; skin graft and flap ~ 15920-15999
pinch graft ~ 15050
pressure ~ 15920-15999
stomach, excision ~ 43610
Ulcerative, cystitis ~ 52260-52265

Ulna ~ see arm, lower; elbow; humerus; radius
  arthrodesis, radioulnar joint, with resection ~ 25830
  arthroplasty, with implant ~ 25442
  centralization or wrist ~ 25335
  craterization ~ 24147, 25150-25151
  cyst, excision ~ 24125-24126, 25120-25126
  diaphysectomy ~ 24147, 25150-25151
  excision ~ 24147
    abscess ~ 24138
    complete ~ 25240
    epiphyseal bar ~ 20150
    partial ~ 25145..2515, 1, 25240
  fracture
    closed treatment ~ 25530-25535
    olecranon ~ 24670-24675
      open treatment ~ 24685
    open treatment ~ 25545
    shaft ~ 25530-25545
      open treatment ~ 25574
    styloid
      closed treatment ~ 25650
      open treatment ~ 25652
      percutaneous fixation ~ 25651
    with dislocation
      closed treatment ~ 24620
      open treatment ~ 24635
    with manipulation ~ 25535
    with radius ~ 25560-25565
      open treatment ~ 25575
    without manipulation ~ 25530
  incision and drainage ~ 25035
  osteoplasty ~ 25390-25393
  prophylactic treatment ~ 25491-25492
  reconstruction, radioulnar ~ 25337
  repair
    epiphyseal arrest ~ 25450-25455
    malunion or nonunion ~ 25400, 25415
    osteotomy ~ 25360, 25370-25375
      and radius ~ 25365
    with graft ~ 25405, 25420-25426
  saucerization ~ 24147, 25150-25151
  sequestrectomy ~ 24138, 25145
  tumor
    cyst ~ 24120
    excision ~ 24125-24126, 25120-25126, 25170
Ulnar arteries ~ see artery, ulnar
Ulnar nerve
  decompression ~ 64718
  neuroplasty ~ 64718-64719
  reconstruction ~ 64718-64719
  release ~ 64718-64719
  repair/suture, motor ~ 64836
  transposition ~ 64718-64719
Ultrasonic ~ see ultrasound
Ultrasonic cardiography ~ see echocardiography
Ultrasonic procedure ~ 52325
Ultrasonography ~ see echography
Ultrasound ~ see echocardiography; echography
  abdomen ~ 76700-76706
  aortic aneurysm screening ~ 76706
  artery
    intracranial ~ 93886-93893
    middle cerebral ~ 76821
    umbilical ~ 76820
  bladder ~ 51798
  bone density study ~ 76977
  breast ~ 76641, 76642
  bronchi
    endobronchial ultrasound (EBUS)~ 31652-31654
  chest ~ 76604
  colon, endoscopic ~ 45391-45392
  colon-sigmoid, endoscopic ~ 45341-45342
  drainage, abscess ~ 75989
  echoencephalography ~ 76506
  esophagus, endoscopy ~ 43231-43232
  extremity(s) ~ 76881-76882
  eye ~ 76510-76513
    biometry ~ 76516-76519
    foreign body ~ 76529
    pachymetry ~ 76514

Ultrasound ~ *continued*
  fetus ~ 76818-76828
  follow-up ~ 76970
  for physical therapy ~ 97035
  gastrointestinal ~ 76975
  gastrointestinal, upper, endoscopic ~ 43237-43238, 43242, 43259
  guidance
    amniocentesis ~ 59001, 76946
    amnioinfusion ~ 59070
    arteriovenous fistulae ~ 76936
    chorionic villus sampling ~ 76945
    cryosurgery ~ 55873
    drainage, fetal fluid ~ 59074
    endometrial ablation ~ 58356
    fetal cordocentesis ~ 76941
    fetal transfusion ~ 76941
    heart biopsy ~ 76932
    needle biopsy ~ 43232, 43238, 43242, 45342, 45392, 76942
    occlusion, umbilical cord ~ 59072
    ova retrieval ~ 76948
    pericardiocentesis ~ 76930
    pseudoaneurysm ~ 76936
    radiation therapy ~ 77387
    radioelement ~ 76965
    shunt placement, fetal ~ 59076
    thoracentesis ~ 76942
    tissue ablation ~ 76490
    uterine fibroid ablation ~ 58674
    vascular access ~ 76937
  head ~ 76506, 76536
  heart, fetal ~ 76825
  hips, infant ~ 76885-76886
  hysteronsonography ~ 76831
  intraoperative ~ 76998
  intravascular, noncoronary ~ 37252, 37253
  kidney ~ 76770-76776
  liver, elastography, shear wave ~ 91200
  MRI-guided high intensity focused ultrasound (MRgFUS) ~ 0398T
    stereotactic lesion ablation ~ 0398T
  neck ~ 76536
  non-coronary, intravascular ~ 37252, 37253
  pelvis ~ 76856-76857
  pregnant uterus ~ 76801-76817
  prostate ~ 76873
  rectal ~ 76872-76873
  retroperitoneal ~ 76770-76775
  scrotum ~ 76870
  sonohysterography ~ 76831
  spine ~ 76800
  stimulation to aid bone healing ~ 20979
  umbilical artery ~ 76820
  unlisted services and procedures ~ 76999
  uterus, tumor ablation ~ 0071T-0072T
  vagina ~ 76830
Ultraviolet light therapy dermatology
  ultraviolet A ~ 96912
  ultraviolet B ~ 96910
  for dermatology ~ 96900
  for physical medicine ~ 97028
Umbilectomy ~ 49250
Umbilical
  artery ultrasound ~ 76820
  hernia ~ 49600-49611
  vein catheterization ~ 36510
Umbilical cord occlusion ~ 59072
Umbilicus
  excision ~ 49250
  repair
    hernia ~ 49580-49587
    omphalocele ~ 49600-49611
Undescended testicle ~ 54550-54560
Unfertilized egg ~ 87177
Unguis ~ see nails
Unilateral simple mastectomy ~ see mastectomy
Unlisted services and procedures ~ 99499, 99600
  abdomen ~ 22999, 49329, 49999
  allergy/immunology ~ 95199
  anal ~ 46999
  anesthesia ~ 01999
  arm ~ 25999

Unlisted services and procedures ~ *continued*

arthroscopy ~ 29999
autopsy ~ 88099
bile duct ~ 47999
brachytherapy ~ 77799
breast ~ 19499
bronchi ~ 31899
cardiac ~ 33999
cardiovascular studies ~ 93799
casting ~ 29799
cervix ~ 58999
chemistry procedure ~ 84999
chemotherapy ~ 96549
chest ~ 32999
coagulation ~ 85999
colon ~ 44799
conjunctiva surgery ~ 68399
craniofacial ~ 21299
CT scan ~ 76497
cytogenetic study ~ 88299
cytopathology ~ 88199
pdermatology ~ 96999
dialysis ~ 90999
diaphragm ~ 39599
ear, external ~ 69399
   inner ~ 69949
   middle ~ 69799
endocrine system ~ 60699
epididymis ~ 55899
esophagus ~ 43289, 43499
evaluation and management services ~ 99499
eye muscle ~ 67399
eye surgery
   anterior segment ~ 66999
   posterior segment ~ 67299
eyelid ~ 67999
fluoroscopy ~ 76496
forearm ~ 25999
gallbladder ~ 47999
gastroenterology test ~ 91299
gum ~ 41899
hand ~ 26989
hemic system ~ 38999
hepatic duct ~ 47999
hip joint ~ 27299
home services ~ 99600
hysteroscopy ~ 58579
immunization ~ 90749
immunology ~ 86849
injection ~ 90799
injection of medication ~ 90799
intestine ~ 44238, 44799
kidney ~ 53899
lacrimal system ~ 68899
laparoscopy ~ 38129, 38589, 43289, 43659, 44238-44239, 44979, 47379, 47579, 49329, 49659, 50549, 50949, 54699, 55559, 58578, 58679, 59898, 60659
larynx ~ 31599
lip ~ 40799
liver ~ 47379, 47399
lungs ~ 32999
lymphatic system ~ 38999
magnetic resonance ~ 76498
maxillofacial ~ 21299
maxillofacial prosthetics ~ 21089
Meckel's diverticulum ~ 44899
mediastinum ~ 39499
mesentery surgery ~ 44899
microbiology ~ 87999
mouth ~ 40899, 41599
musculoskeletal ~ 25999, 26989
musculoskeletal surgery, abdominal wall ~ 22999
   neck ~ 21899
   spine ~ 22899
   thorax ~ 21899
musculoskeletal system ~ 20999
   ankle ~ 27899
   arm, upper ~ 24999
   elbow ~ 24999
   head ~ 21499

Unlisted services and procedures ~ *continued*

   knee ~ 27599
   leg, lower ~ 27899
   leg, upper ~ 27599
necropsy ~ 88099
nervous system surgery ~ 64999
neurology/neuromuscular testing ~ 95999
nose ~ 30999
nuclear medicine ~ 78999
   blood ~ 78199
   bone ~ 78399
   endocrine system ~ 78099
   genitourinary system ~ 78799
   heart ~ 78499
   hematopoietic system ~ 78199
   lymphatic system ~ 78199
   musculoskeletal system ~ 78399
   nervous system ~ 78699
   therapeutic ~ 79999
obstetrical care ~ 59898-59899
omentum ~ 49329, 49999
ophthalmology ~ 92499
orbit ~ 67599
otorhinolaryngology ~ 92700
ovary ~ 58679, 58999
oviduct ~ 58679, 58999
palate ~ 42299
pancreas surgery ~ 48999
pathology ~ 89240
pelvis ~ 27299
penis ~ 55899
peritoneum ~ 49329, 49999
pharynx ~ 42999
physical therapy ~ 97039, 97139, 97799
pleura ~ 32999
pressure ulcer ~ 15999
preventive medicine ~ 99429
prostate ~ 55899
psychiatric ~ 90899
pulmonology ~ 94799
radiation physics ~ 77399
radiation therapy ~ 77499
   planning ~ 77299
radiology, diagnostic ~ 76499
radionuclide therapy ~ 79999
radiopharmaceutical therapy ~ 79999
rectum ~ 44239, 45999
reproductive medicine, lab procedure ~ 89398
salivary gland ~ 42699
scrotum ~ 55899
seminal vesicle ~ 55899
shoulder surgery ~ 23929
sinuses ~ 31299
skin ~ 17999
special services and reports ~ 99199
spine ~ 22899
stomach ~ 43659, 43999
strapping ~ 29799
surgical pathology ~ 88399
temporal bone ~ 69979
testis ~ 54699, 55899
throat ~ 42999
tongue ~ 41599
tonsil/adenoid ~ 42999
trachea ~ 31899
transfusion ~ 86999
ultrasound ~ 76999
ureter ~ 50949
urinary system ~ 53899
uterus ~ 58578-58579, 58999
uvula ~ 42299
vagina ~ 58999
vas deferens ~ 55899
vascular ~ 37799
vascular endoscopy ~ 37501
vascular injection ~ 36299
vascular studies ~ 93799
wrist ~ 25999

Unna paste boot ~ 29580
removal ~ 29700

UPP ~ 51727, 51729

Upper
  digestive system endoscopy ~ see endoscopy, gastrointestinal, upper
  extremity ~ see arm, upper; elbow; humerus
  gastrointestinal bleeding ~ 43255
  gastrointestinal endoscopy, biopsy ~ 43239
    planning ~ 43239
  GI tract ~ 43249
Urachal cyst ~ 51500
Urea breath test ~ 78267-78268, 83014
Urea nitrogen ~ 84520-84525
  clearance ~ 84545
  quantitative ~ 84520
  semiquantitative ~ 84525
  urine ~ 84540
Urea nitrogen, blood ~ 84520-84525
Urecholine supersensitivity test ~ 51725-51726
Ureter
  anastomosis
    to bladder ~ 50780-50785
    to colon ~ 50810-50815
    to intestine ~ 50800, 50820-50825
    to kidney ~ 50740-50750
    to ureter ~ 50760-50770
  biopsy
    endoluminal, non-endoscopic ~ 50606
    endoscopic ~ 50955, 50957, 50974, 50976, 52007
  catheterization ~ 52005
    construction ~ 50840
    via kidney ~ 50693
  continent diversion ~ 50825
  creation, stoma ~ 50860
  destruction
    endoscopic ~ 50957, 50976
  dilation ~ 52341-52342, 52344-52345
    balloon ~ 50706
    endoscopic ~ 50553, 50572, 50953, 50972
  drainage ~ 50600
  embolization ~ 50705
  endoscopy
    biopsy ~ 50955-50957, 50974-50976, 52007, 52354
    catheterization ~ 50953, 50972, 52005
    destruction ~ 50957, 50976, 52354
    dilation ~ 52341-52342, 52344-52345
    excision, tumor ~ 52355
    exploration ~ 52351
    injection of implant material ~ 52327
    insertion, stent ~ 50947, 52332-52334
    lithotripsy ~ 52353
    tmanipulation of ureteral calculus ~ 52330
    removal
      calculus ~ 50961, 50980, 52320-52325, 52352
      foreign body ~ 50961, 50980
    resection ~ 52355
    via incision ~ 50970-50980
    via stoma ~ 50951-50961
  exploration ~ 50600
  incision and drainage ~ 50600
  injection
    drugs ~ 50391
    radiologic ~ 50430, 50431, 50684, 50690
  insertion
    stent ~ 50688, 50693, 50695, 50947, 52332
    tube ~ 50688
  instillation, drugs ~ 50391
  lesion, destruction ~ 52354
  lithotripsy ~ 52353
  lysis, adhesions ~ 50715-50725
  manometric studies, pressure ~ 50686
  meatotomy ~ 52290
  nuclear medicine, reflux study ~ 78740
  occlusion ~ 50705
  postcaval ~ 50725
  reconstruction ~ 50700
    with intestines ~ 50840
  reflux study ~ 78740
  reimplantation ~ 51565
  removal
    anastomosis ~ 50830
    calculus ~ 50610-50630, 50961, 51060-51065, 52320-52325
    foreign body ~ 50961
    stent ~ 50382-50387

Ureter ~ *continued*
  repair ~ 50900
    anastomosis ~ 50740-50825
    continent diversion ~ 50825
    deligation ~ 50940
    fistula ~ 50920-50930
    lysis adhesions ~ 50715-50725
    ureterocele ~ 51535
      ectopic ~ 52301
      orthotopic ~ 52300
    urinary undiversion ~ 50830
  replacement
    stent ~ 50382, 50387
    with intestines ~ 50840
  resection ~ 52355
  revision, anastomosis ~ 50727-50728
  stent
    change ~ 50688
    insertion ~ 50688
    placement
      with nephrostogram ~ 50693-50695
      with ureterogram ~ 50693-50695
  suture ~ 50900
    deligation ~ 50940
    fistula ~ 50920-50930
  tube
    change ~ 50688
    insertion ~ 50688
  tumor resection ~ 52355
  unlisted services and procedures ~ 50949, 53899
  X-ray with contrast
    guide dilation ~ 74485
Ureteral
  catheterization ~ see catheterization, ureter
  guide wire insertion ~ 52334
  meatotomy ~ 52290
  splinting ~ 50400-50405
  stent insertion ~ 52332
Ureterectomy ~ 50650-50660
  partial ~ 50220, 50546
  total ~ 50548
Ureterocalycostomy ~ 50750
Ureterocele
  excision ~ 51535
  fulguration
    ectopic ~ 52301
    orthotopic ~ 52300
  incision ~ 51535
  repair ~ 51535
  resection, ectopic ~ 52301
    orthotopic ~ 52300
Ureterocolon conduit ~ 50815
Ureteroenterostomy ~ 50800
  revision ~ 50830
Ureterography
  injection procedure ~ 50430, 50431, 50684
  with catheter conversion, nephrostomy to nephroureteral ~ 50434
  with nephrostomy catheter exchange ~ 50435
  with pacemement of ureteral stent ~ 50693-50695
Ureteroileal conduit ~ 50820
  cystectomy ~ 51590
  removal ~ 50830
Ureterolithotomy ~ 50610-50630
  laparoscopy ~ 50945
  transvesical ~ 51060
Ureterolysis
  for ovarian vein syndrome ~ 50722
  for retrocaval ureter ~ 50725
  for retroperitoneal fibrosis ~ 50715
Ureteroneocystostomy ~ 50780-50785, 50830, 51565
  laparoscopic ~ 50947-50948
Ureteroplasty ~ 50700
Ureteropyelography ~ 50951, 52005
  injection procedure ~ 50684, 50690
Ureteropyelostomy ~ 50740
Ureteroscopy
  dilation
    intra-renal stricture ~ 52346
    ureter ~ 52344-52345

Ureteroscopy ~ *continued*
  third stage with cystourethroscopy ~ 52351
    biopsy ~ 52354
    destruction ~ 52354
    lithotripsy ~ 52353
    removal, calculus ~ 52352
    tumor excision ~ 52355
Ureterosigmoidostomy ~ 50810
  revision ~ 50830
Ureterostomy ~ 50860, 50951
  injection procedure ~ 50684
  manometric studies ~ 50686
Ureterostomy tube change ~ 50688
Ureterotomy ~ 50600
  insertion indwelling stent ~ 50605
Ureteroureterostomy ~ 50760-50770, 50830
Urethra
  abscess, incision and drainage ~ 53040
  adhesions, lysis ~ 53500
  artificial sphincter, repair ~ 53449
  biopsy ~ 52204, 53200
  cystourethroscopy ~ 52204-52315
  destruction ~ 52214-52224
  dilation ~ 52260-52265, 53600-53621
    general ~ 53665
    suppository and/or instillation ~ 53660-53661
  diverticulum ~ 53240
  drainage, extravasation ~ 53080-53085
  endoscopy ~ 52000
    biopsy ~ 52204, 52354
    catheterization ~ 52010
    destruction ~ 52354, 52400
    evacuation, clot ~ 52001
    excision, tumor ~ 52355
    exploration ~ 52351
    incision, ejaculatory duct ~ 52402
    injection of implant material ~ 51715
    lithotripsy ~ 52353
    removal, calculus ~ 52352
    resection, ejaculatory duct ~ 52402
    vasectomy ~ 52402
    vasotomy ~ 52402
  excision
    diverticulum ~ 53230-53235
    total
      female ~ 53210
      male ~ 53215
  incision ~ 53000-53010
    meatus ~ 53020-53025
  incision and drainage ~ 53060
  insertion, stent ~ 52282, 53855
  lesion
    destruction ~ 53265
    excision ~ 53260
  paraurethral gland, incision and drainage ~ 53060
  polyp
    destruction ~ 53260
    excision ~ 53260
  pressure profile ~ 51727, 51729
  prolapse
    destruction ~ 53275
    excision ~ 53275
    repair ~ 53275
  proximal, micro-remodeling ~ 53860
  radiotracer ~ 52250
  reconstruction ~ 53410-53440, 53445
    and bladder ~ 51800-51820
    complications ~ 54340-54348
    hypospadias
      one stage ~ 54322-54328
      second stage ~ 54308-54316
      third stage ~ 54318
    meatus ~ 53450-53460
  removal
    calculus ~ 52310-52315
    foreign body ~ 52310-52315
    sling ~ 53442
    urethral stent ~ 52310-52315

Urethra ~ *continued*
  repair
    diverticulum ~ 53240, 53400-53405
    fistula ~ 45820-45825, 53400-53405, 53520
    sphincter ~ 57220
    stricture ~ 53400-53405
    urethrocele ~ 57230
    with replantation of penis ~ 54438
    wound ~ 53502-53515
  Skene's gland, incision and drainage ~ 53060
  sphincter ~ 52277
    electromyography ~ 51784-51785
      needle ~ 51785
    insertion, prosthesis ~ 53444
    reconstruction ~ 53445
    removal, prosthesis ~ 53446-53447
    repair, prosthesis ~ 53449
    replacement, prosthesis ~ 53448
  stent
    insertion
      premanent ~ 52282
      temporary ~ 53855
  suture
    fistula ~ 45820-45825, 53520
    to bladder ~ 51840-51841
    wound ~ 53502-53515
  tumor
    destruction ~ 53220
    excision ~ 53220
  unlisted services and procedures ~ 53899
  urethrocystography ~ 74450-74455
  urethrotomy ~ 52270-52276
  X-ray with contrast ~ 74450-74455
Urethral
  diverticulum
    marsupialization ~ 53240
    meatus, dorsal ~ see epispadias
  sphincter
    biofeedback training ~ 90911
    insertion, prosthesis ~ 53444
    removal, prosthesis ~ 53446-53447
    replacement, prosthesis ~ 53448
  stenosis, dilation ~ 52281
  stent
    insertion ~ 0084T, 52282
    removal
      bladder ~ 52310-52315
      urethra ~ 52310-52315
  stricture
    dilation ~ 52281, 53600-53621
    injection, steroids ~ 52283
  syndrome, cystourethroscopy ~ 52285
Urethrectomy total
  female ~ 53210
  male ~ 53215
Urethrocele ~ 53275
Urethrocystography ~ 74450-74455
  contrast and/or chain ~ 51605
  retrograde ~ 51610
  voiding ~ 51600
Urethrocystopexy ~ 51840-51841
Urethromeatoplasty ~ 53450-53460
Urethropexy ~ 51840-51841
Urethroplasty ~ 46744-46746
  first stage ~ 53400
  one stage, hypospadias ~ 54322-54328
  reconstruction
    female urethra ~ 53430
    male anterior urethra ~ 53410
    prostatic/membranous urethra
      first stage ~ 53420
      one stage ~ 53415
      second stage ~ 53425
  second stage ~ 53405
    hypospadias ~ 54308-54316
  third stage, hypospadias ~ 54318
Urethrorrhaphy ~ 53502-53515
Urethroscopy ~ 52000
Urethrostomy ~ 53000-53010

Urethrotomy ~ 53000-53010
  direct vision, with cystourethroscopy ~ 52276
  internal ~ 52601, 52647-52648
  with cystourethroscopy
    female ~ 52270
    male ~ 52275
Uric acid
  blood ~ 84550
  other source ~ 84560
  urine ~ 84560
Uridyltransferase
  galactose-1-phosphate ~ 82775-82776
  galactosephosphate ~ 82775-82776
Urinalysis ~ 81000-81099
  automated ~ 81001, 81003
  glass test ~ 81020
  microalbumin ~ 82043-82044
  microscopic ~ 81015
  pregnancy test ~ 81025
  qualitative ~ 81005
  routine ~ 81002
  screen ~ 81007
  semiquantitative ~ 81005
  unlisted services and procedures ~ 81099
  volume measurement ~ 81050
  without microscopy ~ 81002
Urinary bladder ~ see bladder
Urinary catheter irrigation ~ 62194, 62225
Urinary sphincter, artificial ~ 53444-53449
Urinary system, surgical procedures ~ 50010-53899
Urinary tract X-ray w contrast ~ 74400-74425
Urine
  albumin ~ 82042-82044
  blood ~ 83491
  colony count ~ 87086
  pregnancy test ~ 81025
  tests ~ 81001
Urobilinogen
  feces ~ 84577
  urine ~ 84578-84583
Urodynamic tests
  bladder capacity, ultrasound ~ 51798
  cystometrogram ~ 51725-51729
  electromyography studies, needle ~ 51785
  residual urine, ultrasound ~ 51798
  stimulus evoked response ~ 51792
  urethra pressure profile ~ 51727, 51729
  uroflowmetry ~ 51736-51741
  voiding pressure studies
    bladder ~ 51728, 51729
    intra-abdominal ~ 51797
Uroflowmetry ~ 51736-51741
Urography
  antegrade ~ 74425
  infusion ~ 74410-74415
  intravenous ~ 74400-74415
  retrograde ~ 74420
Uroporphyrin ~ 84120
Urothromboplastin ~ see thromboplastin
Uterine
  adhesion ~ 58559
  cervix ~ see cervix
  endoscopies ~ see endoscopy, uterus
  haemorrhage ~ 59160
Uterus
  ablation
    endometrium ~ 58353-58356
    fibroid
      laparoscopic ~ 58674
      radiofrequency ~ 0404T
    tumor, ultrasound, focused ~ 0071T-0072T
  biopsy
    endometrium ~ 58100-58110
    endoscopic ~ 58558
  catheterization, X-ray ~ 58340
  chromotubation ~ 58350
  curettage ~ 58356
    postpartum ~ 59160
  dilation and curettage ~ 58120
    postpartum ~ 59160

Uterus ~ *continued*
  ectopic pregnancy
    interstitial
      partial resection uterus ~ 59136
      total hysterectomy ~ 59135
  endoscopy
    endometrial ablation ~ 58563
    exploration ~ 58555
    surgery ~ 58558-58565
    treatment ~ 58558-58565
  excision
    laparoscopic ~ 58541-58544, 58550
      with removal of ovaries ~ 58262-58263, 58291-58293, 58552, 58554, 58575
      total ~ 58570-58573, 58575
    partial ~ 58180
    radical
      laparoscopic ~ 58548
      open ~ 58210, 58285
    removal of tubes and/or ovaries ~ 58262-58263, 58291-58293, 58552, 58554
    total ~ 58150-58152, 58200, 58570-58573, 58575, 58953-58956
    vaginal ~ 58260-58270, 58290-58294, 58550-58554
      with colpectomy ~ 58275-58280
      with colpo-urethrocystopexy ~ 58267
      with repair of enterocele ~ 58270, 58294
  hemorrhage, postpartum ~ 59160
  hydatidiform mole, excision ~ 59100
  hydrotubation ~ 58350
  hysterosalpingography ~ 74740
  incision, removal lesion ~ 59100
  insertion
    Heyman capsule, for brachytherapy ~ 58346
    intrauterine device (IUD) ~ 58300
    tandem, for brachytherapy ~ 57155
  laparoscopy ~ 58570-58578
  lesion, excision ~ 58545-58546, 59100
  reconstruction ~ 58540
  removal, intrauterine device (IUD) ~ 58301
  repair
    fistula ~ 51920-51925
    rupture ~ 58520, 59350
    suspension ~ 58400
      with presacral sympathectomy ~ 58410
  sonohysterography ~ 76831
  suture, rupture ~ 59350
  tumor
    ablation, ultrasound, focused ~ 0071T-0072T
    excision
      abdominal approach ~ 58140, 58146
      vaginal approach ~ 58145
  unlisted services and procedures ~ 58578, 58999
  X-ray with contrast ~ 74740
UTP hexose 1 phosphate uridylyltransferase ~ 82775-82776
UV light therapy ~ 96900
Uvula
  abscess, incision and drainage ~ 42000
  biopsy ~ 42100
  excision ~ 42140-42145
  lesion
    destruction ~ 42145
    excision ~ 42104-42107
  unlisted services and procedures ~ 42299
Uvulectomy ~ 42140

V

V flap procedure one stage distal hypospadias repair ~ 54322
V, cranial nerve ~ see trigeminal nerve
V-Y operation, bladder, neck ~ 51845
V-Y plasty ~ 14000-14350
Vaccination ~ see allergen immunotherapy; immunization; vaccines
Vaccines and toxoids
  adenovirus ~ 90476-90477
  anthrax ~ 90581
  chicken pox ~ 90716
  cholera, live, for oral use ~ 90625

Vaccines and toxoids ~ *continued*

dengue vaccine ~ 90587
diphtheria and tetanus toxoids (DT) ~ 90702
diphtheria, tetanus, acellular pertussis (DtaP) (Tdap) ~ 90700, 90715
diphtheria, tetanus toxoids, acellular pertussis, haemophilus influenza ype
    b and inactivated poliovirus (DTaP-IPV/Hib) ~ 90698
diphtheria, tetanus, acellular pertussis, and inactivated poliovirus
    (DTaP-IPV) ~ 90696
diphtheria, tetanus, acellular pertussis, hepatitis B, and inactivated
    poliovirus (DTaP-HepB-IPV) ~ 90723
diphtheria, tetanus toxoids, acellular pertussis, inactivated poliovirus,
    haemophilus influenzae type b PRP-OMP conjugate, and hepatitis b
    (DTaP-IPV-Hib-HepB) ~ 90697
encephalitis, Japanese ~ 90738
haemophilus influenza B (Hib) ~ 90647, 90648
   and meningococcal conjugate, serogroups C and Y (Hib-MenCY) ~
    90644
hepatitis A (HepA) ~ 90632-90634
hepatitis A and hepatitis B (HepA-HepB) ~ 90636
hepatitis B (HepB) ~ 90739-90747
hepatitis B and hemophilus influenza B (HepB-HIB) ~ 90748
human papilloma virus (HPV) ~ 90649, 90650
influenza
   antibiotic free ~ 90756
   cell cultured ~ 90661, 90674, 90756
   DNA derived (RIV3) ~ 90673
   enhanced immunogenicity (IIV) ~ 90662
   for intradermal use ~ 90630, 90654
   for intramuscular use ~ 90653, 90655-90658, 90661, 90662,
    90666-90668, 90673, 90674, 90685-90688, 90756
   for intranasal use ~ 90660, 90664, 90672
   inactivated ~ 90653
   pandemic ~ 90664, 90666-90668
   preservative free ~ 90630, 90654, 90655, 90656, 90661, 90662, 90666,
    90673, 90674, 90685, 90686, 90756
   quadrivalent
    ccIIV3 ~ 90661
    ccIIV4 ~ 90674, 90756
    IIV4 ~ 90630, 90685-90688
    LAIV4 ~ 90672
    RIV4 ~ 90682
   trivalent, DNA derived (RIV3) ~ 90673
   trivalent, live virus (LAIV3) ~ 90660
   trivalent, split virus (IIV3) ~ 90654-90658, 90660, 90673
measles, mumps and rubella (MMR) ~ 90707
measles, mumps and rubella and varicella (MMRV) ~ 90710
meningococcus
   meningococcal conjugate, serogroups A,C,Y,W-135 (MenACWY) ~
    90734
   meningococcal conjugate, serogroups C and Y, haemophilus influenza b
    (Hib-MenCY) ~ 90644
   meningococcal polysaccharide quadrivalent (MPSV4) ~ 90733
   meningococcal, serogroup B (MenB) ~ 90620, 90621
pneumococcal
   13-valent ~ 90670
   polysaccharide 23-valent ~ 90732
poliovirus, inactivate ~ 90713
rabies ~ 90675-90676
rotavirus ~ 90680, 90681
tetanus and diphtheria toxoids (Td) ~ 90714
tetanus, diphtheria, and acellular pertussis (TdaP) ~ 90715
tuberculosis (BCG) ~ 90585-90586
typhoid ~ 90690
unlisted vaccine/toxoid ~ 90749
varicella (chicken pox) ~ 90716
yellow fever ~ 90717
zoster (shingles) (HZV) ~ 90736, 90750

Vagina

abscess, incision and drainage ~ 57010
amines test ~ 82120
biopsy
   colposcopy ~ 57421
   endocervical ~ 57454
   extensive ~ 57105
   simple ~ 57100
closure ~ 57120
colposcopy ~ 57420-57421, 57455-57456, 57461
construction
   without graft ~ 57291
   with graft ~ 57292

Vagina ~ *continued*

cyst, excision ~ 57135
dilation ~ 57400
endocervical
   biopsy ~ 57454
   exploration ~ 57452
excision
   closure ~ 57120
   complete
    with removal of paravaginal tissue ~ 57111
    with removal of paravaginal tissue with lymphadenectomy ~ 57112
    with removal of vaginal wall ~ 57110
   partial
    with removal of paravaginal tissue ~ 57107
    with removal of paravaginal tissue with lymphadenectomy ~ 57109
    with removal of vaginal wall ~ 57106
   total ~ 57110
   with hysterectomy ~ 58275-58280
   with repair of enterocele ~ 58280
exploration
   endocervical ~ 57452
   incision ~ 57000
hematoma, incision and drainage ~ 57022-57023
hemorrhage ~ 57180
hysterectomy ~ 58290, 58550-58554
incision and drainage ~ 57020
insertion
   ovoid, for brachytherapy ~ 57155
   packing for bleeding ~ 57180
   pessary ~ 57160
   radiation afterloading appliance ~ 57156
   sensor, fetal oximetry ~ 0021T
irrigation ~ 57150
lesion
   destruction ~ 57061-57065
   extensive ~ 57065
   simple ~ 57061
prolapse, sacrospinous ligament fixation ~ 57282
removal
   foreign body ~ 57415
   prosthetic graft ~ 57295-57296, 57426
   sling, stress incontinence ~ 57287
repair ~ 56800
   cystocele ~ 57240, 57260
    combined anteroposterior ~ 57260-57265
    posterior ~ 57240
   enterocele ~ 57265
   fistula ~ 51900
    rectovaginal ~ 57300-57308
    transvesical and vaginal approach ~ 57330
    urethrovaginal ~ 57310-57311
    vesicovaginal ~ 51900, 57320-57330
   hysterectomy ~ 58267, 58293
   incontinence ~ 57284, 57288
   obstetric ~ 59300
   paravaginal defect ~ 57284-57285, 57423
   Pereyra Procedure ~ 57289
   prolapse ~ 57282-57284, 57423
   prosthesis insertion ~ 57267
   rectocele
    combined anteroposterior ~ 57260-57265
    posterior ~ 57250
   suspension ~ 57280-57283
    laparoscopic ~ 57425
   urethral sphincter ~ 57220
   wound ~ 57200-57210
    colpoperineorrhaphy ~ 57210
    colporrhaphy ~ 57200
revision
   prosthetic graft ~ 57295-57296, 57426
   sling, stress incontinence ~ 57287
septum, excision ~ 57130
suspension ~ 57280-57283
   laparoscopic ~ 57425
suture
   cystocele ~ 57240, 57260
   enterocele ~ 57265
   fistula ~ 51900, 57300-57330
   rectocele ~ 57250-57260
   wound ~ 57200-57210

Vagina ~ *continued*
  tumor, excision ~ 57135
  ultrasound ~ 76830
  unlisted services and procedures ~ 58999
  X-ray with contrast ~ 74775
Vaginal delivery ~ 59400, 59610-59614
  after previous cesarean delivery ~ 59610-59612
    attempted ~ 59618-59622
  antepartum care ~ 59400
  cesarean delivery after attempted ~ 59618
    delivery only ~ 59620
    postpartum care ~ 59622
  delivery after previous, vaginal delivery only, postpartum care ~ 59614
  delivery only ~ 59409
  external cephalic version ~ 59412
  placenta ~ 59414
  postpartum care ~ 59410
  routine care ~ 59400
Vaginal hysterectomy ~ 58552-58554
Vaginal smear ~ 88141-88155, 88164-88167, 88174-88175
Vaginal suppositories
  induced abortion ~ 59855
    with dilation and curettage ~ 59856
    with hysterectomy ~ 59857
Vaginectomy ~ see colpectomy
Vaginoplasty intersex state ~ 57335
Vaginorrhaphy ~ see colporrhaphy
Vaginoscopy
  biopsy ~ 57454
  exploration ~ 57452
Vaginotomy ~ see colpotomy
Vagotomy
  abdominal ~ 64760
  highly selective ~ 43641
  parietal cell ~ 43641, 64755
  selective ~ 43640
  truncal ~ 43640
  with gastroduodenostomy revision, reconstruction ~ 43855
  with gastrojejunostomy revision, reconstruction ~ 43865
  with partial distal gastrectomy ~ 43635
Vagus nerve
  avulsion
    abdominal ~ 64760
    selective ~ 64755
  incision ~ 43640-43641
    abdominal ~ 64760
    implantation ~ 64568
    selective ~ 64755
  injection, anesthetic ~ 64408
  removal, neurostimulator ~ 64570
  revision or replacement ~ 64569
  transection ~ 43640-43641
    abdominal ~ 64760
    selective ~ 43652, 64755
    truncal ~ 43651
Valentine's test ~ 81020
Valproic acid ~ 80164
Valproic acid measurement ~ 80164
Valsalva sinus ~ 33702-33722
Valva atrioventricularis sinistra (valva mitralis) ~ see mitral valve
Valve
  aortic ~ 33405-33414
  bicuspid ~ see mitral valve
  mitral ~ see mitral valve
  pulmonary ~ 33470-33475
  tricuspid ~ 33460, 33463-33465, 33468
Valve stenoses, aortic ~ 33415, 33417
Valvectomy tricuspid valve ~ 33460
Valvotomy
  mitral valve ~ 33420-33422
  pulmonary valve ~ 33470-33474
  reoperation ~ 33530
Valvuloplasty
  aortic valve ~ 33390, 33391
  femoral vein ~ 34501
  mitral valve ~ 33425-33427
  percutaneous balloon
    aortic valve ~ 92986
    mitral valve ~ 92987
    pulmonary valve ~ 92990

Valvuloplasty ~ *continued*
  prosthetic valve ~ 33496
  reoperation ~ 33530
  tricuspid valve ~ 33463-33465
Van Deen test ~ 82270, 82272
Van Den Bergh test ~ 82247-82248
Vancomycin assay ~ 80202
Vanillylmandelic acid urine ~ 84585
Vanilmandelic acid ~ 84585
Varicella (chicken pox) ~ 90716
Varicella-zoster
  antibody ~ 86787
  antigen detection, direct fluorescence ~ 87290
Varices esophageal ~ 43205, 43400-43401
Varicocele spermatic cord, excision ~ 55530-55540
Varicose vein
  ablation
    chemical adhesive ~ 36482, 36483
    laser ~ 36478, 36479
    mechanochemical ~ 36473, 36474
    radiofrequency ~ 36475, 36476
  removal ~ 37765-37785
  secondary varicosity ~ 37785
  with tissue excision ~ 37735-37761
Vas deferens
  anastomosis
    to epididymis ~ 54900, 54901
  excision ~ 55250
  incision ~ 55200
    for X-ray ~ 55300
  repair, suture ~ 55400
  unlisted services and procedures ~ 55899
  vasography ~ 74440
  X-ray with contrast ~ 74440
Vascular flow check, graft ~ 15860
Vascular injection unlisted services and procedures ~ 36299
Vascular lesion
  cranial, excision ~ 61600-61608, 61615-61616
  cutaneous, destruction ~ 17106-17108
Vascular malformation
  cerebral
    obliteration ~ 61613
    repair ~ 61680, 61682, 61684, 61686, 61690, 61692, 61705, 61708, 61710
  finger, excision ~ 26111-26116
  hand, excision ~ 26111-26116
  spine, occlusion ~ 62294, 63250-63252
Vascular procedure(s)
  angioscopy, non-coronary vessels ~ 35400
  brachytherapy, intracoronary artery ~ 92974
  embolization ~ 37241-37244
  endoscopy, surgical ~ 37500
  harvest, lower extremity vein ~ 35572
  intravascular ultrasound
    coronary vessels ~ 92978-92979
    non-coronary vessels ~ 37252, 37253
  ligation, vena cava ~ 37619
  occlusion ~ 37241-37244
  stent, intracoronary ~ 92928-92929
  thrombolysis
    cerebral ~ 37195
    coronary vessels ~ 92975-92977
    intracranial ~ 61645
    noncoronary ~ 37211-37214
Vascular rehabilitation ~ 93668
Vascular studies ~ see Doppler scan, Duplex, Plethysmography
  angioscopy, non-coronary vessels ~ 35400
  aorta ~ 93978-93979
  arterial studies (non-invasive)
    extracranial ~ 93880-93882
    extremities ~ 93922-93924
    intracranial ~ 93886-93890
    lower extremity ~ 93925-93926
    middle cerebral artery, fetal ~ 76821
    umbilical artery, fetal ~ 76820
  artery studies, upper extremity ~ 93930-93931
  bioimpedance cardiovascular analysis ~ 93701
  blood pressure monitoring, 24 hour ~ 93784-93790
  cardiac catheterization, imaging ~ 93452-93461
  hemodialysis access ~ 93990

Vascular studies ~ *continued*
  kidney
    multiple study, with pharmacological intervention ~ 78709
    single study, with pharmacological intervention ~ 78708
  penile vessels ~ 93980-93981
  spectroscopy, catheter based ~ 0205T
  temperature gradient ~ 93740
  unlisted services and procedures ~ 93799
  venous studies
    extremity ~ 93970, 93971
    venous pressure ~ 93770
  visceral studies ~ 93975-93979
Vascular surgery
  arm, upper, anesthesia ~ 01770-01782
  elbow, anesthesia ~ 01770-01782
  endoscopy ~ 37500
  unlisted services and procedures ~ 37799
Vasectomy ~ 55250
  contact laser vaporization with/without transurethral resection, of prostate ~ 52648
  non-contact laser coagulation of prostate ~ 52647
  reversal ~ 55400
  transurethral, cystourethroscopic ~ 52402
  transurethral electrosurgical resection of prostate ~ 52601, 52648
Vasoactive drugs injection, penis ~ 54231
Vasoactive intestinal peptide ~ 84586
Vasogram ~ 74440
Vasography ~ 74440
Vasointestinal peptide ~ 84586
Vasopneumatic device therapy ~ see physical medicine/therapy/occupational therapy ~ 97016
Vasopressin ~ 84588
Vasotomy ~ 55200, 55300
  transurethral, cystourethroscopic ~ 52402
Vasovasorrhaphy ~ 55400
Vasovasostomy ~ 55400
VATS ~ see thoracoscopy
VDRL ~ 86592-86593
Vein
  ablation, endovenous ~ 36473-36479, 36482, 36483
  adrenal, venography ~ 75840-75842
  anastomosis
    caval to mesenteric ~ 37160
    intrahepatic portosystemic ~ 37182-37183
    portocaval ~ 37140
    reniportal ~ 37145
    saphenopopliteal ~ 34530
    splenorenal ~ 37180-37181
    to vein ~ 37140-37160, 37182-37183
  angioplasty
    transluminal ~ 37248, 37249
  arm
    harvest of vein for bypass graft ~ 35500
    venography ~ 75820-75822
  axillary, thrombectomy ~ 34490
  biopsy, transcatheter ~ 75970
  cannulization
    to artery ~ 36810-36815
    to vein ~ 36800
  catheterization
    central insertion ~ 36555-36558
    organ blood ~ 36500
    peripheral insertion ~ 36568-36569
    removal ~ 36589
    repair ~ 36575
    replacement ~ 36578-36581, 36584
    umbilical ~ 36510
  endoscopic harvest, for bypass graft ~ 33508
  external cannula, declotting ~ 36860-36861
  extremity, non-invasive studies ~ 93970, 93971
  femoral, repair ~ 34501
  femoropopliteal, thrombectomy ~ 34421-34451
  guidance
    fluoroscopic ~ 77001
    ultrasound ~ 76937
  hepatic portal
    splenoportography ~ 75810
    venography ~ 75885-75887
  iliac, thrombectomy ~ 34401-34451
  injection, sclerosing agent ~ 36465, 36466, 36468, 36470, 36471

Vein ~ *continued*
  interrupt
    femoral ~ 37650
    iliac ~ 37660
  jugular, venography ~ 75860
  leg
    harvest for vascular reconstruction ~ 35572
    venography ~ 75820-75822
  ligation
    clusters ~ 37785
    esophagus ~ 43205
    jugular ~ 37565
    perforation ~ 37760-37761
    saphenous ~ 37700-37735, 37780
    secondary ~ 37785
  liver, venography ~ 75889-75891
  neck, venography ~ 75860
  nuclear medicine, thrombosis imaging ~ 78455-78458
  orbit, venography ~ 75880
  portal, catheterization ~ 36481
  pulmonary, repair ~ 33730
  removal
    clusters ~ 37785
    saphenous ~ 37720-37735, 37780
    varicose ~ 37765-37766
  renal, venography ~ 75831-75833
  repair
    angioplasty ~ 37248, 37249
    graft ~ 34520
  sampling, venography ~ 75893
  sinus, venography ~ 75870
  skull, venography ~ 75870-75872
  spermatic
    excision ~ 55530-55540
    ligation ~ 55550
  splenic, splenoportography ~ 75810
  stripping, saphenous ~ 37720-37735
  subclavian, thrombectomy ~ 34471-34490
  thrombectomy, other than hemodialysis graft or fistula ~ 35875-35876
  unlisted services and procedures ~ 37799
  valve transposition ~ 34510
  vena cava
    thrombectomy ~ 34401-34451
    venography ~ 75825-75827
Velpeau cast ~ 29058
Vena cava
  catheterization ~ 36010
  filter
    insertion ~ 37191
    repositioning ~ 37192
    retreival ~ 37193
  ligation ~ 37619
  reconstruction ~ 34502
  resection with reconstruction ~ 37799
Vena caval thrombectomy ~ 50230
Venereal disease research laboratory ~ see VDRL
Venesection ~ 99195
Venipuncture ~ see catheterization ~ 36821
  child/adult
    cutdown ~ 36425
    percutaneous ~ 36410
  infant
    cutdown ~ 36420
    percutaneous ~ 36400-36406
  routine ~ 36415
Venography
  adrenal ~ 75840-75842
  arm ~ 75820-75822
  epidural ~ 75872
  hepatic portal ~ 75885-75887
  injection ~ 36005
  jugular ~ 75860
  leg ~ 75820-75822
  liver ~ 75889-75891
  neck ~ 75860
  nuclear medicine ~ 78445, 78457-78458
  orbit ~ 75880
  renal ~ 75831-75833
  sagittal sinus ~ 75870
  vena cava ~ 75825-75827
  venous sampling ~ 75893

Venorrhaphy ~ see suture, vein
Venotomy ~ 99195
Venous access device
  blood collection ~ 36591-36592
  declotting ~ 36593
  fluoroscopic guidance ~ 77001
  insertion
    central ~ 36560-36566
    peripheral ~ 36570-36571
  irrigation ~ 96523
  obstruction clearance ~ 36595-36596
    guidance ~ 75901-75902
  removal ~ 36590
  repair ~ 36576
  replacement ~ 36582-36583, 36585
    catheter only ~ 36578
Venous blood pressure ~ 93770
Venovenostomy ~ 34530
Ventilating tube
  insertion ~ 69433
  removal ~ 69424
Ventilation assist ~ 94002-94005, 99504
Ventricular assist device (VAD)
  implantable counterpulsation aortic system
    insertion ~ 0451T-0454T
    interrogation device evaluation ~ 0463T
    programming device evaluation ~ 0462T
    relocation ~ 0459T
    removal ~ 0455T-0458T
    repositioning ~ 0460T, 0461T
    replacement ~ 0451T-0454T
  insertion
    extracorporeal ~ 33975, 33976, 33978
    implantable ~ 33979
    percutaneous ~ 33990, 33991
  removal ~ 33977, 33980, 33992
  replacement ~ 33981, 33982
  repositioning ~ 33993
Ventricular puncture ~ 61020-61026, 61105-61120
Ventriculocisternostomy ~ 62180, 62200-62201
Ventriculography
  anesthesia
    brain ~ 00214
    cardiac ~ 01920
  nuclear imaging ~ 78635
Ventriculomyectomy ~ 33416
Ventriculomyotomy ~ 33416
Vermiform appendix ~ see appendix
Vermilionectomy ~ 40500
Verruca plana ~ 17110-17111
Verruca(e) ~ 17110-17111
Version, cephalic ~ 59412
Vertebra ~ see spinal cord; spine; vertebral body ~ 22315
  additional segment, excision ~ 22103, 22116
  arthrodesis
    anterior ~ 22548-22585
    exploration ~ 22830
    lateral extracavitary ~ 22532-22534
    posterior ~ 22590-22802
    spinal deformity
      anterior approach ~ 22808-22812
      posterior approach ~ 22800-22804
  cervical, excision, for tumor ~ 22100, 22110
    fracture ~ 23675-23680
  decompression ~ 62287
  laminotomy/laminectomy ~ 0274T, 0275T
  excision, partial ~ 22100-22103, 22110, 22110, 22112, 22114, 22116
  facetectomy, partial ~ 62380, 63020
  fracture/dislocation
    additional segment, open treatment ~ 22328
    cervical, open treatment ~ 22326
    lumbar, open treatment ~ 22325
    thoracic, open treatment ~ 22327
  kyphectomy ~ 22818-22819
  lumbar
    distraction device ~ 22867-22870
    excision, for tumor ~ 22102, 22114

Vertebra ~ *continued*
  osteoplasty, CT scan ~ 72292
    fluoroscopy ~ 72291
    lumbar ~ 22521-22522
    thoracic ~ 22520-22522
  osteotomy, additional segment, anterior approach ~ 22226
    posterior/posterolateral approach ~ 22216
  cervical, anterior approach ~ 22220
    posterior/posterolateral approach ~ 22210
  lumbar,
    anterior approach ~ 22224
    posterior/posterolateral approach ~ 22214
  thoracic, anterior approach ~ 22222
    posterior/posterolateral approach ~ 22212
  thoracic, excision, for tumor ~ 22101, 22112
Vertebrae ~ see vertebra
  arthrodesis, anterior ~ 22548-22585
    lateral extracavitary ~ 22532-22534
    spinal deformity ~ 22818-22819
Vertebral
  arteries ~ see artery, vertebral
  body
    biopsy
      open ~ 20250-20251
      percutaneous ~ 22510-22512
    excision
      decompression ~ 63081-63103
      lesion ~ 63300-63308
      with skull base surgery ~ 61597
    fracture/dislocation
      closed treatment without manipulation ~ 22310
    insertion
      stabilization device ~ 22869, 22870
    kyphectomy ~ 22818-22819
    repair
      injection
        cervicothoracic ~ 22510, 22512
        lumbosacral ~ 22511, 22512
  column ~ see spine
  corpectomy ~ 63081-63103, 63300-63308
    with insertin of biomechanical device ~ 22854
  fracture ~ see fracture, vertebra
  joint replacement
    lumbar spine ~ 0202T
  process
    fracture/dislocation
      closed treatment
        with manipulation, casting and/or bracing ~ 22315
Vesication ~ see bulla
Vesicle, seminal ~ see seminal vesicle
Vesico-psoas hitch ~ 50785
Vesicostomy cutaneous ~ 51980
Vesicourethropexy ~ 51840-51841
Vesicovaginal fistula ~ 51900, 57320, 57330
Vesiculectomy ~ 55650
Vesiculogram, seminal ~ 55300, 74440
Vesiculography ~ 55300, 74440
Vesiculotomy ~ 55600-55605
  complicated ~ 55605
Vessel, blood ~ see blood vessels
Vessels transposition, great ~ 33770-33781
Vestibular function tests ~ see ear, nose and throat
  additional electrodes ~ 92547
  caloric vestibular tests
    with recording ~ 92537, 92538
    without recording ~ 92533
  foveal stimulation ~ 92540
  nystagmus
    optokinetic ~ 92534, 92544
    positional ~ 92532, 92542
    spontaneous ~ 92531, 92540-92541
  posturography ~ 92548
  sinusoidal rotational testing ~ 92546
  torsion swing test ~ 92546
  tracking test ~ 92545
Vestibular nerve
  section
    transcranial approach ~ 69950
    translabyrinthine approach ~ 69915
Vestibule of mouth ~ see mouth, vestibule of
Vestibuloplasty ~ 40840-40845

Vidal Procedure ~ 55530-55540
Video
  esophagus ~ 74230
  pharynx ~ 70371, 74230
  speech evaluation ~ 70371
  swallowing evaluation ~ 74230
Video-assisted thoracoscopic surgery ~ see thoracoscopy
Videoradiography unlisted services and procedures ~ 76120-76125
VII, coagulation factor ~ 85230
VII, cranial nerve ~ see facial nerve
VIII, coagulation factor ~ 85210-85293
Villus, chorionic ~ 59015
Villusectomy ~ see synovectomy
VIP ~ see vasoactive intestinal peptide
Viral antibodies ~ 86280
Viral warts ~ 17110-17111
Virus
  AIDS ~ 87390
  Burkitt lymphoma ~ 86663-86665
  human immunodeficiency ~ 86689, 86701-86703
  influenza ~ 86710, 87804
  respiratory syncytial ~ see respiratory syncytial virus
  salivary gland ~ see cytomegalovirus
Virus identification immunofluorescence ~ 87254
Virus isolation ~ 87250-87255
Visceral larval migrans ~ 86280
Viscosities, blood ~ 85810
Visit, home ~ 99341-99350
Visual acuity screen ~ 99172-99173
Visual field exam ~ 92081-92083
Visual function screen ~ 99172, 1055F
Visual reinforcement audiometry ~ see audiologic function tests ~ 92579
Visualization ileal conduit ~ 50690
Vital capacity measurement ~ 94150
Vitamin ~ 84591
  A ~ 84590
  B complex ~ 78270-78272
  B-1 ~ 84425
  B-12 ~ 82607-82608
    absorption study ~ 78270-78272
  B-2 ~ 84252
  B-6 ~ 84207
  B-6 measurement ~ 84207
  BC ~ 82747
  C ~ 82180
  D
    25-hydroxy measurement ~ 82306
    1, 25 dihydroxy ~ 82652
    counseling ~ 4019F
  D-2 ~ 82307
  D-3 ~ 82306
  E ~ 84446
  K ~ 84597
  K dependent bone protein ~ 83937
  K-dependent protein S ~ 85305-85306
Vitelline duct ~ 44800
Vitrectomy
  anterior approach, partial ~ 67005
  for retinal detachment ~ 67113
  pars plana approach ~ 67036-67043
  subtotal ~ 67010
  with endolaser panretinal photocoagulation ~ 67040
  with epiretinal membrane stripping ~ 67041-67043
  with focal endolaser photocoagulation ~ 67039
  with implantation or replacement, drug delivery system ~ 67027
Vitreous
  aspiration ~ 67015
  excision
    pars planta approach ~ 67036
    with epiretinal membrane stripping ~ 67041-67043
    with focal endolaser photocoagulation ~ 67039
  implantation, drug delivery system ~ 67027
  incision, strands ~ 67030-67031
  injection
    fluid substitute ~ 67025
    pharmacologic agent ~ 67028
  removal
    anterior approach ~ 67005
    subtotal ~ 67010
  replacement, drug delivery system ~ 67027

Vitreous ~ *continued*
  strands
    discission ~ 67030
    severing ~ 67031
  subtotal ~ 67010
VLDL ~ 83695-83721
VMA ~ 84585
Vocal cords
  injection, endoscopy ~ 31513
    augmentiva ~ 31574
    therapeutic ~ 31570-31571, 31573
  laryngeal medialization ~ 31591
Voice box ~ see larynx
Voice button ~ 31611
Voiding pressure studies
  abdominal ~ 51797
  bladder ~ 51728, 51729
  rectum ~ 51797
Volatiles ~ 84600
Volkman contracture ~ 25315-25316
Volume reduction, lung ~ 32491
Von Kraske proctectomy ~ 45111, 45113-45116, 45123
VP ~ see voiding pressure studies
Vulva
  abscess, incision and drainage ~ 56405
  colposcopy ~ 56820
    biopsy ~ 56821
  excision
    complete ~ 56625, 56633-56640
    partial ~ 56620, 56630-56632
    radical ~ 56630-56631, 56633-56640
      complete ~ 56633-56640
      partial ~ 56630-56632
    simple
      complete ~ 56625
      partial ~ 56620
  lesion, destruction ~ 56501-56515
  perineum
    biopsy ~ 56605-56606
    incision and drainage ~ 56405
  repair, obstetric ~ 59300
Vulvectomy
  complete ~ 56625, 56633-56640
  partial ~ 56620, 56630-56632
  radical ~ 56630-56631, 56633-56640
    complete
      with bilateral inguinofemoral lymphadenectomy ~ 56637
      with inguinofemoral, iliac, and pelvic lymphadenectomy ~ 56640
      with unilateral inguinofemoral lymphadenectomy ~ 56634
    partial
      with bilateral inguinofemoral lymphadenectomy ~ 56632
      with unilateral inguinofemoral lymphadenectomy ~ 56631
  simple, complete ~ 56625
    partial ~ 56620
VZIG ~ 90396

W

W-plasty ~ see skin, adjacent tissue transfer
WADA activation test ~ 95958
WAIS-R ~ 96100
Waldius Procedure ~ 27445
Wall, abdominal ~ see abdominal wall
Walsh modified radical prostatectomy ~ 52601
Warts, flat, destruction ~ 17110-17111
Washing sperm ~ 58323
Wasserman test ~ 86592-86593
Wassmund Procedure osteotomy, maxilla ~ 21206
Water wart ~ 17110-17111, 54050-54065
Waterston Procedure ~ 33755
Watson-Jones Procedure ~ 27695-27698
Wave, ultrasonic shock ~ see ultrasound
WBC ~ see white blood cell
Webbed toe, repair ~ 28280
Wedge excision osteotomy ~ 21122
Wedge resection ovary ~ 58920
Well-baby care ~ 99381, 99391, 99461

Wellness behavior ~ see evaluation and management, health behavior
Wernicke-posadas disease ~ 86490
West Nile virus ~ **86788-86789**
Westergren test ~ 85651-85652
Western blot
  HIV ~ 86689
  protein ~ 84181-84182
  tissue analysis ~ 88371-88372
Wheelchair management/propulsion ~ 97542
  training ~ 97542
Wheeler knife procedure ~ 66820-66821
Wheeler Procedure ~ 15820-15823
  discission secondary membranous cataract ~ 66820
Whipple Procedure ~ 48150
Whirlpool therapy ~ 97022
White blood cell
  alkaline phosphatase ~ 85540
  antibody ~ 86021
  count ~ 85032, 85048, 89055
  differential ~ 85004-85007, 85009
  histamine release test ~ 86343
  injection, autologous concentrate ~ 0481T
  phagocytosis ~ 86344
  transfusion ~ 86950
Whitemead Operation ~ 46260
Whitman astragalectomy ~ 28120, 28130
Whitman Procedure ~ 27120
Wick catheter technique ~ 20950
Widal serum test ~ 86000
Window
  oval ~ 69666
  round ~ 69667
Window technic, pericardial ~ 33015
Windpipe ~ see trachea
Winiwarter Operation ~ 47720-47740
Winter Procedure ~ 54435
Wintrobe test ~ 85651-85652
Wire ~ see pin
  insertion/removal, skeletal traction ~ 20650
  interdental, without fracture ~ 21497
Wiring prophylactic treatment, humerus ~ 24498
Wirsung duct ~ see pancreatic duct
Witzel Operation ~ see incision, stomach, creation, stoma; incision and drainage ~ 43500, 43520, 43830-43832
Womb ~ see uterus
Wood alcohol ~ 84600
Work hardening ~ see physical medicine/therapy/occupational therapy ~ 97545-97546
Work related evaluation services ~ 99455-99456
Worm ~ 86682
Wound
  debridement
    non-selective ~ 97602
    selective ~ 97597-97598
  dehiscence, repair ~ 12020-12021, 13160
  exploration
    penetrating
      abdomen/flank/back ~ 20102
      chest ~ 20101
      extremity ~ 20103
      neck ~ 20100
      penetrating trauma ~ 20100-20103
  infection, incision and drainage, postoperative ~ 10180
  negative pressure therapy ~ 97605-97606
  repair
    complex ~ 13100-13160
    intermediate ~ 12031-12057
    simple ~ 12001-12021
    urethra ~ 53502-53515
  suture
    bladder ~ 51860-51865
    kidney ~ 50500
    trachea
      cervical ~ 31800
      intrathoracic ~ 31805
    urethra ~ 53502-53515
  vagina repair ~ 57200-57210

Wrist ~ **see arm, lower; carpal bone**
  abscess ~ 25028
  arthrocentesis ~ 20605
  arthrodesis ~ 25800
    with graft ~ 25810
    with sliding graft ~ 25805
  arthrography ~ 73115
  arthroplasty ~ 25332, 25443, 25447
    revision ~ 25449
    total replacement ~ 25446
    with implant ~ 25441-25442, 25444-25445
  arthroscopy, diagnostic ~ 29840
    surgical ~ 29843-29848
  arthrotomy ~ 25040, 25100-25105
    for repair ~ 25107
  biopsy ~ 25065-25066, 25100-25101
  bursa
    excision ~ 25115-25116
    incision and drainage ~ 25031
  capsule, incision ~ 25085
  cast ~ 29085
  cyst ~ 25130-25136
  decompression ~ 25020-25025
  disarticulation ~ 25920
    reamputation ~ 25924
    revision ~ 25922
  dislocation
    closed treatment ~ 25660
    intercarpal ~ 25660
      open treatment ~ 25670
    open treatment ~ 25670, 25676
    percutaneous fixation ~ 25671
    radiocarpal ~ 25660
      open treatment ~ 25670
    radioulnar
      closed treatment ~ 25675
      percutaneous fixation ~ 25671
    with fracture
      closed treatment ~ 25680
      open treatment ~ 25685
    with manipulation ~ 25259, 25660, 25675
  excision
    carpal ~ 25210-25215
    cartilage ~ 25107
  exploration ~ 25040, 25101
  fasciotomy ~ 25020-25025
  fracture ~ 25645
    closed treatment ~ 25622, 25630
    open treatment ~ 25628
    with dislocation ~ 25680-25685
    with manipulation ~ 25259, 25624, 25635
  ganglion cyst, excision ~ 25111-25112
  hematoma ~ 25028
  incision ~ 25040, 25100-25105
    tendon sheath ~ 25000-25001
  injection
    carpal tunnel, therapeutic ~ 20526
    X-ray ~ 25246
  joint ~ 25040, 25660
  lesion, tendon sheath, excision ~ 25110
  magnetic resonance imaging (MRI) ~ 73221
  reconstruction
    capsulectomy ~ 25320
    capsulorrhaphy ~ 25320
    carpal bone ~ 25394, 25430
    realign ~ 25335
  removal
    foreign body ~ 25040, 25101, 25248
    implant ~ 25449
    loose body ~ 25101
    prosthesis ~ 25250-25251
  repair ~ 25447
    bone ~ 25440
    carpal bone ~ 25431
    muscle ~ 25260, 25270
      secondary ~ 25263-25265, 25272-25274
    tendon ~ 25260, 25270, 25280-25316
      secondary ~ 25263-25265, 25272-25274
    tendon sheath ~ 25275
  strapping ~ 29260

Wrist ~ *continued*
  synovium, excision ~ 25105, 25115-25119
  tendon sheath, excision ~ 25115-25116
  tenodesis ~ 25300-25301
  tenotomy ~ 25290
  tumor ~ 25130-25136
    excision ~ 25071-25078
  unlisted services and procedures ~ 25999
  X-ray ~ 73100-73110
    with contrast ~ 73115

X

X, coagulation factor ~ 85260
X, cranial nerve ~ see vagus nerve
X-linked ichthyoses ~ 86592-86593
X-ray
  abdomen ~ 74018, 74019, 74021, 74022
  abscess ~ 76080
  acromioclavicular joint ~ 73050
  ankle ~ 73600-73610
  arm, lower ~ 73090
  arm, upper ~ 73092
  auditory meatus ~ 70134
  barium swallow test ~ 3142F, 3200F
  bile duct, guide dilation ~ 74360
  body section ~ 76100
    motion ~ 76101-76102
  bone
    age study ~ 77072
    dual energy absorptiometry ~ 77080-77081
    length study ~ 77073
    osseous survey ~ 77074-77077
    ultrasound ~ 76977
  breast ~ 77065-77067
    tomosynthesis ~ 77061-77063
    with computer-aided detection ~ 77065-77067
  calcaneus ~ 73650
  chest ~ 71045-71048
    with computer-aided detection ~ 0174T, 0175T
  clavicle ~ 73000
  coccyx ~ 72220
  consultation ~ 76140
  duodenum ~ 74260
  elbow ~ 73070-73080
  esophagus ~ 74220
  eye ~ 70030
  facial bones ~ 70140-70150
  fallopian tube ~ 74742
  femur ~ 73551, 73552
    radiostereometric analysis (RSA) ~ 0350T
  fibula ~ 73590
  finger ~ 73140
  fistula ~ 76080
  foot ~ 73620-73630
  gastrointestinal tract ~ 74240-74245
    guide dilation ~ 74360
    guide intubation ~ 74340
    upper ~ 3142F, 3200F
  hand ~ 73120-73130
  head ~ 70350
  heel ~ 73650
  hip
    bilateral ~ 73521-73523
    unilateral ~ 73501-73503
    radiostereometric analysis (RSA) ~ 0350T
  humerus ~ 73060
  intestines, small ~ 74245, 74249-74251
    guide intubation ~ 74355
  jaws ~ 70355
  joint, stress views ~ 77071
  knee ~ 73560-73564, 73580
    bilateral ~ 73565
  larynx ~ 70370
  leg ~ 73592
  lumen dilator ~ 74360

X-ray ~ *continued*
  mandible ~ 70100-70110
  mastoids ~ 70120-70130
  nasal bone ~ 70160
  neck ~ 70360
  nose to rectum, foreign body ~ 76010
  orbit ~ 70190-70200
  pelvis ~ 72170-72190
    with hips ~ 73501-73503, 73521-73523
    manometry ~ 74710
  peritoneum ~ 74190
  pharynx ~ 70370, 74210
  ribs ~ 71100-71111
  sacroiliac joint ~ 72200-72202
  sacrum ~ 72220
  salivary gland ~ 70380
  scapula ~ 73010
  sella turcica ~ 70240
  shoulder ~ 73020-73030, 73050
  sinus tract ~ 76080
  sinuses ~ 70210-70220
  skull ~ 70250, 70260
    with spine ~ 72081-72084
  specimen/surgical ~ 76098
  spine ~ 72020
    cervical ~ 72040, 72050, 72052, 72081-72084
    lumbosacral ~ 72100-72120, 72081-72084
    thoracic ~ 72070-72074, 72081-72084
    thoracolumbar ~ 72080, 72081-72084
    total ~ 72081-72084
  standing
    radiostereometric analysis (RSA) ~ 0348T
  sternum ~ 71120-71130
  teeth ~ 70300-70320
  tibia ~ 73590
  toe ~ 73660
  total body, foreign body ~ 76010
  unlisted services and procedures ~ 76120-76125
  upper GI series ~ 3142F, 3200F
  with contrast
    ankle ~ 73615
    aorta ~ 75600-75630
    artery
      abdominal ~ 75726
      additional vessels ~ 75774
      adrenal ~ 75731-75733
      arm ~ 75710-75716
      head and neck ~ 36221-36226
      leg ~ 75710-75716
      mammary ~ 75756
      pelvic ~ 75736
      pulmonary ~ 75741-75746
      renal ~ 36251-36254
      spine ~ 75705
      transcatheter therapy ~ 75894-75898
    bile duct ~ 47531, 47532, 74300, 74301
      catheterization ~ 75984
      drainage ~ 47533-47540
      guide catheter ~ 74328, 74330
    bladder ~ 74430, 74450-74455
    brain ~ 70010-70015
    bronchi ~ 76499
    colon, barium enema ~ 74270-74280
    corpora cavernosa ~ 74445
    elbow ~ 73085
    epididymis ~ 74440
    gallbladder ~ 74290-74291
    gastrointestinal tract ~ 74246-74249
    hip ~ 73525
    iliofemoral artery ~ 75630
    intervertebral disk
      cervical ~ 72285
      lumbar ~ 72295
      thoracic ~ 72285
    joint, stress views ~ 77071
    kidney
      cyst ~ 74470
    knee ~ 73560-73564, 73580
    lacrimal duct ~ 70170

X-ray ~ *continued*
  lymph vessel
    abdomen ~ 75805-75807
    arm ~ 75801-75803
    leg ~ 75801-75803
  nasolacrimal duct ~ 70170
    guide dilation ~ 74485
  oviduct ~ 74740
  pancreas ~ 47531, 74300, 74301
  pancreatic duct, guide catheter ~ 74329, 74330
  perineum ~ 74775
  peritoneum ~ 74190
  salivary gland ~ 70390
  seminal vesicles ~ 74440
  shoulder ~ 73040
  spine
    cervical ~ 72240
    lumbosacral ~ 72265
    thoracic ~ 72255
    total ~ 72270
  temporomandibular joint (TMJ) ~ 70328-70332
  ureter
    guide dilation ~ 74485
  urethra ~ 74450-74455
  urinary tract ~ 74400-74425
  uterus ~ 74740
  vas deferens ~ 74440
  vein
    adrenal ~ 75840-75842
    arm ~ 75820-75822
    hepatic portal ~ 75810, 75885-75887
    jugular ~ 75860
    leg ~ 75820-75822
    liver ~ 75889-75891
    neck ~ 75860
    orbit ~ 75880
    renal ~ 75831-75833
    sampling ~ 75893
    sinus ~ 75870
    skull ~ 75870-75872
    splenic ~ 75810
    vena cava ~ 75825-75827
  wrist ~ 73115
  wrist ~ 73100-73110
X-ray tomography, computed ~ see CT scan
XA, coagulation factor ~ 85260
Xenoantibodies ~ 86308-86310
XI, coagulation factor ~ 85270
XI, cranial nerve ~ see accessory nerve
XII, coagulation factor ~ 85280
XII, cranial nerve ~ see hypoglossal nerve
XIII, coagulation factor ~ 85290-85291
Xylose absorption test
  blood ~ 84620
  urine ~ 84620

Y

Yeast culture ~ 87106
Yellow fever vaccine ~ 90717
Yersinia antibody ~ 86793

Z

Ziegler Procedure discission secondary membranous cataract ~ 66820
Zinc ~ 84630
Zinc manganese leucine aminopeptidase ~ 83670
Zonisamide
  drug assay ~ 80203
Zygoma ~ see cheekbone
Zygomatic arch fracture
  open treatment ~ 21356-21366
  with manipulation ~ 21355